Official 19

National Football League

Record & Fact Book

A National Football League Book.
Workman Publishing Co., New York.

National Football League, 1993

410 Park Avenue, New York, N.Y. 10022 (212) 758-1500

Commissioner: Paul Tagliabue
President: Neil Austrian

Executive Vice President and League Counsel: Jay Moyer
Vice President of Communications and Development: Joe Browne
Vice President of Broadcasting and Productions: Val Pinchbeck, Jr.
Vice President of Operations: Roger Goodell
Treasurer: Tom Sullivan
Executive Director for Special Events: Jim Steeg

Executive Vice President for Labor Relations/Chairman NFLMC: Harold Henderson
Vice President/General Counsel: Dennis Curran
Vice President for Operations and Compliance: Peter Ruocco

ADMINISTRATION
Director of Administration: John Buzzeo
Comptroller: Joe Siclare

BROADCASTING
Director of Broadcast Services: Dick Maxwell
Director of Broadcasting Research: Joe Ferreira
Assistant Director of Broadcasting/Productions: Nancy Behar

COMMUNICATIONS
Director of Communications: Greg Aiello
Director of International Public Relations: Pete Abitante
Director of Information, AFC: Leslie Hammond
Director of Information, NFC: Reggie Roberts

OFFICIATING
Director of Officiating: Jerry Seeman
Assistant Director of Officiating: Jack Reader
Supervisor of Officials: Leo Miles
Supervisor of Officials: Ron DeSouza

OPERATIONS
Director of Club Administration: Joe Ellis
Director of Game Operations: Jan Van Duser
Director of Planning: Don Weiss
Assistant Director of Game Operations: Tim Davey

PLAYER EMPLOYMENT
Director of Labor Administration: John Jones
Director of Player Personnel: Joel Bussert
Director of Player Programs: Lem Burnham
Labor Relations Counsel: Lal Heneghan
Labor Relations Counsel: Rapheal Prevot

SECURITY
Director of Security: Warren Welsh
Assistant Director of Security: Charles R. Jackson, Jr.

Cover Photograph by Paul Spinelli/NFLP.

Printed in the United States of America.

A National Football League Book.
Compiled by the NFL Communications Department and Seymour Siwoff, Elias Sports Bureau.
Edited by Reggie Roberts, NFL Communications Department and Chuck Garrity, Jr., NFLP Creative Services.
Statistics by Elias Sports Bureau.
Produced by NFL Properties, Inc., Creative Services Division.

Workman Publishing Co.
708 Broadway, New York, N.Y. 10003
Manufactured in the United States of America.
First printing, July 1993.

10 9 8 7 6 5 4 3 2 1

Index

1993 SCHEDULE AND NOTE CALENDAR

(All times local except Barcelona, Berlin, London, and Tokyo which are EDT.)
Nationally televised games in parentheses.

Preseason/First Week

Friday, July 30	Buffalo ___ at Detroit ___	7:30
Saturday, July 31	Hall of Fame Game at Canton, Ohio Los Angeles Raiders ___ vs. Green Bay ___	(ABC) 3:00
	American Bowl '93 at Tokyo New Orleans ___ vs. Philadelphia ___	(ESPN) 10:00*
Sunday, August 1	Minnesota ___ at Dallas ___	7:00
	American Bowl '93 at Barcelona Pittsburgh ___ vs. San Francisco ___	(NBC) 1:00**
Friday, August 6	Miami ___ at Atlanta ___	7:30
Saturday, August 7	American Bowl '93 at Berlin Buffalo ___ vs. Minnesota ___	(NBC) 1:00†
	Denver ___ at Tampa Bay ___	7:30
	Houston ___ vs. New Orleans ___ at San Antonio, Tex.	7:00
	Indianapolis ___ at Seattle ___	6:00
	Kansas City ___ vs. Green Bay ___ at Milwaukee	7:00
	Los Angeles Raiders ___ vs. San Francisco ___ at Palo Alto, Calif.	1:00
	Los Angeles Rams ___ at Phoenix ___	7:30
	New England ___ at San Diego ___	6:00
	New York Giants ___ at Cincinnati ___	7:30
	New York Jets ___ at Pittsburgh ___	6:00
Sunday, August 8	Chicago ___ at Philadelphia ___	(TNT) 8:00
	American Bowl '93 at London Dallas ___ vs. Detroit ___	(CBS) 12:30††
Monday, August 9	Cleveland ___ at Washington ___	(ABC) 8:00

*Tokyo game actual kickoff 11:00 A.M. August 1.
**Barcelona game actual kickoff 7:00 P.M. August 1.
†Berlin game actual kickoff 7:00 P.M. August 7.
††London game actual kickoff 5:30 P.M. August 8.

Preseason/Second Week

Thursday, August 12	Buffalo ___ at Kansas City ___	(TNT) 7:00
Friday, August 13	Philadelphia ___ at New York Jets ___	7:30
Saturday, August 14	Cincinnati ___ at Indianapolis ___	7:00
	Los Angeles Raiders ___ at Dallas ___	(ESPN) 7:00
	New England ___ vs. Cleveland ___ at Toronto, Canada	7:30
	New Orleans ___ vs. Green Bay ___ at Madison, Wis.	12:00
	Phoenix ___ at Chicago ___	7:00
	Pittsburgh ___ at New York Giants ___	8:00
	San Diego ___ at Los Angeles Rams ___	7:00
	Seattle ___ at Minnesota ___	7:00
	Tampa Bay ___ at Atlanta ___	7:30
	Washington ___ at Miami ___	8:00
Monday, August 16	Detroit ___ at Houston ___	8:00
	San Francisco ___ at Denver ___	(ABC) 6:00

Preseason/Third Week

Friday, August 20	Cincinnati ___ at Detroit ___	7:30
	Green Bay ___ at New England ___	7:00
	Los Angeles Raiders ___ at Indianapolis ___	7:00
	Miami ___ at Denver ___	(NBC) 6:00
Saturday, August 21	Atlanta ___ at Philadelphia ___	7:30
	Buffalo ___ vs. Tampa Bay ___ at Orlando, Fla.	7:00
	Dallas ___ vs. Houston ___ at San Antonio, Tex.	(CBS) 12:30
	Los Angeles Rams ___ at Cleveland ___	7:00
	Minnesota ___ at Kansas City ___	7:00
	New York Jets ___ at New York Giants ___	8:00
	Phoenix ___ at San Diego ___	6:00
	San Francisco ___ at Seattle ___	7:00
Sunday, August 22	Washington ___ at Pittsburgh ___	(TNT) 8:00
Monday, August 23	Chicago ___ at New Orleans ___	(ABC) 7:00

Preseason/Fourth Week

Thursday, August 26	Pittsburgh ___ at Minnesota ___	(ESPN) 7:00
Friday, August 27	Atlanta ___ at Buffalo ___	7:30
	Cleveland ___ at Tampa Bay ___	8:00
	Dallas ___ at Chicago ___	7:30
	Denver ___ at Phoenix ___	8:00
	Detroit ___ at New Orleans ___	7:00
	Indianapolis ___ at Green Bay ___	7:00
	Kansas City ___ at New England ___	7:00
	New York Jets ___ at Washington ___	8:00
	Philadelphia ___ at Cincinnati ___	7:30
Saturday, August 28	Los Angeles Raiders ___ at Los Angeles Rams ___	6:00
	New York Giants ___ at Miami ___	8:00
	San Diego ___ at San Francisco ___	(CBS) 5:00
	Seattle ___ at Houston ___	7:00

First Week

Sunday, September 5 (CBS-TV National Weekend)	Atlanta ___ at Detroit ___ 13-30	1:00
	Cincinnati ___ at Cleveland ___ 14-27	1:00
	Denver ___ at New York Jets ___ 26-20	1:00
	Kansas City ___ at Tampa Bay ___ 27-3	1:00
	Los Angeles Rams ___ vs. Green Bay ___ 6-36 at Milwaukee	12:00
	Miami ___ at Indianapolis ___ 24-20	12:00
	Minnesota ___ at Los Angeles Raiders ___ 7-24	1:00
	New England ___ at Buffalo ___ 14-38	1:00
	New York Giants ___ at Chicago ___ 26-20	3:00
	Phoenix ___ at Philadelphia ___ 17-23	1:00
	San Francisco ___ at Pittsburgh ___ 24-13	1:00
	Seattle ___ at San Diego ___ 12-18	1:00
Sunday Night	Houston ___ at New Orleans ___ 21-33	(TNT) 7:00
Monday, September 6	Dallas ___ at Washington ___ 15-35	(ABC) 9:00

Second Week

Sunday, September 12 (NBC-TV National Weekend)	Buffalo ___ at Dallas ___ 13-10	3:00
	Chicago ___ at Minnesota ___ 7-10	12:00
	Detroit ___ at New England ___ 19-16 (OT)	1:00
	Indianapolis ___ at Cincinnati ___ 9-6	1:00
	Kansas City ___ at Houston ___ 0-30	12:00
	New Orleans ___ at Atlanta ___ 34-31	1:00
	New York Jets ___ at Miami ___ 24-14	4:00
	Philadelphia ___ at Green Bay ___ 20-17	12:00
	Phoenix ___ at Washington ___ 17-10	1:00
	Pittsburgh ___ at Los Angeles Rams ___ 0-27	1:00
	San Diego ___ at Denver ___ 17-34	2:00
	Tampa Bay ___ at New York Giants ___ 7-23	1:00
Sunday Night	Los Angeles Raiders ___ at Seattle ___	(TNT) 5:00
Monday, September 13	San Francisco ___ at Cleveland ___	(ABC) 9:00

Third Week

Open Dates: AFC East except New England, NFC Central except Detroit

Sunday, September 19 (NBC-TV National Weekend)	Atlanta ___ at San Francisco ___	1:00
	Cincinnati ___ at Pittsburgh ___	1:00
	Cleveland ___ at Los Angeles Raiders ___	1:00
	Detroit ___ at New Orleans ___	12:00
	Houston ___ at San Diego ___	1:00
	Los Angeles Rams ___ at New York Giants ___	1:00
	Seattle ___ at New England ___	1:00
	Washington ___ at Philadelphia ___	1:00
Sunday Night	Dallas ___ at Phoenix ___	(TNT) 5:00
Monday, September 20	Denver ___ at Kansas City ___	(ABC) 8:00

Fourth Week

Open Dates: AFC West except Seattle, NFC East except Phoenix

Sunday, September 26 (CBS-TV National Weekend)	Cleveland ___ at Indianapolis ___	12:00
	Green Bay ___ at Minnesota ___	12:00
	Los Angeles Rams ___ at Houston ___	12:00
	Miami ___ at Buffalo ___	1:00
	Phoenix ___ at Detroit ___	1:00
	San Francisco ___ at New Orleans ___	3:00
	Seattle ___ at Cincinnati ___	4:00
	Tampa Bay ___ at Chicago ___	12:00
Sunday Night	New England ___ at New York Jets ___	(TNT) 8:00
Monday, September 27	Pittsburgh ___ at Atlanta ___	(ABC) 9:00

Fifth Week

Open Dates: AFC Central, New England, Phoenix

Sunday, October 3 (CBS-TV National Weekend)	Atlanta ___ at Chicago ___	12:00
	Detroit ___ at Tampa Bay ___	1:00
	Green Bay ___ at Dallas ___	12:00
	Indianapolis ___ at Denver ___	2:00
	Los Angeles Raiders ___ at Kansas City ___	12:00
	Minnesota ___ at San Francisco ___	1:00
	New Orleans ___ at Los Angeles Rams ___	1:00
	Philadelphia ___ at New York Jets ___	4:00
	San Diego ___ at Seattle ___	1:00
Sunday Night	New York Giants ___ at Buffalo ___	(TNT) 8:00
Monday, October 4	Washington ___ at Miami ___	(ABC) 9:00

Sixth Week

Open Dates: NFC West, Detroit, Seattle

Sunday, October 10 (NBC-TV National Weekend)	Chicago ___ at Philadelphia ___	1:00
	Cincinnati ___ at Kansas City ___	12:00
	Dallas ___ at Indianapolis ___	12:00
	Miami ___ at Cleveland ___	1:00
	New England ___ at Phoenix ___	1:00
	New York Giants ___ at Washington ___	1:00
	New York Jets ___ at Los Angeles Raiders ___	1:00
	San Diego ___ at Pittsburgh ___	1:00
	Tampa Bay ___ at Minnesota ___	12:00
Sunday Night	Denver ___ at Green Bay ___	(TNT) 6:30
Monday, October 11	Houston ___ at Buffalo ___	(ABC) 9:00

Seventh Week
Open Dates: AFC East except New England, NFC Central except Detroit

Thursday, October 14
Los Angeles Rams ___ at Atlanta ___ (TNT) 7:30

Sunday, October 17 (CBS-TV National Weekend)
Cleveland ___ at Cincinnati ___ 1:00
Houston ___ at New England ___ 1:00
Kansas City ___ at San Diego ___ 1:00
New Orleans ___ at Pittsburgh ___ 1:00
Philadelphia ___ at New York Giants ___ 1:00
San Francisco ___ at Dallas ___ 3:00
Seattle ___ at Detroit ___ 1:00
Washington ___ at Phoenix ___ 1:00

Monday, October 18
Los Angeles Raiders ___ at Denver ___ (ABC) 7:00

Eighth Week
Open Dates: AFC West except Seattle, NFC East except Phoenix

Sunday, October 24 (NBC-TV National Weekend)
Atlanta ___ at New Orleans ___ 12:00
Buffalo ___ at New York Jets ___ 1:00
Cincinnati ___ at Houston ___ 12:00
Detroit ___ at Los Angeles Rams ___ 1:00
Green Bay ___ at Tampa Bay ___ 1:00
New England ___ at Seattle ___ 1:00
Phoenix ___ at San Francisco ___ 1:00
Pittsburgh ___ at Cleveland ___ 1:00

Sunday Night
Indianapolis ___ at Miami ___ (TNT) 7:30

Monday, October 25
Minnesota ___ at Chicago ___ (ABC) 8:00

Ninth Week
Open Dates: AFC Central

Sunday, October 31 (CBS-TV National Weekend)
Chicago ___ at Green Bay ___ 12:00
Dallas ___ at Philadelphia ___ 1:00
Kansas City ___ at Miami ___ 1:00
Los Angeles Rams ___ at San Francisco ___ 1:00
New England ___ at Indianapolis ___ 1:00
New Orleans ___ at Phoenix ___ 2:00
New York Jets ___ at New York Giants ___ 1:00
San Diego ___ at Los Angeles Raiders ___ 1:00
Seattle ___ at Denver ___ 2:00
Tampa Bay ___ at Atlanta ___ 1:00

Sunday Night
Detroit ___ at Minnesota ___ (TNT) 7:00

Monday, November 1
Washington ___ at Buffalo ___ (ABC) 9:00

Tenth Week
Open Dates: NFC West

Sunday, November 7 (NBC-TV National Weekend)
Buffalo ___ at New England ___ 1:00
Denver ___ at Cleveland ___ 1:00
Los Angeles Raiders ___ at Chicago ___ 3:00
Miami ___ at New York Jets ___ 4:00
New York Giants ___ at Dallas ___ 12:00
Philadelphia ___ at Phoenix ___ 2:00
Pittsburgh ___ at Cincinnati ___ 1:00
San Diego ___ at Minnesota ___ 12:00
Seattle ___ at Houston ___ 12:00
Tampa Bay ___ at Detroit ___ 1:00

Sunday Night
Indianapolis ___ at Washington ___ (ESPN) 8:00

Monday, November 8
Green Bay ___ at Kansas City ___ (ABC) 8:00

Eleventh Week
Open Dates: Detroit, New England

Sunday, November 14 (CBS-TV National Weekend)	Atlanta ___ at Los Angeles Rams ___	1:00
	Cleveland ___ at Seattle ___	1:00
	Green Bay ___ at New Orleans ___	12:00
	Houston ___ at Cincinnati ___	1:00
	Kansas City ___ at Los Angeles Raiders ___	1:00
	Miami ___ at Philadelphia ___	1:00
	Minnesota ___ at Denver ___	2:00
	New York Jets ___ at Indianapolis ___	4:00
	Phoenix ___ at Dallas ___	12:00
	San Francisco ___ at Tampa Bay ___	1:00
	Washington ___ at New York Giants ___	1:00
Sunday Night	Chicago ___ at San Diego ___	(ESPN) 5:00
Monday, November 15	Buffalo ___ at Pittsburgh ___	(ABC) 9:00

Twelfth Week
Open Dates: Phoenix, Seattle

Sunday, November 21 (NBC-TV National Weekend)	Chicago ___ at Kansas City ___	12:00
	Cincinnati ___ at New York Jets ___	1:00
	Dallas ___ at Atlanta ___	1:00
	Detroit ___ vs. Green Bay ___ at Milwaukee	12:00
	Houston ___ at Cleveland ___	1:00
	Indianapolis ___ at Buffalo ___	1:00
	Los Angeles Raiders ___ at San Diego ___	1:00
	New England ___ at Miami ___	1:00
	New York Giants ___ at Philadelphia ___	4:00
	Pittsburgh ___ at Denver ___	2:00
	Washington ___ at Los Angeles Rams ___	1:00
Sunday Night	Minnesota ___ at Tampa Bay ___	(ESPN) 8:00
Monday, November 22	New Orleans ___ at San Francisco ___	(ABC) 6:00

Thirteenth Week

Thursday, November 25 Thanksgiving Day	Chicago ___ at Detroit ___	(CBS) 12:30
	Miami ___ at Dallas ___	(NBC) 3:00
Sunday, November 28 (CBS-TV National Weekend)	Buffalo ___ at Kansas City ___	3:00
	Cleveland ___ at Atlanta ___	1:00
	Denver ___ at Seattle ___	1:00
	Los Angeles Raiders ___ at Cincinnati ___	1:00
	New Orleans ___ at Minnesota ___	12:00
	New York Jets ___ at New England ___	1:00
	Philadelphia ___ at Washington ___	1:00
	Phoenix ___ at New York Giants ___	4:00
	San Francisco ___ at Los Angeles Rams ___	1:00
	Tampa Bay ___ at Green Bay ___	12:00
Sunday Night	Pittsburgh ___ at Houston ___	(ESPN) 7:00
Monday, November 29	San Diego ___ at Indianapolis ___	(ABC) 9:00

Fourteenth Week

Sunday, December 5 (NBC-TV National Weekend)	Atlanta ___ at Houston ___	12:00
	Denver ___ at San Diego ___	1:00
	Green Bay ___ at Chicago ___	12:00
	Indianapolis ___ at New York Jets ___	1:00
	Kansas City ___ at Seattle ___	1:00
	Los Angeles Raiders ___ at Buffalo ___	1:00
	Los Angeles Rams ___ at Phoenix ___	2:00
	Minnesota ___ at Detroit ___	1:00
	New England ___ at Pittsburgh ___	1:00
	New Orleans ___ at Cleveland ___	1:00
	New York Giants ___ at Miami ___	4:00
	Washington ___ at Tampa Bay ___	1:00
Sunday Night	Cincinnati ___ at San Francisco ___	(ESPN) 5:00
Monday, December 6	Philadelphia ___ at Dallas ___	(ABC) 8:00

Fifteenth Week

Saturday, December 11	New York Jets ___ at Washington ___	(NBC) 12:30
	San Francisco ___ at Atlanta ___	(CBS) 4:00
Sunday, December 12	Buffalo ___ at Philadelphia ___	1:00
(NBC-TV National Weekend)	Chicago ___ at Tampa Bay ___	1:00
	Cincinnati ___ at New England ___	1:00
	Cleveland ___ at Houston ___	12:00
	Dallas ___ at Minnesota ___	3:00
	Detroit ___ at Phoenix ___	2:00
	Indianapolis ___ at New York Giants ___	1:00
	Kansas City ___ at Denver ___	2:00
	Los Angeles Rams ___ at New Orleans ___	12:00
	Seattle ___ at Los Angeles Raiders ___	1:00
Sunday Night	Green Bay ___ at San Diego ___	(ESPN) 5:00
Monday, December 13	Pittsburgh ___ at Miami ___	(ABC) 9:00

Sixteenth Week

Saturday, December 18	Dallas ___ at New York Jets ___	(CBS) 4:00
	Denver ___ at Chicago ___	(NBC) 11:30
Sunday, December 19	Atlanta ___ at Washington ___	1:00
(CBS-TV National Weekend)	Buffalo ___ at Miami ___	1:00
	Houston ___ at Pittsburgh ___	1:00
	Los Angeles Rams ___ at Cincinnati ___	1:00
	Minnesota ___ vs. Green Bay ___ at Milwaukee	12:00
	New England ___ at Cleveland ___	1:00
	Phoenix ___ at Seattle ___	1:00
	San Diego ___ at Kansas City ___	3:00
	San Francisco ___ at Detroit ___	4:00
	Tampa Bay ___ at Los Angeles Raiders ___	1:00
Sunday Night	Philadelphia ___ at Indianapolis ___	(ESPN) 8:00
Monday, December 20	New York Giants ___ at New Orleans ___	(ABC) 8:00

Seventeenth Week

Saturday, December 25	Houston ___ at San Francisco ___	(NBC) 2:30
Sunday, December 26	Atlanta ___ at Cincinnati ___	1:00
(CBS-TV National Weekend)	Cleveland ___ at Los Angeles Rams ___	1:00
	Detroit ___ at Chicago ___	12:00
	Indianapolis ___ at New England ___	1:00
	Los Angeles Raiders ___ at Green Bay ___	12:00
	New Orleans ___ at Philadelphia ___	1:00
	New York Giants ___ at Phoenix ___	2:00
	New York Jets ___ at Buffalo ___	1:00
	Pittsburgh ___ at Seattle ___	1:00
	Tampa Bay ___ at Denver ___	2:00
	Washington ___ at Dallas ___	3:00
Sunday Night	Kansas City ___ at Minnesota ___	(ESPN) 7:00
Monday, December 27	Miami ___ at San Diego ___	(ABC) 6:00

Eighteenth Week

Friday, December 31	Minnesota ___ at Washington ___	(CBS) 3:00
Sunday, January 2, 1994	Buffalo ___ at Indianapolis ___	1:00
(NBC-TV National Weekend)	Chicago ___ at Los Angeles Rams ___	1:00
	Cincinnati ___ at New Orleans ___	3:00
	Cleveland ___ at Pittsburgh ___	1:00
	Dallas ___ at New York Giants ___	1:00
	Denver ___ at Los Angeles Raiders ___	1:00
	Green Bay ___ at Detroit ___	1:00
	Miami ___ at New England ___	1:00
	Phoenix ___ at Atlanta ___	1:00
	San Diego ___ at Tampa Bay ___	4:00
	Seattle ___ at Kansas City ___	12:00
Sunday Night	New York Jets ___ at Houston ___	(ESPN) 7:00
Monday, January 3, 1994	Philadelphia ___ at San Francisco ___	(ABC) 6:00

Wild Card Playoff Games

Site Priorities
Three Wild Card teams (division non-champions with best three records) from each conference and the division champion with the third-best record in each conference will enter the first round of the playoffs. The division champion with the third-best record will play host to the Wild Card team with the third-best record. The Wild Card team with the best record will play host to the Wild Card team with the second-best record. There are no restrictions on intra-division games.

Saturday, January 8, 1994

American Football Conference

________ at ________ (ABC)

National Football Conference

________ at ________ (ABC)

Sunday, January 9, 1994

American Football Conference

________ at ________ (NBC)

National Football Conference

________ at ________ (CBS)

Divisional Playoff Games

Site Priorities
In each conference, the two division champions with the highest won-lost-tied percentage during the regular season will play host to the Wild Card winners. The division champion with the best record in each conference is assured of playing the Wild Card survivor with the poorest record. There are no restrictions on intra-division games.

Saturday, January 15, 1994

American Football Conference

________ at ________ (NBC)

National Football Conference

________ at ________ (CBS)

Sunday, January 16, 1994

American Football Conference

________ at ________ (NBC)

National Football Conference

________ at ________ (CBS)

Conference Championship Games, Super Bowl XXVIII, and AFC-NFC Pro Bowl

Site Priorities for Championship Games
The home teams will be the surviving playoff winners with the best won-lost-tied percentage during the regular season. A Wild Card team cannot play host unless two Wild Card teams are in the game, in which case the Wild Card team with the best record will play host.

Sunday, January 23, 1994

American Football Conference Championship Game

________ at ________ (NBC)

National Football Conference Championship Game

________ at ________ (CBS)

Sunday, January 30, 1994

Super Bowl XXVIII at Georgia Dome, Atlanta, Georgia

________ vs. ________ (NBC)

Sunday, February 6, 1994

AFC-NFC Pro Bowl at Honolulu, Hawaii

AFC ________ vs. NFC ________ (ESPN)

Postseason Games

Saturday, January 8	AFC and NFC Wild Card Playoffs (ABC)
Sunday, January 9	AFC and NFC Wild Card Playoffs (NBC and CBS)
Saturday, January 15	AFC and NFC Divisional Playoffs (NBC and CBS)
Sunday, January 16	AFC and NFC Divisional Playoffs (NBC and CBS)
Sunday, January 23	AFC and NFC Championship Games (NBC and CBS)
Sunday, January 30	Super Bowl XXVIII at Georgia Dome, Atlanta, Georgia (NBC)
Sunday, February 6	AFC-NFC Pro Bowl at Honolulu, Hawaii (ESPN)

1993 Nationally Televised Games

(All games carried on CBS Radio Network)

Regular Season

Sunday, September 5	Minnesota at Los Angeles Raiders (day, CBS)
	Houston at New Orleans (night, TNT)
Monday, September 6	Dallas at Washington (night, ABC)
Sunday, September 12	Buffalo at Dallas (day, NBC)
	Los Angeles Raiders at Seattle (night, TNT)
Monday, September 13	San Francisco at Cleveland (night, ABC)
Sunday, September 19	Houston at San Diego (day, NBC)
	Dallas at Phoenix (night, TNT)
Monday, September 20	Denver at Kansas City (night, ABC)
Sunday, September 26	San Francisco at New Orleans (day, CBS)
	New England at New York Jets (night, TNT)
Monday, September 27	Pittsburgh at Atlanta (night, ABC)
Sunday, October 3	Minnesota at San Francisco (day, CBS)
	New York Giants at Buffalo (night, TNT)
Monday, October 4	Washington at Miami (night, ABC)
Sunday, October 10	New York Jets at Los Angeles Raiders (day, NBC)
	Denver at Green Bay (night, TNT)
Monday, October 11	Houston at Buffalo (night, ABC)
Thursday, October 14	Los Angeles Rams at Atlanta (night, TNT)
Sunday, October 17	San Francisco at Dallas (day, CBS)
Monday, October 18	Los Angeles Raiders at Denver (night, ABC)
Sunday, October 24	Buffalo at New York Jets (day, NBC)
	Indianapolis at Miami (night, TNT)
Monday, October 25	Minnesota at Chicago (night, ABC)
Sunday, October 31	Los Angeles Rams at San Francisco (day, CBS)
	Detroit at Minnesota (night, TNT)
Monday, November 1	Washington at Buffalo (night, ABC)
Sunday, November 7	Los Angeles Raiders at Chicago (day, NBC)
	Indianapolis at Washington (night, ESPN)
Monday, November 8	Green Bay at Kansas City (night, ABC)
Sunday, November 14	Minnesota at Denver (day, CBS)
	Chicago at San Diego (night, ESPN)
Monday, November 15	Buffalo at Pittsburgh (night, ABC)
Sunday, November 21	Pittsburgh at Denver (day, NBC)
	Minnesota at Tampa Bay (night, ESPN)
Monday, November 22	New Orleans at San Francisco (night, ABC)
Thursday, November 25	Chicago at Detroit (day, CBS)
	Miami at Dallas (day, NBC)
Sunday, November 28	San Francisco at Los Angeles Rams (day, CBS)
	Pittsburgh at Houston (night, ESPN)
Monday, November 29	San Diego at Indianapolis (night, ABC)
Sunday, December 5	Denver at San Diego (day, NBC)
	Cincinnati at San Francisco (night, ESPN)
Monday, December 6	Philadelphia at Dallas (night, ABC)
Saturday, December 11	New York Jets at Washington (day, NBC)
	San Francisco at Atlanta (day, CBS)
Sunday, December 12	Kansas City at Denver (day, NBC)
	Green Bay at San Diego (night, ESPN)
Monday, December 13	Pittsburgh at Miami (night, ABC)
Saturday, December 18	Dallas at New York Jets (day, CBS)
	Denver at Chicago (day, NBC)
Sunday, December 19	San Francisco at Detroit (day, CBS)
	Philadelphia at Indianapolis (night, ESPN)
Monday, December 20	New York Giants at New Orleans (night, ABC)
Saturday, December 25	Houston at San Francisco (day, NBC)
Sunday, December 26	Washington at Dallas (day, CBS)
	Kansas City at Minnesota (night, ESPN)
Monday, December 27	Miami at San Diego (night, ABC)
Friday, December 31	Minnesota at Washington (day, CBS)
Sunday, January 2	Denver at Los Angeles Raiders (day, NBC)
	New York Jets at Houston (night, ESPN)
Monday, January 3	Philadelphia at San Francisco (night, ABC)

1993 AFC-NFC Interconference Games

(All times local.)

September 5	Houston at New Orleans	7:00
	Kansas City at Tampa Bay	1:00
	Minnesota at Los Angeles Raiders	1:00
	San Francisco at Pittsburgh	1:00
September 12	Buffalo at Dallas	3:00
	Detroit at New England	1:00
	Pittsburgh at Los Angeles Rams	1:00
September 13	San Francisco at Cleveland	9:00
September 26	Los Angeles Rams at Houston	12:00
September 27	Pittsburgh at Atlanta	9:00
October 3	New York Giants at Buffalo	8:00
	Philadelphia at New York Jets	4:00
October 4	Washington at Miami	9:00
October 10	Dallas at Indianapolis	12:00
	Denver at Green Bay	7:00
	New England at Phoenix	1:00
October 17	New Orleans at Pittsburgh	1:00
	Seattle at Detroit	1:00
October 31	New York Jets at New York Giants	1:00
November 1	Washington at Buffalo	9:00
November 7	Indianapolis at Washington	8:00
	Los Angeles Raiders at Chicago	3:00
	San Diego at Minnesota	12:00
November 8	Green Bay at Kansas City	8:00
November 14	Chicago at San Diego	5:00
	Miami at Philadelphia	1:00
	Minnesota at Denver	2:00
November 21	Chicago at Kansas City	12:00
November 25	Miami at Dallas	3:00
November 28	Cleveland at Atlanta	1:00
December 5	Atlanta at Houston	12:00
	Cincinnati at San Francisco	5:00
	New Orleans at Cleveland	1:00
	New York Giants at Miami	4:00
December 11	New York Jets at Washington	12:30
December 12	Buffalo at Philadelphia	1:00
	Green Bay at San Diego	5:00
	Indianapolis at New York Giants	1:00
December 18	Dallas at New York Jets	4:00
	Denver at Chicago	11:30
December 19	Los Angeles Rams at Cincinnati	1:00
	Philadelphia at Indianapolis	8:00
	Phoenix at Seattle	1:00
	Tampa Bay at Los Angeles Raiders	1:00
December 25	Houston at San Francisco	2:30
December 26	Atlanta at Cincinnati	1:00
	Cleveland at Los Angeles Rams	1:00
	Kansas City at Minnesota	7:00
	Los Angeles Raiders at Green Bay	12:00
	Tampa Bay at Denver	2:00
January 2, 1994	Cincinnati at New Orleans	3:00
	San Diego at Tampa Bay	4:00

Important Dates

1993 Season

July 6	Claiming period of 24 hours begins in waiver system. All waiver requests for the rest of the year are no-recall and no-withdrawal.
July 11	Los Angeles Raiders are first team to open training camp. Veteran players cannot be required to report earlier than 15 days prior to club's first preseason game or July 15, whichever is later.
July 15	Signing periods ends at 4 P.M., Eastern time, for Unrestricted Veteran Free Agents to whom June 1 tender was made by Old Club. After this date and through 4 P.M., Eastern time, on November 9, Old Club has exclusive negotiating rights with its unsigned Unrestricted Veteran Free Agents.
July 31	Hall of Fame Game, Canton, Ohio: Los Angeles Raiders vs. Green Bay.
August 1	American Bowl, Tokyo, Japan: New Orleans vs. Philadelphia.
August 1	American Bowl, Barcelona, Spain: Pittsburgh vs. San Francisco.
August 6	If a drafted rookie has not signed with his club by this date, he may not be traded to any other club in 1993.
August 7	American Bowl, Berlin, Germany: Buffalo vs. Minnesota.
August 8	American Bowl, London, England: Dallas vs. Detroit.
August 24	Roster cutdown to maximum of 60 players on Active list by 4 P.M., Eastern time.
August 30	Roster cutdown to maximum of 47 players on Active List by 12 noon, Eastern time.
August 31	Beginning at 12 noon, Eastern time, clubs may establish an Inactive List of six additional players by waivers or signing free agents. Clubs may dress 45 players and a third quarterback for each regular-season and postseason game.
August 31	After 4 P.M., Eastern time, clubs may establish a Practice Squad of five players by signing free agents who do not have a season of free-agency credit.
September 3	All clubs are required to identify their 49-player Active List by 7:00 P.M., Eastern time, on this Friday and thereafter on each Friday before a regular-season game or 7:00 P.M., Eastern time, two days prior to non-Sunday games). No later than one hour and 15 minutes prior to kickoff, clubs must identify their 45-player Active List and third quarterback, if any.
September 5-6	Regular-Season opens.
September 21	Priority on multiple waiver claims is now based on the current season's standing.
October 19	All trading ends at 4 P.M., Eastern time.
October 20	Players with at least four previous pension credits are subject to the waiver system for the remainder of the regular season and postseason.
October 26-27	NFL Fall Meeting, Chicago, Illinois.
November 9	Deadline for clubs to sign by 4 P.M., Eastern time, their Unrestricted Veteran Free Agents to whom June 1 tender was made. If still unsigned after this date, such players are prohibited from playing in NFL in 1993.
November 9	Deadline for clubs to sign by 4 P.M., Eastern time, their Restricted Free Agents to whom June 1 tender was made. If such players remain unsigned, they are prohibited from playing in NFL in 1993.
November 9	Deadline for clubs to sign by 4 P.M., Eastern time, their drafted players. If such players remain unsigned, they are prohibited from playing in NFL in 1993.
December 4	Deadline for reinstatement of players in Reserve List categories of Retired and Did Not Report.
December 31	Deadline for waiver requests in 1993, except for "special waiver requests" by teams participating in playoffs.

1994 Season

January 8-9	Wild Card Playoff Games.
January 15-16	Divisional Playoff Games.
January 23	AFC and NFC Championship Games.
January 30	Super Bowl XXVIII, Georgia Dome, Atlanta, Georgia.
January 31	Clubs may begin signing free-agent players for the 1994 season.
February 6	AFC-NFC Pro Bowl, Honolulu, Hawaii.
February 10-14	Combine Timing and Testing, Hoosier Dome, Indianapolis, Indiana.
February 16	Deadline for exercising options for 1994 on all players who have option clauses in their 1993 contracts.
February 16	Deadline for submission of qualifying offers by clubs to their Restricted Free Agents whose contracts have expired and to whom they desire to retain a Right of First Refusal/Compensation.
February 16	Deadline for clubs to submit offer of minimum salary to retain exclusive negotiating rights to their players with fewer than three seasons of free-agency credit whose contracts have expired.
February 17	Trading period begins after expiration of all 1993 contracts.
February 17	Expiration date of all player contracts due to expire in 1994.
March 13-18	NFL Annual Meeting, Orlando, Florida.
Mid-April	Deadline for signing of Offer Sheets by Restricted Free Agents.
April 24-25	Annual Player Selection Meeting, New York, New York.

Waivers

The waiver system is a procedure by which player contracts or NFL rights to players are made available by a club to other clubs in the League. During the procedure, the 27 other clubs either file claims to obtain the players or waive the opportunity to do so — thus the term "waiver." Claiming clubs are assigned players on a priority based on the inverse of won-and-lost standing. The claiming period normally is 10 days during the offseason and 24 hours from early July through December. In some circumstances, another 24 hours is added on to allow the original club to rescind its action (known as a recall of a waiver request) and/or the claiming club to do the same (known as withdrawal of a claim). If a player passes through waivers unclaimed and is not recalled by the original club, he becomes a free agent. All waivers from July through December are no recall and no withdrawal. Under the Collective Bargaining Agreement, from the beginning of the waiver system each year through the trading deadline (October 19, 1993), any veteran who has acquired four years of pension credit is not subject to the waiver system if the club desires to release him. After the trading deadline, such players are subject to the waiver system.

Active/Inactive List

The Active/Inactive List is the principal status for players participating for a club. It consists of all players under contract who are eligible for preseason, regular-season, and postseason games. In 1993, teams will be permitted to open training camp with no more than 80 players under contract and thereafter must meet two mandatory roster reductions prior to the season opener. Teams will be permitted an Active List of 45 players and an Inactive List of eight players for each regular-season and postseason game during the 1993 season. Provided that a club has two quarterbacks on its 45-player Active List, a third quarterback from its Inactive List is permitted to dress for the game, but if he participates in the game, the other two quarterbacks are thereafter prohibited from playing. Teams also are permitted to establish Practice Squads of up to five players who are eligible to participate in practice, but these players remain free agents and are eligible to sign with any other team in the league.

August 24 .... Roster reduction to 60 players
August 30 .... Roster reduction to 47 players
August 31 .... Teams may add six players for an Active/Inactive List total of 53 and establish a Practice Squad of up to five players

In addition to the squad limits described above, there also is an overall roster limit of 80 players that is applicable to players on a team's Active, Inactive, and Exempt Lists, and any players on the Practice Squad and on the Reserve List as Injured, Physically Unable to Perform, Non-Football Illness/Injury, and Suspended.

Reserve List

The Reserve List is a status for players who, for reasons of injury, retirement, military service, or other circumstances, are not immediately available for participation with a club. Players on Reserve/Injured are not eligible to practice or return to the Active/Inactive List in the same season that they are placed on Reserve.

Players in the category of Reserve/Retired or Reserve/Did Not Report may not be reinstated during the period from 30 days before the end of the regular season through the postseason.

Trades

Unrestricted trading between the AFC and NFC is allowed in 1993 through October 19, after which trading will end until 1994.

Annual Active Player Limits

NFL

Year(s)	Limit
1985-93	45
1983-84	49
1982	45†–49
1978–81	45
1975–77	43
1974	47
1964–73	40
1963	37
1961–62	36
1960	38
1959	36
1957–58	35
1951–56	33
1949–50	32
1948	35
1947	35*–34
1945–46	33
1943–44	28
1940–42	33
1938–39	30
1936–37	25
1935	24
1930–34	20
1926–29	18
1925	16

†45 for first two games
*35 for first three games

AFL

Year(s)	Limit
1966–69	40
1965	38
1964	34
1962–63	33
1960–61	35

Tie-Breaking Procedures

The following procedures will be used to break standings ties for postseason playoffs and to determine regular-season schedules.

To Break a Tie Within a Division

If, at the end of the regular season, two or more clubs in the same division finish with identical won-lost-tied percentages, the following steps will be taken until a champion is determined.

Two Clubs

1. Head-to-head (best won-lost-tied percentage in games between the clubs).
2. Best won-lost-tied percentage in games played within the division.
3. Best won-lost-tied percentage in games played within the conference.
4. Best won-lost-tied percentage in common games, if applicable.
5. Best net points in division games.
6. Best net points in all games.
7. Strength of schedule.
8. Best net touchdowns in all games.
9. Coin toss.

Three or More Clubs

(Note: If two clubs remain tied after a third club is eliminated during any step, the tiebreaker reverts back to step 1 of the two-club format).

(Note: If one team wins multiple-team tiebreaker to advance to playoff round, remaining teams revert to step 1 of applicable two-club format, i.e., either in division tiebreaker or Wild Card tiebreaker. If two teams in a multiple-team tie possess superior marks in a tiebreaking step, this pair of teams revert to top of applicable two-club format to break tie. One team advances to playoff round, while other returns to original group and step 1 of applicable tiebreaker).

1. Head-to-head (best won-lost-tied percentage in games among the clubs).
2. Best won-lost-tied percentage in games played within the division.
3. Best won-lost-tied percentage in games played within the conference.
4. Best won-lost-tied percentage in common games.
5. Best net points in division games.
6. Best net points in all games.
7. Strength of schedule.
8. Best net touchdowns in all games.
9. Coin toss.

To Break a Tie for the Wild Card Team

If it is necessary to break ties to determine the three Wild Card clubs from each conference, the following steps will be taken.

1. If the tied clubs are from the same division, apply division tiebreaker.
2. If the tied clubs are from different divisions, apply the following steps.

Two Clubs

1. Head-to-head, if applicable.
2. Best won-lost-tied percentage in games played within the conference.
3. Best won-lost-tied percentage in common games, minimum of four.
4. Best average net points in conference games.
5. Best net points in all games.
6. Strength of schedule.
7. Best net touchdowns in all games.
8. Coin toss.

Three or More Clubs

(Note: If two clubs remain tied after third or other clubs are eliminated, tiebreaker reverts to step 1 of applicable two-club format.)

When the first Wild Card team has been identified, the procedure is repeated to name the second Wild Card, i.e., eliminate all but the highest-ranked club in each division prior to proceeding to step 2, and repeated a third time, if necessary, to identify the third Wild Card. In situations where three or more teams from the same division are involved in the procedure, the original seeding of the teams remains the same for subsequent applications of the tiebreaker if the top-ranked team in that division qualifies for a Wild Card berth.

1. Apply division tiebreaker to eliminate all but the highest ranked club in each division prior to proceeding to a step 2. The original seeding within a division upon application of the division tiebreaker remains the same for all subsequent applications of the procedure that are necessary to identify the three Wild Card participants.
2. Head-to-head sweep (Applicable only if one club has defeated each of the others or if one club has lost to each of the others).
3. Best won-lost-tied percentage in games played within the conference.
4. Best won-lost-tied percentage in common games, minimum of four.
5. Best average net points in all games.
6. Best net points in all games.
7. Strength of schedule.
8. Best net touchdowns in all games.
9. Coin toss.

Other Tie-Breaking Procedures

1. Only one team advances to the playoffs in any tie-breaking step. Remaining tied teams revert to the first step of the division or Wild Card tiebreakers.
2. In comparing division and conference records or records against common opponents among tied teams, the best won-lost-tied percentage is the deciding factor since teams may have played an unequal number of games.
3. To determine home-field priority among division titlists, apply Wild Card tiebreakers.
4. To determine home-field priority for Wild Card qualifiers, apply division tiebreakers (if teams are from the same division) or Wild Card tiebreakers (if teams are from different divisions).

Tie-Breaking Procedure for Selection Meeting

If two or more clubs are tied for selection order, the conventional strength of schedule tiebreaker will be applied, subject to the following exceptions for all playoff teams:

1. The Super Bowl winner will be last and the Super Bowl loser will be next-to-last.
2. Any non-Super Bowl playoff team involved in the tie moves down in drafting priority within its tied segment as follows:
   A. For a loss in the Wild Card Playoffs, a plus-factor of one-half.
   B. For participation, win or lose in the Divisional Playoffs, a plus-factor of one.
   C. For a loss in the Conference Championship, a plus-factor of one.

NFL Passer Rating System

The NFL rates its passers for statistical purposes against a pre-fixed performance standard based on statistical achievements of all qualified pro passers since 1960. The system now being used replaced one that rated passers in relation to their position in a total group based on various criteria. The current system, which was adopted in 1973, removes inequities that existed in the former method and, at the same time, provides a means of comparing passing performances from one season to the next.

It is important to remember that the system is used to rate **passers,** not **quarterbacks.** Statistics do not reflect leadership, play-calling, and other intangible factors that go into making a successful professional quarterback. Four categories are used as a basis for compiling a rating:

- Percentage of touchdown passes per attempt
- Percentage of completions per attempt
- Percentage of interceptions per attempt
- Average yards gained per attempt

The base, or **average** standard, is 1.000. The bottom is .000. To earn a 2.000 rating, a passer must perform at exceptional levels, i.e., 70 percent in completions, 10 percent in touchdowns, 1.5 percent in interceptions, and 11 yards average gain per pass attempt. The **maximum** a passer can receive in any category is 2.375.

For example, to gain a 2.375 in completion percentage, a passer would have to complete 77.5 percent of his passes. The NFL record is 70.55 by Ken Anderson (Cincinnati, 1982). To earn a 2.375 in percentage of touchdowns, a passer would have to achieve an 11.9. The record is 13.9 by Sid Luckman (Chicago, 1943). To gain 2.375 in per centage of interceptions, a passer would have to go the entire season without an interception. The 2.375 figure in average yards is 12.50, compared with the NFL record of 11.17 by Tommy O'Connell (Cleveland, 1957).

In order to make the rating more understandable, the point rating is then converted into a scale of 100. For instance, if a passer completes 11 of 23 passes for 114 yards, with one touchdown and no interceptions, the four components would be:

—**Percentage of Completions**—11 of 23 is 47.8 percent. The point rating is 0.890.

—**Percentage of Touchdown Passes**—1 touchdown in 23 attempts works out to 4.3 percent for a rating of 0.860.

—**Percentage of Interceptions**—You can't do better than zero, so the passer receives a maximum rating of 2.375.

—**Average Yards Gained Per Attempt**—23 attempts divided into 114 yards equals 4.96 yards per attempt for a corresponding rating of 0.490.

The sum of the four components is 4.615, which converts to a rating of 76.9. In order for a passer to achieve 100, his points would have to total 6.000. In rare cases, where statistical performance has been superior, it is possible for a passer to surpass 100.

The following is a list of qualifying passers who had a single-season passer rating of 100 or higher:

Player, Team	Season	Rating	Att.	Comp.	Pct.	Yds.	Avg.	TD	TD Pct.	Int.	Int. Pct.
Joe Montana, San Francisco	1989	112.4	386	271	70.2	3,521	9.12	26	6.7	8	2.1
Milt Plum, Cleveland	1960	110.4	250	151	60.4	2,297	9.19	21	8.4	5	2.0
Sammy Baugh, Washington	1945	109.9	182	128	70.3	1,669	9.17	11	6.0	4	2.2
Dan Marino, Miami	1984	108.9	564	362	64.2	5,084	9.01	48	8.5	17	3.0
Sid Luckman, Chicago Bears	1943	107.5	202	110	54.5	2,194	10.86	28	13.9	12	5.9
Steve Young, San Francisco	1992	107.0	402	268	66.7	3,465	8.62	25	6.2	7	1.7
Bart Starr, Green Bay	1966	105.0	251	156	62.2	2,257	8.99	14	5.6	3	1.2
Roger Staubach, Dallas	1971	104.8	211	126	59.7	1,882	8.92	15	7.1	4	1.9
Y.A. Tittle, N.Y. Giants	1963	104.8	367	221	60.2	3,145	8.57	36	9.8	14	3.8
Bart Starr, Green Bay	1968	104.3	171	109	63.7	1,617	9.46	15	8.8	8	4.7
Ken Stabler, Oakland	1976	103.4	291	194	66.7	2,737	9.41	27	9.3	17	5.8
Joe Montana, San Francisco	1984	102.9	432	279	64.6	3,630	8.40	28	6.5	10	2.3
Charlie Conerly, N.Y. Giants	1959	102.7	194	113	58.2	1,706	8.79	14	7.2	4	2.1
Bert Jones, Baltimore	1976	102.5	343	207	60.3	3,104	9.05	24	7.0	9	2.6
Joe Montana, San Francisco	1987	102.1	398	266	66.8	3,054	7.67	31	7.8	13	3.3
Steve Young, San Francisco	1991	101.8	279	180	64.5	2,517	9.02	17	6.1	8	2.9
Len Dawson, Kansas City	1966	101.7	284	159	56.0	2,527	8.90	26	9.2	10	3.5
Jim Kelly, Buffalo	1990	101.2	346	219	63.3	2,829	8.18	24	6.9	9	2.6

Figuring the 1994 NFL Schedule

As soon as the final game of the 1993 NFL regular season (Philadelphia at San Francisco on January 3) has been completed, it will be possible to determine the 1994 opponents of the 28 teams.

Each 1993 team schedule is based on a "common opponent" formula initiated for the 1978 season and most recently modified in 1987. Under the common opponent format, the first- through fourth-place teams in a division play at least 12 of their 16 games the following season against common opponents, and the fifth-place team in the division plays at least 10 common opponent games. It is not a position scheduling format in which the strong play the strong and the weak play the weak.

For years, the NFL had been seeking a more easily understood and balanced schedule that would provide both competitive equality and a variety of opponents. Under the old rotation scheduling system in effect from 1970-77, non-division opponents were determined by a pre-set formula. This often resulted in competitive imbalances.

With common opponents as the basis for scheduling, a more competitive and equitable method of determining division champions and postseason playoff representatives has developed. Teams battling for a division title are playing at least 75 percent of their games against common opponents.

In 1987, NFL owners passed a bylaw proposal designed to modify the common opponent scheduling format in the hopes of creating even more equity. Since then, the pairings with non-division opponents have been:

Prior Year's Finish in Division	Pairings in Non-Division Games Within Conference	Previous Pairings 1978-86
1	1-1-2-3	1-1-4-4
2	1-2-2-4	2-2-3-3
3	1-3-3-4	2-2-3-3
4	2-3-4-4	1-1-4-4

Under the common opponent format, schedules of any NFL team are figured according to one of the following three formulas. (The reference point for the figuring is the team's final division standing. Ties for a position in divisions are broken according to the tie-breaking procedures outlined on page 14. The chart on the following page is included for use as you go through each step.)

A. First- through fourth-place teams in a five-team division (AFC East, AFC West, NFC East, NFC Central).

1. Home-and-home round-robin within the division (8 games).
2. One game each with the first- through fourth-place teams in a division of the other conference (4 games). In 1994, the AFC East will play the NFC Central, the AFC Central will play the NFC East, and the AFC West will play the NFC West.
3. The first-place team plays the first-place teams in the other divisions within the conference plus a second- and third-place team within the conference. The second-place team plays the second-place teams in the other divisions within the conference plus a first- and fourth-place team within the conference. The third-place team plays the third-place teams in the other divisions within the conference plus a first- and fourth-place team within the conference. The fourth-place team plays the fourth-place teams in the other divisions within the conference plus a second- and third-place team within the conference (4 games).

This completes the 16-game schedule.

B. First- through fourth-place teams in a four-team division (AFC Central, NFC West).

1. Home-and-home round-robin within the division (6 games).
2. One game with each of the fifth-place teams in the conference (2 games).
3. The same procedure that is listed in step A2 (4 games).
4. The same procedure that is listed in step A3 (4 games).

This completes the 16-game schedule.

C. The fifth-place teams in a division (AFC East, AFC West, NFC East, NFC Central).

1. Home-and-home round-robin within the division (8 games).
2. One game with each team in the four-team division of the conference (4 games).
3. A home-and-home with the other fifth-place team in the conference (2 games).
4. One game each with the fifth-place teams in the other conference (2 games).

This completes the 16-game schedule.

The 1994 Opponent Breakdown chart on the following page does not include the round-robin games within the division. Those are automatically scheduled on a home-and-away basis.

1993 NFL Standings

AFC

EAST AE

1 __________
2 __________
3 __________
4 __________
5 __________

CENTRAL AC

1 __________
2 __________
3 __________
4 __________

WEST AW

1 __________
2 __________
3 __________
4 __________
5 __________

NFC

EAST NE

1 __________
2 __________
3 __________
4 __________
5 __________

WEST NW

1 __________
2 __________
3 __________
4 __________

CENTRAL NC

1 __________
2 __________
3 __________
4 __________
5 __________

A Team's 1994 Schedule

Team Name __________

1994 Opponent Breakdown

(Certain game sites for interconference opponents are subject to change under NFL scheduling formulas.)

AE AFC EAST

	HOME	AWAY
AE1	AW1	AC1
	AW3	AC2
	NC2	NC1
	NC4	NC3
AE2	AW2	AC2
	AW1	AC4
	NC1	NC2
	NC3	NC4
AE3	AW3	AC3
	AW4	AC1
	NC2	NC1
	NC4	NC3
AE4	AW4	AC4
	AW2	AC3
	NC1	NC2
	NC3	NC4
AE5	AC1	AC2
	AC3	AC4
	AW5	AW5
	NE5	NC5

AC AFC CENTRAL

	HOME	AWAY
AC1	AE1	AW1
	AE3	AW2
	AW5	AE5
	NE2	NE1
	NE4	NE3
AC2	AE2	AW2
	AE1	AW4
	AE5	AW5
	NE1	NE2
	NE3	NE4
AC3	AE3	AW3
	AE4	AW1
	AW5	AE5
	NE2	NE1
	NE4	NE3
AC4	AE4	AW4
	AE2	AW3
	AE5	AW5
	NE1	NE2
	NE3	NE4

AW AFC WEST

	HOME	AWAY
AW1	AC1	AE1
	AC3	AE2
	NW2	NW1
	NW4	NW3
AW2	AC2	AE2
	AC1	AE4
	NW1	NW2
	NW3	NW4
AW3	AC3	AE3
	AC4	AE1
	NW2	NW1
	NW4	NW3
AW4	AC4	AE4
	AC2	AE3
	NW1	NW2
	NW3	NW4
AW5	AC2	AC1
	AC4	AC3
	AE5	AE5
	NC5	NE5

NE NFC EAST

	HOME	AWAY
NE1	NC1	NW1
	NC3	NW2
	AC1	AC2
	AC3	AC4
NE2	NC2	NW2
	NC1	NW4
	AC2	AC1
	AC4	AC3
NE3	NC3	NW3
	NC4	NW1
	AC1	AC2
	AC3	AC4
NE4	NC4	NW4
	NC2	NW3
	AC2	AC1
	AC4	AC3
NE5	NW1	NW2
	NW3	NW4
	NC5	NC5
	AW5	AE5

NC NFC CENTRAL

	HOME	AWAY
NC1	NW1	NE1
	NW3	NE2
	AE1	AE2
	AE3	AE4
NC2	NW2	NE2
	NW1	NE4
	AE2	AE1
	AE4	AE3
NC3	NW3	NE3
	NW4	NE1
	AE1	AE2
	AE3	AE4
NC4	NW4	NE4
	NW2	NE3
	AE2	AE1
	AE4	AE3
NC5	NW2	NW1
	NW4	NW3
	NE5	NE5
	AE5	AW5

NW NFC WEST

	HOME	AWAY
NW1	NE1	NC1
	NE3	NC2
	NC5	NE5
	AW1	AW2
	AW3	AW4
NW2	NE2	NC2
	NE1	NC4
	NE5	NC5
	AW2	AW1
	AW4	AW3
NW3	NE3	NC3
	NE4	NC1
	NC5	NE5
	AW1	AW2
	AW3	AW4
NW4	NE4	NC4
	NE2	NC3
	NE5	NC5
	AW2	AW1
	AW4	AW3

AFC ACTIVE STATISTICAL LEADERS

LEADING ACTIVE PASSERS, AMERICAN FOOTBALL CONFERENCE

1,000 or more attempts

	Yrs.	Att.	Comp.	Pct. Comp.	Yards	Avg. Gain	TD	Pct. TD	Had Int.	Pct. Int.	Rating Pts.
Joe Montana, K.C.	13	4600	2929	63.7	35124	7.64	244	5.3	123	2.7	93.5
Dan Marino, Mia.	10	5284	3128	59.2	39502	7.48	290	5.5	165	3.1	87.8
Jim Kelly, Buff.	7	3024	1824	60.3	23031	7.62	161	5.3	108	3.6	86.9
Dave Krieg, K.C.	13	3989	2326	58.3	29247	7.33	210	5.3	160	4.0	82.1
Bernie Kosar, Clev.	8	3012	1774	58.9	21097	7.00	111	3.7	78	2.6	81.8
Boomer Esiason, N.Y.J.	9	3378	1897	56.2	25671	7.60	174	5.2	129	3.8	81.8
Warren Moon, Hou.	9	4026	2329	57.8	30200	7.50	175	4.3	145	3.6	81.0
John Elway, Den.	10	4339	2375	54.7	30216	6.96	158	3.6	157	3.6	73.8
Jay Schroeder, Cin.	8	2411	1215	50.4	17721	7.35	105	4.4	99	4.1	72.1
Jeff George, Ind.	3	1125	640	56.9	7025	6.24	33	2.9	40	3.6	70.5
Mike Tomczak, Pitt.	8	1364	702	51.5	9430	6.91	51	3.7	63	4.6	67.0
Jack Trudeau, Ind.	7	1374	727	52.9	8655	6.30	39	2.8	55	4.0	65.2
Vinny Testaverde, Clev.	6	2160	1126	52.1	14820	6.86	77	3.6	112	5.2	64.4
Vince Evans, Raiders	12	1106	541	48.9	7387	6.68	41	3.7	62	5.6	59.7

TOP ACTIVE RUSHERS, AFC

2,000 or more yards

	Yrs.	Att.	Yards	TD
1. Eric Dickerson, Raiders	12	2970	13168	90
2. Marcus Allen, K.C.	11	2090	8545	79
3. Thurman Thomas, Buff.	5	1376	6316	35
4. Kevin Mack, Clev.	8	1281	5090	45
5. Christian Okoye, K.C.	6	1246	4897	40
6. John L. Williams, Sea.	7	1066	4208	14
7. Marion Butts, S.D.	4	846	3551	27
8. Rueben Mayes, Sea.	5	865	3482	23
9. Merril Hoge, Pitt.	6	768	2866	20
10. Bobby Humphrey, Mia.	4	695	2857	15
Lorenzo White, Hou.	5	678	2857	24
Other Leading Rushers				
Kenneth Davis, Buff.	7	623	2741	19
Barry Word, K.C.	5	563	2439	14
Barry Foster, Pitt.	3	522	2381	13
Johnny Johnson, N.Y.J.	3	608	2326	15
John Elway, Den.	10	494	2282	22
Harold Green, Cin.	3	506	2254	5
Gaston Green, Raiders	5	551	2136	6
Ronnie Harmon, S.D.	7	454	2110	7
Mark Higgs, Mia.	5	546	2071	11
Rod Bernstine, Den.	6	407	2007	17

TOP ACTIVE PASS RECEIVERS, AFC

275 or more receptions

	Yrs.	No.	Yards	TD
1. James Lofton, Raiders	15	750	13821	75
2. Andre Reed, Buff.	8	534	7379	52
3. Mark Duper, Mia.	11	511	8869	59
4. Marcus Allen, K.C.	11	446	4258	18
5. Ernest Givins, Hou.	7	438	6527	41
6. John L. Williams, Sea.	7	413	3701	15
7. Bill Brooks, Buff.	7	411	5818	28
8. Vance Johnson, Den.	8	367	5008	32
9. Irving Fryar, Mia.	9	363	5726	38
Pete Holohan, Clev.	12	363	3981	16
10. Louis Lipps, Pitt.	9	359	6019	39
Other Leading Receivers				
Webster Slaughter, Hou.	7	344	5320	31
Brian Brennan, S.D.	11	334	4336	20
Ronnie Harmon, S.D.	7	328	3432	14
Reggie Langhorne, Ind.	8	326	4408	16
Willie Gault, Raiders	10	325	6571	44
Mark Carrier, Clev.	6	321	2559	5
Haywood Jeffires, Hou.	6	320	3899	27
Anthony Miller, S.D.	5	290	4420	30
Keith Jackson, Mia.	5	290	3350	25
Curtis Duncan, Hou.	6	281	3479	17
Eric Dickerson, Raiders	12	275	2079	6

TOP ACTIVE SCORERS, AFC

250 or more points

	Yrs.	TD	FG	PAT	TP
1. Nick Lowery, K.C.	14	0	306	449	1367
2. Jim Breech, Cin.	14	0	243	517	1246
3. Gary Anderson, Pitt.	11	0	257	352	1123
4. Al Del Greco, Hou.	11	0	132	278	674
5. Dean Biasucci, Ind.	8	0	134	203	605
6. Marcus Allen, K.C.	11	98	0	0	588
7. Eric Dickerson, Raiders	12	96	0	0	576
8. James Lofton, Raiders	15	76	0	0	456
9. Jeff Jaeger, Raiders	5	0	96	164	452
10. Pete Stoyanovich, Mia.	4	0	101	137	440
Other Leading Scorers					
David Treadwell, Den.	4	0	99	132	429
Mark Duper, Mia.	11	59	0	0	354
Kevin Mack, Clev.	8	53	0	0	318
Andre Reed, Buff.	8	53	0	0	318
Thurman Thomas, Buff.	5	51	0	0	306
John Carney, S.D.	7	0	66	99	297
Steve Christie, Buff.	3	0	62	92	278
Louis Lipps, Pitt.	9	46	0	0	276
Willie Gault, Raiders	10	45	0	0	270
Irving Fryar, Mia.	9	42	0	0	252
Ernest Givins, Hou.	7	42	0	0	252

TOP ACTIVE INTERCEPTORS, AFC

20 or more interceptions

	Yrs.	No.	Yards	TD
1. Ronnie Lott, N.Y.J.	12	60	695	5
2. Everson Walls, Clev.	14	57	504	1
3. Gill Byrd, S.D.	10	42	546	2
4. Albert Lewis, K.C.	10	32	268	0
5. David Fulcher, Cin.	7	31	246	2
6. Mark Kelso, Buff.	7	30	327	1
7. Eugene Robinson, Sea.	8	29	456	0
8. Kevin Ross, K.C.	9	28	502	2
Lionel Washington, Raid.	10	28	292	2
10. Dennis Smith, Den.	12	27	374	0
Other Leading Interceptors				
Eugene Daniel, Ind.	9	26	223	1
Terry Taylor, Clev.	9	21	228	2
Rod Woodson, Pitt.	6	20	411	1
Frank Minnifield, Clev.	9	20	124	0

TOP ACTIVE QUARTERBACK SACKERS, AFC (since 1982)

50 or more sacks

	Yrs.	No.
1. Greg Townsend, Raiders	10	100.0
2. Bruce Smith, Buff.	8	92.0
3. Andre Tippett, N.E.	10	91.5
4. Lee Williams, Hou.	9	79.5
Leonard Marshall, N.Y.J.	10	79.5
6. Howie Long, Raiders	12	78.0
7. Sean Jones, Hou.	9	75.5
8. Kevin Greene, Pitt.	8	72.5
9. Simon Fletcher, Den.	8	72.0
10. Karl Mecklenburg, Den.	10	68.5
Leslie O'Neal, S.D.	6	68.5
Other Leading Sackers		
Jeff Bryant, Sea.	11	62.0
Ray Childress, Hou.	8	59.5
Keith Willis, Buff.	10	59.0
Derrick Thomas, K.C.	4	58.0
Clay Matthews, Clev.	15	56.5
Bill Pickel, N.Y.J.	10	56.0

TOP ACTIVE PUNT RETURNERS, AFC

40 or more punt returns

	Yrs.	No.	Yards	Avg.	TD
1. Louis Lipps, Pitt.	9	112	1234	11.0	3
2. Clarence Verdin, Ind.	7	125	1364	10.9	4
3. Kelvin Martin, Sea.	6	138	1430	10.4	3
Mitchell Price, Cin.	4	49	510	10.4	2
5. Irving Fryar, Mia.	9	206	2055	10.0	3
6. Tim Brown, Raiders	5	153	1495	9.8	1
7. Rod Woodson, Pitt.	6	176	1705	9.7	2
8. Cliff Hicks, N.Y.J.	8	83	785	9.5	0
9. Eric Metcalf, Clev.	4	56	529	9.4	1
Jeff Query, Cin.	4	76	712	9.4	0
Other Leading Punt Returners					
Kitrick Taylor, Den.	5	63	568	9.0	1
Willie Drewrey, Hou.	8	151	1322	8.8	0
Chris Warren, Sea.	3	94	819	8.7	1
Vance Johnson, Den.	8	81	689	8.5	0
Nesby Glasgow, Sea.	14	80	651	8.1	1
Scott Miller, Mia.	2	52	423	8.1	0
Brian Brennan, S.D.	11	56	438	7.8	1
Bill Brooks, Buff.	7	43	292	6.8	0

TOP ACTIVE KICKOFF RETURNERS, AFC

40 or more kickoff returns

	Yrs.	No.	Yards	Avg.	TD
1. Anthony Miller, S.D.	5	48	1227	25.6	2
Tim Brown, Raiders	5	47	1204	25.6	1
3. Jon Vaughn, N.E.	2	54	1281	23.7	2
4. Nate Lewis, S.D.	3	59	1363	23.1	1
5. Vance Johnson, Den.	8	45	1027	22.8	0
6. Nesby Glasgow, Sea.	14	85	1906	22.4	0
7. Rod Woodson, Pitt.	6	190	4235	22.3	2
8. Al Edwards, Buff.	3	54	1153	21.4	1
9. Steve Tasker, Buff.	10	42	896	21.3	0
10. Eric Ball, Cin.	4	50	1058	21.2	0
Other Leading Kickoff Returners					
Leonard Harris, Hou.	7	57	1193	20.9	0
Alexander Wright, Raiders	5	59	1232	20.9	2
Gaston Green, Raiders	5	47	981	20.9	1
Chris Warren, Sea.	3	86	1794	20.9	0
Willie Drewrey, Hou.	8	87	1804	20.7	0
Harvey Williams, K.C.	2	45	929	20.6	0
Clarence Verdin, Ind.	7	143	2854	20.0	1
Dwight Stone, Pitt.	6	87	1736	20.0	1
Ronnie Harmon, S.D.	7	57	1130	19.8	0
Eric Metcalf, Clev.	4	115	2278	19.8	2
Aaron Craver, Mia.	2	40	789	19.7	0
Robert Delpino, Den.	5	61	1193	19.6	0
Kelvin Martin, Sea.	6	51	997	19.5	0
Terance Mathis, N.Y.J.	3	100	1878	18.8	0

TOP ACTIVE PUNTERS, AFC

50 or more punts

	Yrs.	No.	Avg.	LG
1. Rohn Stark, Ind.	11	829	44.0	72
2. Reggie Roby, Mia.	10	555	43.3	77
3. Greg Montgomery, Hou.	5	256	43.2	66
4. Rick Tuten, Sea.	4	217	42.5	65
5. Mike Horan, Den.	10	557	42.3	75
6. Brian Hansen, Clev.	8	607	42.0	73
7. Lee Johnson, Cin.	12	517	41.5	70
8. Jeff Gossett, Raiders	13	702	41.1	64
9. Mark Royals, Pitt.	6	240	41.0	62
Bryan Barker, K.C.	3	196	41.0	65
Other Leading Punters				
Shawn McCarthy, N.E.	2	169	40.7	93
John Kidd, S.D.	9	651	40.6	67
Louie Aguiar, N.Y.J.	3	137	40.2	65
Chris Mohr, Buff.	4	198	40.0	61

NFC ACTIVE STATISTICAL LEADERS

LEADING ACTIVE PASSERS, NATIONAL FOOTBALL CONFERENCE

1,000 or more attempts

	Yrs.	Att.	Comp.	Pct. Comp.	Yards	Avg. Gain	TD	Pct. TD	Had Int.	Pct. Int.	Rating Pts.
Steve Young, S.F.	8	1506	908	60.3	11877	7.89	76	5.0	42	2.8	90.4
Mark Rypien, Wash.	5	1888	1078	57.1	14414	7.63	97	5.1	65	3.4	84.3
Ken O'Brien, G.B.	9	3465	2039	58.8	24386	7.04	124	3.6	95	2.7	81.0
Randall Cunningham, Phil.	8	2641	1464	55.4	18193	6.89	126	4.8	82	3.1	79.9
Jim Everett, Rams	7	3003	1712	57.0	22106	7.36	134	4.5	111	3.7	79.7
Bobby Hebert, Atl.	7	2055	1202	58.5	14630	7.12	85	4.1	75	3.6	79.1
Jim McMahon, Minn.	11	2194	1265	57.7	15916	7.25	90	4.1	79	3.6	79.0
Phil Simms, N.Y.G.	13	4247	2329	54.8	30424	7.16	184	4.3	148	3.5	77.6
Wade Wilson, N.O.	11	1828	1040	56.9	13501	7.39	79	4.3	79	4.3	76.7
Troy Aikman, Dall.	4	1528	920	60.2	10527	6.89	54	3.5	60	3.9	76.4
Chris Miller, Atl.	6	2023	1097	54.2	13721	6.78	86	4.3	69	3.4	75.5
Jim Harbaugh, Chi.	6	1434	823	57.4	9565	6.67	43	3.0	45	3.1	74.6
Steve DeBerg, T.B.	15	4738	2708	57.2	32165	6.79	186	3.9	193	4.1	74.1
Rich Gannon, Minn.	5	1003	561	55.9	6457	6.44	40	4.0	36	3.6	73.9
Don Majkowski, G.B.	6	1607	889	55.3	10870	6.76	56	3.5	56	3.5	73.5
Mike Pagel, Rams	11	1500	753	50.2	9391	6.26	49	3.3	62	4.1	63.7

TOP ACTIVE RUSHERS, NFC

2,000 or more yards

	Yrs.	Att.	Yards	TD
1. Ottis Anderson, N.Y.G.	16	2562	10273	81
2. Roger Craig, Minn.	10	1953	8070	55
3. Herschel Walker, Phil.	9	1620	6722	54
4. Earnest Byner, Wash.	9	1639	6558	47
5. Barry Sanders, Det.	4	1189	5674	52
6. Neal Anderson, Chi.	7	1313	5520	47
7. Emmitt Smith, Dall.	3	979	4213	41
8. Dalton Hilliard, N.O.	7	1076	3999	37
9. Randall Cunningham, Phil.	8	573	3986	28
10. James Jones, Det.	10	1010	3626	26
Other Leading Rushers				
Gary Anderson, T.B.	7	841	3353	16
John Stephens, G.B.	5	891	3249	17
Keith Byars, Phil.	7	750	2672	17
Rodney Hampton, N.Y.G.	3	622	2655	26
Reggie Cobb, T.B.	3	657	2403	18
Cleveland Gary, Rams	4	588	2341	23
Steve Young, S.F.	8	362	2269	18
Brad Muster, N.O.	5	455	2014	20

TOP ACTIVE PASS RECEIVERS, NFC

275 or more receptions

	Yrs.	No.	Yards	TD
1. Art Monk, Wash.	13	847	11628	63
2. Jerry Rice, S.F.	8	610	10273	103
3. Drew Hill, Atl.	13	600	9447	60
4. Roy Green, Phil.	14	559	8965	66
5. Mark Clayton, G.B.	10	550	8643	81
6. Gary Clark, Phx.	8	549	8742	58
7. Roger Craig, Minn.	10	547	4742	16
8. Henry Ellard, Rams	10	532	8816	46
9. Eric Martin, N.O.	8	466	6904	45
10. Steve Jordan, Minn.	11	439	5742	27
Other Leading Receivers				
Anthony Carter, Minn.	8	418	6861	47
Sterling Sharpe, G.B.	5	389	5741	36
Ottis Anderson, N.Y.G.	16	376	3062	5
Keith Byars, Phil.	7	371	3532	13
Earnest Byner, Wash.	9	362	3417	12
Ricky Sanders, Wash.	7	356	5216	32
Herschel Walker, Phil.	9	335	3277	13
Rodney Holman, Det.	11	318	4329	34
James Jones, Det.	10	318	2641	10
Andre Rison, Atl.	4	308	4123	37
Jeff Chadwick, Rams	12	292	4549	27
Mark Bavaro, Phil.	7	291	4037	30
Gary Anderson, T.B.	7	291	2910	14
Tom Rathman, S.F.	7	284	2404	8
Mark Jackson, N.Y.G.	7	276	4746	24

TOP ACTIVE SCORERS, NFC

250 or more points

	Yrs.	TD	FG	PAT	TP
1. Matt Bahr, N.Y.G.	16	0	237	431	1142
2. Eddie Murray, T.B.	15	0	249	394	1141
3. Morten Andersen, N.O.	11	0	246	347	1085
4. Norm Johnson, Atl.	11	0	196	410	998
5. Kevin Butler, Chi.	8	0	172	297	813
6. Tony Zendejas, Rams	8	0	149	260	707
7. Jerry Rice, S.F.	8	108	0	0	648
8. Chip Lohmiller, Wash.	5	0	139	208	625
9. Mike Cofer, S.F.	6	0	113	235	574
10. Fuad Reveiz, Minn.	9	0	102	266	572
Other Leading Scorers					
Roger Ruzek, Phil.	8	0	112	193	529
Ottis Anderson, N.Y.G.	16	86	0	0	516
Mark Clayton, G.B.	10	82	0	0	492
Greg Davis, Phx.	8	0	101	143	446
Roger Craig, Minn.	10	71	0	0	426
Roy Green, Phil.	14	69	0	0	414
Herschel Walker, Phil.	9	68	0	0	408
Neal Anderson, Chi.	7	67	0	0	402
Chris Jacke, G.B.	4	0	85	131	386
Art Monk, Wash.	13	63	0	0	378
Drew Hill, Atl.	13	61	0	0	366
Earnest Byner, Wash.	9	60	0	0	360
Gary Clark, Phx.	8	58	0	0	348
Barry Sanders, Det.	4	57	0	0	342
Henry Ellard, Rams	10	50	0	0	300
Dalton Hilliard, N.O.	7	50	0	0	300
Anthony Carter, Minn.	8	49	0	0	294
Eric Martin, N.O.	8	45	0	0	270
Emmitt Smith, Dall.	3	43	0	0	258
Ken Willis, N.Y.G.	5	0	55	90	255

TOP ACTIVE INTERCEPTORS, NFC

20 or more interceptions

	Yrs.	No.	Yards	TD
1. Darrell Green, Wash.	10	30	266	2
2. Wes Hopkins, Phil.	9	29	241	1
3. Jerry Gray, T.B.	8	28	374	3
Scott Case, Atl.	9	28	252	1
5. Mike Prior, G.B.	7	27	351	1
Bobby Butler, Atl.	12	27	222	1
Tim McKyer, Atl.	7	27	126	1
8. Carl Lee, Minn.	10	26	329	2
9. Eric Allen, Phil.	5	25	220	1
10. Erik McMillan, Phil.	5	22	608	5
Other Leading Interceptors				
Vencie Glenn, Minn.	9	21	349	1
Wilber Marshall, Wash.	9	21	271	3
Tim McDonald, S.F.	6	20	315	1
Dave Duerson, Phx.	10	20	226	0
Cedric Mack, N.O.	12	20	178	0

TOP ACTIVE QUARTERBACK SACKERS, NFC (since 1982)

50 or more sacks

	Yrs.	No.
1. Lawrence Taylor, N.Y.G.	12	126.5
2. Reggie White, G.B.	8	124.0
3. Richard Dent, Chi.	10	112.0
4. Rickey Jackson, N.O.	12	103.5
5. Steve McMichael, Chi.	13	86.5
6. Charles Mann, Wash.	10	81.0
7. Jim Jeffcoat, Dall.	10	80.5
8. Pat Swilling, Det.	7	76.5
9. Chris Doleman, Minn.	8	76.0
10. Tim Harris, Phil.	7	75.0
Other Leading Sackers		
Clyde Simmons, Phil.	7	71.0
Charles Haley, Dall.	7	69.5
Mike Cofer, Det.	10	62.5
Freddie Joe Nunn, Phx.	8	60.0

TOP ACTIVE PUNT RETURNERS, NFC

40 or more punt returns

	Yrs.	No.	Yards	Avg.	TD
1. Mel Gray, Det.	7	137	1654	12.1	3
2. Brian Mitchell, Wash.	3	86	978	11.4	3
3. Henry Ellard, Rams	10	133	1509	11.3	4
4. Vai Sikahema, Phil.	7	259	2894	11.2	4
5. Darrell Green, Wash.	10	50	549	11.0	0
6. David Meggett, N.Y.G.	4	144	1576	10.9	3
7. John Taylor, S.F.	6	138	1461	10.6	2
8. Johnny Bailey, Phx.	3	92	943	10.3	1
9. Darryl Henley, Rams	4	60	571	9.5	0
10. Mark Clayton, G.B.	10	52	485	9.3	1
Other Leading Punt Returners					
Don Griffin, S.F.	7	74	667	9.0	1
Deion Sanders, Atl.	4	91	768	8.4	2
Vince Buck, N.O.	3	70	569	8.1	0
Eric Martin, N.O.	8	46	368	8.0	0
Vernon Turner, Det.	3	51	408	8.0	0

TOP ACTIVE KICKOFF RETURNERS, NFC

40 or more kickoff returns

	Yrs.	No.	Yards	Avg.	TD
1. Mel Gray, Det.	7	236	5686	24.1	2
2. Deion Sanders, Atl.	4	140	3219	23.0	3
Herschel Walker, Phil.	9	65	1492	23.0	1
4. Charles Wilson, T.B.	3	59	1343	22.8	1
5. Roy Green, Phil.	14	89	2002	22.5	1
6. David Meggett, N.Y.G.	4	93	2038	21.9	1
7. Tim McGee, Wash.	7	58	1249	21.5	0
8. Gene Atkins, N.O.	6	71	1508	21.2	0
Vai Sikahema, Phil.	7	205	4354	21.2	0
10. Jamie Holland, G.B.	6	133	2806	21.1	1
Other Leading Kickoff Returners					
Dexter Carter, S.F.	3	80	1677	21.0	1
Joe Johnson, Minn.	5	53	1111	21.0	1
Marc Logan, S.F.	6	85	1760	20.7	1
Brian Mitchell, Wash.	3	70	1440	20.6	0
Johnny Bailey, Phx.	3	67	1364	20.4	0
Alton Montgomery, Atl.	3	61	1240	20.3	0
Drew Hill, Atl.	13	172	3460	20.1	1
Gary Anderson, T.B.	7	128	2547	19.9	1
Allen Pinkett, N.O.	6	80	1577	19.7	0
Vernon Turner, Det.	3	53	1026	19.4	0
Vince Workman, T.B.	4	56	913	16.3	0

TOP ACTIVE PUNTERS, NFC

50 or more punts

	Yrs.	No.	Avg.	LG
1. Sean Landeta, N.Y.G.	8	493	43.4	71
2. Chris Gardocki, Chi.	2	79	42.9	61
3. Rich Camarillo, Phx.	12	781	42.8	76
4. Tommy Barnhardt, N.O.	8	310	42.6	65
5. Harry Newsome, Minn.	8	593	42.4	84
6. Jim Arnold, Det.	10	748	42.3	71
7. Mike Saxon, Dall.	8	591	41.5	64
8. Scott Fulhage, Atl.	6	399	41.4	65
9. Jeff Feagles, Phil.	5	395	40.5	77
10. Bryan Wagner, G.B.	6	330	40.0	71
Other Leading Punters				
Kelly Goodburn, Wash.	8	346	39.9	66
Don Bracken, Rams	7	444	39.9	65
Dan Stryzinski, T.B.	3	213	39.7	63

DRAFT LIST FOR 1993

58th Annual NFL Draft, April 25-26, 1993

Atlanta Falcons (Drafted alternately 10-9-11)

1. Lincoln Kennedy—9, T, Washington
2. Roger Harper—38, DB, Ohio State
3. Harold Alexander—67, P, Appalachian State
4. Choice to Dallas through Green Bay
5. Ron George—121, LB, Stanford
6. Mitch Lyons—151, TE, Michigan State
7. Darnell Walker—178, DB, Oklahoma
8. Shannon Baker—205, WR, Florida State

Buffalo Bills (Drafted 27)

1. Thomas Smith—28, DB, North Carolina
2. John Parrella—55, DT, Nebraska
3. Choice to Cleveland through Atlanta and Denver
4. Russell Copeland—111, WR, Memphis State
5. Mike Devlin—136, C, Iowa, from Philadelphia
   Sebastian Savage—139, DB, North Carolina State
6. Corbin Lacina—167, T, Augustana (S.D.)
7. Willie Harris—195, WR, Mississippi State
8. Chris Luneberg—223, T, West Chester (Pa.)

Chicago Bears (Drafted alternately 7-6-5-8)

1. Curtis Conway—7, WR, Southern California
2. Carl Simpson—35, DT, Florida State
3. Chris Gedney—61, TE, Syracuse
4. Choice to Indianapolis
   Todd Perry—97, G, Kentucky, from Cleveland
   Myron Baker—100, LB, Louisiana Tech, from Indianapolis
   Albert Fontenot—112, DE, Baylor, from Dallas through Green Bay
5. Choice to Green Bay
6. Dave Hoffmann—146, LB, Washington
7. Keshon Johnson—173, DB, Arizona
8. Choice to Seattle

Cincinnati Bengals (Drafted alternately 5-8-7-6)

1. John Copeland—5, DE, Alabama
2. Tony McGee—37, TE, Michigan
3. Steve Tovar—59, LB, Ohio State, from New York Jets
   Ty Parten—63, DT, Arizona
4. Marcello Simmons—90, DB, Southern Methodist
5. Forey Duckett—117, DB, Nevada-Reno
6. Tom Scott—148, T, East Carolina
7. Lance Gunn—175, DB, Texas
8. Doug Pelfrey—202, K, Kentucky

Cleveland Browns (Drafted alternately 12-13)

1. Choice to Denver
   Steve Everitt—14, C, Michigan, from Denver
2. Dan Footman—42, DE, Florida State
3. Choice to Detroit
   Mike Caldwell—83, LB, Middle Tennessee State, from Buffalo through Atlanta and Denver
4. Choice to Chicago
5. Herman Arvie—124, T, Grambling
6. Rich McKenzie—153, LB, Penn State
7. Travis Hill—180, LB, Nebraska
8. Choice to Los Angeles Rams

Dallas Cowboys (Drafted 28)

1. Choice to Green Bay
2. Kevin Williams—46, WR, Miami, from Green Bay
   Darrin Smith—54, LB, Miami, from San Francisco through Green Bay
3. Choice to Los Angeles Raiders through San Francisco
   Mike Middleton—84, DB, Indiana
4. Derrick Lassic—94, RB, Alabama, from Atlanta through Green Bay
   Ron Stone—96, T, Boston College, from Los Angeles Raiders
   Choice to Chicago through Green Bay
5. Choice to Pittsburgh
6. Barry Minter—168, LB, Tulsa
7. Brock Marion—196, DB, Nevada-Reno
8. Dave Thomas—203, DB, Tennessee, from Tampa Bay
   Reggie Givens—213, DB, Penn State, from Green Bay
   Choice to Tampa Bay

Denver Broncos (Drafted 14)

1. Dan Williams—11, DE, Toledo, from Cleveland
   Choice to Cleveland
2. Glyn Milburn—43, RB, Stanford
3. Rondell Jones—69, DB, North Carolina, from Los Angeles Raiders
   Jason Elam—70, P-K, Hawaii
4. Jeff Robinson—98, DE, Idaho
5. Kevin Williams—126, RB, UCLA
6. Melvin Bonner—154, WR, Baylor
7. Clarence Williams—169, TE, Washington State, from New England through Atlanta
   Antonius Kimbrough—182, WR, Jackson State
8. Brian Stablein—210, WR, Ohio State

Detroit Lions (Drafted alternately 8-7-6-5)

1. Choice to New Orleans
2. Ryan McNeil—33, DB, Miami, from New York Jets
   Choice to New York Jets
3. Antonio London—62, LB, Alabama
   Mike Compton—68, C, West Virginia, from Cleveland
4. Choice to New Orleans
5. Choice to New York Jets
6. Greg Jeffries—147, DB, Virginia
7. Ty Hallock—174, LB, Michigan State
8. Kevin Miniefield—201, DB, Arizona State

Green Bay Packers (Drafted alternately 15-17-16)

1. Wayne Simmons—15, LB, Clemson
   George Teague—29, DB, Alabama, from Dallas
2. Choice to Dallas
3. Choice to Los Angeles Raiders
   Earl Dotson—81, T, Texas A&I, from New Orleans through San Francisco and Los Angeles Raiders
4. Choice to San Diego through New England
5. Mark Brunell—118, QB, Washington, from Tampa Bay
   James Willis—119, LB, Auburn, from Chicago
   Choice to New York Jets
6. Doug Evans—141, DB, Louisiana Tech, from Seattle
   Paul Hutchins—152, T, Western Michigan, from Los Angeles Raiders
   Tim Watson—156, DB, Howard
7. Robert Kuberski—183, DE, Navy
8. Choice to Dallas

Houston Oilers (Drafted alternately 19-18)

1. Brad Hopkins—13, T, Illinois, from Philadelphia
   Choice to Philadelphia
2. Micheal Barrow—47, LB, Miami
3. Choice to Philadelphia
4. Travis Hannah—102, WR, Southern California
5. John Henry Mills—131, TE, Wake Forest
6. Chuck Bradley—158, T, Kentucky
7. Patrick Robinson—187, WR, Tennessee State
8. Blaine Bishop—214, DB, Ball State

Indianapolis Colts (Drafted alternately 16-15-17)

1. Sean Dawkins—16, WR, California
2. Choice to Pittsburgh
   Roosevelt Potts—49, RB, Northeast Louisiana, from Pittsburgh
3. Ray Buchanan—65, DB, Louisville, from Los Angeles Rams
   Choice to Los Angeles Rams
4. Derwin Gray—92, DB, Brigham Young, from Chicago
   Choice to Chicago
   Devon McDonald—107, LB, Notre Dame, from San Diego through Pittsburgh
5. Choice to Los Angeles Rams
6. Carlos Etheredge—157, TE, Miami
7. Lance Lewis—184, RB, Nebraska
8. Marquise Thomas—211, LB, Mississippi

Kansas City Chiefs (Drafted alternately 18-19)

1. Choice to Phoenix through San Francisco
2. Choice exercised in 1992 Supplemental Draft
3. Will Shields—74, G, Nebraska
4. Jaime Fields—103, LB, Washington
5. Lindsay Knapp—130, G, Notre Dame
6. Darius Turner—159, RB, Washington
7. Danan Hughes—186, WR, Iowa
8. Choice to Phoenix

Los Angeles Raiders (Drafted alternately 13-12)

1. Patrick Bates—12, DB, Texas A&M
2. Choice to San Diego through San Francisco
3. Billy Joe Hobert—58, QB, Washington, from Dallas through San Francisco
   Choice to Denver
   James Trapp—72, DB, Clemson, from Green Bay
4. Choice to Dallas
5. Olanda Truitt—125, WR, Mississippi State
6. Choice to Green Bay
7. Greg Biekert—181, LB, Colorado
8. Greg Robinson—208, RB, Northeast Louisiana

Los Angeles Rams (Drafted alternately 11-10-9)

1. Jerome Bettis—10, RB, Notre Dame
2. Troy Drayton—39, TE, Penn State
3. Choice to Indianapolis
   Russell White—73, RB, California, from Indianapolis
4. Choice to San Diego
5. Sean LaChapelle—122, WR, UCLA
   Chuck Belin—127, G, Wisconsin, from Indianapolis
6. Deral Boykin—149, DB, Louisville
7. Brad Fichtel—179, C, Eastern Illinois
8. Jeff Buffaloe—206, P, Memphis State
   Maa Tanuvasa—209, DT, Hawaii, from Cleveland

Miami Dolphins (Drafted alternately 24-23-22-21-20)

1. O.J. McDuffie—25, WR, Penn State
2. Choice to New England
3. Terry Kirby—78, RB, Virginia
4. Ronnie Bradford—105, DB, Colorado
5. Chris Gray—132, G, Auburn
6. Robert O'Neal—164, DB, Clemson
7. David Merritt—191, LB, North Carolina State
8. Dwayne Gordon—218, LB, New Hampshire

Minnesota Vikings (Drafted alternately 20-24-23-22-21)

1. Robert Smith—21, RB, Ohio State
2. Qadry Ismail—52, WR, Syracuse
3. John Gerak—57, G, Penn State, from Seattle
   Gilbert Brown—79, DT, Kansas
4. Ashley Sheppard—106, LB, Clemson
5. Everett Lindsay—133, T, Mississippi
6. Choice to Washington
7. Gino Torretta—192, QB, Miami
8. Choice to San Francisco

New England Patriots (Drafted alternately 1-2)

1. Drew Bledsoe—1, QB, Washington State
2. Chris Slade—31, DE, Virginia
   Todd Rucci—51, T, Penn State, from Miami
   Vincent Brisby—56, WR, Northeast Louisiana
4. Kevin Johnson—86, NT, Texas Southern
   Corwin Brown—110, DB, Michigan, from San Francisco through San Diego
5. Scott Sisson—113, K, Georgia Tech
   Richard Griffith—138, TE, Arizona, from San Francisco through San Diego
6. Lawrence Hatch—142, DB, Florida
7. Choice to Denver through Atlanta
8. Troy Brown—198, KR, Marshall

New Orleans Saints (Drafted 25)

1. Willie Roaf—8, T, Louisiana Tech, from Detroit
   Irv Smith—20, TE, Notre Dame, from Phoenix through San Francisco
   Choice to San Francisco
2. Reggie Freeman—53, LB, Florida State
3. Choice to Green Bay through San Francisco and Los Angeles Raiders
4. Lorenzo Neal—89, RB, Fresno State, from Detroit
   Derek Brown—109, RB, Nebraska
5. Tyrone Hughes—137, DB, Nebraska
6. Ronnie Dixon—165, NT, Cincinnati
7. Othello Henderson—193, DB, UCLA
8. Jon Kirksey—221, NT, Cal State-Sacramento

New York Giants (Drafted alternately 9-11-10)

1. Choice exercised in 1992 Supplemental Draft
2. Michael Strahan—40, DE, Texas Southern
3. Marcus Buckley—66, LB, Texas A&M
4. Greg Bishop—93, T, Pacific
5. Tommy Thigpen—123, LB, North Carolina
6. Scott Davis—150, G, Iowa
7. Todd Peterson—177, K, Georgia
8. Jessie Armstead—207, LB, Miami

New York Jets (Drafted alternately 3-4)

1. Choice to Phoenix
   Marvin Jones—4, LB, Florida State, from Phoenix
2. Choice to Detroit
   Coleman Rudolph—36, DE, Georgia Tech, from Detroit
3. Choice to Cincinnati
4. David Ware—88, T, Virginia
5. Fred Baxter—115, TE, Auburn
   Adrian Murrell—120, RB, West Virginia, from Detroit
   Kenny Shedd—129, WR, Northern Iowa, from Green Bay
6. Richie Anderson—144, RB, Penn State
7. Alec Millen—171, T, Georgia
8. Craig Hentrich—200, K, Notre Dame

Philadelphia Eagles (Drafted alternately 23-22-21-20-24)

*1. Choice to Houston
   Lester Holmes—19, T, Jackson State, from Houston
   Leonard Renfro—24, DT, Colorado
2. Victor Bailey—50, WR, Missouri
3. Derrick Frazier—75, DB, Texas A&M, from Houston
   Mike Reid—77, DB, North Carolina State
4. Choice to Tampa Bay through San Diego
5. Choice to Buffalo
6. Derrick Oden—163, LB, Alabama
7. Joey Mickey—190, TE, Oklahoma
8. Doug Skene—217, T, Michigan

*Compensatory Pick

Phoenix Cardinals (Drafted alternately 4-3)

1. Garrison Hearst—3, RB, Georgia, from New York Jets
   Choice to New York Jets
   Ernest Dye—18, T, South Carolina, from Kansas City through San Francisco
*1. Choice to New Orleans through San Francisco
2. Ben Coleman—32, T, Wake Forest
3. Choice to Tampa Bay
4. Ronald Moore—87, RB, Pittsburg (Kan.)
5. Choice to San Francisco
6. Brett Wallerstedt—143, LB, Arizona State
7. Will White—172, DB, Florida
8. Chad Brown—199, DE, Mississippi
   Steve Anderson—215, WR, Grambling, from Kansas City

*Compensatory Pick

Pittsburgh Steelers (Drafted alternately 22-21-20-24-23)

1. Deon Figures—23, DB, Colorado
2. Chad Brown—44, LB, Colorado, from Indianapolis
   Choice to Indianapolis
3. Andre Hastings—76, WR, Georgia
4. Kevin Henry—108, DE, Mississippi State
5. Lonnie Palelei—135, G, Nevada-Las Vegas
   Marc Woodard—140, LB, Mississippi State, from Dallas
6. Willie Williams—162, DB, Western Carolina
7. Jeff Zgonina—185, DT, Purdue, from Washington
   Craig Keith—189, TE, Lenoir-Rhyne
8. Alex Van Pelt—216, QB, Pittsburgh

San Diego Chargers (Drafted alternately 21-20-24-23-22)

1. Darrien Gordon—22, DB, Stanford
2. Natrone Means—41, RB, North Carolina, from Los Angeles Raiders through San Francisco
   Choice to San Francisco
3. Joe Cocozzo—64, G, Michigan, from Tampa Bay
   Choice to Washington
4. Ray Lee Johnson—95, DE, Arkansas, from Los Angeles Rams
   Lewis Bush—99, LB, Washington State, from Green Bay through New England
   Choice to Indianapolis through Pittsburgh
5. Walter Dunson—134, WR, Middle Tennessee State
6. Eric Castle—161, DB, Oregon
7. Doug Miller—188, LB, South Dakota State
8. Choice to Tampa Bay
   Trent Green—222, QB, Indiana, from San Francisco

San Francisco 49ers (Drafted 26)

1. Dana Stubblefield—26, DT, Kansas, from New Orleans
   Todd Kelly—27, DE, Tennessee
2. Adrian Hardy—48, DB, Northwestern Louisiana, from San Diego
   Choice to Dallas through Green Bay
3. Choice to Tampa Bay through San Diego
4. Choice to New England through San Diego
5. Artie Smith—116, DT, Louisiana Tech, from Phoenix
   Choice to New England through San Diego
6. Chris Dalman—166, G, Stanford
7. Troy Wilson—194, LB, Pittsburg (Kan.)
8. Elvis Grbac—219, QB, Michigan, from Minnesota
   Choice to San Diego

Seattle Seahawks (Drafted alternately 2-1)

1. Rick Mirer—2, QB, Notre Dame
2. Carlton Gray—30, DB, UCLA
3. Choice to Minnesota
4. Dean Wells—85, LB, Kentucky
5. Terrence Warren—114, WR, Hampton
6. Choice to Green Bay
7. Michael McCrary—170, DE, Wake Forest
8. Jeff Blackshear—197, G, Northeast Louisiana
   Antonio Edwards—204, DE, Valdosta State, from Chicago

Tampa Bay Buccaneers (Drafted alternately 6-5-8-7)

1. Eric Curry—6, DE, Alabama
2. Demetrius DuBose—34, LB, Notre Dame
3. Lamar Thomas—60, WR, Miami, from Phoenix
   Choice to San Diego
   John Lynch—82, DB, Stanford, from San Francisco through San Diego
4. Rudy Harris—91, RB, Clemson
   Horace Copeland—104, WR, Miami, from Philadelphia through San Diego
5. Choice to Green Bay
6. Chidi Ahanotu—145, DT, California
7. Tyree Davis—176, WR, Central Arkansas
8. Choice to Dallas
   Darrick Branch—220, WR, Hawaii, from San Diego
   Daron Alcorn—224, K, Akron, from Dallas

Washington Redskins (Drafted alternately 17-16-15)

1. Tom Carter—17, DB, Notre Dame
2. Reggie Brooks—45, RB, Notre Dame
3. Rick Hamilton—71, LB, Central Florida
   Ed Bunn—80, P, Texas-El Paso, from San Diego
4. Sterling Palmer—101, DE, Florida State
5. Greg Huntington—128, C, Penn State
6. Darryl Morrison—155, DB, Arizona
   Frank Wycheck—160, TE, Maryland, from Minnesota
7. Choice to Pittsburgh
8. Lamont Hollinquest—212, LB, Southern California

Active Coaches' Career Records (Order Based on Career Victories)

Start of 1993 Season

Coach	Team(s)	Regular Season Yrs.	Won	Lost	Tied	Pct.	Postseason Won	Lost	Tied	Pct.	Career Won	Lost	Tied	Pct.
Don Shula	Baltimore Colts, Miami Dolphins	30	300	136	6	.686	18	15	0	.545	318	151	6	.676
Chuck Knox	Los Angeles Rams, Buffalo Bills, Seattle Seahawks	20	177	124	1	.588	7	11	0	.389	184	135	1	.577
Dan Reeves	Denver Broncos, New York Giants	12	110	73	1	.604	7	6	0	.538	117	79	1	.597
Marv Levy	Kansas City Chiefs, Buffalo Bills	12	98	77	0	.560	8	5	0	.615	106	82	0	.564
Tom Flores	Oakland-Los Angeles Raiders, Seattle Seahawks	10	85	67	0	.559	8	3	0	.727	93	70	0	.571
Marty Schottenheimer	Cleveland Browns, Kansas City Chiefs	9	83	51	1	.619	3	7	0	.300	86	58	1	.597
Bill Parcells	New York Giants, New England Patriots	8	77	49	1	.610	8	3	0	.727	85	52	1	.620
Jack Pardee	Chicago Bears, Washington Redskins, Houston Oilers	9	74	64	0	.536	1	4	0	.200	75	68	0	.524
Jim Mora	New Orleans Saints	7	69	42	0	.622	0	4	0	.000	69	46	0	.600
Sam Wyche	Cincinnati Bengals, Tampa Bay Buccaneers	9	66	77	0	.462	3	2	0	.600	69	79	0	.466
Jerry Glanville	Houston Oilers, Atlanta Falcons	8	54	59	0	.478	3	4	0	.429	57	63	0	.475
George Seifert	San Francisco 49ers	4	52	12	0	.813	5	2	0	.714	57	14	0	.803
Ted Marchibroda	Baltimore-Indianapolis Colts	6	50	40	0	.556	0	3	0	.000	50	43	0	.538
Art Shell	Los Angeles Raiders	4	35	25	0	.583	1	2	0	.333	36	27	0	.571
Jimmy Johnson	Dallas Cowboys	4	32	32	0	.500	4	1	0	.800	36	33	0	.522
Wayne Fontes	Detroit Lions	4	32	37	0	.464	1	1	0	.500	33	38	0	.465
Rich Kotite	Philadelphia Eagles	2	21	11	0	.656	1	1	0	.500	22	12	0	.647
Bruce Coslet	New York Jets	3	18	30	0	.375	0	1	0	.000	18	31	0	.367
Bill Belichick	Cleveland Browns	2	13	19	0	.406	0	0	0	.000	13	19	0	.406
Joe Bugel	Phoenix Cardinals	3	13	35	0	.271	0	0	0	.000	13	35	0	.271
Bobby Ross	San Diego Chargers	1	11	5	0	.688	1	1	0	.500	12	6	0	.667
Bill Cowher	Pittsburgh Steelers	1	11	5	0	.688	0	1	0	.000	11	6	0	.647
Dennis Green	Minnesota Vikings	1	11	5	0	.688	0	1	0	.000	11	6	0	.647
Mike Holmgren	Green Bay Packers	1	9	7	0	.563	0	0	0	.000	9	7	0	.563
Dave Shula	Cincinnati Bengals	1	5	11	0	.313	0	0	0	.000	5	11	0	.313
Wade Phillips	New Orleans Saints, Denver Broncos	1	1	3	0	.250	0	0	0	.000	1	3	0	.250
Richie Petitbon	Washington Redskins	0	0	0	0	.000	0	0	0	.000	0	0	0	.000
Dave Wannstedt	Chicago Bears	0	0	0	0	.000	0	0	0	.000	0	0	0	.000

Coaches With 100 Career Victories (Order Based on Career Victories)

Start of 1993 Season

Coach	Team(s)	Regular Season Yrs.	Won	Lost	Tied	Pct.	Postseason Won	Lost	Tied	Pct.	Career Won	Lost	Tied	Pct.
George Halas	Chicago Bears	40	318	148	31	.671	6	3	0	.667	324	151	31	.671
Don Shula	Baltimore Colts, Miami Dolphins	30	300	136	6	.686	18	15	0	.545	318	151	6	.676
Tom Landry	Dallas Cowboys	29	250	162	6	.605	20	16	0	.556	270	178	6	.601
Earl (Curly) Lambeau	Green Bay Packers, Chicago Cardinals, Washington Redskins	33	226	132	22	.624	3	2	0	.600	229	134	22	.623
Chuck Noll	Pittsburgh Steelers	23	193	148	1	.566	16	8	0	.667	209	156	1	.572
Chuck Knox	Los Angeles Rams, Buffalo Bills, Seattle Seahawks	20	177	124	1	.588	7	11	0	.389	184	135	1	.577
Paul Brown	Cleveland Browns, Cincinnati Bengals	21	166	100	6	.621	4	8	0	.333	170	108	6	.609
Bud Grant	Minnesota Vikings	18	158	96	5	.620	10	12	0	.455	168	108	5	.607
Steve Owen	New York Giants	23	151	100	17	.595	2	8	0	.200	153	108	17	.581
Joe Gibbs	Washington Redskins	12	124	60	0	.674	16	5	0	.762	140	65	0	.683
Hank Stram	Kansas City Chiefs, New Orleans Saints	17	131	97	10	.571	5	3	0	.625	136	100	10	.573
Weeb Ewbank	Baltimore Colts, New York Jets	20	130	129	7	.502	4	1	0	.800	134	130	7	.507
Sid Gillman	Los Angeles Rams, Los Angeles-San Diego Chargers, Houston Oilers	18	122	99	7	.550	1	5	0	.167	123	104	7	.541
George Allen	Los Angeles Rams, Washington Redskins	12	116	47	5	.705	2	7	0	.222	118	54	5	.681
Don Coryell	St. Louis Cardinals, San Diego Chargers	14	111	83	1	.572	3	6	0	.333	114	89	1	.561
Dan Reeves	Denver Broncos	12	110	73	1	.604	7	6	0	.538	117	79	1	.597
Mike Ditka	Chicago Bears	11	106	62	0	.631	6	6	0	.500	112	68	0	.622
John Madden	Oakland Raiders	10	103	32	7	.750	9	7	0	.563	112	39	7	.731
Ray (Buddy) Parker	Chicago Cardinals, Detroit Lions, Pittsburgh Steelers	15	104	75	9	.577	3	1	0	.750	107	76	9	.581
Marv Levy	Kansas City Chiefs, Buffalo Bills	12	98	77	0	.560	8	5	0	.615	106	82	0	.564
Vince Lombardi	Green Bay Packers, Washington Redskins	10	96	34	6	.728	9	1	0	.900	105	35	6	.740
Bill Walsh	San Francisco 49ers	10	92	59	1	.609	10	4	0	.714	102	63	1	.617

What to Look For in 1993

• **Don Shula,** Miami, enters his thirty-first season as an NFL head coach. Shula, who leads all active coaches with 318 career victories, needs seven victories to become the winningest coach in NFL history. Shula would then surpass George Halas, who recorded 324 career victories during 40 seasons as coach of the Chicago Bears.

• **Derrick Thomas,** Kansas City, has recorded 58 sacks through four NFL seasons. He needs 15 sacks during the 1993 regular season to break Art Still's club career sack record of 72.5.

• **Reggie Cobb,** Tampa Bay, rushed for 1,171 yards on 310 carries in 1992 and became the first Tampa Bay running back since James Wilder (1,300 in 1985) to rush for 1,000 yards. Should Cobb rush for 1,000-or-more yards in 1993, he would become the first Tampa Bay running back to post back-to-back 1,000-yard seasons since Wilder did it in 1984 (1,544) and 1985.

• **Anthony Carter,** Minnesota, has caught 47 touchdown passes during eight NFL seasons. He needs 4 touchdown receptions to surpass Sammy White and become the club's all-time leader for receiving touchdowns.

• **Clay Matthews,** Cleveland, begins his sixteenth NFL season on opening day when the Browns face the Bengals. With one play against the Bengals, Matthews will have seen action in a club-record 217 regular-season games, which will eclipse the club record of 216 he currently shares with Hall of Fame tackle-kicker Lou Groza.

• **Jim Everett,** Los Angeles Rams, has passed for 22,106 yards during his seven-year NFL career. He needs 118 yards to overtake Roman Gabriel (22,223 yards) as the club's all-time leading passer. Everett, who has 134 career touchdown passes, needs 21 to surpass Gabriel's club record of 154.

• **Barry Sanders,** Detroit, has recorded 1,189 carries during his four NFL seasons. He needs 15 more to become the club's all-time leader with 1,204, which would surpass current leader Dexter Bussey.

• **Eric Martin,** New Orleans, is the club's all-time leading receiver with 6,904 yards on 466 catches. Martin, who has caught passes in 89 consecutive games, needs 34 receptions to become the first player in club history to record 500 career receptions.

• **Dalton Hilliard,** New Orleans, is second on the club's all-time rushing list with 3,999 yards. He needs one yard for 4,000 in his career and 269 to surpass George Rogers as the club's career rushing leader.

• **Chip Lohmiller,** Washington, has converted a club-record 198 consecutive extra points during five NFL seasons. He needs 37 more to break the NFL record of 234 held by Tommy Davis. Lohmiller also has a chance to lead the NFC in scoring for the fourth consecutive season. He led the NFC in total points with 131 in 1990, 149 in 1991, and 120 in 1992.

• **Christian Okoye,** Kansas City, has rushed for 4,897 yards during his six NFL seasons. He needs 103 yards to become the first player in club history to record 5,000 career rushing yards.

• **Henry Ellard,** Los Angeles Rams, has 46 career touchdown receptions. He needs eight to surpass Elroy (Crazylegs) Hirsch and become the club's all-time leader with 54.

• **Monte Coleman,** Washington, has played in 185 games during his 14-year NFL career. Should Coleman play in 15 games this season, he would become only the second player in club history to play in 200 games. Former Redskins player Dave Butz is the all-time leader with 203.

• **Art Monk,** Washington, begins his fourteenth NFL season as the league's all-time leading receiver with 847 catches. Monk, who has caught at least one pass in 148 consecutive games, needs one reception in his next three regular-season games for second-place on the all-time consecutive game receptions list ahead of former Cleveland Browns tight end Ozzie Newsome (150).

• **Steve Young,** San Francisco, completed 268 of 402 passes for 3,465 yards, with 25 touchdowns and 7 interceptions for a passer rating of 107.0 in 1992. It marked the second consecutive season that Young had achieved a passer rating greater than 100 (101.8 in 1991). Young, who has 908 career NFL completions, needs 92 to reach 1,000 for his career.

• **Steve McMichael,** Chicago, is a veteran of 13 NFL seasons and 181 games. McMichael needs to play in 10 games to become the club's all-time leader for most games played with 191.

• **Dan Marino,** Miami, has passed for 39,502 yards during his 10 NFL seasons. Marino needs 498 yards to become only the fourth quarterback in NFL history to pass for 40,000 yards. The others are Fran Tarkenton (47,003), Dan Fouts (43,040), and Johnny Unitas (40,239).

• Marino (290) also needs 10 touchdown passes to become only the second player in NFL history to reach 300 touchdown passes during an NFL career. Fran Tarkenton threw 342 scoring strikes during his 18-year NFL career.

• Marino's 17 games with at least 4 touchdown passes tie for the NFL lead with Johnny Unitas. Marino's next 4 touchdown-pass performance will make him the NFL's all-time leader in that category.

• **Darrell Green,** Washington, has intercepted 30 passes during his 10 NFL seasons. Green needs seven more interceptions to become the club's all-time leader, surpassing current leader Brig Owens, who had 36 career interceptions.

• **Andre Tippett,** New England, has 91.5 sacks during his 10-year career. He needs 8.5 sacks to become the first player in club history to record 100.

• **Gary Clark,** Phoenix, has 549 receptions during his eight NFL seasons. Should Clark catch at least 50 passes during the 1993 season, he will have recorded nine consecutive seasons with 50-or-more receptions.

• **Bernie Kosar,** Cleveland, has 21,097 career passing yards. He needs 2,617 to surpass Brian Sipe for the top spot on the Browns' all-time passing list. Kosar (1,774 completions and 3,012 attempts) needs 171 completions and 428 attempts to surpass Sipe for first place in those categories.

• **Joe Montana,** Kansas City, has completed 2,929 passes during his 13 NFL seasons. Montana needs 71 completions to become only the fourth player in NFL history to complete 3,000 passes in a career. The others are Fran Tarkenton (3,686), Dan Fouts (3,297), and Dan Marino (3,128).

• **Dave Krieg,** Kansas City, has passed for 29,247 career yards. He needs 753 to become only the sixteenth quarterback in NFL history to throw for 30,000 career yards. Krieg, who has 2,326 career completions, needs 174 to become just the ninth quarterback in league history to complete 2,500 passes.

• **Vance Johnson,** Denver, has 367 career receptions and needs 33 to become only the second player in club history to record 400 receptions.

• **Eric Dickerson,** Los Angeles Raiders, has rushed for 13,168 yards during his 10 NFL seasons. Dickerson needs 832 yards to become only the second running back in league history to record 14,000 rushing yards. Dickerson, who has scored 96 career touchdowns, needs 4 to become the ninth player in league history to record at least 100 touchdowns.

• **Simon Fletcher,** Denver, enters the 1993 season with 72 career sacks and needs two to surpass Rulon Jones (73.5) as the club's all-time leader.

• **Chris Doleman,** Minnesota, has forced 27 fumbles during his eight-year career. He needs two more to eclipse the club record of 28 set by Hall of Fame defensive tackle Alan Page.

THE AFC

BUFFALO BILLS

American Football Conference Eastern Division

Team Colors: Royal Blue, Scarlet Red, and White

One Bills Drive
Orchard Park, New York 14127
Telephone: (716) 648-1800

Club Officials

President: Ralph C. Wilson
Exec. VP/General Manager: John Butler
VP-Administration: Jerry Foran
Corporate VP: Linda Bogdan
VP/Head Coach: Marv Levy
Treasurer: Jeffrey C. Littmann
Asst. G. M./Business Operations: Bill Munson
Director of Business Operations: Jim Overdorf
Director of Marketing: John Livsey
Director of Merchandising: Christy Wilson Hofmann
Director of Player Personnel: Dwight Adams
Director of Pro Personnel: A.J. Smith
Director of Public/Community Relations: Denny Lynch
Director of Media Relations: Scott Berchtold
Director of Stadium Operations: George Koch
Director of Security: Bill Bambach
Ticket Director: June Foran
Equipment Manager: Dave Hojnowski
Strength/Conditioning Coordinator: Rusty Jones
Trainers: Ed Abramoski, Bud Carpenter, Bill Ford
Video Director: Henry Kunttu

Stadium: Rich Stadium • **Capacity:** 80,290
One Bills Drive
Orchard Park, New York 14127

Playing Surface: AstroTurf

Training Camp: Fredonia State University
Fredonia, New York 14063

1993 Schedule

Preseason

July 30	at Detroit	7:30
Aug. 7	vs. Minnesota at Berlin	1:00
Aug. 12	at Kansas City	7:00
Aug. 21	vs. Tampa Bay at Orlando, Fla.	7:00
Aug. 27	**Atlanta**	7:30

Regular Season

Sept. 5	**New England**	1:00
Sept. 12	at Dallas	3:00
Sept. 19	**Open Date**	
Sept. 26	**Miami**	1:00
Oct. 3	**New York Giants**	8:00
Oct. 11	**Houston** (Monday)	9:00
Oct. 17	**Open Date**	
Oct. 24	at New York Jets	1:00
Nov. 1	**Washington** (Monday)	9:00
Nov. 7	at New England	1:00
Nov. 15	at Pittsburgh (Monday)	9:00
Nov. 21	**Indianapolis**	1:00
Nov. 28	at Kansas City	3:00
Dec. 5	**Los Angeles Raiders**	1:00
Dec. 12	at Philadelphia	1:00
Dec. 19	at Miami	1:00
Dec. 26	**New York Jets**	1:00
Jan. 2	at Indianapolis	1:00

Bills Coaching History

(233-264-8)

1960-61	Buster Ramsey	11-16-1
1962-65	Lou Saban	38-18-3
1966-68	Joe Collier*	13-17-1
1968	Harvey Johnson	1-10-1
1969-70	John Rauch	7-20-1
1971	Harvey Johnson	1-13-0
1972-76	Lou Saban**	32-29-1
1976-77	Jim Ringo	3-20-0
1978-82	Chuck Knox	38-38-0
1983-85	Kay Stephenson***	10-26-0
1985-86	Hank Bullough****	4-17-0
1986-92	Marv Levy	75-40-0

*Released after two games in 1968
**Resigned after five games in 1976
***Released after four games in 1985
****Released after nine games in 1986

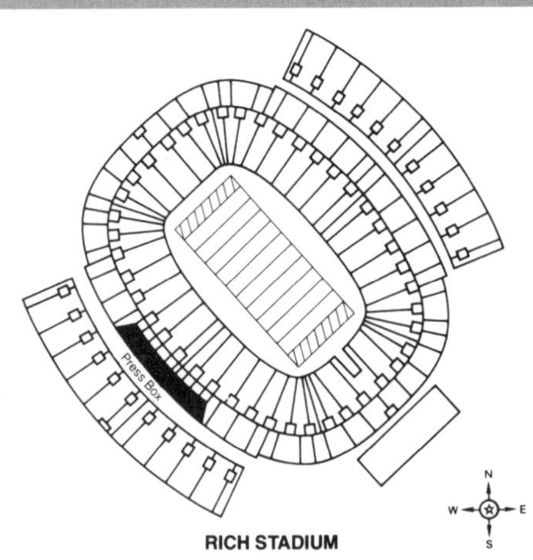

RICH STADIUM

Record Holders

Individual Records — Career

Category	Name	Performance
Rushing (Yds.)	O.J. Simpson, 1969-1977	10,183
Passing (Yds.)	Joe Ferguson, 1973-1984	27,590
Passing (TDs)	Joe Ferguson, 1973-1984	181
Receiving (No.)	Andre Reed, 1985-1992	534
Receiving (Yds.)	Andre Reed, 1985-1992	7,379
Interceptions	George (Butch) Byrd, 1964-1970	40
Punting (Avg.)	Paul Maguire, 1964-1970	42.1
Punt Return (Avg.)	Keith Moody, 1976-79	10.5
Kickoff Return (Avg.)	Wallace Francis, 1973-74	27.2
Field Goals	Scott Norwood, 1985-1991	133
Touchdowns (Tot.)	O.J. Simpson, 1969-1977	70
Points	Scott Norwood, 1985-1991	670

Individual Records — Single Season

Category	Name	Performance
Rushing (Yds.)	O.J. Simpson, 1973	2,003
Passing (Yds.)	Jim Kelly, 1991	3,844
Passing (TDs)	Jim Kelly, 1991	33
Receiving (No.)	Andre Reed, 1989	88
Receiving (Yds.)	Andre Reed, 1989	1,312
Interceptions	Billy Atkins, 1961	10
	Tom Janik, 1967	10
Punting (Avg.)	Billy Atkins, 1961	44.5
Punt Return (Avg.)	Keith Moody, 1977	13.1
Kickoff Return (Avg.)	Ed Rutkowski, 1963	30.2
Field Goals	Scott Norwood, 1988	32
Touchdowns (Tot.)	O.J. Simpson, 1975	23
Points	O.J. Simpson, 1975	138

Individual Records — Single Game

Category	Name	Performance
Rushing (Yds.)	O.J. Simpson, 11-25-76	273
Passing (Yds.)	Joe Ferguson, 10-9-83	419
Passing (TDs)	Jim Kelly, 9-8-91	6
Receiving (No.)	Greg Bell, 9-8-85	13
	Andre Reed, 9-18-89	13
	Thurman Thomas, 9-15-91	13
Receiving (Yds.)	Jerry Butler, 9-23-79	255
Interceptions	Many Times	3
	Last time by Jeff Nixon, 9-7-80	
Field Goals	Pete Gogolak, 12-5-65	5
	Scott Norwood, 9-25-88	5
Touchdowns (Tot.)	Cookie Gilchrist, 12-8-63	5
Points	Cookie Gilchrist, 12-8-63	30

1992 Team Record

Preseason (2-2)

Date	Result		Opponents
8/8	L	3-24	at Minnesota
8/17	W	30-24	Detroit
8/24	L	0-35	at Kansas City
8/28	W	27-21	at Atlanta

Regular Season (11-5)

Date	Result		Opponents	Att.
9/6	W	40- 7	L.A. Rams	78,851
9/13	W	34-31	at San Francisco	65,401
9/20	W	38- 0	Indianapolis	78,997
9/27	W	41- 7	at New England	58,925
10/4	L	10-37	Miami	78,998
10/11	L	3-20	at L.A. Raiders	50,548
10/26	W	24-20	at N.Y. Jets	75,925
11/1	W	16- 7	New England	78,840
11/8	W	28-20	Pittsburgh	78,870
11/16	W	26-20	at Miami	71,274
11/22	W	41-14	Atlanta	78,983
11/29	L	13-16	at Indianapolis (OT)	47,483
12/6	L	17-24	N.Y. Jets	78,752
12/12	W	27- 7	Denver	78,687
12/20	W	20-16	at New Orleans	67,636
12/27	L	3-27	at Houston	62,803

(OT) Overtime

Postseason (3-1)

Date	Result		Opponent	Att.
1/3	W	41-38	Houston (OT)	75,141
1/9	W	24- 3	at Pittsburgh	60,407
1/17	W	29-10	at Miami	72,703
1/31	L	17-52	Dallas	98,374

Score by Periods

Bills	77	118	105	81	8	—	381
Opponents	46	101	72	61	3	—	283

Attendance

Home 630,978 Away 499,995 Total 1,130,973
Single-game home record, 80,366 (9-29-91)
Single-season home record, 635,899 (1991)*
*NFL record

1992 Team Statistics

	Bills	Opp.
Total First Downs	350	278
Rushing	133	77
Passing	192	185
Penalty	25	16
Third Down: Made/Att.	80/202	84/218
Third Down: Pct.	39.6	38.5
Fourth Down: Made/Att.	4/10	7/14
Fourth Down: Pct.	40.0	50.0
Total Net Yards	5893	4604
Avg. Per Game	368.3	287.8
Total Plays	1087	991
Avg. Per Play	5.4	4.6
Net Yards Rushing	2436	1395
Avg. Per Game	152.3	87.2
Total Rushes	549	427
Net Yards Passing	3457	3209
Avg. Per Game	216.1	200.6
Sacked/Yards Lost	29/221	44/351
Gross Yards	3678	3560
Att./Completions	509/293	520/305
Completion Pct.	57.6	58.7
Had Intercepted	21	23
Punts/Avg.	60/42.2	79/43.9
Net Punting Avg.	60/36.8	79/36.5
Penalties/Yards Lost	103/775	118/933
Fumbles/Ball Lost	31/17	29/12
Touchdowns	44	31
Rushing	18	8
Passing	23	19
Returns	3	4
Avg. Time of Possession	28:10	31:50

1992 Individual Statistics

Scoring	TD R	TD P	TD Rt	PAT	FG	Saf	TP
Christie	0	0	0	43/44	24/30	0	115
T. Thomas	9	3	0	0/0	0/0	0	72
K. Davis	6	0	0	0/0	0/0	0	36
Lofton	0	6	0	0/0	0/0	0	36
Metzelaars	0	6	0	0/0	0/0	0	36
Reed	0	3	0	0/0	0/0	0	18
Beebe	0	2	0	0/0	0/0	0	12
Frerotte	0	2	0	0/0	0/0	0	12
Gardner	2	0	0	0/0	0/0	0	12
Jones	0	0	2	0/0	0/0	0	12
Fina	0	1	0	0/0	0/0	0	6
Kelly	1	0	0	0/0	0/0	0	6
Lodish	0	0	1	0/0	0/0	0	6
Hale	0	0	0	0/0	0/0	1	2
Bills	18	23	3	43/44	24/30	1	381
Opponents	8	19	4	31/31	22/30	0	283

Passing	Att.	Comp.	Yds.	Pct.	TD	Int.	Tkld.	Rate
Kelly	462	269	3457	58.2	23	19	20/145	81.2
Reich	47	24	221	51.1	0	2	9/76	46.5
Bills	509	293	3678	57.6	23	21	29/221	78.0
Opponents	520	305	3560	58.7	19	23	44/351	73.2

Rushing	Att.	Yds.	Avg.	LG	TD
T. Thomas	312	1487	4.8	44	9
K. Davis	139	613	4.4	64t	6
Gardner	40	166	4.2	19	2
Reed	8	65	8.1	24	0
Kelly	31	53	1.7	10	1
Fuller	6	39	6.5	15	0
Mohr	1	11	11.0	11	0
Tasker	1	9	9.0	9	0
Edwards	1	8	8.0	8	0
Beebe	1	−6	−6.0	−6	0
Reich	9	−9	−1.0	0	0
Bills	549	2436	4.4	64t	18
Opponents	427	1395	3.3	29	8

Receiving	No.	Yds.	Avg.	LG	TD
Reed	65	913	14.0	51	3
T. Thomas	58	626	10.8	43	3
Lofton	51	786	15.4	50	6
Beebe	33	554	16.8	65t	2
Metzelaars	30	298	9.9	53t	6
K. Davis	15	80	5.3	22	0
McKeller	14	110	7.9	26	0
Lamb	7	139	19.9	53	0
Gardner	7	67	9.6	17	0
Awalt	4	34	8.5	10	0
Edwards	2	25	12.5	20	0
Tasker	2	24	12.0	17	0
Fuller	2	17	8.5	17	0
Frerotte	2	4	2.0	2t	2
Fina	1	1	1.0	1t	1
Bills	293	3678	12.6	65t	23
Opponents	305	3560	11.7	57	19

Interceptions	No.	Yds.	Avg.	LG	TD
Jones	8	263	32.9	82t	2
Kelso	7	21	3.0	13	0
Odomes	5	19	3.8	10	0
Williams	2	15	7.5	15	0
Conlan	1	7	7.0	7	0
Bills	23	325	14.1	82t	2
Opponents	21	423	20.1	103t	2

Punting	No.	Yds.	Avg.	In 20	LG
Mohr	60	2531	42.2	12	61
Bills	60	2531	42.2	12	61
Opponents	79	3465	43.9	20	62

Punt Returns	No.	FC	Yds.	Avg.	LG	TD
Hicks	29	6	289	10.0	42	0
Hale	14	2	175	12.5	27	0
Bills	43	8	464	10.8	42	0
Opponents	22	18	185	8.4	17	0

Kickoff Returns	No.	Yds.	Avg.	LG	TD
K. Davis	14	251	17.9	35	0
Edwards	12	274	22.8	34	0
Frerotte	1	0	0.0	0	0
Fuller	8	134	16.8	28	0
Hicks	1	5	5.0	5	0
Lamb	5	97	19.4	31	0
Bills	41	761	18.6	35	0
Opponents	60	1215	20.3	75t	1

Sacks	No.
Smith	14.0
Hansen	8.0
Wright	6.0
Bennett	4.0
Talley	4.0
Conlan	2.0
M. Patton	2.0
Bailey	1.0
Hicks	1.0
Odomes	1.0
Pike	1.0
Bills	44.0
Opponents	29.0

1993 Draft Choices

Round	Name	Pos.	College
1.	Thomas Smith	DB	North Carolina
2.	John Parrella	DT	Nebraska
4.	Russell Copeland	WR	Memphis State
5.	Mike Devlin	C	Iowa
	Sebastian Savage	DB	North Carolina St.
6.	Corbin Lacina	T	Augustana (S.D.)
7.	Willie Harris	WR	Mississippi State
8.	Chris Luneberg	T	West Chester (Pa.)

Buffalo Bills 1993 Veteran Roster

No.	Name	Pos.	Ht.	Wt.	Birth-date	NFL Exp.	College	Hometown	How Acq.	'92 Games/ Starts
86	Awalt, Rob	TE	6-5	242	4/9/64	7	San Diego State	Sacramento, Calif.	FA-'92	14/1
75	Ballard, Howard	T	6-6	330	11/3/63	6	Alabama A&M	Ashland, Ala.	D11-'87	16/16
77	Barnett, Oliver	DE	6-3	292	4/9/66	4	Kentucky	Louisville, Ky.	RFA(Atl)-'93	16/7*
82	Beebe, Don	WR	5-11	180	12/18/64	5	Chadron State	Sugar Grove, Ill.	D3-'89	12/8
97	Bennett, Cornelius	LB	6-2	238	8/25/66	7	Alabama	Birmingham, Ala.	T(Ind)-'87	15/15
80	Brooks, Bill	WR	6-0	189	4/6/64	8	Boston University	Framingham, Mass.	UFA(Ind)-'93	14/10*
2	Christie, Steve	K	6-0	185	11/13/67	4	William & Mary	Oakville, Canada	PB(TB)-'92	16/0
66	Crafts, Jerry	T	6-6	351	1/6/68	2	Louisville	Tulsa, Okla.	FA-'92	6/0
43	Darby, Matt	S	6-1	200	11/19/68	2	UCLA	Virginia Beach, Va.	D5-'92	16/1
65	Davis, John	G	6-4	310	8/22/65	7	Georgia Tech	Ellijay, Ga.	PB(Hou)-'89	9/0
23	Davis, Kenneth	RB	5-10	208	4/16/62	8	Texas Christian	Temple, Tex.	PB(GB)-'89	16/0
85	Edwards, Al	WR	5-8	173	5/18/67	4	Northwestern Louisiana	Kenner, La.	D11-'90	7/0
70	Fina, John	T-G	6-4	285	3/11/69	2	Arizona	Tucson, Ariz.	D1-'92	16/0
33	Fuller, Eddie	RB	5-9	198	6/22/68	4	Louisiana State	Leesville, La.	D4-'90	14/3
35	Gardner, Carwell	RB	6-2	244	11/27/66	4	Louisville	Louisville, Ky.	D2-'90	16/8
7	Gilbert, Gale	QB	6-3	210	12/20/61	8	California	Red Bluff, Calif.	FA-'89	0*
50	Goganious, Keith	LB	6-2	239	12/7/68	2	Penn State	Virginia Beach, Va.	D3-'92	13/0
26	†Hale, Chris	CB	5-7	179	1/4/66	5	Southern California	Monrovia, Calif.	D7b-'89	14/0
90	Hansen, Phil	DE	6-5	278	6/20/68	3	North Dakota State	Ellendale, N.D.	D2-'91	16/16
52	Harvey, Richard	LB	6-1	242	9/11/66	4	Tulane	Pascagoula, Miss.	FA-'92	12/0
67	Hull, Kent	C	6-5	284	1/13/61	8	Mississippi State	Greenwood, Miss.	FA-'86	16/16
47	Jackson, Kirby	CB	5-10	180	2/2/65	7	Mississippi State	Sturgis, Miss.	FA-'87	15/10
20	Jones, Henry	S	5-11	197	12/29/67	3	Illinois	St. Louis, Mo.	D1-'91	16/16
12	Kelly, Jim	QB	6-3	226	2/14/60	8	Miami	East Brady, Pa.	D1b-'83	16/16
38	Kelso, Mark	S	5-11	180	7/23/63	8	William & Mary	Pittsburgh, Pa.	FA-'86	16/16
81	Lamb, Brad	WR	5-10	177	10/7/67	3	Anderson, Ind.	Middletown, Ohio	D8-'91	7/0
63	Lingner, Adam	C	6-4	268	11/2/60	11	Illinois	Rock Island, Ill.	PB(KC)-'89	16/0
73	Lodish, Mike	NT	6-3	280	8/11/67	4	UCLA	Birmingham, Mich.	D10-'90	16/0
55	Maddox, Mark	LB	6-1	233	3/23/68	3	Northern Michigan	Milwaukee, Wis.	D9-'91	15/1
84	McKeller, Keith	TE	6-4	242	7/9/64	7	Jacksonville State	Fairfield, Ala.	D9-'87	11/8
88	Metzelaars, Pete	TE	6-7	254	5/24/60	12	Wabash	Portage, Mich.	T(Sea)-'85	16/7
9	Mohr, Chris	P	6-5	215	5/11/66	4	Alabama	Thomson, Ga.	FA-'91	15/0
60	Myslinski, Tom	G	6-2	295	12/7/68	2	Tennessee	Rome, N.Y.	FA-'92	1/0*
37	Odomes, Nate	CB	5-10	188	8/25/65	7	Wisconsin	Columbus, Ga.	D2a-'87	16/16
74	†Parker, Glenn	G-T	6-5	305	4/22/66	4	Arizona	Huntington Beach, Calif.	D3-'90	13/13
44	Paterra, Greg	RB	5-11	224	5/11/67	3	Slippery Rock	McKeesport, Pa.	FA-'91	0*
99	Patton, James	DE-NT	6-3	287	1/5/70	2	Texas	Houston, Tex.	D2-'92	0*
53	Patton, Marvcus	LB	6-2	243	5/1/67	4	UCLA	Lawndale, Calif.	D8-'90	16/4
94	Pike, Mark	DE	6-4	272	12/27/63	8	Georgia Tech	Villa Hills, Ky.	D7b-'86	16/0
83	Reed, Andre	WR	6-2	190	1/29/64	9	Kutztown	Allentown, Pa.	D4c-'85	16/16
14	Reich, Frank	QB	6-4	205	12/4/61	9	Maryland	Lebanon, Pa.	D3a-'85	16/0
51	Ritcher, Jim	G	6-3	273	5/21/58	14	North Carolina State	Medina, Ohio	D1-'80	16/16
58	Sanders, Glenell	LB	6-0	235	11/4/66	2	Louisiana Tech	Clinton, La.	FA-'93	0*
24	Schulz, Kurt	S	6-1	208	12/12/68	2	Eastern Washington	Yakima, Wash.	D7-'92	8/1
78	Smith, Bruce	DE	6-4	273	6/18/63	9	Virginia Tech	Norfolk, Va.	D1a-'85	15/15
56	Talley, Darryl	LB	6-4	235	7/10/60	11	West Virginia	Cleveland, Ohio	D2-'83	16/16
89	Tasker, Steve	WR	5-9	181	4/10/62	9	Northwestern	Leoti, Kan.	W(Hou)-'86	15/2
87	Thomas, Ed	TE	6-3	251	5/4/66	4	Houston	New Orleans, La.	PB(TB)-'92	0*
34	Thomas, Thurman	RB	5-10	198	5/16/66	6	Oklahoma State	Missouri City, Tex.	D2-'88	16/16
21	Turner, Nate	RB	6-1	255	5/28/69	2	Nebraska	Chicago, Ill.	D6-'92	0*
25	Washington, Mickey	CB	5-9	191	7/8/68	3	Texas A&M	Beaumont, Tex.	FA-'93	0*
29	Williams, James	CB	5-10	186	3/30/67	4	Fresno State	Coalinga, Calif.	D1-'90	15/8
93	Willis, Keith	DE	6-1	263	7/29/59	12	Northeastern	Newark, N.J.	FA-'92	12/1
22	Wren, Darryl	CB	6-0	188	1/25/67	3	Pittsburg State, Kan.	Tulsa, Okla.	D3-'91	0*
91	Wright, Jeff	NT	6-3	274	6/13/63	6	Central Missouri State	Lawrence, Kan.	D8b-'88	16/16

* Barnett played 16 games with Atlanta in '92; Brooks played 14 games with Indianapolis; Gilbert was active for 2 games but did not play; Myslinski played 1 game with Washington; Paterra, J. Patton, Sanders, E. Thomas, Turner, and Wren missed '92 due to injury; Washington last active with New England in '91.

† Restricted free agent; subject to developments.

Players lost through free agency (6): LB Carlton Bailey (NYG; 16 games in '92), LB Shane Conlan (Rams; 13), G Mitch Frerotte (Sea; 14), CB Clifford Hicks (NYJ; 12), WR James Lofton (Raiders; 16), T Will Wolford (Ind; 16).

Also played with Bills in '92—NT Gary Baldinger (4 games).

COACHING STAFF

Head Coach, Marv Levy

Pro Career: Begins his seventh full season as Bills head coach. Led the Bills to their third consecutive AFC championship in 1992. Under Levy, the Bills recorded 13-3 records in 1990 and 1991, the best regular-season marks in club history. He guided the Bills to their second consecutive AFC East title with a 9-7 record in 1989. Finished 1988 season with a 12-4 record and a berth in the AFC Championship Game. In his first full year with Bills in 1987, he led team to a 7-8 record. Replaced Hank Bullough on November 3, 1986, and compiled a 2-5 record over the final seven weeks of the season. Previously served as head coach of the Kansas City Chiefs from 1978-1982 and produced a 31-42 mark. Levy began his pro coaching career in 1969 as an assistant with the Philadelphia Eagles. He joined George Allen and the Los Angeles Rams as an assistant one year later and followed Allen to Washington, where he remained with the Redskins through the 1972 season when Washington played in Super Bowl VII. He was named head coach of the Montreal Alouettes (CFL) in 1973 and posted a 50-34-4 record and two Grey Cup victories (1974, 1977) in five seasons in Canada. After two seasons away from football, he became head coach of the Chicago Blitz of the USFL in 1984. No pro playing experience. Career NFL record: 106-82.

Background: Running back at Coe College 1948-1950. Coached at high school level for two years before returning to alma mater from 1953-55. Joined New Mexico staff in 1956 and served as head coach there in 1958-59. Head coach at California from 1960-63 before becoming head coach at William & Mary from 1964-68.

Personal: Born August 3, 1928, Chicago, Ill. Levy was Phi Beta Kappa at Coe College and earned master's degree in English history from Harvard. He lives with his wife Mary Frances in Hamburg, N.Y.

Assistant Coaches

Tom Bresnahan, offensive coordinator-offensive line; born January 21, 1935, Springfield, Mass., lives in Hamburg, N.Y. Tackle Holy Cross 1953-55. No pro playing experience. College coach: Williams 1963-67, Columbia 1968-72, Navy 1973-80. Pro coach: Kansas City Chiefs 1981-82, New York Giants 1983-84, St. Louis/Phoenix Cardinals 1986-88, joined Bills in 1989.

Walt Corey, defensive coordinator-linebackers; born May 9, 1938, Latrobe, Pa., lives in West Seneca, N.Y. Defensive end Miami 1957-59. Pro linebacker Kansas City Chiefs 1960-66. College coach: Utah State 1967-69, Miami 1970-71. Pro coach: Kansas City Chiefs 1971-74, 1978-86, Cleveland Browns 1975-77, joined Bills in 1987.

Bruce DeHaven, special teams; born September 6, 1952, Trousdale, Kan., lives in East Aurora, N.Y. No college or pro playing experience. College coach: Kansas 1979-81, New Mexico State 1982. Pro coach: New Jersey Generals (USFL) 1983, Pittsburgh Maulers (USFL) 1984, Orlando Renegades (USFL) 1985, joined Bills in 1987.

Charlie Joiner, receivers; born October 14, 1947, Many, La., lives in Orchard Park, N.Y. Wide receiver Grambling 1965-68. Defensive back-wide receiver Houston Oilers 1969-72, Cincinnati Bengals 1972-75, San Diego Chargers 1976-86. Pro coach: San Diego Chargers 1987-91, joined Bills in 1992.

Rusty Jones, strength and conditioning; born August 14, 1953, Berwick, Maine, lives in Lakeview, N.Y. No college or pro playing experience. College coach: Springfield 1978-79. Pro coach: Pittsburgh Maulers (USFL) 1983-84, joined Bills in 1985.

Buffalo Bills 1993 First-Year Roster

Name	Pos.	Ht.	Wt.	Birth-date	College	Hometown	How Acq.
Bloedorn, Kurt	P	6-5	207	10/20/67	Cal State-Fullerton	Green Bay, Wis.	FA
Brown, Monty	LB	6-0	228	4/13/70	Ferris State	Bridgeport, Conn.	FA
Bryant, Phil	RB	5-10	208	3/27/70	Virginia Tech	Fairfax, Va.	FA
Carthen, Jason	LB	6-3	255	11/16/70	Ohio University	Toledo, Ohio	FA
Copeland, Russ	WR	6-0	200	11/4/71	Memphis State	Tupelo, Miss.	D4
Delvin, Mike	C	6-1	293	11/16/69	Iowa	Marlton, N.J.	D5a
Everett, Malcolm	S	5-10	200	11/16/70	Youngstown State	Lakeland, Fla.	FA
Fieldings, Anthony	LB	6-1	237	7/9/71	Morningside	Eustis, Fla.	FA
Gordon, Bob (1)	WR	5-10	185	7/9/68	Nebraska-Omaha	Papillon, Neb.	FA
Gray, Jim (1)	NT	6-2	277	7/5/69	West Virginia	West Miffin, Pa.	FA
Harris, Willie	WR	6-1	198	11/8/70	Mississippi State	Moss Point, Miss.	D7
Jones, Dean	DE	6-3	274	9/25/70	Morningside	Alvin, Tex.	FA
Jourdain, Yonel	RB	5-11	204	4/20/71	Southern Illinois	Evanston, Ill.	FA
Kratz, Steve	K	6-0	187	12/16/70	Kutztown	Royorsford, Pa.	FA
Lacina, Corbin	G-T	6-4	297	11/2/70	Augustana	Woodbury, Minn.	D6
Love, Sean (1)	G-T	6-3	290	9/6/68	Penn State	Tamaqua, Pa.	FA
Luneberg, Chris	G-T	6-5	290	2/2/70	West Chester	Moorestown, N.J.	D8
O'Brien, Kevin	LB	6-3	230	7/1/70	Bowling Green	Sterling Heights, Mich.	FA
Parrella, John	DE-NT	6-3	296	11/22/69	Nebraska	Topeka, Kan.	D2
Rogers, Matt (1)	QB	6-3	205	1/8/69	Iowa	Walpole, Mass.	D12-'92
Rose, Barry	WR	6-0	185	7/28/68	Wis.-Steven's Point	Baldwin, Wis.	D10-'92
Savage, Sebastian	CB	5-10	189	12/12/69	North Carolina State	Carlisle, S.C.	D5b
Smith, Thomas	CB	5-11	188	12/5/70	North Carolina	Gates, N.C.	D1
Svobodny, Tom	T	6-6	309	4/1/69	Morehead State	Wilmar, Minn.	FA
Walsh, Chris (1)	WR	6-1	185	12/12/68	Stanford	Concord, Calif.	D9-'92
White, David	LB	6-2	235	2/27/70	Nebraska	New Orleans, La.	FA

The term NFL Rookie is defined as a player who is in his first season of professional football and has not been on the roster of another professional football team for any regular-season or postseason games. A Rookie is designated by an "R" on NFL rosters. Players who have been active in another professional football league or players who have NFL experience, including either preseason training camp or being on an Active List or Inactive List, or on Reserve/Injured or Reserve/Physically Unable to Perform for fewer than six regular-season games, are termed NFL First-Year Players. An NFL First-Year Player is designated by a "1" on NFL rosters. Thereafter, a player is credited with an additional year of experience for each season in which he accumulates six games on the Active List or Inactive List, or on Reserve/Injured or Reserve/Physically Unable to Perform.

NOTES

Don Lawrence, offensive quality control-tight ends; born June 4, 1937, Cleveland, Ohio, lives in Orchard Park, N.Y. Offensive-defensive lineman Notre Dame 1957-59. Pro offensive-defensive lineman Washington Redskins 1959-61. College coach: Notre Dame 1961-63, Kansas State 1964-65, Cincinnati 1966, Virginia 1970-73 (head coach 1971-73), Texas Christian 1974-75, Missouri 1976-77. Pro coach: British Columbia Lions (CFL) 1978-79, Kansas City Chiefs 1980-82, 1987-88, Buffalo Bills 1983-84, Tampa Bay Buccaneers 1985-86, Winnipeg Blue Bombers (CFL) 1989, rejoined Bills in 1990.

Chuck Lester, administrative assistant to head coach, assistant linebackers coach; born May 18, 1955, Chicago, Ill., lives in Orchard Park, N.Y. Linebacker Oklahoma 1974. No pro playing experience. College coach: Iowa State 1980-81, Oklahoma 1982-84. Pro coach: Kansas City Chiefs 1984-86 (scout), joined Bills in 1987.

Elijah Pitts, assistant head coach-running backs; born February 3, 1938, Mayflower, Ark., lives in Orchard Park, N.Y. Running back Philander Smith 1957-60. Pro running back Green Bay Packers 1961-69, 1971, Los Angeles Rams 1970, Chicago Bears 1970, New Orleans Saints 1970. Pro coach: Los Angeles Rams 1974-77, Buffalo Bills 1978-80, Houston Oilers 1981-83, Hamilton Tiger-Cats (CFL) 1984, rejoined Bills in 1985.

Dick Roach, defensive backs; born August 23, 1937, Rapid City, S.D., lives in West Seneca, N.Y. Defensive back Black Hills State 1952-55. No pro playing experience. College coach: Montana State 1966-69, Oregon State 1970, Wyoming 1971-72, Fresno State 1973, Washington State 1974-75. Pro coach: Montreal Alouettes (CFL) 1976-77, Kansas City Chiefs 1978-80, New England Patriots 1981, Michigan Panthers (USFL) 1983-84, Tampa Bay Buccaneers 1985-86, joined Bills in 1987.

Dan Sekanovich, defensive line; born July 27, 1933, West Hazelton, Pa., lives in Orchard Park, N.Y. End Tennessee 1951-53. Pro defensive end Montreal Alouettes (CFL) 1954. College coach: Susquehanna 1961-63, Connecticut 1964-67, Pittsburgh 1968, Navy 1969-70, Kentucky 1971-72. Pro coach: Montreal Alouettes (CFL) 1973-76, New York Jets 1977-82, Atlanta Falcons 1983-85, Miami Dolphins 1986-91, joined Bills in 1992.

Jim Shofner, quarterbacks; born December 18, 1935, Grapevine, Tex., lives in Orchard Park, N.Y. Running back Texas Christian 1955-57. Pro defensive back Cleveland Browns 1958-63. College coach: Texas Christian 1964-66, 1974-76 (head coach). Pro coach: San Francisco 49ers 1967-73, 1977, Cleveland Browns 1978-80, 1990-91 (head coach last 7 games in 1990, director of player personnel in 1991), Houston Oilers 1981-82, Dallas Cowboys 1983-85, St. Louis/Phoenix Cardinals 1986-89, joined Bills in 1992.

CINCINNATI BENGALS

American Football Conference Central Division

Team Colors: Black, Orange, and White

200 Riverfront Stadium
Cincinnati, Ohio 45202
Telephone: (513) 621-3550

Club Officials

President: John Sawyer
Vice President/General Manager: Michael Brown
Assistant General Manager, Director of Player Personnel: Pete Brown
Corporate Secretary, Legal Counsel: Katie Brown Blackburn
Scouting: Paul H. Brown
Business Manager: Bill Connelly
Director of Public Relations: Allan Heim
Accountant: Jay Reis
Ticket Manager: Paul Kelly
Consultant: John Murdough, Bill Johnson
Trainer: Paul Sparling
Equipment Manager: Tom Gray
Video Director: Al Davis

Stadium: Riverfront Stadium • **Capacity:** 60,389
200 Riverfront Stadium
Cincinnati, Ohio 45202

Playing Surface: AstroTurf-8

Training Camp: Wilmington College
Wilmington, Ohio 45177

1993 Schedule

Preseason

Aug. 7	**New York Giants**	7:30
Aug. 14	at Indianapolis	7:00
Aug. 20	at Detroit	7:30
Aug. 27	**Philadelphia**	7:30

Regular Season

Sept. 5	at Cleveland	1:00
Sept. 12	**Indianapolis**	1:00
Sept. 19	at Pittsburgh	1:00
Sept. 26	**Seattle**	1:00
Oct. 3	**Open Date**	
Oct. 10	at Kansas City	12:00
Oct. 17	**Cleveland**	1:00
Oct. 24	at Houston	12:00
Oct. 31	**Open Date**	
Nov. 7	**Pittsburgh**	1:00
Nov. 14	**Houston**	1:00
Nov. 21	at New York Jets	1:00
Nov. 28	**Los Angeles Raiders**	1:00
Dec. 5	at San Francisco	5:00
Dec. 12	at New England	1:00
Dec. 19	**Los Angeles Rams**	1:00
Dec. 26	**Atlanta**	1:00
Jan. 2	at New Orleans	3:00

Bengals Coaching History

(184-199-1)

1968-75	Paul Brown	55-59-1
1976-78	Bill Johnson*	18-15-0
1978-79	Homer Rice	8-19-0
1980-83	Forrest Gregg	34-27-0
1984-91	Sam Wyche	64-68-0
1992	Dave Shula	5-11-0

*Resigned after five games in 1978

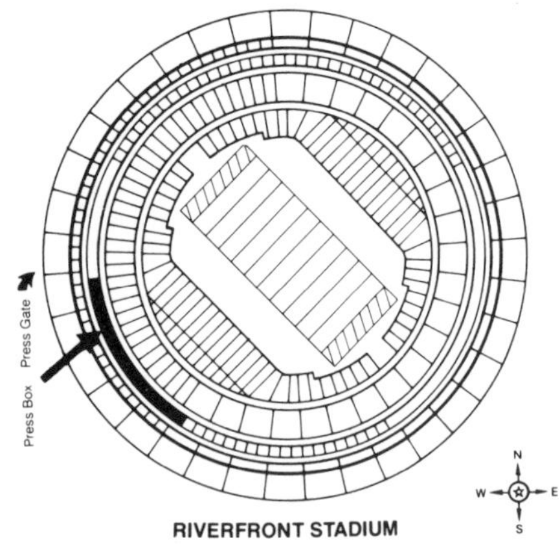

RIVERFRONT STADIUM

Record Holders

Individual Records — Career

Category	Name	Performance
Rushing (Yds.)	James Brooks, 1984-1991	6,393
Passing (Yds.)	Ken Anderson, 1971-1986	32,838
Passing (TDs)	Ken Anderson, 1971-1986	197
Receiving (No.)	Isaac Curtis, 1973-1984	420
Receiving (Yds.)	Isaac Curtis, 1973-1984	7,106
Interceptions	Ken Riley, 1969-1983	63
Punting (Avg.)	Dave Lewis, 1970-73	43.9
Punt Return (Avg.)	Carl Pickens, 1992	12.7
Kickoff Return (Avg.)	Lemar Parrish, 1970-78	24.7
Field Goals	Jim Breech, 1980-1992	203
Touchdowns (Tot.)	Pete Johnson, 1977-1983	70
Points	Jim Breech, 1980-1992	1,059

Individual Records — Single Season

Category	Name	Performance
Rushing (Yds.)	James Brooks, 1989	1,239
Passing (Yds.)	Boomer Esiason, 1986	3,959
Passing (TDs)	Ken Anderson, 1981	29
Receiving (No.)	Dan Ross, 1981	71
Receiving (Yds.)	Eddie Brown, 1988	1,273
Interceptions	Ken Riley, 1976	9
Punting (Avg.)	Dave Lewis, 1970	46.2
Punt Return (Avg.)	Mike Martin, 1984	15.7
Kickoff Return (Avg.)	Lemar Parrish, 1970	30.2
Field Goals	Horst Muhlmann, 1972	27
Touchdowns (Tot.)	Pete Johnson, 1981	16
Points	Jim Breech, 1985	120

Individual Records — Single Game

Category	Name	Performance
Rushing (Yds.)	James Brooks, 12-23-90	201
Passing (Yds.)	Boomer Esiason, 10-7-90	490
Passing (TDs)	Boomer Esiason, 12-21-86	5
Receiving (No.)	Tim McGee, 11-9-89	11
Receiving (Yds.)	Eddie Brown, 11-6-88	216
Interceptions	Many times	3
	Last time by David Fulcher, 12-16-89	
Field Goals	Horst Muhlmann, 11-8-70	5
	Horst Muhlmann, 9-24-72	5
	Jim Breech, 11-1-87	5
Touchdowns (Tot.)	Larry Kinnebrew, 10-28-84	4
Points	Larry Kinnebrew, 10-28-84	24

1992 Team Record

Preseason (2-2)

Date	Result		Opponents
8/9	L	7-13	at N.Y. Giants
8/15	L	17-27	at Philadelphia
8/22	W	20- 0	Indianapolis
8/28	W	34-17	Detroit

Regular Season (5-11)

Date	Result		Opponents	Att.
9/6	W	21- 3	at Seattle	64,601
9/13	W	24-21	L.A. Raiders (OT)	55,551
9/20	L	23-24	at Green Bay	58,500
9/27	L	7-42	Minnesota	55,526
10/11	L	24-38	Houston	59,029
10/19	L	0-38	at Pittsburgh	59,307
10/25	L	10-26	at Houston	61,303
11/1	W	30-26	Cleveland	59,140
11/8	W	31-28	at Chicago (OT)	66,006
11/15	L	14-17	at N.Y. Jets	75,442
11/22	L	13-19	Detroit	58,921
11/29	L	9-21	Pittsburgh	59,123
12/6	L	21-37	at Cleveland	69,609
12/13	L	10-27	at San Diego	48,843
12/20	W	20-10	New England	58,125
12/27	L	17-21	Indianapolis	58,519

(OT) Overtime

Score by Periods

Bengals	48	84	55	81	6	—	274
Opponents	81	98	91	94	0	—	364

Attendance

Home 463,934 Away 503,611 Total 967,545
Single-game home record, 60,284 (10-17-71)
Single-season home record, 473,288 (1990)

1992 Team Statistics

	Bengals	Opp.
Total First Downs	248	319
Rushing	112	126
Passing	114	168
Penalty	22	25
Third Down: Made/Att.	66/205	99/216
Third Down: Pct.	32.2	45.8
Fourth Down: Made/Att.	14/25	10/18
Fourth Down: Pct.	56.0	55.6
Total Net Yards	3919	5333
Avg. Per Game	244.9	333.3
Total Plays	934	1024
Avg. Per Play	4.2	5.2
Net Yards Rushing	1976	2007
Avg. Per Game	123.5	125.4
Total Rushes	454	490
Net Yards Passing	1943	3326
Avg. Per Game	121.4	207.9
Sacked/Yards Lost	45/341	45/294
Gross Yards	2284	3620
Att./Completions	435/227	489/288
Completion Pct.	52.2	58.9
Had Intercepted	17	16
Punts/Avg.	76/42.1	57/41.8
Net Punting Avg.	76/35.9	57/35.1
Penalties/Yards Lost	98/755	95/797
Fumbles/Ball Lost	32/10	36/17
Touchdowns	31	44
Rushing	11	15
Passing	16	24
Returns	4	5
Avg. Time of Possession	27:05	32:55

1992 Individual Statistics

Scoring	TD R	TD P	TD Rt	PAT	FG	Saf	TP
Breech	0	0	0	31/31	19/27	0	88
Fenner	7	1	0	0/0	0/0	0	48
Ball	2	2	0	0/0	0/0	0	24
McGee	0	3	0	0/0	0/0	0	18
Query	0	3	0	0/0	0/0	0	18
Green	2	0	0	0/0	0/0	0	12
Holman	0	2	0	0/0	0/0	0	12
Pickens	0	1	1	0/0	0/0	0	12
Thompson	0	2	0	0/0	0/0	0	12
Bentley	0	0	1	0/0	0/0	0	6
Brennan	0	1	0	0/0	0/0	0	6
Francis	0	0	1	0/0	0/0	0	6
Stegall	0	1	0	0/0	0/0	0	6
Vinson	0	0	1	0/0	0/0	0	6
Johnson	0	0	0	0/0	0/1	0	0
Bengals	11	16	4	31/31	19/28	0	274
Opponents	15	24	5	44/44	18/30	1	364

Passing	Att.	Comp.	Yds.	Pct.	TD	Int.	Tkld.	Rate
Esiason	278	144	1407	51.8	11	15	19/150	57.0
Klingler	98	47	530	48.0	3	2	18/146	66.3
Hollas	58	35	335	60.3	2	0	8/45	87.9
Breech	1	1	12	100.0	0	0	0/0	116.7
Bengals	435	227	2284	52.2	16	17	45/341	63.4
Opponents	489	288	3620	58.9	24	16	45/294	84.7

Rushing	Att.	Yds.	Avg.	LG	TD
Green	265	1170	4.4	53	2
Fenner	112	500	4.5	35t	7
Hollas	20	109	5.5	24	0
Esiason	21	66	3.1	15	0
Ball	16	55	3.4	17	2
Klingler	11	53	4.8	12	0
Miles	8	22	2.8	9	0
Query	1	1	1.0	1	0
Bengals	454	1976	4.4	53	11
Opponents	490	2007	4.1	36t	15

Receiving	No.	Yds.	Avg.	LG	TD
Green	41	214	5.2	19	0
McGee	35	408	11.7	36	3
Pickens	26	326	12.5	38	1
Holman	26	266	10.2	26t	2
Rembert	19	219	11.5	27	0
Thompson	19	194	10.2	32	2
Query	16	265	16.6	83t	3
Brennan	16	166	10.4	21	1
Riggs	11	70	6.4	17	0
Fenner	7	41	5.9	15	1
Ball	6	66	11.0	35t	2
Stegall	3	35	11.7	13	1
Thomason	2	14	7.0	10	0
Bengals	227	2284	10.1	83t	16
Opponents	288	3620	12.6	47	24

Interceptions	No.	Yds.	Avg.	LG	TD
D. Williams	4	65	16.3	30	0
Francis	3	108	36.0	66t	1
Fulcher	3	0	0.0	0	0
R. Jones	2	14	7.0	14	0
Wheeler	1	12	12.0	12	0
Bussey	1	3	3.0	3	0
Mitz	1	3	3.0	3	0
McDonald	1	0	0.0	0	0
Bengals	16	205	12.8	66t	1
Opponents	17	127	7.5	36	0

Punting	No.	Yds.	Avg.	In 20	LG
Johnson	76	3196	42.1	15	64
Bengals	76	3196	42.1	15	64
Opponents	57	2384	41.8	16	70

Punt Returns	No.	FC	Yds.	Avg.	LG	TD
Pickens	18	9	229	12.7	95t	1
Price	6	2	56	9.3	25	0
Bengals	24	11	285	11.9	95t	1
Opponents	32	14	284	8.9	58t	1

Kickoff Returns	No.	Yds.	Avg.	LG	TD
Stegall	25	430	17.2	39	0
Ball	20	411	20.6	48	0
Bussey	1	18	18.0	18	0
Fenner	2	38	19.0	19	0
Miles	8	128	16.0	27	0
Price	2	20	10.0	13	0
Query	1	13	13.0	13	0
Bengals	59	1058	17.9	48	0
Opponents	46	1079	23.5	100t	2

Sacks	No.
A. Williams	10.0
Stubbs	9.0
Francis	6.0
Krumrie	4.0
Rogers	4.0
Mitz	3.0
Ridgle	3.0
D. Williams	2.0
Fulcher	1.0
Gordon	1.0
Nix	1.0
Vinson	1.0
Bengals	45.0
Opponents	45.0

1993 Draft Choices

Round	Name	Pos.	College
1.	John Copeland	DE	Alabama
2.	Tony McGee	TE	Michigan
3.	Steve Tovar	LB	Ohio State
	Ty Parten	DT	Arizona
4.	Marcello Simmons	DB	Southern Methodist
5.	Forey Duckett	DB	Nevada-Reno
6.	Tom Scott	T	East Carolina
7.	Lance Gunn	DB	Texas
8.	Doug Pelfrey	K	Kentucky

Cincinnati Bengals 1993 Veteran Roster

No.	Name	Pos.	Ht.	Wt.	Birth-date	NFL Exp.	College	Hometown	How Acq.	'92 Games/ Starts
65	Arthur, Mike	C	6-3	280	5/7/68	3	Texas A&M	Minneapolis, Minn.	D5-'91	16/13
42	†Ball, Eric	RB	6-0	220	7/1/66	5	UCLA	Ypsilanti, Mich.	D2-'89	16/14
57	Bentley, Ray	LB	6-2	235	11/25/60	8	Central Michigan	Grand Rapids, Mich.	PB(Buff)-'92	2/2
3	Breech, Jim	K	5-6	175	4/11/56	14	California	Sacramento, Calif.	FA-'89	16/0
81	Brown, Eddie	WR	6-0	185	12/17/62	8	Miami	Miami, Fla.	D1-'85	0*
38	Dingle, Mike	RB	6-2	240	1/30/69	3	South Carolina	Moncks Corner, S.C.	D8-'91	0*
29	Dixon, Rickey	S	5-11	191	12/26/66	6	Oklahoma	Dallas, Tex.	D1-'88	14/2
44	Fenner, Derrick	RB	6-3	228	4/6/67	5	North Carolina	Oxon Hill, Md.	PB(Sea)-'92	16/1
50	Francis, James	LB	6-5	252	8/4/68	4	Baylor	Houston, Tex.	D1-'90	14/13
97	Frier, Mike	DE	6-5	299	3/20/69	2	Appalachian State	Jacksonville, N.C.	W(Sea)-'92	15/3
33	Fulcher, David	S	6-3	238	9/28/64	8	Arizona State	Los Angeles, Calif.	D3b-'86	12/11
58	Gordon, Alex	LB	6-5	245	9/14/64	7	Cincinnati	Jacksonville, Fla.	PB(Raid)-'91	15/3
28	†Green, Harold	RB	6-2	222	1/29/68	4	South Carolina	Ladson, S.C.	D2-'90	16/15
12	Hollas, Donald	QB	6-3	215	11/22/67	3	Rice	Kingsville, Tex.	D4-'91	10/1
11	Johnson, Lee	P-K	6-2	200	11/27/61	9	Brigham Young	Conroe, Tex.	W(Clev)-'88	16/0
25	Jones, Rod	CB	6-0	185	3/31/64	8	Southern Methodist	Dallas, Tex.	T(TB)-'90	16/14
55	Kirk, Randy	LB	6-2	231	12/27/64	6	San Diego State	San Diego, Calif.	PB(SD)-'92	15/0
7	Klingler, David	QB	6-2	205	2/17/69	2	Houston	Stratford, Tex.	D1a-'92	4/4
64	Kozerski, Bruce	G	6-4	287	4/2/62	10	Holy Cross	Plains, Pa.	D9-'84	16/16
69	Krumrie, Tim	NT	6-2	274	5/20/60	11	Wisconsin	Eau Claire, Wis.	D10-'83	16/16
56	McDonald, Ricardo	LB	6-2	235	11/8/69	2	Pittsburgh	Kingston, Jamaica	D4-'92	16/13
62	Melander, Jon	G	6-7	280	12/27/66	4	Minnesota	Fridley, Minn.	PB(NE)-'92	15/7
36	Miles, Ostell	RB	6-0	236	8/6/71	2	Houston	Pueblo, Colo.	D9-'92	11/0
99	#Mitz, Alonzo	DE	6-4	278	6/5/63	7	Florida	Ft. Pierce, Fla.	W(SF)-'91	16/14
73	Moyer, Ken	T	6-7	297	11/19/66	4	Toledo	Temperance, Mich.	FA-'89	0*
95	Nix, Roosevelt	DE	6-6	292	4/17/67	2	Central State, Ohio	Toledo, Ohio	D8-'92	6/0
80	Pickens, Carl	WR	6-2	206	3/23/70	2	Tennessee	Murphy, N.C.	D2-'92	16/10
32	Price, Mitchell	CB	5-9	181	5/10/67	4	Tulane	San Antonio, Tex.	FA-'92	4/1
89	Query, Jeff	WR	6-0	165	3/7/67	5	Millikin	Maroa, Ill.	W(Hou)-'92	10/2
61	Rayam, Tom	T	6-6	297	1/3/68	2	Alabama	Orlando, Fla.	W(Wash)-'92	10/5
52	#Reasons, Gary	LB	6-4	234	2/18/62	10	Northwestern Louisiana	Spring, Tex.	FA-'92	12/9
88	†Rembert, Reggie	WR	6-5	200	12/25/66	4	West Virginia	Okeechobee, Fla.	T(NYJ)-'90	9/4
79	Rogers, Lamar	DE	6-4	292	11/5/67	3	Auburn	Opp, Ala.	D2-'91	15/12
77	Sargent, Kevin	T	6-6	284	3/31/69	2	Eastern Washington	Bremerton, Wash.	FA-'92	16/8
98	Savage, Tony	NT	6-3	285	7/7/67	3	Washington State	San Diego, Calif.	FA-'92	1/0
10	Schroeder, Jay	QB	6-4	215	6/28/61	10	UCLA	Pacific Palisades, Calif.	UFA(Raid)-'93	13/9*
76	Scrafford, Kirk	T	6-6	255	3/16/67	4	Montana	Billings, Mont.	FA-'90	8/4
90	Shaw, Eric	LB	6-3	248	9/17/71	2	Louisiana Tech	Pensacola, Fla.	D12-'92	11/1
84	Stegall, Milt	WR	6-0	184	1/25/70	2	Miami, Ohio	Cincinnati, Ohio	FA-'92	16/0
67	Stubbs, Daniel	DE	6-4	264	1/3/65	6	Miami	Red Bank, N.J.	W(Dall)-'91	16/12
49	Thomason, Jeff	TE	6-4	233	12/30/69	2	Oregon	Newport Beach, Calif.	FA-'92	4/0
48	Thompson, Craig	TE	6-2	244	1/13/69	2	North Carolina A&T	Hartsville, S.C.	D5-'92	16/3
34	Vinson, Fernandus	S	5-10	197	11/3/68	3	North Carolina State	Montgomery, Ala.	D7-'91	13/4
59	#Walker, Kevin	LB	6-3	244	12/24/65	6	Maryland	West Milford, N.J.	D3-'88	4/4
63	Walter, Joe	T	6-7	292	6/18/63	9	Texas Tech	Dallas, Tex.	D7a-'85	16/16
37	Wheeler, Leonard	CB	5-11	189	1/15/69	2	Troy State	Toccoa, Ga.	D3-'92	16/2
39	White, Sheldon	CB	5-11	188	3/1/65	6	Miami, Ohio	Dayton, Ohio	UFA(Det)-'93	13/0*
94	Williams, Alfred	LB	6-6	240	11/6/68	3	Colorado	Houston, Tex.	D1-'91	15/6
31	Williams, Darryl	S	6-0	191	1/7/70	2	Miami	Miami, Fla.	D1a-'92	16/12
60	Withycombe, Mike	T	6-5	297	11/18/64	5	Fresno State	Lemoore, Calif.	W(Pitt)-'91	14/3

* Brown, Dingle, and Moyer missed '92 season due to injury; Schroeder played 13 games with L.A. Raiders in '92; White played 13 games with Detroit.

#Unrestricted free agent; subject to developments.

† Restricted free agent; subject to developments.

Traded—QB Boomer Esiason to N.Y. Jets.

Players lost through free agency (5): S Barney Bussey (TB; 9 games in '92), WR Tim McGee (Wash; 16), T Anthony Muñoz (TB; 8), TE Jim Riggs (Wash; 12), CB Eric Thomas (NYJ; 16).

Also played with Bengals in '92—CB-S Antoine Bennett (11 games), WR Brian Brennan (9), QB Boomer Esiason (12), TE Rodney Holman (16), DE Elston Ridgle (7), LB Frank Robinson (3), RB Brian Townsend (3).

COACHING STAFF

Head Coach, Dave Shula

Pro Career: Shula is in his second year as head coach of the Cincinnati Bengals. He became the sixth head coach in Bengals history on December 27, 1991. Shula was offensive coordinator and quarterbacks coach for Dallas in 1989-90 before joining Cincinnati in 1991 as receivers coach. Shula began his coaching career with the Miami Dolphins in 1982. In 1988, Shula was named assistant head coach with the Dolphins. He was a wide receiver and kick return specialist with the Baltimore Colts in 1981. Career record: 5-11.

Background: Outstanding wide receiver at Dartmouth where he was a two-time All-Ivy League selection.

Personal: Born May 28, 1959, Lexington, Ky. Mike and his wife, Leslie, live in Cincinnati, and have three sons—Daniel, Christopher, and Matthew.

Assistant Coaches

Jim Anderson, running backs; born March 27, 1948, Harrisburg, Pa., lives in Cincinnati. Linebacker-defensive end Cal Western (U.S. International) 1967-70. No pro playing experience. College coach: Cal Western 1970-71, Scottsdale, Ariz., Community College 1973, Nevada-Las Vegas 1974-75, Southern Methodist 1976-80, Stanford 1981-83. Pro coach: Joined Bengals in 1984.

Ken Anderson, quarterbacks; born February 15, 1949, Rock Island, Ill., lives in Lakeside Park, Ky. Quarterback Augustana (Ill.) 1967-70. Quarterback Cincinnati Bengals 1971-86. Pro coach: Joined Bengals in 1992.

Marv Braden, special teams; born January 25, 1938, Kansas City, Mo., lives in Cincinnati. Linebacker Southwest Missouri State 1956-59. No pro playing experience. College coach: Parsons 1963-66, Northeast Missouri State 1967-68 (head coach), Cal Western (U.S. International) 1969-72, Iowa State 1973, Southern Methodist 1974-75, Michigan State 1976. Pro coach: Denver Broncos 1977-80, San Diego Chargers 1981-85, St. Louis/Phoenix Cardinals 1986-89, joined Bengals in 1990.

Mike Haluchak, linebackers; born November 28, 1949, Concord, Calif., lives in Cincinnati. Linebacker Southern California 1967-70. No pro playing experience. College coach: Southern California 1976-77, Cal State-Fullerton 1978, Pacific 1979-80, California 1981, North Carolina State 1982. Pro coach: Oakland Invaders (USFL) 1983-85; San Diego Chargers 1986-91, joined Bengals in 1992.

Bob Karmelowicz, defensive line; born July 22, 1949, New Britain, Conn., lives in Cincinnati. Nose tackle Bridgeport 1972. No pro playing experience. College coach: Arizona State 1974-79, Massachusetts 1979-80, Texas-El Paso 1980-81, Illinois 1982-87, Washington State 1987-89, Miami 1990-91. Pro coach: Joined Bengals in 1992.

Ron Lynn, defensive coordinator; born December 6, 1944, Youngstown, Ohio, lives in Cincinnati. Quarterback-defensive back Mt. Union (Ohio) 1963-65. No pro playing experience. College coach: Toledo 1966, Mt. Union (Ohio) 1967-73, Kent State 1974-76, San Jose State 1977-78, Pacific 1979, California 1980-82. Pro coach: Oakland Invaders (USFL) 1983-85, San Diego Chargers 1986-91, joined Bengals in 1992.

Jim McNally, offensive line; born December 13, 1943, Buffalo, N.Y., lives in Cincinnati. Guard Buffalo 1961-65. No pro playing experience. College coach: Buffalo 1966-69, Marshall 1973-75, Boston College 1976-78, Wake Forest 1979. Pro coach: Joined Bengals in 1980.

Ron Meeks, defensive backfield; born August 27, 1954, Jacksonville, Fla., lives in Cincinnati. Defensive back Arkansas State 1975-76. Pro defensive back Hamilton Tiger-Cats (CFL) 1977-79, Ottawa Roughriders (CFL) 1979, Toronto Argonauts (CFL) 1980-81. College coach: Arkansas State 1984-85, Miami 1986-87, New Mexico State 1988, Fresno State 1989-90. Pro coach: Dallas Cowboys 1991, joined Bengals in 1992.

Cincinnati Bengals 1993 First-Year Roster

Name	Pos.	Ht.	Wt.	Birth-date	College	Hometown	How Acq.
Amie, Charmyst	S	5-10	195	6/26/71	Stephen F. Austin	Tyler, Tex.	FA
Anderson, Roman	K	5-10	195	4/19/69	Houston	The Woodlands, Tex.	FA
Benjamin, Ryan	RB	5-7	183	4/23/70	Pacific	Pixley, Calif.	FA
Brumfield, Scott	T	6-8	320	8/19/70	Brigham Young	Spansh Fork, Utah	FA
Casey, Brian	T	6-5	325	11/12/70	Indiana, Pa.	Wexford, Pa.	FA
Casper, Gary	LB	6-2	235	3/25/70	Wisconsin	Downers Grove, Ill.	FA
Copeland, John	NT	6-3	286	9/20/70	Alabama	Lanett, Ala.	D1
Degraffenreid, Allen	WR	6-3	200	5/1/70	Ohio State	Cincinnati, Ohio	FA
Duckett, Forey	CB	6-3	195	2/5/70	Nevada-Reno	Pinole, Calif.	D5
Faulkerson, Mike	RB	6-0	237	9/9/70	North Carolina	Kingsport, Tex.	FA
Fite, Jeff	P	6-1	210	2/1/69	Memphis State	Germantown, Tenn.	FA
Ford, Artis	NT	6-3	275	9/30/71	Mississippi	Pahokee, Fla.	FA
Forehand, Sheldon	WR	6-2	194	8/7/69	Boise State	Fremont, Calif.	FA
Frisch, David	TE	6-7	260	6/22/70	Colorado State	House Springs, Mo.	FA
Gray, Derrick	G-T	6-8	330	7/22/70	Tennessee Tech	Yemassee, S.C.	FA
Greene, Nigel	G-T	6-5	305	2/5/70	Howard	Atlanta, Ga.	FA
Gunn, Lance	S	6-3	222	1/9/70	Texas	Houston, Tex.	D7
Hadley, Darius	CB-S	6-1	190	9/9/71	South Carolina State	Miami, Fla.	FA
Isaiah, Richard (1)	WR	6-0	175	7/17/68	Toledo	Akron, Ohio	FA
Johnson, Donnell	DE	6-7	310	12/24/69	Johnson C. Smith	Miami, Fla.	FA
Lebo, Brad	QB	6-4	210	3/20/70	Montana	Post Falls, Idaho	FA
McGee, Tony	TE	6-3	246	4/21/71	Michigan	Terre Haute, Ind.	D2
McGill, Karmeeleyah	LB	6-3	224	1/11/71	Notre Dame	Clearwater, Fla.	FA
McGowan, Scott	WR	5-11	185	8/22/71	Indiana	Indianapolis, Ind.	FA
Parten, Ty	NT	6-4	272	10/13/69	Arizona	Washington, D.C.	D3a
Pelfrey, Doug	K	5-11	185	9/25/70	Kentucky	Ft. Thomas, Ky.	D8
Scott, Tom	T	6-6	350	6/25/70	East Carolina	Burke County, N.C.	D6
Sevillian, Clarence	WR	5-10	175	4/30/70	Vanderbilt	Saginaw, Mich.	FA
Simmons, Marcello	CB	6-1	180	8/8/71	Southern Methodist	Tomball, Tex.	D4
Smith, Brad	LB	6-2	228	9/5/69	Texas Christian	Houston, Tex.	FA
Staten, Mark	G-T	6-6	300	10/8/70	Miami	Dowagiac, Miss.	FA
Thornton, Reggie	WR	5-11	173	9/26/67	Bowling Green	Indianapolis, Ind.	FA
Tovar, Steve	LB	6-3	244	4/25/70	Ohio State	Elyria, Ohio	D3
Turner, Elbert (1)	WR	5-11	165	3/19/68	Illinois	Gary, Ind.	FA
Williams, Nate (1)	DE	6-2	287	6/11/68	Mississippi State	Houston, Tex.	FA
Williams, Ronald	RB	6-1	203	5/19/72	Clemson	Ninety Six, S.C.	FA

The term NFL Rookie is defined as a player who is in his first season of professional football and has not been on the roster of another professional football team for any regular-season or postseason games. A Rookie is designated by an "R" on NFL rosters. Players who have been active in another professional football league or players who have NFL experience, including either preseason training camp or being on an Active List or Inactive List, or on Reserve/Injured or Reserve/Physically Unable to Perform for fewer than six regular-season games, are termed NFL First-Year Players. An NFL First-Year Player is designated by a "1" on NFL rosters. Thereafter, a player is credited with an additional year of experience for each season in which he accumulates six games on the Active List or Inactive List, or on Reserve/Injured or Reserve/Physically Unable to Perform.

NOTES

Mike Pope, offensive coordinator, tight ends; born March 15, 1942, Monroe, N.C., lives in Cincinnati. Quarterback Lenoir Rhyne 1962-64. No pro playing experience. College coach: Florida State 1970-74, Texas Tech 1975-77, Mississippi 1978-82. Pro coach: New York Giants 1983-91, joined Bengals in 1992.

Richard Williamson, wide receivers, born April 13, 1941, Ft. Deposit, Ala., lives in Cincinnati. Receiver Alabama 1961-62. No pro playing experience. College coach: Alabama 1963-67, 1970-71, Arkansas 1968-69, 1972-74, Memphis State 1975-80 (head coach). Pro coach: Kansas City Chiefs 1983-86, Tampa Bay Buccaneers 1987-91 (interim head coach final three games of 1990 season, head coach 1991), joined Bengals in 1992.

Kim Wood, strength; born July 12, 1945, Barrington, Ill., lives in Cincinnati. Running back Wisconsin 1965-68. No pro playing experience. Pro coach: Joined Bengals in 1975.

CLEVELAND BROWNS

American Football Conference Central Division

Team Colors: Seal Brown, Orange, and White

80 First Avenue
Berea, Ohio 44017
Telephone: (216) 891-5000

Club Officials

President and Owner: Arthur B. Modell
Executive Vice President/Legal and Administration: Jim Bailey
Vice President/Assistant to President: David Modell
Vice President/Public Relations: Kevin Byrne
Director of Player Personnel: Michael Lombardi
Assistant to Head Coach/Offense-Pro Personnel: Ozzie Newsome
Treasurer: Mike Srsen
Director of Operations/Information: Bob Eller
Assistant Director of Public Relations: Francine Lubera
Player Relations/Media Services: Dino Lucarelli
Director of College Scouting: Dom Anile
Scouts: Tom Dimitroff, Pat Hill, Ron Marciniak, Terry McDonough, Scott Pioli, Ernie Plank, Ellis Rainsberger, Bill Shunkwiler, Lionel Vital
Head Trainer: Bill Tessendorf
Facilities Manager: Charley Cusick
Equipment Manager: Ed Carroll

Stadium: Cleveland Stadium • **Capacity:** 78,512
West 3rd Street
Cleveland, Ohio 44114

Playing Surface: Grass

Training Camp: 80 First Avenue
Berea, Ohio 44017

1993 Schedule

Preseason

Aug. 9	at Washington	8:00
Aug. 14	vs. New England at Toronto, Canada	7:30
Aug. 21	**Los Angeles Rams**	7:00
Aug. 27	at Tampa Bay	8:00

Regular Season

Sept. 5	**Cincinnati**	1:00
Sept. 13	**San Francisco** (Monday)	9:00
Sept. 19	at Los Angeles Raiders	1:00
Sept. 26	at Indianapolis	1:00
Oct. 3	**Open Date**	
Oct. 10	**Miami**	1:00
Oct. 17	at Cincinnati	1:00
Oct. 24	**Pittsburgh**	1:00
Oct. 31	**Open Date**	
Nov. 7	**Denver**	1:00
Nov. 14	at Seattle	1:00
Nov. 21	**Houston**	1:00
Nov. 28	at Atlanta	1:00
Dec. 5	**New Orleans**	1:00
Dec. 12	at Houston	12:00
Dec. 19	**New England**	1:00
Dec. 26	at Los Angeles Rams	1:00
Jan. 2	at Pittsburgh	1:00

Browns Coaching History

(361-259-10)

1950-62	Paul Brown	115-49-5
1963-70	Blanton Collier	79-38-2
1971-74	Nick Skorich	30-26-2
1975-77	Forrest Gregg*	18-23-0
1977	Dick Modzelewski	0-1-0
1978-84	Sam Rutigliano**	47-52-0
1984-88	Marty Schottenheimer	46-31-0
1989-90	Bud Carson***	12-14-1
1990	Jim Shofner	1-6-0
1991-92	Bill Belichick	13-19-0

*Resigned after 13 games in 1977
**Released after eight games in 1984
***Released after nine games in 1990

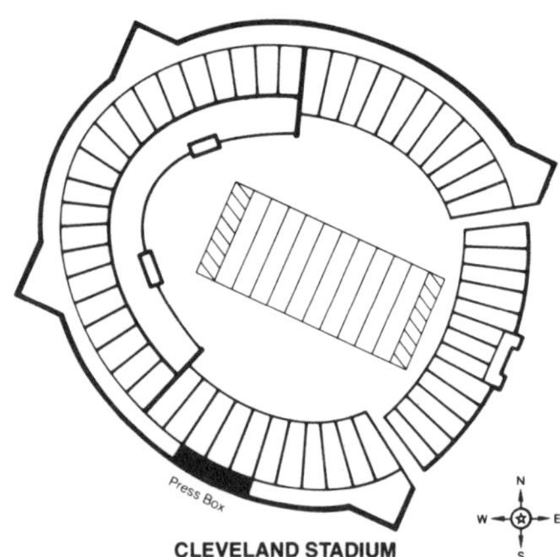

CLEVELAND STADIUM

Record Holders

Individual Records — Career

Category	Name	Performance
Rushing (Yds.)	Jim Brown, 1957-1965	12,312
Passing (Yds.)	Brian Sipe, 1974-1983	23,713
Passing (TDs)	Brian Sipe, 1974-1983	154
Receiving (No.)	Ozzie Newsome, 1978-1990	662
Receiving (Yds.)	Ozzie Newsome, 1978-1990	7,980
Interceptions	Thom Darden, 1972-74, 1976-1981	45
Punting (Avg.)	Horace Gillom, 1950-56	43.8
Punt Return (Avg.)	Greg Pruitt, 1973-1981	11.8
Kickoff Return (Avg.)	Greg Pruitt, 1973-1981	26.3
Field Goals	Lou Groza, 1950-59, 1961-67	234
Touchdowns (Tot.)	Jim Brown, 1957-1965	*126
Points	Lou Groza, 1950-59, 1961-67	1,349

Individual Records — Single Season

Category	Name	Performance
Rushing (Yds.)	Jim Brown, 1963	1,863
Passing (Yds.)	Brian Sipe, 1980	4,132
Passing (TDs)	Brian Sipe, 1980	30
Receiving (No.)	Ozzie Newsome, 1983	89
	Ozzie Newsome, 1984	89
Receiving (Yds.)	Webster Slaughter, 1989	1,236
Interceptions	Thom Darden, 1978	10
Punting (Avg.)	Gary Collins, 1965	46.7
Punt Return (Avg.)	Leroy Kelly, 1965	15.6
Kickoff Return (Avg.)	Billy Reynolds, 1954	29.5
Field Goals	Matt Bahr, 1984	24
	Matt Bahr, 1988	24
Touchdowns (Tot.)	Jim Brown, 1965	21
Points	Jim Brown, 1965	126

Individual Records — Single Game

Category	Name	Performance
Rushing (Yds.)	Jim Brown, 11-24-57	237
	Jim Brown, 11-19-61	237
Passing (Yds.)	Bernie Kosar, 1-3-87	489
Passing (TDs)	Frank Ryan, 12-12-64	5
	Bill Nelsen, 11-2-69	5
	Brian Sipe, 10-7-79	5
Receiving (No.)	Ozzie Newsome, 10-14-84	14
Receiving (Yds.)	Ozzie Newsome, 10-14-84	191
Interceptions	Many times	3
	Last time by Frank Minnifield, 11-22-87	
Field Goals	Don Cockroft, 10-19-75	5
Touchdowns (Tot.)	Dub Jones, 11-25-51	*6
Points	Dub Jones, 11-25-51	36

*NFL Record

1992 Team Record

Preseason (2-2)

Date	Result		Opponents
8/8	W	7- 0	Atlanta
8/15	L	7-16	at N.Y. Giants
8/24	L	3-56	Minnesota
8/28	W	24- 3	at Tampa Bay

Regular Season (7-9)

Date	Result		Opponents	Att.
9/6	L	3-14	at Indianapolis	51,315
9/14	L	23-27	Miami	75,912
9/20	W	28-16	at L.A. Raiders	46,198
9/27	L	0-12	Denver	78,069
10/11	W	17- 9	Pittsburgh	78,256
10/18	W	17- 6	Green Bay	69,682
10/25	W	19-17	at New England	38,442
11/1	L	10-30	at Cincinnati	59,140
11/8	W	24-14	at Houston	61,282
11/15	L	13-14	San Diego	59,610
11/22	L	13-17	at Minnesota	60,798
11/29	W	27-14	Chicago	73,727
12/6	W	37-21	Cincinnati	69,609
12/13	L	14-24	at Detroit	70,746
12/20	L	14-17	Houston	60,060
12/27	L	13-23	at Pittsburgh	59,431

Score by Periods

Browns	63	31	76	102	0	—	272
Opponents	55	47	80	93	0	—	275

Attendance

Home 564,925 Away 447,352 Total 1,012,277
Single-game home record, 85,073 (9-21-70)
Single-season home record, 620,496 (1980)

1992 Team Statistics

	Browns	Opp.
Total First Downs	242	281
Rushing	85	86
Passing	141	170
Penalty	16	25
Third Down: Made/Att.	67/196	76/205
Third Down: Pct.	34.2	37.1
Fourth Down: Made/Att.	9/17	7/14
Fourth Down: Pct.	52.9	50.0
Total Net Yards	4492	4757
Avg. Per Game	280.8	297.3
Total Plays	883	963
Avg. Per Play	5.1	4.9
Net Yards Rushing	1607	1605
Avg. Per Game	100.4	100.3
Total Rushes	451	429
Net Yards Passing	2885	3152
Avg. Per Game	180.3	197.0
Sacked/Yards Lost	34/217	48/315
Gross Yards	3102	3467
Att./Completions	398/238	486/291
Completion Pct.	59.8	59.9
Had Intercepted	16	13
Punts/Avg.	75/41.1	74/44.5
Net Punting Avg.	75/36.1	74/37.6
Penalties/Yards Lost	104/765	93/764
Fumbles/Ball Lost	19/12	33/20
Touchdowns	30	29
Rushing	7	5
Passing	18	23
Returns	5	1
Avg. Time of Possession	30:13	29:47

1992 Individual Statistics

Scoring	TD R	TD P	TD Rt	PAT	FG	Saf	TP
Stover	0	0	0	29/30	21/29	0	92
M. Jackson	0	7	0	0/0	0/0	0	42
Metcalf	1	5	1	0/0	0/0	0	42
Mack	6	0	0	0/0	0/0	0	36
Bavaro	0	2	0	0/0	0/0	0	12
Brandon	0	0	2	0/0	0/0	0	12
Galbraith	0	1	0	0/0	0/0	0	6
Hoard	0	1	0	0/0	0/0	0	6
M. Johnson	0	0	1	0/0	0/0	0	6
J. Jones	0	1	0	0/0	0/0	0	6
Moore	0	0	1	0/0	0/0	0	6
Wolfley	0	1	0	0/0	0/0	0	6
Browns	7	18	5	29/30	21/29	0	272
Opponents	5	23	1	29/29	24/29	0	275

Passing	Att.	Comp.	Yds.	Pct.	TD	Int.	Tkld.	Rate
Tomczak	211	120	1693	56.9	7	7	12/85	80.1
Kosar	155	103	1160	66.5	8	7	21/126	87.0
Philcox	27	13	217	48.1	3	1	1/6	97.3
Goebel	3	2	32	66.7	0	0	0/0	102.1
Metcalf	1	0	0	0.0	0	0	0/0	39.6
Stover	1	0	0	0.0	0	1	0/0	0.0
Browns	398	238	3102	59.8	18	16	34/217	82.7
Opponents	486	291	3467	59.9	23	13	48/315	86.3

Rushing	Att.	Yds.	Avg.	LG	TD
Mack	169	543	3.2	37	6
Vardell	99	369	3.7	35	0
Metcalf	73	301	4.1	31	1
Hoard	54	236	4.4	37	0
Tomczak	24	39	1.6	16	0
Brooks	13	38	2.9	13	0
Baldwin	10	31	3.1	11	0
M. Jackson	1	21	21.0	21	0
Tillman	2	15	7.5	15	0
Kosar	5	12	2.4	8	0
Wolfley	1	2	2.0	2	0
Browns	451	1607	3.6	37	7
Opponents	429	1605	3.7	48	5

Receiving	No.	Yds.	Avg.	LG	TD
M. Jackson	47	755	16.1	69t	7
Metcalf	47	614	13.1	69t	5
Hoard	26	310	11.9	46t	1
Tillman	25	498	19.9	52	0
Bavaro	25	315	12.6	39	2
Holohan	20	170	8.5	24	0
Vardell	13	128	9.8	23	0
Mack	13	81	6.2	23	0
Smith	5	64	12.8	21	0
Galbraith	4	63	15.8	28	1
Collins	3	31	10.3	11	0
Baldwin	2	30	15.0	20	0
Holland	2	27	13.5	16	0
Wolfley	2	8	4.0	6	1
Brooks	2	−1	−0.5	4	0
McCardell	1	8	8.0	8	0
J. Jones	1	1	1.0	1t	1
Browns	238	3102	13.0	69t	18
Opponents	291	3467	11.9	68t	23

Interceptions	No.	Yds.	Avg.	LG	TD
Newsome	3	55	18.3	29	0
Walls	2	26	13.0	24	0
Brandon	2	123	61.5	92t	1
Minnifield	2	6	3.0	5	0
Matthews	1	6	6.0	6	0
Turner	1	6	6.0	6	0
M. Johnson	1	0	0.0	0	0
Taylor	1	0	0.0	0	0
Browns	13	222	17.1	92t	1
Opponents	16	213	13.3	69	1

Punting	No.	Yds.	Avg.	In 20	LG
Hansen	74	3083	41.7	28	73
Browns	75	3083	41.1	28	73
Opponents	74	3293	44.5	19	66

Punt Returns	No.	FC	Yds.	Avg.	LG	TD
Metcalf	44	10	429	9.8	75t	1
Browns	44	10	429	9.8	75t	1
Opponents	27	23	234	8.7	50	0

Kickoff Returns	No.	Yds.	Avg.	LG	TD
Baldwin	30	675	22.5	47	0
Hoard	2	34	17.0	25	0
Metcalf	9	157	17.4	30	0
Vardell	2	14	7.0	13	0
Browns	43	880	20.5	47	0
Opponents	51	907	17.8	30	0

Sacks	No.
Burnett	9.0
Matthews	9.0
Perry	8.5
J. Jones	4.0
Pleasant	4.0
M. Johnson	2.0
B. Johnson	2.0
Moore	2.0
Newsome	2.0
Brandon	1.0
Brown	1.0
Hilliard	1.0
Logan	1.0
Turner	1.0
Walls	0.5
Browns	48.0
Opponents	34.0

1993 Draft Choices

Round	Name	Pos.	College
1.	Steve Everitt	C	Michigan
2.	Dan Footman	DE	Florida State
3.	Mike Caldwell	LB	Mid. Tennessee St.
5.	Herman Arvie	T	Grambling
6.	Rich McKenzie	LB	Penn State
7.	Travis Hill	LB	Nebraska

Cleveland Browns 1993 Veteran Roster

No.	Name	Pos.	Ht.	Wt.	Birth-date	NFL Exp.	College	Hometown	How Acq.	'92 Games/ Starts
23	Baldwin, Randy	RB	5-10	216	8/19/67	3	Mississippi	Griffin, Ga.	FA-'91	15/0
93	t-Ball, Jerry	DT	6-1	300	12/15/64	7	Southern Methodist	Beaumont, Tex.	T(Det)-'93	12/12*
37	†Barnett, Harlon	S	5-11	200	1/2/67	4	Michigan State	Cincinnati, Ohio	D4-'90	16/0
58	Brandon, David	LB	6-4	230	2/9/65	7	Memphis State	Memphis, Tenn.	PB(SD)-'91	16/15
52	#Brown, Richard	LB	6-3	240	9/21/65	6	San Diego State	Westminster, Calif.	PB(SD)-'91	10/10
90	†Burnett, Rob	DE	6-4	270	8/27/67	4	Syracuse	Coram, N.Y.	D5-'90	16/16
83	Carrier, Mark	WR	6-0	185	10/28/65	7	Nicholls State	Lafayette, La.	UFA(TB)-'93	14/12*
80	†Collins, Shawn	WR	6-2	207	2/20/67	5	Northern Arizona	San Diego, Calif.	T(Atl)-'92	0*
72	Dahl, Bob	G-T	6-5	285	11/5/68	2	Notre Dame	Chagrin Falls, Ohio	FA-'92	9/2
79	Davis, Travis	DT	6-2	275	5/10/66	3	Michigan State	Warren, Ohio	FA-'93	0*
53	#Figaro, Cedric	LB	6-3	255	8/17/66	6	Notre Dame	Lafayette, La.	FA-'91	16/0
69	Fike, Dan	G-T	6-7	285	6/16/61	9	Florida	Pensacola, Fla.	FA-'85	16/16
81	†Galbraith, Scott	TE	6-2	255	1/7/67	4	Southern California	Sacramento, Calif.	D7-'90	14/2
8	Goebel, Brad	QB	6-3	198	10/13/67	3	Baylor	Cuero, Tex.	FA-'93	1/0
41	Haddix, Wayne	CB	6-1	204	7/23/65	5	Liberty	Middleton, Tenn.	FA-'93	0*
20	Haller, Alan	CB	5-11	185	8/9/70	2	Michigan State	Lansing, Mich.	W(Pitt)-'92	14/2
11	Hansen, Brian	P	6-2	215	10/26/60	9	Sioux Falls	Hawarden, Iowa	PB(NE)-'91	16/0
53	Hilgenberg, Jay	C	6-3	270	3/21/59	13	Iowa	Iowa City, Iowa	T(Chi)-'92	16/16
39	†Hilliard, Randy	CB	5-11	160	6/2/67	4	Northwestern Louisiana	Metairie, La.	D6-'90	16/4
33	Hoard, Leroy	RB	5-11	230	5/15/68	4	Michigan	New Orleans, La.	D2-'90	16/9
89	Holohan, Pete	TE	6-4	244	7/25/59	13	Notre Dame	Liverpool, N.Y.	PB(KC)-'92	4/3
64	Hoover, Houston	G	6-2	300	2/6/65	6	Jackson State	Yazoo City, Miss.	UFA(Atl)-'93	16/16*
1	Jackson, Michael	WR	6-4	195	4/12/65	3	Southern Mississippi	Kentwood, La.	D6-'91	16/14
94	Johnson, Bill	DE-DT	6-4	295	12/9/68	2	Michigan State	Chicago, Ill.	D3a-'92	16/2
59	Johnson, Mike	LB	6-1	230	11/26/62	8	Virginia Tech	Hyattsville, Md.	SD1b-'84	16/16
96	Jones, James	DT	6-2	290	2/6/69	3	Northern Iowa	Davenport, Iowa	D3-'91	16/16
12	Jones, Selwyn	CB	6-0	185	5/13/70	2	Colorado State	Missouri City, Tex.	D7-'92	0*
66	Jones, Tony	T	6-5	295	5/24/66	6	Western Carolina	Cannesville, Ga.	FA-'88	16/16
88	Kinchen, Brian	TE	6-2	232	8/6/65	5	Louisiana State	Baton Rouge, La.	FA-'91	16/0
68	King, Ed	G-T	6-4	300	12/3/69	3	Auburn	Phenix City, Ala.	D2-'91	16/14
19	Kosar, Bernie	QB	6-5	215	11/15/63	9	Miami	Boardman, Ohio	SD1-'85	7/7
97	Logan, Ernie	DE-DT	6-3	285	5/18/68	3	East Carolina	Fayetteville, N.C.	W(Atl)-'91	16/0
34	#Mack, Kevin	RB	6-0	225	8/9/62	8	Clemson	Kings Mountain, N.C.	SD1a-'84	12/6
57	Matthews, Clay	LB	6-2	245	3/15/56	16	Southern California	New Trier, Ill.	D1a-'78	16/16
87	McCardell, Keenan	WR	6-1	175	1/6/70	2	Nevada-Las Vegas	Houston, Tex.	FA-'92	2/0
21	Metcalf, Eric	RB	5-10	190	1/23/68	5	Texas	Arlington, Va.	D1-'89	16/5
65	Milstead, Rod	G	6-2	290	11/10/69	2	Delaware State	Bryans Road, Md.	T(Dall)-'92	0*
31	#Minnifield, Frank	CB	5-9	180	1/1/60	10	Louisville	Lexington, Ky.	FA-'84	10/8
27	Moore, Stevon	S	5-11	205	2/9/67	5	Mississippi	Wiggins, Miss.	FA-'92	14/4
48	Mustafaa, Najee	CB	6-1	190	6/20/64	7	Georgia Tech	East Point, Ga.	UFA(Minn)-'93	0*
92	Perry, Michael Dean	DT	6-1	285	8/27/65	6	Clemson	Aiken, S.C.	D2-'88	14/14
17	†Philcox, Todd	QB	6-4	225	9/25/66	4	Syracuse	Norwalk, Conn.	PB(Cin)-'91	2/1
98	Pleasant, Anthony	DE	6-5	258	1/27/68	4	Tennessee State	Century, Fla.	D3-'90	16/14
15	Pruitt, James	WR	6-2	198	1/29/64	6	Cal State-Fullerton	Los Angeles, Calif.	FA-'93	0*
70	#Rienstra, John	G	6-5	275	3/22/63	8	Temple	Bryn Athyn, Pa.	PB(Pitt)-'91	7/5
86	Rowe, Patrick	WR	6-1	195	2/17/69	2	San Diego State	San Diego, Calif.	D2-'92	0*
75	Sagapolutele, Pio	G-T	6-6	297	11/28/69	3	San Diego State	Honolulu, Hawaii	D4-'91	14/0
84	Smith, Rico	WR	6-0	185	1/4/69	2	Colorado	Paramount, Calif.	D6-'92	10/1
50	†Stams, Frank	LB	6-2	240	7/17/66	5	Notre Dame	Akron, Ohio	T(Rams)-'92	12/0
3	†Stover, Matt	K	5-11	178	1/27/68	4	Louisiana Tech	Dallas, Tex.	PB(NYG)-'91	16/0
24	Taylor, Terry	CB	5-10	185	7/18/61	9	Southern Illinois	Warren, Ohio	FA-'92	16/16
12	Testaverde, Vinny	QB	6-5	215	11/13/63	7	Miami	Floral Park, N.Y.	UFA(TB)-'93	14/14*
91	Thornton, John	DT	6-3	303	6/28/69	2	Cincinnati	Flint, Mich.	W(NO)-'91	0*
85	Tillman, Lawyer	WR	6-5	230	5/20/66	5	Auburn	Mobile, Ala.	D2-'89	11/9
29	Turner, Eric	S	6-1	207	9/20/68	3	UCLA	Ventura, Calif.	D1-'91	15/13
44	Vardell, Tommy	RB	6-2	233	2/20/69	2	Stanford	El Cajon, Calif.	D1-'92	14/10
28	Walls, Everson	CB-S	6-1	195	12/28/59	13	Grambling	Richardson, Tex.	FA-'92	10/5
95	Williams, George	DT	6-2	297	2/3/69	2	Notre Dame	Willingboro, N.J.	D6b-'92	0*
26	Wolfley, Ron	RB	6-0	230	10/14/62	9	West Virginia	Hamburg, N.Y.	PB(Phx)-'92	15/0
60	Zeno, Lance	C	6-4	279	4/15/67	2	UCLA	Fountain Valley, Calif.	FA-'92	3/0

* Ball played 12 games with Detroit in '92; Carrier played 14 games with Tampa Bay; Collins, S. Jones, Rowe, Thornton, and Williams missed '92 season due to injury; Davis last active with Indianapolis in '91; Haddix last active with Tampa Bay in '91; Hoover played 16 games with Atlanta; Milstead last active with Dallas in '91; Mustafaa last active with Minnesota in '91; Pruitt last active with Miami in '91; Testaverde played 14 games with Tampa Bay.

Unrestricted free agent; subject to developments.

† Restricted free agent; subject to developments.

t- Browns traded for Ball (Detroit).

Players lost through free agency (2): TE Mark Bavaro (Phil; 16 games in '92), QB Mike Tomczak (Pitt; 12).

Also played with Browns in '92 — LB Bobby Abrams (3 games), CB-S Latin Berry (1), RB James Brooks (4), T Freddie Childress (16), CB-S Fred Foggie (2), QB Jeff Francis (2), CB-S Odie Harris (4), WR Jamie Holland (4), CB Alfred Jackson (4), S Vince Newsome (16), C Chris Thome (3), CB Barry Wilburn (6), DT Alvin Wright (3).

COACHING STAFF

Head Coach, Bill Belichick

Pro Career: Became the Browns' tenth head coach on February 5, 1991. Belichick formerly was defensive coordinator of the New York Giants, who defeated the Buffalo Bills 20-19 in Super Bowl XXV. He also coordinated the Giants' defense that won Super Bowl XXI in 1986. Began coaching career at 23 as a special assistant to Ted Marchibroda with the Baltimore Colts in 1975. He tutored the Detroit Lions' tight ends, wide receivers, and special teams in 1976-77, before joining the Denver Broncos in 1978. He joined the Giants in 1979 as a defensive assistant and special teams coach, moved to linebackers in 1981-82, and became defensive coordinator in 1983. Career record: 13-19.

Background: Attended Annapolis (Maryland) High School and Phillips Academy in Andover, Mass. Played football and lacrosse at Wesleyan (Conn.) University. Earned a bachelor's degree in economics from Wesleyan in 1975.

Personal: Born April 16, 1952, in Nashville, Tenn. Bill and his wife, Debby, live in Brecksville, Ohio, and have three children, Amanda, Stephen, and Brian.

Assistant Coaches

Ernie Adams, special assignments; born March 31, 1953, Waltham, Mass., lives in Lakewood, Ohio. No college or pro playing experience. College coach: Northwestern 1972-75. Pro coach: New England Patriots 1975-78, New York Giants 1979-81 (Pro Personnel Director 1982-85), joined Browns in 1991.

Jim Bates, defensive line; born May 31, 1946, Pontiac, Mich., lives in Strongsville, Ohio. Linebacker Tennessee 1964-67. No pro playing experience. College coach: Tennessee 1968, 1989, Southern Mississippi 1972, Villanova 1973-74, Kansas State 1975-76, West Virginia 1977, Texas Tech 1978-83, Florida 1990. Pro coach: San Antonio Gunslingers (USFL) 1984-85 (head coach 1985), Detroit Drive (Arena Football) 1988, joined Browns in 1991.

Steve Crosby, running backs; born July 3, 1950, Great Bend, Kan., lives in Strongsville, Ohio. Running back Fort Hays State 1969-72. Pro running back New York Giants 1974-76. Pro coach: Miami Dolphins 1979-82, Atlanta Falcons 1983-84, 1986-89, Cleveland Browns 1985, New England Patriots 1990, rejoined Browns in 1991.

Kirk Ferentz, offensive line; born August 1, 1955, Royal Oak, Mich., lives in Berea, Ohio. Linebacker Connecticut 1973-76. No pro playing experience. College coach: Connecticut 1977, Pittsburgh 1980, Iowa 1981-89, Maine 1990-92 (head coach). Pro coach: Joined Browns in 1993.

Richard Mann, receivers; born April 20, 1947, Aliquippa, Pa., lives in Shaker Heights, Ohio. Wide receiver Arizona State 1966-68. No pro playing experience. College coach: Arizona State 1974-79, Louisville 1980-81. Pro coach: Baltimore/Indianapolis Colts 1982-84, joined Browns in 1985.

John Mitchell, defensive line; born October 14, 1950, Mobile, Ala., lives in Hinckley, Ohio. Defensive end Eastern Arizona J.C. 1969-70, Alabama 1971-72. No pro playing experience. College coach: Alabama 1973-76, Arkansas 1977-82, Temple 1986, Louisiana State 1987-90. Pro coach: Birmingham Stallions (USFL) 1983-85, joined Browns in 1991.

Scott O'Brien, special teams; born June 25, 1957, Superior, Wis., lives in Strongsville, Ohio. Defensive end Wisconsin-Superior 1975-78. Pro defensive end Green Bay Packers 1979, Toronto Argonauts (CFL) 1979. College coach: Wisconsin-Superior 1980-82, Nevada-Las Vegas 1983-85, Rice 1986, Pittsburgh 1987-90. Pro coach: Joined Browns in 1991.

Nick Saban, defensive coordinator; born October 31, 1951, Fairmont, W. Va., lives in Medina, Ohio. Defensive back Kent State 1969-72. No pro playing experience. College coach: Kent State 1973-76, Syracuse 1977, West Virginia 1978-79, Ohio State 1980-81, Navy 1982, Michigan State 1983-87, Toledo 1990 (head coach). Pro coach: Houston Oilers 1988-89, joined Browns in 1991.

Phil Savage, defensive assistant; born April 7, 1965, Mobile, Ala., lives in North Royalton, Ohio. Quarterback University of the South 1983-86. No pro playing experience. College coach: Alabama 1987-89, UCLA 1990. Pro coach: Joined Browns in 1991.

Mike Sheppard, offensive assistant; born October 29, 1951, Tulsa, Okla., lives in Berea, Ohio. Wide receiver Cal Lutheran 1969-72. No pro playing experience. College coach: Cal Lutheran 1974-76, Brigham Young 1977-78, U.S. International 1979, Idaho State 1980-81, Long Beach State 1982, 1984-86 (head coach), Kansas 1983, New Mexico 1987-91 (head coach), California 1992. Pro coach: Joined Browns in 1993.

Jerry Simmons, strength and conditioning; born June 15, 1954, Elkhart, Kan., lives in Strongsville, Ohio. Linebacker Fort Hays State 1976-77. No pro playing experience. College coach: Fort Hays State 1978, Clemson 1980, Rice 1981-82, Southern California 1983-87. Pro coach: New England Patriots 1988-90, joined Browns in 1991.

Kevin Spencer, offensive assistant; born November 2, 1953, Queens, N.Y., lives in Bay Village, Ohio. No college or pro playing experience. College coach: State University of New York 1975-76, Cornell 1979-80, Ithaca 1981-86, Wesleyan 1987-91 (head coach). Pro coach: Joined Browns in 1991.

Gary Tranquill, quarterbacks; born April 13, 1940, Avella, Pa., lives in Hinckley, Ohio. Quarterback Wittenberg 1959-62. College coach: Wittenberg 1963-69, Ball State 1970, Bowling Green 1971-72, Navy 1973-76, Ohio State 1977-78, West Virginia 1979-81, Navy 1982-86 (head coach), Virginia 1987-90. Pro coach: Joined Browns in 1991.

Woody Widenhofer, linebackers; born January 20, 1943, Butler, Pa., lives in Berea, Ohio. Linebacker Missouri 1961-64. No pro playing experience. College coach: Michigan State 1969-70, Eastern Michigan 1971, Minnesota 1972, Missouri 1985-88 (head coach). Pro coach: Pittsburgh Steelers 1973-83, Oklahoma Outlaws (USFL) 1984 (head coach), Detroit Lions 1989-92, joined Browns in 1993.

Cleveland Browns 1993 First-Year Roster

Name	Pos.	Ht.	Wt.	Birth-date	College	Hometown	How Acq.
Arvie, Herman	T	6-4	320	10/12/70	Grambling	Opelousas, La.	D5
Ashby, Paul	RB	6-1	205	9/29/71	Alabama State	Fulton, Miss.	FA
Brown, Jerome	DE-DT	6-5	270	11/27/65	Mississippi State	Monroe County, Ala.	FA
Caldwell, Mike	LB	6-2	222	8/31/71	Mid. Tennessee St.	Oak Ridge, Tenn.	D3
Cotton, Curtis	CB-S	6-0	210	10/15/69	Nebraska	Omaha, Neb.	FA
Dixon, Gerald	LB	6-3	252	6/20/69	South Carolina	Rock Hill, S.C.	D3b-'92
Everitt, Steve	C-G	6-5	292	8/21/70	Michigan	Miami, Fla.	D1
Ferrell, Kerry	WR	5-11	173	7/8/70	Syracuse	Piscataway, N.J.	FA
Fisher, John (1)	C	6-3	280	9/4/69	Tennessee	Milan, Tenn.	FA
Foggie, Fred	CB-S	6-0	188	6/10/69	Minnesota	Laurens, S.C.	FA
Footman, Dan	DE	6-5	285	1/13/69	Florida State	Tampa, Fla.	D2
Hill, Travis	LB	6-2	231	10/3/69	Nebraska	Houston, Tex.	D7
Jacobs, Tim	CB	5-10	185	4/5/70	Delaware	Landover, Md.	FA
Keen, Robbie (1)	K	6-5	215	8/28/68	California	Orangevale, Calif.	FA
Lawson, Shawn	CB	5-11	175	9/27/70	Baylor	Longview, Tex.	FA
Malone, James (1)	LB	6-2	237	3/13/69	UCLA	Dallas, Tex.	FA
McKenzie, Rich	LB	6-2	230	4/15/71	Penn State	Ft. Lauderdale, Fla.	D6
Pourdanesh, Shahriar	DE-DT	6-6	280	7/19/70	Nevada	Irvine, Calif.	FA
Prince, William	RB	6-2	222	5/8/70	Mississippi State	Vicksburg, Miss.	FA
Spear, Del	CB-S	6-0	196	2/1/70	Florida	Miami, Fla.	FA
Swilling, Ken (1)	LB	6-2	245	9/25/70	Georgia Tech	Toccoa, Ga.	FA
Williams, Wally	C	6-2	300	2/19/71	Florida A&M	Tallahassee, Fla.	FA

The term NFL Rookie is defined as a player who is in his first season of professional football and has not been on the roster of another professional football team for any regular-season or postseason games. A Rookie is designated by an "R" on NFL rosters. Players who have been active in another professional football league or players who have NFL experience, including either preseason training camp or being on an Active List or Inactive List, or on Reserve/Injured or Reserve/Physically Unable to Perform for fewer than six regular-season games, are termed NFL First-Year Players. An NFL First-Year Player is designated by a "1" on NFL rosters. Thereafter, a player is credited with an additional year of experience for each season in which he accumulates six games on the Active List or Inactive List, or on Reserve/Injured or Reserve/Physically Unable to Perform.

NOTES

American Football Conference Western Division

Team Colors: Orange, Royal Blue, and White

13655 Broncos Parkway
Englewood, Colorado 80112
Telephone: (303) 649-9000

Club Officials

President-Chief Executive Officer: Pat Bowlen
General Manager: John Beake
Head Coach: Wade Phillips
Chief Financial Officer-Treasurer: Robert M. Hurley
Director of Football Operations/Player Personnel: Bob Ferguson
Director of Media Relations: Jim Saccomano
Assistant to the General Manager: Fred Fleming
Ticket Manager: Gail Stuckey
Director of Operations: Bill Harpole
Director of Player and Community Relations: Charlie Lee
Trainer: Steve Antonopulos
Equipment Manager: Doug West
Video Director: Kent Erickson

Stadium: Denver Mile High Stadium • **Capacity:** 76,273
1900 West Eliot
Denver, Colorado 80204

Playing Surface: Grass (PAT)

Training Camp: University of Northern Colorado
Greeley, Colorado 80639

1993 Schedule

Preseason

Aug. 7	at Tampa Bay	7:30
Aug. 16	**San Francisco**	6:00
Aug. 20	**Miami**	6:00
Aug. 27	at Phoenix	8:00

Regular Season

Sept. 5	at New York Jets	1:00
Sept. 12	**San Diego**	2:00
Sept. 20	at Kansas City (Monday)	8:00
Sept. 26	**Open Date**	
Oct. 3	**Indianapolis**	2:00
Oct. 10	at Green Bay	6:30
Oct. 18	**L.A. Raiders** (Monday)	7:00
Oct. 24	**Open Date**	
Oct. 31	**Seattle**	2:00
Nov. 7	at Cleveland	1:00
Nov. 14	**Minnesota**	2:00
Nov. 21	**Pittsburgh**	2:00
Nov. 28	at Seattle	1:00
Dec. 5	at San Diego	1:00
Dec. 12	**Kansas City**	2:00
Dec. 18	at Chicago (Saturday)	11:30
Dec. 26	**Tampa Bay**	2:00
Jan. 2	at Los Angeles Raiders	1:00

Broncos Coaching History

(241-251-10)

1960-61	Frank Filchock	7-20-1
1962-64	Jack Faulkner*	9-22-1
1964-66	Mac Speedie**	6-19-1
1966	Ray Malavasi	4-8-0
1967-71	Lou Saban***	20-42-3
1971	Jerry Smith	2-3-0
1972-76	John Ralston	34-33-3
1977-80	Robert (Red) Miller	42-25-0
1981-92	Dan Reeves	117-79-1

*Released after four games in 1964
**Resigned after two games in 1966
***Resigned after nine games in 1971

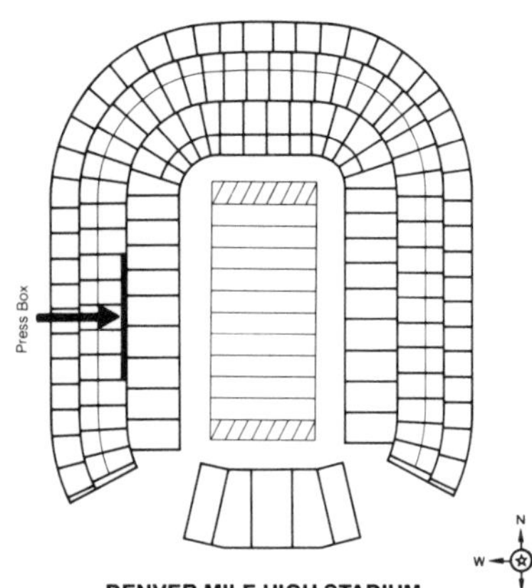

DENVER MILE HIGH STADIUM

Record Holders

Individual Records — Career

Category	Name	Performance
Rushing (Yds.)	Floyd Little, 1967-1975	6,323
Passing (Yds.)	John Elway, 1983-1992	30,216
Passing (TDs)	John Elway, 1983-1992	158
Receiving (No.)	Lionel Taylor, 1960-66	543
Receiving (Yds.)	Lionel Taylor, 1960-66	6,872
Interceptions	Steve Foley, 1976-1986	44
Punting (Avg.)	Jim Fraser, 1962-64	45.2
Punt Return (Avg.)	Rick Upchurch, 1975-1983	12.1
Kickoff Return (Avg.)	Abner Haynes, 1965-66	26.3
Field Goals	Jim Turner, 1971-79	151
Touchdowns (Tot.)	Floyd Little, 1967-1975	54
Points	Jim Turner, 1971-79	742

Individual Records — Single Season

Category	Name	Performance
Rushing (Yds.)	Otis Armstrong, 1974	1,407
Passing (Yds.)	John Elway, 1985	3,891
Passing (TDs)	Frank Tripucka, 1960	24
Receiving (No.)	Lionel Taylor, 1961	100
Receiving (Yds.)	Steve Watson, 1981	1,244
Interceptions	Goose Gonsoulin, 1960	11
Punting (Avg.)	Jim Fraser, 1963	46.1
Punt Return (Avg.)	Floyd Little, 1967	16.9
Kickoff Return (Avg.)	Bill Thompson, 1969	28.5
Field Goals	Gene Mingo, 1962	27
	David Treadwell, 1989, 1991	27
Touchdowns (Tot.)	Sammy Winder, 1986	14
Points	Gene Mingo, 1962	137

Individual Records — Single Game

Category	Name	Performance
Rushing (Yds.)	Otis Armstrong, 12-8-74	183
Passing (Yds.)	Frank Tripucka, 9-15-62	447
Passing (TDs)	Frank Tripucka, 10-28-62	5
	John Elway, 11-18-84	5
Receiving (No.)	Lionel Taylor, 11-29-64	13
	Bobby Anderson, 9-30-73	13
Receiving (Yds.)	Lionel Taylor, 11-27-60	199
Interceptions	Goose Gonsoulin, 9-18-60	*4
	Willie Brown, 11-15-64	*4
Field Goals	Gene Mingo, 10-6-63	5
	Rich Karlis, 11-20-83	5
Touchdowns (Tot.)	Many times	3
	Last time by Gaston Green, 9-22-91	
Points	Gene Mingo, 12-10-60	21

*NFL Record

1992 Team Record

Preseason (1-4)

Date	Result		Opponents
8/3	L	7-13	at San Francisco
8/8	W	31-10	Tampa Bay
8/15	L	27-31	vs. Miami at Berlin
8/22	L	3-17	at Dallas
8/28	L	17-21	Phoenix

Regular Season (8-8)

Date	Result		Opponents	Att.
9/6	W	17-13	L.A. Raiders	74,824
9/13	W	21-13	San Diego	72,180
9/20	L	0-30	at Philadelphia	65,507
9/27	W	12- 0	at Cleveland	78,069
10/4	W	20-19	Kansas City	74,372
10/12	L	17-34	at Washington	55,455
10/18	W	27-21	Houston	73,825
10/25	L	21-24	at San Diego	52,149
11/8	W	27-16	N.Y. Jets	73,036
11/15	W	27-13	N.Y. Giants	74,161
11/22	L	0-24	at L.A. Raiders	47,786
11/30	L	13-16	at Seattle (OT)	64,482
12/6	L	27-31	Dallas	74,929
12/12	L	17-27	at Buffalo	78,687
12/20	W	10- 6	Seattle	72,763
12/27	L	20-42	at Kansas City	76,608

(OT) Overtime

Score by Periods

Broncos	61	40	63	98	0	—	262
Opponents	51	121	74	80	0	—	329

Attendance

Home 590,090 Away 518,743 Total 1,108,833
Single-game home record, 76,105 (1-4-87)
Single-season home record, 598,224 (1981)

1992 Team Statistics

	Broncos	Opp.
Total First Downs	234	283
Rushing	84	105
Passing	135	156
Penalty	15	22
Third Down: Made/Att.	67/208	81/222
Third Down: Pct.	32.2	36.5
Fourth Down: Made/Att.	5/11	5/13
Fourth Down: Pct.	45.5	38.5
Total Net Yards	4430	5083
Avg. Per Game	276.9	317.7
Total Plays	928	1001
Avg. Per Play	4.8	5.1
Net Yards Rushing	1500	1963
Avg. Per Game	93.8	122.7
Total Rushes	403	489
Net Yards Passing	2930	3120
Avg. Per Game	183.1	195.0
Sacked/Yards Lost	52/382	50/317
Gross Yards	3312	3437
Att./Completions	473/258	462/268
Completion Pct.	54.5	58.0
Had Intercepted	29	15
Punts/Avg.	85/43.6	78/43.3
Net Punting Avg.	85/37.7	78/36.2
Penalties/Yards Lost	98/768	96/715
Fumbles/Ball Lost	29/14	33/16
Touchdowns	29	35
Rushing	11	10
Passing	16	21
Returns	2	4
Avg. Time of Possession	28:14	31:46

1992 Individual Statistics

Scoring	TD R	TD P	TD Rt	PAT	FG	Saf	TP
Treadwell	0	0	0	28/28	20/24	0	88
Jackson	0	8	0	0/0	0/0	0	48
Lewis	4	0	0	0/0	0/0	0	24
Rivers	3	1	0	0/0	0/0	0	24
Elway	2	0	0	0/0	0/0	0	12
Green	2	0	0	0/0	0/0	0	12
V. Johnson	0	2	0	0/0	0/0	0	12
Sharpe	0	2	0	0/0	0/0	0	12
Brooks	0	0	1	0/0	0/0	0	6
Henderson	0	0	1	0/0	0/0	0	6
R. Johnson	0	1	0	0/0	0/0	0	6
Marshall	0	1	0	0/0	0/0	0	6
Tillman	0	1	0	0/0	0/0	0	6
Daluiso	0	0	0	0/0	0/1	0	0
Broncos	11	16	2	28/29	20/25	0	262
Opponents	10	21	4	35/35	28/38	0	329

Passing	Att.	Comp.	Yds.	Pct.	TD	Int.	Tkld.	Rate
Elway	316	174	2242	55.1	10	17	36/272	65.7
Maddox	121	66	757	54.5	5	9	10/60	56.4
Moore	34	17	232	50.0	0	3	6/50	35.4
Lewis	1	0	0	0.0	0	0	0/0	39.6
Marshall	1	1	81	100.0	1	0	0/0	158.3
Broncos	473	258	3312	54.5	16	29	52/382	62.4
Opponents	462	268	3437	58.0	21	15	50/317	83.0

Rushing	Att.	Yds.	Avg.	LG	TD
Green	161	648	4.0	67t	2
Rivers	74	282	3.8	48	3
Lewis	73	268	3.7	22	4
Elway	34	94	2.8	9	2
S. Smith	23	94	4.1	15	0
Marshall	11	56	5.1	16	0
Moore	8	39	4.9	11	0
Maddox	9	20	2.2	11	0
R. Johnson	2	7	3.5	8	0
Jackson	3	−1	−0.5	1	0
Perryman	3	−1	−0.5	1	0
Sharpe	2	−6	−3.0	−3	0
Broncos	403	1500	3.7	67t	11
Opponents	489	1963	4.0	37	10

Receiving	No.	Yds.	Avg.	LG	TD
Sharpe	53	640	12.1	55	2
Jackson	48	745	15.5	51t	8
Rivers	45	449	10.0	37	1
Marshall	26	493	19.0	80t	1
V. Johnson	24	294	12.3	40	2
Tillman	12	211	17.6	81t	1
Russell	12	140	11.7	22	0
R. Johnson	10	139	13.9	48	1
Green	10	79	7.9	33	0
Kay	7	56	8.0	15	0
Lewis	4	30	7.5	16	0
Jones	3	17	5.7	16	0
Perryman	2	15	7.5	9	0
Young	1	11	11.0	11	0
Do. Widell	1	−7	−7.0	−7	0
Broncos	258	3312	12.8	81t	16
Opponents	268	3437	12.8	72	21

Interceptions	No.	Yds.	Avg.	LG	TD
Henderson	4	79	19.8	46t	1
D. Smith	4	10	2.5	8	0
Braxton	2	54	27.0	40	0
Atwater	2	22	11.0	22	0
Lang	1	26	26.0	26	0
Brooks	1	17	17.0	17	0
Dimry	1	2	2.0	2	0
Broncos	15	210	14.0	46t	1
Opponents	29	567	19.6	69	3

Punting	No.	Yds.	Avg.	In 20	LG
Horan	37	1681	45.4	7	62
Rodriguez	25	1066	42.6	4	55
Parker	12	491	40.9	1	61
Daluiso	10	467	46.7	3	67
Broncos	85	3705	43.6	15	67
Opponents	78	3380	43.3	19	73

Punt Returns	No.	FC	Yds.	Avg.	LG	TD
Marshall	33	16	349	10.6	47	0
Dimry	1	0	4	4.0	4	0
Broncos	34	16	353	10.4	47	0
Opponents	39	16	382	9.8	42	0

Kickoff Returns	No.	Yds.	Avg.	LG	TD
Montgomery	21	466	22.2	64	0
Green	5	76	15.2	20	0
R. Johnson	2	47	23.5	34	0
Marshall	8	132	16.5	21	0
Oliver	1	20	20.0	20	0
Robinson	4	89	22.3	26	0
Russell	7	154	22.0	33	0
S. Smith	2	31	15.5	21	0
Traylor	1	13	13.0	13	0
Broncos	51	1028	20.2	64	0
Opponents	13	254	19.5	47	0

Sacks	No.
Fletcher	16.0
Mecklenburg	7.5
Dronett	6.5
Kragen	5.5
Croel	5.0
Mills	2.0
Sochia	1.5
Walker	1.5
Atwater	1.0
Lang	1.0
Traylor	1.0
Holmes	0.5
Broncos	50.0
Opponents	52.0

1993 Draft Choices

Round	Name	Pos.	College
1.	Dan Williams	DE	Toledo
2.	Glyn Milburn	RB	Stanford
3.	Rondell Jones	DB	North Carolina
	Jason Elam	P-K	Hawaii
4.	Jeff Robinson	DE	Idaho
5.	Kevin Williams	RB	UCLA
6.	Melvin Bonner	WR	Baylor
7.	Clarence Williams	TE	Washington State
	Antonius Kimbrough	WR	Jackson State
8.	Brian Stablein	WR	Ohio State

Denver Broncos 1993 Veteran Roster

No.	Name	Pos.	Ht.	Wt.	Birth-date	NFL Exp.	College	Hometown	How Acq.	'92 Games/ Starts
27	Atwater, Steve	S	6-3	217	10/28/66	5	Arkansas	Chicago, Ill.	D1-'89	15/15
33	Bernstine, Rod	RB	6-3	238	2/8/65	7	Texas A&M	Bryan, Tex.	UFA(SD)-'93	9/1*
34	#Braxton, Tyrone	CB	5-11	185	12/17/64	7	North Dakota State	Madison, Wis.	D12-'87	16/14
42	Brooks, Michael	S	6-0	189	3/12/67	2	North Carolina State	Greensboro, N.C.	FA-'93	0*
23	Coleman, Eric	CB	6-0	190	12/27/66	3	Wyoming	Denver, Colo.	FA-'93	0*
51	Croel, Mike	LB	6-3	231	6/6/69	3	Nebraska	Detroit, Mich.	D1-'91	16/16
5	Daluiso, Brad	K	6-2	207	12/31/67	3	UCLA	San Diego, Calif.	W(Dall)-'92	16/0
62	Davidson, Jeff	G	6-5	309	10/3/67	4	Ohio State	Akron, Ohio	D5a-'90	16/16
39	Delpino, Robert	RB	6-0	205	11/2/65	6	Missouri	Dodge City, Kan.	UFA(Rams)-'93	10/4*
29	#Dimry, Charles	CB	6-0	175	1/31/66	6	Nevada-Las Vegas	San Diego, Calif.	PB(Atl)-'91	16/6
99	Dronett, Shane	DE	6-6	275	1/12/71	2	Texas	Orange, Tex.	D2-'92	16/2
7	Elway, John	QB	6-3	215	6/28/60	11	Stanford	Port Angeles, Wash.	T(Balt)-'83	12/12
73	Fletcher, Simon	LB	6-5	240	2/18/62	9	Houston	Bay City, Tex.	D2b-'85	16/16
68	†Freeman, Russell	T	6-7	290	9/2/69	2	Georgia Tech	Homestead, Pa.	FA-'92	16/16
92	†Geater, Ron	NT	6-6	270	4/23/69	2	Iowa	Cedar Rapids, Iowa	D7-'92	3/0
75	Habib, Brian	T	6-7	292	12/2/64	6	Washington	Ellensburg, Wash.	UFA(Minn)-'93	16/15*
93	Haliburton, Ronnie	LB	6-4	230	4/14/68	3	Louisiana State	Port Arthur, Tex.	D6-'90	0*
83	Harry, Emile	WR	5-11	186	4/5/63	8	Stanford	Los Angeles, Calif.	UFA(Rams)-'93	11/0*
24	#Henderson, Wymon	CB	5-10	186	12/15/61	8	Nevada-Las Vegas	North Miami Beach, Fla.	FA-'89	15/11
2	Horan, Mike	P	5-11	190	2/1/59	9	Long Beach State	Orange, Calif.	FA-'86	8/0
66	Johnson, Chuck	T	6-5	275	5/22/69	2	Texas	Freeport, Tex.	D4-'92	16/0
89	Johnson, Reggie	TE	6-2	256	1/27/68	3	Florida State	Pensacola, Fla.	D2-'91	15/7
82	Johnson, Vance	WR	5-11	185	3/13/63	9	Arizona	Trenton, N.J.	D2a-'85	11/7
55	†Kacherski, John	LB	6-3	240	6/27/67	2	Ohio State	Riverhead, N.Y.	FA-'92	7/0
72	Kartz, Keith	C	6-4	270	5/5/63	7	California	Las Vegas, Nev.	FA-'87	15/15
71	#Kragen, Greg	NT	6-3	265	3/4/62	9	Utah State	Chicago, Ill.	FA-'85	16/16
21	†Lang, Le-Lo	CB	5-11	185	1/23/67	4	Washington	Los Angeles, Calif.	D5b-'90	16/1
76	†Lanier, Ken	T	6-3	290	7/8/59	13	Florida State	Columbus, Ohio	D5-'81	16/16
20	Lewis, Greg	RB	5-10	214	8/10/69	3	Washington	Port St. Joe, Fla.	D5-'91	16/2
59	†Lucas, Tim	LB	6-3	230	4/3/61	7	California	Stockton, Calif.	FA-'87	9/0
8	Maddox, Tommy	QB	6-4	195	9/2/71	2	UCLA	Shreveport, La.	D1-'92	13/4
78	Maggs, Don	T	6-5	290	11/1/61	8	Tulane	Youngstown, Ohio	UFA(Hou)-'93	16/14*
86	†Marshall, Arthur	WR	5-11	174	4/29/69	2	Georgia	Ft. Gordon, Ga.	FA-'92	16/1
77	Mecklenburg, Karl	LB	6-3	235	9/1/60	11	Minnesota	Edina, Minn.	D12-'83	16/16
61	Meeks, Bob	C	6-2	279	5/28/69	2	Auburn	Andalusia, Ala.	D10-'92	0*
52	†Mills, Jeff	LB	6-3	238	10/8/68	4	Nebraska	Montclair, N.J.	W(SD)-'90	14/0
12	Moore, Shawn	QB	6-2	213	4/4/68	2	Virginia	Martinsville, Va.	D11-'91	3/0
74	Noonan, Danny	NT	6-4	275	7/14/65	7	Nebraska	Lincoln, Neb.	FA-'93	6/0
26	Oliver, Muhammad	CB-S	5-11	170	3/12/69	2	Oregon	Brooklyn, N.Y.	D9-'92	3/0
91	Oshodin, Willie	DE	6-4	260	9/16/69	3	Villanova	Benn City, Nigeria	FA-'92	0*
63	Pollack, Frank	G-T	6-5	285	11/5/67	4	Northern Arizona	Phoenix, Ariz.	PB(SF)-'92	0*
38	Rivers, Reggie	RB	6-1	215	2/22/68	3	Southwest Texas State	Dayton, Ohio	FA-'91	16/3
36	Robinson, Frank	CB	5-11	174	1/11/69	2	Boise State	Newark, N.J.	D5-'92	12/0
85	Russell, Derek	WR	6-0	179	6/22/69	3	Arkansas	Little Rock, Ark.	D4-'91	12/7
30	Sewell, Steve	RB	6-3	210	4/2/63	9	Oklahoma	San Francisco, Calif.	D1-'85	0*
84	Sharpe, Shannon	TE	6-2	230	6/26/68	4	Savannah State	Glennville, Ga.	D7-'90	16/11
49	Smith, Dennis	S	6-3	200	2/3/59	13	Southern California	Santa Monica, Calif.	D1-'81	16/16
50	†Sullins, John	LB	6-1	225	9/7/69	2	Alabama	Oxford, Miss.	FA-'92	6/0
81	Taylor, Kitrick	WR	5-11	189	7/22/64	6	Washington State	Pomona, Calif.	FA-'93	10/0*
87	†Tillman, Cedric	WR	6-2	204	7/22/70	2	Alcorn State	Gulfport, Miss.	D11-'92	9/1
54	†Traylor, Keith	LB	6-2	260	9/3/69	3	Central Oklahoma	Malvern, Ark.	D3-'91	16/3
9	†Treadwell, David	K	6-1	180	2/27/67	5	Clemson	Columbia, S.C.	T(Phx)-'89	16/0
96	Walker, Kenny	DE	6-3	260	4/6/67	3	Nebraska	Crane, Tex.	D8-'91	15/15
79	#Widell, Dave	C-T	6-6	292	5/14/65	6	Boston College	Hartford, Conn.	T(Dall)-'91	16/1
67	Widell, Doug	G	6-4	287	9/23/66	5	Boston College	Hartford, Conn.	D2a-'89	16/16

* Bernstine played 9 games with San Diego in '92; Brooks last active with Dallas '91; Coleman last active with Kansas City '91; Delpino played 10 games with L.A. Rams; Habib played 16 games with Minnesota; Haliburton, Oshodin, Pollack, and Sewell missed '92 season due to injury; Harry played 7 games with Kansas City and 4 with L.A. Rams; Maggs played 16 games with Houston; Meeks active for 6 games but did not play; Taylor played 10 games with Green Bay.

#Unrestricted free agent; subject to developments.

† Restricted free agent; subject to developments.

Retired—NT-DE Brian Sochia, 10-year veteran, 16 games in '92.

Traded—RB Gaston Green to L.A. Raiders, S Alton Montgomery to Atlanta.

Players lost through free agency (2): LB Michael Brooks (NYG; 15 games in '92), WR Mark Jackson (NYG; 16).

Also played with Broncos in '92—RB Jeff Alexander (7 games), WR John Granby (4), TE Clarence Kay (16), WR Ricky Nattiel (4), P Daren Parker (3), RB Robert Perryman (4), P Ruben Rodriguez (5), RB Sammie Smith (3), WR Michael Young (3).

COACHING STAFF

Head Coach, Wade Phillips

Pro Career: Became the tenth head coach in Broncos history on January 25, 1993, moving into the head-coaching slot from his previous position as defensive coordinator. Under Phillips's leadership, the Broncos' defense led the American Football Conference in fewest points allowed in two of the past four seasons (1989 and 1991), and the 1991 Denver team was paced by a defensive unit that led the AFC in 12 different categories. In addition to his role as defensive coordinator with the Broncos, Phillips assumed the capacity of interim head coach during the 1990 preseason posting a win over Indianapolis. Going into his fifth season with Denver, Phillips came to the Broncos from Philadelphia, where he was the defensive coordinator and linebackers coach from 1986-88. He served as defensive coordinator at New Orleans from 1981-85, and was the interim head coach for the final four games of the 1985 season (1-3 record). Prior to joining the Saints, Phillips spent five seasons at Houston, coaching the linebackers (1976) and defensive line (1977-80). Career record: 1-3.

Background: Phillips began his coaching career at his alma mater, the University of Houston, in 1969, and then coached at Orange (Texas) High School for three years (1970-72) before moving to Oklahoma State (1973-74) and Kansas (1975).

Personal: The son of former NFL head coach Bum Phillips, Phillips was born in Orange, Texas on June 21, 1947. He attended Port Neches-Groves High School. He went on to be a three-year starter at linebacker at Houston under head coach Bill Yeoman. Wade and his wife, Laurie, live in Denver and have two children, Tracy and Wesley.

Assistant Coaches

Vernon Banks, strength and conditioning; born May 24, 1956, Alvin, Tex., lives in Denver. Defensive back-running back Blinn Junior College 1976-77, Texas A&M 1978-79. No pro playing experience. College coach: Texas A&M 1981-83, Houston 1985-86, Wyoming 1986-87, 1992, Stanford 1987-90, Colorado 1990-91. Pro coach: Joined Broncos in 1993.

Barney Chavous, defensive assistant; born March 22, 1951, Aiken, S.C., lives in Englewood, Colo. Defensive end South Carolina State 1969-72. Pro defensive end Denver Broncos 1973-85. Pro coach: Joined Broncos in 1989.

Jim Fassel, offensive coordinator-quarterbacks coach; born August 31, 1949, Anaheim, Calif., lives in Greenwood Village, Colo. Quarterback Southern California 1969-70, Long Beach State 1971. Pro quarterback Chicago Bears 1972, Houston Oilers 1972, San Diego Chargers 1972. College coach: Fullerton (Calif.) Junior College 1973, Utah 1976, 1985-89 (head coach), Weber State 1977-78, Stanford 1979-83. Pro coach: Hawaii (WFL) 1974, Portland Breakers (USFL) 1984, New York Giants 1990-92, joined Broncos in 1993.

Mo Forte, wide receivers; born March 1, 1947, Hannibal, Mo., lives in Littleton, Colo. Running back Minnesota 1965-68. No pro playing experience. College coach: Minnesota 1970-75, Duke 1976-77, Michigan State 1978-79, Arizona State 1980-81, North Carolina A&T 1982-87 (head coach). Pro coach: Joined Broncos in 1988.

Bishop Harris, running backs; born November 23, 1941, Phoenix City, Ala., lives in Denver. Defensive back North Carolina College 1960-64. No pro playing experience. College coach: Duke 1972-75, North Carolina State 1977-79, Louisiana State 1980-84, Notre Dame 1984-85, Minnesota 1986-91, North Carolina Central 1991-92. Pro coach: Joined Broncos in 1993.

John Levra, offensive line; born October 2, 1937, Arma, Kan., lives in Englewood, Colo. Guard-linebacker Pittsburg (Kan.) State 1963-65. No pro playing experience. College coach: Stephen F. Austin 1971-74, Kansas 1975-78, North Texas State 1979. Pro coach: British Columbia Lions (CFL) 1980, New Orleans Saints 1981-85, Chicago Bears 1986-92, joined Broncos in 1993.

Denver Broncos 1993 First-Year Roster

Name	Pos.	Ht.	Wt.	Birth-date	College	Hometown	How Acq.
Auer, William	TE	6-4	245	2/24/70	North Carolina State	Eden, N.C.	FA
Bonner, Melvin	WR	6-3	207	2/18/70	Baylor	Hempstead, Tex.	D6
Boudreaux, Frank	DE-NT	6-5	273	6/20/70	Northwestern	Honolulu, Hawaii	FA
Daly, Richard	TE	6-5	240	1/17/70	UCLA	Urbana, Ill.	FA
Elam, Jason	P-K	5-11	192	3/8/70	Hawaii	Ft. Walton Beach, Fla.	D3b
Evans, Jerry (1)	TE	6-4	250	9/28/68	Toledo	Lorain, Ohio	FA
Glover, Deval (1)	WR	6-0	181	9/12/66	Syracuse	Troy, N.Y.	FA
Hall, Darryl	S	6-2	210	8/1/66	Washington	Oscoda, Mich.	FA
Hampel, Olaf	G-T	6-6	305	6/24/67	No College	Essen, Germany	FA
Jones, Rondell	S	6-2	210	5/7/71	North Carolina	Sunderland, Mass.	D3a
Kimbrough, Antonius	WR	6-2	192	9/17/70	Jackson State	Weir, Miss.	D7b
Kirkland, Dean (1)	G	6-2	290	1/4/68	Washington	Vancouver, Wash.	FA
Lynn, Anthony (1)	RB	6-3	230	12/21/68	Texas Tech	McKinney, Tex.	FA
Milburn, Glyn	RB	5-8	171	2/19/71	Stanford	Santa Monica, Calif.	D2
Perez, Michael (1)	QB	6-2	215	3/7/65	San Jose State	Denver, Colo.	FA
Primus, Greg	WR	5-11	185	10/20/70	Colorado State	Denver, Colo.	FA
Robinson, Jeff	DE	6-4	265	2/20/70	Idaho	Kennewick, Wash.	D4
Rouen, Tom (1)	P	6-3	215	6/9/68	Colorado	Hindsdale, Ill.	FA
Sims, Travis	RB	5-10	225	1/28/70	Hawaii	Burien, Wash.	FA
Stablein, Brian	WR	6-1	185	4/14/70	Ohio State	Erie, Pa.	D8
Williams, Clarence	TE	6-2	240	8/7/69	Washington State	Los Angeles, Calif.	D7a
Williams, Dan	DE	6-4	278	12/15/69	Toledo	Ypsilanti, Mich.	D1
Williams, Kevin	RB	6-0	208	2/17/70	UCLA	Spring, Tex.	D5

The term NFL Rookie is defined as a player who is in his first season of professional football and has not been on the roster of another professional football team for any regular-season or postseason games. A Rookie is designated by an "R" on NFL rosters. Players who have been active in another professional football league or players who have NFL experience, including either preseason training camp or being on an Active List or Inactive List, or on Reserve/Injured or Reserve/Physically Unable to Perform for fewer than six regular-season games, are termed NFL First-Year Players. An NFL First-Year Player is designated by a "1" on NFL rosters. Thereafter, a player is credited with an additional year of experience for each season in which he accumulates six games on the Active List or Inactive List, or on Reserve/Injured or Reserve/Physically Unable to Perform.

NOTES

Alvin Reynolds, defensive assistant-quality control; born June 24, 1959, Pineville, La., lives in Aurora, Colo. Safety Indiana State 1978-81. No pro playing experience. College coach: Indiana State 1982-92. Pro coach: Joined Broncos in 1993.

Harold Richardson, quality control-administrative assistant; born September 27, 1944, Houston, Tex., lives in Englewood, Colo. Tight end Southern Methodist 1964-67. No pro playing experience. College coach: Southern Methodist 1971-72, Oklahoma State 1973-76, Texas Christian 1977-78, North Texas State 1979-80, Colorado State 1986-88. Pro coach: New Orleans Saints 1981-85, joined Broncos in 1989.

Richard Smith, special teams; born October 17, 1955, Los Angeles, Calif., lives in Denver. Offensive lineman Rio Hondo (Calif.) Junior College 1975-76, Fresno State 1977-78. No pro playing experience. College coach: Rio Hondo (Calif.) Junior College 1979-80, Cal State-Fullerton 1981-83, California 1984-86, Arizona 1987. Pro coach: Houston Oilers 1988-92, joined Broncos in 1993.

Ernie Stautner, defensive line; born April 20, 1925, Cham, Bavaria, lives in Littleton, Colo. Tackle Boston College 1946-49. Pro defensive tackle Pittsburgh Steelers 1950-63 (player-coach 1963). Inducted into Pro Football Hall of Fame in 1969. Pro coach: Pittsburgh Steelers 1964, Washington Redskins 1965, Dallas Cowboys 1966-88, Dallas Texans (Arena League, head coach) 1990, joined Broncos in 1991.

Les Steckel, tight ends-H-backs; born July 1, 1946, North Hampton, Pa., lives in Louisville, Colo. Running back Kansas 1964-68. No pro playing experience. College coach: Colorado 1972-76, 1991-92, Navy 1977, Brown 1989. Pro coach: San Francisco 49ers 1978, Minnesota Vikings 1979-84 (head coach, 1984), New England Patriots 1985-88, joined Broncos in 1993.

Charlie Waters, defensive coordinator; born September 10, 1948, Miami, Fla., lives in Greenwood Village, Colo. Safety Clemson 1967-69. Pro safety Dallas Cowboys 1970-81. Pro coach: Joined Broncos in 1988.

John Paul Young, linebackers; born December 31, 1939, Dallas, Tex., lives in Denver. Linebacker Texas-El Paso 1959-61. No pro playing experience. College coach: Texas El-Paso 1962-63, Southern Methodist 1967-68, Oklahoma State 1969, Texas A&M 1970-77, Texas Tech 1989-91. Pro coach: Houston Oilers 1978-80, New Orleans Saints 1981-85, Kansas City Chiefs 1986-88, Dallas Texans (Arena League, head coach) 1992, joined Broncos in 1993.

American Football Conference Central Division

Team Colors: Columbia Blue, Scarlet, and White

6910 Fannin Street
Houston, Texas 77030
Telephone: (713) 797-9111

Club Officials

President: K. S. (Bud) Adams, Jr.
Exec. VP/General Manager: Mike Holovak
Exec. VP/Administration: Mike McClure
Exec. VP/Finance: Scott Thompson
Exec. Assistant to President: Thomas S. Smith
General Counsel: Steve Underwood
VP/Marketing and Broadcasting: Don MacLachlan
Assistant General Manager: Floyd Reese
Director of Business Operations: Lewis Mangum
Controller: Gene Peirce
Director of Accounting Services: Marilan Logan
Director of Media Services: Chip Namias
Director of Ticket Administration Services: Mike Mullis
Assistant Ticket Manager: Ralph Stolarski
Director of Security: Grady Sessums
Director of Computer Services: Steve Reese
Director of Player Relations: Willie Alexander
Head Trainer: Brad Brown
Assistant Trainer: Don Moseley
Equipment Manager: Gordon Batty
Video Coordinator: Ken Sparacino

Stadium: Astrodome • **Capacity:** 62,439
Loop 610, Kirby and Fannin Streets
Houston, Texas 77054

Playing Surface: AstroTurf-8

Training Camp: Prassel Residence Hall
Trinity University
San Antonio, Texas 78212

1993 Schedule

Preseason

Aug. 7	vs. New Orleans at San Antonio, Tex.	7:00
Aug. 16	**Detroit**	7:00
Aug. 21	vs. Dallas at San Antonio, Tex.	11:30
Aug. 28	**Seattle**	7:00

Regular Season

Sept. 5	at New Orleans	7:00
Sept. 12	**Kansas City**	12:00
Sept. 19	at San Diego	1:00
Sept. 26	**Los Angeles Rams**	12:00
Oct. 3	**Open Date**	
Oct. 11	at Buffalo (Monday)	9:00
Oct. 17	at New England	1:00
Oct. 24	**Cincinnati**	12:00
Oct. 31	**Open Date**	
Nov. 7	**Seattle**	12:00
Nov. 14	at Cincinnati	1:00
Nov. 21	at Cleveland	1:00
Nov. 28	**Pittsburgh**	7:00
Dec. 5	**Atlanta**	12:00
Dec. 12	**Cleveland**	12:00
Dec. 19	at Pittsburgh	1:00
Dec. 25	at San Francisco (Saturday)	2:30
Jan. 2	**New York Jets**	7:00

Oilers Coaching History

(231-268-6)

1960-61	Lou Rymkus*	12-7-1
1961	Wally Lemm	10-0-0
1962-63	Frank (Pop) Ivy	17-12-0
1964	Sammy Baugh	4-10-0
1965	Hugh Taylor	4-10-0
1966-70	Wally Lemm	28-40-4
1971	Ed Hughes	4-9-1
1972-73	Bill Peterson**	1-18-0
1973-74	Sid Gillman	8-15-0
1975-80	O.A. (Bum) Phillips	59-38-0
1981-83	Ed Biles***	8-23-0
1983	Chuck Studley	2-8-0
1984-85	Hugh Campbell****	8-22-0
1985-89	Jerry Glanville	35-35-0
1990-92	Jack Pardee	31-21-0

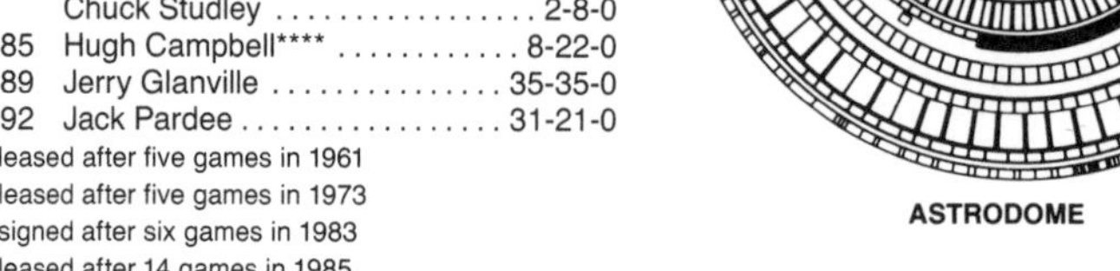

*Released after five games in 1961
**Released after five games in 1973
***Resigned after six games in 1983
****Released after 14 games in 1985

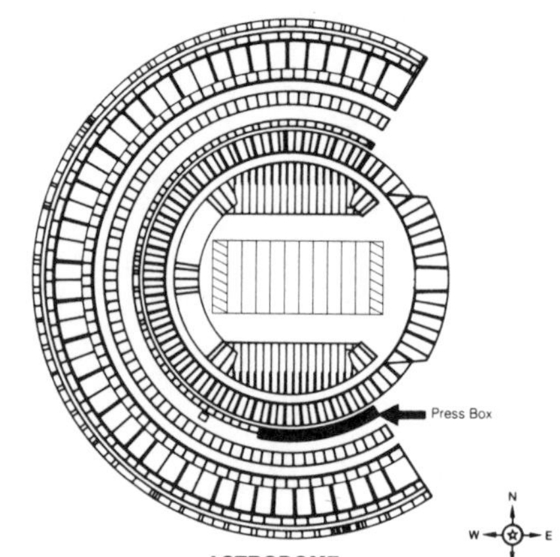

ASTRODOME

Record Holders

Individual Records — Career

Category	Name	Performance
Rushing (Yds.)	Earl Campbell, 1978-1984	8,574
Passing (Yds.)	Warren Moon, 1984-1992	30,200
Passing (TDs)	Warren Moon, 1984-1992	175
Receiving (No.)	Drew Hill, 1985-1991	480
Receiving (Yds.)	Drew Hill, 1985-1991	7,477
Interceptions	Jim Norton, 1960-68	45
Punting (Avg.)	Greg Montgomery, 1988-1992	43.2
Punt Return (Avg.)	Billy Johnson, 1974-1980	13.2
Kickoff Return (Avg.)	Bobby Jancik, 1962-67	26.4
Field Goals	Tony Zendejas, 1985-1990	117
Touchdowns (Tot.)	Earl Campbell, 1978-1984	73
Points	George Blanda, 1960-66	596

Individual Records — Single Season

Category	Name	Performance
Rushing (Yds.)	Earl Campbell, 1980	1,934
Passing (Yds.)	Warren Moon, 1991	4,690
Passing (TDs)	George Blanda, 1961	36
Receiving (No.)	Charlie Hennigan, 1964	101
Receiving (Yds.)	Charlie Hennigan, 1961	*1,746
Interceptions	Fred Glick, 1963	12
	Mike Reinfeldt, 1979	12
Punting (Avg.)	Greg Montgomery, 1992	46.9
Punt Return (Avg.)	Billy Johnson, 1977	15.4
Kickoff Return (Avg.)	Ken Hall, 1960	31.2
Field Goals	Tony Zendejas, 1989	25
Touchdowns (Tot.)	Earl Campbell, 1979	19
Points	George Blanda, 1960	115
	Tony Zendejas, 1989	115

Individual Records — Single Game

Category	Name	Performance
Rushing (Yds.)	Billy Cannon, 12-10-61	216
Passing (Yds.)	Warren Moon, 12-16-90	527
Passing (TDs)	George Blanda, 11-19-61	*7
Receiving (No.)	Charlie Hennigan, 10-13-61	13
	Haywood Jeffires, 10-13-91	13
Receiving (Yds.)	Charlie Hennigan, 10-13-61	272
Interceptions	Many times	3
	Last time by Willie Alexander, 11-14-71	
Field Goals	Skip Butler, 10-12-75	6
Touchdowns (Tot.)	Billy Cannon, 12-10-61	5
Points	Billy Cannon, 12-10-61	30

*NFL Record

1992 Team Record

Preseason (4-1)

Date	Result		Opponents
8/1	W	34-23	vs. Dallas at Tokyo
8/7	W	17- 7	at Detroit
8/15	W	17-16	at Dallas
8/22	W	33- 3	at New Orleans
8/29	L	26-30	at L.A. Raiders

Regular Season (10-6)

Date	Result		Opponents	Att.
9/6	L	24-29	Pittsburgh	63,705
9/13	W	20-10	at Indianapolis	45,274
9/20	W	23-20	Kansas City (OT)	62,672
9/27	W	27- 0	San Diego	59,159
10/11	W	38-24	at Cincinnati	59,029
10/18	L	21-27	at Denver	73,825
10/25	W	26-10	Cincinnati	61,303
11/1	L	20-21	at Pittsburgh	59,504
11/8	L	14-24	Cleveland	61,282
11/15	W	17-13	at Minnesota	61,073
11/22	L	16-19	at Miami	70,439
11/26	W	24-21	at Detroit	76,105
12/7	W	24- 7	Chicago	62,408
12/13	L	14-16	Green Bay	61,115
12/20	W	17-14	at Cleveland	60,060
12/27	W	27- 3	Buffalo	62,803

Postseason (0-1)

Date	Result		Opponent	Att.
1/3	L	38-41	at Buffalo (OT)	75,141

(OT) Overtime

Score by Periods

Oilers	81	75	80	113	3	—	352
Opponents	23	96	50	89	0	—	258

Attendance

Home 494,447 Away 505,309 Total 999,756
Single-game home record, 63,705 (9-6-92)
Single-season home record, 494,447 (1992)

1992 Team Statistics

	Oilers	Opp.
Total First Downs	339	254
Rushing	101	93
Passing	217	139
Penalty	21	22
Third Down: Made/Att.	72/170	68/194
Third Down: Pct.	42.4	35.1
Fourth Down: Made/Att.	3/9	7/14
Fourth Down: Pct.	33.3	50.0
Total Net Yards	5655	4211
Avg. Per Game	353.4	263.2
Total Plays	958	907
Avg. Per Play	5.9	4.6
Net Yards Rushing	1626	1634
Avg. Per Game	101.6	102.1
Total Rushes	353	412
Net Yards Passing	4029	2577
Avg. Per Game	251.8	161.1
Sacked/Yards Lost	32/202	50/321
Gross Yards	4231	2898
Att./Completions	573/373	445/248
Completion Pct.	65.1	55.7
Had Intercepted	23	20
Punts/Avg.	55/45.2	68/43.2
Net Punting Avg.	55/37.3	68/38.6
Penalties/Yards Lost	111/824	114/886
Fumbles/Ball Lost	28/12	24/11
Touchdowns	41	28
Rushing	10	6
Passing	27	20
Returns	4	2
Avg. Time of Possession	31:09	28:51

1992 Individual Statistics

Scoring	TD R	TD P	TD Rt	PAT	FG	Saf	TP
Del Greco	0	0	0	41/41	21/27	0	104
Givins	0	10	0	0/0	0/0	0	60
Jeffires	0	9	0	0/0	0/0	0	54
White	7	1	0	0/0	0/0	0	48
Slaughter	0	4	0	0/0	0/0	0	24
L. Harris	0	2	0	0/0	0/0	0	12
G. Brown	1	0	0	0/0	0/0	0	6
Carlson	1	0	0	0/0	0/0	0	6
Childress	0	0	1	0/0	0/0	0	6
Duncan	0	1	0	0/0	0/0	0	6
Fuller	0	0	1	0/0	0/0	0	6
McDowell	0	0	1	0/0	0/0	0	6
Meads	0	0	1	0/0	0/0	0	6
Moon	1	0	0	0/0	0/0	0	6
Oilers	10	27	4	41/41	21/27	1	352
Opponents	6	20	2	27/28	21/26	0	258

Passing	Att.	Comp.	Yds.	Pct.	TD	Int.	Tkld.	Rate
Moon	346	224	2521	64.7	18	12	16/105	89.3
Carlson	227	149	1710	65.6	9	11	15/90	81.2
Richardson	—	—	—	—	—	—	1/7	—
Oilers	573	373	4231	65.1	27	23	32/202	86.1
Opponents	445	248	2898	55.7	20	20	50/321	71.9

Rushing	Att.	Yds.	Avg.	LG	TD
White	265	1226	4.6	44	7
Moon	27	147	5.4	23	1
G. Brown	19	87	4.6	26	1
Carlson	27	77	2.9	13	1
Givins	7	75	10.7	44	0
Slaughter	3	20	6.7	10	0
L. Harris	1	8	8.0	8	0
Tillman	1	1	1.0	1	0
Richardson	1	−1	−1.0	−1	0
Gr. Montgomery	2	−14	−7.0	0	0
Oilers	353	1626	4.6	44	10
Opponents	412	1634	4.0	67t	6

Receiving	No.	Yds.	Avg.	LG	TD
Jeffires	90	913	10.1	47	9
Duncan	82	954	11.6	72	1
Givins	67	787	11.7	41	10
White	57	641	11.2	69t	1
Slaughter	39	486	12.5	36t	4
L. Harris	35	435	12.4	47	2
Coleman	2	10	5.0	6	0
G. Brown	1	5	5.0	5	0
Oilers	373	4231	11.3	72	27
Opponents	248	2898	11.7	77t	20

Interceptions	No.	Yds.	Avg.	LG	TD
Gray	6	24	4.0	22	0
McDowell	3	52	17.3	26t	1
Dishman	3	34	11.3	17	0
Jackson	3	18	6.0	18	0
Robertson	1	27	27.0	27	0
A. Smith	1	26	26.0	26	0
Dumas	1	0	0.0	0	0
Graf	1	0	0.0	0	0
Jones	1	0	0.0	0	0
Oilers	20	181	9.1	27	1
Opponents	23	367	16.0	57	0

Punting	No.	Yds.	Avg.	In 20	LG
Gr. Montgomery	53	2487	46.9	14	66
Oilers	55	2487	45.2	14	66
Opponents	68	2939	43.2	23	65

Punt Returns	No.	FC	Yds.	Avg.	LG	TD
Slaughter	20	8	142	7.1	20	0
Coleman	7	4	35	5.0	19	0
C. Harris	6	0	17	2.8	13	0
Oilers	33	12	194	5.9	20	0
Opponents	31	2	255	8.2	25	0

Kickoff Returns	No.	Yds.	Avg.	LG	TD
G. Brown	1	15	15.0	15	0
Coleman	14	290	20.7	28	0
Flannery	1	12	12.0	12	0
C. Harris	10	206	20.6	42	0
Lewis	8	171	21.4	26	0
Gl. Montgomery	1	13	13.0	13	0
Slaughter	1	21	21.0	21	0
Tillman	10	157	15.7	33	0
Oilers	46	885	19.2	42	0
Opponents	63	989	15.7	35	0

Sacks	No.
Childress	13.0
L. Williams	11.0
Jones	8.5
Fuller	8.0
Lathon	1.5
McDowell	1.5
Alm	1.0
Graf	1.0
Jackson	1.0
Lewis	1.0
Robinson	1.0
A. Smith	1.0
Gl. Montgomery	0.5
Oilers	50.0
Opponents	32.0

1993 Draft Choices

Round	Name	Pos.	College
1.	Brad Hopkins	T	Illinois
2.	Micheal Barrow	LB	Miami
4.	Travis Hannah	WR	Southern California
5.	John Henry Mills	TE	Wake Forest
6.	Chuck Bradley	T	Kentucky
7.	Patrick Robinson	WR	Tennessee State
8.	Blaine Bishop	DB	Ball State

Houston Oilers 1993 Veteran Roster

No.	Name	Pos.	Ht.	Wt.	Birth-date	NFL Exp.	College	Hometown	How Acq.	'92 Games/ Starts
76	†Alm, Jeff	DT	6-6	272	3/31/68	4	Notre Dame	Orland Park, Ill.	D2-'90	14/7
58	Bowden, Joe	LB	5-11	230	2/25/70	2	Oklahoma	Mesquite, Tex.	D5a-'92	14/0
33	Brown, Gary	RB	5-11	229	7/1/69	3	Penn State	Williamsport, Pa.	D8-'91	16/0
22	Brown, Tony	CB	5-9	183	5/15/70	2	Fresno State	Granada Hills, Calif.	D5b-'92	12/1
14	Carlson, Cody	QB	6-3	202	11/5/63	7	Baylor	San Antonio, Tex.	D3-'87	11/6
79	Childress, Ray	DT-DE	6-6	272	10/20/62	9	Texas A&M	Richardson, Tex.	D1a-'85	16/16
87	Coleman, Pat	WR	5-7	173	4/8/67	3	Mississippi	Cleveland, Miss.	FA-'91	14/0
66	Dawson, Doug	G	6-3	288	12/27/61	7	Texas	Houston, Tex.	FA-'91	16/16
3	Del Greco, Al	K	5-10	200	3/2/62	10	Auburn	Coral Gables, Fla.	FA-'91	16/0
28	Dishman, Cris	CB	6-0	188	8/13/65	6	Purdue	Louisville, Ky.	D5a-'88	15/15
77	Donnalley, Kevin	T	6-5	305	6/10/68	3	North Carolina	Raleigh, N.C.	D3b-'91	16/2
38	Dumas, Mike	S	5-11	181	3/18/69	3	Indiana	Lowell, Mich.	D2a-'91	16/1
80	Duncan, Curtis	WR	5-11	184	1/26/65	7	Northwestern	Detroit, Mich.	D10-'87	16/16
55	Flannery, John	G-C	6-3	304	1/13/69	3	Syracuse	Pottsville, Pa.	D2c-'91	15/2
95	Fuller, William	DE	6-3	274	3/8/62	8	North Carolina	Chesapeake, Va.	T(Rams)-'86	15/14
81	Givins, Ernest	WR	5-9	172	9/3/64	8	Louisville	St. Petersburg, Fla.	D2-'86	16/16
83	#Harris, Leonard	WR	5-8	166	11/27/60	8	Texas Tech	McKinney, Tex.	FA-'87	14/7
24	Jackson, Steve	CB	5-8	182	4/8/69	3	Purdue	Houston, Tex.	D3a-'91	16/1
84	Jeffires, Haywood	WR	6-2	201	12/12/64	7	North Carolina State	Greensboro, N.C.	D1b-'87	16/16
96	Jones, Sean	DE	6-7	268	12/19/62	10	Northeastern	Montclair, N.J.	T(Raid)-'88	15/15
56	†Kozak, Scott	LB	6-3	222	11/28/65	5	Oregon	Colton, Ore.	D2-'89	16/0
57	Lathon, Lamar	LB	6-3	252	12/23/67	4	Houston	Wharton, Tex.	D1-'90	11/11
29	Lewis, Darryll	CB	5-9	188	12/16/68	3	Arizona	La Puente, Calif.	D2b-'91	13/0
74	Matthews, Bruce	C-G	6-5	291	8/8/61	11	Southern California	Arcadia, Calif.	D1-'83	16/16
86	Mays, Damon	WR	5-9	170	5/20/68	2	Missouri	Phoenix, Ariz.	FA-'92	1/0
25	McDowell, Bubba	S	6-1	198	11/4/66	5	Miami	Merritt Island, Fla.	D3-'89	16/16
94	Montgomery, Glenn	DT	6-0	278	3/31/67	5	Houston	Gretna, La.	D5-'89	16/0
9	Montgomery, Greg	P	6-4	215	10/29/64	6	Michigan State	Red Bank, N.J.	D3-'88	16/0
1	Moon, Warren	QB	6-3	212	11/18/56	10	Washington	Los Angeles, Calif.	FA-'84	11/10
63	Munchak, Mike	G	6-3	284	3/5/60	12	Penn State	Scranton, Pa.	D1-'82	15/14
64	Norgard, Erik	C-G	6-1	282	11/4/65	4	Colorado	Arlington, Wash.	FA-'92	15/0
26	Orlando, Bo	S	5-10	180	4/3/66	4	West Virginia	Berwick, Pa.	FA-'90	6/1
7	Richardson, Bucky	QB	6-1	228	2/7/69	2	Texas A&M	Baton Rouge, La.	D8-'92	7/0
68	Roberts, Tim	DT	6-6	318	4/14/69	2	Southern Mississippi	Atlanta, Ga.	D5c-'92	6/0
31	Robertson, Marcus	S-CB	5-11	197	10/2/69	3	Iowa State	Pasadena, Calif.	D4b-'91	16/14
50	Robinson, Eddie	LB	6-1	245	4/13/70	2	Alabama State	New Orleans, La.	D2-'92	9/0
53	Seale, Eugene	LB	5-10	260	6/3/64	7	Lamar	Jasper, Tex.	FA-'87	9/0
89	Slaughter, Webster	WR	6-1	175	10/19/64	8	San Diego State	Stockton, Calif.	FA-'92	12/9
54	Smith, Al	LB	6-1	251	11/26/64	7	Utah State	Los Angeles, Calif.	D5a-'87	16/16
99	#Smith, Doug	DT	6-5	328	6/13/60	9	Auburn	Bayboro, N.C.	D2a-'84	6/6
32	Tillman, Spencer	RB	5-11	206	4/21/64	7	Oklahoma	Tulsa, Okla.	PB(SF)-'92	16/0
88	Wellman, Gary	WR	5-9	173	8/9/67	2	Southern California	Westlake Hills, Calif.	D5-'91	9/0
44	White, Lorenzo	RB	5-11	222	4/12/66	6	Michigan State	Ft. Lauderdale, Fla.	D1-'88	16/16
73	†Williams, David	T	6-5	297	6/21/66	5	Florida	Lakeland, Fla.	D1-'89	16/16
97	Williams, Lee	DE-DT	6-6	271	10/15/62	10	Bethune-Cookman	Ft. Lauderdale, Fla.	T(SD)-'91	16/5

#Unrestricted free agent; subject to developments.

† Restricted free agent; subject to developments.

Players lost through free agency (3): LB Rick Graf (Wash; 16 games in '92), CB Jerry Gray (TB; 16), T Don Maggs (Den; 16).

Also played with Oilers in '92— WR Corey Harris (5 games), CB Richard Johnson (1), LB Johnny Meads (4), DE Willis Peguese (1), DT Craig Veasey (4).

COACHING STAFF

Head Coach,
Jack Pardee

Pro Career: Named the Oilers' fourteenth head coach on January 9, 1990. Houston has qualified for playoffs in each of his three seasons with the Oilers. Accepted post after serving three years (1987-89) as head coach at University of Houston. While at Houston, Cougars set over 100 NCAA/ Southwest Conference records in 1988 and 1989. In 1986, was a scout for the Green Bay Packers. Prior to that, was head coach of successful Houston Gamblers of the USFL from 1984-85 as team led league in total offense and scoring in both seasons. Spent 1982 in private business after serving as defensive coordinator for San Diego Chargers in 1981. That season, Chargers won AFC's Western Division and advanced to AFC Championship Game. From 1978-80, was head coach of the Washington Redskins, earning NFL coach of the year honors in 1979. Was head coach of the Chicago Bears from 1975-77, earning NFC coach of the year accolades in 1976 and leading the club in 1977 to its first playoff berth in 14 years. Was general manager/head coach for Florida Blazers of the World Football League in 1974, winning division title and advancing to WFL title game. Began coaching career as Washington Redskins' assistant in 1973. Drafted by Los Angeles Rams in second round in 1957 and played 15 seasons at linebacker for Rams (1957-64, 1966-70) and Washington Redskins (1971-72). Was an all-pro selection in 1963 and 1971, and is a member of Rams' fortieth anniversary team. Career record: 75-68.

Background: Played linebacker and fullback in All-America and Academic All-America career for coach Paul (Bear) Bryant at Texas A&M (1953-56). Is a member of the Texas A&M Hall of Fame, National Football Foundation Hall of Fame, College Football Hall of Fame, Texas Sports Hall of Fame, and Senior Bowl Hall of Fame.

Personal: Born April 19, 1936, Exira, Iowa. Jack and his wife, Phyllis, live in Missouri City, Tex., and have two sons, Steven and Ted, and three daughters, Judee, Anne, and Susan.

Assistant Coaches

Charlie Baggett, receivers; born January 21, 1953, Fayetteville, N.C., lives in Houston. Quarterback Michigan State 1972-75. No pro playing experience. College coach: Bowling Green 1977-80, Minnesota 1981-82, Michigan State 1983-93. Pro coach: Joined Oilers in 1993.

Tom Bettis, defensive backs; born March 17, 1933, Chicago, Ill., lives in Houston, Tex. Linebacker-guard Purdue 1952-54. Pro linebacker Green Bay Packers 1955-61, Pittsburgh Steelers 1962, Chicago Bears 1963. Pro coach: Chicago Bears 1964-65 (scout), Kansas City Chiefs 1966-77 (interim head coach 1977), 1988, St. Louis Cardinals 1978-84, Cleveland Browns 1985, Houston Oilers 1986-87, Philadelphia Eagles 1989-90, Los Angeles Rams 1991, rejoined Oilers in 1993.

Frank Bush, quality control; born January 10, 1963, Athens, Ga., lives in Houston. Linebacker North Carolina State 1981-84. Pro linebacker Houston Oilers 1985-86. Pro coach: Joined Oilers in 1987 as scout, named assistant coach in 1992.

Kevin Gilbride, offensive coordinator; born August 27, 1951, New Haven, Conn., lives in Missouri City, Tex. Quarterback-tight end Southern Connecticut State 1970-73. No pro playing experience. College coach: Idaho State 1974-75, Tufts 1976-77, American International 1978-79, Southern Connecticut State 1980-84 (head coach), East Carolina 1987-88. Pro coach: Ottawa Rough Riders (CFL) 1985-86, joined Oilers in 1989.

Ronnie Jones, linebackers; born October 17, 1955, Dumas, Tex., lives in Sugar Land, Tex. Running back Northwestern (Okla.) State 1974-77. No pro playing experience. College coach: Northeastern Oklahoma State 1979-83, Tulsa 1984, Arizona State 1985-86. Pro coach: Philadelphia Eagles 1987-90, Los Angeles Rams 1991, Los Angeles Raiders 1992, joined Oilers in 1993.

Frank Novak, running backs; born May 18, 1938, Worcester, Mass., lives in Missouri City, Tex. Quarterback Northern Michigan 1959-61. No pro playing experience. College coach: Northern Michigan 1966-72, East Carolina 1973, Virginia 1974-75, Western Illinois 1976-77, Holy Cross 1978-83, Massachusetts 1986, Missouri 1988. Pro coach: Oklahoma Outlaws (USFL) 1984, Birmingham Stallions (USFL) 1985, joined Oilers in 1989.

Buddy Ryan, defensive coordinator; born February 17, 1934, Frederick, Okla., lives in Houston. Guard Oklahoma State 1952-55. No pro playing experience. College coach: Buffalo 1961-65, Vanderbilt 1966, Pacific 1967. Pro coach: New York Jets 1968-75, Minnesota Vikings 1976-77, Chicago Bears 1978-85, Philadelphia Eagles 1986-90 (head coach), joined Oilers in 1993.

Jim Stanley, defensive line; born June 22, 1934, Dunham, Ky., lives in Houston. Guard-defensive tackle Texas A&M 1954-57. No pro playing experience. College coach: Southern Methodist 1961, Texas-El Paso 1962, Oklahoma State 1963-68, 1972-78 (head coach 1973-78), Navy 1969-70. Pro coach: Winnipeg Blue Bombers (CFL) 1971, New York Giants 1979, Atlanta Falcons 1980-82, Michigan Panthers (USFL) 1983-84 (head coach), Tampa Bay Buccaneers 1986, joined Oilers in 1990.

Steve Watterson, strength and rehabilitation; born November 27, 1956, Newport, R.I., lives in Sugar Land, Tex. Attended Rhode Island. No college or pro playing experience. Pro coach: Philadelphia Eagles 1984-85 (assistant trainer), joined Oilers in 1986 (elevated to assistant coach in 1988).

Gregg Williams, special teams; born July 15, 1958, Excelsior Springs, Mo., lives in Katy, Tex. Quarterback Northeast Missouri State 1976-79. No pro playing experience. College coach: Houston 1988-89. Pro coach: Houston Oilers 1990-92 (quality control coordinator), named assistant coach in 1993.

Bob Young, offensive line; born September 3, 1942, Marshall, Tex., lives in Sugar Land, Tex. Guard Texas 1960-61, Howard Payne 1962-63. Pro guard Denver Broncos 1966-70, Houston Oilers 1971, 1980, St. Louis Cardinals 1972-79, New Orleans Saints 1981. College coach: Houston 1987-89. Pro coach: Houston Gamblers (USFL) 1984-85, joined Oilers in 1990.

Houston Oilers 1993 First-Year Roster

Name	Pos.	Ht.	Wt.	Birth-date	College	Hometown	How Acq.
Aldridge, Melvin	S	6-2	200	7/22/70	Murray State	Pittsburg, Tex.	FA
Barrow, Micheal	LB	6-1	236	4/19/70	Miami	Homestead, Fla.	D2
Benton, Gerald	WR	5-7	155	8/24/70	Kansas State	Bay Shore, Fla.	FA
Bishop, Blaine	CB	5-8	184	7/24/70	Ball State	Indianapolis, Ind.	D8
Bradley, Chuck	T	6-5	296	4/9/70	Kentucky	Fern Creek, Ky.	D6
Brown, Reggie (1)	WR	6-1	187	5/5/70	Alabama State	Miami, Fla.	FA
Burns, Chris (1)	DE	6-4	282	1/9/70	Mid. Tennessee State	Franklin, Tenn.	FA
Campbell, Joe (1)	WR	5-8	174	1/4/68	Mid. Tennessee State	Stratford, Tenn.	FA
Carmer, Steven	S	6-1	207	8/26/69	Nebraska	Wahoo, Neb.	FA
Cavness, Grady	CB	5-10	190	9/13/71	Texas	Sugar Land, Tex.	FA
Cuba, Monte (1)	DT	6-4	305	1/29/69	New Mexico	Gilmer, Tex.	FA
Gilbert, Freddie	WR	5-8	174	9/3/69	Houston	Huntsville, Tex.	FA
Gipson, Paul	CB	5-9	178	7/6/70	Houston	Sugar Land, Tex.	FA
Hannah, Travis	WR	5-7	161	1/31/70	Southern California	Hawthorne, Calif.	D4
Hopkins, Brad	T	6-3	306	9/5/70	Illinois	Moline, Ill.	D1
Huerta, Carlos (1)	K	5-7	172	6/29/69	Miami	Coral Gables, Fla.	FA
Joseph, Dale (1)	CB	6-0	180	3/8/67	Howard Payne	Houston, Tex.	FA
Little, Joseph (1)	WR	5-10	157	11/6/69	Cal State-Sacramento	Stockton, Calif.	FA
Martin, Emanuel (1)	CB	5-11	184	7/31/69	Alabama State	Miami, Fla.	FA
Miller, Eric (1)	DE	6-5	275	5/13/69	Miami	Palm Beach Gardens, Fla.	FA
Mills, John Henry	TE	6-0	222	10/31/69	Wake Forest	Tallahassee, Fla.	D5
Nee, John (1)	T-G	6-5	295	11/21/67	Elon	Highland Mills, N.Y.	FA
O'Bradovich, Ed (1)	LB	6-0	247	7/28/69	Michigan State	Chicago, Ill.	FA
Pierce, Alonzo	TE	6-1	241	9/17/68	Baylor	Houston, Tex.	FA
Power, Mike (1)	QB	6-2	190	3/3/67	Boston College	Westboro, Mass.	FA
Raye, Jimmy (1)	WR	5-9	165	11/24/68	San Diego State	Irvine, Calif.	FA
Robinson, Bo	DE	6-3	260	11/20/69	Texas	Bremond, Tex.	FA
Robinson, Patrick	WR	5-8	176	10/3/69	Tennessee State	Memphis, Tenn.	D7
Smith, Eddie	DT	6-1	356	3/23/70	Texas Southern	Jackson, Tenn.	FA
Teeter, Mike (1)	DT	6-2	260	10/4/67	Michigan	Fruitport, Mich.	FA
Truitt, Leroy (1)	T	6-3	310	5/23/69	Houston	La Marque, Tex.	FA
Wallow, Rob (1)	G-T	6-4	280	10/16/69	Northeast Louisiana	Macintosh, Ga.	FA
Williams, James (1)	CB	5-11	190	10/8/70	Texas Southern	Baton Rouge, La.	FA

The term NFL Rookie is defined as a player who is in his first season of professional football and has not been on the roster of another professional football team for any regular-season or postseason games. A Rookie is designated by an "R" on NFL rosters. Players who have been active in another professional football league or players who have NFL experience, including either preseason training camp or being on an Active List or Inactive List, or on Reserve/Injured or Reserve/ Physically Unable to Perform for fewer than six regular-season games, are termed NFL First-Year Players. An NFL First-Year Player is designated by a "1" on NFL rosters. Thereafter, a player is credited with an additional year of experience for each season in which he accumulates six games on the Active List or Inactive List, or on Reserve/Injured or Reserve/ Physically Unable to Perform.

NOTES

American Football Conference Eastern Division

Team Colors: Royal Blue and White

P.O. Box 535000
Indianapolis, Indiana 46253
Telephone: (317) 297-2658

Club Officials

President-Treasurer: Robert Irsay
Vice President-General Manager: James Irsay
Vice President-General Counsel: Michael G. Chernoff
Assistant General Manager: Bob Terpening
Director of Player Personnel: Jack Bushofsky
Controller: Kurt Humphrey
Director of Operations: Pete Ward
Director of Public Relations: Craig Kelley
Ticket Manager: Larry Hall
Director of Sales: Rene Longoria
Assistant Directors of Public Relations: Rod St. Clair, Todd Stewart
Purchasing Administrator: David Filar
Equipment Manager: Jon Scott
Assistant Equipment Manager: Mike Mays
Video Director: Marty Heckscher
Assistant Video Director: John Starliper
Head Trainer: Hunter Smith
Assistant Trainer: Dave Hammer
Team Physician and Orthopedic Surgeon: K. Donald Shelbourne
Orthopedic Surgeon: Arthur C. Rettig

Stadium: Hoosier Dome • **Capacity:** 60,129
100 South Capitol Avenue
Indianapolis, Indiana 46225

Playing Surface: AstroTurf

Training Camp: Anderson University
Anderson, Indiana 46011

1993 Schedule

Preseason

Aug. 7	at Seattle	6:00
Aug. 14	**Cincinnati**	7:00
Aug. 20	**Los Angeles Raiders**	7:00
Aug. 27	at Green Bay	7:00

Regular Season

Sept. 5	**Miami**	12:00
Sept. 12	at Cincinnati	1:00
Sept. 19	**Open Date**	
Sept. 26	**Cleveland**	12:00
Oct. 3	at Denver	2:00
Oct. 10	**Dallas**	12:00
Oct. 17	**Open Date**	
Oct. 24	at Miami	7:30
Oct. 31	**New England**	1:00
Nov. 7	at Washington	8:00
Nov. 14	**New York Jets**	4:00
Nov. 21	at Buffalo	1:00
Nov. 29	**San Diego** (Monday)	9:00
Dec. 5	at New York Jets	1:00
Dec. 12	at New York Giants	1:00
Dec. 19	**Philadelphia**	8:00
Dec. 26	at New England	1:00
Jan. 2	**Buffalo**	1:00

Colts Coaching History

Baltimore 1953-1983
(285-290-7)

1953	Keith Molesworth	3-9-0
1954-62	Weeb Ewbank	61-52-1
1963-69	Don Shula	73-26-4
1970-72	Don McCafferty*	26-11-1
1972	John Sandusky	4-5-0
1973-74	Howard Schnellenberger**	4-13-0
1974	Joe Thomas	2-9-0
1975-79	Ted Marchibroda	41-36-0
1980-81	Mike McCormack	9-23-0
1982-84	Frank Kush***	11-28-1
1984	Hal Hunter	0-1-0
1985-86	Rod Dowhower****	5-24-0
1986-91	Ron Meyer#	36-36-0
1991	Rick Venturi	1-10-0
1992	Ted Marchibroda	9-7-0

*Released after five games in 1972
**Released after three games in 1974
***Resigned after 15 games in 1984
****Released after 13 games in 1986
#Released after 5 games in 1991

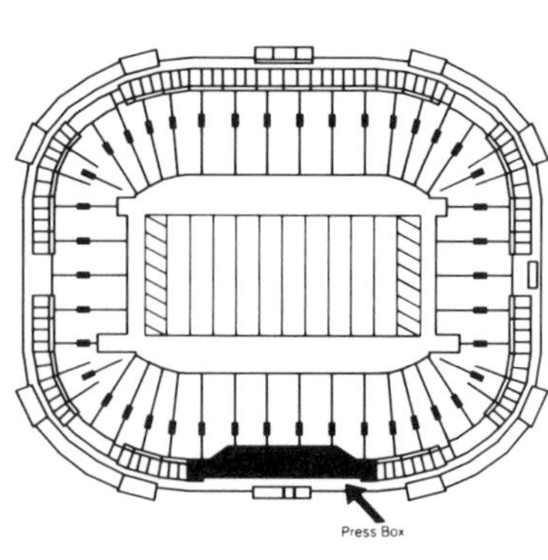

HOOSIER DOME

Record Holders

Individual Records — Career

Category	Name	Performance
Rushing (Yds.)	Lydell Mitchell, 1972-77	5,487
Passing (Yds.)	Johnny Unitas, 1956-1972	39,768
Passing (TDs)	Johnny Unitas, 1956-1972	287
Receiving (No.)	Raymond Berry, 1955-1967	631
Receiving (Yds.)	Raymond Berry, 1955-1967	9,275
Interceptions	Bob Boyd, 1960-68	57
Punting (Avg.)	Rohn Stark, 1982-1992	44.0
Punt Return (Avg.)	Wendell Harris, 1964	12.6
Kickoff Return (Avg.)	Jim Duncan, 1969-1971	32.5
Field Goals	Dean Biasucci 1984, 1986-1992	134
Touchdowns (Tot.)	Lenny Moore, 1956-1967	113
Points	Lenny Moore, 1956-1967	678

Individual Records — Single Season

Category	Name	Performance
Rushing (Yds.)	Eric Dickerson, 1988	1,659
Passing (Yds.)	Johnny Unitas, 1963	3,481
Passing (TDs)	Johnny Unitas, 1959	32
Receiving (No.)	Joe Washington, 1979	82
Receiving (Yds.)	Raymond Berry, 1960	1,298
Interceptions	Tom Keane, 1953	11
Punting (Avg.)	Rohn Stark, 1985	45.9
Punt Return (Avg.)	Clarence Verdin, 1989	12.9
Kickoff Return (Avg.)	Jim Duncan, 1970	35.4
Field Goals	Raul Allegre, 1983	30
Touchdowns (Tot.)	Lenny Moore, 1964	20
Points	Lenny Moore, 1964	120

Individual Records — Single Game

Category	Name	Performance
Rushing (Yds.)	Norm Bulaich, 9-19-71	198
Passing (Yds.)	Johnny Unitas, 9-17-67	401
Passing (TDs)	Gary Cuozzo, 11-14-65	5
	Gary Hogeboom, 10-4-87	5
Receiving (No.)	Lydell Mitchell, 12-15-74	13
	Joe Washington, 9-2-79	13
Receiving (Yds.)	Raymond Berry, 11-10-57	224
Interceptions	Many times	3
	Last time by Mike Prior, 12-20-92	
Field Goals	Many times	5
	Last time by Dean Biasucci, 9-25-88	
Touchdowns (Tot.)	Many times	4
	Last time by Eric Dickerson, 10-31-88	
Points	Many times	24
	Last time by Eric Dickerson, 10-31-88	

1992 Team Record

Preseason (2-2)

Date	Result		Opponents
8/8	W	34-14	New England
8/15	L	10-27	Seattle
8/22	L	0-20	at Cincinnati
8/28	W	21-10	at Kansas City

Regular Season (9-7)

Date	Result		Opponents	Att.
9/6	W	14- 3	Cleveland	51,315
9/13	L	10-20	Houston	45,274
9/20	L	0-38	at Buffalo	78,997
10/4	W	24-14	at Tampa Bay	56,229
10/11	W	6- 3	N.Y. Jets (OT)	45,188
10/18	L	14-34	San Diego	43,805
10/25	W	31-20	at Miami	61,245
11/1	L	0-26	at San Diego	38,832
11/8	L	0-28	Miami	58,599
11/15	L	34-37	New England (OT)	41,426
11/22	L	14-30	at Pittsburgh	58,611
11/29	W	16-13	Buffalo (OT)	47,483
12/6	W	6- 0	at New England	26,196
12/13	W	10- 6	at N.Y. Jets	74,636
12/20	W	16-13	Phoenix	43,135
12/27	W	21-17	at Cincinnati	58,519

(OT) Overtime

Score by Periods

Colts	38	29	58	85	6	—	216
Opponents	80	71	69	79	3	—	302

Attendance

Home 376,225 Away 453,265 Total 829,490
Single-game home record, 61,479 (11-13-83)
Single-season home record, 481,305 (1984)

1992 Team Statistics

	Colts	Opp.
Total First Downs	267	314
Rushing	70	129
Passing	174	164
Penalty	23	21
Third Down: Made/Att.	75/210	70/197
Third Down: Pct.	35.7	35.5
Fourth Down: Made/Att.	5/8	6/15
Fourth Down: Pct.	62.5	40.0
Total Net Yards	4368	5074
Avg. Per Game	273.0	317.1
Total Plays	969	1004
Avg. Per Play	4.5	5.1
Net Yards Rushing	1102	2174
Avg. Per Game	68.9	135.9
Total Rushes	379	495
Net Yards Passing	3266	2900
Avg. Per Game	204.1	181.3
Sacked/Yards Lost	44/318	39/336
Gross Yards	3584	3236
Att./Completions	546/305	470/260
Completion Pct.	55.9	55.3
Had Intercepted	26	20
Punts/Avg.	83/44.8	71/42.5
Net Punting Avg.	83/39.3	71/37.3
Penalties/Yards Lost	122/958	101/836
Fumbles/Ball Lost	24/11	28/15
Touchdowns	24	34
Rushing	8	16
Passing	13	14
Returns	3	4
Avg. Time of Possession	28:17	31:43

1992 Individual Statistics

Scoring	TD R	TD P	TD Rt	PAT	FG	Saf	TP
Biasucci	0	0	0	24/24	16/29	0	72
Culver	7	2	0	0/0	0/0	0	54
Cash	0	3	0	0/0	0/0	0	18
Johnson	0	3	0	0/0	0/0	0	18
Verdin	0	0	2	0/0	0/0	0	12
Arbuckle	0	1	0	0/0	0/0	0	6
Brooks	0	1	0	0/0	0/0	0	6
Emtman	0	0	1	0/0	0/0	0	6
George	1	0	0	0/0	0/0	0	6
Hester	0	1	0	0/0	0/0	0	6
Langhorne	0	1	0	0/0	0/0	0	6
Schultz	0	1	0	0/0	0/0	0	6
Colts	8	13	3	24/24	16/29	0	216
Opponents	16	14	4	33/34	21/28	1	302

Passing	Att.	Comp.	Yds.	Pct.	TD	Int.	Tkld.	Rate
George	306	167	1963	54.6	7	15	27/188	61.5
Trudeau	181	105	1271	58.0	4	8	11/85	68.6
Tupa	33	17	156	51.5	1	2	5/40	49.6
Herrmann	24	15	177	62.5	1	1	1/5	81.4
Johnson	1	0	0	0.0	0	0	0/0	39.6
Stark	1	1	17	100.0	0	0	0/0	118.8
Colts	546	305	3584	55.9	13	26	44/318	64.1
Opponents	470	260	3236	55.3	14	20	39/336	69.1

Rushing	Att.	Yds.	Avg.	LG	TD
Johnson	178	592	3.3	19	0
Culver	121	321	2.7	36t	7
Clark	40	134	3.4	13	0
George	14	26	1.9	13	1
Brooks	2	14	7.0	8	0
Carthon	4	9	2.3	5	0
Tupa	3	9	3.0	10	0
Trudeau	13	6	0.5	5	0
Herrmann	3	−2	−0.7	0	0
Langhorne	1	−7	−7.0	−7	0
Colts	379	1102	2.9	36t	8
Opponents	495	2174	4.4	35t	16

Receiving	No.	Yds.	Avg.	LG	TD
Langhorne	65	811	12.5	34	1
Hester	52	792	15.2	81	1
Johnson	49	517	10.6	57t	3
Brooks	44	468	10.6	26	1
Cash	43	521	12.1	41	3
Culver	26	210	8.1	27	2
Arbuckle	13	152	11.7	23t	1
Clark	5	46	9.2	17	0
Verdin	3	37	12.3	21	0
Carthon	3	10	3.3	6	0
Prior	1	17	17.0	17	0
Schultz	1	3	3.0	3t	1
Colts	305	3584	11.8	81	13
Opponents	260	3236	12.4	69t	14

Interceptions	No.	Yds.	Avg.	LG	TD
Prior	6	44	7.3	19	0
Belser	3	27	9.0	21	0
Goode	2	93	46.5	47	0
Stargell	2	26	13.0	15	0
Emtman	1	90	90.0	90t	1
Bickett	1	14	14.0	14	0
Herrod	1	4	4.0	4	0
Banks	1	3	3.0	3	0
Baylor	1	1	1.0	1	0
Daniel	1	0	0.0	0	0
Radecic	1	0	0.0	0	0
Colts	20	302	15.1	90t	1
Opponents	26	461	17.7	82t	4

Punting	No.	Yds.	Avg.	In 20	LG
Stark	83	3716	44.8	22	64
Colts	83	3716	44.8	22	64
Opponents	71	3021	42.5	24	61

Punt Returns	No.	FC	Yds.	Avg.	LG	TD
Verdin	24	12	268	11.2	84t	2
Prior	1	12	7	7.0	7	0
Colts	25	24	275	11.0	84t	2
Opponents	45	18	313	7.0	24	0

Kickoff Returns	No.	Yds.	Avg.	LG	TD
Verdin	39	815	20.9	42	0
Ambrose	8	126	15.8	26	0
Clark	3	54	18.0	20	0
Vanderbeek	1	6	6.0	6	0
Colts	51	1001	19.6	42	0
Opponents	36	630	17.5	34	0

Sacks	No.
Banks	9.0
Bickett	6.5
Clancy	4.5
Baylor	3.0
Emtman	3.0
Siragusa	3.0
Coryatt	2.0
Daniel	2.0
Herrod	2.0
Hand	1.0
McClendon	1.0
McCoy	1.0
Walker	1.0
Colts	39.0
Opponents	44.0

1993 Draft Choices

Round	Name	Pos.	College
1.	Sean Dawkins	WR	California
2.	Roosevelt Potts	RB	N.E. Louisiana
3.	Ray Buchanan	DB	Louisville
4.	Derwin Gray	DB	Brigham Young
	Devon McDonald	LB	Notre Dame
6.	Carlos Etheredge	TE	Miami
7.	Lance Lewis	RB	Nebraska
8.	Marquise Thomas	LB	Mississippi

Indianapolis Colts 1993 Veteran Roster

No.	Name	Pos.	Ht.	Wt.	Birth-date	NFL Exp.	College	Hometown	How Acq.	'92 Games/ Starts
22	Ambrose, Ashley	CB-S	5-10	177	9/17/70	2	Mississippi Valley State	New Orleans, La.	D2-'92	10/2
81	Arbuckle, Charles	TE	6-3	248	9/13/68	3	UCLA	Beaumont, Tex.	FA-'92	16/3
31	Ball, Michael	CB-S	6-0	220	8/5/64	6	Southern	New Orleans, La.	D4-'88	16/0
51	Banks, Chip	LB	6-4	254	9/18/59	11	Southern California	Augusta, Ga.	T(SD)-'89	16/16
36	Baylor, John	CB-S	6-0	208	3/5/65	6	Southern Mississippi	Meridian, Miss.	D5-'88	16/15
29	Belser, Jason	CB-S	5-9	187	5/28/70	2	Oklahoma	Kansas City, Mo.	D8a-'92	16/2
4	#Bisasucci, Dean	K	6-0	190	7/25/62	9	Western Carolina	Niagara Falls, N.Y.	FA-'86	16/0
50	Bickett, Duane	LB	6-5	251	12/1/62	9	Southern California	Los Angeles, Calif.	D1-'85	15/15
71	Call, Kevin	T	6-7	308	11/13/61	10	Colorado State	Boulder, Colo.	D5b-'84	16/16
88	Cash, Kerry	TE	6-3	252	8/7/69	3	Texas	San Antonio, Tex.	D5-'91	16/16
76	Clancy, Sam	DE	6-7	300	5/29/58	11	Pittsburgh	Pittsburgh, Pa.	PB(Clev)-'89	16/9
32	†Clark, Ken	RB	5-9	204	6/11/66	4	Nebraska	Evergreen, Ala.	FA-'91	13/2
55	Coryatt, Quentin	LB	6-3	250	8/1/70	2	Texas A&M	St. Croix, Virgin Islands	D1b-'92	7/7
80	Cox, Aaron	WR	5-10	178	3/13/65	6	Arizona State	Los Angeles, Calif.	UFA(Rams)-'93	10/4*
35	Culver, Rodney	RB	5-9	224	12/23/69	2	Notre Dame	Detroit, Mich.	D4a-'92	16/2
38	Daniel, Eugene	CB-S	5-11	188	5/4/61	10	Louisiana State	Baton Rouge, La.	D8-'84	14/13
69	Dixon, Randy	G	6-3	305	3/12/65	7	Pittsburgh	Clewiston, Fla.	D4-'87	15/15
90	Emtman, Steve	DE	6-4	290	4/16/70	2	Washington	Spokane, Wash.	D1a-'92	9/9
11	George, Jeff	QB	6-4	227	12/8/67	4	Illinois	Indianapolis, Ind.	D1-'90	10/10
37	Goode, Chris	CB-S	6-0	199	9/17/63	7	Alabama	Town Creek, Ala.	D10-'87	15/15
59	Grant, Stephen	LB	6-0	231	12/23/69	2	West Virginia	Miami, Fla.	D10-'92	16/0
78	Hand, Jon	DE	6-7	301	11/13/63	8	Alabama	Sylacaugua, Ala.	D1-'86	15/9
54	Herrod, Jeff	LB	6-0	249	7/29/66	6	Mississippi	Birmingham, Ala.	D9-'88	16/16
84	Hester, Jessie	WR	5-11	175	1/21/63	8	Florida State	Belle Glade, Fla.	FA-'90	16/16
23	Johnson, Anthony	RB	6-0	222	10/25/67	4	Notre Dame	Indianapolis, Ind.	D2-'90	15/13
85	Langhorne, Reggie	WR	6-2	207	4/7/63	9	Elizabeth City State	Carrollton, Va.	PB(Clev)-'92	16/12
63	Lowdermilk, Kirk	C	6-4	275	4/10/63	9	Ohio State	South Charleston, Va.	UFA(Minn)-'93	16/16*
64	Matich, Trevor	G-T	6-4	297	10/9/61	9	Brigham Young	Sacramento, Calif.	PB(NYJ)-'92	16/1
95	McClendon, Skip	DE-DT	6-7	302	4/9/64	7	Arizona State	Detroit, Mich.	FA-'92	7/4*
61	McCoy, Tony	NT	6-0	279	6/10/69	2	Florida	Orlando, Fla.	D4b-'92	16/3
86	Miller, Eddie	WR	6-0	185	6/20/69	2	South Carolina	Tumison, Ga.	D9-'92	14/0
73	Moss, Zefross	T	6-6	338	8/17/66	5	Alabama State	Tuscaloosa, Ala.	T(Dall)-'89	13/13
96	†Peguese, Willis	DE	6-4	274	12/18/66	4	Miami	Berwick, Pa.	FA-'93	13/1*
97	Radecic, Scott	LB	6-3	240	6/14/62	10	Penn State	Pittsburgh, Pa.	W(Buff)-'90	16/9
74	†Schultz, William	T	6-5	305	5/1/67	4	Southern California	Granada Hills, Calif.	D4b-'90	10/2
98	Siragusa, Tony	NT	6-3	303	5/14/67	4	Pittsburgh	Kenilworth, N.J.	FA-'90	16/12
66	Solt, Ron	G	6-3	280	5/19/62	10	Maryland	Wilkes-Barre, Pa.	PB(Phil)-'92	12/12
45	Stargell, Tony	CB-S	5-11	189	8/7/66	4	Tennessee State	La Grange, Ga.	W(NYJ)-'92	13/3
3	Stark, Rohn	P	6-3	203	5/4/59	12	Florida State	Minneapolis, Minn.	D2b-'82	16/0
79	Staysniak, Joe	T	6-4	296	12/8/66	3	Ohio State	Elyria, Ohio	FA-'92	6/0*
28	Toner, Ed	RB	6-0	240	3/22/68	2	Boston College	Lynn, Mass.	FA-'92	8/0
10	Trudeau, Jack	QB	6-3	227	9/9/62	8	Illinois	Livermore, Calif.	D2-'86	11/5
7	Tupa, Tom	QB	6-4	230	2/6/66	6	Ohio State	Brecksville, Ohio	PB(Phx)-'92	3/0
72	Vander Poel, Mark	T	6-7	303	3/5/88	3	Michigan State	Holland, Mich.	FA-'91	13/0
58	†Vanderbeek, Matt	LB	6-3	258	8/16/67	4	Colorado	Upland, Calif.	D4-'91	15/0
83	Verdin, Clarence	WR	5-8	162	6/14/63	8	Southwestern Louisiana	New Orleans, La.	T(Wash)-'88	16/1
92	Walker, Tony	LB	6-3	246	4/2/68	4	Southeastern Missouri	Birmingham, Ala.	D6-'90	13/1
67	Wolford, Will	T	6-5	296	5/18/64	8	Vanderbilt	Mendham, N.J.	RFA(Buff)-'93	16/16*

* Cox played 10 games with L.A. Rams in '92; Lowdermilk played 16 games with Minnesota; McClendon played 7 games with Indianapolis; Peguese played 1 game with Houston and 12 games with Indianapolis; Staysniak played 6 games with Kansas City; Wolford played 16 games with Buffalo.

#Unrestricted free agent; subject to developments.

† Restricted free agent; subject to developments.

Players lost through free agency (2): WR Bill Brooks (Buff; 14 games in '92); S Mike Prior (GB; 16).

Also played with Colts in '92—DE Mel Agee (1 game), RB Maurice Carthon (16), QB Mark Herrmann (1), CB-S Cornell Holloway (7), T Ron Mattes (5), T Irv Pankey (3), G Tom Ricketts (8).

COACHING STAFF

Head Coach, Ted Marchibroda

Pro Career: Marchibroda ranks as the third-winningest head coach in Colts history with a 50-43 record. He returned to the Colts on January 28, 1992, after serving as head coach with the team from 1975-79. Marchibroda's first tenure produced a 41-36 overall record and three AFC Eastern Divisional titles (1975, 10-4; 1976, 11-3; and 1977, 10-4). He took over a Colts team that was 2-12 in 1974 and produced an eight-game improvement, then the best one-season turnaround in NFL history. It marked the first time a coach had taken a team from last to first place in one season. Marchibroda authored a 9-7 record last year, thus his 1975 and 1992 Colts squads posted two of the four eight-game seasonal turnarounds in NFL history. His three divisional championships represent the most titles won by a Colts head coach. Prior to returning to the Colts, Marchibroda served five years as an assistant with the Buffalo Bills, the last three as offensive coordinator. Marchibroda began his career as backfield coach with the Washington Redskins in 1961. He joined George Allen's staff with the Los Angeles Rams in 1966. He moved with Allen to the Redskins in 1971, where he served as offensive coordinator through the 1974 season. After his stint with the Colts, Marchibroda served as quarterback coach with Chicago in 1981, then moved on to Detroit as offensive coordinator from 1982-83. He served that same role in Philadelphia from 1984-85 before joining Buffalo in 1987. Marchibroda was the first draft pick of the Pittsburgh Steelers in 1953 and played one year before serving in the Army. He returned to Pittsburgh for the 1955-56 seasons. His top year was 1956, completing 124 of 275 passes for 1,585 yards and 12 touchdowns. Marchibroda's playing career ended with the Chicago Cardinals in 1957. Career record: 50-43.

Background: Quarterback at St. Bonaventure 1950-51 and University of Detroit 1952. Led nation in total offense at Detroit. He was a football, basketball (all-state selection), and baseball player at Franklin (Pa.) High School.

Personal: Born March 15, 1931, Franklin, Pa. Ted and his wife, Ann, reside in Indianapolis. They have two daughters, Jodi and Lonni, and two sons, Ted Jr. and Robert.

Assistant Coaches

Ron Blackledge, offensive line; born April 15, 1938, Canton, Ohio, lives in Indianapolis. Tight end-defensive end Bowling Green 1957-59. No pro playing experience. College coach: Ashland 1968-69, Cincinnati 1970-72, Kentucky 1973-75, Princeton 1976, Kent State 1977-81 (head coach 1979-81). Pro coach: Pittsburgh Steelers 1982-91, joined Colts in 1992.

Fred Bruney, offensive assistant; born December 30, 1931, Martins Ferry, Ohio, lives in Indianapolis. Running back-defensive back Ohio State 1950-52. Pro defensive back San Francisco 49ers 1953-56, Pittsburgh Steelers 1957, Los Angeles Rams 1958, and Boston Patriots 1960-62. College coach: Ohio State 1959. Pro coach: Boston Patriots 1962-63, Philadelphia Eagles 1964-68, 1977-85, Atlanta Falcons 1969-76, 1986-89, Tampa Bay Buccaneers 1990, New York Giants 1991-92, joined Colts in 1993.

George Catavolos, secondary; born May 8, 1945, Chicago, Ill., lives in Indianapolis. Defensive back Purdue 1964-66. No pro playing experience. College coach: Purdue 1967-68, 1971-76, Middle Tennessee State 1969, Louisville 1970, Kentucky 1977-81, Tennessee 1982-83. Pro coach: Joined Colts in 1984.

Gene Huey, running backs; born July 20, 1947, Uniontown, Pa., lives in Indianapolis. Defensive back-wide receiver Wyoming 1966-69. No pro playing experience. College coach: Wyoming 1970-74, New Mexico 1975-77, Nebraska 1977-87, Ohio State 1988-91. Pro coach: Joined Colts in 1992.

Indianapolis Colts 1993 First-Year Roster

Name	Pos.	Ht.	Wt.	Birth-date	College	Hometown	How Acq.
Beatty, Eric	LB	6-0	233	4/20/71	Purdue	Oak Park, Mich.	FA
Borgognone, Dirk (1)	K	6-2	220	1/9/68	Pacific	Elko, Nev.	FA
Brandon, Michael (1)	DE	6-4	290	7/30/68	Florida	Berry, Fla.	FA
Buchanan, Ray	CB-S	5-9	193	9/29/71	Louisville	Chicago, Ill.	D3
Cook, Bryan	CB-S	6-3	200	11/13/69	Ohio State	Youngstown, Ohio	FA
Dawkins, Sean	WR	6-4	213	2/3/71	California	Red Bank, N.J.	D1
Etheredge, Carlos	TE	6-5	236	8/10/70	Miami	Albuquerque, N.M.	D6
Garrett, Murray (1)	DE	6-4	285	7/28/69	Eastern New Mexico	Houston, Tex.	FA
Gray, Derwin	CB-S	5-10	190	4/9/71	Brigham Young	San Antonio, Tex.	D4a
Hall, Victor (1)	TE	6-3	288	12/4/68	Auburn	Anniston, Ala.	FA
Hamlet, Anthony (1)	DE	6-3	260	9/4/69	Miami	Delray Beach, Fla.	FA
Heldt, Michael (1)	C	6-2	285	1/2/70	Notre Dame	Cedar Rapids, Iowa	FA
Humphrey, Ronald (1)	RB	5-10	201	3/3/69	Mississippi Valley St.	Marland, Tex.	FA
James, Clint (1)	DE-DT	6-6	288	4/17/67	Louisiana State	New Orleans, La.	FA
Johnson, Hendricks (1)	WR	6-2	185	7/31/68	Northern Arizona	Tucson, Ariz.	FA
Lewis, Lance	RB	5-11	224	3/27/70	Nebraska	Scott City, Kan.	D7
Lowery, Tim	RB	5-11	238	11/29/70	Clark, Ga.	Darlington, S.C.	FA
McCorvey, Derriel	CB-S	6-1	201	3/16/70	Louisiana State	Pensacola, Fla.	FA
McDonald, Devon	LB	6-4	240	11/8/69	Notre Dame	Kingston, Jamaica	D4b
Pesek, Jim	G-T	6-4	293	10/28/69	Illinois	Carmel, Ind.	FA
Potts, Roosevelt	RB	6-0	258	1/8/71	Northeast Louisiana	Rayville, La.	D2
Ratigan, Brian	LB	6-4	226	12/27/70	Notre Dame	Council Bluffs, Iowa	FA
Ray, John (1)	T	6-8	340	4/26/69	West Virginia	South Charleston, W.Va.	FA
Sharp, Jerry	G-T	6-2	289	10/8/69	Syracuse	Rahway, N.J.	FA
Thomas, Marquise	LB	6-4	255	5/25/71	Mississippi	Fresno, Calif.	D8
Toy, Maury (1)	RB	6-0	235	1/27/69	UCLA	Chicago, Ill.	D5-'92
Vickers, Kipp	G-T	6-2	275	8/27/69	Miami	Holiday, Fla.	FA
White, Erik	QB	6-6	215	9/12/70	Bowling Green	Massillon, Ohio	FA
Young, Robbie	CB-S	6-1	191	10/23/71	Vanderbilt	Evansville, Ind.	FA

The term NFL Rookie is defined as a player who is in his first season of professional football and has not been on the roster of another professional football team for any regular-season or postseason games. A Rookie is designated by an "R" on NFL rosters. Players who have been active in another professional football league or players who have NFL experience, including either preseason training camp or being on an Active List, Inactive List, Reserve/Injured or Reserve/Physically Unable to Perform for fewer than six regular season games, are termed NFL First-Year Players. An NFL First-Year Player is designated by a "1" on NFL rosters. Thereafter, a player is credited with an additional year of experience for each season in which he accumulates six games on the Active List, Inactive List, Reserve/Injured, or Reserve/Physically Unable to Perform.

NOTES

Nick Nicolau, offensive coordinator; born May 5, 1933, New York, N.Y., lives in Indianapolis. Running back Southern Connecticut 1957-59. No pro playing experience. College coach: Southern Connecticut 1960, Springfield 1961, Bridgeport 1962-69 (head coach 1965-69), Massachusetts 1970, Connecticut 1971-72, Kentucky 1973-75, Kent State 1976. Pro coach: Hamilton Tiger-Cats (CFL) 1977, Montreal Alouettes (CFL) 1978-79, New Orleans Saints 1980, Denver Broncos 1981-87, Los Angeles Raiders 1988, Buffalo Bills 1989-91, joined Colts in 1992.

Dwain Painter, receivers; born February 13, 1942, Monroeville, Pa., lives in Indianapolis. Quarterback-defensive back Rutgers 1961-64. No pro playing experience. College coach: San Jose State 1971-72, College of San Mateo 1973, Brigham Young 1974-75, UCLA 1976-78, Northern Arizona 1979-81 (head coach), Georgia Tech 1982-85, Texas 1986, Illinois 1987. Pro coach: Pittsburgh Steelers 1988-91, joined Colts in 1992.

Francis Peay, defensive line; born May 23, 1944, Pittsburgh, Pa., lives in Indianapolis. Tackle Missouri 1963-66. Pro tackle New York Giants 1966-67, Green Bay Packers 1968-72, Kansas City Chiefs 1973-74. College coach: Notre Dame 1976-77, California 1978-79, Northwestern 1980-81, 1986-91 (head coach). Pro coach: Joined Colts in 1992.

Jay Robertson, defensive assistant; born February 20, 1940, Chicago, Ill., lives in Indianapolis. Center Northwestern 1959-62. No pro playing experience. College coach: Northwestern 1967-75, Northern Illinois 1976-79, Wisconsin 1980-81, Notre Dame 1982-83, Army 1984-91. Pro coach: Joined Colts in 1992.

Brad Seely, special teams-tight ends; born September 6, 1956, Vinton, Iowa, lives in Indianapolis. Tackle-guard South Dakota State 1974-77. No pro playing experience. College coach: Colorado State 1980, Southern Methodist 1981, North Carolina State 1982, Pacific 1983, Oklahoma State 1984-88. Pro coach: Joined Colts in 1989.

Rick Venturi, defensive coordinator-linebackers; born February 23, 1946, Taylorville, Ill., lives in Indianapolis. Quarterback-defensive back Northwestern 1965-67. No pro playing experience. College coach: Northwestern 1968-72, 1978-80 (head coach), Purdue 1973-76, Illinois 1977. Pro coach: Hamilton Tiger-Cats (CFL) 1981, joined Colts in 1982 (head coach for 11 games in 1991).

Tom Zupancic, strength and conditioning; born September 14, 1955, Indianapolis, lives in Indianapolis. Defensive tackle-offensive tackle Indiana Central 1975-78. No pro playing experience. Pro coach: Joined Colts in 1984.

American Football Conference Western Division

Team Colors: Red, Gold, and White

One Arrowhead Drive
Kansas City, Missouri 64129
Telephone: (816) 924-9300

Club Officials

Founder: Lamar Hunt
Chairman of the Board: Jack Steadman
President/General Manager and Chief Operating Officer: Carl Peterson
Executive Vice President: Tim Connolly
Vice President/Player Personnel: Lynn Stiles
Assistant General Manager: Dennis Thum
Secretary: Jim Seigfreid
Director of Finance/Treasurer: Dale Young
Director of Public Relations: Bob Moore
Director of Operations: Jeff Klein
Director of Marketing & Sales: Dennis Watley
Director of Development: Ken Blume
Assistant Director of Public Relations: Jim Carr
Director of Promotions: Phil Thomas
Community Relations Manager: Brenda Boatright-Sniezek
Ticket Manager: Phil Youtsey
Equipment Manager: Mike Davidson
Assistant Equipment Manager: Allen Wright, Darin Kerns
Trainer: Dave Kendall
Assistant Trainer: Bud Epps
Video Coordinator: Mike Dennis
Assistant Video Coordinator: Mike Kirk

Stadium: Arrowhead Stadium • **Capacity:** 78,067
One Arrowhead Drive
Kansas City, Missouri 64129

Playing Surface: AstroTurf-8

Training Camp: University of Wisconsin-River Falls
River Falls, Wisconsin 54022

1993 Schedule

Preseason

Aug. 7	vs. Green Bay at Milw.	7:00
Aug. 12	**Buffalo**	7:00
Aug. 21	**Minnesota**	7:00
Aug. 27	at New England	7:00

Regular Season

Sept. 5	at Tampa Bay	1:00
Sept. 12	at Houston	12:00
Sept. 20	**Denver** (Monday)	8:00
Sept. 26	**Open Date**	
Oct. 3	**Los Angeles Raiders**	12:00
Oct. 10	**Cincinnati**	12:00
Oct. 17	at San Diego	1:00
Oct. 24	**Open Date**	
Oct. 31	at Miami	1:00
Nov. 8	**Green Bay** (Monday)	8:00
Nov. 14	at Los Angeles Raiders	1:00
Nov. 21	**Chicago**	12:00
Nov. 28	**Buffalo**	3:00
Dec. 5	at Seattle	1:00
Dec. 12	at Denver	2:00
Dec. 19	**San Diego**	3:00
Dec. 26	at Minnesota	7:00
Jan. 2	**Seattle**	12:00

Chiefs Coaching History

Dallas Texans 1960-62
(250-235-12)

1960-74	Hank Stram	129-79-10
1975-77	Paul Wiggin*	11-24-0
1977	Tom Bettis	1-6-0
1978-82	Marv Levy	31-42-0
1983-86	John Mackovic	30-35-0
1987-88	Frank Gansz	8-22-1
1989-92	Marty Schottenheimer	40-27-1

*Released after seven games in 1977

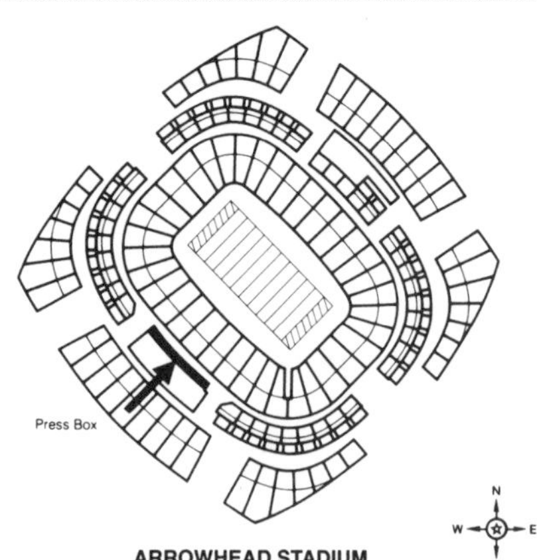

ARROWHEAD STADIUM

Record Holders

Individual Records — Career

Category	Name	Performance
Rushing (Yds.)	Christian Okoye, 1987-1992	4,897
Passing (Yds.)	Len Dawson, 1962-1975	28,507
Passing (TDs)	Len Dawson, 1962-1975	237
Receiving (No.)	Henry Marshall, 1976-1987	416
Receiving (Yds.)	Otis Taylor, 1965-1975	7,306
Interceptions	Emmitt Thomas, 1966-1978	58
Punting (Avg.)	Jerrel Wilson, 1963-1977	43.5
Punt Return (Avg.)	J.T. Smith, 1979-1984	10.6
Kickoff Return (Avg.)	Noland Smith, 1967-69	26.8
Field Goals	Nick Lowery, 1980-1992	306
Touchdowns (Tot.)	Otis Taylor, 1965-1975	60
Points	Nick Lowery, 1980-1992	1,360

Individual Records — Single Season

Category	Name	Performance
Rushing (Yds.)	Christian Okoye, 1989	1,480
Passing (Yds.)	Bill Kenney, 1983	4,348
Passing (TDs)	Len Dawson, 1964	30
Receiving (No.)	Carlos Carson, 1983	80
Receiving (Yds.)	Carlos Carson, 1983	1,351
Interceptions	Emmitt Thomas, 1974	12
Punting (Avg.)	Jerrel Wilson, 1965	46.0
Punt Return (Avg.)	Abner Haynes, 1960	15.4
Kickoff Return (Avg.)	Dave Grayson, 1962	29.7
Field Goals	Nick Lowery, 1990	34
Touchdowns (Tot.)	Abner Haynes, 1962	19
Points	Nick Lowery, 1990	139

Individual Records — Single Game

Category	Name	Performance
Rushing (Yds.)	Barry Word, 10-14-90	200
Passing (Yds.)	Len Dawson, 11-1-64	435
Passing (TDs)	Len Dawson, 11-1-64	6
Receiving (No.)	Ed Podolak, 10-7-73	12
Receiving (Yds.)	Stephone Paige, 12-22-85	309
Interceptions	Bobby Ply, 12-16-62	*4
	Bobby Hunt, 12-4-64	*4
	Deron Cherry, 9-29-85	*4
Field Goals	Many times	5
	Last time by Nick Lowery, 12-29-90	
Touchdowns (Tot.)	Abner Haynes, 11-26-61	5
Points	Abner Haynes, 11-26-61	30

*NFL Record

1992 Team Record

Preseason (1-3)

Date	Result		Opponents
8/8	L	13-21	at Green Bay
8/15	L	0-30	at Minnesota
8/24	W	35- 0	Buffalo
8/28	L	10-21	Indianapolis

Regular Season (10-6)

Date	Result		Opponents	Att.
9/6	W	24-10	at San Diego	43,403
9/13	W	26- 7	Seattle	76,591
9/20	L	20-23	at Houston (OT)	62,672
9/28	W	27- 7	L.A. Raiders	76,607
10/4	L	19-20	at Denver	74,372
10/11	W	24-17	Philadelphia	76,570
10/18	L	10-17	at Dallas	62,775
10/25	L	3-27	Pittsburgh	76,610
11/8	W	16-14	San Diego	76,590
11/15	W	35-16	Washington	76,617
11/22	W	24-14	at Seattle	64,017
11/29	W	23- 7	at N.Y. Jets	75,473
12/6	L	7-28	at L.A. Raiders	44,029
12/13	W	27-20	New England	76,580
12/19	L	21-35	at N.Y. Giants	75,981
12/27	W	42-20	Denver	76,608

(OT) Overtime

Postseason (0-1)

Date	Result		Opponent	Att.
1/2	L	0-17	San Diego	58,278

Score by Periods

Chiefs	53	128	66	101	0	—	348
Opponents	68	57	64	90	3	—	282

Attendance

Home 612,773 Away 502,722 Total 1,115,495
Single-game home record, 82,094 (11-5-72)
Single-season home record, 612,773 (1992)

1992 Team Statistics

	Chiefs	Opp.
Total First Downs	246	256
Rushing	87	97
Passing	134	145
Penalty	25	14
Third Down: Made/Att.	71/207	73/205
Third Down: Pct.	34.3	35.6
Fourth Down: Made/Att.	5/14	6/11
Fourth Down: Pct.	35.7	54.5
Total Net Yards	4324	4324
Avg. Per Game	270.3	270.3
Total Plays	907	949
Avg. Per Play	4.8	4.6
Net Yards Rushing	1532	1787
Avg. Per Game	95.8	111.7
Total Rushes	446	441
Net Yards Passing	2792	2537
Avg. Per Game	174.5	158.6
Sacked/Yards Lost	48/323	50/391
Gross Yards	3115	2928
Att./Completions	413/230	458/253
Completion Pct.	55.7	55.2
Had Intercepted	12	24
Punts/Avg.	86/42.2	80/43.1
Net Punting Avg.	86/35.4	80/36.0
Penalties/Yards Lost	82/675	124/959
Fumbles/Ball Lost	28/9	34/15
Touchdowns	40	34
Rushing	14	12
Passing	15	19
Returns	11	3
Avg. Time of Possession	29:37	30:23

1992 Individual Statistics

Scoring	TD R	TD P	TD Rt	PAT	FG	Saf	TP
Lowery	0	0	0	39/39	22/24	0	105
Okoye	6	0	0	0/0	0/0	0	36
Barnett	0	4	0	0/0	0/0	0	24
Word	4	0	0	0/0	0/0	0	24
Birden	0	3	0	0/0	0/0	0	18
Carter	0	0	3	0/0	0/0	0	18
Davis	0	3	0	0/0	0/0	0	18
Mincy	0	0	3	0/0	0/0	0	18
Cash	0	2	0	0/0	0/0	0	12
Hayes	0	2	0	0/0	0/0	0	12
Krieg	2	0	0	0/0	0/0	0	12
McNair	1	1	0	0/0	0/0	0	12
Marts	0	0	1	0/0	0/0	0	6
Rogers	0	0	1	0/0	0/0	0	6
Ross	0	0	1	0/0	0/0	0	6
N. Smith	0	0	1	0/0	0/0	0	6
Thomas	0	0	1	0/0	0/0	0	6
Williams	1	0	0	0/0	0/0	0	6
Murray	0	0	0	0/0	1/1	0	3
Chiefs	14	15	11	39/40	23/25	0	348
Opponents	12	19	3	33/34	15/21	0	282

Passing	Att.	Comp.	Yds.	Pct.	TD	Int.	Tkld.	Rate
Krieg	413	230	3115	55.7	15	12	48/323	79.9
Chiefs	413	230	3115	55.7	15	12	48/323	79.9
Opponents	458	253	2928	55.2	19	24	50/391	66.7

Rushing	Att.	Yds.	Avg.	LG	TD
Word	163	607	3.7	44t	4
Okoye	144	448	3.1	22	6
Williams	78	262	3.4	11	1
McNair	21	124	5.9	30	1
Krieg	37	74	2.0	17	2
Harry	1	27	27.0	27	0
Anders	1	1	1.0	1	0
Davis	1	−11	−11.0	−11	0
Chiefs	446	1532	3.4	44t	14
Opponents	441	1787	4.1	40t	12

Receiving	No.	Yds.	Avg.	LG	TD
McNair	44	380	8.6	36	1
Birden	42	644	15.3	72t	3
Davis	36	756	21.0	74t	3
Barnett	24	442	18.4	77t	4
F. Jones	18	265	14.7	56	0
Hargain	17	205	12.1	25	0
Cash	12	113	9.4	19	2
Word	9	80	8.9	22	0
Hayes	9	77	8.6	21	2
Anders	5	65	13.0	28	0
Harry	5	46	9.2	13	0
Williams	5	24	4.8	12	0
B. Jones	2	6	3.0	5	0
Dyal	1	7	7.0	7	0
Okoye	1	5	5.0	5	0
Chiefs	230	3115	13.5	77t	15
Opponents	253	2928	11.6	62	19

Interceptions	No.	Yds.	Avg.	LG	TD
Carter	7	65	9.3	36t	1
Mincy	4	128	32.0	39	2
Thompson	4	26	6.5	25	0
Simien	3	18	6.0	10	0
Ross	1	99	99.0	99t	1
Marts	1	36	36.0	36t	1
N. Smith	1	22	22.0	22t	1
Terry	1	9	9.0	9	0
Bayless	1	0	0.0	0	0
A. Lewis	1	0	0.0	0	0
Chiefs	24	403	16.8	99t	6
Opponents	12	162	13.5	38	0

Punting	No.	Yds.	Avg.	In 20	LG
Barker	75	3245	43.3	16	65
Sullivan	6	247	41.2	2	59
Lowery	4	141	35.3	0	39
Chiefs	86	3633	42.2	18	65
Opponents	80	3445	43.1	22	67

Punt Returns	No.	FC	Yds.	Avg.	LG	TD
Carter	38	6	398	10.5	86t	2
Mincy	1	1	4	4.0	4	0
Birden	0	1	0	—	—	0
Chiefs	39	8	402	10.3	86t	2
Opponents	40	15	328	8.2	80t	1

Kickoff Returns	No.	Yds.	Avg.	LG	TD
Williams	21	405	19.3	37	0
Anders	1	20	20.0	20	0
Carter	11	190	17.3	39	0
Cash	1	36	36.0	36	0
F. Jones	3	51	17.0	23	0
McNair	2	20	10.0	14	0
Chiefs	39	722	18.5	39	0
Opponents	64	1203	18.8	42	0

Sacks	No.
N. Smith	14.5
Thomas	14.5
Saleaumua	6.0
Sims	3.0
Griffin	2.5
Phillips	2.5
Maas	1.5
Thompson	1.5
Pearson	1.0
Simien	1.0
Martin	0.5
Ross	0.5
Chiefs	50.0
Opponents	48.0

1993 Draft Choices

Round	Name	Pos.	College
3.	Will Shields	G	Nebraska
4.	Jaime Fields	LB	Washington
5.	Lindsay Knapp	G	Notre Dame
6.	Darius Turner	RB	Washington
7.	Danan Hughes	WR	Iowa

Kansas City Chiefs 1993 Veteran Roster

No.	Name	Pos.	Ht.	Wt.	Birth-date	NFL Exp.	College	Hometown	How Acq.	'92 Games/ Starts
32	Allen, Marcus	RB	6-2	210	3/26/60	12	Southern California	San Diego, Calif.	UFA(Raid)-'93	16/0*
76	Alt, John	T	6-8	303	5/30/62	10	Iowa	Columbia Heights, Minn.	D1b-'84	16/16
38	Anders, Kimble	RB	5-11	221	9/10/66	3	Houston	Galveston, Tex.	FA-'91	11/2
50	Anderson, Erick	LB	6-1	241	10/7/68	2	Michigan	Glenbrook, Ill.	D7-'92	0*
77	Baldinger, Rich	T-G	6-4	293	12/31/59	12	Wake Forest	Long Island, N.Y.	FA-'83	13/11
4	Barker, Bryan	P	6-1	187	6/28/64	4	Santa Clara	Orinda, Calif.	FA-'90	15/0
82	Barnett, Tim	WR	6-1	201	4/19/68	3	Jackson State	Rosedale, Miss.	D3-'91	12/3
30	Bayless, Martin	S	6-2	213	10/11/62	10	Bowling Green	Dayton, Ohio	PB(SD)-'92	16/16
88	†Birden, J.J.	WR	5-9	170	6/16/65	5	Oregon	Portland, Ore.	FA-'90	16/11
14	Blundin, Matt	QB	6-6	230	3/7/69	2	Virginia	Ridley, Pa.	D2-'92	0*
34	Carter, Dale	CB-KR	6-1	188	11/28/69	2	Tennessee	Covington, Ga.	D1-'92	16/9
89	Cash, Keith	TE	6-4	245	8/7/69	2	Texas	San Antonio, Tex.	PB(Pitt)-'92	15/8
24	Dandridge, Gary	S	6-0	213	12/14/68	2	Appalachian State	Bristol, Tenn.	FA-'93	0*
84	Davis, Willie	WR	6-0	170	10/10/67	2	Central Arkansas	Altheimer, Ark.	FA-'92	16/14
71	Dohring, Tom	T	6-6	290	5/24/68	3	Michigan	Dearborn, Mich.	D8-'91	3/1
87	Dyal, Mike	TE	6-2	240	5/20/66	6	Texas A&I	Kerrville, Tex.	PB(Raid)-'92	3/0
94	Evans, Mike	DT-DE	6-3	269	6/2/67	2	Michigan	Roxbury, Mass.	D4-'92	12/1
26	Flagler, Terrence	RB	6-0	200	9/24/64	6	Clemson	Fernandina Beach, Fla.	FA-'93	0*
74	Graham, Derrick	T	6-4	306	3/18/67	4	Appalachian State	Groveland, Fla.	D5a-'90	2/2
98	#Griffin, Leonard	DE	6-4	278	9/22/62	8	Grambling	Lake Providence, La.	D3-'86	15/10
61	Grunhard, Tim	C	6-2	299	5/17/68	4	Notre Dame	Chicago, Ill.	D2-'90	12/12
56	#Hackett, Dino	LB	6-3	230	6/28/64	8	Appalachian State	Greensboro, N.C.	D2-'86	0*
81	Hargain, Tony	WR	6-0	194	12/26/67	2	Oregon	North Highlands, Calif.	PB(SF)-'92	12/0
85	Hayes, Jonathan	TE	6-5	248	8/11/62	9	Iowa	Pittsburgh, Pa.	D2-'85	16/16*
40	Highsmith, Alonzo	RB	6-1	235	2/26/65	6	Miami	Miami, Fla.	FA-'93	5/2*
80	†Jones, Fred	WR	5-9	183	3/6/67	4	Grambling	Decatur, Ga.	D4-'90	14/4
91	Kirksey, William	LB	6-2	237	1/29/66	3	Southern Mississippi	Leeds, Ala.	FA-'92	0*
17	Krieg, Dave	QB	6-1	202	10/20/58	14	Milton	Schofield, Wis.	PB(Sea)-'92	16/16
29	Lewis, Albert	CB	6-2	195	10/6/60	11	Grambling	Mansfield, La.	D3-'83	9/8
21	Lewis, Tahaun	CB	5-10	175	9/29/68	2	Nebraska	Colorado Springs, Colo.	PB(Raid)-'92	9/0
8	Lowery, Nick	K	6-4	205	5/27/56	14	Dartmouth	Washington, D.C.	FA-'80	15/0
51	Marts, Lonnie	LB	6-1	243	11/10/68	4	Tulane	New Orleans, La.	FA-'90	15/3
48	†McNair, Todd	RB	6-1	202	10/7/65	5	Temple	Pennsauken, N.J.	D8b-'89	16/0
92	Mickell, Darren	DE	6-4	268	8/3/70	2	Florida	Miami, Fla.	SD2-'92	1/0
42	†Mincy, Charles	S	5-11	197	12/16/69	3	Washington	Los Angeles, Calif.	D5-'91	16/16
19	t-Montana, Joe	QB	6-2	195	6/11/56	15	Notre Dame	Monongahela, Pa.	T(SF)-'93	1/0*
96	Newton, Tim	DT	6-0	275	3/23/63	8	Florida	Orlando, Fla.	FA-'93	0*
35	Okoye, Christian	RB	6-1	260	8/16/61	7	Azusa Pacific	Enugu, Nigeria	D2-'87	15/5
75	Phillips, Joe	DT	6-5	300	7/15/63	7	Southern Methodist	Vancouver, Wash.	FA-'92	12/10
64	Ricketts, Tom	G	6-5	305	11/21/65	5	Pittsburgh	Murrysville, Pa.	FA-'93	0*
52	†Rogers, Tracy	LB	6-2	241	8/13/67	4	Fresno State	Taft, Calif.	FA-'90	8/0
31	Ross, Kevin	CB	5-9	185	1/16/62	10	Temple	Paulsboro, N.J.	D7-'84	16/16
97	Saleaumua, Dan	DT	6-0	295	11/25/64	7	Arizona State	San Diego, Calif.	PB(Det)-'89	16/16
66	Siglar, Ricky	T-G	6-7	296	6/14/66	2	San Jose State	Manzano, N.M.	FA-'93	0*
54	Simien, Tracy	LB	6-1	250	5/21/67	3	Texas Christian	Bay City, Tex.	FA-'91	15/15
95	Sims, Tom	DT	6-2	291	4/18/67	4	Pittsburgh	Detroit, Mich.	D6-'90	12/0
90	#Smith, Neil	DE	6-4	275	4/10/66	6	Nebraska	New Orleans, La.	D1-'88	16/16
55	Snow, Percy	LB	6-2	250	11/5/67	4	Michigan State	Canton, Ohio	D1-'90	15/1
79	Szott, Dave	G	6-4	290	12/12/67	4	Penn State	Clifton, N.J.	D7-'90	16/16
27	t-Taylor, Jay	CB	5-10	170	11/8/67	5	San Jose State	San Diego, Calif.	T(Phx)-'93	0*
32	Terry, Doug	S	5-11	192	12/12/69	2	Kansas	Liberal, Kan.	FA-'92	16/1
58	Thomas, Derrick	LB	6-3	242	1/1/67	5	Alabama	Miami, Fla.	D1-'89	16/16
60	Thome, Chris	C	6-5	280	1/15/69	3	Minnesota	St. Paul, Minn.	FA-'93	0*
46	Thompson, Bennie	S	6-0	214	2/10/63	4	Grambling	New Orleans, La.	PB(NO)-'92	16/0
73	Valerio, Joe	T-C	6-5	293	2/11/69	3	Pennsylvania	Ridley, Pa.	D2-'91	16/3
41	t-Whitmore, David	S	6-0	217	7/6/67	4	Stephen F. Austin	Daingerfield, Tex.	T(SF)-'93	16/12*
44	Williams, Harvey	RB	6-2	229	4/22/67	3	Louisiana State	Hempstead, Tex.	D1-'91	14/0
23	#Word, Barry	RB	6-2	245	7/17/64	5	Virginia	Long Island, Va.	FA-'90	12/11
15	Young, Michael	WR	6-1	183	2/21/62	9	UCLA	Hanford, Calif.	FA-'93	0*
91	Young, Todd	TE	6-5	269	2/2/67	2	Penn State	Tempe, Ariz.	FA-'92	0*

* Allen played 16 games with L.A. Raiders in '92; Anderson, Dandridge, Hackett, Kirksey, Taylor, and T. Young missed '92 season due to injury; Blundin active for 16 games but did not play; Flagler last active with Phoenix in '91; Highsmith played 5 games with Tampa Bay; Montana played 1 game with San Francisco; Newton last active with Tampa Bay in '91; Ricketts last active with Pittsburgh in '91; Siglar last active with San Francisco in '90; Thome last active with N.Y. Giants in '92; Whitmore played 16 games with San Francisco; M. Young last active with Denver in '91.

#Unrestricted free agent; subject to developments.

† Restricted free agent; subject to developments.

Traded—LB Chris Martin to L.A. Rams.

t- Chiefs traded for Montana (San Francisco), Taylor (Phoenix), Whitmore (San Francisco).

Players lost through free agency (5): C Kani Kauahi (Phx; 16 games in '92), G Dave Lutz (Det; 16), DE Bill Maas (GB; 9), CB-S Jayice Pearson (Minn; 7), QB Mark Vlasic (TB; 0).

Also played with Chiefs in '92—C Mike Baab (3 games), WR Emile Harry (7), RB Bill Jones (7), CB Cedric Mack (1), CB Darrell Malone (4), LB Chris Martin (14), K Eddie Murray (1), S Kevin Porter (13), LB Ervin Randle (8), G Joe Staysniak (7), P Kent Sullivan (1).

COACHING STAFF

Head Coach, Marty Schottenheimer

Pro Career: In four seasons as head coach of the Kansas City Chiefs, Schottenheimer has established the highest winning percentage in franchise history (.614). Moreover, his .619 regular season winning percentage is fifth highest among active NFL coaches with at least four full seasons of experience. He has directed the Chiefs to four of their six winning seasons since 1974 and has taken Kansas City to the playoffs three consecutive years, a team record. He is the only coach that has taken his team to the playoffs seven times since 1985 and has missed the playoffs only once as an NFL head coach. As head coach of the Cleveland Browns from midseason in 1984 through 1988, he led the club to four playoff berths, three AFC Central Division titles, two AFC Championship Game appearances, and captured AFC coach of the years honors (1986). He first joined the Browns in 1980 as defensive coordinator after serving as linebackers coach of the Detroit Lions in 1978-79. His first NFL coaching job came with the New York Giants, where he was linebackers coach and later defensive coordinator from 1975-77. He also served as an assistant coach with the Portland Storm (WFL) in 1974. A seventh-round draft choice of the Buffalo Bills in 1965, he played linebacker with the Bills until 1968 and finished his pro playing career with the Boston Patriots in 1969-70. Career record: 86-58-1.

Background: Schottenheimer was an All-America linebacker at the University of Pittsburgh 1962-64. Following his retirement from pro football, he worked as a real estate developer in both Miami and Denver from 1971-74.

Personal: Born September 23, 1943, Canonsburg, Pa. Marty and his wife, Patricia, live in Overland Park, Kan., and have one daughter, Kristen, and one son, Brian.

Assistant Coaches

Dave Adolph, defensive coordinator-linebackers; born June 6, 1937, Akron, Ohio, lives in Overland Park, Kan. Guard-linebacker Akron 1955-58. No pro playing experience. College coach: Akron 1963-64, Connecticut 1965-68, Kentucky 1969-72, Illinois 1973-76, Ohio State 1977-78. Pro coach: Cleveland Browns 1979-84, 1986-88, San Diego Chargers 1985, Los Angeles Raiders 1989-91, joined Chiefs in 1992.

Russ Ball, assistant strength and conditioning; born August 28, 1959, Moberly, Mo., lives in Kansas City. Center Central Missouri State 1977-80. No pro playing experience. College coach: Missouri 1981-88. Pro coach: Joined Chiefs in 1989.

John Bunting, defensive assistant; born July 15, 1950, Portland, Me., lives in Kansas City. Linebacker North Carolina 1968-71. Pro linebacker Philadelphia Eagles 1972-82, Philadelphia Stars (USFL) 1983-84. College coach: Brown 1986, Rowan College 1987-92 (head coach 1988-92). Pro coach: Baltimore Stars (USFL) 1985, joined Chiefs in 1993.

Herman Edwards, defensive backs; born April 27, 1954, Ft. Monmouth, N.J., lives in Blue Springs, Mo. Defensive back California 1972-75, San Diego State 1976-77. Pro cornerback Philadelphia Eagles 1977-85, Los Angeles Rams 1986, Atlanta Falcons 1986. Pro scout: Kansas City Chiefs 1989-91. Pro coach: Joined Chiefs in 1992.

Alex Gibbs, offensive line; born February 11, 1941, Morganton, N.C., lives in Kansas City. Running back-defensive back Davidson College 1959-63. No pro playing experience. College coach: Duke 1969-70, Kentucky 1971-72, West Virginia 1973-74, Ohio State 1975-78, Auburn 1979-81, Georgia 1982-83. Pro coach: Denver Broncos 1984-87, Los Angeles Raiders 1988-89, San Diego Chargers 1990-91, Indianapolis Colts 1992, joined Chiefs in 1993.

Kansas City Chiefs 1993 First-Year Roster

Name	Pos.	Ht.	Wt.	Birth-date	College	Hometown	How Acq.
Bartrum, Mike	TE	6-4	233	6/23/70	Marshall	Pomeroy, Ohio	FA
Bender, Wes	RB	5-9	232	8/2/70	Southern California	Burbank, Calif.	FA
Cobb, Trevor	RB	5-9	190	11/20/70	Rice	Pasadena, Tex.	FA
Dickerson, Ron	WR	6-0	206	8/31/71	Arkansas	State College, Pa.	FA
Earle, John (1)	G-C	6-5	284	7/3/69	Western Illinois	Keyport, N.J.	FA
Ervin, Corris (1)	CB	5-11	183	8/30/66	Central Florida	Coral Springs, Fla.	FA
Fields, Jaime	LB	5-11	230	8/28/70	Washington	Lynwood, Calif.	D4
Gay, Matt	WR	5-11	180	4/3/70	Kansas	Chicago, Ill.	FA
Hilleary, Chip	QB	6-1	185	2/22/71	Kansas	Westerville, Ohio	FA
Hughes, Danan	WR	6-1	201	12/11/70	Iowa	Bayonne, N.J.	D7
Jackson, Byron (1)	WR	5-7	160	2/16/68	San Jose State	Landover, Md.	FA
Jennings, Jim (1)	G-C	6-4	295	4/4/69	San Diego State	San Marcos, Calif.	FA
Jones, Jeff	WR	5-10	185	10/19/70	California	Irvine, Calif.	FA
Knapp, Lindsay	G-T	6-6	276	2/25/70	Notre Dame	Deerfield, Ill.	D5
Lolar, Morris	CB-S	5-10	176	12/18/70	Friends, Kan.	Wichita, Kan.	FA
Marrow, Vince (1)	TE	6-3	251	8/17/68	Toledo	Youngstown, Ohio	FA
McDaniels, Pellom (1)	DE	6-3	278	2/21/68	Oregon State	San Jose, Calif.	FA
McWright, Robert (1)	CB	5-8	170	11/10/66	Texas Christian	Dallas, Tex.	FA
Pharms, Charles (1)	S	5-11	185	12/15/69	Miami	Houston, Tex.	FA
Shields, Will	G	6-2	299	9/15/71	Nebraska	Lawton, Okla.	D3
Smith, Leroy (1)	LB	6-2	225	1/6/69	Iowa	Sicklerville, N.J.	FA
Smith, Michael (1)	WR	5-8	160	11/21/70	Kansas State	New Orleans, La.	FA
Smith, Tony (1)	WR	6-2	185	10/2/69	Notre Dame	Gary, Ind.	D6-'92
Stephens, Santo (1)	LB	6-4	232	6/16/69	Temple	Capital Heights, Md.	FA
Thompson, Ernie (1)	RB	5-11	230	10/25/69	Indiana	Terre Haute, Ind.	FA
Turner, Darius	RB	5-11	235	1/3/70	Washington	Gardena, Calif.	D6

The term NFL Rookie is defined as a player who is in his first season of professional football and has not been on the roster of another professional football team for any regular-season or postseason games. A Rookie is designated by an "R" on NFL rosters. Players who have been active in another professional football league or players who have NFL experience, including either preseason training camp or being on an Active List or Inactive List, or on Reserve/Injured or Reserve/Physically Unable to Perform for fewer than six regular-season games, are termed NFL First-Year Players. An NFL First-Year Player is designated by a "1" on NFL rosters. Thereafter, a player is credited with an additional year of experience for each season in which he accumulates six games on the Active List or Inactive List, or on Reserve/Injured or Reserve/Physically Unable to Perform.

NOTES

Paul Hackett, offensive coordinator-quarterbacks; born July 5, 1947, Burlington, Vt., lives in Overland Park, Kan. Quarterback Cal-Davis 1965-68. No pro playing experience. College coach: Cal-Davis 1970-71, California 1972-75, Southern California 1976-80, Pittsburgh 1989-92 (head coach 1990-92). Pro coach: Cleveland Browns 1981-82, San Francisco 49ers 1983-85, Dallas Cowboys 1986-88, joined Chiefs in 1993.

Mike McCarthy, offensive assistant-quality control; born November 10, 1963, Pittsburgh, Pa., lives in Overland Park, Kan. Tight end Baker University 1985-86. No pro playing experience. College coach: Fort Hays State 1987-88, Pittsburgh 1989-92. Pro coach: Joined Chiefs in 1993.

Tom Pratt, defensive line; born June 21, 1935, Edgerton, Wis., lives in Overland Park, Kan. Linebacker Miami 1953-56. No pro playing experience. College coach: Miami 1957-59, Southern Mississippi 1960-62. Pro coach: Kansas City Chiefs 1963-77, New Orleans Saints 1978-80, Cleveland Browns 1981-88, rejoined Chiefs in 1989.

Dave Redding, strength and conditioning; born June 14, 1952, North Platte, Neb., lives in Kansas City. Defensive end Nebraska 1972-75. No pro playing experience. College coach: Nebraska 1976, Washington State 1977, Missouri 1978-81. Pro coach: Cleveland Browns 1982-88, joined Chiefs in 1989.

Al Saunders, assistant head coach-receivers; born February 1, 1947, London, England, lives in Kansas City. Defensive back San Jose State 1966-68. No pro playing experience. College coach: Southern California 1970-71, Missouri 1972, Utah State 1973-75, California 1976-81, Tennessee 1982. Pro coach: San Diego Chargers 1983-88 (head coach 1986-88), joined Chiefs in 1989.

Kurt Schottenheimer, special teams; born October 1, 1949, McDonald, Pa., lives in Kansas City. Defensive back Miami 1969-70. No pro playing experience. College coach: William Patterson 1974, Michigan State 1978-82, Tulane 1983, Louisiana State 1984-85, Notre Dame 1986. Pro coach: Cleveland Browns 1987-88, joined Chiefs in 1989.

Darvin Wallis, special assistant-quality control; born February 14, 1949, Ft. Branch, Ind., lives in Overland Park, Kan. Defensive end Arizona 1970-71. No pro playing experience. College coach: Adams State 1976-77, Tulane 1978-79, Mississippi 1980-81. Pro coach: Cleveland Browns 1982-88, joined Chiefs in 1989.

LOS ANGELES RAIDERS

American Football Conference Western Division

Team Colors: Silver and Black

332 Center Street
El Segundo, California 90245
Telephone: (310) 322-3451

Club Officials

President of the Managing General Partner: Al Davis
Executive Assistant: Al LoCasale
Pro Football Scout: George Karras
Finance: Gary Huff
Legal Affairs: Jeff Birren, Amy Trask
Senior Executive: John Herrera
Senior Administrator: Morris Bradshaw
Business Manager: John Novak
Publications: Mike Taylor
Community Relations: Gil Lafferty-Hernandez
Administrative Assistant: John Walsh
Ticket Operations: Peter Eiges
Trainers: George Anderson, H. Rod Martin, Todd Sperber
Equipment Manager: Richard Romanski
Assistant Equipment Manager: Bob Romanski

Stadium: Los Angeles Memorial Coliseum • **Capacity:** 68,000
3911 South Figueroa Street
Los Angeles, California 90037

Playing Surface: Grass

Training Camp: Radisson Hotel
Oxnard, California 93030

1993 Schedule

Preseason

July 31	vs. Green Bay at Canton	3:00
Aug. 8	vs. San Francisco at Stanford Stadium	1:00
Aug. 14	at Dallas	8:00
Aug. 20	at Indianapolis	7:00
Aug. 28	at Los Angeles Rams	6:00

Regular Season

Sept. 5	**Minnesota**	1:00
Sept. 12	at Seattle	5:00
Sept. 19	**Cleveland**	1:00
Sept. 26	**Open Date**	
Oct. 3	at Kansas City	12:00
Oct. 10	**New York Jets**	1:00
Oct. 18	at Denver (Monday)	7:00
Oct. 24	**Open Date**	
Oct. 31	**San Diego**	1:00
Nov. 7	at Chicago	3:00
Nov. 14	**Kansas City**	1:00
Nov. 21	at San Diego	1:00
Nov. 28	at Cincinnati	1:00
Dec. 5	at Buffalo	1:00
Dec. 12	**Seattle**	1:00
Dec. 19	**Tampa Bay**	1:00
Dec. 26	at Green Bay	12:00
Jan. 2	**Denver**	1:00

Raiders Coaching History

Oakland 1960-1981
(314-193-11)

1960-61	Eddie Erdelatz*	6-10-0
1961-62	Marty Feldman**	2-15-0
1962	Red Conkright	1-8-0
1963-65	Al Davis	23-16-3
1966-68	John Rauch	35-10-1
1969-78	John Madden	112-39-7
1979-87	Tom Flores	91-56-0
1988-89	Mike Shanahan***	8-12-0
1989-92	Art Shell	36-27-0

*Released after two games in 1961
**Released after five games in 1962
***Released after four games in 1989

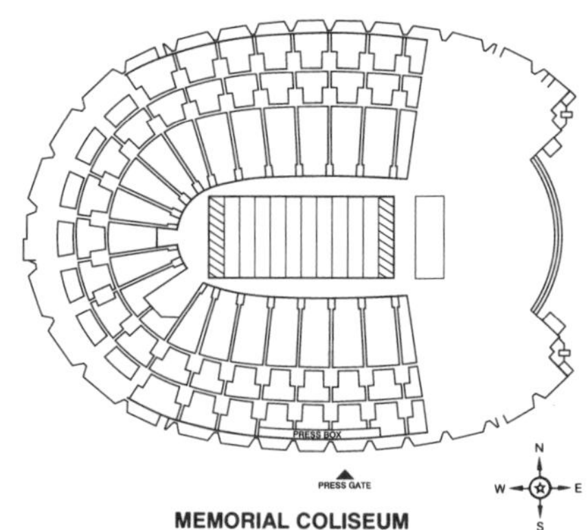

MEMORIAL COLISEUM

Record Holders

Individual Records—Career

Category	Name	Performance
Rushing (Yds.)	Marcus Allen, 1982-1992	8,545
Passing (Yds.)	Ken Stabler, 1970-79	19,078
Passing (TDs)	Ken Stabler, 1970-79	150
Receiving (No.)	Fred Biletnikoff, 1965-1978	589
Receiving (Yds.)	Fred Biletnikoff, 1965-1978	8,974
Interceptions	Willie Brown, 1967-1978	39
	Lester Hayes, 1977-1986	39
Punting (Avg.)	Ray Guy, 1973-1986	42.5
Punt Return (Avg.)	Claude Gibson, 1963-65	12.6
Kickoff Return (Avg.)	Jack Larscheid, 1960-61	28.4
Field Goals	George Blanda, 1967-1975	156
Touchdowns (Tot.)	Marcus Allen, 1982-1992	98
Points	George Blanda, 1967-1975	863

Individual Records—Single Season

Category	Name	Performance
Rushing (Yds.)	Marcus Allen, 1985	1,759
Passing (Yds.)	Ken Stabler, 1979	3,615
Passing (TDs)	Daryle Lamonica, 1969	34
Receiving (No.)	Todd Christensen, 1986	95
Receiving (Yds.)	Art Powell, 1964	1,361
Interceptions	Lester Hayes, 1980	13
Punting (Avg.)	Ray Guy, 1973	45.3
Punt Return (Avg.)	Claude Gibson, 1964	14.4
Kickoff Return (Avg.)	Harold Hart, 1975	30.5
Field Goals	Jeff Jaeger, 1991	29
Touchdowns (Tot.)	Marcus Allen, 1984	18
Points	George Blanda, 1968	117

Individual Records—Single Game

Category	Name	Performance
Rushing (Yds.)	Bo Jackson, 11-30-87	221
Passing (Yds.)	Cotton Davidson, 10-25-64	427
Passing (TDs)	Tom Flores, 12-22-63	6
	Daryle Lamonica, 10-19-69	6
Receiving (No.)	Dave Casper, 10-3-76	12
Receiving (Yds.)	Art Powell, 12-22-63	247
Interceptions	Many times	3
	Last time by Charles Phillips, 12-8-75	
Field Goals	Many times	4
	Last time by Jeff Jaeger, 9-29-91	
Touchdowns (Tot.)	Art Powell, 12-22-63	4
	Marcus Allen, 9-24-84	4
Points	Art Powell, 12-22-63	24
	Marcus Allen, 9-24-84	24

1992 Team Record

Preseason (1-3)

Date	Result		Opponents
8/8	L	10-24	at San Francisco
8/15	L	16-19	at L.A. Rams
8/22	L	23-27	Washington
8/29	W	30-26	Houston

Regular Season (7-9)

Date	Result		Opponents	Att.
9/6	L	13-17	at Denver	74,824
9/13	L	21-24	at Cincinnati (OT)	55,551
9/20	L	16-28	Cleveland	46,198
9/28	L	7-27	at Kansas City	76,607
10/4	W	13-10	N.Y. Giants	49,919
10/11	W	20- 3	Buffalo	50,548
10/18	W	19- 0	at Seattle	64,646
10/25	L	13-28	Dallas	89,985
11/8	L	10-31	at Philadelphia	65,736
11/15	W	20- 3	Seattle	31,805
11/22	W	24- 0	Denver	47,786
11/29	L	3-27	at San Diego	59,224
12/6	W	28- 7	Kansas City	44,029
12/14	L	7-20	at Miami	71,005
12/20	L	14-36	San Diego	37,163
12/26	W	21-20	at Washington	55,460

(OT) Overtime

Score by Periods

Raiders	43	83	61	62	0	—	249
Opponents	48	98	48	84	3	—	281

Attendance

Home 388,433 Away 523,053 Total 911,486
Single-game home record, 91,494 (9-29-91)
Single-season home record, 516,205 (1986)

1992 Team Statistics

	Raiders	Opp.
Total First Downs	259	264
Rushing	99	104
Passing	139	135
Penalty	21	25
Third Down: Made/Att.	80/208	72/219
Third Down: Pct.	38.5	32.9
Fourth Down: Made/Att.	5/13	10/22
Fourth Down: Pct.	38.5	45.5
Total Net Yards	4384	4516
Avg. Per Game	274.0	282.3
Total Plays	953	974
Avg. Per Play	4.6	4.6
Net Yards Rushing	1794	1683
Avg. Per Game	112.1	105.2
Total Rushes	434	478
Net Yards Passing	2590	2833
Avg. Per Game	161.9	177.1
Sacked/Yards Lost	48/360	46/320
Gross Yards	2950	3153
Att./Completions	471/233	450/243
Completion Pct.	49.5	54.0
Had Intercepted	23	12
Punts/Avg.	77/42.3	85/42.5
Net Punting Avg.	77/36.5	85/35.2
Penalties/Yards Lost	113/832	98/755
Fumbles/Ball Lost	25/15	21/7
Touchdowns	29	32
Rushing	7	17
Passing	20	11
Returns	2	4
Avg. Time of Possession	29:06	30:54

1992 Individual Statistics

Scoring	TD R	TD P	TD Rt	PAT	FG	Saf	TP
Jaeger	0	0	0	28/28	15/26	0	73
Brown	0	7	0	0/0	0/0	0	42
Gault	0	4	0	0/0	0/0	0	24
Allen	2	1	0	0/0	0/0	0	18
N. Bell	3	0	0	0/0	0/0	0	18
Dickerson	2	1	0	0/0	0/0	0	18
Horton	0	2	0	0/0	0/0	0	12
A. Wright	0	2	0	0/0	0/0	0	12
Anderson	0	0	1	0/0	0/0	0	6
Glover	0	1	0	0/0	0/0	0	6
Graddy	0	1	0	0/0	0/0	0	6
Patterson	0	0	1	0/0	0/0	0	6
S. Smith	0	1	0	0/0	0/0	0	6
Harrison	0	0	0	0/0	0/0	1	2
Raiders	7	20	2	28/29	15/26	1	249
Opponents	17	11	4	32/32	19/30	0	281

Passing	Att.	Comp.	Yds.	Pct.	TD	Int.	Tkld.	Rate
Schroeder	253	123	1476	48.6	11	11	25/180	63.3
Marinovich	165	81	1102	49.1	5	9	20/154	58.2
Evans	53	29	372	54.7	4	3	3/26	78.5
Raiders	471	233	2950	49.5	20	23	48/360	63.2
Opponents	450	243	3153	54.0	11	12	46/320	73.3

Rushing	Att.	Yds.	Avg.	LG	TD
Dickerson	187	729	3.9	40t	2
N. Bell	81	366	4.5	66t	3
Allen	67	301	4.5	21	2
Schroeder	28	160	5.7	19	0
S. Smith	44	129	2.9	15	0
Evans	11	79	7.2	16	0
Marinovich	9	30	3.3	11	0
Gainer	2	10	5.0	6	0
Gault	1	6	6.0	6	0
Brown	3	−4	−1.3	3	0
Gossett	1	−12	−12.0	−12	0
Raiders	434	1794	4.1	66t	7
Opponents	478	1683	3.5	33	17

Receiving	No.	Yds.	Avg.	LG	TD
Brown	49	693	14.1	68t	7
Horton	33	409	12.4	30	2
Allen	28	277	9.9	40	1
S. Smith	28	217	7.8	19	1
Gault	27	508	18.8	53	4
Glover	15	178	11.9	30	1
Dickerson	14	85	6.1	15	1
A. Wright	12	175	14.6	41t	2
Graddy	10	205	20.5	48	1
Fernandez	9	121	13.4	21	0
N. Bell	4	40	10.0	16	0
D. Jones	2	29	14.5	25	0
McCallum	2	13	6.5	7	0
Raiders	233	2950	12.7	68t	20
Opponents	243	3153	13.0	69t	11

Interceptions	No.	Yds.	Avg.	LG	TD
McDaniel	4	180	45.0	67	0
Anderson	3	131	43.7	102t	1
Washington	2	21	10.5	18	0
Dorn	1	7	7.0	7	0
Land	1	0	0.0	0	0
Lott	1	0	0.0	0	0
Raiders	12	339	28.3	102t	1
Opponents	23	345	15.0	35t	2

Punting	No.	Yds.	Avg.	In 20	LG
Gossett	77	3255	42.3	17	56
Raiders	77	3255	42.3	17	56
Opponents	85	3615	42.5	22	61

Punt Returns	No.	FC	Yds.	Avg.	LG	TD
Brown	37	19	383	10.4	40	0
McCallum	4	1	19	4.8	13	0
Fernandez	0	1	0	—	—	0
Raiders	41	21	402	9.8	40	0
Opponents	40	10	385	9.6	39	0

Kickoff Returns	No.	Yds.	Avg.	LG	TD
N. Bell	1	16	16.0	16	0
Brown	2	14	7.0	14	0
Graddy	5	85	17.0	21	0
Land	2	27	13.5	14	0
McCallum	14	274	19.6	41	0
Turk	1	3	3.0	3	0
A. Wright	18	325	18.0	33	0
Raiders	43	744	17.3	41	0
Opponents	35	690	19.7	47	0

Sacks	No.
A. Smith	13.0
Long	9.0
Townsend	5.0
Wallace	4.0
Bruce	3.5
McGlockton	3.0
Harrison	2.5
Moss	2.0
Anderson	1.0
Broughton	1.0
R. Ellison	1.0
Raiders	46.0
Opponents	48.0

1993 Draft Choices

Round	Name	Pos.	College
1.	Patrick Bates	DB	Texas A&M
3.	Billy Joe Hobert	QB	Washington
	James Trapp	DB	Clemson
5.	Olanda Truitt	WR	Mississippi State
7.	Greg Biekert	LB	Colorado
8.	Greg Robinson	RB	N.E. Louisiana

Los Angeles Raiders 1993 Veteran Roster

No.	Name	Pos.	Ht.	Wt.	Birth-date	NFL Exp.	College	Hometown	How Acq.	'92 Games/ Starts
33	Anderson, Eddie	S	6-1	210	7/22/63	8	Fort Valley State	Warner Robins, Ga.	FA-'87	16/16
59	Bell, Anthony	LB	6-3	240	7/2/64	8	Michigan State	Ft. Lauderdale, Fla.	PB(Det)-'92	16/5
38	Bell, Nick	RB	6-2	255	8/19/68	3	Iowa	Las Vegas, Nev.	D2-'91	16/1
97	Broughton, Willie	DT	6-5	280	9/9/64	7	Miami	Ft. Pierce, Fla.	FA-'92	16/8
81	Brown, Tim	WR	6-0	195	7/22/66	6	Notre Dame	Dallas, Tex.	D1-'88	15/12
56	Bruce, Aundray	DE	6-5	260	1/30/66	6	Auburn	Montgomery, Ala.	PB(Atl)-'92	16/4
29	Dickerson, Eric	RB	6-3	220	9/2/60	11	Southern Methodist	Sealy, Tex.	T(Ind)-'92	16/15
46	†Dorn, Torin	CB	6-0	190	2/29/68	4	North Carolina	Southfield, Mich.	D4-'90	15/0
11	Evans, Vince	QB	6-2	210	6/19/55	13	Southern California	Greensboro, N.C.	FA-'90	5/0
83	#Gault, Willie	WR	6-1	175	9/5/60	11	Tennessee	Griffin, Ga.	T(Chi)-'91	16/16
87	Glover, Andrew	TE	6-6	240	8/12/67	3	Grambling	Geismar, La.	D10-'91	16/2
7	Gossett, Jeff	P	6-2	195	1/25/57	12	Eastern Illinois	Charleston, Ill.	PB(Clev)-'89	16/0
85	#Graddy, Sam	WR	5-10	180	2/10/64	7	Tennessee	Gaffney, S.C.	PB(Den)-'89	7/1
22	t-Green, Gaston	RB	5-11	190	8/1/66	6	UCLA	Los Angeles, Calif.	T(Den)-'93	14/13*
74	Harrison, Nolan	DT	6-5	290	1/25/69	3	Indiana	Flossmoor, Ill.	D6-'91	14/14
88	Horton, Ethan	TE	6-4	240	12/19/62	7	North Carolina	Kannapolis, N.C.	FA-'89	16/16
20	Hoskins, Derrick	S	6-2	205	11/16/70	2	Southern Mississippi	Philadelphia, Pa.	D5-'92	16/0
15	Hostetler, Jeff	QB	6-3	215	4/22/61	10	West Virginia	Johnstown, Pa.	UFA(NYG)-'93	13/9*
18	Jaeger, Jeff	K	5-11	190	11/26/64	7	Washington	Kent, Wash.	PB(Clev)-'89	16/0
58	Jimerson, A.J.	LB	6-3	230	5/12/68	3	Norfolk State	Chesapeake, Va.	FA-'93	0*
82	Jones, David	TE	6-3	225	11/9/68	3	Delaware State	Hillside, N.J.	PB(SD)-'92	16/0
52	Jones, Mike	LB	6-1	230	4/15/69	3	Missouri	Kansas City, Mo.	FA-'91	16/0
57	Kelly, Joe	LB	6-2	235	12/11/64	8	Washington	Los Angeles, Calif.	UFA(NYJ)-'93	9/0*
25	Land, Dan	CB	6-0	195	7/3/65	6	Albany State	Donalsonville, Ga.	FA-'89	16/0
80	Lofton, James	WR	6-3	190	7/5/56	16	Stanford	Los Angeles, Calif.	UFA(Buff)-'93	16/15*
75	Long, Howie	DE	6-5	275	1/6/60	13	Villanova	Charleston, Mass.	D2-'81	16/16
12	Marinovich, Todd	QB	6-4	210	7/4/69	3	Southern California	Mission Viejo, Calif.	D1-'91	7/7
41	†McCallum, Napoleon	RB	6-2	230	10/6/63	5	Navy	Milford, Ohio	T(SD)-'90	13/0
36	McDaniel, Terry	CB	5-10	180	2/8/63	6	Tennessee	Saginaw, Mich.	D1-'88	16/16
91	McGlockton, Chester	DT	6-4	320	9/16/69	2	Clemson	Whiteville, N.C.	D1-'92	10/0
65	Montoya, Max	G	6-5	295	5/2/56	15	UCLA	La Puente, Calif.	PB(Cin)-'90	10/9
72	Mosebar, Don	C	6-6	300	9/11/61	11	Southern California	Visalia, Calif.	D1-'83	16/16
99	Moss, Winston	LB	6-3	249	12/24/65	7	Miami	Miami, Fla.	T(TB)-'91	15/15
43	Patterson, Elvis	S	5-11	195	10/21/60	10	Kansas	Houston, Tex.	PB(SD)-'90	15/0
64	Peat, Todd	G	6-2	310	5/20/64	5	Northern Illinois	Champaign, Ill.	FA-'92	16/8
71	Perry, Gerald	T	6-6	305	11/12/64	6	Southern	Columbia, S.C.	UFA(Rams)-'93	16/16*
78	Skrepenak, Greg	G	6-6	300	1/31/70	2	Michigan	Wilkes-Barre, Pa.	D2-'92	10/0
94	Smith, Anthony	DE	6-3	265	6/28/67	4	Arizona	Elizabeth City, N.J.	D1-'90	15/1
35	Smith, Steve	RB	6-1	235	8/30/64	7	Penn State	Clinton, Md.	D3-'87	16/15
93	Townsend, Greg	DE	6-3	275	11/3/61	11	Texas Christian	Compton, Calif.	D4-'83	14/14
67	Turk, Dan	C	6-4	300	6/25/62	9	Wisconsin	Milwaukee, Wis.	FA-'84	16/0
51	†Wallace, Aaron	LB	6-3	240	4/17/67	4	Texas A&M	New Orleans, La.	D2-'90	16/16
48	Washington, Lionel	CB	6-0	185	10/21/60	11	Tulane	New Orleans, La.	T(StL)-'87	16/16
68	Wilkerson, Bruce	T	6-5	295	7/28/64	7	Tennessee	Philadelphia, Tenn.	D2-'87	15/15
76	†Wisniewski, Steve	G	6-4	285	4/7/67	5	Penn State	Houston, Tex.	D2-'89	16/16
89	†Wright, Alexander	WR	6-0	195	7/19/67	4	Auburn	Albany, Ga.	T(Dall)-'92	10/1
66	Wright, Steve	T	6-6	285	4/18/59	11	Northern Illinois	Wayzata, Minn.	FA-'88	7/4

* Green played 14 games with Denver in '92; Hostetler played 13 games with N.Y. Giants; Jimerson missed '92 season due to injury; Kelly played 9 games with N.Y. Jets; Lofton played 16 games with Buffalo; Perry played 16 games with L.A. Rams.

Unrestricted free agent; subject to developments.

† Restricted free agent; subject to developments.

Traded—WR Mervyn Fernandez to San Francisco.

t- Raiders traded for Green (Denver).

Players lost through free agency (4): RB Marcus Allen (KC; 16 games in '92); S Ronnie Lott (NYJ; 16), T Reggie McElroy (KC; 10), QB Jay Schroeder (Cin; 13).

Also played with Raiders in '92—LB Tom Benson (1 game), LB Riki Ellison (12), WR Mervyn Fernandez (15), RB Derrick Gainer (2), DT Bob Golic (9), CB Sam Seale (5), S Dave Waymer (16).

COACHING STAFF

Head Coach, Art Shell

Pro Career: Named ninth head coach in Raiders' history on October 3, 1989. Had been Raiders' offensive line coach for seven years, including 1983 world championship season. He first joined the coaching staff in 1983 after 15 seasons as one of the greatest offensive tackles in pro football history. Came to Raiders in 1968 as a third-round draft choice out of Maryland State (now Maryland-Eastern Shore). Went on to play in 207 league games, including first 156 in a row, and 24 playoff games for the Raiders. Starting left tackle in Super Bowl XI and XV victories. Selected to Pro Bowl eight times — most by any Raiders player. Inducted into Pro Football Hall of Fame on August 5, 1989. Also named to state of South Carolina Sports Hall of Fame. Career record: 36-27.

Background: All-America tackle as junior and senior and three-year All-Conference on both offense and defense at Maryland State 1965-67. Also lettered in basketball.

Personal: Born November 26, 1946, Charleston, S.C. Art and wife, Janice, live in Palos Verdes, California with their sons Arthur III and Christopher.

Assistant Coaches

Fred Biletnikoff, wide receivers; born February 23, 1943, Erie, Pa., lives in El Segundo, Calif. Wide receiver Florida State 1962-64. Pro wide receiver Oakland Raiders 1965-78, Montreal Alouettes (CFL) 1980. College coach: Palomar, Calif., J.C. 1983, Diablo Valley, Calif., J.C. 1984, 1986. Pro coach: Oakland Invaders (USFL) 1985, Calgary Stampeders (CFL) 1987-88, joined Raiders in 1989.

Gunther Cunningham, defense-linebackers; born June 19, 1946, Munich, Germany, lives in El Segundo, Calif. Linebacker Oregon 1965-67. No pro playing experience. College coach: Oregon 1969-71, Arkansas 1972, Stanford 1973-76, California 1977-80. Pro coach: Hamilton Tiger-Cats (CFL) 1981, Baltimore/Indianapolis Colts 1982-84, San Diego Chargers 1985-90, joined Raiders in 1991.

Ray Hamilton, defensive line; born January 20, 1951, Omaha, Neb., lives in Culver City, Calif. Nose tackle Oklahoma 1969-72. Pro nose tackle-defensive end New England Patriots 1973-81. College coach: Tennessee 1992. Pro coach: New England Patriots 1985-89, Tampa Bay Buccaneers 1991, joined Raiders in 1993.

Jim Haslett, linebackers; born December 9, 1955, Pittsburgh, Pa., lives in El Segundo, Calif. Defensive end Indiana University (Pa.) 1975-78. Linebacker Buffalo Bills 1979-86, New York Jets 1987. College coach: Buffalo 1988-90. Pro coach: Sacramento Surge (WLAF) 1991-92, joined Raiders in 1993.

Odis McKinney, defensive backs; born May 19, 1957, Detroit, Mich., lives in Woodland Hills, Calif. Defensive back Colorado 1976-77. Pro defensive back New York Giants 1978-79, Oakland/Los Angeles Raiders 1980-85, Kansas City Chiefs 1985, Los Angeles Raiders 1986. Pro coach: Joined Raiders in 1990.

Bill Meyers, offensive line; born October 8, 1946, Chippewa Falls, Wis., lives in El Segundo, Calif. Tackle Stanford 1970-71. No pro playing experience. College coach: California 1972-73, 1977-78, Santa Clara 1974-76, Notre Dame 1979-81, Missouri 1985-86, Pittsburgh 1987-92. Pro coach: Green Bay Packers 1982-83, Pittsburgh Steelers 1984, joined Raiders in 1993.

Steve Ortmayer, football operations-special teams; born February 13, 1944, Painesville, Ohio, lives in Palos Verdes Estates, Calif. La Verne College 1966. No college or pro playing experience. College coach: Colorado 1967-73, Georgia Tech 1974. Pro coach: Kansas City Chiefs 1975-77, Oakland/Los Angeles Raiders 1978-86, San Diego Chargers 1987-89 (Director of Football Operations), rejoined Raiders in 1990.

Terry Robiskie, tight ends; born November 12, 1954, New Orleans, La., lives in Beverly Hills, Calif. Running back Louisiana State 1973-76. Pro running back Oakland Raiders 1977-79, Miami Dolphins 1980-81. Pro coach: Joined Raiders in 1982.

Joe Scannella, offensive backfield; born May 22, 1932, Passaic, N.J., lives in El Segundo, Calif. Quarterback Lehigh 1947-50. Pro safety Saskatchewan Roughriders (CFL) 1951-52. College coach: Cornell 1960, C.W. Post 1963-68 (head coach 1964-68), Vermont 1970-71. Pro coach: Montreal Alouettes (CFL) 1969, 1978-81 (head coach), Oakland Raiders 1972-77, Cleveland Browns 1982-84, rejoined Raiders in 1987.

Jack Stanton, defensive backs; born June 6, 1938, Bridgeville, Pa., lives in El Segundo, Calif. Running back North Carolina State 1959-60. Pro running back Pittsburgh Steelers 1961, Toronto Argonauts (CFL) 1962-63. College coach: George Washington 1966, North Carolina State 1968-72, Florida State 1973, 1976-83, North Carolina 1974-75, Purdue 1986, New Mexico 1987-88. Pro coach: Atlanta Falcons 1984-85, joined Raiders in 1989.

Tom Walsh, offense; born April 16, 1949, Vallejo, Calif., lives in Manhattan Beach, Calif. UC-Santa Barbara 1971. No college or pro playing experience. College coach: University of San Diego 1972-76, U.S. International 1979 (head coach), Murray State 1980, Cincinnati 1981. Pro coach: Joined Raiders in 1982.

Mike White, offensive line; born January 4, 1936, Berkeley, Calif., lives in Newport Beach, Calif. Offensive end California 1955-57. No pro playing experience. College coach: California 1958-63, 1972-77 (head coach), Stanford 1964-71, Illinois 1980-87 (head coach). Pro coach: San Francisco 49ers 1978-79, joined Raiders in 1990.

Los Angeles Raiders 1993 First-Year Roster

Name	Pos.	Ht.	Wt.	Birth-date	College	Hometown	How Acq.
Addison, Byron	S	6-0	200	4/13/70	Hawaii	Los Angeles, Calif.	FA
Baker, Jon (1)	DE	6-7	290	3/6/68	Pittsburgh	San Rafael, Calif.	FA
Bates, Patrick	S	6-3	225	11/27/70	Texas A&M	Houston, Tex.	D1
Bierket, Greg	LB	6-3	235	3/14/69	Colorado	Longmont, Colo.	D7
Brabham, Cary	S	5-11	195	8/11/70	Southern Methodist	Hughes Springs, Tex.	FA
Butler, Darren	CB-S	5-10	175	1/19/70	Alcorn State	Tylertown, Miss.	FA
Calhoun, Akill	DT	6-3	275	3/4/67	Hawaii	Granada Hills, Calif.	FA
Celestine, J.J. (1)	WR	5-9	195	9/30/68	Cal State-Fullerton	Riverside, Calif.	FA
Collons, Ferric (1)	DT	6-6	290	12/4/69	California	Sacramento, Calif.	FA
Duff, John (1)	TE	6-7	255	7/31/67	New Mexico	Tustin, Calif.	FA
Freeman, Kyle (1)	LB	6-1	225	11/22/65	Angelo State	Snyder, Tex.	FA
Hobbs, Daryl (1)	WR	6-1	175	5/23/71	Pacific	Los Angeles, Calif.	FA
Hobert, Billy Joe	QB	6-3	230	1/8/71	Washington	Puyallup, Wash.	D3
Jett, James	WR	5-10	165	12/28/70	West Virginia	Kearneysville, W. Va.	FA
Johnson, Dennis (1)	CB	6-1	205	8/22/67	Winston-Salem State	Harrels, N.C.	D12-'91
Jordan, Randy	G	5-10	205	6/6/70	North Carolina	Hanson, N.C.	FA
Montgomery, Tyrone (1)	RB	5-11	190	8/3/70	Mississippi	Greenville, Miss.	FA
Norton, James	WR	6-0	185	9/24/69	Western Michigan	Auburn Hills, Mich.	FA
Ridley, Lester	S	6-0	190	11/15/70	Iowa State	Omaha, Neb.	FA
Robinson, Greg	RB	5-11	205	8/7/69	Northeast Louisiana	Grenada, Miss.	FA
Roth, Tom (1)	C	6-5	285	9/19/68	Florida	Melbourne, Fla.	FA
Smith, Kevin (1)	RB	6-4	255	7/25/69	UCLA	Oakland, Calif.	D7-'92
Stephens, Rich (1)	G	6-7	305	11/1/65	Tulsa	St. Louis, Mo.	FA
Trapp, James	CB	6-0	180	12/28/69	Clemson	Lawton, Okla.	D3
Truitt, Olanda	WR	6-1	190	1/4/71	Mississippi State	Birmingham, Ala.	D5
Young, Glen	LB	6-3	235	5/2/69	Syracuse	Scarboro, Canada	FA

The term NFL Rookie is defined as a player who is in his first season of professional football and has not been on the roster of another professional football team for any regular-season or postseason games. A Rookie is designated by an "R" on NFL rosters. Players who have been active in another professional football league or players who have NFL experience, including either preseason training camp or being on an Active List or Inactive List, or on Reserve/Injured or Reserve/Physically Unable to Perform for fewer than six regular-season games, are termed NFL First-Year Players. An NFL First-Year Player is designated by a "1" on NFL rosters. Thereafter, a player is credited with an additional year of experience for each season in which he accumulates six games on the Active List or Inactive List, or on Reserve/Injured or Reserve/Physically Unable to Perform.

NOTES

American Football Conference
Eastern Division

Team Colors: Aqua, Coral, and White

Joe Robbie Stadium
2269 N.W. 199th Street
Miami, Florida 33056
Telephone: (305) 620-5000

Club Officials

President: Timothy J. Robbie
Executive Vice President: Daniel T. Robbie
Executive Vice President: Janet Robbie
Executive V.P./General Manager: Eddie J. Jones
General Counsel: Jann M. Iliff
Assistant General Manager: Bryan Wiedmeier
Head Coach: Don Shula
Director of Player Personnel: Tom Heckert
Director of College Scouting: Tom Braatz
Director of Media Relations: Harvey Greene
Media Relations Assistant: Scott Stone
Marketing Director: David Evans
Community Relations Director: Fudge Browne
Treasurer: Jill R. Strafaci
Trainer: Ryan Vermillion
Equipment Manager: Bob Monica

Stadium: Joe Robbie Stadium • **Capacity:** 73,000
2269 N.W. 199th Street
Miami, Florida 33056

Playing Surface: Grass (PAT)

Training Camp: Nova University
7500 S.W. 30th Street
Davie, Florida 33314

1993 Schedule

Preseason

Aug. 6	at Atlanta	7:30
Aug. 14	**Washington**	8:00
Aug. 20	at Denver	6:00
Aug. 28	**New York Giants**	8:00

Regular Season

Sept. 5	at Indianapolis	1:00
Sept. 12	**New York Jets**	4:00
Sept. 19	**Open Date**	
Sept. 26	at Buffalo	1:00
Oct. 4	**Washington** (Monday)	9:00
Oct. 10	at Cleveland	1:00
Oct. 17	**Open Date**	
Oct. 24	**Indianapolis**	7:30
Oct. 31	**Kansas City**	1:00
Nov. 7	at New York Jets	4:00
Nov. 14	at Philadelphia	1:00
Nov. 21	**New England**	1:00
Nov. 25	at Dallas (Thanksgiving)	3:00
Dec. 5	**New York Giants**	4:00
Dec. 13	**Pittsburgh** (Monday)	9:00
Dec. 19	**Buffalo**	1:00
Dec. 27	at San Diego (Monday)	6:00
Jan. 2	at New England	1:00

Dolphins Coaching History

(260-164-4)

1966-69	George Wilson	15-39-2
1970-92	Don Shula	245-125-2

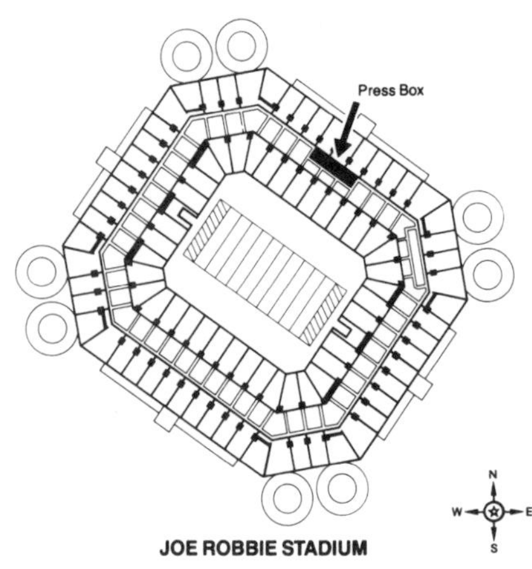

JOE ROBBIE STADIUM

Record Holders

Individual Records — Career

Category	Name	Performance
Rushing (Yds.)	Larry Csonka, 1968-1974, 1979	6,737
Passing (Yds.)	Dan Marino, 1983-1992	39,502
Passing (TDs)	Dan Marino, 1983-1992	290
Receiving (No.)	Mark Clayton, 1983-1992	550
Receiving (Yds.)	Mark Duper, 1982-1992	8,869
Interceptions	Jake Scott, 1970-75	35
Punting (Avg.)	Reggie Roby, 1983-1992	43.3
Punt Return (Avg.)	Freddie Solomon, 1975-77	11.4
Kickoff Return (Avg.)	Mercury Morris, 1969-1975	26.5
Field Goals	Garo Yepremian, 1970-78	165
Touchdowns (Tot.)	Mark Clayton, 1983-1992	82
Points	Garo Yepremian, 1970-78	830

Individual Records — Single Season

Category	Name	Performance
Rushing (Yds.)	Delvin Williams, 1978	1,258
Passing (Yds.)	Dan Marino, 1984	*5,084
Passing (TDs)	Dan Marino, 1984	*48
Receiving (No.)	Mark Clayton, 1988	86
Receiving (Yds.)	Mark Clayton, 1984	1,389
Interceptions	Dick Westmoreland, 1967	10
Punting (Avg.)	Reggie Roby, 1991	45.7
Punt Return (Avg.)	Freddie Solomon, 1975	12.3
Kickoff Return (Avg.)	Duriel Harris, 1976	32.9
Field Goals	Pete Stoyanovich, 1991	31
Touchdowns (Tot.)	Mark Clayton, 1984	18
Points	Pete Stoyanovich, 1992	124

Individual Records — Single Game

Category	Name	Performance
Rushing (Yds.)	Mercury Morris, 9-30-73	197
Passing (Yds.)	Dan Marino, 10-23-88	521
Passing (TDs)	Bob Griese, 11-24-77	6
	Dan Marino, 9-21-86	6
Receiving (No.)	Jim Jensen, 11-6-88	12
Receiving (Yds.)	Mark Duper, 11-10-85	217
Interceptions	Dick Anderson, 12-3-73	*4
Field Goals	Garo Yepremian, 9-26-71	5
Touchdowns (Tot.)	Paul Warfield, 12-15-73	4
Points	Paul Warfield, 12-15-73	24

*NFL Record

1992 Team Record

Preseason (3-2)

Date	Result		Opponents
8/1	W	22-21	vs. Washington at Orlando
8/7	L	24-27	Dallas
8/15	W	31-27	vs. Denver at Berlin
8/22	W	22- 7	Tampa Bay
8/27	L	3-17	vs. New Orleans at Baltimore

Regular Season (11-5)

Date	Result		Opponents	Att.
9/14	W	27-23	at Cleveland	75,912
9/20	W	26-10	L.A. Rams	57,701
9/27	W	19-17	at Seattle	64,629
10/4	W	37-10	at Buffalo	78,998
10/11	W	21-17	Atlanta	70,765
10/18	W	38-17	New England	59,981
10/25	L	20-31	Indianapolis	61,245
11/1	L	14-26	at N.Y. Jets	75,903
11/8	W	28- 0	at Indianapolis	58,599
11/16	L	20-26	Buffalo	71,274
11/22	W	19-16	Houston	70,439
11/29	L	13-24	at New Orleans	67,664
12/6	L	3-27	at San Francisco	65,461
12/14	W	20- 7	L.A. Raiders	71,005
12/20	W	19-17	N.Y. Jets	70,907
12/27	W	16-13	at New England (OT)	41,451

(OT) Overtime

Postseason (1-1)

Date	Result		Opponent	Att.
1/10	W	31- 0	San Diego	71,224
1/17	L	10-29	Buffalo	72,703

Score by Periods

Dolphins	75	85	87	90	3	—	340
Opponents	49	80	71	81	0	—	281

Attendance

Home 533,317 Away 528,617 Total 1,061,934
Single-game home record, 71,274 (11-16-92)
Single-season home record, 533,317 (1992)

1992 Team Statistics

	Dolphins	Opp.
Total First Downs	316	273
Rushing	101	92
Passing	194	168
Penalty	21	13
Third Down: Made/Att.	78/201	88/217
Third Down: Pct.	38.8	40.6
Fourth Down: Made/Att.	8/16	7/20
Fourth Down: Pct.	50.0	35.0
Total Net Yards	5500	4583
Avg. Per Game	343.8	286.4
Total Plays	998	976
Avg. Per Play	5.5	4.7
Net Yards Rushing	1525	1600
Avg. Per Game	95.3	100.0
Total Rushes	407	428
Net Yards Passing	3975	2983
Avg. Per Game	248.4	186.4
Sacked/Yards Lost	28/173	36/283
Gross Yards	4148	3266
Att./Completions	563/332	512/294
Completion Pct.	59.0	57.4
Had Intercepted	17	18
Punts/Avg.	61/39.7	74/40.1
Net Punting Avg.	61/32.5	74/35.7
Penalties/Yards Lost	86/656	89/679
Fumbles/Ball Lost	31/17	25/14
Touchdowns	36	32
Rushing	9	9
Passing	24	16
Returns	3	7
Avg. Time of Possession	30:30	29:30

1992 Individual Statistics

Scoring	TD R	TD P	TD Rt	PAT	FG	Saf	TP
Stoyanovich	0	0	0	34/36	30/37	0	124
Duper	0	7	0	0/0	0/0	0	42
Higgs	7	0	0	0/0	0/0	0	42
K. Jackson	0	5	0	0/0	0/0	0	30
Banks	0	3	0	0/0	0/0	0	18
Clayton	0	3	0	0/0	0/0	0	18
Humphrey	1	1	0	0/0	0/0	0	12
Martin	0	2	0	0/0	0/0	0	12
Paige	1	1	0	0/0	0/0	0	12
Baty	0	1	0	0/0	0/0	0	6
Brown	0	0	1	0/0	0/0	0	6
Edmunds	0	1	0	0/0	0/0	0	6
V. Jackson	0	0	1	0/0	0/0	0	6
Oliver	0	0	1	0/0	0/0	0	6
Dolphins	9	24	3	34/36	30/37	0	340
Opponents	9	16	7	30/32	19/26	1	281

Passing	Att.	Comp.	Yds.	Pct.	TD	Int.	Tkld.	Rate
Marino	554	330	4116	59.6	24	16	28/173	85.1
Mitchell	8	2	32	25.0	0	1	0/0	4.2
Martin	1	0	0	0.0	0	0	0/0	39.6
Dolphins	563	332	4148	59.0	24	17	28/173	83.6
Opponents	512	294	3266	57.4	16	18	36/283	72.3

Rushing	Att.	Yds.	Avg.	LG	TD
Higgs	256	915	3.6	23	7
Humphrey	102	471	4.6	21	1
Marino	20	66	3.3	12	0
Parmalee	6	38	6.3	20	0
Paige	7	11	1.6	6	1
Mitchell	8	10	1.3	8	0
Craver	3	9	3.0	8	0
Saxon	4	7	1.8	4	0
Martin	1	−2	−2.0	−2	0
Dolphins	407	1525	3.7	23	9
Opponents	428	1600	3.7	40	9

Receiving	No.	Yds.	Avg.	LG	TD
Humphrey	54	507	9.4	26	1
K. Jackson	48	594	12.4	42	5
Paige	48	399	8.3	30	1
Duper	44	762	17.3	62t	7
Clayton	43	619	14.4	44t	3
Martin	33	553	16.8	55t	2
Banks	22	319	14.5	39t	3
Higgs	16	142	8.9	21	0
Edmunds	10	91	9.1	15	1
Saxon	5	41	8.2	14	0
Clark	3	59	19.7	45	0
M. Williams	3	43	14.3	18	0
Baty	3	19	6.3	12	1
Dolphins	332	4148	12.5	62t	24
Opponents	294	3266	11.1	60	16

Interceptions	No.	Yds.	Avg.	LG	TD
Oliver	5	200	40.0	103t	1
Brown	4	119	29.8	48	1
V. Jackson	3	63	21.0	30t	1
Vincent	2	47	23.5	32	0
J. Williams	2	29	14.5	25	0
Alexander	1	0	0.0	0	0
Cox	1	0	0.0	0	0
Dolphins	18	458	25.4	103t	3
Opponents	17	446	26.2	102t	4

Punting	No.	Yds.	Avg.	In 20	LG
Roby	35	1443	41.2	11	60
Prokop	24	891	37.1	2	56
Stoyanovich	2	90	45.0	0	48
Dolphins	61	2424	39.7	13	60
Opponents	74	2971	40.1	15	59

Punt Returns	No.	FC	Yds.	Avg.	LG	TD
Miller	24	18	175	7.3	19	0
Vincent	5	0	16	3.2	6	0
Martin	1	0	0	0.0	0	0
J. Williams	1	1	0	0.0	0	0
Dolphins	31	19	191	6.2	19	0
Opponents	33	10	382	11.6	84t	1

Kickoff Returns	No.	Yds.	Avg.	LG	TD
Craver	8	174	21.8	44	0
Humphrey	1	18	18.0	18	0
Paige	2	29	14.5	19	0
Parmalee	14	289	20.6	32	0
M. Williams	19	328	17.3	28	0
Dolphins	44	838	19.0	44	0
Opponents	65	1380	21.2	82	0

Sacks	No.
Cox	14.0
Coleman	6.0
Cross	5.0
Griggs	3.0
Hobley	2.0
Offerdahl	1.5
Webster	1.5
Braggs	1.0
Hollier	1.0
Klingbeil	1.0
Dolphins	36.0
Opponents	28.0

1993 Draft Choices

Round	Name	Pos.	College
1.	O.J. McDuffie	WR	Penn State
3.	Terry Kirby	RB	Virginia
4.	Ronnie Bradford	DB	Colorado
5.	Chris Gray	G	Auburn
6.	Robert O'Neal	DB	Clemson
7.	David Merritt	LB	North Carolina St.
8.	Dwayne Gordon	LB	New Hampshire

Miami Dolphins 1993 Veteran Roster

No.	Name	Pos.	Ht.	Wt.	Birth-date	NFL Exp.	College	Hometown	How Acq.	'92 Games/ Starts
32	Alexander, Bruce	CB	5-8	178	9/17/65	5	Stephen F. Austin	Lufkin, Tex.	PB(Det)-'92	12/1
86	#Banks, Fred	WR	5-10	185	5/26/62	8	Liberty	Columbus, Ga.	FA-'87	16/0
84	Baty, Greg	TE	6-6	240	8/28/64	7	Stanford	Sparta, N.J.	FA-'90	16/0
96	Benson, Mitchell	NT	6-4	300	5/30/67	4	Texas Christian	Ft. Worth, Tex.	FA-'93	0*
66	Blake, Eddie	G	6-3	315	12/18/68	2	Auburn	Fayetteville, Tenn.	D2-'92	0*
53	†Bolcar, Ned	LB	6-2	240	1/12/67	4	Notre Dame	Phillipsburg, N.J.	PB(Sea)-'91	0*
36	#Braggs, Stephen	CB	5-9	177	8/29/65	7	Texas	Houston, Tex.	FA-'92	6/0
37	†Brown, J.B.	CB	6-0	190	1/5/67	5	Maryland	Washington, D.C.	D12-'89	16/16
90	Coleman, Marco	DE	6-3	263	12/18/69	2	Georgia Tech	Dayton, Ohio	D1b-'92	16/15
52	Collins, Roosevelt	LB	6-4	235	1/25/68	2	Texas Christian	Shreveport, La.	D6-'92	10/0
51	Cox, Bryan	LB	6-4	241	2/17/68	3	Western Illinois	East St. Louis, Ill.	D5a-'91	16/16
34	Craver, Aaron	RB	6-0	216	12/18/68	3	Fresno State	Compton, Calif.	D3-'91	6/0
91	Cross, Jeff	DE	6-4	271	3/25/66	6	Missouri	Blythe, Calif.	D9-'88	16/16
65	Dellenbach, Jeff	T-C	6-5	296	2/14/63	9	Wisconsin	Wausau, Wis.	D4b-'85	16/8
74	Dennis, Mark	T	6-6	292	4/15/65	7	Illinois	Washington, Ill.	D8b-'87	16/8
85	Duper, Mark	WR	5-9	192	1/25/59	12	Northwestern Louisiana	Moreauville, La.	D2-'82	16/16
8	Ford, Bernard	WR	5-9	183	2/27/66	4	Central Florida	Cordele, Ga.	FA-'93	0*
35	Glenn, Kerry	CB	5-9	177	1/3/62	9	Minnesota	East St. Louis, Ill.	PB(NYJ)-'90	16/1
96	Golic, Mike	DT	6-5	275	12/12/62	8	Notre Dame	Cleveland, Ohio	UFA(Phil)-'93	16/13*
42	Green, Chris	CB-S	5-11	189	2/26/68	3	Illinois	Lawrenceburg, Ind.	D7-'91	4/2
92	Griggs, David	DE	6-3	250	2/5/67	4	Virginia	Pennsauken, N.J.	FA-'89	16/13
59	Grimsley, John	LB	6-2	236	2/25/62	10	Kentucky	Canton, Ohio	T(Hou)-'91	14/11
45	Harden, Bobby	S	6-0	202	2/8/67	4	Miami	Ft. Lauderdale, Fla.	D12-'90	4/0
21	Higgs, Mark	RB	5-7	198	4/11/66	6	Kentucky	Owensboro, Ky.	PB(Phil)-'90	16/15
29	Hobley, Liffort	S	6-0	207	5/12/62	7	Louisiana State	Shreveport, La.	FA-'87	15/5
50	Hollier, Dwight	LB	6-2	245	4/21/69	2	North Carolina	Hampton, Va.	D4-'92	16/5
27	Holt, Issiac	CB	6-2	201	10/4/62	9	Alcorn State	Birmingham, Ala.	FA-'93	16/11*
44	†Humphrey, Bobby	RB	6-1	201	10/11/65	5	Alabama	Birmingham, Ala.	T(Den)-'92	16/1
97	Hunter, Jeff	DE	6-4	291	4/12/66	4	Albany State	Augusta, Ga.	FA-'92	4/0*
89	Ingram, Mark	WR	5-11	188	8/23/68	7	Michigan State	Flint, Mich.	UFA(NYG)-'93	12/10*
88	Jackson, Keith	TE	6-2	249	4/19/65	6	Oklahoma	Little Rock, Ark.	UFA(Phil)-'92	13/11
24	Jackson, Vestee	CB	6-0	186	8/14/63	8	Washington	Fresno, Calif.	T(Chi)-'91	11/5
9	Johnson, Alex	WR	5-9	173	8/18/68	2	Miami	Homestead, Fla.	FA-'93	0*
99	Klingbeil, Chuck	NT	6-1	288	11/2/65	3	Northern Michigan	Houghton, Mich.	FA-'91	15/15
47	Malone, Darrell	CB	5-10	182	11/23/67	2	Jacksonville State	Jacksonville, Ala.	FA-'92	4/0*
13	Marino, Dan	QB	6-4	224	9/15/61	11	Pittsburgh	Pittsburgh, Pa.	D1-'83	16/16
80	Martin, Tony	WR	6-0	177	9/5/65	4	Mesa, Colo.	Miami, Fla.	FA-'89	16/3
82	Miller, Scott	WR	5-11	179	10/20/68	3	UCLA	El Toro, Calif.	D9-'91	15/0
19	Mitchell, Scott	QB	6-6	230	1/2/68	4	Utah	Springville, Utah	D4-'90	16/0
93	Odom, Cliff	LB	6-2	236	8/15/58	13	Texas-Arlington	Beaumont, Tex.	PB(Ind)-'90	3/0
56	Offerdahl, John	LB	6-3	238	8/17/64	8	Western Michigan	Ft. Atkinson, Wis.	D2-'86	8/8
25	†Oliver, Louis	S	6-2	224	3/9/66	5	Florida	Belle Glade, Fla.	D1b-'89	16/16
30	Parmalee, Bernie	RB	5-11	201	9/16/67	2	Ball State	Jersey City, N.J.	FA-'92	10/0
71	Robbins, Kevin	T	6-6	308	12/12/66	3	Michigan State	Washington, D.C.	FA-'93	0*
4	Roby, Reggie	P	6-2	243	7/30/61	11	Iowa	East Waterloo, Iowa	D6-'83	9/0
58	Sander, Mark	LB	6-2	232	3/21/68	2	Louisville	Louisville, Ky.	FA-'92	12/2
22	Saxon, James	RB	5-11	237	3/23/66	6	San Jose State	Burton, S.C.	PB(KC)-'92	16/0
69	†Sims, Keith	G	6-3	310	6/17/67	4	Iowa State	Watchung, N.J.	D2-'90	16/16
31	Smith, Cedric	RB	5-10	223	5/27/68	3	Florida	Enterprise, La.	FA-'93	0*
10	Stoyanovich, Pete	K	5-10	181	4/28/67	5	Indiana	Dearborn Heights, Mich.	D8-'89	16/0
95	Turner, T.J.	NT	6-4	280	5/16/63	8	Houston	Lufkin, Tex.	D3-'86	16/5
63	†Uhlenhake, Jeff	C	6-3	284	1/28/66	5	Ohio State	Newark, Ohio	D5-'89	13/13
94	Veasey, Craig	NT	6-2	300	12/25/66	4	Houston	Houston, Tex.	FA-'93	4/0*
23	Vincent, Troy	CB	6-0	192	6/8/70	2	Wisconsin	Trenton, N.J.	D1a-'92	15/14
78	Webb, Richmond	T	6-6	298	1/11/67	4	Texas A&M	Dallas, Tex.	D1-'90	16/16
79	Webster, Larry	DT	6-5	285	1/18/69	2	Maryland	Elkton, Md.	D3-'92	16/0
60	Weidner, Bert	G-C	6-2	290	11/20/66	4	Kent State	Eden, N.Y.	D11-'89	16/3
61	Williams, Gene	G	6-3	308	10/14/68	3	Iowa State	Omaha, Neb.	D5b-'91	5/0
26	Williams, Jarvis	S	5-11	200	5/16/65	6	Florida	Palatka, Fla.	D2-'88	16/10
87	Williams, Mike	WR	5-10	183	10/9/66	3	Northeastern	Katonah, N.Y.	FA-'91	15/0

* Benson last active with San Diego in '91; Blake and Bolcar missed '92 season due to injury; Ford last active with Houston in '91; Golic played 16 games with Philadelphia; Hunter played 4 games with Detroit in '92; Holt played 16 games with Dallas; Ingram played 12 games with N.Y. Giants; Johnson last active with New England in '91; Malone played 4 games with Kansas City in '92; Robbins last active with Atlanta in '91; Smith last active with New Orleans in '91; Veasey played 4 games with Houston.

#Unrestricted free agent; subject to developments.

† Restricted free agent; subject to developments.

Retired—Running back Tony Paige, 9-year veteran, 16 games in '92.

Players lost through free agency (3): TE Ferrell Edmunds (Sea; 10 games in '92), G Harry Galbreath (GB; 16), QB Scott Secules (NE; did not play in '92).

Also played with Dolphins in '92—WR Robert Clark (3 games), WR Mark Clayton (13), WR Jim Jensen (3), TE Dave Moore (1), NT Alfred Oglesby (6), P Joe Prokop (7).

COACHING STAFF

Head Coach, Don Shula

Pro Career: Begins his thirty-first season as an NFL head coach, and twenty-fourth with the Dolphins. Miami has won or shared first place in the AFC East in 14 of his 23 years and has earned 14 playoff berths in that span. Has most wins (318) among active NFL coaches and is second only to George Halas's 324. Captured back-to-back NFL championships, defeating Washington 14-7 in Super Bowl VII and Minnesota 24-7 in Super Bowl VIII. Lost to Dallas 24-3 in Super Bowl VI, to Washington 27-17 in Super Bowl XVII, and to San Francisco 38-16 in Super Bowl XIX. His 17-0 team in 1972 is the only team in NFL history to go undefeated throughout the regular season and postseason. Started his pro playing career with Cleveland Browns as defensive back in 1951. After two seasons with Browns, spent 1953-56 with Baltimore Colts and 1957 with Washington Redskins. Joined Detroit Lions as defensive coach in 1960 and was named head coach of the Colts in 1963. Baltimore had a 13-1 record in 1968 and captured NFL championship before losing to New York Jets in Super Bowl III. Career record: 318-151-6.

Background: Outstanding offensive player at John Carroll University in Cleveland before becoming defensive specialist as a pro. His alma mater awarded him a doctorate in humanities in May, 1973. Served as assistant coach at Virginia in 1958 and at Kentucky in 1959.

Personal: Born January 4, 1930, in Painesville, Ohio. Don lives in Miami Lakes, Fla., and has five children — Dave, Donna, Sharon, Annie, and Mike. Dave is Cincinnati's head coach and Mike is tight ends coach with Chicago.

Assistant Coaches

Joe Greene, defensive line; born September 24, 1946, Temple, Tex., lives in Miami. Defensive tackle North Texas State 1966-68. Pro defensive tackle Pittsburgh Steelers 1969-81. Inducted into Pro Football Hall of Fame in 1987. Pro coach: Pittsburgh Steelers 1987-91, joined Dolphins in 1992.

Kim Helton, offensive line; born July 28, 1948, Pensacola, Fla., lives in Miami. Center Florida 1967-69. No pro playing experience. College coach: Florida 1972-78, Miami 1979-82. Pro coach: Tampa Bay Buccaneers 1983-86, Houston Oilers 1987-89, Los Angeles Raiders 1990-92, joined Dolphins in 1993.

George Hill, linebackers; born April 28, 1933, Bay Village, Ohio, lives in Miami. Tackle-fullback Denison 1954-57. No pro playing experience. College coach: Findlay 1959, Denison 1960-64, Cornell 1965, Duke 1966-70, Ohio State 1971-78. Pro coach: Philadelphia Eagles 1979-84, Indianapolis Colts 1985-88, joined Dolphins in 1989.

Tony Nathan, offensive backs; born December 14, 1956, Birmingham, Ala., lives in Miami. Running back Alabama 1975-78. Pro running back Miami Dolphins 1979-87. Pro coach: Joined Dolphins in 1988.

Tom Olivadotti, defense; born September 22, 1945, Long Branch, N.J., lives in Cooper City, Fla. Defensive back-wide receiver Upsala 1963-66. No pro playing experience. College coach: Princeton 1975-77, Boston College 1978-79, Miami 1980-83. Pro coach: Cleveland Browns 1985-86, joined Dolphins in 1987.

Mel Phillips, defensive backs; born January 6, 1942, Shelby, N.C., lives in Miami Lakes, Fla. Defensive back-running back North Carolina A&T 1964-65. Pro defensive back San Francisco 49ers 1966-77. Pro coach: Detroit Lions 1980-84, joined Dolphins in 1985.

John Sandusky, assistant head coach-tight ends; born December 28, 1925, Philadelphia, Pa., lives in Hollywood, Fla. Tackle Villanova 1946-49. Pro tackle Cleveland Browns 1950-55, Green Bay Packers 1956. College coach: Villanova 1957-58. Pro coach: Baltimore Colts 1959-72 (head coach 1972), Philadelphia Eagles 1973-75, joined Dolphins in 1976.

Miami Dolphins 1993 First-Year Roster

Name	Pos.	Ht.	Wt.	Birth-date	College	Hometown	How Acq.
Austin, Elijah (1)	NT	6-2	272	10/3/67	North Carolina State	Attapulgus, Ga.	FA
Barber, Lavaras	CB	5-10	190	4/29/70	California	Rosemead, Calif.	FA
Bell, Coleman	TE	6-2	232	4/22/70	Miami	Tampa, Fla.	FA
Bell, Kameno (1)	RB	5-11	230	4/5/69	Illinois	Chicago, Ill.	FA
Boyd, Daniel	LB	6-0	238	5/1/70	Mississippi State	Memphis, Tenn.	FA
Bradford, Ronnie	CB	5-10	188	10/1/70	Colorado	Commerce City, Colo.	D4
Brothen, Kevin (1)	C	6-1	287	11/16/69	Vanderbilt	Oak Lawn, Ill.	FA
Brown, Reggie (1)	WR	5-11	174	6/1/68	Mesa, Colo.	Denver, Colo.	FA
Bullough, Chuck (1)	LB	6-1	238	3/3/69	Michigan State	Orchard Park, N.Y.	FA
Caesar, Mark	NT	6-2	295	1/12/70	Miami	Newark, N.J.	FA
Campbell, Bo	WR	5-11	186	4/17/70	Virginia Tech	Virginia Beach, Va.	FA
Carswell, Chuck (1)	CB	5-9	186	10/13/69	Georgia	Marietta, Ga.	FA
Coons, Rob	TE	6-5	239	9/18/69	Pittsburgh	El Dorado, Calif.	FA
Cromartie, Tim	NT	6-1	281	11/9/68	Auburn	Godby, Fla.	FA
Gordon, Dwayne	LB	6-1	231	11/2/69	New Hampshire	Poughkeepsie, N.Y.	D8
Gray, Chris	G-T	6-4	286	6/19/70	Auburn	Birmingham, Ala.	D5
Hickerson, Eric (1)	S	6-2	224	10/4/65	Indiana	New Albany, Ind.	FA
Hochertz, Martin (1)	DE	6-5	269	10/21/68	Southern Illinois	Cary, Ill.	FA
Hope, Charles (1)	G	6-3	308	3/12/70	Central State, Ohio	New Castle, Del.	FA
Kirby, Terry	RB	6-1	221	1/20/70	Virginia	Tabb, Va.	D3
Kirchoff, Jay	K	6-2	210	5/28/70	Arizona	Plymouth, Minn.	FA
McDuffie, O.J.	WR	5-10	191	12/2/69	Penn State	Gates Mills, Ohio	D1
Merritt, David	LB	6-1	237	9/8/71	North Carolina State	Raleigh, N.C.	D7
Moore, Brandon	T	6-7	281	6/21/70	Duke	Ardmore, Pa.	FA
O'Neal, Robert	S	6-1	194	2/1/71	Clemson	Clarkston, Ga.	D6
Pederson, Doug (1)	QB	6-3	209	1/31/68	Northeast Louisiana	Ferndale, Wash.	FA
Rasul, Amir (1)	RB	5-11	198	7/3/69	Florida A&M	Tallahassee, Fla.	FA
Rose, Blaine (1)	G	6-5	285	6/13/66	Maryland	Stanton, Ohio	FA
Rowell, Tony (1)	C	6-4	293	7/25/69	Florida	Melbourne, Fla.	FA
Smith, Frankie (1)	CB	5-9	186	10/8/68	Baylor	Groesbeck, Tex.	FA
Turner, Eric	CB	6-0	189	2/13/70	East Texas State	Daingerfield, Tex.	FA
Walker, David	RB	5-9	216	12/4/69	Syracuse	Rochester, N.Y.	FA

The term NFL Rookie is defined as a player who is in his first season of professional football and has not been on the roster of another professional football team for any regular-season or postseason games. A Rookie is designated by an "R" on NFL rosters. Players who have been active in another professional football league or players who have NFL experience, including either preseason training camp or being on an Active List or Inactive List, or on Reserve/Injured or Reserve/Physically Unable to Perform for fewer than six regular-season games, are termed NFL First-Year Players. An NFL First-Year Player is designated by a "1" on NFL rosters. Thereafter, a player is credited with an additional year of experience for each season in which he accumulates six games on the Active List or Inactive List, or on Reserve/Injured or Reserve/Physically Unable to Perform.

NOTES

Larry Seiple, wide receivers; born February 14, 1945, Allentown, Pa., lives in Miami Lakes, Fla. Running back-receiver-punter Kentucky 1964-66. Pro punter-tight end-receiver-running back Miami Dolphins 1967-77. College coach: Miami 1978-79. Pro coach: Detroit Lions 1980-84, Tampa Bay Buccaneers 1985-86, joined Dolphins in 1988.

Gary Stevens, offense-quarterbacks; born March 19, 1943, Cleveland, Ohio, lives in Kendall, Fla. Running back John Carroll 1963-65. No pro playing experience. College coach: Louisville 1971-74, Kent State 1975, West Virginia 1976-79, Miami 1980-88. Pro coach: Joined Dolphins in 1989.

Carl Taseff, staff assistant; born September 28, 1928, Cleveland, Ohio, lives in Miami. Back John Carroll 1947-50. Pro defensive back Cleveland Browns 1951, Baltimore Colts 1953-61, Philadelphia Eagles 1961, Buffalo Bills 1962. Pro coach: Boston Patriots 1964, Detroit Lions 1965-66, joined Dolphins in 1970.

Junior Wade, strength and conditioning; born February 2, 1947, Bath, S.C., lives in Miami. South Carolina State 1969. No college or pro playing experience. Pro coach: Joined Dolphins in 1975, coach since 1983.

Mike Westhoff, special teams; born January 10, 1948, Pittsburgh, Pa., lives in Ft. Lauderdale, Fla. Center-linebacker Wichita State 1967-69. No pro playing experience. College coach: Indiana 1974-75, Dayton 1976, Indiana State 1977, Northwestern 1978-80, Texas Christian 1981. Pro coach: Baltimore/Indianapolis Colts 1982-84, Arizona Outlaws (USFL) 1985, joined Dolphins in 1986.

NEW ENGLAND PATRIOTS

American Football Conference Eastern Division

Team Colors: Blue, Red, Silver, and White

Foxboro Stadium
Route 1
Foxboro, Massachusetts 02035
Telephone: (508) 543-8200

Club Officials

Chairman of the Board/Owner: James B. Orthwein
Vice Chairman: Michael O'Hallaron
Executive Vice President/Football Operations: Patrick Forté
Executive Vice President/Business Operations: James Hausmann
Vice President: Francis J. Kilroy
Director of College Scouting: Charles Armey
Executive Director of Marketing: Ann Parry
Director of Public Relations: Mike Hanson
Assistant Director of Public Relations: Stacey James
Director of Special Projects: Mitch Hardin
Director of Community Relations: Nadine Jackson
Director of Data Processing: Peg Myers
Director of Operations: Mike Quashie
Director of Ticket Sales: Ken Sternfeld
Controller: Virginia Widmann
Head Trainer: Ron O'Neil
Equipment Manager: George Luongo
Video Director: Ken Deininger

Stadium: Foxboro Stadium • **Capacity:** 60,794
Route 1
Foxboro, Massachusetts 02035

Playing Surface: Grass

Training Camp: Bryant College
Route 7
Smithfield, Rhode Island 02917

1993 Schedule

Preseason

Aug. 7	at San Diego	6:00
Aug. 14	vs. Cleveland at Toronto	7:30
Aug. 20	**Green Bay**	7:00
Aug. 27	**Kansas City**	7:00

Regular Season

Sept. 5	at Buffalo	1:00
Sept. 12	**Detroit**	1:00
Sept. 19	**Seattle**	1:00
Sept. 26	at New York Jets	8:00
Oct. 3	**Open Date**	
Oct. 10	at Phoenix	2:00
Oct. 17	**Houston**	1:00
Oct. 24	at Seattle	1:00
Oct. 31	at Indianapolis	1:00
Nov. 7	**Buffalo**	1:00
Nov. 14	**Open Date**	
Nov. 21	at Miami	1:00
Nov. 28	**New York Jets**	1:00
Dec. 5	at Pittsburgh	1:00
Dec. 12	**Cincinnati**	1:00
Dec. 19	at Cleveland	1:00
Dec. 26	**Indianapolis**	1:00
Jan. 2	**Miami**	1:00

Patriots Coaching History

Boston 1960-1970
(220-265-9)

1960-61	Lou Saban*	7-12-0
1961-68	Mike Holovak	53-47-9
1969-70	Clive Rush**	5-16-0
1970-72	John Mazur***	9-21-0
1972	Phil Bengtson	1-4-0
1973-78	Chuck Fairbanks****	46-41-0
1978	Hank Bullough-Ron Erhardt#	0-1-0
1979-81	Ron Erhardt	21-27-0
1982-84	Ron Meyer##	18-16-0
1984-89	Raymond Berry	51-41-0
1990	Rod Rust	1-15-0
1991-92	Dick MacPherson	8-24-0

*Released after five games in 1961
**Released after seven games in 1970
***Resigned after nine games in 1972
****Suspended for final regular season game in 1978
#Co-coaches
##Released after eight games in 1984

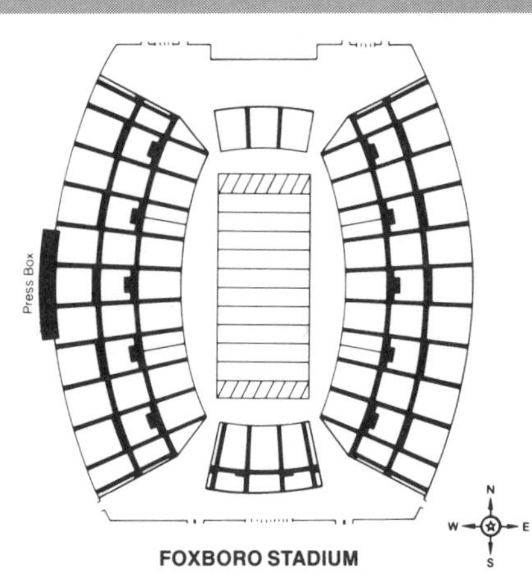

FOXBORO STADIUM

Record Holders

Individual Records — Career

Category	Name	Performance
Rushing (Yds.)	Sam Cunningham, 1973-79, 1981-82	5,453
Passing (Yds.)	Steve Grogan, 1975-1990	26,886
Passing (TDs)	Steve Grogan, 1975-1990	182
Receiving (No.)	Stanley Morgan, 1977-1989	534
Receiving (Yds.)	Stanley Morgan, 1977-1989	10,352
Interceptions	Raymond Clayborn, 1977-1989	36
Punting (Avg.)	Rich Camarillo, 1981-87	42.6
Punt Return (Avg.)	Mack Herron, 1973-75	12.0
Kickoff Return (Avg.)	Horace Ivory, 1977-1981	27.6
Field Goals	Gino Cappelletti, 1960-1970	176
Touchdowns (Tot.)	Stanley Morgan, 1977-1989	68
Points	Gino Cappelletti, 1960-1970	1,130

Individual Records — Single Season

Category	Name	Performance
Rushing (Yds.)	Jim Nance, 1966	1,458
Passing (Yds.)	Vito (Babe) Parilli, 1964	3,465
Passing (TDs)	Vito (Babe) Parilli, 1964	31
Receiving (No.)	Stanley Morgan, 1986	84
Receiving (Yds.)	Stanley Morgan, 1986	1,491
Interceptions	Ron Hall, 1964	11
Punting (Avg.)	Rich Camarillo, 1983	44.6
Punt Return (Avg.)	Mack Herron, 1974	14.8
Kickoff Return (Avg.)	Raymond Clayborn, 1977	31.0
Field Goals	Tony Franklin, 1986	32
Touchdowns (Tot.)	Steve Grogan, 1976	13
	Stanley Morgan, 1979	13
Points	Gino Cappelletti, 1964	155

Individual Records — Single Game

Category	Name	Performance
Rushing (Yds.)	Tony Collins, 9-18-83	212
Passing (Yds.)	Tony Eason, 9-21-86	414
Passing (TDs)	Vito (Babe) Parilli, 11-15-64	5
	Vito (Babe) Parilli, 10-15-67	5
	Steve Grogan, 9-9-79	5
Receiving (No.)	Art Graham, 11-20-66	11
	Tony Collins, 11-29-87	11
Receiving (Yds.)	Stanley Morgan, 11-8-81	182
Interceptions	Many times	3
	Last time by Roland James, 10-23-83	
Field Goals	Gino Cappelletti, 10-4-64	6
Touchdowns (Tot.)	Many times	3
	Last time by Stanley Morgan, 9-21-86	
Points	Gino Cappelletti, 12-18-65	28

1992 Team Record

Preseason (1-3)

Date	Result		Opponents
8/8	L	14-34	at Indianapolis
8/14	L	10-20	San Diego
8/22	L	9-42	at Detroit
8/29	W	24-10	Green Bay

Regular Season (2-14)

Date	Result		Opponents	Att.
9/13	L	0-14	at L.A. Rams	44,000
9/20	L	6-10	Seattle	45,785
9/27	L	7-41	Buffalo	58,925
10/4	L	21-30	at N.Y. Jets	75,004
10/11	L	12-24	San Francisco	59,437
10/18	L	17-38	at Miami	59,981
10/25	L	17-19	Cleveland	38,442
11/1	L	7-16	at Buffalo	78,840
11/8	L	14-31	New Orleans	51,878
11/15	W	37-34	at Indianapolis (OT)	41,426
11/22	W	24- 3	N.Y. Jets	34,301
11/29	L	0-34	at Atlanta	68,416
12/6	L	0- 6	Indianapolis	26,196
12/13	L	20-27	at Kansas City	76,580
12/20	L	10-20	at Cincinnati	58,125
12/27	L	13-16	Miami (OT)	41,451

(OT) Overtime

Score by Periods

Patriots	61	51	32	58	3	—	205
Opponents	84	80	88	108	3	—	363

Attendance

Home 356,415 Away 502,372 Total 858,787
Single-game home record, 61,457 (12-5-71)
Single-season home record, 482,572 (1986)

1992 Team Statistics

	Patriots	Opp.
Total First Downs	215	292
Rushing	71	112
Passing	130	149
Penalty	14	31
Third Down: Made/Att.	72/223	77/214
Third Down: Pct.	32.3	36.0
Fourth Down: Made/Att.	8/19	6/15
Fourth Down: Pct.	42.1	40.0
Total Net Yards	3584	5048
Avg. Per Game	224.0	315.5
Total Plays	928	1000
Avg. Per Play	3.9	5.0
Net Yards Rushing	1550	1951
Avg. Per Game	96.9	121.9
Total Rushes	419	521
Net Yards Passing	2034	3097
Avg. Per Game	127.1	193.6
Sacked/Yards Lost	65/458	20/114
Gross Yards	2492	3211
Att./Completions	444/244	459/258
Completion Pct.	55.0	56.2
Had Intercepted	19	14
Punts/Avg.	103/41.0	75/40.6
Net Punting Avg.	103/35.4	75/35.3
Penalties/Yards Lost	111/1051	90/673
Fumbles/Ball Lost	43/26	30/15
Touchdowns	25	40
Rushing	6	15
Passing	13	22
Returns	6	3
Avg. Time of Possession	28:30	31:30

1992 Individual Statistics

Scoring	TD R	TD P	TD Rt	PAT	FG	Saf	TP
Baumann	0	0	0	22/24	11/17	0	55
Fryar	0	4	0	0/0	0/0	0	24
Coates	0	3	0	0/0	0/0	0	18
V. Brown	0	0	2	0/0	0/0	0	12
Cook	0	2	0	0/0	0/0	0	12
Russell	2	0	0	0/0	0/0	0	12
J. Stephens	2	0	0	0/0	0/0	0	12
Turner	0	2	0	0/0	0/0	0	12
Vaughn	1	0	1	0/0	0/0	0	12
Gash	1	0	0	0/0	0/0	0	6
Goad	0	0	1	0/0	0/0	0	6
McMurtry	0	1	0	0/0	0/0	0	6
Pool	0	0	1	0/0	0/0	0	6
Singleton	0	0	1	0/0	0/0	0	6
Timpson	0	1	0	0/0	0/0	0	6
Patriots	6	13	6	22/25	11/17	0	205
Opponents	15	22	3	40/40	27/41	1	363

Passing	Att.	Comp.	Yds.	Pct.	TD	Int.	Tkld.	Rate
Millen	203	124	1203	61.1	8	10	33/204	70.3
Zolak	100	52	561	52.0	2	4	17/137	58.8
Hodson	91	50	496	54.9	2	2	12/96	68.8
Carlson	49	18	232	36.7	1	3	3/21	33.7
McMurtry	1	0	0	0.0	0	0	0/0	39.6
Patriots	444	244	2492	55.0	13	19	65/458	63.2
Opponents	459	258	3211	56.2	22	14	20/114	81.3

Rushing	Att.	Yds.	Avg.	LG	TD
Vaughn	113	451	4.0	36	1
Russell	123	390	3.2	23	2
J. Stephens	75	277	3.7	19	2
Lockwood	35	162	4.6	23	0
Millen	17	108	6.4	26	0
Zolak	18	71	3.9	19	0
Turner	10	40	4.0	11	0
Carlson	11	32	2.9	7	0
Hodson	5	11	2.2	5	0
Gash	5	7	1.4	4	1
Fryar	1	6	6.0	8	0
McMurtry	2	3	1.5	2	0
Coates	1	2	2.0	2	0
McCarthy	3	−10	−3.3	0	0
Patriots	419	1550	3.7	36	6
Opponents	521	1951	3.7	53	15

Receiving	No.	Yds.	Avg.	LG	TD
Fryar	55	791	14.4	54t	4
Cook	52	413	7.9	27	2
McMurtry	35	424	12.1	65t	1
Timpson	26	315	12.1	25	1
J. Stephens	21	161	7.7	32	0
Coates	20	171	8.6	22t	3
Vaughn	13	84	6.5	28	0
Russell	11	24	2.2	12	0
Turner	7	52	7.4	19t	2
Stanley	3	63	21.0	36	0
Hodson	1	−6	−6.0	−6	0
Patriots	244	2492	10.2	65t	13
Opponents	258	3211	12.4	56	22

Interceptions	No.	Yds.	Avg.	LG	TD
Henderson	3	43	14.3	34	0
Hurst	3	29	9.7	27	0
Pool	2	54	27.0	41t	1
Robbins	2	27	13.5	20	0
Singleton	1	82	82.0	82t	1
V. Brown	1	49	49.0	49t	1
Howard	1	1	1.0	1	0
Smith	1	0	0.0	0	0
Patriots	14	285	20.4	82t	3
Opponents	19	232	12.2	47	0

Punting	No.	Yds.	Avg.	In 20	LG
McCarthy	103	4227	41.0	19	61
Patriots	103	4227	41.0	19	61
Opponents	75	3045	40.6	27	59

Punt Returns	No.	FC	Yds.	Avg.	LG	TD
Stanley	28	17	227	8.1	50	0
Timpson	8	2	47	5.9	14	0
Lambert	1	0	0	0.0	0	0
Fryar	0	1	0	—	—	0
Patriots	37	20	274	7.4	50	0
Opponents	59	21	499	8.5	53t	1

Kickoff Returns	No.	Yds.	Avg.	LG	TD
Vaughn	20	564	28.2	100t	1
Stanley	29	529	18.2	40	0
Hobby	1	11	11.0	11	0
Lockwood	11	233	21.2	36	0
Timpson	2	28	14.0	28	0
Turner	1	11	11.0	11	0
Patriots	64	1376	21.5	100t	1
Opponents	45	749	16.6	39	0

Sacks	No.
Tippett	7.0
B. Williams	4.0
Goad	2.5
Agnew	1.0
Edwards	1.0
Howard	1.0
Lambert	1.0
Rembert	1.0
Sabb	1.0
V. Brown	0.5
Patriots	20.0
Opponents	65.0

1993 Draft Choices

Round	Name	Pos.	College
1.	Drew Bledsoe	QB	Washington State
2.	Chris Slade	DE	Virginia
	Todd Rucci	T	Penn State
	Vincent Brisby	WR	N.E. Louisiana
4.	Kevin Johnson	NT	Texas Southern
	Corwin Brown	DB	Michigan
5.	Scott Sisson	K	Georgia Tech
	Richard Griffith	TE	Arizona
6.	Lawrence Hatch	DB	Florida
8.	Troy Brown	KR	Marshall

New England Patriots 1993 Veteran Roster

No.	Name	Pos.	Ht.	Wt.	Birth-date	NFL Exp.	College	Hometown	How Acq.	'92 Games/ Starts
92	Agnew, Ray	DE	6-3	272	12/9/67	4	North Carolina State	Winston-Salem, N.C.	D1b-'90	14/14
78	Armstrong, Bruce	T	6-4	284	9/7/65	7	Louisville	Miami, Fla.	D1-'87	8/8
8	Baumann, Charlie	K	6-1	203	8/25/67	3	West Virginia	Erie, Pa.	FA-'91	16/0
47	Brown, Roger	S	6-0	196	12/16/66	4	Virginia Tech	Baltimore, Md.	FA-'92	16/3
59	Brown, Vincent	LB	6-2	245	1/9/65	6	Mississippi Valley State	Decatur, Ga.	D2-'88	13/13
17	†Carlson, Jeff	QB	6-3	215	5/23/66	4	Weber State	Garden Grove, Calif.	FA-'92	3/2
63	Chilton, Gene	C	6-3	286	3/27/64	7	Texas	Houston, Tex.	FA-'90	16/16
69	Chung, Eugene	T	6-4	295	6/14/69	2	Virginia Tech	Oakton, Va.	D1-'92	16/14
87	Coates, Ben	TE	6-4	245	8/16/69	3	Livingston	Greenwood, S.C.	D5b-'91	16/2
54	Collins, Ted	LB	6-2	242	5/27/70	2	Carson-Newman	New Market, Tenn.	D3a-'92	10/0
85	Cook, Marv	TE	6-4	234	2/24/66	5	Iowa	West Branch, Iowa	D3a-'89	16/15
98	Edwards, Tim	DE	6-1	270	8/29/68	2	Delta State	Nesoba, Miss.	FA-'92	14/1
81	Farr, Mike	WR	5-10	192	8/8/67	4	UCLA	Birmingham, Mich.	RFA(Det)-'93	13/0*
91	Gannon, Chris	DE	6-6	260	1/20/66	5	Southwestern Louisiana	Orange Park, Fla.	PB(SD)-'90	12/0
33	Gash, Sam	RB	5-11	224	3/7/69	2	Penn State	Hendersonville, N.C.	D8b-'92	15/0
72	Goad, Tim	NT	6-3	280	2/28/66	6	North Carolina	Stuart, Va.	D4a-'88	16/16
41	Gordon, Tim	S	6-0	188	5/7/65	7	Tulsa	Ardmore, Okla.	FA-'90	10/7
77	Harlow, Pat	T	6-6	290	3/16/69	3	Southern California	Norco, Calif.	D1a-'91	16/16
36	Henderson, Jerome	CB	5-10	189	8/8/69	3	Clemson	Statesville, N.C.	D2-'91	16/10
90	†Hobby, Marion	DE	6-4	277	11/7/66	4	Tennessee	Birmingham, Ala.	FA-'90	11/2
13	†Hodson, Tom	QB	6-3	195	1/28/67	4	Louisiana State	Mathews, La.	D3-'90	9/3
99	#Howard, David	LB	6-1	230	12/8/61	9	Long Beach State	Long Beach, Calif.	T(Dall)-'91	16/10
37	†Hurst, Maurice	CB	5-10	185	9/17/67	5	Southern	New Orleans, La.	D4a-'89	16/16
93	Jones, Aaron	DE-DT	6-5	267	12/18/66	6	Eastern Kentucky	Orlando, Fla.	UFA(Pitt)-'93	14/0*
28	Lambert, Dion	CB	6-0	185	2/12/69	2	UCLA	Lake View Terrace, Calif.	D4a-'92	16/0
75	Lewis, Bill	C	6-6	290	7/12/63	8	Nebraska	Sioux City, Iowa	UFA(Phx)-'93	6/6*
51	Lockhart, Eugene	LB	6-2	233	3/8/61	10	Houston	Crockett, Tex.	T(Dall)-'91	16/8
40	Lockwood, Scott	RB	5-10	196	3/23/68	2	Southern California	Boulder, Colo.	FA-'92	4/0
5	McCarthy, Shawn	P	6-6	227	2/22/68	3	Purdue	Fremont, Ohio	FA-'91	16/0
58	†McGovern, Rob	LB	6-2	234	10/1/66	4	Holy Cross	Teaneck, N.J.	FA-'92	4/0
86	McMurtry, Greg	WR	6-2	207	10/15/67	4	Michigan	Brockton, Mass.	D3-'90	16/15
93	Pitts, Mike	DT	6-5	280	9/25/60	11	Alabama	Baltimore, Md.	UFA(Phil)-'93	11/3*
27	Pool, David	CB	5-9	182	12/20/66	4	Carson-Newman	Cincinnati, Ohio	FA-'91	16/14
70	Redding, Reggie	G	6-4	305	9/22/68	4	Cal State-Fullerton	Cincinnati, Ohio	T(Atl)-'92	14/14
32	Russell, Leonard	RB	6-2	235	11/17/69	3	Arizona State	Long Beach, Calif.	D1b-'91	11/10
95	Sabb, Dwayne	LB	6-4	248	10/9/69	2	New Hampshire	Union, N.J.	D5-'92	16/2
10	Secules, Scott	QB	6-3	223	11/8/64	6	Virginia	Newport News, Va.	UFA(Mia)-'93	0*
55	Singleton, Chris	LB	6-2	247	2/20/67	4	Arizona	Parsippany, N.J.	D1a-'90	8/7
22	Smith, Rod	CB	5-11	187	3/12/70	2	Notre Dame	Roseville, Minn.	D2-'92	16/1
68	Stephens, Calvin	G	6-2	285	10/25/67	3	South Carolina	Kings Mountain, N.C.	D3-'91	14/1
21	Thompson, Reyna	CB-S	6-0	193	8/28/63	8	Baylor	Dallas, Tex.	UFA(NYG)-'93	16/0*
83	Timpson, Michael	WR	5-10	175	6/6/67	5	Penn State	Hialeah, Fla.	D4-'89	16/2
56	Tippett, Andre	LB	6-3	241	12/27/59	12	Iowa	Newark, N.J.	D2b-'82	14/13
65	Trapilo, Steve	G-T	6-5	289	9/20/64	7	Boston College	Boston, Mass.	UFA(NO)-'93	5/0*
34	Turner, Kevin	RB	6-0	224	6/12/69	2	Alabama	Prattville, Ala.	D3b-'92	16/1
24	Vaughn, Jon	RB	5-9	203	3/12/70	3	Michigan	Florissant, Mo.	D5a-'91	16/5
76	Washington, John	DE-DT	6-4	290	2/20/63	8	Oklahoma State	Houston, Tex.	UFA(Atl)-'93	15/1*
38	t-White, Adrian	CB-S	6-0	205	4/6/64	7	Florida	Orange Park, Fla.	T(GB)-'93	15/0*
96	Williams, Brent	DE	6-4	275	10/23/64	8	Toledo	Flint, Mich.	D7b-'86	16/15
16	Zolak, Scott	QB	6-5	222	12/13/67	3	Maryland	Monongahela, Pa.	D4-'91	6/4

* Farr played 13 games with Detroit in '92; Jones played 14 games with Pittsburgh; Lewis played 6 games with Phoenix; Pitts played 11 games with Philadelphia; Secules missed '92 season due to injury; Thompson played 16 games with N.Y. Giants; Trapilo played 5 games with New Orleans; Washington played 12 games with N.Y. Giants and 3 games with Atlanta; White played 15 games with Green Bay.

#Unrestricted free agent; subject to developments.

† Restricted free agent; subject to developments.

Traded—WR Irving Fryar to Miami; RB John Stephens to Green Bay.

t- Patriots traded for White (Green Bay).

Also played with Patriots in '92—CB Darren Anderson (1 game), WR Irving Fryar (15), G-T Gregg Rakoczy (16), LB Johnny Rembert (12), S Randy Robbins (15), NT Fred Smerlas (16), WR Walter Stanley (13), RB John Stephens (16), LB Richard Tardits (9), G Larry David Wilson (1).

COACHING STAFF

Head Coach, Bill Parcells

Pro Career: Became twelfth head coach in franchise history on January 21, 1993. Rejoins coaching ranks after spending two seasons as an analyst on NFL broadcasts for NBC. Parcells spent eight years as head coach of the New York Giants (1983-90), leading the team to Super Bowl titles following the 1986 and 1990 seasons. Returns to New England where his pro coaching career began—he was the Patriots' linebackers coach in 1980. Career record: 85-52-1.

Background: Linebacker at Wichita State 1961-63. College assistant Hastings (Neb.) 1964, Wichita State 1965, Army 1966-69, Florida State 1970-72, Vanderbilt 1973-74, Texas Tech 1975-77, Air Force 1978 (head coach).

Personal: Born August 22, 1941, Englewood, N.J. Bill and his wife, Judy, live in Foxboro, Mass., and have three daughters—Suzy, Jill, and Dallas.

Assistant Coaches

David Atkins, offensive backs; born May 18, 1949, Victoria, Tex., lives in Foxboro, Mass. Running back Texas-El Paso 1970-72. Pro running back San Francisco 49ers 1973, Honolulu (WFL) 1974, San Diego Chargers 1975. College coach: Texas-El Paso 1979-80, San Diego State 1981-85. Pro coach: Philadelphia Eagles 1986-91, joined Patriots in 1993.

Romeo Crennel, defensive line; born June 18, 1947, Lynchburg, Va., lives in Foxboro, Mass. Defensive tackle, linebacker Western Kentucky 1966-69. No pro playing experience. College coach: Western Kentucky 1970-74, Texas Tech 1975-77, Mississippi 1978-79, Georgia Tech 1980. Pro coach: New York Giants 1981-92, joined Patriots in 1993.

Al Groh, defensive coordinator; born July 13, 1944, New York City, lives in Foxboro, Mass. Defensive end Virginia 1964-67. No pro playing experience. College coach: Army 1968-69, Virginia 1970-72, North Carolina 1973-77, Air Force 1978-79, Texas Tech 1980, Wake Forest 1981-86 (head coach), South Carolina 1988. Pro coach: Atlanta Falcons 1987, New York Giants 1989-91, Cleveland Browns 1992, joined Patriots in 1993.

Fred Hoaglin, offensive line; born January 28, 1944, Alliance, Ohio, lives in Cumberland, R.I. Center Pittsburgh 1962-65. Pro center Cleveland Browns 1966-72, Baltimore Colts 1973, Houston Oilers 1974-75, Seattle Seahawks 1976. Pro coach: Detroit Lions 1978-84, New York Giants 1985-92, joined Patriots in 1993.

Chris Palmer, wide receivers; born September 23, 1949, Mt. Kisco, N.Y., lives in Foxboro, Mass. Quarterback Southern Connecticut State 1968-71. No pro playing experience. College coach: Connecticut 1972-74, Lehigh 1975, Colgate 1976-82, New Haven 1986-87 (head coach), Boston University 1988-89 (head coach). Pro coach: Montreal Concordes (CFL) 1983, New Jersey Generals (USFL) 1984-85, Houston Oilers 1990-92, joined Patriots in 1993.

Johnny Parker, strength and conditioning; born February 1, 1947, Greenville, S.C., lives in Foxboro, Mass. Graduate of Mississippi, master's degree from Delta State University. No college or pro playing experience. College coach: South Carolina 1974-76, Indiana 1977-79, Louisiana State 1980, Mississippi 1981-83. Pro coach: New York Giants 1984-92, joined Patriots in 1993.

Ray Perkins, offensive coordinator, born November 6, 1941, Mount Olive, Miss., lives in Foxboro, Mass. Wide receiver Alabama 1964-66. Pro receiver Baltimore Colts 1967-71. College coach: Mississippi State 1973, Alabama 1983-86 (head coach), Arkansas State 1992 (head coach). Pro coach: New England Patriots 1974-77, San Diego Chargers 1978, New York Giants 1979-82 (head coach), Tampa Bay Buccaneers 1987-90 (head coach), rejoined Patriots in 1993.

New England Patriots 1993 First-Year Roster

Name	Pos.	Ht.	Wt.	Birth-date	College	Hometown	How Acq.
Ale, Arnold	LB	6-2	230	6/17/70	UCLA	Carson, Calif.	FA
Armstrong, Chris (1)	WR	6-1	205	8/28/67	Arkansas-Fayetteville	Fayetteville, N.C.	FA
Ballard, Keith	T	6-3	298	12/16/70	Minnesota	Detroit, Mich.	FA
Bledsoe, Drew	QB	6-5	233	2/14/72	Washington State	Walla Walla, Wash.	D1
Bolden, Tunji	LB	6-1	247	10/31/70	Texas Christian	Ann Arbor, Mich.	FA
Bomba, Matt	DE-NT	6-5	275	5/22/68	Indiana	Bloomington, Ind.	FA
Brisby, Vincent	WR	6-1	186	1/25/71	Northeast Louisiana	Lake Charles, La.	D2c
Brown, Corwin	CB	6-0	192	4/25/70	Michigan	Chicago, Ill.	D4b
Brown, Troy	WR	5-9	195	7/2/71	Marshall	Blackville, S.C.	D8
Croom, Corey	RB	5-11	212	5/22/71	Ball State	Sandusky, Ohio	FA
Dwight, Reggie (1)	TE	6-3	285	4/4/70	Troy State	Cordele, Ga.	FA
Gallon, Eric	RB	5-11	201	11/22/70	Kansas State	Lakeland, Fla.	FA
Gibson, Don (1)	DE-NT	6-3	275	3/4/68	Southern California	Orange, Calif.	FA
Gilliard, Bo	WR	5-11	180	7/1/71	Prairie View A&M	Houston, Tex.	FA
Gisler, Mike (1)	G-T	6-4	300	8/26/69	Houston	Range, Tex.	FA
Godfrey, Frank	G	6-2	266	2/25/70	Louisiana State	Pascagoula, Miss.	FA
Golden, Al (1)	TE	6-3	240	7/4/69	Penn State	Red Bank, N.J.	FA
Gordon, Steve (1)	C	6-3	279	4/14/69	California	Nevada City, Calif.	D10b-'92
Granby, John (1)	S	6-1	200	11/11/68	Virginia Tech	Virginia Beach, Va.	FA
Griffith, Richard	TE	6-4	250	7/3/69	Arizona	Tucson, Ariz.	D5b
Harris, Ron	WR	5-10	170	6/4/70	Oregon	Granada Hills, Calif.	FA
Hatch, Lawrence	CB	5-11	194	5/22/71	Florida	Gainesville, Fla.	D6
Hawkins, Wayne (1)	WR	5-10	182	8/13/69	Southwest St., Minn.	St. Paul, Minn.	FA
Hopkins, Wade (1)	WR	6-2	195	8/23/68	Southwest Baptist	Houston, Tex.	FA
Johnson, Kevin	NT	6-1	306	10/30/70	Texas Southern	Los Angeles, Calif.	D4a
Legette, Burnie	RB	6-0	243	12/5/70	Michigan	Colorado Springs, Colo.	FA
Lewis, Vernon	CB-S	5-10	192	10/27/70	Pittsburgh	Houston, Tex.	FA
Olberding, Lance (1)	G-T	6-7	310	3/1/71	No College	Apple Valley, Minn.	FA
Perez, Chris (1)	G-T	6-6	305	6/21/69	Kansas	Palatine, Ill.	FA
Rucci, Todd	T	6-5	291	7/14/70	Penn State	Upper Darby, Pa.	D2b
Sisson, Scott	K	6-0	197	7/21/71	Georgia Tech	Marietta, Ga.	D5
Slade, Chris	LB	6-4	232	1/30/71	Virginia	Tabb, Va.	D2a
Sutter, Eddie (1)	LB	6-3	240	10/3/69	Northwestern	Peoria, Ill.	FA
Tudors, Pumpy (1)	P	5-7	203	11/3/69	Tenn.-Chattanooga	Marion County, Tenn.	FA
Van Bellinger, Scott (1)	LB	6-5	245	5/26/69	Northern Illinois	Green Bay, Wis.	FA
Vincent, Tom	T	6-4	278	3/25/70	Vanderbilt	Brownsville, Ky.	FA

The term NFL Rookie is defined as a player who is in his first season of professional football and has not been on the roster of another professional football team for any regular-season or postseason games. A Rookie is designated by an "R" on NFL rosters. Players who have been active in another professional football league or players who have NFL experience, including either preseason training camp or being on an Active List or Inactive List, or on Reserve/Injured or Reserve/Physically Unable to Perform for fewer than six regular-season games, are termed NFL First-Year Players. An NFL First-Year Player is designated by a "1" on NFL rosters. Thereafter, a player is credited with an additional year of experience for each season in which he accumulates six games on the Active List or Inactive List, or on Reserve/Injured or Reserve/Physically Unable to Perform.

NOTES

Dante Scarnecchia, special assistant, born February 15, 1948, Los Angeles, Calif., lives in Wrentham, Mass. Center-guard California Western 1968-70. No pro playing experience. College coach: California Western (now U.S. International) 1970-72, Iowa State 1973, Southern Methodist 1975-76, 1980-81, Pacific 1977-78, Northern Arizona 1979. Pro coach: New England Patriots 1982-89, Indianapolis Colts 1990, rejoined Patriots in 1991.

Mike Sweatman, special teams, born October 23, 1947, Kansas City, Mo., lives in Foxboro, Mass. Linebacker Kansas 1964-67. No pro playing experience. College coach: Kansas 1973-74, 1979-82, Tulsa 1977-78, Tennessee 1983. Pro coach: Minnesota Vikings 1984, New York Giants 1985-92, joined Patriots in 1993.

Bob Trott, defensive backs, born March 19, 1954, Kannapolis, N.C., lives in Franklin, Mass. Defensive back North Carolina 1973-75. No pro playing experience. College coach: North Carolina 1976-77, Air Force 1978-83, Arkansas 1984-89, Clemson 1990. Pro coach: New York Giants 1990-92, joined Patriots in 1993.

Charlie Weis, tight ends, born March 30, 1956, Trenton, N.J., lives in Foxboro, Mass. Graduate of Notre Dame. No college or pro playing experience. College coach: South Carolina 1985-88. Pro coach: New York Giants 1990-92, joined Patriots in 1993.

NEW YORK JETS

American Football Conference Eastern Division

Team Colors: Kelly Green and White

1000 Fulton Avenue
Hempstead, New York 11550
Telephone: (516) 538-6600

Club Officials

Chairman of the Board: Leon Hess
President: Steve Gutman
VP/General Manager: Dick Steinberg
Assistant General Manager: James Harris
Director of Player Personnel: Dick Haley
Pro Personnel Director: Jim Royer
Assistant Pro Personnel Director: Pat Kirwan
Talent Scouts: Joe Collins, Don Grammer, Sid Hall, Ron Nay, Marv Sunderland
College Scouting Coordinator: John Griffin
Director of Public Relations: Frank Ramos
Asst. Director of Public Relations: Brooks Thomas
Public Relations Assistants: Ken Ilchuk, Sharon Kelleher, Doug Miller
Controller: Mike Gerstle
Director of Operations: Mike Kensil
Director of Business Relations: Bob Parente
Marketing Manager: Bruce Popko
Ticket Manager: Gerry Parravano
Video Director: Jim Pons
Assistant Video Director: John Seiter
Trainer: Bob Reese
Assistant Trainers: Joe Patten, Darryl Conway
Equipment Manager: Bill Hampton
Assistant Equipment Managers: Bill Hampton, Jr., Mickey Rendine

Stadium: Giants Stadium • **Capacity:** 76,891
East Rutherford, New Jersey 07073

Playing Surface: AstroTurf

Training Center: 1000 Fulton Avenue
Hempstead, New York 11550
(516) 538-6600

1993 Schedule

Preseason

Aug. 7	at Pittsburgh	6:00
Aug. 13	**Philadelphia**	7:30
Aug. 21	at New York Giants	8:00
Aug. 27	at Washington	8:00

Regular Season

Sept. 5	**Denver**	1:00
Sept. 12	at Miami	4:00
Sept. 19	**Open Date**	
Sept. 26	**New England**	8:00
Oct. 3	**Philadelphia**	4:00
Oct. 10	at Los Angeles Raiders	1:00
Oct. 17	**Open Date**	
Oct. 24	**Buffalo**	1:00
Oct. 31	at New York Giants	1:00
Nov. 7	**Miami**	4:00
Nov. 14	at Indianapolis	4:00
Nov. 21	**Cincinnati**	1:00
Nov. 28	at New England	1:00
Dec. 5	**Indianapolis**	1:00
Dec. 11	at Washington (Saturday)	12:30
Dec. 18	**Dallas** (Saturday)	4:00
Dec. 26	at Buffalo	1:00
Jan. 2	at Houston	7:00

Jets Coaching History

New York Titans 1960-62
(218-269-8)

1960-61	Sammy Baugh	14-14-0
1962	Clyde (Bulldog) Turner	5-9-0
1963-73	Weeb Ewbank	73-78-6
1974-75	Charley Winner*	9-14-0
1975	Ken Shipp	1-4-0
1976	Lou Holtz**	3-10-0
1976	Mike Holovak	0-1-0
1977-82	Walt Michaels	41-49-1
1983-89	Joe Walton	54-59-1
1990-92	Bruce Coslet	18-31-0

*Released after nine games in 1975
**Resigned after 13 games in 1976

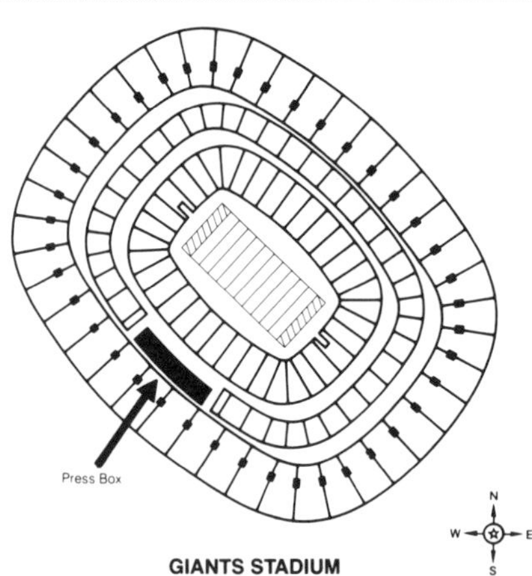

GIANTS STADIUM

Record Holders

Individual Records — Career

Category	Name	Performance
Rushing (Yds.)	Freeman McNeil, 1981-1992	8,074
Passing (Yds.)	Joe Namath, 1965-1976	27,057
Passing (TDs)	Joe Namath, 1965-1976	170
Receiving (No.)	Don Maynard, 1960-1972	627
Receiving (Yds.)	Don Maynard, 1960-1972	11,732
Interceptions	Bill Baird, 1963-69	34
Punting (Avg.)	Curley Johnson, 1961-68	42.8
Punt Return (Avg.)	Dick Christy, 1961-63	16.2
Kickoff Return (Avg.)	Bobby Humphery, 1984-89	22.8
Field Goals	Pat Leahy, 1974-1991	304
Touchdowns (Tot.)	Don Maynard, 1960-1972	88
Points	Pat Leahy, 1974-1991	1,470

Individual Records — Single Season

Category	Name	Performance
Rushing (Yds.)	Freeman McNeil, 1985	1,331
Passing (Yds.)	Joe Namath, 1967	4,007
Passing (TDs)	Al Dorow, 1960	26
	Joe Namath, 1967	26
Receiving (No.)	Al Toon, 1988	93
Receiving (Yds.)	Don Maynard, 1967	1,434
Interceptions	Dainard Paulson, 1964	12
Punting (Avg.)	Curley Johnson, 1965	45.3
Punt Return (Avg.)	Dick Christy, 1961	21.3
Kickoff Return (Avg.)	Bobby Humphery, 1984	30.7
Field Goals	Jim Turner, 1968	34
Touchdowns (Tot.)	Art Powell, 1960	14
	Don Maynard, 1965	14
	Emerson Boozer, 1972	14
Points	Jim Turner, 1968	145

Individual Records — Single Game

Category	Name	Performance
Rushing (Yds.)	Freeman McNeil, 9-15-85	192
Passing (Yds.)	Joe Namath, 9-24-72	496
Passing (TDs)	Joe Namath, 9-24-72	6
Receiving (No.)	Clark Gaines, 9-21-80	17
Receiving (Yds.)	Don Maynard, 11-17-68	228
Interceptions	Many times	3
	Last time by Erik McMillan, 10-23-88	
Field Goals	Jim Turner, 11-3-68	6
	Bobby Howfield, 12-3-72	6
Touchdowns (Tot.)	Wesley Walker, 9-21-86	4
Points	Wesley Walker, 9-21-86	24

1992 Team Record

Preseason (5-0)

Date	Result		Opponents
8/1	W	41-14	vs. Philadelphia at Canton
8/8	W	14-13	Washington
8/16	W	24- 7	vs. Green Bay at Madison
8/22	W	20-14	N.Y. Giants
8/27	W	22-13	at Philadelphia

Regular Season (4-12)

Date	Result		Opponents	Att.
9/6	L	17-20	at Atlanta	69,045
9/13	L	10-27	at Pittsburgh	58,327
9/20	L	14-31	San Francisco	75,945
9/27	L	10-18	at L.A. Rams	45,735
10/4	W	30-21	New England	75,004
10/11	L	3- 6	at Indianapolis (OT)	45,188
10/26	L	20-24	Buffalo	75,925
11/1	W	26-14	Miami	75,903
11/8	L	16-27	at Denver	73,036
11/15	W	17-14	Cincinnati	75,442
11/22	L	3-24	at New England	34,301
11/29	L	7-23	Kansas City	75,473
12/6	W	24-17	at Buffalo	78,752
12/13	L	6-10	Indianapolis	74,636
12/20	L	17-19	at Miami	70,907
12/26	L	0-20	New Orleans	75,291

(OT) Overtime

Score by Periods

Jets	24	80	56	60	0	—	220
Opponents	57	93	58	104	3	—	315

Attendance

Home 603,619 Away 475,291 Total 1,078,910
Single-game home record, 75,945 (9-20-92)
Single-season home record, 603,619 (1992)

1992 Team Statistics

	Jets	Opp.
Total First Downs	252	276
Rushing	94	110
Passing	137	146
Penalty	21	20
Third Down: Made/Att.	65/207	72/201
Third Down: Pct.	31.4	35.8
Fourth Down: Made/Att.	11/28	7/14
Fourth Down: Pct.	39.3	50.0
Total Net Yards	4431	4880
Avg. Per Game	276.9	305.0
Total Plays	958	961
Avg. Per Play	4.6	5.1
Net Yards Rushing	1752	1919
Avg. Per Game	109.5	119.9
Total Rushes	424	460
Net Yards Passing	2679	2961
Avg. Per Game	167.4	185.1
Sacked/Yards Lost	39/283	36/240
Gross Yards	2962	3201
Att./Completions	495/251	465/257
Completion Pct.	50.7	55.3
Had Intercepted	24	21
Punts/Avg.	73/41.0	70/40.9
Net Punting Avg.	73/37.6	70/35.3
Penalties/Yards Lost	107/873	82/808
Fumbles/Ball Lost	28/15	33/18
Touchdowns	23	35
Rushing	8	13
Passing	12	19
Returns	3	3
Avg. Time of Possession	30:24	29:36

1992 Individual Statistics

Scoring	TD R	TD P	TD Rt	PAT	FG	Saf	TP
Blanchard	0	0	0	17/17	16/22	0	65
Baxter	6	0	0	0/0	0/0	0	36
Mathis	1	3	0	0/0	0/0	0	24
Moore	0	4	0	0/0	0/0	0	24
Staurovsky	0	0	0	6/6	3/8	0	15
Toon	0	2	0	0/0	0/0	0	12
Brim	0	0	1	0/0	0/0	0	6
Burkett	0	1	0	0/0	0/0	0	6
Carpenter	0	1	0	0/0	0/0	0	6
Chaffey	1	0	0	0/0	0/0	0	6
Houston	0	0	1	0/0	0/0	0	6
Mitchell	0	1	0	0/0	0/0	0	6
B. Washington	0	0	1	0/0	0/0	0	6
M. Washington	0	0	0	0/0	0/0	1	2
Jets	8	12	3	23/23	19/30	1	220
Opponents	13	19	3	34/35	23/31	1	315

Passing	Att.	Comp.	Yds.	Pct.	TD	Int.	Tkld.	Rate
Nagle	387	192	2280	49.6	7	17	27/215	55.7
O'Brien	98	55	642	56.1	5	6	10/61	67.6
Blake	9	4	40	44.4	0	1	2/7	18.1
Carpenter	1	0	0	0.0	0	0	0/0	39.6
Jets	495	251	2962	50.7	12	24	39/283	57.2
Opponents	465	257	3201	55.3	19	21	36/240	71.6

Rushing	Att.	Yds.	Avg.	LG	TD
Baxter	152	698	4.6	30	6
Thomas	97	440	4.5	19	0
Chaffey	27	186	6.9	32	1
McNeil	43	170	4.0	18	0
Hector	24	67	2.8	14	0
Nagle	24	57	2.4	20	0
Brown	24	42	1.8	9	0
Graham	14	29	2.1	6	0
Mathis	3	25	8.3	10t	1
Moore	1	21	21.0	21	0
Canley	4	9	2.3	4	0
O'Brien	8	8	1.0	7	0
Carpenter	1	2	2.0	2	0
Blake	2	−2	−1.0	1	0
Jets	424	1752	4.1	32	8
Opponents	460	1919	4.2	54t	13

Receiving	No.	Yds.	Avg.	LG	TD
Burkett	57	724	12.7	37t	1
Moore	50	726	14.5	48t	4
Toon	31	311	10.0	32	2
Mathis	22	316	14.4	55t	3
Boyer	19	149	7.8	23	0
Mitchell	16	210	13.1	37t	1
McNeil	16	154	9.6	32	0
Carpenter	13	161	12.4	51	1
Chaffey	7	56	8.0	14	0
Thomas	7	49	7.0	10	0
Baxter	4	32	8.0	12	0
Brown	4	30	7.5	20	0
Hector	2	13	6.5	9	0
Whisenhunt	2	11	5.5	10	0
Sadowski	1	20	20.0	20	0
Jets	251	2962	11.8	55t	12
Opponents	257	3201	12.5	80t	19

Interceptions	No.	Yds.	Avg.	LG	TD
Brim	6	139	23.2	77t	1
B. Washington	6	59	9.8	23t	1
Hasty	2	18	9.0	18	0
Turner	2	15	7.5	14	0
Houston	1	20	20.0	20t	1
Kors	1	16	16.0	16	0
Clifton	1	1	1.0	1	0
Lewis	1	1	1.0	1	0
Price	1	0	0.0	0	0
Jets	21	269	12.8	77t	3
Opponents	24	347	14.5	65t	2

Punting	No.	Yds.	Avg.	In 20	LG
Aguiar	73	2993	41.0	21	65
Jets	73	2993	41.0	21	65
Opponents	70	2866	40.9	13	56

Punt Returns	No.	FC	Yds.	Avg.	LG	TD
Carpenter	28	9	208	7.4	21	0
Mathis	2	0	24	12.0	12	0
Jets	30	9	232	7.7	21	0
Opponents	26	18	189	7.3	46	0

Kickoff Returns	No.	Yds.	Avg.	LG	TD
Mathis	28	492	17.6	32	0
McMillan	22	420	19.1	45	0
Dawkins	1	10	10.0	10	0
Dixon	1	6	6.0	6	0
Duffy	1	7	7.0	7	0
Hector	1	15	15.0	15	0
Jets	54	950	17.6	45	0
Opponents	33	552	16.7	33	0

Sacks	No.
M. Washington	8.5
Frase	5.0
Mersereau	5.0
Houston	4.0
Gunn	2.0
Johnson	2.0
Lewis	2.0
McMillan	2.0
Byrd	1.0
Clifton	1.0
Lageman	1.0
Pickel	1.0
B. Washington	1.0
Barber	0.5
Jets	36.0
Opponents	39.0

1993 Draft Choices

Round	Name	Pos.	College
1.	Marvin Jones	LB	Florida State
2.	Coleman Rudolph	DE	Georgia Tech
4.	David Ware	T	Virginia
5.	Fred Baxter	TE	Auburn
	Adrian Murrell	RB	West Virginia
	Kenny Shedd	WR	Northern Iowa
6.	Richie Anderson	RB	Penn State
7.	Alec Millen	T	Georgia
8.	Craig Hentrich	K	Notre Dame

New York Jets 1993 Veteran Roster

No.	Name	Pos.	Ht.	Wt.	Birth-date	NFL Exp.	College	Hometown	How Acq.	'92 Games/ Starts
4	Aguiar, Louie	P	6-2	215	6/30/66	3	Utah State	Livermore, Calif.	FA-'91	16/0
98	Barber, Kurt	LB	6-4	241	1/5/69	2	Southern California	Paducah, Ky.	D2-'92	16/0
30	†Baxter, Brad	RB	6-1	235	5/5/67	4	Alabama State	Slocomb, Ala.	FA-'89	15/15
9	Blake, Jeff	QB	6-0	202	12/4/70	2	East Carolina	Sanford, Fla.	D6b-'92	3/0
10	Blanchard, Cary	K	6-1	225	11/5/68	2	Oklahoma State	Hurst, Tex.	W(NO)-'92	11/0
18	Boles, Eric	WR	6-3	211	4/29/70	2	Central Washington	Tacoma, Wash.	D11-'92	0*
60	Bruhin, John	G	6-3	290	12/9/64	5	Tennessee	Knoxville, Tenn.	FA-'93	0*
87	#Burkett, Chris	WR	6-4	200	8/21/62	9	Jackson State	Collins, Miss.	FA-'89	16/5
66	Cadigan, Dave	G	6-4	285	4/6/65	6	Southern California	Newport Beach, Calif.	D1-'88	15/12
50	Cadrez, Glenn	LB	6-3	240	1/20/70	2	Houston	El Centro, Calif.	D6a-'92	16/0
82	Carpenter, Rob	WR	6-2	190	8/1/68	3	Syracuse	Amityville, N.Y.	PB(NE)-'92	16/0
28	Chaffey, Pat	RB	6-1	220	4/19/67	3	Oregon State	Aurora, Ore.	PB(Atl)-'92	14/0
59	Clifton, Kyle	LB	6-4	236	8/23/62	10	Texas Christian	Bridgeport, Tex.	D3-'84	16/16
99	Coleman, Keo	LB	6-1	247	5/1/70	2	Mississippi State	Milwaukee, Wis.	D4-'92	6/0
69	Criswell, Jeff	T	6-7	291	3/7/64	6	Graceland	Searsboro, Iowa	FA-'88	14/13
89	†Dawkins, Dale	WR	6-1	190	10/30/66	4	Miami	Vero Beach, Fla.	D9-'90	6/0
52	Dixon, Cal	C	6-4	284	10/11/69	2	Florida	Merritt Island, Fla.	D5-'92	11/0
62	Duffy, Roger	G-C	6-3	285	7/16/67	4	Penn State	Canton, Ohio	D8-'90	16/6
7	t-Esiason, Boomer	QB	6-5	220	4/17/61	10	Maryland	East Islip, N.Y.	T(Cin)-'93	12/11*
91	†Frase, Paul	DT-DE	6-5	270	5/5/65	5	Syracuse	Barrington, N.H.	D6-'88	16/12
96	Gunn, Mark	DT-DE	6-5	279	7/24/68	3	Pittsburgh	Cleveland, Ohio	D4-'91	16/12
40	Hasty, James	CB	6-0	201	5/23/65	6	Washington State	Seattle, Wash.	D3b-'88	16/16
25	Hicks, Clifford	CB-KR	5-10	195	8/18/64	7	Oregon	San Diego, Calif.	UFA(Buff)-'93	12/2*
55	Houston, Bobby	LB	6-2	239	10/26/67	3	North Carolina State	Hyattsville, Md.	PB(Atl)-'91	16/15
39	t-Johnson, Johnny	RB	6-3	220	6/11/68	4	San Jose State	Santa Cruz, Calif.	T(Phx)-'93	12/8*
78	Johnson, Mario	DT	6-3	288	1/30/70	2	Missouri	Florissant, Mo.	D10-'92	14/0
56	Lageman, Jeff	DE	6-5	266	7/18/67	5	Virginia	Great Falls, Va.	D1-'89	2/2
57	Lewis, Mo	LB	6-3	250	10/21/69	3	Georgia	Peachtree, Ga.	D3-'91	16/16
42	Lott, Ronnie	S	6-1	203	5/8/59	13	Southern California	Rialto, Calif.	UFA(Raid)-'93	16/16*
75	Malamala, Siupeli	T	6-5	308	1/15/69	2	Washington	Kalaheo, Hawaii	D3-'92	9/5
70	Marshall, Leonard	DT	6-4	288	10/22/61	11	Louisiana State	Franklin, La.	UFA(NYG)-'93	14/12*
81	Mathis, Terance	WR-KR	5-10	177	6/7/67	4	New Mexico	Stone Mountain, Ga.	D6-'90	10/1
94	#Mersereau, Scott	DT	6-3	275	4/8/65	7	Southern Connecticut	Riverhead, N.Y.	FA-'87	15/15
83	Mitchell, Johnny	TE	6-3	237	1/20/71	2	Nebraska	Chicago, Ill.	D1-'92	11/3
85	Moore, Rob	WR	6-3	205	9/27/68	4	Syracuse	Hempstead, N.Y.	SD1-'90	16/15
8	Nagle, Browning	QB	6-3	225	4/29/68	3	Louisville	Largo, Fla.	D2-'91	14/13
3	Peters, Paul	WR	6-1	206	5/26/68	2	Cal State-Northridge	Santa Ana, Calif.	FA-'93	0*
71	#Pickel, Bill	DT	6-5	265	11/5/59	11	Rutgers	Maspeth, N.Y.	PB(Raid)-'91	11/1
27	Porter, Kevin	S	5-10	214	4/11/66	6	Auburn	Warner Robins, Ga.	W(KC)-'92	2/0
20	#Price, Dennis	CB	6-1	182	6/14/65	6	UCLA	Long Beach, Calif.	T(Raid)-'90	14/0
84	Sadowski, Troy	TE	6-5	250	12/8/65	4	Georgia	Chamblee, Ga.	FA-'93	6/2
53	Sweeney, Jim	C-G	6-4	286	8/8/62	10	Pittsburgh	Pittsburgh, Pa.	D2a-'84	16/16
49	Tate, David	S-CB	6-1	200	11/22/64	6	Colorado	Denver, Colo.	UFA(Chi)-'93	16/3*
32	Thomas, Blair	RB	5-10	202	10/7/67	4	Penn State	Philadelphia, Pa.	D1-'90	9/7
22	Thomas, Eric	CB	5-11	184	9/11/64	7	Tulane	Sacramento, Calif.	UFA(Cin)-'93	16/16*
80	Thornton, James	TE	6-2	242	2/8/65	6	Cal State-Fullerton	Santa Rosa, Calif.	UFA(Chi)-'93	0*
23	Turner, Marcus	CB-S	6-0	190	1/13/66	5	UCLA	Long Beach, Calif.	PB(Phx)-'92	16/0
48	†Washington, Brian	S	6-1	206	9/10/65	5	Nebraska	Richmond, Va.	W(Clev)-'89	16/16
97	†Washington, Marvin	DE	6-6	272	10/22/65	5	Idaho	Dallas, Tex.	D6a-'89	16/14
86	#Whisenhunt, Ken	TE	6-3	235	2/28/62	8	Georgia Tech	Augusta, Ga.	W(Wash)-'91	10/5
67	White, Dwayne	G	6-2	315	2/10/67	4	Alcorn State	Philadelphia, Pa.	D7a-'90	16/16
72	Wilson, Karl	DT-DE	6-5	277	9/10/64	6	Louisiana State	Amite, La.	FA-'93	2/0
31	Young, Lonnie	S-CB	6-1	196	7/18/63	9	Michigan State	Flint, Mich.	T(Phx)-'91	13/13

* Boles and Peters missed '92 season due to injury; Bruhin last active with Philadelphia in '91; Esiason played 12 games with Cincinnati in '92; Hicks played 12 games with Buffalo; J. Johnson played 12 games with Phoenix; Lott played 16 games with L.A. Raiders; Marshall played 14 games with N.Y. Giants; Tate played 16 games with Chicago; E. Thomas played 16 games with Cincinnati; Thornton last active with Chicago in '91.

Unrestricted free agent; subject to developments.

† Restricted free agent; subject to developments.

t- Jets traded for Esiason (Cincinnati), J. Johnson (Phoenix).

Traded—QB Ken O'Brien to Green Bay.

Retired—Freeman McNeil, 12-year running back, 12 games in '92; Al Toon, 8-year wide receiver, 9 games in '92.

Players lost through free agency (5): CB-S Michael Brim (Cin; 16 games in '92), T Irv Eatman (Rams; 12); LB Joe Kelly (Raid; 9), CB-S R.J. Kors (Rams; 14), CB-S Erik McMillan (Phil; 15).

Also played with Jets in '92—TE Mark Boyer (12 games), RB A.B. Brown (7), DE Dennis Byrd (7), S Joe Fishback (5), RB Johnny Hector (5), LB Don Jones (2), TE Eric Kattus (4), QB Ken O'Brien (10), LB-DT Huey Richardson (7), K Jason Staurovsky (4).

COACHING STAFF

Head Coach, Bruce Coslet

Pro Career: Became New York's eighth head coach on February 6, 1990, and is now entering his fourth year as head coach of the Jets. After leading New York back to the playoffs in 1991 for the first time since 1986, the Jets struggled last year and were devastated by injuries. Aside from the 1992 season, Coslet's team showed marked improvement in each of his first three seasons. Coslet entered the pro coaching ranks as tight ends and special teams coach with San Francisco in 1980. He joined the Cincinnati Bengals in 1981 in the same capacity. In 1983, he was given the added responsibility of the passing game. Coslet tutored the Cincinnati receiving corps in 1984-85 before being named offensive coordinator (1986-89). The Bengals had the top-ranked offense in three of those years and went to Super Bowl XXIII. He played tight end for Cincinnati in 1969-76. Career record: 18-31.

Background: Tight end at the University of the Pacific from 1965-67.

Personal: Born August 5, 1946, in Oakdale, Calif. Bruce and his wife, Kathy, live on Long Island, and have two children — J.J. and Amy.

Assistant Coaches

Paul Alexander, offensive assistant-tight ends; born February 12, 1960, Rochester, N.Y., lives on Long Island. Tackle Cortland State 1978-81. No pro playing experience. College coach: Penn State 1982-84, Michigan 1985-86, Central Michigan 1987-91. Pro coach: Joined Jets in 1992.

Larry Beightol, offensive line; born November 21, 1942, Morrisdale, Pa., lives on Long Island. Guard-linebacker Catawba College 1961-63. No pro playing experience. College coach: William & Mary 1968-71, North Carolina State 1972-75, Auburn 1976, Arkansas 1977-78, 1980-82, Louisiana Tech 1979 (head coach), Missouri 1983-84. Pro coach: Atlanta Falcons 1985-86, Tampa Bay Buccaneers 1987-88, San Diego Chargers 1989, joined Jets in 1990.

Pete Carroll, defensive coordinator; born September 15, 1951, San Francisco, Calif., lives on Long Island. Defensive back Pacific 1969-72. No pro playing experience. College coach: Arkansas 1977, Iowa State 1978, Ohio State 1979, North Carolina State 1980-82, Pacific 1983. Pro coach: Buffalo Bills 1984, Minnesota Vikings 1985-89, joined Jets in 1990.

Ed Donatell, defensive assistant-secondary; born February 4, 1957, Akron, Ohio, lives on Long Island. Safety Glenville State 1975-78. No pro playing experience. College coach: Kent State 1979-80, Washington 1981-82, Pacific 1983-85, Idaho 1986-88, Cal State-Fullerton 1989. Pro coach: Joined Jets in 1990.

Foge Fazio, linebackers; born February 28, 1939, Dawmont, W. Va., lives on Long Island. Linebacker-center Pittsburgh 1957-60. No pro playing experience. College coach: Boston University 1967, Harvard 1968, Pittsburgh 1969-72, 1977-81, 1982-85 (head coach), Cincinnati 1973-76, Notre Dame 1986-87. Pro coach: Atlanta Falcons 1988-89, joined Jets in 1990.

Walt Harris, quarterbacks; born November 9, 1946, Modesto, Calif., lives on Long Island. Defensive back Pacific 1966-67. No pro playing experience. College coach: Pacific 1970-73, 1988-91 (head coach), California 1974-77, Michigan State 1978-79, Illinois 1980-82, Tennessee 1983-88. Pro coach: Joined Jets in 1992.

Greg Mackrides, strength and conditioning; born July 9, 1954, Philadelphia, Pa., lives on Long Island. No college or pro playing experience. College coach: Villanova 1984-85, Fairfield 1986-88. U.S. Olympic Wrestling team 1988, U.S. Pan American and World touring teams 1986-88. Pro coach: New York Knicks (NBA) 1987-90, joined Jets in 1990.

Chip Myers, receivers; born July 9, 1945, Panama City, Fla., lives on Long Island. Receiver Northwestern Oklahoma 1964-66. Pro receiver San Francisco 49ers 1967, Cincinnati Bengals 1969-76. College coach: Illinois 1980-82. Pro coach: Tampa Bay Buccaneers 1983-84, Indianapolis Colts 1985-88, joined Jets in 1990.

Al Roberts, special teams coordinator; born January 6, 1944, Fresno, Calif., lives on Long Island. Running back Washington 1964-65, Puget Sound 1967-68. No pro playing experience. College coach: Washington 1977-82, Purdue 1986, Wyoming 1987. Pro coach: Los Angeles Express (USFL) 1983-84, Houston Oilers 1984-85, Philadelphia Eagles 1988-90, joined Jets in 1991.

Greg Robinson, defensive line; born October 9, 1951, Los Angeles, Calif., lives on Long Island. Linebacker-tight end Pacific 1972-73. No pro playing experience. College coach: Cal State-Fullerton 1977-79, North Carolina State 1980-81, UCLA 1982-89. Pro coach: Joined Jets in 1990.

Johnny Roland, running backs; born May 21, 1943, Corpus Christi, Tex., lives on Long Island. Running back Missouri 1963-65. Pro running back St. Louis Cardinals 1966-72, New York Giants 1973. College coach: Notre Dame 1975. Pro coach: Green Bay Packers 1974, Philadelphia Eagles 1976-78, Chicago Bears 1983-92, joined Jets in 1993.

New York Jets 1993 First-Year Roster

Name	Pos.	Ht.	Wt.	Birth-date	College	Hometown	How Acq.
Anderson, Richie	RB	6-2	215	9/13/71	Penn State	Sandy Spring, Md.	D6
Bailey, Mario (1)	WR	5-9	168	11/30/70	Washington	Seattle, Wash.	FA
Baxter, Fred	TE	6-3	250	6/14/71	Auburn	Brundidge, Ala.	D5a
Broady, Bryant	RB	6-0	240	11/4/69	Arkansas State	Uniondale, N.Y.	FA
Brown, James (1)	T	6-6	321	1/3/70	Virginia State	Philadelphia, Pa.	FA
Davis, Robert	DT	6-3	280	12/10/68	Shippensburg, Pa.	District Heights, Md.	FA
Drozdov, Darren	DT	6-3	281	4/7/69	Maryland	Mays Landing, N.J.	FA
Esters, Jeff	DT	6-2	291	7/6/69	Pittsburgh	Dania, Fla.	FA
Graham, Scottie (1)	RB	5-9	215	3/28/69	Ohio State	Long Beach, N.Y.	FA
Green, Victor	CB	5-9	195	12/8/69	Akron	Americus, Ga.	FA
Henderson, Kerry	RB	5-6	167	9/29/69	Texas Southern	Baytown, Tex.	FA
Hentrich, Craig	P-K	6-3	200	5/18/71	Notre Dame	Alton, Ill.	D8
Jones, Don (1)	LB	6-0	231	3/26/69	Washington	Gladys, Va.	FA
Jones, Marvin	LB	6-2	240	6/28/72	Florida State	Miami, Fla.	D1
McCullough, Russ (1)	T	6-10	315	10/31/68	Missouri	Olathe, Kan.	FA
Millen, Alec	T	6-7	285	9/25/70	Georgia	Atlanta, Ga.	D7
Murrell, Adrian	RB	5-11	205	10/16/70	West Virginia	Wahiawa, Hawaii	D5b
Perry, Marcus	T	6-5	288	9/18/70	Murray State	Dyersburg, Tenn.	FA
Pieri, Damon	S	6-0	186	9/25/70	San Diego State	Phoenix, Ariz.	FA
Prior, Anthony	CB-S	5-11	185	3/27/70	Washington State	Riverside, Calif.	FA
Redmond, Jamie	CB	5-9	179	10/1/69	Middle Tennessee St.	Oak Ridge, Tenn.	FA
Richardson, Paul	WR	6-3	204	2/25/69	UCLA	Los Angeles, Calif.	FA
Rudolph, Coleman	DE-DT	6-4	270	10/22/70	Georgia Tech	Valdosta, Ga.	D2
Sayles, Rick	WR	6-5	206	3/26/70	Penn State	McKeesport, Pa.	FA
Shedd, Kenny	WR-KR	5-9	166	2/14/71	Northern Iowa	Davenport, Iowa	D5c
Sherwin, Greg	T	6-5	285	9/4/69	Central Michigan	Traverse City, Mich.	FA
Spencer, Chris	WR	6-4	207	8/31/70	Iowa State	Omaha, Neb.	FA
Spencer, James	DT	6-6	285	1/9/70	Syracuse	Copiague, N.Y.	FA
Ware, David	T	6-6	285	2/21/70	Virginia	Roanoke, Va.	D4
Williams, Shawn	LB	6-2	244	6/19/70	Rutgers	Burlington, N.J.	FA
Willig, Greg	QB	6-6	228	3/11/71	Rice	La Mirada, Calif.	FA
Willig, Matt (1)	T	6-8	305	1/21/69	Southern California	Santa Fe Springs, Calif.	FA

The term NFL Rookie is defined as a player who is in his first season of professional football and has not been on the roster of another professional football team for any regular-season or postseason games. A Rookie is designated by an "R" on NFL rosters. Players who have been active in another professional football league or players who have NFL experience, including either preseason training camp or being on an Active List or Inactive List, or on Reserve/Injured or Reserve/Physically Unable to Perform for fewer than six regular-season games, are termed NFL First-Year Players. An NFL First-Year Player is designated by a "1" on NFL rosters. Thereafter, a player is credited with an additional year of experience for each season in which he accumulates six games on the Active List or Inactive List, or on Reserve/Injured or Reserve/Physically Unable to Perform.

NOTES

PITTSBURGH STEELERS

American Football Conference Central Division

Team Colors: Black and Gold

Three Rivers Stadium
300 Stadium Circle
Pittsburgh, Pennsylvania 15212
Telephone: (412) 323-1200

Club Officials

President: Daniel M. Rooney
Vice President: John R. McGinley
Vice President: Arthur J. Rooney, Jr.
Secretary and Counsel: Arthur J. Rooney II
Administration Advisor: Charles H. Noll
Director of Communications: Joe Gordon
Public Relations Coordinator: Dan Edwards
P.R. Assistant/Community Relations: Ron Miller
Assistant Controller: Dan Ferens
Assistant Controller: Jim Ellenberger
Director of Football Operations: Tom Donahoe
Football Business Manager: James A. Boston
Director of Scouting: Tom Modrak
Pro Personnel Coordinator: Charles Bailey
College Scouts: Phil Kreidler, Bob Lane, Max McCartney, Bob Schmitz
Ticket Sales Manager: Geraldine R. Glenn
Player Development Coordinator: Anthony Griggs
Head Trainer: John Norwig
Equipment Manager: Anthony Parisi
Field Manager: Rodgers Freyvogel

Stadium: Three Rivers Stadium • **Capacity:** 59,600
300 Stadium Circle
Pittsburgh, Pennsylvania 15212

Playing Surface: AstroTurf

Training Camp: St. Vincent College
Latrobe, Pennsylvania 15650

1993 Schedule

Preseason

Aug. 1	vs. San Francisco at Barcelona	1:00
Aug. 7	**New York Jets**	6:00
Aug. 14	at New York Giants	8:00
Aug. 22	**Washington**	8:00
Aug. 26	at Minnesota	7:00

Regular Season

Sept. 5	**San Francisco**	1:00
Sept. 12	at Los Angeles Rams	1:00
Sept. 19	**Cincinnati**	1:00
Sept. 27	at Atlanta (Monday)	9:00
Oct. 3	**Open Date**	
Oct. 10	**San Diego**	1:00
Oct. 17	**New Orleans**	1:00
Oct. 24	at Cleveland	1:00
Oct. 31	**Open Date**	
Nov. 7	at Cincinnati	1:00
Nov. 15	**Buffalo** (Monday)	9:00
Nov. 21	at Denver	2:00
Nov. 28	at Houston	7:00
Dec. 5	**New England**	1:00
Dec. 13	at Miami (Monday)	9:00
Dec. 19	**Houston**	1:00
Dec. 26	at Seattle	1:00
Jan. 2	**Cleveland**	1:00

Steelers Coaching History

Pittsburgh Pirates 1933-1940
(381-417-20)

1933	Forrest (Jap) Douds	3-6-2
1934	Luby DiMelio	2-10-0
1935-36	Joe Bach	10-14-0
1937-39	Johnny Blood (McNally)*	6-19-0
1939-40	Walt Kiesling	3-13-3
1941	Bert Bell**	0-2-0
	Aldo (Buff) Donelli***	0-5-0
1941-44	Walt Kiesling****	13-20-2
1945	Jim Leonard	2-8-0
1946-47	Jock Sutherland	13-10-1
1948-51	Johnny Michelosen	20-26-2
1952-53	Joe Bach	11-13-0
1954-56	Walt Kiesling	14-22-0
1957-64	Raymond (Buddy) Parker	51-47-6
1965	Mike Nixon	2-12-0
1966-68	Bill Austin	11-28-3
1969-91	Chuck Noll	209-156-1
1992	Bill Cowher	11-6-0

*Released after three games in 1939
**Resigned after two games in 1941
***Released after five games in 1941
****Co-coach with Earle (Greasy) Neale in Philadelphia-Pittsburgh merger in 1943 and with Phil Handler in Chicago Cardinals-Pittsburgh merger in 1944

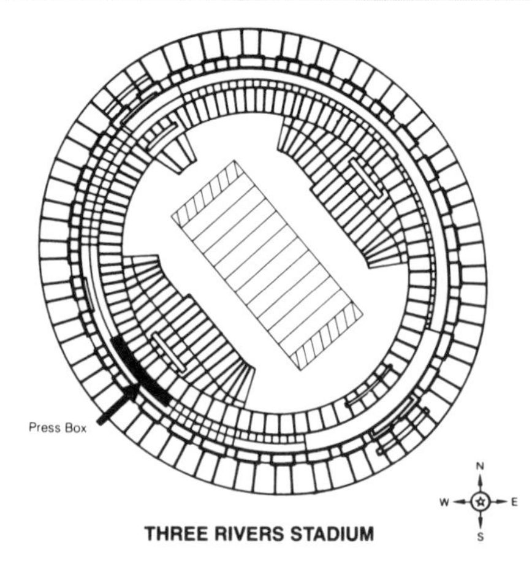

THREE RIVERS STADIUM

Record Holders

Individual Records — Career

Category	Name	Performance
Rushing (Yds.)	Franco Harris, 1972-1983	11,950
Passing (Yds.)	Terry Bradshaw, 1970-1983	27,989
Passing (TDs)	Terry Bradshaw, 1970-1983	212
Receiving (No.)	John Stallworth, 1974-1987	537
Receiving (Yds.)	John Stallworth, 1974-1987	8,723
Interceptions	Mel Blount, 1970-1983	57
Punting (Avg.)	Bobby Joe Green, 1960-61	45.7
Punt Return (Avg.)	Bobby Gage, 1949-1950	14.9
Kickoff Return (Avg.)	Lynn Chandnois, 1950-56	29.6
Field Goals	Gary Anderson, 1982-1992	257
Touchdowns (Tot.)	Franco Harris, 1972-1983	100
Points	Gary Anderson, 1982-1992	1,123

Individual Records — Single Season

Category	Name	Performance
Rushing (Yds.)	Barry Foster, 1992	1,690
Passing (Yds.)	Terry Bradshaw, 1979	3,724
Passing (TDs)	Terry Bradshaw, 1978	28
Receiving (No.)	John Stallworth, 1984	80
Receiving (Yds.)	John Stallworth, 1984	1,395
Interceptions	Mel Blount, 1975	11
Punting (Avg.)	Bobby Joe Green, 1961	47.0
Punt Return (Avg.)	Bobby Gage, 1949	16.0
Kickoff Return (Avg.)	Lynn Chandnois, 1952	35.2
Field Goals	Gary Anderson, 1985	33
Touchdowns (Tot.)	Louis Lipps, 1985	15
Points	Gary Anderson, 1985	139

Individual Records — Single Game

Category	Name	Performance
Rushing (Yds.)	John Fuqua, 12-20-70	218
Passing (Yds.)	Bobby Layne, 12-3-58	409
Passing (TDs)	Terry Bradshaw, 11-15-81	5
	Mark Malone, 9-8-85	5
Receiving (No.)	J.R. Wilburn, 10-22-67	12
Receiving (Yds.)	Buddy Dial, 10-22-61	235
Interceptions	Jack Butler, 12-13-53	*4
Field Goals	Gary Anderson, 10-23-88	6
Touchdowns (Tot.)	Ray Mathews, 10-17-54	4
	Roy Jefferson, 11-3-68	4
Points	Ray Mathews, 10-17-54	24
	Roy Jefferson, 11-3-68	24

*NFL Record

1992 Team Record

Preseason (2-2)

Date	Result		Opponents
8/8	L	33-35	Philadelphia
8/17	L	0-26	at New Orleans
8/23	W	28-17	at Chicago
8/29	W	24- 3	New York Giants

Regular Season (11-5)

Date	Result		Opponents	Att.
9/6	W	29-24	at Houston	63,705
9/13	W	27-10	N.Y. Jets	58,327
9/20	W	23- 6	at San Diego	44,764
9/27	L	3-17	at Green Bay	58,700
10/11	L	9-17	at Cleveland	78,256
10/19	W	20- 0	Cincinnati	59,307
10/25	W	27- 3	at Kansas City	76,610
11/1	W	21-20	Houston	59,504
11/8	L	20-28	at Buffalo	78,870
11/15	W	17-14	Detroit	58,993
11/22	W	30-14	Indianapolis	58,611
11/29	W	21- 9	at Cincinnati	59,123
12/6	W	20-14	Seattle	58,128
12/13	L	6-30	at Chicago	66,034
12/20	L	3- 6	Minnesota	59,005
12/27	W	23-13	Cleveland	59,431

Postseason (0-1)

Date	Result		Opponent	Att.
1/9	L	3-24	Buffalo	60,407

Score by Periods

Steelers	58	90	51	100	0	—	299
Opponents	33	86	56	50	0	—	225

Attendance

Home 471,306 Away 526,062 Total 997,368
Single-game home record, 59,541 (9-30-85)
Single-season home record, 471,306 (1992)

1992 Team Statistics

	Steelers	Opp.
Total First Downs	284	266
Rushing	119	99
Passing	143	146
Penalty	22	21
Third Down: Made/Att.	73/211	65/195
Third Down: Pct.	34.6	33.3
Fourth Down: Made/Att.	6/15	5/17
Fourth Down: Pct.	40.0	29.4
Total Net Yards	4906	4658
Avg. Per Game	306.6	291.1
Total Plays	989	949
Avg. Per Play	5.0	4.9
Net Yards Rushing	2156	1841
Avg. Per Game	134.8	115.1
Total Rushes	518	435
Net Yards Passing	2750	2817
Avg. Per Game	171.9	176.1
Sacked/Yards Lost	40/296	36/248
Gross Yards	3046	3065
Att./Completions	431/249	478/252
Completion Pct.	57.8	52.7
Had Intercepted	14	22
Punts/Avg.	74/42.1	74/42.0
Net Punting Avg.	74/35.6	74/34.4
Penalties/Yards Lost	106/941	104/814
Fumbles/Ball Lost	28/18	34/21
Touchdowns	31	24
Rushing	13	6
Passing	15	15
Returns	3	3
Avg. Time of Possession	32:05	27:55

1992 Individual Statistics

Scoring	TD R	TD P	TD Rt	PAT	FG	Saf	TP
G. Anderson	0	0	0	29/31	28/36	0	113
Foster	11	0	0	0/0	0/0	0	66
Cooper	0	3	0	0/0	0/0	0	18
Mills	0	3	0	0/0	0/0	0	18
Stone	0	3	0	0/0	0/0	0	18
Green	0	2	0	0/0	0/0	0	12
Jorden	0	2	0	0/0	0/0	0	12
Davenport	0	0	1	0/0	0/0	0	6
Graham	0	1	0	0/0	0/0	0	6
Griffin	0	0	1	0/0	0/0	0	6
Hoge	0	1	0	0/0	0/0	0	6
O'Donnell	1	0	0	0/0	0/0	0	6
Thompson	1	0	0	0/0	0/0	0	6
Woodson	0	0	1	0/0	0/0	0	6
Steelers	13	15	3	29/31	28/36	0	299
Opponents	6	15	3	24/24	19/28	0	225

Passing	Att.	Comp.	Yds.	Pct.	TD	Int.	Tkld.	Rate
O'Donnell	313	185	2283	59.1	13	9	27/208	83.6
Brister	116	63	719	54.3	2	5	13/88	61.0
Foster	1	0	0	0.0	0	0	0/0	39.6
Royals	1	1	44	100.0	0	0	0/0	118.8
Steelers	431	249	3046	57.8	15	14	40/296	77.7
Opponents	478	252	3065	52.7	15	22	36/248	64.0

Rushing	Att.	Yds.	Avg.	LG	TD
Foster	390	1690	4.3	69	11
Thompson	35	157	4.5	25	1
Hoge	41	150	3.7	15	0
Stone	12	118	9.8	30	0
Mills	1	20	20.0	20	0
Brister	10	16	1.6	8	0
O'Donnell	27	5	0.2	9	1
W. Williams	2	0	0.0	2	0
Steelers	518	2156	4.2	69	13
Opponents	435	1841	4.2	44	6

Receiving	No.	Yds.	Avg.	LG	TD
Graham	49	711	14.5	51	1
Foster	36	344	9.6	42	0
Stone	34	501	14.7	49	3
Mills	30	383	12.8	22	3
Hoge	28	231	8.3	20	1
Thompson	22	278	12.6	29	0
Cooper	16	197	12.3	27	3
Green	14	152	10.9	24	2
Davenport	9	136	15.1	31	0
Jorden	6	28	4.7	8	2
Didio	3	39	13.0	18	0
W. Williams	1	44	44.0	44	0
Thigpen	1	2	2.0	2	0
Steelers	249	3046	12.2	51	15
Opponents	252	3065	12.2	81	15

Interceptions	No.	Yds.	Avg.	LG	TD
Perry	6	69	11.5	34	0
Johnson	5	67	13.4	35	0
Woodson	4	90	22.5	57	0
Griffin	3	98	32.7	65t	1
Little	2	6	3.0	6	0
Lloyd	1	35	35.0	35	0
J. Williams	1	4	4.0	4	0
Shelton	0	15	—	15	0
Steelers	22	384	17.5	65t	1
Opponents	14	235	16.8	77t	1

Punting	No.	Yds.	Avg.	In 20	LG
Royals	73	3119	42.7	22	58
Steelers	74	3119	42.1	22	58
Opponents	74	3107	42.0	12	84

Punt Returns	No.	FC	Yds.	Avg.	LG	TD
Woodson	32	13	364	11.4	80t	1
Steelers	32	13	364	11.4	80t	1
Opponents	39	7	308	7.9	36	0

Kickoff Returns	No.	Yds.	Avg.	LG	TD
Woodson	25	469	18.8	32	0
Bentley	1	17	17.0	17	0
Campbell	1	0	0.0	0	0
Cooper	1	8	8.0	8	0
Hoge	2	28	14.0	17	0
Mills	1	11	11.0	11	0
Stone	12	219	18.3	28	0
Thigpen	2	44	22.0	29	0
Thompson	2	51	25.5	33	0
W. Williams	1	0	0.0	0	0
Steelers	48	847	17.6	33	0
Opponents	52	1052	20.2	48	0

Sacks	No.
Lloyd	6.5
Woodson	6.0
J. Williams	4.5
Evans	3.0
Little	3.0
G. Williams	3.0
Davidson	2.0
Howe	2.0
A. Jones	2.0
Lake	2.0
Nickerson	2.0
Steelers	36.0
Opponents	40.0

1993 Draft Choices

Round	Name	Pos.	College
1.	Deon Figures	DB	Colorado
2.	Chad Brown	LB	Colorado
3.	Andre Hastings	WR	Georgia
4.	Kevin Henry	DE	Mississippi State
5.	Lonnie Palelei	G	Nevada-Las Vegas
	Marc Woodard	LB	Mississippi State
6.	Willie Williams	DB	Western Carolina
7.	Jeff Zgonina	DT	Purdue
	Craig Keith	TE	Lenoir-Rhyne
8.	Alex Van Pelt	QB	Pittsburgh

Pittsburgh Steelers 1993 Veteran Roster

No.	Name	Pos.	Ht.	Wt.	Birth-date	NFL Exp.	College	Hometown	How Acq.	'92 Games/ Starts
1	Anderson, Gary	K	5-11	181	7/16/59	12	Syracuse	Durban, South Africa	W(Buff)-'82	16/0
85	Campbell, Russ	TE	6-5	259	4/2/69	2	Kansas State	Wichita, Kan.	D7a-'92	7/0
56	Clark, Greg	LB	6-0	225	3/5/65	6	Arizona State	Compton, Calif.	UFA(Sea)-'93	12/0*
87	Cooper, Adrian	TE	6-5	268	4/27/68	3	Oklahoma	Denver, Colo.	D4b-'91	16/15
51	Cooper, Louis	LB	6-1	235	8/5/63	8	Western Carolina	Marion, S.C.	FA-'93	0*
80	Davenport, Charles	WR	6-3	210	11/22/68	2	North Carolina State	Fayetteville, N.C.	D4-'92	15/1
64	#Davidson, Kenny	DE	6-5	277	8/17/67	4	Louisiana State	Shreveport, La.	D2-'90	16/12
63	Dawson, Dermontti	C	6-2	288	6/17/65	6	Kentucky	Lexington, Ky.	D2-'88	16/16
66	Evans, Donald	DE	6-2	275	3/14/64	6	Winston-Salem State	Raleigh, N.C.	FA-'90	16/16
29	Foster, Barry	RB	5-10	217	12/8/68	4	Arkansas	Duncanville, Tex.	D5-'90	16/15
60	Gammon, Kendall	C-G	6-4	273	10/23/68	2	Pittsburg State, Kan.	Wichita, Kan.	D11-'92	16/0
81	Graham, Jeff	WR	6-1	193	2/14/69	3	Ohio State	Dayton, Ohio	D2-'91	14/10
86	Green, Eric	TE	6-5	284	6/22/67	4	Liberty	Savannah, Ga.	D1-'90	7/5
91	Greene, Kevin	LB	6-3	247	7/31/62	9	Auburn	Oxford, Ala.	UFA(Rams)-'93	16/16*
22	Griffin, Larry	S	6-0	199	1/11/63	7	North Carolina	Chesapeake, Va.	FA-'87	14/2
77	Haselrig, Carlton	G	6-1	290	1/22/66	4	Pittsburgh-Johnstown	Johnstown, Pa.	D12-'89	16/16
53	†Hinkle, Bryan	LB	6-2	229	6/4/59	13	Oregon	Silverdale, Wash.	D6-'81	13/1
33	Hoge, Merril	RB	6-2	230	1/26/65	7	Idaho State	Pocatello, Idaho	D10-'87	16/11
36	Holloway, Cornell	CB	5-10	182	1/30/66	4	Pittsburgh	Alliance, Ohio	FA-'93	7/0*
78	Howe, Garry	NT	6-1	298	6/20/68	2	Colorado	Spencer, Iowa	FA-'91	11/2
65	Jackson, John	T	6-6	290	1/4/65	6	Eastern Kentucky	Cincinnati, Ohio	D10-'88	16/13
44	Johnson, D.J.	CB	6-0	184	7/14/66	5	Kentucky	Louisville, Ky.	D7-'89	15/15
25	Jones, Gary	S	6-1	215	11/30/67	4	Texas A&M	Tyler, Tex.	D9-'90	0*
84	Jorden, Tim	TE	6-3	239	10/30/66	4	Indiana	Middletown, Ohio	FA-'92	15/4
99	Kirkland, Levon	LB	6-0	247	2/17/69	2	Clemson	Lamar, S.C.	D2-'92	16/0
37	Lake, Carnell	S	6-1	210	7/15/67	5	UCLA	Inglewood, Calif.	D2-'89	16/16
83	Lipps, Louis	WR	5-10	193	8/9/62	9	Southern Mississippi	Reserve, La.	FA-'93	2/0*
50	Little, David	LB	6-1	239	1/3/59	13	Florida	Miami, Fla.	D7-'81	16/12
95	Lloyd, Greg	LB	6-2	227	5/26/65	7	Ft. Valley State	Ft. Valley, Ga.	D6b-'87	16/16
67	Love, Duval	G	6-3	291	6/24/63	9	UCLA	Fountain Valley, Calif.	PB(Rams)-'92	16/16
89	Mills, Ernie	WR	5-11	186	10/28/68	3	Florida	Dunnellon, Fla.	D3-'91	16/5
14	#O'Donnell, Neil	QB	6-3	230	7/3/66	4	Maryland	Madison, N.J.	D3a-'90	12/12
55	Olsavsky, Jerry	LB	6-1	222	3/29/67	5	Pittsburgh	Youngstown, Ohio	D10-'89	7/0
39	Perry, Darren	S	5-10	194	12/29/68	2	Penn State	Deep Creek, Va.	D8a-'92	16/16
3	Royals, Mark	P	6-5	212	6/22/64	4	Appalachian State	Mathews, Va.	PB(TB)-'92	16/0
72	Searcy, Leon	T	6-3	305	12/21/69	2	Miami	Orlando, Fla.	D1-'92	15/0
24	Shelton, Richard	CB-S	5-9	199	1/2/66	4	Liberty	Marietta, Ga.	FA-'91	16/3
40	Smagala, Stan	S	5-10	177	4/6/68	4	Notre Dame	Burbank, Ill.	PB(Dall)-'92	0*
69	Solomon, Ariel	C-T	6-5	286	7/16/68	3	Colorado	Boulder, Colo.	D10-'91	4/0
93	Steed, Joel	NT	6-2	290	2/17/69	2	Colorado	Denver, Colo.	D3-'92	11/4
20	Stone, Dwight	WR-RB	6-0	187	1/28/64	7	Middle Tennessee State	Florala, Ala.	FA-'87	15/12
11	Strom, Rick	QB	6-2	205	3/11/65	5	Georgia Tech	Pittsburgh, Pa.	FA-'89	0*
73	Strzelczyk, Justin	T	6-5	305	8/18/68	4	Maine	Seneca, N.Y.	D11-'90	16/7
94	Szymanski, Jim	DE	6-5	270	9/7/67	3	Michigan State	Sterling Heights, Mich.	FA-'93	0*
82	Thigpen, Yancey	WR	6-1	203	8/15/69	2	Winston-Salem State	Pinetops, N.C.	FA-'92	12/0
34	Thompson, Leroy	RB	5-10	215	2/3/69	3	Penn State	Knoxville, Tenn.	D6-'91	15/2
18	Tomczak, Mike	QB	6-1	204	10/23/62	9	Ohio State	Calumet City, Ill.	UFA(Clev)-'93	12/8*
71	Viaene, David	G-T	6-5	300	7/14/65	5	Minnesota-Duluth	Kaukauna, Wis.	FA-'93	1/0*
23	Walker, Sammy	CB	5-11	200	1/20/69	3	Texas Tech	McKinney, Tex.	D4a-'91	16/4
92	Webster, Elnardo	LB	6-2	243	12/23/69	2	Rutgers	Jersey City, N.J.	D9-'92	3/0
41	Wilcots, Solomon	S	5-11	202	10/3/64	7	Colorado	Riverside, Calif.	FA-'92	16/0
98	Williams, Gerald	NT	6-3	289	9/8/63	8	Auburn	Lanett, Ala.	D2-'86	10/10
42	Williams, Warren	RB	6-0	214	7/29/65	6	Miami	Ft. Myers, Fla.	D6-'88	16/0
26	Woodson, Rod	CB	6-0	200	3/10/65	7	Purdue	Ft. Wayne, Ind.	D1-'87	16/16
38	Worley, Tim	RB	6-2	218	9/24/66	4	Georgia	Lumberton, N.C.	D1a-'89	0*

* Clark played 12 games with Seattle in '92; Cooper last active with Miami in '91; Greene played 16 games with L.A. Rams; Holloway played 7 games with Indianapolis; Jones last active with Pittsburgh in '91; Lipps played 2 games with New Orleans; Smagala missed '92 season due to injury; Strom active for 4 games but did not play; Szymanski last active with Denver in '91; Tomczak played 12 games with Cleveland; Viaene played 1 game with Green Bay; Worley last active with Pittsburgh in '91.

#Unrestricted free agent; subject to developments.

† Restricted free agent; subject to developments.

Players lost through free agency (4): T Tunch Ilkin (GB; 12 games in '92), DE Aaron Jones (NE; 13), LB Hardy Nickerson (TB; 15), LB Jerrol Williams (SD; 16).

Also played with Steelers in '92—RB Albert Bentley (2 games), QB Bubby Brister (6), LB Darryl Ford (8), CB Alan Haller (3).

COACHING STAFF

Head Coach, Bill Cowher

Pro Career: Became the fifteenth head coach in Steelers' history on January 21, 1992, succeeding the retired Chuck Noll. Cowher is the second-youngest head coach in the NFL. Named AP NFL Coach of the Year last season, after becoming one of only 12 coaches in NFL history to win 11 games in his first season. Began his NFL career as a free agent linebacker with the Philadelphia Eagles in 1979, and then signed with the Cleveland Browns the following year. Cowher played three seasons (1980-82) in Cleveland before being traded back to the Eagles, where he played two more years (1983-84). Cowher began his coaching career in 1985 at age 28 under Marty Schottenheimer at the Cleveland Browns. He was the Browns' special teams coach in 1985-86 and secondary coach in 1987-88 before following Schottenheimer to the Kansas City Chiefs in 1989 as defensive coordinator. Career record: 11-6.

Background: Excelled in football, basketball, and track for Carlynton High in Crafton, Pa. Was a three-year starter at linebacker for North Carolina State, serving as captain and earning team MVP honors as senior. Graduated in 1979 with education degree.

Personal: Born in Pittsburgh, Pa., on May 8, 1957. His wife Kaye, also a North Carolina State graduate, played professional basketball for the New York Stars of the Women's Professional Basketball League with twin sister Faye. Bill and Kaye live in Pittsburgh and have three daughters—Meagan Lyn, Lauren Marie, and Lindsay Morgan.

Assistant Coaches

Dom Capers, defensive coordinator; born August 7, 1950, Cambridge, Ohio, lives in Pittsburgh. Defensive back Mount Union College 1968-71. No pro playing experience. College coach: Hawaii 1975-76, San Jose State 1977, California 1978-79, Tennessee 1980-81, Ohio State 1982-83. Pro coach: Philadelphia/Baltimore Stars (USFL) 1984-85, New Orleans Saints 1986-91, joined Steelers in 1992.

Ron Erhardt, offensive coordinator; born February 27, 1931, Mandan, N.D., lives in Pittsburgh. Quarterback Jamestown (N.D.) College 1951-54. No pro playing experience. College coach: North Dakota State 1963-72 (head coach 1966-72). Pro coach: New England Patriots 1973-81 (head coach 1979-81), New York Giants 1982-91, joined Steelers in 1992.

Steve Furness, defensive line; born December 5, 1950, Warwick, R.I., lives in Pittsburgh. Defensive tackle Rhode Island 1968-71. Pro defensive tackle Pittsburgh Steelers 1972-80, Detroit Lions 1981. College coach: Michigan State 1983-90. Pro coach: Indianapolis Colts 1991, joined Steelers in 1992.

John Guy, special teams; born May 26, 1951, Greensboro, N.C., lives in Pittsburgh. Defensive back-kicker North Carolina A&T 1969-72. No pro playing experience. College coach: North Carolina 1973-77, Virginia Tech 1978, Duke 1978-80, Georgia Tech 1981-86, Alabama 1987-89, Kentucky 1990-91. Pro coach: Joined Steelers in 1992.

Bob Harrison, wide receivers; born September 9, 1941, Cleveland, Ohio, lives in Pittsburgh. Wide receiver Kent State 1960-63. No pro playing experience. College coach: Kent State 1969-70, Iowa 1971-73, Cornell 1974, North Carolina State 1975-76, Tennessee 1977-82, Georgia 1989-91. Pro coach: Atlanta Falcons 1983-86, joined Steelers in 1992.

Dick Hoak, running backs; born December 8, 1939, Jeannette, Pa., lives in Greensburg, Pa. Halfback-quarterback Penn State 1958-60. Pro running back Pittsburgh Steelers 1961-70. Pro coach: Joined Steelers in 1972.

Pittsburgh Steelers 1993 First-Year Roster

Name	Pos.	Ht.	Wt.	Birth-date	College	Hometown	How Acq.
Avery, Steve (1)	RB	6-1	225	8/18/66	Northern Michigan	Brookfield, Wis.	FA
Barnes, Reggie	LB	6-0	232	1/23/69	Oklahoma	Grand Prairie, Tex.	FA
Brown, Chad	LB	6-2	236	7/12/70	Colorado	Pasadena, Calif.	D2
Cuthbert, Randy	RB	6-2	222	1/16/70	Duke	Chalfont, Pa.	FA
Didio, Mark (1)	WR	5-11	181	2/17/69	Connecticut	Syracuse, N.Y.	FA
Figures, Deon	CB	6-0	190	1/10/70	Colorado	Compton, Calif.	D1
Finn, Mike (1)	DE-DT	6-4	296	9/26/67	Arkansas-Pine Bluff	Texarkana, Tex.	FA
Graham, Boris	LB	6-2	236	1/21/69	West Virginia	Pemberton, N.J.	FA
Hargett, David (1)	S	6-1	200	12/2/68	Georgia	Valdosta, Ga.	FA
Hastings, Andre	WR	6-0	185	11/7/70	Georgia	Macon, Ga.	D3
Henry, Kevin	DE	6-4	274	10/23/68	Mississippi State	Mound Bayou, Miss.	D4
Houston, Martin	RB	5-9	234	4/18/70	Alabama	Centre, Ala.	FA
Keith, Craig	TE	6-3	247	4/27/71	Lenoir-Rhyne	Raleigh, N.C.	D7b
Lawrence, Toby	G-T	6-4	298	3/1/70	Kansas State	St. Joseph, Mo.	FA
Owens, Darrick (1)	WR	6-2	195	11/5/70	Mississippi	Tallahassee, Fla.	FA
Palelei, Lonnie	G	6-3	324	10/15/70	Nevada-Las Vegas	American Samoa	D5a
Reid, Gary	DE-DT	6-2	265	1/13/70	Cincinnati	Miami, Fla.	FA
Samec, Tim	C	6-3	288	5/13/70	Virginia	Hazelton, Pa.	FA
Shaw, Rickie (1)	T	6-4	295	12/26/69	North Carolina	Whiteville, N.C.	FA
Shepherd, Leslie (1)	WR	5-11	180	11/3/69	Temple	Forestville, Md.	FA
Simpson, Tim (1)	G-C	6-2	295	3/5/69	Illinois	Peoria, Ill.	FA
Sutton, Ricky	DE-DT	6-2	260	4/27/71	Auburn	Tucker, Ga.	FA
Van Pelt, Alex	QB	6-1	212	5/1/70	Pittsburgh	San Antonio, Tex.	D8
Williams, Willie	CB	5-9	180	12/26/70	Western Carolina	Columbia, S.C.	D6
Woodard, Marc	LB	6-0	235	2/21/70	Mississippi State	Kosciusko, Miss.	D5b
Zgonina, Jeff	DE-DT	6-0	285	5/24/70	Purdue	Lake Grove, Ill.	D7a

The term NFL Rookie is defined as a player who is in his first season of professional football and has not been on the roster of another professional football team for any regular-season or postseason games. A Rookie is designated by an "R" on NFL rosters. Players who have been active in another professional football league or players who have NFL experience, including either preseason training camp or being on an Active List or Inactive List, or on Reserve/Injured or Reserve/Physically Unable to Perform for fewer than six regular-season games, are termed NFL First-Year Players. An NFL First-Year Player is designated by a "1" on NFL rosters. Thereafter, a player is credited with an additional year of experience for each season in which he accumulates six games on the Active List or Inactive List, or on Reserve/Injured or Reserve/Physically Unable to Perform.

NOTES

Pat Hodgson, tight ends; born January 30, 1944, Columbus, Ga., lives in Pittsburgh. Tight end Georgia 1963-65. Pro tight end Washington Redskins 1966, Minnesota Vikings 1967. College coach: Georgia 1968-70, 1972-77, Florida State 1971, Texas Tech 1978. Pro coach: San Diego Chargers 1978, New York Giants 1979-87, joined Steelers in 1992.

Dick LeBeau, defensive backs; born September 9, 1937, London, Ohio, lives in Pittsburgh. Defensive back-offensive back Ohio State 1954-57. Pro cornerback Detroit Lions 1959-72. Pro coach: Philadelphia Eagles 1972-75, Green Bay Packers 1976-79, Cincinnati Bengals 1980-91, joined Steelers in 1992.

Marvin Lewis, linebackers; born September 23, 1958, McDonald, Pa., lives in Pittsburgh. Linebacker Idaho State 1977-80. No pro playing experience. College coach: Idaho State 1981-84, Long Beach State 1985-86, New Mexico 1987-89, Pittsburgh 1990-91. Pro coach: Joined Steelers in 1992.

Kent Stephenson, offensive line; born February 4, 1942, Anita, Iowa, lives in Pittsburgh. Guard-nose tackle Northern Iowa 1962-64. No pro playing experience. College coach: Wayne State 1965-68, North Dakota 1969-71, Southern Methodist 1972-73, Iowa 1974-76, Oklahoma State 1977-78, Kansas 1979-82. Pro coach: Michigan Panthers (USFL) 1983-84, Seattle Seahawks 1985-91, joined Steelers in 1992.

SAN DIEGO CHARGERS

American Football Conference Western Division

Team Colors: Navy Blue, White, and Gold

San Diego Jack Murphy Stadium
P.O. Box 609609
San Diego, California 92160-9609
Telephone: (619) 280-2111

Club Officials

Chairman of the Board/President: Alex G. Spanos
Vice Chairman: Dean A. Spanos
General Manager: Bobby Beathard
Vice President-Finance: Jeremiah T. Murphy
Assistant General Manager: Dick Daniels
Director of Player Personnel: Billy Devaney
Director of Pro Personnel: Rudy Feldman
Director of College Scouting: John Hinek
Coordinator of Football Operations: Marty Hurney
Director of Public Relations: Bill Johnston
Chief Financial Officer: Jeanne Bonk
Business Manager: Pat Curran
Director of Marketing: Rich Israel
Director of Ticket Operations: Joe Scott
Assistant Director of Public Relations: Rob Boulware
Video Director: Gene Leff
Head Trainer: Keoki Kamau
Equipment Manager: Sid Brooks

Stadium: San Diego Jack Murphy Stadium •
Capacity: 60,836
9449 Friars Road
San Diego, California 92108

Playing Surface: Grass

Training Camp: University of California-San Diego
Third College
La Jolla, California 92037

1993 Schedule

Preseason

Aug. 7	**New England**	6:00
Aug. 14	at Los Angeles Rams	7:00
Aug. 21	**Phoenix**	6:00
Aug. 28	at San Francisco	5:00

Regular Season

Sept. 5	**Seattle**	1:00
Sept. 12	at Denver	2:00
Sept. 19	**Houston**	1:00
Sept. 26	**Open Date**	
Oct. 3	at Seattle	1:00
Oct. 10	at Pittsburgh	1:00
Oct. 17	**Kansas City**	1:00
Oct. 24	**Open Date**	
Oct. 31	at Los Angeles Raiders	1:00
Nov. 7	at Minnesota	12:00
Nov. 14	**Chicago**	5:00
Nov. 21	**Los Angeles Raiders**	1:00
Nov. 29	at Indianapolis (Monday)	9:00
Dec. 5	**Denver**	1:00
Dec. 12	**Green Bay**	5:00
Dec. 19	at Kansas City	3:00
Dec. 27	**Miami** (Monday)	6:00
Jan. 2	at Tampa Bay	4:00

Chargers Coaching History

(242-245-11)

1960-69	Sid Gillman*	83-51-6
1969-70	Charlie Waller	9-7-3
1971	Sid Gillman**	4-6-0
1971-73	Harland Svare***	7-17-2
1973	Ron Waller	1-5-0
1974-78	Tommy Prothro****	21-39-0
1978-86	Don Coryell#	72-60-0
1986-88	Al Saunders	17-22-0
1989-91	Dan Henning	16-32-0
1992	Bobby Ross	12-6-0

*Retired after nine games in 1969
**Resigned after 10 games in 1971
***Resigned after eight games in 1973
****Resigned after four games in 1978
#Resigned after eight games in 1986

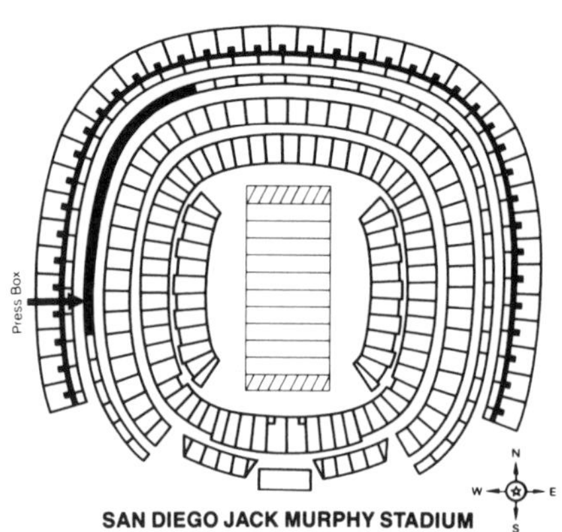

SAN DIEGO JACK MURPHY STADIUM

Record Holders

Individual Records—Career

Category	Name	Performance
Rushing (Yds.)	Paul Lowe, 1960-67	4,963
Passing (Yds.)	Dan Fouts, 1973-1987	43,040
Passing (TDs)	Dan Fouts, 1973-1987	254
Receiving (No.)	Charlie Joiner, 1976-1986	586
Receiving (Yds.)	Lance Alworth, 1962-1970	9,585
Interceptions	Gill Byrd, 1983-1992	42
Punting (Avg.)	Maury Buford, 1982-84	42.7
Punt Return (Avg.)	Leslie (Speedy) Duncan, 1964-1970	12.3
Kickoff Return (Avg.)	Leslie (Speedy) Duncan, 1964-1970	25.2
Field Goals	Rolf Benirschke, 1977-1986	146
Touchdowns (Tot.)	Lance Alworth, 1962-1970	83
Points	Rolf Benirschke, 1977-1986	766

Individual Records—Single Season

Category	Name	Performance
Rushing (Yds.)	Marion Butts, 1990	1,225
Passing (Yds.)	Dan Fouts, 1981	4,802
Passing (TDs)	Dan Fouts, 1981	33
Receiving (No.)	Kellen Winslow, 1980	89
Receiving (Yds.)	Lance Alworth, 1965	1,602
Interceptions	Charlie McNeil, 1961	9
Punting (Avg.)	Dennis Partee, 1969	44.6
Punt Return (Avg.)	Leslie (Speedy) Duncan, 1965	15.5
Kickoff Return (Avg.)	Keith Lincoln, 1962	28.4
Field Goals	John Carney, 1992	26
Touchdowns (Tot.)	Chuck Muncie, 1981	19
Points	Rolf Benirschke, 1980	118

Individual Records—Single Game

Category	Name	Performance
Rushing (Yds.)	Gary Anderson, 12-18-88	217
Passing (Yds.)	Dan Fouts, 10-19-80	444
	Dan Fouts, 12-11-82	444
Passing (TDs)	Dan Fouts, 11-22-81	6
Receiving (No.)	Kellen Winslow, 10-7-84	15
Receiving (Yds.)	Wes Chandler, 12-20-82	260
Interceptions	Many times	3
	Last time by Pete Shaw, 11-2-80	
Field Goals	John Carney, 12-20-92	5
Touchdowns (Tot.)	Kellen Winslow, 11-22-81	5
Points	Kellen Winslow, 11-22-81	30

1992 Team Record

Preseason (2-2)

Date	Result		Opponents
8/8	L	14-35	at Phoenix
8/14	W	20-10	at New England
8/21	L	14-20	San Francisco
8/27	W	30-19	L.A. Rams

Regular Season (11-5)

Date	Result		Opponents	Att.
9/6	L	10-24	Kansas City	43,403
9/13	L	13-21	at Denver	72,180
9/20	L	6-23	Pittsburgh	44,764
9/27	L	0-27	at Houston	59,159
10/4	W	17- 6	Seattle	37,344
10/18	W	34-14	at Indianapolis	43,805
10/25	W	24-21	Denver	52,149
11/1	W	26- 0	Indianapolis	38,832
11/8	L	14-16	at Kansas City	76,590
11/15	W	14-13	at Cleveland	59,610
11/22	W	29-14	Tampa Bay	40,646
11/29	W	27- 3	L.A. Raiders	59,224
12/6	W	27-21	at Phoenix	26,663
12/13	W	27-10	Cincinnati	48,843
12/20	W	36-14	at L.A. Raiders	37,163
12/27	W	31-14	at Seattle	63,834

Postseason (1-1)

Date	Result		Opponent	Att.
1/2	W	17- 0	Kansas City	58,278
1/10	L	0-31	at Miami	71,224

Score by Periods

Chargers	69	92	72	102	0	—	335
Opponents	62	46	59	74	0	—	241

Attendance

Home 365,205 Away 439,004 Total 804,209
Single-game home record, 64,411 (12-15-84)
Single-season home record, 494,103 (1988)

1992 Team Statistics

	Chargers	Opp.
Total First Downs	302	250
Rushing	118	80
Passing	161	157
Penalty	23	13
Third Down: Made/Att.	87/221	73/200
Third Down: Pct.	39.4	36.5
Fourth Down: Made/Att.	6/13	3/12
Fourth Down: Pct.	46.2	25.0
Total Net Yards	5221	4227
Avg. Per Game	326.3	264.2
Total Plays	1018	907
Avg. Per Play	5.1	4.7
Net Yards Rushing	1875	1395
Avg. Per Game	117.2	87.2
Total Rushes	489	365
Net Yards Passing	3346	2832
Avg. Per Game	209.1	177.0
Sacked/Yards Lost	33/268	51/356
Gross Yards	3614	3188
Att./Completions	496/282	491/271
Completion Pct.	56.9	55.2
Had Intercepted	21	25
Punts/Avg.	68/42.6	80/44.6
Net Punting Avg.	68/36.4	80/38.1
Penalties/Yards Lost	91/813	98/798
Fumbles/Ball Lost	26/12	18/11
Touchdowns	36	29
Rushing	18	10
Passing	16	17
Returns	2	2
Avg. Time of Possession	32:03	27:57

1992 Individual Statistics

Scoring	TD R	TD P	TD Rt	PAT	FG	Saf	TP
Carney	0	0	0	35/35	26/32	0	113
Miller	0	7	1	0/0	0/0	0	48
Bernstine	4	0	0	0/0	0/0	0	24
Butts	4	0	0	0/0	0/0	0	24
Harmon	3	1	0	0/0	0/0	0	24
Humphries	4	0	0	0/0	0/0	0	24
Lewis	0	4	0	0/0	0/0	0	24
Bieniemy	3	0	0	0/0	0/0	0	18
Jefferson	0	2	0	0/0	0/0	0	12
Walker	0	2	0	0/0	0/0	0	12
Brennan	0	1	0	0/0	0/0	0	6
Carrington	0	0	1	0/0	0/0	0	6
Grossman	0	0	0	0/0	0/0	2	4
Mims	0	0	0	0/0	0/0	1	2
Chargers	18	16	2	35/36	26/32	3	335
Opponents	10	17	2	28/29	13/16	0	241

Passing	Att.	Comp.	Yds.	Pct.	TD	Int.	Tkld.	Rate
Humphries	454	263	3356	57.9	16	18	28/218	76.4
Gagliano	42	19	258	45.2	0	3	5/50	35.6
Chargers	496	282	3614	56.9	16	21	33/268	72.9
Opponents	491	271	3188	55.2	17	25	51/356	65.5

Rushing	Att.	Yds.	Avg.	LG	TD
Butts	218	809	3.7	22	4
Bernstine	106	499	4.7	25t	4
Bieniemy	74	264	3.6	21	3
Harmon	55	235	4.3	33	3
Humphries	28	79	2.8	25	4
Lewis	2	7	3.5	4	0
Miller	1	−1	−1.0	−1	0
Gagliano	3	−4	−1.3	0	0
Kidd	2	−13	−6.5	0	0
Chargers	489	1875	3.8	33	18
Opponents	365	1395	3.8	52	10

Receiving	No.	Yds.	Avg.	LG	TD
Harmon	79	914	11.6	55	1
Miller	72	1060	14.7	67t	7
Lewis	34	580	17.1	62	4
Walker	34	393	11.6	59	2
Jefferson	29	377	13.0	51	2
Bernstine	12	86	7.2	16	0
Butts	9	73	8.1	22	0
Bieniemy	5	49	9.8	25	0
Young	4	45	11.3	14	0
Brennan	3	22	7.3	12	0
Claiborne	1	15	15.0	15	0
Chargers	282	3614	12.8	67t	16
Opponents	271	3188	11.8	83t	17

Interceptions	No.	Yds.	Avg.	LG	TD
Carrington	6	152	25.3	69	1
Byrd	4	88	22.0	44	0
Frank	4	37	9.3	33	0
Richard	3	26	8.7	20	0
Seau	2	51	25.5	29	0
Plummer	2	40	20.0	38	0
Blaylock	2	0	0.0	0	0
Vanhorse	1	11	11.0	11	0
Fields	1	0	0.0	0	0
Chargers	25	405	16.2	69	1
Opponents	21	241	11.5	99t	1

Punting	No.	Yds.	Avg.	In 20	LG
Kidd	68	2899	42.6	22	65
Chargers	68	2899	42.6	22	65
Opponents	80	3565	44.6	18	62

Punt Returns	No.	FC	Yds.	Avg.	LG	TD
Bieniemy	30	3	229	7.6	21	0
Lewis	13	5	127	9.8	25	0
Brennan	1	1	3	3.0	3	0
Byrd	0	3	0	—	—	0
Chargers	44	12	359	8.2	25	0
Opponents	24	19	244	10.2	46t	1

Kickoff Returns	No.	Yds.	Avg.	LG	TD
Bieniemy	15	257	17.1	30	0
Brennan	1	10	10.0	10	0
Harmon	7	96	13.7	30	0
Hendrickson	2	14	7.0	8	0
Lewis	19	402	21.2	62	0
Miller	1	33	33.0	33	0
Chargers	45	812	18.0	62	0
Opponents	54	962	17.8	52	0

Sacks	No.
O'Neal	17.0
Mims	10.0
Grossman	8.0
Winter	6.0
Seau	4.5
Thornton	2.0
D. Hall	1.0
Rolling	1.0
White	1.0
Lee	0.5
Chargers	51.0
Opponents	33.0

1993 Draft Choices

Round	Name	Pos.	College
1.	Darrien Gordon	DB	Stanford
2.	Natrone Means	RB	North Carolina
3.	Joe Cocozzo	G	Michigan
4.	Ray Lee Johnson	DE	Arkansas
	Lewis Bush	LB	Washington State
5.	Walter Dunson	WR	Mid. Tennessee St.
6.	Eric Castle	DB	Oregon
7.	Doug Miller	LB	South Dakota State
8.	Trent Green	QB	Indiana

San Diego Chargers 1993 Veteran Roster

No.	Name	Pos.	Ht.	Wt.	Birth-date	NFL Exp.	College	Hometown	How Acq.	'92 Games/ Starts
52	# Anno, Sam	LB	6-3	240	1/26/65	7	Southern California	Santa Monica, Calif.	PB(TB)-'92	16/0
85	Barnes, Johnnie	WR	6-1	180	7/21/68	2	Hampton	Suffolk, Va.	D9-'92	1/0
32	Bieniemy, Eric	RB	5-7	198	8/15/69	3	Colorado	West Covina, Calif.	D2b-'91	15/0
13	# Brennan, Brian	WR	5-10	185	2/15/62	10	Boston College	Bloomfield, Mich.	W(Cin)-'92	15/0
35	Butts, Marion	RB	6-1	248	8/1/66	5	Florida State	Sylvester, Ga.	D7a-'89	15/14
22	Byrd, Gill	CB-S	5-11	198	2/20/61	11	San Jose State	San Francisco, Calif.	D1c-'83	16/16
3	† Carney, John	K	5-11	170	4/20/64	6	Notre Dame	West Palm Beach, Fla.	FA-'90	16/0
29	† Carrington, Darren	S	6-2	200	10/10/66	5	Northern Arizona	Bronx, N.Y.	FA-'91	16/4
59	Clark, Reggie	LB	6-3	238	10/17/67	2	North Carolina	Charlotte, N.C.	FA-'92	0*
31	Davis, Brian	CB	6-2	190	8/31/63	7	Nebraska	Phoenix, Ariz.	UFA(Sea)-'93	13/0*
28	Elder, Donnie	CB	5-9	178	12/13/62	9	Memphis State	Chattanooga, Tenn.	FA-'90	0*
26	Fields, Floyd	S	6-0	208	1/7/69	3	Arizona State	South Holland, Ill.	D5b-'91	16/14
27	† Frank, Donald	CB	6-0	192	10/24/65	4	Winston-Salem State	Tarboro, N.C.	FA-'90	16/0
17	Friesz, John	QB	6-4	218	5/19/67	4	Idaho	Coeur d'Alene, Idaho	D6a-'90	0*
56	Grayson, David	LB	6-3	233	2/27/64	7	Fresno State	San Diego, Calif.	FA-'91	0*
21	Griffith, Howard	RB	5-11	230	11/17/67	2	Illinois	Chicago, Ill.	FA-'92	0*
92	Grossman, Burt	DE	6-4	270	4/10/67	5	Pittsburgh	Bala-Cynwyd, Pa.	D1-'89	15/14
53	Hall, Courtney	C-G	6-1	281	8/26/68	5	Rice	Wilmington, Calif.	D2a-'89	16/16
36	Hall, Delton	S	6-1	211	1/16/65	7	Clemson	Greensboro, N.C.	PB(Pitt)-'92	16/1
33	Harmon, Ronnie	RB	5-11	207	5/7/64	8	Iowa	Queens, N.Y.	PB(Buff)-'90	16/2
34	Hendrickson, Steve	RB-LB	6-0	250	8/30/66	5	California	Napa, Calif.	FA-'90	16/2
12	Humphries, Stan	QB	6-2	223	4/14/65	5	Northeast Louisiana	Shreveport, La.	T(Wash)-'92	16/15
80	Jefferson, Shawn	WR	5-11	172	2/22/69	3	Central Florida	Jacksonville, Fla.	T(Hou)-'91	16/1
10	# Kidd, John	P	6-3	208	8/22/61	10	Northwestern	Findlay, Ohio	PB(Buff)-'90	16/0
98	# Lee, Shawn	DT	6-2	300	10/24/66	6	North Alabama	Brooklyn, N.Y.	FA-'92	9/1
81	Lewis, Nate	WR	5-11	198	10/19/66	4	Oregon Tech	Moultrie, Ga.	D7c-'90	15/7
88	May, Deems	TE	6-4	250	3/6/69	2	North Carolina	Lexington, N.C.	D7-'92	16/6
75	Milinichik, Joe	G	6-5	290	3/30/63	8	North Carolina State	Emmaus, Pa.	UFA(Rams)-'93	16/16*
83	Miller, Anthony	WR	5-11	189	4/15/65	6	Tennessee	Pasadena, Calif.	D1-'88	16/16
94	Mims, Chris	DE	6-5	270	9/29/70	2	Tennessee	Los Angeles, Calif.	D1-'92	16/4
73	Mooney, Mike	T	6-6	320	5/31/69	2	Georgia Tech	Sykesville, Md.	W(Hou)-'92	0*
77	Moten, Eric	G	6-2	306	4/11/68	3	Michigan State	Cleveland Heights, Ohio	D2c-'91	16/16
4	O'Hara, Pat	QB	6-3	205	9/27/68	3	Southern California	Santa Monica, Calif.	PB(TB)-'92	0*
91	O'Neal, Leslie	DE	6-4	259	5/7/64	8	Oklahoma State	Little Rock, Ark.	D1a-'86	15/15
50	# Plummer, Gary	LB	6-2	244	1/26/60	8	California	Fremont, Calif.	FA-'86	16/13
30	Pope, Marquez	CB	5-10	188	10/29/70	2	Fresno State	Moreno Valley, Calif.	D2-'92	7/0
86	Pupunu, Alfred	TE	6-2	252	10/17/69	2	Weber State	Salt Lake City, Utah	W(KC)-'92	15/2
24	Richard, Stanley	S	6-2	197	10/21/67	3	Texas	Hawkins, Tex.	D1-'91	14/14
55	Seau, Junior	LB	6-3	250	1/19/69	4	Southern California	Oceanside, Calif.	D1-'90	15/15
23	Shelton, Anthony	S	6-1	195	9/4/67	4	Tennessee State	Fayetteville, Tenn.	W(SF)-'90	0*
72	Swayne, Harry	T	6-5	295	2/2/65	7	Rutgers	Philadelphia, Pa.	PB(TB)-'91	16/16
93	Thornton, George	DT	6-3	305	4/27/68	3	Alabama	Montgomery, Ala.	D2a-'91	16/13
43	Tuipulotu, Peter	RB	5-11	210	2/20/69	2	Brigham Young	San Mateo, Calif.	FA-'92	6/0
25	Vanhorse, Sean	CB	5-10	180	7/22/68	3	Howard	Baltimore, Md.	PB(Det)-'92	16/9
89	† Walker, Derrick	TE	6-5	244	6/23/67	4	Michigan	Chicago Heights, Ill.	D6d-'90	16/16
90	White, Reggie	DT	6-4	291	3/22/70	2	North Carolina A&T	Mulford Mills, Md.	D6-'92	3/0
64	Whitley, Curtis	C	6-1	288	5/10/69	2	Clemson	Smithfield, N.C.	D5a-'92	3/0
57	Williams, Jerrol	LB	6-4	240	7/5/67	5	Purdue	Las Vegas, Nev.	RFA(Pitt)-'93	16/16*
96	# Winter, Blaise	DT	6-4	278	1/31/62	9	Syracuse	Tappan, N.Y.	FA-'92	16/15
87	Young, Duane	TE	6-1	260	5/29/68	3	Michigan State	Kalamazoo, Mich.	D5-'91	16/12
70	† Zandofsky, Mike	C-G	6-2	305	11/30/65	5	Washington	Corvallis, Ore.	T(Phx)-'90	15/0

* Clark spent '92 season on San Diego's practice squad; Davis played 13 games with Seattle in '92; Elder last active with San Diego in '91; Friesz, Grayson, Griffith, Mooney, O'Hara, and Shelton missed '92 season due to injury; Milinichik played 16 games with L.A. Rams; Williams played 16 games with Pittsburgh.

Unrestricted free agent; subject to developments.

† Restricted free agent; subject to developments.

Traded—G-T Broderick Thompson to Philadelphia.

Players lost through free agency (5): RB Rod Bernstine (Den; 9 games in '92), CB Tony Blaylock (Chi; 11), LB Kevin Murphy (Sea; 14), G Dave Richards (Det; 16), LB Henry Rolling (Rams; 15).

Also played with Chargers in '92—WR Robert Claiborne (9 games), QB Bob Gagliano (5), G-T Leo Goeas (16), LB Eugene Marve (16), NT Tony Savage (2), DE Jim Skow (1), LB Billy Ray Smith (1), WR Walter Stanley (1), G-T Broderick Thompson (12).

COACHING STAFF

Head Coach, Bobby Ross

Pro Career: Begins second season as San Diego's head coach after leading the Chargers to an 11-5 regular-season record and the team's first AFC Western Division title since 1981. Named ninth head coach in Chargers' history on January 2, 1992. Ross began his pro coaching career in 1978 as an assistant with the Kansas City Chiefs, where he coached special teams and defense in 1978-79 and offensive backs in 1980-81. No pro playing experience. Career record: 12-6.

Background: Played quarterback and defensive back for Virginia Military Institute. Began coaching career in 1965 at VMI. Moved on as an assistant at William & Mary 1967-70, Rice 1971, and Maryland 1972. Head coach at The Citadel 1973-77. Compiled 39-19-1 (.672) record as he led Maryland (1982-86) to three Atlantic Coast Conference titles and made four bowl game appearances in five seasons. Guided Georgia Tech (1987-91) to first ACC title in school history. Under Ross, the Yellow Jackets won first national championship as country's only undefeated team (11-0-1) in 1990. Named consensus national coach of the year in 1990. Career collegiate head coaching record: 94-76-2.

Personal: Born December 23, 1936, Richmond, Va. Bobby and wife, Alice, live in San Diego and have five children — Chris, Kevin, Robbie, Mary, and Teresa.

Assistant Coaches

Bill Arnsparger, defensive coordinator; born December 16, 1926, Paris, Ky., lives in San Diego. Tackle Miami (Ohio) 1946-49. No pro playing experience. College coach: Miami (Ohio) 1950, Ohio State 1951-53, Kentucky 1954-61, Tulane 1962-63, Louisiana State 1984-86, Florida 1987-91 (athletic director). Pro coach: Baltimore Colts 1964-69, Miami Dolphins 1970-73, 1976-83, New York Giants 1974-76 (head coach), joined Chargers in 1992.

Sylvester Croom, offensive backs; born September 25, 1954, Tuscaloosa, Ala., lives in San Diego. Center Alabama 1971-74. Pro center New Orleans Saints 1975. College coach: Alabama 1976-86. Pro coach: Tampa Bay Buccaneers 1987-90, Indianapolis Colts 1991, joined Chargers in 1992.

John Dunn, strength and conditioning; born July 22, 1956, Hillsdale, N.Y., lives in San Diego. Guard Penn State 1974-77. No pro playing experience. College coach: Penn State 1978. Pro coach: Washington Redskins 1984-86, Los Angeles Raiders 1987-89, joined Chargers in 1990.

John Fox, defensive backs; born February 8, 1955, Virginia Beach, Va., lives in San Diego. Defensive back San Diego State 1975-77. No pro playing experience. College coach: U.S. International 1979, Boise State 1980, Long Beach State 1981, Utah 1982, Kansas 1983, 1985, Iowa State 1984, Pittsburgh 1986-88. Pro coach: Los Angeles Express (USFL) 1985, Pittsburgh Steelers 1989-91, joined Chargers in 1992.

Ralph Friedgen, tight ends-running game coordinator; born April 4, 1947, Harrison, N.Y., lives in San Diego. Guard Maryland 1967-68. No pro playing experience. College coach: The Citadel 1973-79, William & Mary 1980, Murray State 1981, Maryland 1982-86, Georgia Tech 1987-91. Pro coach: Joined Chargers in 1992.

Dale Lindsey, linebackers; born January 18, 1943, Bedford, Ind., lives in San Diego. Linebacker Western Kentucky 1961-64. Pro linebacker Cleveland Browns 1965-73. College coach: Southern Methodist 1988-89. Pro coach: Cleveland Browns 1974, Portland Storm (WFL) 1975, Toronto Argonauts (CFL) 1979-82, Boston Breakers (USFL) 1983, New Jersey Generals (USFL) 1984-85, Green Bay Packers 1986-87, New England Patriots 1990, Tampa Bay Buccaneers 1991, joined Chargers in 1992.

San Diego Chargers 1993 First-Year Roster

Name	Pos.	Ht.	Wt.	Birth-date	College	Hometown	How Acq.
Amos, Anthony	CB	5-11	182	4/7/70	Mississippi	Jackson, Miss.	FA
Balady, Louis	WR	5-10	190	7/7/70	Rice	Dallas, Tex.	FA
Brasher, Robert	RB	6-5	244	4/30/70	Arizona State	San Diego, Calif.	FA
Bush, Lewis	LB	6-2	245	12/2/69	Washington State	Tacoma, Wash.	D4b
Butler, Wayde	WR	6-0	180	12/25/69	S.W. Louisiana	Beaumont, Tex.	FA
Castle, Eric	S	6-3	212	3/15/70	Oregon	Lebanon, Ore.	D6
Cocozzo, Joe	G	6-4	300	8/7/70	Michigan	Mechanicville, N.Y.	D3
Cornelius, Shannon	DT	6-2	285	4/30/70	Louisiana Tech	Minden, La.	FA
Dark, Stephen	RB-TE	6-2	238	11/11/69	Mid. Tennessee State	Chattanooga, Tenn.	FA
Davidson, Reginald	G-T	6-2	305	7/15/70	Jackson State	Tuscaloosa, Ala.	FA
Dunson, Walter	WR	5-9	173	10/24/70	Mid. Tennessee State	Carrollton, Ga.	D5
Habersham, Shaun (1)	WR	5-11	183	12/4/68	Tenn.-Chattanooga	Louisville, Ga.	FA
Embray, Keith	LB	6-4	255	11/29/69	Utah	Spring Valley, Calif.	FA
Gordon, Darrien	CB	5-11	182	11/14/70	Stanford	Shawnee, Okla.	D1
Green, Trent	QB	6-3	211	7/9/70	Indiana	St. Louis, Mo.	D8
Hardwick, Jesse	T	6-5	287	7/21/70	Fresno State	Garden Grove, Calif.	FA
Harrison, Ted	C-G	6-4	295	10/20/69	Minnesota	New Hope, Minn.	FA
Johnson, James	RB	5-11	210	3/28/70	Jackson State	Forest, Miss.	FA
Johnson, Raylee	DE	6-3	245	6/1/70	Arkansas	Fordyce, Ark.	D4a
Kaplan, Scott	K	6-0	190	2/17/70	Pittsburgh	Coral Springs, Fla.	FA
Lavin, Jim (1)	G	6-4	275	12/25/68	Georgia Tech	New Orleans, La.	FA
Malone, Art (1)	CB-S	5-10	190	8/21/66	Washington	Ventura, Calif.	FA
McIver, Everett	DT	6-6	335	8/5/70	Elizabeth City State	Fayetteville, N.C.	FA
Means, Natrone	RB	5-10	245	4/26/72	North Carolina	Harrisburg, N.C.	D2
Miller, Doug	LB	6-3	232	10/29/69	South Dakota State	Sturgis, S.D.	D7
Miller, Reggie	WR	5-9	168	10/20/69	Baylor	Waco, Tex.	FA
Parks, Vincent	WR	5-9	163	1/30/70	Mid. Tennessee State	Carrollton, Ga.	FA
Paul, Arthur (1)	DT	6-6	294	8/23/68	Arizona State	Washington, D.C.	D10-'92
Sims, Kenny	RB	5-11	191	2/24/69	James Madison	Purcellville, Va.	FA
Smoot, Raymond	G-T	6-4	300	7/24/70	Louisiana State	Leesville, La.	FA
Snisky, Eugene	T	6-6	295	1/14/70	Missouri	Lansford, Pa.	FA
Stanley, Israel	LB	6-2	250	4/21/70	Arizona State	San Diego, Calif.	FA
Staten, Ray	WR	6-1	175	3/5/69	Pittsburg State, Kan.	Parsons, Kan.	FA
Stephens, Ralph (1)	P	6-3	210	12/17/65	Georgia Southwestern	Orange Park, Fla.	FA
Thomas, Chris	WR	6-1	180	7/16/71	Cal Poly-SLO	Ventura, Calif.	FA
Williams, Michael	CB-S	5-10	185	5/28/70	UCLA	Los Angeles, Calif.	FA
Youngblood, Jason	G-T	6-3	288	12/18/70	Houston	Refugio, Tex.	FA

The term NFL Rookie is defined as a player who is in his first season of professional football and has not been on the roster of another professional football team for any regular-season or postseason games. A Rookie is designated by an "R" on NFL rosters. Players who have been active in another professional football league or players who have NFL experience, including either preseason training camp or being on an Active List or Inactive List, or on Reserve/Injured or Reserve/Physically Unable to Perform for fewer than six regular-season games, are termed NFL First-Year Players. An NFL First-Year Player is designated by a "1" on NFL rosters. Thereafter, a player is credited with an additional year of experience for each season in which he accumulates six games on the Active List or Inactive List, or on Reserve/Injured or Reserve/Physically Unable to Perform.

NOTES

Carl Mauck, offensive line; born July 7, 1947, McLeansboro, Ill., lives in San Diego. Linebacker-center Southern Illinois 1966-68. Pro center Baltimore Colts 1969, Miami Dolphins 1970, San Diego Chargers 1971-74, Houston Oilers 1975-81. Pro coach: New Orleans Saints 1982-85, Kansas City Chiefs 1986-88, Tampa Bay Buccaneers 1991, joined Chargers in 1992.

John Misciagna, quality control; born December 11, 1954, Brooklyn, N.Y., lives in San Diego. Guard Dickinson College 1973-76. No pro playing experience. College coach: Indiana (Pa.) University 1977, Columbia 1978-79, Maryland 1980-88, Georgia Tech 1989-91. Pro coach: Joined Chargers in 1992.

George O'Leary, defensive line; born August 17, 1946, New York, N.Y., lives in San Diego. Offensive lineman-fullback New Hampshire 1964-67. No pro playing experience. College coach: Syracuse 1980-86, Georgia Tech 1987-91. Pro coach: Joined Chargers in 1992.

Chuck Priefer, special teams; born July 26, 1941, Cleveland, Ohio, lives in San Diego. No college or pro playing experience. College coach: Miami (Ohio) 1977, North Carolina 1978-83, Kent State 1986, Georgia Tech 1987-91. Pro coach: Green Bay Packers 1984-85, joined Chargers in 1992.

Jack Reilly, quarterbacks-passing game coordinator; born May 22, 1945, Boston, Mass., lives in San Diego. Quarterback Washington State 1963, Santa Monica, Calif., College 1964, Long Beach State 1965-66. No pro playing experience. College coach: El Camino, Calif., J.C. 1980-84, Utah 1985-89 (head coach). Pro coach: Joined Chargers in 1990.

Jerry Sullivan, wide receivers; born July 13, 1944, Miami, Fla., lives in San Diego. Quarterback Florida State 1963-64. No pro playing experience. College coach: Kansas State 1971-72, Texas Tech 1973-75, South Carolina 1976-82, Indiana 1983, Louisiana State 1984-90, Ohio State 1991. Pro coach: Joined Chargers in 1992.

American Football Conference Western Division

Team Colors: Blue, Green, and Silver

11220 N.E. 53rd Street
Kirkland, Washington 98033
Telephone: (206) 827-9777

Club Officials

Owner: Ken Behring
President: David Behring
General Manager/Head Coach: Tom Flores
Executive Vice President: Mickey Loomis
Vice President/Football Operations: Chuck Allen
Vice President/Administration and Public Relations: Gary Wright
Player Personnel Director: Mike Allman
Publicity Director: Dave Neubert
Community Relations Director: Sandy Gregory
Sales and Marketing Director: Reggie McKenzie
Data Processing Director: Tom Monroe
Ticket Manager: James Nagaoka
Trainer: Jim Whitesel
Equipment Manager: Terry Sinclair
Team Physicians: Dr. Kevin Auld, Dr. Pierce Scranton, Dr. James Trombold, Dr. Pete Van Patten

Stadium: Kingdome • **Capacity:** 66,000
201 South King Street
Seattle, Washington 98104

Playing Surface: AstroTurf

Training Camp: 11220 N.E. 53rd Street
Kirkland, Washington 98033

1993 Schedule

Preseason

Aug. 7	**Indianapolis**	6:00
Aug. 14	at Minnesota	7:00
Aug. 21	**San Francisco**	7:00
Aug. 28	at Houston	7:00

Regular Season

Sept. 5	at San Diego	1:00
Sept. 12	**Los Angeles Raiders**	5:00
Sept. 19	at New England	1:00
Sept. 26	at Cincinnati	1:00
Oct. 3	**San Diego**	1:00
Oct. 10	**Open Date**	
Oct. 17	at Detroit	1:00
Oct. 24	**New England**	1:00
Oct. 31	at Denver	2:00
Nov. 7	at Houston	12:00
Nov. 14	**Cleveland**	1:00
Nov. 21	**Open Date**	
Nov. 28	**Denver**	1:00
Dec. 5	**Kansas City**	1:00
Dec. 12	at Los Angeles Raiders	1:00
Dec. 19	**Phoenix**	1:00
Dec. 26	**Pittsburgh**	1:00
Jan. 2	at Kansas City	12:00

Seahawks Coaching History

(124-143-0)

1976-82	Jack Patera*	35-59-0
1982	Mike McCormack	4-3-0
1983-91	Chuck Knox	83-67-0
1992	Tom Flores	2-14-0

*Released after two games in 1982

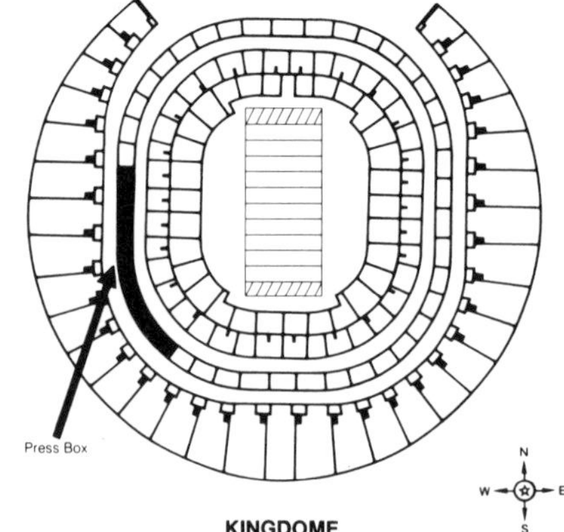

KINGDOME

Record Holders

Individual Records — Career

Category	Name	Performance
Rushing (Yds.)	Curt Warner, 1983-89	6,705
Passing (Yds.)	Dave Krieg, 1980-1991	26,132
Passing (TDs)	Dave Krieg, 1980-1991	195
Receiving (No.)	Steve Largent, 1976-1989	819
Receiving (Yds.)	Steve Largent, 1976-1989	13,089
Interceptions	Dave Brown, 1976-1986	50
Punting (Avg.)	Rick Tuten, 1991-92	43.7
Punt Return (Avg.)	Paul Johns, 1981-84	11.4
Kickoff Return (Avg.)	Bobby Joe Edmonds, 1986-88	22.1
Field Goals	Norm Johnson, 1982-1990	159
Touchdowns (Tot.)	Steve Largent, 1976-1989	101
Points	Norm Johnson, 1982-1990	810

Individual Records — Single Season

Category	Name	Performance
Rushing (Yds.)	Curt Warner, 1986	1,481
Passing (Yds.)	Dave Krieg, 1984	3,671
Passing (TDs)	Dave Krieg, 1984	32
Receiving (No.)	Steve Largent, 1985	79
Receiving (Yds.)	Steve Largent, 1985	1,287
Interceptions	John Harris, 1981	10
	Kenny Easley, 1984	10
Punting (Avg.)	Rick Tuten, 1992	44.1
Punt Return (Avg.)	Bobby Joe Edmonds, 1987	12.6
Kickoff Return (Avg.)	Al Hunter, 1978	24.1
Field Goals	John Kasay, 1991	25
Touchdowns (Tot.)	David Sims, 1978	15
	Sherman Smith, 1979	15
	Derrick Fenner, 1990	15
Points	Norm Johnson, 1984	110

Individual Records — Single Game

Category	Name	Performance
Rushing (Yds.)	Curt Warner, 11-27-83	207
Passing (Yds.)	Dave Krieg, 11-20-83	418
Passing (TDs)	Dave Krieg, 12-2-84	5
	Dave Krieg, 9-15-85	5
	Dave Krieg, 11-28-88	5
Receiving (No.)	Steve Largent, 10-18-87	15
Receiving (Yds.)	Steve Largent, 10-18-87	261
Interceptions	Kenny Easley, 9-3-84	3
	Eugene Robinson, 12-6-92	3
Field Goals	Norm Johnson, 9-20-87	5
	Norm Johnson, 12-18-88	5
Touchdowns (Tot.)	Daryl Turner, 9-15-85	4
	Curt Warner, 12-11-88	4
Points	Daryl Turner, 9-15-85	24
	Curt Warner, 12-11-88	24

*NFL Record

1992 Team Record

Preseason (2-2)

Date	Result		Opponents
8/6	L	7-21	L.A. Rams
8/15	W	27-10	at Indianapolis
8/22	W	17-10	Phoenix
8/28	L	17-24	at San Francisco

Regular Season (2-14)

Date	Result		Opponents	Att.
9/6	L	3-21	Cincinnati	64,601
9/13	L	7-26	at Kansas City	76,591
9/20	W	10- 6	at New England	45,785
9/27	L	17-19	Miami	64,629
10/4	L	6-17	at San Diego	37,344
10/11	L	0-27	at Dallas	62,569
10/18	L	0-19	L.A. Raiders	64,646
10/25	L	10-23	at N.Y. Giants	76,021
11/8	L	3-16	Washington	64,673
11/15	L	3-20	at L.A. Raiders	31,805
11/22	L	14-24	Kansas City	64,017
11/30	W	16-13	Denver (OT)	64,482
12/6	L	14-20	at Pittsburgh	58,128
12/13	L	17-20	Philadelphia (OT)	64,102
12/20	L	6-10	at Denver	72,763
12/27	L	14-31	San Diego	63,834

(OT) Overtime

Score by Periods

Seahawks	20	53	34	30	3	—	140
Opponents	63	87	74	85	3	—	312

Attendance

Home 514,984 Away 461,006 Total 975,990
Single-game home record, 64,673 (11-8-92)
Single-season home record, 514,984 (1992)

1992 Team Statistics

	Seahawks	Opp.
Total First Downs	208	247
Rushing	77	96
Passing	114	129
Penalty	17	22
Third Down: Made/Att.	59/222	75/230
Third Down: Pct.	26.6	32.6
Fourth Down: Made/Att.	5/17	6/9
Fourth Down: Pct.	29.4	66.7
Total Net Yards	3374	4583
Avg. Per Game	210.9	286.4
Total Plays	945	987
Avg. Per Play	3.6	4.6
Net Yards Rushing	1596	1922
Avg. Per Game	99.8	120.1
Total Rushes	402	513
Net Yards Passing	1778	2661
Avg. Per Game	111.1	166.3
Sacked/Yards Lost	67/545	46/317
Gross Yards	2323	2978
Att./Completions	476/230	428/251
Completion Pct.	48.3	58.6
Had Intercepted	23	20
Punts/Avg.	108/44.1	96/41.8
Net Punting Avg.	108/38.7	96/36.8
Penalties/Yards Lost	111/918	100/776
Fumbles/Ball Lost	37/18	25/11
Touchdowns	14	32
Rushing	4	14
Passing	9	11
Returns	1	7
Avg. Time of Possession	29:01	30:59

1992 Individual Statistics

Scoring	TD R	TD P	TD Rt	PAT	FG	Saf	TP
Kasay	0	0	0	14/14	14/22	0	56
Kane	0	3	0	0/0	0/0	0	18
Warren	3	0	0	0/0	0/0	0	18
Williams	1	2	0	0/0	0/0	0	18
Blades	0	1	0	0/0	0/0	0	6
L. Clark	0	1	0	0/0	0/0	0	6
P. Green	0	1	0	0/0	0/0	0	6
Harper	0	0	1	0/0	0/0	0	6
Junkin	0	1	0	0/0	0/0	0	6
Seahawks	4	9	1	14/14	14/22	0	140
Opponents	14	11	7	29/32	29/36	2	312

Passing	Att.	Comp.	Yds.	Pct.	TD	Int.	Tkld.	Rate
Gelbaugh	255	121	1307	47.5	6	11	34/265	52.9
Stouffer	190	92	900	48.4	3	9	26/222	47.7
McGwire	30	17	116	56.7	0	3	7/58	25.8
Tuten	1	0	0	0.0	0	0	0/0	39.6
Seahawks	476	230	2323	48.3	9	23	67/545	48.9
Opponents	428	251	2978	58.6	11	20	46/317	69.0

Rushing	Att.	Yds.	Avg.	LG	TD
Warren	223	1017	4.6	52	3
Williams	114	339	3.0	14	1
Gelbaugh	16	79	4.9	22	0
Mayes	28	74	2.6	14	0
Stouffer	9	37	4.1	11	0
Johnson	3	26	8.7	19	0
McGwire	3	13	4.3	11	0
D. Thomas	3	7	2.3	8	0
Blades	1	5	5.0	5	0
Tuten	1	0	0.0	0	0
R. Thomas	1	−1	−1.0	−1	0
Seahawks	402	1596	4.0	52	4
Opponents	513	1922	3.7	66t	14

Receiving	No.	Yds.	Avg.	LG	TD
Williams	74	556	7.5	27	2
Kane	27	369	13.7	31	3
J. Jones	21	190	9.0	30	0
L. Clark	20	290	14.5	33	1
Blades	19	256	13.5	37	1
Warren	16	134	8.4	33	0
Heller	12	85	7.1	17	0
R. Thomas	11	136	12.4	31	0
P. Green	9	67	7.4	15	1
D. Thomas	8	85	10.6	19	0
Daniels	5	99	19.8	57	0
Junkin	3	25	8.3	13	1
M. Jones	3	18	6.0	7	0
Mayes	2	13	6.5	7	0
Seahawks	230	2323	10.1	57	9
Opponents	251	2978	11.9	72t	11

Interceptions	No.	Yds.	Avg.	LG	TD
E. Robinson	7	126	18.0	49	0
Harper	3	74	24.7	41	0
Davis	2	36	18.0	36	0
Cain	2	3	1.5	3	0
P. Hunter	2	0	0.0	0	0
Blackmon	1	69	69.0	69	0
Dodge	1	13	13.0	13	0
Wooden	1	3	3.0	3	0
Tuatagaloa	1	0	0.0	0	0
Seahawks	20	324	16.2	69	0
Opponents	23	231	10.0	40	4

Punting	No.	Yds.	Avg.	In 20	LG
Tuten	108	4760	44.1	29	65
Seahawks	108	4760	44.1	29	65
Opponents	96	4015	41.8	23	65

Punt Returns	No.	FC	Yds.	Avg.	LG	TD
Warren	34	25	252	7.4	16	0
Treggs	4	2	31	7.8	13	0
Seahawks	38	27	283	7.4	16	0
Opponents	56	26	416	7.4	86t	1

Kickoff Returns	No.	Yds.	Avg.	LG	TD
Warren	28	524	18.7	34	0
Johnson	1	15	15.0	15	0
J. Jones	1	16	16.0	16	0
Mayes	19	311	16.4	29	0
D. Thomas	1	19	19.0	19	0
Seahawks	50	885	17.7	34	0
Opponents	36	685	19.0	64	0

Sacks	No.
Kennedy	14.0
Porter	9.5
Bryant	4.5
Nash	4.5
Blackmon	3.5
Tuatagaloa	3.0
Woods	3.0
Dodge	1.0
Glasgow	1.0
K. Millard	1.0
Sinclair	1.0
Seahawks	46.0
Opponents	67.0

1993 Draft Choices

Round	Name	Pos.	College
1.	Rick Mirer	QB	Notre Dame
2.	Carlton Gray	DB	UCLA
4.	Dean Wells	LB	Kentucky
5.	Terrence Warren	WR	Hampton
7.	Michael McCrary	DE	Wake Forest
8.	Jeff Blackshear	G	N.E. Louisiana
	Antonio Edwards	DE	Valdosta State

Seattle Seahawks 1993 Veteran Roster

No.	Name	Pos.	Ht.	Wt.	Birth-date	NFL Exp.	College	Hometown	How Acq.	'92 Games/ Starts
61	Adams, Theo	G	6-4	298	4/24/66	2	Hawaii	Honolulu, Hawaii	FA-'91	10/0
25	†Blackmon, Robert	S	6-0	197	5/12/67	4	Baylor	Van Vleck, Tex.	D2b-'90	15/15
89	Blades, Brian	WR	5-11	189	7/24/66	6	Miami	Ft. Lauderdale, Fla.	D2-'88	6/5
64	Brilz, Darrick	G	6-3	287	2/14/64	7	Oregon State	Pinole Valley, Calif.	FA-'89	16/16
77	Bryant, Jeff	DE	6-5	281	5/22/60	12	Clemson	Decatur, Ga.	D1-'82	16/16
88	Daniels, David	WR	6-1	190	9/16/69	3	Penn State	Sarasota, Fla.	D3-'91	13/1
33	Dodge, Dedrick	S	6-2	184	6/14/67	3	Florida State	Mulberry, Fla.	FA-'91	14/0
53	Donaldson, Ray	C	6-3	300	5/18/58	14	Georgia	Rome, Ga.	FA-'93	16/16*
82	Edmunds, Ferrell	TE	6-6	254	4/16/65	6	Maryland	Danville, Va.	UFA(Mia)-'93	10/6*
54	Feasel, Grant	C	6-7	283	6/28/60	11	Abilene Christian	Barstow, Calif.	FA-'87	16/0
31	Frank, Malcolm	CB	5-8	182	12/5/68	2	Baylor	Beaumont, Tex.	FA-'92	15/0
51	Frerotte, Mitch	G	6-3	286	3/30/65	6	Penn State	Kittanning, Pa.	UFA(Buff)-'93	14/3*
18	†Gelbaugh, Stan	QB	6-3	207	12/4/62	5	Maryland	Mechanicsburg, Pa.	PB(Phx)-'92	10/8
68	Gibson, Tom	DT	6-8	279	12/20/63	5	Northern Arizona	Saugus, Calif.	FA-'93	0*
7	Graham, Jeff	QB	6-5	220	2/5/66	2	Long Beach State	Costa Mesa, Calif.	FA-'92	0*
87	Green, Paul	TE	6-3	230	10/8/66	2	Southern California	Clovis, Calif.	FA-'92	4/4
35	Hagy, John	S	6-0	190	12/9/65	4	Texas	San Antonio, Tex.	FA-'93	0*
29	Harper, Dwayne	CB	5-11	174	3/29/66	6	South Carolina State	Orangeburg, S.C.	D11b-'88	16/16
66	Heck, Andy	T	6-6	298	1/1/67	5	Notre Dame	Fairfax, Va.	D1-'89	13/13
76	Hitchcock, Bill	G	6-6	291	8/26/65	3	Purdue	Kirkland, Canada	FA-'91	16/11
27	Hunter, Patrick	CB	5-11	186	10/24/64	8	Nevada	San Francisco, Calif.	D3-'86	16/16
20	†Jefferson, James	CB	6-1	199	11/18/63	5	Texas A&I	Kingsville, Tex.	FA-'89	1/0
43	Johnson, Tracy	RB	6-0	230	11/29/66	5	Clemson	Kannapolis, N.C.	PB(Atl)-'92	16/0
93	Junior, E.J.	LB	6-3	242	12/8/59	13	Alabama	Nashville, Tenn.	FA-'92	2/0*
83	#Junkin, Trey	TE	6-2	237	1/23/61	11	Louisiana Tech	Winfield, La.	FA-'90	16/1
81	Kane, Tommy	WR	5-11	181	1/14/64	6	Syracuse	Montreal, Canada	D3-'88	11/11
4	Kasay, John	K	5-10	189	10/27/69	3	Georgia	Athens, Ga.	D4-'91	16/0
96	Kennedy, Cortez	DT	6-3	293	8/23/68	4	Miami	Rivercrest, Ark.	D1-'90	16/16
63	#Lee, Ronnie	T	6-3	296	12/24/56	15	Baylor	Tyler, Tex.	T(Atl)-'90	9/5
84	Martin, Kelvin	WR	5-9	162	5/14/65	7	Boston College	Jacksonville, Fla.	UFA(Dall)-'93	16/1*
36	Mayes, Rueben	RB	5-11	201	6/6/63	7	Washington State	North Battleford, Canada	T(NO)-'92	16/0
44	McCloughan, Dave	S	6-1	185	11/20/66	3	Colorado	Loveland, Colo.	T(GB)-'93	5/0*
10	McGwire, Dan	QB	6-8	239	12/18/67	3	San Diego State	Claremont, Calif.	D1-'91	2/1
71	Millard, Bryan	G	6-5	277	12/2/60	10	Texas	Dumas, Tex.	FA-'84	0*
98	Murphy, Kevin	LB	6-2	235	9/8/63	8	Oklahoma	Richardson, Tex.	UFA(SD)-'93	14/1*
72	Nash, Joe	DT	6-3	278	10/11/60	12	Boston College	Dorchester, Mass.	FA-'82	16/16
97	Porter, Rufus	LB	6-1	227	5/18/65	6	Southern	Baton Rouge, La.	FA-'88	16/16
73	Roberts, Ray	T	6-6	304	6/3/69	2	Virginia	Asheville, N.C.	D1-'92	16/16
41	Robinson, Eugene	S	6-0	191	5/28/63	9	Colgate	Hartford, Conn.	FA-'85	16/16
37	Robinson, Rafael	S	5-11	200	6/19/69	2	Wisconsin	Jefferson, Tex.	FA-'92	6/0
91	Rodgers, Tyrone	DT	6-3	266	4/27/69	2	Washington	Carson, Calif.	FA-'92	16/0
70	Sinclair, Michael	DE	6-4	271	1/31/68	2	Eastern New Mexico	Beaumont, Tex.	D6-'91	12/1
59	Spitulski, Bob	LB	6-3	235	9/10/69	2	Central Florida	Orlando, Fla.	D3-'92	4/0
48	Stayner, Larry	TE	6-5	241	6/4/69	2	Boise State	Marysville, Wash.	D9-'92	0*
94	†Stephens, Rod	LB	6-1	237	6/14/66	4	Georgia Tech	Atlanta, Ga.	FA-'90	16/5
85	Thomas, Doug	WR	5-10	178	9/18/69	3	Clemson	Hamlet, N.C.	D2-'91	12/4
86	†Thomas, Robb	WR	5-11	175	3/29/66	5	Oregon State	Corvallis, Ore.	FA-'92	15/0
56	†Tofflemire, Joe	C	6-3	273	7/7/65	5	Arizona	Post Falls, Idaho	D2-'89	16/16
99	†Tuatagaloa, Natu	DE	6-4	274	5/25/66	5	California	San Rafael, Calif.	FA-'92	14/0
14	Tuten, Rick	P	6-2	218	1/5/65	5	Florida State	Ocala, Fla.	FA-'91	16/0
42	†Warren, Chris	RB	6-2	225	1/24/67	4	Ferrum	Burke, Va.	D4-'90	16/16
32	Williams, John L.	RB	5-11	231	11/23/64	8	Florida	Palatka, Fla.	D1-'86	16/16
90	†Wooden, Terry	LB	6-3	239	1/14/67	4	Syracuse	Farmington, Conn.	D2a-'90	8/8
57	#Woods, Tony	DE	6-4	269	9/11/65	7	Pittsburgh	Newark, N.J.	D1-'87	15/15
92	#Wyman, David	LB	6-2	248	3/31/64	7	Stanford	Reno, Nev.	D2-'87	11/11

* Donaldson played 16 games with Indianapolis in '92; Edmunds played 10 with Miami; Frerotte played 14 games with Buffalo; Gibson last active with L.A. Rams in '91; Graham last active with San Diego in '91; Hagy, Millard, and Stayner missed '92 season due to injury; Junior played 2 games with Tampa Bay; Martin played 16 games with Dallas; McCloughan played 5 games with Green Bay; Murphy played 14 games with San Diego.

\# Unrestricted free agent; subject to developments.

† Restricted free agent; subject to developments.

Retired—Safety Nesby Glasgow, 14-year veteran, 13 games in '92; Safety Vann McElroy, 10-year veteran, 0 games in '92.

Players lost through free agency (5): LB Joe Cain (Chi; 16 games in '92), LB Greg Clark (Pitt; 12), WR Louis Clark (GB; 10), CB Brian Davis (SD; 13), RB James Jones (Det; 16).

Also played with Seahawks in '92—G Sean Farrell (6 games), C Grant Feasel (16), TE Ron Heller (16), G John Hunter (5), TE Mike Jones (4), T Mike Keim (1), DT Keith Millard (2), LB Richard Newbill (7), QB Kelly Stouffer (9), WR Brian Treggs (2).

COACHING STAFF

Head Coach, Tom Flores

Pro Career: Named the fourth head coach in the history of the Seahawks on January 6, 1992. Had served as president and general manager from February 22, 1989. Flores previously served as the head coach of the Oakland/Los Angeles Raiders from 1979 through 1987. He won two Super Bowl titles with the Raiders, 27-10 over the Philadelphia Eagles in Super Bowl XV after the 1980 season, and 38-9 over the Washington Redskins in Super Bowl XVIII in 1983. Those are the only Super Bowl triumphs by an AFC team in the 1980s. The 1980 Raiders are the only Wild Card team to win the Super Bowl. Flores was a member of the Raiders' organization for 22 seasons, as a quarterback (1960-61, 1963-66), assistant coach (1972-78), and head coach (1979-87). Also played for the Buffalo Bills (1967-68) and Kansas City Chiefs (1969-70), and coached with the Bills (1971) before returning to the Raiders as a coach. Is one of two players in league history to have Super Bowl rings as a player (Kansas City, Super Bowl IV), assistant coach (Raiders, Super Bowl XI) and head coach (Raiders, Super Bowls XV and XVIII). Still holds the Raiders' record with six touchdown passes in a 1963 game. Career record: 93-70-0.

Background: Quarterback at Fresno, California, Junior College 1954-55 and the College of the Pacific 1956-57. Coached at his alma mater in 1959 before joining the Raiders as a quarterback in 1960.

Personal: Born March 21, 1937, in Fresno, California. Tom and his wife, Barbara, live in Kirkland, Washington, and have twin sons, Mark and Scott, and a daughter, Kim.

Assistant Coaches

Tommy Brasher, defensive line; born December 30, 1940, El Dorado, Ark., lives in Redmond, Wash. Linebacker Arkansas 1962-63. No pro playing experience. College coach: Arkansas 1970, Virginia Tech 1971, Northeast Louisiana 1974, 1976, Southern Methodist 1977-81. Pro coach: Shreveport Steamer (WFL) 1975, New England Patriots 1982-84, Philadelphia Eagles 1985, Atlanta Falcons 1986-89, Tampa Bay Buccaneers 1990, joined Seahawks in 1992.

Bob Bratkowski, wide receivers; born December 2, 1955, San Angelo, Tex., lives in Redmond, Wash. Wide receiver Washington State 1974, 1976-77. No pro playing experience. College coach: Missouri 1978-80, Weber State 1981-85, Wyoming 1986, Washington State 1987-88, Miami 1989-91. Pro coach: Joined Seahawks in 1992.

Dave Brown, defensive assistant; born January 16, 1953, Akron, Ohio, lives in Woodinville, Wash. Defensive back Michigan 1972-74. Pro defensive back Pittsburgh Steelers 1975, Seattle Seahawks 1976-86, Green Bay Packers 1987-90. Pro coach: Joined Seahawks in 1992.

Tom Catlin, assistant head coach; born September 8, 1931, Ponca City, Okla., lives in Redmond, Wash. Center-linebacker Oklahoma 1950-52. Pro linebacker Cleveland Browns 1953-54, 1957-58, Philadelphia Eagles 1959. College coach: Army 1956. Pro coach: Dallas Texans-Kansas City Chiefs 1960-65, Los Angeles Rams 1966-77, Buffalo Bills 1978-82, joined Seahawks in 1983.

Larry Kennan, offensive coordinator-quarterbacks; born June 13, 1944, Pomona, Calif., lives in Kirkland, Wash. Quarterback La Verne College 1962-65. No pro playing experience. College coach: Colorado 1969-71, Nevada-Las Vegas 1973-75, Southern Methodist 1976-78, Lamar 1979-81 (head coach). Pro coach: Los Angeles Raiders 1982-87, Denver Broncos 1988, Indianapolis Colts 1989-90, London Monarchs (World League) 1991 (head coach), joined Seahawks in 1992.

Paul Moyer, defensive backfield; born July 26, 1961, Villa Park, Calif., lives in Renton, Wash. Safety Fullerton, Calif., J.C. 1979-80, Arizona State 1981-82. Pro safety Seattle Seahawks 1983-89. Pro coach: Joined Seahawks in 1990.

Seattle Seahawks 1993 First-Year Roster

Name	Pos.	Ht.	Wt.	Birth-date	College	Hometown	How Acq.
Bates, Michael (1)	WR	5-10	189	12/19/69	Arizona	Tucson, Ariz.	D6-'92
Blackshear, Jeff	G	6-6	325	3/29/69	Northeast Louisiana	Ft. Pierce, Fla.	D8a
Brown, Norris	CB	5-9	188	12/14/69	Clemson	Conway, S.C.	FA
Burress, Ken	CB	5-11	175	2/16/70	Bowling Green	Middletown, Ohio	FA
Davis, Anthony (1)	LB	6-0	231	3/7/69	Utah	Pasco, Wash	FA
Davis, C.J.	WR	5-11	191	9/4/69	Washington State	Tacoma, Wash.	FA
Dees, Andrew (1)	T	6-6	274	12/1/69	Syracuse	Babylon, N.Y.	FA
De Hoog, Mike	T	6-4	296	2/14/69	Utah	Ontario, Calif.	FA
Dugan, Chris	K	5-10	170	5/4/65	Arizona State	Indianapolis, Ind.	FA
Edwards, Antonio	DE	6-3	270	3/10/70	Valdosta State	Moultrie, Ga.	D8b
Evans, Marcus	LB	6-2	248	1/1/70	Youngstown State	Forest Park, Ill.	FA
Gardere, Peter	P	6-0	190	9/28/69	Texas	Houston, Tex.	FA
Gray, Carlton	CB	6-0	191	6/26/71	UCLA	Cincinnati, Ohio	D2
Green, Anthony (1)	WR	5-11	190	6/12/67	Western Kentucky	Dallas, Tex.	FA
Hairston, Stacey (1)	CB	5-9	180	8/16/67	Northern Ohio	Columbus, Ohio	FA
Keim, Mike (1)	T	6-7	285	11/12/65	Brigham Young	Springerville, Ariz.	FA
Long, Paul	C	6-3	282	4/9/69	Ohio State	Mayfield, Ohio	FA
Lustyk, Mike	DT	6-3	270	6/24/70	Washington	Bellevue, Wash.	FA
McCrary, Michael	DE	6-4	250	7/7/70	Wake Forest	Vienna, Va.	D7
McKinley, Mike	RB	6-0	226	11/30/68	Oklahoma	Perrytown, Tex.	FA
McKinney, Darian (1)	TE	6-6	240	11/11/69	Central Michigan	Lansing, Mich.	FA
Mirer, Rick	QB	6-2	216	3/3/70	Notre Dame	Goshen, Ind.	D1
Oliver, David	T	6-6	282	7/2/70	Northern Colorado	Colorado Springs, Colo.	FA
Rees, Bob	T	6-6	267	2/3/70	Iowa	Sioux City, Iowa	FA
Shamsid-Deen, Muhammad (1)	RB	5-11	200	11/16/69	Tenn.-Chattanooga	Decatur, Ga.	D8-'92
Smith, Alex	RB	5-10	211	8/10/69	Auburn	College Park, Ga.	FA
Smith, Tommie	S	6-1	212	8/7/71	Washington	Lancaster, Calif.	FA
Stayner, Larry (1)	TE	6-5	241	6/4/69	Boise State	Marysville, Wash.	D9-'92
Strong, Mack	RB	6-0	211	9/11/71	Georgia	Columbus, Ga.	FA
Treggs, Brian (1)	WR	5-9	161	6/11/70	California	Carson, Calif.	FA
Velicer, Ted	G	6-3	287	10/15/69	Iowa	Green Bay, Wis.	FA
Warren, Terrence	WR	6-1	200	8/2/69	Hampton	Suffolk, Va.	D5
Webb, David	LB	6-4	227	11/14/69	Southern California	Irvine, Calif.	FA
Wells, Dean	LB	6-3	238	7/20/70	Kentucky	Louisville, Ky.	D4
Wisdom, Terrence	G	6-4	297	12/4/71	Syracuse	Roosevelt, N.Y.	FA

The term NFL Rookie is defined as a player who is in his first season of professional football and has not been on the roster of another professional football team for any regular-season or postseason games. A Rookie is designated by an "R" on NFL rosters. Players who have been active in another professional football league or players who have NFL experience, including either preseason training camp or being on an Active List or Inactive List, or on Reserve/Injured or Reserve/Physically Unable to Perform for fewer than six regular-season games, are termed NFL First-Year Players. An NFL First-Year Player is designated by a "1" on NFL rosters. Thereafter, a player is credited with an additional year of experience for each season in which he accumulates six games on the Active List or Inactive List, or on Reserve/Injured or Reserve/Physically Unable to Perform.

NOTES

Howard Mudd, offensive line; born February 10, 1942, Midland, Mich., lives in Kirkland, Wash. Guard Hillsdale College 1961-63. Pro guard San Francisco 49ers 1964-69, Chicago Bears 1969-71. College coach: California 1972-73. Pro coach: San Diego Chargers 1974-76, San Francisco 49ers 1977, Seattle Seahawks 1978-82, Cleveland Browns 1983-88, Kansas City Chiefs 1989-92, rejoined Seahawks in 1993.

Russ Purnell, special teams-tight ends; born June 12, 1948, Chicago, Ill., lives in Bellevue, Wash. Center Orange Coast, Calif., J.C. 1966-67, Whittier College 1968-69. No pro playing experience. College coach: Whittier 1970-71, Southern California 1982-85. Pro coach: Joined Seahawks in 1986.

Frank Raines, strength and conditioning; born November 29, 1960, Portsmouth, Va., lives in Renton, Wash. No college or pro playing experience. Pro coach: Washington Redskins 1986-89, joined Seahawks in 1990.

Clarence Shelmon, running backs; born September 17, 1952, Bossier, La., lives in Kirkland, Wash. Running back Houston 1971-75. No pro playing experience. College coach: Army 1978-80, Indiana 1981-83, Arizona 1984-86, Southern California 1987-90. Pro coach: Los Angeles Rams 1991, joined Seahawks in 1992.

Rusty Tillman, defensive coordinator-linebackers; born February 27, 1948, Beloit, Wis., lives in Redmond, Wash. Linebacker Northern Arizona 1967-69. Pro linebacker Washington Redskins 1970-77. Pro coach: Joined Seahawks in 1979.

THE NFC

National Football Conference Western Division

Team Colors: Black, Red, Silver, and White

2745 Burnette Road
Suwanee, Georgia 30174
Telephone: (404) 945-1111

Club Officials

Chairman of the Board: Rankin M. Smith, Sr.
President: Taylor Smith
Vice President & Chief Financial Officer: Jim Hay
Vice President of Player Personnel: Ken Herock
Director of Player Development: Tommy Nobis
Director of Public Relations: Charlie Taylor
Director of Administration: Rob Jackson
Asst. Director of Public Relations: Frank Kleha
Public Relations Assistant: Todd Marble
Director of Community Relations: Carol Breeding
Director of Ticket Operations: Jack Ragsdale
Asst. Director of Ticket Operations: Luci Bailey
Administrative Asst./Finance: Kevin Anthony
Administrative Asst./Player Personnel: Danny Mock
Scouts: Bill Baker, Scott Campbell, Dick Corrick, Elbert Dubenion, Bill Groman
Director of Pro Personnel: Chuck Connor
Controller: Wallace Norman
Trainer: Jerry Rhea
Assistant Trainer: Billy Brooks
Equipment Manager: Whitey Zimmerman
Assistant Equipment Manager: Horace Daniel
Equipment Assistant: Craig Campanozzi
Video Director: Tom Atcheson
Assistant Video Director: Lou Crocker

Stadium: Georgia Dome • **Capacity:** 71,594
One Georgia Dome Drive
Atlanta, Georgia 30313

Playing Surface: Artificial turf

Training Camp: 2745 Burnette Road
Suwanee, Georgia 30174

1993 Schedule

Preseason

Aug. 6	**Miami**	7:30
Aug. 14	**Tampa Bay**	7:30
Aug. 21	at Philadelphia	7:30
Aug. 27	at Buffalo	8:00

Regular Season

Sept. 5	at Detroit	1:00
Sept. 12	**New Orleans**	1:00
Sept. 19	at San Francisco	1:00
Sept. 27	**Pittsburgh** (Monday)	9:00
Oct. 3	at Chicago	12:00
Oct. 10	**Open Date**	
Oct. 14	**L.A. Rams** (Thursday)	7:30
Oct. 24	at New Orleans	12:00
Oct. 31	**Tampa Bay**	1:00
Nov. 7	**Open Date**	
Nov. 14	at Los Angeles Rams	1:00
Nov. 21	**Dallas**	1:00
Nov. 28	**Cleveland**	1:00
Dec. 5	at Houston	12:00
Dec. 11	**San Francisco** (Saturday)	4:00
Dec. 19	at Washington	1:00
Dec. 26	at Cincinnati	1:00
Jan. 2	**Phoenix**	1:00

Falcons Coaching History

(152-249-5)

1966-68	Norb Hecker*	4-26-1
1968-74	Norm Van Brocklin**	37-49-3
1974-76	Marion Campbell***	6-19-0
1976	Pat Peppler	3-6-0
1977-82	Leeman Bennett	47-44-0
1983-86	Dan Henning	22-41-1
1987-89	Marion Campbell****	11-32-0
1989	Jim Hanifan	0-4-0
1990-92	Jerry Glanville	22-28-0

*Released after three games in 1968
**Released after eight games in 1974
***Released after five games in 1976
****Retired after 12 games in 1989

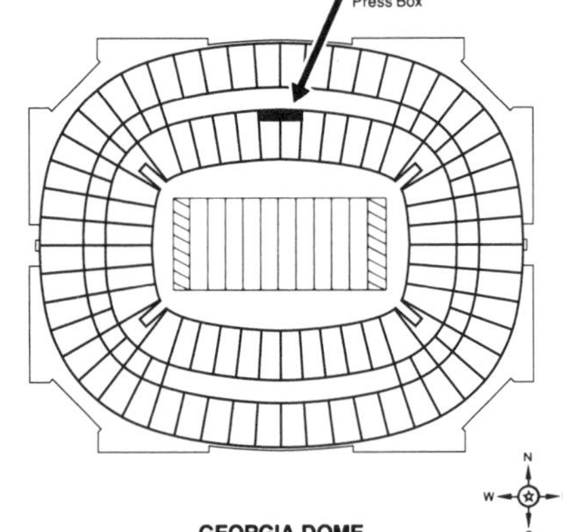

GEORGIA DOME

Record Holders

Individual Records — Career

Category	Name	Performance
Rushing (Yds.)	Gerald Riggs, 1982-88	6,631
Passing (Yds.)	Steve Bartkowski, 1975-1985	23,468
Passing (TDs)	Steve Bartkowski, 1975-1985	154
Receiving (No.)	Alfred Jenkins, 1975-1983	359
Receiving (Yds.)	Alfred Jenkins, 1975-1983	6,257
Interceptions	Rolland Lawrence, 1973-1980	39
Punting (Avg.)	Rick Donnelly, 1985-89	42.6
Punt Return (Avg.)	Al Dodd, 1973-74	11.8
Kickoff Return (Avg.)	Ron Smith, 1966-67	24.3
Field Goals	Mick Luckhurst, 1981-87	115
Touchdowns (Tot.)	Gerald Riggs, 1982-88	48
Points	Mick Luckhurst, 1981-87	558

Individual Records — Single Season

Category	Name	Performance
Rushing (Yds.)	Gerald Riggs, 1985	1,719
Passing (Yds.)	Steve Bartkowski, 1981	3,830
Passing (TDs)	Steve Bartkowski, 1980	31
Receiving (No.)	Andre Rison, 1992	93
Receiving (Yds.)	Alfred Jenkins, 1981	1,358
Interceptions	Scott Case, 1988	10
Punting (Avg.)	Billy Lothridge, 1968	44.3
Punt Return (Avg.)	Gerald Tinker, 1974	13.9
Kickoff Return (Avg.)	Sylvester Stamps, 1987	27.5
Field Goals	Nick Mike-Mayer, 1973	26
Touchdowns (Tot.)	Alfred Jenkins, 1981	13
	Gerald Riggs, 1984	13
Points	Mick Luckhurst, 1981	114

Individual Records — Single Game

Category	Name	Performance
Rushing (Yds.)	Gerald Riggs, 9-2-84	202
Passing (Yds.)	Steve Bartkowski, 11-15-81	416
Passing (TDs)	Wade Wilson, 12-13-92	5
Receiving (No.)	William Andrews, 11-15-81	15
Receiving (Yds.)	Alfred Jackson, 12-2-84	193
Interceptions	Many times	2
	Last time by Deion Sanders, 11-29-92	
Field Goals	Nick Mike-Mayer, 11-4-73	5
	Tim Mazzetti, 10-30-78	5
Touchdowns (Tot.)	Many times	3
	Last time by Andre Rison, 9-27-92	
Points	Many times	18
	Last time by Andre Rison, 9-27-92	

1992 Team Record

Preseason (1-3)

Date	Result		Opponents
8/8	L	0- 7	at Cleveland
8/15	L	28-40	at Tampa Bay
8/23	W	20-10	Philadelphia
8/28	L	21-27	Buffalo

Regular Season (6-10)

Date	Result		Opponents	Att.
9/6	W	20-17	N.Y. Jets	69,045
9/13	L	17-24	at Washington	55,459
9/20	L	7-10	New Orleans	69,820
9/27	L	31-41	at Chicago	66,094
10/4	W	24-10	Green Bay	69,120
10/11	L	17-21	at Miami	70,765
10/18	L	17-56	at San Francisco	65,446
11/1	W	30-28	L.A. Rams	69,503
11/9	L	3-41	San Francisco	69,898
11/15	W	20-17	Phoenix	68,377
11/22	L	14-41	at Buffalo	78,983
11/29	W	34- 0	New England	68,416
12/3	L	14-22	at New Orleans	67,604
12/13	W	35- 7	at Tampa Bay	42,783
12/21	L	17-41	Dallas	69,800
12/27	L	27-38	at L.A. Rams	44,627

Score by Periods

Falcons	94	96	55	82	0	—	327
Opponents	100	137	96	81	0	—	414

Attendance

Home 553,979 Away 491,761 Total 1,045,740
Single-game home record, 69,898 (11-9-92)
Single-season home record, 553,979 (1992)

1992 Team Statistics

	Falcons	Opp.
Total First Downs	273	304
Rushing	67	109
Passing	194	172
Penalty	12	23
Third Down: Made/Att.	73/190	81/189
Third Down: Pct.	38.4	42.9
Fourth Down: Made/Att.	5/14	1/6
Fourth Down: Pct.	35.7	16.7
Total Net Yards	4903	5549
Avg. Per Game	306.4	346.8
Total Plays	910	934
Avg. Per Play	5.4	5.9
Net Yards Rushing	1270	2294
Avg. Per Game	79.4	143.4
Total Rushes	322	464
Net Yards Passing	3633	3255
Avg. Per Game	227.1	203.4
Sacked/Yards Lost	40/259	31/241
Gross Yards	3892	3496
Att./Completions	548/336	439/277
Completion Pct.	61.3	63.1
Had Intercepted	15	11
Punts/Avg.	70/40.8	61/41.5
Net Punting Avg.	70/33.0	61/36.7
Penalties/Yards Lost	78/656	92/761
Fumbles/Ball Lost	30/14	24/12
Touchdowns	39	51
Rushing	3	20
Passing	33	24
Returns	3	7
Avg. Time of Possession	28:36	31:24

1992 Individual Statistics

Scoring	TD R	TD P	TD Rt	PAT	FG	Saf	TP
Johnson	0	0	0	39/39	18/22	0	93
Rison	0	11	0	0/0	0/0	0	66
Haynes	0	10	0	0/0	0/0	0	60
Pritchard	0	5	0	0/0	0/0	0	30
Hill	0	3	0	0/0	0/0	0	18
Sanders	0	1	2	0/0	0/0	0	18
Broussard	1	1	0	0/0	0/0	0	12
T. Smith	2	0	0	0/0	0/0	0	12
T. Jones	0	1	0	0/0	0/0	0	6
Phillips	0	1	0	0/0	0/0	0	6
Tuggle	0	0	1	0/0	0/0	0	6
Falcons	3	33	3	39/39	18/22	0	327
Opponents	20	24	7	51/51	19/31	0	414

Passing	Att.	Comp.	Yds.	Pct.	TD	Int.	Tkld.	Rate
Miller	253	152	1739	60.1	15	6	16/103	90.7
Wilson	163	111	1366	68.1	13	4	8/58	110.1
Tolliver	131	73	787	55.7	5	5	16/98	70.4
K. Jones	1	0	0	0.0	0	0	0/0	39.6
Falcons	548	336	3892	61.3	33	15	40/259	91.4
Opponents	439	277	3496	63.1	24	11	31/241	95.6

Rushing	Att.	Yds.	Avg.	LG	TD
Broussard	84	363	4.3	27	1
T. Smith	87	329	3.8	32	2
K. Jones	79	278	3.5	26	0
Miller	23	89	3.9	16	0
Pegram	21	89	4.2	15	0
Wilson	15	62	4.1	12	0
Pritchard	5	37	7.4	22	0
Tolliver	4	15	3.8	15	0
Solomon	2	12	6.0	12	0
Fulhage	1	0	0.0	0	0
Sanders	1	−4	−4.0	−4	0
Falcons	322	1270	3.9	32	3
Opponents	464	2294	4.9	64t	20

Receiving	No.	Yds.	Avg.	LG	TD
Rison	93	1119	12.0	71t	11
Pritchard	77	827	10.7	38t	5
Hill	60	623	10.4	43	3
Haynes	48	808	16.8	89t	10
T. Jones	14	138	9.9	24	1
K. Jones	12	94	7.8	15	0
Broussard	11	96	8.7	24	1
Thomas	6	54	9.0	18	0
Phillips	4	26	6.5	8	1
Sanders	3	45	15.0	37t	1
Milling	3	25	8.3	15	0
Pegram	2	25	12.5	19	0
T. Smith	2	14	7.0	8	0
Hinton	1	−2	−2.0	−2	0
Falcons	336	3892	11.6	89t	33
Opponents	277	3496	12.6	80t	24

Interceptions	No.	Yds.	Avg.	LG	TD
Sanders	3	105	35.0	55	0
Pickens	2	16	8.0	16	0
Case	2	0	0.0	0	0
Solomon	1	13	13.0	13	0
Tuggle	1	1	1.0	1	0
McKyer	1	0	0.0	0	0
Mitchell	1	0	0.0	0	0
Falcons	11	135	12.3	55	0
Opponents	15	246	16.4	48t	3

Punting	No.	Yds.	Avg.	In 20	LG
Fulhage	68	2818	41.4	11	56
Johnson	1	37	37.0	1	37
Falcons	70	2855	40.8	12	56
Opponents	61	2534	41.5	20	61

Punt Returns	No.	FC	Yds.	Avg.	LG	TD
T. Smith	16	4	155	9.7	45	0
Sanders	13	9	41	3.2	14	0
Phillips	0	1	0	—	—	0
Falcons	29	14	196	6.8	45	0
Opponents	44	10	482	11.0	61t	4

Kickoff Returns	No.	Yds.	Avg.	LG	TD
Sanders	40	1067	26.7	99t	2
Barnett	1	13	13.0	13	0
Fortin	1	5	5.0	5	0
K. Jones	6	114	19.0	29	0
Pegram	9	161	17.9	42	0
T. Smith	7	172	24.6	60	0
Falcons	64	1532	23.9	99t	2
Opponents	55	1059	19.3	39	0

Sacks	No.
Conner	7.0
Gardner	4.5
Solomon	4.5
Green	3.0
Tippins	3.0
Gann	2.0
C. Smith	2.0
Donaldson	1.0
McKyer	1.0
Pickens	1.0
Riddick	1.0
Tuggle	1.0
Falcons	31.0
Opponents	40.0

1993 Draft Choices

Round	Name	Pos.	College
1.	Lincoln Kennedy	T	Washington
2.	Roger Harper	DB	Ohio State
3.	Harold Alexander	P	Appalachian State
5.	Ron George	LB	Stanford
6.	Mitch Lyons	TE	Michigan State
7.	Darnell Walker	DB	Oklahoma
8.	Shannon Baker	WR	Florida State

Atlanta Falcons 1993 Veteran Roster

No.	Name	Pos.	Ht.	Wt.	Birth-date	NFL Exp.	College	Hometown	How Acq.	'92 Games/ Starts
68	Agee, Mel	DE-DT	6-5	298	11/22/68	2	Illinois	Chicago, Ill.	FA-'92	0*
44	Broussard, Steve	RB	5-7	201	2/22/67	4	Washington State	Los Angeles, Calif.	D1-'90	15/1
77	Bryan, Rick	DE	6-4	265	3/20/62	10	Oklahoma	Coweta, Okla.	D1-'84	0*
25	Case, Scott	S	6-1	188	5/17/62	10	Oklahoma	Edmond, Okla.	D2-'84	12/11
27	t-Clark, Vinnie	CB	6-0	194	1/22/69	3	Ohio State	Cincinnati, Ohio	T(GB)-'93	16/11*
56	†Conner, Darion	LB	6-2	245	9/28/67	4	Jackson State	Prairie Point, Miss.	D2-'90	16/16
51	Dinkins, Howard	LB	6-1	223	4/26/69	2	Florida State	Jacksonville, Fla.	D3-'92	0*
42	#Donaldson, Jeff	S	6-1	190	4/19/62	10	Colorado	Ft. Collins, Colo.	PB(Hou)-'91	16/16
64	Dukes, Jamie	C	6-1	285	6/14/64	8	Florida State	Orlando, Fla.	FA-'86	16/16
32	#Eaton, Tracey	S	6-1	195	7/19/65	6	Portland State	Medford, Ore.	PB(Hou)-'91	0*
74	Epps, Tory	NT	6-1	280	5/29/67	4	Memphis State	Uniontown, Pa.	D8-'90	16/5
29	Fishback, Joe	S	6-0	212	11/29/67	4	Carson-Newman	Knoxville, Tenn.	FA-'92	8/0
53	Forde, Brian	LB	6-3	235	11/1/63	6	Washington State	Montreal, Canada	PB(NO)-'92	0*
65	Fortin, Roman	G	6-5	285	2/26/67	4	San Diego State	Ventura, Calif.	PB(Det)-'92	16/1
17	Fulhage, Scott	P	6-1	193	11/17/61	7	Kansas State	Beloit, Kan.	FA-'89	16/0
76	Gann, Mike	DE	6-5	270	10/19/63	9	Notre Dame	Lakewood, Colo.	D2-'85	13/13
67	Gardner, Moe	NT	6-2	258	8/10/68	3	Illinois	Indianapolis, Ind.	D4-'91	16/14
97	Geathers, Jumpy	DT	6-7	290	6/26/60	10	Wichita State	Lafayette Hills, Pa.	UFA(Wash)-'93	16/0*
99	#Green, Tim	DE	6-2	245	12/16/63	8	Syracuse	Liverpool, N.Y.	D1-'86	12/11
81	Haynes, Michael	WR	6-1	180	12/24/65	6	Northern Arizona	New Orleans, La.	D7-'88	14/14
3	Hebert, Bobby	QB	6-4	215	8/19/60	8	Northwestern Louisiana	Mandeville, La.	UFA(NO)-'93	16/16*
85	Hill, Drew	WR	5-9	172	10/5/56	15	Georgia Tech	Newnan, Ga.	PB(Hou)-'92	16/14
75	Hinton, Chris	T	6-4	300	7/31/61	11	Northwestern	Chicago, Ill.	T(Ind)-'90	16/16
95	Holt, Pierce	DE	6-4	280	1/1/62	6	Angelo State	Marlin, Tex.	RFA(SF)-'93	16/16*
20	Jenkins, Melvin	CB	5-10	173	6/16/62	7	Cincinnati	Jacksonville, Miss.	UFA(Det)-'93	16/16*
9	Johnson, Norm	K	6-2	203	5/31/60	12	UCLA	Garden Grove, Calif.	FA-'91	16/0
38	†Jones, Keith	RB	6-1	210	3/20/66	5	Illinois	Rock Hills, Mo.	D3-'89	16/8
83	Jones, Tony	WR	5-7	145	12/30/65	4	Texas	Grapeland, Tex.	PB(Hou)-'92	10/4
78	Kenn, Mike	T	6-7	280	2/9/56	16	Michigan	Evanston, Ill.	D1-'87	16/16
88	†Le Bel, Harper	TE	6-4	245	7/14/63	5	Colorado State	Sherman Oaks, Calif.	PB(Phil)-'91	16/2
12	Miller, Chris	QB	6-2	205	8/9/65	7	Oregon	Eugene, Ore.	D1-'87	8/8
87	Milling, James	WR	5-9	160	2/14/65	5	Maryland	Oxon Hill, Md.	PB(NYG)-'92	5/0
24	Mitchell, Brian	CB	5-9	164	12/13/68	3	Brigham Young	Waco, Tex.	FA-'93	16/0*
22	t-Montgomery, Alton	S	6-0	195	6/16/68	4	Houston	Griffin, Ga.	T(Den)-'93	12/1*
36	Moore, Derrick	RB	6-1	227	10/13/67	2	Northeast Oklahoma St.	Albany, Ga.	D8a-'92	0*
33	Pegram, Erric	RB	5-9	188	1/7/69	3	North Texas State	Dallas, Tex.	D6-'91	16/1
82	Phillips, Jason	WR	5-7	166	10/11/66	5	Houston	Houston, Tex.	PB(Det)-'91	12/0
39	Pickens, Bruce	CB	5-11	190	5/9/68	3	Nebraska	Kansas City, Mo.	D1a-'91	16/4
35	Pritchard, Mike	WR	5-11	180	10/25/69	3	Colorado	Las Vegas, Nev.	D1b-'91	16/15
30	Ray, Terry	S	6-1	187	10/12/69	2	Oklahoma	Killeen, Tex.	D6-'92	10/2
26	Riddick, Louis	S	6-2	216	3/15/69	2	Pittsburgh	Quakertown, Pa.	FA-'92	16/4
80	Rison, Andre	WR	6-1	188	3/18/67	5	Michigan State	Flint, Mich.	T(Ind)-'90	15/13
41	Rouse, James	RB	6-0	220	12/18/66	4	Arkansas	Mundelein, Ill.	FA-'93	0*
55	Ruether, Mike	C	6-4	286	9/20/62	8	Texas	Shawnee Mission, Kan.	FA-'90	16/0
21	Sanders, Deion	CB	6-1	185	8/9/67	5	Florida State	Ft. Myers, Fla.	D1-'89	13/12
37	#Shelley, Elbert	CB	5-11	185	12/24/64	7	Arkansas State	Tyronza, Ark.	D11-'87	13/0
90	Smith, Chuck	DE	6-2	242	12/21/69	2	Tennessee	Athens, Ga.	D2-'92	16/0
28	Smith, Tony	RB	6-1	214	6/29/70	2	Southern Mississippi	Vicksburg, Miss.	D1b-'92	14/6
54	#Solomon, Jesse	LB	6-0	235	11/4/63	8	Florida State	Madison, Fla.	FA-'92	16/14
49	Stonebreaker, Michael	LB	6-0	235	1/14/67	2	Notre Dame	Glencoe, Ill.	FA-'93	0*
52	Tippins, Ken	LB	6-1	230	7/22/66	5	Middle Tennessee State	Adel, Ga.	FA-'90	16/15
11	†Tolliver, Billy Joe	QB	6-1	218	2/7/66	5	Texas Tech	Boyd, Tex.	T(SD)-'91	9/5
58	Tuggle, Jessie	LB	5-11	230	2/14/65	7	Valdosta State	Spalding, Ga.	FA-'87	15/15
70	Whitfield, Bob	T	6-5	291	10/18/71	2	Stanford	Carson, Calif.	D1a-'92	11/0

* Agee was active for 1 game in '92 but did not play; Bryan, Dinkins, Eaton, Forde, Moore, Rouse, and Stonebreaker missed '92 season due to injury; Clark played 16 games with Green Bay in '92; Geathers played 16 games with Washington; Hebert played 16 games with New Orleans; Holt played 16 games with San Francisco; Jenkins played 16 games with Detroit; Mitchell last active with Dallas in '91; Montgomery played 12 games with Denver.

Unrestricted free agent; subject to developments.

† Restricted free agent; subject to developments.

t- Falcons traded for Clark (Green Bay), Montgomery (Denver).

Players lost through free agency (5): DE Oliver Barnett (Buff; 16 games in '92), G Bill Fralic (Det; 16), G Houston Hoover (Clev; 16), DE John Washington (NE; 3), QB Wade Wilson (NO; 9).

Also played with Falcons in '92—CB Bobby Butler (15 games), NT Bill Goldberg (4), CB Tim McKyer (16), LB Michael Reid (16).

COACHING STAFF

Head Coach, Jerry Glanville

Pro Career: Led Atlanta to a 10-6 regular-season record in 1991 and a spot in the NFC playoffs for first time since 1982. Named Falcons' head coach on January 14, 1990. Served as Houston Oilers' head coach from the last two games of the 1985 season through 1989. Guided Oilers to three consecutive playoff berths (1987-89), posting a 28-19 mark in the process. Under his direction, Houston was one of only four NFL teams to make the playoffs during those years. The 51-year-old Glanville took over a team that had suffered five consecutive losing seasons and turned the club into winners in his second season at the helm. As an assistant coach, he was part of three playoff teams and one division title winner in Atlanta. He helped the 1977 team establish the modern-day record for fewest points allowed in a season (129 over 14 games) with his attacking "Gritz Blitz" defense. Career record: 57-63.

Background: Attended Montana State in 1960 before transferring to Northern Michigan, where he played linebacker from 1961-63. He coached in the Ohio high school system from 1964-66 before accepting an assistant coaching post at Western Kentucky in 1967. From 1968-73, he was an assistant at Georgia Tech, helping the Yellow Jackets to three bowl games.

Personal: Born October 14, 1941, in Detroit, Mich. Jerry and his wife, Brenda, live in Roswell, Ga., with their son, Justin.

Assistant Coaches

Bobby April, Jr., special teams, tight ends; born April 15, 1953, New Orleans, La., lives in Atlanta. Linebacker Nicholls State 1972-75. No pro playing experience. College coach: Tulane 1979, Arizona 1980-86, Southern California 1987-90. Pro coach: Joined Falcons in 1991.

Jimmy Carr, secondary; born March 25, 1933, Kayford, W. Va., lives in Atlanta. Running back-defensive back-linebacker Morris Harvey (now University of Charleston, W. Va.) 1951-54. Pro running back-defensive back-linebacker Chicago Cardinals 1955-57, Montreal Alouettes (CFL) 1958, Philadelphia Eagles 1959-63, Washington Redskins 1964-65. Pro coach: Minnesota Vikings 1966-68, 1979-81, Chicago Bears 1969, 1973-74, Philadelphia Eagles 1970-72, Detroit Lions 1975-76, Buffalo Bills 1977, San Francisco 49ers 1978, Denver Gold (USFL) 1983-84, New England Patriots 1985-89, joined Falcons in 1990.

June Jones, assistant head coach-offense; born February 19, 1953, Portland, Ore., lives in Atlanta. Quarterback Hawaii 1973-74, Portland State 1975-76. Pro quarterback Atlanta Falcons 1977-81, Toronto Argonauts (CFL) 1982. College coach: Hawaii 1983. Pro coach: Toronto Argonauts (CFL) 1982, Houston Gamblers (USFL) 1984, Denver Gold (USFL) 1985, Houston Oilers 1987-88, Detroit Lions 1989-90, joined Falcons in 1991.

Tim Jorgensen, strength and conditioning; born April 21, 1955, St. Louis, Mo., lives in Snellville, Ga. Guard Southwest Missouri State 1974-76. No pro playing experience. College coach: Southwest Missouri State 1977-78, Alabama 1979, Louisiana State 1980-83. Pro coach: Philadelphia Eagles 1984-86, joined Falcons in 1987.

Bill Kollar, defensive line; born November 12, 1952, Warren, Ohio, lives in Atlanta. Defensive end Montana State 1971-74. Pro defensive end Cincinnati Bengals 1974-76, Tampa Bay Buccaneers 1977-81. College coach: Illinois 1985-87, Purdue 1988-89. Pro coach: Tampa Bay Buccaneers 1984, joined Falcons in 1990.

Jimmy Robinson, wide receivers; born January 3, 1953, Atlanta, lives in Atlanta. Wide receiver Georgia Tech 1972-74. Pro wide receiver Atlanta Falcons 1975, New York Giants 1976-79, San Francisco 49ers 1980, Denver Broncos 1981. College coach: Georgia Tech 1986-89. Pro coach: Memphis Showboats (USFL) 1984-85, joined Falcons in 1990.

Atlanta Falcons 1993 First-Year Roster

Name	Pos.	Ht.	Wt.	Birth-date	College	Hometown	How Acq.
Alex, Keith (1)	G	6-4	315	6/9/69	Texas A&M	Beaumont, Tex.	FA
Alexander, Harold	P	6-2	224	10/20/70	Appalachian State	Pickens, S.C.	D3
Avila, Estevan	NT	6-3	285	10/27/69	Stanford	Sebastopol, Calif.	FA
Baker, Shannon	WR	5-9	185	7/20/71	Florida State	Lakeland, Fla.	D8
Baldwin, Derek	WR	6-0	175	7/30/71	Portland State	Portland, Ore.	FA
Beatty, Greg	WR	5-11	185	7/1/70	Ohio State	Houston, Tex.	FA
Brooks, Horace	WR	5-8	170	12/12/70	Alabama State	Tuskegee, Ala.	FA
Buddenberg, John (1)	G-T	6-6	285	10/9/65	Akron	Bellaire, Ohio	FA
Charles, John	QB	5-11	211	8/18/71	Portland State	Mountain View, Calif.	FA
Davis, Darrick	CB	5-8	153	9/29/69	Idaho	Gardena, Calif.	FA
George, Ron	LB	6-2	225	3/20/70	Stanford	Heidelberg, Germany	D5
Giannetti, Frank (1)	LB	6-2	267	3/14/68	Penn State	University Park, Pa.	FA
Giles, Oscar (1)	LB	6-2	246	9/27/68	Texas	Dallas, Tex.	FA
Goldberg, Bill (1)	NT	6-2	266	12/27/66	Georgia	Tulsa, Okla.	FA
Grant, Marcus (1)	WR	5-9	172	9/12/70	Houston	Dallas, Tex.	FA
Hall, Les	T	6-6	313	8/8/70	Clemson	Columbia, S.C.	FA
Hardy, Darryl (1)	LB	6-2	220	11/22/68	Tennessee	Cincinnati, Ohio	D10-'92
Harper, Roger	S	6-2	223	10/26/70	Ohio State	Columbus, Ohio	D2
Kalal, Tim	P	6-3	205	9/13/67	Miami	Longview, Wash.	FA
Kennedy, Lincoln	T-G	6-6	340	2/12/71	Washington	San Diego, Calif.	D1
Lyons, Mitch	TE	6-4	255	6/13/70	Michigan State	Grand Rapids, Mich.	D6
Mims, David	WR	5-8	191	7/7/70	Baylor	Daingerfield, Tex.	FA
Ostroski, Jerry (1)	G	6-3	316	7/12/70	Tulsa	Collegeville, Pa.	FA
Rollins, Baron	G	6-4	330	7/23/70	Louisiana Tech	Winnsboro, La.	FA
Sims, Kelly (1)	CB	5-10	200	11/10/70	Cincinnati	St. Petersburg, Fla.	FA
Spencer, Darryl	WR	5-8	173	3/21/70	Miami	Merritt Island, Fla.	FA
Stevenson, Robert	C	6-1	281	12/20/69	Florida State	Pensacola, Fla.	FA
Styles, Lorenzo	G	6-5	282	10/19/70	West Virginia	Miami, Fla.	FA
Tobeck, Robbie	C	6-4	275	3/6/70	Washington State	Tarpon Springs, Fla.	FA
Walker, Darnell	CB	5-8	164	1/17/70	Oklahoma	St. Louis, Mo.	D7
Wallace, Anthony (1)	RB	6-0	191	7/8/69	California	Pasadena, Calif.	FA

The term NFL Rookie is defined as a player who is in his first season of professional football and has not been on the roster of another professional football team for any regular-season or postseason games. A Rookie is designated by an "R" on NFL rosters. Players who have been active in another professional football league or players who have NFL experience, including either preseason training camp or being on an Active List or Inactive List, or on Reserve/Injured or Reserve/Physically Unable to Perform for fewer than six regular-season games, are termed NFL First-Year Players. An NFL First-Year Player is designated by a "1" on NFL rosters. Thereafter, a player is credited with an additional year of experience for each season in which he accumulates six games on the Active List or Inactive List, or on Reserve/Injured or Reserve/Physically Unable to Perform.

NOTES

Keith Rowen, offensive line; born September 2, 1952, New York, N.Y., lives in Atlanta. Offensive tackle Stanford 1972-74. No pro playing experience. College coach: Stanford 1975-76, Long Beach State 1977-78, Arizona 1979-82. Pro coach: Boston/New Orleans Breakers (USFL) 1983-84, Cleveland Browns 1984, Indianapolis Colts 1985-88, New England Patriots 1989, joined Falcons in 1990.

Doug Shively, assistant head coach-defense; born March 18, 1938, Lexington, Ky., lives in Atlanta. End Kentucky 1955-58. No pro playing experience. College coach: Virginia Tech 1960-66, Kentucky 1967-70, Clemson 1971-72, North Carolina 1973. Pro coach: New Orleans Saints 1974-76, Atlanta Falcons 1977-82, Arizona Wranglers (USFL) 1983 (head coach), San Diego Chargers 1984, Tampa Bay Buccaneers 1985, Houston Oilers 1986-89, rejoined Falcons in 1990.

Ollie Wilson, running backs; born March 31, 1951, Worcester, Mass., lives in Atlanta. Wide receiver Springfield 1971-73. No pro playing experience. College coach: Springfield 1975, Northeastern 1976-82, California 1983-90. Pro coach: Joined Falcons in 1991.

CHICAGO BEARS

National Football Conference Central Division

Team Colors: Navy Blue, Orange, and White

Halas Hall, 250 North Washington
Lake Forest, Illinois 60045
Telephone: (708) 295-6600

Club Officials

Chairman of the Board: Edward W. McCaskey
President and CEO: Michael B. McCaskey
Secretary: Virginia H. McCaskey
Vice President: Tim McCaskey
Vice President of Operations: Ted Phillips
Dir. of College Scouting: Rod Graves
Dir. of Administration: Tim LeFevour
Dir. of Community Relations: Pat McCaskey
Player Liaison: Brian McCaskey
Dir. of Marketing/Communications: Ken Valdiserri
Dir. of Public Relations: Bryan Harlan
Asst. Director of Public Relations: John Bostrom
Public Relations Assistant: Doug Green
Ticket Manager: George McCaskey
Computer Systems: Greg Gershuny
Video Director: Mitch Friedman
Trainer: Fred Caito
Strength Coordinator: Clyde Emrich
Physical Dev. Coordinator: Russ Reiderer
Equipment Manager: Gary Haeger
Assistant Equipment Manager: Tony Medlin
Scouts: Gary Smith, Ken Geiger, Jeff Shiver, Charlie Mackey, Bobby Riggle

Stadium: Soldier Field • **Capacity:** 66,950
425 McFetridge Place
Chicago, Illinois 60605

Playing Surface: Grass

Training Camp: University of Wisconsin-Platteville
Platteville, Wisconsin 53818

1993 Schedule

Preseason

Aug. 8	at Philadelphia	8:00
Aug. 14	**Phoenix**	7:00
Aug. 23	at New Orleans	7:00
Aug. 27	**Dallas**	7:30

Regular Season

Sept. 5	**New York Giants**	3:00
Sept. 12	at Minnesota	12:00
Sept. 19	**Open Date**	
Sept. 26	**Tampa Bay**	12:00
Oct. 3	**Atlanta**	12:00
Oct. 10	at Philadelphia	1:00
Oct. 17	**Open Date**	
Oct. 25	**Minnesota** (Monday)	8:00
Oct. 31	at Green Bay	12:00
Nov. 7	**Los Angeles Raiders**	3:00
Nov. 14	at San Diego	5:00
Nov. 21	at Kansas City	12:00
Nov. 25	at Detroit (Thanksgiving)	12:30
Dec. 5	**Green Bay**	12:00
Dec. 12	at Tampa Bay	1:00
Dec. 18	**Denver** (Saturday)	11:30
Dec. 26	**Detroit**	12:00
Jan. 2	at Los Angeles Rams	1:00

Bears Coaching History

Decatur Staleys 1920
Chicago Staleys 1921
(579-375-42)

1920-29	George Halas	84-31-19
1930-32	Ralph Jones	24-10-7
1933-42	George Halas*	88-24-4
1942-45	Hunk Anderson-Luke Johnsos**	24-12-2
1946-55	George Halas	76-43-2
1956-57	John (Paddy) Driscoll	14-10-1
1958-67	George Halas	76-53-6
1968-71	Jim Dooley	20-36-0
1972-74	Abe Gibron	11-30-1
1975-77	Jack Pardee	20-23-0
1978-81	Neill Armstrong	30-35-0
1982-92	Mike Ditka	112-68-0

*Retired after five games to enter U.S. Navy
**Co-coaches

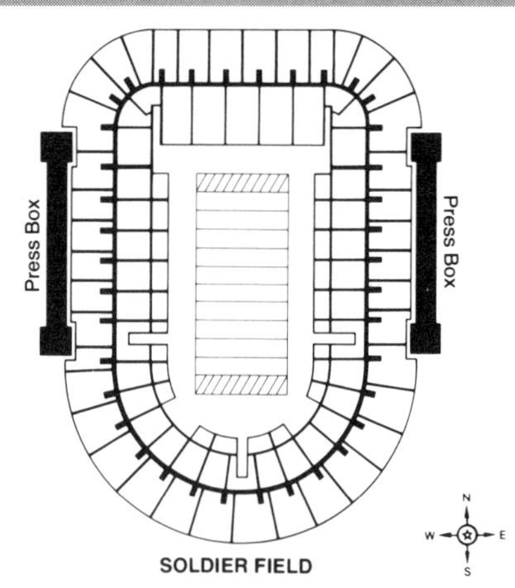

SOLDIER FIELD

Record Holders

Individual Records — Career

Category	Name	Performance
Rushing (Yds.)	Walter Payton, 1975-1987	*16,726
Passing (Yds.)	Sid Luckman, 1939-1950	14,686
Passing (TDs)	Sid Luckman, 1939-1950	137
Receiving (No.)	Walter Payton, 1975-1987	492
Receiving (Yds.)	Johnny Morris, 1958-1967	5,059
Interceptions	Gary Fencik, 1976-1987	38
Punting (Avg.)	George Gulyanics, 1947-1952	44.5
Punt Return (Avg.)	Ray (Scooter) McLean, 1940-47	14.8
Kickoff Return (Avg.)	Gale Sayers, 1965-1971	30.6
Field Goals	Kevin Butler, 1985-1992	172
Touchdowns (Tot.)	Walter Payton, 1975-1987	125
Points	Kevin Butler, 1985-1992	813

Individual Records — Single Season

Category	Name	Performance
Rushing (Yds.)	Walter Payton, 1977	1,852
Passing (Yds.)	Bill Wade, 1962	3,172
Passing (TDs)	Sid Luckman, 1943	28
Receiving (No.)	Johnny Morris, 1964	93
Receiving (Yds.)	Johnny Morris, 1964	1,200
Interceptions	Mark Carrier, 1990	10
Punting (Avg.)	Bobby Joe Green, 1963	46.5
Punt Return (Avg.)	Harry Clark, 1943	15.8
Kickoff Return (Avg.)	Gale Sayers, 1967	37.7
Field Goals	Kevin Butler, 1985	31
Touchdowns (Tot.)	Gale Sayers, 1965	**22
Points	Kevin Butler, 1985	**144

Individual Records — Single Game

Category	Name	Performance
Rushing (Yds.)	Walter Payton, 11-20-77	*275
Passing (Yds.)	Johnny Lujack, 12-11-49	468
Passing (TDs)	Sid Luckman, 11-14-43	*7
Receiving (No.)	Jim Keane, 10-23-49	14
Receiving (Yds.)	Harlon Hill, 10-31-54	214
Interceptions	Many times	3
	Last time by Mark Carrier, 12-9-90	
Field Goals	Roger LeClerc, 12-3-61	5
	Mac Percival, 10-20-68	5
Touchdowns (Tot.)	Gale Sayers, 12-12-65	*6
Points	Gale Sayers, 12-12-65	36

*NFL Record
**NFL Rookie Record

1992 Team Record

Preseason (1-3)

Date	Result		Opponents
8/8	L	31-34	New Orleans
8/15	L	17-20	at Phoenix
8/23	L	17-28	Pittsburgh
8/28	W	20-13	at Dallas

Regular Season (5-11)

Date	Result		Opponents	Att.
9/6	W	27-24	Detroit	66,101
9/13	L	6-28	at New Orleans	67,633
9/21	L	14-27	N.Y. Giants	66,091
9/27	W	41-31	Atlanta	66,094
10/4	L	20-21	at Minnesota	62,510
10/18	W	31-14	Tampa Bay	65,973
10/25	W	30-10	at Green Bay	58,672
11/2	L	10-38	Minnesota	66,091
11/8	L	28-31	Cincinnati (OT)	66,006
11/15	L	17-20	at Tampa Bay	72,607
11/22	L	3-17	Green Bay	66,075
11/29	L	14-27	at Cleveland	73,727
12/7	L	7-24	at Houston	62,408
12/13	W	30- 6	Pittsburgh	66,034
12/20	L	3-16	at Detroit	75,804
12/27	L	14-27	at Dallas	63,208

(OT) Overtime

Score by Periods

Bears	57	98	51	89	0	—	295
Opponents	58	83	93	124	3	—	361

Attendance

Home 528,465 Away 536,569 Total 1,165,034
Single-game home record, 66,475 (9-17-89)
Single-season home record, 528,465 (1992)

1992 Team Statistics

	Bears	Opp.
Total First Downs	282	274
Rushing	101	109
Passing	157	144
Penalty	24	21
Third Down: Made/Att.	72/198	69/194
Third Down: Pct.	36.4	35.6
Fourth Down: Made/Att.	5/16	9/20
Fourth Down: Pct.	31.3	45.0
Total Net Yards	4941	4952
Avg. Per Game	308.8	309.5
Total Plays	951	953
Avg. Per Play	5.2	5.2
Net Yards Rushing	1871	1948
Avg. Per Game	116.9	121.8
Total Rushes	427	468
Net Yards Passing	3070	3004
Avg. Per Game	191.9	187.8
Sacked/Yards Lost	45/264	43/286
Gross Yards	3334	3290
Att./Completions	479/266	442/261
Completion Pct.	55.5	59.0
Had Intercepted	24	14
Punts/Avg.	79/42.9	70/40.6
Net Punting Avg.	79/36.2	70/35.2
Penalties/Yards Lost	93/776	90/780
Fumbles/Ball Lost	23/10	34/16
Touchdowns	34	43
Rushing	15	14
Passing	17	20
Returns	2	9
Avg. Time of Possession	29:15	30:45

1992 Individual Statistics

Scoring	TD R	TD P	TD Rt	PAT	FG	Saf	TP
Butler	0	0	0	34/34	19/26	0	91
Anderson	5	6	0	0/0	0/0	0	66
Lewis	4	0	1	0/0	0/0	0	30
Muster	3	2	0	0/0	0/0	0	30
Waddle	0	4	0	0/0	0/0	0	24
Davis	0	2	0	0/0	0/0	0	12
Green	2	0	0	0/0	0/0	0	12
Morgan	0	2	0	0/0	0/0	0	12
Harbaugh	1	0	0	0/0	0/0	0	6
Jennings	0	1	0	0/0	0/0	0	6
Zorich	0	0	1	0/0	0/0	0	6
Bears	15	17	2	34/34	19/26	0	295
Opponents	14	20	9	43/43	20/25	0	361

Passing	Att.	Comp.	Yds.	Pct.	TD	Int.	Tkld.	Rate
Harbaugh	358	202	2486	56.4	13	12	31/167	76.2
Willis	92	54	716	58.7	4	8	10/58	61.7
Furrer	25	9	89	36.0	0	3	4/39	7.3
Gardocki	3	1	43	33.3	0	0	0/0	81.9
Muster	1	0	0	0.0	0	1	0/0	0.0
Bears	479	266	3334	55.5	17	24	45/264	68.3
Opponents	442	261	3290	59.0	20	14	43/286	84.2

Rushing	Att.	Yds.	Avg.	LG	TD
Anderson	156	582	3.7	49t	5
Muster	98	414	4.2	35	3
Lewis	90	382	4.2	33	4
Harbaugh	47	272	5.8	17	1
Green	23	107	4.7	18	2
Morgan	3	68	22.7	35	0
Davis	4	42	10.5	21	0
Gentry	5	2	0.4	3	0
Willis	1	2	2.0	2	0
Bears	427	1871	4.4	49t	15
Opponents	468	1948	4.2	44	14

Receiving	No.	Yds.	Avg.	LG	TD
Davis	54	734	13.6	40	2
Waddle	46	674	14.7	68t	4
Anderson	42	399	9.5	30t	6
Muster	34	389	11.4	44t	2
Jennings	23	264	11.5	23	1
Lewis	18	175	9.7	30	0
Morgan	14	323	23.1	83t	2
Gentry	12	114	9.5	18	0
Green	7	85	12.1	43	0
Wright	5	56	11.2	24	0
Blackwell	5	54	10.8	18	0
Morris	4	44	11.0	26	0
Wagner	1	16	16.0	16	0
Kozlowski	1	7	7.0	7	0
Bears	266	3334	12.5	83t	17
Opponents	261	3290	12.6	72t	20

Interceptions	No.	Yds.	Avg.	LG	TD
Woolford	7	67	9.6	32	0
Stinson	2	46	23.0	46	0
Gayle	2	39	19.5	30	0
Morrissey	1	22	22.0	22	0
Paul	1	10	10.0	10	0
Singletary	1	4	4.0	4	0
Bears	14	188	13.4	46	0
Opponents	24	612	25.5	92t	6

Punting	No.	Yds.	Avg.	In 20	LG
Gardocki	79	3393	42.9	19	61
Bears	79	3393	42.9	19	61
Opponents	70	2840	40.6	18	61

Punt Returns	No.	FC	Yds.	Avg.	LG	TD
Woolford	12	3	127	10.6	36	0
Waddle	8	10	28	3.5	13	0
Morgan	3	1	21	7.0	13	0
Bears	23	14	176	7.7	36	0
Opponents	38	15	351	9.2	75t	1

Kickoff Returns	No.	Yds.	Avg.	LG	TD
Lewis	23	511	22.2	97t	1
Gentry	16	330	20.6	66	0
Green	11	224	20.4	29	0
Leeuwenburg	1	7	7.0	7	0
Morgan	4	71	17.8	30	0
Rivera	1	0	0.0	0	0
Bears	56	1143	20.4	97t	1
Opponents	50	1027	20.5	55	0

Sacks	No.
McMichael	10.5
Dent	8.5
Armstrong	6.5
Spellman	4.0
Ryan	3.0
Roper	2.5
Perry	2.0
Zorich	2.0
Cox	1.0
Morrissey	1.0
Rivera	1.0
Singletary	1.0
Bears	43.0
Opponents	45.0

1993 Draft Choices

Round	Name	Pos.	College
1.	Curtis Conway	WR	Southern California
2.	Carl Simpson	DT	Florida State
3.	Chris Gedney	TE	Syracuse
4.	Todd Perry	G	Kentucky
	Myron Baker	LB	Louisiana Tech
	Albert Fontenot	DE	Baylor
6.	Dave Hoffmann	LB	Washington
7.	Keshon Johnson	DB	Arizona

Chicago Bears 1993 Veteran Roster

No.	Name	Pos.	Ht.	Wt.	Birth-date	NFL Exp.	College	Hometown	How Acq.	'92 Games/ Starts
79	Age, Louis	T	6-7	350	2/1/70	2	Southwestern Louisiana	New Orleans, La.	D11-'92	6/0
35	Anderson, Neal	RB	5-11	215	8/14/64	8	Florida	Graceville, Fla.	D1-'86	16/11
93	Armstrong, Trace	DE	6-4	265	10/5/65	5	Florida	Birmingham, Ala.	D1b-'89	14/14
70	Auzenne, Troy	T	6-7	290	6/26/69	2	California	Baldwin Park, Calif.	D2-'92	16/16
89	Blackwell, Kelly	TE	6-1	225	2/13/69	2	Texas Christian	Ft. Worth, Tex.	FA-'92	16/2
47	Blaylock, Anthony	CB	5-10	185	2/21/65	6	Winston-Salem State	Raleigh, N.C.	UFA(SD)-'93	11/10*
62	Bortz, Mark	G	6-6	282	2/12/61	11	Iowa	Pardeeville, Wis.	D8-'83	12/12
6	Butler, Kevin	K	6-1	190	7/24/62	9	Georgia	Redan, Ga.	D4-'85	16/0
95	Cain, Joe	LB	6-1	233	6/11/65	5	Oregon Tech	Compton, Calif.	RFA(Sea)-'93	16/8*
20	Carrier, Mark	S	6-1	192	4/28/68	4	Southern California	Long Beach, Calif.	D1-'90	16/14
96	Cooper, Reggie	LB	6-2	215	7/11/68	2	Nebraska	Slidell, La.	FA-'93	2/0
54	Cox, Ron	LB	6-2	235	2/27/68	4	Fresno State	Fresno, Calif.	D2b-'90	16/3
82	Davis, Wendell	WR	5-11	188	1/3/66	6	Louisiana State	Shreveport, La.	D1-'88	16/15
95	Dent, Richard	DE	6-5	265	12/13/60	11	Tennessee State	Atlanta, Ga.	D8-'83	16/16
37	#Douglass, Maurice	CB	5-11	202	2/12/64	7	Kentucky	Dayton, Ohio	D8-'86	16/0
24	Fain, Richard	CB	5-10	180	2/29/68	3	Florida	Ft. Myers, Fla.	PB(Phx)-'92	16/6
67	†Fontenot, Jerry	G-C	6-3	287	11/21/66	5	Texas A&M	Lafayette, La.	D3-'89	16/16
2	Furrer, Will	QB	6-3	209	2/5/68	2	Virginia Tech	Pullman, Wash.	D4-'92	2/1
17	Gardocki, Chris	P-K	6-1	196	2/7/70	3	Clemson	Stone Mountain, Ga.	D3-'91	16/0
23	Gayle, Shaun	S	5-11	202	3/8/62	10	Ohio State	Bethel, Va.	D10-'84	11/11
31	Green, Mark	RB	5-11	190	3/22/67	5	Notre Dame	Technic, Calif.	D5a-'89	15/0
4	Harbaugh, Jim	QB	6-3	215	12/23/64	7	Michigan	Ann Arbor, Mich.	D1-'87	16/13
45	Heyward, Craig	RB	5-11	260	9/26/66	6	Pittsburgh	Passaic, N.J.	UFA(NO)-'93	16/13*
85	Jennings, Keith	TE	6-4	260	5/19/66	4	Clemson	Summerville, S.C.	FA-'91	16/14
53	Jones, Dante	LB	6-2	238	3/23/65	6	Oklahoma	Dallas, Tex.	D2-'88	13/0
64	Jurkovic, Mirko	G	6-3	290	5/19/70	2	Notre Dame	Calumet, Ill.	D9-'92	0*
88	#Kozlowski, Glen	WR	6-1	210	12/31/62	7	Brigham Young	Carlsbad, Calif.	D11-'86	4/0
58	Leeuwenburg, Jay	C	6-2	290	6/18/69	2	Colorado	Kirkwood, Mo.	W(KC)-'92	12/0
33	Lewis, Darren	RB	5-10	225	11/7/68	3	Texas A&M	Dallas, Tex.	D6-'91	16/5
39	Lincoln, Jeremy	CB	5-10	184	4/7/69	2	Tennessee	Toledo, Ohio	D3-'92	0*
26	†Mangum, John	CB	5-10	178	3/16/67	4	Alabama	Magee, Miss.	FA-'90	5/1
76	McMichael, Steve	DT	6-2	268	10/17/57	14	Texas	Freer, Tex.	FA-'81	16/16
81	Morgan, Anthony	WR	6-1	195	11/15/67	3	Tennessee	Cleveland, Ohio	D5-'91	12/4
84	Morris, Ron	WR	6-1	198	11/4/64	7	Southern Methodist	Cooper, Tex.	D2-'87	4/0
51	Morrissey, Jim	LB	6-3	225	12/24/62	9	Michigan State	Flint Powers, Mich.	D11-'85	16/14
36	Paul, Markus	S	6-2	200	4/1/66	5	Syracuse	Osceloa, Fla.	D4-'89	16/5
72	Perry, William	DT	6-2	335	12/16/62	9	Clemson	Aiken, S.C.	D1-'85	15/14
59	#Rivera, Ron	LB	6-3	234	1/7/62	10	California	Seaside, Calif.	D2-'84	16/0
55	†Roper, John	LB	6-1	235	10/4/65	5	Texas A&M	Houston, Tex.	D2a-'89	16/13
99	Ryan, Tim	DT	6-4	265	9/8/67	4	Southern California	Oak Grove, Calif.	D3a-'90	16/1
69	Smith, Vernice	G	6-3	298	10/24/65	5	Florida A&M	Orlando, Fla.	RFA(Phx)-'93	12/2*
90	Spellman, Alonzo	DE	6-4	282	9/27/71	2	Ohio State	Rancocas, N.J.	D1-'92	15/0
32	#Stinson, Lemuel	CB	5-9	180	5/10/66	6	Texas Tech	Houston, Tex.	D6-'88	16/11
57	Thayer, Tom	G	6-4	284	8/16/61	9	Notre Dame	Catholic, Ill.	D4-'83	16/16
60	Thomas, Stan	T	6-5	295	10/28/68	3	Texas	El Centro, Calif.	D1-'91	11/0
78	#Van Horne, Keith	T	6-6	290	11/6/57	13	Southern California	Fullerton, Calif.	D1-'81	16/16
87	Waddle, Tom	WR	6-0	185	2/20/67	4	Boston College	Cincinnati, Ohio	FA-'89	12/12
71	Williams, James	DT	6-7	335	3/29/68	3	Cheyney State	Allderdice, Pa.	FA-'91	5/0
10	†Willis, Peter Tom	QB	6-2	204	1/4/67	4	Florida State	Morris, Ala.	D3b-'90	9/2
73	#Wojciechowski, John	G	6-4	280	7/30/63	7	Michigan State	Fitzgerald, Mich.	FA-'87	16/4
21	Woolford, Donnell	CB	5-9	185	1/6/66	5	Clemson	Byrd, N.C.	D1a-'89	16/16
83	Wright, Eric	WR	6-0	203	8/4/69	2	Stephen F. Austin	Pittsburgh, Tex.	FA-'91	13/0
97	Zorich, Chris	DT	6-1	284	3/13/69	3	Notre Dame	Chicago, Ill.	D2-'91	16/2

* Blaylock played 11 games with San Diego in '92; Cain played 16 games with Seattle; Heyward played 16 games with New Orleans; Jurkovic and Lincoln missed '92 season due to injury; Smith played 12 games with Phoenix.

Unrestricted free agent; subject to developments.

† Restricted free agent; subject to developments.

Retired — Dennis Gentry, 11-year wide receiver, 15 games in '92; Mike Singletary, 12-year linebacker, 16 games in '92.

Players lost through free agency (3): RB Brad Muster (NO; 16 games in '92), S David Tate (NYJ; 16), TE Jim Thornton (NYJ; 0).

Also played with Bears in '92—RB Bob Christian (2 games), LB Jim Schwantz (1).

COACHING STAFF

Head Coach, Dave Wannstedt

Pro Career: Named Chicago's head coach on January 19, 1993. He was an integral part of one of the most successful turnarounds in NFL history, helping the 1989 Dallas Cowboys, which finished the season 1-15, into Super Bowl champions four years later. In January, 1992, he was named Dallas's assistant head coach and defensive coordinator. He was the defensive coordinator for the Cowboys in 1989. Selected by the Green Bay Packers in the fifteenth round of the 1974 draft, but spent the entire season on injured reserve.

Background: Played offensive tackle at the University of Pittsburgh from 1970-73. Began coaching career at Pittsburgh in 1975 and was part of the staff that led the Panthers to a 12-0 record and the NCAA championship in 1976. In 1979, he took a job with Jimmy Johnson at Oklahoma State as defensive line coach. After two seasons, he was promoted to defensive coordinator. In 1983, Wannstedt was the defensive line coach for Southern California before rejoining Johnson at the University of Miami as the Hurricanes defensive coordinator. In his first year (1986), Miami went 11-0 before losing to Penn State in the Fiesta Bowl. The following season Miami was crowned NCAA champion with a perfect 12-0 record.

Personal: Born May 21, 1952, Pittsburgh, Pa. Dave and his wife, Jan, live in Lake Forest, Ill. and have two children—Keri and Jami.

Assistant Coaches

Danny Abramowicz, special teams; born July 13, 1945, Steubenville, Ohio, lives in Lake Forest, Ill. Wide receiver Xavier 1964-66. Pro wide receiver New Orleans Saints 1967-73, San Francisco 49ers 1973-74. Pro coach: Joined Bears in 1992.

Clarence Brooks, defensive line; born May 20, 1951, New York, N.Y., lives in Lake Forest, Ill. Guard Massachusetts 1970-73. No pro playing experience. College coach: Massachusetts 1976-80, Syracuse 1981-89, Arizona 1990-92. Pro coach: Joined Bears in 1993.

Ivan Fears, wide receivers; born November 15, 1954, Portsmouth, Va., lives in Lake Forest, Ill. Running back William and Mary 1973-75. No pro playing experience. College coach: William and Mary 1977-80, Syracuse 1981-90. Pro coach: New England Patriots 1991-92, joined Bears in 1993.

Carlos Mainord, defensive assistant; born August 26, 1944, Greenville, Tex., lives in Lake Forest, Ill. Linebacker Navarro (Tex.) Junior College 1962-63, McMurry College 1964-65. No pro playing experience. College coach: McMurry College 1966-68, Texas Tech 1969, 1983-85, 1987-92, Ranger (Tex.) Junior College 1970-71, 1972-77 (head coach), Rice 1978-82, Miami 1986. Pro coach: Joined Bears in 1993.

David McGinnis, linebackers; born August 7, 1951, Independence, Kan., lives in Lake Forest, Ill. Defensive back Texas Christian 1970-72. No pro playing experience. College coach: Texas Christian 1973-74, 1982, Missouri 1975-77, Indiana State 1978-81, Kansas State 1983-85. Pro coach: Joined Bears in 1986.

Joe Pendry, running backs; born August 5, 1947, Matheny, W. Va., lives in Lake Forest, Ill. Tight end West Virginia 1966-67. No pro playing experience. College coach: West Virginia 1967-74, 1976-77, Kansas State 1975, Pittsburgh 1978-79, Michigan State 1980-81. Pro coach: Philadelphia Stars (USFL) 1983, Pittsburgh Maulers (USFL) 1984 (head coach), Cleveland Browns 1985-88, Kansas City Chiefs 1989-92, joined Bears in 1993.

Mike Shula, tight ends; born June 23, 1965, Baltimore, Md., lives in Lake Forest, Ill. Quarterback Alabama 1984-87. Pro quarterback Tampa Bay Buccaneers 1987. Pro coach: Tampa Bay Buccaneers 1988-90, Miami Dolphins 1991-92, joined Bears in 1993.

Bob Slowik, defensive coordinator-defensive backs; born May 16, 1954, Pittsburgh, Pa., lives in Lake Forest, Ill. Cornerback Delaware 1973-76. No pro playing experience. College coach: Delaware 1977, Florida 1978-81, Drake 1982, Rutgers 1983, East Carolina 1984-91. Pro coach: Dallas Cowboys 1992, joined Bears in 1993.

Ron Turner, offensive coordinator-quarterbacks; born December 5, 1953, Martinez, Calif., lives in Lake Forest, Ill. Running back-defensive back Pacific 1973-76. No pro playing experience. College coach: Pacific 1977, Arizona 1978-80, Northwestern 1981-82, Pittsburgh 1983-84, Southern California 1985-87, Texas A&M 1988, Stanford 1989-91, San Jose State 1992 (head coach). Pro coach: Joined Bears in 1993.

Tony Wise, offensive line; born December 28, 1951, Albany, N.Y., lives in Lake Forest, Ill. Offensive lineman Ithaca College 1971-72. No pro playing experience. College coach: Albany State 1973, Bridgeport 1974, Central Connecticut State 1975, Washington State 1976, Pittsburgh 1977-78, Oklahoma State 1979-83, Syracuse 1984, Miami 1985-88. Pro coach: Dallas Cowboys 1989-92, joined Bears in 1993.

Chicago Bears 1993 First-Year Roster

Name	Pos.	Ht.	Wt.	Birth-date	College	Hometown	How Acq.
Baker, Myron	LB	6-1	221	1/6/71	Louisiana Tech	Haughton, La.	D4b
Bonnell, Scott	K	5-10	167	10/14/69	Indiana	Newburgh, Ind.	FA
Brewer, Dewell	RB	5-8	203	4/22/70	Oklahoma	Lawton, Okla.	FA
Burger, Todd	G	6-3	266	3/20/70	Penn State	Clark, N.J.	FA
Conway, Curtis	WR-KR	6-0	185	3/13/71	Southern California	Hawthorne, Calif.	D1
Ellisor, John	G	6-4	270	9/5/69	Texas A&M	Kinwood, Tex.	FA
Fleeks, Carlos	RB	6-0	200	6/24/71	Hampton	Wichita Falls, Tex.	FA
Fontenot, Albert	DE	6-4	260	9/17/70	Baylor	Houston, Tex.	D4c
Gedney, Chris	TE	6-5	254	8/9/70	Syracuse	Liverpool, N.Y.	D3
Goodwin, Matt	CB	6-1	223	7/15/70	Iowa State	Ames, Iowa	FA
Govi, Mark	G	6-4	287	8/11/70	Tulsa	Jeannette, Pa.	FA
Hawkins, Garland	DE	6-3	232	2/19/70	Syracuse	Hyattsville, Md.	FA
Hoffman, Dave	LB	6-2	229	7/24/70	Washington	San Jose, Calif.	D6
Ivlow, John	RB	5-11	226	1/26/70	Colorado State	Joliet, Ill.	FA
Johnson, Antonio	WR-KR	5-8	195	4/18/69	Syracuse	Detroit, Mich.	FA
Johnson, Keshon	CB	5-10	177	7/17/70	Arizona	Fresno, Calif.	D7
Mack, Rico	LB	6-4	226	2/22/71	Appalachian State	Statham, Ga.	FA
Matthews, Shane	QB	6-3	192	6/1/70	Florida	Pascagoula, Miss.	FA
Miller, Maurice	LB	6-3	217	9/5/69	Wake Forest	Richmond, Va.	FA
Nichols, Tony	T	6-4	290	9/11/70	San Diego State	Sonora, Calif.	FA
Pace, Stephon	S	5-10	191	6/5/70	Southern California	La Puente, Calif.	FA
Perry, Todd	G	6-5	291	11/28/70	Kentucky	Elizabethtown, Ky.	D4a
Saul, Tracy	S	5-10	179	9/15/70	Texas Tech	Lubbock, Tex.	FA
Scott, Jim	C	6-2	268	7/4/70	Nebraska	Ansley, Neb.	FA
Simpson, Carl	DT	6-2	278	4/18/70	Florida State	Appling County, Ga.	D2
Wetnight, Ryan	TE	6-2	225	11/5/70	Stanford	Fresno, Calif.	FA
Wilhite, Kenny	CB	5-8	189	7/26/70	Nebraska	St. Louis, Mo.	FA
Wynn, Larry	WR	6-1	181	10/8/71	Northern Illinois	Centreville, Ill.	FA
Zomalt, Greg	RB	6-2	210	1/16/71	California	Monroe Valley, Calif.	FA

The term NFL Rookie is defined as a player who is in his first season of professional football and has not been on the roster of another professional football team for any regular-season or postseason games. A Rookie is designated by an "R" on NFL rosters. Players who have been active in another professional football league or players who have NFL experience, including either preseason training camp or being on an Active List or Inactive List, or on Reserve/Injured or Reserve/Physically Unable to Perform for fewer than six regular-season games, are termed NFL First-Year Players. An NFL First-Year Player is designated by a "1" on NFL rosters. Thereafter, a player is credited with an additional year of experience for each season in which he accumulates six games on the Active List or Inactive List, or on Reserve/Injured or Reserve/Physically Unable to Perform.

NOTES

DALLAS COWBOYS

National Football Conference Eastern Division

Team Colors: Royal Blue, Metallic Silver Blue, and White

Cowboys Center
One Cowboys Parkway
Irving, Texas 75063
Telephone: (214) 556-9900

Club Officials

Owner/President/General Manager: Jerry Jones
Vice President: Stephen Jones
Vice President: Mike McCoy
Vice President/Marketing: George Hays
Treasurer: Jack Dixon
Marketing and Special Events Coordinator: Charlotte Anderson
Public Relations Director: Rich Dalrymple
Assistant Director of Public Relations: Brett Daniels
Director of College Scouting: Larry Lacewell
Director of Operations: Bruce Mays
Trainer: Kevin O'Neill
Equipment Manager: Buck Buchanan
Video Director: Robert Blackwell
Cheerleader Director: Kelli McGonagill

Stadium: Texas Stadium • **Capacity:** 65,024
Irving, Texas 75062

Playing Surface: Texas Turf

Training Camp: St. Edward's University
Austin, Texas 78704

1993 Schedule

Preseason

Aug. 1	**Minnesota**	7:00
Aug. 8	vs. Detroit at London	12:30
Aug. 14	**Los Angeles Raiders**	8:00
Aug. 21	vs. Houston at San Antonio	12:30
Aug. 27	at Chicago	7:30

Regular Season

Sept. 6	at Washington (Monday)	9:00
Sept. 12	**Buffalo**	3:00
Sept. 19	at Phoenix	6:00
Sept. 26	**Open Date**	
Oct. 3	**Green Bay**	12:00
Oct. 10	at Indianapolis	1:00
Oct. 17	**San Francisco**	3:00
Oct. 24	**Open Date**	
Oct. 31	at Philadelphia	1:00
Nov. 7	**New York Giants**	12:00
Nov. 14	**Phoenix**	12:00
Nov. 21	at Atlanta	1:00
Nov. 25	**Miami** (Thanksgiving)	3:00
Dec. 6	**Philadelphia** (Monday)	8:00
Dec. 12	at Minnesota	3:00
Dec. 18	at New York Jets (Saturday)	4:00
Dec. 26	**Washington**	3:00
Jan. 2	at New York Giants	1:00

Cowboys Coaching History

(306-211-6)

1960-88	Tom Landry	270-178-6
1989-92	Jimmy Johnson	36-33-0

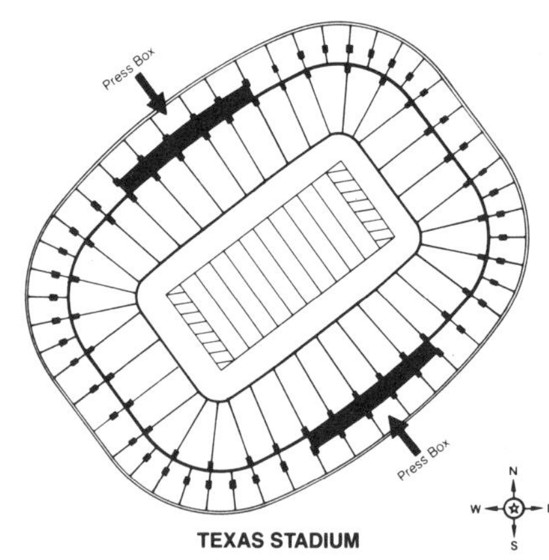

Record Holders

Individual Records — Career

Category	Name	Performance
Rushing (Yds.)	Tony Dorsett, 1977-1987	12,036
Passing (Yds.)	Roger Staubach, 1969-1979	22,700
Passing (TDs)	Danny White, 1976-1988	155
Receiving (No.)	Drew Pearson, 1973-1983	489
Receiving (Yds.)	Tony Hill, 1977-1986	7,988
Interceptions	Mel Renfro, 1964-1977	52
Punting (Avg.)	Mike Saxon, 1985-1992	41.5
Punt Return (Avg.)	Bob Hayes, 1965-1974	11.1
Kickoff Return (Avg.)	Mel Renfro, 1964-1977	26.4
Field Goals	Rafael Septien, 1978-1986	162
Touchdowns (Tot.)	Tony Dorsett, 1977-1987	86
Points	Rafael Septien, 1978-1986	874

Individual Records — Single Season

Category	Name	Performance
Rushing (Yds.)	Emmitt Smith, 1992	1,713
Passing (Yds.)	Danny White, 1983	3,980
Passing (TDs)	Danny White, 1983	29
Receiving (No.)	Michael Irvin, 1991	93
Receiving (Yds.)	Michael Irvin, 1991	1,523
Interceptions	Everson Walls, 1981	11
Punting (Avg.)	Sam Baker, 1962	45.4
Punt Return (Avg.)	Bob Hayes, 1968	20.8
Kickoff Return (Avg.)	Mel Renfro, 1965	30.0
Field Goals	Rafael Septien, 1981	27
	Ken Willis, 1991	27
Touchdowns (Tot.)	Emmitt Smith, 1992	19
Points	Rafael Septien, 1983	123

Individual Records — Single Game

Category	Name	Performance
Rushing (Yds.)	Tony Dorsett, 12-4-77	206
Passing (Yds.)	Don Meredith, 11-10-63	460
Passing (TDs)	Many times	5
	Last time by Danny White, 10-30-83	
Receiving (No.)	Lance Rentzel, 11-19-67	13
Receiving (Yds.)	Bob Hayes, 11-13-66	246
Interceptions	Herb Adderley, 9-26-71	3
	Lee Roy Jordan, 11-4-73	3
	Dennis Thurman, 12-13-81	3
Field Goals	Roger Ruzek, 12-21-87	5
Touchdowns (Tot.)	Many times	4
	Last time by Emmitt Smith, 11-18-90	
Points	Many times	24
	Last time by Emmitt Smith, 11-18-90	

1992 Team Record

Preseason (2-3)

Date	Result		Opponents
8/1	L	23-34	vs. Houston at Tokyo
8/7	W	27-24	at Miami
8/15	L	16-17	Houston
8/22	W	17- 3	Denver
8/28	L	13-20	Chicago

Regular Season (13-3)

Date	Result		Opponents	Att.
9/7	W	23-10	Washington	62,652
9/13	W	34-28	at N.Y. Giants	76,034
9/20	W	31-20	Phoenix	62,200
10/5	L	7-31	at Philadelphia	65,740
10/11	W	27- 0	Seattle	62,569
10/18	W	17-10	Kansas City	62,775
10/25	W	28-13	at L.A. Raiders	89,985
11/1	W	20-10	Philadelphia	63,290
11/8	W	37- 3	at Detroit	78,815
11/15	L	23-27	L.A. Rams	62,993
11/22	W	16-10	at Phoenix	71,628
11/26	W	30- 3	N.Y. Giants	62,974
12/6	W	31-27	at Denver	74,929
12/13	L	17-20	at Washington	55,455
12/21	W	41-17	at Atlanta	69,800
12/27	W	27-14	Chicago	63,208

Postseason (3-0)

Date	Result		Opponent	Att.
1/10	W	34-10	Philadelphia	63,721
1/17	W	30-20	at San Francisco	64,920
1/31	W	52-17	Buffalo	98,374

Score by Periods

Cowboys	108	116	134	51	0	—	409
Opponents	54	53	51	85	0	—	243

Attendance

Home 502,661 Away 582,386 Total 1,085,047
Single-game home record, 80,259 (11-24-66)
Single-season home record, 511,541 (1981)

1992 Team Statistics

	Cowboys	Opp.
Total First Downs	324	241
Rushing	119	68
Passing	183	147
Penalty	22	26
Third Down: Made/Att.	87/208	50/184
Third Down: Pct.	41.8	27.2
Fourth Down: Made/Att.	8/12	7/15
Fourth Down: Pct.	66.7	46.7
Total Net Yards	5606	3931
Avg. Per Game	350.4	245.7
Total Plays	1014	873
Avg. Per Play	5.5	4.5
Net Yards Rushing	2121	1244
Avg. Per Game	132.6	77.8
Total Rushes	500	345
Net Yards Passing	3485	2687
Avg. Per Game	217.8	167.9
Sacked/Yards Lost	23/112	44/347
Gross Yards	3597	3034
Att./Completions	491/314	484/263
Completion Pct.	64.0	54.3
Had Intercepted	15	17
Punts/Avg.	61/43.0	87/42.1
Net Punting Avg.	61/33.5	87/35.1
Penalties/Yards Lost	91/650	94/727
Fumbles/Ball Lost	16/9	25/14
Touchdowns	48	29
Rushing	20	11
Passing	23	16
Returns	5	2
Avg. Time of Possession	33:57	26:03

1992 Individual Statistics

Scoring	TD R	TD P	TD Rt	PAT	FG	Saf	TP
Elliott	0	0	0	47/48	24/35	0	119
E. Smith	18	1	0	0/0	0/0	0	114
Irvin	0	7	0	0/0	0/0	0	42
Novacek	0	6	0	0/0	0/0	0	36
Martin	0	3	2	0/0	0/0	0	30
Harper	0	4	0	0/0	0/0	0	24
Johnston	0	2	0	0/0	0/0	0	12
Aikman	1	0	0	0/0	0/0	0	6
Horton	0	0	1	0/0	0/0	0	6
Maryland	0	0	1	0/0	0/0	0	6
Richards	1	0	0	0/0	0/0	0	6
R. Williams	0	0	1	0/0	0/0	0	6
Holt	0	0	0	0/0	0/0	1	2
Cowboys	20	23	5	47/48	24/35	1	409
Opponents	11	16	2	27/29	14/17	0	243

Passing	Att.	Comp.	Yds.	Pct.	TD	Int.	Tkld.	Rate
Aikman	473	302	3445	63.8	23	14	23/112	89.5
Beuerlein	18	12	152	66.7	0	1	0/0	69.7
Cowboys	491	314	3597	64.0	23	15	23/112	88.8
Opponents	484	263	3034	54.3	16	17	44/347	69.9

Rushing	Att.	Yds.	Avg.	LG	TD
E. Smith	373	1713	4.6	68t	18
Richards	49	176	3.6	15	1
Aikman	37	105	2.8	19	1
Johnston	17	61	3.6	14	0
Agee	16	54	3.4	10	0
Harper	1	15	15.0	15	0
Martin	2	13	6.5	8	0
Beuerlein	4	−7	−1.7	−1	0
Irvin	1	−9	−9.0	−9	0
Cowboys	500	2121	4.2	68t	20
Opponents	345	1244	3.6	28	11

Receiving	No.	Yds.	Avg.	LG	TD
Irvin	78	1396	17.9	87t	7
Novacek	68	630	9.3	34	6
E. Smith	59	335	5.7	26t	1
Harper	35	562	16.1	52	4
Martin	32	359	11.2	27	3
Johnston	32	249	7.8	18	2
Roberts	3	36	12.0	18	0
Agee	3	18	6.0	8	0
Richards	3	8	2.7	6	0
Gesek	1	4	4.0	4	0
Cowboys	314	3597	11.5	87t	23
Opponents	263	3034	11.5	81t	16

Interceptions	No.	Yds.	Avg.	LG	TD
Washington	3	31	10.3	16	0
Gant	3	19	6.3	11	0
Everett	2	28	14.0	17	0
Horton	2	15	7.5	15t	1
Holt	2	11	5.5	8	0
K. Smith	2	10	5.0	7	0
Brown	1	30	30.0	30	0
Myles	1	13	13.0	13	0
Harper	1	1	1.0	1	0
Cowboys	17	158	9.3	30	1
Opponents	15	300	20.0	59	0

Punting	No.	Yds.	Avg.	In 20	LG
Saxon	61	2620	43.0	19	58
Cowboys	61	2620	43.0	19	58
Opponents	87	3660	42.1	17	73

Punt Returns	No.	FC	Yds.	Avg.	LG	TD
Martin	42	18	532	12.7	79t	2
K. Smith	1	0	17	17.0	17	0
Horton	1	0	1	1.0	1	0
Cowboys	44	18	550	12.5	79t	2
Opponents	34	6	397	11.7	65	0

Kickoff Returns	No.	Yds.	Avg.	LG	TD
Martin	24	503	21.0	59	0
Edwards	1	0	0.0	0	0
Holmes	3	70	23.3	28	0
K. Smith	1	9	9.0	9	0
Wright	8	117	14.6	21	0
Cowboys	37	699	18.9	59	0
Opponents	60	1217	20.3	42	0

Sacks	No.
Jeffcoat	10.5
Tolbert	8.5
Haley	6.0
J. Jones	4.0
Lett	3.5
Casillas	3.0
Gant	3.0
Maryland	2.5
R. Jones	1.0
V. Smith	1.0
Woodson	1.0
Cowboys	44.0
Opponents	23.0

1993 Draft Choices

Round	Name	Pos.	College
2.	Kevin Williams	WR	Miami
	Darrin Smith	LB	Miami
3.	Mike Middleton	DB	Indiana
4.	Derrick Lassic	RB	Alabama
	Ron Stone	T	Boston College
6.	Barry Minter	LB	Tulsa
7.	Brock Marion	DB	Nevada-Reno
8.	Dave Thomas	DB	Tennessee
	Reggie Givens	DB	Penn State

Dallas Cowboys 1993 Veteran Roster

No.	Name	Pos.	Ht.	Wt.	Birth-date	NFL Exp.	College	Hometown	How Acq.	'92 Games/ Starts
50	Abrams, Bobby	LB	6-3	230	4/12/67	4	Michigan	Detroit, Mich.	FA-'93	3/0
34	Agee, Tommie	RB	6-0	227	2/22/64	7	Auburn	Maplesville, Ala.	PB(KC)-'90	16/0
8	Aikman, Troy	QB	6-4	222	11/21/66	5	UCLA	Henryetta, Okla.	D1-'89	16/16
40	†Bates, Bill	S	6-1	203	6/6/61	11	Tennessee	Knoxville, Tenn.	FA-'83	5/0
42	Briggs, Greg	S	6-3	212	10/19/68	2	Texas Southern	Meadville, Miss.	D5a-'92	0*
24	Brown, Larry	CB	5-11	185	11/30/69	3	Texas Christian	Los Angeles, Calif.	D12-'91	16/15
75	Casillas, Tony	DT	6-3	273	10/26/63	8	Oklahoma	Tulsa, Okla.	T(Atl)-'91	15/15
68	Cornish, Frank	C-G	6-4	285	9/24/67	4	UCLA	Chicago, Ill.	PB(SD)-'92	11/2
3	Daniel, Tim	WR	5-11	192	9/14/69	2	Florida A&M	Atlanta, Ga.	D11-'92	0*
58	Edwards, Dixon	LB	6-1	224	3/25/68	3	Michigan State	Cincinnati, Ohio	D2-'91	16/1
2	Elliott, Lin	K	6-0	182	11/11/68	2	Texas Tech	Waco, Tex.	FA-'92	16/0
60	Evans, Melvin	G	6-2	303	1/29/69	2	Texas Southern	Trenton, N.J.	FA-'92	0*
27	Everett, Thomas	S	5-9	183	11/21/64	7	Baylor	Daingerfield, Tex.	T(Pitt)-'92	11/9
39	Gainer, Derrick	RB	5-11	240	8/15/66	3	Florida A&M	Plant City, Fla.	FA-'92	5/0
29	#Gant, Kenneth	S	5-11	191	4/18/67	4	Albany State	Lakeland, Fla.	D9-'90	16/4
63	Gesek, John	G	6-5	282	2/18/63	7	Cal State-Sacramento	Danville, Calif.	T(Raid)-'90	16/16
66	Gogan, Kevin	G-T	6-7	319	11/2/64	7	Washington	Pacifica, Calif.	D8-'87	16/1
94	Haley, Charles	DE	6-5	245	1/6/64	8	James Madison	Campbell County, Va.	T(SF)-'92	15/13
80	Harper, Alvin	WR	6-3	207	7/6/67	3	Tennessee	Frostproof, Fla.	D1b-'91	16/13
70	†Hellestrae, Dale	C-G	6-5	283	7/11/62	9	Southern Methodist	Scottsdale, Ariz.	T(Raid)-'90	16/0
95	Hennings, Chad	DE-DT	6-6	267	10/20/65	2	Air Force	Elberon, Iowa	D11-'88	8/0
90	Hill, Tony	DE	6-6	255	10/23/68	3	Tennessee-Chattanooga	Warren County, Ga.	D4c-'91	5/0
47	Holmes, Clayton	CB	5-10	181	8/23/69	2	Carson-Newman	Florence, S.C.	D3a-'92	15/0
88	Irvin, Michael	WR	6-2	199	3/5/66	6	Miami	Ft. Lauderdale, Fla.	D1-'88	16/14
77	Jeffcoat, Jim	DE	6-5	276	4/1/61	11	Arizona State	Cliffwood, N.J.	D1-'83	16/3
48	#Johnston, Daryl	RB	6-2	238	2/10/66	5	Syracuse	Youngstown, N.Y.	D2-'89	16/16
97	Jones, Jimmie	DE-DT	6-4	276	1/9/66	4	Miami	Okeechobee, Fla.	D3-'90	16/2
55	Jones, Robert	LB	6-2	238	9/27/69	2	East Carolina	Nottoway, Va.	D1b-'92	15/13
69	Jones, Todd	T	6-3	295	7/3/67	2	Henderson State	Little Rock, Ark.	FA-'92	0*
78	Lett, Leon	DE-DT	6-6	292	10/12/68	3	Emporia State	Fair Hope, Ala.	D7-'91	16/0
67	Maryland, Russell	DT	6-1	275	3/22/69	3	Miami	Chicago, Ill.	D1a-'91	14/13
7	t-Millen, Hugh	QB	6-5	216	11/22/63	8	Washington	Seattle, Wash.	T(NE)-'93	7/7*
98	Myles, Godfrey	LB	6-1	242	9/22/68	3	Florida	Miami, Fla.	D3a-'91	16/0
61	Newton, Nate	G	6-3	303	12/20/61	8	Florida A&M	Orlando, Fla.	FA-'86	15/15
51	Norton, Ken	LB	6-2	241	9/29/66	6	UCLA	Los Angeles, Calif.	D2-'88	16/16
84	Novacek, Jay	TE	6-4	231	10/24/62	9	Wyoming	Gothenburg, Neb.	PB(Phx)-'90	16/16
52	†Pruitt, Mickey	LB	6-1	218	1/10/65	6	Colorado	Chicago, Ill.	W(Chi)-'91	6/0
87	Roberts, Alfredo	TE	6-3	251	3/17/65	6	Miami	Hollywood, Fla.	PB(KC)-'91	16/4
4	Saxon, Mike	P	6-3	200	7/10/62	9	San Diego State	Arcadia, Calif.	FA-'85	16/0
22	#Smith, Emmitt	RB	5-9	209	5/15/69	4	Florida	Escambia, Fla.	D1-'90	16/16
82	Smith, Jimmy	WR	6-1	205	2/9/69	2	Jackson State	Jackson, Miss.	D2a-'92	7/0
26	Smith, Kevin	CB	5-11	177	4/7/70	2	Texas A&M	Orange, Tex.	D1a-'92	16/6
57	Smith, Vinson	LB	6-2	237	7/3/65	6	East Carolina	Statesville, N.C.	PB(Pitt)-'90	16/13
53	Stepnoski, Mark	C	6-2	269	1/20/67	5	Pittsburgh	Erie, Pa.	D3a-'89	14/14
92	Tolbert, Tony	DE	6-6	265	12/29/67	5	Texas-El Paso	Englewood, N.J.	D4-'89	16/16
71	Tuinei, Mark	T	6-5	298	3/31/60	11	Hawaii	Honolulu, Hawaii	FA-'83	15/15
76	Veingrad, Alan	G-T	6-5	280	7/24/63	8	East Texas State	Miami, Fla.	PB(GB)-'91	11/1
37	Washington, James	S	6-1	203	1/10/65	6	UCLA	Los Angeles, Calif.	PB(Rams)-'90	16/15
79	Williams, Erik	T	6-6	321	9/7/68	3	Central State, Ohio	Philadelphia, Pa.	D3c-'91	16/16
23	Williams, Robert	CB	5-10	186	10/2/62	7	Baylor	Galveston, Tex.	FA-'87	9/0
28	Woodson, Darren	S	6-1	215	4/25/69	2	Arizona State	Phoenix, Ariz.	D2b-'92	16/2

* Briggs, Daniel, Evans, and T. Jones missed '92 season due to injury; Millen played 7 games with New England in '92.

#Unrestricted free agent; subject to developments.

† Restricted free agent; subject to developments.

t- Cowboys traded for Millen (New England)

Players lost through free agency (2); QB Steve Beuerlein (Phx; 16 games in '92), WR Kelvin Martin (Sea; 16).

Also played with Cowboys in '92—CB Issiac Holt (16 games), DT Danny Noonan (2), RB Curvin Richards (9), WR Alexander Wright (3).

COACHING STAFF

Head Coach, Jimmy Johnson

Pro Career: Led Cowboys to Super Bowl XXVII victory over the Buffalo Bills in January, 1993. Dallas finished the 1992 regular season with a 13-3 record (second best in the NFL). Named second head coach in Cowboys' history on February 25, 1989. Named NFL coach of the year in 1990. No pro playing experience. Career record: 36-33.

Background: All-Southwest Conference defensive lineman on Arkansas's 1964 undefeated national championship team. Began coaching career in 1965 at Louisiana Tech. Moved on as an assistant at Wichita State 1967, Iowa State 1968-69, Oklahoma 1970-72, Arkansas 1973-76, and Pittsburgh 1977-78. Head coach at Oklahoma State from 1979-83. Compiled 52-9 (.853) record in five seasons as head coach at the University of Miami. Under Johnson, the Hurricanes won the national championship in 1987 and 34 of 36 games from 1986-88. Career collegiate record: 81-34-3.

Personal: Born July 16, 1943, Port Arthur, Tex. Jimmy lives in Irving, Tex., and has two sons, Brent and Chad.

Assistant Coaches

Hubbard Alexander, wide receivers; born February 14, 1939, Winston-Salem, N.C., lives in Coppell, Tex. Center Tennessee State 1958-61. No pro playing experience. College coach: Tennessee State 1962-63, Vanderbilt 1974-78, Miami 1979-88. Pro coach: Joined Cowboys in 1989.

Joe Avezzano, special teams; born November 17, 1943, Yonkers, N.Y., lives in Coppell, Tex. Guard Florida State 1961-65. Pro center Boston Patriots 1966. College coach: Florida State 1968, Iowa State 1969-72, Pittsburgh 1973-76, Tennessee 1977-79, Oregon State 1980-84 (head coach), Texas 1985-88. Pro coach: Joined Cowboys in 1990.

John Blake, defensive line; born March 6, 1961, Sand Springs, Okla., lives in Irving, Tex. Nose tackle Oklahoma 1980-83. No pro playing experience. College coach: Oklahoma 1986-87, 1989-92, Tulsa 1988. Pro coach: Joined Cowboys in 1993.

Joe Brodsky, running backs; born June 9, 1934, Miami, Fla., lives in Coppell, Tex. Fullback-linebacker Florida 1953-56. No pro playing experience. College coach: Miami 1978-88. Pro coach: Joined Cowboys in 1989.

Dave Campo, defensive backs; born July 18, 1947, New London, Conn., lives in Coppell, Tex. Defensive back Central Connecticut State 1967-70. No pro playing experience. College coach: Central Connecticut State 1971-72, Albany State 1973, Bridgeport 1974, Pittsburgh 1975, Washington State 1976, Boise State 1977-79, Oregon State 1980, Weber State 1981-82, Iowa State 1983, Syracuse 1984-86, Miami 1987-88. Pro coach: Joined Cowboys in 1989.

Butch Davis, defensive coordinator-linebackers; born November 17, 1951, Tahlequah, Okla., lives in Coppell, Tex. Defensive end Arkansas 1971-74. No pro playing experience. College coach: Oklahoma State 1979-83, Miami 1984-88. Pro coach: Joined Cowboys in 1989.

Jim Eddy, defensive assistant; born May 2, 1939, Checotah, Okla., lives in Irving, Tex. Defensive back-running back New Mexico State 1956-59. No pro playing experience. College coach: New Mexico State 1965-70, Texas El-Paso 1971-72, Houston 1987-89. Pro coach: Saskatchewan Rough Riders (CFL) 1974-78 (head coach 1977-78), Hamilton Tiger Cats (CFL) 1979-80, Montreal Alouettes (CFL) 1981 (head coach), Toronto Argonauts (CFL) 1982-83, Houston Gamblers (USFL) 1984-85, Houston Oilers 1990-92, joined Cowboys in 1993.

Robert Ford, tight ends; born June 21, 1951, Belton, Tex., lives in Coppell, Tex. Wide receiver Houston 1970-72. No pro playing experience. College coach: Western Illinois 1974-76, New Mexico 1977-79, Oregon State 1980-81, Mississippi State 1982-83, Kansas 1986, Texas Tech 1987-88, Texas A&M 1989-90. Pro coach: Houston Gamblers (USFL) 1985, joined Cowboys in 1991.

Dallas Cowboys 1993 First-Year Roster

Name	Pos.	Ht.	Wt.	Birth-date	College	Hometown	How Acq.
Beasley, Michael (1)	RB	5-10	195	5/27/69	West Virginia	Pottstown, Pa.	FA
Biggins, Milton (1)	TE	6-4	273	12/29/69	Western Kentucky	Chicago, Ill.	FA
Bretz, Brad	QB	6-4	208	8/17/70	Cal State-Hayward	San Jose, Calif.	FA
Burleson, Jason	TE	6-5	243	11/9/68	Texas	Sherman, Tex.	FA
Domingos, Steve (1)	P	6-3	200	4/15/67	San Francisco State	Visalia, Calif.	FA
Garrett, Jason (1)	QB	6-2	195	3/28/66	Princeton	Chagrin, Ohio	FA
Garrett, Judd (1)	RB	6-1	205	6/25/67	Princeton	Monmouth Beach, N.J.	FA
Givens, Reggie	S	6-0	219	10/3/71	Penn State	Sussex, Va.	D8b
Hall, Chris (1)	S	6-2	184	4/25/70	East Carolina	Pemberton, N.J.	FA
Jett, John (1)	P	6-0	184	11/11/68	East Carolina	Reedville, Va.	FA
Jones, Anthony	WR	5-11	190	2/20/70	Oregon	Cerritos, Calif.	FA
Kennedy, Tony	RB	5-11	212	8/3/70	Virginia Tech	Upper Marlboro, Md.	FA
Lassic, Derrick	RB	5-10	192	1/26/70	Alabama	North Rockland, N.Y.	D4a
Luther, Alan	G	6-3	305	9/29/69	Texas	Houston, Tex.	FA
Marion, Brock	CB	5-11	178	6/11/70	Nevada-Reno	Bakersfield, Calif.	D7
Middleton, Mike	S	5-10	211	12/4/69	Indiana	Cincinnati, Ohio	D3
Minter, Barry	LB	6-2	236	1/28/70	Tulsa	Mt. Pleasant, Tex.	D6
Payton, Michael	QB	6-0	225	3/5/70	Marshall	Harrisburg, Pa.	FA
Rankin, Alex (1)	G	6-9	312	11/24/68	Angelo State	Laredo, Tex.	FA
Reed, Greg	WR	6-1	183	3/31/71	Southern Mississippi	Gulfport, Miss.	FA
Richards, James (1)	G	6-4	288	11/7/69	California	Antelope Valley, Calif.	FA
Smith, Darrin	LB	6-1	237	4/15/70	Miami	Miami, Fla.	D2b
Stone, Ron	T	6-5	306	7/20/71	Boston College	West Roxbury, Mass.	D4b
Thomas, Dave	CB	6-2	205	8/25/68	Tennessee	Miami, Fla.	D8a
Wacasey, Fallon (1)	TE	6-7	241	2/8/69	Tulsa	Kansas, Okla.	D6-'92
Williams, Kevin	WR	5-9	190	1/25/71	Miami	Dallas, Tex.	D2a
Williams, Tyrone (1)	WR	6-5	207	3/26/70	Western Ontario	Halifax, Nova Scotia	FA

The term NFL Rookie is defined as a player who is in his first season of professional football and has not been on the roster of another professional football team for any regular-season or postseason games. A Rookie is designated by an "R" on NFL rosters. Players who have been active in another professional football league or players who have NFL experience, including either preseason training camp or being on an Active List or Inactive List, or on Reserve/Injured or Reserve/Physically Unable to Perform for fewer than six regular-season games, are termed NFL First-Year Players. An NFL First-Year Player is designated by a "1" on NFL rosters. Thereafter, a player is credited with an additional year of experience for each season in which he accumulates six games on the Active List or Inactive List, or on Reserve/Injured or Reserve/Physically Unable to Perform.

NOTES

Steve Hoffman, kickers-research and development; born September 8, 1958, Camden, N.J., lives in Coppell, Tex. Quarterback-running back-wide receiver Dickinson College 1979-82. Pro punter Washington Federals (USFL) 1983. College coach: Miami 1985-87. Pro coach: Joined Cowboys in 1989.

Hudson Houck, offensive line; born January 7, 1943, Los Angeles, Calif., lives in Irving, Tex. Center Southern California 1962-64. No pro playing experience. College coach: Southern California 1970-72, 1976-82, Stanford 1973-75. Pro coach: Los Angeles Rams 1983-91, Seattle Seahawks 1992, joined Cowboys in 1993.

Norv Turner, assistant head coach-offensive coordinator-quarterbacks; born May 17, 1952, Martinez, Calif., lives in Coppell, Tex. Quarterback Oregon 1972-74. No pro playing experience. College coach: Oregon 1975, Southern California 1976-84. Pro coach: L.A. Rams 1985-90, joined Cowboys in 1991.

Mike Woicik, strength and conditioning; born September 26, 1956, Westwood, Mass., lives in Coppell, Tex. Boston College 1974-78. No college or pro playing experience. College coach: Springfield 1978-80, Syracuse 1980-89. Pro coach: Joined Cowboys in 1990.

National Football Conference Central Division

Team Colors: Honolulu Blue and Silver

Pontiac Silverdome
1200 Featherstone Road
Pontiac, Michigan 48342
Telephone: (313) 335-4131

Club Officials

President-Owner: William Clay Ford
Executive Vice President-COO: Chuck Schmidt
VP Administration/General Counsel: Michael Huyghue
Director of Player Personnel: Ron Hughes
Director of Pro Personnel: Kevin Colbert
Scouts: Milt Davis, Dirk Dierking, Allen Hughes, Scott McEwen, Jim Owens, Rick Spielman, John Trump
Director of Player Relations: Otis Canty
Controller/Travel Coordinator: Tom Lesnau
Director of Marketing, Broadcasting, and Communications: Bill Keenist
Director of Marketing, Sales, and Ticket Operations: Fred Otto
Director of Community Relations and Detroit Lions Charities: Tim Pendell
Media Relations Coordinator: Mike Murray
Media Relations Assistant: James Petrylka
Strength and Conditioning: Bert Hill
Trainer: Kent Falb
Equipment Manager: Dan Jaroshewich
Video Director: Steve Hermans

Stadium: Pontiac Silverdome • **Capacity:** 80,500
1200 Featherstone Road
Pontiac, Michigan 48342

Playing Surface: AstroTurf

Training Camp: Pontiac Silverdome
1200 Featherstone Road
Pontiac, Michigan 48342

1993 Schedule

Preseason

July 30	**Buffalo**	7:30
Aug. 8	vs. Dallas at London	12:30
Aug. 16	at Houston	8:00
Aug. 20	**Cincinnati**	7:30
Aug. 27	at New Orleans	7:00

Regular Season

Sept. 5	**Atlanta**	1:00
Sept. 12	at New England	1:00
Sept. 19	at New Orleans	12:00
Sept. 26	**Phoenix**	1:00
Oct. 3	at Tampa Bay	1:00
Oct. 10	**Open Date**	
Oct. 17	**Seattle**	1:00
Oct. 24	at Los Angeles Rams	1:00
Oct. 31	at Minnesota	7:00
Nov. 7	**Tampa Bay**	1:00
Nov. 14	**Open Date**	
Nov. 21	vs. Green Bay at Milw.	12:00
Nov. 25	**Chicago** (Thanksgiving)	12:30
Dec. 5	**Minnesota**	1:00
Dec. 12	at Phoenix	2:00
Dec. 19	**San Francisco**	4:00
Dec. 26	at Chicago	12:00
Jan. 2	**Green Bay**	1:00

Lions Coaching History

Portsmouth Spartans 1930-33
(399-414-32)

1930	Hal (Tubby) Griffen	5-6-3
1931-36	George (Potsy) Clark	49-20-6
1937-38	Earl (Dutch) Clark	14-8-0
1939	Elmer (Gus) Henderson	6-5-0
1940	George (Potsy) Clark	5-5-1
1941-42	Bill Edwards*	4-9-1
1942	John Karcis	0-8-0
1943-47	Charles (Gus) Dorais	20-31-2
1948-50	Alvin (Bo) McMillin	12-24-0
1951-56	Raymond (Buddy) Parker	50-24-2
1957-64	George Wilson	55-45-6
1965-66	Harry Gilmer	10-16-2
1967-72	Joe Schmidt	43-35-7
1973	Don McCafferty	6-7-1
1974-76	Rick Forzano**	15-17-0
1976-77	Tommy Hudspeth	11-13-0
1978-84	Monte Clark	43-63-1
1985-88	Darryl Rogers***	18-40-0
1988-92	Wayne Fontes	33-38-0

*Released after three games in 1942
**Resigned after four games in 1976
***Released after 11 games in 1988

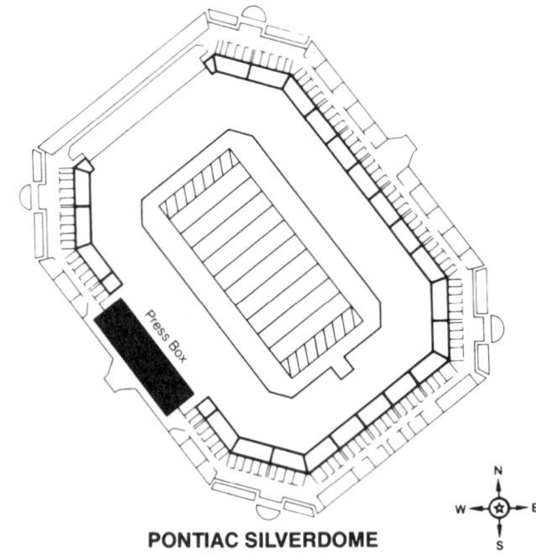

PONTIAC SILVERDOME

Record Holders

Individual Records — Career

Category	Name	Performance
Rushing (Yds.)	Barry Sanders, 1989-1992	5,674
Passing (Yds.)	Bobby Layne, 1950-58	15,710
Passing (TDs)	Bobby Layne, 1950-58	118
Receiving (No.)	Charlie Sanders, 1968-1977	336
Receiving (Yds.)	Gail Cogdill, 1960-68	5,220
Interceptions	Dick LeBeau, 1959-1972	62
Punting (Avg.)	Yale Lary, 1952-53, 1956-1964	44.3
Punt Return (Avg.)	Jack Christiansen, 1951-58	12.8
Kickoff Return (Avg.)	Pat Studstill, 1961-67	25.7
Field Goals	Eddie Murray, 1980-1991	243
Touchdowns (Tot.)	Barry Sanders, 1989-1992	57
Points	Eddie Murray, 1980-1991	1,113

Individual Records — Single Season

Category	Name	Performance
Rushing (Yds.)	Barry Sanders, 1991	1,548
Passing (Yds.)	Gary Danielson, 1980	3,223
Passing (TDs)	Bobby Layne, 1951	26
Receiving (No.)	James Jones, 1984	77
Receiving (Yds.)	Pat Studstill, 1966	1,266
Interceptions	Don Doll, 1950	12
	Jack Christiansen, 1953	12
Punting (Avg.)	Yale Lary, 1963	48.9
Punt Return (Avg.)	Jack Christiansen, 1952	21.5
Kickoff Return (Avg.)	Tom Watkins, 1965	34.4
Field Goals	Eddie Murray, 1980	27
Touchdowns (Tot.)	Barry Sanders, 1991	17
Points	Doak Walker, 1950	128

Individual Records — Single Game

Category	Name	Performance
Rushing (Yds.)	Barry Sanders, 11-24-91	220
Passing (Yds.)	Bobby Layne, 11-5-50	374
Passing (TDs)	Gary Danielson, 12-9-78	5
Receiving (No.)	Cloyce Box, 12-3-50	12
	James Jones, 9-28-86	12
Receiving (Yds.)	Cloyce Box, 12-3-50	302
Interceptions	Don Doll, 10-23-49	*4
Field Goals	Garo Yepremian, 11-13-66	6
Touchdowns (Tot.)	Cloyce Box, 12-3-50	4
Points	Cloyce Box, 12-3-50	24

*NFL Record

1992 Team Record

Preseason (1-3)

Date	Result		Opponents
8/8	L	7-17	Houston
8/17	L	24-30	at Buffalo
8/22	W	42- 9	New England
8/28	L	17-34	at Cincinnati

Regular Season (5-11)

Date	Result		Opponents	Att.
9/6	L	24-27	at Chicago	66,101
9/13	W	31-17	Minnesota	57,353
9/20	L	10-13	at Washington	55,482
9/27	L	23-27	Tampa Bay	52,779
10/4	L	7-13	New Orleans	68,428
10/15	L	14-31	at Minnesota	61,010
10/25	W	38- 7	at Tampa Bay	58,649
11/1	L	13-27	Green Bay	62,372
11/8	L	3-37	Dallas	78,815
11/15	L	14-17	at Pittsburgh	58,993
11/22	W	19-13	at Cincinnati	58,921
11/26	L	21-24	Houston	76,105
12/6	L	10-38	vs. G.B. at Milw.	54,681
12/13	W	24-14	Cleveland	70,746
12/20	W	16- 3	Chicago	75,804
12/28	L	6-24	at San Francisco	65,432

Score by Periods

Lions	37	99	65	72	0	—	273
Opponents	83	82	34	133	0	—	332

Attendance

Home 542,402 Away 479,269 Total 1,021,671
Single-game home record, 80,444 (12-20-81)
Single-season home record, 622,593 (1980)

1992 Team Statistics

	Lions	Opp.
Total First Downs	241	308
Rushing	83	119
Passing	133	168
Penalty	25	21
Third Down: Made/Att.	60/175	84/200
Third Down: Pct.	34.3	42.0
Fourth Down: Made/Att.	3/7	4/9
Fourth Down: Pct.	42.9	44.4
Total Net Yards	4440	5058
Avg. Per Game	277.5	316.1
Total Plays	843	976
Avg. Per Play	5.3	5.2
Net Yards Rushing	1644	1841
Avg. Per Game	102.8	115.1
Total Rushes	378	460
Net Yards Passing	2796	3217
Avg. Per Game	174.8	201.1
Sacked/Yards Lost	59/354	29/185
Gross Yards	3150	3402
Att./Completions	406/231	487/296
Completion Pct.	56.9	60.8
Had Intercepted	21	21
Punts/Avg.	66/43.1	55/41.1
Net Punting Avg.	66/34.7	55/33.3
Penalties/Yards Lost	122/903	111/871
Fumbles/Ball Lost	26/15	25/11
Touchdowns	30	38
Rushing	9	14
Passing	16	20
Returns	5	4
Avg. Time of Possession	27:36	32:24

1992 Individual Statistics

Scoring	TD R	TD P	TD Rt	PAT	FG	Saf	TP
Hanson	0	0	0	30/30	21/26	0	93
B. Sanders	9	1	0	0/0	0/0	0	60
Green	0	5	0	0/0	0/0	0	30
Moore	0	4	0	0/0	0/0	0	24
Perriman	0	4	0	0/0	0/0	0	24
Gray	0	0	2	0/0	0/0	0	12
Ball	0	0	1	0/0	0/0	0	6
Barrett	0	1	0	0/0	0/0	0	6
Blades	0	0	1	0/0	0/0	0	6
Campbell	0	1	0	0/0	0/0	0	6
Jenkins	0	0	1	0/0	0/0	0	6
Lions	9	16	5	30/30	21/26	0	273
Opponents	14	20	4	38/38	22/35	0	332

Passing	Att.	Comp.	Yds.	Pct.	TD	Int.	Tkld.	Rate
Peete	213	123	1702	57.7	9	9	28/170	80.0
Kramer	106	58	771	54.7	4	8	15/80	59.1
Ware	86	50	677	58.1	3	4	16/104	75.6
B. Sanders	1	0	0	0.0	0	0	0/0	39.6
Lions	406	231	3150	56.9	16	21	59/354	73.4
Opponents	487	296	3402	60.8	20	21	29/185	77.6

Rushing	Att.	Yds.	Avg.	LG	TD
B. Sanders	312	1352	4.3	55t	9
Ware	20	124	6.2	32	0
Peete	21	83	4.0	12	0
Stradford	9	29	3.2	11	0
Kramer	12	34	2.8	11	0
Tillison	4	22	5.5	10	0
Lions	378	1644	4.3	55t	9
Opponents	460	1841	4.0	25	14

Receiving	No.	Yds.	Avg.	LG	TD
Perriman	69	810	11.7	40t	4
Moore	51	966	18.9	77t	4
Green	33	586	17.8	73t	5
B. Sanders	29	225	7.8	48	1
Farr	15	115	7.7	14	0
Matthews	9	137	15.2	24	0
Campbell	8	155	19.4	78t	1
J. Johnson	6	34	5.7	9	0
Barrett	4	67	16.8	24	1
Hinnant	3	28	9.3	13	0
Stradford	2	15	7.5	12	0
McLemore	2	12	6.0	6	0
Lions	231	3150	13.6	78t	16
Opponents	296	3402	11.5	69t	20

Interceptions	No.	Yds.	Avg.	LG	TD
W. White	4	54	13.5	28	0
Crockett	4	50	12.5	35	0
Scott	4	35	8.8	26	0
Jenkins	4	34	8.5	14	0
Blades	3	56	18.7	34	0
S. White	2	26	13.0	20	0
Lions	21	255	12.1	35	0
Opponents	21	294	14.0	66t	1

Punting	No.	Yds.	Avg.	In 20	LG
Arnold	65	2846	43.8	12	71
Lions	66	2846	43.1	12	71
Opponents	55	2263	41.1	21	60

Punt Returns	No.	FC	Yds.	Avg.	LG	TD
Gray	18	9	175	9.7	58t	1
Campbell	3	0	15	5.0	9	0
Lions	21	9	190	9.0	58t	1
Opponents	30	5	356	11.9	48	0

Kickoff Returns	No.	Yds.	Avg.	LG	TD
Gray	42	1006	24.0	89t	1
Campbell	4	61	15.3	21	0
J. Johnson	1	0	0.0	0	0
Perriman	4	59	14.8	22	0
Scott	3	5	1.7	3	0
Stradford	4	35	8.8	16	0
Tillison	1	27	27.0	27	0
Lions	59	1193	20.2	89t	1
Opponents	45	948	21.1	39	0

Sacks	No.
Scroggins	7.5
Pritchett	6.5
Ball	2.5
Spindler	2.5
Cofer	2.0
Jamison	2.0
Owens	2.0
Crockett	1.0
Pete	1.0
Porcher	1.0
Spielman	1.0
Lions	29.0
Opponents	59.0

1993 Draft Choices

Round	Name	Pos.	College
2.	Ryan McNeil	DB	Miami
3.	Antonio London	LB	Alabama
	Mike Compton	C	West Virginia
6.	Greg Jeffries	DB	Virginia
7.	Ty Hallock	LB	Michigan State
8.	Kevin Miniefield	DB	Arizona State

Detroit Lions 1993 Veteran Roster

No.	Name	Pos.	Ht.	Wt.	Birth-date	NFL Exp.	College	Hometown	How Acq.	'92 Games/ Starts
6	Arnold, Jim	P	6-3	211	1/31/61	11	Vanderbilt	Dalton, Ga.	FA-'86	16/0
40	Barrett, Reggie	WR	6-3	215	8/14/69	3	Texas-El Paso	Corpus Christi, Tex.	D3-'91	8/6
33	Bennett, Antoine	CB	5-11	185	11/29/67	2	Florida A&M	Miami, Fla.	FA-'93	0*
36	Blades, Bennie	S	6-1	221	9/3/66	6	Miami	Ft. Lauderdale, Fla.	D1-'88	16/16
66	Bouwens, Shawn	G	6-4	290	5/25/68	3	Nebraska Wesleyan	Lincoln, Neb.	FA-'91	16/16
75	Brown, Lomas	T	6-4	287	3/30/63	9	Florida	Miami, Fla.	D1-'85	16/16
68	#Burton, Leonard	C	6-3	275	6/18/64	8	South Carolina	Memphis, Tenn.	FA-'92	2/2
87	Campbell, Jeff	WR	5-8	173	3/29/68	4	Colorado	Vail, Colo.	D5-'90	15/0
50	Caston, Toby	LB	6-1	243	7/17/65	7	Louisiana State	Monroe, La.	FA-'89	15/0
32	Clay, Willie	CB	5-9	184	9/5/70	2	Georgia Tech	Pittsburgh, Pa.	D8-'92	6/0
55	Cofer, Michael	LB	6-5	244	4/7/60	11	Tennessee	Knoxville, Tenn.	D3-'83	8/0
48	Coleman, Sidney	LB	6-2	250	1/14/64	5	Southern Mississippi	Gulfport, Miss.	FA-'93	0*
21	Colon, Harry	S	6-0	203	2/14/69	3	Missouri	Kansas City, Kan.	FA-'92	16/0
76	Conover, Scott	T	6-4	285	9/27/68	3	Purdue	Freehold, N.J.	D5-'91	15/15
39	Crockett, Ray	CB	5-9	181	1/5/67	5	Baylor	Duncanville, Tex.	D4-'89	15/15
97	Ford, Darryl	LB	6-1	225	6/22/66	2	New Mexico State	Dallas, Tex.	FA-'92	1/0
79	Fralic, Bill	G	6-5	280	10/31/62	9	Pittsburgh	Penn Hills, Pa.	UFA(Atl)-'93	16/16*
98	Gibson, Dennis	LB	6-2	243	2/8/64	7	Iowa State	Ankeny, Iowa	D8-'87	16/16
53	Glover, Kevin	C	6-2	282	6/17/63	9	Maryland	Upper Marlboro, Md.	D2-'85	7/7
23	Gray, Mel	WR-KR	5-9	171	3/16/61	8	Purdue	Williamsburgh, Va.	FA-'89	15/0
86	Green, Willie	WR	6-2	181	4/2/66	4	Mississippi	Athens, Ga.	D8a-'90	15/13
4	Hanson, Jason	K	5-11	183	6/17/70	2	Washington State	Spokane, Wash.	D2b-'92	16/0
99	Hayworth, Tracy	LB	6-3	260	12/18/67	4	Tennessee	Franklin, Tenn.	D7-'90	4/0
81	Holman, Rodney	TE	6-3	238	4/20/60	12	Tulane	Ypsilanti, Mich.	FA-'93	13/0*
44	Iaquaniello, Mike	S	6-3	208	2/13/68	2	Michigan State	Dearborn, Mich.	FA-'93	0*
58	Jamison, George	LB	6-1	235	9/30/63	8	Cincinnati	Bridgeton, N.J.	SD2-'84	16/16
89	Johnson, Jimmie	TE	6-2	255	10/6/66	6	Howard	Augusta, Ga.	FA-'92	16/5
30	Jones, James	RB	6-3	232	3/21/61	11	Florida	Pompano Beach, Fla.	UFA(Sea)-'93	16/1*
57	#Jones, Victor	LB	6-2	250	10/19/66	6	Virginia Tech	Rockville, Md.	FA-'89	16/0
12	Kramer, Erik	QB	6-1	199	11/6/64	4	North Carolina State	Encino, Calif.	FA-'91	7/3
72	Linn, Jack	G-T	6-5	285	6/10/67	2	West Virginia	Rochester, Pa.	FA-'92	4/4
16	Long, Chuck	QB	6-4	217	2/18/63	7	Iowa	Wheaton, Ill.	FA-'91	12/3
73	Lutz, Dave	G-T	6-6	305	12/20/59	11	Georgia Tech	Peachland, N.C.	UFA(KC)-'93	16/16*
83	#Matthews, Aubrey	WR	5-7	165	9/15/62	8	Delta State	Pascaguola, Miss.	FA-'90	13/0
82	McLemore, Thomas	TE	6-5	245	3/14/70	2	Southern	Shreveport, La.	D3-'92	11/1
84	Moore, Herman	WR	6-3	210	10/20/69	3	Virginia	Danville, Va.	D1-'91	12/11
90	†Owens, Dan	DE	6-3	280	3/16/67	4	Southern California	Whittier, Calif.	D2-'90	16/4
9	Peete, Rodney	QB	6-0	207	3/16/66	5	Southern California	Tucson, Ariz.	D6-'89	10/10
80	Perriman, Brett	WR	5-9	180	10/10/65	6	Miami	Miami, Fla.	T(NO)-'91	16/16
96	†Pete, Lawrence	NT	6-0	275	1/18/66	5	Nebraska	Wichita, Kan.	D5-'89	13/4
91	Porcher, Robert	DE	6-3	283	7/30/69	2	South Carolina State	Wendo, S.C.	D1-'92	16/1
94	Pritchett, Kelvin	DE	6-2	281	10/24/69	3	Mississippi	Atlanta, Ga.	T(Dall)-'91	16/15
28	Richards, Curvin	RB	5-9	195	12/26/68	3	Pittsburgh	Houston, Tex.	FA-'93	9/0*
63	Richards, Dave	G	6-5	310	4/11/66	6	UCLA	Dallas, Tex.	UFA(SD)-'93	16/16*
27	Robinson, Junior	CB	5-9	181	2/3/68	3	East Carolina	Wingate, N.C.	FA-'92	10/0
64	Rodenhauser, Mark	C	6-5	280	6/1/61	6	Illinois State	Addison, Ill.	FA-'93	0*
20	Sanders, Barry	RB	5-8	203	7/16/68	5	Oklahoma State	Wichita, Kan.	D1-'89	16/16
38	Scott, Kevin	CB	5-9	175	5/19/69	3	Stanford	Phoenix, Ariz.	D4-'91	16/1
59	Scroggins, Tracy	LB	6-2	255	9/11/69	2	Tulsa	Chectah, Okla.	D2a-'92	16/7
54	Spielman, Chris	LB	6-0	247	10/11/65	6	Ohio State	Massilon, Ohio	D2b-'88	16/16
93	†Spindler, Marc	DE	6-5	290	11/28/69	4	Pittsburgh	West Scranton, Pa.	D3-'90	13/13
56	t-Swilling, Pat	LB	6-3	242	10/25/64	8	Georgia Tech	Toccoa, Ga.	T(NO)-'93	16/16*
71	Tharpe, Larry	T	6-4	299	11/19/70	2	Tennessee State	Macon, Ga.	D6-'92	11/10
34	Tillison, Ed	RB	6-0	225	2/12/69	3	Northwest Missouri State	Pearl River, La.	D11-'92	6/0
8	Turner, Vernon	WR	5-8	185	1/6/67	3	Carson-Newman	Staten Island, N.Y.	FA-'93	6/0
11	Ware, Andre	QB	6-2	205	7/31/68	4	Houston	Dickinson, Tex.	D1-'90	4/3
35	#White, William	S	5-10	191	2/19/66	6	Ohio State	Lima, Ohio	D4-'88	16/16

* Bennett last active with Cincinnati in '91; Coleman last active with Phoenix in '91; Fralic played 16 games with Atlanta in '92; Holman played 13 games with Cincinnati; Iaquaniello last active with Miami in '91; J. Jones played 16 games with Seattle; Lutz played 16 games with Kansas City; C. Richards played 9 games with Dallas; D. Richards played 16 games with San Diego; Rodenhauser last active with Chicago in '91; Swilling played 16 games with New Orleans.

Unrestricted free agent; subject to developments.

† Restricted free agent; subject to developments.

Traded—NT Jerry Ball to Cleveland.

t- Lions traded for Swilling (New Orleans).

Players lost through free agency (2): CB Melvin Jenkins (Atl; 16 games in '92), S Sheldon White (Cin; 16).

Also played with Lions in '92—NT Jerry Ball (12 games), G Ken Dallafior (12), LB John Derby (1), WR Mike Farr (14), G Mike Haight (2), TE Mike Hinnant (15), DE Jeff Hunter (4), TE Jimmie Johnson (16), LB Troy Johnson (9), LB Andre Jones (9), G Eric Lynch (4), LB Mike McDonald (1), C Dennis McKnight (12), C Blake Miller (14), RB Don Overton (1), T Eric Sanders (6), RB Troy Stradford (6), CB Sheldon White (13).

COACHING STAFF

Head Coach, Wayne Fontes

Pro Career: Became the Lions' seventeenth head coach on December 22, 1988, after serving five weeks as interim head coach (2-3 record). Fontes led the Lions to a 7-9 record in 1989, including five consecutive season-ending wins, and a 6-10 record in 1990. Under Fontes, the Lions finished 12-4 and won the NFC Central Division in 1991. The Lions notched their first playoff victory since 1957 and made their first appearance in the NFC Championship Game in 1991. He began the 1988 season as Detroit's defensive coordinator and secondary coach, following a nine-year stint with the Tampa Bay Buccaneers. A former defensive back with the New York Jets, Fontes advanced from secondary coach to defensive coordinator to assistant head coach of the Buccaneers during his years with Tampa Bay. As a player with the Jets, his brief pro career was cut short by a broken leg after two seasons (1963-64). However, his 83-yard interception return against Houston (12-15-63) did stand as the Jets' team record until it was broken in 1989 by Erik McMillan's 93-yard return. Career record: 33-38.

Background: A former two-sport star (football and baseball) at Michigan State, Fontes earned all-Big Ten honors at defensive back for the Spartans. He earned his bachelor's degree in education and biological science and later earned his master's degree in administration, all from Michigan State. Fontes became defensive backfield coach at Dayton in 1968. He also served in the same capacity at Iowa (1969-71) and Southern California (1972-75).

Personal: Born February 17, 1939, New Bedford, Mass. Fontes and his wife, Evelyn, live in Rochester Hills, Mich., and have three children – Mike, Scott, and Kim.

Assistant Coaches

Hank Bullough, defensive coordinator; born January 24, 1934, Scranton, Pa., lives in Okemos, Mich. Linebacker Michigan State 1952-54. Pro linebacker Green Bay Packers 1955, 1958. College coach: Michigan State 1959-69. Pro coach: Baltimore Colts 1970-72, New England Patriots 1973-79, Cincinnati Bengals 1980-84, Buffalo Bills 1985-86 (head coach from October 1985 through November, 1986), Green Bay Packers 1988-91, joined Lions in 1993.

Don Clemons, outside linebackers; born February 15, 1954, Newark, N.J., lives in Rochester, Mich. Defensive end Muehlenberg College 1973-76. No pro playing experience. College coach: Kutztown State 1977-78, New Mexico 1979, Arizona State 1980-84. Pro coach: Joined Lions in 1985.

Frank Gansz, special teams; born November 22, 1938, Altoona, Pa., lives in Rochester Hills, Mich. Center-linebacker Navy 1957-59. No pro playing experience. College coach: Air Force 1964, Colgate 1968, Navy 1969, Oklahoma State 1973, 1975, Army 1974, UCLA 1976-77. Pro coach: San Francisco 49ers 1978, Cincinnati Bengals 1979-80, Kansas City Chiefs 1981-82, 1986-88 (head coach 1987-88), Philadelphia Eagles 1983-85, joined Lions in 1989.

Dan Henning, offensive coordinator; born June 21, 1942, Bronx, N.Y., lives in Rochester Hills, Mich. Quarterback William & Mary 1960-63. Pro quarterback San Diego Chargers 1966. College coach: Florida State 1968-70, 1974, Virginia Tech 1971, 1973. Pro coach: Houston Oilers 1972, New York Jets 1976-78, Miami Dolphins 1979-80, Washington Redskins 1981-82, 1987-88, Atlanta Falcons 1983-86 (head coach), San Diego Chargers 1989-91 (head coach), joined Lions in 1992.

Lamar Leachman, defensive line; born August 7, 1934, Cartersville, Ga., lives in Pontiac, Mich. Center-linebacker Tennessee 1952-55. No pro playing experience. College coach: Richmond 1966-67, Georgia Tech 1968-71, Memphis State 1972, South Carolina 1973. Pro coach: New York Stars (WFL) 1974, Toronto Argonauts (CFL) 1975-77, Montreal Alouettes (CFL) 1978-79, New York Giants 1980-89, joined Lions in 1990.

Dave Levy, assistant head coach; born October 25, 1932, Carrollton, Mo., lives in Southfield, Mich. Guard UCLA 1952-53. No pro playing experience. College coach: UCLA 1954, Long Beach City College 1955, Southern California 1960-75. Pro coach: San Diego Chargers 1980-88, joined Lions in 1989.

Billie Matthews, running backs; born March 15, 1930, Houston, Tex., lives in Rochester, Mich. Quarterback Southern University 1948-51. No pro playing experience. College coach: Kansas 1970, UCLA 1971-78. Pro coach: San Francisco 49ers 1979-82, Philadelphia Eagles 1983-84, Indianapolis Colts 1985-86, Kansas City Chiefs 1987-88, joined Lions in 1989.

Herb Paterra, inside linebackers; born November 8, 1940, Glassport, Pa., lives in Rochester Hills, Mich. Offensive guard-linebacker Michigan State 1960-62. Pro linebacker Buffalo Bills 1963-64, Hamilton Tiger-Cats (CFL) 1965-68. College coach: Michigan State 1969-71, Wyoming 1972-74. Pro coach: Charlotte Hornets (WFL) 1975, Hamilton Tiger-Cats (CFL) 1978-79, Los Angeles Rams 1980-82, Edmonton Eskimos (CFL) 1983, Green Bay Packers 1984-85, Buffalo Bills 1986, Tampa Bay Buccaneers 1987-88, joined Lions in 1989.

Charlie Sanders, receivers; born August 25, 1946, Greensboro, N.C., lives in Rochester, Mich. Tight end Minnesota 1966-67. Pro tight end Detroit Lions 1968-77. Pro coach: Joined Lions in 1989.

Jerry Wampfler, offensive line; born August 6, 1932, New Philadelphia, Ohio, lives in Lake Orion, Mich. Tackle Miami, Ohio 1951-54. No pro playing experience. College coach: Presbyterian 1955, Miami, Ohio 1963-65, Notre Dame 1966-69, Colorado State 1970-72 (head coach). Pro coach: Philadelphia Eagles 1973-75, 1979-83, Buffalo Bills 1976-77, New York Giants 1978, Green Bay Packers 1984-87, San Diego Chargers 1988, joined Lions in 1989.

Detroit Lions 1993 First-Year Roster

Name	Pos.	Ht.	Wt.	Birth-date	College	Hometown	How Acq.
Compton, Mike	C-G	6-6	297	9/18/70	West Virginia	Glenwood, Iowa	D3b
Conley, Sean	K	6-1	183	2/1/70	Pittsburgh	Erie, Pa.	FA
Derby, John (1)	LB	6-0	232	3/24/68	Iowa	Oconomowoc, Wis.	FA
Hallock, Ty	LB	6-3	249	4/30/71	Michigan State	Greenville, Mich.	D7
Jeffries, Greg	CB	5-9	184	10/16/71	Virginia	High Point, N.C.	D6
Johnson, Demeris	WR	5-11	181	8/26/68	Western Illinois	Detroit, Mich.	FA
Kent, Phillip (1)	LB	6-1	244	9/19/70	Mississippi	Kansas City, Mo.	FA
Logo, Ricky	NT	5-11	304	5/6/70	North Carolina State	Ft. Benning, Ga.	FA
London, Antonio	LB	6-2	234	4/14/71	Alabama	Tullahoma, Tenn.	D3a
Lynch, Eric (1)	RB	5-11	224	5/16/70	Grand Valley State	Woodhaven, Mich.	FA
McNeil, Ryan	CB	6-0	175	10/4/70	Miami	Ft. Pierce, Fla.	D2
Miniefield, Kevin	CB	5-9	178	3/2/70	Arizona State	Phoenix, Ariz.	D8
Moore, Kyle	DE	6-3	250	2/27/71	Kansas	Newark, N.J.	FA
Reynolds, Don (1)	DE	6-3	278	11/25/69	Virginia	Martinsville, Va.	FA
Riley, Mike (1)	P	6-0	217	9/27/68	Mississippi State	Dumas, Ariz.	FA
Ryans, Larry	WR	5-11	182	7/28/71	Clemson	Greenwood, S.C.	FA
Thompson, Marty	TE	6-3	243	12/9/69	Fresno State	Mammoth Lakes, Calif.	FA
Travis, Mack	NT	6-1	280	7/3/70	California	Las Vegas, Nev.	FA
Vercheval, Pierre (1)	C-G	6-1	275	11/22/64	Western Ontario	Quebec City, Canada	FA
Ware, Dwayne	CB-S	5-11	193	11/12/69	Michigan	Bloomington, Ill.	FA
White, Mark (1)	G	6-5	298	1/27/69	Florida	Pensacola, Fla.	FA
Wilson, Bernard (1)	NT	6-2	295	8/17/70	Tennessee State	Nashville, Tenn.	FA
Wright-Fair, Shaumbe	RB	5-11	214	6/29/70	Washington State	Seaside, Calif.	FA

The term NFL Rookie is defined as a player who is in his first season of professional football and has not been on the roster of another professional football team for any regular-season or postseason games. A Rookie is designated by an "R" on NFL rosters. Players who have been active in another professional football league or players who have NFL experience, including either preseason training camp or being on an Active List or Inactive List, or on Reserve/Injured or Reserve/Physically Unable to Perform for fewer than six regular-season games, are termed NFL First-Year Players. An NFL First-Year Player is designated by a "1" on NFL rosters. Thereafter, a player is credited with an additional year of experience for each season in which he accumulates six games on the Active List or Inactive List, or on Reserve/Injured or Reserve/Physically Unable to Perform.

NOTES

National Football Conference Central Division

Team Colors: Dark Green, Gold, and White

1265 Lombardi Avenue
Green Bay, Wisconsin 54307-0628
Telephone: (414) 496-5700

Club Officials

President, CEO: Bob Harlan
Vice President: John Fabry
Secretary: Peter M. Platten III
Treasurer: John R. Underwood
Chief Financial Officer: Michael R. Reinfeldt
Exec. V.P. and General Manager: Ron Wolf
Exec. Assistant to the President: Phil Pionek
Exec. Director of Public Relations: Lee Remmel
Director of Marketing: Jeff Cieply
Asst. Director of Public Relations: Jeff Blumb
Dir. of Community Relations: Mark Schiefelbein
Director of Pro Personnel: Jesse Kaye
Director of College Scouting: John Math
Green Bay Ticket Director: Mark Wagner
Milwaukee Ticket Director: Marge Paget
Controller: Dick Blasczyk
Dir. of Computer Operations: Wayne A. Wichlacz
Video Director: Al Treml
Trainer: Pepper Burruss
Equipment Manager: Bob Noel
Corporate Security Officer: Jerry Parins
Stadium Supervisor: Ted Eisenreich

Stadium: Lambeau Field • **Capacity:** 59,543
1265 Lombardi Avenue
Green Bay, Wisconsin 54307-0628
Milwaukee County Stadium •
Capacity: 56,051 • Highway I-94
Milwaukee, Wisconsin 53214

Playing Surfaces: Grass

Training Camp: St. Norbert College
West DePere, Wisconsin 54115

1993 Schedule

Preseason

July 31	vs. Raiders at Canton	3:00
Aug. 7	vs. Kansas City at Milw.	7:00
Aug. 14	vs. N.O. at Madison, Wis.	12:00
Aug. 21	at New England	7:00
Aug. 27	**Indianapolis**	7:00

Regular Season

Sept. 5	**L.A. Rams** at Milwaukee	12:00
Sept. 12	**Philadelphia**	12:00
Sept. 19	**Open Date**	
Sept. 26	at Minnesota	12:00
Oct. 3	at Dallas	12:00
Oct. 10	**Denver**	6:30
Oct. 17	**Open Date**	
Oct. 24	at Tampa Bay	1:00
Oct. 31	**Chicago**	12:00
Nov. 8	at Kansas City (Monday)	8:00
Nov. 14	at New Orleans	12:00
Nov. 21	**Detroit** at Milwaukee	12:00
Nov. 28	**Tampa Bay**	12:00
Dec. 5	at Chicago	12:00
Dec. 12	at San Diego	5:00
Dec. 19	**Minnesota** at Milwaukee	12:00
Dec. 26	**Los Angeles Raiders**	12:00
Jan. 2	at Detroit	1:00

Packers Coaching History

(498-420-36)

1921-49	Earl (Curly) Lambeau	212-106-21
1950-53	Gene Ronzani*	14-31-1
1953	Hugh Devore- Ray (Scooter) McLean**	0-2-0
1954-57	Lisle Blackbourn	17-31-0
1958	Ray (Scooter) McLean	1-10-1
1959-67	Vince Lombardi	98-30-4
1968-70	Phil Bengtson	20-21-1
1971-74	Dan Devine	25-28-4
1975-83	Bart Starr	53-77-3
1984-87	Forrest Gregg	25-37-1
1988-91	Lindy Infante	24-40-0
1992	Mike Holmgren	9-7-0

*Released after 10 games in 1953
**Co-coaches

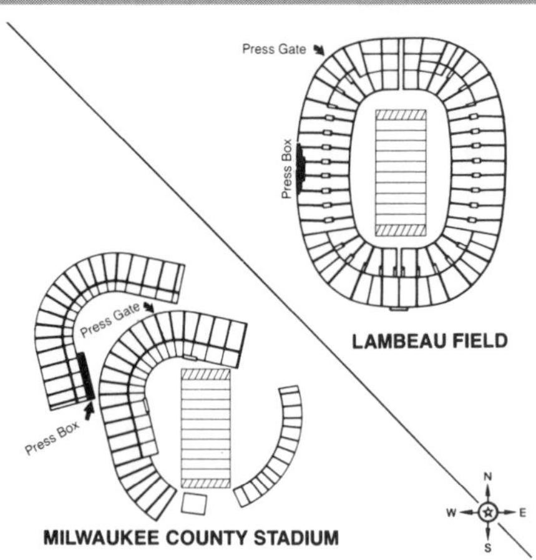

Record Holders

Individual Records — Career

Category	Name	Performance
Rushing (Yds.)	Jim Taylor, 1958-1966	8,207
Passing (Yds.)	Bart Starr, 1956-1971	23,718
Passing (TDs)	Bart Starr, 1956-1971	152
Receiving (No.)	James Lofton, 1978-1986	530
Receiving (Yds.)	James Lofton, 1978-1986	9,656
Interceptions	Bobby Dillon, 1952-59	52
Punting (Avg.)	Dick Deschaine, 1955-57	42.6
Punt Return (Avg.)	Billy Grimes, 1950-52	13.2
Kickoff Return (Avg.)	Travis Williams, 1967-1970	26.7
Field Goals	Chester Marcol, 1972-1980	120
Touchdowns (Tot.)	Don Hutson, 1935-1945	105
Points	Don Hutson, 1935-1945	823

Individual Records — Single Season

Category	Name	Performance
Rushing (Yds.)	Jim Taylor, 1962	1,407
Passing (Yds.)	Lynn Dickey, 1983	4,458
Passing (TDs)	Lynn Dickey, 1983	32
Receiving (No.)	Sterling Sharpe, 1992	108
Receiving (Yds.)	Sterling Sharpe, 1992	1,461
Interceptions	Irv Comp, 1943	10
Punting (Avg.)	Jerry Norton, 1963	44.7
Punt Return (Avg.)	Billy Grimes, 1950	19.1
Kickoff Return (Avg.)	Travis Williams, 1967	41.1
Field Goals	Chester Marcol, 1972	33
Touchdowns (Tot.)	Jim Taylor, 1962	19
Points	Paul Hornung, 1960	*176

Individual Records — Single Game

Category	Name	Performance
Rushing (Yds.)	Jim Taylor, 12-3-61	186
Passing (Yds.)	Lynn Dickey, 10-12-80	418
Passing (TDs)	Many times	5
	Last time by Lynn Dickey, 9-4-83	
Receiving (No.)	Don Hutson, 11-22-42	14
Receiving (Yds.)	Bill Howton, 10-21-56	257
Interceptions	Bobby Dillon, 11-26-53	*4
	Willie Buchanon, 9-24-78	*4
Field Goals	Chris Jacke, 11-11-90	5
Touchdowns (Tot.)	Paul Hornung, 12-12-65	5
Points	Paul Hornung, 10-8-61	33

*NFL Record

1992 Team Record

Preseason (1-3)

Date	Result		Opponents
8/8	W	21-13	Kansas City
8/16	L	7-24	vs. N.Y. Jets at Madison
8/22	L	13-16	at L.A. Rams
8/29	L	10-24	New England at Milw.

Regular Season (9-7)

Date	Result		Opponents	Att.
9/6	L	20-23	Minnesota (OT)	58,704
9/13	L	3-31	at Tampa Bay	50,725
9/20	W	24-23	Cincinnati	58,500
9/27	W	17- 3	Pittsburgh	58,700
10/4	L	10-24	at Atlanta	69,120
10/18	L	6-17	at Cleveland	69,682
10/25	L	10-30	Chicago	58,672
11/1	W	27-13	at Detroit	62,372
11/8	L	7-27	at N.Y. Giants	76,069
11/15	W	27-24	Phil. at Milw.	54,867
11/22	W	17- 3	at Chicago	66,075
11/29	W	19-14	T.B. at Milw.	54,172
12/6	W	38-10	Detroit at Milw.	54,681
12/13	W	16-14	at Houston	61,115
12/20	W	28-13	L.A. Rams	58,648
12/27	L	7-27	at Minnesota	62,597

(OT) Overtime

Score by Periods

Packers	48	115	25	88	0	—	276
Opponents	73	73	71	76	3	—	296

Attendance

Home 456,944 Away 517,755 Total 974,699
Single-game home record, 58,895 (11-3-85, Lambeau Field), 56,258 (9-28-80, Milwaukee County Stadium)
Single-season home record, 456,944 (1992)

1992 Team Statistics

	Packers	Opp.
Total First Downs	291	277
Rushing	101	89
Passing	171	170
Penalty	19	18
Third Down: Made/Att.	91/214	71/189
Third Down: Pct.	42.5	37.6
Fourth Down: Made/Att.	6/11	7/16
Fourth Down: Pct.	54.5	43.8
Total Net Yards	4785	5098
Avg. Per Game	299.1	318.6
Total Plays	990	923
Avg. Per Play	4.8	5.5
Net Yards Rushing	1555	1821
Avg. Per Game	97.2	113.8
Total Rushes	420	406
Net Yards Passing	3230	3277
Avg. Per Game	201.9	204.8
Sacked/Yards Lost	43/268	34/219
Gross Yards	3498	3496
Att./Completions	527/340	483/277
Completion Pct.	64.5	57.3
Had Intercepted	15	15
Punts/Avg.	68/38.4	68/43.3
Net Punting Avg.	68/32.3	68/33.9
Penalties/Yards Lost	88/749	98/830
Fumbles/Ball Lost	41/21	32/19
Touchdowns	30	32
Rushing	7	12
Passing	20	16
Returns	3	4
Avg. Time of Possession	32:30	27:30

1992 Individual Statistics

Scoring	TD R	TD P	TD Rt	PAT	FG	Saf	TP
Jacke	0	0	0	30/30	22/29	0	96
Sharpe	0	13	0	0/0	0/0	0	78
Sydney	2	1	0	0/0	0/0	0	18
Thompson	2	1	0	0/0	0/0	0	18
Buckley	0	0	2	0/0	0/0	0	12
J. Harris	0	2	0	0/0	0/0	0	12
Workman	2	0	0	0/0	0/0	0	12
Beach	0	1	0	0/0	0/0	0	6
T. Bennett	0	0	1	0/0	0/0	0	6
Brooks	0	1	0	0/0	0/0	0	6
Favre	1	0	0	0/0	0/0	0	6
Taylor	0	1	0	0/0	0/0	0	6
Packers	7	20	3	30/30	22/29	0	276
Opponents	12	16	4	32/32	24/27	0	296

Passing	Att.	Comp.	Yds.	Pct.	TD	Int.	Tkld.	Rate
Favre	471	302	3227	64.1	18	13	34/208	85.3
Majkowski	55	38	271	69.1	2	2	9/60	77.2
McJulien	1	0	0	0.0	0	0	0/0	39.6
Packers	527	340	3498	64.5	20	15	43/268	84.3
Opponents	483	277	3496	57.3	16	15	34/219	78.1

Rushing	Att.	Yds.	Avg.	LG	TD
Workman	159	631	4.0	44	2
Thompson	76	254	3.3	33	2
E. Bennett	61	214	3.5	18	0
Favre	47	198	4.2	19	1
Sydney	51	163	3.2	19	2
Majkowski	8	33	4.1	8	0
McGee	8	19	2.4	4	0
Brooks	2	14	7.0	8	0
McNabb	2	11	5.5	8	0
C. Harris	2	10	5.0	7	0
Sharpe	4	8	2.0	14	0
Packers	420	1555	3.7	44	7
Opponents	406	1821	4.5	71	12

Receiving	No.	Yds.	Avg.	LG	TD
Sharpe	108	1461	13.5	76t	13
J. Harris	55	595	10.8	40	2
Sydney	49	384	7.8	20	1
Workman	47	290	6.2	21	0
Beach	17	122	7.2	20	1
Lewis	13	152	11.7	27	0
Thompson	13	129	9.9	43	1
E. Bennett	13	93	7.2	22	0
Brooks	12	126	10.5	18	1
McGee	6	60	10.0	15	0
West	4	30	7.5	10	0
Taylor	2	63	31.5	35t	1
Favre	1	−7	−7.0	−7	0
Packers	340	3498	10.3	76t	20
Opponents	277	3496	12.6	75t	16

Interceptions	No.	Yds.	Avg.	LG	TD
Cecil	4	52	13.0	29	0
Buckley	3	33	11.0	33t	1
Holland	3	27	9.0	22	0
Clark	2	70	35.0	43	0
Mitchell	2	40	20.0	35	0
Butler	1	0	0.0	0	0
Packers	15	222	14.8	43	1
Opponents	15	198	13.2	69t	1

Punting	No.	Yds.	Avg.	In 20	LG
McJulien	36	1386	38.5	8	67
Wagner	30	1222	40.7	10	52
Packers	68	2608	38.4	18	67
Opponents	68	2941	43.3	14	71

Punt Returns	No.	FC	Yds.	Avg.	LG	TD
Buckley	21	5	211	10.0	58t	1
Brooks	11	1	102	9.3	22	0
C. Harris	6	0	17	2.8	13	0
Lewis	4	0	23	5.8	9	0
Hauck	1	0	2	2.0	2	0
Cecil	1	0	0	0.0	0	0
Clark	1	0	0	0.0	0	0
Packers	35	6	315	9.0	58t	1
Opponents	26	10	230	8.8	95t	1

Kickoff Returns	No.	Yds.	Avg.	LG	TD
C. Harris	23	485	21.1	50	0
E. Bennett	5	104	20.8	33	0
Brooks	18	338	18.8	30	0
Davey	1	8	8.0	8	0
Jurkovic	3	39	13.0	14	0
McNabb	1	15	15.0	15	0
Sims	1	11	11.0	11	0
West	1	0	0.0	0	0
Workman	1	17	17.0	17	0
Packers	54	1017	18.8	50	0
Opponents	57	901	15.8	48	0

Sacks	No.
T. Bennett	13.5
Paup	6.5
Brock	4.0
Jurkovic	2.0
Noble	2.0
Koonce	1.5
Archambeau	1.0
Brown	1.0
Dent	1.0
Jackson	1.0
Millard	1.0
Tuaolo	1.0
Holland	0.5
Packers	34.0
Opponents	43.0

1993 Draft Choices

Round	Name	Pos.	College
1.	Wayne Simmons	LB	Clemson
	George Teague	DB	Alabama
3.	Earl Dotson	T	Texas A&I
5.	Mark Brunell	QB	Washington
	James Willis	LB	Auburn
6.	Doug Evans	DB	Louisiana Tech
	Paul Hutchins	T	Western Michigan
	Tim Watson	DB	Howard
7.	Robert Kuberski	DE	Navy

Green Bay Packers 1993 Veteran Roster

No.	Name	Pos.	Ht.	Wt.	Birth-date	NFL Exp.	College	Hometown	How Acq.	'92 Games/ Starts
43	Anderson, Jesse	TE	6-2	255	7/26/66	3	Mississippi State	West Point, Miss.	FA-'93	0*
74	Archambeau, Lester	DE	6-5	275	6/27/67	4	Stanford	Montville, N.J.	D7-'90	16/0
78	Barrie, Sebastian	DE	6-2	270	5/26/70	2	Liberty	Dallas, Tex.	FA-'92	3/0
82	Beach, Sanjay	WR	6-1	194	2/21/66	3	Colorado State	Chandler, Ariz.	PB(SF)-'92	16/11
34	Bennett, Edgar	RB	6-0	223	2/15/69	2	Florida State	Jacksonville, Fla.	D4-'92	16/2
90	#Bennett, Tony	LB	6-2	243	7/1/67	4	Mississippi	Clarksdale, Miss.	D1a-'90	16/16
35	Berry, Latin	RB	5-10	196	1/13/67	3	Oregon	Lakeview Terrace, Calif.	W(Clev)-'93	1/0*
97	Bethune, George	DE	6-4	255	3/30/67	3	Alabama	Ft. Walton Beach, Fla.	FA-'93	0*
51	Brady, Jeff	LB	6-1	235	1/9/68	3	Kentucky	Newport, Ky.	PB(Pitt)-'92	8/0
62	#Brock, Matt	DE	6-5	290	1/14/66	5	Oregon	San Diego, Calif.	D3a-'89	16/16
87	Brooks, Robert	WR	6-0	171	6/23/70	2	South Carolina	Greenwood, S.C.	D3-'92	16/1
27	Buckley, Terrell	CB	5-9	174	6/7/71	2	Florida State	Pascagoula, Miss.	D1-'92	14/12
36	Butler, LeRoy	S	6-0	200	7/19/68	4	Florida State	Jacksonville, Fla.	D2-'90	15/15
63	†Campen, James	C	6-2	280	6/11/64	7	Tulane	Sacramento, Calif.	PB(NO)-'89	13/13
21	Carter, Carl	CB	5-11	190	3/7/64	8	Texas Tech	Ft. Worth, Tex.	FA-'92	7/1
87	Clayton, Mark	WR	5-9	181	4/8/61	11	Louisville	Indianapolis, Ind.	UFA(Mia)-'93	13/13*
55	Collins, Brett	LB	6-1	226	10/8/68	2	Washington	Hillsboro, Ore.	D12-'92	11/0
49	Crews, Terry	LB	6-2	240	7/30/68	2	Western Michigan	Flint, Mich.	FA-'93	0*
99	Davey, Don	DE	6-4	280	4/8/68	3	Wisconsin	Manitowoc, Wis.	D3a-'91	9/0
4	Favre, Brett	QB	6-2	220	10/10/69	3	Southern Mississippi	Kiln, Miss.	T(Atl)-'92	15/13
76	Galbreath, Harry	G	6-1	271	1/1/65	6	Tennessee	Clarksville, Tenn.	UFA(Mia)-'93	16/16*
70	Grant, David	NT	6-4	275	9/17/65	5	West Virginia	Belleville, N.J.	FA-'92	0*
71	Gray, Cecil	T	6-4	292	2/16/68	4	North Carolina	Norfolk, Va.	FA-'92	2/0
65	†Hallstrom, Ron	G	6-6	310	6/11/59	12	Iowa	Moline, Ill.	D1-'82	16/16
30	Harris, Corey	CB-S	5-11	195	10/25/69	2	Vanderbilt	Indianapolis, Ind.	W(Hou)-'92	5/0*
80	Harris, Jackie	TE	6-3	243	1/4/68	4	Northeast Louisiana	Pine Bluff, Ark.	D4-'90	16/11
24	#Hauck, Tim	S	5-10	181	12/20/66	4	Montana	Big Timber, Mont.	PB(NE)-'91	16/0
40	Holland, Jamie	WR-KR	6-1	195	2/1/64	7	Ohio State	Wake Forest, N.C.	FA-'93	0*
50	†Holland, Johnny	LB	6-2	235	3/11/65	7	Texas A&M	Hempstead, Tex.	D2-'87	14/14
79	Ilkin, Tunch	T	6-3	272	9/23/57	13	Indiana State	Highland Park, Ill.	UFA(Pitt)-'93	12/12*
88	Ingram, Darryl	TE	6-3	250	5/2/66	3	California	Newhall, Calif.	FA-'92	16/0
13	Jacke, Chris	K	6-0	197	3/12/66	5	Texas-El Paso	Richardson, Tex.	D6-'89	16/0
64	Jurkovic, John	NT	6-2	300	8/18/67	3	Eastern Illinois	Calumet City, Ill.	FA-'91	16/12
53	Koonce, George	LB	6-1	238	10/15/68	2	East Carolina	Vanceboro, N.C.	FA-'92	16/10
85	#Lewis, Ron	WR	5-11	180	3/25/68	3	Florida State	Jacksonville, Fla.	W(SF)-'92	6/4*
77	Maas, Bill	NT	6-5	275	3/2/62	10	Pittsburgh	Newton Square, Pa.	UFA(KC)-'93	9/5*
7	†Majkowski, Don	QB	6-2	203	2/25/64	7	Virginia	Depew, N.Y.	D10-'87	14/3
44	McNabb, Dexter	RB	6-1	245	7/9/69	2	Florida	De Funiak Springs, Fla.	D5a-'92	16/0
47	†Mitchell, Roland	CB	5-11	195	3/15/64	7	Texas Tech	Bay City, Tex.	PB(Atl)-'91	15/8
57	Moran, Rich	G	6-3	280	3/19/62	9	San Diego State	Pleasanton, Calif.	D3-'85	8/8
51	Neville, Tom	G	6-5	288	9/4/61	6	Fresno State	Fairbanks, Alaska	FA-'92	8/0
91	Noble, Brian	LB	6-2	250	9/6/62	9	Arizona State	Anaheim, Calif.	D5-'85	13/9
8	t-O'Brien, Ken	QB	6-4	212	11/27/60	11	California-Davis	Sacramento, Calif.	T(NYJ)-'93	10/3*
98	Oglesby, Alfred	NT	6-3	285	1/27/67	4	Houston	Weimer, Tex.	FA-'92	7/0
96	†Patterson, Shawn	DE	6-5	273	6/13/64	6	Arizona State	Tempe, Ariz.	D2-'88	0*
95	Paup, Bryce	LB	6-5	247	2/29/68	4	Northern Iowa	Scranton, Iowa	D6-'90	16/10
45	Prior, Mike	S	6-0	210	11/14/63	8	Illinois State	Chicago Heights, Ill.	UFA(Ind)-'93	16/16*
54	Randle, Ervin	LB	6-1	251	10/12/62	9	Baylor	Hearne, Tex.	FA-'93	13/0*
75	Ruettgers, Ken	T	6-6	286	8/20/62	9	Southern California	Bakersfield, Calif.	D1-'85	16/16
84	Sharpe, Sterling	WR	6-1	205	4/6/65	6	South Carolina	Glennville, Ga.	D1-'88	16/16
68	Sims, Joe	T-G	6-3	294	3/1/69	3	Nebraska	Sudbury, Mass.	FA-'92	15/0
32	t-Stephens, John	RB	6-1	215	2/23/66	6	Northwestern Louisiana	Springhill, La.	T(NE)-'92	16/16*
42	Sydney, Harry	RB	6-0	217	6/29/59	7	Kansas	Fayetteville, N.C.	W(SF)-'92	16/10
39	#Thompson, Darrell	RB	6-0	222	11/23/67	4	Minnesota	Rochester, Minn.	D1b-'90	7/4
9	Wagner, Bryan	P	6-2	200	3/28/62	7	Cal State-Northridge	Chula Vista, Calif.	FA-'92	7/0
86	West, Ed	TE	6-1	244	8/2/61	10	Auburn	Leighton, Ala.	FA-'84	16/8
92	White, Reggie	DE	6-5	285	12/19/61	9	Tennessee	Chattanooga, Tenn.	UFA(Phil)-'93	16/16*
29	Wilson, Marcus	RB	6-1	210	4/16/68	2	Virginia	Rochester, N.Y.	FA-'92	6/0
20	Wilson, Robert	RB	6-0	245	1/31/69	2	Texas A&M	Houston, Tex.	FA-'93	0*
52	Winters, Frank	C-G	6-3	290	1/23/64	7	Western Illinois	Union City, N.J.	PB(KC)-'92	16/11

* Anderson last active with Pittsburgh in '91; Berry played 1 game with Cleveland in '92; Bethune last active with Houston in '91; Clayton played 13 games with Miami; Crews, Patterson, and R. Wilson missed '92 season due to injury; Galbreath played 16 games with Miami; Grant last active with Cincinnati in '91; C. Harris played 5 games with Houston; Jamie Holland last active with L.A. Raiders in '91; Ilkin played 12 games with Pittsburgh; Lewis played 6 games with San Francisco; Maas played 9 games with Kansas City; O'Brien played 10 games with the N.Y. Jets; Prior played 16 games with Indianapolis; Randle played 13 games with Kansas City; Stephens played 16 games with New England; White played 16 games with Philadelphia.

#Unrestricted free agent; subject to developments.

† Restricted free agent; subject to developments.

t- Packers traded for O'Brien (New York Jets), Stephens (New England).

Traded—CB Vinnie Clark to Atlanta, S Dave McCloughan to Seattle, S Adrian White to New England.

Players lost through free agency (3): S Chuck Cecil (Phx; 16 games in '92), T Tootie Robbins (NO; 15), RB Vince Workman (TB; 10).

Also played with Packers in '92—CB Lewis Billups (5 games), LB Robert Brown (16), LB Burnell Dent (15), S Johnnie Jackson (1), CB Dave McCloughan (5), RB Buford McGee (4), P Paul McJulien (9), DE Keith Millard (2), NT Danny Noonan (6), G Harvey Salem (4), WR-KR Kitrick Taylor (10), NT Esera Tuaolo (4), T David Viaene (1), S Adrian White (15).

COACHING STAFF

Head Coach, Mike Holmgren

Pro Career: Became Packers' eleventh head coach on January 11, 1992, and led them to a 9-7 record, their second-best mark since 1972, including a six-game winning streak, Green Bay's longest since 1965. Holmgren was offensive coordinator for the San Francisco 49ers under George Seifert (1989-91) after spending previous three seasons (1986-88) as quarterbacks coach under Bill Walsh. During his six-year tenure with San Francisco, the 49ers won five consecutive NFC Western Division championships (1986-90) and back-to-back Super Bowls (XXIII and XXIV). In that span, San Francisco compiled the NFL's best overall record (71-23-1, a .753 percentage). The 49ers' never ranked lower than third overall in his three years as offensive coordinator. Career record: 9-7.

Background: Quarterback at Southern California (1966-69) and was drafted by the St. Louis Cardinals in the eighth round of the 1970 NFL draft. He served as an assistant coach at San Francisco State (1981) and Brigham Young (1982-85) before his tenure with the 49ers. Earned his bachelor of science degree in business finance at Southern California (1970).

Personal: Born June 15, 1948, in San Francisco. He and his wife, Kathy, live in Green Bay and have four daughters—Calla, Jenny, Emily, and Gretchen.

Assistant Coaches

Greg Blache, defensive line; born March 9, 1949, New Orleans, La., lives in Green Bay. No college or pro playing experience. College coach: Notre Dame 1973-75, 1981-83, Tulane 1976-80, Southern University 1986, Kansas 1987. Pro coach: Jacksonville Bulls (USFL) 1984-85, joined Packers in 1988.

Nolan Cromwell, special teams; born January 30, 1955, Smith Center, Kan., lives in Green Bay. Quarterback-safety Kansas 1973-76. Pro defensive back Los Angeles Rams 1977-87. Pro coach: Los Angeles Rams 1991, joined Packers in 1992.

Jon Gruden, wide receivers; born August 17, 1963, Sandusky, Ohio, lives in Green Bay. Quarterback Dayton 1983-85. No pro playing experience. College coach: Tennessee 1986-87, Southeast Missouri 1988, Pacific 1989, Pittsburgh 1991. Pro coach: San Francisco 49ers 1990, joined Packers in 1992.

Gil Haskell, running backs; born September 24, 1943, San Francisco, Calif., lives in Green Bay. Defensive back San Francisco State 1961, 1963-65. No pro playing exprience. College coach: Southern California 1978-82. Pro coach: Los Angeles Rams 1983-91, joined Packers in 1992.

Dick Jauron, defensive backs; born October 7, 1950, Peoria, Ill., lives in Green Bay. Defensive back Yale 1970-72. Pro defensive back Detroit Lions 1973-77, Cincinnati Bengals 1978-80. Pro coach: Buffalo Bills 1985, joined Packers in 1986.

Kent Johnston, strength and conditioning; born February 21, 1956, Mexia, Tex., lives in Green Bay. Defensive back Stephen F. Austin 1974-77. No pro playing experience. College coach: Northeast Louisiana 1979, Northwestern Louisiana 1980-81, Alabama 1983-86. Pro coach: Tampa Bay Buccaneers 1987-91, joined Packers in 1992.

Sherman Lewis, offensive coordinator-receivers; born June 29, 1942, Louisville, Ky., lives in Green Bay. Running back Michigan State 1961-63. Pro running back Toronto Argonauts (CFL) 1964-65, New York Jets 1966. College coach: Michigan State 1969-82. Pro coach: San Francisco 49ers 1983-91, joined Packers in 1992.

Jim Lind, defensive assistant-quality control; born November 11, 1947, Isle, Minn., lives in Green Bay. Linebacker Bethel College 1965-66; defensive back Bemidji State 1971-72. No pro playing experience. College coach: St. Cloud State 1977-78, St. John's (Minn.) 1979-80, Brigham Young 1981-82, Minnesota-Morris 1983-86 (head coach), Wisconsin-Eau Claire 1987-91 (head coach). Pro coach: Joined Packers in 1992.

Green Bay Packers 1993 First-Year Roster

Name	Pos.	Ht.	Wt.	Birth-date	College	Hometown	How Acq.
Beauford, Terry (1)	G	6-1	296	3/27/68	Florida A&M	Ft. Pierce, Fla.	FA
Brunell, Mark	QB	6-1	208	9/17/70	Washington	Santa Maria, Calif.	D5a
Chmura, Mark (1)	TE	6-5	240	2/22/69	Boston College	South Deerfield, Mass.	D6-'92
Crawford, Lionell	WR	5-11	185	12/24/69	Wisconsin	Houston, Tex.	FA
Detmer, Ty (1)	QB	6-0	183	10/30/67	Brigham Young	San Antonio, Tex.	D9a-'92
D'Onofrio, Mark (1)	LB	6-2	235	3/17/69	Penn State	North Bergen, N.J.	D2-'92
Dotson, Earl	T	6-3	319	2/17/71	Texas A&I	Beaumont, Tex.	D3
Evans, Doug	CB-S	6-0	188	5/13/70	Louisiana Tech	Haynesville, La.	D6a
Greer, Casey	S	6-1	204	11/28/69	Miami	Memphis, Tenn.	FA
Hall, Justin	T	6-3	291	12/20/69	Notre Dame	Plano, Tex.	FA
Holder, Chris (1)	WR	6-0	182	10/23/68	Tuskegee	Prichard, Ala.	D7-'92
Hutchins, Paul	T	6-4	342	2/11/70	Western Michigan	Chicago, Ill.	D6b
Kuberski, Bob	DE	6-4	283	4/5/71	Navy	Folsom, Pa.	D7
McKay, Orlando (1)	WR	5-10	175	10/2/69	Washington	Mesa, Ariz.	D5b-'92
Miller, Josh	P	6-2	214	7/14/70	Arizona	East Brunswick, N.J.	FA
Rohrscheib, Steve	QB	6-1	193	10/13/69	Wisconsin-Eau Claire	Mondovi, Wis.	FA
Sanders, Tracey	CB	6-0	180	5/16/66	Florida State	Bradenton, Fla.	FA
Shavers, Tyrone	WR	6-3	205	7/14/67	Lamar	Texarkana, Tex.	FA
Showell, Malcolm	DE	6-6	270	10/1/68	Delaware State	Baltimore, Md.	FA
Simmons, Wayne	LB	6-1	236	12/15/69	Clemson	Hilton Head, S.C.	D1a
Slay, Steve	G-T	6-7	295	4/6/67	Wyoming	Mt. Clemens, Mich.	FA
Smith, Nick	LB	6-1	227	6/24/71	Notre Dame	Cincinnati, Ohio	FA
Smith, Tracy	CB-S	5-9	190	8/5/69	Tennessee	Jonesboro, Ga.	FA
Teague, George	CB-S	6-1	187	2/18/71	Alabama	Montgomery, Ala.	D1b
Thompson, Rich	K	6-0	210	2/28/70	Wisconsin	Skiatook, Okla.	FA
Watson, Tim	CB-S	6-1	213	8/13/70	Howard	Ft. Valley, Ga.	FA
Willis, James	LB	6-1	230	9/2/72	Auburn	Huntsville, Ala.	D5b

The term NFL Rookie is defined as a player who is in his first season of professional football and has not been on the roster of another professional football team for any regular-season or postseason games. A Rookie is designated by an "R" on NFL rosters. Players who have been active in another professional football league or players who have NFL experience, including either preseason training camp or being on an Active List or Inactive List, or on Reserve/Injured or Reserve/Physically Unable to Perform for fewer than six regular-season games, are termed NFL First-Year Players. An NFL First-Year Player is designated by a "1" on NFL rosters. Thereafter, a player is credited with an additional year of experience for each season in which he accumulates six games on the Active List or Inactive List, or on Reserve/Injured or Reserve/Physically Unable to Perform.

NOTES

Tom Lovat, offensive line; born December 28, 1938, Bingham, Utah, lives in Green Bay. Guard-linebacker Utah 1958-60. No pro playing experience. College coach: Utah 1967, 1972-76 (head coach 1974-76), Idaho State 1968-70, Stanford 1977-79, Wyoming 1989. Pro coach: Saskatchewan Roughriders (CFL) 1971, Green Bay Packers 1980, St. Louis-Phoenix Cardinals 1981-84, 1990-91, Indianapolis Colts 1985-88, rejoined Packers in 1992.

Steve Mariucci, quarterbacks; born November 4, 1955, Iron Mountain, Mich., lives in Green Bay. Quarterback Northern Michigan 1974-77. No pro playing experience. College coach: Northern Michigan 1978-79, Cal State-Fullerton 1980-82, Louisville 1983-84, Southern California 1986, California 1987-91. Pro coach: Orlando Renegades (USFL) 1985, Los Angeles Rams 1985, joined Packers in 1992.

Andy Reid, tight ends-offensive line assistant; born March 19, 1958, Los Angeles, Calif., lives in Green Bay. Offensive tackle-guard Brigham Young 1978-80. No pro playing experience. College coach: San Francisco State 1983-85, Northern Arizona 1986, Texas-El Paso 1987, Missouri 1988-91. Pro coach: Joined Packers in 1992.

Ray Rhodes, defensive coordinator; born October 20, 1950, Mexia, Tex., lives in Green Bay. Running back-wide receiver Texas Christian 1969-70, Tulsa 1972-73. Pro defensive back New York Giants 1974-79, San Francisco 49ers 1980. Pro coach: San Francisco 49ers 1981-91, joined Packers in 1992.

Bob Valesente, linebackers; born July 19, 1940, Seneca Falls, N.Y., lives in Green Bay. Halfback Ithaca College 1958-61. No pro playing experience. College coach: Cornell 1964-74, Cincinnati 1975-76, Arizona 1977-79, Mississippi State 1980-81, Kansas 1984-87 (head coach, 1986-87), Maryland 1988, Pittsburgh 1989. Pro coach: Baltimore Colts 1982-83, Pittsburgh Steelers 1990-91, joined Packers in 1992.

National Football Conference Western Division

Team Colors: Royal Blue, Gold, and White

Business Address:
2327 West Lincoln Avenue
Anaheim, California 92801
Telephone: (714) 535-7267

Ticket Office:
Anaheim Stadium
1900 State College Boulevard
Anaheim, California 92806
Telephone: (714) 937-6767

Club Officials

Owner/President: Georgia Frontiere
Executive Vice President: John Shaw
Senior Vice President: Jay Zygmunt
Vice President-Media and Community Relations: Marshall Klein
Vice President-Head Coach: Chuck Knox
Administrator-Football Operations: Jack Faulkner
General Counsel: Steve Novak
Director of Player Personnel: John Becker
Director of Player Relations: Paul (Tank) Younger
Director of Promotions/Sales: Pete Donovan
Director of Public Relations: Rick Smith
Trainers: Jim Anderson, Blynn DeNiro, George Menefee
Equipment Managers: Don Hewitt, Todd Hewitt

Stadium: Anaheim Stadium • **Capacity:** 69,008
Anaheim, California 92806

Playing Surface: Grass

Training Camp: California State University-Fullerton
Fullerton, California 92634

1993 Schedule

Preseason

Aug. 7	at Phoenix	7:30
Aug. 14	**San Diego**	7:00
Aug. 21	at Cleveland	4:00
Aug. 28	**Los Angeles Raiders**	6:00

Regular Season

Sept. 5	vs. Green Bay at Milw.	12:00
Sept. 12	**Pittsburgh**	1:00
Sept. 19	at New York Giants	1:00
Sept. 26	at Houston	12:00
Oct. 3	**New Orleans**	1:00
Oct. 10	**Open Date**	
Oct. 14	at Atlanta (Thursday)	7:30
Oct. 24	**Detroit**	1:00
Oct. 31	at San Francisco	1:00
Nov. 7	**Open Date**	
Nov. 14	**Atlanta**	1:00
Nov. 21	**Washington**	1:00
Nov. 28	**San Francisco**	1:00
Dec. 5	at Phoenix	2:00
Dec. 12	at New Orleans	12:00
Dec. 19	at Cincinnati	1:00
Dec. 26	**Cleveland**	1:00
Jan. 2	**Chicago**	1:00

Rams Coaching History

Cleveland 1937-1945 (402-346-20)

1937-38	Hugo Bezdek*	1-13-0
1938	Art Lewis	4-4-0
1939-42	Earl (Dutch) Clark	16-26-2
1944	Aldo (Buff) Donelli	4-6-0
1945-46	Adam Walsh	16-5-1
1947	Bob Snyder	6-6-0
1948-49	Clark Shaughnessy	14-8-3
1950-52	Joe Stydahar**	19-9-0
1952-54	Hamp Pool	23-11-2
1955-59	Sid Gillman	28-32-1
1960-62	Bob Waterfield***	9-24-1
1962-65	Harland Svare	14-31-3
1966-70	George Allen	49-19-4
1971-72	Tommy Prothro	14-12-2
1973-77	Chuck Knox	57-20-1
1978-82	Ray Malavasi	43-36-0
1983-91	John Robinson	79-74-0
1992	Chuck Knox	6-10-0

*Released after three games in 1938
**Resigned after one game in 1952
***Resigned after eight games in 1962

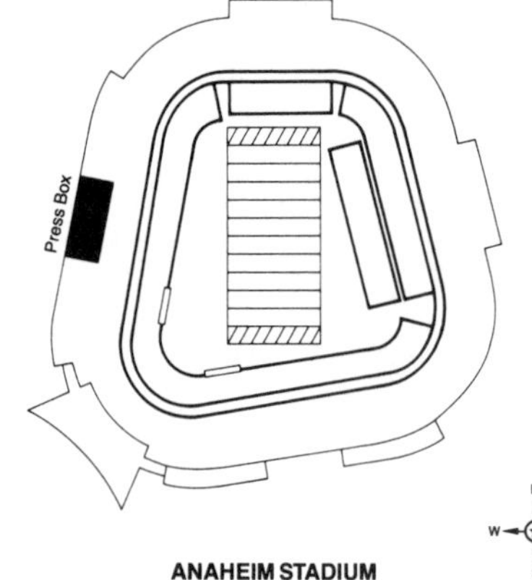

ANAHEIM STADIUM

Record Holders

Individual Records — Career

Category	Name	Performance
Rushing (Yds.)	Eric Dickerson, 1983-87	7,245
Passing (Yds.)	Roman Gabriel, 1962-1972	22,223
Passing (TDs)	Roman Gabriel, 1962-1972	154
Receiving (No.)	Henry Ellard, 1983-1992	532
Receiving (Yds.)	Henry Ellard, 1983-1992	8,816
Interceptions	Ed Meador, 1959-1970	46
Punting (Avg.)	Danny Villanueva, 1960-64	44.2
Punt Return (Avg.)	Henry Ellard, 1983-1992	11.3
Kickoff Return (Avg.)	Tom Wilson, 1956-1961	27.1
Field Goals	Mike Lansford, 1982-1990	158
Touchdowns (Tot.)	Eric Dickerson, 1983-87	58
Points	Mike Lansford, 1982-1990	789

Individual Records — Single Season

Category	Name	Performance
Rushing (Yds.)	Eric Dickerson, 1984	*2,105
Passing (Yds.)	Jim Everett, 1989	4,310
Passing (TDs)	Jim Everett, 1988	31
Receiving (No.)	Henry Ellard, 1988	86
Receiving (Yds.)	Elroy (Crazylegs) Hirsch, 1951	1,425
Interceptions	Dick (Night Train) Lane, 1952	*14
Punting (Avg.)	Danny Villanueva, 1962	45.5
Punt Return (Avg.)	Woodley Lewis, 1952	18.5
Kickoff Return (Avg.)	Verda (Vitamin T) Smith, 1950	33.7
Field Goals	David Ray, 1973	30
Touchdowns (Tot.)	Eric Dickerson, 1983	20
Points	David Ray, 1973	130

Individual Records — Single Game

Category	Name	Performance
Rushing (Yds.)	Eric Dickerson, 1-4-86	248
Passing (Yds.)	Norm Van Brocklin, 9-28-51	*554
Passing (TDs)	Many times	5
	Last time by Jim Everett, 9-25-88	
Receiving (No.)	Tom Fears, 12-3-50	*18
Receiving (Yds.)	Willie Anderson, 11-26-89	*336
Interceptions	Many times	3
	Last time by Pat Thomas, 10-7-79	
Field Goals	Bob Waterfield, 12-9-51	5
Touchdowns (Tot.)	Bob Shaw, 12-11-49	4
	Elroy (Crazylegs) Hirsch, 9-28-51	4
	Harold Jackson, 10-14-73	4
Points	Bob Shaw, 12-11-49	24
	Elroy (Crazylegs) Hirsch, 9-28-51	24
	Harold Jackson, 10-14-73	24

*NFL Record

1992 Team Record

Preseason (3-1)

Date	Result		Opponents
8/6	W	21- 7	at Seattle
8/15	W	19-16	L.A. Raiders
8/22	W	16-13	Green Bay
8/27	L	19-30	at San Diego

Regular Season (6-10)

Date	Result		Opponents	Att.
9/6	L	7-40	at Buffalo	78,851
9/13	W	14- 0	New England	44,000
9/20	L	10-26	at Miami	57,701
9/27	W	18-10	N.Y. Jets	45,735
10/4	L	24-27	at San Francisco	65,340
10/11	L	10-13	at New Orleans	67,591
10/18	W	38-17	N.Y. Giants	56,549
11/1	L	28-30	at Atlanta	69,503
11/8	L	14-20	Phoenix	44,241
11/15	W	27-23	at Dallas	62,993
11/22	L	10-27	San Francisco	67,461
11/29	L	17-31	Minnesota	58,882
12/6	W	31-27	at Tampa Bay	39,056
12/13	L	14-37	New Orleans	53,007
12/20	L	13-28	at Green Bay	58,648
12/27	W	38-27	Atlanta	44,627

Score by Periods

Rams	42	73	86	112	0	—	313
Opponents	94	151	57	81	0	—	383

Attendance

Home 414,502 Away 499,683 Total 914,185
Single-game home record, 67,461 (11-22-92)
Single-season home record, 500,403 (1980)

1992 Team Statistics

	Rams	Opp.
Total First Downs	278	319
Rushing	83	130
Passing	174	175
Penalty	21	14
Third Down: Made/Att.	69/186	91/204
Third Down: Pct.	37.1	44.6
Fourth Down: Made/Att.	1/7	2/5
Fourth Down: Pct.	14.3	40.0
Total Net Yards	4877	5523
Avg. Per Game	304.8	345.2
Total Plays	914	1005
Avg. Per Play	5.3	5.5
Net Yards Rushing	1659	2230
Avg. Per Game	103.7	139.4
Total Rushes	393	467
Net Yards Passing	3218	3293
Avg. Per Game	201.1	205.8
Sacked/Yards Lost	26/204	31/188
Gross Yards	3422	3481
Att./Completions	495/289	507/305
Completion Pct.	58.4	60.2
Had Intercepted	20	18
Punts/Avg.	76/41.1	66/42.1
Net Punting Avg.	76/33.2	66/34.7
Penalties/Yards Lost	79/592	102/778
Fumbles/Ball Lost	30/17	26/15
Touchdowns	38	43
Rushing	12	22
Passing	23	18
Returns	3	3
Avg. Time of Possession	28:31	31:29

1992 Individual Statistics

Scoring	TD R	TD P	TD Rt	PAT	FG	Saf	TP
Zendejas	0	0	0	38/38	15/20	0	83
Gary	7	3	0	0/0	0/0	0	60
Anderson	0	7	0	0/0	0/0	0	42
Lang	5	1	0	0/0	0/0	0	36
Carter	0	3	0	0/0	0/0	0	18
Chadwick	0	3	0	0/0	0/0	0	18
Ellard	0	3	0	0/0	0/0	0	18
Kinchen	0	0	2	0/0	0/0	0	12
Price	0	2	0	0/0	0/0	0	12
Bailey	0	0	1	0/0	0/0	0	6
Delpino	0	1	0	0/0	0/0	0	6
Greene	0	0	0	0/0	0/0	1	2
Rams	12	23	3	38/38	15/20	1	313
Opponents	22	18	3	41/43	28/34	0	383

Passing	Att.	Comp.	Yds.	Pct.	TD	Int.	Tkld.	Rate
Everett	475	281	3323	59.2	22	18	26/204	80.2
Pagel	20	8	99	40.0	1	2	0/0	33.1
Rams	495	289	3422	58.4	23	20	26/204	78.2
Opponents	507	305	3481	60.2	18	18	31/188	77.9

Rushing	Att.	Yds.	Avg.	LG	TD
Gary	279	1125	4.0	63	7
Lang	33	203	6.2	71	5
Everett	32	133	4.2	22	0
Delpino	32	115	3.6	31	0
Thompson	11	57	5.2	12	0
Turner	2	14	7.0	9	0
Stradford	3	12	4.0	5	0
Pagel	1	0	0.0	0	0
Rams	393	1659	4.2	71	12
Opponents	467	2230	4.8	39t	22

Receiving	No.	Yds.	Avg.	LG	TD
Gary	52	293	5.6	22	3
Ellard	47	727	15.5	33t	3
Anderson	38	657	17.3	51	7
Price	34	324	9.5	25	2
Chadwick	29	362	12.5	27t	3
Carter	20	232	11.6	25	3
Lang	18	283	15.7	67t	1
Cox	18	261	14.5	26	0
Delpino	18	139	7.7	12t	1
Turner	5	42	8.4	16	0
Thompson	5	11	2.2	7	0
McNeal	4	79	19.8	38	0
Harry	1	12	12.0	12	0
Rams	289	3422	11.8	67t	23
Opponents	305	3481	11.4	81t	18

Interceptions	No.	Yds.	Avg.	LG	TD
Henley	4	41	10.3	25	0
Newman	4	33	8.3	17	0
Lyght	3	80	26.7	39	0
Bailey	3	61	20.3	37	1
White	2	49	24.5	40	0
Kelm	1	16	16.0	16	0
Phifer	1	3	3.0	3	0
Rams	18	283	15.7	40	1
Opponents	20	305	15.3	67	1

Punting	No.	Yds.	Avg.	In 20	LG
Bracken	76	3122	41.1	20	59
Rams	76	3122	41.1	20	59
Opponents	66	2776	42.1	14	58

Punt Returns	No.	FC	Yds.	Avg.	LG	TD
Turner	28	6	207	7.4	23	0
Harry	6	4	34	5.7	11	0
Kinchen	4	1	103	25.8	61t	2
Stradford	1	0	1	1.0	1	0
Rams	39	11	345	8.8	61t	2
Opponents	48	11	522	10.9	74t	1

Kickoff Returns	No.	Yds.	Avg.	LG	TD
Turner	29	569	19.6	35	0
Anderson	1	9	9.0	9	0
Delpino	6	83	13.8	18	0
Israel	1	−3	−3.0	−3	0
Kinchen	4	63	15.8	19	0
Lang	13	228	17.5	26	0
Stephen	2	12	6.0	7	0
Stradford	3	59	19.7	21	0
Thompson	4	34	8.5	14	0
Rams	63	1054	16.7	35	0
Opponents	55	1128	20.5	60	0

Sacks	No.
Greene	10.0
Gilbert	5.0
Robinson	5.0
Piel	3.0
Hawkins	2.0
Stewart	2.0
Young	2.0
Boutte	1.0
Rams	31.0
Opponents	26.0

1993 Draft Choices

Round	Name	Pos.	College
1.	Jerome Bettis	RB	Notre Dame
2.	Troy Drayton	TE	Penn State
3.	Russell White	RB	California
5.	Sean LaChapelle	WR	UCLA
	Chuck Belin	G	Wisconsin
6.	Deral Boykin	DB	Louisville
7.	Brad Fichtel	C	Eastern Illinois
8.	Jeff Buffaloe	P	Memphis State
	Maa Tanuvasa	DT	Hawaii

Los Angeles Rams 1993 Veteran Roster

No.	Name	Pos.	Ht.	Wt.	Birth-date	NFL Exp.	College	Hometown	How Acq.	'92 Games/ Starts
83	Anderson, Willie	WR	6-0	172	3/7/65	6	UCLA	Paulsboro, N.J.	D2b-'88	15/9
28	Bailey, Robert	CB	5-9	176	9/3/68	3	Miami	Miami, Fla.	D4-'91	16/6
96	Boutte, Marc	DT	6-4	298	7/26/69	2	Louisiana State	Lake Charles, La.	D3a-'92	16/15
17	#Bracken, Don	P	6-1	211	2/16/62	8	Michigan	Thermopolis, Wyo.	FA-'92	16/0
61	Brostek, Bern	C	6-3	300	9/11/66	4	Washington	Honolulu, Hawaii	D1-'90	16/16
51	#Bush, Blair	C	6-3	275	11/25/56	16	Washington	Palos Verdes, Calif.	PB(GB)-'92	16/0
88	Carter, Pat	TE	6-4	250	8/1/66	6	Florida State	Sarasota, Fla.	T(Det)-'89	16/16
89	Chadwick, Jeff	WR	6-3	185	12/16/60	11	Grand Valley State	Dearborn, Mich.	PB(Sea)-'92	16/16
56	Conlan, Shane	LB	6-3	235	3/4/64	7	Penn State	Frewsburg, N.Y.	UFA(Buff)-'93	13/12*
25	Crooms, Chris	S	6-2	211	2/4/69	2	Texas A&M	Baytown, Tex.	D5-'92	16/0
77	Eatman, Irv	T	6-7	300	1/1/61	8	UCLA	Dayton, Ohio	UFA(NYJ)-'93	12/12*
80	Ellard, Henry	WR	5-11	182	7/21/61	11	Fresno State	Fresno, Calif.	D2-'83	16/15
11	Everett, Jim	QB	6-5	212	1/3/63	8	Purdue	Albuquerque, N.M.	T(Hou)-'86	16/16
43	†Gary, Cleveland	RB	6-0	226	5/4/66	5	Miami	Indiantown, Fla.	D1b-'89	16/16
90	Gilbert, Sean	DT	6-4	315	4/10/70	2	Pittsburgh	Aliquippa, Pa.	D1-'92	16/16
79	t-Goeas, Leo	G-T	6-4	292	8/15/66	4	Hawaii	Honolulu, Hawaii	T(SD)-'93	16/16*
70	†Hawkins, Bill	DE	6-6	269	5/9/66	5	Miami	Miami, Fla.	D1a-'89	8/7
20	Henley, Darryl	CB	5-9	172	10/30/66	5	UCLA	LaVerne, Calif.	D2c-'89	16/15
31	Israel, Steve	CB	5-11	186	3/16/69	2	Pittsburgh	Lawnside, N.J.	D2-'92	16/1
72	Jenkins, Robert	T	6-5	285	12/30/63	8	UCLA	Dublin, Calif.	D6-'86	9/0
86	Johnson, Damone	TE	6-4	250	3/2/62	9	Cal Poly-SLO	Santa Monica, Calif.	D6-'85	16/15
52	Kelm, Larry	LB	6-4	240	11/29/64	7	Texas A&M	Corpus Christi, Tex.	D4-'87	16/15
81	Kinchen, Todd	WR	6-0	187	1/7/69	2	Louisiana State	Baton Rouge, La.	D3b-'92	14/0
22	Kors, R.J.	S	6-0	195	6/27/66	3	Long Beach State	Woodland Hills, Calif.	RFA(NYJ)-'93	14/3*
38	Lang, David	RB	5-11	213	3/28/67	3	Northern Arizona	San Bernardino, Calif.	D12-'90	11/0
34	Lester, Tim	RB	5-9	215	6/15/68	2	Eastern Kentucky	Miami, Fla.	D10-'92	9/0
27	Lilly, Sammy	CB	5-11	175	2/12/65	6	Georgia Tech	Augusta, Ga.	FA-'92	12/0
41	Lyght, Todd	CB	6-0	186	2/9/69	3	Notre Dame	Flint, Mich.	D1-'91	12/12
53	t-Martin, Chris	LB	6-2	241	12/19/60	11	Auburn	Huntsville, Ala.	T(KC)-'93	14/12*
82	†McNeal, Travis	TE	6-3	244	1/10/67	5	Tennessee-Chattanooga	Birmingham, Ala.	FA-'92	12/0
66	Newberry, Tom	G	6-2	285	12/20/62	8	Wisconsin-LaCrosse	Onalaska, Wis.	D2-'86	16/16
26	Newman, Anthony	S	6-0	199	11/25/65	6	Oregon	Beaverton, Ore.	D2a-'88	16/16
14	#Pagel, Mike	QB	6-2	220	9/13/60	12	Arizona State	Phoenix, Ariz.	FA(Clev)-'91	16/0
69	Pahukoa, Jeff	G-T	6-2	298	2/2/69	3	Washington	Marysville, Wash.	D12a-'91	16/0
58	Phifer, Roman	LB	6-2	230	3/5/68	3	UCLA	Pineville, N.C.	D2-'91	16/14
95	Piel, Mike	DT	6-4	270	9/21/65	5	Illinois	El Toro, Calif.	D3-'88	15/5
98	Powers, Warren	DE	6-6	287	2/4/65	5	Maryland	Baltimore, Md.	W(Den)-'92	7/0
87	Price, Jim	TE	6-4	247	10/2/66	3	Stanford	Englewood, N.J.	FA-'91	15/3
97	Robinson, Gerald	DE	6-3	262	5/4/63	6	Auburn	Notasulga, Ala.	PB(SD)-'91	16/16
92	Rocker, David	DT	6-4	267	3/12/69	3	Auburn	Atlanta, Ga.	FA-'91	3/0
59	Rolling, Henry	LB	6-2	225	9/8/65	6	Nevada-Reno	Henderson, Nev.	UFA(SD)-'93	15/15*
12	Rubley, T.J.	QB	6-3	205	11/29/68	2	Tulsa	Davenport, Iowa	D9-'92	0*
78	Slater, Jackie	T	6-4	285	5/27/54	18	Jackson State	Jackson, Miss.	D3-'76	16/16
50	Stephen, Scott	LB	6-3	243	6/18/64	7	Arizona State	Los Angeles, Calif.	W(GB)-'92	16/0
23	Stewart, Michael	S	6-0	195	7/12/65	7	Fresno State	Bakersfield, Calif.	D8-'87	11/6
60	Stokes, Fred	DE	6-3	274	3/14/64	7	Georgia Southern	Vidalia, Ga.	UFA(Wash)-'93	16/11*
65	Subis, Nick	T	6-4	278	12/24/67	2	San Diego State	Torrance, Calif.	FA-'93	0*
37	Terrell, Pat	S	6-0	195	3/18/68	4	Notre Dame	Memphis, Tenn.	D2-'90	15/11
32	†Thompson, Anthony	RB	6-0	210	4/8/67	4	Indiana	Terre Haute, Ind.	W(Phx)-'92	7/0
54	Townsend, Brian	LB	6-3	242	11/7/68	2	Michigan	Cincinnati, Ohio	FA-'93	3/0*
55	#White, Leon	LB	6-3	242	10/4/63	8	Brigham Young	La Mesa, Calif.	FA-'92	1/1
76	Young, Robert	DE	6-6	273	1/29/69	3	Mississippi State	Jackson, Miss.	D5-'91	11/1
10	#Zendejas, Tony	K	5-8	165	5/15/60	9	Nevada-Reno	Chino, Calif.	PB(Hou)-'91	16/0

* Conlan played 13 games with Buffalo in '92; Eatman played 12 games with N.Y. Jets; Goeas played 16 games with San Diego; Kors played 14 games with N.Y. Jets; Martin played 14 games with Kansas City; Rolling played 15 games with San Diego; Rubley was on practice squad for entire '92 season; Stokes played 16 games with Washington; Subis last active with Denver in '91; Townsend played 3 games with Cincinnati.

\# Unrestricted free agent; subject to developments.

† Restricted free agent; subject to developments.

t- Rams traded for G-T Leo Goeas (San Diego).

Players lost through free agency (7): WR Aaron Cox (Ind; 10 games in '92), RB Robert Delpino (Den; 10), LB Kevin Greene (16; Pitt), WR Emile Harry (Den; 4), G Joe Milinichik (SD; 16), T Gerald Perry (Raid; 16); LB Fred Strickland (Minn; 15).

Also played with Rams in '92—DT Eric Hayes (1 game), DE Jim Skow (4), RB Troy Stradford (2), WR-KR Vernon Turner (12).

COACHING STAFF

Head Coach, Chuck Knox

Pro Career: Started his second tour of duty as Rams head coach on January 8, 1992, after serving as Seattle's head coach from 1983-91 and leading the Seahawks into the playoffs four times, including the AFC Western Division title in 1988. Previously served as head coach of Buffalo Bills 1978-82, leading them to the AFC East title in 1980. Led the Rams to five consecutive NFC West titles (1973-77) before taking over Bills. Pro assistant with New York Jets 1963-66, coaching offensive line, before moving to Detroit in 1967. Served Lions as offensive line coach until named head coach of Rams in 1973. No pro playing experience. Career record: 184-135-1.

Background: Played tackle for Juniata College in Huntingdon, Pa., 1950-53. Was an assistant coach at his alma mater in 1954, then spent 1955 season at Tyrone High in Tyrone, Pa. Was head coach at Ellwood City (Pa.) High School from 1956-58. Moved to Wake Forest as an assistant coach in 1959-60, then Kentucky in 1961-62.

Personal: Born April 27, 1932, in Sewickley, Pa. Chuck and his wife, Shirley live in Villa Park, Calif., and have four children — Chris, Kathy, Colleen, and Chuck.

Assistant Coaches

Chris Clausen, strength and conditioning coordinator; born February 21, 1958, Evergreen Park, Ill., lives in Huntington Beach, Calif. Cornerback Indiana 1976-79. No pro playing experience. College coach: San Diego State 1987-89. Pro coach: San Diego Chargers 1989-91, joined Rams in 1992.

George Dyer, defensive coordinator; born May 4, 1940, Alhambra, Calif., lives in Villa Park, Calif. Center-linebacker U.C. Santa Barbara 1961-63. No pro playing experience. College coach: Humboldt State 1964-66, Coalinga (Calif.) J.C. 1967 (head coach), Portland State 1968-71, Idaho 1972, San Jose State 1973, Michigan State 1977-79, Arizona State 1980-81. Pro coach: Winnipeg Blue Bombers (CFL) 1974-76, Buffalo Bills 1982, Seattle Seahawks 1983-91, joined Rams in 1992.

Jim Erkenbeck, offensive line; born September 10, 1929, Los Angeles, Calif., lives in Anaheim Hills, Calif. Linebacker-end San Diego State 1949-52. No pro playing experience. College coach: San Diego State 1960-63, Grossmont (Calif.) J.C. 1964-67, Utah State 1968, Washington State 1969-71, California 1972-76. Pro coach: Winnipeg Blue Bombers (CFL) 1977, Montreal Alouettes (CFL) 1978-81, Calgary Stampeders (CFL) 1982, Philadelphia/Baltimore Stars (USFL) 1983-85, New Orleans Saints 1986, Dallas Cowboys 1987-88, Kansas City Chiefs 1989-91, joined Rams in 1992.

Greg Gaines, defensive assistant; born October 16, 1958, Martinsville, Va., lives in Mission Viejo, Calif. Linebacker Tennessee 1976-80. Pro linebacker Seattle Seahawks 1981-88, Kansas City Chiefs 1989. Pro coach: Joined Rams in 1992.

Chick Harris, running backs; born September 21, 1945, Durham, N.C., lives in Irvine, Calif. Running back Northern Arizona 1966-69. No pro playing experience. College coach: Colorado State 1970-72, Long Beach State 1973-74, Washington 1975-80. Pro coach: Buffalo Bills 1981-82, Seattle Seahawks 1983-91, joined Rams in 1992.

Milt Jackson, receivers; born October 16, 1943, Groesbeck, Tex., lives in Anaheim Hills, Calif. Defensive back Tulsa 1965-66. Pro defensive back San Francisco 49ers 1967. College coach: Oregon State 1973, Rice 1974, California 1975-76, Oregon 1977-78, UCLA 1979. Pro coach: San Francisco 49ers 1980-82, Buffalo Bills 1983-84, Philadelphia Eagles 1985, Houston Oilers 1986-88, Indianapolis Colts 1989-91, joined Rams in 1992.

Los Angeles Rams 1993 First-Year Roster

Name	Pos.	Ht.	Wt.	Birth-date	College	Hometown	How Acq.
Ashmore, Darryl (1)	T	6-7	300	11/1/69	Northwestern	Peoria, Ill.	D7
Barry, Jay	RB	5-10	185	10/29/69	Washington	Northglenn, Colo.	FA
Belin, Charles	G	6-2	312	6/26/70	Wisconsin	Milwaukee, Wis.	D5b
Beltis, Jerome	RB	5-11	243	2/16/72	Notre Dame	Detroit, Mich.	D1
Bobo, Phillip	WR	5-11	186	12/6/71	Washington State	Moreno Valley, Calif.	FA
Boykin, Deral	S	5-11	196	9/2/70	Louisville	Kent, Ohio	D6
Buchanan, Richard (1)	WR	5-10	178	5/8/69	Northwestern	Maywood, Ill.	FA
Buckley, Eric (1)	S	5-11	212	6/4/69	Central Florida	Lakeview, Fla.	FA
Buffaloe, Jeff	P	6-1	194	9/18/70	Memphis State	Memphis, Tenn.	D8a
Carter, Kaleaph	RB	6-0	230	5/29/70	UCLA	Huntington Beach, Calif.	FA
Cummins, Jeff	DT	6-6	270	5/25/69	Oregon	Torrance, Calif.	FA
Davison, Jerone	RB	5-11	217	9/16/70	Arizona State	Picayune, Miss.	FA
Drayton, Troy	TE	6-3	255	6/29/70	Penn State	Steelton, Pa.	D2
Fichel, Brad	C	6-2	285	3/10/70	Eastern Illinois	Oswego, Ill.	D7
Foster, Sean (1)	WR	6-1	190	12/22/67	Long Beach State	Los Angeles, Calif.	FA
Garten, Joe (1)	G	6-2	290	8/13/68	Colorado	Valencia, Calif.	FA
Gaspard, Curtis (1)	WR	6-0	180	2/23/68	Washington	New Orleans, La.	FA
Geter, Eric	CB	5-10	193	6/24/70	Clemson	Newnan, Ga.	FA
Goodwin, Malcolm	LB	6-1	226	7/15/70	Iowa State	Ames, Iowa	FA
Griffin, Courtney (1)	CB	5-10	180	12/19/66	Fresno State	Fresno, Calif.	FA
Harper, Shawn (1)	T	6-4	292	7/9/68	Indiana	Columbus, Ohio	D4-'92
Harris, Kevin (1)	C	6-2	272	5/17/69	Miami	Ft. Myers, Fla.	D12-'92
Homco, Thomas (1)	LB	6-0	245	1/8/70	Northwestern	Highland, Tenn.	FA
James, John	T	6-3	300	3/28/70	Mississippi State	Atlanta, Ga.	FA
Jordan, Al	CB	5-10	180	2/25/70	UCLA	Beltsville, Md.	FA
LaChapelle, Sean	WR	6-3	205	7/29/70	UCLA	Napa, Calif.	D5a
Loneker, Keith	G	6-3	330	6/21/71	Kansas	Roselle Park, N.J.	FA
Martin, Jamie	QB	6-2	215	2/8/70	Weber State	Arroyo Grande, Calif.	FA
Miles, Carlton	LB	6-2	245	2/24/70	Florida	Daytona Beach, Fla.	FA
Moore, Reggie (1)	WR	5-9	181	3/23/68	UCLA	Houston, Tex.	FA
Perez, Louis	K	5-9	197	4/11/71	UCLA	Carson, Calif.	FA
Tanuvasa, Maa	DT	6-2	277	11/6/70	Hawaii	Mililani, Hawaii	D8b
White, Russell	RB	5-11	216	12/15/70	California	Encino, Calif.	D3
Williams, Anthony (1)	LB	6-2	245	6/1/70	Alabama A&M	Waco, Tex.	FA

The term NFL Rookie is defined as a player who is in his first season of professional football and has not been on the roster of another professional football team for any regular-season or postseason games. A Rookie is designated by an "R" on NFL rosters. Players who have been active in another professional football league or players who have NFL experience, including either preseason training camp or being on an Active List or Inactive List, or on Reserve/Injured or Reserve/Physically Unable to Perform for fewer than six regular-season games, are termed NFL First-Year Players. An NFL First-Year Player is designated by a "1" on NFL rosters. Thereafter, a player is credited with an additional year of experience for each season in which he accumulates six games on the Active List or Inactive List, or on Reserve/Injured or Reserve/Physically Unable to Perform.

NOTES

Mike Martz, offensive assistant; born May 13, 1951, Sioux Falls, S.D., lives in Huntington Beach, Calif. Tight end San Diego Mesa (Calif.) Junior College 1969-70, U.C.-Santa Barbara 1971, Fresno State 1972. No pro playing experience. College coach: San Diego Mesa (Calif.) Junior College 1974, 1976-78, San Jose State 1975, Santa Ana (Calif.) Junior College 1978-79, Fresno State 1979, Pacific 1980-82, Minnesota 1982-83, Arizona State 1984-91. Pro coach: Joined Rams in 1992.

Rod Perry, defensive backfield; born September 11, 1953, Fresno, Calif., lives in Anaheim Hills, Calif. Defensive back Colorado 1972-74. Pro cornerback Los Angeles Rams 1975-82, Cleveland Browns 1983-84. College coach: Columbia 1985, Fresno City College 1986, Fresno State 1987-88. Pro coach: Seattle Seahawks 1989-91, joined Rams in 1992.

Howard Tippett, special teams-tight ends; born September 23, 1938, Tallassee, Ala., lives in Huntington Beach, Calif. Quarterback-safety East Tennessee State 1956-58. No pro playing experience. College coach: Tulane 1963-65, West Virginia 1966, 1970-71, Houston 1967-69, Wake Forest 1972, Mississippi State 1973, 1979, Washington State 1976, Oregon 1977-78, UCLA 1980, Illinois 1987. Pro coach: Jacksonville, Express (WFL) 1974-75, Tampa Bay Buccaneers 1981-86, Green Bay Packers 1988-91, joined Rams in 1992.

Ted Tollner, quarterbacks; born May 29, 1940, San Francisco, Calif., lives in Huntington Beach, Calif. Quarterback Cal Poly-SLO 1959-61. No pro playing experience. College coach: College of San Mateo 1971-72 (head coach), San Diego State 1973-80, Brigham Young 1981, Southern California 1982-86 (head coach 1983-86). Pro coach: Buffalo Bills 1987-88, San Diego Chargers 1989-91, joined Rams in 1992.

Joe Vitt, assistant head coach-safeties; born August 23, 1954, Camden, N.J., lives in Mission Viejo, Calif. Linebacker Towson State 1973-75. No pro playing experience. Pro coach: Baltimore Colts 1979-81, Seattle Seahawks 1982-91, joined Rams in 1992.

Ernie Zampese, offensive coordinator; born March 12, 1936, Santa Barbara, Calif., lives in Mission Viejo, Calif. Halfback Southern California 1956-58. No pro playing experience. College coach: Hancock, Calif., J.C. 1962-65, Cal Poly-SLO 1966, San Diego State 1967-75. Pro coach: San Diego Chargers 1976, 1979-86, New York Jets 1977-78 (scout), joined Rams in 1987.

National Football Conference Central Division

Team Colors: Purple, Gold, and White

9520 Viking Drive
Eden Prairie, Minnesota 55344
Telephone: (612) 828-6500

Club Officers
Chairman of the Board: John C. Skoglund
Vice Chairmen: Jaye F. Dyer, Philip S. Maas
Directors: N. Bud Grossman, Roger L. Headrick, Elizabeth MacMillan, Carol S. Sperry, Wheelock Whitney

Club Officials
President/CEO: Roger L. Headrick
VP Administration/Team Operations: Jeff Diamond
VP Finance/Commercial Operations: James D. Miller
Director of Finance: Nick Valentine
Director of Research and Dev.: Mike Eayrs
Director of Marketing: Kernal Buhler
Community Relations Coordinator: Mary Bednarz
Director of Public Relations: David Pelletier
Director of Team Operations: Breck Spinner
Ticket Manager: Harry Randolph
Asst. G.M., Player Personnel: Jerry Reichow
Director of Player Personnel: Frank Gilliam
Director of Pro Personnel: Paul Wiggin
Director of Security: Steve Rollins
Player Personnel Coordinator: Scott Studwell
Equipment Manager: Dennis Ryan
Trainer: Fred Zamberletti
Video Director: Larry Kohout

Stadium: Hubert H. Humphrey Metrodome • **Capacity:** 63,000
500 11th Avenue South
Minneapolis, Minnesota 55415

Playing Surface: AstroTurf

Training Camp: Mankato State University
Mankato, Minnesota 56001

1993 Schedule

Preseason

Aug. 1	at Dallas	7:00
Aug. 7	vs. Buffalo at Berlin	1:00
Aug. 14	**Seattle**	7:00
Aug. 21	at Kansas City	7:00
Aug. 26	**Pittsburgh**	7:00

Regular Season

Sept. 5	at Los Angeles Raiders	1:00
Sept. 12	**Chicago**	12:00
Sept. 19	**Open Date**	
Sept. 26	**Green Bay**	12:00
Oct. 3	at San Francisco	1:00
Oct. 10	**Tampa Bay**	12:00
Oct. 17	**Open Date**	
Oct. 25	at Chicago (Monday)	8:00
Oct. 31	**Detroit**	7:00
Nov. 7	**San Diego**	12:00
Nov. 14	at Denver	2:00
Nov. 21	at Tampa Bay	8:00
Nov. 28	**New Orleans**	12:00
Dec. 5	at Detroit	1:00
Dec. 12	**Dallas**	3:00
Dec. 19	vs. Green Bay at Milw.	12:00
Dec. 26	**Kansas City**	7:00
Dec. 31	at Washington (Friday)	3:00

Vikings Coaching History

(266-224-9)

1961-66	Norm Van Brocklin	29-51-4
1967-83	Bud Grant	161-99-5
1984	Les Steckel	3-13-0
1985	Bud Grant	7-9-0
1986-91	Jerry Burns	55-46-0
1992	Dennis Green	11-6-0

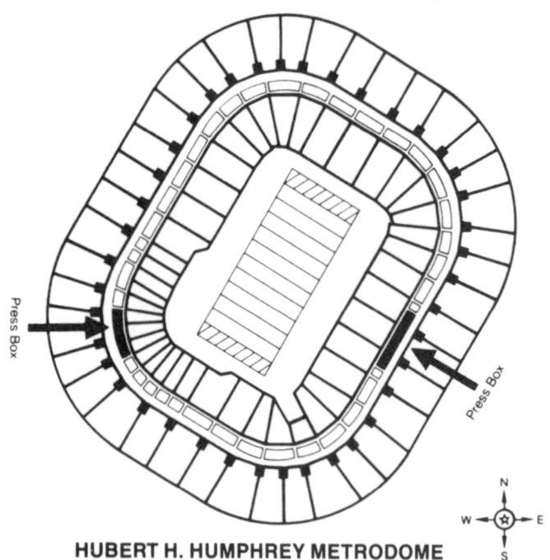

HUBERT H. HUMPHREY METRODOME

Record Holders

Individual Records — Career

Category	Name	Performance
Rushing (Yds.)	Chuck Foreman, 1973-79	5,879
Passing (Yds.)	Fran Tarkenton, 1961-66, 1972-78	33,098
Passing (TDs)	Fran Tarkenton, 1961-66, 1972-78	239
Receiving (No.)	Steve Jordan 1982-1992	439
Receiving (Yds.)	Anthony Carter, 1985-1992	6,861
Interceptions	Paul Krause, 1968-1979	53
Punting (Avg.)	Harry Newsome, 1990-92	44.2
Punt Return (Avg.)	Tommy Mason, 1961-66	10.4
Kickoff Return (Avg.)	Bob Reed, 1962-63	27.1
Field Goals	Fred Cox, 1963-1977	282
Touchdowns (Tot.)	Bill Brown, 1962-1974	76
Points	Fred Cox, 1963-1977	1,365

Individual Records — Single Season

Category	Name	Performance
Rushing (Yds.)	Terry Allen, 1992	1,201
Passing (Yds.)	Tommy Kramer, 1981	3,912
Passing (TDs)	Tommy Kramer, 1981	26
Receiving (No.)	Rickey Young, 1978	88
Receiving (Yds.)	Anthony Carter, 1988	1,225
Interceptions	Paul Krause, 1975	10
Punting (Avg.)	Bobby Walden, 1964	46.4
Punt Return (Avg.)	Leo Lewis, 1987	12.5
Kickoff Return (Avg.)	John Gilliam, 1972	26.3
Field Goals	Rich Karlis, 1989	31
Touchdowns (Tot.)	Chuck Foreman, 1975	22
Points	Chuck Foreman, 1975	132

Individual Records — Single Game

Category	Name	Performance
Rushing (Yds.)	Chuck Foreman, 10-24-76	200
Passing (Yds.)	Tommy Kramer, 11-2-86	490
Passing (TDs)	Joe Kapp, 9-28-69	*7
Receiving (No.)	Rickey Young, 12-16-79	15
Receiving (Yds.)	Sammy White, 11-7-76	210
Interceptions	Many times	3
	Last time by Vencie Glenn, 12-27-92	
Field Goals	Rich Karlis, 11-5-89	*7
Touchdowns (Tot.)	Chuck Foreman, 12-20-75	4
	Ahmad Rashad, 9-2-79	4
Points	Chuck Foreman, 12-20-75	24
	Ahmad Rashad, 9-2-79	24

*NFL Record

1992 Team Record

Preseason (4-0)

Date	Result		Opponents
8/8	W	24- 3	Buffalo
8/15	W	30- 0	Kansas City
8/24	W	56- 3	at Cleveland
8/29	W	30- 0	at Washington

Regular Season (11-5)

Date	Result		Opponents	Att.
9/6	W	23-20	at Green Bay (OT)	58,704
9/13	L	17-31	at Detroit	57,353
9/20	W	26-20	Tampa Bay	53,371
9/27	W	42- 7	at Cincinnati	55,526
10/4	W	21-20	Chicago	62,510
10/15	W	31-14	Detroit	61,010
10/25	L	13-15	Washington	61,801
11/2	W	38-10	at Chicago	66,091
11/8	W	35- 7	at Tampa Bay	51,658
11/15	L	13-17	Houston	61,073
11/22	W	17-13	Cleveland	60,798
11/29	W	31-17	at L.A. Rams	58,882
12/6	L	17-28	at Philadelphia	65,698
12/13	L	17-20	San Francisco	62,456
12/20	W	6- 3	at Pittsburgh	59,005
12/27	W	27- 7	Green Bay	62,597

(OT) Overtime

Postseason (0-1)

Date	Result		Opponent	Att.
1/2	L	7-24	Washington	57,353

Score by Periods

Vikings	87	91	64	129	3	—	374
Opponents	57	92	31	69	0	—	249

Attendance

Home 485,616 Away 472,917 Total 958,533
Single-game home record, 62,851 (10-19-86)
Single-season home record, 485,616 (1992)

1992 Team Statistics

	Vikings	Opp.
Total First Downs	288	293
Rushing	115	113
Passing	157	154
Penalty	16	26
Third Down: Made/Att.	94/212	79/207
Third Down: Pct.	44.3	38.2
Fourth Down: Made/Att.	6/11	4/14
Fourth Down: Pct.	54.5	28.6
Total Net Yards	4899	4515
Avg. Per Game	306.2	282.2
Total Plays	995	997
Avg. Per Play	4.9	4.5
Net Yards Rushing	2030	1733
Avg. Per Game	126.9	108.3
Total Rushes	497	438
Net Yards Passing	2869	2782
Avg. Per Game	179.3	173.9
Sacked/Yards Lost	40/293	51/342
Gross Yards	3162	3124
Att./Completions	458/258	508/320
Completion Pct.	56.3	63.0
Had Intercepted	15	28
Punts/Avg.	73/44.4	76/41.9
Net Punting Avg.	73/35.7	76/35.3
Penalties/Yards Lost	99/809	98/768
Fumbles/Ball Lost	29/17	23/14
Touchdowns	45	27
Rushing	19	11
Passing	18	12
Returns	8	4
Avg. Time of Possession	29:18	30:42

1992 Individual Statistics

Scoring

Scoring	TD R	TD P	TD Rt	PAT	FG	Saf	TP
Reveiz	0	0	0	45/45	19/25	0	102
Allen	13	2	0	0/0	0/0	0	90
C. Carter	0	6	0	0/0	0/0	0	36
Craig	4	0	0	0/0	0/0	0	24
Jones	0	4	0	0/0	0/0	0	24
A. Carter	1	2	0	0/0	0/0	0	18
Jenkins	0	0	2	0/0	0/0	0	12
Jordan	0	2	0	0/0	0/0	0	12
McMillian	0	0	2	0/0	0/0	0	12
Doleman	0	0	1	0/0	0/0	1	8
Del Rio	0	0	1	0/0	0/0	0	6
Henderson	1	0	0	0/0	0/0	0	6
J. Johnson	0	1	0	0/0	0/0	0	6
Parker	0	0	1	0/0	0/0	0	6
Scott	0	0	1	0/0	0/0	0	6
Tice	0	1	0	0/0	0/0	0	6
Vikings	19	18	8	45/45	19/25	1	374
Opponents	11	12	4	27/27	20/25	0	249

Passing

Passing	Att.	Comp.	Yds.	Pct.	TD	Int.	Tkld.	Rate
Gannon	279	159	1905	57.0	12	13	25/177	72.9
Salisbury	175	97	1203	55.4	5	2	15/116	81.7
A. Carter	1	0	0	0.0	0	0	0/0	39.6
Henderson	1	1	36	100.0	1	0	0/0	158.3
Jones	1	1	18	100.0	0	0	0/0	118.8
Newsome	1	0	0	0.0	0	0	0/0	39.6
Vikings	458	258	3162	56.3	18	15	40/293	77.2
Opponents	508	320	3124	63.0	12	28	51/342	65.1

Rushing

Rushing	Att.	Yds.	Avg.	LG	TD
Allen	266	1201	4.5	51	13
Craig	105	416	4.0	21	4
Gannon	45	187	4.2	14	0
Henderson	34	113	3.3	12	1
A. Carter	16	66	4.1	14	1
J. Johnson	4	26	6.5	9	0
C. Carter	5	15	3.0	6	0
Nelson	10	5	0.5	9	0
Jones	1	1	1.0	1	0
Salisbury	11	0	0.0	4	0
Vikings	497	2030	4.1	51	19
Opponents	438	1733	4.0	43	11

Receiving

Receiving	No.	Yds.	Avg.	LG	TD
C. Carter	53	681	12.8	44	6
Allen	49	478	9.8	36t	2
A. Carter	41	580	14.1	54	2
Jordan	28	394	14.1	60t	2
Jones	22	308	14.0	43t	4
Craig	22	164	7.5	22	0
J. Johnson	21	211	10.0	37	1
Reed	6	142	23.7	51	0
Tice	5	65	13.0	34t	1
Novoselsky	4	63	15.8	34	0
Henderson	4	60	15.0	23	0
Tennell	2	12	6.0	8	0
Whitaker	1	4	4.0	4	0
Vikings	258	3162	12.3	60t	18
Opponents	320	3124	9.8	52	12

Interceptions

Interceptions	No.	Yds.	Avg.	LG	TD
McMillian	8	157	19.6	51t	2
Scott	5	79	15.8	35t	1
Glenn	5	65	13.0	39	0
Parker	3	23	7.7	23	0
Del Rio	2	92	46.0	84t	1
Lee	2	20	10.0	20	0
Doleman	1	27	27.0	27t	1
Wright	1	20	20.0	20	0
Jenkins	1	19	19.0	19t	1
Vikings	28	502	17.9	84t	6
Opponents	15	164	10.9	43	1

Punting

Punting	No.	Yds.	Avg.	In 20	LG
Newsome	72	3243	45.0	19	84
Vikings	73	3243	44.4	19	84
Opponents	76	3182	41.9	14	61

Punt Returns

Punt Returns	No.	FC	Yds.	Avg.	LG	TD
Parker	33	17	336	10.2	42	0
J. Johnson	0	1	0	—	—	0
Vikings	33	18	336	10.2	42	0
Opponents	34	13	339	10.0	58t	1

Kickoff Returns

Kickoff Returns	No.	Yds.	Avg.	LG	TD
Nelson	29	626	21.6	53	0
Adams	1	0	0.0	0	0
Henderson	5	111	22.2	29	0
J. Johnson	5	79	15.8	25	0
Parker	2	30	15.0	15	0
Reed	1	1	1.0	1	0
West	2	27	13.5	27	0
Vikings	45	874	19.4	53	0
Opponents	50	925	18.5	47	0

Sacks

Sacks	No.
Doleman	14.5
Randle	11.5
Noga	9.0
Thomas	6.0
Jenkins	4.0
Merriweather	3.0
Del Rio	2.0
Scott	1.0
Tuaolo	1.0
Vikings	51.0
Opponents	40.0

1993 Draft Choices

Round	Name	Pos.	College
1.	Robert Smith	RB	Ohio State
2.	Qadry Ismail	WR	Syracuse
3.	John Gerak	G	Penn State
	Gilbert Brown	DT	Kansas
4.	Ashley Sheppard	LB	Clemson
5.	Everett Lindsay	T	Mississippi
7.	Gino Torretta	QB	Miami

Minnesota Vikings 1993 Veteran Roster

No.	Name	Pos.	Ht.	Wt.	Birth-date	NFL Exp.	College	Hometown	How Acq.	'92 Games/ Starts
72	Adams, Scott	G-T	6-5	281	9/28/66	2	Georgia	Lake City, Fla.	FA-'91	15/0
21	Allen, Terry	RB	5-10	197	2/21/68	3	Clemson	Commerce, Ga.	D9-'90	16/16
92	Barker, Roy	DT	6-4	292	2/14/69	2	North Carolina	Central Issip, N.Y.	PB(Wash)-'92	8/0
52	Bavaro, David	LB	6-0	228	3/27/67	3	Syracuse	Danvers, Mass.	D4-'92	5/0
50	Berry, Ray	LB	6-2	230	10/28/63	7	Baylor	Abilene, Tex.	D2-'87	8/0
81	Carter, Anthony	WR	5-11	181	9/17/60	9	Michigan	Riviera Beach, Fla.	T(Mia)-'85	16/14
80	Carter, Cris	WR	6-3	197	11/25/65	7	Ohio State	Middletown, Ohio	W(Phil)-'90	12/12
94	Conover, Frank	DT	6-5	325	4/6/68	3	Syracuse	Englishtown, N.J.	FA-'93	15/15*
33	Craig, Roger	RB	6-0	219	7/10/60	11	Nebraska	Davenport, Iowa	PB(Raid)-'92	15/1
77	Culpepper, Brad	DT	6-1	267	5/8/68	2	Florida	Tallahassee, Fla.	D10-'92	11/2
75	Dafney, Bernard	G	6-5	317	11/1/69	2	Tennessee	Los Angeles, Calif.	FA-'92	2/0
55	Del Rio, Jack	LB	6-4	250	4/4/63	9	Southern California	Castro Valley, Calif.	PB(Dall)-'92	16/16
56	Doleman, Chris	DE	6-5	275	10/16/61	9	Pittsburgh	York, Pa.	D1-'85	16/16
16	Gannon, Rich	QB	6-3	208	12/20/65	7	Delaware	Philadelphia, Pa.	T(NE)-'87	12/12
25	Glenn, Vencie	S	6-0	189	10/26/64	8	Indiana State	Silver Spring, Md.	PB(NO)-'92	16/3
90	Harris, Robert	DE	6-4	285	6/13/69	2	Southern	Riviera Beach, Fla.	D2-'92	7/0
30	Henderson, Keith	RB	6-1	230	8/4/66	4	Georgia	Carterville, Ga.	T(SF)-'92	13/0
98	Hinkle, George	DT	6-5	288	3/17/65	6	Arizona	Pacific, Mo.	T(Wash)-'92	9/0
76	Irwin, Tim	T	6-7	297	12/13/58	13	Tennessee	Knoxville, Tenn.	D3-'81	16/16
51	Jenkins, Carlos	LB	6-3	219	7/12/68	3	Michigan State	Lantana, Fla.	D3a-'91	16/12
28	Jenkins, Izel	CB	5-10	190	5/27/64	6	North Carolina State	Wilson, N.C.	UFA(Phil)-'93	15/6*
83	Jordan, Steve	TE	6-3	240	1/10/61	12	Brown	Phoenix, Ariz.	D7-'82	14/12
69	Kalis, Todd	G	6-5	291	5/10/65	6	Arizona State	Phoenix, Ariz.	D4-'88	0*
39	Lee, Carl	CB	5-11	182	4/6/61	11	Marshall	South Charleston, W. Va.	D7-'83	16/16
91	#Manusky, Greg	LB	6-1	237	8/12/66	6	Colgate	Wilkes Barre, Pa.	PB(Wash)-'91	11/0
58	McDaniel, Ed	LB	5-11	232	2/2/69	2	Clemson	Leesville, S.C.	D5-'92	8/0
64	McDaniel, Randall	G	6-3	280	12/19/64	6	Arizona State	Avondale, Ariz.	D1-'88	16/16
9	McMahon, Jim	QB	6-1	195	8/21/59	12	Brigham Young	Jersey City, N.J.	UFA(Phil)-'93	4/1*
26	McMillian, Audray	CB	6-0	190	8/13/62	8	Houston	Carthage, Tex.	PB(Hou)-'89	16/16
68	Morris, Mike	C	6-5	273	2/22/61	6	Northeast Missouri State	Centerville, Iowa	FA-'91	16/0
18	Newsome, Harry	P	6-0	185	1/25/63	9	Wake Forest	Cheraw, S.C.	PB(Pitt)-'90	16/0
85	Novoselsky, Brent	TE	6-2	237	1/8/66	6	Pennsylvania	Niles, Ill.	FA-'89	16/1
82	Paige, Stephone	WR	6-2	188	10/15/61	10	Fresno State	Long Beach, Calif.	FA-'93	0*
27	Parker, Anthony	CB	5-10	179	2/11/66	3	Arizona State	Tempe, Ariz.	PB(Ind)-'92	16/2
23	Pearson, Jayice	CB	5-11	186	8/17/63	7	Washington	Oceanside, Calif.	UFA(KC)-'93	7/0*
93	Randle, John	DT	6-1	270	12/12/67	4	Texas A&I	Hearne, Tex.	FA-'90	16/14
86	Reed, Jake	WR	6-3	220	9/28/67	2	Grambling	Covington, Ga.	D3b-'91	16/0
7	Reveiz, Fuad	K	5-11	226	2/24/63	9	Tennessee	Miami, Fla.	FA-'90	16/0
12	Salisbury, Sean	QB	6-5	217	3/9/63	5	Southern California	Escondido, Calif.	FA-'90	10/4
60	Schreiber, Adam	C-G	6-4	290	2/20/62	10	Texas	Huntsville, Ala.	PB(NYJ)-'90	16/1
38	Scott, Todd	S	5-10	191	1/23/68	3	Southwestern Louisiana	Galveston, Tex.	D6-'91	16/16
63	Smith, Daryle	T	6-5	276	1/18/64	6	Tennessee	Hawkins County, Tenn.	UFA(Phil)-'93	16/4*
53	Strickland, Fred	LB	6-2	250	8/15/64	6	Purdue	Wanaque, N.J.	UFA(Rams)-'93	15/11*
46	Tennell, Derek	TE	6-2	258	2/12/64	6	UCLA	West Covina, Calif.	FA-'93	3/2*
87	Tice, Mike	TE	6-7	253	2/2/59	12	Maryland	Central Islip, N.Y.	PB(Sea)-'92	12/9
97	Thomas, Henry	DT	6-2	285	1/12/65	7	Louisiana State	Houston, Tex.	D3-'87	16/16
95	#Tuaolo, Esera	DT	6-2	275	7/11/68	3	Oregon State	Honolulu, Hawaii	FA-'92	5/0
35	West, Ronnie	WR	6-2	215	6/23/68	2	Pittsburg State, Kan.	Wilcox, Ga.	D9b-'92	13/0
24	Wilson, David	S	5-10	192	6/10/70	2	California	Los Angeles, Calif.	D7-'92	3/0
65	Zimmerman, Gary	T	6-6	294	12/13/61	8	Oregon	Walnut, Calif.	T(NYG)-'86	16/16

* Conover last active with Cleveland in '91; I. Jenkins played 16 games with Philadelphia in '92; McMahon played 4 games with Philadelphia; Kalis and Paige missed '92 season due to injury; Pearson played 7 games with Kansas City; Smith played 16 games with Philadelphia; Strickland played 15 games with L.A. Rams; Tennell played 3 games with Minnesota.

Unrestricted free agent; subject to developments.

† Restricted free agent; subject to developments.

Players lost through free agency (4): G Brian Habib (Den; 16 games in '92), C Kirk Lowdermilk (Ind; 16), CB Najee Mustafaa (Clev; 5), DE Al Noga (Wash; 16).

Also played with Vikings in '92—CB Eric Everett (16 games), WR Joe Johnson (15), WR Hassan Jones (9), DE Skip McClendon (3), LB Mike Merriweather (16), RB Darrin Nelson (16), LB Van Waiters (16), WR Ronnie West (2), WR Danta Whitaker (12), S Felix Wright (13).

COACHING STAFF

Head Coach, Dennis Green

Pro Career: Named the fifth head coach in Vikings history on January 10, 1992. Led Minnesota to an 11-5 regular-season record and the NFC Central Division title. Coached special teams and receivers for the San Francisco 49ers in 1979. Returned to San Francisco from 1986-88 as receivers coach. Credited with the development of two of the game's premier wide receivers — Jerry Rice and John Taylor. Coached with 49ers in Super Bowl XXIII. Played one season for British Columbia Lions (CFL). Career record: 11-6.

Background: Running back at Iowa 1968-70. Began coaching career at Iowa as a graduate assistant in 1972. Moved to Dayton in 1973 as running backs and receivers coach before returning to Iowa from 1974-76 to coach receivers and quarterbacks. Running backs coach at Stanford from 1977-78. Returned to Stanford in 1980 as offensive coordinator. Head coach at Northwestern from 1981-85. Green earned Big Ten coach-of-the-year honors in 1982. In 1989, Green was named head coach at Stanford where he was 16-16 in three seasons.

Personal: Born February 17, 1949, in Harrisburg, Pa. Graduated from Iowa with bachelor of science degree in recreation. Dennis, and his wife, Margie, live in Eden Prairie, Minn., and have two children — Patti and Jeremy.

Assistant Coaches

Tom Batta, special teams; born October 6, 1942, Youngstown, Ohio, lives in Bloomington, Minn. Offensive-defensive lineman Kent State 1961-63. No pro playing experience. College coach: Akron 1973, Colorado 1974-78, Kansas 1979-82, North Carolina State 1983. Pro coach: Joined Vikings in 1984.

Brian Billick, tight ends; born February 28, 1954, Redlands, Calif., lives in Eden Prairie, Minn. Tight end Brigham Young 1974-76. Pro tight end Dallas Cowboys 1977. College coach: Brigham Young 1978, Redlands 1979, San Diego State 1981-85, Utah State 1986-88, Stanford 1989-91. Pro coach: Joined Vikings in 1992.

Jack Burns, offensive coordinator; born January 3, 1949, Tampa, Fla., lives in Eden Prairie, Minn. Safety Florida 1967-71. No pro playing experience. College coach: Florida 1971-73, 1975, Louisville 1974, 1985-88, Texas 1976, Vanderbilt 1977-78, Auburn 1979-80. Pro coach: Tampa Bay Bandits (USFL) 1981-83 (scout), Washington Redskins 1989-91, joined Vikings in 1992.

Tony Dungy, defensive coordinator; born October 6, 1955, Jackson, Mich., lives in Eden Prairie, Minn. Quarterback Minnesota 1973-76. Pro safety Pittsburgh Steelers 1977-78, San Francisco 49ers 1979. College coach: Minnesota 1980. Pro coach: Pittsburgh Steelers 1981-88, Kansas City Chiefs 1989-91, joined Vikings in 1992.

Monte Kiffin, inside linebackers; born February 29, 1940, Lexington, Ky., lives in Bloomington, Minn. Offensive-defensive tackle Nebraska 1958-61. Pro defensive end Winnipeg Blue Bombers (CFL) 1965-66. College coach: Nebraska 1966-76, Arkansas 1977-79, North Carolina State 1980-82 (head coach). Pro coach: Green Bay Packers 1983, Buffalo Bills 1984-85, Minnesota Vikings 1986-89, New York Jets 1990, rejoined Vikings in 1991.

John Michels, offensive line; born February 15, 1931, Philadelphia, Pa., lives in Bloomington, Minn. Guard Tennessee 1949-52. Pro guard Philadelphia Eagles 1953, 1956, Winnipeg Blue Bombers (CFL) 1957. College coach: Texas A&M 1958. Pro coach: Winnipeg Blue Bombers (CFL) 1959-66, joined Vikings in 1967.

Minnesota Vikings 1993 First-Year Roster

Name	Pos.	Ht.	Wt.	Birth-date	College	Hometown	How Acq.
Brown, Gilbert	DT	6-2	330	2/22/71	Kansas	Detroit, Mich.	D3b
Boyd, Tracy (1)	T	6-4	296	8/27/67	Elizabeth City State	Crowley, La.	FA
Carpenter, Ron	S	6-1	188	1/20/70	Miami, Ohio	Cincinnati, Ohio	FA
Christy, Jeff (1)	C	6-3	289	2/2/69	Pittsburgh	Freeport, Pa.	FA
Dixon, David (1)	G	6-5	350	1/5/69	Arizona State	Auckland, New Zealand	FA
Eller, Matt	DE	6-6	280	1/30/70	Bethel College	Radcliffe, Iowa	FA
Evans, Patt (1)	TE	6-6	261	3/14/69	Minnesota	Swarthmore, Pa.	FA
Evans, Chuck (1)	RB	6-1	217	4/16/67	Clark, Ga.	Augusta, Ga.	D11-'92
Fisher, Luke (1)	TE	6-2	235	11/21/68	East Carolina	Mount Holly, N.J.	D8-'92
Gaddis, Mike (1)	RB	6-0	217	3/4/69	Oklahoma	Midwest City, Okla.	D6-'92
Garnett, Dave	LB	6-2	225	12/6/70	Stanford	Naperville, Ill.	FA
Gerak, John	G	6-3	292	1/6/70	Penn State	Struthers, Ohio	D3a
Graham, Lorenzo (1)	RB	5-11	200	3/25/65	Livingston	Perdido, Ala.	FA
Guliford, Eric	WR	5-8	160	10/25/69	Arizona State	Peoria, Ill.	FA
Harris, James (1)	DE	6-4	275	5/13/68	Temple	East St. Louis, Ill.	FA
Holmes, Bruce (1)	LB	6-2	237	10/24/65	Minnesota	Detroit, Mich.	FA
Hooks, Bryan	DE	6-3	286	9/15/70	Arizona State	Tempe, Ariz.	FA
Ismail, Qadry	WR	6-0	192	11/8/70	Syracuse	Newark, N.J.	D2
Johnson, Brad (1)	QB	6-4	218	9/13/68	Florida State	Black Mountain, N.C.	D9a-'92
Jones, Shawn	S	6-1	200	6/16/70	Georgia Tech	Thomasville, Ga.	FA
Lenseigne, Tony (1)	TE	6-4	235	8/7/69	Eastern Washington	Yakima, Wash.	FA
Lindsay, Everett	G	6-4	296	9/18/70	Mississippi	Raleigh, N.C.	D5
Randolph, Joe (1)	WR	5-7	155	4/30/71	Elon	Washington, N.Y.	D12-'92
Sheppard, Ashley	LB	6-3	258	1/21/69	Clemson	Greenville, N.C.	D4
Sims, William	LB	6-3	265	12/30/70	S.W. Louisiana	Brooks County, Ga.	FA
Smith, Robert	RB	6-0	195	3/4/72	Ohio State	Euclid, Ohio	D1
Staten, Robert	RB	5-11	235	11/23/69	Jackson State	Shubuta, Miss.	FA
Torretta, Gino	QB	6-2	219	8/10/70	Miami	Pinole Valley, Calif.	D7
Watkins, Slip (1)	WR	5-9	173	9/29/67	Louisiana State	Ft. Lauderdale, Fla.	FA
Welborne, Tripp (1)	S	6-0	205	11/20/68	Michigan	Reidsville, N.C.	D7b-'91

The term NFL Rookie is defined as a player who is in his first season of professional football and has not been on the roster of another professional football team for any regular-season or postseason games. A Rookie is designated by an "R" on NFL rosters. Players who have been active in another professional football league or players who have NFL experience, including either preseason training camp or being on an Active List or Inactive List, or on Reserve/Injured or Reserve/Physically Unable to Perform for fewer than six regular-season games, are termed NFL First-Year Players. An NFL First-Year Player is designated by a "1" on NFL rosters. Thereafter, a player is credited with an additional year of experience for each season in which he accumulates six games on the Active List or Inactive List, or on Reserve/Injured or Reserve/Physically Unable to Perform.

NOTES

Tom Moore, wide receivers; born November 7, 1938, Owatanna, Minn., lives in Bloomington, Minn. Quarterback Iowa 1957-60. No pro playing experience. College coach: Iowa 1961-62, Dayton 1965-68, Wake Forest 1969, Georgia Tech 1970-71, Minnesota 1972-73, 1975-76. Pro coach: New York Stars (WFL) 1974, Pittsburgh Steelers 1977-89, joined Vikings in 1990.

John Teerlinck, defensive line; born April 9, 1951, Rochester, N.Y., lives in Eden Prairie, Minn. Defensive lineman Western Illinois 1970-73. Pro defensive tackle San Diego Chargers 1974-76. College coach: Iowa Lakes J.C. 1977, Eastern Illinois 1978-79, Illinois 1980-82. Pro coach: Chicago Blitz (USFL) 1984, Cleveland Browns 1989-90, Los Angeles Rams 1991, joined Vikings in 1992.

Willie Shaw, defensive backs; born January 11, 1944, San Diego, Calif., lives in Eden Prairie, Minn. Cornerback New Mexico 1966-68. No pro playing experience. College coach: San Diego City College 1970-73, Stanford 1974-76, 1989-91, Long Beach State 1977-78, Oregon 1979, Arizona State 1980-84. Pro coach: Detroit Lions 1985-88, joined Vikings in 1992.

Richard Solomon, outside linebackers; born December 8, 1949, New Orleans, La., lives in Eden Prairie, Minn. Running back-defensive back Iowa 1970-73. No pro playing experience. College coach: Dubuque 1973-75, Southern Illinois 1976, Iowa 1977-78, Syracuse 1979, Illinois 1980-86. Pro coach: New York Giants 1987-91 (scout), joined Vikings in 1992.

Tyrone Willingham, running backs; born December 30, 1953, Jacksonville, N.C., lives in Deephaven, Minn. Quarterback Michigan State 1974-77. No pro playing experience. College coach: Michigan State 1977, 1980-82, Central Michigan 1978-79, North Carolina State 1983-85, Rice 1986-88, Stanford 1989-91. Pro coach: Joined Vikings in 1992.

Steve Wetzel, strength and conditioning; born May 11, 1963, Washington D.C., lives in Eden Prairie, Minn. No college or pro playing experience. College coach: Maryland 1985-89, George Mason 1990. Pro coach: Washington Redskins 1990-91, joined Vikings in 1992.

NEW ORLEANS SAINTS

National Football Conference
Western Division

Team Colors: Old Gold, Black, and White

1500 Poydras Street
New Orleans, Louisiana 70112
Telephone: (504) 733-0255

Club Officials

Owner/General Partner: Tom Benson
President/General Manager: Jim Finks
Vice President/Administration: Jim Miller
Business Manager/Controller: Bruce Broussard
Director of Player Personnel: Bill Kuharich
Director of Marketing: Greg Suit
Assistant Director of Marketing: Bill Ferrante
Director of Media Relations: Rusty Kasmiersky
Assistant Director of Media Relations: Neal Gulkis
Director of Travel/Entertainment: Barra Birrcher
Director of Community Relations: Chanel Lagarde
Player Personnel Scouts: Bill Baker, Hamp Cook, Hokie Gajan, Tom Marino, Carmen Piccone
Ticket Manager: Sandy King
Trainer: Dean Kleinschmidt
Equipment Manager: Dan Simmons
Video Director: Albert Aucoin

Stadium: Louisiana Superdome • **Capacity:** 69,056
1500 Poydras Street
New Orleans, Louisiana 70112

Playing Surface: AstroTurf

Training Camp: University of Wisconsin-La Crosse
La Crosse, Wisconsin 54601

1993 Schedule

Preseason

July 31	vs. Philadelphia at Tokyo	9:00
Aug. 7	vs. Houston at San Antonio	7:00
Aug. 14	vs. Green Bay at Madison	12:00
Aug. 23	**Chicago**	7:00
Aug. 27	**Detroit**	7:00

Regular Season

Sept. 5	**Houston**	7:00
Sept. 12	at Atlanta	1:00
Sept. 19	**Detroit**	12:00
Sept. 26	**San Francisco**	3:00
Oct. 3	at Los Angeles Rams	1:00
Oct. 10	**Open Date**	
Oct. 17	at Pittsburgh	1:00
Oct. 24	**Atlanta**	12:00
Oct. 31	at Phoenix	2:00
Nov. 7	**Open Date**	
Nov. 14	**Green Bay**	12:00
Nov. 22	at San Francisco (Monday)	6:00
Nov. 28	at Minnesota	12:00
Dec. 5	at Cleveland	1:00
Dec. 12	**Los Angeles Rams**	12:00
Dec. 20	**New York Giants** (Monday)	8:00
Dec. 26	at Philadelphia	1:00
Jan. 2	**Cincinnati**	3:00

Saints Coaching History

(152-233-5)

1967-70	Tom Fears*	13-34-2
1970-72	J.D. Roberts	7-25-3
1973-75	John North**	11-23-0
1975	Ernie Hefferle	1-7-0
1976-77	Hank Stram	7-21-0
1978-80	Dick Nolan***	15-29-0
1980	Dick Stanfel	1-3-0
1981-85	O.A. (Bum) Phillips****	27-42-0
1985	Wade Phillips	1-3-0
1986-92	Jim Mora	69-46-0

*Released after seven games in 1970
**Released after six games in 1975
***Released after 12 games in 1980
****Resigned after 12 games in 1985

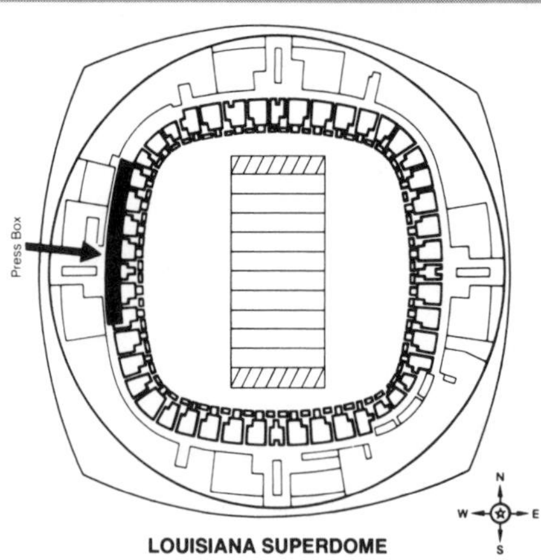

LOUISIANA SUPERDOME

Record Holders

Individual Records — Career

Category	Name	Performance
Rushing (Yds.)	George Rogers, 1981-84	4,267
Passing (Yds.)	Archie Manning, 1971-1982	21,734
Passing (TDs)	Archie Manning, 1971-1982	115
Receiving (No.)	Eric Martin, 1985-1992	466
Receiving (Yds.)	Eric Martin, 1985-1992	6,904
Interceptions	Dave Waymer, 1980-89	37
Punting (Avg.)	Tommy Barnhardt, 1987, 1989-1992	42.7
Punt Return (Avg.)	Mel Gray, 1986-88	13.4
Kickoff Return (Avg.)	Walter Roberts, 1967	26.3
Field Goals	Morten Andersen, 1982-1992	346
Touchdowns (Tot.)	Dalton Hilliard, 1986-1992	50
Points	Morten Andersen, 1982-1992	1,085

Individual Records — Single Season

Category	Name	Performance
Rushing (Yds.)	George Rogers, 1981	1,674
Passing (Yds.)	Archie Manning, 1980	3,716
Passing (TDs)	Archie Manning, 1980	23
Receiving (No.)	Eric Martin, 1988	85
Receiving (Yds.)	Eric Martin, 1989	1,090
Interceptions	Dave Whitsell, 1967	10
Punting (Avg.)	Tommy Barnhardt, 1992	44.0
Punt Return (Avg.)	Mel Gray, 1987	14.7
Kickoff Return (Avg.)	Don Shy, 1969	27.9
Field Goals	Morten Andersen, 1985	31
Touchdowns (Tot.)	Dalton Hilliard, 1989	18
Points	Morten Andersen, 1987	121

Individual Records — Single Game

Category	Name	Performance
Rushing (Yds.)	George Rogers, 9-4-83	206
Passing (Yds.)	Archie Manning, 12-7-80	377
Passing (TDs)	Billy Kilmer, 11-2-69	6
Receiving (No.)	Tony Galbreath, 9-10-78	14
Receiving (Yds.)	Wes Chandler, 9-2-79	205
Interceptions	Tommy Myers, 9-3-78	3
	Dave Waymer, 10-6-85	3
	Reggie Sutton, 10-18-87	3
	Gene Atkins, 12-22-91	3
Field Goals	Morten Andersen, 12-1-85	5
	Morten Andersen, 11-15-87	5
	Morten Anderson, 12-3-92	5
Touchdowns (Tot.)	Many times	3
	Last time by Rueben Mayes, 9-23-90	
Points	Many times	18
	Last time by Rueben Mayes, 9-23-90	

1992 Team Record

Preseason (3-1)

Date	Result		Opponents
8/10	W	34-31	at Chicago
8/17	W	26- 0	Pittsburgh
8/22	L	3-33	Houston
8/27	W	17- 3	vs. Miami at Baltimore

Regular Season (12-4)

Date	Result		Opponents	Att.
9/6	L	13-15	at Philadelphia	65,418
9/13	W	28- 6	Chicago	67,633
9/20	W	10- 7	at Atlanta	69,820
9/27	L	10-16	San Francisco	67,627
10/4	W	13- 7	at Detroit	68,428
10/11	W	13-10	L.A. Rams	67,591
10/18	W	30-21	at Phoenix	28,117
11/1	W	23-21	Tampa Bay	67,601
11/8	W	31-14	at New England	51,878
11/15	L	20-21	at San Francisco	65,484
11/23	W	20- 3	Washington	67,723
11/29	W	24-13	Miami	67,664
12/3	W	22-14	Atlanta	67,604
12/13	W	37-14	at L.A. Rams	53,007
12/20	L	16-20	Buffalo	67,636
12/26	W	20- 0	at N.Y. Jets	75,291

Postseason (0-1)

Date	Result		Opponent	Att.
1/3	L	20-36	Philadelphia	68,893

Score by Periods

Saints	70	86	91	83	0	—	330
Opponents	26	64	31	81	0	—	202

Attendance

Home 541,079 Away 477,443 Total 1,018,522
Single-game home record, 70,940 (11-4-79)
Single-season home record, 548,655 (1991)

1992 Team Statistics

	Saints	Opp.
Total First Downs	267	246
Rushing	92	86
Passing	155	146
Penalty	20	14
Third Down: Made/Att.	75/197	71/209
Third Down: Pct.	38.1	34.0
Fourth Down: Made/Att.	3/8	8/18
Fourth Down: Pct.	37.5	44.4
Total Net Yards	4806	4075
Avg. Per Game	300.4	254.7
Total Plays	895	949
Avg. Per Play	5.4	4.3
Net Yards Rushing	1628	1605
Avg. Per Game	101.8	100.3
Total Rushes	454	381
Net Yards Passing	3178	2470
Avg. Per Game	198.6	154.4
Sacked/Yards Lost	15/119	57/376
Gross Yards	3297	2846
Att./Completions	426/251	511/287
Completion Pct.	58.9	56.2
Had Intercepted	16	18
Punts/Avg.	67/44.0	89/41.2
Net Punting Avg.	67/37.7	89/37.0
Penalties/Yards Lost	60/567	77/729
Fumbles/Ball Lost	27/13	37/20
Touchdowns	35	24
Rushing	10	8
Passing	19	13
Returns	6	3
Avg. Time of Possession	31:10	28:50

1992 Individual Statistics

Scoring	TD R	TD P	TD Rt	PAT	FG	Saf	TP
Andersen	0	0	0	33/34	29/34	0	120
Hilliard	3	4	0	0/0	0/0	0	42
Early	0	5	0	0/0	0/0	0	30
E. Martin	0	5	0	0/0	0/0	0	30
Dunbar	3	0	0	0/0	0/0	0	18
Heyward	3	0	0	0/0	0/0	0	18
Small	0	3	0	0/0	0/0	0	18
Carroll	0	2	0	0/0	0/0	0	12
Goff	0	0	2	0/0	0/0	0	12
V. Buck	0	0	1	0/0	0/0	0	6
Cook	0	0	1	0/0	0/0	0	6
Jones	0	0	1	0/0	0/0	0	6
McAfee	1	0	0	0/0	0/0	0	6
Mills	0	0	1	0/0	0/0	0	6
Saints	10	19	6	33/35	29/34	0	330
Opponents	8	13	3	22/24	12/17	0	202

Passing	Att.	Comp.	Yds.	Pct.	TD	Int.	Tkld.	Rate
Hebert	422	249	3287	59.0	19	16	15/119	82.9
M. Buck	4	2	10	50.0	0	0	0/0	56.3
Saints	426	251	3297	58.9	19	16	15/119	82.6
Opponents	511	287	2846	56.2	13	18	57/376	65.9

Rushing	Att.	Yds.	Avg.	LG	TD
Dunbar	154	565	3.7	25	3
Hilliard	115	445	3.9	22	3
Heyward	104	416	4.0	23	3
McAfee	39	114	2.9	19	1
Hebert	32	95	3.0	18	0
Early	3	−1	−0.3	7	0
Barnhardt	4	−2	−0.5	12	0
M. Buck	3	−4	−1.3	−1	0
Saints	454	1628	3.6	25	10
Opponents	381	1605	4.2	41	8

Receiving	No.	Yds.	Avg.	LG	TD
E. Martin	68	1041	15.3	52t	5
Hilliard	48	465	9.7	41	4
Early	30	566	18.9	59t	5
Small	23	278	12.1	33	3
Heyward	19	159	8.4	21	0
Carroll	18	292	16.2	72t	2
Brenner	12	161	13.4	23	0
Wainright	9	143	15.9	29	0
Dunbar	9	62	6.9	13	0
Turner	5	43	8.6	18	0
Stowers	4	23	5.8	8	0
Newman	3	21	7.0	8	0
McAfee	1	16	16.0	16	0
Dowdell	1	6	6.0	6	0
Lipps	1	1	1.0	1	0
Cooper	0	20	—	20	0
Saints	251	3297	13.1	72t	19
Opponents	287	2846	9.9	44	13

Interceptions	No.	Yds.	Avg.	LG	TD
Cook	6	90	15.0	48t	1
Atkins	3	0	0.0	0	0
Jones	2	71	35.5	71t	1
V. Buck	2	51	25.5	34t	1
Taylor	2	20	10.0	20	0
Maxie	2	12	6.0	8	0
Mills	1	10	10.0	10	0
Saints	18	254	14.1	71t	3
Opponents	16	280	17.5	56t	2

Punting	No.	Yds.	Avg.	In 20	LG
Barnhardt	67	2947	44.0	19	62
Saints	67	2947	44.0	19	62
Opponents	89	3666	41.2	18	59

Punt Returns	No.	FC	Yds.	Avg.	LG	TD
Newman	23	10	158	6.9	18	0
Dowdell	12	6	37	3.1	34	0
Lipps	5	1	22	4.4	16	0
Turner	3	0	10	3.3	5	0
V. Buck	2	4	4	2.0	3	0
Saints	45	21	231	5.1	34	0
Opponents	31	21	218	7.0	34	0

Kickoff Returns	No.	Yds.	Avg.	LG	TD
Dunbar	10	187	18.7	27	0
Heyward	1	14	14.0	14	0
Hilliard	7	130	18.6	48	0
Jordan	1	18	18.0	18	0
Kennard	1	11	11.0	11	0
McAfee	19	393	20.7	38	0
Newman	3	62	20.7	29	0
Saints	42	815	19.4	48	0
Opponents	40	923	23.1	60	0

Sacks	No.
W. Martin	15.5
Jackson	13.5
Swilling	10.5
Warren	4.0
Wilks	4.0
Mills	3.0
Turnbull	1.5
Cook	1.0
Johnson	1.0
Maxie	1.0
Miller	1.0
V. Buck	0.5
Smeenge	0.5
Saints	57.0
Opponents	15.0

1993 Draft Choices

Round	Name	Pos.	College
1.	Willie Roaf	T	Louisiana Tech
	Irv Smith	TE	Notre Dame
2.	Reggie Freeman	LB	Florida State
4.	Lorenzo Neal	RB	Fresno State
	Derek Brown	RB	Nebraska
5.	Tyrone Hughes	DB	Nebraska
6.	Ronnie Dixon	NT	Cincinnati
7.	Othello Henderson	DB	UCLA
8.	Jon Kirksey	NT	Cal St.-Sacramento

New Orleans Saints 1993 Veteran Roster

No.	Name	Pos.	Ht.	Wt.	Birth-date	NFL Exp.	College	Hometown	How Acq.	'92 Games/ Starts
7	Andersen, Morten	K	6-2	221	8/19/60	12	Michigan State	Indianapolis, Ind.	D4-'82	16/0
28	Atkins, Gene	S	6-1	200	11/22/64	7	Florida A&M	Tallahassee, Fla.	D7-'87	16/16
6	#Barnhardt, Tommy	P	6-2	207	6/11/63	7	North Carolina	China Grove, N.C.	FA-'89	16/0
74	Bowles, Scott	G-T	6-5	280	12/27/67	3	North Texas State	Wichita Falls, Tex.	FA-'93	0*
64	Brennan, Mike	G-T	6-5	285	3/22/67	3	Notre Dame	Baltimore, Md.	FA-'93	0*
85	#Brenner, Hoby	TE	6-5	245	6/2/59	13	Southern California	Fullerton, Calif.	D3b-'81	15/13
16	†Buck, Mike	QB	6-3	227	4/22/67	4	Maine	Sayville, N.Y.	D6a-'90	2/0
26	Buck, Vince	CB	6-0	198	1/12/68	4	Central State, Ohio	Owensboro, Ky.	D2-'90	10/5
80	Carroll, Wesley	WR	6-0	183	9/6/67	3	Miami	Cleveland, Ohio	D2-'91	16/5
41	Cook, Toi	CB	5-11	188	12/3/64	7	Stanford	Van Nuys, Calif.	D8-'87	16/15
71	†Cooper, Richard	T	6-5	290	11/1/64	4	Tennessee	Memphis, Tenn.	FA-'89	16/16
72	Dombrowski, Jim	T	6-5	298	10/19/63	8	Virginia	Williamsville, N.Y.	D1-'86	16/16
63	Dunbar, Karl	DE	6-4	275	5/18/67	2	Louisiana State	Opelousas, La.	FA-'92	0*
32	Dunbar, Vaughn	RB	5-10	204	9/4/68	2	Indiana	Ft. Wayne, Ind.	D1-'92	16/8
89	Early, Quinn	WR	6-0	188	4/13/65	6	Iowa	South Great Neck, N.Y.	PB(SD)-'91	16/16
91	#Goff, Robert	NT	6-3	270	10/2/65	6	Auburn	Bradenton, Fla.	T(TB)-'90	16/0
61	Hilgenberg, Joel	C-G	6-2	252	7/10/62	10	Iowa	Iowa City, Iowa	D4-'84	16/16
21	#Hilliard, Dalton	RB	5-8	204	1/21/64	8	Louisiana State	Patterson, La.	D2-'86	16/4
57	Jackson, Rickey	LB	6-2	243	3/20/58	13	Pittsburgh	Pahokee, Fla.	D2-'81	16/16
68	Jetton, Paul	C-G	6-4	288	10/6/64	6	Texas	Houston, Tex.	PB(Cin)-'92	2/0
53	Johnson, Vaughan	LB	6-3	235	3/24/62	8	North Carolina State	Morehead City, N.C.	SD1-'84	16/14
27	Jones, Reginald	CB	6-1	202	1/11/69	3	Memphis State	West Memphis, Ark.	D5-'91	15/15
60	Kennard, Derek	G	6-3	300	9/9/62	8	Nevada-Reno	Stockton, Calif.	T(Phx)-'91	16/16
43	Legette, Tyrone	CB	5-9	177	2/15/70	2	Nebraska	Columbia, S.C.	D3-'92	8/0
62	Leggett, Brad	C	6-4	270	1/16/66	2	Southern California	Fountain Valley, Calif.	FA-'93	0*
46	Lumpkin, Sean	S	6-0	206	1/4/70	2	Minnesota	St. Louis Park, Minn.	D4b-'92	16/0
47	#Mack, Cedric	CB	5-11	190	9/14/60	11	Baylor	Freeport, Tex.	FA-'92	14/2
84	#Martin, Eric	WR	6-1	207	11/8/61	9	Louisiana State	Van Vleck, Tex.	D7-'85	16/11
42	Martin, Sammy	WR	5-11	182	8/21/65	5	Louisiana State	New Orleans, La.	FA-'93	0*
93	Martin, Wayne	DE	6-5	275	10/26/65	5	Arkansas	Cherry Valley, Ark.	D1-'89	16/16
39	Maxie, Brett	S	6-2	194	1/13/62	9	Texas Southern	Dallas, Tex.	FA-'85	10/10
25	McAfee, Fred	RB	5-10	193	6/20/68	3	Mississippi College	Philadelphia, Miss.	D6-'91	14/1
76	McGuire, Gene	C	6-2	284	7/17/70	2	Notre Dame	Panama City, Fla.	D4a-'92	0*
69	Miller, Les	DE	6-7	285	3/1/65	7	Fort Hays State	Arkansas City, Kan.	PB(SD)-'91	16/2
51	Mills, Sam	LB	5-9	225	6/3/59	8	Montclair State	Long Branch, N.J.	FA-'86	16/16
22	Muster, Brad	RB	6-4	235	4/11/65	6	Stanford	Santa Rosa, Calif.	UFA(Chi)-'93	16/16*
86	†Newman, Patrick	WR	5-11	189	9/10/68	4	Utah State	San Diego, Calif.	PB(Minn)-'91	10/0
70	Port, Chris	G-T	6-5	290	11/2/67	3	Duke	Wanaque, N.J.	FA-'90	16/0
66	Robbins, Tootie	T	6-5	310	6/2/58	12	East Carolina	Windsor, N.C.	UFA(GB)-'93	15/15*
83	Small, Torrance	WR	6-3	201	9/6/70	2	Alcorn State	Tampa, Fla.	D5-'92	13/2
99	†Smeenge, Joel	DE	6-5	250	4/1/68	3	Western Michigan	Grand Rapids, Mich.	D3-'90	11/0
37	Spencer, Jimmy	CB	5-9	180	3/29/69	2	Florida	South Bay, Fla.	FA-'92	16/4
49	Stowers, Tommie	TE	6-3	240	11/18/66	2	Missouri	Kansas City, Mo.	FA-'92	12/0
20	Taylor, Craig	RB	6-0	228	1/3/66	4	West Virginia	Linden, N.J.	FA-'93	0*
29	Taylor, Keith	S	5-11	206	12/21/64	6	Illinois	Pennsauken, N.J.	PB(Ind)-'92	16/4
97	Turnbull, Renaldo	DE	6-4	255	1/5/66	4	West Virginia	St. Thomas, Virgin Islands	D1-'90	14/0
88	†Turner, Floyd	WR	5-11	188	5/29/66	5	Northwestern Louisiana	Mansfield, La.	D6-'89	2/2
87	Wainright, Frank	TE	6-3	236	10/10/67	3	Northern Colorado	Arvada, Colo.	D8-'91	13/4
4	†Walsh, Steve	QB	6-3	210	12/1/66	5	Miami	St. Paul, Minn.	T(Dall)-'90	0*
73	Warren, Frank	DE	6-4	290	9/14/59	12	Auburn	Birmingham, Ala.	D3a-'81	16/16
94	#Wilks, Jim	NT	6-5	275	3/12/58	13	San Diego State	Pasadena, Calif.	D12-'81	12/9
90	Williams, James	LB	6-0	230	10/10/68	4	Mississippi State	North Natchez, Miss.	D6b-'90	16/0
48	Williams, Ronnie	TE	6-4	260	1/9/66	2	Oklahoma State	Wichita Falls, Tex.	FA-'93	0*
18	Wilson, Wade	QB	6-3	206	2/1/59	13	East Texas State	Commerce, Tex.	UFA(Atl)-'93	9/3*
92	Winston, DeMond	LB	6-2	239	9/14/68	4	Vanderbilt	Lansing, Mich.	D4-'90	15/0

* Bowles active with New England for 5 games in '92 but did not play; Brennan last active with Buffalo in '91; K. Dunbar was on New Orleans' practice squad; Leggett active for 2 games with Detroit but did not play; S. Martin last active with Indianapolis in '91; McGuire active for 12 games but did not play; Muster played 16 games with Chicago; Robbins played 15 games with Green Bay; C. Taylor last active with Cincinnati in '91; Walsh was active for 2 games but did not play; R. Williams last active with Kansas City in '90; Wilson played 9 games with Atlanta.

#Unrestricted free agent; subject to developments.

† Restricted free agent; subject to developments.

Traded—Linebacker Pat Swilling to Detroit.

Players lost through free agency (4): T Stan Brock (SD, 16 games in '92), RB Craig Heyward (Chi; 16), QB Bobby Hebert (Atl; 16), G Steve Trapilo (NE; 5).

Also played with Saints in '92—WR Marcus Dowdell (4 games), S Antonio Gibson (6), RB Buford Jordan (2), WR Louis Lipps (2), LB Pat Swilling (16), TE John Tice (3).

COACHING STAFF

Head Coach,
Jim Mora

Pro Career: Begins eighth year as an NFL head coach, after leading Saints to a 12-4 record and their third straight playoff appearance in 1992. Guided Saints to an 11-5 mark and the club's first-ever NFC West title. Was named 1987 NFL coach of the year after leading Saints to a 12-4 record and the team's first playoff appearance. Came to New Orleans following a three-year career as the winningest coach in USFL history as head coach of the Philadelphia/Baltimore Stars. Directed Stars to championship game in each of his three seasons and won league championship in 1984 and 1985. He won USFL coach of the year honors following the 1984 season. Mora began his pro coaching career in 1978 as defensive line coach of the Seattle Seahawks. In 1982, he became defensive coordinator of the New England Patriots and played a vital role in the Patriots' march to the playoffs that year. No pro playing experience. Career record: 69-46.

Background: Played tight end and defensive end at Occidental College. Assistant coach at Occidental from 1960-63 and head coach from 1964-66. Linebacker coach at Stanford (1967) on a staff that included former Eagles head coach Dick Vermeil. Defensive assistant at Colorado 1968-73. Linebacker coach under Vermeil at UCLA 1974. Defensive coordinator at Washington 1975-77. Received bachelor's degree in physical education from Occidental in 1957. Also holds master's degree in education from Southern California.

Personal: Born May 24, 1935, in Glendale, Calif. Jim and his wife, Connie, live in Metairie, La., and have three sons — Michael, Stephen, and Jim (defensive backs coach for the Saints).

Assistant Coaches

Paul Boudreau, offensive line; born December 30, 1949, Somerville, Mass., lives in Destrehan, La. Guard Boston College 1971-73. No pro playing experience. College coach: Boston College 1974-76, Maine 1977-78, Dartmouth 1979-81, Navy 1983. Pro coach: Edmonton Eskimos (CFL) 1983-86, joined Saints in 1987.

Vic Fangio, outside linebackers; born August 22, 1958, Dunmore, Pa., lives in Destrehan, La. Defensive back East Stroudsburg 1976-78. No pro playing experience. College coach: North Carolina 1983. Pro coach: Philadelphia/Baltimore Stars (USFL) 1984-85, joined Saints in 1986.

Joe Marciano, tight ends-special teams; born February 10, 1954, Scranton, Pa., lives in Kenner, La. Quarterback Temple 1972-75. No pro playing experience. College coach: East Stroudsburg 1977, Rhode Island 1978-79, Villanova 1980, Penn State 1981, Temple 1982. Pro coach: Philadelphia/Baltimore Stars (USFL) 1983-85, joined Saints in 1986.

Jim Mora, defensive backs; born November 19, 1961, Los Angeles, Calif., lives in New Orleans. Defensive back Washington 1980-83. No pro playing experience. College coach: Washington 1984. Pro coach: San Diego Chargers 1985-91, joined Saints in 1992.

Russell Paternostro, strength and conditioning; born July 21, 1940, New Orleans, La., lives in Covington, La. San Diego State. No college or pro playing experience. Pro coach: Joined Saints in 1981.

John Pease, defensive line; born October 14, 1943, Pittsburgh, Pa., lives in Kenner, La. Wingback Utah 1963-64. No pro playing experience. College coach: Fullerton, Calif., J.C. 1970-73, Long Beach State 1974-76, Utah 1977, Washington 1978-83. Pro coach: Philadelphia/Baltimore Stars (USFL) 1983-85, joined Saints in 1986.

Steve Sidwell, defensive coordinator-inside linebackers; born August 30, 1944, Winfield, Kan., lives in New Orleans. Linebacker Colorado 1962-65. No pro playing experience. College coach: Colorado 1966-73, Nevada-Las Vegas 1974-75, Southern Methodist 1976-81. Pro coach: New England Patriots 1982-84, Indianapolis Colts 1985, joined Saints in 1986.

Jim Skipper, running backs; born January 23, 1949, Breaux Bridge, La., lives in Kenner, La. Defensive back Whittier College 1971-72. No pro playing experience. College coach: Cal Poly-Pomona 1974-76, San Jose State 1977-78, Pacific 1979, Oregon 1980-82. Pro coach: Philadelphia/Baltimore Stars (USFL) 1983-85, joined Saints in 1986.

Carl Smith, offensive coordinator-quarterbacks; born April 26, 1948, Wasco, Calif., lives in Kenner, La. Defensive back Cal Poly-SLO 1968-70. No pro playing experience. College coach: Cal Poly-SLO 1971, Colorado 1972-73, Southwestern Louisiana 1974-78, Lamar 1979-81, North Carolina State 1982. Pro coach: Philadelphia/Baltimore Stars (USFL) 1983-85, joined Saints in 1986.

Steve Walters, wide receivers; born June 16, 1948, Jonesboro, Ark., lives in Destrehan, La. Quarterback-defensive back Arkansas 1967-70. No pro playing experience. College coach: Tampa 1973, Northeast Louisiana 1974-75, Morehead State 1976, Tulsa 1977-78, Memphis State 1979, Southern Methodist 1980-81, Alabama 1985. Pro coach: New England Patriots 1982-84, joined Saints in 1986.

New Orleans Saints 1993 First-Year Roster

Name	Pos.	Ht.	Wt.	Birth-date	College	Hometown	How Acq.
Bockes, Tom (1)	T	6-4	273	3/19/68	Oklahoma	El Paso, Tex.	FA
Blount, Eric	LB	5-11	234	4/20/70	Houston	Memphis, Tenn.	FA
Brown, Derek	RB	5-9	186	4/15/71	Nebraska	Anaheim, Calif.	D4b
Byrd, Israel	CB	5-11	184	2/1/71	Utah State	St. Louis, Mo.	FA
Coghill, George	S	6-2	196	3/30/70	Wake Forest	Fredericksburg, Va.	FA
Dixon, Ronnie	NT	6-2	292	5/10/71	Cincinnati	Clinton, N.C.	D6
Dolly, Rick	DE	6-4	259	11/21/69	West Virginia	New Crock, W. Va.	FA
Dowdell, Marcus (1)	WR	5-10	179	5/22/70	Tennessee State	Birmingham, Ala.	D10-'92
Eldridge, J.J.	CB	5-11	182	7/2/70	NW Louisiana	Dallas, Tex.	FA
Evans, Fernando	WR	6-1	188	10/12/69	Alcorn State	Wiggins, Miss.	FA
Everett, Tre	WR	5-10	172	12/10/69	Florida	Washington, D.C.	FA
Freeman, Reggie	LB	6-1	233	5/8/70	Florida State	Clewiston, Fla.	D2
Henderson, Othello	S	6-0	192	8/23/72	UCLA	Killeen, Tex.	D7
Hughes, Tyrone	CB	5-9	175	1/14/70	Nebraska	New Orleans, La.	D5
Kirksey, Jon	NT	6-3	360	2/21/70	Cal State-Sacramento	Greer, S.C.	D8
McCleskey, J.J.	WR	5-7	177	4/10/70	Tennessee	Knoxville, Tenn.	FA
McManus, Tom	LB	6-2	236	7/3/70	Boston College	Wheeling, Ill.	FA
Neal, Lorenzo	RB	5-10	228	12/27/70	Fresno State	Lemoore, Calif.	D4a
Ned, Derrick (1)	RB	6-1	210	1/5/69	Grambling	Eunice, La.	FA
Nelson, Royce	G	6-4	315	8/9/70	Nicholls State	New Orleans, La.	FA
Pahukoa, Shane	S	6-2	202	11/25/70	Washington	Marysville, Calif.	FA
Roaf, Willie	T	6-4	299	4/18/70	Louisiana Tech	Pine Bluff, Ark.	D1a
Sally, Lamar	DE	6-4	271	8/11/70	Central Michigan	Detroit, Mich.	FA
Shufelt, Pete	LB	6-2	241	10/28/69	Texas-El Paso	Tucson, Ariz.	FA
Smith, Irv	TE	6-3	246	10/13/71	Notre Dame	Pemberton, N.J.	D1b
Stigge, Mike	P	6-2	191	10/31/69	Nebraska	Washington, Kan.	FA
Turner, Ken	LB	6-0	237	3/10/71	Angelo State	Texas City, Tex.	FA
Verdugo, Kevin (1)	QB	6-3	211	9/16/68	Colorado State	Pittsburg, Kan.	FA

The term NFL Rookie is defined as a player who is in his first season of professional football and has not been on the roster of another professional football team for any regular-season or postseason games. A Rookie is designated by an "R" on NFL rosters. Players who have been active in another professional football league or players who have NFL experience, including either preseason training camp or being on an Active List, Inactive List, Reserve/Injured or Reserve/Physically Unable to Perform for fewer than six regular season games, are termed NFL First-Year Players. An NFL First-Year Player is designated by a "1" on NFL rosters. Thereafter, a player is credited with an additional year of experience for each season in which he accumulates six games on the Active List, Inactive List, Reserve/Injured, or Reserve/Physically Unable to Perform.

NOTES

NEW YORK GIANTS

National Football Conference Eastern Division

Team Colors: Blue, Red, and White

Giants Stadium
East Rutherford, New Jersey 07073
Telephone: (201) 935-8111

Club Officials

President/Co-CEO: Wellington T. Mara
Chairman/Co-CEO: Preston Robert Tisch
Executive Vice President/General Counsel: John K. Mara, Esq.
Treasurer: Jonathan Tisch
Vice President-General Manager: George Young
Assistant General Manager: Harry Hulmes
Controller: John Pasquali
Director of Player Personnel: Tom Boisture
Director of Pro Personnel: Tim Rooney
Director of Administration: Tom Power
Senior Director of Marketing: Rusty Hawley
Director of Promotion: Frank Mara
Ticket Manager: John Gorman
Director of Public Relations: Pat Hanlon
Head Trainer: Ronnie Barnes
Assistant Trainers: John Johnson, Mike Ryan, Steve Kennelly
Equipment Manager: Ed Wagner, Jr.

Stadium: Giants Stadium • **Capacity:** 77,311
East Rutherford, New Jersey 07073

Playing Surface: AstroTurf

Training Camp: Fairleigh Dickinson-Madison
Florham Park, N.J. 07932

1993 Schedule

Preseason

Aug. 7	at Cincinnati	7:30
Aug. 14	**Pittsburgh**	8:00
Aug. 21	**New York Jets**	8:00
Aug. 28	at Miami	8:00

Regular Season

Sept. 5	at Chicago	3:00
Sept. 12	**Tampa Bay**	1:00
Sept. 19	**Los Angeles Rams**	1:00
Sept. 26	**Open Date**	
Oct. 3	at Buffalo	8:00
Oct. 10	at Washington	1:00
Oct. 17	**Philadelphia**	1:00
Oct. 24	**Open Date**	
Oct. 31	**New York Jets**	1:00
Nov. 7	at Dallas	12:00
Nov. 14	**Washington**	1:00
Nov. 21	at Philadelphia	4:00
Nov. 28	**Phoenix**	4:00
Dec. 5	at Miami	4:00
Dec. 12	**Indianapolis**	1:00
Dec. 20	at New Orleans (Monday)	8:00
Dec. 26	at Phoenix	2:00
Jan. 2	**Dallas**	1:00

Giants Coaching History

(494-408-32)

1925	Bob Folwell	8-4-0
1926	Joe Alexander	8-4-1
1927-28	Earl Potteiger	15-8-3
1929-30	LeRoy Andrews*	24-5-1
1930	Benny Friedman	2-0-0
1931-53	Steve Owen	153-108-17
1954-60	Jim Lee Howell	54-29-4
1961-68	Allie Sherman	57-54-4
1969-73	Alex Webster	29-40-1
1974-76	Bill Arnsparger**	7-28-0
1976-78	John McVay	14-23-0
1979-82	Ray Perkins	24-35-0
1983-90	Bill Parcells	85-52-1
1991-92	Ray Handley	14-18-0

*Released after 15 games in 1930
**Released after seven games in 1976

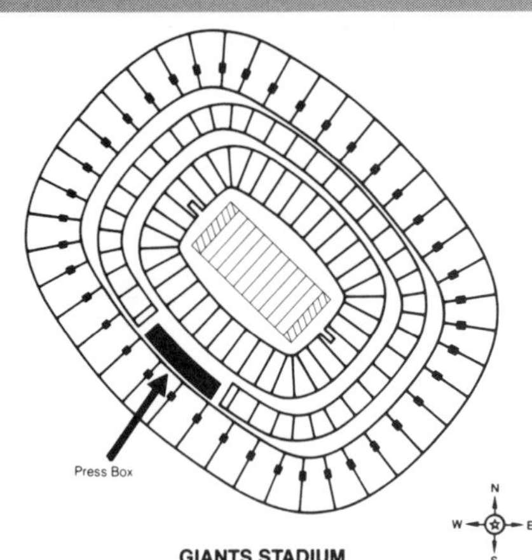

GIANTS STADIUM

Record Holders

Individual Records — Career

Category	Name	Performance
Rushing (Yds.)	Joe Morris, 1982-88	5,296
Passing (Yds.)	Phil Simms, 1979-1992	30,424
Passing (TDs)	Phil Simms, 1979-1992	184
Receiving (No.)	Joe Morrison, 1959-1972	395
Receiving (Yds.)	Frank Gifford, 1952-1960, 1962-64	5,434
Interceptions	Emlen Tunnell, 1948-1958	74
Punting (Avg.)	Don Chandler, 1956-1964	43.8
Punt Return (Avg.)	David Meggett, 1989-1992	10.9
Kickoff Return (Avg.)	Rocky Thompson, 1971-72	27.2
Field Goals	Pete Gogolak, 1966-1974	126
Touchdowns (Tot.)	Frank Gifford, 1952-1960, 1962-64	78
Points	Pete Gogolak, 1966-1974	646

Individual Records — Single Season

Category	Name	Performance
Rushing (Yds.)	Joe Morris, 1986	1,516
Passing (Yds.)	Phil Simms, 1984	4,044
Passing (TDs)	Y.A. Tittle, 1963	36
Receiving (No.)	Earnest Gray, 1983	78
Receiving (Yds.)	Homer Jones, 1967	1,209
Interceptions	Otto Schnellbacher, 1951	11
	Jim Patton, 1958	11
Punting (Avg.)	Don Chandler, 1959	46.6
Punt Return (Avg.)	Merle Hapes, 1942	15.5
Kickoff Return (Avg.)	John Salscheider, 1949	31.6
Field Goals	Ali Haji-Sheikh, 1983	*35
Touchdowns (Tot.)	Joe Morris, 1985	21
Points	Ali Haji-Sheikh, 1983	127

Individual Records — Single Game

Category	Name	Performance
Rushing (Yds.)	Gene Roberts, 11-12-50	218
Passing (Yds.)	Phil Simms, 10-13-85	513
Passing (TDs)	Y.A. Tittle, 10-28-62	*7
Receiving (No.)	Mark Bavaro, 10-13-85	12
Receiving (Yds.)	Del Shofner, 10-28-62	269
Interceptions	Many times	3
	Last time by Terry Kinard, 9-27-87	
Field Goals	Joe Danelo, 10-18-81	6
Touchdowns (Tot.)	Ron Johnson, 10-2-72	4
	Earnest Gray, 9-7-80	4
Points	Ron Johnson, 10-2-72	24
	Earnest Gray, 9-7-80	24

*NFL Record

1992 Team Record

Preseason (2-2)

Date	Result		Opponents
8/9	W	13- 7	Cincinnati
8/15	W	16- 7	Cleveland
8/22	L	14-20	at N.Y. Jets
8/29	L	3-24	at Pittsburgh

Regular Season (6-10)

Date	Result		Opponents	Att.
9/6	L	14-31	San Francisco	76,241
9/13	L	28-34	Dallas	76,034
9/21	W	27-14	at Chicago	66,091
10/4	L	10-13	at L.A. Raiders	40,919
10/11	W	31-21	Phoenix	76,007
10/18	L	17-38	at L.A. Rams	56,549
10/25	W	23-10	Seattle	76,021
11/1	W	24- 7	at Washington	55,458
11/8	W	27- 7	Green Bay	76,069
11/15	L	13-27	at Denver	74,161
11/22	L	34-47	Philadelphia	76,191
11/26	L	3-30	at Dallas	62,974
12/6	L	10-28	Washington	76,162
12/12	L	0-19	at Phoenix	31,905
12/19	W	35-21	Kansas City	75,981
12/27	L	10-20	at Philadelphia	65,655

Score by Periods

Giants	51	104	86	65	0	— 306
Opponents	83	110	95	79	0	— 367

Attendance

Home 608,706 Away 453,712 Total 1,062,418
Single-game home record, 77,025 (1-31-91)
Single-season home record, 608,706 (1992)

1992 Team Statistics

	Giants	Opp.
Total First Downs	271	287
Rushing	120	115
Passing	119	155
Penalty	32	17
Third Down: Made/Att.	70/203	76/180
Third Down: Pct.	34.5	42.2
Fourth Down: Made/Att.	8/13	4/15
Fourth Down: Pct.	61.5	26.7
Total Net Yards	4421	5043
Avg. Per Game	276.3	315.2
Total Plays	936	923
Avg. Per Play	4.7	5.5
Net Yards Rushing	2077	2012
Avg. Per Game	129.8	125.8
Total Rushes	458	458
Net Yards Passing	2344	3031
Avg. Per Game	146.5	189.4
Sacked/Yards Lost	45/284	25/197
Gross Yards	2628	3228
Att./Completions	433/232	440/270
Completion Pct.	53.6	61.4
Had Intercepted	10	14
Punts/Avg.	85/40.6	64/38.7
Net Punting Avg.	85/31.8	64/33.7
Penalties/Yards Lost	87/647	93/744
Fumbles/Ball Lost	25/13	27/12
Touchdowns	36	46
Rushing	20	17
Passing	14	22
Returns	2	7
Avg. Time of Possession	29:22	30:38

1992 Individual Statistics

Scoring	TD R	TD P	TD Rt	PAT	FG	Saf	TP
Hampton	14	0	0	0/0	0/0	0	84
Bahr	0	0	0	29/29	16/21	0	77
Willis	0	0	0	7/7	2/2	0	13
McCaffrey	0	5	0	0/0	0/0	0	30
Bunch	3	1	0	0/0	0/0	0	24
Hostetler	3	0	0	0/0	0/0	0	18
Meggett	0	2	1	0/0	0/0	0	18
Baker	0	2	0	0/0	0/0	0	12
Cross	0	2	0	0/0	0/0	0	12
Calloway	0	1	0	0/0	0/0	0	6
Ingram	0	1	0	0/0	0/0	0	6
Thompson	0	0	1	0/0	0/0	0	6
Giants	20	14	2	36/36	18/23	0	306
Opponents	17	22	7	44/46	15/21	1	367

Passing	Att.	Comp.	Yds.	Pct.	TD	Int.	Tkld.	Rate
Hostetler	192	103	1225	53.6	8	3	24/149	80.8
Simms	137	83	912	60.6	5	3	10/67	83.3
Graham	97	42	470	43.3	1	4	7/49	44.6
Da. Brown	7	4	21	57.1	0	0	4/19	62.2
Giants	433	232	2628	53.6	14	10	45/284	73.2
Opponents	440	270	3228	61.4	22	14	25/197	87.2

Rushing	Att.	Yds.	Avg.	LG	TD
Hampton	257	1141	4.4	63t	14
Bunch	104	501	4.8	37	3
Hostetler	35	172	4.9	27	3
Meggett	32	167	5.2	30	0
Graham	6	36	6.0	15	0
Anderson	10	31	3.1	6	0
Simms	6	17	2.8	7	0
Tillman	6	13	2.2	6	0
Da. Brown	2	−1	−.5	1	0
Giants	458	2077	4.5	63t	20
Opponents	458	2012	4.4	68t	17

Receiving	No.	Yds.	Avg.	LG	TD
McCaffrey	49	610	12.4	44	5
Meggett	38	229	6.0	24	2
Hampton	28	215	7.7	31	0
Ingram	27	408	15.1	34	1
Cross	27	357	13.2	29	2
Calloway	27	335	12.4	28	1
Baker	17	333	19.6	46	2
Bunch	11	50	4.5	13	1
De. Brown	4	31	7.8	9	0
Smith	3	45	15.0	22	0
Tillman	1	15	15.0	15	0
Giants	232	2628	11.3	46	14
Opponents	270	3228	12.0	77t	22

Interceptions	No.	Yds.	Avg.	LG	TD
Jackson	4	71	17.8	36	0
Thompson	2	69	34.5	69t	1
Johnson	2	42	21.0	38	0
Miller	2	10	5.0	10	0
Collins	1	0	0.0	0	0
Sparks	1	0	0.0	0	0
Walls	1	0	0.0	0	0
P. Williams	1	0	0.0	0	0
Giants	14	192	13.7	69t	1
Opponents	10	190	19.0	56t	2

Punting	No.	Yds.	Avg.	In 20	LG
Landeta	53	2317	43.7	13	71
Rodriguez	21	841	40.0	5	55
Prokop	8	293	36.6	0	43
Giants	85	3451	40.6	18	71
Opponents	64	2477	38.7	22	55

Punt Returns	No.	FC	Yds.	Avg.	LG	TD
Meggett	27	11	240	8.9	39	0
Giants	27	11	240	8.9	39	0
Opponents	46	11	548	11.9	87t	2

Kickoff Returns	No.	Yds.	Avg.	LG	TD
Meggett	20	455	22.8	92t	1
Smith	30	564	18.8	35	0
Calloway	2	29	14.5	17	0
Bunch	2	27	13.5	17	0
Sparks	2	23	11.5	14	0
Giants	56	1098	19.6	92t	1
Opponents	64	1207	18.9	56	0

Sacks	No.
Taylor	5.0
Banks	4.0
Marshall	4.0
K. Hamilton	3.5
Fox	2.5
Dorsey	2.0
Miller	2.0
Johnson	1.0
Raymond	1.0
Giants	25.0
Opponents	45.0

1993 Draft Choices

Round	Name	Pos.	College
2.	Michael Strahan	DE	Texas Southern
3.	Marcus Buckley	LB	Texas A&M
4.	Greg Bishop	T	Pacific
5.	Tommy Thigpen	LB	North Carolina
6.	Scott Davis	G	Iowa
7.	Todd Peterson	K	Georgia
8.	Jessie Armstead	LB	Miami

New York Giants 1993 Veteran Roster

No.	Name	Pos.	Ht.	Wt.	Birth-date	NFL Exp.	College	Hometown	How Acq.	'92 Games/ Starts
41	Allred, Brian	CB-S	5-10	175	3/16/69	2	Cal State-Sacramento	Washington, D.C.	FA-'92	0*
24	Anderson, Ottis	RB	6-2	225	1/19/57	15	Miami	West Palm Beach, Fla.	T(StL)-'86	13/0
9	†Bahr, Matt	K	5-10	175	7/6/56	15	Penn State	Langhorne, Pa.	FA-'90	12/0
54	Bailey, Carlton	LB	6-3	235	12/15/64	6	North Carolina	Baltimore, Md.	UFA(Buff)-'93	16/0*
85	†Baker, Stephen	WR	5-8	160	8/30/64	7	Fresno State	San Antonio, Tex.	D3-'87	16/11
82	Brandes, John	TE	6-2	249	4/2/64	6	Cameron	Arlington, Tex.	FA-'92	5/0*
94	Brooks, Michael	LB	6-1	235	10/2/64	7	Louisiana State	Rustin, La.	UFA(Den)-'93	15/14*
17	Brown, Dave	QB	6-5	215	2/25/70	2	Duke	Westfield, N.J.	SD1-'92	2/0
86	Brown, Derek	TE	6-6	252	3/31/70	2	Notre Dame	Fairfax, Va.	D1-'92	16/7
33	Bunch, Jarrod	RB	6-2	248	8/9/68	3	Michigan	Ashtabula, Ohio	D1-'91	16/13
80	Calloway, Chris	WR	5-10	185	3/29/68	4	Michigan	Chicago, Ill.	FA-'92	16/1
37	Campbell, Jesse	S	6-1	215	4/11/69	2	North Carolina State	Vanceboro, N.C.	FA-'92	11/0
25	Collins, Mark	CB	5-10	190	1/16/64	8	Cal State-Fullerton	San Bernardino, Calif.	D2-'86	14/14
87	#Cross, Howard	TE	6-5	245	8/8/67	5	Alabama	Huntsville, Ala.	D6-'89	16/16
99	†DeOssie, Steve	LB	6-2	248	11/22/62	10	Boston College	Tacoma, Wash.	T(Dall)-'89	12/11
71	Dillard, Stacey	DE	6-5	288	9/17/68	2	Oklahoma	Clarksville, Tex.	D6-'92	12/0
77	Dorsey, Eric	DE	6-5	280	8/5/64	8	Notre Dame	McLean, Va.	D1-'86	16/16
76	†Elliott, John	T	6-7	305	4/1/65	6	Michigan	Lake Ronkonkoma, N.Y.	D2-'88	16/16
93	#Fox, Mike	DE	6-6	275	8/5/67	4	West Virginia	Akron, Ohio	D2-'90	16/4
10	Graham, Kent	QB	6-5	220	11/1/68	2	Ohio State	Wheaton, Ill.	D8-'92	6/3
29	#Guyton, Myron	S	6-1	205	8/26/67	5	Eastern Kentucky	Metcalf, Ga.	D8-'89	4/4
75	Hamilton, Keith	DE	6-6	280	5/25/71	2	Pittsburgh	Lynchburg, Va.	D4-'92	16/0
27	Hampton, Rodney	RB	5-11	215	4/3/69	4	Georgia	Houston, Tex.	D1-'90	16/16
74	Howard, Erik	NT	6-4	268	11/12/64	8	Washington State	San Jose, Calif.	D2a-'86	16/15
47	Jackson, Greg	S	6-1	200	8/20/66	5	Louisiana State	Hialeah, Fla.	D3a-'89	16/16
18	Jackson, Mark	WR	5-9	180	7/23/63	8	Purdue	Chicago, Ill.	UFA(Den)-'93	16/13*
52	Johnson, Pepper	LB	6-3	248	6/29/64	8	Ohio State	Detroit, Mich.	D2b-'86	16/16
68	Jones, Clarence	T	6-6	280	5/6/68	3	Maryland	Brooklyn, N.Y.	D4-'92	3/0
21	Jones, Victor	RB	5-8	220	12/5/67	4	Louisiana State	Zachary, La.	FA-'92	16/1*
26	#Kaumeyer, Thom	S	5-11	190	3/17/67	4	Oregon	La Jolla, Calif.	FA-'91	0*
61	Kratch, Bob	G	6-3	288	1/6/66	5	Iowa	Mahwah, N.J.	D3-'89	16/7
5	Landeta, Sean	P	6-0	210	1/6/62	9	Towson State	Baltimore, Md.	FA-'85	11/0
81	McCaffrey, Ed	WR	6-5	215	8/17/68	3	Stanford	Allentown, Pa.	D3-'91	16/3
96	McGhee, Kanavis	LB	6-4	257	10/4/68	3	Colorado	Houston, Tex.	D2-'91	14/1
38	McGriggs, Lamar	CB-S	6-3	210	5/9/68	3	Western Illinois	Chicago, Ill.	D8-'91	16/10
30	#Meggett, David	RB-KR	5-7	180	4/30/66	5	Towson State	Charleston, S.C.	D5-'89	16/0
57	Miller, Corey	LB	6-2	255	10/25/68	3	South Carolina	Pageland, S.C.	D6-'91	16/7
60	Moore, Eric	T	6-5	290	1/21/65	6	Indiana	Berkeley, Mo.	D1-'88	10/10
65	Oates, Bart	C	6-3	265	12/16/58	9	Brigham Young	Albany, Ga.	FA-'85	16/15
84	Pierce, Aaron	TE	6-5	246	9/6/69	2	Washington	Seattle, Wash.	D3-'92	1/0
39	Raymond, Corey	S	5-11	180	7/28/69	2	Louisiana State	New Iberia, La.	FA-'92	1/0
95	Reynolds, Ed	LB	6-5	242	9/23/61	11	Virginia	Ridgeway, Va.	FA-'92	16/5
72	Riesenberg, Doug	T	6-5	275	7/22/65	7	California	Moscow, Idaho	D6a-'87	16/16
66	Roberts, William	G	6-5	280	8/5/62	9	Ohio State	Miami, Fla.	D1a-'84	16/15
91	Rooks, George	DE	6-4	275	8/9/70	2	Syracuse	White Plains, N.Y.	D10-'92	0*
19	Sherrard, Mike	WR	6-2	187	6/21/63	6	UCLA	Los Angeles, Calif.	UFA(SF)-'93	16/8*
11	Simms, Phil	QB	6-3	214	11/3/56	15	Morehead State	Louisville, Ky.	D1-'79	4/4
88	Smith, Joey	WR	5-10	177	5/30/69	3	Louisville	Knoxville, Tenn.	FA-'91	16/1
22	Sparks, Phillippi	CB	5-11	186	4/15/69	2	Arizona State	Glendale, Calif.	D2-'92	16/2
56	Taylor, Lawrence	LB	6-3	243	2/4/59	13	North Carolina	Williamsburg, Va.	D1-'81	9/9
34	Tillman, Lewis	RB	6-0	195	4/16/66	5	Jackson State	Oklahoma City, Okla.	D4-'89	16/0
90	Widmer, Corey	DE	6-3	276	12/25/68	2	Montana State	Bozeman, Mont.	D7-'92	8/0
59	†Williams, Brian	C-G	6-5	300	6/8/66	5	Minnesota	Mt. Lebanon, Pa.	D1-'89	13/1
23	Williams, Perry	CB	6-2	203	5/12/61	10	North Carolina State	Hamlet, N.C.	D7-'83	16/16
3	#Willis, Ken	K	5-11	190	10/6/66	4	Kentucky	Owensboro, Ky.	FA-'92	9/0*
36	Wright, Mike	CB	6-0	182	9/25/69	2	Washington State	Seattle, Wash.	D5-'92	0*

* Allred, Kaumeyer, Rooks, and Wright missed '92 season because of injury; Bailey played 16 games with Buffalo in '92; Brooks played 15 games with Denver; Brandes played 1 game with Washington, 4 games with N.Y. Giants; M. Jackson played 16 games with Denver; V. Jones played 16 games with Denver; Sherrard played 16 games with San Francisco; Willis played 9 games with Tampa Bay.

Unrestricted free agent; subject to developments.

† Restricted free agent; subject to developments.

Players lost through free agency (5): LB Carl Banks (Wash; 15 games '92), QB Jeff Hostetler (Raid; 13), WR Mark Ingram (Mia; 12), DE Leonard Marshall (NYJ; 14), CB-S Reyna Thompson (NE; 16).

Also played with Giants in '92 — LB Bobby Abrams (1 game), P Joe Prokop (1), P Ruben Rodriguez (4), CB-S Everson Walls (6), DE John Washington (12).

COACHING STAFF

Head Coach, Dan Reeves

Pro Career: Became the fourteenth head coach in Giants' history on January 27, 1993, after 12 years as head coach of the Denver Broncos. He compiled a 117-79-1 record with the Broncos, including an 8-8 mark in 1992. In 1991, Reeves led the Broncos to a 14-4 record, the AFC Western Division title, and a berth in the AFC Championship Game. Reeves took the Broncos to five first- and three second-place finishes in the division, along with six playoff berths and four AFC Championship Game appearances. He comes into the 1993 season in fifteenth place on the all-time pro coaching victory list. Denver was 5-11 in 1990, but Reeves's Broncos won the AFC championship in 1986, 1987, and 1989, making Denver the only AFC team to reach three Super Bowls during the decade of the 1980s. Denver posted regular-season records of 11-5 (1986), 10-4-1 (1987), and 11-5 (1989) in those championship seasons. Reeves has played or coached in eight Super Bowls, the most by any single participant in the NFL's Championship Game. He led Denver to an 11-5 record in 1985, barely missing a playoff berth. Reeves also guided the Broncos to an AFC West championship with a 13-3 record in 1984, and a 9-7 mark and playoff berth in 1983. His teams were 10-6 in 1981 and 2-7 in 1982. He joined the Dallas Cowboys as a free-agent running back in 1965 and became a member of the coaching staff in 1970 when he undertook the dual role of player-coach for two seasons. Reeves was the Cowboys' offensive backfield coach in 1972 and from 1974-76, and became offensive coordinator in 1977. Reeves was an all-purpose running back during his eight seasons as a player, rushing for 1,990 yards and catching 129 passes for 1,693. Career record 117-79-1.

Background: Quarterback at South Carolina from 1962-64. He was inducted into the school's Hall of Fame in 1978.

Personal: Born January 19, 1944, Rome, Ga. Dan and his wife, Pam, live in East Rutherford, N.J., and have three children, Dan, Laura, and Lee.

Assistant Coaches

Dave Brazil, defensive quality control; born March 25, 1936, Detroit, Mich., lives in East Rutherford, N.J. No college or pro playing experience. College coach: Holy Cross 1968-69, Tulsa 1970-71, Eastern Michigan 1972-74, Boston College 1978-79, Kent State 1980-82. Pro coach: Detroit Wheel (WFL) 1975, Chicago Fire (WFL) 1976, Kansas City Chiefs 1984-88, Pittsburgh Steelers 1989-91, joined Giants in 1992.

Joe DeCamillis, special teams; born June 29, 1965, Arvada, Colo., lives in East Rutherford, N.J. No college or pro playing experience. Wrestler Wyoming 1983-87. Pro coach: Denver Broncos 1989-92, joined Giants 1993.

James Daniel, tight ends; born January 17, 1953, Wetumpka, Ala., lives in East Rutherford, N.J. Offensive guard Alabama State 1970-73. No pro playing experience. College coach: Auburn 1981-92. Pro coach: Joined Giants in 1993.

Kerry Goode, assistant strength and conditioning; born July 28, 1965, Town Creek, Ala., lives in East Rutherford, N.J. Tailback Alabama 1983-87. Pro running back Tampa Bay Buccaneers 1988, Denver Broncos 1989, Miami Dolphins 1990. Pro coach: Joined Giants in 1993.

George Henshaw, offensive coordinator-quarterbacks; born January 22, 1948, Richmond, Va., lives in East Rutherford, N.J. Defensive tackle West Virginia 1967-69. No pro playing experience. College coach: West Virginia 1970-75, Florida State 1976-82, Alabama 1983-86, Tulsa 1987 (head coach). Pro coach: Denver Broncos 1988-92, joined Giants in 1993.

New York Giants 1993 First-Year Roster

Name	Pos.	Ht.	Wt.	Birth-date	College	Hometown	How Acq.
Armstead, Jessie	LB	6-1	238	10/26/70	Miami	Dallas, Tex.	D8
Bailey, Hassan	CB-S	6-0	205	1/28/71	Kansas	Gahanna, Ohio	FA
Bailey, Walter	CB-S	5-11	190	3/16/70	Washington	Portland, Ohio	FA
Beamon, Willie	CB-S	5-11	170	6/14/70	Northern Iowa	Riviera Beach, Fla.	FA
Bishop, Greg	T	6-5	298	5/2/71	Pacific	Lodi, Calif.	D4
Bradley, Shazzon (1)	DE	6-1	270	2/22/70	Tennessee	Athens, Tenn.	FA
Brannon, Steve	DE	6-3	265	11/27/68	Hampton	Georgetown, S.C.	FA
Bruun, Eric (1)	P	6-2	215	11/16/68	Purdue	Oakland, Calif.	FA
Buckley, Marcus	LB	6-3	235	2/3/71	Texas	Ft. Worth, Tex.	D3
Crawford, Keith	WR	6-2	180	11/21/70	Howard Payne	Palestine, Tex.	FA
Crysdale, Jamie	C	6-4	281	12/14/68	Cincinnati	Toronto, Canada	FA
Davis, Scott	G	6-3	289	1/29/70	Iowa	Glenwood, Iowa	D6
Duckett, Tico	RB	5-10	195	2/4/70	Michigan State	Kalamazoo, Mich.	FA
Flythe, Mark	DE	6-7	290	10/4/68	Penn State	Philadelphia, Pa.	FA
Fox, Brian	QB	6-4	214	12/23/70	Florida	Winter Garden, Fla.	FA
Jeffcoat, Jerold	NT	6-2	280	8/30/69	Temple	Matawan, N.J.	FA
Johnson, Jim (1)	T	6-5	305	6/20/68	Michigan State	Grand Rapids, Mich.	FA
Kozlowski, Brian	TE	6-3	245	10/4/70	Connecticut	Rochester, N.Y.	FA
Latson, Lawann	WR	5-8	170	3/11/71	N.W. Louisiana	Shreveport, La.	FA
McFarland, Mike	CB-S	5-10	178	12/29/70	Baylor	Jasper, Tex.	FA
Mitter, Craig	RB	5-9	203	2/3/70	Rutgers	Matawan, N.J.	FA
Myles, Lee	WR	5-6	156	9/18/69	Baylor	Mart, Tex.	FA
Nash, Harold	CB-S	5-9	178	5/5/70	S.W. Louisiana	New Orleans, La.	FA
Novak, Jeff (1)	T	6-6	300	7/27/67	S.W. Texas State	Cook County, Ill.	FA
Peterson, Todd	K	5-10	175	2/4/70	Georgia	Valdosta, Ga.	D7
Pope, Marcus	TE	6-3	250	6/16/71	Southern Mississippi	Hattiesburg, Miss.	FA
Powell, Andre (1)	LB	6-1	226	6/5/69	Penn State	York, Pa.	FA
Preston, Jerome	CB-S	6-5	288	5/4/71	Virginia Tech	Martinsville, Va.	FA
Rasheed, Kenyon	RB	5-10	245	8/23/70	Oklahoma	Kansas City, Mo.	FA
Roseman, Scott	LB	6-4	235	1/2/70	California	Benicia, Calif.	FA
Strahan, Michael	DE	6-4	253	11/21/71	Texas Southern	Westbury, Tex.	D2
Thigpen, Tommy	LB	6-2	242	3/17/71	North Carolina	Dunfries, Va.	D5
Thomas, Norris	CB-S	5-11	190	1/16/69	Wisconsin-LaCrosse	Milwaukee, Wis.	FA
Thornton, Joel	CB-S	5-10	170	9/11/71	Pittsburg State, Kan.	Tulsa, Okla.	FA
Weir, Eric	WR	6-2	175	7/15/70	Vanderbilt	Houston, Tex.	FA

The term NFL Rookie is defined as a player who is in his first season of professional football and has not been on the roster of another professional football team for any regular-season or postseason games. A Rookie is designated by an "R" on NFL rosters. Players who have been active in another professional football league or players who have NFL experience, including either preseason training camp or being on an Active List or Inactive List, or on Reserve/Injured or Reserve/Physically Unable to Perform for fewer than six regular-season games, are termed NFL First-Year Players. An NFL First-Year Player is designated by a "1" on NFL rosters. Thereafter, a player is credited with an additional year of experience for each season in which he accumulates six games on the Active List or Inactive List, or on Reserve/Injured or Reserve/Physically Unable to Perform.

NOTES

Earl Leggett, defensive line, born May 5, 1933, Jacksonville, Fla., lives in East Rutherford, N.J. Tackle Hinds J.C. 1953-54, Louisiana State 1955-56. Pro defensive tackle Chicago Bears 1957-65, Los Angeles Rams 1966, New Orleans Saints 1967-68. College coach: Nicholls State 1971, Texas Christian 1972-73. Pro coach: Southern California Sun (WFL) 1974-75, Seattle Seahawks 1976-77, San Francisco 49ers 1978, Oakland/Los Angeles Raiders 1980-88, Denver Broncos 1989-92, joined Giants in 1993.

Pete Mangurian, offensive line; born June 17, 1955, Los Angeles, Calif., lives in East Rutherford, N.J. Defensive lineman Louisiana State 1975-78. No pro playing experience. College coach: Southern Methodist 1979-80, New Mexico State 1981, Stanford 1982-83, Louisiana State 1984-87. Pro coach: Denver Broncos 1988-92, joined Giants in 1993.

Al Miller, strength and conditioning; born August 29, 1947, El Dorado, Ark., lives in East Rutherford, N.J. Wide receiver Northeast Louisiana 1966-69. No pro playing experience. College coach: Northwestern Louisiana 1974-78, Mississippi State 1980. Northeast Louisiana 1981, Alabama 1982-84. Pro coach: Denver Broncos 1987-92, joined Giants in 1993.

Mike Nolan, defensive coordinator, born March 7, 1959, Baltimore, Md., lives in East Rutherford, N.J. Safety Oregon 1977-80. No pro playing experience. College coach: Stanford 1982-83, Rice 1984-85, Louisiana State 1986. Pro coach: Denver Broncos 1987-92, joined Giants in 1993.

Dick Rehbein, wide receivers; born November 22, 1955, Green Bay, Wis., lives in East Rutherford, N.J. Center Ripon 1973-77. No pro playing experience. Pro coach: Green Bay Packers 1979-83, Los Angeles Express (USFL) 1984, Minnesota Vikings 1984-91, joined Giants in 1992.

George Sefcik, running backs, born December 27, 1939, Cleveland, Ohio, lives in East Rutherford, N.J. Halfback Notre Dame 1959-61. No pro playing experience. College coach: Notre Dame 1963-68, Kentucky 1969-72. Pro coach: Baltimore Colts 1973-74, Cleveland Browns 1975-77, 1989-90, Cincinnati Bengals 1979-83, Green Bay Packers 1984-87, Kansas City Chiefs 1988, joined Giants in 1991.

Zaven Yaralian, defensive backs, born February 5, 1952, Syria, lives in East Rutherford, N.J. Defensive back Nebraska 1972-73. Pro defensive back Green Bay Packers 1974, Philadelphia Bell (WFL) 1975. College coach: Nebraska 1975, Washington State 1976-77, Missouri 1978-83, Florida 1984-87, Colorado 1988-89. Pro coach: Chicago Bears 1990-92, joined Giants in 1993.

PHILADELPHIA EAGLES

National Football Conference Eastern Division

Team Colors: Kelly Green, Silver, and White

Veterans Stadium
Broad Street and Pattison Avenue
Philadelphia, Pennsylvania 19148
Telephone: (215) 463-2500

Club Officials
Owner: Norman Braman
President-Chief Operating Officer: Harry Gamble
Vice President: Suzi Braman
V.P.-Chief Financial Officer: Mimi Box
V.P.-Sales and Development: Decker Uhlhorn
Asst. to Pres.: George Azar
Asst. to Pres.-General Counsel: Bob Wallace
Director of Player Personnel: Joe Woolley
Director of Pro Scouting: Tom Gamble
Director of Public Relations: Ron Howard
Asst. Director of Public Relations: Michael Gilbert
Director of Marketing: Leslie Stephenson-Matz
Dir. of Alumni Relations/Traveling Sec.: Jim Gallagher
Director of Administration: Vicki Chatley
Ticket Manager: Leo Carlin
Penthouse Suites Sales: Andrea Minassian
Asst. Director of Penthouse Sales: Ken Iman
Dir. Penthouse Suites Operations: Christiana Noyalas
Trainer: Otho Davis
Asst. Trainer: David Price
Equipment Manager: Rusty Sweeney
Video Director: Mike Dougherty

Stadium: Veterans Stadium •
Capacity: 65,178
3501 South Broad Street
Philadelphia, Pennsylvania 19148

Playing Surface: AstroTurf-8

Training Camp: West Chester University
West Chester, Pennsylvania 19382

1993 Schedule

Preseason

July 31	vs. New Orleans at Tokyo	10:00
Aug. 8	**Chicago**	8:00
Aug. 13	at New York Jets	7:30
Aug. 21	**Atlanta**	7:30
Aug. 27	at Cincinnati	7:30

Regular Season

Sept. 5	**Phoenix**	1:00
Sept. 12	at Green Bay	12:00
Sept. 19	**Washington**	1:00
Sept. 26	**Open Date**	
Oct. 3	at New York Jets	4:00
Oct. 10	**Chicago**	1:00
Oct. 17	at New York Giants	1:00
Oct. 24	**Open Date**	
Oct. 31	**Dallas**	1:00
Nov. 7	at Phoenix	2:00
Nov. 14	**Miami**	1:00
Nov. 21	**New York Giants**	4:00
Nov. 28	at Washington	1:00
Dec. 6	at Dallas (Monday)	8:00
Dec. 12	**Buffalo**	1:00
Dec. 19	at Indianapolis	8:00
Dec. 26	**New Orleans**	1:00
Jan. 3	at San Francisco (Monday)	6:00

Eagles Coaching History

(355-426-24)

1933-35	Lud Wray	9-21-1
1936-40	Bert Bell	10-44-2
1941-50	Earle (Greasy) Neale*	66-44-5
1951	Alvin (Bo) McMillin**	2-0-0
1951	Wayne Millner	2-8-0
1952-55	Jim Trimble	25-20-3
1956-57	Hugh Devore	7-16-1
1958-60	Lawrence (Buck) Shaw	20-16-1
1961-63	Nick Skorich	15-24-3
1964-68	Joe Kuharich	28-41-1
1969-71	Jerry Williams***	7-22-2
1971-72	Ed Khayat	8-15-2
1973-75	Mike McCormack	16-25-1
1976-82	Dick Vermeil	57-51-0
1983-85	Marion Campbell****	17-29-1
1985	Fred Bruney	1-0-0
1986-90	Buddy Ryan	43-38-1
1991-92	Rich Kotite	22-12-0

*Co-coach with Walt Kiesling in Philadelphia-Pittsburgh merger in 1943
**Retired after two games in 1951
***Released after three games in 1971
****Released after 15 games in 1985

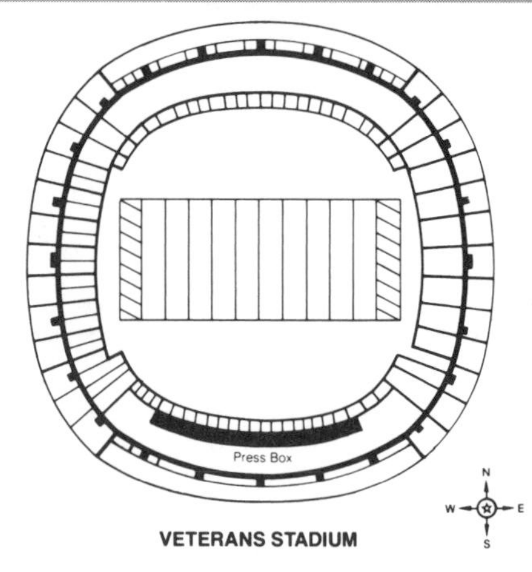

VETERANS STADIUM

Record Holders

Individual Records — Career

Category	Name	Performance
Rushing (Yds.)	Wilbert Montgomery, 1977-1984	6,538
Passing (Yds.)	Ron Jaworski, 1977-1986	26,963
Passing (TDs)	Ron Jaworski, 1977-1986	175
Receiving (No.)	Harold Carmichael, 1971-1983	589
Receiving (Yds.)	Harold Carmichael, 1971-1983	8,978
Interceptions	Bill Bradley, 1969-1976	34
Punting (Avg.)	Joe Muha, 1946-1950	42.9
Punt Return (Avg.)	Steve Van Buren, 1944-1951	13.9
Kickoff Return (Avg.)	Steve Van Buren, 1944-1951	26.7
Field Goals	Paul McFadden, 1984-87	91
Touchdowns (Tot.)	Harold Carmichael, 1971-1983	79
Points	Bobby Walston, 1951-1962	881

Individual Records — Single Season

Category	Name	Performance
Rushing (Yds.)	Wilbert Montgomery, 1979	1,512
Passing (Yds.)	Randall Cunningham, 1988	3,808
Passing (TDs)	Sonny Jurgensen, 1961	32
Receiving (No.)	Keith Jackson, 1988	81
	Keith Byars, 1990	81
Receiving (Yds.)	Mike Quick, 1983	1,409
Interceptions	Bill Bradley, 1971	11
Punting (Avg.)	Joe Muha, 1948	47.2
Punt Return (Avg.)	Steve Van Buren, 1944	15.3
Kickoff Return (Avg.)	Al Nelson, 1972	29.1
Field Goals	Paul McFadden, 1984	30
Touchdowns (Tot.)	Steve Van Buren, 1945	18
Points	Paul McFadden, 1984	116

Individual Records — Single Game

Category	Name	Performance
Rushing (Yds.)	Steve Van Buren, 11-27-49	205
Passing (Yds.)	Bobby Thomason, 11-18-53	437
Passing (TDs)	Adrian Burk, 10-17-54	*7
Receiving (No.)	Don Looney, 12-1-40	14
Receiving (Yds.)	Tommy McDonald, 12-10-60	237
Interceptions	Russ Craft, 9-24-50	*4
Field Goals	Tom Dempsey, 11-12-72	6
Touchdowns (Tot.)	Many times	4
	Last time by Wilbert Montgomery, 10-7-79	
Points	Bobby Walston, 10-17-54	25

*NFL Record

1992 Team Record

Preseason (2-3)

Date	Result		Opponents
8/1	L	14-41	vs. N.Y. Jets at Canton
8/8	W	35-33	at Pittsburgh
8/15	W	27-17	Cincinnati
8/23	L	10-20	at Atlanta
8/27	L	13-22	N.Y. Jets

Regular Season (11-5)

Date	Result		Opponents	Att.
9/6	W	15-13	New Orleans	65,418
9/13	W	31-14	at Phoenix	44,120
9/20	W	31- 0	Denver	65,507
10/5	W	31- 7	Dallas	65,740
10/11	L	17-24	at Kansas City	76,570
10/18	L	12-16	at Washington	55,454
10/25	W	7- 3	Phoenix	65,438
11/1	L	10-20	at Dallas	63,290
11/8	W	31-10	L.A. Raiders	65,736
11/15	L	24-27	vs. G.B. at Milw.	54,867
11/22	W	47-34	at N.Y. Giants	76,191
11/29	L	14-20	at San Francisco	65,486
12/6	W	28-17	Minnesota	65,698
12/13	W	20-17	at Seattle (OT)	64,102
12/20	W	17-13	Washington	65,809
12/27	W	20-10	N.Y. Giants	65,655

(OT) Overtime

Postseason (1-1)

Date	Result		Opponent	Att.
1/3	W	36-20	at New Orleans	68,893
1/10	L	10-34	at Dallas	63,721

Score by Periods

Eagles	45	109	89	108	3	— 354
Opponents	47	87	30	81	0	— 245

Attendance

Home 525,001 Away 500,080 Total 1,025,081
Single-game home record, 72,111 (11-1-81)
Single-season home record, 557,325 (1980)

1992 Team Statistics

	Eagles	Opp.
Total First Downs	292	242
Rushing	138	73
Passing	138	146
Penalty	16	23
Third Down: Made/Att.	80/208	74/222
Third Down: Pct.	38.5	33.3
Fourth Down: Made/Att.	7/14	13/20
Fourth Down: Pct.	50.0	65.0
Total Net Yards	4980	4411
Avg. Per Game	311.3	275.7
Total Plays	1009	959
Avg. Per Play	4.9	4.6
Net Yards Rushing	2388	1481
Avg. Per Game	149.3	92.6
Total Rushes	516	387
Net Yards Passing	2592	2930
Avg. Per Game	162.0	183.1
Sacked/Yards Lost	64/462	55/386
Gross Yards	3054	3316
Att./Completions	429/255	517/263
Completion Pct.	59.4	50.9
Had Intercepted	13	24
Punts/Avg.	82/42.2	85/41.5
Net Punting Avg.	82/36.9	85/34.3
Penalties/Yards Lost	101/807	86/683
Fumbles/Ball Lost	25/15	27/13
Touchdowns	44	26
Rushing	19	4
Passing	20	20
Returns	5	2
Avg. Time of Possession	31:47	28:13

1992 Individual Statistics

Scoring	TD R	TD P	TD Rt	PAT	FG	Saf	TP
Ruzek	0	0	0	40/44	16/25	0	88
Walker	8	2	0	0/0	0/0	0	60
Williams	0	7	0	0/0	0/0	0	42
Barnett	0	6	0	0/0	0/0	0	36
Sherman	5	1	0	0/0	0/0	0	36
Cunningham	5	0	0	0/0	0/0	0	30
Byars	1	2	0	0/0	0/0	0	18
Beach	0	2	0	0/0	0/0	0	12
Joyner	0	0	2	0/0	0/0	0	12
Rose	0	0	1	0/0	0/0	0	6
Sikahema	0	0	1	0/0	0/0	0	6
White	0	0	1	0/0	0/0	0	6
Eagles	19	20	5	40/44	16/25	1	354
Opponents	4	20	2	26/26	21/32	0	245

Passing	Att.	Comp.	Yds.	Pct.	TD	Int.	Tkld.	Rate
Cunningham	384	233	2775	60.7	19	11	60/437	87.3
McMahon	43	22	279	51.2	1	2	4/25	60.1
Byars	1	0	0	0.0	0	0	0/0	39.6
Walker	1	0	0	0.0	0	0	0/0	39.6
Eagles	429	255	3054	59.4	20	13	64/462	84.2
Opponents	517	263	3316	50.9	20	24	55/386	64.8

Rushing	Att.	Yds.	Avg.	LG	TD
Walker	267	1070	4.0	38	8
Sherman	112	583	5.2	34	5
Cunningham	87	549	6.3	30	5
Byars	41	176	4.3	23	1
McMahon	6	23	3.8	11	0
Sikahema	2	2	1.0	1	0
Barnett	1	−15	−15.0	−15	0
Eagles	516	2388	4.6	38	19
Opponents	387	1481	3.8	51	4

Receiving	No.	Yds.	Avg.	LG	TD
Barnett	67	1083	16.2	71t	6
Byars	56	502	9.0	46	2
Williams	42	598	14.2	49t	7
Walker	38	278	7.3	41	2
Sherman	18	219	12.2	75t	1
Sikahema	13	142	10.9	22	0
Green	8	105	13.1	21	0
Beach	8	75	9.4	16	2
F. Dixon	3	36	12.0	19	0
Johnson	2	16	8.0	13	0
Eagles	255	3054	12.0	75t	20
Opponents	263	3316	12.6	74t	20

Interceptions	No.	Yds.	Avg.	LG	TD
Joyner	4	88	22.0	43t	2
Evans	4	76	19.0	43	0
Allen	4	49	12.3	36	0
Booty	3	22	7.3	22	0
Hopkins	3	6	2.0	4	0
Thomas	2	4	2.0	4	0
Miano	1	39	39.0	39	0
Waters	1	23	23.0	23	0
McMillian	1	0	0.0	0	0
O. Smith	1	0	0.0	0	0
Eagles	24	307	12.8	49	2
Opponents	13	77	5.9	30	0

Punting	No.	Yds.	Avg.	In 20	LG
Feagles	82	3459	42.2	26	68
Eagles	82	3459	42.2	26	68
Opponents	85	3531	41.5	22	66

Punt Returns	No.	FC	Yds.	Avg.	LG	TD
Sikahema	40	10	503	12.6	87t	1
Sydner	7	5	52	7.4	17	0
Eagles	47	15	555	11.8	87t	1
Opponents	36	20	295	8.2	47	0

Kickoff Returns	No.	Yds.	Avg.	LG	TD
Sikahema	26	528	20.3	41	0
Booty	1	11	11.0	11	0
Brooks	1	11	11.0	11	0
Sydner	17	368	21.6	45	0
Walker	3	69	23.0	34	0
Eagles	48	987	20.6	45	0
Opponents	53	1027	19.4	92t	1

Sacks	No.
Simmons	19.0
White	14.0
Harmon	7.0
Joyner	6.5
Pitts	4.0
Golic	2.0
Thomas	1.5
Eagles	55.0
Opponents	64.0

1993 Draft Choices

Round	Name	Pos.	College
1.	Lester Holmes	T	Jackson State
	Leonard Renfro	DT	Colorado
2.	Victor Bailey	WR	Missouri
3.	Derrick Frazier	DB	Texas A&M
	Mike Reid	DB	North Carolina St.
6.	Derrick Oden	LB	Alabama
7.	Joey Mickey	TE	Oklahoma
8.	Doug Skene	T	Michigan

Philadelphia Eagles 1993 Veteran Roster

No.	Name	Pos.	Ht.	Wt.	Birth-date	NFL Exp.	College	Hometown	How Acq.	'92 Games/ Starts
72	Alexander, David	C	6-3	275	7/28/64	7	Tulsa	Broken Arrow, Okla.	D5-'87	16/16
21	Allen, Eric	CB	5-10	180	11/22/65	6	Arizona State	San Diego, Calif.	D2-'88	16/16
62	Baldinger, Brian	G-T	6-4	278	1/7/60	12	Duke	Indianapolis, Ind.	FA-'92	12/3
86	Barnett, Fred	WR	6-0	199	6/17/66	4	Arkansas State	Gunnison, Miss.	D3-'90	16/16
50	Bartley, Ephesians	LB	6-2	213	8/9/69	2	Florida	Jacksonville, Fla.	D9-'92	6/0
88	Bavaro, Mark	TE	6-4	245	4/28/63	9	Notre Dame	Danvers, Mass.	UFA(Clev)-'93	16/16*
83	Beach, Pat	TE	6-4	250	12/28/59	12	Washington State	Pullman, Wash.	FA-'92	16/7
39	Brooks, Tony	RB	6-0	230	8/17/69	2	Notre Dame	Tulsa, Okla.	D4a-'92	5/0
41	#Byars, Keith	TE-RB	6-1	238	10/14/63	8	Ohio State	Dayton, Ohio	D1-'86	15/15
12	Cunningham, Randall	QB	6-4	205	3/27/63	9	Nevada-Las Vegas	Santa Barbara, Calif.	D2-'85	15/15
78	Davis, Antone	T	6-4	325	2/28/67	3	Tennessee	Ft. Valley, Ga.	D1-'91	15/15
56	Evans, Byron	LB	6-2	235	2/23/64	7	Arizona	Phoenix, Ariz.	D4-'87	16/16
5	Feagles, Jeff	P	6-1	205	3/7/66	6	Miami	Scottsdale, Ariz.	W(NE)-'90	16/0
95	Flores, Mike	DE	6-3	256	12/1/66	3	Louisville	Youngstown, Ohio	D11-'91	15/0
61	Floyd, Eric	G	6-5	310	10/28/65	4	Auburn	Rome, Ga.	PB(SD)-'92	16/16
33	Frizzell, William	S	6-3	206	9/8/62	10	North Carolina Central	Greenville, N.C.	FA-'92	10/1
81	#Green, Roy	WR	6-1	195	6/30/57	15	Henderson State	Magnolia, Ark.	FA-'91	9/0
54	†Hager, Britt	LB	6-1	225	2/20/66	5	Texas	Odessa, Tex.	D3b-'89	10/0
91	Harmon, Andy	DT	6-4	265	4/6/69	3	Kent State	Centerville, Ohio	D6-'91	16/13
97	Harris, Tim	DE	6-6	258	9/10/64	8	Memphis State	Memphis, Tenn.	UFA(SF)-'93	16/15*
48	#Hopkins, Wes	S	6-1	215	9/26/61	11	Southern Methodist	Birmingham, Ala.	D2a-'83	10/10
76	†Hudson, John	G-C	6-2	275	1/29/68	2	Auburn	Memphis, Tenn.	D11a-'90	3/0
98	Jeter, Tommy	DT	6-5	282	9/20/69	2	Texas	Nacogdoches, Tex.	D3-'92	15/0
87	Johnson, Maurice	TE	6-2	243	1/9/67	3	Temple	Washington, D.C.	FA-'91	11/3
32	Joseph, James	RB	6-2	222	10/28/67	3	Auburn	Phenix City, Ala.	D7-'91	16/0
59	Joyner, Seth	LB	6-2	235	11/18/64	8	Texas-El Paso	El Paso, Tex.	D8-'86	16/16
57	Kowalkowski, Scott	LB	6-2	228	8/23/68	3	Notre Dame	Orchard Lake, Mich.	D8-'91	16/0
42	McMillan, Erik	S	6-2	200	5/3/65	6	Missouri	Silver Spring, Md.	UFA(NYJ)-'93	16/0*
29	McMillian, Mark	CB	5-7	162	4/29/70	2	Alabama	Los Angeles, Calif.	D10-'92	16/3
38	Miano, Rich	S	6-1	200	9/3/62	8	Hawaii	Honolulu, Hawaii	FA-'91	16/11
77	Millard, Keith	DT	6-5	263	3/18/62	9	Washington State	Pleasanton, Calif.	FA-'93	2/0*
55	#Rose, Ken	LB	6-1	215	6/9/62	7	Nevada-Las Vegas	Sacramento, Calif.	FA-'90	16/0
7	Ruzek, Roger	K	6-1	200	12/17/60	7	Weber State	San Francisco, Calif.	FA-'89	16/0
79	#Schad, Mike	G	6-5	290	10/2/63	5	Queens College, Canada	Bellville, Canada	PB(Rams)-'89	14/14
75	Selby, Rob	G	6-3	286	10/11/67	3	Auburn	Birmingham, Ala.	D3-'91	16/1
23	†Sherman, Heath	RB	6-0	205	3/27/67	5	Texas A&I	El Campo, Tex.	D6-'89	16/7
22	Sikahema, Vai	WR-KR	5-9	196	8/29/62	8	Brigham Young	Mesa, Ariz.	PB(GB)-'92	16/0
96	Simmons, Clyde	DE	6-6	280	8/4/64	8	Western Carolina	Wilmington, N.C.	D9-'86	16/16
26	Smith, Ben	CB	5-11	185	5/14/67	4	Georgia	Warner Robins, Ga.	D1-'90	0*
30	Smith, Otis	CB	5-11	184	10/22/65	4	Missouri	Metairie, La.	FA-'90	16/1
27	Stacy, Siran	RB	5-11	203	8/6/68	2	Alabama	Geneva, Ala.	D2-'92	16/0
85	Sydner, Jeff	WR-KR	5-6	170	11/11/69	2	Hawaii	Columbus, Ohio	D6-'92	15/0
51	Thomas, William	LB	6-2	218	8/13/68	3	Texas A&M	Amarillo, Tex.	D4-'91	16/15
71	t-Thompson, Broderick	T-G	6-5	295	8/14/60	8	Kansas	Cerritos, Calif.	T(SD)-'93	12/12*
34	Walker, Herschel	RB	6-1	225	3/3/62	8	Georgia	Wrightsville, Ga.	FA-'92	16/16
20	Waters, Andre	S	5-11	200	3/10/62	10	Cheyney State	Pahokee, Fla.	FA-'84	6/6
89	Williams, Calvin	WR	5-11	190	3/3/67	4	Purdue	Baltimore, Md.	D5-'90	16/15

* Bavaro played 16 games with Cleveland in '92; Harris played 16 games with San Francisco; McMillan played 16 games with N.Y. Jets; Millard played 2 games with Seattle; B. Smith missed '92 season due to injury; Thompson played 12 games with San Diego.

#Unrestricted free agent; subject to developments.

† Restricted free agent; subject to developments.

t- Eagles traded for Thompson (San Diego).

Players lost through free agency (9): CB-S John Booty (Phx; 16 games in '92), DT Mike Golic (Mia; 16), T Ron Heller (Mia; 12), CB-S Izel Jenkins (Minn; 16), QB Jim McMahon (Minn; 4), DT Mike Pitts (NE; 11), DT Leon Seals (NE; 5), T Daryle Smith (Minn; 16), DE Reggie White (GB; 16).

Also played with Eagles in '92—QB David Archer (active for 3 games but did not play), WR Floyd Dixon (7).

COACHING STAFF

Head Coach, Rich Kotite

Pro Career: Became the eighteenth head coach in Eagles' history on January 8, 1991. After a 3-5 start in his rookie year as head coach, marked by a season-ending injury to quarterback Randall Cunningham on opening day and subsequent injuries to backup Jim McMahon, Kotite rallied the Eagles. Philadelphia narrowly missed the playoffs after winning seven of their last eight games on the strength of the league's best defense. In his second season, the Eagles returned to the playoffs for the fourth time in five years, recording an 11-5 mark along the way to give the club five consecutive seasons of 10-or-more wins. Kotite originally served as the team's offensive coordinator in 1990 when the club led the NFL in rushing and time of possession, and also topped the NFC in scoring and touchdown passes. Kotite had previously served as the New York Jets' offensive coordinator and receivers coach from 1985-89 after originally joining the club as receivers coach in 1983. In each of Kotite's years at the helm of the New York offense, the Jets finished near the top in the AFC in total offense, including a third-place ranking in 1985. Kotite began his pro coaching career with New Orleans in 1977 before joining Cleveland the following year. Kotite was the Browns' receivers coach from 1978-82. He aided in the development of Cleveland's perennial all-pro tight end Ozzie Newsome. During his playing career, he was known as a scrappy tight end and outstanding special teams performer with the New York Giants (1967, 1969-72) and Steelers (1968). Career record: 22-12.

Background: Attended Poly Prep in Brooklyn, N.Y. After a brief boxing career at the University of Miami where he was the school's heavyweight champ, he served as a sparring partner for Cassius Clay, later known as Muhammad Ali. Kotite became a Little All-America tight end at Wagner College in Staten Island, N.Y.

Personal: Born in Brooklyn on October 13, 1942. He and his wife, Elizabeth, live in Mt. Laurel, N.J. and have one daughter— Alexandra.

Assistant Coaches

Zeke Bratkowski, offensive coordinator-quarterbacks; born October 20, 1931, Danville, Ill., lives in Mt. Laurel, N.J. Quarterback Georgia 1951-53. Pro quarterback Chicago Bears 1954, 1957-60, Los Angeles Rams 1961-63, Green Bay Packers 1963-68, 1971. Pro coach: Green Bay Packers 1969-70, 1975-81, Chicago Bears 1972-74, Baltimore-Indianapolis Colts 1982-84, New York Jets 1985-89, Cleveland Browns 1990, joined Eagles in 1991.

Lew Carpenter, receivers-tight ends; born January 12, 1932, Hayti, Mo., lives in Mt. Laurel, N.J. Running back-end Arkansas 1950-52. Pro running back-defensive back-end Detroit Lions 1953-55, Cleveland Browns 1957-58, Green Bay Packers 1959-63. College coach: Southwest Texas State 1989. Pro coach: Minnesota Vikings 1964-66, Atlanta Falcons 1967-68, Washington Redskins 1969-70, St. Louis Cardinals 1971-72, Houston Oilers 1973-74, Green Bay Packers 1975-85, Detroit Lions 1986-88, joined Eagles in 1990.

Bud Carson, defensive coordinator-secondary; born April 28, 1931, Freeport, Pa., lives in Mt. Laurel, N.J. Defensive back North Carolina 1950-52. No pro playing experience. College coach: North Carolina 1957-64, South Carolina 1965, Georgia Tech 1966-71 (head coach 1967-71), Kansas 1984. Pro coach: Pittsburgh Steelers 1972-77, Los Angeles Rams 1978-81, Baltimore Colts 1982, Kansas City Chiefs 1983, New York Jets 1985-88, Cleveland Browns 1989-90 (head coach), joined Eagles in 1991.

Peter Giunta, defensive assistant; born August 11, 1956, Salem, Mass., lives in Bensalem, Pa. Running back-defensive back Northeastern 1974-77. No pro playing experience. College coach: Penn State 1981-83, Brown 1984-87, Lehigh 1988-90. Pro coach: Joined Eagles in 1991.

Philadelphia Eagles 1993 First-Year Roster

Name	Pos.	Ht.	Wt.	Birth-date	College	Hometown	How Acq.
Bailey, Victor	WR	6-2	196	7/30/70	Missouri	Fort Worth, Tex.	D2
Barlow, Corey (1)	CB	5-9	182	11/1/70	Auburn	Atlanta, Ga.	D5-'92
Baskerville, Cliff	CB-S	5-11	178	8/27/71	North Carolina	Union, N.J.	FA
Bradford, Jack (1)	LB	6-1	227	5/8/68	Maryland	Columbia, Md.	FA
Branum, Matt	G-T	6-1	274	8/12/70	Kentucky	Lexington, Ky.	FA
Britten, Danny	G-T	6-4	268	1/30/70	Boston College	Tewksbury, Mo.	FA
Brooks, Anthony	WR	5-10	171	8/3/68	East Texas State	Dallas, Tex.	FA
Brown, Curt	DE-DT	6-4	233	4/5/70	North Carolina	Virginia Beach, Va.	FA
Bruton, Tim (1)	TE	6-3	260	9/14/67	Missouri	Indianapolis, Ind.	FA
Caeser, Ivan	LB	6-2	239	1/7/67	Boston College	Boston, Mass.	FA
Chalenski, Mike	DE-DT	6-4	260	1/28/70	UCLA	Elizabeth, N.J.	FA
Chaney, Don	WR	6-6	225	7/14/70	South Carolina	Florida City, Fla.	FA
Crawford, Xavier	RB	5-9	212	3/17/70	Memphis State	Memphis, Tenn.	FA
Crespina, Keita	CB-S	5-8	190	2/25/71	Temple	Philadelphia, Pa.	FA
Erwin, Brian	G-T	6-1	266	11/24/70	Temple	Philadelphia, Pa.	FA
Frazier, Derrick	CB	5-10	178	4/29/70	Texas A&M	Sugar Land, Tex.	D3a
Gardner, Donnie (1)	DE-DT	6-4	270	2/17/68	Kentucky	Louisville, Ky.	FA
Garlick, Tom	WR	5-10	180	9/22/71	Fordham	Philadelphia, Pa.	FA
Gerhart, Tom (1)	S	6-1	195	6/4/65	Ohio University	Lebanon, Pa.	FA
Greco, Tony	G-T	6-4	280	6/2/70	Mansfield	Bergenfield, N.J.	FA
Hebron, Vaughn	RB	5-8	196	10/7/70	Virginia Tech	Baltimore, Md.	FA
Hess, Bill (1)	WR	5-8	171	2/6/66	West Chester	West Chester, Pa.	FA
Holmes, Lester	G	6-3	301	9/27/69	Jackson State	Tylertown, Miss.	D1a
Houston, Brandon (1)	T	6-4	284	4/2/69	Oklahoma	Abernathy, Tex.	D11-'92
Kirschhoff, Tom	QB	6-3	210	12/4/70	Lafayette	Lemoyne, Pa.	FA
Lewis, Greg	CB-S	5-11	180	6/29/71	New Hampshire	Newburgh, N.Y.	FA
McKenzie, Mike	TE	6-2	247	9/18/70	Baylor	San Antonio, Tex.	FA
Mickey, Joey	TE	6-5	288	11/29/70	Oklahoma	Oklahoma City, Okla.	D7
Minor, Billy	WR	6-1	196	6/27/70	East Texas State	Paris, Tex.	FA
Mokwah, Gabe (1)	LB	6-2	254	11/28/70	American International	Springfield, Mass.	FA
Montgomery, Fred	WR	5-10	187	8/30/71	New Mexico State	Greenville, Miss.	FA
Murphy, Chris	WR	6-0	175	3/11/71	Georgetown	Staten Island, N.Y.	FA
Oden, Derrick	LB	5-11	230	9/29/70	Alabama	Hillcrest, Ala.	D6
Perry, Ron	LB	6-1	226	12/28/70	Grambling	Grambling, La.	FA
Petetti, Carl (1)	K	5-7	195	8/27/69	Miami	Holland, Pa.	FA
Pohopek, Jason	LB	6-1	220	8/26/70	Boston College	Barrington, N.H.	FA
Presbury, Robert (1)	DE-DT	6-3	275	7/18/65	Delaware State	Aberdeen, Md.	FA
Quast, Brad (1)	LB	6-2	246	6/5/68	Iowa	Des Plaines, Iowa	FA
Reid, Mike	S	6-1	218	11/24/70	North Carolina State	Spartanburg, S.C.	D3b
Renfro, Leonard	DT	6-2	291	6/29/70	Colorado	Detroit, Mich.	D1b
Rizzi, Darren	TE	6-2	235	7/21/70	Rhode Island	Emerson, N.J.	FA
Roberts, Dave	CB-S	5-11	200	7/1/71	Youngstown State	Glassport, Pa.	FA
Schrock, Chris	P	6-2	225	10/18/70	Boston University	Hamilton, Mass.	FA
Skene, Doug	G	6-6	294	6/17/70	Michigan	Fairview, Tex.	D8
Thomas, Marcus	RB	5-10	192	7/12/70	Eastern Kentucky	Cincinnati, Ohio	FA
Titley, Mike	TE	6-1	243	5/5/68	Iowa	Brooklyn, N.Y.	FA
Turner, Aaron	WR	5-11	178	5/4/71	Pacific	Vallejo, Calif.	FA
Wagner, Steve	G-T	6-7	309	5/2/70	Delaware Valley	Landsdale, Pa.	FA

The term NFL Rookie is defined as a player who is in his first season of professional football and has not been on the roster of another professional football team for any regular-season or postseason games. A Rookie is designated by an "R" on NFL rosters. Players who have been active in another professional football league or players who have NFL experience, including either preseason training camp or being on an Active List, Inactive List, Reserve/Injured or Reserve/Physically Unable to Perform for fewer than six regular season games, are termed NFL First-Year Players. An NFL First-Year Player is designated by a "1" on NFL rosters. Thereafter, a player is credited with an additional year of experience for each season in which he accumulates six games on the Active List, Inactive List, Reserve/Injured, or Reserve/Physically Unable to Perform.

Dale Haupt, defensive line; born April 12, 1929, Manitowoc, Wis., lives in Cherry Hill, N.J. Defensive lineman-linebacker Wyoming 1950-53. No pro playing experience. College coach: Tennessee 1960-63, Iowa State 1964-65, Richmond 1966-71, North Carolina State 1972-76, Duke 1977. Pro coach: Chicago Bears 1978-85, joined Eagles in 1986.

Bill Muir, offensive line; born October 26, 1942, Pittsburgh, Pa., lives in Mt. Laurel, N.J. Tackle Susquehanna 1962-64. No pro playing experience. College coach: Susquehanna 1965, Delaware Valley 1966-67, Rhode Island 1970-71, Idaho State 1972-73, Southern Methodist 1976-77. Pro coach: Orlando (Continental Football League) 1968-69, Houston-Shreveport Steamer (WFL) 1975, New England Patriots 1982-84, Detroit Lions 1985-88, Indianapolis Colts 1989-91, joined Eagles in 1992.

Larry Pasquale, special teams coordinator; born April 21, 1941, Brooklyn, N.Y., lives in Mt. Laurel, N.J. Quarterback Bridgeport 1961-63. No pro playing experience. College coach: Slippery Rock State 1967, Boston University 1968, Navy 1969-70, Massachusetts 1971-75, Idaho State 1976. Pro coach: Montreal Alouettes (CFL) 1977-78, Detroit Lions 1979, New York Jets 1980-89, San Diego Chargers 1990-91, joined Eagles in 1992.

Jim Vechiarella, linebackers; born February 20, 1937, Youngstown, Ohio, lives in Mt. Laurel, N.J. Linebacker Youngstown State 1955-57. No pro playing experience. College coach: Youngstown State 1964-74, Southern Illinois 1976-77, Tulane 1978-80. Pro coach: Charlotte (WFL) 1975, Los Angeles Rams 1981-82, Kansas City Chiefs 1983-85, New York Jets 1986-89, Cleveland Browns 1990, joined Eagles in 1991.

Jim Williams, strength and conditioning; born March 29, 1948, Kingston, Pa., lives in Mt. Laurel, N.J. No college or pro playing experience. College coach: Nebraska 1972-74, Arkansas 1974-77, Wyoming 1977-79. Pro coach: New York Giants 1979-81, New York Jets 1982-89, joined Eagles in 1991.

Richard Wood, running backs; born February 2, 1936, Lanett, Ala., lives in Mt. Laurel, N.J. Quarterback Auburn 1956-59. Pro quarterback Baltimore Colts 1960-61, San Diego Chargers 1962, Denver Broncos 1962, New York Jets 1963-64, Oakland Raiders 1965, Miami Dolphins 1966. College coach: Georgia 1967-68, Mississippi 1971-73, Auburn 1986. Pro coach: Oakland Raiders 1969-70, Cleveland Browns 1974, New Orleans Saints 1976-77, Atlanta Falcons 1978-82, Philadelphia Eagles 1983, Kansas City Chiefs 1987-88, New England Patriots 1989-90, rejoined Eagles in 1991.

PHOENIX CARDINALS

National Football Conference
Eastern Division

Team Colors: Cardinal Red, Black, and White

P.O. Box 888
Phoenix, Arizona 85001-0888
Telephone: (602) 379-0101

Club Officials

President: William V. Bidwill
Executive Vice President: Joe Rhein
Vice President/General Manager: Larry Wilson
Secretary and General Counsel: Thomas J. Guilfoil
Treasurer and Chief Financial Officer: Charley Schlegel
Director of Pro Personnel: Erik Widmark
Director of College Scouting: Bob Ackles
Public Relations Director: Paul Jensen
Media Coordinator: Greg Gladysiewski
Director of Community Relations: Adele Harris
Director of Marketing: Joe Castor
Ticket Manager: Steve Walsh
Trainer: John Omohundro
Assistant Trainers: Jim Shearer, Jeff Herndon
Equipment Manager: Mark Ahlemeier
Assistant Equipment Manager: Steve Christensen

Stadium: Sun Devil Stadium • **Capacity:** 73,521
Fifth Street
Tempe, Arizona 85287

Playing Surface: Grass

Training Camp: Northern Arizona University
Flagstaff, Arizona 86011

1993 Schedule

Preseason

Aug. 7	**Los Angeles Rams**	7:30
Aug. 14	at Chicago	7:00
Aug. 21	at San Diego	6:00
Aug. 27	**Denver**	8:00

Regular Season

Sept. 5	at Philadelphia	1:00
Sept. 12	at Washington	1:00
Sept. 19	**Dallas**	5:00
Sept. 26	at Detroit	1:00
Oct. 3	**Open Date**	
Oct. 10	**New England**	1:00
Oct. 17	**Washington**	1:00
Oct. 24	at San Francisco	1:00
Oct. 31	**New Orleans**	2:00
Nov. 7	**Philadelphia**	2:00
Nov. 14	at Dallas	12:00
Nov. 21	**Open Date**	
Nov. 28	at New York Giants	4:00
Dec. 5	**Los Angeles Rams**	2:00
Dec. 12	**Detroit**	2:00
Dec. 19	at Seattle	1:00
Dec. 26	**New York Giants**	2:00
Jan. 2	at Atlanta	1:00

Cardinals Coaching History

Chicago 1920-1959
St. Louis 1960-1987
(379-517-39)

1920-22	John (Paddy) Driscoll	17-8-4
1923-24	Arnold Horween	13-8-1
1925-26	Norman Barry	16-8-2
1927	Guy Chamberlin	3-7-1
1928	Fred Gillies	1-5-0
1929	Dewey Scanlon	6-6-1
1930	Ernie Nevers	5-6-2
1931	LeRoy Andrews*	0-1-0
1931	Ernie Nevers	5-3-0
1932	Jack Chevigny	2-6-2
1933-34	Paul Schissler	6-15-1
1935-38	Milan Creighton	16-26-4
1939	Ernie Nevers	1-10-0
1940-42	Jimmy Conzelman	8-22-3
1943-45	Phil Handler**	1-29-0
1946-48	Jimmy Conzelman	27-10-0
1949	Phil Handler-Buddy Parker***	2-4-0
1949	Raymond (Buddy) Parker	4-1-1
1950-51	Earl (Curly) Lambeau****	7-15-0
1951	Phil Handler-Cecil Isbell#	1-1-0
1952	Joe Kuharich	4-8-0
1953-54	Joe Stydahar	3-20-1
1955-57	Ray Richards	14-21-1
1958-61	Frank (Pop) Ivy##	17-29-2
1961	Chuck Drulis-Ray Prochaska-Ray Willsey###	2-0-0
1962-65	Wally Lemm	27-26-3
1966-70	Charley Winner	35-30-5
1971-72	Bob Hollway	8-18-2
1973-77	Don Coryell	42-29-1
1978-79	Bud Wilkinson####	9-20-0
1979	Larry Wilson	2-1-0
1980-85	Jim Hanifan	39-50-1
1986-89	Gene Stallings@	23-34-1
1989	Hank Kuhlmann	0-5-0
1990-92	Joe Bugel	13-35-0

*Resigned after one game in 1931
**Co-coach with Walt Kiesling in Chicago Cardinals-Pittsburgh merger in 1944
***Co-coaches for first six games in 1949
****Resigned after 10 games in 1951
#Co-coaches
##Resigned after 12 games in 1961
###Co-coaches
####Released after 13 games in 1979
@Released after 11 games in 1989

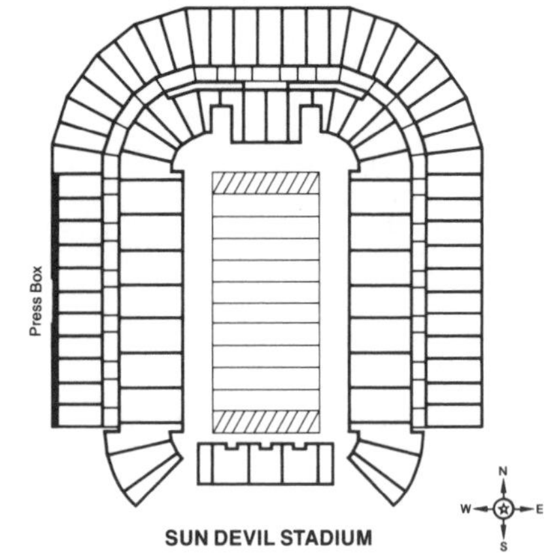

SUN DEVIL STADIUM

Record Holders

Individual Records — Career

Category	Name	Performance
Rushing (Yds.)	Ottis Anderson, 1979-1986	7,999
Passing (Yds.)	Jim Hart, 1966-1983	34,639
Passing (TDs)	Jim Hart, 1966-1983	209
Receiving (No.)	Roy Green, 1979-1990	522
Receiving (Yds.)	Roy Green, 1979-1990	8,497
Interceptions	Larry Wilson, 1960-1972	52
Punting (Avg.)	Jerry Norton, 1959-1961	44.9
Punt Return (Avg.)	Charley Trippi, 1947-1955	13.7
Kickoff Return (Avg.)	Ollie Matson, 1952, 1954-58	28.5
Field Goals	Jim Bakken, 1962-1978	282
Touchdowns (Tot.)	Roy Green, 1979-1990	70
Points	Jim Bakken, 1962-1978	1,380

Individual Records — Single Season

Category	Name	Performance
Rushing (Yds.)	Ottis Anderson, 1979	1,605
Passing (Yds.)	Neil Lomax, 1984	4,614
Passing (TDs)	Charley Johnson, 1963	28
	Neil Lomax, 1984	28
Receiving (No.)	J.T. Smith, 1987	91
Receiving (Yds.)	Roy Green, 1984	1,555
Interceptions	Bob Nussbaumer, 1949	12
Punting (Avg.)	Jerry Norton, 1960	45.6
Punt Return (Avg.)	John (Red) Cochran, 1949	20.9
Kickoff Return (Avg.)	Ollie Matson, 1958	35.5
Field Goals	Jim Bakken, 1967	27
Touchdowns (Tot.)	John David Crow, 1962	17
Points	Jim Bakken, 1967	117
	Neil O'Donoghue, 1984	117

Individual Records — Single Game

Category	Name	Performance
Rushing (Yds.)	John David Crow, 12-18-60	203
Passing (Yds.)	Neil Lomax, 12-16-84	468
Passing (TDs)	Jim Hardy, 10-2-50	6
	Charley Johnson, 9-26-65	6
	Charley Johnson, 11-2-69	6
Receiving (No.)	Sonny Randle, 11-4-62	16
Receiving (Yds.)	Sonny Randle, 11-4-62	256
Interceptions	Bob Nussbaumer, 11-13-49	*4
	Jerry Norton, 11-20-60	*4
Field Goals	Jim Bakken, 9-24-67	*7
Touchdowns (Tot.)	Ernie Nevers, 11-28-29	*6
Points	Ernie Nevers, 11-28-29	*40

*NFL Record

1992 Team Record

Preseason (3-1)

Date	Result		Opponents
8/8	W	35-14	San Diego
8/15	W	20-17	Chicago
8/22	L	10-17	at Seattle
8/28	W	21-17	at Denver

Regular Season (4-12)

Date	Result		Opponents	Att.
9/6	L	7-23	at Tampa Bay	44,779
9/13	L	14-31	Philadelphia	44,120
9/20	L	20-31	at Dallas	62,200
10/4	W	27-24	Washington	37,657
10/11	L	21-31	at N.Y. Giants	76,007
10/18	L	21-30	New Orleans	28,117
10/25	L	3- 7	at Philadelphia	65,438
11/1	W	24-14	San Francisco	50,482
11/8	W	20-14	at L.A. Rams	44,241
11/15	L	17-20	at Atlanta	68,377
11/22	L	10-16	Dallas	71,628
11/29	L	3-41	at Washington	55,455
12/6	L	21-27	San Diego	26,663
12/12	W	19- 0	N.Y. Giants	31,905
12/20	L	13-16	at Indianapolis	43,135
12/27	L	3- 7	Tampa Bay	28,790

Score by Periods

Cardinals	58	70	43	72	0	—	243
Opponents	62	108	88	74	0	—	332

Attendance

Home 319,362 Away 459,632 Total 778,994
Single-game home record, 71,628 (11-22-92)
Single-season home record, 472,937 (1988)

1992 Team Statistics

	Cardinals	Opp.
Total First Downs	277	281
Rushing	88	101
Passing	161	163
Penalty	28	17
Third Down: Made/Att.	79/204	67/185
Third Down: Pct.	38.7	36.2
Fourth Down: Made/Att.	10/24	2/5
Fourth Down: Pct.	41.7	40.0
Total Net Yards	4577	5126
Avg. Per Game	286.1	320.4
Total Plays	948	915
Avg. Per Play	4.8	5.6
Net Yards Rushing	1491	1635
Avg. Per Game	93.2	102.2
Total Rushes	395	436
Net Yards Passing	3086	3491
Avg. Per Game	192.9	218.2
Sacked/Yards Lost	36/258	27/196
Gross Yards	3344	3687
Att./Completions	517/298	452/276
Completion Pct.	57.6	61.1
Had Intercepted	24	16
Punts/Avg.	58/42.8	62/42.8
Net Punting Avg.	58/39.4	62/34.7
Penalties/Yards Lost	85/722	100/826
Fumbles/Ball Lost	26/18	25/12
Touchdowns	29	40
Rushing	11	13
Passing	15	24
Returns	3	3
Avg. Time of Possession	31:01	28:59

1992 Individual Statistics

Scoring	TD R	TD P	TD Rt	PAT	FG	Saf	TP
G. Davis	0	0	0	28/28	13/26	0	67
Johnson	6	0	0	0/0	0/0	0	36
E. Jones	0	4	0	0/0	0/0	0	24
R. Hill	0	3	0	0/0	0/0	0	18
Massey	0	0	3	0/0	0/0	0	18
Proehl	0	3	0	0/0	0/0	0	18
Bailey	1	1	0	0/0	0/0	0	12
Brown	2	0	0	0/0	0/0	0	12
Centers	0	2	0	0/0	0/0	0	12
Chandler	1	0	0	0/0	0/0	0	6
Edwards	0	1	0	0/0	0/0	0	6
Jackson	0	1	0	0/0	0/0	0	6
Thompson	1	0	0	0/0	0/0	0	6
Swann	0	0	0	0/0	0/0	1	2
Camarillo	0	0	0	0/1	0/0	0	0
Cardinals	11	15	3	28/29	13/26	1	243
Opponents	13	24	3	38/40	18/28	0	332

Passing	Att.	Comp.	Yds.	Pct.	TD	Int.	Tkld.	Rate
Chandler	413	245	2832	59.3	15	15	29/226	77.1
Rosenbach	92	49	483	53.3	0	6	7/32	41.2
Sacca	11	4	29	36.4	0	2	0/0	5.3
Proehl	1	0	0	0.0	0	1	0/0	0.0
Cardinals	517	298	3344	57.6	15	24	36/258	67.4
Opponents	452	276	3687	61.1	24	16	27/196	89.9

Rushing	Att.	Yds.	Avg.	LG	TD
Johnson	178	734	4.1	42t	6
Bailey	52	233	4.5	15	1
Brown	68	194	2.9	13	2
Chandler	36	149	4.1	18	1
Centers	37	139	3.8	28	0
Proehl	3	23	7.7	10	0
Rosenbach	9	11	1.2	10	0
Thompson	8	8	1.0	6	1
R. Hill	1	4	4.0	4	0
Blount	1	−1	−1.0	−1	0
E. Jones	2	−3	−1.5	1	0
Cardinals	395	1491	3.8	42t	11
Opponents	436	1635	3.8	63t	13

Receiving	No.	Yds.	Avg.	LG	TD
Proehl	60	744	12.4	63t	3
R. Hill	58	861	14.8	49	3
Centers	50	417	8.3	26	2
E. Jones	38	559	14.7	72t	4
Bailey	33	331	10.0	34	1
Edwards	14	147	10.5	25t	1
Johnson	14	103	7.4	26	0
Rolle	13	64	4.9	12	0
Brown	7	54	7.7	18	0
Reeves	6	28	4.7	12	0
Blount	3	18	6.0	18	0
Ware	1	13	13.0	13	0
Jackson	1	5	5.0	5t	1
Cardinals	298	3344	11.2	72t	15
Opponents	276	3687	13.4	87t	24

Interceptions	No.	Yds.	Avg.	LG	TD
Massey	5	147	29.4	46t	3
Zordich	3	37	12.3	23	0
A. Williams	3	25	8.3	23	0
McDonald	2	35	17.5	20	0
D. Davis	2	27	13.5	27	0
J. Jones	1	27	27.0	27	0
Cardinals	16	298	18.6	46t	3
Opponents	24	279	11.6	65	1

Punting	No.	Yds.	Avg.	In 20	LG
Camarillo	54	2317	42.9	23	73
G. Davis	4	167	41.8	0	52
Cardinals	58	2484	42.8	23	73
Opponents	62	2656	42.8	13	62

Punt Returns	No.	FC	Yds.	Avg.	LG	TD
Bailey	20	8	263	13.2	65	0
Blount	13	4	101	7.8	16	0
Cardinals	33	12	364	11.0	65	0
Opponents	22	11	141	6.4	26	0

Kickoff Returns	No.	Yds.	Avg.	LG	TD
Bailey	28	690	24.6	63	0
Blount	11	251	22.8	52	0
Edwards	8	143	17.9	24	0
Jackson	1	17	17.0	17	0
Rolle	1	10	10.0	10	0
L. Smith	2	16	8.0	13	0
Cardinals	51	1127	22.1	63	0
Opponents	42	767	18.3	43	0

Sacks	No.
Harvey	6.0
M. Jones	6.0
Nunn	4.0
Bankston	2.0
R. Davis	2.0
Rucker	2.0
Swann	2.0
Hyche	1.0
J. Jones	1.0
Faulkner	0.5
McDonald	0.5
Cardinals	27.0
Opponents	36.0

1993 Draft Choices

Round	Name	Pos.	College
1.	Garrison Hearst	RB	Georgia
	Ernest Dye	T	South Carolina
2.	Ben Coleman	T	Wake Forest
4.	Ronald Moore	RB	Pittsburg (Kan.)
6.	Brett Wallerstedt	LB	Arizona State
7.	Will White	DB	Florida
8.	Chad Brown	DE	Mississippi
	Steve Anderson	WR	Grambling

Phoenix Cardinals 1993 Veteran Roster

No.	Name	Pos.	Ht.	Wt.	Birth-date	NFL Exp.	College	Hometown	How Acq.	'92 Games/ Starts
20	Bailey, Johnny	RB	5-8	180	3/17/67	4	Texas A&I	Houston, Tex.	PB(Chi)-'92	12/2
63	Bankston, Michael	DE-DT	6-2	290	3/12/70	2	Sam Houston State	East Bernard, Tex.	D4b-'92	16/6
70	Baxley, Rob	T	6-5	287	3/14/69	2	Iowa	Oswego, Ill.	D11-'92	6/0
7	Beuerlein, Steve	QB	6-2	209	3/7/65	7	Notre Dame	Hollywood, Calif.	UFA(Dall)-'93	16/0*
25	Blount, Eric	RB-KR	5-9	190	9/22/70	2	North Carolina	Ayden, N.C.	D8-'92	4/0
42	Booty, John	S	6-0	180	10/9/65	6	Texas Christian	Carthage, Tex.	UFA(Phil)-'93	16/11*
54	#Braxton, David	LB	6-2	230	5/26/65	5	Wake Forest	Jacksonville, N.C.	FA-'90	16/2
33	†Brown, Ivory Lee	RB	6-2	230	8/17/69	2	Arkansas-Pine Bluff	Palestine, Tex.	D7-'91	7/5
16	Camarillo, Rich	P	5-11	195	11/29/59	13	Washington	Pico Rivera, Calif.	FA-'89	15/0
26	Cecil, Chuck	S	6-0	190	11/8/64	6	Arizona	San Diego, Calif.	UFA(GB)-'93	16/16*
37	Centers, Larry	RB	6-0	200	6/1/68	4	Stephen F. Austin	Tatum, Tex.	D5-'90	16/1
17	Chandler, Chris	QB	6-4	220	10/12/65	6	Washington	Everett, Wash.	W(TB)-'91	15/13
84	Clark, Gary	WR	5-9	173	5/1/62	9	James Madison	Dublin, Va.	UFA(Wash)-'93	16/14*
59	Cunningham, Ed	C	6-3	290	8/17/69	2	Washington	Alexandria, Va.	D3-'92	10/5
64	Cunningham, Rick	T	6-6	307	1/4/67	3	Texas A&M	Los Angeles, Calif.	FA-'92	8/6
21	Davis, Dexter	CB	5-10	190	3/20/70	3	Clemson	Brooklyn, N.Y.	D4-'91	16/2
5	#Davis, Greg	K	6-0	200	10/29/65	6	Citadel	Atlanta, Ga.	PB(Atl)-'91	16/0
93	Davis, Reuben	DE-DT	6-4	292	5/7/65	6	North Carolina	Greensboro, N.C.	T(TB)-'92	11/5
22	#Duerson, Dave	S	6-1	208	11/28/60	11	Notre Dame	Muncie, Ind.	FA-'91	15/0
83	Edwards, Anthony	WR	5-9	190	5/26/66	5	New Mexico Highlands	Casa Grande, Ariz.	FA-'91	16/0
94	Faulkner, Jeff	DE	6-4	305	4/4/64	4	Southern	Miami, Fla.	PB(Ind)-'91	16/5
31	#Harris, Odie	S	6-0	190	4/1/66	6	Sam Houston State	Bryan, Tex.	W(Clev)-'92	8/0
56	Harvey, Ken	LB	6-3	230	5/6/65	6	California	Austin, Tex.	D1-'88	10/10
58	#Hill, Eric	LB	6-2	250	11/14/66	5	Louisiana State	Galveston, Tex.	D1-'89	16/16
81	Hill, Randal	WR	5-10	177	9/21/69	3	Miami	Miami, Fla.	T(Mia)-'91	16/14
97	†Hyche, Steve	LB	6-2	226	6/12/63	4	Livingston	Cordova, Ala.	FA-'91	16/1
53	#Jax, Garth	LB	6-3	240	9/16/63	8	Florida State	Houston, Tex.	PB(Dall)-'89	16/0
86	Jones, Ernie	WR	6-0	200	12/15/64	6	Indiana	Elkhart, Ind.	D7-'88	11/5
55	Jones, Jock	LB	6-2	227	3/13/68	4	Virginia Tech	Ashland, Va.	FA-'91	14/2
75	Jones, Mike	DE-DT	6-4	285	8/25/69	3	North Carolina State	Columbia, S.C.	D2-'91	15/15
57	Kauahi, Kani	C	6-3	275	9/6/59	11	Hawaii	Kekaha, Hawaii	UFA(KC)-'93	16/0*
28	†Lofton, Steve	CB	5-9	180	11/26/68	3	Texas A&M	Jacksonville, Miss.	FA-'91	4/0
29	Lynch, Lorenzo	CB	5-10	200	4/6/63	7	Cal State-Sacramento	Oakland, Calif.	PB(Chi)-'90	16/9
40	#Massey, Robert	CB	5-10	185	2/17/67	5	North Carolina Central	Charlotte, N.C.	T(NO)-'91	15/12
73	May, Mark	G	6-6	290	11/2/59	13	Pittsburgh	Oneonta, N.Y.	PB(SD)-'92	16/16
50	Nunn, Freddie Joe	LB	6-4	250	4/9/62	9	Mississippi	Louisville, Miss.	D1-'85	11/9
27	†Oldham, Chris	CB	5-9	183	10/28/68	3	Oregon	Sacramento, Calif.	FA-'92	1/0
87	Proehl, Ricky	WR	6-0	190	3/7/68	4	Wake Forest	Hillsboro, N.J.	D3-'90	16/15
89	Reeves, Walter	TE	6-3	266	12/15/65	5	Auburn	Eufala, Ala.	D2-'89	16/16
82	Rolle, Butch	TE	6-4	245	8/19/64	8	Michigan State	Hallandale, Fla.	PB(Buff)-'92	16/14
3	Rosenbach, Timm	QB	6-1	210	10/27/66	4	Washington State	Pullman, Wash.	SD1-'89	8/3
79	Rucker, Keith	DE-DT	6-3	325	11/20/68	3	Ohio Wesleyan	University Park, Ill.	FA-'92	14/5
19	Sacca, Tony	QB	6-5	230	4/17/70	2	Penn State	Delran, N.J.	D2-'92	2/0
67	#Sharpe, Luis	T	6-5	295	6/16/60	12	UCLA	Detroit, Mich.	D1-'82	15/15
52	#Small, Jessie	LB	6-3	240	11/30/66	5	Eastern Kentucky	Boston, Ga.	PB(Phil)-'92	6/0
61	Smith, Lance	G	6-3	290	11/1/63	9	Louisiana State	Kannapolis, N.C.	D3-'85	16/16
90	Stowe, Tyronne	LB	6-1	249	5/30/65	7	Rutgers	Passaic, N.J.	PB(Pitt)-'91	15/15
98	Swann, Eric	DE-DT	6-4	310	8/16/70	3	No College	Swann Station, N.C.	D1-'91	16/11
85	Ware, Derek	RB-TE	6-2	255	9/17/67	2	Central State, Ohio	Sacramento, Calif.	D7-'92	15/0
35	Williams, Aeneas	CB	5-10	187	1/29/69	3	Southern	New Orleans, La.	D3-'91	16/16
60	†Williams, Willie	T	6-6	300	8/6/67	3	Louisiana State	Houston, Tex.	SD9-'90	0*
68	#Wolf, Joe	G	6-6	295	12/28/66	5	Boston College	Allentown, Pa.	D1b-'89	3/2
60	Wright, Willie	TE	6-4	239	3/9/68	2	Wyoming	Riverton, Wyo.	FA-'91	9/0
38	#Zordich, Michael	S	6-1	200	10/12/63	7	Penn State	Youngstown, Ohio	PB(NYJ)-'89	16/16

* Beuerlein played 16 games with Dallas in '92; Booty played 16 games with Philadelphia; Cecil played 16 games with Green Bay; Clark played 16 games with Washington; Kauahi played 16 games with Kansas City; W. Williams missed '92 season due to injury.

Unrestricted free agent; subject to developments.

† Restricted free agent; subject to developments.

Traded—RB Johnny Johnson to New York Jets, CB-S Jay Taylor to Kansas City.

Players lost through free agency (4): C Bill Lewis (NE; 6 games in '92), S Tim McDonald (SF; 16), G Vernice Smith (Chi; 12), G-T Danny Villa (KC; 16).

Also played with Cardinals in '92—WR John Jackson (6 games), RB Johnny Johnson (12), CB-S Mitchell Price (2), NT Jim Wahler (5).

Coaching Staff

Head Coach, Joe Bugel

Pro Career: Named head coach on February 7, 1990. Became thirty-first head coach in the history of the franchise dating back to 1920. Assistant head coach-offense under Joe Gibbs with Washington Redskins from 1981-89. Tutored the famous "Hogs" as Redskins' offensive line coach during his tenure with Washington. The Redskins reached the playoffs five times in nine seasons, posting an 11-3 (.786) postseason record. Washington won three NFL championships and four division titles in that span. Four Redskin offensive linemen earned Pro Bowl recognition under Bugel's tutelage — Jeff Bostic, Russ Grimm, Joe Jacoby, and Mark May. He coached Houston Oilers' offensive line from 1977-80 when team set rushing and passing records (1980). He began his professional coaching career with the Detroit Lions in 1975-76. Career record: 13-35.

Background: Offensive guard at Western Kentucky (1960-62). He served as an assistant coach at Western Kentucky (1964-68), Navy (1969), Iowa State (1973), and Ohio State (1974).

Personal: Born March 10, 1940, in Pittsburgh, Pa. Joe and wife Brenda, live in Phoenix, and have three daughters — Angie, Holly, and Jennifer.

Assistant Coaches

Ted Cottrell, defensive line; born June 13, 1947, Chester, Pa., lives in Phoenix. Linebacker Delaware Valley College 1966-68. Pro linebacker Atlanta Falcons 1969-70, Winnipeg Blue Bombers (CFL) 1971. College coach: Rutgers 1973-80, 1983. Pro coach: Kansas City Chiefs 1981-82, New Jersey Generals (USFL) 1983-84, Buffalo Bills 1986-89, joined Cardinals in 1990.

Bobby Jackson, running backs; born February 16, 1940, Forsyth, Ga., lives in Phoenix. Linebacker-running back Samford (Ga.) 1959-62. No pro playing experience. College coach: Florida State 1965-69, Kansas State 1970-74, Louisville 1975-76, Tennessee 1977-82. Pro coach: Atlanta Falcons 1983-86, San Diego Chargers 1987-91, joined Cardinals in 1992.

Jim Johnson, defensive secondary; born May 26, 1941, Maywood, Ill., lives in Phoenix. Quarterback Missouri 1959-62. Pro tight end Buffalo Bills 1963-64. College coach: Missouri Southern 1967-68 (head coach), Drake 1969-72, Indiana 1973-76, Notre Dame 1977-80. Pro coach: Oklahoma Outlaws (USFL) 1984, Jacksonville Bulls (USFL) 1985, joined Cardinals in 1986.

John Matsko, offensive line; born February 2, 1951, Cleveland, Ohio, lives in Phoenix. Fullback Kent State 1970-73. No pro playing experience. College coach: Kent State 1973, Miami, Ohio 1974-75, 1977, North Carolina 1978-84, Navy 1985, Arizona 1986, Southern California 1987-91. Pro coach: Joined Cardinals in 1992.

LeCharls McDaniel, wide receivers; born October 15, 1958, Fort Bragg, N.C., lives in Phoenix, Ariz. Defensive back Cal Poly-San Luis Obispo 1977-80. Pro defensive back Washington Redskins 1981-82. New York Giants 1983-84. College coach: Hartnell (Calif.) Junior College 1986-88, Cal Poly-SLO 1992. Pro coach: San Diego Chargers 1989-91, joined Cardinals in 1993.

Mike Murphy, defensive assistant-quality control; born September 25, 1944, New York, N.Y., lives in Phoenix. Guard-linebacker Huron, S.D., College 1962-65. No pro playing experience. College coach: Vermont 1970-73, Idaho State 1974-76, Western Illinois 1977-78. Pro coach: Saskatchewan Roughriders (CFL) 1979-83, Chicago Blitz (USFL) 1984, Detroit Lions 1985-89, joined Cardinals in 1990.

Phoenix Cardinals 1993 First-Year Roster

Name	Pos.	Ht.	Wt.	Birth-date	College	Hometown	How Acq.
Anderson, Stevie	WR	6-4	210	5/12/70	Grambling	Jonesboro, La.	D8b
Bair, Cameron	K	5-10	182	6/30/70	Illinois State	Tempe, Ariz.	FA
Bonds, John	QB	6-4	230	2/6/70	Northern Arizona	Phoenix, Ariz.	FA
Brown, Chad	DE	6-6	268	7/9/71	Mississippi	Thomasville, Ga.	D8a
Butcher, Dexter	WR	5-10	171	9/6/68	Grambling	Jonesville, La.	FA
Coleman, Ben	T	6-5	329	5/18/71	Wake Forest	South Hill, Va.	D2
Cook, Mike	WR	6-4	200	3/20/71	Stanford	Fountain Valley, Calif.	FA
Dye, Ernest	T	6-4	317	7/15/71	South Carolina	Greenwood, S.C.	D1b
Fann, Chad	TE	6-3	240	6/7/70	Florida A&M	Jacksonville, Fla.	FA
Franklin, Keith	LB	6-3	230	3/4/70	South Carolina	Los Angeles, Calif.	FA
Garman, Robert	G	6-3	290	12/7/68	Washington State	Bremerton, Wash.	FA
Hearst, Garrison	RB	5-9	199	1/4/71	Georgia	Lincolnton, Ga.	D1a
Henson, David (1)	DE-DT	6-2	280	11/28/67	Arkansas Central	Maumelle, Ark.	D9a-'92
Jackson, Robert (1)	WR	6-1	190	6/10/69	Central State, Ohio	Gaithersburg, Md.	FA
Johnson, Chuckie	DT	6-3	280	3/5/69	Auburn	Fayetteville, N.C.	FA
LaDuke, Nathan (1)	S	5-11	200	10/8/68	Arizona State	Phoenix, Ariz.	FA
Malcolm, Marty	G	6-4	287	2/24/70	Central Michigan	Sterling, Mich.	FA
Moody, Mike	T	6-5	285	5/9/69	Southern California	San Francisco, Calif.	FA
Moore, Ron	RB	5-10	226	1/26/70	Pittsburg State, Kan.	Spencer, Okla.	D4
Pay, Garry	C	6-5	273	1/20/68	Brigham Young	Glendale, Ariz.	FA
Richards, Willie	DE	6-2	245	12/10/68	Tennessee	Griffin, Ga.	FA
Searcy, George (1)	RB	5-11	225	11/22/68	East Tennessee State	Jacksonville, Fla.	FA
Snyder, Sean	P	6-0	187	9/21/69	Kansas State	Greenville, Tex.	FA
Stohlmann, Darren	WR	6-3	213	11/25/68	Nebraska Wesleyan	Omaha, Neb.	FA
Sullivan, Ed	WR	5-9	177	10/21/70	Catholic University	Adelphia, Md.	FA
Taylor, Alphonso (1)	DE-DT	6-1	325	9/7/69	Temple	Trenton, N.J.	FA
Tremble, Carl	RB	5-9	193	1/19/71	Furman	Jacksonville, Fla.	FA
Wallerstedt, Brett	LB	6-1	226	11/24/70	Arizona State	Manhattan, Kan.	D6
White, Will	S	6-0	202	6/25/70	Florida	Tallahassee, Fla.	D7
Wooden, Edward	LB	6-0	245	10/14/69	Syracuse	Hartford, Conn.	FA

The term NFL Rookie is defined as a player who is in his first season of professional football and has not been on the roster of another professional football team for any regular-season or postseason games. A Rookie is designated by an "R" on NFL rosters. Players who have been active in another professional football league or players who have NFL experience, including either preseason training camp or being on an Active List or Inactive List, or on Reserve/Injured or Reserve/Physically Unable to Perform for fewer than six regular-season games, are termed NFL First-Year Players. An NFL First-Year Player is designated by a "1" on NFL rosters. Thereafter, a player is credited with an additional year of experience for each season in which he accumulates six games on the Active List or Inactive List, or on Reserve/Injured or Reserve/Physically Unable to Perform.

NOTES

Joe Pascale, outside linebackers; born April 4, 1946, New York, N.Y., lives in Phoenix. Linebacker Connecticut 1963-66. No pro playing experience. College coach: Connecticut 1967-68, Rhode Island 1969-73, Idaho State 1974-76 (head coach 1976), Princeton 1977-79. Pro coach: Montreal Alouettes (CFL) 1980-81, Ottawa Rough Riders (CFL) 1982-83, New Jersey Generals (USFL) 1984-85, joined Cardinals in 1986.

Ted Plumb, tight ends; born August 20, 1939, Reno, Nev., lives in Phoenix. Wide receiver Baylor 1960-61. Pro wide receiver Buffalo Bills 1962. College coach: Cerritos, Calif., J.C. 1966-67, Texas Christian 1968-70, Tulsa 1971, Kansas 1972-73. Pro coach: New York Giants 1974-76, Atlanta Falcons 1977-79, Chicago Bears 1980-85, Philadelphia Eagles 1986-89, joined Cardinals in 1990.

Jerry Rhome, offensive coordinator; born March 6, 1942, Dallas, Tex., lives in Phoenix. Quarterback Southern Methodist 1960-61, Tulsa 1963-64. Pro quarterback Dallas Cowboys 1965-68, Cleveland Browns 1969, Houston Oilers 1970, Los Angeles Rams 1971-72. College coach: Tulsa 1973-75. Pro coach: Seattle Seahawks 1976-82, Washington Redskins 1983-87, San Diego Chargers 1988, Dallas Cowboys 1989, joined Cardinals in 1990.

Pete Rodriguez, special teams; born July 25, 1940, Chicago, Ill., lives in Phoenix. Guard-linebacker Denver University 1959-60, Western State, Colo. 1961-63. No pro playing experience. College coach: Western State, Colo. 1964, Arizona 1968-69, Western Illinois 1970-73, 1979-82 (head coach), Florida State 1974-75, Iowa State 1976-78, Northern Iowa 1986. Pro coach: Michigan Panthers (USFL) 1983-84, Denver Gold (USFL) 1985, Jacksonville Bulls (USFL) 1986, Ottawa Rough Riders (CFL) 1987, Los Angeles Raiders 1988-89, joined Cardinals in 1990.

Bob Rogucki, strength and conditioning; born September 27, 1953, Clarksburg, W. Va., lives in Phoenix. No college or pro playing experience. College coach: Penn State 1981, Weber State 1982, Army 1983-89. Pro coach: Joined Cardinals in 1990.

Fritz Shurmur, defensive coordinator; born July 15, 1932, Riverview, Mich., lives in Phoenix. Center Albion 1951-53. No pro playing experience. College coach: Albion 1956-61, Wyoming 1962-74 (head coach 1971-74). Pro coach: Detroit Lions 1975-77, New England Patriots 1978-81, Los Angeles Rams 1982-90, joined Cardinals in 1991.

SAN FRANCISCO 49ERS

National Football Conference Western Division

Team Colors: Forty Niners Gold and Scarlet

4949 Centennial Boulevard
Santa Clara, California 95054
Telephone: (408) 562-4949

Club Officials

Owner: Edward J. DeBartolo, Jr.
President: Carmen Policy
Vice President-Football Administration: John McVay
Vice President-Business Operations & C.F.O.: Keith Simon
Coordinator of Football Operations/Player Personnel: Dwight Clark
Director of Pro Personnel: Allan Webb
Director of College Scouting: Vinny Cerrato
Director of Public/Community Relations: Rodney Knox
Director of Marketing/Promotions: Laurie Albrecht
Coordinator of Football Operations: Neal Dahlen
Ticket Manager: Lynn Carrozzi
Director of Stadium Operations: Murlan (Mo) Fowell
Video Director: Robert Yanagi
Trainer: Lindsy McLean
Equipment Manager: Bronco Hinek

Stadium: Candlestick Park • **Capacity:** 66,513
San Francisco, California 94124

Playing Surface: Grass

Training Camp: Sierra Community College
Rockin, California 95677

1993 Schedule

Preseason

Aug. 1	vs. Pittsburgh at Barcelona	1:00
Aug. 8	vs. Los Angeles Raiders at Stanford Stadium	1:00
Aug. 16	at Denver	5:00
Aug. 21	at Seattle	7:00
Aug. 28	**San Diego**	6:00

Regular Season

Sept. 5	at Pittsburgh	1:00
Sept. 13	at Cleveland (Monday)	9:00
Sept. 19	**Atlanta**	1:00
Sept. 26	at New Orleans	3:00
Oct. 3	**Minnesota**	1:00
Oct. 10	**Open Date**	
Oct. 17	at Dallas	3:00
Oct. 24	**Phoenix**	1:00
Oct. 31	**Los Angeles Rams**	1:00
Nov. 7	**Open Date**	
Nov. 14	at Tampa Bay	1:00
Nov. 22	**New Orleans** (Monday)	6:00
Nov. 28	at Los Angeles Rams	1:00
Dec. 5	**Cincinnati**	5:00
Dec. 11	at Atlanta (Saturday)	4:00
Dec. 19	at Detroit	4:00
Dec. 25	**Houston** (Saturday)	2:30
Jan. 3	**Philadelphia** (Monday)	6:00

49ers Coaching History

(339-277-13)

1950-54	Lawrence (Buck) Shaw	33-25-2
1955	Norman (Red) Strader	4-8-0
1956-58	Frankie Albert	19-17-1
1959-63	Howard (Red) Hickey*	27-27-1
1963-67	Jack Christiansen	26-38-3
1968-75	Dick Nolan	56-56-5
1976	Monte Clark	8-6-0
1977	Ken Meyer	5-9-0
1978	Pete McCulley**	1-8-0
1978	Fred O'Connor	1-6-0
1979-88	Bill Walsh	102-63-1
1989-92	George Seifert	57-14-0

*Resigned after three games in 1963
**Released after nine games in 1978

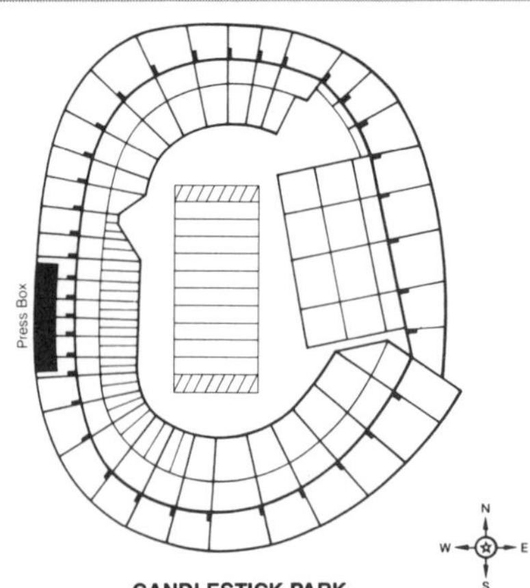

CANDLESTICK PARK

Record Holders

Individual Records—Career

Category	Name	Performance
Rushing (Yds.)	Joe Perry, 1950-1960, 1963	7,344
Passing (Yds.)	Joe Montana, 1979-1992	35,124
Passing (TDs)	Joe Montana, 1979-1992	244
Receiving (No.)	Jerry Rice, 1985-1992	610
Receiving (Yds.)	Jerry Rice, 1985-1992	10,273
Interceptions	Ronnie Lott, 1981-1990	51
Punting (Avg.)	Tommy Davis, 1959-1969	44.7
Punt Return (Avg.)	Manfred Moore, 1974-75	14.7
Kickoff Return (Avg.)	Abe Woodson, 1958-1964	29.4
Field Goals	Ray Wersching, 1977-1987	190
Touchdowns (Tot.)	Jerry Rice, 1985-1992	108
Points	Ray Wersching, 1977-1987	979

Individual Records—Single Season

Category	Name	Performance
Rushing (Yds.)	Roger Craig, 1988	1,502
Passing (Yds.)	Joe Montana, 1990	3,944
Passing (TDs)	Joe Montana, 1987	31
Receiving (No.)	Jerry Rice, 1990	100
Receiving (Yds.)	Jerry Rice, 1986	1,570
Interceptions	Dave Baker, 1960	10
	Ronnie Lott, 1986	10
Punting (Avg.)	Tommy Davis, 1965	45.8
Punt Return (Avg.)	Dana McLemore, 1982	22.3
Kickoff Return (Avg.)	Joe Arenas, 1953	34.4
Field Goals	Mike Cofer, 1989	29
Touchdowns (Tot.)	Jerry Rice, 1987	23
Points	Jerry Rice, 1987	138

Individual Records—Single Game

Category	Name	Performance
Rushing (Yds.)	Delvin Williams, 10-31-76	194
Passing (Yds.)	Joe Montana, 10-14-90	476
Passing (TDs)	Joe Montana, 10-14-90	6
Receiving (No.)	Jerry Rice, 10-14-90	13
Receiving (Yds.)	John Taylor, 12-11-89	286
Interceptions	Dave Baker, 12-4-60	*4
Field Goals	Ray Wersching, 10-16-83	6
Touchdowns (Tot.)	Jerry Rice, 10-14-90	5
Points	Jerry Rice, 10-14-90	30

*NFL Record

1992 Team Record

Preseason (5-0)

Date	Result		Opponents
8/3	W	13- 7	Denver
8/8	W	24-10	L.A. Raiders
8/16	W	17-15	vs. Washington at London
8/21	W	20-14	at San Diego
8/28	W	24-17	Seattle

Regular Season (14-2)

Date	Result		Opponents	Att.
9/6	W	31-14	at N.Y. Giants	76,241
9/13	L	31-34	Buffalo	65,401
9/20	W	31-14	at N.Y. Jets	75,945
9/27	W	16-10	at New Orleans	67,627
10/4	W	27-24	L.A. Rams	65,340
10/11	W	24-12	at New England	59,437
10/18	W	56-17	Atlanta	65,446
11/1	L	14-24	at Phoenix	50,482
11/9	W	41- 3	at Atlanta	69,898
11/15	W	21-20	New Orleans	65,484
11/22	W	27-10	at L.A. Rams	67,461
11/29	W	20-14	Philadelphia	65,486
12/6	W	27- 3	Miami	65,461
12/13	W	20-17	at Minnesota	52,456
12/19	W	21-14	Tampa Bay	65,305
12/28	W	24- 6	Detroit	65,432

Postseason (1-1)

Date	Result		Opponent	Att.
1/9	W	20-13	Washington	64,991
1/17	L	20-30	Dallas	64,920

Score by Periods

49ers	87	135	78	131	0	— 431
Opponents	37	56	74	69	0	— 236

Attendance

Home 523,355 Away 529,547 Total 1,052,902
Single-game home record, 66,334 (1-20-91)
Single-season home record, 523,355 (1992)

1992 Team Statistics

	49ers	Opp.
Total First Downs	344	277
Rushing	135	90
Passing	192	174
Penalty	17	13
Third Down: Made/Att.	87/187	75/199
Third Down: Pct.	46.5	37.7
Fourth Down: Made/Att.	5/13	8/17
Fourth Down: Pct.	38.5	47.1
Total Net Yards	6195	4787
Avg. Per Game	387.2	299.2
Total Plays	994	943
Avg. Per Play	6.2	5.1
Net Yards Rushing	2315	1418
Avg. Per Game	144.7	88.6
Total Rushes	482	351
Net Yards Passing	3880	3369
Avg. Per Game	242.5	210.6
Sacked/Yards Lost	32/174	41/273
Gross Yards	4054	3642
Att./Completions	480/319	551/320
Completion Pct.	66.5	58.1
Had Intercepted	9	17
Punts/Avg.	49/39.1	76/41.2
Net Punting Avg.	49/34.7	76/34.3
Penalties/Yards Lost	80/636	79/651
Fumbles/Ball Lost	29/13	23/12
Touchdowns	54	27
Rushing	22	5
Passing	29	20
Returns	3	2
Avg. Time of Possession	32:19	27:41

1992 Individual Statistics

Scoring	TD R	TD P	TD Rt	PAT	FG	Saf	TP
Cofer	0	0	0	53/54	18/27	0	107
Rice	1	10	0	0/0	0/0	0	66
Watters	9	2	0	0/0	0/0	0	66
Rathman	5	4	0	0/0	0/0	0	54
Jones	0	4	0	0/0	0/0	0	24
Lee	2	2	0	0/0	0/0	0	24
Young	4	0	0	0/0	0/0	0	24
Taylor	0	3	0	0/0	0/0	0	18
Turner	0	2	0	0/0	0/0	0	12
D. Carter	0	1	0	0/0	0/0	0	6
Hanks	0	0	1	0/0	0/0	0	6
Johnson	0	0	1	0/0	0/0	0	6
Logan	1	0	0	0/0	0/0	0	6
Sherrard	0	0	1	0/0	0/0	0	6
Williams	0	1	0	0/0	0/0	0	6
49ers	22	29	3	53/54	18/27	0	431
Opponents	5	20	2	26/27	16/20	0	236

Passing	Att.	Comp.	Yds.	Pct.	TD	Int.	Tkld.	Rate
Young	402	268	3465	66.7	25	7	29/152	107.0
Bono	56	36	463	64.3	2	2	2/14	87.1
Montana	21	15	126	71.4	2	0	1/8	118.4
Watters	1	0	0	0.0	0	0	0/0	39.6
49ers	480	319	4054	66.5	29	9	32/174	105.0
Opponents	551	320	3642	58.1	20	17	41/273	77.3

Rushing	Att.	Yds.	Avg.	LG	TD
Watters	206	1013	4.9	43	9
Young	76	537	7.1	39t	4
Lee	91	362	4.0	43	2
Rathman	57	194	3.4	17	5
Rice	9	58	6.4	26t	1
Logan	8	44	5.5	26	1
Henderson	10	37	3.7	9	0
Montana	3	28	9.3	16	0
Bono	15	23	1.5	19	0
Taylor	1	10	10.0	10	0
D. Carter	4	9	2.3	6	0
Wilmsmeyer	2	0	0.0	10	0
49ers	482	2315	4.8	43	22
Opponents	351	1418	4.0	35	5

Receiving	No.	Yds.	Avg.	LG	TD
Rice	84	1201	14.3	80t	10
Jones	45	628	14.0	43	4
Rathman	44	343	7.8	27t	4
Watters	43	405	9.4	35	2
Sherrard	38	607	16.0	56	0
Taylor	25	428	17.1	54t	3
Lee	20	102	5.1	17	2
Turner	9	200	22.2	57	2
Williams	7	76	10.9	21	1
Logan	2	17	8.5	13	0
D. Carter	1	43	43.0	43t	1
Henderson	1	4	4.0	4	0
49ers	319	4054	12.7	80t	29
Opponents	320	3642	11.4	55t	20

Interceptions	No.	Yds.	Avg.	LG	TD
Griffin	5	4	0.8	2	0
Davis	3	52	17.3	37	0
Hall	2	34	17.0	34	0
Hanks	2	5	2.5	4	0
Johnson	1	56	56.0	56t	1
Roberts	1	19	19.0	19	0
DeLong	1	2	2.0	2	0
Brown	1	0	0.0	0	0
Whitmore	1	0	0.0	0	0
49ers	17	172	10.1	56t	1
Opponents	9	126	14.0	51t	2

Punting	No.	Yds.	Avg.	In 20	LG
Wilmsmeyer	49	1918	39.1	19	58
49ers	49	1918	39.1	19	58
Opponents	76	3134	41.2	23	71

Punt Returns	No.	FC	Yds.	Avg.	LG	TD
Grant	29	10	249	8.6	46	0
Griffin	6	2	69	11.5	29	0
R. Lewis	4	0	23	5.8	9	0
Hanks	1	0	48	48.0	48t	1
49ers	40	12	389	9.7	48t	1
Opponents	23	9	177	7.7	27	0

Kickoff Returns	No.	Yds.	Avg.	LG	TD
Logan	22	478	21.7	82	0
D. Carter	2	55	27.5	32	0
Grant	3	70	23.3	47	0
Lee	14	276	19.7	33	0
Turner	1	0	0.0	0	0
49ers	42	879	20.9	82	0
Opponents	66	1273	19.3	45	0

Sacks	No.
Harris	17.0
Holt	5.5
Brown	3.5
Harrison	3.5
Washington	2.0
Wilkins	1.5
M. Carter	1.0
Fagan	1.0
Hall	1.0
Jackson	1.0
Johnson	1.0
Roberts	1.0
Romanowski	1.0
Walter	1.0
49ers	41.0
Opponents	32.0

1993 Draft Choices

Round	Name	Pos.	College
1.	Dana Stubblefield	DT	Kansas
	Todd Kelly	DE	Tennessee
2.	Adrian Hardy	DB	N.W. Louisiana
5.	Artie Smith	DT	Louisiana Tech
6.	Chris Dalman	G	Stanford
7.	Troy Wilson	LB	Pittsburg (Kan.)
8.	Elvis Grbac	QB	Michigan

San Francisco 49ers 1993 Veteran Roster

No.	Name	Pos.	Ht.	Wt.	Birth-date	NFL Exp.	College	Hometown	How Acq.	'92 Games/ Starts
21	Alexander, Mike	WR	6-3	190	3/19/65	3	Penn State	Piscataway, N.J.	FA-'93	0*
79	Barton, Harris	G	6-4	286	4/19/64	7	North Carolina	Atlanta, Ga.	D1a-'87	13/13
65	Boatswain, Harry	T	6-4	295	6/26/69	3	New Haven	Brooklyn, N.Y.	D5b-'91	16/2
71	Bollinger, Brian	G	6-5	285	11/21/68	2	North Carolina	Indialantic, Fla.	D3-'92	16/0
13	Bono, Steve	QB	6-4	211	5/11/62	9	UCLA	Norristown, Pa.	FA-'89	16/0
96	Brown, Dennis	DE	6-4	290	11/6/67	4	Washington	Long Beach, Calif.	D2a-'90	16/3
35	Carter, Dexter	RB	5-9	174	9/15/67	4	Florida State	Appling County, Ga.	D1-'90	3/0
95	†Carter, Michael	NT	6-2	285	10/29/60	10	Southern Methodist	Dallas, Tex.	D5a-'84	12/11
6	†Cofer, Mike	K	6-1	190	2/19/62	6	North Carolina State	Charlotte, N.C.	FA-'88	16/0
85	Covington, Tom	TE	6-3	241	5/1/69	2	Georgia Tech	Brookville, N.Y.	D11-'92	0*
25	#Davis, Eric	CB	5-11	178	1/26/68	4	Jacksonville State	Anniston, Ala.	D2b-'90	16/16
63	Deese, Derrick	G	6-3	270	5/17/70	2	Southern California	Culver City, Calif.	FA-'92	0*
59	#DeLong, Keith	LB	6-2	250	8/14/67	5	Tennessee	Knoxville, Tenn.	D1-'89	14/9
54	Donahue, Mitch	LB	6-2	254	2/4/68	3	Wyoming	Billings, Mont.	D4-'91	2/0
75	Fagan, Kevin	DE	6-3	265	4/25/63	7	Miami	Lake Worth, Fla.	D4c-'86	15/13
17	Faison, Derrick	WR	6-4	210	8/24/67	2	Howard	Lake City, S.C.	FA-'93	0*
57	Faryniarz, Brett	LB	6-3	230	7/23/65	5	San Diego State	Rancho Cordova, Calif.	FA-'93	0*
88	t-Fernandez, Mervyn	WR	6-3	200	12/29/59	7	San Jose State	San Jose, Calif.	T(Raid)-'93	15/1*
67	Foster, Roy	G	6-4	290	5/24/60	12	Southern California	Shawnee Mission, Kan.	PB(Mia)-'91	16/16
31	Gash, Thane	S	5-11	198	9/1/65	6	East Tennessee State	Hendersonville, N.C.	PB(Clev)-'92	16/3
98	#Goss, Antonio	LB	6-4	228	8/11/66	4	North Carolina	Randleman, N.C.	D12a-'89	16/0
24	Grant, Alan	CB	5-10	187	10/1/66	4	Stanford	Pasadena, Calif.	FA-'92	15/0
29	Griffin, Don	CB	6-0	180	3/17/64	8	Middle Tennessee State	Pelham, Ga.	D6-'86	16/16
77	Haggins, Odell	NT	6-2	275	2/27/67	2	Florida State	Bartow, Fla.	FA-'93	0*
28	Hall, Dana	S	6-2	206	7/8/69	2	Washington	Diamond Bar, Calif.	D1-'92	15/15
36	Hanks, Merton	CB	6-2	185	3/12/68	3	Iowa	Dallas, Tex.	D5a-'91	16/5
56	Harrison, Martin	LB	6-5	240	9/20/67	3	Washington	Bellevue, Wash.	D10-'90	16/1
23	Johnson, Barry	WR	6-2	197	2/1/68	2	Maryland	Herndon, Va.	FA-'93	0*
55	Johnson, John	LB	6-3	230	5/8/68	3	Clemson	LaGrange, Ga.	D2c-'91	16/2
84	Jones, Brent	TE	6-4	230	2/12/63	7	Santa Clara	San Jose, Calif.	FA-'87	15/15
90	Jordan, Darin	LB	6-2	245	12/4/64	4	Northeastern	Stoughton, Mass.	PB(Raid)-'91	15/1
22	Lee, Amp	RB	5-11	200	10/1/71	2	Florida State	Chipley, Fla.	D2-'92	16/3
43	†Logan, Marc	RB	6-0	212	5/9/65	7	Kentucky	Lexington, Ky.	PB(Mia)-'92	16/1
20	Loville, Derek	RB	5-10	205	7/4/68	3	Oregon	San Francisco, Calif.	FA-'93	0*
46	McDonald, Tim	S	6-2	215	1/26/65	7	Southern California	Fresno, Calif.	UFA(Phx)-'93	16/16*
26	McGruder, Michael	CB	5-10	190	5/6/64	4	Kent State	Cleveland, Ohio	FA-'92	9/2
62	McIntyre, Guy	G	6-3	276	2/17/61	10	Georgia	Thomasville, Ga.	D3-'84	16/16
51	Mott, Joe	LB	6-4	255	10/6/65	4	Iowa	Endicott, N.Y.	FA-'93	0*
14	Musgrave, Bill	QB	6-2	205	11/11/67	3	Oregon	Grand Junction, Colo.	FA-'91	0*
44	Rathman, Tom	RB	6-1	232	10/7/62	8	Nebraska	Grand Island, Neb.	D3a-'86	15/15
80	Rice, Jerry	WR	6-2	200	10/13/62	9	Mississippi Valley State	Crawford, Miss.	D1-'85	16/16
91	†Roberts, Larry	DE	6-3	275	6/2/63	8	Alabama	Dothan, Ala.	D2-'86	3/0
53	Romanowski, Bill	LB	6-4	240	4/2/66	6	Boston College	Vernon, Conn.	D3-'88	16/16
38	Russell, Damien	S	6-1	204	8/20/70	2	Virginia Tech	Washington, D.C.	D6-'92	0*
61	Sapolu, Jesse	C	6-4	278	3/10/61	11	Hawaii	Honolulu, Hawaii	D11-'83	16/16
65	Stewart, Andrew	DE	6-6	275	11/20/65	4	Cincinnati	West Hempstead, N.Y.	FA-'93	0*
64	Tamm, Ralph	G-C	6-4	280	3/11/66	6	West Chester	Philadelphia, Pa.	PB(Cin)-'92	14/1
47	Taylor, Brian	S	5-10	195	10/1/67	3	Oregon State	New Orleans, La.	FA-'93	0*
82	Taylor, John	WR	6-1	185	3/31/62	8	Delaware State	Pennsauken, N.J.	D3c-'86	9/8
72	Thomas, Mark	DE	6-5	273	5/6/69	2	North Carolina State	Lilburn, Ga.	D4a-'92	0*
86	Turner, Odessa	WR	6-3	215	10/12/64	7	Northwestern Louisiana	Monroe, La.	PB(NYG)-'92	16/0
93	Veris, Garin	DE	6-4	255	2/27/63	9	Stanford	Chillicothe, Ohio	FA-'92	10/0
27	Walker, Adam	RB	6-1	210	6/7/68	2	Pittsburgh	Munhall, Pa.	FA-'91	1/0
74	Wallace, Steve	T	6-5	280	12/27/64	8	Auburn	Atlanta, Ga.	D4b-'86	16/16
89	Walls, Wesley	TE	6-5	254	2/26/66	5	Mississippi	Pontotic, Miss.	D2-'89	0*
99	Walter, Michael	LB	6-3	246	11/30/60	11	Oregon	Eugene, Ore.	FA-'84	15/13
97	Washington, Ted	NT	6-4	295	4/13/68	3	Louisville	Tampa, Fla.	D1-'91	16/6
32	Watters, Ricky	RB	6-1	212	4/7/69	3	Notre Dame	Harrisburg, Pa.	D2a-'91	14/13
66	Wilkins, David	LB	6-4	240	2/24/69	2	Eastern Kentucky	Cincinnati, Ohio	FA-'92	13/0
81	Williams, Jamie	TE	6-4	245	2/25/60	10	Nebraska	Houston, Tex.	PB(Hou)-'89	16/1
10	Wilmsmeyer, Klaus	P	6-1	210	12/4/67	2	Louisville	Mississauga, Canada	FA-'92	15/0
8	Young, Steve	QB	6-2	205	10/11/61	9	Brigham Young	Greenwich, Conn.	T(TB)-'87	16/16

* Alexander last active with Buffalo in '91; Covington, Deese, Russell, Stewart, and Walls missed '92 season because of injury; Faison last active with L.A. Rams in '90; Faryniarz last active with L.A. Rams in '91; Fernandez played 15 games with L.A. Raiders; Haggins last active with Buffalo in '91; B. Johnson last active with Denver in '91; Loville last active with Seattle in '91; McDonald played 16 games with Phoenix; Mott last active with N.Y. Jets in '91; Musgrave was active for 1 game but did not play; B. Taylor last active with Buffalo in '91; M. Thomas spent entire '92 season on practice squad.

\# Restricted free agent; subject to developments.

† Unrestricted free agent; subject to developments.

Traded—QB Joe Montana to Kansas City; S David Whitmore to Kansas City.

t- 49ers traded for Fernandez (L.A. Raiders).

Players lost through free agency (3); DE Tim Harris (Phil; 16 games in '92), DE Pierce Holt (Atl; 16), WR Mike Sherrard (NYG; 16).

Also played with 49ers in '92—TE Chris Dressel (1 game), DE Jacob Green (2), RB Keith Henderson (2), S Johnnie Jackson (5), WR Ron Lewis (5), G-T Reggie McKenzie (2), QB Joe Montana (1), C Chuck Thomas (2), S David Whitmore (16).

COACHING STAFF

Head Coach, George Seifert

Pro Career: Named 49ers' head coach on January 26, 1989, after serving as the team's defensive coordinator since 1983. Immediately earned a place in league history, winning a record 17 games his first year and becoming only the second rookie head coach to lead his team to a Super Bowl title (Don McCafferty of Baltimore in 1970 was the first). Recorded the NFL's best won-loss mark in 1990, posting a 14-2 record and guided San Francisco to its fifth consecutive NFC West title. In 1991, the 49ers recorded a 10-6 mark, missing the playoffs for the first time since 1982. Again posted the NFL's best won-loss record in 1992, going 14-2 and advancing to the NFC Championship Game. Joined 49ers as secondary coach in 1980. In only his second season in the pro ranks, San Francisco had the second best defense in the league and won a Super Bowl (XVI) title, despite starting three rookies in the defensive backfield. Appointed the team's defensive coordinator in 1983. Finished 1987 with the top defense in the NFL and a 13-2 record. No pro playing experience. Career record: 57-14.

Background: Linebacker at University of Utah (1960-62). Served a six-month tour of duty with the U.S. Army following graduation. Returned to Utah as a graduate assistant in 1964. Named head coach at Westminster College in Salt Lake City in 1965. Assistant at Iowa (1966), Oregon (1967-71), and Stanford (1972-74). Left Stanford to become head coach at Cornell (1975-76). Joined Bill Walsh's staff at Stanford in 1977 and helped the Cardinal to a two-year mark of 17-7, including victories in the Sun and Bluebonnet Bowls. Received bachelor's degree in zoology (1963) and master's degree in physical education (1966) from Utah.

Personal: Born January 22, 1940, in San Francisco. He and his wife, Linda, have two children—Eve and Jason—and live in Los Altos, Calif.

Assistant Coaches

Jerry Attaway, conditioning; born January 3, 1946, Susanville, Calif., lives in San Jose, Calif. Defensive back Yuba, Calif., J.C. 1964-65, Cal-Davis 1967. No pro playing experience. College coach: Cal-Davis 1970-71, Idaho 1972-74, Utah State 1975-77, Southern California 1978-82. Pro coach: Joined 49ers in 1983.

Dwaine Board, defensive assistant; born November 29, 1956, Rocky Mount, Va., lives in Redwood City, Calif. Defensive lineman North Carolina A&T 1974-77. Pro defensive lineman San Francisco 49ers 1979-87, New Orleans Saints 1988. Pro coach: Joined 49ers in 1991.

Jeff Fisher, defensive backs; born February 25, 1958, Culver City, Calif., lives in Danville, Calif. Defensive back Southern California 1978-80. Pro defensive back-punt returner Chicago Bears 1981-85. Pro coach: Philadelphia Eagles 1986-90, Los Angeles Rams 1991, joined 49ers in 1992.

Carl Jackson, running backs; born August 16, 1940, Bay City, Tex., lives in San Jose, Calif. Quarterback Prairie View A&M 1959-62. No pro playing experience. College coach: North Texas State 1976-78, Iowa 1979-91. Pro coach: Joined 49ers in 1992.

Alan Lowry, special teams; born November 21, 1950, Irving, Tex., lives in Danville, Calif. Defensive back-quarterback Texas 1970-72. No pro playing experience. College coach: Virginia Tech 1974, Wyoming 1975, Texas 1976-81. Pro coach: Dallas Cowboys 1982-90, Tampa Bay Buccaneers 1991, joined 49ers in 1992.

John Marshall, defensive line; born October 2, 1945, Arroyo Grande, Calif., lives in Pleasanton, Calif. Linebacker Washington State 1964. No pro playing experience. College coach: Oregon 1970-76, Southern California 1977-79. Pro coach: Green Bay Packers 1980-82, Atlanta Falcons 1983-85, Indianapolis Colts 1986-88, joined 49ers in 1989.

San Francisco 49ers 1993 First-Year Roster

Name	Pos.	Ht.	Wt.	Birth-date	College	Hometown	How Acq.
Barnes, Tomur	CB	5-10	188	9/8/70	North Texas State	Baytown, Tex.	FA
Birch, Swift (1)	DE	6-4	270	5/8/69	Temple	Washington, D.C.	FA
Bridewell, Jeff (1)	QB	6-5	220	5/13/67	Cal-Davis	Napa, Calif.	FA
Brown, Hurlie (1)	S	6-0	195	6/21/69	Miami	Merritt Island, Fla.	FA
Bryant, Junior	DE	6-4	275	1/16/71	Notre Dame	Omaha, Neb.	FA
Childs, Jason (1)	T	6-4	285	1/6/69	North Dakota	Plymouth, Minn.	FA
Dalman, Chris	G-C	6-3	285	3/15/70	Stanford	Salinas, Calif.	D6
Downing, Tim (1)	DE	6-5	284	4/9/67	Washington State	Durham, Calif.	FA
Dressel, Robert (1)	C	6-4	290	8/19/69	Purdue	Portland, Ind.	FA
Evans, Kevin (1)	WR	6-4	190	8/16/68	San Jose State	Ft. Worth, Tex.	FA
Grbac, Elvis	QB	6-5	232	8/13/70	Michigan	Willoughby Hills, Ohio	D8
Hardy, Adrian	CB	5-11	194	8/16/70	N.W. Louisiana	New Orleans, La.	D2
Hillman, Jay (1)	RB	6-0	230	3/10/68	Boston University	Oxford, Conn.	FA
Holland, John Robert (1)	CB	5-10	186	7/18/65	Cal State-Sacramento	Seaside, Calif.	FA
Jarmolowich, Mike	LB	6-1	240	12/24/69	Maryland	Union, N.J.	FA
Kelly, Todd	LB	6-2	259	11/27/70	Tennessee	Hampton, Va.	D1b
LaBounty, Matt (1)	DE	6-4	254	1/3/69	Oregon	Novato, Calif.	D12-'92
McGuire, Steve	RB	5-11	216	11/20/69	Miami	Brooklyn, N.Y.	FA
Moss, Anthony (1)	LB	6-4	238	10/12/67	Florida State	Miami, Fla.	FA
Parrish, James (1)	T	6-6	315	5/19/68	Temple	Baltimore, Md.	FA
Peery, Ryan (1)	DE	6-5	265	5/15/69	California	Morgan Hill, Calif.	FA
Popson, Ted (1)	TE	6-4	250	9/10/66	Portland State	Lake Tahoe, Calif.	FA
Seay, Mark (1)	WR	6-0	175	4/11/67	Long Beach State	San Bernardino, Calif.	FA
Singleton, Nate (1)	WR	5-11	190	7/5/68	Grambling	Marrero, La.	FA
Smith, Artie	DE	6-4	303	5/15/70	Louisiana Tech	Stillwater, Okla.	D5
Stubblefield, Dana	DE	6-2	302	11/14/70	Kansas	Cleves, Ohio	D1a
Sullivan, Kent (1)	P	6-0	206	5/15/64	Cal Lutheran	Middlebury, Ind.	FA
Wilson, Troy	DE	6-4	235	11/20/70	Pittsburg State, Kan.	Topeka, Kan.	D7
Young, Charlie (1)	RB	6-1	205	8/21/68	Stanford	Winnetka, Ill.	FA

The term NFL Rookie is defined as a player who is in his first season of professional football and has not been on the roster of another professional football team for any regular-season or postseason games. A Rookie is designated by an "R" on NFL rosters. Players who have been active in another professional football league or players who have NFL experience, including either preseason training camp or being on an Active List or Inactive List, or on Reserve/Injured or Reserve/Physically Unable to Perform for fewer than six regular-season games, are termed NFL First-Year Players. An NFL First-Year Player is designated by a "1" on NFL rosters. Thereafter, a player is credited with an additional year of experience for each season in which he accumulates six games on the Active List or Inactive List, or on Reserve/Injured or Reserve/Physically Unable to Perform.

NOTES

Bobb McKittrick, offensive line; born December 29, 1935, Baker, Ore., lives in San Mateo, Calif. Guard Oregon State 1955-57. No pro playing experience. College coach: Oregon State 1961-64, UCLA 1965-70. Pro coach: Los Angeles Rams 1971-72, San Diego Chargers 1974-78, joined 49ers in 1979.

Bill McPherson, defensive coordinator; born October 24, 1931, Santa Clara, Calif., lives in San Jose, Calif. Tackle Santa Clara 1950-52. No pro playing experience. College coach: Santa Clara 1963-74, UCLA 1975-77. Pro coach: Philadelphia Eagles 1978, joined 49ers in 1979.

Mike Shanahan, offensive coordinator-quarterbacks; born August 24, 1952, Oak Park, Ill., lives in Saratoga, Calif. Quarterback Eastern Illinois 1970-73. No pro playing experience. College coach: Oklahoma 1975-76, Northern Arizona 1977, Eastern Illinois 1978, Minnesota 1979, Florida 1980-83. Pro coach: Denver Broncos 1984-87, 1989-91, Los Angeles Raiders 1988-89 (head coach), joined 49ers in 1992.

Ray Sherman, receivers; born November 27, 1951, Berkeley, Calif., lives in Dublin, Calif. Wide receiver Laney, Calif., J.C. 1969-70, Fresno State 1971-72. Pro defensive back Green Bay Packers 1973. College coach: San Jose State 1974, California 1975, 1981, Michigan State 1976-77, Wake Forest 1978-80, Purdue 1982-85, Georgia 1986-87. Pro coach: Houston Oilers 1988-89, Atlanta Falcons 1990, joined 49ers in 1991.

Mike Solari, tight ends-offensive line assistant; born January 16, 1955, Daly City, Calif., lives in Pleasanton, Calif. Offensive lineman San Diego State 1975-76. No pro playing experience. College coach: Mira Vista (Calif.) Junior College 1977-78, U.S. International 1979, Boise State 1980, Cincinnati 1981-82, Kansas 1983-85, Pittsburgh 1986, Alabama 1990-91. Pro coach: Dallas Cowboys 1987-88, Phoenix Cardinals 1989, joined 49ers in 1992.

Eric Wright, defensive backs assistant; born April 18, 1959, St. Louis, Mo., lives in San Jose, Calif. Defensive back Missouri 1978-80. Pro defensive back San Francisco 49ers 1981-90. Pro coach: Joined 49ers in 1991.

Bob Zeman, linebackers; born February 22, 1937, Wheaton, Ill., lives in Boulder Creek, Calif. Fullback/halfback Wisconsin 1957-59. Pro defensive back Los Angeles/San Diego Chargers 1960-61, 1965-66, Denver Broncos 1962-63. College coach: Northwestern 1968-69, Wisconsin 1970. Pro coach: Oakland Raiders 1971-77, 1984-86, Denver Broncos 1978-82, Buffalo Bills 1983, joined 49ers in 1989.

National Football Conference
Central Division

Team Colors: Florida Orange, White, and Red

One Buccaneer Place
Tampa, Florida 33607
Telephone: (813) 870-2700

Club Officials

Owner: Hugh F. Culverhouse
President: Gay Culverhouse
VP-Football Administration: Rich McKay
Assistant to the President: Terry Wooten
Director of Player Personnel: Jerry Angelo
Director of College Scouting: Tim Ruskell
Director of Public Relations: Rick Odioso
Director of Corp. Sales/Broadcasting: Jim Overton
Director of Advertising & Sales: Paul Sickmon
Controller: Patrick Smith
College Scouts: Mike Ackerley, Brian Gardner Ruston Webster, Mike Yowarsky
Pro Personnel Asst.: John Garrett, John Idzik
Office Manager: Deb Matzke
Asst. Director/Ticket Operations: Lori Grimm
Asst. Director/Public Relations: Cheryl Harden
Computer Services Coordinator: Terri Kimbell
Community Relations Asst.: Sherry Gruden
Media Relations Assistant: Scott Smith
Advertising Sales Assistant: Jayne Portnoy
Corporate Sales Assistant: Roy Collins
Trainer: Chris Smith
Assistant Trainer: Joe Joe Petrone
Equipment Manager: Frank Pupello
Video Director: Davy Levy
Assistant Video Director: Pat Brazil

Stadium: Tampa Stadium • **Capacity:** 74,296
Tampa, Florida 33607

Playing Surface: Grass

Training Camp: University of Tampa
Tampa, Florida 33606

1993 Schedule

Preseason

Aug. 7	**Denver**	7:30
Aug. 14	at Atlanta	7:30
Aug. 21	vs. Buffalo at Orlando, Fla.	7:00
Aug. 27	**Cleveland**	8:00

Regular Season

Sept. 5	**Kansas City**	1:00
Sept. 12	at New York Giants	1:00
Sept. 19	**Open Date**	
Sept. 26	at Chicago	12:00
Oct. 3	**Detroit**	1:00
Oct. 10	at Minnesota	12:00
Oct. 17	**Open Date**	
Oct. 24	**Green Bay**	1:00
Oct. 31	at Atlanta	1:00
Nov. 7	at Detroit	1:00
Nov. 14	**San Francisco**	1:00
Nov. 21	**Minnesota**	8:00
Nov. 28	at Green Bay	12:00
Dec. 5	**Washington**	1:00
Dec. 12	**Chicago**	1:00
Dec. 19	at Los Angeles Raiders	1:00
Dec. 26	at Denver	2:00
Jan. 2	**San Diego**	4:00

Buccaneers Coaching History

(77-186-1)

1976-84	John McKay	45-91-1
1985-86	Leeman Bennett	4-28-0
1987-90	Ray Perkins*	19-41-0
1990-91	Richard Williamson	4-15-0
1992	Sam Wyche	5-11-0

*Released after 13 games in 1990

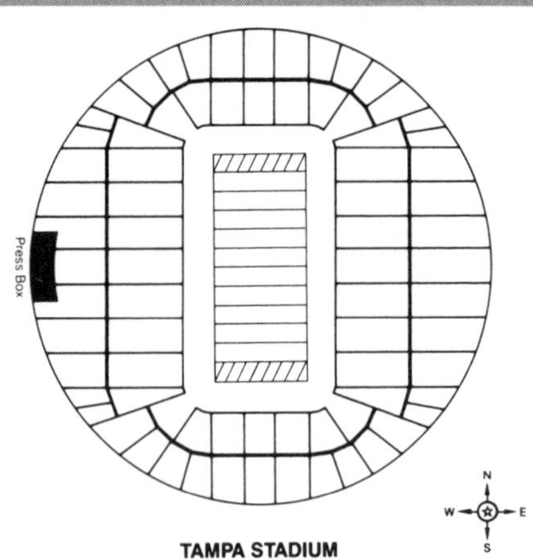

TAMPA STADIUM

Record Holders

Individual Records — Career

Category	Name	Performance
Rushing (Yds.)	James Wilder, 1981-89	5,957
Passing (Yds.)	Vinny Testaverde, 1987-1992	14,820
Passing (TDs)	Vinny Testaverde, 1987-1992	77
Receiving (No.)	James Wilder, 1981-89	430
Receiving (Yds.)	Mark Carrier, 1987-1992	5,018
Interceptions	Cedric Brown, 1977-1984	29
Punting (Avg.)	Frank Garcia, 1983-87	41.1
Punt Return (Avg.)	Willie Drewrey, 1989-1992	9.4
Kickoff Return (Avg.)	Isaac Hagins, 1976-1980	21.9
Field Goals	Donald Igwebuike, 1985-89	94
Touchdowns (Tot.)	James Wilder, 1981-89	46
Points	Donald Igwebuike, 1985-89	416

Individual Records — Single Season

Category	Name	Performance
Rushing (Yds.)	James Wilder, 1984	1,544
Passing (Yds.)	Doug Williams, 1981	3,563
Passing (TDs)	Doug Williams, 1980	20
	Vinny Testaverde, 1989	20
Receiving (No.)	James Wilder, 1984	85
Receiving (Yds.)	Kevin House, 1981	1,176
Interceptions	Cedric Brown, 1981	9
Punting (Avg.)	Larry Swider, 1981	42.7
Punt Return (Avg.)	Willie Drewrey, 1989	11.0
Kickoff Return (Avg.)	Isaac Hagins, 1977	23.5
Field Goals	Steve Christie, 1990	23
Touchdowns (Tot.)	James Wilder, 1984	13
Points	Donald Igwebuike, 1989	99

Individual Records — Single Game

Category	Name	Performance
Rushing (Yds.)	James Wilder, 11-6-83	219
Passing (Yds.)	Doug Williams, 11-16-80	486
Passing (TDs)	Steve DeBerg, 9-13-87	5
Receiving (No.)	James Wilder, 9-15-85	13
Receiving (Yds.)	Mark Carrier, 12-6-87	212
Interceptions	Many times	2
	Last time by Joe King and Milton Mack, 12-27-92	
Field Goals	Many times	4
	Last time by Steve Christie, 12-16-90	4
Touchdowns (Tot.)	Jimmie Giles, 10-20-85	4
Points	Jimmie Giles, 10-20-85	24

1992 Team Record

Preseason (1-3)

Date	Result		Opponents
8/8	L	10-31	at Denver
8/15	W	40-28	Atlanta
8/22	L	7-22	at Miami
8/28	L	3-24	Cleveland

Regular Season (5-11)

Date	Result		Opponents	Att.
9/6	W	23- 7	Phoenix	44,779
9/13	W	31- 3	Green Bay	50,725
9/20	L	20-26	at Minnesota	53,371
9/27	W	27-23	at Detroit	52,779
10/4	L	14-24	Indianapolis	56,229
10/18	L	14-31	at Chicago	65,973
10/25	L	7-38	Detroit	58,649
11/1	L	21-23	at New Orleans	67,601
11/8	L	7-35	Minnesota	51,658
11/15	W	20-17	Chicago	72,607
11/22	L	14-29	at San Diego	40,646
11/29	L	14-19	vs. G.B. at Milw.	54,172
12/6	L	27-31	L.A. Rams	39,056
12/13	L	7-35	Atlanta	42,783
12/19	L	14-21	at San Francisco	65,305
12/27	W	7- 3	at Phoenix	28,790

Score by Periods

Buccaneers	60	107	31	69	0	—	267
Opponents	88	70	112	95	0	—	365

Attendance

Home 416,486 Away 428,637 Total 845,123
Single-game home record, 72,077 (10-8-89)
Single-season home record, 545,980 (1979)

1992 Team Statistics

	Buccaneers	Opp.
Total First Downs	281	296
Rushing	100	100
Passing	165	175
Penalty	16	21
Third Down: Made/Att.	78/210	92/212
Third Down: Pct.	37.1	43.4
Fourth Down: Made/Att.	8/21	7/12
Fourth Down: Pct.	38.1	58.3
Total Net Yards	4771	5185
Avg. Per Game	298.2	324.1
Total Plays	994	985
Avg. Per Play	4.8	5.3
Net Yards Rushing	1706	1675
Avg. Per Game	106.6	104.7
Total Rushes	438	441
Net Yards Passing	3065	3510
Avg. Per Game	191.6	219.4
Sacked/Yards Lost	45/334	36/230
Gross Yards	3399	3740
Att./Completions	511/299	508/293
Completion Pct.	58.5	57.7
Had Intercepted	20	20
Punts/Avg.	74/40.7	64/41.3
Net Punting Avg.	74/36.2	64/36.3
Penalties/Yards Lost	91/754	74/563
Fumbles/Ball Lost	19/9	19/13
Touchdowns	33	43
Rushing	12	15
Passing	17	25
Returns	4	3
Avg. Time of Possession	29:15	30:45

1992 Individual Statistics

Scoring	TD R	TD P	TD Rt	PAT	FG	Saf	TP
Cobb	9	0	0	0/0	0/0	0	54
Willis	0	0	0	20/20	8/14	0	44
Murray	0	0	0	13/13	4/8	0	25
Carrier	0	4	0	0/0	0/0	0	24
Ro. Hall	0	4	0	0/0	0/0	0	24
Drewrey	0	2	0	0/0	0/0	0	12
Hawkins	0	2	0	0/0	0/0	0	12
McDowell	0	2	0	0/0	0/0	0	12
Testaverde	2	0	0	0/0	0/0	0	12
G. Anderson	1	0	0	0/0	0/0	0	6
Armstrong	0	1	0	0/0	0/0	0	6
Dawsey	0	1	0	0/0	0/0	0	6
Dotson	0	0	1	0/0	0/0	0	6
Jennings	0	1	0	0/0	0/0	0	6
Jones	0	0	1	0/0	0/0	0	6
Reynolds	0	0	1	0/0	0/0	0	6
B. Thomas	0	0	1	0/0	0/0	0	6
Buccaneers	12	17	4	33/33	12/22	0	267
Opponents	15	25	3	43/43	20/30	2	365

Passing	Att.	Comp.	Yds.	Pct.	TD	Int.	Tkld.	Rate
Testaverde	358	206	2554	57.4	14	16	35/259	74.2
DeBerg	125	76	710	60.8	3	4	8/66	71.1
Erickson	26	15	121	57.5	0	0	2/9	69.6
Stryzinski	2	2	14	100.0	0	0	0/0	95.8
Buccaneers	511	299	3399	58.5	17	20	45/334	73.3
Opponents	508	293	3740	57.7	25	20	36/230	80.8

Rushing	Att.	Yds.	Avg.	LG	TD
Cobb	310	1171	3.8	25	9
Testaverde	36	197	5.5	18	2
G. Anderson	55	194	3.5	18	1
McDowell	14	81	5.8	23	0
Jennings	5	25	5.0	10	0
Highsmith	8	23	2.9	5	0
Stryzinski	1	7	7.0	7	0
Brooks	5	6	1.2	4	0
DeBerg	3	3	1.0	4	0
Erickson	1	−1	−1.0	−1	0
Buccaneers	438	1706	3.9	25	12
Opponents	441	1675	3.8	55t	15

Receiving	No.	Yds.	Avg.	LG	TD
Dawsey	60	776	12.9	41	1
Carrier	56	692	12.4	40	4
Ro. Hall	39	351	9.0	32	4
G. Anderson	34	284	8.4	34	0
McDowell	27	258	9.6	51t	2
Cobb	21	156	7.4	27	0
Hawkins	20	336	16.8	49	2
Drewrey	16	237	14.8	32	2
Jennings	9	69	7.7	20t	1
Armstrong	7	138	19.7	81t	1
G. Thomas	6	54	9.0	18	0
Highsmith	5	28	5.6	11	0
Brooks	2	−1	−.5	4	0
M. Barber	1	32	32.0	32	0
Fullington	1	12	12.0	12	0
Parker	1	12	12.0	12	0
Moore	1	10	10.0	10	0
Royster	1	8	8.0	8	0
Buccaneers	299	3399	11.4	81t	17
Opponents	293	3740	12.8	83t	25

Interceptions	No.	Yds.	Avg.	LG	TD
Fullington	3	25	8.3	16	0
Carter	3	1	0.3	1	0
Mack	3	0	0.0	0	0
Pollard	2	99	49.5	75	0
B. Thomas	2	81	40.5	56t	1
King	2	24	12.0	24	0
Williams	2	4	2.0	3	0
Reynolds	2	0	0.0	0	0
Lewis	1	0	0.0	0	0
Buccaneers	20	234	11.7	75	1
Opponents	20	211	10.6	46	1

Punting	No.	Yds.	Avg.	In 20	LG
Stryzinski	74	3015	40.7	15	57
Buccaneers	74	3015	40.7	15	57
Opponents	64	2645	41.3	16	60

Punt Returns	No.	FC	Yds.	Avg.	LG	TD
Hawkins	13	8	53	4.1	17	0
Drewrey	7	6	62	8.9	17	0
G. Anderson	6	1	45	7.5	13	0
Buccaneers	26	15	160	6.2	17	0
Opponents	22	26	117	5.3	16	0

Kickoff Returns	No.	Yds.	Avg.	LG	TD
G. Anderson	29	564	19.4	39	0
Brooks	3	49	16.3	24	0
Chamblee	1	9	9.0	9	0
Hawkins	9	118	13.1	18	0
Mayfield	2	22	11.0	15	0
Ryan	2	24	12.0	13	0
G. Thomas	3	72	24.0	37	0
Wilson	1	23	23.0	23	0
Buccaneers	50	881	17.6	39	0
Opponents	49	1236	25.2	89t	1

Sacks	No.
Dotson	10.0
McCants	5.0
Seals	5.0
B. Thomas	5.0
Wheeler	5.0
Carter	2.0
Williams	2.0
Chamblee	1.0
Reynolds	1.0
Buccaneers	36.0
Opponents	45.0

1993 Draft Choices

Round	Name	Pos.	College
1.	Eric Curry	DE	Alabama
2.	Demetrius DuBose	LB	Notre Dame
3.	Lamar Thomas	WR	Miami
	John Lynch	DB	Stanford
4.	Rudy Harris	RB	Clemson
	Horace Copeland	WR	Miami
6.	Chidi Ahanotu	DT	California
7.	Tyree Davis	WR	Central Arkansas
8.	Darrick Branch	WR	Hawaii
	Daron Alcorn	K	Akron

Tampa Bay Buccaneers 1993 Veteran Roster

No.	Name	Pos.	Ht.	Wt.	Birth-date	NFL Exp.	College	Hometown	How Acq.	'92 Games/ Starts
59	Alexander, Elijah	LB	6-2	230	8/8/70	2	Kansas State	Ft. Worth, Tex.	D10-'92	12/0
40	Anderson, Gary	RB	6-1	190	4/18/61	8	Arkansas	Columbia, Mo.	T(SD)-'90	15/4
86	Armstrong, Tyji	TE	6-4	255	10/3/70	2	Mississippi	Inkster, Mich.	D3b-'92	15/7
36	Barber, Chris	CB	6-0	190	1/15/64	3	North Carolina A&T	Winston-Salem, N.C.	FA-'92	3/0*
62	Beckles, Ian	G	6-1	295	7/20/67	4	Indiana	Montreal, Canada	D5-'90	11/7
53	Brady, Ed	LB	6-2	235	6/17/62	10	Illinois	Morris, Ill.	PB(Cin)-'92	16/0
55	Brownlow, Darrick	LB	6-0	235	12/28/68	4	Illinois	Indianapolis, Ind.	FA-'92	16/4
50	Burnette, Reggie	LB	6-2	240	10/4/68	3	Houston	Rayville, La.	PB(GB)-'92	15/2
28	Bussey, Barney	S	6-0	210	5/20/62	9	South Carolina State	Lincolnton, Ga.	UFA(Cin)-'93	16/4*
23	†Carter, Marty	S	6-1	200	12/17/69	3	Middle Tennessee State	La Grange, Ga.	D8-'91	16/16
57	Chamblee, Al	DE	6-1	240	11/17/68	3	Virginia Tech	Virginia Beach, Va.	D12-'91	13/3
15	Claiborne, Robert	WR	5-10	175	7/10/67	2	San Diego State	Spring Valley, Calif.	FA-'93	0*
34	Cobb, Reggie	RB	6-0	215	7/7/68	4	Tennessee	Knoxville, Tenn.	D2-'90	16/13
25	†Covington, Tony	S	5-11	190	12/26/67	2	Virginia	Winston-Salem, N.C.	D4-'91	1/1
80	†Dawsey, Lawrence	WR	6-0	195	11/16/67	3	Florida State	Dothan, Ala.	D3a-'91	15/12
17	DeBerg, Steve	QB	6-3	215	1/19/54	17	San Jose State	Anaheim, Calif.	PB(KC)-'92	6/2
76	Dill, Scott	T	6-5	285	4/5/66	5	Memphis State	Birmingham, Ala.	PB(Phx)-'90	4/3
71	Dotson, Santana	DE	6-5	270	12/19/69	2	Baylor	Houston, Tex.	D5b-'92	16/16
7	Erickson, Craig	QB	6-2	200	5/17/69	2	Miami	West Palm Beach, Fla.	D4-'92	6/2
27	†Fullington, Darrell	S	6-1	200	4/17/64	6	Miami	New Smyrna Beach, Fla.	FA-'91	16/13
20	Gray, Jerry	CB	6-0	185	12/16/62	9	Texas	Lubbock, Tex.	UFA(Hou)-'93	16/16*
60	†Grimes, Randy	C	6-4	275	7/20/60	10	Baylor	Tyler, Tex.	D2-'83	2/0
74	Gruber, Paul	T	6-5	290	2/24/65	6	Wisconsin	Prairie Du Sac, Wis.	D1-'88	16/16
91	†Hall, Rhett	DE-NT	6-2	260	12/5/68	2	California	Morgan Hill, Calif.	D6-'91	4/0
82	Hall, Ron	TE	6-4	245	3/15/64	7	Hawaii	Escondido, Calif.	D4-'87	12/11
85	Hawkins, Courtney	WR-KR	5-9	180	12/12/69	2	Michigan State	Flint, Mich.	D2-'92	16/5
95	Hayes, Eric	DE-NT	6-3	290	11/12/67	3	Florida State	Tampa, Fla.	FA-'93	1/0*
8	Howfield, Ian	K	6-2	195	5/4/66	2	Tennessee	Littleton, Colo.	FA-'93	0*
24	Jones, Roger	CB	5-9	175	4/22/69	3	Tennessee State	Nashville, Tenn.	FA-'92	9/1
41	†King, Joe	S	6-2	200	5/7/68	3	Oklahoma State	Dallas, Tex.	PB(Clev)-'92	14/2
22	Lewis, Garry	CB	5-11	185	8/25/67	4	Alcorn State	New Orleans, La.	T(Dall)-'92	16/2
21	Mack, Milton	CB	5-11	185	9/20/63	7	Alcorn State	Jackson, Miss.	PB(NO)-'92	16/16
61	Mayberry, Tony	C	6-4	290	12/8/67	4	Wake Forest	Springfield, Va.	D4-'90	16/16
78	Mayfield, Corey	DE-NT	6-3	280	2/25/70	2	Oklahoma	Tyler, Tex.	FA-'92	11/0
35	Mayhew, Martin	CB	5-8	175	10/8/65	7	Florida State	Tallahassee, Fla.	UFA(Wash)-'93	10/10*
52	McCants, Keith	DE	6-3	265	4/19/68	4	Alabama	Mobile, Ala.	D1-'90	16/15
37	McDowell, Anthony	RB	5-11	230	11/12/68	2	Texas Tech	Killeen, Tex.	D8a-'92	12/8
73	McHale, Tom	G	6-4	290	2/25/63	7	Cornell	Gaithersburg, Md.	FA-'87	9/3
70	McRae, Charles	T	6-7	300	9/16/68	3	Tennessee	Clinton, Tenn.	D1-'91	16/16
78	Muñoz, Anthony	T	6-6	284	8/19/58	14	Southern California	Ontario, Calif.	UFA(Cin)-'93	7/7*
3	†Murray, Eddie	K	5-11	185	8/29/56	14	Tulane	Victoria, British Columbia	FA-'92	7/0
56	Nickerson, Hardy	LB	6-2	225	9/1/65	8	California	Los Angeles, Calif.	UFA(Pitt)-'93	15/15*
31	Pollard, Darryl	CB	5-11	185	5/11/64	6	Weber State	Colorado Springs, Colo.	FA-'92	16/2
66	Reimers, Bruce	G	6-7	300	9/28/60	10	Iowa State	Humboldt, Iowa	PB(Cin)-'92	16/16
29	Reynolds, Ricky	CB	5-11	190	1/19/65	7	Washington State	Sacramento, Calif.	D2-'87	16/16
64	†Ryan, Tim	G	6-2	280	9/2/68	3	Notre Dame	Kansas City, Mo.	D5b-'91	16/1
98	Seals, Ray	DE	6-3	270	6/17/65	4	No College	Syracuse, N.Y.	FA-'90	11/8
4	Stryzinski, Dan	P	6-1	195	5/15/65	4	Indiana	Indianapolis, Ind.	PB(Pitt)-'92	16/0
67	Sullivan, Mike	G	6-3	290	12/22/67	2	Miami	Chicago, Ill.	FA-'92	9/0
72	Taylor, Rob	T	6-6	290	11/14/60	8	Northwestern	Fairmont, Ohio	FA-'86	9/6
51	Thomas, Broderick	LB	6-4	250	2/20/67	5	Nebraska	Houston, Tex.	D1-'89	16/16
58	†Tiggle, Calvin	LB	6-1	235	11/10/68	3	Georgia Tech	Ft. Washington, Md.	D7-'91	8/4
68	Tomberlin, Pat	G-T	6-2	300	1/29/66	4	Florida State	Jacksonville, Fla.	FA-'93	0*
13	Vlasic, Mark	QB	6-3	205	10/25/63	6	Iowa	Central Township, Pa.	UFA(KC)-'93	0*
77	Wheeler, Mark	NT	6-2	280	4/1/70	2	Texas A&M	San Marcos, Tex.	D3a-'92	16/16
54	#Williams, Jimmy	LB	6-3	220	11/15/60	12	Nebraska	Washington, D.C.	T(Minn)-'92	16/16
84	†Wilson, Charles	WR	5-10	180	7/1/68	3	Memphis State	Tallahassee, Fla.	FA-'92	2/0
19	Wilson, Walter	WR	5-10	185	10/6/66	2	East Carolina	Baltimore, Md.	FA-'93	0*
46	Workman, Vince	RB	5-10	205	5/9/68	5	Ohio State	Dublin, Ohio	RFA(GB)-'93	10/0*

* Barber played 16 games with Cincinnati in '92; Bussey played 16 games with Cincinnati; Claiborne was on San Diego's practice squad; Gray played 16 games with Houston; Hayes played 1 game with L.A. Rams; Howfield last active with Houston in '91; Mayhew played 10 games with Washington; Muñoz played 7 games with Cincinnati; Nickerson played 15 games with Pittsburgh; Tomberlin missed '92 season due to injury; Vlasic active for 16 games with Kansas City but did not play; W. Wilson last active with San Diego in '90; Workman played 10 games with Green Bay.

Unrestricted free agent; subject to developments.

† Restricted free agent; subject to developments.

Players lost through free agency (2): WR Mark Carrier (Clev; 14 games in '92), QB Vinny Testaverde (Clev; 14).

Also played with Buccaneers in '92—CB Darren Anderson (1 game), TE Jesse Anderson (1), WR Mike Barber (2), G Brian Blados (2), RB James Brooks (2), S Joey Browner (7), LB Sidney Coleman (1), WR Willie Culpepper (3), DE-NT Reuben Davis (3), WR Willie Drewrey (9), DE-NT Mark Duckens (5), DE-NT David Grant (2), RB Alonzo Highsmith (5), RB Stanford Jennings (11), LB E.J. Junior (2), WR Jeff Parker (3), DE-NT Reggie Rogers (2), WR George Thomas (5), K Ken Willis (9).

COACHING STAFF

Head Coach, Sam Wyche

Pro Career: Became the Buccaneers' fifth head coach on January 10, 1992, after eight seasons with the Cincinnati Bengals. Led the Bengals to the AFC championship in 1988 and Super Bowl XXIII against the San Francisco 49ers. Played quarterback with the Bengals 1968-70, Washington Redskins 1971-73, Detroit Lions 1974-75, St. Louis Cardinals 1976, and Buffalo Bills 1977. Quarterback coach with the San Francisco 49ers 1979-82. Career record 69-79.

Background: Attended North Fulton High School in Atlanta. Quarterback at Furman University from 1963-65. Assistant coach at South Carolina in 1967. Head coach at Indiana in 1983.

Personal: Born January 5, 1945, in Atlanta, Georgia. Sam and wife, Jane, live in Tampa, and have two children—Zak and Kerry.

Assistant Coaches

Maxie Baughan, linebackers; born August 3, 1938, Forkland, Ala., lives in Tampa. Center-linebacker Georgia Tech 1956-60. Pro linebacker Philadelphia Eagles 1960-65, Los Angeles Rams 1966-70, Washington Redskins 1971, 1974. College coach: Georgia Tech 1972-73, Cornell 1983-88 (head coach). Pro coach: Baltimore Colts 1975-79, Detroit Lions 1980-82, Minnesota Vikings 1990-91, joined Buccaneers in 1992.

Jeff Fitzgerald, defensive assistant; born April 18, 1960, Burbank, Calif., lives in Tampa. No college or pro playing experience. College coach: Cincinnati 1985-86, Alabama 1986-90. Pro coach: Joined Buccaneers in 1990.

Harold Jackson, receivers; born January 6, 1946, Quincy, Miss., lives in Tampa. Wide receiver Jackson State 1964-67. Pro wide receiver Los Angeles Rams 1968, 1973-77, Philadelphia Eagles 1969-72, New England Patriots 1978-81, Seattle Seahawks 1983. Pro coach: New England Patriots 1985-89, joined Buccaneers in 1992.

Ed Khayat, defensive line; born September 14, 1935, Moss Point, Miss., lives in Tampa. Offensive-defensive end Millsaps 1953, Perkinston J.C. 1954, Tulane 1955-56. Pro defensive end-tackle Washington Redskins 1957, 1962-63, Philadelphia Eagles 1958-61, 1964-65, Boston Patriots 1966. Pro coach: New Orleans Saints 1967-70, Philadelphia Eagles 1971-72 (head coach), Detroit Lions 1973-74, 1982-84, Atlanta Falcons 1975-76, Baltimore Colts 1977-81, New England Patriots 1985-89, joined Buccaneers in 1992.

Willie Peete, running backs; born July 14, 1937, Mesa, Ariz., lives in Tampa. Fullback Arizona 1956-59. No pro playing experience. College coach: Arizona 1960-62, 1971-82. Pro coach: Kansas City Chiefs 1983-86, Green Bay Packers 1987-91, joined Buccaneers in 1992.

Floyd Peters, defensive coordinator; born May 21, 1936, Council Bluffs, Iowa; lives in Tampa. Defensive lineman San Francisco State 1954-57. Defensive tackle Baltimore Colts 1958, Cleveland Browns 1959-62, Detroit Lions 1963, Philadelphia Eagles 1964-69, Washington Redskins 1970. Pro coach: Miami Dolphins 1971-73 (scout), New York Giants 1974-75, San Francisco 49ers 1976-77, Detroit Lions 1978-81, St. Louis Cardinals 1982-85, Minnesota Vikings 1986-90, joined Buccaneers in 1991.

Turk Schonert, quarterbacks; born January 15, 1957, Placentia, Calif., lives in Tampa. Quarterback Stanford 1976-79. Pro quarterback Cincinnati Bengals 1981-85, 1988-89, Atlanta Falcons 1986. Pro coach: Joined Buccaneers in 1992.

Steve Shafer, defensive backs, born December 8, 1940, Glendale, Calif., lives in Tampa. Quarterback Utah State 1961-62. No pro playing experience. College coach: College of San Mateo 1968-74, San Diego State 1975-82. Pro coach: Los Angeles Rams 1983-90, joined Buccaneers in 1991.

Tampa Bay Buccaneers 1993 First-Year Roster

Name	Pos.	Ht.	Wt.	Birth-date	College	Hometown	How Acq.
Ahanotu, Chidi	DE-DT	6-2	270	10/11/70	California	Berkeley, Calif.	D6
Alcorn, Daron	K	6-2	240	5/12/71	Akron	Vancouver, Wash.	D8b
Anderson, Darren (1)	CB	5-10	180	1/11/69	Toledo	Cincinnati, Ohio	FA
Bennett, Tracy	K	6-0	180	6/29/68	Mesa State, Colo.	Grand Junction, Colo.	FA
Branch, Darrick	WR	5-11	195	2/10/70	Hawaii	Dallas, Tex.	D8a
Copeland, Horace	WR	6-2	195	1/1/71	Miami	Orlando, Fla.	D4b
Crouch, Jim	K	6-3	180	9/13/68	Cal St.-Sacramento	Sacramento, Calif.	FA
Curry, Eric	DE	6-5	265	2/3/70	Alabama	Thomasville, Ga.	D1
Davis, Tyree	WR	5-9	165	9/23/70	Central Arkansas	Altheimer, Ark.	D7
Doyle, Philip	K	6-0	210	4/20/69	Alabama	Birmingham, Ala.	FA
DuBose, Demetrius	LB	6-1	235	3/23/71	Notre Dame	Seattle, Wash.	D2
Green, Rogerick (1)	CB	5-10	180	12/15/69	Kansas State	San Antonio, Tex.	D5a-'92
Harris, Rudy	RB	6-1	255	9/18/71	Clemson	Brockton, Mass.	D4a
Harrison, Todd (1)	TE	6-4	260	3/20/69	North Carolina State	Gainesville, Fla.	FA
Humphries, Leonard	CB	5-9	175	6/19/70	Penn State	Akron, Ohio	FA
Lynch, John	S	6-1	220	9/25/71	Stanford	Solana Beach, Calif.	D3b
Mayfield, Curtis	WR	5-11	175	3/23/68	Oklahoma State	Dallas, Tex.	FA
McAlister, Scott	P	6-2	210	3/30/69	North Carolina	Greensboro, N.C.	FA
McClendon, Willie	RB	6-0	225	6/11/69	Florida	Jacksonville, Fla.	FA
Moore, Dave (1)	TE	6-2	245	11/11/69	Pittsburgh	Roxbury, N.J.	FA
Pawlawski, Mike (1)	QB	6-1	205	7/18/69	California	Yorba Linda, Calif.	D8b-'92
Royster, Mazio (1)	RB	6-1	205	8/3/70	Southern California	Pomona, Calif.	D11-'92
Thomas, Lamar	WR	6-1	165	2/12/70	Miami	Gainesville, Fla.	D3a

The term NFL Rookie is defined as a player who is in his first season of professional football and has not been on the roster of another professional football team for any regular-season or postseason games. A Rookie is designated by an "R" on NFL rosters. Players who have been active in another professional football league or players who have NFL experience, including either preseason training camp or being on an Active List, Inactive List, Reserve/Injured or Reserve/Physically Unable to Perform for fewer than six regular season games, are termed NFL First-Year Players. An NFL First-Year Player is designated by a "1" on NFL rosters. Thereafter, a player is credited with an additional year of experience for each season in which he accumulates six games on the Active List, Inactive List, Reserve/Injured, or Reserve/Physically Unable to Perform.

NOTES

George Stewart, special teams; born December 29, 1958, Little Rock, Ark., lives in Tampa. Guard Arkansas 1977-80. No pro playing experience. College coach: Minnesota 1984-85, Notre Dame 1986-88. Pro coach: Pittsburgh Steelers 1989-91, joined Buccaneers in 1992.

Richard Wood, defensive assistant, born May 31, 1953, Elizabeth, N.J., lives in Tampa. Linebacker Southern California 1972-74. Pro linebacker New York Jets 1975, Tampa Bay Buccaneers 1976-84. Pro coach: Joined Buccaneers in 1991.

Bob Wylie, offensive line; born February 16, 1951, Providence, R.I., lives in Tampa. Linebacker Colorado 1969-71. No pro playing experience. College coach: Brown 1980-82, Holy Cross 1983-84, Ohio University 1985-87, Colorado State 1988-89. Pro coach: New York Jets 1990-91, joined Buccaneers in 1992.

WASHINGTON REDSKINS

National Football Conference Eastern Division

Team Colors: Burgundy and Gold

Redskin Park, P.O. Box 17247
Washington, D.C. 20041
Telephone: (703) 478-8900

Club Officials

Chairman of the Board-CEO: Jack Kent Cooke
Executive Vice President: John Kent Cooke
Secretary: Stuart Haney
Controller: Gregory Dillon
Board of Directors: Jack Kent Cooke, John Kent Cooke, Ralph Kent Cooke, James Lacher
General Manager: Charley Casserly
Assistant General Manager: Bobby Mitchell
Director of Pro Player Personnel: Kirk Mee
Director of Pro Scouting: Joe Mack
Director of College Scouting: George Saimes
Scouts: Chuck Banker, Gene Bates, Larry Bryan, Scott Cohen, Mike Hagen, Mel Kaufman, Miller McCalmon, Joe Mendes
V.P./Communications: Charlie Dayton
Director of Media Relations: Mike McCall
Director of Information: John Autry
Dir. of Stadium Op./Club Promo.: John Kent Cooke, Jr.
Asst. Promotions/Advertising Dir.: John Wagner
Video Director: Donnie Schoenmann
Asst. Video Director: Hugh McPhillips
Ticket Manager: Sue Barton
Asst. Ticket Mgrs.: Larry Desautels, Tony Lyman
Head Trainer: Bubba Tyer
Assistant Trainers: Al Bellamy, Kevin Bastin
Equipment Manager: Jay Brunetti
Asst. Equipment Manager: Jeff Parsons

Stadium: RFK Stadium • **Capacity:** 56,454
Washington, D.C. 20003

Playing Surface: Grass

Training Camp: Dickinson College
Carlisle, Pennsylvania 17013

1993 Schedule

Preseason

Aug. 9	**Cleveland**	8:00
Aug. 14	at Miami	8:00
Aug. 22	at Pittsburgh	8:00
Aug. 27	**New York Jets**	8:00

Regular Season

Sept. 6	**Dallas** (Monday)	9:00
Sept. 12	**Phoenix**	1:00
Sept. 19	at Philadelphia	1:00
Sept. 26	**Open Date**	
Oct. 4	at Miami (Monday)	9:00
Oct. 10	**New York Giants**	1:00
Oct. 17	at Phoenix	2:00
Oct. 24	**Open Date**	
Nov. 1	at Buffalo (Monday)	9:00
Nov. 7	**Indianapolis**	8:00
Nov. 14	at New York Giants	1:00
Nov. 21	at Los Angeles Rams	1:00
Nov. 28	**Philadelphia**	1:00
Dec. 5	at Tampa Bay	1:00
Dec. 11	**New York Jets** (Saturday)	12:30
Dec. 19	**Atlanta**	1:00
Dec. 26	at Dallas	3:00
Dec. 31	**Minnesota** (Friday)	3:00

Redskins Coaching History

Boston 1932-36 (446-365-26)

1932	Lud Wray	4-4-2
1933-34	William (Lone Star) Dietz	11-11-2
1935	Eddie Casey	2-8-1
1936-42	Ray Flaherty	56-23-3
1943	Arthur (Dutch) Bergman	7-4-1
1944-45	Dudley DeGroot	14-6-1
1946-48	Glen (Turk) Edwards	16-18-1
1949	John Whelchel*	3-3-1
1949-51	Herman Ball**	4-16-0
1951	Dick Todd	5-4-0
1952-53	Earl (Curly) Lambeau	10-13-1
1954-58	Joe Kuharich	26-32-2
1959-60	Mike Nixon	4-18-2
1961-65	Bill McPeak	21-46-3
1966-68	Otto Graham	17-22-3
1969	Vince Lombardi	7-5-2
1970	Bill Austin	6-8-0
1971-77	George Allen	69-35-1
1978-80	Jack Pardee	24-24-0
1981-92	Joe Gibbs	140-65-0

*Released after seven games in 1949
**Released after three games in 1951

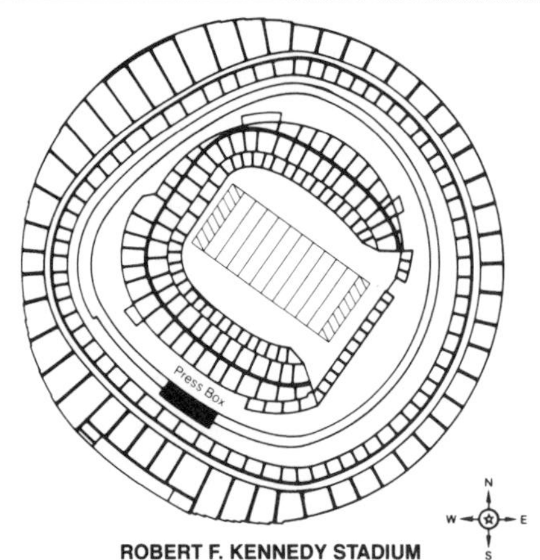

ROBERT F. KENNEDY STADIUM

Record Holders

Individual Records — Career

Category	Name	Performance
Rushing (Yds.)	John Riggins, 1976-79, 1981-85	7,472
Passing (Yds.)	Joe Theismann, 1974-1985	25,206
Passing (TDs)	Sammy Baugh, 1937-1952	187
Receiving (No.)	Art Monk, 1980-1992	*847
Receiving (Yds.)	Art Monk, 1980-1992	11,627
Interceptions	Brig Owens, 1966-1977	36
Punting (Avg.)	Sammy Baugh, 1937-1952	*45.1
Punt Return (Avg.)	Johnny Williams, 1952-53	12.8
Kickoff Return (Avg.)	Bobby Mitchell, 1962-68	28.5
Field Goals	Mark Moseley, 1974-1986	263
Touchdowns (Tot.)	Charley Taylor, 1964-1977	90
Points	Mark Moseley, 1974-1986	1,206

Individual Records — Single Season

Category	Name	Performance
Rushing (Yds.)	John Riggins, 1983	1,347
Passing (Yds.)	Jay Schroeder, 1986	4,109
Passing (TDs)	Sonny Jurgensen, 1967	31
Receiving (No.)	Art Monk, 1984	106
Receiving (Yds.)	Bobby Mitchell, 1963	1,436
Interceptions	Dan Sandifer, 1948	13
Punting (Avg.)	Sammy Baugh, 1940	*51.4
Punt Return (Avg.)	Johnny Williams, 1952	15.3
Kickoff Return (Avg.)	Mike Nelms, 1981	29.7
Field Goals	Mark Moseley, 1983	33
Touchdowns (Tot.)	John Riggins, 1983	*24
Points	Mark Moseley, 1983	161

Individual Records — Single Game

Category	Name	Performance
Rushing (Yds.)	Gerald Riggs, 9-17-89	221
Passing (Yds.)	Sammy Baugh, 10-31-43	446
Passing (TDs)	Sammy Baugh, 10-31-43	6
	Sammy Baugh, 11-23-47	6
	Mark Rypien, 11-10-91	6
Receiving (No.)	Art Monk, 12-15-85	13
	Kelvin Bryant, 12-7-86	13
	Art Monk, 11-4-90	13
Receiving (Yds.)	Anthony Allen, 10-4-87	255
Interceptions	Sammy Baugh, 11-14-43	*4
	Dan Sandifer, 10-31-48	*4
Field Goals	Many times	5
	Last time by Chip Lohmiller, 10-25-92	
Touchdowns (Tot.)	Dick James, 12-17-61	4
	Larry Brown, 12-4-73	4
Points	Dick James, 12-17-61	24
	Larry Brown, 12-4-73	24

*NFL Record

1992 Team Record

Preseason (1-4)

Date	Result		Opponents
8/1	L	21-22	vs. Miami at Orlando
8/8	L	13-14	at N.Y. Jets
8/16	L	15-17	vs. San Francisco at London
8/22	W	27-23	at L.A. Raiders
8/29	L	0-30	Minnesota

Regular Season (9-7)

Date	Result		Opponents	Att.
9/7	L	10-23	at Dallas	62,652
9/13	W	24-17	Atlanta	55,456
9/20	W	13-10	Detroit	55,482
10/4	L	24-27	at Phoenix	37,657
10/12	W	34- 3	Denver	55,455
10/18	W	16-12	Philadelphia	55,454
10/25	W	15-13	at Minnesota	61,801
11/1	L	7-24	N.Y. Giants	55,458
11/8	W	16- 3	at Seattle	64,673
11/15	L	16-35	at Kansas City	76,617
11/23	L	3-20	at New Orleans	67,723
11/29	W	41- 3	Phoenix	55,455
12/6	W	28-10	at N.Y. Giants	76,162
12/13	W	20-17	Dallas	55,455
12/20	L	13-17	at Philadelphia	65,809
12/26	L	20-21	L.A. Raiders	55,460

Postseason (1-1)

Date	Result		Opponent	Att.
1/2	W	24- 7	at Minnesota	57,353
1/9	L	13-20	at San Francisco	64,991

Score by Periods

Redskins	79	92	63	66	0	—	300
Opponents	32	103	40	80	0	—	255

Attendance

Home 443,678 Away 513,094 Total 956,772
Single-game home record, 55,750 (11-10-85)
Single-season home record, 443,678 (1992)

1992 Team Statistics

	Redskins	Opp.
Total First Downs	276	249
Rushing	104	89
Passing	160	138
Penalty	12	22
Third Down: Made/Att.	98/226	72/202
Third Down: Pct.	43.4	35.6
Fourth Down: Made/Att.	8/13	9/19
Fourth Down: Pct.	61.5	47.4
Total Net Yards	4890	4438
Avg. Per Game	305.6	277.4
Total Plays	991	911
Avg. Per Play	4.9	4.9
Net Yards Rushing	1727	1696
Avg. Per Game	107.9	106.0
Total Rushes	483	406
Net Yards Passing	3163	2742
Avg. Per Game	197.7	171.4
Sacked/Yards Lost	23/176	39/279
Gross Yards	3339	3021
Att./Completions	485/272	466/258
Completion Pct.	56.1	55.4
Had Intercepted	17	23
Punts/Avg.	65/39.3	73/42.8
Net Punting Avg.	65/32.7	73/37.2
Penalties/Yards Lost	84/741	85/709
Fumbles/Ball Lost	18/7	23/11
Touchdowns	30	30
Rushing	10	11
Passing	15	15
Returns	5	4
Avg. Time of Possession	31:04	28:56

1992 Individual Statistics

Scoring	TD R	TD P	TD Rt	PAT	FG	Saf	TP
Lohmiller	0	0	0	30/30	30/40	0	120
Byner	6	1	0	0/0	0/0	0	42
Clark	0	5	0	0/0	0/0	0	30
Monk	0	3	0	0/0	0/0	0	18
Orr	0	3	0	0/0	0/0	0	18
Sanders	0	3	0	0/0	0/0	0	18
Ervins	2	0	0	0/0	0/0	0	12
Rypien	2	0	0	0/0	0/0	0	12
Copeland	0	0	1	0/0	0/0	0	6
Edwards	0	0	1	0/0	0/0	0	6
Howard	0	0	1	0/0	0/0	0	6
Marshall	0	0	1	0/0	0/0	0	6
Mitchell	0	0	1	0/0	0/0	0	6
Redskins	10	15	5	30/30	30/40	0	300
Opponents	11	15	4	29/30	14/21	2	255

Passing	Att.	Comp.	Yds.	Pct.	TD	Int.	Tkld.	Rate
Rypien	479	269	3282	56.2	13	17	23/176	71.7
Byner	3	1	41	33.3	1	0	0/0	121.5
Conklin	2	2	16	100.0	1	0	0/0	139.6
Mitchell	1	0	0	0.0	0	0	0/0	39.6
Redskins	485	272	3339	56.1	15	17	23/176	73.2
Opponents	466	258	3021	55.4	15	23	39/279	65.4

Rushing	Att.	Yds.	Avg.	LG	TD
Byner	262	998	3.8	23	6
Ervins	151	495	3.3	25	2
Mitchell	6	70	11.7	33	0
Rypien	36	50	1.4	11	2
R. Green	8	46	5.8	23	0
Monk	6	45	7.5	16	0
Clark	2	18	9.0	12	0
Howard	3	14	4.7	7	0
Goodburn	2	1	0.5	5	0
Conklin	3	−4	−1.3	−1	0
Sanders	4	−6	−1.5	3	0
Redskins	483	1727	3.6	33	10
Opponents	406	1696	4.2	36	11

Receiving	No.	Yds.	Avg.	LG	TD
Clark	64	912	14.3	47	5
Sanders	51	707	13.9	62t	3
Monk	46	644	14.0	49t	3
Byner	39	338	8.7	29	1
Ervins	32	252	7.9	19	0
Orr	22	356	16.2	58	3
Middleton	7	50	7.1	16	0
Warren	4	25	6.3	11	0
Dixon	3	36	12.0	19	0
Mitchell	3	30	10.0	17	0
Howard	3	20	6.7	8	0
R. Green	1	5	5.0	5	0
Redskins	272	3339	12.3	62t	15
Opponents	258	3021	11.7	89t	15

Interceptions	No.	Yds.	Avg.	LG	TD
Edwards	6	157	26.2	53t	1
Mayhew	3	58	19.3	33	0
Gouveia	3	43	14.3	28	0
A. Johnson	3	38	12.7	29	0
Marshall	2	20	10.0	20t	1
Mays	2	18	9.0	13	0
Bowles	1	65	65.0	65	0
A. Collins	1	59	59.0	59	0
D. Green	1	15	15.0	15	0
S. Johnson	1	12	12.0	12	0
Redskins	23	485	21.1	65	2
Opponents	17	318	18.7	49	2

Punting	No.	Yds.	Avg.	In 20	LG
Goodburn	64	2555	39.9	17	66
Redskins	65	2555	39.3	17	66
Opponents	73	3128	42.8	18	58

Punt Returns	No.	FC	Yds.	Avg.	LG	TD
Mitchell	29	9	271	9.3	84t	1
Howard	6	3	84	14.0	55t	1
S. Johnson	1	0	0	0.0	0	0
Thomas	1	0	0	0.0	0	0
Redskins	37	12	355	9.6	84t	2
Opponents	27	13	332	12.3	79t	1

Kickoff Returns	No.	Yds.	Avg.	LG	TD
Mitchell	23	492	21.4	47	0
Howard	22	462	21.0	42	0
Gouveia	1	7	7.0	7	0
R. Green	1	9	9.0	9	0
Orr	1	3	3.0	3	0
Redskins	48	973	20.3	47	0
Opponents	54	1074	19.9	99t	1

Sacks	No.
T. Johnson	6.0
Marshall	6.0
Geathers	5.0
Mann	4.5
Stokes	3.5
Buck	3.0
Coleman	3.0
A. Collins	2.0
Wilson	2.0
S. Collins	1.0
Copeland	1.0
Gouveia	1.0
Mays	1.0
Redskins	39.0
Opponents	23.0

1993 Draft Choices

Round	Name	Pos.	College
1.	Tom Carter	DB	Notre Dame
2.	Reggie Brooks	RB	Notre Dame
3.	Rick Hamilton	LB	Central Florida
	Ed Bunn	P	Texas-El Paso
4.	Sterling Palmer	DE	Florida State
5.	Greg Huntington	C	Penn State
6.	Darryl Morrison	DB	Arizona
	Frank Wycheck	TE	Maryland
8.	Lamont Hollinquest	LB	Southern California

Washington Redskins 1993 Veteran Roster

No.	Name	Pos.	Ht.	Wt.	Birth-date	NFL Exp.	College	Hometown	How Acq.	'92 Games/ Starts
	t-Banks, Carl	LB	6-4	235	8/29/62	10	Michigan State	Washington, D.C.	UFA(NYG)-'93	15/15*
98	Barker, Tony	LB	6-2	230	9/9/68	2	Rice	Wichita, Kan.	D10-'92	8/2
57	†Bingham, Guy	C	6-3	260	2/25/58	14	Montana	Aberdeen, Wash.	FA-'92	15/0
53	Bostic, Jeff	C	6-2	278	9/18/58	14	Clemson	Greensboro, N.C.	FA-'80	4/4
22	†Bowles, Todd	S	6-2	205	11/18/63	8	Temple	Elizabeth, N.J.	FA-'92	16/4
59	Brantley, John	LB	6-3	240	10/23/65	2	Georgia	Wildwood, Fla.	FA-'92	12/2
67	Brown, Ray	T	6-5	280	12/12/62	8	Arkansas State	Marion, Ark.	PB(Phx)-'89	16/8
99	†Buck, Jason	DE	6-4	265	7/27/63	7	Brigham Young	St. Anthony, Idaho	FA-'91	16/5
21	Byner, Earnest	RB	5-10	218	9/15/62	10	East Carolina	Milledgeville, Ga.	T(Clev)-'89	16/16
50	†Caldwell, Ravin	LB	6-3	240	8/4/63	8	Arkansas	Ft. Smith, Ark.	D5-'86	4/0
51	†Coleman, Monte	LB	6-2	245	11/4/57	15	Central Arkansas	Pine Bluff, Ark.	D11-'79	16/14
55	#Collins, Andre	LB	6-1	233	5/4/68	4	Penn State	Cinnaminson, N.J.	D2-'90	14/14
91	Collins, Shane	DE	6-3	267	4/11/69	2	Arizona State	Bozeman, Mont.	D2-'92	16/5
12	Conklin, Cary	QB	6-4	215	2/29/68	2	Washington	Yakima, Wash.	D4-'90	1/0
26	†Copeland, Danny	S	6-2	213	1/24/66	5	Eastern Kentucky	Thomasville, Ga.	PB(KC)-'91	13/13
27	†Edwards, Brad	S	6-2	207	3/22/66	6	South Carolina	Fayetteville, N.C.	PB(Minn)-'90	16/16
25	Eilers, Pat	S	5-11	195	9/3/66	3	Notre Dame	St. Paul, Minn.	FA-'93	1/0*
64	#Elewonibi, Mo	T	6-4	282	12/16/65	4	Brigham Young	British Columbia, Canada	D3-'90	5/4
52	Elliott, Matt	C	6-1	265	10/1/68	2	Michigan	Carmel, Ind.	D12-'92	16/2
32	Ervins, Ricky	RB	5-7	200	12/7/68	3	Southern California	Pasadena, Calif.	D3-'91	16/0
2	†Goodburn, Kelly	P	6-2	199	4/14/62	7	Emporia State	Correctionville, Iowa	FA-'91	16/0
54	Gouveia, Kurt	LB	6-1	228	9/14/64	7	Brigham Young	Honolulu, Hawaii	D8-'86	16/14
90	Graf, Rick	LB	6-5	244	8/29/64	7	Wisconsin	Madison, Wis.	UFA(Hou)-'93	16/16*
28	Green, Darrell	CB	5-8	170	2/15/60	11	Texas A&I	Houston, Tex.	D1-'83	8/7
39	Greene, Robert	RB	5-8	207	9/10/70	2	William & Mary	Ft. Washington, Md.	FA-'92	15/0
29	Gulledge, David	S	6-1	203	10/26/67	2	Jacksonville State	Pell City, Ala.	D11-'91	4/0
6	Hakel, Chris	QB	6-2	230	8/9/69	2	William & Mary	Mechanicsburg, Pa.	D4-'92	0*
34	Hoage, Terry	S	6-2	201	4/11/62	10	Georgia	Huntsville, Tex.	PB(Phil)-'91	16/13
86	Hobbs, Stephen	WR	5-11	200	11/14/65	6	North Alabama	Mendenhall, Miss.	PB(KC)-'89	2/0
80	Howard, Desmond	WR	5-9	183	5/15/70	2	Michigan	Cleveland, Ohio	D1-'92	16/1
66	Jacoby, Joe	G-T	6-6	314	7/6/59	13	Louisville	Louisville, Ky.	FA-'81	13/9
88	Jenkins, James	TE	6-2	234	8/17/67	3	Rutgers	Staten Island, N.Y.	FA-'91	5/1
47	Johnson, AJ	CB	5-8	170	6/22/67	5	Southwest Texas State	San Antonio, Tex.	D6-'89	14/11
45	Johnson, Sidney	CB	5-9	175	3/7/65	6	California	Cerritos, Calif.	FA-'91	8/0
78	†Johnson, Tim	DT	6-3	283	1/29/65	7	Penn State	Sarasota, Fla.	T(Pitt)-'90	16/16
79	Lachey, Jim	T	6-6	294	6/4/63	9	Ohio State	St. Henry, Ohio	T(Raid)-'89	10/10
8	Lohmiller, Chip	K	6-3	210	7/16/66	6	Minnesota	Minneapolis, Minn.	D2-'88	16/0
71	Mann, Charles	DE	6-6	272	4/12/61	11	Nevada-Reno	Sacramento, Calif.	D3-'83	16/16
58	Marshall, Wilber	LB	6-1	231	4/18/62	10	Florida	Titusville, Fla.	FA-'88	16/16
20	Mays, Alvoid	CB	5-9	180	7/10/66	4	West Virginia	Bradenton, Fla.	FA-'90	16/3
85	McGee, Tim	WR	5-10	183	8/7/64	8	Tennessee	Cleveland, Ohio	UFA(Cin)-'93	16/16*
63	McKenzie, Raleigh	C-G	6-2	279	2/8/63	9	Tennessee	Knoxville, Tenn.	D11-'85	16/16
87	Middleton, Ron	TE	6-2	270	7/17/65	8	Auburn	Atmore, Ala.	PB(Clev)-'90	16/12
30	Mitchell, Brian	RB	5-10	209	8/18/68	4	Southwestern Louisiana	Plaquemine, La.	D5-'90	16/0
81	†Monk, Art	WR	6-3	210	12/5/57	14	Syracuse	White Plains, N.Y.	D1-'80	16/14
62	Moore, Darryl	G	6-2	292	1/27/69	2	Texas-El Paso	Minden, La.	D8-'92	0*
97	Noga, Al	DE	6-1	269	9/16/65	6	Hawaii	Honolulu, Hawaii	UFA(Minn)-'93	16/16*
89	Orr, Terry	TE	6-2	235	9/27/61	9	Texas	Savannah, Ga.	FA-'91	16/7
56	Powell, Boone	LB	6-3	237	9/4/68	2	Texas	Duncanville, Tex.	D9-'92	0*
95	Rogers, Ted	LB	6-2	240	11/10/69	2	Williams	Bethesda, Md.	FA-'91	0*
82	Rowe, Ray	TE	6-2	256	7/28/69	2	San Diego State	San Diego, Calif.	D6-'92	3/0
11	Rypien, Mark	QB	6-4	234	10/2/62	7	Washington State	Spokane, Wash.	D6-'86	16/16
83	Sanders, Ricky	WR	5-11	180	8/30/62	8	Southwest Texas State	Temple, Tex.	T(NE)-'86	15/5
69	Schlereth, Mark	G	6-3	283	1/25/66	5	Idaho	Anchorage, Alaska	D10-'89	16/16
74	Siever, Paul	G	6-5	293	8/10/69	2	Penn State	Coatesville, Pa.	D3-'92	0*
76	Simmons, Ed	T	6-5	300	12/31/63	7	Eastern Washington	Seattle, Wash.	D6-'87	16/11
21	Stock, Mark	WR	6-0	185	4/27/66	3	Virginia Military	Canton, Ohio	FA-'92	0*
41	Thomas, Johnny	CB	5-9	191	8/3/64	5	Baylor	Houston, Tex.	FA-'92	16/0
77	#Wahler, Jim	DT	6-4	275	7/29/66	5	UCLA	San Jose, Calif.	FA-'92	5/0
75	†Williams, Eric	DT	6-4	290	2/24/62	10	Washington State	Stockton, Calif.	T(Det)-'90	6/6
94	Wilson, Bobby	DT	6-2	283	3/4/68	3	Michigan State	Chicago, Ill.	D1-'91	5/5

* Banks played 15 games with N.Y. Giants in '92; Eilers played 1 game with Washington; Graf played 16 games with Houston; Hakel, Moore, Powell, Rogers, Siever, and Stock missed '92 season due to injury; McGee played 16 games with Cincinnati; Noga played 16 games with Minnesota.

#Unrestricted free agent; subject to developments.

† Restricted free agent; subject to developments.

Players lost through free agency (4): WR Gary Clark (Phx; 16 games in '92), DT James Geathers (Atl; 16), CB Martin Mayhew (TB; 10), DE Fred Stokes (L.A. Rams; 16).

Also played with Redskins in '92—TE John Brandes (1 game), T Mike Haight (7), WR Carl Harry (1), LB Johnny Meads (2), G Tom Myslinski (1), LB Huey Richardson (4), TE Don Warren (11), CB Mickey Washington (3).

COACHING STAFF

Head Coach, Richie Petitbon

Pro Career: Enters his first season as head coach of the Redskins after serving as Washington's assistant head coach-defense. He has been on the Redskins' coaching staff since 1978, coming to Washington from the Houston Oilers where he coached from 1974-78. Began coaching career in 1974 following successful NFL playing career with the Chicago Bears (1959-67), Los Angeles Rams (1969-70), and Washington Redskins (1971-73). A second-round draft pick by the Bears in 1959, he played 10 seasons in Chicago, starting on the 1963 world championship team. He was traded to the Los Angeles Rams in 1969, playing two seasons before joining the Redskins in 1971. He was a member of the Redskins' 1972 Super Bowl team. He has been a member of every Redskins Super Bowl team (5) as either a player or a coach. As a player, he had 48 career interceptions and made four Pro Bowl appearances.

Background: Petitbon was an all-Southeastern Conference quarterback at Tulane before switching to safety in the NFL. He began his collegiate career at Loyola in New Orleans where he was an outstanding track star, transferring to Tulane after his freshman year.

Personal: Born April 18, 1938, New Orleans, La. Richie and his wife, Beverly, live in Vienna, Va., and have three children—Hope, Richie, and Vicki Leigh.

Assistant Coaches

Jason Arapoff, assistant conditioning; born July 8, 1965, Weymouth, Mass., lives in Centreville, Va. Defensive back Springfield College 1985-88. No pro playing experience. Pro coach: Joined Redskins in 1992.

Don Breaux, running backs; born August 3, 1940, Jennings, La., lives in Centreville, Va. Quarterback McNeese State 1959-61. Pro quarterback Denver Broncos 1963, San Diego Chargers 1964-65. College coach: Florida State 1966-67, Arkansas 1968-71, 1977-80, Florida 1973-74, Texas 1975-76. Pro coach: Joined Redskins in 1981.

Bobby DePaul, administrative assistant-defensive line; born January 29, 1963, Cheverly, Md., lives in Bowie, Md. Linebacker Maryland 1982-83. No pro playing experience. College coach: Catholic University 1986-88. Pro coach: Joined Redskins in 1989.

Rod Dowhower, offensive coordinator; born April 15, 1943, Ord, Neb., lives in Ashburn, Va. Quarterback San Diego State 1963-65. No pro playing experience. College coach: San Diego State 1966-72, UCLA 1974-75, Boise State 1976, Stanford 1977-79 (head coach 1979). Pro coach: St. Louis Cardinals 1973, 1982-84, Denver Broncos 1980-81, Indianapolis Colts 1985-86 (head coach), Atlanta Falcons 1987-89, joined Redskins in 1990.

Jim Hanifan, offensive line; born September 21, 1933, Compton, Calif., lives in Reston, Va. Tight end California 1952-54. Pro tight end Toronto Argonauts (CFL) 1955. College coach: Glendale, Calif., J.C. 1964-66, Utah 1967-70, California 1971-72, San Diego State 1972-73. Pro coach: St. Louis Cardinals 1974-85 (head coach 1980-85), Atlanta Falcons 1987-89 (interim head coach last four games of 1989), joined Redskins in 1990.

Larry Peccatiello, assistant head coach; born December 21, 1935, Newark, N.J., lives in Warrenton, Va. Receiver William & Mary 1955-58. No pro playing experience. College coach: William & Mary 1961-68, Navy 1969-70, Rice 1971. Pro coach: Houston Oilers 1972-75, Seattle Seahawks 1976-80, joined Redskins in 1981.

Dan Riley, conditioning; born October 19, 1949, Syracuse, N.Y., lives in Ashburn, Va. No college or pro playing experience. College coach: Army 1973-76, Penn State 1977-81. Pro coach: Joined Redskins in 1982.

Wayne Sevier, special teams; born July 3, 1941, San Diego, Calif., lives in Broad Run, Va. Quarterback Chaffey, Calif., J.C. 1960, San Diego State 1961-62. No pro playing experience. College coach: California Western 1968-69. Pro coach: St. Louis Cardinals 1974-75, Atlanta Falcons 1976, San Diego Chargers 1979-80, 1987-88, Washington Redskins 1981-86, rejoined Redskins in 1989.

Warren Simmons, offensive line; born February 25, 1942, Poughkeepsie, N.Y., lives in Ashburn, Va. Center San Diego State 1963-65. No pro playing experience. College coach: Cal State-Fullerton 1972-75, Cerritos, Calif., J.C. 1976-80. Pro coach: Joined Redskins in 1981.

Charley Taylor, research and development-receivers; born September 28, 1942, Grand Prairie, Tex., lives in Reston, Va. Running back Arizona State 1961-63. Pro running back-wide receiver Washington Redskins 1964-76. Pro coach: Joined Redskins in 1982.

Emmitt Thomas, defensive coordinator; born June 4, 1943, Angleton,Tex., lives in Reston, Va. Quarterback-wide receiver Bishop (Tex.) College 1963-65. Pro defensive back Kansas City Chiefs 1966-78. College coach: Central Missouri State 1979-80. Pro coach: St. Louis Cardinals 1981-85, joined Redskins in 1986.

LaVern Torgeson, defensive line; born February 28, 1929, LaCrosse, Wash., lives in Fairfax, Va. Center-linebacker Washington State 1948-50. Pro linebacker Detroit Lions 1951-54, Washington Redskins 1955-58. Pro coach: Washington Redskins 1959-61, 1971-77, Pittsburgh Steelers 1962-68, Los Angeles Rams 1969-70, 1978-80, rejoined Redskins in 1981.

Washington Redskins 1993 First-Year Roster

Name	Pos.	Ht.	Wt.	Birth-date	College	Hometown	How Acq.
Brooks, Reggie	RB	5-8	205	1/9/71	Notre Dame	Tulsa, Okla.	D2
Bunn, Ed	P	6-3	195	6/25/68	Texas-El Paso	Alexandria, Va.	D3b
Carter, Tom	CB	5-11	185	9/5/72	Notre Dame	St. Petersburg, Fla.	D1
Clifton, Gregory	WR	5-11	178	2/6/68	Johnson C. Smith	Charlotte, N.C.	FA
Cochrane, Chris (1)	QB	6-3	220	6/6/69	Cornell	Bronxville, N.Y.	FA
Cross, Alan	TE	6-3	235	8/27/70	Iowa	Moline, Ill.	FA
Dillon, Jerry	LB	6-3	227	9/17/69	East Carolina	Lake Placid, Fla.	FA
Dukes, Charles	RB	5-9	190	5/16/70	Boston College	Albany, N.Y.	FA
Earle, Guy	T	6-4	290	4/1/68	Chadron State	Red Bank, N.J.	FA
Fuhler, Tom (1)	C-G	6-4	290	3/4/69	Tennessee	Champaign, Ill.	FA
Hamilton, Rick	LB	6-2	238	4/19/70	Central Florida	Inverness, Fla.	D3a
Harry, Carl (1)	WR	5-9	170	10/27/67	Utah	Fountain Valley, Calif.	FA
Hollinquest, Lamont	LB	6-3	225	10/24/70	Southern California	Downey, Calif.	D8
Huntington, Greg	C	6-3	278	9/22/70	Penn State	Birmingham, Ala.	D5
Jackson, Yonnie	TE	6-2	255	2/28/71	Southern California	Stockton, Calif.	FA
Jordan, Vince	WR	6-2	185	10/9/70	Central Missouri	Boynton Beach, Fla.	FA
LeSure, Michael	WR	6-1	185	10/23/69	Ball State	South Bend, Ind.	FA
Loertscher, Kurt	LB	6-5	230	5/14/70	Washington State	Aberdeen, Wash.	FA
Monior, Greg	RB	6-1	245	12/26/69	North Carolina State	Savannah, Ga.	FA
Morrison, Darryl	S	5-11	185	5/19/71	Arizona	Phoenix, Ariz.	D6a
Orte, Ralph	DT	6-3	275	12/15/69	Maryland	Jersey City, N.J.	FA
Palmer, Sterling	DE	6-5	268	2/4/71	Florida State	Ft. Lauderdale, Fla.	D4
Parsons, Randall	C	6-3	278	11/28/69	North Carolina	Wilkesboro, N.C.	FA
Steele, Derek	DE	6-3	265	12/27/68	Maryland	Newport News, Va.	FA
Wycheck, Frank	TE	6-3	235	10/14/71	Maryland	Philadelphia, Pa.	D6b

The term NFL Rookie is defined as a player who is in his first season of professional football and has not been on the roster of another professional football team for any regular-season or postseason games. A Rookie is designated by an "R" on NFL rosters. Players who have been active in another professional football league or players who have NFL experience, including either preseason training camp or being on an Active List or Inactive List, or on Reserve/Injured or Reserve/Physically Unable to Perform for fewer than six regular-season games, are termed NFL First-Year Players. An NFL First-Year Player is designated by a "1" on NFL rosters. Thereafter, a player is credited with an additional year of experience for each season in which he accumulates six games on the Active List or Inactive List, or on Reserve/Injured or Reserve/Physically Unable to Perform.

NOTES

1992 SEASON IN REVIEW

Trades

1992 Interconference Trades

Wide receiver **Stacey Simmons** from Tampa Bay to the Los Angeles Raiders for past consideration. (6/19)

Wide receiver **Paul Richardson** from the Los Angeles Raiders to Green Bay for past consideration. (6/20)

Tight end **Corwin Anthony** from the New York Jets to Green Bay for a draft choice. (8/4)

Quarterback **Stan Humphries** from Washington to San Diego for a draft choice. (8/13)

Defensive back **David McCloughan** from Indianapolis to Green Bay for a draft choice. (8/19)

Quarterback **Brad Goebel** from Philadelphia to Cleveland for a draft choice. (8/19)

Linebacker **Frank Stams** from the Los Angeles Rams to Cleveland for a draft choice. (8/24)

Guard **Ron Milstead** from Dallas to Cleveland for a draft choice. (8/25)

Linebacker **Kevin Murphy** from Tampa Bay to San Diego for a draft choice. (8/26)

Center **Jay Hilgenberg** from Chicago to Cleveland for a draft choice. (8/28)

Defensive end **Leon Seals** from Buffalo to Philadelphia for a draft choice. (9/1)

Linebacker **Huey Richardson** from Pittsburgh to Washington for a draft choice. (9/2)

Wide receiver **Shawn Collins** from Atlanta to Cleveland for a draft choice. (9/12)

Defensive back **Thomas Everett** from Pittsburgh to Dallas for a draft choice. (9/21)

Wide receiver **Alexander Wright** from Dallas to the Los Angeles Raiders for a draft choice. (10/13)

1993 Interconference Trades

Running back **John Stephens** from New England to Green Bay for a draft choice. (3/31)

Quarterback **Ken O'Brien** from the New York Jets to Green Bay for a draft choice. (4/5)

Defensive back **Jay Taylor** from Phoenix to Kansas City for a draft choice. (4/8)

Defensive back **Alton Montgomery** from Denver to Atlanta for draft choices. (4/13)

Tackle **Leo Goeas** from San Diego to the Los Angeles Rams for a draft choice. (4/15)

Quarterback **Joe Montana,** safety **David Whitmore,** and the 49ers' third-round choice in 1994 from San Francisco to Kansas City for the Chiefs' first-round choice in 1993. (4/22)

Defensive tackle **Jerry Ball** from Detroit to Cleveland for a draft choice. (4/23)

The New York Jets' first-round choice in 1993 to Phoenix for the Cardinals' first-round choice in 1993 and running back **Johnny Johnson.** Phoenix selected running back **Garrison Hearst** (Georgia). New York selected linebacker **Marvin Jones** (Florida State). (4/25)

Philadelphia's compensatory first-round choice in 1993 to Houston for the Oilers' first- and third-round choices in 1993. Houston selected guard **Brad Hopkins** (Illinois). Philadelphia selected tackle **Lester Holmes** (Jackson State) and defensive back **Derrick Frazier** (Texas A&M). (4/25)

The New York Jets' second-round choice in 1993 to Detroit for the Lions' second- and fifth-round choices. Detroit selected defensive back **Ryan McNeil** (Miami). New York selected defensive end **Coleman Rudolph** (Georgia Tech) and running back **Adrian Murrell** (West Virginia). (4/25)

The Los Angeles Raiders' second-round choice in 1993 to San Francisco for the Cowboys' second-round choice and the Saints' third-round choice, each previously obtained by the 49ers. San Francisco subsequently traded Los Angeles's choice to San Diego. The Raiders selected quarterback **Billy Joe Hobert** (Washington) and traded the Saints' third-round choice to Green Bay. (4/25)

The Los Angeles Raiders' second-round choice and San Francisco's third-, fourth-, and fifth-round choices in 1993 to San Diego for the Chargers' second-round choice in 1993 and first-round choice in 1994. San Diego selected running back **Natrone Means** (North Carolina), traded the third-round choice to Tampa Bay, and traded the fourth-round choice to New England. San Francisco selected defensive back **Adrian Hardy** (Northwestern Louisiana). (4/25)

Tackle **Broderick Thompson** from San Diego to Philadelphia for the Eagles' fourth-round choice in 1993. The Chargers traded that choice to Tampa Bay. (4/25)

Tampa Bay's third-round choice in 1993 to San Diego for San Francisco's third-round choice and Philadelphia's fourth-round choice. The Chargers selected guard **Joe Cocozzo** (Michigan). Tampa Bay selected defensive back **John Lynch** (Stanford) and wide receiver **Horace Copeland** (Miami). (4/25)

Indianapolis's third- and fifth-round choices in 1993 to the Los Angeles Rams for the Rams' third-round choice in 1993. The Rams selected running back **Russell White** (California) and guard **Charles Belin** (Wisconsin). The Colts selected defensive back **Ray Buchanan** (Louisville). (4/25)

Green Bay's third-round choice in 1993 to the Los Angeles Raiders for the Raiders' third-round choice in 1993 previously obtained from New Orleans and the Raiders' sixth-round choice in 1993. The Raiders selected defensive back **James Trapp** (Clemson). The Packers selected tackle **Earl Dotson** (Texas A&E) and tackle **Paul Hutchins** (Western Michigan). (4/25)

Green Bay defensive back **Adrian White** to New England for a future choice in 1994. (4/25)

Chicago's fourth-round draft choice in 1993 to Indianapolis for the Colts' fourth-round choice in 1993 and sixth-round choice in 1993 previously obtained from Green Bay. The Bears selected linebacker **Myron Baker** (Louisiana Tech), and traded its sixth-round choice to Green Bay. The Colts selected defensive back **Derwin Gray** (Brigham Young). (4/25)

Defensive back **David McCloughan** from Green Bay to Seattle for the Seahawks' sixth-round choice in 1993. Green Bay selected defensive back **Doug Evans** (Louisiana Tech). (4/26)

1992 AFC Trades

Running back **Bobby Humphrey** from Denver to Miami for running back **Sammie Smith.** (5/26)

1993 AFC Trades

Quarterback **Boomer Esiason** from Cincinnati to the New York Jets for draft choices. (3/17)

Wide receiver **Irving Fryar** from New England to Miami for draft choices. (4/5)

Running back **Gaston Green** from Denver to the Los Angeles Raiders for a draft choice. (4/14)

Cleveland's first-round choice in 1993 to Denver for the Broncos' first-round choice in 1993 and Buffalo's third-round choice in 1993. Denver selected defensive end **Dan Williams** (Toledo). Cleveland selected center **Steve Everitt** (Michigan) and linebacker **Michael Caldwell** (Middle Tennessee State). (4/25)

Indianapolis' second-round choice in 1993 to Pittsburgh for the Steelers' second-round choice and the Chargers' fourth-round choice previously obtained by Pittsburgh. Pittsburgh selected linebacker **Chad Brown** (Colorado). Indianapolis selected running back **Roosevelt Potts** (Northeast Louisiana) and linebacker **Devon McDonald** (Notre Dame). (4/25)

Green Bay's fourth-round choice in 1993 from New England to San Diego for San Francisco's fourth- and fifth-round choices in 1993.

1992 NFC Trades

Wide receiver **Joe Johnson** and defensive tackle **George Hinkle** from Washington to Minnesota for a draft choice. (8/25)

Defensive back **Garry Lewis** from Dallas to Tampa Bay for a draft choice. (8/26)

Defensive end **Charles Haley** from San Francisco to Dallas for a draft choice. (8/27)

Running back **Keith Henderson** from San Francisco to Minnesota for a draft choice. (9/16)

Defensive tackle **Reuben Davis** from Tampa Bay to Phoenix for a draft choice. (10/13)

1993 NFC Trades

Defensive back **Vinnie Clark** from Green Bay to Atlanta for a draft choice. (4/2)

Linebacker **Pat Swilling** from New Orleans to Detroit for the Lions' first- and fourth-round choices in 1993. New Orleans selected tackle **Willie Roaf** (Louisiana Tech) and running back **Lorenzo Neal** (Fresno State). (4/25)

Phoenix's first-round choice in 1993 from San Francisco to New Orleans for the Saints' first- and third-round choices. The Saints selected tight end **Irv Smith** (Notre Dame). The 49ers selected defensive tackle **Dana Stubblefield** (Kansas) and subsequently traded the third-round choice to the Los Angeles Raiders, which traded the choice to Green Bay. (4/25)

Dallas' first- and fourth-round choices in 1993 to Green Bay for the Packers' second-round choice, San Francisco's second-round choice, Atlanta's fourth-round selection, and Green Bay's eighth-round choice. The Packers selected defensive back **George Teague** (Alabama) and traded the eighth-round choice to Chicago. Dallas selected wide receiver **Kevin Williams** (Miami), linebacker **Darrin Smith** (Miami), running back **Derrick Lassic** (Alabama), and defensive back **Reggie Givens** (Penn State). (4/25)

Kansas City's first-round choice in 1993 from San Francisco to Phoenix for the Cardinals' compensatory first-round and their fifth-round choices in 1993. Phoenix selected tackle **Ernest Dye** (South Carolina). The 49ers subsequently traded the Cardinals' first-round choice to the Saints and selected defensive tackle **Artie Smith** (Louisiana Tech) with Phoenix's fifth-round choice. (4/25)

Dallas' fourth-round choice in 1993 from Green Bay to Chicago for the Bears' fifth-round choice and the Packers' sixth-round choice in 1993.

1992 PRESEASON STANDINGS

American Football Conference

Eastern Division

	W	L	T	Pct.	Pts.	OP
N.Y. Jets*	5	0	0	1.000	121	61
Miami***	3	2	0	.600	102	99
Buffalo	2	2	0	.500	60	104
Indianapolis	2	2	0	.500	65	71
New England	1	3	0	.250	57	106

Central Division

	W	L	T	Pct.	Pts.	OP
Houston†	4	1	0	.800	127	79
Pittsburgh	2	2	0	.500	85	81
Cleveland	2	2	0	.500	41	75
Cincinnati	2	2	0	.500	78	57

Western Division

	W	L	T	Pct.	Pts.	OP
San Diego	2	2	0	.500	78	84
Seattle	2	2	0	.500	68	65
Kansas City	1	3	0	.250	58	72
L.A. Raiders	1	3	0	.250	79	96
Denver***	1	4	0	.200	85	92

National Football Conference

Eastern Division

	W	L	T	Pct.	Pts.	OP
Phoenix	3	1	0	.750	86	65
N.Y. Giants	2	2	0	.500	46	58
Dallas†	2	3	0	.400	96	98
Philadelphia*	2	3	0	.400	99	133
Washington**	1	4	0	.200	76	106

Central Division

	W	L	T	Pct.	Pts.	OP
Minnesota	4	0	0	1.000	140	6
Chicago	1	3	0	.250	85	95
Detroit	1	3	0	.250	90	90
Green Bay	1	3	0	.250	51	77
Tampa Bay	1	3	0	.250	60	105

Western Division

	W	L	T	Pct.	Pts.	OP
San Fran.**	5	0	0	1.000	98	63
New Orleans	3	1	0	.750	80	67
L.A. Rams	3	1	0	.750	75	66
Atlanta	1	3	0	.250	69	84

**Includes Hall of Fame Game*
***Includes American Bowl '92 in London*
****Includes American Bowl '92 in Berlin*
†Includes American Bowl '92 in Tokyo

AFC Preseason Results — Team By Team

Eastern Division

BUFFALO (2-2)

3	Minnesota	24
30	*Detroit	24
0	Kansas City	35
27	Atlanta	21
60		104

INDIANAPOLIS (2-2)

34	*New England	14
10	*Seattle	27
0	Cincinnati	20
21	Kansas City	10
65		71

MIAMI (3-2)

22	Washington	21
24	*Dallas	27
31	Denver (ABB)	27
22	*Tampa Bay	7
3	New Orleans	17
102		99

NEW ENGLAND (1-3)

14	Indianapolis	34
10	*San Diego	20
9	Detroit	42
24	Green Bay	10
57		106

N.Y. JETS (5-0)

41	Phil. (HOF)	14
14	*Washington	13
24	Green Bay	7
20	*N.Y. Giants	14
22	Philadelphia	13
121		61

Central Division

CINCINNATI (2-2)

7	N.Y. Giants	13
17	Philadelphia	27
20	*Indianapolis	0
34	*Detroit	17
78		57

CLEVELAND (2-2)

7	*Atlanta	0
7	N.Y. Giants	16
3	*Minnesota	56
24	Tampa Bay	3
41		75

HOUSTON (4-1)

34	Dallas (ABT)	23
17	Detroit	7
17	Dallas	16
33	New Orleans	3
26	L.A. Raiders	30
127		79

PITTSBURGH (2-2)

33	*Philadelphia	35
0	New Orleans	26
28	Chicago	17
24	*N.Y. Giants	3
85		81

Western Division

DENVER (1-4)

7	San Francisco	13
31	*Tampa Bay	10
27	Miami (ABB)	31
3	Dallas	17
17	*Phoenix	21
85		92

KANSAS CITY (1-3)

13	Green Bay	21
0	Minnesota	30
35	*Buffalo	0
10	*Indianapolis	21
58		72

L.A. RAIDERS (1-3)

10	San Francisco	24
16	L.A. Rams	19
23	*Washington	27
30	*Houston	26
79		96

SAN DIEGO (2-2)

14	Phoenix	35
20	New England	10
14	*San Francisco	20
30	*L.A. Rams	19
78		84

SEATTLE (2-2)

7	*L.A. Rams	21
27	Indianapolis	10
17	*Phoenix	10
17	San Francisco	24
68		65

NFC Preseason Results — Team By Team

Eastern Division

DALLAS (2-3)

23	Houston (ABT)	34
27	Miami	24
16	*Houston	17
17	*Denver	3
13	*Chicago	20
96		98

N.Y. GIANTS (2-2)

13	*Cincinnati	7
16	*Cleveland	7
14	N.Y. Jets	20
3	Pittsburgh	24
46		58

PHILADELPHIA (2-3)

14	N.Y. Jets (HOF)	41
35	Pittsburgh	33
27	*Cincinnati	17
10	Atlanta	20
13	*N.Y. Jets	22
99		133

PHOENIX (3-1)

35	*San Diego	14
20	*Chicago	17
10	Seattle	17
21	Denver	17
86		65

WASHINGTON (1-4)

21	Miami	22
13	N.Y. Jets	14
15	San Fran. (ABL)	17
27	L.A. Raiders	23
0	*Minnesota	30
76		106

Central Division

CHICAGO (1-3)

31	*New Orleans	34
17	Phoenix	20
17	*Pittsburgh	28
20	Dallas	13
85		95

DETROIT (1-3)

7	*Houston	17
24	Buffalo	30
42	*New England	9
17	Cincinnati	34
90		90

GREEN BAY (1-3)

21	*Kansas City	13
7	*N.Y. Jets	24
13	L.A. Rams	16
10	*New England	24
51		77

MINNESOTA (4-0)

24	*Buffalo	3
30	*Kansas City	0
56	Cleveland	3
30	Washington	0
140		6

TAMPA BAY (1-3)

10	Denver	31
40	*Atlanta	28
7	Miami	22
3	*Cleveland	24
60		105

Western Division

ATLANTA (1-3)

0	Cleveland	7
28	Tampa Bay	40
20	*Philadelphia	10
21	*Buffalo	27
69		84

L.A. RAMS (3-1)

21	Seattle	7
19	*L.A. Raiders	16
16	*Green Bay	13
19	San Diego	30
75		66

NEW ORLEANS (3-1)

34	Chicago	31
26	*Pittsburgh	0
3	*Houston	33
17	Miami	3
80		67

SAN FRANCISCO (5-0)

13	*Denver	7
24	*L.A. Raiders	10
17	Wash. (ABL)	15
20	San Diego	14
24	*Seattle	17
98		63

**denotes home game*
(OT) denotes overtime
(HOF) denotes Hall of Fame Game
(ABB) denotes American Bowl '92 in Berlin
(ABL) denotes American Bowl '92 in London
(ABT) denotes American Bowl '92 in Tokyo

1992 NFL STANDINGS

American Football Conference

Eastern Division

	W	L	T	Pct.	Pts.	OP
Miami	11	5	0	.688	340	281
Buffalo*	11	5	0	.688	381	283
Indianapolis	9	7	0	.563	216	302
N.Y. Jets	4	12	0	.250	220	315
New England	2	14	0	.125	205	363

Central Division

	W	L	T	Pct.	Pts.	OP
Pittsburgh	11	5	0	.688	299	225
Houston*	10	6	0	.625	352	258
Cleveland	7	9	0	.438	272	275
Cincinnati	5	11	0	.313	274	364

Western Division

	W	L	T	Pct.	Pts.	OP
San Diego	11	5	0	.688	335	241
Kansas City*	10	6	0	.625	348	282
Denver	8	8	0	.500	262	329
L.A. Raiders	7	9	0	.438	249	281
Seattle	2	14	0	.125	140	312

National Football Conference

Eastern Division

	W	L	T	Pct.	Pts.	OP
Dallas	13	3	0	.813	409	243
Philadelphia*	11	5	0	.688	354	245
Washington*	9	7	0	.563	300	255
N.Y. Giants	6	10	0	.375	306	367
Phoenix	4	12	0	.250	243	332

Central Division

	W	L	T	Pct.	Pts.	OP
Minnesota	11	5	0	.688	374	249
Green Bay	9	7	0	.563	276	296
Tampa Bay	5	11	0	.313	267	365
Chicago	5	11	0	.313	295	361
Detroit	5	11	0	.313	273	332

Western Division

	W	L	T	Pct.	Pts.	OP
San Francisco	14	2	0	.875	431	236
New Orleans*	12	4	0	.750	330	202
Atlanta	6	10	0	.375	327	414
L.A. Rams	6	10	0	.375	313	383

**Wild Card Team*

Miami finished ahead of Buffalo based on better conference record (9-3 to 7-5). Tampa Bay finished ahead of Chicago and Detroit based on better conference record (5-9 to Bears' 4-8 and Lions' 3-9). Atlanta finished ahead of L.A. Rams based on better record versus common opponents (5-7 to 4-8).

Wild Card Playoffs

AFC .... San Diego 17, Kansas City 0, January 2, at San Diego
Buffalo 41, Houston 38 (OT), January 3, at Buffalo

NFC .... Washington 24, Minnesota 7, January 2, at Minneapolis
Philadelphia 36, New Orleans 20, January 3, at New Orleans

Divisional Playoffs

AFC .... Buffalo 24, Pittsburgh 3, January 9, at Pittsburgh
Miami 31, San Diego 0, January 10, at Miami

NFC .... San Francisco 20, Washington 13, January 9, at San Francisco
Dallas 34, Philadelphia 10, January 10, at Dallas

Championship Games

AFC .... Buffalo 29, Miami 10, January 17, at Miami

NFC .... Dallas 30, San Francisco 20, January 17, at San Francisco

SUPER BOWL XXVII .... Dallas 52, Buffalo 17, January 31, at Rose Bowl, Pasadena, California

AFC-NFC PRO BOWL .... AFC 23, NFC 20 (OT), February 7, at Aloha Stadium, Honolulu, Hawaii

AFC Season Records — Team by Team

BUFFALO (11-5)

40	*L.A. Rams	7
34	at San Francisco	31
38	*Indianapolis	0
41	at New England	7
10	*Miami	37
3	at L.A. Raiders	20
	OPEN DATE	
24	at N.Y. Jets	20
16	*New England	7
28	*Pittsburgh	20
26	at Miami	20
41	*Atlanta	14
13	at Ind. (OT)	16
17	*N.Y. Jets	24
27	*Denver	17
20	at New Orleans	16
3	at Houston	27
381		283

CINCINNATI (5-11)

21	at Seattle	3
24	*L.A. Raiders (OT)	21
23	at Green Bay	24
7	*Minnesota	42
	OPEN DATE	
24	*Houston	38
0	at Pittsburgh	20
10	at Houston	26
30	*Cleveland	10
31	at Chicago (OT)	28
14	at N.Y. Jets	17
13	*Detroit	19
9	*Pittsburgh	21
21	at Cleveland	37
10	at San Diego	27
20	*New England	10
17	*Indianapolis	21
274		364

CLEVELAND (7-9)

3	at Indianapolis	14
23	*Miami	27
28	at L.A. Raiders	16
0	*Denver	12
	OPEN DATE	
17	*Pittsburgh	9
17	*Green Bay	6
19	at New England	17
10	at Cincinnati	30
24	at Houston	14
13	*San Diego	14
13	at Minnesota	17
27	*Chicago	14
37	*Cincinnati	21
14	at Detroit	24
14	*Houston	17
13	at Pittsburgh	23
272		275

DENVER (8-8)

17	*L.A. Raiders	13
21	*San Diego	13
0	at Philadelphia	30
12	at Cleveland	0
20	*Kansas City	19
3	at Washington	34
27	*Houston	21
21	at San Diego	24
	OPEN DATE	
27	*N.Y. Jets	16
27	*N.Y. Giants	13
0	at L.A. Raiders	24
13	at Seattle (OT)	16
27	*Dallas	31
17	at Buffalo	27
10	*Seattle	6
20	at Kansas City	42
262		329

HOUSTON (10-6)

24	*Pittsburgh	29
20	at Indianapolis	10
23	*Kansas City (OT)	20
27	*San Diego	0
	OPEN DATE	
38	at Cincinnati	24
21	at Denver	27
26	*Cincinnati	10
20	at Pittsburgh	21
14	*Cleveland	24
17	at Minnesota	13
16	at Miami	19
24	at Detroit	21
24	*Chicago	7
14	*Green Bay	16
17	at Cleveland	14
27	*Buffalo	3
352		258

INDIANAPOLIS (9-7)

14	*Cleveland	3
10	*Houston	20
0	at Buffalo	38
	OPEN DATE	
24	at Tampa Bay	14
6	*N.Y. Jets (OT)	3
14	*San Diego	34
31	at Miami	20
0	at San Diego	26
0	*Miami	28
34	*New Eng. (OT)	37
14	at Pittsburgh	30
16	*Buffalo (OT)	13
6	at New England	0
10	at N.Y. Jets	6
16	*Phoenix	13
21	at Cincinnati	17
216		302

KANSAS CITY (10-6)

24	at San Diego	10
26	*Seattle	7
20	at Houston (OT)	23
27	*L.A. Raiders	7
19	at Denver	20
24	*Philadelphia	17
10	at Dallas	17
3	*Pittsburgh	27
	OPEN DATE	
16	*San Diego	14
35	*Washington	16
24	at Seattle	14
23	at N.Y. Jets	7
7	at L.A. Raiders	28
27	*New England	20
21	at N.Y. Giants	35
42	*Denver	20
348		282

L.A. RAIDERS (7-9)

13	at Denver	17
21	at Cincinnati (OT)	24
16	*Cleveland	28
7	at Kansas City	27
13	*N.Y. Giants	10
20	*Buffalo	3
19	at Seattle	0
13	*Dallas	28
	OPEN DATE	
10	at Philadelphia	31
20	*Seattle	3
24	*Denver	0
3	at San Diego	27
28	*Kansas City	7
7	at Miami	20
14	*San Diego	36
21	at Washington	20
249		281

MIAMI (11-5)

	OPEN DATE	
27	at Cleveland	23
26	*L.A. Rams	10
19	at Seattle	17
37	at Buffalo	10
21	*Atlanta	17
38	*New England	17
20	*Indianapolis	31
14	at N.Y. Jets	26
28	at Indianapolis	0
20	*Buffalo	26
19	*Houston	16
13	at New Orleans	24
3	at San Francisco	27
20	*L.A. Raiders	7
19	*N.Y. Jets	17
16	at New Eng. (OT)	13
340		281

NEW ENGLAND (2-14)

	OPEN DATE	
0	at L.A. Rams	14
6	*Seattle	10
7	*Buffalo	41
21	at N.Y. Jets	30
12	*San Francisco	24
17	at Miami	38
17	*Cleveland	19
7	at Buffalo	16
14	*New Orleans	31
37	at Ind. (OT)	34
24	*N.Y. Jets	3
0	at Atlanta	34
0	*Indianapolis	6
20	at Kansas City	27
10	at Cincinnati	20
13	*Miami (OT)	16
205		363

N.Y. JETS (4-12)

17	at Atlanta	20
10	at Pittsburgh	27
14	*San Francisco	31
10	at L.A. Rams	18
30	*New England	21
3	at Ind. (OT)	6
	OPEN DATE	
20	*Buffalo	24
26	*Miami	14
16	at Denver	27
17	*Cincinnati	14
3	at New England	24
7	*Kansas City	23
24	at Buffalo	17
6	*Indianapolis	10
17	at Miami	19
0	*New Orleans	20
220		315

PITTSBURGH (11-5)

29	at Houston	24
27	*N.Y. Jets	10
23	at San Diego	6
3	at Green Bay	17
	OPEN DATE	
9	at Cleveland	17
20	*Cincinnati	0
27	at Kansas City	3
21	*Houston	20
20	at Buffalo	28
17	*Detroit	14
30	*Indianapolis	14
21	at Cincinnati	9
20	*Seattle	14
6	at Chicago	30
3	*Minnesota	6
23	*Cleveland	13
299		225

SAN DIEGO (11-5)

10	*Kansas City	24
13	at Denver	21
6	*Pittsburgh	23
0	at Houston	27
17	*Seattle	6
	OPEN DATE	
34	at Indianapolis	14
24	*Denver	21
26	*Indianapolis	0
14	at Kansas City	16
14	at Cleveland	13
29	*Tampa Bay	14
27	*L.A. Raiders	3
27	at Phoenix	21
27	*Cincinnati	10
36	at L.A. Raiders	14
31	at Seattle	14
335		241

SEATTLE (2-14)

3	*Cincinnati	21
7	at Kansas City	26
10	at New England	6
17	*Miami	19
6	at San Diego	17
0	at Dallas	27
0	*L.A. Raiders	19
10	at N.Y. Giants	23
	OPEN DATE	
3	*Washington	16
3	at L.A. Raiders	20
14	*Kansas City	24
16	*Denver (OT)	13
14	at Pittsburgh	20
17	*Philadelphia (OT)	20
6	at Denver	10
14	*San Diego	31
140		312

NFC Season Records — Team by Team

ATLANTA (6-10)

20	*N.Y. Jets	17
17	at Washington	24
7	*New Orleans	10
31	at Chicago	41
24	*Green Bay	10
17	at Miami	21
17	at San Francisco	56
	OPEN DATE	
30	*L.A. Rams	28
3	*San Francisco	41
20	*Phoenix	17
14	at Buffalo	41
34	*New England	0
14	at New Orleans	22
35	at Tampa Bay	7
17	*Dallas	41
27	at L.A. Rams	38
327		414

CHICAGO (5-11)

27	*Detroit	24
6	at New Orleans	28
14	*N.Y. Giants	27
41	*Atlanta	31
20	at Minnesota	21
	OPEN DATE	
31	*Tampa Bay	14
30	at Green Bay	10
10	*Minnesota	38
28	*Cincinnati (OT)	31
17	at Tampa Bay	20
3	*Green Bay	17
14	at Cleveland	27
7	at Houston	24
30	*Pittsburgh	6
3	at Detroit	16
14	at Dallas	27
295		361

DALLAS (13-3)

23	*Washington	10
34	at N.Y. Giants	28
31	*Phoenix	20
	OPEN DATE	
7	at Philadelphia	31
27	*Seattle	0
17	*Kansas City	10
28	at L.A. Raiders	13
20	*Philadelphia	10
37	at Detroit	3
23	*L.A. Rams	27
16	at Phoenix	10
30	*N.Y. Giants	3
31	at Denver	27
17	at Washington	20
41	at Atlanta	17
27	*Chicago	14
409		243

DETROIT (5-11)

24	at Chicago	27
31	*Minnesota	17
10	at Washington	13
23	*Tampa Bay	27
7	*New Orleans	13
	OPEN DATE	
14	at Minnesota	31
38	at Tampa Bay	7
13	*Green Bay	27
3	*Dallas	37
14	at Pittsburgh	17
19	at Cincinnati	13
21	*Houston	24
10	at Green Bay	38
24	*Cleveland	14
16	*Chicago	3
6	at San Francisco	24
273		332

GREEN BAY (9-7)

20	*Minnesota (OT)	23
3	at Tampa Bay	31
24	*Cincinnati	23
17	*Pittsburgh	3
10	at Atlanta	24
	OPEN DATE	
6	at Cleveland	17
10	*Chicago	30
27	at Detroit	13
7	at N.Y. Giants	27
27	*Philadelphia	24
17	at Chicago	3
19	*Tampa Bay	14
38	*Detroit	10
16	at Houston	14
28	*L.A. Rams	13
7	at Minnesota	27
276		296

L.A. RAMS (6-10)

7	at Buffalo	40
14	*New England	0
10	at Miami	26
18	*N.Y. Jets	10
24	at San Francisco	27
10	at New Orleans	13
38	*N.Y. Giants	17
	OPEN DATE	
28	at Atlanta	30
14	*Phoenix	20
27	at Dallas	23
10	*San Francisco	27
17	*Minnesota	31
31	at Tampa Bay	27
14	*New Orleans	37
13	at Green Bay	28
38	*Atlanta	27
313		383

MINNESOTA (11-5)

23	at Green Bay (OT)	20
17	at Detroit	31
26	*Tampa Bay	20
42	at Cincinnati	7
21	*Chicago	20
	OPEN DATE	
31	*Detroit	14
13	*Washington	15
38	at Chicago	10
35	at Tampa Bay	7
13	*Houston	17
17	*Cleveland	13
31	at L.A. Rams	17
17	at Philadelphia	28
17	*San Francisco	20
6	at Pittsburgh	3
27	*Green Bay	7
374		249

NEW ORLEANS (12-4)

13	at Philadelphia	15
28	*Chicago	6
10	at Atlanta	7
10	*San Francisco	16
13	at Detroit	7
13	*L.A. Rams	10
30	at Phoenix	21
	OPEN DATE	
23	*Tampa Bay	21
31	at New England	14
20	at San Francisco	21
20	*Washington	3
24	*Miami	13
22	*Atlanta	14
37	at L.A. Rams	14
16	*Buffalo	20
20	at N.Y. Jets	0
330		202

N.Y. GIANTS (6-10)

14	*San Francisco	31
28	*Dallas	34
27	at Chicago	14
	OPEN DATE	
10	at L.A. Raiders	13
31	*Phoenix	21
17	at L.A. Rams	38
23	*Seattle	10
24	at Washington	7
27	*Green Bay	7
13	at Denver	27
34	*Philadelphia	47
3	at Dallas	30
10	*Washington	28
0	at Phoenix	19
35	*Kansas City	21
10	at Philadelphia	20
306		367

PHILADELPHIA (11-5)

15	*New Orleans	13
31	at Phoenix	14
30	*Denver	0
	OPEN DATE	
31	*Dallas	7
17	at Kansas City	24
12	at Washington	16
7	*Phoenix	3
10	at Dallas	20
31	*L.A. Raiders	10
24	at Green Bay	27
47	at N.Y. Giants	34
14	at San Francisco	20
28	*Minnesota	17
20	at Seattle (OT)	17
17	*Washington	13
20	*N.Y. Giants	10
354		245

PHOENIX (4-12)

7	at Tampa Bay	23
14	*Philadelphia	31
20	at Dallas	31
	OPEN DATE	
27	*Washington	24
21	at N.Y. Giants	31
21	*New Orleans	30
3	at Philadelphia	7
24	*San Francisco	14
20	at L.A. Rams	14
17	at Atlanta	20
10	*Dallas	16
3	at Washington	41
21	*San Diego	27
19	*N.Y. Giants	0
13	at Indianapolis	16
3	*Tampa Bay	7
243		332

SAN FRANCISCO (14-2)

31	at N.Y. Giants	14
31	*Buffalo	34
31	at N.Y. Jets	14
16	at New Orleans	10
27	*L.A. Rams	24
24	at New England	12
56	*Atlanta	17
	OPEN DATE	
14	at Phoenix	24
41	at Atlanta	3
21	*New Orleans	20
27	at L.A. Rams	10
20	*Philadelphia	14
27	*Miami	3
20	at Minnesota	17
21	*Tampa Bay	14
24	*Detroit	6
431		236

TAMPA BAY (5-11)

23	*Phoenix	7
31	*Green Bay	3
20	at Minnesota	26
27	at Detroit	23
14	*Indianapolis	24
	OPEN DATE	
14	at Chicago	31
7	*Detroit	38
21	at New Orleans	23
7	*Minnesota	35
20	*Chicago	17
14	at San Diego	29
14	at Green Bay	19
27	*L.A. Rams	31
7	*Atlanta	35
14	at San Francisco	21
7	at Phoenix	3
267		365

WASHINGTON (9-7)

10	at Dallas	23
24	*Atlanta	17
13	*Detroit	10
	OPEN DATE	
24	at Phoenix	27
34	*Denver	3
16	*Philadelphia	12
15	at Minnesota	13
7	*N.Y. Giants	24
16	at Seattle	3
16	at Kansas City	35
3	at New Orleans	20
41	*Phoenix	3
28	at N.Y. Giants	10
20	*Dallas	17
13	at Philadelphia	17
20	*L.A. Raiders	21
300		255

** denotes home game*
(OT) denotes overtime

Attendance figures as they appear in the following, and in the club-by-club sections starting on page 26, are turnstile counts and not paid attendance. Paid attendance totals are on page 210.

First Week Summaries

Standings

American Football Conference

Eastern Division

	W	L	T	Pct.	Pts.	OP
Buffalo	1	0	0	1.000	40	7
Indianapolis	1	0	0	1.000	14	3
Miami	0	0	0	.000	0	0
New England	0	0	0	.000	0	0
N.Y. Jets	0	1	0	.000	17	20
Central Division						
Pittsburgh	1	0	0	1.000	29	24
Cincinnati	1	0	0	1.000	21	3
Cleveland	0	1	0	.000	3	14
Houston	0	1	0	.000	24	29
Western Division						
Denver	1	0	0	1.000	17	13
Kansas City	1	0	0	1.000	24	10
L.A. Raiders	0	1	0	.000	13	17
San Diego	0	1	0	.000	10	24
Seattle	0	1	0	.000	3	21

National Football Conference

Eastern Division

	W	L	T	Pct.	Pts.	OP
Dallas	1	0	0	1.000	23	10
Philadelphia	1	0	0	1.000	15	13
N.Y. Giants	0	1	0	.000	14	31
Phoenix	0	1	0	.000	7	23
Washington	0	1	0	.000	10	23
Central Division						
Chicago	1	0	0	1.000	27	24
Minnesota	1	0	0	1.000	23	20
Tampa Bay	1	0	0	1.000	23	7
Detroit	0	1	0	.000	24	27
Green Bay	0	1	0	.000	20	23
Western Division						
Atlanta	1	0	0	1.000	20	17
San Francisco	1	0	0	1.000	31	14
L.A. Rams	0	1	0	.000	7	40
New Orleans	0	1	0	.000	13	15

Sunday, September 6

Cincinnati 21, Seattle 3—at Kingdome, attendance 65,851. Linebacker Ray Bentley and safety Fernandus Vinson each returned fumbles for touchdowns to help give 33-year-old Dave Shula a victory in his first game as head coach. Seattle led 3-0 in the second quarter until wide receiver Doug Thomas fumbled when hit by Bengals linebacker James Francis. Bentley, a Plan B free agent playing in his first game with the Bengals, picked up the loose ball and ran 75 yards for the only points Cincinnati would need. The Bengals put the game away with 2 touchdowns in a span of 3:15 of the fourth quarter, the final score coming on Vinson's 22-yard fumble return with 8:17 left. Cincinnati's Harold Green mustered most of the day's offense, rushing for 123 yards on 21 carries and catching 5 passes for 18 yards.

Cincinnati	0	7	0	14	—	21
Seattle	3	0	0	0	—	3

Sea — FG Kasay 40
Cin — Bentley 75 fumble recovery return (Breech kick)
Cin — Ball 1 run (Breech kick)
Cin — Vinson 22 fumble recovery return (Breech kick)

Indianapolis 14, Cleveland 3—at Hoosier Dome, attendance 50,766. Linebacker Chip Banks had 4 sacks as a relentless defense lifted the Colts to their first season-opening victory since 1983. Quentin Coryatt, the second overall pick in the 1992 draft, added 2 sacks and Steve Emtman, the top pick, had 1 as Indianapolis tied a club record by dropping Browns quarterback Bernie Kosar 11 times. The Colts only had 29 sacks the entire 1991 season. Aided by 72 yards in losses on sacks, Indianapolis limited Cleveland to only 13 first downs and 145 total yards.

Cleveland	0	0	3	0	—	3
Indianapolis	7	0	7	0	—	14

Ind — Culver 1 run (Biasucci kick)
Cleve — FG Stover 20
Ind — Langhorne 26 pass from Herrmann (Biasucci kick)

Chicago 27, Detroit 24—at Soldier Field, attendance 63,672. Jim Harbaugh's 6-yard, fourth-down touchdown pass to Tom Waddle with one second left capped a wild fourth quarter and gave the Bears their ninth consecutive opening-day victory. The score was tied 10-10 when the fourth-quarter dramatics started. The Lions' Barry Sanders, apparently stopped after a short gain, gave his team the lead when he broke free and scored on a 43-yard run with 9:56 left. The Bears countered with Kevin Butler's 38-yard field goal and Neal Anderson's 18-yard touchdown run with 2:55 to go for a 20-17 advantage. But Detroit quarterback Rodney Peete, who passed for 273 yards and 2 touchdowns, drove the Lions 80 yards in four plays, passing 27 yards to Willie Green to make it 24-20 with 1:02 to go. The Bears rallied by marching 74 yards in 9 plays to the winning touchdown. Harbaugh passed for 227 yards and 2 touchdowns and had a key 14-yard scramble on the final drive. Sanders led all rushers with 109 yards on 19 carries.

Detroit	0	10	0	14	—	24
Chicago	7	3	0	17	—	27

Chi — Anderson 11 pass from Harbaugh (Butler kick)
Chi — FG Butler 34
Det — Perriman 40 pass from Peete (Hanson kick)
Det — FG Hanson 38
Det — Sanders 43 run (Hanson kick)
Chi — FG Butler 38
Chi — Anderson 18 run (Butler kick)
Det — W. Green 27 pass from Peete (Hanson kick)
Chi — Waddle 6 pass from Harbaugh (Butler kick)

Kansas City 24, San Diego 10—at Jack Murphy Stadium, attendance 45,024. Rookie cornerback Dale Carter raced 46 yards for a touchdown on his first NFL punt return and also intercepted a pass as the Chiefs beat San Diego for the fifth consecutive time. Carter's punt return came just 1:39 into the game, and gave Kansas City a quick 7-0 advantage. But neither team could generate much offense, and the Chiefs led just 10-3 until late in the third quarter. The Chargers drove to the Kansas City 18-yard line before Chiefs cornerback Kevin Ross intercepted a tipped pass from Bob Gagliano at the 1-yard line and raced 99 yards down the left sideline to make it 17-3. The defenses for both teams dominated the game, as Kansas City managed only 188 total yards and San Diego just 155.

Kansas City	7	3	7	7	—	24
San Diego	3	0	0	7	—	10

KC — Carter 46 punt return (Lowery kick)
SD — FG Carney 45
KC — FG Lowery 21
KC — Ross 99 interception return (Lowery kick)
SD — Bernstine 2 run (Carney kick)
KC — Word 1 run (Lowery kick)

Buffalo 40, L.A. Rams 7—at Rich Stadium, attendance 79,001. Running back Thurman Thomas scored 4 touchdowns and wide receiver James Lofton became the NFL's career leader in receiving yards during the Bills' rout. Thomas, who scored on touchdown runs of 10, 6, and 1 yard and caught a 10-yard pass for another touchdown, ran for 103 yards and totaled 136 yards from scrimmage. His third touchdown came early in the second quarter to give Buffalo a 21-0 lead, and the Bills never were seriously threatened. Defensive backs Henry Jones and Nate Odomes each intercepted 2 passes to help keep the game out of reach and spoil Chuck Knox's debut in his second tenure as Rams head coach. Lofton entered the game needing 55 yards to break former Seahawks star Steve Largent's NFL record of 13,089 career receiving yards. He broke the record on his sixth and final catch of the day, a 6-yard reception midway through the fourth quarter, and finished the day at 13,091 yards.

L.A. Rams	0	7	0	0	—	7
Buffalo	14	13	7	6	—	40

Buff — Thomas 10 pass from Kelly (Christie kick)
Buff — Thomas 1 run (Christie kick)
Buff — Thomas 6 run (Christie kick)
Rams — Delpino 12 pass from Everett (Zendejas kick)
Buff — Frerotte 2 pass from Kelly (kick failed)
Buff — Thomas 10 run (Christie kick)
Buff — FG Christie 49
Buff — FG Christie 38

Minnesota 23, Green Bay 20—at Lambeau Field, attendance 58,617. Terry Allen's 45-yard run positioned Fuad Reveiz for his game-winning 25-yard field goal with 4:40 remaining in overtime. The Packers had forced the extra period on Chris Jacke's 24-yard field goal with 1:57 left in regulation. Allen, who also had a 51-yard run to set up the Vikings' go-ahead touchdown in the fourth quarter but fumbled following a 17-yard gain earlier in overtime, finished with 140 yards on only 12 carries. Minnesota quarterback Rich Gannon passed for 266 yards as the Vikings amassed 425 total yards. Don Majkowski completed 27 of 38 passes for 189 yards and running back Vince Workman had 89 rushing yards and caught 12 passes for Green Bay. The game marked the head-coaching debuts of the Vikings' Dennis Green and the Packers' Mike Holmgren.

Minnesota	0	10	3	7	3	—	23
Green Bay	7	3	0	10	0	—	20

GB — Sharpe 12 pass from Majkowski (Jacke kick)
Minn — FG Reveiz 50
GB — FG Jacke 25
Minn — Jones 11 pass from Gannon (Reveiz kick)
Minn — FG Reveiz 38
GB — Beach 4 pass from Majkowski (Jacke kick)
Minn — Jones 4 pass from Gannon (Reveiz kick)
GB — FG Jacke 24
Minn — FG Reveiz 25

Philadelphia 15, New Orleans 13—at Veterans Stadium, attendance 63,513. Free-agent running back Herschel Walker, playing in his first game for the Eagles, rushed for 114 yards on 26 carries and caught a 2-yard touchdown pass as Philadelphia edged the Saints. Eagles quarterback Randall Cunningham, back after missing nearly all of the 1991 season with a knee injury, passed for 165 yards and 2 touchdowns despite being sacked 6 times and fumbling 3 times. Philadelphia, which in 1991 became only the fifth team in NFL history to lead the league in rushing defense, passing defense, and total defense, held the Saints to only 8 first downs and 202 total yards. New Orleans quarterback Bobby Hebert completed just 12 of 30 passes for 156 yards and was intercepted twice, but did throw a 10-yard touchdown pass to Wesley Carroll with 3:14 left in the game to pull his team within two points.

New Orleans	3	3	0	7	—	13
Philadelphia	6	3	0	6	—	15

Phil — Walker 2 pass from Cunningham (kick failed)
NO — FG Andersen 39
NO — FG Andersen 31
Phil — FG Ruzek 18
Phil — Barnett 20 pass from Cunningham (kick failed)
NO — Carroll 10 pass from Hebert (Andersen kick)

Atlanta 20, N.Y. Jets 17—at Georgia Dome, attendance 65,585. The Falcons built a 17-0 advantage in the first quarter, then hung on for the victory in their first regular-season game at the new Georgia Dome. Norm Johnson kicked a 25-yard field goal on Atlanta's first possession and Chris Miller completed touchdown passes of 14 and 11 yards to Michael Haynes to give the Falcons their early lead. But the Jets rallied behind 366 passing yards from Browning Nagle in his first NFL start. Nagle's 37-yard touchdown pass to Chris Burkett with 7:14 left in the third quarter pulled New York within three points. However, despite totaling 411 yards in offense, the Jets could not score again, losing a fumble inside the Atlanta 10-yard line and missing field-goal attempts of 42 and 41 yards in the second half.

N.Y. Jets	0	10	7	0	—	17
Atlanta	17	3	0	0	—	20

Atl — FG Johnson 25
Atl — Haynes 14 pass from Miller (Johnson kick)
Atl — Haynes 11 pass from Miller (Johnson kick)
Jets — FG Staurovsky 43
Atl — FG Johnson 54
Jets — Toon 15 pass from Nagle (Staurovsky kick)
Jets — Burkett 37 pass from Nagle (Staurovsky kick)

Tampa Bay 23, Phoenix 7—at Tampa Stadium, attendance 41,315. Vinny Testaverde passed for 167 yards and 1 touchdown and Ken Willis kicked 3 field goals as the Buccaneers made Sam Wyche a winner in his first game as Tampa Bay's new head coach. Reggie Cobb's 1-yard touchdown run with 50 seconds left in the first half capped an 80-yard drive and gave the Buccaneers the lead for good at 10-7. Willis, a Plan B signee in the offseason, kicked a 40-yard field goal in the first half and added kicks of 45 and 23 yards in the second half to help put the game out of reach.

	1	2	3	4		F
Phoenix	0	7	0	0	—	7
Tampa Bay	3	7	10	3	—	23

TB — FG Willis 40
Phx — Thompson 3 run (Davis kick)
TB — Cobb 1 run (Willis kick)
TB — FG Willis 45
TB — Hall 1 pass from Testaverde (Willis kick)
TB — FG Willis 23

Pittsburgh 29, Houston 24—at Astrodome, attendance 63,713. Neil O'Donnell's 9-yard touchdown pass to tight end Adrian Cooper with 8:06 left to play gave the Steelers and rookie head coach Bill Cowher an upset over the Oilers. Houston jumped out to a 14-0 lead in the opening 10 minutes of the game and still had a 24-16 advantage at halftime. After a pair of Gary Anderson field goals trimmed Pittsburgh's deficit to 24-22, the Oilers marched to the Steelers' 3-yard line early in the fourth quarter. But on second-and-goal, Warren Moon scrambled to his right and threw across the field to his left. Pittsburgh's Rod Woodson intercepted the pass at the goal line and returned it 57 yards. The Steelers scored five plays later. O'Donnell passed for 223 yards and 2 touchdowns, while Barry Foster added 107 rushing yards for Pittsburgh. Lorenzo White rushed for 100 yards for the Oilers and Moon completed 29 of 45 passes for 330 yards, but was intercepted 5 times.

	1	2	3	4		F
Pittsburgh	7	9	6	7	—	29
Houston	14	10	0	0	—	24

Hou — Meads 15 fumble recovery return (Del Greco kick)
Hou — Givins 11 pass from Moon (Del Greco kick)
Pitt — Foster 1 run (Anderson kick)
Pitt — FG Anderson 30
Hou — FG Del Greco 36
Pitt — Graham 26 pass from O'Donnell (kick blocked)
Hou — Givins 8 pass from Moon (Del Greco kick)
Pitt — FG Anderson 25
Pitt — FG Anderson 37
Pitt — Cooper 9 pass from O'Donnell (Anderson kick)

San Francisco 31, N.Y. Giants 14—at Giants Stadium, attendance 74,519. Steve Bono relieved injured Steve Young and passed for 187 yards and 2 touchdowns to key the 49ers' victory. Fullback Tom Rathman, a short-yardage rushing specialist who had caught only 4 touchdown passes in his previous six seasons in the league, caught both touchdown passes from Bono as well as 1 from Young, who was knocked out in the first quarter with a concussion. Ricky Watters ran for 100 yards on 13 carries in his NFL debut after missing all of the 1991 season with a broken foot. The victory was the seventh consecutive regular-season triumph for San Francisco, which closed 1991 with six straight wins and also won all five of its preseason games in 1992.

	1	2	3	4		F
San Francisco	7	10	7	7	—	31
N.Y. Giants	0	7	7	0	—	14

SF — Rathman 3 pass from Young (Cofer kick)
Giants — Hampton 11 run (Bahr kick)
SF — FG Cofer 36
SF — Rathman 15 pass from Bono (Cofer kick)
Giants — Hampton 3 run (Bahr kick)
SF — Rathman 4 pass from Bono (Cofer kick)
SF — Johnson 56 interception return (Cofer kick)

Sunday Night, September 6

Denver 17, L.A. Raiders 13—at Mile High Stadium, attendance 75,418. Reggie Rivers ran 1 yard for a touchdown with 55 seconds remaining to lift the Broncos past the Raiders. Rivers's run came on his only carry of the game and capped a dramatic 85-yard drive as Denver snapped a five-game losing streak to the Raiders. The five losses had come by a combined total of only 15 points, and the Broncos appeared headed for another narrow defeat in this game when they were mired on their own 15-yard line and trailing 13-10 with 2:51 left. But Broncos quarterback John Elway, who had completed only 7 of 20 passes for 99 yards to that point, connected on 3 of his next 4 attempts, including a 48-yard pass to Arthur Marshall that moved the ball to the Raiders' 8. A pass interference penalty in the end zone positioned the ball at the 1 and set up Rivers's game-winning score.

	1	2	3	4		F
L.A. Raiders	0	10	3	0	—	13
Denver	7	0	3	7	—	17

Den — Brooks 54 fumble recovery return (Treadwell kick)
Raid — Bell 1 run (Jaeger kick)
Raid — FG Jaeger 41
Raid — FG Jaeger 34
Den — FG Treadwell 39
Den — Rivers 1 run (Treadwell kick)

Monday, September 7

Dallas 23, Washington 10—at Texas Stadium, attendance 63,538. Emmitt Smith rushed for 139 yards and Dallas's special teams played a big role as the Cowboys overwhelmed the defending Super Bowl-champion Redskins. Issiac Holt blocked a punt out of the end zone for a safety on Washington's first possession, and Smith, who broke the 100-yard mark for the fourth consecutive game against the Redskins, ran 5 yards for a touchdown to give Dallas a 9-0 lead in the first quarter. It was 16-7 midway through the third period when Kelvin Martin put the game out of reach by returning a punt 79 yards for a touchdown. Washington, which finished fourth in the NFL in total offense en route to its victory in Super Bowl XXVI, was limited to only 264 total yards. The Cowboys, meanwhile, rolled up 390, including 216 through the air from quarterback Troy Aikman.

	1	2	3	4		F
Washington	0	7	0	3	—	10
Dallas	9	7	7	0	—	23

Dall — Safety, Holt blocked punt out of end zone
Dall — E. Smith 5 run (Elliott kick)
Wash — Clark 30 pass from Rypien (Lohmiller kick)
Dall — Harper 26 pass from Aikman (Elliott kick)
Dall — Martin 79 punt return (Elliott kick)
Wash — FG Lohmiller 49

Second Week Summaries

Standings

American Football Conference

Eastern Division

	W	L	T	Pct.	Pts.	OP
Buffalo	2	0	0	1.000	74	38
Miami	1	0	0	1.000	27	23
Indianapolis	1	1	0	.500	24	23
New England	0	1	0	.000	0	14
N.Y. Jets	0	2	0	.000	27	47

Central Division

	W	L	T	Pct.	Pts.	OP
Cincinnati	2	0	0	1.000	45	24
Pittsburgh	2	0	0	1.000	56	34
Houston	1	1	0	.500	44	39
Cleveland	0	2	0	.000	26	41

Western Division

	W	L	T	Pct.	Pts.	OP
Denver	2	0	0	1.000	38	26
Kansas City	2	0	0	1.000	50	17
L.A. Raiders	0	2	0	.000	34	41
San Diego	0	2	0	.000	23	45
Seattle	0	2	0	.000	10	47

National Football Conference

Eastern Division

	W	L	T	Pct.	Pts.	OP
Dallas	2	0	0	1.000	57	38
Philadelphia	2	0	0	1.000	46	27
Washington	1	1	0	.500	34	40
N.Y. Giants	0	2	0	.000	42	65
Phoenix	0	2	0	.000	21	54

Central Division

	W	L	T	Pct.	Pts.	OP
Tampa Bay	2	0	0	1.000	54	10
Chicago	1	1	0	.500	33	52
Detroit	1	1	0	.500	55	44
Minnesota	1	1	0	.500	40	51
Green Bay	0	2	0	.000	23	54

Western Division

	W	L	T	Pct.	Pts.	OP
Atlanta	1	1	0	.500	37	41
L.A. Rams	1	1	0	.500	21	40
New Orleans	1	1	0	.500	41	21
San Francisco	1	1	0	.500	62	48

Sunday, September 13

Washington 24, Atlanta 17—at RFK Stadium, attendance 54,343. Rookie Desmond Howard returned a punt 55 yards for a touchdown to spark the defending Super Bowl-champion Redskins to their first victory of the season. Washington, which beat Atlanta in the divisional playoffs en route to its Super Bowl XXVI triumph, led 7-0 early in the second quarter when Howard took a cross-field lateral from teammate Brian Mitchell, who had fielded a Falcons' punt, and sprinted for the first touchdown of his career. Atlanta's Deion Sanders returned the ensuing kickoff 99 yards for a touchdown, but the Falcons never could get closer than 7 points. Redskins linebacker Kurt Gouveia ended Atlanta's last chance with a diving interception in the end zone with 3:41 to go.

	1	2	3	4		F
Atlanta	0	14	0	3	—	17
Washington	0	21	3	0	—	24

Wash — Byner 5 pass from Rypien (Lohmiller kick)
Wash — Howard 55 punt return (Lohmiller kick)
Atl — Sanders 99 kickoff return (Johnson kick)
Wash — Clark 16 pass from Rypien (Lohmiller kick)
Atl — Haynes 89 pass from Miller (Johnson kick)
Wash — FG Lohmiller 41
Atl — FG Johnson 24

Buffalo 34, San Francisco 31—at Candlestick Park, attendance 64,053. Thurman Thomas ran 11 yards for a touchdown with 3:04 left in the game and the Bills held on to win when the 49ers' Mike Cofer missed a potential game-tying 47-yard field goal with 54 seconds remaining. The wide-open game featured 1,086 yards of total offense, the fourth-highest single-game total in NFL history. Neither team punted, the first time in league annals that happened. San Francisco amassed 598 total yards but could not hold first-half leads of 14-3 and 24-13. Buffalo rallied from an 11-point halftime deficit on a pair of third-quarter touchdown passes from Jim Kelly to tight end Pete Metzelaars. The 49ers countered with a 54-yard touchdown pass from Steve Young to John Taylor to regain the lead at 31-27 before Thomas capped a 72-yard drive with his sixth touchdown of the young season. Kelly completed 22 of 33 passes for 403 yards and 3 touchdowns. Young was 26 of 37 for 449 yards and 3 scores. Four players caught passes for more than 100 yards: the Bills' Andre Reed (10 for 144) and Metzelaars (4 for 113), and the 49ers' Mike Sherrard (6 for 159) and Taylor (5 for 112).

	1	2	3	4		F
Buffalo	3	10	14	7	—	34
San Francisco	7	17	7	0	—	31

SF — Turner 23 pass from Young (Cofer kick)
Buff — FG Christie 41
SF — Rathman 2 run (Cofer kick)
Buff — Thomas 20 pass from Kelly (Christie kick)
SF — FG Cofer 24
Buff — FG Christie 28
SF — Taylor 7 pass from Young (Cofer kick)
Buff — Metzelaars 53 pass from Kelly (Christie kick)
Buff — Metzelaars 24 pass from Kelly (Christie kick)
SF — Taylor 54 pass from Young (Cofer kick)
Buff — Thomas 11 run (Christie kick)

New Orleans 28, Chicago 6—at Louisiana Superdome, attendance 68,591. Bobby Hebert threw a pair of long touchdown passes in the second half and the Saints' defense tacked on 2 more scores as New Orleans beat the Bears. Chicago led 6-0 until Hebert, who had been just 3 of 14 passing for 23 yards in the first half, teamed with Eric Martin on a 52-yard touchdown pass early in the third quarter. Fifty-eight seconds into the fourth quarter, he found Wesley Carroll on a 72-yard scoring play to put the Saints ahead 14-6. Hebert was 10 of 11 for 241 yards and the 2 touchdowns in the second half. New Orleans's 2 defensive touchdowns came only 81 seconds apart late in the game and sealed the Bears' fate.

	1	2	3	4		F
Chicago	0	6	0	0	—	6
New Orleans	0	0	7	21	—	28

Chi — FG Butler 39
Chi — FG Butler 30
NO — Martin 52 pass from Hebert (Andersen kick)
NO — Carroll 72 pass from Hebert (Andersen kick)
NO — Goff 19 fumble recovery return (Andersen kick)
NO — Jones 71 interception return (Andersen kick)

Dallas 34, N.Y. Giants 28—at Giants Stadium, attendance 76,430. The Cowboys built a 34-0 advantage in the third quarter, then withstood a furious rally by the Giants to hang on for the victory. Dallas jumped to a 17-0 lead in the first quarter in part by blocking 1 punt (which Robert Williams returned 3 yards for a touchdown) and deflecting another (to set up a field goal) on New York's first two possessions. The Cowboys took a 34-point lead when Troy Aikman threw a 27-yard touchdown pass to Michael Irvin 1:30 into the second half. But behind Phil Simms, who tossed 3 touchdown passes, the Giants scored 4 times in a span of 17:15 of the third and fourth quarters to pull within six points. But after the last touchdown, a 2-yard pass from Simms to Howard Cross with 6:52 left, New York got the ball back only once, and was forced to punt. Simms passed for 273 yards and became the thirteenth player in NFL history to pass for 30,000 yards in his career. He finished the day at 30,008.

	1	2	3	4		F
Dallas	17	10	7	0	—	34
N.Y. Giants	0	0	14	14	—	28

Dall — E. Smith 5 run (Elliott kick)
Dall — R. Williams 3 blocked punt return (Elliott kick)
Dall — FG Elliott 39
Dall — FG Elliott 35
Dall — Novacek 2 pass from Aikman (Elliott kick)
Dall — Irvin 27 pass from Aikman (Elliott kick)
Giants — Hampton 5 run (Bahr kick)
Giants — Bunch 1 pass from Simms (Bahr kick)
Giants — Baker 6 pass from Simms (Bahr kick)
Giants — Cross 2 pass from Simms (Bahr kick)

Tampa Bay 31, Green Bay 3—at Tampa Stadium, attendance 50,051. Vinny Testaverde completed 22 of 25 passes for 363 yards and 2 touchdowns, and the

Buccaneers improved to 2-0 for the first time in 12 years by routing the Packers. The game's outcome never was in doubt after cornerback Ricky Reynolds forced and recovered a fumble that he returned 15 yards for Tampa Bay's first touchdown 6:02 into the game. Just 2:30 later, Testaverde threw an 8-yard touchdown pass to Mark Carrier to make it 14-0. Testaverde, who completed his first 9 passes, also closed the day's scoring with a 2-yard touchdown run early in the fourth quarter. Carrier caught 7 passes for 115 yards.

Green Bay	0	0	3	0	—	3
Tampa Bay	14	3	7	7	—	31

TB — Reynolds 15 fumble recovery return (Willis kick)
TB — Carrier 8 pass from Testaverde (Willis kick)
TB — FG Willis 22
GB — FG Jacke 33
TB — Drewrey 13 pass from Testaverde (Willis kick)
TB — Testaverde 2 run (Willis kick)

Houston 20, Indianapolis 10—at Hoosier Dome, attendance 44,851. Warren Moon passed for 361 yards and 2 touchdowns and the Oilers shook off an opening-day upset at the hands of the Steelers to beat the Colts. The game was not as close as the score would indicate. Houston outgained Indianapolis 419-162 and built a 20-3 lead until the Colts scored in the closing seconds. Moon completed 29 of 39 passes, including a 69-yard touchdown to running back Lorenzo White midway through the first quarter and a 2-yard touchdown to Haywood Jeffires to open a 17-3 advantage with 6:41 left in the third period. White caught 4 passes for a career-high 106 yards.

Houston	7	3	7	3	—	20
Indianapolis	0	3	0	7	—	10

Hou — White 69 pass from Moon (Del Greco kick)
Ind — FG Biasucci 37
Hou — FG Del Greco 27
Hou — Jeffires 2 pass from Moon (Del Greco kick)
Hou — FG Del Greco 20
Ind — Johnson 3 pass from Tupa (Biasucci kick)

Cincinnati 24, L.A. Raiders 21—at Riverfront Stadium, attendance 54,240. Jim Breech kicked a 34-yard field goal just 1:01 into overtime to give the Bengals the victory. The Raiders drove 90 yards to the tying touchdown—Marcus Allen's 1-yard run with 1:55 left in regulation—then won the coin toss to receive possession in overtime. But Dan Land fumbled the kickoff return when he collided with teammate Sam Graddy and Antoine Bennett recovered for Cincinnati at the 21.

L.A. Raiders	7	7	0	7	0	—	21
Cincinnati	7	7	7	0	3	—	24

Raid — Brown 33 pass from Schroeder (Jaeger kick)
Cin — Green 20 run (Breech kick)
Raid — Graddy 37 pass from Schroeder (Jaeger kick)
Cin — Fenner 9 pass from Esiason (Breech kick)
Cin — Ball 1 run (Breech kick)
Raid — Allen 1 run (Jaeger kick)
Cin — FG Breech 34

Detroit 31, Minnesota 17—at Pontiac Silverdome, attendance 57,519. The Lions' special teams scored 2 touchdowns and the defense added another to key the rout of the Vikings. Detroit could muster only 169 yards of total offense, but still breezed to victory, building a 31-3 advantage through three quarters. Mel Gray returned a punt following Minnesota's first possession 58 yards for a touchdown, and Melvin Jenkins scooped up a loose ball and returned it 56 yards for another score when Marc Spindler blocked a Vikings' field-goal attempt midway through the second quarter. Nose tackle Jerry Ball helped put the game out of reach by returning a fumble 21 yards for a touchdown just 21 seconds into the second half.

Minnesota	0	3	0	14	—	17
Detroit	7	10	14	0	—	31

Det — Gray 58 punt return (Hanson kick)
Minn — FG Reveiz 52
Det — Jenkins 56 blocked field goal return (Hanson kick)
Det — FG Hanson 35
Det — Ball 21 fumble recovery return (Hanson kick)
Det — W. Green 16 pass from Peete (Hanson kick)
Minn — Allen 3 run (Reveiz kick)
Minn — A. Carter 11 pass from Gannon (Reveiz kick)

L.A. Rams 14, New England 0—at Anaheim Stadium, attendance 40,402. Cleveland Gary capped 2 short drives following turnovers with touchdown runs and the Rams snapped an 11-game losing streak dating back to the 1991 season. The game was scoreless until late in the third quarter, when Los Angeles linebacker Roman Phifer recovered a fumble by Patriots quarterback Hugh Millen at the New England 39-yard line. A pass interference penalty in the end zone moved the ball to the 1, and Gary scored on the next play. In the fourth quarter, cornerback Todd Lyght intercepted Millen's pass at the Patriots' 34 and returned it to the 11, setting up Gary's 9-yard touchdown run with 2:08 left in the game. Lyght's theft was 1 of 4 for the Rams' defense, which also recorded 7 sacks. Los Angeles kicker Tony Zendejas entered the game with a string of 23 consecutive field goals made, 1 short of tying the NFL record, but missed all 3 of his tries.

New England	0	0	0	0	—	0
L.A. Rams	0	0	7	7	—	14

Rams — Gary 1 run (Zendejas kick)
Rams — Gary 9 run (Zendejas kick)

Pittsburgh 27, N.Y. Jets 10—at Three Rivers Stadium, attendance 56,050. Barry Foster ran for 190 yards and the Steelers' defense forced 7 turnovers in an error-plagued game. Pittsburgh turned over the ball 5 times itself, including 3 on fumbles by Foster. But it was the third-year running back's 54-yard run 55 seconds into the fourth quarter that broke a 10-10 tie and gave the Steelers the lead for good. The Jets' comeback efforts were thwarted by 4 interceptions, 1 of which was returned by Pittsburgh safety Larry Griffin 65 yards for the clinching score with 3:40 left. Steelers wide receiver Jeff Graham totaled 146 yards on 6 catches.

N.Y. Jets	3	7	0	0	—	10
Pittsburgh	0	10	0	17	—	27

Jets — FG Staurovsky 32
Pitt — Foster 23 run (Anderson kick)
Jets — Brim 77 interception return (Staurovsky kick)
Pitt — FG Anderson 28
Pitt — Foster 54 run (Anderson kick)
Pitt — FG Anderson 35
Pitt — Griffin 65 interception return (Anderson kick)

Denver 21, San Diego 13—at Mile High Stadium, attendance 74,367. John Elway passed for 2 touchdowns and ran for another in the Broncos' victory. The Chargers lost despite outgaining Denver 355-226, totaling 27 first downs to the Broncos' 12, and controlling the ball for more than 35 minutes. They maintained possession for more than 11 minutes of the second quarter while scoring 10 points for a 10-7 halftime lead. But Elway's 8-yard run 4:25 into the third quarter gave Denver the lead for good, and his 34-yard touchdown pass to Shannon Sharpe with 25 seconds left in the period provided the final points.

San Diego	0	10	3	0	—	13
Denver	7	0	14	0	—	21

Den — Jackson 32 pass from Elway (Treadwell kick)
SD — FG Carney 20
SD — Lewis 2 pass from Humphries (Carney kick)
Den — Elway 8 run (Treadwell kick)
SD — FG Carney 27
Den — Sharpe 34 pass from Elway (Treadwell kick)

Kansas City 26, Seattle 7—at Arrowhead Stadium, attendance 75,125. Dave Krieg, playing his first game against his former teammates, passed for 231 yards and 1 touchdown, and the Chiefs limited the Seahawks to 189 total yards en route to the victory. Krieg, the leading passer in Seattle history, signed with Kansas City as a Plan B free agent prior to the 1992 season after 12 years with the Seahawks. He threw a 72-yard touchdown pass to J.J. Birden just 1:39 into the game and went on to complete 13 of 19 passes. Nick Lowery broke a 7-7 tie with a pair of field goals 1:02 apart late in the second quarter. Kelly Stouffer, Krieg's replacement in Seattle, completed only 13 of 31 passes for 106 yards and was intercepted twice, 1 of which was returned 36 yards for a touchdown by linebacker Lonnie Marts in the third quarter. Chiefs running back Christian Okoye gained 63 yards and surpassed Ed Podolak as the leading rusher in franchise history.

Seattle	0	7	0	0	—	7
Kansas City	7	6	7	6	—	26

KC — Birden 72 pass from Krieg (Lowery kick)
Sea — Green 3 pass from Stouffer (Kasay kick)
KC — FG Lowery 26
KC — FG Lowery 32
KC — Marts 36 interception return (Lowery kick)
KC — Word 2 run (kick failed)

Sunday Night, September 13

Philadelphia 31, Phoenix 14—at Sun Devil Stadium, attendance 42,533. Randall Cunningham passed for 267 yards and 3 touchdowns and Herschel Walker had his second consecutive 100-yard rushing day in the Eagles' victory. Philadelphia trailed 14-10 until Cunningham passed 10 yards to Calvin Williams for a touchdown just 15 seconds before halftime. Cunningham and Fred Barnett teamed on a 71-yard score late in the third quarter to put the game out of reach. Walker, who rushed for 114 yards in the Eagles' season-opening victory over the Saints, gained 115 yards on 28 carries against the Cardinals. Barnett caught 8 passes for 193 yards. Phoenix quarterback Timm Rosenbach, who missed all of the 1991 season with a knee injury and suffered a concussion in the 1992 opener, was knocked out in the second quarter of this game with a separated right shoulder.

Philadelphia	3	14	7	7	—	31
Phoenix	0	14	0	0	—	14

Phil — FG Ruzek 33
Phil — Barnett 17 pass from Cunningham (Ruzek kick)
Phx — Proehl 10 pass from Chandler (Davis kick)
Phx — Jones 46 pass from Chandler (Davis kick)
Phil — Williams 10 pass from Cunningham (Ruzek kick)
Phil — Barnett 71 pass from Cunningham (Ruzek kick)
Phil — White 37 fumble recovery return (Ruzek kick)

Monday, September 14

Miami 27, Cleveland 23—at Cleveland Stadium, attendance 74,765. Mark Higgs dived 1 yard for a touchdown with seven seconds remaining to give the Dolphins a season-opening victory and spoil a brilliant fourth-quarter comeback by the Browns. Miami was playing its first game of the season after hurricane damage in the south Florida area forced its scheduled opener against the Patriots on September 6 to be moved to October 18. The Dolphins appeared to be breezing to the victory, leading 20-3 midway through the fourth quarter. But Cleveland rallied, scoring 2 touchdowns in a span of 67 seconds to trim the deficit to 20-17. First, Bernie Kosar threw a fourth-down, 6-yard touchdown pass to Michael Jackson with 7:46 left in the game. Then, on Miami's next series, Browns linebacker Mike Johnson stripped the ball from Higgs. Linebacker Mike Brandon scooped up the loose ball and ran 32 yards for a touchdown with 6:39 to go. After the Dolphins punted, Cleveland marched 77 yards to Kosar's 3-yard touchdown pass to Mark Bavaro for a 23-20 advantage with 1:18 to go. But the Browns' lead was short-lived, as Miami marched 84 yards to the winning score. Dan Marino, who passed for 322 yards in all, completed each of his 4 attempts for 68 yards on the drive. The Dolphins also were aided by a roughing-the-passer call.

Miami	14	0	3	10	—	27
Cleveland	0	0	3	20	—	23

Mia — Duper 25 pass from Marino (Stoyanovich kick)
Mia — Higgs 7 run (Stoyanovich kick)
Cleve — FG Stover 28
Mia — FG Stoyanovich 22
Mia — FG Stoyanovich 32
Cleve — M. Jackson 6 pass from Kosar (Stover kick)
Cleve — Brandon 32 fumble recovery return (Stover kick)
Cleve — Bavaro 3 pass from Kosar (kick failed)
Mia — Higgs 1 run (Stoyanovich kick)

Third Week Summaries

Standings

American Football Conference

Eastern Division

	W	L	T	Pct.	Pts.	OP
Buffalo	3	0	0	1.000	112	38
Miami	2	0	0	1.000	53	33
Indianapolis	1	2	0	.333	24	61
New England	0	2	0	.000	6	24
N.Y. Jets	0	3	0	.000	41	78

Central Division

	W	L	T	Pct.	Pts.	OP
Pittsburgh	3	0	0	1.000	79	40
Cincinnati	2	1	0	.667	68	48
Houston	2	1	0	.667	67	59
Cleveland	1	2	0	.333	54	57

Western Division

	W	L	T	Pct.	Pts.	OP
Denver	2	1	0	.667	38	56
Kansas City	2	1	0	.667	70	40
Seattle	1	2	0	.333	20	53
L.A. Raiders	0	3	0	.000	50	69
San Diego	0	3	0	.000	29	68

National Football Conference

Eastern Division

	W	L	T	Pct.	Pts.	OP
Dallas	3	0	0	1.000	88	58
Philadelphia	3	0	0	1.000	76	27
Washington	2	1	0	.667	47	50
N.Y. Giants	1	2	0	.333	69	79
Phoenix	0	3	0	.000	41	85

Central Division

Minnesota	2	1	0	.667	66	71
Tampa Bay	2	1	0	.667	74	36
Chicago	1	2	0	.333	65	57
Detroit	1	2	0	.333	65	57
Green Bay	1	2	0	.333	47	77

Western Division

New Orleans	2	1	0	.667	51	28
San Francisco	2	1	0	.667	93	62
Atlanta	1	2	0	.333	44	51
L.A. Rams	1	2	0	.333	31	66

Sunday, September 20

Green Bay 24, Cincinnati 23—at Lambeau Field, attendance 57,272. Brett Favre's 35-yard touchdown pass to Kitrick Taylor with 13 seconds left lifted the Packers to a dramatic victory and gave rookie head coach Mike Holmgren his first win. The touchdown pass capped a furious fourth-quarter rally by Green Bay, which trailed 17-3 early in the period. But rookie cornerback Terrell Buckley, playing in his first NFL game, got the comeback started by returning a punt 58 yards for a touchdown with 12:43 remaining. Late in the game, Jim Breech's third field goal, a 41-yarder, gave the Bengals a 23-17 advantage with 1:07 left. But Favre, working with no timeouts, marched the Packers 92 yards in only five plays. The key gain was a 42-yard completion to Sterling Sharpe. Favre was in the game only because starter Don Majkowski injured an ankle in the first quarter. Taylor was in the game because Sharpe injured his ribs on the final drive. Harold Green rushed for 101 yards on 21 carries for Cincinnati.

Cincinnati	0	10	7	6	—	23
Green Bay	0	3	0	21	—	24

Cin — FG Breech 20
Cin — Pickens 95 punt return (Breech kick)
GB — FG Jacke 37
Cin — Ball 17 pass from Esiason (Breech kick)
GB — Buckley 58 punt return (Jacke kick)
Cin — FG Breech 34
GB — Sharpe 5 pass from Favre (Jacke kick)
Cin — FG Breech 41
GB — Taylor 35 pass from Favre (Jacke kick)

Cleveland 28, L.A. Raiders 16—at Los Angeles Memorial Coliseum, attendance 48,102. Eric Metcalf caught 3 touchdown passes and ran for another score as the Browns, playing without injured starting quarterback Bernie Kosar, beat the Raiders. Kosar, who played much of the previous Monday night against the Dolphins on a broken ankle, was replaced by Todd Philcox. Philcox completed 10 of 20 passes for 200 yards and the 3 touchdowns in his first NFL start. Two of the scores were short passes that Metcalf turned into long touchdowns. The most critical came late in the third quarter, after the Raiders pulled within 14-13 on Jeff Jaeger's 30-yard field goal. But on the next play from scrimmage, Metcalf caught a pass from Philcox and turned it into a 69-yard touchdown. Todd Marinovich made his first start of the season for the struggling Raiders and completed 33 of a club-record 59 passes for 395 yards, but was intercepted 3 times. Los Angeles had 464 total yards to only 231 for Cleveland, but suffered 5 turnovers and 5 sacks. The Browns did not turn the ball over and did not permit a sack.

Cleveland	14	0	7	7	—	28
L.A. Raiders	0	3	10	3	—	16

Cleve — Metcalf 4 pass from Philcox (Stover kick)
Cleve — Metcalf 6 run (Stover kick)
Raid — FG Jaeger 27
Raid — Gault 25 pass from Marinovich (Jaeger kick)
Raid — FG Jaeger 30
Cleve — Metcalf 69 pass from Philcox (Stover kick)
Cleve — Metcalf 63 pass from Philcox (Stover kick)
Raid — FG Jaeger 43

Philadelphia 30, Denver 0—at Veterans Stadium, attendance 65,833. Randall Cunningham threw 3 touchdown passes, but the Eagles' defense was the big story as Philadelphia routed the Broncos. The Eagles allowed Denver only 4 first downs and 82 total yards, while limiting Broncos quarterback John Elway to 8 completions in 18 attempts for 59 yards. Denver had only 40 plays from scrimmage and was 0-for-11 on third-down opportunities. Cunningham completed 18 of 25 passes for 270 yards. He threw touchdown passes of 24 yards to Calvin Williams and 34 yards to Fred Barnett as Philadelphia built a 17-0 halftime advantage, then added a 49-yard score to Williams late in the third quarter. Williams caught 5 passes for 108 yards.

Denver	0	0	0	0	—	0
Philadelphia	3	14	10	3	—	30

Phil — FG Ruzek 50
Phil — Williams 24 pass from Cunningham (Ruzek kick)
Phil — Barnett 34 pass from Cunningham (Ruzek kick)
Phil — FG Ruzek 27
Phil — Williams 49 pass from Cunningham (Ruzek kick)
Phil — FG Ruzek 35

Washington 13, Detroit 10—at RFK Stadium, attendance 55,818. Earnest Byner rushed for 120 yards on 30 carries to give the Redskins their sixteenth consecutive victory over the Lions. Byner capped a 13-play, 80-yard drive on Washington's first possession with a 6-yard touchdown run. The Redskins led 13-3 before Detroit made it close on a 67-yard touchdown pass from Rodney Peete to Willie Green with 9:45 to go. The Lions had a chance to tie the game with 1:42 remaining but rookie Jason Hanson, who earlier had kicked a 52-yard field goal, missed from 49 yards. Washington held Detroit to only 8 first downs and 206 total yards, and kept running back Barry Sanders in check, limiting him to only 34 yards on 14 carries.

Detroit	0	3	0	7	—	10
Washington	7	3	0	3	—	13

Wash — Byner 6 run (Lohmiller kick)
Det — FG Hanson 52
Wash — FG Lohmiller 53
Wash — FG Lohmiller 27
Det — Green 67 pass from Peete (Hanson kick)

Houston 23, Kansas City 20—at Astrodome, attendance 60,955. Al Del Greco's 39-yard field goal after 1:55 of overtime gave the Oilers the victory. The winning kick came only two plays after Houston cornerback Cris Dishman jarred the ball loose from Chiefs wide receiver J.J. Birden and Oilers defensive tackle Doug Smith recovered at the Kansas City 23. Del Greco's field goal was his third of the game, 1 of which was a career-best 54-yarder on the final play of the first half. Quarterback Warren Moon completed 19 of 28 passes for 279 yards and a pair of fourth-quarter touchdowns that rallied the Oilers from a seven-point deficit to a 20-13 lead. But the Chiefs tied the game with an 85-yard drive capped by Todd McNair's 4-yard run with 23 seconds remaining in regulation. Barry Word rushed for 114 yards on 22 carries for Kansas City.

Kansas City	3	10	0	7	0	—	20
Houston	3	3	0	14	3	—	23

KC — FG Lowery 31
Hou — FG Del Greco 21
KC — FG Lowery 52
KC — McNair 5 pass from Krieg (Lowery kick)
Hou — FG Del Greco 54
Hou — L. Harris 8 pass from Moon (Del Greco kick)
Hou — Givins 21 pass from Moon (Del Greco kick)
KC — McNair 4 run (Lowery kick)
Hou — FG Del Greco 39

Miami 26, L.A. Rams 10—at Joe Robbie Stadium, attendance 55,945. Dan Marino threw a pair of touchdown passes in the first quarter as the Dolphins built a 17-0 lead in the first 15 minutes and won handily. Miami drove 76 yards on its first possession and 60 yards on its second for a quick 14-0 advantage. Pete Stoyanovich added a 36-yard field goal late in the first quarter. The Rams got as close as 20-10 when Tony Zendejas kicked a 31-yard field goal 26 seconds into the fourth quarter, but the Dolphins quelled any comeback hopes by eating up more than seven minutes on a 71-yard drive en route to the third of Stoyanovich's 4 field goals. Miami ran for 158 yards, including 111 on 23 carries by Mark Higgs.

L.A. Rams	0	0	7	3	—	10
Miami	17	0	3	6	—	26

Mia — Edmunds 1 pass from Marino (Stoyanovich kick)
Mia — Duper 38 pass from Marino (Stoyanovich kick)
Mia — FG Stoyanovich 36
Rams — Anderson 23 pass from Everett (Zendejas kick)
Mia — FG Stoyanovich 44
Rams — FG Zendejas 31
Mia — FG Stoyanovich 27
Mia — FG Stoyanovich 20

New Orleans 10, Atlanta 7—at Georgia Dome, attendance 67,328. Morten Andersen's 47-yard field goal with 1:51 remaining in the game gave the Saints the victory in a taut defensive struggle. Andersen's field goal capped a 44-yard drive in which the key 21-yard gain came on a screen pass from Bobby Hebert to Craig Heyward. The Falcons had taken a 7-0 lead on a 14-yard touchdown pass from Chris Miller to Mike Pritchard just 24 seconds before halftime. But New Orleans, which gained only 69 yards in the first half, marched 64 yards to the tying touchdown after taking the second-half kickoff.

New Orleans	0	0	7	3	—	10
Atlanta	0	7	0	0	—	7

Atl — Pritchard 14 pass from Miller (Johnson kick)
NO — Early 11 pass from Hebert (Andersen kick)
NO — FG Andersen 47

Dallas 31, Phoenix 20—at Texas Stadium, attendance 62,575. Michael Irvin caught 8 passes for a career-high 210 yards and 3 touchdowns as the Cowboys handed the Cardinals their eleventh consecutive defeat dating back to the 1991 season. Irvin set the tone for his day by catching a short pass from Troy Aikman and breaking loose for an 87-yard touchdown just 1:01 into the game. Before the first quarter ended, he also had a 41-yard touchdown catch, and he added a 4-yarder to put the game out of reach at 28-10 midway through the third quarter. Emmitt Smith rushed for 112 yards, 56 of which came on a 90-yard, second-quarter scoring drive that he capped with a 1-yard touchdown run. Phoenix quarterback Chris Chandler completed 28 of 43 passes for 383 yards and 1 touchdown. The Cardinals amassed 438 total yards, the Cowboys 413.

Phoenix	7	3	3	7	—	20
Dallas	14	7	7	3	—	31

Dall — Irvin 87 pass from Aikman (Elliott kick)
Phx — Hill 34 pass from Chandler (G. Davis kick)
Dall — Irvin 41 pass from Aikman (Elliott kick)
Dall — E. Smith 1 run (Elliott kick)
Phx — FG G. Davis 22
Dall — Irvin 4 pass from Aikman (Elliott kick)
Phx — FG G. Davis 42
Dall — FG Elliott 29
Phx — Brown 1 run (G. Davis kick)

Pittsburgh 23, San Diego 6—at San Diego Jack Murphy Stadium, attendance 46,127. Neil O'Donnell threw 2 touchdown passes and ran for another and Bill Cowher became the first head coach in Steelers history to begin his career 3-0 when his team downed the Chargers. San Diego trailed only 7-6 midway through the third quarter before the game got out of reach. First, kicker John Carney missed a 25-yard field-goal try that would have given San Diego the lead. Then Pittsburgh took possession and drove 80 yards to O'Donnell's 6-yard touchdown pass to Dwight Stone 46 seconds into the fourth quarter. Linebacker David Little's interception on the next play from scrimmage set up O'Donnell's 1-yard run that increased the Steelers' advantage to 20-6.

Pittsburgh	0	7	0	16	—	23
San Diego	3	3	0	0	—	6

SD — FG Carney 24
Pitt — Cooper 24 pass from O'Donnell (Anderson kick)
SD — FG Carney 43
Pitt — Stone 6 pass from O'Donnell (kick failed)
Pitt — O'Donnell 1 run (Anderson kick)
Pitt — FG Anderson 42

San Francisco 31, N.Y. Jets 14—at Giants Stadium, attendance 71,020. Steve Young passed for 2 touchdowns and ran for another, all in the first half, and the 49ers built a 31-0 lead midway through the third quarter and coasted to the victory. It was San Francisco's second win in three weeks at Giants Stadium by the same score. The 49ers beat the Giants 31-14 on Opening Day. Young threw a 5-yard touchdown pass to Jerry Rice in the first quarter and passed 8 yards for a score to tight end Jamie Williams just 40 seconds before halftime. In between, he also ran 10 yards for a touchdown as the 49ers took a 24-0 halftime advantage. Ken O'Brien completed 23 of 42 passes for 264 yards for New York. Terance Mathis totaled 111 yards on 4 receptions, including a 55-yard touchdown late in the game. San Francisco linebacker Tim Harris had 3 sacks.

San Francisco	7	17	7	0	—	31
N.Y. Jets	0	0	0	14	—	14

SF — Rice 5 pass from Young (Cofer kick)
SF — Young 10 run (Cofer kick)
SF — FG Cofer 45
SF — Williams 8 pass from Young (Cofer kick)
SF — Watters 1 run (Cofer kick)
Jets — Carpenter 7 pass from O'Brien (Staurovsky kick)
Jets — Mathis 55 pass from O'Brien (Staurovsky kick)

Seattle 10, New England 6—at Foxboro Stadium, attendance 42,327. Cornerback Patrick Hunter's interception in the end zone with 35 seconds left secured the Seahawks' first victory under new head coach Tom Flores. Quarterback Hugh Millen had driven the Patriots from their 20-yard line to the Seattle 25, but underthrew intended receiver Irving Fryar on the deciding play. New England could not tie the game with a field goal on its final drive because of a costly missed extra-point attempt following its lone touchdown. Seahawks running back Chris Warren rushed for a career-high 122 yards and 1 touchdown on 24 carries. Defensive tackle Cortez Kennedy had 2½ sacks and forced a pair of fumbles. The Seahawks forced 3 turnovers while not committing any miscues of their own.

Seattle	7	0	0	3	—	10
New England	0	0	6	0	—	6

Sea — Warren 2 run (Kasay kick)
NE — Fryar 36 pass from Millen (kick failed)
Sea — FG Kasay 25

Minnesota 26, Tampa Bay 20—at Metrodome, attendance 48,113. Backup quarterback Sean Salisbury, playing in his first NFL game since 1987, threw a 29-yard touchdown pass to Cris Carter in the third quarter to spark the Vikings' victory. Salisbury replaced starter Rich Gannon, who was knocked from the game with an injured wrist, which he suffered when he threw a 30-yard scoring pass to Carter in the first quarter. After Carter's score, Minnesota fell behind 13-7. But Terry Allen, who rushed for 87 yards, ran 1 yard for the go-ahead touchdown with 9:28 left in the third quarter. Six minutes later, Salisbury teamed with Carter for what turned out to be the deciding points. Tampa Bay also lost its starting quarterback when Vinny Testaverde injured his arm in the second quarter. Steve DeBerg replaced him and passed for 213 yards and 2 touchdowns.

Tampa Bay	3	10	0	7	—	20
Minnesota	7	0	14	5	—	26

Minn — C. Carter 30 pass from Gannon (Reveiz kick)
TB — FG Willis 40
TB — Hawkins 28 pass from DeBerg (Willis kick)
TB — FG Willis 29
Minn — Allen 1 run (Reveiz kick)
Minn — C. Carter 29 pass from Salisbury (Reveiz kick)
Minn — FG Reveiz 36
Minn — Safety, DeBerg stepped out of end zone
TB — Dawsey 14 pass from DeBerg (Willis kick)

Sunday Night, September 20

Buffalo 38, Indianapolis 0—at Rich Stadium, attendance 77,781. Jim Kelly passed for 211 yards and 2 touchdowns and safety Henry Jones returned a pair of interceptions for touchdowns in the Bills' rout. Buffalo, which allowed a club-record 598 total yards to the 49ers the previous week, permitted the Colts only 9 first downs and 140 total yards. Indianapolis gained only 37 rushing yards on 24 attempts. Kelly threw 1-yard touchdown passes to tight end Pete Metzelaars and rookie John Fina on a tackle-eligible play. Jones's interception returns covered 23 and 82 yards and broke the game open in the second half. Buffalo defensive end Bruce Smith had 2½ sacks.

Indianapolis	0	0	0	0	—	0
Buffalo	7	3	14	14	—	38

Buff — Metzelaars 1 pass from Kelly (Christie kick)
Buff — FG Christie 52
Buff — Gardner 1 run (Christie kick)
Buff — Jones 23 interception return (Christie kick)
Buff — Fina 1 pass from Kelly (Christie kick)
Buff — Jones 82 interception return (Christie kick)

Monday, September 21

N.Y. Giants 27, Chicago 14—at Soldier Field, attendance 63,444. Phil Simms passed for 220 yards and 2 touchdowns and the Giants broke open a close game by dominating the third quarter in the victory over the Bears. Each team traded touchdowns in a first half that ended with the score tied 14-14. But New York took the second-half kickoff and marched 80 yards to the go-ahead touchdown, a 13-yard pass from Simms to Stephen Baker. Matt Bahr's 2 field goals accounted for the rest of the scoring. The Giants totaled 155 yards and maintained possession for 12:17 of the decisive third quarter while allowing Chicago only 3 yards and 2:43 of possession time. New York rushed for 172 yards in the game, topped by Rodney Hampton's 94 yards on 22 carries. Baker caught 7 passes for 109 yards.

N.Y. Giants	7	7	10	3	—	27
Chicago	7	7	0	0	—	14

Chi — Anderson 8 pass from Harbaugh (Butler kick)
Giants — Cross 15 pass from Simms (Bahr kick)
Chi — Muster 44 pass from Harbaugh (Butler kick)
Giants — Hampton 1 run (Bahr kick)
Giants — Baker 13 pass from Simms (Bahr kick)
Giants — FG Bahr 31
Giants — FG Bahr 32

Fourth Week Summaries

Standings

American Football Conference

Eastern Division	W	L	T	Pct.	Pts.	OP
Buffalo	4	0	0	1.000	153	45
Miami	3	0	0	1.000	72	50
Indianapolis	1	2	0	.333	24	61
New England	0	3	0	.000	13	65
N.Y. Jets	0	4	0	.000	51	96
Central Division						
Houston	3	1	0	.750	94	59
Pittsburgh	3	1	0	.750	82	57
Cincinnati	2	2	0	.500	75	90
Cleveland	1	3	0	.250	54	69
Western Division						
Denver	3	1	0	.750	50	56
Kansas City	3	1	0	.750	97	47
Seattle	1	3	0	.250	37	72
L.A. Raiders	0	4	0	.000	57	96
San Diego	0	4	0	.000	29	95

National Football Conference

Eastern Division	W	L	T	Pct.	Pts.	OP
Dallas	3	0	0	1.000	88	58
Philadelphia	3	0	0	1.000	76	27
Washington	2	1	0	.667	47	50
N.Y. Giants	1	2	0	.333	69	79
Phoenix	0	3	0	.000	41	85
Central Division						
Minnesota	3	1	0	.750	108	78
Tampa Bay	3	1	0	.750	101	59
Chicago	2	2	0	.500	88	110
Green Bay	2	2	0	.500	64	89
Detroit	1	3	0	.250	88	84
Western Division						
San Francisco	3	1	0	.750	109	72
L.A. Rams	2	2	0	.500	49	76
New Orleans	2	2	0	.500	61	44
Atlanta	1	3	0	.250	75	92

Sunday, September 27

Chicago 41, Atlanta 31—at Soldier Field, attendance 63,528. Neal Anderson rushed for 2 touchdowns and Jim Harbaugh passed for 2 as the Bears built a 31-7 halftime lead and held on for the victory. Anderson's 49-yard run and Harbaugh's 41-yard touchdown pass to Tom Waddle, sandwiched around a 20-yard field goal by Kevin Butler, gave Chicago a 17-0 lead before Atlanta could muster a first down. The Falcons made a game of it in the second half, pulling within 31-21 on Chris Miller's 23-yard touchdown pass to Tony Jones with 6:30 left in the third quarter. But the Bears countered, marching 80 yards in seven plays to put the game out of reach at 38-21 on Brad Muster's 14-yard run late in the period. Harbaugh completed 18 of 24 passes for 280 yards as Chicago amassed 489 total yards. Muster ran for 96 yards and Anderson added 74 as the Bears had a whopping 217-24 advantage in rushing yards. Miller completed 30 of 48 passes for 381 yards and 4 touchdowns for Atlanta. Andre Rison caught 10 passes for 177 yards and 3 scores.

Atlanta	7	0	14	10	—	31
Chicago	17	14	7	3	—	41

Chi — Anderson 49 run (Butler kick)
Chi — FG Butler 20
Chi — Waddle 41 pass from Harbaugh (Butler kick)
Atl — Rison 71 pass from Miller (Johnson kick)
Chi — Anderson 14 run (Butler kick)
Chi — Davis 11 pass from Harbaugh (Butler kick)
Atl — Rison 6 pass from Miller (Johnson kick)
Atl — Jones 23 pass from Miller (Johnson kick)
Chi — Muster 14 run (Butler kick)
Atl — FG Johnson 46
Chi — FG Butler 21
Atl — Rison 10 pass from Miller (Johnson kick)

Buffalo 41, New England 7—at Foxboro Stadium, attendance 52,527. Jim Kelly passed for 308 yards and 3 touchdowns as the Bills broke open a close game in the second half to rout the Patriots. Buffalo led 6-0 at halftime on a pair of field goals by Steve Christie. The Bills took the second-half kickoff and marched 84 yards in eight plays, capped by Kelly's 29-yard touchdown pass to James Lofton. Buffalo went on to score on each of their next three drives and built a 41-0 advantage before New England scored its lone touchdown midway through the fourth quarter. Thurman Thomas rushed for 120 yards on 18 carries for the Bills, who outgained the Patriots 490-265. Andre Reed caught 9 passes for 168 yards and 1 touchdown, while Lofton added 4 catches for 113 yards and 2 scores. New England's Hugh Millen completed his first 14 passes and finished 24 of 33 for 202 yards.

Buffalo	3	3	21	14	—	41
New England	0	0	0	7	—	7

Buff — FG Christie 42
Buff — FG Christie 30
Buff — Lofton 29 pass from Kelly (Christie kick)
Buff — Thomas 1 run (Christie kick)
Buff — Reed 45 pass from Kelly (Christie kick)
Buff — Lofton 22 pass from Kelly (Christie kick)
Buff — Lodish 18 fumble recovery return (Christie kick)
NE — Cook 4 pass from Millen (Baumann kick)

Denver 12, Cleveland 0—at Cleveland Stadium, attendance 78,064. David Treadwell accounted for all the scoring by kicking 4 field goals for the Broncos. Interceptions by linebacker Michael Brooks and safety Dennis Smith set up Treadwell's second and third field goals, and Denver put the game away by driving 94 yards to the final three-pointer with 3:28 left in the game. Reggie Rivers got that drive on track by breaking a 48-yard run from the Broncos' 5-yard line. The Browns used free-agent signee Mike Tomczak at quarterback after Todd Philcox, who had been filling in for injured starter Bernie Kosar, broke his thumb in a victory over the Raiders one week earlier. Tomczak completed only 9 of 19 passes for 75 yards and 2 interceptions. Anthony Pleasant and Rob Burnett each had 1½ sacks for Cleveland, which dropped Denver quarterback John Elway 5 times.

Denver	3	0	3	6	—	12
Cleveland	0	0	0	0	—	0

Den — FG Treadwell 23
Den — FG Treadwell 44
Den — FG Treadwell 32
Den — FG Treadwell 20

Miami 19, Seattle 17—at Kingdome, attendance 59,674. Dan Marino shook off a mild concussion and completed a 15-yard touchdown pass to Fred Banks with 2:45 left in the game to give the Dolphins the victory. The Miami quarterback was injured when hit while throwing an incomplete pass on the winning drive, which covered 80 yards in 12 plays. He left the game and was replaced by first-year quarterback Scott Mitchell, who converted a key third-down-and-10 with an 18-yard completion on his first NFL pass. Marino, who completed 24 of 39 passes for 260 yards, then came back in the game and found Banks for the winning score three plays later. Pete Stoyanovich kept the Dolphins in position to win by making all 4 of his field-goal tries, including a 27-yarder 1:24 into the fourth quarter to give Miami a 12-10 lead. But minutes later, linebacker Terry Wooden's interception set up a 4-yard touchdown run by John L. Williams that gave the Seahawks a 17-12 advantage with 9:51 to go.

Miami	3	3	3	10	—	19
Seattle	0	10	0	7	—	17

Mia — FG Stoyanovich 53
Sea — Clark 26 pass from Stouffer (Kasay kick)
Sea — FG Kasay 35
Mia — FG Stoyanovich 31
Mia — FG Stoyanovich 37
Mia — FG Stoyanovich 27
Sea — J.L. Williams 4 run (Kasay kick)
Mia — Banks 15 pass from Marino (Stoyanovich kick)

Minnesota 42, Cincinnati 7—at Riverfront Stadium, attendance 53,847. Quarterback Rich Gannon, a questionable starter throughout the week because of a chipped bone in his throwing hand, passed for 318 yards and 4 touchdowns, and Terry Allen scored 3 times in the Vikings' rout. Safety Todd Scott intercepted 3 passes and wide receiver Cris Carter caught a career-high 11 passes for 124 yards and 2 touchdowns as the Vikings dominated the game. Minnesota scored on four of its first five possessions to build a 28-0 halftime lead. Gannon completed 19 of 22 passes for 212 yards in the first half, and he finished with 25 completions in 32 attempts. Defensive end Chris Doleman had 2 of 5 sacks for the Vikings, who limited the Bengals to 178 total yards. Minnesota piled up 423 yards.

Minnesota	14	14	7	7	—	42
Cincinnati	0	0	0	7	—	7

Minn — Allen 15 pass from Gannon (Reveiz kick)
Minn — C. Carter 15 pass from Gannon (Reveiz kick)
Minn — Allen 2 run (Reveiz kick)
Minn — Allen 1 run (Reveiz kick)
Minn — C. Carter 30 pass from Gannon (Reveiz kick)
Cin — Fenner 1 run (Breech kick)
Minn — Jones 32 pass from Gannon (Reveiz kick)

L.A. Rams 18, N.Y. Jets 10—at Anaheim Stadium, attendance 42,005. The Rams' defense forced 4 turnovers and recorded a safety to key Los Angeles's victory over the winless Jets. Two of the turnovers resulted in field goals as the Rams overcame a 10-point first-half deficit. Jim Everett's 31-yard touchdown pass to Willie Anderson 3:55 into the second half gave Los Angeles the lead for good at 12-10. Tony Zendejas kicked a pair of field goals in the fourth quarter to put the game out of reach. New York, which made the playoffs as a wild-card team in 1991, fell to 0-4 despite outgaining the Rams 330-269. Jets quarterback Browning Nagle passed for 200 yards but was intercepted twice.

N.Y. Jets	3	7	0	0	—	10
L.A. Rams	0	5	7	6	—	18

Jets — FG Staurovsky 19
Jets — Baxter 1 run (Staurovsky kick)
Rams — FG Zendejas 49
Rams — Safety, Greene tackled Nagle in end zone

Rams — Anderson 31 pass from Everett (Zendejas kick)
Rams — FG Zendejas 22
Rams — FG Zendejas 20

Green Bay 17, Pittsburgh 3—at Lambeau Field, attendance 58,743. Brett Favre threw a pair of touchdown passes in his first NFL start as the Packers snapped the Steelers' three-game winning streak. Both of Green Bay's touchdowns came on one-play drives. With the score tied 3-3 in the second quarter, the Packers' Vinnie Clark blocked a 20-yard field-goal try by Gary Anderson. On the next play, Favre hit Sterling Sharpe on a 76-yard touchdown pass for a 10-3 lead. Early in the fourth quarter, Green Bay fell on Rod Woodson's fumbled punt return at Pittsburgh's 8-yard line. Favre's 8-yard touchdown pass to rookie wide receiver Robert Brooks provided the final points. The Steelers drove 57 yards to Anderson's 35-yard field goal on their first possession of the game, but could not score after that. Pittsburgh's Barry Foster ran for 117 yards on 12 carries, his third 100-yard effort in four games, and Dwight Stone caught 5 passes for 101 yards. Favre completed 14 of 19 passes for 210 yards for the Packers.

Pittsburgh 3 0 0 0 — 3
Green Bay 0 10 0 7 — 17
Pitt — FG Anderson 35
GB — FG Jacke 47
GB — Sharpe 76 pass from Favre (Jacke kick)
GB — Brooks 8 pass from Favre (Jacke kick)

Houston 27, San Diego 0—at Astrodome, attendance 57,491. Warren Moon threw a 3-yard touchdown pass to Haywood Jeffires on the opening series of the game, igniting the Oilers' easy victory over the Chargers. Moon, who had a key 33-yard completion to Curtis Duncan on the 80-yard drive, also ran for a touchdown early in the fourth quarter to make the score 24-0. Stan Humphries completed 22 of 38 passes for 219 yards for San Diego, but was intercepted 3 times. The Chargers fell to 0-4 for the first time since 1971.

San Diego 0 0 0 0 — 0
Houston 10 0 7 10 — 27
Hou — Jeffires 3 pass from Moon (Del Greco kick)
Hou — FG Del Greco 49
Hou — White 5 run (Del Greco kick)
Hou — Moon 5 run (Del Greco kick)
Hou — FG Del Greco 46

Tampa Bay 27, Detroit 23—at Pontiac Silverdome, attendance 51,374. Vinny Testaverde's 14-yard touchdown pass to tight end Ron Hall with 49 seconds left gave the Buccaneers their first road victory after 15 consecutive losses and ended the Lions' 11-game winning streak at home. Tampa Bay's win wasn't secured, however, until cornerback Milton Mack tackled Detroit wide receiver Brett Perriman at the Buccaneers' 3-yard line as time expired. The lead changed hands three times in the final 6:01. First, Tampa Bay rookie defensive tackle Santana Dotson caught a fumble out of the air and returned it 42 yards for a touchdown to put the Buccaneers on top 20-16. The Lions' Mel Gray returned the ensuing kickoff 89 yards for a touchdown and a 23-20 lead for Detroit. But Tampa Bay marched 80 yards in 14 plays, converting three third-down opportunities along the way, to the winning score. Testaverde passed for 248 yards and Reggie Cobb rushed for 107 for the Buccaneers, who rolled up 395 total yards. The Lions nearly matched that, recording 368. Rodney Peete passed for 323 yards and Perriman caught 9 passes for 117 yards.

Tampa Bay 3 7 0 17 — 27
Detroit 0 3 13 7 — 23
TB — FG Willis 42
Det — FG Hanson 42
TB — Cobb 1 run (Willis kick)
Det — Campbell 78 pass from Peete (Hanson kick)
Det — FG Hanson 35
Det — FG Hanson 36
TB — FG Willis 31
TB — Dotson 42 fumble recovery return (Willis kick)
Det — Gray 89 kickoff return (Hanson kick)
TB — Hall 14 pass from Testaverde (Willis kick)

Sunday Night, September 27

San Francisco 16, New Orleans 10—at Louisiana Superdome, attendance 68,591. Struggling kicker Mike Cofer connected on 3 field goals and Eric Davis intercepted a pass in the end zone in the closing seconds to preserve the 49ers' victory. Cofer, who came into the game only 3 of 7 on field-goal attempts for the year, successfully converted all 3 of his kicks, including a pair in the fourth quarter to break a 10-10 tie. After his 42-yarder with 6:54 left gave San Francisco a six-point lead, the Saints drove to the 49ers' 24-yard line before fumbling the ball away. New Orleans had one more chance and reached the 2 in the final minute until a holding penalty pushed the ball back to the 12 and Davis intercepted Bobby Hebert's pass in the end zone with 10 seconds to go. Hebert completed 25 of 40 passes for 267 yards, but was intercepted 3 times. The Saints outgained San Francisco 336-333, but turned over the ball 5 times. 49ers rookie running back Ricky Watters rushed for 76 yards and caught 7 passes for 52 more.

San Francisco 7 3 0 6 — 16
New Orleans 7 3 0 0 — 10
NO — Martin 11 pass from Hebert (Andersen kick)
SF — Rathman 1 run (Cofer kick)
SF — FG Cofer 40
NO — FG Andersen 42
SF — FG Cofer 26
SF — FG Cofer 42

Monday, September 28

Kansas City 27, L.A. Raiders 7—at Arrowhead Stadium, attendance 77,486. Dave Krieg ran for 2 touchdowns as the Chiefs kept pace with the Broncos for the AFC Western Division lead and dropped the Raiders to 0-4 for the first time in 28 years. Los Angeles took the lead 14 seconds into the second quarter on Eric Dickerson's 40-yard run, his first touchdown as a Raider. But the first of Krieg's 2 touchdown runs, a 3-yarder 6:03 before halftime, tied the score, and Nick Lowery's 22-yard field goal with 1:03 left in the half gave Kansas City the lead for good. Rookie safety Charles Mincy intercepted his first NFL pass and returned it 25 yards for a touchdown to close the scoring late in the fourth quarter. The Chiefs' Barry Word rushed for 125 yards on 27 carries.

L.A. Raiders 0 7 0 0 — 7
Kansas City 0 10 0 17 — 27
Raid — Dickerson 40 run (Jaeger kick)
KC — Krieg 3 run (Lowery kick)
KC — FG Lowery 22
KC — Krieg 7 run (Lowery kick)
KC — FG Lowery 41
KC — Mincy 25 interception return (Lowery kick)

Fifth Week Summaries

Standings

American Football Conference

Eastern Division

	W	L	T	Pct.	Pts.	OP
Miami	4	0	0	1.000	109	60
Buffalo	4	1	0	.800	163	82
Indianapolis	2	2	0	.500	48	75
N.Y. Jets	1	4	0	.200	81	117
New England	0	4	0	.000	34	95

Central Division

	W	L	T	Pct.	Pts.	OP
Houston	3	1	0	.750	94	59
Pittsburgh	3	1	0	.750	82	57
Cincinnati	2	2	0	.500	75	90
Cleveland	1	3	0	.250	54	69

Western Division

	W	L	T	Pct.	Pts.	OP
Denver	4	1	0	.800	70	75
Kansas City	3	2	0	.600	116	67
L.A. Raiders	1	4	0	.200	70	106
San Diego	1	4	0	.200	46	101
Seattle	1	4	0	.200	43	89

National Football Conference

Eastern Division

	W	L	T	Pct.	Pts.	OP
Philadelphia	4	0	0	1.000	107	34
Dallas	3	1	0	.750	95	89
Washington	2	2	0	.500	71	77
N.Y. Giants	1	3	0	.250	79	92
Phoenix	1	3	0	.250	68	109

Central Division

	W	L	T	Pct.	Pts.	OP
Minnesota	4	1	0	.800	129	98
Tampa Bay	3	2	0	.600	115	83
Chicago	2	3	0	.400	108	131
Green Bay	2	3	0	.400	74	104
Detroit	1	4	0	.200	95	97

Western Division

	W	L	T	Pct.	Pts.	OP
San Francisco	4	1	0	.800	136	96
New Orleans	3	2	0	.600	74	51
Atlanta	2	3	0	.400	99	102
L.A. Rams	2	3	0	.400	73	103

Sunday, October 4

Minnesota 21, Chicago 20—at Metrodome, attendance 60,992. Roger Craig's 1-yard touchdown run with 1:46 left in the game capped a stirring fourth-quarter comeback in which the Vikings erased a 20-point deficit to beat the Bears. The victory, coupled with the Buccaneers' loss to the Colts, lifted Minnesota into sole possession of first place in the NFC Central Division. Chicago appeared to be in complete control after taking the second-half kickoff and holding the ball for 10:27 on a 91-yard touchdown drive that lifted its advantage to 20-0. But safety Todd Scott intercepted a Jim Harbaugh pass and returned it 35 yards for a touchdown 57 seconds into the fourth quarter to ignite the Vikings' comeback. Minnesota's Rich Gannon completed 20 of 25 passes for 187 yards, including a 16-yard touchdown pass to Cris Carter that trimmed the deficit to 20-14 with 9:37 to play. Gannon connected on all 7 of his attempts on the Vikings' 2 touchdown drives. By winning, Minnesota improved its record to 4-1 for the first time in 15 years.

Chicago 3 10 7 0 — 20
Minnesota 0 0 0 21 — 21
Chi — FG Butler 50
Chi — FG Butler 37
Chi — Waddle 28 pass from Harbaugh (Butler kick)
Chi — Harbaugh 6 run (Butler kick)
Minn — Scott 35 interception return (Reveiz kick)
Minn — C. Carter 16 pass from Gannon (Reveiz kick)
Minn — Craig 1 run (Reveiz kick)

Atlanta 24, Green Bay 10—at Georgia Dome, attendance 63,769. Chris Miller's 3 touchdown passes made the difference as the Falcons beat the Packers. Two of Miller's scoring tosses went to Andre Rison, giving the wide receiver 5 touchdown receptions in two weeks. The pair teamed on a 10-yard score late in the first quarter, and on a 21-yard score to secure the outcome with 6:07 left in the game. Former Falcon Brett Favre completed 33 of 43 passes for 276 yards for Green Bay. Wide receiver Sterling Sharpe had 9 catches for 107 yards, including a 15-yard touchdown in the third quarter.

Green Bay 0 0 7 3 — 10
Atlanta 14 0 3 7 — 24
Atl — Pritchard 2 pass from Miller (Johnson kick)
Atl — Rison 10 pass from Miller (Johnson kick)
Atl — FG Johnson 49
GB — Sharpe 15 pass from Favre (Jacke kick)
GB — FG Jacke 41
Atl — Rison 21 pass from Miller (Johnson kick)

Indianapolis 24, Tampa Bay 14—at Tampa Stadium, attendance 56,585. Jeff George, playing in his first game since injuring the thumb on his throwing hand in the preseason, passed for 2 touchdowns in the second half as the Colts came back to beat the Buccaneers. Indianapolis controlled the ball for only 30 seconds in the first quarter and for 6:30 of the first half, but found itself trailing just 14-7 at the intermission, thanks to a 46-yard interception return by Chris Goode that set up Rodney Culver's 2-yard touchdown run. The Colts then marched 71 yards with their first possession of the second half, tying the score on George's 34-yard touchdown pass to Jessie Hester. Dean Biasucci's 45-yard field goal with 5:49 left in the third quarter put Indianapolis ahead for good, and George added a 14-yard touchdown pass to tight end Kerry Cash midway through the fourth quarter. After a slow start (2 of his first 3 passes were intercepted), George finished with 15 completions in 33 attempts for 234 yards. Tampa Bay's Vinny Testaverde was 23 of 47 for 286 yards.

Indianapolis 7 0 10 7 — 24
Tampa Bay 7 7 0 0 — 14
TB — Jennings 20 pass from Testaverde (Willis kick)
Ind — Culver 2 run (Biasucci kick)
TB — Cobb 1 run (Willis kick)
Ind — Hester 34 pass from George (Biasucci kick)
Ind — FG Biasucci 45
Ind — Cash 14 pass from George (Biasucci kick)

Denver 20, Kansas City 19—at Mile High Stadium, attendance 75,629. John Elway's 2 touchdown passes in the final two minutes, including a 12-yard completion to Vance Johnson with 38 seconds to go, gave the Broncos a dramatic victory and sole possession of first place in the AFC Western Division. After Nick Lowery's fourth field goal of the game gave the Chiefs a 19-6 lead with five minutes remaining, Elway jumpstarted a lackluster Denver offense that had not scored a touchdown in 12 quarters. First, the Broncos moved 80 yards in 14 plays to trim the deficit to 19-13 on a 25-yard touchdown pass from Elway to Mark Jackson. After Kansas City failed to make a first down, rookie Arthur Marshall returned a punt 28 yards to the Chiefs' 27-yard line to set up the winning touchdown pass. Elway shook off 5 sacks, including 3 by defensive end Neil Smith, to complete 23 of 38 passes for 311 yards, including 9 for 118 yards to tight end Shannon Sharpe. Kansas City's Dave Krieg was 22 of 31 for 301 yards, including a 50-yard touchdown to wide receiver Willie Davis in the second quarter. Davis caught 5 passes for 127 yards.

Kansas City 0 10 3 6 — 19
Denver 0 3 3 14 — 20
KC — Davis 50 pass from Krieg (Lowery kick)
Den — FG Treadwell 41
KC — FG Lowery 44
KC — FG Lowery 36
Den — FG Treadwell 22

KC	— FG Lowery 26
KC	— FG Lowery 33
Den	— Jackson 25 pass from Elway (Treadwell kick)
Den	— V. Johnson 12 pass from Elway (Treadwell kick)

San Francisco 27, L.A. Rams 24—at Candlestick Park, attendance 63,071. Mike Cofer kicked a 21-yard field goal with one second remaining to give the 49ers the victory after a furious fourth quarter. San Francisco entered the period leading 10-7 but the Rams rallied, tying the score on a 33-yard field goal by Tony Zendejas with 12:56 left. Los Angeles then took the lead on cornerback Robert Bailey's 24-yard interception return just 26 seconds later. The 49ers countered with touchdown runs of 8 and 39 yards by quarterback Steve Young, the latter coming at the 3:55 mark. The Rams drove 69 yards to tie it again on a 9-yard touchdown pass from Jim Everett to Willie Anderson with 1:50 left. But Young passed 43 yards to Brent Jones and 26 yards to Jerry Rice on the ensuing 77-yard march that set up Cofer's winning field goal.

L.A. Rams	0	7	0	17	—	24
San Francisco	7	3	0	17	—	27

SF	— Watters 3 run (Cofer kick)
Rams	— Carter 11 pass from Everett (Zendejas kick)
SF	— FG Cofer 26
Rams	— FG Zendejas 33
Rams	— Bailey 24 interception return (Zendejas kick)
SF	— Young 8 run (Cofer kick)
SF	— Young 39 run (Cofer kick)
Rams	— Anderson 9 pass from Everett (Zendejas kick)
SF	— FG Cofer 21

Miami 37, Buffalo 10—at Rich Stadium, attendance 80,368. Safety Louis Oliver returned 1 of his 3 interceptions an NFL record-tying 103 yards for a touchdown to help lead the Dolphins past the previously undefeated Bills. Oliver's interception return equaled the league record established by San Diego's Vencie Glenn against Denver in 1987, and gave Miami an insurmountable 31-10 advantage with 4:38 left in the third quarter. Oliver finished with 170 return yards on his thefts, and cornerback J.B. Brown added 48 more yards on a second-quarter interception return that set up a touchdown. Dan Marino passed for 282 yards and 3 touchdowns, including a 24-yard pass to tight end Keith Jackson, who had signed as a free agent earlier in the week. Buffalo's Jim Kelly completed 25 of 48 passes for 306 yards, but was victimized by the 4 interceptions.

Miami	3	14	17	3	—	37
Buffalo	3	7	0	0	—	10

Buff	— FG Christie 40
Mia	— FG Stoyanovich 30
Mia	— Jackson 24 pass from Marino (Stoyanovich kick)
Mia	— Paige 5 pass from Marino (Stoyanovich kick)
Buff	— Reed 16 pass from Kelly (Christie kick)
Mia	— Humphrey 9 pass from Marino (Stoyanovich kick)
Mia	— Oliver 103 interception return (Stoyanovich kick)
Mia	— FG Stoyanovich 43
Mia	— FG Stoyanovich 34

New Orleans 13, Detroit 7—at Pontiac Silverdome, attendance 66,971. The Saints' defense registered 6 sacks and limited the Lions to 187 total yards while handing the defending NFC Central Division champions their fourth loss in five games. New Orleans also converted the game's lone turnover into the deciding touchdown midway through the third quarter. Defensive end Frank Warren recovered a fumbled handoff at the Detroit 17-yard line, and four plays later rookie Vaughn Dunbar ran 1 yard for the touchdown that gave the Saints the lead. New Orleans made the advantage stand up by controlling the ball for more than 40 of the game's 60 minutes, and by not allowing the Lions to move the ball past the Detroit 34 in the second half. Linebacker Pat Swilling and defensive end Wayne Martin each had 2 sacks for the Saints. Kicker Morten Andersen had a 50-yard field goal, his NFL record-tying nineteenth career three-pointer of 50 or more yards.

New Orleans	0	3	7	3	—	13
Detroit	0	7	0	0	—	7

NO	— FG Andersen 50
Det	— Perriman 7 pass from Peete (Hanson kick)
NO	— Dunbar 1 run (Andersen kick)
NO	— FG Andersen 20

L.A. Raiders 13, N.Y. Giants 10—at Los Angeles Memorial Coliseum, attendance 43,103. Jeff Jaeger atoned for a pair of missed field-goal attempts earlier in the game by kicking a career-best 54-yarder with 7:15 remaining to give the Raiders the victory, their first after seven consecutive regular-season defeats dating back to the 1991 season. The Giants led 10-0 at halftime, though it could have have been more—they were forced to settle for Matt Bahr's 18-yard field goal two seconds before intermission after driving 79 yards, only to be turned away at the 1. Jaeger's 26-yard field goal and a 68-yard touchdown pass from Todd Marinovich to Tim Brown, who outleaped New York cornerback Mark Collins for a short pass and then sprinted to the end zone, tied the score before Los Angeles drove 44 yards to the go-ahead field goal. Marinovich, who completed 14 of 23 passes for 216 yards with no interceptions, passed 33 yards to Willie Gault for the key play on the winning drive. The Raiders' defense held after that, allowing the Giants to get no closer than Los Angeles's 42.

N.Y. Giants	0	10	0	0	—	10
L.A. Raiders	0	0	10	3	—	13

Giants	— Bunch 5 run (Bahr kick)
Giants	— FG Bahr 18
Raid	— FG Jaeger 26
Raid	— T. Brown 68 pass from Marinovich (Jaeger kick)
Raid	— FG Jaeger 54

San Diego 17, Seattle 6—at San Diego Jack Murphy Stadium, attendance 36,783. Anthony Miller caught a 67-yard touchdown pass from Stan Humphries just five plays into the game to spark the Chargers to their first victory of the season. Miller, who had 9 receptions for 142 yards, also caught a 5-yard scoring pass 12 seconds before halftime to give San Diego a 17-3 lead at the intermission. The Chargers' defense limited the Seahawks to 11 first downs and 180 total yards. Seattle quarterback Kelly Stouffer suffered a dislocated shoulder when sacked by Chargers defensive end Leslie O'Neal in the second quarter. Stouffer's replacement, Dan McGwire, completed 12 of 21 passes, but for only 70 yards. He was intercepted 3 times and sacked 3 times.

Seattle	0	3	3	0	—	6
San Diego	10	7	0	0	—	17

SD	— Miller 67 pass from Humphries (Carney kick)
SD	— FG Carney 49
Sea	— FG Kasay 27
SD	— Miller 5 pass from Humphries (Carney kick)
Sea	— FG Kasay 29

Phoenix 27, Washington 24—at Sun Devil Stadium, attendance 34,488. Chris Chandler's 9-yard touchdown pass to running back Larry Centers with 41 seconds left gave the Cardinals a stunning come-from-behind victory. Phoenix cornerback Robert Massey ignited the rally by returning a pair of fourth-quarter interceptions for touchdowns. Washington led 24-6 through three quarters. But Massey struck on the first play of the fourth quarter, stepping in front of a pass intended for Art Monk and returning it 31 yards to make it 24-13 nine seconds into the period. He returned his second theft 41 yards to trim the deficit to 24-20 with 8:05 to play. After a Redskins' punt, Chandler marched the Cardinals 85 yards to the winning score, completing all 6 of his attempts along the way. The Redskins still had a chance to tie, but Chip Lohmiller's 40-yard field-goal try failed as time expired.

Washington	14	3	7	0	—	24
Phoenix	0	0	6	21	—	27

Wash	— Sanders 19 pass from Rypien (Lohmiller kick)
Wash	— Byner 9 run (Lohmiller kick)
Wash	— FG Lohmiller 33
Phx	— Brown 1 run (kick failed)
Wash	— Byner 3 run (Lohmiller kick)
Phx	— Massey 31 interception return (Davis kick)
Phx	— Massey 41 interception return (Davis kick)
Phx	— Centers 9 pass from Chandler (Davis kick)

Sunday Night, October 4

N.Y. Jets 30, New England 21—at Giants Stadium, attendance 60,180. Browning Nagle passed for 2 touchdowns and Cary Blanchard, claimed on waivers from New Orleans earlier in the week, kicked 3 field goals in his first game with the Jets. The victory was the first of the season for New York, and left the Patriots as the NFL's lone team without a win in 1992. Nagle's 7-yard touchdown pass to Terance Mathis gave the Jets a 17-0 lead 31 seconds before halftime. His 19-yard touchdown pass to Rob Moore put the game out of reach at 30-14 with four minutes remaining. Hugh Millen completed 23 of 33 passes for 259 yards for the Patriots, but was intercepted 2 times and sacked 7 times, twice each by Marvin Washington and Paul Frase. The Patriots' Irving Fryar caught 8 passes for 165 yards, including touchdowns of 38 and 20 yards.

New England	0	0	7	14	—	21
N.Y. Jets	3	14	0	13	—	30

Jets	— FG Blanchard 37
Jets	— Baxter 2 run (Blanchard kick)
Jets	— Mathis 7 pass from Nagle (Blanchard kick)
NE	— Fryar 20 pass from Millen (Baumann kick)
Jets	— FG Blanchard 40
Jets	— FG Blanchard 47
NE	— Fryar 38 pass from Millen (Baumann kick)
Jets	— Moore 19 pass from Nagle (Blanchard kick)
NE	— Cook 5 pass from Millen (Baumann kick)

Monday, October 5

Philadelphia 31, Dallas 7—at Veterans Stadium, attendance 66,572. Former Cowboys running back Herschel Walker rushed for 86 yards and 2 touchdowns, and the Eagles forced 4 turnovers en route to their victory over Dallas. Philadelphia's 3 interceptions and 1 fumble recovery led to 3 Eagles touchdowns. Walker helped capitalize on 2 of the miscues by rushing 9 yards for a touchdown in the third quarter and 16 yards for a score in the fourth. Those runs turned a tight 10-7 game into a 24-7 rout. In addition to intercepting Dallas quarterback Troy Aikman 3 times, Philadelphia recorded 4 sacks. Despite constant pressure, Aikman managed to complete 19 of 38 passes for 256 yards. Michael Irvin totaled 105 yards on 4 catches.

Dallas	7	0	0	0	—	7
Philadelphia	10	0	7	14	—	31

Phil	— Cunningham 2 run (Ruzek kick)
Dall	— Martin 7 pass from Aikman (Elliott kick)
Phil	— FG Ruzek 40
Phil	— Walker 9 run (Ruzek kick)
Phil	— Walker 16 run (Ruzek kick)
Phil	— Byars 12 run (Ruzek kick)

Sixth Week Summaries

Standings

American Football Conference

Eastern Division	W	L	T	Pct.	Pts.	OP
Miami	5	0	0	1.000	130	77
Buffalo	4	2	0	.667	166	102
Indianapolis	3	2	0	.600	54	78
N.Y. Jets	1	5	0	.167	84	123
New England	0	5	0	.000	46	119
Central Division						
Houston	4	1	0	.800	132	83
Pittsburgh	3	2	0	.600	91	74
Cincinnati	2	3	0	.400	99	128
Cleveland	2	3	0	.400	71	78
Western Division						
Denver	4	2	0	.667	73	109
Kansas City	4	2	0	.667	140	84
L.A. Raiders	2	4	0	.333	90	109
San Diego	1	4	0	.200	46	101
Seattle	1	5	0	.167	43	116

National Football Conference

Eastern Division	W	L	T	Pct.	Pts.	OP
Dallas	4	1	0	.800	122	89
Philadelphia	4	1	0	.800	124	58
Washington	3	2	0	.600	105	80
N.Y. Giants	2	3	0	.400	110	113
Phoenix	1	4	0	.200	89	140
Central Division						
Minnesota	4	1	0	.800	129	98
Tampa Bay	3	2	0	.600	115	83
Chicago	2	3	0	.400	108	131
Green Bay	2	3	0	.400	74	104
Detroit	1	4	0	.200	95	97
Western Division						
San Francisco	5	1	0	.833	160	108
New Orleans	4	2	0	.667	87	61
Atlanta	2	4	0	.333	116	123
L.A. Rams	2	4	0	.333	83	116

Sunday, October 11

Miami 21, Atlanta 17—at Joe Robbie Stadium, attendance 68,633. Mark Higgs ran 1 yard for a touchdown with 5:01 left in the game as the Dolphins averted an upset to stand as the lone undefeated team in the NFL. The Falcons were in control, leading 17-7 late in the third quarter, until Miami safety Vestee Jackson intercepted a pass from Chris Miller and returned it 30 yards to trim the margin to 17-14. Higgs's winning run concluded a 77-yard drive, the key play a 46-yard pass completion from Dan Marino to Tony Martin. Marino passed for 250 yards and Higgs, who also had a 14-yard touchdown run in the first quarter, scored twice. Miller completed 26 of 41 passes for 254 yards and 2 touchdowns for the Falcons. Andre Rison caught 7 passes for 101 yards, including a 22-yard touchdown to give Atlanta its 10-point lead midway through the third quarter.

Atlanta	0	10	7	0	—	17
Miami	7	0	7	7	—	21

Mia — Higgs 14 run (Stoyanovich kick)
Atl — Pritchard 18 pass from Miller (Johnson kick)
Atl — FG Johnson 52
Atl — Rison 22 pass from Miller (Johnson kick)
Mia — V. Jackson 30 interception return (Stoyanovich kick)
Mia — Higgs 1 run (Stoyanovich kick)

L.A. Raiders 20, Buffalo 3—at Los Angeles Memorial Coliseum, attendance 52,287. Todd Marinovich passed for 2 touchdowns and the Raiders didn't allow the NFL's top-ranked offense to reach the end zone. Marinovich's 2-yard scoring toss to running back Eric Dickerson put Los Angeles ahead 7-0 in the first quarter, and the Raiders built a 14-3 cushion in the second period when Tim Brown took a short pass from Marinovich and bolted 52 yards for a touchdown. The Bills got 302 passing yards from Jim Kelly and amassed 350 total yards, but had a pair of fourth-quarter drives stall deep in Los Angeles territory. The Raiders also got to Kelly for 5 sacks, including 2 each by defensive ends Howie Long and Anthony Smith. The Bill's scoring output was their lowest since they scored 3 points against the Bears in 1988.

Buffalo	0	3	0	0	—	3
L.A. Raiders	7	10	3	0	—	20

Raid — Dickerson 2 pass from Marinovich (Jaeger kick)
Buff — FG Christie 25
Raid — T. Brown 52 pass from Marinovich (Jaeger kick)
Raid — FG Jaeger 45
Raid — FG Jaeger 36

Houston 38, Cincinnati 24—at Riverfront Stadium, attendance 54,254. Warren Moon threw 5 touchdown passes and Lorenzo White rushed for a career-high 149 yards to help the Oilers breeze past the Bengals. Haywood Jeffires caught 3 of the touchdown passes and Ernest Givins grabbed the other 2 as Houston won its fourth consecutive game and moved into sole possession of first place in the AFC Central. Cincinnati entered the game with the poorest pass defense in the NFL and decided to take the long pass away from Moon. Though the Oilers' quarterback was held in check with 216 yards on his 32 pass attempts, he matched his career mark for touchdown passes, throwing his fifth with 8:25 to play in the third quarter, by which time his team led 38-10. Houston amassed 418 total yards, including 202 rushing.

Houston	10	14	14	0	—	38
Cincinnati	0	10	7	7	—	24

Hou — FG Del Greco 39
Hou — Jeffires 8 pass from Moon (Del Greco kick)
Hou — Givins 2 pass from Moon (Del Greco kick)
Hou — Jeffires 14 pass from Moon (Del Greco kick)
Cin — McGee 21 pass from Esiason (Breech kick)
Cin — FG Breech 29
Hou — Givins 7 pass from Moon (Del Greco kick)
Hou — Jeffires 3 pass from Moon (Del Greco kick)
Cin — McGee 26 pass from Esiason (Breech kick)
Cin — Stegall 12 pass from Hollas (Breech kick)

Indianapolis 6, N.Y. Jets 3—at Hoosier Dome, attendance 48,393. Dean Biasucci's 47-yard field goal 3:01 into overtime gave the Colts—who won only one game all of 1991—their third victory of the season. After Jets rookie Cary Blanchard tied the game on a 35-yard field goal with 30 seconds left in regulation, Indianapolis took the kickoff in the extra session and marched 34 yards in 8 plays to the winning kick. The Colts had big advantages in most statistical categories: 22-8 in first downs, 282-147 in total yards, and 39:10-23:51 in time of possession. They were particularly dominant in the first half, running 46 plays to New York's 13. The Jets also were whistled for 10 penalties. But until the overtime, Indianapolis couldn't capitalize as Biasucci missed 3 field-goal tries, and quarterback Jeff George threw an interception in the end zone when his receiver turned the wrong way

N.Y. Jets	0	0	0	3	0	—	3
Indianapolis	0	3	0	0	3	—	6

Ind — FG Biasucci 31
Jets — FG Blanchard 35
Ind — FG Biasucci 47

Kansas City 24, Philadelphia 17—at Arrowhead Stadium, attendance 76,626. The run-oriented Chiefs took to the air to hand the Eagles their first loss of the season, as quarterback Dave Krieg passed for 272 yards and 3 touchdowns. Philadelphia entered the game with the league's best defense overall and against the run, so Kansas City came out firing. Krieg threw passes on each of the game's first five plays, the fifth a 43-yard touchdown to J.J. Birden. He added a 24-yard touchdown to Birden just 20 seconds before halftime, then gave the Chiefs what proved to be an insurmountable 21-3 advantage with a 74-yard bomb to Willie Davis midway through the third quarter. Eagles quarterback Randall Cunningham, who was sacked 6 times and threw 2 interceptions, rallied his team with a pair of fourth-quarter touchdown passes to tight end Pat Beach, but it wasn't enough. Davis caught 5 passes for 167 yards for Kansas City. Outside linebacker Derrick Thomas had 3 sacks and defensive end Neil Smith added 2. Krieg's 3 touchdown passes gave him 201 for his career. He was the fifteenth player in league history to reach the 200 mark.

Philadelphia	0	3	0	14	—	17
Kansas City	7	7	7	3	—	24

KC — Birden 43 pass from Krieg (Lowery kick)
Phil — FG Ruzek 49
KC — Birden 24 pass from Krieg (Lowery kick)
KC — Davis 74 pass from Krieg (Lowery kick)
KC — FG Lowery 20
Phil — Beach 3 pass from Cunningham (Ruzek kick)
Phil — Beach 3 pass from Cunningham (Ruzek kick)

N.Y. Giants 31, Phoenix 21—at Giants Stadium, attendance 70,042. Rodney Hampton rushed for a career-high 167 yards to lead the Giants to their ninth consecutive win over the Cardinals. Jeff Hostetler, making his first start of the season in place of injured Phil Simms, passed for 142 yards, including a 25-yard touchdown to Ed McCaffrey. Hostetler also scrambled 16 yards for a touchdown midway through the third quarter to give the Giants a 28-14 lead. The Cardinals' Ernie Jones caught a 72-yard touchdown pass on the fourth play of the game to give his team an early lead. But Hampton responded with a 63-yard touchdown run to pull New York even, and the Giants scored on each of their next two possessions to build a 21-7 advantage. New York finished the game with 260 rushing yards and 399 total yards.

Phoenix	7	7	0	7	—	21
N.Y. Giants	7	14	10	0	—	31

Phx — E. Jones 72 pass from Chandler (G. Davis kick)
Giants — Hampton 63 run (Bahr kick)
Giants — Bunch 6 run (Bahr kick)
Giants — McCaffrey 25 pass from Hostetler (Bahr kick)
Phx — Chandler 1 run (G. Davis kick)
Giants — Hostetler 16 run (Bahr kick)
Giants — FG Bahr 32
Phx — Bailey 7 pass from Chandler (G. Davis kick)

Cleveland 17, Pittsburgh 9—at Cleveland Stadium, attendance 78,080. Kevin Mack's 1-yard touchdown run capped a 90-yard, third-quarter touchdown drive and provided the winning points in the Browns' victory. Mack's run gave Cleveland a 10-6 advantage with 5:20 remaining in the third quarter. After the Steelers' Gary Anderson kicked his third field goal of the game, a 40-yarder with 13:52 left to pull his team within one point, the Browns added an insurance touchdown on Mike Tomczak's 47-yard touchdown pass to Michael Jackson with 10:44 to go. Pittsburgh dominated the game statistically, recording 20 first downs to Cleveland's 12, totaling 350 yards to 253, and maintaining possession for nearly 35 minutes. But the Steelers had a touchdown called back by a penalty, had 1 field-goal attempt hit the upright, and were forced to settle for three-pointers on 3 other occasions. Steelers quarterback Neil O'Donnell, who completed his first 11 passes, finished 25 of 32 for 241 yards. Barry Foster gained 133 yards rushing and receiving.

Pittsburgh	3	3	0	3	—	9
Cleveland	0	3	7	7	—	17

Pitt — FG Anderson 25
Pitt — FG Anderson 36
Cleve — FG Stover 51
Cleve — Mack 1 run (Stover kick)
Pitt — FG Anderson 40
Cleve — Jackson 47 pass from Tomczak (Stover kick)

San Francisco 24, New England 12—at Foxboro Stadium, attendance 54,126. Ricky Watters's 2 fourth-quarter touchdowns lifted the 49ers past the stubborn Patriots. New England, still winless in 1992, took a 12-10 advantage—their first lead of the season—on Hugh Millen's 11-yard touchdown pass to tight end Ben Coates late in the third quarter. But Watters began a 75-yard march to the go-ahead score with a 30-yard run, and ended it by catching a 2-yard touchdown pass from Steve Young with 8:52 left in the game. He put the game out of reach by running 1 yard for the clinching score with 2:21 to go. Young passed for 234 yards and also had a 32-yard scoring toss to Jerry Rice in the second quarter. Watters ran for 104 yards on 19 carries and caught 8 passes for 84 yards. The Patriots scored all of their points following special-teams mistakes by San Francisco: the touchdown and a field goal after fumbled punt returns, and another field goal after a bobbled snap aborted a punt attempt.

San Francisco	0	10	0	14	—	24
New England	0	3	9	0	—	12

SF — Rice 32 pass from Young (Cofer kick)
SF — FG Cofer 36
NE — FG Baumann 24
NE — FG Baumann 44
NE — Coates 11 pass from Millen (kick failed)
SF — Watters 2 pass from Young (Cofer kick)
SF — Watters 1 run (Cofer kick)

Dallas 27, Seattle 0—at Texas Stadium, attendance 62,311. The Cowboys set a club record by limiting the Seahawks to only 62 total yards while recording their first regular-season shutout since 1978. Dallas's defense recorded 7 sacks, including 2 each by ends Tony Tolbert and Jim Jeffcoat, recovered 2 fumbles, and intercepted a pass, which safety Ray Horton returned 15 yards for a touchdown. Seattle managed only 6 first downs and 24 net yards passing. The Seahawks, already playing without injured starting quarterback Kelly Stouffer, suffered another blow when his replacement, Dan McGwire, was knocked out of the game with hip and shoulder injuries. Emmitt Smith rushed for 78 yards and a pair of short touchdowns for the Cowboys. Michael Irvin caught 6 passes for 113 yards.

Seattle	0	0	0	0	—	0
Dallas	7	13	7	0	—	27

Dall — E. Smith 2 run (Elliott kick)
Dall — E. Smith 1 run (Elliott kick)
Dall — FG Elliott 31
Dall — FG Elliott 51
Dall — Horton 15 interception return (Elliott kick)

Sunday Night, October 11

New Orleans 13, L.A. Rams 10—at Louisiana Superdome, attendance 68,591. Morten Andersen's 30-yard field goal with 3:37 left was the difference as the Saints edged the Rams. Los Angeles was poised for an upset after Cleveland Gary capped a 75-yard drive with a 1-yard touchdown run late in the third quarter to tie the game at 10-10. But New Orleans rookie Marcus Dowdell, playing in his first NFL game, returned a punt 34 yards to the Rams' 37-yard line to position his team for the winning drive. The Saints allowed Los Angeles only 196 total yards while sacking quarterback Jim Everett 4 times. Linebacker Rickey Jackson had 3 of the sacks. New Orleans wide receiver Eric Martin caught 6 passes for 103 yards, including a 5-yard touchdown catch in the first quarter.

L.A. Rams	0	3	7	0	—	10
New Orleans	7	3	0	3	—	13

NO — E. Martin 5 pass from Hebert (Andersen kick)
Rams — FG Zendejas 30
NO — FG Andersen 26
Rams — Gary 1 run (Zendejas kick)
NO — FG Andersen 30

Monday, October 12

Washington 34, Denver 3—at RFK Stadium, attendance 56,371. Quarterback Mark Rypien accounted for 3 touchdowns and wide receiver Art Monk became the NFL's all-time leading pass catcher during the Redskins' rout. Rypien completed 16 of 26 passes for 245 yards, including a 44-yard touchdown to Gary Clark in the second quarter. He also twice sneaked 1 yard for scores. Meanwhile, Washington's defense was allowing the Broncos only 7 first downs and 128 total yards while forcing 4 turnovers and making 5 sacks. Linebacker Wilber Marshall returned an interception 20 yards for a touchdown 42 seconds before halftime to put the Redskins ahead 24-3. Monk caught 7 passes (for 69 yards) to give him 820 receptions for his career, 1 better than Steve Largent, the previous record holder. He caught 3 consecutive passes on a fourth-quarter drive, the record-breaker coming on a 10-yard catch with 3:12 left.

Denver	3	0	0	0	—	3
Washington	17	7	7	3	—	34

Wash — Rypien 1 run (Lohmiller kick)
Den — FG Treadwell 38
Wash — FG Lohmiller 43
Wash — Marshall 20 interception return (Lohmiller kick)
Wash — Clark 44 pass from Rypien (Lohmiller kick)
Wash — Rypien 1 run (Lohmiller kick)
Wash — FG Lohmiller 36

Seventh Week Summaries

Standings

American Football Conference

Eastern Division

	W	L	T	Pct.	Pts.	OP
Miami	6	0	0	1.000	168	94
Buffalo	4	2	0	.667	166	102
Indianapolis	3	3	0	.500	68	112
N.Y. Jets	1	5	0	.167	84	123
New England	0	6	0	.000	63	157

Central Division						
Houston	4	2	0	.667	153	110
Pittsburgh	4	2	0	.667	111	74
Cleveland	3	3	0	.500	88	84
Cincinnati	2	4	0	.333	99	148
Western Division						
Denver	5	2	0	.714	100	130
Kansas City	4	3	0	.571	150	101
L.A. Raiders	3	4	0	.429	109	109
San Diego	2	4	0	.333	80	115
Seattle	1	6	0	.143	43	135

National Football Conference

Eastern Division	W	L	T	Pct.	Pts.	OP
Dallas	5	1	0	.833	139	99
Philadelphia	4	2	0	.667	136	74
Washington	4	2	0	.667	121	92
N.Y. Giants	2	4	0	.333	127	151
Phoenix	1	5	0	.167	110	170
Central Division						
Minnesota	5	1	0	.833	160	112
Chicago	3	3	0	.500	139	145
Tampa Bay	3	3	0	.500	129	114
Green Bay	2	4	0	.333	80	121
Detroit	1	5	0	.167	109	128
Western Division						
San Francisco	6	1	0	.857	216	125
New Orleans	5	2	0	.714	117	82
L.A. Rams	3	4	0	.429	121	133
Atlanta	2	5	0	.286	133	179

Thursday, October 15

Minnesota 31, Detroit 14—at Metrodome, attendance 52,816. The Vikings scored touchdowns on their first three possessions, added a field goal on their fourth, and cruised past the Lions. Quarterback Rich Gannon threw touchdown passes of 47 yards to Anthony Carter and 43 yards to Hassan Jones, and after an interception by cornerback Carl Lee, Terry Allen ran 1 yard to give Minnesota a 21-0 lead in the first quarter. Gannon left the game early in the second quarter with a hyperextended knee and was replaced by Sean Salisbury, who threw a 29-yard touchdown pass to Cris Carter in the fourth quarter. Anthony Carter had 109 yards on 5 catches for the Vikings, who totaled 393 yards of offense. Brett Perriman caught 8 passes for 124 yards for the defending NFC Central Division-champion Lions, who lost their fourth straight.

Detroit	0	7	0	7	—	14
Minnesota	21	3	0	7	—	31

Minn — A. Carter 47 pass from Gannon (Reveiz kick)
Minn — Jones 43 pass from Gannon (Reveiz kick)
Minn — Allen 1 run (Reveiz kick)
Minn — FG Reveiz 20
Det — Sanders 11 run (Hanson kick)
Minn — C. Carter 29 pass from Salisbury (Reveiz kick)
Det — Moore 47 pass from Kramer (Hanson kick)

Sunday, October 18

San Francisco 56, Atlanta 17—at Candlestick Park, attendance 63,302. Steve Young passed for 399 yards and 3 touchdowns, and wide receiver Jerry Rice and running back Ricky Watters each scored 3 touchdowns as the 49ers blasted the Falcons. San Francisco rolled up 590 total yards en route to setting a club single-game scoring record, eclipsing the old mark established in its 55-10 victory over the Broncos in Super Bowl XXIV. Young, who completed 18 of 28 passes, had 336 passing yards in the first half alone as the 49ers built a 42-10 lead by intermission. Rice caught 7 passes for 183 yards and ran 26 yards for a touchdown on a reverse in the third quarter. He became only the eighth player in NFL history to score 100 career touchdowns and finished the day with 102, good for sixth on the all-time list. His 2 touchdown receptions gave him 97 for his career, only 3 behind Steve Largent's league-record 100. Watters, the first-year player, scored 3 touchdowns in a game for the first time and had 132 rushing and receiving yards.

Atlanta	7	3	0	7	—	17
San Francisco	21	21	14	0	—	56

SF — Rathman 1 run (Cofer kick)
SF — Watters 8 run (Cofer kick)
Atl — Haynes 44 pass from Miller (Johnson kick)
SF — Rice 80 pass from Young (Cofer kick)
SF — Watters 4 run (Cofer kick)
SF — Watters 1 run (Cofer kick)
Atl — FG Johnson 51
SF — Rice 40 pass from Young (Cofer kick)
SF — Rice 26 run (Cofer kick)
SF — B. Jones 11 pass from Young (Cofer kick)
Atl — Phillips 6 pass from Wilson (Johnson kick)

Cleveland 17, Green Bay 6—at Cleveland Stadium, attendance 69,268. Kevin Mack capped a pair of long scoring drives with touchdown runs to lead the Browns to their third victory in four games. Mack's 4-yard run at the end of a 73-yard drive broke a 3-3 tie and gave Cleveland the lead for good at 10-3 with 3:54 left in the third quarter. Midway through the fourth period, the Browns marched 80 yards to Mack's 5-yard run to put the game away. Meanwhile, Cleveland's defense stretched its string to 13 consecutive quarters without allowing a touchdown. The Packers managed 5 trips inside the Browns' 30-yard line, but could come away with only a pair of field goals.

Green Bay	0	0	3	3	—	6
Cleveland	3	0	7	7	—	17

Cleve — FG Stover 26
GB — FG Jacke 44
Cleve — Mack 4 run (Stover kick)
GB — FG Jacke 37
Cleve — Mack 5 run (Stover kick)

Denver 27, Houston 21—at Mile High Stadium, attendance 74,827. Reggie Rivers's 20-yard touchdown run with 1:34 remaining capped another John Elway-led comeback that gave the Broncos the victory. The Oilers had taken a 21-20 lead on a 7-yard touchdown pass from Warren Moon to Haywood Jeffires at the end of a 94-yard drive with 1:56 to play. But Elway, the Denver quarterback who already had engineered 30 game-winning drives in the fourth-quarter or overtime in his career, including an 87-yard march to beat the Oilers in a 1991 divisional playoff game, marched Denver 80 yards in only 22 seconds for the winning score. From the Broncos' 20-yard line, Elway passed 39 yards to Mark Jackson, then found Vance Johnson for 21 yards to position Rivers for the winning run. It was Rivers's only rushing attempt of the day. Moon completed 23 of 39 passes for 321 yards and wide receiver Curtis Duncan had 133 yards on 5 receptions for the Oilers. But Moon, who had been sacked only 4 times all season entering the game, was dropped 4 times by the Broncos' defense, including 2½ times by linebacker Simon Fletcher. Denver's Gaston Green ran for 98 yards on only 8 carries, including a 67-yard touchdown run in the second quarter.

Houston	7	0	7	7	—	21
Denver	0	10	7	10	—	27

Hou — Givins 8 pass from Moon (Del Greco kick)
Den — FG Treadwell 45
Den — Green 67 run (Treadwell kick)
Hou — White 3 run (Del Greco kick)
Den — Jackson 42 pass from Elway (Treadwell kick)
Den — FG Treadwell 28
Hou — Jeffires 7 pass from Moon (Del Greco kick)
Den — Rivers 20 run (Treadwell kick)

Dallas 17, Kansas City 10—at Texas Stadium, attendance 64,115. The Cowboys took over sole possession of first place in the NFC Eastern Division for the first time since 1986 by beating the Chiefs. Emmitt Smith's 2-yard touchdown run early in the second quarter gave Dallas a 14-3 lead and what proved to be all the points the Cowboys would need. Kansas City pulled within 14-10 at halftime on a 2-yard run by Barry Word, but Lin Elliott's third-quarter field goal for Dallas was the only scoring of the second half. The Chiefs' best chance to tie came after rookie defensive back Dale Carter intercepted a pass from Troy Aikman at the Cowboys' 47-yard line late in the game. But after reaching the 26, Kansas City was turned away by Dallas safety Ray Horton, who stepped in front of a pass from Dave Krieg to make an interception at the 8 with 3:27 to play, and the Cowboys held on for their tenth consecutive victory at Texas Stadium.

Kansas City	3	7	0	0	—	10
Dallas	7	7	3	0	—	17

KC — FG Lowery 32
Dall — Johnston 2 pass from Aikman (Elliott kick)
Dall — E. Smith 2 run (Elliott kick)
KC — Word 2 run (Lowery kick)
Dall — FG Elliott 39

L.A. Raiders 19, Seattle 0—at Kingdome, attendance 56,904. The Raiders' defense recorded 6 sacks and a safety en route to shutting out the injury-riddled Seahawks. End Anthony Smith had 4 of the sacks as Los Angeles harassed Seattle quarterback Stan Gelbaugh, the team's third starting quarterback in as many weeks, into only 17 completions in 41 attempts. The Seahawks were just as ineffective on the ground, gaining only 41 rushing yards while getting shut out for the second straight week, the first time that had happened in franchise history. It also was their third consecutive game without a touchdown. The Raiders lost starting quarterback Todd Marinovich in the first quarter after he suffered a sprained knee while being sacked by Seattle defensive tackle Cortez Kennedy. But backup Jay Schroeder passed 4 yards to Willie Gault for a touchdown in the second quarter and Nick Bell ran 66 yards for a score in the fourth period. Bell finished with 97 yards on only 10 carries. Fellow running back Eric Dickerson gained only 24 yards on 9 carries, but moved past Tony Dorsett into second place on the NFL's career rushing list with 12,744 yards.

L.A. Raiders	0	12	0	7	—	19
Seattle	0	0	0	0	—	0

Raid — Gault 4 pass from Schroeder (Jaeger kick)
Raid — FG Jaeger 53
Raid — Safety, Harrison tackled Hitchcock in end zone
Raid — Bell 66 run (Jaeger kick)

Miami 38, New England 17—at Joe Robbie Stadium, attendance 57,282. Dan Marino passed for 294 yards and 4 touchdowns in only three quarters of play and the Dolphins overcame a slow start to remain unbeaten and keep the Patriots winless. After spotting New England a 10-0 lead in the first quarter, Miami responded with 5 touchdowns and a field goal on its next 6 possessions. Marino tossed scoring passes of 44 yards to Mark Clayton and 43 yards to Mark Duper, and hit tight end Keith Jackson with 6- and 11-yard scores. It was the seventeenth time in his career that Marino passed for 4 touchdowns in a game, equaling Johnny Unitas's NFL record. The game originally was scheduled to be played on the opening weekend of the season, but was shifted to the teams' bye weekend after a hurricane struck south Florida and forced a postponement. With the victory, the Dolphins raised their record to 6-0, their best start since 1984, their last Super Bowl season.

New England	10	0	0	7	—	17
Miami	0	17	21	0	—	38

NE — FG Baumann 19
NE — Fryar 54 pass from Hodson (Baumann kick)
Mia — Clayton 44 pass from Marino (Stoyanovich kick)
Mia — FG Stoyanovich 34
Mia — K. Jackson 6 pass from Marino (Stoyanovich kick)
Mia — Duper 43 pass from Marino (Stoyanovich kick)
Mia — K. Jackson 11 pass Marino (Stoyanovich kick)
Mia — Higgs 3 run (Stoyanovich kick)
NE — Timpson 14 pass from Hodson (Baumann kick)

New Orleans 30, Phoenix 21—at Sun Devil Stadium, attendance 27,735. Bobby Hebert passed for a career-high 355 yards and 3 touchdowns and the Saints overcame an 11-point deficit to beat the Cardinals. Chris Chandler's 7-yard touchdown pass to Ernie Jones midway through the second quarter gave Phoenix a 14-3 advantage. But Hebert countered with an 11-yard touchdown pass to Eric Martin 1:04 before halftime to trim the margin to 14-10 at intermission. He connected with running back Dalton Hilliard (15 yards) and wide receiver Quinn Early (59 yards) in the third quarter to give New Orleans the lead for good. Martin finished with 8 receptions for 151 yards. The Saints, who had not scored more than 2 touchdowns in any of their previous six games, had 399 yards of total offense.

New Orleans	0	10	13	7	—	30
Phoenix	7	7	0	7	—	21

Phx — Bailey 1 run (G. Davis kick)
NO — FG Andersen 52
Phx — E. Jones 7 pass from Chandler (G. Davis kick)
NO — Martin 11 pass from Hebert (Andersen kick)
NO — Hilliard 15 pass from Hebert (kick failed)
NO — Early 59 pass from Hebert (Andersen kick)
NO — Heyward 6 run (Andersen kick)
Phx — Edwards 25 pass from Chandler (G. Davis kick)

L.A. Rams 38, N.Y. Giants 17—at Anaheim Stadium, attendance 53,541. Jim Everett completed 18 of 21 passes for 242 yards and 2 touchdowns to lead the Rams to a surprisingly easy victory over the Giants. Leading 14-10 at halftime, Los Angeles broke the game open by scoring 24 points in the second half. The Rams scored on a 46-yard field goal by Tony Zendejas and a 19-yard pass from Everett to Jeff Chadwick in the third quarter. The scoring pass capped an 81-yard drive that took 12 plays and made the score 24-10. Cleveland Gary, who ran for a pair of touchdowns, gained 126 yards on 31 carries, both career highs.

N.Y. Giants	0	10	0	7	—	17
L.A. Rams	7	7	10	14	—	38

Rams — Gary 1 run (Zendejas kick)
Giants — Hampton 10 run (Bahr kick)
Rams — Carter 9 pass from Everett (Zendejas kick)
Giants — FG Bahr 31

Rams — FG Zendejas 46
Rams — Chadwick 19 pass from Everett (Zendejas kick)
Rams — Gary 5 run (Zendejas kick)
Giants — Hampton 2 run (Bahr kick)
Rams — Lang 1 run (Zendejas kick)

Washington 16, Philadelphia 12—at RFK Stadium, attendance 55,198. The Redskins drove to a touchdown on the game's opening possession, then used 3 Chip Lohmiller field goals and a stifling defense to upend the Eagles in an NFC Eastern Division showdown. Earnest Byner carried eight consecutive plays on the 11-play, 61-yard drive to open the game, and Mark Rypien hit Gary Clark with a 10-yard touchdown pass after 7:21 to give Washington a 7-0 advantage. Though the Redskins were able to penetrate deep into Philadelphia territory the rest of the game, a missed field goal and an end-zone interception helped limit them to only 9 points after that. But the Eagles fared no better, totaling just 78 yards in the first half and getting only a concession safety and touchdown in the closing seconds of the second half. Philadelphia's Randall Cunningham gained 39 yards on 5 rushes to become the NFL's career leader in rushing yards by a quarterback. But he was under constant pressure all day, suffering 5 sacks.

Philadelphia	0	3	0	9	—	12
Washington	7	3	3	3	—	16

Wash — Clark 10 pass from Rypien (Lohmiller kick)
Phil — FG Ruzek 39
Wash — FG Lohmiller 18
Wash — FG Lohmiller 21
Wash — FG Lohmiller 28
Phil — Safety, Goodburn stepped out of end zone
Phil — C. Williams 6 pass from Cunningham (Ruzek kick)

San Diego 34, Indianapolis 14—at Hoosier Dome, attendance 48,552. Rod Bernstine ran for a career-high 150 yards and 2 touchdowns on 23 carries to help the Chargers beat the Colts. Bernstine had to leave the game with a shoulder injury one minute into the fourth quarter, however, and was expected to miss about six weeks. San Diego entered the game without a first-quarter touchdown in any of its five previous games and having scored only 46 points in all. But the Chargers took the opening kickoff and marched 81 yards in 8 plays to a touchdown and a 7-0 lead. Bernstine carried 5 times for 53 yards and capped the drive by scoring from 25 yards out. His 2-yard run the next time San Diego had the ball made it 14-0 and the Chargers never were threatened after that. San Diego finished with 212 rushing yards and 392 total yards. Indianapolis quarterback Jeff George completed 27 of 39 passes for 318 yards (Jessie Hester had 9 catches for 126 yards), but was intercepted twice and sacked 5 times. The Colts also lost 3 fumbles.

San Diego	14	0	3	17	—	34
Indianapolis	7	0	7	0	—	14

SD — Bernstine 25 run (Carney kick)
SD — Bernstine 2 run (Carney kick)
Ind — Johnson 8 pass from George (Biasucci kick)
SD — FG Carney 23
Ind — Schultz 3 pass from George (Biasucci kick)
SD — Bieniemy 2 run (Carney kick)
SD — Humphries 2 run (Carney kick)
SD — FG Carney 27

Chicago 31, Tampa Bay 14—at Soldier Field, attendance 61,412. Jim Harbaugh passed for a career-high 304 yards and a pair of touchdowns in the Bears' victory. Chicago opened the game by driving 85 yards and 74 yards to touchdowns on its first two possessions for a 14-0 lead. Running back Brad Muster scored both touchdowns from 1 yard out, the first on a run and the second on a pass from Harbaugh. In the third quarter, Harbaugh connected with Anthony Morgan over the middle, and when two defenders collided, Morgan raced to the end zone to complete an 83-yard touchdown play that made it 21-7. The Buccaneers stayed close on Reggie Cobb's 1-yard touchdown run on the first play of the fourth quarter, but they could not generate the tying score. Kevin Butler's 26-yard field goal with 2:59 left in the game and Darren Lewis's 7-yard run 1:05 later, after Tampa Bay turned the ball over on downs at its 9-yard line, completed the scoring. Cobb finished with 109 yards on 24 carries, while Buccaneers rookie wide receiver Courtney Hawkins caught 5 passes for 102 yards and a touchdown. Chicago wide receiver Tom Waddle had 114 receiving yards on just 3 catches.

Tampa Bay	0	7	0	7	—	14
Chicago	7	7	7	10	—	31

Chi — Muster 1 run (Butler kick)
Chi — Muster 1 pass from Harbaugh (Butler kick)
TB — Hawkins 12 pass from Testaverde (Willis kick)
Chi — Morgan 83 pass from Harbaugh (Butler kick)
TB — Cobb 1 run (Willis kick)
Chi — FG Butler 26
Chi — Lewis 7 run (Butler kick)

Monday, October 19

Pittsburgh 20, Cincinnati 0—at Three Rivers Stadium, attendance 55,411. Dwight Stone caught a pair of touchdown passes and the Steelers dominated the Bengals en route to handing Cincinnati its fourth consecutive defeat. Pittsburgh gained 424 yards to only 118 for the Bengals, had 26 first downs to only 6, and controlled the ball for more than 38 minutes. Steelers quarterback Neil O'Donnell completed 23 of 37 passes for 287 yards, and running back Barry Foster gained 108 yards on 24 carries. Stone caught 6 passes and set up the first of his 2 touchdowns by running 30 yards on a reverse. Jeff Graham added 7 catches for 115 yards. Nothing went right for the Bengals, who also were penalized 8 times for 49 yards. Cincinnati kicker Jim Breech, who missed a 47-yard field-goal attempt, had his NFL-record scoring streak snapped at 186 games.

Cincinnati	0	0	0	0	—	0
Pittsburgh	3	7	0	10	—	20

Pitt — FG Anderson 21
Pitt — Stone 24 pass from O'Donnell (Anderson kick)
Pitt — Stone 5 pass from O'Donnell (Anderson kick)
Pitt — FG Anderson 27

Eighth Week Summaries

Standings

American Football Conference

Eastern Division	W	L	T	Pct.	Pts.	OP
Miami	6	1	0	.857	188	125
Buffalo	5	2	0	.714	190	122
Indianapolis	4	3	0	.571	99	132
N.Y. Jets	1	6	0	.143	104	147
New England	0	7	0	.000	80	176
Central Division						
Houston	5	2	0	.714	179	120
Pittsburgh	5	2	0	.714	138	77
Cleveland	4	3	0	.571	107	101
Cincinnati	2	5	0	.286	109	174
Western Division						
Denver	5	3	0	.625	121	154
Kansas City	4	4	0	.500	153	128
San Diego	3	4	0	.429	104	136
L.A. Raiders	3	5	0	.375	122	137
Seattle	1	7	0	.125	53	158

National Football Conference

Eastern Division	W	L	T	Pct.	Pts.	OP
Dallas	6	1	0	.857	167	112
Philadelphia	5	2	0	.714	143	77
Washington	5	2	0	.714	136	105
N.Y. Giants	3	4	0	.429	150	161
Phoenix	1	6	0	.143	113	177
Central Division						
Minnesota	5	2	0	.714	173	127
Chicago	4	3	0	.571	169	155
Tampa Bay	3	4	0	.429	136	152
Detroit	2	5	0	.286	144	135
Green Bay	2	5	0	.286	90	151
Western Division						
San Francisco	6	1	0	.857	216	125
New Orleans	5	2	0	.714	117	82
L.A. Rams	3	4	0	.429	121	133
Atlanta	2	5	0	.286	133	179

Sunday, October 25

Chicago 30, Green Bay 10—at Lambeau Field, attendance 59,435. Chris Gardocki threw a 43-yard pass to Mark Green from punt formation to set up the key score as the Bears posted back-to-back victories for the first time this season. The punter's pass came on fourth-and-6 from the Packers' 48-yard line with the score tied 3-3 midway through the second quarter. Moments later, Brad Muster ran 1 yard for the touchdown that gave Chicago the lead for good. Jim Harbaugh's 4-yard touchdown pass to tight end Keith Jennings with 1:54 left in the first half opened up a 17-3 advantage and Green Bay could get no closer than seven points after that. Harbaugh, who completed 16 of 23 passes for 194 yards and 1 touchdown and was not intercepted, had a string of 13 completions at one point to equal a 28-year-old club record. Sterling Sharpe had 9 catches for 144 yards and a touchdown for the Packers.

Chicago	3	17	3	7	—	30
Green Bay	0	10	0	0	—	10

Chi — FG Butler 18
GB — FG Jacke 51
Chi — Muster 1 run (Butler kick)
Chi — Jennings 4 pass from Harbaugh (Butler kick)
GB — Sharpe 10 pass from Favre (Jacke kick)
Chi — FG Butler 30
Chi — FG Butler 21
Chi — Lewis 30 run (Butler kick)

Houston 26, Cincinnati 10—at Astrodome, attendance 58,701. Warren Moon passed for 342 yards and 2 touchdowns, and the Oilers dominated the second half to beat the Bengals for the second time in three weeks. Boomier Esiason's 17-yard touchdown pass to Brian Brennan and Jim Breech's short field goal had helped Cincinnati, which had lost four straight games, tie Houston 10-10 at halftime. But the Bengals managed only 1 first down and 8 total yards in the second half while failing to move the ball past their 31-yard line. Meanwhile, the Oilers mounted a lengthy 15-play, 85-yard touchdown drive that consumed 9:33 to take the lead on Lorenzo White's 1-yard touchdown run with 1:12 left in the third quarter. One minute into the fourth period, Moon teamed with Webster Slaughter on a 36-yard touchdown pass to make it 24-10. It was the first touchdown catch as an Oiler for Slaughter, who had signed with the team as a free agent one month earlier. Moon finished with 27 completions in 40 attempts. Curtis Duncan caught 9 passes for 84 yards and Ernest Givins had 8 receptions for 100 yards, including a 30-yard touchdown in the first quarter.

Cincinnati	0	10	0	0	—	10
Houston	7	3	7	9	—	26

Hou — Givins 30 pass from Moon (Del Greco kick)
Cin — Brennan 17 pass from Esiason (Breech kick)
Hou — FG Del Greco 27
Cin — FG Breech 24
Hou — White 1 run (Del Greco kick)
Hou — Slaughter 36 pass from Moon (Del Greco kick)
Hou — Safety, Esiason ran out of end zone

Cleveland 19, New England 17—at Foxboro Stadium, attendance 32,219. Mike Tomczak's 6-yard, fourth-down touchdown pass to tight end Scott Galbraith with 31 seconds remaining rallied the Browns to their fourth victory in five games. Two touchdown passes by Hugh Millen and a field goal had given the winless Patriots a 17-9 edge entering the fourth quarter. But Cleveland capitalized on a New England fumble to pull within 17-12 on Matt Stover's fourth field goal of the game, a 32-yarder with 12:33 to play. Later in the period, Millen fumbled when sacked by linebacker Mike Johnson. Johnson recovered at the Patriots' 40, and the Browns drove eight plays to the winning score. The loss dropped New England to 0-7, equaling the worst start in club history.

Cleveland	6	3	0	10	—	19
New England	0	7	10	0	—	17

Cleve — FG Stover 29
Cleve — FG Stover 28
Cleve — FG Stover 21
NE — Turner 19 pass from Millen (Baumann kick)
NE — Coates 22 pass from Millen (Baumann kick)
NE — FG Baumann 30
Cleve — FG Stover 32
Cleve — Galbraith 6 pass from Tomczak (Stover kick)

Dallas 28, L.A. Raiders 13—at Los Angeles Memorial Coliseum, attendance 91,505. Emmitt Smith rushed for 152 yards and 3 touchdowns, and the Cowboys remained atop the NFC East by snapping the Raiders' three-game winning streak. Los Angeles drove 83 yards to a touchdown on the game's opening possession, but Dallas's defense stiffened after that. Offensively, the Cowboys countered Los Angeles's opening drive with an 80-yard march of their own, capped by Smith's 6-yard touchdown run. His 4-yard run midway through the third quarter put Dallas ahead for good, and he added a 26-yard touchdown with 3:26 to play to seal the outcome. Troy Aikman completed 16 of 25 passes for 234 yards for the Cowboys, who outgained the Raiders 369-165. More than 91,000 fans jammed the Los Angeles Memorial Coliseum, the largest crowd to see an NFL game this season.

Dallas	7	0	7	14	—	28
L.A. Raiders	6	0	7	0	—	13

Raid — Allen 1 run (pass failed)
Dall — E. Smith 6 run (Elliott kick)
Raid — Gault 31 pass from Marinovich (Jaeger kick)
Dall — E. Smith 4 run (Elliott kick)
Dall — Aikman 3 run (Elliott kick)
Dall — E. Smith 26 run (Elliott kick)

San Diego 24, Denver 21—at San Diego Jack Murphy Stadium, attendance 53,576. Stan Humphries passed for a career-high 349 yards and 2 touchdowns, and the

Chargers thwarted John Elway's comeback bid to win their third straight. Humphries, who completed 20 of 27 passes and also ran 2 yards for a touchdown, threw a 27-yard scoring toss to tight end Derrick Walker to give San Diego a 21-7 lead in the third quarter. But Elway, the Broncos' quarterback who had brought his team from behind to win three times in the final two minutes already this season, ran 5 yards for a touchdown early in the fourth quarter to cap an 80-yard drive and trim the deficit to 21-14. After the Chargers' John Carney kicked a 37-yard field goal, Elway passed to Mark Jackson for a 28-yard touchdown that pulled his team within 24-21. Moments later, when Denver safety Dennis Smith recovered a fumble at the San Diego 34, it appeared another winning rally was in store. But on the next play, cornerback Tony Blaylock intercepted Elway's pass in the end zone with three minutes left to preserve the win. Elway finished with 260 passing yards and 2 touchdowns, but was intercepted 3 times. Jackson caught 5 passes for 113 yards. Chargers safety Gill Byrd had a pair of thefts. Wide receiver Anthony Miller caught 6 passes for 129 yards and Walker had 104 yards on his 4 catches to give San Diego two 100-yard receivers in the same game for the first time since 1985.

Denver	0	7	0	14	—	21
San Diego	7	0	14	3	—	24

SD — Miller 38 pass from Humphries (Carney kick)
Den — Jackson 32 pass from Elway (Treadwell kick)
SD — Humphries 2 run (Carney kick)
SD — Walker 27 pass from Humphries (Carney kick)
Den — Elway 5 run (Treadwell kick)
SD — FG Carney 37
Den — Jackson 28 pass from Elway (Treadwell kick)

Detroit 38, Tampa Bay 7—at Tampa Stadium, attendance 53,985. Rodney Peete threw 3 touchdown passes, Barry Sanders rushed for 122 yards and 2 scores, and the Lions snapped a four-game losing streak by routing the Buccaneers. Peete, who attempted only 19 passes, completed 11 for 208 yards, including scoring tosses of 31 yards to Willie Green and 63 yards to Herman Moore in the game's first nine minutes. And when Sanders ran 1 yard for a touchdown early in the second quarter, Detroit led 21-0. Tampa Bay tried to rally with an 80-yard touchdown drive engineered by backup quarterback Steve DeBerg, culminating with Reggie Cobb's 1-yard run 32 seconds before halftime. But any comeback hopes immediately were thwarted when Mel Gray returned the ensuing kickoff 89 yards, and Jason Hanson kicked a 27-yard field goal on the final play of the half to put the Lions ahead 24-7 at intermission. Sanders, who had a 55-yard touchdown run in the third quarter, carried 21 times and recorded his first 100-yard rushing day since the season opener. Moore had 108 yards on 3 catches as Detroit amassed a season-high 400 total yards.

Detroit	14	10	7	7	—	38
Tampa Bay	0	7	0	0	—	7

Det — Green 29 pass from Peete (Hanson kick)
Det — Moore 63 pass from Peete (Hanson kick)
Det — Sanders 1 run (Hanson kick)
TB — Cobb 1 run (Willis kick)
Det — FG Hanson 27
Det — Sanders 55 run (Hanson kick)
Det — Perriman 4 pass from Peete (Hanson kick)

Indianapolis 31, Miami 20—at Joe Robbie Stadium, attendance 61,117. Quarterback Jeff George ran 1 yard for the go-ahead touchdown with 1:32 left in the game, and the Colts went on to stun the previously undefeated Dolphins. The victory wasn't secured, however, until Indianapolis rookie defensive end Steve Emtman intercepted Dan Marino's pass on the final play of the game and lumbered 90 yards for a touchdown. Miami had driven to the Colts' 7-yard line and was facing fourth-and-goal. Earlier, the Dolphins had taken a 20-17 lead on Marino's 12-yard touchdown pass to Tony Martin with 6:01 left in the game. But the extra-point attempt failed, a miss that would prove critical because the Dolphins trailed by four points instead of three after George drove Indianapolis 73 yards in the next 10 plays to the winning score. Marino passed for 355 yards and 2 touchdowns, but was intercepted 3 times. Miami also lost 2 fumbles. The Colts, who were outgained 413 total yards to 262, got an 84-yard punt return for a touchdown by Clarence Verdin to forge a 14-14 tie late in the third quarter.

Indianapolis	0	7	7	17	—	31
Miami	0	7	7	6	—	20

Mia — Higgs 2 run (Stoyanovich kick)
Ind — Culver 4 run (Biasucci kick)
Mia — Duper 48 pass from Marino (Stoyanovich kick)
Ind — Verdin 84 punt return (Biasucci kick)
Ind — FG Biasucci 32
Mia — Martin 12 pass from Marino (kick failed)
Ind — George 1 run (Biasucci kick)
Ind — Emtman 90 interception return (Biasucci kick)

Philadelphia 7, Phoenix 3—at Veterans Stadium, attendance 64,676. Calvin Williams caught a 40-yard pass in the second quarter for the game's only touchdown, and the Eagles' defense executed a stellar goal-line stand as Philadelphia beat the Cardinals. After Phoenix cornerback Aeneas Williams intercepted Randall Cunningham's pass and returned it 23 yards to the 3-yard line late in the second quarter, running back Johnny Bailey ran two yards to the 1. But on six plays from there (the Eagles were penalized for being offsides three times), the Cardinals could not punch it in. Bailey tried four more times, and quarterback Chris Chandler tried to sneak it in twice when the penalties pushed the ball to within inches of the goal line. Philadelphia never did allow Phoenix in the end zone, limiting the Cardinals to Greg Davis's 34-yard field goal 17 seconds into the fourth quarter. Herschel Walker had his third 100-yard rushing day of the season for the Eagles, gaining 112 yards on 20 carries. Phoenix held Philadelphia to only 84 net passing yards. Five players each had 1 sack of Cunningham.

Phoenix	0	0	0	3	—	3
Philadelphia	0	7	0	0	—	7

Phil — C. Williams 40 pass from Cunningham (Ruzek kick)
Phx — FG G. Davis 34

N.Y. Giants 23, Seattle 10—at Giants Stadium, attendance 67,399. Quarterback Jeff Hostetler ran 7 yards for a touchdown and passed 7 yards to Ed McCaffrey for another to help the Giants overcome a four-point deficit in the third quarter. The Seahawks had taken a 10-6 advantage by scoring their first touchdown in 14 quarters, a 13-yard pass from Stan Gelbaugh to Tommy Kane early in the second half. But a 36-yard pass interference penalty led to Hostetler's scoring run with 8:05 to go in the third period. Seven minutes later, the pass to McCaffrey capped a 72-yard drive that made the score 20-10. Hostetler's 46-yard completion to Stephen Baker was the key play of that drive. Hostetler attempted only 9 passes, completing 5 for 94 yards, as New York kept the ball on the ground. Jarrod Bunch rushed for 77 yards and Rodney Hampton had 69. Seattle's Gelbaugh completed 22 of 32 passes, but for only 130 yards. Running back John L. Williams had 11 receptions for 45 yards. The Seahawks, who had suffered two consecutive shutouts, finally ended their scoring drought when John Kasay kicked a 33-yard field goal midway through the second quarter.

Seattle	0	3	7	0	—	10
N.Y. Giants	0	6	14	3	—	23

Giants — FG Bahr 36
Sea — FG Kasay 33
Giants — FG Bahr 25
Sea — Kane 13 pass from Gelbaugh (Kasay kick)
Giants — Hostetler 7 run (Bahr kick)
Giants — McCaffrey 7 pass from Hostetler (Bahr kick)
Giants — FG Bahr 30

Washington 15, Minnesota 13—at Metrodome, attendance 59,098. The last of Chip Lohmiller's 5 field goals, a 49-yarder with 1:09 left to play, gave the Redskins the victory. Lohmiller kicked 4 field goals in the first half, 3 of them following Vikings turnovers, as Washington took a 12-0 halftime lead. Minnesota rallied in the second half, however, and took a 13-12 advantage on Fuad Reveiz's 41-yard field goal with 2:28 left in the game. But Reveiz's ensuing squib kickoff went out of bounds and gave the Redskins possession on their 35-yard line. From there, Mark Rypien passed 20 yards to Art Monk and scrambled 11 yards to position Lohmiller for the winning kick.

Washington	3	9	0	3	—	15
Minnesota	0	0	3	10	—	13

Wash — FG Lohmiller 22
Wash — FG Lohmiller 52
Wash — FG Lohmiller 25
Wash — FG Lohmiller 45
Minn — FG Reveiz 26
Minn — Allen 1 run (Reveiz kick)
Minn — FG Reveiz 41
Wash — FG Lohmiller 49

Sunday Night, October 25

Pittsburgh 27, Kansas City 3—at Arrowhead Stadium, attendance 76,175. Barry Foster ran for 105 yards and the Steelers kept pace with Houston, remaining in a tie for first place in the AFC Central by beating the Chiefs. Foster, who broke the 100-yard barrier for the fifth time in seven games, ran 4 yards for a touchdown to break open the game late in the third quarter. His scoring run came two plays after cornerback D.J. Johnson's 31-yard interception return to the 2. That was 1 of 3 interceptions for Pittsburgh's defense, which held Kansas City quarterback Dave Krieg in check, limiting him to only 9 completions in 27 attempts for 82 yards. Linebacker Greg Lloyd also got to Krieg for a pair of sacks. Rod Woodson had an 80-yard punt return for a touchdown midway through the first quarter for the Steelers. Eddie Murray, signed the day before the game to replace injured Nick Lowery, kicked a 52-yard field goal in the closing seconds of the first half to account for the Chiefs' only points.

Pittsburgh	7	6	7	7	—	27
Kansas City	0	3	0	0	—	3

Pitt — Woodson 80 punt return (Anderson kick)
Pitt — FG Anderson 49
Pitt — FG Anderson 30
KC — FG Murray 52
Pitt — Foster 4 run (Anderson kick)
Pitt — Green 4 pass from O'Donnell (Anderson kick)

Monday, October 26

Buffalo 24, N.Y. Jets 20—at Giants Stadium, attendance 68,181. The Bills averted a third consecutive defeat when Jim Kelly passed 12 yards to running back Thurman Thomas for the game-winning touchdown with 51 seconds remaining. The Jets had rallied to take a 20-17 advantage when Brad Baxter's 1-yard run with 1:50 to go capped a 77-yard drive. But it took Buffalo only 59 seconds to go 75 yards to the winning score. Kelly and wide receiver Don Beebe teamed on 34- and 19-yard completions, and Thomas ran for 18 yards to set up the touchdown pass. Thomas finished with 142 yards on 21 carries, while Beebe had 6 catches for 106 yards. The victory was the Bills' tenth straight over the Jets.

Buffalo	0	14	3	7	—	24
N.Y. Jets	3	3	7	7	—	20

Jets — FG Blanchard 42
Buff — K. Davis 2 run (Christie kick)
Jets — FG Blanchard 40
Buff — Lofton 16 pass from Kelly (Christie kick)
Jets — Chaffey 1 run (Blanchard kick)
Buff — FG Christie 33
Jets — Baxter 1 run (Blanchard kick)
Buff — T. Thomas 12 pass from Kelly (Christie kick)

Ninth Week Summaries

Standings

American Football Conference

Eastern Division	W	L	T	Pct.	Pts.	OP
Buffalo	6	2	0	.750	206	129
Miami	6	2	0	.750	202	151
Indianapolis	4	4	0	.500	99	158
N.Y. Jets	2	6	0	.250	130	161
New England	0	8	0	.000	87	192
Central Division						
Pittsburgh	6	2	0	.750	159	97
Houston	5	3	0	.625	199	141
Cleveland	4	4	0	.500	117	131
Cincinnati	3	5	0	.375	139	184
Western Division						
Denver	5	3	0	.625	121	154
Kansas City	4	4	0	.500	153	128
San Diego	4	4	0	.500	130	136
L.A. Raiders	3	5	0	.375	122	137
Seattle	1	7	0	.125	53	158

National Football Conference

Eastern Division	W	L	T	Pct.	Pts.	OP
Dallas	7	1	0	.875	187	122
Philadelphia	5	3	0	.625	153	97
Washington	5	3	0	.625	143	129
N.Y. Giants	4	4	0	.500	174	168
Phoenix	2	6	0	.250	137	191
Central Division						
Minnesota	6	2	0	.750	211	137
Chicago	4	4	0	.500	179	193
Green Bay	3	5	0	.375	117	164
Tampa Bay	3	5	0	.375	157	175
Detroit	2	6	0	.250	160	162
Western Division						
New Orleans	6	2	0	.750	140	103
San Francisco	6	2	0	.750	230	149
Atlanta	3	5	0	.375	163	207
L.A. Rams	3	5	0	.375	149	163

Sunday, November 1

Cincinnati 30, Cleveland 10—at Riverfront Stadium, attendance 54,765. The Bengals snapped a five-game losing streak behind Boomer Esiason's 3 touchdown passes and a crucial goal-line stand. Esiason threw scoring tosses to tight ends Craig Thompson (1 yard) and Rodney Holman (4 yards) as Cincinnati built a 14-3 halftime advantage. It would have been closer but the Bengals stopped the Browns four times from inside the 5-yard line—the last two from inside the 1—shortly before halftime. And when Esiason connected with Tim McGee on a 24-yard touchdown pass to cap an 82-yard drive on

Cincinnati's opening possession of the second half, the Bengals had broken the game open at 21-3. Mike Tomczak passed for 252 yards for Cleveland, which outgained Cincinnati 328-300 but could not crack the end zone until the issue had been decided in the fourth quarter. The defeat was the Browns' sixth in the last seven games against the Bengals.

Cleveland	3	0	0	7	—	10
Cincinnati	7	7	10	6	—	30

Cleve — FG Stover 39
Cin — Thompson 1 pass from Esiason (Breech kick)
Cin — Holman 4 pass from Esiason (Breech kick)
Cin — McGee 24 pass from Esiason (Breech kick)
Cin — FG Breech 26
Cin — FG Breech 21
Cleve — Jackson 30 pass from Tomczak (Stover kick)
Cin — FG Breech 32

Green Bay 27, Detroit 13—at Pontiac Silverdome, attendance 60,594. Brett Favre threw a pair of touchdown passes and Vince Workman became the first Packer to rush for more than 100 yards in a game in three years as Green Bay overwhelmed the Lions. The Packers amassed 25 first downs and 347 total yards to only 9 first downs and 190 total yards for Detroit, the defending NFC Central Division champions who fell to last place. Still, the Lions made a game of it after falling behind 20-3 early in the second half. Jason Hanson's field goal and Bennie Blades's 7-yard return of a blocked punt trimmed the Lions' deficit to 20-13 with 1:30 left in the third quarter. But Green Bay responded with a 12-play, 77-yard drive that consumed more than six-and-a-half minutes, capped by Favre's 30-yard touchdown pass to Sterling Sharpe with 9:59 left in the game. Favre completed three third-down passes to keep the final drive alive, and finished the day with 22 completions in 37 attempts. Workman carried 23 times for 101 yards. The Packers also got their first rushing touchdown of the season when Harry Sydney carried 1 yard for a score in the first quarter.

Green Bay	7	10	3	7	—	27
Detroit	3	0	10	0	—	13

Det — FG Hanson 32
GB — Sydney 1 run (Jacke kick)
GB — FG Jacke 53
GB — Harris 14 pass from Favre (Jacke kick)
GB — FG Jacke 25
Det — FG Hanson 34
Det — Blades 7 blocked punt return (Hanson kick)
GB — Sharpe 30 pass from Favre (Jacke kick)

Pittsburgh 21, Houston 20—at Three Rivers Stadium, attendance 58,074. Neil O'Donnell threw a pair of fourth-quarter touchdown passes and Pittsburgh held on to win when the Oilers' Al Del Greco misfired on a 39-yard field-goal attempt with one second left in the game. The victory was the second of the season for the Steelers over defending AFC Central Division champion Houston and lifted them into sole possession of first place. The Oilers trailed by a point at halftime and lost quarterback Warren Moon for the remainder of the game when he sustained a concussion on the second play of the third quarter. But backup Cody Carlson threw an 11-yard touchdown pass to Webster Slaughter to give Houston the lead 4:59 into the second half, and just 63 seconds later, defensive tackle Ray Childress picked up a fumble by O'Donnell and returned it 8 yards for a touchdown and a 20-7 lead. Pittsburgh rallied when O'Donnell passed 2 yards to tight end Adrian Cooper and 5 yards to tight end Eric Green for touchdowns. The latter came after linebacker Greg Lloyd recovered Carlson's fumble at the Oilers' 38-yard line, and it gave the Steelers the lead with 7:13 to go. Houston marched 64 yards to the Pittsburgh 22 in the closing moments but came away empty when Del Greco's kick went wide left. The Steelers' Barry Foster rushed for 118 yards on 31 carries. It was his sixth 100-yard rushing day of the season, just 1 short of Franco Harris's club record.

Houston	3	3	14	0	—	20
Pittsburgh	0	7	0	14	—	21

Hou — FG Del Greco 29
Hou — FG Del Greco 19
Pitt — Foster 1 run (Anderson kick)
Hou — Slaughter 11 pass from Carlson (Del Greco kick)
Hou — Childress 8 fumble recovery return (Del Greco kick)
Pitt — Cooper 2 pass from O'Donnell (Anderson kick)
Pitt — Green 5 pass from O'Donnell (Anderson kick)

San Diego 26, Indianapolis 0—at San Diego Jack Murphy Stadium, attendance 40,324. The Chargers limited the Colts to only 8 first downs and 99 total yards en route to posting their first shutout in six years and winning their fourth consecutive game. After starting the season 0-4, San Diego evened its record at 4-4 and pulled within one game of first-place Denver in the AFC Western Division. The Chargers led just 5-0 at halftime despite holding Indianapolis to minus-5 yards from scrimmage. But San Diego put the game away by marching to touchdowns on each of its first two possessions of the second half, each culminated by scoring passes from Stan Humphries to Nate Lewis. Humphries finished with 22 completions in 33 attempts for 256 yards, while Marion Butts rushed for 120 yards on 27 carries. Anthony Miller caught 6 passes for 105 yards. The Chargers rolled up 26 first downs and 400 total yards while controlling the ball for nearly 43 of the game's 60 minutes. The defense also recorded 7 sacks, including 2 each by Burt Grossman (1 for a safety), Chris Mims, and Leslie O'Neal.

Indianapolis	0	0	0	0	—	0
San Diego	0	5	14	7	—	26

SD — Safety, Grossman tackled George in end zone
SD — FG Carney 33
SD — Lewis 17 pass from Humphries (Carney kick)
SD — Lewis 9 pass from Humphries (Carney kick)
SD — Butts 3 run (Carney kick)

Atlanta 30, L.A. Rams 28—at Georgia Dome, attendance 62,168. Backup quarterback Billy Joe Tolliver's 13-yard, fourth-quarter touchdown pass to Michael Haynes overcame a comeback effort by the Rams and lifted the Falcons to the victory. Los Angeles had rallied from a 17-0 second-quarter deficit behind the passing of Jim Everett (253 yards and 4 touchdowns) and the running of Cleveland Gary (144 yards on 18 carries), taking the lead on Everett's 5-yard touchdown pass to tight end Jim Price with 5:55 left in the third quarter. But Tolliver, in the game because starting quarterback Chris Miller went down with a knee injury in the third quarter, directed an 81-yard march to the winning score, which came with 12:51 left in the game. A day later, Atlanta learned that Miller's knee injury would sideline him the rest of the season. The Rams' defeat was their twelfth in a row on the road, and their thirteenth consecutive setback against an NFC Western Division opponent.

L.A. Rams	0	14	14	0	—	28
Atlanta	14	6	3	7	—	30

Atl — T. Smith 2 run (Johnson kick)
Atl — Haynes 38 pass from Miller (Johnson kick)
Atl — FG Johnson 49
Rams — Gary 3 pass from Everett (Zendejas kick)
Atl — FG Johnson 26
Rams — Gary 2 pass from Everett (Zendejas kick)
Atl — FG Johnson 37
Rams — Lang 67 pass from Everett (Zendejas kick)
Rams — Price 5 pass from Everett (Zendejas kick)
Atl — Haynes 13 pass from Tolliver (Johnson kick)

N.Y. Jets 26, Miami 14—at Giants Stadium, attendance 69,313. Ken O'Brien, subbing for injured starter Browning Nagle, threw 3 touchdown passes in the first half as the Jets beat the Dolphins. O'Brien's third scoring toss, a 20-yarder to Rob Moore with 21 seconds left in the second quarter, gave New York a 23-0 advantage at intermission. But perhaps his most important effort came after Miami had scored a pair of second-half touchdowns in a span of 69 seconds—the latter on a 39-yard pass from Dan Marino to Mark Duper just 18 seconds into the fourth quarter. O'Brien, who finished with 21 completions in 29 attempts for 240 yards, then marched the Jets 52 yards on a time-consuming (8:09), 13-play drive that resulted in Cary Blanchard's 47-yard field goal with 6:33 to go. New York's Brad Baxter ran for a career-high 103 yards on 20 carries to help the Jets outgain the Dolphins 363 to 296.

Miami	0	0	7	7	—	14
N.Y. Jets	9	14	0	3	—	26

Jets — Mitchell 37 pass from O'Brien (Blanchard kick)
Jets — Safety, M. Washington sacked Marino in end zone
Jets — Toon 4 pass from O'Brien (Blanchard kick)
Jets — Moore 20 pass from O'Brien (Blanchard kick)
Mia — K. Jackson 5 pass from Marino (Stoyanovich kick)
Mia — Duper 39 pass from Marino (Stoyanovich kick)
Jets — FG Blanchard 47

Buffalo 16, New England 7—at Rich Stadium, attendance 78,268. The Bills' Jim Kelly threw 2 touchdown passes in the second half to thwart the Patriots' upset bid. Winless New England took a 7-0 halftime lead when linebacker Dwayne Sabb forced a fumble that teammate Vincent Brown picked up and returned 25 yards for a touchdown 1:23 before the intermission. But Buffalo rallied on Kelly's 3-yard touchdown pass to Pete Metzelaars and a third-quarter safety for a 9-7 lead, then overcame a potentially costly turnover early in the fourth quarter. New England safety Randy Robbins intercepted Kelly's pass and returned it 20 yards to the Bills' 25-yard line. But Bills linebacker Cornelius Bennett sacked Patriots quarterback Tom Hodson, nose tackle Jeff Wright recovered at the 27, and 10 plays later Kelly threw a 13-yard touchdown pass to James Lofton to secure the victory with 5:05 left.

New England	0	7	0	0	—	7
Buffalo	0	0	9	7	—	16

NE — Brown 25 fumble recovery return (Baumann kick)
Buff — Metzelaars 3 pass from Kelly (Christie kick)
Buff — Safety, Hale tackled McCarthy in end zone
Buff — Lofton 13 pass from Kelly (Christie kick)

Dallas 20, Philadelphia 10—at Texas Stadium, attendance 65,015. The Cowboys avenged their only loss of the season and opened a two-game advantage in the NFC Eastern Division by beating the Eagles. Rookie Lin Elliott's 48-yard field goal and Troy Aikman's 14-yard touchdown pass to Daryl Johnston broke a 10-10 tie in the fourth quarter. Elliott's three-pointer was set up by running back Emmitt Smith, who broke off a 51-yard run just one play after Philadelphia's Roger Ruzek had forged the tie with an 18-yard field goal. Smith, whose runs also were pivotal on the subsequent 78-yard touchdown drive, carried 30 times for 163 yards. Aikman completed 19 of 33 passes for 214 yards and 2 touchdowns, and Dallas rolled up 389 total yards to only 190 for the Eagles. Jim McMahon replaced an ineffective Randall Cunningham at quarterback to start the second half and immediately drove Philadelphia to its only touchdown, a 2-yard run by Herschel Walker to cap an 80-yard drive 4:36 into the third quarter.

Philadelphia	0	0	10	0	—	10
Dallas	0	3	7	10	—	20

Dall — FG Elliott 35
Phil — Walker 2 run (Ruzek kick)
Dall — Martin 22 pass from Aikman (Elliott kick)
Phil — FG Ruzek 18
Dall — FG Elliott 48
Dall — Johnson 14 pass from Aikman (Elliott kick)

Phoenix 24, San Francisco 14—at Sun Devil Stadium, attendance 47,642. Chris Chandler threw 3 touchdown passes to give the Cardinals a stunning upset of the 49ers, who entered the game with a five-game winning streak. Phoenix's Johnny Johnson, recovered from a chest injury and making his first start of the season, ran for 102 yards on 26 carries and helped the Cardinals control the ball for more than 36 minutes, thus keeping the NFL's top-ranked offense off the field for much of the game. San Francisco was further hampered by the loss of starting quarterback Steve Young, who left the game in the second quarter because of the flu. Phoenix led 10-0 at halftime and Chandler's 23-yard touchdown pass to Randal Hill 4:40 into the second half increased the advantage to 17-0. The 49ers tried to rally, pulling within 10 again less than three minutes later when wide receiver Mike Sherrard stripped the ball from Cardinals linebacker Eric Hill—who had recovered tight end Brent Jones's fumble—and raced 39 yards for a touchdown. But Chandler countered with a 22-yard touchdown pass to Ricky Proehl to make it 24-7 with 3:23 left in the third quarter.

San Francisco	0	0	7	7	—	14
Phoenix	0	10	14	0	—	24

Phx — R. Hill 4 pass from Chandler (G. Davis kick)
Phx — FG G. Davis 33
Phx — R. Hill 23 pass from Chandler (G. Davis kick)
SF — Sherrard 39 fumble recovery return (Cofer kick)
Phx — Proehl 22 pass from Chandler (G. Davis kick)
SF — Watters 4 run (Cofer kick)

New Orleans 23, Tampa Bay 21—at Louisiana Superdome, attendance 68,591. Morten Andersen's 50-yard field goal with 9:14 left lifted the Saints past the Buccaneers. New Orleans won despite 3 interceptions and a lost fumble that led to all of Tampa Bay's points. The Buccaneers, who finished with only 154 total yards, had just 1 first down in the first half but trailed only 10-7 because of linebacker Broderick Thomas's 56-yard interception return for a touchdown in the second quarter. Late in the third period, with the Buccaneers trailing 20-7, Thomas recovered Vaughn Dunbar's fumble at the Saints' 37-yard line to set up Steve DeBerg's 4-yard touchdown pass to Willie Drewrey. Moments later, safety Marty Carter intercepted a Bobby Hebert pass to set up Reggie Cobb's 4-yard touchdown run that gave Tampa Bay its first lead, at 21-20 with 13:03 left in the game. But New Orleans, aided by a key personal foul penalty, mounted a short drive to the winning field goal on its next possession.

Tampa Bay	0	7	7	7	—	21
New Orleans	7	3	10	3	—	23

NO	— Hilliard 8 pass from Hebert (Andersen kick)
TB	— Thomas 56 interception return (Willis kick)
NO	— FG Andersen 31
NO	— Hilliard 17 run (Andersen kick)
NO	— FG Andersen 45
TB	— Drewrey 4 pass from DeBerg (Willis kick)
TB	— Cobb 4 run (Willis kick)
NO	— FG Andersen 50

Sunday Night, November 1

N.Y. Giants 24, Washington 7—at RFK Stadium, attendance 53,647. Jeff Hostetler threw a pair of touchdown passes in a span of 2:28 late in the second quarter to break a 7-7 tie and ignite the Giants' victory. Rodney Hampton ran for 138 yards as New York amassed 241 rushing yards with a ball-control attack, maintaining possession for 39:20. The Giants dominated the first half, but still were tied at 7-7 late in the second quarter because of an 84-yard punt return for a touchdown by the Redskins' Brian Mitchell. But Hostetler threw a 17-yard touchdown pass to Ed McCaffrey with 2:36 left in the first half, then directed a 67-yard drive that culminated in his 4-yard touchdown toss to David Meggett with eight seconds to go. Giants linebacker Lawrence Taylor helped keep the game out of reach by thwarting a Washington drive with a fumble-causing sack in New York territory. Teammate Leonard Marshall recovered and the Giants marched to Matt Bahr's 19-yard field goal with 8:07 to go.

N.Y. Giants	7	14	0	3	—	24
Washington	7	0	0	0	—	7

Wash	— Mitchell 84 punt return (Lohmiller kick)
Giants	— Bunch 8 run (Bahr kick)
Giants	— McCaffrey 17 pass from Hostetler (Bahr kick)
Giants	— Meggett 4 pass from Hostetler (Bahr kick)
Giants	— FG Bahr 19

Monday, November 2

Minnesota 38, Chicago 10—at Soldier Field, attendance 61,257. Linebackers Jack Del Rio and Carlos Jenkins returned interceptions for touchdowns and the Vikings took control of the NFC Central Division race by beating the Bears. The victory was Minnesota's second of the year against Chicago and gave the Vikings a two-game lead over the second-place Bears. Minnesota led 14-3 at halftime, then broke the game open in the second half. Del Rio's 84-yard interception return came just 36 seconds into the third quarter and made it 21-3. Rich Gannon's 60-yard touchdown pass to tight end Steve Jordan in the first minute of the fourth quarter made it 31-3 and Jenkins added a 19-yard interception return for a touchdown five minutes later.

Minnesota	7	7	10	14	—	38
Chicago	0	3	0	7	—	10

Minn	— Craig 1 run (Reveiz kick)
Minn	— Allen 1 run (Reveiz kick)
Chi	— FG Butler 28
Minn	— Del Rio 84 interception return (Reveiz kick)
Minn	— FG Reveiz 28
Minn	— Jordan 60 pass from Gannon (Reveiz kick)
Minn	— Jenkins 19 interception return (Reveiz kick)
Chi	— Davis 14 pass from Willis (Butler kick)

Tenth Week Summaries

Standings

American Football Conference

Eastern Division	W	L	T	Pct.	Pts.	OP
Buffalo	7	2	0	.778	234	149
Miami	7	2	0	.778	230	151
Indianapolis	4	5	0	.444	99	186
N.Y. Jets	2	7	0	.222	146	188
New England	0	9	0	.000	101	223
Central Division						
Pittsburgh	6	3	0	.667	179	125
Cleveland	5	4	0	.556	141	145
Houston	5	4	0	.556	213	165
Cincinnati	4	5	0	.444	170	212
Western Division						
Denver	6	3	0	.667	148	170
Kansas City	5	4	0	.556	169	142
San Diego	4	5	0	.444	144	152
L.A. Raiders	3	6	0	.333	132	168
Seattle	1	8	0	.111	56	174

National Football Conference

Eastern Division	W	L	T	Pct.	Pts.	OP
Dallas	8	1	0	.889	224	125
Philadelphia	6	3	0	.667	184	107
Washington	6	3	0	.667	159	132
N.Y. Giants	5	4	0	.556	201	175
Phoenix	3	6	0	.333	157	205
Central Division						
Minnesota	7	2	0	.778	246	144
Chicago	4	5	0	.444	207	224
Green Bay	3	6	0	.333	124	191
Tampa Bay	3	6	0	.333	164	210
Detroit	2	7	0	.222	163	199
Western Division						
New Orleans	7	2	0	.778	171	117
San Francisco	7	2	0	.778	271	152
Atlanta	3	6	0	.333	166	248
L.A. Rams	3	6	0	.333	163	183

Sunday, November 8

Cleveland 24, Houston 14—at Astrodome, attendance 57,348. The Browns vaulted back into the AFC Central Division race by stifling the Oilers' Run-and-Shoot offense. Cleveland's Mike Tomczak passed for 219 yards and 2 touchdowns and safety Stevon Moore returned a fumble 73 yards for another touchdown. Moore's big play came with the Browns leading 10-0 late in the third quarter. Houston, which had been forced to punt on its first eight possessions, apparently had successfully converted a fourth-and-2 opportunity when Warren Moon completed a pass to Ernest Givins. But Givins fumbled when hit by cornerback Everson Walls and Moore's recovery and return broke the game open at 17-0. Cody Carlson replaced an ineffective Moon (12 of 25 for 70 yards) and rallied the Oilers with a pair of fourth-quarter touchdowns passes, but it wasn't enough. The victory lifted Cleveland into a second-place tie with Houston, just one game behind division-leading Pittsburgh.

Cleveland	3	7	7	7	—	24
Houston	0	0	0	14	—	14

Cleve	— FG Stover 44
Cleve	— Hoard 46 pass from Tomczak (Stover kick)
Cleve	— Moore 73 fumble recovery return (Stover kick)
Hou	— Slaughter 12 pass from Carlson (Del Greco kick)
Cleve	— Bavaro 17 pass from Tomczak (Stover kick)
Hou	— Givins 18 pass from Carlson (Del Greco kick)

Dallas 37, Detroit 3—at Pontiac Silverdome, attendance 74,816. Emmitt Smith rushed for 3 touchdowns as the Cowboys handed the Lions their worst home loss in 28 years. Smith ran for a pair of scores late in the first quarter to help Dallas build a 20-3 halftime advantage. His 1-yard run on the Cowboys' first possession of the second half made it 27-3 and gave him 12 touchdowns for the season, equaling the club record. Troy Aikman passed for 214 yards and Michael Irvin caught 5 passes for 114 yards and 1 touchdown for Dallas, which rolled up 398 total yards. Barry Sanders accounted for most of Detroit's 201 yards of offense by rushing for 108 yards.

Dallas	14	6	14	3	—	37
Detroit	0	3	0	0	—	3

Dall	— E. Smith 7 run (Elliott kick)
Dall	— E. Smith 1 run (Elliott kick)
Det	— FG Hanson 36
Dall	— FG Elliott 25
Dall	— FG Elliott 42
Dall	— E. Smith 1 run (Elliott kick)
Dall	— Irvin 15 pass from Aikman (Elliott kick)
Dall	— FG Elliott 30

N.Y. Giants 27, Green Bay 7—at Giants Stadium, attendance 72,038. The Giants broke open a close game late in the fourth quarter to post their third consecutive victory. Rodney Hampton's 2-yard touchdown run in the second quarter and a pair of Matt Bahr field goals had given New York a 13-7 lead. But the Packers mounted a late drive and reached the Giants' 33-yard line with less than four minutes left in the game. From there, however, quarterback Brett Favre's pass was intercepted by New York cornerback Reyna Thompson, who returned it 69 yards for the clinching touchdown with 3:38 to go. The Giants added another touchdown in the final minute after safety Greg Jackson's interception and 36-yard return positioned Hampton for an 8-yard touchdown run. Favre finished with 27 completions in 44 attempts for 279 yards, but was intercepted 3 times. Green Bay wide receiver Sterling Sharpe caught 11 passes for 160 yards. Giants linebacker Lawrence Taylor, who had announced that this was his last season, suffered a season-ending Achilles tendon injury in the third quarter.

Green Bay	0	7	0	0	—	7
N.Y. Giants	6	7	0	14	—	27

Giants	— FG Bahr 47
Giants	— FG Bahr 38
GB	— Workman 3 run (Jacke kick)
Giants	— Hampton 2 run (Bahr kick)
Giants	— Thompson 69 interception return (Bahr kick)
Giants	— Hampton 8 run (Bahr kick)

Philadelphia 31, L.A. Raiders 10—at Veterans Stadium, attendance 65,388. Jim McMahon replaced slumping starter Randall Cunningham and, aided by a defense that forced 5 turnovers, led the Eagles to the victory. McMahon completed 12 of 24 passes for 157 yards and helped break open the game with a 42-yard touchdown pass to Fred Barnett with 1:53 left in the first half. That came shortly after the Raiders had pulled within 10-3 on a 22-yard field goal by Jeff Jaeger. But Philadelphia's Vai Sikahema returned the ensuing kickoff 40 yards, and McMahon hit Barnett with a 12-yard completion before the two connected again on the long bomb. Cornerback Eric Allen had 2 interceptions for the Eagles, who had 4 thefts in all and also recovered a fumble. Raiders starting quarterback Todd Marinovich completed only 3 of 10 passes for 25 yards and was intercepted 3 times in less than two quarters before being lifted in favor of Jay Schroeder.

L.A. Raiders	0	3	0	7	—	10
Philadelphia	3	14	7	7	—	31

Phil	— FG Ruzek 24
Phil	— Walker 1 run (Ruzek kick)
Raid	— FG Jaeger 22
Phil	— Barnett 42 pass from McMahon (Ruzek kick)
Phil	— Sherman 30 run (Ruzek kick)
Phil	— Walker 2 run (Ruzek kick)
Raid	— T. Brown 6 pass from Schroeder (Jaeger kick)

Miami 28, Indianapolis 0—at Hoosier Dome, attendance 59,892. Mark Higgs rushed for 107 yards and 1 touchdown as the Dolphins avenged an upset loss to the Colts two weeks earlier. Normally pass-happy Miami used a combination of a strong running game and a stifling defense to post the shutout. The Dolphins amassed 212 rushing yards on 40 carries, while the defense limited Indianapolis to 193 total yards. Still, Miami quarterback Dan Marino added 245 passing yards on 22 completions in 28 attempts. The Dolphins scored on their opening possession and never looked back. Higgs had a 13-yard run and a 19-yard reception on the 69-yard, 10-play drive following the opening kickoff. Marino's 2-yard touchdown pass to tight end Keith Jackson capped the 6:03 march.

Miami	14	7	0	7	—	28
Indianapolis	0	0	0	0	—	0

Mia	— Jackson 2 pass from Marino (Stoyanovich kick)
Mia	— Higgs 3 run (Stoyanovich kick)
Mia	— Banks 3 pass from Marino (Stoyanovich kick)
Mia	— Paige 1 run (Stoyanovich kick)

Minnesota 35, Tampa Bay 7—at Tampa Stadium, attendance 49,095. Roger Craig ran for 2 touchdowns and the Vikings' defense scored twice for the second consecutive week as Minnesota pounded the Buccaneers. The previous week, linebackers Jack Del Rio and Carlos Jenkins returned interceptions for touchdowns in Minnesota's 38-10 victory over the Bears. Against Tampa Bay, Jenkins scooped up a fumble and returned it 22 yards for a touchdown in the first quarter, and end Chris Doleman returned an interception 27 yards for a touchdown just 13 seconds before halftime to break the game open at 28-0. Both plays were set up by pressure on Buccaneers quarterback Steve DeBerg from end Al Noga. Tampa Bay outgained the Vikings 354-296, but was victimized by 3 turnovers and numerous missed opportunities. On six trips inside the Minnesota 35-yard line, the Buccaneers could come away with only a fourth-quarter touchdown long after the issue was decided.

Minnesota	14	14	0	7	—	35
Tampa Bay	0	0	0	7	—	7

Minn	— Craig 5 run (Reveiz kick)
Minn	— Jenkins 22 fumble recovery return (Reveiz kick)
Minn	— A. Carter 10 run (Reveiz kick)
Minn	— Doleman 27 interception return (Reveiz kick)
Minn	— Craig 2 run (Reveiz kick)
TB	— Anderson 4 run (Willis kick)

New Orleans 31, New England 14—at Foxboro Stadium, attendance 45,413. Bobby Hebert threw 2 touchdown passes to Quinn Early in the first quarter and the Saints cruised to a victory over the winless Patriots. Hebert, who also had a 12-yard touchdown pass to running back Dalton Hilliard in the second quarter, completed 14 of 26 passes for 198 yards to lead New Orleans's efficient offense. The Saints' defense, meanwhile, harrassed New England into 4 turnovers. Five different players each recorded 1 sack, and defensive backs Gene Atkins and Toi Cook intercepted passes. The Patriots played without head coach Dick MacPherson, who was hospitalized earlier in the week with an intestinal disorder. Assistant coach Dante Scarnecchia took over MacPherson's duties.

	1	2	3	4		
New Orleans	14	7	7	3	—	31
New England	0	7	0	7	—	14

NO — Early 9 pass from Hebert (Andersen kick)
NO — Early 39 pass from Hebert (Andersen kick)
NE — Russell 8 run (Baumann kick)
NO — Hilliard 12 pass from Hebert (Andersen kick)
NO — Dunbar 1 run (Andersen kick)
NO — FG Andersen 46
NE — Brown 49 interception return (Baumann kick)

Denver 27, N.Y. Jets 16—at Mile High Stadium, attendance 74,678. John Elway passed for 261 yards and the Broncos used a pair of big plays in the second quarter to down the Jets. New York had tied the score at 3-3 early in the second period on a 27-yard field goal by Cary Blanchard. But three plays later, Elway teamed with Arthur Marshall on an 80-yard touchdown pass—the longest regular-season completion of the Denver quarterback's career— to give the Broncos the lead for good. It was 10-6 late in the quarter when cornerback Wymon Henderson returned an interception 46 yards for a touchdown just 1:28 before halftime. The Jets rallied to within 20-16 in the second half, then recovered a fumble near midfield early in the fourth quarter. But two plays later, New York fumbled the ball back to Denver, and the Broncos drove to Greg Lewis's game-clinching 1-yard touchdown run with 6:54 to play. Elway, who called his own plays for the first time this season, finished with 18 completions in 33 attempts. Marshall caught 5 passes for 134 yards. The Jets' Brad Baxter ran for 96 yards on 12 carries.

	1	2	3	4		
N.Y. Jets	0	6	7	3	—	16
Denver	3	14	3	7	—	27

Den — FG Treadwell 37
Jets — FG Blanchard 27
Den — Marshall 80 pass from Elway (Treadwell kick)
Jets — FG Blanchard 19
Den — Henderson 46 interception return (Treadwell kick)
Den — FG Treadwell 23
Jets — Moore 25 pass from Nagle (Blanchard kick)
Jets — FG Blanchard 36
Den — Lewis 1 run (Treadwell kick)

Phoenix 20, L.A. Rams 14—at Anaheim Stadium, attendance 40,788. Johnny Johnson's 10-yard touchdown run with 2:04 left to play gave the Cardinals the victory. The Rams, ahead 14-13 late in the game, were driving to the apparent clinching score when running back Cleveland Gary fumbled at the Cardinals' 31. Phoenix cornerback Aeneas Williams scooped up the loose ball and raced 69 yards to the end zone, only to have part of his return negated by an illegal block. Phoenix took over possession at the Rams' 40 and Johnson scored six plays later. Johnson, who ran for 91 yards on 24 carries, also scored on a 6-yard run to give the Cardinals the lead at 13-7 in the third quarter. That touchdown also was set up when the Cardinals recovered a fumble by Gary. But the Los Angeles running back, who ran for 55 yards and caught 7 passes for 60 yards, put the Rams back in front by running 1 yard for a score 2:45 into the fourth quarter. Jim Everett completed 21 of 32 passes for 248 yards and 1 touchdown for Los Angeles. Phoenix wide receiver Ricky Proehl caught a career-high 9 passes for 126 yards.

	1	2	3	4		
Phoenix	3	0	10	7	—	20
L.A. Rams	0	7	0	7	—	14

Phx — FG Davis 21
Rams — Ellard 33 pass from Everett (Zendejas kick)
Phx — FG Davis 31
Phx — Johnson 6 run (Davis kick)
Rams — Gary 1 run (Zendejas kick)
Phx — Johnson 10 run (Davis kick)

Buffalo 28, Pittsburgh 20—at Rich Stadium, attendance 80,294. Jim Kelly passed for 3 touchdowns, Thurman Thomas rushed for 155 yards, and the Bills broke out of a scoring slump to beat the Steelers. Buffalo's high-powered offense, which had scored only 53 points in its previous four games, recorded 31 first downs and 458 total yards in this one. Kelly, who completed 26 of 33 passes for 290 yards and was not intercepted, threw a 22-yard touchdown pass to James Lofton and a 2-yard toss to tackle-eligible Mitch Frerotte as the Bills built a 21-6 halftime lead. His 45-yard touchdown to Lofton midway through the third quarter provided the clinching score. Thomas, who carried a career-high 37 times, had a 1-yard touchdown run in the second quarter. Wide receiver Don Beebe caught 8 passes for 101 yards. Pittsburgh's Neil O'Donnell kept the game close with a pair of third-quarter touchdown passes.

	1	2	3	4		
Pittsburgh	0	6	14	0	—	20
Buffalo	7	14	7	0	—	28

Buff — Lofton 22 pass from Kelly (Christie kick)
Pitt — FG Anderson 28
Buff — Frerotte 2 pass from Kelly (Christie kick)
Buff — Thomas 1 run (Christie kick)
Pitt — FG Anderson 49
Pitt — Mills 12 pass from O'Donnell (Anderson kick)
Buff — Lofton 45 pass from Kelly (Christie kick)
Pitt — Hoge 11 pass from O'Donnell (Anderson kick)

Kansas City 16, San Diego 14—at Arrowhead Stadium, attendance 72,876. Nick Lowery's 36-yard field goal with 54 seconds remaining lifted the Chiefs to the victory and snapped the Chargers' four-game winning streak. Lowery's kick spoiled a second-half comeback by San Diego, which rallied from a 13-0 halftime deficit to a 14-13 lead by driving 80 and 90 yards to touchdowns late in the third quarter and early in the fourth. But Kansas City forced a punt late in the game and took over at its 33-yard line. Chiefs quarterback Dave Krieg, only 7 of 25 passing before the winning drive, marched his team into field-goal range by completing 3 consecutive attempts, including a 25-yarder to Willie Davis. Kansas City had forged its first-half lead by taking advantage of a furious pass rush supplied by Derrick Thomas. The outside linebacker sacked Chargers quarterback Stan Humphries 4 times before intermission, twice causing fumbles that the Chiefs converted into a touchdown and a field goal. Humphries had a strong second half to finish with 20 completions in 35 attempts for 294 yards and a touchdown. Lowery, who also had field goals of 47 and 35 yards, became only the sixth player in NFL history to record 300 career three-pointers when he made his winning kick.

	1	2	3	4		
San Diego	0	0	7	7	—	14
Kansas City	3	10	0	3	—	16

KC — FG Lowery 47
KC — Okoye 2 run (Lowery kick)
KC — FG Lowery 35
SD — Walker 14 pass from Humphries (Carney kick)
SD — Butts 1 run (Carney kick)
KC — FG Lowery 36

Washington 16, Seattle 3—at Kingdome, attendance 53,616. Mark Rypien passed for a touchdown and Chip Lohmiller kicked 3 field goals to lift the Redskins past the Seahawks. Lohmiller, who had a 48-yard field goal to tie the game at 3-3 just before halftime, booted kicks of 33 and 37 yards in the third quarter. Washington then scored its first offensive touchdown in 15 quarters when Rypien and tight end Terry Orr teamed on a 26-yard pass 4:32 into the fourth quarter. Earnest Byner had 108 yards rushing and receiving for the Redskins, who outgained Seattle 330-183. Chris Warren ran for 103 yards for the Seahawks, who dropped their sixth consecutive game and fell to 1-8, the worst start in franchise history.

	1	2	3	4		
Washington	0	3	6	7	—	16
Seattle	0	3	0	0	—	3

Sea — FG Kasay 22
Wash — FG Lohmiller 48
Wash — FG Lohmiller 33
Wash — FG Lohmiller 37
Wash — Orr 26 pass from Rypien (Lohmiller kick)

Sunday Night, November 8

Cincinnati 31, Chicago 28—at Soldier Field, attendance 56,120. Boomer Esiason's 23-yard touchdown pass to Carl Pickens with 59 seconds left in regulation tied the game, and Jim Breech's 36-yard field goal 8:39 into overtime won it as the Bengals rallied to beat the Bears. Cincinnati trailed 28-14 before closing the deficit to seven points on Esiason's 1-yard touchdown pass to tight end Craig Thompson with five seconds left in the third quarter. The Bengals then got the opportunity to tie the game in the fourth quarter when rookie cornerback Leonard Wheeler intercepted a Jim Harbaugh pass and returned it 12 yards to the Bears' 35-yard line. Eleven plays later, Esiason lofted a fourth-down pass to the 6-foot-2 Pickens, who outjumped 5-foot-9 cornerback Lemuel Stinson in the end zone. After holding the Bears on the opening possession of overtime, Cincinnati marched 65 yards to the winning field goal. Esiason finished with 3 touchdown passes and Harold Green rushed for 117 yards for the Bengals. Chicago's Darren Lewis ran for 72 yards and 1 touchdown, and returned a third-quarter kickoff 97 yards for another score.

	1	2	3	4	OT		
Cincinnati	7	0	14	7	3	—	31
Chicago	7	14	7	0	0	—	28

Cin — Fenner 2 run (Breech kick)
Chi — Lewis 15 run (Butler kick)
Chi — Morgan 46 pass from Harbaugh (Butler kick)
Chi — Green 1 run (Butler kick)
Cin — Ball 35 pass from Esiason (Breech kick)
Chi — Lewis 97 kickoff return (Butler kick)
Cin — Thompson 1 pass from Esiason (Breech kick)
Cin — Pickens 23 pass from Esiason (Breech kick)
Cin — FG Breech 36

Monday, November 9

San Francisco 41, Atlanta 3—at Georgia Dome, attendance 67,404. Steve Young threw 3 touchdown passes and the 49ers took advantage of 6 turnovers to blast the Falcons for the second time this season. Three weeks earlier, San Francisco beat Atlanta 56-17 at Candlestick Park. This time, the 49ers actually were outgained by the Falcons, 304 total yards to 303, but converted 3 fumbles and 3 interceptions into 24 points. San Francisco led 14-3 at halftime, then put the game away in the third quarter. After Mike Cofer's 40-yard field goal made it 17-3, cornerback Don Griffin stripped the ball from Atlanta wide receiver Andre Rison and Michael McGruder recovered at the Falcons' 35-yard line to set up another three-pointer. The 49ers' Amp Lee then recovered Deion Sanders's fumble on the ensuing kickoff, and four plays later, Tom Rathman ran 2 yards for a touchdown to make it 27-3.

	1	2	3	4		
San Francisco	7	7	13	14	—	41
Atlanta	0	3	0	0	—	3

SF — Turner 12 pass from Young (Cofer kick)
SF — Watters 21 pass from Young (Cofer kick)
Atl — FG Johnson 33
SF — FG Cofer 40
SF — FG Cofer 32
SF — Rathman 2 run (Cofer kick)
SF — Rice 19 pass from Young (Cofer kick)
SF — Hanks 48 punt return (Cofer kick)

Eleventh Week Summaries

Standings

American Football Conference

Eastern Division

	W	L	T	Pct.	Pts.	OP
Buffalo	8	2	0	.800	260	169
Miami	7	3	0	.700	250	177
Indianapolis	4	6	0	.400	133	223
N.Y. Jets	3	7	0	.300	163	202
New England	1	9	0	.100	138	257

Central Division

	W	L	T	Pct.	Pts.	OP
Pittsburgh	7	3	0	.700	196	139
Houston	6	4	0	.600	230	178
Cleveland	5	5	0	.500	154	159
Cincinnati	4	6	0	.400	184	229

Western Division

	W	L	T	Pct.	Pts.	OP
Denver	7	3	0	.700	175	183
Kansas City	6	4	0	.600	204	158
San Diego	5	5	0	.500	158	165
L.A. Raiders	4	6	0	.400	152	171
Seattle	1	9	0	.100	59	194

National Football Conference

Eastern Division

	W	L	T	Pct.	Pts.	OP
Dallas	8	2	0	.800	247	152
Philadelphia	6	4	0	.600	208	134
Washington	6	4	0	.600	175	167
N.Y. Giants	5	5	0	.500	214	202
Phoenix	3	7	0	.300	174	225

Central Division

	W	L	T	Pct.	Pts.	OP
Minnesota	7	3	0	.700	259	161
Chicago	4	6	0	.400	224	244
Green Bay	4	6	0	.400	151	215
Tampa Bay	4	6	0	.400	184	227
Detroit	2	8	0	.200	177	216

Western Division

	W	L	T	Pct.	Pts.	OP
San Francisco	8	2	0	.800	292	172
New Orleans	7	3	0	.700	191	138
Atlanta	4	6	0	.400	186	265
L.A. Rams	4	6	0	.400	190	206

Sunday, November 15

Tampa Bay 20, Chicago 17—at Tampa Stadium, attendance 69,102. Reggie Cobb rushed for 114 yards and 1 touchdown and the Buccaneers built a 20-0 halftime lead, then held on to snap a five-game losing streak while handing the Bears their third consecutive defeat. Vinny Testaverde, back in the starting lineup after two weeks on the bench, completed 12 of 21 passes for 182 yards, including a 12-yard touchdown pass to tight end Ron Hall with 1:53 left in the first half. But Kevin Butler's 27-yard field goal and a pair of touchdowns by running back Neal Anderson pulled Chicago within three points. The Bears had a chance to tie after getting the ball back on their 27-yard line with 1:37 left and marching 47 yards. But Butler's 44-yard field-goal try with one second remaining was wide left.

	1	2	3	4		
Chicago	0	0	3	14	—	17
Tampa Bay	10	10	0	0	—	20

TB — FG Murray 31
TB — Cobb 1 run (Murray kick)

TB — FG Murray 40
TB — Hall 12 pass from Testaverde (Murray kick)
Chi — FG Butler 27
Chi — Anderson 1 run (Butler kick)
Chi — Anderson 11 pass from Harbaugh (Butler kick)

N.Y. Jets 17, Cincinnati 14—at Giants Stadium, attendance 60,196. Brad Baxter and Terance Mathis scored on touchdown runs and the Jets held off a late rally to beat the Bengals. New York, playing without injured running back Blair Thomas and injured wide receiver Al Toon, built a 17-0 advantage in the third quarter, then turned it over to its defense, which allowed only 227 total yards. Much of that was in the fourth quarter, however, when Cincinnati scored on a pair of runs by Derrick Fenner to trim its deficit to only three points with 5:21 left in the game. But the Bengals could not get the ball back again until only 1:06 remained. Fenner finished with 92 rushing yards, all of them in the fourth quarter.

Cincinnati	0	0	0	14	—	14
N.Y. Jets	0	10	7	0	—	17

Jets — FG Blanchard 42
Jets — Baxter 1 run (Blanchard kick)
Jets — Mathis 10 run (Blanchard kick)
Cin — Fenner 5 run (Breech kick)
Cin — Fenner 17 run (Breech kick)

Pittsburgh 17, Detroit 14—at Three Rivers Stadium, attendance 52,242. Backup quarterback Bubby Brister, playing in his first game of the season, threw a 1-yard touchdown pass to tight end Tim Jorden with 2:50 remaining to give the Steelers the victory. The Lions had rallied from a 10-0 deficit to take a 14-10 lead on Barry Sanders's 1-yard run seven seconds into the fourth quarter. Detroit was threatening to widen its lead when Sanders, who had a 42-yard run earlier on the drive, lost a fumble near the Pittsburgh goal line. Late in the game, Steelers cornerback Rod Woodson sacked Lions quarterback Erik Kramer, forcing a fumble that safety Carnell Lake returned 12 yards to the Detroit 3 with 3:33 to play. Brister, who entered the game one series earlier when starter Neil O'Donnell pulled a hamstring muscle, tossed the winning touchdown pass two plays later. Pittsburgh running back Barry Foster had his seventh 100-yard rushing day of the season. He gained 106 yards on 25 attempts to become the first player this season to reach the 1,000-yard mark. Kramer completed 20 of 37 passes for 304 yards, but was intercepted twice. The Lions had 6 turnovers.

Detroit	0	7	0	7	—	14
Pittsburgh	7	3	0	7	—	17

Pitt — Mills 11 pass from O'Donnell (Anderson kick)
Pitt — FG Anderson 20
Det — Green 73 pass from Kramer (Hanson kick)
Det — Sanders 1 run (Hanson kick)
Pitt — Jorden 1 pass from Brister (Anderson kick)

Houston 17, Minnesota 13—at Metrodome, attendance 56,726. Lorenzo White's 1-yard run with 48 seconds left was the difference as the Oilers beat the Vikings. White's run capped an 80-yard, 13-play drive on which Houston starting quarterback Warren Moon was injured while making the key play. Moon, who completed 28 of 38 passes for 243 yards, escaped trouble on third-and-4 at the Minnesota 26-yard line by scrambling 5 yards. But he was hit by safety Vencie Glenn while diving for the first down at the end of his run, and broke his left (nonthrowing) arm. He was expected to miss three to six weeks. Backup Cody Carlson came on and completed his only 2 attempts for 13 yards, including an 8-yard pass to White that positioned the ball on the 1. White finished with 81 yards on 18 carries as the Oilers amassed 342 total yards to only 174 for Minnesota. The Vikings' lone touchdown came in the second quarter, when linebacker Carlos Jenkins sacked Moon, forcing a fumble that cornerback Anthony Parker returned 58 yards for Minnesota's fifth defensive score in three weeks. Vikings defensive end Chris Doleman had 2½ sacks and forced a pair of fumbles. Moon upped his career total to 30,120 passing yards to become the fourteenth player in NFL history to surpass 30,000 passing yards.

Houston	0	10	0	7	—	17
Minnesota	0	10	0	3	—	13

Hou — FG Del Greco 30
Minn — Parker 58 fumble recovery return (Reveiz kick)
Minn — FG Reveiz 42
Hou — Givins 5 pass from Moon (Del Greco kick)
Minn — FG Reveiz 51
Hou — White 1 run (Del Greco kick)

L.A. Rams 27, Dallas 23—at Texas Stadium, attendance 63,690. Running back Cleveland Gary accounted for 154 yards from scrimmage and scored 2 touchdowns as the Rams snapped the Cowboys' 11-game winning streak at home. Gary, who carried 29 times for 110 yards, opened the scoring with a 1-yard run midway through the first quarter. He also caught 7 passes for 44 yards, including a 3-yard touchdown just 18 seconds before halftime to put Los Angeles ahead 21-13. Dallas rallied to take a 23-21 lead on Lin Elliott's third field goal of the game and Kelvin Martin's 74-yard punt return late in the third quarter. But the Rams regained the lead on 2 field goals by Tony Zendejas, the second field goal coming with 1:54 to play. Dallas took the subsequent kickoff and marched to Los Angeles's 14-yard line, but quarterback Troy Aikman threw incomplete in the end zone on the final two plays of the game. Rams quarterback Jim Everett completed 22 of 37 passes for 251 yards and 2 touchdowns. Aikman was 22 of 37 for 272 yards, with 8 of his throws for 168 yards to wide receiver Michael Irvin. Emmitt Smith's 3-yard touchdown run in the second quarter was his thirteenth of the season, a Cowboys' record.

L.A. Rams	7	14	0	6	—	27
Dallas	3	10	10	0	—	23

Rams — Gary 1 run (Zendejas kick)
Dall — FG Elliott 37
Dall — E. Smith 3 run (Elliott kick)
Dall — FG Elliott 42
Rams — Chadwick 8 pass from Everett (Zendejas kick)
Rams — Gary 3 pass from Everett (Zendejas kick)
Dall — FG Elliott 36
Dall — Martin 74 punt return (Elliott kick)
Rams — FG Zendejas 33
Rams — FG Zendejas 44

New England 37, Indianapolis 34—at Hoosier Dome, attendance 42,631. Charlie Baumann's 18-yard field goal 3:25 into overtime gave the Patriots their first victory of the season. Baumann had forced the extra session by kicking a 44-yard field goal on the final play of regulation. Then in overtime, New England cornerback Jerome Henderson intercepted a pass from Jeff George and returned it 9 yards to the Colts' 29-yard line to set up the winning kick. Patriots quarterback Scott Zolak, making his first NFL start, completed 20 of 29 passes for 261 yards and 2 touchdowns as he repeatedly brought his team from behind. Indianapolis led most of the way and took a 31-21 advantage on Rodney Culver's 1-yard run on the first play of the fourth quarter. But New England linebacker Chris Singleton returned an interception 82 yards for a touchdown three-and-a-half minutes later and, after an exchange of field goals, the Patriots marched 67 yards in 10 plays to the tying field goal. George completed 18 of 35 passes for 330 yards and 2 touchdowns, but suffered 3 costly interceptions (New England cornerback David Pool also returned a theft for a score). Running back Anthony Johnson had 77 rushing yards and 163 receiving yards on 7 catches to help the Colts amass 417 total yards.

New England	14	7	0	13	3	—	37
Indianapolis	14	7	3	10	0	—	34

Ind — Verdin 53 punt return (Biasucci kick)
NE — Pool 41 interception return (Baumann kick)
Ind — Culver 1 pass from George (Biasucci kick)
NE — Coates 2 pass from Zolak (Baumann kick)
Ind — Cash 23 pass from George (Biasucci kick)
NE — McMurtry 65 pass from Zolak (Baumann kick)
Ind — FG Biasucci 48
Ind — Culver 1 run (Biasucci kick)
NE — Singleton 82 interception return (Baumann kick)
NE — FG Baumann 36
Ind — FG Biasucci 33
NE — FG Baumann 44
NE — FG Baumann 18

San Francisco 21, New Orleans 20—at Candlestick Park, attendance 64,895. Steve Young tossed a pair of fourth-quarter touchdown passes to tight end Brent Jones, including the 8-yard game-winner with 46 seconds remaining, to lift the 49ers past the Saints and into sole possession of first place in the NFC Western Division. San Francisco trailed 20-7 in the fourth quarter until the 49ers went to a No-Huddle offense. With Young calling most of the plays, the 49ers drove 65 yards, capped by Young's 14-yard touchdown pass to Jones with 10:16 left to make it 20-14. The subsequent winning drive covered 74 yards in 13 plays. Young converted a trio of third-down opportunities along the way, 2 with completions to Jerry Rice and another on his 8-yard run. He finished the game with 205 passing yards and 58 rushing yards, including a 10-yard touchdown run late in the first half. 49ers running back Ricky Watters gained 115 yards on 21 carries. New Orleans quarterback Bobby Hebert completed 22 of 35 passes for 301 yards, including a 22-yard touchdown pass to Torrance Small in the second quarter. The victory was the fiftieth of San Francisco head coach George Seifert's career. He reached that plateau in his sixty-third game, faster than any other head coach in NFL history.

New Orleans	3	7	10	0	—	20
San Francisco	0	7	0	14	—	21

NO — FG Andersen 29
NO — Small 22 pass from Hebert (Andersen kick)
SF — Young 10 run (Cofer kick)
NO — FG Andersen 42
NO — Hilliard 11 pass from Hebert (Andersen kick)
SF — Jones 14 pass from Young (Cofer kick)
SF — Jones 8 pass from Young (Cofer kick)

Green Bay 27, Philadelphia 24—at Milwaukee County Stadium, attendance 52,689. Chris Jacke kicked a pair of field goals in the final 1:31, including the game-winner as time expired to lift the Packers over the Eagles. Jacke's 31-yard field goal, which tied the score at 24-24, followed a 57-yard drive that started after Green Bay cornerback LeRoy Butler recovered Heath Sherman's fumble deep in Packers territory. Two plays after the tying kick, Philadelphia's Herschel Walker fumbled and Green Bay linebacker Johnny Holland pounced on it at the Eagles' 23-yard line with 43 seconds left to set up Jacke's winning kick. Earlier in the fourth quarter, Sherman and Walker had rallied Philadelphia from a 21-10 deficit. Sherman took a short swing pass and rambled 75 yards for a touchdown, and Walker scored on a 2-yard run to give the Eagles a 24-21 lead. Green Bay quarterback Brett Favre completed 23 of 33 passes for 275 yards and 2 touchdowns. Sterling Sharpe, the league's leading receiver, caught 7 passes for 116 yards. Philadelphia's Randall Cunningham returned to the starting lineup and completed 14 of 23 passes for 169 yards.

Philadelphia	3	0	7	14	—	24
Green Bay	0	14	0	13	—	27

Phil — FG Ruzek 34
GB — Sharpe 5 pass from Favre (Jacke kick)
GB — Workman 1 run (Jacke kick)
Phil — Sherman 17 run (Ruzek kick)
GB — Thompson 3 pass from Favre (Jacke kick)
Phil — Sherman 75 pass from Cunningham (Ruzek kick)
Phil — Walker 2 run (Ruzek kick)
GB — FG Jacke 31
GB — FG Jacke 41

Atlanta 20, Phoenix 17—at Georgia Dome, attendance 58,477. Norm Johnson's 35-yard field goal with 50 seconds remaining lifted the Falcons to the victory. Phoenix had tied the score at 17-17 when cornerback Robert Massey returned an interception 46 yards for a touchdown with 7:39 left in the game, his third theft and third touchdown return of the season. But backup quarterback Wade Wilson entered the game with 4:22 remaining and completed all 3 of his passes for 31 yards while marching Atlanta 48 yards to the winning field goal. Starting quarterback Billy Joe Tolliver completed 16 of 24 passes for 209 yards and 2 touchdowns, both to Andre Rison, before being lifted in favor of Wilson. Cardinals quarterback Chris Chandler passed for 261 yards, including as 5-yard touchdown pass to John Jackson.

Phoenix	0	10	0	7	—	17
Atlanta	7	3	0	10	—	20

Atl — Rison 30 pass from Tolliver (Johnson kick)
Atl — FG Johnson 27
Phx — J. Jackson 5 pass from Chandler (G. Davis kick)
Phx — FG G. Davis 49
Atl — Rison 7 pass from Tolliver (Johnson kick)
Phx — Massey 46 interception return (G. Davis kick)
Atl — FG Johnson 35

San Diego 14, Cleveland 13—at Cleveland Stadium, attendance 58,396. Anthony Miller caught a 45-yard touchdown pass from Stan Humphries with 2:05 left in the game to give the Chargers their fifth victory in their last six outings. The Browns had taken a 10-7 lead early in the fourth quarter when Mike Tomczak tossed a 24-yard touchdown pass to Michael Jackson to cap a 99-yard drive. Matt Stover then kicked his second field goal of the game, a 28-yarder with 5:00 left, to increase Cleveland's advantage to 13-7. But Humphries, who completed 19 of 32 passes for 234 yards and 2 touchdowns, directed the winning 72-yard, 6-play march. Miller caught 7 passes for 110 yards, his fourth 100-yard receiving day in a five-game span. The Browns' Lawyer Tillman had a career-high 148 yards on 8 catches.

San Diego	7	0	0	7	—	14
Cleveland	0	3	0	10	—	13

SD — Jefferson 26 pass from Humphries (Carney kick)
Cleve — FG Stover 36
Cleve — Jackson 24 pass from Tomczak (Stover kick)
Cleve — FG Stover 28
SD — Miller 45 pass from Humphries (Carney kick)

L.A. Raiders 20, Seattle 3—at Los Angeles Memorial Coliseum, attendance 46,862. Jay Schroeder returned to the starting lineup and threw a touchdown pass in the Raiders' victory. Schroeder, starting for the first time after losing his job to Todd Marinovich two games into the season, completed just 10 of 23 passes for 108 yards, but his 9-yard touchdown pass to tight end Ethan Horton 58 seconds before halftime gave the Raiders a 13-0 lead. That advantage was just about insurmountable considering that the Seahawks entered the game having scored only 5 touchdowns all year. Their only points in this one came on a 43-yard field goal by John Kasay with 4:25 left in the game. Los Angeles managed 188 total yards to Seattle's 159.

Seattle	0	0	0	3	—	3
L.A. Raiders	6	7	7	0	—	20

Raid — FG Jaeger 47
Raid — FG Jaeger 43
Raid — Horton 9 pass from Schroeder (Jaeger kick)
Raid — Dickerson 1 run (Jaeger kick)
Sea — FG Kasay 43

Kansas City 35, Washington 16—at Arrowhead Stadium, attendance 75,238. Dave Krieg passed for 232 of his season-high 302 yards in the first half as the Chiefs built a 28-0 lead en route to beating the Redskins. Krieg finished with 19 completions in 29 attempts and 2 touchdown passes, including a 35-yarder to Tim Barnett in the fourth quarter. Barnett's catch came after 3 field goals by Chip Lohmiller and Ricky Ervins's 5-yard touchdown run trimmed Washington's deficit to 28-16. Barnett, who also caught a 44-yard touchdown pass in the second quarter, finished with 6 catches for 148 yards. Harvey Williams ran for 88 yards and Christian Okoye had a pair of short touchdown runs for Kansas City, which outgained the Redskins 385-280.

Washington	0	0	13	3	—	16
Kansas City	7	21	0	7	—	35

KC — Okoye 2 run (Lowery kick)
KC — Barnett 44 pass from Krieg (Lowery kick)
KC — Okoye 3 run (Lowery kick)
KC — Williams 5 run (Lowery kick)
Wash — Ervins 5 run (Lohmiller kick)
Wash — FG Lohmiller 40
Wash — FG Lohmiller 26
Wash — FG Lohmiller 38
KC — Barnett 35 pass from Krieg (Lowery kick)

Sunday Night, November 15

Denver 27, N.Y. Giants 13—at Mile High Stadium, attendance 75,269. Veteran quarterback John Elway and rookie Tommy Maddox teamed up to help beat the Giants. Elway helped stake Denver to a 14-6 halftime lead by throwing for 96 yards, including a 51-yard touchdown pass to Mark Jackson. But he also injured his shoulder while scrambling for a first down in the second quarter. Enter Maddox, who played the entire second half, and kept the game out of reach by leading the Broncos to scores on three of their first four possessions after the intermission. Greg Lewis's 2-yard touchdown run with 5:44 left clinched Denver's ninth consecutive home victory. Maddox completed 9 of 13 passes for 134 yards and Gaston Green rushed for 92 yards as the Broncos rolled up 379 total yards. New York managed only 159 total yards, including just 39 passing. Denver recorded 5 sacks, including 2 each by Greg Kragen and Simon Fletcher.

N.Y. Giants	0	6	0	7	—	13
Denver	14	0	3	10	—	27

Den — Rivers 2 run (Treadwell kick)
Den — Jackson 51 pass from Elway (Treadwell kick)
Giants — FG Bahr 30
Giants — FG Bahr 38
Den — FG Treadwell 25
Den — FG Treadwell 46
Giants — Hostetler 5 run (Bahr kick)
Den — Lewis 2 run (Treadwell kick)

Monday, November 16

Buffalo 26, Miami 20—at Joe Robbie Stadium, attendance 70,629. Kenneth Davis ran for 2 touchdowns and Steve Christie kicked 4 field goals as the Bills rallied from an 11-point first-half deficit to beat the Dolphins and take over first place in the AFC Eastern Division. Miami's Dan Marino, who completed his first 11 passes, capped the Dolphins' first two possessions with touchdown throws to tight end Greg Baty and wide receiver Mark Clayton for a 14-3 lead. But Buffalo began to pressure the Miami quarterback after that, getting to him for 4 sacks. The Bills, down 17-13 at halftime, took a 20-17 lead when Davis ran 1 yard for a score on their opening drive of the second half, then added a pair of short field goals by Christie following Dolphins turnovers. Christie's 2 first-half field goals included a club-record 54-yarder. Buffalo quarterback Jim Kelly completed 19 of 32 passes for 212 yards, and running back Thurman Thomas totaled 139 yards from scrimmage. Marino finished 22 of 33 for 321 yards. Miami's Mark Duper caught 5 passes for 100 yards and Clayton had 5 receptions for 98 yards.

Buffalo	3	10	13	0	—	26
Miami	7	10	0	3	—	20

Mia — Baty 1 pass from Marino (Stoyanovich kick)
Buff — FG Christie 26
Mia — Clayton 19 pass from Marino (Stoyanovich kick)
Buff — FG Christie 54
Buff — K. Davis 5 run (Christie kick)
Mia — FG Stoyanovich 21
Buff — K. Davis 1 run (Christie kick)
Buff — FG Christie 23
Buff — FG Christie 19
Mia — FG Stoyanovich 50

Twelfth Week Summaries

Standings

American Football Conference

Eastern Division	W	L	T	Pct.	Pts.	OP
Buffalo	9	2	0	.818	301	183
Miami	8	3	0	.727	269	193
Indianapolis	4	7	0	.364	147	253
N.Y. Jets	3	8	0	.273	166	226
New England	2	9	0	.182	162	260
Central Division						
Pittsburgh	8	3	0	.727	226	153
Houston	6	5	0	.545	246	197
Cleveland	5	6	0	.455	167	176
Cincinnati	4	7	0	.364	197	249
Western Division						
Denver	7	4	0	.636	175	207
Kansas City	7	4	0	.636	228	172
San Diego	6	5	0	.545	187	179
L.A. Raiders	5	6	0	.455	176	171
Seattle	1	10	0	.091	73	218

National Football Conference

Eastern Division	W	L	T	Pct.	Pts.	OP
Dallas	9	2	0	.818	263	162
Philadelphia	7	4	0	.636	255	168
Washington	6	5	0	.545	178	187
N.Y. Giants	5	6	0	.455	248	249
Phoenix	3	8	0	.273	184	241
Central Division						
Minnesota	8	3	0	.727	276	174
Green Bay	5	6	0	.455	168	218
Chicago	4	7	0	.364	227	261
Tampa Bay	4	7	0	.364	198	256
Detroit	3	8	0	.273	196	229
Western Division						
San Francisco	9	2	0	.818	319	182
New Orleans	8	3	0	.727	211	141
Atlanta	4	7	0	.364	200	306
L.A. Rams	4	7	0	.400	200	233

Sunday, November 22

Buffalo 41, Atlanta 14—at Rich Stadium, attendance 80,004. The Bills scored touchdowns on each of their first five possessions to open a 35-0 lead only 16 minutes into the game and cruise past the Falcons. Kenneth Davis rushed for a career-high 181 yards on 20 carries and scored twice, and Thurman Thomas ran for 103 yards on 13 attempts, all in the first half, as Buffalo amassed a whopping 315 yards on the ground. Atlanta was never in the game, allowing a club-record 28 first-quarter points and failing to score until falling behind 38-0. That came with only 12 seconds left in the first half, when Deion Sanders took a lateral on a kickoff and sprinted 73 yards for a touchdown. The Bills outgained the Falcons 412-174, including 310-49 in the first half alone.

Atlanta	0	7	0	7	—	14
Buffalo	28	10	0	3	—	41

Buff — Gardner 2 run (Christie kick)
Buff — Metzelaars 3 pass from Kelly (Christie kick)
Buff — Reed 15 pass from Kelly (Christie kick)
Buff — K. Davis 1 run (Christie kick)
Buff — K. Davis 64 run (Christie kick)
Buff — FG Christie 47
Atl — Sanders 75 kickoff return (Johnson kick)
Buff — FG Christie 18
Atl — Hill 1 pass from Wilson (Johnson kick)

Minnesota 17, Cleveland 13—at Metrodome, attendance 53,323. The Vikings scored 2 touchdowns in a span of 16 seconds in the fourth quarter to come from behind and beat the Browns. Cleveland led 13-0 at halftime and still had a 13-3 advantage in the final period. But backup quarterback Sean Salisbury, subbing for an ineffective Rich Gannon, tossed a 3-yard touchdown pass to tight end Joe Johnson to make it 13-10 with 9:21 remaining. On the Browns' first play following the ensuing kickoff, Vikings cornerback Audray McMillian picked off a Todd Philcox pass and returned it 25 yards for the decisive score with 9:05 to go. It was McMillian's third interception of the day and the seventh touchdown scored by Minnesota's defense this season, equaling the club record set in 1988. Six of the scores came in the past four weeks. Despite the victory, the Vikings struggled on offense, completing only 9 of 25 passes and gaining just 141 total yards. Wide receiver Anthony Carter failed to catch a pass, ending his streak at 105 games.

Cleveland	10	3	0	0	—	13
Minnesota	0	0	3	14	—	17

Cleve — FG Stover 19
Cleve — Mack 1 run (Stover kick)
Cleve — FG Stover 30
Minn — FG Reveiz 40
Minn — Johnson 3 pass from Salisbury (Reveiz kick)
Minn — McMillian 25 interception return (Reveiz kick)

Dallas 16, Phoenix 10—at Sun Devil Stadium, attendance 72,439. Troy Aikman threw a pair of touchdown passes to lead the Cowboys past the stubborn Cardinals. Phoenix took a 7-0 lead in the first quarter after Johnny Bailey's 65-yard punt return set up Chris Chandler's 2-yard touchdown pass to running back Larry Centers. But Chandler, who completed 5 of 7 passes, suffered bruised ribs while scrambling late in the first period, and left the game. The Cardinals struggled after that, and finished the game with only 9 first downs and 149 total yards. Meanwhile, Aikman was throwing touchdown passes of 7 yards to tight end Jay Novacek and 37 yards to wide receiver Alvin Harper. His scoring toss to Novacek came with only 14 seconds left in the first half and gave Dallas the lead for good. The Cowboys' quarterback finished with 25 completions in 36 attempts for 237 yards. Emmitt Smith rushed for 84 yards to surpass the 1,000-yard mark for the season and also caught 12 passes for 67 yards.

Dallas	0	10	6	0	—	16
Phoenix	7	0	0	3	—	10

Phx — Centers 2 pass from Chandler (Davis kick)
Dall — FG Elliott 28
Dall — Novacek 7 pass from Aikman (Elliott kick)
Dall — Harper 37 pass from Aikman (kick failed)
Phx — FG Davis 20

L.A. Raiders 24, Denver 0—at Los Angeles Memorial Coliseum, attendance 50,011. Jay Schroeder threw 3 touchdown passes and the Raiders' defense took advantage of the inexperience of Broncos quarterback Tommy Maddox to post the shutout. The 21-year-old Maddox, making his first NFL start in place of injured John Elway, completed 18 of 26 passes for 207 yards, but also fumbled 3 times (1 was recovered by the Raiders), was sacked 3 times, and intercepted twice. Los Angeles cornerback Terry McDaniel recorded both thefts, returning each one 67 yards. The first came late in the first quarter and set up Schroeder's 1-yard scoring toss to tight end Andrew Glover on the first play of the second period for a 10-0 Raiders lead. Schroeder, who completed 16 of 30 passes for 160 yards, also had touchdown passes of 11 yards to Tim Brown and 10 yards to Marcus Allen. Eric Dickerson recorded his first 100-yard rushing day as a Raider, gaining 107 yards on 16 carries.

Denver	0	0	0	0	—	0
L.A. Raiders	3	14	0	7	—	24

Raid — FG Jaeger 51
Raid — Glover 1 pass from Schroeder (Jaeger kick)
Raid — T. Brown 11 pass from Schroeder (Jaeger kick)
Raid — Allen 10 pass from Schroeder (Jaeger kick)

Detroit 19, Cincinnati 13—at Riverfront Stadium, attendance 48,574. Barry Sanders rushed for 151 yards and became the Lions' all-time leading rusher during Detroit's victory over the Bengals. Sanders, who carried 29 times, broke Billy Sims's club mark of 5,106 yards with an 18-yard run late in the first half. The fourth-year running back finished the day at 5,202 yards. Jason Hanson gave the Lions a 9-6 lead with his third field goal of the game, a 20-yarder six seconds before halftime. Sanders then gave Detroit the remaining points it needed with a 5-yard touchdown run early in the fourth quarter. Hanson added a fourth field goal late in the game. The Lions' defense did the rest, permitting Cincinnati only 95 total yards, including just 43 through the air. Bengals linebacker James Francis had a pair of sacks and returned a fourth-quarter interception 66 yards for a touchdown.

Detroit	0	9	0	10	—	19
Cincinnati	3	3	0	7	—	13

Cin — FG Breech 40
Det — FG Hanson 35
Det — FG Hanson 27
Cin — FG Breech 20
Det — FG Hanson 20

Det	— Sanders 5 run (Hanson kick)
Cin	— Francis 66 interception return (Breech kick)
Det	— FG Hanson 29

Green Bay 17, Chicago 3—at Soldier Field, attendance 56,170. Quarterback Brett Favre passed for 1 touchdown and ran for another as the Packers handed the Bears their fourth consecutive loss. Favre, playing with a separated left (nonthrowing) shoulder, completed 16 of 24 passes for 209 yards, including a 49-yard bomb to Sterling Sharpe late in the first quarter to break a 3-3 tie and give Green Bay the lead for good. He capped a 74-yard, 13-play drive with his 5-yard touchdown run 2:28 into the fourth quarter. Packers rookie Edgar Bennett, making his first NFL start because of injuries to Vince Workman and Darrell Thompson, rushed for 107 yards on 29 carries. Chicago quarterback Peter Tom Willis replaced ineffective starter Jim Harbaugh in the fourth quarter and completed 16 of 23 passes for 160 yards. Wendell Davis caught 8 passes for 106 yards for the Bears.

Green Bay	10	0	0	7	—	17
Chicago	3	0	0	0	—	3

Chi	— FG Butler 36
GB	— FG Jacke 39
GB	— Sharpe 49 pass from Favre (Jacke kick)
GB	— Favre 5 run (Jacke kick)

Miami 19, Houston 16—at Joe Robbie Stadium, attendance 63,597. Pete Stoyanovich kicked a 52-yard field goal with two seconds left to give the Dolphins the victory. Stoyanovich's field goal was his fourth of the game and came 1:47 after the Oilers' Al Del Greco, who made his first 3 attempts, missed from 41 yards. Miami quarterback Dan Marino struggled most of the day, misfiring on his first 6 attempts and failing to complete his first pass until 2:45 remained in the second quarter. But he marched his team 42 yards in seven plays to the winning score, and also drove the Dolphins 80 yards in 9 plays as time wound down in the first half, capping the drive with a 39-yard touchdown pass to Fred Banks. Marino finished 19 of 40 for 237 yards. Houston's Cody Carlson, filling in for injured Warren Moon, completed 22 of 35 passes for 228 yards.

Houston	10	3	3	0	—	16
Miami	0	10	3	6	—	19

Hou	— FG Del Greco 24
Hou	— Jeffires 5 pass from Carlson (Del Greco kick)
Mia	— FG Stoyanovich 38
Hou	— FG Del Greco 41
Mia	— Banks 39 pass from Marino (Stoyanovich kick)
Mia	— FG Stoyanovich 40
Hou	— FG Del Greco 23
Mia	— FG Stoyanovich 29
Mia	— FG Stoyanovich 52

Pittsburgh 30, Indianapolis 14—at Three Rivers Stadium, attendance 51,501. Barry Foster rushed for 168 yards and 2 touchdowns to lead the Steelers past the Colts. Foster, who leads the NFL in both rushing yards and total yards from scrimmage, broke Pro Football Hall of Fame member Franco Harris's club-record with his eighth 100-yard rushing game of the season. He had 98 yards by halftime as Pittsburgh built a 13-0 advantage, then helped put the game away in the third quarter with a 13-yard touchdown run after Indianapolis had pulled within six points. Jack Trudeau passed for 266 yards for the Colts, but was intercepted 3 times. Indianapolis lost its fourth consecutive game.

Indianapolis	0	0	7	7	—	14
Pittsburgh	7	6	14	3	—	30

Pitt	— Foster 20 run (Anderson kick)
Pitt	— FG Anderson 31
Pitt	— FG Anderson 22
Ind	— Culver 1 run (Biasucci kick)
Pitt	— Foster 13 run (Anderson kick)
Pitt	— Thompson 2 run (Anderson kick)
Ind	— Culver 4 pass from Trudeau (Biasucci kick)
Pitt	— FG Anderson 36

New England 24, N.Y. Jets 3—at Foxboro Stadium, attendance 27,642. Jon Vaughn rushed for 110 yards and John Stephens scored a pair of touchdowns as the Patriots won for the second straight week after losing their first nine games. New England took the opening kickoff, marched 80 yards to a touchdown, and never trailed. Vaughn had runs of 24 and 15 yards on the drive, and Stephens capped it with a 13-yard scoring run 4:40 into the game. Stephens's second touchdown, a 1-yard run with 2:48 left in the first half, increased the Patriots' advantage to 24-0. The Jets never threatened, and were limited to only 11 first downs and 166 total yards.

N.Y. Jets	0	3	0	0	—	3
New England	10	14	0	0	—	24

NE	— Stephens 13 run (Baumann kick)
NE	— FG Baumann 32
NE	— Vaughn 9 run (Baumann kick)
NE	— Stephens 1 run (Baumann kick)
Jets	— FG Blanchard 27

Philadelphia 47, N.Y. Giants 34—at Giants Stadium, attendance 68,153. Linebacker Seth Joyner returned an interception 43 yards for a touchdown to spark the Eagles, who rallied from a 14-point first-half deficit to a wild victory over the Giants. New York led 20-6 until Joyner's touchdown trimmed the margin to 7 points with 9:35 left in the first half. That began a run of 34 unanswered points that lifted Philadelphia to a 40-20 advantage midway through the third quarter. Randall Cunningham's 38-yard touchdown pass to Keith Byars 1:51 into the second half gave the Eagles the lead for good, and special teams provided the next 2 scores. Linebacker Ken Rose blocked a punt and returned it 3 yards for a touchdown, and Vai Sikahema returned a punt a club-record 87 yards for a touchdown. Sikahema also had a pair of long kickoff returns to set up touchdowns in the first half.

Philadelphia	0	20	20	7	—	47
N.Y. Giants	10	10	7	7	—	34

Giants	— FG Bahr 35
Giants	— Meggett 14 pass from Hostetler (Bahr kick)
Phil	— Walker 21 pass from Cunningham (kick failed)
Giants	— Meggett 92 kickoff return (Bahr kick)
Giants	— FG Bahr 44
Phil	— Joyner 43 interception return (Ruzek kick)
Phil	— Walker 11 run (Ruzek kick)
Phil	— Byars 38 pass from Cunningham (Ruzek kick)
Phil	— Rose 3 blocked punt return (Ruzek kick)
Phil	— Sikahema 87 punt return (kick failed)
Giants	— McCaffrey 18 pass from Graham (Bahr kick)
Phil	— Sherman 30 run (Ruzek kick)
Giants	— Hampton 2 run (Bahr kick)

San Francisco 27, L.A. Rams 10—at Anaheim Stadium, attendance 65,858. Steve Young's 42-yard touchdown pass to Jerry Rice broke open a close game midway through the fourth quarter and the 49ers went on to beat the Rams for the sixth consecutive time at Anaheim Stadium. San Francisco led only 13-10 until Young and Rice collaborated on the scoring bomb with 6:36 left in the game. It was Rice's ninety-ninth career touchdown catch, leaving him just one short of Steve Largent's NFL record. The 49ers then put the game away with a time-consuming, 61-yard drive capped by Ricky Watters's 3-yard touchdown run with 1:11 to go. Watters carried 26 times for 163 yards and a pair of touchdowns.

San Francisco	7	3	3	14	—	27
L.A. Rams	0	0	7	3	—	10

SF	— Watters 3 run (Cofer kick)
SF	— FG Cofer 34
Rams	— Ellard 31 pass from Everett (Zendejas kick)
SF	— FG Cofer 40
Rams	— FG Zendejas 35
SF	— Rice 42 pass from Young (Cofer kick)
SF	— Watters 3 run (Cofer kick)

San Diego 29, Tamps Bay 14—at San Diego Jack Murphy Stadium, attendance 43,197. Ronnie Harmon scored 2 touchdowns, Marion Butts rushed for 104 yards, and the Chargers won for the sixth time in their last seven games to move above .500 for the first time since late in the 1987 season. San Diego got to Buccaneers quarterback Vinny Testaverde for 6 sacks. Rookie defensive end Chris Mims had 3 of the sacks, including 1 for a safety in the first quarter. Harmon opened the scoring by catching a 3-yard touchdown pass from Stan Humphries late in the first quarter, and gave the Chargers a 22-7 advantage at halftime by running 6 yards for a score with 14 seconds left in the second period. Tampa Bay pulled within 22-14 on Testaverde's 1-yard run 1:32 into the fourth quarter, but Humphries provided the final points on a 4-yard bootleg with 1:12 left in the game.

Tampa Bay	0	7	0	7	—	14
San Diego	12	10	0	7	—	29

SD	— Harmon 3 pass from Humphries (Carney kick)
SD	— Safety, Mims tackled Testaverde in end zone
SD	— FG Carney 28
TB	— Hall 10 pass from Testaverde (Murray kick)
SD	— FG Carney 31
SD	— Harmon 6 run (Carney kick)
TB	— Testaverde 1 run (Murray kick)
SD	— Humphries 4 run (Carney kick)

Sunday Night, November 22

Kansas City 24, Seattle 14—at Kingdome, attendance 49,867. Defensive end Neil Smith and defensive back Dale Carter each scored touchdowns as the Chiefs forced 6 turnovers while handing the Seahawks their tenth loss in 11 outings. Carter returned a punt 86 yards for a score late in the second quarter to give Kansas City a 17-7 halftime lead. Smith then put the game out of reach by bringing back an interception 22 yards for a touchdown midway through the third quarter. The Chiefs also got a 44-yard touchdown run from Barry Word, while quarterback Dave Krieg, who played his first 12 NFL seasons with the Seahawks, completed 11 of 15 passes for 103 yards in his return to the Kingdome. Seattle recorded 20 first downs to only 11 for Kansas City, and outgained the Chiefs 310-190, but was victimized by 4 interceptions and a pair of lost fumbles. Seahawks running back Chris Warren ran for a career-high 154 yards and 1 touchdown.

Kansas City	10	7	7	0	—	24
Seattle	0	7	7	0	—	14

KC	— Word 44 run (Lowery kick)
KC	— FG Lowery 20
Sea	— Kane 25 pass from Stouffer (Kasay kick)
KC	— Carter 86 punt return (Lowery kick)
KC	— N. Smith 22 interception return (Lowery kick)
Sea	— Warren 6 run (Kasay kick)

Monday, November 23

New Orleans 20, Washington 3—at Louisiana Superdome, attendance 68,591. Running back Dalton Hilliard and wide receiver Quinn Early scored second-quarter touchdowns to lead the Saints past the Redskins, who continue to experience offensive woes. Hilliard's 18-yard run with 4:12 left in the first half gave New Orleans the lead for good and 3:06 later, Early caught a 5-yard scoring toss from Bobby Hebert. That was enough against the defending Super Bowl champions, who failed to score a touchdown and who have produced just 2 touchdowns offensively in the last 23 quarters. Hebert completed 14 of 18 passes for 142 yards for the Saints. Washington quarterback Mark Rypien was 21 of 38 for 207 yards, but was sacked 4 times, twice by linebacker Rickey Jackson.

Washington	3	0	0	0	—	3
New Orleans	0	14	3	3	—	20

Wash	— FG Lohmiller 34
NO	— Hilliard 18 run (Andersen kick)
NO	— Early 5 pass from Hebert (Andersen kick)
NO	— FG Andersen 43
NO	— FG Andersen 45

Thirteenth Week Summaries

Standings

American Football Conference

Eastern Division

	W	L	T	Pct.	Pts.	OP
Buffalo	9	3	0	.750	314	199
Miami	8	4	0	.667	282	217
Indianapolis	5	7	0	.417	163	266
N.Y. Jets	3	9	0	.250	173	249
New England	2	10	0	.167	162	294

Central Division

	W	L	T	Pct.	Pts.	OP
Pittsburgh	9	3	0	.750	247	162
Houston	7	5	0	.583	270	218
Cleveland	6	6	0	.500	194	190
Cincinnati	4	8	0	.333	206	269

Western Division

	W	L	T	Pct.	Pts.	OP
Kansas City	8	4	0	.667	251	179
Denver	7	5	0	.583	188	223
San Diego	7	5	0	.583	214	182
L.A. Raiders	5	7	0	.417	179	198
Seattle	2	10	0	.167	89	231

National Football Conference

Eastern Division

	W	L	T	Pct.	Pts.	OP
Dallas	10	2	0	.833	293	165
Philadelphia	7	5	0	.571	269	188
Washington	7	5	0	.571	219	190
N.Y. Giants	5	7	0	.417	251	279
Phoenix	3	9	0	.250	187	282

Central Division

	W	L	T	Pct.	Pts.	OP
Minnesota	9	3	0	.750	307	191
Green Bay	6	6	0	.500	187	232
Chicago	4	8	0	.333	241	288
Tampa Bay	4	8	0	.333	212	275
Detroit	3	9	0	.250	217	253

Western Division

	W	L	T	Pct.	Pts.	OP
San Francisco	10	2	0	.833	339	196
New Orleans	9	3	0	.750	235	154
Atlanta	5	7	0	.417	234	306
L.A. Rams	4	8	0	.333	217	264

Thursday, November 26

Houston 24, Detroit 21—at Pontiac Silverdome, attendance 73,711. Lorenzo White's 8-yard touchdown run with 1:17 left to play gave the Oilers the Thanksgiving-Day victory over the Lions. The lead changed hands five times in a dramatic second half, with Detroit taking the advantage for the last time at 21-17 on Erik Kramer's 8-yard touchdown pass to Barry Sanders with 2:57 to go.

That score was set up when Lions safety Bennie Blades broke through and dropped Houston punter Greg Montgomery at the Oilers' 13-yard line before he could get a kick off. But the Oilers responded quickly to Sanders's score, marching 83 yards in only five plays. Cody Carlson completed 4 consecutive passes for 75 yards, then White scored on a draw play up the middle. Carlson finished with 24 completions in 33 attempts for 338 yards. Wide receiver Ernest Givins totaled 100 yards on 4 catches as Houston outgained Detroit 383-214.

Houston	0	3	7	14	—	24
Detroit	0	7	7	7	—	21

Det — Sanders 1 run (Hanson kick)
Hou — FG Del Greco 30
Hou — Fuller 10 fumble recovery return (Del Greco kick)
Det — Moore 77 pass from Kramer (Hanson kick)
Hou — Jeffires 4 pass from Carlson (Del Greco kick)
Det — Sanders 8 pass from Kramer (Hanson kick)
Hou — White 8 run (Del Greco kick)

Dallas 30, N.Y. Giants 3—at Texas Stadium, attendance 62,416. Emmitt Smith rushed for 120 yards and scored a pair of touchdowns as the Cowboys raised their record to 17-7-1 on Thanksgiving Day. Smith, held in check during the first half, helped break open the game in the third quarter. Dallas led just 9-3 when Smith took a swing pass from Troy Aikman and went 26 yards for a touchdown 8:57 into the second half. Two minutes later, he broke free for a 68-yard touchdown run to give the Cowboys a 23-3 advantage. Dallas's defense, which permitted the Giants only a field goal by Matt Bahr three seconds before halftime, limited New York to 207 total yards.

N.Y. Giants	0	3	0	0	—	3
Dallas	3	6	14	7	—	30

Dall — FG Elliott 45
Dall — FG Elliott 33
Dall — FG Elliott 53
Giants — FG Bahr 42
Dall — E. Smith 26 pass from Aikman (Elliott kick)
Dall — E. Smith 68 run (Elliott kick)
Dall — Harper 4 pass from Aikman (Elliott kick)

Sunday, November 29

Indianapolis 16, Buffalo 13—at Hoosier Dome, attendance 50,221. The Colts shocked the Bills when Dean Biasucci kicked a 40-yard field goal 3:51 into overtime. Indianapolis had rallied from a 10-point deficit in the fourth quarter to force the extra session. Rodney Culver ran 4 yards for a touchdown with 5:54 remaining to trim the Colts' deficit to 13-10, and Biasucci tied the game with a 23-yard field goal with 1:07 to go. Indianapolis then took the overtime kickoff and marched 56 yards to the winning kick. Jack Trudeau, who passed for 337 yards, made the key play, completing a 26-yard pass to Jessie Hester to move the ball to the Buffalo 27-yard line. Trudeau, starting in place of injured Jeff George, completed 26 of 41 pass attempts. Free agent tight end Charles Arbuckle, who had not caught an NFL pass entering the game, had 9 receptions for 106 yards. The Bills' Jim Kelly was limited to 11 completions in 33 attempts and was intercepted twice. Buffalo's Thurman Thomas rushed for 102 yards on 21 carries, while Don Beebe caught 4 passes for 110 yards, including a 65-yard touchdown early in the third quarter.

Buffalo	0	3	7	3	0	—	13
Indianapolis	0	3	0	10	3	—	16

Ind — FG Biasucci 52
Buff — FG Christie 52
Buff — Beebe 65 pass from Kelly (Christie kick)
Buff — FG Christie 44
Ind — Culver 4 run (Biasucci kick)
Ind — FG Biasucci 23
Ind — FG Biasucci 40

Cleveland 27, Chicago 14—at Cleveland Stadium, attendance 73,578. Linebacker David Brandon returned a first-quarter interception 92 yards for a touchdown, and the Browns went on to hand the Bears their fifth consecutive defeat. Despite a sizable advantage in total yards (320-178), Chicago lost because it turned the ball over 4 times. Cleveland, which did not turn the ball over, converted those miscues into 17 points, and also scored on Eric Metcalf's 75-yard punt return, which put the Browns ahead 20-7 with 2:07 to play in the third quarter. The Bears pulled within 6 points again on the next play from scrimmage, a 68-yard touchdown pass from Peter Tom Willis to Tom Waddle, but Brandon recovered a fumble on the Chicago 28-yard line early in the fourth quarter, and Kevin Mack's 1-yard run with 10:35 left in the game sealed Cleveland's victory. Willis completed 19 of 26 passes for 285 yards and 2 touchdowns in his first NFL start, but was intercepted twice. The Browns' Bernie Kosar played for the first time since breaking an ankle in week two and completed 8 of 17 passes for 59 yards.

Chicago	0	7	7	0	—	14
Cleveland	7	6	7	7	—	27

Cleve — Brandon 92 interception return (Stover kick)
Cleve — FG Stover 27
Cleve — FG Stover 43
Chi — Anderson 30 pass from Willis (Butler kick)
Cleve — Metcalf 75 punt return (Stover kick)
Chi — Waddle 68 pass from Willis (Butler kick)
Cleve — Mack 1 run (Stover kick)

Kansas City 23, N.Y. Jets 7—at Giants Stadium, attendance 57,375. Dave Krieg threw a pair of third-quarter touchdown passes to lead the Chiefs to their fourth consecutive victory. Kansas City led just 6-0 until Krieg capped a 75-yard drive with a 2-yard touchdown pass to tight end Keith Cash 4:27 into the third quarter. The Chiefs then recovered the ensuing onside kickoff and marched 45 yards to Krieg's 4-yard touchdown pass to Tim Barnett, increasing their advantage to 20-0 with 5:17 left in the third quarter. Krieg completed passes to 10 different receivers en route to a 17-of-21, 222-yard day. The victory was Kansas City's first in Giants Stadium after 6 losses and a tie to the Jets and Giants. The game was marred by an injury to Jets defensive tackle Dennis Byrd, who broke his vetebra when he collided with teammate Scott Mersereau in the third quarter.

Kansas City	3	3	14	3	—	23
N.Y. Jets	0	0	0	7	—	7

KC — FG Lowery 20
KC — FG Lowery 27
KC — Cash 2 pass from Krieg (Lowery kick)
KC — Barnett 4 pass from Krieg (Lowery kick)
Jets — Mathis 10 pass from Nagle (Blanchard kick)
KC — FG Lowery 38

New Orleans 24, Miami 13—at Louisiana Superdome, attendance 68,591. The Saints turned a fumble recovery and an interception into second-half touchdowns to beat the Dolphins. The Saints' Morten Andersen kicked a 26-yard field goal 10:55 into the third quarter to tie the game at 10-10. Just 1:34 later, linebacker Pat Swilling sacked Miami quarterback Dan Marino, forcing a fumble that was recovered by nose tackle Robert Goff, who returned it 28 yards for the touchdown that gave the Saints the lead for good. It was 17-13 in the fourth quarter when cornerback Vince Buck picked off a pass from Marino and returned it 34 yards for the clinching score with 9:55 left. The Dolphins outgained New Orleans 281-252, but Marino was sacked a career-high 5 times, twice by defensive end Wayne Martin. Marino finished with 259 passing yards, most of it in the second quarter, when he completed 13 of 14 passes for 142 yards. The Saints' Dalton Hilliard recorded a touchdown for the sixth consecutive game, running 1 yard for a score in the first quarter.

Miami	0	7	3	3	—	13
New Orleans	7	0	10	7	—	24

NO — Hilliard 1 run (Andersen kick)
Mia — Duper 2 pass from Marino (Stoyanovich kick)
Mia — FG Stoyanovich 48
NO — FG Andersen 26
NO — Goff 28 fumble recovery return (Andersen kick)
Mia — FG Stoyanovich 34
NO — Buck 34 interception return (Andersen kick)

Minnesota 31, L.A. Rams 17—at Anaheim Stadium, attendance 54,831. Terry Allen scored 3 touchdowns and Sean Salisbury passed for 238 yards in first NFL start as the Vikings eased past the Rams. Allen ran for 2 touchdowns and also caught a 36-yard option pass from running back Keith Henderson. The latter came 4:08 into the second quarter and broke a 7-7 tie. Minnesota never trailed after that. Allen finished with 88 rushing yards and caught 10 passes for 110 yards. The 29-year-old Salisbury, a veteran of four NFL seasons and four more in the Canadian Football League, had thrown only 12 NFL passes entering 1992. But he got the starting nod over Rich Gannon and completed 23 of 34 passes for 238 yards while leading the Vikings to 408 yards of total offense.

Minnesota	7	10	14	0	—	31
L.A. Rams	7	3	0	7	—	17

Minn — Allen 1 run (Reveiz kick)
Rams — Anderson 17 pass from Everett (Zendejas kick)
Minn — Allen 36 pass from Henderson (Reveiz kick)
Rams — FG Zendejas 30
Minn — FG Reveiz 38
Minn — Allen 12 run (Reveiz kick)
Minn — Henderson 8 run (Reveiz kick)
Rams — Price 16 pass from Pagel (Zendejas kick)

Atlanta 34, New England 0—at Georgia Dome, attendance 54,494. Billy Joe Tolliver threw a pair of touchdown passes and the Falcons limited the Patriots to 105 total yards while recording their first shutout since 1988. Tolliver completed scoring tosses of 10 yards to Drew Hill and 18 yards to Steve Broussard as Atlanta built a 24-0 advantage at halftime. The latter came three plays after linebacker Darion Conner sacked New England quarterback Scott Zolak, forcing a fumble that teammate Mike Gann recovered. On the Patriots' next possession, Falcons safety Jeff Donaldson forced another fumble, and cornerback Deion Sanders recovered to set up a field goal. Atlanta's defense, which entered the game ranked last in the NFL, forced 4 turnovers and sacked Zolak 5 times. New England's first-year quarterback threw for only 58 yards, and 43 yards in sacks reduced the Patriots' passing output to only 15 yards. Conner had 3 of the sacks and Sanders intercepted a pair of passes in the fourth quarter. Rookie Tony Smith ran for 81 yards on 10 carries, including a 29-yard scoring run in the third quarter.

New England	0	0	0	0	—	0
Atlanta	14	10	7	3	—	34

Atl — Broussard 8 run (Johnson kick)
Atl — D. Hill 10 pass from Tolliver (Johnson kick)
Atl — Broussard 18 pass from Tolliver (Johnson kick)
Atl — FG Johnson 26
Atl — T. Smith 29 run (Johnson kick)
Atl — FG Johnson 54

San Francisco 20, Philadelphia 14—at Candlestick Park, attendance 64,374. Jerry Rice caught the 100th touchdown pass of his career and the 49ers held off the Eagles to become the first team to clinch a playoff berth this season. Rice's 22-yard touchdown catch in the first quarter gave San Francisco a lead it would never relinquish and gave him a share of the NFL record for career touchdown catches, equaling the mark set by former Seattle Seahawk Steve Largent. Rice finished with 8 catches for 133 yards. Steve Young, who completed 24 of 35 passes for 342 yards, fired a 43-yard touchdown pass to running back Dexter Carter early in the fourth quarter to give the 49ers a 20-7 lead. But Philadelphia fought back, pulling to within six points when Randall Cunningham—who completed 28 of 42 for 257 yards and 2 touchdowns—threw an 11-yard touchdown pass to Keith Byars with 8:58 remaining. San Francisco's victory wasn't secured until Cunningham's fourth-and-15 pass to Calvin Williams came up an inch short of a first down at the 49ers' 11-yard line with 36 seconds remaining.

Philadelphia	0	0	7	7	—	14
San Francisco	7	3	3	7	—	20

SF — Rice 22 pass from Young (Cofer kick)
SF — FG Cofer 22
Phil — Barnett 23 pass from Cunningham (Ruzek kick)
SF — FG Cofer 28
SF — D. Carter 43 pass from Young (Cofer kick)
Phil — Byars 11 pass from Cunningham (Ruzek kick)

Washington 41, Phoenix 3—at RFK Stadium, attendance 53,541. Safety Brad Edwards intercepted 3 passes, returning 1 for a touchdown, as the defending Super Bowl-champion Redskins snapped a two-game losing streak and remained in contention for a playoff berth. Washington, which had struggled on offense for most of the season, spotted the Cardinals an early field goal, but countered with a 67-yard touchdown drive on its first possession to take the lead for good. Quarterback Mark Rypien threw a 13-yard touchdown pass to Ricky Sanders to cap that drive, and Edwards intercepted a Timm Rosenbach pass on Phoenix's next possession and returned it 53 yards for a touchdown. Rypien also had a 31-yard touchdown pass to Gary Clark in the fourth quarter, and backup Cary Conklin threw his first NFL touchdown pass, a 10-yarder to Art Monk, late in the game. Rosenbach completed 19 of 34 passes for 262 yards for the Cardinals, but was intercepted 4 times. Phoenix's Ricky Proehl caught 7 passes for 104 yards. The victory was the Redskins' fourteenth in a row over the Cardinals at RFK Stadium.

Phoenix	3	0	0	0	—	3
Washington	14	6	7	14	—	41

Phx — FG G. Davis 42
Wash — Sanders 13 pass from Rypien (Lohmiller kick)
Wash — Edwards 53 interception return (Lohmiller kick)
Wash — FG Lohmiller 32
Wash — FG Lohmiller 18
Wash — Byner 3 run (Lohmiller kick)
Wash — Clark 31 pass from Rypien (Lohmiller kick)
Wash — Monk 10 pass from Conklin (Lohmiller kick)

Pittsburgh 21, Cincinnati 9—at Riverfront Stadium, attendance 54,253. Barry Foster scored 2 touchdowns and set a club single-season rushing record as the Steelers spoiled Bengals quarterback David Klingler's NFL debut. Pittsburgh never trailed, taking the lead when a fake punt went awry on Cincinnati's first possession.

Up-back Eric Ball fumbled the snap and the Steelers' Charles Davenport scooped up the loose ball and went 34 yards for a touchdown. Foster ran for 102 yards on 25 carries to up his league-leading total to 1,319 yards. That broke Pro Football Hall of Fame member Franco Harris's Pittsburgh record of 1,246 yards, set in 1975. Klingler, the Bengals' first-round draft pick, started in place of Boomer Esiason and completed 16 of 34 passes for 140 yards, with no interceptions. But the Steelers, blitzing liberally, sacked him 10 times, including 3 by linebacker David Little. Bengals running back Harold Green had 116 yards on 16 carries and Klingler managed to scramble for 44 yards.

Pittsburgh	7	7	7	0	—	21
Cincinnati	0	6	0	3	—	9

Pitt — Davenport 34 fumble recovery return (Anderson kick)
Cin — FG Breech 33
Pitt — Foster 2 run (Anderson kick)
Cin — FG Breech 42
Pitt — Foster 1 run (Anderson kick)
Cin — FG Breech 38

Green Bay 19, Tampa Bay 14—at Milwaukee County Stadium, attendance 52,347. Brett Favre tossed a 9-yard touchdown pass to tight end Jackie Harris for the winning points as the Packers won for the fourth time in five games and raised their record to .500. Favre, who completed 26 of 41 passes for 223 yards, erased a 14-12 deficit with his scoring toss to Harris with 10:09 left in the game. To that point, all of Green Bay's scoring had come from kicker Chris Jacke, who booted 4 field goals. Vinny Testaverde threw 2 touchdown passes for the Buccaneers, but could not rally his team in the final quarter. Packers defensive back Roland Mitchell intercepted a pair of Testaverde's passes, the last to thwart Tampa Bay's final chance with 1:32 remaining. Green Bay intercepted 3 passes in all and recovered a pair of fumbles.

Tampa Bay	7	0	7	0	—	14
Green Bay	3	6	3	7	—	19

GB — FG Jacke 34
TB — Carrier 20 pass from Testaverde (Murray kick)
GB — FG Jacke 33
GB — FG Jacke 29
GB — FG Jacke 48
TB — McDowell 15 pass from Testaverde (Murray kick)
GB — J. Harris 9 pass from Favre (Jacke kick)

Sunday Night, November 29

San Diego 27, L.A. Raiders 3—at San Diego Jack Murphy Stadium, attendance 59,894. The Chargers won for the seventh time in their last eight games by taking advantage of Raiders mistakes to build a 21-3 first-half lead. Los Angeles moved the ball effectively against the top-ranked rushing defense in the league, as running back Eric Dickerson compiled 100 yards by halftime. But the Raiders managed only 3 points despite moving into San Diego territory on all four first-half possessions. Their first possession ended in a blocked field goal and their second in safety Stanley Richards's interception and 20-yard return. The Chargers then marched 55 yards to a touchdown, scoring when wide receiver Anthony Miller recovered running back Marion Butts's fumble in the end zone. Butts had a 1-yard touchdown run later in the half and a fumble recovery by San Diego safety Darren Carrington led to Stan Humphries's 15-yard touchdown pass to Shawn Jefferson just 16 seconds before halftime. The Raiders never mounted a challenge in the second half, and John Carney added a pair of field goals for the Chargers. Dickerson carried only 1 time in the second half and finished with 103 yards.

L.A. Raiders	0	3	0	0	—	3
San Diego	7	14	0	6	—	27

SD — Miller fumble recovery in end zone (Carney kick)
Raid — FG Jaeger 36
SD — Butts 1 run (Carney kick)
SD — Jefferson 15 pass from Humphries (Carney kick)
SD — FG Carney 27
SD — FG Carney 21

Monday, November 30

Seattle 16, Denver 13—at Kingdome, attendance 51,612. John Kasay kicked a 32-yard field goal with 3:50 left in overtime as the Seahawks stunned the Broncos. The victory was only the second of the season for Seattle and knocked Denver out of a share of first place in the AFC Western Division. The Broncos, playing without injured starting quarterback John Elway, struggled on offense, gaining only 196 total yards. But Denver still had an apparently comfortable 13-3 lead over the low-scoring Seahawks late in the game. Kasay kicked a 33-yard field goal with 5:20 remaining in regulation, and backup quarterback Stan Gelbaugh threw a 3-yard touchdown pass to Brian Blades as time expired to tie the score and force the extra session. Kasay missed a 33-yard field-goal try early in the overtime, but got a second chance. Gelbaugh was 12 of 21 for 164 yards despite not entering the game until only 9:27 remained in the fourth quarter. The victory snapped Seattle's eight-game losing streak.

Denver	10	0	3	0	0	—	13
Seattle	0	3	0	10	3	—	16

Den — Jackson 6 pass from Maddox (Treadwell kick)
Den — FG Treadwell 28
Sea — FG Kasay 30
Den — FG Treadwell 36
Sea — FG Kasay 33
Sea — Blades 3 pass from Gelbaugh (Kasay kick)
Sea — FG Kasay 32

Fourteenth Week Summaries

Standings

American Football Conference

Eastern Division

	W	L	T	Pct.	Pts.	OP
Buffalo	9	4	0	.692	331	223
Miami	8	5	0	.615	285	244
Indianapolis	6	7	0	.462	169	266
N.Y. Jets	4	9	0	.308	197	266
New England	2	11	0	.154	162	300

Central Division

	W	L	T	Pct.	Pts.	OP
Pittsburgh	10	3	0	.769	267	176
Houston	8	5	0	.615	294	225
Cleveland	7	6	0	.538	231	211
Cincinnati	4	9	0	.308	227	306

Western Division

	W	L	T	Pct.	Pts.	OP
Kansas City	8	5	0	.615	258	207
San Diego	8	5	0	.615	241	203
Denver	7	6	0	.538	215	254
L.A. Raiders	6	7	0	.462	207	205
Seattle	2	11	0	.154	103	251

National Football Conference

Eastern Division

	W	L	T	Pct.	Pts.	OP
Dallas	11	2	0	.846	324	192
Philadelphia	8	5	0	.615	297	205
Washington	8	5	0	.615	247	200
N.Y. Giants	5	8	0	.385	261	307
Phoenix	3	10	0	.231	208	309

Central Division

	W	L	T	Pct.	Pts.	OP
Minnesota	9	4	0	.692	324	219
Green Bay	7	6	0	.538	225	242
Chicago	4	9	0	.308	248	312
Tampa Bay	4	9	0	.308	239	306
Detroit	3	10	0	.231	227	291

Western Division

	W	L	T	Pct.	Pts.	OP
San Francisco	11	2	0	.846	366	199
New Orleans	10	3	0	.769	257	168
Atlanta	5	8	0	.385	248	328
L.A. Rams	5	8	0	.385	248	291

Thursday, December 3

New Orleans 22, Atlanta 14—at Louisiana Superdome, attendance 68,591. Morten Andersen's 5 field goals helped the Saints clinch a playoff berth. Andersen's final field goal, a 37-yarder, gave New Orleans a 15-14 lead with 1:56 left in the game. Cornerback Toi Cook sealed the victory by returning an interception 48 yards for a touchdown with 52 seconds to go. The Saints dominated the game statistically, outgaining the Falcons 388 yards to 168 and maintaining possession for more than 40 minutes. But New Orleans's offense could not reach the end zone and Atlanta took a 14-12 advantage when Wade Wilson tossed a 13-yard touchdown pass to Michael Haynes with 4:25 left in the game.

Atlanta	0	0	7	7	—	14
New Orleans	3	6	0	13	—	22

NO — FG Andersen 20
NO — FG Andersen 31
NO — FG Andersen 24
Atl — Tuggle 69 fumble recovery return (Johnson kick)
NO — FG Andersen 26
Atl — Haynes 13 pass from Wilson (Johnson kick)
NO — FG Andersen 37
NO — Cook 48 interception return (Andersen kick)

Sunday, December 6

Cleveland 37, Cincinnati 21—at Cleveland Stadium, attendance 68,368. The Browns scored 3 touchdowns in a span of 96 seconds of the third quarter to break open their game against the Bengals and keep alive their wild-card playoff hopes. Bernie Kosar threw a 35-yard touchdown pass to running back Eric Metcalf 5:06 into the second half to make it 20-7. Just 1:19 later, Kosar found Michael Jackson on a 45-yard touchdown pass to make it 27-7. Linebacker Mike Johnson finished the scoring spurt 17 seconds after that when he recovered Cincinnati quarterback David Klingler's fumble in the end zone for a touchdown. Kosar completed 19 of 23 passes (a club-record 82.6 percent) for 239 yards and the 2 touchdowns, while Metcalf accumulated 210 yards rushing, receiving, and returning kicks. Bengals wide receiver Jeff Query caught 6 passes for 85 yards and 2 scores.

Cincinnati	0	7	7	7	—	21
Cleveland	10	3	21	3	—	37

Cleve — Mack 7 run (Stover kick)
Cleve — FG Stover 34
Cin — Holman 26 pass from Klingler (Breech kick)
Cleve — FG Stover 30
Cleve — Metcalf 35 pass from Kosar (Stover kick)
Cleve — Jackson 45 pass from Kosar (Stover kick)
Cleve — M. Johnson recovered fumble in end zone (Stover kick)
Cin — Query 10 pass from Klingler (Breech kick)
Cleve — FG Stover 27
Cin — Query 24 pass from Hollas (Breech kick)

Dallas 31, Denver 27—at Mile High Stadium, attendance 74,946. Emmitt Smith's 3-yard touchdown run with 2:47 left in the game gave the Cowboys a wild victory and at least a wild-card playoff berth. The Broncos, who lost their third consecutive game but their first at home after eight straight regular-season victories, used alternating quarterbacks to replace injured starter John Elway. Tommy Maddox and Shawn Moore shuffled in and out on nearly every play and each threw for 104 yards. Maddox tossed 3 touchdown passes but also was intercepted 4 times and lost a fumble, leading to 3 Dallas touchdowns. The rookie had his first 2 passes picked off, and the Cowboys converted each into Troy Aikman touchdown passes to Michael Irvin to build a 14-0 advantage less than seven minutes into the game. But Denver battled back, and when Maddox threw a 23-yard touchdown pass to running back Reggie Rivers late in the third quarter, the Broncos trailed just 24-20. In the fourth quarter, Maddox tossed a lateral to rookie wide receiver Arthur Marshall, who connected with rookie Cedric Tillman on an 81-yard touchdown pass to give Denver a 27-24 lead with 9:05 remaining. But Dallas countered with an 11-play, 77-yard drive to win the game. Aikman converted a key third-and-14 with a 14-yard pass to Irvin, and also had 22- and 18-yard strikes to tight end Jay Novacek along the way. The Cowboys' quarterback completed 25 of 35 passes for 231 yards in all. The Broncos fell to third place in the AFC West with the loss.

Dallas	14	3	7	7	—	31
Denver	7	6	7	7	—	27

Dall — Irvin 6 pass from Aikman (Elliott kick)
Dall — Irvin 4 pass from Aikman (Elliott kick)
Den — V. Johnson 18 pass from Maddox (Treadwell kick)
Den — Jackson 12 pass from Maddox (kick failed)
Dall — FG Elliott 53
Dall — Novacek 1 pass from Aikman (Elliott kick)
Den — Rivers 23 pass from Maddox (Treadwell kick)
Den — Tillman 81 pass from Marshall (Treadwell kick)
Dall — E. Smith 3 run (Elliott kick)

Green Bay 38, Detroit 10—at Milwaukee County Stadium, attendance 49,469. Brett Favre threw 3 first-half touchdown passes and the Packers breezed to their fourth consecutive victory. Snow flurries throughout the game couldn't slow Green Bay's offense, which amassed 374 total yards. Favre completed 15 of 19 passes for 214 yards. Two of his touchdown passes went to Sterling Sharpe, who had 6 receptions for 107 yards. Linebacker Tony Bennett recovered Lions quarterback Andre Ware's fumble and ran 18 yards for another score. Ware, Detroit's first-round draft pick in 1990, had played sparingly in his career. He replaced injured Rodney Peete early in the second quarter and had his first pass intercepted, then fumbled when sacked by defensive end Matt Brock on the play that Bennett scored. But Ware rebounded to complete 13 of 23 passes for 133 yards, including an 11-yard touchdown to Herman Moore in the second quarter. Moore caught 8 passes for 114 yards and Barry Sanders rushed for 114 yards for the Lions. Sanders finished the day with a season total of 1,048 rushing yards, and thus joined Eric Dickerson, Tony Dorsett, and Earl Campbell as the only players to rush for 1,000 or more yards in each of their first four NFL seasons. The Packers four-game winning streak was their longest since winning four in a row in 1984.

Detroit	0	10	0	0	—	10
Green Bay	14	21	0	3	—	38

GB — Thompson 1 run (Jacke kick)
GB — Sharpe 65 pass from Favre (Jacke kick)
GB — Sydney 9 pass from Favre (Jacke kick)

GB — T. Bennett 18 fumble recovery return (Jacke kick)
Det — Moore 11 pass from Ware (Hanson kick)
GB — Sharpe 9 pass from Favre (Jacke kick)
Det — FG Hanson 44
GB — FG Jacke 46

Indianapolis 6, New England 0—at Foxboro Stadium, attendance 19,429. Dean Biasucci kicked a pair of first-half field goals in the cold and the wind for the only points in the Colts' victory. The Patriots, shut out a week earlier by the Falcons, were blanked in back-to-back games for the first time in franchise history. New England managed only 9 first downs and 94 yards in total offense. Patriots quarterbacks were victimized by 8 sacks, including 3½ by Indianapolis linebacker Duane Bickett. The Colts fared a little better on offense, accumulating 265 total yards, most of it behind quarterback Jack Trudeau, who completed 23 of 35 passes for 209 yards. Neither team could move the ball inside the other team's 10-yard line. The wind chill factor was minus-5 at kickoff.

Indianapolis	3	3	0	0	—	6
New England	0	0	0	0	—	0

Ind — FG Biasucci 30
Ind — FG Biasucci 48

L.A. Raiders 28, Kansas City 7—at Los Angeles Memorial Coliseum, attendance 45,227. Jay Schroeder threw 3 touchdown passes and the Raiders knocked the Chiefs into a tie with San Diego for first place in the AFC West. Schroeder threw for only 93 yards and had 2 of his 18 attempts (he completed 12) intercepted, but he spread scoring tosses around to tight end Ethan Horton, running back Steve Smith, and wide receiver Willie Gault. His 6-yarder to Horton gave Los Angeles the lead 7:34 into the game, and when Elvis Patterson blocked Bryan Barker's punt and recovered it in the end zone for a touchdown following Kansas City's next possession, the Raiders had all the points they would need. The Chiefs outgained Los Angeles 265-230, but managed only 17 rushing yards while playing catch-up. Dave Krieg passed for 276 yards.

Kansas City	0	7	0	0	—	7
L.A. Raiders	14	7	7	0	—	28

Raid — Horton 6 pass from Schroeder (Jaeger kick)
Raid — Patterson blocked punt recovery in end zone (Jaeger kick)
Raid — S. Smith 11 pass from Schroeder (Jaeger kick)
KC — Cash 2 pass from Krieg (Lowery kick)
Raid — Gault 17 pass from Schroeder (Jaeger kick)

San Francisco 27, Miami 3—at Candlestick Park, attendance 58,474. Jerry Rice set an NFL record for career touchdown catches and the 49ers maintained their one-game lead over the Saints in the NFC West by routing the Dolphins. Rice caught a 12-yard touchdown pass from Steve Young 6:04 into the fourth quarter. It was the 101st touchdown reception of his career, breaking former Seattle Seahawk Steve Largent's league mark. Young completed 19 of 27 passes for 220 yards, and San Francisco's pass defense, ranked last in the NFL, limited Miami quarterback Dan Marino to 192 yards. Rookie Amp Lee started at running back for injured Ricky Watters and ran 1 yard for his first NFL touchdown midway through the third quarter to give the 49ers a 20-3 lead. San Francisco won its fifth consecutive game and tenth in the past 11.

Miami	0	0	3	0	—	3
San Francisco	0	13	7	7	—	27

SF — Rathman 27 pass from Young (kick blocked)
SF — Rathman 1 run (Cofer kick)
Mia — FG Stoyanovich 32
SF — Lee 1 run (Cofer kick)
SF — Rice 12 pass from Young (Cofer kick)

Philadelphia 28, Minnesota 17—at Veterans Stadium, attendance 65,280. Quarterback Randall Cunningham rushed for a season-high 121 yards and scored 2 touchdowns to pace the Eagles' victory. Cunningham, playing perhaps his best game since returning from the knee injury that kept him out nearly all of 1991, averaged better than 10 yards on his 12 carries. He also completed 16 of 23 passes for 164 yards. Philadelphia trailed 3-0 until Cunningham scrambled for 30 and 18 yards on a 70-yard drive that he capped by sneaking 1 yard for a touchdown late in the first quarter. After the Vikings rallied with the first of Terry Allen's 2 touchdown runs, Heath Sherman gave the Eagles the lead for good with a 1-yard run with 2:54 left in the first half. Cunningham sneaked 1 yard again for a touchdown late in the third quarter, and linebacker Seth Joyner secured the victory with a one-handed interception that he returned 24 yards for a touchdown with 4:35 left in the game. Philadelphia rushed for 225 yards and had a sizable advantage in total yards, 370-219. Eagles defensive tackle Andy Harmon recorded 3 sacks.

Minnesota	3	7	0	7	—	17
Philadelphia	7	7	7	7	—	28

Minn — FG Reveiz 32
Phil — Cunningham 1 run (Ruzek kick)
Minn — Allen 3 run (Reveiz kick)
Phil — Sherman 1 run (Ruzek kick)
Phil — Cunningham 1 run (Ruzek kick)
Minn — Allen 1 run (Reveiz kick)
Phil — Joyner 24 interception return (Ruzek kick)

N.Y. Jets 24, Buffalo 17—at Rich Stadium, attendance 75,876. Jets safety Brian Washington intercepted a Jim Kelly pass and returned it 23 yards for the winning touchdown with 1:41 remaining. Washington then sealed the victory by picking off Kelly's desperation pass in the closing seconds. New York entered the fourth quarter ahead 17-10 on the strength of 2 touchdown runs by Brad Baxter that erased a 10-3 halftime deficit. But Kelly tossed a 1-yard touchdown pass to tight end Pete Metzelaars to tie the game with 8:55 left. The Bills took possession at their 19-yard line with 1:53 to go. Two plays later, Washington provided the winning points. A fumble and Washington's second interception ended Buffalo's final two possessions. Baxter ran for 98 yards and Browning Nagle completed 14 of 22 passes for 176 yards for the Jets. Thurman Thomas rushed for 116 yards for the Bills, who amassed 345 total yards, but turned the ball over 4 times.

N.Y. Jets	3	0	14	7	—	24
Buffalo	3	7	0	7	—	17

Jets — FG Blanchard 41
Buff — FG Christie 26
Buff — K. Davis 6 run (Christie kick)
Jets — Baxter 1 run (Blanchard kick)
Jets — Baxter 9 run (Blanchard kick)
Buff — Metzelaars 1 pass from Kelly (Christie kick)
Jets — B. Washington 23 interception return (Blanchard kick)

San Diego 27, Phoenix 21—at Sun Devil Stadium, attendance 26,880. The Chargers continued their dramatic charge by rallying from a 14-point deficit to beat the Cardinals. After starting the season 0-4, San Diego won for the eighth time in nine games and moved into a first-place tie with Kansas City in the AFC West. No team in NFL history has started a season with four consecutive losses and gone on to make the playoffs. Phoenix jumped out to a 14-0 lead before the game was eight minutes old and still had a 21-10 advantage after quarterback Chris Chandler teamed with wide receiver Ricky Proehl on a 63-yard touchdown pass midway through the third quarter. But the Chargers' Stan Humphries had 25- and 26-yard completions on a 55-yard drive that was capped by Eric Bieniemy's 5-yard touchdown run to trim the deficit to 21-17 with 43 seconds left in the third quarter. San Diego then marched 63 yards to the go-ahead touchdown on Ronnie Harmon's 1-yard run with 8:44 left in the game. That drive started when cornerback Gill Byrd recovered a fumble at the Chargers' 37-yard line. Byrd later forced a fumble that thwarted the Cardinals' last threat.

San Diego	0	10	7	10	—	27
Phoenix	14	0	7	0	—	21

Phx — E. Jones 4 pass from Chandler (G. Davis kick)
Phx — Johnson 6 run (G. Davis kick)
SD — Miller 23 pass from Humphries (Carney kick)
SD — FG Carney 50
Phx — Proehl 63 pass from Chandler (G. Davis kick)
SD — Bieniemy 5 run (Carney kick)
SD — Harmon 1 run (Carney kick)
SD — FG Carney 43

Pittsburgh 20, Seattle 14—at Three Rivers Stadium, attendance 47,015. The Steelers became the first AFC team to clinch a playoff berth when they overcame 5 interceptions to beat the Seahawks. Barry Foster, who rushed for 125 yards on 33 carries (his tenth 100-yard effort of the season), ran 4 yards to put Pittsburgh ahead 17-14 with 2:22 to play. Gary Anderson added a 39-yard field goal in the final minute. Stan Gelbaugh had given Seattle its four-point lead with touchdown passes of 28 yards to Tommy Kane and 3 yards to John L. Williams. But backup quarterback Bubby Brister, who entered the game in the third quarter when starter Neil O'Donnell was injured, directed a 13-play, 80-yard march to the go-ahead score. O'Donnell threw interceptions on 3 of his first 4 pass attempts, but the Seahawks could not convert any of the thefts into scores. Brister threw 2 interceptions, but again Seattle could not convert. Seahawks kicker John Kasay missed field-goal attempts of 40, 44, and 38 yards. Safety Eugene Robinson had 3 interceptions.

Seattle	0	7	7	0	—	14
Pittsburgh	7	3	0	10	—	20

Pitt — Mills 19 pass from O'Donnell (Anderson kick)
Pitt — FG Anderson 38
Sea — Kane 28 pass from Gelbaugh (Kasay kick)
Sea — J.L. Williams 3 pass from Gelbaugh (Kasay kick)
Pitt — Foster 4 run (Anderson kick)
Pitt — FG Anderson 39

Washington 28, N.Y. Giants 10—at Giants Stadium, attendance 62,998. Earnest Byner ran for 100 yards and a pair of touchdowns as the Redskins handed the Giants their fourth consecutive defeat. Byner's scoring runs of 1 yard and 11 yards gave Washington a 14-3 halftime advantage. After New York pulled within 14-10 on Rodney Hampton's 1-yard scoring run 8:37 into the second half, the Redskins countered with an 80-yard touchdown march. Mark Rypien, who was 15 of 18 for 216 yards in the game, completed 4 consecutive passes on the drive, the last a 20-yard touchdown to tight end Terry Orr with 46 seconds left in the third quarter. Rypien added a 42-yard touchdown pass to Art Monk early in the fourth quarter. It was Monk's only catch of the day and extended his streak of consecutive games with a reception to 145. Washington amassed 393 total yards, including 177 on the ground. The Giants managed only 165 total yards while being all but eliminated from playoff contention.

Washington	7	7	7	7	—	28
N.Y. Giants	0	3	7	0	—	10

Wash — Byner 1 run (Lohmiller kick)
Wash — Byner 11 run (Lohmiller kick)
Giants — FG Willis 43
Giants — Hampton 1 run (Willis kick)
Wash — Orr 20 pass from Rypien (Lohmiller kick)
Wash — Monk 42 pass from Rypien (Lohmiller kick)

Sunday Night, December 6

L.A. Rams 31, Tampa Bay 27—at Tampa Stadium, attendance 38,387. Jim Everett's 8-yard touchdown pass to tight end Pat Carter with 5:40 remaining capped a dramatic rally that saw the Rams erase a 24-point halftime deficit to beat the Buccaneers. Vinny Testaverde's 81-yard scoring toss to tight end Tyji Armstrong highlighted the first half for Tampa Bay, which led 27-3 at intermission. But Los Angeles marched 70 yards to a touchdown following the second-half kickoff, then converted a fumble recovery and an interception into touchdowns to pull within 27-24 only 7:41 into the third quarter. Everett then capped a 69-yard drive with his scoring toss to Carter, the Rams quarterback's third touchdown pass of the second half. He finished with 25 completions in 38 attempts for 342 yards and was not intercepted. Los Angeles rolled up 405 yards of total offense. Buccaneers running back Reggie Cobb gained 100 yards on 26 carries and surpassed the 1,000-yard mark for the season. He is the first Tampa Bay running back to do so since 1985.

L.A. Rams	0	3	21	7	—	31
Tampa Bay	6	21	0	0	—	27

TB — FG Murray 34
TB — FG Murray 47
TB — Armstrong 81 pass from Testaverde (Murray kick)
TB — Jones 26 fumble recovery return (Murray kick)
Rams — FG Zendejas 18
TB — Carrier 10 pass from Testaverde (Murray kick)
Rams — W. Anderson 40 pass from Everett (Zendejas kick)
Rams — Chadwick 27 pass from Everett (Zendejas kick)
Rams — Lang 1 run (Zendejas kick)
Rams — P. Carter 8 pass from Everett (Zendejas kick)

Monday, December 7

Houston 24, Chicago 7—at Astrodome, attendance 62,193. The Oilers converted a pair of turnovers into touchdowns to break open a defensive struggle and hand the Bears their sixth consecutive defeat. Houston, still in the hunt for a wild-card playoff berth, led only 3-0 until safety Bubba McDowell intercepted a Peter Tom Willis pass and returned it 26 yards for the touchdown that made the score 10-0 just 44 seconds before halftime. In the third quarter, defensive tackle Ray Childress recovered a fumble at Chicago's 43-yard line, and five plays later Cody Carlson passed 6 yards to Webster Slaughter to put the Oilers ahead 17-0.

Chicago	0	0	0	7	—	7
Houston	0	10	7	7	—	24

Hou — FG Del Greco 19
Hou — McDowell 26 interception return (Del Greco kick)
Hou — Slaughter 6 pass from Carlson (Del Greco kick)
Chi — Anderson 17 pass from Willis (Butler kick)
Hou — White 1 run (Del Greco kick)

Fifteenth Week Summaries

Standings

American Football Conference

Eastern Division

	W	L	T	Pct.	Pts.	OP
Buffalo	10	4	0	.714	358	240
Miami	9	5	0	.643	305	251
Indianapolis	7	7	0	.500	179	272
N.Y. Jets	4	10	0	.286	203	276
New England	2	12	0	.143	182	327

Central Division

	W	L	T	Pct.	Pts.	OP
Pittsburgh	10	4	0	.714	273	206
Houston	8	6	0	.571	308	241
Cleveland	7	7	0	.500	245	235
Cincinnati	4	10	0	.286	237	333

Western Division

	W	L	T	Pct.	Pts.	OP
Kansas City	9	5	0	.643	285	227
San Diego	9	5	0	.643	268	213
Denver	7	7	0	.500	232	281
L.A. Raiders	6	8	0	.429	214	225
Seattle	2	12	0	.143	120	271

National Football Conference

Eastern Division

	W	L	T	Pct.	Pts.	OP
Dallas	11	3	0	.786	341	212
Philadelphia	9	5	0	.643	317	222
Washington	9	5	0	.643	267	217
N.Y. Giants	5	9	0	.357	261	326
Phoenix	4	10	0	.286	227	309

Central Division

	W	L	T	Pct.	Pts.	OP
Minnesota	9	5	0	.643	341	239
Green Bay	8	6	0	.571	241	256
Chicago	5	9	0	.357	278	318
Detroit	4	10	0	.286	251	305
Tampa Bay	4	10	0	.286	246	341

Western Division

	W	L	T	Pct.	Pts.	OP
San Francisco	12	2	0	.857	386	216
New Orleans	11	3	0	.786	294	182
Atlanta	6	8	0	.429	283	335
L.A. Rams	5	9	0	.357	262	328

Saturday, December 12

Buffalo 27, Denver 17—at Rich Stadium, attendance 71,740. The Bills built a 24-0 third-quarter lead, then held off a furious rally by the Broncos to snap a two-game losing streak and send Denver to its fourth consecutive defeat. Buffalo broke a scoreless tie midway through the second quarter on a flea-flicker that started with quarterback Jim Kelly handing off to running back Thurman Thomas, who handed off to wide receiver Andre Reed on a reverse. But Reed pitched the ball back to Kelly, who found wide receiver Don Beebe alone behind the Broncos' secondary for a 64-yard touchdown. Denver could not get on the board until Tommy Maddox threw a 1-yard touchdown pass to Shannon Sharpe to make the score 24-7 late in the third quarter. But kicker Brad Daluiso recovered his ensuing onside kickoff, and the Broncos drove to a field goal. And when Greg Lewis ran 1 yard for a touchdown with 6:13 remaining, Denver trailed only 24-17. But the Bills responded with a 62-yard, 10-play drive that resulted in Steve Christie's 25-yard field goal to insure the victory. Thurman Thomas rushed for 120 yards for Buffalo and Beebe caught 4 passes for 104 yards. Sharpe had 7 receptions for 109 yards for the Broncos.

Denver	0	0	7	10	—	17
Buffalo	0	21	3	3	—	27

Buff — Beebe 64 pass from Kelly (Christie kick)
Buff — Kelly 2 run (Christie kick)
Buff — Thomas 11 run (Christie kick)
Buff — FG Christie 29
Den — Sharpe 1 pass from Maddox (Treadwell kick)
Den — FG Treadwell 26
Den — Lewis 1 run (Treadwell kick)
Buff — FG Christie 25

Phoenix 19, N.Y. Giants 0—at Sun Devil Stadium, attendance 28,452. Johnny Johnson rushed for a career-high 156 yards and 2 touchdowns as the Cardinals ended an eight-game losing streak to their division rivals. Phoenix's victory was its first over New York since 1988 and extended the Giants' losing streak to five games. Johnson, who equaled a club record with 36 carries, scored on a 5-yard run in the second quarter, then raced 42 yards on the first play of the fourth quarter to put the game out of reach. The Cardinals finished with 179 rushing yards, while limiting New York to 8 first downs and 131 total yards, and maintaining possession for more than 40 minutes. Phoenix recorded its first shutout since the 1981 season, while the Giants were blanked during the regular season for the first time since 1980.

N.Y. Giants	0	0	0	0	—	0
Phoenix	0	9	3	7	—	19

Phx — Safety, Swann tackled Brown in end zone
Phx — J. Johnson 5 run (G. Davis kick)
Phx — FG G.Davis 26
Phx — J. Johnson 42 run (G. Davis kick)

Sunday, December 13

Atlanta 35, Tampa Bay 7—at Tampa Stadium, attendance 38,208. Wade Wilson, given the starting nod over injured Billy Joe Tolliver shortly before game time, responded by throwing a club-record 5 touchdown passes in the Falcons' rout. Wilson completed 19 of 26 passes for 324 yards, including scoring tosses to Michael Haynes (2), Andre Rison, Mike Pritchard, and Deion Sanders. A starting cornerback and part-time wide receiver, Sanders caught a 37-yard pass with 8:45 left in the game for his first touchdown reception as a pro. Haynes finished with 113 yards on 5 catches. The Buccaneers set a dubious NFL record by becoming the first team to lose at least 10 games for the tenth consecutive season.

Atlanta	7	7	14	7	—	35
Tampa Bay	0	7	0	0	—	7

Atl — Haynes 8 pass from Wilson (Johnson kick)
TB — Cobb 1 run (Murray kick)
Atl — Rison 20 pass from Wilson (Johnson kick)
Atl — Pritchard 38 pass from Wilson (Johnson kick)
Atl — Haynes 60 pass from Wilson (Johnson kick)
Atl — Sanders 37 pass from Wilson (Johnson kick)

San Diego 27, Cincinnati 10—at San Diego Jack Murphy Stadium, attendance 50,579. The Chargers remained tied for first place in the AFC Western Division by winning for the ninth time in their last 10 games. The score was tied at 10-10 late in the third quarter before San Diego broke it open. First, quarterback Stan Humphries scored from 1 yard out on a fourth-down bootleg with 4:19 left in the period. Three minutes later, Rod Bernstine, playing for the first time after missing seven games because of an injury, scored on a 7-yard run to cap an 18-yard drive that was set up by linebacker Gary Plummer's interception. Safety Darren Carrington's interception on the Bengals' next drive set up the Chargers' final points, a 48-yard field goal by John Carney 1:14 into the fourth quarter. San Diego controlled the ball for nearly 40 minutes while recording 161 yards on the ground and 370 in all. The Chargers marched 77 yards to a field goal following the opening kickoff, holding the ball for 9:11. The Bengals answered with an 83-yard touchdown pass from David Klingler to Jeff Query on their first play from scrimmage.

Cincinnati	7	3	0	0	—	10
San Diego	3	7	14	3	—	27

SD — FG Carney 21
Cin — Query 83 pass from Klingler (Breech kick)
Cin — FG Breech 48
SD — Miller 11 pass from Humphries (Carney kick)
SD — Humphries 1 run (Carney kick)
SD — Bernstine 7 run (Carney kick)
SD — FG Carney 48

Detroit 24, Cleveland 14—at Pontiac Silverdome, attendance 65,970. Andre Ware passed for a pair of touchdowns to lead the Lions over the Browns. Ware, making his first start since 1990, completed 10 of 14 passes for 138 yards and also ran for 68 yards on 5 carries. He threw touchdown passes of 13 yards to Brett Perriman and 19 yards to Reggie Barrett as Detroit built a 21-0 lead. Bernie Kosar, who completed 20 of 28 passes for 276 yards, tried to rally Cleveland with a pair of fourth-quarter touchdown passes. But he also was intercepted twice as the Browns, who entered the game with a turnover margin of plus-11, second-best in the NFL, gave the ball away 3 times and did not register any takeaways.

Cleveland	0	0	0	14	—	14
Detroit	7	0	14	3	—	24

Det — Perriman 13 pass from Ware (Hanson kick)
Det — Sanders 14 run (Hanson kick)
Det — Barrett 19 pass from Ware (Hanson kick)
Cleve — M. Jackson 69 pass from Kosar (Stover kick)
Det — FG Hanson 46
Cleve — Metcalf 5 pass from Kosar (Stover kick)

Washington 20, Dallas 17—at RFK Stadium, attendance 56,437. Safety Danny Copeland fell on a fumble in the end zone with 3:14 remaining to give the Redskins a dramatic victory. The win bolstered Washington's playoff chances and prevented the Cowboys from clinching their first NFC Eastern Division title since 1985. Dallas dominated much of the game, but only led 17-10 in the fourth quarter. The Cowboys drove to the Redskins' 2-yard line early in the final period, but Washington linebacker Andre Collins stepped in front of a Troy Aikman pass at the goal line, and returned the interception 59 yards to set up a field goal with 7:02 remaining. On the Cowboys' next possession, Copeland recovered a fumble and returned it 15 yards to Dallas's 24, but the Redskins' drive stalled at the 2 when Mark Rypien's fourth-down pass was incomplete. Two plays later, the Cowboys were at the 5 when Aikman was sacked by defensive end Jason Buck in the end zone. Dallas running back Emmitt Smith picked up the ball briefly, but when he also fumbled, Copeland fell on the ball for the winning points.

Dallas	3	14	0	0	—	17
Washington	0	7	3	10	—	20

Dall — FG Elliott 23
Dall — Novacek 5 pass from Aikman (Elliott kick)
Wash — Orr 41 pass from Byner (Lohmiller kick)
Dall — Novacek 5 pass from Aikman (Elliott kick)
Wash — FG Lohmiller 32
Wash — FG Lohmiller 22
Wash — Copeland fumble recovery in end zone (Lohmiller kick)

Indianapolis 10, N.Y. Jets 6—at Giants Stadium, attendance 33,684. Jack Trudeau came off the bench to throw a 23-yard touchdown pass to tight end Charles Arbuckle with 2:29 left to lift the Colts to victory. Trudeau, who had led Indianapolis to victories each of the last two weeks as a starter, was back on the bench after Jeff George returned from an injury to start against the Jets. But George could not produce a touchdown and Trudeau replaced him with 8:23 to go in the game. He directed the winning 71-yard drive, converting a key third down with a 41-yard pass to tight end Kerry Cash. The subsequent touchdown to Arbuckle was the first scoring catch of the reserve tight end's career. Cash, meanwhile, finished with 7 receptions for 104 yards. New York's Chris Burkett caught 6 passes for 110 yards. The game was marred by 7 turnovers, including 5 by the Jets.

Indianapolis	0	0	3	7	—	10
N.Y. Jets	0	6	0	0	—	6

Jets — FG Blanchard 35
Jets — FG Blanchard 19
Ind — FG Biasucci 31
Ind — Arbuckle 23 pass from Trudeau (Biasucci kick)

Kansas City 27, New England 20—at Arrowhead Stadium, attendance 52,208. Safety Charles Mincy scooped up a fumble and returned it 30 yards for a touchdown 22 seconds into the fourth quarter, breaking a 13-13 tie and sending the Chiefs on their way to the victory. The game featured 10 fumbles, thanks largely to a steady downpour. The Patriots had opened the game by scoring on a fumble return of their own, when nose tackle Tim Goad picked up Christian Okoye's fumble and went 19 yards for a touchdown on the first play from scrimmage. Okoye rebounded to rush for 86 yards, including a 1-yard touchdown run that tied the game in the third quarter. After Mincy returned Jon Vaughn's fumble for the go-ahead score, Dave Krieg put Kansas City ahead 27-13 with a 43-yard touchdown pass to Willie Davis five minutes into the fourth quarter. Krieg completed only 10 passes (for 196 yards), but spread them around to 9 different receivers.

New England	13	0	0	7	—	20
Kansas City	3	3	7	14	—	27

NE — Goad 19 fumble recovery return (Baumann kick)
KC — FG Lowery 30
NE — Russell 3 run (kick failed)
KC — FG Lowery 26
KC — Okoye 1 run (Lowery kick)
KC — Mincy 30 fumble recovery return (Lowery kick)
KC — W. Davis 43 pass from Krieg (Lowery kick)
NE — Turner 6 pass from Carlson (Baumann kick)

New Orleans 37, L.A. Rams 14—at Anaheim Stadium, attendance 47,355. Bobby Hebert passed for a pair of first-half touchdowns as the Saints dominated the Rams in an easy victory. New Orleans forced 6 turnovers and the game's outcome never was in doubt. The Saints led 23-0 by halftime and 37-0 midway through the fourth quarter before Los Angeles scored. New Orleans's offense, normally overshadowed by the team's stifling defense, amassed 399 yards. Hebert completed 15 of 25 passes for 238 yards, and rookie running back Vaughn Dunbar had 91 yards on 13 carries. Rams quarterback Jim Everett passed for 226 yards and a pair of fourth-quarter touchdowns, but was intercepted 3 times.

New Orleans	6	17	7	7	—	37
L.A. Rams	0	0	0	14	—	14

NO — Martin 12 pass from Hebert (kick failed)
NO — McAfee 1 run (Andersen kick)
NO — Small 16 pass from Hebert (Andersen kick)

NO — FG Andersen 21
NO — Dunbar 1 run (Andersen kick)
NO — Heyward 9 run (Andersen kick)
Rams — Anderson 17 pass from Everett (Zendejas kick)
Rams — Ellard 32 pass from Everett (Zendejas kick)

Philadelphia 20, Seattle 17—at Kingdome, attendance 65,902. Roger Ruzek kicked a 44-yard field goal with no time left in overtime as the Eagles survived a scare to beat the Seahawks. Philadelphia dominated Seattle (2-12) statistically, compiling 25 first downs to only 11 and outgaining the Seahawks 466-87. But 10 sacks and a club-record 191 yards in penalties prevented the Eagles from winning in regulation. In fact, Philadelphia had to rally to tie, doing so when Herschel Walker ran 8 yards for a touchdown with 4:52 left in the game. Late in the overtime, the Eagles marched 53 yards to the winning field goal. Randall Cunningham's 21-yard shovel pass to Keith Byars was the key play. Cunningham finished with 27 completions in 44 attempts for 365 yards. Fred Barnett had 9 catches for 161 yards and Walker ran for 111 yards on 23 carries. Safety Robert Blackmon and linebacker Rufus Porter each had 2½ sacks for Seattle.

Philadelphia	3	7	0	7	3	— 20
Seattle	3	7	0	7	0	— 17

Sea — FG Kasay 39
Phil — FG Ruzek 42
Phil — Cunningham 4 run (Ruzek kick)
Sea — J.L. Williams 11 pass from Gelbaugh (Kasay kick)
Sea — Harper 52 fumble recovery return (Kasay kick)
Phil — Walker 8 run (Ruzek kick)
Phil — FG Ruzek 44

Chicago 30, Pittsburgh 6—at Soldier Field, attendance 52,904. Running back Neal Anderson scored twice and the Bears snapped a six-game losing streak in linebacker Mike Singletary's final home game. Singletary, a nine-time Pro Bowl pick had 3 tackles while helping Chicago's defense limit Barry Foster, the NFL's leading rusher, to only 25 yards on 12 carries. The Bears never trailed, and put the game away when Anderson scored twice in the second half. His 15-yard touchdown catch from Jim Harbaugh midway through the third quarter put his team ahead 20-3, and his 6-yard run with 3:02 left in the game closed the scoring.

Pittsburgh	0	3	0	3	— 6
Chicago	3	10	7	10	— 30

Chi — FG Butler 37
Chi — Lewis 3 run (Butler kick)
Chi — FG Butler 26
Pitt — FG Anderson 38
Chi — Anderson 15 pass from Harbaugh (Butler kick)
Chi — FG Butler 38
Pitt — FG Anderson 38
Chi — Anderson 6 run (Butler kick)

San Francisco 20, Minnesota 17—at Metrodome, attendance 60,685. Rookie Amp Lee, playing in place of injured starter Ricky Watters, rushed for 134 yards and scored a pair of touchdowns to lead the 49ers to their sixth consecutive victory. San Francisco also got a couple of big defensive plays down the stretch to secure the victory. After pulling to within three points on Terry Allen's 1-yard run with 9:29 left in the game, the Vikings made a bid for the tying or winning score, driving to the 49ers' 35-yard line. But defensive end Pierce Holt and linebacker Tim Harris combined to sack Minnesota quarterback Rich Gannon on second down, and Harris added another sack on third down to push the Vikings out of field-goal range. Lee, whose 43-yard run set up what proved to be the decisive field goal in the closing seconds of the third quarter, then helped San Francisco run out the final 2:13. The 49ers' top-rated offense was limited to 287 total yards, far below its season average of 401. But Minnesota managed only 185. Harris had 2½ sacks for the 49ers, while the Vikings' Al Noga had 3 of his team's 7 sacks. Cornerback Audray McMillian's 51-yard interception return for a touchdown was Minnesota's club-record eighth defensive touchdown of the season.

San Francisco	3	14	3	0	— 20
Minnesota	7	0	3	7	— 17

SF — FG Cofer 46
Minn — McMillian 51 interception return (Reveiz kick)
SF — Lee 3 pass from Young (Cofer kick)
SF — Lee 2 run (Cofer kick)
Minn — FG Reveiz 44
SF — FG Cofer 26
Minn — Allen 1 run (Reveiz kick)

Sunday Night, December 13

Green Bay 16, Houston 14—at Astrodome, attendance 57,285. The surging Packers won their fifth consecutive game to match their longest winning streak since 1966 and keep their NFC Central Division title hopes alive. Chris Jacke kicked 3 field goals, Brett Favre threw a 6-yard touchdown pass to Sterling Sharpe, and Green Bay's defense forced 4 critical turnovers. The Packers converted 2 fumble recoveries and 2 interceptions into 13 points. Houston's final turnover, a fumbled snap by quarterback Cody Carlson after the Oilers had reached the Green Bay 37-yard line while trailing only 9-7 in the fourth quarter, led to Sharpe's touchdown catch, which proved to be the decisive score. Carlson completed 25 of 36 passes for 330 yards for Houston, which outgained the Packers 387-215. The Oilers' Curtis Duncan caught 6 passes for 100 yards.

Green Bay	0	3	6	7	— 16
Houston	0	0	7	7	— 14

GB — FG Jacke 39
GB — FG Jacke 36
GB — FG Jacke 20
Hou — Carlson 1 run (Del Greco kick)
GB — Sharpe 6 pass from Favre (Jacke kick)
Hou — White 2 run (Del Greco kick)

Monday, December 14

Miami 20, L.A. Raiders 7—at Joe Robbie Stadium, attendance 67,098. Mark Duper caught a 62-yard flea-flicker touchdown pass from Dan Marino and cornerback J.B. Brown returned an interception 35 yards for a touchdown to highlight the Dolphins' victory. The game was scoreless until Miami's Pete Stoyanovich kicked a 26-yard field goal 4:53 before halftime. Just 20 seconds later, Brown's interception return made it 10-0. In the third quarter, Marino handed off to Mark Higgs, who lateraled back to the Dolphins quarterback. Marino then fired a strike to Duper for the score that broke the game open. The Raiders rarely threatened on offense, totaling only 151 yards. Los Angeles's lone score came when safety Eddie Anderson returned a fourth-quarter interception 102 yards for a touchdown. It was the longest interception return in club history and equaled the third-longest in NFL annals.

L.A. Raiders	0	0	0	7	— 7
Miami	0	10	7	3	— 20

Mia — FG Stoyanovich 26
Mia — J.B.Brown 35 interception return (Stoyanovich kick)
Mia — Duper 62 pass from Marino (Stoyanovich kick)
Raid — Anderson 102 interception return (Jaeger kick)
Mia — FG Stoyanovich 25

Sixteenth Week Summaries

Standings

American Football Conference

Eastern Division	W	L	T	Pct.	Pts.	OP
Buffalo	11	4	0	.733	378	256
Miami	10	5	0	.667	324	268
Indianapolis	8	7	0	.533	195	285
N.Y. Jets	4	11	0	.267	220	295
New England	2	13	0	.133	192	347
Central Division						
Pittsburgh	10	5	0	.667	276	212
Houston	9	6	0	.600	325	255
Cleveland	7	8	0	.467	259	252
Cincinnati	5	10	0	.333	257	343
Western Division						
San Diego	10	5	0	.667	304	227
Kansas City	9	6	0	.600	306	262
Denver	8	7	0	.533	242	287
L.A. Raiders	6	9	0	.400	228	261
Seattle	2	13	0	.133	126	281

National Football Conference

Eastern Division	W	L	T	Pct.	Pts.	OP
Dallas	12	3	0	.800	382	229
Philadelphia	10	5	0	.667	334	235
Washington	9	6	0	.600	280	234
N.Y. Giants	6	9	0	.400	296	347
Phoenix	4	11	0	.267	240	325
Central Division						
Minnesota	10	5	0	.667	347	242
Green Bay	9	6	0	.600	269	269
Chicago	5	10	0	.333	281	334
Detroit	5	10	0	.333	267	308
Tampa Bay	4	11	0	.267	260	362
Western Division						
San Francisco	13	2	0	.867	407	230
New Orleans	11	4	0	.733	310	202
Atlanta	6	9	0	.400	300	376
L.A. Rams	5	10	0	.333	275	356

Saturday, December 19

N.Y. Giants 35, Kansas City 21—at Giants Stadium, attendance 53,418. Rodney Hampton rushed for 3 touchdowns and Jeff Hostetler passed for 2 as the Giants knocked the Chiefs out of a first-place tie in the AFC Western Division and prevented Kansas City from clinching a playoff berth. New York, which snapped a five-game losing streak, ground out 217 rushing yards, including 84 each by Hampton and Jarrod Bunch. The Giants led 21-7 at halftime, forcing the ground-oriented Chiefs to take to the air to try to catch up. Dave Krieg passed for 259 yards, including a 77-yard touchdown to Tim Barnett in the third quarter, but also was intercepted twice. Hostetler completed 10 of 16 passes for 131 yards and scrambled for 23 yards on 6 carries in his return to the lineup after missing three with a severe concussion. The Giants scored only a combined 13 points in the three weeks he missed, but had 14 in the first quarter alone against Kansas City. The Chiefs' loss, coupled with Denver's victory over Seattle a day later, set up a regular-season ending showdown between the Broncos and Chiefs for the AFC's final playoff spot.

Kansas City	0	7	7	7	— 21
N.Y. Giants	14	7	14	0	— 35

Giants — Ingram 21 pass from Hostetler (Willis kick)
Giants — Hampton 2 run (Willis kick)
KC — Okoye 1 run (Lowery kick)
Giants — Calloway 15 pass from Hostetler (Willis kick)
Giants — Hampton 1 run (Willis kick)
Giants — Hampton 20 run (Willis kick)
KC — Barnett 77 pass from Krieg (Lowery kick)
KC — Rogers recovered blocked punt in end zone (Lowery kick)

San Francisco 21, Tampa Bay 14—at Candlestick Park, attendance 60,519. Steve Young threw 3 touchdown passes, 2 of them to Jerry Rice, as the 49ers won the NFC West for the sixth time in the past seven seasons and clinched home-field advantage throughout the playoffs. Young, who completed 18 of 31 passes for 270 yards and was not intercepted, broke a 7-7 tie with a 32-yard touchdown pass to Rice early in the second half. After the Buccaneers' Reggie Cobb tied the game with a 1-yard touchdown run 53 seconds into the fourth quarter, San Francisco drove 64 yards in six plays to the winning score on Young's 30-yard pass to Rice. Tampa Bay had a first-and-goal at the 49ers' 3-yard line late in the game but could not score, and San Francisco rookie safety Dana Hall knocked down Vinny Testaverde's desperation pass in the end zone on the game's final play. Buccaneers wide receiver Mark Carrier had 28 yards on 3 receptions to finish the day with 4,930 career receiving yards, a club record.

Tampa Bay	7	0	0	7	— 14
San Francisco	7	0	7	7	— 21

TB — McDowell 51 pass from Testaverde (Murray kick)
SF — Taylor 9 pass from Young (Cofer kick)
SF — Rice 32 pass from Young (Cofer kick)
TB — Cobb 1 run (Murray kick)
SF — Rice 30 pass from Young (Cofer kick)

Sunday, December 20

Buffalo 20, New Orleans 16—at Louisiana Superdome, attendance 68,591. Thurman Thomas ran for 115 yards and 2 touchdowns as the Bills improved to 11-4, best in the AFC. Buffalo, playing without injured defensive stars Bruce Smith and Cornelius Bennett, still limited the Saints to 205 total yards. New Orleans quarterback Bobby Hebert, who had been sacked only 11 times all season, was dropped 4 times, including twice by nose tackle Jeff Wright and twice by defensive end Phil Hansen, who was starting in place of the injured Smith. Still, the Bills found themselves trailing 16-10 entering the fourth quarter. But an 85-yard drive was kept alive by a critical fourth-down pass interference penalty, and Thomas scored from 2 yards to give Buffalo the lead for good with 7:19 to play. The Bills recovered a fumble on the ensuing kickoff and added an insurance field goal with 3:36 to go.

Buffalo	3	0	7	10	— 20
New Orleans	6	7	3	0	— 16

Buff — FG Christie 25
NO — FG Andersen 35
NO — FG Andersen 27
NO — Small 20 pass from Hebert (Andersen kick)
Buff — Thomas 6 run (Christie kick)
NO — FG Andersen 42
Buff — Thomas 2 run (Christie kick)
Buff — FG Christie 29

Detroit 16, Chicago 3—at Pontiac Silverdome, attendance 72,777. Andre Ware passed for 290 yards, Barry Sanders rushed for 113 yards and a touchdown, and the Lions won back-to-back games for the first time this season. Ware completed only 12 passes but many were long-range. His 31-yard pass to Brett Perriman and his 43-yard pass to Herman Moore set up Detroit's first score, a 22-yard field goal by Jason Hanson 3:53 into the game. He had a 35-yard pass to Perriman on a 93-yard drive that culminated in Sanders's 6-yard touchdown run

52 seconds into the second quarter. Ware's 59-yard strike to Moore helped Hanson make it 13-0 at intermission with a 38-yard field goal in the final minute of the first half. The Bears never got on track, managing only a 24-yard field goal by Kevin Butler in the third quarter. The Lions finished with 399 total yards to only 242 for Chicago. Moore totaled 108 yards on just 3 receptions.

Chicago	0	0	3	0	—	3
Detroit	3	10	0	3	—	16

Det — FG Hanson 22
Det — Sanders 6 run (Hanson kick)
Det — FG Hanson 38
Chi — FG Butler 24
Det — FG Hanson 30

Houston 17, Cleveland 14—at Cleveland Stadium, attendance 59,898. Cody Carlson's 3-yard touchdown pass to Ernest Givins with 34 seconds remaining gave the Oilers a come-from-behind victory. Houston's win, coupled with Miami's victory over the Jets later in the day, gave the Oilers a wild-card playoff berth while eliminating the Browns from postseason contention. Cleveland led 14-3 until late in the game, when Carlson capped an 85-yard drive by teaming with Curtis Duncan on a 2-yard touchdown pass with 2:58 to go. Moments later, running back Lorenzo White turned a screen pass from Carlson into a 65-yard gain to position Houston for the winning points. Carlson finished with 248 passing yards, much of it on the final two drives. White caught 6 passes for 105 yards. The Browns' Kevin Mack rushed for 95 yards on 21 carries.

Houston	0	3	0	14	—	17
Cleveland	7	0	7	0	—	14

Cleve — Wolfley 2 pass from Kosar (Stover kick)
Hou — FG Del Greco 47
Cleve — Jones 1 pass from Kosar (Stover kick)
Hou — Duncan 2 pass from Carlson (Del Greco kick)
Hou — Givins 3 pass from Carlson (Del Greco kick)

Green Bay 28, L.A. Rams 13—at Lambeau Field, attendance 57,796. The Packers overcame a 10-point second-quarter deficit by scoring 4 touchdowns in a span of 6:33. Darrell Thompson began the onslaught by running 2 yards for a touchdown with 6:48 remaining in the first half. Just 1:18 later, rookie cornerback Terrell Buckley intercepted a Jim Everett pass and returned it 33 yards for a touchdown to give Green Bay a 14-10 advantage, a lead it never relinquished. Quarterback Brett Favre and wide receiver Sterling Sharpe then teamed on a pair of scoring passes 65 seconds apart, a 17-yarder with 1:20 left in the half and a 16-yarder at the 15-second mark. Sharpe caught 8 passes for 110 yards to became the sixth player in NFL history to reach the century mark in a single season. He finished the day with 102 catches, just 4 away from the NFL record of 106, set by Washington's Art Monk in 1984. Everett completed 24 of 44 passes for 222 yards for the Rams, but was intercepted 3 times. Though Minnesota clinched the NFC Central Division title with its victory over Pittsburgh, the Packers' triumph kept their own wild-card playoff hopes alive.

L.A. Rams	7	3	3	0	—	13
Green Bay	0	28	0	0	—	28

Rams — Anderson 16 pass from Everett (Zendejas kick)
Rams — FG Zendejas 19
GB — Thompson 2 run (Jacke kick)
GB — Buckley 33 interception return (Jacke kick)
GB — Sharpe 17 pass from Favre (Jacke kick)
GB — Sharpe 16 pass from Favre (Jacke kick)
Rams — FG Zendejas 39

Minnesota 6, Pittsburgh 3—at Three Rivers Stadium, attendance 53,613. Fuad Reveiz kicked 2 fourth-quarter field goals, including the game-winner from 36 yards on the final play, as the Vikings won the NFC Central Division title. Both teams generated considerable yardage on the ground, but neither could crack the end zone. Minnesota's Terry Allen rushed for 172 yards on 33 carries, but the Vikings fumbled the ball away 3 times and a had a field-goal attempt aborted by a bad snap. The Steelers' Barry Foster rushed for 118 yards on 24 carries—his eleventh 100-yard outing of the season—but left the game in the fourth quarter with a back injury. Pittsburgh's lone score came on Gary Anderson's 23-yard field goal five seconds before halftime. After Reveiz's 38-yard field goal tied the game at 3-3 with 7:08 left, Minnesota marched 61 yards on its next possession to set up the winning kick. The key play was Sean Salisbury's third-down, 35-yard pass to Jake Reed.

Minnesota	0	0	0	6	—	6
Pittsburgh	0	3	0	0	—	3

Pitt — FG Anderson 23
Minn — FG Reveiz 38
Minn — FG Reveiz 36

Cincinnati 20, New England 10—at Riverfront Stadium, attendance 45,355. Harold Green rushed for a career-high 190 yards on 31 carries as the Bengals broke a five-game losing streak and handed the Patriots their fourth consecutive defeat. Green, who surpassed the 1,000-yard mark for the season (he finished the day at 1,131), started the scoring with a 6-yard touchdown run with 3:50 to go in the first quarter. Cincinnati quickly extended its lead to 14-0 on Derrick Fenner's 1-yard run only 25 seconds later. Fenner's run was set up after the Bengals recovered an onside kick at midfield, then got the ball at the New England 1-yard line after a pass interference penalty in the end zone. That would be all the points they'd need against the Patriots, who managed only 10 first downs and 176 total yards. New England's lone touchdown came on Jon Vaughn's 100-yard kickoff return following Fenner's touchdown.

New England	7	0	0	3	—	10
Cincinnati	14	0	3	3	—	20

Cin — Green 6 run (Breech kick)
Cin — Fenner 1 run (Breech kick)
NE — Vaughn 100 kickoff return (Baumann kick)
Cin — FG Breech 21
NE — FG Baumann 27
Cin — FG Breech 39

Indianapolis 16, Phoenix 13—at Hoosier Dome, attendance 46,763. Though Miami's victory later in the day eliminated them from playoff contention, the Colts completed an unprecedented turnaround by beating the Cardinals. With the victory, Indianapolis improved to 8-7 on the season, thus becoming the first team to win as many as eight games the year after going 1-15. Dean Biasucci kicked 3 field goals in this one, including the game-winner from 42 yards with 49 seconds to go. The Colts rallied from a 10-0 first-half deficit behind the passing of Jeff George, who completed 25 of 41 attempts for 328 yards, including a 57-yard touchdown to running back Anthony Johnson. Johnny Johnson ran for 146 yards on 28 carries for Phoenix, which had its final chance to win or tie thwarted when safety Mike Prior intercepted Chris Chandler's pass at the Indianapolis 36-yard line with 19 seconds left. It was Prior's club-record-tying third theft of the day.

Phoenix	7	3	0	3	—	13
Indianapolis	0	3	7	6	—	16

Phx — J. Johnson 10 run (G. Davis kick)
Phx — FG G. Davis 28
Ind — FG Biasucci 26
Ind — A. Johnson 57 pass from George (Biasucci kick)
Ind — FG Biasucci 28
Phx — FG G. Davis 48
Ind — FG Biasucci 42

San Diego 36, L.A. Raiders 14—at Los Angeles Memorial Coliseum, attendance 40,152. The Chargers scored on their first five possessions en route to blasting the Raiders and becoming the first team in NFL history to reach the playoffs after starting the season with four consecutive losses. San Diego, which won its sixth straight and tenth in the last 11 games, moved into first place in the AFC Western Division and clinched at least a wild-card playoff spot, its first postseason berth since 1982. The Chargers limited Los Angeles to only 30 total yards in the decisive first half, which ended with San Diego ahead 23-0. John Carney kicked 3 of his club-record 5 field goals before halftime and Stan Humphries threw touchdown passes of 14 yards to Anthony Miller and 50 yards to Nate Lewis to break the game open. Vince Evans threw a pair of second-half touchdown passes for the Raiders.

San Diego	3	20	3	10	—	36
L.A. Raiders	0	0	7	7	—	14

SD — FG Carney 42
SD — FG Carney 23
SD — Miller 14 pass from Humphries (Carney kick)
SD — Lewis 50 pass from Humphries (Carney kick)
SD — FG Carney 25
SD — FG Carney 28
Raid — Wright 21 pass from Evans (Jaeger kick)
SD — Bieniemy 1 run (Carney kick)
Raid — T. Brown 5 pass from Evans (Jaeger kick)
SD — FG Carney 23

Denver 10, Seattle 6—at Mile High Stadium, attendance 72,570. John Elway returned to the lineup after missing four weeks with a bruised throwing shoulder and the Broncos won for the first time since his injury. The veteran quarterback completed 19 of 28 passes for 213 yards and became the fifteenth player in NFL history to surpass the 30,000-yard mark for his career (30,008). But on this day, he also was intercepted 3 times, as Denver turned the ball over 5 times in an error-plagued first half. But the Seahawks could not capitalize, and led only 3-0 at halftime on John Kasay's 34-yard field goal midway through the second quarter. That came after safety Robert Blackmon recovered Reggie Rivers's fumble at the Broncos' 40-yard line and returned it 9 yards. But Denver got a turnover of its own on the first play of the second half to set up the game's lone touchdown: Kenny Walker's fumble recovery at Seattle's 23 led to Gaston Green's 1-yard run just 1:20 into the third quarter. That provided the Broncos with all the points they would need and set up a showdown with the Chiefs one week later in Kansas City for the AFC's lone remaining playoff berth.

Seattle	0	3	3	0	—	6
Denver	0	0	7	3	—	10

Sea — FG Kasay 34
Den — Green 1 run (Treadwell kick)
Sea — FG Kasay 36
Den — FG Treadwell 30

Philadelphia 17, Washington 13—at Veterans Stadium, attendance 65,841. The Eagles clinched at least a wild-card playoff berth when cornerback Eric Allen tipped away Mark Rypien's pass to Gary Clark in the end zone on the final play. Roger Ruzek kicked a 23-yard field goal with 3:35 left in the game to put Philadelphia ahead by four points. Starting at their 10-yard line, the Redskins drove to the Eagles' 5 behind Rypien, who converted three third downs and a pair of fourth downs along the way. But Allen saved the victory by batting away Rypien's pass as time ran out. Rypien completed 22 of 38 passes for 272 yards, including a 62-yard touchdown to give Washington a 10-7 lead in the second quarter. It was 13-7 at halftime, but Randall Cunningham's 28-yard touchdown pass to Calvin Williams 4:15 into the third quarter put Philadelphia ahead for good. The Eagles' Heath Sherman rushed for 96 yards, including a 21-yard touchdown run in the second quarter. Sanders caught 7 passes for 114 yards for the Redskins, who had 364 total yards to Philadelphia's 299.

Washington	0	13	0	0	—	13
Philadelphia	0	7	7	3	—	17

Wash — FG Lohmiller 29
Phil — Sherman 21 run (Ruzek kick)
Wash — Sanders 62 pass from Rypien (Lohmiller kick)
Wash — FG Lohmiller 41
Phil — Williams 28 pass from Cunningham (Ruzek kick)
Phil — FG Ruzek 23

Sunday Night, December 20

Miami 19, N.Y. Jets 17—at Joe Robbie Stadium, attendance 68,275. Pete Stoyanovich, who missed a crucial extra-point attempt two minutes earlier, lifted the Dolphins to the victory and a spot in the AFC playoffs by kicking a 37-yard field goal with seven seconds remaining. After Cary Blanchard had given the Jets a 17-10 lead on a 35-yard field goal with 4:16 left in the game, Miami's Tony Martin took a short fourth-down pass from Dan Marino and broke free for a 55-yard touchdown with 2:30 to go. But the Dolphins still trailed by a point when Stoyanovich pushed the conversion attempt to the right. After holding New York without a first down and forcing a short punt, Miami got the ball back on the Jets' 45-yard line with 1:05 remaining. Marino completed passes of 11 yards to Fred Banks and 17 yards to Mark Duper to position the Dolphins for the winning kick. With the win, Miami clinched at least a wild-card playoff berth and kept alive its hopes for winning the AFC Eastern Division title.

N.Y. Jets	0	0	14	3	—	17
Miami	7	0	0	12	—	19

Mia — Clayton 39 pass from Marino (Stoyanovich kick)
Jets — Moore 48 pass from Nagle (Blanchard kick)
Jets — Houston 20 interception return (Blanchard kick)
Mia — FG Stoyanovich 32
Jets — FG Blanchard 35
Mia — Martin 55 pass from Marino (kick failed)
Mia — FG Stoyanovich 37

Monday, December 21

Dallas 41, Atlanta 17—at Georgia Dome, attendance 67,036. The Cowboys wrapped up their first NFC Eastern Division title since 1985 by pummeling the Falcons. Dallas led 20-10 at halftime, then broke the game open by recovering a pair of fumbles and turning them into touchdowns in a 25-second span of the third quarter. First, Cowboys cornerback Larry Brown recovered Steve Broussard's fumble. That set up Troy Aikman's 23-yard touchdown pass to Alvin Harper three plays later. Then, Atlanta's Deion Sanders fumbled the ensuing kickoff. Dallas safety Thomas Everett recovered at the Falcons' 29-yard line, and Emmitt Smith ran for a score on the next play to make it 34-10. Smith added another 29-yard touchdown run in the fourth quarter and finished with 174 yards on 24 carries. Aikman was 18 of 21 for 239 yards and 3 touchdowns and was not intercepted as the Cowboys amassed 435 total yards. Wade Wilson completed 30 of 41 passes for 342 yards and a pair of scores for Atlanta. The Falcons had a pair of receivers eclipse the 100-yard mark–Mike Pritchard with 105 (on 9 catches) and Michael Haynes with 100 (on 5). By winning, Dallas assured itself of a bye in the first round of the NFL playoffs.

	1	2	3	4		
Dallas	3	17	14	7	—	41
Atlanta	7	3	0	7	—	17

Dall — FG Elliott 47
Atl — Hill 6 pass from Wilson (Johnson kick)
Dall — Martin 11 pass from Aikman (Elliott kick)
Dall — FG Elliott 22
Dall — Novacek 18 pass from Aikman (Elliott kick)
Atl — FG Johnson 27
Dall — Harper 23 pass from Aikman (Elliott kick)
Dall — E. Smith 29 run (Elliott kick)
Dall — E. Smith 29 run (Elliott kick)
Atl — Rison 10 pass from Wilson (Johnson kick)

Seventeenth Week Summaries

Standings

American Football Conference

Eastern Division

	W	L	T	Pct.	Pts.	OP
Miami	11	5	0	.688	340	281
Buffalo	11	5	0	.688	381	283
Indianapolis	9	7	0	.563	216	302
N.Y. Jets	4	12	0	.250	220	315
New England	2	14	0	.125	205	363

Central Division

	W	L	T	Pct.	Pts.	OP
Pittsburgh	11	5	0	.688	299	225
Houston	10	6	0	.625	352	258
Cleveland	7	9	0	.438	272	275
Cincinnati	5	11	0	.313	274	364

Western Division

	W	L	T	Pct.	Pts.	OP
San Diego	11	5	0	.688	335	241
Kansas City	10	6	0	.625	348	282
Denver	8	8	0	.500	262	329
L.A. Raiders	7	9	0	.438	249	281
Seattle	2	14	0	.125	140	312

National Football Conference

Eastern Division

	W	L	T	Pct.	Pts.	OP
Dallas	13	3	0	.813	409	243
Philadelphia	11	5	0	.688	354	245
Washington	9	7	0	.563	300	255
N.Y. Giants	6	10	0	.375	306	367
Phoenix	4	12	0	.250	243	332

Central Division

	W	L	T	Pct.	Pts.	OP
Minnesota	11	5	0	.688	374	249
Green Bay	9	7	0	.563	276	296
Tampa Bay	5	11	0	.313	267	365
Chicago	5	11	0	.313	295	361
Detroit	5	11	0	.313	273	332

Western Division

	W	L	T	Pct.	Pts.	OP
San Francisco	14	2	0	.875	431	236
New Orleans	12	4	0	.750	330	202
Atlanta	6	10	0	.375	327	414
L.A. Rams	6	10	0	.375	313	383

Saturday, December 26

L.A. Raiders 21, Washington 20—at RFK Stadium, attendance 53,032. Vince Evans threw a 3-yard touchdown pass to Tim Brown with 13 seconds remaining to give the Raiders the upset victory. Despite the defeat, the defending Super Bowl-champion Redskins still made the playoffs as the NFC's last wild-card entrant when the Packers lost the following day at Minnesota. The lead changed hands five times in this one, including three times in the closing minutes. Nick Bell gave Los Angeles a 14-13 advantage with 4:03 to go on a 5-yard touchdown run that capped a 67-yard drive. Washington responded by marching 55 yards in only four plays—the key gain a 43-yard pass from Mark Rypien to Art Monk—to take a 20-14 lead on Ricky Ervins's 1-yard run with 1:57 to play. But the Raiders took over on their 20-yard line, moved into scoring position when Evans teamed with Willie Gault on a 50-yard bomb, and scored the winning touchdown on fourth-and-goal. The 37-year-old Evans, who entered the game in the second quarter in relief of injured starter Jay Schroeder, completed 15 of 22 passes for 214 yards and 2 touchdowns. Brown caught 8 passes for 88 yards.

	1	2	3	4		
L.A. Raiders	0	0	7	14	—	21
Washington	0	3	7	10	—	20

Wash — FG Lohmiller 39
Raid — Wright 41 pass from Evans (Jaeger kick)
Wash — Monk 49 pass from Rypien (Lohmiller kick)
Wash — FG Lohmiller 22
Raid — N. Bell 5 run (Jaeger kick)
Wash — Ervins 1 run (Lohmiller kick)
Raid — T. Brown 3 pass from Evans (Jaeger kick)

New Orleans 20, N.Y. Jets 0—at Giants Stadium, attendance 45,614. Linebacker Sam Mills returned a fumble a club-record 76 yards for a touchdown as the Saints ensured themselves of home-field advantage in the opening round of the playoffs. The Jets maintained possession for all but 1:51 of the first quarter, but New Orleans came out of the period with the lead after Mills knocked the ball out of quarterback Browning Nagle's hands deep in Saints' territory. The ball bounced up to Mills and he returned it for his first career touchdown. New York didn't threaten much after that, and finished with only 10 first downs and 172 total yards. New Orleans's Morten Andersen kicked a pair of field goals to give him 20 consecutive successful attempts. The NFL record is 24, by the Bears' Kevin Butler.

	1	2	3	4		
New Orleans	7	3	7	3	—	20
N.Y. Jets	0	0	0	0	—	0

NO — Mills 76 fumble recovery return (Andersen kick)
NO — FG Andersen 27
NO — Heyward 2 run (Andersen kick)
NO — FG Andersen 36

Sunday, December 27

L.A. Rams 38, Atlanta 27—at Anaheim Stadium, attendance 37,706. David Lang ran for 3 touchdowns and Todd Kinchen tied an NFL record when he returned a pair of punts for touchdowns in the Rams' victory. Los Angeles jumped out to a 14-0 lead just 6:29 into the game on the first of Lang's two 1-yard touchdown runs and Kinchen's 61-yard touchdown on the first punt return of his career. The Falcons countered with 20 second-quarter points and led 20-17 entering the fourth quarter. But Lang's 1-yard touchdown run 41 seconds into the period gave the Rams the lead for good, and his 37-yarder for a score put Los Angeles ahead 31-20 with 8:54 to go. Kinchen's 35-yard punt return for a touchdown (only five other players in NFL history have returned 2 punts for scores in the same game) 1:46 later put the game out of reach. Wade Wilson completed 31 of 47 passes for 374 yards—his third consecutive week of more than 300 yards—and 3 touchdowns for Atlanta.

	1	2	3	4		
Atlanta	0	20	0	7	—	27
L.A. Rams	14	0	3	21	—	38

Rams — Lang 1 run (Zendejas kick)
Rams — Kinchen 61 punt return (Zendejas kick)
Atl — Rison 29 pass from Wilson (Johnson kick)
Atl — FG Johnson 44
Atl — Pritchard 11 pass from Wilson (Johnson kick)
Atl — FG Johnson 38
Rams — FG Zendéjas 24
Rams — Lang 1 run (Zendejas kick)
Rams — Lang 37 run (Zendejas kick)
Rams — Kinchen 35 punt return (Zendejas kick)
Atl — Haynes 21 pass from Wilson (Johnson kick)

Dallas 27, Chicago 14—at Texas Stadium, attendance 63,101. Emmitt Smith ran for 131 yards to clinch his second consecutive NFL rushing title and the Cowboys won for a club-record thirteenth time this season. Smith's 31-yard touchdown run 3:55 into the second half gave Dallas a 10-0 lead and enabled him to edge the Steelers' Barry Foster for the rushing crown by 23 yards. He did not return to the game after the scoring run and finished the year with 1,713 yards. He became only the ninth player to win back-to-back rushing titles and also set a franchise single-season record, eclipsing Tony Dorsett's previous mark of 1,646 yards. The Cowboys, already assured of the NFC Eastern Division title and a bye in the first round of the playoffs, put the game away when defensive tackle Russell Maryland returned a fumble 26 yards for a touchdown just 31 seconds after Smith's run. Rookie quarterback Will Furrer made his first start for the Bears but completed only 9 of 23 passes for 89 yards and was intercepted 3 times.

	1	2	3	4		
Chicago	0	0	0	14	—	14
Dallas	0	3	24	0	—	27

Dall — FG Elliott 21
Dall — E. Smith 31 run (Elliott kick)
Dall — Maryland 26 fumble recovery return (Elliott kick)
Dall — Richards 3 run (Elliott kick)
Dall — FG Elliott 34
Chi — Green 6 run (Butler kick)
Chi — Zorich 42 fumble recovery return (Butler kick)

Pittsburgh 23, Cleveland 13—at Three Rivers Stadium, attendance 53,776. The AFC Central Division-champion Steelers assured themselves of home-field advantage throughout the playoffs with the victory and Buffalo's loss later in the day. Bubby Brister completed 18 of 25 passes for 223 yards and 1 touchdown, a 2-yarder to tight end Tim Jorden 30 seconds before halftime. That gave Pittsburgh a 14-3 lead, and the Steelers increased it to 17-3 at intermission after recovering a fumble on the ensuing kickoff and converting it into Gary Anderson's 26-yard field goal as the first half ended. The Browns pulled within seven points twice, the last time at 20-13 on Matt Stover's 22-yard field goal with 11:18 remaining, but Pittsburgh responded with a 17-play drive that consumed 8:43 and resulted in Gary Anderson's 28-yard field goal for the final points. The Steelers' Barry Foster ran for 103 yards on 26 carries, his twelfth 100-yard effort of the season. That tied Eric Dickerson's NFL record, set in 1984.

	1	2	3	4		
Cleveland	0	3	7	3	—	13
Pittsburgh	7	10	3	3	—	23

Pitt — Foster 7 run (Anderson kick)
Cleve — FG Stover 22
Pitt — Jorden 2 pass from Brister (Anderson kick)
Pitt — FG Anderson 26
Cleve — M. Jackson 38 pass from Tomczak (Stover kick)
Pitt — FG Anderson 29
Cleve — FG Stover 22
Pitt — FG Anderson 28

Kansas City 42, Denver 20—at Arrowhead Stadium, attendance 76,240. The Chiefs' defense accounted for 3 touchdowns and set up a fourth as Kansas City beat the Broncos in a showdown for the final AFC wild-card playoff spot. The Chiefs' managed only 220 total yards, but got big plays from safety Charles Mincy (who took a lateral from teammate Bennie Thompson, who had intercepted a pass, and returned it 32 yards for a touchdown), cornerback Dale Carter (who picked off a pass from John Elway and returned it 36 yards for a score), and linebacker Derrick Thomas (who had 3 sacks, 1 of which resulted in a fumble that he recovered in the end zone for a touchdown). Thomas also recovered a fumble at the Broncos' 13-yard line to set up Dave Krieg's 5-yard touchdown pass to tight end Jonathan Hayes midway through the fourth quarter. Hayes also caught a 12-yard strike from Krieg in the second period.

	1	2	3	4		
Denver	7	0	3	10	—	20
Kansas City	0	14	7	21	—	42

Den — R. Johnson 12 pass from Elway (Treadwell kick)
KC — Hayes 12 pass from Krieg (Lowery kick)
KC — Mincy 32 interception return (Lowery kick)
KC — Carter 36 interception return (Lowery kick)
Den — FG Treadwell 27
Den — FG Treadwell 19
KC — Thomas fumble recovery in end zone (Lowery kick)
KC — Hayes 5 pass from Krieg (Lowery kick)
Den — Lewis 1 run (Treadwell kick)
KC — Okoye 8 run (Lowery kick)

Minnesota 27, Green Bay 7—at Metrodome, attendance 61,461. The Vikings snapped the Packers' six-game winning streak and in the process knocked their division rivals out of the playoffs. After the Redskins were upset by the Raiders the previous day, Green Bay entered this game needing only a victory to clinch the NFC's remaining wild-card berth. But Minnesota, which already had won the Central Division, got a career-high 292 passing yards from Sean Salisbury and 3 interceptions from safety Vencie Glenn to win easily. Salisbury, the four-year veteran making only his fourth career start, completed 20 of 33 passes, including scoring strikes of 13 yards to tight end Steve Jordan and 34 yards to tight end Mike Tice. Terry Allen ran for 100 yards on 20 carries to give him a club-record 1,201 rushing yards for the season. Packers wide receiver Sterling Sharpe caught 6 passes and finished the year with an NFL-record 108 receptions, breaking Redskins wide receiver Art Monk's mark of 106, set in 1984.

	1	2	3	4		
Green Bay	7	0	0	0	—	7
Minnesota	7	13	7	0	—	27

GB — Sydney 2 run (Jacke kick)
Minn — Jordan 13 pass from Salisbury (Reveiz kick)
Minn — FG Reveiz 46
Minn — Tice 34 pass from Salisbury (Reviez kick)
Minn — FG Reveiz 32
Minn — Allen 1 run (Reveiz kick)

Indianapolis 21, Cincinnati 17—at Riverfront Stadium, attendance 47,837. Jack Trudeau came off the bench to throw a pair of second-half touchdowns and rally the Colts from a 17-point deficit to the victory. Derrick Fenner's scoring runs of 12 and 35 yards in the second quarter helped stake the Bengals to a 17-0 advantage at halftime. But Trudeau came on in the third quarter to replace starting quarterback Jeff George, who suffered a concussion while being sacked. Trudeau directed scoring drives of 87 and 84 yards, finishing them off with touchdown passes to Kerry Cash and Bill Brooks, to pull Indianapolis within 17-14 with 11:14 left in the game. Rodney Culver provided the winning points on a 36-yard touchdown run with 7:31 to go. That came four plays after Colts nose tackle Tony Siragusa recovered Cincinnati quarterback Donald Hollas's fumble at the Bengals' 44-yard line. Trudeau finished with 15 completions in 19 attempts for 183 yards, while Culver ran for 92 yards on 14 carries. Indianapolis finished the season at 9-7, a dramatic improvement over its 1-15 disaster of 1991. The Colts' eight-game improvement equaled the second-best one-season turnaround in NFL history.

	1	2	3	4		
Indianapolis	0	0	7	14	—	21
Cincinnati	3	14	0	0	—	17

Cin — FG Breech 25
Cin — Fenner 12 run (Breech kick)
Cin — Fenner 35 run (Breech kick)
Ind — Cash 7 pass from Trudeau (Biasucci kick)
Ind — Brooks 19 pass from Trudeau (Biasucci kick)
Ind — Culver 36 run (Biasucci kick)

Miami 16, New England 13—at Foxboro Stadium, attendance 34,726. Pete Stoyanovich's 35-yard field goal 8:17 into overtime, coupled with the Oilers' victory over the Bills later in the day, gave the Dolphins the AFC Eastern Division title and a first-round bye in the playoffs. The stubborn Patriots made it difficult, however, building a 13-3 advantage on Sam Gash's 1-yard scoring run and a pair of field goals by Charlie Baumann. It was 13-6 when Miami quarterback Dan Marino directed a 75-yard, nine-play drive late in the game, capped by Bobby Humphrey's 1-yard run with 2:53 to play that forced overtime. In the extra session, Marino completed all 3 of his passes for 32 yards as the Dolphins marched from their own 35-yard line to New England's 18 to position Stoyanovich for the winning kick. Marino finished with 217 passing yards, while Humphrey rushed for 88. Scott Lockwood carried 30 times for 123 yards for the Patriots. New England benefited from the return of head coach Dick MacPherson, who was back on the sidelines after missing seven games because of an intestinal ailment.

	1	2	3	4	OT		
Miami	3	0	3	7	3	—	16
New England	7	6	0	0	0	—	13

Mia — FG Stoyanovich 38
NE — Gash 1 run (Baumann kick)
NE — FG Baumann 25
NE — FG Baumann 29
Mia — FG Stoyanovich 23
Mia — Humphrey 1 run (Stoyanovich kick)
Mia — FG Stoyanovich 35

Philadelphia 20, N.Y. Giants 10—at Veterans Stadium, attendance 64,266. The Eagles tuned up for the playoffs by completing their first perfect season at home since 1949. Philadelphia dominated the first half, building a 17-0 advantage while preventing the Giants from making a first down and limiting them to 40 total yards. New York pulled within seven points on Ken Willis's 20-yard field goal and Jeff Hostetler's 13-yard touchdown pass to Ed McCaffrey with 10:05 left in the game, but the Eagles countered with Roger Ruzek's 46-yard field goal for the final points less than three minutes later. Philadelphia's Herschel Walker ran for 104 yards on 16 carries and finished the season with 1,070 yards, his first 1,000-yard season since 1988, when he played for Dallas.

	1	2	3	4		
N.Y. Giants	0	0	3	7	—	10
Philadelphia	7	10	0	3	—	20

Phil — Williams 34 pass from Cunningham (Ruzek kick)
Phil — Cunningham 20 run (Ruzek kick)
Phil — FG Ruzek 45
Giants — FG Willis 20
Giants — McCaffrey 13 pass from Hostetler (Willis kick)
Phil — FG Ruzek 46

San Diego 31, Seattle 14—at Kingdome, attendance 49,324. Backup quarterback Bob Gagliano directed the go-ahead field-goal drive, then the defense took over to secure the Chargers' twelfth victory in the last 13 games and their first AFC West title since 1981. Gagliano, who had not thrown a pass since the third week of the season, took over after starting quarterback Stan Humphries dislocated his left (non-throwing) shoulder late in the first half. San Diego trailed 14-13 until beginning a fourth-quarter drive at its 3-yard line. Gagliano completed passes of 22 yards to Anthony Miller and 19 yards to Shawn Jefferson to position John Carney for a 47-yard field goal that put the Chargers ahead with 5:17 remaining. San Diego then added 15 more points in a span of 1:52: Ronnie Harmon's 5-yard touchdown run three plays after linebacker Gary Plummer intercepted a pass and returned it 38 yards, defensive end Burt Grossman's sack of quarterback Stan Gelbaugh in the end zone for a safety, and safety Darren Carrington's 26-yard interception return for a touchdown. The Seahawks finished 2-14, the worst season in franchise history. They scored only 140 points, the lowest 16-game total in NFL annals, 3 points fewer than the 143 scored by the 1991 Colts.

	1	2	3	4		
San Diego	0	6	7	18	—	31
Seattle	7	0	7	0	—	14

Sea — Warren 30 run (Kasay kick)
SD — FG Carney 31
SD — FG Carney 38
SD — Butts 7 run (Carney kick)
Sea — Junkin 2 pass from Gelbaugh (Kasay kick)
SD — FG Carney 47
SD — Harmon 5 run (Carney kick)
SD — Safety, Grossman sacked Gelbaugh in end zone
SD — Carrington 26 interception return (kick failed)

Tampa Bay 7, Phoenix 3—at Sun Devil Stadium, attendance 29,645. Vinny Testaverde threw a 23-yard pass to Mark Carrier in the second quarter for the game's only touchdown, and cornerback Milton Mack intercepted a pass in the end zone in the closing seconds to preserve the Buccaneers' victory. The game was marred by poor footing on a sloppy field, a factor that contributed to 6 missed field goals, 3 by each team. Tampa Bay's Eddie Murray missed from 40, 33, and 36 yards, while the Cardinals' Greg Davis failed to connect from 47, 43, and 33 yards. Davis did make a 21-yard field goal in the first quarter, and Phoenix still had a chance to win after driving to the Buccaneers' 17-yard line with 17 seconds left. But quarterback Timm Rosenbach replaced Chris Chandler, who was injured while passing, and had his only pass of the day intercepted in the end zone by Mack. It was Mack's second theft of the day, the fifth by Tampa Bay. Testaverde finished with 24 completions in 41 attempts for 228 yards.

	1	2	3	4		
Tampa Bay	0	7	0	0	—	7
Phoenix	3	0	0	0	—	3

Phx — FG G. Davis 21
TB — Carrier 23 pass from Testaverde (Murray kick)

Sunday Night, December 27

Houston 27, Buffalo 3—at Astrodome, attendance 61,742. Cody Carlson and Warren Moon each threw touchdown passes as the Oilers prevented the Bills from winning their fifth consecutive AFC Eastern Division title. Houston, already in the playoffs as a wild-card team, set up a first-round playoff against the Bills in Buffalo the following week because the Bills were knocked into a first-place tie with Miami. Tiebreakers gave the division nod to the Dolphins, while dropping Buffalo to wild-card status. Moon, who had not played in five games because of a broken arm, threw a 17-yard touchdown pass to Haywood Jeffires late in the second quarter to put the Oilers ahead 17-3. Earlier, Cody Carlson had thrown a 13-yard scoring pass to Leonard Harris. The Bills couldn't get back in it after starting quarterback Jim Kelly went down with a sprained knee ligament while being sacked by tackle Ray Childress in the second quarter. Buffalo's Thurman Thomas ran for 97 yards and caught 3 passes for 8 yards to finish the season with an NFL-high 2,113 yards from scrimmage. He led the league in that category for a record fourth consecutive season.

	1	2	3	4		
Buffalo	3	0	0	0	—	3
Houston	10	10	0	7	—	27

Buff — FG Christie 40
Hou — FG Del Greco 28
Hou — L. Harris 13 pass from Carlson (Del Greco kick)
Hou — Jeffires 17 pass from Moon (Del Greco kick)
Hou — FG Del Greco 18
Hou — G. Brown 1 run (Del Greco kick)

Monday, December 28

San Francisco 24, Detroit 6—at Candlestick Park, attendance 55,907. Joe Montana, who hadn't played in a regular-season or playoff game since the NFC Championship Game in January of 1991, completed 15 of 21 passes for 126 yards while directing the 49ers during the second half of their Monday-night victory over the Lions. Montana had been sidelined since the start of the 1991 season while recovering from surgery to repair a torn tendon in his throwing elbow. He led San Francisco to 17 fourth-quarter points, throwing scoring tosses of 9 yards to tight end Brent Jones and 8 yards to running back Amp Lee. He also scrambled for 28 yards on 3 carries, and his first completion (a four-yarder to running back Marc Logan) made him only the fifth player to pass for more than 35,000 yards in his career. Starting quarterback Steve Young passed for 153 yards in the first half before giving way to Montana. Logan's 1-yard touchdown run with 3:14 left in the second quarter gave the 49ers the lead for good.

	1	2	3	4		
Detroit	3	3	0	0	—	6
San Francisco	0	7	0	17	—	24

Det — FG Hanson 44
Det — FG Hanson 50
SF — Logan 1 run (Cofer kick)
SF — FG Cofer 37
SF — Jones 9 pass from Montana (Cofer kick)
SF — Lee 8 pass from Montana (Cofer kick)

Eighteenth Week Summaries

Saturday, January 2, 1993

San Diego 17, Kansas City 0—at San Diego Jack Murphy Stadium, attendance 58,278. Marion Butts broke a scoreless tie with a 54-yard touchdown run in the third quarter and the Chargers ground out a victory over the Chiefs. San Diego, whose lone loss over the final 12 weeks of the regular season came against Kansas City, rushed for 192 yards while limiting the Chiefs to 61. Butts had 119 yards on 15 carries, including his scoring run with 5:53 left in the third quarter. On Kansas City's next possession, Chargers defensive tackle Blaise Winter tipped a Dave Krieg pass, and end Leslie O'Neal intercepted it to set up John Carney's 34-yard field goal. San Diego put the game away in the fourth quarter with a 10-play, 90-yard drive capped by Steve Hendrickson's 5-yard touchdown run with 4:57 left in the game. Hendrickson, a linebacker who doubles as a blocking back in goal-line situations, carried for the first time all year. The Chargers' defense did the rest, limiting the Chiefs to 251 total yards. Krieg passed for 233 yards, but completed only 16 of 34 attempts, was sacked 7 times, and was intercepted twice. San Diego defensive end Burt Grossman had 2½ sacks, while O'Neal and tackle Shawn Lee added 2 each.

	1	2	3	4		
Kansas City	0	0	0	0	—	0
San Diego	0	0	10	7	—	17

SD — Butts 54 run (Carney kick)
SD — FG Carney 34
SD — Hendrickson 5 run (Carney kick)

Washington 24, Minnesota 7—at Metrodome, attendance 57,353. Third-string running back Brian Mitchell ran for 109 yards and added 100 yards on punt returns and receptions as the Redskins, the NFC's lowest seed in the playoffs, upset the Central Division-champion Vikings. Mitchell had carried the ball only 6 times during the regular season and 18 times in his three-year NFL career, but with backup Ricky Ervins injured, he had 16 rushes in this game. The key play was his 36-yard run from Washington's 44-yard line line on a fake punt late in the second quarter. Moments later, he scored on an 8-yard run to increase the Redskins' lead to 17-7 at intermission. Minnesota took the game's opening kickoff and marched 79 yards to a touchdown, Terry Allen's 1-yard run, but then managed only 69 total yards the rest of the way. Quarterback Sean Salisbury completed 42- and 14-yard passes to Cris Carter to key the first drive, but finished only 6 of 20 for 113 yards, with a pair of interceptions. Meanwhile, Washington's offense controlled the ball on the ground, rushing for 196 yards on 47 attempts and maintaining possession for 42:43 of the game's 60 minutes. The Redskins improved their postseason record to 16-4 under head coach Joe Gibbs.

	1	2	3	4		
Washington	3	14	7	0	—	24
Minnesota	7	0	0	0	—	7

Minn — Allen 1 run (Reveiz kick)
Wash — FG Lohmiller 44
Wash — Byner 3 run (Lohmiller kick)
Wash — Mitchell 8 run (Lohmiller kick)
Wash — Clark 24 pass from Rypien (Lohmiller kick)

Sunday, January 3, 1993

Buffalo 41, Houston 38—at Rich Stadium, attendance 75,141. Frank Reich threw 4 second-half touchdown passes and Steve Christie kicked a 32-yard field goal 3:06 into overtime as the Bills mounted the greatest comeback in NFL history to stun the Oilers. Houston led 35-3 after Warren Moon threw 4 first-half touchdown passes and safety Bubba McDowell returned an interception 58 yards for a score 1:41 into the third quarter. Then Reich, who as a collegian had rallied Maryland from a 31-0 halftime deficit to a 42-40 victory over Miami, began the dramatic rally by engineering a 50-yard drive capped by Kenneth Davis's 1-yard run with 8:54 left in the third quarter. Christie recovered his ensuing onside kickoff and Reich's 38-yard touchdown pass four plays later made it 38-17. After a short punt by the Oilers, Reich took only four more plays to march his team 59 yards to a touchdown on his 26-yard pass to Andre Reed. Houston's next possession ended in an interception by Buffalo safety Henry Jones, which set up Reich's 18-yard pass to Reed, the Bills' fourth touchdown in a span of 6:54. It stayed 35-31 until late in the game, when Buffalo drove 74 yards in seven plays. The drive was capped by Reed's third touchdown, a 17-yard throw from Reich that gave the Bills the lead for the first time. Moon rallied the Oilers to a short field goal with 12 seconds left in regulation to tie the score, but was intercepted by cornerback Henry Odomes on the first possession of overtime. Odomes's 2-yard return and a 15-yard facemask penalty on Houston wide receiver Haywood Jeffires positioned Buffalo for the winning field goal three plays later. Reich, subbing for injured starter Jim Kelly, completed 21 of 34 passes for 389 yards, including 8 for 136 yards to Reed. Moon, who was 19 of 22 as the Oilers built their first-half advantage, finished 36 of 50 for 371 yards. Ernest Givins caught 9 passes for 117 yards and Jeffires had 8 receptions for 98 yards and 2 touchdowns. Previously, the largest deficit any NFL team had overcome to win was 28 points, when the 49ers rallied to a 38-35 victory over the Saints after trailing 35-7 in a game in 1980. The largest postseason comeback came when the Lions erased a 27-7 deficit to the 49ers to win 31-27 in a Western Conference playoff in 1957.

	1	2	3	4	OT		
Houston	7	21	7	3	0	—	38
Buffalo	3	0	28	7	3	—	41

Hou — Jeffires 3 pass from Moon (Del Greco kick)
Buff — FG Christie 36
Hou — Slaughter 7 pass from Moon (Del Greco kick)
Hou — Duncan 26 pass from Moon (Del Greco kick)
Hou — Jeffires 27 pass from Moon (Del Greco kick)
Hou — McDowell 58 interception return (Del Greco kick)
Buff — K. Davis 1 run (Christie kick)
Buff — Beebe 38 pass from Reich (Christie kick)
Buff — Reed 26 pass from Reich (Christie kick)
Buff — Reed 18 pass from Reich (Christie kick)
Buff — Reed 17 pass from Reich (Christie kick)
Hou — FG Del Greco 26
Buff — FG Christie 32

Philadelphia 36, New Orleans 20—at Louisiana Superdome, attendance 68,591. The Eagles exploded for 26 points in the fourth quarter to rally past the Saints and win a playoff game for the first time since the 1980 NFL Championship Game. New Orleans, the only NFL team that has never won a postseason game, led 20-7 until Philadelphia's Roger Ruzek kicked a 40-yard field goal late in the third quarter to trim the margin to 10 points. In the fourth period, Randall Cunningham's 35-yard touchdown pass to Fred Barnett with 10:37 remaining sparked an Eagles' scoring frenzy against the Saints, who had allowed the fewest points in the NFL during the regular season and had not permitted any opponent more than 21 points in a game all year. On the first play from scrimmage following Barnett's touchdown, Eagles linebacker Seth Joyner intercepted a Bobby Hebert pass and returned it 14 yards to the Saints' 26-yard line. That set up a 6-yard touchdown run by Heath Sherman for a 24-20 Philadelphia lead with 6:48 left in the game. Seventy-two seconds later, defensive end Reggie White sacked Hebert in the end zone to make it 26-20, and Roger Ruzek's 39-yard field goal at the 2:36 mark made it 29-20. Cornerback Eric Allen sealed the victory 19 seconds later with his second interception of the game, returning it 18 yards for a touchdown. Sherman finished with 105 yards on 21 carries, while Cunningham passed for 219 yards and 2 touchdowns, both to Barnett. Hebert completed 23 of 39 passes for 291 yards and a touchdown, but was intercepted 3 times.

Philadelphia	7	0	3	26	—	36
New Orleans	7	10	3	0	—	20

NO — Heyward 1 run (Andersen kick)
Phil — Barnett 57 pass from Cunningham (Ruzek kick)
NO — FG Andersen 35
NO — Early 7 pass from Hebert (Andersen kick)
NO — FG Andersen 42
Phil — FG Ruzek 40
Phil — Barnett 35 pass from Cunningham (Ruzek kick)
Phil — Sherman 6 run (Ruzek kick)
Phil — Safety, White sacked Hebert in end zone
Phil — FG Ruzek 39
Phil — Allen 18 interception return (Ruzek kick)

Ninteenth Week Summaries

Saturday, January 9, 1993

Buffalo 24, Pittsburgh 3—at Three Rivers Stadium, attendance 60,407. Frank Reich passed for 2 touchdowns to lead the Bills to a methodical victory over the Steelers. Reich, playing for injured starter Jim Kelly, completed 16 of 23 passes for 160 yards and was not intercepted, while running back Kenneth Davis added 104 yards on the ground. Pittsburgh, which led the NFL with 43 takeaways during the regular season, did not register any in this one while turning the ball over 4 times. Trailing 3-0 in the second quarter, Buffalo drove 59 yards to a touchdown after defensive end Phil Hansen recovered Neil O'Donnell's fumble at the Bills' 41-yard line. Reich's 1-yard touchdown pass to tackle-eligible Mitch Frerotte capped that drive and gave Buffalo the lead for good. Reich's 17-yard touchdown pass to James Lofton 11 minutes into the second half gave the Bills all the cushion they would need. O'Donnell, who missed the last three games of the regular season, was rusty in his return, completing 15 of 29 passes for 163 yards, with 2 interceptions. Steelers running back Barry Foster gained 104 yards on 20 carries.

Buffalo	0	7	7	10	—	24
Pittsburgh	3	0	0	0	—	3

Pitt — FG Anderson 38
Buff — Frerotte 1 pass from Reich (Christie kick)
Buff — Lofton 17 pass from Reich (Christie kick)
Buff — FG Christie 43
Buff — Gardner 1 run (Christie kick)

San Francisco 20, Washington 13—at Candlestick Park, attendance 64,991. Steve Young threw 2 touchdown passes and survived 4 turnovers as the 49ers eliminated the Super Bowl XXVI champions. Young completed 20 of 30 passes for 227 yards, including scoring strikes of 5 yards to wide receiver John Taylor and 16 yards to tight end Brent Jones that helped San Francisco build a 17-3 advantage in the first half. But the 49ers' quarterback also lost 3 fumbles, the last of which the Redskins converted into a 15-yard drive capped by quarterback Mark Rypien's 1-yard sneak for a touchdown that trimmed the margin to 17-13 with 14:36 left in the game. Moments later, Washington was driving again, and reached San Francisco's 23-yard line before Rypien fumbled while trying to hand off. The 49ers took over and ate up more than seven minutes on a 59-yard, 14-play drive that culminated in Mike Cofer's 33-yard field goal with 2:22 remaining. Ricky Watters ran for 83 yards and Young added 73 yards on only 8 carries for San Francisco, which amassed 401 total yards. The Redskins had 323 total yards, but also were victimized by 4 turnovers. 49ers defensive end Pierce Holt recorded 3 of his team's 5 sacks.

Washington	3	0	3	7	—	13
San Francisco	7	10	0	3	—	20

SF — Taylor 5 pass from Young (Cofer kick)
Wash — FG Lohmiller 19
SF — FG Cofer 23
SF — Jones 16 pass from Young (Cofer kick)
Wash — FG Lohmiller 32
Wash — Rypien 1 run (Lohmiller kick)
SF — FG Cofer 33

Sunday, January 10, 1993

Dallas 34, Philadelphia 10—at Texas Stadium, attendance 63,721. The Cowboys converted a balanced offense and a stingy defense into an easy victory over the Eagles. Philadelphia took a 3-0 lead on Roger Ruzek's 32-yard field goal 7:15 into the game, but Dallas countered with Troy Aikman's 1-yard touchdown pass to tight end Derek Tennell and never was headed after that. Aikman's second touchdown pass, a 6-yarder to tight end Jay Novacek, gave the Cowboys a 14-3 advantage just 47 seconds before intermission. On the ensuing kickoff, Vai Sikahema fumbled, and Dallas converted the turnover into a 20-yard field goal by Lin Elliott as time ran out in the half. The Cowboys went on to build a 34-3 advantage in the fourth quarter before the Eagles got their lone touchdown in the final minute. Emmitt Smith ran for 114 yards, including a 23-yard touchdown run, as Dallas amassed 160 rushing yards. The Cowboys added 185 yards through the air as Aikman completed 15 of 25 passes. Philadelphia managed only 178 total yards. Randall Cunningham completed 17 of 30 passes, but was sacked 5 times and accumulated most of his 160 yards in the final period, long after the issue had been decided.

Philadelphia	3	0	0	7	—	10
Dallas	7	10	10	7	—	34

Phil — FG Ruzek 32
Dall — Tennell 1 pass from Aikman (Elliott kick)
Dall — Novacek 6 pass from Aikman (Elliott kick)
Dall — FG Elliott 20
Dall — E. Smith 23 run (Elliott kick)
Dall — FG Elliott 43
Dall — Gainer 1 run (Elliott kick)
Phil — C. Williams 18 pass from Cunningham (Ruzek kick)

Miami 31, San Diego 0—at Joe Robbie Stadium, attendance 71,224. Dan Marino threw 3 first-half touchdown passes, including 2 just 79 seconds apart late in the second quarter to break open a close game with the Chargers. Cornerback Troy Vincent's interception and two-yard return to San Diego's 48-yard line set up Miami's first touchdown, a 1-yard pass from Marino to running back Tony Paige 6:30 before halftime. Minutes later, Vincent intercepted another pass, and it took Marino only two plays to put the Dolphins in the end zone again, this time on his 9-yard strike to tight end Keith Jackson with 1:46 left in the half. Chargers quarterback Stan Humphries then was intercepted for the third time in the second quarter, this time by linebacker Bryan Cox, who picked off Humphries's pass and returned it seven yards to the San Diego 42. Marino's 30-yard touchdown pass to Jackson with 27 seconds to go in the half put the game out of reach. Miami controlled the ball on the ground for most of the second half, with Aaron Craver adding a 25-yard touchdown run in the fourth quarter. Craver finished with 72 rushing yards, while Bobby Humphrey had 71. San Diego managed only 10 first downs and 202 total yards, and Humphries suffered 4 interceptions in all. The Chargers entered the game with victories in each of their last eight games and 12 of their last 13.

San Diego	0	0	0	0	—	0
Miami	0	21	0	10	—	31

Mia — Paige 1 pass from Marino (Stoyanovich kick)
Mia — K. Jackson 9 pass from Marino (Stoyanovich kick)
Mia — K. Jackson 30 pass from Marino (Stoyanovich kick)
Mia — FG Stoyanovich 22
Mia — Craver 25 run (Stoyanovich kick)

Twentieth Week Summaries

Sunday, January 17, 1993

Buffalo 29, Miami 10—at Joe Robbie Stadium, attendance 72,703. The Bills forced 5 turnovers en route to an easy victory over the Dolphins. Buffalo thus qualified for its third consecutive Super Bowl, a feat equaled only by Miami, which appeared in games VI, VII, and VIII. The Bills' defense was a big factor in this one, recovering 3 fumbles, intercepting 2 passes, and sacking Dolphins quarterback Dan Marino 4 times. Buffalo's offense, meanwhile, converted the miscues into 13 points, then controlled the ball on the ground, rushing for 182 yards (Miami had only 33) and maintaining possession for 36:19. Kicker Steve Christie kept the Bills comfortably ahead by tying an NFL postseason record with 5 field goals. Thurman Thomas rushed for 96 yards and caught 5 passes for 70 more, including a 17-yard touchdown 40 seconds into the second quarter that broke a 3-3 tie and gave Buffalo the lead for good. It was 13-3 at halftime, and the Bills broke the game open after recovering a fumble at the Dolphins' 24-yard line on the second-half kickoff. Five plays later, Kenneth Davis ran 2 yards for the touchdown that made it 20-3. Jim Kelly, playing for the first time since spraining his knee in Buffalo's final regular-season game, completed 17 of 24 passes for 177 yards, with 2 interceptions. Miami's Dan Marino was 22 of 45 for 268 yards and had 2 passes picked off. His 15-yard touchdown pass to Mark Duper midway through the fourth quarter gave him an NFL record-tying 10 consecutive postseason games with at least 1 touchdown pass.

Buffalo	3	10	10	6	—	29
Miami	3	0	0	7	—	10

Buff — FG Christie 21
Mia — FG Stoyanovich 51
Buff — Thomas 17 pass from Kelly (Christie kick)
Buff — FG Christie 33
Buff — K. Davis 2 run (Christie kick)
Buff — FG Christie 21
Buff — FG Christie 31
Mia — Duper 15 pass from Marino (Stoyanovich kick)
Buff — FG Christie 38

Dallas 30, San Francisco 20—at Candlestick Park, attendance 64,920. Troy Aikman passed for 322 yards and 2 touchdowns and Emmitt Smith rushed for 114 yards as the Cowboys qualified for their first Super Bowl in 14 years and their record sixth overall. Aikman was particularly effective in the second half, completing 13 of 16 passes and directing Dallas on 3 long touchdown drives to clinch the victory. The game was tied at 10-10 at intermission, but Aikman marched the Cowboys 78 yards in eight plays following the second-half kickoff. His 38-yard pass to Alvin Harper moved the ball into 49ers territory, and Daryl Johnston's 4-yard run gave Dallas a lead it would never relinquish. Smith, who also had 7 receptions for 59 yards, caught a 16-yard touchdown pass 2:35 into the fourth quarter to make it 24-13 after the Cowboys had eaten up more than nine minutes off the clock. Steve Young's 5-yard touchdown pass to Jerry Rice pulled San Francisco within 24-20 with 4:22 to go, but Harper turned Aikman's short pass into a back-breaking 70-yard gain on the next play from scrimmage, Three plays later, Aikman teamed with Kelvin Martin on a 6-yard touchdown for the clinching score with 3:43 remaining. The two teams were even in most offensive statistics, including first downs (24 each) and total yards (Dallas had 416, the 49ers 415). But the glaring difference was in turnovers, where San Francisco had 4 and the Cowboys none. Dallas turned 2 fumble recoveries into all 10 of their points in the first half, then intercepted a pair of Young passes as San Francisco tried to rally in the fourth quarter. Young finished with 313 passing yards and Rice caught 8 passes for 123 yards. Harper had 117 yards on only 3 receptions for the Cowboys.

Dallas	3	7	7	13	—	30
San Francisco	7	3	3	7	—	20

Dall — FG Elliott 20
SF — Young 1 run (Cofer kick)
Dall — E. Smith 5 run (Elliott kick)
SF — FG Cofer 28
Dall — Johnston 4 run (Elliott kick)
SF — FG Cofer 42
Dall — E. Smith 16 pass from Aikman (Elliott kick)
SF — Rice 5 pass from Young (Cofer kick)
Dall — K. Martin 6 pass from Aikman (kick failed)

Twenty-First Week Summary

Sunday, January 31, 1993
Super Bowl XXVII
Pasadena, California

Dallas 52, Buffalo 17—at Rose Bowl, attendance 98,374. Troy Aikman threw 4 touchdown passes, Emmitt Smith rushed for 108 yards, and the Cowboys converted 9 turnovers into 35 points while coasting to the victory.

Dallas's win was its third in its record sixth Super Bowl appearance; the Bills became the first team to drop three in succession. Buffalo led 7-0 until the first 2 of its record number of turnovers helped the Cowboys take the lead for good late in the opening quarter. First, Dallas safety James Washington intercepted a Jim Kelly pass and returned it 13 yards to the Bills' 47, setting up Aikman's 23-yard touchdown pass to tight end Jay Novacek with 1:36 remaining in the period. On the next play from scrimmage, Kelly fumbled when sacked by Charles Haley at the Bills' 2-yard line, and the Cowboys' Jimmie Jones picked up the loose ball and ran 2 yards for the touchdown. Dallas, which recovered 5 fumbles and intercepted 4 passes in all, struck just as quickly late in the first half, when Aikman tossed 19- and 18-yard touchdown passes to Michael Irvin 15 seconds apart to give the Cowboys a 28-10 lead at intermission. The second score was set up when Bills running back Thurman Thomas lost a fumble at his own 19-yard line. Buffalo had one last glimpse at the game when backup quarterback Frank Reich, playing because Kelly was injured while attempting to pass midway through the second quarter, threw a 40-yard touchdown pass to Don Beebe on the final play of the third period to trim the deficit to 31-17. But Dallas put the game out of reach by scoring three times in a span of 2:33 of the fourth quarter. Aikman, the game's most valuable player, completed 22 of 30 passes for 273 yards and was not intercepted. Novacek caught 7 passes and Smith and Irvin had 6 each. The Bills' Andre Reed had 8 receptions for 152 yards. The victory was the ninth in succession for NFC teams over AFC teams in the Super Bowl.

Buffalo	7	3	7	0	—	17
Dallas	14	14	3	21	—	52

Buff — Thomas 2 run (Christie kick)
Dall — Novacek 23 pass from Aikman (Elliott kick)
Dall — J. Jones 2 fumble recovery return (Elliott kick)
Buff — FG Christie 21
Dall — Irvin 19 pass from Aikman (Elliott kick)
Dall — Irvin 18 pass from Aikman (Elliott kick)
Dall — FG Elliott 20
Buff — Beebe 40 pass from Reich (Christie kick)
Dall — Harper 45 pass from Aikman (Elliott kick)
Dall — E. Smith 10 run (Elliott kick)
Dall — Norton 9 fumble recovery return (Elliott kick)

Twenty-Second Week Summary

Sunday, February 7, 1993
Pro Bowl
Honolulu, Hawaii

AFC 23, NFC 20—at Aloha Stadium, attendance 50,007. Nick Lowery's 33-yard field goal 4:09 into overtime gave the American Conference all-stars an unlikely 23-20 victory over the National Conference. Despite being overwhelmed by the NFC in first downs (30-9), total yards (472-114), and time of possession (40:19-23:50), the AFC won because it forced 6 turnovers, blocked a pair of field goals (1 of which was returned for a touchdown), and returned an interception for a score. Special-teams star Steve Tasker of the Bills earned the Dan McGuire Trophy as the player of the game for making 4 tackles, forcing a fumble, and blocking a field goal. The block came with eight minutes left in regulation and the game tied at 13-13. The Raiders' Terry McDaniel picked up the loose ball and ran 28 yards for a touchdown and a 20-13 AFC lead. The NFC rallied behind 49ers quarterback Steve Young, whose fourth-down, 23-yard touchdown pass to Giants running back Rodney Hampton tied the game at 20-20 with 10 seconds left in regulation. Young completed 18 of 32 passes for 196 yards but was intercepted 3 times and lost a fumble when sacked in overtime. Raiders defensive end Howie Long fell on that fumble at the NFC 28-yard line, and five plays later, Lowery converted the winning field goal.

AFC	0	10	3	7	3	—	23
NFC	3	10	0	7	0	—	20

NFC — FG Andersen 27
AFC — Seau 31 interception return (Lowery kick)
NFC — FG Andersen 37
NFC — Irvin 9 pass from Aikman (Andersen kick)
AFC — FG Lowery 42
AFC — FG Lowery 29
AFC — McDaniel 28 return of blocked field goal (Lowery kick)
NFC — Hampton 23 pass from Young (Andersen kick)
AFC — FG Lowery 33

1992 Professional Football Awards

	NFL	AFC	NFC
Professional Football Writers of America			
Most Valuable Player	Steve Young		
Rookie of the Year	Dale Carter		
Coach of the Year	Bobby Ross		
Associated Press			
Most Valuable Player	Steve Young		
Offensive Player of the Year	Steve Young		
Defensive Player of the Year	Cortez Kennedy		
Rookie of the Year — Offensive	Carl Pickens		
Rookie of the Year — Defensive	Dale Carter		
Coach of the Year	Bill Cowher		
United Press International			
Offensive Player of the Year		Barry Foster	Steve Young
Defensive Player of the Year		Junior Seau	Chris Doleman
Coach of the Year		Bobby Ross	Dennis Green
Rookie of the Year		Dale Carter	Robert Jones
The Sporting News			
Player of the Year	Steve Young		
Rookie of the Year	Santana Dotson		
Coach of the Year	Bill Cowher		
Football News			
Player of the Year		Barry Foster	Steve Young
Coach of the Year		Bobby Ross	Mike Holmgren
Pro Football Weekly			
Offensive Player of the Year	Steve Young		
Defensive Player of the Year	Cortez Kennedy		
Rookie of the Year — Offensive	Jason Hanson		
Rookie of the Year — Defensive	Dale Carter		
Coach of the Year	Bobby Ross		
Football Digest			
Player of the Year	Steve Young		
Defensive Player of the Year	Junior Seau		
Rookie of the Year — Offensive	Carl Pickens		
Rookie of the Year — Defensive	Santana Dotson		
Coach of the Year	Bobby Ross		
Maxwell Club Player of the Year			
(Bert Bell Trophy)	Steve Young		
Super Bowl XXVII Most Valuable Player			
(Pete Rozelle Trophy)	Troy Aikman		
AFC-NFC Pro Bowl Player of the Game			
(Dan McGuire Award)	Steve Tasker		

AFC-NFC Players of the Week:

	AFC Offense	AFC Defense	NFC Offense	NFC Defense
Week 1	QB John Elway, Den.	LB Chip Banks, Ind.	RB Emmitt Smith, Dall.	DE Chris Doleman, Minn.
Week 2	QB Jim Kelly, Buff.	CB Rod Woodson, Pitt.	QB Vinny Testaverde, T.B.	CB Todd Lyght, Rams
Week 3	RB Eric Metcalf, Clev.	DT Cortez Kennedy, Sea.	WR Michael Irvin, Dall.	LB Johnny Holland, G.B.
Week 4	QB Jim Kelly, Buff.	LB Bryan Cox, Mia.	QB Rich Gannon, Minn.	DT Santana Dotson, T.B.
Week 5	QB John Elway, Den.	S Louis Oliver, Mia.	RB Herschel Walker, Phil.	CB Robert Massey, Phx.
Week 6	QB Dave Krieg, K.C.	CB Terry McDaniel, Raiders	WR Art Monk, Wash.	LB Rickey Jackson, N.O.
Week 7	TE-RB Rod Bernstine, S.D.	DE Anthony Smith, Raiders	WR Jerry Rice, S.F.	LB Wilber Marshall, Wash.
Week 8	QB Stan Humphries, S.D.	DE Steve Emtman, Ind.	RB Emmitt Smith, Dall.	LB Seth Joyner, Phil.
Week 9	QB Ken O'Brien, N.Y.J.	LB Alfred Williams, Cin.	T Erik Williams, Dall.	LB Jack Del Rio, Minn.
Week 10	RB Thurman Thomas, Buff.	LB Derrick Thomas, K.C.	RB Johnny Johnson, Phx.	LB Mike Merriweather, Minn.
Week 11	QB Scott Zolak, N.E.	S Darren Carrington, S.D.	QB Steve Young, S.F.	S Scott Case, Atl.
Week 12	RB Barry Foster, Pitt.	LB James Francis, Cin.	RB Ricky Watters, S.F.	CB Audray McMillian, Minn.
Week 13	QB Cody Carlson, Hou.	LB David Little, Pitt.	WR Jerry Rice, S.F.	S Brad Edwards, Wash.
Week 14	QB Bernie Kosar, Clev.	S Brian Washington, N.Y.J.	QB Jim Everett, Rams	DE Wayne Martin, N.O.
Week 15	RB Thurman Thomas, Buff.	LB Bryan Cox, Mia.	RB Amp Lee, S.F.	S Danny Copeland, Wash.
Week 16	RB Lorenzo White, Hou.	NT Jeff Wright, Buff.	WR Sterling Sharpe, G.B.	LB Seth Joyner, Phil.
Week 17	QB Vince Evans, Raiders	DT Ray Childress, Hou.	RB Emmitt Smith, Dall.	S Vencie Glenn, Minn.

AFC-NFC Players of the Month:

	AFC Offense	AFC Defense	NFC Offense	NFC Defense
Sept.	QB Jim Kelly, Buff.	LB Bryan Cox, Mia.	QB Randall Cunningham, Phil.	DE Chris Doleman, Minn.
Oct.	QB Stan Humphries, S.D.	LB Mike Johnson, Clev.	QB Steve Young, S.F.	LB Wilber Marshall, Wash.
Nov.	RB Barry Foster, Pitt.	DE Chris Mims, S.D.	RB Emmitt Smith, Dall.	LB Tony Bennett, G.B.
Dec.	RB Lorenzo White, Hou.	DE Leslie O'Neal, S.D.	RB Emmitt Smith, Dall.	LB Tim Harris, S.F.

1992 ALL-PRO TEAMS

1992 PFWA All-Pro Teams

Selected by the Professional Football Writers of America

Offense

Jerry Rice, San Francisco .... Wide Receiver
Sterling Sharpe, Green Bay .... Wide Receiver
Jay Novacek, Dallas .... Tight End
Steve Wallace, San Francisco .... Tackle
Harris Barton, San Francisco .... Tackle
Randall McDaniel, Minnesota .... Guard
Steve Wisniewski, Los Angeles Raiders .... Guard
Bruce Matthews, Houston .... Center
Steve Young, San Francisco .... Quarterback
Emmitt Smith, Dallas .... Running Back
Barry Foster, Pittsburgh .... Running Back

Defense

Reggie White, Philadelphia .... End
Chris Doleman, Minnesota .... End
Cortez Kennedy, Seattle .... Tackle
Ray Childress, Houston .... Tackle
Rickey Jackson, New Orleans .... Outside Linebacker
Wilber Marshall, Washington .... Outside Linebacker
Sam Mills, New Orleans .... Inside Linebacker
Junior Seau, San Diego .... Inside Linebacker
Audray McMillian, Minnesota .... Cornerback
Rod Woodson, Pittsburgh .... Cornerback
Henry Jones, Buffalo .... Safety
Steve Atwater, Denver .... Safety

Specialists

Morten Andersen, New Orleans .... Kicker
Rich Camarillo, Phoenix .... Punter
Deion Sanders, Atlanta .... Kick Returner
Kelvin Martin, Dallas .... Punt Returner
Steve Tasker, Buffalo .... Special Teamer

1992 Associated Press All-Pro Team

Offense

Sterling Sharpe, Green Bay .... Wide Receiver
Jerry Rice, San Francisco .... Wide Receiver
Jay Novacek, Dallas .... Tight End
Harris Barton, San Francisco .... Tackle
Richmond Webb, Miami .... Tackle
Randall McDaniel, Minnesota .... Guard
Steve Wisniewski, Los Angeles Raiders .... Guard
Bruce Matthews, Houston .... Center
Steve Young, San Francisco .... Quarterback
Emmitt Smith, Dallas .... Running Back
Barry Foster, Pittsburgh .... Running Back
Pete Stoyanovich, Miami .... Kicker
Deion Sanders, Atlanta .... Kick Returner

Defense

Clyde Simmons, Philadelphia .... End
Chris Doleman, Minnesota .... End
Cortez Kennedy, Seattle .... Tackle
Ray Childress, Houston .... Nose Tackle
Wilber Marshall, Washington .... Outside Linebacker
Pat Swilling, New Orleans .... Outside Linebacker
Junior Seau, San Diego .... Inside Linebacker
Al Smith, Houston .... Inside Linebacker
Rod Woodson, Pittsburgh .... Cornerback
Audray McMillian, Minnesota .... Cornerback
Henry Jones, Buffalo .... Safety
Steve Atwater, Denver .... Safety
Rich Camarillo, Phoenix .... Punter

1992 All-NFL Team

Selected by the Associated Press and Professional Football Writers of America

Offense

Jerry Rice, San Francisco (AP, PFWA) .... Wide Receiver
Sterling Sharpe, Green Bay (AP, PFWA) .... Wide Receiver
Jay Novacek, Dallas (AP, PFWA) .... Tight End
Harris Barton, San Francisco (AP, PFWA) .... Tackle
Richmond Webb, Miami (AP) .... Tackle
Steve Wallace, San Francisco (PFWA) .... Tackle
Randall McDaniel, Minnesota (AP, PFWA) .... Guard
Steve Wisniewski, Los Angeles Raiders (AP, PFWA) .... Guard
Bruce Matthews, Houston (AP, PFWA) .... Center
Steve Young, San Francisco (AP, PFWA) .... Quarterback
Emmitt Smith, Dallas (AP, PFWA) .... Running Back
Barry Foster, Pittsburgh (AP, PFWA) .... Running Back

Defense

Chris Doleman, Minnesota (AP, PFWA) .... Defensive End
Clyde Simmons, Philadelphia (AP) .... Defensive End
Reggie White, Philadelphia (PFWA) .... Defensive End
Cortez Kennedy, Seattle (AP, PFWA) .... Defensive Tackle
Ray Childress, Houston (AP, PFWA) .... Defensive Tackle
Wilber Marshall, Washington (AP, PFWA) .... Outside Linebacker
Pat Swilling, New Orleans (AP) .... Outside Linebacker
Rickey Jackson, New Orleans (PFWA) .... Outside Linebacker
Junior Seau, San Diego (AP, PFWA) .... Inside Linebacker
Al Smith, Houston (AP) .... Inside Linebacker
Sam Mills, New Orleans (PFWA) .... Inside Linebacker
Rod Woodson, Pittsburgh (AP, PFWA) .... Cornerback
Audray McMillian, Minnesota (AP, PFWA) .... Cornerback
Henry Jones, Buffalo (AP, PFWA) .... Safety
Steve Atwater, Denver (AP, PFWA) .... Safety

Specialists

Pete Stoyanovich, Miami (AP) .... Kicker
Morten Andersen, New Orleans (PFWA) .... Kicker
Rich Camarillo, Phoenix (AP, PFWA) .... Punter
Deion Sanders, Atlanta (AP, PFWA) .... Kick Returner
Kelvin Martin, Dallas (PFWA) .... Punt Returner
Steve Tasker, Buffalo (PFWA) .... Special Teamer

1992 UPI All-AFC Team

Selected by United Press International

Offense

Anthony Miller, San Diego . . . Wide Receiver
Haywood Jeffires, Houston . . . Wide Receiver
Keith Jackson, Miami . . . Tight End
Richmond Webb, Miami . . . Tackle
Howard Ballard, Buffalo . . . Tackle
Mike Munchak, Houston . . . Guard
Carlton Haselrig, Pittsburgh . . . Guard
Bruce Matthews, Houston . . . Center
Dan Marino, Miami . . . Quarterback
Thurman Thomas, Buffalo . . . Running Back
Barry Foster, Pittsburgh . . . Running Back

Defense

Bruce Smith, Buffalo . . . End
Leslie O'Neal, San Diego . . . End
Cortez Kennedy, Seattle . . . Tackle
Bryan Cox, Miami . . . Outside Linebacker
Derrick Thomas, Kansas City . . . Outside Linebacker
Junior Seau, San Diego . . . Inside Linebacker
Vincent Brown, New England . . . Inside Linebacker
Rod Woodson, Pittsburgh . . . Cornerback
Gill Byrd, San Diego . . . Cornerback
Henry Jones, Buffalo . . . Safety
Louis Oliver, Miami . . . Safety

Specialists

Pete Stoyanovich, Miami . . . Kicker
Greg Montgomery, Houston . . . Punter
Clarence Verdin, Indianapolis . . . Kick Returner

1992 UPI All-NFC Team

Selected by United Press International

Offense

Jerry Rice, San Francisco . . . Wide Receiver
Sterling Sharpe, Green Bay . . . Wide Receiver
Jay Novacek, Dallas . . . Tight End
Gary Zimmerman, Minnesota . . . Tackle
Steve Wallace, San Francisco . . . Tackle
Nate Newton, Dallas . . . Guard
Guy McIntyre, San Francisco . . . Guard
Mark Stepnoski, Dallas . . . Center
Steve Young, San Francisco . . . Quarterback
Barry Sanders, Detroit . . . Running Back
Emmitt Smith, Dallas . . . Running Back

Defense

Reggie White, Philadelphia . . . End
Chris Doleman, Minnesota . . . End
Pierce Holt, San Francisco . . . Tackle
Rickey Jackson, New Orleans . . . Outside Linebacker
Wilber Marshall, Washington . . . Outside Linebacker
Sam Mills, New Orleans . . . Inside Linebacker
Vaughan Johnson, New Orleans . . . Inside Linebacker
Audray McMillian, Minnesota . . . Cornerback
Eric Allen, Philadelphia . . . Cornerback
Todd Scott, Minnesota . . . Safety
Brad Edwards, Washington . . . Safety

Specialists

Morten Andersen, New Orleans . . . Kicker
Rich Camarillo, Phoenix . . . Punter
Johnny Bailey, Phoenix . . . Kick Returner

1992 PFWA All-Rookie Team

Selected by the Professional Football Writers of America

Offense

Carl Pickens, Cincinnati . . . Wide Receiver
Arthur Marshall, Denver . . . Wide Receiver
Johnny Mitchell, New York Jets . . . Tight End
Troy Auzenne, Chicago . . . Tackle
Eugene Chung, New England . . . Tackle
No Selection . . . Guard
Matt Elliott, Washington . . . Center
David Klingler, Cincinnati . . . Quarterback
Amp Lee, San Francisco . . . Running Back
Vaughn Dunbar, New Orleans . . . Running Back

Defense

Santana Dotson, Tampa Bay . . . End
Chris Mims, San Diego . . . End
Steve Emtman, Indianapolis . . . Tackle
Sean Gilbert, Los Angeles Rams . . . Tackle
Quentin Coryatt, Indianapolis . . . Outside Linebacker
Marco Coleman, Miami . . . Outside Linebacker
Robert Jones, Dallas . . . Inside Linebacker
Ricardo McDonald, Cincinnati . . . Inside Linebacker
Dale Carter, Kansas City . . . Cornerback
Troy Vincent, Miami . . . Cornerback
Dana Hall, San Francisco . . . Safety
Darren Perry, Pittsburgh . . . Safety

Specialists

Jason Hanson, Detroit . . . Kicker
Klaus Wilmsmeyer, San Francisco . . . Punter
Desmond Howard, Washington . . . Kickoff Returner
Dale Carter, Kansas City . . . Punt Returner
Darren Woodson, Dallas . . . Special Teamer

Ten Best Rushing Performances, 1992

		Attempts	Yards	TD
1.	Barry Foster Pittsburgh vs. N.Y. Jets, September 13	33	190	2
	Harold Green Cincinnati vs. New England, December 20	31	190	1
3.	Kenneth Davis Buffalo vs. Atlanta, November 22	20	181	2
4.	Emmitt Smith Dallas vs. Atlanta, December 21	24	174	2
5.	Terry Allen Minnesota vs. Pittsburgh, December 20	33	172	0
6.	Barry Foster Pittsburgh vs. Indianapolis, November 22	28	168	2
7.	Rodney Hampton N.Y. Giants vs. Phoenix, October 11	21	167	1
8.	Emmitt Smith Dallas vs. Philadelphia, November 1	30	163	0
	Ricky Watters San Francisco vs. L.A. Rams, November 22	26	163	2
10.	Johnny Johnson Phoenix vs. N.Y. Giants, December 12	36	156	2

100-Yard Rushing Performances, 1992

First Week

Terry Allen, Minnesota	140 yards vs. Green Bay
Emmitt Smith, Dallas	140 yards vs. Washington
Harold Green, Cincinnati	123 yards vs. Seattle
Herschel Walker, Philadelphia	114 yards vs. New Orleans
Barry Sanders, Detroit	109 yards vs. Chicago
Barry Foster, Pittsburgh	107 yards vs. Houston
Thurman Thomas, Buffalo	103 yards vs. L.A. Rams
Ricky Watters, San Francisco	100 yards vs. N.Y. Giants
Lorenzo White, Houston	100 yards vs. Pittsburgh

Second Week

Barry Foster, Pittsburgh	190 yards vs. N.Y. Jets
Herschel Walker, Philadelphia	115 yards vs. Phoenix

Third Week

Chris Warren, Seattle	122 yards vs. New England
Earnest Byner, Washington	120 yards vs. Detroit
Barry Word, Kansas City	114 yards vs. Houston
Emmitt Smith, Dallas	112 yards vs. Phoenix
Mark Higgs, Miami	111 yards vs. L.A. Rams
Harold Green, Cincinnati	101 yards vs. Green Bay

Fourth Week

Barry Word, Kansas City	125 yards vs. L.A. Raiders
Thurman Thomas, Buffalo	120 yards vs. New England
Barry Foster, Pittsburgh	117 yards vs. Green Bay
Reggie Cobb, Tampa Bay	107 yards vs. Detroit

Fifth Week

Cleveland Gary, L.A. Rams	110 yards vs. San Francisco

Sixth Week

Rodney Hampton, N.Y. Giants	167 yards vs. Phoenix
Lorenzo White, Houston	149 yards vs. Cincinnati
Ricky Watters, San Francisco	104 yards vs. New England

Seventh Week

Rod Bernstine, San Diego	150 yards vs. Indianapolis
Cleveland Gary, L.A. Rams	126 yards vs. N.Y. Giants
Reggie Cobb, Tampa Bay	109 yards vs. Chicago
Barry Foster, Pittsburgh	108 yards vs. Cincinnati

Eighth Week

Emmitt Smith, Dallas	152 yards vs. L.A. Raiders
Thurman Thomas, Buffalo	142 yards vs. N.Y. Jets
Barry Sanders, Detroit	122 yards vs. Tampa Bay
Herschel Walker, Philadelphia	112 yards vs. Phoenix
Barry Foster, Pittsburgh	105 yards vs. Kansas City

Ninth Week

Emmitt Smith, Dallas	163 yards vs. Philadelphia
Cleveland Gary, L.A. Rams	144 yards vs. Atlanta
Rodney Hampton, N.Y. Giants	138 yards vs. Washington
Marion Butts, San Diego	120 yards vs. Indianapolis
Barry Foster, Pittsburgh	118 yards vs. Houston
Brad Baxter, N.Y. Jets	103 yards vs. Miami
Johnny Johnson, Phoenix	102 yards vs. San Francisco
Vince Workman, Green Bay	101 yards vs. Detroit

Tenth Week

Thurman Thomas, Buffalo	155 yards vs. Pittsburgh
Harold Green, Cincinnati	117 yards vs. Chicago
Barry Sanders, Detroit	108 yards vs. Dallas
Mark Higgs, Miami	107 yards vs. Indianapolis
Chris Warren, Seattle	103 yards vs. Washington

Eleventh Week

Ricky Watters, San Francisco	115 yards vs. New Orleans
Reggie Cobb, Tampa Bay	114 yards vs. Chicago
Cleveland Gary, L.A. Rams	110 yards vs. Dallas
Barry Foster, Pittsburgh	106 yards vs. Detroit

Twelfth Week

Kenneth Davis, Buffalo	181 yards vs. Atlanta
Barry Foster, Pittsburgh	168 yards vs. Indianapolis
Ricky Watters, San Francisco	163 yards vs. L.A. Rams
Chris Warren, Seattle	154 yards vs. Kansas City
Barry Sanders, Detroit	151 yards vs. Cincinnati
Jon Vaughn, New England	110 yards vs. N.Y. Jets
Heath Sherman, Philadelphia	109 yards vs. N.Y. Giants
Edgar Bennett, Green Bay	107 yards vs. Chicago
Eric Dickerson, L.A. Raiders	107 yards vs. Denver
Marion Butts, San Diego	104 yards vs. Tampa Bay
Thurman Thomas, Buffalo	103 yards vs. Atlanta

Thirteenth Week

Emmitt Smith, Dallas	120 yards vs. N.Y. Giants
Harold Green, Cincinnati	116 yards vs. Pittsburgh
Eric Dickerson, L.A. Raiders	103 yards vs. San Diego
Barry Foster, Pittsburgh	102 yards vs. Cincinnati
Thurman Thomas, Buffalo	102 yards vs. Indianapolis

Fourteenth Week

Barry Foster, Pittsburgh	125 yards vs. Seattle
Randall Cunningham, Phil.	121 yards vs. Minnesota
Thurman Thomas, Buffalo	116 yards vs. N.Y. Jets
Lorenzo White, Houston	116 yards vs. Chicago
Barry Sanders, Detroit	114 yards vs. Green Bay
Earnest Byner, Washington	100 yards vs. N.Y. Giants
Reggie Cobb, Tampa Bay	100 yards vs. L.A. Rams

Fifteenth Week

Johnny Johnson, Phoenix	156 yards vs. N.Y. Giants
Amp Lee, San Francisco	134 yards vs. Minnesota
Thurman Thomas, Buffalo	120 yards vs. Denver
Herschel Walker, Philadelphia	111 yards vs. Seattle

Sixteenth Week

Harold Green, Cincinnati	190 yards vs. New England
Emmitt Smith, Dallas	174 yards vs. Atlanta
Terry Allen, Minnesota	172 yards vs. Pittsburgh
Johnny Johnson, Phoenix	146 yards vs. Indianapolis
Barry Foster, Pittsburgh	118 yards vs. Minnesota
Thurman Thomas, Buffalo	115 yards vs. New Orleans
Barry Sanders, Detroit	113 yards vs. Chicago

Seventeenth Week

Emmitt Smith, Dallas	131 yards vs. Chicago
Scott Lockwood, New England	123 yards vs. Miami
Barry Sanders, Detroit	104 yards vs. San Francisco
Herschel Walker, Philadelphia	104 yards vs. N.Y. Giants
Barry Foster, Pittsburgh	103 yards vs. Cleveland
Terry Allen, Minnesota	100 yards vs. Green Bay

Times 100 or More (91)
Foster, 12; T. Thomas, 9; B. Sanders, E. Smith, 7; H. Green, H. Walker, 5; Cobb, Gary, Watters, 4; J. Johnson, Warren, L. White, 3; Allen, Butts, Byner, Dickerson, Hampton, Higgs, Word, 2.

Ten Best Passing Performances, 1992

		Att.	Comp.	Yards	TD
1.	Steve Young San Francisco vs. Buffalo, September 13	37	26	449	3
2.	Jim Kelly Buffalo vs. San Francisco, September 13	33	22	403	3
3.	Steve Young San Francisco vs. Atlanta, October 18	28	18	399	3
4.	Todd Marinovich L.A. Raiders vs. Cleveland, September 20	59	33	395	1
5.	Chris Chandler Phoenix vs. Dallas, September 20	43	28	383	1
6.	Browning Nagle New York Jets vs. Atlanta, September 6	37	21	381	2
7.	Jay Schroeder L.A. Raiders vs. Cincinnati, September 13	40	25	380	2
8.	Randall Cunningham Philadelphia vs. Seattle, December 13	44	27	365	0
9.	Wade Wilson Atlanta vs. L.A. Rams, December 27	47	31	374	3
10.	Vinny Testaverde Tampa Bay vs. Green Bay, September 13	25	22	363	2

300-Yard Passing Performances, 1992

First Week
Browning Nagle, N.Y. Jets — 381 yards vs. Atlanta
Warren Moon, Houston — 330 yards vs. Pittsburgh

Second Week
Steve Young, San Francisco — 449 yards vs. Buffalo
Jim Kelly, Buffalo — 403 yards vs. San Francisco
Jay Schroeder, L.A. Raiders — 380 yards vs. Cincinnati
Vinny Testaverde, Tampa Bay — 363 yards vs. Green Bay
Warren Moon, Houston — 361 yards vs. Indianapolis
Dan Marino, Miami — 322 yards vs. Cleveland

Third Week
Todd Marinovich, L.A. Raiders — 395 yards vs. Cleveland
Chris Chandler, Phoenix — 383 yards vs. Dallas

Fourth Week
Chris Miller, Atlanta — 351 yards vs. Chicago
Rodney Peete, Detroit — 323 yards vs. Tampa Bay
Rich Gannon, Minnesota — 318 yards vs. Cincinnati
Jim Kelly, Buffalo — 308 yards vs. New England

Fifth Week
John Elway, Denver — 311 yards vs. Kansas City
Jim Kelly, Buffalo — 306 yards vs. Miami
Dave Krieg, Kansas City — 301 yards vs. Denver

Sixth Week
Jim Kelly, Buffalo — 302 yards vs. L.A. Raiders

Seventh Week
Steve Young, San Francisco — 399 yards vs. Atlanta
Bobby Hebert, New Orleans — 355 yards vs. Phoenix
Warren Moon, Houston — 321 yards vs. Denver
Jeff George, Indianapolis — 318 yards vs. San Diego
Jim Harbaugh, Chicago — 304 yards vs. Tampa Bay

Eighth Week
Dan Marino, Miami — 355 yards vs. Indianapolis
Stan Humphries, San Diego — 349 yards vs. Denver
Warren Moon, Houston — 342 yards vs. Cincinnati

Ninth Week
None

Tenth Week
None

Eleventh Week
Jeff George, Indianapolis — 330 yards vs. New England
Mike Tomczak, Cleveland — 322 yards vs. San Diego
Dan Marino, Miami — 321 yards vs. Buffalo
Erik Kramer, Detroit — 304 yards vs. Pittsburgh
Dave Krieg, Kansas City — 302 yards vs. Washington
Bobby Hebert, New Orleans — 301 yards vs. San Francisco

Twelfth Week
None

Thirteenth Week
Steve Young, San Francisco — 342 yards vs. Philadelphia
Cody Carlson, Houston — 338 yards vs. Detroit
Jack Trudeau, Indianapolis — 337 yards vs. Buffalo

Fourteenth Week
Jim Everett, L.A. Rams — 342 yards vs. Tampa Bay

Fifteenth Week
Randall Cunningham, Phil. — 365 yards vs. Seattle
Cody Carlson, Houston — 330 yards vs. Green Bay
Wade Wilson, Atlanta — 324 yards vs. Tampa Bay

Sixteenth Week
Wade Wilson, Atlanta — 342 yards vs. Dallas
Jeff George, Indianapolis — 328 yards vs. Phoenix

Seventeenth Week
Wade Wilson, Atlanta — 374 yards vs. L.A. Rams

Times 300 or More (42)
Kelly, Moon, 4; George, Marino, Wilson, Young, 3; Carlson, Hebert, Krieg, 2.

Ten Best Receiving Performances, 1992

	Yards	No.	TD
1. Michael Irvin Dallas vs. Phoenix, September 20	210	8	3
2. Jerry Rice San Francisco vs. Atlanta, October 18	183	7	2
3. Eric Metcalf Cleveland vs. L.A. Raiders, September 20	177	5	3
Andre Rison Atlanta vs. Chicago, September 27	177	10	3
5. Andre Reed Buffalo vs. New England, September 27	168	9	1
Michael Irvin Dallas vs. L.A. Rams, November 15	168	8	0
7. Willie Davis Kansas City vs. Philadelphia, October 11	167	5	1
8. Irving Fryar New England vs. N.Y. Jets, October 4	165	8	2
9. Anthony Johnson Indianapolis vs. New England, November 15	163	7	0
10. Fred Barnett Philadelphia vs. Seattle, December 13	161	9	0

100-Yard Receiving Performances, 1992

(Number in parentheses is receptions.)

First Week

Haywood Jeffires, Houston — 117 yards (7) vs. Pittsburgh
Willie Green, Detroit — 114 yards (5) vs. Chicago
Rob Carpenter, N.Y. Jets — 109 yards (6) vs. Atlanta

Second Week

Fred Barnett, Philadelphia — 193 yards (8) vs. Phoenix
Mike Sherrard, San Francisco — 159 yards (6) vs. Buffalo
Jeff Graham, Pittsburgh — 146 yards (6) vs. N.Y. Jets
Andre Reed, Buffalo — 144 yards (10) vs. San Francisco
Mark Carrier, Tampa Bay — 115 yards (7) vs. Green Bay
Pete Metzelaars, Buffalo — 113 yards (4) vs. San Francisco
John Taylor, San Francisco — 112 yards (5) vs. Buffalo
Randal Hill, Phoenix — 109 yards (5) vs. Philadelphia
Lawrence Dawsey, Tampa Bay — 107 yards (7) vs. Green Bay
Lorenzo White, Houston — 106 yards (4) vs. Indianapolis
Tim Brown, L.A. Raiders — 104 yards (6) vs. Cincinnati

Third Week

Michael Irvin, Dallas — 210 yards (8) vs. Phoenix
Eric Metcalf, Cleveland — 177 yards (5) vs. L.A. Raiders
Sam Graddy, L.A. Raiders — 114 yards (6) vs. Cleveland
Terance Mathis, N.Y. Jets — 111 yards (4) vs. San Francisco
Stephen Baker, N.Y. Giants — 109 yards (7) vs. Chicago
Sterling Sharpe, Green Bay — 109 yards (7) vs. Cincinnati
Calvin Williams, Philadelphia — 108 yards (5) vs. Denver
Fred Barnett, Philadelphia — 102 yards (5) vs. Denver
Irving Fryar, New England — 101 yards (6) vs. Seattle

Fourth Week

Andre Rison, Atlanta — 177 yards (10) vs. Chicago
Andre Reed, Buffalo — 168 yards (9) vs. New England
Cris Carter, Minnesota — 124 yards (11) vs. Cincinnati
Brett Perriman, Detroit — 117 yards (9) vs. Tampa Bay
James Lofton, Buffalo — 113 yards (4) vs. New England
Dwight Stone, Pittsburgh — 101 yards (5) vs. Green Bay

Fifth Week

Irving Fryar, New England — 165 yards (8) vs. N.Y. Jets
Anthony Miller, San Diego — 142 yards (9) vs. Seattle
Willie Davis, Kansas City — 127 yards (5) vs. Denver
Shannon Sharpe, Denver — 118 yards (9) vs. Kansas City
Sterling Sharpe, Green Bay — 107 yards (9) vs. Atlanta
Gary Clark, Washington — 106 yards (4) vs. Phoenix
Michael Irvin, Dallas — 105 yards (4) vs. Philadelphia

Sixth Week

Willie Davis, Kansas City — 167 yards (5) vs. Philadelphia
Ernie Jones, Phoenix — 125 yards (6) vs. N.Y. Giants
Michael Irvin, Dallas — 113 yards (6) vs. Seattle
Eric Martin, New Orleans — 103 yards (6) vs. L.A. Rams
Andre Rison, Atlanta — 101 yards (7) vs. Miami

Seventh Week

Jerry Rice, San Francisco — 183 yards (7) vs. Atlanta
Eric Martin, New Orleans — 151 yards (8) vs. Phoenix
Curtis Duncan, Houston — 133 yards (5) vs. Denver
Brett Perriman, Detroit — 124 yards (8) vs. Minnesota
Anthony Carter, Minnesota — 109 yards (5) vs. Detroit
Jeff Graham, Pittsburgh — 115 yards (7) vs. Cincinnati
Tom Waddle, Chicago — 114 yards (3) vs. Tampa Bay
Jessie Hester, Indianapolis — 105 yards (9) vs. San Diego
Courtney Hawkins, Tampa Bay — 102 yards (5) vs. Chicago
Willie Davis, Kansas City — 100 yards (6) vs. Dallas

Eighth Week

Sterling Sharpe, Green Bay — 144 yards (9) vs. Chicago
Anthony Miller, San Diego — 129 yards (6) vs. Denver
Mark Jackson, Denver — 113 yards (5) vs. San Diego
Herman Moore, Detroit — 108 yards (3) vs. Tampa Bay
Don Beebe, Buffalo — 106 yards (6) vs. N.Y. Jets
Derrick Walker, San Diego — 104 yards (4) vs. Denver
Ernest Givins, Houston — 100 yards (8) vs. Cincinnati

Ninth Week

Anthony Miller, San Diego — 105 yards (6) vs. Indianapolis

Tenth Week

Sterling Sharpe, Green Bay — 160 yards (11) vs. N.Y. Giants
Arthur Marshall, Denver — 134 yards (5) vs. N.Y. Jets
Ricky Proehl, Phoenix — 126 yards (9) vs. L.A. Rams
Michael Irvin, Dallas — 114 yards (5) vs. Detroit
Don Beebe, Buffalo — 101 yards (8) vs. Pittsburgh

Eleventh Week

Michael Irvin, Dallas — 168 yards (8) vs. L.A. Rams
Anthony Johnson, Indianapolis — 163 yards (7) vs. New England
Lawyer Tillman, Cleveland — 148 yards (8) vs. San Diego
Tim Barnett, Kansas City — 148 yards (6) vs. Washington
Sterling Sharpe, Green Bay — 116 yards (7) vs. Philadelphia
Willie Green, Detroit — 115 yards (6) vs. Pittsburgh
Anthony Miller, San Diego — 110 yards (7) vs. Cleveland
Mark Jackson, Denver — 108 yards (3) vs. N.Y. Giants
Mark Duper, Miami — 100 yards (5) vs. Buffalo

Twelfth Week

Wendell Davis, Chicago — 106 yards (8) vs. Green Bay

Thirteenth Week

Jerry Rice, San Francisco — 133 yards (8) vs. Philadelphia
Don Beebe, Buffalo — 110 yards (4) vs. Indianapolis
Terry Allen, Minnesota — 110 yards (10) vs. L.A. Rams
Charles Arbuckle, Indianapolis — 106 yards (9) vs. Buffalo
Ed McCaffrey, N.Y. Giants — 105 yards (6) vs. Dallas
Ricky Proehl, Phoenix — 104 yards (7) vs. Washington
Ernest Givins, Houston — 100 yards (4) vs. Detroit
Tom Waddle, Chicago — 100 yards (4) vs. Cleveland

Fourteenth Week

Herman Moore, Detroit — 114 yards (8) vs. Green Bay
Ricky Proehl, Phoenix — 112 yards (6) vs. San Diego
Sterling Sharpe, Green Bay — 107 yards (6) vs. Detroit

Fifteenth Week

Fred Barnett, Philadelphia — 161 yards (9) vs. Seattle
Michael Haynes, Atlanta — 113 yards (5) vs. Tampa Bay
Chris Burkett, N.Y. Jets — 110 yards (6) vs. Indianapolis
Shannon Sharpe, Denver — 109 yards (7) vs. Buffalo
Michael Irvin, Dallas — 105 yards (5) vs. Washington
Don Beebe, Buffalo — 104 yards (4) vs. Denver
Kerry Cash, Indianapolis — 104 yards (7) vs. N.Y. Jets
Curtis Duncan, Houston — 100 yards (6) vs. Green Bay

Sixteenth Week

Jerry Rice, San Francisco	118 yards (7) vs. Tampa Bay
Ricky Sanders, Washington	114 yards (7) vs. Philadelphia
Sterling Sharpe, Green Bay	110 yards (8) vs. L.A. Rams
Herman Moore, Detroit	108 yards (3) vs. Chicago
Mike Pritchard, Atlanta	105 yards (9) vs. Dallas
Lorenzo White, Houston	105 yards (6) vs. Cleveland
Michael Haynes, Atlanta	100 yards (5) vs. Dallas

Seventeenth Week

Drew Hill, Atlanta	107 yards (8) vs. L.A. Rams
Brian Blades, Seattle	103 yards (6) vs. San Diego

Times 100 or More (102)
Sterling Sharpe, 7; Irvin, 6; Beebe, Miller, 4; Barnett, W. Davis, Moore, Proehl, Rice, 3; A. Carter, K. Davis, Duncan, Fryar, Green, Givins, Graham, M. Haynes, M. Jackson, E. Martin, Perriman, Rison, Reed, Shannon Sharpe, Waddle, L. White, 2.

Top Quarterback Sack Performances, 1992

(2.5 or More Sacks Per Game Needed to Qualify)

First Week

Chip Banks, Indianapolis	4.0 vs. Cleveland

Second Week

Kevin Greene, L.A. Rams	3.0 vs. New England
Clyde Simmons, Philadelphia	3.0 vs. Phoenix
Mike Croel, Denver	2.5 vs. San Diego

Third Week

Tim Harris, San Francisco	3.0 vs. N.Y. Jets
Cortez Kennedy, Seattle	2.5 vs. New England
Bruce Smith, Buffalo	2.5 vs. Indianapolis
Broderick Thomas, Tampa Bay	2.5 vs. Minnesota

Fourth Week

None

Fifth Week

Neil Smith, Kansas City	3.0 vs. Denver

Sixth Week

Rickey Jackson, New Orleans	3.0 vs. L.A. Rams
Derrick Thomas, Kansas City	3.0 vs. Philadelphia

Seventh Week

Anthony Smith, L.A. Raiders	4.0 vs. Seattle
Simon Fletcher, Denver	2.5 vs. Houston

Eighth Week

None

Ninth Week

John Randle, Minnesota	3.0 vs. Chicago
Cornelius Bennett, Buffalo	2.5 vs. New England

Tenth Week

Derrick Thomas, Kansas City	4.0 vs. San Diego
Tony Bennett, Green Bay	2.5 vs. N.Y. Giants

Eleventh Week

Neil Smith, Kansas City	3.0 vs. Washington
John Randle, Minnesota	2.5 vs. Houston

Twelfth Week

Reggie White, Philadelphia	3.5 vs. N.Y. Giants
Chris Mims, San Diego	3.0 vs. Tampa Bay

Thirteenth Week

Simon Fletcher, Denver	3.5 vs. Seattle
Sean Jones, Houston	3.0 vs. Detroit
David Little, Pittsburgh	3.0 vs. Cincinnati

Fourteenth Week

Wayne Martin, New Orleans	4.5 vs. Atlanta
Duane Bickett, Indianapolis	3.5 vs. New England
Andy Harmon, Philadelphia	3.0 vs. Minnesota
Leslie O'Neal, San Diego	3.0 vs. Phoenix

Fifteenth Week

Al Noga, Minnesota	3.0 vs. San Francisco
James Blackmon, Seattle	2.5 vs. Philadelphia
Tim Harris, San Francisco	2.5 vs. Minnesota
Rufus Porter, Seattle	2.5 vs. Philadelphia

Sixteenth Week

None

Seventeenth Week

Tim Harris, San Francisco	3.0 vs. Detroit
Derrick Thomas, Kansas City	3.0 vs. Denver
Lee Williams, Houston	3.0 vs. Buffalo

American Football Conference Offense

	Buff.	Cin.	Clev.	Den.	Hou.	Ind.	K.C.	Raid.	Mia.	N.E.	N.Y.J.	Pitt.	S.D.	Sea.
First Downs	350	248	242	234	339	267	246	259	316	215	252	284	302	208
Rushing	133	112	85	84	101	70	87	99	101	71	94	119	118	77
Passing	192	114	141	135	217	174	134	139	194	130	137	143	161	114
Penalty	25	22	16	15	21	23	25	21	21	14	21	22	23	17
Rushes	549	454	451	403	353	379	446	434	407	419	424	518	489	402
Net Yds. Gained	2436	1976	1607	1500	1626	1102	1532	1794	1525	1550	1752	2156	1875	1596
Avg. Gain	4.4	4.4	3.6	3.7	4.6	2.9	3.4	4.1	3.7	3.7	4.1	4.2	3.8	4.0
Avg. Yds. per Game	152.3	123.5	100.4	93.8	101.6	68.9	95.8	112.1	95.3	96.9	109.5	134.8	117.2	99.8
Passes Attempted	509	435	398	473	573	546	413	471	563	444	495	431	496	476
Completed	293	227	238	258	373	305	230	233	332	244	251	249	282	230
% Completed	57.6	52.2	59.8	54.5	65.1	55.9	55.7	49.5	59.0	55.0	50.7	57.8	56.9	48.3
Total Yds. Gained	3678	2284	3102	3312	4231	3584	3115	2950	4148	2492	2962	3046	3614	2323
Times Sacked	29	45	34	52	32	44	48	48	28	65	39	40	33	67
Yds. Lost	221	341	217	382	202	318	323	360	173	458	283	296	268	545
Net Yds. Gained	3457	1943	2885	2930	4029	3266	2792	2590	3975	2034	2679	2750	3346	1778
Avg. Yds. per Game	216.1	121.4	180.3	183.1	251.8	204.1	174.5	161.9	248.4	127.1	167.4	171.9	209.1	111.1
Net Yds. per Pass Play	6.43	4.05	6.68	5.58	6.66	5.54	6.06	4.99	6.73	4.00	5.02	5.84	6.33	3.27
Yds. Gained per Comp.	12.55	10.06	13.03	12.84	11.34	11.75	13.54	12.66	12.49	10.21	11.80	12.23	12.82	10.10
Combined Net Yds. Gained	5893	3919	4492	4430	5655	4368	4324	4384	5500	3584	4431	4906	5221	3374
% Total Yds. Rushing	41.3	50.4	35.8	33.9	28.8	25.2	35.4	40.9	27.7	43.2	39.5	43.9	35.9	47.3
% Total Yds. Passing	58.7	49.6	64.2	66.1	71.2	74.8	64.6	59.1	72.3	56.8	60.5	56.1	64.1	52.7
Avg. Yds. per Game	368.3	244.9	280.8	276.9	353.4	273.0	270.3	274.0	343.8	224.0	276.9	306.6	326.3	210.9
Ball Control Plays	1087	934	883	928	958	969	907	953	998	928	958	989	1018	945
Avg. Yds. per Play	5.4	4.2	5.1	4.8	5.9	4.5	4.8	4.6	5.5	3.9	4.6	5.0	5.1	3.6
Avg. Time of Poss.	28:10	27:05	30:13	28:14	31:09	28:17	29:37	29:06	30:30	28:30	30:24	32:05	32:03	29:01
Third Down Efficiency	39.6	32.2	34.2	32.2	42.4	35.7	34.3	38.5	38.8	32.3	31.4	34.6	39.4	26.6
Had Intercepted	21	17	16	29	23	26	12	23	17	19	24	14	21	23
Yds. Opp Returned	423	127	213	567	367	461	162	345	446	232	347	235	241	231
Ret. by Opp. for TD	2	0	1	3	0	4	0	2	4	0	2	1	1	4
Punts	60	76	75	85	55	83	86	77	61	103	73	74	68	108
Yds. Punted	2531	3196	3083	3705	2487	3716	3633	3255	2424	4227	2993	3119	2899	4760
Avg. Yds. per Punt	42.2	42.1	41.1	43.6	45.2	44.8	42.2	42.3	39.7	41.0	41.0	42.1	42.6	44.1
Punt Returns	43	24	44	34	33	25	39	41	31	37	30	32	44	38
Yds. Returned	464	285	429	353	194	275	402	402	191	274	232	364	359	283
Avg. Yds. per Return	10.8	11.9	9.8	10.4	5.9	11.0	10.3	9.8	6.2	7.4	7.7	11.4	8.2	7.4
Returned for TD	0	1	1	0	0	2	2	0	0	0	0	1	0	0
Kickoff Returns	41	59	43	51	46	51	39	43	44	64	54	48	45	50
Yds. Returned	761	1058	880	1028	885	1001	722	744	838	1376	950	847	812	885
Avg. Yds. per Return	18.6	17.9	20.5	20.2	19.2	19.6	18.5	17.3	19.0	21.5	17.6	17.6	18.0	17.7
Returned for TD	0	0	0	0	0	0	0	0	0	1	0	0	0	0
Fumbles	31	32	19	29	28	24	28	25	31	43	28	28	26	37
Lost	17	10	12	14	12	11	9	15	17	26	15	18	12	18
Out of Bounds	1	0	1	2	1	1	3	2	1	0	1	0	1	2
Own Rec. for TD	0	0	0	0	0	0	0	0	0	0	0	0	1	0
Opp. Rec. by	12	17	20	16	11	15	15	7	14	15	18	21	11	11
Opp. Rec. for TD	1	2	3	1	3	0	2	0	0	2	0	1	0	1
Penalties	103	98	104	98	111	122	82	113	86	111	107	106	91	111
Yds. Penalized	775	755	765	768	824	958	675	832	656	1051	873	941	813	918
Total Points Scored	381	274	272	262	352	216	348	249	340	205	220	299	335	140
Total TDs	44	31	30	29	41	24	40	29	36	25	23	31	36	14
TDs Rushing	18	11	7	11	10	8	14	7	9	6	8	13	18	4
TDs Passing	23	16	18	16	27	13	15	20	24	13	12	15	16	9
TDs on Ret. and Rec.	3	4	5	2	4	3	11	2	3	6	3	3	2	1
Extra Points	43	31	29	28	41	24	39	28	34	22	23	29	35	14
Safeties	1	0	0	0	1	0	0	1	0	0	1	0	3	0
Field Goals Made	24	19	21	20	21	16	23	15	30	11	19	28	26	14
Field Goals Attempted	30	28	29	25	27	29	25	26	37	17	30	36	32	22
% Successful	80.0	67.9	72.4	80.0	77.8	55.2	92.0	57.7	81.1	64.7	63.3	77.8	81.3	63.6

American Football Conference Defense

	Buff.	Cin.	Clev.	Den.	Hou.	Ind.	K.C.	Raid.	Mia.	N.E.	N.Y.J.	Pitt.	S.D.	Sea.
First Downs	278	319	281	283	254	314	256	264	273	292	276	266	250	247
Rushing	77	126	86	105	93	129	97	104	92	112	110	99	80	96
Passing	185	168	170	156	139	164	145	135	168	149	146	146	157	129
Penalty	16	25	25	22	22	21	14	25	13	31	20	21	13	22
Rushes	427	490	429	489	412	495	441	478	428	521	460	435	365	513
Net Yds. Gained	1395	2007	1605	1963	1634	2174	1787	1683	1600	1951	1919	1841	1395	1922
Avg. Gain	3.3	4.1	3.7	4.0	4.0	4.4	4.1	3.5	3.7	3.7	4.2	4.2	3.8	3.7
Avg. Yds. per Game	87.2	125.4	100.3	122.7	102.1	135.9	111.7	105.2	100.0	121.9	119.9	115.1	87.2	120.1
Passes Attempted	520	489	486	462	445	470	458	450	512	459	465	478	491	428
Completed	305	288	291	268	248	260	253	243	294	258	257	252	271	251
% Completed	58.7	58.9	59.9	58.0	55.7	55.3	55.2	54.0	57.4	56.2	55.3	52.7	55.2	58.6
Total Yds. Gained	3560	3620	3467	3437	2898	3236	2928	3153	3266	3211	3201	3065	3188	2978
Times Sacked	44	45	48	50	50	39	50	46	36	20	36	36	51	46
Yds. Lost	351	294	315	317	321	336	391	320	283	114	240	248	356	317
Net Yds. Gained	3209	3326	3152	3120	2577	2900	2537	2833	2983	3097	2961	2817	2832	2661
Avg. Yds. per Game	200.6	207.9	197.0	195.0	161.1	181.3	158.6	177.1	186.4	193.6	185.1	176.1	177.0	166.3
Net Yds. per Pass Play	5.69	6.23	5.90	6.09	5.21	5.70	4.99	5.71	5.44	6.47	5.91	5.48	5.23	5.61
Yds. Gained per Comp.	11.67	12.57	11.91	12.82	11.69	12.45	11.57	12.98	11.11	12.45	12.46	12.16	11.76	11.86
Combined Net Yds. Gained	4604	5333	4757	5083	4211	5074	4324	4516	4583	5048	4880	4658	4227	4583
% Total Yds. Rushing	30.3	37.6	33.7	38.6	38.8	42.8	41.3	37.3	34.9	38.6	39.3	39.5	33.0	41.9
% Total Yds. Passing	69.7	62.4	66.3	61.4	61.2	57.2	58.7	62.7	65.1	61.4	60.7	60.5	67.0	58.1
Avg. Yds. per Game	287.8	333.3	297.3	317.7	263.2	317.1	270.3	282.3	286.4	315.5	305.0	291.1	264.2	286.4
Ball Control Plays	991	1024	963	1001	907	1004	949	974	976	1000	961	949	907	987
Avg. Yds. per Play	4.6	5.2	4.9	5.1	4.6	5.1	4.6	4.6	4.7	5.0	5.1	4.9	4.7	4.6
Avg. Time of Poss.	31:50	32:55	29:47	31:46	28:51	31:43	30:23	30:54	29:30	31:30	29:36	27:55	27:57	30:59
Third Down Efficiency	38.5	45.8	37.1	36.5	35.1	35.5	35.6	32.9	40.6	36.0	35.8	33.3	36.5	32.6
Intercepted by	23	16	13	15	20	20	24	12	18	14	21	22	25	20
Yds. Returned By	325	205	222	210	181	302	403	339	458	285	269	384	405	324
Returned for TD	2	1	1	1	1	1	6	1	3	3	3	1	1	0
Punts	79	57	74	78	68	71	80	85	74	75	70	74	80	96
Yds. Punted	3465	2384	3293	3380	2939	3021	3445	3615	2971	3045	2866	3107	3565	4015
Avg. Yds. per Punt	43.9	41.8	44.5	43.3	43.2	42.5	43.1	42.5	40.1	40.6	40.9	42.0	44.6	41.8
Punt Returns	22	32	27	39	31	45	40	40	33	59	26	39	24	56
Yds. Returned	185	284	234	382	255	313	328	385	382	499	189	308	244	416
Avg. Yds. per Return	8.4	8.9	8.7	9.8	8.2	7.0	8.2	9.6	11.6	8.5	7.3	7.9	10.2	7.4
Returned for TD	0	1	0	0	0	0	1	0	1	1	0	0	1	1
Kickoff Returns	60	46	51	13	63	36	64	35	65	45	33	52	54	36
Yds. Returned	1215	1079	907	254	989	630	1203	690	1380	749	552	1052	962	685
Avg. Yds. per Return	20.3	23.5	17.8	19.5	15.7	17.5	18.8	19.7	21.2	16.6	16.7	20.2	17.8	19.0
Returned for TD	1	2	0	0	0	0	0	0	0	0	0	0	0	0
Fumbles	29	36	33	33	24	28	34	21	25	30	33	34	18	25
Lost	12	17	20	16	11	15	15	7	14	15	18	21	11	11
Out of Bounds	2	2	1	1	0	1	2	0	0	1	1	5	0	3
Own Rec. for TD	0	0	0	0	0	0	0	1	0	0	0	0	0	0
Opp. Rec. by	17	10	12	14	12	11	9	15	17	26	15	18	12	18
Opp. Rec. for TD	1	2	0	1	2	0	1	1	2	2	1	2	0	2
Penalties	118	95	93	96	114	101	124	98	89	90	82	104	98	100
Yds. Penalized	933	797	764	715	886	836	959	755	679	673	808	814	798	776
Total Points Scored	283	364	275	329	258	302	282	281	281	363	315	225	241	312
Total TDs	31	44	29	35	28	34	34	32	32	40	35	24	29	32
TDs Rushing	8	15	5	10	6	16	12	17	9	15	13	6	10	14
TDs Passing	19	24	23	21	20	14	19	11	16	22	19	15	17	11
TDs on Ret. and Rec.	4	5	1	4	2	4	3	4	7	3	3	3	2	7
Extra Points	31	44	29	35	27	33	33	32	30	40	34	24	28	29
Safeties	0	1	0	0	0	1	0	0	1	1	1	0	0	2
Field Goals Made	22	18	24	28	21	21	15	19	19	27	23	19	13	29
Field Goals Attempted	30	30	29	38	26	28	21	30	26	41	31	28	16	36
% Successful	73.3	60.0	82.8	73.7	80.8	75.0	71.4	63.3	73.1	65.9	74.2	67.9	81.3	80.6

National Football Conference Offense

	Atl.	Chi.	Dall.	Det.	G.B.	Rams	Minn.	N.O.	N.Y.G.	Phil.	Phoe.	S.F.	T.B.	Wash.
First Downs	273	282	324	241	291	278	288	267	271	292	277	344	281	276
Rushing	67	101	119	83	101	83	115	92	120	138	88	135	100	104
Passing	194	157	183	133	171	174	157	155	119	138	161	192	165	160
Penalty	12	24	22	25	19	21	16	20	32	16	28	17	16	12
Rushes	322	427	500	378	420	393	497	454	458	516	395	482	438	483
Net Yds. Gained	1270	1871	2121	1644	1555	1659	2030	1628	2077	2388	1491	2315	1706	1727
Avg. Gain	3.9	4.4	4.2	4.3	3.7	4.2	4.1	3.6	4.5	4.6	3.8	4.8	3.9	3.6
Avg. Yds. per Game	79.4	116.9	132.6	102.8	97.2	103.7	126.9	101.8	129.8	149.3	93.2	144.7	106.6	107.9
Passes Attempted	548	479	491	406	527	495	458	426	433	429	517	480	511	485
Completed	336	266	314	231	340	289	258	251	232	255	298	319	299	272
% Completed	61.3	55.5	64.0	56.9	64.5	58.4	56.3	58.9	53.6	59.4	57.6	66.5	58.5	56.1
Total Yds. Gained	3892	3334	3597	3150	3498	3422	3162	3297	2628	3054	3344	4054	3399	3339
Times Sacked	40	45	23	59	43	26	40	15	45	64	36	32	45	23
Yds. Lost	259	264	112	354	268	204	293	119	283	462	258	174	334	176
Net Yds. Gained	3633	3070	3485	2796	3230	3218	2869	3178	2345	2592	3086	3880	3065	3163
Avg. Yds. per Game	227.1	191.9	217.8	174.8	201.9	201.1	179.3	198.6	146.6	162.0	192.9	242.5	191.6	197.7
Net Yds. per Pass Play	6.18	5.86	6.78	6.01	5.67	6.18	5.76	7.21	4.91	5.26	5.58	7.58	5.51	6.23
Yds. Gained per Comp.	11.58	12.53	11.46	13.64	10.29	11.84	12.26	13.14	11.33	11.98	11.22	12.71	11.37	12.28
Combined Net Yds. Gained	4903	4941	5606	4440	4785	4877	4899	4806	4422	4980	4577	6195	4771	4890
% Total Yds. Rushing	25.9	37.9	37.8	37.0	32.5	34.0	41.4	33.9	47.0	48.0	32.6	37.4	35.8	35.3
% Total Yds. Passing	74.1	62.1	62.2	63.0	67.5	66.0	58.6	66.1	53.0	52.0	67.4	62.6	64.2	64.7
Avg. Yds. per Game	306.4	308.8	350.4	277.5	299.1	304.8	306.2	300.4	276.4	311.3	286.1	387.2	298.2	305.6
Ball Control Plays	910	951	1014	843	990	914	995	895	936	1009	948	994	994	991
Avg. Yds. per Play	5.4	5.2	5.5	5.3	4.8	5.3	4.9	5.4	4.7	4.9	4.8	6.2	4.8	4.9
Avg. Time of Poss.	28:36	29:15	33:57	27:36	32:30	28:31	29:18	31:10	29:22	31:47	31:01	32:19	29:15	31:04
Third Down Efficiency	38.4	36.4	41.8	34.3	42.5	37.1	44.3	38.1	34.5	38.5	38.7	46.5	37.1	43.4
Had Intercepted	15	24	15	21	15	20	15	16	10	13	24	9	20	17
Yds. Opp Returned	246	612	300	294	198	305	164	280	190	77	279	126	211	318
Ret. by Opp. for TD	3	6	0	1	1	1	1	2	2	0	1	2	1	2
Punts	70	79	61	66	68	76	73	67	85	82	58	49	74	65
Yds. Punted	2855	3393	2620	2846	2608	3122	3243	2947	3451	3459	2484	1918	3015	2555
Avg. Yds. per Punt	40.8	42.9	43.0	43.1	38.4	41.1	44.4	44.0	40.6	42.2	42.8	39.1	40.7	39.3
Punt Returns	29	23	44	21	35	39	33	45	27	47	33	40	26	37
Yds. Returned	196	176	550	190	315	345	336	231	240	555	364	389	160	355
Avg. Yds. per Return	6.8	7.7	12.5	9.0	9.0	8.8	10.2	5.1	8.9	11.8	11.0	9.7	6.2	9.6
Returned for TD	0	0	2	1	1	2	0	0	0	1	0	1	0	2
Kickoff Returns	64	56	37	59	54	63	45	42	56	48	51	42	50	48
Yds. Returned	1532	1143	699	1193	1017	1054	874	815	1098	987	1127	879	881	973
Avg. Yds. per Return	23.9	20.4	18.9	20.2	18.8	16.7	19.4	19.4	19.6	20.6	22.1	20.9	17.6	20.3
Returned for TD	2	1	0	1	0	0	0	0	1	0	0	0	0	0
Fumbles	30	23	16	26	41	30	29	27	25	25	26	29	19	18
Lost	14	10	9	15	21	17	17	13	13	15	18	13	9	7
Out of Bounds	0	3	0	2	2	1	1	2	0	1	1	4	1	1
Own Rec. for TD	0	0	0	0	0	0	0	0	0	0	0	0	0	0
Opp. Rec. by	12	16	14	11	19	15	14	20	12	13	12	12	13	11
Opp. Rec. for TD	1	1	1	1	1	0	2	3	0	1	0	1	3	1
Penalties	78	93	91	122	88	79	99	60	87	101	85	80	91	84
Yds. Penalized	656	776	650	903	749	592	809	567	647	807	722	636	754	741
Total Points Scored	327	295	409	273	276	313	374	330	306	354	243	431	267	300
Total TDs	39	34	48	30	30	38	45	35	36	44	29	54	33	30
TDs Rushing	3	15	20	9	7	12	19	10	20	19	11	22	12	10
TDs Passing	33	17	23	16	20	23	18	19	14	20	15	29	17	15
TDs on Ret. and Rec.	3	2	5	5	3	3	8	6	2	5	3	3	4	5
Extra Points	39	34	47	30	30	38	45	33	36	40	28	53	33	30
Safeties	0	0	1	0	0	1	1	0	0	1	1	0	0	0
Field Goals Made	18	19	24	21	22	15	19	29	18	16	13	18	12	30
Field Goals Attempted	22	26	35	26	29	20	25	34	23	25	26	27	22	40
% Successful	81.8	73.1	68.6	80.8	75.9	75.0	76.0	85.3	78.3	64.0	50.0	66.7	54.5	75.0

National Football Conference Defense

	Atl.	Chi.	Dall.	Det.	G.B.	Rams	Minn.	N.O.	N.Y.G.	Phil.	Phoe.	S.F.	T.B.	Wash.
First Downs	304	274	241	308	277	319	293	246	287	242	281	277	296	249
Rushing	109	109	68	119	89	130	113	86	115	73	101	90	100	89
Passing	172	144	147	168	170	175	154	146	155	146	163	174	175	138
Penalty	23	21	26	21	18	14	26	14	17	23	17	13	21	22
Rushes	464	468	345	460	406	467	438	381	458	387	436	351	441	406
Net Yds. Gained	2294	1948	1244	1841	1821	2230	1733	1605	2012	1481	1635	1418	1675	1696
Avg. Gain	4.9	4.2	3.6	4.0	4.5	4.8	4.0	4.2	4.4	3.8	3.8	4.0	3.8	4.2
Avg. Yds. per Game	143.4	121.8	77.8	115.1	113.8	139.4	108.3	100.3	125.8	92.6	102.2	88.6	104.7	106.0
Passes Attempted	439	442	484	487	483	507	508	511	440	517	452	551	508	466
Completed	277	261	263	296	277	305	320	287	270	263	276	320	293	258
% Completed	63.1	59.0	54.3	60.8	57.3	60.2	63.0	56.2	61.4	50.9	61.1	58.1	57.7	55.4
Total Yds. Gained	3496	3290	3034	3402	3496	3481	3124	2846	3228	3316	3687	3642	3740	3021
Times Sacked	31	43	44	29	34	31	51	57	25	55	27	41	36	39
Yds. Lost	241	286	347	185	219	188	342	376	197	385	196	273	230	279
Net Yds. Gained	3255	3004	2687	3217	3277	3293	2782	2470	3031	2931	3491	3369	3510	2742
Avg. Yds. per Game	203.4	187.8	167.9	201.1	204.8	205.8	173.9	154.4	189.4	183.2	218.2	210.6	219.4	171.4
Net Yds. per Pass Play	6.93	6.19	5.09	6.23	6.34	6.12	4.98	4.35	6.52	5.12	7.29	5.69	6.45	5.43
Yds. Gained per Comp.	12.62	12.61	11.54	11.49	12.62	11.41	9.76	9.92	11.96	12.61	13.36	11.38	12.76	11.71
Combined Net Yds. Gained	5549	4952	3931	5058	5098	5523	4515	4075	5043	4412	5126	4787	5185	4438
% Total Yds. Rushing	41.3	39.3	31.6	36.4	35.7	40.4	38.4	39.4	39.9	33.6	31.9	29.6	32.3	38.2
% Total Yds. Passing	58.7	60.7	68.4	63.6	64.3	59.6	61.6	60.6	60.1	66.4	68.1	70.4	67.7	61.8
Avg. Yds. per Game	346.8	309.5	245.7	316.1	318.6	345.2	282.2	254.7	315.2	275.8	320.4	299.2	324.1	277.4
Ball Control Plays	934	953	873	976	923	1005	997	949	923	959	915	943	985	911
Avg. Yds. per Play	5.9	5.2	4.5	5.2	5.5	5.5	4.5	4.3	5.5	4.6	5.6	5.1	5.3	4.9
Avg. Time of Poss.	31:24	30:45	26:03	32:24	27:30	31:29	30:42	28:50	30:38	28:13	28:59	27:41	30:45	28:56
Third Down Efficiency	42.9	35.6	27.2	42.0	37.6	44.6	38.2	34.0	42.2	33.3	36.2	37.7	43.4	35.6
Intercepted By	11	14	17	21	15	18	28	18	14	24	16	17	20	23
Yds. Returned By	135	188	158	255	222	283	502	254	192	307	298	172	234	485
Returned for TD	0	0	1	0	1	1	6	3	1	2	3	1	1	2
Punts	61	70	87	55	68	66	76	89	64	85	62	76	64	73
Yds. Punted	2534	2840	3660	2263	2941	2776	3182	3666	2477	3531	2656	3134	2645	3128
Avg. Yds. per Punt	41.5	40.6	42.1	41.1	43.3	42.1	41.9	41.2	38.7	41.5	42.8	41.2	41.3	42.8
Punt Returns	44	38	34	30	26	48	34	31	46	36	22	23	22	27
Yds. Returned	482	351	397	356	230	522	339	218	548	295	141	177	117	332
Avg. Yds. per Return	11.0	9.2	11.7	11.9	8.8	10.9	10.0	7.0	11.9	8.2	6.4	7.7	5.3	12.3
Returned for TD	4	1	0	0	1	1	1	0	2	0	0	0	0	1
Kickoff Returns	55	50	60	45	57	55	50	40	64	53	42	66	49	54
Yds. Returned	1059	1027	1217	948	901	1128	925	923	1207	1027	767	1273	1236	1074
Avg. Yds. per Return	19.3	20.5	20.3	21.1	15.8	20.5	18.5	23.1	18.9	19.4	18.3	19.3	25.2	19.9
Returned for TD	0	0	0	0	0	0	0	0	0	1	0	0	1	1
Fumbles	24	34	25	25	32	26	23	37	27	27	25	23	19	23
Lost	12	16	14	11	19	15	14	20	12	13	12	12	13	11
Out of Bounds	1	1	1	1	0	1	2	0	2	2	1	2	1	1
Own Rec. for TD	0	0	0	0	0	0	0	0	0	0	0	0	0	0
Opp. Rec. by	14	10	9	15	21	17	17	13	13	15	18	13	9	7
Opp. Rec. for TD	0	2	2	3	1	1	1	1	0	1	2	0	1	0
Penalties	92	90	94	111	98	102	98	77	93	86	100	79	74	85
Yds. Penalized	761	780	727	871	830	778	768	729	744	683	826	651	563	709
Total Points Scored	414	361	243	332	296	383	249	202	367	245	332	236	365	255
Total TDs	51	43	29	38	32	43	27	24	46	26	40	27	43	30
TDs Rushing	20	14	11	14	12	22	11	8	17	4	13	5	15	11
TDs Passing	24	20	16	20	16	18	12	13	22	20	24	20	25	15
TDs on Ret. and Rec.	7	9	2	4	4	3	4	3	7	2	3	2	3	4
Extra Points	51	43	27	38	32	41	27	22	44	26	38	26	43	29
Safeties	0	0	0	0	0	0	0	0	1	0	0	0	2	2
Field Goals Made	19	20	14	22	24	28	20	12	15	21	18	16	20	14
Field Goals Attempted	31	25	17	35	27	34	25	17	21	32	28	20	30	21
% Successful	61.3	80.0	82.4	62.9	88.9	82.4	80.0	70.6	71.4	65.6	64.3	80.0	66.7	66.7

AFC, NFC, and NFL Summary

	AFC Offense Total	AFC Offense Average	AFC Defense Total	AFC Defense Average	NFC Offense Total	NFC Offense Average	NFC Defense Total	NFC Defense Average	NFL Total	NFL Average
First Downs	3762	268.7	3853	275.2	3985	284.6	3894	278.1	7747	276.7
Rushing	1351	96.5	1406	100.4	1446	103.3	1391	99.4	2797	99.9
Passing	2125	151.8	2157	154.1	2259	161.4	2227	159.1	4384	156.6
Penalty	286	20.4	290	20.7	280	20.0	276	19.7	566	20.2
Rushes	6128	437.7	6383	455.9	6163	440.2	5908	422.0	12291	439.0
Net Yds. Gained	24027	1716.2	24876	1776.9	25482	1820.1	24633	1759.5	49509	1768.2
Avg. Gain	—	3.9	—	3.9	—	4.1	—	4.2	—	4.0
Avg. Yds. per Game	—	107.3	—	111.1	—	113.8	—	110.0	—	110.5
Passes Attempted	6723	480.2	6613	472.4	6685	477.5	6795	485.4	13408	478.9
Completed	3745	267.5	3739	267.1	3960	282.9	3966	283.3	7705	275.2
% Completed	—	55.7	—	56.5	—	59.2	—	58.4	—	57.5
Total Yds. Gained	44841	3202.9	45208	3229.1	47170	3369.3	46803	3343.1	92011	3286.1
Times Sacked	604	43.1	597	42.6	536	38.3	543	38.8	1140	40.7
Yds. Lost	4387	313.4	4203	300.2	3560	254.3	3744	267.4	7947	283.8
Net Yds. Gained	40454	2889.6	41005	2928.9	43610	3115.0	43059	3075.6	84064	3002.3
Avg. Yds. per Game	—	180.6	—	183.1	—	194.7	—	192.2	—	187.6
Net Yds. per Pass Play	—	5.52	—	5.69	—	6.04	—	5.87	—	5.78
Yds. Gained per Comp.	—	11.97	—	12.09	—	11.91	—	11.80	—	11.94
Combined Net Yds. Gained	64481	4605.8	65881	4705.8	69092	4935.1	67692	4835.1	133573	4770.5
% Total Yds. Rushing	—	37.3	—	37.8	—	36.9	—	36.4	—	37.1
% Total Yds. Passing	—	62.7	—	62.2	—	63.1	—	63.6	—	62.9
Avg. Yds. per Game	—	287.9	—	294.1	—	308.4	—	302.2	—	298.2
Ball Control Plays	13455	961.1	13593	970.9	13384	956.0	13246	946.1	26839	958.5
Avg. Yds. per Play	—	4.8	—	4.8	—	5.2	—	5.1	—	5.0
Third Down Efficiency	—	35.0	—	36.6	—	39.5	—	37.9	—	37.2
Interceptions	285	20.4	263	18.8	234	16.7	256	18.3	519	18.5
Yds. Returned	4397	314.1	4312	308.0	3600	257.1	3685	263.2	7997	285.6
Returned for TD	24	1.7	25	1.8	23	1.6	22	1.6	47	1.7
Punts	1084	77.4	1061	75.8	973	69.5	996	71.1	2057	73.5
Yds. Punted	46028	3287.7	45111	3222.2	40516	2894.0	41433	2959.5	86544	3090.9
Avg. Yds. per Punt	—	42.5	—	42.5	—	41.6	—	41.6	—	42.1
Punt Returns	495	35.4	513	36.6	479	34.2	461	32.9	974	34.8
Yds. Returned	4507	321.9	4404	314.6	4402	314.4	4505	321.8	8909	318.2
Avg. Yds. per Return	—	9.1	—	8.6	—	9.2	—	9.8	—	9.1
Returned for TD	7	0.5	6	0.4	10	0.7	11	0.8	17	0.6
Kickoff Returns	678	48.4	653	46.6	715	51.1	740	52.9	1393	49.8
Yds. Returned	12787	913.4	12347	881.9	14272	1019.4	14712	1050.9	27059	966.4
Avg. Yds. per Return	—	18.9	—	18.9	—	20.0	—	19.9	—	19.4
Returned for TD	1	0.1	3	0.2	5	0.4	3	0.2	6	0.2
Fumbles	409	29.2	403	28.8	364	26.0	370	26.4	773	27.6
Lost	206	14.7	203	14.5	191	13.6	194	13.9	397	14.2
Out of Bounds	16	1.1	19	1.4	19	1.4	16	1.1	35	1.3
Own Rec. for TD	1	0.1	1	0.1	0	0.0	0	0.0	1	0.0
Opp. Rec.	203	14.5	206	14.7	194	13.9	191	13.6	397	14.2
Opp. Rec. for TD	16	1.1	17	1.2	16	1.1	15	1.1	32	1.1
Penalties	1443	103.1	1402	100.1	1238	88.4	1279	91.4	2681	95.8
Yds. Penalized	11604	828.9	11193	799.5	10009	714.9	10420	744.3	21613	771.9
Total Points Scored	3893	278.1	4111	293.6	4498	321.3	4280	305.7	8391	299.7
Total TDs	433	30.9	459	32.8	525	37.5	499	35.6	958	34.2
TDs Rushing	144	10.3	156	11.1	189	13.5	177	12.6	333	11.9
TDs Passing	237	16.9	251	17.9	279	19.9	265	18.9	516	18.4
TDs on Ret. and Rec.	52	3.7	52	3.7	57	4.1	57	4.1	109	3.9
Extra Points	420	30.0	449	32.1	516	36.9	487	34.8	936	33.4
Safeties	7	0.5	7	0.5	5	0.4	5	0.4	12	0.4
Field Goals Made	287	20.5	298	21.3	274	19.6	263	18.8	561	20.0
Field Goals Attempted	393	28.1	410	29.3	380	27.1	363	25.9	773	27.6
% Successful	—	73.0	—	72.7	—	72.1	—	72.5	—	72.6

Club Leaders

	Offense	Defense
First Downs	Buff. 350	Dall. 241
Rushing	Phil. 138	Dall. 68
Passing	Hou. 217	Sea. 129
Penalty	N.Y.G. 32	Mia., S.D., & S.F. 13
Rushes	Buff. 549	Dall. 345
Net Yds. Gained	Buff. 2436	Dall. 1244
Avg. Gain	S.F. 4.8	Buff. 3.3
Passes Attempted	Hou. 573	Sea. 428
Completed	Hou. 373	Raid. 243
% Completed	S.F. 66.5	Phil. 50.9
Total Yds. Gained	Hou. 4231	N.O. 2846
Times Sacked	N.O. 15	N.O. 57
Yds. Lost	Dall. 112	K.C. 391
Net Yds. Gained	Hou. 4029	N.O. 2470
Net Yds. per Pass Play	S.F. 7.58	N.O. 4.35
Yds. Gained per Comp.	Det. 13.64	Minn. 9.76
Combined Net Yds. Gained	S.F. 6195	Dall. 3931
% Total Yds. Rushing	Cin. 50.4	S.F. 29.6
% Total Yds. Passing	Hou. 74.8	Ind. 57.2
Ball Control Plays	Buff. 1087	Dall. 873
Avg. Yds. per Play	S.F. 6.23	N.O. 4.29
Avg. Time of Poss.	Dall. 33:57	—
Third Down Efficiency	S.F. 46.5	Dall. 27.2
Interceptions	—	Minn. 28
Yds. Returned	—	Minn. 502
Returned for TD	—	K.C. & Minn. 6
Punts	Sea. 108	—
Yds. Punted	Sea. 4760	—
Avg. Yds. per Punt	Hou. 45.2	—
Punt Returns	Phil. 47	Buff., Pho., & T.B. 22
Yds. Returned	Phil. 555	T.B. 117
Avg. Yds. per Return	Dall. 12.5	T.B. 5.3
Returned for TD	Five with 2	—
Kickoff Returns	Atl. & N.E. 64	Den. 13
Yds. Returned	Atl. 1532	Den. 254
Avg. Yds. per Return	Atl. 23.9	Hou. 15.7
Returned for TD	Atl. 2	—
Total Points Scored	S.F. 431	N.O. 202
Total TDs	S.F. 54	N.O. & Pitt. 24
TDs Rushing	S.F. 22	Phil. 4
TDs Passing	S.F. 29	Raid. & Sea. 11
TDs on Ret. and Rec.	K.C. 11	Clev. 1
Extra Points	S.F. 53	N.O. 22
Safeties	S.D. 3	—
Field Goals Made	Mia. & Wash. 30	N.O. 12
Field Goals Attempted	Wash. 40	S.D. 16
% Successful	K.C. 92.0	Cin. 60.0

National Football League Club Ranking By Yards

	Offense			Defense		
	Total	Rush	Pass	Total	Rush	Pass
Atlanta	10	27	4	28	28	22
Buffalo	2	*1	6	12	2T	20
Chicago	8	10	14	17	21	15
Cincinnati	26	8	27	26	24	25
Cleveland	18	19	17	14	7T	19
Dallas	4	5	5	*1	*1	5
Denver	21	25	16	22	23	18
Detroit	19	16	19	20	17T	21
Green Bay	15	21	9	23	16	23
Houston	3	18	*1	3	9	3
Indianapolis	24	28	8	21	26	11
Kansas City	25	23	20	5	15	2
L.A. Rams	13	15	10	27	27	24
L.A. Raiders	23	11	24	9	12	10
Miami	5	24	2	10T	6	14
Minnesota	11	7	18	8	14	7
New England	27	22	26	19	22	17
New Orleans	14	17	11	2	7T	*1
N.Y. Giants	22	6	25	18	25	16
N.Y. Jets	20	12	22	16	19	13
Philadelphia	7	2	23	6	5	12
Phoenix	17	26	13	24	10	27
Pittsburgh	9	4	21	13	17T	8
San Diego	6	9	7	4	2T	9
San Francisco	*1	3	3	15	4	26
Seattle	28	20	28	10T	20	4
Tampa Bay	16	14	15	25	11	28
Washington	12	13	12	7	13	6

T = Tied for position
** = League Leader*

AFC Takeaways/Giveaways

	Takeaways			Giveaways			Net
	Int	Fum	Total	Int	Fum	Total	Diff.
Kansas City	24	15	39	12	9	21	18
Pittsburgh	22	21	43	14	18	32	11
Cincinnati	16	17	33	17	10	27	6
Cleveland	13	20	33	16	12	28	5
San Diego	25	11	36	21	12	33	3
N.Y. Jets	21	18	39	24	15	39	0
Miami	18	14	32	17	17	34	-2
Indianapolis	20	15	35	26	11	37	-2
Buffalo	23	12	35	21	17	38	-3
Houston	20	11	31	23	12	35	-4
Seattle	20	12	32	23	18	41	-9
Denver	15	16	31	29	15	44	-13
New England	14	15	29	19	26	45	-16
L.A. Raiders	12	7	19	23	15	38	-19

NFC Takeaways/Giveaways

	Takeaways			Giveaways			Net
	Int	Fum	Total	Int	Fum	Total	Diff.
Minnesota	28	14	42	15	17	32	10
Washington	23	11	34	17	7	24	10
New Orleans	18	20	38	16	13	29	9
Philadelphia	24	13	37	13	15	28	9
San Francisco	17	12	29	9	13	22	7
Dallas	17	14	31	15	9	24	7
Tampa Bay	20	13	33	20	9	29	4
N.Y. Giants	14	12	26	10	13	23	3
Green Bay	15	19	34	15	21	36	-2
L.A. Rams	18	15	33	20	17	37	-4
Detroit	21	11	32	21	15	6	-4
Chicago	14	16	30	24	10	34	-4
Atlanta	11	12	23	15	14	29	-6
Phoenix	16	12	28	24	18	42	-14

Scoring

Points

AFC: 124—Pete Stoyanovich, Miami
NFC: 120—Morten Andersen, New Orleans
Chip Lohmiller, Washington

Touchdowns

NFC: 19—Emmitt Smith, Dallas
AFC: 12—Thurman Thomas, Buffalo

Extra Points

NFC: 53—Mike Cofer, San Francisco
AFC: 43—Steve Christie, Buffalo

Field Goals

AFC: 30—Pete Stoyanovich, Miami
NFC: 30—Chip Lohmiller, Washington

Field Goal Attempts

NFC: 40—Chip Lohmiller, Washington
AFC: 37—Pete Stoyanovich, Miami

Longest Field Goal

AFC: 54—Al Del Greco, Houston vs. Kansas City, September 20
Jaeger, Raiders vs. Giants, October 4
Christie, Buffalo at Miami, November 16
NFC: 54—Norm Johnson, Atlanta vs. Jets, September 6
Norm Johnson, Atlanta vs. New England, November 29

Most Points, Game

AFC: 24—Thurman Thomas, Buffalo vs. Rams, September 6 (4 TD)
Eric Metcalf, Cleveland at Raiders, September 20 (4 TD)
NFC: 18—Tom Rathman, San Francisco at Giants, September 6 (3 TD)
Michael Irvin, Dallas vs. Phoenix, September 20 (3 TD)
Andre Rison, Atlanta at Chicago, September 27 (3 TD)
Terry Allen, Minnesota at Cincinnati, September 27 (3 TD)
Jerry Rice, San Francisco vs. Atlanta, October 18 (3 TD)
Ricky Watters, San Francisco vs. Atlanta, October 18 (3 TD)
Emmitt Smith, Dallas at Raiders, October 25 (3 TD)
Emmitt Smith, Dallas at Detroit, November 8 (3 TD)
Terry Allen, Minnesota at Rams, November 29 (3 TD)
Rodney Hampton, Giants vs. Kansas City, December 19 (3 TD)

Team Leaders, Points

AFC: BUFFALO: 115, Steve Christie; CINCINNATI: 88, Jim Breech; CLEVELAND: 92, Matt Stover; DENVER: 88, David Treadwell; HOUSTON: 104, Al Del Greco; INDIANAPOLIS: 72, Dean Biasucci; KANSAS CITY: 105, Nick Lowery; L.A. RAIDERS: 73, Jeff Jaeger; MIAMI: 124, Pete Stoyanovich; NEW ENGLAND: 55, Charlie Baumann; N.Y. JETS: 65, Cary Blanchard; PITTSBURGH: 113, Gary Anderson; SAN DIEGO: 113, John Carney; SEATTLE: 56, John Kasay

NFC: ATLANTA: 93, Norm Johnson; CHICAGO: 91, Kevin Butler; DALLAS: 119, Lin Elliott; DETROIT: 93, Jason Hanson; GREEN BAY: 96, Chris Jacke; L.A. RAMS: 83, Tony Zendejas; MINNESOTA: 102, Fuad Reveiz; NEW ORLEANS: 120, Morten Andersen; N.Y. GIANTS: 84, Rodney Hampton; PHILADELPHIA: 88, Roger Ruzek; PHOENIX: 67, Greg Davis; SAN FRANCISCO: 107, Mike Cofer; TAMPA BAY: 54, Reggie Cobb; WASHINGTON: 120, Chip Lohmiller

Team Champion

NFC: 431—San Francisco
AFC: 381—Buffalo

AFC Scoring—Team

	TD	TDR	TDP	TDM	XP	XPA	FG	FGA	SAF	TP
Buffalo	44	18	23	3	43	44	24	30	1	381
Houston	41	10	27	4	41	41	21	27	1	352
Kansas City	40	14	15	11	39	40	23	25	0	348
Miami	36	9	24	3	34	36	30	37	0	340
San Diego	36	18	16	2	35	36	26	32	3	335
Pittsburgh	31	13	15	3	29	31	28	36	0	299
Cincinnati	31	11	16	4	31	31	19	28	0	274
Cleveland	30	7	18	5	29	30	21	29	0	272
Denver	29	11	16	2	28	29	20	25	0	262
L.A. Raiders	29	7	20	2	28	29	15	26	1	249
N.Y. Jets	23	8	12	3	23	23	19	30	1	220
Indianapolis	24	8	13	3	24	24	16	29	0	216
New England	25	6	13	6	22	25	11	17	0	205
Seattle	14	4	9	1	14	14	14	22	0	140
AFC Total	433	144	237	52	420	433	287	393	7	3893
AFC Average	30.9	10.3	16.9	3.7	30.0	30.9	20.5	28.1	0.5	278.1

NFC Scoring—Team

	TD	TDR	TDP	TDM	XP	XPA	FG	FGA	SAF	TP
San Francisco	54	22	29	3	53	54	18	27	0	431
Dallas	48	20	23	5	47	48	24	35	1	409
Minnesota	45	19	18	8	45	45	19	25	1	374
Philadelphia	44	19	20	5	40	44	16	25	1	354
New Orleans	35	10	19	6	33	35	29	34	0	330
Atlanta	39	3	33	3	39	39	18	22	0	327
L.A. Rams	38	12	23	3	38	38	15	20	1	313
N.Y. Giants	36	20	14	2	36	36	18	23	0	306
Washington	30	10	15	5	30	30	30	40	0	300
Chicago	34	15	17	2	34	34	19	26	0	295
Green Bay	30	7	20	3	30	30	22	29	0	276
Detroit	30	9	16	5	30	30	21	26	0	273
Tampa Bay	33	12	17	4	33	33	12	22	0	267
Phoenix	29	11	15	3	28	29	13	26	1	243
NFC Total	525	189	279	57	516	525	274	380	5	4498
NFC Average	37.5	13.5	19.9	4.1	36.9	37.5	19.6	27.1	0.4	321.3
NFL Total	958	333	516	109	936	958	561	773	12	8391
NFL Average	34.2	11.9	18.4	3.9	33.4	34.2	20.0	27.6	0.4	299.7

NFL Top 10 Scorers—Touchdowns

	TD	TDR	TDP	TDM	PTS
Smith, Emmitt, Dal.	19	18	1	0	114
Allen, Terry, Min.	15	13	2	0	90
Hampton, Rodney, NY-G	14	14	0	0	84
Sharpe, Sterling, G.B.	13	0	13	0	78
Thomas, Thurman, Buf.	12	9	3	0	72
Foster, Barry, Pit.	11	11	0	0	66
Rice, Jerry, S.F.	11	1	10	0	66
Rison, Andre, Atl.	11	0	11	0	66
Anderson, Neal, Chi.	11	5	6	0	66
Watters, Ricky, S.F.	11	9	2	0	66

NFL Top 10 Scorers—Kicking

	XP	XPA	FG	FGA	PTS
Stoyanovich, Pete, Mia.	34	36	30	37	124
Lohmiller, Chip, Was.	30	30	30	40	120
Andersen, Morten, N.O.	33	34	29	34	120
Elliott, Lin, Dal.	47	48	24	35	119
Christie, Steve, Buf.	43	44	24	30	115
Carney, John, S.D.	35	35	26	32	113
Anderson, Gary, Pit.	29	31	28	36	113
Cofer, Mike, S.F.	53	54	18	27	107
Lowery, Nick, K.C.	39	39	22	24	105
Del Greco, Al, Hou.	41	41	21	27	104

AFC Scoring—Individual

Kickers	XP	XPA	FG	FGA	PTS
Stoyanovich, Pete, Mia.	34	36	30	37	124
Christie, Steve, Buf.	43	44	24	30	115
Anderson, Gary, Pit.	29	31	28	36	113
Carney, John, S.D.	35	35	26	32	113
Lowery, Nick, K.C.	39	39	22	24	105
Del Greco, Al, Hou.	41	41	21	27	104
Stover, Matt, Cle.	29	30	21	29	92
Breech, Jim, Cin.	31	31	19	27	88
Treadwell, David, Den.	28	28	20	24	88
Jaeger, Jeff, Rai.	28	28	15	26	73
Biasucci, Dean, Ind.	24	24	16	29	72
Blanchard, Cary, NY-J	17	17	16	22	65
Kasay, John, Sea.	14	14	14	22	56
Baumann, Charlie, N.E.	22	24	11	17	55
Staurovsky, Jason, NY-J	6	6	3	8	15
Daluiso, Brad, Den.	0	0	0	1	0
Johnson, Lee, Cin.	0	0	0	1	0

Non-kickers	TD	TDR	TDP	TDM	PTS
Thomas, Thurman, Buf.	12	9	3	0	72
Foster, Barry, Pit.	11	11	0	0	66
Givins, Earnest, Hou.	10	0	10	0	60
Culver, Rodney, Ind.	9	7	2	0	54
Jeffires, Haywood, Hou.	9	0	9	0	54
Fenner, Derrick, Cin.	8	7	1	0	48
Jackson, Mark, Den.	8	0	8	0	48
Miller, Anthony, S.D.	8	0	7	1	48
White, Lorenzo, Hou.	8	7	1	0	48
Brown, Tim, Rai.	7	0	7	0	42
Duper, Mark, Mia.	7	0	7	0	42
Higgs, Mark, Mia.	7	7	0	0	42
Jackson, Michael, Cle.	7	0	7	0	42
Metcalf, Eric, Cle.	7	1	5	1	42
Baxter, Brad, NY-J	6	6	0	0	36
Davis, Kenneth, Buf.	6	6	0	0	36
Lofton, James, Buf.	6	0	6	0	36
Mack, Kevin, Cle.	6	6	0	0	36
Metzelaars, Pete, Buf.	6	0	6	0	36
Okoye, Christian, K.C.	6	6	0	0	36
Jackson, Keith, Mia.	5	0	5	0	30
Ball, Eric, Cin.	4	2	2	0	24
Barnett, Tim, K.C.	4	0	4	0	24
Bernstine, Rod, S.D.	4	4	0	0	24
Butts, Marion, S.D.	4	4	0	0	24
Fryar, Irving, N.E.	4	0	4	0	24
Gault, Willie, Rai.	4	0	4	0	24

	TD	TDR	TDP	TDM	PTS
Harmon, Ronnie, S.D.	4	3	1	0	24
Humphries, Stan, S.D.	4	4	0	0	24
Lewis, Greg, Den.	4	4	0	0	24
Lewis, Nate, S.D.	4	0	4	0	24
Mathis, Terance, NY-J	4	1	3	0	24
Moore, Rob, NY-J	4	0	4	0	24
Rivers, Reggie, Den.	4	3	1	0	24
Slaughter, Webster, Hou.	4	0	4	0	24
Word, Barry, K.C.	4	4	0	0	24
Allen, Marcus, Rai.	3	2	1	0	18
Banks, Fred, Mia.	3	0	3	0	18
Bell, Nick, Rai.	3	3	0	0	18
Bieniemy, Eric, S.D.	3	3	0	0	18
Birden, J.J., K.C.	3	0	3	0	18
Carter, Dale, K.C.	3	0	0	3	18
Cash, Kerry, Ind.	3	0	3	0	18
Clayton, Mark, Mia.	3	0	3	0	18
Coates, Ben, N.E.	3	0	3	0	18
Cooper, Adrian, Pit.	3	0	3	0	18
Davis, Willie, K.C.	3	0	3	0	18
Dickerson, Eric, Rai.	3	2	1	0	18
Johnson, Anthony, Ind.	3	0	3	0	18
Kane, Tommy, Sea.	3	0	3	0	18
McGee, Tim, Cin.	3	0	3	0	18
Mills, Ernie, Pit.	3	0	3	0	18
Mincy, Charles, K.C.	3	0	0	3	18
Query, Jeff, Cin.	3	0	3	0	18
Reed, Andre, Buf.	3	0	3	0	18
Stone, Dwight, Pit.	3	0	3	0	18
Warren, Chris, Sea.	3	3	0	0	18
Williams, John L., Sea.	3	1	2	0	18
Bavaro, Mark, Cle.	2	0	2	0	12
Beebe, Don, Buf.	2	0	2	0	12
Brandon, David, Cle.	2	0	0	2	12
Brown, Vincent, N.E.	2	0	0	2	12
Cash, Keith, K.C.	2	0	2	0	12
Cook, Marv, N.E.	2	0	2	0	12
Elway, John, Den.	2	2	0	0	12
Frerotte, Mitch, Buf.	2	0	2	0	12
Gardner, Carwell, Buf.	2	2	0	0	12
Green, Eric, Pit.	2	0	2	0	12
Green, Gaston, Den.	2	2	0	0	12
Green, Harold, Cin.	2	2	0	0	12
Harris, Leonard, Hou.	2	0	2	0	12
Hayes, Jonathan, K.C.	2	0	2	0	12
Holman, Rodney, Cin.	2	0	2	0	12
Horton, Ethan, Rai.	2	0	2	0	12
Humphrey, Bobby, Mia.	2	1	1	0	12
Jefferson, Shawn, S.D.	2	0	2	0	12
Johnson, Vance, Den.	2	0	2	0	12
Jones, Henry, Buf.	2	0	0	2	12
Jorden, Tim, Pit.	2	0	2	0	12
Krieg, Dave, K.C.	2	2	0	0	12
Martin, Tony, Mia.	2	0	2	0	12
McNair, Todd, K.C.	2	1	1	0	12
Paige, Tony, Mia.	2	1	1	0	12
Pickens, Carl, Cin.	2	0	1	1	12
Russell, Leonard, N.E.	2	2	0	0	12
Sharpe, Shannon, Den.	2	0	2	0	12
Stephens, John, N.E.	2	2	0	0	12
Thompson, Craig, Cin.	2	0	2	0	12
Toon, Al, NY-J	2	0	2	0	12
Turner, Kevin, N.E.	2	0	2	0	12
Vaughn, Jon, N.E.	2	1	0	1	12
Verdin, Clarence, Ind.	2	0	0	2	12
Walker, Derrick, S.D.	2	0	2	0	12
Wright, Alexander, Rai.	2	0	2	0	12
Anderson, Eddie, Rai.	1	0	0	1	6
Arbuckle, Charles, Ind.	1	0	1	0	6
Baty, Greg, Mia.	1	0	1	0	6
Bentley, Ray, Cin.	1	0	0	1	6
Blades, Brian, Sea.	1	0	1	0	6
Brennan, Brian, Cin.	1	0	1	0	6
Brim, Michael, NY-J	1	0	0	1	6
Brooks, Michael, Den.	1	0	0	1	6
Brooks, Bill, Ind.	1	0	1	0	6
Brown, Gary, Hou.	1	1	0	0	6
Brown, J.B., Mia.	1	0	0	1	6
Burkett, Chris, NY-J	1	0	1	0	6
Carlson, Cody, Hou.	1	1	0	0	6
Carpenter, Rob, NY-J	1	0	1	0	6
Carrington, Darren, S.D.	1	0	0	1	6
Chaffey, Pat, NY-J	1	1	0	0	6
Childress, Ray, Hou.	1	0	0	1	6
Clark, Louis, Sea.	1	0	1	0	6
Davenport, Charles, Pit.	1	0	0	1	6
Duncan, Curtis, Hou.	1	0	1	0	6
Edmunds, Ferrell, Mia.	1	0	1	0	6
Emtman, Steve, Ind.	1	0	0	1	6

	TD	TDR	TDP	TDM	PTS
Fina, John, Buf.	1	0	1	0	6
Francis, James, Cin.	1	0	0	1	6
Fuller, William, Hou.	1	0	0	1	6
Galbraith, Scott, Cle.	1	0	1	0	6
Gash, Sam, N.E.	1	1	0	0	6
George, Jeff, Ind.	1	1	0	0	6
Glover, Andrew, Rai.	1	0	1	0	6
Goad, Tim, N.E.	1	0	0	1	6
Graddy, Sam, Rai.	1	0	1	0	6
Graham, Jeff, Pit.	1	0	1	0	6
Green, Paul, Sea.	1	0	1	0	6
Griffin, Larry, Pit.	1	0	0	1	6
Harper, Dwayne, Sea.	1	0	0	1	6
Henderson, Wymon, Den.	1	0	0	1	6
Hester, Jessie, Ind.	1	0	1	0	6
Hoard, Leroy, Cle.	1	0	1	0	6
Hoge, Merril, Pit.	1	0	1	0	6
Houston, Bobby, NY-J	1	0	0	1	6
Jackson, Vestee, Mia.	1	0	0	1	6
Johnson, Mike, Cle.	1	0	0	1	6
Johnson, Reggie, Den.	1	0	1	0	6
Jones, James, Cle.	1	0	1	0	6
Junkin, Trey, Sea.	1	0	1	0	6
Kelly, Jim, Buf.	1	1	0	0	6
Langhorne, Reggie, Ind.	1	0	1	0	6
Lodish, Mike, Buf.	1	0	0	1	6
Marshall, Arthur, Den.	1	0	1	0	6
Marts, Lonnie, K.C.	1	0	0	1	6
McDowell, Bubba, Hou.	1	0	0	1	6
McMurtry, Greg, N.E.	1	0	1	0	6
Meads, Johnny, Hou.	1	0	0	1	6
Mitchell, Johnny, NY-J	1	0	1	0	6
Moon, Warren, Hou.	1	1	0	0	6
Moore, Stevon, Cle.	1	0	0	1	6
O'Donnell, Neil, Pit.	1	1	0	0	6
Oliver, Louis, Mia.	1	0	0	1	6
Patterson, Elvis, Rai.	1	0	0	1	6
Pool, David, N.E.	1	0	0	1	6
Rogers, Tracy, K.C.	1	0	0	1	6
Ross, Kevin, K.C.	1	0	0	1	6
Schultz, William, Ind.	1	0	1	0	6
Singleton, Chris, N.E.	1	0	0	1	6
Smith, Neil, K.C.	1	0	0	1	6
Smith, Steve, Rai.	1	0	1	0	6
Stegall, Milt, Cin.	1	0	1	0	6
Thomas, Derrick, K.C.	1	0	0	1	6
Thompson, Leroy, Pit.	1	1	0	0	6
Tillman, Cedric, Den.	1	0	1	0	6
Timpson, Michael, N.E.	1	0	1	0	6
Vinson, Fernandus, Cin.	1	0	0	1	6
Washington, Brian, NY-J	1	0	0	1	6
Williams, Harvey, K.C.	1	1	0	0	6
Wolfley, Ron, Cle.	1	0	1	0	6
Woodson, Rod, Pit.	1	0	0	1	6
Grossman, Burt, S.D.	0	0	0	0	*4
Hale, Chris, Buf.	0	0	0	0	*2
Harrison, Nolan, Rai.	0	0	0	0	*2
Mims, Chris, S.D.	0	0	0	0	*2
Washington, Marvin, NY-J	0	0	0	0	*2

** indicates safety*
Team safety credited to Houston

NFC Scoring—Individual

Kickers	XP	XPA	FG	FGA	PTS
Andersen, Morten, N.O.	33	34	29	34	120
Lohmiller, Chip, Was.	30	30	30	40	120
Elliott, Lin, Dal.	47	48	24	35	119
Cofer, Mike, S.F.	53	54	18	27	107
Reveiz, Fuad, Min.	45	45	19	25	102
Jacke, Chris, G.B.	30	30	22	29	96
Hanson, Jason, Det.	30	30	21	26	93
Johnson, Norm, Atl.	39	39	18	22	93
Butler, Kevin, Chi.	34	34	19	26	91
Ruzek, Roger, Phi.	40	44	16	25	88
Zendejas, Tony, Rams	38	38	15	20	83
Bahr, Matt, NY-G	29	29	16	21	77
Davis, Greg, Pho.	28	28	13	26	67
Willis, Ken, T.B.-NY-G	27	27	10	16	57
Murray, Eddie, K.C.-T.B.	13	13	5	9	28
Camarillo, Rich, Pho.	0	1	0	0	0

Non-kickers	TD	TDR	TDP	TDM	PTS
Smith, Emmitt, Dal.	19	18	1	0	114
Allen, Terry, Min.	15	13	2	0	90
Hampton, Rodney, NY-G	14	14	0	0	84
Sharpe, Sterling, G.B.	13	0	13	0	78
Anderson, Neal, Chi.	11	5	6	0	66

	TD	TDR	TDP	TDM	PTS
Rice, Jerry, S.F.	11	1	10	0	66
Rison, Andre, Atl.	11	0	11	0	66
Watters, Ricky, S.F.	11	9	2	0	66
Gary, Cleveland, Rams	10	7	3	0	60
Haynes, Michael, Atl.	10	0	10	0	60
Sanders, Barry, Det.	10	9	1	0	60
Walker, Herschel, Phi.	10	8	2	0	60
Cobb, Reggie, T.B.	9	9	0	0	54
Rathman, Tom, S.F.	9	5	4	0	54
Anderson, Willie, Rams	7	0	7	0	42
Byner, Earnest, Was.	7	6	1	0	42
Hilliard, Dalton, N.O.	7	3	4	0	42
Irvin, Michael, Dal.	7	0	7	0	42
Williams, Calvin, Phi.	7	0	7	0	42
Barnett, Fred, Phi.	6	0	6	0	36
Carter, Cris, Min.	6	0	6	0	36
Johnson, Johnny, Pho.	6	6	0	0	36
Lang, David, Rams	6	5	1	0	36
Novacek, Jay, Dal.	6	0	6	0	36
Sherman, Heath, Phi.	6	5	1	0	36
Clark, Gary, Was.	5	0	5	0	30
Cunningham, Randall, Phi.	5	5	0	0	30
Early, Quinn, N.O.	5	0	5	0	30
Green, Willie, Det.	5	0	5	0	30
Lewis, Darren, Chi.	5	4	0	1	30
Martin, Eric, N.O.	5	0	5	0	30
Martin, Kelvin, Dal.	5	0	3	2	30
McCaffrey, Ed, NY-G	5	0	5	0	30
Muster, Brad, Chi.	5	3	2	0	30
Pritchard, Mike, Atl.	5	0	5	0	30
Bunch, Jarrod, NY-G	4	3	1	0	24
Carrier, Mark, T.B.	4	0	4	0	24
Craig, Roger, Min.	4	4	0	0	24
Hall, Ron, T.B.	4	0	4	0	24
Harper, Alvin, Dal.	4	0	4	0	24
Jones, Brent, S.F.	4	0	4	0	24
Jones, Ernie, Pho.	4	0	4	0	24
Jones, Hassan, Min.	4	0	4	0	24
Lee, Amp, S.F.	4	2	2	0	24
Moore, Herman, Det.	4	0	4	0	24
Perriman, Brett, Det.	4	0	4	0	24
Waddle, Tom, Chi.	4	0	4	0	24
Young, Steve, S.F.	4	4	0	0	24
Byars, Keith, Phi.	3	1	2	0	18
Carter, Anthony, Min.	3	1	2	0	18
Carter, Pat, Rams	3	0	3	0	18
Chadwick, Jeff, Rams	3	0	3	0	18
Dunbar, Vaughn, N.O.	3	3	0	0	18
Ellard, Henry, Rams	3	0	3	0	18
Heyward, Craig, N.O.	3	3	0	0	18
Hill, Drew, Atl.	3	0	3	0	18
Hill, Randal, Pho.	3	0	3	0	18
Hostetler, Jeff, NY-G	3	3	0	0	18
Massey, Robert, Pho.	3	0	0	3	18
Meggett, David, NY-G	3	0	2	1	18
Monk, Art, Was.	3	0	3	0	18
Orr, Terry, Was.	3	0	3	0	18
Proehl, Ricky, Pho.	3	0	3	0	18
Sanders, Deion, Atl.	3	0	1	2	18
Sanders, Ricky, Was.	3	0	3	0	18
Small, Torrance, N.O.	3	0	3	0	18
Sydney, Harry, G.B.	3	2	1	0	18
Taylor, John, S.F.	3	0	3	0	18
Thompson, Darrell, G.B.	3	2	1	0	18
Bailey, Johnny, Pho.	2	1	1	0	12
Baker, Stephen, NY-G	2	0	2	0	12
Beach, Pat, Phi.	2	0	2	0	12
Broussard, Steve, Atl.	2	1	1	0	12
Brown, Ivory Lee, Pho.	2	2	0	0	12
Buckley, Terrell, G.B.	2	0	0	2	12
Carroll, Wesley, N.O.	2	0	2	0	12
Centers, Larry, Pho.	2	0	2	0	12
Cross, Howard, NY-G	2	0	2	0	12
Davis, Wendell, Chi.	2	0	2	0	12
Drewrey, Willie, T.B.	2	0	2	0	12
Ervins, Ricky, Was.	2	2	0	0	12
Goff, Robert, N.O.	2	0	0	2	12
Gray, Mel, Det.	2	0	0	2	12
Green, Mark, Chi.	2	2	0	0	12
Harris, Jackie, G.B.	2	0	2	0	12
Hawkins, Courtney, T.B.	2	0	2	0	12
Jenkins, Carlos, Min.	2	0	0	2	12
Johnston, Daryl, Dal.	2	0	2	0	12
Jordan, Steve, Min.	2	0	2	0	12
Joyner, Seth, Phi.	2	0	0	2	12
Kinchen, Todd, Rams	2	0	0	2	12
McDowell, Anthony, T.B.	2	0	2	0	12
McMillian, Audray, Min.	2	0	0	2	12
Morgan, Anthony, Chi.	2	0	2	0	12
Price, Jim, Rams	2	0	2	0	12
Rypien, Mark, Was.	2	2	0	0	12
Smith, Tony, Atl.	2	2	0	0	12
Testaverde, Vinny, T.B.	2	2	0	0	12
Turner, Odessa, S.F.	2	0	2	0	12
Workman, Vince, G.B.	2	2	0	0	12
Doleman, Chris, Min.	1	0	0	1	*8
Aikman, Troy, Dal.	1	1	0	0	6
Anderson, Gary, T.B.	1	1	0	0	6
Armstrong, Tyji, T.B.	1	0	1	0	6
Bailey, Robert, Rams	1	0	0	1	6
Ball, Jerry, Det.	1	0	0	1	6
Barrett, Reggie, Det.	1	0	1	0	6
Beach, Sanjay, G.B.	1	0	1	0	6
Bennett, Tony, G.B.	1	0	0	1	6
Blades, Bennie, Det.	1	0	0	1	6
Brooks, Robert, G.B.	1	0	1	0	6
Buck, Vince, N.O.	1	0	0	1	6
Calloway, Chris, NY-G	1	0	1	0	6
Campbell, Jeff, Det.	1	0	1	0	6
Carter, Dexter, S.F.	1	0	1	0	6
Chandler, Chris, Pho.	1	1	0	0	6
Cook, Toi, N.O.	1	0	0	1	6
Copeland, Danny, Was.	1	0	0	1	6
Dawsey, Lawrence, T.B.	1	0	1	0	6
Delpino, Robert, Rams	1	0	1	0	6
Del Rio, Jack, Min.	1	0	0	1	6
Dotson, Santana, T.B.	1	0	0	1	6
Edwards, Anthony, Pho.	1	0	1	0	6
Edwards, Brad, Was.	1	0	0	1	6
Favre, Brett, G.B.	1	1	0	0	6
Hanks, Merton, S.F.	1	0	0	1	6
Harbaugh, Jim, Chi.	1	1	0	0	6
Henderson, Keith, Min.	1	1	0	0	6
Horton, Ray, Dal.	1	0	0	1	6
Howard, Desmond, Was.	1	0	0	1	6
Ingram, Mark, NY-G	1	0	1	0	6
Jackson, John, Pho.	1	0	1	0	6
Jenkins, Mel, Det.	1	0	0	1	6
Jennings, Keith, Chi.	1	0	1	0	6
Jennings, Stanford, T.B.	1	0	1	0	6
Johnson, John, S.F.	1	0	0	1	6
Johnson, Joe, Min.	1	0	1	0	6
Jones, Tony, Atl.	1	0	1	0	6
Jones, Reggie, N.O.	1	0	0	1	6
Jones, Roger, T.B.	1	0	0	1	6
Logan, Marc, S.F.	1	1	0	0	6
Marshall, Wilber, Was.	1	0	0	1	6
Maryland, Russell, Dal.	1	0	0	1	6
McAfee, Fred, N.O.	1	1	0	0	6
Mills, Sam, N.O.	1	0	0	1	6
Mitchell, Brian, Was.	1	0	0	1	6
Parker, Anthony, Min.	1	0	0	1	6
Phillips, Jason, Atl.	1	0	1	0	6
Reynolds, Ricky, T.B.	1	0	0	1	6
Richards, Curvin, Dal.	1	1	0	0	6
Rose, Ken, Phi.	1	0	0	1	6
Scott, Todd, Min.	1	0	0	1	6
Sherrard, Mike, S.F.	1	0	0	1	6
Sikahema, Vai, Phi.	1	0	0	1	6
Taylor, Kitrick, G.B.	1	0	1	0	6
Thomas, Broderick, T.B.	1	0	0	1	6
Thompson, Anthony, Pho.	1	1	0	0	6
Thompson, Reyna, NY-G	1	0	0	1	6
Tice, Mike, Min.	1	0	1	0	6
Tuggle, Jessie, Atl.	1	0	0	1	6
White, Reggie, Phi.	1	0	0	1	6
Williams, Jamie, S.F.	1	0	1	0	6
Williams, Robert, Dal.	1	0	0	1	6
Zorich, Chris, Chi.	1	0	0	1	6
Greene, Kevin, Rams	0	0	0	0	*2
Holt, Issiac, Dal.	0	0	0	0	*2
Swann, Eric, Pho.	0	0	0	0	*2

** indicates safety*
Team safety credited to Philadelphia

Field Goals

Field Goal Percentage

AFC: .917—Nick Lowery, Kansas City
NFC: .853—Morten Andersen, New Orleans

Field Goals

AFC: 30—Pete Stoyanovich, Miami
NFC: 30—Chip Lohmiller, Washington

Field Goal Attempts

NFC: 40—Chip Lohmiller, Washington
AFC: 37—Pete Stoyanovich, Miami

Longest Field Goal

AFC: 54—Al Del Greco, Houston vs. Kansas City, September 20
Jeff Jaeger, Raiders vs. Giants, October 4
Steve Christie, Buffalo at Miami, November 16
NFC: 54—Norm Johnson, Atlanta vs. Jets, September 6
Norm Johnson, Atlanta vs. New England, November 29

Average Yards Made

AFC: 39.2—Jeff Jaeger, Raiders
NFC: 38.7—Norm Johnson, Atlanta

AFC Field Goals—Team

	FG	FGA	Pct	Long
Kansas City	23	25	.920	52
San Diego	26	32	.813	50
Miami	30	37	.811	53
Buffalo	24	30	.800	54
Denver	20	25	.800	46
Pittsburgh	28	36	.778	49
Houston	21	27	.778	54
Cleveland	21	29	.724	51
Cincinnati	19	28	.679	48
New England	11	17	.647	44
Seattle	14	22	.636	43
N.Y. Jets	19	30	.633	47
L.A. Raiders	15	26	.577	54
Indianapolis	16	29	.552	52
AFC Total	287	393	——	54
AFC Average	20.5	28.1	.730	—

NFC Field Goals—Team

	FG	FGA	Pct	Long
New Orleans	29	34	.853	52
Atlanta	18	22	.818	54
Detroit	21	26	.808	52
N.Y. Giants	18	23	.783	47
Minnesota	19	25	.760	52
Green Bay	22	29	.759	53
L.A. Rams	15	20	.750	49
Washington	30	40	.750	53
Chicago	19	26	.731	50
Dallas	24	35	.686	53
San Francisco	18	27	.667	46
Philadelphia	16	25	.640	50
Tampa Bay	12	22	.545	47
Phoenix	13	26	.500	49
NFC Total	274	380	——	54
NFC Average	19.6	27.1	.721	—
NFL Total	561	773	——	54
NFL Average	20.0	27.6	.726	—

AFC Field Goals—Individual

	1-19 Yards	20-29 Yards	30-39 Yards	40-49 Yards	50 or Longer	Totals	Avg. Yds. Att.	Avg Yds Made	Avg. Yds. Miss	Long
Lowery, Nick, K.C.	0-0	9-10	9-9	3-4	1-1	22-24	31.6	31.6	34.5	52
	—	.900	1.000	.750	1.000	.917				
Treadwell, David, Den.	1-1	9-10	6-8	4-5	0-0	20-24	31.9	31.5	34.0	46
	1.000	.900	.750	.800	—	.833				
Carney, John, S.D.	0-0	13-14	5-7	7-8	1-3	26-32	34.4	32.8	41.2	50
	—	.929	.714	.875	.333	.813				
Stoyanovich, Pete, Mia.	0-0	9-9	14-16	4-4	3-8	30-37	36.8	34.3	47.1	53
	—	1.000	.875	1.000	.375	.811				
Christie, Steve, Buf.	2-2	9-9	3-6	7-8	3-5	24-30	36.5	34.8	43.3	54
	1.000	1.000	.500	.875	.600	.800				
Anderson, Gary, Pit.	0-0	12-13	12-15	4-6	0-2	28-36	33.8	32.3	38.9	49
	—	.923	.800	.667	.000	.778				
Del Greco, Al, Hou.	3-3	8-9	5-6	4-8	1-1	21-27	33.7	31.7	40.8	54
	1.000	.889	.833	.500	1.000	.778				
Blanchard, Cary, NY-J	2-2	2-3	5-7	7-9	0-1	16-22	36.4	35.6	38.7	47
	1.000	.667	.714	.778	.000	.727				
Stover, Matt, Cle.	1-1	11-11	6-8	2-6	1-3	21-29	33.9	30.3	43.5	51
	1.000	1.000	.750	.333	.333	.724				
Breech, Jim, Cin.	0-0	8-8	7-7	4-11	0-1	19-27	36.0	31.7	46.0	48
	—	1.000	1.000	.364	.000	.704				
Baumann, Charlie, N.E.	2-2	4-4	3-7	2-4	0-0	11-17	33.6	29.8	40.7	44
	1.000	1.000	.429	.500	—	.647				
Kasay, John, Sea.	0-0	4-5	8-11	2-6	0-0	14-22	34.2	32.7	36.9	43
	—	.800	.727	.333	—	.636				
Jaeger, Jeff, Rai.	0-0	3-5	4-6	5-9	3-6	15-26	41.0	39.2	43.5	54
	—	.600	.667	.556	.500	577				
Biasucci, Dean, Ind.	0-0	3-3	6-11	6-12	1-3	16-29	39.6	37.1	42.6	52
	—	1.000	.545	.500	.333	.552				
Nonqualifiers:										
Staurovsky, Jason, NY-J	1-1	0-0	1-2	1-5	0-0	3-8	38.5	31.3	42.8	43
	1.000	—	.500	.200	—	.375				
Daluiso, Brad, Den.	0-0	0-0	0-0	0-0	0-1	0-1	54.0	0.0	54.0	—
	—	—	—	—	.000	.000				
Johnson, Lee, Cin.	0-0	0-0	0-0	0-0	0-1	0-1	59.0	0.0	59.0	—
	—	—	—	—	.000	.000				
AFC Total	12-12	104-113	94-126	62-105	15-37	287-393	35.6	33.2	41.9	54
	1.000	.920	.746	.590	.405	.730				
NFL Total	21-21	181-201	192-253	131-226	36-72	561-773	36.1	34.0	41.6	54
	1.000	.900	.759	.580	.500	.726				

Leader based on percentage, minimum 16 field goal attempts

NFC Field Goals—Individual

	1-19 Yards	20-29 Yards	30-39 Yards	40-49 Yards	50 or Longer	Totals	Avg. Yds. Att.	Avg Yds Made	Avg. Yds. Miss	Long
Andersen, Morten, N.O.	0-0	10-10	8-10	8-11	3-3	29-34	36.1	35.2	41.2	52
	—	1.000	.800	.727	1.000	.853				
Johnson, Norm, Atl.	0-0	6-6	4-5	4-7	4-4	18-22	39.0	38.7	40.5	54
	—	1.000	.800	.571	1.000	.818				
Hanson, Jason, Det.	0-0	5-5	10-10	4-6	2-5	21-26	38.8	35.8	51.4	52
	—	1.000	1.000	.667	.400	.808				
Bahr, Matt, NY-G	2-2	1-1	10-11	3-5	0-2	16-21	36.0	32.9	45.8	47
	1.000	1.000	.909	.600	.000	.762				
Reveiz, Fuad, Min.	0-0	4-6	7-7	5-8	3-4	19-25	37.8	37.6	38.3	52
	—	.667	1.000	.625	.750	.760				
Jacke, Chris, G.B.	0-0	5-7	9-10	6-9	2-3	22-29	37.6	37.0	39.4	53
	—	.714	.900	.667	.667	.759				
Lohmiller, Chip, Was.	2-2	9-9	9-15	8-12	2-2	30-40	35.9	34.4	40.3	53
	1.000	1.000	.600	.667	1.000	.750				
Zendejas, Tony, Rams	2-2	3-4	7-9	3-5	0-0	15-20	33.3	31.5	38.6	49
	1.000	.750	.778	.600	—	.750				
Butler, Kevin, Chi.	1-1	8-8	9-10	0-4	1-3	19-26	34.7	30.5	45.9	50
	1.000	1.000	.900	.000	.333	.731				
Elliott, Lin, Dal.	0-0	6-7	10-14	5-10	3-4	24-35	37.7	36.6	40.0	53
	—	.857	.714	.500	.750	.686				
Cofer, Mike, S.F.	0-0	7-8	5-8	6-10	0-1	18-27	35.6	33.4	39.9	46
	—	.875	.625	.600	.000	.667				
Ruzek, Roger, Phi.	2-2	3-3	4-6	6-13	1-1	16-25	37.7	35.4	41.8	50
	1.000	1.000	.667	.462	1.000	.640				
Willis, Ken, T.B.-NY-G	0-0	4-4	1-4	5-8	0-0	10-16	36.5	33.5	41.5	45
	—	1.000	.250	.625	—	.625				
Davis, Greg, Pho.	0-0	6-10	3-4	4-9	0-3	13-26	36.5	32.1	40.9	49
	—	.600	.750	.444	.000	.500				
Nonqualifiers:										
Murray, Eddie, K.C.-T.B.	0-0	0-0	2-4	2-4	1-1	5-9	39.4	40.8	37.8	52
	—	—	.500	.500	1.000	.556				
NFC Total	9-9	77-88	98-127	69-121	21-35	274-380	36.7	34.9	41.4	54
	1.000	.875	.772	.570	.600	.721				
NFL Total	21-21	181-201	192-253	131-226	36-72	561-773	36.1	34.0	41.6	54
	1.000	.900	.759	.580	.500	.726				

Leader based on percentage, minimum 16 field goal attempts

Rushing

Yards
NFC: 1713—Emmitt Smith, Dallas
AFC: 1690—Barry Foster, Pittsburgh

Yards, Game
AFC: 190—Barry Foster, Pittsburgh vs. Jets, September 13, (33 attempts, 2 TD)
Harold Green, Cincinnati vs. New England, December 20, (31 attempts, TD)
NFC: 174—Emmitt Smith, Dallas at Atlanta, December 21, (24 attempts, 2 TD)

Longest
NFC: 71—David Lang, Rams at Green Bay, December 20
AFC: 69—Barry Foster, Pittsburgh at Green Bay, September 27

Attempts
AFC: 390—Barry Foster, Pittsburgh
NFC: 373—Emmitt Smith, Dallas

Attempts, Game
AFC: 37—Thurman Thomas, Buffalo vs. Pittsburgh, November 8 (155 yards)
NFC: 36—Johnny Johnson, Phoenix vs. Giants, December 12 (156 yards)

Yards per Attempt
NFC: 5.2—Heath Sherman, Philadelphia
AFC: 4.8—Thurman Thomas, Buffalo

Touchdown
NFC: 18—Emmitt Smith, Dallas
AFC: 11—Barry Foster, Pittsburgh

Team Leaders, Yards
AFC: BUFFALO: 1487, Thurman Thomas; CINCINNATI: 1170, Harold Green; CLEVELAND: 543, Kevin Mack; DENVER: 648, Gaston Green; HOUSTON: 1226, Lorenzo White; INDIANAPOLIS: 592, Anthony Johnson; KANSAS CITY: 607, Barry Word; L.A. RAIDERS: 729, Eric Dickerson; MIAMI: 915, Mark Higgs; NEW ENGLAND: 451, Jon Vaughn; N.Y. JETS: 698, Brad Baxter; PITTSBURGH: 1690, Barry Foster; SAN DIEGO: 809, Marion Butts; SEATTLE: 1017, Chris Warren
NFC: ATLANTA: 363, Steve Broussard; CHICAGO: 582, Neal Anderson; DALLAS: 1713, Emmitt Smith; DETROIT: 1352, Barry Sanders; GREEN BAY: 631, Vince Workman; L.A. RAMS: 1125, Cleveland Gary; MINNESOTA: 1201, Terry Allen; NEW ORLEANS: 565, Vaughn Dunbar; N.Y. GIANTS: 1141, Rodney Hampton; PHILADELPHIA: 1070, Herschel Walker; PHOENIX: 734, Johnny Johnson; SAN FRANCISCO: 1013, Ricky Watters; TAMPA BAY: 1171, Reggie Cobb; WASHINGTON: 998, Earnest Byner

Team Champion
AFC: 2436—Buffalo
NFC: 2388—Philadelphia

AFC Rushing—Team

	Att.	Yards	Avg.	Long	TD
Buffalo	549	2436	4.4	64t	18
Pittsburgh	518	2156	4.2	69	13
Cincinnati	454	1976	4.4	53	11
San Diego	489	1875	3.8	33	18
L.A. Raiders	434	1794	4.1	66t	7
N.Y. Jets	424	1752	4.1	32	8
Houston	353	1626	4.6	44	10
Cleveland	451	1607	3.6	37	7
Seattle	402	1596	4.0	52	4
New England	419	1550	3.7	36	6
Kansas City	446	1532	3.4	44t	14
Miami	407	1525	3.7	23	9
Denver	403	1500	3.7	67t	11
Indianapolis	379	1102	2.9	36t	8
AFC Total	6128	24027	3.9	69	144
AFC Average	437.7	1716.2	3.9	—	10.3

NFC Rushing—Team

	Att.	Yards	Avg.	Long	TD
Philadelphia	516	2388	4.6	38	19
San Francisco	482	2315	4.8	43	22
Dallas	500	2121	4.2	68t	20
N.Y. Giants	458	2077	4.5	63t	20
Minnesota	497	2030	4.1	51	19
Chicago	427	1871	4.4	49t	15
Washington	483	1727	3.6	33	10
Tampa Bay	438	1706	3.9	25	12
L.A. Rams	393	1659	4.2	71	12
Detroit	378	1644	4.3	55t	9
New Orleans	454	1628	3.6	25	10
Green Bay	420	1555	3.7	44	7
Phoenix	395	1491	3.8	42t	11
Atlanta	322	1270	3.9	32	3
NFC Total	6163	25482	4.1	71	189
NFC Average	440.2	1820.1	4.1	—	13.5
NFL Total	12291	49509	—	71	333
NFL Average	439.0	1768.2	4.0	—	11.9

NFL Top 10 Rushers

	Att	Yards	Avg	Long	TD
Smith, Emmitt, Dal.	373	1713	4.6	68t	18
Foster, Barry, Pit.	390	1690	4.3	69	11
Thomas, Thurman, Buf.	312	1487	4.8	44	9
Sanders, Barry, Det.	312	1352	4.3	55t	9
White, Lorenzo, Hou.	265	1226	4.6	44	7
Allen, Terry, Min.	266	1201	4.5	51	13
Cobb, Reggie, T.B.	310	1171	3.8	25	9
Green, Harold, Cin.	265	1170	4.4	53	2
Hampton, Rodney, NY-G	257	1141	4.4	63t	14
Gary, Cleveland, Rams	279	1125	4.0	63	7

AFC Rushing—Individual

	Att	Yards	Avg	Long	TD
Foster, Barry, Pit.	390	1690	4.3	69	11
Thomas, Thurman, Buf.	312	1487	4.8	44	9
White, Lorenzo, Hou.	265	1226	4.6	44	7
Green, Harold, Cin.	265	1170	4.4	53	2
Warren, Chris, Sea.	223	1017	4.6	52	3
Higgs, Mark, Mia.	256	915	3.6	23	7
Butts, Marion, S.D.	218	809	3.7	22	4
Dickerson, Eric, Rai.	187	729	3.9	40t	2
Baxter, Brad, NY-J	152	698	4.6	30	6
Green, Gaston, Den.	161	648	4.0	67t	2
Davis, Kenneth, Buf.	139	613	4.4	64t	6
Word, Barry, K.C.	163	607	3.7	44t	4
Johnson, Anthony, Ind.	178	592	3.3	19	0
Mack, Kevin, Cle.	169	543	3.2	37	6
Fenner, Derrick, Cin.	112	500	4.5	35t	7
Bernstine, Rod, S.D.	106	499	4.7	25t	4
Humphrey, Bobby, Mia.	102	471	4.6	21	1
Vaughn, Jon, N.E.	113	451	4.0	36	1
Okoye, Christian, K.C.	144	448	3.1	22	6
Thomas, Blair, NY-J	97	440	4.5	19	0
Russell, Leonard, N.E.	123	390	3.2	23	2
Vardell, Tommy, Cle.	99	369	3.7	35	0
Bell, Nick, Rai.	81	366	4.5	66t	3
Williams, John L., Sea.	114	339	3.0	14	1
Culver, Rodney, Ind.	121	321	2.7	36t	7
Allen, Marcus, Rai.	67	301	4.5	21	2
Metcalf, Eric, Cle.	73	301	4.1	31	1
Rivers, Reggie, Den.	74	282	3.8	48	3
Stephens, John, N.E.	75	277	3.7	19	2
Lewis, Greg, Den.	73	268	3.7	22	4
Bieniemy, Eric, S.D.	74	264	3.6	21	3
Williams, Harvey, K.C.	78	262	3.4	11	1
Hoard, Leroy, Cle.	54	236	4.4	37	0
Harmon, Ronnie, S.D.	55	235	4.3	33	3
Chaffey, Pat, NY-J	27	186	6.9	32	1
McNeil, Freeman, NY-J	43	170	4.0	18	0
Gardner, Carwell, Buf.	40	166	4.2	19	2
Lockwood, Scott, N.E.	35	162	4.6	23	0
Schroeder, Jay, Rai.	28	160	5.7	19	0
Thompson, Leroy, Pit.	35	157	4.5	25	1
Hoge, Merril, Pit.	41	150	3.7	15	0
Moon, Warren, Hou.	27	147	5.4	23	1
Clark, Ken, Ind.	40	134	3.4	13	0
Smith, Steve, Rai.	44	129	2.9	15	0
McNair, Todd, K.C.	21	124	5.9	30	1
Stone, Dwight, Pit.	12	118	9.8	30	0
Hollas, Donald, Cin.	20	109	5.5	24	0
Millen, Hugh, N.E.	17	108	6.4	26	0
Elway, John, Den.	34	94	2.8	9	2
Smith, Sammie, Den.	23	94	4.1	15	0
Brown, Gary, Hou.	19	87	4.6	26	1
Evans, Vince, Rai.	11	79	7.2	16	0
Gelbaugh, Stan, Sea.	16	79	4.9	22	0
Humphries, Stan, S.D.	28	79	2.8	25	4
Carlson, Cody, Hou.	27	77	2.9	13	1
Givins, Earnest, Hou.	7	75	10.7	44	0
Krieg, Dave, K.C.	37	74	2.0	17	2
Mayes, Rueben, Sea.	28	74	2.6	14	0
Zolak, Scott, N.E.	18	71	3.9	19	0
Hector, Johnny, NY-J	24	67	2.8	14	0
Esiason, Boomer, Cin.	21	66	3.1	15	0
Marino, Dan, Mia.	20	66	3.3	12	0
Reed, Andre, Buf.	8	65	8.1	24	0
Nagle, Browning, NY-J	24	57	2.4	20	0
Marshall, Arthur, Den.	11	56	5.1	16	0
Ball, Eric, Cin.	16	55	3.4	17	2
Kelly, Jim, Buf.	31	53	1.7	10	1
Klingler, David, Cin.	11	53	4.8	12	0
Brown, A.B., NY-J	24	42	1.8	9	0
Turner, Kevin, N.E.	10	40	4.0	11	0
Fuller, Eddie, Buf.	6	39	6.5	15	0
Moore, Shawn, Den.	8	39	4.9	11	0
Tomczak, Mike, Cle.	24	39	1.6	16	0
Parmalee, Bernie, Mia.	6	38	6.3	20	0
Stouffer, Kelly, Sea.	9	37	4.1	11	0
Carlson, Jeff, N.E.	11	32	2.9	7	0
Baldwin, Randy, Cle.	10	31	3.1	11	0
Marinovich, Todd, Rai.	9	30	3.3	11	0
Graham, Scottie, NY-J	14	29	2.1	6	0
Harry, Emile, K.C.	1	27	27.0	27	0
George, Jeff, Ind.	14	26	1.9	13	1
Johnson, Tracy, Sea.	3	26	8.7	19	0
Mathis, Terance, NY-J	3	25	8.3	10t	1
Miles, Ostell, Cin.	8	22	2.8	9	0
Jackson, Michael, Cle.	1	21	21.0	21	0
Moore, Rob, NY-J	1	21	21.0	21	0
Maddox, Tommy, Den.	9	20	2.2	11	0
Mills, Ernie, Pit.	1	20	20.0	20	0
Slaughter, Webster, Hou.	3	20	6.7	10	0
Brister, Bubby, Pit.	10	16	1.6	8	0
Tillman, Lawyer, Cle.	2	15	7.5	15	0
Brooks, Bill, Ind.	2	14	7.0	8	0
McGwire, Dan, Sea.	3	13	4.3	11	0
Kosar, Bernie, Cle.	5	12	2.4	8	0
Hodson, Tom, N.E.	5	11	2.2	5	0
Mohr, Chris, Buf.	1	11	11.0	11	0
Paige, Tony, Mia.	7	11	1.6	6	1
Gainer, Derrick, Rai.	2	10	5.0	6	0
Mitchell, Scott, Mia.	8	10	1.3	8	0
Canley, Sheldon, NY-J	4	9	2.3	4	0
Carthon, Maurice, Ind.	4	9	2.3	5	0
Craver, Aaron, Mia.	3	9	3.0	8	0
Tasker, Steve, Buf.	1	9	9.0	9	0
Tupa, Tom, Ind.	3	9	3.0	10	0
Edwards, Al, Buf.	1	8	8.0	8	0
Harris, Leonard, Hou.	1	8	8.0	8	0
O'Brien, Ken, NY-J	8	8	1.0	7	0
Gash, Sam, N.E.	5	7	1.4	4	1
Johnson, Reggie, Den.	2	7	3.5	8	0
Lewis, Nate, S.D.	2	7	3.5	4	0
Saxon, James, Mia.	4	7	1.8	4	0
Thomas, Doug, Sea.	3	7	2.3	8	0
Fryar, Irving, N.E.	1	6	6.0	8	0
Gault, Willie, Rai.	1	6	6.0	6	0
Trudeau, Jack, Ind.	13	6	0.5	5	0
Blades, Brian, Sea.	1	5	5.0	5	0
O'Donnell, Neil, Pit.	27	5	0.2	9	1
McMurtry, Greg, N.E.	2	3	1.5	2	0
Carpenter, Rob, NY-J	1	2	2.0	2	0
Coates, Ben, N.E.	1	2	2.0	2	0
Wolfley, Ron, Cle.	1	2	2.0	2	0
Anders, Kimble, K.C.	1	1	1.0	1	0
Query, Jeff, Cin.	1	1	1.0	1	0
Tillman, Spencer, Hou.	1	1	1.0	1	0
Tuten, Rick, Sea.	1	0	0.0	0	0
Williams, Warren, Pit.	2	0	0.0	2	0
Jackson, Mark, Den.	3	-1	-0.3	1	0
Miller, Anthony, S.D.	1	-1	-1.0	-1	0
Perryman, Bob, Den.	3	-1	-0.3	1	0
Richardson, Bucky, Hou.	1	-1	-1.0	-1	0
Thomas, Robb, Sea.	1	-1	-1.0	-1	0
Blake, Jeff, NY-J	2	-2	-1.0	1	0
Herrmann, Mark, Ind.	3	-2	-0.7	0	0
Martin, Tony, Mia.	1	-2	-2.0	-2	0
Brown, Tim, Rai.	3	-4	-1.3	3	0
Gagliano, Bob, S.D.	3	-4	-1.3	0	0
Beebe, Don, Buf.	1	-6	-6.0	-6	0
Sharpe, Shannon, Den.	2	-6	-3.0	-3	0
Langhorne, Reggie, Ind.	1	-7	-7.0	-7	0
Reich, Frank, Buf.	9	-9	-1.0	0	0
McCarthy, Shawn, N.E.	3	-10	-3.3	0	0
Davis, Willie, K.C.	1	-11	-11.0	-11	0
Gossett, Jeff, Rai.	1	-12	-12.0	-12	0
Kidd, John, S.D.	2	-13	-6.5	0	0
Montgomery, Greg, Hou.	2	-14	-7.0	0	0

t *indicates touchdown*
Leader based on most yards gained

NFC Rushing—Individual

	Att	Yards	Avg	Long	TD
Smith, Emmitt, Dal.	373	1713	4.6	68t	18
Sanders, Barry, Det.	312	1352	4.3	55t	9
Allen, Terry, Min.	266	1201	4.5	51	13
Cobb, Reggie, T.B.	310	1171	3.8	25	9
Hampton, Rodney, NY-G	257	1141	4.4	63t	14
Gary, Cleveland, Rams	279	1125	4.0	63	7
Walker, Herschel, Phi.	267	1070	4.0	38	8
Watters, Ricky, S.F.	206	1013	4.9	43	9
Byner, Earnest, Was.	262	998	3.8	23	6
Johnson, Johnny, Pho.	178	734	4.1	42t	6
Workman, Vince, G.B.	159	631	4.0	44	2
Sherman, Heath, Phi.	112	583	5.2	34	5
Anderson, Neal, Chi.	156	582	3.7	49t	5

	Att	Yards	Avg	Long	TD
Dunbar, Vaughn, N.O.	154	565	3.7	25	3
Cunningham, Randall, Phi.	87	549	6.3	30	5
Young, Steve, S.F.	76	537	7.1	39t	4
Bunch, Jarrod, NY-G	104	501	4.8	37	3
Ervins, Ricky, Was.	151	495	3.3	25	2
Hilliard, Dalton, N.O.	115	445	3.9	22	3
Craig, Roger, Min.	105	416	4.0	21	4
Heyward, Craig, N.O.	104	416	4.0	23	3
Muster, Brad, Chi.	98	414	4.2	35	3
Lewis, Darren, Chi.	90	382	4.2	33	4
Broussard, Steve, Atl.	84	363	4.3	27	1
Lee, Amp, S.F.	91	362	4.0	43	2
Smith, Tony, Atl.	87	329	3.8	32	2
Jones, Keith, Atl.	79	278	3.5	26	0
Harbaugh, Jim, Chi.	47	272	5.8	17	1
Thompson, Darrell, G.B.	76	254	3.3	33	2
Bailey, Johnny, Pho.	52	233	4.5	15	1
Bennett, Edgar, G.B.	61	214	3.5	18	0
Lang, David, Rams	33	203	6.2	71	5
Favre, Brett, G.B.	47	198	4.2	19	1
Testaverde, Vinny, T.B.	36	197	5.5	18	2
Anderson, Gary, T.B.	55	194	3.5	18	1
Rathman, Tom, S.F.	57	194	3.4	17	5
Brown, Ivory Lee, Pho.	68	194	2.9	13	2
Gannon, Rich, Min.	45	187	4.2	14	0
Byars, Keith, Phi.	41	176	4.3	23	1
Richards, Curvin, Dal.	49	176	3.6	15	1
Hostetler, Jeff, NY-G	35	172	4.9	27	3
Meggett, David, NY-G	32	167	5.2	30	0
Sydney, Harry, G.B.	51	163	3.2	19	2
Henderson, Keith, S.F.-Min.	44	150	3.4	12	1
Chandler, Chris, Pho.	36	149	4.1	18	1
Centers, Larry, Pho.	37	139	3.8	28	0
Everett, Jim, Rams	32	133	4.2	22	0
Ware, Andre, Det.	20	124	6.2	32	0
Delpino, Robert, Rams	32	115	3.6	31	0
McAfee, Fred, N.O.	39	114	2.9	19	1
Green, Mark, Chi.	23	107	4.7	18	2
Aikman, Troy, Dal.	37	105	2.8	19	1
Hebert, Bobby, N.O.	32	95	3.0	18	0
Miller, Chris, Atl.	23	89	3.9	16	0
Pegram, Erric, Atl.	21	89	4.2	15	0
Peete, Rodney, Det.	21	83	4.0	12	0
McDowell, Anthony, T.B.	14	81	5.8	23	0
Mitchell, Brian, Was.	6	70	11.7	33	0
Morgan, Anthony, Chi.	3	68	22.7	35	0
Carter, Anthony, Min.	16	66	4.1	14	1
Thompson, Anthony, Pho.-Rams	19	65	3.4	12	1
Wilson, Wade, Atl.	15	62	4.1	12	0
Johnston, Daryl, Dal.	17	61	3.6	14	0
Rice, Jerry, S.F.	9	58	6.4	26t	1
Agee, Tommie, Dal.	16	54	3.4	10	0
Rypien, Mark, Was.	36	50	1.4	11	2
Green, Robert, Was.	8	46	5.8	23	0
Monk, Art, Was.	6	45	7.5	16	0
Brooks, James, Cle.-T.B.	18	44	2.4	13	0
Logan, Marc, S.F.	8	44	5.5	26	1
Davis, Wendell, Chi.	4	42	10.5	21	0
Stradford, Troy, Rams-Det.	12	41	3.4	11	0
Pritchard, Mike, Atl.	5	37	7.4	22	0
Graham, Kent, NY-G	6	36	6.0	15	0
Kramer, Erik, Det.	12	34	2.8	11	0
Majkowski, Don, G.B.	8	33	4.1	8	0
Anderson, Ottis, NY-G	10	31	3.1	6	0
Montana, Joe, S.F.	3	28	9.3	16	0
Johnson, Joe, Min.	4	26	6.5	9	0
Jennings, Stanford, T.B.	5	25	5.0	10	0
Bono, Steve, S.F.	15	23	1.5	19	0
Highsmith, Alonzo, T.B.	8	23	2.9	5	0
McMahon, Jim, Phi.	6	23	3.8	11	0
Proehl, Ricky, Pho.	3	23	7.7	10	0
Tillison, Ed, Det.	4	22	5.5	10	0
McGee, Buford, G.B.	8	19	2.4	4	0
Clark, Gary, Was.	2	18	9.0	12	0
Simms, Phil, NY-G	6	17	2.8	7	0
Carter, Cris, Min.	5	15	3.0	6	0
Harper, Alvin, Dal.	1	15	15.0	15	0
Tolliver, Billy Joe, Atl.	4	15	3.8	15	0
Brooks, Robert, G.B.	2	14	7.0	8	0
Howard, Desmond, Was.	3	14	4.7	7	0
Turner, Vernon, Rams	2	14	7.0	9	0
Martin, Kelvin, Dal.	2	13	6.5	8	0
Tillman, Lewis, NY-G	6	13	2.2	6	0
Solomon, Jesse, Atl.	2	12	6.0	12	0
McNabb, Dexter, G.B.	2	11	5.5	8	0
Rosenbach, Timm, Pho.	9	11	1.2	10	0
Harris, Corey, G.B.	2	10	5.0	7	0
Taylor, John, S.F.	1	10	10.0	10	0
Carter, Dexter, S.F.	4	9	2.3	6	0
Sharpe, Sterling, G.B.	4	8	2.0	14	0
Stryzinski, Dan, T.B.	1	7	7.0	7	0
Nelson, Darrin, Min.	10	5	0.5	9	0
Hill, Randal, Pho.	1	4	4.0	4	0
DeBerg, Steve, T.B.	3	3	1.0	4	0
Gentry, Dennis, Chi.	5	2	0.4	3	0
Sikahema, Vai, Phi.	2	2	1.0	1	0
Willis, Peter Tom, Chi.	1	2	2.0	2	0
Goodburn, Kelly, Was.	2	1	0.5	5	0
Jones, Hassan, Min.	1	1	1.0	1	0
Fulhage, Scott, Atl.	1	0	0.0	0	0
Pagel, Mike, Rams	1	0	0.0	0	0
Salisbury, Sean, Min.	11	0	0.0	4	0
Wilmsmeyer, Klaus, S.F.	2	0	0.0	10	0
Blount, Eric, Pho.	1	-1	-1.0	-1	0
Brown, Dave, NY-G	2	-1	-0.5	1	0
Early, Quinn, N.O.	3	-1	-0.3	7	0
Erickson, Craig, T.B.	1	-1	-1.0	-1	0
Barnhardt, Tommy, N.O.	4	-2	-0.5	12	0
Jones, Ernie, Pho.	2	-3	-1.5	1	0
Buck, Mike, N.O.	3	-4	-1.3	-1	0
Conklin, Cary, Was.	3	-4	-1.3	-1	0
Sanders, Deion, Atl.	1	-4	-4.0	-4	0
Sanders, Ricky, Was.	4	-6	-1.5	3	0
Beuerlein, Steve, Dal.	4	-7	-1.7	-1	0
Irvin, Michael, Dal.	1	-9	-9.0	-9	0
Barnett, Fred, Phi.	1	-15	-15.0	-15	0

t indicates touchdown
Leader based on most yards gained

Passing

Highest Rating
NFC: 107.0—Steve Young, San Francisco
AFC: 89.3—Warren Moon, Houston

Completion Percentage
NFC: 66.7—Steve Young, San Francisco
AFC: 65.6—Cody Carlson, Houston

Attempts
AFC: 554—Dan Marino, Miami
NFC: 479—Mark Rypien, Washington

Completions
AFC: 330—Dan Marino, Miami
NFC: 302—Troy Aikman, Dallas
Brett Favre, Green Bay

Yards
AFC: 4116—Dan Marino, Miami
NFC: 3465—Steve Young, San Francisco

Yards, Game
NFC: 449—Steve Young, San Francisco vs. Buffalo, September 13, (26-37, 3 TD)
AFC: 403—Jim Kelly, Buffalo at San Francisco, September 13, (22-33, 3 TD)

Longest
NFC: 89—Chris Miller (to Michael Haynes), Atlanta at Washington, September 13 - TD
AFC: 83—David Klingler (to Jeff Query), Cincinnati at San Diego, December 13 - TD

Yards per Attempt
NFC: 8.62—Steve Young, San Francisco
AFC: 7.54—Dave Krieg, Kansas City

Touchdown Passes
NFC: 25—Steve Young, San Francisco
AFC: 24—Dan Marino, Miami

Touchdown Passes, Game
AFC: 5—Warren Moon, Houston at Cincinnati, October 11, (21-32, 216 yards)
NFC: 5—Wade Wilson, Atlanta at Tampa Bay, December 13, (19-26, 324 yards)

Lowest Interception Percentage
NFC: 1.7—Steve Young, San Francisco
AFC: 2.9—Neil O'Donnell, Pittsburgh

Team Champion (Most Net Yards)
AFC: 4029—Houston
NFC: 3880—San Francisco

AFC Passing—Team

	Att	Comp	Pct Comp	Gross Yards	Yds/ Att	Yds/ Comp	Sacked	Yds Lost	Net Yards	TD	Pct TD	Long	Int	Pct Int
Houston	573	373	65.1	4231	7.38	11.34	32	202	4029	27	4.71	72	23	4.0
Miami	563	332	59.0	4148	7.37	12.49	28	173	3975	24	4.26	62t	17	3.0
Buffalo	509	293	57.6	3678	7.23	12.55	29	221	3457	23	4.52	65t	21	4.1
San Diego	496	282	56.9	3614	7.29	12.82	33	268	3346	16	3.23	67t	21	4.2
Indianapolis	546	305	55.9	3584	6.56	11.75	44	318	3266	13	2.38	81	26	4.8
Denver	473	258	54.5	3312	7.00	12.84	52	382	2930	16	3.38	81t	29	6.1
Kansas City	413	230	55.7	3115	7.54	13.54	48	323	2792	15	3.63	77t	12	2.9
Cleveland	398	238	59.8	3102	7.79	13.03	34	217	2885	18	4.52	69t	16	4.0
Pittsburgh	431	249	57.8	3046	7.07	12.23	40	296	2750	15	3.48	51	14	3.2
N.Y. Jets	495	251	50.7	2962	5.98	11.80	39	283	2679	12	2.42	55t	24	4.8
L.A. Raiders	471	233	49.5	2950	6.26	12.66	48	360	2590	20	4.25	68t	23	4.9
New England	444	244	55.0	2492	5.61	10.21	65	458	2034	13	2.93	65t	19	4.3
Seattle	476	230	48.3	2323	4.88	10.10	67	545	1778	9	1.89	57	23	4.8
Cincinnati	435	227	52.2	2284	5.25	10.06	45	341	1943	16	3.68	83t	17	3.9
AFC Total	6723	3745	—	44841	—	—	604	4387	40454	237	—	83t	285	—
AFC Average	480.2	267.5	55.7	3202.9	6.67	11.97	43.1	313.4	2889.6	16.9	3.5	—	20.4	4.2

NFC Passing—Team

	Att	Comp	Pct Comp	Gross Yards	Yds/ Att	Yds/ Comp	Sacked	Yds Lost	Net Yards	TD	Pct TD	Long	Int	Pct Int
San Francisco	480	319	66.5	4054	8.45	12.71	32	174	3880	29	6.04	80t	9	1.9
Atlanta	548	336	61.3	3892	7.10	11.58	40	259	3633	33	6.02	89t	15	2.7
Dallas	491	314	64.0	3597	7.33	11.46	23	112	3485	23	4.68	87t	15	3.1
Green Bay	527	340	64.5	3498	6.64	10.29	43	268	3230	20	3.80	76t	15	2.8
L.A. Rams	495	289	58.4	3422	6.91	11.84	26	204	3218	23	4.65	67t	20	4.0
Tampa Bay	511	299	58.5	3399	6.65	11.37	45	334	3065	17	3.33	81t	20	3.9
Phoenix	517	298	57.6	3344	6.47	11.22	36	258	3086	15	2.90	72t	24	4.6
Washington	485	272	56.1	3339	6.88	12.28	23	176	3163	15	3.09	62t	17	3.5
Chicago	479	266	55.5	3334	6.96	12.53	45	264	3070	17	3.55	83t	24	5.0
New Orleans	426	251	58.9	3297	7.74	13.14	15	119	3178	19	4.46	72t	16	3.8
Minnesota	458	258	56.3	3162	6.90	12.26	40	293	2869	18	3.93	60t	15	3.3
Detroit	406	231	56.9	3150	7.76	13.64	59	354	2796	16	3.94	78t	21	5.2
Philadelphia	429	255	59.4	3054	7.12	11.98	64	462	2592	20	4.66	75t	13	3.0
N.Y. Giants	433	232	53.6	2628	6.07	11.33	45	283	2345	14	3.23	46	10	2.3
NFC Total	6685	3960	—	47170	—	—	536	3560	43610	279	—	89t	234	—
NFC Average	477.5	282.9	59.2	3369.3	7.06	11.91	38.3	254.3	3115.0	19.9	4.2	—	16.7	3.5
NFL Total	13408	7705	—	92011	—	—	1140	7947	84064	516	—	89t	519	—
NFL Average	478.9	275.2	57.5	3286.1	6.86	11.94	40.7	283.8	3002.3	18.4	3.8	—	18.5	3.9

Leader based on net yards

NFL Top 10 Passers

	Att	Comp	Pct Comp	Yds	Avg Gain	TD	Pct TD	Long	Int	Pct Int	Sack	Yds Lost	Rating Points
Young, Steve, S.F.	402	268	66.7	3465	8.62	25	6.2	80t	7	1.7	29	152	107.0
Miller, Chris, Atl.	253	152	60.1	1739	6.87	15	5.9	89t	6	2.4	16	103	90.7
Aikman, Troy, Dal.	473	302	63.8	3445	7.28	23	4.9	87t	14	3.0	23	112	89.5
Moon, Warren, Hou.	346	224	64.7	2521	7.29	18	5.2	72	12	3.5	16	105	89.3
Cunningham, Randall, Phi.	384	233	60.7	2775	7.23	19	4.9	75t	11	2.9	60	437	87.3
Favre, Brett, G.B.	471	302	64.1	3227	6.85	18	3.8	76t	13	2.8	34	208	85.3
Marino, Dan, Mia.	554	330	59.6	4116	7.43	24	4.3	62t	16	2.9	28	173	85.1
O'Donnell, Neil, Pit.	313	185	59.1	2283	7.29	13	4.2	51	9	2.9	27	208	83.6
Hebert, Bobby, N.O.	422	249	59.0	3287	7.79	19	4.5	72t	16	3.8	15	119	82.9
Kelly, Jim, Buf.	462	269	58.2	3457	7.48	23	5.0	65t	19	4.1	20	145	81.2

AFC Passing—Individual

	Att	Comp	Pct Comp	Yds	Avg Gain	TD	Pct TD	Long	Int	Pct Int	Sack	Yds Lost	Rating Points
Moon, Warren, Hou.	346	224	64.7	2521	7.29	18	5.2	72	12	3.5	16	105	89.3
Marino, Dan, Mia.	554	330	59.6	4116	7.43	24	4.3	62t	16	2.9	28	173	85.1
O'Donnell, Neil, Pit.	313	185	59.1	2283	7.29	13	4.2	51	9	2.9	27	208	83.6
Kelly, Jim, Buf.	462	269	58.2	3457	7.48	23	5.0	65t	19	4.1	20	145	81.2
Carlson, Cody, Hou.	227	149	65.6	1710	7.53	9	4.0	65	11	4.8	15	90	81.2
Krieg, Dave, K.C.	413	230	55.7	3115	7.54	15	3.6	77t	12	2.9	48	323	79.9
Humphries, Stan, S.D.	454	263	57.9	3356	7.39	16	3.5	67t	18	4.0	28	218	76.4
Elway, John, Den.	316	174	55.1	2242	7.09	10	3.2	80t	17	5.4	36	272	65.7
Schroeder, Jay, Rai.	253	123	48.6	1476	5.83	11	4.3	53	11	4.3	25	180	63.3
George, Jeff, Ind.	306	167	54.6	1963	6.42	7	2.3	57t	15	4.9	27	188	61.5
Esiason, Boomer, Cin.	278	144	51.8	1407	5.06	11	4.0	38	15	5.4	19	150	57.0
Nagle, Browning, NY-J	387	192	49.6	2280	5.89	7	1.8	51	17	4.4	27	215	55.7
Gelbaugh, Stan, Sea.	255	121	47.5	1307	5.13	6	2.4	57	11	4.3	34	265	52.9
Nonqualifiers													
Philcox, Todd, Cle.	27	13	48.1	217	8.04	3	11.1	69t	1	3.7	1	6	97.3
Hollas, Donald, Cin.	58	35	60.3	335	5.78	2	3.4	24t	0	0.0	8	45	87.9

	Att	Comp	Pct Comp	Yds	Avg Gain	TD	Pct TD	Long	Int	Pct Int	Sack	Yds Lost	Rating Points
Kosar, Bernie, Cle.	155	103	66.5	1160	7.48	8	5.2	69t	7	4.5	21	126	87.0
Herrmann, Mark, Ind.	24	15	62.5	177	7.38	1	4.2	27	1	4.2	1	5	81.4
Tomczak, Mike, Cle.	211	120	56.9	1693	8.02	7	3.3	52	7	3.3	12	85	80.1
Evans, Vince, Rai.	53	29	54.7	372	7.02	4	7.5	50	3	5.7	3	26	78.5
Millen, Hugh, N.E.	203	124	61.1	1203	5.93	8	3.9	39	10	4.9	33	204	70.3
Hodson, Tom, N.E.	91	50	54.9	496	5.45	2	2.2	54t	2	2.2	12	96	68.8
Trudeau, Jack, Ind.	181	105	58.0	1271	7.02	4	2.2	81	8	4.4	11	85	68.6
O'Brien, Ken, NY-J	98	55	56.1	642	6.55	5	5.1	55t	6	6.1	10	61	67.6
Klingler, David, Cin.	98	47	48.0	530	5.41	3	3.1	83t	2	2.0	18	146	66.3
Brister, Bubby, Pit.	116	63	54.3	719	6.20	2	1.7	42	5	4.3	13	88	61.0
Zolak, Scott, N.E.	100	52	52.0	561	5.61	2	2.0	65t	4	4.0	17	137	58.8
Marinovich, Todd, Rai.	165	81	49.1	1102	6.68	5	3.0	68t	9	5.5	20	154	58.2
Maddox, Tommy, Den.	121	66	54.5	757	6.26	5	4.1	38	9	7.4	10	60	56.4
Tupa, Tom, Ind.	33	17	51.5	156	4.73	1	3.0	19	2	6.1	5	40	49.6
Stouffer, Kelly, Sea.	190	92	48.4	900	4.74	3	1.6	33	9	4.7	26	222	47.7
Reich, Frank, Buf.	47	24	51.1	221	4.70	0	0.0	21	2	4.3	9	76	46.5
Gagliano, Bob, S.D.	42	19	45.2	258	6.14	0	0.0	55	3	7.1	5	50	35.6
Moore, Shawn, Den.	34	17	50.0	232	6.82	0	0.0	40	3	8.8	6	50	35.4
Carlson, Jeff, N.E.	49	18	36.7	232	4.73	1	2.0	40	3	6.1	3	21	33.7
McGwire, Dan, Sea.	30	17	56.7	116	3.87	0	0.0	20	3	10.0	7	58	25.8
Fewer than 10 attempts													
Blake, Jeff, NY-J	9	4	44.4	40	4.44	0	0.0	19	1	11.1	2	7	18.1
Breech, Jim, Cin.	1	1	100.0	12	12.00	0	0.0	12	0	0.0	0	0	116.7
Carpenter, Rob, NY-J	1	0	0.0	0	0.00	0	0.0	0	0	0.0	0	0	39.6
Foster, Barry, Pit.	1	0	0.0	0	0.00	0	0.0	0	0	0.0	0	0	39.6
Goebel, Brad, Cle.	3	2	66.7	32	10.67	0	0.0	22	0	0.0	0	0	102.1
Johnson, Anthony, Ind.	1	0	0.0	0	0.00	0	0.0	0	0	0.0	0	0	39.6
Lewis, Greg, Den.	1	0	0.0	0	0.00	0	0.0	0	0	0.0	0	0	39.6
Marshall, Arthur, Den.	1	1	100.0	81	81.00	1	100.0	81t	0	0.0	0	0	158.3
Martin, Tony, Mia.	1	0	0.0	0	0.00	0	0.0	0	0	0.0	0	0	39.6
McMurtry, Greg, N.E.	1	0	0.0	0	0.00	0	0.0	0	0	0.0	0	0	39.6
Metcalf, Eric, Cle.	1	0	0.0	0	0.00	0	0.0	0	0	0.0	0	0	39.6
Mitchell, Scott, Mia.	8	2	25.0	32	4.00	0	0.0	18	1	12.5	0	0	4.2
Richardson, Bucky, Hou.	0	0	—	0	—	0	—	—	0	—	1	7	—
Royals, Mark, Pit.	1	1	100.0	44	44.00	0	0.0	44	0	0.0	0	0	118.8
Stark, Rohn, Ind.	1	1	100.0	17	17.00	0	0.0	17	0	0.0	0	0	118.8
Stover, Matt, Cle.	1	0	0.0	0	0.00	0	0.0	0	1	100.0	0	0	0.0
Tuten, Rick, Sea.	1	0	0.0	0	0.00	0	0.0	0	0	0.0	0	0	39.6

t indicates touchdown
Leader based on rating points, minimum 224 attempts

NFC Passing—Individual

	Att	Comp	Pct Comp	Yds	Avg Gain	TD	Pct TD	Long	Int	Pct Int	Sack	Yds Lost	Rating Points
Young, Steve, S.F.	402	268	66.7	3465	8.62	25	6.2	80t	7	1.7	29	152	107.0
Miller, Chris, Atl.	253	152	60.1	1739	6.87	15	5.9	89t	6	2.4	16	103	90.7
Aikman, Troy, Dal.	473	302	63.8	3445	7.28	23	4.9	87t	14	3.0	23	112	89.5
Cunningham, Randall, Phi.	384	233	60.7	2775	7.23	19	4.9	75t	11	2.9	60	437	87.3
Favre, Brett, G.B.	471	302	64.1	3227	6.85	18	3.8	76t	13	2.8	34	208	85.3
Hebert, Bobby, N.O.	422	249	59.0	3287	7.79	19	4.5	72t	16	3.8	15	119	82.9
Everett, Jim, Rams	475	281	59.2	3323	7.00	22	4.6	67t	18	3.8	26	204	80.2
Chandler, Chris, Pho.	413	245	59.3	2832	6.86	15	3.6	72t	15	3.6	29	226	77.1
Harbaugh, Jim, Chi.	358	202	56.4	2486	6.94	13	3.6	83t	12	3.4	31	167	76.2
Testaverde, Vinny, T.B.	358	206	57.5	2554	7.13	14	3.9	81t	16	4.5	35	259	74.2
Gannon, Rich, Min.	279	159	57.0	1905	6.83	12	4.3	60t	13	4.7	25	177	72.9
Rypien, Mark, Was.	479	269	56.2	3282	6.85	13	2.7	62t	17	3.5	23	176	71.7
Nonqualifiers													
Montana, Joe, S.F.	21	15	71.4	126	6.00	2	9.5	17	0	0.0	1	8	118.4
Wilson, Wade, Atl.	163	111	68.1	1366	8.38	13	8.0	60t	4	2.5	8	58	110.1
Bono, Steve, S.F.	56	36	64.3	463	8.27	2	3.6	36	2	3.6	2	14	87.1
Simms, Phil, NY-G	137	83	60.6	912	6.66	5	3.6	38	3	2.2	10	67	83.3
Salisbury, Sean, Min.	175	97	55.4	1203	6.87	5	2.9	51	2	1.1	15	116	81.7
Hostetler, Jeff, NY-G	192	103	53.6	1225	6.38	8	4.2	46	3	1.6	24	148	80.8
Peete, Rodney, Det.	213	123	57.7	1702	7.99	9	4.2	78t	9	4.2	28	170	80.0
Majkowski, Don, G.B.	55	38	69.1	271	4.93	2	3.6	32	2	3.6	9	60	77.2
Ware, Andre, Det.	86	50	58.1	677	7.87	3	3.5	59	4	4.7	16	104	75.6
DeBerg, Steve, T.B.	125	76	60.8	710	5.68	3	2.4	28t	4	3.2	8	66	71.1
Tolliver, Billy Joe, Atl.	131	73	55.7	787	6.01	5	3.8	30t	5	3.8	16	98	70.4
Beuerlein, Steve, Dal.	18	12	66.7	152	8.44	0	0.0	27	1	5.6	0	0	69.7
Erickson, Craig, T.B.	26	15	57.7	121	4.65	0	0.0	24	0	0.0	2	9	69.6
Willis, Peter Tom, Chi.	92	54	58.7	716	7.78	4	4.3	68t	8	8.7	10	58	61.7
McMahon, Jim, Phi.	43	22	51.2	279	6.49	1	2.3	42t	2	4.7	4	25	60.1
Kramer, Erik, Det.	106	58	54.7	771	7.27	4	3.8	77t	8	7.5	15	80	59.1
Graham, Kent, NY-G	97	42	43.3	470	4.85	1	1.0	44	4	4.1	7	49	44.6
Rosenbach, Timm, Pho.	92	49	53.3	483	5.25	0	0.0	45	6	6.5	7	32	41.2
Pagel, Mike, Rams	20	8	40.0	99	4.95	1	5.0	22	2	10.0	0	0	33.1
Furrer, Will, Chi.	25	9	36.0	89	3.56	0	0.0	16	3	12.0	4	39	7.3
Sacca, Tony, Pho.	11	4	36.4	29	2.64	0	0.0	16	2	18.2	0	0	5.3
Fewer than 10 attempts													
Brown, Dave, NY-G	7	4	57.1	21	3.00	0	0.0	8	0	0.0	4	19	62.2
Buck, Mike, N.O.	4	2	50.0	10	2.50	0	0.0	10	0	0.0	0	0	56.3
Byars, Keith, Phi.	1	0	0.0	0	0.00	0	0.0	0	0	0.0	0	0	39.6

	Att	Comp	Pct Comp	Yds	Avg Gain	TD	Pct TD	Long	Int	Pct Int	Sack	Yds Lost	Rating Points
Byner, Earnest, Was.	3	1	33.3	41	13.67	1	33.3	41t	0	0.0	0	0	121.5
Carter, Anthony, Min.	1	0	0.0	0	0.00	0	0.0	0	0	0.0	0	0	39.6
Conklin, Cary, Was.	2	2	100.0	16	8.00	1	50.0	10t	0	0.0	0	0	139.6
Gardocki, Chris, Chi.	3	1	33.3	43	14.33	0	0.0	43	0	0.0	0	0	81.9
Henderson, Keith, Min.	1	1	100.0	36	36.00	1	100.0	36t	0	0.0	0	0	158.3
Jones, Hassan, Min.	1	1	100.0	18	18.00	0	0.0	18	0	0.0	0	0	118.8
Jones, Keith, Atl.	1	0	0.0	0	0.00	0	0.0	0	0	0.0	0	0	39.6
McJulien, Paul, G.B.	1	0	0.0	0	0.00	0	0.0	0	0	0.0	0	0	39.6
Mitchell, Brian, Was.	1	0	0.0	0	0.00	0	0.0	0	0	0.0	0	0	39.6
Muster, Brad, Chi.	1	0	0.0	0	0.00	0	0.0	0	1	100.0	0	0	0.0
Newsome, Harry, Min.	1	0	0.0	0	0.00	0	0.0	0	0	0.0	0	0	39.6
Proehl, Ricky, Pho.	1	0	0.0	0	0.00	0	0.0	0	1	100.0	0	0	0.0
Sanders, Barry, Det.	1	0	0.0	0	0.00	0	0.0	0	0	0.0	0	0	39.6
Stryzinski, Dan, T.B.	2	2	100.0	14	7.00	0	0.0	12	0	0.0	0	0	95.8
Walker, Herschel, Phi.	1	0	0.0	0	0.00	0	0.0	0	0	0.0	0	0	39.6
Watters, Ricky, S.F.	1	0	0.0	0	0.00	0	0.0	0	0	0.0	0	0	39.6

t indicates touchdown
Leader based on rating points, minimum 224 attempts

Pass Receiving

Receptions
NFC: 108—Sterling Sharpe, Green Bay
AFC: 90—Haywood Jeffires, Houston

Receptions, Game
NFC: 12—Vince Workman, Green Bay vs. Minnesota, September 6, (50 yards) (OT)
Emmitt Smith, Dallas at Phoenix, November 22, (67 yards)
AFC: 11—John L. Williams, Seattle at Giants, October 25, (45 yards)

Yards
NFC: 1461—Sterling Sharpe, Green Bay
AFC: 1060—Anthony Miller, San Diego

Yards, Game
NFC: 210—Michael Irvin, Dallas vs. Phoenix, September 20, (8 receptions - 3 TD)
AFC: 177—Eric Metcalf, Cleveland at Raiders, Septmeber 20, (5 receptions - 3 TD)

Longest
NFC: 89—Michael Haynes (from Chris Miller), Atlanta at Washington, September 13 - TD
AFC: 83—Jeff Query (from David Klingler), Cincinnati at San Diego, December 13 - TD

Yards per Reception
AFC: 21.0—Willie Davis, Kansas City
NFC: 18.9—Herman Moore, Detroit

Touchdowns
NFC: 13—Sterling Sharpe, Green Bay
AFC: 10—Ernest Givins, Houston

Team Leaders, Receptions
AFC: BUFFALO: 65, Andre Reed; CINCINNATI: 41, Harold Green; CLEVELAND: 47, Michael Jackson, Eric Metcalf; DENVER: 53, Shannon Sharpe; HOUSTON: 90, Haywood Jeffires; INDIANAPOLIS: 65, Reggie Langhorne; KANSAS CITY: 44, Todd McNair; L.A. RAIDERS: 49, Tim Brown; MIAMI: 54, Bobby Humphrey; NEW ENGLAND: 55, Irving Fryar; N.Y. JETS: 57, Chris Burkett; PITTSBURGH: 49, Jeff Graham; SAN DIEGO: 79, Ronnie Harmon; SEATTLE: 74, John L. Williams
NFC: ATLANTA: 93, Andre Rison; CHICAGO: 54, Wendell Davis; DALLAS: 78, Michael Irvin; DETROIT: 69, Brett Perriman; GREEN BAY: 108, Sterling Sharpe; L.A. RAMS: 52, Cleveland Gary; MINNESOTA: 53, Cris Carter; NEW ORLEANS: 68, Eric Martin; N.Y. GIANTS: 49, Ed McCaffrey; PHILADELPHIA: 67, Fred Barnett; PHOENIX: 60, Ricky Proehl; SAN FRANCISCO: 84, Jerry Rice; TAMPA BAY: 60, Lawrence Dawsey; WASHINGTON: 64, Gary Clark

NFL Top 10 Pass Receivers

	No.	Yards	Avg	Long	TD
Sharpe, Sterling, G.B.	108	1461	13.5	76t	13
Rison, Andre, Atl.	93	1119	12.0	71t	11
Jeffires, Haywood, Hou.	90	913	10.1	47	9
Rice, Jerry, S.F.	84	1201	14.3	80t	10
Duncan, Curtis, Hou.	82	954	11.6	72	1
Harmon, Ronnie, S.D.	79	914	11.6	55	1
Irvin, Michael, Dal.	78	1396	17.9	87t	7
Pritchard, Mike, Atl.	77	827	10.7	38t	5
Williams, John L., Sea.	74	556	7.5	27	2
Miller, Anthony, S.D.	72	1060	14.7	67t	7

NFL Top 10 Receivers By Yards

	Yards	No	Avg	Long	TD
Sharpe, Sterling, G.B.	1461	108	13.5	76t	13
Irvin, Michael, Dal.	1396	78	17.9	87t	7
Rice, Jerry, S.F.	1201	84	14.3	80t	10
Rison, Andre, Atl.	1119	93	12.0	71t	11
Barnett, Fred, Phi.	1083	67	16.2	71t	6
Miller, Anthony, S.D.	1060	72	14.7	67t	7
Martin, Eric, N.O.	1041	68	15.3	52t	5
Moore, Herman, Det.	966	51	18.9	77t	4
Duncan, Curtis, Hou.	954	82	11.6	72	1
Harmon, Ronnie, S.D.	914	79	11.6	55	1

AFC Pass Receiving—Individual

	No	Yards	Avg	Long	TD
Jeffires, Haywood, Hou.	90	913	10.1	47	9
Duncan, Curtis, Hou.	82	954	11.6	72	1
Harmon, Ronnie, S.D.	79	914	11.6	55	1
Williams, John L., Sea.	74	556	7.5	27	2
Miller, Anthony, S.D.	72	1060	14.7	67t	7
Givins, Earnest, Hou.	67	787	11.7	41	10
Reed, Andre, Buf.	65	913	14.0	51	3
Langhorne, Reggie, Ind.	65	811	12.5	34	1
Thomas, Thurman, Buf.	58	626	10.8	43	3
Burkett, Chris, NY-J	57	724	12.7	37t	1
White, Lorenzo, Hou.	57	641	11.2	69t	1
Fryar, Irving, N.E.	55	791	14.4	54t	4
Humphrey, Bobby, Mia.	54	507	9.4	26	1
Sharpe, Shannon, Den.	53	640	12.1	55	2
Hester, Jessie, Ind.	52	792	15.2	81	1
Cook, Marv, N.E.	52	413	7.9	27	2
Lofton, James, Buf.	51	786	15.4	50	6
Moore, Rob, NY-J	50	726	14.5	48t	4
Graham, Jeff, Pit.	49	711	14.5	51	1
Brown, Tim, Rai.	49	693	14.1	68t	7
Johnson, Anthony, Ind.	49	517	10.6	57t	3
Jackson, Mark, Den.	48	745	15.5	51t	8
Jackson, Keith, Mia.	48	594	12.4	42	5
Paige, Tony, Mia.	48	399	8.3	30	1
Jackson, Michael, Cle.	47	755	16.1	69t	7
Metcalf, Eric, Cle.	47	614	13.1	69t	5
Rivers, Reggie, Den.	45	449	10.0	37	1
Duper, Mark, Mia.	44	762	17.3	62t	7
Brooks, Bill, Ind.	44	468	10.6	26	1
McNair, Todd, K.C.	44	380	8.6	36	1
Clayton, Mark, Mia.	43	619	14.4	44t	3
Cash, Kerry, Ind.	43	521	12.1	41	3
Birden, J.J., K.C.	42	644	15.3	72t	3
Green, Harold, Cin.	41	214	5.2	19	0
Slaughter, Webster, Hou.	39	486	12.5	36t	4
Davis, Willie, K.C.	36	756	21.0	74t	3
Foster, Barry, Pit.	36	344	9.6	42	0
Harris, Leonard, Hou.	35	435	12.4	47	2
McMurtry, Greg, N.E.	35	424	12.1	65t	1
McGee, Tim, Cin.	35	408	11.7	36	3
Lewis, Nate, S.D.	34	580	17.1	62	4
Stone, Dwight, Pit.	34	501	14.7	49	3
Walker, Derrick, S.D.	34	393	11.6	59	2
Beebe, Don, Buf.	33	554	16.8	65t	2
Martin, Tony, Mia.	33	553	16.8	55t	2
Horton, Ethan, Rai.	33	409	12.4	30	2
Toon, Al, NY-J	31	311	10.0	32	2
Mills, Ernie, Pit.	30	383	12.8	22	3
Metzelaars, Pete, Buf.	30	298	9.9	53t	6
Jefferson, Shawn, S.D.	29	377	13.0	51	2
Allen, Marcus, Rai.	28	277	9.9	40	1
Hoge, Merril, Pit.	28	231	8.3	20	1
Smith, Steve, Rai.	28	217	7.8	19	1
Gault, Willie, Rai.	27	508	18.8	53	4
Kane, Tommy, Sea.	27	369	13.7	31	3
Marshall, Arthur, Den.	26	493	19.0	80t	1
Pickens, Carl, Cin.	26	326	12.5	38	1
Timpson, Michael, N.E.	26	315	12.1	25	1
Hoard, Leroy, Cle.	26	310	11.9	46t	1
Holman, Rodney, Cin.	26	266	10.2	26t	2
Culver, Rodney, Ind.	26	210	8.1	27	2
Tillman, Lawyer, Cle.	25	498	19.9	52	0

	No	Yards	Avg	Long	TD
Bavaro, Mark, Cle.	25	315	12.6	39	2
Barnett, Tim, K.C.	24	442	18.4	77t	4
Johnson, Vance, Den.	24	294	12.3	40	2
Banks, Fred, Mia.	22	319	14.5	39t	3
Mathis, Terance, NY-J	22	316	14.4	55t	3
Thompson, Leroy, Pit.	22	278	12.6	29	0
Jones, James, Sea.	21	190	9.0	30	0
Stephens, John, N.E.	21	161	7.7	32	0
Clark, Louis, Sea.	20	290	14.5	33	1
Coates, Ben, N.E.	20	171	8.6	22t	3
Holohan, Pete, Cle.	20	170	8.5	24	0
Blades, Brian, Sea.	19	256	13.5	37	1
Rembert, Reggie, Cin.	19	219	11.5	27	0
Thompson, Craig, Cin.	19	194	10.2	32	2
Brennan, Brian, Cin.-S.D.	19	188	9.9	21	1
Boyer, Mark, NY-J	19	149	7.8	23	0
Jones, Fred, K.C.	18	265	14.7	56	0
Hargain, Tony, K.C.	17	205	12.1	25	0
Query, Jeff, Cin.	16	265	16.6	83t	3
Mitchell, Johnny, NY-J	16	210	13.1	37t	1
Cooper, Adrian, Pit.	16	197	12.3	27	3
McNeil, Freeman, NY-J	16	154	9.6	32	0
Higgs, Mark, Mia.	16	142	8.9	21	0
Warren, Chris, Sea.	16	134	8.4	33	0
Glover, Andrew, Rai.	15	178	11.9	30	1
Davis, Kenneth, Buf.	15	80	5.3	22	0
Green, Eric, Pit.	14	152	10.9	24	2
McKeller, Keith, Buf.	14	110	7.9	26	0
Dickerson, Eric, Rai.	14	85	6.1	15	1
Carpenter, Rob, NY-J	13	161	12.4	51	1
Arbuckle, Charles, Ind.	13	152	11.7	23t	1
Vardell, Tommy, Cle.	13	128	9.8	23	0
Vaughn, Jon, N.E.	13	84	6.5	28	0
Mack, Kevin, Cle.	13	81	6.2	23	0
Tillman, Cedric, Den.	12	211	17.6	81t	1
Wright, Alexander, Rai.	12	175	14.6	41t	2
Russell, Derek, Den.	12	140	11.7	22	0
Cash, Keith, K.C.	12	113	9.4	19	2
Bernstine, Rod, S.D.	12	86	7.2	16	0
Heller, Ron, Sea.	12	85	7.1	17	0
Thomas, Robb, Sea.	11	136	12.4	31	0
Riggs, Jim, Cin.	11	70	6.4	17	0
Russell, Leonard, N.E.	11	24	2.2	12	0
Graddy, Sam, Rai.	10	205	20.5	48	1
Johnson, Reggie, Den.	10	139	13.9	48	1
Edmunds, Ferrell, Mia.	10	91	9.1	15	1
Green, Gaston, Den.	10	79	7.9	33	0
Davenport, Charles, Pit.	9	136	15.1	31	0
Fernandez, Mervyn, Rai.	9	121	13.4	21	0
Word, Barry, K.C.	9	80	8.9	22	0
Hayes, Jonathan, K.C.	9	77	8.6	21	2
Butts, Marion, S.D.	9	73	8.1	22	0
Green, Paul, Sea.	9	67	7.4	15	1
Thomas, Doug, Sea.	8	85	10.6	19	0
Lamb, Brad, Buf.	7	139	19.9	53	0
Gardner, Carwell, Buf.	7	67	9.6	17	0
Chaffey, Pat, NY-J	7	56	8.0	14	0
Kay, Clarence, Den.	7	56	8.0	15	0
Turner, Kevin, N.E.	7	52	7.4	19t	2
Thomas, Blair, NY-J	7	49	7.0	10	0
Fenner, Derrick, Cin.	7	41	5.9	15	1
Ball, Eric, Cin.	6	66	11.0	35t	2
Jorden, Tim, Pit.	6	28	4.7	8	2
Daniels, David, Sea.	5	99	19.8	57	0
Anders, Kimble, K.C.	5	65	13.0	28	0
Smith, Rico, Cle.	5	64	12.8	21	0
Bieniemy, Eric, S.D.	5	49	9.8	25	0
Clark, Ken, Ind.	5	46	9.2	17	0
Saxon, James, Mia.	5	41	8.2	14	0
Williams, Harvey, K.C.	5	24	4.8	12	0
Galbraith, Scott, Cle.	4	63	15.8	28	1
Young, Duane, S.D.	4	45	11.3	14	0
Bell, Nick, Rai.	4	40	10.0	16	0
Awalt, Robert, Buf.	4	34	8.5	10	0
Baxter, Brad, NY-J	4	32	8.0	12	0
Brown, A.B., NY-J	4	30	7.5	20	0
Lewis, Greg, Den.	4	30	7.5	16	0
Stanley, Walter, N.E.	3	63	21.0	36	0
Clark, Robert, Mia.	3	59	19.7	45	0
Williams, Mike, Mia.	3	43	14.3	18	0
Didio, Mark, Pit.	3	39	13.0	18	0
Verdin, Clarence, Ind.	3	37	12.3	21	0
Stegall, Milt, Cin.	3	35	11.7	13	1
Collins, Shawn, Cle.	3	31	10.3	11	0
Junkin, Trey, Sea.	3	25	8.3	13	1
Baty, Greg, Mia.	3	19	6.3	12	1
Jones, Mike, Sea.	3	18	6.0	7	0
Jones, Victor, Den.	3	17	5.7	16	0
Carthon, Maurice, Ind.	3	10	3.3	6	0
Baldwin, Randy, Cle.	2	30	15.0	20	0
Jones, David, Rai.	2	29	14.5	25	0
Holland, Jamie, Cle.	2	27	13.5	16	0
Edwards, Al, Buf.	2	25	12.5	20	0
Tasker, Steve, Buf.	2	24	12.0	17	0
Fuller, Eddie, Buf.	2	17	8.5	17	0
Perryman, Bob, Den.	2	15	7.5	9	0
Thomason, Jeff, Cin.	2	14	7.0	10	0
Hector, Johnny, NY-J	2	13	6.5	9	0
Mayes, Rueben, Sea.	2	13	6.5	7	0
McCallum, Napoleon, Rai.	2	13	6.5	7	0
Whisenhunt, Ken, NY-J	2	11	5.5	10	0
Coleman, Pat, Hou.	2	10	5.0	6	0
Wolfley, Ron, Cle.	2	8	4.0	6	1
Jones, Bill, K.C.	2	6	3.0	5	0
Frerotte, Mitch, Buf.	2	4	2.0	2t	2
Brooks, James, Cle.	2	-1	-0.5	4	0
Williams, Warren, Pit.	1	44	44.0	44	0
Sadowski, Troy, NY-J	1	20	20.0	20	0
Prior, Mike, Ind.	1	17	17.0	17	0
Claiborne, Robert, S.D.	1	15	15.0	15	0
Young, Mike, Den.	1	11	11.0	11	0
McCardell, Keenan, Cle.	1	8	8.0	8	0
Dyal, Mike, K.C.	1	7	7.0	7	0
Brown, Gary, Hou.	1	5	5.0	5	0
Okoye, Christian, K.C.	1	5	5.0	5	0
Schultz, William, Ind.	1	3	3.0	3t	1
Thigpen, Yancey, Pit.	1	2	2.0	2	0
Fina, John, Buf.	1	1	1.0	1t	1
Jones, James, Cle.	1	1	1.0	1t	1
Hodson, Tom, N.E.	1	-6	-6.0	-6	0
Widell, Doug, Den.	1	-7	-7.0	-7	0

t indicates touchdown
Leader based on receptions

NFC Pass Receiving—Individual

	No	Yards	Avg	Long	TD
Sharpe, Sterling, G.B.	108	1461	13.5	76t	13
Rison, Andre, Atl.	93	1119	12.0	71t	11
Rice, Jerry, S.F.	84	1201	14.3	80t	10
Irvin, Michael, Dal.	78	1396	17.9	87t	7
Pritchard, Mike, Atl.	77	827	10.7	38t	5
Perriman, Brett, Det.	69	810	11.7	40t	4
Martin, Eric, N.O.	68	1041	15.3	52t	5
Novacek, Jay, Dal.	68	630	9.3	34	6
Barnett, Fred, Phi.	67	1083	16.2	71t	6
Clark, Gary, Was.	64	912	14.3	47	5
Dawsey, Lawrence, T.B.	60	776	12.9	41	1
Proehl, Ricky, Pho.	60	744	12.4	63t	3
Hill, Drew, Atl.	60	623	10.4	43	3
Smith, Emmitt, Dal.	59	335	5.7	26t	1
Hill, Randal, Pho.	58	861	14.8	49	3
Carrier, Mark, T.B.	56	692	12.4	40	4
Byars, Keith, Phi.	56	502	9.0	46	2
Harris, Jackie, G.B.	55	595	10.8	40	2
Davis, Wendell, Chi.	54	734	13.6	40	2
Carter, Cris, Min.	53	681	12.8	44	6
Gary, Cleveland, Rams	52	293	5.6	22	3
Moore, Herman, Det.	51	966	18.9	77t	4
Sanders, Ricky, Was.	51	707	13.9	62t	3
Centers, Larry, Pho.	50	417	8.3	26	2
McCaffrey, Ed, NY-G	49	610	12.4	44	5
Allen, Terry, Min.	49	478	9.8	36t	2
Sydney, Harry, G.B.	49	384	7.8	20	1
Haynes, Michael, Atl.	48	808	16.8	89t	10
Hilliard, Dalton, N.O.	48	465	9.7	41	4
Ellard, Henry, Rams	47	727	15.5	33t	3
Workman, Vince, G.B.	47	290	6.2	21	0
Waddle, Tom, Chi.	46	674	14.7	68t	4
Monk, Art, Was.	46	644	14.0	49t	3
Jones, Brent, S.F.	45	628	14.0	43	4
Rathman, Tom, S.F.	44	343	7.8	27t	4
Watters, Ricky, S.F.	43	405	9.4	35	2
Williams, Calvin, Phi.	42	598	14.2	49t	7
Anderson, Neal, Chi.	42	399	9.5	30t	6
Carter, Anthony, Min.	41	580	14.1	54	2
Hall, Ron, T.B.	39	351	9.0	32	4
Byner, Earnest, Was.	39	338	8.7	29	1
Anderson, Willie, Rams	38	657	17.3	51	7
Sherrard, Mike, S.F.	38	607	16.0	56	0
Jones, Ernie, Pho.	38	559	14.7	72t	4
Walker, Herschel, Phi.	38	278	7.3	41	2
Meggett, David, NY-G	38	229	6.0	24	2
Harper, Alvin, Dal.	35	562	16.1	52	4
Muster, Brad, Chi.	34	389	11.4	44t	2

	No	Yards	Avg	Long	TD
Price, Jim, Rams	34	324	9.5	25	2
Anderson, Gary, T.B.	34	284	8.4	34	0
Green, Willie, Det.	33	586	17.8	73t	5
Bailey, Johnny, Pho.	33	331	10.0	34	1
Martin, Kelvin, Dal.	32	359	11.2	27	3
Ervins, Ricky, Was.	32	252	7.9	19	0
Johnston, Daryl, Dal.	32	249	7.8	18	2
Early, Quinn, N.O.	30	566	18.9	59t	5
Chadwick, Jeff, Rams	29	362	12.5	27t	3
Sanders, Barry, Det.	29	225	7.8	48	1
Jordan, Steve, Min.	28	394	14.1	60t	2
Hampton, Rodney, NY-G	28	215	7.7	31	0
Ingram, Mark, NY-G	27	408	15.1	34	1
Cross, Howard, NY-G	27	357	13.2	29	2
Calloway, Chris, NY-G	27	335	12.4	28	1
McDowell, Anthony, T.B.	27	258	9.6	51t	2
Taylor, John, S.F.	25	428	17.1	54t	3
Small, Torrance, N.O.	23	278	12.1	33	3
Jennings, Keith, Chi.	23	264	11.5	23	1
Orr, Terry, Was.	22	356	16.2	58	3
Jones, Hassan, Min.	22	308	14.0	43t	4
Craig, Roger, Min.	22	164	7.5	22	0
Johnson, Joe, Min.	21	211	10.0	37	1
Cobb, Reggie, T.B.	21	156	7.4	27	0
Hawkins, Courtney, T.B.	20	336	16.8	49	2
Carter, Pat, Rams	20	232	11.6	25	3
Lee, Amp, S.F.	20	102	5.1	17	2
Heyward, Craig, N.O.	19	159	8.4	21	0
Carroll, Wesley, N.O.	18	292	16.2	72t	2
Lang, David, Rams	18	283	15.7	67t	1
Cox, Aaron, Rams	18	261	14.5	26	0
Sherman, Heath, Phi.	18	219	12.2	75t	1
Lewis, Darren, Chi.	18	175	9.7	30	0
Delpino, Robert, Rams	18	139	7.7	12t	1
Baker, Stephen, NY-G	17	333	19.6	46	2
Beach, Sanjay, G.B.	17	122	7.2	20	1
Drewrey, Willie, T.B.	16	237	14.8	32	2
Farr, Mike, Det.	15	115	7.7	14	0
Morgan, Anthony, Chi.	14	323	23.1	83t	2
Edwards, Anthony, Pho.	14	147	10.5	25t	1
Jones, Tony, Atl.	14	138	9.9	24	1
Johnson, Johnny, Pho.	14	103	7.4	26	0
Lewis, Ronald, G.B.	13	152	11.7	27	0
Sikahema, Vai, Phi.	13	142	10.9	22	0
Thompson, Darrell, G.B.	13	129	9.9	43	1
Bennett, Edgar, G.B.	13	93	7.2	22	0
Rolle, Butch, Pho.	13	64	4.9	12	0
Brenner, Hoby, N.O.	12	161	13.4	23	0
Brooks, Robert, G.B.	12	126	10.5	18	1
Gentry, Dennis, Chi.	12	114	9.5	18	0
Jones, Keith, Atl.	12	94	7.8	15	0
Broussard, Steve, Atl.	11	96	8.7	24	1
Bunch, Jarrod, NY-G	11	50	4.5	13	1
Turner, Odessa, S.F.	9	200	22.2	57	2
Wainright, Frank, N.O.	9	143	15.9	29	0
Matthews, Aubrey, Det.	9	137	15.2	24	0
Jennings, Stanford, T.B.	9	69	7.7	20t	1
Dunbar, Vaughn, N.O.	9	62	6.9	13	0
Campbell, Jeff, Det.	8	155	19.4	78t	1
Green, Roy, Phi.	8	105	13.1	21	0
Beach, Pat, Phi.	8	75	9.4	16	2
Armstrong, Tyji, T.B.	7	138	19.7	81t	1
Green, Mark, Chi.	7	85	12.1	43	0
Williams, Jamie, S.F.	7	76	10.9	21	1
Brown, Ivory Lee, Pho.	7	54	7.7	18	0
Middleton, Ron, Was.	7	50	7.1	16	0
Reed, Jake, Min.	6	142	23.7	51	0
McGee, Buford, G.B.	6	60	10.0	15	0
Harry, Emile, K.C.-Rams	6	58	9.7	13	0
Thomas, George, Atl.	6	54	9.0	18	0
Johnson, Jimmy, Det.	6	34	5.7	9	0
Reeves, Walter, Pho.	6	28	4.7	12	0
Tice, Mike, Min.	5	65	13.0	34t	1
Henderson, Keith, S.F.-Min.	5	64	12.8	23	0
Wright, Eric, Chi.	5	56	11.2	24	0
Blackwell, Kelly, Chi.	5	54	10.8	18	0
Turner, Floyd, N.O.	5	43	8.6	18	0
Turner, Vernon, Rams	5	42	8.4	16	0
Highsmith, Alonzo, T.B.	5	28	5.6	11	0
Thompson, Anthony, Rams	5	11	2.2	7	0
McNeal, Travis, Rams	4	79	19.8	38	0
Barrett, Reggie, Det.	4	67	16.8	24	1
Novoselsky, Brent, Min.	4	63	15.8	34	0
Morris, Ron, Chi.	4	44	11.0	26	0
Brown, Derek, NY-G	4	31	7.8	9	0
West, Ed, G.B.	4	30	7.5	10	0
Phillips, Jason, Atl.	4	26	6.5	8	1
Warren, Don, Was.	4	25	6.3	11	0
Stowers, Tommie, N.O.	4	23	5.8	8	0
Sanders, Deion, Atl.	3	45	15.0	37t	1
Smith, Joey, NY-G	3	45	15.0	22	0
Dixon, Floyd, Phi.	3	36	12.0	19	0
Roberts, Alfredo, Dal.	3	36	12.0	18	0
Mitchell, Brian, Was.	3	30	10.0	17	0
Hinnant, Mike, Det.	3	28	9.3	13	0
Milling, James, Atl.	3	25	8.3	15	0
Newman, Pat, N.O.	3	21	7.0	8	0
Howard, Desmond, Was.	3	20	6.7	8	0
Agee, Tommie, Dal.	3	18	6.0	8	0
Blount, Eric, Pho.	3	18	6.0	18	0
Richards, Curvin, Dal.	3	8	2.7	6	0
Taylor, Kitrick, G.B.	2	63	31.5	35t	1
Pegram, Erric, Atl.	2	25	12.5	19	0
Logan, Marc, S.F.	2	17	8.5	13	0
Johnson, Maurice, Phi.	2	16	8.0	13	0
Stradford, Troy, Det.	2	15	7.5	12	0
Smith, Tony, Atl.	2	14	7.0	8	0
McLemore, Thomas, Det.	2	12	6.0	6	0
Tennell, Derek, Min.	2	12	6.0	8	0
Carter, Dexter, S.F.	1	43	43.0	43t	1
Barber, Mike, T.B.	1	32	32.0	32	0
McAfee, Fred, N.O.	1	16	16.0	16	0
Wagner, Barry, Chi.	1	16	16.0	16	0
Tillman, Lewis, NY-G	1	15	15.0	15	0
Ware, Derek, Pho.	1	13	13.0	13	0
Fullington, Darrell, T.B.	1	12	12.0	12	0
Parker, Jeff, T.B.	1	12	12.0	12	0
Moore, Dave, T.B.	1	10	10.0	10	0
Royster, Mazio, T.B.	1	8	8.0	8	0
Kozlowski, Glen, Chi.	1	7	7.0	7	0
Dowdell, Marcus, N.O.	1	6	6.0	6	0
Green, Robert, Was.	1	5	5.0	5	0
Jackson, John, Pho.	1	5	5.0	5t	1
Gesek, John, Dal.	1	4	4.0	4	0
Whitaker, Danta, Min.	1	4	4.0	4	0
Lipps, Louis, N.O.	1	1	1.0	1	0
Hinton, Chris, Atl.	1	-2	-2.0	-2	0
Favre, Brett, G.B.	1	-7	-7.0	-7	0
Cooper, Richard, N.O.	0	20	—	20	0

t indicates touchdown
Leader based on receptions

Interceptions

Interceptions
AFC: 8—Henry Jones, Buffalo
NFC: 8—Audray McMillian, Minnesota

Interceptions, Game
AFC: 3—Louis Oliver, Miami at Buffalo, October 4 - TD
Eugene Robinson, Seattle at Pittsburgh, December 6
Mark Kelso, Buffalo vs. Denver, December 12
Mike Prior, Indianapolis vs. Phoenix, December 20
NFC: 3—Todd Scott, Minnesota at Cincinnati, September 27
Audray McMillian, Minnesota vs. Cleveland, November 22 - TD
Brad Edwards, Washington vs. Phoenix, November 29 - TD
Vencie Glenn, Minnesota vs. Green Bay, December 27

Yards
AFC: 263—Henry Jones, Buffalo
NFC: 157—Brad Edwards, Washington
Audray McMillian, Minnesota

Longest
AFC: 103—Louis Oliver, Miami at Buffalo, October 4 - TD
NFC: 84—Jack Del Rio, Minnesota at Chicago, November 2 - TD

Touchdowns
NFC: 3—Robert Massey, Phoenix
AFC: 2—Henry Jones, Buffalo
Charles Mincy, Kansas City

Team Leaders, Interception
AFC: BUFFALO: 8, Henry Jones; CINCINNATI: 4, Darryl Williams; CLEVELAND: 3, Vince Newsome; DENVER: 4, Wymon Henderson, Dennis Smith; HOUSTON: 6, Jerry Gray; INDIANAPOLIS: 6, Mike Prior; KANSAS CITY: 7, Dale Carter; L.A. RAIDERS: 4, Terry McDaniel; MIAMI: 5, Louis Oliver; NEW ENGLAND: 3, Jerome Henderson, Maurice Hurst; N.Y. JETS: 6, Mike Brim, Brian Washington; PITTSBURGH: 6, Darren Perry; SAN DIEGO: 6, Darren Carrington; SEATTLE: 7, Eugene Robinson
NFC: ATLANTA: 3, Deion Sanders; CHICAGO: 7, Donnell Woolford; DALLAS: 3, Kenneth Gant, James Washington; DETROIT: 4, Ray Crockett, Mel Jenkins, Kevin Scott, William White; GREEN BAY: 4, Chuck Cecil; L.A. RAMS: 4, Darryl Henley, Anthony Newman; MINNESOTA: 8, Audray McMillian; NEW ORLEANS: 6, Toi Cook; N.Y. GIANTS: 4, Greg Jackson; PHILADELPHIA: 4, Eric Allen, Byron Evans, Seth Joyner; PHOENIX: 5, Robert Massey; SAN FRANCISCO: 5, Don Griffin; TAMPA BAY: 3, Marty Carter, Darrell Fullington, Milton Mack; WASHINGTON: 6, Brad Edwards

Team Champion
NFC: 28—Minnesota
AFC: 25—San Diego

AFC Interceptions—Team

	No	Yards	Avg	Long	TD
San Diego	25	405	16.2	69	1
Kansas City	24	403	16.8	99t	6
Buffalo	23	325	14.1	82t	2
Pittsburgh	22	384	17.5	65t	1
N.Y. Jets	21	269	12.8	77t	3
Indianapolis	20	302	15.1	90t	1
Houston	20	181	9.1	27	1
Seattle	20	324	16.2	69	0
Miami	18	458	25.4	103t	3
Cincinnati	16	205	12.8	66t	1
Denver	15	210	14.0	46t	1
New England	14	285	20.4	82t	3
Cleveland	13	222	17.1	92t	1
L.A. Raiders	12	339	28.3	102t	1
AFC Total	263	4312	16.4	103t	25
AFC Average	18.8	308.0	16.4	—	1.8

NFC Interceptions—Team

	No	Yards	Avg	Long	TD
Minnesota	28	502	17.9	84t	6
Philadelphia	24	307	12.8	49	2
Washington	23	485	21.1	65	2
Detroit	21	255	12.1	35	0
Tampa Bay	20	234	11.7	75	1
New Orleans	18	254	14.1	71t	3
L.A. Rams	18	283	15.7	40	1
San Francisco	17	172	10.1	56t	1
Dallas	17	158	9.3	30	1
Phoenix	16	298	18.6	46t	3
Green Bay	15	222	14.8	43	1
N.Y. Giants	14	192	13.7	69t	1
Chicago	14	188	13.4	46	0
Atlanta	11	135	12.3	55	0
NFC Total	256	3685	14.4	84t	22
NFC Average	18.3	263.2	14.4	—	1.6
NFL Total	519	7997	—	103t	47
NFL Average	18.5	285.6	15.4	—	1.7

NFL Top 10 Interceptors

	No	Yards	Avg	Long	TD
Jones, Henry, Buf.	8	263	32.9	82t	2
McMillian, Audray, Min.	8	157	19.6	51t	2
Carter, Dale, K.C.	7	65	9.3	36t	1
Kelso, Mark, Buf.	7	21	3.0	13	0
Robinson, Eugene, Sea.	7	126	18.0	49	0
Woolford, Donnell, Chi.	7	67	9.6	32	0
Brim, Michael, NY-J	6	139	23.2	77t	1
Carrington, Darren, S.D.	6	152	25.3	69	1
Cook, Toi, N.O.	6	90	15.0	48t	1
Edwards, Brad, Was.	6	157	26.2	53t	1
Gray, Jerry, Hou.	6	24	4.0	22	0
Perry, Darren, Pit.	6	69	11.5	34	0
Prior, Mike, Ind.	6	44	7.3	19	0
Washington, Brian, NY-J	6	59	9.8	23t	1

AFC Interceptions—Individual

	No	Yards	Avg	Long	TD
Jones, Henry, Buf.	8	263	32.9	82t	2
Robinson, Eugene, Sea.	7	126	18.0	49	0
Carter, Dale, K.C.	7	65	9.3	36t	1
Kelso, Mark, Buf.	7	21	3.0	13	0
Carrington, Darren, S.D.	6	152	25.3	69	1
Brim, Michael, NY-J	6	139	23.2	77t	1
Perry, Darren, Pit.	6	69	11.5	34	0
Washington, Brian, NY-J	6	59	9.8	23t	1
Prior, Mike, Ind.	6	44	7.3	19	0
Gray, Jerry, Hou.	6	24	4.0	22	0
Oliver, Louis, Mia.	5	200	40.0	103t	1
Johnson, David, Pit.	5	67	13.4	35	0
Odomes, Nate, Buf.	5	19	3.8	10	0
McDaniel, Terry, Rai.	4	180	45.0	67	0
Mincy, Charles, K.C.	4	128	32.0	39	2
Brown, J.B., Mia.	4	119	29.8	48	1
Woodson, Rod, Pit.	4	90	22.5	57	0
Byrd, Gill, S.D.	4	88	22.0	44	0
Henderson, Wymon, Den.	4	79	19.8	46t	1
Williams, Darryl, Cin.	4	65	16.3	30	0
Frank, Donald, S.D.	4	37	9.3	33	0
Thompson, Bennie, K.C.	4	26	6.5	25	0
Smith, Dennis, Den.	4	10	2.5	8	0
Anderson, Eddie, Rai.	3	131	43.7	102t	1
Francis, James, Cin.	3	108	36.0	66t	1
Griffin, Larry, Pit.	3	98	32.7	65t	1
Harper, Dwayne, Sea.	3	74	24.7	41	0
Jackson, Vestee, Mia.	3	63	21.0	30t	1
Newsome, Vince, Cle.	3	55	18.3	29	0
McDowell, Bubba, Hou.	3	52	17.3	26t	1
Henderson, Jerome, N.E.	3	43	14.3	34	0
Dishman, Cris, Hou.	3	34	11.3	17	0
Hurst, Maurice, N.E.	3	29	9.7	27	0
Belser, Jason, Ind.	3	27	9.0	21	0
Richard, Stanley, S.D.	3	26	8.7	20	0
Walls, Everson, NY-G-Cle.	3	26	8.7	24	0
Jackson, Steve, Hou.	3	18	6.0	18	0
Simien, Tracy, K.C.	3	18	6.0	10	0
Fulcher, David, Cin.	3	0	0.0	0	0
Brandon, David, Cle.	2	123	61.5	92t	1
Goode, Chris, Ind.	2	93	46.5	47	0
Braxton, Tyrone, Den.	2	54	27.0	40	0
Pool, David, N.E.	2	54	27.0	41t	1
Seau, Junior, S.D.	2	51	25.5	29	0
Vincent, Troy, Mia.	2	47	23.5	32	0
Plummer, Gary, S.D.	2	40	20.0	38	0
Davis, Brian, Sea.	2	36	18.0	36	0
Williams, Jarvis, Mia.	2	29	14.5	25	0
Robbins, Randy, N.E.	2	27	13.5	20	0
Stargell, Tony, Ind.	2	26	13.0	15	0
Atwater, Steve, Den.	2	22	11.0	22	0
Washington, Lionel, Rai.	2	21	10.5	18	0
Hasty, James, NY-J	2	18	9.0	18	0
Turner, Marcus, NY-J	2	15	7.5	14	0
Williams, James, Buf.	2	15	7.5	15	0
Jones, Rod, Cin.	2	14	7.0	14	0
Little, David, Pit.	2	6	3.0	6	0
Minnifield, Frank, Cle.	2	6	3.0	5	0
Cain, Joseph, Sea.	2	3	1.5	3	0
Blaylock, Anthony, S.D.	2	0	0.0	0	0
Hunter, Patrick, Sea.	2	0	0.0	0	0
Ross, Kevin, K.C.	1	99	99.0	99t	1
Emtman, Steve, Ind.	1	90	90.0	90t	1
Singleton, Chris, N.E.	1	82	82.0	82t	1
Blackmon, Robert, Sea.	1	69	69.0	69	0
Brown, Vincent, N.E.	1	49	49.0	49t	1
Marts, Lonnie, K.C.	1	36	36.0	36t	1
Lloyd, Greg, Pit.	1	35	35.0	35	0
Robertson, Marcus, Hou.	1	27	27.0	27	0
Lang, Le-Lo, Den.	1	26	26.0	26	0
Smith, Al, Hou.	1	26	26.0	26	0
Smith, Neil, K.C.	1	22	22.0	22t	1
Houston, Bobby, NY-J	1	20	20.0	20t	1
Brooks, Michael, Den.	1	17	17.0	17	0
Kors, R.J., NY-J	1	16	16.0	16	0
Bickett, Duane, Ind.	1	14	14.0	14	0
Dodge, Dedrick, Sea.	1	13	13.0	13	0
Wheeler, Leonard, Cin.	1	12	12.0	12	0
Vanhorse, Sean, S.D.	1	11	11.0	11	0
Terry, Doug, K.C.	1	9	9.0	9	0
Conlan, Shane, Buf.	1	7	7.0	7	0
Dorn, Torin, Rai.	1	7	7.0	7	0
Matthews, Clay, Cle.	1	6	6.0	6	0
Turner, Eric, Cle.	1	6	6.0	6	0
Herrod, Jeff, Ind.	1	4	4.0	4	0
Williams, Jerrol, Pit.	1	4	4.0	4	0
Banks, Chip, Ind.	1	3	3.0	3	0
Bussey, Barney, Cin.	1	3	3.0	3	0
Mitz, Alonzo, Cin.	1	3	3.0	3	0
Wooden, Terry, Sea.	1	3	3.0	3	0
Dimry, Charles, Den.	1	2	2.0	2	0
Baylor, John, Ind.	1	1	1.0	1	0
Clifton, Kyle, NY-J	1	1	1.0	1	0
Howard, David, N.E.	1	1	1.0	1	0
Lewis, Mo, NY-J	1	1	1.0	1	0
Alexander, Bruce, Mia.	1	0	0.0	0	0
Bayless, Martin, K.C.	1	0	0.0	0	0
Cox, Bryan, Mia.	1	0	0.0	0	0
Daniel, Eugene, Ind.	1	0	0.0	0	0
Dumas, Mike, Hou.	1	0	0.0	0	0
Fields, Floyd, S.D.	1	0	0.0	0	0
Graf, Rick, Hou.	1	0	0.0	0	0
Johnson, Mike, Cle.	1	0	0.0	0	0
Jones, Sean, Hou.	1	0	0.0	0	0
Land, Dan, Rai.	1	0	0.0	0	0
Lewis, Albert, K.C.	1	0	0.0	0	0
Lott, Ronnie, Rai.	1	0	0.0	0	0
McDonald, Ricardo, Cin.	1	0	0.0	0	0
Price, Dennis, NY-J	1	0	0.0	0	0
Radecic, Scott, Ind.	1	0	0.0	0	0
Smith, Rod, N.E.	1	0	0.0	0	0
Taylor, Terry, Cle.	1	0	0.0	0	0

Tuatagaloa, Natu, Sea.	1	0	0.0	0	0
Shelton, Richard, Pit.	0	15	—	15	0

t indicates touchdown
Leader based on interceptions

NFC Interceptions—Individual

	No	Yards	Avg	Long	TD
McMillian, Audray, Min.	8	157	19.6	51t	2
Woolford, Donnell, Chi.	7	67	9.6	32	0
Edwards, Brad, Was.	6	157	26.2	53t	1
Cook, Toi, N.O.	6	90	15.0	48t	1
Massey, Robert, Pho.	5	147	29.4	46t	3
Scott, Todd, Min.	5	79	15.8	35t	1
Glenn, Vencie, Min.	5	65	13.0	39	0
Griffin, Don, S.F.	5	4	0.8	2	0
Joyner, Seth, Phi.	4	88	22.0	43t	2
Evans, Byron, Phi.	4	76	19.0	43	0
Jackson, Greg, NY-G	4	71	17.8	36	0
White, William, Det.	4	54	13.5	28	0
Cecil, Chuck, G.B.	4	52	13.0	29	0
Crockett, Ray, Det.	4	50	12.5	35	0
Allen, Eric, Phi.	4	49	12.3	36	0
Henley, Darryl, Rams	4	41	10.3	25	0
Scott, Kevin, Det.	4	35	8.8	26	0
Jenkins, Mel, Det.	4	34	8.5	14	0
Newman, Anthony, Rams	4	33	8.3	17	0
Sanders, Deion, Atl.	3	105	35.0	55	0
Lyght, Todd, Rams	3	80	26.7	39	0
Bailey, Robert, Rams	3	61	20.3	37	1
Mayhew, Martin, Was.	3	58	19.3	33	0
Blades, Bennie, Det.	3	56	18.7	34	0
Davis, Eric, S.F.	3	52	17.3	37	0
Gouveia, Kurt, Was.	3	43	14.3	28	0
Johnson, A.J., Was.	3	38	12.7	29	0
Zordich, Mike, Pho.	3	37	12.3	23	0
Buckley, Terrell, G.B.	3	33	11.0	33t	1
Washington, James, Dal.	3	31	10.3	16	0
Holland, Johnny, G.B.	3	27	9.0	22	0
Fullington, Darrell, T.B.	3	25	8.3	16	0
Williams, Aeneas, Pho.	3	25	8.3	23	0
Parker, Anthony, Min.	3	23	7.7	23	0
Booty, John, Phi.	3	22	7.3	22	0
Gant, Kenneth, Dal.	3	19	6.3	11	0
Hopkins, Wes, Phi.	3	6	2.0	4	0
Carter, Marty, T.B.	3	1	0.3	1	0
Atkins, Gene, N.O.	3	0	0.0	0	0
Mack, Milton, T.B.	3	0	0.0	0	0
Pollard, Darryl, T.B.	2	99	49.5	75	0
Del Rio, Jack, Min.	2	92	46.0	84t	1
Thomas, Broderick, T.B.	2	81	40.5	56t	1
Jones, Reggie, N.O.	2	71	35.5	71t	1
Clark, Vinnie, G.B.	2	70	35.0	43	0
Thompson, Reyna, NY-G	2	69	34.5	69t	1
Buck, Vince, N.O.	2	51	25.5	34t	1
White, Leon, Rams	2	49	24.5	40	0
Stinson, Lemuel, Chi.	2	46	23.0	46	0
Johnson, Pepper, NY-G	2	42	21.0	38	0
Mitchell, Roland, G.B.	2	40	20.0	35	0
Gayle, Shaun, Chi.	2	39	19.5	30	0
McDonald, Tim, Pho.	2	35	17.5	20	0
Hall, Dana, S.F.	2	34	17.0	34	0
Everett, Thomas, Dal.	2	28	14.0	17	0
Davis, Dexter, Pho.	2	27	13.5	27	0
White, Sheldon, Det.	2	26	13.0	20	0
King, Joe, T.B.	2	24	12.0	24	0
Lee, Carl, Min.	2	20	10.0	20	0
Marshall, Wilber, Was.	2	20	10.0	20t	1
Taylor, Keith, N.O.	2	20	10.0	20	0
Mays, Alvoid, Was.	2	18	9.0	13	0
Pickens, Bruce, Atl.	2	16	8.0	16	0
Horton, Ray, Dal.	2	15	7.5	15t	1
Maxie, Brett, N.O.	2	12	6.0	8	0
Holt, Issiac, Dal.	2	11	5.5	8	0
Miller, Corey, NY-G	2	10	5.0	10	0
Smith, Kevin, Dal.	2	10	5.0	7	0
Hanks, Merton, S.F.	2	5	2.5	4	0
Thomas, William, Phi.	2	4	2.0	4	0
Williams, Jimmy, T.B.	2	4	2.0	3	0
Case, Scott, Atl.	2	0	0.0	0	0
Reynolds, Ricky, T.B.	2	0	0.0	0	0
Bowles, Todd, Was.	1	65	65.0	65	0
Collins, Andre, Was.	1	59	59.0	59	0
Johnson, John, S.F.	1	56	56.0	56t	1
Miano, Rich, Phi.	1	39	39.0	39	0
Brown, Larry, Dal.	1	30	30.0	30	0
Doleman, Chris, Min.	1	27	27.0	27t	1
Jones, Jock, Pho.	1	27	27.0	27	0
Waters, Andre, Phi.	1	23	23.0	23	0
Morrissey, Jim, Chi.	1	22	22.0	22	0
Wright, Felix, Min.	1	20	20.0	20	0
Jenkins, Carlos, Min.	1	19	19.0	19t	1
Roberts, Larry, S.F.	1	19	19.0	19	0
Kelm, Larry, Rams	1	16	16.0	16	0
Green, Darrell, Was.	1	15	15.0	15	0
Myles, Godfrey, Dal.	1	13	13.0	13	0
Solomon, Jesse, Atl.	1	13	13.0	13	0
Johnson, Sidney, Was.	1	12	12.0	12	0
Mills, Sam, N.O.	1	10	10.0	10	0
Paul, Markus, Chi.	1	10	10.0	10	0
Singletary, Mike, Chi.	1	4	4.0	4	0
Phifer, Roman, Rams	1	3	3.0	3	0
DeLong, Keith, S.F.	1	2	2.0	2	0
Harper, Alvin, Dal.	1	1	1.0	1	0
Tuggle, Jessie, Atl.	1	1	1.0	1	0
Brown, Dennis, S.F.	1	0	0.0	0	0
Butler, Leroy, G.B.	1	0	0.0	0	0
Collins, Mark, NY-G	1	0	0.0	0	0
Lewis, Garry, T.B.	1	0	0.0	0	0
McKyer, Tim, Atl.	1	0	0.0	0	0
McMillian, Mark, Phi.	1	0	0.0	0	0
Mitchell, Brian, Atl.	1	0	0.0	0	0
Smith, Otis, Phi.	1	0	0.0	0	0
Sparks, Phillipi, NY-G	1	0	0.0	0	0
Whitmore, David, S.F.	1	0	0.0	0	0
Williams, Perry, NY-G	1	0	0.0	0	0

t indicates touchdown
Leader based on interceptions

Punting

Average Yards per Punt
AFC: 46.9—Greg Montgomery, Houston
NFC: 45.0—Harry Newsome, Minnesota

Net Average Yards per Punt
NFC: 39.6—Rich Camarillo, Phoenix
AFC: 39.3—Rohn Stark, Indianapolis

Longest
NFC: 84—Harry Newsome, Minnesota at Pittsburgh, December 20
AFC: 73—Brian Hansen, Cleveland vs. Denver, September 27

Punts
AFC: 108—Rick Tuten, Seattle
NFC: 82—Jeff Feagles, Philadelphia

Punts, Game
AFC: 11—Shawn McCarthy, New England vs. New Orleans, November 8 (395 yards)
Rich Rodriguez, Denver at Seattle, November 30 (445 yards) (OT)
Rick Tuten, Seattle vs. Philadelphia, December 13 (506 yards) (OT)
NFC: 10—Jeff Feagles, Philadelphia at Seattle, December 13 (425 yards) (OT)

Team Champion
AFC: 45.2—Houston
NFC: 44.4—Minnesota

AFC Punting—Team

	Total Punts	Yards	Long	Gross Avg	TB	Blk	Opp. Ret	Ret. Yards	In 20	Net Avg
Houston	55	2487	66	45.2	9	2	31	255	14	37.3
Indianapolis	83	3716	64	44.8	7	0	45	313	22	39.3
Seattle	108	4760	65	44.1	8	0	56	416	29	38.7
Denver	85	3705	67	43.6	6	1	39	382	15	37.7
San Diego	68	2899	65	42.6	9	0	24	244	22	36.4
L.A. Raiders	77	3255	56	42.3	3	0	40	385	17	36.5
Kansas City	86	3633	65	42.2	13	1	40	328	18	35.4
Buffalo	60	2531	61	42.2	7	0	22	185	12	36.8
Pittsburgh	74	3119	58	42.1	9	1	39	308	22	35.6
Cincinnati	76	3196	64	42.1	9	0	32	284	15	35.9
Cleveland	75	3083	73	41.1	7	1	27	234	28	36.1
New England	103	4227	61	41.0	4	0	59	499	19	35.4
N.Y. Jets	73	2993	65	41.0	3	0	26	189	21	37.6
Miami	61	2424	60	39.7	3	0	33	382	13	32.5
AFC Total	1084	46028	73	—	97	6	513	4404	267	—
AFC Average	77.4	3287.7	—	42.5	6.9	0.4	36.6	314.6	19.1	36.6

NFC Punting—Team

	Total Punts	Yards	Long	Gross Avg	TB	Blk	Opp. Ret	Ret. Yards	In 20	Net Avg
Minnesota	73	3243	84	44.4	15	1	34	339	19	35.7
New Orleans	67	2947	62	44.0	10	0	31	218	19	37.7
Detroit	66	2846	71	43.1	10	1	30	356	12	34.7
Dallas	61	2620	58	43.0	9	0	34	397	19	33.5
Chicago	79	3393	61	42.9	9	0	38	351	19	36.2
Phoenix	58	2484	73	42.8	3	0	22	141	23	39.4
Philadelphia	82	3459	68	42.2	7	0	36	295	26	36.9
L.A. Rams	76	3122	59	41.1	4	0	48	522	20	33.2
Atlanta	70	2855	56	40.8	3	1	44	482	12	33.0
Tampa Bay	74	3015	57	40.7	11	0	22	117	15	36.2
N.Y. Giants	85	3451	71	40.6	10	3	46	548	18	31.8
Washington	65	2555	66	39.3	5	1	27	332	17	32.7
San Francisco	49	1918	58	39.1	2	0	23	177	19	34.7
Green Bay	68	2608	67	38.4	9	2	26	230	18	32.3
NFC Total	973	40516	84	—	107	9	461	4505	256	—
NFC Average	69.5	2894.0	—	41.6	7.6	0.6	32.9	321.8	18.3	34.8
NFL Total	2057	86544	84	—	204	15	974	8909	523	—
NFL Average	73.5	3090.9	—	42.1	7.3	0.5	34.8	318.2	18.7	35.8

NFL Top 10 Punters

	No	Yards	Long	Gross Avg	Total Punts	TB	Blk	Opp Ret	Ret Yds	In 20	Net Avg
Montgomery, Greg, Hou.	53	2487	66	46.9	55	9	2	31	255	14	37.3
Newsome, Harry, Min.	72	3243	84	45.0	73	15	1	34	339	19	35.7
Stark, Rohn, Ind.	83	3716	64	44.8	83	7	0	45	313	22	39.3
Tuten, Rick, Sea.	108	4760	65	44.1	108	8	0	56	416	29	38.7
Barnhardt, Tommy, N.O.	67	2947	62	44.0	67	10	0	31	218	19	37.7
Arnold, Jim, Det.	65	2846	71	43.8	66	10	1	30	356	12	34.7
Landeta, Sean, NY-G	53	2317	71	43.7	55	9	2	30	406	13	31.5
Barker, Bryan, K.C.	75	3245	65	43.3	76	13	1	35	300	16	35.3
Saxon, Mike, Dal.	61	2620	58	43.0	61	9	0	34	397	19	33.5
Gardocki, Chris, Chi.	79	3393	61	42.9	79	9	0	38	351	19	36.2

AFC Punters—Individual

	No	Yards	Long	Gross Avg	Total Punts	TB	Blk	Opp Ret	Ret Yds	In 20	Net Avg
Montgomery, Greg, Hou.	53	2487	66	46.9	55	9	2	31	255	14	37.3
Stark, Rohn, Ind.	83	3716	64	44.8	83	7	0	45	313	22	39.3
Tuten, Rick, Sea.	108	4760	65	44.1	108	8	0	56	416	29	38.7
Barker, Bryan, K.C.	75	3245	65	43.3	76	13	1	35	300	16	35.3
Royals, Mark, Pit.	73	3119	58	42.7	74	9	1	39	308	22	35.6
Kidd, John, S.D.	68	2899	65	42.6	68	9	0	24	244	22	36.4
Gossett, Jeff, Rai.	77	3255	56	42.3	77	3	0	40	385	17	36.5
Mohr, Chris, Buf.	60	2531	61	42.2	60	7	0	22	185	12	36.8
Johnson, Lee, Cin.	76	3196	64	42.1	76	9	0	32	284	15	35.9
Hansen, Brian, Cle.	74	3083	73	41.7	75	7	1	27	234	28	36.1
McCarthy, Shawn, N.E.	103	4227	61	41.0	103	4	0	59	499	19	35.4
Aguiar, Louie, NY-J	73	2993	65	41.0	73	3	0	26	189	21	37.6
Nonqualifiers											
Horan, Mike, Den.	37	1681	62	45.4	38	1	1	14	132	7	40.2
Roby, Reggie, Mia.	35	1443	60	41.2	35	3	0	16	183	11	34.3
Parker, Daren, Den.	12	491	61	40.9	12	1	0	7	88	1	31.9
Daluiso, Brad, Den.	10	467	67	46.7	10	1	0	6	40	3	40.7
Sullivan, Kent, K.C.	6	247	59	41.2	6	0	0	4	18	2	38.2
Lowery, Nick, K.C.	4	141	39	35.3	4	0	0	1	10	0	32.8
Stoyanovich, Pete, Mia.	2	90	48	45.0	2	0	0	0	0	0	45.0

Leader based on gross average, minimum 40 punts

NFC Punters—Individual

	No	Yards	Long	Gross Avg	Total Punts	TB	Blk	Opp Ret	Ret Yds	In 20	Net Avg
Newsome, Harry, Min.	72	3243	84	45.0	73	15	1	34	339	19	35.7
Barnhardt, Tommy, N.O.	67	2947	62	44.0	67	10	0	31	218	19	37.7
Arnold, Jim, Det.	65	2846	71	43.8	66	10	1	30	356	12	34.7
Landeta, Sean, NY-G	53	2317	71	43.7	55	9	2	30	406	13	31.5
Saxon, Mike, Dal.	61	2620	58	43.0	61	9	0	34	397	19	33.5
Gardocki, Chris, Chi.	79	3393	61	42.9	79	9	0	38	351	19	36.2
Camarillo, Rich, Pho.	54	2317	73	42.9	54	2	0	22	141	23	39.6
Feagles, Jeff, Phi.	82	3459	68	42.2	82	7	0	36	295	26	36.9
Rodriguez, Ruben, Den.-NY-G	46	1907	55	41.5	47	4	1	23	205	9	34.5
Fulhage, Scott, Atl.	68	2818	56	41.4	69	3	1	44	482	11	33.0
Bracken, Don, Rams	76	3122	59	41.1	76	4	0	48	522	20	33.2
Stryzinski, Dan, T.B.	74	3015	57	40.7	74	11	0	22	117	15	36.2
Goodburn, Kelly, Was.	64	2555	66	39.9	65	5	1	27	332	17	32.7
Wilmsmeyer, Klaus, S.F.	49	1918	58	39.1	49	2	0	23	177	19	34.7
Nonqualifiers											
McJulien, Paul, G.B.	36	1386	67	38.5	38	4	2	10	157	8	30.2
Prokop, Joe, Mia.-NY-G	32	1184	56	37.0	32	0	0	22	258	2	28.9
Wagner, Bryan, G.B.	30	1222	52	40.7	30	5	0	16	73	10	35.0
Davis, Greg, Pho.	4	167	52	41.8	4	1	0	0	0	0	36.8
Johnson, Norm, Atl.	1	37	37	37.0	1	0	0	0	0	1	37.0

Leader based on gross average, minimum 40 punts

Punt Returns

Yards per Return
- **NFC:** 13.2—Johnny Bailey, Phoenix
- **AFC:** 11.4—Rod Woodson, Pittsburgh

Yards
- **NFC:** 532—Kelvin Martin, Dallas
- **AFC:** 429—Eric Metcalf, Cleveland

Yards, Game
- **NFC:** 111—Vai Sikahema, Philadelphia at Giants, November 22 (4 returns - TD))
- **AFC:** 100—Carl Pickens, Cincinnati at Green Bay, September 20 (2 returns - TD)
  Dale Carter, Kansas City at Seattle, November 22 (4 returns - TD)
  Eric Metcalf, Cleveland vs. Chicago, November 29 (5 returns - TD)

Longest
- **AFC:** 95—Carl Pickens, Cincinnati at Green Bay, September 20 - TD
- **NFC:** 87—Vai Sikahema, Philadelphia at Giants, November 22 -TD

Returns
- **AFC:** 44—Eric Metcalf, Cleveland
- **NFC:** 42—Kelvin Martin, Dallas

Returns, Game
- **NFC:** 8—Vai Sikahema, Philadelphia at Seattle, December 13 (57 yards) (OT)
- **AFC:** 7—Chris Hale, Buffalo vs. Indianapolis, September 20 (83 yards)
  Eric Metcalf, Cleveland at Houston, November 8 (87 yards)

Fair Catches
- **AFC:** 25—Chris Warren, Seattle
- **NFC:** 18—Kelvin Martin, Dallas

Touchdowns
- **AFC:** 2—Dale Carter, Kansas City
  Clarence Verdin, Indianapolis
- **NFC:** 2—Todd Kinchen, Rams
  Kelvin Martin, Dallas

Team Champion
- **NFC:** 12.5—Dallas
- **AFC:** 11.9—Cincinnati

AFC Punt Returns—Team

	No	FC	Yards	Avg	Long	TD
Cincinnati	24	11	285	11.9	95t	1
Pittsburgh	32	13	364	11.4	80t	1
Indianapolis	25	24	275	11.0	84t	2
Buffalo	43	8	464	10.8	42	0
Denver	34	16	353	10.4	47	0
Kansas City	39	8	402	10.3	86t	2
L.A. Raiders	41	21	402	9.8	40	0
Cleveland	44	10	429	9.8	75t	1
San Diego	44	12	359	8.2	25	0
N.Y. Jets	30	9	232	7.7	21	0
Seattle	38	27	283	7.4	16	0
New England	37	20	274	7.4	50	0
Miami	31	19	191	6.2	19	0
Houston	33	12	194	5.9	20	0
AFC Total	495	210	4507	9.1	95t	7
AFC Average	35.4	15.0	321.9	9.1	—	0.5

NFC Punt Returns—Team

	No	FC	Yards	Avg	Long	TD
Dallas	44	18	550	12.5	79t	2
Philadelphia	47	15	555	11.8	87t	1
Phoenix	33	12	364	11.0	65	0
Minnesota	33	18	336	10.2	42	0
San Francisco	40	12	389	9.7	48t	1
Washington	37	12	355	9.6	84t	2
Detroit	21	9	190	9.0	58t	1
Green Bay	35	6	315	9.0	58t	1
N.Y. Giants	27	11	240	8.9	39	0
L.A. Rams	39	11	345	8.8	61t	2
Chicago	23	14	176	7.7	36	0
Atlanta	29	14	196	6.8	45	0
Tampa Bay	26	15	160	6.2	17	0
New Orleans	45	21	231	5.1	34	0
NFC Total	479	188	4402	9.2	87t	10
NFC Average	34.2	13.4	314.4	9.2	—	0.7
NFL Total	974	398	8909	—	95t	17
NFL Average	34.8	14.2	318.2	9.1	—	0.6

NFL Top 10 Punt Returners

	No	FC	Yards	Avg	Long	TD
Bailey, Johnny, Pho.	20	8	263	13.2	65	0
Martin, Kelvin, Dal.	42	18	532	12.7	79t	2
Sikahema, Vai, Phi.	40	10	503	12.6	87t	1
Woodson, Rod, Pit.	32	13	364	11.4	80t	1
Verdin, Clarence, Ind.	24	12	268	11.2	84t	2
Marshall, Arthur, Den.	33	16	349	10.6	47	0
Carter, Dale, K.C.	38	6	398	10.5	86t	2
Brown, Tim, Rai.	37	19	383	10.4	40	0
Parker, Anthony, Min.	33	17	336	10.2	42	0
Buckley, Terrell, G.B.	21	5	211	10.0	58t	1

AFC Punt Returns—Individual

	No	FC	Yards	Avg	Long	TD
Woodson, Rod, Pit.	32	13	364	11.4	80t	1
Verdin, Clarence, Ind.	24	12	268	11.2	84t	2
Marshall, Arthur, Den.	33	16	349	10.6	47	0
Carter, Dale, K.C.	38	6	398	10.5	86t	2
Brown, Tim, Rai.	37	19	383	10.4	40	0
Hicks, Cliff, Buf.	29	6	289	10.0	42	0
Metcalf, Eric, Cle.	44	10	429	9.8	75t	1
Stanley, Walter, N.E.	28	17	227	8.1	50	0
Bieniemy, Eric, S.D.	30	3	229	7.6	21	0
Carpenter, Rob, NY-J	28	9	208	7.4	21	0
Warren, Chris, Sea.	34	25	252	7.4	16	0
Miller, Scott, Mia.	24	18	175	7.3	19	0
Slaughter, Webster, Hou.	20	8	142	7.1	20	0
Nonqualifiers						
Pickens, Carl, Cin.	18	9	229	12.7	95t	1
Hale, Chris, Buf.	14	2	175	12.5	27	0
Lewis, Nate, S.D.	13	5	127	9.8	25	0
Timpson, Michael, N.E.	8	2	47	5.9	14	0
Coleman, Pat, Hou.	7	4	35	5.0	19	0
Price, Mitchell, Cin.	6	2	56	9.3	25	0
Harris, Corey, Hou.	6	0	17	2.8	13	0
Vincent, Troy, Mia.	5	0	16	3.2	6	0
Treggs, Brian, Sea.	4	2	31	7.8	13	0
McCallum, Napoleon, Rai.	4	1	19	4.8	13	0
Mathis, Terance, NY-J	2	0	24	12.0	12	0
Prior, Mike, Ind.	1	12	7	7.0	7	0
Dimry, Charles, Den.	1	0	4	4.0	4	0
Mincy, Charles, K.C.	1	1	4	4.0	4	0
Brennan, Brian, S.D.	1	1	3	3.0	3	0
Lambert, Dion, N.E.	1	0	0	0.0	0	0
Martin, Tony, Mia.	1	0	0	0.0	0	0
Williams, Jarvis, Mia.	1	1	0	0.0	0	0
Birden, J.J., K.C.	0	1	0	—	—	0
Byrd, Gill, S.D.	0	3	0	—	—	0
Fernandez, Mervyn, Rai.	0	1	0	—	—	0
Fryar, Irving, N.E.	0	1	0	—	—	0

t indicates touchdown
Leader based on average return, minimum 20 returns

NFC Punt Returns—Individual

	No	FC	Yards	Avg	Long	TD
Bailey, Johnny, Pho.	20	8	263	13.2	65	0
Martin, Kelvin, Dal.	42	18	532	12.7	79t	2
Sikahema, Vai, Phi.	40	10	503	12.6	87t	1
Parker, Anthony, Min.	33	17	336	10.2	42	0
Buckley, Terrell, G.B.	21	5	211	10.0	58t	1
Mitchell, Brian, Was.	29	9	271	9.3	84t	1
Meggett, David, NY-G	27	11	240	8.9	39	0
Grant, Alan, S.F.	29	10	249	8.6	46	0
Turner, Vernon, Rams	28	6	207	7.4	23	0
Newman, Pat, N.O.	23	10	158	6.9	18	0
Nonqualifiers						
Gray, Mel, Det.	18	9	175	9.7	58t	1
Smith, Tony, Atl.	16	4	155	9.7	45	0
Blount, Eric, Pho.	13	4	101	7.8	16	0
Hawkins, Courtney, T.B.	13	8	53	4.1	17	0
Sanders, Deion, Atl.	13	9	41	3.2	14	0
Woolford, Donnell, Chi.	12	3	127	10.6	36	0
Dowdell, Marcus, N.O.	12	6	37	3.1	34	0
Brooks, Robert, G.B.	11	1	102	9.3	22	0
Waddle, Tom, Chi.	8	10	28	3.5	13	0
Drewrey, Willie, T.B.	7	6	62	8.9	17	0
Sydner, Jeff, Phi.	7	5	52	7.4	17	0
Howard, Desmond, Was.	6	3	84	14.0	55t	1
Griffin, Don, S.F.	6	2	69	11.5	29	0
Anderson, Gary, T.B.	6	1	45	7.5	13	0
Harry, Emile, Rams	6	4	34	5.7	11	0
Lipps, Louis, N.O.	5	1	22	4.4	16	0
Kinchen, Todd, Rams	4	1	103	25.8	61t	2
Lewis, Ronald, S.F.	4	0	23	5.8	9	0
Morgan, Anthony, Chi.	3	1	21	7.0	13	0
Campbell, Jeff, Det.	3	0	15	5.0	9	0
Turner, Floyd, N.O.	3	0	10	3.3	5	0
Buck, Vince, N.O.	2	4	4	2.0	3	0

	No	FC	Yards	Avg	Long	TD
Hanks, Merton, S.F.	1	0	48	48.0	48t	1
Smith, Kevin, Dal.	1	0	17	17.0	17	0
Hauck, Tim, G.B.	1	0	2	2.0	2	0
Horton, Ray, Dal.	1	0	1	1.0	1	0
Stradford, Troy, Rams	1	0	1	1.0	1	0
Cecil, Chuck, G.B.	1	0	0	0.0	0	0
Clark, Vinnie, G.B.	1	0	0	0.0	0	0
Johnson, Sidney, Was.	1	0	0	0.0	0	0
Thomas, Johnny, Was.	1	0	0	0.0	0	0
Johnson, Joe, Min.	0	1	0	—	—	0
Phillips, Jason, Atl.	0	1	0	—	—	0

t indicates touchdown
Leader based on average return, minimum 20 returns

Kickoff Returns

Yards per Return
AFC: 28.2—Jon Vaughn, New England
NFC: 26.7—Deion Sanders, Atlanta

Yards
NFC: 1067—Deion Sanders, Atlanta
AFC: 815—Clarence Verdin, Indianapolis

Yards, Game
NFC: 190—Deion Sanders, Atlanta at New Orleans, December 3 (6 returns)
AFC: 125—Scott Lockwood, New England at Kansas City, December 13 (6 returns)

Longest
AFC: 100—Jon Vaughn, New England at Cincinnati, December 20 - TD
NFC: 99—Deion Sanders, Atlanta at Washington, September 13 - TD

Returns
NFC: 42—Mel Gray, Detroit
AFC: 39—Clarence Verdin, Indianapolis

Returns, Game
NFC: 8—Mel Gray, Detroit vs. Dallas, November 8 (178 yards)
AFC: 7—Walter Stanley, New England at Atlanta, November 29 (120 yards)

Touchdown
NFC: 2—Deion Sanders, Atlanta
AFC: 1—Jon Vaughn, New England

Team Champion
NFC: 23.9—Atlanta
AFC: 21.5—New England

AFC Kickoff Returns—Team

	No	Yards	Avg	Long	TD
New England	64	1376	21.5	100t	1
Cleveland	43	880	20.5	47	0
Denver	51	1028	20.2	64	0
Indianapolis	51	1001	19.6	42	0
Houston	46	885	19.2	42	0
Miami	44	838	19.0	44	0
Buffalo	41	761	18.6	35	0
Kansas City	39	722	18.5	39	0
San Diego	45	812	18.0	62	0
Cincinnati	59	1058	17.9	48	0
Seattle	50	885	17.7	34	0
Pittsburgh	48	847	17.6	33	0
N.Y. Jets	54	950	17.6	45	0
L.A. Raiders	43	744	17.3	41	0
AFC Total	678	12787	18.9	100t	1
AFC Average	48.4	913.4	18.9	—	0.1

NFC Kickoff Returns—Team

	No	Yards	Avg	Long	TD
Atlanta	64	1532	23.9	99t	2
Phoenix	51	1127	22.1	63	0
San Francisco	42	879	20.9	82	0
Philadelphia	48	987	20.6	45	0
Chicago	56	1143	20.4	97t	1
Washington	48	973	20.3	47	0
Detroit	59	1193	20.2	89t	1
N.Y. Giants	56	1098	19.6	92t	1
Minnesota	45	874	19.4	53	0
New Orleans	42	815	19.4	48	0
Dallas	37	699	18.9	59	0
Green Bay	54	1017	18.8	50	0
Tampa Bay	50	881	17.6	39	0
L.A. Rams	63	1054	16.7	35	0
NFC Total	715	14272	20.0	99t	5
NFC Average	51.1	1019.4	20.0	—	0.4
NFL Total	1393	27059	—	100t	6
NFL Average	49.8	966.4	19.4	—	0.2

NFL Top 10 Kickoff Returners

	No	Yards	Avg	Long	TD
Vaughn, Jon, N.E.	20	564	28.2	100t	1
Sanders, Deion, Atl.	40	1067	26.7	99t	2
Bailey, Johnny, Pho.	28	690	24.6	63	0
Gray, Mel, Det.	42	1006	24.0	89t	1
Meggett, David, NY-G	20	455	22.8	92t	1
Baldwin, Randy, Cle.	30	675	22.5	47	0
Lewis, Darren, Chi.	23	511	22.2	97t	1
Montgomery, Alton, Den.	21	466	22.2	64	0
Logan, Marc, S.F.	22	478	21.7	82	0
Nelson, Darrin, Min.	29	626	21.6	53	0

AFC Kickoff Returns—Individual

	No	Yards	Avg	Long	TD
Vaughn, Jon, N.E.	20	564	28.2	100t	1
Baldwin, Randy, Cle.	30	675	22.5	47	0
Montgomery, Alton, Den.	21	466	22.2	64	0
Verdin, Clarence, Ind.	39	815	20.9	42	0
Ball, Eric, Cin.	20	411	20.6	48	0
Williams, Harvey, K.C.	21	405	19.3	37	0
McMillan, Erik, NY-J	22	420	19.1	45	0
Woodson, Rod, Pit.	25	469	18.8	32	0
Warren, Chris, Sea.	28	524	18.7	34	0
Stanley, Walter, N.E.	29	529	18.2	40	0
Mathis, Terance, NY-J	28	492	17.6	32	0
Stegall, Milt, Cin.	25	430	17.2	39	0
Wright, Alexander, Dal.-Rai.	26	442	17.0	33	0
Nonqualifiers					
Lewis, Nate, S.D.	19	402	21.2	62	0
Williams, Mike, Mia.	19	328	17.3	28	0
Mayes, Rueben, Sea.	19	311	16.4	29	0
Bieniemy, Eric, S.D.	15	257	17.1	30	0
Coleman, Pat, Hou.	14	290	20.7	28	0
Parmalee, Bernie, Mia.	14	289	20.6	32	0
McCallum, Napoleon, Rai.	14	274	19.6	41	0
Davis, Kenneth, Buf.	14	251	17.9	35	0
Edwards, Al, Buf.	12	274	22.8	34	0
Stone, Dwight, Pit.	12	219	18.3	28	0
Lockwood, Scott, N.E.	11	233	21.2	36	0
Carter, Dale, K.C.	11	190	17.3	39	0
Tillman, Spencer, Hou.	10	157	15.7	33	0
Metcalf, Eric, Cle.	9	157	17.4	30	0
Craver, Aaron, Mia.	8	174	21.8	44	0
Lewis, Darryll, Hou.	8	171	21.4	26	0
Fuller, Eddie, Buf.	8	134	16.8	28	0
Marshall, Arthur, Den.	8	132	16.5	21	0
Miles, Ostell, Cin.	8	128	16.0	27	0
Ambrose, Ashley, Ind.	8	126	15.8	26	0
Russell, Derek, Den.	7	154	22.0	33	0
Harmon, Ronnie, S.D.	7	96	13.7	30	0
Lamb, Brad, Buf.	5	97	19.4	31	0
Graddy, Sam, Rai.	5	85	17.0	21	0
Green, Gaston, Den.	5	76	15.2	20	0
Robinson, Frank, Cin.-Den.	4	89	22.3	26	0
Clark, Ken, Ind.	3	54	18.0	20	0
Jones, Fred, K.C.	3	51	17.0	23	0
Thompson, Leroy, Pit.	2	51	25.5	33	0
Johnson, Reggie, Den.	2	47	23.5	34	0
Thigpen, Yancey, Pit.	2	44	22.0	29	0
Fenner, Derrick, Cin.	f2	38	19.0	19	0
Hoard, Leroy, Cle.	2	34	17.0	25	0
Smith, Sammie, Den.	2	31	15.5	21	0
Paige, Tony, Mia.	2	29	14.5	19	0
Hoge, Merril, Pit.	2	28	14.0	17	0
Timpson, Michael, N.E.	2	28	14.0	28	0
Land, Dan, Rai.	2	27	13.5	14	0
McNair, Todd, K.C.	2	20	10.0	14	0
Price, Mitchell, Cin.	2	20	10.0	13	0
Brown, Tim, Rai.	2	14	7.0	14	0
Hendrickson, Steve, S.D.	2	14	7.0	8	0
Vardell, Tommy, Cle.	2	14	7.0	13	0
Cash, Keith, K.C.	1	36	36.0	36	0
Miller, Anthony, S.D.	1	33	33.0	33	0
Slaughter, Webster, Hou.	1	21	21.0	21	0
Anders, Kimble, K.C.	1	20	20.0	20	0
Oliver, Muhammad, Den.	1	20	20.0	20	0
Thomas, Doug, Sea.	1	19	19.0	19	0
Bussey, Barney, Cin.	1	18	18.0	18	0
Humphrey, Bobby, Mia.	1	18	18.0	18	0
Bentley, Albert, Pit.	1	17	17.0	17	0
Bell, Nick, Rai.	1	16	16.0	16	0
Jones, James, Sea.	1	16	16.0	16	0
Brown, Gary, Hou.	1	15	15.0	15	0
Hector, Johnny, NY-J	1	15	15.0	15	0
Johnson, Tracy, Sea.	1	15	15.0	15	0
Montgomery, Glenn, Hou.	1	13	13.0	13	0
Query, Jeff, Cin.	1	13	13.0	13	0
Traylor, Keith, Den.	1	13	13.0	13	0

	No	Yards	Avg	Long	TD
Flannery, John, Hou.	1	12	12.0	12	0
Hobby, Marion, N.E.	1	11	11.0	11	0
Mills, Ernie, Pit.	1	11	11.0	11	0
Turner, Kevin, N.E.	f1	11	11.0	11	0
Brennan, Brian, S.D.	1	10	10.0	10	0
Dawkins, Dale, NY-J	1	10	10.0	10	0
Cooper, Adrian, Pit.	1	8	8.0	8	0
Duffy, Roger, NY-J	1	7	7.0	7	0
Dixon, Cal, NY-J	1	6	6.0	6	0
Vanderbeek, Matt, Ind.	1	6	6.0	6	0
Hicks, Cliff, Buf.	1	5	5.0	5	0
Turk, Daniel, Rai.	1	3	3.0	3	0
Campbell, Russ, Pit.	1	0	0.0	0	0
Frerotte, Mitch, Buf.	1	0	0.0	0	0
Williams, Warren, Pit.	1	0	0.0	0	0
Anderson, Jesse, Pit.	f0	0	—	—	0
Awalt, Robert, Buf.	f0	0	—	—	0
Whisenhunt, Ken, NY-J	f0	0	—	—	0

t indicates touchdown
f indicates fair catch (Kevin Turner, N.E.: 2 fair catches)
Leader based on average return, minimum 20 returns

NFC Kickoff Returns—Individual

	No	Yards	Avg	Long	TD
Sanders, Deion, Atl.	40	1067	26.7	99t	2
Bailey, Johnny, Pho.	28	690	24.6	63	0
Gray, Mel, Det.	f42	1006	24.0	89t	1
Meggett, David, NY-G	20	455	22.8	92t	1
Lewis, Darren, Chi.	23	511	22.2	97t	1
Logan, Marc, S.F.	22	478	21.7	82	0
Nelson, Darrin, Min.	29	626	21.6	53	0
Mitchell, Brian, Was.	23	492	21.4	47	0
Howard, Desmond, Was.	22	462	21.0	42	0
Martin, Kelvin, Dal.	24	503	21.0	59	0
Harris, Corey, Hou.-G.B.	33	691	20.9	50	0
Sikahema, Vai, Phi.	26	528	20.3	41	0
Turner, Vernon, Rams	29	569	19.6	35	0
Anderson, Gary, T.B.	29	564	19.4	39	0
Smith, Joey, NY-G	30	564	18.8	35	0
Nonqualifiers					
McAfee, Fred, N.O.	19	393	20.7	38	0
Brooks, Robert, G.B.	18	338	18.8	30	0
Sydner, Jeff, Phi.	17	368	21.6	45	0
Gentry, Dennis, Chi.	16	330	20.6	66	0
Lee, Amp, S.F.	14	276	19.7	33	0
Lang, David, Rams	13	228	17.5	26	0
Blount, Eric, Pho.	11	251	22.8	52	0
Green, Mark, Chi.	11	224	20.4	29	0
Dunbar, Vaughn, N.O.	10	187	18.7	27	0
Pegram, Erric, Atl.	9	161	17.9	42	0
Hawkins, Courtney, T.B.	9	118	13.1	18	0
Edwards, Anthony, Pho.	8	143	17.9	24	0
Smith, Tony, Atl.	7	172	24.6	60	0
Hilliard, Dalton, N.O.	7	130	18.6	48	0
Stradford, Troy, Rams-Det.	7	94	13.4	21	0
Jones, Keith, Atl.	6	114	19.0	29	0
Delpino, Robert, Rams	6	83	13.8	18	0
Henderson, Keith, Min.	5	111	22.2	29	0
Bennett, Edgar, G.B.	5	104	20.8	33	0
Johnson, Joe, Min.	5	79	15.8	25	0
Morgan, Anthony, Chi.	4	71	17.8	30	0
Kinchen, Todd, Rams	4	63	15.8	19	0
Campbell, Jeff, Det.	4	61	15.3	21	0
Perriman, Brett, Det.	4	59	14.8	22	0
Thompson, Anthony, Rams	4	34	8.5	14	0
Thomas, George, T.B.	3	72	24.0	37	0
Grant, Alan, S.F.	3	70	23.3	47	0
Holmes, Clayton, Dal.	3	70	23.3	28	0
Walker, Herschel, Phi.	3	69	23.0	34	0
Newman, Pat, N.O.	3	62	20.7	29	0
Brooks, James, T.B.	3	49	16.3	24	0
Jurkovic, John, G.B.	3	39	13.0	14	0
Scott, Kevin, Det.	3	5	1.7	3	0
Carter, Dexter, S.F.	2	55	27.5	32	0
Parker, Anthony, Min.	2	30	15.0	15	0
Calloway, Chris, NY-G	2	29	14.5	17	0
Bunch, Jarrod, NY-G	2	27	13.5	17	0
West, Ronnie, Min.	2	27	13.5	27	0
Ryan, Tim, T.B.	2	24	12.0	13	0
Sparks, Phillipi, NY-G	2	23	11.5	14	0
Mayfield, Corey, T.B.	2	22	11.0	15	0
Smith, Lance, Pho.	2	16	8.0	13	0
Stephen, Scott, Rams	2	12	6.0	7	0
Tillison, Ed, Det.	1	27	27.0	27	0
Wilson, Charles, T.B.	1	23	23.0	23	0
Jordan, Buford, N.O.	1	18	18.0	18	0
Jackson, John, Pho.	1	17	17.0	17	0
Workman, Vince, G.B.	1	17	17.0	17	0

	No	Yards	Avg	Long	TD
McNabb, Dexter, G.B.	1	15	15.0	15	0
Heyward, Craig, N.O.	1	14	14.0	14	0
Barnett, Oliver, Atl.	1	13	13.0	13	0
Booty, John, Phi.	1	11	11.0	11	0
Brooks, Tony, Phi.	1	11	11.0	11	0
Kennard, Derek, N.O.	1	11	11.0	11	0
Sims, Joe, G.B.	1	11	11.0	11	0
Rolle, Butch, Pho.	1	10	10.0	10	0
Anderson, Willie, Rams	1	9	9.0	9	0
Chamblee, Al, T.B.	1	9	9.0	9	0
Green, Robert, Was.	1	9	9.0	9	0
Smith, Kevin, Dal.	1	9	9.0	9	0
Davey, Don, G.B.	1	8	8.0	8	0
Gouveia, Kurt, Was.	1	7	7.0	7	0
Leeuwenburg, Jay, Chi.	1	7	7.0	7	0
Fortin, Roman, Atl.	1	5	5.0	5	0
Orr, Terry, Was.	1	3	3.0	3	0
Reed, Jake, Min.	1	1	1.0	1	0
Adams, Scott, Min.	1	0	0.0	0	0
Edwards, Dixon, Dal.	1	0	0.0	0	0
Johnson, Jimmy, Det.	1	0	0.0	0	0
Rivera, Ron, Chi.	1	0	0.0	0	0
Turner, Odessa, S.F.	f1	0	0.0	0	0
West, Ed, G.B.	1	0	0.0	0	0
Israel, Steve, Rams	1	-3	-3.0	-3	0
Epps, Tory, Atl.	f0	0	—	—	0
Gash, Thane, S.F.	f0	0	—	—	0

t indicates touchdown
f Fair Catch (Mel Gray, Det.: 2 fair catches)
Leader based on average return, minimum 20 returns

Fumbles

Most Fumbles

NFC: 13—Randall Cunningham, Philadelphia
AFC: 12—John Elway, Denver
Boomer Esiason, Cincinnati
Browning Nagle, Jets
Kelly Stouffer, Seattle

Most Fumbles, Game

NFC: 5—Andre Ware, Detroit at Green Bay, December 6
AFC: 3—John Elway, Denver vs. Raiders, September 6
Barry Foster, Pittsburgh vs. Jets, September 13
Browning Nagle, Jets at Rams, September 27
John Elway, Denver vs. Kansas City, October 4
Stan Gelbaugh, Seattle vs. Raiders, October 18
Stan Humphries, San Diego vs. Denver, October 25
Mike Tomczak, Cleveland at Cincinnati, November 1
Stan Humphries, San Diego at Kansas City, November 8
Warren Moon, Houston at Minnesota, November 15
Boomer Esiason, Cincinnati vs. Detroit, November 22
Tommy Maddox, Denver at Raiders, November 22
Kelly Stouffer, Seattle vs. Denver, November 30 (OT)
Dave Krieg, Kansas City at Raiders, December 6
Browning Nagle, Jets at Buffalo, December 6
Cody Carlson, Houston vs. Chicago, December 7
John Elway, Denver at Kansas City, December 27
Donald Hollas, Cincinnati vs. Indianapolis, December 27

Own Fumbles Recovered

AFC: 6—Boomer Esiason, Cincinnati
Dave Krieg, Kansas City
NFC: 4—Vinny Testaverde, Tampa Bay

Most Own Fumbles Recovered, Game

NFC: 3—Don Majkowski, Green Bay vs. Minnesota, September 6 (OT)
Marcus Dowdell, New Orleans at Phoenix, October 18
AFC: 2—Victor Jones, Denver at Philadelphia, September 20
Kelly Stouffer, Seattle at New England, September 20
John Flannery, Houston at Denver, October 18
Boomer Esiason, Cincinnati at Chicago, November 8 (OT)
Tommy Maddox, Denver at Raiders, November 22
Dave Krieg, Kansas City at Raiders, December 6
Cody Carlson, Houston vs. Chicago, December 7
Bubby Brister, Pittsburgh vs. Minnesota, December 20
Donald Hollas, Cincinnati vs. Indianapolis, December 27

Opponents' Fumbles Recovered

AFC: 5—Mike Johnson, Cleveland
NFC: 4—Kevin Greene, Rams

Most Opponents' Fumbles Recovered, Game

AFC: 2—Brian Washington, Jets vs. Miami, November 1
NFC: 2—Danny Copeland, Washington vs. Dallas, December 13
Thomas Everett, Dallas at Atlanta, December 21

Yards

AFC: 115—Stevon Moore, Cleveland
NFC: 76—Sam Mills, New Orleans

Longest

NFC: 76—Sam Mills, New Orleans at Jets, December 26 - TD
AFC: 75—Ray Bentley, Cincinnati at Seattle, September 6 - TD

AFC Fumbles—Team

	Fum	Own Rec	Fum OB	TD	Opp Rec	TD	Fum Yards	Tot Rec
Cleveland	19	6	1	0	20	3	152	26
Indianapolis	24	12	1	0	15	0	-32	27
L.A. Raiders	25	8	2	0	7	0	35	15
San Diego	26	13	1	1	11	0	19	24
Pittsburgh	28	10	0	0	21	1	86	31
N.Y. Jets	28	12	1	0	18	0	16	30
Kansas City	28	16	3	0	15	2	17	31
Houston	28	15	1	0	11	3	7	26
Denver	29	13	2	0	16	1	117	29
Buffalo	31	13	1	0	12	1	8	25
Miami	31	13	1	0	14	0	-17	27
Cincinnati	32	22	0	0	17	2	58	39
Seattle	37	17	2	0	11	1	69	28
New England	43	17	0	0	15	2	-41	32
AFC Total	409	187	16	1	203	16	494	390
AFC Average	29.2	13.4	1.1	0.1	14.5	1.1	35.3	27.9

NFC Fumbles—Team

	Fum	Own Rec	Fum OB	TD	Opp Rec	TD	Fum Yards	Tot Rec
Dallas	16	7	0	0	14	1	44	21
Washington	18	10	1	0	11	1	114	21
Tampa Bay	19	9	1	0	13	3	63	22
Chicago	23	10	3	0	16	1	42	26
Philadelphia	25	9	1	0	13	1	39	22
N.Y. Giants	25	12	0	0	12	0	-19	24
Phoenix	26	7	1	0	12	0	28	19
Detroit	26	9	2	0	11	1	8	20
New Orleans	27	12	2	0	20	3	135	32
San Francisco	29	12	4	0	12	1	36	24
Minnesota	29	11	1	0	14	2	85	25
L.A. Rams	30	12	1	0	15	0	-8	27
Atlanta	30	16	0	0	12	1	31	28
Green Bay	41	18	2	0	19	1	57	37
NFC Total	364	154	19	0	194	16	655	348
NFC Average	26.0	11.0	1.4	0.0	13.9	1.1	46.8	24.9
NFL Total	773	341	35	1	397	32	1149	738
NFL Average	27.6	12.2	1.3	0.0	14.2	1.1	41.0	26.4

Fum OB= Fumbled out of bounds, includes fumbled through the end zone. Yards includes aborted plays, own recoveries, and oppponents' recoveries. Fumbled through the end zone, ball awarded to opponents: Denver (possession awarded to Seattle).

AFC Fumbles—Individual

	Fum.	Own Rec.	Opp. Rec.	Yds	Tot. Rec.
Agnew, Ray, N.E.	0	0	1	0	1
Allen, Marcus, Rai.	1	0	0	0	0
Ambrose, Ashley, Ind.	2	0	0	0	0
Anders, Kimble, K.C.	1	0	0	0	0
Armstrong, Bruce, N.E.	0	1	0	0	1
Arthur, Mike, Cin.	4	0	0	-33	0
Atwater, Steve, Den.	0	0	2	1	2
Baldwin, Randy, Cle.	1	0	0	0	0
Ball, Eric, Cin.	1	0	2	-6	2
Banks, Chip, Ind.	0	0	1	0	1
Barnett, Tim, K.C.	1	0	0	0	0
Baty, Greg, Mia.	0	0	1	0	1
Baumann, Charlie, N.E.	0	0	1	0	1
Baxter, Brad, NY-J	3	1	0	0	1
Baylor, John, Ind.	0	0	2	0	2
Beebe, Don, Buf.	1	0	0	0	0
Bell, Nick, Rai.	2	1	0	0	1
Belser, Jason, Ind.	1	1	1	0	2
Bennett, Antoine, Cin.	0	0	1	0	1
Bennett, Cornelius, Buf.	0	0	3	0	3
Bentley, Ray, Cin.	0	0	1	75	1
Bernstine, Rod, S.D.	2	0	0	0	0
Bickett, Duane, Ind.	0	0	2	0	2
Bieniemy, Eric, S.D.	4	1	0	0	1
Birden, J.J., K.C.	3	1	0	0	1
Blackmon, Robert, Sea.	0	0	1	9	1
Blades, Brian, Sea.	1	0	0	0	0
Blake, Jeff, NY-J	1	0	0	0	0
Brandon, David, Cle.	0	0	3	32	3
Brister, Bubby, Pit.	2	2	0	-2	2
Brooks, Michael, Den.	0	0	2	55	2
Brooks, Bill, Ind.	0	1	0	0	1
Brown, A.B., NY-J	1	1	0	0	1
Brown, Gary, Hou.	0	1	0	0	1
Brown, J.B., Mia.	0	0	1	0	1
Brown, Roger, N.E.	0	0	1	0	1
Brown, Tim, Rai.	6	1	0	0	1
Brown, Vincent, N.E.	0	0	2	25	2
Bryant, Jeff, Sea.	0	0	1	0	1
Burkett, Chris, NY-J	1	0	0	0	0
Burnett, Rob, Cle.	0	0	2	0	2
Butts, Marion, S.D.	4	0	1	0	1
Byrd, Gill, S.D.	0	0	2	0	2
Cadrez, Glenn, NY-J	0	0	1	0	1
Cain, Joseph, Sea.	0	0	1	0	1
Call, Kevin, Ind.	0	1	0	0	1
Carlson, Jeff, N.E.	2	1	0	-4	1
Carlson, Cody, Hou.	8	3	0	-9	3
Carpenter, Rob, NY-J	3	0	0	0	0
Carter, Dale, K.C.	7	2	0	0	2
Cash, Keith, K.C.	0	1	0	0	1
Cash, Kerry, Ind.	0	2	0	0	2
Chaffey, Pat, NY-J	0	1	0	0	1
Childress, Ray, Hou.	0	0	2	8	2
Chilton, Gene, N.E.	1	2	0	0	2
Clayton, Mark, Mia.	1	1	0	0	1
Clifton, Kyle, NY-J	0	0	4	0	4
Coates, Ben, N.E.	1	0	0	0	0
Collins, Shawn, Cle.	0	1	0	0	1
Collins, Todd, N.E.	0	0	2	0	2
Cook, Marv, N.E.	3	1	0	-26	1
Cooper, Adrian, Pit.	1	0	0	0	0
Coryatt, Quentin, Ind.	0	0	1	0	1
Cox, Bryan, Mia.	0	0	1	0	1

	Fum.	Own Rec.	Opp. Rec.	Yds	Tot. Rec.
Croel, Mike, Den.	0	0	1	0	1
Culver, Rodney, Ind.	2	1	0	0	1
Darby, Matt, Buf.	0	1	0	0	1
Davenport, Charles, Pit.	0	0	1	34	1
Davidson, Jeff, Den.	0	1	0	0	1
Davis, Kenneth, Buf.	5	2	0	0	2
Dawson, Doug, Hou.	0	1	0	0	1
Dellenbach, Jeff, Mia.	0	1	0	0	1
Dickerson, Eric, Rai.	1	0	0	0	0
Donaldson, Ray, Ind.	1	0	0	-17	0
Dronett, Shane, Den.	0	0	2	-5	2
Duffy, Roger, NY-J	0	1	0	0	1
Dumas, Mike, Hou.	0	0	1	0	1
Duncan, Curtis, Hou.	0	1	0	0	1
Duper, Mark, Mia.	2	0	0	0	0
Edwards, Al, Buf.	1	0	0	0	0
Ellison, Riki, Rai.	0	0	2	0	2
Elway, John, Den.	12	1	0	0	1
Esiason, Boomer, Cin.	12	6	0	-9	6
Evans, Donald, Pit.	0	0	2	0	2
Evans, Vince, Rai.	1	0	0	0	0
Farrell, Sean, Sea.	0	1	0	0	1
Fenner, Derrick, Cin.	1	1	0	0	1
Figaro, Cedric, Cle.	0	1	0	0	1
Flannery, John, Hou.	0	2	0	0	2
Foster, Barry, Pit.	9	2	0	-20	2
Francis, James, Cin.	0	0	2	3	2
Fuller, William, Hou.	0	0	1	10	1
Gagliano, Bob, S.D.	1	1	0	0	1
Gannon, Chris, N.E.	1	0	0	-12	0
Gardner, Carwell, Buf.	0	2	0	0	2
Gash, Sam, N.E.	1	1	1	0	2
Gelbaugh, Stan, Sea.	9	2	0	-11	2
George, Jeff, Ind.	6	1	0	-2	1
Givins, Earnest, Hou.	3	1	0	0	1
Glover, Andrew, Rai.	1	1	0	0	1
Goad, Tim, N.E.	0	0	1	19	1
Goeas, Leo, S.D.	0	1	0	0	1
Gordon, Alex, Cin.	0	0	1	0	1
Gossett, Jeff, Rai.	1	0	0	0	0
Gray, Jerry, Hou.	0	0	2	4	2
Green, Harold, Cin.	1	1	0	0	1
Griffin, Leonard, K.C.	0	0	1	0	1
Griggs, David, Mia.	0	0	3	-5	3
Grunhard, Tim, K.C.	0	2	0	0	2
Hansen, Brian, Cle.	1	1	0	0	1
Harden, Bobby, Mia.	0	0	1	0	1
Harmon, Ronnie, S.D.	4	2	0	0	2
Harper, Dwayne, Sea.	1	1	1	52	2
Harvey, Richard, Buf.	0	0	1	0	1
Haselrig, Carlton, Pit.	0	1	0	4	1
Hasty, James, NY-J	0	0	2	0	2
Hector, Johnny, NY-J	1	1	0	0	1
Hicks, Cliff, Buf.	2	0	0	0	0
Higgs, Mark, Mia.	5	0	0	0	0
Hilliard, Randy, Cle.	0	0	1	0	1
Hitchcock, Bill, Sea.	0	2	0	0	2
Hoard, Leroy, Cle.	3	1	0	0	1
Hobley, Liffort, Mia.	0	0	1	0	1
Hodson, Tom, N.E.	2	1	0	0	1
Hoge, Merril, Pit.	3	0	0	0	0
Hollas, Donald, Cin.	6	5	0	-5	5
Hollier, Dwight, Mia.	0	1	2	0	3
Horton, Ethan, Rai.	1	2	0	0	2
Howard, David, N.E.	0	0	1	0	1
Hull, Kent, Buf.	0	2	0	0	2
Humphrey, Bobby, Mia.	2	1	0	0	1
Humphries, Stan, S.D.	9	3	0	0	3
Hunter, Patrick, Sea.	0	0	1	2	1
Jackson, Keith, Mia.	2	0	0	0	0
Jeffires, Haywood, Hou.	1	0	0	0	0
Johnson, Anthony, Ind.	6	2	2	0	4
Johnson, David, Pit.	0	0	2	0	2
Johnson, Mike, Cle.	0	0	5	0	5
Johnson, Reggie, Den.	0	1	0	0	1
Johnson, Tracy, Sea.	0	0	1	10	1
Johnson, Vance, Den.	1	0	0	0	0
Jones, Aaron, Pit.	0	0	1	0	1
Jones, Henry, Buf.	0	0	2	0	2
Jones, James, Cle.	0	0	1	0	1
Jones, James, Sea.	0	0	1	0	1
Jones, Rod, Cin.	0	0	1	0	1
Jones, Victor, Den.	0	2	0	0	2
Jorden, Tim, Pit.	0	1	0	0	1
Kartz, Keith, Den.	0	1	0	0	1
Kelly, Jim, Buf.	8	0	0	-18	0
Kennedy, Cortez, Sea.	1	0	1	19	1
Kidd, John, S.D.	1	1	0	-9	1
Kirk, Randy, Cin.	0	1	1	7	2
Klingler, David, Cin.	3	0	0	0	0
Kosar, Bernie, Cle.	1	0	0	0	0
Krieg, Dave, K.C.	10	6	0	-15	6
Krumrie, Tim, Cin.	0	0	1	0	1
Lake, Carnell, Pit.	0	0	1	12	1
Lambert, Dion, N.E.	0	0	1	0	1
Land, Dan, Rai.	1	0	0	0	0
Lang, Le-Lo, Den.	0	0	1	0	1
Lee, Ronnie, Sea.	0	1	0	0	1
Lee, Shawn, S.D.	0	0	1	0	1
Lewis, Darryll, Hou.	0	0	1	0	1
Lewis, Greg, Den.	2	0	0	0	0
Lewis, Mo, NY-J	0	0	4	22	4
Lewis, Nate, S.D.	1	2	0	0	2
Lloyd, Greg, Pit.	1	0	4	0	4
Lockhart, Eugene, N.E.	0	0	1	0	1
Lockwood, Scott, N.E.	1	0	1	0	1
Lodish, Mike, Buf.	0	0	1	18	1
Lott, Ronnie, Rai.	0	0	1	0	1
Love, Duval, Pit.	0	1	0	7	1
Lutz, Dave, K.C.	0	1	0	0	1
Mack, Kevin, Cle.	1	0	0	0	0
Maddox, Tommy, Den.	4	2	0	0	2
Marino, Dan, Mia.	5	2	0	-12	2
Marinovich, Todd, Rai.	4	2	0	-5	2
Marshall, Arthur, Den.	3	1	0	0	1
Martin, Tony, Mia.	2	1	0	0	1
Marts, Lonnie, K.C.	0	0	1	2	1
Mathis, Terance, NY-J	2	1	0	0	1
Mayes, Rueben, Sea.	1	0	0	0	0
McCarthy, Shawn, N.E.	1	1	0	0	1
McCoy, Tony, Ind.	0	0	1	0	1
McDaniel, Terry, Rai.	0	0	1	40	1
McDonald, Ricardo, Cin.	0	0	1	4	1
McGee, Tim, Cin.	0	2	0	0	2
McGwire, Dan, Sea.	1	0	0	-1	0
McKeller, Keith, Buf.	1	0	0	0	0
McMillan, Erik, NY-J	1	1	1	0	2
McNair, Todd, K.C.	1	1	0	0	1
McNeil, Freeman, NY-J	1	1	0	0	1
Meads, Johnny, Hou.	0	0	1	15	1
Metcalf, Eric, Cle.	6	2	0	0	2
Millen, Hugh, N.E.	8	0	0	-6	0
Miller, Eddie, Ind.	0	0	1	0	1
Miller, Anthony, S.D.	0	1	0	0	1
Miller, Scott, Mia.	2	1	0	0	1
Mills, Ernie, Pit.	2	0	0	0	0
Mills, Jeff, Den.	0	0	2	0	2
Mims, Chris, S.D.	0	0	1	0	1
Mincy, Charles, K.C.	0	0	1	30	1
Minnifield, Frank, Cle.	0	0	1	0	1
Mitchell, Scott, Mia.	1	0	0	-1	0
Mitz, Alonzo, Cin.	0	0	2	0	2
Mohr, Chris, Buf.	0	0	1	0	1
Montgomery, Alton, Den.	1	0	2	66	2
Montgomery, Glenn, Hou.	0	0	2	0	2
Montgomery, Greg, Hou.	1	1	0	-15	1
Moon, Warren, Hou.	7	0	0	-6	0
Moore, Shawn, Den.	3	0	0	0	0
Moore, Stevon, Cle.	0	0	3	115	3
Nagle, Browning, NY-J	12	3	0	-14	3
Nickerson, Hardy, Pit.	0	0	2	44	2
Odomes, Nate, Buf.	0	0	1	12	1
O'Donnell, Neil, Pit.	6	3	1	-20	4
Okoye, Christian, K.C.	2	0	0	0	0
Oliver, Louis, Mia.	0	0	1	0	1
O'Neal, Leslie, S.D.	0	0	1	0	1
Paige, Tony, Mia.	1	0	0	0	0
Parker, Glenn, Buf.	0	1	0	0	1
Parmalee, Bernie, Mia.	3	0	0	0	0
Perry, Darren, Pit.	0	0	1	0	1
Phillips, Joe, K.C.	0	0	1	0	1
Pickel, Bill, NY-J	0	0	1	0	1
Pickens, Carl, Cin.	3	2	0	0	2
Plummer, Gary, S.D.	0	1	1	0	2
Prior, Mike, Ind.	0	0	1	0	1
Radecic, Scott, Ind.	0	0	1	0	1
Rakoczy, Gregg, N.E.	1	0	0	-13	0
Reasons, Gary, Cin.	0	0	1	0	1
Redding, Reggie, N.E.	0	1	0	0	1
Reed, Andre, Buf.	4	0	0	0	0
Reich, Frank, Buf.	3	2	0	-4	2
Richard, Stanley, S.D.	0	0	1	0	1
Ritcher, Jim, Buf.	0	1	0	0	1
Rivers, Reggie, Den.	2	1	0	0	1
Robbins, Randy, N.E.	0	0	1	0	1
Robinson, Eugene, Sea.	0	0	1	0	1

	Fum.	Own Rec.	Opp. Rec.	Yds	Tot. Rec.
Robinson, Frank, Den.	0	1	0	0	1
Rogers, Tracy, K.C.	0	0	1	0	1
Rolling, Henry, S.D.	0	0	1	0	1
Ross, Kevin, K.C.	0	0	2	0	2
Russell, Leonard, N.E.	3	0	0	0	0
Saleaumua, Dan, K.C.	0	0	1	0	1
Sargent, Kevin, Cin.	0	2	0	0	2
Schroeder, Jay, Rai.	5	0	0	0	0
Schulz, Kurt, Buf.	0	1	1	0	2
Seau, Junior, S.D.	0	0	1	10	1
Sharpe, Shannon, Den.	1	0	0	0	0
Shelton, Richard, Pit.	0	0	2	0	2
Sims, Tom, K.C.	0	0	1	0	1
Siragusa, Tony, Ind.	0	0	1	0	1
Slaughter, Webster, Hou.	3	2	0	0	2
Smith, Al, Hou.	1	0	0	0	0
Smith, Dennis, Den.	0	0	2	0	2
Smith, Doug, Hou.	0	0	1	0	1
Smith, Neil, K.C.	0	0	2	0	2
Stanley, Walter, N.E.	5	2	0	0	2
Stegall, Milt, Cin.	1	0	0	0	0
Stephens, John, N.E.	0	1	0	0	1
Stouffer, Kelly, Sea.	12	4	0	-8	4
Stubbs, Danny, Cin.	0	0	1	0	1
Tasker, Steve, Buf.	0	0	1	0	1
Taylor, Terry, Cle.	0	0	1	7	1
Thomas, Blair, NY-J	2	0	0	0	0
Thomas, Derrick, K.C.	0	0	3	0	3
Thomas, Doug, Sea.	1	0	0	0	0
Thomas, Robb, Sea.	1	0	0	0	0
Thomas, Thurman, Buf.	6	1	0	0	1
Thompson, Leroy, Pit.	2	0	0	0	0
Thornton, George, S.D.	0	0	1	0	1
Tillman, Lawyer, Cle.	1	0	0	0	0
Tillman, Spencer, Hou.	2	0	0	0	0
Tofflemire, Joe, Sea.	1	0	0	0	0
Tomczak, Mike, Cle.	5	0	0	-7	0
Townsend, Greg, Rai.	0	0	1	0	1
Treggs, Brian, Sea.	0	1	0	0	1
Trudeau, Jack, Ind.	3	2	0	-12	2
Tupa, Tom, Ind.	1	1	0	-1	1
Turner, Eric, Cle.	0	0	2	0	2
Turner, Marcus, NY-J	0	0	1	0	1
Turner, Kevin, N.E.	2	1	1	0	2
Turner, T.J., Mia.	0	0	2	0	2
Tuten, Rick, Sea.	2	2	0	-9	2
Uhlenhake, Jeff, Mia.	1	2	0	-4	2
Vaughn, Jon, N.E.	6	0	0	-3	0
Verdin, Clarence, Ind.	2	0	0	0	0
Vincent, Troy, Mia.	2	2	0	0	2
Vinson, Fernandus, Cin.	0	0	1	22	1
Walker, Kenny, Den.	0	0	2	0	2
Walker, Sammy, Pit.	0	0	1	0	1
Walker, Tony, Ind.	0	0	1	0	1
Wallace, Aaron, Rai.	0	0	2	0	2
Walter, Joe, Cin.	0	1	0	0	1
Warren, Chris, Sea.	2	2	0	0	2
Washington, Brian, NY-J	0	0	2	0	2
White, Dwayne, NY-J	0	1	0	-1	1
White, Lorenzo, Hou.	2	2	0	0	2
Widell, Doug, Den.	0	2	0	0	2
Wilburn, Barry, Cle.	0	0	1	5	1
Wilkerson, Bruce, Rai.	0	1	0	0	1
Williams, Darryl, Cin.	0	0	1	0	1
Williams, David, Hou.	0	1	0	0	1
Williams, Harvey, K.C.	1	0	0	0	0
Williams, Jarvis, Mia.	1	0	1	5	1
Williams, Jerrol, Pit.	0	0	2	18	2
Williams, John L., Sea.	4	1	0	0	1
Williams, Larry, N.E.	0	1	0	0	1
Williams, Mike, Mia.	1	1	0	0	1
Withycombe, Mike, Cin.	0	1	0	0	1
Woodson, Rod, Pit.	2	0	1	9	1
Word, Barry, K.C.	2	2	1	0	3
Wright, Alexander, Rai.	1	0	0	0	0
Wright, Jeff, Buf.	0	0	1	0	1
Wyman, David, Sea.	0	0	1	6	1
Young, Lonnie, NY-J	0	0	2	9	2
Zolak, Scott, N.E.	5	3	0	-21	3

Yards includes aborted plays, own recoveries, and opponents' recoveries.

NFC Fumbles—Individual

	Fum.	Own Rec.	Opp. Rec.	Yds	Tot. Rec.
Adams, Scott, Min.	1	0	0	0	0
Aikman, Troy, Dal.	4	1	0	0	1
Allen, Eric, Phi.	0	0	2	0	2
Allen, Terry, Min.	9	2	0	0	2
Anderson, Neal, Chi.	6	0	0	0	0
Anderson, Gary, T.B.	3	1	0	0	1
Anderson, Willie, Rams	1	0	0	0	0
Armstrong, Trace, Chi.	0	0	1	0	1
Atkins, Gene, N.O.	0	0	1	9	1
Auzenne, Troy, Chi.	0	1	0	0	1
Bailey, Johnny, Pho.	2	2	0	0	2
Ball, Jerry, Det.	0	0	3	21	3
Barnett, Fred, Phi.	1	0	0	0	0
Barnhardt, Tommy, N.O.	2	0	0	-16	0
Beach, Sanjay, G.B.	1	0	1	0	1
Bennett, Edgar, G.B.	2	0	0	0	0
Bennett, Tony, G.B.	0	0	3	18	3
Billups, Lewis, G.B.	0	0	1	0	1
Bingham, Guy, Was.	0	0	1	0	1
Bono, Steve, S.F.	2	1	0	-3	1
Booty, John, Phi.	0	0	1	0	1
Bostic, Jeff, Was.	1	0	0	-2	0
Bouwens, Shawn, Det.	0	1	0	0	1
Bowles, Todd, Was.	0	1	0	0	1
Brady, Ed, T.B.	0	0	1	0	1
Brandes, John, NY-G	1	0	0	0	0
Brantley, John, Was.	0	0	1	0	1
Brenner, Hoby, N.O.	0	1	0	0	1
Brock, Matt, G.B.	0	0	2	34	2
Brooks, James, T.B.	1	0	0	0	0
Brostek, Bern, Rams	0	1	0	0	1
Broussard, Steve, Atl.	3	1	0	-2	1
Brown, Larry, Dal.	0	0	1	0	1
Brown, Robert, G.B.	0	0	1	0	1
Buckley, Terrell, G.B.	7	3	1	0	4
Bunch, Jarrod, NY-G	3	1	0	0	1
Butler, LeRoy, G.B.	0	0	1	17	1
Byars, Keith, Phi.	1	1	0	0	1
Byner, Earnest, Was.	1	0	0	0	0
Campbell, Jeff, Det.	1	0	0	0	0
Campbell, Jesse, NY-G	0	0	1	0	1
Campen, James, G.B.	0	1	0	0	1
Carrier, Mark, T.B.	1	0	0	0	0
Carrier, Mark, Chi.	0	0	2	0	2
Carroll, Wesley, N.O.	1	0	0	0	0
Carter, Anthony, Min.	1	0	0	0	0
Carter, Cris, Min.	1	0	0	0	0
Case, Scott, Atl.	0	0	2	0	2
Casillas, Tony, Dal.	0	0	1	3	1
Cecil, Chuck, G.B.	1	0	0	0	0
Centers, Larry, Pho.	1	0	0	0	0
Chadwick, Jeff, Rams	1	0	0	0	0
Chandler, Chris, Pho.	9	2	0	-11	2
Clark, Gary, Was.	1	0	0	0	0
Cobb, Reggie, T.B.	3	1	0	0	1
Coleman, Monte, Was.	1	0	0	0	0
Collins, Andre, Was.	0	0	1	40	1
Colon, Harry, Det.	0	0	2	0	2
Cooper, Richard, N.O.	0	1	0	0	1
Copeland, Danny, Was.	0	0	3	15	3
Cox, Ron, Chi.	0	0	1	0	1
Craig, Roger, Min.	2	0	0	0	0
Crockett, Ray, Det.	0	0	1	15	1
Cross, Howard, NY-G	2	1	0	0	1
Cunningham, Randall, Phi.	13	3	0	0	3
Davis, Eric, S.F.	0	0	2	0	2
Dawsey, Lawrence, T.B.	1	1	0	0	1
DeBerg, Steve, T.B.	2	0	0	-7	0
DeLong, Keith, S.F.	0	0	1	6	1
Delpino, Robert, Rams	2	2	0	0	2
Del Rio, Jack, Min.	0	0	2	0	2
Dent, Richard, Chi.	0	0	1	0	1
Doleman, Chris, Min.	0	0	3	0	3
Dombrowski, Jim, N.O.	0	1	0	0	1
Dotson, Santana, T.B.	0	0	2	42	2
Dowdell, Marcus, N.O.	4	3	0	0	3
Duckens, Mark, T.B.	0	0	1	0	1
Dukes, Jaime, Atl.	0	2	0	0	2
Dunbar, Vaughn, N.O.	3	0	0	0	0
Epps, Tory, Atl.	0	0	1	0	1
Ervins, Ricky, Was.	1	1	0	0	1
Everett, Jim, Rams	5	0	0	-9	0
Everett, Thomas, Dal.	0	0	2	15	2
Favre, Brett, G.B.	12	3	0	-12	3
Fontenot, Jerry, Chi.	1	0	0	-2	0
Fortin, Roman, Atl.	0	1	0	0	1
Fralic, Bill, Atl.	0	2	0	0	2
Fulhage, Scott, Atl.	0	1	0	0	1
Furrer, Will, Chi.	1	0	0	0	0
Gann, Mike, Atl.	0	0	2	0	2
Gannon, Rich, Min.	5	0	0	0	0
Gant, Kenneth, Dal.	0	0	1	0	1

	Fum.	Own Rec.	Opp. Rec.	Yds	Tot. Rec.
Gardocki, Chris, Chi.	0	0	1	0	1
Gary, Cleveland, Rams	9	1	0	0	1
Gayle, Shaun, Chi.	0	0	3	0	3
Gesek, John, Dal.	1	0	0	0	0
Gilbert, Sean, Rams	0	0	1	0	1
Glover, Kevin, Det.	0	1	0	0	1
Goff, Robert, N.O.	0	0	3	47	3
Golic, Mike, Phi.	0	0	1	0	1
Graham, Kent, NY-G	1	1	0	0	1
Grant, Alan, S.F.	1	0	0	0	0
Green, Tim, Atl.	0	0	1	0	1
Green, Willie, Det.	1	0	0	0	0
Greene, Kevin, Rams	0	0	4	2	4
Griffin, Don, S.F.	1	0	0	0	0
Gruber, Paul, T.B.	0	1	0	0	1
Hall, Dana, S.F.	0	0	1	0	1
Hamilton, Keith, NY-G	0	0	1	4	1
Hampton, Rodney, NY-G	1	2	0	0	2
Harbaugh, Jim, Chi.	6	3	0	0	3
Harmon, Andy, Phi.	0	0	1	0	1
Harper, Alvin, Dal.	1	0	0	0	0
Harris, Jackie, G.B.	1	0	0	0	0
Harris, Tim, S.F.	0	0	1	0	1
Harvey, Ken, Pho.	0	0	2	0	2
Hawkins, Courtney, T.B.	2	1	0	0	1
Hebert, Bobby, N.O.	3	1	0	0	1
Heller, Ron, Phi.	0	2	0	0	2
Henderson, Keith, S.F.-Min.	4	1	0	0	1
Heyward, Craig, N.O.	1	1	0	0	1
Hill, Drew, Atl.	1	0	0	0	0
Hill, Eric, Pho.	1	0	1	-2	1
Hill, Randal, Pho.	2	0	0	0	0
Hilliard, Dalton, N.O.	6	1	0	0	1
Holland, Johnny, G.B.	2	1	2	0	3
Holmes, Clayton, Dal.	0	1	0	0	1
Hoover, Houston, Atl.	0	1	0	0	1
Hostetler, Jeff, NY-G	6	0	0	-3	0
Howard, Desmond, Was.	1	0	0	0	0
Howard, Erik, NY-G	0	0	3	7	3
Hyche, Steve, Pho.	0	0	1	0	1
Ingram, Mark, NY-G	0	1	0	0	1
Irvin, Michael, Dal.	1	1	0	0	1
Israel, Steve, Rams	0	0	1	0	1
Jackson, Greg, NY-G	0	0	1	0	1
Jackson, Johnnie, S.F.	0	0	1	0	1
Jackson, Rickey, N.O.	0	0	3	15	3
Jamison, George, Det.	0	0	1	0	1
Jenkins, Carlos, Min.	0	0	1	22	1
Jenkins, Mel, Det.	0	0	1	0	1
Jennings, Stanford, T.B.	1	0	0	0	0
Johnson, Johnny, Pho.	2	0	0	0	0
Johnson, Sidney, Was.	1	0	0	0	0
Johnson, Pepper, NY-G	1	0	2	0	2
Johnson, Tim, Was.	0	0	1	0	1
Johnston, Daryl, Dal.	0	1	0	0	1
Jones, Tony, Atl.	0	1	0	1	1
Jones, Brent, S.F.	1	0	0	0	0
Jones, Jock, Pho.	0	0	1	0	1
Jones, Keith, Atl.	2	0	0	0	0
Jones, Robert, Dal.	0	0	1	0	1
Jones, Roger, T.B.	0	0	2	26	2
Jordan, Buford, N.O.	1	0	1	0	1
Joyner, Seth, Phi.	0	0	1	0	1
Kelm, Larry, Rams	0	0	2	0	2
Kennard, Derek, N.O.	0	1	0	0	1
Koonce, George, G.B.	0	0	1	0	1
Kramer, Erik, Det.	4	1	0	-1	1
Lang, David, Rams	5	2	0	0	2
LeBel, Harper, Atl.	1	0	0	-37	0
Lee, Amp, S.F.	1	2	1	0	3
Lee, Carl, Min.	0	1	1	0	2
Lett, Leon, Dal.	0	0	1	0	1
Lewis, Darren, Chi.	4	1	0	0	1
Lewis, Ron, S.F.	2	0	0	0	0
Lipps, Louis, N.O.	1	0	0	0	0
Lumpkin, Sean, N.O.	0	1	0	0	1
Lynch, Lorenzo, Pho.	0	0	1	0	1
Majkowski, Don, G.B.	4	3	0	0	3
Marshall, Leonard, NY-G	0	0	2	0	2
Marshall, Wilber, Was.	0	1	2	35	3
Martin, Eric, N.O.	1	1	0	0	1
Martin, Kelvin, Dal.	2	0	0	0	0
Martin, Wayne, N.O.	0	0	2	0	2
Maryland, Russell, Dal.	0	0	2	26	2
Maxie, Brett, N.O.	0	0	1	0	1
Mayhew, Martin, Was.	0	0	1	0	1
McCaffrey, Ed, NY-G	2	0	0	0	0
McCants, Keith, T.B.	0	0	1	0	1
McDonald, Tim, Pho.	0	0	3	2	3
McDowell, Anthony, T.B.	1	0	0	0	0
McGriggs, Lamar, NY-G	0	0	1	0	1
McGruder, Michael, S.F.	0	0	1	7	1
McIntyre, Guy, S.F.	0	1	0	0	1
McJulien, Paul, G.B.	0	1	0	0	1
McMichael, Steve, Chi.	0	0	2	2	2
Meggett, David, NY-G	5	3	0	0	3
Merriweather, Mike, Min.	0	0	2	3	2
Miano, Rich, Phi.	0	0	2	0	2
Milinichik, Joe, Rams	0	1	0	0	1
Millard, Keith, Sea.-G.B.	0	0	2	0	2
Miller, Chris, Atl.	6	1	0	-1	1
Miller, Les, N.O.	0	0	1	0	1
Mills, Sam, N.O.	0	0	3	76	3
Mitchell, Brian, Was.	4	2	0	0	2
Mitchell, Brian, Atl.	0	0	1	0	1
Mitchell, Roland, G.B.	0	0	1	0	1
Monk, Art, Was.	1	0	0	0	0
Moran, Rich, G.B.	0	1	0	0	1
Muster, Brad, Chi.	2	0	0	0	0
Nelson, Darrin, Min.	2	2	0	0	2
Newberry, Tom, Rams	0	1	0	0	1
Newman, Anthony, Rams	0	0	3	0	3
Newman, Pat, N.O.	2	0	0	0	0
Newton, Nate, Dal.	0	1	0	0	1
Noble, Brian, G.B.	0	0	2	0	2
Noga, Al, Min.	0	0	1	3	1
Norton, Ken, Dal.	0	0	2	0	2
Novoselsky, Brent, Min.	0	0	2	0	2
Nunn, Freddie Joe, Pho.	0	0	1	0	1
Oates, Bart, NY-G	2	0	0	-29	0
Orr, Terry, Was.	1	2	0	0	2
Owens, Dan, Det.	0	0	1	0	1
Pagel, Mike, Rams	1	1	0	-1	1
Parker, Anthony, Min.	2	1	1	58	2
Paup, Bryce, G.B.	0	0	2	0	2
Peete, Rodney, Det.	6	2	0	-7	2
Pegram, Erric, Atl.	0	3	0	1	3
Perriman, Brett, Det.	1	0	0	0	0
Perry, William, Chi.	0	0	1	0	1
Pete, Lawrence, Det.	0	0	1	0	1
Phifer, Roman, Rams	0	0	2	0	2
Price, Jim, Rams	2	2	0	0	2
Pritchard, Mike, Atl.	3	0	0	0	0
Proehl, Ricky, Pho.	5	0	0	0	0
Randle, John, Min.	0	0	1	0	1
Rathman, Tom, S.F.	1	0	0	0	0
Ray, Terry, Atl.	0	0	1	0	1
Reeves, Walter, Pho.	0	2	0	0	2
Reid, Michael, Atl.	0	0	1	0	1
Reynolds, Ricky, T.B.	0	0	2	11	2
Rice, Jerry, S.F.	2	0	0	0	0
Richards, Curvin, Dal.	3	0	0	0	0
Riesenberg, Doug, NY-G	0	2	0	0	2
Rison, Andre, Atl.	2	0	0	0	0
Rivera, Ron, Chi.	0	1	1	0	2
Robinson, Gerald, Rams	0	0	1	0	1
Rodriguez, Ruben, NY-G	0	1	0	0	1
Romanowski, Bill, S.F.	0	0	1	0	1
Rosenbach, Timm, Pho.	4	0	0	0	0
Rypien, Mark, Was.	4	2	0	0	2
Salisbury, Sean, Min.	4	3	0	-5	3
Sanders, Barry, Det.	6	2	0	0	2
Sanders, Deion, Atl.	3	1	1	0	2
Schreiber, Adam, Min.	0	1	0	0	1
Sharpe, Sterling, G.B.	2	1	0	0	1
Sherman, Heath, Phi.	3	1	1	0	2
Sherrard, Mike, S.F.	1	1	1	39	2
Simmons, Clyde, Phi.	1	0	1	0	1
Small, Jessie, Pho.	0	0	1	0	1
Smeenge, Joel, N.O.	0	0	1	0	1
Smith, Emmitt, Dal.	4	1	0	0	1
Smith, Joey, NY-G	1	0	0	0	0
Smith, Lance, Pho.	0	1	0	0	1
Smith, Tony, Atl.	4	1	0	0	1
Smith, Vinson, Dal.	0	0	2	0	2
Spencer, Jimmy, N.O.	0	0	1	0	1
Spielman, Chris, Det.	0	0	1	0	1
Stepnoski, Mark, Dal.	0	1	0	0	1
Stewart, Michael, Rams	0	0	1	0	1
Stokes, Fred, Was.	0	0	1	0	1
Swilling, Pat, N.O.	0	0	1	0	1
Sydner, Jeff, Phi.	1	0	0	0	0
Sydney, Harry, G.B.	2	2	0	0	2
Tate, David, Chi.	0	0	1	0	1
Taylor, Lawrence, NY-G	0	0	1	2	1
Testaverde, Vinny, T.B.	4	4	0	-8	4

	Fum.	Own Rec.	Opp. Rec.	Yds	Tot. Rec.
Thomas, Broderick, T.B.	0	0	3	-1	3
Thomas, Johnny, Was.	1	1	0	0	1
Thomas, William, Phi.	0	0	2	2	2
Thompson, Anthony, Rams	1	1	0	0	1
Thompson, Darrell, G.B.	2	0	0	0	0
Tice, Mike, Min.	0	1	0	4	1
Tippins, Kenny, Atl.	0	0	1	0	1
Tolliver, Billy Joe, Atl.	5	0	0	0	0
Tuggle, Jessie, Atl.	0	0	1	69	1
Turner, Floyd, N.O.	2	0	0	0	0
Turner, Odessa, S.F.	1	0	0	0	0
Turner, Vernon, Rams	3	0	0	0	0
Van Horne, Keith, Chi.	0	1	0	0	1
Waddle, Tom, Chi.	1	2	0	0	2
Walker, Herschel, Phi.	6	2	0	0	2
Wallace, Steve, S.F.	0	1	0	0	1
Walter, Michael, S.F.	0	0	2	0	2
Ware, Andre, Det.	6	2	0	-20	2
Warren, Frank, N.O.	0	0	1	0	1
Washington, Charles, Atl.	0	1	0	0	1
Washington, James, Dal.	0	0	1	0	1
Watters, Ricky, S.F.	2	1	0	0	1
West, Ronnie, Min.	1	0	0	0	0
White, Reggie, Phi.	0	0	1	37	1
White, William, Det.	1	0	0	0	0
Wilks, Jimmy, N.O.	0	0	1	4	1
Williams, Aeneas, Pho.	0	0	1	39	1
Williams, Jimmy, T.B.	0	0	1	0	1
Williams, Jamie, S.F.	1	0	0	0	0
Wilmsmeyer, Klaus, S.F.	1	1	0	0	1
Winters, Frank, G.B.	1	0	0	0	0
Wojciechowski, John, Chi.	0	0	1	0	1
Woolford, Donnell, Chi.	2	1	0	0	1
Workman, Vince, G.B.	4	2	0	0	2
Young, Steve, S.F.	9	3	0	-13	3
Zorich, Chris, Chi.	0	0	1	42	1

Yards includes aborted plays, own recoveries, and opponents' recoveries.

Sacks

Most Sacks
NFC: 19.0—Clyde Simmons, Philadelphia
AFC: 17.0—Leslie O'Neal, San Diego

Most Sacks, Game
AFC: 4.0—Chip Banks, Indianapolis vs. Cleveland, September 6
Anthony Smith, Raiders at Seattle, October 18
Derrick Thomas, Kansas City vs. San Diego, November 8
Leslie O'Neal, San Diego at Phoenix, December 6
NFC: 4.0—Wayne Martin, New Orleans vs. Atlanta, December 3

Team Champion
NFC: 57—New Orleans
AFC: 51—San Diego

AFC Sacks—Team

	Sacks	Yards
San Diego	51	356
Kansas City	50	391
Houston	50	321
Denver	50	317
Cleveland	48	315
Seattle	46	317
L.A. Raiders	46	320
Cincinnati	45	294
Buffalo	44	351
Indianapolis	39	336
Pittsburgh	36	248
N.Y. Jets	36	240
Miami	36	283
New England	20	114
AFC Total	597	4203
AFC Average	42.6	300.2

NFC Sacks—Team

	Sacks	Yards
New Orleans	57	376
Philadelphia	55	385
Minnesota	51	342
Dallas	44	347
Chicago	43	286
San Francisco	41	273
Washington	39	279
Tampa Bay	36	230
Green Bay	34	219
Atlanta	31	241
L.A. Rams	31	188
Detroit	29	185
Phoenix	27	196
N.Y. Giants	25	197
NFC Total	543	3744
NFC Average	38.8	267.4
NFL Total	1140	7947
NFL Average	40.7	283.8

NFL Top 10 Leaders—Sacks

	Total
Simmons, Clyde, Phi.	19.0
Harris, Tim, S.F.	17.0
O'Neal, Leslie, S.D.	17.0
Fletcher, Simon, Den.	16.0
Martin, Wayne, N.O.	15.5
Doleman, Chris, Min.	14.5
Smith, Neil, K.C.	14.5
Thomas, Derrick, K.C.	14.5
Cox, Bryan, Mia.	14.0
Kennedy, Cortez, Sea.	14.0
Smith, Bruce, Buf.	14.0
White, Reggie, Phi.	14.0

AFC Sacks—Individual

O'Neal, Leslie, S.D.	17.0
Fletcher, Simon, Den.	16.0
Smith, Neil, K.C.	14.5
Thomas, Derrick, K.C.	14.5
Cox, Bryan, Mia.	14.0
Kennedy, Cortez, Sea.	14.0
Smith, Bruce, Buf.	14.0
Childress, Ray, Hou.	13.0
Smith, Anthony, Rai.	13.0
Williams, Lee, Hou.	11.0
Mims, Chris, S.D.	10.0
Williams, Alfred, Cin.	10.0
Porter, Rufus, Sea.	9.5
Banks, Chip, Ind.	9.0
Burnett, Rob, Cle.	9.0
Long, Howie, Rai.	9.0
Matthews, Clay, Cle.	9.0
Stubbs, Danny, Cin.	9.0
Jones, Sean, Hou.	8.5
Perry, Michael Dean, Cle.	8.5
Washington, Marvin, NY-J	8.5
Fuller, William, Hou.	8.0
Grossman, Burt, S.D.	8.0
Hansen, Phil, Buf.	8.0
Mecklenburg, Karl, Den.	7.5
Tippett, Andre, N.E.	7.0
Bickett, Duane, Ind.	6.5
Dronett, Shane, Den.	6.5
Lloyd, Greg, Pit.	6.5
Coleman, Marco, Mia.	6.0
Francis, James, Cin.	6.0
Saleaumua, Dan, K.C.	6.0
Winter, Blaise, S.D.	6.0
Woodson, Rod, Pit.	6.0
Wright, Jeff, Buf.	6.0
Kragen, Greg, Den.	5.5
Croel, Mike, Den.	5.0
Cross, Jeff, Mia.	5.0
Frase, Paul, NY-J	5.0
Mersereau, Scott, NY-J	5.0
Townsend, Greg, Rai.	5.0
Bryant, Jeff, Sea.	4.5
Clancy, Sam, Ind.	4.5
Nash, Joe, Sea.	4.5
Seau, Junior, S.D.	4.5
Williams, Jerrol, Pit.	4.5
Bennett, Cornelius, Buf.	4.0
Houston, Bobby, NY-J	4.0
Jones, James, Cle.	4.0
Krumrie, Tim, Cin.	4.0
Pleasant, Anthony, Cle.	4.0
Rogers, Lamar, Cin.	4.0
Talley, Darryl, Buf.	4.0
Wallace, Aaron, Rai.	4.0
Williams, Brent, N.E.	4.0
Blackmon, Robert, Sea.	3.5
Bruce, Aundray, Rai.	3.5
Baylor, John, Ind.	3.0
Emtman, Steve, Ind.	3.0
Evans, Donald, Pit.	3.0
Griggs, David, Mia.	3.0
Little, David, Pit.	3.0
McGlockton, Chester, Rai.	3.0
Mitz, Alonzo, Cin.	3.0
Ridgle, Elston, Cin.	3.0
Sims, Tom, K.C.	3.0
Siragusa, Tony, Ind.	3.0
Tuatagaloa, Natu, Sea.	3.0
Williams, Gerald, Pit.	3.0
Woods, Tony, Sea.	3.0
Goad, Tim, N.E.	2.5
Griffin, Leonard, K.C.	2.5
Harrison, Nolan, Rai.	2.5
Phillips, Joe, K.C.	2.5
Conlan, Shane, Buf.	2.0
Coryatt, Quentin, Ind.	2.0
Daniel, Eugene, Ind.	2.0
Davidson, Kenny, Pit.	2.0
Gunn, Mark, NY-J	2.0
Herrod, Jeff, Ind.	2.0
Hobley, Liffort, Mia.	2.0
Howe, Garry, Pit.	2.0
Johnson, Mario, NY-J	2.0
Johnson, Mike, Cle.	2.0
Johnson, Bill, Cle.	2.0
Jones, Aaron, Pit.	2.0
Lake, Carnell, Pit.	2.0
Lewis, Mo, NY-J	2.0
McMillan, Erik, NY-J	2.0
Mills, Jeff, Den.	2.0
Moore, Stevon, Cle.	2.0
Moss, Winston, Rai.	2.0
Newsome, Vince, Cle.	2.0
Nickerson, Hardy, Pit.	2.0
Patton, Marvcus, Buf.	2.0
Thornton, George, S.D.	2.0
Williams, Darryl, Cin.	2.0
Lathon, Lamar, Hou.	1.5
Maas, Bill, K.C.	1.5
McDowell, Bubba, Hou.	1.5
Offerdahl, John, Mia.	1.5
Sochia, Brian, Den.	1.5
Thompson, Bennie, K.C.	1.5
Walker, Kenny, Den.	1.5
Webster, Larry, Mia.	1.5
Agnew, Ray, N.E.	1.0
Alm, Jeff, Hou.	1.0
Anderson, Eddie, Rai.	1.0
Atwater, Steve, Den.	1.0
Bailey, Carlton, Buf.	1.0
Braggs, Stephen, Mia.	1.0
Brandon, David, Cle.	1.0
Broughton, Willie, Rai.	1.0
Brown, Richard, Cle.	1.0
Byrd, Dennis, NY-J	1.0
Clifton, Kyle, NY-J	1.0
Dodge, Dedrick, Sea.	1.0
Edwards, Tim, N.E.	1.0
Ellison, Riki, Rai.	1.0
Fulcher, David, Cin.	1.0
Glasgow, Nesby, Sea.	1.0
Gordon, Alex, Cin.	1.0
Graf, Rick, Hou.	1.0
Hall, Delton, S.D.	1.0
Hand, Jon, Ind.	1.0
Hicks, Cliff, Buf.	1.0
Hilliard, Randy, Cle.	1.0
Hollier, Dwight, Mia.	1.0
Howard, David, N.E.	1.0
Jackson, Steve, Hou.	1.0
Klingbeil, Chuck, Mia.	1.0
Lageman, Jeff, NY-J	1.0
Lambert, Dion, N.E.	1.0
Lang, Le-Lo, Den.	1.0
Lewis, Darryll, Hou.	1.0
Logan, Ernie, Cle.	1.0
McClendon, Skip, Ind.	1.0
McCoy, Tony, Ind.	1.0
Millard, Keith, Sea.	1.0
Nix, Roosevelt, Cin.	1.0
Odomes, Nate, Buf.	1.0
Pearson, J.C., K.C.	1.0
Pickel, Bill, NY-J	1.0
Pike, Mark, Buf.	1.0
Rembert, Johnny, N.E.	1.0
Robinson, Eddie, Hou.	1.0
Rolling, Henry, S.D.	1.0
Sabb, Dwayne, N.E.	1.0
Simien, Tracy, K.C.	1.0
Sinclair, Mike, Sea.	1.0
Smith, Al, Hou.	1.0
Traylor, Keith, Den.	1.0
Turner, Eric, Cle.	1.0
Vinson, Fernandus, Cin.	1.0
Walker, Tony, Ind.	1.0
Washington, Brian, NY-J	1.0
White, Reggie, S.D.	1.0
Barber, Kurt, NY-J	0.5
Brown, Vincent, N.E.	0.5
Holmes, Ron, Den.	0.5
Lee, Shawn, S.D.	0.5
Martin, Chris, K.C.	0.5
Montgomery, Glenn, Hou.	0.5
Ross, Kevin, K.C.	0.5
Walls, Everson, Cle.	0.5

NFC Sacks—Individual

Simmons, Clyde, Phi.	19.0
Harris, Tim, S.F.	17.0
Martin, Wayne, N.O.	15.5
Doleman, Chris, Min.	14.5
White, Reggie, Phi.	14.0
Bennett, Tony, G.B.	13.5
Jackson, Rickey, N.O.	13.5
Randle, John, Min.	11.5
Jeffcoat, Jim, Dal.	10.5
McMichael, Steve, Chi.	10.5
Swilling, Pat, N.O.	10.5
Dotson, Santana, T.B.	10.0
Greene, Kevin, Rams	10.0
Noga, Al, Min.	9.0
Dent, Richard, Chi.	8.5
Tolbert, Tony, Dal.	8.5
Scroggins, Tracy, Det.	7.5
Conner, Darion, Atl.	7.0
Harmon, Andy, Phi.	7.0
Armstrong, Trace, Chi.	6.5
Joyner, Seth, Phi.	6.5
Paup, Bryce, G.B.	6.5
Pritchett, Kelvin, Det.	6.5
Haley, Charles, Dal.	6.0
Harvey, Ken, Pho.	6.0
Johnson, Tim, Was.	6.0
Jones, Mike, Pho.	6.0
Marshall, Wilber, Was.	6.0
Thomas, Henry, Min.	6.0
Holt, Pierce, S.F.	5.5
Geathers, James, Was.	5.0
Gilbert, Sean, Rams	5.0
McCants, Keith, T.B.	5.0
Robinson, Gerald, Rams	5.0
Seals, Ray, T.B.	5.0
Taylor, Lawrence, NY-G	5.0
Thomas, Broderick, T.B.	5.0
Wheeler, Mark, T.B.	5.0
Gardner, Moe, Atl.	4.5
Mann, Charles, Was.	4.5
Solomon, Jesse, Atl.	4.5
Banks, Carl, NY-G	4.0
Brock, Matt, G.B.	4.0
Jenkins, Carlos, Min.	4.0
Jones, Jimmie, Dal.	4.0
Marshall, Leonard, NY-G	4.0
Nunn, Freddie Joe, Pho.	4.0
Pitts, Mike, Phi.	4.0
Spellman, Alonzo, Chi.	4.0
Warren, Frank, N.O.	4.0
Wilks, Jimmy, N.O.	4.0
Brown, Dennis, S.F.	3.5
Hamilton, Keith, NY-G	3.5
Harrison, Martin, S.F.	3.5
Lett, Leon, Dal.	3.5
Stokes, Fred, Was.	3.5
Buck, Jason, Was.	3.0
Casillas, Tony, Dal.	3.0
Coleman, Monte, Was.	3.0
Gant, Kenneth, Dal.	3.0
Green, Tim, Atl.	3.0
Merriweather, Mike, Min.	3.0
Mills, Sam, N.O.	3.0
Piel, Mike, Rams	3.0
Ryan, Tim, Chi.	3.0
Tippins, Kenny, Atl.	3.0
Ball, Jerry, Det.	2.5
Fox, Mike, NY-G	2.5
Maryland, Russell, Dal.	2.5
Roper, John, Chi.	2.5
Spindler, Marc, Det.	2.5
Bankston, Michael, Pho.	2.0
Carter, Marty, T.B.	2.0
Cofer, Mike, Det.	2.0
Collins, Andre, Was.	2.0
Davis, Reuben, Pho.	2.0
Del Rio, Jack, Min.	2.0
Dorsey, Eric, NY-G	2.0
Gann, Mike, Atl.	2.0
Golic, Mike, Phi.	2.0
Hawkins, Bill, Rams	2.0
Jamison, George, Det.	2.0
Jurkovic, John, G.B.	2.0
Miller, Corey, NY-G	2.0
Noble, Brian, G.B.	2.0
Owens, Dan, Det.	2.0
Perry, William, Chi.	2.0
Rucker, Keith, Pho.	2.0
Smith, Chuck, Atl.	2.0
Stewart, Michael, Rams	2.0
Swann, Eric, Pho.	2.0
Washington, Ted, S.F.	2.0
Williams, Jimmy, T.B.	2.0
Wilson, Bobby, Was.	2.0
Young, Robert, Rams	2.0
Zorich, Chris, Chi.	2.0
Koonce, George, G.B.	1.5
Thomas, William, Phi.	1.5
Turnbull, Renaldo, N.O.	1.5
Wilkins, David, S.F.	1.5
Archambeau, Lester, G.B.	1.0
Boutte, Marc, Rams	1.0
Brown, Robert, G.B.	1.0
Carter, Michael, S.F.	1.0
Chamblee, Al, T.B.	1.0
Collins, Shane, Was.	1.0
Cook, Toi, N.O.	1.0
Copeland, Danny, Was.	1.0
Cox, Ron, Chi.	1.0
Crockett, Ray, Det.	1.0
Dent, Burnell, G.B.	1.0
Donaldson, Jeff, Atl.	1.0
Fagan, Kevin, S.F.	1.0
Gouveia, Kurt, Was.	1.0
Hall, Dana, S.F.	1.0
Hyche, Steve, Pho.	1.0
Jackson, Johnny, S.F.-G.B.	1.0
Johnson, John, S.F.	1.0
Johnson, Pepper, NY-G	1.0
Johnson, Vaughan, N.O.	1.0
Jones, Jock, Pho.	1.0
Jones, Robert, Dal.	1.0
Maxie, Brett, N.O.	1.0
Mays, Alvoid, Was.	1.0
McKyer, Tim, Atl.	1.0
Miller, Les, N.O.	1.0
Morrissey, Jim, Chi.	1.0
Pete, Lawrence, Det.	1.0
Pickens, Bruce, Atl.	1.0
Porcher, Robert, Det.	1.0
Raymond, Corey, NY-G	1.0
Reynolds, Ricky, T.B.	1.0
Riddick, Louis, Atl.	1.0
Rivera, Ron, Chi.	1.0
Roberts, Larry, S.F.	1.0
Romanowski, Bill, S.F.	1.0
Scott, Todd, Min.	1.0
Singletary, Mike, Chi.	1.0
Smith, Vinson, Dal.	1.0
Spielman, Chris, Det.	1.0
Tuaolo, Esera, G.B.	1.0
Tuggle, Jessie, Atl.	1.0
Walter, Michael, S.F.	1.0
Woodson, Darren, Dal.	1.0
Buck, Vince, N.O.	0.5
Faulkner, Jeff, Pho.	0.5
Holland, Johnny, G.B.	0.5
McDonald, Tim, Pho.	0.5
Smeenge, Joel, N.O.	0.5

1992 NFL Paid Attendance Breakdown

	Games	Attendance	Average
AFC Preseason	8	377,135	47,142
NFC Preseason	8	428,033	53,504
AFC-NFC Preseason, Interconference	44	2,334,389	53,054
NFL Preseason Total	**60**	**3,139,557**	**52,326**
AFC Regular Season	86	5,272,686	61,310
NFC Regular Season	86	5,248,520	61,029
AFC-NFC Regular Season, Interconference	52	3,307,681	63,609
NFL Regular Season Total	**224**	**13,828,887**	**61,736**
AFC Wild Card Playoffs	2		
(Kansas City at San Diego)		59,934	
(Houston at Buffalo)		76,253	
AFC Divisional Playoffs	2		
(Buffalo at Pittsburgh)		60,725	
(San Diego at Miami)		71,797	
AFC Championship Game	1		
(Buffalo at Miami)		73,760	
NFC Wild Card Playoffs	2		
(Washington at Minnesota)		61,070	
(Philadelphia at New Orleans)		68,393	
NFC Divisional Playoffs	2		
(Philadelphia at Dallas)		63,820	
(Washington at San Francisco)		65,413	
NFC Championship Game	1		
(Dallas at San Francisco)		66,364	
Super Bowl XXVII at Pasadena, California	1		
(Buffalo vs. Dallas)		98,374	
AFC-NFC Pro Bowl at Honolulu, Hawaii	1	50,007	
NFL Postseason Total	**12**	**815,910**	**67,993**
NFL All Games	**296**	**17,784,354**	**60,082**

One Million Plus Club

During the 1992 season, 14 clubs drew a combined home and away paid attendance of more than one million. The Buffalo Bills drew an NFL-leading 1,130,973 fans in 1992.

Team	Total Paid Home Attendance	Total Paid Visiting Attendance	Total Paid Attendance
Buffalo	630,978	499,995	1,130,973
Kansas City	612,773	502,722	1,115,495
Denver	590,090	518,743	1,108,833
Dallas	502,661	582,386	1,085,047
New York Jets	603,619	475,291	1,078,910
Chicago	528,465	536,569	1,065,034
New York Giants	608,706	453,712	1,062,418
Miami	533,317	528,617	1,061,934
San Francisco	523,355	529,547	1,052,902
Atlanta	553,979	491,761	1,045,740
Philadelphia	525,001	500,080	1,025,081
Detroit	542,402	479,269	1,021,671
New Orleans	541,079	477,443	1,018,522
Cleveland	564,925	447,352	1,012,277

INSIDE THE NUMBERS

The NFL: Past, Present, and Future

AFC	PAST	PRESENT	FUTURE
BUFFALO	Cookie Gilchrist rushed for 243 yards in game in 1963, the all-time AFL high	Has led AFC in scoring in each of the past four seasons	Could become first team in history to play in 4 consecutive Super Bowls
CINCINNATI	Began in 1968, reached playoffs in 1970, quickest by an expansion team	Only team that gained more yards rushing than passing in 1992	Faces Boomer Esiason November 21, 52 weeks after last Bengals start
CLEVELAND	Set NFL record by scoring in 274 consecutive games, 1950-1971	Bernie Kosar's career interception rate (one every 38.6 passes) is NFL's best	Steve Everitt is first center since 1955 taken by Browns in first round
DENVER	Defeated Patriots, 13-10 (Sept. 9, 1960) in first game in AFL history	Only AFC team to win division title 5 times in last 10 seasons	John Elway needs 125 completions to become ninth NFL quarterback with 2,500
HOUSTON	Bill Groman gained 1,473 yards on receptions in 1960, a rookie record	The only NFL team that has reached the playoffs in each of the last 6 years	Warren Moon needs 25 TD passes to reach 200 for his NFL career
INDIANAPOLIS	Colts' Tom Matte averaged a record 10.5 yards per rush in Super Bowl III	Finished last season with five-game winning streak, longest since 1988	Plays road games at Giants Stadium 2 consecutive weeks, December 5 and 12
KANSAS CITY	Led league in interceptions for a record 5 consecutive years, 1966-1970	Led NFL in 1992 with 11 touchdowns on various recoveries and returns	Joe Montana needs 71 completions to become fourth NFL player with 3,000
LOS ANGELES RAIDERS	Led league in sacks 5 times, most by any team over past 30 years	29-10-1 record on Monday Night Football is best among NFL teams	Six wins shy of 300 mark, covering 33 seasons in AFL and NFL
MIAMI	Set NFL record by scoring 70 touchdowns in 1984	99-60 (.623) record is best in AFC over last 10 seasons	Dan Marino needs 10 TD passes to become second NFL player to reach 300
NEW ENGLAND	Gino Cappelletti was all-time scoring leader in AFL history (1,100 points)	Jon Vaughn led NFL in kickoff returns in 1992 with 28.2-yard average	1993 finale will be 500th game for Patriots and 7 other AFL originals
NEW YORK JETS	First team to win regular-season game in overtime (26-20 vs. Giants in 1974)	Ronnie Lott shares NFL record with 9 interceptions in postseason games	Only team that finishes '93 with 4 games in row vs. '92 playoff teams
PITTSBURGH	Won its first NFL title in fortieth year in NFL, won three more in next five	Allowed only 50 points in fourth quarter last season, fewest for any NFL team	Play NFC opponents 4 times within first 6 games of 1993 season
SAN DIEGO	Forced 66 turnovers in 1961, still an all-time 1-year record	Finished 1992 with 7 wins in a row, longest winning streak since 1987	First Monday Night home game since 1984 upcoming on December 27
SEATTLE	Steve Largent had 1,000 yards on receptions in 8 years, an NFL record	Has forced NFL-high 397 turnovers over the last 10 years	Rick Mirer and Drew Bledsoe face each other on Sept. 19 and Oct. 24

NFC	PAST	PRESENT	FUTURE
ATLANTA	6-0 vs. California teams in 1991, most wins without a loss in NFL history	Norm Johnson led NFL in field goals of 50 or more yards in 1992 (4-for-4)	First time as host team for Super Bowl, January 30, 1994
CHICAGO	Set NFL record with 72 sacks in 1984 season	9 consecutive opening-day wins, longest current streak in NFL	Neal Anderson needs 138 yards to be second-leading rusher in team history
DALLAS	Played in 41 postseason games and six Super Bowls, NFL records	Opponents converted only 27 percent of third-down plays, lowest in NFL	Open 1993 season on Monday night for an NFL-record ninth time
DETROIT	1934 Thanksgiving Day game vs. Bears was first NFL national TV broadcast	Averaged 13.6 yards per completion in 1992, highest in NFL	NFL-low 4 games this season vs. last year's playoff teams
GREEN BAY	Only team to win 3 consecutive NFL championships (1929-1931, 1965-67)	Sterling Sharpe became first Green Bay player since 1956 to lead NFL in catches	Reggie White (124) could surpass Lawrence Taylor (126.5) in sacks
LOS ANGELES RAMS	Gained 300+ yards in NFL-record 29 consecutive games, 1949-1951	Todd Kinchen had two punt-return TDs in 1992 season finale vs. Atlanta	Need 11 wins to reach total of 400 in franchise history
MINNESOTA	13 division titles in last 25 years, most by any NFL team over that span	Defense made 28 interceptions in 1992, highest total by any NFL team	Seeking second consecutive division title for first time since 1977-78
NEW ORLEANS	Never had a winning record until 1987, haven't had a losing record since	Led NFL in 1992 in most sacks (57) and in fewest sacks allowed (15)	Looking to extend club record to four straight years in playoffs
NEW YORK GIANTS	Had 10 consecutive shutouts in 1927 to tie NFL mark set by Pottsville in '26	Committed NFL-low 90 turnovers in 64 games over last four seasons	NFL-high 9 games this season vs. last year's playoff teams
PHILADELPHIA	Had first draft pick in NFL history: halfback Jay Berwanger in 1936	Heath Sherman led NFL with 5.2-yard average per carry in 1992	Randall Cunningham needs 14 yards to be first NFL quarterback to rush for 4,000
PHOENIX	Cardinals scored 5 TDs on punt returns in 1959, still an NFL record	Gary Clark is the only NFL player with 50 or more receptions for 8 consecutive years	Needs 3 more games to reach 100 straight games without an overtime
SAN FRANCISCO	Won 18 consecutive road games, 1989-1990, longest such streak in NFL history	Jerry Rice is the only player in NFL history with 4 straight 80-catch years	Steve Young could be first to lead NFL in passing 3 years in a row
TAMPA BAY	Division winner reached NFC Championship Game in 1979 in only fourth year in NFL	Santana Dotson had 10 sacks in 1992, sharing NFL lead among rookies	Host to Joe Montana's first game with Chiefs, Sept. 5
WASHINGTON	35 points in second quarter of Super Bowl XXII set an NFL postseason record	Chip Lohmiller is NFL's top scorer for last 2 (269 points), 3 (400), and 4 (528) seasons	Will try to beat Cowboys in season opener for first time in 7 tries

Comparison of Joe Montana's Career Statistics With Hall of Fame Quarterbacks Whose Careers Ended Since 1945

Passing

	Att.	Comp.	Pct.	Yds.	Avg.	Lng.	TD	Pct.	Int.	Pct.	Rating
Joe Montana	4600	2929	63.7	35,124	7.64	96t	244	5.3	123	2.7	93.5
Sammy Baugh	2995	1693	56.5	21,886	7.31	86t	187	6.2	203	6.8	72.0
George Blanda	4007	1911	47.7	26,920	6.72	95t	236	5.9	277	6.9	60.8
Terry Bradshaw	3901	2025	51.9	27,989	7.17	90t	212	5.4	210	5.4	70.9
Len Dawson	3741	2136	57.1	28,711	7.67	92t	239	6.4	183	4.9	82.6
Dan Fouts	5604	3297	58.8	43,040	7.68	81t	254	4.5	242	4.3	80.2
Otto Graham	1565	872	55.7	13,499	8.63	81t	88	5.6	94	6.0	78.1
Bob Griese	3429	1926	56.2	25,092	7.32	86t	192	5.6	172	5.0	77.1
Arnie Herber*	1175	481	40.9	8,041	6.84	92t	78	6.6	106	9.0	49.3
Sonny Jurgensen	4262	2433	57.1	32,224	7.56	99t	255	6.0	189	4.4	82.8
Bobby Layne	3700	1814	49.0	26,768	7.23	97t	196	5.3	243	6.6	63.4
Sid Luckman	1744	904	51.8	14,686	8.42	86t	137	7.9	132	7.6	75.0
Joe Namath	3762	1886	50.1	27,663	7.35	91	173	4.6	220	5.8	65.6
Bart Starr	3149	1808	57.4	24,718	7.85	91t	152	4.8	138	4.4	80.5
Roger Staubach	2958	1685	57.0	22,700	7.67	91t	153	5.2	109	3.7	83.4
Fran Tarkenton	6467	3686	57.0	47,003	7.27	89t	342	5.3	266	4.1	80.4
Y.A. Tittle	3817	2118	55.5	28,339	7.42	78t	212	5.6	221	5.8	73.8
Johnny Unitas	5186	2830	54.6	40,239	7.76	89t	290	5.6	253	4.9	78.2
Norm Van Brocklin	2895	1553	53.6	23,611	8.16	91t	173	6.0	178	6.1	75.3
Bob Waterfield	1617	814	50.3	11,849	7.33	91t	97	6.0	128	7.9	61.6

Rushing

	Yrs.	Last Year	G	Att.	Yds.	Avg.	Lng.	TD
Joe Montana	13	1992	167	414	1595	3.9	21	20
Sammy Baugh	16	1952	165	324	325	1.0	41t	9
George Blanda	26	1975	340	135	344	2.5	19	9
Terry Bradshaw	14	1983	168	444	2257	5.1	39	32
Len Dawson	19	1975	211	294	1293	4.4	43	9
Dan Fouts	15	1987	142	224	476	2.1	32	13
Otto Graham	6	1955	72	306	682	2.2	36	33
Bob Griese	14	1980	161	261	994	3.8	35	7
Arnie Herber*	13	1945	x	250	116	0.5	x	2
Sonny Jurgensen	18	1974	218	181	492	2.7	33	15
Bobby Layne	15	1962	175	611	2451	4.0	36	25
Sid Luckman	12	1950	128	204	−239	−1.2	40t	4
Joe Namath	13	1977	140	71	140	2.0	39	7
Bart Starr	16	1971	196	247	1308	5.3	39	15
Roger Staubach	11	1979	131	410	2264	5.5	33	20
Fran Tarkenton	18	1978	246	675	3674	5.4	52t	32
Y.A. Tittle	15	1964	178	291	999	3.4	45	33
Johnny Unitas	18	1973	211	450	1777	3.9	34	13
Norm Van Brocklin	12	1960	140	102	40	0.4	16	11
Bob Waterfield	8	1952	91	75	21	0.3	25	13

*statistics do not include 1930-31 seasons. xUnavailable.

Joe Montana's Game-by-Game Postseason Career

Date	Game	Opponent	Att.	Comp.	Pct.	Yds.	Avg.	TD	Int.	Rating
Jan. 3, 1982	NFC Divisional Playoff	N.Y. Giants	31	20	64.5	304	9.81	2	1	104.8
Jan. 10, 1982	NFC Championship Game	Dallas	35	22	62.9	286	8.17	3	3	81.4
Jan. 24, 1982	Super Bowl XVI	Cincinnati	22	14	63.6	157	7.14	1	0	100.0
Dec. 31, 1983	NFC Divisional Playoff	Detroit	31	18	58.1	201	6.48	1	1	74.8
Jan. 8, 1984	NFC Championship Game	Washington	48	27	56.3	347	7.23	3	1	91.2
Dec. 29, 1984	NFC Divisional Playoff	N.Y. Giants	39	25	64.1	309	7.92	3	3	82.1
Jan. 6, 1985	NFC Championship Game	Chicago	34	18	52.9	233	6.85	1	2	60.0
Jan. 20, 1985	Super Bowl XIX	Miami	35	24	68.6	331	9.46	3	0	127.2
Dec. 29, 1985	NFC First-Round Game	N.Y. Giants	47	26	55.3	296	6.30	0	1	65.6
Jan. 4, 1987	NFC Divisional Playoff	N.Y. Giants	15	8	53.3	98	6.53	0	2	34.2
Jan. 9, 1988	NFC Divisional Playoff	Minnesota	26	12	46.2	109	4.19	0	1	42.0
Jan. 1, 1989	NFC Divisional Playoff	Minnesota	27	16	59.3	178	6.59	3	1	100.5
Jan. 8, 1989	NFC Championship Game	Chicago	27	17	63.0	288	10.67	3	0	136.0
Jan. 22, 1989	Super Bowl XXIII	Cincinnati	36	23	63.9	357	9.92	2	0	115.2
Jan. 6, 1990	NFC Divisional Playoff	Minnesota	24	17	70.8	241	10.04	4	0	142.5
Jan. 14, 1990	NFC Championship Game	L.A. Rams	30	26	86.7	262	8.73	2	0	125.3
Jan. 28, 1990	Super Bowl XXIV	Denver	29	22	75.9	297	10.24	5	0	147.6
Jan. 12, 1991	NFC Divisional Playoff	Washington	31	22	71.0	274	8.84	2	1	106.1
Jan. 20, 1991	NFC Championship Game	N.Y. Giants	26	18	69.2	190	7.31	1	0	103.0
Totals (19 games)			593	375	63.2	4758	8.02	39	17	98.2

Highest NFL Postseason Passer Ratings (Minimum: 100 Attempts)

	Games	Att.	Comp.	Pct.	Yds.	Avg. Gain	TD	Int.	Rating
Troy Aikman	4	105	72	68.6	909	8.66	8	1	116.7
Bart Starr	10	213	130	61.0	1753	8.23	15	3	104.8
Joe Montana	19	593	375	63.2	4758	8.02	39	17	98.2
Ken Anderson	6	166	110	66.3	1321	7.96	9	6	93.5
Joe Theismann	10	211	128	60.7	1782	8.45	11	7	91.4
Warren Moon	8	308	198	64.3	2272	7.38	14	11	86.7
Ken Stabler	13	351	203	57.8	2641	7.52	19	13	84.2
Terry Bradshaw	19	456	261	57.2	3833	8.41	30	26	83.0
Phil Simms	8	228	128	56.1	1461	6.41	10	4	82.9
Jim Plunkett	10	272	162	59.6	2293	8.43	11	12	81.9

Highest NFL Postseason Passer Ratings, Active Players (Minimum: 100 Attempts)

	Games	Att.	Comp.	Pct.	Yds.	Avg. Gain	TD	Int.	Rating
Troy Aikman	4	105	72	68.6	909	8.66	8	1	116.7
Joe Montana	19	593	375	63.2	4758	8.02	39	17	98.2
Warren Moon	8	308	198	64.3	2272	7.38	14	11	86.7
Phil Simms	8	228	128	56.1	1461	6.41	10	4	82.9
Bernie Kosar	7	260	146	56.2	1860	7.15	15	10	81.9
Dan Marino	10	387	212	54.8	2659	6.87	22	14	80.2
Wade Wilson	6	185	99	53.5	1322	7.15	7	6	75.6
Jim McMahon	7	130	70	53.8	967	7.44	4	4	75.4
Mark Rypien	7	222	121	54.5	1699	7.65	8	9	74.5
John Elway	13	384	200	52.1	3019	7.86	16	17	73.7

All-Time Rankings of Players in Four Categories That Determine NFL Passer Rating

Minimum: 1500 Attempts

Completion Percentage

	Pct.	Att.	Comp.
Joe Montana	63.67	4600	2929
Jim Kelly	60.32	3024	1824
Steve Young	60.29	1506	908
Troy Aikman	60.21	1528	920
Ken Stabler	59.85	3793	2270
Danny White	59.69	2950	1761
Ken Anderson	59.31	4475	2654
Dan Marino	59.20	5284	3128
Bernie Kosar	58.90	3012	1774
Ken O'Brien	58.85	3465	2039

Touchdown Percentage

	Pct.	Att.	TD
Sid Luckman	7.86	1744	137
Frank Ryan	6.99	2133	149
Len Dawson	6.39	3741	239
Daryle Lamonica	6.31	2601	164
Sammy Baugh	6.24	2995	187
Charley Conerly	6.11	2833	173
Bob Waterfield	6.00	1617	97
Earl Morrall	5.99	2689	161
Sonny Jurgensen	5.98	4262	255
Norm Van Brocklin	5.98	2895	173

Average Yards Per Pass

	Avg.	Att.	Yards
Otto Graham	8.63	1565	13,499
Sid Luckman	8.42	1744	14,686
Norm Van Brocklin	8.16	2895	23,611
Steve Young	7.89	1506	11,877
Ed Brown	7.85	1987	15,600
Bart Starr	7.85	3149	24,718
Johnny Unitas	7.76	5186	40,239
Earl Morrall	7.74	2689	20,809
Dan Fouts	7.68	5604	43,040
Len Dawson	7.67	3741	28,711

Interception Percentage

	Pct.	Att.	Int.
Bernie Kosar	2.59	3012	78
Joe Montana	2.67	4600	123
Ken O'Brien	2.74	3465	95
Steve Young	2.79	1506	42
Neil Lomax	2.85	3153	90
Randall Cunningham	3.10	2641	82
Dan Marino	3.12	5284	165
Tony Eason	3.26	1564	51
Roman Gabriel	3.31	4498	149
Chris Miller	3.41	2023	69

Teams That Finished In First Place In Their Division the Season After Finishing in Last Place

Season	Team	Record	Previous Season
1967	Houston	9-4-1	*3-11
1968	Minnesota	8-6	3-8-3
1970	Cincinnati	8-6	4-9-1
1970	San Francisco	10-3-1	4-8-2
1972	Green Bay	10-4	4-8-2
1975	Baltimore	10-4	2-12
1979	Tampa Bay	10-6	5-11
1981	Cincinnati	12-4	6-10
1987	Indianapolis	9-6	3-13
1988	Cincinnati	12-4	4-11
1990	Cincinnati	9-7	8-8
1991	Denver	12-4	5-11
1992	San Diego	11-5	4-12

*tied for last place

Records of NFL Teams, 1983-92

AFC	W-L-T	Pct.	Division Titles	Playoff Berths	Postseason Record	Super Bowl Record
Miami	99- 60-0	.623	4	5	5-5	0-1
Denver	98- 60-1	.619	5	6	7-6	0-3
L.A. Raiders	91- 68-0	.572	3	5	4-4	1-0
Seattle	82- 77-0	.516	1	4	3-4	0-0
Buffalo	81- 78-0	.509	4	5	8-5	0-3
Pittsburgh	81- 78-0	.509	3	4	2-4	0-0
Cleveland	79- 79-1	.500	4	5	3-5	0-0
Kansas City	77- 80-2	.491	0	4	1-4	0-0
Cincinnati	73- 86-0	.459	2	2	3-2	0-1
Houston	73- 86-0	.459	1	6	3-6	0-0
N.Y. Jets	71- 87-1	.450	0	3	1-3	0-0
New England	70- 89-0	.440	1	2	3-2	0-1
San Diego	66- 93-0	.415	1	1	1-1	0-0
Indianapolis	62- 97-0	.390	1	1	0-1	0-0

NFC	W-L-T	Pct.	Division Titles	Playoff Berths	Postseason Record	Super Bowl Record
San Francisco	120- 38-1	.758	8	9	12-6	3-0
Washington	108- 51-0	.679	4	7	12-5	2-1
Chicago	103- 56-0	.648	6	7	6-6	1-0
N.Y. Giants	91- 67-1	.575	3	5	8-3	2-0
New Orleans	89- 70-0	.560	1	4	0-4	0-0
Philadelphia	82- 75-2	.522	1	4	1-4	0-0
L.A. Rams	81- 78-0	.509	1	6	4-6	0-0
Minnesota	81- 78-0	.509	2	4	3-4	0-0
Dallas	80- 79-0	.503	2	4	4-3	1-0
Green Bay	66- 92-1	.418	0	0	0-0	0-0
Detroit	63- 95-1	.399	2	2	1-2	0-0
Phoenix	58- 99-2	.371	0	0	0-0	0-0
Atlanta	54-104-1	.343	0	1	1-1	0-0
Tampa Bay	40-119-0	.252	0	0	0-0	0-0

Indianapolis totals include Baltimore, 1983
Phoenix totals include St. Louis, 1983-87

Home Records, 1983-92

AFC	W-L-T	Pct.	NFC	W-L-T	Pct.
Denver	63-17-0	.788	Washington	60-19-0	.759
Miami	56-23-0	.709	Chicago	60-20-0	.750
Kansas City	52-27-0	.658	San Francisco	58-21-0	.734
L.A. Raiders	51-29-0	.638	N.Y. Giants	54-26-0	.675
Pittsburgh	49-30-0	.620	New Orleans	48-31-0	.608
Buffalo	49-31-0	.613	Minnesota	47-33-0	.588
Seattle	49-31-0	.613	Philadelphia	45-34-1	.569
Houston	48-31-0	.608	Dallas	43-36-0	.544
Cleveland	44-34-1	.563	L.A. Rams	43-36-0	.544
Cincinnati	45-35-0	.563	Green Bay	37-42-1	.469
New England	41-39-0	.513	Detroit	36-42-1	.462
San Diego	39-40-0	.494	Phoenix	34-44-1	.437
N.Y. Jets	37-42-1	.469	Atlanta	34-45-1	.431
Indianapolis	33-47-0	.413	Tampa Bay	27-52-0	.342

Road Records, 1983-92

AFC	W-L-T	Pct.	NFC	W-L-T	Pct.
Miami	43-37-0	.538	San Francisco	62-17-1	.781
L.A. Raiders	40-39-0	.506	Washington	48-32-0	.600
Denver	35-43-1	.449	Chicago	43-36-0	.544
Cleveland	35-45-0	.438	New Orleans	41-39-0	.513
N.Y. Jets	34-45-0	.430	L.A. Rams	38-42-0	.475
Seattle	33-46-0	.418	N.Y. Giants	37-41-1	.475
Buffalo	32-47-0	.405	Philadelphia	37-41-1	.475
Pittsburgh	32-48-0	.400	Dallas	37-43-0	.463
Indianapolis	29-50-0	.367	Minnesota	34-45-0	.430
New England	29-50-0	.367	Green Bay	29-50-0	.367
Cincinnati	28-51-0	.354	Detroit	27-53-0	.338
San Diego	27-53-0	.338	Phoenix	24-55-1	.306
Kansas City	25-53-2	.325	Atlanta	20-59-0	.253
Houston	25-55-0	.313	Tampa Bay	13-67-0	.163

Records by Months, 1983-92

AFC	Sept. W-L-T	Oct. W-L-T	Nov. W-L-T	Dec. W-L-T	Total W-L-T	Pct.
Miami	23-15	26-15	26-17	24-13	99- 60-0	.623
Denver	26-12-1	28-13	24-18	20-17	98- 60-1	.619
L.A. Raiders	23-16	26-16	22-19	20-17	91- 68-0	.572
Seattle	18-20	25-18	19-22	20-17	82- 77-0	.516
Buffalo	23-16	21-19	23-20	14-23	81- 78-0	.509
Pittsburgh	16-21	23-20	22-21	20-16	81- 78-0	.509
Cleveland	17-21	23-19	22-19-1	17-20	79- 79-1	.500
Kansas City	22-17	14-27-1	17-23-1	24-13	77- 80-2	.491
Cincinnati	16-20	19-25	18-24	20-17	73- 86-0	.459
Houston	15-23	19-23	21-21	18-19	73- 86-0	.459
N.Y. Jets	21-18	19-21-1	20-24	11-24	71- 87-1	.450
New England	15-23	19-22	21-22	15-22	70- 89-0	.440
San Diego	12-27	15-27	23-19	16-20	66- 93-0	.415
Indianapolis	9-29	19-22	15-28	19-18	62- 97-0	.390

NFC	Sept. W-L-T	Oct. W-L-T	Nov. W-L-T	Dec. W-L-T	Total W-L-T	Pct.
San Francisco	28-10	30-10-1	28-14	34- 4	120- 38-1	.758
Washington	25-13	28-13	29-15	26-10	108- 51-0	.679
Chicago	29-10	28-12	29-15	17-19	103- 56-0	.648
N.Y. Giants	23-15	23-17-1	25-17	20-18	91- 67-1	.575
New Orleans	21-17	22-19	26-17	20-17	89- 70-0	.560
Philadelphia	16-22	22-19	23-19-1	21-15-1	82- 75-2	.522
L.A. Rams	24-14	20-21	20-23	17-20	81- 78-0	.509
Minnesota	23-16	17-24	25-19	16-19	81- 78-0	.509
Dallas	24-14	21-21	21-24	14-20	80- 79-0	.503
Green Bay	10-28-1	16-24	21-22	19-18	66- 92-1	.418
Detroit	13-26	17-23	17-27-1	16-19	63- 95-1	.399
Phoenix	15-23	16-25-1	15-29	12-22-1	58- 99-2	.371
Atlanta	15-23	13-27-1	14-29	12-25	54-104-1	.343
Tampa Bay	13-26	7-34	12-31	8-28	40-119-0	.252

Indianapolis totals include Baltimore, 1983
Phoenix totals include St. Louis, 1983-87

Takeaways/Giveaways in 1983-92

	Takeaways			Giveaways			
AFC	Int.	Fum.	Total	Int.	Fum.	Total	Net Diff.
Kansas City	221	170	391	174	147	321	70
Denver	213	168	381	198	139	337	44
Pittsburgh	232	155	387	198	153	351	36
Seattle	208	189	397	214	158	372	25
N.Y. Jets	193	153	346	175	162	337	9
Cincinnati	189	150	339	182	149	331	8
Cleveland	189	135	324	168	151	319	5
Indianapolis	170	168	338	206	132	338	0
New England	175	170	345	201	163	364	−19
Miami	182	130	312	184	151	335	−23
Houston	185	152	337	213	161	374	−37
Buffalo	178	148	326	215	171	386	−60
San Diego	193	140	333	235	159	394	−61
L.A. Raiders	174	134	308	212	163	375	−67

	Takeaways			Giveaways			
NFC	Int.	Fum.	Total	Int.	Fum.	Total	Net Diff.
San Francisco	220	144	364	132	144	276	88
Philadelphia	221	164	385	182	146	328	57
Washington	232	137	369	177	136	313	56
Minnesota	229	162	391	206	133	339	52
N.Y. Giants	196	140	336	166	148	314	22
New Orleans	206	168	374	202	153	355	19
Chicago	234	141	375	195	163	358	17
L.A. Rams	198	156	354	180	177	357	−3
Atlanta	177	145	322	185	161	346	−24
Dallas	185	153	338	225	142	367	−29
Detroit	183	159	342	212	159	371	−29
Green Bay	190	171	361	232	178	410	−49
Phoenix	167	145	312	205	160	365	−53
Tampa Bay	186	168	354	252	156	408	−54

Indianapolis totals include Baltimore, 1983
Phoenix totals include St. Louis, 1983-87

High and Low Single-Game Yardage Totals, 1983-92

Most Total Yards, Game
676 Washington vs. Detroit, Nov. 4, 1990 (OT)
621 Cincinnati vs. N.Y. Jets, Dec. 21, 1986
598 San Francisco vs. Buffalo, Sept. 13, 1992
597 N.Y. Jets vs. Miami, Nov. 27, 1988
593 San Diego vs. L.A. Raiders, Nov. 10, 1985 (OT)

Fewest Total Yards, Game
53 Pittsburgh vs. Cleveland, Sept. 10, 1989
60 Detroit vs. Minnesota, Nov. 24, 1988
62 Seattle vs. Dallas, Oct. 11, 1992
65 Tampa Bay vs. Green Bay, Dec. 1, 1985
65 Seattle vs. New England, Dec. 4, 1988

Most Yards Rushing, Game
356 L.A. Raiders vs. Seattle, Nov. 30, 1987
328 New England vs. N.Y. Jets, Sept. 18, 1983
315 Buffalo vs. Atlanta, Nov. 22, 1992
310 Kansas City vs. Detroit, Oct. 14, 1990
307 Washington vs. Atlanta, Nov. 3, 1985

Fewest Yards Rushing, Game
0 Buffalo vs. Chicago, Oct. 2, 1988
1 Tampa Bay vs. Washington, Oct. 22, 1989
2 New England vs. New Orleans, Nov. 30, 1986
4 Indianapolis vs. Detroit, Sept. 22, 1991
6 N.Y. Giants vs. L.A. Rams, Nov. 12, 1989

Most Yards Passing, Game
521 Miami vs. N.Y. Jets, Oct. 23, 1988
505 Houston vs. Kansas City, Dec. 16, 1990
494 San Diego vs. Seattle, Sept. 15, 1985
483 Cincinnati vs. L.A. Rams, Oct. 7, 1990
482 Washington vs. Detroit, Nov. 4, 1990 (OT)

Fewest Yards Passing, Game
−22 Atlanta vs. Chicago, Nov. 24, 1985
−13 Cincinnati vs. San Diego, Oct. 4, 1987
1 Denver vs. Pittsburgh, Sept. 4, 1983
2 Seattle vs. L.A. Raiders, Oct. 16, 1983
4 St. Louis vs. New Orleans, Oct. 11, 1987

NFL Individual Leaders, 1983-92

Points
1,074, Nick Lowery
1,073, Morten Andersen
1,071, Gary Anderson
955, Norm Johnson
946, Jim Breech

Rushes
2,970, Eric Dickerson
1,953, Roger Craig
1,930, Marcus Allen
1,911, Gerald Riggs
1,698, Curt Warner

Passes
5,284, Dan Marino
4,339, John Elway
4,026, Warren Moon
3,797, Dave Krieg
3,470, Joe Montana

TD Passes
290, Dan Marino
201, Dave Krieg
192, Joe Montana
175, Warren Moon
174, Boomer Esiason

Receiving TDs
103, Jerry Rice
81, Mark Clayton
60, Mike Quick
59, Mark Duper
59, Roy Green

Touchdowns
108, Jerry Rice
96, Eric Dickerson
84, Marcus Allen
82, Mark Clayton
71, Roger Craig

Rushing Yards
13,168, Eric Dickerson
8,070, Roger Craig
7,889, Gerald Riggs
7,848, Marcus Allen
7,007, James Brooks

Completions
3,128, Dan Marino
2,375, John Elway
2,329, Warren Moon
2,216, Joe Montana
2,213, Dave Krieg

Receptions
698, Art Monk
610, Jerry Rice
554, Drew Hill
550, Mark Clayton
549, Gary Clark

Interceptions
51, Ronnie Lott
49, Deron Cherry
44, Dave Waymer
42, Gill Byrd
39, Everson Walls

Field Goals
247, Gary Anderson
244, Morten Andersen
241, Nick Lowery
186, Norm Johnson
186, Eddie Murray

Rushing TDs
90, Eric Dickerson
68, Marcus Allen
64, Gerald Riggs
56, Curt Warner
55, Roger Craig

Passing Yards
39,502, Dan Marino
30,216, John Elway
30,200, Warren Moon
27,903, Dave Krieg
27,055, Joe Montana

Reception Yards
10,273, Jerry Rice
9,490, Art Monk
8,869, Mark Duper
8,819, James Lofton
8,816, Henry Ellard

Sacks
124, Reggie White
119, Lawrence Taylor
112, Richard Dent
100, Greg Townsend
99, Rickey Jackson

Records for Each Current NFL Team for Most Points in a Game (Regular Season Only)

Note: When the record has been achieved more than once, only the most recent game is shown; summaries are listed in alphabetical order by conference. Bold face indicates team holding record.

BUFFALO BILLS
September 18, 1966, at Buffalo
Miami .... 3 7 0 14 — 24
Buffalo .... 21 27 3 7 — 58
TDs: Buff — Bobby Burnett 2, Butch Byrd 2, Jack Spikes 2, Bobby Crockett, Jack Kemp; Mia — Dave Kocourek, Bo Roberson, John Roderick. TD Passes: Buff — Jack Kemp, Daryle Lamonica; Mia — George Wilson 3. FGs: Buff — Booth Lusteg; Mia — Gene Mingo.

CINCINNATI BENGALS
December 17, 1989, at Cincinnati
Houston .... 0 0 0 7 — 7
Cincinnati .... 21 10 21 9 — 61
TDs: Cin — Eddie Brown 2, Eric Ball, James Brooks, Ira Hillary, Rodney Holman, Tim McGee, Craig Taylor; Hou — Lorenzo White. TD Passes: Cin — Boomer Esiason 4, Erik Wilhelm. FGs: Cin — Jim Breech 2.

CLEVELAND BROWNS
November 7, 1954, at Cleveland
Washington .... 0 3 0 0 — 3
Cleveland .... 13 14 21 14 — 62
TDs: Clev — Darrell Brewster 2, Mo Bassett, Ken Gorgal, Otto Graham, Dub Jones, Dante Lavelli, Curley Morrison. TD Passes: Clev — George Ratterman 3, Otto Graham. FGs: Clev — Lou Groza 2; Wash — Vic Janowicz.

DENVER BRONCOS
October 6, 1963, at Denver
San Diego .... 13 7 0 14 — 34
Denver .... 3 14 9 24 — 50
TDs: Den — Lionel Taylor 2, Goose Gonsoulin, Gene Prebola, Donnie Stone; SD — Keith Lincoln 2, Lance Alworth, Paul Lowe, Jacque MacKinnon. TD Passes: Den — John McCormick 3; SD — Tobin Rote 3, John Hadl 2. FGs: Den — Gene Mingo 5.

HOUSTON OILERS
December 9, 1990, at Houston
Cleveland .... 0 7 7 0 — 14
Houston .... 14 31 7 6 — 58
TDs: Hou — Lorenzo White 4, Ernest Givins, Leonard Harris, Tony Jones, Terry Kinard; Clev — Eric Metcalf 2. TD Passes: Hou — Warren Moon 2, Cody Carlson; Clev — Bernie Kosar. FG: Hou — Teddy Garcia.

INDIANAPOLIS COLTS
December 12, 1976, at Baltimore
Buffalo .... 3 3 7 7 — 20
Baltimore Colts .... 7 13 28 10 — 58
TDs: Balt — Roger Carr, Raymond Chester, Glenn Doughty, Roosevelt Leaks, Derrel Luce, Lydell Mitchell, Howard Stevens; Buff — Bob Chandler, O.J. Simpson. TD Passes: Balt — Bert Jones 3; Buff — Gary Marangi. FGs: Balt — Toni Linhart 3; Buff — George Jakowenko 2.

KANSAS CITY CHIEFS
September 7, 1963, at Denver
Kansas City .... 14 14 21 10 — 59
Denver .... 0 7 0 0 — 7
TDs: KC — Chris Burford 2, Frank Jackson 2, Dave Grayson, Abner Haynes, Sherrill Headrick, Curtis McClinton; Den — Lionel Taylor. TD Passes: KC — Len Dawson 4, Curtis McClinton; Den — Mickey Slaughter. FG: KC — Tommy Brooker.

LOS ANGELES RAIDERS
December 22, 1963, at Oakland
Houston .... 14 21 14 0 — 49
Oakland Raiders .... 7 28 7 10 — 52
TDs: Oak — Art Powell 4, Clem Daniels, Claude Gibson, Ken Herock; Hou — Willard Dewveall 2, Dave Smith 2, Charley Hennigan, Bob McLeod, Charley Tolar. TD Passes: Oak — Tom Flores 6; Hou — George Blanda 5. FG: Oak — Mike Mercer.

MIAMI DOLPHINS
November 24, 1977, at St. Louis
Miami .... 14 14 20 7 — 55
St. Louis .... 7 0 0 7 — 14
TDs: Mia — Nat Moore 3, Gary Davis, Duriel Harris, Leroy Harris, Benny Malone, Andre Tillman; StL — Ike Harris, Terry Metcalf. TD Passes: Mia — Bob Griese 6; StL — Jim Hart.

NEW ENGLAND PATRIOTS
September 9, 1979, at New England
New York Jets .... 3 0 0 0 — 3
New England .... 14 21 7 14 — 56
TDs: NE — Harold Jackson 3, Stanley Morgan 2, Allan Clark, Andy Johnson, Don Westbrook. TD Passes: NE — Steve Grogan 5, Tom Owen. FG: NYJ — Pat Leahy.

NEW YORK JETS
November 17, 1985, at New York
Tampa Bay .... 14 7 7 0 — 28
New York Jets .... 17 24 14 7 — 62
TDs: NYJ — Mickey Shuler 3, Johnny Hector 2, Tony Paige, Al Toon, Wesley Walker; TB — James Wilder 2, Kevin House, Calvin Magee. TD Passes: NYJ — Ken O'Brien 5; TB — Steve DeBerg 2. FGs: NYJ — Pat Leahy 2.

PITTSBURGH STEELERS
November 30, 1952, at Pittsburgh
New York Giants .... 0 0 7 0 — 7
Pittsburgh .... 14 14 7 28 — 63
TDs: Pitt — Lynn Chandnois 2, Dick Hensley 2, Jack Butler, George Hays, Ray Mathews, Ed Modzelewski, Elbie Nickel; NYG — Bill Stribling. TD Passes: Pitt — Jim Finks 4, Gary Kerkorian; NYG — Tom Landry.

SAN DIEGO CHARGERS
December 22, 1963, at San Diego
Denver .... 7 10 3 0 — 20
San Diego .... 10 16 10 22 — 58
TDs: SD — Paul Lowe 2, Chuck Allen, Bobby Jackson, Dave Kocourek, Keith Lincoln, Jacque MacKinnon; Den — Billy Joe, Donnie Stone. TD Passes: SD — John Hadl, Tobin Rote; Den — Don Breaux. FGs: SD — George Blair 3; Den — Gene Mingo 2.

SEATTLE SEAHAWKS
October 30, 1977, at Seattle
Buffalo .... 3 0 7 7 — 17
Seattle .... 14 28 7 7 — 56
TDs: Sea — Steve Largent 2, Duke Fergerson, Al Hunter, David Sims, Sherman Smith, Don Testerman, Jim Zorn; Buff — Joe Ferguson, John Kimbrough. TD Passes: Sea — Jim Zorn 4; Buff — Joe Ferguson. FG: Buff — Carson Long.

ATLANTA FALCONS
September 16, 1973, at New Orleans
Atlanta .... 0 24 21 17 — 62
New Orleans .... 0 0 7 0 — 7
TDs: Atl — Ken Burrow 2, Eddie Ray 2, Wes Chesson, Tom Hayes, Art Malone, Joe Profit; NO — Bill Butler. TD Passes: Atl — Dick Shiner 3, Bob Lee; NO — Archie Manning. FGs: Atl — Nick Mike-Mayer.

CHICAGO BEARS
December 7, 1980, at Chicago
Green Bay .... 0 7 0 0 — 7
Chicago .... 0 28 13 20 — 61
TDs: Chi — Walter Payton 3, Brian Baschnagel, Robin Earl, Roland Harper, Willie McClendon, Len Walterscheid, Rickey Watts; GB — James Lofton. TD Passes: Chi — Vince Evans 3; GB — Lynn Dickey.

DALLAS COWBOYS
October 12, 1980, at Dallas
San Francisco .... 0 7 0 7 — 14
Dallas .... 14 24 14 7 — 59
TDs: Dall — Drew Pearson 3, Ron Springs 2, Tony Dorsett, Billy Joe DuPree, Robert Newhouse; SF — Dwight Clark 2. TD Passes: Dall — Danny White 4; SF — Steve DeBerg 2. FG: Dall — Rafael Septien.

DETROIT LIONS
October 26, 1952, at Green Bay
Detroit .... 14 14 14 10 — 52
Green Bay .... 7 3 7 0 — 17
TDs: Det — Jug Girard 2, Bob Hoernschemeyer 2, Jack Christiansen, Jim Smith, Bill Swiacki; GB — Billy Howton, Jim Keane. TD Passes: Det — Bobby Layne 3; GB — Babe Parilli, Tobin Rote. FGs: Det — Pat Harder; GB — Bill Reichardt.

GREEN BAY PACKERS
October 7, 1945, at Milwaukee
Detroit .... 0 7 7 7 — 21
Green Bay .... 0 41 9 7 — 57
TDs: GB — Don Hutson 4, Charley Brock, Irv Comp, Ted Fritsch, Clyde Goodnight; Det — Chuck Fenenbock, John Greene, Bob Westfall. TD Passes: GB — Tex McKay 4, Lou Brock, Irv Comp; Det — Dave Ryan.

LOS ANGELES RAMS
October 22, 1950, at Los Angeles
Baltimore .... 13 0 7 7 — 27
Los Angeles .... 21 14 14 21 — 70
TDs: LA — Bob Boyd 2, Vitamin T. Smith 2, Tom Fears, Elroy (Crazylegs) Hirsch, Dick Hoerner, Ralph Pasquariello, Dan Towler, Bob Waterfield; Balt — Chet Mutryn 2, Adrian Burk, Billy Stone. TD Passes: LA — Norm Van Brocklin 2, Bob Waterfield 2, Glenn Davis; Balt — Adrian Burk 3.

MINNESOTA VIKINGS
October 18, 1970, at Minnesota
Dallas .... 3 3 0 7 — 13
Minnesota .... 14 20 17 3 — 54
TDs: Minn — Clint Jones 2, Ed Sharockman 2, John Beasley, Dave Osborn; Dall — Calvin Hill. TD Pass: Minn — Gary Cuozzo. FGs: Minn — Fred Cox 4; Dall — Mike Clark 2.

NEW ORLEANS SAINTS
November 21, 1976, at Seattle
New Orleans .... 3 17 28 3 — 51
Seattle .... 6 0 7 14 — 27
TDs: NO — Bobby Douglass 2, Tony Galbreath, Chuck Muncie, Tom Myers, Elex Price; Sea — Sherman Smith 2, Steve Largent, Jim Zorn. TD Pass: Sea — Bill Munson. FGs: NO — Rich Szaro 3.

NEW YORK GIANTS
November 26, 1972, at New York
Philadelphia .... 3 7 0 0 — 10
New York Giants .... 14 24 10 14 — 62
TDs: NYG — Don Herrmann 2, Ron Johnson 2, Bob Tucker 2, Randy Johnson; Phil — Harold Jackson. TD Passes: NYG — Norm Snead 3, Randy Johnson 2; Phil — John Reaves. FGs: NYG — Pete Gogolak 2; Phil — Tom Dempsey.

PHILADELPHIA EAGLES
November 6, 1934, at Philadelphia
Cincinnati Reds .... 0 0 0 0 — 0
Philadelphia .... 26 6 12 20 — 64
TDs: Phil — Joe Carter 3, Swede Hanson 3, Marvin Ellstrom, Roger Kirkman, Ed Matesic, Ed Storm. TD Passes: Phil — Ed Matesic 2, Albert Weiner 2, Marvin Elstrom.

PHOENIX CARDINALS
November 13, 1949, at New York
Chicago Cardinals ...... 7 31 14 13 — 65
New York Bulldogs .... 7 0 6 7 — 20
TDs: Chi — Red Cochran 2, Pat Harder 2, Bill Dewell, Mel Kutner, Bob Ravensburg, Vic Schwall, Charlie Trippi; NY — Joe Golding, Frank Muehlheuser, Johnny Rauch. TD Passes: Chi — Paul Christman 3, Jim Hardy 3; NY — Bobby Layne. FG: Chi — Pat Harder.

SAN FRANCISCO 49ERS
October 18, 1992, at San Francisco
Atlanta .... 7 3 0 7 — 17
San Francisco .... 21 21 14 0 — 56
TDs: SF — Jerry Rice 3, Ricky Watters 3, Brent Jones, Tom Rathman; Atl — Michael Haynes, Jason Phillips. TD Passes: SF — Steve Young 3; Atl — Chris Miller, Wade Wilson. FG: Atl — Norm Johnson.

TAMPA BAY BUCCANEERS
September 13, 1987, at Tampa Bay
Atlanta .... 0 3 0 7 — 10
Tampa Bay .... 14 13 7 14 — 48
TDs: TB — Gerald Carter 2, Cliff Austin, Steve Bartalo, Mark Carrier, Phil Freeman, Calvin Magee; Atl — Stacey Bailey. TD Passes: TB — Steve DeBerg 5; Atl — Scott Campbell. FG: Atl — Mick Luckhurst.

WASHINGTON REDSKINS
November 27, 1966, at Washington
New York Giants .... 0 14 14 13 — 41
Washington .... 13 21 14 24 — 72
TDs: Wash — A. D. Whitfield 3, Brig Owens 2, Charley Taylor 2, Rickie Harris, Joe Don Looney, Bobby Mitchell; NYG — Allen Jacobs, Homer Jones, Dan Lewis, Joe Morrison, Aaron Thomas, Gary Wood. TD Passes: Wash — Sonny Jurgensen 3; NYG — Gary Wood 2, Tom Kennedy. FG: Wash — Charlie Gogolak.

NFL Games In Which a Team Has Scored 60 or More Points

(Home team in capitals)

Regular Season

WASHINGTON 72, New York Giants 41 .... November 27, 1966
LOS ANGELES RAMS 70, Baltimore 27 .... October 22, 1950
Chicago Cardinals 65, NEW YORK BULLDOGS 20 .... November 13, 1949
LOS ANGELES RAMS 65, Detroit 24 .... October 29, 1950
PHILADELPHIA 64, Cincinnati 0 .... November 6, 1934
CHICAGO CARDINALS 63, New York Giants 35 .... October 17, 1948
AKRON 62, Oorang 0 .... October 29,1922
PITTSBURGH 62, New York Giants 7 .... November 30, 1952
CLEVELAND 62, New York Giants 14 .... December 6, 1953
CLEVELAND 62, Washington 3 .... November 7, 1954
NEW YORK GIANTS 62, Philadelphia 10 .... November 26, 1972
Atlanta 62, NEW ORLEANS 7 .... September 16, 1973
NEW YORK JETS 62, Tampa Bay 28 .... November 17, 1985
CHICAGO 61, San Francisco 20 .... December 12, 1965
Cincinnati 61, HOUSTON 17 .... December 17, 1972
CHICAGO 61, Green Bay 7 .... December 7, 1980
CINCINNATI 61, Houston 7 .... December 17, 1989
ROCK ISLAND 60, Evansville 0 .... October 15, 1922
CHICAGO CARDINALS 60, Rochester 0 .... October 7, 1923

Postseason

Chicago Bears 73, WASHINGTON 0 .... December 8, 1940

Youngest and Oldest Players in NFL in 1992

Ten Youngest Players

	Birthdate	Games	Starts	Position
Bob Whitfield, Atlanta	10/18/71	11	0	T
Amp Lee, San Francisco	10/1/71	16	3	RB
Alonzo Spellman, Chicago	9/27/71	15	0	DE
Eric Shaw, Cincinnati	9/17/71	11	1	LB
Tommy Maddox, Denver	9/2/71	13	4	QB
Terrell Buckley, Green Bay	6/7/71	14	12	CB
Keith Hamilton, N.Y. Giants	5/25/71	16	0	DE
Johnny Mitchell, N.Y. Jets	1/20/71	11	3	TE
Shane Dronett, Denver	1/12/71	16	2	DE
Jeff Blake, N.Y. Jets	12/4/70	3	0	QB

Ten Oldest Players

	Birthdate	Games	Starts	Position
Steve DeBerg, Tampa Bay	1/19/54	6	2	QB
Jackie Slater, L.A. Rams	5/27/54	16	16	T
Vince Evans, L.A. Raiders	6/14/55	5	0	QB
Phil Simms, N.Y. Giants	11/3/55	4	4	QB
Mike Kenn, Atlanta	2/9/56	16	16	T
Clay Matthews, Cleveland	3/15/56	16	16	LB
Jim Breech, Cincinnati	4/11/56	16	0	K
Don Warren, Washington	5/5/56	11	10	TE
Max Montoya, L.A. Raiders	5/12/56	10	9	G
Nick Lowery, Kansas City	5/27/56	15	0	K

Youngest and Oldest Regular Starters By Position in 1992

Minimum: 8 Games Started

	Youngest	Oldest
QB	10/10/69 Brett Favre, G.B.	11/18/56 Warren Moon, Hou.
RB	11/17/69 Leonard Russell, N.E.	6/26/59 Harry Sydney, G.B.
WR	3/23/70 Carl Pickens, Cin.	7/5/56 James Lofton, Buff.
TE	8/7/69 Keith Cash, K.C. Kerry Cash, Ind.	5/5/56 Don Warren, Wash.
C	8/26/68 Courtney Hall, S.D.	5/18/58 Ray Donaldson, Ind.
G	12/3/69 Ed King, Clev.	5/12/56 Max Montoya, Raiders
T	9/2/69 Russell Freeman, Den.	5/27/54 Jackie Slater, Rams
DE	12/18/69 Marco Coleman, Mia.	5/29/58 Sam Clancy, Ind.
DT	8/16/70 Eric Swann, Phoe.	10/17/57 Steve McMichael, Chi.
LB	4/13/70 Eddie Robinson, Hou.	3/15/56 Clay Matthews, Clev.
CB	6/7/71 Terrell Buckley, G.B.	1/1/60 Frank Minnifield, Clev.
S	1/1/70 Darryl Williams, Cin.	2/3/59 Dennis Smith, Den.

Eric Dickerson's Career Rushing vs. Each Opponent

Opponent	Games	Rushes	Yards	Yards Per Rush	Yards Per Game	TD
Atlanta	9	179	852	4.8	94.7	9
Buffalo	8	166	632	3.8	79.0	3
Chicago	4	115	482	4.2	120.5	5
Cincinnati	4	85	412	4.8	103.0	3
Cleveland	7	131	631	4.8	90.1	2
Dallas	3	57	286	5.0	95.3	1
Denver	5	81	414	5.1	82.8	4
Detroit	3	67	346	5.2	115.3	5
Green Bay	4	95	426	4.5	106.5	2
Houston	4	105	609	5.8	152.3	4
Indianapolis	1	25	121	4.8	121.0	1
Kansas City	3	61	214	3.5	71.3	2
L.A. Raiders	2	45	175	3.9	87.5	0
L.A. Rams	1	21	116	5.5	116.0	1
Miami	11	231	1065	4.6	96.8	6
Minnesota	3	73	217	3.0	72.3	1
New England	10	224	758	3.4	75.8	4
New Orleans	9	192	907	4.7	100.8	6
N.Y. Giants	5	98	390	4.0	78.0	1
N.Y. Jets	9	196	787	4.0	87.4	8
Philadelphia	3	54	189	3.5	63.0	0
Phoenix	4	96	585	6.1	146.3	4
Pittsburgh	2	36	73	2.0	36.5	0
San Diego	6	128	566	4.4	94.3	0
San Francisco	9	170	832	4.9	92.4	3
Seattle	4	63	247	3.9	61.8	4
Tampa Bay	6	154	768	5.0	128.0	10
Washington	3	22	68	3.1	22.7	1
Totals	142	2970	13,168	4.4	92.7	90

Phoenix totals include three games vs. St. Louis

Roger Craig's Career Rushing vs. Each Opponent

Opponent	Games	Rushes	Yards	Yards Per Rush	Yards Per Game	TD
Atlanta	16	214	1012	4.7	63.3	6
Buffalo	3	49	190	3.9	63.3	1
Chicago	7	61	219	3.6	31.3	2
Cincinnati	5	61	241	4.0	48.2	1
Cleveland	3	28	107	3.8	35.7	2
Dallas	4	57	235	4.1	58.8	2
Denver	4	87	417	4.8	104.3	0
Detroit	5	56	230	4.1	46.0	1
Green Bay	6	65	221	3.4	36.8	0
Houston	5	42	171	4.1	34.2	1
Indianapolis	3	45	210	4.7	70.0	2
Kansas City	2	32	114	3.6	57.0	1
L.A. Raiders	2	27	92	3.4	46.0	0
L.A. Rams	17	248	1026	4.1	60.4	9
Miami	2	29	154	5.3	77.0	2
Minnesota	5	71	247	3.5	49.4	3
New England	3	56	206	3.7	68.7	2
New Orleans	16	200	796	4.0	49.8	5
N.Y. Giants	5	66	256	3.9	51.2	0
N.Y. Jets	3	42	190	4.5	63.3	2
Philadelphia	5	55	227	4.1	45.4	0
Phoenix	4	51	277	5.4	69.3	2
Pittsburgh	3	21	72	3.4	24.0	0
San Diego	2	24	126	5.3	63.0	2
San Francisco	2	17	76	4.5	38.0	0
Seattle	3	48	190	4.0	63.3	0
Tampa Bay	8	97	384	4.0	48.0	9
Washington	6	92	334	3.6	55.7	0
Totals	151	1953	8070	4.1	53.4	55

Phoenix totals include three games vs. St. Louis

Joe Montana's Career Passing vs. Each Opponent

Opponent	Games	Att.	Cmp.	Pct.	Yards	Avg. Gain	TD	Int.	Sacked
Atlanta	21	567	370	65.3	4436	7.82	36	17	33/235
Buffalo	2	64	43	67.2	381	5.95	2	0	6/46
Chicago	7	162	90	55.6	1023	6.31	5	4	20/144
Cincinnati	4	141	90	63.8	923	6.55	7	6	9/75
Cleveland	4	140	88	62.9	1003	7.16	7	6	6/48
Dallas	5	126	84	66.7	1114	8.84	9	3	7/48
Denver	4	106	58	54.7	779	7.35	4	3	6/50
Detroit	6	141	89	63.1	839	5.95	4	2	10/63
Green Bay	5	149	104	69.8	1264	8.48	7	2	8/50
Houston	4	135	95	70.4	1164	8.62	10	4	5/31
Indianapolis	1	26	15	57.7	233	8.96	1	0	3/29
Kansas City	2	69	43	62.3	488	7.07	2	2	3/16
L.A. Raiders	4	96	51	53.1	659	6.86	4	1	11/92
L.A. Rams	23	693	446	64.4	5632	8.13	37	15	47/297
Miami	2	30	19	63.3	267	8.90	1	0	3/22
Minnesota	5	104	66	63.5	829	7.97	9	3	7/28
New England	4	108	69	63.9	791	7.32	6	2	6/39
New Orleans	20	508	314	61.8	3704	7.29	31	14	38/225
N.Y. Giants	8	210	132	62.9	1435	6.83	10	3	7/38
N.Y. Jets	3	79	48	60.8	538	6.81	3	3	3/17
Philadelphia	3	54	35	64.8	546	10.11	5	2	9/52
Phoenix	6	141	95	67.4	1389	9.85	13	5	7/53
Pittsburgh	4	150	100	66.7	919	6.13	4	8	3/20
San Diego	3	68	45	66.2	627	9.22	6	2	2/13
Seattle	3	62	37	59.7	539	8.69	6	4	3/17
Tampa Bay	8	254	176	69.3	1860	7.32	8	6	11/70
Washington	6	217	127	58.5	1742	8.03	7	6	9/84
Totals	167	4600	2929	63.7	35,124	7.64	244	123	282/1902

L.A. Raiders totals include one game vs. Oakland
Phoenix totals include six games vs. St. Louis

Phil Simms's Career Passing vs. Each Opponent

Opponent	Games	Att.	Cmp.	Pct.	Yards	Avg. Gain	TD	Int.	Sacked
Atlanta	4	116	66	56.9	910	7.84	4	3	12/81
Buffalo	1	10	6	60.0	59	5.90	0	0	1/0
Chicago	2	57	34	59.6	401	7.04	3	0	9/61
Cincinnati	2	106	66	62.3	809	7.63	4	2	10/88
Cleveland	1	37	23	62.2	289	7.81	1	2	4/22
Dallas	21	558	294	52.7	4442	7.96	36	31	52/385
Denver	3	78	43	55.1	519	6.65	1	1	8/64
Detroit	4	112	78	69.6	935	8.35	6	0	11/73
Green Bay	5	156	97	62.2	1302	8.35	11	4	16/111
Houston	2	41	28	68.3	434	10.59	3	1	1/8
Indianapolis	2	35	24	68.6	239	6.83	1	5	5/33
Kansas City	3	82	42	51.2	587	7.16	5	5	7/52
L.A. Raiders	3	84	50	59.5	604	7.19	2	3	8/62
L.A. Rams	7	235	131	55.7	1565	6.66	7	6	27/224
Miami	1	25	13	52.0	182	7.28	0	0	1/3
Minnesota	3	58	33	56.9	428	7.38	1	2	4/27
New Orleans	5	155	90	58.1	1011	6.52	5	7	13/88
N.Y. Jets	4	135	78	57.8	928	6.87	5	2	21/167
Philadelphia	19	551	272	49.4	3776	6.85	22	20	55/381
Phoenix	16	438	220	50.2	2853	6.51	28	10	44/275
Pittsburgh	1	16	10	62.5	106	6.63	1	1	3/24
San Diego	3	99	54	54.5	667	6.74	1	4	8/72
San Francisco	8	295	163	55.3	2025	6.86	8	9	35/212
Seattle	3	78	43	55.1	487	6.24	3	5	9/59
Tampa Bay	7	191	111	58.1	1060	5.55	6	5	19/197
Washington	18	499	260	52.1	3806	7.63	22	22	57/432
Totals	148	4247	2329	54.8	30,424	7.16	184	148	440/3201

Indianapolis totals include one game vs. Baltimore
Phoenix totals include 12 games vs. St. Louis

Dan Marino's Career Passing vs. Each Opponent

Opponent	Games	Att.	Cmp.	Pct.	Yards	Avg. Gain	TD	Int.	Sacked
Atlanta	2	80	40	50.0	553	6.91	2	4	1/2
Buffalo	19	649	412	63.5	5093	7.85	38	26	24/203
Chicago	3	79	39	49.4	566	7.16	5	3	6/36
Cincinnati	4	136	84	61.8	1026	7.54	7	1	5/39
Cleveland	5	186	112	60.2	1500	8.06	10	5	3/22
Dallas	3	115	66	57.4	860	7.48	6	3	4/36
Denver	1	43	25	58.1	390	9.07	3	0	3/25
Detroit	2	78	39	50.0	421	5.40	2	2	3/28
Green Bay	4	146	95	65.1	1151	7.88	9	6	4/22
Houston	7	220	116	52.7	1464	6.65	10	11	7/36
Indianapolis	20	647	390	60.3	4872	7.53	34	10	16/115
Kansas City	4	148	84	56.8	1031	6.97	8	3	2/20
L.A. Raiders	6	204	116	56.9	1469	7.20	12	6	8/70
L.A. Rams	3	121	75	62.0	905	7.48	9	3	1/4
Minnesota	1	37	20	54.1	264	7.14	2	3	0/0
New England	19	649	376	57.9	4544	7.00	30	29	13/101
New Orleans	3	105	65	61.9	650	6.19	5	2	6/42
N.Y. Giants	1	30	14	46.7	115	3.83	0	2	1/7
N.Y. Jets	18	683	398	58.3	5438	7.96	47	22	24/134
Philadelphia	3	127	72	56.7	987	7.77	6	2	5/45
Phoenix	2	61	42	68.9	634	10.39	5	0	1/9
Pittsburgh	6	175	110	62.9	1333	7.62	9	9	1/4
San Diego	4	163	103	63.2	1243	7.63	9	2	6/42
San Francisco	3	106	61	57.5	687	6.48	3	4	4/36
Seattle	2	68	40	58.8	504	7.41	3	4	3/21
Tampa Bay	3	117	74	63.2	875	7.48	7	1	1/10
Washington	3	111	60	54.1	927	8.35	9	2	1/2
Totals	151	5284	3128	59.2	39,502	7.48	290	165	153/1115

Indianapolis totals include two games vs. Baltimore
Phoenix totals include one game vs. St. Louis

John Elway's Career Passing vs. Each Opponent

Opponent	Games	Att.	Cmp.	Pct.	Yards	Avg. Gain	TD	Int.	Sacked
Atlanta	2	64	35	54.7	526	8.22	4	2	4/26
Buffalo	4	109	55	50.5	739	6.78	5	4	8/70
Chicago	4	94	51	54.3	650	6.91	3	4	9/65
Cincinnati	3	75	48	64.0	617	8.23	6	1	2/13
Cleveland	7	187	100	53.5	1412	7.55	9	7	14/109
Dallas	1	24	12	50.0	200	8.33	3	0	1/2
Detroit	3	88	56	63.6	699	7.94	2	2	7/72
Green Bay	3	94	55	58.5	546	5.81	1	4	1/4
Houston	3	98	54	55.1	749	7.64	6	4	11/109
Indianapolis	6	183	98	53.6	1315	7.19	6	2	16/127
Kansas City	18	551	293	53.2	3790	6.88	13	26	50/371
L.A. Raiders	17	494	265	53.6	3262	6.60	17	22	44/350
L.A. Rams	2	74	39	52.7	501	6.77	5	2	3/24
Miami	1	37	18	48.6	250	6.76	0	1	3/24
Minnesota	4	90	54	60.0	633	7.03	8	1	9/60
New England	6	192	108	56.3	1286	6.70	7	4	8/54
New Orleans	2	79	46	58.2	519	6.57	4	2	4/35
N.Y. Giants	3	103	58	56.3	724	7.03	2	3	3/19
N.Y. Jets	2	61	31	50.8	406	6.66	1	3	5/27
Philadelphia	4	102	52	51.0	626	6.14	4	6	16/119
Phoenix	2	62	39	62.9	492	7.94	3	5	3/16
Pittsburgh	6	167	87	52.1	1090	6.53	5	5	12/90
San Diego	19	580	319	55.0	3862	6.66	15	24	44/296
San Francisco	2	81	41	50.6	425	5.25	3	3	5/43
Seattle	18	583	326	55.9	4487	7.70	25	18	41/293
Washington	2	67	35	52.2	410	6.12	1	2	8/59
Totals	144	4339	2375	54.7	30,216	6.96	158	157	331/2477

Boomer Esiason's Career Passing vs. Each Opponent

Opponent	Games	Att.	Cmp.	Pct.	Yards	Avg. Gain	TD	Int.	Sacked
Atlanta	3	67	34	50.7	367	5.48	1	2	3/3
Buffalo	6	127	73	57.5	989	7.79	6	4	5/42
Chicago	3	95	48	50.5	568	5.98	5	5	9/88
Cleveland	16	369	198	53.7	2561	6.94	18	13	19/134
Dallas	3	85	48	56.5	661	7.78	6	2	4/22
Denver	2	50	32	64.0	512	10.24	4	4	2/17
Detroit	3	91	55	60.4	630	6.92	3	4	5/24
Green Bay	2	47	26	55.3	335	7.13	4	2	3/24
Houston	16	435	255	58.6	3621	8.32	25	20	32/235
Indianapolis	4	93	51	54.8	658	7.08	4	3	9/72
Kansas City	4	121	67	55.4	940	7.77	5	3	7/71
L.A. Raiders	5	107	60	56.1	813	7.60	5	2	5/44
L.A. Rams	1	45	31	68.9	490	10.89	3	0	1/7
Miami	3	86	47	54.7	617	7.17	2	1	6/69
Minnesota	3	100	59	59.0	747	7.47	4	8	9/78
New England	6	190	101	53.2	1571	8.27	12	7	10/71
New Orleans	3	75	33	44.0	309	4.12	3	2	9/71
N.Y. Giants	2	54	32	59.3	397	7.35	4	0	4/36
N.Y. Jets	7	180	93	51.7	1410	7.83	12	8	16/123
Philadelphia	2	50	30	60.0	473	9.46	5	3	5/45
Phoenix	2	38	24	63.2	356	9.37	4	1	3/22
Pittsburgh	16	437	261	59.7	3589	8.21	18	17	28/230
San Diego	3	97	56	57.7	748	7.71	8	5	10/84
San Francisco	2	49	26	53.1	294	6.00	2	2	5/28
Seattle	6	167	90	53.9	1093	6.54	2	6	14/109
Tampa Bay	1	28	17	60.7	197	7.04	5	0	1/1
Washington	3	95	50	52.6	756	7.96	4	3	8/65
Totals	127	3378	1897	56.2	25,671	7.60	174	129	230/1815

Phoenix totals include one game vs. St. Louis

Warren Moon's Career Passing vs. Each Opponent

Opponent	Games	Att.	Cmp.	Pct.	Yards	Avg. Gain	TD	Int.	Sacked
Atlanta	3	114	63	55.3	847	7.43	8	5	7/37
Buffalo	6	147	80	54.4	1090	7.41	6	6	9/73
Chicago	2	55	28	50.9	521	9.47	3	3	5/49
Cincinnati	17	541	310	57.3	4130	7.63	29	21	34/289
Cleveland	16	493	284	57.6	3706	7.52	21	18	36/277
Dallas	3	111	67	60.4	873	7.86	2	4	16/105
Denver	3	87	50	57.5	777	8.93	5	2	9/66
Detroit	2	76	51	67.1	743	9.78	3	4	0/0
Green Bay	1	21	14	66.7	218	10.38	2	1	0/0
Indianapolis	7	255	160	62.7	2156	8.45	13	7	14/97
Kansas City	7	232	144	62.1	1802	7.77	9	6	24/166
L.A. Raiders	4	138	68	49.3	1004	7.28	6	5	13/115
L.A. Rams	3	115	66	57.4	853	7.42	3	5	6/49
Miami	5	111	76	68.5	910	8.20	5	6	9/97
Minnesota	3	95	58	61.1	592	6.23	2	2	14/106
New England	2	73	34	46.6	495	6.78	3	4	3/25
New Orleans	3	81	42	51.9	496	6.12	2	2	5/37
N.Y. Giants	2	83	48	57.8	566	6.82	3	2	5/46
N.Y. Jets	3	121	85	70.2	1011	8.36	6	2	7/60
Philadelphia	1	46	24	52.2	262	5.70	0	0	4/36
Phoenix	2	61	31	50.8	453	7.43	4	2	3/21
Pittsburgh	17	519	293	56.5	3645	7.02	20	26	37/284
San Diego	5	164	89	54.3	1163	7.09	6	2	7/53
San Francisco	3	102	60	58.8	745	7.30	6	5	6/39
Seattle	2	60	37	61.7	414	6.90	2	2	2/12
Tampa Bay	1	23	14	60.9	149	6.48	2	0	0/0
Washington	3	102	53	52.0	579	5.68	4	3	6/46
Totals	126	4026	2329	57.8	30,200	7.50	175	145	281/2185

Phoenix totals include one game vs. St. Louis

Jim Kelly's Career Passing vs. Each Opponent

Opponent	Games	Att.	Cmp.	Pct.	Yards	Avg. Gain	TD	Int.	Sacked
Atlanta	2	37	24	64.9	324	8.76	4	2	3/18
Chicago	2	66	39	59.1	576	8.73	3	1	9/79
Cincinnati	4	99	65	65.7	1008	10.18	10	7	5/49
Cleveland	3	93	56	60.2	737	7.93	5	0	6/31
Dallas	3	111	67	60.4	873	7.86	2	4	16/105
Denver	4	124	71	57.3	813	6.56	3	7	8/58
Green Bay	2	49	27	55.1	312	6.37	3	2	5/23

Opponent	Games	Att.	Cmp.	Pct.	Yards	Avg. Gain	TD	Int.	Sacked
Indianapolis	13	353	207	58.6	2616	7.41	23	9	12/99
Kansas City	3	95	58	61.1	670	7.05	3	4	10/82
L.A. Raiders	5	178	105	59.0	1274	7.16	7	4	12/89
L.A. Rams	1	19	13	68.4	106	5.58	2	1	1/0
Miami	12	381	246	64.6	2914	7.65	15	9	18/150
Minnesota	1	31	17	54.8	204	6.58	0	1	1/8
New England	13	358	210	58.7	2751	7.68	15	18	38/300
New Orleans	2	63	30	47.6	346	5.49	2	4	3/16
N.Y. Giants	1	11	7	63.6	115	10.46	1	0	0/0
N.Y. Jets	13	406	239	58.9	3086	7.60	26	14	23/162
Philadelphia	2	71	39	54.9	488	6.87	4	3	2/20
Phoenix	2	26	17	65.4	270	10.39	4	1	5/34
Pittsburgh	2	76	57	75.0	653	8.59	9	2	3/26
San Francisco	2	75	48	64.0	668	8.91	3	4	5/32
Seattle	2	48	26	54.2	324	6.75	1	2	2/21
Tampa Bay	3	114	72	63.2	913	8.01	4	3	5/54
Washington	1	43	25	58.1	292	6.79	1	3	3/33
Totals	102	3024	1824	60.3	23,031	7.62	161	108	201/1544

Phoenix totals include one game vs. St. Louis

Jerry Rice's Career Receiving vs. Each Opponent

Opponent	Games	Rec.	Yards	Yards Per Rec.	Yards Per Game	TD
Atlanta	15	80	1385	17.3	92.3	17
Buffalo	2	6	72	12.0	36.0	1
Chicago	5	24	424	17.7	84.8	7
Cincinnati	2	12	187	15.6	93.5	2
Cleveland	2	13	193	14.8	96.5	4
Dallas	3	21	286	13.6	95.3	2
Denver	2	7	145	20.7	72.5	0
Detroit	4	13	135	10.4	33.8	1
Green Bay	4	23	432	18.8	108.0	4
Houston	2	13	155	11.9	77.5	2
Indianapolis	2	12	335	27.9	167.5	4
Kansas City	2	8	100	12.5	50.0	2
L.A. Raiders	3	11	193	17.5	64.3	0
L.A. Rams	16	70	1298	18.5	81.1	9
Miami	2	10	155	15.5	77.5	3
Minnesota	6	30	492	16.4	82.0	5
New England	3	13	207	15.9	69.0	3
New Orleans	16	75	1123	15.0	70.2	7
N.Y. Giants	6	27	454	16.8	75.7	4
N.Y. Jets	3	15	265	17.7	88.3	2
Philadelphia	4	19	371	19.5	92.8	4
Phoenix	4	16	310	19.4	77.5	3
Pittsburgh	2	11	137	12.5	68.5	1
San Diego	2	15	321	21.4	160.5	4
Seattle	3	14	272	19.4	90.7	4
Tampa Bay	5	31	453	14.6	90.6	6
Washington	4	21	383	18.2	95.8	2
Totals	124	610	10,273	16.8	82.8	103

Phoenix totals include one game vs. St. Louis

James Lofton's Career Receiving vs. Each Opponent

Opponent	Games	Rec.	Yards	Yards Per Rec.	Yards Per Game	TD
Atlanta	7	25	595	23.8	85.0	4
Buffalo	4	14	343	24.5	85.8	2
Chicago	18	72	1312	18.2	72.9	5
Cincinnati	6	23	443	19.3	73.8	4
Cleveland	5	16	295	18.4	59.0	2
Dallas	3	4	37	9.3	12.3	0
Denver	7	25	423	16.9	60.4	1
Detroit	19	68	1123	16.5	59.1	5
Green Bay	2	8	146	18.3	73.0	0
Houston	6	20	305	15.3	50.8	1
Indianapolis	10	20	270	13.5	27.0	2
Kansas City	4	12	220	18.3	55.0	0
L.A. Raiders	5	16	265	16.6	53.0	2
L.A. Rams	10	40	704	17.6	70.4	3
Miami	10	31	488	15.7	48.8	2
Minnesota	18	68	1312	19.3	72.9	7
New England	10	24	492	20.5	49.2	3
New Orleans	9	27	539	20.0	59.9	6
N.Y. Giants	7	27	524	19.4	74.9	1
N.Y. Jets	12	34	675	19.9	56.3	4
Philadelphia	3	12	269	22.4	89.7	2
Phoenix	3	16	244	15.3	81.3	1
Pittsburgh	5	18	423	23.5	84.6	6
San Diego	5	15	337	22.5	67.4	2
San Francisco	6	21	309	14.7	51.5	0
Seattle	8	21	448	21.3	56.0	6
Tampa Bay	17	63	1089	17.3	64.1	4
Washington	4	10	191	19.1	47.8	0
Totals	223	750	13,821	18.4	62.0	75

Indianapolis totals include one game vs. Baltimore
L.A. Raiders totals include one game vs. Oakland
Phoenix totals include two games vs. St. Louis

Art Monk's Career Receiving vs. Each Opponent

Opponent	Games	Rec.	Yards	Yards Per Rec.	Yards Per Game	TD
Atlanta	8	39	583	14.9	72.9	7
Buffalo	4	28	263	9.4	65.8	2
Chicago	7	36	496	13.8	70.9	4
Cincinnati	3	21	366	17.4	122.0	1
Cleveland	3	11	146	13.3	48.7	1
Dallas	22	90	1264	14.0	57.5	2
Denver	4	21	261	12.4	65.3	2
Detroit	8	39	426	10.9	53.3	2
Green Bay	3	10	148	14.8	49.3	1
Houston	3	16	147	9.2	49.0	0
Indianapolis	3	19	340	17.9	113.3	5
Kansas City	1	2	19	9.5	19.0	0
L.A. Raiders	5	14	258	18.4	51.6	1
L.A. Rams	4	15	306	20.4	76.5	2
Miami	3	17	188	11.1	62.7	2
Minnesota	4	18	226	12.6	56.5	1
New England	3	9	100	11.1	33.3	0
New Orleans	7	32	440	13.8	62.9	2
N.Y. Giants	24	95	1251	13.2	52.1	3
N.Y. Jets	1	3	70	23.3	70.0	0
Philadelphia	25	96	1245	13.0	49.8	8
Phoenix	25	106	1496	14.1	59.8	14
Pittsburgh	3	23	281	12.2	93.7	1
San Diego	4	23	361	15.7	90.3	0
San Francisco	6	40	583	14.6	97.2	2
Seattle	4	12	226	18.8	56.5	0
Tampa Bay	2	12	138	11.5	69.0	0
Totals	189	847	11,628	13.7	61.5	63

Indianapolis totals include one game vs. Baltimore
L.A. Raiders totals include one game vs. Oakland
Phoenix totals include 15 games vs. St. Louis

Starting Records of Active NFL Quarterbacks
Minimum: 10 starts

	W-L-T	Pct.
Joe Montana	100-39	.719
Jim McMahon	59-25	.702
Stan Humphries	14- 6	.700
Mark Rypien	42-20	.677
Cody Carlson	8- 4	.667
Bobby Hebert	49-26	.653
Jay Schroeder	57-31	.648
Jeff Hostetler	16- 9	.640
Steve Beuerlein	12- 7	.632
John Elway	89-52-1	.630
Jim Kelly	64-38	.627
Dan Marino	93-56	.624
Brett Favre	8- 5	.615
Erik Kramer	8- 5	.615
Randall Cunningham	51-33-1	.606
Dave Krieg	80-55	.593
Phil Simms	84-59	.587
Mike Tomczak	27-19	.587
Jim Harbaugh	28-22	.560
Neil O'Donnell	11- 9	.550
Wade Wilson	28-23	.549
Rich Gannon	19-16	.543
Bob Gagliano	7- 6	.538
Steve Young	29-26	.527
Bernie Kosar	50-48-1	.510
Troy Aikman	27-27	.500
Boomer Esiason	58-60	.492
Bubby Brister	28-29	.491
Warren Moon	60-65	.480
Ken O'Brien	50-55-1	.476
Don Majkowski	22-26-1	.459
Jim Everett	43-53	.448
Steve Walsh	10-13	.435
Billy Joe Tolliver	11-15	.423
Rodney Peete	15-22	.405
Steve DeBerg	51-82-1	.384
Jack Trudeau	16-26	.381
Chris Chandler	14-23	.378
Chris Miller	23-41	.359
Rusty Hilger	5- 9	.357
Vinny Testaverde	24-48	.333
Mike Pagel	17-36-1	.324
Jeff George	12-26	.316
Kelly Stouffer	5-11	.313
Tom Tupa	4- 9	.308
Hugh Millen	7-16	.304

Timm Rosenbach	5-15	.250
Jeff Rutledge	2- 7-1	.250
John Friesz	4-13	.235
Browning Nagle	3-10	.231
Chuck Long	4-17	.190
Tom Hodson	1-11	.083
Stan Gelbaugh	0-11	.000

Individual NFL Leaders Over Recent Seasons

Last 2 Seasons	Last 3 Seasons	Last 4 Seasons
Points		
269, Chip Lohmiller	400, Chip Lohmiller	528, Chip Lohmiller
245, Pete Stoyanovich	354, Nick Lowery	460, Nick Lowery
233, Morten Andersen	345, Pete Stoyanovich	445, Mike Cofer
215, Nick Lowery	325, Morten Andersen	440, Pete Stoyanovich
213, Gary Anderson	309, Mike Cofer	429, Morten Andersen
	309, David Treadwell	429, David Treadwell
Touchdowns		
32, Emmitt Smith	43, Barry Sanders	57, Barry Sanders
27, Barry Sanders	43, Emmitt Smith	55, Jerry Rice
25, Jerry Rice	38, Jerry Rice	49, Thurman Thomas
24, Rodney Hampton	37, Thurman Thomas	48, Neal Anderson
24, Thurman Thomas	33, Neal Anderson	43, Emmitt Smith
	33, Andre Rison	
Field Goals		
61, Chip Lohmiller	91, Chip Lohmiller	120, Chip Lohmiller
61, Pete Stoyanovich	82, Pete Stoyanovich	105, Nick Lowery
54, Morten Andersen	81, Nick Lowery	101, Pete Stoyanovich
51, Gary Anderson	75, Morten Andersen	99, David Treadwell
47, Nick Lowery	72, David Treadwell	95, Morten Andersen
47, David Treadwell		
Rushes		
738, Emmitt Smith	979, Emmitt Smith	1189, Barry Sanders
654, Barry Sanders	909, Barry Sanders	1169, Thurman Thomas
600, Thurman Thomas	871, Thurman Thomas	984, Christian Okoye
536, Earnest Byner	833, Earnest Byner	979, Emmitt Smith
513, Rodney Hampton	676, Marion Butts	967, Earnest Byner
Rushing Yards		
3276, Emmitt Smith	4213, Emmitt Smith	5674, Barry Sanders
2900, Barry Sanders	4204, Barry Sanders	5435, Thurman Thomas
2894, Thurman Thomas	4191, Thurman Thomas	4213, Emmitt Smith
2200, Rodney Hampton	3265, Earnest Byner	3845, Earnest Byner
2178, Barry Foster	2868, Marion Butts	3764, Christian Okoye
Rushing TDs		
30, Emmitt Smith	41, Emmitt Smith	52, Barry Sanders
25, Barry Sanders	38, Barry Sanders	41, Emmitt Smith
24, Rodney Hampton	27, Thurman Thomas	34, Christian Okoye
18, Herschel Walker	26, Rodney Hampton	33, Thurman Thomas
17, Brad Baxter	25, Derrick Fenner	32, Neal Anderson
Passes		
1103, Dan Marino	1634, Dan Marino	2184, Dan Marino
1001, Warren Moon	1585, Warren Moon	2049, Warren Moon
965, Jim Everett	1519, Jim Everett	2037, Jim Everett
936, Jim Kelly	1282, Jim Kelly	1685, John Elway
900, Mark Rypien	1269, John Elway	1680, Mark Rypien
Completions		
648, Dan Marino	990, Warren Moon	1270, Warren Moon
628, Warren Moon	954, Dan Marino	1262, Dan Marino
573, Jim Kelly	865, Jim Everett	1169, Jim Everett
558, Jim Everett	792, Jim Kelly	1020, Jim Kelly
539, Troy Aikman	765, Troy Aikman	968, Dave Krieg
Passing Yards		
8086, Dan Marino	11900, Warren Moon	15646, Dan Marino
7301, Jim Kelly	11649, Dan Marino	15531, Warren Moon
7211, Warren Moon	10750, Jim Everett	15060, Jim Everett
6846, Mark Rypien	10130, Jim Kelly	13260, Jim Kelly
6761, Jim Everett	9021, John Elway	12684, Mark Rypien
TD Passes		
56, Jim Kelly	80, Jim Kelly	105, Jim Kelly
49, Dan Marino	74, Warren Moon	97, Warren Moon
42, Steve Young	70, Dan Marino	94, Dan Marino
41, Chris Miller	58, Chris Miller	85, Jim Everett
41, Warren Moon	57, Mark Rypien	79, Mark Rypien
41, Mark Rypien		
Receptions		
190, Haywood Jeffires	264, Haywood Jeffires	346, Jerry Rice
177, Sterling Sharpe	264, Jerry Rice	334, Sterling Sharpe
174, Andre Rison	256, Andre Rison	311, Haywood Jeffires
171, Michael Irvin	244, Sterling Sharpe	308, Andre Rison
164, Jerry Rice	224, Drew Hill	305, Andre Reed
Reception Yards		
2919, Michael Irvin	3909, Jerry Rice	5392, Jerry Rice
2422, Sterling Sharpe	3527, Sterling Sharpe	4950, Sterling Sharpe
2407, Jerry Rice	3364, Gary Clark	4593, Gary Clark
2252, Gary Clark	3332, Michael Irvin	4455, Henry Ellard
2095, Andre Rison	3303, Andre Rison	4283, Andre Reed

Last 2 Seasons	Last 3 Seasons	Last 4 Seasons
Receiving TDs		
24, Jerry Rice	37, Jerry Rice	54, Jerry Rice
23, Andre Rison	33, Andre Rison	37, Andre Rison
21, Michael Haynes	24, Ernest Givins	35, Sterling Sharpe
17, Sterling Sharpe	24, Haywood Jeffires	32, Gary Clark
16, Haywood Jeffires	23, Gary Clark	30, Andre Reed
	23, Sterling Sharpe	
Interceptions		
12, Audray McMillian	17, Gill Byrd	24, Gill Byrd
12, Eugene Robinson	15, Audray McMillian	20, Eric Allen
10, six players	15, Louis Oliver	20, Eugene Robinson
	15, Eugene Robinson	19, David Fulcher
	13, five players	19, Louis Oliver
Sacks		
32.0, Clyde Simmons	48.0, Derrick Thomas	58.0, Derrick Thomas
29.5, Simon Fletcher	43.0, Reggie White	55.0, Clyde Simmons
29.0, Reggie White	40.5, Simon Fletcher	55.0, Pat Swilling
28.0, Derrick Thomas	39.5, Leslie O'Neal	54.0, Reggie White
27.5, Pat Swilling	39.5, Clyde Simmons	53.5, Chris Doleman

NFL Team Leaders Over Recent Seasons

Last 2 Seasons	Last 3 Seasons	Last 4 Seasons
Highest Won-Lost Percentage		
.750, Buffalo	.792, San Francisco	.813, San Francisco
.750, Dallas	.771, Buffalo	.719, Buffalo
.750, San Francisco	.688, Washington	.672, Washington
.719, New Orleans	.646, five teams	.656, Philadelphia
.719, Washington		.625, New Orleans
Most Points		
839, Buffalo	1267, Buffalo	1676, Buffalo
824, San Francisco	1177, San Francisco	1619, San Francisco
785, Washington	1166, Washington	1552, Washington
751, Dallas	1143, Houston	1508, Houston
738, Houston	1039, Kansas City	1377, Minnesota
		1377, Philadelphia
Most Total Yards		
12145, Buffalo	17948, San Francisco	24216, San Francisco
12053, San Francisco	17864, Houston	23291, Houston
11642, Houston	17421, Buffalo	23274, Buffalo
10741, Miami	16193, Washington	22446, Washington
10707, Dallas	15788, Miami	21334, Miami
Most Rushing Yards		
4817, Buffalo	6897, Buffalo	9161, Buffalo
4231, Minnesota	6380, San Diego	8548, Philadelphia
4176, San Francisco	6340, Philadelphia	8543, Chicago
4141, N.Y. Giants	6256, Chicago	8390, Cincinnati
4123, San Diego	6190, N.Y. Giants	8253, San Diego
Most Passing Yards		
8650, Houston	13455, Houston	16954, Houston
7877, San Francisco	12054, San Francisco	16356, San Francisco
7864, Miami	11376, Miami	15592, Miami
7328, Buffalo	10543, Atlanta	14683, Washington
7082, Atlanta	10524, Buffalo	14579, L.A. Rams
Fewest Turnovers		
43, Kansas City	60, N.Y. Giants	90, N.Y. Giants
45, Cleveland	62, Kansas City	103, Kansas City
46, N.Y. Giants	75, Washington	108, San Francisco
47, Washington	81, Dallas	112, Washington
48, Dallas	83, San Francisco	121, Cleveland
Fewest Points Allowed		
413, New Orleans	688, New Orleans	967, San Francisco
475, San Francisco	714, San Francisco	989, New Orleans
479, Washington	780, Washington	1062, Philadelphia
489, Philadelphia	788, Philadelphia	1077, Kansas City
509, Houston	791, Kansas City	1088, Washington
Fewest Total Yards Allowed		
7960, Philadelphia	12620, Philadelphia	17514, Philadelphia
8008, New Orleans	12886, New Orleans	18072, New Orleans
8731, Washington	13461, Washington	18232, San Francisco
8968, Houston	13603, Houston	18376, Washington
8997, Dallas	13612, Dallas	18432, Minnesota
Fewest Rushing Yards Allowed		
2617, Philadelphia	3786, Philadelphia	5391, Philadelphia
2815, Dallas	4188, San Francisco	5571, San Francisco
2818, New Orleans	4377, New Orleans	5703, New Orleans
2930, San Francisco	4576, San Diego	5973, Washington
3042, Washington	4629, Washington	6389, San Diego
Fewest Passing Yards Allowed		
5190, New Orleans	8509, New Orleans	11105, Minnesota
5343, Philadelphia	8604, Minnesota	11533, Kansas City
5680, Seattle	8652, N.Y. Giants	11777, N.Y. Giants
5689, Washington	8684, Seattle	11781, Seattle
5700, Indianapolis	8804, Miami	12869, L.A. Raiders

Last 2 Seasons	Last 3 Seasons	Last 4 Seasons
Most Opponents' Turnovers		
86, New Orleans	117, Kansas City	171, Philadelphia
85, Philadelphia	115, Philadelphia	157, Pittsburgh
76, N.Y. Jets	115, Pittsburgh	152, New Orleans
74, Washington	113, New Orleans	150, Kansas City
73, Pittsburgh	107, Buffalo	149, Washington
	107, Washington	

Records of Teams on Opening Day, 1933-92

AFC	W	L	T	Pct.	Longest W Strk.	Longest L Strk.	Current Streak
Denver	20	12	1	.625	3	4	W-2
L.A. Raiders	19	14	0	.576	5	5	L-2
Cleveland	24	19	0	.558	5	5	L-2
Kansas City	18	15	0	.545	5	4	W-3
San Diego	18	15	0	.545	6	6	L-6
Pittsburgh	29	25	4	.537	4	3	W-2
Indianapolis	21	19	0	.525	8	8	W-1
Cincinnati	13	12	0	.520	4	4	W-1
Houston	17	16	0	.515	4	3	L-1
New England	16	17	0	.485	6	3	L-1
Miami	12	14	1	.462	4	5	W-1
Buffalo	14	19	0	.424	5	5	W-5
N.Y. Jets	14	19	0	.424	3	5	L-1
Seattle	4	13	0	.235	3	8	L-4

NFC	W	L	T	Pct.	Longest W Strk.	Longest L Strk.	Current Streak
Dallas	25	7	1	.781	17	3	W-3
Chicago	35	24	1	.593	9	6	W-9
N.Y. Giants	33	23	4	.589	4	3	L-1
Minnesota	18	13	1	.581	4	2	W-1
Atlanta	15	12	0	.556	5	3	W-1
L.A. Rams	29	26	0	.527	5	6	L-3
Washington	29	27	4	.518	6	5	L-1
Detroit	30	28	2	.517	7	4	L-4
Green Bay	29	28	3	.509	5	6	L-2
San Francisco	20	22	1	.476	4	3	W-1
Phoenix	26	32	1	.448	6	6	L-1
Philadelphia	24	34	1	.414	5	9	W-2
Tampa Bay	7	10	0	.412	3	5	W-1
New Orleans	6	20	0	.231	1	6	L-1

NOTE: All tied games occurred prior to 1972, when calculation of ties in percentages as half-win, half-loss was begun.

Oldest Individual Single-Season or Single-Game Records in NFL Record & Fact Book

Regular-Season Records That Have Not Been Surpassed or Tied

Most Points, Game — 40, Ernie Nevers, Chi. Cardinals vs. Chi. Bears, Nov. 28, 1929 (6-td, 4-pat)

Most Touchdowns Rushing, Game — 6, Ernie Nevers, Chi. Cardinals vs. Chi. Bears, Nov. 28, 1929

Highest Punting Average, Season (Qualifiers) — 51.40, Sammy Baugh, Washington, 1940 (35-1,799)

Highest Punting Average, Game (minimum: 4 punts) — 61.75, Bob Cifers, Detroit vs. Chi. Bears, Nov. 24, 1946 (4-247)

Highest Average Gain, Pass Receptions, Season (minimum: 24 receptions) — 32.58, Don Currivan, Boston, 1947 (24-782)

Highest Average Gain, Passing, Game (minimum: 20 passes) — 18.58, Sammy Baugh, Washington vs. Boston, Oct. 31, 1948 (24-446)

Most Touchdowns, Fumble Recoveries, Game — 2, Fred (Dippy) Evans, Chi. Bears vs. Washington, Nov. 28, 1948

Most Yards Gained, Intercepted Passes, Rookie, Season — 301, Don Doll, Detroit, 1949

Most Passes Had Intercepted, Game — 8, Jim Hardy, Chi. Cardinals vs. Philadelphia, Sept. 24, 1950

Highest Average Gain, Rushing, Game (minimum: 10 attempts) — 17.09, Marion Motley, Cleveland vs. Pittsburgh, Oct. 29, 1950 (11-188)

Most Yards Gained, Kickoff Returns, Game — 294, Wally Triplett, Detroit vs. Los Angeles, Oct. 29, 1950

Highest Kickoff Return Average, Game (minimum: 3 returns) — 73.50, Wally Triplett, Detroit vs. Los Angeles, Oct. 29, 1950 (4-294)

Most Pass Receptions, Game — 18, Tom Fears, Los Angeles vs. Green Bay, Dec. 3, 1950

Highest Punt Return Average, Season (Qualifiers) — 23.00, Herb Rich, Baltimore, 1950 (12-276)

Highest Punt Return Average, Rookie, Season (Qualifiers) — 23.00, Herb Rich, Baltimore, 1950 (12-276)

Most Yards Passing, Game — 554, Norm Van Brocklin, Los Angeles vs. N.Y. Yanks, Sept. 28, 1951

Most Touchdowns, Punt Returns, Rookie, Season — 4, Jack Christiansen, Detroit, 1951

Most Interceptions By, Season — 14, Dick (Night Train) Lane, Los Angeles, 1952

Most Interceptions By, Rookie, Season — 14, Dick (Night Train) Lane, Los Angeles, 1952

Highest Average Gain, Passing, Season (Qualifiers) — 11.17, Tommy O'Connell, Cleveland, 1957 (110-1,229)

Most Points, Season — 176, Paul Hornung, Green Bay, 1960 (15-td, 41-pat, 15-fg)

Most Yards Gained, Pass Receptions, Rookie, Season — 1,473, Bill Groman, Houston, 1960

Largest Trades in NFL History

(Based on number of players or draft choices involved)

18 — October 13, 1989 — RB Herschel Walker from the Dallas Cowboys to Minnesota. Dallas also traded its third-round choice in 1990, its tenth-round choice in 1990, and its third-round choice in 1991 to Minnesota. Minnesota traded LB Jesse Solomon, LB David Howard, CB Issiac Holt, and DE Alex Stewart along with its first-round choice in 1990, its second-round choice in 1990, its sixth-round choice in 1990, its first-round choice in 1991, its second-round choice in 1991, its first-round choice in 1992, its second-round choice in 1992, and its third-round choice in 1992 to Dallas. Minnesota traded RB Darrin Nelson to Dallas, which traded Nelson to San Diego for the Chargers' fifth-round choice in 1990, which Dallas then sent to Minnesota.

15 — March 26, 1953 — T Mike McCormack, DT Don Colo, LB Tom Catlin, DB John Petitbon, and G Herschell Forester from Baltimore to Cleveland for DB Don Shula, DB Bert Rechichar, DB Carl Taseff, LB Ed Sharkey, E Gern Nagler, QB Harry Agganis, T Dick Batten, T Stu Sheets, G Art Spinney, and G Elmer Willhoite.

15 — January 28, 1971 — LB Marlin McKeever, first- and third-round choices in 1971, and third-, fourth-, fifth-, sixth-, and seventh-round choices in 1972 from Washington to the Los Angeles Rams for LB Maxie Baughan, LB Jack Pardee, LB Myron Pottios, RB Jeff Jordan, G John Wilbur, DT Diron Talbert, and a fifth-round choice in 1971.

12 — June 13, 1952 — Selection rights to Les Richter from the Dallas Texans to the Los Angeles Rams for RB Dick Hoerner, DB Tom Keane, DB George Sims, C Joe Reid, HB Billy Baggett, T Jack Halliday, FB Dick McKissack, LB Vic Vasicek, E Richard Wilkins, C Aubrey Phillips, and RB Dave Anderson.

10 — March 23, 1959 — HB Ollie Matson from the Chicago Cardinals to the Los Angeles Rams for T Frank Fuller, DE Glenn Holtzman, T Ken Panfil, DT Art Hauser, E John Tracey, FB Larry Hickman, HB Don Brown, the Rams second-round choice in 1960, and a player to be delivered during the 1959 training camp.

10 — October 31, 1987 — RB Eric Dickerson from the Los Angeles Rams to Indianapolis. The rights to LB Cornelius Bennett from Indianapolis to Buffalo. Indianapolis running back Owen Gill and the Colts' first- and second-round choices in 1988 and second-round choice in 1989, plus Bills running back Greg Bell and Buffalo's first-round choice in 1988 and first- and second-round choices in 1989 to the Rams.

Retired Uniform Numbers in NFL

AFC

Team	Player	No.
Buffalo:	None	
Cincinnati:	Bob Johnson	54
Cleveland:	Otto Graham	14
	Jim Brown	32
	Ernie Davis	45
	Don Fleming	46
	Lou Groza	76
Denver:	Frank Tripucka	18
	Floyd Little	44
Houston:	Earl Campbell	34
	Jim Norton	43
	Elvin Bethea	65
Indianapolis:	Johnny Unitas	19
	Buddy Young	22
	Lenny Moore	24
	Art Donovan	70
	Jim Parker	77
	Raymond Berry	82
	Gino Marchetti	89
Kansas City:	Jan Stenerud	3
	Len Dawson	16
	Abner Haynes	28
	Stone Johnson	33
	Mack Lee Hill	36
	Bobby Bell	78
	Buck Buchanan	86
Los Angeles Raiders:	None	
Miami:	Bob Griese	12
New England:	Gino Cappelletti	20
	Steve Nelson	57
	John Hannah	73
	Jim Hunt	79
	Bob Dee	89
New York Jets:	Joe Namath	12
	Don Maynard	13
Pittsburgh:	None	
San Diego:	Dan Fouts	14
Seattle:	"Fans/the twelfth man"	12

NFC

Team	Player	No.
Atlanta:	William Andrews	31
	Jeff Van Note	57
	Tommy Nobis	60
Chicago:	Bronko Nagurski	3
	George McAfee	5
	Willie Galimore	28
	Walter Payton	34
	Brian Piccolo	41

Chicago:	Sid Luckman	42
	Bill Hewitt	56
	Bill George	61
	Bulldog Turner	66
	Red Grange	77
Dallas:	None	
Detroit:	Dutch Clark	7
	Bobby Layne	22
	Doak Walker	37
	Joe Schmidt	56
	Chuck Hughes	85
	Charlie Sanders	88
Green Bay:	Tony Canadeo	3
	Don Hutson	14
	Bart Starr	15
	Ray Nitschke	66
Los Angeles Rams:	Bob Waterfield	7
	Merlin Olsen	74
Minnesota:	Fran Tarkenton	10
	Alan Page	88
New Orleans:	Jim Taylor	31
	Doug Atkins	81
New York Giants:	Ray Flaherty	1
	Mel Hein	7
	Y.A. Tittle	14
	Al Blozis	32
	Joe Morrison	40
	Charlie Conerly	42
	Ken Strong	50
Philadelphia:	Steve Van Buren	15
	Tom Brookshier	40
	Pete Retzlaff	44
	Chuck Bednarik	60
	Al Wistert	70
	Jerome Brown	99
Phoenix:	Larry Wilson	8
	Stan Mauldin	77
	J.V. Cain	88
	Marshall Goldberg	99
San Francisco:	John Brodie	12
	Joe Perry	34
	Jimmy Johnson	37
	Hugh McElhenny	39
	Charlie Krueger	70
	Leo Nomellini	73
	Dwight Clark	87
Tampa Bay:	Lee Roy Selmon	63
Washington:	Sammy Baugh	33

1992 NFL Score by Quarters

AFC Offense	1	2	3	4	OT	PTS
Buffalo	77	118	105	81	0	381
Houston	81	75	80	113	3	352
Kansas City	53	128	66	101	0	348
Miami	75	85	87	90	3	340
San Diego	69	92	72	102	0	335
Pittsburgh	58	90	51	100	0	299
Cincinnati	48	84	55	81	6	274
Cleveland	63	31	76	102	0	272
Denver	61	40	63	98	0	262
L.A. Raiders	43	83	61	62	0	249
N.Y. Jets	24	80	56	60	0	220
Indianapolis	38	29	58	85	6	216
New England	61	51	32	58	3	205
Seattle	20	53	34	30	3	140

NFC Offense	1	2	3	4	OT	PTS
San Francisco	87	135	78	131	0	431
Dallas	108	116	134	51	0	409
Minnesota	87	91	64	129	3	374
Philadelphia	45	109	89	108	3	354
New Orleans	70	86	91	83	0	330
Atlanta	94	96	55	82	0	327
L.A. Rams	42	73	86	112	0	313
N.Y. Giants	51	104	86	65	0	306
Washington	79	92	63	66	0	300
Chicago	57	98	51	89	0	295
Green Bay	48	115	25	88	0	276
Detroit	37	99	65	72	0	273
Tampa Bay	60	107	31	69	0	267
Phoenix	58	70	43	72	0	243

AFC Defense	1	2	3	4	OT	PTS
Pittsburgh	33	86	56	50	0	225
San Diego	62	46	59	74	0	241
Houston	23	96	50	89	0	258
Cleveland	55	47	80	93	0	275
L.A. Raiders	48	98	48	84	3	281
Miami	49	80	71	81	0	281
Kansas City	68	57	64	90	3	282
Buffalo	46	101	72	61	3	283
Indianapolis	80	71	69	79	3	302
Seattle	63	87	74	85	3	312
N.Y. Jets	57	93	58	104	3	315
Denver	51	121	74	80	3	329
New England	84	80	88	108	3	363
Cincinnati	81	98	91	94	0	364

NFC Defense	1	2	3	4	OT	PTS
New Orleans	26	64	31	81	0	202
San Francisco	37	56	74	69	0	236
Dallas	54	53	51	85	0	243
Philadelphia	47	87	30	81	0	245
Minnesota	57	92	31	69	0	249
Washington	32	103	40	80	0	255
Green Bay	73	73	71	76	3	296
Detroit	83	82	34	133	0	332
Phoenix	62	108	88	74	0	332
Chicago	58	83	93	124	3	361
Tampa Bay	88	70	112	95	0	365
N.Y. Giants	83	110	95	79	0	367
L.A. Rams	94	151	57	81	0	383
Atlanta	100	137	96	81	0	414

NFL TOTALS	1	2	3	4	OT	PTS
	1694	2430	1857	2380	30	8391

Team Leaders

Offense	Most Scored	Fewest Scored
1st Quarter	108, Dallas	20, Seattle
2nd Quarter	135, San Francisco	29, Indianapolis
3rd Quarter	134, Dallas	25, Green Bay
4th Quarter	131, San Francisco	30, Seattle

Defense	Most Allowed	Fewest Allowed
1st Quarter	100, Atlanta	23, Houston
2nd Quarter	151, L.A. Rams	46, San Diego
3rd Quarter	112, Tampa Bay	30, Philadelphia
4th Quarter	133, Detroit	50, Pittsburgh

Greatest Comebacks in NFL History (Most Points Overcome To Win Game)

Regular-Season Games

From 28 points behind to win:
December 7, 1980, at San Francisco

New Orleans	14	21	0	0	0	— 35
San Francisco	0	7	14	14	3	— 38

NO — Harris 33 pass from Manning (Ricardo kick)
NO — Childs 21 pass from Manning (Ricardo kick)
NO — Holmes 1 run (Ricardo kick)
SF — Solomon 57 punt return (Wersching kick)
NO — Holmes 1 run (Ricardo kick)
NO — Harris 41 pass from Manning (Ricardo kick)
SF — Montana 1 run (Wersching kick)
SF — Clark 71 pass from Montana (Wersching kick)
SF — Solomon 14 pass from Montana (Wersching kick)
SF — Elliott 7 run (Wersching kick)
SF — FG Wersching 36

	N.O.	S.F.
First Downs	27	24
Total Yards	519	430
Yards Rushing	143	176
Yards Passing	376	254
Turnovers	3	0

From 25 points behind to win:
November 8, 1987, at St. Louis

Tampa Bay	7	7	14	0	— 28
St. Louis	0	3	0	28	— 31

TB — Carrier 5 pass from DeBerg (Igwebuike kick)
TB — Carter 3 pass from DeBerg (Igwebuike kick)
StL — FG Gallery 31
TB — Smith 34 pass from DeBerg (Igwebuike kick)
TB — Smith 3 run (Igwebuike kick)
StL — Awalt 4 pass from Lomax (Gallery kick)
StL — Noga 23 fumble recovery (Gallery kick)
StL — J. Smith 11 pass from Lomax (Gallery kick)
StL — J. Smith 17 pass from Lomax (Gallery kick)

	T.B.	St.L.
First Downs	26	26
Total Yards	377	415
Yards Rushing	83	137
Yards Passing	294	278
Turnovers	1	2

From 24 points behind to win:
October 27, 1946, at Washington

Philadelphia	0	0	14	14	— 28
Washington	10	14	0	0	— 24

Wash — Rosato 2 run (Poillon kick)
Wash — FG Poillon 28
Wash — Rosato 4 run (Poillon kick)
Wash — Lapka recovered fumble in end zone (Poillon kick)
Phil — Steele 1 run (Lio kick)
Phil — Pritchard 45 pass from Thompson (Lio kick)
Phil — Steinke 7 pass from Thompson (Lio kick)
Phil — Ferrante 30 pass from Thompson (Lio kick)

	Phil.	Wash.
First Downs	14	8
Total Yards	262	127
Yards Rushing	34	66
Yards Passing	228	61
Turnovers	6	3

From 24 points behind to win:
October 20, 1957, at Detroit

Baltimore	7	14	6	0	— 27
Detroit	0	3	7	21	— 31

Balt —Mutscheller 15 pass from Unitas (Rechichar kick)
Det —FG Martin 47
Balt —Moore 72 pass from Unitas (Rechichar kick)
Balt —Mutscheller 52 pass from Unitas (Rechichar kick)
Balt —Moore 4 pass from Unitas (kick failed)
Det —Junker 14 pass from Rote (Layne kick)
Det —Cassady 26 pass from Layne (Layne kick)
Det —Johnson 1 run (Layne kick)
Det —Cassady 29 pass from Layne (Layne kick)

	Balt.	Det.
First Downs	15	20
Total Yards	322	369
Yards Rushing	117	178
Yards Passing	205	191
Turnovers	6	4

From 24 points behind to win:
October 25, 1959, at Chicago

Philadelphia	0	0	21	7	— 28
Chi. Cardinals	7	10	7	0	— 24

Chi —Crow 10 pass from Roach (Conrad kick)
Chi —J. Hill 77 blocked field goal return (Conrad kick)
Chi —FG Conrad 15
Chi —Lane 37 interception return (Conrad kick)
Phil —Barnes 1 run (Walston kick)
Phil —McDonald 29 pass from Van Brocklin (Walston kick)
Phil —Barnes 2 run (Walston kick)
Phil —McDonald 22 pass from Van Brocklin (Walston kick)

	Phil.	Chi.
First Downs	22	14
Total Yards	399	313
Yards Rushing	168	163
Yards Passing	231	150
Turnovers	2	6

From 24 points behind to win:
October 23, 1960, at Denver

Boston	10	7	7	0	— 24
Denver	0	0	14	17	— 31

Bos — FG Cappelletti 12
Bos — Colclough 10 pass from Songin (Cappelletti kick)
Bos — Wells 6 pass from Songin (Cappelletti kick)
Bos — Miller 47 pass from Songin (Cappelletti kick)
Den — Carmichael 21 pass from Tripucka (Mingo kick)
Den — Jessup 19 pass from Tripucka (Mingo kick)
Den — Carmichael 35 lateral from Taylor, pass from Tripucka (Mingo kick)
Den — Taylor 8 pass from Tripucka (Mingo kick)
Den — FG Mingo 9

	Bos.	Den.
First Downs	19	16
Total Yards	434	326
Yards Rushing	211	65
Yards Passing	223	261
Turnovers	7	4

From 24 points behind to win:
December 15, 1974, at Miami

New England	21	3	0	3	— 27
Miami	0	17	7	10	— 34

NE — Hannah recovered fumble in end zone (J. Smith kick)
NE — Sanders 23 interception return (J. Smith kick)
NE — Herron 4 pass from Plunkett (J. Smith kick)
NE — FG J. Smith 46
Mia — Nottingham 1 run (Yepremian kick)
Mia — Baker 37 pass from Morrall (Yepremian kick)
Mia — FG Yepremian 28
Mia — Baker 46 pass from Morrall (Yepremian kick)
NE — FG J. Smith 34
Mia — Nottingham 2 run (Yepremian kick)
Mia — FG Yepremian 40

	N.E.	Mia.
First Downs	18	18
Total Yards	333	333
Yards Rushing	114	61
Yards Passing	219	272
Turnovers	3	4

From 24 points behind to win:
December 4, 1977, at Minnesota

San Francisco	0	10	14	3	— 27
Minnesota	0	0	7	21	— 28

SF — Delvin Williams 2 run (Wersching kick)
SF — FG Wersching 31
SF — Dave Williams 80 kickoff return (Wersching kick)
SF — Delvin Williams 5 run (Wersching kick)
Minn — McClanahan 15 pass from Lee (Cox kick)
Minn — Rashad 8 pass from Kramer (Cox kick)
Minn — Tucker 9 pass from Kramer (Cox kick)
SF — FG Wersching 31
Minn — S. White 69 pass from Kramer (Cox kick)

	S.F.	Minn.
First Downs	19	18
Total Yards	243	309
Yards Rushing	196	52
Yards Passing	47	257
Turnovers	2	5

From 24 points behind to win:
September 23, 1979, at Denver

Seattle	10	10	14	0	— 34
Denver	0	10	21	6	— 37

Sea — FG Herrera 28
Sea — Doornink 5 run (Herrera kick)
Den — FG Turner 27
Sea — Doornink 5 run (Herrera kick)
Den — Armstrong 2 run (Turner kick)
Sea — FG Herrera 22
Sea — McCullum 13 pass from Zorn (Herrera kick)
Sea — Smith 1 run (Herrera kick)
Den — Studdard 2 pass from Morton (Turner kick)
Den — Moses 11 pass from Morton (Turner kick)
Den — Upchurch 35 pass from Morton (Turner kick)
Den — Lytle 1 run (kick failed)

	Sea.	Den.
First Downs	22	23
Total Yards	350	344
Yards Rushing	153	90
Yards Passing	197	254
Turnovers	4	3

From 24 points behind to win:
September 23, 1979, at Cincinnati

Houston	0	10	17	0	3	— 30
Cincinnati	14	10	0	3	0	— 27

Cin — Johnson 1 run (Bahr kick)
Cin — Alexander 2 run (Bahr kick)
Cin — Johnson 1 run (Bahr kick)
Cin — FG Bahr 52
Hou — Burrough 35 pass from Pastorini (Fritsch kick)
Hou — FG Fritsch 33
Hou — Campbell 8 run (Fritsch kick)
Hou — Caster 22 pass from Pastorini (Fritsch kick)
Hou — FG Fritsch 47
Cin — FG Bahr 55
Hou — FG Fritsch 29

	Hou.	Cin.
First Downs	19	21
Total Yards	361	265
Yards Rushing	177	165
Yards Passing	184	100
Turnovers	3	2

From 24 points behind to win:
November 22, 1982, at Los Angeles

San Diego	10	14	0	0	— 24
L.A. Raiders	0	7	14	7	— 28

SD — FG Benirschke 19
SD — Scales 29 pass from Fouts (Benirschke kick)
SD — Muncie 2 run (Benirschke kick)
SD — Muncie 1 run (Benirschke kick)
Raiders — Christensen 1 pass from Plunkett (Bahr kick)
Raiders — Allen 3 run (Bahr kick)
Raiders — Allen 6 run (Bahr kick)
Raiders — Hawkins 1 run (Bahr kick)

	S.D.	Raiders
First Downs	26	23
Total Yards	411	326
Yards Rushing	72	181
Yards Passing	339	145
Turnovers	4	2

From 24 points behind to win:
September 26, 1988, at Denver

L.A. Raiders	0	0	14	13	3 — 30
Denver	7	17	0	3	0 — 27

Den — Dorsett 1 run (Karlis kick)
Den — Dorsett 1 run (Karlis kick)
Den — Sewell 7 pass from Elway (Karlis kick)
Den — FG Karlis 39
Raiders — Smith 40 pass from Schroeder (Bahr kick)
Raiders — Smith 42 pass from Schroeder (Bahr kick)
Raiders — FG Bahr 28
Raiders — Allen 4 run (Bahr kick)
Den — FG Karlis 25
Raiders — FG Bahr 44
Raiders — FG Bahr 35

	Raiders	Den.
First Downs	20	23
Total Yards	363	398
Yards Rushing	128	189
Yards Passing	235	209
Turnovers	1	5

From 24 points behind to win:
December 6, 1992, at Tampa

L.A. Rams	0	3	21	7 — 31
Tampa Bay	6	21	0	0 — 27

TB — FG Murray 34
TB — FG Murray 47
TB — Armstrong 81 pass from Testaverde (Murray kick)
TB — Jones 26 fumble recovery (Murray kick)
Rams — FG Zendejas 18
TB — Carrier 10 pass from Testaverde (Murray kick)
Rams — Anderson 40 pass from Everett (Zendejas kick)
Rams — Chadwick 27 pass from Everett (Zendejas kick)
Rams — Lang 1 run (Zendejas kick)
Rams — Carter 8 pass from Everett (Zendejas kick)

	Rams	T.B.
First Downs	21	16
Total Yards	405	313
Yards Rushing	63	150
Yards Passing	342	163
Turnovers	3	3

Postseason Games

From 32 points behind to win:
AFC First-Round Playoff Game
January 3, 1993, at Buffalo

Houston	7	21	7	3	0 — 38
Buffalo	3	0	28	7	3 — 41

Hou — Jeffires 3 pass from Moon (Del Greco kick)
Buff — FG Christie 36
Hou — Slaughter 7 pass from Moon (Del Greco kick)
Hou — Duncan 26 pass from Moon (Del Greco kick)
Hou — Jeffires 27 pass from Moon (Del Greco kick)
Hou — McDowell 58 interception return (Del Greco kick)
Buff — Davis 1 run (Christie kick)
Buff — Beebe 38 pass from Reich (Christie kick)
Buff — Reed 26 pass from Reich (Christie kick)
Buff — Reed 18 pass from Reich (Christie kick)
Buff — Reed 17 pass from Reich (Christie kick)
Hou — FG Del Greco 26
Buff — FG Christie 32

	Hou.	Buff.
First Downs	27	19
Total Yards	429	366
Yards Rushing	82	98
Yards Passing	347	268
Turnovers	2	1

From 20 points behind to win:
Western Conference Playoff Game
December 22, 1957, at San Francisco

Detroit	0	7	14	10 — 31
San Francisco	14	10	3	0 — 27

SF — Owens 34 pass from Tittle (Soltau kick)
SF — McElhenny 47 pass from Tittle (Soltau kick)
Det — Junker 4 pass from Rote (Martin kick)
SF — Wilson 12 pass from Tittle (Soltau kick)
SF — FG Soltau 25
SF — FG Soltau 10
Det — Tracy 2 run (Martin kick)
Det — Tracy 58 run (Martin kick)
Det — Gedman 3 run (Martin kick)
Det — FG Martin 14

	Det.	S.F.
First Downs	22	20
Total Yards	324	351
Yards Rushing	129	127
Yards Passing	195	224
Turnovers	5	4

From 18 points behind to win:
NFC Divisional Playoff Game
December 23, 1972, at San Francisco

Dallas	3	10	0	17 — 30
San Francisco	7	14	7	0 — 28

SF — Washington 97 kickoff return (Gossett kick)
Dall — FG Fritsch 37
SF — Schreiber 1 run (Gossett kick)
SF — Schreiber 1 run (Gossett kick)
Dall — FG Fritsch 45
Dall — Alworth 28 pass from Morton (Fritsch kick)
SF — Schreiber 1 run (Gossett kick)
Dall — FG Fritsch 27
Dall — Parks 20 pass from Staubach (Fritsch kick)
Dall — Sellers 10 pass from Staubach (Fritsch kick)

	Dall.	S.F.
First Downs	22	13
Total Yards	402	255
Yards Rushing	165	105
Yards Passing	237	150
Turnovers	5	3

From 18 points behind to win:
AFC Divisional Playoff Game
January 4, 1986, at Miami

Cleveland	7	7	7	0 — 21
Miami	3	0	14	7 — 24

Mia — FG Reveiz 51
Clev — Newsome 16 pass from Kosar (Bahr kick)
Clev — Byner 21 run (Bahr kick)
Clev — Byner 66 run (Bahr kick)
Mia — Moore 6 pass from Marino (Reveiz kick)
Mia — Davenport 31 run (Reveiz kick)
Mia — Davenport 1 run (Reveiz kick)

	Clev.	Mia.
First Downs	17	20
Total Yards	313	330
Yards Rushing	251	92
Yards Passing	62	238
Turnovers	1	1

Records of NFL Teams Since 1970 AFL-NFL Merger

AFC	W-L-T	Pct.	Division Titles	Playoff Berths	Post-season Record	Super Bowl Record
Miami	229-113-2	.669	10	14	16-12	2-3
L.A. Raiders	217-121-6	.641	9	14	17-11	3-0
Pittsburgh	203-140-1	.592	10	13	16-9	4-0
Denver	193-145-6	.570	7	9	9-9	0-4
Cleveland	171-170-3	.501	6	9	3-9	0-0
Cincinnati	172-172-0	.500	5	7	5-7	0-2
Kansas City	157-180-7	.466	1	5	1-5	0-0
Seattle*	121-139-0	.465	1	4	3-4	0-0
Buffalo	157-185-2	.459	5	8	9-8	0-3
San Diego	151-188-5	.446	4	5	4-5	0-0
New England	153-191-0	.445	2	5	3-5	0-1
Houston	152-190-2	.444	1	9	7-9	0-0
N.Y. Jets	144-198-2	.422	0	5	3-5	0-0
Indianapolis	144-198-2	.421	5	6	4-5	1-0

NFC	W-L-T	Pct.	Division Titles	Playoff Berths	Post-season Record	Super Bowl Record
Washington	221-122-1	.644	5	13	18-10	3-2
Dallas	215-129-0	.625	10	16	23-13	3-3
San Francisco	202-139-3	.592	12	13	17-9	4-0
Minnesota	201-141-2	.587	11	14	11-14	0-3
L.A. Rams	198-142-4	.582	8	14	10-14	0-1
Chicago	179-164-1	.522	6	9	6-8	1-0
Philadelphia	163-175-6	.482	2	8	4-8	0-1
N.Y. Giants	158-184-2	.462	3	6	9-4	2-0
Detroit	150-190-4	.442	2	4	1-4	0-0
Phoenix	144-194-6	.427	2	3	0-3	0-0
Green Bay	141-195-8	.421	1	2	1-2	0-0
New Orleans	140-200-4	.412	1	4	0-4	0-0
Atlanta	138-202-4	.406	1	4	2-4	0-0
Tampa Bay*	76-183-1	.294	2	3	1-3	0-0

*entered NFL in 1976.
Indianapolis totals include Baltimore, 1970-83.

L.A. Raiders totals include Oakland, 1970-81.
Phoenix totals include St. Louis, 1970-87.

Tie games before 1972 are not calculated in won-lost percentage.

In 1982, due to players' strike, the divisional format was abandoned. (L.A. Raiders and Washington won regular-season conference titles, not included in "Division Titles" totals listed above. Sixteen teams were awarded playoff berths, included in totals listed above.)

Longest Winning Streaks Since 1970

Regular-season games

16	Miami, 1971-73	(1 in 1971, 14 in 1972, 1 in 1973)
16	Miami, 1983-84	(5 in 1983, 11 in 1984)
15	San Francisco, 1989-90	(5 in 1989, 10 in 1990)
14	Oakland, 1976-77	(10 in 1976, 4 in 1977)
13	Chicago, 1984-85	(1 in 1984, 12 in 1985)
13	Minnesota, 1974-75	(3 in 1974, 10 in 1975)
13	N.Y. Giants, 1989-90	(3 in 1989, 10 in 1990)
12	Washington, 1990-91	(1 in 1990, 11 in 1991)
11	Pittsburgh, 1975	
11	Baltimore, 1975-76	(9 in 1975, 2 in 1976)
11	Chicago, 1986-87	(7 in 1986, 4 in 1987)
10	Miami, 1973	
10	Pittsburgh, 1976-77	(9 in 1976, 1 in 1977)
10	Denver, 1984	

NFL Playoff Appearances by Seasons

Team	Number of Seasons in Playoffs
Cleveland	22
Los Angeles Rams	22
New York Giants	22
Chicago	20
Dallas	20
Washington	19
Los Angeles Raiders	17
Minnesota	16
Houston	14
Miami	14
Pittsburgh	14
San Francisco	14
Green Bay	13
Buffalo	12
Philadelphia	12
Indianapolis	11
San Diego	10
Denver	9
Detroit	9
Kansas City	9
Cincinnati	7
New York Jets	7
New England	6
Phoenix	5
Atlanta	4
New Orleans	4
Seattle	4
Tampa Bay	3

Teams in Super Bowl Contention, 1978-92

	With 3 Weeks to Play	With 2 Weeks to Play	With 1 Week to Play
1992	20	16	14
1991	20	18	13
1990	23	20	15
1989	21	18	17
1988	21	18	15
1987	19	19	15
1986	19	17	14
1985	21	18	13
1984	18	14	13
1983	24	19	15
1982	20	17	12
1981	21	20	16
1980	20	14	12
1979	19	15	13
1978	20	17	12

Games Decided by 7 Points or Less and 3 Points or Less (1970-92)

	Games Decided by 7 Points or Less	Games Decided by 3 Points or Less
1970	59 of 182 (32.4%)	34 of 182 (18.7%)
1971	76 of 182 (41.8%)	35 of 182 (19.2%)
1972	71 of 182 (39.0%)	38 of 182 (20.9%)
1973	60 of 182 (32.9%)	28 of 182 (15.4%)
1974	91 of 182 (50.0%)	37 of 182 (20.3%)
1975	62 of 182 (34.1%)	35 of 182 (19.2%)
1976	73 of 196 (37.2%)	38 of 196 (19.4%)
1977	85 of 196 (43.4%)	36 of 196 (18.4%)
1978	108 of 224 (48.2%)	49 of 224 (21.9%)
1979	104 of 224 (46.4%)	51 of 224 (22.8%)
1980	108 of 224 (48.2%)	58 of 224 (25.9%)
1981	91 of 224 (40.6%)	60 of 224 (26.8%)
1982	61 of 126 (48.4%)	33 of 126 (26.2%)
1983	106 of 224 (47.3%)	54 of 224 (24.1%)
1984	95 of 224 (42.4%)	58 of 224 (25.9%)
1985	87 of 224 (38.8%)	38 of 224 (17.0%)
1986	106 of 224 (47.3%)	48 of 224 (21.4%)
1987	99 of 210 (47.1%)	40 of 210 (19.0%)
1988	113 of 224 (50.4%)	62 of 224 (27.7%)
1989	107 of 224 (47.8%)	55 of 224 (24.6%)
1990	97 of 224 (43.3%)	54 of 224 (24.1%)
1991	112 of 224 (50.0%)	57 of 224 (25.4%)
1992	88 of 224 (39.3%)	48 of 224 (21.4%)

1992 Records of Teams in Close Games

AFC	Overall Record	Decided by 7 Pts. or Less	Decided By 3 Pts. or Less
Buffalo	11-5	4-2	1-1
Cincinnati	5-11	2-4	2-2
Cleveland	7-9	1-4	1-2
Denver	8-8	4-3	1-2
Houston	10-6	4-5	3-3
Indianapolis	9-7	6-1	3-1
Kansas City	10-6	3-3	1-2
L.A. Raiders	7-9	2-2	2-1
Miami	11-5	6-1	4-0
New England	2-14	1-5	1-2
N.Y. Jets	4-12	2-5	1-3
Pittsburgh	11-5	4-1	2-1
San Diego	11-5	3-1	2-1
Seattle	2-14	2-4	1-2
NFC	**Overall Record**	**Decided by 7 Pts. or Less**	**Decided By 3 Pts. or Less**
Atlanta	6-10	3-3	3-1
Chicago	5-11	1-3	1-3
Dallas	13-3	4-2	0-1
Detroit	5-11	1-6	0-4
Green Bay	9-7	4-1	3-1
L.A. Rams	6-10	2-4	0-3
Minnesota	11-5	5-3	3-2
New Orleans	12-4	4-4	3-2
N.Y. Giants	6-10	0-2	0-1
Philadelphia	11-5	4-4	2-1
Phoenix	4-12	2-6	1-2
San Francisco	14-2	6-1	3-1
Tampa Bay	5-11	3-5	1-1
Washington	9-7	5-3	3-2

Super Bowl Champions Who Did Not Make Playoffs The Following Year

N.Y. Giants — Super Bowl XXV champions did not make playoffs in the 1991 season.
Washington — Super Bowl XXII champions did not make playoffs in the 1988 season.
N.Y. Giants — Super Bowl XXI champions did not make playoffs in the 1987 season.
San Francisco — Super Bowl XVI champions did not make playoffs in the 1982 season.
Oakland — Super Bowl XV champions did not make playoffs in the 1981 season.
Pittsburgh — Super Bowl XIV champions did not make playoffs in the 1980 season.
Kansas City — Super Bowl IV champions did not make playoffs in the 1970 season.
Green Bay — Super Bowl II champions did not make playoffs in the 1968 season.

All-Time Records of Current NFL Teams

Buffalo Bills

	All Games			Home Games			Road Games		
Season	W	L	T	W	L	T	W	L	T
1960	5	8	1	3	4		2	4	1
1961	6	8		2	5		4	3	
1962	7	6	1	3	3	1	4	3	
1963	7	6	1	4	2	1	3	4	
1964	12	2		6	1		6	1	
1965	10	3	1	5	2		5	1	1
1966	9	4	1	4	2	1	5	2	
1967	4	10		2	5		2	5	
1968	1	12	1	1	6		0	6	1
1969	4	10		4	3		0	7	
1970	3	10	1	1	6		2	4	1
1971	1	13		1	6		0	7	
1972	4	9	1	2	4	1	2	5	
1973	9	5		5	2		4	3	
1974	9	5		5	2		4	3	
1975	8	6		3	4		5	2	
1976	2	12		1	6		1	6	
1977	3	11		1	6		2	5	
1978	5	11		4	4		1	7	
1979	7	9		3	5		4	4	
1980	11	5		6	2		5	3	
1981	10	6		7	1		3	5	
1982	4	5		4	1		0	4	
1983	8	8		3	5		5	3	
1984	2	14		2	6		0	8	
1985	2	14		2	6		0	8	
1986	4	12		3	5		1	7	
1987	7	8		4	4		3	4	
1988	12	4		8	0		4	4	
1989	9	7		6	2		3	5	
1990	13	3		8	0		5	3	
1991	13	3		7	1		6	2	
1992	11	5		6	2		5	3	
Total	222	254	8	126	113	4	96	141	4

Cincinnati Bengals

	All Games			Home Games			Road Games		
Season	W	L	T	W	L	T	W	L	T
1968	3	11		2	5		1	6	
1969	4	9	1	4	3		0	6	1
1970	8	6		5	2		3	4	
1971	4	10		3	4		1	6	
1972	8	6		4	3		4	3	
1973	10	4		7	0		3	4	
1974	7	7		4	3		3	4	
1975	11	3		6	1		5	2	
1976	10	4		6	1		4	3	
1977	8	6		5	2		3	4	
1978	4	12		3	5		1	7	
1979	4	12		4	4		0	8	
1980	6	10		3	5		3	5	
1981	12	4		6	2		6	2	
1982	7	2		4	0		3	2	
1983	7	9		4	4		3	5	
1984	8	8		5	3		3	5	
1985	7	9		5	3		2	6	
1986	10	6		6	2		4	4	
1987	4	11		1	7		3	4	
1988	12	4		8	0		4	4	
1989	8	8		5	3		3	5	
1990	9	7		5	3		4	4	
1991	3	13		3	5		0	8	
1992	5	11		3	5		2	6	
Total	179	192	1	111	75		68	117	1

Cleveland Browns

	All Games			Home Games			Road Games		
Season	W	L	T	W	L	T	W	L	T
1950	10	2		5	1		5	1	
1951	11	1		6	0		5	1	
1952	8	4		4	2		4	2	
1953	11	1		6	0		5	1	
1954	9	3		5	1		4	2	
1955	9	2	1	5	1		4	1	1
1956	5	7		1	5		4	2	
1957	9	2	1	6	0		3	2	1
1958	9	3		4	2		5	1	
1959	7	5		3	3		4	2	
1960	8	3	1	4	2		4	1	1
1961	8	5	1	4	3		4	2	1
1962	7	6	1	4	2	1	3	4	
1963	10	4		5	2		5	2	
1964	10	3	1	5	1	1	5	2	
1965	11	3		5	2		6	1	
1966	9	5		5	2		4	3	
1967	9	5		6	1		3	4	
1968	10	4		5	2		5	2	
1969	10	3	1	5	1	1	5	2	
1970	7	7		4	3		3	4	
1971	9	5		4	3		5	2	
1972	10	4		4	3		6	1	
1973	7	5	2	5	1	1	2	4	1
1974	4	10		3	4		1	6	
1975	3	11		3	4		0	7	
1976	9	5		6	1		3	4	
1977	6	8		2	5		4	3	
1978	8	8		5	3		3	5	
1979	9	7		5	3		4	4	
1980	11	5		6	2		5	3	
1981	5	11		3	5		2	6	
1982	4	5		2	2		2	3	
1983	9	7		6	2		3	5	
1984	5	11		2	6		3	5	
1985	8	8		5	3		3	5	
1986	12	4		6	2		6	2	
1987	10	5		5	2		5	3	
1988	10	6		6	2		4	4	
1989	9	6	1	5	2	1	4	4	
1990	3	13		2	6		1	7	
1991	6	10		3	5		3	5	
1992	7	9		4	4		3	5	
Total	351	241	10	189	106	5	162	135	5

Denver Broncos

	All Games			Home Games			Road Games		
Season	W	L	T	W	L	T	W	L	T
1960	4	9	1	2	4	1	2	5	
1961	3	11		2	5		1	6	
1962	7	7		3	4		4	3	
1963	2	11	1	2	5		0	6	1
1964	2	11	1	2	4	1	0	7	
1965	4	10		2	5		2	5	
1966	4	10		3	4		1	6	
1967	3	11		1	6		2	5	
1968	5	9		3	4		2	5	
1969	5	8	1	4	2	1	1	6	
1970	5	8	1	3	3	1	2	5	
1971	4	9	1	2	4	1	2	5	
1972	5	9		3	4		2	5	
1973	7	5	2	3	3	1	4	2	1
1974	7	6	1	3	3	1	4	3	
1975	6	8		5	2		1	6	
1976	9	5		6	1		3	4	
1977	12	2		6	1		6	1	
1978	10	6		6	2		4	4	
1979	10	6		6	2		4	4	
1980	8	8		4	4		4	4	
1981	10	6		8	0		2	6	
1982	2	7		1	4		1	3	
1983	9	7		6	2		3	5	
1984	13	3		7	1		6	2	
1985	11	5		6	2		5	3	
1986	11	5		7	1		4	4	
1987	10	4	1	7	1		3	3	1
1988	8	8		6	2		2	6	
1989	11	5		6	2		5	3	
1990	5	11		4	4		1	7	
1991	12	4		7	1		5	3	
1992	8	8		7	1		1	7	
Total	232	242	10	143	93	7	89	149	3

Houston Oilers

	All Games			Home Games			Road Games		
Season	W	L	T	W	L	T	W	L	T
1960	10	4		6	1		4	3	
1961	10	3	1	6	1		4	2	1
1962	11	3		6	1		5	2	
1963	6	8		4	3		2	5	
1964	4	10		3	4		1	6	
1965	4	10		3	4		1	6	
1966	3	11		3	4		0	7	
1967	9	4	1	5	2		4	2	1
1968	7	7		3	4		4	3	
1969	6	6	2	4	2	1	2	4	1
1970	3	10	1	1	6		2	4	1
1971	4	9	1	3	3	1	1	6	
1972	1	13		1	6		0	7	
1973	1	13		0	7		1	6	
1974	7	7		3	4		4	3	
1975	10	4		5	2		5	2	
1976	5	9		3	4		2	5	
1977	8	6		5	2		3	4	
1978	10	6		5	3		5	3	
1979	11	5		6	2		5	3	
1980	11	5		6	2		5	3	
1981	7	9		5	3		2	6	
1982	1	8		1	4		0	4	
1983	2	14		2	6		0	8	
1984	3	13		2	6		1	7	
1985	5	11		4	4		1	7	
1986	5	11		4	4		1	7	
1987	9	6		5	2		4	4	
1988	10	6		7	1		3	5	
1989	9	7		6	2		3	5	
1990	9	7		6	2		3	5	
1991	11	5		7	1		4	4	
1992	10	6		5	3		5	3	
Total	222	256	6	135	105	2	87	151	4

Indianapolis Colts*

	All Games			Home Games			Road Games		
Season	W	L	T	W	L	T	W	L	T
1953	3	9		2	4		1	5	
1954	3	9		2	4		1	5	
1955	5	6	1	4	1	1	1	5	
1956	5	7		4	2		1	5	
1957	7	5		4	2		3	3	
1958	9	3		6	0		3	3	
1959	9	3		4	2		5	1	
1960	6	6		4	2		2	4	
1961	8	6		5	2		3	4	
1962	7	7		3	4		4	3	
1963	8	6		4	3		4	3	
1964	12	2		7	1		5	1	
1965	10	3	1	5	2		5	1	1
1966	9	5		5	2		4	3	
1967	11	1	2	6	0	1	5	1	1
1968	13	1		6	1		7	0	
1969	8	5	1	4	2	1	4	3	
1970	11	2	1	5	1	1	6	1	
1971	10	4		5	2		5	2	
1972	5	9		2	5		3	4	
1973	4	10		3	4		1	6	
1974	2	12		0	7		2	5	
1975	10	4		5	2		5	2	
1976	11	3		6	1		5	2	
1977	10	4		6	1		4	3	
1978	5	11		2	6		3	5	
1979	5	11		3	5		2	6	
1980	7	9		2	6		5	3	
1981	2	14		1	7		1	7	
1982	0	8	1	0	3	1	0	5	
1983	7	9		3	5		4	4	
1984	4	12		2	6		2	6	
1985	5	11		4	4		1	7	
1986	3	13		1	7		2	6	
1987	9	6		4	4		5	2	
1988	9	7		6	2		3	5	
1989	8	8		6	2		2	6	
1990	7	9		3	5		4	4	
1991	1	15		0	8		1	7	
1992	9	7		4	4		5	3	
Total	277	282	7	148	131	5	129	151	2

*includes Baltimore Colts (1953-83).

Kansas City Chiefs*

	All Games			Home Games			Road Games		
Season	W	L	T	W	L	T	W	L	T
1960	8	6		5	2		3	4	
1961	6	8		4	3		2	5	
1962	11	3		6	1		5	2	
1963	5	7	2	4	3		1	4	2
1964	7	7		4	3		3	4	
1965	7	5	2	5	2		2	3	2
1966	11	2	1	4	2	1	7	0	
1967	9	5		4	3		5	2	
1968	12	2		6	1		6	1	
1969	11	3		6	1		5	2	
1970	7	5	2	4	1	2	3	4	
1971	10	3	1	7	0		3	3	1
1972	8	6		3	4		5	2	
1973	7	5	2	5	1	1	2	4	1
1974	5	9		1	6		4	3	
1975	5	9		3	4		2	5	
1976	5	9		1	6		4	3	
1977	2	12		1	6		1	6	
1978	4	12		3	5		1	7	
1979	7	9		3	5		4	4	
1980	8	8		3	5		5	3	
1981	9	7		5	3		4	4	
1982	3	6		2	2		1	4	
1983	6	10		5	3		1	7	
1984	8	8		5	3		3	5	

Season	All Games			Home Games			Road Games		
	W	L	T	W	L	T	W	L	T
1985	6	10		5	3		1	7	
1986	10	6		6	2		4	4	
1987	4	11		3	4		1	7	
1988	4	11	1	4	4		0	7	1
1989	8	7	1	5	3		3	4	1
1990	11	5		6	2		5	3	
1991	10	6		6	2		4	4	
1992	10	6		7	1		3	5	
Total	244	228	12	141	96	4	103	132	8

*includes Dallas Texans (1960-62).

Los Angeles Raiders*

Season	All Games			Home Games			Road Games		
	W	L	T	W	L	T	W	L	T
1960	6	8		3	4		3	4	
1961	2	12		1	6		1	6	
1962	1	13		1	6		0	7	
1963	10	4		6	1		4	3	
1964	5	7	2	5	2		0	5	2
1965	8	5	1	5	2		3	3	1
1966	8	5	1	3	3	1	5	2	
1967	13	1		7	0		6	1	
1968	12	2		6	1		6	1	
1969	12	1	1	7	0		5	1	1
1970	8	4	2	6	1		2	3	2
1971	8	4	2	5	1	1	3	3	1
1972	10	3	1	5	1	1	5	2	
1973	9	4	1	5	2		4	2	1
1974	12	2		6	1		6	1	
1975	11	3		6	1		5	2	
1976	13	1		7	0		6	1	
1977	11	3		6	1		5	2	
1978	9	7		4	4		5	3	
1979	9	7		6	2		3	5	
1980	11	5		6	2		5	3	
1981	7	9		4	4		3	5	
1982	8	1		4	0		4	1	
1983	12	4		6	2		6	2	
1984	11	5		6	2		5	3	
1985	12	4		7	1		5	3	
1986	8	8		3	5		5	3	
1987	5	10		3	5		2	5	
1988	7	9		3	5		4	4	
1989	8	8		7	1		1	7	
1990	12	4		6	2		6	2	
1991	9	7		5	3		4	4	
1992	7	9		5	3		2	6	
Total	294	179	11	165	74	3	129	105	8

*includes Oakland Raiders (1960-81).

Miami Dolphins

Season	All Games			Home Games			Road Games		
	W	L	T	W	L	T	W	L	T
1966	3	11		2	5		1	6	
1967	4	10		4	3		0	7	
1968	5	8	1	1	5	1	4	3	
1969	3	10	1	2	4	1	1	6	
1970	10	4		6	1		4	3	
1971	10	3	1	6	1		4	2	1
1972	14	0		7	0		7	0	
1973	12	2		7	0		5	2	
1974	11	3		7	0		4	3	
1975	10	4		5	2		5	2	
1976	6	8		3	4		3	4	
1977	10	4		6	1		4	3	
1978	11	5		7	1		4	4	
1979	10	6		6	2		4	4	
1980	8	8		5	3		3	5	
1981	11	4	1	6	1	1	5	3	
1982	7	2		4	0		3	2	
1983	12	4		7	1		5	3	
1984	14	2		7	1		7	1	
1985	12	4		8	0		4	4	
1986	8	8		4	4		4	4	
1987	8	7		4	3		4	4	
1988	6	10		4	4		2	6	
1989	8	8		4	4		4	4	
1990	12	4		7	1		5	3	
1991	8	8		5	3		3	5	
1992	11	5		6	2		5	3	
Total	244	152	4	140	56	3	104	96	1

New England Patriots*

Season	All Games			Home Games			Road Games		
	W	L	T	W	L	T	W	L	T
1960	5	9		3	4		2	5	
1961	9	4	1	4	2	1	5	2	
1962	9	4	1	6	1		3	3	1
1963	7	6	1	5	1	1	2	5	
1964	10	3	1	4	2	1	6	1	
1965	4	8	2	1	4	2	3	4	
1966	8	4	2	4	2	1	4	2	1
1967	3	10	1	2	4		1	6	1
1968	4	10		2	5		2	5	
1969	4	10		2	5		2	5	
1970	2	12		1	6		1	6	
1971	6	8		5	2		1	6	
1972	3	11		2	5		1	6	
1973	5	9		3	4		2	5	
1974	7	7		3	4		4	3	
1975	3	11		2	5		1	6	
1976	11	3		6	1		5	2	
1977	9	5		6	1		3	4	
1978	11	5		5	3		6	2	
1979	9	7		6	2		3	5	
1980	10	6		6	2		4	4	
1981	2	14		2	6		0	8	
1982	5	4		3	1		2	3	
1983	8	8		5	3		3	5	
1984	9	7		5	3		4	4	
1985	11	5		7	1		4	4	
1986	11	5		4	4		7	1	
1987	8	7		5	3		3	4	
1988	9	7		7	1		2	6	
1989	5	11		3	5		2	6	
1990	1	15		0	8		1	7	
1991	6	10		4	4		2	6	
1992	2	14		1	7		1	7	
Total	216	259	9	124	111	6	92	148	3

*includes Boston Patriots (1960-70).

New York Jets*

Season	All Games			Home Games			Road Games		
	W	L	T	W	L	T	W	L	T
1960	7	7		3	4		4	3	
1961	7	7		5	2		2	5	
1962	5	9		2	5		3	4	
1963	5	8	1	4	2	1	1	6	
1964	5	8	1	5	1	1	0	7	
1965	5	8	1	3	3	1	2	5	
1966	6	6	2	4	3		2	3	2
1967	8	5	1	4	2	1	4	3	
1968	11	3		6	1		5	2	
1969	10	4		5	2		5	2	
1970	4	10		2	5		2	5	
1971	6	8		4	3		2	5	
1972	7	7		4	3		3	4	
1973	4	10		2	4		2	6	
1974	7	7		3	4		4	3	
1975	3	11		1	6		2	5	
1976	3	11		2	5		1	6	
1977	3	11		1	6		2	5	
1978	8	8		4	4		4	4	
1979	8	8		6	2		2	6	
1980	4	12		2	6		2	6	
1981	10	5	1	6	2		4	3	1
1982	6	3		3	1		3	2	
1983	7	9		2	6		5	3	
1984	7	9		3	5		4	4	
1985	11	5		7	1		4	4	
1986	10	6		5	3		5	3	
1987	6	9		4	4		2	5	
1988	8	7	1	5	2	1	3	5	
1989	4	12		1	7		3	5	
1990	6	10		3	5		3	5	
1991	8	8		4	4		4	4	
1992	4	12		3	5		1	7	
Total	213	263	8	118	118	5	95	145	3

*includes New York Titans (1960-62).

Pittsburgh Steelers*

Season	All Games			Home Games			Road Games		
	W	L	T	W	L	T	W	L	T
1933	3	6	2	2	3		1	3	2
1934	2	10		1	5		1	5	
1935	4	8		2	5		2	3	
1936	6	6		4	1		2	5	
1937	4	7		2	4		2	3	
1938	2	9		0	5		2	4	
1939	1	9	1	1	4		0	5	1
1940	2	7	2	1	2	2	1	5	
1941	1	9	1	1	4		0	5	1
1942	7	4		3	2		4	2	
1945	2	8		1	4		1	4	
1946	5	5	1	4	1		1	4	1
1947	8	4		5	1		3	3	
1948	4	8		4	2		0	6	
1949	6	5	1	3	2	1	3	3	
1950	6	6		2	4		4	2	
1951	4	7	1	1	4	1	3	3	
1952	5	7		2	4		3	3	
1953	6	6		3	3		3	3	
1954	5	7		4	2		1	5	
1955	4	8		3	2		1	6	
1956	5	7		3	3		2	4	
1957	6	6		4	2		2	4	
1958	7	4	1	5	1		2	3	1
1959	6	5	1	3	2	1	3	3	
1960	5	6	1	4	2		1	4	1
1961	6	8		4	3		2	5	
1962	9	5		4	3		5	2	
1963	7	4	3	5	0	2	2	4	1
1964	5	9		2	5		3	4	
1965	2	12		1	6		1	6	
1966	5	8	1	3	3	1	2	5	
1967	4	9	1	1	6		3	3	1
1968	2	11	1	1	6		1	5	1
1969	1	13		1	6		0	7	
1970	5	9		4	3		1	6	
1971	6	8		5	2		1	6	
1972	11	3		7	0		4	3	
1973	10	4		7	1		3	3	
1974	10	3	1	5	2		5	1	1
1975	12	2		6	1		6	1	
1976	10	4		6	1		4	3	
1977	9	5		6	1		3	4	
1978	14	2		7	1		7	1	
1979	12	4		8	0		4	4	
1980	9	7		6	2		3	5	
1981	8	8		5	3		3	5	
1982	6	3		4	0		2	3	
1983	10	6		4	4		6	2	
1984	9	7		6	2		3	5	
1985	7	9		5	3		2	6	
1986	6	10		4	4		2	6	
1987	8	7		4	3		4	4	
1988	5	11		4	4		1	7	
1989	9	7		4	4		5	3	
1990	9	7		6	2		3	5	
1991	7	9		5	3		2	6	
1992	11	5		7	1		4	4	
Total	360	393	19	215	159	8	145	234	11

*includes Pittsburgh Pirates (1933-40).

San Diego Chargers*

Season	All Games			Home Games			Road Games		
	W	L	T	W	L	T	W	L	T
1960	10	4		5	2		5	2	
1961	12	2		6	1		6	1	
1962	4	10		3	4		1	6	
1963	11	3		6	1		5	2	
1964	8	5	1	4	3		4	2	1
1965	9	2	3	4	1	2	5	1	1
1966	7	6	1	5	2		2	4	1
1967	8	5	1	5	2	1	3	3	
1968	9	5		4	3		5	2	
1969	8	6		5	2		3	4	
1970	5	6	3	2	3	2	3	3	1
1971	6	8		6	1		0	7	
1972	4	9	1	2	5		2	4	1
1973	2	11	1	2	5		0	6	1
1974	5	9		3	4		2	5	
1975	2	12		1	6		1	6	
1976	6	8		3	4		3	4	
1977	7	7		3	4		4	3	
1978	9	7		5	3		4	4	
1979	12	4		7	1		5	3	
1980	11	5		6	2		5	3	
1981	10	6		5	3		5	3	
1982	6	3		3	1		3	2	
1983	6	10		4	4		2	6	
1984	7	9		4	4		3	5	
1985	8	8		6	2		2	6	
1986	4	12		2	6		2	6	
1987	8	7		4	3		4	4	
1988	6	10		3	5		3	5	
1989	6	10		4	4		2	6	
1990	6	10		3	5		3	5	
1991	4	12		3	5		1	7	
1992	11	5		6	2		5	3	
Total	237	236	11	134	103	5	103	133	6

*includes Los Angeles Chargers (1960).

Seattle Seahawks

Season	All Games			Home Games			Road Games		
	W	L	T	W	L	T	W	L	T
1976	2	12		1	6		1	6	
1977	5	9		3	4		2	5	
1978	9	7		5	3		4	4	
1979	9	7		5	3		4	4	
1980	4	12		0	8		4	4	

Season	All Games W	L	T	Home Games W	L	T	Road Games W	L	T
1981	6	10		5	3		1	7	
1982	4	5		3	2		1	3	
1983	9	7		5	3		4	4	
1984	12	4		7	1		5	3	
1985	8	8		5	3		3	5	
1986	10	6		7	1		3	5	
1987	9	6		6	2		3	4	
1988	9	7		5	3		4	4	
1989	7	9		3	5		4	4	
1990	9	7		5	3		4	4	
1991	7	9		5	3		2	6	
1992	2	14		1	7		1	7	
Total	121	139		71	60		50	79	

Atlanta Falcons

Season	All Games W	L	T	Home Games W	L	T	Road Games W	L	T
1966	3	11		1	6		2	5	
1967	1	12	1	1	5	1	0	7	
1968	2	12		1	6		1	6	
1969	6	8		4	3		2	5	
1970	4	8	2	3	4		1	4	2
1971	7	6	1	4	3		3	3	1
1972	7	7		4	3		3	4	
1973	9	5		4	3		5	2	
1974	3	11		2	5		1	6	
1975	4	10		3	4		1	6	
1976	4	10		3	4		1	6	
1977	7	7		4	3		3	4	
1978	9	7		7	1		2	6	
1979	6	10		3	5		3	5	
1980	12	4		6	2		6	2	
1981	7	9		4	4		3	5	
1982	5	4		2	3		3	1	
1983	7	9		4	4		3	5	
1984	4	12		2	6		2	6	
1985	4	12		3	5		1	7	
1986	7	8	1	2	5	1	5	3	
1987	3	12		2	6		1	6	
1988	5	11		2	6		3	5	
1989	3	13		3	5		0	8	
1990	5	11		5	3		0	8	
1991	10	6		6	2		4	4	
1992	6	10		5	3		1	7	
Total	150	245	5	90	109	2	60	136	3

Chicago Bears*

Season	All Games W	L	T	Home Games W	L	T	Road Games W	L	T
1920	10	1	2	6	0	1	4	1	1
1921	9	1	1	9	1	1	0	0	
1922	9	3		7	1		2	2	
1923	9	2	1	7	1	1	2	1	
1924	6	1	4	5	0	3	1	1	1
1925	9	5	3	7	1	1	2	4	2
1926	12	1	3	10	0	2	2	1	1
1927	9	3	2	7	1	1	2	2	1
1928	7	5	1	6	3		1	2	1
1929	4	9	2	1	5	2	3	4	
1930	9	4	1	5	2	1	4	2	
1931	8	5		6	3		2	2	
1932	7	1	6	6	1	1	1	0	5
1933	10	2	1	6	0		4	2	1
1934	13	0		5	0		8	0	
1935	6	4	2	1	2	2	5	2	
1936	9	3		3	1		6	2	
1937	9	1	1	4	1		5	0	1
1938	6	5		2	3		4	2	
1939	8	3		4	1		4	2	
1940	8	3		5	0		3	3	
1941	10	1		5	1		5	0	
1942	11	0		6	0		5	0	
1943	8	1	1	5	0		3	1	1
1944	6	3	1	4	0	1	2	3	
1945	3	7		2	3		1	4	
1946	8	2	1	4	1	1	4	1	
1947	8	4		4	2		4	2	
1948	10	2		5	1		5	1	
1949	9	3		5	1		4	2	
1950	9	3		6	0		3	3	
1951	7	5		3	3		4	2	
1952	5	7		3	3		2	4	
1953	3	8	1	1	4	1	2	4	
1954	8	4		4	2		4	2	
1955	8	4		5	1		3	3	
1956	9	2	1	6	0		3	2	1
1957	5	7		2	4		3	3	
1958	8	4		5	1		3	3	
1959	8	4		4	2		4	2	
1960	5	6	1	4	2		1	4	1
1961	8	6		5	2		3	4	
1962	9	5		4	3		5	2	
1963	11	1	2	6	0	1	5	1	1
1964	5	9		2	5		3	4	
1965	9	5		5	2		4	3	
1966	5	7	2	4	1	2	1	6	
1967	7	6	1	3	3	1	4	3	
1968	7	7		2	5		5	2	
1969	1	13		1	6		0	7	
1970	6	8		3	4		3	4	
1971	6	8		4	3		2	5	
1972	4	9	1	1	5	1	3	4	
1973	3	11		1	6		2	5	
1974	4	10		4	3		0	7	
1975	4	10		3	4		1	6	
1976	7	7		4	3		3	4	
1977	9	5		5	2		4	3	
1978	7	9		4	4		3	5	
1979	10	6		6	2		4	4	
1980	7	9		5	3		2	6	
1981	6	10		4	4		2	6	
1982	3	6		2	2		1	4	
1983	8	8		5	3		3	5	
1984	10	6		6	2		4	4	
1985	15	1		8	0		7	1	
1986	14	2		7	1		7	1	
1987	11	4		6	2		5	2	
1988	12	4		7	1		5	3	
1989	6	10		4	4		2	6	
1990	11	5		7	1		4	4	
1991	11	5		6	2		5	3	
1992	5	11		4	4		1	7	
Total	566	362	42	333	150	24	233	212	18

*includes Decatur Staleys (1920) and Chicago Staleys (1921).

Dallas Cowboys

Season	All Games W	L	T	Home Games W	L	T	Road Games W	L	T
1960	0	11	1	0	6		0	5	1
1961	4	9	1	2	4	1	2	5	
1962	5	8	1	2	4	1	3	4	
1963	4	10		3	4		1	6	
1964	5	8	1	2	4	1	3	4	
1965	7	7		5	2		2	5	
1966	10	3	1	6	1		4	2	1
1967	9	5		5	2		4	3	
1968	12	2		5	2		7	0	
1969	11	2	1	6	0	1	5	2	
1970	10	4		6	1		4	3	
1971	11	3		6	1		5	2	
1972	10	4		5	2		5	2	
1973	10	4		6	1		4	3	
1974	8	6		5	2		3	4	
1975	10	4		5	2		5	2	
1976	11	3		6	1		5	2	
1977	12	2		6	1		6	1	
1978	12	4		7	1		5	3	
1979	11	5		6	2		5	3	
1980	12	4		8	0		4	4	
1981	12	4		8	0		4	4	
1982	6	3		3	2		3	1	
1983	12	4		6	2		6	2	
1984	9	7		5	3		4	4	
1985	10	6		7	1		3	5	
1986	7	9		3	5		4	4	
1987	7	8		3	4		4	4	
1988	3	13		1	7		2	6	
1989	1	15		0	8		1	7	
1990	7	9		5	3		2	6	
1991	11	5		6	2		5	3	
1992	13	3		7	1		6	2	
Total	282	194	6	156	81	4	126	113	2

Detroit Lions*

Season	All Games W	L	T	Home Games W	L	T	Road Games W	L	T
1930	5	6	3	5	1	2	0	5	1
1931	11	3		8	0		3	3	
1932	6	2	4	3	0	2	3	2	2
1933	6	5		4	1		2	4	
1934	10	3		6	2		4	1	
1935	7	3	2	5	0	1	2	3	1
1936	8	4		5	1		3	3	
1937	7	4		4	2		3	2	
1938	7	4		4	3		3	1	
1939	6	5		4	2		2	3	
1940	5	5	1	3	3		2	2	1
1941	4	6	1	3	2		1	4	1
1942	0	11		0	7		0	4	
1943	3	6	1	2	2	1	1	4	
1944	6	3	1	4	2		2	1	1
1945	7	3		4	1		3	2	
1946	1	10		1	5		0	5	
1947	3	9		2	4		1	5	
1948	2	10		2	4		0	6	
1949	4	8		2	4		2	4	
1950	6	6		4	2		2	4	
1951	7	4	1	3	3	1	4	1	
1952	9	3		6	1		3	2	
1953	10	2		5	1		5	1	
1954	9	2	1	5	0	1	4	2	
1955	3	9		3	4		0	5	
1956	9	3		5	1		4	2	
1957	8	4		5	1		3	3	
1958	4	7	1	2	4		2	3	1
1959	3	8	1	2	4		1	4	1
1960	7	5		5	1		2	4	
1961	8	5	1	2	5		6	0	1
1962	11	3		7	0		4	3	
1963	5	8	1	3	3	1	2	5	
1964	7	5	2	3	3	1	4	2	1
1965	6	7	1	2	4	1	4	3	
1966	4	9	1	3	4		1	5	1
1967	5	7	2	3	4		2	3	2
1968	4	8	2	1	4	2	3	4	
1969	9	4	1	5	2		4	2	1
1970	10	4		6	1		4	3	
1971	7	6	1	3	4		4	2	1
1972	8	5	1	5	2		3	3	1
1973	6	7	1	4	3		2	4	1
1974	7	7		5	2		2	5	
1975	7	7		4	3		3	4	
1976	6	8		5	2		1	6	
1977	6	8		5	2		1	6	
1978	7	9		5	3		2	6	
1979	2	14		2	6		0	8	
1980	9	7		6	2		3	5	
1981	8	8		7	1		1	7	
1982	4	5		2	3		2	2	
1983	9	7		6	2		3	5	
1984	4	11	1	2	5	1	2	6	
1985	7	9		6	2		1	7	
1986	5	11		1	7		4	4	
1987	4	11		1	6		3	5	
1988	4	12		2	6		2	6	
1989	7	9		4	4		3	5	
1990	6	10		3	5		3	5	
1991	12	4		8	0		4	4	
1992	5	11		3	5		2	6	
Total	392	409	32	240	173	14	152	236	18

*includes Portsmouth Spartans (1930-33)

Green Bay Packers

Season	All Games W	L	T	Home Games W	L	T	Road Games W	L	T
1921	3	2	1	2	1		1	1	1
1922	4	3	3	4	1	1	0	2	2
1923	7	2	1	4	2	1	3	0	
1924	7	4		5	0		2	4	
1925	8	5		6	0		2	5	
1926	7	3	3	4	1	2	3	2	1
1927	7	2	1	6	1		1	1	1
1928	6	4	3	2	2	2	4	2	1
1929	12	0	1	5	0		7	0	1
1930	10	3	1	6	0		4	3	1
1931	12	2		8	0		4	2	
1932	10	3	1	5	0	1	5	3	
1933	5	7	1	3	2	1	2	5	
1934	7	6		4	2		3	4	
1935	8	4		5	2		3	2	
1936	10	1	1	5	1		5	0	1
1937	7	4		3	2		4	2	
1938	8	3		4	2		4	1	
1939	9	2		4	1		5	1	
1940	6	4	1	4	2		2	2	1
1941	10	1		4	1		6	0	
1942	8	2	1	4	1		4	1	1
1943	7	2	1	2	1	1	5	1	
1944	8	2		5	0		3	2	
1945	6	4		4	1		2	3	
1946	6	5		2	3		4	2	
1947	6	5	1	4	2		2	3	1
1948	3	9		2	4		1	5	
1949	2	10		1	5		1	5	
1950	3	9		3	3		0	6	
1951	3	9		2	4		1	5	
1952	6	6		3	3		3	3	
1953	2	9	1	1	5		1	4	1
1954	4	8		2	4		2	4	

Season	All Games W	L	T	Home Games W	L	T	Road Games W	L	T
1955	6	6		5	1		1	5	
1956	4	8		2	4		2	4	
1957	3	9		1	5		2	4	
1958	1	10	1	1	4	1	0	6	
1959	7	5		4	2		3	3	
1960	8	4		4	2		4	2	
1961	11	3		6	1		5	2	
1962	13	1		7	0		6	1	
1963	11	2	1	6	1		5	1	1
1964	8	5	1	4	3		4	2	1
1965	10	3	1	6	1		4	2	1
1966	12	2		6	1		6	1	
1967	9	4	1	4	2	1	5	2	
1968	6	7	1	2	5		4	2	1
1969	8	6		5	2		3	4	
1970	6	8		4	3		2	5	
1971	4	8	2	3	3	1	1	5	1
1972	10	4		4	3		6	1	
1973	5	7	2	3	2	2	2	5	
1974	6	8		4	3		2	5	
1975	4	10		3	4		1	6	
1976	5	9		4	3		1	6	
1977	4	10		2	5		2	5	
1978	8	7	1	5	2	1	3	5	
1979	5	11		4	4		1	7	
1980	5	10	1	4	4		1	6	1
1981	8	8		4	4		4	4	
1982	5	3	1	3	1		2	2	1
1983	8	8		5	3		3	5	
1984	8	8		5	3		3	5	
1985	8	8		5	3		3	5	
1986	4	12		1	7		3	5	
1987	5	9	1	2	5	1	3	4	
1988	4	12		2	6		2	6	
1989	10	6		6	2		4	4	
1990	6	10		3	5		3	5	
1991	4	12		2	6		2	6	
1992	9	7		6	2		3	5	
Total	485	415	36	275	176	16	210	239	20

Los Angeles Rams*

Season	All Games W	L	T	Home Games W	L	T	Road Games W	L	T
1937	1	10		0	5		1	5	
1938	4	7		2	2		2	5	
1939	5	5	1	3	2	1	2	3	
1940	4	6	1	3	1	1	1	5	
1941	2	9		1	4		1	5	
1942	5	6		3	2		2	4	
1944	4	6		1	2		3	4	
1945	9	1		4	0		5	1	
1946	6	4	1	3	2		3	2	1
1947	6	6		3	3		3	3	
1948	6	5	1	3	2	1	3	3	
1949	8	2	2	5	1		3	1	2
1950	9	3		5	1		4	2	
1951	8	4		5	2		3	2	
1952	9	3		5	1		4	2	
1953	8	3	1	5	1		3	2	1
1954	6	5	1	3	2	1	3	3	
1955	8	3	1	5	1		3	2	1
1956	4	8		4	2		0	6	
1957	6	6		5	1		1	5	
1958	8	4		4	2		4	2	
1959	2	10		0	6		2	4	
1960	4	7	1	2	3	1	2	4	
1961	4	10		4	3		0	7	
1962	1	12	1	0	7		1	5	1
1963	5	9		3	4		2	5	
1964	5	7	2	3	2	2	2	5	
1965	4	10		3	4		1	6	
1966	8	6		5	2		3	4	
1967	11	1	2	5	1	1	6	0	1
1968	10	3	1	5	2		5	1	1
1969	11	3		5	2		6	1	
1970	9	4	1	3	3	1	6	1	
1971	8	5	1	4	2	1	4	3	
1972	6	7	1	4	3		2	4	1
1973	12	2		7	0		5	2	
1974	10	4		6	1		4	3	
1975	12	2		6	1		6	1	
1976	10	3	1	5	2		5	1	1
1977	10	4		7	0		3	4	
1978	12	4		6	2		6	2	
1979	9	7		4	4		5	3	
1980	11	5		6	2		5	3	
1981	6	10		4	4		2	6	
1982	2	7		1	4		1	3	
1983	9	7		5	3		4	4	
1984	10	6		5	3		5	3	
1985	11	5		6	2		5	3	
1986	10	6		6	2		4	4	
1987	6	9		3	4		3	5	
1988	10	6		4	4		6	2	
1989	11	5		6	2		5	3	
1990	5	11		2	6		3	5	
1991	3	13		2	6		1	7	
1992	6	10		4	4		2	6	
Total	389	326	20	213	139	10	176	187	10

*includes Cleveland Rams (1937-42, 1944-45).

Minnesota Vikings

Season	All Games W	L	T	Home Games W	L	T	Road Games W	L	T
1961	3	11		3	4		0	7	
1962	2	11	1	1	5	1	1	6	
1963	5	8	1	3	4		2	4	1
1964	8	5	1	4	3		4	2	1
1965	7	7		2	5		5	2	
1966	4	9	1	2	5		2	4	1
1967	3	8	3	1	4	2	2	4	1
1968	8	6		4	3		4	3	
1969	12	2		7	0		5	2	
1970	12	2		7	0		5	2	
1971	11	3		5	2		6	1	
1972	7	7		3	4		4	3	
1973	12	2		7	0		5	2	
1974	10	4		4	3		6	1	
1975	12	2		7	0		5	2	
1976	11	2	1	6	0	1	5	2	
1977	9	5		5	2		4	3	
1978	8	7	1	5	3		3	4	1
1979	7	9		5	3		2	6	
1980	9	7		5	3		4	4	
1981	7	9		5	3		2	6	
1982	5	4		4	1		1	3	
1983	8	8		3	5		5	3	
1984	3	13		2	6		1	7	
1985	7	9		4	4		3	5	
1986	9	7		5	3		4	4	
1987	8	7		5	3		3	4	
1988	11	5		7	1		4	4	
1989	10	6		8	0		2	6	
1990	6	10		4	4		2	6	
1991	8	8		4	4		4	4	
1992	11	5		5	3		6	2	
Total	253	208	9	142	90	4	111	118	5

New Orleans Saints

Season	All Games W	L	T	Home Games W	L	T	Road Games W	L	T
1967	3	11		2	5		1	6	
1968	4	9	1	3	4		1	5	1
1969	5	9		3	4		2	5	
1970	2	11	1	2	5		0	6	1
1971	4	8	2	2	4	1	2	4	1
1972	2	11	1	2	5		0	6	1
1973	5	9		5	2		0	7	
1974	5	9		4	3		1	6	
1975	2	12		2	5		0	7	
1976	4	10		2	5		2	5	
1977	3	11		2	5		1	6	
1978	7	9		3	5		4	4	
1979	8	8		3	5		5	3	
1980	1	15		0	8		1	7	
1981	4	12		2	6		2	6	
1982	4	5		2	3		2	2	
1983	8	8		5	3		3	5	
1984	7	9		3	5		4	4	
1985	5	11		3	5		2	6	
1986	7	9		4	4		3	5	
1987	12	3		6	1		6	2	
1988	10	6		5	3		5	3	
1989	9	7		5	3		4	4	
1990	8	8		5	3		3	5	
1991	11	5		6	2		5	3	
1992	12	4		6	2		6	2	
Total	152	229	5	87	105	1	65	124	4

New York Giants

Season	All Games W	L	T	Home Games W	L	T	Road Games W	L	T
1925	8	4		7	2		1	2	
1926	8	4	1	5	2	1	3	2	
1927	11	1	1	7	1		4	0	1
1928	4	7	2	1	2	2	3	5	
1929	13	1	1	7	1		6	0	1
1930	13	4		6	2		7	2	
1931	7	6	1	4	2	1	3	4	
1932	4	6	2	3	2	1	1	4	1
1933	11	3		7	0		4	3	
1934	8	5		5	1		3	4	
1935	9	3		4	2		5	1	
1936	5	6	1	3	3	1	2	3	
1937	6	3	2	4	2	1	2	1	1
1938	8	2	1	6	1		2	1	1
1939	9	1	1	6	0		3	1	1
1940	6	4	1	4	3		2	1	1
1941	8	3		5	2		3	1	
1942	5	5	1	3	2	1	2	3	
1943	6	3	1	4	2		2	1	1
1944	8	1	1	5	1		3	0	1
1945	3	6	1	2	4		1	2	1
1946	7	3	1	5	1	1	2	2	
1947	2	8	2	2	3	1	0	5	1
1948	4	8		2	4		2	4	
1949	6	6		2	4		4	2	
1950	10	2		5	1		5	1	
1951	9	2	1	5	1		4	1	1
1952	7	5		2	4		5	1	
1953	3	9		2	4		1	5	
1954	7	5		4	2		3	3	
1955	6	5	1	4	1	1	2	4	
1956	8	3	1	4	1	1	4	2	
1957	7	5		3	3		4	2	
1958	9	3		5	1		4	2	
1959	10	2		5	1		5	1	
1960	6	4	2	1	3	2	5	1	
1961	10	3	1	4	2	1	6	1	
1962	12	2		6	1		6	1	
1963	11	3		5	2		6	1	
1964	2	10	2	2	5		0	5	2
1965	7	7		3	4		4	3	
1966	1	12	1	1	6		0	6	1
1967	7	7		5	2		2	5	
1968	7	7		3	4		4	3	
1969	6	8		5	2		1	6	
1970	9	5		5	2		4	3	
1971	4	10		1	6		3	4	
1972	8	6		4	3		4	3	
1973	2	11	1	2	4	1	0	7	
1974	2	12		0	7		2	5	
1975	5	9		2	5		3	4	
1976	3	11		3	4		0	7	
1977	5	9		3	4		2	5	
1978	6	10		5	3		1	7	
1979	6	10		4	4		2	6	
1980	4	12		2	6		2	6	
1981	9	7		4	4		5	3	
1982	4	5		2	3		2	2	
1983	3	12	1	1	7		2	5	1
1984	9	7		6	2		3	5	
1985	10	6		6	2		4	4	
1986	14	2		8	0		6	2	
1987	6	9		5	3		1	6	
1988	10	6		5	3		5	3	
1989	12	4		7	1		5	3	
1990	13	3		7	1		6	2	
1991	8	8		5	3		3	5	
1992	6	10		4	4		2	6	
Total	482	391	32	274	180	16	208	211	16

Philadelphia Eagles

Season	All Games W	L	T	Home Games W	L	T	Road Games W	L	T
1933	3	5	1	2	3	1	1	2	
1934	4	7		2	4		2	3	
1935	2	9		0	5		2	4	
1936	1	11		1	6		0	5	
1937	2	8	1	0	5	1	2	3	
1938	5	6		2	3		3	3	
1939	1	9	1	1	3	1	0	6	
1940	1	10		1	4		0	6	
1941	2	8	1	1	4	1	1	4	
1942	2	9		0	5		2	4	
1944	7	1	2	3	1	2	4	0	
1945	7	3		6	0		1	3	
1946	6	5		3	2		3	3	
1947	8	4		6	1		2	3	
1948	9	2	1	6	0		3	2	1
1949	11	1		6	0		5	1	
1950	6	6		2	4		4	2	
1951	4	8		1	5		3	3	
1952	7	5		4	2		3	3	
1953	7	4	1	5	0	1	2	4	
1954	7	4	1	5	1		2	3	1
1955	4	7	1	4	2		0	5	1
1956	3	8	1	2	3	1	1	5	
1957	4	8		3	3		1	5	

Season	All Games W	L	T	Home Games W	L	T	Road Games W	L	T
1958	2	9	1	2	4		0	5	1
1959	6	5		4	1		2	4	
1960	10	2		5	1		5	1	
1961	10	4		5	2		5	2	
1962	3	10	1	2	5		1	5	1
1963	2	10	2	1	5	1	1	5	1
1964	6	8		3	4		3	4	
1965	5	9		2	5		3	4	
1966	9	5		5	2		4	3	
1967	6	7	1	5	2		1	5	1
1968	2	12		1	6		1	6	
1969	4	9	1	2	5		2	4	1
1970	3	10	1	3	3	1	0	7	
1971	6	7	1	3	4		3	3	1
1972	2	11	1	0	6	1	2	5	
1973	5	8	1	4	3		1	5	1
1974	7	7		5	2		2	5	
1975	4	10		2	5		2	5	
1976	4	10		2	5		2	5	
1977	5	9		4	3		1	6	
1978	9	7		5	3		4	4	
1979	11	5		5	3		6	2	
1980	12	4		7	1		5	3	
1981	10	6		6	2		4	4	
1982	3	6		1	4		2	2	
1983	5	11		1	7		4	4	
1984	6	9	1	5	3		1	6	1
1985	7	9		4	4		3	5	
1986	5	10	1	2	5	1	3	5	
1987	7	8		4	4		3	4	
1988	10	6		5	3		5	3	
1989	11	5		6	2		5	3	
1990	10	6		6	2		4	4	
1991	10	6		4	4		6	2	
1992	11	5		8	0		3	5	
Total	341	413	23	195	186	12	146	227	11

Phoenix Cardinals*

Season	All Games W	L	T	Home Games W	L	T	Road Games W	L	T
1920	6	2	2	5	1	1	1	1	1
1921	3	3	2	3	3	1	0	0	1
1922	8	3		8	3		0	0	
1923	8	4		8	3		0	1	
1924	5	4	1	5	3	1	0	1	
1925	11	2	1	11	2		0	0	1
1926	5	6	1	3	3		2	3	1
1927	3	7	1	2	3	1	1	4	
1928	1	5		1	1		0	4	
1929	6	6	1	3	2		3	4	1
1930	5	6	2	3	2		2	4	2
1931	5	4		3	0		2	4	
1932	2	6	2	1	2	1	1	4	1
1933	1	9	1	0	4	1	1	5	
1934	5	6		2	2		3	4	
1935	6	4	2	2	2		4	2	2
1936	3	8	1	3	1	1	0	7	
1937	5	5	1	1	3		4	2	1
1938	2	9		1	4		1	5	
1939	1	10		0	4		1	6	
1940	2	7	2	2	1	1	0	6	1
1941	3	7	1	0	3	1	3	4	
1942	3	8		2	2		1	6	
1943	0	10		0	3		0	7	
1945	1	9		0	3		1	6	
1946	6	5		2	2		4	3	
1947	9	3		5	0		4	3	
1948	11	1		5	1		6	0	
1949	6	5	1	2	3	1	4	2	
1950	5	7		3	3		2	4	
1951	3	9		1	5		2	4	
1952	4	8		2	4		2	4	
1953	1	10	1	0	5	1	1	5	
1954	2	10		2	4		0	6	
1955	4	7	1	3	2	1	1	5	
1956	7	5		4	2		3	3	
1957	3	9		0	6		3	3	
1958	2	9	1	1	4	1	1	5	
1959	2	10		2	4		0	6	
1960	6	5	1	3	2	1	3	3	
1961	7	7		3	4		4	3	
1962	4	9	1	2	4	1	2	5	
1963	9	5		3	4		6	1	
1964	9	3	2	4	1	1	5	2	1
1965	5	9		2	5		3	4	
1966	8	5	1	5	1	1	3	4	
1967	6	7	1	3	3	1	3	4	
1968	9	4	1	4	2	1	5	2	
1969	4	9	1	3	4		1	5	1
1970	8	5	1	6	1		2	4	1
1971	4	9	1	1	5	1	3	4	
1972	4	9	1	2	5		2	4	1
1973	4	9	1	2	4	1	2	5	
1974	10	4		5	2		5	2	
1975	11	3		6	1		5	2	
1976	10	4		6	1		4	3	
1977	7	7		4	3		3	4	
1978	6	10		3	5		3	5	
1979	5	11		3	5		2	6	
1980	5	11		2	6		3	5	
1981	7	9		5	3		2	6	
1982	5	4		1	3		4	1	
1983	8	7	1	4	3	1	4	4	
1984	9	7		5	3		4	4	
1985	5	11		4	4		1	7	
1986	4	11	1	3	5		1	6	1
1987	7	8		4	3		3	5	
1988	7	9		4	4		3	5	
1989	5	11		2	6		3	5	
1990	5	11		3	5		2	6	
1991	4	12		2	6		2	6	
1992	4	12		3	5		1	7	
Total	376	505	39	213	223	22	163	282	17

*includes Chicago Cardinals (1920-59) and St. Louis Cardinals (1960-87).

San Francisco 49ers

Season	All Games W	L	T	Home Games W	L	T	Road Games W	L	T
1950	3	9		3	3		0	6	
1951	7	4	1	5	1		2	3	1
1952	7	5		3	3		4	2	
1953	9	3		5	1		4	2	
1954	7	4	1	4	2		3	2	1
1955	4	8		2	4		2	4	
1956	5	6	1	3	3		2	3	1
1957	8	4		5	1		3	3	
1958	6	6		4	2		2	4	
1959	7	5		4	2		3	3	
1960	7	5		3	3		4	2	
1961	7	6	1	5	1	1	2	5	
1962	6	8		1	6		5	2	
1963	2	12		2	5		0	7	
1964	4	10		3	4		1	6	
1965	7	6	1	4	2	1	3	4	
1966	6	6	2	4	2	1	2	4	1
1967	7	7		3	4		4	3	
1968	7	6	1	3	3	1	4	3	
1969	4	8	2	3	3	1	1	5	1
1970	10	3	1	5	1	1	5	2	
1971	9	5		4	3		5	2	
1972	8	5	1	4	2	1	4	3	
1973	5	9		3	4		2	5	
1974	6	8		3	4		3	4	
1975	5	9		2	5		3	4	
1976	8	6		4	3		4	3	
1977	5	9		3	4		2	5	
1978	2	14		2	6		0	8	
1979	2	14		2	6		0	8	
1980	6	10		4	4		2	6	
1981	13	3		7	1		6	2	
1982	3	6		0	5		3	1	
1983	10	6		4	4		6	2	
1984	15	1		7	1		8	0	
1985	10	6		5	3		5	3	
1986	10	5	1	6	2		4	3	1
1987	13	2		6	1		7	1	
1988	10	6		4	4		6	2	
1989	14	2		6	2		8	0	
1990	14	2		6	2		8	0	
1991	10	6		7	1		3	5	
1992	14	2		7	1		7	1	
Total	322	267	13	170	124	7	152	143	6

Tampa Bay Buccaneers

Season	All Games W	L	T	Home Games W	L	T	Road Games W	L	T
1976	0	14		0	7		0	7	
1977	2	12		1	6		1	6	
1978	5	11		3	5		2	6	
1979	10	6		5	3		5	3	
1980	5	10	1	2	5	1	3	5	
1981	9	7		6	2		3	5	
1982	5	4		4	1		1	3	
1983	2	14		1	7		1	7	
1984	6	10		6	2		0	8	
1985	2	14		2	6		0	8	
1986	2	14		1	7		1	7	
1987	4	11		2	5		2	6	
1988	5	11		3	5		2	6	
1989	5	11		2	6		3	5	
1990	6	10		4	4		2	6	
1991	3	13		3	5		0	8	
1992	5	11		3	5		2	6	
Total	76	183	1	48	81	1	28	102	

Washington Redskins*

Season	All Games W	L	T	Home Games W	L	T	Road Games W	L	T
1932	4	4	2	2	3	1	2	1	1
1933	5	5	2	4	2		1	3	2
1934	6	6		4	3		2	3	
1935	2	8	1	2	5		0	3	1
1936	7	5		4	3		3	2	
1937	8	3		4	2		4	1	
1938	6	3	2	3	1	1	3	2	1
1939	8	2	1	5	0	1	3	2	
1940	9	2		6	0		3	2	
1941	6	5		4	2		2	3	
1942	10	1		5	1		5	0	
1943	6	3	1	4	2		2	1	1
1944	6	3	1	4	2		2	1	1
1945	8	2		6	0		2	2	
1946	5	5	1	3	2	1	2	3	
1947	4	8		4	2		0	6	
1948	7	5		4	2		3	3	
1949	4	7	1	3	3		1	4	1
1950	3	9		1	5		2	4	
1951	5	7		2	4		3	3	
1952	4	8		1	5		3	3	
1953	6	5	1	3	3		3	2	1
1954	3	9		3	3		0	6	
1955	8	4		3	3		5	1	
1956	6	6		4	2		2	4	
1957	5	6	1	2	3	1	3	3	
1958	4	7	1	3	2	1	1	5	
1959	4	8		2	4		2	4	
1960	1	9	2	1	4	1	0	5	1
1961	1	12	1	1	6		0	6	1
1962	5	7	2	3	4		2	3	2
1963	3	11		1	6		2	5	
1964	6	8		4	3		2	5	
1965	6	8		3	4		3	4	
1966	7	7		4	3		3	4	
1967	5	6	3	2	4	1	3	2	2
1968	5	9		3	4		2	5	
1969	7	5	2	4	2	1	3	3	1
1970	6	8		4	3		2	5	
1971	9	4	1	4	2	1	5	2	
1972	11	3		6	1		5	2	
1973	10	4		7	0		3	4	
1974	10	4		6	1		4	3	
1975	8	6		5	2		3	4	
1976	10	4		5	2		5	2	
1977	9	5		5	2		4	3	
1978	8	8		5	3		3	5	
1979	10	6		6	2		4	4	
1980	6	10		4	4		2	6	
1981	8	8		5	3		3	5	
1982	8	1		3	1		5	0	
1983	14	2		7	1		7	1	
1984	11	5		7	1		4	4	
1985	10	6		5	3		5	3	
1986	12	4		7	1		5	3	
1987	11	4		6	1		5	3	
1988	7	9		4	4		3	5	
1989	10	6		4	4		6	2	
1990	10	6		7	1		3	5	
1991	14	2		7	1		7	1	
1992	9	7		6	2		3	5	
Total	426	350	26	246	154	10	180	196	16

*includes Boston Braves (1932) and Boston Redskins (1933-36).

HISTORY

PRO FOOTBALL HALL OF FAME

The Professional Football Hall of Fame is located in Canton, Ohio, site of the organizational meeting on September 17, 1920, from which the National Football League evolved. The NFL recognized Canton as the Hall of Fame site on April 27, 1961. Canton area individuals, foundations, and companies donated almost $400,000 in cash and services to provide funds for the construction of the original two-building complex, which was dedicated on September 7, 1963. The original Hall of Fame complex was almost doubled in size with the completion of a $620,000 expansion project that was dedicated on May 10, 1971. A second expansion project was completed on November 20, 1978. It now features four exhibition areas and a theater twice the size of the original one.

The Hall represents the sport of pro football in many ways—through four large and colorful exhibition galleries, in the twin enshrinement halls, with numerous fan-participation electronic devices, a research library, and a museum store.

In recent years, the Pro Football Hall of Fame has become an extremely popular tourist attraction. At the end of 1992, a total of 5,270,887 fans had visited the Hall of Fame.

New members of the Pro Football Hall of Fame are elected annually by a 34-member National Board of Selectors, made up of media representatives from every league city, five at-large representatives, and a representative of the Pro Football Writers of America. Between four and seven new members are elected each year. An affirmative vote of approximately 80 percent is needed for election.

Any fan may nominate any eligible player or contributor simply by writing to the Pro Football Hall of Fame. Players must be retired five years to be eligible, while a coach need only to be retired with no time limit specified. Contributors (administrators, owners, *et al.*) may be elected while they are still active.

The charter class of 17 enshrinees was elected in 1963 and the honor roll now stands at 169 with the election of a five-man class in 1993. That class consists of Dan Fouts, Larry Little, Chuck Noll, Walter Payton, and Bill Walsh.

Roster of Members

HERB ADDERLEY
Defensive back. 6-1, 200. Born in Philadelphia, Pennsylvania, June 8, 1939. Michigan State. Inducted in 1980. 1961-69 Green Bay Packers, 1970-72 Dallas Cowboys.

LANCE ALWORTH
Wide receiver. 6-0, 184. Born in Houston, Texas, August 3, 1940. Arkansas. Inducted in 1978. 1962-70 San Diego Chargers, 1971-72 Dallas Cowboys.

DOUG ATKINS
Defensive end. 6-8, 275. Born in Humboldt, Tennessee, May 8, 1930. Tennessee. Inducted in 1982. 1953-54 Cleveland Browns, 1955-66 Chicago Bears, 1967-69 New Orleans Saints.

MORRIS (RED) BADGRO
End. 6-0, 190. Born in Orilla, Washington, December 1, 1902. Southern California. Inducted in 1981. 1927 New York Yankees, 1930-35 New York Giants, 1936 Brooklyn Dodgers.

LEM BARNEY
Cornerback. 6-0, 190. Born in Gulfport, Mississippi, September 9, 1945. Jackson State. Inducted in 1992. 1967-77 Detroit Lions.

CLIFF BATTLES
Halfback. 6-1, 201. Born in Akron, Ohio, May 1, 1910. Died April 28, 1981. West Virginia Wesleyan. Inducted in 1968. 1932 Boston Braves, 1933-36 Boston Redskins, 1937 Washington Redskins.

SAMMY BAUGH
Quarterback. 6-2, 180. Born in Temple, Texas, March 17, 1914. Texas Christian. Inducted in 1963. 1937-52 Washington Redskins.

CHUCK BEDNARIK
Center-linebacker. 6-3, 230. Born in Bethlehem, Pennsylvania, May 1, 1925. Pennsylvania. Inducted in 1967. 1949-62 Philadelphia Eagles.

BERT BELL
Team owner. Commissioner. Born in Philadelphia, Pennsylvania, February 25, 1895. Died October 11, 1959. Pennsylvania. Inducted in 1963. 1933-40 Philadelphia Eagles, 1941-42 Pittsburgh Steelers, 1943 Phil-Pitt, 1944-46 Pittsburgh Steelers. Commissioner, 1946-59.

BOBBY BELL
Linebacker. 6-4, 225. Born in Shelby, North Carolina, June 17, 1940. Minnesota. Inducted in 1983. 1963-74 Kansas City Chiefs.

RAYMOND BERRY
End. 6-2, 187. Born in Corpus Christi, Texas, February 27, 1933. Southern Methodist. Inducted in 1973. 1955-67 Baltimore Colts.

CHARLES W. BIDWILL, SR.
Team owner. Born in Chicago, Illinois, September 16, 1895. Died April 19, 1947. Loyola of Chicago. Inducted in 1967. 1933-43 Chicago Cardinals, 1944 Card-Pitt, 1945-47 Chicago Cardinals.

FRED BILETNIKOFF
Wide receiver. 6-1, 190. Born in Erie, Pennsylvania, February 23, 1943. Florida State. Inducted in 1988. 1965-78 Oakland Raiders.

GEORGE BLANDA
Quarterback-kicker. 6-2, 215. Born in Youngwood, Pennsylvania, September 17, 1927. Kentucky. Inducted in 1981. 1949-58 Chicago Bears, 1950 Baltimore Colts, 1960-66 Houston Oilers, 1967-75 Oakland Raiders.

MEL BLOUNT
Cornerback. 6-3, 205. Born in Vidalia, Georgia, April 10, 1948. Southern University. Inducted in 1989. 1970-83 Pittsburgh Steelers.

TERRY BRADSHAW
Quarterback. 6-3, 210. Born in Shreveport, Louisiana, September 2, 1948. Louisiana Tech. Inducted in 1989. 1970-83 Pittsburgh Steelers.

JIM BROWN
Fullback. 6-2, 232. Born in St. Simons, Georgia, February 17, 1936. Syracuse. Inducted in 1971. 1957-65 Cleveland Browns.

PAUL BROWN
Coach. Born in Norwalk, Ohio, September 7, 1908. Died August 5, 1991. Miami, Ohio. Inducted in 1967. 1946-49 Cleveland Browns (AAFC), 1950-62 Cleveland Browns, 1968-75 Cincinnati Bengals.

ROOSEVELT BROWN
Tackle. 6-3, 255. Born in Charlottesville, Virginia, October 20, 1932. Morgan State. Inducted in 1975. 1953-65 New York Giants.

WILLIE BROWN
Defensive back. 6-1, 210. Born in Yazoo City, Mississippi, December 2, 1940. Grambling. Inducted in 1984. 1963-66 Denver Broncos, 1967-78 Oakland Raiders.

BUCK BUCHANAN
Defensive tackle. 6-7, 274. Born in Gainesville, Alabama, September 10, 1940. Grambling. Inducted in 1990. 1963-75 Kansas City Chiefs.

DICK BUTKUS
Linebacker. 6-3, 245. Born in Chicago, Illinois, December 9, 1942. Illinois. Inducted in 1979. 1965-73 Chicago Bears.

EARL CAMPBELL
Running back. 5-11, 233. Born in Tyler, Texas, March 29, 1955. Texas. Inducted in 1991. 1978-84 Houston Oilers, 1984-85 New Orleans Saints.

TONY CANADEO
Halfback. 5-11, 195. Born in Chicago, Illinois, May 5, 1919. Gonzaga. Inducted in 1974. 1941-44, 1946-52 Green Bay Packers.

JOE CARR
NFL president. Born in Columbus, Ohio, October 22, 1880. Died May 20, 1939. Did not attend college. Inducted in 1963. President, 1921-39 National Football League.

GUY CHAMBERLIN
End. Coach. 6-2, 210. Born in Blue Springs, Nebraska, January 16, 1894. Died April 4, 1967. Nebraska. Inducted in 1965. 1920 Decatur Staleys, 1921 Chicago Staleys, player-coach 1922-23 Canton Bulldogs, 1924 Cleveland Bulldogs, 1925-26 Frankford Yellow Jackets, 1927 Chicago Cardinals.

JACK CHRISTIANSEN
Defensive back. 6-1, 185. Born in Sublette, Kansas, December 20, 1928. Died June 29, 1986. Colorado State. Inducted in 1970. 1951-58 Detroit Lions.

EARL (DUTCH) CLARK
Quarterback. 6-0, 185. Born in Fowler, Colorado, October 11, 1906. Died August 5, 1978. Colorado College. Inducted in 1963. 1931-32 Portsmouth Spartans, 1934-38 Detroit Lions.

GEORGE CONNOR
Tackle-linebacker. 6-3, 240. Born in Chicago, Illinois, January 21, 1925. Holy Cross, Notre Dame. Inducted in 1975. 1948-55 Chicago Bears.

JIMMY CONZELMAN
Quarterback. Coach. Team owner. 6-0, 180. Born in St. Louis, Missouri, March 6, 1898. Died July 31, 1970. Washington, Missouri. Inducted in 1964. 1920 Decatur Staleys, 1921-22 Rock Island, Ill., Independents, 1923-24 Milwaukee Badgers; owner-coach, 1925-26 Detroit Panthers; player-coach 1927-29, coach 1930 Providence Steam Roller; coach, 1940-42 Chicago Cardinals, 1946-48 Chicago Cardinals.

LARRY CSONKA
Running back. 6-3, 235. Born in Stow, Ohio, December 25, 1946. Syracuse. Inducted in 1987. Miami Dolphins 1968-74, 1979, New York Giants 1976-78.

AL DAVIS
Team, League Administrator. Born in Brockton, Massachusetts, July 4, 1929. Wittenberg, Syracuse. Inducted in 1992. 1963-81 Oakland Raiders, 1982-92 Los Angeles Raiders, 1966 American Football League.

WILLIE DAVIS
Defensive end. 6-3, 245. Born in Lisbon, Louisiana, July 24, 1934. Grambling. Inducted in 1981. 1958-59 Cleveland Browns, 1960-69 Green Bay Packers.

LEN DAWSON
Quarterback. 6-0, 190. Born in Alliance, Ohio, June 20, 1935. Purdue. Inducted in 1987. Pittsburgh Steelers 1957-59, Cleveland Browns 1960-61, Dallas Texans 1962, Kansas City Chiefs 1963-75.

MIKE DITKA
Tight end. 6-3, 225. Born in Carnegie, Pennsylvania, October 18, 1939. Pittsburgh. Inducted in 1988. 1961-66 Chicago Bears, 1967-68 Philadelphia Eagles, 1969-72 Dallas Cowboys.

ART DONOVAN
Defensive tackle. 6-3, 265. Born in Bronx, New York, June 5, 1925. Boston College. Inducted in 1968. 1950 Baltimore Colts, 1951 New York Yanks, 1952 Dallas Texans, 1953-61 Baltimore Colts.

JOHN (PADDY) DRISCOLL
Quarterback. 5-11, 160. Born in Evanston, Illinois, January 11, 1896. Died June 29, 1968. Northwestern. Inducted in 1965. 1920 Decatur Staleys, 1920-25 Chicago Cardinals, 1926-29 Chicago Bears. Coach, 1956-57 Chicago Bears.

BILL DUDLEY
Halfback. 5-10, 176. Born in Bluefield, Virginia, December 24, 1921. Virginia. Inducted in 1966. 1942, 1945-46 Pittsburgh Steelers, 1947-49 Detroit Lions, 1950-51, 1953 Washington Redskins.

GLEN (TURK) EDWARDS
Tackle. 6-2, 260. Born in Mold, Washington, September 28, 1907. Died January 12, 1973. Washington State. Inducted in 1969. 1932 Boston Braves, 1933-36 Boston Redskins, 1937-40 Washington Redskins.

WEEB EWBANK
Coach. Born in Richmond, Indiana, May 6, 1907. Miami, Ohio. Inducted in 1978. 1954-62 Baltimore Colts, 1963-73 New York Jets.

TOM FEARS
End. 6-2, 215. Born in Los Angeles, California, December 3, 1923. Santa Clara, UCLA. Inducted in 1970. 1948-56 Los Angeles Rams.

RAY FLAHERTY
End. Coach. Born in Spokane, Washington, September 1, 1904. Gonzaga. Inducted in 1976. 1926 Los Angeles Wildcats (AFL), 1927-28 New York Yankees, 1928-29, 1931-35 New York Giants. Coach, 1936 Boston Redskins, 1937-42 Washington Redskins, 1946-48 New York Yankees (AAFC), 1949 Chicago Hornets (AAFC).

LEN FORD
End. 6-5, 260. Born in Washington, D.C., February 18, 1926. Died March 14, 1972. Michigan. Inducted in 1976. 1948-49 Los Angeles Dons (AAFC), 1950-57 Cleveland Browns, 1958 Green Bay Packers.

DAN FORTMANN
Guard. 6-0, 207. Born in Pearl River, New York, April 11, 1916. Colgate. Inducted in 1965. 1936-43 Chicago Bears.

DAN FOUTS
Quarterback. 6-3, 210. Born in San Francisco, California, June 10, 1951. Oregon. Inducted in 1993. 1973-1987 San Diego Chargers.

FRANK GATSKI
Center. 6-3, 240. Born in Farmington, West Virginia, March 18, 1922. Marshall, Auburn. Inducted in 1985. 1946-49 Cleveland Browns (AAFC), 1950-56 Cleveland Browns, 1957 Detroit Lions.

BILL GEORGE
Linebacker. 6-2, 230. Born in Waynesburg, Pennsylvania, October 27, 1930. Died September 30, 1982. Wake Forest. Inducted in 1974. 1952-65 Chicago Bears, 1966 Los Angeles Rams.

FRANK GIFFORD
Halfback. 6-1, 195. Born in Santa Monica, California, August 16, 1930. Southern California. Inducted in 1977. 1952-60, 1962-64 New York Giants.

SID GILLMAN
Coach. Born in Minneapolis, Minnesota, October 26, 1911. Ohio State. Inducted in 1983. 1955-59 Los Angeles Rams, 1960 Los Angeles Chargers, 1961-69 San Diego Chargers, 1973-74 Houston Oilers.

OTTO GRAHAM
Quarterback. 6-1, 195. Born in Waukegan, Illinois, December 6, 1921. Northwestern. Inducted in 1965. 1946-49 Cleveland Browns (AAFC), 1950-55 Cleveland Browns.

HAROLD (RED) GRANGE
Halfback. 6-0, 185. Born in Forksville, Pennsylvania, June 13, 1903. Died January 28, 1991. Illinois. Inducted in 1963. 1925 Chicago Bears, 1926 New York Yankees (AFL), 1927 New York Yankees, 1929-34 Chicago Bears.

JOE GREENE
Defensive tackle. 6-4, 260. Born in Temple, Texas, September 24, 1946. North Texas State. Inducted in 1987. 1969-81 Pittsburgh Steelers.

FORREST GREGG
Tackle. 6-4, 250. Born in Birthright, Texas, October 18, 1933. Southern Methodist. Inducted in 1977. 1956, 1958-70 Green Bay Packers, 1971 Dallas Cowboys.

BOB GRIESE
Quarterback. 6-1, 190. Born in Evansville, Indiana, February 3, 1945. Purdue. Inducted in 1990. 1967-80 Miami Dolphins.

LOU GROZA
Tackle-kicker. 6-3, 250. Born in Martin's Ferry, Ohio, January 25, 1924. Ohio State. Inducted in 1974. 1946-49 Cleveland Browns (AAFC), 1950-59, 1961-67 Cleveland Browns.

JOE GUYON
Halfback. 6-1, 180. Born in Mahnomen, Minnesota, November 26, 1892. Died November 27, 1971. Carlisle, Georgia Tech. Inducted in 1966. 1920 Canton Bulldogs, 1921 Cleveland Indians, 1922-23 Oorang Indians, 1924 Rock Island, Ill., Independents, 1924-25 Kansas City Cowboys, 1927 New York Giants.

GEORGE HALAS
End. Coach. Team owner. Born in Chicago, Illinois, February 2, 1895. Died October 31, 1983. Illinois. Inducted in 1963. 1920 Decatur Staleys, 1921 Chicago Staleys, 1922-29 Chicago Bears; coach, 1933-42, 1946-55, 1958-67 Chicago Bears.

JACK HAM
Linebacker. 6-1, 225. Born in Johnstown, Pennsylvania, December 23, 1948. Penn State. Inducted in 1988. 1971-82 Pittsburgh Steelers.

JOHN HANNAH
Guard. 6-3, 265. Born in Canton, Georgia, April 4, 1951. Alabama. Inducted in 1991. 1973-85 New England Patriots.

FRANCO HARRIS
Running back. 6-2, 225. Born in Fort Dix, New Jersey, March 7, 1950. Penn State. Inducted in 1990. 1972-83 Pittsburgh Steelers, 1984 Seattle Seahawks.

ED HEALEY
Tackle. 6-3, 220. Born in Indian Orchard, Massachusetts, December 28, 1894. Died December 9, 1978. Dartmouth. Inducted in 1964. 1920-22 Rock Island, Ill., Independents, 1922-27 Chicago Bears.

MEL HEIN
Center. 6-2, 225. Born in Redding, California, August 22, 1909. Died January 31, 1992. Washington State. Inducted in 1963. 1931-45 New York Giants.

TED HENDRICKS
Linebacker. 6-7, 235. Born in Guatemala City, Guatemala, November 1, 1947. Miami. Inducted in 1990. 1969-73 Baltimore Colts, 1974 Green Bay Packers, 1975-81 Oakland Raiders, 1982-83 Los Angeles Raiders.

WILBUR (PETE) HENRY
Tackle. 6-0, 250. Born in Mansfield, Ohio, October 31, 1897. Died February 7, 1952. Washington & Jefferson. Inducted in 1963. 1920-23, 1925-26 Canton Bulldogs, 1927 New York Giants, 1927-28 Pottsville Maroons.

ARNIE HERBER
Quarterback. 6-1, 200. Born in Green Bay, Wisconsin, April 2, 1910. Died October 14, 1969. Wisconsin, Regis College. Inducted in 1966. 1930-40 Green Bay Packers, 1944-45 New York Giants.

BILL HEWITT
End. 5-11, 191. Born in Bay City, Michigan, October 8, 1909. Died January 14, 1947. Michigan. Inducted in 1971. 1932-36 Chicago Bears, 1937-39 Philadelphia Eagles, 1943 Phil-Pitt.

CLARKE HINKLE
Fullback. 5-11, 201. Born in Toronto, Ohio, April 10, 1909. Died November 9, 1988. Bucknell. Inducted in 1964. 1932-41 Green Bay Packers.

ELROY (CRAZYLEGS) HIRSCH
Halfback-end. 6-2, 190. Born in Wausau, Wisconsin, June 17, 1923. Wisconsin, Michigan. Inducted in 1968. 1946-48 Chicago Rockets (AAFC), 1949-57 Los Angeles Rams.

PAUL HORNUNG
Halfback. 6-2, 220. Born in Louisville, Kentucky, December 23, 1935. Notre Dame. Inducted in 1986. 1957-62, 1964-66 Green Bay Packers.

KEN HOUSTON
Safety. 6-3, 198. Born in Lufkin, Texas, November 12, 1944. Prairie View A&M. Inducted in 1986. 1967-72 Houston Oilers, 1973-80 Washington Redskins.

CAL HUBBARD
Tackle. 6-5, 250. Born in Keytesville, Missouri, October 31, 1900. Died October 17, 1977. Centenary, Geneva. Inducted in 1963. 1927-28 New York Giants, 1929-33, 1935 Green Bay Packers, 1936 New York Giants, 1936 Pittsburgh Pirates.

SAM HUFF
Linebacker. 6-1, 230. Born in Morgantown, West Virginia, October 4, 1934. West Virginia. Inducted in 1982. 1956-63 New York Giants, 1964-67, 1969 Washington Redskins.

LAMAR HUNT
Team owner. Born in El Dorado, Arkansas, August 2, 1932. Southern Methodist. Inducted in 1972. 1960-62 Dallas Texans, 1963-90 Kansas City Chiefs.

DON HUTSON
End. 6-1, 180. Born in Pine Bluff, Arkansas, January 31, 1913. Alabama. Inducted in 1963. 1935-45 Green Bay Packers.

JOHN HENRY JOHNSON
Fullback. 6-2, 225. Born in Waterproof, Louisiana, November 24, 1929. St. Mary's, Arizona State. Inducted in 1987. 1954-56 San Francisco 49ers, 1957-59 Detroit Lions, 1960-65 Pittsburgh Steelers, 1966 Houston Oilers.

DAVID (DEACON) JONES
Defensive end. 6-5, 250. Born in Eatonville, Florida, December 9, 1938. Mississippi Vocational. Inducted in 1980. 1961-71 Los Angeles Rams, 1972-73 San Diego Chargers, 1974 Washington Redskins.

STAN JONES
Guard-defensive tackle. 6-1, 250. Born in Altoona, Pennsylvania, November 24, 1931. Maryland. Inducted in 1991. 1954-65 Chicago Bears, 1966 Washington Redskins.

SONNY JURGENSEN
Quarterback. 6-0, 203. Born in Wilmington, North Carolina, August 23, 1934. Duke. Inducted in 1983. 1957-63 Philadelphia Eagles, 1964-74 Washington Redskins.

WALT KIESLING
Guard. Coach. 6-2, 245. Born in St. Paul, Minnesota, March 27, 1903. Died March 2, 1962. St. Thomas (Minnesota). Inducted in 1966. 1926-27 Duluth Eskimos, 1928 Pottsville Maroons, 1929-33 Chicago Cardinals, 1934 Chicago Bears, 1935-36 Green Bay Packers, 1937-38 Pittsburgh Pirates; coach, 1939-42 Pittsburgh Steelers; co-coach, 1943 Phil-Pitt, 1944 Card-Pitt; coach, 1954-56 Pittsburgh Steelers.

FRANK (BRUISER) KINARD
Tackle. 6-1, 210. Born in Pelahatchie, Mississippi, October 23, 1914. Died September 7, 1985. Mississippi. Inducted in 1971. 1938-44 Brooklyn Dodgers-Tigers, 1946-47 New York Yankees (AAFC).

EARL (CURLY) LAMBEAU
Coach. Born in Green Bay, Wisconsin, April 9, 1898. Died June 1, 1965. Notre Dame. Inducted in 1963. 1919-49 Green Bay Packers, 1950-51 Chicago Cardinals, 1952-53 Washington Redskins.

JACK LAMBERT
Linebacker. 6-4, 220. Born in Mantua, Ohio, July 8, 1952. Kent State. Inducted in 1990. 1974-84 Pittsburgh Steelers.

TOM LANDRY
Coach. Born in Mission, Texas, September 11, 1924. Texas. Inducted in 1990. 1960-88 Dallas Cowboys.

DICK (NIGHT TRAIN) LANE
Defensive back. 6-2, 210. Born in Austin, Texas, April 16, 1928. Scottsbluff Junior College. Inducted in 1974. 1952-53 Los Angeles Rams, 1954-59 Chicago Cardinals, 1960-65 Detroit Lions.

JIM LANGER
Center. 6-2, 255. Born in Little Falls, Minnesota, May 16, 1948. South Dakota State. Inducted in 1987. Miami Dolphins 1970-79, Minnesota Vikings 1980-81.

WILLIE LANIER
Linebacker. 6-1, 245. Born in Clover, Virginia, August 21, 1945. Morgan State. Inducted in 1986. 1967-77 Kansas City Chiefs.

YALE LARY
Defensive back-punter. 5-11, 189. Born in Fort Worth, Texas, November 24, 1930. Texas A&M. Inducted in 1979. 1952-53, 1956-64 Detroit Lions.

DANTE LAVELLI
End. 6-0, 199. Born in Hudson, Ohio, February 23, 1923. Ohio State. Inducted in 1975. 1946-49 Cleveland Browns (AAFC), 1950-56 Cleveland Browns.

BOBBY LAYNE
Quarterback. 6-2, 190. Born in Santa Anna, Texas, December 19, 1926. Died December 1, 1986. Texas. Inducted in 1967. 1948 Chicago Bears, 1949 New York Bulldogs, 1950-58 Detroit Lions, 1958-62 Pittsburgh Steelers.

ALPHONSE (TUFFY) LEEMANS
Fullback. 6-0, 200. Born in Superior, Wisconsin, November 12, 1912. Died January 19, 1979. George Washington. Inducted in 1978. 1936-43 New York Giants.

BOB LILLY
Defensive tackle. 6-5, 260. Born in Olney, Texas, July 26, 1939. Texas Christian. Inducted in 1980. 1961-74 Dallas Cowboys.

LARRY LITTLE
Guard. 6-1, 255. Born in Groveland, Georgia, November 2, 1945. Bethune-Cookman. Inducted in 1993. 1967-68 San Diego Chargers, 1969-80 Miami Dolphins.

VINCE LOMBARDI
Coach. Born in Brooklyn, New York, June 11, 1913. Died September 3, 1970. Fordham. Inducted in 1971. 1959-67 Green Bay Packers, 1969 Washington Redskins.

SID LUCKMAN
Quarterback. 6-0, 195. Born in Brooklyn, New York, November 21, 1916. Columbia. Inducted in 1965. 1939-50 Chicago Bears.

ROY (LINK) LYMAN
Tackle. 6-2, 252. Born in Table Rock, Nebraska, November 30, 1898. Died December 16, 1972. Nebraska. Inducted in 1964. 1922-23, 1925 Canton Bulldogs, 1924 Cleveland Bulldogs, 1925 Frankford Yellow Jackets, 1926-28, 1930-31, 1933-34 Chicago Bears.

JOHN MACKEY
Tight end. 6-2, 224. Born in New York, New York, September 24, 1941. Syracuse. Inducted in 1992. 1963-71 Baltimore Colts, 1972 San Diego Chargers.

TIM MARA
Team owner. Born in New York, New York, July 29, 1887. Died February 17, 1959. Did not attend college. Inducted in 1963. 1925-59 New York Giants.

GINO MARCHETTI
Defensive end. 6-4, 245. Born in Smithers, West Virginia, January 2, 1927. San Francisco. Inducted in 1972. 1952 Dallas Texans, 1953-64, 1966 Baltimore Colts.

GEORGE PRESTON MARSHALL
Team owner. Born in Grafton, West Virginia, October 11, 1897. Died August 9, 1969. Randolph-Macon. Inducted in 1963. 1932 Boston Braves, 1933-36 Boston Redskins, 1937-69 Washington Redskins.

OLLIE MATSON
Halfback. 6-2, 220. Born in Trinity, Texas, May 1, 1930. San Francisco. Inducted in 1972. 1952, 1954-58 Chicago Cardinals, 1959-62 Los Angeles Rams, 1963 Detroit Lions, 1964-66 Philadelphia Eagles.

DON MAYNARD
Wide receiver. 6-1, 175. Born in Crosbyton, Texas, January 25, 1935. Texas Western. Inducted in 1987. New York Giants 1958, New York Titans 1960-62, New York Jets 1963-72, St. Louis Cardinals 1973.

GEORGE McAFEE
Halfback. 6-0, 177. Born in Ironton, Ohio, March 13, 1918. Duke. Inducted in 1966. 1940-41, 1945-50 Chicago Bears.

MIKE McCORMACK
Tackle. 6-4, 248. Born in Chicago, Illinois, June 21, 1930. Kansas. Inducted in 1984. 1951 New York Yanks, 1954-62 Cleveland Browns.

HUGH McELHENNY
Halfback. 6-1, 198. Born in Los Angeles, California, December 31, 1928. Washington. Inducted in 1970. 1952-60 San Francisco 49ers, 1961-62 Minnesota Vikings, 1963 New York Giants, 1964 Detroit Lions.

JOHNNY BLOOD (McNALLY)
Halfback. 6-0, 185. Born in New Richmond, Wisconsin, November 27, 1903. Died November 28, 1985. St. John's (Minnesota). Inducted in 1963. 1925-26 Milwaukee Badgers, 1926-27 Duluth Eskimos, 1928 Pottsville Maroons, 1929-33, 1935-36 Green Bay Packers, 1934 Pittsburgh Pirates; player-coach, 1937-39 Pittsburgh Pirates.

MIKE MICHALSKE
Guard. 6-0, 209. Born in Cleveland, Ohio, April 24, 1903. Died October 26, 1983. Penn State. Inducted in 1964. 1926 New York Yankees (AFL), 1927-28 New York Yankees, 1929-35, 1937 Green Bay Packers.

WAYNE MILLNER
End. 6-0, 191. Born in Roxbury, Massachusetts, January 31, 1913. Died November 19, 1976. Notre Dame. Inducted in 1968. 1936 Boston Redskins, 1937-41, 1945 Washington Redskins.

BOBBY MITCHELL
Running back-wide receiver. 6-0, 195. Born in Hot Springs, Arkansas, June 6, 1935. Illinois. Inducted in 1983. 1958-61 Cleveland Browns, 1962-68 Washington Redskins.

RON MIX
Tackle. 6-4, 250. Born in Los Angeles, California, March 10, 1938. Southern California. Inducted in 1979. 1960 Los Angeles Chargers, 1961-69 San Diego Chargers, 1971 Oakland Raiders.

LENNY MOORE
Back. 6-1, 198. Born in Reading, Pennsylvania, November 25, 1933. Penn State. Inducted in 1975. 1956-67 Baltimore Colts.

MARION MOTLEY
Fullback. 6-1, 238. Born in Leesburg, Georgia, June 5, 1920. South Carolina State, Nevada. Inducted in 1968. 1946-49 Cleveland Browns (AAFC), 1950-53 Cleveland Browns, 1955 Pittsburgh Steelers.

GEORGE MUSSO
Guard-tackle. 6-2, 270. Born in Collinsville, Illinois. April 8, 1910. Millikin. Inducted in 1982. 1933-44 Chicago Bears.

BRONKO NAGURSKI
Fullback. 6-2, 225. Born in Rainy River, Ontario, Canada, November 3, 1908. Died January 7, 1990. Minnesota. Inducted in 1963. 1930-37, 1943 Chicago Bears.

JOE NAMATH
Quarterback. 6-2, 200. Born in Beaver Falls, Pennsylvania, May 31, 1943. Alabama. Inducted in 1985. 1965-76 New York Jets, 1977 Los Angeles Rams.

EARLE (GREASY) NEALE
Coach. Born in Parkersburg, West Virginia, November 5, 1891. Died November 2, 1973. West Virginia Wesleyan. Inducted in 1969. 1941-42, 1944-50 Philadelphia Eagles; co-coach, Phil-Pitt 1943.

ERNIE NEVERS
Fullback. 6-1, 205. Born in Willow River, Minnesota, June 11, 1903. Died May 3, 1976. Stanford. Inducted in 1963. 1926-27 Duluth Eskimos, 1929-31 Chicago Cardinals.

RAY NITSCHKE
Linebacker. 6-3, 235. Born in Elmwood Park, Illinois, December 29, 1936. Illinois. Inducted in 1978. 1958-72 Green Bay Packers.

CHUCK NOLL
Coach. Born in Cleveland, Ohio, January 5, 1932. Dayton. Inducted in 1993. 1969-91 Pittsburgh Steelers.

LEO NOMELLINI
Defensive tackle. 6-3, 250. Born in Lucca, Italy, June 19, 1924. Minnesota. Inducted in 1969. 1950-63 San Francisco 49ers.

MERLIN OLSEN
Defensive tackle. 6-5, 270. Born in Logan, Utah, September 15, 1940. Utah State. Inducted in 1982. 1962-76 Los Angeles Rams.

JIM OTTO
Center. 6-2, 255. Born in Wausau, Wisconsin, January 5, 1938. Miami. Inducted in 1980. 1960-74 Oakland Raiders.

STEVE OWEN
Tackle. Coach. 6-0, 235. Born in Cleo Springs, Oklahoma, April 21, 1898. Died May 17, 1964. Phillips. Inducted in 1966. 1924-25 Kansas City Cowboys, 1926-30 New York Giants; coach, 1931-53 New York Giants.

ALAN PAGE
Defensive tackle. 6-4, 225. Born in Canton, Ohio, August 7, 1945. Notre Dame. Inducted in 1988. 1967-78 Minnesota Vikings, 1978-81 Chicago Bears.

CLARENCE (ACE) PARKER
Quarterback. 5-11, 168. Born in Portsmouth, Virginia, May 17, 1912. Duke. Inducted in 1972. 1937-41 Brooklyn Dodgers, 1945 Boston Yanks, 1946 New York Yankees (AAFC).

JIM PARKER
Guard-tackle. 6-3, 273. Born in Macon, Georgia, April 3, 1934. Ohio State. Inducted in 1973. 1957-67 Baltimore Colts.

WALTER PAYTON
Running back. 5-10, 202. Born in Columbia, Mississippi, July 25, 1954. Jackson State. Inducted in 1993. 1975-87 Chicago Bears.

JOE PERRY
Fullback. 6-0, 200. Born in Stevens, Arkansas, January 22, 1927. Compton Junior College. Inducted in 1969. 1948-49 San Francisco 49ers (AAFC), 1950-60, 1963 San Francisco 49ers, 1961-62 Baltimore Colts.

PETE PIHOS
End. 6-1, 210. Born in Orlando, Florida, October 22, 1923. Indiana. Inducted in 1970. 1947-55 Philadelphia Eagles.

HUGH (SHORTY) RAY
Supervisor of officials 1938-56. Born in Highland Park, Illinois, September 21, 1884. Died September 16, 1956. Illinois. Inducted in 1966.

DAN REEVES
Team owner. Born in New York, New York, June 30, 1912. Died April 15, 1971. Georgetown. Inducted in 1967. 1941-45 Cleveland Rams, 1946-71 Los Angeles Rams.

JOHN RIGGINS
Running back. 6-2, 240. Born in Seneca, Kansas, August 4, 1949. Kansas. Inducted in 1992. 1971-75 New York Jets, 1976-79, 1981-85 Washington Redskins.

JIM RINGO
Center. 6-1, 235. Born in Orange, New Jersey, November 21, 1931. Syracuse. Inducted in 1981. 1953-63 Green Bay Packers, 1964-67 Philadelphia Eagles.

ANDY ROBUSTELLI
Defensive end. 6-0, 230. Born in Stamford, Connecticut, December 6, 1925. Arnold College. Inducted in 1971. 1951-55 Los Angeles Rams, 1956-64 New York Giants.

ART ROONEY
Team owner. Born in Coulterville, Pennsylvania, January 27, 1901. Died August 25, 1988. Georgetown, Duquesne. Inducted in 1964. 1933-40 Pittsburgh Pirates, 1941-42, 1945-88 Pittsburgh Steelers, 1943 Phil-Pitt, 1944 Card-Pitt.

PETE ROZELLE
Commissioner. Born in South Gate, California, March 1, 1926. San Francisco. Inducted in 1985. Commissioner, 1960-89.

BOB ST. CLAIR
Tackle. 6-9, 265. Born in San Francisco, California, February 18, 1931. San Francisco, Tulsa. Inducted in 1990. 1953-63 San Francisco 49ers.

GALE SAYERS
Running back. 6-0, 200. Born in Wichita, Kansas, May 30, 1943. Kansas. Inducted in 1977. 1965-71 Chicago Bears.

JOE SCHMIDT
Linebacker. 6-0, 222. Born in Pittsburgh, Pennsylvania, January 19, 1932. Pittsburgh. Inducted in 1973. 1953-65 Detroit Lions.

TEX SCHRAMM
Team president-general manager. Born in San Gabriel, California, June 2, 1920. Texas. Inducted in 1991. 1947-57 Los Angeles Rams. 1960-88 Dallas Cowboys.

ART SHELL
Tackle. 6-5, 285. Born in Charleston, South Carolina, November 25, 1946. Maryland State-Eastern Shore. Inducted in 1989. 1968-81 Oakland Raiders, 1982 Los Angeles Raiders.

O.J. SIMPSON
Running back. 6-1, 212. Born in San Francisco, California, July 9, 1947. Southern California. Inducted in 1985. 1969-77 Buffalo Bills, 1978-79 San Francisco 49ers.

BART STARR
Quarterback. 6-1, 200. Born in Montgomery, Alabama, January 9, 1934. Alabama. Inducted in 1977. 1956-71 Green Bay Packers.

ROGER STAUBACH
Quarterback. 6-3, 202. Born in Cincinnati, Ohio, February 5, 1942. Navy. Inducted in 1985. 1969-79 Dallas Cowboys.

ERNIE STAUTNER
Defensive tackle. 6-2, 235. Born in Prinzing-by-Cham, Bavaria, Germany, April 20, 1925. Boston College. Inducted in 1969. 1950-63 Pittsburgh Steelers.

JAN STENERUD
Kicker. 6-2, 190. Born in Fetsund, Norway, November 26, 1942. Montana State. Inducted in 1991. 1967-79 Kansas City Chiefs, 1980-83 Green Bay Packers, 1984-85 Minnesota Vikings.

KEN STRONG
Halfback. 5-11, 210. Born in New Haven, Connecticut, August 6, 1906. Died October 5, 1979. New York University. Inducted in 1967. 1929-32 Staten Island Stapletons, 1933-35, 1939, 1944-47 New York Giants, 1936-37 New York Yanks (AFL).

JOE STYDAHAR
Tackle. 6-4, 230. Born in Kaylor, Pennsylvania, March 3, 1912. Died March 23, 1977. West Virginia. Inducted in 1967. 1936-42, 1945-46 Chicago Bears.

FRAN TARKENTON
Quarterback. 6-0, 185. Born in Richmond, Virginia, February 3, 1940. Georgia. Inducted in 1986. 1961-66, 1972-78 Minnesota Vikings, 1967-71 New York Giants.

CHARLEY TAYLOR
Running back-wide receiver. 6-3, 210. Born in Grand Prairie, Texas, September 28, 1941. Arizona State. Inducted in 1984. 1964-75, 1977 Washington Redskins.

JIM TAYLOR
Fullback. 6-0, 216. Born in Baton Rouge, Louisiana, September 20, 1935. Louisiana State. Inducted in 1976. 1958-66 Green Bay Packers, 1967 New Orleans Saints.

JIM THORPE
Halfback. 6-1, 190. Born in Prague, Oklahoma, May 28, 1888. Died March 28, 1953. Carlisle. Inducted in 1963. 1915-17, 1919-20, 1926 Canton Bulldogs, 1921 Cleveland Indians, 1922-23 Oorang Indians, 1924 Rock Island, Ill., Independents, 1925 New York Giants, 1928 Chicago Cardinals.

Y.A. TITTLE
Quarterback. 6-0, 200. Born in Marshall, Texas, October 24, 1926. Louisiana State. Inducted in 1971. 1948-49 Baltimore Colts (AAFC), 1950 Baltimore Colts, 1951-60 San Francisco 49ers, 1961-64 New York Giants.

GEORGE TRAFTON
Center. 6-2, 235. Born in Chicago, Illinois, December 6, 1896. Died September 5, 1971. Notre Dame. Inducted in 1964. 1920 Decatur Staleys, 1921 Chicago Staleys, 1922-32 Chicago Bears.

CHARLEY TRIPPI
Halfback. 6-0, 185. Born in Pittston, Pennsylvania, December 14, 1922. Georgia. Inducted in 1968. 1947-55 Chicago Cardinals.

EMLEN TUNNELL
Safety. 6-1, 200. Born in Bryn Mawr, Pennsylvania, March 29, 1925. Died July 23, 1975. Toledo, Iowa. Inducted in 1967. 1948-58 New York Giants, 1959-61 Green Bay Packers.

CLYDE (BULLDOG) TURNER
Center. 6-2, 235. Born in Sweetwater, Texas, November 10, 1919. Hardin-Simmons. Inducted in 1966. 1940-52 Chicago Bears.

JOHNNY UNITAS
Quarterback. 6-1, 195. Born in Pittsburgh, Pennsylvania, May 7, 1933. Louisville. Inducted in 1979. 1956-72 Baltimore Colts, 1973 San Diego Chargers.

GENE UPSHAW
Guard. 6-5, 255. Born in Robstown, Texas, August 15, 1945. Texas A & I. Inducted in 1987. Oakland Raiders 1967-81.

NORM VAN BROCKLIN
Quarterback. 6-1, 190. Born in Eagle Butte, South Dakota, March 15, 1926. Died May 2, 1983. Oregon. Inducted in 1971. 1949-57 Los Angeles Rams, 1958-60 Philadelphia Eagles.

STEVE VAN BUREN
Halfback. 6-1, 200. Born in La Ceiba, Honduras, December 28, 1920. Louisiana State. Inducted in 1965. 1944-51 Philadelphia Eagles.

DOAK WALKER
Halfback. 5-10, 172. Born in Dallas, Texas, January 1, 1927. Southern Methodist. Inducted in 1986. 1950-55 Detroit Lions.

BILL WALSH
Coach. Born in Los Angeles, California, November 30, 1931. San Jose State. Inducted in 1993. 1979-88 San Francisco 49ers.

PAUL WARFIELD
Wide receiver. 6-0, 188. Born in Warren, Ohio, November 28, 1942. Ohio State. Inducted in 1983. 1964-69, 1976-77 Cleveland Browns, 1970-74 Miami Dolphins.

BOB WATERFIELD
Quarterback. 6-2, 200. Born in Elmira, New York, July 26, 1920. Died March 25, 1983. UCLA. Inducted in 1965. 1945 Cleveland Rams, 1946-52 Los Angeles Rams.

ARNIE WEINMEISTER
Defensive tackle. 6-4, 235. Born in Rhein, Saskatchewan, Canada, March 23, 1923. Washington. Inducted in 1984. 1948-49 New York Yankees (AAFC), 1950-53 New York Giants.

BILL WILLIS
Guard. 6-2, 215. Born in Columbus, Ohio, October 5, 1921. Ohio State. Inducted in 1977. 1946-49 Cleveland Browns (AAFC), 1950-53 Cleveland Browns.

LARRY WILSON
Safety. 6-0, 190. Born in Rigby, Idaho, March 24, 1938. Utah. Inducted in 1978. 1960-72 St. Louis Cardinals.

ALEX WOJCIECHOWICZ
Center. 6-0, 235. Born in South River, New Jersey, August 12, 1915. Fordham. Inducted in 1968. 1938-46 Detroit Lions, 1946-50 Philadelphia Eagles.

WILLIE WOOD
Safety. 5-10, 190. Born in Washington, D.C., December 23, 1936. Southern California. Inducted in 1989. 1960-71 Green Bay Packers.

A CHRONOLOGY OF PROFESSIONAL FOOTBALL

1869 Rutgers and Princeton played a college soccer football game, the first ever, November 6. The game used modified London Football Association rules. During the next seven years, rugby gained favor with the major eastern schools over soccer, and modern football began to develop from rugby.
1876 At the Massasoit convention, the first rules for American football were written. Walter Camp, who would become known as the father of American football, first became involved with the game.
1892 In an era in which football was a major attraction of local athletic clubs, an intense competition between two Pittsburgh-area clubs, the Allegheny Athletic Association (AAA) and the Pittsburgh Athletic Club (PAC), led to the making of the first professional football player. Former Yale All-America guard William (Pudge) Heffelfinger was paid $500 by the AAA to play in a game against the PAC, becoming the first person to be paid to play football, November 12. The AAA won the game 4-0 when Heffelfinger picked up a PAC fumble and ran 35 yards for a touchdown.
1893 The Pittsburgh Athletic Club signed one of its players, probably halfback Grant Dibert, to the first-known pro football contract, which covered all of the PAC's games for the year.
1895 John Brallier became the first football player to openly turn pro, accepting $10 and expenses to play for the Latrobe YMCA against the Jeannette Athletic Club.
1896 The Allegheny Athletic Association team fielded the first completely professional team for its abbreviated two-game season.
1897 The Latrobe Athletic Association football team went entirely professional, becoming the first team to play a full season with only professionals.
1898 A touchdown was changed from four points to five.
1899 Chris O'Brien formed a neighborhood team, which played under the name the Morgan Athletic Club, on the south side of Chicago. The team later became known as the Normals, then the Racine (for a street in Chicago) Cardinals, the Chicago Cardinals, the St. Louis Cardinals, and, in 1988, the Phoenix Cardinals. The team remains the oldest continuing operation in pro football.
1900 William C. Temple took over the team payments for the Duquesne Country and Athletic Club, becoming the first known individual club owner.
1902 Baseball's Philadelphia Athletics, managed by Connie Mack, and the Philadelphia Phillies formed professional football teams, joining the Pittsburgh Stars in the first attempt at a pro football league, named the National Football League. The Athletics won the first night football game ever played, 39-0 over Kanaweola AC at Elmira, New York, November 21.

All three teams claimed the pro championship for the year, but the league president, Dave Berry, named the Stars the champions. Pitcher Rube Waddell was with the Athletics, and pitcher Christy Mathewson a fullback for Pittsburgh.

The first World Series of pro football, actually a five-team tournament, was played among a team made up of players from both the Athletics and the Phillies, but simply named New York; the New York Knickerbockers; the Syracuse AC; the Warlow AC; and the Orange (New Jersey) AC at New York's original Madison Square Garden. New York and Syracuse played the first indoor football game before 3,000, December 28. Syracuse, with Glen (Pop) Warner at guard, won 6-0 and went on to win the tournament.
1903 The Franklin (Pa.) Athletic Club won the second and last World Series of pro football over the Oreos AC of Asbury Park, New Jersey; the Watertown Red and Blacks; and the Orange AC.

Pro football was popularized in Ohio when the Massillon Tigers, a strong amateur team, hired four Pittsburgh pros to play in the season-ending game against Akron. At the same time, pro football declined in the Pittsburgh area, and the emphasis on the pro game moved west from Pennsylvania to Ohio.
1904 A field goal was changed from five points to four.

Ohio had at least seven pro teams, with Massillon winning the Ohio Independent Championship, that is, the pro title. Talk surfaced about forming a state-wide league to end spiraling salaries brought about by constant bidding for players and to write universal rules for the game. The feeble attempt to start the league failed.

Halfback Charles Follis signed a contract with the Shelby AC, making him the first-known black pro football player.
1905 The Canton AC, later to become known as the Bulldogs, became a professional team. Massillon again won the Ohio League championship.
1906 The forward pass was legalized. The first authenticated pass completion in a pro game came on October 27, when George (Peggy) Parratt of Massillon threw a completion to Dan (Bullet) Riley in a victory over a combined Benwood-Moundsville team.

Arch-rivals Canton and Massillon, the two best pro teams in America, played twice, with Canton winning the first game but Massillon winning the second and the Ohio League championship. A betting scandal and the financial disaster wrought upon the two clubs by paying huge salaries caused a temporary decline in interest in pro football in the two cities and, somewhat, throughout Ohio.
1909 A field goal dropped from four points to three.
1912 A touchdown was increased from five points to six.

Jack Cusack revived a strong pro team in Canton.
1913 Jim Thorpe, a former football and track star at the Carlisle Indian School (Pa.) and a double gold medal winner at the 1912 Olympics in Stockholm, played for the Pine Village Pros in Indiana.
1915 Massillon again fielded a major team, reviving the old rivalry with Canton. Cusack signed Thorpe to play for Canton for $250 a game.
1916 With Thorpe and former Carlisle teammate Pete Calac starring, Canton went 9-0-1, won the Ohio League championship, and was acclaimed the pro football champion.
1917 Despite an upset by Massillon, Canton again won the Ohio League championship.
1919 Canton again won the Ohio League championship, despite the team having been turned over from Cusack to Ralph Hay. Thorpe and Calac were joined in the backfield by Joe Guyon.

Earl (Curly) Lambeau and George Calhoun organized the Green Bay Packers. Lambeau's employer at the Indian Packing Company provided $500 for equipment and allowed the team to use the company field for practices. The Packers went 10-1.
1920 Pro football was in a state of confusion due to three major problems: dramatically rising salaries; players continually jumping from one team to another following the highest offer; and the use of college players still enrolled in school. A league in which all the members would follow the same rules seemed the answer. An organizational meeting, at which the Akron Pros, Canton Bulldogs, Cleveland Indians, and Dayton Triangles were represented, was held in Canton, Ohio, August 20. This meeting resulted in the formation of the American Professional Football Conference.

A second organizational meeting was held in Canton, September 17. The teams were from four states—Akron, Canton, Cleveland, and Dayton from Ohio; the Hammond Pros and Muncie Flyers from Indiana; the Rochester Jeffersons from New York; and the Rock Island Independents, Decatur Staleys, and Racine Cardinals from Illinois. The name of the league was changed to the American Professional Football Association. Hoping to capitalize on his fame, the members elected Thorpe president; Stanley Cofall of Cleveland was elected vice president. A membership fee of $100 per team was charged to give an appearance of respectability, but no team ever paid it. Scheduling was left up to the teams, and there were wide variations, both in the overall number of games played and in the number played against APFA member teams.

Four other teams—the Buffalo All-Americans, Chicago Tigers, Columbus Panhandles, and Detroit Heralds—joined the league sometime during the year. On September 26, the first game featuring an APFA team was played at Rock Island's Douglas Park. A crowd of 800 watched the Independents defeat the St. Paul Ideals 48-0. A week later, October 3, the first game matching two APFA teams was held. At Triangle Park, Dayton defeated Columbus 14-0, with Lou Partlow of Dayton scoring the first touchdown in a game between Association teams. The same day, Rock Island defeated Muncie 45-0.

By the beginning of December, most of the teams in the APFA had abandoned their hopes for a championship, and some of them, including the Chicago Tigers and the Detroit Heralds, had finished their seasons, disbanded, and had their franchises canceled by the Association. Four teams—Akron, Buffalo, Canton, and Decatur—still had championship aspirations, but a series of late-season games among them left Akron as the only undefeated team in the Association. At one of these games, Akron sold tackle Bob Nash to Buffalo for $300 and five percent of the gate receipts—the first APFA player deal.
1921 At the league meeting in Akron, April 30, the championship of the 1920 season was awarded to the Akron Pros. The APFA was reorganized, with Joe Carr of the Columbus Panhandles named president and Carl Storck of Dayton secretary-treasurer. Carr moved the Association's headquarters to Columbus, drafted a league constitution and by-laws, gave teams territorial rights, restricted player movements, developed membership criteria for the franchises, and issued standings for the first time, so that the APFA would have a clear champion.

The Association's membership increased to 22 teams, including the Green Bay Packers, who were awarded to John Clair of the Acme Packing Company.

Thorpe moved from Canton to the Cleveland Indians, but he was hurt early in the season and played very little.

A.E. Staley turned the Decatur Staleys over to player-coach George Halas, who moved the team to Cubs Park in Chicago. Staley paid Halas $5,000 to keep the name Staleys for one more year. Halas made halfback Ed (Dutch) Sternaman his partner.

The Staleys claimed the APFA championship with a 9-1-1 record, as did Buffalo at 9-1-2. Carr ruled in favor of the Staleys, giving Halas his first championship.
1922 After admitting the use of players who had college eligibility remaining during the 1921 season, Clair and the Green Bay management withdrew from the APFA, January 28. Curly Lambeau promised to obey league rules and then used $50 of his own money to buy back the franchise. Bad weather and low attendance plagued the Packers, and Lambeau went broke, but local merchants arranged a $2,500 loan for the club. A public nonprofit corporation was set up to operate the team, with Lambeau as head coach and manager.

The American Professional Football Association changed its name to the National Football League, June 24. The Chicago Staleys became the Chicago Bears.

The NFL fielded 18 teams, including the new Oorang Indians of Marion, Ohio, an all-Indian team featuring Thorpe, Joe Guyon, and Pete Calac, and sponsored by the Oorang dog kennels.

Canton, led by player-coach Guy Chamberlin and tackles Link Lyman and Wilbur (Pete) Henry, emerged as the league's first true powerhouse, going 10-0-2.
1923 For the first time, all of the franchises considered to be part of the NFL fielded teams. Thorpe played first for Oorang, then for the Toledo Maroons. Against the Bears, Thorpe fumbled, and Halas picked up the ball and returned it 98 yards for a touchdown, a record that would last until 1972.

Canton had its second consecutive undefeated season, going 11-0-1 for the NFL title.

1924 The league had 18 franchises, including new ones in Kansas City, Kenosha, and Frankford, a section of Philadelphia. League champion Canton, successful on the field but not at the box office, was purchased by the owner of the Cleveland franchise, who kept the Canton franchise inactive, while using the best players for his Cleveland team, which he renamed the Bulldogs. Cleveland won the title with a 7-1-1 record.

1925 Five new franchises were admitted to the NFL — the New York Giants, who were awarded to Tim Mara and Billy Gibson for $500; the Detroit Panthers, featuring Jimmy Conzelman as owner, coach, and tailback; the Providence Steam Roller; a new Canton Bulldogs team; and the Pottsville Maroons, who had been perhaps the most successful independent pro team. The NFL established its first player limit, at 16 players.

Late in the season, the NFL made its greatest coup in gaining national recognition. Shortly after the University of Illinois season ended in November, All-America halfback Harold (Red) Grange signed a contract to play with the Chicago Bears. On Thanksgiving Day, a crowd of 36,000 — the largest in pro football history — watched Grange and the Bears play the Chicago Cardinals to a scoreless tie at Wrigley Field. At the beginning of December, the Bears left on a barnstorming tour that saw them play eight games in 12 days, in St. Louis, Philadelphia, New York City, Washington, Boston, Pittsburgh, Detroit, and Chicago. A crowd of 73,000 watched the game against the Giants at the Polo Grounds, helping assure the future of the troubled NFL franchise in New York. The Bears then played nine more games in the South and West, including a game in Los Angeles, in which 75,000 fans watched them defeat the Los Angeles Tigers in the Los Angeles Memorial Coliseum.

Pottsville and the Chicago Cardinals were the top contenders for the league title, with Pottsville winning a late-season meeting 21-7. Pottsville scheduled a game against a team of former Notre Dame players for Shibe Park in Philadelphia. Frankford lodged a protest not only because the game was in Frankford's protected territory, but because it was being played the same day as a Yellow Jackets home game. Carr gave three different notices forbidding Pottsville to play the game, but Pottsville played anyway, December 12. That day, Carr fined the club, suspended it from all rights and privileges (including the right to play for the NFL championship), and returned its franchise to the league. The Cardinals, who ended the season with the best record in the league, were named the 1925 champions.

1926 Grange's manager, C.C. Pyle, told the Bears that Grange wouldn't play for them unless he was paid a five-figure salary and given one-third ownership of the team. The Bears refused. Pyle leased Yankee Stadium in New York City, then petitioned for an NFL franchise. After he was refused, he started the first American Football League. It lasted one season and included Grange's New York Yankees and eight other teams. The AFL champion Philadelphia Quakers played a December game against the New York Giants, seventh in the NFL, and the Giants won 31-0. At the end of the season, the AFL folded.

Halas pushed through a rule that prohibited any team from signing a player whose college class had not graduated.

The NFL grew to 22 teams, including the Duluth Eskimos, who signed All-America fullback Ernie Nevers of Stanford, giving the league a gate attraction to rival Grange. The 15-member Eskimos, dubbed the Iron Men of the North, played 29 exhibition and league games, 28 on the road, and Nevers played in all but 29 minutes of them.

Frankford edged the Bears for the championship, despite Halas having obtained John (Paddy) Driscoll from the Cardinals. On December 4, the Yellow Jackets scored in the final two minutes to defeat the Bears 7-6 and move ahead of them in the standings.

1927 At a special meeting in Cleveland, April 23, Carr decided to secure the NFL's future by eliminating the financially weaker teams and consolidating the quality players onto a limited number of more successful teams. The new-look NFL dropped to 12 teams, and the center of gravity of the league left the Midwest, where the NFL had started, and began to emerge in the large cities of the East. One of the new teams was Grange's New York Yankees, but Grange suffered a knee injury and the Yankees finished in the middle of the pack. The NFL championship was won by the cross-town rival New York Giants, who posted 10 shutouts in 13 games.

1928 Grange and Nevers both retired from pro football, and Duluth disbanded, as the NFL was reduced to only 10 teams. The Providence Steam Roller of Jimmy Conzelman and Pearce Johnson won the championship, playing in the Cycledrome, a 10,000-seat oval that had been built for bicycle races.

1929 Chris O'Brien sold the Chicago Cardinals to David Jones, July 27.

The NFL added a fourth official, the field judge, July 28.

Grange and Nevers returned to the NFL. Nevers scored six rushing touchdowns and four extra points as the Cardinals beat Grange's Bears 40-6, November 28. The 40 points set a record that remains the NFL's oldest.

Providence became the first NFL team to host a game at night under floodlights, against the Cardinals, November 3.

The Packers added back Johnny Blood (McNally), tackle Cal Hubbard, and guard Mike Michalske, and won their first NFL championship, edging the Giants, who featured quarterback Benny Friedman.

1930 Dayton, the last of the NFL's original franchises, was purchased by John Dwyer, moved to Brooklyn, and renamed the Dodgers. The Portsmouth, Ohio, Spartans entered the league.

The Packers edged the Giants for the title, but the most improved team was the Bears. Halas retired as a player and replaced himself as coach of the Bears with Ralph Jones, who refined the T-formation by introducing wide ends and a halfback in motion. Jones also introduced rookie All-America fullback-tackle Bronko Nagurski.

The Giants defeated a team of former Notre Dame players coached by Knute Rockne 22-0 before 55,000 at the Polo Grounds, December 14. The proceeds went to the New York Unemployment Fund to help those suffering because of the Great Depression, and the easy victory helped give the NFL credibility with the press and the public.

1931 The NFL decreased to 10 teams, and halfway through the season the Frankford franchise folded. Carr fined the Bears, Packers, and Portsmouth $1,000 each for using players whose college classes had not graduated.

The Packers won an unprecedented third consecutive title, beating out the Spartans, who were led by rookie backs Earl (Dutch) Clark and Glenn Presnell.

1932 George Preston Marshall, Vincent Bendix, Jay O'Brien, and M. Dorland Doyle were awarded a franchise for Boston, July 9. Despite the presence of two rookies — halfback Cliff Battles and tackle Glen (Turk) Edwards — the new team, named the Braves, lost money and Marshall was left as the sole owner at the end of the year.

NFL membership dropped to eight teams, the lowest in history. Official statistics were kept for the first time. The Bears and the Spartans finished the season in the first-ever tie for first place. After the season finale, the league office arranged for the first playoff game in NFL history. The game was moved indoors to Chicago Stadium because of bitter cold and heavy snow. The arena allowed only an 80-yard field that came right to the walls. The goal posts were moved from the end lines to the goal lines and, for safety, inbounds lines or hashmarks where the ball would be put in play were drawn 10 yards from the walls that butted against the sidelines. The Bears won 9-0, December 18, scoring the winning touchdown on a two-yard pass from Nagurski to Grange. The Spartans claimed Nagurski's pass was thrown from less than five yards behind the line of scrimmage, violating the existing passing rule, but the play stood.

1933 The NFL, which long had followed the rules of college football, made a number of significant changes from the college game for the first time and began to independently develop rules serving its needs and the style of play it preferred. The innovations from the 1932 championship game — inbounds line or hashmarks and goal posts on the goal lines — were adopted. Also the forward pass was legalized from anywhere behind the line of scrimmage, February 25.

Marshall and Halas pushed through a proposal that divided the NFL into two divisions, with the winners to meet in an annual championship game, July 8.

Three new franchises joined the league — the Pittsburgh Pirates of Art Rooney, the Philadelphia Eagles of Bert Bell and Lud Wray, and the Cincinnati Reds. The Staten Island Stapletons suspended operations for a year, but never returned to the league.

Halas bought out Sternaman, became sole owner of the Bears, and reinstated himself as head coach. Marshall changed the name of the Boston Braves to the Redskins. David Jones sold the Chicago Cardinals to Charles W. Bidwill.

In the first NFL Championship Game scheduled before the season, the Western Division champion Bears defeated the Eastern Division champion Giants 23-21 at Wrigley Field, December 17.

1934 G.A. (Dick) Richards purchased the Portsmouth Spartans, moved them to Detroit, and renamed them the Lions.

Professional football gained new prestige when the Bears were matched against the best college football players in the first Chicago College All-Star Game, August 31. The game ended in a scoreless tie before 79,432 at Soldier Field.

The Cincinnati Reds lost their first eight games, then were suspended from the league for defaulting on payments. The St. Louis Gunners, an independent team, joined the NFL by buying the Cincinnati franchise and went 1-2 the last three weeks.

Rookie Beattie Feathers of the Bears became the NFL's first 1,000-yard rusher, gaining 1,004 on 101 carries. The Thanksgiving Day game between the Bears and the Lions became the first NFL game broadcast nationally, with Graham McNamee the announcer for CBS radio.

In the championship game, on an extremely cold and icy day at the Polo Grounds, the Giants trailed the Bears 13-3 in the third quarter before changing to basketball shoes for better footing. The Giants won 30-13 in what has come to be known as the Sneakers Game, December 9.

The player waiver rule was adopted, December 10.

1935 The NFL adopted Bert Bell's proposal to hold an annual draft of college players, to begin in 1936, with teams selecting in an inverse order of finish, May 19. The inbounds line or hashmarks were moved nearer the center of the field, 15 yards from the sidelines.

All-America end Don Hutson of Alabama joined Green Bay. The Lions defeated the Giants 26-7 in the NFL Championship Game, December 15.

1936 There were no franchise transactions for the first year since the formation of the NFL. It also was the first year in which all member teams played the same number of games.

The Eagles made University of Chicago halfback and Heisman Trophy winner Jay Berwanger the first player ever selected in the NFL draft, February 8. The Eagles traded his rights to the Bears, but Berwanger never played pro football. The first player selected to actually sign was the number-two pick, Riley Smith of Alabama, who was selected by Boston.

A rival league was formed, and it became the second to call itself the American Football League. The Boston Shamrocks were its champions.

Due to poor attendance, Marshall, the owner of the host team, moved the Championship Game from Boston to the Polo Grounds in New York. Green Bay defeated the Redskins 21-6, December 13.

1937 Homer Marshman was granted a Cleveland franchise, named the Rams, February 12. Marshall moved the Redskins to Washington, D.C., February 13. The Redskins signed

TCU All-America tailback Sammy Baugh, who led them to a 28-21 victory over the Bears in the NFL Championship Game, December 12.

The Los Angeles Bulldogs had an 8-0 record to win the AFL title, but then the two-year-old league folded.

1938 At the suggestion of Halas, Hugh (Shorty) Ray became a technical advisor on rules and officiating to the NFL. A new rule called for a 15-yard penalty for roughing the passer.

Rookie Byron (Whizzer) White of the Pittsburgh Pirates led the NFL in rushing. The Giants defeated the Packers 23-17 for the NFL title, December 11.

Marshall, *Los Angeles Times* sports editor Bill Henry, and promoter Tom Gallery established the Pro Bowl game between the NFL champion and a team of pro all-stars.

1939 The New York Giants defeated the Pro All-Stars 13-10 in the first Pro Bowl, at Wrigley Field, Los Angeles, January 15.

Carr, NFL president since 1921, died in Columbus, May 20. Carl Storck was named acting president, May 25.

An NFL game was televised for the first time when NBC broadcast the Brooklyn Dodgers-Philadelphia Eagles game from Ebbets Field to the approximately 1,000 sets then in New York.

Green Bay defeated New York 27-0 in the NFL Championship Game, December 10 at Milwaukee. NFL attendance exceeded one million in a season for the first time, reaching 1,071,200.

1940 A six-team rival league, the third to call itself the American Football League, was formed, and the Columbus Bullies won its championship.

Halas's Bears, with additional coaching by Clark Shaughnessy of Stanford, defeated the Redskins 73-0 in the NFL Championship Game, December 8. The game, which was the most decisive victory in NFL history, popularized the Bears' T-formation with a man-in-motion. It was the first championship carried on network radio, broadcast by Red Barber to 120 stations of the Mutual Broadcasting System, which paid $2,500 for the rights.

Art Rooney sold the Pittsburgh franchise to Alexis Thompson, December 9, then bought part interest in the Philadelphia Eagles.

1941 Elmer Layden was named the first Commissioner of the NFL, March 1; Storck, the acting president, resigned, April 5. NFL headquarters were moved to Chicago.

Bell and Rooney traded the Eagles to Thompson for the Pirates, then renamed their new team the Steelers. Homer Marshman sold the Rams to Daniel F. Reeves and Fred Levy, Jr.

The league by-laws were revised to provide for playoffs in case there were ties in division races, and sudden-death overtimes in case a playoff game was tied after four quarters. An official *NFL Record Manual* was published for the first time.

Columbus again won the championship of the AFL, but the two-year-old league then folded.

The Bears and the Packers finished in a tie for the Western Division championship, setting up the first divisional playoff game in league history. The Bears won 33-14, then defeated the Giants 37-9 for the NFL championship, December 21.

1942 Players departing for service in World War II depleted the rosters of NFL teams. Halas left the Bears in midseason to join the Navy, and Luke Johnsos and Heartley (Hunk) Anderson served as co-coaches as the Bears went 11-0 in the regular season. The Redskins defeated the Bears 14-6 in the NFL Championship Game, December 13.

1943 The Cleveland Rams, with co-owners Reeves and Levy in the service, were granted permission to suspend operations for one season, April 6. Levy transferred his stock in the team to Reeves, April 16.

The NFL adopted free substitution, April 7. The league also made the wearing of helmets mandatory and approved a 10-game schedule for all teams.

Philadelphia and Pittsburgh were granted permission to merge for one season, June 19. The team, known as Phil-Pitt (and called the Steagles by fans), divided home games between the two cities, and Earle (Greasy) Neale of Philadelphia and Walt Kiesling of Pittsburgh served as co-coaches. The merger automatically dissolved the last day of the season, December 5.

Ted Collins was granted a franchise for Boston, to become active in 1944.

Sammy Baugh led the league in passing, punting, and interceptions. He led the Redskins to a tie with the Giants for the Eastern Division title, and then to a 28-0 victory in a divisional playoff game. The Bears beat the Redskins 41-21 in the NFL Championship Game, December 26.

1944 Collins, who had wanted a franchise in Yankee Stadium in New York, named his new team in Boston the Yanks. Cleveland resumed operations. The Brooklyn Dodgers changed their name to the Tigers.

Coaching from the bench was legalized, April 20.

The Cardinals and the Steelers were granted permission to merge for one year under the name Card-Pitt, April 21. Phil Handler of the Cardinals and Walt Kiesling of the Steelers served as co-coaches. The merger automatically dissolved the last day of the season, December 3.

In the NFL Championship Game, Green Bay defeated the New York Giants 14-7, December 17.

1945 The inbounds lines or hashmarks were moved from 15 yards away from the sidelines to nearer the center of the field — 20 yards from the sidelines.

Brooklyn and Boston merged into a team that played home games in both cities and was known simply as The Yanks. The team was coached by former Boston head coach Herb Kopf. In December, the Brooklyn franchise withdrew from the NFL to join the new All-America Football Conference; all the players on its active and reserve lists were assigned to The Yanks, who once again became the Boston Yanks.

Halas rejoined the Bears late in the season after service with the U.S. Navy. Although Halas took over much of the coaching duties, Anderson and Johnsos remained the coaches of record throughout the season.

Steve Van Buren of Philadelphia led the NFL in rushing, kickoff returns, and scoring.

After the Japanese surrendered ending World War II, a count showed that the NFL service roster, limited to men who had played in league games, totaled 638, 21 of whom had died in action.

Rookie quarterback Bob Waterfield led Cleveland to a 15-14 victory over Washington in the NFL Championship Game, December 16.

1946 The contract of Commissioner Layden was not renewed, and Bert Bell, the co-owner of the Steelers, replaced him, January 11. Bell moved the league headquarters from Chicago to the Philadelphia suburb of Bala-Cynwyd.

Free substitution was withdrawn and substitutions were limited to no more than three men at a time. Forward passes were made automatically incomplete upon striking the goal posts, January 11.

The NFL took on a truly national appearance for the first time when Reeves was granted permission by the league to move his NFL champion Rams to Los Angeles.

The rival All-America Football Conference began play with eight teams. The Cleveland Browns, coached by Paul Brown, won the AAFC's first championship, defeating the New York Yankees 14-9.

Bill Dudley of the Steelers led the NFL in rushing, interceptions, and punt returns, and won the league's most valuable player award.

Backs Frank Filchock and Merle Hapes of the Giants were questioned about an attempt by a New York man to fix the championship game with the Bears. Bell suspended Hapes but allowed Filchock to play; he played well, but Chicago won 24-14, December 15.

1947 The NFL added a fifth official, the back judge.

A bonus choice was made for the first time in the NFL draft. One team each year would select the special choice before the first round began. The Chicago Bears won a lottery and the rights to the first choice and drafted back Bob Fenimore of Oklahoma A&M.

The Cleveland Browns again won the AAFC title, defeating the New York Yankees 14-3.

Charles Bidwill, Sr., owner of the Cardinals, died April 19, but his wife and sons retained ownership of the team. On December 28, the Cardinals won the NFL Championship Game 28-21 over the Philadelphia Eagles, who had beaten Pittsburgh 21-0 in a playoff.

1948 Plastic helmets were prohibited. A flexible artificial tee was permitted at the kickoff. Officials other than the referee were equipped with whistles, not horns, January 14.

Fred Mandel sold the Detroit Lions to a syndicate headed by D. Lyle Fife, January 15.

Halfback Fred Gehrke of the Los Angeles Rams painted horns on the Rams' helmets, the first modern helmet emblems in pro football.

The Cleveland Browns won their third straight championship in the AAFC, going 14-0 and then defeating the Buffalo Bills 49-7.

In a blizzard, the Eagles defeated the Cardinals 7-0 in the NFL Championship Game, December 19.

1949 Alexis Thompson sold the champion Eagles to a syndicate headed by James P. Clark, January 15. The Boston Yanks became the New York Bulldogs, sharing the Polo Grounds with the Giants.

Free substitution was adopted for one year, January 20.

The NFL had two 1,000-yard rushers in the same season for the first time — Steve Van Buren of Philadelphia and Tony Canadeo of Green Bay.

The AAFC played its season with a one-division, seven-team format. On December 9, Bell announced a merger agreement in which three AAFC franchises — Cleveland, San Francisco, and Baltimore — would join the NFL in 1950. The Browns won their fourth consecutive AAFC title, defeating the 49ers 21-7, December 11.

In a heavy rain, the Eagles defeated the Rams 14-0 in the NFL Championship Game, December 18.

1950 Unlimited free substitution was restored, opening the way for the era of two platoons and specialization in pro football, January 20.

Curly Lambeau, founder of the franchise and Green Bay's head coach since 1921, resigned under fire, February 1.

The name National Football League was restored after about three months as the National-American Football League. The American and National conferences were created to replace the Eastern and Western divisions, March 3.

The New York Bulldogs became the Yanks and divided the players of the former AAFC Yankees with the Giants. A special allocation draft was held in which the 13 teams drafted the remaining AAFC players, with special consideration for Baltimore, which received 15 choices compared to 10 for other teams.

The Los Angeles Rams became the first NFL team to have all of its games — both home and away — televised. The Washington Redskins followed the Rams in arranging to televise their games; other teams made deals to put selected games on television.

In the first game of the season, former AAFC champion Cleveland defeated NFL champion Philadelphia 35-10. For the first time, deadlocks occurred in both conferences and playoffs were necessary. The Browns defeated the Giants in the American and the Rams defeated the Bears in the National. Cleveland defeated Los Angeles 30-28 in the NFL Championship Game, December 24.

1951 The Pro Bowl game, dormant since 1942, was revived under a new format matching the all-stars of each conference at the Los Angeles Memorial Coliseum. The American Conference defeated the National Conference 28-27, January 14.

Abraham Watner returned the Baltimore franchise and its player contracts back to the NFL for $50,000. Baltimore's former players were made available for drafting at the same time as college players, January 18.

A rule was passed that no tackle, guard, or center would be eligible to catch a forward pass, January 18.

The Rams reversed their television policy and televised only road games.

The NFL Championship Game was televised coast-to-coast for the first time, December 23. The DuMont Network paid $75,000 for the rights to the game, in which the Rams

defeated the Browns 24-17.
1952 Ted Collins sold the New York Yanks' franchise back to the NFL, January 19. A new franchise was awarded to a group in Dallas after it purchased the assets of the Yanks, January 24. The new Texans went 1-11, with the owners turning the franchise back to the league in midseason. For the last five games of the season, the commissioner's office operated the Texans as a road team, using Hershey, Pennsylvania, as a home base. At the end of the season the franchise was canceled, the last time an NFL team failed.

The Pittsburgh Steelers abandoned the Single-Wing for the T-formation, the last pro team to do so.

The Detroit Lions won their first NFL championship in 17 years, defeating the Browns 17-7 in the title game, December 28.
1953 A Baltimore group headed by Carroll Rosenbloom was granted a franchise and was awarded the holdings of the defunct Dallas organization, January 23. The team, named the Colts, put together the largest trade in league history, acquiring 10 players from Cleveland in exchange for five.

The names of the American and National conferences were changed to the Eastern and Western conferences, January 24.

Jim Thorpe died, March 28.

Mickey McBride, founder of the Cleveland Browns, sold the franchise to a syndicate headed by Dave R. Jones, June 10.

The NFL policy of blacking out home games was upheld by Judge Allan K. Grim of the U.S. District Court in Philadelphia, November 12.

The Lions again defeated the Browns in the NFL Championship Game, winning 17-16, December 27.
1954 The Canadian Football League began a series of raids on NFL teams, signing quarterback Eddie LeBaron and defensive end Gene Brito of Washington and defensive tackle Arnie Weinmeister of the Giants, among others.

Fullback Joe Perry of the 49ers became the first player in league history to gain 1,000 yards rushing in consecutive seasons.

Cleveland defeated Detroit 56-10 in the NFL Championship Game, December 26.
1955 The sudden-death overtime rule was used for the first time in a preseason game between the Rams and Giants at Portland, Oregon, August 28. The Rams won 23-17 three minutes into overtime.

A rule change declared the ball dead immediately if the ball carrier touched the ground with any part of his body except his hands or feet while in the grasp of an opponent.

The NFL Players Association was founded.

The Baltimore Colts made an 80-cent phone call to Johnny Unitas and signed him as a free agent. Another quarterback, Otto Graham, played his last game as the Browns defeated the Rams 38-14 in the NFL Championship Game, December 26. Graham had quarterbacked the Browns to 10 championship-game appearances in 10 years.

NBC replaced DuMont as the network for the title game, paying a rights fee of $100,000.
1956 Grabbing an opponent's facemask (other than the ball carrier) was made illegal. Using radio receivers to communicate with players on the field was prohibited. A natural leather ball with white end stripes replaced the white ball with black stripes for night games.

The Giants moved from the Polo Grounds to Yankee Stadium.

Halas retired as coach of the Bears, and was replaced by Paddy Driscoll.

CBS became the first network to broadcast some NFL regular-season games to selected television markets across the nation.

The Giants routed the Bears 47-7 in the NFL Championship Game, December 30.
1957 Pete Rozelle was named general manager of the Rams. Anthony J. Morabito, founder and co-owner of the 49ers, died of a heart attack during a game against the Bears at Kezar Stadium, October 28. An NFL-record crowd of 102,368 saw the 49ers-Rams game at the Los Angeles Memorial Coliseum, November 10.

The Lions came from 20 points down to post a 31-27 playoff victory over the 49ers, December 22. Detroit defeated Cleveland 59-14 in the NFL Championship Game, December 29.
1958 The bonus selection in the draft was eliminated, January 29. The last selection was quarterback King Hill of Rice by the Chicago Cardinals.

Halas reinstated himself as coach of the Bears.

Jim Brown of Cleveland gained an NFL-record 1,527 yards rushing. In a divisional playoff game, the Giants held Brown to eight yards and defeated Cleveland 10-0.

Baltimore, coached by Weeb Ewbank, defeated the Giants 23-17 in the first sudden-death overtime in an NFL Championship Game, December 28. The game ended when Colts fullback Alan Ameche scored on a one-yard touchdown run after 8:15 of overtime.
1959 Vince Lombardi was named head coach of the Green Bay Packers, January 28. Tim Mara, the co-founder of the Giants, died, February 17.

Lamar Hunt of Dallas announced his intentions to form a second pro football league. The first meeting was held in Chicago, August 14, and consisted of Hunt representing Dallas; Bob Howsam, Denver; K.S. (Bud) Adams, Houston; Barron Hilton, Los Angeles; Max Winter and Bill Boyer, Minneapolis; and Harry Wismer, New York City. They made plans to begin play in 1960.

The new league was named the American Football League, August 22. Buffalo, owned by Ralph Wilson, became the seventh franchise, October 28. Boston, owned by William H. Sullivan, became the eighth team, November 22. The first AFL draft, lasting 33 rounds, was held, November 22. Joe Foss was named AFL Commissioner, November 30. An additional draft of 20 rounds was held by the AFL, December 2.

NFL Commissioner Bert Bell died of a heart attack suffered at Franklin Field, Philadelphia, during the last two minutes of a game between the Eagles and the Steelers, October 11. Treasurer Austin Gunsel was named president in the office of the commissioner, October 14.

The Colts again defeated the Giants in the NFL Championship Game, 31-16, December 27.
1960 Pete Rozelle was elected NFL Commissioner as a compromise choice on the twenty-third ballot, January 26. Rozelle moved the league offices to New York City.

Hunt was elected AFL president for 1960, January 26. Minneapolis withdrew from the AFL, January 27, and the same ownership was given an NFL franchise for Minnesota (to start in 1961), January 28. Dallas received an NFL franchise for 1960, January 28. Oakland received an AFL franchise, January 30.

The AFL adopted the two-point option on points after touchdown, January 28. A no-tampering verbal pact, relative to players' contracts, was agreed to between the NFL and AFL, February 9.

The NFL owners voted to allow the transfer of the Chicago Cardinals to St. Louis, March 13.

The AFL signed a five-year television contract with ABC, June 9.

The Boston Patriots defeated the Buffalo Bills 28-7 before 16,000 at Buffalo in the first AFL preseason game, July 30. The Denver Broncos defeated the Patriots 13-10 before 21,597 at Boston in the first AFL regular-season game, September 9.

Philadelphia defeated Green Bay 17-13 in the NFL Championship Game, December 26.
1961 The Houston Oilers defeated the Los Angeles Chargers 24-16 before 32,183 in the first AFL Championship Game, January 1.

Detroit defeated Cleveland 17-16 in the first Playoff Bowl, or Bert Bell Benefit Bowl, between second-place teams in each conference in Miami, January 7.

End Willard Dewveall of the Bears played out his option and joined the Oilers, becoming the first player to deliberately move from one league to the other, January 14.

Ed McGah, Wayne Valley, and Robert Osborne bought out their partners in the ownership of the Raiders, January 17. The Chargers were transferred to San Diego, February 10. Dave R. Jones sold the Browns to a group headed by Arthur B. Modell, March 22. The Howsam brothers sold the Broncos to a group headed by Calvin Kunz and Gerry Phipps, May 26.

NBC was awarded a two-year contract for radio and television rights to the NFL Championship Game for $615,000 annually, $300,000 of which was to go directly into the NFL Player Benefit Plan, April 5.

Canton, Ohio, where the league that became the NFL was formed in 1920, was chosen as the site of the Pro Football Hall of Fame, April 27. Dick McCann, a former Redskins executive, was named executive director.

A bill legalizing single-network television contracts by professional sports leagues was introduced in Congress by Representative Emanuel Celler. It passed the House and Senate and was signed into law by President John F. Kennedy, September 30.

Houston defeated San Diego 10-3 for the AFL championship, December 24. Green Bay won its first NFL championship since 1944, defeating the New York Giants 37-0, December 31.
1962 The Western Division defeated the Eastern Division 47-27 in the first AFL All-Star Game, played before 20,973 in San Diego, January 7.

Both leagues prohibited grabbing any player's facemask. The AFL voted to make the scoreboard clock the official timer of the game.

The NFL entered into a single-network agreement with CBS for telecasting all regular-season games for $4,650,000 annually, January 10.

Judge Roszel Thompson of the U.S. District Court in Baltimore ruled against the AFL in its antitrust suit against the NFL, May 21. The AFL had charged the NFL with monopoly and conspiracy in areas of expansion, television, and player signings. The case lasted two and a half years, the trial two months.

McGah and Valley acquired controlling interest in the Raiders, May 24. The AFL assumed financial responsibility for the New York Titans, November 8. With Commissioner Rozelle as referee, Daniel F. Reeves regained the ownership of the Rams, outbidding his partners in sealed-envelope bidding for the team, November 27.

The Dallas Texans defeated the Oilers 20-17 for the AFL championship at Houston after 17 minutes, 54 seconds of overtime on a 25-yard field goal by Tommy Brooker, December 23. The game lasted a record 77 minutes, 54 seconds.

Judge Edward Weinfeld of the U.S. District Court in New York City upheld the legality of the NFL's television blackout within a 75-mile radius of home games and denied an injunction that would have forced the championship game between the Giants and the Packers to be televised in the New York City area, December 28. The Packers beat the Giants 16-7 for the NFL title, December 30.
1963 The Dallas Texans transferred to Kansas City, becoming the Chiefs, February 8. The New York Titans were sold to a five-man syndicate headed by David (Sonny) Werblin, March 28. Weeb Ewbank became the Titans' new head coach and the team's name was changed to the Jets, April 15. They began play in Shea Stadium.

NFL Properties, Inc., was founded to serve as the licensing arm of the NFL.

Rozelle indefinitely suspended Green Bay halfback Paul Hornung and Detroit defensive tackle Alex Karras for placing bets on their own teams and on other NFL games; he also fined five other Detroit players $2,000 each for betting on one game in which they did not participate, and the Detroit Lions Football Company $2,000 on each of two counts for failure to report information promptly and for lack of sideline supervision.

Paul Brown, head coach of the Browns since their inception, was fired and replaced by Blanton Collier. Don Shula replaced Weeb Ewbank as head coach of the Colts.

The AFL allowed the Jets and Raiders to select players from other franchises in hopes of giving the league more competitive balance, May 11.

NBC was awarded exclusive network broadcasting rights for the 1963 AFL Championship Game for $926,000, May 23.

The Pro Football Hall of Fame was dedicated at Canton, Ohio, September 7.

The U.S. Fourth Circuit Court of Appeals reaffirmed the lower court's finding for the NFL in the $10-million suit brought by the AFL, ending three and a half years of litigation, November 21.

Jim Brown of Cleveland rushed for an NFL single-season record 1,863 yards.

Boston defeated Buffalo 26-8 in the first divisional playoff game in AFL history, December 28.

The Bears defeated the Giants 14-10 in the NFL Championship Game, a record sixth and last title for Halas in his thirty-sixth season as the Bears' coach, December 29.

1964 The Chargers defeated the Patriots in the AFL Championship Game, January 5.

William Clay Ford, the Lions' president since 1961, purchased the team, January 10. A group representing the late James P. Clark sold the Eagles to a group headed by Jerry Wolman, January 21. Carroll Rosenbloom, the majority owner of the Colts since 1953, acquired complete ownership of the team, January 23.

CBS submitted the winning bid of $14.1 million per year for the NFL regular-season television rights for 1964 and 1965, January 24. CBS acquired the rights to the championship games for 1964 and 1965 for $1.8 million per game, April 17.

The AFL signed a five-year, $36-million television contract with NBC to begin with the 1965 season, January 29.

Hornung and Karras were reinstated by Rozelle, March 16.

Pete Gogolak of Cornell signed a contract with Buffalo, becoming the first soccer-style kicker in pro football.

Buffalo defeated San Diego 20-7 in the AFL Championship Game, December 26. Cleveland defeated Baltimore 27-0 in the NFL Championship Game, December 27.

1965 The NFL teams pledged not to sign college seniors until completion of all their games, including bowl games, and empowered the Commissioner to discipline the clubs up to as much as the loss of an entire draft list for a violation of the pledge, February 15.

The NFL added a sixth official, the line judge, February 19. The color of the officials' penalty flags was changed from white to bright gold, April 5.

Atlanta was awarded an NFL franchise for 1966, with Rankin Smith, Sr., as owner, June 30. Miami was awarded an AFL franchise for 1966, with Joe Robbie and Danny Thomas as owners, August 16.

Green Bay defeated Baltimore 13-10 in sudden-death overtime in a Western Conference playoff game. Don Chandler kicked a 25-yard field goal for the Packers after 13 minutes, 39 seconds of overtime, December 26. The Packers then defeated the Browns 23-12 in the NFL Championship Game, January 2.

In the AFL Championship Game, the Bills again defeated the Chargers, 23-0, December 26.

CBS acquired the rights to the NFL regular-season games in 1966 and 1967, with an option for 1968, for $18.8 million per year, December 29.

1966 The AFL-NFL war reached its peak, as the leagues spent a combined $7 million to sign their 1966 draft choices. The NFL signed 75 percent of its 232 draftees, the AFL 46 percent of its 181. Of the 111 common draft choices, 79 signed with the NFL, 28 with the AFL, and 4 went unsigned.

The rights to the 1966 and 1967 NFL Championship Games were sold to CBS for $2 million per game, February 14.

Foss resigned as AFL Commissioner, April 7. Al Davis, the head coach and general manager of the Raiders, was named to replace him, April 8.

Goal posts offset from the goal line, painted bright yellow, and with uprights 20 feet above the crossbar were made standard in the NFL, May 16.

A series of secret meetings regarding a possible AFL-NFL merger were held in the spring between Hunt of Kansas City and Tex Schramm of Dallas. Rozelle announced the merger, June 8. Under the agreement, the two leagues would combine to form an expanded league with 24 teams, to be increased to 26 in 1968 and to 28 by 1970 or soon thereafter. All existing franchises would be retained, and no franchises would be transferred outside their metropolitan areas. While maintaining separate schedules through 1969, the leagues agreed to play an annual AFL-NFL World Championship Game beginning in January, 1967, and to hold a combined draft, also beginning in 1967. Preseason games would be held between teams of each league starting in 1967. Official regular-season play would start in 1970 when the two leagues would officially merge to form one league with two conferences. Rozelle was named Commissioner of the expanded league setup.

Davis rejoined the Raiders, and Milt Woodard was named president of the AFL, July 25.

The St. Louis Cardinals moved into newly constructed Busch Memorial Stadium.

Barron Hilton sold the Chargers to a group headed by Eugene Klein and Sam Schulman, August 25.

Congress approved the AFL-NFL merger, passing legislation exempting the agreement itself from antitrust action, October 21.

New Orleans was awarded an NFL franchise to begin play in 1967, November 1. John Mecom, Jr., of Houston was designated majority stockholder and president of the franchise, December 15.

The NFL was realigned for the 1967-69 seasons into the Capitol and Century Divisions in the Eastern Conference and the Central and Coastal Divisions in the Western Conference, December 2. New Orleans and the New York Giants agreed to switch divisions in 1968 and return to the 1967 alignment in 1969.

The rights to the Super Bowl for four years were sold to CBS and NBC for $9.5 million, December 13.

1967 Green Bay earned the right to represent the NFL in the first AFL-NFL World Championship Game by defeating Dallas 34-27, January 1. The same day, Kansas City defeated Buffalo 31-7 to represent the AFL. The Packers defeated the Chiefs 35-10 before 61,946 fans at the Los Angeles Memorial Coliseum in the first game between AFL and NFL teams, January 15. The winning players' share for the Packers was $15,000 each, and the losing players' share for the Chiefs was $7,500 each. The game was televised by both CBS and NBC.

The "sling-shot" goal post and a six-foot-wide border around the field were made standard in the NFL, February 22.

Baltimore made Bubba Smith, a Michigan State defensive lineman, the first choice in the first combined AFL-NFL draft, March 14.

The AFL awarded a franchise to begin play in 1968 to Cincinnati, May 24. A group with Paul Brown as part owner, general manager, and head coach, was awarded the Cincinnati franchise, September 27.

Arthur B. Modell, the president of the Cleveland Browns, was elected president of the NFL, May 28.

An AFL team defeated an NFL team for the first time, when Denver beat Detroit 13-7 in a preseason game, August 5.

Green Bay defeated Dallas 21-17 for the NFL championship on a last-minute one-yard quarterback sneak by Bart Starr in 13-below-zero temperature at Green Bay, December 31. The same day, Oakland defeated Houston 40-7 for the AFL championship.

1968 Green Bay defeated Oakland 33-14 in Super Bowl II at Miami, January 14. The game had the first $3-million gate in pro football history.

Vince Lombardi resigned as head coach of the Packers, but remained as general manager, January 28.

Werblin sold his shares in the Jets to his partners Don Lillis, Leon Hess, Townsend Martin, and Phil Iselin, May 21. Lillis assumed the presidency of the club, but then died July 23. Iselin was appointed president, August 6.

Halas retired for the fourth and last time as head coach of the Bears, May 27.

The Oilers left Rice Stadium for the Astrodome and became the first NFL team to play its home games in a domed stadium.

The movie "Heidi" became a footnote in sports history when NBC didn't show the last 1:05 of the Jets-Raiders game in order to permit the children's special to begin on time. The Raiders scored two touchdowns in the last 42 seconds to win 43-32, November 17.

Ewbank became the first coach to win titles in both the NFL and AFL when his Jets defeated the Raiders 27-23 for the AFL championship, December 29. The same day, Baltimore defeated Cleveland 34-0.

1969 The AFL established a playoff format for the 1969 season, with the winner in one division playing the runner-up in the other, January 11.

An AFL team won the Super Bowl for the first time, as the Jets defeated the Colts 16-7 at Miami, January 12 in Super Bowl III. The title Super Bowl was recognized by the NFL for the first time.

Vince Lombardi became part owner, executive vice-president, and head coach of the Washington Redskins, Feb. 7.

Wolman sold the Eagles to Leonard Tose, May 1.

Baltimore, Cleveland, and Pittsburgh agreed to join the AFL teams to form the 13-team American Football Conference of the NFL in 1970, May 17. The NFL also agreed on a playoff format that would include one "wild-card" team per conference — the second-place team with the best record.

Monday Night Football was signed for 1970. ABC acquired the rights to televise 13 NFL regular-season Monday night games in 1970, 1971, and 1972.

George Preston Marshall, president emeritus of the Redskins, died at 72, August 9.

The NFL marked its fiftieth year by the wearing of a special patch by each of the 16 teams.

1970 Kansas City defeated Minnesota 23-7 in Super Bowl IV at New Orleans, January 11. The gross receipts of approximately $3.8 million were the largest ever for a one-day sports event.

Four-year television contracts, under which CBS would televise all NFC games and NBC all AFC games (except Monday night games) and the two would divide televising the Super Bowl and AFC-NFC Pro Bowl games, were announced, January 26.

Art Modell resigned as president of the NFL, March 12. Milt Woodard resigned as president of the AFL, March 13. Lamar Hunt was elected president of the AFC and George Halas was elected president of the NFC, March 19.

The merged 26-team league adopted rules changes putting names on the backs of players' jerseys, making a point after touchdown worth only one point, and making the scoreboard clock the official timing device of the game, March 18.

The Players Negotiating Committee and the NFL Players Association announced a four-year agreement guaranteeing approximately $4,535,000 annually to player pension and insurance benefits, August 3. The owners also agreed to contribute $250,000 annually to improve or implement items such as disability payments, widows' benefits, maternity benefits, and dental benefits. The agreement also provided for increased preseason game and per diem payments, averaging approximately $2.6 million annually.

The Pittsburgh Steelers moved into Three Rivers Stadium. The Cincinnati Bengals moved to Riverfront Stadium.

Lombardi died of cancer at 57, September 3.

Tom Dempsey of New Orleans kicked a game-winning NFL-record 63-yard field goal against Detroit, November 8.

1971 Baltimore defeated Dallas 16-13 on Jim O'Brien's 32-yard field goal with five seconds to go in Super Bowl V at Miami, January 17. The NBC telecast was viewed in an estimated 23,980,000 homes, the largest audience ever for a one-day sports event.

The NFC defeated the AFC 27-6 in the first AFC-NFC Pro Bowl at Los Angeles, January 24.

The Boston Patriots changed their name to the New England Patriots, March 25. Their new stadium, Schaefer Stadium, was dedicated in a 20-14 preseason victory over the Giants.

The Philadelphia Eagles left Franklin Field and played their games at the new Veterans Stadium.

The San Francisco 49ers left Kezar Stadium and moved their games to Candlestick Park.

Daniel F. Reeves, the president

and general manager of the Rams, died at 58, April 15.

The Dallas Cowboys moved from the Cotton Bowl into their new home, Texas Stadium, October 24.

Miami defeated Kansas City 27-24 in sudden-death overtime in an AFC Divisional Playoff Game, December 25. Garo Yepremian kicked a 37-yard field goal for the Dolphins after 22 minutes, 40 seconds of overtime, as the game lasted 82 minutes, 40 seconds overall, making it the longest game in history.

1972 Dallas defeated Miami 24-3 in Super Bowl VI at New Orleans, January 16. The CBS telecast was viewed in an estimated 27,450,000 homes, the top-rated one-day telecast ever.

The inbounds lines or hashmarks were moved nearer the center of the field, 23 yards, 1 foot, 9 inches from the sidelines, March 23. The method of determining won-lost percentage in standings changed. Tie games, previously not counted in the standings, were made equal to a half-game won and a half-game lost, May 24.

Robert Irsay purchased the Los Angeles Rams and transferred ownership of the club to Carroll Rosenbloom in exchange for the Baltimore Colts, July 13.

William V. Bidwill purchased the stock of his brother Charles (Stormy) Bidwill to become the sole owner of the St. Louis Cardinals, September 2.

The National District Attorneys Association endorsed the position of professional leagues in opposing proposed legalization of gambling on professional team sports, September 28.

Franco Harris's "Immaculate Reception" gave the Steelers their first postseason win ever, 13-7 over the Raiders, December 23.

1973 Rozelle announced that all Super Bowl VII tickets were sold and that the game would be telecast in Los Angeles, the site of the game, on an experimental basis, January 3.

Miami defeated Washington 14-7 in Super Bowl VII at Los Angeles, completing a 17-0 season, the first perfect-record regular-season and postseason mark in NFL history, January 14. The NBC telecast was viewed by approximately 75 million people.

The AFC defeated the NFC 33-28 in the Pro Bowl in Dallas, the first time since 1942 that the game was played outside Los Angeles, January 21.

A jersey numbering system was adopted, April 5: 1-19 for quarterbacks and specialists, 20-49 for running backs and defensive backs, 50-59 for centers and linebackers, 60-79 for defensive linemen and interior offensive linemen other than centers, and 80-89 for wide receivers and tight ends. Players who had been in the NFL in 1972 could continue to use old numbers.

NFL Charities, a nonprofit organization, was created to derive an income from monies generated from NFL Properties' licensing of NFL trademarks and team names, June 26. NFL Charities was set up to support education and charitable activities and to supply economic support to persons formerly associated with professional football who were no longer able to support themselves.

Congress adopted experimental legislation (for three years) requiring any NFL game that had been declared a sellout 72 hours prior to kickoff to be made available for local televising, September 14. The legislation provided for an annual review to be made by the Federal Communications Commission.

The Buffalo Bills moved their home games from War Memorial Stadium to Rich Stadium in nearby Orchard Park. The Giants tied the Eagles 23-23 in the final game in Yankee Stadium, September 23. The Giants played the rest of their home games at the Yale Bowl in New Haven, Connecticut.

A rival league, the World Football League, was formed and was reported in operation, October 2. It had plans to start play in 1974.

O.J. Simpson of Buffalo became the first player to rush for more than 2,000 yards in a season, gaining 2,003.

1974 Miami defeated Minnesota 24-7 in Super Bowl VIII at Houston, the second consecutive Super Bowl championship for the Dolphins, January 13. The CBS telecast was viewed by approximately 75 million people.

Rozelle was given a 10-year contract effective January 1, 1973, February 27.

Tampa Bay was awarded a franchise to begin operation in 1976, April 24.

Sweeping rules changes were adopted to add action and tempo to games: one sudden-death overtime period was added for preseason and regular-season games; the goal posts were moved from the goal line to the end lines; kickoffs were moved from the 40- to the 35-yard line; after missed field goals from beyond the 20, the ball was to be returned to the line of scrimmage; restrictions were placed on members of the punting team to open up return possibilities; roll-blocking and cutting of wide receivers was eliminated; the extent of downfield contact a defender could have with an eligible receiver was restricted; the penalties for offensive holding, illegal use of the hands, and tripping were reduced from 15 to 10 yards; wide receivers blocking back toward the ball within three yards of the line of scrimmage were prevented from blocking below the waist, April 25.

The Toronto Northmen of the WFL signed Larry Csonka, Jim Kiick, and Paul Warfield of Miami, March 31.

Seattle was awarded an NFL franchise to begin play in 1976, June 4. Lloyd W. Nordstrom, president of the Seattle Seahawks, and Hugh Culverhouse, president of the Tampa Bay Buccaneers, signed franchise agreements, December 5.

The Birmingham Americans defeated the Florida Blazers 22-21 in the WFL World Bowl, winning the league championship, December 5.

1975 Pittsburgh defeated Minnesota 16-6 in Super Bowl IX at New Orleans, the Steelers' first championship since entering the NFL in 1933. The NBC telecast was viewed by approximately 78 million people.

The divisional winners with the highest won-loss percentage were made the home team for the divisional playoffs, and the surviving winners with the highest percentage made home teams for the championship games, June 26.

Referees were equipped with wireless microphones for all preseason, regular-season, and playoff games.

The Lions moved to the new Pontiac Silverdome. The Giants played their home games in Shea Stadium. The Saints moved into the Louisiana Superdome.

The World Football League folded, October 22.

1976 Pittsburgh defeated Dallas 21-17 in Super Bowl X in Miami. The Steelers joined Green Bay and Miami as the only teams to win two Super Bowls; the Cowboys became the first wild-card team to play in the Super Bowl. The CBS telecast was viewed by an estimated 80 million people, the largest television audience in history.

Lloyd Nordstrom, the president of the Seahawks, died at 66, January 20. His brother Elmer succeeded him as majority representative of the team.

The owners awarded Super Bowl XII, to be played on January 15, 1978, to New Orleans. They also adopted the use of two 30-second clocks for all games, visible to both players and fans to note the official time between the ready-for-play signal and snap of the ball, March 16.

A veteran player allocation was held to stock the Seattle and Tampa Bay franchises with 39 players each, March 30-31. In the college draft, Seattle and Tampa Bay each received eight extra choices, April 8-9.

The Giants moved into new Giants Stadium in East Rutherford, New Jersey.

The Steelers defeated the College All-Stars in a storm-shortened Chicago College All-Star Game, the last of the series, July 23. St. Louis defeated San Diego 20-10 in a preseason game before 38,000 in Korakuen Stadium, Tokyo, in the first NFL game outside of North America, August 16.

1977 Oakland defeated Minnesota 32-14 before a record crowd of 100,421 in Super Bowl XI at Pasadena, January 9. The paid attendance was a pro record 103,438. The NBC telecast was viewed by 81.9 million people, the largest ever to view a sports event. The victory was the fifth consecutive for the AFC in the Super Bowl.

The NFL Players Association and the NFL Management Council ratified a collective bargaining agreement extending until 1982, covering five football seasons while continuing the pension plan—including years 1974, 1975, and 1976—with contributions totaling more than $55 million. The total cost of the agreement was estimated at $107 million. The agreement called for a college draft at least through 1986; contained a no-strike, no-suit clause; established a 43-man active player limit; reduced pension vesting to four years; provided for increases in minimum salaries and preseason and postseason pay; improved insurance, medical, and dental benefits; modified previous practices in player movement and control; and reaffirmed the NFL Commissioner's disciplinary authority. Additionally, the agreement called for the NFL member clubs to make payments totaling $16 million the next 10 years to settle various legal disputes, February 25.

The San Francisco 49ers were sold to Edward J. DeBartolo, Jr., March 28.

A 16-game regular season, 4-game preseason was adopted to begin in 1978, March 29. A second wild-card team was adopted for the playoffs beginning in 1978, with the wild-card teams to play each other and the winners advancing to a round of eight postseason series.

The Seahawks were permanently aligned in the AFC Western Division and the Buccaneers in the NFC Central Division, March 31.

The owners awarded Super Bowl XIII, to be played on January 21, 1979, to Miami, to be played in the Orange Bowl; Super Bowl XIV, to be played January 20, 1980, was awarded to Pasadena, to be played in the Rose Bowl, June 14.

Rules changes were adopted to open up the passing game and to cut down on injuries. Defenders were permitted to make contact with eligible receivers only once; the head slap was outlawed; offensive linemen were prohibited from thrusting their hands to an opponent's neck, face, or head; and wide receivers were prohibited from clipping, even in the legal clipping zone.

Rozelle negotiated contracts with the three television networks to televise all NFL regular-season and postseason games, plus selected preseason games, for four years beginning with the 1978 season. ABC was awarded yearly rights to 16 Monday night games, four prime-time games, the AFC-NFC Pro Bowl, and the Hall of Fame games. CBS received the rights to all NFC regular-season and postseason games (except those in the ABC package) and to Super Bowls XIV and XVI. NBC received the rights to all AFC regular-season and postseason games (except those in the ABC package) and to Super Bowls XIII and XV. Industry sources considered it the largest single television package ever negotiated, October 12.

Chicago's Walter Payton set a single-game rushing record with 275 yards (40 carries) against Minnesota, November 20.

1978 Dallas defeated Denver 27-10 in Super Bowl XII, held indoors for the first time, at the Louisiana Superdome in New Orleans, January 15. The CBS telecast was viewed by more than 102 million people, meaning the game was watched by more viewers than any other show of any kind in the history of television. Dallas's victory was the first for the NFC in six years.

According to a Louis Harris Sports Survey, 70 percent of the nation's sports fans said they followed football, compared to 54 percent who followed baseball. Football increased its lead as the country's favorite, 26 percent to 16 percent for baseball, January 19.

A seventh official, the side judge, was added to the officiating crew, March 14.

The NFL continued a trend toward opening up the game. Rules changes permitted a defender to maintain contact with a receiver within five yards of the line of scrimmage, but restricted contact beyond that point. The pass-blocking rule was interpreted to permit the extending of arms and open hands, March 17.

A study on the use of instant replay as an officiating aid was made during seven nationally televised preseason games.

The NFL played for the first time in

Mexico City, with the Saints defeating the Eagles 14-7 in a preseason game, August 5.

Bolstered by the expansion of the regular-season schedule from 14 to 16 weeks, NFL paid attendance exceeded 12 million (12,771,800) for the first time. The per-game average of 57,017 was the third-highest in league history and the most since 1973.

1979 Pittsburgh defeated Dallas 35-31 in Super Bowl XIII at Miami to become the first team ever to win three Super Bowls, January 21. The NBC telecast was viewed in 35,090,000 homes, by an estimated 96.6 million fans.

The owners awarded three future Super Bowl sites: Super Bowl XV to the Louisiana Superdome in New Orleans, to be played on January 25, 1981; Super Bowl XVI to the Pontiac Silverdome in Pontiac, Michigan, to be played on January 24, 1982; and Super Bowl XVII to Pasadena's Rose Bowl, to be played on January 30, 1983, March 13.

NFL rules changes emphasized additional player safety. The changes prohibited players on the receiving team from blocking below the waist during kickoffs, punts, and field-goal attempts; prohibited the wearing of torn or altered equipment and exposed pads that could be hazardous; extended the zone in which there could be no crackback blocks; and instructed officials to quickly whistle a play dead when a quarterback was clearly in the grasp of a tackler, March 16.

Rosenbloom, the president of the Rams, drowned at 72, April 2. His widow, Georgia, assumed control of the club.

1980 Pittsburgh defeated the Los Angeles Rams 31-19 in Super Bowl XIV at Pasadena to become the first team to win four Super Bowls, January 20. The game was viewed in a record 35,330,000 homes.

The AFC-NFC Pro Bowl, won 37-27 by the NFC, was played before 48,060 fans at Aloha Stadium in Honolulu, Hawaii. It was the first time in the 30-year history of the Pro Bowl that the game was played in a non-NFL city.

Rules changes placed greater restrictions on contact in the area of the head, neck, and face. Under the heading of "personal foul," players were prohibited from directly striking, swinging, or clubbing on the head, neck, or face. Starting in 1980, a penalty could be called for such contact whether or not the initial contact was made below the neck area.

CBS, with a record bid of $12 million, won the national radio rights to 26 NFL regular-season games and all 10 postseason games for the 1980-83 seasons.

The Los Angeles Rams moved their home games to Anaheim Stadium in nearby Orange County, California.

The Oakland Raiders joined the Los Angeles Coliseum Commission's antitrust suit against the NFL. The suit contended the league violated antitrust laws in declining to approve a proposed move by the Raiders from Oakland to Los Angeles.

NFL regular-season attendance of nearly 13.4 million set a record for the third year in a row. The average paid attendance for the 224-game 1980 regular season was 59,787, the highest in the league's 61-year history. NFL games in 1980 were played before 92.4 percent of total stadium capacity.

Television ratings in 1980 were the second-best in NFL history, trailing only the combined ratings of the 1976 season. All three networks posted gains, and NBC's 15.0 rating was its best ever. CBS and ABC had their best ratings since 1977, with 15.3 and 20.8 ratings, respectively. CBS Radio reported a record audience of 7 million for Monday night and special games.

1981 Oakland defeated Philadelphia 27-10 in Super Bowl XV at the Louisiana Superdome in New Orleans, to become the first wild-card team to win a Super Bowl, January 25.

Edgar F. Kaiser, Jr., purchased the Denver Broncos from Gerald and Allan Phipps, February 26.

The owners adopted a disaster plan for re-stocking a team should the club be involved in a fatal accident, March 20.

The owners awarded Super Bowl XVIII to Tampa, to be played in Tampa Stadium on January 22, 1984, June 3.

A CBS-New York Times poll showed that 48 percent of sports fans preferred football to 31 percent for baseball.

The NFL teams hosted 167 representatives from 44 predominantly black colleges during training camps for a total of 289 days. The program was adopted for renewal during each training camp period.

NFL regular-season attendance—13.6 million for an average of 60,745—set a record for the fourth year in a row. It also was the first time the per-game average exceeded 60,000. NFL games in 1981 were played before 93.8 percent of total stadium capacity.

ABC and CBS set all-time rating highs. ABC finished with a 21.7 rating and CBS with a 17.5 rating. NBC was down slightly to 13.9.

1982 San Francisco defeated Cincinnati 26-21 in Super Bowl XVI at the Pontiac Silverdome, in the first Super Bowl held in the North, January 24. The CBS telecast achieved the highest rating of any televised sports event ever, 49.1 with a 73.0 share. The game was viewed by a record 110.2 million fans. CBS Radio reported a record 14 million listeners for the game.

The NFL signed a five-year contract with the three television networks (ABC, CBS, and NBC) to televise all NFL regular-season and postseason games starting with the 1982 season.

The owners awarded the 1983, 1984, and 1985 AFC-NFC Pro Bowls to Honolulu's Aloha Stadium.

A jury ruled against the NFL in the antitrust trial brought by the Los Angeles Coliseum Commission and the Oakland Raiders, May 7. The verdict cleared the way for the Raiders to move to Los Angeles, where they defeated Green Bay 24-3 in their first preseason game, August 29.

The 1982 season was reduced from a 16-game schedule to nine as the result of a 57-day players' strike. The strike was called by the NFLPA at midnight on Monday, September 20, following the Green Bay at New York Giants game. Play resumed November 21-22 following ratification of the Collective Bargaining Agreement by NFL owners, November 17 in New York.

Under the Collective Bargaining Agreement, which was to run through the 1986 season, the NFL draft was extended through 1992 and the veteran free-agent system was left basically unchanged. A minimum salary schedule for years of experience was established; training camp and postseason pay were increased; players' medical, insurance, and retirement benefits were increased; and a severance-pay system was introduced to aid in career transition, a first in professional sports.

Despite the players' strike, the average paid attendance in 1982 was 58,472, the fifth-highest in league history.

The owners awarded the sites of two Super Bowls, December 14: Super Bowl XIX, to be played on January 20, 1985, to Stanford University Stadium in Stanford, California, with San Francisco as host team; and Super Bowl XX, to be played on January 26, 1986, to the Louisiana Superdome in New Orleans.

1983 Because of the shortened season, the NFL adopted a format of 16 teams competing in a Super Bowl Tournament for the 1982 playoffs. The NFC's number-one seed, Washington, defeated the AFC's number-two seed, Miami, 27-17 in Super Bowl XVII at the Rose Bowl in Pasadena, January 30.

Super Bowl XVII was the second-highest rated live television program of all time, giving the NFL a sweep of the top 10 live programs in television history. The game was viewed in more than 40 million homes, the largest ever for a live telecast.

Halas, the owner of the Bears and the last surviving member of the NFL's second organizational meeting, died at 88, October 31.

1984 The Los Angeles Raiders defeated Washington 38-9 in Super Bowl XVIII at Tampa Stadium, January 22. The game achieved a 46.4 rating and 71.0 share.

An 11-man group headed by H.R. (Bum) Bright purchased the Dallas Cowboys from Clint Murchison, Jr., March 20. Club president Tex Schramm was designated as managing general partner.

Patrick Bowlen purchased a majority interest in the Denver Broncos from Edgar Kaiser, Jr., March 21.

The Colts relocated to Indianapolis, March 28. Their new home became the Hoosier Dome.

The owners awarded two Super Bowl sites at their May 23-25 meetings: Super Bowl XXI, to be played on January 25, 1987, to the Rose Bowl in Pasadena; and Super Bowl XXII, to be played on January 31, 1988, to San Diego Jack Murphy Stadium.

The New York Jets moved their home games to Giants Stadium in East Rutherford, New Jersey.

Alex G. Spanos purchased a majority interest in the San Diego Chargers from Eugene V. Klein, August 28.

Houston defeated Pittsburgh 23-20 to mark the one-hundredth overtime game in regular-season play since overtime was adopted in 1974, December 2.

On the field, many all-time records were set: Dan Marino of Miami passed for 5,084 yards and 48 touchdowns; Eric Dickerson of the Los Angeles Rams rushed for 2,105 yards; Art Monk of Washington caught 106 passes; and Walter Payton of Chicago broke Jim Brown's career rushing mark, finishing the season with 13,309 yards.

According to a CBS Sports/New York Times survey, 53 percent of the nation's sports fans said they most enjoyed watching football, compared to 18 percent for baseball, December 2-4.

NFL paid attendance exceeded 13 million for the fifth consecutive complete regular season when 13,398,112, an average of 59,813, attended games. The figure was the second-highest in league history. Teams averaged 42.4 points per game, the second-highest total since the 1970 merger.

1985 San Francisco defeated Miami 38-16 in Super Bowl XIX at Stanford Stadium in Stanford, California, January 20. The game was viewed on television by more people than any other live event in history. President Ronald Reagan, who took his second oath of office before tossing the coin for the game, was one of 115,936,000 viewers. The game drew a 46.4 rating and a 63.0 share. In addition, 6 million people watched the Super Bowl in the United Kingdom and a similar number in Italy. Super Bowl XIX had a direct economic impact of $113.5 million on the San Francisco Bay area.

NBC Radio and the NFL entered into a two-year agreement granting NBC the radio rights to a 37-game package in each of the 1985-86 seasons, March 6. The package included 27 regular-season games and 10 postseason games.

The owners awarded two Super Bowl sites at their annual meeting, March 10-15: Super Bowl XXIII, to be played on January 22, 1989, to the proposed Dolphins Stadium in Miami; and Super Bowl XXIV, to be played on January 28, 1990, to the Louisiana Superdome in New Orleans.

Norman Braman, in partnership with Edward Leibowitz, bought the Philadelphia Eagles from Leonard Tose, April 29.

Bruce Smith, a Virginia Tech defensive lineman selected by Buffalo, was the first player chosen in the fiftieth NFL draft, April 30.

A group headed by Tom Benson, Jr., was approved to purchase the New Orleans Saints from John W. Mecom, Jr., June 3.

The NFL owners adopted a resolution calling for a series of overseas preseason games, beginning in 1986, with one game to be played in England/Europe and/or one game in Japan each year. The game would be a fifth preseason game for the clubs involved and all arrangements and selection of the clubs would be under the control of the Commissioner, May 23.

The league-wide conversion to videotape from movie film for coaching study was approved.

Commissioner Rozelle was authorized to extend the commitment to Honolulu's Aloha Stadium for the AFC-NFC Pro Bowl for 1988, 1989, and 1990, October 15.

The NFL set a single-weekend paid attendance record when 902,657 tickets were sold for the weekend of October 27-28.

A Louis Harris poll in December revealed that pro football remained the sport most followed by Americans. Fifty-nine percent of those surveyed followed pro football, compared with 54 percent who followed baseball.

The Chicago-Miami Monday game had the highest rating, 29.6, and share, 46.0, of any prime-time game in NFL history, December 2. The game was viewed in more than 25 million homes.

The NFL showed a ratings increase on all three networks for the season, gaining 4 percent on NBC, 10 on CBS, and 16 on ABC.

1986 Chicago defeated New England 46-10 in Super Bowl XX at the Louisiana Superdome, January 26. The Patriots had earned the right to play the Bears by becoming the first wild-card team to win three consecutive games on the road. The NBC telecast replaced the final episode of M*A*S*H as the most-viewed television program in history, with an audience of 127 million viewers, according to A.C. Nielsen figures. In addition to drawing a 48.3 rating and a 70 percent share in the United States, Super Bowl XX was televised to 59 foreign countries and beamed via satellite to the QE II. An estimated 300 million Chinese viewed a tape delay of the game in March. NBC Radio figures indicated an audience of 10 million for the game.

Super Bowl XX injected more than $100 million into the New Orleans-area economy, and fans spent $250 per day and a record $17.69 per person on game day.

The owners adopted limited use of instant replay as an officiating aid, prohibited players from wearing or otherwise displaying equipment, apparel, or other items that carry commercial names, names of organizations, or personal messages of any type, March 11.

After an 11-week trial, a jury in U.S. District Court in New York awarded the United States Football League one dollar in its $1.7 billion antitrust suit against the NFL. The jury rejected all of the USFL's television-related claims, which were the self-proclaimed heart of the USFL's case, July 29.

Chicago defeated Dallas 17-6 at Wembley Stadium in London in the first American Bowl. The game drew a sellout crowd of 82,699 and the NBC national telecast in this country produced a 12.4 rating and 36 percent share, making it the second-highest-rated daytime preseason game and highest daytime preseason television audience ever with 10,650,000 viewers, August 3.

Monday Night Football became the longest-running prime-time series in the history of the ABC network.

Instant replay was used to reverse two plays in 31 preseason games. During the regular season, 374 plays were closely reviewed by replay officials, leading to 38 reversals in 224 games. Eighteen plays were closely reviewed by instant replay in 10 postseason games with three reversals.

1987 The New York Giants defeated Denver 39-20 in Super Bowl XXI and captured their first NFL title since 1956. The game, played in Pasadena's Rose Bowl, drew a sellout crowd of 101,063. According to A.C. Nielsen figures, the CBS broadcast of the game was viewed in the U.S. on television by 122,640,000 people, making the telecast the second most-watched television show of all-time behind Super Bowl XX. The game was watched live or on tape in 55 foreign countries and NBC Radio's broadcast of the game was heard by a record 10.1 million people.

The NFL set an all-time paid attendance mark of 17,304,463 for all games, including preseason, regular-season, and postseason. Average regular-season game attendance (60,663) exceeded the 60,000 figure for only the second time in league history.

New three-year TV contracts with ABC, CBS, and NBC were announced for 1987-89 at the NFL annual meeting in Maui, Hawaii, March 15. Commissioner Rozelle and Broadcast Committee Chairman Art Modell also announced a three-year contract with ESPN to televise 13 prime-time games each season. The ESPN contract was the first with a cable network. However, NFL games on ESPN also were scheduled for regular television in the city of the visiting team and in the home city if the game was sold out 72 hours in advance.

Owners also voted to continue in effect for one year the instant replay system used during the 1986 season.

A special payment program was adopted to benefit nearly 1,000 former NFL players who participated in the League before the current Bert Bell NFL Pension Plan was created and made retroactive to the 1959 season. Players covered by the new program spent at least five years in the League and played all or part of their career prior to 1959. Each vested player would receive $60 per month for each year of service in the League for life.

Possible sites for Super Bowl XXV were reduced to five locations by the NFL Super Bowl XXV Site Selection Committee: Anaheim Stadium, Los Angeles Memorial Coliseum, Joe Robbie Stadium, San Diego Jack Murphy Stadium, and Tampa Stadium.

NFL and CBS Radio jointly announced agreement granting CBS the radio rights to a 40-game package in each of the next three NFL seasons, 1987-89, April 7.

NFL owners awarded Super Bowl XXV, to be played on January 27, 1991, to Tampa Stadium, May 20.

Over 400 former NFL players from the pre-1959 era received first payments from NFL owners, July 1.

The NFL's debut on ESPN produced the two highest-rated and most-watched sports programs in basic cable history. The Chicago at Miami game on August 16 drew an 8.9 rating in 3.81 million homes. Those records fell two weeks later when the Los Angeles Raiders at Dallas game achieved a 10.2 cable rating in 4.36 million homes.

Fifty-eight preseason games drew a record paid attendance of 3,116,870.

The 1987 season was reduced from a 16-game season to 15 as the result of a 24-day players' strike. The strike was called by the NFLPA on Tuesday, September 22, following the New England at New York Jets game. Games scheduled for the third weekend were canceled but the games of weeks four, five, and six were played with replacement teams. Striking players returned for the seventh week of the season, October 25.

In a three-team deal involving 10 players and/or draft choices, the Los Angeles Rams traded running back Eric Dickerson to the Indianapolis Colts for six draft choices and two players. Buffalo obtained the rights to linebacker Cornelius Bennett from Indianapolis, sending Greg Bell and three draft choices to the Rams. The Colts added Owen Gill and three draft choices of their own to complete the deal with the Rams, October 31.

The Chicago at Minnesota game became the highest-rated and most-watched sports program in basic cable history when it drew a 14.4 cable rating in 6.5 million homes, December 6.

Instant replay was used to reverse eight plays in 52 preseason games. During the strike-shortened 210-game regular season, 490 plays were closely reviewed by replay officials, leading to 57 reversals. Eighteen plays were closely reviewed by instant replay in 10 postseason games, with three reversals.

1988 Washington defeated Denver 42-10 in Super Bowl XXII to earn its second victory this decade in the NFL Championship Game. The game, played for the first time in San Diego Jack Murphy Stadium, drew a sellout crowd of 73,302. According to A.C. Nielsen figures, the ABC broadcast of the game was viewed in the U.S. on television by 115,000,000 people. The game was seen live or on tape in 60 foreign countries, including the People's Republic of China, and CBS's radio broadcast of the game was heard by 13.7 million people.

A total of 811 players shared in the postseason pool of $16.9 million, the most ever distributed in a single season.

In a unanimous 3-0 decision, the 2nd Circuit Court of Appeals in New York upheld the verdict of the jury that in July, 1986, had awarded the United States Football League one dollar in its $1.7 billion antitrust suit against the NFL. In a 91-page opinion, Judge Ralph K. Winter said the USFL sought through court decree the success it failed to gain among football fans, March 10.

By a 23-5 margin, owners voted to continue the instant replay system for the third consecutive season with the Instant Replay Official to be assigned to a regular seven-man, on-the-field crew. At the NFL annual meeting in Phoenix, Arizona, a 45-second clock was also approved to replace the 30-second clock. For a normal sequence of plays, the interval between plays was changed to 45 seconds from the time the ball is signaled dead until it is snapped on the succeeding play.

NFL owners approved the transfer of the Cardinals' franchise from St. Louis to Phoenix; approved two supplemental drafts each year—one prior to training camp and one prior to the regular season; and voted to initiate an annual series of games in Japan/Asia as early as the 1989 preseason, March 14-18.

The NFL Annual Selection Meeting returned to a separate two-day format and for the first time originated on a Sunday. ESPN drew a 3.6 rating during their seven-hour coverage of the draft, which was viewed in 1.6 million homes, April 24-25.

Art Rooney, founder and owner of the Steelers, died at 87, August 25.

Paid and average attendance of 934,271 and 66,734 at 14 games on October 16-17 set single weekend records.

Commissioner Rozelle announced that two teams would play a preseason game as part of the American Bowl series on August 6, 1989, in the Korakuen Tokyo Dome in Japan, December 16.

NFL regular-season paid attendance of 13,535,335 and the average of 60,427 was the third highest all-time. Buffalo set an NFL team single-season, in-house attendance mark of 622,793.

1989 San Francisco defeated Cincinnati 20-16 in Super Bowl XXIII. The game, played for the first time at Joe Robbie Stadium in Miami, was attended by a sellout crowd of 75,129. NBC's telecast of the game was watched by an estimated 110,780,000 viewers, according to A.C. Nielsen, making it the sixth most-watched program in television history. The game was seen live or on tape in 60 foreign countries, including an estimated 300 million in China. The CBS Radio broadcast of the game was heard by 11.2 million people.

Commissioner Rozelle announced his retirement, pending the naming of a successor, March 22 at the NFL annual meeting in Palm Desert, California.

Following the announcement, AFC president Lamar Hunt and NFC president Wellington Mara announced the formation of a six-man search committee composed of Art Modell, Robert Parins, Dan Rooney, and Ralph Wilson. Hunt and Mara served as co-chairmen.

By a 24-4 margin, owners voted to continue the instant replay system for the fourth straight season. A strengthened policy regarding anabolic steroids and masking agents was announced by Commissioner Rozelle. NFL clubs called for strong disciplinary measures in cases of feigned injuries and adopted a joint proposal by the Long-Range Planning and Finance committees regarding player personnel rules, March 19-23.

Two hundred twenty-nine unconditional free agents signed with new teams under management's Plan B system, April 1.

Jerry Jones purchased a majority interest in the Dallas Cowboys from H.R. (Bum) Bright, April 18.

Tex Schramm was named president of the new World League of American Football to work with a six-man committee of Dan Rooney, chairman; Norman Braman, Lamar Hunt, Victor Kiam, Mike Lynn, and Bill Walsh, April 18.

NFL and CBS Radio jointly announced agreement extending CBS's radio rights to an annual 40-game package through the 1994 season, April 18.

NFL owners awarded Super Bowl XXVI, to be played on January 26, 1992, to Minneapolis, May 24.

As of opening day, September 10, of the 229 Plan B free agents, 111 were active and 23 others were on teams' reserve lists. Ninety-two others were waived and three retired.

Art Shell was named head coach

of the Los Angeles Raiders making him the NFL's first black head coach since Fritz Pollard coached the Akron Pros in 1921, October 3.

The site of the New England Patriots at San Francisco 49ers game scheduled for Candlestick Park on October 22 was switched to Stanford Stadium in the aftermath of the Bay Area Earthquake of October 17. The change was announced on October 19.

Paul Tagliabue became the seventh chief executive of the NFL on October 26 when he was chosen to succeed Commissioner Pete Rozelle on the sixth ballot of a three-day meeting in Cleveland, Ohio.

In all, 12 ballots were required to select Tagliabue. Two were conducted at a meeting in Chicago on July 6, and four at a meeting in Dallas on October 10-11. On the twelfth ballot, with Seattle absent, Tagliabue received more than the 19 affirmative votes required for election from among the 27 clubs present.

The transfer from Commissioner Rozelle to Commissioner Tagliabue took place at 12:01 A.M. on Sunday, November 5.

NFL Charities donated $1 million through United Way to benefit Bay Area earthquake victims, November 6.

NFL paid attendance of 17,399,538 was the highest total in league history. This included a total of 13,625,662 for an average of 60,829 — both NFL records — for the 224-game regular season.

1990 San Francisco defeated Denver 55-10 in Super Bowl XXIV at the Louisiana Superdome, January 28. San Francisco joined Pittsburgh as the NFL's only teams to win four Super Bowls.

The NFL announced revisions in its 1990 draft eligibility rules. College juniors became eligible but must renounce their collegiate football eligibility before applying for the NFL Draft, February 16.

Commissioner Tagliabue announced NFL teams will play their 16-game schedule over 17 weeks in 1990 and 1991 and 16 games over 18 weeks in 1992 and 1993, February 27.

The NFL revised its playoff format to include two additional wild-card teams (one per conference).

Commissioner Tagliabue and Broadcast Committee Chairman Art Modell announced a four-year contract with Turner Broadcasting to televise nine Sunday-night games.

New four-year TV agreements were ratified for 1990-93 for ABC, CBS, NBC, ESPN, and TNT at the NFL annual meeting in Orlando, Florida, March 12. The contracts totaled $3.6 billion, the largest in TV history.

The NFL announced plans to expand its American Bowl series of preseason games. In addition to games in London and Tokyo, American Bowl games were scheduled for Berlin, Germany, and Montreal, Canada, in 1990.

For the fifth straight year, NFL owners voted to continue a limited system of Instant Replay. Beginning in 1990, the replay official will have a two-minute time limit to make a decision. The vote was 21-7, March 12.

Commissioner Tagliabue announced the formation of a Committee on Expansion and Realignment, March 13. He also named a Player Advisory Council, comprised of 12 former NFL players, March 14.

One-hundred eighty-four Plan B unconditional free agents signed with new teams, April 2.

Commissioner Tagliabue appointed Dr. John Lombardo as the League's Drug Advisor for Anabolic Steroids, April 25 and named Dr. Lawrence Brown as the League's Advisor for Drugs of Abuse, May 17.

NFL owners awarded Super Bowl XXVIII, to be played in 1994, to the proposed Georgia Dome, May 23.

Commissioner Tagliabue named NFL referee Jerry Seeman as NFL Director of Officiating, replacing Art McNally, who announced his retirement, July 12.

NFL International Week was celebrated with four preseason games in seven days in Tokyo, London, Berlin, and Montreal. More than 200,000 fans on three continents attended the four games, August 4-11.

Commissioner Tagliabue announced the NFL Teacher of the Month program in which the League furnishes grants and scholarships in recognition of teachers who provided a positive influence upon NFL players in elementary and secondary schools, Sept. 20.

For the first time since 1957, every NFL club won at least one of its first four games, Oct. 1.

NFL total paid attendance of 17,665,671 was the highest total in League history. The regular-season total paid attendance of 13,959,896 and average of 62,321 for 224 games were the highest ever, surpassing the previous records set in the 1989 season.

1991 The New York Giants defeated Buffalo 20-19 in Super Bowl XXV to capture their second title in five years. The game was played before a sellout crowd of 73,813 at Tampa Stadium and became the first Super Bowl decided by one point, January 26. The ABC broadcast of the game was seen by more than 112,000,000 people in the United States and was seen live or taped in 60 other countries.

NFL playoff games earned the top television rating spot of the week for each week of the month-long playoffs, January 29.

A total of 693 players shared in the postseason pool of $14.9 million.

New York businessman Robert Tisch purchased a 50 percent interest in the New York Giants from Mrs. Helen Mara Nugent and her children, Tim Mara and Maura Mara Concannon, February 2.

Commissioner Tagliabue named Neil Austrian to the newly created position of President of the NFL to be chief operating officer for League-wide business and financial operations, February 27.

NFL owners voted to continue a limited system of Instant Replay for the sixth consecutive year. The vote was 21-7, March 19.

The NFL launched the World League of American Football, the first sports league to operate on a weekly basis on two separate continents, March 23.

One-hundred thirty-nine Plan B unconditional free agents signed with new teams, April 1.

NFL Charities presented a $250,000 donation to the United Service Organization. The donation was the second largest single grant ever by NFL Charities, April 5.

Commissioner Tagliabue named Harold Henderson as Executive Vice President for Labor Relations and Chairman of the NFL Management Council Executive Committee, April 8.

Russell Maryland, a University of Miami defensive lineman, was selected by Dallas, becoming the first player chosen in the 1991 NFL draft, April 21.

NFL owners approved a recommendation by the Expansion and Realignment Committee to add two teams for the 1994 season, resulting in six divisions of five teams each, May 22.

NFL owners awarded Super Bowl XXIX, to be played on January 29, 1995, to Miami, May 23.

"NFL International Week" featured six 1990 playoff teams playing nationally televised games in London, Berlin, and Tokyo on July 28 and August 3-4. The games drew more than 150,000 fans.

Paul Brown, founder of the Cleveland Browns and Cincinnati Bengals, died at age 82, August 5.

NFL owners approved a resolution establishing an international division, reporting to the President of the NFL. A three-year financial plan for the World League was approved by NFL clubs at a meeting in Dallas, October 23.

1992 The NFL agreed to provide a minimum of $2.5 million in financial support to the NFL Alumni Association and assistance to NFL Alumni-related programs. The agreement included contributions from NFL Charities to the Pre-59ers and Dire Need Programs for former players, January 25.

The Washington Redskins defeated the Buffalo Bills 37-24 in Super Bowl XXVI to capture their third world championship in 10 years, January 26. The game was played before a sellout crowd of 63,130 at the Hubert H. Humphrey Metrodome in Minneapolis and attracted the second largest television audience in Super Bowl history. The CBS broadcast was seen by more than 120,000,000 people nationally, second only to the 127,000,000 who viewed Super Bowl XX.

For the third consecutive season, NFL total paid attendance reached a record level. Total paid attendance was 17,752,139 for the 296 preseason, regular-season, and postseason games, February 3.

The use in officiating of a limited system of Instant Replay for a seventh consecutive year was not approved. The vote was 17-11 in favor of approval (21 votes were required), March 18.

One-hundred sixty-six Plan B unconditional free agents signed with new teams, April 1.

Steve Emtman, a University of Washington defensive lineman, was selected by Indianapolis, becoming the first player chosen in the 1992 NFL draft, April 26.

St. Louis businessman James Orthwein purchased controlling interest in the New England Patriots from Victor Kiam, May 11.

In the final Nielsen ratings for the 1991-92 television season, ABC's *NFL Monday Night Football* tied for eleventh place out of 132 prime-time shows with a 16.8 rating, meaning it was watched in an average of 15.5 million homes each week in its twenty-second season, May 17.

In a *Harris Poll* taken during the NFL offseason, professional football again was declared the nation's most popular sport. Professional football finished atop similar surveys conducted by Harris in 1985 and 1989, May 23.

NFL clubs accepted the report of the Expansion Committee at a league meeting in Pasadena. The report names fives cities as finalists for the two expansion teams — Baltimore, Charlotte, Jacksonville, Memphis, and St. Louis, May 19.

At a league meeting in Dallas, NFL clubs approved a proposal by the World League Board of Directors to restructure the World League and place future emphasis on its international success. The league announced it will not select its two NFL expansion teams in October, as originally scheduled, because of unresolved labor-management issues, September 17.

The NFL announced several moves to broaden its international presence and reaffirm its commitment to expand American football in Europe. The league opened the first NFL International office on the European continent in Frankfurt, Germany; hired World League executive of the year Oliver Luck to head that office; planned a series of NFL/World League instructional camps for next spring throughout Europe; and announced a record fourth overseas American Bowl to be played in Spain in the summer of 1993, October 29.

The NFL announced that underclassmen who wish to petition for entry into the 1993 NFL draft must submit a written application by January 6. It is the third time in three years the NFL revised the declaration date for underclassmen, December 2.

1993 The NFL and lawyers for the players announced a settlement of various lawsuits and an agreement on the terms of a seven-year deal that included a new player system to be in place through the 1999 season, January 6.

Commissioner Tagliabue announced the establishment of the "NFL World Partnership Program" which will develop amateur football internationally through a series of clinics conducted by former NFL players and coaches, January 14.

The NFL began construction of Youth Education Town, a 20,000-square-foot youth facility located in south central Los Angeles for mostly inner city youth. The facility, constructed to commemorate the playing of Super Bowl XXVII, will be completed by May 15. The educational and recreational facility, the only one of its kind constructed by a professional sports league, will contain a library, computer room, and athletic facilities, January 25.

The Dallas Cowboys defeated the Buffalo Bills 52-17 in Super Bowl XXVII to capture their first NFL title since 1978. The game was played before a crowd of 98,374 at the Rose Bowl in Pasadena, California. The NBC broadcast of the game was the most watched program in television history and was seen by more than 133,400,000 people in the United States. The game also was seen live or taped in more than 100 other countries. The rating for the game was 45.1, the tenth highest for any televised sports event, January 31.

A total of 695 players shared in the postseason pool of $14.9 million, February 15.

The signing period for restricted free agents and unrestricted veterans began, March 1, for all players who completed five accrued seasons and whose contracts expired.

For the fourth consecutive season, the NFL total paid attendance reached a record level. Total paid attendance was 17,784,354 for the 296 preseason, regular-season, and postseason games, March 4.

NFL owners, at their annual meeting in Palm Desert, California, continued to find ways to improve the game. The owners amended several rules and voted to reduce the 45-second play clock to 40 seconds and reduced the ineligible receiver downfield foul from 10 to 5 yards. Both rules changes will be in effect for the 1993 season, March 22.

NFL owners awarded Super Bowl XXX to the city of Phoenix and Cardinals owner Bill Bidwill. The game will be played on January 28, 1996, at Sun Devil Stadium, March 23.

Drew Bledsoe, a quarterback from Washington State, was selected by New England, becoming the first player chosen in the 1993 NFL draft, April 25.

NFL COMMISSIONERS AND PRESIDENTS*

1920 . . . . Jim Thorpe, President
1921-39 . . . . Joe Carr, President
1939-41 . . . . . Carl Storck, President
1941-46 . . . . Elmer Layden, Commissioner
1946-59 . . . Bert Bell, Commissioner
1960-89 . . . . Pete Rozelle, Commissioner
1989-present . . . . Paul Tagliabue, Commissioner

*NFL treasurer Austin Gunsel served as president in the office of the commissioner following the death of Bert Bell (Oct. 11, 1959) until the election of Pete Rozelle (Jan. 26, 1960).

PAST STANDINGS

1992

American Conference

Eastern Division

	W	L	T	Pct.	Pts.	OP
Miami	11	5	0	.688	340	281
Buffalo*	11	5	0	.688	381	283
Indianapolis	9	7	0	.563	216	302
N.Y. Jets	4	12	0	.250	220	315
New England	2	14	0	.125	205	363

Central Division

	W	L	T	Pct.	Pts.	OP
Pittsburgh	11	5	0	.688	299	225
Houston*	10	6	0	.625	352	258
Cleveland	7	9	0	.438	272	275
Cincinnati	5	11	0	.313	274	364

Western Division

	W	L	T	Pct.	Pts.	OP
San Diego	11	5	0	.688	335	241
Kansas City*	10	6	0	.625	348	282
Denver	8	8	0	.500	262	329
L.A. Raiders	7	9	0	.438	249	281
Seattle	2	14	0	.125	140	312

National Conference

Eastern Division

	W	L	T	Pct.	Pts.	OP
Dallas	13	3	0	.813	409	243
Philadelphia*	11	5	0	.688	354	245
Washington*	9	7	0	.563	300	255
N.Y. Giants	6	10	0	.375	306	367
Phoenix	4	12	0	.250	243	332

Central Division

	W	L	T	Pct.	Pts.	OP
Minnesota	11	5	0	.688	374	249
Green Bay	9	7	0	.563	276	296
Tampa Bay	5	11	0	.313	267	365
Chicago	5	11	0	.313	295	361
Detroit	5	11	0	.313	273	332

Western Division

	W	L	T	Pct.	Pts.	OP
San Francisco	14	2	0	.875	431	236
New Orleans*	12	4	0	.750	330	202
Atlanta	6	10	0	.375	327	414
L.A. Rams	6	10	0	.375	313	383

**Wild Card qualifier for playoffs*

Miami finished ahead of Buffalo based on better conference record (9-3 to 7-5). Tampa Bay finished ahead of Chicago and Detroit based on better conference record (5-9 to Bears' 4-8 and Lions' 3-9). Atlanta finished ahead of L.A. Rams based on better record versus common opponents (5-7 to 4-8).

First round playoffs: SAN DIEGO 17, Kansas City 0; BUFFALO 41, Houston 38 (OT)
Divisional playoffs: Buffalo 24, PITTSBURGH 3; MIAMI 31, San Diego 0
AFC championship: Buffalo 29, MIAMI 10
First round playoffs: Washington 24, MINNESOTA 7; Philadelphia 36, NEW ORLEANS 20
Divisional playoffs: SAN FRANCISCO 20, Washington 13; DALLAS 34, Philadelphia 10
NFC championship: Dallas 30, SAN FRANCISCO 20
Super Bowl XXVII: Dallas (NFC) 52, Buffalo (AFC) 17, at Rose Bowl, Pasadena, California.
In Past Standings section, home teams in playoff games are indicated by capital letters.

1991

American Conference

Eastern Division

	W	L	T	Pct.	Pts.	OP
Buffalo	13	3	0	.813	458	318
N.Y. Jets*	8	8	0	.500	314	293
Miami	8	8	0	.500	343	349
New England	6	10	0	.375	211	305
Indianapolis	1	15	0	.063	143	381

Central Division

	W	L	T	Pct.	Pts.	OP
Houston	11	5	0	.688	386	251
Pittsburgh	7	9	0	.438	292	344
Cleveland	6	10	0	.375	293	298
Cincinnati	3	13	0	.188	263	435

Western Division

	W	L	T	Pct.	Pts.	OP
Denver	12	4	0	.750	304	235
Kansas City*	10	6	0	.625	322	252
L.A. Raiders*	9	7	0	.563	298	297
Seattle	7	9	0	.438	276	261
San Diego	4	12	0	.250	274	342

National Conference

Eastern Division

	W	L	T	Pct.	Pts.	OP
Washington	14	2	0	.875	485	224
Dallas*	11	5	0	.688	342	310
Philadelphia	10	6	0	.625	285	244
N.Y. Giants	8	8	0	.500	281	297
Phoenix	4	12	0	.250	196	344

Central Division

	W	L	T	Pct.	Pts.	OP
Detroit	12	4	0	.750	339	295
Chicago*	11	5	0	.688	299	269
Minnesota	8	8	0	.500	301	306
Green Bay	4	12	0	.250	273	313
Tampa Bay	3	13	0	.188	199	365

Western Division

	W	L	T	Pct.	Pts.	OP
New Orleans	11	5	0	.688	341	211
Atlanta*	10	6	0	.625	361	338
San Francisco	10	6	0	.625	393	239
L.A. Rams	3	13	0	.188	234	390

**Wild Card qualifiers for playoffs*

New York Jets finished ahead of Miami based on head-to-head sweep (2-0). Atlanta finished ahead of San Francisco based on head-to-head sweep (2-0).

First round playoffs: KANSAS CITY 10, Los Angeles Raiders 6; HOUSTON 17, N.Y. Jets 10
Divisional playoffs: DENVER 26, Houston 24; BUFFALO 37, Kansas City 14
AFC championship: BUFFALO 10, Denver 7
First round playoffs: Atlanta 27, NEW ORLEANS 20; Dallas 17, CHICAGO 13
Divisional playoffs: WASHINGTON 24, Atlanta 7; DETROIT 38, Dallas 6
NFC championship: WASHINGTON 41, Detroit 10
Super Bowl XXVI: Washington (NFC) 37, Buffalo (AFC) 24, at Hubert H. Humphrey Metrodome, Minneapolis, Minnesota.

1990

American Conference

Eastern Division

	W	L	T	Pct.	Pts.	OP
Buffalo	13	3	0	.813	428	263
Miami*	12	4	0	.750	336	242
Indianapolis	7	9	0	.438	281	353
N.Y. Jets	6	10	0	.375	295	345
New England	1	15	0	.063	181	446

Central Division

	W	L	T	Pct.	Pts.	OP
Cincinnati	9	7	0	.563	360	352
Houston*	9	7	0	.563	405	307
Pittsburgh	9	7	0	.563	292	240
Cleveland	3	13	0	.188	228	462

Western Division

	W	L	T	Pct.	Pts.	OP
L.A. Raiders	12	4	0	.750	337	268
Kansas City*	11	5	0	.688	369	257
Seattle	9	7	0	.563	306	286
San Diego	6	10	0	.375	315	281
Denver	5	11	0	.313	331	374

National Conference

Eastern Division

	W	L	T	Pct.	Pts.	OP
N.Y. Giants	13	3	0	.813	335	211
Philadelphia*	10	6	0	.625	396	299
Washington*	10	6	0	.625	381	301
Dallas	7	9	0	.438	244	308
Phoenix	5	11	0	.313	268	396

Central Division

	W	L	T	Pct.	Pts.	OP
Chicago	11	5	0	.688	348	280
Tampa Bay	6	10	0	.375	264	367
Detroit	6	10	0	.375	373	413
Green Bay	6	10	0	.375	271	347
Minnesota	6	10	0	.375	351	326

Western Division

	W	L	T	Pct.	Pts.	OP
San Francisco	14	2	0	.875	353	239
New Orleans*	8	8	0	.500	274	275
L.A. Rams	5	11	0	.313	345	412
Atlanta	5	11	0	.313	348	365

**Wild Card qualifiers for playoffs*

Cincinnati won AFC Central title based on best head-to-head record (3-1) vs. Houston (2-2) and Pittsburgh (1-3). Houston was Wild Card based on better conference record (8-4) than Seattle (7-5) and Pittsburgh (6-6). Philadelphia finished second in the NFC East based on better division record (5-3) than Washington (4-4). Tampa Bay was second in NFC Central based on 5-1 record vs. Detroit, Green Bay, and Minnesota. Detroit finished third based on best net division points (minus 8) vs. Green Bay (minus 40) in fourth. Minnesota was fifth based on 4-8 conference record. The Los Angeles Rams finished third in NFC West based on net points in division (plus 1) vs. Atlanta (minus 31).

First round playoffs: MIAMI 17, Kansas City 16; CINCINNATI 41, Houston 14
Divisional playoffs: BUFFALO 44, Miami 34; L.A. RAIDERS 20, Cincinnati 10
AFC championship: BUFFALO 51, L.A. Raiders 3
First round playoffs: Washington 20, PHILADELPHIA 6; CHICAGO 16, New Orleans 6
Divisional playoffs: SAN FRANCISCO 28, Washington 10; N.Y. GIANTS 31, Chicago 3
NFC championship: N.Y. Giants 15, SAN FRANCISCO 13
Super Bowl XXV: N.Y. Giants (NFC) 20, Buffalo (AFC) 19, at Tampa Stadium, Tampa, Florida.

1989

American Conference

Eastern Division

	W	L	T	Pct.	Pts.	OP
Buffalo	9	7	0	.563	409	317
Indianapolis	8	8	0	.500	298	301
Miami	8	8	0	.500	331	379
New England	5	11	0	.313	297	391
N.Y. Jets	4	12	0	.250	253	411

Central Division

	W	L	T	Pct.	Pts.	OP
Cleveland	9	6	1	.594	334	254
Houston*	9	7	0	.563	365	412
Pittsburgh*	9	7	0	.563	265	326
Cincinnati	8	8	0	.500	404	285

Western Division

	W	L	T	Pct.	Pts.	OP
Denver	11	5	0	.688	362	226
Kansas City	8	7	1	.531	318	286
L.A. Raiders	8	8	0	.500	315	297
Seattle	7	9	0	.438	241	327
San Diego	6	10	0	.375	266	290

National Conference

Eastern Division

	W	L	T	Pct.	Pts.	OP
N.Y. Giants	12	4	0	.750	348	252
Philadelphia*	11	5	0	.688	342	274
Washington	10	6	0	.625	386	308
Phoenix	5	11	0	.313	258	377
Dallas	1	15	0	.063	204	393

Central Division

	W	L	T	Pct.	Pts.	OP
Minnesota	10	6	0	.625	351	275
Green Bay	10	6	0	.625	362	356
Detroit	7	9	0	.438	312	364
Chicago	6	10	0	.375	358	377
Tampa Bay	5	11	0	.313	320	419

Western Division

	W	L	T	Pct.	Pts.	OP
San Francisco	14	2	0	.875	442	253
L.A. Rams*	11	5	0	.688	426	344
New Orleans	9	7	0	.563	386	301
Atlanta	3	13	0	.188	279	437

**Wild Card qualifiers for playoffs*

Indianapolis finished ahead of Miami in AFC East because of better conference record (7-5 vs. 6-8). Houston finished ahead of Pittsburgh in AFC Central because of head-to-head sweep (2-0). Minnesota finished ahead of Green Bay in NFC Central because of better division record (6-2 vs. 5-3).

First round playoff: Pittsburgh 26, HOUSTON 23 (OT)
Divisional playoffs: CLEVELAND 34, Buffalo 30; DENVER 24, Pittsburgh 23
AFC championship: DENVER 37, Cleveland 21
First round playoff: L.A. Rams 21, PHILADELPHIA 7
Divisional playoffs: L.A. Rams 19, N.Y. GIANTS 13 (OT); SAN FRANCISCO 41, Minnesota 13
NFC championship: SAN FRANCISCO 30, L.A. Rams 3
Super Bowl XXIV: San Francisco (NFC) 55, Denver (AFC) 10, at Louisiana Superdome, New Orleans, Louisiana.

1988

American Conference

Eastern Division

	W	L	T	Pct.	Pts.	OP
Buffalo	12	4	0	.750	329	237
Indianapolis	9	7	0	.563	354	315
New England	9	7	0	.563	250	284
N.Y. Jets	8	7	1	.531	372	354
Miami	6	10	0	.375	319	380

Central Division

	W	L	T	Pct.	Pts.	OP
Cincinnati	12	4	0	.750	448	329
Cleveland*	10	6	0	.625	304	288
Houston*	10	6	0	.625	424	365
Pittsburgh	5	11	0	.313	336	421

Western Division

	W	L	T	Pct.	Pts.	OP
Seattle	9	7	0	.563	339	329
Denver	8	8	0	.500	327	352
L.A. Raiders	7	9	0	.438	325	369
San Diego	6	10	0	.375	231	332
Kansas City	4	11	1	.281	254	320

National Conference

Eastern Division

	W	L	T	Pct.	Pts.	OP
Philadelphia	10	6	0	.625	379	319
N.Y. Giants	10	6	0	.625	359	304
Washington	7	9	0	.438	345	387
Phoenix	7	9	0	.438	344	398
Dallas	3	13	0	.188	265	381

Central Division

	W	L	T	Pct.	Pts.	OP
Chicago	12	4	0	.750	312	215
Minnesota*	11	5	0	.688	406	233
Tampa Bay	5	11	0	.313	261	350
Detroit	4	12	0	.250	220	313
Green Bay	4	12	0	.250	240	315

Western Division

	W	L	T	Pct.	Pts.	OP
San Francisco	10	6	0	.625	369	294
L.A. Rams*	10	6	0	.625	407	293
New Orleans	10	6	0	.625	312	283
Atlanta	5	11	0	.313	244	315

**Wild Card qualifiers for playoffs*

Indianapolis finished second in AFC East on basis of better record versus common opponents (7-5) over New England (6-6). Cleveland gained first AFC Wild Card position based on better division record (4-2) over Houston (3-3). Philadelphia finished first in NFC East on basis of head-to-head sweep over New York Giants. Washington finished third in NFC East on basis of better division record (4-4) over Phoenix (3-5). Detroit finished fourth in NFC Central on basis of head-to-head sweep over Green Bay. San Francisco finished first in NFC West based on better head-to-head record (3-1) over Los Angeles Rams (2-2) and New Orleans (1-3). Los Angeles Rams finished second in NFC West on basis of better division record (4-2) over New Orleans (3-3) and earned Wild Card position based on better conference record (8-4) over New York Giants (9-5) and New Orleans (6-6).

First round playoff: Houston 24, CLEVELAND 23
Divisional playoffs: CINCINNATI 21, Seattle 13; BUFFALO 17, Houston 10
AFC championship: CINCINNATI 21, Buffalo 10
First round playoff: MINNESOTA 28, Los Angeles Rams 17
Divisional playoffs: CHICAGO 20, Philadelphia 12; SAN FRANCISCO 34, Minnesota 9
NFC championship: San Francisco 28, CHICAGO 3
Super Bowl XXIII: San Francisco (NFC) 20, Cincinnati (AFC) 16, at Joe Robbie Stadium, Miami, Florida.

1987

American Conference

Eastern Division

	W	L	T	Pct.	Pts.	OP
Indianapolis	9	6	0	.600	300	238
New England	8	7	0	.533	320	293
Miami	8	7	0	.533	362	335
Buffalo	7	8	0	.467	270	305
N.Y. Jets	6	9	0	.400	334	360

Central Division

	W	L	T	Pct.	Pts.	OP
Cleveland	10	5	0	.667	390	239
Houston*	9	6	0	.600	345	349
Pittsburgh	8	7	0	.533	285	299
Cincinnati	4	11	0	.267	285	370

Western Division

	W	L	T	Pct.	Pts.	OP
Denver	10	4	1	.700	379	288
Seattle*	9	6	0	.600	371	314
San Diego	8	7	0	.533	253	317
L.A. Raiders	5	10	0	.333	301	289
Kansas City	4	11	0	.267	273	388

National Conference

Eastern Division

	W	L	T	Pct.	Pts.	OP
Washington	11	4	0	.733	379	285
Dallas	7	8	0	.467	340	348
St. Louis	7	8	0	.467	362	368
Philadelphia	7	8	0	.467	337	380
N.Y. Giants	6	9	0	.400	280	312

Central Division

	W	L	T	Pct.	Pts.	OP
Chicago	11	4	0	.733	356	282
Minnesota*	8	7	0	.533	336	335
Green Bay	5	9	1	.367	255	300
Tampa Bay	4	11	0	.267	286	360
Detroit	4	11	0	.267	269	384

Western Division

	W	L	T	Pct.	Pts.	OP
San Francisco	13	2	0	.867	459	253
New Orleans*	12	3	0	.800	422	283
L.A. Rams	6	9	0	.400	317	361
Atlanta	3	12	0	.200	205	436

**Wild Card qualifiers for playoffs*

Houston gained first AFC Wild Card position on better conference record (7-4) over Seattle (5-6).

First round playoff: HOUSTON 23, Seattle 20 (OT)
Divisional playoffs: CLEVELAND 38, Indianapolis 21
DENVER 34, Houston 10
AFC championship: DENVER 38, Cleveland 33
First round playoff: Minnesota 44, NEW ORLEANS 10
Divisional playoffs: Minnesota 36, SAN FRANCISCO 24
Washington 21, CHICAGO 17
NFC championship: WASHINGTON 17, Minnesota 10
Super Bowl XXII: Washington (NFC) 42, Denver (AFC) 10, at San Diego Jack Murphy Stadium, San Diego, California.

Note: 1987 regular season was reduced from 16 to 15 games for each team due to players' strike.

1986

American Conference

Eastern Division

	W	L	T	Pct.	Pts.	OP
New England	11	5	0	.688	412	307
N.Y. Jets*	10	6	0	.625	364	386
Miami	8	8	0	.500	430	405
Buffalo	4	12	0	.250	287	348
Indianapolis	3	13	0	.188	229	400

Central Division

	W	L	T	Pct.	Pts.	OP
Cleveland	12	4	0	.750	391	310
Cincinnati	10	6	0	.625	409	394
Pittsburgh	6	10	0	.375	307	336
Houston	5	11	0	.313	274	329

Western Division

	W	L	T	Pct.	Pts.	OP
Denver	11	5	0	.688	378	327
Kansas City*	10	6	0	.625	358	326
Seattle	10	6	0	.625	366	293
L.A. Raiders	8	8	0	.500	323	346
San Diego	4	12	0	.250	335	396

National Conference

Eastern Division

	W	L	T	Pct.	Pts.	OP
N.Y. Giants	14	2	0	.875	371	236
Washington*	12	4	0	.750	368	296
Dallas	7	9	0	.438	346	337
Philadelphia	5	10	1	.344	256	312
St. Louis	4	11	1	.281	218	351

Central Division

	W	L	T	Pct.	Pts.	OP
Chicago	14	2	0	.875	352	187
Minnesota	9	7	0	.563	398	273
Detroit	5	11	0	.313	277	326
Green Bay	4	12	0	.250	254	418
Tampa Bay	2	14	0	.125	239	473

Western Division

	W	L	T	Pct.	Pts.	OP
San Francisco	10	5	1	.656	374	247
L.A. Rams*	10	6	0	.625	309	267
Atlanta	7	8	1	.469	280	280
New Orleans	7	9	0	.438	288	287

**Wild Card qualifiers for playoffs*

New York Jets gained first AFC Wild Card position on better conference record (8-4) over Kansas City (9-5), Seattle (7-5), and Cincinnati (7-5). Kansas City gained second Wild Card based on better conference record (9-5) over Seattle (7-5) and Cincinnati (7-5).

First round playoff: NEW YORK JETS 35, Kansas City 15
Divisional playoffs: CLEVELAND 23, New York Jets 20 (OT)
DENVER 22, New England 17
AFC championship: Denver 23, CLEVELAND 20 (OT)
First round playoff: WASHINGTON 19, Los Angeles Rams 7
Divisional playoffs: Washington 27, CHICAGO 13
NEW YORK GIANTS 49, San Francisco 3
NFC championship: NEW YORK GIANTS 17, Washington 0
Super Bowl XXI: New York Giants (NFC) 39, Denver (AFC) 20, at Rose Bowl, Pasadena, California.

1985

American Conference

Eastern Division

	W	L	T	Pct.	Pts.	OP
Miami	12	4	0	.750	428	320
N.Y. Jets*	11	5	0	.688	393	264
New England*	11	5	0	.688	362	290
Indianapolis	5	11	0	.313	320	386
Buffalo	2	14	0	.125	200	381

Central Division

	W	L	T	Pct.	Pts.	OP
Cleveland	8	8	0	.500	287	294
Cincinnati	7	9	0	.438	441	437
Pittsburgh	7	9	0	.438	379	355
Houston	5	11	0	.313	284	412

Western Division

	W	L	T	Pct.	Pts.	OP
L.A. Raiders	12	4	0	.750	354	308
Denver	11	5	0	.688	380	329
Seattle	8	8	0	.500	349	303
San Diego	8	8	0	.500	467	435
Kansas City	6	10	0	.375	317	360

National Conference

Eastern Division

	W	L	T	Pct.	Pts.	OP
Dallas	10	6	0	.625	357	333
N.Y. Giants*	10	6	0	.625	399	283
Washington	10	6	0	.625	297	312
Philadelphia	7	9	0	.438	286	310
St. Louis	5	11	0	.313	278	414

Central Division

	W	L	T	Pct.	Pts.	OP
Chicago	15	1	0	.938	456	198
Green Bay	8	8	0	.500	337	355
Minnesota	7	9	0	.438	346	359
Detroit	7	9	0	.438	307	366
Tampa Bay	2	14	0	.125	294	448

Western Division

	W	L	T	Pct.	Pts.	OP
L.A. Rams	11	5	0	.688	340	277
San Francisco*	10	6	0	.625	411	263
New Orleans	5	11	0	.313	294	401
Atlanta	4	12	0	.250	282	452

**Wild Card qualifiers for playoffs*

New York Jets gained first AFC Wild Card position on better conference record (9-3) over New England (8-4) and Denver (8-4). New England gained second AFC Wild Card position based on better record vs. common opponents (4-2) than Denver (3-3). Dallas won NFC Eastern Division title based on better record (4-0) vs. New York Giants (1-3) and Washington (1-3). New York Giants gained first NFC Wild Card position based on better conference record (8-4) over San Francisco (7-5) and Washington (6-6). San Francisco gained second NFC Wild Card position based on head-to-head victory over Washington.

First round playoff: New England 26, NEW YORK JETS 14
Divisional playoffs: MIAMI 24, Cleveland 21;
New England 27, LOS ANGELES RAIDERS 20
AFC championship: New England 31, MIAMI 14
First round playoff: NEW YORK GIANTS 17, San Francisco 3
Divisional playoffs: LOS ANGELES RAMS 20, Dallas 0;
CHICAGO 21, New York Giants 0
NFC championship: CHICAGO 24, Los Angeles Rams 0
Super Bowl XX: Chicago (NFC) 46, New England (AFC) 10, at Louisiana Superdome, New Orleans, Louisiana.

1984

American Conference

Eastern Division

	W	L	T	Pct.	Pts.	OP
Miami	14	2	0	.875	513	298
New England	9	7	0	.563	362	352
N.Y. Jets	7	9	0	.438	332	364
Indianapolis	4	12	0	.250	239	414
Buffalo	2	14	0	.125	250	454

Central Division

	W	L	T	Pct.	Pts.	OP
Pittsburgh	9	7	0	.563	387	310
Cincinnati	8	8	0	.500	339	339
Cleveland	5	11	0	.313	250	297
Houston	3	13	0	.188	240	437

Western Division

	W	L	T	Pct.	Pts.	OP
Denver	13	3	0	.813	353	241
Seattle*	12	4	0	.750	418	282
L.A. Raiders*	11	5	0	.688	368	278
Kansas City	8	8	0	.500	314	324
San Diego	7	9	0	.438	394	413

National Conference

Eastern Division

	W	L	T	Pct.	Pts.	OP
Washington	11	5	0	.688	426	310
N.Y. Giants*	9	7	0	.563	299	301
St. Louis	9	7	0	.563	423	345
Dallas	9	7	0	.563	308	308
Philadelphia	6	9	1	.406	278	320

Central Division

	W	L	T	Pct.	Pts.	OP
Chicago	10	6	0	.625	325	248
Green Bay	8	8	0	.500	390	309
Tampa Bay	6	10	0	.375	335	380
Detroit	4	11	1	.281	283	408
Minnesota	3	13	0	.188	276	484

Western Division

	W	L	T	Pct.	Pts.	OP
San Francisco	15	1	0	.938	475	227
L.A. Rams*	10	6	0	.625	346	316
New Orleans	7	9	0	.438	298	361
Atlanta	4	12	0	.250	281	382

**Wild Card qualifiers for playoffs*

New York Giants clinched Wild Card berth based on 3-1 record vs. St. Louis's 2-2 and Dallas's 1-3. St. Louis finished ahead of Dallas based on better division record (5-3 to 3-5).

First round playoff: SEATTLE 13, Los Angeles Raiders 7
Divisional playoffs: MIAMI 31, Seattle 10; Pittsburgh 24, DENVER 17
AFC championship: MIAMI 45, Pittsburgh 28
First round playoff: New York Giants 16, LOS ANGELES RAMS 13
Divisional playoffs: SAN FRANCISCO 21, New York Giants 10; Chicago 23, WASHINGTON 19
NFC championship: SAN FRANCISCO 23, Chicago 0
Super Bowl XIX: San Francisco (NFC) 38, Miami (AFC) 16, at Stanford Stadium, Stanford, California.

1983

American Conference

Eastern Division

	W	L	T	Pct.	Pts.	OP
Miami	12	4	0	.750	389	250
New England	8	8	0	.500	274	289
Buffalo	8	8	0	.500	283	351
Baltimore	7	9	0	.438	264	354
N.Y. Jets	7	9	0	.438	313	331

Central Division

	W	L	T	Pct.	Pts.	OP
Pittsburgh	10	6	0	.625	355	303
Cleveland	9	7	0	.563	356	342
Cincinnati	7	9	0	.438	346	302
Houston	2	14	0	.125	288	460

Western Division

	W	L	T	Pct.	Pts.	OP
L.A. Raiders	12	4	0	.750	442	338
Seattle*	9	7	0	.563	403	397
Denver*	9	7	0	.563	302	327
San Diego	6	10	0	.375	358	462
Kansas City	6	10	0	.375	386	367

National Conference

Eastern Division

	W	L	T	Pct.	Pts.	OP
Washington	14	2	0	.875	541	332
Dallas*	12	4	0	.750	479	360
St. Louis	8	7	1	.531	374	428
Philadelphia	5	11	0	.313	233	322
N.Y. Giants	3	12	1	.219	267	347

Central Division

	W	L	T	Pct.	Pts.	OP
Detroit	9	7	0	.563	347	286
Green Bay	8	8	0	.500	429	439
Chicago	8	8	0	.500	311	301
Minnesota	8	8	0	.500	316	348
Tampa Bay	2	14	0	.125	241	380

Western Division

	W	L	T	Pct.	Pts.	OP
San Francisco	10	6	0	.625	432	293
L.A. Rams*	9	7	0	.563	361	344
New Orleans	8	8	0	.500	319	337
Atlanta	7	9	0	.438	370	389

**Wild Card qualifiers for playoffs*

Seattle and Denver gained Wild Card berths over Cleveland because of their victories over the Browns.

First round playoff: SEATTLE 31, Denver 7
Divisional playoffs: Seattle 27, MIAMI 20; LOS ANGELES RAIDERS 38, Pittsburgh 10
AFC championship: LOS ANGELES RAIDERS 30, Seattle 14
First round playoff: Los Angeles Rams 24, DALLAS 17
Divisional playoffs: SAN FRANCISCO 24, Detroit 23; WASHINGTON 51, L.A. Rams 7
NFC championship: WASHINGTON 24, San Francisco 21
Super Bowl XVIII: Los Angeles Raiders (AFC) 38, Washington (NFC) 9, at Tampa Stadium, Tampa, Florida.

1982

American Conference

	W	L	T	Pct.	Pts.	OP
L.A. Raiders	8	1	0	.889	260	200
Miami	7	2	0	.778	198	131
Cincinnati	7	2	0	.778	232	177
Pittsburgh	6	3	0	.667	204	146
San Diego	6	3	0	.667	288	221
N.Y. Jets	6	3	0	.667	245	166
New England	5	4	0	.556	143	157
Cleveland	4	5	0	.444	140	182
Buffalo	4	5	0	.444	150	154
Seattle	4	5	0	.444	127	147
Kansas City	3	6	0	.333	176	184
Denver	2	7	0	.222	148	226
Houston	1	8	0	.111	136	245
Baltimore	0	8	1	.056	113	236

National Conference

	W	L	T	Pct.	Pts.	OP
Washington	8	1	0	.889	190	128
Dallas	6	3	0	.667	226	145
Green Bay	5	3	1	.611	226	169
Minnesota	5	4	0	.556	187	198
Atlanta	5	4	0	.556	183	199
St. Louis	5	4	0	.556	135	170
Tampa Bay	5	4	0	.556	158	178
Detroit	4	5	0	.444	181	176
New Orleans	4	5	0	.444	129	160
N.Y. Giants	4	5	0	.444	164	160
San Francisco	3	6	0	.333	209	206
Chicago	3	6	0	.333	141	174
Philadelphia	3	6	0	.333	191	195
L.A. Rams	2	7	0	.222	200	250

As the result of a 57-day players' strike, the 1982 NFL regular season schedule was reduced from 16 weeks to 9. At the conclusion of the regular season, the NFL conducted a 16-team postseason Super Bowl Tournament. Eight teams from each conference were seeded 1-8 based on their records during the season.

Miami finished ahead of Cincinnati based on better conference record (6-1 to 6-2). Pittsburgh won common games tie-breaker with San Diego (3-1 to 2-1) after New York Jets were eliminated from three-way tie based on conference record (Pittsburgh and San Diego 5-3 vs. Jets 2-3). Cleveland finished ahead of Buffalo and Seattle based on better conference record (4-3 to 3-3 to 3-5). Minnesota (4-1), Atlanta (4-3), St. Louis (5-4), Tampa Bay (3-3) seeds were determined by best won-lost record in conference games. Detroit finished ahead of New Orleans and the New York Giants based on better conference record (4-4 to 3-5 to 3-5).

First round playoff: MIAMI 28, New England 13
LOS ANGELES RAIDERS 27, Cleveland 10
New York Jets 44, CINCINNATI 17
San Diego 31, PITTSBURGH 28
Second round playoff: New York Jets 17, LOS ANGELES RAIDERS 14
MIAMI 34, San Diego 13
AFC championship: MIAMI 14, New York Jets 0
First round playoff: WASHINGTON 31, Detroit 7
GREEN BAY 41, St. Louis 16
MINNESOTA 30, Atlanta 24
DALLAS 30, Tampa Bay 17
Second round playoff: WASHINGTON 21, Minnesota 7
DALLAS 37, Green Bay 26
NFC championship: WASHINGTON 31, Dallas 17
Super Bowl XVII: Washington (NFC) 27, Miami (AFC) 17, at Rose Bowl, Pasadena, California.

1981

American Conference

Eastern Division

	W	L	T	Pct.	Pts.	OP
Miami	11	4	1	.719	345	275
N.Y. Jets*	10	5	1	.656	355	287
Buffalo*	10	6	0	.625	311	276
Baltimore	2	14	0	.125	259	533
New England	2	14	0	.125	322	370

Central Division

	W	L	T	Pct.	Pts.	OP
Cincinnati	12	4	0	.750	421	304
Pittsburgh	8	8	0	.500	356	297
Houston	7	9	0	.438	281	355
Cleveland	5	11	0	.313	276	375

Western Division

	W	L	T	Pct.	Pts.	OP
San Diego	10	6	0	.625	478	390
Denver	10	6	0	.625	321	289
Kansas City	9	7	0	.563	343	290
Oakland	7	9	0	.438	273	343
Seattle	6	10	0	.375	322	388

National Conference

Eastern Division

	W	L	T	Pct.	Pts.	OP
Dallas	12	4	0	.750	367	277
Philadelphia*	10	6	0	.625	368	221
N.Y. Giants*	9	7	0	.563	295	257
Washington	8	8	0	.500	347	349
St. Louis	7	9	0	.438	315	408

Central Division

	W	L	T	Pct.	Pts.	OP
Tampa Bay	9	7	0	.563	315	268
Detroit	8	8	0	.500	397	322
Green Bay	8	8	0	.500	324	361
Minnesota	7	9	0	.438	325	369
Chicago	6	10	0	.375	253	324

Western Division

	W	L	T	Pct.	Pts.	OP
San Francisco	13	3	0	.813	357	250
Atlanta	7	9	0	.438	426	355
Los Angeles	6	10	0	.375	303	351
New Orleans	4	12	0	.250	207	378

**Wild Card qualifiers for playoffs*

San Diego won AFC Western title over Denver on the basis of a better division record (6-2 to 5-3). Buffalo won a Wild Card playoff berth over Denver as the result of a 9-7 victory in head-to-head competition.

First round playoff: Buffalo 31, NEW YORK JETS 27
Divisional playoffs: San Diego 41, MIAMI 38 (OT); CINCINNATI 28, Buffalo 21
AFC championship: CINCINNATI 27, San Diego 7
First round playoff: New York Giants 27, PHILADELPHIA 21
Divisional playoffs: DALLAS 38, Tampa Bay 0; SAN FRANCISCO 38, New York Giants 24
NFC championship: SAN FRANCISCO 28, Dallas 27
Super Bowl XVI: San Francisco (NFC) 26, Cincinnati (AFC) 21, at Silverdome, Pontiac, Michigan.

1980

American Conference

Eastern Division	W	L	T	Pct.	Pts.	OP
Buffalo	11	5	0	.688	320	260
New England	10	6	0	.625	441	325
Miami	8	8	0	.500	266	305
Baltimore	7	9	0	.438	355	387
N.Y. Jets	4	12	0	.250	302	395

Central Division	W	L	T	Pct.	Pts.	OP
Cleveland	11	5	0	.688	357	310
Houston*	11	5	0	.688	295	251
Pittsburgh	9	7	0	.563	352	313
Cincinnati	6	10	0	.375	244	312

Western Division	W	L	T	Pct.	Pts.	OP
San Diego	11	5	0	.688	418	327
Oakland*	11	5	0	.688	364	306
Kansas City	8	8	0	.500	319	336
Denver	8	8	0	.500	310	323
Seattle	4	12	0	.250	291	408

National Conference

Eastern Division	W	L	T	Pct.	Pts.	OP
Philadelphia	12	4	0	.750	384	222
Dallas*	12	4	0	.750	454	311
Washington	6	10	0	.375	261	293
St. Louis	5	11	0	.313	299	350
N.Y. Giants	4	12	0	.250	249	425

Central Division	W	L	T	Pct.	Pts.	OP
Minnesota	9	7	0	.563	317	308
Detroit	9	7	0	.563	334	272
Chicago	7	9	0	.438	304	264
Tampa Bay	5	10	1	.344	271	341
Green Bay	5	10	1	.344	231	371

Western Division	W	L	T	Pct.	Pts.	OP
Atlanta	12	4	0	.750	405	272
Los Angeles*	11	5	0	.688	424	289
San Francisco	6	10	0	.375	320	415
New Orleans	1	15	0	.063	291	487

**Wild Card qualifiers for playoffs*

Philadelphia won division title over Dallas on the basis of best net points in division games (plus 84 net points to plus 50). Minnesota won division title because of a better conference record than Detroit (8-4 to 9-5). Cleveland won division title because of a better conference record than Houston (8-4 to 7-5). San Diego won division title over Oakland on the basis of best net points in division games (plus 60 net points to plus 37).

First round playoff: OAKLAND 27, Houston 7
Divisional playoffs: SAN DIEGO 20, Buffalo 14; Oakland 14, CLEVELAND 12
AFC championship: Oakland 34, SAN DIEGO 27
First round playoff: DALLAS 34, Los Angeles 13
Divisional playoffs: PHILADELPHIA 31, Minnesota 16; Dallas 30, ATLANTA 27
NFC championship: PHILADELPHIA 20, Dallas 7
Super Bowl XV: Oakland (AFC) 27, Philadelphia (NFC) 10, at Louisiana Superdome, New Orleans, Louisiana.

1979

American Conference

Eastern Division	W	L	T	Pct.	Pts.	OP
Miami	10	6	0	.625	341	257
New England	9	7	0	.563	411	326
N.Y. Jets	8	8	0	.500	337	383
Buffalo	7	9	0	.438	268	279
Baltimore	5	11	0	.313	271	351

Central Division	W	L	T	Pct.	Pts.	OP
Pittsburgh	12	4	0	.750	416	262
Houston*	11	5	0	.688	362	331
Cleveland	9	7	0	.563	359	352
Cincinnati	4	12	0	.250	337	421

Western Division	W	L	T	Pct.	Pts.	OP
San Diego	12	4	0	.750	411	246
Denver*	10	6	0	.625	289	262
Seattle	9	7	0	.563	378	372
Oakland	9	7	0	.563	365	337
Kansas City	7	9	0	.438	238	262

National Conference

Eastern Division	W	L	T	Pct.	Pts.	OP
Dallas	11	5	0	.688	371	313
Philadelphia*	11	5	0	.688	339	282
Washington	10	6	0	.625	348	295
N.Y. Giants	6	10	0	.375	237	323
St. Louis	5	11	0	.313	307	358

Central Division	W	L	T	Pct.	Pts.	OP
Tampa Bay	10	6	0	.625	273	237
Chicago*	10	6	0	.625	306	249
Minnesota	7	9	0	.438	259	337
Green Bay	5	11	0	.313	246	316
Detroit	2	14	0	.125	219	365

Western Division	W	L	T	Pct.	Pts.	OP
Los Angeles	9	7	0	.563	323	309
New Orleans	8	8	0	.500	370	360
Atlanta	6	10	0	.375	300	388
San Francisco	2	14	0	.125	308	416

**Wild Card qualifiers for playoffs*

Dallas won division title because of a better conference record than Philadelphia (10-2 to 9-3). Tampa Bay won division title because of a better division record than Chicago (6-2 to 5-3). Chicago won a Wild Card berth over Washington on the basis of best net points in all games (plus 57 net points to plus 53).

First round playoff: HOUSTON 13, Denver 7
Divisional playoffs: Houston 17, SAN DIEGO 14; PITTSBURGH 34, Miami 14
AFC championship: PITTSBURGH 27, Houston 13
First round playoff: PHILADELPHIA 27, Chicago 17
Divisional playoffs: TAMPA BAY 24, Philadelphia 17; Los Angeles 21, DALLAS 19
NFC championship: Los Angeles 9, TAMPA BAY 0
Super Bowl XIV: Pittsburgh (AFC) 31, Los Angeles (NFC) 19, at Rose Bowl, Pasadena, California.

1978

American Conference

Eastern Division	W	L	T	Pct.	Pts.	OP
New England	11	5	0	.688	358	286
Miami*	11	5	0	.688	372	254
N.Y. Jets	8	8	0	.500	359	364
Buffalo	5	11	0	.313	302	354
Baltimore	5	11	0	.313	239	421

Central Division	W	L	T	Pct.	Pts.	OP
Pittsburgh	14	2	0	.875	356	195
Houston*	10	6	0	.625	283	298
Cleveland	8	8	0	.500	334	356
Cincinnati	4	12	0	.250	252	284

Western Division	W	L	T	Pct.	Pts.	OP
Denver	10	6	0	.625	282	198
Oakland	9	7	0	.563	311	283
Seattle	9	7	0	.563	345	358
San Diego	9	7	0	.563	355	309
Kansas City	4	12	0	.250	243	327

National Conference

Eastern Division	W	L	T	Pct.	Pts.	OP
Dallas	12	4	0	.750	384	208
Philadelphia*	9	7	0	.563	270	250
Washington	8	8	0	.500	273	283
St. Louis	6	10	0	.375	248	296
N.Y. Giants	6	10	0	.375	264	298

Central Division	W	L	T	Pct.	Pts.	OP
Minnesota	8	7	1	.531	294	306
Green Bay	8	7	1	.531	249	269
Detroit	7	9	0	.438	290	300
Chicago	7	9	0	.438	253	274
Tampa Bay	5	11	0	.313	241	259

Western Division	W	L	T	Pct.	Pts.	OP
Los Angeles	12	4	0	.750	316	245
Atlanta*	9	7	0	.563	240	290
New Orleans	7	9	0	.438	281	298
San Francisco	2	14	0	.125	219	350

**Wild Card qualifiers for playoffs*

New England won division title on the basis of a better division record than Miami (6-2 to 5-3). Minnesota won division title because of a better head-to-head record against Green Bay (1-0-1).

First round playoff: Houston 17, MIAMI 9
Divisional playoffs: Houston 31, NEW ENGLAND 14; PITTSBURGH 33, Denver 10
AFC championship: PITTSBURGH 34, Houston 5
First round playoff: ATLANTA 14, Philadelphia 13
Divisional playoffs: DALLAS 27, Atlanta 20; LOS ANGELES 34, Minnesota 10
NFC championship: Dallas 28, LOS ANGELES 0
Super Bowl XIII: Pittsburgh (AFC) 35, Dallas (NFC) 31, at Orange Bowl, Miami, Florida.

1977

American Conference

Eastern Division	W	L	T	Pct.	Pts.	OP
Baltimore	10	4	0	.714	295	221
Miami	10	4	0	.714	313	197
New England	9	5	0	.643	278	217
N.Y. Jets	3	11	0	.214	191	300
Buffalo	3	11	0	.214	160	313

Central Division	W	L	T	Pct.	Pts.	OP
Pittsburgh	9	5	0	.643	283	243
Houston	8	6	0	.571	299	230
Cincinnati	8	6	0	.571	238	235
Cleveland	6	8	0	.429	269	267

Western Division	W	L	T	Pct.	Pts.	OP
Denver	12	2	0	.857	274	148
Oakland*	11	3	0	.786	351	230
San Diego	7	7	0	.500	222	205
Seattle	5	9	0	.357	282	373
Kansas City	2	12	0	.143	225	349

National Conference

Eastern Division	W	L	T	Pct.	Pts.	OP
Dallas	12	2	0	.857	345	212
Washington	9	5	0	.643	196	189
St. Louis	7	7	0	.500	272	287
Philadelphia	5	9	0	.357	220	207
N.Y. Giants	5	9	0	.357	181	265

Central Division	W	L	T	Pct.	Pts.	OP
Minnesota	9	5	0	.643	231	227
Chicago*	9	5	0	.643	255	253
Detroit	6	8	0	.429	183	252
Green Bay	4	10	0	.286	134	219
Tampa Bay	2	12	0	.143	103	223

Western Division	W	L	T	Pct.	Pts.	OP
Los Angeles	10	4	0	.714	302	146
Atlanta	7	7	0	.500	179	129
San Francisco	5	9	0	.357	220	260
New Orleans	3	11	0	.214	232	336

**Wild Card qualifier for playoffs*

Baltimore won division title on the basis of a better conference record than Miami (9-3 to 8-4). Chicago won a Wild Card berth over Washington on the basis of best net points in conference games (plus 48 net points to plus 4).

Divisional playoffs: DENVER 34, Pittsburgh 21; Oakland 37, BALTIMORE 31 (OT)
AFC championship: DENVER 20, Oakland 17
Divisional playoffs: DALLAS 37, Chicago 7; Minnesota 14, LOS ANGELES 7
NFC championship: DALLAS 23, Minnesota 6
Super Bowl XII: Dallas (NFC) 27, Denver (AFC) 10, at Louisiana Superdome, New Orleans, Louisiana.

1976

American Conference

Eastern Division	W	L	T	Pct.	Pts.	OP
Baltimore	11	3	0	.786	417	246
New England*	11	3	0	.786	376	236
Miami	6	8	0	.429	263	264
N.Y. Jets	3	11	0	.214	169	383
Buffalo	2	12	0	.143	245	363

Central Division	W	L	T	Pct.	Pts.	OP
Pittsburgh	10	4	0	.714	342	138
Cincinnati	10	4	0	.714	335	210
Cleveland	9	5	0	.643	267	287
Houston	5	9	0	.357	222	273

Western Division	W	L	T	Pct.	Pts.	OP
Oakland	13	1	0	.929	350	237
Denver	9	5	0	.643	315	206
San Diego	6	8	0	.429	248	285
Kansas City	5	9	0	.357	290	376
Tampa Bay	0	14	0	.000	125	412

National Conference

Eastern Division	W	L	T	Pct.	Pts.	OP
Dallas	11	3	0	.786	296	194
Washington*	10	4	0	.714	291	217
St. Louis	10	4	0	.714	309	267
Philadelphia	4	10	0	.286	165	286
N.Y. Giants	3	11	0	.214	170	250

Central Division	W	L	T	Pct.	Pts.	OP
Minnesota	11	2	1	.821	305	176
Chicago	7	7	0	.500	253	216
Detroit	6	8	0	.429	262	220
Green Bay	5	9	0	.357	218	299

Western Division	W	L	T	Pct.	Pts.	OP
Los Angeles	10	3	1	.750	351	190
San Francisco	8	6	0	.571	270	190
Atlanta	4	10	0	.286	172	312
New Orleans	4	10	0	.286	253	346
Seattle	2	12	0	.143	229	429

**Wild Card qualifier for playoffs*

Baltimore won division title on the basis of a better division record than New England (7-1 to 6-2). Pittsburgh won division title because of a two-game sweep over Cincinnati. Washington won Wild Card berth over St. Louis because of a two-game sweep over Cardinals.

Divisional playoffs: OAKLAND 24, New England 21; Pittsburgh 40, BALTIMORE 14
AFC championship: OAKLAND 24, Pittsburgh 7
Divisional playoffs: MINNESOTA 35, Washington 20; Los Angeles 14, DALLAS 12
NFC championship: MINNESOTA 24, Los Angeles 13
Super Bowl XI: Oakland (AFC) 32, Minnesota (NFC) 14, at Rose Bowl, Pasadena, California.

1975

American Conference

Eastern Division

	W	L	T	Pct.	Pts.	OP
Baltimore	10	4	0	.714	395	269
Miami	10	4	0	.714	357	222
Buffalo	8	6	0	.571	420	355
New England	3	11	0	.214	258	358
N.Y. Jets	3	11	0	.214	258	433

Central Division

	W	L	T	Pct.	Pts.	OP
Pittsburgh	12	2	0	.857	373	162
Cincinnati*	11	3	0	.786	340	246
Houston	10	4	0	.714	293	226
Cleveland	3	11	0	.214	218	372

Western Division

	W	L	T	Pct.	Pts.	OP
Oakland	11	3	0	.786	375	255
Denver	6	8	0	.429	254	307
Kansas City	5	9	0	.357	282	341
San Diego	2	12	0	.143	189	345

National Conference

Eastern Division

	W	L	T	Pct.	Pts.	OP
St. Louis	11	3	0	.786	356	276
Dallas*	10	4	0	.714	350	268
Washington	8	6	0	.571	325	276
N.Y. Giants	5	9	0	.357	216	306
Philadelphia	4	10	0	.286	225	302

Central Division

	W	L	T	Pct.	Pts.	OP
Minnesota	12	2	0	.857	377	180
Detroit	7	7	0	.500	245	262
Chicago	4	10	0	.286	191	379
Green Bay	4	10	0	.286	226	285

Western Division

	W	L	T	Pct.	Pts.	OP
Los Angeles	12	2	0	.857	312	135
San Francisco	5	9	0	.357	255	286
Atlanta	4	10	0	.286	240	289
New Orleans	2	12	0	.143	165	360

**Wild Card qualifier for playoffs*

Baltimore won division title on the basis of a two-game sweep over Miami.

Divisional playoffs: PITTSBURGH 28, Baltimore 10; OAKLAND 31, Cincinnati 28
AFC championship: PITTSBURGH 16, Oakland 10
Divisional playoffs: LOS ANGELES 35, St. Louis 23; Dallas 17, MINNESOTA 14
NFC championship: Dallas 37, LOS ANGELES 7
Super Bowl X: Pittsburgh (AFC) 21, Dallas (NFC) 17, at Orange Bowl, Miami, Florida.

1974

American Conference

Eastern Division

	W	L	T	Pct.	Pts.	OP
Miami	11	3	0	.786	327	216
Buffalo*	9	5	0	.643	264	244
New England	7	7	0	.500	348	289
N.Y. Jets	7	7	0	.500	279	300
Baltimore	2	12	0	.143	190	329

Central Division

	W	L	T	Pct.	Pts.	OP
Pittsburgh	10	3	1	.750	305	189
Cincinnati	7	7	0	.500	283	259
Houston	7	7	0	.500	236	282
Cleveland	4	10	0	.286	251	344

Western Division

	W	L	T	Pct.	Pts.	OP
Oakland	12	2	0	.857	355	228
Denver	7	6	1	.536	302	294
Kansas City	5	9	0	.357	233	293
San Diego	5	9	0	.357	212	285

National Conference

Eastern Division

	W	L	T	Pct.	Pts.	OP
St. Louis	10	4	0	.714	285	218
Washington*	10	4	0	.714	320	196
Dallas	8	6	0	.571	297	235
Philadelphia	7	7	0	.500	242	217
N.Y. Giants	2	12	0	.143	195	299

Central Division

	W	L	T	Pct.	Pts.	OP
Minnesota	10	4	0	.714	310	195
Detroit	7	7	0	.500	256	270
Green Bay	6	8	0	.429	210	206
Chicago	4	10	0	.286	152	279

Western Division

	W	L	T	Pct.	Pts.	OP
Los Angeles	10	4	0	.714	263	181
San Francisco	6	8	0	.429	226	236
New Orleans	5	9	0	.357	166	263
Atlanta	3	11	0	.214	111	271

**Wild Card qualifier for playoffs*

St. Louis won division title because of a two-game sweep over Washington.

Divisional playoffs: OAKLAND 28, Miami 26; PITTSBURGH 32, Buffalo 14
AFC championship: Pittsburgh 24, OAKLAND 13
Divisional playoffs: MINNESOTA 30, St. Louis 14; LOS ANGELES 19, Washington 10
NFC championship: MINNESOTA 14, Los Angeles 10
Super Bowl IX: Pittsburgh (AFC) 16, Minnesota (NFC) 6, at Tulane Stadium, New Orleans, Louisiana.

1973

American Conference

Eastern Division

	W	L	T	Pct.	Pts.	OP
Miami	12	2	0	.857	343	150
Buffalo	9	5	0	.643	259	230
New England	5	9	0	.357	258	300
Baltimore	4	10	0	.286	226	341
N.Y. Jets	4	10	0	.286	240	306

Central Division

	W	L	T	Pct.	Pts.	OP
Cincinnati	10	4	0	.714	286	231
Pittsburgh*	10	4	0	.714	347	210
Cleveland	7	5	2	.571	234	255
Houston	1	13	0	.071	199	447

Western Division

	W	L	T	Pct.	Pts.	OP
Oakland	9	4	1	.679	292	175
Denver	7	5	2	.571	354	296
Kansas City	7	5	2	.571	231	192
San Diego	2	11	1	.179	188	386

National Conference

Eastern Division

	W	L	T	Pct.	Pts.	OP
Dallas	10	4	0	.714	382	203
Washington*	10	4	0	.714	325	198
Philadelphia	5	8	1	.393	310	393
St. Louis	4	9	1	.321	286	365
N.Y. Giants	2	11	1	.179	226	362

Central Division

	W	L	T	Pct.	Pts.	OP
Minnesota	12	2	0	.857	296	168
Detroit	6	7	1	.464	271	247
Green Bay	5	7	2	.429	202	259
Chicago	3	11	0	.214	195	334

Western Division

	W	L	T	Pct.	Pts.	OP
Los Angeles	12	2	0	.857	388	178
Atlanta	9	5	0	.643	318	224
New Orleans	5	9	0	.357	163	312
San Francisco	5	9	0	.357	262	319

**Wild Card qualifier for playoffs*

Cincinnati won division title on the basis of a better conference record than Pittsburgh (8-3 to 7-4). Dallas won division title on the basis of a better point differential vs. Washington (net 13 points).

Divisional playoffs: OAKLAND 33, Pittsburgh 14; MIAMI 34, Cincinnati 16
AFC championship: MIAMI 27, Oakland 10
Divisional playoffs: MINNESOTA 27, Washington 20; DALLAS 27, Los Angeles 16
NFC championship: Minnesota 27, DALLAS 10
Super Bowl VIII: Miami (AFC) 24, Minnesota (NFC) 7, at Rice Stadium, Houston, Texas.

1972

American Conference

Eastern Division

	W	L	T	Pct.	Pts.	OP
Miami	14	0	0	1.000	385	171
N.Y. Jets	7	7	0	.500	367	324
Baltimore	5	9	0	.357	235	252
Buffalo	4	9	1	.321	257	377
New England	3	11	0	.214	192	446

Central Division

	W	L	T	Pct.	Pts.	OP
Pittsburgh	11	3	0	.786	343	175
Cleveland*	10	4	0	.714	268	249
Cincinnati	8	6	0	.571	299	229
Houston	1	13	0	.071	164	380

Western Division

	W	L	T	Pct.	Pts.	OP
Oakland	10	3	1	.750	365	248
Kansas City	8	6	0	.571	287	254
Denver	5	9	0	.357	325	350
San Diego	4	9	1	.321	264	344

National Conference

Eastern Division

	W	L	T	Pct.	Pts.	OP
Washington	11	3	0	.786	336	218
Dallas*	10	4	0	.714	319	240
N.Y. Giants	8	6	0	.571	331	247
St. Louis	4	9	1	.321	193	303
Philadelphia	2	11	1	.179	145	352

Central Division

	W	L	T	Pct.	Pts.	OP
Green Bay	10	4	0	.714	304	226
Detroit	8	5	1	.607	339	290
Minnesota	7	7	0	.500	301	252
Chicago	4	9	1	.321	225	275

Western Division

	W	L	T	Pct.	Pts.	OP
San Francisco	8	5	1	.607	353	249
Atlanta	7	7	0	.500	269	274
Los Angeles	6	7	1	.464	291	286
New Orleans	2	11	1	.179	215	361

**Wild Card qualifier for playoffs*

Divisional playoffs: PITTSBURGH 13, Oakland 7; MIAMI 20, Cleveland 14
AFC championship: Miami 21, PITTSBURGH 17
Divisional playoffs: Dallas 30, SAN FRANCISCO 28; WASHINGTON 16, Green Bay 3
NFC championship: WASHINGTON 26, Dallas 3
Super Bowl VII: Miami (AFC) 14, Washington (NFC) 7, at Memorial Coliseum, Los Angeles, California.

1971

American Conference

Eastern Division

	W	L	T	Pct.	Pts.	OP
Miami	10	3	1	.769	315	174
Baltimore*	10	4	0	.714	313	140
New England	6	8	0	.429	238	325
N.Y. Jets	6	8	0	.429	212	299
Buffalo	1	13	0	.071	184	394

Central Division

	W	L	T	Pct.	Pts.	OP
Cleveland	9	5	0	.643	285	273
Pittsburgh	6	8	0	.429	246	292
Houston	4	9	1	.308	251	330
Cincinnati	4	10	0	.286	284	265

Western Division

	W	L	T	Pct.	Pts.	OP
Kansas City	10	3	1	.769	302	208
Oakland	8	4	2	.667	344	278
San Diego	6	8	0	.429	311	341
Denver	4	9	1	.308	203	275

National Conference

Eastern Division

	W	L	T	Pct.	Pts.	OP
Dallas	11	3	0	.786	406	222
Washington*	9	4	1	.692	276	190
Philadelphia	6	7	1	.462	221	302
St. Louis	4	9	1	.308	231	279
N.Y. Giants	4	10	0	.286	228	362

Central Division

	W	L	T	Pct.	Pts.	OP
Minnesota	11	3	0	.786	245	139
Detroit	7	6	1	.538	341	286
Chicago	6	8	0	.429	185	276
Green Bay	4	8	2	.333	274	298

Western Division

	W	L	T	Pct.	Pts.	OP
San Francisco	9	5	0	.643	300	216
Los Angeles	8	5	1	.615	313	260
Atlanta	7	6	1	.538	274	277
New Orleans	4	8	2	.333	266	347

**Wild Card qualifier for playoffs*

Divisional playoffs: Miami 27, KANSAS CITY 24 (OT); Baltimore 20, CLEVELAND 3
AFC championship: MIAMI 21, Baltimore 0
Divisional playoffs: Dallas 20, MINNESOTA 12; SAN FRANCISCO 24, Washington 20
NFC championship: DALLAS 14, San Francisco 3
Super Bowl VI: Dallas (NFC) 24, Miami (AFC) 3, at Tulane Stadium, New Orleans, Louisiana.

1970

American Conference

Eastern Division

	W	L	T	Pct.	Pts.	OP
Baltimore	11	2	1	.846	321	234
Miami*	10	4	0	.714	297	228
N.Y. Jets	4	10	0	.286	255	286
Buffalo	3	10	1	.231	204	337
Boston Patriots	2	12	0	.143	149	361

Central Division

	W	L	T	Pct.	Pts.	OP
Cincinnati	8	6	0	.571	312	255
Cleveland	7	7	0	.500	286	265
Pittsburgh	5	9	0	.357	210	272
Houston	3	10	1	.231	217	352

Western Division

	W	L	T	Pct.	Pts.	OP
Oakland	8	4	2	.667	300	293
Kansas City	7	5	2	.583	272	244
San Diego	5	6	3	.455	282	278
Denver	5	8	1	.385	253	264

National Conference

Eastern Division

	W	L	T	Pct.	Pts.	OP
Dallas	10	4	0	.714	299	221
N.Y. Giants	9	5	0	.643	301	270
St. Louis	8	5	1	.615	325	228
Washington	6	8	0	.429	297	314
Philadelphia	3	10	1	.231	241	332

Central Division

	W	L	T	Pct.	Pts.	OP
Minnesota	12	2	0	.857	335	143
Detroit*	10	4	0	.714	347	202
Chicago	6	8	0	.429	256	261
Green Bay	6	8	0	.429	196	293

Western Division

	W	L	T	Pct.	Pts.	OP
San Francisco	10	3	1	.769	352	267
Los Angeles	9	4	1	.692	325	202
Atlanta	4	8	2	.333	206	261
New Orleans	2	11	1	.154	172	347

**Wild Card qualifier for playoffs*

Divisional playoffs: BALTIMORE 17, Cincinnati 0; OAKLAND 21, Miami 14
AFC championship: BALTIMORE 27, Oakland 17
Divisional playoffs: DALLAS 5, Detroit 0; San Francisco 17, MINNESOTA 14
NFC championship: Dallas 17, SAN FRANCISCO 10
Super Bowl V: Baltimore (AFC) 16, Dallas (NFC) 13, at Orange Bowl, Miami, Florida.

1969 NFL

Eastern Conference

Capitol Division

Team	W	L	T	Pct.	Pts.	OP
Dallas	11	2	1	.846	369	223
Washington	7	5	2	.583	307	319
New Orleans	5	9	0	.357	311	393
Philadelphia	4	9	1	.308	279	377

Century Division

Team	W	L	T	Pct.	Pts.	OP
Cleveland	10	3	1	.769	351	300
N.Y. Giants	6	8	0	.429	264	298
St. Louis	4	9	1	.308	314	389
Pittsburgh	1	13	0	.071	218	404

Western Conference

Coastal Division

Team	W	L	T	Pct.	Pts.	OP
Los Angeles	11	3	0	.786	320	243
Baltimore	8	5	1	.615	279	268
Atlanta	6	8	0	.429	276	268
San Francisco	4	8	2	.333	277	319

Central Division

Team	W	L	T	Pct.	Pts.	OP
Minnesota	12	2	0	.857	379	133
Detroit	9	4	1	.692	259	188
Green Bay	8	6	0	.571	269	221
Chicago	1	13	0	.071	210	339

Conference championships: Cleveland 38, DALLAS 14; MINNESOTA 23, Los Angeles 20
NFL championship: MINNESOTA 27, Cleveland 7
Super Bowl IV: Kansas City (AFL) 23, Minnesota (NFL) 7, at Tulane Stadium, New Orleans, Louisiana.

1969 AFL

Eastern Division

Team	W	L	T	Pct.	Pts.	OP
N.Y. Jets	10	4	0	.714	353	269
Houston	6	6	2	.500	278	279
Boston Patriots	4	10	0	.286	266	316
Buffalo	4	10	0	.286	230	359
Miami	3	10	1	.231	233	332

Western Division

Team	W	L	T	Pct.	Pts.	OP
Oakland	12	1	1	.923	377	242
Kansas City	11	3	0	.786	359	177
San Diego	8	6	0	.571	288	276
Denver	5	8	1	.385	297	344
Cincinnati	4	9	1	.308	280	367

Divisional Playoffs: Kansas City 13, N.Y. JETS 6; OAKLAND 56, Houston 7
AFL championship: Kansas City 17, OAKLAND 7

1968 NFL

Eastern Conference

Capitol Division

Team	W	L	T	Pct.	Pts.	OP
Dallas	12	2	0	.857	431	186
N.Y. Giants	7	7	0	.500	294	325
Washington	5	9	0	.357	249	358
Philadelphia	2	12	0	.143	202	351

Century Division

Team	W	L	T	Pct.	Pts.	OP
Cleveland	10	4	0	.714	394	273
St. Louis	9	4	1	.692	325	289
New Orleans	4	9	1	.308	246	327
Pittsburgh	2	11	1	.154	244	397

Western Conference

Coastal Division

Team	W	L	T	Pct.	Pts.	OP
Baltimore	13	1	0	.929	402	144
Los Angeles	10	3	1	.769	312	200
San Francisco	7	6	1	.538	303	310
Atlanta	2	12	0	.143	170	389

Central Division

Team	W	L	T	Pct.	Pts.	OP
Minnesota	8	6	0	.571	282	242
Chicago	7	7	0	.500	250	333
Green Bay	6	7	1	.462	281	227
Detroit	4	8	2	.333	207	241

Conference championships: CLEVELAND 31, Dallas 20; BALTIMORE 24, Minnesota 14
NFL championship: Baltimore 34, CLEVELAND 0
Super Bowl III: N.Y. Jets (AFL) 16, Baltimore (NFL) 7, at Orange Bowl, Miami, Florida.

1968 AFL

Eastern Division

Team	W	L	T	Pct.	Pts.	OP
N.Y. Jets	11	3	0	.786	419	280
Houston	7	7	0	.500	303	248
Miami	5	8	1	.385	276	355
Boston Patriots	4	10	0	.286	229	406
Buffalo	1	12	1	.077	199	367

Western Division

Team	W	L	T	Pct.	Pts.	OP
Oakland	12	2	0	.857	453	233
Kansas City	12	2	0	.857	371	170
San Diego	9	5	0	.643	382	310
Denver	5	9	0	.357	255	404
Cincinnati	3	11	0	.214	215	329

Western Division playoff: OAKLAND 41, Kansas City 6
AFL championship: N.Y. JETS 27, Oakland 23

1967 NFL

Eastern Conference

Capitol Division

Team	W	L	T	Pct.	Pts.	OP
Dallas	9	5	0	.643	342	268
Philadelphia	6	7	1	.462	351	409
Washington	5	6	3	.455	347	353
New Orleans	3	11	0	.214	233	379

Century Division

Team	W	L	T	Pct.	Pts.	OP
Cleveland	9	5	0	.643	334	297
N.Y. Giants	7	7	0	.500	369	379
St. Louis	6	7	1	.462	333	356
Pittsburgh	4	9	1	.308	281	320

Western Conference

Coastal Division

Team	W	L	T	Pct.	Pts.	OP
Los Angeles	11	1	2	.917	398	196
Baltimore	11	1	2	.917	394	198
San Francisco	7	7	0	.500	273	337
Atlanta	1	12	1	.077	175	422

Central Division

Team	W	L	T	Pct.	Pts.	OP
Green Bay	9	4	1	.692	332	209
Chicago	7	6	1	.538	239	218
Detroit	5	7	2	.417	260	259
Minnesota	3	8	3	.273	233	294

Los Angeles won division title on the basis of advantage in points (58-34) in two games vs. Baltimore.
Conference championships: DALLAS 52, Cleveland 14; GREEN BAY 28, Los Angeles 7
NFL championship: GREEN BAY 21, Dallas 17
Super Bowl II: Green Bay (NFL) 33, Oakland (AFL) 14, at Orange Bowl, Miami, Florida.

1967 AFL

Eastern Division

Team	W	L	T	Pct.	Pts.	OP
Houston	9	4	1	.692	258	199
N.Y. Jets	8	5	1	.615	371	329
Buffalo	4	10	0	.286	237	285
Miami	4	10	0	.286	219	407
Boston Patriots	3	10	1	.231	280	389

Western Division

Team	W	L	T	Pct.	Pts.	OP
Oakland	13	1	0	.929	468	233
Kansas City	9	5	0	.643	408	254
San Diego	8	5	1	.615	360	352
Denver	3	11	0	.214	256	409

AFL championship: OAKLAND 40, Houston 7

1966 NFL

Eastern Conference

Team	W	L	T	Pct.	Pts.	OP
Dallas	10	3	1	.769	445	239
Cleveland	9	5	0	.643	403	259
Philadelphia	9	5	0	.643	326	340
St. Louis	8	5	1	.615	264	265
Washington	7	7	0	.500	351	355
Pittsburgh	5	8	1	.385	316	347
Atlanta	3	11	0	.214	204	437
N.Y. Giants	1	12	1	.077	263	501

Western Conference

Team	W	L	T	Pct.	Pts.	OP
Green Bay	12	2	0	.857	335	163
Baltimore	9	5	0	.643	314	226
Los Angeles	8	6	0	.571	289	212
San Francisco	6	6	2	.500	320	325
Chicago	5	7	2	.417	234	272
Detroit	4	9	1	.308	206	317
Minnesota	4	9	1	.308	292	304

NFL championship: Green Bay 34, DALLAS 27
Super Bowl I: Green Bay (NFL) 35, Kansas City (AFL) 10, at Memorial Coliseum, Los Angeles, California.

1966 AFL

Eastern Division

Team	W	L	T	Pct.	Pts.	OP
Buffalo	9	4	1	.692	358	255
Boston Patriots	8	4	2	.677	315	283
N.Y. Jets	6	6	2	.500	322	312
Houston	3	11	0	.214	335	396
Miami	3	11	0	.214	213	362

Western Division

Team	W	L	T	Pct.	Pts.	OP
Kansas City	11	2	1	.846	448	276
Oakland	8	5	1	.615	315	288
San Diego	7	6	1	.538	335	284
Denver	4	10	0	.286	196	381

AFL championship: Kansas City 31, BUFFALO 7

1965 NFL

Eastern Conference

Team	W	L	T	Pct.	Pts.	OP
Cleveland	11	3	0	.786	363	325
Dallas	7	7	0	.500	325	280
N.Y. Giants	7	7	0	.500	270	338
Washington	6	8	0	.429	257	301
Philadelphia	5	9	0	.357	363	359
St. Louis	5	9	0	.357	296	309
Pittsburgh	2	12	0	.143	202	397

Western Conference

Team	W	L	T	Pct.	Pts.	OP
Green Bay	10	3	1	.769	316	224
Baltimore	10	3	1	.769	389	284
Chicago	9	5	0	.643	409	275
San Francisco	7	6	1	.538	421	402
Minnesota	7	7	0	.500	383	403
Detroit	6	7	1	.462	257	295
Los Angeles	4	10	0	.286	269	328

Western Conference playoff: GREEN BAY 13, Baltimore 10 (OT)
NFL championship: GREEN BAY 23, Cleveland 12

1965 AFL

Eastern Division

Team	W	L	T	Pct.	Pts.	OP
Buffalo	10	3	1	.769	313	226
N.Y. Jets	5	8	1	.385	285	303
Boston Patriots	4	8	2	.333	244	302
Houston	4	10	0	.286	298	429

Western Division

Team	W	L	T	Pct.	Pts.	OP
San Diego	9	2	3	.818	340	227
Oakland	8	5	1	.615	298	239
Kansas City	7	5	2	.583	322	285
Denver	4	10	0	.286	303	392

AFL championship: Buffalo 23, SAN DIEGO 0

1964 NFL

Eastern Conference

Team	W	L	T	Pct.	Pts.	OP
Cleveland	10	3	1	.769	415	293
St. Louis	9	3	2	.750	357	331
Philadelphia	6	8	0	.429	312	313
Washington	6	8	0	.429	307	305
Dallas	5	8	1	.385	250	289
Pittsburgh	5	9	0	.357	253	315
N.Y. Giants	2	10	2	.167	241	399

Western Conference

Team	W	L	T	Pct.	Pts.	OP
Baltimore	12	2	0	.857	428	225
Green Bay	8	5	1	.615	342	245
Minnesota	8	5	1	.615	355	296
Detroit	7	5	2	.583	280	260
Los Angeles	5	7	2	.417	283	339
Chicago	5	9	0	.357	260	379
San Francisco	4	10	0	.286	236	330

NFL championship: CLEVELAND 27, Baltimore 0

1964 AFL

Eastern Division

Team	W	L	T	Pct.	Pts.	OP
Buffalo	12	2	0	.857	400	242
Boston Patriots	10	3	1	.769	365	297
N.Y. Jets	5	8	1	.385	278	315
Houston	4	10	0	.286	310	355

Western Division

Team	W	L	T	Pct.	Pts.	OP
San Diego	8	5	1	.615	341	300
Kansas City	7	7	0	.500	366	306
Oakland	5	7	2	.417	303	350
Denver	2	11	1	.154	240	438

AFL championship: BUFFALO 20, San Diego 7

1963 NFL

Eastern Conference

Team	W	L	T	Pct.	Pts.	OP
N.Y. Giants	11	3	0	.786	448	280
Cleveland	10	4	0	.714	343	262
St. Louis	9	5	0	.643	341	283
Pittsburgh	7	4	3	.636	321	295
Dallas	4	10	0	.286	305	378
Washington	3	11	0	.214	279	398
Philadelphia	2	10	2	.167	242	381

Western Conference

Team	W	L	T	Pct.	Pts.	OP
Chicago	11	1	2	.917	301	144
Green Bay	11	2	1	.846	369	206
Baltimore	8	6	0	.571	316	285
Detroit	5	8	1	.385	326	265
Minnesota	5	8	1	.385	309	390
Los Angeles	5	9	0	.357	210	350
San Francisco	2	12	0	.143	198	391

NFL championship: CHICAGO 14, N.Y. Giants 10

1963 AFL

Eastern Division

Team	W	L	T	Pct.	Pts.	OP
Boston Patriots	7	6	1	.538	327	257
Buffalo	7	6	1	.538	304	291
Houston	6	8	0	.429	302	372
N.Y. Jets	5	8	1	.385	249	399

Western Division

Team	W	L	T	Pct.	Pts.	OP
San Diego	11	3	0	.786	399	256
Oakland	10	4	0	.714	363	288
Kansas City	5	7	2	.417	347	263
Denver	2	11	1	.154	301	473

Eastern Division playoff: Boston 26, BUFFALO 8
AFL championship: SAN DIEGO 51, Boston 10

1962 NFL

Eastern Conference

	W	L	T	Pct.	Pts.	OP
N.Y. Giants	12	2	0	.857	398	283
Pittsburgh	9	5	0	.643	312	363
Cleveland	7	6	1	.538	291	257
Washington	5	7	2	.417	305	376
Dallas Cowboys	5	8	1	.385	398	402
St. Louis	4	9	1	.308	287	361
Philadelphia	3	10	1	.231	282	356

Western Conference

	W	L	T	Pct.	Pts.	OP
Green Bay	13	1	0	.929	415	148
Detroit	11	3	0	.786	315	177
Chicago	9	5	0	.643	321	287
Baltimore	7	7	0	.500	293	288
San Francisco	6	8	0	.429	282	331
Minnesota	2	11	1	.154	254	410
Los Angeles	1	12	1	.077	220	334

NFL championship: Green Bay 16, N.Y. GIANTS 7

1962 AFL

Eastern Division

	W	L	T	Pct.	Pts.	OP
Houston	11	3	0	.786	387	270
Boston Patriots	9	4	1	.692	346	295
Buffalo	7	6	1	.538	309	272
N.Y. Titans	5	9	0	.357	278	423

Western Division

	W	L	T	Pct.	Pts.	OP
Dallas Texans	11	3	0	.786	389	233
Denver	7	7	0	.500	353	334
San Diego	4	10	0	.286	314	392
Oakland	1	13	0	.071	213	370

AFL championship: Dallas Texans 20, HOUSTON 17 (OT)

1961 NFL

Eastern Conference

	W	L	T	Pct.	Pts.	OP
N.Y. Giants	10	3	1	.769	368	220
Philadelphia	10	4	0	.714	361	297
Cleveland	8	5	1	.615	319	270
St. Louis	7	7	0	.500	279	267
Pittsburgh	6	8	0	.429	295	287
Dallas Cowboys	4	9	1	.308	236	380
Washington	1	12	1	.077	174	392

Western Conference

	W	L	T	Pct.	Pts.	OP
Green Bay	11	3	0	.786	391	223
Detroit	8	5	1	.615	270	258
Baltimore	8	6	0	.571	302	307
Chicago	8	6	0	.571	326	302
San Francisco	7	6	1	.538	346	272
Los Angeles	4	10	0	.286	263	333
Minnesota	3	11	0	.214	285	407

NFL championship: GREEN BAY 37, N.Y. Giants 0

1961 AFL

Eastern Division

	W	L	T	Pct.	Pts.	OP
Houston	10	3	1	.769	513	242
Boston Patriots	9	4	1	.692	413	313
N.Y. Titans	7	7	0	.500	301	390
Buffalo	6	8	0	.429	294	342

Western Division

	W	L	T	Pct.	Pts.	OP
San Diego	12	2	0	.857	396	219
Dallas Texans	6	8	0	.429	334	343
Denver	3	11	0	.214	251	432
Oakland	2	12	0	.143	237	458

AFL championship: Houston 10, SAN DIEGO 3

1960 NFL

Eastern Conference

	W	L	T	Pct.	Pts.	OP
Philadelphia	10	2	0	.833	321	246
Cleveland	8	3	1	.727	362	217
N.Y. Giants	6	4	2	.600	271	261
St. Louis	6	5	1	.545	288	230
Pittsburgh	5	6	1	.455	240	275
Washington	1	9	2	.100	178	309

Western Conference

	W	L	T	Pct.	Pts.	OP
Green Bay	8	4	0	.667	332	209
Detroit	7	5	0	.583	239	212
San Francisco	7	5	0	.583	208	205
Baltimore	6	6	0	.500	288	234
Chicago	5	6	1	.455	194	299
L.A. Rams	4	7	1	.364	265	297
Dallas Cowboys	0	11	1	.000	177	369

NFL championship: PHILADELPHIA 17, Green Bay 13

1960 AFL

Eastern Conference

	W	L	T	Pct.	Pts.	OP
Houston	10	4	0	.714	379	285
N.Y. Titans	7	7	0	.500	382	399
Buffalo	5	8	1	.385	296	303
Boston	5	9	0	.357	286	349

Western Conference

	W	L	T	Pct.	Pts.	OP
L.A. Chargers	10	4	0	.714	373	336
Dallas Texans	8	6	0	.571	362	253
Oakland	6	8	0	.429	319	388
Denver	4	9	1	.308	309	393

AFL championship: HOUSTON 24, L.A. Chargers 16

1959

Eastern Conference

	W	L	T	Pct.	Pts.	OP
N.Y. Giants	10	2	0	.833	284	170
Cleveland	7	5	0	.583	270	214
Philadelphia	7	5	0	.583	268	278
Pittsburgh	6	5	1	.545	257	216
Washington	3	9	0	.250	185	350
Chi. Cardinals	2	10	0	.167	234	324

Western Conference

	W	L	T	Pct.	Pts.	OP
Baltimore	9	3	0	.750	374	251
Chi. Bears	8	4	0	.667	252	196
Green Bay	7	5	0	.583	248	246
San Francisco	7	5	0	.583	255	237
Detroit	3	8	1	.273	203	275
Los Angeles	2	10	0	.167	242	315

NFL championship: BALTIMORE 31, N.Y. Giants 16

1958

Eastern Conference

	W	L	T	Pct.	Pts.	OP
N.Y. Giants	9	3	0	.750	246	183
Cleveland	9	3	0	.750	302	217
Pittsburgh	7	4	1	.636	261	230
Washington	4	7	1	.364	214	268
Chi. Cardinals	2	9	1	.182	261	356
Philadelphia	2	9	1	.182	235	306

Western Conference

	W	L	T	Pct.	Pts.	OP
Baltimore	9	3	0	.750	381	203
Chi. Bears	8	4	0	.667	298	230
Los Angeles	8	4	0	.667	344	278
San Francisco	6	6	0	.500	257	324
Detroit	4	7	1	.364	261	276
Green Bay	1	10	1	.091	193	382

Eastern Conference playoff: N.Y. GIANTS 10, Cleveland 0
NFL championship: Baltimore 23, N.Y. GIANTS 17 (OT)

1957

Eastern Conference

	W	L	T	Pct.	Pts.	OP
Cleveland	9	2	1	.818	269	172
N.Y. Giants	7	5	0	.583	254	211
Pittsburgh	6	6	0	.500	161	178
Washington	5	6	1	.455	251	230
Philadelphia	4	8	0	.333	173	230
Chi. Cardinals	3	9	0	.250	200	299

Western Conference

	W	L	T	Pct.	Pts.	OP
Detroit	8	4	0	.667	251	231
San Francisco	8	4	0	.667	260	264
Baltimore	7	5	0	.583	303	235
Los Angeles	6	6	0	.500	307	278
Chi. Bears	5	7	0	.417	203	211
Green Bay	3	9	0	.250	218	311

Western Conference playoff: Detroit 31, SAN FRANCISCO 27
NFL championship: DETROIT 59, Cleveland 14

1956

Eastern Conference

	W	L	T	Pct.	Pts.	OP
N.Y. Giants	8	3	1	.727	264	197
Chi. Cardinals	7	5	0	.583	240	182
Washington	6	6	0	.500	183	225
Cleveland	5	7	0	.417	167	177
Pittsburgh	5	7	0	.417	217	250
Philadelphia	3	8	1	.273	143	215

Western Conference

	W	L	T	Pct.	Pts.	OP
Chi. Bears	9	2	1	.818	363	246
Detroit	9	3	0	.750	300	188
San Francisco	5	6	1	.455	233	284
Baltimore	5	7	0	.417	270	322
Green Bay	4	8	0	.333	264	342
Los Angeles	4	8	0	.333	291	307

NFL championship: N.Y. GIANTS 47, Chi. Bears 7

1955

Eastern Conference

	W	L	T	Pct.	Pts.	OP
Cleveland	9	2	1	.818	349	218
Washington	8	4	0	.667	246	222
N.Y. Giants	6	5	1	.545	267	223
Chi. Cardinals	4	7	1	.364	224	252
Philadelphia	4	7	1	.364	248	231
Pittsburgh	4	8	0	.333	195	285

Western Conference

	W	L	T	Pct.	Pts.	OP
Los Angeles	8	3	1	.727	260	231
Chi. Bears	8	4	0	.667	294	251
Green Bay	6	6	0	.500	258	276
Baltimore	5	6	1	.455	214	239
San Francisco	4	8	0	.333	216	298
Detroit	3	9	0	.250	230	275

NFL championship: Cleveland 38, LOS ANGELES 14

1954

Eastern Conference

	W	L	T	Pct.	Pts.	OP
Cleveland	9	3	0	.750	336	162
Philadelphia	7	4	1	.636	284	230
N.Y. Giants	7	5	0	.583	293	184
Pittsburgh	5	7	0	.417	219	263
Washington	3	9	0	.250	207	432
Chi. Cardinals	2	10	0	.167	183	347

Western Conference

	W	L	T	Pct.	Pts.	OP
Detroit	9	2	1	.818	337	189
Chi. Bears	8	4	0	.667	301	279
San Francisco	7	4	1	.636	313	251
Los Angeles	6	5	1	.545	314	285
Green Bay	4	8	0	.333	234	251
Baltimore	3	9	0	.250	131	279

NFL championship: CLEVELAND 56, Detroit 10

1953

Eastern Conference

	W	L	T	Pct.	Pts.	OP
Cleveland	11	1	0	.917	348	162
Philadelphia	7	4	1	.636	352	215
Washington	6	5	1	.545	208	215
Pittsburgh	6	6	0	.500	211	263
N.Y. Giants	3	9	0	.250	179	277
Chi. Cardinals	1	10	1	.091	190	337

Western Conference

	W	L	T	Pct.	Pts.	OP
Detroit	10	2	0	.833	271	205
San Francisco	9	3	0	.750	372	237
Los Angeles	8	3	1	.727	366	236
Chi. Bears	3	8	1	.273	218	262
Baltimore	3	9	0	.250	182	350
Green Bay	2	9	1	.182	200	338

NFL championship: DETROIT 17, Cleveland 16

1952

American Conference

	W	L	T	Pct.	Pts.	OP
Cleveland	8	4	0	.667	310	213
N.Y. Giants	7	5	0	.583	234	231
Philadelphia	7	5	0	.583	252	271
Pittsburgh	5	7	0	.417	300	273
Chi. Cardinals	4	8	0	.333	172	221
Washington	4	8	0	.333	240	287

National Conference

	W	L	T	Pct.	Pts.	OP
Detroit	9	3	0	.750	344	192
Los Angeles	9	3	0	.750	349	234
San Francisco	7	5	0	.583	285	221
Green Bay	6	6	0	.500	295	312
Chi. Bears	5	7	0	.417	245	326
Dallas Texans	1	11	0	.083	182	427

National Conference playoff: DETROIT 31, Los Angeles 21
NFL championship: Detroit 17, CLEVELAND 7

1951

American Conference

	W	L	T	Pct.	Pts.	OP
Cleveland	11	1	0	.917	331	152
N.Y. Giants	9	2	1	.818	254	161
Washington	5	7	0	.417	183	296
Pittsburgh	4	7	1	.364	183	235
Philadelphia	4	8	0	.333	234	264
Chi. Cardinals	3	9	0	.250	210	287

National Conference

	W	L	T	Pct.	Pts.	OP
Los Angeles	8	4	0	.667	392	261
Detroit	7	4	1	.636	336	259
San Francisco	7	4	1	.636	255	205
Chi. Bears	7	5	0	.583	286	282
Green Bay	3	9	0	.250	254	375
N.Y. Yanks	1	9	2	.100	241	382

NFL championship: LOS ANGELES 24, Cleveland 17

1950

American Conference

	W	L	T	Pct.	Pts.	OP
Cleveland	10	2	0	.833	310	144
N.Y. Giants	10	2	0	.833	268	150
Philadelphia	6	6	0	.500	254	141
Pittsburgh	6	6	0	.500	180	195
Chi. Cardinals	5	7	0	.417	233	287
Washington	3	9	0	.250	232	326

National Conference

	W	L	T	Pct.	Pts.	OP
Los Angeles	9	3	0	.750	466	309
Chi. Bears	9	3	0	.750	279	207
N.Y. Yanks	7	5	0	.583	366	367
Detroit	6	6	0	.500	321	285
Green Bay	3	9	0	.250	244	406
San Francisco	3	9	0	.250	213	300
Baltimore	1	11	0	.083	213	462

American Conference playoff: CLEVELAND 8, N.Y. Giants 3
National Conference playoff: LOS ANGELES 24, Chi. Bears 14
NFL championship: CLEVELAND 30, Los Angeles 28

1949

Eastern Division

	W	L	T	Pct.	Pts.	OP
Philadelphia	11	1	0	.917	364	134
Pittsburgh	6	5	1	.545	224	214
N.Y. Giants	6	6	0	.500	287	298
Washington	4	7	1	.364	268	339
N.Y. Bulldogs	1	10	1	.091	153	365

Western Division

	W	L	T	Pct.	Pts.	OP
Los Angeles	8	2	2	.800	360	239
Chi. Bears	9	3	0	.750	332	218
Chi. Cardinals	6	5	1	.545	360	301
Detroit	4	8	0	.333	237	259
Green Bay	2	10	0	.167	114	329

NFL championship: Philadelphia 14, LOS ANGELES 0

1948

Eastern Division

	W	L	T	Pct.	Pts.	OP
Philadelphia	9	2	1	.818	376	156
Washington	7	5	0	.583	291	287
N.Y. Giants	4	8	0	.333	297	388
Pittsburgh	4	8	0	.333	200	243
Boston	3	9	0	.250	174	372

Western Division

	W	L	T	Pct.	Pts.	OP
Chi. Cardinals	11	1	0	.917	395	226
Chi. Bears	10	2	0	.833	375	151
Los Angeles	6	5	1	.545	327	269
Green Bay	3	9	0	.250	154	290
Detroit	2	10	0	.167	200	407

NFL championship: PHILADELPHIA 7, Chi. Cardinals 0

1947

Eastern Division

	W	L	T	Pct.	Pts.	OP
Philadelphia	8	4	0	.667	308	242
Pittsburgh	8	4	0	.667	240	259
Boston	4	7	1	.364	168	256
Washington	4	8	0	.333	295	367
N.Y. Giants	2	8	2	.200	190	309

Western Division

	W	L	T	Pct.	Pts.	OP
Chi. Cardinals	9	3	0	.750	306	231
Chi. Bears	8	4	0	.667	363	241
Green Bay	6	5	1	.545	274	210
Los Angeles	6	6	0	.500	259	214
Detroit	3	9	0	.250	231	305

Eastern Division playoff: Philadelphia 21, PITTSBURGH 0
NFL championship: CHI. CARDINALS 28, Philadelphia 21

1946

Eastern Division

	W	L	T	Pct.	Pts.	OP
N.Y. Giants	7	3	1	.700	236	162
Philadelphia	6	5	0	.545	231	220
Washington	5	5	1	.500	171	191
Pittsburgh	5	5	1	.500	136	117
Boston	2	8	1	.200	189	273

Western Division

	W	L	T	Pct.	Pts.	OP
Chi. Bears	8	2	1	.800	289	193
Los Angeles	6	4	1	.600	277	257
Green Bay	6	5	0	.545	148	158
Chi. Cardinals	6	5	0	.545	260	198
Detroit	1	10	0	.091	142	310

NFL championship: Chi. Bears 24, N.Y. GIANTS 14

1945

Eastern Division

	W	L	T	Pct.	Pts.	OP
Washington	8	2	0	.800	209	121
Philadelphia	7	3	0	.700	272	133
N.Y. Giants	3	6	1	.333	179	198
Boston	3	6	1	.333	123	211
Pittsburgh	2	8	0	.200	79	220

Western Division

	W	L	T	Pct.	Pts.	OP
Cleveland	9	1	0	.900	244	136
Detroit	7	3	0	.700	195	194
Green Bay	6	4	0	.600	258	173
Chi. Bears	3	7	0	.300	192	235
Chi. Cardinals	1	9	0	.100	98	228

NFL championship: CLEVELAND 15, Washington 14

1944

Eastern Division

	W	L	T	Pct.	Pts.	OP
N.Y. Giants	8	1	1	.889	206	75
Philadelphia	7	1	2	.875	267	131
Washington	6	3	1	.667	169	180
Boston	2	8	0	.200	82	233
Brooklyn	0	10	0	.000	69	166

Western Division

	W	L	T	Pct.	Pts.	OP
Green Bay	8	2	0	.800	238	141
Chi. Bears	6	3	1	.667	258	172
Detroit	6	3	1	.667	216	151
Cleveland	4	6	0	.400	188	224
Card-Pitt	0	10	0	.000	108	328

NFL championship: Green Bay 14, N.Y. GIANTS 7

1943

Eastern Division

	W	L	T	Pct.	Pts.	OP
Washington	6	3	1	.667	229	137
N.Y. Giants	6	3	1	.667	197	170
Phil-Pitt	5	4	1	.556	225	230
Brooklyn	2	8	0	.200	65	234

Western Division

	W	L	T	Pct.	Pts.	OP
Chi. Bears	8	1	1	.889	303	157
Green Bay	7	2	1	.778	264	172
Detroit	3	6	1	.333	178	218
Chi. Cardinals	0	10	0	.000	95	238

Eastern Division playoff: Washington 28, N.Y. GIANTS 0
NFL championship: CHI. BEARS 41, Washington 21

1942

Eastern Division

	W	L	T	Pct.	Pts.	OP
Washington	10	1	0	.909	227	102
Pittsburgh	7	4	0	.636	167	119
N.Y. Giants	5	5	1	.500	155	139
Brooklyn	3	8	0	.273	100	168
Philadelphia	2	9	0	.182	134	239

Western Division

	W	L	T	Pct.	Pts.	OP
Chi. Bears	11	0	0	1.000	376	84
Green Bay	8	2	1	.800	300	215
Cleveland	5	6	0	.455	150	207
Chi. Cardinals	3	8	0	.273	98	209
Detroit	0	11	0	.000	38	263

NFL championship: WASHINGTON 14, Chi. Bears 6

1941

Eastern Division

	W	L	T	Pct.	Pts.	OP
N.Y. Giants	8	3	0	.727	238	114
Brooklyn	7	4	0	.636	158	127
Washington	6	5	0	.545	176	174
Philadelphia	2	8	1	.200	119	218
Pittsburgh	1	9	1	.100	103	276

Western Division

	W	L	T	Pct.	Pts.	OP
Chi. Bears	10	1	0	.909	396	147
Green Bay	10	1	0	.909	258	120
Detroit	4	6	1	.400	121	195
Chi. Cardinals	3	7	1	.300	127	197
Cleveland	2	9	0	.182	116	244

Western Division playoff: CHI. BEARS 33, Green Bay 14
NFL championship: CHI. BEARS 37, N.Y. Giants 9

1940

Eastern Division

	W	L	T	Pct.	Pts.	OP
Washington	9	2	0	.818	245	142
Brooklyn	8	3	0	.727	186	120
N.Y. Giants	6	4	1	.600	131	133
Pittsburgh	2	7	2	.222	60	178
Philadelphia	1	10	0	.091	111	211

Western Division

	W	L	T	Pct.	Pts.	OP
Chi. Bears	8	3	0	.727	238	152
Green Bay	6	4	1	.600	238	155
Detroit	5	5	1	.500	138	153
Cleveland	4	6	1	.400	171	191
Chi. Cardinals	2	7	2	.222	139	222

NFL championship: Chi. Bears 73, WASHINGTON 0

1939

Eastern Division

	W	L	T	Pct.	Pts.	OP
N.Y. Giants	9	1	1	.900	168	85
Washington	8	2	1	.800	242	94
Brooklyn	4	6	1	.400	108	219
Philadelphia	1	9	1	.100	105	200
Pittsburgh	1	9	1	.100	114	216

Western Division

	W	L	T	Pct.	Pts.	OP
Green Bay	9	2	0	.818	233	153
Chi. Bears	8	3	0	.727	298	157
Detroit	6	5	0	.545	145	150
Cleveland	5	5	1	.500	195	164
Chi. Cardinals	1	10	0	.091	84	254

NFL championship: GREEN BAY 27, N.Y. Giants 0

1938

Eastern Division

	W	L	T	Pct.	Pts.	OP
N.Y. Giants	8	2	1	.800	194	79
Washington	6	3	2	.667	148	154
Brooklyn	4	4	3	.500	131	161
Philadelphia	5	6	0	.455	154	164
Pittsburgh	2	9	0	.182	79	169

Western Division

	W	L	T	Pct.	Pts.	OP
Green Bay	8	3	0	.727	223	118
Detroit	7	4	0	.636	119	108
Chi. Bears	6	5	0	.545	194	148
Cleveland	4	7	0	.364	131	215
Chi. Cardinals	2	9	0	.182	111	168

NFL championship: N.Y. GIANTS 23, Green Bay 17

1937

Eastern Division

	W	L	T	Pct.	Pts.	OP
Washington	8	3	0	.727	195	120
N.Y. Giants	6	3	2	.667	128	109
Pittsburgh	4	7	0	.364	122	145
Brooklyn	3	7	1	.300	82	174
Philadelphia	2	8	1	.200	86	177

Western Division

	W	L	T	Pct.	Pts.	OP
Chi. Bears	9	1	1	.900	201	100
Green Bay	7	4	0	.636	220	122
Detroit	7	4	0	.636	180	105
Chi. Cardinals	5	5	1	.500	135	165
Cleveland	1	10	0	.091	75	207

NFL championship: Washington 28, CHI. BEARS 21

1936

Eastern Division

	W	L	T	Pct.	Pts.	OP
Boston	7	5	0	.583	149	110
Pittsburgh	6	6	0	.500	98	187
N.Y. Giants	5	6	1	.455	115	163
Brooklyn	3	8	1	.273	92	161
Philadelphia	1	11	0	.083	51	206

Western Division

	W	L	T	Pct.	Pts.	OP
Green Bay	10	1	1	.909	248	118
Chi. Bears	9	3	0	.750	222	94
Detroit	8	4	0	.667	235	102
Chi. Cardinals	3	8	1	.273	74	143

NFL championship: Green Bay 21, Boston 6, at Polo Grounds, N.Y.

1935

Eastern Division

	W	L	T	Pct.	Pts.	OP
N. Y. Giants	9	3	0	.750	180	96
Brooklyn	5	6	1	.455	90	141
Pittsburgh	4	8	0	.333	100	209
Boston	2	8	1	.200	65	123
Philadelphia	2	9	0	.182	60	179

Western Division

	W	L	T	Pct.	Pts.	OP
Detroit	7	3	2	.700	191	111
Green Bay	8	4	0	.667	181	96
Chi. Bears	6	4	2	.600	192	106
Chi. Cardinals	6	4	2	.600	99	97

NFL championship: DETROIT 26, N.Y. Giants 7
One game between Boston and Philadelphia was canceled.

1934

Eastern Division

	W	L	T	Pct.	Pts.	OP
N.Y. Giants	8	5	0	.615	147	107
Boston	6	6	0	.500	107	94
Brooklyn	4	7	0	.364	61	153
Philadelphia	4	7	0	.364	127	85
Pittsburgh	2	10	0	.167	51	206

Western Division

	W	L	T	Pct.	Pts.	OP
Chi. Bears	13	0	0	1.000	286	86
Detroit	10	3	0	.769	238	59
Green Bay	7	6	0	.538	156	112
Chi. Cardinals	5	6	0	.455	80	84
St. Louis	1	2	0	.333	27	61
Cincinnati	0	8	0	.000	10	243

NFL championship: N.Y. GIANTS 30, Chi. Bears 13

1933

Eastern Division

	W	L	T	Pct.	Pts.	OP
N.Y. Giants	11	3	0	.786	244	101
Brooklyn	5	4	1	.556	93	54
Boston	5	5	2	.500	103	97
Philadelphia	3	5	1	.375	77	158
Pittsburgh	3	6	2	.333	67	208

Western Division

	W	L	T	Pct.	Pts.	OP
Chi. Bears	10	2	1	.833	133	82
Portsmouth	6	5	0	.545	128	87
Green Bay	5	7	1	.417	170	107
Cincinnati	3	6	1	.333	38	110
Chi. Cardinals	1	9	1	.100	52	101

NFL championship: CHI. BEARS 23, N.Y. Giants 21

1932

	W	L	T	Pct.
Chicago Bears	7	1	6	.875
Green Bay Packers	10	3	1	.769
Portsmouth Spartans	6	2	4	.750
Boston Braves	4	4	2	.500
New York Giants	4	6	2	.400
Brooklyn Dodgers	3	9	0	.250
Chicago Cardinals	2	6	2	.250
Staten Island Stapletons	2	7	3	.222

Chicago Bears and Portsmouth finished regularly scheduled games tied for first place. Bears won playoff game, which counted in standings, 9-0.

1931

	W	L	T	Pct.
Green Bay Packers	12	2	0	.857
Portsmouth Spartans	11	3	0	.786
Chicago Bears	8	5	0	.615
Chicago Cardinals	5	4	0	.556
New York Giants	7	6	1	.538
Providence Steam Roller	4	4	3	.500
Staten Island Stapletons	4	6	1	.400
Cleveland Indians	2	8	0	.200
Brooklyn Dodgers	2	12	0	.143
Frankford Yellow Jackets	1	6	1	.143

1930

	W	L	T	Pct.
Green Bay Packers	10	3	1	.769
New York Giants	13	4	0	.765
Chicago Bears	9	4	1	.692
Brooklyn Dodgers	7	4	1	.636
Providence Steam Roller	6	4	1	.600
Staten Island Stapletons	5	5	2	.500
Chicago Cardinals	5	6	2	.455
Portsmouth Spartans	5	6	3	.455
Frankford Yellow Jackets	4	13	1	.222
Minneapolis Red Jackets	1	7	1	.125
Newark Tornadoes	1	10	1	.091

1929

	W	L	T	Pct.
Green Bay Packers	12	0	1	1.000
New York Giants	13	1	1	.929
Frankford Yellow Jackets	9	4	5	.692
Chicago Cardinals	6	6	1	.500
Boston Bulldogs	4	4	0	.500
Orange Tornadoes	3	4	4	.429
Staten Island Stapletons	3	4	3	.429
Providence Steam Roller	4	6	2	.400
Chicago Bears	4	9	2	.308
Buffalo Bisons	1	7	1	.125
Minneapolis Red Jackets	1	9	0	.100
Dayton Triangles	0	6	0	.000

1928

	W	L	T	Pct.
Providence Steam Roller	8	1	2	.889
Frankford Yellow Jackets	11	3	2	.786
Detroit Wolverines	7	2	1	.778
Green Bay Packers	6	4	3	.600
Chicago Bears	7	5	1	.583
New York Giants	4	7	2	.364
New York Yankees	4	8	1	.333
Pottsville Maroons	2	8	0	.200
Chicago Cardinals	1	5	0	.167
Dayton Triangles	0	7	0	.000

1927

	W	L	T	Pct.
New York Giants	11	1	1	.917
Green Bay Packers	7	2	1	.778
Chicago Bears	9	3	2	.750
Cleveland Bulldogs	8	4	1	.667
Providence Steam Roller	8	5	1	.615
New York Yankees	7	8	1	.467
Frankford Yellow Jackets	6	9	3	.400
Pottsville Maroons	5	8	0	.385
Chicago Cardinals	3	7	1	.300
Dayton Triangles	1	6	1	.143
Duluth Eskimos	1	8	0	.111
Buffalo Bisons	0	5	0	.000

1926

	W	L	T	Pct.
Frankford Yellow Jackets	14	1	1	.933
Chicago Bears	12	1	3	.923
Pottsville Maroons	10	2	1	.833
Kansas City Cowboys	8	3	0	.727
Green Bay Packers	7	3	3	.700
Los Angeles Buccaneers	6	3	1	.667
New York Giants	8	4	1	.667
Duluth Eskimos	6	5	3	.545
Buffalo Rangers	4	4	2	.500
Chicago Cardinals	5	6	1	.455
Providence Steam Roller	5	7	1	.417
Detroit Panthers	4	6	2	.400
Hartford Blues	3	7	0	.300
Brooklyn Lions	3	8	0	.273
Milwaukee Badgers	2	7	0	.222
Akron Pros	1	4	3	.200
Dayton Triangles	1	4	1	.200
Racine Tornadoes	1	4	0	.200
Columbus Tigers	1	6	0	.143
Canton Bulldogs	1	9	3	.100
Hammond Pros	0	4	0	.000
Louisville Colonels	0	4	0	.000

1925

	W	L	T	Pct.
Chicago Cardinals	11	2	1	.846
Pottsville Maroons	10	2	0	.833
Detroit Panthers	8	2	2	.800
New York Giants	8	4	0	.667
Akron Indians	4	2	2	.667
Frankford Yellow Jackets	13	7	0	.650
Chicago Bears	9	5	3	.643
Rock Island Independents	5	3	3	.625
Green Bay Packers	8	5	0	.615
Providence Steam Roller	6	5	1	.545
Canton Bulldogs	4	4	0	.500
Cleveland Bulldogs	5	8	1	.385
Kansas City Cowboys	2	5	1	.286
Hammond Pros	1	4	0	.250
Buffalo Bisons	1	6	2	.143
Duluth Kelleys	0	3	0	.000
Rochester Jeffersons	0	6	1	.000
Milwaukee Badgers	0	6	0	.000
Dayton Triangles	0	7	1	.000
Columbus Tigers	0	9	0	.000

1924

	W	L	T	Pct.
Cleveland Bulldogs	7	1	1	.875
Chicago Bears	6	1	4	.857
Frankford Yellow Jackets	11	2	1	.846
Duluth Kelleys	5	1	0	.833
Rock Island Independents	6	2	2	.750
Green Bay Packers	7	4	0	.636
Racine Legion	4	3	3	.571
Chicago Cardinals	5	4	1	.556
Buffalo Bisons	6	5	0	.545
Columbus Tigers	4	4	0	.500
Hammond Pros	2	2	1	.500
Milwaukee Badgers	5	8	0	.385
Akron Indians	2	6	0	.333
Dayton Triangles	2	6	0	.333
Kansas City Blues	2	7	0	.222
Kenosha Maroons	0	5	1	.000
Minneapolis Marines	0	6	0	.000
Rochester Jeffersons	0	7	0	.000

1923

	W	L	T	Pct.
Canton Bulldogs	11	0	1	1.000
Chicago Bears	9	2	1	.818
Green Bay Packers	7	2	1	.778
Milwaukee Badgers	7	2	3	.778
Cleveland Indians	3	1	3	.750
Chicago Cardinals	8	4	0	.667
Duluth Kelleys	4	3	0	.571
Columbus Tigers	5	4	1	.556
Buffalo All-Americans	4	4	3	.500
Racine Legion	4	4	2	.500
Toledo Maroons	2	3	2	.400
Rock Island Independents	2	3	3	.400
Minneapolis Marines	2	5	2	.286
St. Louis All-Stars	1	4	2	.200
Hammond Pros	1	5	1	.167
Dayton Triangles	1	6	1	.143
Akron Indians	1	6	0	.143
Oorang Indians	1	10	0	.091
Rochester Jeffersons	0	2	0	.000
Louisville Brecks	0	3	0	.000

1922

	W	L	T	Pct.
Canton Bulldogs	10	0	2	1.000
Chicago Bears	9	3	0	.750
Chicago Cardinals	8	3	0	.727
Toledo Maroons	5	2	2	.714
Rock Island Independents	4	2	1	.667
Racine Legion	6	4	1	.600
Dayton Triangles	4	3	1	.571
Green Bay Packers	4	3	3	.571
Buffalo All-Americans	5	4	1	.556
Akron Pros	3	5	2	.375
Milwaukee Badgers	2	4	3	.333
Oorang Indians	2	6	0	.250
Minneapolis Marines	1	3	0	.250
Louisville Brecks	1	3	0	.250
Evansville Crimson Giants	0	3	0	.000
Rochester Jeffersons	0	4	1	.000
Hammond Pros	0	5	1	.000
Columbus Panhandles	0	7	0	.000

1921

	W	L	T	Pct.
Chicago Staleys	9	1	1	.900
Buffalo All-Americans	9	1	2	.900
Akron Pros	8	3	1	.727
Canton Bulldogs	5	2	3	.714
Rock Island Independents	4	2	1	.667
Evansville Crimson Giants	3	2	0	.600
Green Bay Packers	3	2	1	.600
Dayton Triangles	4	4	1	.500
Chicago Cardinals	3	3	2	.500
Rochester Jeffersons	2	3	0	.400
Cleveland Indians	3	5	0	.375
Washington Senators	1	2	0	.333
Cincinnati Celts	1	3	0	.250
Hammond Pros	1	3	1	.250
Minneapolis Marines	1	3	1	.250
Detroit Heralds	1	5	1	.167
Columbus Panhandles	1	8	0	.111
Tonawanda Kardex	0	1	0	.000
Muncie Flyers	0	2	0	.000
Louisville Brecks	0	2	0	.000
New York Giants	0	2	0	.000

1920

	W	L	T	Pct.
Akron Pros	8	0	3	1.000
Decatur Staleys	10	1	2	.909
Buffalo All-Americans	9	1	1	.900
Chicago Cardinals	6	2	2	.750
Rock Island Independents	6	2	2	.750
Dayton Triangles	5	2	2	.714
Rochester Jeffersons	6	3	2	.667
Canton Bulldogs	7	4	2	.636
Detroit Heralds	2	3	3	.400
Cleveland Tigers	2	4	2	.333
Chicago Tigers	2	5	1	.286
Hammond Pros	2	5	0	.286
Columbus Panhandles	2	6	2	.250
Muncie Flyers	0	1	0	.000

ALL-TIME TEAM VS. TEAM RESULTS

RS = REGULAR SEASON
PS = POSTSEASON

ATLANTA vs. BUFFALO
RS: Series tied, 3-3
1973 — Bills, 17-6 (A)
1977 — Bills, 3-0 (B)
1980 — Falcons, 30-14 (B)
1983 — Falcons, 31-14 (A)
1989 — Falcons, 30-28 (A)
1992 — Bills, 41-14 (B)
(RS Pts. — Bills 117, Falcons 111)

ATLANTA vs. CHICAGO
RS: Falcons lead series, 9-8
1966 — Bears, 23-6 (C)
1967 — Bears, 23-14 (A)
1968 — Falcons, 16-13 (C)
1969 — Falcons, 48-31 (A)
1970 — Bears, 23-14 (A)
1972 — Falcons, 37-21 (C)
1973 — Falcons, 46-6 (A)
1974 — Falcons, 13-10 (A)
1976 — Falcons, 10-0 (C)
1977 — Falcons, 16-10 (C)
1978 — Bears, 13-7 (C)
1980 — Falcons, 28-17 (A)
1983 — Falcons, 20-17 (C)
1985 — Bears, 36-0 (C)
1986 — Bears, 13-10 (A)
1990 — Bears, 30-24 (C)
1992 — Bears, 41-31 (C)
(RS Pts. — Falcons 340, Bears 327)

ATLANTA vs. CINCINNATI
RS: Bengals lead series, 5-2
1971 — Falcons, 9-6 (C)
1975 — Bengals, 21-14 (A)
1978 — Bengals, 37-7 (C)
1981 — Bengals, 30-28 (A)
1984 — Bengals, 35-14 (C)
1987 — Bengals, 16-10 (A)
1990 — Falcons, 38-17 (A)
(RS Pts. — Bengals 162, Falcons 120)

ATLANTA vs. CLEVELAND
RS: Browns lead series, 8-1
1966 — Browns, 49-17 (A)
1968 — Browns, 30-7 (C)
1971 — Falcons, 31-14 (C)
1976 — Browns, 20-17 (A)
1978 — Browns, 24-16 (A)
1981 — Browns, 28-17 (C)
1984 — Browns, 23-7 (A)
1987 — Browns, 38-3 (C)
1990 — Browns, 13-10 (C)
(RS Pts. — Browns 239, Falcons 125)

ATLANTA vs. DALLAS
RS: Cowboys lead series, 9-5
PS: Cowboys lead series, 2-0
1966 — Cowboys, 47-14 (A)
1967 — Cowboys, 37-7 (D)
1969 — Cowboys, 24-17 (A)
1970 — Cowboys, 13-0 (D)
1974 — Cowboys, 24-0 (A)
1976 — Falcons, 17-10 (A)
1978 — *Cowboys, 27-20 (D)
1980 — *Cowboys, 30-27 (A)
1985 — Cowboys, 24-10 (D)
1986 — Falcons, 37-35 (D)
1987 — Falcons, 21-10 (D)
1988 — Cowboys, 26-20 (D)
1989 — Falcons 27-21 (A)
1990 — Falcons, 26-7 (A)
1991 — Cowboys, 31-27 (D)
1992 — Cowboys 41-17 (A)
(RS Pts. — Cowboys 350, Falcons 240)
(PS Pts. — Cowboys 57, Falcons 47)
**NFC Divisional Playoff*

ATLANTA vs. DENVER
RS: Broncos lead series, 4-3
1970 — Broncos, 24-10 (D)
1972 — Falcons, 23-20 (A)
1975 — Falcons, 35-21 (A)
1979 — Broncos, 20-17 (A) OT
1982 — Falcons, 34-27 (D)
1985 — Broncos, 44-28 (A)
1988 — Broncos, 30-14 (D)
(RS Pts. — Broncos 186, Falcons 161)

ATLANTA vs. DETROIT
RS: Lions lead series, 16-5
1966 — Lions, 28-10 (D)
1967 — Lions, 24-3 (D)
1968 — Lions, 24-7 (A)
1969 — Lions, 27-21 (D)
1971 — Lions, 41-38 (D)
1972 — Lions, 26-23 (A)
1973 — Lions, 31-6 (D)
1975 — Lions, 17-14 (A)
1976 — Lions, 24-10 (D)
1977 — Falcons, 17-6 (A)
1978 — Falcons, 14-0 (A)
1979 — Lions, 24-23 (D)
1980 — Falcons, 43-28 (A)
1983 — Falcons, 30-14 (D)
1984 — Lions, 27-24 (A) OT
1985 — Lions, 28-27 (A)
1986 — Falcons, 20-6 (D)
1987 — Lions, 30-13 (A)
1988 — Lions, 31-17 (D)
1989 — Lions, 31-24 (A)
1990 — Lions, 21-14 (D)
(RS Pts. — Lions 488, Falcons 398)

ATLANTA vs. GREEN BAY
RS: Series tied, 9-9
1966 — Packers, 56-3 (Mil)
1967 — Packers, 23-0 (Mil)
1968 — Packers, 38-7 (A)
1969 — Packers, 28-10 (GB)
1970 — Packers, 27-24 (GB)
1971 — Falcons, 28-21 (A)
1972 — Falcons, 10-9 (Mil)
1974 — Falcons, 10-3 (A)
1975 — Packers, 22-13 (GB)
1976 — Packers, 24-20 (A)
1979 — Falcons, 25-7 (A)
1981 — Falcons, 31-17 (GB)
1982 — Packers, 38-7 (A)
1983 — Falcons, 47-41 (A) OT
1988 — Falcons, 20-0 (A)
1989 — Packers, 23-21 (Mil)
1991 — Falcons, 35-31 (A)
1992 — Falcons, 24-10 (A)
(RS Pts. — Packers 418, Falcons 335)

ATLANTA vs. HOUSTON
RS: Falcons lead series, 5-2
1972 — Falcons, 20-10 (A)
1976 — Oilers, 20-14 (H)
1978 — Falcons, 20-14 (A)
1981 — Falcons, 31-27 (H)
1984 — Falcons, 42-10 (A)
1987 — Oilers, 37-33 (H)
1990 — Falcons, 47-27 (A)
(RS Pts. — Falcons 207, Oilers 145)

ATLANTA vs. *INDIANAPOLIS
RS: Colts lead series, 10-0
1966 — Colts, 19-7 (A)
1967 — Colts, 38-31 (B)
Colts, 49-7 (A)
1968 — Colts, 28-20 (A)
Colts, 44-0 (B)
1969 — Colts, 21-14 (A)
Colts, 13-6 (B)
1974 — Colts, 17-7 (A)
1986 — Colts, 28-23 (A)
1989 — Colts, 13-9 (I)
(RS Pts. — Colts 270, Falcons 124)
**Franchise in Baltimore prior to 1984*

ATLANTA vs. KANSAS CITY
RS: Chiefs lead series, 3-0
1972 — Chiefs, 17-14 (A)
1985 — Chiefs, 38-10 (KC)
1991 — Chiefs, 14-3 (KC)
(RS Pts. — Chiefs 69, Falcons 27)

ATLANTA vs. *L.A. RAIDERS
RS: Raiders lead series, 4-3
1971 — Falcons, 24-13 (A)
1975 — Raiders, 37-34 (O) OT
1979 — Raiders, 50-19 (O)
1982 — Raiders, 38-14 (A)
1985 — Raiders, 34-24 (A)
1988 — Falcons, 12-6 (LA)
1991 — Falcons, 21-17 (A)
(RS Pts. — Raiders 195, Falcons 148)
**Franchise in Oakland prior to 1982*

ATLANTA vs. L.A. RAMS
RS: Rams lead series, 36-14-2
1966 — Rams, 19-14 (A)
1967 — Rams, 31-3 (A)
Rams, 20-3 (LA)
1968 — Rams, 27-14 (LA)
Rams, 17-10 (A)
1969 — Rams, 17-7 (LA)
Rams, 38-6 (A)
1970 — Tie, 10-10 (LA)
Rams, 17-7 (A)
1971 — Tie, 20-20 (LA)
Rams, 24-16 (A)
1972 — Falcons, 31-3 (A)
Rams, 20-7 (LA)
1973 — Rams, 31-0 (LA)
Falcons, 15-13 (A)
1974 — Rams, 21-0 (LA)
Rams, 30-7 (A)
1975 — Rams, 22-7 (LA)
Rams, 16-7 (A)
1976 — Rams, 30-14 (A)
Rams, 59-0 (LA)
1977 — Falcons, 17-6 (A)
Rams, 23-7 (LA)
1978 — Rams, 10-0 (LA)
Falcons, 15-7 (A)
1979 — Rams, 20-14 (LA)
Rams, 34-13 (A)
1980 — Falcons, 13-10 (A)
Rams, 20-17 (LA) OT
1981 — Rams, 37-35 (A)
Rams, 21-16 (LA)
1982 — Falcons, 34-17 (A)
1983 — Rams, 27-21 (LA)
Rams, 36-13 (A)
1984 — Falcons, 30-28 (LA)
Rams, 24-10 (A)
1985 — Rams, 17-6 (LA)
Falcons, 30-14 (A)
1986 — Falcons, 26-14 (A)
Rams, 14-7 (LA)
1987 — Falcons, 24-20 (A)
Rams, 33-0 (LA)
1988 — Rams, 33-0 (A)
Rams, 22-7 (LA)
1989 — Rams, 31-21 (A)
Rams, 26-14 (LA)
1990 — Rams, 44-24 (LA)
Falcons, 20-13 (A)
1991 — Falcons, 31-14 (A)
Falcons, 31-14 (LA)
1992 — Falcons, 30-28 (A)
Rams, 38-27 (LA)
(RS Pts. — Rams 1,180, Falcons 751)

ATLANTA vs. MIAMI
RS: Dolphins lead series, 5-1
1970 — Dolphins, 20-7 (A)
1974 — Dolphins, 42-7 (M)
1980 — Dolphins, 20-17 (A)
1983 — Dolphins, 31-24 (M)
1986 — Falcons, 20-14 (M)
1992 — Dolphins, 21-17 (M)
(RS Pts. — Dolphins 148, Falcons 92)

ATLANTA vs. MINNESOTA
RS: Vikings lead series, 11-6
PS: Vikings lead series, 1-0
1966 — Falcons, 20-13 (M)
1967 — Falcons, 21-20 (A)
1968 — Vikings, 47-7 (M)
1969 — Falcons, 10-3 (A)
1970 — Vikings, 37-7 (A)
1971 — Vikings, 24-7 (M)
1973 — Falcons, 20-14 (A)
1974 — Vikings, 23-10 (M)
1975 — Vikings, 38-0 (M)
1977 — Vikings, 14-7 (A)
1980 — Vikings, 24-23 (M)
1981 — Falcons, 31-30 (A)
1982 — *Vikings, 30-24 (M)
1984 — Vikings, 27-20 (M)
1985 — Falcons, 14-13 (A)
1987 — Vikings, 24-13 (M)
1989 — Vikings, 43-17 (M)
1991 — Vikings, 20-19 (A)
(RS Pts. — Vikings 414, Falcons 246)
(PS Pts. — Vikings 30, Falcons 24)
**NFC First Round Playoff*

ATLANTA vs. NEW ENGLAND
RS: Falcons lead series, 4-3
1972 — Patriots, 21-20 (NE)
1977 — Patriots, 16-10 (A)
1980 — Falcons, 37-21 (NE)
1983 — Falcons, 24-13 (A)
1986 — Patriots, 25-17 (NE)
1989 — Falcons, 16-15 (A)
1992 — Falcons, 34-0 (A)
(RS Pts. — Falcons 158, Patriots 111)

ATLANTA vs. NEW ORLEANS
RS: Falcons lead series, 26-21
PS: Falcons lead series, 1-0
1967 — Saints, 27-24 (NO)
1969 — Falcons, 45-17 (A)
1970 — Falcons, 14-3 (NO)
Falcons, 32-14 (A)
1971 — Falcons, 28-6 (A)
Falcons, 24-20 (NO)
1972 — Falcons, 21-14 (NO)
Falcons, 36-20 (A)
1973 — Falcons, 62-7 (NO)
Falcons, 14-10 (A)
1974 — Saints, 14-13 (NO)
Saints, 13-3 (A)
1975 — Falcons, 14-7 (A)
Saints, 23-7 (NO)
1976 — Saints, 30-0 (NO)
Falcons, 23-20 (A)
1977 — Saints, 21-20 (NO)
Falcons, 35-7 (A)
1978 — Falcons, 20-17 (NO)
Falcons, 20-17 (A)
1979 — Falcons, 40-34 (NO) OT
Saints, 37-6 (A)
1980 — Falcons, 41-14 (NO)
Falcons, 31-13 (A)
1981 — Falcons, 27-0 (A)
Falcons, 41-10 (NO)
1982 — Falcons, 35-0 (A)
Saints, 35-6 (NO)
1983 — Saints, 19-17 (A)
Saints, 27-10 (NO)
1984 — Falcons, 36-28 (NO)
Saints, 17-13 (A)
1985 — Falcons, 31-24 (A)
Falcons, 16-10 (NO)
1986 — Falcons, 31-10 (NO)
Saints, 14-9 (A)
1987 — Saints, 38-0 (A)
1988 — Saints, 29-21 (A)
Saints, 10-9 (NO)
1989 — Saints, 20-13 (NO)
Saints, 26-17 (A)
1990 — Falcons, 28-27 (A)
Saints, 10-7 (NO)
1991 — Saints, 27-6 (A)
Falcons, 23-20 (NO) OT
*Falcons, 27-20 (NO)
1992 — Saints, 10-7 (A)
Saints, 22-14 (NO)
(RS Pts. — Falcons 990, Saints 838)
(PS Pts. — Falcons 27, Saints 20)
**NFC First Round Playoff*

ATLANTA vs. N.Y. GIANTS
RS: Series tied, 6-6
1966 — Falcons, 27-16 (NY)
1968 — Falcons, 24-21 (A)
1971 — Giants, 21-17 (A)
1974 — Falcons, 14-7 (New Haven)
1977 — Falcons, 17-3 (A)
1978 — Falcons, 23-20 (A)
1979 — Giants, 24-3 (NY)
1981 — Giants, 27-24 (A) OT
1982 — Falcons, 16-14 (NY)
1983 — Giants, 16-13 (A) OT
1984 — Giants, 19-7 (A)
1988 — Giants, 23-16 (A)
(RS Pts. — Giants 211, Falcons 201)

ATLANTA vs. N.Y. JETS
RS: Series tied, 3-3
1973 — Falcons, 28-20 (NY)
1980 — Jets, 14-7 (A)
1983 — Falcons, 27-21 (NY)
1986 — Jets, 28-14 (A)
1989 — Jets, 27-7 (NY)
1992 — Falcons, 20-17 (A)
(RS Pts. — Jets 127, Falcons 103)

ATLANTA vs. PHILADELPHIA
RS: Eagles lead series, 8-6-1
PS: Falcons lead series, 1-0
1966 — Eagles, 23-10 (P)
1967 — Eagles, 38-7 (A)
1969 — Falcons, 27-3 (P)
1970 — Tie, 13-13 (P)
1973 — Falcons, 44-27 (P)
1976 — Eagles, 14-13 (A)
1978 — *Falcons, 14-13 (A)
1979 — Falcons, 14-10 (P)
1980 — Falcons, 20-17 (P)
1981 — Eagles, 16-13 (P)
1983 — Eagles, 28-24 (A)
1984 — Falcons, 26-10 (A)
1985 — Eagles, 23-17 (P) OT
1986 — Eagles, 16-0 (A)
1988 — Falcons, 27-24 (P)
1990 — Eagles, 24-23 (A)
(RS Pts. — Eagles 286, Falcons 278)
(PS Pts. — Falcons 14, Eagles 13)
**NFC First Round Playoff*

ATLANTA vs. *PHOENIX
RS: Cardinals lead series, 10-5
1966 — Falcons, 16-10 (A)
1968 — Cardinals, 17-12 (StL)
1971 — Cardinals, 26-9 (A)
1973 — Cardinals, 32-10 (A)
1975 — Cardinals, 23-20 (StL)
1978 — Cardinals, 42-21 (StL)
1980 — Falcons, 33-27 (StL) OT
1981 — Falcons, 41-20 (A)
1982 — Cardinals, 23-20 (A)
1986 — Falcons, 33-13 (A)
1987 — Cardinals, 34-21 (A)
1989 — Cardinals, 34-20 (P)
1990 — Cardinals, 24-13 (A)
1991 — Cardinals, 16-10 (P)
1992 — Falcons, 20-17 (A)
(RS Pts. — Cardinals 358, Falcons 299)
**Franchise in St. Louis prior to 1988*

ATLANTA vs. PITTSBURGH
RS: Steelers lead series, 8-1
1966 — Steelers, 57-33 (A)
1968 — Steelers, 41-21 (A)
1970 — Falcons, 27-16 (A)
1974 — Steelers, 24-17 (P)
1978 — Steelers, 31-7 (P)
1981 — Steelers, 34-20 (A)

1984 — Steelers, 35-10 (P)
1987 — Steelers, 28-12 (A)
1990 — Steelers, 21-9 (P)
(RS Pts. — Steelers 287, Falcons 156)

ATLANTA vs. SAN DIEGO
RS: Falcons lead series, 3-1
1973 — Falcons, 41-0 (SD)
1979 — Falcons, 28-26 (SD)
1988 — Chargers, 10-7 (A)
1991 — Falcons, 13-10 (SD)
(RS Pts. — Falcons 89, Chargers 46)

ATLANTA vs. SAN FRANCISCO
RS: 49ers lead series, 31-20-1
1966 — 49ers, 44-7 (A)
1967 — 49ers, 38-7 (SF)
49ers, 34-28 (A)
1968 — 49ers, 28-13 (SF)
49ers, 14-12 (A)
1969 — Falcons, 24-12 (A)
Falcons, 21-7 (SF)
1970 — Falcons, 21-20 (A)
49ers, 24-20 (SF)
1971 — Falcons, 20-17 (A)
49ers, 24-3 (SF)
1972 — 49ers, 49-14 (A)
49ers, 20-0 (SF)
1973 — 49ers, 13-9 (A)
Falcons, 17-3 (SF)
1974 — 49ers, 16-10 (A)
49ers, 27-0 (SF)
1975 — Falcons, 17-3 (SF)
Falcons, 31-9 (A)
1976 — 49ers, 15-0 (SF)
Falcons, 21-16 (A)
1977 — Falcons, 7-0 (SF)
49ers, 10-3 (A)
1978 — Falcons, 20-17 (SF)
Falcons, 21-10 (A)
1979 — 49ers, 20-15 (SF)
Falcons, 31-21 (A)
1980 — Falcons, 20-17 (SF)
Falcons, 35-10 (A)
1981 — Falcons, 34-17 (A)
49ers, 17-14 (SF)
1982 — Falcons, 17-7 (SF)
1983 — 49ers, 24-20 (SF)
Falcons, 28-24 (A)
1984 — 49ers, 14-5 (SF)
49ers, 35-17 (A)
1985 — 49ers, 35-16 (SF)
49ers, 38-17 (A)
1986 — Tie, 10-10 (A) OT
49ers, 20-0 (SF)
1987 — 49ers, 25-17 (A)
49ers, 35-7 (SF)
1988 — Falcons, 34-17 (SF)
49ers, 13-3 (A)
1989 — 49ers, 45-3 (SF)
49ers, 23-10 (A)
1990 — 49ers, 19-13 (SF)
49ers, 45-35 (A)
1991 — Falcons, 39-34 (SF)
Falcons, 17-14 (A)
1992 — 49ers, 56-17 (SF)
49ers, 41-3 (A)
(RS Pts. — 49ers 1,146, Falcons 823)

ATLANTA vs. SEATTLE
RS: Seahawks lead series, 4-1
1976 — Seahawks, 30-13 (S)
1979 — Seahawks, 31-28 (A)
1985 — Seahawks, 30-26 (S)
1988 — Seahawks, 31-20 (A)
1991 — Falcons, 26-13 (A)
(RS Pts. — Seahawks 135, Falcons 113)

ATLANTA vs. TAMPA BAY
RS: Falcons lead series, 6-5
1977 — Falcons, 17-0 (TB)
1978 — Buccaneers, 14-9 (TB)
1979 — Falcons, 17-14 (A)
1981 — Buccaneers, 24-23 (TB)
1984 — Buccaneers, 23-6 (TB)
1986 — Falcons, 23-20 (TB) OT
1987 — Buccaneers, 48-10 (TB)
1988 — Falcons, 17-10 (A)
1990 — Buccaneers, 23-17 (TB)
1991 — Falcons, 43-7 (A)
1992 — Falcons, 35-7 (TB)
(RS Pts. — Falcons 217, Buccaneers 190)

ATLANTA vs. WASHINGTON
RS: Redskins lead series, 12-3-1
PS: Redskins lead series, 1-0
1966 — Redskins, 33-20 (W)
1967 — Tie, 20-20 (A)
1969 — Redskins, 27-20 (W)
1972 — Redskins, 24-13 (W)
1975 — Redskins, 30-27 (A)
1977 — Redskins, 10-6 (W)
1978 — Falcons, 20-17 (A)
1979 — Redskins, 16-7 (A)
1980 — Falcons, 10-6 (A)
1983 — Redskins, 37-21 (W)
1984 — Redskins, 27-14 (W)
1985 — Redskins, 44-10 (A)
1987 — Falcons, 21-20 (A)
1989 — Redskins, 31-30 (A)
1991 — Redskins, 56-17 (W)
*Redskins, 24-7 (W)
1992 — Redskins, 24-17 (W)
(RS Pts. — Redskins 422, Falcons 273)
(PS Pts. — Redskins 24, Falcons 7)
**NFC Divisional Playoff*

BUFFALO vs. ATLANTA
RS: Series tied 3-3;
See Atlanta vs. Buffalo

BUFFALO vs. CHICAGO
RS: Bears lead series, 3-2
1970 — Bears, 31-13 (C)
1974 — Bills, 16-6 (B)
1979 — Bears, 7-0 (B)
1988 — Bears, 24-3 (C)
1991 — Bills, 35-20 (B)
(RS Pts. — Bears 88, Bills 67)

BUFFALO vs. CINCINNATI
RS: Bengals lead series, 9-7
PS: Bengals lead series, 2-0
1968 — Bengals, 34-23 (C)
1969 — Bills, 16-13 (B)
1970 — Bengals, 43-14 (B)
1973 — Bengals, 16-13 (B)
1975 — Bengals, 33-24 (C)
1978 — Bills, 5-0 (B)
1979 — Bills, 51-24 (B)
1980 — Bills, 14-0 (C)
1981 — Bengals, 27-24 (C) OT
*Bengals, 28-21 (C)
1983 — Bills, 10-6 (C)
1984 — Bengals, 52-21 (C)
1985 — Bengals, 23-17 (B)
1986 — Bengals, 36-33 (C) OT
1988 — Bengals, 35-21 (C)
**Bengals, 21-10 (C)
1989 — Bills, 24-7 (B)
1991 — Bills, 35-16 (B)
(RS Pts. — Bengals 365, Bills 345)
(PS Pts. — Bengals 49, Bills 31)
**AFC Divisional Playoff*
***AFC Championship*

BUFFALO vs. CLEVELAND
RS: Browns lead series, 7-3
PS: Browns lead series, 1-0
1972 — Browns, 27-10 (C)
1974 — Bills, 15-10 (C)
1977 — Browns, 27-16 (B)
1978 — Browns, 41-20 (C)
1981 — Bills, 22-13 (B)
1984 — Browns, 13-10 (B)
1985 — Browns, 17-7 (C)
1986 — Browns, 21-17 (B)
1987 — Browns, 27-21 (C)
1989 — *Browns, 34-30 (C)
1990 — Bills, 42-0 (C)
(RS Pts. — Browns 196, Bills 180)
(PS Pts. — Browns 34, Bills 30)
**AFC Divisional Playoff*

BUFFALO vs. DALLAS
RS: Cowboys lead series, 3-1
PS: Cowboys lead series, 1-0
1971 — Cowboys, 49-37 (B)
1976 — Cowboys, 17-10 (D)
1981 — Cowboys, 27-14 (D)
1984 — Bills, 14-3 (B)
1992 — *Cowboys, 52-17 (Pasadena)
(RS Pts. — Cowboys 96, Bills 75)
(PS Pts. — Cowboys 52, Bills 17)
**Super Bowl XXVII*

BUFFALO vs. DENVER
RS: Bills lead series, 16-10-1
PS: Bills lead series, 1-0
1960 — Broncos, 27-21 (B)
Tie, 38-38 (D)
1961 — Broncos, 22-10 (B)
Bills, 23-10 (D)
1962 — Broncos, 23-20 (B)
Bills, 45-38 (D)
1963 — Bills, 30-28 (D)
Bills, 27-17 (B)
1964 — Bills, 30-13 (B)
Bills, 30-19 (D)
1965 — Bills, 30-15 (D)
Bills, 31-13 (B)
1966 — Bills, 38-21 (B)
1967 — Bills, 17-16 (D)
Broncos, 21-20 (B)
1968 — Broncos, 34-32 (D)
1969 — Bills, 41-28 (B)
1970 — Broncos, 25-10 (B)
1975 — Bills, 38-14 (B)
1977 — Broncos, 26-6 (D)
1979 — Broncos, 19-16 (B)
1981 — Bills, 9-7 (B)
1984 — Broncos, 37-7 (B)
1987 — Bills, 21-14 (B)
1989 — Broncos, 28-14 (B)
1990 — Bills, 29-28 (B)
1991 — *Bills, 10-7 (B)
1992 — Bills, 27-17 (B)
(RS Pts. — Bills 660, Broncos 598)
(PS Pts. — Bills 10, Broncos 7)
**AFC Championship*

BUFFALO vs. DETROIT
RS: Lions lead series, 2-1-1
1972 — Tie, 21-21 (B)
1976 — Lions, 27-14 (D)
1979 — Bills, 20-17 (D)
1991 — Lions, 17-14 (B) OT
(RS Pts. — Lions 82, Bills 69)

BUFFALO vs. GREEN BAY
RS: Bills lead series, 4-1
1974 — Bills, 27-7 (GB)
1979 — Bills, 19-12 (B)
1982 — Packers, 33-21 (Mil)
1988 — Bills, 28-0 (B)
1991 — Bills, 34-24 (Mil)
(RS Pts. — Bills 129, Packers 76)

BUFFALO vs. HOUSTON
RS: Oilers lead series, 20-11
PS: Bills lead series, 2-0
1960 — Bills, 25-24 (B)
Oilers, 31-23 (H)
1961 — Bills, 22-12 (H)
Oilers, 28-16 (B)
1962 — Oilers, 28-23 (B)
Oilers, 17-14 (H)
1963 — Oilers, 31-20 (B)
Oilers, 28-14 (H)
1964 — Bills, 48-17 (H)
Bills, 24-10 (B)
1965 — Oilers, 19-17 (B)
Bills, 29-18 (H)
1966 — Bills, 27-20 (B)
Bills, 42-20 (H)
1967 — Oilers, 20-3 (B)
Oilers, 10-3 (H)
1968 — Oilers, 30-7 (B)
Oilers, 35-6 (H)
1969 — Oilers, 17-3 (B)
Oilers, 28-14 (H)
1971 — Oilers, 20-14 (B)
1974 — Oilers, 21-9 (B)
1976 — Oilers, 13-3 (B)
1978 — Oilers, 17-10 (H)
1983 — Bills, 30-13 (B)
1985 — Bills, 20-0 (B)
1986 — Oilers, 16-7 (H)
1987 — Bills, 34-30 (B)
1988 — *Bills, 17-10 (B)
1989 — Bills, 47-41 (H) OT
1990 — Oilers, 27-24 (H)
1992 — Oilers, 27-3 (H)
**Bills, 41-38 (B) OT
(RS Pts. — Oilers 668, Bills 581)
(PS Pts. — Bills 58, Oilers 48)
**AFC Divisional Playoff*
***AFC First Round Game*

BUFFALO vs. *INDIANAPOLIS
RS: Bills lead series, 24-20-1
1970 — Tie, 17-17 (Balt)
Colts, 20-14 (Buff)
1971 — Colts, 43-0 (Buff)
Colts, 24-0 (Balt)
1972 — Colts, 17-0 (Buff)
Colts, 35-7 (Balt)
1973 — Bills, 31-13 (Buff)
Bills, 24-17 (Balt)
1974 — Bills, 27-14 (Balt)
Bills, 6-0 (Buff)
1975 — Bills, 38-31 (Balt)
Colts, 42-35 (Buff)
1976 — Colts, 31-13 (Buff)
Colts, 58-20 (Balt)
1977 — Colts, 17-14 (Balt)
Colts, 31-13 (Buff)
1978 — Bills, 24-17 (Buff)
Bills, 21-14 (Balt)
1979 — Bills, 31-13 (Balt)
Colts, 14-13 (Buff)
1980 — Colts, 17-12 (Buff)
Colts, 28-24 (Balt)
1981 — Bills, 35-3 (Balt)
Bills, 23-17 (Buff)
1982 — Bills, 20-0 (Buff)
1983 — Bills, 28-23 (Buff)
Bills, 30-7 (Balt)
1984 — Colts, 31-17 (I)
Bills, 21-15 (Buff)
1985 — Colts, 49-17 (I)
Bills, 21-9 (Buff)
1986 — Bills, 24-13 (Buff)
Colts, 24-14 (I)
1987 — Colts, 47-6 (Buff)
Bills, 27-3 (I)
1988 — Bills, 34-23 (Buff)
Colts, 17-14 (I)
1989 — Colts, 37-14 (I)
Bills, 30-7 (Buff)
1990 — Bills, 26-10 (Buff)
Bills, 31-7 (I)
1991 — Bills, 42-6 (Buff)
Bills, 35-7 (I)
1992 — Bills, 38-0 (Buff)
Colts, 16-13 (I) OT
(RS Pts. — Bills 944, Colts 884)
**Franchise in Baltimore prior to 1984*

BUFFALO vs. *KANSAS CITY
RS: Bills lead series, 15-12-1
PS: Series tied, 1-1
1960 — Texans, 45-28 (B)
Texans, 24-7 (D)
1961 — Bills, 27-24 (B)
Bills, 30-20 (D)
1962 — Texans, 41-21 (D)
Bills, 23-14 (B)
1963 — Tie, 27-27 (B)
Bills, 35-26 (KC)
1964 — Bills, 34-17 (B)
Bills, 35-22 (KC)
1965 — Bills, 23-7 (KC)
Bills, 34-25 (B)
1966 — Chiefs, 42-20 (B)
Bills, 29-14 (KC)
**Chiefs, 31-7 (B)
1967 — Chiefs, 23-13 (KC)
1968 — Chiefs, 18-7 (B)
1969 — Chiefs, 29-7 (B)
Chiefs, 22-19 (KC)
1971 — Chiefs, 22-9 (KC)
1973 — Bills, 23-14 (B)
1976 — Bills, 50-17 (B)
1978 — Bills, 28-13 (B)
Chiefs, 14-10 (KC)
1982 — Bills, 14-9 (B)
1983 — Bills, 14-9 (KC)
1986 — Chiefs, 20-17 (B)
Bills, 17-14 (KC)
1991 — Chiefs, 33-6 (KC)
***Bills, 37-14 (B)
(RS Pts. — Chiefs 610, Bills 602)
(PS Pts. — Chiefs 45, Bills 44)
**Franchise in Dallas prior to 1963 and known as Texans*
***AFL Championship*
****AFC Divisional Playoff*

BUFFALO vs. *L.A. RAIDERS
RS: Series tied, 14-14
PS: Bills lead series, 1-0
1960 — Bills, 38-9 (B)
Raiders, 20-7 (O)
1961 — Raiders, 31-22 (B)
Bills, 26-21 (O)
1962 — Bills, 14-6 (B)
Bills, 10-6 (O)
1963 — Raiders, 35-17 (O)
Bills, 12-0 (B)
1964 — Bills, 23-20 (B)
Raiders, 16-13 (O)
1965 — Bills, 17-12 (B)
Bills, 17-14 (O)
1966 — Bills, 31-10 (O)
1967 — Raiders, 24-20 (B)
Raiders, 28-21 (O)
1968 — Raiders, 48-6 (B)
Raiders, 13-10 (O)
1969 — Raiders, 50-21 (O)
1972 — Raiders, 28-16 (O)
1974 — Bills, 21-20 (B)
1977 — Raiders, 34-13 (O)
1980 — Bills, 24-7 (B)
1983 — Raiders, 27-24 (B)
1987 — Raiders, 34-21 (LA)
1988 — Bills, 37-21 (B)
1990 — Bills, 38-24 (B)
**Bills, 51-3 (B)
1991 — Bills, 30-27 (LA) OT
1992 — Raiders, 20-3 (LA)
(RS Pts. — Raiders 605, Bills 552)
(PS Pts. — Bills 51, Raiders 3)
**Franchise in Oakland prior to 1982*
***AFC Championship*

BUFFALO vs. L.A. RAMS
RS: Series tied, 3-3
1970 — Rams, 19-0 (B)
1974 — Rams, 19-14 (LA)
1980 — Bills, 10-7 (B) OT
1983 — Rams, 41-17 (LA)
1989 — Bills, 23-20 (B)
1992 — Bills, 40-7 (B)
(RS Pts. — Rams 113, Bills 104)

BUFFALO vs. MIAMI
RS: Dolphins lead series, 36-17-1
PS: Bills lead series, 2-0
1966 — Bills, 58-24 (B)
Bills, 29-0 (M)
1967 — Bills, 35-13 (B)
Dolphins, 17-14 (M)
1968 — Tie, 14-14 (M)
Dolphins, 21-17 (B)
1969 — Dolphins, 24-6 (M)
Bills, 28-3 (B)
1970 — Dolphins, 33-14 (B)
Dolphins, 45-7 (M)
1971 — Dolphins, 29-14 (B)

Dolphins, 34-0 (M)
1972 — Dolphins, 24-23 (M)
Dolphins, 30-16 (B)
1973 — Dolphins, 27-6 (M)
Dolphins, 17-0 (B)
1974 — Dolphins, 24-16 (B)
Dolphins, 35-28 (M)
1975 — Dolphins, 35-30 (B)
Dolphins, 31-21 (M)
1976 — Dolphins, 30-21 (B)
Dolphins, 45-27 (M)
1977 — Dolphins, 13-0 (B)
Dolphins, 31-14 (M)
1978 — Dolphins, 31-24 (M)
Dolphins, 25-24 (B)
1979 — Dolphins, 9-7 (B)
Dolphins, 17-7 (M)
1980 — Bills, 17-7 (B)
Dolphins, 17-14 (M)
1981 — Bills, 31-21 (B)
Dolphins, 16-6 (M)
1982 — Dolphins, 9-7 (B)
Dolphins, 27-10 (M)
1983 — Dolphins, 12-0 (B)
Bills, 38-35 (M) OT
1984 — Dolphins, 21-17 (B)
Dolphins, 38-7 (M)
1985 — Dolphins, 23-14 (B)
Dolphins, 28-0 (M)
1986 — Dolphins, 27-14 (M)
Dolphins, 34-24 (B)
1987 — Bills, 34-31 (M) OT
Bills, 27-0 (B)
1988 — Bills, 9-6 (B)
Bills, 31-6 (M)
1989 — Bills, 27-24 (M)
Bills, 31-17 (B)
1990 — Dolphins, 30-7 (M)
Bills, 24-14 (B)
*Bills, 44-34 (B)
1991 — Bills, 35-31 (B)
Bills, 41-27 (M)
1992 — Dolphins, 37-10 (B)
Bills, 26-20 (M)
**Bills, 29-10 (M)
(RS Pts. — Dolphins 1,239, Bills 1,001)
(PS Pts. — Bills 73, Dolphins 44)
AFC Divisional Playoff
***AFC Championship*

BUFFALO vs. MINNESOTA
RS: Vikings lead series, 4-2
1971 — Vikings, 19-0 (M)
1975 — Vikings, 35-13 (B)
1979 — Vikings, 10-3 (M)
1982 — Bills, 23-22 (B)
1985 — Vikings, 27-20 (B)
1988 — Bills, 13-10 (B)
(RS Pts. — Vikings 123, Bills 72)

BUFFALO vs. *NEW ENGLAND
RS: Patriots lead series, 33-31-1
PS: Patriots lead series, 1-0
1960 — Bills, 13-0 (Bos)
Bills, 38-14 (Buff)
1961 — Patriots, 23-21 (Buff)
Patriots, 52-21 (Bos)
1962 — Tie, 28-28 (Buff)
Patriots, 21-10 (Bos)
1963 — Bills, 28-21 (Buff)
Patriots, 17-7 (Bos)
**Patriots, 26-8 (Buff)
1964 — Patriots, 36-28 (Buff)
Bills, 24-14 (Bos)
1965 — Bills, 24-7 (Buff)
Bills, 23-7 (Bos)
1966 — Patriots, 20-10 (Buff)
Patriots, 14-3 (Bos)
1967 — Patriots, 23-0 (Buff)
Bills, 44-16 (Bos)
1968 — Patriots, 16-7 (Buff)
Patriots, 23-6 (Bos)
1969 — Bills, 23-16 (Buff)
Patriots, 35-21 (Bos)
1970 — Bills, 45-10 (Bos)
Patriots, 14-10 (Buff)
1971 — Patriots, 38-33 (NE)
Bills, 27-20 (Buff)
1972 — Bills, 38-14 (Buff)
Bills, 27-24 (NE)
1973 — Bills, 31-13 (NE)
Bills, 37-13 (Buff)
1974 — Bills, 30-28 (Buff)
Bills, 29-28 (NE)
1975 — Bills, 45-31 (Buff)
Bills, 34-14 (NE)
1976 — Patriots, 26-22 (Buff)
Patriots, 20-10 (NE)
1977 — Bills, 24-14 (NE)
Patriots, 20-7 (Buff)
1978 — Patriots, 14-10 (Buff)
Patriots, 26-24 (NE)
1979 — Patriots, 26-6 (Buff)
Bills, 16-13 (NE) OT
1980 — Bills, 31-13 (Buff)
Patriots, 24-2 (NE)
1981 — Bills, 20-17 (Buff)
Bills, 19-10 (NE)
1982 — Patriots, 30-19 (NE)
1983 — Patriots, 31-0 (Buff)
Patriots, 21-7 (NE)
1984 — Patriots, 21-17 (Buff)
Patriots, 38-10 (NE)
1985 — Patriots, 17-14 (Buff)
Patriots, 14-3 (NE)
1986 — Patriots, 23-3 (Buff)
Patriots, 22-19 (NE)
1987 — Patriots, 14-7 (NE)
Patriots, 13-7 (Buff)
1988 — Bills, 16-14 (NE)
Bills, 23-20 (Buff)
1989 — Bills, 31-10 (Buff)
Patriots, 33-24 (NE)
1990 — Bills, 27-10 (NE)
Bills, 14-0 (Buff)
1991 — Bills, 22-17 (Buff)
Patriots, 16-13 (NE)
1992 — Bills, 41-7 (NE)
Bills, 16-7 (Buff)
(RS Pts. — Bills 1,289, Patriots 1,251)
(PS Pts. — Patriots 26, Bills 8)
**Franchise in Boston prior to 1971*
***Division Playoff*

BUFFALO vs. NEW ORLEANS
RS: Bills lead series, 3-2
1973 — Saints, 13-0 (NO)
1980 — Bills, 35-26 (NO)
1983 — Bills, 27-21 (B)
1989 — Saints, 22-19 (B)
1992 — Bills, 20-16 (NO)
(RS Pts. — Bills 101, Saints 98)

BUFFALO vs. N.Y. GIANTS
RS: Bills lead series, 3-2
PS: Giants lead series, 1-0
1970 — Giants, 20-6 (NY)
1975 — Giants, 17-14 (B)
1978 — Bills, 41-17 (B)
1987 — Bills, 6-3 (B) OT
1990 — Bills, 17-13 (NY)
*Giants, 20-19 (Tampa)
(RS Pts. — Bills 84, Giants 70)
(PS Pts. — Giants 20, Bills 19)
**Super Bowl XXV*

BUFFALO vs. *N.Y. JETS
RS: Bills lead series, 35-29
PS: Bills lead series, 1-0
1960 — Titans, 27-3 (NY)
Titans, 17-13 (B)
1961 — Bills, 41-31 (B)
Titans, 21-14 (NY)
1962 — Titans, 17-6 (B)
Bills, 20-3 (NY)
1963 — Bills, 45-14 (B)
Bills, 19-10 (NY)
1964 — Bills, 34-24 (B)
Bills, 20-7 (NY)
1965 — Bills, 33-21 (B)
Jets, 14-12 (NY)
1966 — Bills, 33-23 (NY)
Bills, 14-3 (B)
1967 — Bills, 20-17 (B)
Jets, 20-10 (NY)
1968 — Bills, 37-35 (B)
Jets, 25-21 (NY)
1969 — Jets, 33-19 (B)
Jets, 16-6 (NY)
1970 — Bills, 34-31 (B)
Bills, 10-6 (NY)
1971 — Jets, 28-17 (NY)
Jets, 20-7 (B)
1972 — Jets, 41-24 (B)
Jets, 41-3 (NY)
1973 — Bills, 9-7 (B)
Bills, 34-14 (NY)
1974 — Bills, 16-12 (B)
Jets, 20-10 (NY)
1975 — Bills, 42-14 (B)
Bills, 24-23 (NY)
1976 — Jets, 17-14 (NY)
Jets, 19-14 (B)
1977 — Jets, 24-19 (B)
Bills, 14-10 (NY)
1978 — Jets, 21-20 (B)
Jets, 45-14 (NY)
1979 — Bills, 46-31 (B)
Bills, 14-12 (NY)
1980 — Bills, 20-10 (B)
Bills, 31-24 (NY)
1981 — Bills, 31-0 (B)
Jets, 33-14 (NY)
**Bills, 31-27 (NY)
1983 — Jets, 34-10 (B)
Bills, 24-17 (NY)
1984 — Jets, 28-26 (B)
Jets, 21-17 (NY)
1985 — Jets, 42-3 (NY)
Jets, 27-7 (B)
1986 — Jets, 28-24 (B)
Jets, 14-13 (NY)
1987 — Jets, 31-28 (B)
Bills, 17-14 (NY)
1988 — Bills, 37-14 (NY)
Bills, 9-6 (B) OT
1989 — Bills, 34-3 (B)
Bills, 37-0 (NY)
1990 — Bills, 30-7 (NY)
Bills, 30-27 (B)
1991 — Bills, 23-20 (NY)
Bills, 24-13 (B)
1992 — Bills, 24-20 (NY)
Jets, 24-17 (B)
(RS Pts. — Bills, 1,335, Jets 1,271)
(PS Pts. — Bills 31, Jets 27)
**Jets known as Titans prior to 1963*
***AFC First Round Playoff*

BUFFALO vs. PHILADELPHIA
RS: Eagles lead series, 4-2
1973 — Bills, 27-26 (B)
1981 — Eagles, 20-14 (B)
1984 — Eagles, 27-17 (B)
1985 — Eagles, 21-17 (P)
1987 — Eagles, 17-7 (P)
1990 — Bills, 30-23 (B)
(RS Pts. — Eagles 134, Bills 112)

BUFFALO vs. *PHOENIX
RS: Series tied, 3-3
1971 — Cardinals, 28-23 (B)
1975 — Bills, 32-14 (StL)
1981 — Cardinals, 24-0 (StL)
1984 — Cardinals, 37-7 (StL)
1986 — Bills, 17-10 (B)
1990 — Bills, 45-14 (B)
(RS Pts. — Cardinals 127, Bills 124)
**Franchise in St. Louis prior to 1988*

BUFFALO vs. PITTSBURGH
RS: Bills lead series, 7-5
PS: Series tied, 1-1
1970 — Steelers, 23-10 (P)
1972 — Steelers, 38-21 (B)
1974 — *Steelers, 32-14 (P)
1975 — Bills, 30-21 (P)
1978 — Steelers, 28-17 (B)
1979 — Steelers, 28-0 (P)
1980 — Bills, 28-13 (B)
1982 — Bills, 13-0 (B)
1985 — Steelers, 30-24 (P)
1986 — Bills, 16-12 (B)
1988 — Bills, 36-28 (B)
1991 — Bills, 52-34 (B)
1992 — Bills, 28-20 (B)
*Bills, 24-3 (P)
(RS Pts. — Bills 275, Steelers 275)
(PS Pts. — Bills 38, Steelers 35)
**AFC Divisional Playoff*

BUFFALO vs. *SAN DIEGO
RS: Chargers lead series, 16-7-2
PS: Bills lead series, 2-1
1960 — Chargers, 24-10 (B)
Bills, 32-3 (LA)
1961 — Chargers, 19-11 (B)
Chargers, 28-10 (SD)
1962 — Bills, 35-10 (B)
Bills, 40-20 (SD)
1963 — Chargers, 14-10 (SD)
Chargers, 23-13 (B)
1964 — Bills, 30-3 (B)
Bills, 27-24 (SD)
**Bills, 20-7 (B)
1965 — Chargers, 34-3 (B)
Tie, 20-20 (SD)
**Bills, 23-0 (SD)
1966 — Chargers, 27-7 (SD)
Tie, 17-17 (B)
1967 — Chargers, 37-17 (B)
1968 — Chargers, 21-6 (B)
1969 — Chargers, 45-6 (SD)
1971 — Chargers, 20-3 (SD)
1973 — Chargers, 34-7 (SD)
1976 — Chargers, 34-13 (B)
1979 — Chargers, 27-19 (SD)
1980 — Bills, 26-24 (SD)
***Chargers, 20-14 (SD)
1981 — Bills, 28-27 (SD)
1985 — Chargers, 14-9 (B)
Chargers, 40-7 (SD)
(RS Pts. — Chargers 589, Bills 406)
(PS Pts. — Bills 57, Chargers 27)
**Franchise in Los Angeles prior to 1961*
***AFL Championship*
****AFC Divisional Playoff*

BUFFALO vs. SAN FRANCISCO
RS: Bills lead series 3-2
1972 — Bills, 27-20 (B)
1980 — Bills, 18-13 (SF)
1983 — 49ers, 23-10 (B)
1989 — 49ers, 21-10 (SF)
1992 — Bills, 34-31 (SF)
(RS Pts. — 49ers 108, Bills 99)

BUFFALO vs. SEATTLE
RS: Seahawks lead series, 3-1
1977 — Seahawks, 56-17 (S)
1984 — Seahawks, 31-28 (S)
1988 — Bills, 13-3 (S)
1989 — Seahawks, 17-16 (S)
(RS Pts. — Seahawks 107, Bills 74)

BUFFALO vs. TAMPA BAY
RS: Buccaneers lead series, 4-2
1976 — Bills, 14-9 (TB)
1978 — Buccaneers, 31-10 (TB)
1982 — Buccaneers, 24-23 (TB)
1986 — Buccaneers, 34-28 (TB)
1988 — Buccaneers, 10-5 (TB)
1991 — Bills, 17-10 (TB)
(RS Pts. — Buccaneers 118, Bills 97)

BUFFALO vs. WASHINGTON
RS: Redskins lead series, 4-2
PS: Redskins lead series, 1-0
1972 — Bills, 24-17 (W)
1977 — Redskins, 10-0 (B)
1981 — Bills, 21-14 (B)
1984 — Redskins, 41-14 (W)
1987 — Redskins, 27-7 (B)
1990 — Redskins, 29-14 (W)
1991 — *Redskins, 37-24 (Minneapolis)
(RS Pts. — Redskins 138, Bills 80)
(PS Pts. — Redskins 37, Bills 24)
*Super Bowl XXVI

CHICAGO vs. ATLANTA
RS: Falcons lead series, 9-8;
See Atlanta vs. Chicago

CHICAGO vs. BUFFALO
RS: Bears lead series, 3-2;
See Buffalo vs. Chicago

CHICAGO vs. CINCINNATI
RS: Bengals lead series, 3-2
1972 — Bengals, 13-3 (Chi)
1980 — Bengals, 17-14 (Chi) OT
1986 — Bears, 44-7 (Cin)
1989 — Bears, 17-14 (Chi)
1992 — Bengals, 31-28 (Chi) OT
(RS Pts. — Bears 106, Bengals 82)

CHICAGO vs. CLEVELAND
RS: Browns lead series, 8-3
1951 — Browns, 42-21 (Cle)
1954 — Browns, 39-10 (Chi)
1960 — Browns, 42-0 (Cle)
1961 — Bears, 17-14 (Chi)
1967 — Browns, 24-0 (Cle)
1969 — Browns, 28-24 (Chi)
1972 — Bears, 17-0 (Cle)
1980 — Browns, 27-21 (Cle)
1986 — Bears, 41-31 (Chi)
1989 — Browns, 27-7 (Cle)
1992 — Browns, 27-14 (Cle)
(RS Pts. — Browns 301, Bears 172)

CHICAGO vs. DALLAS
RS: Cowboys lead series, 8-6
PS: Cowboys lead series, 2-0
1960 — Bears, 17-7 (C)
1962 — Bears, 34-33 (D)
1964 — Cowboys, 24-10 (C)
1968 — Cowboys, 34-3 (C)
1971 — Bears, 23-19 (C)
1973 — Cowboys, 20-17 (C)
1976 — Cowboys, 31-21 (D)
1977 — *Cowboys, 37-7 (D)
1979 — Cowboys, 24-20 (D)
1981 — Cowboys, 10-9 (D)
1984 — Cowboys, 23-14 (C)
1985 — Bears, 44-0 (D)
1986 — Bears, 24-10 (D)
1988 — Bears, 17-7 (C)
1991 — **Cowboys, 17-13 (C)
1992 — Cowboys, 27-14 (D)
(RS Pts. — Cowboys 269, Bears 267)
(PS Pts. — Cowboys 54, Bears 20)
**NFC Divisional Playoff*
***NFC First Round Playoff*

CHICAGO vs. DENVER
RS: Bears lead series, 5-4
1971 — Broncos, 6-3 (D)
1973 — Bears, 33-14 (D)
1976 — Broncos, 28-14 (C)
1978 — Broncos, 16-7 (D)
1981 — Bears, 35-24 (C)
1983 — Bears, 31-14 (C)
1984 — Bears, 27-0 (C)
1987 — Broncos, 31-29 (D)
1990 — Bears, 16-13 (D) OT
(RS Pts. — Bears 195, Broncos 146)

CHICAGO vs. *DETROIT
RS: Bears lead series, 73-48-5
1930 — Spartans, 7-6 (P)
Bears, 14-6 (C)
1931 — Bears, 9-6 (C)
Spartans, 3-0 (P)
1932 — Tie, 13-13 (C)
Tie, 7-7 (P)
Bears, 9-0 (C)
1933 — Bears, 17-14 (C)
Bears, 17-7 (P)
1934 — Bears, 19-16 (D)
Bears, 10-7 (C)

1935 — Tie, 20-20 (C)
Lions, 14-2 (D)
1936 — Bears, 12-10 (C)
Lions, 13-7 (D)
1937 — Bears, 28-20 (C)
Bears, 13-0 (D)
1938 — Lions, 13-7 (C)
Lions, 14-7 (D)
1939 — Lions, 10-0 (C)
Bears, 23-13 (D)
1940 — Bears, 7-0 (C)
Lions, 17-14 (D)
1941 — Bears, 49-0 (C)
Bears, 24-7 (D)
1942 — Bears, 16-0 (C)
Bears, 42-0 (D)
1943 — Bears, 27-21 (D)
Bears, 35-14 (C)
1944 — Tie, 21-21 (C)
Lions, 41-21 (D)
1945 — Lions, 16-10 (D)
Lions, 35-28 (C)
1946 — Bears, 42-6 (C)
Bears, 45-24 (D)
1947 — Bears, 33-24 (C)
Bears, 34-14 (D)
1948 — Bears, 28-0 (C)
Bears, 42-14 (D)
1949 — Bears, 27-24 (C)
Bears, 28-7 (D)
1950 — Bears, 35-21 (D)
Bears, 6-3 (C)
1951 — Bears, 28-23 (D)
Lions, 41-28 (C)
1952 — Bears, 24-23 (C)
Lions, 45-21 (D)
1953 — Lions, 20-16 (C)
Lions, 13-7 (D)
1954 — Lions, 48-23 (D)
Bears, 28-24 (C)
1955 — Bears, 24-14 (D)
Bears, 21-20 (C)
1956 — Lions, 42-10 (D)
Bears, 38-21 (C)
1957 — Bears, 27-7 (D)
Lions, 21-13 (C)
1958 — Bears, 20-7 (D)
Bears, 21-16 (C)
1959 — Bears, 24-14 (D)
Bears, 25-14 (C)
1960 — Bears, 28-7 (C)
Lions, 36-0 (D)
1961 — Bears, 31-17 (D)
Lions, 16-15 (C)
1962 — Lions, 11-3 (D)
Bears, 3-0 (C)
1963 — Bears, 37-21 (D)
Bears, 24-14 (C)
1964 — Lions, 10-0 (C)
Bears, 27-24 (D)
1965 — Bears, 38-10 (C)
Bears, 17-10 (D)
1966 — Lions, 14-3 (D)
Tie, 10-10 (C)
1967 — Bears, 14-3 (C)
Bears, 27-13 (D)
1968 — Lions, 42-0 (D)
Lions, 28-10 (C)
1969 — Lions, 13-7 (D)
Lions, 20-3 (C)
1970 — Lions, 28-14 (D)
Lions, 16-10 (C)
1971 — Bears, 28-23 (D)
Lions, 28-3 (C)
1972 — Lions, 38-24 (C)
Lions, 14-0 (D)
1973 — Lions, 30-7 (C)
Lions, 40-7 (D)
1974 — Bears, 17-9 (C)
Lions, 34-17 (D)
1975 — Lions, 27-7 (D)
Bears, 25-21 (C)
1976 — Bears, 10-3 (C)
Lions, 14-10 (D)
1977 — Bears, 30-20 (C)
Bears, 31-14 (D)
1978 — Bears, 19-0 (D)
Lions, 21-17 (C)
1979 — Bears, 35-7 (C)
Lions, 20-0 (D)
1980 — Bears, 24-7 (C)
Bears, 23-17 (D) OT
1981 — Lions, 48-17 (D)
Lions, 23-7 (C)
1982 — Lions, 17-10 (D)
Bears, 20-17 (C)
1983 — Lions, 31-17 (D)
Lions, 38-17 (C)
1984 — Bears, 16-14 (C)
Bears, 30-13 (D)
1985 — Bears, 24-3 (C)
Bears, 37-17 (D)
1986 — Bears, 13-7 (C)
Bears, 16-13 (D)
1987 — Bears, 30-10 (C)
1988 — Bears, 24-7 (D)
Bears, 13-12 (C)
1989 — Bears, 47-27 (D)
Lions, 27-17 (C)
1990 — Bears, 23-17 (C) OT
Lions, 38-21 (D)
1991 — Bears, 20-10 (C)
Lions, 16-6 (D)
1992 — Bears, 27-24 (C)
Lions, 16-3 (D)
(RS Pts. — Bears 2,362, Lions 2,130)
**Franchise in Portsmouth prior to 1934 and known as the Spartans*

***CHICAGO vs. GREEN BAY**
RS: Bears lead series, 80-58-6
PS: Bears lead series, 1-0
1921 — Staleys, 20-0 (C)
1923 — Bears, 3-0 (GB)
1924 — Bears, 3-0 (C)
1925 — Packers, 14-10 (GB)
Bears, 21-0 (C)
1926 — Tie, 6-6 (GB)
Bears, 19-13 (C)
Tie, 3-3 (C)
1927 — Bears, 7-6 (GB)
Bears, 14-6 (C)
1928 — Tie, 12-12 (GB)
Packers, 16-6 (C)
Packers, 6-0 (C)
1929 — Packers, 23-0 (GB)
Packers, 14-0 (C)
Packers, 25-0 (C)
1930 — Packers, 7-0 (GB)
Packers, 13-12 (C)
Bears, 21-0 (C)
1931 — Packers, 7-0 (GB)
Packers, 6-2 (C)
Bears, 7-6 (C)
1932 — Tie, 0-0 (GB)
Packers, 2-0 (C)
Bears, 9-0 (C)
1933 — Bears, 14-7 (GB)
Bears, 10-7 (C)
Bears, 7-6 (C)
1934 — Bears, 24-10 (GB)
Bears, 27-14 (C)
1935 — Packers, 7-0 (GB)
Packers, 17-14 (C)
1936 — Bears, 30-3 (GB)
Packers, 21-10 (C)
1937 — Bears, 14-2 (GB)
Packers, 24-14 (C)
1938 — Bears, 2-0 (GB)
Packers, 24-17 (C)
1939 — Packers, 21-16 (GB)
Bears, 30-27 (C)
1940 — Bears, 41-10 (GB)
Bears, 14-7 (C)
1941 — Bears, 25-17 (GB)
Packers, 16-14 (C)
**Bears, 33-14 (C)
1942 — Bears, 44-28 (GB)
Bears, 38-7 (C)
1943 — Tie, 21-21 (GB)
Bears, 21-7 (C)
1944 — Packers, 42-28 (GB)
Bears, 21-0 (C)
1945 — Packers, 31-21 (GB)
Bears, 28-24 (C)
1946 — Bears, 30-7 (GB)
Bears, 10-7 (C)
1947 — Packers, 29-20 (GB)
Bears, 20-17 (C)
1948 — Bears, 45-7 (GB)
Bears, 7-6 (C)
1949 — Bears, 17-0 (GB)
Bears, 24-3 (C)
1950 — Packers, 31-21 (GB)
Bears, 28-14 (C)
1951 — Bears, 31-20 (GB)
Bears, 24-13 (C)
1952 — Bears, 24-14 (GB)
Packers, 41-28 (C)
1953 — Bears, 17-13 (GB)
Tie, 21-21 (C)
1954 — Bears, 10-3 (GB)
Bears, 28-23 (C)
1955 — Packers, 24-3 (GB)
Bears, 52-31 (C)
1956 — Bears, 37-21 (GB)
Bears, 38-14 (C)
1957 — Packers, 21-17 (GB)
Bears, 21-14 (C)
1958 — Bears, 34-20 (GB)
Bears, 24-10 (C)
1959 — Packers, 9-6 (GB)
Bears, 28-17 (C)
1960 — Bears, 17-14 (GB)
Packers, 41-13 (C)
1961 — Packers, 24-0 (GB)
Packers, 31-28 (C)
1962 — Packers, 49-0 (GB)
Packers, 38-7 (C)
1963 — Bears, 10-3 (GB)
Bears, 26-7 (C)
1964 — Packers, 23-12 (GB)
Packers, 17-3 (C)
1965 — Packers, 23-14 (GB)
Bears, 31-10 (C)
1966 — Packers, 17-0 (C)
Packers, 13-6 (GB)
1967 — Packers, 13-10 (GB)
Packers, 17-13 (C)
1968 — Bears, 13-10 (GB)
Packers, 28-27 (C)
1969 — Packers, 17-0 (GB)
Packers, 21-3 (C)
1970 — Packers, 20-19 (GB)
Bears, 35-17 (C)
1971 — Packers, 17-14 (C)
Packers, 31-10 (GB)
1972 — Packers, 20-17 (GB)
Packers, 23-17 (C)
1973 — Bears, 31-17 (GB)
Packers, 21-0 (C)
1974 — Bears, 10-9 (C)
Packers, 20-3 (Mil)
1975 — Bears, 27-14 (C)
Packers, 28-7 (GB)
1976 — Bears, 24-13 (C)
Bears, 16-10 (GB)
1977 — Bears, 26-0 (GB)
Bears, 21-10 (C)
1978 — Packers, 24-14 (GB)
Bears, 14-0 (C)
1979 — Bears, 6-3 (C)
Bears, 15-14 (GB)
1980 — Packers, 12-6 (GB) OT
Bears, 61-7 (C)
1981 — Packers, 16-9 (C)
Packers, 21-17 (GB)
1983 — Packers, 31-28 (GB)
Bears, 23-21 (C)
1984 — Bears, 9-7 (GB)
Packers, 20-14 (C)
1985 — Bears, 23-7 (C)
Bears, 16-10 (GB)
1986 — Bears, 25-12 (GB)
Bears, 12-10 (C)
1987 — Bears, 26-24 (GB)
Bears, 23-10 (C)
1988 — Bears, 24-6 (GB)
Bears, 16-0 (C)
1989 — Packers, 14-13 (GB)
Packers, 40-28 (C)
1990 — Bears, 31-13 (GB)
Bears, 27-13 (C)
1991 — Bears, 10-0 (GB)
Bears, 27-13 (C)
1992 — Bears, 30-10 (GB)
Packers, 17-3 (C)
(RS Pts. — Bears 2,445, Packers 2,096)
(PS Pts. — Bears 33, Packers 14)
**Bears known as Staleys prior to 1922*
***Division Playoff*

CHICAGO vs. HOUSTON
RS: Oilers lead series, 4-2
1973 — Bears, 35-14 (C)
1977 — Oilers, 47-0 (H)
1980 — Oilers, 10-6 (C)
1986 — Bears, 20-7 (H)
1989 — Oilers, 33-28 (C)
1992 — Oilers, 24-7 (H)
(RS Pts. — Oilers 135, Bears 96)

CHICAGO vs. *INDIANAPOLIS
RS: Colts lead series, 21-16
1953 — Colts, 13-9 (B)
Colts, 16-14 (C)
1954 — Bears, 28-9 (C)
Bears, 28-13 (B)
1955 — Colts, 23-17 (B)
Bears, 38-10 (C)
1956 — Colts, 28-21 (B)
Bears, 58-27 (C)
1957 — Colts, 21-10 (B)
Colts, 29-14 (C)
1958 — Colts, 51-38 (B)
Colts, 17-0 (C)
1959 — Bears, 26-21 (B)
Colts, 21-7 (C)
1960 — Colts, 42-7 (B)
Colts, 24-20 (C)
1961 — Bears, 24-10 (C)
Bears, 21-20 (B)
1962 — Bears, 35-15 (C)
Bears, 57-0 (B)
1963 — Bears, 10-3 (C)
Bears, 17-7 (B)
1964 — Colts, 52-0 (B)
Colts, 40-24 (C)
1965 — Colts, 26-21 (C)
Bears, 13-0 (B)
1966 — Bears, 27-17 (C)
Colts, 21-16 (B)
1967 — Colts, 24-3 (C)
1968 — Colts, 28-7 (B)
1969 — Colts, 24-21 (C)
1970 — Colts, 21-20 (B)
1975 — Colts, 35-7 (C)
1983 — Colts, 22-19 (B) OT
1985 — Bears, 17-10 (C)
1988 — Bears, 17-13 (I)
1991 — Bears, 31-17 (I)
(RS Pts. — Colts 770, Bears 742)
**Franchise in Baltimore prior to 1984*

CHICAGO vs. KANSAS CITY
RS: Bears lead series, 3-2
1973 — Chiefs, 19-7 (KC)
1977 — Bears, 28-27 (C)
1981 — Bears, 16-13 (KC) OT
1987 — Bears, 31-28 (C)
1990 — Chiefs, 21-10 (C)
(RS Pts. — Chiefs 108, Bears 92)

CHICAGO vs. *L.A. RAIDERS
RS: Raiders lead series, 4-3
1972 — Raiders, 28-21 (O)
1976 — Raiders, 28-27 (C)
1978 — Raiders, 25-19 (C) OT
1981 — Bears, 23-6 (O)
1984 — Bears, 17-6 (C)
1987 — Bears, 6-3 (LA)
1990 — Raiders, 24-10 (LA)
(RS Pts. — Bears 123, Raiders 120)
**Franchise in Oakland prior to 1982*

CHICAGO vs. *L.A. RAMS
RS: Bears lead series, 44-28-3
PS: Series tied, 1-1
1937 — Bears, 20-2 (Clev)
Bears, 15-7 (C)
1938 — Rams, 14-7 (C)
Rams, 23-21 (Clev)
1939 — Bears, 30-21 (Clev)
Bears, 35-21 (C)
1940 — Bears, 21-14 (Clev)
Bears, 47-25 (C)
1941 — Bears, 48-21 (Clev)
Bears, 31-13 (C)
1942 — Bears, 21-7 (Clev)
Bears, 47-0 (C)
1944 — Rams, 19-7 (Clev)
Bears, 28-21 (C)
1945 — Rams, 17-0 (Clev)
Rams, 41-21 (C)
1946 — Tie, 28-28 (C)
Bears, 27-21 (LA)
1947 — Bears, 41-21 (LA)
Rams, 17-14 (C)
1948 — Bears, 42-21 (C)
Bears, 21-6 (LA)
1949 — Rams, 31-16 (C)
Rams, 27-24 (LA)
1950 — Bears, 24-20 (LA)
Bears, 24-14 (C)
**Rams, 24-14 (LA)
1951 — Rams, 42-17 (C)
1952 — Rams, 31-7 (LA)
Rams, 40-24 (C)
1953 — Rams, 38-24 (LA)
Bears, 24-21 (C)
1954 — Rams, 42-38 (LA)
Bears, 24-13 (C)
1955 — Bears, 31-20 (LA)
Bears, 24-3 (C)
1956 — Bears, 35-24 (LA)
Bears, 30-21 (C)
1957 — Bears, 34-26 (C)
Bears, 16-10 (LA)
1958 — Bears, 31-10 (C)
Rams, 41-35 (LA)
1959 — Rams, 28-21 (C)
Bears, 26-21 (LA)
1960 — Bears, 34-27 (C)
Tie, 24-24 (LA)
1961 — Bears, 21-17 (LA)
Bears, 28-24 (C)
1962 — Bears, 27-23 (LA)
Bears, 30-14 (C)
1963 — Bears, 52-14 (LA)
Bears, 6-0 (C)
1964 — Bears, 38-17 (C)
Bears, 34-24 (LA)
1965 — Rams, 30-28 (LA)
Bears, 31-6 (C)
1966 — Rams, 31-17 (LA)
Bears, 17-10 (C)
1967 — Rams, 28-17 (C)
1968 — Bears, 17-16 (LA)
1969 — Rams, 9-7 (C)
1971 — Rams, 17-3 (LA)
1972 — Tie, 13-13 (C)
1973 — Rams, 26-0 (C)
1975 — Rams, 38-10 (LA)
1976 — Rams, 20-12 (LA)
1977 — Bears, 24-23 (C)
1979 — Bears, 27-23 (C)
1981 — Rams, 24-7 (C)
1982 — Bears, 34-26 (LA)

1983 — Rams, 21-14 (LA)
1984 — Rams, 29-13 (LA)
1985 — ***Bears, 24-0 (C)
1986 — Rams, 20-17 (C)
1988 — Rams, 23-3 (LA)
1989 — Bears, 20-10 (C)
1990 — Bears, 38-9 (C)
(RS Pts. — Bears 1,764, Rams 1,539)
(PS Pts. — Bears 38, Rams 24)
Franchise in Cleveland prior to 1946
***Conference Playoff*
****NFC Championship*

CHICAGO vs. MIAMI
RS: Dolphins lead series, 5-1
1971 — Dolphins, 34-3 (M)
1975 — Dolphins, 46-13 (C)
1979 — Dolphins, 31-16 (M)
1985 — Dolphins, 38-24 (M)
1988 — Bears, 34-7 (C)
1991 — Dolphins, 16-13 (C) OT
(RS Pts. — Dolphins 172, Bears 103)

CHICAGO vs. MINNESOTA
RS: Vikings lead series, 32-29-2
1961 — Vikings, 37-13 (M)
Bears, 52-35 (C)
1962 — Bears, 13-0 (M)
Bears, 31-30 (C)
1963 — Bears, 28-7 (M)
Tie, 17-17 (C)
1964 — Bears, 34-28 (M)
Vikings, 41-14 (C)
1965 — Bears, 45-37 (M)
Vikings, 24-17 (C)
1966 — Bears, 13-10 (M)
Bears, 41-28 (C)
1967 — Bears, 17-7 (M)
Tie, 10-10 (C)
1968 — Bears, 27-17 (M)
Bears, 26-24 (C)
1969 — Vikings, 31-0 (C)
Vikings, 31-14 (M)
1970 — Vikings, 24-0 (C)
Vikings, 16-13 (M)
1971 — Bears, 20-17 (M)
Vikings, 27-10 (C)
1972 — Bears, 13-10 (C)
Vikings, 23-10 (M)
1973 — Vikings, 22-13 (C)
Vikings, 31-13 (M)
1974 — Vikings, 11-7 (M)
Vikings, 17-0 (C)
1975 — Vikings, 28-3 (M)
Vikings, 13-9 (C)
1976 — Vikings, 20-19 (M)
Bears, 14-13 (C)
1977 — Vikings, 22-16 (M) OT
Bears, 10-7 (C)
1978 — Vikings, 24-20 (C)
Vikings, 17-14 (M)
1979 — Bears, 26-7 (C)
Vikings, 30-27 (M)
1980 — Vikings, 34-14 (C)
Vikings, 13-7 (M)
1981 — Vikings, 24-21 (M)
Bears, 10-9 (C)
1982 — Vikings, 35-7 (M)
1983 — Vikings, 23-14 (C)
Bears, 19-13 (M)
1984 — Bears, 16-7 (C)
Bears, 34-3 (M)
1985 — Bears, 33-24 (M)
Bears, 27-9 (C)
1986 — Bears, 23-0 (C)
Vikings, 23-7 (M)
1987 — Bears, 27-7 (C)
Bears, 30-24 (M)
1988 — Vikings, 31-7 (C)
Vikings, 28-27 (M)
1989 — Bears, 38-7 (C)
Vikings, 27-16 (M)
1990 — Bears, 19-16 (C)
Vikings, 41-13 (M)
1991 — Bears, 10-6 (C)
Bears, 34-17 (M)
1992 — Vikings, 21-20 (M)
Vikings, 38-10 (C)
(RS Pts. — Vikings 1,273, Bears 1,152)

CHICAGO vs. NEW ENGLAND
RS: Patriots lead series, 3-2
PS: Bears lead series, 1-0
1973 — Patriots, 13-10 (C)
1979 — Patriots, 27-7 (C)
1982 — Bears, 26-13 (C)
1985 — Bears, 20-7 (C)
*Bears, 46-10 (New Orleans)
1988 — Patriots, 30-7 (NE)
(RS Pts. — Patriots 100, Bears 70)
(PS Pts. — Bears 46, Patriots 10)
**Super Bowl XX*

CHICAGO vs. NEW ORLEANS
RS: Bears lead series, 8-6
PS: Bears lead series, 1-0
1968 — Bears, 23-17 (NO)
1970 — Bears, 24-3 (NO)
1971 — Bears, 35-14 (C)
1973 — Saints, 21-16 (NO)
1974 — Bears, 24-10 (C)
1975 — Bears, 42-17 (NO)
1977 — Saints, 42-24 (C)
1980 — Bears, 22-3 (C)
1982 — Saints, 10-0 (C)
1983 — Saints, 34-31 (NO) OT
1984 — Bears, 20-7 (C)
1987 — Saints, 19-17 (C)
1990 — *Bears, 16-6 (C)
1991 — Bears, 20-17 (NO)
1992 — Saints, 28-6 (NO)
(RS Pts. — Bears 304, Saints 242)
(PS Pts. — Bears 16, Saints 6)
**NFC First Round Playoff*

CHICAGO vs. N.Y. GIANTS
RS: Bears lead series, 24-15-2
PS: Bears lead series, 5-3
1925 — Bears, 19-7 (NY)
Giants, 9-0 (C)
1926 — Bears, 7-0 (C)
1927 — Giants, 13-7 (NY)
1928 — Bears, 13-0 (C)
1929 — Giants, 26-14 (C)
Giants, 34-0 (NY)
Giants, 14-9 (C)
1930 — Giants, 12-0 (C)
Bears, 12-0 (NY)
1931 — Bears, 6-0 (C)
Bears, 12-6 (NY)
Giants, 25-6 (C)
1932 — Bears, 28-8 (NY)
Bears, 6-0 (C)
1933 — Bears, 14-10 (C)
Giants, 3-0 (NY)
*Bears, 23-21 (C)
1934 — Bears, 27-7 (C)
Bears, 10-9 (NY)
*Giants, 30-13 (NY)
1935 — Bears, 20-3 (NY)
Giants, 3-0 (C)
1936 — Bears, 25-7 (NY)
1937 — Tie, 3-3 (NY)
1939 — Giants, 16-13 (NY)
1940 — Bears, 37-21 (NY)
1941 — *Bears, 37-9 (C)
1942 — Bears, 26-7 (NY)
1943 — Bears, 56-7 (NY)
1946 — Giants, 14-0 (NY)
*Bears, 24-14 (NY)
1948 — Bears, 35-14 (C)
1949 — Giants, 35-28 (NY)
1956 — Tie, 17-17 (NY)
*Giants, 47-7 (NY)
1962 — Giants, 26-24 (C)
1963 — *Bears, 14-10 (C)
1965 — Bears, 35-14 (NY)
1967 — Bears, 34-7 (C)
1969 — Giants, 28-24 (NY)
1970 — Bears, 24-16 (NY)
1974 — Bears, 16-13 (C)
1977 — Bears, 12-9 (NY) OT
1985 — **Bears, 21-0 (C)
1987 — Bears, 34-19 (C)
1990 — **Giants, 31-3 (NY)
1991 — Bears, 20-17 (C)
1992 — Giants, 27-14 (C)
(RS Pts. — Bears 687, Giants 506)
(PS Pts. — Giants 162, Bears 142)
**NFL Championship*
***NFC Divisional Playoff*

CHICAGO vs. N.Y. JETS
RS: Bears lead series, 3-1
1974 — Jets, 23-21 (C)
1979 — Bears, 23-13 (C)
1985 — Bears, 19-6 (NY)
1991 — Bears, 19-13 (C) OT
(RS Pts. — Bears 82, Jets 55)

CHICAGO vs. PHILADELPHIA
RS: Bears lead series, 22-3-1
PS: Series tied, 1-1
1933 — Tie, 3-3 (P)
1935 — Bears, 39-0 (P)
1936 — Bears, 17-0 (P)
Bears, 28-7 (P)
1938 — Bears, 28-6 (P)
1939 — Bears, 27-14 (C)
1941 — Bears, 49-14 (P)
1942 — Bears, 45-14 (C)
1944 — Bears, 28-7 (P)
1946 — Bears, 21-14 (C)
1947 — Bears, 40-7 (C)
1948 — Eagles, 12-7 (P)
1949 — Bears, 38-21 (C)
1955 — Bears, 17-10 (C)
1961 — Eagles, 16-14 (P)
1963 — Bears, 16-7 (C)
1968 — Bears, 29-16 (P)
1970 — Bears, 20-16 (C)
1972 — Bears, 21-12 (P)
1975 — Bears, 15-13 (C)
1979 — *Eagles, 27-17 (P)
1980 — Eagles, 17-14 (P)
1983 — Bears, 7-6 (P)
Bears, 17-14 (C)
1986 — Bears, 13-10 (C) OT
1987 — Bears, 35-3 (P)
1988 — **Bears, 20-12 (C)
1989 — Bears, 27-13 (C)
(RS Pts. — Bears 615, Eagles 272)
(PS Pts. — Eagles 39, Bears 37)
**NFC First Round Playoff*
***NFC Divisional Playoff*

***CHICAGO vs. **PHOENIX**
RS: Bears lead series, 51-25-6
(NP denotes Normal Park;
Wr denotes Wrigley Field;
Co denotes Comiskey Park;
So denotes Soldier Field;
all Chicago)
1920 — Cardinals, 7-6 (NP)
Staleys, 10-0 (Wr)
1921 — Tie, 0-0 (Wr)
1922 — Cardinals, 6-0 (Co)
Cardinals, 9-0 (Co)
1923 — Bears, 3-0 (Wr)
1924 — Bears, 6-0 (Wr)
Bears, 21-0 (Co)
1925 — Cardinals, 9-0 (Co)
Tie, 0-0 (Wr)
1926 — Bears, 16-0 (Wr)
Bears, 10-0 (So)
Tie, 0-0 (Wr)
1927 — Bears, 9-0 (NP)
Cardinals, 3-0 (Wr)
1928 — Bears, 15-0 (NP)
Bears, 34-0 (Wr)
1929 — Tie, 0-0 (Wr)
Cardinals, 40-6 (Co)
1930 — Bears, 32-6 (Co)
Bears, 6-0 (Wr)
1931 — Bears, 26-13 (Wr)
Bears, 18-7 (Wr)
1932 — Tie, 0-0 (Wr)
Bears, 34-0 (Wr)
1933 — Bears, 12-9 (Wr)
Bears, 22-6 (Wr)
1934 — Bears, 20-0 (Wr)
Bears, 17-6 (Wr)
1935 — Tie, 7-7 (Wr)
Bears, 13-0 (Wr)
1936 — Bears, 7-3 (Wr)
Cardinals, 14-7 (Wr)
1937 — Bears, 16-7 (Wr)
Bears, 42-28 (Wr)
1938 — Bears, 16-13 (So)
Bears, 34-28 (Wr)
1939 — Bears, 44-7 (Wr)
Bears, 48-7 (Co)
1940 — Cardinals, 21-7 (Co)
Bears, 31-23 (Wr)
1941 — Bears, 53-7 (Wr)
Bears, 34-24 (Co)
1942 — Bears, 41-14 (Wr)
Bears, 21-7 (Co)
1943 — Bears, 20-0 (Wr)
Bears, 35-24 (Co)
1945 — Cardinals, 16-7 (Wr)
Bears, 28-20 (Co)
1946 — Bears, 34-17 (Co)
Cardinals, 35-28 (Wr)
1947 — Cardinals, 31-7 (Co)
Cardinals, 30-21 (Wr)
1948 — Bears, 28-17 (Co)
Cardinals, 24-21 (Wr)
1949 — Bears, 17-7 (Co)
Bears, 52-21 (Wr)
1950 — Bears, 27-6 (Wr)
Cardinals, 20-10 (Co)
1951 — Cardinals, 28-14 (Co)
Cardinals, 24-14 (Wr)
1952 — Cardinals, 21-10 (Co)
Bears, 10-7 (Wr)
1953 — Cardinals, 24-17 (Wr)
1954 — Bears, 29-7 (Co)
1955 — Cardinals, 53-14 (Co)
1956 — Bears, 10-3 (Wr)
1957 — Bears, 14-6 (Co)
1958 — Bears, 30-14 (Wr)
1959 — Bears, 31-7 (So)
1965 — Bears, 34-13 (Wr)
1966 — Cardinals, 24-17 (StL)
1967 — Bears, 30-3 (Wr)
1969 — Cardinals, 20-17 (StL)
1972 — Bears, 27-10 (StL)
1975 — Cardinals, 34-20 (So)
1977 — Cardinals, 16-13 (StL)
1978 — Bears, 17-10 (So)
1979 — Bears, 42-6 (So)
1982 — Cardinals, 10-7 (So)
1984 — Cardinals, 38-21 (StL)
1990 — Bears, 31-21 (P)
(RS Pts. — Bears 1,548, Cardinals 998)
**Franchise in Decatur prior to 1921; Bears known as Staleys prior to 1922*
***Franchise in St. Louis prior to 1988 and in Chicago prior to 1960*

CHICAGO vs. *PITTSBURGH
RS: Bears lead series, 16-4-1
1934 — Bears, 28-0 (P)
1935 — Bears, 23-7 (P)
1936 — Bears, 27-9 (P)
Bears, 26-6 (C)
1937 — Bears, 7-0 (P)
1939 — Bears, 32-0 (P)
1941 — Bears, 34-7 (C)
1945 — Bears, 28-7 (P)
1947 — Bears, 49-7 (C)
1949 — Bears, 30-21 (C)
1958 — Steelers, 24-10 (P)
1959 — Bears, 27-21 (C)
1963 — Tie, 17-17 (P)
1967 — Steelers, 41-13 (P)
1969 — Bears, 38-7 (C)
1971 — Bears, 17-15 (C)
1975 — Steelers, 34-3 (P)
1980 — Steelers, 38-3 (P)
1986 — Bears, 13-10 (C) OT
1989 — Bears, 20-0 (P)
1992 — Bears, 30-6 (C)
(RS Pts. — Bears 475, Steelers 277)
**Steelers known as Pirates prior to 1941*

CHICAGO vs. SAN DIEGO
RS: Chargers lead series, 4-1
1970 — Chargers, 20-7 (C)
1974 — Chargers, 28-21 (SD)
1978 — Chargers, 40-7 (SD)
1981 — Bears, 20-17 (C) OT
1984 — Chargers, 20-7 (SD)
(RS Pts. — Chargers 125, Bears 62)

CHICAGO vs. SAN FRANCISCO
RS: Series tied, 25-25-1
PS: 49ers lead series, 2-0
1950 — Bears, 32-20 (SF)
Bears, 17-0 (C)
1951 — Bears, 13-7 (C)
1952 — 49ers, 40-16 (C)
Bears, 20-17 (SF)
1953 — 49ers, 35-28 (C)
49ers, 24-14 (SF)
1954 — 49ers, 31-24 (C)
Bears, 31-27 (SF)
1955 — 49ers, 20-19 (C)
Bears, 34-23 (SF)
1956 — Bears, 31-7 (C)
Bears, 38-21 (SF)
1957 — 49ers, 21-17 (C)
49ers, 21-17 (SF)
1958 — Bears, 28-6 (C)
Bears, 27-14 (SF)
1959 — 49ers, 20-17 (SF)
Bears, 14-3 (C)
1960 — Bears, 27-10 (C)
49ers, 25-7 (SF)
1961 — Bears, 31-0 (C)
49ers, 41-31 (SF)
1962 — Bears, 30-14 (SF)
49ers, 34-27 (C)
1963 — 49ers, 20-14 (SF)
Bears, 27-7 (C)
1964 — 49ers, 31-21 (SF)
Bears, 23-21 (C)
1965 — 49ers, 52-24 (SF)
Bears, 61-20 (C)
1966 — Tie, 30-30 (C)
49ers, 41-14 (SF)
1967 — Bears, 28-14 (SF)
1968 — Bears, 27-19 (C)
1969 — 49ers, 42-21 (SF)
1970 — 49ers, 37-16 (C)
1971 — 49ers, 13-0 (SF)
1972 — 49ers, 34-21 (C)
1974 — 49ers, 34-0 (C)
1975 — 49ers, 31-3 (SF)
1976 — Bears, 19-12 (SF)
1978 — Bears, 16-13 (SF)
1979 — Bears, 28-27 (SF)
1981 — 49ers, 28-17 (SF)
1983 — Bears, 13-3 (C)
1984 — *49ers, 23-0 (SF)
1985 — Bears, 26-10 (SF)
1987 — 49ers, 41-0 (SF)
1988 — Bears, 10-9 (C)
*49ers, 28-3 (C)
1989 — 49ers, 26-0 (SF)
1991 — 49ers, 52-14 (SF)
(RS Pts. — 49ers 1,148, Bears 1,063)
(PS Pts. — 49ers 51, Bears 3)
**NFC Championship*

CHICAGO vs. SEATTLE
RS: Seahawks lead series, 4-2
1976 — Bears, 34-7 (S)
1978 — Seahawks, 31-29 (C)
1982 — Seahawks, 20-14 (S)
1984 — Seahawks, 38-9 (S)
1987 — Seahawks, 34-21 (C)
1990 — Bears, 17-0 (C)

(RS Pts. — Seahawks 130, Bears 124)
CHICAGO vs. TAMPA BAY
RS: Bears lead series, 23-7
1977 — Bears, 10-0 (TB)
1978 — Buccaneers, 33-19 (TB)
Bears, 14-3 (C)
1979 — Buccaneers, 17-13 (C)
Bears, 14-0 (TB)
1980 — Bears, 23-0 (C)
Bears, 14-13 (TB)
1981 — Bears, 28-17 (C)
Buccaneers, 20-10 (TB)
1982 — Buccaneers, 26-23 (TB) OT
1983 — Bears, 17-10 (C)
Bears, 27-0 (TB)
1984 — Bears, 34-14 (C)
Bears, 44-9 (TB)
1985 — Bears, 38-28 (C)
Bears, 27-19 (TB)
1986 — Bears, 23-3 (TB)
Bears, 48-14 (C)
1987 — Bears, 20-3 (C)
Bears, 27-26 (TB)
1988 — Bears, 28-10 (C)
Bears, 27-15 (TB)
1989 — Buccaneers, 42-35 (TB)
Buccaneers, 32-31 (C)
1990 — Bears, 26-6 (TB)
Bears, 27-14 (C)
1991 — Bears, 21-20 (TB)
Bears, 27-0 (C)
1992 — Bears, 31-14 (C)
Buccaneers, 20-17 (TB)
(RS Pts. — Bears 743, Buccaneers 428)
CHICAGO vs. *WASHINGTON
RS: Bears lead series, 18-12-1
PS: Redskins lead series, 4-3
1932 — Tie, 7-7 (B)
1933 — Bears, 7-0 (C)
Redskins, 10-0 (B)
1934 — Bears, 21-0 (B)
1935 — Bears, 30-14 (B)
1936 — Bears, 26-0 (B)
1937 — **Redskins, 28-21 (C)
1938 — Bears, 31-7 (C)
1940 — Redskins, 7-3 (W)
**Bears, 73-0 (W)
1941 — Bears, 35-21 (C)
1942 — **Redskins, 14-6 (W)
1943 — Redskins, 21-7 (W)
**Bears, 41-21 (C)
1945 — Redskins, 28-21 (W)
1946 — Bears, 24-20 (C)
1947 — Bears, 56-20 (W)
1948 — Bears, 48-13 (C)
1949 — Bears, 31-21 (W)
1951 — Bears, 27-0 (W)
1953 — Bears, 27-24 (W)
1957 — Redskins, 14-3 (C)
1964 — Redskins, 27-20 (W)
1968 — Redskins, 38-28 (C)
1971 — Bears, 16-15 (C)
1974 — Redskins, 42-0 (W)
1976 — Bears, 33-7 (C)
1978 — Bears, 14-10 (W)
1980 — Bears, 35-21 (C)
1981 — Redskins, 24-7 (C)
1984 — ***Bears, 23-19 (W)
1985 — Bears, 45-10 (C)
1986 — ***Redskins, 27-13 (C)
1987 — ***Redskins, 21-17 (C)
1988 — Bears, 34-14 (W)
1989 — Redskins, 38-14 (W)
1990 — Redskins, 10-9 (W)
1991 — Redskins, 20-7 (C)
(RS Pts. — Bears 666, Redskins 503)
(PS Pts. — Bears 194, Redskins 130)
Franchise in Boston prior to 1937 and known as Braves prior to 1933
***NFL Championship*
****NFC Divisional Playoff*

CINCINNATI vs. ATLANTA
RS: Bengals lead series, 5-2;
See Atlanta vs. Cincinnati
CINCINNATI vs. BUFFALO
RS: Bengals lead series, 9-7
PS: Bengals lead series, 2-0;
See Buffalo vs. Cincinnati
CINCINNATI vs. CHICAGO
RS: Bengals lead series, 3-2;
See Chicago vs. Cincinnati
CINCINNATI vs. CLEVELAND
RS: Bengals lead series, 24-21
1970 — Browns, 30-27 (Cle)
Bengals, 14-10 (Cin)
1971 — Browns, 27-24 (Cin)
Browns, 31-27 (Cle)
1972 — Browns, 27-6 (Cle)
Browns, 27-24 (Cin)
1973 — Browns, 17-10 (Cle)
Bengals, 34-17 (Cin)
1974 — Bengals, 33-7 (Cin)
Bengals, 34-24 (Cle)
1975 — Bengals, 24-17 (Cin)
Browns, 35-23 (Cle)
1976 — Bengals, 45-24 (Cle)
Bengals, 21-6 (Cin)
1977 — Browns, 13-3 (Cin)
Bengals, 10-7 (Cle)
1978 — Browns, 13-10 (Cle) OT
Bengals, 48-16 (Cin)
1979 — Browns, 28-27 (Cle)
Bengals, 16-12 (Cin)
1980 — Browns, 31-7 (Cle)
Browns, 27-24 (Cin)
1981 — Browns, 20-17 (Cin)
Bengals, 41-21 (Cle)
1982 — Bengals, 23-10 (Cin)
1983 — Browns, 17-7 (Cle)
Bengals, 28-21 (Cin)
1984 — Bengals, 12-9 (Cin)
Bengals, 20-17 (Cle) OT
1985 — Bengals, 27-10 (Cin)
Browns, 24-6 (Cle)
1986 — Bengals, 30-13 (Cle)
Browns, 34-3 (Cin)
1987 — Browns, 34-0 (Cin)
Browns, 38-24 (Cle)
1988 — Bengals, 24-17 (Cin)
Browns, 23-16 (Cle)
1989 — Bengals, 21-14 (Cin)
Bengals, 21-0 (Cle)
1990 — Bengals, 34-13 (Cle)
Bengals, 21-14 (Cin)
1991 — Browns, 14-13 (Cle)
Bengals, 23-21 (Cin)
1992 — Bengals, 30-10 (Cin)
Browns, 37-21 (Cle)
(RS Pts. — Bengals 953, Browns 877)
CINCINNATI vs. DALLAS
RS: Cowboys lead series, 3-2
1973 — Cowboys, 38-10 (D)
1979 — Cowboys, 38-13 (D)
1985 — Bengals, 50-24 (C)
1988 — Bengals, 38-24 (D)
1991 — Cowboys, 35-23 (D)
(RS Pts. — Cowboys 159, Bengals 134)
CINCINNATI vs. DENVER
RS: Broncos lead series, 10-6
1968 — Bengals, 24-10 (C)
Broncos, 10-7 (D)
1969 — Broncos, 30-23 (C)
Broncos, 27-16 (D)
1971 — Bengals, 24-10 (D)
1972 — Bengals, 21-10 (C)
1973 — Broncos, 28-10 (D)
1975 — Bengals, 17-16 (D)
1976 — Bengals, 17-7 (C)
1977 — Broncos, 24-13 (C)
1979 — Broncos, 10-0 (D)
1981 — Bengals, 38-21 (C)
1983 — Broncos, 24-17 (D)
1984 — Broncos, 20-17 (D)
1986 — Broncos, 34-28 (D)
1991 — Broncos, 45-14 (D)
(RS Pts. — Broncos 326, Bengals 286)
CINCINNATI vs. DETROIT
RS: Series tied, 3-3
1970 — Lions, 38-3 (D)
1974 — Lions, 23-19 (C)
1983 — Bengals, 17-9 (C)
1986 — Bengals, 24-17 (D)
1989 — Bengals, 42-7 (C)
1992 — Lions, 19-13 (C)
(RS Pts. — Bengals 118, Lions 113)
CINCINNATI vs. GREEN BAY
RS: Bengals lead series, 4-3
1971 — Packers, 20-17 (GB)
1976 — Bengals, 28-7 (C)
1977 — Bengals, 17-7 (Mil)
1980 — Packers, 14-9 (GB)
1983 — Bengals, 34-14 (C)
1986 — Bengals, 34-28 (Mil)
1992 — Packers, 24-23 (GB)
(RS Pts. — Bengals 162, Packers 114)
CINCINNATI vs. HOUSTON
RS: Bengals lead series, 24-23-1
PS: Bengals lead series, 1-0
1968 — Oilers, 27-17 (C)
1969 — Tie, 31-31 (H)
1970 — Oilers, 20-13 (C)
Bengals, 30-20 (H)
1971 — Oilers, 10-6 (H)
Bengals, 28-13 (C)
1972 — Bengals, 30-7 (C)
Bengals, 61-17 (H)
1973 — Bengals, 24-10 (C)
Bengals, 27-24 (H)
1974 — Oilers, 34-21 (C)
Oilers, 20-3 (H)
1975 — Bengals, 21-19 (H)
Bengals, 23-19 (C)
1976 — Bengals, 27-7 (H)
Bengals, 31-27 (C)
1977 — Bengals, 13-10 (C) OT
Oilers, 21-16 (H)
1978 — Bengals, 28-13 (C)
Oilers, 17-10 (H)
1979 — Oilers, 30-27 (C) OT
Oilers, 42-21 (H)
1980 — Oilers, 13-10 (C)
Oilers, 23-3 (H)
1981 — Oilers, 17-10 (H)
Bengals, 34-21 (C)
1982 — Bengals, 27-6 (C)
Bengals, 35-27 (H)
1983 — Bengals, 55-14 (H)
Bengals, 38-10 (C)
1984 — Bengals, 13-3 (C)
Bengals, 31-13 (H)
1985 — Oilers, 44-27 (H)
Bengals, 45-27 (C)
1986 — Bengals, 31-28 (C)
Oilers, 32-28 (H)
1987 — Oilers, 31-29 (C)
Oilers, 21-17 (H)
1988 — Bengals, 44-21 (C)
Oilers, 41-6 (H)
1989 — Oilers, 26-24 (H)
Bengals, 61-7 (C)
1990 — Oilers, 48-17 (H)
Bengals, 40-20 (C)
*Bengals, 41-14 (C)
1991 — Oilers, 30-7 (C)
Oilers, 35-3 (H)
1992 — Oilers, 38-24 (C)
Oilers, 26-10 (H)
(RS Pts. — Bengals 1,177, Oilers 1,060)
(PS Pts. — Bengals 41, Oilers 14)
**AFC First Round Playoff*
CINCINNATI vs.*INDIANAPOLIS
RS: Colts lead series, 7-5
PS: Colts lead series, 1-0
1970 — **Colts, 17-0 (B)
1972 — Colts, 20-19 (C)
1974 — Bengals, 24-14 (B)
1976 — Colts, 28-27 (B)
1979 — Colts, 38-28 (B)
1980 — Bengals, 34-33 (C)
1981 — Bengals, 41-19 (B)
1982 — Bengals, 20-17 (B)
1983 — Colts, 34-31 (C)
1987 — Bengals, 23-21 (I)
1989 — Colts, 23-12 (C)
1990 — Colts, 34-20 (C)
1992 — Colts, 21-17 (C)
(RS Pts. — Colts 302, Bengals 296)
(PS Pts. — Colts 17, Bengals 0)
**Franchise in Baltimore prior to 1984*
***AFC Divisional Playoff*
CINCINNATI vs. KANSAS CITY
RS: Chiefs lead series, 10-9
1968 — Chiefs, 13-3 (KC)
Chiefs, 16-9 (C)
1969 — Bengals, 24-19 (C)
Chiefs, 42-22 (KC)
1970 — Chiefs, 27-19 (C)
1972 — Bengals, 23-16 (KC)
1973 — Bengals, 14-6 (C)
1974 — Bengals, 33-6 (C)
1976 — Bengals, 27-24 (KC)
1977 — Bengals, 27-7 (KC)
1978 — Chiefs, 24-23 (C)
1979 — Chiefs, 10-7 (C)
1980 — Bengals, 20-6 (KC)
1983 — Chiefs, 20-15 (KC)
1984 — Chiefs, 27-22 (C)
1986 — Chiefs, 24-14 (KC)
1987 — Bengals, 30-27 (C) OT
1988 — Chiefs, 31-28 (KC)
1989 — Bengals, 21-17 (KC)
(RS Pts. — Bengals 381, Chiefs 362)
CINCINNATI vs. *L.A. RAIDERS
RS: Raiders lead series, 14-6
PS: Raiders lead series, 2-0
1968 — Raiders, 31-10 (O)
Raiders, 34-0 (C)
1969 — Bengals, 31-17 (C)
Raiders, 37-17 (O)
1970 — Bengals, 31-21 (C)
1971 — Raiders, 31-27 (O)
1972 — Raiders, 20-14 (C)
1974 — Raiders, 30-27 (O)
1975 — Bengals, 14-10 (C)
**Raiders, 31-28 (O)
1976 — Raiders, 35-20 (O)
1978 — Raiders, 34-21 (C)
1980 — Raiders, 28-17 (O)
1982 — Bengals, 31-17 (C)
1983 — Raiders, 20-10 (C)
1985 — Raiders, 13-6 (LA)
1988 — Bengals, 45-21 (LA)
1989 — Raiders, 28-7 (LA)
1990 — Raiders, 24-7 (LA)
**Raiders, 20-10 (LA)
1991 — Raiders, 38-14 (C)
1992 — Bengals, 24-21 (C) OT
(RS Pts. — Raiders 510, Bengals 373)
(PS Pts. — Raiders 51, Bengals 38)
**Franchise in Oakland prior to 1982*
***AFC Divisional Playoff*
CINCINNATI vs. L.A. RAMS
RS: Bengals lead series, 4-2
1972 — Rams, 15-12 (LA)
1976 — Bengals, 20-12 (C)
1978 — Bengals, 20-19 (LA)
1981 — Bengals, 24-10 (C)
1984 — Rams, 24-14 (C)
1990 — Bengals, 34-31 (LA) OT
(RS Pts. — Bengals 124, Rams 111)
CINCINNATI vs. MIAMI
RS: Dolphins lead series, 9-3
PS: Dolphins lead series, 1-0
1968 — Dolphins, 24-22 (C)
Bengals, 38-21 (M)
1969 — Bengals, 27-21 (C)
1971 — Dolphins, 23-13 (C)
1973 — *Dolphins, 34-16 (M)
1974 — Dolphins, 24-3 (M)
1977 — Bengals, 23-17 (C)
1978 — Dolphins, 21-0 (M)
1980 — Dolphins, 17-16 (M)
1983 — Dolphins, 38-14 (M)
1987 — Dolphins, 20-14 (C)
1989 — Dolphins, 20-13 (C)
1991 — Dolphins, 37-13 (M)
(RS Pts. — Dolphins 317, Bengals 212)
(PS Pts. — Dolphins 34, Bengals 16)
**AFC Divisional Playoff*
CINCINNATI vs. MINNESOTA
RS: Vikings lead series, 4-3
1973 — Bengals, 27-0 (C)
1977 — Vikings, 42-10 (M)
1980 — Bengals, 14-0 (C)
1983 — Vikings, 20-14 (M)
1986 — Bengals, 24-20 (C)
1989 — Vikings, 29-21 (M)
1992 — Vikings, 42-7 (C)
(RS Pts. — Vikings 153, Bengals 117)
CINCINNATI vs. *NEW ENGLAND
RS: Series tied, 7-7
1968 — Patriots, 33-14 (B)
1969 — Patriots, 25-14 (C)
1970 — Bengals, 45-7 (C)
1972 — Bengals, 31-7 (NE)
1975 — Bengals, 27-10 (C)
1978 — Patriots, 10-3 (C)
1979 — Patriots, 20-14 (C)
1984 — Patriots, 20-14 (NE)
1985 — Patriots, 34-23 (NE)
1986 — Bengals, 31-7 (NE)
1988 — Patriots, 27-21 (NE)
1990 — Bengals, 41-7 (C)
1991 — Bengals, 29-7 (C)
1992 — Bengals, 20-10 (C)
(RS Pts. — Bengals 327, Patriots 224)
**Franchise in Boston prior to 1971*
CINCINNATI vs. NEW ORLEANS
RS: Saints lead series, 4-3
1970 — Bengals, 26-6 (C)
1975 — Bengals, 21-0 (NO)
1978 — Saints, 20-18 (C)
1981 — Saints, 17-7 (NO)
1984 — Bengals, 24-21 (NO)
1987 — Saints, 41-24 (C)
1990 — Saints, 21-7 (C)
(RS Pts. — Bengals 127, Saints 126)
CINCINNATI vs. N.Y. GIANTS
RS: Bengals lead series, 4-0
1972 — Bengals, 13-10 (C)
1977 — Bengals, 30-13 (C)
1985 — Bengals, 35-30 (C)
1991 — Bengals, 27-24 (C)
(RS Pts. — Bengals 105, Giants 77)
CINCINNATI vs. N.Y. JETS
RS: Jets lead series, 8-6
PS: Jets lead series, 1-0
1968 — Jets, 27-14 (NY)
1969 — Jets, 21-7 (C)
Jets, 40-7 (NY)
1971 — Jets, 35-21 (NY)
1973 — Bengals, 20-14 (C)
1976 — Bengals, 42-3 (NY)
1981 — Bengals, 31-30 (NY)
1982 — *Jets, 44-17 (C)
1984 — Jets, 43-23 (NY)
1985 — Jets, 29-20 (C)
1986 — Bengals, 52-21 (C)
1987 — Jets, 27-20 (NY)
1988 — Bengals, 36-19 (C)
1990 — Bengals, 25-20 (C)
1992 — Jets, 17-14 (NY)
(RS Pts. — Jets 346, Bengals 332)
(PS Pts. — Jets 44, Bengals 17)
**AFC First Round Playoff*
CINCINNATI vs. PHILADELPHIA
RS: Bengals lead series, 5-1
1971 — Bengals, 37-14 (C)
1975 — Bengals, 31-0 (P)
1979 — Bengals, 37-13 (C)
1982 — Bengals, 18-14 (P)

1988 — Bengals, 28-24 (P)
1991 — Eagles, 17-10 (P)
(RS Pts. — Bengals 161, Eagles 82)

CINCINNATI vs. *PHOENIX
RS: Bengals lead series, 3-1
1973 — Bengals, 42-24 (C)
1979 — Bengals, 34-28 (C)
1985 — Cardinals, 41-27 (StL)
1988 — Bengals, 21-14 (C)
(RS Pts. — Bengals 124, Cardinals 107)
Franchise in St. Louis prior to 1988

CINCINNATI vs. PITTSBURGH
RS: Steelers lead series, 24-21
1970 — Steelers, 21-10 (P)
Bengals, 34-7 (C)
1971 — Steelers, 21-10 (P)
Steelers, 21-13 (C)
1972 — Bengals, 15-10 (C)
Steelers, 40-17 (P)
1973 — Bengals, 19-7 (C)
Steelers, 20-13 (P)
1974 — Bengals, 17-10 (C)
Steelers, 27-3 (P)
1975 — Steelers, 30-24 (C)
Steelers, 35-14 (P)
1976 — Steelers, 23-6 (P)
Steelers, 7-3 (C)
1977 — Steelers, 20-14 (P)
Bengals, 17-10 (C)
1978 — Steelers, 28-3 (C)
Steelers, 7-6 (P)
1979 — Bengals, 34-10 (C)
Steelers, 37-17 (P)
1980 — Bengals, 30-28 (C)
Bengals, 17-16 (P)
1981 — Bengals, 34-7 (C)
Bengals, 17-10 (P)
1982 — Steelers, 26-20 (P) OT
1983 — Steelers, 24-14 (C)
Bengals, 23-10 (P)
1984 — Steelers, 38-17 (P)
Bengals, 22-20 (C)
1985 — Bengals, 37-24 (P)
Bengals, 26-21 (C)
1986 — Bengals, 24-22 (C)
Steelers, 30-9 (P)
1987 — Steelers, 23-20 (P)
Steelers, 30-16 (C)
1988 — Bengals, 17-12 (P)
Bengals, 42-7 (C)
1989 — Bengals, 41-10 (C)
Bengals, 26-16 (P)
1990 — Bengals, 27-3 (C)
Bengals, 16-12 (P)
1991 — Steelers, 33-27 (C) OT
Steelers, 17-10 (P)
1992 — Steelers, 20-0 (P)
Steelers, 21-9 (C)
(RS Pts. — Steelers 871, Bengals 830)

CINCINNATI vs. SAN DIEGO
RS: Chargers lead series, 12-8
PS: Bengals lead series, 1-0
1968 — Chargers, 29-13 (SD)
Chargers, 31-10 (C)
1969 — Bengals, 34-20 (C)
Chargers, 21-14 (SD)
1970 — Bengals, 17-14 (SD)
1971 — Bengals, 31-0 (C)
1973 — Bengals, 20-13 (SD)
1974 — Chargers, 20-17 (C)
1975 — Bengals, 47-17 (C)
1977 — Chargers, 24-3 (SD)
1978 — Chargers, 22-13 (SD)
1979 — Chargers, 26-24 (C)
1980 — Chargers, 31-14 (C)
1981 — Bengals, 40-17 (SD)
*Bengals, 27-7 (C)
1982 — Chargers, 50-34 (SD)
1985 — Chargers, 44-41 (C)
1987 — Chargers, 10-9 (C)
1988 — Bengals, 27-10 (C)
1990 — Bengals, 21-16 (SD)
1992 — Chargers, 27-10 (SD)
(RS Pts. — Chargers 442, Bengals 439)
(PS Pts. — Bengals 27, Chargers 7)
AFC Championship

CINCINNATI vs. SAN FRANCISCO
RS: 49ers lead series, 5-1
PS: 49ers lead series, 2-0
1974 — Bengals, 21-3 (SF)
1978 — 49ers, 28-12 (SF)
1981 — 49ers, 21-3 (C)
*49ers, 26-21 (Detroit)
1984 — 49ers, 23-17 (SF)
1987 — 49ers, 27-26 (C)
1988 — **49ers, 20-16 (Miami)
1990 — 49ers, 20-17 (C)
(RS Pts. — 49ers 122, Bengals 96)
(PS Pts. — 49ers 46, Bengals 37)
Super Bowl XVI
***Super Bowl XXIII*

CINCINNATI vs. SEATTLE
RS: Bengals lead series 6-5
PS: Bengals lead series, 1-0
1977 — Bengals, 42-20 (C)
1981 — Bengals, 27-21 (C)
1982 — Bengals, 24-10 (C)
1984 — Seahawks, 26-6 (C)
1985 — Seahawks, 28-24 (C)
1986 — Bengals, 34-7 (C)
1987 — Bengals, 17-10 (S)
1988 — *Bengals, 21-13 (C)
1989 — Seahawks, 24-17 (C)
1990 — Seahawks, 31-16 (S)
1991 — Seahawks, 13-7 (C)
1992 — Bengals, 21-3 (S)
(RS Pts. — Bengals 235, Seahawks 193)
(PS Pts. — Bengals 21, Seahawks 13)
AFC Divisional Playoff

CINCINNATI vs. TAMPA BAY
RS: Bengals lead series, 3-1
1976 — Bengals, 21-0 (C)
1980 — Buccaneers, 17-12 (C)
1983 — Bengals, 23-17 (TB)
1989 — Bengals, 56-23 (C)
(RS Pts. — Bengals 112, Buccaneers 57)

CINCINNATI vs. WASHINGTON
RS: Redskins lead series, 4-2
1970 — Redskins, 20-0 (W)
1974 — Bengals, 28-17 (C)
1979 — Redskins, 28-14 (W)
1985 — Redskins, 27-24 (W)
1988 — Bengals, 20-17 (C) OT
1991 — Redskins, 34-27 (C)
(RS Pts. — Redskins 143, Bengals 113)

CLEVELAND vs. ATLANTA
RS: Browns lead series, 8-1;
See Atlanta vs. Cleveland

CLEVELAND vs. BUFFALO
RS: Browns lead series, 7-3
PS: Browns lead series, 1-0;
See Buffalo vs. Cleveland

CLEVELAND vs. CHICAGO
RS: Browns lead series, 8-3;
See Chicago vs. Cleveland

CLEVELAND vs. CINCINNATI
RS: Bengals lead series, 24-21;
See Cincinnati vs. Cleveland

CLEVELAND vs. DALLAS
RS: Browns lead series, 14-9
PS: Browns lead series, 2-1
1960 — Browns, 48-7 (D)
1961 — Browns, 25-7 (C)
Browns, 38-17 (D)
1962 — Browns, 19-10 (C)
Cowboys, 45-21 (D)
1963 — Browns, 41-24 (D)
Browns, 27-17 (C)
1964 — Browns, 27-6 (C)
Browns, 20-16 (D)
1965 — Browns, 23-17 (C)
Browns, 24-17 (D)
1966 — Browns, 30-21 (C)
Cowboys, 26-14 (D)
1967 — Cowboys, 21-14 (C)
*Cowboys, 52-14 (D)
1968 — Cowboys, 28-7 (C)
*Browns, 31-20 (C)
1969 — Browns, 42-10 (C)
*Browns, 38-14 (D)
1970 — Cowboys, 6-2 (C)
1974 — Cowboys, 41-17 (D)
1979 — Browns, 26-7 (C)
1982 — Cowboys, 31-14 (D)
1985 — Cowboys, 20-7 (D)
1988 — Browns, 24-21 (C)
1991 — Cowboys, 26-14 (C)
(RS Pts. — Browns 524, Cowboys 441)
(PS Pts. — Cowboys 86, Browns 83)
Conference Championship

CLEVELAND vs. DENVER
RS: Broncos lead series, 11-5
PS: Broncos lead series, 3-0
1970 — Browns, 27-13 (D)
1971 — Broncos, 27-0 (C)
1972 — Browns, 27-20 (D)
1974 — Browns, 23-21 (C)
1975 — Broncos, 16-15 (D)
1976 — Broncos, 44-13 (D)
1978 — Broncos, 19-7 (C)
1980 — Broncos, 19-16 (C)
1981 — Broncos, 23-20 (D) OT
1983 — Broncos, 27-6 (D)
1984 — Broncos, 24-14 (C)
1986 — *Broncos, 23-20 (C) OT
1987 — *Broncos, 38-33 (D)
1988 — Broncos, 30-7 (D)
1989 — Browns, 16-13 (C)
*Broncos, 37-21 (D)
1990 — Browns, 30-29 (D)
1991 — Broncos, 17-7 (C)
1992 — Broncos, 12-0 (C)
(RS Pts. — Broncos 354, Browns 228)
(PS Pts. — Broncos 98, Browns 74)
AFC Championship

CLEVELAND vs. DETROIT
RS: Lions lead series, 11-3
PS: Lions lead series, 3-1
1952 — Lions, 17-6 (D)
*Lions, 17-7 (C)
1953 — *Lions, 17-16 (D)
1954 — Lions, 14-10 (C)
*Browns, 56-10 (C)
1957 — Lions, 20-7 (D)
*Lions, 59-14 (D)
1958 — Lions, 30-10 (C)
1963 — Lions, 38-10 (D)
1964 — Browns, 37-21 (C)
1967 — Lions, 31-14 (D)
1969 — Lions, 28-21 (C)
1970 — Lions, 41-24 (C)
1975 — Lions, 21-10 (D)
1983 — Browns, 31-26 (D)
1986 — Browns, 24-21 (C)
1989 — Lions, 13-10 (D)
1992 — Lions, 24-14 (D)
(RS Pts. — Lions 345, Browns 228)
(PS Pts. — Lions 103, Browns 93)
NFL Championship

CLEVELAND vs. GREEN BAY
RS: Packers lead series, 7-6
PS: Packers lead series, 1-0
1953 — Browns, 27-0 (Mil)
1955 — Browns, 41-10 (C)
1956 — Browns, 24-7 (Mil)
1961 — Packers, 49-17 (C)
1964 — Packers, 28-21 (Mil)
1965 — *Packers, 23-12 (GB)
1966 — Packers, 21-20 (C)
1967 — Packers, 55-7 (Mil)
1969 — Browns, 20-7 (C)
1972 — Packers, 26-10 (C)
1980 — Browns, 26-21 (C)
1983 — Packers, 35-21 (Mil)
1986 — Packers, 17-14 (C)
1992 — Browns, 17-6 (C)
(RS Pts. — Packers 282, Browns 265)
(PS Pts. — Packers 23, Browns 12)
NFL Championship

CLEVELAND vs. HOUSTON
RS: Browns lead series, 27-18
PS: Oilers lead series, 1-0
1970 — Browns, 28-14 (C)
Browns, 21-10 (H)
1971 — Browns, 31-0 (C)
Browns, 37-24 (H)
1972 — Browns, 23-17 (H)
Browns, 20-0 (C)
1973 — Browns, 42-13 (C)
Browns, 23-13 (H)
1974 — Browns, 20-7 (C)
Oilers, 28-24 (H)
1975 — Oilers, 40-10 (C)
Oilers, 21-10 (H)
1976 — Browns, 21-7 (H)
Browns, 13-10 (C)
1977 — Browns, 24-23 (H)
Oilers, 19-15 (C)
1978 — Oilers, 16-13 (C)
Oilers, 14-10 (H)
1979 — Oilers, 31-10 (H)
Browns, 14-7 (C)
1980 — Oilers, 16-7 (C)
Browns, 17-14 (H)
1981 — Oilers, 9-3 (C)
Oilers, 17-13 (H)
1982 — Browns, 20-14 (H)
1983 — Browns, 25-19 (C) OT
Oilers, 34-27 (H)
1984 — Browns, 27-10 (C)
Browns, 27-20 (H)
1985 — Browns, 21-6 (H)
Browns, 28-21 (C)
1986 — Browns, 23-20 (H)
Browns, 13-10 (C) OT
1987 — Oilers, 15-10 (C)
Browns, 40-7 (H)
1988 — Oilers, 24-17 (H)
Browns, 28-23 (C)
*Oilers, 24-23 (C)
1989 — Browns, 28-17 (C)
Browns, 24-20 (H)
1990 — Oilers 35-23 (C)
Oilers 58-14 (H)
1991 — Oilers, 28-24 (H)
Oilers, 17-14 (C)
1992 — Browns, 24-14 (H)
Oilers, 17-14 (C)
(RS Pts. — Browns 920, Oilers 799)
(PS Pts. — Oilers 24, Browns 23)
AFC First Round Playoff

CLEVELAND vs. *INDIANAPOLIS
RS: Browns lead series, 12-6
PS: Series tied, 2-2
1956 — Colts, 21-7 (C)
1959 — Browns, 38-31 (B)
1962 — Colts, 36-14 (C)
1964 — **Browns, 27-0 (C)
1968 — Browns, 30-20 (B)
**Colts, 34-0 (C)
1971 — Browns, 14-13 (B)
***Colts, 20-3 (C)
1973 — Browns, 24-14 (C)
1975 — Colts, 21-7 (B)
1978 — Browns, 45-24 (B)
1979 — Browns, 13-10 (C)
1980 — Browns, 28-27 (B)
1981 — Browns, 42-28 (C)
1983 — Browns, 41-23 (C)
1986 — Browns, 24-9 (I)
1987 — Colts, 9-7 (C)
***Browns, 38-21 (C)
1988 — Browns, 23-17 (C)
1989 — Colts, 23-17 (I) OT
1991 — Browns, 31-0 (I)
1992 — Colts, 14-3 (I)
(RS Pts. — Browns 408, Colts 340)
(PS Pts. — Colts 75, Browns 68)
Franchise in Baltimore prior to 1984
***NFL Championship*
****AFC Divisional Playoff*

CLEVELAND vs. KANSAS CITY
RS: Browns lead series, 7-6-2
1971 — Chiefs, 13-7 (KC)
1972 — Chiefs, 31-7 (C)
1973 — Tie, 20-20 (KC)
1975 — Browns, 40-14 (C)
1976 — Chiefs, 39-14 (KC)
1977 — Browns, 44-7 (C)
1978 — Chiefs, 17-3 (KC)
1979 — Browns, 27-24 (KC)
1980 — Browns, 20-13 (C)
1984 — Chiefs, 10-6 (KC)
1986 — Browns, 20-7 (C)
1988 — Browns, 6-3 (KC)
1989 — Tie, 10-10 (C) OT
1990 — Chiefs, 34-0 (KC)
1991 — Browns, 20-15 (C)
(RS Pts. — Chiefs 257, Browns 244)

CLEVELAND vs. *L.A.RAIDERS
RS: Raiders lead series, 8-3
PS: Raiders lead series, 2-0
1970 — Raiders, 23-20 (O)
1971 — Raiders, 34-20 (C)
1973 — Browns, 7-3 (O)
1974 — Raiders, 40-24 (C)
1975 — Raiders, 38-17 (O)
1977 — Raiders, 26-10 (C)
1979 — Raiders, 19-14 (O)
1980 — **Raiders, 14-12 (C)
1982 — ***Raiders, 27-10 (LA)
1985 — Raiders, 21-20 (C)
1986 — Raiders, 27-14 (LA)
1987 — Browns, 24-17 (LA)
1992 — Browns, 28-16 (LA)
(RS Pts. — Raiders 264, Browns 198)
(PS Pts. — Raiders 41, Browns 22)
Franchise in Oakland prior to 1982
***AFC Divisional Playoff*
****AFC First Round Playoff*

CLEVELAND vs. L.A. RAMS
RS: Series tied, 7-7
PS: Browns lead series, 2-1
1950 — *Browns, 30-28 (C)
1951 — Browns, 38-23 (LA)
*Rams, 24-17 (LA)
1952 — Browns, 37-7 (C)
1955 — *Browns, 38-14 (LA)
1957 — Browns, 45-31 (C)
1958 — Browns, 30-27 (LA)
1963 — Browns, 20-6 (C)
1965 — Rams, 42-7 (LA)
1968 — Rams, 24-6 (C)
1973 — Rams, 30-17 (LA)
1977 — Rams, 9-0 (C)
1978 — Browns, 30-19 (C)
1981 — Rams, 27-16 (LA)
1984 — Rams, 20-17 (LA)
1987 — Browns, 30-17 (C)
1990 — Rams, 38-23 (C)
(RS Pts. — Rams 320, Browns 316)
(PS Pts. — Browns 85, Rams 66)
NFL Championship

CLEVELAND vs. MIAMI
RS: Dolphins lead series, 5-4
PS: Dolphins lead series, 2-0
1970 — Browns, 28-0 (M)
1972 — *Dolphins, 20-14 (M)
1973 — Dolphins, 17-9 (C)
1976 — Browns, 17-13 (C)
1979 — Browns, 30-24 (C) OT
1985 — *Dolphins, 24-21 (M)
1986 — Browns, 26-16 (C)
1988 — Dolphins, 38-31 (M)
1989 — Dolphins, 13-10 (M) OT
1990 — Dolphins, 30-13 (C)
1992 — Dolphins, 27-23 (C)
(RS Pts. — Browns 187, Dolphins 178)
(PS Pts. — Dolphins 44, Browns 35)
AFC Divisional Playoff

CLEVELAND vs. MINNESOTA
RS: Vikings lead series, 7-3
PS: Vikings lead series, 1-0
1965 — Vikings, 27-17 (C)
1967 — Browns, 14-10 (C)
1969 — Vikings, 51-3 (M)
*Vikings, 27-7 (M)
1973 — Vikings, 26-3 (M)
1975 — Vikings, 42-10 (C)
1980 — Vikings, 28-23 (M)
1983 — Vikings, 27-21 (C)
1986 — Browns, 23-20 (M)
1989 — Browns, 23-17 (C) OT
1992 — Vikings, 17-13 (M)
(RS Pts. — Vikings 265, Browns 150)
(PS Pts. — Vikings 27, Browns 7)
NFL Championship
CLEVELAND vs. NEW ENGLAND
RS: Browns lead series, 9-2
1971 — Browns, 27-7 (C)
1974 — Browns, 21-14 (NE)
1977 — Browns, 30-27 (C) OT
1980 — Patriots, 34-17 (NE)
1982 — Browns, 10-7 (C)
1983 — Browns, 30-0 (NE)
1984 — Patriots, 17-16 (C)
1985 — Browns, 24-20 (C)
1987 — Browns, 20-10 (NE)
1991 — Browns, 20-0 (NE)
1992 — Browns, 19-17 (NE)
(RS Pts. — Browns 234, Patriots 153)
CLEVELAND vs. NEW ORLEANS
RS: Browns lead series, 8-3
1967 — Browns, 42-7 (NO)
1968 — Browns, 24-10 (NO)
Browns, 35-17 (C)
1969 — Browns, 27-17 (NO)
1971 — Browns, 21-17 (NO)
1975 — Browns, 17-16 (C)
1978 — Browns, 24-16 (NO)
1981 — Browns, 20-17 (C)
1984 — Saints, 16-14 (C)
1987 — Saints, 28-21 (NO)
1990 — Saints, 25-20 (NO)
(RS Pts. — Browns 265, Saints 186)
CLEVELAND vs. N.Y. GIANTS
RS: Browns lead series, 25-16-2
PS: Series tied, 1-1
1950 — Giants, 6-0 (C)
Giants, 17-13 (NY)
*Browns, 8-3 (C)
1951 — Browns, 14-13 (C)
Browns, 10-0 (NY)
1952 — Giants, 17-9 (C)
Giants, 37-34 (NY)
1953 — Browns, 7-0 (NY)
Browns, 62-14 (C)
1954 — Browns, 24-14 (C)
Browns, 16-7 (NY)
1955 — Browns, 24-14 (C)
Tie, 35-35 (NY)
1956 — Giants, 21-9 (C)
Browns, 24-7 (NY)
1957 — Browns, 6-3 (C)
Browns, 34-28 (NY)
1958 — Giants, 21-17 (C)
Giants, 13-10 (NY)
*Giants, 10-0 (NY)
1959 — Giants, 10-6 (C)
Giants, 48-7 (NY)
1960 — Giants, 17-13 (C)
Browns, 48-34 (NY)
1961 — Giants, 37-21 (C)
Tie, 7-7 (NY)
1962 — Browns, 17-7 (C)
Giants, 17-13 (NY)
1963 — Browns, 35-24 (NY)
Giants, 33-6 (C)
1964 — Browns, 42-20 (C)
Browns, 52-20 (NY)
1965 — Browns, 38-14 (NY)
Browns, 34-21 (C)
1966 — Browns, 28-7 (NY)
Browns, 49-40 (C)
1967 — Giants, 38-34 (NY)
Browns, 24-14 (C)
1968 — Browns, 45-10 (C)
1969 — Browns, 28-17 (C)
Giants, 27-14 (NY)
1973 — Browns, 12-10 (C)
1977 — Browns, 21-7 (NY)
1985 — Browns, 35-33 (NY)
1991 — Giants, 13-10 (NY)
(RS Pts. — Browns 987, Giants 792)
(PS Pts. — Giants 13, Browns 8)
Conference Playoff
CLEVELAND vs. N.Y. JETS
RS: Browns lead series, 8-6
PS: Browns lead series, 1-0
1970 — Browns, 31-21 (C)
1972 — Browns, 26-10 (NY)
1976 — Browns, 38-17 (C)
1978 — Browns, 37-34 (C) OT
1979 — Browns, 25-22 (NY) OT
1980 — Browns, 17-14 (C)
1981 — Jets, 14-13 (C)
1983 — Browns, 10-7 (C)
1984 — Jets, 24-20 (C)
1985 — Jets, 37-10 (NY)
1986 — *Browns, 23-20 (C) OT
1988 — Jets, 23-3 (C)
1989 — Browns, 38-24 (C)
1990 — Jets, 24-21 (NY)
1991 — Jets, 17-14 (C)
(RS Pts. — Browns 303, Jets 288)
(PS Pts. — Browns 23, Jets 20)
AFC Divisional Playoff
CLEVELAND vs. PHILADELPHIA
RS: Browns lead series, 30-12-1
1950 — Browns, 35-10 (P)
Browns, 13-7 (C)
1951 — Browns, 20-17 (C)
Browns, 24-9 (P)
1952 — Browns, 49-7 (P)
Eagles, 28-20 (C)
1953 — Browns, 37-13 (C)
Eagles, 42-27 (P)
1954 — Eagles, 28-10 (P)
Browns, 6-0 (C)
1955 — Browns, 21-17 (C)
Eagles, 33-17 (P)
1956 — Browns, 16-0 (P)
Browns, 17-14 (C)
1957 — Browns, 24-7 (C)
Eagles, 17-7 (P)
1958 — Browns, 28-14 (C)
Browns, 21-14 (P)
1959 — Browns, 28-7 (C)
Browns, 28-21 (P)
1960 — Browns, 41-24 (P)
Eagles, 31-29 (C)
1961 — Eagles, 27-20 (P)
Browns, 45-24 (C)
1962 — Eagles, 35-7 (P)
Tie, 14-14 (C)
1963 — Browns, 37-7 (C)
Browns, 23-17 (P)
1964 — Browns, 28-20 (P)
Browns, 38-24 (C)
1965 — Browns, 35-17 (P)
Browns, 38-34 (C)
1966 — Browns, 27-7 (C)
Eagles, 33-21 (P)
1967 — Eagles, 28-24 (P)
1968 — Browns, 47-13 (C)
1969 — Browns, 27-20 (P)
1972 — Browns, 27-17 (P)
1976 — Browns, 24-3 (C)
1979 — Browns, 24-19 (P)
1982 — Eagles, 24-21 (C)
1988 — Browns, 19-3 (C)
1991 — Eagles, 32-30 (C)
(RS Pts. — Browns 1,094, Eagles 778)
CLEVELAND vs. *PHOENIX
RS: Browns lead series, 31-10-3
1950 — Browns, 34-24 (Cle)
Browns, 10-7 (Chi)
1951 — Browns, 34-17 (Chi)
Browns, 49-28 (Cle)
1952 — Browns, 28-13 (Cle)
Browns, 10-0 (Chi)
1953 — Browns, 27-7 (Chi)
Browns, 27-16 (Cle)
1954 — Browns, 31-7 (Cle)
Browns, 35-3 (Chi)
1955 — Browns, 26-20 (Chi)
Browns, 35-24 (Cle)
1956 — Cardinals, 9-7 (Chi)
Cardinals, 24-7 (Cle)
1957 — Browns, 17-7 (Chi)
Browns, 31-0 (Cle)
1958 — Browns, 35-28 (Cle)
Browns, 38-24 (Chi)
1959 — Browns, 34-7 (Chi)
Browns, 17-7 (Cle)
1960 — Browns, 28-27 (Cle)
Tie, 17-17 (StL)
1961 — Browns, 20-17 (Cle)
Browns, 21-10 (StL)
1962 — Browns, 34-7 (StL)
Browns, 38-14 (Cle)
1963 — Cardinals, 20-14 (Cle)
Browns, 24-10 (StL)
1964 — Tie, 33-33 (Cle)
Cardinals, 28-19 (StL)
1965 — Cardinals, 49-13 (Cle)
Browns, 27-24 (StL)
1966 — Cardinals, 34-28 (Cle)
Browns, 38-10 (StL)
1967 — Browns, 20-16 (Cle)
Browns, 20-16 (StL)
1968 — Cardinals, 27-21 (Cle)
Cardinals, 27-16 (StL)
1969 — Tie, 21-21 (Cle)
Browns, 27-21 (StL)
1974 — Cardinals, 29-7 (StL)
1979 — Browns, 38-20 (StL)
1985 — Cardinals, 27-24 (Cle) OT
1988 — Browns, 29-21 (P)
(RS Pts. — Browns 1,109, Cardinals 797)
**Franchise in St. Louis prior to 1988, and in Chicago prior to 1960*
CLEVELAND vs. PITTSBURGH
RS: Browns lead series, 51-35
1950 — Browns, 30-17 (P)
Browns, 45-7 (C)
1951 — Browns, 17-0 (C)
Browns, 28-0 (P)
1952 — Browns, 21-20 (P)
Browns, 29-28 (C)
1953 — Browns, 34-16 (C)
Browns, 20-16 (P)
1954 — Steelers, 55-27 (P)
Browns, 42-7 (C)
1955 — Browns, 41-14 (C)
Browns, 30-7 (P)
1956 — Browns, 14-10 (P)
Steelers, 24-16 (C)
1957 — Browns, 23-12 (P)
Browns, 24-0 (C)
1958 — Browns, 45-12 (P)
Browns, 27-10 (C)
1959 — Steelers, 17-7 (P)
Steelers, 21-20 (C)
1960 — Browns, 28-20 (C)
Steelers, 14-10 (P)
1961 — Browns, 30-28 (P)
Steelers, 17-13 (C)
1962 — Browns, 41-14 (P)
Browns, 35-14 (C)
1963 — Browns, 35-23 (C)
Steelers, 9-7 (P)
1964 — Steelers, 23-7 (C)
Browns, 30-17 (P)
1965 — Browns, 24-19 (C)
Browns, 42-21 (P)
1966 — Browns, 41-10 (C)
Steelers, 16-6 (P)
1967 — Browns, 21-10 (C)
Browns, 34-14 (P)
1968 — Browns, 31-24 (C)
Browns, 45-24 (P)
1969 — Browns, 42-31 (C)
Browns, 24-3 (P)
1970 — Browns, 15-7 (C)
Steelers, 28-9 (P)
1971 — Browns, 27-17 (C)
Steelers, 26-9 (P)
1972 — Browns, 26-24 (C)
Steelers, 30-0 (P)
1973 — Steelers, 33-6 (P)
Browns, 21-16 (C)
1974 — Steelers, 20-16 (P)
Steelers, 26-16 (C)
1975 — Steelers, 42-6 (C)
Steelers, 31-17 (P)
1976 — Steelers, 31-14 (P)
Browns, 18-16 (C)
1977 — Steelers, 28-14 (C)
Steelers, 35-31 (P)
1978 — Steelers, 15-9 (P) OT
Steelers, 34-14 (C)
1979 — Steelers, 51-35 (C)
Steelers, 33-30 (P) OT
1980 — Browns, 27-26 (C)
Steelers, 16-13 (P)
1981 — Steelers, 13-7 (P)
Steelers, 32-10 (C)
1982 — Browns, 10-9 (C)
Steelers, 37-21 (P)
1983 — Steelers, 44-17 (P)
Browns, 30-17 (C)
1984 — Browns, 20-10 (C)
Steelers, 23-20 (P)
1985 — Browns, 17-7 (C)
Steelers, 10-9 (P)
1986 — Browns, 27-24 (P)
Browns, 37-31 (C) OT
1987 — Browns, 34-10 (C)
Browns, 19-13 (P)
1988 — Browns, 23-9 (P)
Browns, 27-7 (C)
1989 — Browns, 51-0 (P)
Steelers, 17-7 (C)
1990 — Browns, 13-3 (C)
Steelers, 35-0 (P)
1991 — Browns, 17-14 (C)
Steelers, 17-10 (P)
1992 — Browns, 17-9 (C)
Steelers, 23-13 (P)
(RS Pts. — Browns 1,915, Steelers 1,643)
CLEVELAND vs. SAN DIEGO
RS: Chargers lead series, 8-6-1
1970 — Chargers, 27-10 (C)
1972 — Browns, 21-17 (SD)
1973 — Tie, 16-16 (C)
1974 — Chargers, 36-35 (SD)
1976 — Browns, 21-17 (C)
1977 — Chargers, 37-14 (SD)
1981 — Chargers, 44-14 (C)
1982 — Chargers, 30-13 (C)
1983 — Browns, 30-24 (SD) OT
1985 — Browns, 21-7 (SD)
1986 — Browns, 47-17 (C)
1987 — Chargers, 27-24 (SD) OT
1990 — Chargers, 24-14 (C)
1991 — Browns, 30-24 (SD) OT
1992 — Chargers, 14-13 (C)
(RS Pts. — Chargers 361, Browns 323)
CLEVELAND vs. SAN FRANCISCO
RS: Browns lead series, 8-6
1950 — Browns, 34-14 (C)
1951 — 49ers, 24-10 (SF)
1953 — Browns, 23-21 (C)
1955 — Browns, 38-3 (SF)
1959 — 49ers, 21-20 (C)
1962 — Browns, 13-10 (SF)
1968 — Browns, 33-21 (SF)
1970 — 49ers, 34-31 (SF)
1974 — Browns, 7-0 (C)
1978 — Browns, 24-7 (C)
1981 — Browns, 15-12 (SF)
1984 — 49ers, 41-7 (C)
1987 — 49ers, 38-24 (SF)
1990 — 49ers, 20-17 (SF)
(RS Pts. — Browns 296, 49ers 266)
CLEVELAND vs. SEATTLE
RS: Seahawks lead series, 8-3
1977 — Seahawks, 20-19 (S)
1978 — Seahawks, 47-24 (S)
1979 — Seahawks, 29-24 (C)
1980 — Browns, 27-3 (S)
1981 — Seahawks, 42-21 (S)
1982 — Browns, 21-7 (S)
1983 — Seahawks, 24-9 (C)
1984 — Seahawks, 33-0 (S)
1985 — Seahawks, 31-13 (S)
1988 — Seahawks, 16-10 (C)
1989 — Browns, 17-7 (S)
(RS Pts. — Seahawks 259, Browns 185)
CLEVELAND vs. TAMPA BAY
RS: Browns lead series, 4-0
1976 — Browns, 24-7 (TB)
1980 — Browns, 34-27 (TB)
1983 — Browns, 20-0 (C)
1989 — Browns, 42-31 (TB)
(RS Pts. — Browns 120, Buccaneers 65)
CLEVELAND vs. WASHINGTON
RS: Browns lead series, 32-9-1
1950 — Browns, 20-14 (C)
Browns, 45-21 (W)
1951 — Browns, 45-0 (C)
1952 — Browns, 19-15 (C)
Browns, 48-24 (W)
1953 — Browns, 30-14 (W)
Browns, 27-3 (C)
1954 — Browns, 62-3 (C)
Browns, 34-14 (W)
1955 — Redskins, 27-17 (C)
Browns, 24-14 (W)
1956 — Redskins, 20-9 (W)
Redskins, 20-17 (C)
1957 — Browns, 21-17 (C)
Tie, 30-30 (W)
1958 — Browns, 20-10 (W)
Browns, 21-14 (C)
1959 — Browns, 34-7 (C)
Browns, 31-17 (W)
1960 — Browns, 31-10 (W)
Browns, 27-16 (C)
1961 — Browns, 31-7 (C)
Browns, 17-6 (W)
1962 — Redskins, 17-16 (C)
Redskins, 17-9 (W)
1963 — Browns, 37-14 (C)
Browns, 27-20 (W)
1964 — Browns, 27-13 (W)
Browns, 34-24 (C)
1965 — Browns, 17-7 (W)
Browns, 24-16 (C)
1966 — Browns, 38-14 (W)
Browns, 14-3 (C)
1967 — Browns, 42-37 (C)
1968 — Browns, 24-21 (W)
1969 — Browns, 27-23 (C)
1971 — Browns, 20-13 (W)
1975 — Redskins, 23-7 (C)
1979 — Redskins, 13-9 (C)
1985 — Redskins, 14-7 (C)
1988 — Browns, 17-13 (W)
1991 — Redskins, 42-17 (W)
(RS Pts. — Browns 1,073, Redskins 667)

DALLAS vs. ATLANTA
RS: Cowboys lead series, 9-5
PS: Cowboys lead series, 2-0;
See Atlanta vs. Dallas
DALLAS vs. BUFFALO
RS: Cowboys lead series, 3-1
PS: Cowboys lead series, 1-0;
See Buffalo vs. Dallas

DALLAS vs. CHICAGO
RS: Cowboys lead series, 8-6
PS: Cowboys lead series, 2-0;
See Chicago vs. Dallas
DALLAS vs. CINCINNATI
RS: Cowboys lead series, 3-2;
See Cincinnati vs. Dallas
DALLAS vs. CLEVELAND
RS: Browns lead series, 14-9
PS: Browns lead series, 2-1;
See Cleveland vs. Dallas
DALLAS vs. DENVER
RS: Cowboys lead series, 3-2
PS: Cowboys lead series, 1-0
1973 — Cowboys, 22-10 (Den)
1977 — Cowboys, 14-6 (Dal)
*Cowboys, 27-10 (New Orleans)
1980 — Broncos, 41-20 (Den)
1986 — Broncos, 29-14 (Den)
1992 — Cowboys, 31-27 (Den)
(RS Pts. — Broncos 113, Cowboys 101)
(PS Pts. — Cowboys 27, Broncos 10)
**Super Bowl XII*
DALLAS vs. DETROIT
RS: Cowboys lead series, 7-5
PS: Series tied, 1-1
1960 — Lions, 23-14 (Det)
1963 — Cowboys, 17-14 (Dal)
1968 — Cowboys, 59-13 (Dal)
1970 — *Cowboys, 5-0 (Dal)
1972 — Cowboys, 28-24 (Dal)
1975 — Cowboys, 36-10 (Det)
1977 — Cowboys, 37-0 (Dal)
1981 — Lions, 27-24 (Det)
1985 — Lions, 26-21 (Det)
1986 — Cowboys, 31-7 (Det)
1987 — Lions, 27-17 (Det)
1991 — Lions, 34-10 (Det)
*Lions, 38-6 (Det)
1992 — Cowboys, 37-3 (Det)
(RS Pts. — Cowboys 331, Lions 208)
(PS Pts. — Lions 38, Cowboys 11)
**NFC Divisional Playoff*
DALLAS vs. GREEN BAY
RS: Packers lead series, 8-5
PS: Packers lead series, 2-1
1960 — Packers, 41-7 (GB)
1964 — Packers, 45-21 (D)
1965 — Packers, 13-3 (Mil)
1966 — *Packers, 34-27 (D)
1967 — *Packers, 21-17 (GB)
1968 — Packers, 28-17 (D)
1970 — Cowboys, 16-3 (D)
1972 — Packers, 16-13 (Mil)
1975 — Packers, 19-17 (D)
1978 — Cowboys, 42-14 (Mil)
1980 — Cowboys, 28-7 (Mil)
1982 — **Cowboys, 37-26 (D)
1984 — Cowboys, 20-6 (D)
1989 — Packers, 31-13 (GB)
Packers, 20-10 (D)
1991 — Cowboys, 20-17 (Mil)
(RS Pts. — Packers 260, Cowboys 227)
(PS Pts. — Cowboys 81, Packers 81)
**NFL Championship*
***NFC Second Round Playoff*
DALLAS vs. HOUSTON
RS: Cowboys lead series, 4-3
1970 — Cowboys, 52-10 (D)
1974 — Cowboys, 10-0 (H)
1979 — Oilers, 30-24 (D)
1982 — Cowboys, 37-7 (H)
1985 — Cowboys, 17-10 (H)
1988 — Oilers, 25-17 (D)
1991 — Oilers, 26-23 (H) OT
(RS Pts. — Cowboys 180, Oilers 108)
DALLAS vs. *INDIANAPOLIS
RS: Cowboys lead series, 6-2
PS: Colts lead series, 1-0
1960 — Colts, 45-7 (D)
1967 — Colts, 23-17 (B)
1969 — Cowboys, 27-10 (D)
1970 — **Colts, 16-13 (Miami)
1972 — Cowboys, 21-0 (B)
1976 — Cowboys, 30-27 (D)
1978 — Cowboys, 38-0 (D)
1981 — Cowboys, 37-13 (B)
1984 — Cowboys, 22-3 (D)
(RS Pts. — Cowboys 199, Colts 121)
(PS Pts. — Colts 16, Cowboys 13)
**Franchise in Baltimore prior to 1984*
***Super Bowl V*
DALLAS vs. KANSAS CITY
RS: Cowboys lead series, 3-2
1970 — Cowboys, 27-16 (KC)
1975 — Chiefs, 34-31 (D)
1983 — Cowboys, 41-21 (D)
1989 — Chiefs, 36-28 (KC)
1992 — Cowboys, 17-10 (D)
(RS Pts. — Cowboys 144, Chiefs 117)
DALLAS vs. *L.A. RAIDERS
RS: Raiders lead series, 3-2
1974 — Raiders, 27-23 (O)
1980 — Cowboys, 19-13 (O)
1983 — Raiders, 40-38 (D)
1986 — Raiders, 17-13 (D)
1992 — Cowboys, 28-13 (LA)
(RS Pts. — Cowboys 121, Raiders 110)
**Franchise in Oakland prior to 1982*
DALLAS vs. L.A. RAMS
RS: Rams lead series, 9-8
PS: Series tied, 4-4
1960 — Rams, 38-13 (D)
1962 — Cowboys, 27-17 (LA)
1967 — Rams, 35-13 (D)
1969 — Rams, 24-23 (LA)
1971 — Cowboys, 28-21 (D)
1973 — Rams, 37-31 (LA)
*Cowboys, 27-16 (D)
1975 — Cowboys, 18-7 (D)
**Cowboys, 37-7 (LA)
1976 — *Rams, 14-12 (D)
1978 — Rams, 27-14 (LA)
**Cowboys, 28-0 (LA)
1979 — Cowboys, 30-6 (D)
*Rams, 21-19 (D)
1980 — Rams, 38-14 (LA)
***Cowboys, 34-13 (D)
1981 — Cowboys, 29-17 (D)
1983 — ***Rams, 24-17 (D)
1984 — Cowboys, 20-13 (LA)
1985 — *Rams, 20-0 (LA)
1986 — Rams, 29-10 (LA)
1987 — Cowboys, 29-21 (LA)
1989 — Rams, 35-31 (D)
1990 — Cowboys, 24-21 (LA)
1992 — Rams, 27-23 (D)
(RS Pts. — Rams 413, Cowboys 377)
(PS Pts. — Cowboys 174, Rams 115)
**NFC Divisional Playoff*
***NFC Championship*
****NFC First Round Playoff*
DALLAS vs. MIAMI
RS: Dolphins lead series, 5-1
PS: Cowboys lead series, 1-0
1971 — *Cowboys, 24-3 (New Orleans)
1973 — Dolphins, 14-7 (D)
1978 — Dolphins, 23-16 (M)
1981 — Cowboys, 28-27 (D)
1984 — Dolphins, 28-21 (M)
1987 — Dolphins, 20-14 (D)
1989 — Dolphins, 17-14 (D)
(RS Pts. — Dolphins 129, Cowboys 100)
(PS Pts. — Cowboys 24, Dolphins 3)
**Super Bowl VI*
DALLAS vs. MINNESOTA
RS: Cowboys lead series, 7-6
PS: Cowboys lead series, 3-1
1961 — Cowboys, 21-7 (D)
Cowboys, 28-0 (M)
1966 — Cowboys, 28-17 (D)
1968 — Cowboys, 20-7 (M)
1970 — Vikings, 54-13 (M)
1971 — *Cowboys, 20-12 (M)
1973 — **Vikings, 27-10 (D)
1974 — Vikings, 23-21 (D)
1975 — *Cowboys, 17-14 (M)
1977 — Cowboys, 16-10 (M) OT
**Cowboys, 23-6 (D)
1978 — Vikings, 21-10 (D)
1979 — Cowboys, 36-20 (M)
1982 — Vikings, 31-27 (M)
1983 — Cowboys, 37-24 (M)
1987 — Vikings, 44-38 (D) OT
1988 — Vikings, 43-3 (D)
(RS Pts. — Vikings 301, Cowboys 298)
(PS Pts. — Cowboys 70, Vikings 59)
**NFC Divisional Playoff*
***NFC Championship*
DALLAS vs. NEW ENGLAND
RS: Cowboys lead series, 6-0
1971 — Cowboys, 44-21 (D)
1975 — Cowboys, 34-31 (NE)
1978 — Cowboys, 17-10 (D)
1981 — Cowboys, 35-21 (NE)
1984 — Cowboys, 20-17 (D)
1987 — Cowboys, 23-17 (NE) OT
(RS Pts. — Cowboys 173, Patriots 117)
DALLAS vs. NEW ORLEANS
RS: Cowboys lead series, 13-3
1967 — Cowboys, 14-10 (D)
Cowboys, 27-10 (NO)
1968 — Cowboys, 17-3 (NO)
1969 — Cowboys, 21-17 (NO)
Cowboys, 33-17 (D)
1971 — Saints, 24-14 (NO)
1973 — Cowboys, 40-3 (D)
1976 — Cowboys, 24-6 (NO)
1978 — Cowboys, 27-7 (D)
1982 — Cowboys, 21-7 (D)
1983 — Cowboys, 21-20 (D)
1984 — Cowboys, 30-27 (D) OT
1988 — Saints, 20-17 (NO)
1989 — Saints, 28-0 (NO)
1990 — Cowboys, 17-13 (D)
1991 — Cowboys, 23-14 (D)
(RS Pts. — Cowboys 346, Saints 226)
DALLAS vs. N.Y. GIANTS
RS: Cowboys lead series, 38-21-2
1960 — Tie, 31-31 (NY)
1961 — Giants, 31-10 (D)
Cowboys, 17-16 (NY)
1962 — Giants, 41-10 (D)
Giants, 41-31 (NY)
1963 — Giants, 37-21 (NY)
Giants, 34-27 (D)
1964 — Tie, 13-13 (D)
Cowboys, 31-21 (NY)
1965 — Cowboys, 31-2 (D)
Cowboys, 38-20 (NY)
1966 — Cowboys, 52-7 (D)
Cowboys, 17-7 (NY)
1967 — Cowboys, 38-24 (D)
1968 — Giants, 27-21 (D)
Cowboys, 28-10 (NY)
1969 — Cowboys, 25-3 (D)
1970 — Cowboys, 28-10 (D)
Giants, 23-20 (NY)
1971 — Cowboys, 20-13 (D)
Cowboys, 42-14 (NY)
1972 — Cowboys, 23-14 (NY)
Giants, 23-3 (D)
1973 — Cowboys, 45-28 (D)
Cowboys, 23-10 (New Haven)
1974 — Giants, 14-6 (D)
Cowboys, 21-7 (New Haven)
1975 — Cowboys, 13-7 (NY)
Cowboys, 14-3 (D)
1976 — Cowboys, 24-14 (NY)
Cowboys, 9-3 (D)
1977 — Cowboys, 41-21 (D)
Cowboys, 24-10 (NY)
1978 — Cowboys, 34-24 (NY)
Cowboys, 24-3 (D)
1979 — Cowboys, 16-14 (NY)
Cowboys, 28-7 (D)
1980 — Cowboys, 24-3 (D)
Giants, 38-35 (NY)
1981 — Cowboys, 18-10 (D)
Giants, 13-10 (NY) OT
1983 — Cowboys, 28-13 (D)
Cowboys, 38-20 (NY)
1984 — Giants, 28-7 (NY)
Giants, 19-7 (D)
1985 — Cowboys, 30-29 (NY)
Cowboys, 28-21 (D)
1986 — Cowboys, 31-28 (D)
Giants, 17-14 (NY)
1987 — Cowboys, 16-14 (NY)
Cowboys, 33-24 (D)
1988 — Giants, 12-10 (D)
Giants, 29-21 (NY)
1989 — Giants, 30-13 (D)
Giants, 15-0 (NY)
1990 — Giants, 28-7 (D)
Giants, 31-17 (NY)
1991 — Cowboys, 21-16 (D)
Giants, 22-9 (NY)
1992 — Cowboys, 34-28 (NY)
Cowboys, 30-3 (D)
(RS Pts. — Cowboys 1,380, Giants 1,118)
DALLAS vs. N.Y. JETS
RS: Cowboys lead series, 4-1
1971 — Cowboys, 52-10 (D)
1975 — Cowboys, 31-21 (NY)
1978 — Cowboys, 30-7 (NY)
1987 — Cowboys, 38-24 (NY)
1990 — Jets, 24-9 (NY)
(RS Pts. — Cowboys 160, Jets 86)
DALLAS vs. PHILADELPHIA
RS: Cowboys lead series, 38-26
PS: Series tied, 1-1
1960 — Eagles, 27-25 (D)
1961 — Eagles, 43-7 (D)
Eagles, 35-13 (P)
1962 — Cowboys, 41-19 (D)
Eagles, 28-14 (P)
1963 — Eagles, 24-21 (P)
Cowboys, 27-20 (D)
1964 — Eagles, 17-14 (D)
Eagles, 24-14 (P)
1965 — Eagles, 35-24 (D)
Cowboys, 21-19 (P)
1966 — Cowboys, 56-7 (D)
Eagles, 24-23 (P)
1967 — Eagles, 21-14 (P)
Cowboys, 38-17 (D)
1968 — Cowboys, 45-13 (P)
Cowboys, 34-14 (D)
1969 — Cowboys, 38-7 (P)
Cowboys, 49-14 (D)
1970 — Cowboys, 17-7 (P)
Cowboys, 21-17 (D)
1971 — Cowboys, 42-7 (P)
Cowboys, 20-7 (D)
1972 — Cowboys, 28-6 (D)
Cowboys, 28-7 (P)
1973 — Eagles, 30-16 (P)
Cowboys, 31-10 (D)
1974 — Eagles, 13-10 (P)
Cowboys, 31-24 (D)
1975 — Cowboys, 20-17 (P)
Cowboys, 27-17 (D)
1976 — Cowboys, 27-7 (D)
Cowboys, 26-7 (P)
1977 — Cowboys, 16-10 (P)
Cowboys, 24-14 (D)
1978 — Cowboys, 14-7 (D)
Cowboys, 31-13 (P)
1979 — Eagles, 31-21 (D)
Cowboys, 24-17 (P)
1980 — Eagles, 17-10 (P)
Cowboys, 35-27 (D)
*Eagles, 20-7 (P)
1981 — Cowboys, 17-14 (P)
Cowboys, 21-10 (D)
1982 — Eagles, 24-20 (D)
1983 — Cowboys, 37-7 (D)
Cowboys, 27-20 (P)
1984 — Cowboys, 23-17 (D)
Cowboys, 26-10 (P)
1985 — Eagles, 16-14 (P)
Cowboys, 34-17 (D)
1986 — Cowboys, 17-14 (P)
Eagles, 23-21 (D)
1987 — Cowboys, 41-22 (D)
Eagles, 37-20 (P)
1988 — Eagles, 24-23 (P)
Eagles, 23-7 (D)
1989 — Eagles, 27-0 (D)
Eagles, 20-10 (P)
1990 — Eagles, 21-20 (D)
Eagles, 17-3 (P)
1991 — Eagles, 24-0 (D)
Cowboys, 25-13 (P)
1992 — Eagles, 31-7 (P)
Cowboys, 20-10 (D)
**Cowboys, 34-10 (D)
(RS Pts. — Cowboys 1,470, Eagles 1,161)
(PS Pts. — Cowboys 41, Eagles 30)
**NFC Championship*
***NFC Divisional Playoff*
DALLAS vs. *PHOENIX
RS: Cowboys lead series, 38-22-1
1960 — Cardinals, 12-10 (StL)
1961 — Cardinals, 31-17 (D)
Cardinals, 31-13 (StL)
1962 — Cardinals, 28-24 (D)
Cardinals, 52-20 (StL)
1963 — Cardinals, 34-7 (D)
Cowboys, 28-24 (StL)
1964 — Cardinals, 16-6 (D)
Cowboys, 31-13 (StL)
1965 — Cardinals, 20-13 (StL)
Cowboys, 27-13 (D)
1966 — Tie, 10-10 (StL)
Cowboys, 31-17 (D)
1967 — Cowboys, 46-21 (D)
1968 — Cowboys, 27-10 (StL)
1969 — Cowboys, 24-3 (D)
1970 — Cardinals, 20-7 (StL)
Cardinals, 38-0 (D)
1971 — Cowboys, 16-13 (StL)
Cowboys, 31-12 (D)
1972 — Cowboys, 33-24 (D)
Cowboys, 27-6 (StL)
1973 — Cowboys, 45-10 (D)
Cowboys, 30-3 (StL)
1974 — Cardinals, 31-28 (StL)
Cowboys, 17-14 (D)
1975 — Cowboys, 37-31 (D) OT
Cardinals, 31-17 (StL)
1976 — Cardinals, 21-17 (StL)
Cowboys, 19-14 (D)
1977 — Cowboys, 30-24 (StL)
Cardinals, 24-17 (D)
1978 — Cowboys, 21-12 (D)
Cowboys, 24-21 (StL) OT
1979 — Cowboys, 22-21 (StL)
Cowboys, 22-13 (D)
1980 — Cowboys, 27-24 (StL)
Cowboys, 31-21 (D)
1981 — Cowboys, 30-17 (D)
Cardinals, 20-17 (StL)
1982 — Cowboys, 24-7 (StL)
1983 — Cowboys, 34-17 (StL)
Cowboys, 35-17 (D)
1984 — Cardinals, 31-20 (D)
Cowboys, 24-17 (StL)
1985 — Cardinals, 21-10 (StL)
Cowboys, 35-17 (D)
1986 — Cowboys, 31-7 (StL)
Cowboys, 37-6 (D)
1987 — Cardinals, 24-13 (StL)
Cowboys, 21-16 (D)
1988 — Cowboys, 17-14 (P)
Cardinals, 16-10 (D)
1989 — Cardinals, 19-10 (D)
Cardinals, 24-20 (P)
1990 — Cardinals, 20-3 (P)
Cowboys, 41-10 (D)
1991 — Cowboys, 17-9 (P)

Cowboys, 27-7 (D)
1992 — Cowboys, 31-20 (D)
Cowboys, 16-10 (P)
(RS Pts. — Cowboys 1,375, Cardinals 1,129)
Franchise in St. Louis prior to 1988

DALLAS vs. PITTSBURGH
RS: Cowboys lead series, 12-11
PS: Steelers lead series, 2-0
1960 — Steelers, 35-28 (D)
1961 — Cowboys, 27-24 (D)
Steelers, 37-7 (P)
1962 — Steelers, 30-28 (D)
Cowboys, 42-27 (P)
1963 — Steelers, 27-21 (P)
Steelers, 24-19 (D)
1964 — Steelers, 23-17 (P)
Cowboys, 17-14 (D)
1965 — Steelers, 22-13 (P)
Cowboys, 24-17 (D)
1966 — Cowboys, 52-21 (D)
Cowboys, 20-7 (P)
1967 — Cowboys, 24-21 (P)
1968 — Cowboys, 28-7 (D)
1969 — Cowboys, 10-7 (P)
1972 — Cowboys, 17-13 (D)
1975 — *Steelers, 21-17 (Miami)
1977 — Steelers, 28-13 (P)
1978 — **Steelers, 35-31 (Miami)
1979 — Steelers, 14-3 (P)
1982 — Steelers, 36-28 (D)
1985 — Cowboys, 27-13 (D)
1988 — Steelers, 24-21 (P)
1991 — Cowboys, 20-10 (D)
(RS Pts. — Cowboys 506, Steelers 481)
(PS Pts. — Steelers 56, Cowboys 48)
*Super Bowl X
**Super Bowl XIII

DALLAS vs. SAN DIEGO
RS: Cowboys lead series, 4-1
1972 — Cowboys, 34-28 (SD)
1980 — Cowboys, 42-31 (D)
1983 — Chargers, 24-23 (SD)
1986 — Cowboys, 24-21 (SD)
1990 — Cowboys, 17-14 (D)
(RS Pts. — Cowboys 140, Chargers 118)

DALLAS vs. SAN FRANCISCO
RS: 49ers lead series, 9-5-1
PS: Cowboys lead series, 4-1
1960 — 49ers, 26-14 (D)
1963 — 49ers, 31-24 (SF)
1965 — Cowboys, 39-31 (D)
1967 — 49ers, 24-16 (SF)
1969 — Tie, 24-24 (D)
1970 — *Cowboys, 17-10 (SF)
1971 — *Cowboys, 14-3 (D)
1972 — 49ers, 31-10 (D)
**Cowboys, 30-28 (SF)
1974 — Cowboys, 20-14 (D)
1977 — Cowboys, 42-35 (SF)
1979 — Cowboys, 21-13 (SF)
1980 — Cowboys, 59-14 (D)
1981 — 49ers, 45-14 (SF)
*49ers, 28-27 (SF)
1983 — 49ers, 42-17 (SF)
1985 — 49ers, 31-16 (SF)
1989 — 49ers, 31-14 (D)
1990 — 49ers, 24-6 (D)
1992 — *Cowboys, 30-20 (SF)
(RS Pts. — 49ers 416, Cowboys 336)
(PS Pts. — Cowboys 118, 49ers 89)
*NFC Championship
**NFC Divisional Playoff

DALLAS vs. SEATTLE
RS: Cowboys lead series, 4-1
1976 — Cowboys, 28-13 (S)
1980 — Cowboys, 51-7 (D)
1983 — Cowboys, 35-10 (S)
1986 — Seahawks, 31-14 (D)
1992 — Cowboys, 27-0 (D)
(RS Pts. — Cowboys 155, Seahawks 61)

DALLAS vs. TAMPA BAY
RS: Cowboys lead series, 6-0
PS: Cowboys lead series, 2-0
1977 — Cowboys, 23-7 (D)
1980 — Cowboys, 28-17 (D)
1981 — *Cowboys, 38-0 (D)
1982 — Cowboys, 14-9 (D)
**Cowboys, 30-17 (D)
1983 — Cowboys, 27-24 (D) OT
1990 — Cowboys, 14-10 (D)
Cowboys 17-13 (TB)
(RS Pts. — Cowboys 123, Buccaneers 80)
(PS Pts. — Cowboys 68, Buccaneers 17)
*NFC Divisional Playoff
**NFC First Round Playoff

DALLAS vs. WASHINGTON
RS: Cowboys lead series, 36-26-2
PS: Redskins lead series, 2-0
1960 — Redskins, 26-14 (W)
1961 — Tie, 28-28 (D)
Redskins, 34-24 (W)
1962 — Tie, 35-35 (D)
Cowboys, 38-10 (W)
1963 — Redskins, 21-17 (W)
Cowboys, 35-20 (D)
1964 — Cowboys, 24-18 (D)
Redskins, 28-16 (W)
1965 — Cowboys, 27-7 (D)
Redskins, 34-31 (W)
1966 — Cowboys, 31-30 (W)
Redskins, 34-31 (D)
1967 — Cowboys, 17-14 (W)
Redskins, 27-20 (D)
1968 — Cowboys, 44-24 (W)
Cowboys, 29-20 (D)
1969 — Cowboys, 41-28 (W)
Cowboys, 20-10 (D)
1970 — Cowboys, 45-21 (W)
Cowboys, 34-0 (D)
1971 — Redskins, 20-16 (D)
Cowboys, 13-0 (W)
1972 — Redskins, 24-20 (W)
Cowboys, 34-24 (D)
*Redskins, 26-3 (W)
1973 — Redskins, 14-7 (W)
Cowboys, 27-7 (D)
1974 — Redskins, 28-21 (W)
Cowboys, 24-23 (D)
1975 — Redskins, 30-24 (W) OT
Cowboys, 31-10 (D)
1976 — Cowboys, 20-7 (W)
Redskins, 27-14 (D)
1977 — Cowboys, 34-16 (D)
Cowboys, 14-7 (W)
1978 — Redskins, 9-5 (W)
Cowboys, 37-10 (D)
1979 — Redskins, 34-20 (W)
Cowboys, 35-34 (D)
1980 — Cowboys, 17-3 (W)
Cowboys, 14-10 (D)
1981 — Cowboys, 26-10 (W)
Cowboys, 24-10 (D)
1982 — Cowboys, 24-10 (W)
*Redskins, 31-17 (W)
1983 — Cowboys, 31-30 (W)
Redskins, 31-10 (D)
1984 — Redskins, 34-14 (W)
Redskins, 30-28 (D)
1985 — Cowboys, 44-14 (D)
Cowboys, 13-7 (W)
1986 — Cowboys, 30-6 (D)
Redskins, 41-14 (W)
1987 — Redskins, 13-7 (D)
Redskins, 24-20 (W)
1988 — Redskins, 35-17 (D)
Cowboys, 24-17 (W)
1989 — Redskins, 30-7 (D)
Cowboys, 13-3 (W)
1990 — Redskins, 19-15 (W)
Cowboys, 27-17 (D)
1991 — Redskins, 33-31 (D)
Cowboys, 24-21 (W)
1992 — Cowboys, 23-10 (D)
Redskins, 20-17 (W)
(RS Pts. — Cowboys, 1,511, Redskins 1,271)
(PS Pts. — Redskins 57, Cowboys 20)
*NFC Championship

DENVER vs. ATLANTA
RS: Broncos lead series, 4-3;
See Atlanta vs. Denver

DENVER vs. BUFFALO
RS: Bills lead series, 16-10-1
PS: Bills lead series, 1-0;
See Buffalo vs. Denver

DENVER vs. CHICAGO
RS: Bears lead series, 5-4;
See Chicago vs. Denver

DENVER vs. CINCINNATI
RS: Broncos lead series, 10-6;
See Cincinnati vs. Denver

DENVER vs. CLEVELAND
RS: Broncos lead series, 11-5
PS: Broncos lead series, 3-0;
See Cleveland vs. Denver

DENVER vs. DALLAS
RS: Cowboys lead series, 3-2
PS: Cowboys lead series, 1-0;
See Dallas vs. Denver

DENVER vs. DETROIT
RS: Broncos lead series, 4-3
1971 — Lions, 24-20 (Den)
1974 — Broncos, 31-27 (Det)
1978 — Lions, 17-14 (Det)
1981 — Broncos, 27-21 (Den)
1984 — Broncos, 28-7 (Det)
1987 — Broncos, 34-0 (Den)
1990 — Lions, 40-27 (Det)
(RS Pts. — Broncos 181, Lions 136)

DENVER vs. GREEN BAY
RS: Broncos lead series, 4-1-1
1971 — Packers, 34-13 (Mil)
1975 — Broncos, 23-13 (D)
1978 — Broncos, 16-3 (D)
1984 — Broncos, 17-14 (D)
1987 — Tie, 17-17 (Mil) OT
1990 — Broncos, 22-13 (D)
(RS Pts. — Broncos 108, Packers 94)

DENVER vs. HOUSTON
RS: Oilers lead series, 19-11-1
PS: Broncos lead series, 2-1
1960 — Oilers, 45-25 (D)
Oilers, 20-10 (H)
1961 — Oilers, 55-14 (D)
Oilers, 45-14 (H)
1962 — Broncos, 20-10 (D)
Oilers, 34-17 (H)
1963 — Oilers, 20-14 (H)
Oilers, 33-24 (D)
1964 — Oilers, 38-17 (D)
Oilers, 34-15 (H)
1965 — Broncos, 28-17 (D)
Broncos, 31-21 (H)
1966 — Oilers, 45-7 (H)
Broncos, 40-38 (D)
1967 — Oilers, 10-6 (H)
Oilers, 20-18 (D)
1968 — Oilers, 38-17 (H)
1969 — Oilers, 24-21 (H)
Tie, 20-20 (D)
1970 — Oilers, 31-21 (H)
1972 — Broncos, 30-17 (D)
1973 — Broncos, 48-20 (H)
1974 — Broncos, 37-14 (D)
1976 — Oilers, 17-3 (H)
1977 — Broncos, 24-14 (H)
1979 — *Oilers, 13-7 (H)
1980 — Oilers, 20-16 (D)
1983 — Broncos, 26-14 (H)
1985 — Broncos, 31-20 (D)
1987 — Oilers, 40-10 (D)
**Broncos, 34-10 (D)
1991 — Oilers, 42-14 (H)
**Broncos, 26-24 (D)
1992 — Broncos, 27-21 (D)
(RS Pts. — Oilers 837, Broncos 645)
(PS Pts. — Broncos 67, Oilers 47)
*AFC First Round Playoff
**AFC Divisional Playoff

DENVER vs. *INDIANAPOLIS
RS: Broncos lead series, 8-2
1974 — Broncos, 17-6 (B)
1977 — Broncos, 27-13 (D)
1978 — Colts, 7-6 (B)
1981 — Broncos, 28-10 (D)
1983 — Broncos, 17-10 (B)
Broncos, 21-19 (D)
1985 — Broncos, 15-10 (I)
1988 — Colts, 55-23 (I)
1989 — Broncos, 14-3 (D)
1990 — Broncos, 27-17 (I)
(RS Pts. — Broncos 195, Colts 150)
Franchise in Baltimore prior to 1984

DENVER vs. *KANSAS CITY
RS: Chiefs lead series, 37-28
1960 — Texans, 17-14 (D)
Texans, 34-7 (Da)
1961 — Texans, 19-12 (D)
Texans, 49-21 (Da)
1962 — Texans, 24-3 (D)
Texans, 17-10 (Da)
1963 — Chiefs, 59-7 (D)
Chiefs, 52-21 (KC)
1964 — Broncos, 33-27 (D)
Chiefs, 49-39 (KC)
1965 — Chiefs, 31-23 (D)
Chiefs, 45-35 (KC)
1966 — Chiefs, 37-10 (KC)
Chiefs, 56-10 (D)
1967 — Chiefs, 52-9 (KC)
Chiefs, 38-24 (D)
1968 — Chiefs, 34-2 (KC)
Chiefs, 30-7 (D)
1969 — Chiefs, 26-13 (D)
Chiefs, 31-17 (KC)
1970 — Broncos, 26-13 (D)
Chiefs, 16-0 (KC)
1971 — Chiefs, 16-3 (D)
Chiefs, 28-10 (KC)
1972 — Chiefs, 45-24 (D)
Chiefs, 24-21 (KC)
1973 — Chiefs, 16-14 (KC)
Broncos, 14-10 (D)
1974 — Broncos, 17-14 (KC)
Chiefs, 42-34 (D)
1975 — Broncos, 37-33 (D)
Chiefs, 26-13 (KC)
1976 — Broncos, 35-26 (KC)
Broncos, 17-16 (D)
1977 — Broncos, 23-7 (D)
Broncos, 14-7 (KC)
1978 — Broncos, 23-17 (KC) OT
Broncos, 24-3 (D)
1979 — Broncos, 24-10 (KC)
Broncos, 20-3 (D)
1980 — Chiefs, 23-17 (D)
Chiefs, 31-14 (KC)
1981 — Chiefs, 28-14 (KC)
Broncos, 16-13 (D)
1982 — Chiefs, 37-16 (D)
1983 — Broncos, 27-24 (D)
Chiefs, 48-17 (KC)
1984 — Broncos, 21-0 (D)
Chiefs, 16-13 (KC)
1985 — Broncos, 30-10 (KC)
Broncos, 14-13 (D)
1986 — Broncos, 38-17 (D)
Chiefs, 37-10 (KC)
1987 — Broncos, 26-17 (KC)
Broncos, 20-17 (D)
1988 — Chiefs, 20-13 (KC)
Broncos, 17-11 (D)
1989 — Broncos, 34-20 (D)
Broncos, 16-13 (KC)
1990 — Broncos, 24-23 (D)
Chiefs, 31-20 (KC)
1991 — Broncos, 19-16 (D)
Broncos, 24-20 (KC)
1992 — Broncos, 20-19 (D)
Chiefs, 42-20 (KC)
(RS Pts. — Chiefs 1,645, Broncos 1,210)
Franchise in Dallas prior to 1963 and known as Texans

DENVER vs. *L.A. RAIDERS
RS: Raiders lead series, 44-19-2
PS: Broncos lead series, 1-0
1960 — Broncos, 31-14 (D)
Raiders, 48-10 (O)
1961 — Raiders, 33-19 (O)
Broncos, 27-24 (D)
1962 — Broncos, 44-7 (D)
Broncos, 23-6 (O)
1963 — Raiders, 26-10 (D)
Raiders, 35-31 (O)
1964 — Raiders, 40-7 (O)
Tie, 20-20 (D)
1965 — Raiders, 28-20 (D)
Raiders, 24-13 (O)
1966 — Raiders, 17-3 (D)
Raiders, 28-10 (O)
1967 — Raiders, 51-0 (O)
Raiders, 21-17 (D)
1968 — Raiders, 43-7 (D)
Raiders, 33-27 (O)
1969 — Raiders, 24-14 (D)
Raiders, 41-10 (O)
1970 — Raiders, 35-23 (O)
Raiders, 24-19 (D)
1971 — Raiders, 27-16 (D)
Raiders, 21-13 (O)
1972 — Broncos, 30-23 (O)
Raiders, 37-20 (D)
1973 — Tie, 23-23 (D)
Raiders, 21-17 (O)
1974 — Raiders, 28-17 (D)
Broncos, 20-17 (O)
1975 — Raiders, 42-17 (D)
Raiders, 17-10 (O)
1976 — Raiders, 17-10 (D)
Raiders, 19-6 (O)
1977 — Broncos, 30-7 (O)
Raiders, 24-14 (D)
**Broncos, 20-17 (D)
1978 — Broncos, 14-6 (D)
Broncos, 21-6 (O)
1979 — Raiders, 27-3 (O)
Raiders, 14-10 (D)
1980 — Raiders, 9-3 (O)
Raiders, 24-21 (D)
1981 — Broncos, 9-7 (D)
Broncos, 17-0 (O)
1982 — Raiders, 27-10 (LA)
1983 — Raiders, 22-7 (D)
Raiders, 22-20 (LA)
1984 — Broncos, 16-13 (D)
Broncos, 22-19 (LA) OT
1985 — Raiders, 31-28 (LA) OT
Raiders, 17-14 (D) OT
1986 — Broncos, 38-36 (D)
Broncos, 21-10 (LA)
1987 — Broncos, 30-14 (D)
Broncos, 23-17 (LA)
1988 — Raiders, 30-27 (D) OT
Raiders, 21-20 (LA)
1989 — Broncos, 31-21 (D)
Raiders, 16-13 (LA) OT
1990 — Raiders, 14-9 (LA)
Raiders, 23-20 (D)
1991 — Raiders, 16-13 (LA)
Raiders, 17-16 (D)
1992 — Broncos, 17-13 (D)
Raiders, 24-0 (LA)
(RS Pts. — Raiders 1,461, Broncos 1,121)
(PS Pts. — Broncos 20, Raiders 17)
*Franchise in Oakland prior to 1982
**AFC Championship

DENVER vs. L.A. RAMS
RS: Series tied, 3-3
1972 — Broncos, 16-10 (LA)
1974 — Rams, 17-10 (D)
1979 — Rams, 13-9 (D)
1982 — Broncos, 27-24 (LA)

1985 — Rams, 20-16 (LA)
1988 — Broncos, 35-24 (D)
(RS Pts. — Broncos 113, Rams 108)
DENVER vs. MIAMI
RS: Dolphins lead series, 5-2-1
1966 — Dolphins, 24-7 (M)
Broncos, 17-7 (D)
1967 — Dolphins, 35-21 (M)
1968 — Broncos, 21-14 (D)
1969 — Dolphins, 27-24 (M)
1971 — Tie, 10-10 (D)
1975 — Dolphins, 14-13 (M)
1985 — Dolphins, 30-26 (D)
(RS Pts. — Dolphins 161, Broncos 139)
DENVER vs. MINNESOTA
RS: Vikings lead series, 4-3
1972 — Vikings, 23-20 (D)
1978 — Vikings, 12-9 (M) OT
1981 — Broncos, 19-17 (D)
1984 — Broncos, 42-21 (D)
1987 — Vikings, 34-27 (M)
1990 — Vikings, 27-22 (M)
1991 — Broncos, 13-6 (M)
(RS Pts. — Broncos 152, Vikings 140)
DENVER vs. *NEW ENGLAND
RS: Broncos lead series, 16-12
PS: Broncos lead series, 1-0
1960 — Broncos, 13-10 (B)
Broncos, 31-24 (D)
1961 — Patriots, 45-17 (B)
Patriots, 28-24 (D)
1962 — Patriots, 41-16 (B)
Patriots, 33-29 (D)
1963 — Broncos, 14-10 (D)
Patriots, 40-21 (B)
1964 — Patriots, 39-10 (D)
Patriots, 12-7 (B)
1965 — Broncos, 27-10 (B)
Patriots, 28-20 (D)
1966 — Patriots, 24-10 (D)
Broncos, 17-10 (B)
1967 — Broncos, 26-21 (D)
1968 — Patriots, 20-17 (D)
Broncos, 35-14 (B)
1969 — Broncos, 35-7 (D)
1972 — Broncos, 45-21 (D)
1976 — Patriots, 38-14 (NE)
1979 — Broncos, 45-10 (D)
1980 — Patriots, 23-14 (NE)
1984 — Broncos, 26-19 (D)
1986 — Broncos, 27-20 (D)
**Broncos, 22-17 (D)
1987 — Broncos, 31-20 (D)
1988 — Broncos, 21-10 (D)
1991 — Broncos, 9-6 (NE)
Broncos, 20-3 (D)
(RS Pts. — Broncos 621, Patriots 586)
(PS Pts. — Broncos 22, Patriots 17)
**Franchise in Boston prior to 1971*
***AFC Divisional Playoff*
DENVER vs. NEW ORLEANS
RS: Broncos lead series, 4-1
1970 — Broncos, 31-6 (NO)
1974 — Broncos, 33-17 (D)
1979 — Broncos, 10-3 (D)
1985 — Broncos, 34-23 (D)
1988 — Saints, 42-0 (NO)
(RS Pts. — Broncos 108, Saints 91)
DENVER vs. N.Y. GIANTS
RS: Series tied, 3-3
PS: Giants lead series, 1-0
1972 — Giants, 29-17 (NY)
1976 — Broncos, 14-13 (D)
1980 — Broncos, 14-9 (NY)
1986 — Giants, 19-16 (NY)
*Giants, 39-20 (Pasadena)
1989 — Giants, 14-7 (D)
1992 — Broncos, 27-13 (D)
(RS Pts. — Giants 97, Broncos 95)
(PS Pts. — Giants 39, Broncos 20)
**Super Bowl XXI*
DENVER vs. *N.Y. JETS
RS: Series tied, 11-11-1
1960 — Titans, 28-24 (NY)
Titans, 30-27 (D)
1961 — Titans, 35-28 (NY)
Broncos, 27-10 (D)
1962 — Broncos, 32-10 (NY)
Titans, 46-45 (D)
1963 — Tie, 35-35 (NY)
Jets, 14-9 (D)
1964 — Jets, 30-6 (NY)
Broncos, 20-16 (D)
1965 — Broncos, 16-13 (D)
Jets, 45-10 (NY)
1966 — Jets, 16-7 (D)
1967 — Jets, 38-24 (D)
Broncos, 33-24 (NY)
1968 — Broncos, 21-13 (NY)
1969 — Broncos, 21-19 (D)
1973 — Broncos, 40-28 (NY)
1976 — Broncos, 46-3 (D)
1978 — Jets, 31-28 (D)
1980 — Broncos, 31-24 (D)
1986 — Jets, 22-10 (NY)
1992 — Broncos, 27-16 (D)
(RS Pts. — Broncos 567, Jets 546)
**Jets known as Titans prior to 1963*
DENVER vs. PHILADELPHIA
RS: Eagles lead series, 5-2
1971 — Eagles, 17-16 (P)
1975 — Broncos, 25-10 (D)
1980 — Eagles, 27-6 (P)
1983 — Eagles, 13-10 (D)
1986 — Broncos, 33-7 (P)
1989 — Eagles, 28-24 (D)
1992 — Eagles, 30-0 (P)
(RS Pts. — Eagles 132, Broncos 114)
DENVER vs. *PHOENIX
RS: Broncos lead series, 3-0-1
1973 — Tie, 17-17 (StL)
1977 — Broncos, 7-0 (D)
1989 — Broncos, 37-0 (P)
1991 — Broncos, 24-19 (D)
(RS Pts. — Broncos 85, Cardinals 36)
**Franchise in St. Louis prior to 1988*
DENVER vs. PITTSBURGH
RS: Broncos lead series, 9-5-1
PS: Series tied, 2-2
1970 — Broncos, 16-13 (D)
1971 — Broncos, 22-10 (P)
1973 — Broncos, 23-13 (P)
1974 — Tie, 35-35 (D) OT
1975 — Steelers, 20-9 (P)
1977 — Broncos, 21-7 (D)
*Broncos, 34-21 (D)
1978 — Steelers, 21-17 (D)
*Steelers, 33-10 (P)
1979 — Steelers, 42-7 (P)
1983 — Broncos, 14-10 (P)
1984 — *Steelers, 24-17 (D)
1985 — Broncos, 31-23 (P)
1986 — Broncos, 21-10 (P)
1988 — Steelers, 39-21 (P)
1989 — Broncos, 34-7 (D)
*Broncos, 24-23 (D)
1990 — Steelers, 34-17 (D)
1991 — Broncos, 20-13 (D)
(RS Pts. — Broncos 308, Steelers 297)
(PS Pts. — Steelers 101, Broncos 85)
**AFC Divisional Playoff*
DENVER vs. *SAN DIEGO
RS: Broncos lead series, 34-31-1
1960 — Chargers, 23-19 (D)
Chargers, 41-33 (LA)
1961 — Chargers, 37-0 (SD)
Chargers, 19-16 (D)
1962 — Broncos, 30-21 (D)
Broncos, 23-20 (SD)
1963 — Broncos, 50-34 (D)
Chargers, 58-20 (SD)
1964 — Chargers, 42-14 (SD)
Chargers, 31-20 (D)
1965 — Chargers, 34-31 (SD)
Chargers, 33-21 (D)
1966 — Chargers, 24-17 (SD)
Broncos, 20-17 (D)
1967 — Chargers, 38-21 (D)
Chargers, 24-20 (SD)
1968 — Chargers, 55-24 (SD)
Chargers, 47-23 (D)
1969 — Broncos, 13-0 (D)
Chargers, 45-24 (SD)
1970 — Chargers, 24-21 (SD)
Tie, 17-17 (D)
1971 — Broncos, 20-16 (D)
Chargers, 45-17 (SD)
1972 — Chargers, 37-14 (SD)
Broncos, 38-13 (D)
1973 — Broncos, 30-19 (D)
Broncos, 42-28 (SD)
1974 — Broncos, 27-7 (D)
Chargers, 17-0 (SD)
1975 — Broncos, 27-17 (SD)
Broncos, 13-10 (D) OT
1976 — Broncos, 26-0 (D)
Broncos, 17-0 (SD)
1977 — Broncos, 17-14 (SD)
Broncos, 17-9 (D)
1978 — Broncos, 27-14 (D)
Chargers, 23-0 (SD)
1979 — Broncos, 7-0 (D)
Chargers, 17-7 (SD)
1980 — Chargers, 30-13 (D)
Broncos, 20-13 (SD)
1981 — Broncos, 42-24 (D)
Chargers, 34-17 (SD)
1982 — Chargers, 23-3 (D)
Chargers, 30-20 (SD)
1983 — Broncos, 14-6 (D)
Chargers, 31-7 (SD)
1984 — Broncos, 16-13 (SD)
Broncos, 16-13 (D)
1985 — Chargers, 30-10 (SD)
Broncos, 30-24 (D) OT
1986 — Broncos, 31-14 (SD)
Chargers, 9-3 (D)
1987 — Broncos, 31-17 (SD)
Broncos, 24-0 (D)
1988 — Broncos, 34-3 (D)
Broncos, 12-0 (SD)
1989 — Broncos, 16-10 (D)
Chargers, 19-16 (SD)
1990 — Chargers, 19-7 (SD)
Broncos, 20-10 (D)
1991 — Broncos, 27-19 (D)
Broncos, 17-14 (SD)
1992 — Broncos, 21-13 (D)
Chargers, 24-21 (SD)
(RS Pts. — Chargers 1,412, Broncos 1,311)
**Franchise in Los Angeles prior to 1961*
DENVER vs. SAN FRANCISCO
RS: Broncos lead series, 4-2
PS: 49ers lead series, 1-0
1970 — 49ers, 19-14 (SF)
1973 — 49ers, 36-34 (D)
1979 — Broncos, 38-28 (SF)
1982 — Broncos, 24-21 (D)
1985 — Broncos, 17-16 (D)
1988 — Broncos, 16-13 (SF) OT
1989 — *49ers, 55-10 (New Orleans)
(RS Pts. — Broncos 143, 49ers 133)
(PS Pts. — 49ers 55, Broncos 10)
**Super Bowl XXIV*
DENVER vs. SEATTLE
RS: Broncos lead series, 18-13
PS: Seahawks lead series, 1-0
1977 — Broncos, 24-13 (S)
1978 — Broncos, 28-7 (D)
Broncos, 20-17 (S) OT
1979 — Broncos, 37-34 (D)
Seahawks, 28-23 (S)
1980 — Broncos, 36-20 (D)
Broncos, 25-17 (S)
1981 — Seahawks, 13-10 (S)
Broncos, 23-13 (D)
1982 — Seahawks, 17-10 (D)
Seahawks, 13-11 (S)
1983 — Seahawks, 27-19 (S)
Broncos, 38-27 (D)
*Seahawks, 31-7 (S)
1984 — Seahawks, 27-24 (D)
Broncos, 31-14 (S)
1985 — Broncos, 13-10 (D) OT
Broncos, 27-24 (S)
1986 — Broncos, 20-13 (D)
Seahawks, 41-16 (S)
1987 — Broncos, 40-17 (D)
Seahawks, 28-21 (S)
1988 — Seahawks, 21-14 (D)
Seahawks, 42-14 (S)
1989 — Broncos, 24-21 (S) OT
Broncos, 41-14 (D)
1990 — Broncos, 34-31 (D) OT
Seahawks, 17-12 (S)
1991 — Broncos, 16-10 (D)
Seahawks, 13-10 (S)
1992 — Seahawks, 16-13 (S) OT
Broncos, 10-6 (D)
(RS Pts. — Broncos 684, Seahawks 611)
(PS Pts. — Seahawks 31, Broncos 7)
**AFC First Round Playoff*
DENVER vs. TAMPA BAY
RS: Broncos lead series, 2-0
1976 — Broncos, 48-13 (D)
1981 — Broncos, 24-7 (TB)
(RS Pts. — Broncos 72, Buccaneers 20)
DENVER vs. WASHINGTON
RS: Series tied, 3-3
PS: Redskins lead series, 1-0
1970 — Redskins, 19-3 (D)
1974 — Redskins, 30-3 (W)
1980 — Broncos, 20-17 (D)
1986 — Broncos, 31-30 (D)
1987 — *Redskins, 42-10 (San Diego)
1989 — Broncos, 14-10 (W)
1992 — Redskins, 34-3 (W)
(RS Pts. — Redskins 140, Broncos 74)
(PS Pts. — Redskins 42, Broncos 10)
**Super Bowl XXII*

DETROIT vs. ATLANTA
RS: Lions lead series, 16-5;
See Atlanta vs. Detroit
DETROIT vs. BUFFALO
RS: Lions lead series, 2-1-1;
See Buffalo vs. Detroit
DETROIT vs. CHICAGO
RS: Bears lead series, 73-48-5;
See Chicago vs. Detroit
DETROIT vs. CINCINNATI
RS: Series tied, 3-3;
See Cincinnati vs. Detroit
DETROIT vs. CLEVELAND
RS: Lions lead series, 11-3
PS: Lions lead series, 3-1;
See Cleveland vs. Detroit
DETROIT vs. DALLAS
RS: Cowboys lead series, 7-5
PS: Series tied, 1-1;
See Dallas vs. Detroit
DETROIT vs. DENVER
RS: Broncos lead series, 4-3;
See Denver vs. Detroit
***DETROIT vs. GREEN BAY**
RS: Packers lead series, 63-55-7
1930 — Packers, 47-13 (GB)
Tie, 6-6 (P)
1932 — Packers, 15-10 (GB)
Spartans, 19-0 (P)
1933 — Packers, 17-0 (GB)
Spartans, 7-0 (P)
1934 — Lions, 3-0 (GB)
Packers, 3-0 (D)
1935 — Packers, 13-9 (GB)
Packers, 31-7 (GB)
Lions, 20-10 (D)
1936 — Packers, 20-18 (GB)
Packers, 26-17 (D)
1937 — Packers, 26-6 (GB)
Packers, 14-13 (D)
1938 — Lions, 17-7 (GB)
Packers, 28-7 (D)
1939 — Packers, 26-7 (GB)
Packers, 12-7 (D)
1940 — Lions, 23-14 (GB)
Packers, 50-7 (D)
1941 — Packers, 23-0 (GB)
Packers, 24-7 (D)
1942 — Packers, 38-7 (Mil)
Packers, 28-7 (D)
1943 — Packers, 35-14 (GB)
Packers, 27-6 (D)
1944 — Packers, 27-6 (GB)
Packers, 14-0 (D)
1945 — Packers, 57-21 (Mil)
Lions, 14-3 (D)
1946 — Packers, 10-7 (Mil)
Packers, 9-0 (D)
1947 — Packers, 34-17 (GB)
Packers, 35-14 (D)
1948 — Packers, 33-21 (GB)
Lions, 24-20 (D)
1949 — Packers, 16-14 (GB)
Lions, 21-7 (D)
1950 — Lions, 45-7 (GB)
Lions, 24-21 (D)
1951 — Lions, 24-17 (GB)
Lions, 52-35 (D)
1952 — Lions, 52-17 (GB)
Lions, 48-24 (D)
1953 — Lions, 14-7 (GB)
Lions, 34-15 (D)
1954 — Lions, 21-17 (GB)
Lions, 28-24 (D)
1955 — Packers, 20-17 (GB)
Lions, 24-10 (D)
1956 — Lions, 20-16 (GB)
Packers, 24-20 (D)
1957 — Lions, 24-14 (GB)
Lions, 18-6 (D)
1958 — Tie, 13-13 (GB)
Lions, 24-14 (D)
1959 — Packers, 28-10 (GB)
Packers, 24-17 (D)
1960 — Packers, 28-9 (GB)
Lions, 23-10 (D)
1961 — Lions, 17-13 (Mil)
Packers, 17-9 (D)
1962 — Packers, 9-7 (GB)
Lions, 26-14 (D)
1963 — Packers, 31-10 (Mil)
Tie, 13-13 (D)
1964 — Packers, 14-10 (D)
Packers, 30-7 (GB)
1965 — Packers, 31-21 (D)
Lions, 12-7 (GB)
1966 — Packers, 23-14 (GB)
Packers, 31-7 (D)
1967 — Tie, 17-17 (GB)
Packers, 27-17 (D)
1968 — Lions, 23-17 (GB)
Tie, 14-14 (D)
1969 — Packers, 28-17 (D)
Lions, 16-10 (GB)
1970 — Lions, 40-0 (GB)
Lions, 20-0 (D)
1971 — Lions, 31-28 (D)
Tie, 14-14 (Mil)
1972 — Packers, 24-23 (D)
Packers, 33-7 (GB)
1973 — Tie, 13-13 (GB)
Lions, 34-0 (D)
1974 — Packers, 21-19 (Mil)
Lions, 19-17 (D)
1975 — Lions, 30-16 (Mil)
Lions, 13-10 (D)
1976 — Packers, 24-14 (GB)
Lions, 27-6 (D)
1977 — Lions, 10-6 (D)
Packers, 10-9 (GB)
1978 — Packers, 13-7 (D)

Packers, 35-14 (Mil)
1979 — Packers, 24-16 (Mil)
Packers, 18-13 (D)
1980 — Lions, 29-7 (Mil)
Lions, 24-3 (D)
1981 — Lions, 31-27 (D)
Packers, 31-17 (GB)
1982 — Lions, 30-10 (GB)
Lions, 27-24 (D)
1983 — Lions, 38-14 (D)
Lions, 23-20 (Mil) OT
1984 — Packers, 41-9 (GB)
Lions, 31-28 (D)
1985 — Packers, 43-10 (GB)
Packers, 26-23 (D)
1986 — Lions, 21-14 (GB)
Packers, 44-40 (D)
1987 — Lions, 19-16 (GB) OT
Packers, 34-33 (D)
1988 — Lions, 19-9 (Mil)
Lions, 30-14 (D)
1989 — Packers, 23-20 (Mil) OT
Lions, 31-22 (D)
1990 — Packers, 24-21 (D)
Lions, 24-17 (GB)
1991 — Lions, 23-14 (D)
Lions, 21-17 (GB)
1992 — Packers, 27-13 (D)
Packers, 38-10 (Mil)
(RS Pts. — Packers 2,441, Lions 2,224)
Franchise in Portsmouth prior to 1934 and known as the Spartans

DETROIT vs. HOUSTON
RS: Oilers lead series, 4-2
1971 — Lions, 31-7 (H)
1975 — Oilers, 24-8 (H)
1983 — Oilers, 27-17 (H)
1986 — Lions, 24-13 (D)
1989 — Oilers, 35-31 (H)
1992 — Oilers, 24-21 (D)
(RS Pts. — Lions 132, Oilers 130)

DETROIT vs. *INDIANAPOLIS
RS: Series tied, 17-17-2
1953 — Lions, 27-17 (B)
Lions, 17-7 (D)
1954 — Lions, 35-0 (D)
Lions, 27-3 (B)
1955 — Colts, 28-13 (B)
Lions, 24-14 (D)
1956 — Lions, 31-14 (B)
Lions, 27-3 (D)
1957 — Colts, 34-14 (B)
Lions, 31-27 (D)
1958 — Colts, 28-15 (B)
Colts, 40-14 (D)
1959 — Colts, 21-9 (B)
Colts, 31-24 (D)
1960 — Lions, 30-17 (D)
Lions, 20-15 (B)
1961 — Lions, 16-15 (B)
Colts, 17-14 (D)
1962 — Lions, 29-20 (B)
Lions, 21-14 (D)
1963 — Colts, 25-21 (D)
Colts, 24-21 (B)
1964 — Colts, 34-0 (D)
Lions, 31-14 (B)
1965 — Colts, 31-7 (B)
Tie, 24-24 (D)
1966 — Colts, 45-14 (B)
Lions, 20-14 (D)
1967 — Colts, 41-7 (B)
1968 — Colts, 27-10 (D)
1969 — Tie, 17-17 (B)
1973 — Colts, 29-27 (D)
1977 — Lions, 13-10 (B)
1980 — Colts, 10-9 (D)
1985 — Colts, 14-6 (I)
1991 — Lions, 33-24 (I)
(RS Pts. — Colts 748, Lions 698)
Franchise in Baltimore prior to 1984

DETROIT vs. KANSAS CITY
RS: Chiefs lead series, 4-3
1971 — Lions, 32-21 (D)
1975 — Chiefs, 24-21 (KC) OT
1980 — Chiefs, 20-17 (KC)
1981 — Lions, 27-10 (D)
1987 — Chiefs, 27-20 (D)
1988 — Lions, 7-6 (KC)
1990 — Chiefs, 43-24 (KC)
(RS Pts. — Chiefs 151, Lions 148)

DETROIT vs. *L.A. RAIDERS
RS: Raiders lead series, 5-2
1970 — Lions, 28-14 (D)
1974 — Raiders, 35-13 (O)
1978 — Raiders, 29-17 (O)
1981 — Lions, 16-0 (D)
1984 — Raiders, 24-3 (D)
1987 — Raiders, 27-7 (LA)
1990 — Raiders, 38-31 (D)
(RS Pts. — Raiders 167, Lions 115)
Franchise in Oakland prior to 1982

DETROIT vs. *L.A. RAMS
RS: Rams lead series, 39-34-1
PS: Lions lead series, 1-0
1937 — Lions, 28-0 (C)
Lions, 27-7 (D)
1938 — Rams, 21-17 (C)
Lions, 6-0 (D)
1939 — Lions, 15-7 (D)
Rams, 14-3 (C)
1940 — Lions, 6-0 (D)
Rams, 24-0 (C)
1941 — Lions, 17-7 (D)
Lions, 14-0 (C)
1942 — Rams, 14-0 (D)
Rams, 27-7 (C)
1944 — Rams, 20-17 (D)
Lions, 26-14 (C)
1945 — Rams, 28-21 (D)
1946 — Rams, 35-14 (LA)
Rams, 41-20 (D)
1947 — Rams, 27-13 (D)
Rams, 28-17 (LA)
1948 — Rams, 44-7 (LA)
Rams, 34-27 (D)
1949 — Rams, 27-24 (LA)
Rams, 21-10 (D)
1950 — Rams, 30-28 (D)
Rams, 65-24 (LA)
1951 — Rams, 27-21 (D)
Lions, 24-22 (LA)
1952 — Lions, 17-14 (LA)
Lions, 24-16 (D)
**Lions, 31-21 (D)
1953 — Rams, 31-19 (D)
Rams, 37-24 (LA)
1954 — Lions, 21-3 (D)
Lions, 27-24 (LA)
1955 — Rams, 17-10 (D)
Rams, 24-13 (LA)
1956 — Lions, 24-21 (D)
Lions, 16-7 (LA)
1957 — Lions, 10-7 (D)
Rams, 35-17 (LA)
1958 — Rams, 42-28 (D)
Lions, 41-24 (LA)
1959 — Lions, 17-7 (LA)
Lions, 23-17 (D)
1960 — Rams, 48-35 (LA)
Lions, 12-10 (D)
1961 — Lions, 14-13 (D)
Lions, 28-10 (LA)
1962 — Lions, 13-10 (D)
Lions, 12-3 (LA)
1963 — Lions, 23-2 (LA)
Rams, 28-21 (D)
1964 — Tie, 17-17 (LA)
Lions, 37-17 (D)
1965 — Lions, 20-0 (D)
Lions, 31-7 (LA)
1966 — Rams, 14-7 (D)
Rams, 23-3 (LA)
1967 — Rams, 31-7 (D)
1968 — Rams, 10-7 (LA)
1969 — Lions, 28-0 (D)
1970 — Lions, 28-23 (LA)
1971 — Rams, 21-13 (D)
1972 — Lions, 34-17 (LA)
1974 — Rams, 16-13 (LA)
1975 — Rams, 20-0 (D)
1976 — Rams, 20-17 (D)
1980 — Lions, 41-20 (LA)
1981 — Rams, 20-13 (LA)
1982 — Lions, 19-14 (LA)
1983 — Rams, 21-10 (LA)
1986 — Rams, 14-10 (LA)
1987 — Rams, 37-16 (D)
1988 — Rams, 17-10 (LA)
1991 — Lions, 21-10 (D)
(RS Pts. — Rams 1,423, Lions 1,324)
(PS Pts. — Lions 31, Rams 21)
Franchise in Cleveland prior to 1946
**Conference Playoff*

DETROIT vs. MIAMI
RS: Series tied, 2-2
1973 — Dolphins, 34-7 (M)
1979 — Dolphins, 28-10 (D)
1985 — Lions, 31-21 (D)
1991 — Lions, 17-13 (D)
(RS Pts. — Dolphins 96, Lions 65)

DETROIT vs. MINNESOTA
RS: Vikings lead series, 39-22-2
1961 — Lions, 37-10 (M)
Lions, 13-7 (D)
1962 — Lions, 17-6 (M)
Lions, 37-23 (D)
1963 — Lions, 28-10 (D)
Vikings, 34-31 (M)
1964 — Lions, 24-20 (M)
Tie, 23-23 (D)
1965 — Lions, 31-29 (M)
Vikings, 29-7 (D)
1966 — Lions, 32-31 (M)
Vikings, 28-16 (D)
1967 — Tie, 10-10 (M)
Lions, 14-3 (D)
1968 — Vikings, 24-10 (M)
Vikings, 13-6 (D)
1969 — Vikings, 24-10 (M)
Vikings, 27-0 (D)
1970 — Vikings, 30-17 (D)
Vikings, 24-20 (M)
1971 — Vikings, 16-13 (D)
Vikings, 29-10 (M)
1972 — Vikings, 34-10 (D)
Vikings, 16-14 (M)
1973 — Vikings, 23-9 (D)
Vikings, 28-7 (M)
1974 — Vikings, 7-6 (D)
Lions, 20-16 (M)
1975 — Vikings, 25-19 (M)
Lions, 17-10 (D)
1976 — Vikings, 10-9 (D)
Vikings, 31-23 (M)
1977 — Vikings, 14-7 (M)
Vikings, 30-21 (D)
1978 — Vikings, 17-7 (M)
Lions, 45-14 (D)
1979 — Vikings, 13-10 (D)
Vikings, 14-7 (M)
1980 — Lions, 27-7 (D)
Vikings, 34-0 (M)
1981 — Vikings, 26-24 (M)
Lions, 45-7 (D)
1982 — Vikings, 34-31 (D)
1983 — Vikings, 20-17 (M)
Lions, 13-2 (D)
1984 — Vikings, 29-28 (D)
Lions, 16-14 (M)
1985 — Vikings, 16-13 (M)
Lions, 41-21 (D)
1986 — Lions, 13-10 (M)
Vikings, 24-10 (D)
1987 — Vikings, 34-19 (M)
Vikings, 17-14 (D)
1988 — Vikings, 44-17 (M)
Vikings, 23-0 (D)
1989 — Vikings, 24-17 (M)
Vikings, 20-7 (D)
1990 — Lions, 34-27 (M)
Vikings, 17-7 (D)
1991 — Lions, 24-20 (D)
Lions, 34-14 (M)
1992 — Lions, 31-17 (D)
Vikings, 31-14 (M)
(RS Pts. — Vikings 1,287, Lions 1,133)

DETROIT vs. NEW ENGLAND
RS: Series tied, 2-2
1971 — Lions, 34-7 (NE)
1976 — Lions, 30-10 (D)
1979 — Patriots, 24-17 (NE)
1985 — Patriots, 23-6 (NE)
(RS Pts. — Lions 87, Patriots 64)

DETROIT vs. NEW ORLEANS
RS: Series tied, 6-6-1
1968 — Tie, 20-20 (D)
1970 — Saints, 19-17 (NO)
1972 — Lions, 27-14 (D)
1973 — Saints, 20-13 (NO)
1974 — Lions, 19-14 (D)
1976 — Saints, 17-16 (NO)
1977 — Lions, 23-19 (D)
1979 — Saints, 17-7 (NO)
1980 — Lions, 24-13 (D)
1988 — Saints, 22-14 (D)
1989 — Lions, 21-14 (D)
1990 — Lions, 27-10 (NO)
1992 — Saints, 13-7 (D)
(RS Pts. — Lions 235, Saints 212)

***DETROIT vs. N.Y. GIANTS**
RS: Lions lead series, 17-15-1
PS: Lions lead series, 1-0
1930 — Giants, 19-6 (P)
1931 — Spartans, 14-6 (P)
Giants, 14-0 (NY)
1932 — Spartans, 7-0 (P)
Spartans, 6-0 (NY)
1933 — Spartans, 17-7 (P)
Giants, 13-10 (NY)
1934 — Lions, 9-0 (D)
1935 — **Lions, 26-7 (D)
1936 — Giants, 14-7 (NY)
Lions, 38-0 (D)
1937 — Lions, 17-0 (NY)
1939 — Lions, 18-14 (D)
1941 — Giants, 20-13 (NY)
1943 — Tie, 0-0 (D)
1945 — Giants, 35-14 (NY)
1947 — Lions, 35-7 (D)
1949 — Lions, 45-21 (NY)
1953 — Lions, 27-16 (NY)
1955 — Giants, 24-19 (D)
1958 — Giants, 19-17 (D)
1962 — Giants, 17-14 (NY)
1964 — Lions, 26-3 (D)
1967 — Lions, 30-7 (NY)
1969 — Lions, 24-0 (D)
1972 — Lions, 30-16 (D)
1974 — Lions, 20-19 (D)
1976 — Giants, 24-10 (NY)
1982 — Giants, 13-6 (D)
1983 — Lions, 15-9 (D)
1988 — Giants, 30-10 (NY)
Giants, 13-10 (D) OT
1989 — Giants, 24-14 (NY)
1990 — Giants, 20-0 (NY)
(RS Pts. — Lions, 528, Giants 424)
(PS Pts. — Lions 26, Giants 7)
Franchise in Portsmouth prior to 1934 and known as the Spartans
**NFL Championship*

DETROIT vs. N.Y. JETS
RS: Series tied, 3-3
1972 — Lions, 37-20 (D)
1979 — Jets, 31-10 (NY)
1982 — Jets, 28-13 (D)
1985 — Lions, 31-20 (D)
1988 — Jets, 17-10 (D)
1991 — Lions, 34-20 (D)
(RS Pts. — Jets 136, Lions 135)

***DETROIT vs. PHILADELPHIA**
RS: Lions lead series, 12-9-2
1933 — Spartans, 25-0 (P)
1934 — Lions, 10-0 (P)
1935 — Lions, 35-0 (D)
1936 — Lions, 23-0 (P)
1938 — Eagles, 21-7 (D)
1940 — Lions, 21-0 (P)
1941 — Lions, 21-17 (D)
1945 — Lions, 28-24 (D)
1948 — Eagles, 45-21 (P)
1949 — Eagles, 22-14 (D)
1951 — Lions, 28-10 (P)
1954 — Tie, 13-13 (D)
1957 — Lions, 27-16 (P)
1960 — Eagles, 28-10 (P)
1961 — Eagles, 27-24 (D)
1965 — Lions, 35-28 (P)
1968 — Eagles, 12-0 (D)
1971 — Eagles, 23-20 (D)
1974 — Eagles, 28-17 (P)
1977 — Lions, 17-13 (D)
1979 — Eagles, 44-7 (P)
1984 — Tie, 23-23 (D) OT
1986 — Lions, 13-11 (P)
(RS Pts. — Lions 439, Eagles 405)
Franchise in Portsmouth prior to 1934 and known as the Spartans

***DETROIT vs. **PHOENIX**
RS: Lions lead series, 25-16-5
1930 — Tie, 0-0 (P)
Cardinals, 23-0 (C)
1931 — Cardinals, 20-19 (C)
1932 — Tie, 7-7 (P)
1933 — Spartans, 7-6 (P)
1934 — Lions, 6-0 (D)
Lions, 17-13 (C)
1935 — Tie, 10-10 (D)
Lions, 7-6 (C)
1936 — Lions, 39-0 (D)
Lions, 14-7 (C)
1937 — Lions, 16-7 (C)
Lions, 16-7 (D)
1938 — Lions, 10-0 (D)
Lions, 7-3 (C)
1939 — Lions, 21-3 (D)
Lions, 17-3 (C)
1940 — Tie, 0-0 (Buffalo)
Lions, 43-14 (C)
1941 — Tie, 14-14 (C)
Lions, 21-3 (D)
1942 — Cardinals, 13-0 (C)
Cardinals, 7-0 (D)
1943 — Lions, 35-17 (D)
Lions, 7-0 (C)
1945 — Lions, 10-0 (C)
Lions, 26-0 (D)
1946 — Cardinals, 34-14 (C)
Cardinals, 36-14 (D)
1947 — Cardinals, 45-21 (C)
Cardinals, 17-7 (D)
1948 — Cardinals, 56-20 (C)
Cardinals, 28-14 (D)
1949 — Lions, 24-7 (C)
Cardinals, 42-19 (D)
1959 — Lions, 45-21 (D)
1961 — Lions, 45-14 (StL)
1967 — Cardinals, 38-28 (StL)
1969 — Lions, 20-0 (D)
1970 — Lions, 16-3 (D)
1973 — Lions, 20-16 (StL)
1975 — Cardinals, 24-13 (D)
1978 — Cardinals, 21-14 (StL)
1980 — Lions, 20-7 (D)
Cardinals, 24-23 (StL)
1989 — Cardinals, 16-13 (D)
(RS Pts. — Lions 759, Cardinals 642)
Franchise in Portsmouth prior to 1934 and known as the Spartans
***Franchise in St. Louis prior to 1988 and in Chicago prior to 1960*

DETROIT vs. *PITTSBURGH
RS: Lions lead series, 13-11-1
1934 — Lions, 40-7 (D)
1936 — Lions, 28-3 (D)
1937 — Lions, 7-3 (D)
1938 — Lions, 16-7 (D)
1940 — Pirates, 10-7 (D)
1942 — Steelers, 35-7 (D)
1946 — Lions, 17-7 (D)
1947 — Steelers, 17-10 (P)
1948 — Lions, 17-14 (D)
1949 — Steelers, 14-7 (P)
1950 — Lions, 10-7 (D)
1952 — Lions, 31-6 (P)
1953 — Lions, 38-21 (D)
1955 — Lions, 31-28 (P)
1956 — Lions, 45-7 (D)
1959 — Tie, 10-10 (P)
1962 — Lions, 45-7 (D)
1966 — Steelers, 17-3 (P)
1967 — Steelers, 24-14 (D)
1969 — Steelers, 16-13 (P)
1973 — Steelers, 24-10 (P)
1983 — Lions, 45-3 (D)
1986 — Steelers, 27-17 (P)
1989 — Steelers, 23-3 (D)
1992 — Steelers, 17-14 (P)
(RS Pts. — Lions 485, Steelers 354)
**Steelers known as Pirates prior to 1941*
DETROIT vs. SAN DIEGO
RS: Lions lead series, 3-2
1972 — Lions, 34-20 (D)
1977 — Lions, 20-0 (D)
1978 — Lions, 31-14 (D)
1981 — Chargers, 28-23 (SD)
1984 — Chargers, 27-24 (SD)
(RS Pts. — Lions 132, Chargers 89)
DETROIT vs. SAN FRANCISCO
RS: Series tied, 25-25-1
PS: Series tied, 1-1
1950 — Lions, 24-7 (D)
49ers, 28-27 (SF)
1951 — 49ers, 20-10 (D)
49ers, 21-17 (SF)
1952 — 49ers, 17-3 (SF)
49ers, 28-0 (D)
1953 — Lions, 24-21 (D)
Lions, 14-10 (SF)
1954 — 49ers, 37-31 (SF)
Lions, 48-7 (D)
1955 — 49ers, 27-24 (D)
49ers, 38-21 (SF)
1956 — Lions, 20-17 (D)
Lions, 17-13 (SF)
1957 — 49ers, 35-31 (SF)
Lions, 31-10 (D)
*Lions, 31-27 (SF)
1958 — 49ers, 24-21 (SF)
Lions, 35-21 (D)
1959 — 49ers, 34-13 (D)
49ers, 33-7 (SF)
1960 — 49ers, 14-10 (D)
Lions, 24-0 (SF)
1961 — 49ers, 49-0 (D)
Tie, 20-20 (SF)
1962 — Lions, 45-24 (D)
Lions, 38-24 (SF)
1963 — Lions, 26-3 (D)
Lions, 45-7 (SF)
1964 — Lions, 26-17 (SF)
Lions, 24-7 (D)
1965 — 49ers, 27-21 (D)
49ers, 17-14 (SF)
1966 — 49ers, 27-24 (SF)
49ers, 41-14 (D)
1967 — Lions, 45-3 (SF)
1968 — 49ers, 14-7 (D)
1969 — Lions, 26-14 (SF)
1970 — Lions, 28-7 (D)
1971 — 49ers, 31-27 (SF)
1973 — Lions, 30-20 (D)
1974 — Lions, 17-13 (D)
1975 — Lions, 28-17 (SF)
1977 — 49ers, 28-7 (SF)
1978 — Lions, 33-14 (D)
1980 — Lions, 17-13 (D)
1981 — Lions, 24-17 (D)
1983 — **49ers, 24-23 (SF)
1984 — 49ers, 30-27 (D)
1985 — Lions, 23-21 (D)
1988 — 49ers, 20-13 (SF)
1991 — 49ers, 35-3 (SF)
1992 — 49ers, 24-6 (SF)
(RS Pts. — Lions 1,110, 49ers 1,046)
(PS Pts. — Lions 54, 49ers 51)
**Conference Playoff*
***NFC Divisional Playoff*
DETROIT vs. SEATTLE
RS: Seahawks lead series, 4-1
1976 — Lions, 41-14 (S)
1978 — Seahawks, 28-16 (S)
1984 — Seahawks, 38-17 (S)
1987 — Seahawks, 37-14 (D)
1990 — Seahawks, 30-10 (S)
(RS Pts. — Seahawks 147, Lions 98)
DETROIT vs. TAMPA BAY
RS: Series tied, 15-15
1977 — Lions, 16-7 (D)
1978 — Lions, 15-7 (TB)
Lions, 34-23 (D)
1979 — Buccaneers, 31-16 (TB)
Buccaneers, 16-14 (D)
1980 — Lions, 24-10 (TB)
Lions, 27-14 (D)
1981 — Buccaneers, 28-10 (TB)
Buccaneers, 20-17 (D)
1982 — Buccaneers, 23-21 (TB)
1983 — Lions, 11-0 (TB)
Lions, 23-20 (D)
1984 — Buccaneers, 21-17 (TB)
Lions, 13-7 (D) OT
1985 — Lions, 30-9 (D)
Buccaneers, 19-16 (TB) OT
1986 — Buccaneers, 24-20 (D)
Lions, 38-17 (TB)
1987 — Buccaneers, 31-27 (D)
Lions, 20-10 (TB)
1988 — Buccaneers, 23-20 (D)
Buccaneers, 21-10 (TB)
1989 — Lions, 17-16 (TB)
Lions, 33-7 (D)
1990 — Buccaneers, 38-21 (D)
Buccaneers, 23-20 (TB)
1991 — Lions, 31-3 (D)
Buccaneers, 30-21 (TB)
1992 — Buccaneers, 27-23 (D)
Lions, 38-7 (TB)
(RS Pts. — Lions 643, Buccaneers 532)
***DETROIT vs. **WASHINGTON**
RS: Redskins lead series, 22-8
PS: Redskins lead series, 2-0
1932 — Spartans, 10-0 (P)
1933 — Spartans, 13-0 (B)
1934 — Lions, 24-0 (D)
1935 — Lions, 17-7 (B)
Lions, 14-0 (D)
1938 — Redskins, 7-5 (D)
1939 — Redskins, 31-7 (W)
1940 — Redskins, 20-14 (D)
1942 — Redskins, 15-3 (D)
1943 — Redskins, 42-20 (W)
1946 — Redskins, 17-16 (W)
1947 — Lions, 38-21 (D)
1948 — Redskins, 46-21 (W)
1951 — Lions, 35-17 (D)
1956 — Redskins, 18-17 (W)
1965 — Lions, 14-10 (D)
1968 — Redskins, 14-3 (W)
1970 — Redskins, 31-10 (W)
1973 — Redskins, 20-0 (D)
1976 — Redskins, 20-7 (W)
1978 — Redskins, 21-19 (D)
1979 — Redskins, 27-24 (D)
1981 — Redskins, 33-31 (W)
1982 — ***Redskins, 31-7 (W)
1983 — Redskins, 38-17 (W)
1984 — Redskins, 28-14 (W)
1985 — Redskins, 24-3 (W)
1987 — Redskins, 20-13 (W)
1990 — Redskins, 41-38 (D)
1991 — Redskins, 45-0 (W)
****Redskins, 41-10 (W)
1992 — Redskins, 13-10 (W)
(RS Pts. — Redskins 626, Lions 457)
(PS Pts. — Redskins 72, Lions 17)
**Franchise in Portsmouth prior to 1934 and known as the Spartans.*
***Franchise in Boston prior to 1937*
****NFC First Round Playoff*
*****NFC Championship*

GREEN BAY vs. ATLANTA
RS: Series tied, 9-9;
See Atlanta vs. Green Bay
GREEN BAY vs. BUFFALO
RS: Bills lead series, 4-1;
See Buffalo vs. Green Bay
GREEN BAY vs. CHICAGO
RS: Bears lead series, 80-58-6
PS: Bears lead series, 1-0;
See Chicago vs. Green Bay
GREEN BAY vs. CINCINNATI
RS: Bengals lead series, 4-3;
See Cincinnati vs. Green Bay
GREEN BAY vs. CLEVELAND
RS: Packers lead series, 7-6
PS: Packers lead series, 1-0;
See Cleveland vs. Green Bay
GREEN BAY vs. DALLAS
RS: Packers lead series, 8-5
PS: Packers lead series, 2-1;
See Dallas vs. Green Bay
GREEN BAY vs. DENVER
RS: Broncos lead series, 4-1-1;
See Denver vs. Green Bay
GREEN BAY vs. DETROIT
RS: Packers lead series, 63-55-7;
See Detroit vs. Green Bay
GREEN BAY vs. HOUSTON
RS: Series tied, 3-3
1972 — Packers, 23-10 (H)
1977 — Oilers, 16-10 (GB)
1980 — Oilers, 22-3 (GB)
1983 — Packers, 41-38 (H) OT
1986 — Oilers, 31-3 (GB)
1992 — Packers, 16-14 (H)
(RS Pts. — Oilers 131, Packers 96)
GREEN BAY vs. *INDIANAPOLIS
RS: Series tied, 18-18-1
PS: Packers lead series, 1-0
1953 — Packers, 37-14 (GB)
Packers, 35-24 (B)
1954 — Packers, 7-6 (B)
Packers, 24-13 (Mil)
1955 — Colts, 24-20 (Mil)
Colts, 14-10 (B)
1956 — Packers, 38-33 (Mil)
Colts, 28-21 (B)
1957 — Colts, 45-17 (Mil)
Packers, 24-21 (B)
1958 — Colts, 24-17 (Mil)
Colts, 56-0 (B)
1959 — Colts, 38-21 (B)
Colts, 28-24 (Mil)
1960 — Packers, 35-21 (GB)
Colts, 38-24 (B)
1961 — Packers, 45-7 (GB)
Colts, 45-21 (B)
1962 — Packers, 17-6 (B)
Packers, 17-13 (GB)
1963 — Packers, 31-20 (GB)
Packers, 34-20 (B)
1964 — Colts, 21-20 (GB)
Colts, 24-21 (B)
1965 — Packers, 20-17 (Mil)
Packers, 42-27 (B)
**Packers, 13-10 (GB) OT
1966 — Packers, 24-3 (Mil)
Packers, 14-10 (B)
1967 — Colts, 13-10 (B)
1968 — Colts, 16-3 (GB)
1969 — Colts, 14-6 (B)
1970 — Colts, 13-10 (Mil)
1974 — Packers, 20-13 (B)
1982 — Tie, 20-20 (B) OT
1985 — Colts, 37-10 (I)
1988 — Colts, 20-13 (GB)
1991 — Packers, 14-10 (Mil)
(RS Pts. — Colts 796, Packers 766)
(PS Pts. — Packers 13, Colts 10)
**Franchise in Baltimore prior to 1984*
***Conference Playoff*
GREEN BAY vs. KANSAS CITY
RS: Chiefs lead series, 3-1-1
PS: Packers lead series, 1-0
1966 — *Packers, 35-10 (Los Angeles)
1973 — Tie, 10-10 (Mil)
1977 — Chiefs, 20-10 (KC)
1987 — Packers, 23-3 (KC)
1989 — Chiefs, 21-3 (GB)
1990 — Chiefs, 17-3 (GB)
(RS Pts. — Chiefs 71, Packers 49)
(PS Pts. — Packers 35, Chiefs 10)
**Super Bowl I*
GREEN BAY vs. *L.A. RAIDERS
RS: Raiders lead series, 5-1
PS: Packers lead series, 1-0
1967 — **Packers, 33-14 (Miami)
1972 — Raiders, 20-14 (GB)
1976 — Raiders, 18-14 (O)
1978 — Raiders, 28-3 (GB)
1984 — Raiders, 28-7 (LA)
1987 — Raiders, 20-0 (GB)
1990 — Packers, 29-16 (LA)
(RS Pts. — Raiders 130, Packers 67)
(PS Pts. — Packers 33, Raiders 14)
**Franchise in Oakland prior to 1982*
***Super Bowl II*
GREEN BAY vs. *L.A. RAMS
RS: Rams lead series, 42-35-2
PS: Packers lead series, 1-0
1937 — Packers, 35-10 (C)
Packers, 35-7 (GB)
1938 — Packers, 26-17 (GB)
Packers, 28-7 (C)
1939 — Rams, 27-24 (GB)
Packers, 7-6 (C)
1940 — Packers, 31-14 (GB)
Tie, 13-13 (C)
1941 — Packers, 24-7 (Mil)
Packers, 17-14 (C)
1942 — Packers, 45-28 (GB)
Packers, 30-12 (C)
1944 — Packers, 30-21 (GB)
Packers, 42-7 (C)
1945 — Rams, 27-14 (GB)
Rams, 20-7 (C)
1946 — Rams, 21-17 (Mil)
Rams, 38-17 (LA)
1947 — Packers, 17-14 (Mil)
Packers, 30-10 (LA)
1948 — Packers, 16-0 (GB)
Rams, 24-10 (LA)
1949 — Rams, 48-7 (GB)
Rams, 35-7 (LA)
1950 — Rams, 45-14 (Mil)
Rams, 51-14 (LA)
1951 — Rams, 28-0 (Mil)
Rams, 42-14 (LA)
1952 — Rams, 30-28 (Mil)
Rams, 45-27 (LA)
1953 — Rams, 38-20 (Mil)
Rams, 33-17 (LA)
1954 — Packers, 35-17 (Mil)
Rams, 35-27 (LA)
1955 — Packers, 30-28 (Mil)
Rams, 31-17 (LA)
1956 — Packers, 42-17 (Mil)
Rams, 49-21 (LA)
1957 — Rams, 31-27 (Mil)
Rams, 42-17 (LA)
1958 — Rams, 20-7 (GB)
Rams, 34-20 (LA)
1959 — Rams, 45-6 (Mil)
Packers, 38-20 (LA)
1960 — Rams, 33-31 (Mil)
Packers, 35-2 (LA)
1961 — Packers, 35-17 (GB)
Packers, 24-17 (LA)
1962 — Packers, 41-10 (Mil)
Packers, 20-17 (LA)
1963 — Packers, 42-10 (GB)
Packers, 31-14 (LA)
1964 — Rams, 27-17 (Mil)
Tie, 24-24 (LA)
1965 — Packers, 6-3 (Mil)
Rams, 21-10 (LA)
1966 — Packers, 24-13 (GB)
Packers, 27-23 (LA)
1967 — Rams, 27-24 (LA)
**Packers, 28-7 (Mil)
1968 — Rams, 16-14 (Mil)
1969 — Rams, 34-21 (LA)
1970 — Rams, 31-21 (GB)
1971 — Rams, 30-13 (LA)
1973 — Rams, 24-7 (LA)
1974 — Packers, 17-6 (Mil)
1975 — Rams, 22-5 (LA)
1977 — Rams, 24-6 (Mil)
1978 — Rams, 31-14 (LA)
1980 — Rams, 51-21 (LA)
1981 — Rams, 35-23 (LA)
1982 — Packers, 35-23 (Mil)
1983 — Packers, 27-24 (Mil)
1984 — Packers, 31-6 (Mil)
1985 — Rams, 34-17 (LA)
1988 — Rams, 34-7 (GB)
1989 — Rams, 41-38 (LA)
1990 — Packers, 36-24 (GB)
1991 — Rams, 23-21 (LA)
1992 — Packers, 28-13 (GB)
(RS Pts. — Rams 1,911, Packers 1,743)
(PS Pts. — Packers 28, Rams 7)
**Franchise in Cleveland prior to 1946*
***Conference Championship*
GREEN BAY vs. MIAMI
RS: Dolphins lead series, 7-0
1971 — Dolphins, 27-6 (Mia)
1975 — Dolphins, 31-7 (GB)
1979 — Dolphins, 27-7 (Mia)
1985 — Dolphins, 34-24 (GB)
1988 — Dolphins, 24-17 (Mia)
1989 — Dolphins, 23-20 (Mil)
1991 — Dolphins, 16-13 (Mia)
(RS Pts. — Dolphins 182, Packers 94)
GREEN BAY vs. MINNESOTA
RS: Series tied, 31-31-1
1961 — Packers, 33-7 (Minn)
Packers, 28-10 (Mil)
1962 — Packers, 34-7 (GB)
Packers, 48-21 (Minn)
1963 — Packers, 37-28 (Minn)
Packers, 28-7 (GB)
1964 — Vikings, 24-23 (GB)
Packers, 42-13 (Minn)
1965 — Packers, 38-13 (Minn)
Packers, 24-19 (GB)
1966 — Vikings, 20-17 (GB)
Packers, 28-16 (Minn)
1967 — Vikings, 10-7 (Mil)
Packers, 30-27 (Minn)
1968 — Vikings, 26-13 (Mil)
Vikings, 14-10 (Minn)
1969 — Vikings, 19-7 (Minn)
Vikings, 9-7 (Mil)
1970 — Packers, 13-10 (Mil)
Vikings, 10-3 (Minn)
1971 — Vikings, 24-13 (GB)
Vikings, 3-0 (Minn)
1972 — Vikings, 27-13 (GB)
Packers, 23-7 (Minn)

1973 — Vikings, 11-3 (Minn)
Vikings, 31-7 (GB)
1974 — Vikings, 32-17 (GB)
Packers, 19-7 (Minn)
1975 — Vikings, 28-17 (GB)
Vikings, 24-3 (Minn)
1976 — Vikings, 17-10 (Mil)
Vikings, 20-9 (Minn)
1977 — Vikings, 19-7 (Minn)
Vikings, 13-6 (GB)
1978 — Vikings, 21-7 (Minn)
Tie, 10-10 (GB) OT
1979 — Vikings, 27-21 (Minn) OT
Packers, 19-7 (Mil)
1980 — Packers, 16-3 (GB)
Packers, 25-13 (Minn)
1981 — Vikings, 30-13 (Mil)
Packers, 35-23 (Minn)
1982 — Packers, 26-7 (Mil)
1983 — Vikings, 20-17 (GB) OT
Packers, 29-21 (Minn)
1984 — Packers, 45-17 (Mil)
Packers, 38-14 (Minn)
1985 — Packers, 20-17 (Mil)
Packers, 27-17 (Minn)
1986 — Vikings, 42-7 (Minn)
Vikings, 32-6 (GB)
1987 — Packers, 23-16 (Minn)
Packers, 16-10 (Mil)
1988 — Packers, 34-14 (Minn)
Packers, 18-6 (GB)
1989 — Vikings, 26-14 (Minn)
Packers, 20-19 (Mil)
1990 — Packers, 24-10 (Mil)
Vikings, 23-7 (Minn)
1991 — Vikings, 35-21 (GB)
Packers, 27-7 (Minn)
1992 — Vikings, 23-20 (GB) OT
Vikings, 27-7 (Minn)
(RS Pts. — Packers 1,209, Vikings 1,110)

GREEN BAY vs. NEW ENGLAND
RS: Series tied, 2-2
1973 — Patriots, 33-24 (NE)
1979 — Packers, 27-14 (GB)
1985 — Patriots, 26-20 (NE)
1988 — Packers, 45-3 (Mil)
(RS Pts. — Packers 116, Patriots 76)

GREEN BAY vs. NEW ORLEANS
RS: Packers lead series, 11-4
1968 — Packers, 29-7 (Mil)
1971 — Saints, 29-21 (Mil)
1972 — Packers, 30-20 (NO)
1973 — Packers, 30-10 (Mil)
1975 — Saints, 20-19 (NO)
1976 — Packers, 32-27 (Mil)
1977 — Packers, 24-20 (NO)
1978 — Packers, 28-17 (Mil)
1979 — Packers, 28-19 (Mil)
1981 — Packers, 35-7 (NO)
1984 — Packers, 23-13 (NO)
1985 — Packers, 38-14 (Mil)
1986 — Saints, 24-10 (NO)
1987 — Saints, 33-24 (NO)
1989 — Packers, 35-34 (GB)
(RS Pts. — Packers 406, Saints 294)

GREEN BAY vs. N.Y. GIANTS
RS: Packers lead series, 21-20-2
PS: Packers lead series, 4-1
1928 — Giants, 6-0 (GB)
Packers, 7-0 (NY)
1929 — Packers, 20-6 (NY)
1930 — Packers, 14-7 (GB)
Giants, 13-6 (NY)
1931 — Packers, 27-7 (GB)
Packers, 14-10 (NY)
1932 — Packers, 13-0 (GB)
Giants, 6-0 (NY)
1933 — Giants, 10-7 (Mil)
Giants, 17-6 (NY)
1934 — Packers, 20-6 (Mil)
Giants, 17-3 (NY)
1935 — Packers, 16-7 (GB)
1936 — Packers, 26-14 (NY)
1937 — Giants, 10-0 (NY)
1938 — Giants, 15-3 (NY)
*Giants, 23-17 (NY)
1939 — *Packers, 27-0 (Mil)
1940 — Giants, 7-3 (NY)
1942 — Tie, 21-21 (NY)
1943 — Packers, 35-21 (NY)
1944 — Giants, 24-0 (NY)
*Packers, 14-7 (NY)
1945 — Packers, 23-14 (NY)
1947 — Tie, 24-24 (NY)
1948 — Giants, 49-3 (Mil)
1949 — Giants, 30-10 (GB)
1952 — Packers, 17-3 (NY)
1957 — Giants, 31-17 (GB)
1959 — Giants, 20-3 (NY)
1961 — Packers, 20-17 (Mil)
*Packers, 37-0 (GB)
1962 — *Packers, 16-7 (NY)
1967 — Packers, 48-21 (NY)
1969 — Packers, 20-10 (Mil)
1971 — Giants, 42-40 (GB)
1973 — Packers, 16-14 (New Haven)
1975 — Packers, 40-14 (Mil)
1980 — Giants, 27-21 (NY)
1981 — Packers, 27-14 (NY)
Packers, 26-24 (Mil)
1982 — Packers, 27-19 (NY)
1983 — Giants, 27-3 (NY)
1985 — Packers, 23-20 (GB)
1986 — Giants, 55-24 (NY)
1987 — Giants, 20-10 (NY)
1992 — Giants, 27-7 (NY)
(RS Pts. — Giants 746, Packers 690)
(PS Pts. — Packers 111, Giants 37)
**NFL Championship*

GREEN BAY vs. N.Y. JETS
RS: Jets lead series, 5-1
1973 — Packers, 23-7 (Mil)
1979 — Jets, 27-22 (GB)
1981 — Jets, 28-3 (NY)
1982 — Jets, 15-13 (NY)
1985 — Jets, 24-3 (Mil)
1991 — Jets, 19-16 (NY) OT
(RS Pts. — Jets 120, Packers 80)

GREEN BAY vs. PHILADELPHIA
RS: Packers lead series, 19-6
PS: Eagles lead series, 1-0
1933 — Packers, 35-9 (GB)
Packers, 10-0 (P)
1934 — Packers, 19-6 (GB)
1935 — Packers, 13-6 (P)
1937 — Packers, 37-7 (Mil)
1939 — Packers, 23-16 (P)
1940 — Packers, 27-20 (GB)
1942 — Packers, 7-0 (P)
1946 — Packers, 19-7 (P)
1947 — Eagles, 28-14 (P)
1951 — Packers, 37-24 (GB)
1952 — Packers, 12-10 (Mil)
1954 — Packers, 37-14 (P)
1958 — Packers, 38-35 (GB)
1960 — *Eagles, 17-13 (P)
1962 — Packers, 49-0 (P)
1968 — Packers, 30-13 (GB)
1970 — Packers, 30-17 (Mil)
1974 — Eagles, 36-14 (P)
1976 — Packers, 28-13 (GB)
1978 — Eagles, 10-3 (P)
1979 — Eagles, 21-10 (GB)
1987 — Packers, 16-10 (GB) OT
1990 — Eagles, 31-0 (P)
1991 — Eagles, 20-3 (GB)
1992 — Packers, 27-24 (Mil)
(RS Pts. — Packers 538, Eagles 377)
(PS Pts. — Eagles 17, Packers 13)
**NFL Championship*

GREEN BAY vs. *PHOENIX
RS: Packers lead series, 39-21-4
PS: Packers lead series, 1-0
1921 — Tie, 3-3 (C)
1922 — Cardinals, 16-3 (C)
1924 — Cardinals, 3-0 (C)
1925 — Cardinals, 9-6 (C)
1926 — Cardinals, 13-7 (GB)
Packers, 3-0 (C)
1927 — Packers, 13-0 (GB)
Tie, 6-6 (C)
1928 — Packers, 20-0 (GB)
1929 — Packers, 9-2 (GB)
Packers, 7-6 (C)
Packers, 12-0 (C)
1930 — Packers, 14-0 (GB)
Cardinals, 13-6 (C)
1931 — Packers, 26-7 (GB)
Cardinals, 21-13 (C)
1932 — Packers, 15-7 (GB)
Packers, 19-9 (C)
1933 — Packers, 14-6 (C)
1934 — Packers, 15-0 (GB)
Cardinals, 9-0 (Mil)
Cardinals, 6-0 (C)
1935 — Cardinals, 7-6 (GB)
Cardinals, 3-0 (Mil)
Cardinals, 9-7 (C)
1936 — Packers, 10-7 (GB)
Packers, 24-0 (Mil)
Tie, 0-0 (C)
1937 — Cardinals, 14-7 (GB)
Packers, 34-13 (Mil)
1938 — Packers, 28-7 (Mil)
Packers, 24-22 (Buffalo)
1939 — Packers, 14-10 (GB)
Packers, 27-20 (Mil)
1940 — Packers, 31-6 (Mil)
Packers, 28-7 (C)
1941 — Packers, 14-13 (Mil)
Packers, 17-9 (GB)
1942 — Packers, 17-13 (C)
Packers, 55-24 (GB)
1943 — Packers, 28-7 (C)
Packers, 35-14 (Mil)
1945 — Packers, 33-14 (GB)
1946 — Packers, 19-7 (C)
Cardinals, 24-6 (GB)
1947 — Cardinals, 14-10 (GB)
Cardinals, 21-20 (C)
1948 — Cardinals, 17-7 (Mil)
Cardinals, 42-7 (C)
1949 — Cardinals, 39-17 (Mil)
Cardinals, 41-21 (C)
1955 — Packers, 31-14 (GB)
1956 — Packers, 24-21 (C)
1962 — Packers, 17-0 (Mil)
1963 — Packers, 30-7 (StL)
1967 — Packers, 31-23 (StL)
1969 — Packers, 45-28 (GB)
1971 — Tie, 16-16 (StL)
1973 — Packers, 25-21 (GB)
1976 — Cardinals, 29-0 (StL)
1982 — **Packers, 41-16 (GB)
1984 — Packers, 24-23 (GB)
1985 — Cardinals, 43-28 (StL)
1988 — Packers, 26-17 (P)
1990 — Packers, 24-21 (P)
(RS Pts. — Packers 1,082, Cardinals 823)
(PS Pts. — Packers 41, Cardinals 16)
**Franchise in St. Louis prior to 1988, and in Chicago prior to 1960*
***NFC First Round Playoff*

GREEN BAY vs. *PITTSBURGH
RS: Packers lead series, 17-11
1933 — Packers, 47-0 (GB)
1935 — Packers, 27-0 (GB)
Packers, 34-14 (P)
1936 — Packers, 42-10 (Mil)
1938 — Packers, 20-0 (GB)
1940 — Packers, 24-3 (Mil)
1941 — Packers, 54-7 (P)
1942 — Packers, 24-21 (Mil)
1946 — Packers, 17-7 (GB)
1947 — Steelers, 18-17 (Mil)
1948 — Steelers, 38-7 (P)
1949 — Steelers, 30-7 (Mil)
1951 — Packers, 35-33 (Mil)
Steelers, 28-7 (P)
1953 — Steelers, 31-14 (P)
1954 — Steelers, 21-20 (GB)
1957 — Packers, 27-10 (P)
1960 — Packers, 19-13 (P)
1963 — Packers, 33-14 (Mil)
1965 — Packers, 41-9 (P)
1967 — Steelers, 24-17 (GB)
1969 — Packers, 38-34 (P)
1970 — Packers, 20-12 (P)
1975 — Steelers, 16-13 (Mil)
1980 — Steelers, 22-20 (P)
1983 — Steelers, 25-21 (GB)
1986 — Steelers, 27-3 (P)
1992 — Packers, 17-3 (GB)
(RS Pts. — Packers 665, Steelers 470)
**Steelers known as Pirates prior to 1941*

GREEN BAY vs. SAN DIEGO
RS: Packers lead series, 3-1
1970 — Packers, 22-20 (SD)
1974 — Packers, 34-0 (GB)
1978 — Packers, 24-3 (SD)
1984 — Chargers, 34-28 (GB)
(RS Pts. — Packers 108, Chargers 57)

GREEN BAY vs. SAN FRANCISCO
RS: 49ers lead series, 25-21-1
1950 — Packers, 25-21 (GB)
49ers, 30-14 (SF)
1951 — 49ers, 31-19 (SF)
1952 — 49ers, 24-14 (SF)
1953 — 49ers, 37-7 (Mil)
49ers, 48-14 (SF)
1954 — 49ers, 23-17 (Mil)
49ers, 35-0 (SF)
1955 — Packers, 27-21 (Mil)
Packers, 28-7 (SF)
1956 — 49ers, 17-16 (GB)
49ers, 38-20 (SF)
1957 — 49ers, 24-14 (Mil)
49ers, 27-20 (SF)
1958 — 49ers, 33-12 (Mil)
49ers, 48-21 (SF)
1959 — Packers, 21-20 (GB)
Packers, 36-14 (SF)
1960 — Packers, 41-14 (Mil)
Packers, 13-0 (SF)
1961 — Packers, 30-10 (GB)
49ers, 22-21 (SF)
1962 — Packers, 31-13 (Mil)
Packers, 31-21 (SF)
1963 — Packers, 28-10 (Mil)
Packers, 21-17 (SF)
1964 — Packers, 24-14 (Mil)
49ers, 24-14 (SF)
1965 — Packers, 27-10 (GB)
Tie, 24-24 (SF)
1966 — 49ers, 21-20 (SF)
Packers, 20-7 (Mil)
1967 — Packers, 13-0 (GB)
1968 — 49ers, 27-20 (SF)
1969 — Packers, 14-7 (Mil)
1970 — 49ers, 26-10 (SF)
1972 — Packers, 34-24 (Mil)
1973 — 49ers, 20-6 (SF)
1974 — 49ers, 7-6 (SF)
1976 — 49ers, 26-14 (GB)
1977 — Packers, 16-14 (Mil)
1980 — Packers, 23-16 (Mil)
1981 — 49ers, 13-3 (Mil)
1986 — 49ers, 31-17 (Mil)
1987 — 49ers, 23-12 (GB)
1989 — Packers, 21-17 (SF)
1990 — 49ers, 24-20 (GB)
(RS Pts. — 49ers 980, Packers 899)

GREEN BAY vs. SEATTLE
RS: Series tied, 3-3
1976 — Packers, 27-20 (Mil)
1978 — Packers, 45-28 (Mil)
1981 — Packers, 34-24 (GB)
1984 — Seahawks, 30-24 (Mil)
1987 — Seahawks, 24-13 (S)
1990 — Seahawks, 20-14 (Mil)
(RS Pts. — Packers 157, Seahawks 146)

GREEN BAY vs. TAMPA BAY
RS: Packers lead series, 15-12-1
1977 — Packers, 13-0 (TB)
1978 — Packers, 9-7 (GB)
Packers, 17-7 (TB)
1979 — Buccaneers, 21-10 (GB)
Buccaneers, 21-3 (TB)
1980 — Tie, 14-14 (TB) OT
Buccaneers, 20-17 (Mil)
1981 — Buccaneers, 21-10 (GB)
Buccaneers, 37-3 (TB)
1983 — Packers, 55-14 (GB)
Packers, 12-9 (TB) OT
1984 — Buccaneers, 30-27 (TB) OT
Packers, 27-14 (GB)
1985 — Packers, 21-0 (GB)
Packers, 20-17 (TB)
1986 — Packers, 31-7 (Mil)
Packers, 21-7 (TB)
1987 — Buccaneers, 23-17 (Mil)
1988 — Buccaneers, 13-10 (GB)
Buccaneers, 27-24 (TB)
1989 — Buccaneers, 23-21 (GB)
Packers, 17-16 (TB)
1990 — Buccaneers, 26-14 (TB)
Packers, 20-10 (Mil)
1991 — Packers, 15-13 (GB)
Packers, 27-0 (TB)
1992 — Buccaneers, 31-3 (TB)
Packers, 19-14 (Mil)
(RS Pts. — Packers 497, Buccaneers 441)

GREEN BAY vs. *WASHINGTON
RS: Packers lead series, 13-12-1
PS: Series tied, 1-1
1932 — Packers, 21-0 (B)
1933 — Tie, 7-7 (GB)
Redskins, 20-7 (B)
1934 — Packers, 10-0 (B)
1936 — Packers, 31-2 (GB)
Packers, 7-3 (B)
**Packers, 21-6 (New York)
1937 — Redskins, 14-6 (W)
1939 — Packers, 24-14 (Mil)
1941 — Packers, 22-17 (W)
1943 — Redskins, 33-7 (Mil)
1946 — Packers, 20-7 (W)
1947 — Packers, 27-10 (Mil)
1948 — Redskins, 23-7 (Mil)
1949 — Redskins, 30-0 (W)
1950 — Packers, 35-21 (Mil)
1952 — Packers, 35-20 (Mil)
1958 — Redskins, 37-21 (W)
1959 — Packers, 21-0 (GB)
1968 — Packers, 27-7 (W)
1972 — Redskins, 21-16 (W)
***Redskins, 16-3 (W)
1974 — Redskins, 17-6 (GB)
1977 — Redskins, 10-9 (W)
1979 — Redskins, 38-21 (W)
1983 — Packers, 48-47 (GB)
1986 — Redskins, 16-7 (GB)
1988 — Redskins, 20-17 (Mil)
(RS Pts. — Packers 459, Redskins 434)
(PS Pts. — Packers 24, Redskins 22)
**Franchise in Boston prior to 1937 and known as Braves prior to 1933*
***NFL Championship*
****NFC Divisional Playoff*

HOUSTON vs. ATLANTA
RS: Falcons lead series, 5-2;
See Atlanta vs. Houston

HOUSTON vs. BUFFALO
RS: Oilers lead series, 20-11
PS: Bills lead series, 2-0;
See Buffalo vs. Houston

HOUSTON vs. CHICAGO
RS: Oilers lead series, 4-2;
See Chicago vs. Houston

HOUSTON vs. CINCINNATI
RS: Bengals lead series, 24-23-1

PS: Bengals lead series, 1-0;
See Cincinnati vs. Houston
HOUSTON vs. CLEVELAND
RS: Browns lead series, 27-18
PS: Oilers lead series, 1-0;
See Cleveland vs. Houston
HOUSTON vs. DALLAS
RS: Cowboys lead series, 4-3;
See Dallas vs. Houston
HOUSTON vs. DENVER
RS: Oilers lead series, 19-11-1
PS: Broncos lead series, 2-1;
See Denver vs. Houston
HOUSTON vs. DETROIT
RS: Oilers lead series, 4-2;
See Detroit vs. Houston
HOUSTON vs. GREEN BAY
RS: Series tied, 3-3;
See Green Bay vs. Houston
HOUSTON vs. *INDIANAPOLIS
RS: Oilers lead series, 7-6
1970 — Colts, 24-20 (H)
1973 — Oilers, 31-27 (B)
1976 — Colts, 38-14 (B)
1979 — Oilers, 28-16 (B)
1980 — Oilers, 21-16 (H)
1983 — Colts, 20-10 (B)
1984 — Colts, 35-21 (H)
1985 — Colts, 34-16 (I)
1986 — Oilers, 31-17 (H)
1987 — Colts, 51-27 (I)
1988 — Oilers, 17-14 (I) OT
1990 — Oilers 24-10 (H)
1992 — Oilers, 20-10 (I)
(RS Pts. — Colts 312, Oilers 280)
**Franchise in Baltimore prior to 1984*
HOUSTON vs. *KANSAS CITY
RS: Chiefs lead series, 21-16
PS: Chiefs lead series, 1-0
1960 — Oilers, 20-10 (H)
Texans, 24-0 (D)
1961 — Texans, 26-21 (D)
Oilers, 38-7 (H)
1962 — Texans, 31-7 (H)
Oilers, 14-6 (D)
**Texans, 20-17 (H) OT
1963 — Chiefs, 28-7 (KC)
Oilers, 28-7 (H)
1964 — Chiefs, 28-7 (KC)
Chiefs, 28-19 (H)
1965 — Chiefs, 52-21 (KC)
Oilers, 38-36 (H)
1966 — Chiefs, 48-23 (KC)
1967 — Chiefs, 25-20 (H)
Oilers, 24-19 (KC)
1968 — Chiefs, 26-21 (H)
Chiefs, 24-10 (KC)
1969 — Chiefs, 24-0 (KC)
1970 — Chiefs, 24-9 (KC)
1971 — Chiefs, 20-16 (H)
1973 — Chiefs, 38-14 (KC)
1974 — Chiefs, 17-7 (H)
1975 — Oilers, 17-13 (KC)
1977 — Oilers, 34-20 (H)
1978 — Oilers, 20-17 (KC)
1979 — Oilers, 20-6 (H)
1980 — Chiefs, 21-20 (KC)
1981 — Chiefs, 23-10 (KC)
1983 — Chiefs, 13-10 (H) OT
1984 — Oilers, 17-16 (KC)
1985 — Oilers, 23-20 (H)
1986 — Chiefs, 27-13 (KC)
1988 — Oilers, 7-6 (H)
1989 — Chiefs, 34-0 (KC)
1990 — Oilers 27-10 (KC)
1991 — Oilers, 17-7 (H)
1992 — Oilers, 23-20 (H) OT
(RS Pts. — Chiefs 801, Oilers 622)
(PS Pts. — Chiefs 20, Oilers 17)
**Franchise in Dallas prior to 1963 and known as Texans*
***AFL Championship*
HOUSTON vs. *L.A. RAIDERS
RS: Raiders lead series, 19-13
PS: Raiders lead series, 3-0
1960 — Oilers, 37-22 (O)
Raiders, 14-13 (H)
1961 — Oilers, 55-0 (H)
Oilers, 47-16 (O)
1962 — Oilers, 28-20 (O)
Oilers, 32-17 (H)
1963 — Raiders, 24-13 (H)
Raiders, 52-49 (O)
1964 — Oilers, 42-28 (H)
Raiders, 20-10 (O)
1965 — Raiders, 21-17 (O)
Raiders, 33-21 (H)
1966 — Oilers, 31-0 (H)
Raiders, 38-23 (O)
1967 — Raiders, 19-7 (H)
**Raiders, 40-7 (O)
1968 — Raiders, 24-15 (H)
1969 — Raiders, 21-17 (O)
***Raiders, 56-7 (O)
1971 — Raiders, 41-21 (O)
1972 — Raiders, 34-0 (H)
1973 — Raiders, 17-6 (H)
1975 — Oilers, 27-26 (O)
1976 — Raiders, 14-13 (H)
1977 — Raiders, 34-29 (O)
1978 — Raiders, 21-17 (O)
1979 — Oilers, 31-17 (H)
1980 — ****Raiders, 27-7 (O)
1981 — Oilers, 17-16 (H)
1983 — Raiders, 20-6 (LA)
1984 — Raiders, 24-14 (H)
1986 — Raiders, 28-17 (H)
1988 — Oilers, 38-35 (H)
1989 — Oilers, 23-7 (H)
1991 — Oilers, 47-17 (H)
(RS Pts. — Oilers 763, Raiders 720)
(PS Pts. — Raiders 123, Oilers 21)
**Franchise in Oakland prior to 1982*
***AFL Championship*
****Inter-Divisional Playoff*
*****AFC First Round Playoff*
HOUSTON vs. L.A. RAMS
RS: Rams lead series, 4-2
1973 — Rams, 31-26 (H)
1978 — Rams, 10-6 (H)
1981 — Oilers, 27-20 (LA)
1984 — Rams, 27-16 (LA)
1987 — Oilers, 20-16 (H)
1990 — Rams, 17-13 (LA)
(RS Pts. — Rams 121, Oilers 108)
HOUSTON vs. MIAMI
RS: Series tied, 11-11
PS: Oilers lead series, 1-0
1966 — Dolphins, 20-13 (H)
Dolphins, 29-28 (M)
1967 — Oilers, 17-14 (H)
Oilers, 41-10 (M)
1968 — Oilers, 24-10 (M)
Dolphins, 24-7 (H)
1969 — Oilers, 22-10 (H)
Oilers, 32-7 (M)
1970 — Dolphins, 20-10 (H)
1972 — Dolphins, 34-13 (M)
1975 — Oilers, 20-19 (H)
1977 — Dolphins, 27-7 (M)
1978 — Oilers, 35-30 (H)
*Oilers, 17-9 (M)
1979 — Oilers, 9-6 (M)
1981 — Dolphins, 16-10 (H)
1983 — Dolphins, 24-17 (H)
1984 — Dolphins, 28-10 (M)
1985 — Oilers, 26-23 (H)
1986 — Dolphins, 28-7 (M)
1989 — Oilers, 39-7 (H)
1991 — Oilers, 17-13 (M)
1992 — Dolphins, 19-16 (M)
(RS Pts. — Oilers 420, Dolphins 418)
(PS Pts. — Oilers 17, Dolphins 9)
**AFC First Round Playoff*
HOUSTON vs. MINNESOTA
RS: Series tied, 3-3
1974 — Vikings, 51-10 (M)
1980 — Oilers, 20-16 (H)
1983 — Vikings, 34-14 (M)
1986 — Oilers, 23-10 (H)
1989 — Vikings, 38-7 (M)
1992 — Oilers, 17-13 (M)
(RS Pts. — Vikings 162, Oilers 91)
HOUSTON vs. *NEW ENGLAND
RS: Patriots lead series, 17-13-1
PS: Oilers lead series, 1-0
1960 — Oilers, 24-10 (B)
Oilers, 37-21 (H)
1961 — Tie, 31-31 (B)
Oilers, 27-15 (H)
1962 — Patriots, 34-21 (B)
Oilers, 21-17 (H)
1963 — Patriots, 45-3 (B)
Patriots, 46-28 (H)
1964 — Patriots, 25-24 (B)
Patriots, 34-17 (H)
1965 — Oilers, 31-10 (H)
Patriots, 42-14 (B)
1966 — Patriots, 27-21 (B)
Patriots, 38-14 (H)
1967 — Patriots, 18-7 (B)
Oilers, 27-6 (H)
1968 — Oilers, 16-0 (B)
Oilers, 45-17 (H)
1969 — Patriots, 24-0 (B)
Oilers, 27-23 (H)
1971 — Patriots, 28-20 (NE)
1973 — Patriots, 32-0 (H)
1975 — Oilers, 7-0 (NE)
1978 — Oilers, 26-23 (NE)
**Oilers, 31-14 (NE)
1980 — Oilers, 38-34 (H)
1981 — Patriots, 38-10 (NE)
1982 — Patriots, 29-21 (NE)
1987 — Patriots, 21-7 (H)
1988 — Oilers, 31-6 (H)
1989 — Patriots, 23-13 (NE)
1991 — Patriots, 24-20 (NE)
(RS Pts. — Patriots 741, Oilers 628)
(PS Pts. — Oilers 31, Patriots 14)
**Franchise in Boston prior to 1971*
***AFC Divisional Playoff*
HOUSTON vs. NEW ORLEANS
RS: Series tied, 3-3-1
1971 — Tie, 13-13 (H)
1976 — Oilers, 31-26 (NO)
1978 — Oilers, 17-12 (NO)
1981 — Saints, 27-24 (H)
1984 — Saints, 27-10 (H)
1987 — Saints, 24-10 (NO)
1990 — Oilers 23-10 (H)
(RS Pts. — Saints 139, Oilers 128)
HOUSTON vs. N.Y. GIANTS
RS: Giants lead series, 4-0
1973 — Giants, 34-14 (NY)
1982 — Giants, 17-14 (NY)
1985 — Giants, 35-14 (H)
1991 — Giants, 24-20 (NY)
(RS Pts. — Giants 110, Oilers 62)
HOUSTON vs. *N.Y. JETS
RS: Oilers lead series, 16-12-1
PS: Oilers lead series, 1-0
1960 — Oilers, 27-21 (H)
Oilers, 42-28 (NY)
1961 — Oilers, 49-13 (H)
Oilers, 48-21 (NY)
1962 — Oilers, 56-17 (H)
Oilers, 44-10 (NY)
1963 — Jets, 24-17 (NY)
Oilers, 31-27 (H)
1964 — Jets, 24-21 (NY)
Oilers, 33-17 (H)
1965 — Oilers, 27-21 (H)
Jets, 41-14 (NY)
1966 — Jets, 52-13 (NY)
Oilers, 24-0 (H)
1967 — Tie, 28-28 (NY)
1968 — Jets, 20-14 (H)
Jets, 26-7 (NY)
1969 — Jets, 26-17 (NY)
Jets, 34-26 (H)
1972 — Oilers, 26-20 (H)
1974 — Oilers, 27-22 (NY)
1977 — Oilers, 20-0 (H)
1979 — Oilers, 27-24 (H) OT
1980 — Jets, 31-28 (NY) OT
1981 — Jets, 33-17 (NY)
1984 — Oilers, 31-20 (H)
1988 — Jets, 45-3 (NY)
1990 — Jets, 17-12 (H)
1991 — Oilers, 23-20 (NY)
**Oilers, 17-10 (H)
(RS Pts. — Oilers 752, Jets 682)
(PS Pts. — Oilers 17, Jets 10)
**Jets known as Titans prior to 1963*
***AFC First Round Playoff*
HOUSTON vs. PHILADELPHIA
RS: Eagles lead series, 5-0
1972 — Eagles, 18-17 (H)
1979 — Eagles, 26-20 (H)
1982 — Eagles, 35-14 (P)
1988 — Eagles, 32-23 (P)
1991 — Eagles, 13-6 (H)
(RS Pts. — Eagles 124, Oilers 80)
HOUSTON vs. *PHOENIX
RS: Cardinals lead series, 3-2
1970 — Cardinals, 44-0 (StL)
1974 — Cardinals, 31-27 (H)
1979 — Cardinals, 24-17 (H)
1985 — Oilers, 20-10 (StL)
1988 — Oilers, 38-20 (H)
(RS Pts. — Cardinals 129, Oilers 102)
**Franchise in St. Louis prior to 1988*
HOUSTON vs. PITTSBURGH
RS: Steelers lead series, 29-16
PS: Steelers lead series, 3-0
1970 — Oilers, 19-7 (P)
Steelers, 7-3 (H)
1971 — Steelers, 23-16 (P)
Oilers, 29-3 (H)
1972 — Steelers, 24-7 (P)
Steelers, 9-3 (H)
1973 — Steelers, 36-7 (H)
Steelers, 33-7 (P)
1974 — Steelers, 13-7 (H)
Oilers, 13-10 (P)
1975 — Steelers, 24-17 (P)
Steelers, 32-9 (H)
1976 — Steelers, 32-16 (P)
Steelers, 21-0 (H)
1977 — Oilers, 27-10 (H)
Steelers, 27-10 (P)
1978 — Oilers, 24-17 (P)
Steelers, 13-3 (H)
*Steelers, 34-5 (P)
1979 — Steelers, 38-7 (P)
Oilers, 20-17 (H)
*Steelers, 27-13 (P)
1980 — Steelers, 31-17 (P)
Oilers, 6-0 (H)
1981 — Steelers, 26-13 (P)
Oilers, 21-20 (H)
1982 — Steelers, 24-10 (H)
1983 — Steelers, 40-28 (H)
Steelers, 17-10 (P)
1984 — Steelers, 35-7 (P)
Oilers, 23-20 (H) OT
1985 — Steelers, 20-0 (P)
Steelers, 30-7 (H)
1986 — Steelers, 22-16 (H) OT
Steelers, 21-10 (P)
1987 — Oilers, 23-3 (P)
Oilers, 24-16 (H)
1988 — Oilers, 34-14 (P)
Steelers, 37-34 (H)
1989 — Oilers, 27-0 (H)
Oilers, 23-16 (P)
**Steelers, 26-23 (H)
1990 — Steelers, 20-9 (P)
Oilers 34-14 (H)
1991 — Steelers, 26-14 (P)
Oilers, 31-6 (H)
1992 — Steelers, 29-24 (H)
Steelers, 21-20 (P)
(RS Pts. — Steelers 904, Oilers 709)
(PS Pts. — Steelers 87, Oilers 41)
**AFC Championship*
***AFC First Round Playoff*
HOUSTON vs. *SAN DIEGO
RS: Chargers lead series, 17-13-1
PS: Oilers lead series, 3-0
1960 — Oilers, 38-28 (H)
Chargers, 24-21 (LA)
**Oilers, 24-16 (H)
1961 — Chargers, 34-24 (SD)
Oilers, 33-13 (H)
**Oilers, 10-3 (SD)
1962 — Oilers, 42-17 (SD)
Oilers, 33-27 (H)
1963 — Chargers, 27-0 (SD)
Chargers 20-14 (H)
1964 — Chargers, 27-21 (SD)
Chargers, 20-17 (H)
1965 — Chargers, 31-14 (SD)
Chargers, 37-26 (H)
1966 — Chargers, 28-22 (H)
1967 — Chargers, 13-3 (SD)
Oilers, 24-17 (H)
1968 — Chargers, 30-14 (SD)
1969 — Chargers, 21-17 (H)
1970 — Tie, 31-31 (SD)
1971 — Oilers, 49-33 (H)
1972 — Chargers, 34-20 (SD)
1974 — Oilers, 21-14 (H)
1975 — Oilers, 33-17 (H)
1976 — Chargers, 30-27 (SD)
1978 — Chargers, 45-24 (H)
1979 — ***Oilers, 17-14 (SD)
1984 — Chargers, 31-14 (SD)
1985 — Oilers, 37-35 (H)
1986 — Chargers, 27-0 (SD)
1987 — Oilers, 33-18 (H)
1989 — Oilers, 34-27 (SD)
1990 — Oilers 17-7 (SD)
1992 — Oilers, 27-0 (H)
(RS Pts. — Chargers 763, Oilers 730)
(PS Pts. — Oilers 51, Chargers 33)
**Franchise in Los Angeles prior to 1961*
***AFL Championship*
****AFC Divisional Playoff*
HOUSTON vs. SAN FRANCISCO
RS: 49ers lead series, 5-2
1970 — 49ers, 30-20 (H)
1975 — Oilers, 27-13 (SF)
1978 — Oilers, 20-19 (H)
1981 — 49ers, 28-6 (SF)
1984 — 49ers, 34-21 (H)
1987 — 49ers, 27-20 (SF)
1990 — 49ers, 24-21 (H)
(RS Pts. — 49ers 175, Oilers 135)
HOUSTON vs. SEATTLE
RS: Seahawks lead series, 4-3
PS: Oilers lead series, 1-0
1977 — Oilers, 22-10 (S)
1979 — Seahawks, 34-14 (S)
1980 — Seahawks, 26-7 (H)
1981 — Oilers, 35-17 (H)
1982 — Oilers, 23-21 (H)
1987 — *Oilers, 23-20 (H) OT
1988 — Seahawks, 27-24 (S)
1990 — Seahawks, 13-10 (S) OT
(RS Pts. — Seahawks 148, Oilers 135)
(PS Pts. — Oilers 23, Seahawks 20)
**AFC First Round Playoff*
HOUSTON vs. TAMPA BAY
RS: Oilers lead series, 3-1
1976 — Oilers, 20-0 (H)
1980 — Oilers, 20-14 (H)
1983 — Buccaneers, 33-24 (TB)
1989 — Oilers, 20-17 (H)
(RS Pts. — Oilers 84, Buccaneers 64)

HOUSTON vs. WASHINGTON
RS: Series tied, 3-3
1971 — Redskins, 22-13 (W)
1975 — Oilers, 13-10 (H)
1979 — Oilers, 29-27 (W)
1985 — Redskins, 16-13 (W)
1988 — Oilers, 41-17 (H)
1991 — Redskins, 16-13 (W) OT
(RS Pts. — Oilers 122, Redskins 108)

INDIANAPOLIS vs. ATLANTA
RS: Colts lead series, 10-0;
See Atlanta vs. Indianapolis
INDIANAPOLIS vs. BUFFALO
RS: Bills lead series, 24-20-1;
See Buffalo vs. Indianapolis
INDIANAPOLIS vs. CHICAGO
RS: Colts lead series, 21-16;
See Chicago vs. Indianapolis
INDIANAPOLIS vs. CINCINNATI
RS: Colts lead series, 7-5
PS: Colts lead series, 1-0;
See Cincinnati vs. Indianapolis
INDIANAPOLIS vs. CLEVELAND
RS: Browns lead series, 12-6
PS: Series tied, 2-2;
See Cleveland vs. Indianapolis
INDIANAPOLIS vs. DALLAS
RS: Cowboys lead series, 6-2
PS: Colts lead series, 1-0;
See Dallas vs. Indianapolis
INDIANAPOLIS vs. DENVER
RS: Broncos lead series, 8-2;
See Denver vs. Indianapolis
INDIANAPOLIS vs. DETROIT
RS: Series tied, 17-17-2;
See Detroit vs. Indianapolis
INDIANAPOLIS vs. GREEN BAY
RS: Series tied, 18-18-1
PS: Packers lead series, 1-0;
See Green Bay vs. Indianapolis
INDIANAPOLIS vs. HOUSTON
RS: Oilers lead series, 7-6;
See Houston vs. Indianapolis
***INDIANAPOLIS vs. KANSAS CITY**
RS: Chiefs lead series, 6-4
1970 — Chiefs, 44-24 (B)
1972 — Chiefs, 24-10 (KC)
1975 — Colts, 28-14 (B)
1977 — Colts, 17-6 (KC)
1979 — Chiefs, 14-0 (KC)
Chiefs, 10-7 (B)
1980 — Colts, 31-24 (KC)
Chiefs, 38-28 (B)
1985 — Chiefs, 20-7 (KC)
1990 — Colts, 23-19 (I)
(RS Pts. — Chiefs 213, Colts 175)
**Franchise in Baltimore prior to 1984*
***INDIANAPOLIS vs **L.A. RAIDERS**
RS: Raiders lead series, 4-2
PS: Series tied, 1-1
1970 — ***Colts, 27-17 (B)
1971 — Colts, 37-14 (O)
1973 — Raiders, 34-21 (B)
1975 — Raiders, 31-20 (B)
1977 — ****Raiders, 37-31 (B) OT
1984 — Raiders, 21-7 (LA)
1986 — Colts, 30-24 (LA)
1991 — Raiders, 16-0 (LA)
(RS Pts. — Raiders 140, Colts 115)
(PS Pts. — Colts 58, Raiders 54)
**Franchise in Baltimore prior to 1984*
***Franchise in Oakland prior to 1982*
****AFC Championship*
*****AFC Divisional Playoff*
***INDIANAPOLIS vs. L.A. RAMS**
RS: Colts lead series, 20-16-2
1953 — Rams, 21-13 (B)
Rams, 45-2 (LA)
1954 — Rams, 48-0 (B)
Colts, 22-21 (LA)
1955 — Tie, 17-17 (B)
Rams, 20-14 (LA)
1956 — Colts, 56-21 (B)
Rams, 31-7 (LA)
1957 — Colts, 31-14 (B)
Rams, 37-21 (LA)
1958 — Colts, 34-7 (B)
Rams, 30-28 (LA)
1959 — Colts, 35-21 (B)
Colts, 45-26 (LA)
1960 — Colts, 31-17 (B)
Rams, 10-3 (LA)
1961 — Colts, 27-24 (B)
Rams, 34-17 (LA)
1962 — Colts, 30-27 (B)
Colts, 14-2 (LA)
1963 — Rams, 17-16 (LA)
Colts, 19-16 (B)
1964 — Colts, 35-20 (B)
Colts, 24-7 (LA)
1965 — Colts, 35-20 (B)
Colts, 20-17 (LA)
1966 — Colts, 17-3 (LA)
Rams, 23-7 (B)
1967 — Tie, 24-24 (B)
Rams, 34-10 (LA)
1968 — Colts, 27-10 (B)
Colts, 28-24 (LA)
1969 — Rams, 27-20 (B)
Colts, 13-7 (LA)
1971 — Colts, 24-17 (B)
1975 — Rams, 24-13 (LA)
1986 — Rams, 24-7 (I)
1989 — Rams, 31-17 (LA)
(RS Pts. — Rams 818, Colts 803)
**Franchise in Baltimore prior to 1984*
***INDIANAPOLIS vs. MIAMI**
RS: Dolphins lead series, 32-14
PS: Dolphins lead series, 1-0
1970 — Colts, 35-0 (B)
Dolphins, 34-17 (M)
1971 — Dolphins, 17-14 (M)
Colts, 14-3 (B)
**Dolphins, 21-0 (M)
1972 — Dolphins, 23-0 (B)
Dolphins, 16-0 (M)
1973 — Dolphins, 44-0 (M)
Colts, 16-3 (B)
1974 — Dolphins, 17-7 (M)
Dolphins, 17-16 (B)
1975 — Colts, 33-17 (M)
Colts, 10-7 (B) OT
1976 — Colts, 28-14 (B)
Colts, 17-16 (M)
1977 — Colts, 45-28 (B)
Dolphins, 17-6 (M)
1978 — Dolphins, 42-0 (B)
Dolphins, 26-8 (M)
1979 — Dolphins, 19-0 (M)
Dolphins, 28-24 (B)
1980 — Colts, 30-17 (M)
Dolphins, 24-14 (B)
1981 — Dolphins, 31-28 (B)
Dolphins, 27-10 (M)
1982 — Dolphins, 24-20 (M)
Dolphins, 34-7 (B)
1983 — Dolphins, 21-7 (B)
Dolphins, 37-0 (M)
1984 — Dolphins, 44-7 (M)
Dolphins, 35-17 (I)
1985 — Dolphins, 30-13 (M)
Dolphins, 34-20 (I)
1986 — Dolphins, 30-10 (M)
Dolphins, 17-13 (I)
1987 — Dolphins, 23-10 (I)
Colts, 40-21 (M)
1988 — Colts, 15-13 (I)
Colts, 31-28 (M)
1989 — Dolphins, 19-13 (M)
Colts, 42-13 (I)
1990 — Dolphins, 27-7 (I)
Dolphins, 23-17 (M)
1991 — Dolphins, 17-6 (M)
Dolphins, 10-6 (I)
1992 — Colts, 31-20 (M)
Dolphins, 28-0 (I)
(RS Pts. — Dolphins 1,035, Colts 704)
(PS Pts. — Dolphins 21, Colts 0)
**Franchise in Baltimore prior to 1984*
***AFC Championship*
***INDIANAPOLIS vs. MINNESOTA**
RS: Colts lead series, 11-6-1
PS: Colts lead series, 1-0
1961 — Colts, 34-33 (B)
Vikings, 28-20 (M)
1962 — Colts, 34-7 (M)
Colts, 42-17 (B)
1963 — Colts, 37-34 (M)
Colts, 41-10 (B)
1964 — Vikings, 34-24 (M)
Colts, 17-14 (B)
1965 — Colts, 35-16 (B)
Colts, 41-21 (M)
1966 — Colts, 38-23 (M)
Colts, 20-17 (B)
1967 — Tie, 20-20 (M)
1968 — Colts, 21-9 (B)
**Colts, 24-14 (B)
1969 — Vikings, 52-14 (M)
1971 — Vikings, 10-3 (M)
1982 — Vikings, 13-10 (M)
1988 — Vikings, 12-3 (M)
(RS Pts. — Colts 454, Vikings 370)
(PS Pts. — Colts 24, Vikings 14)
**Franchise in Baltimore prior to 1984*
***Conference Championship*
***INDIANAPOLIS vs. **NEW ENGLAND**
RS: Patriots lead series, 26-19
1970 — Colts, 14-6 (Bos)
Colts, 27-3 (Balt)
1971 — Colts, 23-3 (NE)
Patriots, 21-17 (Balt)
1972 — Colts, 24-17 (NE)
Colts, 31-0 (Balt)
1973 — Patriots, 24-16 (NE)
Colts, 18-13 (Balt)
1974 — Patriots, 42-3 (NE)
Patriots, 27-17 (Balt)
1975 — Patriots, 21-10 (NE)
Colts, 34-21 (Balt)
1976 — Colts, 27-13 (NE)
Patriots, 21-14 (Balt)
1977 — Patriots, 17-3 (NE)
Colts, 30-24 (Balt)
1978 — Colts, 34-27 (NE)
Patriots, 35-14 (Balt)
1979 — Colts, 31-26 (Balt)
Patriots, 50-21 (NE)
1980 — Patriots, 37-21 (Balt)
Patriots, 47-21 (NE)
1981 — Colts, 29-28 (NE)
Colts, 23-21 (Balt)
1982 — Patriots, 24-13 (Balt)
1983 — Colts, 29-23 (NE) OT
Colts, 12-7 (B)
1984 — Patriots, 50-17 (I)
Patriots, 16-10 (NE)
1985 — Patriots, 34-15 (NE)
Patriots, 38-31 (I)
1986 — Patriots, 33-3 (NE)
Patriots, 30-21 (I)
1987 — Colts, 30-16 (I)
Patriots, 24-0 (NE)
1988 — Patriots, 21-17 (NE)
Colts, 24-21 (I)
1989 — Patriots, 23-20 (I) OT
Patriots, 22-16 (NE)
1990 — Patriots, 16-14 (I)
Colts, 13-10 (NE)
1991 — Patriots, 16-7 (I)
Patriots, 23-17 (NE) OT
1992 — Patriots, 37-34 (I) OT
Colts, 6-0 (NE)
(RS Pts. — Patriots 1,028, Colts 851)
**Franchise in Baltimore prior to 1984*
***Franchise in Boston prior to 1971*
***INDIANAPOLIS vs. NEW ORLEANS**
RS: Colts lead series, 3-2
1967 — Colts, 30-10 (B)
1969 — Colts, 30-10 (NO)
1973 — Colts, 14-10 (B)
1986 — Saints, 17-14 (I)
1989 — Saints, 41-6 (NO)
(RS Pts. — Colts 94, Saints 88)
**Franchise in Baltimore prior to 1984*
***INDIANAPOLIS vs. N.Y. GIANTS**
RS: Colts lead series, 5-4
PS: Colts lead series, 2-0
1954 — Colts, 20-14 (B)
1955 — Giants, 17-7 (NY)
1958 — Giants, 24-21 (NY)
**Colts, 23-17 (NY) OT
1959 — **Colts, 31-16 (B)
1963 — Giants, 37-28 (B)
1968 — Colts, 26-0 (NY)
1971 — Colts, 31-7 (NY)
1975 — Colts, 21-0 (NY)
1979 — Colts, 31-7 (NY)
1990 — Giants, 24-7 (I)
(RS Pts. — Colts 192, Giants 130)
(PS Pts. — Colts 54, Giants 33)
**Franchise in Baltimore prior to 1984*
***NFL Championship*
***INDIANAPOLIS vs. N.Y. JETS**
RS: Colts lead series, 26-19
PS: Jets lead series, 1-0
1968 — **Jets 16-7 (Miami)
1970 — Colts, 29-22 (NY)
Colts, 35-20 (B)
1971 — Colts, 22-0 (B)
Colts, 14-13 (NY)
1972 — Jets, 44-34 (B)
Jets, 24-20 (NY)
1973 — Jets, 34-10 (B)
Jets, 20-17 (NY)
1974 — Colts, 35-20 (NY)
Jets, 45-38 (B)
1975 — Colts, 45-28 (NY)
Colts, 52-19 (B)
1976 — Colts, 20-0 (NY)
Colts, 33-16 (B)
1977 — Colts, 20-12 (NY)
Colts, 33-12 (B)
1978 — Jets, 33-10 (B)
Jets, 24-16 (NY)
1979 — Colts, 10-8 (B)
Jets, 30-17 (NY)
1980 — Colts, 17-14 (NY)
Colts, 35-21 (B)
1981 — Jets, 41-14 (B)
Jets, 25-0 (NY)
1982 — Jets, 37-0 (NY)
1983 — Colts, 17-14 (NY)
Jets, 10-6 (B)
1984 — Jets, 23-14 (I)
Colts, 9-5 (NY)
1985 — Jets, 25-20 (NY)
Jets, 35-17 (I)
1986 — Jets, 26-7 (I)
Jets, 31-16 (NY)
1987 — Colts, 6-0 (I)
Colts, 19-14 (NY)
1988 — Colts, 38-14 (I)
Jets, 34-16 (NY)
1989 — Colts, 17-10 (NY)
Colts, 27-10 (I)
1990 — Colts, 17-14 (I)
Colts, 29-21 (NY)
1991 — Jets, 17-6 (I)
Colts, 28-27 (NY)
1992 — Colts, 6-3 (I) OT
Colts, 10-6 (NY)
(RS Pts. — Colts 901, Jets 901)
(PS Pts. — Jets 16, Colts 7)
**Franchise in Baltimore prior to 1984*
***Super Bowl III*
***INDIANAPOLIS vs. PHILADELPHIA**
RS: Colts lead series, 6-5
1953 — Eagles, 45-14 (P)
1965 — Colts, 34-24 (B)
1967 — Colts, 38-6 (P)
1969 — Colts, 24-20 (B)
1970 — Colts, 29-10 (B)
1974 — Eagles, 30-10 (P)
1978 — Eagles, 17-14 (B)
1981 — Eagles, 38-13 (P)
1983 — Colts, 22-21 (P)
1984 — Eagles, 16-7 (P)
1990 — Colts, 24-23 (P)
(RS Pts. — Eagles 250, Colts 229)
**Franchise in Baltimore prior to 1984*
***INDIANAPOLIS vs. **PHOENIX**
RS: Cardinals lead series, 6-5
1961 — Colts, 16-0 (B)
1964 — Colts, 47-27 (B)
1968 — Colts, 27-0 (B)
1972 — Cardinals, 10-3 (B)
1976 — Cardinals, 24-17 (StL)
1978 — Colts, 30-17 (StL)
1980 — Cardinals, 17-10 (B)
1981 — Cardinals, 35-24 (B)
1984 — Cardinals, 34-33 (I)
1990 — Cardinals, 20-17 (P)
1992 — Colts, 16-13 (I)
(RS Pts. — Colts 240, Cardinals 197)
**Franchise in Baltimore prior to 1984*
***Franchise in St. Louis prior to 1988*
***INDIANAPOLIS vs. PITTSBURGH**
RS: Steelers lead series, 10-4
PS: Steelers lead series, 2-0
1957 — Steelers, 19-13 (B)
1968 — Colts, 41-7 (P)
1971 — Colts, 34-21 (B)
1974 — Steelers, 30-0 (B)
1975 — **Steelers, 28-10 (P)
1976 — **Steelers, 40-14 (B)
1977 — Colts, 31-21 (B)
1978 — Steelers, 35-13 (P)
1979 — Steelers, 17-13 (P)
1980 — Steelers, 20-17 (B)
1983 — Steelers, 24-13 (B)
1984 — Colts, 17-16 (I)
1985 — Steelers, 45-3 (P)
1987 — Steelers, 21-7 (P)
1991 — Steelers, 21-3 (I)
1992 — Steelers, 30-14 (P)
(RS Pts. — Steelers 327, Colts 219)
(PS Pts. — Steelers 68, Colts 24)
**Franchise in Baltimore prior to 1984*
***AFC Divisional Playoff*
***INDIANAPOLIS vs. SAN DIEGO**
RS: Chargers lead series, 8-5
1970 — Colts, 16-14 (SD)
1972 — Chargers, 23-20 (B)
1976 — Colts, 37-21 (SD)
1981 — Chargers, 43-14 (B)
1982 — Chargers, 44-26 (SD)
1984 — Chargers, 38-10 (I)
1986 — Chargers, 17-3 (I)
1987 — Chargers, 16-13 (I)
Colts, 20-7 (SD)
1988 — Colts, 16-0 (SD)
1989 — Colts, 10-6 (I)
1992 — Chargers, 34-14 (I)
Chargers, 26-0 (SD)
(RS Pts. — Chargers 289, Colts 199)
**Franchise in Baltimore prior to 1984*
***INDIANAPOLIS vs. SAN FRANCISCO**
RS: Colts lead series, 21-16
1953 — 49ers, 38-21 (B)
49ers, 45-14 (SF)
1954 — Colts, 17-13 (B)
49ers, 10-7 (SF)
1955 — Colts, 26-14 (B)
49ers, 35-24 (SF)
1956 — 49ers, 20-17 (B)
49ers, 30-17 (SF)
1957 — Colts, 27-21 (B)
49ers, 17-13 (SF)
1958 — Colts, 35-27 (B)
49ers, 21-12 (SF)

1959 — Colts, 45-14 (B)
Colts, 34-14 (SF)
1960 — 49ers, 30-22 (B)
49ers, 34-10 (SF)
1961 — Colts, 20-17 (B)
Colts, 27-24 (SF)
1962 — 49ers, 21-13 (B)
Colts, 22-3 (SF)
1963 — Colts, 20-14 (SF)
Colts, 20-3 (B)
1964 — Colts, 37-7 (B)
Colts, 14-3 (SF)
1965 — Colts, 27-24 (B)
Colts, 34-28 (SF)
1966 — Colts, 36-14 (B)
Colts, 30-14 (SF)
1967 — Colts, 41-7 (B)
Colts, 26-9 (SF)
1968 — Colts, 27-10 (B)
Colts, 42-14 (SF)
1969 — 49ers, 24-21 (B)
49ers, 20-17 (SF)
1972 — 49ers, 24-21 (SF)
1986 — 49ers, 35-14 (SF)
1989 — 49ers, 30-24 (I)
(RS Pts. — Colts 874, 49ers 728)
Franchise in Baltimore prior to 1984

***INDIANAPOLIS vs. SEATTLE**
RS: Colts lead series, 2-1
1977 — Colts, 29-14 (S)
1978 — Colts, 17-14 (S)
1991 — Seahawks, 31-3 (S)
(RS Pts. — Seahawks 59, Colts 49)
**Franchise in Baltimore prior to 1984*

***INDIANAPOLIS vs. TAMPA BAY**
RS: Colts lead series, 5-2
1976 — Colts, 42-17 (B)
1979 — Buccaneers, 29-26 (B) OT
1985 — Colts, 31-23 (TB)
1987 — Colts, 24-6 (I)
1988 — Colts, 35-31 (I)
1991 — Buccaneers, 17-3 (TB)
1992 — Colts, 24-14 (TB)
(RS Pts. — Colts 185, Buccaneers 137)
**Franchise in Baltimore prior to 1984*

***INDIANAPOLIS vs. WASHINGTON**
RS: Colts lead series, 16-6
1953 — Colts, 27-17 (B)
1954 — Redskins, 24-21 (W)
1955 — Redskins, 14-13 (B)
1956 — Colts, 19-17 (B)
1957 — Colts, 21-17 (W)
1958 — Colts, 35-10 (B)
1959 — Redskins, 27-24 (W)
1960 — Colts, 20-0 (B)
1961 — Colts, 27-6 (W)
1962 — Colts, 34-21 (B)
1963 — Colts, 36-20 (W)
1964 — Colts, 45-17 (B)
1965 — Colts, 38-7 (W)
1966 — Colts, 37-10 (B)
1967 — Colts, 17-13 (W)
1969 — Colts, 41-17 (B)
1973 — Redskins, 22-14 (W)
1977 — Colts, 10-3 (B)
1978 — Colts, 21-17 (B)
1981 — Redskins, 38-14 (W)
1984 — Redskins, 35-7 (I)
1990 — Colts, 35-28 (I)
(RS Pts. — Colts 556, Redskins 380)
**Franchise in Baltimore prior to 1984*

KANSAS CITY vs. ATLANTA
RS: Chiefs lead series, 3-0;
See Atlanta vs. Kansas City

KANSAS CITY vs. BUFFALO
RS: Bills lead series, 15-12-1
PS: Series tied, 1-1;
See Buffalo vs. Kansas City

KANSAS CITY vs. CHICAGO
RS: Bears lead series, 3-2;
See Chicago vs. Kansas City

KANSAS CITY vs. CINCINNATI
RS: Chiefs lead series, 10-9;
See Cincinnati vs. Kansas City

KANSAS CITY vs. CLEVELAND
RS: Browns lead, 7-6-2;
See Cleveland vs. Kansas City

KANSAS CITY vs. DALLAS
RS: Cowboys lead series, 3-2;
See Dallas vs. Kansas City

KANSAS CITY vs. DENVER
RS: Chiefs lead series, 37-28;
See Denver vs. Kansas City

KANSAS CITY vs. DETROIT
RS: Chiefs lead series, 4-3;
See Detroit vs. Kansas City

KANSAS CITY vs. GREEN BAY
RS: Chiefs lead series, 3-1-1
PS: Packers lead series, 1-0;
See Green Bay vs. Kansas City

KANSAS CITY vs. HOUSTON
RS: Chiefs lead series, 21-16
PS: Chiefs lead series, 1-0;
See Houston vs. Kansas City

KANSAS CITY vs. INDIANAPOLIS
RS: Chiefs lead series, 6-4;
See Indianapolis vs. Kansas City

***KANSAS CITY vs. **L.A. RAIDERS**
RS: Raiders lead series, 35-28-2
PS: Chiefs lead series, 2-1
1960 — Texans, 34-16 (O)
Raiders, 20-19 (D)
1961 — Texans, 42-35 (O)
Texans, 43-11 (D)
1962 — Texans, 26-16 (O)
Texans, 35-7 (D)
1963 — Raiders, 10-7 (O)
Raiders, 22-7 (KC)
1964 — Chiefs, 21-9 (O)
Chiefs, 42-7 (KC)
1965 — Raiders, 37-10 (O)
Chiefs, 14-7 (KC)
1966 — Chiefs, 32-10 (O)
Raiders, 34-13 (KC)
1967 — Raiders, 23-21 (O)
Raiders, 44-22 (KC)
1968 — Chiefs, 24-10 (KC)
Raiders, 38-21 (O)
***Raiders, 41-6 (O)
1969 — Raiders, 27-24 (KC)
Raiders, 10-6 (O)
****Chiefs, 17-7 (O)
1970 — Tie, 17-17 (KC)
Raiders, 20-6 (O)
1971 — Tie, 20-20 (O)
Chiefs, 16-14 (KC)
1972 — Chiefs, 27-14 (KC)
Raiders, 26-3 (O)
1973 — Chiefs, 16-3 (KC)
Raiders, 37-7 (O)
1974 — Raiders, 27-7 (O)
Raiders, 7-6 (KC)
1975 — Chiefs, 42-10 (KC)
Raiders, 28-20 (O)
1976 — Raiders, 24-21 (KC)
Raiders, 21-10 (O)
1977 — Raiders, 37-28 (KC)
Raiders, 21-20 (O)
1978 — Raiders, 28-6 (O)
Raiders, 20-10 (KC)
1979 — Chiefs, 35-7 (KC)
Chiefs, 24-21 (O)
1980 — Raiders, 27-14 (KC)
Chiefs, 31-17 (O)
1981 — Chiefs, 27-0 (KC)
Chiefs, 28-17 (O)
1982 — Raiders, 21-16 (KC)
1983 — Raiders, 21-20 (LA)
Raiders, 28-20 (KC)
1984 — Raiders, 22-20 (KC)
Raiders, 17-7 (LA)
1985 — Chiefs, 36-20 (KC)
Raiders, 19-10 (LA)
1986 — Raiders, 24-17 (KC)
Chiefs, 20-17 (LA)
1987 — Raiders, 35-17 (LA)
Chiefs, 16-10 (KC)
1988 — Raiders, 27-17 (KC)
Raiders, 17-10 (LA)
1989 — Chiefs, 24-19 (KC)
Raiders, 20-14 (LA)
1990 — Chiefs, 9-7 (KC)
Chiefs, 27-24 (LA)
1991 — Chiefs, 24-21 (KC)
Chiefs, 27-21 (LA)
†Chiefs, 10-6 (KC)
1992 — Chiefs, 27-7 (KC)
Raiders, 28-7 (LA)
(RS Pts. — Chiefs 1,289, Raiders 1,281)
(PS Pts. — Raiders 54, Chiefs 33)
**Franchise in Dallas prior to 1963 and known as Texans*
***Franchise in Oakland prior to 1982*
****Division Playoff*
*****AFL Championship*
†AFC First Round Playoff

KANSAS CITY vs. L.A. RAMS
RS: Rams lead series, 3-1
1973 — Rams, 23-13 (KC)
1982 — Rams, 20-14 (LA)
1985 — Rams, 16-0 (KC)
1991 — Chiefs, 27-20 (LA)
(RS Pts. — Rams 79, Chiefs 54)

KANSAS CITY vs. MIAMI
RS: Chiefs lead series, 10-6
PS: Dolphins lead series, 2-0
1966 — Chiefs, 34-16 (KC)
Chiefs, 19-18 (M)
1967 — Chiefs, 24-0 (M)
Chiefs, 41-0 (KC)
1968 — Chiefs, 48-3 (M)
1969 — Chiefs, 17-10 (KC)
1971 — *Dolphins, 27-24 (KC) OT
1972 — Dolphins, 20-10 (KC)
1974 — Dolphins, 9-3 (M)
1976 — Chiefs, 20-17 (M) OT
1981 — Dolphins, 17-7 (KC)
1983 — Dolphins, 14-6 (M)
1985 — Dolphins, 31-0 (M)
1987 — Dolphins, 42-0 (M)
1989 — Chiefs, 26-21 (KC)
Chiefs, 27-24 (M)
1990 — **Dolphins, 17-16 (M)
1991 — Chiefs, 42-7 (KC)
(RS Pts. — Chiefs 324, Dolphins 249)
(PS Pts. — Dolphins 44, Chiefs 40)
**AFC Divisional Playoff*
***AFC First Round Playoff*

KANSAS CITY vs. MINNESOTA
RS: Series tied, 2-2
PS: Chiefs lead series, 1-0
1969 — *Chiefs, 23-7 (New Orleans)
1970 — Vikings, 27-10 (M)
1974 — Vikings, 35-15 (KC)
1981 — Chiefs, 10-6 (M)
1990 — Chiefs, 24-21 (KC)
(RS Pts. — Vikings 89, Chiefs 59)
(PS Pts. — Chiefs 23, Vikings 7)
**Super Bowl IV*

***KANSAS CITY vs. **NEW ENGLAND**
RS: Chiefs lead series, 13-7-3
1960 — Patriots, 42-14 (B)
Texans, 34-0 (D)
1961 — Patriots, 18-17 (D)
Patriots, 28-21 (B)
1962 — Texans, 42-28 (D)
Texans, 27-7 (B)
1963 — Tie, 24-24 (B)
Chiefs, 35-3 (KC)
1964 — Patriots, 24-7 (B)
Patriots, 31-24 (KC)
1965 — Chiefs, 27-17 (KC)
Tie, 10-10 (B)
1966 — Chiefs, 43-24 (B)
Tie, 27-27 (KC)
1967 — Chiefs, 33-10 (B)
1968 — Chiefs, 31-17 (KC)
1969 — Chiefs, 31-0 (B)
1970 — Chiefs, 23-10 (KC)
1973 — Chiefs, 10-7 (NE)
1977 — Patriots, 21-17 (NE)
1981 — Patriots, 33-17 (NE)
1990 — Chiefs, 37-7 (NE)
1992 — Chiefs, 27-20 (KC)
(RS Pts. — Chiefs 578, Patriots 408)
**Franchise located in Dallas prior to 1963 and known as Texans*
***Franchise in Boston prior to 1971*

KANSAS CITY vs. NEW ORLEANS
RS: Saints lead series, 3-2
1972 — Chiefs, 20-17 (NO)
1976 — Saints, 27-17 (KC)
1982 — Saints, 27-17 (NO)
1985 — Chiefs, 47-27 (NO)
1991 — Saints, 17-10 (KC)
(RS Pts. — Saints 115, Chiefs 111)

KANSAS CITY vs. N.Y. GIANTS
RS: Giants lead series, 6-1
1974 — Giants, 33-27 (KC)
1978 — Giants, 26-10 (NY)
1979 — Giants, 21-17 (KC)
1983 — Chiefs, 38-17 (KC)
1984 — Giants, 28-27 (NY)
1988 — Giants, 28-12 (NY)
1992 — Giants, 35-21 (NY)
(RS Pts. — Giants 188, Chiefs 152)

***KANSAS CITY vs. **N.Y. JETS**
RS: Chiefs lead series, 14-12-1
PS: Series tied, 1-1
1960 — Titans, 37-35 (D)
Titans, 41-35 (NY)
1961 — Titans, 28-7 (NY)
Texans, 35-24 (D)
1962 — Texans, 20-17 (D)
Texans, 52-31 (NY)
1963 — Jets, 17-0 (NY)
Chiefs, 48-0 (KC)
1964 — Jets, 27-14 (NY)
Chiefs, 24-7 (KC)
1965 — Chiefs, 14-10 (NY)
Jets, 13-10 (KC)
1966 — Chiefs, 32-24 (NY)
1967 — Chiefs, 42-18 (KC)
Chiefs, 21-7 (NY)
1968 — Jets, 20-19 (KC)
1969 — Chiefs, 34-16 (NY)
***Chiefs, 13-6 (NY)
1971 — Jets, 13-10 (NY)
1974 — Chiefs, 24-16 (KC)
1975 — Jets, 30-24 (KC)
1982 — Chiefs, 37-13 (KC)
1984 — Jets, 17-16 (KC)
Jets, 28-7 (NY)
1986 — ****Jets, 35-15 (NY)
1987 — Jets, 16-9 (KC)
1988 — Tie, 17-17 (NY)
Chiefs, 38-34 (KC)
1992 — Chiefs, 23-7 (NY)
(RS Pts. — Chiefs 647, Jets 528)
(PS Pts. — Jets 41, Chiefs 28)
**Franchise in Dallas prior to 1963 and known as Texans*
***Jets known as Titans prior to 1963*
****Inter-Divisional Playoff*
*****AFC First Round Playoff*

KANSAS CITY vs. PHILADELPHIA
RS: Series tied, 1-1
1972 — Eagles, 21-20 (KC)
1992 — Chiefs, 24-17 (KC)
(RS Pts. — Chiefs 44, Eagles 38)

KANSAS CITY vs. *PHOENIX
RS: Chiefs lead series, 3-1-1
1970 — Tie, 6-6 (KC)
1974 — Chiefs, 17-13 (StL)
1980 — Chiefs, 21-13 (StL)
1983 — Chiefs, 38-14 (KC)
1986 — Cardinals, 23-14 (StL)
(RS Pts. — Chiefs 96, Cardinals 69)
**Franchise in St. Louis prior to 1988*

KANSAS CITY vs. PITTSBURGH
RS: Steelers lead series, 13-5
1970 — Chiefs, 31-14 (P)
1971 — Chiefs, 38-16 (KC)
1972 — Steelers, 16-7 (P)
1974 — Steelers, 34-24 (KC)
1975 — Steelers, 28-3 (P)
1976 — Steelers, 45-0 (KC)
1978 — Steelers, 27-24 (P)
1979 — Steelers, 30-3 (KC)
1980 — Steelers, 21-16 (P)
1981 — Chiefs, 37-33 (P)
1982 — Steelers, 35-14 (P)
1984 — Chiefs, 37-27 (P)
1985 — Steelers, 36-28 (KC)
1986 — Chiefs, 24-19 (P)
1987 — Steelers, 17-16 (KC)
1988 — Steelers, 16-10 (P)
1989 — Steelers, 23-17 (P)
1992 — Steelers, 27-3 (KC)
(RS Pts. — Steelers 464, Chiefs 332)

***KANSAS CITY vs. **SAN DIEGO**
RS: Chiefs lead series, 33-31-1
PS: Chargers lead series, 1-0
1960 — Chargers, 21-20 (LA)
Texans, 17-0 (D)
1961 — Chargers, 26-10 (D)
Chargers, 24-14 (SD)
1962 — Chargers, 32-28 (SD)
Texans, 26-17 (D)
1963 — Chargers, 24-10 (SD)
Chargers, 38-17 (KC)
1964 — Chargers, 28-14 (KC)
Chiefs, 49-6 (SD)
1965 — Tie, 10-10 (SD)
Chiefs, 31-7 (KC)
1966 — Chiefs, 24-14 (KC)
Chiefs, 27-17 (SD)
1967 — Chargers, 45-31 (SD)
Chargers, 17-16 (KC)
1968 — Chiefs, 27-20 (KC)
Chiefs, 40-3 (SD)
1969 — Chiefs, 27-9 (SD)
Chiefs, 27-3 (KC)
1970 — Chiefs, 26-14 (KC)
Chargers, 31-13 (SD)
1971 — Chargers, 21-14 (SD)
Chiefs, 31-10 (KC)
1972 — Chiefs, 26-14 (SD)
Chargers, 27-17 (KC)
1973 — Chiefs, 19-0 (SD)
Chiefs, 33-6 (KC)
1974 — Chiefs, 24-14 (SD)
Chargers, 14-7 (KC)
1975 — Chiefs, 12-10 (SD)
Chargers, 28-20 (KC)
1976 — Chargers, 30-16 (KC)
Chiefs, 23-20 (SD)
1977 — Chargers, 23-7 (KC)
Chiefs, 21-16 (SD)
1978 — Chargers, 29-23 (SD) OT
Chiefs, 23-0 (KC)
1979 — Chargers, 20-14 (KC)
Chargers, 28-7 (SD)
1980 — Chargers, 24-7 (KC)
Chargers, 20-7 (SD)
1981 — Chargers, 42-31 (KC)
Chargers, 22-20 (SD)
1982 — Chiefs, 19-12 (KC)
1983 — Chargers, 17-14 (KC)
Chargers, 41-38 (SD)
1984 — Chiefs, 31-13 (KC)
Chiefs, 42-21 (SD)
1985 — Chargers, 31-20 (SD)
Chiefs, 38-34 (KC)
1986 — Chiefs, 42-41 (KC)
Chiefs, 24-23 (SD)
1987 — Chiefs, 20-13 (KC)
Chargers, 42-21 (SD)
1988 — Chargers, 24-23 (KC)
Chargers, 24-13 (SD)
1989 — Chargers, 21-6 (SD)

Chargers, 20-13 (KC)
1990 — Chiefs, 27-10 (KC)
Chiefs, 24-21 (SD)
1991 — Chiefs, 14-13 (SD)
Chiefs, 20-17 (KC) OT
1992 — Chiefs, 24-10 (SD)
Chiefs, 16-14 (KC)
***Chargers, 17-0 (SD)
(RS Pts. — Chiefs 1,395, Chargers 1,286)
(PS Pts. — Chargers 17, Chiefs 0)
Franchise in Dallas prior to 1963 and known as Texans
***Franchise in Los Angeles prior to 1961*
****AFC First Round Playoff*

KANSAS CITY vs. SAN FRANCISCO
RS: 49ers lead series, 4-1
1971 — Chiefs, 26-17 (SF)
1975 — 49ers, 20-3 (KC)
1982 — 49ers, 26-13 (KC)
1985 — 49ers, 31-3 (SF)
1991 — 49ers, 28-14 (SF)
(RS Pts. — 49ers 122, Chiefs 59)

KANSAS CITY vs. SEATTLE
RS: Chiefs lead series, 17-12
1977 — Seahawks, 34-31 (KC)
1978 — Seahawks, 13-10 (KC)
Seahawks, 23-19 (S)
1979 — Chiefs, 24-6 (S)
Chiefs, 37-21 (KC)
1980 — Seahawks, 17-16 (KC)
Chiefs, 31-30 (S)
1981 — Chiefs, 20-14 (S)
Chiefs, 40-13 (KC)
1983 — Chiefs, 17-13 (KC)
Seahawks, 51-48 (S) OT
1984 — Seahawks, 45-0 (S)
Chiefs, 34-7 (KC)
1985 — Chiefs, 28-7 (KC)
Seahawks, 24-6 (S)
1986 — Seahawks, 23-17 (S)
Chiefs, 27-7 (KC)
1987 — Seahawks, 43-14 (S)
Chiefs, 41-20 (KC)
1988 — Seahawks, 31-10 (S)
Chiefs, 27-24 (KC)
1989 — Chiefs, 20-16 (S)
Chiefs, 20-10 (KC)
1990 — Seahawks, 19-7 (S)
Seahawks, 17-16 (KC)
1991 — Chiefs, 20-13 (KC)
Chiefs, 19-6 (S)
1992 — Chiefs, 26-7 (KC)
Chiefs, 24-14 (S)
(RS Pts. — Chiefs 649, Seahawks 568)

KANSAS CITY vs. TAMPA BAY
RS: Chiefs lead series, 4-2
1976 — Chiefs, 28-19 (TB)
1978 — Buccaneers, 30-13 (KC)
1979 — Buccaneers, 3-0 (TB)
1981 — Chiefs, 19-10 (KC)
1984 — Chiefs, 24-20 (KC)
1986 — Chiefs, 27-20 (KC)
(RS Pts. — Chiefs 111, Buccaneers 102)

KANSAS CITY vs. WASHINGTON
RS: Chiefs lead series, 3-1
1971 — Chiefs, 27-20 (KC)
1976 — Chiefs, 33-30 (W)
1983 — Redskins, 27-12 (W)
1992 — Chiefs, 35-16 (KC)
(RS Pts. — Chiefs 107, Redskins 93)

L.A. RAIDERS vs. ATLANTA
RS: Raiders lead series, 4-3;
See Atlanta vs. L.A. Raiders

L.A. RAIDERS vs. BUFFALO
RS: Series tied, 14-14
PS: Bills lead series, 1-0;
See Buffalo vs. L.A. Raiders

L.A. RAIDERS vs. CHICAGO
RS: Raiders lead series, 4-3;
See Chicago vs. L.A. Raiders

L.A. RAIDERS vs. CINCINNATI
RS: Raiders lead series, 14-6
PS: Raiders lead series, 2-0;
See Cincinnati vs. L.A. Raiders

L.A. RAIDERS vs. CLEVELAND
RS: Raiders lead series, 8-3
PS: Raiders lead series, 2-0;
See Cleveland vs. L.A. Raiders

L.A. RAIDERS vs. DALLAS
RS: Raiders lead series, 3-2;
See Dallas vs. L.A. Raiders

L.A. RAIDERS vs. DENVER
RS: Raiders lead series, 44-19-2
PS: Broncos lead series, 1-0;
See Denver vs. L.A. Raiders

L.A. RAIDERS vs. DETROIT
RS: Raiders lead series, 5-2;
See Detroit vs. L.A. Raiders

L.A. RAIDERS vs. GREEN BAY
RS: Raiders lead series, 5-1
PS: Packers lead series, 1-0;
See Green Bay vs. L.A. Raiders

L.A. RAIDERS vs. HOUSTON
RS: Raiders lead series, 19-13
PS: Raiders lead series, 3-0;
See Houston vs. L.A. Raiders

L.A. RAIDERS vs. INDIANAPOLIS
RS: Raiders lead series, 4-2
PS: Series tied, 1-1;
See Indianapolis vs. L.A. Raiders

L.A. RAIDERS vs. KANSAS CITY
RS: Raiders lead series, 35-28-2
PS: Chiefs lead series, 2-1;
See Kansas City vs. L.A. Raiders

***L.A. RAIDERS vs. L.A. RAMS**
RS: Raiders lead series, 5-2
1972 — Raiders, 45-17 (O)
1977 — Rams, 20-14 (LA)
1979 — Raiders, 24-17 (LA)
1982 — Raiders, 37-31 (LA Raiders)
1985 — Raiders, 16-6 (LA Rams)
1988 — Rams, 22-17 (LA Raiders)
1991 — Raiders, 20-17 (LA Raiders)
(RS Pts. — Raiders 173, Rams 130)
**Franchise in Oakland prior to 1982*

***L.A. RAIDERS vs. MIAMI**
RS: Raiders lead series, 14-4-1
PS: Raiders lead series, 2-1
1966 — Raiders, 23-14 (M)
Raiders, 21-10 (O)
1967 — Raiders, 31-17 (O)
1968 — Raiders, 47-21 (M)
1969 — Raiders, 20-17 (O)
Tie, 20-20 (M)
1970 — Dolphins, 20-13 (M)
**Raiders, 21-14 (O)
1973 — Raiders, 12-7 (O)
***Dolphins, 27-10 (M)
1974 — **Raiders, 28-26 (O)
1975 — Raiders, 31-21 (M)
1978 — Dolphins, 23-6 (M)
1979 — Raiders, 13-3 (O)
1980 — Raiders, 16-10 (O)
1981 — Raiders, 33-17 (M)
1983 — Raiders, 27-14 (LA)
1984 — Raiders, 45-34 (M)
1986 — Raiders, 30-28 (M)
1988 — Dolphins, 24-14 (LA)
1990 — Raiders, 13-10 (M)
1992 — Dolphins, 20-7 (M)
(RS Pts. — Raiders 422, Dolphins 330)
(PS Pts. — Dolphins 67, Raiders 59)
**Franchise in Oakland prior to 1982*
***AFC Divisional Playoff*
****AFC Championship*

***L.A. RAIDERS vs. MINNESOTA**
RS: Raiders lead series, 5-2
PS: Raiders lead series, 1-0
1973 — Vikings, 24-16 (M)
1976 — **Raiders, 32-14 (Pasadena)
1977 — Raiders, 35-13 (O)
1978 — Raiders, 27-20 (O)
1981 — Raiders, 36-10 (M)
1984 — Raiders, 23-20 (LA)
1987 — Vikings, 31-20 (M)
1990 — Raiders, 28-24 (M)
(RS Pts. — Raiders 185, Vikings 142)
(PS Pts. — Raiders 32, Vikings 14)
**Franchise in Oakland prior to 1982*
***Super Bowl XI*

***L.A. RAIDERS vs. **NEW ENGLAND**
RS: Series tied, 12-12-1
PS: Series tied, 1-1
1960 — Raiders, 27-14 (O)
Patriots, 34-28 (B)
1961 — Patriots, 20-17 (B)
Patriots, 35-21 (O)
1962 — Patriots, 26-16 (B)
Raiders, 20-0 (O)
1963 — Patriots, 20-14 (O)
Patriots, 20-14 (B)
1964 — Patriots, 17-14 (O)
Tie, 43-43 (B)
1965 — Raiders, 24-10 (B)
Raiders, 30-21 (O)
1966 — Patriots, 24-21 (B)
1967 — Raiders, 35-7 (O)
Raiders, 48-14 (B)
1968 — Raiders, 41-10 (O)
1969 — Raiders, 38-23 (B)
1971 — Patriots, 20-6 (NE)
1974 — Raiders, 41-26 (O)
1976 — Patriots, 48-17 (NE)
***Raiders, 24-21 (O)
1978 — Patriots, 21-14 (O)
1981 — Raiders, 27-17 (O)
1985 — Raiders, 35-20 (NE)
***Patriots, 27-20 (LA)
1987 — Patriots, 26-23 (NE)
1989 — Raiders, 24-21 (LA)
(RS Pts. — Raiders 638, Patriots 537)
(PS Pts. — Patriots 48, Raiders 44)
**Franchise in Oakland prior to 1982*
***Franchise in Boston prior to 1971*
****AFC Divisional Playoff*

***L.A. RAIDERS vs. NEW ORLEANS**
RS: Raiders lead series, 3-2-1
1971 — Tie, 21-21 (NO)
1975 — Raiders, 48-10 (O)
1979 — Raiders, 42-35 (NO)
1985 — Raiders, 23-13 (LA)
1988 — Saints, 20-6 (NO)
1991 — Saints, 27-0 (NO)
(RS Pts. — Raiders 140, Saints 126)
**Franchise in Oakland prior to 1982*

***L.A. RAIDERS vs. N.Y. GIANTS**
RS: Raiders lead series, 4-2
1973 — Raiders, 42-0 (O)
1980 — Raiders, 33-17 (NY)
1983 — Raiders, 27-12 (LA)
1986 — Giants, 14-9 (LA)
1989 — Giants, 34-17 (NY)
1992 — Raiders, 13-10 (LA)
(RS Pts. — Raiders 141, Giants 87)
**Franchise in Oakland prior to 1982*

***L.A. RAIDERS vs. **N.Y. JETS**
RS: Raiders lead series, 13-9-2
PS: Jets lead series, 2-0
1960 — Raiders, 28-27 (NY)
Titans, 31-28 (O)
1961 — Titans, 14-6 (O)
Titans, 23-12 (NY)
1962 — Titans, 28-17 (O)
Titans, 31-21 (NY)
1963 — Jets, 10-7 (NY)
Raiders, 49-26 (O)
1964 — Jets, 35-13 (NY)
Raiders, 35-26 (O)
1965 — Tie, 24-24 (NY)
Raiders, 24-14 (O)
1966 — Raiders, 24-21 (NY)
Tie, 28-28 (O)
1967 — Jets, 27-14 (NY)
Raiders, 38-29 (O)
1968 — Raiders, 43-32 (O)
***Jets, 27-23 (NY)
1969 — Raiders, 27-14 (NY)
1970 — Raiders, 14-13 (NY)
1972 — Raiders, 24-16 (O)
1977 — Raiders, 28-27 (NY)
1979 — Jets, 28-19 (NY)
1982 — ****Jets, 17-14 (LA)
1985 — Raiders, 31-0 (LA)
1989 — Raiders, 14-7 (NY)
(RS Pts. — Raiders 568, Jets 531)
(PS Pts. — Jets 44, Raiders 37)
**Franchise in Oakland prior to 1982*
***Jets known as Titans prior to 1963*
****AFL Championship*
*****AFC Second Round Playoff*

***L.A. RAIDERS vs. PHILADELPHIA**
RS: Eagles lead series, 4-2
PS: Raiders lead series, 1-0
1971 — Raiders, 34-10 (O)
1976 — Raiders, 26-7 (P)
1980 — Eagles, 10-7 (P)
**Raiders, 27-10 (NO)
1986 — Eagles, 33-27 (LA) OT
1989 — Eagles, 10-7 (P)
1992 — Eagles, 31-10 (P)
(RS Pts. — Raiders 111, Eagles 101)
(PS Pts. — Raiders 27, Eagles 10)
**Franchise in Oakland prior to 1982*
***Super Bowl XV*

***L.A. RAIDERS vs. **PHOENIX**
RS: Raiders lead series, 2-1
1973 — Raiders, 17-10 (StL)
1983 — Cardinals, 34-24 (LA)
1989 — Raiders, 16-14 (LA)
(RS Pts. — Cardinals 58, Raiders 57)
**Franchise in Oakland prior to 1982*
***Franchise in St. Louis prior to 1988*

***L.A. RAIDERS vs. PITTSBURGH**
RS: Raiders lead series, 7-3
PS: Series tied, 3-3
1970 — Raiders, 31-14 (O)
1972 — Steelers, 34-28 (P)
**Steelers, 13-7 (P)
1973 — Steelers, 17-9 (O)
**Raiders, 33-14 (O)
1974 — Raiders, 17-0 (P)
***Steelers, 24-13 (O)
1975 — ***Steelers, 16-10 (P)
1976 — Raiders, 31-28 (O)
***Raiders, 24-7 (O)
1977 — Raiders, 16-7 (P)
1980 — Raiders, 45-34 (P)
1981 — Raiders, 30-27 (O)
1983 — **Raiders, 38-10 (LA)
1984 — Steelers, 13-7 (LA)
1990 — Raiders, 20-3 (LA)
(RS Pts. — Raiders 234, Steelers 177)
(PS Pts. — Raiders 125, Steelers 84)
**Franchise in Oakland prior to 1982*
***AFC Divisional Playoff*
****AFC Championship*

***L.A. RAIDERS vs. **SAN DIEGO**
RS: Raiders lead series, 40-24-2
PS: Raiders lead series, 1-0
1960 — Chargers, 52-28 (LA)
Chargers, 41-17 (O)
1961 — Chargers, 44-0 (SD)
Chargers, 41-10 (O)
1962 — Chargers, 42-33 (O)
Chargers, 31-21 (SD)
1963 — Raiders, 34-33 (SD)
Raiders, 41-27 (O)
1964 — Chargers, 31-17 (O)
Raiders, 21-20 (SD)
1965 — Chargers, 17-6 (O)
Chargers, 24-14 (SD)
1966 — Chargers, 29-20 (O)
Raiders, 41-19 (SD)
1967 — Raiders, 51-10 (O)
Raiders, 41-21 (SD)
1968 — Chargers, 23-14 (O)
Raiders, 34-27 (SD)
1969 — Raiders, 24-12 (SD)
Raiders, 21-16 (O)
1970 — Tie, 27-27 (SD)
Raiders, 20-17 (O)
1971 — Raiders, 34-0 (SD)
Raiders, 34-33 (O)
1972 — Tie, 17-17 (O)
Raiders, 21-19 (SD)
1973 — Raiders, 27-17 (SD)
Raiders, 31-3 (O)
1974 — Raiders, 14-10 (SD)
Raiders, 17-10 (O)
1975 — Raiders, 6-0 (SD)
Raiders, 25-0 (O)
1976 — Raiders, 27-17 (SD)
Raiders, 24-0 (O)
1977 — Raiders, 24-0 (O)
Chargers, 12-7 (SD)
1978 — Raiders, 21-20 (SD)
Chargers, 27-23 (O)
1979 — Chargers, 30-10 (SD)
Raiders, 45-22 (O)
1980 — Chargers, 30-24 (SD) OT
Raiders, 38-24 (O)
***Raiders, 34-27 (SD)
1981 — Chargers, 55-21 (O)
Chargers, 23-10 (SD)
1982 — Raiders, 28-24 (LA)
Raiders, 41-34 (SD)
1983 — Raiders, 42-10 (SD)
Raiders, 30-14 (LA)
1984 — Raiders, 33-30 (LA)
Raiders, 44-37 (SD)
1985 — Raiders, 34-21 (LA)
Chargers, 40-34 (SD) OT
1986 — Raiders, 17-13 (LA)
Raiders, 37-31 (SD) OT
1987 — Chargers, 23-17 (LA)
Chargers, 16-14 (SD)
1988 — Raiders, 24-13 (LA)
Raiders, 13-3 (SD)
1989 — Raiders, 40-14 (LA)
Chargers, 14-12 (SD)
1990 — Raiders, 24-9 (SD)
Raiders, 17-12 (LA)
1991 — Chargers, 21-13 (LA)
Raiders, 9-7 (SD)
1992 — Chargers, 27-3 (SD)
Chargers, 36-14 (LA)
(RS Pts. — Raiders 1,575, Chargers, 1,422)
(PS Pts. — Raiders 34, Chargers 27)
**Franchise in Oakland prior to 1982*
***Franchise in Los Angeles prior to 1961*
****AFC Championship*

***L.A. RAIDERS vs. SAN FRANCISCO**
RS: Raiders lead series, 5-2
1970 — 49ers, 38-7 (O)
1974 — Raiders, 35-24 (SF)
1979 — Raiders, 23-10 (O)
1982 — Raiders, 23-17 (SF)
1985 — 49ers, 34-10 (LA)
1988 — Raiders, 9-3 (SF)
1991 — Raiders, 12-6 (LA)
(RS Pts. — 49ers 132, Raiders 119)
**Franchise in Oakland prior to 1982*

***L.A. RAIDERS vs. SEATTLE**
RS: Raiders lead series, 16-14
PS: Series tied, 1-1
1977 — Raiders, 44-7 (O)
1978 — Seahawks, 27-7 (S)
Seahawks, 17-16 (O)
1979 — Seahawks, 27-10 (S)
Seahawks, 29-24 (O)
1980 — Raiders, 33-14 (O)
Raiders, 19-17 (S)
1981 — Raiders, 20-10 (O)
Raiders, 32-31 (S)
1982 — Raiders, 28-23 (LA)
1983 — Seahawks, 38-36 (S)
Seahawks, 34-21 (LA)
**Raiders, 30-14 (LA)
1984 — Raiders, 28-14 (LA)

Seahawks, 17-14 (S)
***Seahawks, 13-7 (S)
1985 — Seahawks, 33-3 (S)
Raiders, 13-3 (LA)
1986 — Raiders, 14-10 (LA)
Seahawks, 37-0 (S)
1987 — Seahawks, 35-13 (LA)
Raiders, 37-14 (S)
1988 — Seahawks, 35-27 (S)
Seahawks, 43-37 (LA)
1989 — Seahawks, 24-20 (LA)
Seahawks, 23-17 (S)
1990 — Raiders, 17-13 (S)
Raiders, 24-17 (LA)
1991 — Raiders, 23-20 (S) OT
Raiders, 31-7 (LA)
1992 — Raiders, 19-0 (S)
Raiders, 20-3 (LA)
(RS Pts. — Raiders 647, Seahawks 622)
(PS Pts. — Raiders 37, Seahawks 27)
Franchise in Oakland prior to 1982
***AFC Championship*
****AFC First Round Playoff*

***L.A. RAIDERS vs. TAMPA BAY**
RS: Raiders lead series, 2-0
1976 — Raiders, 49-16 (O)
1981 — Raiders, 18-16 (O)
(RS Pts. — Raiders 67, Buccaneers 32)
Franchise in Oakland prior to 1982

***L.A. RAIDERS vs. WASHINGTON**
RS: Raiders lead series, 5-2
PS: Raiders lead series, 1-0
1970 — Raiders, 34-20 (O)
1975 — Raiders, 26-23 (W) OT
1980 — Raiders, 24-21 (O)
1983 — Redskins, 37-35 (W)
**Raiders, 38-9 (Tampa)
1986 — Redskins, 10-6 (W)
1989 — Raiders, 37-24 (LA)
1992 — Raiders, 21-20 (W)
(RS Pts. — Raiders 183, Redskins 155)
(PS Pts. — Raiders 38, Redskins 9)
Franchise in Oakland prior to 1982
***Super Bowl XVIII*

L.A. RAMS vs. ATLANTA
RS: Rams lead series, 36-14-2;
See Atlanta vs. L.A. Rams

L.A. RAMS vs. BUFFALO
RS: Series tied, 3-3;
See Buffalo vs. L.A. Rams

L.A. RAMS vs. CHICAGO
RS: Bears lead series, 44-28-3
PS: Series tied, 1-1;
See Chicago vs. L.A. Rams

L.A. RAMS vs. CINCINNATI
RS: Bengals lead series, 4-2;
See Cincinnati vs. L.A. Rams

L.A. RAMS vs. CLEVELAND
RS: Series tied, 7-7
PS: Browns lead series, 2-1;
See Cleveland vs. L.A. Rams

L.A. RAMS vs. DALLAS
RS: Rams lead series, 9-8
PS: Series tied, 4-4;
See Dallas vs. L.A. Rams

L.A. RAMS vs. DENVER
RS: Series tied, 3-3;
See Denver vs. L.A. Rams

L.A. RAMS vs. DETROIT
RS: Rams lead series, 39-34-1
PS: Lions lead series, 1-0;
See Detroit vs. L.A. Rams

L.A. RAMS vs. GREEN BAY
RS: Rams lead series, 42-35-2
PS: Packers lead series, 1-0;
See Green Bay vs. L.A. Rams

L.A. RAMS vs. HOUSTON
RS: Rams lead series, 4-2;
See Houston vs. L.A. Rams

L.A. RAMS vs. INDIANAPOLIS
RS: Colts lead series, 20-16-2;
See Indianapolis vs. L.A. Rams

L.A. RAMS vs. KANSAS CITY
RS: Rams lead series, 3-1;
See Kansas City vs. L.A. Rams

L.A. RAMS VS. L.A. RAIDERS
RS: Raiders lead series, 5-2;
See L.A. Raiders vs. L.A. Rams

L.A. RAMS vs. MIAMI
RS: Dolphins lead series, 5-1
1971 — Dolphins, 20-14 (LA)
1976 — Rams, 31-28 (M)
1980 — Dolphins, 35-14 (LA)
1983 — Dolphins, 30-14 (M)
1986 — Dolphins 37-31 (LA) OT
1992 — Dolphins, 26-10 (M)
(RS Pts. — Dolphins 176, Rams 114)

L.A. RAMS vs. MINNESOTA
RS: Vikings lead series, 15-11-2
PS: Vikings lead series, 5-1
1961 — Rams, 31-17 (LA)
Vikings, 42-21 (M)
1962 — Vikings, 38-14 (LA)
Tie, 24-24 (M)
1963 — Rams, 27-24 (LA)
Vikings, 21-13 (M)
1964 — Rams, 22-13 (LA)
Vikings, 34-13 (M)
1965 — Vikings, 38-35 (LA)
Vikings, 24-13 (M)
1966 — Vikings, 35-7 (M)
Rams, 21-6 (LA)
1967 — Rams, 39-3 (LA)
1968 — Rams, 31-3 (M)
1969 — Vikings, 20-13 (LA)
*Vikings, 23-20 (M)
1970 — Vikings, 13-3 (M)
1972 — Vikings, 45-41 (LA)
1973 — Vikings, 10-9 (M)
1974 — Rams, 20-17 (LA)
**Vikings, 14-10 (M)
1976 — Tie, 10-10 (M) OT
**Vikings, 24-13 (M)
1977 — Rams, 35-3 (LA)
***Vikings, 14-7 (LA)
1978 — Rams, 34-17 (M)
***Rams, 34-10 (LA)
1979 — Rams, 27-21 (LA) OT
1985 — Rams, 13-10 (LA)
1987 — Vikings, 21-16 (LA)
1988 — ****Vikings, 28-17 (M)
1989 — Vikings, 23-21 (M) OT
1991 — Vikings, 20-14 (M)
1992 — Vikings, 31-17 (LA)
(RS Pts. — Rams 584, Vikings 583)
(PS Pts. — Vikings 113, Rams 101)
**Conference Championship*
***NFC Championship*
****NFC Divisional Playoff*
*****NFC First Round Playoff*

L.A. RAMS vs. NEW ENGLAND
RS: Series tied, 3-3
1974 — Patriots, 20-14 (NE)
1980 — Rams, 17-14 (NE)
1983 — Patriots, 21-7 (LA)
1986 — Patriots, 30-28 (LA)
1989 — Rams, 24-20 (NE)
1992 — Rams, 14-0 (LA)
(RS Pts. — Patriots 105, Rams 104)

L.A. RAMS vs. NEW ORLEANS
RS: Rams lead series, 26-20
1967 — Rams, 27-13 (NO)
1969 — Rams, 36-17 (LA)
1970 — Rams, 30-17 (NO)
Rams, 34-16 (LA)
1971 — Saints, 24-20 (NO)
Rams, 45-28 (LA)
1972 — Rams, 34-14 (LA)
Saints, 19-16 (NO)
1973 — Rams, 29-7 (LA)
Rams, 24-13 (NO)
1974 — Rams, 24-0 (LA)
Saints, 20-7 (NO)
1975 — Rams, 38-14 (LA)
Rams, 14-7 (NO)
1976 — Rams, 16-10 (NO)
Rams, 33-14 (LA)
1977 — Rams, 14-7 (LA)
Saints, 27-26 (NO)
1978 — Rams, 26-20 (NO)
Saints, 10-3 (LA)
1979 — Rams, 35-17 (NO)
Saints, 29-14 (LA)
1980 — Rams, 45-31 (LA)
Rams, 27-7 (NO)
1981 — Saints, 23-17 (NO)
Saints, 21-13 (LA)
1983 — Rams, 30-27 (LA)
Rams, 26-24 (NO)
1984 — Rams, 28-10 (NO)
Rams, 34-21 (LA)
1985 — Rams, 28-10 (LA)
Saints, 29-3 (NO)
1986 — Saints, 6-0 (NO)
Rams, 26-13 (LA)
1987 — Saints, 37-10 (NO)
Saints, 31-14 (LA)
1988 — Rams, 12-10 (NO)
Saints, 14-10 (LA)
1989 — Saints, 40-21 (LA)
Rams, 20-17 (NO) OT
1990 — Saints, 24-20 (LA)
Saints, 20-17 (NO)
1991 — Saints, 24-7 (NO)
Saints, 24-17 (LA)
1992 — Saints, 13-10 (NO)
Saints, 37-14 (LA)
(RS Pts. — Rams 994, Saints 856)

***L.A. RAMS vs. N.Y. GIANTS**
RS: Rams lead series, 20-8
PS: Series tied, 1-1
1938 — Giants, 28-0 (NY)
1940 — Rams, 13-0 (NY)
1941 — Giants, 49-14 (NY)
1945 — Rams, 21-17 (NY)
1946 — Rams, 31-21 (NY)
1947 — Rams, 34-10 (LA)
1948 — Rams, 52-37 (NY)
1953 — Rams, 21-7 (LA)
1954 — Rams, 17-16 (NY)
1959 — Giants, 23-21 (LA)
1961 — Giants, 24-14 (NY)
1966 — Rams, 55-14 (LA)
1968 — Rams, 24-21 (LA)
1970 — Rams, 31-3 (NY)
1973 — Rams, 40-6 (LA)
1976 — Rams, 24-10 (LA)
1978 — Rams, 20-17 (NY)
1979 — Giants, 20-14 (LA)
1980 — Rams, 28-7 (NY)
1981 — Giants, 10-7 (NY)
1983 — Rams, 16-6 (NY)
1984 — Rams, 33-12 (LA)
**Giants, 16-13 (LA)
1985 — Giants, 24-19 (NY)
1988 — Rams, 45-31 (NY)
1989 — Rams, 31-10 (LA)
***Rams, 19-13 (NY) OT
1990 — Giants, 31-7 (LA)
1991 — Rams, 19-13 (NY)
1992 — Rams, 38-17 (LA)
(RS Pts. — Rams 689, Giants 484)
(PS Pts. — Rams 32, Giants 29)
Franchise in Cleveland prior to 1946
***NFC First Round Playoff*
****NFC Divisional Playoff*

L.A. RAMS vs. N.Y. JETS
RS: Rams lead series, 5-2
1970 — Jets, 31-20 (LA)
1974 — Rams, 20-13 (NY)
1980 — Rams, 38-13 (LA)
1983 — Jets, 27-24 (NY) OT
1986 — Rams, 17-3 (NY)
1989 — Rams, 38-14 (LA)
1992 — Rams, 18-10 (LA)
(RS Pts. — Rams 175, Jets 111)

***L.A. RAMS vs. PHILADELPHIA**
RS: Rams lead series, 15-11-1
PS: Series tied, 1-1
1937 — Rams, 21-3 (P)
1939 — Rams, 35-13 (Colorado Springs)
1940 — Rams, 21-13 (C)
1942 — Rams, 24-14 (Akron)
1944 — Eagles, 26-13 (P)
1945 — Eagles, 28-14 (P)
1946 — Eagles, 25-14 (LA)
1947 — Eagles, 14-7 (P)
1948 — Tie, 28-28 (LA)
1949 — Eagles, 38-14 (P)
**Eagles, 14-0 (LA)
1950 — Eagles, 56-20 (P)
1955 — Rams, 23-21 (P)
1956 — Rams, 27-7 (LA)
1957 — Rams, 17-13 (LA)
1959 — Eagles, 23-20 (P)
1964 — Rams, 20-10 (LA)
1967 — Rams, 33-17 (LA)
1969 — Rams, 23-17 (P)
1972 — Rams, 34-3 (P)
1975 — Rams, 42-3 (P)
1977 — Rams, 20-0 (LA)
1978 — Rams, 16-14 (P)
1983 — Eagles, 13-9 (P)
1985 — Rams, 17-6 (P)
1986 — Eagles, 34-20 (P)
1988 — Eagles, 30-24 (P)
1989 — ***Rams, 21-7 (P)
1990 — Eagles, 27-21 (LA)
(RS Pts. — Rams 577, Eagles 496)
(PS Pts. — Rams 21, Eagles 21)
Franchise in Cleveland prior to 1946
***NFL Championship*
****NFC First Round Playoff*

***L.A. RAMS vs. **PHOENIX**
RS: Rams lead series, 22-18-2
PS: Rams lead series, 1-0
1937 — Cardinals, 6-0 (Clev)
Cardinals, 13-7 (Chi)
1938 — Cardinals, 7-6 (Clev)
Cardinals, 31-17 (Chi)
1939 — Rams, 24-0 (Chi)
Rams, 14-0 (Clev)
1940 — Rams, 26-14 (Clev)
Cardinals, 17-7 (Chi)
1941 — Rams, 10-6 (Clev)
Cardinals, 7-0 (Chi)
1942 — Cardinals, 7-0 (Chi)
Rams, 7-3 (Clev)
1945 — Rams, 21-0 (Clev)
Rams, 35-21 (Chi)
1946 — Cardinals, 34-10 (Chi)
Rams, 17-14 (LA)
1947 — Rams, 27-7 (LA)
Cardinals, 17-10 (Chi)
1948 — Cardinals, 27-22 (LA)
Cardinals, 27-24 (Chi)
1949 — Tie, 28-28 (Chi)
Cardinals, 31-27 (LA)
1951 — Rams, 45-21 (LA)
1953 — Tie, 24-24 (Chi)
1954 — Rams, 28-17 (LA)
1958 — Rams, 20-14 (Chi)
1960 — Cardinals, 43-21 (LA)
1965 — Rams, 27-3 (StL)
1968 — Rams, 24-13 (StL)
1970 — Rams, 34-13 (LA)
1972 — Cardinals, 24-14 (StL)
1975 — ***Rams, 35-23 (LA)
1976 — Cardinals, 30-28 (LA)
1979 — Rams, 21-0 (LA)
1980 — Rams, 21-13 (StL)
1984 — Rams, 16-13 (StL)
1985 — Rams, 46-14 (LA)
1986 — Rams, 16-10 (StL)
1987 — Rams, 27-24 (StL)
1988 — Cardinals, 41-27 (LA)
1989 — Rams, 37-14 (LA)
1991 — Cardinals, 24-14 (LA)
1992 — Cardinals, 20-14 (LA)
(RS Pts. — Rams 843, Cardinals 692)
(PS Pts. — Rams 35, Cardinals 23)
Franchise in Cleveland prior to 1946
***Franchise in St. Louis prior to 1988 and in Chicago prior to 1960*
****NFC Divisional Playoff*

***L.A. RAMS vs. **PITTSBURGH**
RS: Rams lead series, 13-4-2
PS: Steelers lead series, 1-0
1938 — Rams, 13-7 (New Orleans)
1939 — Tie, 14-14 (C)
1941 — Rams, 17-14 (Akron)
1947 — Rams, 48-7 (P)
1948 — Rams, 31-14 (LA)
1949 — Tie, 7-7 (P)
1952 — Rams, 28-14 (LA)
1955 — Rams, 27-26 (LA)
1956 — Steelers, 30-13 (P)
1961 — Rams, 24-14 (LA)
1964 — Rams, 26-14 (P)
1968 — Rams, 45-10 (LA)
1971 — Rams, 23-14 (P)
1975 — Rams, 10-3 (LA)
1978 — Rams, 10-7 (LA)
1979 — ***Steelers, 31-19 (Pasadena)
1981 — Steelers, 24-0 (P)
1984 — Steelers, 24-14 (P)
1987 — Rams, 31-21 (LA)
1990 — Steelers, 41-10 (P)
(RS Pts. — Rams 391, Steelers 305)
(PS Pts. — Steelers 31, Rams 19)
Franchise in Cleveland prior to 1946
***Steelers known as Pirates prior to 1941*
****Super Bowl XIV*

L.A. RAMS vs. SAN DIEGO
RS: Rams lead series, 3-2
1970 — Rams, 37-10 (LA)
1975 — Rams, 13-10 (SD) OT
1979 — Chargers, 40-16 (LA)
1988 — Chargers, 38-24 (LA)
1991 — Rams, 30-24 (LA)
(RS Pts. — Chargers 122, Rams 120)

L.A. RAMS vs. SAN FRANCISCO
RS: Rams lead series, 48-36-2
PS: 49ers lead series, 1-0
1950 — Rams, 35-14 (SF)
Rams, 28-21 (LA)
1951 — 49ers, 44-17 (SF)
Rams, 23-16 (LA)
1952 — Rams, 35-9 (LA)
Rams, 34-21 (SF)
1953 — 49ers, 31-30 (SF)
49ers, 31-27 (LA)
1954 — Tie, 24-24 (LA)
Rams, 42-34 (SF)
1955 — Rams, 23-14 (SF)
Rams, 27-14 (LA)
1956 — 49ers, 33-30 (SF)
Rams, 30-6 (LA)
1957 — 49ers, 23-20 (SF)
Rams, 37-24 (LA)
1958 — Rams, 33-3 (SF)
Rams, 56-7 (LA)
1959 — 49ers, 34-0 (SF)
49ers, 24-16 (LA)
1960 — 49ers, 13-9 (SF)
49ers, 23-7 (LA)
1961 — 49ers, 35-0 (SF)
Rams, 17-7 (LA)
1962 — Rams, 28-14 (SF)
49ers, 24-17 (LA)
1963 — Rams, 28-21 (LA)
Rams, 21-17 (SF)
1964 — Rams, 42-14 (LA)
49ers, 28-7 (SF)
1965 — 49ers, 45-21 (LA)
49ers, 30-27 (SF)
1966 — Rams, 34-3 (LA)
49ers, 21-13 (SF)
1967 — 49ers, 27-24 (LA)
Rams, 17-7 (SF)
1968 — Rams, 24-10 (LA)

Tie, 20-20 (SF)
1969 — Rams, 27-21 (SF)
Rams, 41-30 (LA)
1970 — 49ers, 20-6 (LA)
Rams, 30-13 (SF)
1971 — Rams, 20-13 (SF)
Rams, 17-6 (LA)
1972 — Rams, 31-7 (LA)
Rams, 26-16 (SF)
1973 — Rams, 40-20 (SF)
Rams, 31-13 (LA)
1974 — Rams, 37-14 (LA)
Rams, 15-13 (SF)
1975 — Rams, 23-14 (SF)
49ers, 24-23 (LA)
1976 — 49ers, 16-0 (LA)
Rams, 23-3 (SF)
1977 — Rams, 34-14 (LA)
Rams, 23-10 (SF)
1978 — Rams, 27-10 (LA)
Rams, 31-28 (SF)
1979 — Rams, 27-24 (LA)
Rams, 26-20 (SF)
1980 — Rams, 48-26 (LA)
Rams, 31-17 (SF)
1981 — 49ers, 20-17 (SF)
49ers, 33-31 (LA)
1982 — 49ers, 30-24 (LA)
Rams, 21-20 (SF)
1983 — Rams, 10-7 (SF)
49ers, 45-35 (LA)
1984 — 49ers, 33-0 (LA)
49ers, 19-16 (SF)
1985 — 49ers, 28-14 (LA)
Rams, 27-20 (SF)
1986 — Rams, 16-13 (LA)
49ers, 24-14 (SF)
1987 — 49ers, 31-10 (LA)
49ers, 48-0 (SF)
1988 — 49ers, 24-21 (LA)
Rams, 38-16 (SF)
1989 — Rams, 13-12 (SF)
49ers, 30-27 (LA)
*49ers, 30-3 (SF)
1990 — Rams, 28-17 (SF)
49ers, 26-10 (LA)
1991 — 49ers, 27-10 (SF)
49ers, 33-10 (LA)
1992 — 49ers, 27-24 (SF)
49ers, 27-10 (LA)
(RS Pts. — Rams 1,986, 49ers 1,788)
(PS Pts. — 49ers 30, Rams 3)
NFC Championship

L.A. RAMS vs. SEATTLE
RS: Rams lead series, 4-1
1976 — Rams, 45-6 (LA)
1979 — Rams, 24-0 (S)
1985 — Rams, 35-24 (S)
1988 — Rams, 31-10 (LA)
1991 — Seahawks, 23-9 (S)
(RS Pts. — Rams 144, Seahawks 63)

L.A. RAMS vs. TAMPA BAY
RS: Rams lead series, 8-2
PS: Rams lead series, 1-0
1977 — Rams, 31-0 (LA)
1978 — Rams, 26-23 (LA)
1979 — Buccaneers, 21-6 (TB)
*Rams, 9-0 (TB)
1980 — Buccaneers, 10-9 (TB)
1984 — Rams, 34-33 (TB)
1985 — Rams, 31-27 (TB)
1986 — Rams, 26-20 (LA) OT
1987 — Rams, 35-3 (LA)
1990 — Rams, 35-14 (TB)
1992 — Rams, 31-27 (TB)
(RS Pts. — Rams 264, Buccaneers 178)
(PS Pts. — Rams 9, Buccaneers 0)
NFC Championship

***L.A. RAMS vs. WASHINGTON**
RS: Redskins lead series, 14-4-1
PS: Series tied, 2-2
1937 — Redskins, 16-7 (C)
1938 — Redskins, 37-13 (W)
1941 — Redskins, 17-13 (W)
1942 — Redskins, 33-14 (W)
1944 — Redskins, 14-10 (W)
1945 — **Rams, 15-14 (C)
1948 — Rams, 41-13 (W)
1949 — Rams, 53-27 (LA)
1951 — Redskins, 31-21 (W)
1962 — Redskins, 20-14 (W)
1963 — Redskins, 37-14 (LA)
1967 — Tie, 28-28 (LA)
1969 — Rams, 24-13 (W)
1971 — Redskins, 38-24 (LA)
1974 — Redskins, 23-17 (LA)
***Rams, 19-10 (LA)
1977 — Redskins, 17-14 (W)
1981 — Redskins, 30-7 (LA)
1983 — Redskins, 42-20 (LA)
***Redskins, 51-7 (W)
1986 — ****Redskins, 19-7 (W)
1987 — Rams, 30-26 (W)
1991 — Redskins, 27-6 (LA)
(RS Pts. — Redskins 489, Rams 370)
(PS Pts. — Redskins 94, Rams 48)
*Franchise in Cleveland prior to 1946
**NFL Championship
***NFC Divisional Playoff
****NFC First Round Playoff*

MIAMI vs. ATLANTA
RS: Dolphins lead series, 5-1;
See Atlanta vs. Miami

MIAMI vs. BUFFALO
RS: Dolphins lead series, 36-17-1
PS: Bills lead series, 2-0;
See Buffalo vs. Miami

MIAMI vs. CHICAGO
RS: Dolphins lead series, 5-1;
See Chicago vs. Miami

MIAMI vs. CINCINNATI
RS: Dolphins lead series, 9-3
PS: Dolphins lead series, 1-0;
See Cincinnati vs. Miami

MIAMI vs. CLEVELAND
RS: Dolphins lead series, 5-4
PS: Dolphins lead series, 2-0;
See Cleveland vs. Miami

MIAMI vs. DALLAS
RS: Dolphins lead series, 5-1
PS: Cowboys lead series, 1-0;
See Dallas vs. Miami

MIAMI vs. DENVER
RS: Dolphins lead series, 5-2-1;
See Denver vs. Miami

MIAMI vs. DETROIT
RS: Series tied, 2-2;
See Detroit vs. Miami

MIAMI vs. GREEN BAY
RS: Dolphins lead series, 7-0;
See Green Bay vs. Miami

MIAMI vs. HOUSTON
RS: Series tied, 11-11
PS: Oilers lead series, 1-0;
See Houston vs. Miami

MIAMI vs. INDIANAPOLIS
RS: Dolphins lead series, 32-14
PS: Dolphins lead series, 1-0;
See Indianapolis vs. Miami

MIAMI vs. KANSAS CITY
RS: Chiefs lead series, 10-6
PS: Dolphins lead series, 2-0;
See Kansas City vs. Miami

MIAMI vs. L.A. RAIDERS
RS: Raiders lead series, 14-4-1
PS: Raiders lead series, 2-1;
See L.A. Raiders vs. Miami

MIAMI vs. L.A. RAMS
RS: Dolphins lead series, 5-1;
See L.A. Rams vs. Miami

MIAMI vs. MINNESOTA
RS: Dolphins lead series, 4-1
PS: Dolphins lead series, 1-0
1972 — Dolphins, 16-14 (Minn)
1973 — *Dolphins, 24-7 (Houston)
1976 — Vikings, 29-7 (Mia)
1979 — Dolphins, 27-12 (Minn)
1982 — Dolphins, 22-14 (Mia)
1988 — Dolphins, 24-7 (Mia)
(RS Pts. — Dolphins 96, Vikings 76)
(PS Pts. — Dolphins 24, Vikings 7)
Super Bowl VIII

MIAMI vs. *NEW ENGLAND
RS: Dolphins lead series, 32-20
PS: Series tied, 1-1
1966 — Patriots, 20-14 (M)
1967 — Patriots, 41-10 (B)
Dolphins, 41-32 (M)
1968 — Dolphins, 34-10 (B)
Dolphins, 38-7 (M)
1969 — Dolphins, 17-16 (B)
Patriots, 38-23 (Tampa)
1970 — Patriots, 27-14 (B)
Dolphins, 37-20 (M)
1971 — Dolphins, 41-3 (M)
Patriots, 34-13 (NE)
1972 — Dolphins, 52-0 (M)
Dolphins, 37-21 (NE)
1973 — Dolphins, 44-23 (M)
Dolphins, 30-14 (NE)
1974 — Patriots, 34-24 (NE)
Dolphins, 34-27 (M)
1975 — Dolphins, 22-14 (NE)
Dolphins, 20-7 (M)
1976 — Patriots, 30-14 (NE)
Dolphins, 10-3 (M)
1977 — Dolphins, 17-5 (M)
Patriots, 14-10 (NE)
1978 — Patriots, 33-24 (NE)
Dolphins, 23-3 (M)
1979 — Patriots, 28-13 (NE)
Dolphins, 39-24 (M)
1980 — Patriots, 34-0 (NE)
Dolphins, 16-13 (M) OT
1981 — Dolphins, 30-27 (NE) OT
Dolphins, 24-14 (M)
1982 — Patriots, 3-0 (NE)
**Dolphins, 28-13 (M)
1983 — Dolphins, 34-24 (M)
Patriots, 17-6 (NE)
1984 — Dolphins, 28-7 (M)
Dolphins, 44-24 (NE)
1985 — Patriots, 17-13 (NE)
Dolphins, 30-27 (M)
***Patriots, 31-14 (M)
1986 — Patriots, 34-7 (NE)
Patriots, 34-27 (M)
1987 — Patriots, 28-21 (NE)
Patriots, 24-10 (M)
1988 — Patriots, 21-10 (NE)
Patriots, 6-3 (M)
1989 — Dolphins, 24-10 (NE)
Dolphins, 31-10 (M)
1990 — Dolphins, 27-24 (NE)
Dolphins, 17-10 (M)
1991 — Dolphins, 20-10 (NE)
Dolphins, 30-20 (M)
1992 — Dolphins, 38-17 (M)
Dolphins, 16-13 (NE) OT
(RS Pts. — Dolphins 1,201, Patriots 996)
(PS Pts. — Patriots 44, Dolphins 42)
*Franchise in Boston prior to 1971
**AFC First Round Playoff
***AFC Championship*

MIAMI vs. NEW ORLEANS
RS: Dolphins lead series, 4-2
1970 — Dolphins, 21-10 (M)
1974 — Dolphins, 21-0 (NO)
1980 — Dolphins, 21-16 (M)
1983 — Saints, 17-7 (NO)
1986 — Dolphins, 31-27 (NO)
1992 — Saints, 24-13 (NO)
(RS Pts. — Dolphins 114, Saints 94)

MIAMI vs. N.Y. GIANTS
RS: Series tied, 1-1
1972 — Dolphins, 23-13 (NY)
1990 — Giants, 20-3 (NY)
(RS Pts. — Giants 33, Dolphins 26)

MIAMI vs. N.Y. JETS
RS: Dolphins lead series, 27-26-1
PS: Dolphins lead series, 1-0
1966 — Jets, 19-14 (M)
Jets, 30-13 (NY)
1967 — Jets, 29-7 (NY)
Jets, 33-14 (M)
1968 — Jets, 35-17 (NY)
Jets, 31-7 (M)
1969 — Jets, 34-31 (NY)
Jets, 27-9 (M)
1970 — Dolphins, 20-6 (NY)
Dolphins, 16-10 (M)
1971 — Jets, 14-10 (M)
Dolphins, 30-14 (NY)
1972 — Dolphins, 27-17 (NY)
Dolphins, 28-24 (M)
1973 — Dolphins, 31-3 (M)
Dolphins, 24-14 (NY)
1974 — Dolphins, 21-17 (M)
Jets, 17-14 (NY)
1975 — Dolphins, 43-0 (NY)
Dolphins, 27-7 (M)
1976 — Dolphins, 16-0 (M)
Dolphins, 27-7 (NY)
1977 — Dolphins, 21-17 (M)
Dolphins, 14-10 (NY)
1978 — Jets, 33-20 (NY)
Jets, 24-13 (M)
1979 — Jets, 33-27 (NY)
Jets, 27-24 (M)
1980 — Jets, 17-14 (NY)
Jets, 24-17 (M)
1981 — Tie, 28-28 (M) OT
Jets, 16-15 (NY)
1982 — Dolphins, 45-28 (NY)
Dolphins, 20-19 (M)
*Dolphins, 14-0 (M)
1983 — Dolphins, 32-14 (NY)
Dolphins, 34-14 (M)
1984 — Dolphins, 31-17 (NY)
Dolphins, 28-17 (M)
1985 — Jets, 23-7 (NY)
Dolphins, 21-17 (M)
1986 — Jets, 51-45 (NY) OT
Dolphins, 45-3 (M)
1987 — Jets, 37-31 (NY) OT
Dolphins, 37-28 (M)
1988 — Jets, 44-30 (M)
Jets, 38-34 (NY)
1989 — Jets, 40-33 (M)
Dolphins, 31-23 (NY)
1990 — Dolphins, 20-16 (M)
Dolphins, 17-3 (NY)
1991 — Jets, 41-23 (NY)
Jets, 23-20 (M) OT
1992 — Jets, 26-14 (NY)
Dolphins, 19-17 (M)
(RS Pts. — Dolphins 1,256, Jets 1,156)
(PS Pts. — Dolphins 14, Jets 0)
AFC Championship

MIAMI vs. PHILADELPHIA
RS: Dolphins lead series, 5-2
1970 — Eagles, 24-17 (P)
1975 — Dolphins, 24-16 (M)
1978 — Eagles, 17-3 (P)
1981 — Dolphins, 13-10 (M)
1984 — Dolphins, 24-23 (M)
1987 — Dolphins, 28-10 (P)
1990 — Dolphins, 23-20 (M) OT
(RS Pts. — Dolphins 132, Eagles 120)

MIAMI vs. *PHOENIX
RS: Dolphins lead series, 6-0
1972 — Dolphins, 31-10 (M)
1977 — Dolphins, 55-14 (StL)
1978 — Dolphins, 24-10 (M)
1981 — Dolphins, 20-7 (StL)
1984 — Dolphins, 36-28 (StL)
1990 — Dolphins, 23-3 (M)
(RS Pts. — Dolphins 189, Cardinals 72)
Franchise in St. Louis prior to 1988

MIAMI vs. PITTSBURGH
RS: Dolphins lead series, 7-4
PS: Dolphins lead series, 2-1
1971 — Dolphins, 24-21 (M)
1972 — *Dolphins, 21-17 (P)
1973 — Dolphins, 30-26 (M)
1976 — Steelers, 14-3 (P)
1979 — **Steelers, 34-14 (P)
1980 — Steelers, 23-10 (P)
1981 — Dolphins, 30-10 (M)
1984 — Dolphins, 31-7 (P)
*Dolphins, 45-28 (M)
1985 — Dolphins, 24-20 (M)
1987 — Dolphins, 35-24 (M)
1988 — Steelers, 40-24 (P)
1989 — Steelers, 34-14 (M)
1990 — Dolphins, 28-6 (P)
(RS Pts. — Dolphins 253, Steelers 225)
(PS Pts. — Dolphins 80, Steelers 79)
*AFC Championship
**AFC Divisional Playoff*

MIAMI vs. SAN DIEGO
RS: Chargers lead series, 9-5
PS: Dolphins lead series, 2-1
1966 — Chargers, 44-10 (SD)
1967 — Chargers, 24-0 (SD)
Dolphins, 41-24 (M)
1968 — Chargers, 34-28 (SD)
1969 — Chargers, 21-14 (M)
1972 — Dolphins, 24-10 (M)
1974 — Dolphins, 28-21 (SD)
1977 — Chargers, 14-13 (M)
1978 — Dolphins, 28-21 (SD)
1980 — Chargers, 27-24 (M) OT
1981 — *Chargers, 41-38 (M) OT
1982 — **Dolphins, 34-13 (M)
1984 — Chargers, 34-28 (SD) OT
1986 — Chargers, 50-28 (SD)
1988 — Dolphins, 31-28 (M)
1991 — Chargers, 38-30 (SD)
1992 — *Dolphins, 31-0 (M)
(RS Pts. — Chargers 390, Dolphins 327)
(PS Pts. — Dolphins 103, Chargers 54)
*AFC Divisional Playoff
**AFC Second Round Playoff*

MIAMI vs. SAN FRANCISCO
RS: Dolphins lead series, 4-2
PS: 49ers lead series, 1-0
1973 — Dolphins, 21-13 (M)
1977 — Dolphins, 19-15 (SF)
1980 — Dolphins, 17-13 (M)
1983 — Dolphins, 20-17 (SF)
1984 — *49ers, 38-16 (Stanford)
1986 — 49ers, 31-16 (M)
1992 — 49ers, 27-3 (SF)
(RS Pts. — 49ers 116, Dolphins 96)
(PS Pts. — 49ers 38, Dolphins 16)
Super Bowl XIX

MIAMI vs. SEATTLE
RS: Dolphins lead series, 4-1
PS: Series tied, 1-1
1977 — Dolphins, 31-13 (M)
1979 — Dolphins, 19-10 (M)
1983 — *Seahawks, 27-20 (M)
1984 — *Dolphins, 31-10 (M)
1987 — Seahawks, 24-20 (S)
1990 — Dolphins, 24-17 (M)
1992 — Dolphins, 19-17 (S)
(RS Pts. — Dolphins 113, Seahawks 81)
(PS Pts. — Dolphins 51, Seahawks 37)
AFC Divisional Playoff

MIAMI vs. TAMPA BAY
RS: Dolphins lead series, 4-1
1976 — Dolphins, 23-20 (TB)
1982 — Buccaneers, 23-17 (TB)
1985 — Dolphins, 41-38 (M)
1988 — Dolphins, 17-14 (TB)
1991 — Dolphins, 33-14 (M)
(RS Pts. — Dolphins 131, Buccaneers 109)

MIAMI vs. WASHINGTON
RS: Dolphins lead series, 4-2
PS: Series tied, 1-1

1972 — *Dolphins, 14-7 (Los Angeles)
1974 — Redskins, 20-17 (W)
1978 — Dolphins, 16-0 (W)
1981 — Dolphins, 13-10 (M)
1982 — **Redskins, 27-17 (Pasadena)
1984 — Dolphins, 35-17 (W)
1987 — Dolphins, 23-21 (M)
1990 — Redskins, 42-20 (W)
(RS Pts. — Dolphins 124, Redskins 110)
(PS Pts. — Redskins 34, Dolphins 31)
Super Bowl VII
**Super Bowl XVII*

MINNESOTA vs. ATLANTA
RS: Vikings lead series, 11-6
PS: Vikings lead series, 1-0;
See Atlanta vs. Minnesota
MINNESOTA vs. BUFFALO
RS: Vikings lead series, 4-2;
See Buffalo vs. Minnesota
MINNESOTA vs. CHICAGO
RS: Vikings lead series, 32-29-2;
See Chicago vs. Minnesota
MINNESOTA vs. CINCINNATI
RS: Vikings lead series, 4-3;
See Cincinnati vs. Minnesota
MINNESOTA vs. CLEVELAND
RS: Vikings lead series, 7-3
PS: Vikings lead series, 1-0;
See Cleveland vs. Minnesota
MINNESOTA vs. DALLAS
RS: Cowboys lead series, 7-6
PS: Cowboys lead series, 3-1;
See Dallas vs. Minnesota
MINNESOTA vs. DENVER
RS: Vikings lead series, 4-3;
See Denver vs. Minnesota
MINNESOTA vs. DETROIT
RS: Vikings lead series, 39-22-2;
See Detroit vs. Minnesota
MINNESOTA vs. GREEN BAY
RS: Series tied, 31-31-1;
See Green Bay vs. Minnesota
MINNESOTA vs. HOUSTON
RS: Series tied, 3-3;
See Houston vs. Minnesota
MINNESOTA vs. INDIANAPOLIS
RS: Colts lead series, 11-6-1
PS: Colts lead series, 1-0;
See Indianapolis vs. Minnesota
MINNESOTA vs. KANSAS CITY
RS: Series tied, 2-2
PS: Chiefs lead series, 1-0;
See Kansas City vs. Minnesota
MINNESOTA vs. L.A. RAIDERS
RS: Raiders lead series, 5-2
PS: Raiders lead series, 1-0;
See L.A. Raiders vs. Minnesota
MINNESOTA vs. L.A. RAMS
RS: Vikings lead series, 15-11-2
PS: Vikings lead series, 5-1;
See L.A. Rams vs. Minnesota
MINNESOTA vs. MIAMI
RS: Dolphins lead series, 4-1
PS: Dolphins lead series, 1-0;
See Miami vs. Minnesota
MINNESOTA vs. *NEW ENGLAND
RS: Patriots lead series, 3-2
1970 — Vikings, 35-14 (B)
1974 — Patriots, 17-14 (M)
1979 — Patriots, 27-23 (NE)
1988 — Vikings, 36-6 (M)
1991 — Patriots, 26-23 (NE) OT
(RS Pts. — Vikings 131, Patriots 90)
Franchise in Boston prior to 1971
MINNESOTA vs. NEW ORLEANS
RS: Vikings lead series, 11-5
PS: Vikings lead series, 1-0
1968 — Saints, 20-17 (NO)
1970 — Vikings, 26-0 (M)
1971 — Vikings, 23-10 (NO)
1972 — Vikings, 37-6 (M)
1974 — Vikings, 29-9 (M)
1975 — Vikings, 20-7 (NO)
1976 — Vikings, 40-9 (NO)
1978 — Saints, 31-24 (NO)
1980 — Vikings, 23-20 (NO)
1981 — Vikings, 20-10 (M)
1983 — Saints, 17-16 (NO)
1985 — Saints, 30-23 (M)
1986 — Vikings, 33-17 (M)
1987 — *Vikings, 44-10 (NO)
1988 — Vikings, 45-3 (M)
1990 — Vikings, 32-3 (M)
1991 — Saints, 26-0 (NO)
(RS Pts. — Vikings 408, Saints 218)
(PS Pts. — Vikings 44, Saints 10)
NFC First Round Playoff
MINNESOTA vs. N.Y. GIANTS
RS: Vikings lead series, 6-4
1964 — Vikings, 30-21 (NY)
1965 — Vikings, 40-14 (M)
1967 — Vikings, 27-24 (M)
1969 — Giants, 24-23 (NY)
1971 — Vikings, 17-10 (NY)
1973 — Vikings, 31-7 (New Haven)
1976 — Vikings, 24-7 (M)
1986 — Giants, 22-20 (M)
1989 — Giants, 24-14 (NY)
1990 — Giants, 23-15 (NY)
(RS Pts. — Vikings 241, Giants 176)
MINNESOTA vs. N.Y. JETS
RS: Jets lead series, 3-1
1970 — Jets, 20-10 (NY)
1975 — Vikings, 29-21 (M)
1979 — Jets, 14-7 (NY)
1982 — Jets 42-14 (M)
(RS Pts. — Jets 97, Vikings 60)
MINNESOTA vs. PHILADELPHIA
RS: Vikings lead series, 10-6
PS: Eagles lead series, 1-0
1962 — Vikings, 31-21 (M)
1963 — Vikings, 34-13 (P)
1968 — Vikings, 24-17 (P)
1971 — Vikings, 13-0 (P)
1973 — Vikings, 28-21 (M)
1976 — Vikings, 31-12 (P)
1978 — Vikings, 28-27 (M)
1980 — Eagles, 42-7 (M)
*Eagles, 31-16 (P)
1981 — Vikings, 35-23 (M)
1984 — Eagles, 19-17 (P)
1985 — Vikings, 28-23 (P)
Eagles, 37-35 (M)
1988 — Vikings, 23-21 (M)
1989 — Eagles, 10-9 (P)
1990 — Eagles, 32-24 (P)
1992 — Eagles, 28-17 (P)
(RS Pts. — Vikings 384, Eagles 346)
(PS Pts. — Eagles 31, Vikings 16)
NFC Divisional Playoff
MINNESOTA vs. *PHOENIX
RS: Cardinals lead series, 7-4
PS: Vikings lead series, 1-0
1963 — Cardinals, 56-14 (M)
1967 — Cardinals, 34-24 (M)
1969 — Vikings, 27-10 (StL)
1972 — Cardinals, 19-17 (M)
1974 — Vikings, 28-24 (StL)
**Vikings, 30-14 (M)
1977 — Cardinals, 27-7 (M)
1979 — Cardinals, 37-7 (StL)
1981 — Cardinals, 30-17 (StL)
1983 — Cardinals, 41-31 (StL)
1991 — Vikings, 34-7 (M)
Vikings, 28-0 (P)
(RS Pts. — Cardinals 285, Vikings 234)
(PS Pts. — Vikings 30, Cardinals 14)
Franchise in St. Louis prior to 1988
**NFC Divisional Playoff*
MINNESOTA vs. PITTSBURGH
RS: Vikings lead series, 7-4
PS: Steelers lead series, 1-0
1962 — Steelers, 39-31 (P)
1964 — Vikings, 30-10 (M)
1967 — Vikings, 41-27 (P)
1969 — Vikings, 52-14 (M)
1972 — Steelers, 23-10 (P)
1974 — *Steelers, 16-6 (New Orleans)
1976 — Vikings, 17-6 (M)
1980 — Steelers, 23-17 (M)
1983 — Vikings, 17-14 (P)
1986 — Vikings, 31-7 (M)
1989 — Steelers, 27-14 (P)
1992 — Vikings, 6-3 (P)
(RS Pts. — Vikings 266, Steelers 193)
(PS Pts. — Steelers 16, Vikings 6)
Super Bowl IX
MINNESOTA vs. SAN DIEGO
RS: Series tied, 3-3
1971 — Chargers, 30-14 (SD)
1975 — Vikings, 28-13 (M)
1978 — Chargers, 13-7 (M)
1981 — Vikings, 33-31 (SD)
1984 — Chargers, 42-13 (M)
1985 — Vikings, 21-17 (M)
(RS Pts. — Chargers 146, Vikings 116)
MINNESOTA vs. SAN FRANCISCO
RS: Vikings lead series, 15-14-1
PS: 49ers lead series, 3-1
1961 — 49ers, 38-24 (M)
49ers, 38-28 (SF)
1962 — 49ers, 21-7 (SF)
49ers, 35-12 (M)
1963 — Vikings, 24-20 (SF)
Vikings, 45-14 (M)
1964 — Vikings, 27-22 (SF)
Vikings, 24-7 (M)
1965 — Vikings, 42-41 (SF)
49ers, 45-24 (M)
1966 — Tie, 20-20 (SF)
Vikings, 28-3 (SF)
1967 — 49ers, 27-21 (M)
1968 — Vikings, 30-20 (SF)
1969 — Vikings, 10-7 (M)
1970 — *49ers, 17-14 (M)
1971 — 49ers, 13-9 (M)
1972 — 49ers, 20-17 (SF)
1973 — Vikings, 17-13 (SF)
1975 — Vikings, 27-17 (M)
1976 — 49ers, 20-16 (SF)
1977 — Vikings, 28-27 (M)
1979 — Vikings, 28-22 (M)
1983 — 49ers, 48-17 (M)
1984 — 49ers, 51-7 (SF)
1985 — Vikings, 28-21 (M)
1986 — Vikings, 27-24 (SF) OT
1987 — *Vikings, 36-24 (SF)
1988 — 49ers, 24-21 (SF)
*49ers, 34-9 (SF)
1989 — *49ers, 41-13 (SF)
1990 — 49ers, 20-17 (M)
1991 — Vikings, 17-14 (M)
1992 — 49ers, 20-17 (M)
(RS Pts. — 49ers 712, Vikings 659)
(PS Pts. — 49ers 116, Vikings 72)
NFC Divisional Playoff
MINNESOTA vs. SEATTLE
RS: Seahawks lead series, 3-2
1976 — Vikings, 27-21 (M)
1978 — Seahawks, 29-28 (S)
1984 — Seahawks, 20-12 (M)
1987 — Seahawks, 28-17 (S)
1990 — Vikings, 24-21 (S)
(RS Pts. — Seahawks 119, Vikings 108)
MINNESOTA vs. TAMPA BAY
RS: Vikings lead series, 22-8
1977 — Vikings, 9-3 (TB)
1978 — Buccaneers, 16-10 (M)
Vikings, 24-7 (TB)
1979 — Buccaneers, 12-10 (M)
Vikings, 23-22 (TB)
1980 — Vikings, 38-30 (M)
Vikings, 21-10 (TB)
1981 — Buccaneers, 21-13 (TB)
Vikings, 25-10 (M)
1982 — Vikings, 17-10 (M)
1983 — Vikings, 19-16 (TB) OT
Buccaneers, 17-12 (M)
1984 — Buccaneers, 35-31 (TB)
Vikings, 27-24 (M)
1985 — Vikings, 31-16 (TB)
Vikings, 26-7 (M)
1986 — Vikings, 23-10 (TB)
Vikings, 45-13 (M)
1987 — Buccaneers, 20-10 (TB)
Vikings, 23-17 (M)
1988 — Vikings, 14-13 (M)
Vikings, 49-20 (TB)
1989 — Vikings, 17-3 (M)
Vikings, 24-10 (TB)
1990 — Buccaneers, 23-20 (M) OT
Buccaneers, 26-13 (TB)
1991 — Vikings, 28-13 (M)
Vikings, 26-24 (TB)
1992 — Vikings, 26-20 (M)
Vikings, 35-7 (TB)
(RS Pts. — Vikings 689, Buccaneers 475)
MINNESOTA vs. WASHINGTON
RS: Redskins lead series, 6-3
PS: Redskins lead series, 3-2
1968 — Vikings, 27-14 (M)
1970 — Vikings, 19-10 (W)
1972 — Redskins, 24-21 (M)
1973 — *Vikings, 27-20 (M)
1975 — Redskins, 31-30 (W)
1976 — *Vikings, 35-20 (M)
1980 — Vikings, 39-14 (W)
1982 — **Redskins, 21-7 (W)
1984 — Redskins, 31-17 (M)
1986 — Redskins, 44-38 (W) OT
1987 — Redskins, 27-24 (M) OT
***Redskins, 17-10 (W)
1992 — Redskins, 15-13 (M)
****Redskins, 24-7 (M)
(RS Pts. — Vikings 228, Redskins 210)
(PS Pts. — Redskins 102, Vikings 86)
NFC Divisional Playoff
**NFC Second Round Playoff*
***NFC Championship*
****NFC First Round Playoff*

NEW ENGLAND vs. ATLANTA
RS: Falcons lead series, 4-3;
See Atlanta vs. New England
NEW ENGLAND vs. BUFFALO
RS: Patriots lead series, 33-31-1
PS: Patriots lead series, 1-0;
See Buffalo vs. New England
NEW ENGLAND vs. CHICAGO
RS: Patriots lead series, 3-2
PS: Bears lead series, 1-0;
See Chicago vs. New England
NEW ENGLAND vs. CINCINNATI
RS: Series tied, 7-7;
See Cincinnati vs. New England
NEW ENGLAND vs. CLEVELAND
RS: Browns lead series, 9-2;
See Cleveland vs. New England
NEW ENGLAND vs. DALLAS
RS: Cowboys lead series, 6-0;
See Dallas vs. New England
NEW ENGLAND vs. DENVER
RS: Broncos lead series, 16-12
PS: Broncos lead series, 1-0;
See Denver vs. New England
NEW ENGLAND vs. DETROIT
RS: Series tied, 2-2;
See Detroit vs. New England
NEW ENGLAND vs. GREEN BAY
RS: Series tied, 2-2;
See Green Bay vs. New England
NEW ENGLAND vs. HOUSTON
RS: Patriots lead series, 17-13-1
PS: Oilers lead series, 1-0;
See Houston vs. New England
NEW ENGLAND vs. INDIANAPOLIS
RS: Patriots lead series, 26-19;
See Indianapolis vs. New England
NEW ENGLAND vs. KANSAS CITY
RS: Chiefs lead series, 13-7-3;
See Kansas City vs. New England
NEW ENGLAND vs. L.A. RAIDERS
RS: Series tied, 12-12-1
PS: Series tied, 1-1;
See L.A. Raiders vs. New England
NEW ENGLAND vs. L.A. RAMS
RS: Series tied, 3-3;
See L.A. Rams vs. New England
NEW ENGLAND vs. MIAMI
RS: Dolphins lead series, 32-20
PS: Series tied, 1-1;
See Miami vs. New England
NEW ENGLAND vs. MINNESOTA
RS: Patriots lead series, 3-2;
See Minnesota vs. New England
NEW ENGLAND vs. NEW ORLEANS
RS: Patriots lead series, 5-2
1972 — Patriots, 17-10 (NO)
1976 — Patriots, 27-6 (NE)
1980 — Patriots, 38-27 (NO)
1983 — Patriots, 7-0 (NE)
1986 — Patriots, 21-20 (NO)
1989 — Saints, 28-24 (NE)
1992 — Saints, 31-14 (NE)
(RS Pts. — Patriots 148, Saints 122)
***NEW ENGLAND vs. N.Y. GIANTS**
RS: Giants lead series, 3-1
1970 — Giants, 16-0 (B)
1974 — Patriots, 28-20 (New Haven)
1987 — Giants, 17-10 (NY)
1990 — Giants, 13-10 (NE)
(RS Pts. — Giants 66, Patriots 48)
Franchise in Boston prior to 1971
***NEW ENGLAND vs. **N.Y. JETS**
RS: Jets lead series, 36-28-1
PS: Patriots lead series, 1-0
1960 — Patriots, 28-24 (NY)
Patriots, 38-21 (B)
1961 — Titans, 21-20 (B)
Titans, 37-30 (NY)
1962 — Patriots, 43-14 (NY)
Patriots, 24-17 (B)
1963 — Patriots, 38-14 (B)
Jets, 31-24 (NY)
1964 — Patriots, 26-10 (B)
Jets, 35-14 (NY)
1965 — Jets, 30-20 (B)
Patriots, 27-23 (NY)
1966 — Tie, 24-24 (B)
Jets, 38-28 (NY)
1967 — Jets, 30-23 (NY)
Jets, 29-24 (B)
1968 — Jets, 47-31 (Birmingham)
Jets, 48-14 (NY)
1969 — Jets, 23-14 (B)
Jets, 23-17 (NY)
1970 — Jets, 31-21 (B)
Jets, 17-3 (NY)
1971 — Patriots, 20-0 (NE)
Jets, 13-6 (NY)
1972 — Jets, 41-13 (NE)
Jets, 34-10 (NY)
1973 — Jets, 9-7 (NE)
Jets, 33-13 (NY)
1974 — Patriots, 24-0 (NY)
Jets, 21-16 (NE)
1975 — Jets, 36-7 (NY)
Jets, 30-28 (NE)
1976 — Patriots, 41-7 (NE)
Patriots, 38-24 (NY)
1977 — Jets, 30-27 (NY)
Patriots, 24-13 (NE)
1978 — Patriots, 55-21 (NE)
Patriots, 19-17 (NY)
1979 — Patriots, 56-3 (NE)
Jets, 27-26 (NY)
1980 — Patriots, 21-11 (NY)
Patriots, 34-21 (NE)
1981 — Jets, 28-24 (NY)
Jets, 17-6 (NE)
1982 — Jets, 31-7 (NE)

1983 — Patriots, 23-13 (NE)
Jets, 26-3 (NY)
1984 — Patriots, 28-21 (NY)
Patriots, 30-20 (NE)
1985 — Patriots, 20-13 (NE)
Jets, 16-13 (NY) OT
***Patriots, 26-14 (NY)
1986 — Patriots, 20-6 (NY)
Jets, 31-24 (NE)
1987 — Jets, 43-24 (NY)
Patriots, 42-20 (NE)
1988 — Patriots, 28-3 (NE)
Patriots, 14-13 (NY)
1989 — Patriots, 27-24 (NY)
Jets, 27-26 (NE)
1990 — Jets, 37-13 (NE)
Jets, 42-7 (NY)
1991 — Jets, 28-21 (NE)
Patriots, 6-3 (NY)
1992 — Jets, 30-21 (NY)
Patriots, 24-3 (NE)
(RS Pts. — Jets 1,473, Patriots 1,467)
(PS Pts. — Patriots 26, Jets 14)
Franchise in Boston prior to 1971
***Jets known as Titans prior to 1963*
****AFC First Round Playoff*
NEW ENGLAND vs. PHILADELPHIA
RS: Eagles lead series, 5-2
1973 — Eagles, 24-23 (P)
1977 — Patriots, 14-6 (NE)
1978 — Patriots, 24-14 (NE)
1981 — Eagles, 13-3 (P)
1984 — Eagles, 27-17 (P)
1987 — Eagles, 34-31 (NE) OT
1990 — Eagles, 48-20 (P)
(RS Pts. — Eagles 166, Patriots 132)
***NEW ENGLAND vs. **PHOENIX**
RS: Cardinals lead series, 6-1
1970 — Cardinals, 31-0 (StL)
1975 — Cardinals, 24-17 (StL)
1978 — Patriots, 16-6 (StL)
1981 — Cardinals, 27-20 (NE)
1984 — Cardinals, 33-10 (NE)
1990 — Cardinals, 34-14 (P)
1991 — Cardinals, 24-10 (P)
(RS Pts. — Cardinals 179, Patriots 87)
Franchise in Boston prior to 1971
***Franchise in St. Louis prior to 1988*
NEW ENGLAND vs. PITTSBURGH
RS: Steelers lead series, 8-3
1972 — Steelers, 33-3 (P)
1974 — Steelers, 21-17 (NE)
1976 — Patriots, 30-27 (P)
1979 — Steelers, 16-13 (NE) OT
1981 — Steelers, 27-21 (P) OT
1982 — Steelers, 37-14 (P)
1983 — Patriots, 28-23 (P)
1986 — Patriots, 34-0 (P)
1989 — Steelers, 28-10 (P)
1990 — Steelers, 24-3 (P)
1991 — Steelers, 20-6 (P)
(RS Pts. — Steelers 256, Patriots 179)
***NEW ENGLAND vs. **SAN DIEGO**
RS: Patriots lead series, 13-11-2
PS: Chargers lead series, 1-0
1960 — Patriots, 35-0 (LA)
Chargers, 45-16 (B)
1961 — Chargers, 38-27 (B)
Patriots, 41-0 (SD)
1962 — Patriots, 24-20 (B)
Patriots, 20-14 (SD)
1963 — Chargers, 17-13 (SD)
Chargers, 7-6 (B)
***Chargers, 51-10 (SD)
1964 — Patriots, 33-28 (SD)
Chargers, 26-17 (B)
1965 — Tie, 10-10 (B)
Patriots, 22-6 (SD)
1966 — Chargers, 24-0 (SD)
Patriots, 35-17 (B)
1967 — Chargers, 28-14 (SD)
Tie, 31-31 (SD)
1968 — Chargers, 27-17 (B)
1969 — Chargers, 13-10 (B)
Chargers, 28-18 (SD)
1970 — Chargers, 16-14 (B)
1973 — Patriots, 30-14 (NE)
1975 — Patriots, 33-19 (SD)
1977 — Patriots, 24-20 (SD)
1978 — Patriots, 28-23 (NE)
1979 — Patriots, 27-21 (NE)
1983 — Patriots, 37-21 (NE)
(RS Pts. — Patriots 582, Chargers 513)
(PS Pts. — Chargers 51, Patriots 10)
Franchise in Boston prior to 1971
***Franchise in Los Angeles prior to 1961*
****AFL Championship*
NEW ENGLAND vs. SAN FRANCISCO
RS: 49ers lead series, 6-1
1971 — 49ers, 27-10 (SF)
1975 — Patriots, 24-16 (NE)
1980 — 49ers, 21-17 (SF)
1983 — 49ers, 33-13 (NE)
1986 — 49ers, 29-24 (NE)
1989 — 49ers, 37-20 (SF)
1992 — 49ers, 24-12 (NE)
(RS Pts. — 49ers 187, Patriots 120)
NEW ENGLAND vs. SEATTLE
RS: Patriots lead series, 6-5
1977 — Patriots, 31-0 (NE)
1980 — Patriots, 37-31 (S)
1982 — Patriots, 16-0 (S)
1983 — Seahawks, 24-6 (S)
1984 — Patriots, 38-23 (NE)
1985 — Patriots, 20-13 (S)
1986 — Seahawks, 38-31 (NE)
1988 — Patriots, 13-7 (NE)
1989 — Seahawks, 24-3 (NE)
1990 — Seahawks, 33-20 (NE)
1992 — Seahawks, 10-6 (NE)
(RS Pts. — Patriots 221, Seahawks 203)
NEW ENGLAND vs. TAMPA BAY
RS: Patriots lead series, 3-0
1976 — Patriots, 31-14 (TB)
1985 — Patriots, 32-14 (TB)
1988 — Patriots, 10-7 (NE) OT
(RS Pts. — Patriots 73, Buccaneers 35)
NEW ENGLAND vs. WASHINGTON
RS: Redskins lead series, 4-1
1972 — Patriots, 24-23 (NE)
1978 — Redskins, 16-14 (NE)
1981 — Redskins, 24-22 (W)
1984 — Redskins, 26-10 (NE)
1990 — Redskins, 25-10 (NE)
(RS Pts. — Redskins 114, Patriots 80)

NEW ORLEANS vs. ATLANTA
RS: Falcons lead series, 26-21
PS: Falcons lead series, 1-0;
See Atlanta vs. New Orleans
NEW ORLEANS vs. BUFFALO
RS: Bills lead series, 3-2;
See Buffalo vs. New Orleans
NEW ORLEANS vs. CHICAGO
RS: Bears lead series, 8-6
PS: Bears lead series, 1-0;
See Chicago vs. New Orleans
NEW ORLEANS vs. CINCINNATI
RS: Saints lead series, 4-3;
See Cincinnati vs. New Orleans
NEW ORLEANS vs. CLEVELAND
RS: Browns lead series, 8-3;
See Cleveland vs. New Orleans
NEW ORLEANS vs. DALLAS
RS: Cowboys lead series, 13-3;
See Dallas vs. New Orleans
NEW ORLEANS vs. DENVER
RS: Broncos lead series, 4-1;
See Denver vs. New Orleans
NEW ORLEANS vs. DETROIT
RS: Series tied, 6-6-1;
See Detroit vs. New Orleans
NEW ORLEANS vs. GREEN BAY
RS: Packers lead series, 11-4;
See Green Bay vs. New Orleans
NEW ORLEANS vs. HOUSTON
RS: Series tied, 3-3-1;
See Houston vs. New Orleans
NEW ORLEANS vs. INDIANAPOLIS
RS: Colts lead series, 3-2;
See Indianapolis vs. New Orleans
NEW ORLEANS vs. KANSAS CITY
RS: Saints lead series, 3-2;
See Kansas City vs. New Orleans
NEW ORLEANS vs. L.A. RAIDERS
RS: Raiders lead series, 3-2-1;
See L.A. Raiders vs. New Orleans
NEW ORLEANS vs. L.A. RAMS
RS: Rams lead series, 26-20;
See L.A. Rams vs. New Orleans
NEW ORLEANS vs. MIAMI
RS: Dolphins lead series, 4-2;
See Miami vs. New Orleans
NEW ORLEANS vs. MINNESOTA
RS: Vikings lead series, 11-5
PS: Vikings lead series, 1-0;
See Minnesota vs. New Orleans
NEW ORLEANS vs. NEW ENGLAND
RS: Patriots lead series, 5-2;
See New England vs. New Orleans
NEW ORLEANS vs. N.Y. GIANTS
RS: Giants lead series, 8-6
1967 — Giants, 27-21 (NY)
1968 — Giants, 38-21 (NY)
1969 — Saints, 25-24 (NY)
1970 — Saints, 14-10 (NO)
1972 — Giants, 45-21 (NY)
1975 — Giants, 28-14 (NY)
1978 — Saints, 28-17 (NO)
1979 — Saints, 24-14 (NO)
1981 — Giants, 20-7 (NY)
1984 — Saints, 10-3 (NY)
1985 — Giants, 21-13 (NO)
1986 — Giants, 20-17 (NY)
1987 — Saints, 23-14 (NO)
1988 — Giants, 13-12 (NO)
(RS Pts. — Giants 294, Saints 250)
NEW ORLEANS vs. N.Y. JETS
RS: Jets lead series, 4-3
1972 — Jets, 18-17 (NY)
1977 — Jets, 16-13 (NO)
1980 — Saints, 21-20 (NY)
1983 — Jets, 31-28 (NO)
1986 — Jets, 28-23 (NY)
1989 — Saints, 29-14 (NO)
1992 — Saints, 20-0 (NY)
(RS Pts. — Saints 151, Jets 127)
NEW ORLEANS vs. PHILADELPHIA
RS: Eagles lead series, 10-8
PS: Eagles lead series, 1-0
1967 — Saints, 31-24 (NO)
Eagles, 48-21 (P)
1968 — Eagles, 29-17 (P)
1969 — Eagles, 13-10 (P)
Saints, 26-17 (NO)
1972 — Saints, 21-3 (NO)
1974 — Saints, 14-10 (NO)
1977 — Eagles, 28-7 (P)
1978 — Eagles, 24-17 (NO)
1979 — Eagles, 26-14 (NO)
1980 — Eagles, 34-21 (NO)
1981 — Eagles, 31-14 (NO)
1983 — Saints, 20-17 (P) OT
1985 — Saints, 23-21 (NO)
1987 — Eagles, 27-17 (P)
1989 — Saints, 30-20 (NO)
1991 — Saints, 13-6 (P)
1992 — Eagles, 15-13 (P)
*Eagles, 36-20 (NO)
(RS Pts. — Eagles 393, Saints 329)
(PS Pts. — Eagles 36, Saints 20)
NFC First Round Playoff
NEW ORLEANS vs. *PHOENIX
RS: Cardinals lead series, 10-8
1967 — Cardinals, 31-20 (StL)
1968 — Cardinals, 21-20 (NO)
Cardinals, 31-17 (StL)
1969 — Saints, 51-42 (StL)
1970 — Cardinals, 24-17 (StL)
1974 — Saints, 14-0 (NO)
1977 — Cardinals, 49-31 (StL)
1980 — Cardinals, 40-7 (NO)
1981 — Cardinals, 30-3 (StL)
1982 — Cardinals, 21-7 (NO)
1983 — Saints, 28-17 (NO)
1984 — Saints, 34-24 (NO)
1985 — Cardinals, 28-16 (StL)
1986 — Saints, 16-7 (StL)
1987 — Cardinals, 24-19 (StL)
1990 — Saints, 28-7 (NO)
1991 — Saints, 27-3 (P)
1992 — Saints, 30-21 (P)
(RS Pts. — Cardinals 420, Saints 385)
Franchise in St. Louis prior to 1988
NEW ORLEANS vs. PITTSBURGH
RS: Series tied, 5-5
1967 — Steelers, 14-10 (NO)
1968 — Saints, 16-12 (P)
Saints, 24-14 (NO)
1969 — Saints, 27-24 (NO)
1974 — Steelers, 28-7 (NO)
1978 — Steelers, 20-14 (P)
1981 — Steelers, 20-6 (NO)
1984 — Saints, 27-24 (NO)
1987 — Saints, 20-16 (P)
1990 — Steelers, 9-6 (NO)
(RS Pts. — Steelers 181, Saints 157)
NEW ORLEANS vs. SAN DIEGO
RS: Chargers lead series, 4-1
1973 — Chargers, 17-14 (SD)
1977 — Chargers, 14-0 (NO)
1979 — Chargers, 35-0 (NO)
1988 — Saints, 23-17 (SD)
1991 — Chargers, 24-21 (SD)
(RS Pts. — Chargers 107, Saints 58)
NEW ORLEANS vs. SAN FRANCISCO
RS: 49ers lead series, 32-13-2
1967 — 49ers, 27-13 (SF)
1969 — Saints, 43-38 (NO)
1970 — Tie, 20-20 (SF)
49ers, 38-27 (NO)
1971 — 49ers, 38-20 (NO)
Saints, 26-20 (SF)
1972 — 49ers, 37-2 (NO)
Tie, 20-20 (SF)
1973 — 49ers, 40-0 (SF)
Saints, 16-10 (NO)
1974 — 49ers, 17-13 (NO)
49ers, 35-21 (SF)
1975 — 49ers, 35-21 (SF)
49ers, 16-6 (NO)
1976 — 49ers, 33-3 (SF)
49ers, 27-7 (NO)
1977 — 49ers, 10-7 (NO) OT
49ers, 20-17 (SF)
1978 — Saints, 14-7 (SF)
Saints, 24-13 (NO)
1979 — Saints, 30-21 (SF)
Saints, 31-20 (NO)
1980 — 49ers, 26-23 (NO)
49ers, 38-35 (SF) OT
1981 — 49ers, 21-14 (SF)
49ers, 21-17 (NO)
1982 — Saints, 23-20 (SF)
1983 — 49ers, 32-13 (NO)
49ers, 27-0 (SF)
1984 — 49ers, 30-20 (SF)
49ers, 35-3 (NO)
1985 — Saints, 20-17 (SF)
49ers, 31-19 (NO)
1986 — 49ers, 26-17 (SF)
Saints, 23-10 (NO)
1987 — 49ers, 24-22 (NO)
Saints, 26-24 (SF)
1988 — 49ers, 34-33 (NO)
49ers, 30-17 (SF)
1989 — 49ers, 24-20 (NO)
49ers, 31-13 (SF)
1990 — 49ers, 13-12 (NO)
Saints, 13-10 (SF)
1991 — Saints, 10-3 (NO)
49ers, 38-24 (SF)
1992 — 49ers, 16-10 (NO)
49ers, 21-20 (SF)
(RS Pts. — 49ers, 1,144, Saints 828)
NEW ORLEANS vs. SEATTLE
RS: Saints lead series, 3-2
1976 — Saints, 51-27 (S)
1979 — Seahawks, 38-24 (S)
1985 — Seahawks, 27-3 (NO)
1988 — Saints, 20-19 (S)
1991 — Saints, 27-24 (NO)
(RS Pts. — Seahawks 135, Saints 125)
NEW ORLEANS vs. TAMPA BAY
RS: Saints lead series, 11-4
1977 — Buccaneers, 33-14 (NO)
1978 — Saints, 17-10 (TB)
1979 — Saints, 42-14 (TB)
1981 — Buccaneers, 31-14 (NO)
1982 — Buccaneers, 13-10 (NO)
1983 — Saints, 24-21 (TB)
1984 — Saints, 17-13 (NO)
1985 — Saints, 20-13 (NO)
1986 — Saints, 38-7 (NO)
1987 — Saints, 44-34 (NO)
1988 — Saints, 13-9 (NO)
1989 — Buccaneers, 20-10 (TB)
1990 — Saints, 35-7 (NO)
1991 — Saints, 23-7 (NO)
1992 — Saints, 23-21 (NO)
(RS Pts. — Saints 344, Buccaneers 253)
NEW ORLEANS vs. WASHINGTON
RS: Redskins lead series, 11-5
1967 — Redskins, 30-10 (NO)
Saints, 30-14 (W)
1968 — Saints, 37-17 (NO)
1969 — Redskins, 26-20 (NO)
Redskins, 17-14 (W)
1971 — Redskins, 24-14 (W)
1973 — Saints, 19-3 (NO)
1975 — Redskins, 41-3 (W)
1979 — Saints, 14-10 (W)
1980 — Redskins, 22-14 (W)
1982 — Redskins, 27-10 (NO)
1986 — Redskins, 14-6 (NO)
1988 — Redskins, 27-24 (W)
1989 — Redskins, 16-14 (NO)
1990 — Redskins, 31-17 (W)
1992 — Saints, 20-3 (NO)
(RS Pts. — Redskins 322, Saints 266)

N.Y. GIANTS vs. ATLANTA
RS: Series tied, 6-6;
See Atlanta vs. N.Y. Giants
N.Y. GIANTS vs. BUFFALO
RS: Bills lead series, 3-2
PS: Giants lead series, 1-0;
See Buffalo vs. N.Y. Giants
N.Y. GIANTS vs. CHICAGO
RS: Bears lead series, 24-15-2
PS: Bears lead series, 5-3;
See Chicago vs. N.Y. Giants
N.Y. GIANTS vs. CINCINNATI
RS: Bengals lead series, 4-0;
See Cincinnati vs. N.Y. Giants
N.Y. GIANTS vs. CLEVELAND
RS: Browns lead series, 25-16-2
PS: Series tied, 1-1;
See Cleveland vs. N.Y. Giants
N.Y. GIANTS vs. DALLAS
RS: Cowboys lead series, 38-21-2;
See Dallas vs. N.Y. Giants
N.Y. GIANTS vs. DENVER
RS: Series tied, 3-3
PS: Giants lead series, 1-0;
See Denver vs. N.Y. Giants
N.Y. GIANTS vs. DETROIT
RS: Lions lead series, 17-15-1
PS: Lions lead series, 1-0;
See Detroit vs. N.Y. Giants
N.Y. GIANTS vs. GREEN BAY
RS: Packers lead series, 21-20-2

PS: Packers lead series, 4-1;
See Green Bay vs. N.Y. Giants
N.Y. GIANTS vs. HOUSTON
RS: Giants lead series, 4-0;
See Houston vs. N.Y. Giants
N.Y. GIANTS vs. INDIANAPOLIS
RS: Colts lead series, 5-4
PS: Colts lead series, 2-0;
See Indianapolis vs. N.Y. Giants
N.Y. GIANTS vs. KANSAS CITY
RS: Giants lead series, 6-1;
See Kansas City vs. N.Y. Giants
N.Y. GIANTS vs. L.A. RAIDERS
RS: Raiders lead series, 4-2;
See L.A. Raiders vs. N.Y. Giants
N.Y. GIANTS vs. L.A. RAMS
RS: Rams lead series, 20-8
PS: Series tied, 1-1;
See L.A. Rams vs. N.Y. Giants
N.Y. GIANTS vs. MIAMI
RS: Series tied, 1-1;
See Miami vs. N.Y. Giants
N.Y. GIANTS vs. MINNESOTA
RS: Vikings lead series, 6-4;
See Minnesota vs. N.Y. Giants
N.Y. GIANTS vs. NEW ENGLAND
RS: Giants lead series, 3-1;
See New England vs. N.Y. Giants
N.Y. GIANTS vs. NEW ORLEANS
RS: Giants lead series, 8-6;
See New Orleans vs. N.Y. Giants
N.Y. GIANTS vs. N.Y. JETS
RS: Series tied, 3-3
1970 — Giants, 22-10 (NYJ)
1974 — Jets, 26-20 (New Haven) OT
1981 — Jets, 26-7 (NYG)
1984 — Giants, 20-10 (NYJ)
1987 — Giants, 20-7 (NYG)
1988 — Jets, 27-21 (NYJ)
(RS Pts. — Giants 110, Jets 106)
N.Y. GIANTS vs. PHILADELPHIA
RS: Giants lead series, 60-54-2
PS: Giants lead series, 1-0
1933 — Giants, 56-0 (NY)
Giants, 20-14 (P)
1934 — Giants, 17-0 (NY)
Eagles, 6-0 (P)
1935 — Giants, 10-0 (NY)
Giants, 21-14 (P)
1936 — Eagles, 10-7 (P)
Giants, 21-17 (NY)
1937 — Giants, 16-7 (P)
Giants, 21-0 (NY)
1938 — Eagles, 14-10 (P)
Giants, 17-7 (NY)
1939 — Giants, 13-3 (P)
Giants, 27-10 (NY)
1940 — Giants, 20-14 (P)
Giants, 17-7 (NY)
1941 — Giants, 24-0 (P)
Giants, 16-0 (NY)
1942 — Giants, 35-17 (NY)
Giants, 14-0 (P)
1944 — Eagles, 24-17 (NY)
Tie, 21-21 (P)
1945 — Eagles, 38-17 (P)
Giants, 28-21 (NY)
1946 — Eagles, 24-14 (P)
Giants, 45-17 (NY)
1947 — Eagles, 23-0 (P)
Eagles, 41-24 (NY)
1948 — Eagles, 45-0 (P)
Eagles, 35-14 (NY)
1949 — Eagles, 24-3 (NY)
Eagles, 17-3 (P)
1950 — Giants, 7-3 (NY)
Giants, 9-7 (P)
1951 — Giants, 26-24 (NY)
Giants, 23-7 (P)
1952 — Giants, 31-7 (P)
Eagles, 14-10 (NY)
1953 — Eagles, 30-7 (P)
Giants, 37-28 (NY)
1954 — Giants, 27-14 (NY)
Eagles, 29-14 (P)
1955 — Eagles, 27-17 (P)
Giants, 31-7 (NY)
1956 — Giants, 20-3 (NY)
Giants, 21-7 (P)
1957 — Giants, 24-20 (P)
Giants, 13-0 (NY)
1958 — Eagles, 27-24 (P)
Giants, 24-10 (NY)
1959 — Eagles, 49-21 (P)
Giants, 24-7 (NY)
1960 — Eagles, 17-10 (NY)
Eagles, 31-23 (P)
1961 — Giants, 38-21 (NY)
Giants, 28-24 (P)
1962 — Giants, 29-13 (P)
Giants, 19-14 (NY)
1963 — Giants, 37-14 (P)
Giants, 42-14 (NY)
1964 — Eagles, 38-7 (P)
Eagles, 23-17 (NY)
1965 — Giants, 16-14 (P)
Giants, 35-27 (NY)
1966 — Eagles, 35-17 (P)
Eagles, 31-3 (NY)
1967 — Giants, 44-7 (NY)
1968 — Giants, 34-25 (P)
Giants, 7-6 (NY)
1969 — Eagles, 23-20 (NY)
1970 — Giants, 30-23 (NY)
Eagles, 23-20 (P)
1971 — Eagles, 23-7 (P)
Eagles, 41-28 (NY)
1972 — Giants, 27-12 (P)
Giants, 62-10 (NY)
1973 — Tie, 23-23 (NY)
Eagles, 20-16 (P)
1974 — Eagles, 35-7 (P)
Eagles, 20-7 (New Haven)
1975 — Giants, 23-14 (P)
Eagles, 13-10 (NY)
1976 — Eagles, 20-7 (P)
Eagles, 10-0 (NY)
1977 — Eagles, 28-10 (NY)
Eagles, 17-14 (P)
1978 — Eagles, 19-17 (NY)
Eagles, 20-3 (P)
1979 — Eagles, 23-17 (P)
Eagles, 17-13 (NY)
1980 — Eagles, 35-3 (P)
Eagles, 31-16 (NY)
1981 — Eagles, 24-10 (NY)
Giants, 20-10 (P)
*Giants, 27-21 (P)
1982 — Giants, 23-7 (NY)
Giants, 26-24 (P)
1983 — Eagles, 17-13 (NY)
Giants, 23-0 (P)
1984 — Giants, 28-27 (NY)
Eagles, 24-10 (P)
1985 — Giants, 21-0 (NY)
Giants, 16-10 (P) OT
1986 — Giants, 35-3 (NY)
Giants, 17-14 (P)
1987 — Giants, 20-17 (P)
Giants, 23-20 (NY) OT
1988 — Eagles, 24-13 (P)
Eagles, 23-17 (NY) OT
1989 — Eagles, 21-19 (P)
Eagles, 24-17 (NY)
1990 — Giants, 27-20 (NY)
Eagles, 31-13 (P)
1991 — Eagles, 30-7 (P)
Eagles, 19-14 (NY)
1992 — Eagles, 47-34 (NY)
Eagles, 20-10 (P)
(RS Pts. — Giants 2,220, Eagles 2,100)
(PS Pts. — Giants 27, Eagles 21)
NFC First Round Playoff
N.Y. GIANTS vs. *PHOENIX
RS: Giants lead series, 64-34-2
1926 — Giants, 20-0 (NY)
1927 — Giants, 28-7 (NY)
1929 — Giants, 24-21 (NY)
1930 — Giants, 25-12 (NY)
Giants, 13-7 (C)
1935 — Cardinals, 14-13 (NY)
1936 — Giants, 14-6 (NY)
1938 — Giants, 6-0 (NY)
1939 — Giants, 17-7 (NY)
1941 — Cardinals, 10-7 (NY)
1942 — Giants, 21-7 (NY)
1943 — Giants, 24-13 (NY)
1946 — Giants, 28-24 (NY)
1947 — Giants, 35-31 (NY)
1948 — Cardinals, 63-35 (NY)
1949 — Giants, 41-38 (C)
1950 — Cardinals, 17-3 (C)
Giants, 51-21 (NY)
1951 — Giants, 28-17 (NY)
Giants, 10-0 (C)
1952 — Cardinals, 24-23 (NY)
Giants, 28-6 (C)
1953 — Giants, 21-7 (NY)
Giants, 23-20 (C)
1954 — Giants, 41-10 (C)
Giants, 31-17 (NY)
1955 — Cardinals, 28-17 (C)
Giants, 10-0 (NY)
1956 — Cardinals, 35-27 (C)
Giants, 23-10 (NY)
1957 — Giants, 27-14 (NY)
Giants, 28-21 (C)
1958 — Giants, 37-7 (Buffalo)
Cardinals, 23-6 (NY)
1959 — Giants, 9-3 (NY)
Giants, 30-20 (Minn)
1960 — Giants, 35-14 (StL)
Cardinals, 20-13 (NY)
1961 — Cardinals, 21-10 (NY)
Giants, 24-9 (StL)
1962 — Giants, 31-14 (StL)
Giants, 31-28 (NY)
1963 — Giants, 38-21 (StL)
Cardinals, 24-17 (NY)
1964 — Giants, 34-17 (NY)
Tie, 10-10 (StL)
1965 — Giants, 14-10 (NY)
Giants, 28-15 (StL)
1966 — Cardinals, 24-19 (StL)
Cardinals, 20-17 (NY)
1967 — Giants, 37-20 (StL)
Giants, 37-14 (NY)
1968 — Cardinals, 28-21 (NY)
1969 — Cardinals, 42-17 (StL)
Giants, 49-6 (NY)
1970 — Giants, 35-17 (NY)
Giants, 34-17 (StL)
1971 — Giants, 21-20 (StL)
Cardinals, 24-7 (NY)
1972 — Giants, 27-21 (NY)
Giants, 13-7 (StL)
1973 — Cardinals, 35-27 (StL)
Giants, 24-13 (New Haven)
1974 — Cardinals, 23-21 (New Haven)
Cardinals, 26-14 (StL)
1975 — Cardinals, 26-14 (StL)
Cardinals, 20-13 (NY)
1976 — Cardinals, 27-21 (StL)
Cardinals, 17-14 (NY)
1977 — Cardinals, 28-0 (StL)
Giants, 27-7 (NY)
1978 — Cardinals, 20-10 (StL)
Giants, 17-0 (NY)
1979 — Cardinals, 27-14 (NY)
Cardinals, 29-20 (StL)
1980 — Giants, 41-35 (StL)
Cardinals, 23-7 (NY)
1981 — Giants, 34-14 (NY)
Giants, 20-10 (StL)
1982 — Cardinals, 24-21 (StL)
1983 — Tie, 20-20 (StL) OT
Cardinals, 10-6 (NY)
1984 — Giants, 16-10 (NY)
Cardinals, 31-21 (StL)
1985 — Giants, 27-17 (NY)
Giants, 34-3 (StL)
1986 — Giants, 13-6 (StL)
Giants, 27-7 (NY)
1987 — Giants, 30-7 (NY)
Cardinals, 27-24 (StL)
1988 — Cardinals, 24-17 (P)
Giants, 44-7 (NY)
1989 — Giants, 35-7 (NY)
Giants, 20-13 (P)
1990 — Giants, 20-19 (NY)
Giants, 24-21 (P)
1991 — Giants, 20-9 (NY)
Giants, 21-14 (P)
1992 — Giants, 31-21 (NY)
Cardinals, 19-0 (P)
(RS Pts. — Giants 2,252, Cardinals 1,719)
Franchise in St. Louis prior to 1988 and in Chicago prior to 1960
N.Y. GIANTS vs. *PITTSBURGH
RS: Giants lead series, 42-26-3
1933 — Giants, 23-2 (P)
Giants, 27-3 (NY)
1934 — Giants, 14-12 (P)
Giants, 17-7 (NY)
1935 — Giants, 42-7 (P)
Giants, 13-0 (NY)
1936 — Pirates, 10-7 (P)
1937 — Giants, 10-7 (P)
Giants, 17-0 (NY)
1938 — Giants, 27-14 (P)
Pirates, 13-10 (NY)
1939 — Giants, 14-7 (P)
Giants, 23-7 (NY)
1940 — Tie, 10-10 (P)
Giants, 12-0 (NY)
1941 — Giants, 37-10 (P)
Giants, 28-7 (NY)
1942 — Steelers, 13-10 (P)
Steelers, 17-9 (NY)
1945 — Giants, 34-6 (P)
Steelers, 21-7 (NY)
1946 — Giants, 17-14 (P)
Giants, 7-0 (NY)
1947 — Steelers, 38-21 (NY)
Steelers, 24-7 (P)
1948 — Giants, 34-27 (NY)
Steelers, 38-28 (P)
1949 — Steelers, 28-7 (P)
Steelers, 21-17 (NY)
1950 — Giants, 18-7 (P)
Steelers, 17-6 (NY)
1951 — Tie, 13-13 (P)
Giants, 14-0 (NY)
1952 — Steelers, 63-7 (P)
1953 — Steelers, 24-14 (P)
Steelers, 14-10 (NY)
1954 — Giants, 30-6 (P)
Giants, 24-3 (NY)
1955 — Steelers, 30-23 (P)
1956 — Steelers, 19-17 (NY)
1956 — Giants, 38-10 (NY)
Giants, 17-14 (P)
1957 — Giants, 35-0 (NY)
Steelers, 21-10 (P)
1958 — Giants, 17-6 (NY)
Steelers, 31-10 (P)
1959 — Giants, 21-16 (P)
Steelers, 14-9 (NY)
1960 — Giants, 19-17 (P)
Giants, 27-24 (NY)
1961 — Giants, 17-14 (P)
Giants, 42-21 (NY)
1962 — Giants, 31-27 (P)
Steelers, 20-17 (NY)
1963 — Steelers, 31-0 (P)
Giants, 33-17 (NY)
1964 — Steelers, 27-24 (P)
Steelers, 44-17 (NY)
1965 — Giants, 23-13 (P)
Giants, 35-10 (NY)
1966 — Tie, 34-34 (P)
Steelers, 47-28 (NY)
1967 — Giants, 27-24 (P)
Giants, 28-20 (NY)
1968 — Giants, 34-20 (P)
1969 — Giants, 10-7 (NY)
Giants, 21-17 (P)
1971 — Steelers, 17-13 (P)
1976 — Steelers, 27-0 (NY)
1985 — Giants, 28-10 (NY)
1991 — Giants, 23-20 (P)
(RS Pts. — Giants 1,393, Steelers 1,179)
Steelers known as Pirates prior to 1941
N.Y. GIANTS vs. SAN DIEGO
RS: Giants lead series, 4-2
1971 — Giants, 35-17 (NY)
1975 — Giants, 35-24 (NY)
1980 — Chargers, 44-7 (SD)
1983 — Chargers, 41-34 (NY)
1986 — Giants, 20-7 (NY)
1989 — Giants, 20-13 (SD)
(RS Pts. — Giants 151, Chargers 146)
N.Y. GIANTS vs. SAN FRANCISCO
RS: Giants lead series, 11-10
PS: Giants lead series, 3-2
1952 — Giants, 23-14 (NY)
1956 — Giants, 38-21 (SF)
1957 — 49ers, 27-17 (NY)
1960 — Giants, 21-19 (SF)
1963 — Giants, 48-14 (NY)
1968 — 49ers, 26-10 (NY)
1972 — Giants, 23-17 (SF)
1975 — Giants, 26-23 (SF)
1977 — Giants, 20-17 (NY)
1978 — Giants, 27-10 (NY)
1979 — Giants, 32-16 (NY)
1980 — 49ers, 12-0 (SF)
1981 — 49ers, 17-10 (SF)
*49ers, 38-24 (SF)
1984 — 49ers, 31-10 (NY)
*49ers, 21-10 (SF)
1985 — **Giants, 17-3 (NY)
1986 — Giants, 21-17 (SF)
*Giants, 49-3 (NY)
1987 — 49ers, 41-21 (NY)
1988 — 49ers, 20-17 (NY)
1989 — 49ers, 34-24 (SF)
1990 — 49ers, 7-3 (SF)
***Giants, 15-13 (SF)
1991 — Giants, 16-14 (NY)
1992 — 49ers, 31-14 (NY)
(RS Pts. — 49ers 431, Giants 421)
(PS Pts. — Giants 115, 49ers 75)
NFC Divisional Playoff
***NFC First Round Playoff*
****NFC Championship*
N.Y. GIANTS vs. SEATTLE
RS: Giants lead series, 5-2
1976 — Giants, 28-16 (NY)
1980 — Giants, 27-21 (S)
1981 — Giants, 32-0 (S)
1983 — Seahawks, 17-12 (NY)
1986 — Seahawks, 17-12 (S)
1989 — Giants, 15-3 (NY)
1992 — Giants, 23-10 (NY)
(RS Pts. — Giants 149, Seahawks 84)
N.Y. GIANTS vs. TAMPA BAY
RS: Giants lead series, 7-3
1977 — Giants, 10-0 (TB)
1978 — Giants, 19-13 (TB)
Giants, 17-14 (NY)
1979 — Giants, 17-14 (NY)
Buccaneers, 31-3 (TB)
1980 — Buccaneers, 30-13 (TB)
1984 — Giants, 17-14 (NY)
Buccaneers, 20-17 (TB)
1985 — Giants, 22-20 (NY)
1991 — Giants, 21-14 (TB)
(RS Pts. — Buccaneers 170, Giants 156)
N.Y. GIANTS vs. *WASHINGTON
RS: Giants lead series, 67-50-3
PS: Series tied, 1-1

1932 — Braves, 14-6 (B)
Tie, 0-0 (NY)
1933 — Redskins, 21-20 (B)
Giants, 7-0 (NY)
1934 — Giants, 16-13 (B)
Giants, 3-0 (NY)
1935 — Giants, 20-12 (B)
Giants, 17-6 (NY)
1936 — Giants, 7-0 (B)
Redskins, 14-0 (NY)
1937 — Redskins, 13-3 (W)
Redskins, 49-14 (NY)
1938 — Giants, 10-7 (W)
Giants, 36-0 (NY)
1939 — Tie, 0-0 (W)
Giants, 9-7 (NY)
1940 — Redskins, 21-7 (W)
Giants, 21-7 (NY)
1941 — Giants, 17-10 (W)
Giants, 20-13 (NY)
1942 — Giants, 14-7 (W)
Redskins, 14-7 (NY)
1943 — Giants, 14-10 (NY)
Giants, 31-7 (W)
**Redskins, 28-0 (NY)
1944 — Giants, 16-13 (NY)
Giants, 31-0 (W)
1945 — Redskins, 24-14 (NY)
Redskins, 17-0 (W)
1946 — Redskins, 24-14 (W)
Giants, 31-0 (NY)
1947 — Redskins, 28-20 (W)
Giants, 35-10 (NY)
1948 — Redskins, 41-10 (W)
Redskins, 28-21 (NY)
1949 — Giants, 45-35 (W)
Giants, 23-7 (NY)
1950 — Giants, 21-17 (W)
Giants, 24-21 (NY)
1951 — Giants, 35-14 (W)
Giants, 28-14 (NY)
1952 — Giants, 14-10 (W)
Redskins, 27-17 (NY)
1953 — Redskins, 13-9 (W)
Redskins, 24-21 (NY)
1954 — Giants, 51-21 (W)
Giants, 24-7 (NY)
1955 — Giants, 35-7 (NY)
Giants, 27-20 (W)
1956 — Redskins, 33-7 (W)
Giants, 28-14 (NY)
1957 — Giants, 24-20 (W)
Redskins, 31-14 (NY)
1958 — Giants, 21-14 (W)
Giants, 30-0 (NY)
1959 — Giants, 45-14 (NY)
Giants, 24-10 (W)
1960 — Tie, 24-24 (NY)
Giants, 17-3 (W)
1961 — Giants, 24-21 (W)
Giants, 53-0 (NY)
1962 — Giants, 49-34 (NY)
Giants, 42-24 (W)
1963 — Giants, 24-14 (W)
Giants, 44-14 (NY)
1964 — Giants, 13-10 (NY)
Redskins, 36-21 (W)
1965 — Redskins, 23-7 (NY)
Giants, 27-10 (W)
1966 — Giants, 13-10 (NY)
Redskins, 72-41 (W)
1967 — Redskins, 38-34 (W)
1968 — Giants, 48-21 (NY)
Giants, 13-10 (W)
1969 — Redskins, 20-14 (W)
1970 — Giants, 35-33 (NY)
Giants, 27-24 (W)
1971 — Redskins, 30-3 (NY)
Redskins, 23-7 (W)
1972 — Redskins, 23-16 (NY)
Redskins, 27-13 (W)
1973 — Redskins, 21-3 (New Haven)
Redskins, 27-24 (W)
1974 — Redskins, 13-10 (New Haven)
Redskins, 24-3 (W)
1975 — Redskins, 49-13 (W)
Redskins, 21-13 (NY)
1976 — Redskins, 19-17 (W)
Giants, 12-9 (NY)
1977 — Giants, 20-17 (NY)
Giants, 17-6 (W)
1978 — Giants, 17-6 (NY)
Redskins, 16-13 (W) OT
1979 — Redskins, 27-0 (W)
Giants, 14-6 (NY)
1980 — Redskins, 23-21 (NY)
Redskins, 16-13 (W)
1981 — Giants, 17-7 (W)
Redskins, 30-27 (NY) OT
1982 — Redskins, 27-17 (NY)
Redskins, 15-14 (W)
1983 — Redskins, 33-17 (NY)
Redskins, 31-22 (W)
1984 — Redskins, 30-14 (W)
Giants, 37-13 (NY)
1985 — Giants, 17-3 (NY)
Redskins, 23-21 (W)
1986 — Giants, 27-20 (NY)
Giants, 24-14 (W)
***Giants, 17-0 (NY)
1987 — Redskins, 38-12 (NY)
Redskins, 23-19 (W)
1988 — Giants, 27-20 (NY)
Giants, 24-23 (W)
1989 — Giants, 27-24 (W)
Giants, 20-17 (NY)
1990 — Giants, 24-20 (W)
Giants, 21-10 (NY)
1991 — Redskins, 17-13 (NY)
Redskins, 34-17 (W)
1992 — Giants, 24-7 (W)
Redskins, 28-10 (NY)
(RS Pts. — Giants 2,369, Redskins 2,154)
(PS Pts. — Redskins 28, Giants 17)
Franchise in Boston prior to 1937 and known as Braves prior to 1933
***Division Playoff*
****NFC Championship*

N.Y. JETS vs. ATLANTA
RS: Series tied, 3-3;
See Atlanta vs. N.Y. Jets
N.Y. JETS vs. BUFFALO
RS: Bills lead series, 35-29
PS: Bills lead series, 1-0;
See Buffalo vs. N.Y. Jets
N.Y. JETS vs. CHICAGO
RS: Bears lead series, 3-1;
See Chicago vs. N.Y. Jets
N.Y. JETS vs. CINCINNATI
RS: Jets lead series, 8-6
PS: Jets lead series, 1-0;
See Cincinnati vs. N.Y. Jets
N.Y. JETS vs. CLEVELAND
RS: Browns lead series, 8-6
PS: Browns lead series, 1-0;
See Cleveland vs. N.Y. Jets
N.Y. JETS vs. DALLAS
RS: Cowboys lead series, 4-1;
See Dallas vs. N.Y. Jets
N.Y. JETS vs. DENVER
RS: Series tied, 11-11-1;
See Denver vs. N.Y. Jets
N.Y. JETS vs. DETROIT
RS: Series tied, 3-3;
See Detroit vs. N.Y. Jets
N.Y. JETS vs. GREEN BAY
RS: Jets lead series, 5-1;
See Green Bay vs. N.Y. Jets
N.Y. JETS vs. HOUSTON
RS: Oilers lead series, 16-12-1
PS: Oilers lead series, 1-0;
See Houston vs. N.Y. Jets
N.Y. JETS vs. INDIANAPOLIS
RS: Colts lead series, 26-19
PS: Jets lead series, 1-0;
See Indianapolis vs. N.Y. Jets
N.Y. JETS vs. KANSAS CITY
RS: Chiefs lead series, 14-12-1
PS: Series tied, 1-1;
See Kansas City vs. N.Y. Jets
N.Y. JETS vs. L.A. RAIDERS
RS: Raiders lead series, 13-9-2
PS: Jets lead series, 2-0;
See L.A. Raiders vs. N.Y. Jets
N.Y. JETS vs. L.A. RAMS
RS: Rams lead series, 5-2;
See L.A. Rams vs. N.Y. Jets
N.Y. JETS vs. MIAMI
RS: Dolphins lead series, 27-26-1
PS: Dolphins lead series, 1-0;
See Miami vs. N.Y. Jets
N.Y. JETS vs. MINNESOTA
RS: Jets lead series, 3-1;
See Minnesota vs. N.Y. Jets
N.Y. JETS vs. NEW ENGLAND
RS: Jets lead series, 36-28-1
PS: Patriots lead series, 1-0;
See New England vs. N.Y. Jets
N.Y. JETS vs. NEW ORLEANS
RS: Jets lead series, 4-3;
See New Orleans vs. N.Y. Jets
N.Y. JETS vs. N.Y. GIANTS
RS: Series tied, 3-3;
See N.Y. Giants vs. N.Y. Jets
N.Y. JETS vs. PHILADELPHIA
RS: Eagles lead series, 4-0
1973 — Eagles, 24-23 (P)
1977 — Eagles, 27-0 (P)
1978 — Eagles, 17-9 (P)
1987 — Eagles, 38-27 (NY)
(RS Pts. — Eagles 106, Jets 59)
N.Y. JETS vs. *PHOENIX
RS: Cardinals lead series, 2-1
1971 — Cardinals, 17-10 (StL)
1975 — Cardinals 37-6 (NY)
1978 — Jets, 23-10 (NY)
(RS Pts. — Cardinals 64, Jets 39)
Franchise in St. Louis prior to 1988
N.Y. JETS vs. PITTSBURGH
RS: Steelers lead series, 12-1
1970 — Steelers, 21-17 (P)
1973 — Steelers, 26-14 (P)
1975 — Steelers, 20-7 (NY)
1977 — Steelers, 23-20 (NY)
1978 — Steelers, 28-17 (NY)
1981 — Steelers, 38-10 (P)
1983 — Steelers, 34-7 (NY)
1984 — Steelers, 23-17 (NY)
1986 — Steelers, 45-24 (NY)
1988 — Jets, 24-20 (NY)
1989 — Steelers, 13-0 (NY)
1990 — Steelers, 24-7 (NY)
1992 — Steelers, 27-10 (P)
(RS Pts. — Steelers 342, Jets 174)
***N.Y. JETS vs. **SAN DIEGO**
RS: Chargers lead series, 16-9-1
1960 — Chargers, 21-7 (NY)
Chargers, 50-43 (LA)
1961 — Chargers, 25-10 (NY)
Chargers, 48-13 (SD)
1962 — Chargers, 40-14 (SD)
Titans, 23-3 (NY)
1963 — Chargers, 24-20 (SD)
Chargers, 53-7 (NY)
1964 — Tie, 17-17 (NY)
Chargers, 38-3 (SD)
1965 — Chargers, 34-9 (NY)
Chargers, 38-7 (SD)
1966 — Jets, 17-16 (NY)
Chargers, 42-27 (SD)
1967 — Jets, 42-31 (SD)
1968 — Jets, 23-20 (NY)
Jets, 37-15 (SD)
1969 — Chargers, 34-27 (SD)
1971 — Chargers, 49-21 (SD)
1974 — Jets, 27-14 (NY)
1975 — Chargers, 24-16 (SD)
1983 — Jets, 41-29 (SD)
1989 — Jets, 20-17 (SD)
1990 — Chargers, 39-3 (NY)
Chargers, 38-17 (SD)
1991 — Jets, 24-3 (NY)
(RS Pts. — Chargers 762, Jets 515)
Jets known as Titans prior to 1963
***Franchise in Los Angeles prior to 1961*
N.Y. JETS vs. SAN FRANCISCO
RS: 49ers lead series, 6-1
1971 — 49ers, 24-21 (NY)
1976 — 49ers, 17-6 (SF)
1980 — 49ers, 37-27 (NY)
1983 — Jets, 27-13 (SF)
1986 — 49ers, 24-10 (SF)
1989 — 49ers, 23-10 (NY)
1992 — 49ers, 31-14 (NY)
(RS Pts. — 49ers 169, Jets 115)
N.Y. JETS vs. SEATTLE
RS: Seahawks lead series, 8-3
1977 — Seahawks, 17-0 (NY)
1978 — Seahawks, 24-17 (NY)
1979 — Seahawks, 30-7 (S)
1980 — Seahawks, 27-17 (NY)
1981 — Seahawks, 19-3 (NY)
Seahawks, 27-23 (S)
1983 — Seahawks, 17-10 (NY)
1985 — Jets, 17-14 (NY)
1986 — Jets, 38-7 (S)
1987 — Jets, 30-14 (NY)
1991 — Seahawks, 20-13 (S)
(RS Pts. — Seahawks 216, Jets 175)
N.Y. JETS vs. TAMPA BAY
RS: Jets lead series, 5-1
1976 — Jets, 34-0 (NY)
1982 — Jets, 32-17 (NY)
1984 — Buccaneers, 41-21 (TB)
1985 — Jets, 62-28 (NY)
1990 — Jets, 16-14 (TB)
1991 — Jets, 16-13 (NY)
(RS Pts. — Jets 181, Buccaneers 113)
N.Y. JETS vs. WASHINGTON
RS: Redskins lead series, 4-0
1972 — Redskins, 35-17 (NY)
1976 — Redskins, 37-16 (NY)
1978 — Redskins, 23-3 (W)
1987 — Redskins, 17-16 (W)
(RS Pts. — Redskins 112, Jets 52)

PHILADELPHIA vs. ATLANTA
RS: Eagles lead series, 8-6-1
PS: Falcons lead series, 1-0;
See Atlanta vs. Philadelphia
PHILADELPHIA vs. BUFFALO
RS: Eagles lead series, 4-2;
See Buffalo vs. Philadelphia
PHILADELPHIA vs. CHICAGO
RS: Bears lead series, 22-3-1
PS: Series tied, 1-1;
See Chicago vs. Philadelphia
PHILADELPHIA vs. CINCINNATI
RS: Bengals lead series, 5-1;
See Cincinnati vs. Philadelphia
PHILADELPHIA vs. CLEVELAND
RS: Browns lead series, 30-12-1;
See Cleveland vs. Philadelphia
PHILADELPHIA vs. DALLAS
RS: Cowboys lead series, 38-26
PS: Series tied, 1-1;
See Dallas vs. Philadelphia
PHILADELPHIA vs. DENVER
RS: Eagles lead series, 5-2;
See Denver vs. Philadelphia
PHILADELPHIA vs. DETROIT
RS: Lions lead series, 12-9-2;
See Detroit vs. Philadelphia
PHILADELPHIA vs. GREEN BAY
RS: Packers lead series, 19-6
PS: Eagles lead series, 1-0;
See Green Bay vs. Philadelphia
PHILADELPHIA vs. HOUSTON
RS: Eagles lead series, 5-0;
See Houston vs. Philadelphia
PHILADELPHIA vs. INDIANAPOLIS
RS: Colts lead series, 6-5;
See Indianapolis vs. Philadelphia
PHILADELPHIA vs. KANSAS CITY
RS: Series tied, 1-1;
See Kansas City vs. Philadelphia
PHILADELPHIA vs. L.A. RAIDERS
RS: Eagles lead series, 4-2
PS: Raiders lead series, 1-0;
See L.A. Raiders vs. Philadelphia
PHILADELPHIA vs. L.A. RAMS
RS: Rams lead series, 15-11-1
PS: Series tied, 1-1;
See L.A. Rams vs. Philadelphia
PHILADELPHIA vs. MIAMI
RS: Dolphins lead series, 5-2;
See Miami vs. Philadelphia
PHILADELPHIA vs. MINNESOTA
RS: Vikings lead series, 10-6
PS: Eagles lead series, 1-0;
See Minnesota vs. Philadelphia
PHILADELPHIA vs. NEW ENGLAND
RS: Eagles lead series, 5-2;
See New England vs. Philadelphia
PHILADELPHIA vs. NEW ORLEANS
RS: Eagles lead series, 10-8
PS; Eagles lead series, 1-0;
See New Orleans vs. Philadelphia
PHILADELPHIA vs. N.Y. GIANTS
RS: Giants lead series, 60-54-2
PS: Giants lead series, 1-0;
See N.Y. Giants vs. Philadelphia
PHILADELPHIA vs. N.Y. JETS
RS: Eagles lead series, 4-0;
See N.Y. Jets vs. Philadelphia
PHILADELPHIA vs. *PHOENIX
RS: Cardinals lead series, 43-42-5
PS: Series tied, 1-1
1935 — Cardinals, 12-3 (C)
1936 — Cardinals, 13-0 (C)
1937 — Tie, 6-6 (P)
1938 — Eagles, 7-0 (Erie, Pa.)
1941 — Eagles, 21-14 (P)
1945 — Eagles, 21-6 (P)
1947 — Cardinals, 45-21 (P)
**Cardinals, 28-21 (C)
1948 — Cardinals, 21-14 (C)
**Eagles, 7-0 (P)
1949 — Eagles, 28-3 (P)
1950 — Eagles, 45-7 (C)
Cardinals, 14-10 (P)
1951 — Eagles, 17-14 (C)
1952 — Eagles, 10-7 (P)
Cardinals, 28-22 (C)
1953 — Eagles, 56-17 (C)
Eagles, 38-0 (P)
1954 — Eagles, 35-16 (C)
Eagles, 30-14 (P)
1955 — Tie, 24-24 (C)
Eagles, 27-3 (P)
1956 — Cardinals, 20-6 (P)
Cardinals, 28-17 (C)
1957 — Eagles, 38-21 (C)
Cardinals, 31-27 (P)
1958 — Tie, 21-21 (C)
Eagles, 49-21 (P)
1959 — Eagles, 28-24 (Minn)
Eagles, 27-17 (P)
1960 — Eagles, 31-27 (P)
Eagles, 20-6 (StL)
1961 — Cardinals, 30-27 (P)
Eagles, 20-7 (StL)
1962 — Cardinals, 27-21 (P)
Cardinals, 45-35 (StL)
1963 — Cardinals, 28-24 (P)
Cardinals, 38-14 (StL)
1964 — Cardinals, 38-13 (P)
Cardinals, 36-34 (StL)
1965 — Eagles, 34-27 (P)
Eagles, 28-24 (StL)

1966 — Cardinals, 16-13 (StL)
Cardinals, 41-10 (P)
1967 — Cardinals, 48-14 (StL)
1968 — Cardinals, 45-17 (P)
1969 — Eagles, 34-30 (StL)
1970 — Cardinals, 35-20 (P)
Cardinals, 23-14 (StL)
1971 — Eagles, 37-20 (StL)
Eagles, 19-7 (P)
1972 — Tie, 6-6 (P)
Cardinals, 24-23 (StL)
1973 — Cardinals, 34-23 (P)
Eagles, 27-24 (StL)
1974 — Cardinals, 7-3 (StL)
Cardinals, 13-3 (P)
1975 — Cardinals, 31-20 (StL)
Cardinals, 24-23 (P)
1976 — Cardinals, 33-14 (StL)
Cardinals, 17-14 (P)
1977 — Cardinals, 21-17 (P)
Cardinals, 21-16 (StL)
1978 — Cardinals, 16-10 (P)
Eagles, 14-10 (StL)
1979 — Eagles, 24-20 (StL)
Eagles, 16-13 (P)
1980 — Cardinals, 24-14 (StL)
Eagles, 17-3 (P)
1981 — Eagles, 52-10 (StL)
Eagles, 38-0 (P)
1982 — Cardinals, 23-20 (P)
1983 — Cardinals, 14-11 (P)
Cardinals, 31-7 (StL)
1984 — Cardinals, 34-14 (P)
Cardinals, 17-16 (StL)
1985 — Eagles, 30-7 (P)
Eagles, 24-14 (StL)
1986 — Cardinals, 13-10 (StL)
Tie, 10-10 (P) OT
1987 — Eagles, 28-23 (StL)
Cardinals, 31-19 (P)
1988 — Eagles, 31-21 (P)
Eagles, 23-17 (Phx)
1989 — Eagles, 17-5 (Phx)
Eagles, 31-14 (P)
1990 — Cardinals, 23-21 (P)
Eagles, 23-21 (Phx)
1991 — Cardinals, 26-10 (P)
Eagles, 34-14 (Phx)
1992 — Eagles, 31-14 (Phx)
Eagles, 7-3 (P)
(RS Pts. — Eagles 1,946, Cardinals 1,799)
Franchise in St. Louis prior to 1988 and in Chicago prior to 1960
***NFL Championship*

PHILADELPHIA vs. *PITTSBURGH
RS: Eagles lead series, 43-25-3
PS: Eagles lead series, 1-0
1933 — Eagles, 25-6 (Phila)
1934 — Eagles, 17-0 (Pitt)
Pirates, 9-7 (Phila)
1935 — Pirates, 17-7 (Phila)
Eagles, 17-6 (Pitt)
1936 — Pirates, 17-0 (Pitt)
Pirates, 6-0 (Johnstown, Pa.)
1937 — Pirates, 27-14 (Pitt)
Pirates, 16-7 (Phila)
1938 — Eagles, 27-7 (Buffalo)
Eagles, 14-7 (Charleston, W. Va.)
1939 — Eagles, 17-14 (Phila)
Pirates, 24-12 (Pitt)
1940 — Pirates, 7-3 (Pitt)
Eagles, 7-0 (Phila)
1941 — Eagles, 10-7 (Pitt)
Tie, 7-7 (Phila)
1942 — Eagles, 24-14 (Pitt)
Steelers, 14-0 (Phila)
1945 — Eagles, 45-3 (Pitt)
Eagles, 30-6 (Phila)
1946 — Steelers, 10-7 (Pitt)
Eagles, 10-7 (Phila)
1947 — Steelers, 35-24 (Pitt)
Eagles, 21-0 (Phila)
**Eagles, 21-0 (Pitt)
1948 — Eagles, 34-7 (Pitt)
Eagles, 17-0 (Phila)
1949 — Eagles, 38-7 (Pitt)
Eagles, 34-17 (Phila)
1950 — Eagles, 17-10 (Pitt)
Steelers, 9-7 (Phila)
1951 — Eagles, 34-13 (Pitt)
Steelers, 17-13 (Phila)
1952 — Eagles, 31-25 (Pitt)
Eagles, 26-21 (Phila)
1953 — Eagles, 23-17 (Phila)
Eagles, 35-7 (Pitt)
1954 — Eagles, 24-22 (Phila)
Steelers, 17-7 (Pitt)
1955 — Steelers, 13-7 (Pitt)
Eagles, 24-0 (Phila)
1956 — Eagles, 35-21 (Pitt)
Eagles, 14-7 (Phila)
1957 — Steelers, 6-0 (Pitt)
Eagles, 7-6 (Phila)
1958 — Steelers, 24-3 (Pitt)
Steelers, 31-24 (Phila)
1959 — Eagles, 28-24 (Phila)
Steelers, 31-0 (Pitt)
1960 — Eagles, 34-7 (Phila)
Steelers, 27-21 (Pitt)
1961 — Eagles, 21-16 (Phila)
Eagles, 35-24 (Pitt)
1962 — Steelers, 13-7 (Pitt)
Steelers, 26-17 (Phila)
1963 — Tie, 21-21 (Phila)
Tie, 20-20 (Pitt)
1964 — Eagles, 21-7 (Phila)
Eagles, 34-10 (Pitt)
1965 — Steelers, 20-14 (Phila)
Eagles, 47-13 (Pitt)
1966 — Eagles, 31-14 (Pitt)
Eagles, 27-23 (Phila)
1967 — Eagles, 34-24 (Phila)
1968 — Steelers, 6-3 (Pitt)
1969 — Eagles, 41-27 (Phila)
1970 — Eagles, 30-20 (Phila)
1974 — Steelers, 27-0 (Pitt)
1979 — Eagles, 17-14 (Phila)
1988 — Eagles, 27-26 (Pitt)
1991 — Eagles, 23-14 (Phila)
(RS Pts. — Eagles 1,359, Steelers 1,007)
(PS Pts. — Eagles 21, Steelers 0)
**Steelers known as Pirates prior to 1941*
***Division Playoff*

PHILADELPHIA vs. SAN DIEGO
RS: Chargers lead series, 3-2
1974 — Eagles, 13-7 (SD)
1980 — Chargers, 22-21 (SD)
1985 — Chargers, 20-14 (SD)
1986 — Eagles, 23-7 (P)
1989 — Chargers, 20-17 (SD)
(RS Pts. — Eagles 88, Chargers 76)

PHILADELPHIA vs. SAN FRANCISCO
RS: 49ers lead series, 13-4-1
1951 — Eagles, 21-14 (P)
1953 — 49ers, 31-21 (SF)
1956 — Tie, 10-10 (P)
1958 — 49ers, 30-24 (P)
1959 — 49ers, 24-14 (SF)
1964 — 49ers, 28-24 (P)
1966 — Eagles, 35-34 (SF)
1967 — 49ers, 28-27 (P)
1969 — 49ers, 14-13 (SF)
1971 — 49ers, 31-3 (P)
1973 — 49ers, 38-28 (SF)
1975 — Eagles, 27-17 (P)
1983 — Eagles, 22-17 (SF)
1984 — 49ers, 21-9 (P)
1985 — 49ers, 24-13 (SF)
1989 — 49ers, 38-28 (P)
1991 — 49ers, 23-7 (P)
1992 — 49ers, 20-14 (SF)
(RS Pts. — 49ers 442, Eagles 340)

PHILADELPHIA vs. SEATTLE
RS: Eagles lead series, 4-1
1976 — Eagles, 27-10 (P)
1980 — Eagles, 27-20 (S)
1986 — Seahawks, 24-20 (S)
1989 — Eagles, 31-7 (P)
1992 — Eagles, 20-17 (S) OT
(RS Pts. — Eagles 125, Seahawks 78)

PHILADELPHIA vs. TAMPA BAY
RS: Eagles lead series, 3-1
PS: Buccaneers lead series, 1-0
1977 — Eagles, 13-3 (P)
1979 — *Buccaneers, 24-17 (TB)
1981 — Eagles, 20-10 (P)
1988 — Eagles, 41-14 (TB)
1991 — Buccaneers, 14-13 (TB)
(RS Pts. — Eagles 87, Buccaneers 41)
(PS Pts. — Buccaneers 24, Eagles 17)
**NFC Divisional Playoff*

PHILADELPHIA vs. *WASHINGTON
RS: Redskins lead series, 66-44-5
PS: Redskins lead series, 1-0
1934 — Redskins, 6-0 (B)
Redskins, 14-7 (P)
1935 — Eagles, 7-6 (B)
1936 — Redskins, 26-3 (P)
Redskins, 17-7 (B)
1937 — Eagles, 14-0 (W)
Redskins, 10-7 (P)
1938 — Redskins, 26-23 (P)
Redskins, 20-14 (W)
1939 — Redskins, 7-0 (P)
Redskins, 7-6 (W)
1940 — Redskins, 34-17 (P)
Redskins, 13-6 (W)
1941 — Redskins, 21-17 (P)
Redskins, 20-14 (W)
1942 — Redskins, 14-10 (P)
Redskins, 30-27 (W)
1944 — Tie, 31-31 (P)
Eagles, 37-7 (W)
1945 — Redskins, 24-14 (W)
Eagles, 16-0 (P)
1946 — Eagles, 28-24 (W)
Redskins, 27-10 (P)
1947 — Eagles, 45-42 (P)
Eagles, 38-14 (W)
1948 — Eagles, 45-0 (W)
Eagles, 42-21 (P)
1949 — Eagles, 49-14 (P)
Eagles, 44-21 (W)
1950 — Eagles, 35-3 (P)
Eagles, 33-0 (W)
1951 — Redskins, 27-23 (P)
Eagles, 35-21 (W)
1952 — Eagles, 38-20 (P)
Redskins, 27-21 (W)
1953 — Tie, 21-21 (P)
Redskins, 10-0 (W)
1954 — Eagles, 49-21 (W)
Eagles, 41-33 (P)
1955 — Redskins, 31-30 (P)
Redskins, 34-21 (W)
1956 — Eagles, 13-9 (P)
Redskins, 19-17 (W)
1957 — Eagles, 21-12 (P)
Redskins, 42-7 (W)
1958 — Redskins, 24-14 (P)
Redskins, 20-0 (W)
1959 — Eagles, 30-23 (P)
Eagles, 34-14 (W)
1960 — Eagles, 19-13 (P)
Eagles, 38-28 (W)
1961 — Eagles, 14-7 (P)
Eagles, 27-24 (W)
1962 — Redskins, 27-21 (P)
Eagles, 37-14 (W)
1963 — Eagles, 37-24 (W)
Redskins, 13-10 (P)
1964 — Redskins, 35-20 (W)
Redskins, 21-10 (P)
1965 — Redskins, 23-21 (W)
Eagles, 21-14 (P)
1966 — Redskins, 27-13 (P)
Eagles, 37-28 (W)
1967 — Eagles, 35-24 (P)
Tie, 35-35 (W)
1968 — Redskins, 17-14 (W)
Redskins, 16-10 (P)
1969 — Tie, 28-28 (W)
Redskins, 34-29 (P)
1970 — Redskins, 33-21 (P)
Redskins, 24-6 (W)
1971 — Tie, 7-7 (W)
Redskins, 20-13 (P)
1972 — Redskins, 14-0 (W)
Redskins, 23-7 (P)
1973 — Redskins, 28-7 (P)
Redskins, 38-20 (W)
1974 — Redskins, 27-20 (P)
Redskins, 26-7 (W)
1975 — Eagles, 26-10 (P)
Eagles, 26-3 (W)
1976 — Redskins, 20-17 (P) OT
Redskins, 24-0 (W)
1977 — Redskins, 23-17 (W)
Redskins, 17-14 (P)
1978 — Redskins, 35-30 (W)
Eagles, 17-10 (P)
1979 — Eagles, 28-17 (P)
Redskins, 17-7 (W)
1980 — Eagles, 24-14 (P)
Eagles, 24-0 (W)
1981 — Eagles, 36-13 (P)
Redskins, 15-13 (W)
1982 — Redskins, 37-34 (P) OT
Redskins, 13-9 (W)
1983 — Redskins, 23-13 (P)
Redskins, 28-24 (W)
1984 — Redskins, 20-0 (W)
Eagles, 16-10 (P)
1985 — Eagles, 19-6 (W)
Redskins, 17-12 (P)
1986 — Redskins, 41-14 (W)
Redskins, 21-14 (P)
1987 — Redskins, 34-24 (W)
Eagles, 31-27 (P)
1988 — Redskins, 17-10 (W)
Redskins, 20-19 (P)
1989 — Eagles, 42-37 (W)
Redskins, 10-3 (P)
1990 — Redskins, 13-7 (W)
Eagles, 28-14 (P)
**Redskins, 20-6 (P)
1991 — Redskins, 23-0 (W)
Eagles, 24-22 (P)
1992 — Redskins, 16-12 (W)
Eagles, 17-13 (P)
(RS Pts. — Eagles 2,296, Redskins 2,279)
(PS Pts. — Redskins 20, Eagles 6)
**Franchise in Boston prior to 1937*
***NFC First Round Playoff*

PHOENIX vs. ATLANTA
RS: Cardinals lead series, 10-5;
See Atlanta vs. Phoenix

PHOENIX vs. BUFFALO
RS: Series tied, 3-3;
See Buffalo vs. Phoenix

PHOENIX vs. CHICAGO
RS: Bears lead series, 51-25-6;
See Chicago vs. Phoenix

PHOENIX vs. CINCINNATI
RS: Bengals lead series, 3-1;
See Cincinnati vs. Phoenix

PHOENIX vs. CLEVELAND
RS: Browns lead series, 31-10-3;
See Cleveland vs. Phoenix

PHOENIX vs. DALLAS
RS: Cowboys lead series, 38-22-1;
See Dallas vs. Phoenix

PHOENIX vs. DENVER
RS: Broncos lead series, 3-0-1;
See Denver vs. Phoenix

PHOENIX vs. DETROIT
RS: Lions lead series, 25-16-5;
See Detroit vs. Phoenix

PHOENIX vs. GREEN BAY
RS: Packers lead series, 39-21-4
PS: Packers lead series, 1-0;
See Green Bay vs. Phoenix

PHOENIX vs. HOUSTON
RS: Cardinals lead series, 3-2;
See Houston vs. Phoenix

PHOENIX vs. INDIANAPOLIS
RS: Cardinals lead series, 6-5;
See Indianapolis vs. Phoenix

PHOENIX vs. KANSAS CITY
RS: Chiefs lead series, 3-1-1;
See Kansas City vs. Phoenix

PHOENIX vs. L.A. RAIDERS
RS: Raiders lead series, 2-1;
See L.A. Raiders vs. Phoenix

PHOENIX vs. L.A. RAMS
RS: Rams lead series, 22-18-2
PS: Rams lead series, 1-0;
See L.A. Rams vs. Phoenix

PHOENIX vs. MIAMI
RS: Dolphins lead series, 6-0;
See Miami vs. Phoenix

PHOENIX vs. MINNESOTA
RS: Cardinals lead series, 7-4
PS: Vikings lead series, 1-0;
See Minnesota vs. Phoenix

PHOENIX vs. NEW ENGLAND
RS: Cardinals lead series, 6-1;
See New England vs. Phoenix

PHOENIX vs. NEW ORLEANS
RS: Cardinals lead series, 10-8;
See New Orleans vs. Phoenix

PHOENIX vs. N.Y. GIANTS
RS: Giants lead series, 64-34-2;
See N.Y. Giants vs. Phoenix

PHOENIX vs. N.Y. JETS
RS: Cardinals lead series, 2-1;
See N.Y. Jets vs. Phoenix

PHOENIX vs. PHILADELPHIA
RS: Cardinals lead series, 43-42-5
PS: Series tied, 1-1;
See Philadelphia vs. Phoenix

***PHOENIX vs. **PITTSBURGH**
RS: Steelers lead series, 29-21-3
1933 — Pirates, 14-13 (C)
1935 — Pirates, 17-13 (P)
1936 — Cardinals, 14-6 (C)
1937 — Cardinals, 13-7 (P)
1939 — Cardinals, 10-0 (P)
1940 — Tie, 7-7 (P)
1942 — Steelers, 19-3 (P)
1945 — Steelers, 23-0 (P)
1946 — Steelers, 14-7 (P)
1948 — Cardinals, 24-7 (P)
1950 — Steelers, 28-17 (C)
Steelers, 28-7 (P)
1951 — Steelers, 28-14 (C)
1952 — Steelers, 34-28 (C)
Steelers, 17-14 (P)
1953 — Steelers, 31-28 (P)
Steelers, 21-17 (C)
1954 — Cardinals, 17-14 (C)
Steelers, 20-17 (P)
1955 — Steelers, 14-7 (P)
Cardinals, 27-13 (C)
1956 — Steelers, 14-7 (P)
Cardinals, 38-27 (C)
1957 — Steelers, 29-20 (P)
Steelers, 27-2 (C)
1958 — Steelers, 27-20 (C)
Steelers, 38-21 (P)
1959 — Cardinals, 45-24 (C)
Steelers, 35-20 (P)
1960 — Steelers, 27-14 (P)
Cardinals, 38-7 (StL)
1961 — Steelers, 30-27 (P)
Cardinals, 20-0 (StL)
1962 — Steelers, 26-17 (StL)
Steelers, 19-7 (P)
1963 — Steelers, 23-10 (P)
Cardinals, 24-23 (StL)

1964 — Cardinals, 34-30 (StL)
Cardinals, 21-20 (P)
1965 — Cardinals, 20-7 (P)
Cardinals, 21-17 (StL)
1966 — Steelers, 30-9 (P)
Cardinals, 6-3 (StL)
1967 — Cardinals, 28-14 (P)
Tie, 14-14 (StL)
1968 — Tie, 28-28 (StL)
Cardinals, 20-10 (P)
1969 — Cardinals, 27-14 (P)
Cardinals, 47-10 (StL)
1972 — Steelers, 25-19 (StL)
1979 — Steelers, 24-21 (StL)
1985 — Steelers, 23-10 (P)
1988 — Cardinals, 31-14 (Phx)
(RS Pts. — Steelers 1,021, Cardinals 983)
**Franchise in St. Louis prior to 1988 and in Chicago prior to 1960*
***Steelers known as Pirates prior to 1941*

***PHOENIX vs. SAN DIEGO**
RS: Chargers lead series, 5-1
1971 — Chargers, 20-17 (SD)
1976 — Chargers, 43-24 (SD)
1983 — Cardinals, 44-14 (StL)
1987 — Chargers, 28-24 (SD)
1989 — Chargers, 24-13 (P)
1992 — Chargers, 27-21 (P)
(RS Pts. — Chargers 156, Cardinals 143)
**Franchise in St. Louis prior to 1988*

***PHOENIX vs. SAN FRANCISCO**
RS: Series tied, 9-9
1951 — Cardinals, 27-21 (SF)
1957 — Cardinals, 20-10 (SF)
1962 — 49ers, 24-17 (StL)
1964 — Cardinals, 23-13 (SF)
1968 — 49ers, 35-17 (SF)
1971 — 49ers, 26-14 (StL)
1974 — Cardinals, 34-9 (SF)
1976 — Cardinals, 23-20 (StL) OT
1978 — Cardinals, 16-10 (SF)
1979 — Cardinals, 13-10 (StL)
1980 — 49ers, 24-21 (SF) OT
1982 — 49ers, 31-20 (StL)
1983 — 49ers, 42-27 (StL)
1986 — 49ers, 43-17 (SF)
1987 — 49ers, 34-28 (SF)
1988 — Cardinals, 24-23 (P)
1991 — 49ers, 14-10 (SF)
1992 — Cardinals, 24-14 (P)
(RS Pts. — 49ers 403, Cardinals 375)
**Franchise in St. Louis prior to 1988 and in Chicago prior to 1960*

***PHOENIX vs. SEATTLE**
RS: Cardinals lead series, 3-0
1976 — Cardinals, 30-24 (S)
1983 — Cardinals, 33-28 (StL)
1989 — Cardinals, 34-24 (S)
(RS Pts. — Cardinals 97, Seahawks 76)
**Franchise in St. Louis prior to 1988*

***PHOENIX vs. TAMPA BAY**
RS: Series tied, 6-6
1977 — Buccaneers, 17-7 (TB)
1981 — Buccaneers, 20-10 (TB)
1983 — Cardinals, 34-27 (TB)
1985 — Buccaneers, 16-0 (TB)
1986 — Cardinals, 30-19 (TB)
Cardinals, 21-17 (StL)
1987 — Cardinals, 31-28 (StL)
Cardinals, 31-14 (TB)
1988 — Cardinals, 30-24 (TB)
1989 — Buccaneers, 14-13 (P)
1992 — Buccaneers, 23-7 (TB)
Buccaneers, 7-3 (P)
(RS Pts. — Buccaneers 226, Cardinals 217)
**Franchise in St. Louis prior to 1988*

***PHOENIX vs. **WASHINGTON**
RS: Redskins lead series, 61-34-2
1932 — Cardinals, 9-0 (B)
Braves, 8-6 (C)
1933 — Redskins, 10-0 (C)
Tie, 0-0 (B)
1934 — Redskins, 9-0 (B)
1935 — Cardinals, 6-0 (B)
1936 — Redskins, 13-10 (B)
1937 — Cardinals, 21-14 (W)
1939 — Redskins, 28-7 (W)
1940 — Redskins, 28-21 (W)
1942 — Redskins, 28-0 (W)
1943 — Redskins, 13-7 (W)
1945 — Redskins, 24-21 (W)
1947 — Redskins, 45-21 (W)
1949 — Cardinals, 38-7 (C)
1950 — Cardinals, 38-28 (W)
1951 — Redskins, 7-3 (C)
Redskins, 20-17 (W)
1952 — Redskins, 23-7 (C)
Cardinals, 17-6 (W)
1953 — Redskins, 24-13 (C)
Redskins, 28-17 (W)
1954 — Cardinals, 38-16 (C)
Redskins, 37-20 (W)
1955 — Cardinals, 24-10 (W)
Redskins, 31-0 (C)
1956 — Cardinals, 31-3 (W)
Redskins, 17-14 (C)
1957 — Redskins, 37-14 (C)
Cardinals, 44-14 (W)
1958 — Cardinals, 37-10 (C)
Redskins, 45-31 (W)
1959 — Cardinals, 49-21 (C)
Redskins, 23-14 (W)
1960 — Cardinals, 44-7 (StL)
Cardinals, 26-14 (W)
1961 — Cardinals, 24-0 (W)
Cardinals, 38-24 (StL)
1962 — Redskins, 24-14 (W)
Tie, 17-17 (StL)
1963 — Cardinals, 21-7 (W)
Cardinals, 24-20 (StL)
1964 — Cardinals, 23-17 (W)
Cardinals, 38-24 (StL)
1965 — Cardinals, 37-16 (W)
Redskins, 24-20 (StL)
1966 — Cardinals, 23-7 (StL)
Redskins, 26-20 (W)
1967 — Cardinals, 27-21 (W)
1968 — Cardinals, 41-14 (StL)
1969 — Redskins, 33-17 (W)
1970 — Cardinals, 27-17 (StL)
Redskins, 28-27 (W)
1971 — Redskins, 24-17 (StL)
Redskins, 20-0 (W)
1972 — Redskins, 24-10 (W)
Redskins, 33-3 (StL)
1973 — Cardinals, 34-27 (StL)
Redskins, 31-13 (W)
1974 — Cardinals, 17-10 (W)
Cardinals, 23-20 (StL)
1975 — Redskins, 27-17 (W)
Cardinals, 20-17 (StL) OT
1976 — Redskins, 20-10 (W)
Redskins, 16-10 (StL)
1977 — Redskins, 24-14 (W)
Redskins, 26-20 (StL)
1978 — Redskins, 28-10 (StL)
Cardinals, 27-17 (W)
1979 — Redskins, 17-7 (StL)
Redskins, 30-28 (W)
1980 — Redskins, 23-0 (W)
Redskins, 31-7 (StL)
1981 — Cardinals, 40-30 (StL)
Redskins, 42-21 (W)
1982 — Redskins, 12-7 (StL)
Redskins, 28-0 (W)
1983 — Redskins, 38-14 (StL)
Redskins, 45-7 (W)
1984 — Cardinals, 26-24 (StL)
Redskins, 29-27 (W)
1985 — Redskins, 27-10 (W)
Redskins, 27-16 (StL)
1986 — Redskins, 28-21 (W)
Redskins, 20-17 (StL)
1987 — Redskins, 28-21 (W)
Redskins, 34-17 (StL)
1988 — Cardinals, 30-21 (P)
Redskins, 33-17 (W)
1989 — Redskins, 30-28 (W)
Redskins, 29-10 (P)
1990 — Redskins, 31-0 (W)
Redskins, 38-10 (P)
1991 — Redskins, 34-0 (W)
Redskins, 20-14 (P)
1992 — Cardinals, 27-24 (P)
Redskins, 41-3 (W)
(RS Pts. — Redskins 2,145, Cardinals 1,773)
**Franchise in St. Louis prior to 1988 and in Chicago prior to 1960*
***Franchise in Boston prior to 1937 and known as Braves prior to 1933*

PITTSBURGH vs. ATLANTA
RS: Steelers lead series, 8-1;
See Atlanta vs. Pittsburgh

PITTSBURGH vs. BUFFALO
RS: Bills lead series, 7-5
PS: Series tied, 1-1;
See Buffalo vs. Pittsburgh

PITTSBURGH vs. CHICAGO
RS: Bears lead series, 16-4-1;
See Chicago vs. Pittsburgh

PITTSBURGH vs. CINCINNATI
RS: Steelers lead series, 24-21;
See Cincinnati vs. Pittsburgh

PITTSBURGH vs. CLEVELAND
RS: Browns lead series, 51-35;
See Cleveland vs. Pittsburgh

PITTSBURGH vs. DALLAS
RS: Cowboys lead series, 12-11
PS: Steelers lead series, 2-0;
See Dallas vs. Pittsburgh

PITTSBURGH vs. DENVER
RS: Broncos lead series, 9-5-1
PS: Series tied, 2-2;
See Denver vs. Pittsburgh

PITTSBURGH vs. DETROIT
RS: Lions lead series, 13-11-1;
See Detroit vs. Pittsburgh

PITTSBURGH vs. GREEN BAY
RS: Packers lead series, 17-11;
See Green Bay vs. Pittsburgh

PITTSBURGH vs. HOUSTON
RS: Steelers lead series, 29-16
PS: Steelers lead series, 3-0;
See Houston vs. Pittsburgh

PITTSBURGH vs. INDIANAPOLIS
RS: Steelers lead series, 10-4
PS: Steelers lead series, 2-0;
See Indianapolis vs. Pittsburgh

PITTSBURGH vs. KANSAS CITY
RS: Steelers lead series, 13-5;
See Kansas City vs. Pittsburgh

PITTSBURGH vs. L.A. RAIDERS
RS: Raiders lead series, 7-3
PS: Series tied, 3-3;
See L.A. Raiders vs. Pittsburgh

PITTSBURGH vs. L.A. RAMS
RS: Rams lead series, 13-4-2
PS: Steelers lead series, 1-0;
See L.A. Rams vs. Pittsburgh

PITTSBURGH vs. MIAMI
RS: Dolphins lead series, 7-4
PS: Dolphins lead series, 2-1;
See Miami vs. Pittsburgh

PITTSBURGH vs. MINNESOTA
RS: Vikings lead series, 7-4
PS: Steelers lead series, 1-0;
See Minnesota vs. Pittsburgh

PITTSBURGH vs. NEW ENGLAND
RS: Steelers lead series, 8-3;
See New England vs. Pittsburgh

PITTSBURGH vs. NEW ORLEANS
RS: Series tied, 5-5;
See New Orleans vs. Pittsburgh

PITTSBURGH vs. N.Y. GIANTS
RS: Giants lead series, 42-26-3;
See N.Y. Giants vs. Pittsburgh

PITTSBURGH vs. N.Y. JETS
RS: Steelers lead series, 12-1;
See N.Y. Jets vs. Pittsburgh

PITTSBURGH vs. PHILADELPHIA
RS: Eagles lead series, 43-25-3
PS: Eagles lead series, 1-0;
See Philadelphia vs. Pittsburgh

PITTSBURGH vs. PHOENIX
RS: Steelers lead series, 29-21-3;
See Phoenix vs. Pittsburgh

PITTSBURGH vs. SAN DIEGO
RS: Steelers lead series, 13-4
PS: Chargers lead series, 1-0
1971 — Steelers, 21-17 (P)
1972 — Steelers, 24-2 (SD)
1973 — Steelers, 38-21 (P)
1975 — Steelers, 37-0 (SD)
1976 — Steelers, 23-0 (P)
1977 — Steelers, 10-9 (SD)
1979 — Chargers, 35-7 (SD)
1980 — Chargers, 26-17 (SD)
1982 — *Chargers, 31-28 (P)
1983 — Steelers, 26-3 (P)
1984 — Steelers, 52-24 (P)
1985 — Chargers, 54-44 (SD)
1987 — Steelers, 20-16 (SD)
1988 — Chargers, 20-14 (SD)
1989 — Steelers, 20-17 (P)
1990 — Steelers, 36-14 (P)
1991 — Steelers, 26-20 (P)
1992 — Steelers, 23-6 (SD)
(RS Pts. — Steelers 438, Chargers 284)
(PS Pts. — Chargers 31, Steelers 28)
**AFC First Round Playoff*

PITTSBURGH vs. SAN FRANCISCO
RS: Series tied, 7-7
1951 — 49ers, 28-24 (P)
1952 — Steelers, 24-7 (SF)
1954 — 49ers, 31-3 (SF)
1958 — 49ers, 23-20 (SF)
1961 — Steelers, 20-10 (P)
1965 — 49ers, 27-17 (SF)
1968 — 49ers, 45-28 (P)
1973 — Steelers, 37-14 (SF)
1977 — Steelers, 27-0 (P)
1978 — Steelers, 24-7 (SF)
1981 — 49ers, 17-14 (P)
1984 — Steelers, 20-17 (SF)
1987 — Steelers, 30-17 (P)
1990 — 49ers, 27-7 (SF)
(RS Pts. — Steelers 295, 49ers 270)

PITTSBURGH vs. SEATTLE
RS: Steelers lead series, 5-4
1977 — Steelers, 30-20 (P)
1978 — Steelers, 21-10 (P)
1981 — Seahawks, 24-21 (S)
1982 — Seahawks, 16-0 (S)
1983 — Steelers, 27-21 (S)
1986 — Seahawks, 30-0 (S)
1987 — Steelers, 13-9 (P)
1991 — Seahawks, 27-7 (P)
1992 — Steelers, 20-14 (P)
(RS Pts. — Seahawks 171, Steelers 139)

PITTSBURGH vs. TAMPA BAY
RS: Steelers lead series, 4-0
1976 — Steelers, 42-0 (P)
1980 — Steelers, 24-21 (TB)
1983 — Steelers, 17-12 (P)
1989 — Steelers, 31-22 (TB)
(RS Pts. — Steelers 114, Buccaneers 55)

***PITTSBURGH vs. **WASHINGTON**
RS: Redskins lead series, 42-27-3
1933 — Redskins, 21-6 (P)
Pirates, 16-14 (B)
1934 — Redskins, 7-0 (P)
Redskins, 39-0 (B)
1935 — Pirates, 6-0 (P)
Redskins, 13-3 (B)
1936 — Pirates, 10-0 (P)
Redskins, 30-0 (B)
1937 — Redskins, 34-20 (W)
Pirates, 21-13 (P)
1938 — Redskins, 7-0 (P)
Redskins, 15-0 (W)
1939 — Redskins, 44-14 (W)
Redskins, 21-14 (P)
1940 — Redskins, 40-10 (P)
Redskins, 37-10 (W)
1941 — Redskins, 24-20 (P)
Redskins, 23-3 (W)
1942 — Redskins, 28-14 (W)
Redskins, 14-0 (P)
1945 — Redskins, 14-0 (P)
Redskins, 24-0 (W)
1946 — Tie, 14-14 (W)
Steelers, 14-7 (P)
1947 — Redskins, 27-26 (W)
Steelers, 21-14 (P)
1948 — Redskins, 17-14 (W)
Steelers, 10-7 (P)
1949 — Redskins, 27-14 (P)
Redskins, 27-14 (W)
1950 — Steelers, 26-7 (W)
Redskins, 24-7 (P)
1951 — Redskins, 22-7 (P)
Steelers, 20-10 (W)
1952 — Redskins, 28-24 (P)
Steelers, 24-23 (W)
1953 — Redskins, 17-9 (P)
Steelers, 14-13 (W)
1954 — Steelers, 37-7 (P)
Redskins, 17-14 (W)
1955 — Redskins, 23-14 (P)
Redskins, 28-17 (W)
1956 — Steelers, 30-13 (P)
Steelers, 23-0 (W)
1957 — Steelers, 28-7 (P)
Redskins, 10-3 (W)
1958 — Steelers, 24-16 (P)
Tie, 14-14 (W)
1959 — Redskins, 23-17 (P)
Steelers, 27-6 (W)
1960 — Tie, 27-27 (W)
Steelers, 22-10 (P)
1961 — Steelers, 20-0 (P)
Steelers, 30-14 (W)
1962 — Steelers, 23-21 (P)
Steelers, 27-24 (W)
1963 — Steelers, 38-27 (P)
Steelers, 34-28 (W)
1964 — Redskins, 30-0 (P)
Steelers, 14-7 (W)
1965 — Redskins, 31-3 (P)
Redskins, 35-14 (W)
1966 — Redskins, 33-27 (P)
Redskins, 24-10 (W)
1967 — Redskins, 15-10 (P)
1968 — Redskins, 16-13 (W)
1969 — Redskins, 14-7 (P)
1973 — Steelers, 21-16 (P)
1979 — Steelers, 38-7 (P)
1985 — Redskins, 30-23 (P)
1988 — Redskins, 30-29 (W)
1991 — Redskins, 41-14 (P)
(RS Pts. — Redskins 1,390, Steelers 1,117)
**Steelers known as Pirates prior to 1941*
***Franchise in Boston prior to 1937*

SAN DIEGO vs. ATLANTA
RS: Falcons lead series, 3-1;
See Atlanta vs. San Diego

SAN DIEGO vs. BUFFALO
RS: Chargers lead series, 16-7-2
PS: Bills lead series, 2-1;
See Buffalo vs. San Diego

SAN DIEGO vs. CHICAGO
RS: Chargers lead series, 4-1;
See Chicago vs. San Diego

SAN DIEGO vs. CINCINNATI
RS: Chargers lead series, 12-8
PS: Bengals lead series, 1-0;
See Cincinnati vs. San Diego

SAN DIEGO vs. CLEVELAND
RS: Chargers lead series, 8-6-1;

See Cleveland vs. San Diego
SAN DIEGO vs. DALLAS
RS: Cowboys lead series, 4-1;
See Dallas vs. San Diego
SAN DIEGO vs. DENVER
RS: Broncos lead series, 34-31-1;
See Denver vs. San Diego
SAN DIEGO vs. DETROIT
RS: Lions lead series, 3-2;
See Detroit vs. San Diego
SAN DIEGO vs. GREEN BAY
RS: Packers lead series, 3-1;
See Green Bay vs. San Diego
SAN DIEGO vs. HOUSTON
RS: Chargers lead series, 17-13-1
PS: Oilers lead series, 3-0;
See Houston vs. San Diego
SAN DIEGO vs. INDIANAPOLIS
RS: Chargers lead series, 8-5;
See Indianapolis vs. San Diego
SAN DIEGO vs. KANSAS CITY
RS: Chiefs lead series, 33-31-1
PS: Chargers lead series, 1-0;
See Kansas City vs. San Diego
SAN DIEGO vs. L.A. RAIDERS
RS: Raiders lead series, 40-24-2
PS: Raiders lead series, 1-0;
See L.A. Raiders vs. San Diego
SAN DIEGO vs. L.A. RAMS
RS: Rams lead series, 3-2;
See L.A. Rams vs. San Diego
SAN DIEGO vs. MIAMI
RS: Chargers lead series, 9-5
PS: Dolphins lead series, 2-1;
See Miami vs. San Diego
SAN DIEGO vs. MINNESOTA
RS: Series tied, 3-3;
See Minnesota vs. San Diego
SAN DIEGO vs. NEW ENGLAND
RS: Patriots lead series, 13-11-2
PS: Chargers lead series, 1-0;
See New England vs. San Diego
SAN DIEGO vs. NEW ORLEANS
RS: Chargers lead series, 4-1;
See New Orleans vs. San Diego
SAN DIEGO vs. N.Y. GIANTS
RS: Giants lead series, 4-2;
See N.Y. Giants vs. San Diego
SAN DIEGO vs. N.Y. JETS
RS: Chargers lead series, 16-9-1;
See N.Y. Jets vs. San Diego
SAN DIEGO vs. PHILADELPHIA
RS: Chargers lead series, 3-2;
See Philadelphia vs. San Diego
SAN DIEGO vs. PHOENIX
RS: Chargers lead series, 5-1;
See Phoenix vs. San Diego
SAN DIEGO vs. PITTSBURGH
RS: Steelers lead series, 13-4
PS: Chargers lead series, 1-0;
See Pittsburgh vs. San Diego
SAN DIEGO vs. SAN FRANCISCO
RS: Series tied, 3-3
1972 — 49ers, 34-3 (SF)
1976 — Chargers, 13-7 (SD) OT
1979 — Chargers, 31-9 (SD)
1982 — Chargers, 41-37 (SF)
1988 — 49ers, 48-10 (SD)
1991 — 49ers, 34-14 (SF)
(RS Pts. — 49ers 169, Chargers 112)
SAN DIEGO vs. SEATTLE
RS: Series tied, 14-14
1977 — Chargers, 30-28 (S)
1978 — Chargers, 24-20 (S)
Chargers, 37-10 (SD)
1979 — Chargers, 33-16 (S)
Chargers, 20-10 (SD)
1980 — Chargers, 34-13 (S)
Chargers, 21-14 (SD)
1981 — Chargers, 24-10 (SD)
Seahawks, 44-23 (S)
1983 — Seahawks, 34-31 (S)
Chargers, 28-21 (SD)
1984 — Seahawks, 31-17 (S)
Seahawks, 24-0 (SD)
1985 — Seahawks, 49-35 (SD)
Seahawks, 26-21 (S)
1986 — Seahawks, 33-7 (S)
Seahawks, 34-24 (SD)
1987 — Seahawks, 34-3 (S)
1988 — Chargers, 17-6 (SD)
Seahawks, 17-14 (S)
1989 — Seahawks, 17-16 (SD)
Seahawks, 10-7 (S)
1990 — Chargers, 31-14 (S)
Seahawks, 13-10 (SD) OT
1991 — Seahawks, 20-9 (S)
Chargers, 17-14 (SD)
1992 — Chargers, 17-6 (SD)
Chargers, 31-14 (S)
(RS Pts. — Seahawks 582, Chargers 581)
SAN DIEGO vs. TAMPA BAY
RS: Chargers lead series, 5-0
1976 — Chargers, 23-0 (TB)
1981 — Chargers, 24-23 (TB)
1987 — Chargers, 17-13 (TB)
1990 — Chargers, 41-10 (SD)
1992 — Chargers, 29-14 (SD)
(RS Pts. — Chargers 134, Buccaneers 60)
SAN DIEGO vs. WASHINGTON
RS: Redskins lead series, 5-0
1973 — Redskins, 38-0 (W)
1980 — Redskins, 40-17 (W)
1983 — Redskins, 27-24 (SD)
1986 — Redskins, 30-27 (SD)
1989 — Redskins, 26-21 (W)
(RS Pts. — Redskins 161, Chargers 89)

SAN FRANCISCO vs. ATLANTA
RS: 49ers lead series, 31-20-1;
See Atlanta vs. San Francisco
SAN FRANCISCO vs. BUFFALO
RS: Bills lead series, 3-2;
See Buffalo vs. San Francisco
SAN FRANCISCO vs. CHICAGO
RS: Series tied, 25-25-1
PS: 49ers lead series, 2-0;
See Chicago vs. San Francisco
SAN FRANCISCO vs. CINCINNATI
RS: 49ers lead series, 5-1
PS: 49ers lead series, 2-0;
See Cincinnati vs. San Francisco
SAN FRANCISCO vs. CLEVELAND
RS: Browns lead series, 8-6;
See Cleveland vs. San Francisco
SAN FRANCISCO vs. DALLAS
RS: 49ers lead series, 9-5-1
PS: Cowboys lead series, 4-1;
See Dallas vs. San Francisco
SAN FRANCISCO vs. DENVER
RS: Broncos lead series, 4-2
PS: 49ers lead series, 1-0;
See Denver vs. San Francisco
SAN FRANCISCO vs. DETROIT
RS: Series tied, 25-25-1
PS: Series tied, 1-1;
See Detroit vs. San Francisco
SAN FRANCISCO vs. GREEN BAY
RS: 49ers lead series, 25-21-1;
See Green Bay vs. San Francisco
SAN FRANCISCO vs. HOUSTON
RS: 49ers lead series, 5-2;
See Houston vs. San Francisco
SAN FRANCISCO vs. INDIANAPOLIS
RS: Colts lead series, 21-16;
See Indianapolis vs. San Francisco
SAN FRANCISCO vs. KANSAS CITY
RS: 49ers lead series, 4-1;
See Kansas City vs. San Francisco
SAN FRANCISCO vs. L.A RAIDERS
RS: Raiders lead series, 5-2;
See L.A. Raiders vs. San Francisco
SAN FRANCISCO vs. L.A. RAMS
RS: Rams lead series, 48-36-2
PS: 49ers lead series, 1-0;
See L.A. Rams vs. San Francisco
SAN FRANCISCO vs. MIAMI
RS: Dolphins lead series, 4-2
PS: 49ers lead series, 1-0;
See Miami vs. San Francisco
SAN FRANCISCO vs. MINNESOTA
RS: Vikings lead series, 15-14-1
PS: 49ers lead series, 3-1;
See Minnesota vs. San Francisco
SAN FRANCISCO vs. NEW ENGLAND
RS: 49ers lead series, 6-1;
See New England vs. San Francisco
SAN FRANCISCO vs. NEW ORLEANS
RS: 49ers lead series, 32-13-2;
See New Orleans vs. San Francisco
SAN FRANCISCO vs. N.Y. GIANTS
RS: Giants lead series, 11-10
PS: Giants lead series, 3-2;
See N.Y. Giants vs. San Francisco
SAN FRANCISCO vs. N.Y. JETS
RS: 49ers lead series, 6-1;
See N.Y. Jets vs. San Francisco
SAN FRANCISCO vs. PHILADELPHIA
RS: 49ers lead series, 13-4-1;
See Philadelphia vs. San Francisco
SAN FRANCISCO vs. PHOENIX
RS: Series tied, 9-9;
See Phoenix vs. San Francisco
SAN FRANCISCO vs. PITTSBURGH
RS: Series tied, 7-7;
See Pittsburgh vs. San Francisco
SAN FRANCISCO vs. SAN DIEGO
RS: Series tied, 3-3;
See San Diego vs. San Francisco
SAN FRANCISCO vs. SEATTLE
RS: 49ers lead series, 4-1
1976 — 49ers, 37-21 (S)
1979 — Seahawks, 35-24 (SF)
1985 — 49ers, 19-6 (SF)
1988 — 49ers, 38-7 (S)
1991 — 49ers, 24-22 (S)
(RS Pts. — 49ers 142, Seahawks 91)
SAN FRANCISCO vs. TAMPA BAY
RS: 49ers lead series, 10-1
1977 — 49ers, 20-10 (SF)
1978 — 49ers, 6-3 (SF)
1979 — 49ers, 23-7 (SF)
1980 — Buccaneers, 24-23 (SF)
1983 — 49ers, 35-21 (SF)
1984 — 49ers, 24-17 (SF)
1986 — 49ers, 31-7 (TB)
1987 — 49ers, 24-10 (TB)
1989 — 49ers, 20-16 (TB)
1990 — 49ers, 31-7 (SF)
1992 — 49ers, 21-14 (SF)
(RS. Pts. — 49ers 258, Buccaneers 136)
SAN FRANCISCO vs. WASHINGTON
RS: 49ers lead series, 9-6-1
PS: 49ers lead series, 3-1
1952 — 49ers, 23-17 (W)
1954 — 49ers, 41-7 (SF)
1955 — Redskins, 7-0 (W)
1961 — 49ers, 35-3 (SF)
1967 — Redskins, 31-28 (W)
1969 — Tie, 17-17 (SF)
1970 — 49ers, 26-17 (SF)
1971 — *49ers, 24-20 (SF)
1973 — Redskins, 33-9 (W)
1976 — Redskins, 24-21 (SF)
1978 — Redskins, 38-20 (W)
1981 — 49ers, 30-17 (W)
1983 — **Redskins, 24-21 (W)
1984 — 49ers, 37-31 (SF)
1985 — 49ers, 35-8 (W)
1986 — Redskins, 14-6 (W)
1988 — 49ers, 37-21 (SF)
1990 — 49ers, 26-13 (SF)
*49ers, 28-10 (SF)
1992 — *49ers, 20-13 (SF)
(RS Pts. — 49ers 391, Redskins 298)
(PS Pts. — 49ers 93, Redskins 67)
**NFC Divisional Playoff*
***NFC Championship*

SEATTLE vs. ATLANTA
RS: Seahawks lead series, 4-1;
See Atlanta vs. Seattle
SEATTLE vs. BUFFALO
RS: Seahawks lead series, 3-1;
See Buffalo vs. Seattle
SEATTLE vs. CHICAGO
RS: Seahawks lead series, 4-2;
See Chicago vs. Seattle
SEATTLE vs. CINCINNATI
RS: Bengals lead series, 6-5
PS: Bengals lead series, 1-0;
See Cincinnati vs. Seattle
SEATTLE vs. CLEVELAND
RS: Seahawks lead series, 8-3;
See Cleveland vs. Seattle
SEATTLE vs. DALLAS
RS: Cowboys lead series, 4-1;
See Dallas vs. Seattle
SEATTLE vs. DENVER
RS: Broncos lead series, 18-13
PS: Seahawks lead series, 1-0;
See Denver vs. Seattle
SEATTLE vs. DETROIT
RS: Seahawks lead series, 4-1;
See Detroit vs. Seattle
SEATTLE vs. GREEN BAY
RS: Series tied, 3-3;
See Green Bay vs. Seattle
SEATTLE vs. HOUSTON
RS: Seahawks lead series, 4-3
PS: Oilers lead series, 1-0;
See Houston vs. Seattle
SEATTLE vs. INDIANAPOLIS
RS: Colts lead series, 2-1;
See Indianapolis vs. Seattle
SEATTLE vs. KANSAS CITY
RS: Chiefs lead series, 17-12;
See Kansas City vs. Seattle
SEATTLE vs. L.A. RAIDERS
RS: Raiders lead series, 16-14
PS: Series tied, 1-1;
See L.A. Raiders vs. Seattle
SEATTLE vs. L.A. RAMS
RS: Rams lead series, 4-1;
See L.A. Rams vs. Seattle
SEATTLE vs. MIAMI
RS: Dolphins lead series, 4-1
PS: Series tied, 1-1;
See Miami vs. Seattle
SEATTLE vs. MINNESOTA
RS: Seahawks lead series, 3-2;
See Minnesota vs. Seattle
SEATTLE vs. NEW ENGLAND
RS: Patriots lead series, 6-5;
See New England vs. Seattle
SEATTLE vs. NEW ORLEANS
RS: Saints lead series, 3-2;
See New Orleans vs. Seattle
SEATTLE vs. N.Y. GIANTS
RS: Giants lead series, 5-2;
See N.Y. Giants vs. Seattle
SEATTLE vs. N.Y. JETS
RS: Seahawks lead series, 8-3;
See N.Y. Jets vs. Seattle
SEATTLE vs. PHILADELPHIA
RS: Eagles lead series, 4-1;
See Philadelphia vs. Seattle
SEATTLE vs. PHOENIX
RS: Cardinals lead series, 3-0;
See Phoenix vs. Seattle
SEATTLE vs. PITTSBURGH
RS: Steelers lead series, 5-4;
See Pittsburgh vs. Seattle
SEATTLE vs. SAN DIEGO
RS: Series tied, 14-14;
See San Diego vs. Seattle
SEATTLE vs. SAN FRANCISCO
RS: 49ers lead series, 4-1;
See San Francisco vs. Seattle
SEATTLE vs. TAMPA BAY
RS: Seahawks lead series, 2-0
1976 — Seahawks, 13-10 (TB)
1977 — Seahawks, 30-23 (S)
(RS Pts. — Seahawks 43, Buccaneers 33)
SEATTLE vs. WASHINGTON
RS: Redskins lead series, 5-1
1976 — Redskins, 31-7 (W)
1980 — Seahawks, 14-0 (W)
1983 — Redskins, 27-17 (S)
1986 — Redskins, 19-14 (W)
1989 — Redskins, 29-0 (S)
1992 — Redskins, 16-3 (S)
(RS Pts. — Redskins 122, Seahawks 55)

TAMPA BAY vs. ATLANTA
RS: Falcons lead series, 6-5;
See Atlanta vs. Tampa Bay
TAMPA BAY vs. BUFFALO
RS: Buccaneers lead series, 4-2;
See Buffalo vs. Tampa Bay
TAMPA BAY vs. CHICAGO
RS: Bears lead series, 23-7;
See Chicago vs. Tampa Bay
TAMPA BAY vs. CINCINNATI
RS: Bengals lead series, 3-1;
See Cincinnati vs. Tampa Bay
TAMPA BAY vs. CLEVELAND
RS: Browns lead series, 4-0;
See Cleveland vs. Tampa Bay
TAMPA BAY vs. DALLAS
RS: Cowboys lead series, 6-0
PS: Cowboys lead series, 2-0;
See Dallas vs. Tampa Bay
TAMPA BAY vs. DENVER
RS: Broncos lead series, 2-0;
See Denver vs. Tampa Bay
TAMPA BAY vs. DETROIT
RS: Series tied, 15-15;
See Detroit vs. Tampa Bay
TAMPA BAY vs. GREEN BAY
RS: Packers lead series, 15-12-1;
See Green Bay vs. Tampa Bay
TAMPA BAY vs. HOUSTON
RS: Oilers lead series, 3-1;
See Houston vs. Tampa Bay
TAMPA BAY vs. INDIANAPOLIS
RS: Colts lead series, 5-2;
See Indianapolis vs. Tampa Bay
TAMPA BAY vs. KANSAS CITY
RS: Chiefs lead series, 4-2;
See Kansas City vs. Tampa Bay
TAMPA BAY vs. L.A RAIDERS
RS: Raiders lead series, 2-0;
See L.A. Raiders vs. Tampa Bay
TAMPA BAY vs. L.A. RAMS
RS: Rams lead series, 8-2
PS: Rams lead series, 1-0;
See L.A. Rams vs. Tampa Bay
TAMPA BAY vs. MIAMI
RS: Dolphins lead series, 4-1;
See Miami vs. Tampa Bay
TAMPA BAY vs. MINNESOTA
RS: Vikings lead series, 22-8;
See Minnesota vs. Tampa Bay
TAMPA BAY vs. NEW ENGLAND
RS: Patriots lead series, 3-0;
See New England vs. Tampa Bay
TAMPA BAY vs. NEW ORLEANS
RS: Saints lead series, 11-4;
See New Orleans vs. Tampa Bay
TAMPA BAY vs. N.Y. GIANTS
RS: Giants lead series, 7-3;
See N.Y. Giants vs. Tampa Bay
TAMPA BAY vs. N.Y. JETS
RS: Jets lead series, 5-1;
See N.Y. Jets vs. Tampa Bay
TAMPA BAY vs. PHILADELPHIA
RS: Eagles lead series, 3-1
PS: Buccaneers lead series, 1-0;
See Philadelphia vs. Tampa Bay
TAMPA BAY vs. PHOENIX
RS: Series tied, 6-6;

See Phoenix vs. Tampa Bay
TAMPA BAY vs. PITTSBURGH
RS: Steelers lead series, 4-0;
See Pittsburgh vs. Tampa Bay
TAMPA BAY vs. SAN DIEGO
RS: Chargers lead series, 5-0;
See San Diego vs. Tampa Bay
TAMPA BAY vs. SAN FRANCISCO
RS: 49ers lead series, 10-1;
See San Francisco vs. Tampa Bay
TAMPA BAY vs. SEATTLE
RS: Seahawks lead series, 2-0;
See Seattle vs. Tampa Bay
TAMPA BAY vs. WASHINGTON
RS: Redskins lead series, 3-0
1977 — Redskins, 10-0 (TB)
1982 — Redskins, 21-13 (TB)
1989 — Redskins, 32-28 (W)
(RS Pts. — Redskins 63, Buccaneers 41)

WASHINGTON vs. ATLANTA
RS: Redskins lead series, 12-3-1
PS: Redskins lead series, 1-0;
See Atlanta vs. Washington
WASHINGTON vs. BUFFALO
RS: Redskins lead series, 4-2
PS: Redskins lead series, 1-0;
See Buffalo vs. Washington
WASHINGTON vs. CHICAGO
RS: Bears lead series, 18-12-1
PS: Redskins lead series, 4-3;
See Chicago vs. Washington
WASHINGTON vs. CINCINNATI
RS: Redskins lead series, 4-2;
See Cincinnati vs. Washington
WASHINGTON vs. CLEVELAND
RS: Browns lead series, 32-9-1;
See Cleveland vs. Washington
WASHINGTON vs. DALLAS
RS: Cowboys lead series, 36-26-2
PS: Redskins lead series, 2-0;
See Dallas vs. Washington
WASHINGTON vs. DENVER
RS: Series tied, 3-3
PS: Redskins lead series, 1-0;
See Denver vs. Washington
WASHINGTON vs. DETROIT
RS: Redskins lead series, 22-8
PS: Redskins lead series, 2-0;
See Detroit vs. Washington
WASHINGTON vs. GREEN BAY
RS: Packers lead series, 13-12-1
PS: Series tied, 1-1;
See Green Bay vs. Washington
WASHINGTON vs. HOUSTON
RS: Series tied, 3-3;
See Houston vs. Washington
WASHINGTON vs. INDIANAPOLIS
RS: Colts lead series, 16-6;
See Indianapolis vs. Washington
WASHINGTON vs. KANSAS CITY
RS: Chiefs lead series, 3-1;
See Kansas City vs. Washington
WASHINGTON vs. L.A. RAIDERS
RS: Raiders lead series, 5-2
PS: Raiders lead series, 1-0;
See L.A. Raiders vs. Washington
WASHINGTON vs. L.A. RAMS
RS: Redskins lead series, 14-4-1
PS: Series tied, 2-2;
See L.A. Rams vs. Washington
WASHINGTON vs. MIAMI
RS: Dolphins lead series, 4-2
PS: Series tied, 1-1;
See Miami vs. Washington
WASHINGTON vs. MINNESOTA
RS: Redskins lead series, 6-3
PS: Redskins lead series, 3-2;
See Minnesota vs. Washington
WASHINGTON vs. NEW ENGLAND
RS: Redskins lead series, 4-1;
See New England vs. Washington
WASHINGTON vs. NEW ORLEANS
RS: Redskins lead series, 11-5;
See New Orleans vs. Washington
WASHINGTON vs. N.Y. GIANTS
RS: Giants lead series, 67-50-3
PS: Series tied, 1-1;
See N.Y. Giants vs. Washington
WASHINGTON vs. N.Y. JETS
RS: Redskins lead series, 4-0;
See N.Y. Jets vs. Washington
WASHINGTON vs. PHILADELPHIA
RS: Redskins lead series, 66-44-5
PS: Redskins lead series, 1-0;
See Philadelphia vs. Washington
WASHINGTON vs. PHOENIX
RS: Redskins lead series, 61-34-2;
See Phoenix vs. Washington
WASHINGTON vs. PITTSBURGH
RS: Redskins lead series, 42-27-3;
See Pittsburgh vs. Washington
WASHINGTON vs. SAN DIEGO
RS: Redskins lead series, 5-0;
See San Diego vs. Washington
WASHINGTON vs. SAN FRANCISCO
RS: 49ers lead series, 9-6-1
PS: 49ers lead series, 3-1;
See San Francisco vs. Washington
WASHINGTON vs. SEATTLE
RS: Redskins lead series, 5-1;
See Seattle vs. Washington
WASHINGTON vs. TAMPA BAY
RS: Redskins lead series, 3-0;
See Tampa Bay vs. Washington

Results

Season	Date	Winner (Share)	Loser (Share)	Score	Site	Attendance
XXVII	1-31-93	Dallas ($36,000)	Buffalo ($18,000)	52-17	Pasadena	98,374
XXVI	1-26-92	Washington ($36,000)	Buffalo ($18,000)	37-24	Minneapolis	63,130
XXV	1-27-91	N.Y. Giants ($36,000)	Buffalo ($18,000)	20-19	Tampa	73,813
XXIV	1-28-90	San Francisco ($36,000)	Denver ($18,000)	55-10	New Orleans	72,919
XXIII	1-22-89	San Francisco ($36,000)	Cincinnati ($18,000)	20-16	Miami	75,129
XXII	1-31-88	Washington ($36,000)	Denver ($18,000)	42-10	San Diego	73,302
XXI	1-25-87	N.Y. Giants ($36,000)	Denver ($18,000)	39-20	Pasadena	101,063
XX	1-26-86	Chicago ($36,000)	New England ($18,000)	46-10	New Orleans	73,818
XIX	1-20-85	San Francisco ($36,000)	Miami ($18,000)	38-16	Stanford	84,059
XVIII	1-22-84	L.A. Raiders ($36,000)	Washington ($18,000)	38-9	Tampa	72,920
XVII	1-30-83	Washington ($36,000)	Miami ($18,000)	27-17	Pasadena	103,667
XVI	1-24-82	San Francisco ($18,000)	Cincinnati ($9,000)	26-21	Pontiac	81,270
XV	1-25-81	Oakland ($18,000)	Philadelphia ($9,000)	27-10	New Orleans	76,135
XIV	1-20-80	Pittsburgh ($18,000)	Los Angeles ($9,000)	31-19	Pasadena	103,985
XIII	1-21-79	Pittsburgh ($18,000)	Dallas ($9,000)	35-31	Miami	79,484
XII	1-15-78	Dallas ($18,000)	Denver ($9,000)	27-10	New Orleans	75,583
XI	1-9-77	Oakland ($15,000)	Minnesota ($7,500)	32-14	Pasadena	103,438
X	1-18-76	Pittsburgh ($15,000)	Dallas ($7,500)	21-17	Miami	80,187
IX	1-12-75	Pittsburgh ($15,000)	Minnesota ($7,500)	16-6	New Orleans	80,997
VIII	1-13-74	Miami ($15,000)	Minnesota ($7,500)	24-7	Houston	71,882
VII	1-14-73	Miami ($15,000)	Washington ($7,500)	14-7	Los Angeles	90,182
VI	1-16-72	Dallas ($15,000)	Miami ($7,500)	24-3	New Orleans	81,023
V	1-17-71	Baltimore ($15,000)	Dallas ($7,500)	16-13	Miami	79,204
IV	1-11-70	Kansas City ($15,000)	Minnesota ($7,500)	23-7	New Orleans	80,562
III	1-12-69	N.Y. Jets ($15,000)	Baltimore ($7,500)	16-7	Miami	75,389
II	1-14-68	Green Bay ($15,000)	Oakland ($7,500)	33-14	Miami	75,546
I	1-15-67	Green Bay ($15,000)	Kansas City ($7,500)	35-10	Los Angeles	61,946

Super Bowl Composite Standings

	W	L	Pct.	Pts.	OP
Pittsburgh Steelers	4	0	1.000	103	73
San Francisco 49ers	4	0	1.000	139	63
Green Bay Packers	2	0	1.000	68	24
New York Giants	2	0	1.000	59	39
Chicago Bears	1	0	1.000	46	10
New York Jets	1	0	1.000	16	7
Oakland/L.A. Raiders	3	1	.750	111	66
Washington Redskins	3	2	.600	122	103
Dallas Cowboys	3	3	.500	164	102
Baltimore Colts	1	1	.500	23	29
Kansas City Chiefs	1	1	.500	33	42
Miami Dolphins	2	3	.400	74	103
Los Angeles Rams	0	1	.000	19	31
New England Patriots	0	1	.000	10	46
Philadelphia Eagles	0	1	.000	10	27
Cincinnati Bengals	0	2	.000	37	46
Buffalo Bills	0	3	.000	60	109
Denver Broncos	0	4	.000	50	163
Minnesota Vikings	0	4	.000	34	95

Past Super Bowl Most Valuable Players

Super Bowl I — QB Bart Starr, Green Bay
Super Bowl II — QB Bart Starr, Green Bay
Super Bowl III — QB Joe Namath, New York Jets
Super Bowl IV — QB Len Dawson, Kansas City
Super Bowl V — LB Chuck Howley, Dallas
Super Bowl VI — QB Roger Staubach, Dallas
Super Bowl VII — S Jake Scott, Miami
Super Bowl VIII — RB Larry Csonka, Miami
Super Bowl IX — RB Franco Harris, Pittsburgh
Super Bowl X — WR Lynn Swann, Pittsburgh
Super Bowl XI — WR Fred Biletnikoff, Oakland
Super Bowl XII — DT Randy White and DE Harvey Martin, Dallas
Super Bowl XIII — QB Terry Bradshaw, Pittsburgh
Super Bowl XIV — QB Terry Bradshaw, Pittsburgh
Super Bowl XV — QB Jim Plunkett, Oakland
Super Bowl XVI — QB Joe Montana, San Francisco
Super Bowl XVII — RB John Riggins, Washington
Super Bowl XVIII — RB Marcus Allen, Los Angeles Raiders
Super Bowl XIX — QB Joe Montana, San Francisco
Super Bowl XX — DE Richard Dent, Chicago
Super Bowl XXI — QB Phil Simms, New York Giants
Super Bowl XXII — QB Doug Williams, Washington
Super Bowl XXIII — WR Jerry Rice, San Francisco
Super Bowl XXIV — QB Joe Montana, San Francisco
Super Bowl XXV — RB Ottis Anderson, New York Giants
Super Bowl XXVI — QB Mark Rypien, Washington
Super Bowl XXVII — QB Troy Aikman, Dallas Cowboys

Super Bowl XXVII

Rose Bowl, Pasadena, California — January 31, 1993
Attendance: 98,374

DALLAS 52, BUFFALO 17 — Troy Aikman threw 4 touchdown passes, Emmitt Smith rushed for 108 yards, and the Cowboys converted 9 turnovers into 35 points while coasting to the victory. Dallas's win was its third in its record sixth Super Bowl appearance; the Bills became the first team to drop three in succession. Buffalo led 7-0 until the first 2 of its record number of turnovers helped the Cowboys take the lead for good late in the opening quarter. First, Dallas safety James Washington intercepted a Jim Kelly pass and returned it 13 yards to the Bills' 47, setting up Aikman's 23-yard touchdown pass to tight end Jay Novacek with 1:36 remaining in the period. On the next play from scrimmage, Kelly was sacked by Charles Haley and fumbled at the Bills' 2-yard line where the Cowboys' Jimmie Jones picked up the loose ball and ran 2 yards for a touchdown. Dallas, which recovered 5 fumbles and intercepted 4 passes, struck just as quickly late in the first half, when Aikman tossed 19- and 18-yard touchdown passes to Michael Irvin 15 seconds apart to give the Cowboys a 28-10 lead at intermission. The second score was set up when Bills running back Thurman Thomas lost a fumble at his 19-yard line. Buffalo scored for the last time when backup quarterback Frank Reich, playing because Kelly was injured while attempting to pass midway through the second quarter, threw a 40-yard touchdown pass to Don Beebe on the final play of the third period to trim the deficit to 31-17. But Dallas put the game out of reach by scoring three times in a span of 2:33 of the fourth quarter. Aikman, the game's most valuable player, completed 22 of 30 passes for 273 yards and was not intercepted. Novacek caught 7 passes and Smith and Irvin had 6 each. The Bills' Andre Reed had 8 receptions for 152 yards. The victory was the ninth in succession for the NFC over AFC teams in the Super Bowl.

Buffalo (17)	Offense	Dallas (52)
James Lofton	WR	Alvin Harper
Will Wolford	LT	Mark Tuinei
Jim Ritcher	LG	Nate Newton
Kent Hull	C	Mark Stepnoski
Glenn Parker	RG	John Gesek
Howard Ballard	RT	Erik Williams
Pete Metzelaars	TE	Jay Novacek
Andre Reed	WR	Michael Irvin
Jim Kelly	QB	Troy Aikman
Thurman Thomas	RB	Emmitt Smith
Don Beebe	WR-RB	Daryl Johnston
	Defense	
Phil Hansen	LE	Tony Tolbert
Jeff Wright	NT-LT	Tony Casillas
Bruce Smith	RE-RT	Russell Maryland
Marvcus Patton	LOLB-RE	Charles Haley
Shane Conlan	LILB-LLB	Vinson Smith
Cornelius Bennett	RILB-MLB	Robert Jones
Darryl Talley	ROLB-RLB	Ken Norton
James Williams	LCB	Kevin Smith
Nate Odomes	RCB	Larry Brown
Henry Jones	SS	Thomas Everett
Mark Kelso	FS	James Washington

Substitutions

Buffalo — Offense: K — Steve Christie. P — Chris Mohr. QB — Frank Reich. RB — Kenneth Davis, Carwell Gardner. WR — Brad Lamb, Steve Tasker. TE — Rob Awalt, Keith McKeller. T — John Fina. G — John Davis, Mitch Frerotte. C — Adam Lingner. Defense: E — Mark Pike. T — Mike Lodish. LB — Carlton Bailey, Keith Goganious, Mark Maddox. CB — Chris Hale, Clifford Hicks, Kirby Jackson. S — Matt Darby. DNP: DE — Keith Willis. Inactive: QB — Gale Gilbert. S — Kurt Schulz.

Dallas — Offense: K — Lin Elliott. P — Mike Saxon. QB — Steve Beuerlein. RB — Tommie Agee, Derrick Gainer. WR — Kelvin Martin, Jimmy Smith. TE — Derek Tennell. G — Kevin Gogan. C — Frank Cornish, Dale Hellestrae. Defense: E — Jim Jeffcoat. T — Chad Hennings, Jimmie Jones, Leon Lett. LB — Dixon Edwards, Godfrey Myles, Mickey Pruitt. CB — Clayton Holmes, Issiac Holt. S — Kenneth Gant, Ray Horton, Darren Woodson. DNP: None. Inactive: T — Alan Veingrad. S — Robert Williams.

Officials

Referee — Dick Hantak. Umpire — Ron Botchan. Head Linesman — Ron Phares. Line Judge — Dick McKenzie. Back Judge — Jim Poole. Field Judge — Donnie Hampton. Side Judge — Dean Look.

Scoring

Buffalo (AFC)	7	3	7	0	— 17
Dallas (NFC)	14	14	3	21	— 52

Buff — Thomas 2 run (Christie kick)
Dall — Novacek 23 pass from Aikman (Elliott kick)
Dall — J. Jones 2 fumble recovery return (Elliott kick)
Buff — FG Christie 21
Dall — Irvin 19 pass from Aikman (Elliott kick)
Dall — Irvin 18 pass from Aikman (Elliott kick)
Dall — FG Elliott 20
Buff — Beebe 40 pass from Reich (Christie kick)
Dall — Harper 45 pass from Aikman (Elliott kick)
Dall — E. Smith 10 run (Elliott kick)
Dall — Norton 9 fumble recovery return (Elliott kick)

Team Statistics

	Buffalo	Dallas
Total First Downs	22	20
First Downs Rushing	7	9
First Downs Passing	11	11
First Downs Penalty	4	0
Total Net Yardage	362	408
Total Offensive Plays	71	60
Average Gain per Offensive Play	5.1	6.8
Rushes	29	29
Yards Gained Rushing (Net)	108	137
Average Yards per Rush	3.7	4.7
Passes Attempted	38	30
Passes Completed	22	22
Had Intercepted	4	0
Tackled Attempting to Pass	4	1
Yards Lost Attempting to Pass	22	2
Yards Gained Passing (Net)	254	271
Punts	3	4
Average Distance	45.3	32.8
Punt Returns	1	3
Punt Return Yardage	0	35
Kickoff Returns	4	4
Kickoff Return Yardage	90	79
Interception Return Yardage	0	35
Total Return Yardage	90	149
Fumbles	8	4
Own Fumbles Recovered	3	2
Opponent Fumbles Recovered	2	5
Penalties	4	8
Yards Penalized	30	53
Total Points Scored	17	52
Touchdowns	2	7
Touchdowns Rushing	1	1
Touchdowns Passing	1	4
Touchdowns Returns	0	2
Extra Points	2	7
Field Goals	1	1
Field Goals Attempted	1	1
Safeties	0	0
Third Down Efficiency	5/11	5/11
Fourth Down Efficiency	0/2	0/1
Time of Possession	28:48	31:12

Individual Statistics

Rushing

Buffalo	No.	Yds.	LG	TD
K. Davis	15	86	14	0
Thomas	11	19	9	1
Gardner	1	3	3	0
Reich	2	0	0	0
Dallas	**No.**	**Yds.**	**LG**	**TD**
E. Smith	22	108	38	1
Aikman	3	28	19	0
Gainer	2	1	1	0
Beuerlein	1	0	0	0
Johnston	1	0	0	0

Passing

Buff.	Att.	Comp.	Yds.	TD	Int.
Reich	31	18	194	1	2
Kelly	7	4	82	0	2
Dallas	**Att.**	**Comp.**	**Yds.**	**TD**	**Int.**
Aikman	30	22	273	4	0

Receiving

Buffalo	No.	Yds.	LG	TD
Reed	8	152	40	0
Thomas	4	10	7	0
K. Davis	3	16	13	0
Beebe	2	50	40t	1
Tasker	2	30	16	0
Metzelaars	2	12	7	0
McKeller	1	6	6	0
Dallas	**No.**	**Yds.**	**LG**	**TD**
Novacek	7	72	23t	1
Irvin	6	114	25	2
E. Smith	6	27	18	0
Johnston	2	15	8	0
Harper	1	45	45t	1

Interceptions

Buffalo	No.	Yds.	LG	TD
None				
Dallas	**No.**	**Yds.**	**LG**	**TD**
Everett	2	22	22	0
Washington	1	13	13	0
Brown	1	0	0	0

Punting

Buffalo	No.	Avg.	LG	Blk.
Mohr	3	45.3	48	0
Dallas	**No.**	**Avg.**	**LG**	**Blk.**
Saxon	3	43.7	57	1

Punt Returns

Buffalo	No.	FC	Yds.	LG	TD
Hicks	1	1	0	0	0
Dallas	**No.**	**FC**	**Yds.**	**LG**	**TD**
Martin	3	0	35	30	0

Kickoff Returns

Buffalo	No.	Yds.	LG	TD
Lamb	2	49	33	0
K. Davis	1	21	21	0
Hick	1	20	20	0
Dallas	**No.**	**Yds.**	**LG**	**TD**
Martin	4	79	22	0

Super Bowl XXVI

Metrodome, Minneapolis, Minnesota — January 26, 1992

Attendance: 63,130

WASHINGTON 37, BUFFALO 24 — Mark Rypien passed for 292 yards and 2 touchdowns as the Redskins overwhelmed the Bills to win their third Super Bowl in the past 10 years. Rypien, the game's most valuable player, completed 18 of 33 passes, including a 10-yard scoring strike to Earnest Byner and a 30-yard touchdown to Gary Clark. The latter came late in the third quarter after Buffalo had trimmed a 24-0 deficit to 24-10, and effectively put the game out of reach. Washington went on to lead by as much as 37-10 before the Bills made it close with a pair of touchdowns in the final six minutes. Though the Redskins struggled early, converting their first three drives inside the Bills' 20-yard line into only 3 points, they built a 17-0 halftime lead. And they made it 24-0 just 16 seconds into the second half, after Kurt Gouveia intercepted Buffalo quarterback Jim Kelly's pass on the first play of the third quarter and returned it 23 yards to the Bills' 2. One play later, Gerald Riggs scored his second touchdown of the game to make it 24-0. Kelly, forced to bring Buffalo from behind, completed 28 of a Super Bowl-record 58 passes for 275 yards and 2 touchdowns, but was intercepted 4 times. Bills running back Thurman Thomas, who had an AFC-high 1,407 yards rushing and an NFL-best 2,038 total yards from scrimmage during the regular season, ran for only 13 yards on 10 carries and was limited to 27 yards on 4 receptions. Clark had 7 catches for 114 yards and Art Monk added 7 for 113 for the Redskins, who amassed 417 yards of total offense while limiting the explosive Bills to 283. Washington's Joe Gibbs became only the third head coach to win as many as three Super Bowls.

Washington (NFC)	0	17	14	6	— 37
Buffalo (AFC)	0	0	10	14	— 24

Wash — FG Lohmiller 34
Wash — Byner 10 pass from Rypien (Lohmiller kick)
Wash — Riggs 1 run (Lohmiller kick)
Wash — Riggs 2 run (Lohmiller kick)
Buff — FG Norwood 21
Buff — Thomas 1 run (Norwood kick)
Wash — Clark 30 pass from Rypien (Lohmiller kick)
Wash — FG Lohmiller 25
Wash — FG Lohmiller 39
Buff — Metzelaars 2 pass from Kelly (Norwood kick)
Buff — Beebe 4 pass from Kelly (Norwood kick)

Super Bowl XXV

Tampa Stadium, Tampa, Florida — January 27, 1991

Attendance: 73,813

NEW YORK GIANTS 20, BUFFALO 19 — The NFC champion New York Giants won their second Super Bowl in five years with a 20-19 victory over AFC titlist Buffalo. New York, employing its ball-control offense, had possession for 40 minutes, 33 seconds, a Super Bowl record. The Bills, who scored 95 points in their previous two playoff games leading to Super Bowl XXV, had the ball for less than eight minutes in the second half and just 19:27 for the game. Fourteen of New York's 73 plays came on its initial drive of the third quarter, which covered 75 yards and consumed a Super Bowl-record 9:29 before running back Ottis Anderson ran one yard for a touchdown. Giants quarterback Jeff Hostetler kept the long drive going by converting three third-down plays — an

11-yard pass to running back David Meggett on third-and-eight, a 14-yard toss to wide receiver Mark Ingram on third-and-13, and a nine-yard pass to Howard Cross on third-and-four—to give New York a 17-12 lead in the third quarter. Buffalo jumped to a 12-3 lead midway through the second quarter before Hostetler completed a 14-yard scoring strike to wide receiver Stephen Baker to close the score to 12-10 at halftime. Buffalo's Thurman Thomas ran 31 yards for a touchdown on the opening play of the fourth quarter to help Buffalo recapture the lead 19-17. Giants kicker Matt Bahr's 21-yard field goal gave the Giants a 20-19 lead, but Buffalo's Scott Norwood had a chance to win the game with seconds remaining before his 47-yard field-goal attempt sailed wide right. Hostetler completed 20 of 32 passes for 222 yards and one touchdown for the game. Wide receiver Mark Ingram caught five passes for 74 yards; tight end Mark Bavaro five for 50. Anderson rushed 21 times for 102 yards and one touchdown to capture the most-valuable-player honors. Thomas totaled 190 scrimmage yards, rushing 15 times for 135 yards and catching five passes for 55 yards.

Buffalo (AFC)	3	9	0	7	— 19
N.Y. Giants (NFC)	3	7	7	3	— 20

NYG—FG Bahr 28
Buff —FG Norwood 23
Buff —D. Smith, 1 run (Norwood kick)
Buff —Safety, B. Smith (tackled Hostetler in end zone)
NYG—Baker 14 pass from Hostetler (Bahr kick)
NYG—Anderson 1 run (Bahr kick)
Buff —Thomas 31 run (Norwood kick)
NYG—FG Bahr 21

Super Bowl XXIV

Louisiana Superdome, New Orleans, Louisiana January 28, 1990
Attendance: 72,919

SAN FRANCISCO 55, DENVER 10—NFC titlist San Francisco won its fourth Super Bowl championship with a 55-10 victory over AFC champion Denver. The 49ers, who also won Super Bowls XVI, XIX, and XXIII, tied the Pittsburgh Steelers for most Super Bowl victories. The Steelers captured Super Bowls IX, X, XIII, and XIV. San Francisco's 55 points broke the previous Super Bowl scoring mark of 46 points by Chicago in Super Bowl XX. San Francisco scored touchdowns on four of its six first-half possessons to hold a 27-3 lead at halftime. The 49ers' first-half scoring drives were lengthy and time-consuming (10 plays for 66 yards, 10 for 54, 14 for 69, and 5 for 59). Interceptions by Michael Walter and Chet Brooks ended the Broncos' first two possessions of the second half. San Francisco quarterback Joe Montana was named the Super Bowl most valuable player for a record third time. Montana completed 22 of 29 passes for 297 yards and a Super Bowl-record five touchdowns (old record: four, Terry Bradshaw, Pittsburgh, Super Bowl XIII, and Doug Williams, Washington, Super Bowl XXII). Jerry Rice, Super Bowl XXIII most valuable player, caught seven passes for 148 yards and three touchdowns. The 49ers' domination included first downs (28 to 12), net yards (461 to 167), and time of possession (39:31 to 20:29).

San Francisco (NFC)	13	14	14	14	— 55
Denver (AFC)	3	0	7	0	— 10

SF —Rice 20 pass from Montana (Cofer kick)
Den—FG Treadwell 42
SF —Jones 7 pass from Montana (kick failed)
SF —Rathman 1 run (Cofer kick)
SF —Rice 38 pass from Montana (Cofer kick)
SF —Rice 28 pass from Montana (Cofer kick)
SF —Taylor 35 pass from Montana (Cofer kick)
Den—Elway 3 run (Treadwell kick)
SF —Rathman 3 run (Cofer kick)
SF —Craig 1 run (Cofer kick)

Super Bowl XXIII

Joe Robbie Stadium, Miami, Florida January 22, 1989
Attendance: 75,129

SAN FRANCISCO 20, CINCINNATI 16—NFC champion San Francisco captured its third Super Bowl of the 1980s by defeating AFC champion Cincinnati 20-16. The 49ers, who also won Super Bowls XVI and XIX, are the first NFC team to win three Super Bowls. Pittsburgh with four Super Bowl titles (IX, X, XIII, and XIV) and the Oakland/Los Angeles Raiders with three (XI, XV, and XVIII) lead AFC franchises. Even though San Francisco held an advantage in total net yards (453 to 229), the 49ers found themselves trailing the Bengals late in the game. With the score tied 13-13, Cincinnati took a 16-13 lead on Jim Breech's 40-yard field goal with 3:20 remaining. It was Breech's third field goal of the day, following earlier successes from 34 and 43 yards. The 49ers started their winning drive at their own 8-yard line. Over the next 11 plays, San Francisco covered 92 yards with the decisive score coming on a 10-yard pass from quarterback Joe Montana to wide receiver John Taylor with 34 seconds remaining. At halftime, the score was 3-3, the first time in Super Bowl history the game was tied at intermission. After the teams traded third-period field goals, the Bengals jumped ahead 13-6 on Stanford Jennings's 93-yard kickoff return for a touchdown with 34 seconds remaining in the quarter. The 49ers didn't waste any time coming back as they covered 85 yards in four plays, concluding with Montana's 14-yard scoring pass to Jerry Rice 57 seconds into the final stanza. Rice was named the game's most valuable player after compiling 11 catches for a Super Bowl-record 215 yards. Montana completed 23 of 36 passes for a Super Bowl-record 357 yards and two touchdowns.

Cincinnati (AFC)	0	3	10	3	— 16
San Francisco (NFC)	3	0	3	14	— 20

SF —FG Cofer 41
Cin—FG Breech 34
Cin—FG Breech 43
SF —FG Cofer 32
Cin—Jennings 93 kickoff return (Breech kick)
SF —Rice 14 pass from Montana (Cofer kick)
Cin—FG Breech 40
SF —Taylor 10 pass from Montana (Cofer kick)

Super Bowl XXII

San Diego Jack Murphy Stadium, San Diego, California January 31, 1988
Attendance: 73,302

WASHINGTON 42, DENVER 10—NFC champion Washington won Super Bowl XXII and its second NFL championship of the 1980s with a 42-10 decision over AFC champion Denver. The Redskins, who also won Super Bowl XVII, enjoyed a record-setting second quarter en route to the victory. The Broncos broke in front 10-0 when quarterback John Elway threw a 56-yard touchdown pass to wide receiver Ricky Nattiel on the Broncos' first play from scrimmage. Following a Washington punt, Denver's Rich Karlis kicked a 24-yard field goal to cap a seven-play, 61-yard scoring drive. The Redskins then erupted for 35 points on five straight possessions in the second period and coasted thereafter. The 35 points established an NFL postseason mark for most points scored in a period, bettering the previous total of 21 by San Francisco in Super Bowl XIX and Chicago in Super Bowl XX. Redskins quarterback Doug Williams led the second-period explosion by throwing a Super Bowl record-tying four touchdown passes, including 80- and 50-yarders to wide receiver Ricky Sanders, a 27-yarder to wide receiver Gary Clark, and an 8-yarder to tight end Clint Didier. Washington scored five touchdowns in 18 plays with total time of possession of only 5:47. Overall, Williams completed 18 of 29 passes for 340 yards and was named the game's most valuable player. His pass-yardage total eclipsed the previous Super Bowl record of 331 yards by Joe Montana of San Francisco in Super Bowl XIX. Sanders ended with 193 yards on eight catches, breaking the previous Super Bowl yardage record of 161 yards by Lynn Swann of Pittsburgh in Game X. Rookie running back Timmy Smith was the game's leading rusher with 22 carries for a Super Bowl-record 204 yards, breaking the previous mark of 191 yards by Marcus Allen of the Raiders in Game XVIII. Smith also scored twice on runs of 58 and four yards. Washington's six touchdowns and 602 total yards gained also set Super Bowl records. Redskins cornerback Barry Wilburn had two of the team's three interceptions, and strong safety Alvin Walton had two of Washington's five sacks.

Washington (NFC)	0	35	0	7	— 42
Denver (AFC)	10	0	0	0	— 10

Den —Nattiel 56 pass from Elway (Karlis kick)
Den —FG Karlis 24
Wash—Sanders 80 pass from Williams (Haji-Sheikh kick)
Wash—Clark 27 pass from Williams (Haji-Sheikh kick)
Wash—Smith 58 run (Haji-Sheikh kick)
Wash—Sanders 50 pass from Williams (Haji-Sheikh kick)
Wash—Didier 8 pass from Williams (Haji-Sheikh kick)
Wash—Smith 4 run (Haji-Sheikh kick)

Super Bowl XXI

Rose Bowl, Pasadena, California January 25, 1987
Attendance: 101,063

NEW YORK GIANTS 39, DENVER 20—The NFC champion New York Giants captured their first NFL title since 1956 when they downed the AFC champion Denver Broncos 39-20 in Super Bowl XXI. The victory marked the NFC's fifth NFL title in the past six seasons. The Broncos, behind the passing of quarterback John Elway, who was 13 of 20 for 187 yards in the first half, held a 10-9 lead at intermission, the narrowest halftime margin in Super Bowl history. Denver's Rich Karlis opened the scoring with a Super Bowl record-tying 48-yard field goal. New York drove 78 yards in nine plays on the next series to take a 7-3 lead on quarterback Phil Simms's six-yard touchdown pass to tight end Zeke Mowatt. The Broncos came right back with a 58-yard scoring drive on six plays capped by Elway's four-yard touchdown run. The only scoring in the second period was the sack of Elway in the end zone by defensive end George Martin for a New York safety. The Giants produced a key defensive stand early in the second quarter when the Broncos had a first down at the New York one-yard line, but failed to score on three running plays and Karlis's 23-yard missed field-goal attempt. The Giants took command of the game in the third period en route to a 30-point second half, the most ever scored in one half of Super Bowl play. New York took the lead for good on tight end Mark Bavaro's 13-yard touchdown catch 4:52 into the third period. The nine-play, 63-yard scoring drive included the successful conversion of a fourth down and one play on the New York 46-yard line. Denver was limited to only two net yards on 10 offensive plays in the third period. Simms set Super Bowl records for most consecutive completions (10) and highest completion percentage (88 percent on 22 completions in 25 attempts). He also passed for 268 yards and three touchdowns and was named the game's most valuable player. New York running back Joe Morris was the game's leading rusher with 20 carries for 67 yards. Denver wide receiver Vance Johnson led all receivers with five catches for 121 yards. The Giants defeated their three playoff opponents by a cumulative total of 82 points (New York 105, opponents 23), the largest such margin by a Super Bowl winner.

Denver (AFC)	10	0	0	10	— 20
N.Y. Giants (NFC)	7	2	17	13	— 39

Den —FG Karlis 48
NYG—Mowatt 6 pass from Simms (Allegre kick)
Den —Elway 4 run (Karlis kick)

NYG—Safety, Martin tackled Elway in end zone
NYG—Bavaro 13 pass from Simms (Allegre kick)
NYG—FG Allegre 21
NYG—Morris 1 run (Allegre kick)
NYG—McConkey 6 pass from Simms (Allegre kick)
Den —FG Karlis 28
NYG—Anderson 2 run (kick failed)
Den —V. Johnson 47 pass from Elway (Karlis kick)

Super Bowl XX

Louisiana Superdome, New Orleans, Louisiana — January 26, 1986
Attendance: 73,818

CHICAGO 46, NEW ENGLAND 10—The NFC champion Chicago Bears, seeking their first NFL title since 1963, scored a Super Bowl-record 46 points in downing AFC champion New England 46-10 in Super Bowl XX. The previous record for most points in a Super Bowl was 38, shared by San Francisco in XIX and the Los Angeles Raiders in XVIII. The Bears' league-leading defense tied the Super Bowl record for sacks (seven) and limited the Patriots to a record-low seven yards rushing. New England took the quickest lead in Super Bowl history when Tony Franklin kicked a 36-yard field goal with 1:19 elapsed in the first period. The score came about because of Larry McGrew's fumble recovery at the Chicago 19-yard line. However, the Bears rebounded for a 23-3 first-half lead, while building a yardage advantage of 236 total yards to New England's minus 19. Running back Matt Suhey rushed eight times for 37 yards, including an 11-yard touchdown run, and caught one pass for 24 yards in the first half. After the Patriots first drive of the second half ended with a punt to the Bears' 4-yard line, Chicago marched 96 yards in nine plays with quarterback Jim McMahon's one-yard scoring run capping the drive. McMahon became the first quarterback in Super Bowl history to rush for a pair of touchdowns. The Bears completed their scoring via a 28-yard interception return by reserve cornerback Reggie Phillips, a one-yard run by defensive tackle/fullback William Perry, and a safety when defensive end Henry Waechter tackled Patriots quarterback Steve Grogan in the end zone. Bears defensive end Richard Dent became the fourth defender to be named the game's most valuable player after contributing 1½ sacks. The Bears' victory margin of 36 points was the largest in Super Bowl history, bettering the previous mark of 29 by the Los Angeles Raiders when they topped Washington 38-9 in Game XVIII. McMahon completed 12 of 20 passes for 256 yards before leaving the game in the fourth period with a wrist injury. The NFL's all-time leading rusher, Bears running back Walter Payton, carried 22 times for 61 yards. Wide receiver Willie Gault caught four passes for 129 yards, the fourth-most receiving yards in a Super Bowl. Chicago coach Mike Ditka became the second man (Tom Flores of Raiders was the other) who played in a Super Bowl and coached a team to a victory in the game.

Chicago (NFC)	13	10	21	2	— 46
New England (AFC)	3	0	0	7	— 10

NE—FG Franklin 36
Chi—FG Butler 28
Chi—FG Butler 24
Chi—Suhey 11 run (Butler kick)
Chi—McMahon 2 run (Butler kick)
Chi—FG Butler 24
Chi—McMahon 1 run (Butler kick)
Chi—Phillips 28 interception return (Butler kick)
Chi—Perry 1 run (Butler kick)
NE—Fryar 8 pass from Grogan (Franklin kick)
Chi—Safety, Waechter tackled Grogan in end zone

Super Bowl XIX

Stanford Stadium, Stanford, California — January 20, 1985
Attendance: 84,059

SAN FRANCISCO 38, MIAMI 16—The San Francisco 49ers captured their second Super Bowl title with a dominating offense and a defense that tamed Miami's explosive passing attack. The Dolphins held a 10-7 lead at the end of the first period, which represented the most points scored by two teams in an opening quarter of a Super Bowl. However, the 49ers used excellent field position in the second period to build a 28-16 halftime lead. Running back Roger Craig set a Super Bowl record by scoring three touchdowns on pass receptions of 8 and 16 yards and a run of 2 yards. San Francisco's Joe Montana was voted the game's most valuable player. He joined Green Bay's Bart Starr and Pittsburgh's Terry Bradshaw as the only two-time Super Bowl most valuable players. Montana completed 24 of 35 passes for a Super Bowl-record 331 yards and three touchdowns, and rushed five times for 59 yards, including a six-yard touchdown. Craig had 58 yards on 15 carries and caught seven passes for 77 yards. Wendell Tyler rushed 13 times for 65 yards and had four catches for 70 yards. Dwight Clark had six receptions for 77 yards, while Russ Francis had five for 60. San Francisco's 537 total net yards bettered the previous Super Bowl record of 429 yards by Oakland in Super Bowl XI. The 49ers also held a time of possession advantage over the Dolphins of 37:11 to 22:49.

Miami (AFC)	10	6	0	0	— 16
San Francisco (NFC)	7	21	10	0	— 38

Mia—FG von Schamann 37
SF —Monroe 33 pass from Montana (Wersching kick)
Mia—D. Johnson 2 pass from Marino (von Schamann kick)
SF —Craig 8 pass from Montana (Wersching kick)
SF —Montana 6 run (Wersching kick)
SF —Craig 2 run (Wersching kick)
Mia—FG von Schamann 31
Mia—FG von Schamann 30
SF —FG Wersching 27
SF —Craig 16 pass from Montana (Wersching kick)

Super Bowl XVIII

Tampa Stadium, Tampa, Florida — January 22, 1984
Attendance: 72,920

LOS ANGELES RAIDERS 38, WASHINGTON 9—The Los Angeles Raiders dominated the Washington Redskins from the beginning in Super Bowl XVIII and achieved the most lopsided victory in Super Bowl history, surpassing Green Bay's 35-10 win over Kansas City in Super Bowl I. The Raiders took a 7-0 lead 4:52 into the game when Derrick Jensen blocked a Jeff Hayes punt and recovered it in the end zone for a touchdown. With 9:14 remaining in the first half, Raiders quarterback Jim Plunkett threw a 12-yard touchdown pass to wide receiver Cliff Branch to complete a three-play, 65-yard drive. Washington cut the Raiders' lead to 14-3 on a 24-yard field goal by Mark Moseley. With seven seconds left in the first half, Raiders linebacker Jack Squirek intercepted a Joe Theismann pass at the Redskins' 5-yard line and ran it in for a touchdown to give Los Angeles a 21-3 halftime lead. In the third period, running back Marcus Allen, who rushed for a Super Bowl-record 191 yards on 20 carries, increased the Raiders' lead to 35-9 on touchdown runs of five and 74 yards, the latter erasing the previous Super Bowl record of 58 yards set by Baltimore's Tom Matte in Game III. Allen was named the game's most valuable player. The victory over Washington raised Raiders coach Tom Flores' playoff record to 8-1, including a 27-10 win against Philadelphia in Super Bowl XV. The 38 points scored by the Raiders were the highest total by a Super Bowl team. The previous high was 35 points by Green Bay in Game I.

Washington (NFC)	0	3	6	0	— 9
L.A. Raiders (AFC)	7	14	14	3	— 38

Raiders—Jensen recovered blocked punt in end zone (Bahr kick)
Raiders—Branch 12 pass from Plunkett (Bahr kick)
Wash —FG Moseley 24
Raiders—Squirek 5 interception return (Bahr kick)
Wash —Riggins 1 run (kick blocked)
Raiders—Allen 5 run (Bahr kick)
Raiders—Allen 74 run (Bahr kick)
Raiders—FG Bahr 21

Super Bowl XVII

Rose Bowl, Pasadena, California — January 30, 1983
Attendance: 103,667

WASHINGTON 27, MIAMI 17—Fullback John Riggins's Super Bowl-record 166 yards on 38 carries sparked Washington to a 27-17 victory over AFC champion Miami. It was Riggins's fourth straight 100-yard rushing game during the playoffs, also a record. The win marked Washington's first NFL title since 1942, and was only the second time in Super Bowl history NFL/NFC teams scored consecutive victories (Green Bay did it in Super Bowls I and II and San Francisco won Super Bowl XVI). The Redskins, under second-year head coach Joe Gibbs, used a balanced offense that accounted for 400 total yards (a Super Bowl-record 276 yards rushing and 124 passing), second in Super Bowl history to 429 yards by Oakland in Super Bowl XI. The Dolphins built a 17-10 halftime lead on a 76-yard touchdown pass from quarterback David Woodley to wide receiver Jimmy Cefalo 6:49 into the first period, a 20-yard field goal by Uwe von Schamann with 6:00 left in the half, and a Super Bowl-record 98-yard kickoff return by Fulton Walker with 1:38 remaining. Washington had tied the score at 10-10 with 1:51 left on a four-yard touchdown pass from Joe Theismann to wide receiver Alvin Garrett. Mark Moseley started the Redskins' scoring with a 31-yard field goal late in the first period, and added a 20-yarder midway through the third period to cut the Dolphins' lead to 17-13. Riggins, who was voted the game's most valuable player, gave Washington its first lead of the game with 10:01 left when he ran 43 yards off left tackle for a touchdown on a fourth-and-one situation. Wide receiver Charlie Brown caught a six-yard scoring pass from Theismann with 1:55 left to complete the scoring. The Dolphins managed only 176 yards (142 in first half). Theismann completed 15 of 23 passes for 143 yards, with two touchdowns and two interceptions. For Miami, Woodley was 4 of 14 for 97 yards, with one touchdown, and one interception. Don Strock was 0 for 3 in relief.

Miami (AFC)	7	10	0	0	— 17
Washington (NFC)	0	10	3	14	— 27

Mia —Cefalo 76 pass from Woodley (von Schamann kick)
Wash—FG Moseley 31
Mia —FG von Schamann 20
Wash—Garrett 4 pass from Theismann (Moseley kick)
Mia —Walker 98 kickoff return (von Schamann kick)
Wash—FG Moseley 20
Wash—Riggins 43 run (Moseley kick)
Wash—Brown 6 pass from Theismann (Moseley kick)

Super Bowl XVI

Pontiac Silverdome, Pontiac, Michigan — January 24, 1982
Attendance: 81,270

SAN FRANCISCO 26, CINCINNATI 21—Ray Wersching's Super Bowl record-tying four field goals and Joe Montana's controlled passing helped lift the San Francisco 49ers to their first NFL championship with a 26-21 victory over Cincinnati. The 49ers built a game-record 20-0 halftime lead via Montana's one-yard touchdown run, which capped an 11-play, 68-yard drive; fullback Earl Cooper's 11-yard scoring pass from Montana, which climaxed a Super Bowl record 92-yard drive on 12 plays; and Wersching's 22- and 26-yard field goals. The Bengals rebounded in the second half, closing the gap to 20-14 on quarterback Ken Anderson's five-yard run and Dan Ross's four-yard reception from

Anderson, who established Super Bowl passing records for completions (25) and completion percentage (73.5 percent on 25 of 34). Wersching added early fourth-period field goals of 40 and 23 yards to increase the 49ers' lead to 26-14. The Bengals managed to score on an Anderson-to-Ross three-yard pass with only 16 seconds remaining. Ross set a Super Bowl record with 11 receptions for 104 yards. Montana, the game's most valuable player, completed 14 of 22 passes for 157 yards. Cincinnati compiled 356 yards to San Francisco's 275, which marked the first time in Super Bowl history that the team that gained the most yards from scrimmage lost the game.

San Francisco (NFC)	7	13	0	6	— 26
Cincinnati (AFC)	0	0	7	14	— 21

SF — Montana 1 run (Wersching kick)
SF — Cooper 11 pass from Montana (Wersching kick)
SF — FG Wersching 22
SF — FG Wersching 26
Cin — Anderson 5 run (Breech kick)
Cin — Ross 4 pass from Anderson (Breech kick)
SF — FG Wersching 40
SF — FG Wersching 23
Cin — Ross 3 pass from Anderson (Breech kick)

Super Bowl XV

Louisiana Superdome, New Orleans, Louisiana — January 25, 1981
Attendance: 76,135

OAKLAND 27, PHILADELPHIA 10 — Jim Plunkett threw three touchdown passes, including an 80-yarder to Kenny King, as the Raiders became the first wild-card team to win the Super Bowl. Plunkett's touchdown bomb to King — the longest play in Super Bowl history — gave Oakland a decisive 14-0 lead with nine seconds left in the first period. Linebacker Rod Martin had set up Oakland's first touchdown, a two-yard reception by Cliff Branch, with a 17-yard interception return to the Eagles' 30 yard line. The Eagles never recovered from that early deficit, managing only a Tony Franklin field goal (30 yards) and an eight-yard touchdown pass from Ron Jaworski to Keith Krepfle the rest of the game. Plunkett, who became a starter in the sixth game of the season, completed 13 of 21 for 261 yards and was named the game's most valuable player. Oakland won nine of 11 games with Plunkett starting, but that was good enough only for second place in the AFC West, although they tied division winner San Diego with an 11-5 record. The Raiders, who had previously won Super Bowl XI over Minnesota, had to win three playoff games to get to the championship game. Oakland defeated Houston 27-7 at home followed by road victories over Cleveland (14-12) and San Diego (34-27). Oakland's Mark van Eeghen was the game's leading rusher with 75 yards on 18 carries. Philadelphia's Wilbert Montgomery led all receivers with six receptions for 91 yards. Branch had five for 67 and Harold Carmichael of Philadelphia five for 83. Martin finished the game with three interceptions, a Super Bowl record.

Oakland (AFC)	14	0	10	3	— 27
Philadelphia (NFC)	0	3	0	7	— 10

Oak — Branch 2 pass from Plunkett (Bahr kick)
Oak — King 80 pass from Plunkett (Bahr kick)
Phil — FG Franklin 30
Oak — Branch 29 pass from Plunkett (Bahr kick)
Oak — FG Bahr 46
Phil — Krepfle 8 pass from Jaworski (Franklin kick)
Oak — FG Bahr 35

Super Bowl XIV

Rose Bowl, Pasadena, California — January 20, 1980
Attendance: 103,985

PITTSBURGH 31, LOS ANGELES 19 — Terry Bradshaw completed 14 of 21 passes for 309 yards and set two passing records as the Steelers became the first team to win four Super Bowls. Despite three interceptions by the Rams, Bradshaw kept his poise and brought the Steelers from behind twice in the second half. Trailing 13-10 at halftime, Pittsburgh went ahead 17-13 when Bradshaw hit Lynn Swann with a 47-yard touchdown pass after 2:48 of the third quarter. On the Rams' next possession Vince Ferragamo, who completed 15 of 25 passes for 212 yards, responded with a 50-yard pass to Billy Waddy that moved Los Angeles from its own 26 to the Steelers' 24. On the following play, Lawrence McCutcheon connected with Ron Smith on a halfback option pass that gave the Rams a 19-17 lead. On Pittsburgh's initial possession of the final period, Bradshaw lofted a 73-yard scoring pass to John Stallworth to put the Steelers in front to stay, 24-19. Franco Harris scored on a one-yard run later in the quarter to seal the verdict. A 45-yard pass from Bradshaw to Stallworth was the key play in the drive to Harris's score. Bradshaw, the game's most valuable player for the second straight year, set career Super Bowl records for most touchdown passes (nine) and most passing yards (932). Larry Anderson gave the Steelers excellent field position throughout the game with five kickoff returns for a record 162 yards.

Los Angeles (NFC)	7	6	6	0	— 19
Pittsburgh (AFC)	3	7	7	14	— 31

Pitt — FG Bahr 41
LA — Bryant 1 run (Corral kick)
Pitt — Harris 1 run (Bahr kick)
LA — FG Corral 31
LA — FG Corral 45
Pitt — Swann 47 pass from Bradshaw (Bahr kick)
LA — Smith 24 pass from McCutcheon (kick failed)
Pitt — Stallworth 73 pass from Bradshaw (Bahr kick)
Pitt — Harris 1 run (Bahr kick)

Super Bowl XIII

Orange Bowl, Miami, Florida — January 21, 1979
Attendance: 79,484

PITTSBURGH 35, DALLAS 31 — Terry Bradshaw threw a record four touchdown passes to lead the Steelers to victory. The Steelers became the first team to win three Super Bowls, mostly because of Bradshaw's accurate arm. Bradshaw, voted the game's most valuable player, completed 17 of 30 passes for 318 yards, a personal high. Four of those passes went for touchdowns — two to John Stallworth and the third, with 26 seconds remaining in the second period, to Rocky Bleier for a 21-14 halftime lead. The Cowboys scored twice before intermission on Roger Staubach's 39-yard pass to Tony Hill and a 37-yard fumble return by linebacker Mike Hegman, who stole the ball from Bradshaw. The Steelers broke open the contest with two touchdowns in a span of 19 seconds midway through the final period. Franco Harris rambled 22 yards up the middle to give the Steelers a 28-17 lead with 7:10 left. Pittsburgh got the ball right back when Randy White fumbled the kickoff and Dennis Winston recovered for the Steelers. On first down, Bradshaw fired his fourth touchdown pass, an 18-yarder to Lynn Swann to boost the Steelers' lead to 35-17 with 6:51 to play. The Cowboys refused to let the Steelers run away with the contest. Staubach connected with Billy Joe DuPree on a seven-yard scoring pass with 2:23 left. Then the Cowboys recovered an onside kick and Staubach took them in for another score, passing four yards to Butch Johnson with 22 seconds remaining. Bleier recovered another onside kick with 17 seconds left to seal the victory for the Steelers.

Pittsburgh (AFC)	7	14	0	14	— 35
Dallas (NFC)	7	7	3	14	— 31

Pitt — Stallworth 28 pass from Bradshaw (Gerela kick)
Dall — Hill 39 pass from Staubach (Septien kick)
Dall — Hegman 37 fumble recovery return (Septien kick)
Pitt — Stallworth 75 pass from Bradshaw (Gerela kick)
Pitt — Bleier 7 pass from Bradshaw (Gerela kick)
Dall — FG Septien 27
Pitt — Harris 22 run (Gerela kick)
Pitt — Swann 18 pass from Bradshaw (Gerela kick)
Dall — DuPree 7 pass from Staubach (Septien kick)
Dall — B. Johnson 4 pass from Staubach (Septien kick)

Super Bowl XII

Louisiana Superdome, New Orleans, Louisiana — January 15, 1978
Attendance: 75,583

DALLAS 27, DENVER 10 — The Cowboys evened their Super Bowl record at 2-2 by defeating Denver before a sellout crowd of 75,583, plus 102,010,000 television viewers, the largest audience ever to watch a sporting event. Dallas converted two interceptions into 10 points and Efren Herrera added a 35-yard field goal for a 13-0 halftime advantage. In the third period Craig Morton engineered a drive to the Cowboys' 30 and Jim Turner's 47-yard field goal made the score 13-3. After an exchange of punts, Butch Johnson made a spectacular diving catch in the end zone to complete a 45-yard pass from Roger Staubach and put the Cowboys ahead 20-3. Following Rick Upchurch's 67-yard kickoff return, Norris Weese guided the Broncos to a touchdown to cut the Dallas lead to 20-10. Dallas clinched the victory when running back Robert Newhouse threw a 29-yard touchdown pass to Golden Richards with 7:04 remaining in the game. It was the first pass thrown by Newhouse since 1975. Harvey Martin and Randy White, who were named co-most valuable players, led the Cowboys' defense, which recovered four fumbles and intercepted four passes.

Dallas (NFC)	10	3	7	7	— 27
Denver (AFC)	0	0	10	0	— 10

Dall — Dorsett 3 run (Herrera kick)
Dall — FG Herrera 35
Dall — FG Herrera 43
Den — FG Turner 47
Dall — Johnson 45 pass from Staubach (Herrera kick)
Den — Lytle 1 run (Turner kick)
Dall — Richards 29 pass from Newhouse (Herrera kick)

Super Bowl XI

Rose Bowl, Pasadena, California — January 9, 1977
Attendance: 103,438

OAKLAND 32, MINNESOTA 14 — The Raiders won their first NFL championship before a record Super Bowl crowd plus 81 million television viewers, the largest audience ever to watch a sporting event. The Raiders gained a record-breaking 429 yards, including running back Clarence Davis's 137 yards rushing. Wide receiver Fred Biletnikoff made four key receptions, which earned him the game's most valuable player trophy. Oakland scored on three successive possessions in the second quarter to build a 16-0 halftime lead. Errol Mann's 24-yard field goal opened the scoring, then the AFC champions put together drives of 64 and 35 yards, scoring on a one-yard pass from Ken Stabler to Dave Casper and a one-yard run by Pete Banaszak. The Raiders increased their lead to 19-0 on a 40-yard field goal in the third quarter, but Minnesota responded with a 12-play, 58-yard drive late in the period, with Fran Tarkenton passing eight yards to wide receiver Sammy White to cut the deficit to 19-7. Two fourth-quarter interceptions clinched the title for the Raiders. One set up Banaszak's second touchdown run, the other resulted in cornerback Willie Brown's Super Bowl-record 75-yard interception return.

Oakland (AFC)	0	16	3	13	— 32
Minnesota (NFC)	0	0	7	7	— 14

Oak — FG Mann 24
Oak — Casper 1 pass from Stabler (Mann kick)

Oak — Banaszak 1 run (kick failed)
Oak — FG Mann 40
Minn— S. White 8 pass from Tarkenton (Cox kick)
Oak — Banaszak 2 run (Mann kick)
Oak — Brown 75 interception return (kick failed)
Minn— Voigt 13 pass from Lee (Cox kick)

Super Bowl X

Orange Bowl, Miami, Florida — January 18, 1976
Attendance: 80,187

PITTSBURGH 21, DALLAS 17 — The Steelers won the Super Bowl for the second year in a row on Terry Bradshaw's 64-yard touchdown pass to Lynn Swann and an aggressive defense that snuffed out a late rally by the Cowboys with an end-zone interception on the final play of the game. In the fourth quarter, Pittsburgh ran on fourth down and gave up the ball on the Cowboys' 39 with 1:22 to play. Roger Staubach ran and passed for two first downs but his last desperation pass was picked off by Glen Edwards. Dallas's scoring was the result of two touchdown passes by Staubach, one to Drew Pearson for 29 yards and the other to Percy Howard for 34 yards. Toni Fritsch had a 36-yard field goal. The Steelers scored on two touchdown passes by Bradshaw, one to Randy Grossman for seven yards and the long bomb to Swann. Roy Gerela had 36- and 18-yard field goals. Reggie Harrison blocked a punt through the end zone for a safety. Swann set a Super Bowl record by gaining 161 yards on his four receptions.

Dallas (NFC)	7	3	0	7	— 17
Pittsburgh (AFC)	7	0	0	14	— 21

Dall— D. Pearson 29 pass from Staubach (Fritsch kick)
Pitt — Grossman 7 pass from Bradshaw (Gerela kick)
Dall— FG Fritsch 36
Pitt — Safety, Harrison blocked Hoopes's punt through end zone
Pitt — FG Gerela 36
Pitt — FG Gerela 18
Pitt — Swann 64 pass from Bradshaw (kick failed)
Dall— P. Howard 34 pass from Staubach (Fritsch kick)

Super Bowl IX

Tulane Stadium, New Orleans, Louisiana — January 12, 1975
Attendance: 80,997

PITTSBURGH 16, MINNESOTA 6 — AFC champion Pittsburgh, in its initial Super Bowl appearance, and NFC champion Minnesota, making a third bid for its first Super Bowl title, struggled through a first half in which the only score was produced by the Steelers' defense when Dwight White downed Vikings' quarterback Fran Tarkenton in the end zone for a safety 7:49 into the second period. The Steelers forced another break and took advantage on the second-half kickoff when Minnesota's Bill Brown fumbled and Marv Kellum recovered for Pittsburgh on the Vikings' 30. After Rocky Bleier failed to gain on first down, Franco Harris carried three consecutive times for 24 yards, a loss of 3, and a 9-yard touchdown and a 9-0 lead. Though its offense was completely stymied by Pittsburgh's defense, Minnesota managed to move into a threatening position after 4:27 of the final period when Matt Blair blocked Bobby Walden's punt and Terry Brown recovered the ball in the end zone for a touchdown. Fred Cox's kick failed and the Steelers led 9-6. Pittsburgh wasted no time putting the victory away. The Steelers took the ensuing kickoff and marched 66 yards in 11 plays, climaxed by Terry Bradshaw's four-yard scoring pass to Larry Brown with 3:31 left. Pittsburgh's defense permitted Minnesota only 119 yards total offense, including a Super Bowl low of 17 rushing yards. The Steelers, meanwhile, gained 333 yards, including Harris's record 158 yards on 34 carries.

Pittsburgh (AFC)	0	2	7	7	— 16
Minnesota (NFC)	0	0	0	6	— 6

Pitt — Safety, White downed Tarkenton in end zone
Pitt — Harris 9 run (Gerela kick)
Minn— T. Brown recovered blocked punt in end zone (kick failed)
Pitt — L. Brown 4 pass from Bradshaw (Gerela kick)

Super Bowl VIII

Rice Stadium, Houston, Texas — January 13, 1974
Attendance: 71,882

MIAMI 24, MINNESOTA 7 — The defending NFL champion Dolphins, representing the AFC for the third straight year, scored the first two times they had possession on marches of 62 and 56 yards while the Miami defense limited the Vikings to only seven plays in the first period. Larry Csonka climaxed the initial 10-play drive with a five-yard touchdown bolt through right guard after 5:27 had elapsed. Four plays later, Miami began another 10-play scoring drive, which ended with Jim Kiick bursting one yard through the middle for another touchdown after 13:38 of the period. Garo Yepremian added a 28-yard field goal midway in the second period for a 17-0 Miami lead. Minnesota then drove from its 20 to a second-and-two situation on the Miami 7 yard line with 1:18 left in the half. But on two plays, Miami limited Oscar Reed to one yard. On fourth-and-one from the 6, Reed went over right tackle, but Dolphins middle linebacker Nick Buoniconti jarred the ball loose and Jake Scott recovered for Miami to halt the Minnesota threat. The Vikings were unable to muster enough offense in the second half to threaten the Dolphins. Csonka rushed 33 times for a Super Bowl-record 145 yards. Bob Griese of Miami completed six of seven passes for 73 yards.

Minnesota (NFC)	0	0	0	7	— 7
Miami (AFC)	14	3	7	0	— 24

Mia — Csonka 5 run (Yepremian kick)
Mia — Kiick 1 run (Yepremian kick)
Mia — FG Yepremian 28
Mia — Csonka 2 run (Yepremian kick)
Minn— Tarkenton 4 run (Cox kick)

Super Bowl VII

Memorial Coliseum, Los Angeles, California — January 14, 1973
Attendance: 90,182

MIAMI 14, WASHINGTON 7 — The Dolphins played virtually perfect football in the first half as their defense permitted the Redskins to cross midfield only once and their offense turned good field position into two touchdowns. On its third possession, Miami opened its first scoring drive from the Dolphins' 37 yard line. An 18-yard pass from Bob Griese to Paul Warfield preceded by three plays Griese's 28-yard touchdown pass to Howard Twilley. After Washington moved from its 17 to the Miami 48 with two minutes remaining in the first half, Dolphins linebacker Nick Buoniconti intercepted a Billy Kilmer pass at the Miami 41 and returned it to the Washington 27. Jim Kiick ran for three yards, Larry Csonka for three, Griese passed to Jim Mandich for 19, and Kiick gained one to the 1-yard line. With 18 seconds left until intermission, Kiick scored from the 1. Washington's only touchdown came with 2:07 left in the game and resulted from a misplayed field-goal attempt and fumble by Garo Yepremian, with the Redskins' Mike Bass picking the ball out of the air and running 49 yards for the score. Dolphins safety Jake Scott, who had two interceptions, including one in the end zone to kill a Redskins' drive, was voted the game's most valuable player.

Miami (AFC)	7	7	0	0	— 14
Washington (NFC)	0	0	0	7	— 7

Mia — Twilley 28 pass from Griese (Yepremian kick)
Mia — Kiick 1 run (Yepremian kick)
Wash— Bass 49 fumble recovery return (Knight kick)

Super Bowl VI

Tulane Stadium, New Orleans, Louisiana — January 16, 1972
Attendance: 81,023

DALLAS 24, MIAMI 3 — The Cowboys rushed for a record 252 yards and their defense limited the Dolphins to a low of 185 yards while not permitting a touchdown for the first time in Super Bowl history. Dallas converted Chuck Howley's recovery of Larry Csonka's first fumble of the season into a 3-0 advantage and led at halftime 10-3. After Dallas received the second-half kickoff, Duane Thomas led a 71-yard march in eight plays for a 17-3 margin. Howley intercepted Bob Griese's pass at the 50 and returned it to the Miami 9 early in the fourth period, and three plays later Roger Staubach passed seven yards to Mike Ditka for the final touchdown. Thomas rushed for 95 yards and Walt Garrison gained 74. Staubach, voted the game's most valuable player, completed 12 of 19 passes for 119 yards and two touchdowns.

Dallas (NFC)	3	7	7	7	— 24
Miami (AFC)	0	3	0	0	— 3

Dall— FG Clark 9
Dall— Alworth 7 pass from Staubach (Clark kick)
Mia— FG Yepremian 31
Dall— D. Thomas 3 run (Clark kick)
Dall— Ditka 7 pass from Staubach (Clark kick)

Super Bowl V

Orange Bowl, Miami, Florida — January 17, 1971
Attendance: 79,204

BALTIMORE 16, DALLAS 13 — A 32-yard field goal by first-year kicker Jim O'Brien brought the Baltimore Colts a victory over the Dallas Cowboys in the final five seconds of Super Bowl V. The game between the champions of the AFC and NFC was played on artificial turf for the first time. Dallas led 13-6 at the half but interceptions by Rick Volk and Mike Curtis set up a Baltimore touchdown and O'Brien's decisive kick in the fourth period. Earl Morrall relieved an injured Johnny Unitas late in the first half, although Unitas completed the Colts' only scoring pass. It caromed off receiver Eddie Hinton's fingertips, off Dallas defensive back Mel Renfro, and finally settled into the grasp of John Mackey, who went 45 yards to score on a 75-yard play.

Baltimore (AFC)	0	6	0	10	— 16
Dallas (NFC)	3	10	0	0	— 13

Dall— FG Clark 14
Dall— FG Clark 30
Balt— Mackey 75 pass from Unitas (kick blocked)
Dall— Thomas 7 pass from Morton (Clark kick)
Balt— Nowatzke 2 run (O'Brien kick)
Balt— FG O'Brien 32

Super Bowl IV

Tulane Stadium, New Orleans, Louisiana — January 11, 1970
Attendance: 80,562

KANSAS CITY 23, MINNESOTA 7 — The AFL squared the Super Bowl at two games apiece with the NFL, building a 16-0 halftime lead behind Len Dawson's superb quarterbacking and a powerful defense. Dawson, the fourth consecutive quarterback to be chosen the Super Bowl's top player, called an almost flawless game, completing 12 of 17 passes and hitting Otis Taylor on a 46-yard play for the final Chiefs touchdown. The Kansas City defense limited Minnesota's strong rushing game to 67 yards and had three interceptions and two fumble recoveries. The crowd of 80,562 set a Super Bowl record, as did the gross receipts of $3,817,872.69.

Minnesota (NFL)	0	0	7	0	— 7
Kansas City (AFL)	3	13	7	0	— 23

KC —FG Stenerud 48
KC —FG Stenerud 32
KC —FG Stenerud 25
KC —Garrett 5 run (Stenerud kick)
Minn—Osborn 4 run (Cox kick)
KC —Taylor 46 pass from Dawson (Stenerud kick)

Super Bowl III

Orange Bowl, Miami, Florida — January 12, 1969
Attendance: 75,389

NEW YORK JETS 16, BALTIMORE 7—Jets quarterback Joe Namath "guaranteed" victory on the Thursday before the game, then went out and led the AFL to its first Super Bowl victory over a Baltimore team that had lost only once in 16 games all season. Namath, chosen the outstanding player, completed 17 of 28 passes for 206 yards and directed a steady attack that dominated the NFL champions after the Jets' defense had intercepted Colts quarterback Earl Morrall three times in the first half. The Jets had 337 total yards, including 121 yards rushing by Matt Snell. Johnny Unitas, who had missed most of the season with a sore elbow, came off the bench and led Baltimore to its only touchdown late in the fourth quarter after New York led 16-0.

New York Jets (AFL)	0	7	6	3	— 16
Baltimore (NFL)	0	0	0	7	— 7

NYJ—Snell 4 run (Turner kick)
NYJ—FG Turner 32
NYJ—FG Turner 30
NYJ—FG Turner 9
Balt—Hill 1 run (Michaels kick)

Super Bowl II

Orange Bowl, Miami, Florida — January 14, 1968
Attendance: 75,546

GREEN BAY 33, OAKLAND 14—Green Bay, after winning its third consecutive NFL championship, won the Super Bowl title for the second straight year 33-14 over the AFL champion Raiders in a game that drew the first $3-million gate in football history. Bart Starr again was chosen the game's most valuable player as he completed 13 of 24 passes for 202 yards and one touchdown and directed a Packers attack that was in control all the way after building a 16-7 halftime lead. Don Chandler kicked four field goals and all-pro cornerback Herb Adderley capped the Green Bay scoring with a 60-yard run with an interception. The game marked the last for Vince Lombardi as Packers coach, ending nine years at Green Bay in which he won six Western Conference championships, five NFL championships, and two Super Bowls.

Green Bay (NFL)	3	13	10	7	— 33
Oakland (AFL)	0	7	0	7	— 14

GB —FG Chandler 39
GB —FG Chandler 20
GB —Dowler 62 pass from Starr (Chandler kick)
Oak—Miller 23 pass from Lamonica (Blanda kick)
GB —FG Chandler 43
GB —Anderson 2 run (Chandler kick)
GB —FG Chandler 31
GB —Adderley 60 interception return (Chandler kick)
Oak—Miller 23 pass from Lamonica (Blanda kick)

Super Bowl I

Memorial Coliseum, Los Angeles, California — January 15, 1967
Attendance: 61,946

GREEN BAY 35, KANSAS CITY 10—The Green Bay Packers opened the Super Bowl series by defeating Kansas City's American Football League champions 35-10 behind the passing of Bart Starr, the receiving of Max McGee, and a key interception by all-pro safety Willie Wood. Green Bay broke open the game with three second-half touchdowns, the first of which was set up by Wood's 50-yard return of an interception to the Chiefs' 5 yard line. McGee, filling in for ailing Boyd Dowler after having caught only four passes all season, caught seven from Starr for 138 yards and two touchdowns. Elijah Pitts ran for two other scores. The Chiefs' 10 points came in the second quarter, the only touchdown on a seven-yard pass from Len Dawson to Curtis McClinton. Starr completed 16 of 23 passes for 250 yards and two touchdowns and was chosen the most valuable player. The Packers collected $15,000 per man and the Chiefs $7,500—the largest single-game shares in the history of team sports.

Kansas City (AFL)	0	10	0	0	— 10
Green Bay (NFL)	7	7	14	7	— 35

GB—McGee 37 pass from Starr (Chandler kick)
KC—McClinton 7 pass from Dawson (Mercer kick)
GB—Taylor 14 run (Chandler kick)
KC—FG Mercer 31
GB—Pitts 5 run (Chandler kick)
GB—McGee 13 pass from Starr (Chandler kick)
GB—Pitts 1 run (Chandler kick)

AFC Championship Game

Includes AFL Championship Games (1960-69)

Results

Season	Date	Winner (Share)	Loser (Share)	Score	Site	Attendance
1992	Jan. 17	Buffalo ($18,000)	Miami ($18,000)	29-10	Miami	72,703
1991	Jan. 12	Buffalo ($18,000)	Denver ($18,000)	10-7	Buffalo	80,272
1990	Jan. 20	Buffalo ($18,000)	L.A. Raiders ($18,000)	51-3	Buffalo	80,325
1989	Jan. 14	Denver ($18,000)	Cleveland ($18,000)	37-21	Denver	76,046
1988	Jan. 8	Cincinnati ($18,000)	Buffalo ($18,000)	21-10	Cincinnati	59,747
1987	Jan. 17	Denver ($18,000)	Cleveland ($18,000)	38-33	Denver	76,197
1986	Jan. 11	Denver ($18,000)	Cleveland ($18,000)	23-20*	Cleveland	79,973
1985	Jan. 12	New England ($18,000)	Miami ($18,000)	31-14	Miami	75,662
1984	Jan. 6	Miami ($18,000)	Pittsburgh ($18,000)	45-28	Miami	76,029
1983	Jan. 8	L.A. Raiders ($18,000)	Seattle ($18,000)	30-14	Los Angeles	91,445
1982	Jan. 23	Miami ($18,000)	N.Y. Jets ($18,000)	14-0	Miami	67,396
1981	Jan. 10	Cincinnati ($9,000)	San Diego ($9,000)	27-7	Cincinnati	46,302
1980	Jan. 11	Oakland ($9,000)	San Diego ($9,000)	34-27	San Diego	52,675
1979	Jan. 6	Pittsburgh ($9,000)	Houston ($9,000)	27-13	Pittsburgh	50,475
1978	Jan. 7	Pittsburgh ($9,000)	Houston ($9,000)	34-5	Pittsburgh	50,725
1977	Jan. 1	Denver ($9,000)	Oakland ($9,000)	20-17	Denver	75,044
1976	Dec. 26	Oakland ($8,500)	Pittsburgh ($5,500)	24-7	Oakland	53,821
1975	Jan. 4	Pittsburgh ($8,500)	Oakland ($5,500)	16-10	Pittsburgh	50,609
1974	Dec. 29	Pittsburgh ($8,500)	Oakland ($5,500)	24-13	Oakland	53,800
1973	Dec. 30	Miami ($8,500)	Oakland ($5,500)	27-10	Miami	79,325
1972	Dec. 31	Miami ($8,500)	Pittsburgh ($5,500)	21-17	Pittsburgh	50,845
1971	Jan. 2	Miami ($8,500)	Baltimore ($5,500)	21-0	Miami	76,622
1970	Jan. 3	Baltimore ($8,500)	Oakland ($5,500)	27-17	Baltimore	54,799
1969	Jan. 4	Kansas City ($7,755)	Oakland ($6,252)	17-7	Oakland	53,564
1968	Dec. 29	N.Y. Jets ($7,007)	Oakland ($5,349)	27-23	New York	62,627
1967	Dec. 31	Oakland ($6,321)	Houston ($4,996)	40-7	Oakland	53,330
1966	Jan. 1	Kansas City ($5,309)	Buffalo ($3,799)	31-7	Buffalo	42,080
1965	Dec. 26	Buffalo ($5,189)	San Diego ($3,447)	23-0	San Diego	30,361
1964	Dec. 26	Buffalo ($2,668)	San Diego ($1,738)	20-7	Buffalo	40,242
1963	Jan. 5	San Diego ($2,498)	Boston ($1,596)	51-10	San Diego	30,127
1962	Dec. 23	Dallas ($2,206)	Houston ($1,471)	20-17*	Houston	37,981
1961	Dec. 24	Houston ($1,792)	San Diego ($1,111)	10-3	San Diego	29,556
1960	Jan. 1	Houston ($1,025)	L.A. Chargers ($718)	24-16	Houston	32,183

**Sudden death overtime.*

AFC Championship Game Composite Standings

	W	L	Pct.	Pts.	OP
Kansas City Chiefs*	3	0	1.000	68	31
Cincinnati Bengals	2	0	1.000	48	17
Denver Broncos	4	1	.800	125	101
Buffalo Bills	5	2	.714	150	79
Miami Dolphins	5	2	.714	152	115
Pittsburgh Steelers	4	3	.571	153	131
Baltimore Colts	1	1	.500	27	38
New England Patriots**	1	1	.500	41	65
New York Jets	1	1	.500	27	37
Houston Oilers	2	4	.333	76	140
Oakland/L.A. Raiders	4	8	.333	228	264
San Diego Chargers***	1	6	.143	111	148
Seattle Seahawks	0	1	.000	14	30
Cleveland Browns	0	3	.000	74	98

**One game played when franchise was in Dallas (Texans). (Won 20-17)*
***One game played when franchise was in Boston. (Lost 51-10)*
****One game played when franchise was in Los Angeles. (Lost 24-16)*

1992 American Football Conference Championship Game

Joe Robbie Stadium, Miami, Florida — January 17, 1993

Attendance: 72,703

The Bills forced 5 turnovers en route to an easy victory over the Dolphins. Buffalo thus qualified for its third consecutive Super Bowl, a feat equaled only by Miami, which appeared in games VI, VII, and VIII. The Bills' defense was a big factor in this one, recovering 3 fumbles, intercepting 2 passes, and sacking Dolphins quarterback Dan Marino 4 times. Buffalo's offense, meanwhile, converted the miscues into 13 points, then controlled the ball on the ground, rushing for 182 yards (Miami had only 33) and maintaining possession for 36:19. Kicker Steve Christie kept the Bills comfortably ahead by tying an NFL postseason record with 5 field goals. Thurman Thomas rushed for 96 yards and caught 5 passes for 70 more, including a 17-yard touchdown 40 seconds into the second quarter that broke a 3-3 tie and gave Buffalo the lead for good. It was 13-3 at halftime, and the Bills broke the game open after recovering a fumble at the Dolphins' 24-yard line on the second-half kickoff. Five plays later, Kenneth Davis ran 2 yards for the touchdown that made it 20-3. Jim Kelly, playing for the first time since spraining his knee in Buffalo's final regular-season game, completed 17 of 24 passes for 177 yards, with 2 interceptions. Miami's Dan Marino was 22 of 45 for 268 yards and had 2 passes picked off. His 15-yard touchdown pass to Mark Duper midway through the fourth quarter gave him an NFL record-tying 10 consecutive postseason games with at least 1 touchdown pass.

Buffalo (29)	Offense	Miami (10)
James Lofton	WR	Mark Duper
Will Wolford	LT	Richmond Webb
Jim Ritcher	LG	Keith Sims
Kent Hull	C	Jeff Uhlenhake
Glenn Parker	RG	Harry Galbreath
Howard Ballard	RT	Jeff Dellenbach
Pete Metzelaars	TE	Keith Jackson
Andre Reed	WR	Mark Clayton
Jim Kelly	QB	Dan Marino
Thurman Thomas	RB	Bobby Humphrey
Don Beebe	WR-FB	Tony Paige
	Defense	
Phil Hansen	LE	Jeff Cross
Jeff Wright	NT	Chuck Klingbeil
Bruce Smith	RE	Marco Coleman
Marvcus Patton	LOLB	David Griggs
Shane Conlan	LILB	Liffort Hobley
Cornelius Bennett	RILB	Dwight Hollier
Darryl Talley	ROLB	Bryan Cox
James Williams	LCB	Troy Vincent
Nate Odomes	RCB	J.B. Brown
Henry Jones	SS	Stephen Braggs
Mark Kelso	FS	Louis Oliver

Substitutions

Buffalo — Offense: K — Steve Christie. P — Chris Mohr. QB — Frank Reich. RB — Kenneth Davis, Carwell Gardner. WR — Brad Lamb, Steve Tasker. TE — Rob Awalt, Keith McKeller. T — John Fina. G — John Davis, Mitch Frerotte. C — Adam Lingner. Defense: E — Mark Pike, Keith Willis. NT — Mike Lodish. LB — Carlton Bailey, Keith Goganious, Mark Maddox. CB — Chris Hale, Clifford Hicks, Kirby Jackson. S — Matt Darby. DNP: None. Inactive: QB — Gale Gilbert. S — Kurt Schulz.

Miami — Offense: K — Pete Stoyanovich. P — Reggie Roby. QB — Scott Mitchell. RB — Aaron Craver, James Saxon. WR — Fred Banks, Tony Martin, Scott Miller, Mike Williams. TE — Greg Baty, Ferrell Edmunds. T — Mark Dennis. G — Bert Weidner. Defense: E — Jeff Hunter, Larry Webster. NT — T.J. Turner. LB — Roosevelt Collins, John Grimsley, Cliff Odom. CB — Bruce Alexander, Kerry Glenn, Darrell Malone. S — Jarvis Williams. DNP: None. Inactive: QB — Scott Secules. G — Gene Williams.

Officials

Referee — Bob McElwee. Umpire — John Keck. Head Linesman — Earnie Frantz. Line Judge — Ron Blum. Back Judge — Roy Clymer. Field Judge — Don Orr. Side Judge — Bill Carollo.

Scoring

Buffalo	3	10	10	6	— 29
Miami	3	0	0	7	— 10

Buff—FG Christie 21
Mia—FG Stoyanovich 51
Buff—Thomas 17 pass from Kelly (Christie kick)
Buff—FG Christie 33
Buff—K. Davis 2 run (Christie kick)
Buff—FG Christie 21
Buff—FG Christie 31
Mia—Duper 15 pass from Marino (Stoyanovich kick)
Buff—FG Christie 38

Team Statistics

	Buffalo	Miami
Total First Downs	20	15
First Downs Rushing	10	1
First Downs Passing	8	14
First Downs Penalty	2	0
Total Net Yardage	358	276
Total Offensive Plays	73	60
Average Gain per Offensive Play	4.9	4.6
Rushes	48	11
Yards Gained Rushing (net)	182	33
Average Yards per Rush	3.8	3.0
Passes Attempted	24	45
Passes Completed	17	22
Had Intercepted	2	2
Tackled Attempting to Pass	1	4
Yards Lost Attempting to Pass	1	25
Yards Gained Passing (net)	176	243
Punts	2	4
Average Distance	34.5	37.0
Punt Returns	1	1
Punt Return Yardage	16	14
Kickoff Returns	2	7
Kickoff Return Yardage	59	112
Interception Return Yardage	31	32
Total Return Yardage	106	158
Fumbles	1	4
Own Fumbles Recovered	1	1
Opponents Fumbles Recovered	3	0
Penalties	3	5
Yards Penalized	20	40
Total Points Scored	29	10
Touchdowns	2	1
Touchdowns Rushing	1	0
Touchdowns Passing	1	1
Touchdowns Returns	0	0
Extra Points	2	1
Field Goals	5	1
Field Goals Attempted	6	1
Safeties	0	0
Third Down Efficiency	11/19	3/12
Fourth Down Efficiency	0/0	1/2
Time of Possession	36:19	23:41

Individual Statistics

Rushing

Buffalo	No.	Yds.	LG	TD
Thomas	20	96	24	0
K. Davis	19	61	12	1
Lamb	1	16	16	0
Reed	2	6	4	0
Kelly	3	4	4	0
Gardner	3	−1	1	0
Miami	**No.**	**Yds.**	**LG**	**TD**
Humphrey	8	22	6	0
Craver	2	13	11	0
Marino	1	−2	−2	0

Passing

Buffalo	Att.	Comp.	Yds.	TD	Int.
Kelly	24	17	177	1	2
Miami	**Att.**	**Comp.**	**Yds.**	**TD**	**Int.**
Marino	45	22	268	1	2

Receiving

Buffalo	No.	Yds.	LG	TD
Thomas	5	70	19	1
K. Davis	4	52	30	0
Reed	3	25	9	0
Lofton	2	19	10	0
McKeller	1	11	11	0
Metzelaars	1	6	6	0
Gardner	1	−6	−6	0
Miami	**No.**	**Yds.**	**LG**	**TD**
Jackson	5	71	24	0
Humphrey	5	41	16	0
Martin	3	55	22	0
Clayton	3	32	16	0
Duper	2	36	21	1
Banks	2	18	13	0
Craver	2	15	9	0

Interceptions

Buffalo	No.	Yds.	LG	TD
Hicks	1	31	31	0
Hansen	1	0	0	0
Miami	**No.**	**Yds.**	**LG**	**TD**
Brown	1	32	32	0
Oliver	1	0	0	0

Punting

Buffalo	No.	Avg.	LG	Blk.
Mohr	2	34.5	39	0
Miami	**No.**	**Avg.**	**LG**	**Blk.**
Roby	4	37.0	51	0

Punt Returns

Buffalo	No.	FC	Yds.	LG	TD
Hicks	1	0	16	16	0
Hale	0	1	0	0	0
Miami	**No.**	**FC**	**Yds.**	**LG**	**TD**
Miller	1	1	14	14	0

Kickoff Returns

Buffalo	No.	Yds.	LG	TD
Lamb	1	36	36	0
K. Davis	1	23	23	0
Miami	**No.**	**Yds.**	**LG**	**TD**
Craver	4	48	22	0
M. Williams	3	64	25	0

NFC Championship Game

Includes NFL Championship Games (1933-69)

Results

Season	Date	Winner (Share)	Loser (Share)	Score	Site	Attendance
1992	Jan. 17	Dallas ($18,000)	San Francisco ($18,000)	30-20	San Francisco	64,920
1991	Jan. 12	Washington ($18,000)	Detroit ($18,000)	41-10	Washington	55,585
1990	Jan. 20	N.Y. Giants ($18,000)	San Francisco ($18,000)	15-13	San Francisco	65,750
1989	Jan. 14	San Francisco ($18,000)	L.A. Rams ($18,000)	30-3	San Francisco	65,634
1988	Jan. 8	San Francisco ($18,000)	Chicago ($18,000)	28-3	Chicago	66,946
1987	Jan. 17	Washington ($18,000)	Minnesota ($18,000)	17-10	Washington	55,212
1986	Jan. 11	New York Giants ($18,000)	Washington ($18,000)	17-0	New York	76,891
1985	Jan. 12	Chicago ($18,000)	L.A. Rams ($18,000)	24-0	Chicago	66,030
1984	Jan. 6	San Francisco ($18,000)	Chicago ($18,000)	23-0	San Francisco	61,336
1983	Jan. 8	Washington ($18,000)	San Francisco ($18,000)	24-21	Washington	55,363
1982	Jan. 22	Washington ($18,000)	Dallas ($18,000)	31-17	Washington	55,045
1981	Jan. 10	San Francisco ($9,000)	Dallas ($9,000)	28-27	San Francisco	60,525
1980	Jan. 11	Philadelphia ($9,000)	Dallas ($9,000)	20-7	Philadelphia	71,522
1979	Jan. 6	Los Angeles ($9,000)	Tampa Bay ($9,000)	9-0	Tampa Bay	72,033
1978	Jan. 7	Dallas ($9,000)	Los Angeles ($9,000)	28-0	Los Angeles	71,086
1977	Jan. 1	Dallas ($9,000)	Minnesota ($9,000)	23-6	Dallas	64,293
1976	Dec. 26	Minnesota ($8,500)	Los Angeles ($5,500)	24-13	Minnesota	48,379
1975	Jan. 4	Dallas ($8,500)	Los Angeles ($5,500)	37-7	Los Angeles	88,919
1974	Dec. 29	Minnesota ($8,500)	Los Angeles ($5,500)	14-10	Minnesota	48,444
1973	Dec. 30	Minnesota ($8,500)	Dallas ($5,500)	27-10	Dallas	64,422
1972	Dec. 31	Washington ($8,500)	Dallas ($5,500)	26-3	Washington	53,129
1971	Jan. 2	Dallas ($8,500)	San Francisco ($5,500)	14-3	Dallas	63,409
1970	Jan. 3	Dallas ($8,500)	San Francisco ($5,500)	17-10	San Francisco	59,364
1969	Jan. 4	Minnesota ($7,930)	Cleveland ($5,118)	27-7	Minnesota	46,503
1968	Dec. 29	Baltimore ($9,306)	Cleveland ($5,963)	34-0	Cleveland	78,410
1967	Dec. 31	Green Bay ($7,950)	Dallas ($5,299)	21-17	Green Bay	50,861
1966	Jan. 1	Green Bay ($9,813)	Dallas ($6,527)	34-27	Dallas	74,152
1965	Jan. 2	Green Bay ($7,819)	Cleveland ($5,288)	23-12	Green Bay	50,777
1964	Dec. 27	Cleveland ($8,052)	Baltimore ($5,571)	27-0	Cleveland	79,544
1963	Dec. 29	Chicago ($5,899)	New York ($4,218)	14-10	Chicago	45,801
1962	Dec. 30	Green Bay ($5,888)	New York ($4,166)	16-7	New York	64,892
1961	Dec. 31	Green Bay ($5,195)	New York ($3,339)	37-0	Green Bay	39,029
1960	Dec. 26	Philadelphia ($5,116)	Green Bay ($3,105)	17-13	Philadelphia	67,325
1959	Dec. 27	Baltimore ($4,674)	New York ($3,083)	31-16	Baltimore	57,545
1958	Dec. 28	Baltimore ($4,718)	New York ($3,111)	23-17*	New York	64,185
1957	Dec. 29	Detroit ($4,295)	Cleveland ($2,750)	59-14	Detroit	55,263
1956	Dec. 30	New York ($3,779)	Chi. Bears ($2,485)	47-7	New York	56,836
1955	Dec. 26	Cleveland ($3,508)	Los Angeles ($2,316)	38-14	Los Angeles	85,693

Season	Date	Winner (Share)	Loser (Share)	Score	Site	Attendance
1954	Dec. 26	Cleveland ($2,478)	Detroit ($1,585)	56-10	Cleveland	43,827
1953	Dec. 27	Detroit ($2,424)	Cleveland ($1,654)	17-16	Detroit	54,577
1952	Dec. 28	Detroit ($2,274)	Cleveland ($1,712)	17-7	Cleveland	50,934
1951	Dec. 23	Los Angeles ($2,108)	Cleveland ($1,483)	24-17	Los Angeles	57,522
1950	Dec. 24	Cleveland ($1,113)	Los Angeles ($686)	30-28	Cleveland	29,751
1949	Dec. 18	Philadelphia ($1,094)	Los Angeles ($739)	14-0	Los Angeles	27,980
1948	Dec. 19	Philadelphia ($1,540)	Chi. Cardinals ($874)	7-0	Philadelphia	36,309
1947	Dec. 28	Chi. Cardinals ($1,132)	Philadelphia ($754)	28-21	Chicago	30,759
1946	Dec. 15	Chi. Bears ($1,975)	New York ($1,295)	24-14	New York	58,346
1945	Dec. 16	Cleveland ($1,469)	Washington ($902)	15-14	Cleveland	32,178
1944	Dec. 17	Green Bay ($1,449)	New York ($814)	14-7	New York	46,016
1943	Dec. 26	Chi. Bears ($1,146)	Washington ($765)	41-21	Chicago	34,320
1942	Dec. 13	Washington ($965)	Chi. Bears ($637)	14-6	Washington	36,006
1941	Dec. 21	Chi. Bears ($430)	New York ($288)	37-9	Chicago	13,341
1940	Dec. 8	Chi. Bears ($873)	Washington ($606)	73-0	Washington	36,034
1939	Dec. 10	Green Bay ($703.97)	New York ($455.57)	27-0	Milwaukee	32,279
1938	Dec. 11	New York ($504.45)	Green Bay ($368.81)	23-17	New York	48,120
1937	Dec. 12	Washington ($225.90)	Chi. Bears ($127.78)	28-21	Chicago	15,870
1936	Dec. 13	Green Bay ($250)	Boston ($180)	21-6	New York	29,545
1935	Dec. 15	Detroit ($313.35)	New York ($200.20)	26-7	Detroit	15,000
1934	Dec. 9	New York ($621)	Chi. Bears ($414.02)	30-13	New York	35,059
1933	Dec. 17	Chi. Bears ($210.34)	New York ($140.22)	23-21	Chicago	26,000

Sudden death overtime.

NFC Championship Game Composite Standings

	W	L	Pct.	Pts.	OP
Green Bay Packers	8	2	.800	223	116
Philadelphia Eagles	4	1	.800	79	48
Baltimore Colts	3	1	.750	88	60
Detroit Lions	4	2	.667	139	141
Minnesota Vikings	4	2	.667	108	80
Washington Redskins*	7	5	.583	222	255
Chicago Bears	7	6	.538	286	245
Phoenix Cardinals**	1	1	.500	28	28
Dallas Cowboys	6	7	.462	257	233
San Francisco 49ers	4	5	.444	176	133
Cleveland Browns	4	7	.364	224	253
New York Giants	5	11	.313	240	322
Los Angeles Rams***	3	9	.250	123	270
Tampa Bay Buccaneers	0	1	.000	0	9

**One game played when franchise was in Boston. (Lost 21-6)*
***Both games played when franchise was in Chicago. (Won 28-21, lost 7-0)*
****One game played when franchise was in Cleveland. (Won 15-14)*

1992 National Football Conference Championship Game

Candlestick Park, San Francisco, California — January 17, 1993
Attendance: 64,920

DALLAS 30, SAN FRANCISCO 20 — Troy Aikman passed for 322 yards and 2 touchdowns and Emmitt Smith rushed for 114 yards as the Cowboys qualified for their first Super Bowl in 14 years and their record sixth overall. Aikman was particularly effective in the second half, completing 13 of 16 passes and directing Dallas on 3 long touchdown drives to clinch the victory. The game was tied at 10-10 at intermission, but Aikman marched the Cowboys 78 yards in eight plays following the second-half kickoff. His 38-yard pass to Alvin Harper moved the ball into 49ers territory, and Daryl Johnston's 3-yard run gave Dallas a lead it would never relinquish. Smith, who also had 7 receptions for 59 yards, caught a 16-yard touchdown pass 2:35 into the fourth quarter to make it 24-13 after the Cowboys had eaten up more than nine minutes off the clock. Steve Young's 5-yard touchdown pass to Jerry Rice pulled San Francisco within 24-20 with 4:22 to go, but Harper turned Aikman's short pass into a backbreaking 70-yard gain on the next play from scrimmage. Three plays later, Aikman teamed with Kelvin Martin on a 6-yard touchdown for the clinching score with 3:43 remaining. The two teams were even in most offensive statistics, including first downs (24 each) and total yards (Dallas had 416, the 49ers 415). But the glaring difference was in turnovers, where San Francisco had 4 and the Cowboys none. Dallas turned 2 fumble recoveries into all 10 of their points in the first half, then intercepted a pair of Young passes as San Francisco tried to rally in the fourth quarter. Young finished with 313 passing yards and Rice caught 8 passes for 123 yards. Harper had 117 yards on only 3 receptions for the Cowboys.

Dallas (30)	Offense	San Francisco (20)
Alvin Harper	WR	John Taylor
Mark Tuinei	LT	Steve Wallace
Nate Newton	LG	Guy McIntyre
Mark Stepnoski	C	Jesse Sapolu
John Gesek	RG	Roy Foster
Erik Williams	RT	Harris Barton
Jay Novacek	TE	Brent Jones
Michael Irvin	WR	Jerry Rice
Troy Aikman	QB	Steve Young
Emmitt Smith	RB	Ricky Watters
Daryl Johnston	FB	Tom Rathman

	Defense	
Tony Tolbert	LE	Pierce Holt
Tony Casillas	LT-NT	Michael Carter
Russell Maryland	RT-RE	Kevin Fagan
Charles Haley	RE-LOLB	Tim Harris
Vinson Smith	LLB-LILB	Keith DeLong
Robert Jones	MLB-RILB	Mike Walter
Ken Norton	RLB-ROLB	Bill Romanowski
Kevin Smith	LCB	Eric Davis
Larry Brown	RCB	Don Griffin
Thomas Everett	SS	David Whitmore
James Washington	FS	Dana Hall

Substitutions

Dallas — Offense: K — Lin Elliott. P — Mike Saxon. QB — Steve Beuerlein. RB — Tommie Agee, Derrick Gainer. WR — Kelvin Martin, Jimmy Smith. TE — Derek Tennell. G — Kevin Gogan. C — Frank Cornish, Dale Hellestrae. Defense: E — Jim Jeffcoat. T — Chad Hennings, Jimmie Jones, Leon Lett. LB — Dixon Edwards, Godfrey Myles, Mickey Pruitt. CB — Clayton Holmes, Issiac Holt. S — Kenneth Gant, Ray Horton, Darren Woodson. DNP: None. Inactive: T — Alan Veingrad. S — Robert Williams.

San Francisco — Offense: K — Mike Cofer. P — Klaus Wilmsmeyer. QB — Steve Bono. RB — Amp Lee, Marc Logan. WR — Mike Sherrard, Odessa Turner. TE — Jamie Williams. T — Harry Boatswain. G — Brian Bollinger, Ralph Tamm. Defense: DE — Dennis Brown. NT — Ted Washington. LB — Antonio Goss, Martin Harrison, John Johnson, Darin Jordan. CB — Alan Grant, Merton Hanks, Michael McGruder. S — Thane Gash. DNP: QB — Joe Montana. DE — Garin Veris. Inactive: RB — Adam Walker. TE — Wesley Walls.

Officials

Referee — Jerry Markbreit. Umpire — Al Conway. Head Linesman — Paul Weidner. Line Judge — Tom Barnes. Back Judge — Al Jury. Field Judge — Don Hakes. Side Judge — Ron Spitler.

Scoring

Dallas	3	7	7	13	— 30
San Francisco	7	3	3	7	— 20

Dall — FG Elliott 20
SF — Young 1 run (Cofer kick)
Dall — E. Smith 4 run (Elliott kick)
SF — FG Cofer 28
Dall — Johnston 3 run (Elliott kick)
SF — FG Cofer 42
Dall — E. Smith 16 pass from Aikman (Elliott kick)
SF — Rice 5 pass from Young (Cofer kick)
Dall — Martin 6 pass from Aikman (kick blocked)

Team Statistics

	Dallas	San Francisco
Total First Downs	24	24
First Downs Rushing	7	8
First Downs Passing	16	16
First Downs Penalty	1	0
Total Net Yardage	416	415
Total Offensive Plays	68	59
Average Gain per Offensive Play	6.1	7.0
Rushes	30	21
Yards Gained Rushing (net)	121	114
Average Yards per Rush	4.0	5.4
Passes Attempted	34	35
Passes Completed	24	25
Had Intercepted	0	2
Tackled Attempting to Pass	4	3

	Dallas	San Francisco
Yards Lost Attempting to Pass	27	12
Yards Gained Passing (net)	295	301
Punts	4	1
Average Distance	35.8	57.0
Punt Returns	1	3
Punt Return Yardage	8	30
Kickoff Returns	4	5
Kickoff Return Yardage	73	114
Interception Return Yardage	35	0
Total Return Yardage	116	144
Fumbles	1	2
Own Fumbles Recovered	1	0
Opponents Fumbles Recovered	2	0
Penalties	4	4
Yards Penalized	25	38
Total Points Scored	30	20
Touchdowns	4	2
Touchdowns Rushing	2	1
Touchdowns Passing	2	1
Touchdowns Returns	0	0
Extra Points	3	2
Field Goals	1	2
Field Goals Attempted	2	3
Safeties	0	0
Third Down Efficiency	7/13	4/8
Fourth Down Efficiency	0/1	0/0
Time of Possession	35:20	24:40

Individual Statistics

Rushing

Dallas	No.	Yds.	LG	TD
E. Smith	24	114	28	1
Johnston	2	7	4	1
Harper	1	3	3	0
Aikman	3	−3	−1	0
San Francisco	**No.**	**Yds.**	**LG**	**TD**
Watters	11	69	16	0
Young	8	33	10	1
Lee	1	6	6	0
Rathman	1	6	6	0

Passing

Dallas	Att.	Comp.	Yds.	TD	Int.
Aikman	34	24	322	2	0
San Fran.	**Att.**	**Comp.**	**Yds.**	**TD**	**Int.**
Young	35	25	313	1	2

Receiving

Dallas	No.	Yds.	LG	TD
E. Smith	7	59	16t	1
Irvin	6	86	21	0
Johnston	4	26	10	0
Harper	3	117	70	0
Novacek	3	28	11	0
Martin	1	6	6t	1
San Francisco	**No.**	**Yds.**	**LG**	**TD**
Rice	8	123	36	1
Watters	6	69	17	0
Rathman	4	33	12	0
Jones	3	40	17	0
Taylor	3	33	18	0
Sherrard	1	15	15	0

Interceptions

Dallas	No.	Yds.	LG	TD
Washington	1	21	21	0
Norton	1	14	14	0
San Francisco	**No.**	**Yds.**	**LG**	**TD**
None				

Punting

Dallas	No.	Avg.	LG	Blk.
Saxon	4	35.8	49	0
San Fran.	**No.**	**Avg.**	**LG**	**Blk.**
Wilmsmeyer	1	57.0	57	0

Punt Returns

Dallas	No.	FC	Yds.	LG	TD
Martin	1	0	8	8	0
San Fran.	**No.**	**FC**	**Yds.**	**LG**	**TD**
Grant	3	1	30	15	0

Kickoff Returns

Dallas	No.	Yds.	LG	TD
Martin	3	62	31	0
K. Smith	1	11	11	0
San Francisco	**No.**	**Yds.**	**LG**	**TD**
Logan	3	79	50	0
Grant	2	35	21	0

AFC Divisional Playoffs

Includes Second-Round Playoff Games (1982), AFC Inter-Divisional Games (1969), and special playoff games to break ties for AFL Division Championships (1963, 1968)

Results

Season	Date	Winner (Share)	Loser (Share)	Score	Site	Attendance
1992	Jan. 10	Miami ($10,000)	San Diego ($10,000)	31-0	Miami	71,224
	Jan. 9	Buffalo ($10,000)	Pittsburgh ($10,000)	24-3	Pittsburgh	60,407
1991	Jan. 5	Buffalo ($10,000)	Kansas City ($10,000)	37-14	Buffalo	80,182
	Jan. 4	Denver ($10,000)	Houston ($10,000)	26-24	Denver	75,301
1990	Jan. 13	L.A. Raiders ($10,000)	Cincinnati ($10,000)	20-10	Los Angeles	92,045
	Jan. 12	Buffalo ($10,000)	Miami ($10,000)	44-34	Buffalo	77,087
1989	Jan. 7	Denver ($10,000)	Pittsburgh ($10,000)	24-23	Denver	75,477
	Jan. 6	Cleveland ($10,000)	Buffalo ($10,000)	34-30	Cleveland	78,921
1988	Jan. 1	Buffalo ($10,000)	Houston ($10,000)	17-10	Buffalo	79,532
	Dec. 31	Cincinnati ($10,000)	Seattle ($10,000)	21-13	Cincinnati	58,560
1987	Jan. 10	Denver ($10,000)	Houston ($10,000)	34-10	Denver	75,440
	Jan. 9	Cleveland ($10,000)	Indianapolis ($10,000)	38-21	Cleveland	79,372
1986	Jan. 4	Denver ($10,000)	New England ($10,000)	22-17	Denver	75,262
	Jan. 3	Cleveland ($10,000)	N.Y. Jets ($10,000)	23-20*	Cleveland	79,720
1985	Jan. 5	New England ($10,000)	L.A. Raiders ($10,000)	27-20	Los Angeles	87,163
	Jan. 4	Miami ($10,000)	Cleveland ($10,000)	24-21	Miami	74,667
1984	Dec. 30	Pittsburgh ($10,000)	Denver ($10,000)	24-17	Denver	74,981
	Dec. 29	Miami ($10,000)	Seattle ($10,000)	31-10	Miami	73,469
1983	Jan. 1	L.A. Raiders ($10,000)	Pittsburgh ($10,000)	38-10	Los Angeles	90,380
	Dec. 31	Seattle ($10,000)	Miami ($10,000)	27-20	Miami	74,136
1982	Jan. 16	Miami ($10,000)	San Diego ($10,000)	34-13	Miami	71,383
	Jan. 15	N.Y. Jets ($10,000)	L.A. Raiders ($10,000)	17-14	Los Angeles	90,038
1981	Jan. 3	Cincinnati ($5,000)	Buffalo ($5,000)	28-21	Cincinnati	55,420
	Jan. 2	San Diego ($5,000)	Miami ($5,000)	41-38*	Miami	73,735
1980	Jan. 4	Oakland ($5,000)	Cleveland ($5,000)	14-12	Cleveland	78,245
	Jan. 3	San Diego ($5,000)	Buffalo ($5,000)	20-14	San Diego	52,253
1979	Dec. 30	Pittsburgh ($5,000)	Miami ($5,000)	34-14	Pittsburgh	50,214
	Dec. 29	Houston ($5,000)	San Diego ($5,000)	17-14	San Diego	51,192
1978	Dec. 31	Houston ($5,000)	New England ($5,000)	31-14	New England	60,735
	Dec. 30	Pittsburgh ($5,000)	Denver ($5,000)	33-10	Pittsburgh	50,230
1977	Dec. 24	Oakland ($5,000)	Baltimore ($5,000)	37-31*	Baltimore	59,925
	Dec. 24	Denver ($5,000)	Pittsburgh ($5,000)	34-21	Denver	75,059
1976	Dec. 19	Pittsburgh ($)	Baltimore ($)	40-14	Baltimore	59,296
	Dec. 18	Oakland ($)	New England ($)	24-21	Oakland	53,050
1975	Dec. 28	Oakland ($)	Cincinnati ($)	31-28	Oakland	53,030
	Dec. 27	Pittsburgh ($)	Baltimore ($)	28-10	Pittsburgh	49,557
1974	Dec. 22	Pittsburgh ($)	Buffalo ($)	32-14	Pittsburgh	49,841
	Dec. 21	Oakland ($)	Miami ($)	28-26	Oakland	53,023
1973	Dec. 23	Miami ($)	Cincinnati ($)	34-16	Miami	78,928
	Dec. 22	Oakland ($)	Pittsburgh ($)	33-14	Oakland	52,646
1972	Dec. 24	Miami ($)	Cleveland ($)	20-14	Miami	78,916
	Dec. 23	Pittsburgh ($)	Oakland ($)	13-7	Pittsburgh	50,327
1971	Dec. 26	Baltimore ($)	Cleveland ($)	20-3	Cleveland	70,734
	Dec. 25	Miami ($)	Kansas City ($)	27-24*	Kansas City	45,822
1970	Dec. 27	Oakland ($)	Miami ($)	21-14	Oakland	52,594
	Dec. 26	Baltimore ($)	Cincinnati ($)	17-0	Baltimore	49,694
1969	Dec. 21	Oakland ($)	Houston ($)	56-7	Oakland	53,539
	Dec. 20	Kansas City ($)	N.Y. Jets ($)	13-6	New York	62,977
1968	Dec. 22	Oakland ($)	Kansas City ($)	41-6	Oakland	53,605
1963	Dec. 28	Boston ($)	Buffalo ($)	26-8	Buffalo	33,044

**Sudden Death Overtime.*

$ Players received 1/14 of annual salary for playoff appearances.

1992 AFC Divisional Playoff Games

Three Rivers Stadium, Pittsburgh, Pennsylvania January 9, 1993
Attendance: 60,407

BUFFALO 24, PITTSBURGH 3 — Frank Reich passed for 2 touchdowns to lead the Bills to a methodical victory over the Steelers. Reich, playing for injured starter Jim Kelly, completed 16 of 23 passes for 160 yards and was not intercepted, while running back Kenneth Davis added 104 yards on the ground. Pittsburgh, which led the NFL with 43 takeaways during the regular season, did not register any in this one while turning the ball over 4 times. Trailing 3-0 in the second quarter, Buffalo drove 59 yards to a touchdown after defensive end Phil Hansen recovered O'Donnell's fumble at the Bills' 41-yard line. Reich's 1-yard touchdown pass to tackle-eligible Mitch Frerotte capped that drive and gave Buffalo the lead for good. Reich's 17-yard touchdown pass to James Lofton 11 minutes into the second half gave the Bills all the cushion they would need. O'Donnell, who missed the last three games of the regular season, was rusty in his return, completing 15 of 29 passes for 163 yards, with 2 interceptions. Steelers running back Barry Foster gained 104 yards on 20 carries.

Buffalo	0	7	7	10	— 24
Pittsburgh	3	0	0	0	— 3

Pitt — FG Anderson 38
Buff — Frerotte 1 pass from Reich (Christie kick)
Buff — Lofton 17 pass from Reich (Christie kick)
Buff — FG Christie 43
Buff — Gardner 1 run (Christie kick)

Joe Robbie Stadium, Miami, Florida January 10, 1993
Attendance: 71,224

MIAMI 31, SAN DIEGO 0 — Dan Marino threw 3 first-half touchdown passes, including 2 just 79 seconds apart late in the second quarter, to break open a close game with the Chargers. Cornerback Troy Vincent's interception and 2-yard return to San Diego's 48-yard line set up Miami's first touchdown, a 1-yard pass from Marino to running back Tony Paige 6:30 before halftime. Minutes later, Vincent intercepted another pass, and it took Marino only two plays to put the Dolphins in the end zone again, this time on his 9-yard strike to tight end Keith Jackson with 1:46 left in the half. Chargers quarterback Stan Humphries then was intercepted for the third time in the second quarter, this time by linebacker Bryan Cox, who picked off Humphries's pass and returned it seven yards to the San Diego 42. Marino's 30-yard touchdown pass to Jackson with 27 seconds to go in the half put the game out of reach. Miami controlled the ball on the ground for most of the second half, with Aaron Craver adding a 25-yard touchdown run in the fourth quarter. Craver finished with 72 rushing yards, while Bobby Humphrey had 71. San Diego managed only 10 first downs and 202 total yards, and Humphries suffered 4 interceptions in all. The Chargers entered the game with victories in each of their last eight games and 12 of their last 13.

San Diego	0	0	0	0	— 0
Miami	0	21	0	10	— 31

Mia — Paige 1 pass from Marino (Stoyanovich kick)
Mia — K. Jackson 9 pass from Marino (Stoyanovich kick)
Mia — K. Jackson 30 pass from Marino (Stoyanovich kick)
Mia — FG Stoyanovich 22
Mia — Craver 25 run (Stoyanovich kick)

NFC Divisional Playoffs

Includes Second-Round Playoff Games (1982), NFL Conference Championship Games (1967-69), and special playoff games to break ties for NFL Division or Conference Championships (1941, 1943, 1947, 1950, 1952, 1957, 1958, 1965)

Results

Season	Date	Winner (Share)	Loser (Share)	Score	Site	Attendance
1992	Jan. 10	Dallas ($10,000)	Philadelphia ($10,000)	34-10	Dallas	63,721
	Jan. 9	San Francisco ($10,000)	Washington ($10,000)	20-13	San Francisco	64,991
1991	Jan. 5	Detroit ($10,000)	Dallas ($10,000)	38-6	Detroit	78,290
	Jan. 4	Washington ($10,000)	Atlanta ($10,000)	24-7	Washington	55,181
1990	Jan. 13	N.Y. Giants ($10,000)	Chicago ($10,000)	31-3	East Rutherford	77,025
	Jan. 12	San Francisco ($10,000)	Washington ($10,000)	28-10	San Francisco	65,292
1989	Jan. 7	L.A. Rams ($10,000)	N.Y. Giants ($10,000)	19-13*	East Rutherford	76,526
	Jan. 6	San Francisco ($10,000)	Minnesota ($10,000)	41-13	San Francisco	64,918
1988	Jan. 1	San Francisco ($10,000)	Minnesota ($10,000)	34-9	San Francisco	61,848
	Dec. 31	Chicago ($10,000)	Philadelphia ($10,000)	20-12	Chicago	65,534
1987	Jan. 10	Washington ($10,000)	Chicago ($10,000)	21-17	Chicago	65,268
	Jan. 9	Minnesota ($10,000)	San Francisco ($10,000)	36-24	San Francisco	63,008
1986	Jan. 4	N.Y. Giants ($10,000)	San Francisco ($10,000)	49-3	East Rutherford	75,691
	Jan. 3	Washington ($10,000)	Chicago ($10,000)	27-13	Chicago	65,524
1985	Jan. 5	Chicago ($10,000)	N.Y. Giants ($10,000)	21-0	Chicago	65,670
	Jan. 4	L.A. Rams ($10,000)	Dallas ($10,000)	20-0	Anaheim	66,581
1984	Dec. 30	Chicago ($10,000)	Washington ($10,000)	23-19	Washington	55,431
	Dec. 29	San Francisco ($10,000)	N.Y. Giants ($10,000)	21-10	San Francisco	60,303
1983	Jan. 1	Washington ($10,000)	L.A. Rams ($10,000)	51-7	Washington	54,440
	Dec. 31	San Francisco ($10,000)	Detroit ($10,000)	24-23	San Francisco	59,979
1982	Jan. 16	Dallas ($10,000)	Green Bay ($10,000)	37-26	Dallas	63,972
	Jan. 15	Washington ($10,000)	Minnesota ($10,000)	21-7	Washington	54,593
1981	Jan. 3	San Francisco ($5,000)	N.Y. Giants ($5,000)	38-24	San Francisco	58,360
	Jan. 2	Dallas ($5,000)	Tampa Bay ($5,000)	38-0	Dallas	64,848
1980	Jan. 4	Dallas ($5,000)	Atlanta ($5,000)	30-27	Atlanta	59,793
	Jan. 3	Philadelphia ($5,000)	Minnesota ($5,000)	31-16	Philadelphia	70,178
1979	Dec. 30	Los Angeles ($5,000)	Dallas ($5,000)	21-19	Dallas	64,792
	Dec. 29	Tampa Bay ($5,000)	Philadelphia ($5,000)	24-17	Tampa Bay	71,402
1978	Dec. 31	Los Angeles ($5,000)	Minnesota ($5,000)	34-10	Los Angeles	70,436
	Dec. 30	Dallas ($5,000)	Atlanta ($5,000)	27-20	Dallas	63,406
1977	Dec. 26	Dallas ($5,000)	Chicago ($5,000)	37-7	Dallas	63,260
	Dec. 26	Minnesota ($5,000)	Los Angeles ($5,000)	14-7	Los Angeles	70,203
1976	Dec. 19	Los Angeles ($)	Dallas ($)	14-12	Dallas	63,283
	Dec. 18	Minnesota ($)	Washington ($)	35-20	Minnesota	47,466
1975	Dec. 28	Dallas ($)	Minnesota ($)	17-14	Minnesota	48,050
	Dec. 27	Los Angeles ($)	St. Louis ($)	35-23	Los Angeles	73,459
1974	Dec. 22	Los Angeles ($)	Washington ($)	19-10	Los Angeles	77,925
	Dec. 21	Minnesota ($)	St. Louis ($)	30-14	Minnesota	48,150
1973	Dec. 23	Dallas ($)	Los Angeles ($)	27-16	Dallas	63,272
	Dec. 22	Minnesota ($)	Washington ($)	27-20	Minnesota	48,040
1972	Dec. 24	Washington ($)	Green Bay ($)	16-3	Washington	52,321
	Dec. 23	Dallas ($)	San Francisco ($)	30-28	San Francisco	59,746
1971	Dec. 26	San Francisco ($)	Washington ($)	24-20	San Francisco	45,327
	Dec. 25	Dallas ($)	Minnesota ($)	20-12	Minnesota	47,307
1970	Dec. 27	San Francisco ($)	Minnesota ($)	17-14	Minnesota	45,103
	Dec. 26	Dallas ($)	Detroit ($)	5-0	Dallas	69,613
1969	Dec. 28	Cleveland ($)	Dallas ($)	38-14	Dallas	69,321
	Dec. 27	Minnesota ($)	Los Angeles ($)	23-20	Minnesota	47,900
1968	Dec. 22	Baltimore ($)	Minnesota ($)	24-14	Baltimore	60,238
	Dec. 21	Cleveland ($)	Dallas ($)	31-20	Cleveland	81,497
1967	Dec. 24	Dallas ($)	Cleveland ($)	52-14	Dallas	70,786
	Dec. 23	Green Bay ($)	Los Angeles ($)	28-7	Milwaukee	49,861
1965	Dec. 26	Green Bay ($)	Baltimore ($)	13-10*	Green Bay	50,484

Season	Date	Winner (Share)	Loser (Share)	Score	Site	Attendance
1958	Dec. 21	N.Y. Giants (#)	Cleveland (#)	10-0	New York	61,274
1957	Dec. 22	Detroit (#)	San Francisco (#)	31-27	San Francisco	60,118
1952	Dec. 21	Detroit (#)	Los Angeles (#)	31-21	Detroit	47,645
1950	Dec. 17	Los Angeles (#)	Chicago Bears (#)	24-14	Los Angeles	83,501
	Dec. 17	Cleveland (#)	N.Y. Giants (#)	8-3	Cleveland	33,054
1947	Dec. 21	Philadelphia (#)	Pittsburgh (#)	21-0	Pittsburgh	35,729
1943	Dec. 19	Washington (¢)	N.Y. Giants (¢)	28-0	New York	42,800
1941	Dec. 14	Chicago Bears (¢)	Green Bay (¢)	33-14	Chicago	43,425

**Sudden Death Overtime.*
$ Players received 1/14 of annual salary for playoff appearances.
 # Players received 1/12 of annual salary for playoff appearances.
¢ Players received 1/10 of annual salary for playoff appearances.

1992 NFC Divisional Playoff Games

Candlestick Park, San Francisco, California — January 9, 1993
Attendance: 64,991

SAN FRANCISCO 20, WASHINGTON 13—Steve Young threw 2 touchdown passes and survived 4 turnovers as the 49ers eliminated the Super Bowl XXVI champions. Young completed 20 of 30 passes for 227 yards, including scoring strikes of 5 yards to wide receiver John Taylor and 16 yards to tight end Brent Jones that helped San Francisco build a 17-3 advantage in the first half. But the 49ers' quarterback also lost 3 fumbles, the last of which the Redskins converted into a 15-yard drive capped by quarterback Mark Rypien's 1-yard sneak for a touchdown that trimmed the margin to 17-13 with 14:36 left in the game. Moments later, Washington was driving again, and reached San Francisco's 23-yard line before Rypien fumbled while trying to hand off. The 49ers took over and ate up more than seven minutes on a 59-yard, 14-play drive that culiminated in Mike Cofer's 33-yard field goal with 2:22 remaining. Ricky Watters ran for 83 yards and Young added 73 yards on only 8 carries for San Francisco, which amassed 401 total yards. The Redskins had 323 total yards, but also were victimized by 4 turnovers. 49ers defensive end Pierce Holt recorded 3 of his team's 5 sacks.

Washington	3	0	3	7	— 13
San Francisco	7	10	0	3	— 20

SF —Taylor 5 pass from Young (Cofer kick)
Wash—FG Lohmiller 19
SF —FG Cofer 23
SF —Jones 16 pass from Young (Cofer kick)
Wash—FG Lohmiller 32
Wash—Rypien 1 run (Lohmiller kick)
SF —FG Cofer 33

Texas Stadium, Irving, Texas — January 10, 1993
Attendance: 63,721

DALLAS 34, PHILADELPHIA 10—The Cowboys converted a balanced offense and a stingy defense into an easy victory over the Eagles. Philadelphia took a 3-0 lead on Roger Ruzek's 32-yard field goal 7:15 into the game, but Dallas countered with Troy Aikman's 1-yard touchdown pass to tight end Derek Tennell and a 7-3 advantage. Aikman's second touchdown pass, a 6-yarder to tight end Jay Novacek, gave the Cowboys a 14-3 advantage just 47 seconds before intermission. On the ensuing kickoff, Vai Sikahema fumbled, and Dallas converted the turnover into a 20-yard field goal by Lin Elliott as time ran out in the half. The Cowboys went on to build a 34-3 advantage in the fourth quarter before the Eagles got their lone touchdown in the final minute. Emmitt Smith ran for 114 yards, including a 23-yard touchdown run, as Dallas amassed 160 rushing yards. The Cowboys added 185 yards through the air as Aikman completed 15 of 25 passes. Philadelphia managed only 178 total yards. Randall Cunningham completed 17 of 30 passes, but was sacked 5 times and accumulated most of his 160 yards in the final period, long after the game had been decided.

Philadelphia	3	0	0	7	— 10
Dallas	7	10	10	7	— 34

Phil—FG Ruzek 32
Dall—Tennell 1 pass from Aikman (Elliott kick)
Dall—Novacek 6 pass from Aikman (Elliott kick)
Dall—FG Elliott 20
Dall—E. Smith 23 run (Elliott kick)
Dall—FG Elliott 43
Dall—Gainer 1 run (Elliott kick)
Phil—C. Williams 18 pass from Cunningham (Ruzek kick)

AFC Wild Card Playoff Games

Results

Season	Date	Winner (Share)	Loser (Share)	Score	Site	Attendance
1992	Jan. 3	Buffalo ($6,000)	Houston ($6,000)	41-38*	Buffalo	75,141
	Jan. 2	San Diego ($10,000)	Kansas City ($6,000)	17-0	San Diego	58,278
1991	Dec. 29	Houston ($10,000)	N.Y. Jets ($6,000)	17-10	Houston	61,485
	Dec. 28	Kansas City ($6,000)	L.A. Raiders ($6,000)	10-6	Kansas City	75,827
1990	Jan. 6	Cincinnati ($10,000)	Houston ($6,000)	41-14	Cincinnati	60,012
	Jan. 5	Miami ($6,000)	Kansas City ($6,000)	17-16	Miami	67,276
1989	Dec. 31	Pittsburgh ($6,000)	Houston ($6,000)	26-23*	Houston	59,406
1988	Dec. 26	Houston ($6,000)	Cleveland ($6,000)	24-23	Cleveland	75,896
1987	Jan. 3	Houston ($6,000)	Seattle ($6,000)	23-20*	Houston	50,519
1986	Dec. 28	N.Y. Jets ($6,000)	Kansas City ($6,000)	35-15	East Rutherford	75,210
1985	Dec. 28	New England ($6,000)	N.Y. Jets ($6,000)	26-14	East Rutherford	75,945
1984	Dec. 22	Seattle ($6,000)	L.A. Raiders ($6,000)	13-7	Seattle	62,049
1983	Dec. 24	Seattle ($6,000)	Denver ($6,000)	31-7	Seattle	64,275
1982	Jan. 9	N.Y. Jets ($6,000)	Cincinnati ($6,000)	44-17	Cincinnati	57,560
	Jan. 9	San Diego ($6,000)	Pittsburgh ($6,000)	31-28	Pittsburgh	53,546
	Jan. 8	L.A. Raiders ($6,000)	Cleveland ($6,000)	27-10	Los Angeles	56,555
	Jan. 8	Miami ($6,000)	New England ($6,000)	28-13	Miami	68,842
1981	Dec. 27	Buffalo ($3,000)	N.Y. Jets ($3,000)	31-27	New York	57,050
1980	Dec. 28	Oakland ($3,000)	Houston ($3,000)	27-7	Oakland	53,333
1979	Dec. 23	Houston ($3,000)	Denver ($3,000)	13-7	Houston	48,776
1978	Dec. 24	Houston ($3,000)	Miami ($3,000)	17-9	Miami	72,445

**Sudden death overtime.*

1992 AFC Wild Card Playoff Games

San Diego Jack Murphy Stadium, San Diego, California — January 2, 1993
Attendance: 58,278

SAN DIEGO 17, KANSAS CITY 0 — Marion Butts broke a scoreless tie with a 54-yard touchdown run in the third quarter and the Chargers ground out a victory over the Chiefs. San Diego, whose lone loss over the final 12 weeks of the regular season came against Kansas City, rushed for 192 yards while limiting the Chiefs to 61. Butts had 119 yards on 15 carries, including his scoring run with 5:53 left in the third quarter. On Kansas City's next possession, Chargers defensive tackle Blaise Winter tipped a Dave Krieg pass, and end Leslie O'Neal intercepted it to set up John Carney's 34-yard field goal. San Diego put the game away in the fourth quarter with a 10-play, 90-yard drive capped by Steve Hendrickson's 5-yard touchdown run with 4:57 left in the game. Hendrickson, a linebacker who doubles as a blocking back in goal-line situations, carried for the first time all year. The Chargers' defense did the rest, limiting the Chiefs to 251 total yards. Krieg passed for 233 yards, but completed only 16 of 34 attempts, was sacked 7 times, and was intercepted twice. San Diego defensive end Burt Grossman had 2½ sacks, while O'Neal and tackle Shawn Lee added 2 each.

Kansas City	0	0	0	0	— 0
San Diego	0	0	10	7	— 17

SD— Butts 54 run (Carney kick)
SD— FG Carney 34
SD— Hendrickson 5 run (Carney kick)

Rich Stadium, Orchard Park, New York — January 3, 1993
Attendance: 75,141

BUFFALO 41, HOUSTON 38 — Frank Reich threw 4 second-half touchdown passes and Steve Christie kicked a 32-yard field goal 3:06 into overtime as the Bills mounted the greatest comeback in NFL history to stun the Oilers. Houston led 35-3 after Warren Moon threw 4 first-half touchdown passes and safety Bubba McDowell returned an interception 58 yards for a score 1:41 into the third quarter. Then Reich, who as a collegian had rallied Maryland from a 31-0 halftime deficit to a 42-40 victory over Miami, began the dramatic rally by engineering a 50-yard drive capped by Kenneth Davis's 1-yard run with 8:54 left in the third quarter. Christie recovered his ensuing onside kickoff and Reich's 38-yard touchdown pass four plays later made it 38-17. After a short punt by the Oilers, Reich took only four more plays to march his team 59 yards to a touchdown on his 26-yard pass to Andre Reed. Houston's next possession ended in an interception by Buffalo safety Henry Jones, which set up Reich's 18-yard pass to Reed, the Bills' fourth touchdown in a span of 6:54. It stayed 35-31 until late in the game, when Buffalo drove 74 yards in seven plays. The drive was capped by Reed's third touchdown, a 17-yard throw from Reich that gave the Bills the lead for the first time. Moon rallied the Oilers to a short field goal with 12 seconds left in regulation to tie the score, but was intercepted by cornerback Henry Odomes on the first possession of overtime. Odomes's 2-yard return and a 15-yard facemask penalty on Houston wide receiver Haywood Jeffires positioned Buffalo for the winning field goal three plays later. Reich, subbing for injured starter Jim Kelly, completed 21 of 34 passes for 389 yards, including 8 for 136 yards to Reed. Moon, who was 19 of 22 as the Oilers built their first-half advantage, finished 36 of 50 for 371 yards. Ernest Givins caught 9 passes for 117 yards and Jeffires had 8 receptions for 98 yards and 2 touchdowns. Previously, the largest deficit any NFL team had overcome to win was 28 points, when the 49ers rallied to a 38-35 victory over the Saints after trailing 35-7 in a game in 1980. The largest postseason comeback came when the Lions erased a 27-7 deficit to the 49ers to win 31-27 in a Western Conference playoff in 1957.

Houston	7	21	7	3	0	— 38
Buffalo	3	0	28	7	3	— 41

Hou— Jeffires 3 pass from Moon (Del Greco kick)
Buff— FG Christie 36
Hou— Slaughter 7 pass from Moon (Del Greco kick)
Hou— Duncan 26 pass from Moon (Del Greco kick)
Hou— Jeffires 27 pass from Moon (Del Greco kick)
Hou— McDowell 58 interception return (Del Greco kick)
Buff— K. Davis 1 run (Christie kick)
Buff— Beebe 38 pass from Reich (Christie kick)
Buff— Reed 26 pass from Reich (Christie kick)
Buff— Reed 18 pass from Reich (Christie kick)
Buff— Reed 17 pass from Reich (Christie kick)
Hou— FG Del Greco 26
Buff— FG Christie 32

NFC Wild Card Playoff Games

Results

Season	Date	Winner (Share)	Loser (Share)	Score	Site	Attendance
1992	Jan. 3	Philadelphia ($6,000)	New Orleans ($6,000)	36-20	New Orleans	68,893
	Jan. 2	Washington ($6,000)	Minnesota ($10,000)	24-7	Minneapolis	57,353
1991	Dec. 29	Dallas ($6,000)	Chicago ($6,000)	17-13	Chicago	62,594
	Dec. 28	Atlanta ($6,000)	New Orleans ($6,000)	27-20	New Orleans	68,794
1990	Jan. 6	Chicago ($10,000)	New Orleans ($10,000)	16-6	Chicago	60,767
	Jan. 5	Washington ($6,000)	Philadelphia ($6,000)	20-6	Philadelphia	65,287
1989	Dec. 31	L.A. Rams ($6,000)	Philadelphia ($6,000)	21-7	Philadelphia	65,479
1988	Dec. 26	Minnesota ($6,000)	L.A. Rams ($6,000)	28-17	Minnesota	61,204
1987	Jan. 3	Minnesota ($6,000)	New Orleans ($6,000)	44-10	New Orleans	68,546
1986	Dec. 28	Washington ($6,000)	L.A. Rams ($6,000)	19-7	Washington	54,567
1985	Dec. 29	N.Y. Giants ($6,000)	San Francisco ($6,000)	17-3	East Rutherford	75,131
1984	Dec. 23	N.Y. Giants ($6,000)	L.A. Rams ($6,000)	16-3	Anaheim	67,037
1983	Dec. 26	L.A. Rams ($6,000)	Dallas ($6,000)	24-17	Dallas	62,118
1982	Jan. 9	Dallas ($6,000)	Tampa Bay ($6,000)	30-17	Dallas	65,042
	Jan. 9	Minnesota ($6,000)	Atlanta ($6,000)	30-24	Minnesota	60,560
	Jan. 8	Green Bay ($6,000)	St. Louis ($6,000)	41-16	Green Bay	54,282
	Jan. 8	Washington ($6,000)	Detroit ($6,000)	31-7	Washington	55,045
1981	Dec. 27	N.Y. Giants ($3,000)	Philadelphia ($3,000)	27-21	Philadelphia	71,611
1980	Dec. 28	Dallas ($3,000)	Los Angeles ($3,000)	34-13	Dallas	63,052
1979	Dec. 23	Philadelphia ($3,000)	Chicago ($3,000)	27-17	Philadelphia	69,397
1978	Dec. 24	Atlanta ($3,000)	Philadelphia ($3,000)	14-13	Atlanta	59,403

1992 NFC Wild Card Playoff Games

Metrodome, Minneapolis, Minnesota — January 2, 1993
Attendance: 57,353

WASHINGTON 24, MINNESOTA 7 — Third-string running back Brian Mitchell ran for 109 yards and added 100 yards on punt returns and receptions as the Redskins, the NFC's lowest seed in the playoffs, upset the Central Division-champion Vikings. Mitchell had carried the ball only 6 times during the regular season and 18 times in his three-year NFL career, but with backup Ricky Ervins injured, he had 16 rushes in this game. The key play was his 36-yard run from Washington's 44-yard line on a fake punt late in the second quarter. Moments later, he scored on an 8-yard run to increase the Redskins' lead to 17-7 at intermission. Minnesota took the game's opening kickoff and marched 79 yards to a touchdown, Terry Allen's 1-yard run, but then managed only 69 total yards the rest of the way. Quarterback Sean Salisbury completed 42- and 14-yard passes to Cris Carter to key the first drive, but finished only 6 of 20 for 113 yards, with a pair of interceptions. Meanwhile, Washington's offense controlled the ball on the ground, rushing for 196 yards on 47 attempts and maintaining possession for 42:43 of the game's 60 minutes. The Redskins improved their postseason record to 16-4 under head coach Joe Gibbs.

Washington	3	14	7	0	— 24
Minnesota	7	0	0	0	— 7

Minn — Allen 1 run (Reveiz kick)
Wash — FG Lohmiller 44
Wash — Byner 3 run (Lohmiller kick)
Wash — Mitchell 8 run (Lohmiller kick)
Wash — Clark 24 pass from Rypien (Lohmiller kick)

Louisiana Superdome, New Orleans, Louisiana — January 3, 1993
Attendance: 68,893

PHILADELPHIA 36, NEW ORLEANS 20 — The Eagles exploded for 26 points in the fourth quarter to rally past the Saints and win a playoff game for the first time since the 1980 NFL Championship Game. New Orleans, the only NFL team that has never won a postseason game, led 20-7 until Philadelphia's Roger Ruzek kicked a 40-yard field goal late in the third quarter to trim the margin to 10 points. In the fourth period, Randall Cunningham's 35-yard touchdown pass to Fred Barnett with 10:37 remaining sparked an Eagles' scoring frenzy against the Saints, who had allowed the fewest points in the NFL during the regular season and had not permitted any opponent more than 21 points in a game all year. On the first play from scrimmage following Barnett's touchdown, Eagles linebacker Seth Joyner intercepted a Bobby Hebert pass and returned it 14 yards to the Saints' 26-yard line. That set up a 6-yard touchdown run by Heath Sherman for a 24-20 Philadelphia lead with 6:48 left in the game. Seventy-two seconds later, defensive end Reggie White sacked Hebert in the end zone to make it 26-20, and Roger Ruzek's 39-yard field goal at the 2:36 mark made it 29-20. Cornerback Eric Allen sealed the victory 19 seconds later with his second interception of the game, returning it 18 yards for a touchdown. Sherman finished with 105 yards on 21 carries, while Cunningham passed for 219 yards and 2 touchdowns, both to Barnett. Hebert completed 23 of 39 passes for 291 yards and a touchdown, but was intercepted 3 times.

Philadelphia	7	0	3	26	— 36
New Orleans	7	10	3	0	— 20

NO — Heyward 1 run (Andersen kick)
Phil — Barnett 57 pass from Cunningham (Ruzek kick)
NO — FG Andersen 35
NO — Early 7 pass from Hebert (Andersen kick)
NO — FG Andersen 42
Phil — FG Ruzek 40
Phil — Barnett 35 pass from Cunningham (Ruzek kick)
Phil — Sherman 6 run (Ruzek kick)
Phil — Safety, White sacked Hebert in end zone
Phil — FG Ruzek 39
Phil — Allen 18 interception return (Ruzek kick)

AFC-NFC PRO BOWL SUMMARIES

AFC-NFC Pro Bowl At A Glance (1971-1993)

NFC leads series, 13-10

Results

Year	Date	Winner (Share)	Loser (Share)	Score	Site	Attendance
1993	Feb. 7	AFC ($10,000)	NFC ($5,000)	23-20 (OT)	Honolulu	50,007
1992	Feb. 2	NFC ($10,000)	AFC ($5,000)	21-15	Honolulu	50,209
1991	Feb. 3	AFC ($10,000)	NFC ($5,000)	23-21	Honolulu	50,345
1990	Feb. 4	NFC ($10,000)	AFC ($5,000)	27-21	Honolulu	50,445
1989	Jan. 29	NFC ($10,000)	AFC ($5,000)	34-3	Honolulu	50,113
1988	Feb. 7	AFC ($10,000)	NFC ($5,000)	15-6	Honolulu	50,113
1987	Feb. 1	AFC ($10,000)	NFC ($5,000)	10-6	Honolulu	50,101
1986	Feb. 2	NFC ($10,000)	AFC ($5,000)	28-24	Honolulu	50,101
1985	Jan. 27	AFC ($10,000)	NFC ($5,000)	22-14	Honolulu	50,385
1984	Jan. 29	NFC ($10,000)	AFC ($5,000)	45-3	Honolulu	50,445
1983	Feb. 6	NFC ($10,000)	AFC ($5,000)	20-19	Honolulu	49,883
1982	Jan. 31	AFC ($5,000)	NFC ($2,500)	16-13	Honolulu	50,402
1981	Feb. 1	NFC ($5,000)	AFC ($2,500)	21-7	Honolulu	50,360
1980	Jan. 27	NFC ($5,000)	AFC ($2,500)	37-27	Honolulu	49,800
1979	Jan. 29	NFC ($5,000)	AFC ($2,500)	13-7	Los Angeles	46,281
1978	Jan. 23	NFC ($5,000)	AFC ($2,500)	14-13	Tampa	51,337
1977	Jan. 17	AFC ($2,000)	NFC ($1,500)	24-14	Seattle	64,752
1976	Jan. 26	NFC ($2,000)	AFC ($1,500)	23-20	New Orleans	30,546
1975	Jan. 20	NFC ($2,000)	AFC ($1,500)	17-10	Miami	26,484
1974	Jan. 20	AFC ($2,000)	NFC ($1,500)	15-13	Kansas City	66,918
1973	Jan. 21	AFC ($2,000)	NFC ($1,500)	33-28	Irving	37,091
1972	Jan. 23	AFC ($2,000)	NFC ($1,500)	26-13	Los Angeles	53,647
1971	Jan. 24	NFC ($2,000)	AFC ($1,500)	27-6	Los Angeles	48,222

1993 AFC-NFC Pro Bowl

Aloha Stadium, Honolulu, Hawaii — February 7, 1993

Attendance: 50,007

AFC 23, NFC 20 — Nick Lowery's 33-yard field goal 4:09 into overtime gave the American Conference all-stars an unlikely 23-20 victory over the National Conference. Despite being overwhelmed by the NFC in first downs (30-9), total yards (472-114), and time of possession (40:19-23:50), the AFC won because it forced 6 turnovers, blocked a pair of field goals (1 of which was returned for a touchdown), and returned an interception for a score. Special-teams star Steve Tasker of the Bills earned the Dan McGuire Trophy as the player of the game for making 4 tackles, forcing a fumble, and blocking a field goal. The block came with eight minutes left in regulation and the game tied at 13-13. The Raiders' Terry McDaniel picked up the loose ball and ran 28 yards for a touchdown and a 20-13 AFC lead. The NFC rallied behind 49ers quarterback Steve Young, whose fourth-down, 23-yard touchdown pass to Giants running back Rodney Hampton tied the game at 20-20 with 10 seconds left in regulation. Young completed 18 of 32 passes for 196 yards but was intercepted 3 times and lost a fumble when sacked in overtime. Raiders defensive end Howie Long fell on that fumble at the NFC 28-yard line, and five plays later, Lowery converted the winning field goal.

AFC (23)	Offense	NFC (20)
Anthony Miller (San Diego)	WR	Jerry Rice (San Francisco)
Howard Ballard (Buffalo)	LT	Gary Zimmerman (Minnesota)
Mike Munchak (Houston)	LG	Guy McIntyre (San Francisco)
Bruce Matthews (Houston)	C	Joel Hilgenberg (New Orleans)
Carlton Haselrig (Pittsburgh)	RG	Randall McDaniel (Minnesota)
Richmond Webb (Miami)	RT	Lomas Brown (Detroit)
Marv Cook (New England)	TE	Jay Novacek (Dallas)
Haywood Jeffires (Houston)	WR	Sterling Sharpe (Green Bay)
Dan Marino (Miami)	QB	Steve Young (San Francisco)
Barry Foster (Pittsburgh)	RB	Barry Sanders (Detroit)
Harold Green (Cincinnati)	RB	Emmitt Smith (Dallas)
	Defense	
Neil Smith (Kansas City)	LE	Reggie White (Philadelphia)
Cortez Kennedy (Seattle)	NT	Pierce Holt (San Francisco)
Leslie O'Neal (San Diego)	RE	Chris Doleman (Minnesota)
Derrick Thomas (Kansas City)	LOLB	Rickey Jackson (New Orleans)
Al Smith (Houston)	LILB	Sam Mills (New Orleans)
Junior Seau (San Diego)	RILB	Jessie Tuggle (Atlanta)
Bryan Cox (Miami)	ROLB	Pat Swilling (New Orleans)
Terry McDaniel (L.A. Raiders)	LCB	Deion Sanders (Atlanta)
Rod Woodson (Pittsburgh)	RCB	Eric Allen (Philadelphia)
Henry Jones (Buffalo)	SS	Tim McDonald (Phoenix)
Steve Atwater (Denver)	FS	Chuck Cecil (Green Bay)

Substitutions

AFC — Offense: K — Nick Lowery (Kansas City). P — Rohn Stark (Indianapolis). QB — Warren Moon (Houston), Neil O'Donnell (Pittsburgh). RB — Ronnie Harmon (San Diego), Lorenzo White (Houston). WR — Curtis Duncan (Houston), Ernest Givins (Houston), Andre Reed (Buffalo). TE — Shannon Sharpe (Denver). ST — Steve Tasker (Buffalo). KR — Clarence Verdin (Indianapolis). T — John Alt (Kansas City). G — Jim Ritcher (Buffalo). C — Dermontti Dawson (Pittsburgh). Defense: E — Howie Long (L.A. Raiders). NT — Ray Childress (Houston). LB — Cornelius Bennett (Buffalo), Michael Brooks (Denver), Greg Lloyd (Pittsburgh). CB — Nate Odomes (Buffalo). S — Eugene Robinson (Seattle). DNP — None.

NFC — Offense: K — Morten Andersen (New Orleans). P — Rich Camarillo (Phoenix). QB — Troy Aikman (Dallas), Brett Favre (Green Bay). RB — Rodney Hampton (N.Y. Giants), Ricky Watters (San Francisco). WR — Fred Barnett (Philadelphia), Michael Irvin (Dallas), Andre Rison (Atlanta). TE — Brent Jones (San Francisco). ST — Elbert Shelley (Atlanta). KR — Johnny Bailey (Phoenix). C — Mark Stepnoski (Dallas). G — Nate Newton (Dallas). T — Steve Wallace (San Francisco). Defense: E — Clyde Simmons (Philadelphia). NT — Henry Thomas (Minnesota). LB — Vaughan Johnson (New Orleans), Wilber Marshall (Washington), Mike Singletary (Chicago). CB — Robert Massey (Phoenix). S — Todd Scott (Minnesota). DNP — None.

Head Coaches

AFC — Don Shula (Miami)

NFC — George Seifert (San Francisco)

Officials

Referee — Howard Roe. Umpire — Neil Gereb. Head Linesman — Aaron Pointer. Line Judge — John Alderton. Back Judge — Banks Williams. Field Judge — Phil Luckett. Side Judge — Mike Borgard.

Scoring

AFC	0	10	3	7	3 — 23
NFC	3	10	0	7	0 — 20

NFC — FG Andersen 27

AFC — Seau 31 interception return (Lowery kick)

NFC — FG Andersen 37

NFC — Irvin 9 pass from Aikman (Andersen kick)

AFC — FG Lowery 42

AFC — FG Lowery 29

AFC — McDaniel 28 blocked field goal return (Lowery kick)

NFC — Hampton 23 pass from Young (Andersen kick)

AFC — FG Lowery 33

Team Statistics

	AFC	NFC
Total First Downs	9	30
First Downs Rushing	2	6
First Downs Passing	6	21
First Downs Penalty	1	3
Total Net Yardage	114	472
Total Offensive Plays	50	90
Average Gain per Offensive Play	2.3	5.2
Rushes	23	29
Yards Gained Rushing (net)	67	103
Average Yards per Rush	2.9	3.6
Passes Attempted	24	55
Passes Completed	9	32
Had Intercepted	1	4
Tackled Attempting to Pass	3	6
Yards Lost Attempting to Pass	24	21
Yards Gained Passing (net)	47	369
Punts	7	1
Average Distance	45.3	46.0

Punt Returns	1	6
Punt Return Yardage	20	59
Kickoff Returns	4	5
Kickoff Return Yardage	86	126
Interception Return Yardage	76	−6
Total Return Yardage	182	179
Fumbles	1	3
Own Fumbles Recovered	1	1
Opponent Fumbles Recovered	2	0
Penalties	9	9
Yards Penalized	73	60
Total Points Scored	23	20
Touchdowns	2	2
Touchdowns Rushing	0	0
Touchdowns Passing	0	2
Touchdowns Returns	2	0
Extra Points	2	2
Field Goals	3	2
Field Goals Attempted	4	4
Safeties	0	0
Third Down Efficiency	3/12	11/19
Fourth Down Efficiency	0/0	1/3
Time of Possession	23:50	40:19

Individual Statistics

Rushing

AFC	No.	Yds.	LG	TD
Foster	15	57	8	0
Green	4	9	7	0
Harmon	1	1	1	0
White	2	1	2	0
Marino	1	−1	−1	0
NFC	**No.**	**Yds.**	**LG**	**TD**
Young	6	34	10	0
E. Smith	5	27	23	0
B. Sanders	7	19	8	0
Hampton	3	11	6	0
Watters	6	9	6	0
Rice	1	3	3	0
Favre	1	0	0	0

Passing

AFC	Att.	Comp.	Yds.	TD	Int.
Marino	9	3	31	0	0
Moon	8	2	17	0	0
O'Donnell	7	4	23	0	1
NFC	**Att.**	**Comp.**	**Yds.**	**TD**	**Int.**
Young	32	18	196	1	3
Aikman	15	10	120	1	1
Favre	8	4	74	0	0

Receiving

AFC	No.	Yds.	LG	TD
Jeffires	3	26	11	0
Miller	2	23	16	0
Reed	2	11	9	0
Sh. Sharpe	1	6	6	0
Givins	1	5	5	0
NFC	**No.**	**Yds.**	**LG**	**TD**
Rison	8	80	18	0
Irvin	5	59	19	1
Rice	4	78	48	0
Novacek	4	43	26	0
B. Jones	3	43	16	0
Hampton	3	35	23t	1
B. Sanders	2	23	19	0
Barnett	1	16	16	0
St. Sharpe	1	7	7	0
E. Smith	1	6	6	0

Interceptions

AFC	No.	Yds.	LG	TD
H. Jones	1	32	32	0
Seau	1	31	31t	1
Odomes	1	13	13	0
Atwater	1	0	0	0
NFC	**No.**	**Yds.**	**LG**	**TD**
McDonald	1	−6	−6	0

Punting

AFC	No.	Avg.	LG	Blk.
Stark	7	45.3	53	0
NFC	**No.**	**Avg.**	**LG**	**Blk.**
Camarillo	1	46.0	46	0

Punt Returns

AFC	No.	FC	Yds.	LG	TD
Verdin	1	0	20	20	0
NFC	**No.**	**FC**	**Yds.**	**LG**	**TD**
Bailey	5	1	45	20	0
D. Sanders	0	0	14	14	0

Kickoff Returns

AFC	No.	Yds.	LG	TD
Verdin	3	64	38	0
Miller	1	22	22	0
NFC	**No.**	**Yds.**	**LG**	**TD**
D. Sanders	3	84	46	0
Bailey	2	42	22	0

1992 AFC-NFC Pro Bowl

Aloha Stadium, Honolulu, Hawaii — February 2, 1992

Attendance: 50,209

NFC 21, AFC 15 — Atlanta's Chris Miller threw an 11-yard touchdown pass to San Francisco's Jerry Rice with 4:04 remaining in the game to lift the NFC over the AFC. It was the NFC's thirteenth win in the 22-game series. The AFC had taken a 15-14 lead when the Raiders' Jeff Jaeger kicked a 27-yard field goal 1:49 into the fourth quarter. But the NFC, aided by a key roughing-the-passer penalty on a third-down incompletion from the AFC 24-yard line, drove 85 yards to the winning score. The Cowboys' Michael Irvin, playing in his first Pro Bowl, caught 8 passes for 125 yards, including a 13-yard touchdown in the first quarter, and was named the player of the game. Rice had 7 catches for 77 yards. Mark Rypien of Washington, the Super Bowl most valuable player one week earlier, completed 11 of 18 passes for 165 yards and 2 touchdowns for the NFC, including a 35-yarder to Redskins teammate Gary Clark just 26 seconds before halftime. Miller completed 7 of his 10 attempts for 85 yards.

NFC	7	7	0	7	— 21
AFC	7	5	0	3	— 15

AFC — Clayton 4 pass from Kelly (Jaeger kick)
NFC — Irvin 13 pass from Rypien (Lohmiller kick)
AFC — Safety, Townsend tackled Byner in end zone
AFC — FG Jaeger 48
NFC — Clark 35 pass from Rypien (Lohmiller kick)
AFC — FG Jaeger 27
NFC — Rice 11 pass from Miller (Lohmiller kick)

1991 AFC-NFC Pro Bowl

Aloha Stadium, Honolulu, Hawaii — February 3, 1991

Attendance: 50,345

AFC 23, NFC 21 — Buffalo's Jim Kelly and Houston's Ernest Givins combined for a 13-yard scoring pass late in the fourth quarter to rally the AFC over the NFC. Phoenix rookie Johnny Johnson scored on runs of one and nine yards to put the NFC ahead 14-3 in the third quarter. Buffalo's Andre Reed, who led all receivers with four catches for 80 yards, caught a 20-yard scoring reception from Kelly early in the fourth quarter to move the AFC to within one point. Barry Sanders ran 22 yards for a touchdown to increase the NFC's lead to 21-13. Miami's Jeff Cross blocked a 46-yard field-goal attempt by New Orleans's Morten Andersen with seven seconds remaining to preserve the win. Buffalo's Bruce Smith recorded three sacks and also had a blocked field goal. Kelly, who completed 13 of 19 passes for 210 yards and two touchdowns, was presented the Dan McGuire Award as player of the game. The AFC's victory narrowed the NFC's Pro Bowl series lead to 12-9.

AFC	3	0	3	17	— 23
NFC	0	7	7	7	— 21

AFC — FG Lowery 26
NFC — J. Johnson 1 run (Andersen kick)
AFC — FG Lowery 43
NFC — J. Johnson 9 run (Andersen kick)
AFC — Reed 20 pass from Kelly (Lowery kick)
NFC — Sanders 22 run (Andersen kick)
AFC — FG Lowery 34
AFC — Givins 13 pass from Kelly (Lowery kick)

1990 AFC-NFC Pro Bowl

Aloha Stadium, Honolulu, Hawaii — February 4, 1990

Attendance: 50,445

NFC 27, AFC 21 — The NFC captured its second straight Pro Bowl as the defense accounted for a pair of touchdowns and forced five turnovers before the eleventh consecutive sellout crowd at Aloha Stadium. The AFC held a 7-6 halftime edge on a one-yard scoring run by Christian Okoye of the Chiefs. The NFC then rallied with 21 unanswered points in the third quarter. David Meggett of the Giants began the comeback with an 11-yard touchdown reception from Philadelphia's Randall Cunningham. The Rams' Jerry Gray followed with a 51-yard interception return for a score and the Vikings' Keith Millard added an eight-yard fumble return for a touchdown four minutes later to give the NFC a commanding 27-7 lead. Seattle's Dave Krieg rallied the AFC with a five-yard touchdown pass to Miami's Ferrell Edmunds. Cleveland's Mike Johnson then returned an interception 22 yards for a score to pull the AFC to within six points 27-21. Gray, who was credited with seven tackles, was given the Dan McGuire Award as player of the game. Krieg led all quarterbacks by completing 15 of 23 for 148 yards and one touchdown. Buffalo's Thurman Thomas topped all receivers with five catches for 47 yards, while Indianapolis's Eric Dickerson led all rushers with 46 yards on 15 carries. The win gave the NFC a 12-8 advantage in Pro Bowl games since 1971.

NFC	3	3	21	0	— 27
AFC	0	7	0	14	— 21

NFC — FG Murray 23
NFC — FG Murray 41
AFC — Okoye 1 run (Treadwell kick)
NFC — Meggett 11 pass from Cunningham (Murray kick)
NFC — Gray 51 interception return (Murray kick)
NFC — Millard 8 fumble recovery return (Murray kick)
AFC — Edmunds 5 pass from Krieg (Treadwell kick)
AFC — M. Johnson 22 interception return (Treadwell kick)

1989 AFC-NFC Pro Bowl

Aloha Stadium, Honolulu, Hawaii — January 29, 1989

Attendance: 50,113

NFC 34, AFC 3 — The NFC scored 34 unanswered points to snap a two-game losing streak to the AFC before the tenth straight sellout crowd in Honolulu's Aloha Stadium. Bills kicker Scott Norwood provided the AFC's only points on a 38-yard field goal 6:23 into the game. Touchdown runs by Dallas's Herschel Walker (four yards) and Atlanta's John Settle (one) brought the NFC a 14-3 half-time lead. Walker added a seven-yard scoring run, the Saints' Morten Andersen kicked field goals of 27 and 51 yards, and Los Angeles Rams' wide receiver Henry Ellard caught an eight-yard scoring pass from Minnesota quarterback Wade Wilson in the second half to complete the scoring. Chicago running back Neal Anderson and Philadelphia quarterback Randall Cunningham, who were both appearing in their first Pro Bowl, also played major roles in the NFC's victory. Anderson rushed 13 times for 85 yards and had two receptions for 17. Cunningham, who was voted the game's outstanding player, completed 10 of 14 passes for 63 yards and rushed for 49 yards. The NFC, which had five takeaways, outgained the AFC 355 yards to 167 and held a time-of-possession advantage of 35:18 to 24:42. Houston quarterback Warren Moon completed 13 of 20 passes for 134 yards for the AFC. The win gave the NFC an 11-8 advantage in Pro Bowl games.

AFC	3	0	0	0	— 3
NFC	7	7	10	10	— 34

AFC — FG Norwood 38
NFC — Walker 4 run (Andersen kick)
NFC — Settle 1 run (Andersen kick)
NFC — FG Andersen 27
NFC — Walker 7 run (Andersen kick)
NFC — FG Andersen 51
NFC — Ellard 8 pass from Wilson (Andersen kick)

1988 AFC-NFC Pro Bowl

Aloha Stadium, Honolulu, Hawaii — February 7, 1988

Attendance: 50,113

AFC 15, NFC 6—Led by a tenacious pass rush, the AFC defeated the NFC for the second consecutive year before the ninth straight sellout crowd in Honolulu's Aloha Stadium. Buffalo quarterback Jim Kelly scored the game's lone touchdown on a one-yard run for a 7-6 halftime lead. Colts kicker Dean Biasucci added field goals from 37 and 30 yards to complete the AFC's scoring. Saints kicker Morten Andersen had 25- and 36-yard field goals to account for the NFC's points. AFC defenders held the NFC to 213 yards and recorded eight sacks. Bills defensive end Bruce Smith, who had five tackles and two sacks, was voted the game's outstanding player. Oilers running back Mike Rozier led all rushers with 49 yards on nine carries. Jets wide receiver Al Toon had five receptions for 75 yards. The AFC generated 341 yards total offense and held a time-of-possession advantage of 34:14 to 25:46. By winning, the AFC cut the NFC's lead in the Pro Bowl series to 10-8.

NFC	0	6	0	0	— 6
AFC	0	7	6	2	— 15

NFC—FG Andersen 25
AFC—Kelly 1 run (Biasucci kick)
NFC—FG Andersen 36
AFC—FG Biasucci 37
AFC—FG Biasucci 30
AFC—Safety, Montana forced out of end zone

1987 AFC-NFC Pro Bowl

Aloha Stadium, Honolulu, Hawaii — February 1, 1987

Attendance: 50,101

AFC 10, NFC 6—The AFC defeated the NFC in the lowest-scoring game in AFC-NFC Pro Bowl history. The AFC took a 10-0 halftime lead on Broncos quarterback John Elway's 10-yard touchdown pass to Raiders tight end Todd Christensen and Patriots kicker Tony Franklin's 26-yard field goal. The AFC defense made the lead stand up by forcing the NFC to settle for a pair of field goals from 38 and 19 yards by Saints kicker Morten Andersen after the NFC had first downs at the AFC 31-, 7-, 16-, 15-, 5-, and 7-yard lines. Both AFC scores were set up by fumble recoveries by Seahawks linebacker Fredd Young and Dolphins linebacker John Offerdahl, respectively. Eagles defensive end Reggie White, who tied a Pro Bowl record with four sacks and also contributed seven solo tackles, was voted the game's outstanding player. The AFC victory cut the NFC's lead in the Pro Bowl series to 10-7.

AFC	7	3	0	0	— 10
NFC	0	0	3	3	— 6

AFC—Christensen 10 pass from Elway (Franklin kick)
AFC—FG Franklin 26
NFC—FG Andersen 38
NFC—FG Andersen 19

1986 AFC-NFC Pro Bowl

Aloha Stadium, Honolulu, Hawaii — February 2, 1986

Attendance: 50,101

NFC 28, AFC 24—New York Giants quarterback Phil Simms brought the NFC back from a 24-7 halftime deficit to defeat the AFC. Simms, who completed 15 of 27 passes for 212 yards and three touchdowns, was named the most valuable player of the game. The AFC had taken its first-half lead behind a two-yard run by Los Angeles Raiders running back Marcus Allen, who also threw a 51-yard scoring pass to San Diego wide receiver Wes Chandler, an 11-yard touchdown catch by Pittsburgh wide receiver Louis Lipps, and a 34-yard field goal by Steelers kicker Gary Anderson. Minnesota's Joey Browner accounted for the NFC's only score before halftime with a 48-yard interception return for a touchdown. After intermission, the NFC blanked the AFC while scoring three touchdowns via a 15-yard catch by Washington wide receiver Art Monk, a 2-yard reception by Dallas tight end Doug Cosbie, and a 15-yard catch by Tampa Bay tight end Jimmie Giles with 2:47 remaining in the game. The victory gave the NFC a 10-6 Pro Bowl record vs. the AFC.

NFC	0	7	7	14	— 28
AFC	7	17	0	0	— 24

AFC—Allen 2 run (Anderson kick)
NFC—Browner 48 interception return (Andersen kick)
AFC—Chandler 51 pass from Allen (Anderson kick)
AFC—FG Anderson 34
AFC—Lipps 11 pass from O'Brien (Anderson kick)
NFC—Monk 15 pass from Simms (Andersen kick)
NFC—Cosbie 2 pass from Simms (Andersen kick)
NFC—Giles 15 pass from Simms (Andersen kick)

1985 AFC-NFC Pro Bowl

Aloha Stadium, Honolulu, Hawaii — January 27, 1985

Attendance: 50,385

AFC 22, NFC 14—Defensive end Art Still of the Kansas City Chiefs recovered a fumble and returned it 83 yards for a touchdown to clinch the AFC's victory over the NFC. Still's touchdown came in the fourth period with the AFC trailing 14-12 and was one of several outstanding defensive plays in a Pro Bowl dominated by two record-breaking defenses. The teams combined for a Pro Bowl-record 17 sacks, including four by New York Jets defensive end Mark Gastineau, who was named the game's outstanding player. The AFC's first score came on a safety when Gastineau tackled running back Eric Dickerson of the Los Angeles Rams in the end zone. The AFC's second score, a six-yard pass from Miami's Dan Marino to Los Angeles Raiders running back Marcus Allen, was set up by a partial block of a punt by Seahawks linebacker Fredd Young. The NFC leads the series 9-6.

AFC	0	9	0	13	— 22
NFC	0	0	7	7	— 14

AFC—Safety, Gastineau tackled Dickerson in end zone
AFC—Allen 6 pass from Marino (Johnson kick)
NFC—Lofton 13 pass from Montana (Stenerud kick)
NFC—Payton 1 run (Stenerud kick)
AFC—FG Johnson 33
AFC—Still 83 fumble recovery return (Johnson kick)
AFC—FG Johnson 22

1984 AFC-NFC Pro Bowl

Aloha Stadium, Honolulu, Hawaii — January 29, 1984

Attendance: 50,445

NFC 45, AFC 3—The NFC won its sixth Pro Bowl in the last seven seasons by routing the AFC. The NFC was led by the passing of most valuable player Joe Theismann of Washington, who completed 21 of 27 passes for 242 yards and three touchdowns. Theismann set Pro Bowl records for completions and touchdown passes. The NFC established Pro Bowl marks for most points scored and fewest points allowed. Running back William Andrews of Atlanta had six carries for 43 yards and caught four passes for 49 yards, including scoring receptions of 16 and 2 yards. Los Angeles Rams rookie Eric Dickerson gained 46 yards on 11 carries, including a 14-yard touchdown run, and had 45 yards on five catches. Rams safety Nolan Cromwell had a 44-yard interception return for a touchdown early in the third period to give the NFC a commanding 24-3 lead. Green Bay wide receiver James Lofton caught an eight-yard touchdown pass, while tight end teammate Paul Coffman had a six-yard scoring catch.

NFC	3	14	14	14	— 45
AFC	0	3	0	0	— 3

NFC—FG Haji-Sheikh 23
NFC—Andrews 16 pass from Theismann (Haji-Sheikh kick)
NFC—Andrews 2 pass from Montana (Haji-Sheikh kick)
AFC—FG Anderson 43
NFC—Cromwell 44 interception return (Haji-Sheikh kick)
NFC—Lofton 8 pass from Theismann (Haji-Sheikh kick)
NFC—Coffman 6 pass from Theismann (Haji-Sheikh kick)
NFC—Dickerson 14 run (Haji-Sheikh kick)

1983 AFC-NFC Pro Bowl

Aloha Stadium, Honolulu, Hawaii — February 6, 1983

Attendance: 49,883

NFC 20, AFC 19—Dallas's Danny White threw an 11-yard touchdown pass to the Packers' John Jefferson with 35 seconds remaining to rally the NFC over the AFC. White, who completed 14 of 26 passes for 162 yards, kept the winning 65-yard drive alive with a 14-yard completion to Jefferson on a fourth-and-seven play at the AFC 25. The AFC was ahead 12-10 at halftime and increased the lead to 19-10 in the third period, when Marcus Allen scored on a one-yard run. San Diego's Dan Fouts, who attempted 30 passes, set Pro Bowl records for most completions (17) and yards (274). Pittsburgh's John Stallworth was the AFC's leading receiver with seven catches for 67 yards. William Andrews topped the NFC with five receptions for 48 yards. Fouts and Jefferson were voted co-winners of the player of the game award.

AFC	9	3	7	0	— 19
NFC	0	10	0	10	— 20

AFC—Walker 34 pass from Fouts (Benirschke kick)
AFC—Safety, Still tackled Theismann in end zone
NFC—Andrews 3 run (Moseley kick)
NFC—FG Moseley 35
AFC—FG Benirschke 29
AFC—Allen 1 run (Benirschke kick)
NFC—FG Moseley 41
NFC—Jefferson 11 pass from D. White (Moseley kick)

1982 AFC-NFC Pro Bowl

Aloha Stadium, Honolulu, Hawaii — January 31, 1982

Attendance: 50,402

AFC 16, NFC 13—Nick Lowery of Kansas City kicked a 23-yard field goal with three seconds remaining to give the AFC a last-second victory over the NFC. Lowery's kick climaxed a 69-yard drive directed by quarterback Dan Fouts. The NFC gained a 13-13 tie with 2:43 to go when Dallas's Tony Dorsett ran four yards for a touchdown. In the drive to the game-winning field goal, Fouts completed three passes, including a 23-yarder to San Diego teammate Kellen Winslow that put the ball on the NFC's 5-yard line. Two plays later, Lowery kicked the field goal. Winslow, who caught six passes for 86 yards, was named co-player of the game along with Tampa Bay defensive end Lee Roy Selmon.

NFC	0	6	0	7	— 13
AFC	0	0	13	3	— 16

NFC—Giles 4 pass from Montana (kick blocked)
AFC—Muncie 2 run (kick failed)
AFC—Campbell 1 run (Lowery kick)
NFC—Dorsett 4 run (Septien kick)
AFC—FG Lowery 23

1981 AFC-NFC Pro Bowl

Aloha Stadium, Honolulu, Hawaii — February 1, 1981

Attendance: 50,360

NFC 21, AFC 7— Ed Murray kicked four field goals and Steve Bartkowski fired a 55-yard scoring pass to Alfred Jenkins to lead the NFC to its fourth straight victory over the AFC and a 7-4 edge in the series. Murray was named the game's most valuable player and missed tying Garo Yepremian's Pro Bowl record of five field goals when a 37-yard attempt hit the crossbar with 22 seconds remaining. The AFC's only score came on a nine-yard pass from Brian Sipe to Stanley Morgan in the second period. Bartkowski completed 9 of 21 passes for 173 yards, while Sipe connected on 10 of 15 for 142 yards. Ottis Anderson led all rushers with 70 yards on 10 carries. Earl Campbell, the NFL's leading rusher in 1980, was limited to 24 yards on eight attempts.

AFC	0	7	0	0	— 7
NFC	3	6	0	12	— 21

NFC — FG Murray 31
AFC — Morgan 9 pass from Sipe (J. Smith kick)
NFC — FG Murray 31
NFC — FG Murray 34
NFC — Jenkins 55 pass from Bartkowski (Murray kick)
NFC — FG Murray 36
NFC — Safety, Shell called for holding in end zone

1980 AFC-NFC Pro Bowl

Aloha Stadium, Honolulu, Hawaii — January 27, 1980

Attendance: 49,800

NFC 37, AFC 27— Running back Chuck Muncie of New Orleans ran for two touchdowns and threw a 25-yard option pass for another score to give the NFC its third consecutive victory over the AFC. Muncie, who was selected the game's most valuable player, snapped a 3-3 tie on a one-yard touchdown run at 1:41 of the second quarter, then scored on an 11-yard run in the fourth quarter for the NFC's final touchdown. Two scoring records were set in the game — 37 points by the NFC, eclipsing the 33 by the AFC in 1973, and the 64 points by both teams, surpassing the 61 scored in 1973.

NFC	3	20	7	7	— 37
AFC	3	7	10	7	— 27

NFC — FG Moseley 37
AFC — FG Fritsch 19
NFC — Muncie 1 run (Moseley kick)
AFC — Pruitt 1 pass from Bradshaw (Fritsch kick)
NFC — D. Hill 13 pass from Manning (kick failed)
NFC — T. Hill 25 pass from Muncie (Moseley kick)
NFC — Henry 86 punt return (Moseley kick)
AFC — Campbell 2 run (Fritsch kick)
AFC — FG Fritsch 29
NFC — Muncie 11 run (Moseley kick)
AFC — Campbell 1 run (Fritsch kick)

1979 AFC-NFC Pro Bowl

Memorial Coliseum, Los Angeles, California — January 29, 1979

Attendance: 46,281

NFC 13, AFC 7— Roger Staubach completed 9 of 15 passes for 125 yards, including the winning touchdown on a 19-yard strike to Dallas Cowboys teammate Tony Hill in the third period. The winning drive began at the AFC's 45 yard line after a shanked punt. Staubach hit Ahmad Rashad with passes of 15 and 17 yards to set up Hill's decisive catch. The victory gave the NFC a 5-4 advantage in Pro Bowl games. Rashad, who accounted for 89 yards on five receptions, was named the player of the game. The AFC led 7-6 at halftime on Bob Griese's eight-yard scoring toss to Steve Largent late in the second quarter. Largent finished the game with five receptions for 75 yards. The NFC scored first as Archie Manning marched his team 70 yards in 11 plays, capped by Wilbert Montgomery's two-yard touchdown run. The AFC's Earl Campbell was the game's leading rusher with 66 yards on 12 carries.

AFC	0	7	0	0	— 7
NFC	0	6	7	0	— 13

NFC — Montgomery 2 run (kick failed)
AFC — Largent 8 pass from Griese (Yepremian kick)
NFC — T. Hill 19 pass from Staubach (Corral kick)

1978 AFC-NFC Pro Bowl

Tampa Stadium, Tampa, Florida — January 23, 1978

Attendance: 51,337

NFC 14, AFC 13 — Walter Payton, the NFL's leading rusher in 1977, sparked a second-half comeback to give the NFC the win and tie the series between the two conferences at four victories each. Payton, who was the game's most valuable player, gained 77 yards on 13 carries and scored the tying touchdown on a one-yard burst with 7:37 left in the game. Efren Herrera kicked the winning extra point. The AFC dominated the first half of the game, taking a 13-0 lead on field goals of 21 and 39 yards by Toni Linhart and a 10-yard touchdown pass from Ken Stabler to Oakland teammate Cliff Branch. On the NFC's first possession of the second half, Pat Haden put together the first touchdown drive after Eddie Brown returned Ray Guy's punt to the AFC 46-yard line. Haden connected on all four of his passes on that drive, finally hitting Terry Metcalf with a four-yard scoring toss. The NFC continued to rally and, with Jim Hart at quarterback, moved 63 yards in 12 plays for the go-ahead score. During the winning drive, Hart completed five of six passes for 38 yards and Payton picked up 20 more on the ground.

AFC	3	10	0	0	— 13
NFC	0	0	7	7	— 14

AFC — FG Linhart 21
AFC — Branch 10 pass from Stabler (Linhart kick)
AFC — FG Linhart 39
NFC — Metcalf 4 pass from Haden (Herrera kick)
NFC — Payton 1 run (Herrera kick)

1977 AFC-NFC Pro Bowl

Kingdome, Seattle, Washington — January 17, 1977

Attendance: 64,752

AFC 24, NFC 14 — O.J. Simpson's three-yard touchdown burst at 7:03 of the first quarter gave the AFC a lead it would not surrender, the victory breaking a two-game NFC win streak and giving the American Conference stars a 4-3 series lead. The AFC took a 17-7 lead midway through the second period on the first of two Ken Anderson touchdown passes, a 12-yarder to Charlie Joiner. But the NFC mounted a 73-yard drive capped by Lawrence McCutcheon's one-yard touchdown plunge to pull within 17-14 at the half. Following a scoreless third quarter, player of the game Mel Blount thwarted a possible NFC score when he intercepted Jim Hart's pass in the end zone. Less than three minutes later, Blount again picked off a Hart pass, returning it 16 yards to the NFC 27. That set up Anderson's 27-yard touchdown strike to the Raiders' Cliff Branch for the final score.

NFC	0	14	0	0	— 14
AFC	10	7	0	7	— 24

AFC — Simpson 3 run (Linhart kick)
AFC — FG Linhart 31
NFC — Thomas 15 run (Bakken kick)
AFC — Joiner 12 pass from Anderson (Linhart kick)
NFC — McCutcheon 1 run (Bakken kick)
AFC — Branch 27 pass from Anderson (Linhart kick)

1976 AFC-NFC Pro Bowl

Superdome, New Orleans, Louisiana — January 26, 1976

Attendance: 30,546

NFC 23, AFC 20 — Mike Boryla, a late substitute who did not enter the game until 5:39 remained, lifted the National Football Conference to the victory over the American Football Conference with two touchdown passes in the final minutes. It was the second straight NFC win, squaring the series at 3-3. Until Boryla started firing the ball the AFC was in control, leading 13-0 at the half. Boryla entered the game after Billy Johnson had raced 90 yards with a punt to make the score 20-9 in favor of the AFC. He floated a 14-yard pass to Terry Metcalf and later fired an eight-yarder to Mel Gray for the winner.

AFC	0	13	0	7	— 20
NFC	0	0	9	14	— 23

AFC — FG Stenerud 20
AFC — FG Stenerud 35
AFC — Burrough 64 pass from Pastorini (Stenerud kick)
NFC — FG Bakken 42
NFC — Foreman 4 pass from Hart (kick blocked)
AFC — Johnson 90 punt return (Stenerud kick)
NFC — Metcalf 14 pass from Boryla (Bakken kick)
NFC — Gray 8 pass from Boryla (Bakken kick)

1975 AFC-NFC Pro Bowl

Orange Bowl, Miami, Florida — January 20, 1975

Attendance: 26,484

NFC 17, AFC 10 — Los Angeles quarterback James Harris, who took over the NFC offense after Jim Hart of St. Louis suffered a laceration above his right eye in the second period, threw a pair of touchdown passes early in the fourth period to pace the NFC to its second victory in the five-game Pro Bowl series. The NFC win snapped a three-game AFC victory string. Harris, who was named the player of the game, connected with St. Louis's Mel Gray for an eight-yard touchdown 2:03 into the final period. One minute and 24 seconds later, following a recovery by Washington's Ken Houston of a fumble by Franco Harris of Pittsburgh, Harris tossed another eight-yard scoring pass to Washington's Charley Taylor for the decisive points.

NFC	0	3	0	14	— 17
AFC	0	0	10	0	— 10

NFC — FG Marcol 33
AFC — Warfield 32 pass from Griese (Gerela kick)
AFC — FG Gerela 33
NFC — Gray 8 pass from J. Harris (Marcol kick)
NFC — Taylor 8 pass from J. Harris (Marcol kick)

1974 AFC-NFC Pro Bowl

Arrowhead Stadium, Kansas City, Missouri — January 20, 1974

Attendance: 66,918

AFC 15, NFC 13 — Miami's Garo Yepremian kicked his fifth consecutive field goal, a 42-yard kick with 21 seconds remaining, to give the AFC its third straight victory since the NFC won the inaugural game following the 1970 season. The field goal by Yepremian, who was voted the game's outstanding player, offset a 21-yard field goal by Atlanta's Nick Mike-Mayer that had given the NFC a 13-12 advantage with 1:41 remaining. The only touchdown in the game was scored by the NFC on a 14-yard pass from Philadelphia's Roman Gabriel to Lawrence McCutcheon of the Los Angeles Rams.

NFC	0	10	0	3	— 13
AFC	3	3	3	6	— 15

AFC — FG Yepremian 16
NFC — FG Mike-Mayer 27
NFC — McCutcheon 14 pass from Gabriel (Mike-Mayer kick)

AFC — FG Yepremian 37
AFC — FG Yepremian 27
AFC — FG Yepremian 41
NFC — FG Mike-Mayer 21
AFC — FG Yepremian 42

1973 AFC-NFC Pro Bowl

Texas Stadium, Irving, Texas — January 21, 1973
Attendance: 37,091

AFC 33, NFC 28 — Paced by the rushing and receiving of player of the game O.J. Simpson, the AFC erased a 14-0 first period deficit and built a commanding 33-14 lead midway through the fourth period before the NFC managed two touchdowns in the final minute of play. Simpson rushed for 112 yards and caught three passes for 58 more to gain unanimous recognition in the balloting for player of the game. John Brockington scored three touchdowns for the NFC.

AFC	0	10	10	13	— 33
NFC	14	0	0	14	— 28

NFC — Brockington 1 run (Marcol kick)
NFC — Brockington 3 pass from Kilmer (Marcol kick)
AFC — Simpson 7 run (Gerela kick)
AFC — FG Gerela 18
AFC — FG Gerela 22
AFC — Hubbard 11 run (Gerela kick)
AFC — O. Taylor 5 pass from Lamonica (kick failed)
AFC — Bell 12 interception return (Gerela kick)
NFC — Brockington 1 run (Marcol kick)
NFC — Kwalick 12 pass from Snead (Marcol kick)

1972 AFC-NFC Pro Bowl

Memorial Coliseum, Los Angeles, California — January 23, 1972
Attendance: 53,647

AFC 26, NFC 13 — Four field goals by Jan Stenerud of Kansas City, including a 6-6 tie-breaker from 48 yards, helped lift the AFC from a 6-0 deficit to a 19-6 advantage early in the fourth period. The AFC defense picked off three interceptions. Stenerud was selected as the outstanding offensive player and his Kansas City teammate, linebacker Willie Lanier, was the game's outstanding defensive player.

AFC	0	3	13	10	— 26
NFC	0	6	0	7	— 13

NFC — Grim 50 pass from Landry (kick failed)
AFC — FG Stenerud 25
AFC — FG Stenerud 23
AFC — FG Stenerud 48
AFC — Morin 5 pass from Dawson (Stenerud kick)
AFC — FG Stenerud 42
NFC — V. Washington 2 run (Knight kick)
AFC — F. Little 6 run (Stenerud kick)

1971 AFC-NFC Pro Bowl

Memorial Coliseum, Los Angeles, California — January 24, 1971
Attendance: 48,222

NFC 27, AFC 6 — Mel Renfro of Dallas broke open the first meeting between the American Football Conference and National Football Conference all-star teams as he returned a pair of punts 82 and 56 yards for touchdowns in the final period to clinch the NFC victory over the AFC. Renfro was voted the game's outstanding back and linebacker Fred Carr of Green Bay the outstanding lineman.

AFC	0	3	3	0	— 6
NFC	0	3	10	14	— 27

AFC — FG Stenerud 37
NFC — FG Cox 13
NFC — Osborn 23 pass from Brodie (Cox kick)
NFC — FG Cox 35
AFC — FG Stenerud 16
NFC — Renfro 82 punt return (Cox kick)
NFC — Renfro 56 punt return (Cox kick)

Pro Bowl All-Time Results

Date	Result	Site (attendance)	Honored players
Jan. 15, 1939	New York Giants 13, Pro All-Stars 10	Wrigley Field, Los Angeles (20,000)	
Jan. 14, 1940	Green Bay 16, NFL All-Stars 7	Gilmore Stadium, Los Angeles (18,000)	
Dec. 29, 1940	Chicago Bears 28, NFL All-Stars 14	Gilmore Stadium, Los Angeles (21,624)	
Jan. 4, 1942	Chicago Bears 35, NFL All-Stars 24	Polo Grounds, New York (17,725)	
Dec. 27, 1942	NFL All-Stars 17, Washington 14	Shibe Park, Philadelphia (18,671)	
Jan. 14, 1951	American Conf. 28, National Conf. 27	Los Angeles Memorial Coliseum (53,676)	Otto Graham, Cleveland, player of the game
Jan. 12, 1952	National Conf. 30, American Conf. 13	Los Angeles Memorial Coliseum (19,400)	Dan Towler, Los Angeles, player of the game
Jan. 10, 1953	National Conf. 27, American Conf. 7	Los Angeles Memorial Coliseum (34,208)	Don Doll, Detroit, player of the game
Jan. 17, 1954	East 20, West 9	Los Angeles Memorial Coliseum (44,214)	Chuck Bednarik, Philadelphia, player of the game
Jan. 16, 1955	West 26, East 19	Los Angeles Memorial Coliseum (43,972)	Billy Wilson, San Francisco, player of the game
Jan. 15, 1956	East 31, West 30	Los Angeles Memorial Coliseum (37,867)	Ollie Matson, Chi. Cardinals, player of the game
Jan. 13, 1957	West 19, East 10	Los Angeles Memorial Coliseum (44,177)	Bert Rechichar, Baltimore, outstanding back Ernie Stautner, Pittsburgh, outstanding lineman
Jan. 12, 1958	West 26, East 7	Los Angeles Memorial Coliseum (66,634)	Hugh McElhenny, San Francisco, outstanding back Gene Brito, Washington, outstanding lineman
Jan. 11, 1959	East 28, West 21	Los Angeles Memorial Coliseum (72,250)	Frank Gifford, N.Y. Giants, outstanding back Doug Atkins, Chi. Bears, outstanding lineman
Jan. 17, 1960	West 38, East 21	Los Angeles Memorial Coliseum (56,876)	Johnny Unitas, Baltimore, outstanding back Gene (Big Daddy) Lipscomb, Baltimore, outstanding lineman
Jan. 15, 1961	West 35, East 31	Los Angeles Memorial Coliseum (62,971)	Johnny Unitas, Baltimore, outstanding back Sam Huff, N.Y. Giants, outstanding lineman
Jan. 7, 1962	AFL West 47, East 27	Balboa Stadium, San Diego (20,973)	Cotton Davidson, Dallas Texans, player of the game
Jan. 14, 1962	NFL West 31, East 30	Los Angeles Memorial Coliseum (57,409)	Jim Brown, Cleveland, outstanding back Henry Jordan, Green Bay, outstanding lineman
Jan. 13, 1963	AFL West 21, East 14	Balboa Stadium, San Diego (27,641)	Curtis McClinton, Dallas Texans, outstanding offensive player Earl Faison, San Diego, outstanding defensive player
Jan. 13, 1963	NFL East 30, West 20	Los Angeles Memorial Coliseum (61,374)	Jim Brown, Cleveland, outstanding back Gene (Big Daddy) Lipscomb, Pittsburgh, outstanding lineman
Jan. 12, 1964	NFL West 31, East 17	Los Angeles Memorial Coliseum (67,242)	Johnny Unitas, Baltimore, player of the game Gino Marchetti, Baltimore, outstanding lineman
Jan. 19, 1964	AFL West 27, East 24	Balboa Stadium, San Diego (20,016)	Keith Lincoln, San Diego, outstanding offensive player Archie Matsos, Oakland, outstanding defensive player
Jan. 10, 1965	NFL West 34, East 14	Los Angeles Memorial Coliseum (60,598)	Fran Tarkenton, Minnesota, outstanding back Terry Barr, Detroit, outstanding lineman
Jan. 16, 1965	AFL West 38, East 14	Jeppesen Stadium, Houston (15,446)	Keith Lincoln, San Diego, outstanding offensive player Willie Brown, Denver, outstanding defensive player
Jan. 15, 1966	AFL All-Stars 30, Buffalo 19	Rice Stadium, Houston (35,572)	Joe Namath, N.Y. Jets, most valuable player, offense Frank Buncom, San Diego, most valuable player, defense
Jan. 15, 1966	NFL East 36, West 7	Los Angeles Memorial Coliseum (60,124)	Jim Brown, Cleveland, outstanding back Dale Meinert, St. Louis, outstanding lineman
Jan. 21, 1967	AFL East 30, West 23	Oakland-Alameda County Coliseum (18,876)	Babe Parilli, Boston, outstanding offensive player Verlon Biggs, N.Y. Jets, outstanding defensive player
Jan. 22, 1967	NFL East 20, West 10	Los Angeles Memorial Coliseum (15,062)	Gale Sayers, Chicago, outstanding back Floyd Peters, Philadelphia, outstanding lineman
Jan. 21, 1968	AFL East 25, West 24	Gator Bowl, Jacksonville, Fla. (40,103)	Joe Namath and Don Maynard, N.Y. Jets, out. off. players Leslie (Speedy) Duncan, San Diego, out. def. player
Jan. 21, 1968	NFL West 38, East 20	Los Angeles Memorial Coliseum (53,289)	Gale Sayers, Chicago, outstanding back Dave Robinson, Green Bay, outstanding lineman
Jan. 19, 1969	AFL West 38, East 25	Gator Bowl, Jacksonville, Fla. (41,058)	Len Dawson, Kansas City, outstanding offensive player George Webster, Houston, outstanding defensive player
Jan. 19, 1969	NFL West 10, East 7	Los Angeles Memorial Coliseum (32,050)	Roman Gabriel, Los Angeles, outstanding back Merlin Olsen, Los Angeles, outstanding lineman
Jan. 17, 1970	AFL West 26, East 3	Astrodome, Houston (30,170)	John Hadl, San Diego, player of the game
Jan. 18, 1970	NFL West 16, East 13	Los Angeles Memorial Coliseum (57,786)	Gale Sayers, Chicago, outstanding back George Andrie, Dallas, outstanding lineman
Jan. 24, 1971	NFC 27, AFC 6	Los Angeles Memorial Coliseum (48,222)	Mel Renfro, Dallas, outstanding back Fred Carr, Green Bay, outstanding lineman
Jan. 23, 1972	AFC 26, NFC 13	Los Angeles Memorial Coliseum (53,647)	Jan Stenerud, Kansas City, outstanding offensive player Willie Lanier, Kansas City, outstanding defensive player
Jan. 21, 1973	AFC 33, NFC 28	Texas Stadium, Irving (37,091)	O.J. Simpson, Buffalo, player of the game
Jan. 20, 1974	AFC 15, NFC 13	Arrowhead Stadium, Kansas City (66,918)	Garo Yepremian, Miami, player of the game
Jan. 20, 1975	NFC 17, AFC 10	Orange Bowl, Miami (26,484)	James Harris, Los Angeles, player of the game
Jan. 26, 1976	NFC 23, AFC 20	Louisiana Superdome, New Orleans (30,546)	Billy Johnson, Houston, player of the game
Jan. 17, 1977	AFC 24, NFC 14	Kingdome, Seattle (64,752)	Mel Blount, Pittsburgh, player of the game
Jan. 23, 1978	NFC 14, AFC 13	Tampa Stadium (51,337)	Walter Payton, Chicago, player of the game
Jan. 29, 1979	NFC 13, AFC 7	Los Angeles Memorial Coliseum (46,281)	Ahmad Rashad, Minnesota, player of the game
Jan. 27, 1980	NFC 37, AFC 27	Aloha Stadium, Honolulu (49,800)	Chuck Muncie, New Orleans, player of the game
Feb. 1, 1981	NFC 21, AFC 7	Aloha Stadium, Honolulu (50,360)	Eddie Murray, Detroit, player of the game
Jan. 31, 1982	AFC 16, NFC 13	Aloha Stadium, Honolulu (50,402)	Kellen Winslow, San Diego, and Lee Roy Selmon, Tampa Bay, players of the game
Feb. 6, 1983	NFC 20, AFC 19	Aloha Stadium, Honolulu (49,883)	Dan Fouts, San Diego, and John Jefferson, Green Bay, players of the game
Jan. 29, 1984	NFC 45, AFC 3	Aloha Stadium, Honolulu (50,445)	Joe Theismann, Washington, player of the game
Jan. 27, 1985	AFC 22, NFC 14	Aloha Stadium, Honolulu (50,385)	Mark Gastineau, N.Y. Jets, player of the game
Feb. 2, 1986	NFC 28, AFC 24	Aloha Stadium, Honolulu (50,101)	Phil Simms, N.Y. Giants, player of the game
Feb. 1, 1987	AFC 10, NFC 6	Aloha Stadium, Honolulu (50,101)	Reggie White, Philadelphia, player of the game
Feb. 7, 1988	AFC 15, NFC 6	Aloha Stadium, Honolulu (50,113)	Bruce Smith, Buffalo, player of the game
Jan. 29, 1989	NFC 34, AFC 3	Aloha Stadium, Honolulu (50,113)	Randall Cunningham, Philadelphia, player of the game
Feb. 4, 1990	NFC 27, AFC 21	Aloha Stadium, Honolulu (50,445)	Jerry Gray, L.A. Rams, player of the game
Feb. 3, 1991	AFC 23, NFC 21	Aloha Stadium, Honolulu (50,345)	Jim Kelly, Buffalo, player of the game
Feb. 2, 1992	NFC 21, AFC 15	Aloha Stadium, Honolulu (50,209)	Michael Irvin, Dallas, player of the game
Feb. 7, 1993	AFC 23, NFC 20 (OT)	Aloha Stadium, Honolulu (50,007)	Steve Tasker, Buffalo, player of the game

Pro Football Hall of Fame Game

1962	New York Giants 21, St. Louis Cardinals 21
1963	Pittsburgh Steelers 16, Cleveland Browns 7
1964	Baltimore Colts 48, Pittsburgh Steelers 17
1965	Washington Redskins 20, Detroit Lions 3
1966	No game
1967	Philadelphia Eagles 28, Cleveland Browns 13
1968	Chicago Bears 30, Dallas Cowboys 24
1969	Green Bay Packers 38, Atlanta Falcons 24
1970	New Orleans Saints 14, Minnesota Vikings 13
1971	Los Angeles Rams (NFC) 17, Houston Oilers (AFC) 6
1972	Kansas City Chiefs (AFC) 23, New York Giants (NFC) 17
1973	San Francisco 49ers (NFC) 20, New England Patriots (AFC) 7
1974	St. Louis Cardinals (NFC) 21, Buffalo Bills (AFC) 13
1975	Washington Redskins (NFC) 17, Cincinnati Bengals (AFC) 9
1976	Denver Broncos (AFC) 10, Detroit Lions (NFC) 7
1977	Chicago Bears (NFC) 20, New York Jets (AFC) 6
1978	Philadelphia Eagles (NFC) 17, Miami Dolphins (AFC) 3
1979	Oakland Raiders (AFC) 20, Dallas Cowboys (NFC) 13
1980*	San Diego Chargers (AFC) 0, Green Bay Packers (NFC) 0
1981	Cleveland Browns (AFC) 24, Atlanta Falcons (NFC) 10
1982	Minnesota Vikings (NFC) 30, Baltimore Colts (AFC) 14
1983	Pittsburgh Steelers (AFC) 27, New Orleans Saints (NFC) 14
1984	Seattle Seahawks (AFC) 38, Tampa Bay Buccaneers (NFC) 0
1985	New York Giants (NFC) 21, Houston Oilers (AFC) 20
1986	New England Patriots (AFC) 21, St. Louis Cardinals (NFC) 16
1987	San Francisco 49ers (NFC) 20, Kansas City Chiefs (AFC) 7
1988	Cincinnati Bengals (AFC) 14, Los Angeles Rams (NFC) 7
1989	Washington Redskins (NFC) 31, Buffalo Bills (AFC) 6
1990	Chicago Bears (NFC) 13, Cleveland Browns (AFC) 0
1991	Detroit Lions (NFC) 14, Denver Broncos (AFC) 3
1992	New York Jets (AFC) 41, Philadelphia Eagles (NFC) 14

*Game called with 5:29 remaining due to severe thunder and lightning.

NFL International Games

Date	Site	Teams
Aug. 12, 1950	Ottawa, Canada	N.Y. Giants 27, Ottawa Roughriders 6
Aug. 11, 1951	Ottawa, Canada	N.Y. Giants 41, Ottawa Roughriders 18
Aug. 5, 1959	Toronto, Canada	Chi. Cardinals 55, Tor. Argonauts 26
Aug. 3, 1960	Toronto, Canada	Pittsburgh 43, Toronto Argonauts 16
Aug. 15, 1960	Toronto, Canada	Chicago Bears 16, N.Y. Giants 7
Aug. 2, 1961	Toronto, Canada	St. Louis 36, Toronto Argonauts 7
Aug. 5, 1961	Montreal, Canada	Chi. Bears 34, Montreal Allouettes 16
Aug. 8, 1961	Hamilton, Canada	Hamilton Tiger-Cats 38, Buffalo 21
Sept. 11, 1969	Montreal, Canada	Pittsburgh 17, N.Y. Giants 13
Aug. 25, 1969	Montreal, Canada	Detroit 22, Boston Patriots 9
Aug. 16, 1976	Tokyo, Japan	St. Louis 20, San Diego 10
Aug. 5, 1978	Mexico City, Mexico	New Orleans 14, Philadelphia 7
Aug. 6, 1983	London, England	Minnesota 28, St. Louis 10
Aug. 3, 1986	London, England	Chicago Bears 17, Dallas 6
Aug. 9, 1987	London, England	L.A. Rams 28, Denver 27
July 31, 1988	London, England	Miami 27, San Francisco 21
Aug. 14, 1988	Goteborg, Sweden	Minnesota 28, Chicago 21
Aug. 18, 1988	Montreal, Canada	N.Y. Jets 11, Cleveland 7
Aug. 5, 1989	Tokyo, Japan	L.A. Rams 16, San Francisco 13 (OT)
Aug. 6, 1989	London, England	Philadelphia 17, Cleveland 13
Aug. 4, 1990	Tokyo, Japan	Denver 10, Seattle 7
Aug. 5, 1990	London, England	New Orleans 17, L.A. Raiders 10
Aug. 9, 1990	Montreal, Canada	Pittsburgh 30, New England 14
Aug. 11, 1990	Berlin, Germany	L.A. Rams 19, Kansas City 3
July 28, 1991	London, England	Buffalo 17, Philadelphia 13
Aug. 3, 1991	Berlin, Germany	San Francisco 21, Chicago 7
Aug. 3, 1991	Tokyo, Japan	Miami 19, L.A. Raiders 17
Aug. 1, 1992	Tokyo, Japan	Houston 34, Dallas 23
Aug. 15, 1992	Berlin, Germany	Miami 31, Denver 27
Aug. 16, 1992	London, England	San Francisco 17, Washington 15

Chicago All-Star Game

Pro teams won 31, lost 9, and tied 2. The game was discontinued after 1976.

Year	Date	Winner	Loser	Attendance
1976*	July 23	Pittsburgh 24	All-Stars 0	52,895
1975	Aug. 1	Pittsburgh 21	All-Stars 14	54,103
1974		No game was played		
1973	July 27	Miami 14	All-Stars 3	54,103
1972	July 28	Dallas 20	All-Stars 7	54,162
1971	July 30	Baltimore 24	All-Stars 17	52,289
1970	July 31	Kansas City 24	All-Stars 3	69,940
1969	Aug. 1	N.Y. Jets 26	All-Stars 24	74,208
1968	Aug. 2	Green Bay 34	All-Stars 17	69,917
1967	Aug. 4	Green Bay 27	All-Stars 0	70,934
1966	Aug. 5	Green Bay 38	All-Stars 0	72,000
1965	Aug. 6	Cleveland 24	All-Stars 16	68,000
1964	Aug. 7	Chicago 28	All-Stars 17	65,000
1963	Aug. 2	All-Stars 20	Green Bay 17	65,000
1962	Aug. 3	Green Bay 42	All-Stars 20	65,000
1961	Aug. 4	Philadelphia 28	All-Stars 14	66,000
1960	Aug. 12	Baltimore 32	All-Stars 7	70,000
1959	Aug. 14	Baltimore 29	All-Stars 0	70,000
1958	Aug. 15	All-Stars 35	Detroit 19	70,000
1957	Aug. 9	N.Y. Giants 22	All-Stars 12	75,000
1956	Aug. 10	Cleveland 26	All-Stars 0	75,000
1955	Aug. 12	All-Stars 30	Cleveland 27	75,000
1954	Aug. 13	Detroit 31	All-Stars 6	93,470
1953	Aug. 14	Detroit 24	All-Stars 10	93,818
1952	Aug. 15	Los Angeles 10	All-Stars 7	88,316
1951	Aug. 17	Cleveland 33	All-Stars 0	92,180
1950	Aug. 11	All-Stars 17	Philadelphia 7	88,885
1949	Aug. 12	Philadelphia 38	All-Stars 0	93,780
1948	Aug. 20	Chi. Cardinals 28	All-Stars 0	101,220
1947	Aug. 22	All-Stars 16	Chi. Bears 0	105,840
1946	Aug. 23	All-Stars 16	Los Angeles 0	97,380
1945	Aug. 30	Green Bay 19	All-Stars 7	92,753
1944	Aug. 30	Chi. Bears 24	All-Stars 21	48,769
1943	Aug. 25	All-Stars 27	Washington 7	48,471
1942	Aug. 28	Chi. Bears 21	All-Stars 0	101,100
1941	Aug. 28	Chi. Bears 37	All-Stars 13	98,203
1940	Aug. 29	Green Bay 45	All-Stars 28	84,567
1939	Aug. 30	N.Y. Giants 9	All-Stars 0	81,456
1938	Aug. 31	All-Stars 28	Washington 16	74,250
1937	Sept. 1	All-Stars 6	Green Bay 0	84,560
1936	Sept. 3	All-Stars 7	Detroit 7 (tie)	76,000
1935	Aug. 29	Chi. Bears 5	All-Stars 0	77,450
1934	Aug. 31	Chi. Bears 0	All-Stars 0 (tie)	79,432

*Game shortened due to thunderstorms.

NFL Playoff Bowl

Western Conference won 8, Eastern Conference won 2. All games played at Miami's Orange Bowl.

1970	Los Angeles Rams 31, Dallas Cowboys 0
1969	Dallas Cowboys 17, Minnesota Vikings 13
1968	Los Angeles Rams 30, Cleveland Browns 6
1967	Baltimore Colts 20, Philadelphia Eagles 14
1966	Baltimore Colts 35, Dallas Cowboys 3
1965	St. Louis Cardinals 24, Green Bay Packers 17
1964	Green Bay Packers 40, Cleveland Browns 23
1963	Detroit Lions 17, Pittsburgh Steelers 10
1962	Detroit Lions 28, Philadelphia Eagles 10
1961	Detroit Lions 17, Cleveland Browns 16

AFC VS. NFC (REGULAR SEASON), 1970-1992

	1970	1971	1972	1973	1974	1975	1976	1977	1978	1979	1980	1981	1982	1983	1984	1985	1986	1987	1988	1989	1990	1991	1992	Totals
Miami	2-1	3-0	3-0	3-0	2-1	3-0	0-2	2-0	3-1	4-0	4-0	3-1	1-1	3-1	4-0	3-1	2-2	3-0	3-1	2-0	2-2	3-1	2-2	60-17
L.A. Raiders	1-2	1-1-1	3-0	2-1	3-0	3-0	3-0	1-1	4-0	4-0	2-2	2-2	3-0	2-2	3-1	3-1	1-3	2-2	1-3	2-2	3-1	2-2	2-2	53-28-1
Pittsburgh	0-3	1-2	2-1	3-0	3-0	2-1	1-1	2-0	3-1	3-1	4-0	3-1	1-0	2-2	3-1	1-3	2-2	2-2	1-3	3-1	3-1	0-4	1-3	46-33
Cincinnati	1-2	1-2	2-1	2-1	2-1	3-0	2-0	2-1	2-2	2-2	2-2	2-2	1-0	3-1	2-2	2-2	3-1	1-2	4-0	2-2	1-3	1-3	1-3	44-35
Denver	2-2	1-3	1-3	0-3-1	2-2	2-1	2-0	1-1	2-2	3-1	3-1	3-1	2-1	0-2	3-1	3-1	3-1	2-1-1	3-1	2-2	1-3	2-0	1-3	44-36-2
Cleveland	0-3	2-1	1-2	1-2	1-2	1-3	2-0	1-1	4-0	3-1	3-1	3-1	0-2	2-2	1-3	1-3	2-2	2-2	4-0	3-1	1-3	0-4	2-2	40-41
San Diego	1-2	2-1	0-3	1-2	1-2	0-3	2-0	1-1	2-2	3-1	2-2	2-2	1-0	2-2	4-0	1-1	0-4	2-0	2-2	2-2	1-1	1-3	2-0	35-36
Kansas City	0-2-1	2-1	2-1	1-1-1	1-2	2-1	1-1	1-1	0-2	0-2	2-0	2-2	0-3	2-2	1-1	2-2	1-1	1-2	0-2	2-0	4-0	2-2	2-2	31-33-2
Seattle								1-0	3-1	3-1	1-3	0-2	1-0	1-3	4-0	2-2	3-1	4-0	1-3	0-4	2-2	1-3	0-4	27-29
Buffalo	0-3	0-3	2-0-1	2-1	2-1	1-2	0-2	1-1	1-1	2-2	3-1	1-3	1-2	1-3	1-3	0-2	1-1	1-2	2-2	1-3	3-1	3-1	4-0	33-40-1
Indianapolis	3-0	2-1	0-3	2-1	1-2	2-1	0-2	1-1	2-2	1-1	1-1	0-4	0-1-1	2-0	0-4	3-1	1-3	1-0	2-2	1-3	2-2	0-4	2-0	29-39-1
N.Y. Jets	2-1	0-3	1-2	0-3	2-1	0-3	0-2	1-1	1-3	3-1	1-3	2-0	4-0	3-1	0-2	2-2	2-2	0-4	2-0	1-3	2-0	2-2	0-4	31-43
Houston	0-3	0-2-1	0-3	0-3	0-3	3-0	2-0	2-0	2-2	2-2	4-0	1-3	0-3	1-3	0-4	1-3	2-2	2-2	3-1	3-1	1-3	1-3	3-1	33-47-1
New England	0-3	0-3	3-0	2-1	3-0	1-2	1-1	2-0	2-2	3-1	1-3	0-4	0-1	2-2	0-4	3-1	3-1	0-3	2-2	0-4	0-4	1-1	0-4	29-47
Tampa Bay							0-1																	0-1
TOTALS	12-27-1	15-23-2	20-19-1	19-19-2	23-17	23-17	16-12	19-9	31-21	36-16	33-19	24-28	15-14-1	26-26	26-26	27-25	26-26	23-22-1	30-22	24-28	26-26	19-33	22-30	535-505-8

NFC VS. AFC (REGULAR SEASON), 1970-1992

	1970	1971	1972	1973	1974	1975	1976	1977	1978	1979	1980	1981	1982	1983	1984	1985	1986	1987	1988	1989	1990	1991	1992	Totals
Dallas	3-0	3-0	3-0	2-1	2-1	2-1	2-0	1-1	3-1	1-3	3-1	4-0	2-1	2-2	2-2	3-1	1-3	2-1	0-4	0-2	1-1	3-1	4-0	49-27
Washington	2-1	1-2	1-2	2-1	2-1	1-2	1-1	1-1	2-2	2-2	1-3	2-2		4-0	3-1	4-0	3-1	2-1	1-3	2-2	3-1	4-0	2-2	46-31
Philadelphia	2-1	1-2	2-1	2-1	2-1	0-3	0-2	1-1	3-1	2-2	3-1	3-1	2-1	1-1	3-1	1-1	2-2	3-1	2-2	3-1	1-3	4-0	3-1	46-31
San Francisco	4-0	2-1	2-1	1-2	0-3	1-2	1-1	0-2	1-3	0-4	2-2	3-1	1-3	2-2	3-1	3-1	4-0	3-1	2-2	4-0	4-0	3-1	3-1	49-34
L.A. Rams	2-1	1-2	1-2	3-0	3-1	3-0	1-1	2-0	2-2	2-2	2-2	1-3	1-2	1-3	3-1	3-1	2-2	1-2	2-2	3-1	2-2	1-3	2-2	44-37
N.Y. Giants	3-0	1-2	1-2	1-2	1-2	2-1	0-2	0-2	1-1	1-1	1-3	1-1	1-0	0-4	2-0	2-2	3-1	2-1	1-1	4-0	3-1	3-1	2-2	36-32
Minnesota	2-1	2-1	1-2	2-1	2-1	4-0	2-0	1-1	1-3	1-3	1-3	1-3	1-3	4-0	0-4	2-0	1-3	2-1	2-2	2-2	2-2	0-2	3-1	39-39
Phoenix	2-0-1	2-1	1-2	0-2-1	2-1	2-1	1-1	0-2	0-4	1-3	1-1	3-1		3-1	3-1	2-2	1-1	0-1	1-3	1-3	2-2	1-1	0-2	29-36-2
Chicago	1-2	1-2	1-2	2-2	0-3	0-3	0-2	1-1	0-4	2-2	0-4	4-0	1-1	1-1	2-2	3-1	4-0	2-2	3-1	2-2	2-2	2-2	1-3	35-44
Detroit	3-0	4-0	2-0-1	0-3	1-2	1-2	2-0	2-0	2-2	0-4	0-2	2-2	0-1	1-3	0-4	2-2	1-3	0-4	1-1	1-3	1-3	4-0	2-2	32-43-1
New Orleans	0-3	0-1-2	0-3	1-2	0-3	0-3	1-2	0-2	1-3	0-4	1-3	2-2	1-0	1-3	3-1	0-4	1-3	4-0	4-0	4-0	2-2	3-1	3-1	32-46-2
Atlanta	1-2	3-0	2-2	2-1	0-3	1-2	0-2	0-2	1-3	1-3	2-2	1-3	1-1	3-1	1-3	0-4	1-3	0-4	1-3	2-2	2-2	3-1	2-2	30-51
Green Bay	2-1	2-1	2-1	1-1-1	2-1	0-3	0-2	0-3	2-2	1-3	1-3	1-1	1-1-1	2-2	0-4	0-4	1-3	1-2-1	1-3	0-2	1-3	1-3	3-1	25-50-3
Tampa Bay								0-1	2-0	2-0	1-3	0-4	2-1	1-3	1-1	0-4	1-1	0-2	1-3	0-4	0-2	1-3	0-2	12-34
Seattle							1-0																	1-0
TOTALS	27-12-1	23-15-2	19-20-1	19-19-2	17-23	17-23	12-16	9-19	21-31	16-36	19-33	28-24	14-15-1	26-26	26-26	25-27	26-26	22-23-1	22-30	28-24	26-26	33-19	30-22	505-535-8

1992 Interconference Games
(Home Team in capital letters)

NFC 30, AFC 22

AFC Victories

BUFFALO 40, Los Angeles Rams 7
Buffalo 34, SAN FRANCISCO 31
MIAMI 26, Los Angeles Rams 10
Indianapolis 24, TAMPA BAY 14
LOS ANGELES RAIDERS 13, New York Giants 10
MIAMI 21, Atlanta 17
KANSAS CITY 24, Philadelphia 17
CLEVELAND 17, Green Bay 6
Cincinnati 31, CHICAGO 28 (OT)
PITTSBURGH 17, Detroit 14
Houston 17, MINNESOTA 13
KANSAS CITY 35, Washington 16
DENVER 27, New York Giants 13
BUFFALO 41, Atlanta 14
SAN DIEGO 29, Tampa Bay 14
Houston 24, DETROIT 21
CLEVELAND 27, Chicago 14
San Diego 27, PHOENIX 21
HOUSTON 24, Chicago 7
Buffalo 20, NEW ORLEANS 16
INDIANAPOLIS 16, Phoenix 13
Los Angeles Raiders 21, WASHINGTON 20

NFC Victories

ATLANTA 20, New York Jets 17
LOS ANGELES RAMS 14, New England 0
GREEN BAY 24, Cincinnati 23
PHILADELPHIA 30, Denver 0
San Francisco 31, NEW YORK JETS 14
Minnesota 42, CINCINNATI 7
LOS ANGELES RAMS 18, New York Jets 10
GREEN BAY 17, Pittsburgh 3
San Francisco 24, NEW ENGLAND 12
DALLAS 27, Seattle 0
WASHINGTON 34, Denver 3
DALLAS 17, Kansas City 10
Dallas 28, LOS ANGELES RAIDERS 13
NEW YORK GIANTS 23, Seattle 10
PHILADELPHIA 31, Los Angeles Raiders 10
New Orleans 31, NEW ENGLAND 14
Washington 16, SEATTLE 3
MINNESOTA 17, Cleveland 13
Detroit 19, CINCINNATI 13
NEW ORLEANS 24, Miami 13
ATLANTA 34, New England 0
Dallas 31, DENVER 27
SAN FRANCISCO 27, Miami 3
DETROIT 24, Cleveland 14
Philadelphia 20, SEATTLE 17 (OT)
CHICAGO 30, Pittsburgh 6
Green Bay 16, HOUSTON 14
NEW YORK GIANTS 35, Kansas City 21
Minnesota 6, PITTSBURGH 3
New Orleans 20, NEW YORK JETS 0

Regular Season Interconference Records, 1970-1992

American Football Conference

Eastern Division	W	L	T	Pct.
Miami	60	17	0	.779
Buffalo	33	40	1	.453
Indianapolis	29	39	1	.428
New York Jets	31	43	0	.419
New England	29	47	0	.382
Central Division				
Pittsburgh	46	33	0	.582
Cincinnati	44	35	0	.557
Cleveland	40	41	0	.494
Houston	33	47	1	.414
Western Division				
Los Angeles Raiders	53	28	1	.652
Denver	44	36	2	.549
San Diego	35	36	0	.493
Kansas City	31	33	2	.485
Seattle	27	29	0	.482

National Football Conference

Eastern Division	W	L	T	Pct.
Dallas	49	27	0	.645
Philadelphia	46	31	0	.597
Washington	46	31	0	.597
New York Giants	36	32	0	.529
Phoenix	29	36	2	.446
Central Division				
Minnesota	39	39	0	.500
Chicago	35	44	0	.443
Detroit	32	43	1	.428
Green Bay	25	50	3	.340
Tampa Bay	12	34	0	.261
Western Division				
San Francisco	49	34	0	.590
Los Angeles Rams	44	37	0	.543
New Orleans	32	46	2	.413
Atlanta	30	51	0	.370

Interconference Victories, 1970-1992

Regular Season

	AFC	NFC	Tie
1970	12	27	1
1971	15	23	2
1972	20	19	1
1973	19	19	2
1974	23	17	0
1975	23	17	0
1976	16	12	0
1977	19	9	0
1978	31	21	0
1979	36	16	0
1980	33	19	0
1981	24	28	0
1982	15	14	1
1983	26	26	0
1984	26	26	0
1985	27	25	0
1986	26	26	0
1987	23	22	1
1988	30	22	0
1989	24	28	0
1990	26	26	0
1991	19	33	0
1992	22	30	0
Total	535	505	8

Preseason

	AFC	NFC	Tie
1970	21	28	1
1971	28	28	3
1972	27	25	4
1973	23	35	2
1974	35	25	0
1975	30	26	1
1976	30	31	0
1977	38	25	0
1978	20	19	0
1979	25	18	0
1980	22	20	1
1981	18	19	0
1982	25	16	0
1983	15	24	0
1984	16	19	0
1985	10	22	1
1986	22	17	0
1987	22	22	0
1988	23	16	1
1989	16	27	0
1990	15	29	0
1991	19	27	0
1992	30	22	0
Total	530	540	14

Monday Night Football, 1970-1992

(Home Team in capitals, games listed in chronological order.)

1992
DALLAS 23, Washington 10
Miami 27, CLEVELAND 23
New York Giants 27, CHICAGO 14
KANSAS CITY 27, Los Angeles Raiders 7
PHILADELPHIA 31, Dallas 7
WASHINGTON 34, Denver 3
PITTSBURGH 20, Cincinnati 0
Buffalo 24, NEW YORK JETS 20
Minnesota 38, CHICAGO 10
San Francisco 41, ATLANTA 3
Buffalo 26, MIAMI 20
NEW ORLEANS 20, Washington 3
SEATTLE 16, Denver 13 (OT)
HOUSTON 24, Chicago 7
MIAMI 20, Los Angeles Raiders 7
Dallas 41, ATLANTA 17
SAN FRANCISCO 24, Detroit 6

1991
NEW YORK GIANTS 16, San Francisco 14
Washington 33, DALLAS 31
HOUSTON 17, Kansas City 7
CHICAGO 19, New York Jets 13 (OT)
WASHINGTON 23, Philadelphia 0
KANSAS CITY 33, Buffalo 6
New York Giants 23, PITTSBURGH 20
BUFFALO 35, Cincinnati 16
KANSAS CITY 24, Los Angeles Raiders 21
PHILADELPHIA 30, New York Giants 7
Chicago 34, MINNESOTA 17
Buffalo 41, MIAMI 27
San Francisco 33, LOS ANGELES RAMS 10
Philadelphia 13, HOUSTON 6
MIAMI 37, Cincinnati 13
NEW ORLEANS 27, Los Angeles Raiders 0
SAN FRANCISCO 52, Chicago 14

1990
San Francisco 13, NEW ORLEANS 12
DENVER 24, Kansas City 23
Buffalo 30, NEW YORK JETS 7
SEATTLE 31, Cincinnati 16
Cleveland 30, DENVER 29
PHILADELPHIA 32, Minnesota 24
Cincinnati 34, CLEVELAND 13
PITTSBURGH 41, Los Angeles Rams 10
New York Giants 24, INDIANAPOLIS 7
PHILADELPHIA 28, Washington 14
Los Angeles Raiders 13, MIAMI 10
HOUSTON 27, Buffalo 24
SAN FRANCISCO 7, New York Giants 3
Los Angeles Raiders 38, DETROIT 31
San Francisco 26, LOS ANGELES RAMS 10
NEW ORLEANS 20, Los Angeles Rams 17

1989
New York Giants 27, WASHINGTON 24
Denver 28, BUFFALO 14
CINCINNATI 21, Cleveland 14
CHICAGO 27, Philadelphia 13
Los Angeles Raiders 14, NEW YORK JETS 7
BUFFALO 23, Los Angeles Rams 20
CLEVELAND 27, Chicago 7
NEW YORK GIANTS 24, Minnesota 14
SAN FRANCISCO 31, New Orleans 13
HOUSTON 26, Cincinnati 24
Denver 14, WASHINGTON 10
SAN FRANCISCO 34, New York Giants 24
SEATTLE 17, Buffalo 16
San Francisco 30, LOS ANGELES RAMS 27
NEW ORLEANS 30, Philadelphia 20
MINNESOTA 29, Cincinnati 21

1988
NEW YORK GIANTS 27, Washington 20
Dallas 17, PHOENIX 14
CLEVELAND 23, Indianapolis 17
Los Angeles Raiders 30, DENVER 27 (OT)
NEW ORLEANS 20, Dallas 17
PHILADELPHIA 24, New York Giants 13
Buffalo 37, NEW YORK JETS 14
CHICAGO 10, San Francisco 9
INDIANAPOLIS 55, Denver 23
HOUSTON 24, Cleveland 17
Buffalo 31, MIAMI 6
SAN FRANCISCO 37, Washington 21
SEATTLE 35, Los Angeles Raiders 27
LOS ANGELES RAMS 23, Chicago 3
MIAMI 38, Cleveland 31
MINNESOTA 28, Chicago 27

1987
CHICAGO 34, New York Giants 19
NEW YORK JETS 43, New England 24
San Francisco 41, NEW YORK GIANTS 21
DENVER 30, Los Angeles Raiders 14
Washington 13, DALLAS 7
CLEVELAND 30, Los Angeles Rams 17
MINNESOTA 34, Denver 27
DALLAS 33, New York Giants 24
NEW YORK JETS 30, Seattle 14
DENVER 31, Chicago 29
Los Angeles Rams 30, WASHINGTON 26
Los Angeles Raiders 37, SEATTLE 14
MIAMI 37, New York Jets 28
SAN FRANCISCO 41, Chicago 0
Dallas 29, LOS ANGELES RAMS 21
New England 24, MIAMI 10

1986
DALLAS 31, New York Giants 28
Denver 21, PITTSBURGH 10
Chicago 25, GREEN BAY 12
Dallas 31, ST. LOUIS 7
SEATTLE 33, San Diego 7
CINCINNATI 24, Pittsburgh 22
NEW YORK JETS 22, Denver 10
NEW YORK GIANTS 27, Washington 20
Los Angeles Rams 20, CHICAGO 17
CLEVELAND 26, Miami 16
WASHINGTON 14, San Francisco 6
MIAMI 45, New York Jets 3
New York Giants 21, SAN FRANCISCO 17
SEATTLE 37, Los Angeles Raiders 0
Chicago 16, DETROIT 13
New England 34, MIAMI 27

1985
DALLAS 44, Washington 14
CLEVELAND 17, Pittsburgh 7
Los Angeles Rams 35, SEATTLE 24
Cincinnati 37, PITTSBURGH 24
WASHINGTON 27, St. Louis 10
NEW YORK JETS 23, Miami 7
CHICAGO 23, Green Bay 7
LOS ANGELES RAIDERS 34, San Diego 21
ST. LOUIS 21, Dallas 10
DENVER 17, San Francisco 16
WASHINGTON 23, New York Giants 21
SAN FRANCISCO 19, Seattle 6
MIAMI 38, Chicago 24
Los Angeles Rams 27, SAN FRANCISCO 20
MIAMI 30, New England 27
L.A. Raiders 16, L.A. RAMS 6

1984
Dallas 20, LOS ANGELES RAMS 13
SAN FRANCISCO 37, Washington 31
Miami 21, BUFFALO 17
LOS ANGELES RAIDERS 33, San Diego 30
PITTSBURGH 38, Cincinnati 17
San Francisco 31, NEW YORK GIANTS 10
DENVER 17, Green Bay 14
Los Angeles Rams 24, ATLANTA 10
Seattle 24, SAN DIEGO 0
WASHINGTON 27, Atlanta 14
SEATTLE 17, Los Angeles Raiders 14
NEW ORLEANS 27, Pittsburgh 24
MIAMI 28, New York Jets 17
SAN DIEGO 20, Chicago 7
Los Angeles Raiders 24, DETROIT 3
MIAMI 28, Dallas 21

1983
Dallas 31, WASHINGTON 30
San Diego 17, KANSAS CITY 14
LOS ANGELES RAIDERS 27, Miami 14
NEW YORK GIANTS 27, Green Bay 3
New York Jets 34, BUFFALO 10
Pittsburgh 24, CINCINNATI 14
GREEN BAY 48, Washington 47
ST. LOUIS 20, New York Giants 20 (OT)
Washington 27, SAN DIEGO 24
DETROIT 15, New York Giants 9
Los Angeles Rams 36, ATLANTA 13
New York Jets 31, NEW ORLEANS 28
MIAMI 38, Cincinnati 14
DETROIT 13, Minnesota 2
Green Bay 12, TAMPA BAY 9 (OT)
SAN FRANCISCO 42, Dallas 17

1982
Pittsburgh 36, DALLAS 28
Green Bay 27, NEW YORK GIANTS 19
LOS ANGELES RAIDERS 28, San Diego 24
TAMPA BAY 23, Miami 17
New York Jets 28, DETROIT 13
Dallas 37, HOUSTON 7
SAN DIEGO 50, Cincinnati 34
MIAMI 27, Buffalo 10
MINNESOTA 31, Dallas 27

1981
San Diego 44, CLEVELAND 14
Oakland 36, MINNESOTA 10
Dallas 35, NEW ENGLAND 21
Los Angeles 24, CHICAGO 7
PHILADELPHIA 16, Atlanta 13
BUFFALO 31, Miami 21
DETROIT 48, Chicago 17
PITTSBURGH 26, Houston 13
DENVER 19, Minnesota 17
DALLAS 27, Buffalo 14
SEATTLE 44, San Diego 23
ATLANTA 31, Minnesota 30
MIAMI 13, Philadelphia 10
OAKLAND 30, Pittsburgh 27
LOS ANGELES 21, Atlanta 16
SAN DIEGO 23, Oakland 10

1980
Dallas 17, WASHINGTON 3
Houston 16, CLEVELAND 7
PHILADELPHIA 35, New York Giants 3
NEW ENGLAND 23, Denver 14
CHICAGO 23, Tampa Bay 0
DENVER 20, Washington 17
Oakland 45, PITTSBURGH 34
NEW YORK JETS 17, Miami 14
CLEVELAND 27, Chicago 21
HOUSTON 38, New England 34
Oakland 19, SEATTLE 17
Los Angeles 27, NEW ORLEANS 7
OAKLAND 9, Denver 3
MIAMI 16, New England 13 (OT)
LOS ANGELES 38, Dallas 14
SAN DIEGO 26, Pittsburgh 17

1979
Pittsburgh 16, NEW ENGLAND 13 (OT)
Atlanta 14, PHILADELPHIA 10
WASHINGTON 27, New York Giants 0
CLEVELAND 26, Dallas 7
GREEN BAY 27, New England 14
OAKLAND 13, Miami 3
NEW YORK JETS 14, Minnesota 7
PITTSBURGH 42, Denver 7
Seattle 31, ATLANTA 28
Houston 9, MIAMI 6
Philadelphia 31, DALLAS 21
LOS ANGELES 20, Atlanta 14
SEATTLE 30, New York Jets 7
Oakland 42, NEW ORLEANS 35
HOUSTON 20, Pittsburgh 17
SAN DIEGO 17, Denver 7

1978
DALLAS 38, Baltimore 0
MINNESOTA 12, Denver 9 (OT)
Baltimore 34, NEW ENGLAND 27
Minnesota 24, CHICAGO 20
WASHINGTON 9, Dallas 5
MIAMI 21, Cincinnati 0
DENVER 16, Chicago 7
Houston 24, PITTSBURGH 17
ATLANTA 15, Los Angeles 7
BALTIMORE 21, Washington 17
Oakland 34, CINCINNATI 21
HOUSTON 35, Miami 30
Pittsburgh 24, SAN FRANCISCO 7
SAN DIEGO 40, Chicago 7
Cincinnati 20, LOS ANGELES 19
MIAMI 23, New England 3

1977
PITTSBURGH 27, San Francisco 0
CLEVELAND 30, New England 27 (OT)
Oakland 37, KANSAS CITY 28
CHICAGO 24, Los Angeles 23
PITTSBURGH 20, Cincinnati 14
LOS ANGELES 35, Minnesota 3
ST. LOUIS 28, New York Giants 0
BALTIMORE 10, Washington 3
St. Louis 24, DALLAS 17
WASHINGTON 10, Green Bay 9
OAKLAND 34, Buffalo 13
MIAMI 17, Baltimore 6
Dallas 42, SAN FRANCISCO 35

1976
Miami 30, BUFFALO 21
Oakland 24, KANSAS CITY 21
Washington 20, PHILADELPHIA 17 (OT)
MINNESOTA 17, Pittsburgh 6
San Francisco 16, LOS ANGELES 0
NEW ENGLAND 41, New York Jets 7
WASHINGTON 20, St. Louis 10
BALTIMORE 38, Houston 14
CINCINNATI 20, Los Angeles 12
DALLAS 17, Buffalo 10
Baltimore 17, MIAMI 16
SAN FRANCISCO 20, Minnesota 16
OAKLAND 35, Cincinnati 20

1975
Oakland 31, MIAMI 21
DENVER 23, Green Bay 13
Dallas 36, DETROIT 10
WASHINGTON 27, St. Louis 17
New York Giants 17, BUFFALO 14
Minnesota 13, CHICAGO 9
Los Angeles 42, PHILADELPHIA 3
Kansas City 34, DALLAS 31
CINCINNATI 33, Buffalo 24
Pittsburgh 32, HOUSTON 9
MIAMI 20, New England 7
OAKLAND 17, Denver 10
SAN DIEGO 24, New York Jets 16

1974
BUFFALO 21, Oakland 20
PHILADELPHIA 13, Dallas 10
WASHINGTON 30, Denver 3
MIAMI 21, New York Jets 17
DETROIT 17, San Francisco 13
CHICAGO 10, Green Bay 9
PITTSBURGH 24, Atlanta 17
Los Angeles 15, SAN FRANCISCO 13
Minnesota 28, ST. LOUIS 24
Kansas City 42, DENVER 34
Pittsburgh 28, NEW ORLEANS 7
MIAMI 24, Cincinnati 3
Washington 23, LOS ANGELES 17

1973
GREEN BAY 23, New York Jets 7
DALLAS 40, New Orleans 3
DETROIT 31, Atlanta 6
WASHINGTON 14, Dallas 7
Miami 17, CLEVELAND 9
DENVER 23, Oakland 23
BUFFALO 23, Kansas City 14
PITTSBURGH 21, Washington 16
KANSAS CITY 19, Chicago 7
ATLANTA 20, Minnesota 14
SAN FRANCISCO 20, Green Bay 6
MIAMI 30, Pittsburgh 26
LOS ANGELES 40, New York Giants 6

1972
Washington 24, MINNESOTA 21
Kansas City 20, NEW ORLEANS 17
New York Giants 27, PHILADELPHIA 12
Oakland 34, HOUSTON 0
Green Bay 24, DETROIT 23
CHICAGO 13, Minnesota 10
DALLAS 28, Detroit 24
Baltimore 24, NEW ENGLAND 17
Cleveland 21, SAN DIEGO 17
WASHINGTON 24, Atlanta 13
MIAMI 31, St. Louis 10
Los Angeles 26, SAN FRANCISCO 16
OAKLAND 24, New York Jets 16

1971
Minnesota 16, DETROIT 13
ST. LOUIS 17, New York Jets 10
Oakland 34, CLEVELAND 20
DALLAS 20, New York Giants 13
KANSAS CITY 38, Pittsburgh 16
MINNESOTA 10, Baltimore 3
GREEN BAY 14, Detroit 14
BALTIMORE 24, Los Angeles 17
SAN DIEGO 20, St. Louis 17
ATLANTA 28, Green Bay 21
MIAMI 34, Chicago 3
Kansas City 26, SAN FRANCISCO 17
Washington 38, LOS ANGELES 24

1970
CLEVELAND 31, New York Jets 21
Kansas City 44, BALTIMORE 24
DETROIT 28, Chicago 14
Green Bay 22, SAN DIEGO 20
OAKLAND 34, Washington 20
MINNESOTA 13, Los Angeles 3
PITTSBURGH 21, Cincinnati 10
Baltimore 13, GREEN BAY 10
St. Louis 38, DALLAS 0
PHILADELPHIA 23, New York Giants 20
Miami 20, ATLANTA 7
Cleveland 21, HOUSTON 10
Detroit 28, LOS ANGELES 23

Monday Night Syndrome

1992

Of the 16 winning teams:	11 won the next week 4 lost the next week 0 tied the next week 1 had an Open Date the next week
Of the 16 losing teams:	11 won the next week 5 lost the next week 0 tied the next week 0 had an Open Date the next week
Of the 32 NFL teams:	22 won the next week 9 lost the next week 0 tied the next week 1 had an Open Date the next week

1970-1992

Of the 321 winning teams:	187 won the next week 127 lost the next week 3 tied the next week 4 had Open Dates the next week
Of the 321 losing teams:	175 won the next week 143 lost the next week 1 tied the next week 2 had Open Dates the next week
Of the 6 tying teams:	5 won the next week 1 lost the next week 0 tied the next week
Of the 648 NFL teams:	367 won the next week 271 lost the next week 4 tied the next week 6 had Open Dates the next week

Monday Night Won-Lost Records, 1970-1992

American Football Conference

	Buff.	Cin.	Clev.	Den.	Hou.	Ind.	K.C.	Raid.	Mia.	N.E.	N.Y.J.	Pitt.	S.D.	Sea.
Total	11-13	7-16	12-9	12-15-1	11-7	9-6	10-6	29-10-1	27-17	4-12	9-16	16-14	10-9	11-5
1992	2-0	0-1	0-1	0-2	1-0		1-0	0-2	2-1		0-1	1-0		1-0
1991	2-1	0-2			1-1		2-1	0-2	1-1		0-1	0-1		
1990	1-1	1-1	1-1	1-1	1-0	0-1	0-1	2-0	0-1		0-1	1-0		1-0
1989	1-2	1-2	1-1	2-0	1-0			1-0			0-1			1-0
1988	2-0		1-2	0-2	1-0	1-1		1-1	1-1		0-1			1-0
1987			1-0	2-1				1-1	1-1	1-1	2-1			0-2
1986		1-0	1-0	1-1				0-1	1-2	1-0	1-1	0-2	0-1	2-0
1985		1-0	1-0	1-0				2-0	2-1	0-1	1-0	0-2	0-1	0-2
1984	0-1	0-1		1-0				2-1	3-0		0-1	1-1	1-2	2-0
1983	0-1	0-2					0-1	1-0	1-1		2-0	1-0	1-1	
1982	0-1	0-1			0-1			1-0	1-1		1-0	1-0	1-1	
1981	1-1		0-1	1-0	0-1			2-1	1-1	0-1		1-1	2-1	1-0
1980			1-1	1-2	2-0			3-0	1-1	1-2	1-0	0-2	1-0	0-1
1979			1-0	0-2	2-0			2-0	0-2	0-2	1-1	2-1	1-0	2-0
1978		1-2		1-1	2-0	2-1		1-0	2-1	0-2		1-1	1-0	
1977	0-1	0-1	1-0			1-1	0-1	2-0	1-0	0-1		2-0		
1976	0-2	1-1			0-1	2-0	0-1	2-0	1-1	1-0	0-1	0-1		
1975	0-2	1-0		1-1	0-1		1-0	2-0	1-1	0-1	0-1	1-0	1-0	
1974	1-0	0-1		0-2			1-0	0-1	2-0		0-1	2-0		
1973	1-0		0-1	0-0-1			1-1	0-0-1	2-0		0-1	1-1		
1972			1-0		0-1	1-0	1-0	2-0	1-0	0-1	0-1		0-1	
1971			0-1			1-1	2-0	1-0	1-0		0-1	0-1	1-0	
1970		0-1	2-0		0-1	1-1	1-0	1-0	1-0		0-1	1-0	0-1	

National Football Conference

	Atl.	Chi.	Dall.	Det.	G.B.	Rams	Minn.	N.O.	N.Y.G.	Phil.	Phx.	S.F.	T.B.	Wash.
Total	5-13	12-22	21-18	7-9-1	7-10-1	17-20	13-13	6-8	12-18-1	11-8	5-8-1	20-12	1-2	21-19
1992	0-2	0-3	2-1	0-1			1-0	1-0	1-0	1-0		2-0		1-2
1991		2-1	0-1			0-1	0-1	1-0	2-1	2-1		2-1		2-0
1990				0-1		0-3	0-1	1-1	1-1	2-0		3-0		0-1
1989		1-1				0-2	1-1	1-1	2-1	0-2		3-0		0-2
1988		1-2	1-1			1-0	1-0	1-0	1-1	1-0	0-1	1-1		0-2
1987		1-2	2-1			1-2	1-0		0-3			2-0		1-1
1986		2-1	2-0	0-1	0-1	1-0			2-1		0-1	0-2		1-1
1985		1-1	1-1		0-1	2-1			0-1		1-1	1-2		2-1
1984	0-2	0-1	1-1	0-1	0-1	1-1		1-0	0-1			2-0		1-1
1983	0-1		1-1	2-0	2-1	1-0	0-1	0-1	1-1-1		0-0-1	1-0	0-1	1-2
1982			1-2	0-1	1-0		1-0		0-1				1-0	
1981	1-2	0-2	2-0	1-0		2-0	0-3			1-1				
1980		1-1	1-1			2-0		0-1	0-1	1-0			0-1	0-2
1979	1-2		0-2		1-0	1-0	0-1	0-1	0-1	1-1				1-0
1978	1-0	0-3	1-1			0-2	2-0				2-0	0-1		1-1
1977		1-0	1-1		0-1	1-1	0-1		0-1		0-1	0-2		1-1
1976			1-0			0-2	1-1			0-1	0-1	2-0		2-0
1975		0-1	1-1	0-1	0-1	1-0	1-0		1-0	0-1	0-1			1-0
1974	0-1	1-0	0-1	1-0	0-1	1-1	1-0	0-1		1-0		0-2		2-0
1973	1-1	0-1	1-1	1-0	1-1	1-0	0-1	0-1	0-1		0-1	1-0		1-1
1972	0-1	1-0	1-0	0-2	1-0	1-0	0-2	0-1	1-0	0-1	1-1	0-1		2-0
1971	1-0	0-1	1-0	0-1-1	0-1-1	0-2	2-0		0-1		1-0	0-1		1-0
1970	0-1	0-1	0-1	2-0	1-1	0-2	1-0		0-1	1-0				0-1

Thursday-Sunday Night Football, 1974-1992

(Home Team in capitals, games listed in chronological order.)

1992
DENVER 17, Los Angeles Raiders 13 (Sun.)
Philadelphia 31, PHOENIX 14 (Sun.)
BUFFALO 38, Indianapolis 0 (Sun.)
San Francisco 16, NEW ORLEANS 10 (Sun.)
NEW YORK JETS 30, New England 21 (Sun.)
NEW ORLEANS 13, Los Angeles Rams 10 (Sun.)
MINNESOTA 31, Detroit 14 (Thurs.)
Pittsburgh 27, KANSAS CITY 3 (Sun.)
New York Giants 24, WASHINGTON 7 (Sun.)
Cincinnati 31, CHICAGO 28 (OT) (Sun.)
DENVER 27, New York Giants 13 (Sun.)
Kansas City 24, SEATTLE 14 (Sun.)
Houston 24, DETROIT 21 (Thurs.)
DALLAS 30, N.Y. Giants 3 (Thurs.)
SAN DIEGO 27, Los Angeles Raiders 3 (Sun.)
NEW ORLEANS 22, Atlanta 14 (Thurs.)
Los Angeles Rams 31, TAMPA BAY 27 (Sun.)
Green Bay 16, HOUSTON 14 (Sun.)
MIAMI 19, New York Jets 17 (Sun.)
Los Angeles Raiders 21, WASHINGTON 20 (Sat.)
HOUSTON 27, Buffalo 3 (Sun.)

1991
WASHINGTON 45, Detroit 0 (Sun.)
Houston 30, CINCINNATI 7 (Sun.)
NEW ORLEANS 24, Los Angeles Rams 7 (Sun.)
Dallas 17, PHOENIX 9 (Sun.)
Denver 13, MINNESOTA 6 (Sun.)
Pittsburgh 21, INDIANAPOLIS 3 (Sun.)
Los Angeles Raiders 23, SEATTLE 20 (Sun.)
Chicago 10, GREEN BAY 0 (Thurs.)
Washington 17, NEW YORK GIANTS 13 (Sun.)
DENVER 20, Pittsburgh 13 (Sun.)
MIAMI 30, New England 20 (Sun.)
HOUSTON 28, Cleveland 24 (Sun.)
Atlanta 23, NEW ORLEANS 20 (OT) (Sun.)
Los Angeles Raiders 9, SAN DIEGO 7 (Sun.)
Minnesota 26, TAMPA BAY 24 (Sun.)
Buffalo 35, INDIANAPOLIS 7 (Sun.)
SEATTLE 23, Los Angeles Rams 9 (Sun.)

1990
NEW YORK GIANTS 27, Philadelphia 20 (Sun.)
PITTSBURGH 20, Houston 9 (Sun.)
TAMPA BAY 23, Detroit 20 (Sun.)
Washington 38, PHOENIX 10 (Sun.)
BUFFALO 38, Los Angeles Raiders 24 (Sun.)
CHICAGO 38, Los Angeles Rams 9 (Sun.)
MIAMI 17, New England 10 (Thurs.)
ATLANTA 38, Cincinnati 17 (Sun.)
MINNESOTA 27, Denver 22 (Sun.)
San Francisco 24, DALLAS 6 (Sun.)
CINCINNATI 27, Pittsburgh 3 (Sun.)
Seattle 13, SAN DIEGO 10 (Sun.)
MINNESOTA 23, Green Bay 7 (Sun.)
MIAMI 23, Philadelphia 20 (Sun.)
DETROIT 38, Chicago 21 (Sun.)
INDIANAPOLIS 35, Washington 28 (Sat.)
SEATTLE 17, Denver 12 (Sun.)
HOUSTON 34, Pittsburgh 14 (Sun.)

1989
Dallas 13, WASHINGTON 3 (Sun.)
SAN DIEGO 14, Los Angeles Raiders 12 (Sun.)
INDIANAPOLIS 27, New York Jets 10 (Sun.)
Los Angeles Rams 20, NEW ORLEANS 17 (Sun.)
MINNESOTA 27, Chicago 16 (Sun.)
MIAMI 31, New England 10 (Sun.)
SEATTLE 23, Los Angeles Raiders 17 (Sun.)
Cleveland 24, HOUSTON 20 (Sat.)

1988
HOUSTON 41, Washington 17 (Sun.)
Los Angeles Raiders 13, SAN DIEGO 3 (Sun.)
Minnesota 34, DALLAS 3 (Sun.)
New England 6, MIAMI 3 (Sun.)
New York Giants 13, NEW ORLEANS 12 (Sun.)
Pittsburgh 37, HOUSTON 34 (Sun.)
SEATTLE 42, Denver 14 (Sun.)
Los Angeles Rams 38, SAN FRANCISCO 16 (Sun.)

1987
NEW YORK GIANTS 17, New England 10 (Sun.)
SAN DIEGO 16, Los Angeles Raiders 14 (Sun.)
Miami 20, DALLAS 14 (Sun.)
SAN FRANCISCO 38, Cleveland 24 (Sun.)
Chicago 30, MINNESOTA 24 (Sun.)
SEATTLE 28, Denver 21 (Sun.)
MIAMI 23, Washington 21 (Sun.)
SAN FRANCISCO 48, Los Angeles Rams 0 (Sun.)

1986
New England 20, NEW YORK JETS 6 (Thurs.)
Cincinnati 30, CLEVELAND 13 (Thurs.)
Los Angeles Raiders 37, SAN DIEGO 31 (OT) (Thurs.)
LOS ANGELES RAMS 29, Dallas 10 (Sun.)
SAN FRANCISCO 24, Los Angeles Rams 14 (Fri.)

1985
KANSAS CITY 36, Los Angeles Raiders 20 (Thurs.)
Chicago 33, MINNESOTA 24 (Thurs.)
Dallas 30, NEW YORK GIANTS 29 (Sun.)
SAN DIEGO 54, Pittsburgh 44 (Sun.)
Denver 27, SEATTLE 24 (Fri.)

1984
Pittsburgh 23, NEW YORK JETS 17 (Thurs.)
Denver 24, CLEVELAND 14 (Sun.)
DALLAS 30, New Orleans 27 (Sun.)
Washington 31, MINNESOTA 17 (Thurs.)
SAN FRANCISCO 19, Los Angeles Rams 16 (Fri.)

1983
San Francisco 48, MINNESOTA 17 (Thurs.)
CLEVELAND 17, Cincinnati 7 (Thurs.)
Los Angeles Raiders 40, DALLAS 38 (Sun.)
Los Angeles Raiders 42, SAN DIEGO 10 (Thurs.)
MIAMI 34, New York Jets 14 (Fri.)

1982
BUFFALO 23, Minnesota 22 (Thurs.)
SAN FRANCISCO 30, Los Angeles Rams 24 (Thurs.)
ATLANTA 17, San Francisco 7 (Sun.)

1981
MIAMI 30, Pittsburgh 10 (Thurs.)
Philadelphia 20, BUFFALO 14 (Thurs.)
DALLAS 29, Los Angeles 17 (Sun.)
HOUSTON 17, Cleveland 13 (Thurs.)

1980
TAMPA BAY 10, Los Angeles 9 (Thurs.)
DALLAS 42, San Diego 31 (Sun.)
San Diego 27, MIAMI 24 (OT) (Thurs.)
HOUSTON 6, Pittsburgh 0 (Thurs.)

1979
Los Angeles 13, DENVER 9 (Thurs.)
DALLAS 30, Los Angeles 6 (Sun.)
OAKLAND 45, San Diego 22 (Thurs.)
MIAMI 39, New England 24 (Thurs.)

1978
New England 21, OAKLAND 14 (Sun.)
Minnesota 21, DALLAS 10 (Thurs.)
LOS ANGELES 10, Pittsburgh 7 (Sun.)
Denver 21, OAKLAND 6 (Sun.)

1977
Minnesota 30, DETROIT 21 (Sat.)

1976
Los Angeles 20, DETROIT 17 (Sat.)

1975
LOS ANGELES 10, Pittsburgh 3 (Sat.)

1974
OAKLAND 27, Dallas 23 (Sat.)

History of Overtime Games

Preseason

Aug. 28, 1955	Los Angeles 23, New York Giants 17, at Portland, Oregon
Aug. 24, 1962	Denver 27, Dallas Texans 24, at Fort Worth, Texas
Aug. 10, 1974	San Diego 20, New York Jets 14, at San Diego
Aug. 17, 1974	Pittsburgh 33, Philadelphia 30, at Philadelphia
Aug. 17, 1974	Dallas 19, Houston 13, at Dallas
Aug. 17, 1974	Cincinnati 13, Atlanta 7, at Atlanta
Sept. 6, 1974	Buffalo 23, New York Giants 17, at Buffalo
Aug. 9, 1975	Baltimore 23, Denver 20, at Denver
Aug. 30, 1975	New England 20, Green Bay 17, at Milwaukee
Sept. 13, 1975	Minnesota 14, San Diego 14, at San Diego
Aug. 1, 1976	New England 13, New York Giants 7, at New England
Aug. 2, 1976	Kansas City 9, Houston 3, at Kansas City
Aug. 20, 1976	New Orleans 26, Baltimore 20, at Baltimore
Sept. 4, 1976	Dallas 26, Houston 20, at Dallas
Aug. 13, 1977	Seattle 23, Dallas 17, at Seattle
Aug. 28, 1977	New England 13, Pittsburgh 10, at New England
Aug. 28, 1977	New York Giants 24, Buffalo 21, at East Rutherford, N.J.
Aug. 2, 1979	Seattle 12, Minnesota 9, at Minnesota
Aug. 4, 1979	Los Angeles 20, Oakland 14, at Los Angeles
Aug. 24, 1979	Denver 20, New England 17, at Denver
Aug. 23, 1980	Tampa Bay 20, Cincinnati 14, at Tampa Bay
Aug. 5, 1981	San Francisco 27, Seattle 24, at Seattle
Aug. 29, 1981	New Orleans 20, Detroit 17, at New Orleans
Aug. 28, 1982	Miami 17, Kansas City 17, at Kansas City
Sept. 3, 1982	Miami 16, New York Giants 13, at Miami
Aug. 6, 1983	L.A. Raiders 26, San Francisco 23, at Los Angeles
Aug. 6, 1983	Atlanta 13, Washington 10, at Atlanta
Aug. 13, 1983	St. Louis 27, Chicago 24, at St. Louis
Aug. 18, 1983	New York Jets 20, Cincinnati 17, at Cincinnati
Aug. 27, 1983	Chicago 20, Kansas City 17, at Chicago
Aug. 11, 1984	Pittsburgh 20, Philadelphia 17, at Pittsburgh
Aug. 9, 1985	Buffalo 10, Detroit 10, at Pontiac, Mich.
Aug. 10, 1985	Minnesota 16, Miami 13, at Miami
Aug. 17, 1985	Dallas 27, San Diego 24, at San Diego
Aug. 24, 1985	N.Y. Giants 34, N.Y. Jets 31, at East Rutherford, N.J.
Aug. 15, 1986	Washington 27, Pittsburgh 24, at Washington
Aug. 15, 1986	Detroit 30, Seattle 27, at Detroit
Aug. 23, 1986	Los Angeles Rams 20, San Diego 17, at Anaheim
Aug. 30, 1986	Minnesota 23, Indianapolis 20, at Indianapolis
Aug. 23, 1987	Philadelphia 19, New England 13, at New England
Sept. 5, 1987	Cleveland 30, Green Bay 24, at Milwaukee
Sept. 6, 1987	Kansas City 13, St. Louis 10, at Memphis, Tenn.
Aug. 11, 1988	Seattle 16, Detroit 13, at Detroit
Aug. 19, 1988	Miami 16, Denver 13, at Miami
Aug. 19, 1988	Green Bay 21, Kansas City 21, at Milwaukee
Aug. 20, 1988	Houston 20, Los Angeles Rams 17, at Anaheim
Aug. 21, 1988	Minnesota 19, Phoenix 16, at Phoenix
Aug. 5, 1989	Los Angeles Rams 16, San Francisco 13, at Tokyo, Japan
Aug. 26, 1989	Denver 24, Dallas 21, at Denver
Sept. 1, 1989	N.Y. Jets 15, Kansas City 13, at Kansas City
Aug. 24, 1990	Cincinnati 13, New England 10, at New England
Aug. 16, 1991	Cleveland 24, Washington 21, at Washington
Aug. 17, 1991	Cincinnati 27, Minnesota 24, at Cincinnati
Aug. 23, 1991	Dallas 20, Atlanta 17, at Dallas
Aug. 24, 1991	Cincinnati 19, Green Bay 16, at Green Bay
Aug. 22, 1992	Los Angeles Rams 16, Green Bay 13, at Anaheim

Regular Season

Sept. 22, 1974 — Pittsburgh 35, Denver 35, at Denver; Steelers win toss. Gilliam's pass intercepted and returned by Rowser to Denver's 42. Turner misses 41-yard field goal. Walden punts and Greer returns to Broncos' 39. Van Heusen punts and Edwards returns to Steelers' 16. Game ends with Steelers on own 26.

Nov. 10, 1974 — New York Jets 26, New York Giants 20, at New Haven, Conn.; Giants win toss. Gogolak misses 42-yard field goal. Namath passes to Boozer for five yards and touchdown at 6:53.

Sept. 28, 1975 — Dallas 37, St. Louis 31, at Dallas; Cardinals win toss. Hart's pass intercepted and returned by Jordan to Cardinals' 37. Staubach passes to DuPree for three yards and touchdown at 7:53.

Oct. 12, 1975 — Los Angeles 13, San Diego 10, at San Diego; Chargers win toss. Partee punts to Rams' 14. Dempsey kicks 22-yard field goal at 9:27.

Nov. 2, 1975 — Washington 30, Dallas 24, at Washington; Cowboys win toss. Staubach's pass intercepted and returned by Houston to Cowboys' 35. Kilmer runs one yard for touchdown at 6:34.

Nov. 16, 1975 — St. Louis 20, Washington 17, at St. Louis; Cardinals win toss. Bakken kicks 37-yard field goal at 7:00.

Nov. 23, 1975 — Kansas City 24, Detroit 21, at Kansas City; Lions win toss. Chiefs take over on downs at own 38. Stenerud kicks 26-yard field goal at 6:44.

Nov. 23, 1975 — Oakland 26, Washington 23, at Washington; Redskins win toss. Bragg punts to Raiders' 42. Blanda kicks 27-yard field goal at 7:13.

Nov. 30, 1975 — Denver 13, San Diego 10, at Denver; Broncos win toss. Turner kicks 25-yard field goal at 4:13.

Nov. 30, 1975 — Oakland 37, Atlanta 34, at Oakland; Falcons win toss. James punts to Raiders' 16. Guy punts and Herron returns to Falcons' 41. Nick Mike-Mayer misses 45-yard field goal. Guy punts into Falcons' end zone. James punts to Raiders' 39. Blanda kicks 36-yard field goal at 15:00.

Dec. 14, 1975 — Baltimore 10, Miami 7, at Baltimore; Dolphins win toss. Seiple punts to Colts' 4. Linhart kicks 31-yard field goal at 12:44.

Sept. 19, 1976 — Minnesota 10, Los Angeles 10, at Minnesota; Vikings win toss. Tarkenton's pass intercepted by Monte Jackson and returned to Minnesota 16. Allen blocks Dempsey's 30-yard field goal attempt, ball rolls into end zone for touchback. Clabo punts and Scribner returns to Rams' 20. Rusty Jackson punts to Vikings' 35. Tarkenton's pass intercepted by Kay at Rams' 1, no return. Game ends with Rams on own 3.

***Sept. 27, 1976 — Washington 20, Philadelphia 17,** at Philadelphia; Eagles win toss. Jones punts and E. Brown loses one yard on return to Redskins' 40. Bragg punts 51 yards into end zone for touchback. Jones punts and E. Brown returns to Redskins' 42. Bragg punts and Marshall returns to Eagles' 41. Boryla's pass intercepted by Dusek at Redskins' 37, no return. Bragg punts and Bradley returns. Philadelphia holding penalty moves ball back to Eagles' 8. Boryla pass intercepted by E. Brown and returned to Eagles' 22. Moseley kicks 29-yard field goal at 12:49.

Oct. 17, 1976 — Kansas City 20, Miami 17, at Miami; Chiefs win toss. Wilson punts into end zone for touchback. Bulaich fumbles into Kansas City end zone, Collier recovers for touchback. Stenerud kicks 34-yard field goal at 14:48.

Oct. 31, 1976 — St. Louis 23, San Francisco 20, at St. Louis; Cardinals win toss. Joyce punts and Leonard fumbles on return, Jones recovers at 49ers' 43. Bakken kicks 21-yard field goal at 6:42.

Dec. 5, 1976 — San Diego 13, San Francisco 7, at San Diego; Chargers win toss. Morris runs 13 yards for touchdown at 5:12.

Sept. 18, 1977 — Dallas 16, Minnesota 10, at Minnesota; Vikings win toss. Dallas starts on Vikings' 47 after a punt early in the overtime period. Staubach scores seven plays later on a four-yard run at 6:14.

***Sept. 26, 1977 — Cleveland 30, New England 27,** at Cleveland; Browns win toss. Sipe throws a 22-yard pass to Logan at Patriots' 19. Cockroft kicks 35-yard field goal at 4:45.

Oct. 16, 1977 — Minnesota 22, Chicago 16, at Minnesota; Bears win toss. Parsons punts 53 yards to Vikings' 18. Minnesota drives to Bears' 11. On a first-and-10, Vikings fake a field goal and holder Krause hits Voigt with a touchdown pass at 6:45.

Oct. 30, 1977 — Cincinnati 13, Houston 10, at Cincinnati; Bengals win toss. Bahr kicks a 22-yard field goal at 5:51.

Nov. 13, 1977 — San Francisco 10, New Orleans 7, at New Orleans; Saints win toss. Saints fail to move ball and Blanchard punts to 49ers' 41. Wersching kicks a 33-yard field goal at 6:33.

Dec. 18, 1977 — Chicago 12, New York Giants 9, at East Rutherford, N.J.; Giants win toss. The ball changes hands eight times before Thomas kicks a 28-yard field goal at 14:51.

Sept. 10, 1978 — Cleveland 13, Cincinnati 10, at Cleveland; Browns win toss. Collins returns kickoff 41 yards to Browns' 47. Cockroft kicks 27-yard field goal at 4:30.

***Sept. 11, 1978 — Minnesota 12, Denver 9,** at Minnesota; Vikings win toss. Danmeier kicks 44-yard field goal at 2:56.

Sept. 24, 1978 — Pittsburgh 15, Cleveland 9, at Pittsburgh; Steelers win toss. Cunningham scores on a 37-yard "gadget" pass from Bradshaw at 3:43. Steelers start winning drive on their 21.

Sept. 24, 1978 — Denver 23, Kansas City 17, at Kansas City; Broncos win toss. Dilts punts to Kansas City. Chiefs advance to Broncos' 40 where Reed fails to make first down on fourth-and-one situation. Broncos march downfield. Preston scores two-yard touchdown at 10:28.

Oct. 1, 1978 — Oakland 25, Chicago 19, at Chicago; Bears win toss. Both teams punt on first possession. On Chicago's second offensive series, Colzie intercepts Avellini's pass and returns it to Bears' 3. Three plays later, Whittington runs two yards for a touchdown at 5:19.

Oct. 15, 1978 — Dallas 24, St. Louis 21, at St. Louis; Cowboys win toss. Dallas drives from its 23 into field goal range. Septien kicks 27-yard field goal at 3:28.

Oct. 29, 1978 — Denver 20, Seattle 17, at Seattle; Broncos win toss. Ball changes hands four times before Turner kicks 18-yard field goal at 12:59.

Nov. 12, 1978 — San Diego 29, Kansas City 23, at San Diego; Chiefs win toss. Fouts hits Jefferson for decisive 14-yard touchdown pass on the last play (15:00) of overtime period.

Nov. 12, 1978 — Washington 16, New York Giants 13, at Washington; Redskins win toss. Moseley kicks winning 45-yard field goal at 8:32 after missing first down field goal attempt of 35 yards at 4:50.

Nov. 26, 1978 — Green Bay 10, Minnesota 10, at Green Bay; Packers win toss. Both teams have possession of the ball four times.

Dec. 9, 1978 — Cleveland 37, New York Jets 34, at Cleveland; Browns win toss. Cockroft kicks 22-yard field goal at 3:07.

Sept. 2, 1979 — Atlanta 40, New Orleans 34, at New Orleans; Falcons win toss. Bartkowski's pass intercepted by Myers and returned to Falcons' 46. Erxleben punts to Falcons' 4. James punts to Chandler on Saints' 43. Erxleben punts and Ryckman returns to Falcons' 28. James punts and Chandler returns to Saints' 36. Erxleben retrieves punt snap on Saints' 1 and attempts pass. Mayberry intercepts and returns six yards for touchdown at 8:22.

Sept. 2, 1979 — Cleveland 25, New York Jets 22, at New York; Jets win toss. Leahy's 43-yard field goal attempt goes wide right at 4:41. Evans's punt blocked by Dykes is recovered by Newton. Ramsey punts into end zone for touchback. Evans punts and Harper returns to Jets' 24. Robinson's pass intercepted by Davis and returned 33 yards to Jets' 31. Cockroft kicks 27-yard field goal at 14:45.

***Sept. 3, 1979 — Pittsburgh 16, New England 13,** at Foxboro; Patriots win toss. Hare punts to Swann at Steelers' 31. Bahr kicks 41-yard field goal at 5:10.

Sept. 9, 1979 — Tampa Bay 29, Baltimore 26, at Baltimore; Colts win toss. Landry fumbles, recovered by Kollar at Colts' 14. O'Donoghue kicks 31-yard, first-down field goal at 1:41.

Sept. 16, 1979 — Denver 20, Atlanta 17, at Atlanta; Broncos win toss. Broncos march 65 yards to Falcons' 7. Turner kicks 24-yard field goal at 6:15.

Sept. 23, 1979 — Houston 30, Cincinnati 27, at Cincinnati; Oilers win toss. Parsley punts and Lusby returns to Bengals' 33. Bahr's 32-yard field goal attempt is wide right at 8:05. Parsley's punt downed on Bengals' 5. McInally punts and Ellender returns to Bengals' 42. Fritsch's third down, 29-yard field goal attempt hits left upright and bounces through at 14:28.

Sept. 23, 1979 — Minnesota 27, Green Bay 21, at Minnesota; Vikings win toss. Kramer throws 50-yard touchdown pass to Rashad at 3:18.

Oct. 28, 1979 — Houston 27, New York Jets 24, at Houston; Oilers win toss. Oilers march 58 yards to Jets' 18. Fritsch kicks 35-yard field goal at 5:10.

Nov. 18, 1979 — Cleveland 30, Miami 24, at Cleveland; Browns win toss. Sipe passes 39 yards to Rucker for touchdown at 1:59.

Nov. 25, 1979 — Pittsburgh 33, Cleveland 30, at Pittsburgh; Browns win toss. Sipe's pass intercepted by Blount on Steelers' 4. Bradshaw pass intercepted by Bolton on Browns' 12. Evans punts and Bell returns to Steelers' 17. Bahr kicks 37-yard field goal at 14:51.

Nov. 25, 1979 — Buffalo 16, New England 13, at Foxboro; Patriots win toss. Hare's punt downed on Bills' 38. Jackson punts and Morgan returns to Patriots' 20. Grogan's pass intercepted by Haslett and returned to Bills' 42. Ferguson's 51-yard pass to Butler sets up N. Mike-Mayer's 29-yard field goal at 9:15.

Dec. 2, 1979 — Los Angeles 27, Minnesota 21, at Los Angeles; Rams win toss. Clark punts and Miller returns to Vikings' 25. Kramer's pass intercepted by Brown and returned to Rams' 40. Cromwell, holding for 22-yard field goal attempt, runs around left end untouched for winning score at 6:53.

Sept. 7, 1980 — Green Bay 12, Chicago 6, at Green Bay; Bears win toss. Parsons punts and Nixon returns 16 yards. Five plays later, Marcol returns own blocked field goal attempt 24 yards for touchdown at 6:00.

Sept. 14, 1980 — San Diego 30, Oakland 24, at San Diego; Raiders win toss. Pastorini's first-down pass intercepted by Edwards. Millen intercepts Fouts' first-down pass and returns to San Diego 46. Bahr's 50-yard field goal attempt partially blocked by Williams and recovered on Chargers' 32. Eight plays later, Fouts throws 24-yard touchdown pass to Jefferson at 8:09.

Sept. 14, 1980 — San Francisco 24, St. Louis 21, at San Francisco; Cardinals win toss. Swider punts and Robinson returns to 49ers' 32. San Francisco drives 52 yards to St. Louis 16, where Wersching kicks 33-yard field goal at 4:12.

Oct. 12, 1980 — Green Bay 14, Tampa Bay 14, at Tampa Bay; Packers win toss. Teams trade punts twice. Lee returns second Tampa Bay punt to Green Bay 42. Dickey completes three passes to Buccaneers' 18, where Birney's 36-yard field goal attempt is wide right as time expires.

Nov. 9, 1980 — Atlanta 33, St. Louis 27, at St. Louis; Falcons win toss. Strong runs 21 yards for touchdown at 4:20.

#**Nov. 20, 1980 — San Diego 27, Miami 24,** at Miami; Chargers win toss. Partridge punts into end zone, Dolphins take over on their own 20. Woodley's pass for Nathan intercepted by Lowe and returned 28 yards to Dolphins' 12. Benirschke kicks 28-yard field goal at 7:14.

Nov. 23, 1980 — New York Jets 31, Houston 28, at New York; Jets win toss. Leahy kicks 38-yard field goal at 3:58.

Nov. 27, 1980 — Chicago 23, Detroit 17, at Detroit; Bears win toss. Williams returns kickoff 95 yards for touchdown at 0:21.

Dec. 7, 1980 — Buffalo 10, Los Angeles 7, at Buffalo; Rams win toss. Corral punts and Hooks returns to Bills' 34. Ferguson's 30-yard pass to Lewis sets up N. Mike-Mayer's 30-yard field goal at 5:14.

Dec. 7, 1980 — San Francisco 38, New Orleans 35, at San Francisco; Saints win toss. Erxleben's punt downed by Hardy on 49ers' 27. Wersching kicks 36-yard field goal at 7:40.

***Dec. 8, 1980 — Miami 16, New England 13,** at Miami; Dolphins win toss. Von Schamann kicks 23-yard field goal at 3:20.

Dec. 14, 1980 — Cincinnati 17, Chicago 14, at Chicago; Bengals win toss. Breech kicks 28-yard field goal at 4:23.

Dec. 21, 1980 — Los Angeles 20, Atlanta 17, at Los Angeles; Rams win toss. Corral's punt downed at Rams' 37. James punts into end zone for touchback. Corral's punt downed on Falcons' 17. Bartkowski fumbles when hit by Harris, recovered by Delaney. Corral kicks 23-yard field goal on first play of possession at 7:00.

Sept. 27, 1981 — Cincinnati 27, Buffalo 24, at Cincinnati; Bills win toss. Cater punts into end zone for touchback. Bengals drive to the Bills' 10 where Breech kicks 28-yard field goal at 9:33.

Sept. 27, 1981 — Pittsburgh 27, New England 21, at Pittsburgh; Patriots win toss. Hubach punts and Smith returns five yards to midfield. Four plays later Bradshaw throws 24-yard touchdown pass to Swann at 3:19.

Oct. 4, 1981 — Miami 28, New York Jets 28, at Miami; Jets win toss. Teams trade punts twice. Leahy's 48-yard field goal attempt is wide right as time expires.

Oct. 25, 1981 — New York Giants 27, Atlanta 24, at Atlanta; Giants win toss. Jennings' punt goes out of bounds at New York 47. Bright returns Atlanta punt to Giants' 14. Woerner fair catches punt at own 28. Andrews fumbles on first play, recovered by Van Pelt. Danelo kicks 40-yard field goal four plays later at 9:20.

Oct. 25, 1981 — Chicago 20, San Diego 17, at Chicago; Bears win toss. Teams trade punts. Bears' second punt returned by Brooks to Chargers' 33. Fouts pass intercepted by Fencik and returned 32 yards to San Diego 27. Roveto kicks 27-yard field goal seven plays later at 9:30.

Nov. 8, 1981 — Chicago 16, Kansas City 13, at Kansas City; Bears win toss. Teams trade punts. Kansas City takes over on downs on its own 38. Fuller's fumble recovered by Harris on Chicago 36. Roveto's 37-yard field goal wide, but Chiefs penalized for leverage. Roveto's 22-yard field goal attempt three plays later is good at 13:07.

Nov. 8, 1981 — Denver 23, Cleveland 20, at Denver; Browns win toss. D. Smith recovers Hill's fumble at Denver 48. Morton's 33-yard pass to Upchurch and six-yard run by Preston set up Steinfort's 30-yard field goal at 4:10.

Nov. 8, 1981 — Miami 30, New England 27, at New England; Dolphins win toss. Orosz punts and Morgan returns six yards to New England 26. Grogan's pass intercepted by Brudzinski who returns 19 yards to Patriots' 26. Von Schamann kicks 30-yard field goal on first down at 7:09.

Nov. 15, 1981 — Washington 30, New York Giants 27, at New York; Giants win toss. Nelms returns Giants' punt 26 yards to New York 47. Five plays later Moseley kicks 48-yard field goal at 3:44.

Dec. 20, 1981 — New York Giants 13, Dallas 10, at New York; Cowboys win toss and kick off. Jennings punts to Dallas 40. Taylor recovers Dorsett's fumble on second down. Danelo's 33-yard field goal attempt hits right upright and bounces back. White's pass for Pearson intercepted by Hunt and returned seven yards to Dallas 24. Four plays later Danelo kicks 35-yard field goal at 6:19.

Sept. 12, 1982 — Washington 37, Philadelphia 34, at Philadelphia; Redskins win toss. Theismann completes five passes for 63 yards to set up Moseley's 26-yard field goal at 4:47.

Sept. 19, 1982 — Pittsburgh 26, Cincinnati 20, at Pittsburgh; Bengals win toss. Anderson's pass intended for Kreider intercepted by Woodruff and returned 30 yards to Cincinnati 2. Bradshaw completes two-yard touchdown pass to Stallworth on first down at 1:08.

Dec. 19, 1982 — Baltimore 20, Green Bay 20, at Baltimore; Packers win toss. K. Anderson intercepts Dickey's first-down pass and returns to Packers' 42. Miller's 44-yard field goal attempt blocked by G. Lewis. Teams trade punts before Stenerud's 47-yard field goal attempt is wide right. Teams trade punts again before time expires in Colts possession.

Jan. 2, 1983 — Tampa Bay 26, Chicago 23, at Tampa; Bears win toss. Parsons punts to T. Bell at Buccaneers' 40. Capece kicks 33-yard field goal at 3:14.

Sept. 4, 1983 — Baltimore 29, New England 23, at New England; Patriots win toss. Cooks runs 52 yards with fumble recovery three plays into overtime at 0:30.

Sept. 4, 1983 — Green Bay 41, Houston 38, at Houston; Packers win toss. Stenerud kicks 42-yard field goal at 5:55.

Sept. 11, 1983 — New York Giants 16, Atlanta 13, at Atlanta; Giants win toss. Dennis returns kickoff 54 yards to Atlanta 41. Haji-Sheikh kicks 30-yard field goal at 3:38.

Sept. 18, 1983 — New Orleans 34, Chicago 31, at New Orleans; Bears win toss. Parsons punts and Groth returns five yards to New Orleans 34. Stabler pass intercepted by Schmidt at Chicago 47. Parsons punt downed by Gentry at New Orleans 2. Stabler gains 36 yards in four passes; Wilson 38 on six carries. Andersen kicks 41-yard field goal at 10:57.

Sept. 18, 1983 — Minnesota 19, Tampa Bay 16, at Tampa; Vikings win toss. Coleman punts and Bell returns eight yards to Tampa Bay 47. Capece's 33-yard field goal attempt sails wide at 7:26. Dils and Young combine for 48-yard gain to Tampa Bay 27. Ricardo kicks 42-yard field goal at 9:27.

Sept. 25, 1983 — Baltimore 22, Chicago 19, at Baltimore; Colts win toss. Allegre kicks 33-yard field goal nine plays later at 4:51.

Sept. 25, 1983 — Cleveland 30, San Diego 24, at San Diego; Browns win toss. Walker returns kickoff 33 yards to Cleveland 37. Sipe completes 48-yard touchdown pass to Holt four plays later at 1:53.

Sept. 25, 1983 — New York Jets 27, Los Angeles Rams 24, at New York; Jets win toss. Ramsey punts to Irvin who returns to 25 but penalty puts Rams on own 13. Holmes 30-yard interception return sets up Leahy's 26-yard field goal at 3:22.

Oct. 9, 1983 — Buffalo 38, Miami 35, at Miami; Dolphins win toss. Von Schamann's 52-yard field goal attempt goes wide at 12:36. Cater punts to Clayton who loses 11 to own 13. Von Schamann's 43-yard field goal attempt sails wide at 5:15. Danelo kicks 36-yard field goal nine plays later at 13:58.

Oct. 9, 1983 — Dallas 27, Tampa Bay 24, at Dallas; Cowboys win toss. Septien's 51-yard field goal attempt goes wide but Buccaneers penalized for roughing kicker. Septien kicks 42-yard field goal at 4:38.

Oct. 23, 1983 — Kansas City 13, Houston 10, at Houston; Chiefs win toss. Lowery kicks 41-yard field goal 13 plays later at 7:41.

Oct. 23, 1983 — Minnesota 20, Green Bay 17, at Green Bay; Packers win toss. Scribner's punt downed on Vikings' 42. Ricardo kicks 32-yard field goal eight plays later at 5:05.

***Oct. 24, 1983 — New York Giants 20, St. Louis 20,** at St. Louis; Cardinals win toss. Teams trade punts before O'Donoghue's 44-yard field goal attempt is wide left. Jennings' punt returned by Bird to St. Louis 21. Lomax pass intercepted by Haynes who loses six yards to New York 33. Jennings' punt downed on St. Louis 17. O'Donoghue's 19-yard field goal attempt is wide right. Rutledge's pass intercepted by L. Washington who returns 25 yards to New York 25. O'Donoghue's 42-yard field goal attempt is wide right. Rutledge's pass intercepted by W. Smith at St. Louis 33 to end game.

Oct. 30, 1983 — Cleveland 25, Houston 19, at Cleveland; Oilers win toss. Teams trade punts. Nielsen's pass intercepted by Whitwell who returns to Houston 20. Green runs 20 yards for touchdown on first down at 6:34.

Nov. 20, 1983 — Detroit 23, Green Bay 20, at Milwaukee; Packers win toss. Scribner punts and Jenkins returns 14 yards to Green Bay 45. Murray's 33-yard field goal attempt is wide left at 9:32. Whitehurst's pass intercepted by Watkins and returned to Green Bay 27. Murray kicks 37-yard field goal four plays later at 8:30.

Nov. 27, 1983 — Atlanta 47, Green Bay 41, at Atlanta; Packers win toss. K. Johnson returns interception 31 yards for touchdown at 2:13.

Nov. 27, 1983 — Seattle 51, Kansas City 48, at Seattle; Seahawks win toss. Dixon's 47-yard kickoff return sets up N. Johnson's 42-yard field goal at 1:36.

Dec. 11, 1983 — New Orleans 20, Philadelphia 17, at Philadelphia; Eagles win toss. Runager punts to Groth who fair catches on New Orleans 32. Stabler completes two passes for 36 yards to Goodlow to set up Andersen's 50-yard field goal at 5:30.

***Dec. 12, 1983 — Green Bay 12, Tampa Bay 9,** at Tampa; Packers win toss. Stenerud kicks 23-yard field goal 11 plays later at 4:07.

Sept. 9, 1984 — Detroit 27, Atlanta 24, at Atlanta; Lions win toss. Murray kicks 48-yard field goal nine plays later at 5:06.

Sept. 30, 1984 — Tampa Bay 30, Green Bay 27, at Tampa; Packers win toss. Scribner punts 44 yards to Tampa Bay 2. Epps returns Garcia's punt three yards to Green Bay 27. Scribner's punt downed on Buccaneers' 33. Ariri kicks 46-yard field goal 11 plays later at 10:32.

Oct. 14, 1984 — Detroit 13, Tampa Bay 7, at Detroit; Buccaneers win toss. Tampa Bay drives to Lions' 39 before Wilder fumbles. Five plays later Danielson hits Thompson with 37-yard touchdown pass at 4:34.

Oct. 21, 1984 — Dallas 30, New Orleans 27, at Dallas; Cowboys win toss. Septien kicks 41-yard field goal eight plays later at 3:42.

Oct. 28, 1984 — Denver 22, Los Angeles Raiders 19, at Los Angeles; Raiders win toss. Hawkins fumble recovered by Foley at Denver 7. Teams trade punts. Karlis's 42-yard field goal attempt is wide left. Teams trade punts. Wilson pass intercepted by R. Jackson at Los Angeles 45, returned 23 yards to Los Angeles 22. Karlis kicks 35-yard field goal two plays later at 15:00.

Nov. 4, 1984 — Philadelphia 23, Detroit 23, at Detroit; Lions win toss. Lions drive to Eagles' 3 in eight plays. Murray's 21-yard field goal attempt hits right upright and bounces back. Jaworski's pass intercepted by Watkins at Detroit 5. Teams trade punts. Cooper returns Black's punt five yards to Eagles' 14. Time expires four plays later with Eagles on own 21.

Nov. 18, 1984 — San Diego 34, Miami 28, at San Diego; Chargers win toss. McGee scores eight plays later on a 25-yard run at 3:17.

Dec. 2, 1984 — Cincinnati 20, Cleveland 17, at Cleveland; Browns win toss. Simmons returns Cox's punt 30 yards to Cleveland 35. Breech kicks 35-yard field goal seven plays later at 4:34.

Dec. 2, 1984 — Houston 23, Pittsburgh 20, at Houston; Oilers win toss. Cooper kicks 30-yard field goal 16 plays later at 5:53.

Sept. 8, 1985 — St. Louis 27, Cleveland 24, at Cleveland; Cardinals win toss. O'Donoghue kicks 35-yard field goal nine plays later at 5:27.

Sept. 29, 1985 — New York Giants 16, Philadelphia 10, at Philadelphia; Eagles win toss. Jaworski's pass tipped by Quick and intercepted by Patterson who returns 29 yards for touchdown at 0:55.

Oct. 20, 1985 — Denver 13, Seattle 10, at Denver; Seahawks win toss. Teams trade punts twice. Krieg's pass intercepted by Hunter and returned to Seahawks' 15. Karlis kicks 24-yard field goal four plays later at 9:19.

Nov. 10, 1985 — Philadelphia 23, Atlanta 17, at Philadelphia; Falcons win toss. Donnelly's 62-yard punt goes out of bounds at Eagles' 1. Jaworski completes 99-yard touchdown pass to Quick two plays later at 1:49.

Nov. 10, 1985 — San Diego 40, Los Angeles Raiders 34, at San Diego; Chargers win toss. James scores on 17-yard run seven plays later at 3:44.

Nov. 17, 1985 — Denver 30, San Diego 24, at Denver; Chargers win toss. Thomas' 40-yard field goal attempt blocked by Smith and returned 60 yards by Wright for touchdown at 4:45.

Nov. 24, 1985 — New York Jets 16, New England 13, at New York; Jets win toss. Teams trade punts twice. Patriots' second punt returned 46 yards by Sohn to Patriots' 15. Leahy kicks 32-yard field goal one play later at 10:05.

Nov. 24, 1985 — Tampa Bay 19, Detroit 16, at Tampa; Lions win toss. Teams trade punts. Lions' punt downed on Buccaneers' 38. Igwebuike kicks 24-yard field goal 11 plays later at 12:31.

Nov. 24, 1985 — Los Angeles Raiders 31, Denver 28, at Los Angeles; Raiders win toss. Bahr kicks 32-yard field goal six plays later at 2:42.

Dec. 8, 1985 — Los Angeles Raiders 17, Denver 14, at Denver; Broncos win toss. Teams trade punts twice. Elway's fumble recovered by Townsend at Broncos' 8. Bahr kicks 26-yard field goal one play later at 4:55.

Sept. 14, 1986 — Chicago 13, Philadelphia 10, at Chicago; Eagles win toss. Crawford's fumble of kickoff recovered by Jackson at Eagles' 35. Butler kicks 23-yard field goal 10 plays later at 5:56.

Sept. 14, 1986 — Cincinnati 36, Buffalo 33, at Cincinnati; Bills win toss. Zander intercepts Kelly's first-down pass and returns it to Bills' 17. Breech kicks 20-yard field goal two plays later at 0:56.

Sept. 21, 1986 — New York Jets 51, Miami 45, at New York; Jets win toss. O'Brien completes 43-yard touchdown pass to Walker five plays later at 2:35.

Sept. 28, 1986 — Pittsburgh 22, Houston 16, at Houston; Oilers win toss. Johnson's punt returned 41 yards by Woods to Oilers' 15. Abercrombie scores on three-yard run three plays later at 2:35.

Sept. 28, 1986 — Atlanta 23, Tampa Bay 20, at Tampa; Falcons win toss. Teams trade punts. Luckhurst kicks 34-yard field goal 10 plays later at 12:35.

Oct. 5, 1986 — Los Angeles Rams 26, Tampa Bay 20, at Anaheim; Rams win toss. Dickerson scores four plays later on 42-yard run at 2:16.

Oct. 12, 1986 — Minnesota 27, San Francisco 24, at San Francisco; Vikings win toss. C. Nelson kicks 28-yard field goal nine plays later at 4:27.

Oct. 19, 1986 — San Francisco 10, Atlanta 10, at Atlanta; Falcons win toss. Teams trade punts twice. Donnelly punts to 49ers' 27. The following play Wilson recovers Rice's fumble at 49ers' 46 as time expires.

Nov. 2, 1986 — Washington 44, Minnesota 38, at Washington; Redskins win toss. Schroeder completes 38-yard touchdown pass to Clark four plays later at 1:46.

Nov. 20, 1986 — Los Angeles Raiders 37, San Diego 31, at San Diego; Raiders win toss. Teams trade punts. Allen scores five plays later on 28-yard run at 8:33.

Nov. 23, 1986 — Cleveland 37, Pittsburgh 31, at Cleveland; Browns win toss. Teams trade punts. Six plays later Kosar hits Slaughter with 36-yard touchdown pass at 6:37.

Nov. 30, 1986 — Chicago 13, Pittsburgh 10, at Chicago; Bears win toss and kick off. Newsome's punt returned by Barnes to Chicago 49. Butler kicks 42-yard field goal five plays later at 3:55.

Nov. 30, 1986 — Philadelphia 33, Los Angeles Raiders 27, at Los Angeles; Eagles win toss. Teams trade punts. Long recovers Cunningham's fumble at Philadelphia 42. Waters returns Allen's fumble 81 yards to Los Angeles 4. Cunningham scores on one-yard run two plays later at 6:53.

Nov. 30, 1986 — Cleveland 13, Houston 10, at Cleveland; Oilers win toss and kick off. Gossett punts to Houston 39. Luck's pass intercepted by Minnifield at Cleveland 21. Gossett punts to Houston 34. Luck's pass intercepted by Minnifield at Cleveland 43 who returns 20 yards to Houston 37. Moseley kicks 29-yard field goal nine plays later at 14:44.

Dec. 7, 1986 — St. Louis 10, Philadelphia 10, at Philadelphia; Cardinals win toss. White blocks Schubert's 40-yard field goal attempt. Teams trade punts. McFadden's 43-yard field goal attempt is wide left. Schubert's 37-yard field goal attempt is wide right. Cavanaugh's pass intercepted by Carter and returned to Eagles' 48 to end game.

Dec. 14, 1986 — Miami 37, Los Angeles Rams 31, at Anaheim; Dolphins win toss. Marino completes 20-yard touchdown pass to Duper six plays later at 3:04.

Sept. 20, 1987 — Denver 17, Green Bay 17, at Milwaukee; Packers win toss. Del Greco's 47-yard field goal attempt is short. Teams trade punts. Elway intercepted by Noble who returns 10 yards to Green Bay 34. Davis fumbles on next play and Smith recovers. Two plays later, Karlis's 40-yard field goal attempt is wide left. Time expires two plays later with Packers on own 23.

Oct. 11, 1987 — Detroit 19, Green Bay 16, at Green Bay; Lions win toss. Prindle's 42-yard field goal attempt is wide left. Packers punt downed on Detroit 17. Prindle kicks 31-yard field goal 16 plays later at 12:26.

Oct. 18, 1987 — New York Jets 37, Miami 31, at New York; Jets win toss. Teams trade punts. Ryan intercepted by Hooper at Jets' 47 who returns 11 yards. Mackey intercepted by Haslett at Jets' 37 who returns 9 yards. Jets punt. Mackey intercepted by Radachowsky who returns 45 yards to Miami 24. Ryan completes eight-yard touchdown pass to Hunter five plays later at 14:26.

Oct. 18, 1987 — Green Bay 16, Philadelphia 10, at Green Bay; Packers win toss. Hargrove scores on seven-yard run 10 plays later at 5:04.

Oct. 18, 1987 — Buffalo 6, New York Giants 3, at Buffalo; Bills win toss. Schlopy's 28-yard field goal attempt is wide left. Teams trade punts. Rutledge intercepted by Clark who returns 23 yards to Buffalo 40. Schlopy kicks 27-yard field goal nine plays later at 14:41.

Oct. 25, 1987 — Buffalo 34, Miami 31, at Miami; Bills win toss. Norwood kicks 27-yard field goal seven plays later at 4:12.

Nov. 1, 1987 — San Diego 27, Cleveland 24, at San Diego; Browns win toss. Kosar intercepted by Glenn who returns 20 yards to Browns' 25. Abbott kicks 33-yard field goal three plays later at 2:16.

Nov. 15, 1987 — Dallas 23, New England 17, at New England; Cowboys win toss. Walker scores on 60-yard run four plays later at 1:50.

Nov. 26, 1987 — Minnesota 44, Dallas 38, at Dallas; Vikings win toss. Coleman's punt downed by Hilton at Cowboys' 37. White intercepted by Studwell who returns 12 yards to Vikings' 37. D. Nelson scores on 24-yard run seven plays later at 7:51.

Nov. 29, 1987 — Philadelphia 34, New England 31, at New England; Patriots win toss. Ramsey intercepted by Joyner who returns 29 yards to Eagles' 32. Fryar fair catches Teltschik's punt at Patriots' 13. Franklin's 46-yard field goal attempt is short. McFadden's 39-yard field goal attempt is wide left. Tatupu fumbles on next play and Cobb recovers. McFadden kicks 38-yard field goal four plays later at 12:16.

Dec. 6, 1987 — New York Giants 23, Philadelphia 20, at New York; Giants win toss and kick off. Teams trade punts twice. Teltschik's punt is returned 16 yards by McConkey to Eagles' 33. Three plays later, Allegre's 50-yard field goal attempt is blocked by Joyner and returned 25 yards by Hoage to Eagles' 30. McConkey returns Teltschik's punt four yards to Giants' 44. Allegre kicks 28-yard field goal four plays later at 10:42.

Dec. 6, 1987 — Cincinnati 30, Kansas City 27, at Cincinnati; Bengals win toss. Teams trade punts. Breech kicks 32-yard field goal 16 plays later at 9:44.

Dec. 26, 1987 — Washington 27, Minnesota 24, at Minnesota; Redskins win toss. Haji-Sheikh kicks 26-yard field goal six plays later at 2:09.

Sept. 4, 1988 — Houston 17, Indianapolis 14, at Indianapolis; Colts win toss. Dickerson fumble recovered by Lyles who returns six yards to Colts' 42. Zendejas kicks 35-yard field goal six plays later at 3:51.

***Sept. 26, 1988 — Los Angeles Raiders 30, Denver 27,** at Denver; Broncos win toss. Teams trade punts twice. Elway intercepted by Lee who returns 20 yards to Broncos' 31. Bahr kicks 35-yard field goal four plays later at 12:35.

Oct. 2, 1988 — New York Jets 17, Kansas City 17, at New York; Chiefs win toss. Chiefs punt goes into end zone for touchback. Leahy's 44-yard field goal attempt is wide right. Chiefs punt is returned by Townsell to Jets' 26. Burruss recovers McNeil's fumble at Chiefs' 11. DeBerg intercepted by Humphery at Jets' 49. Three plays later, time expires.

Oct. 9, 1988 — Denver 16, San Francisco 13, at San Francisco; Broncos win toss and kick off. Young intercepted by Haynes at Broncos' 32. Denver punt downed at 49ers' 5. Young intercepted by Wilson who returns seven yards to 49ers' 5. Karlis kicks 22-yard field goal two plays later at 8:11.

Oct. 30, 1988 — New York Giants 13, Detroit 10, at Detroit; Lions win toss. James's fumble recovered by Taylor at Lions' 22. Three plays later, McFadden kicks 33-yard field goal at 1:13.

Nov. 20, 1988 — Buffalo 9, New York Jets 6, at Buffalo; Jets win toss. Vick's fumble recovered by Bennett at Bills' 32. Norwood kicks 30-yard field goal five plays later at 3:47.

Nov. 20, 1988 — Philadelphia 23, New York Giants 17, at New York; Eagles win toss. Philadelphia's punt goes into end zone for touchback. Hostetler intercepted by Hoage who returns 11 yards to Giants' 41. Six plays later, Zendejas's 30-yard field-goal attempt is blocked and ball is recovered behind line of scrimmage by Eagles' Simmons, who runs 15 yards for touchdown at 3:09.

Dec. 11, 1988 — New England 10, Tampa Bay 7, at New England; Buccaneers win toss and kick off. Staurovsky kicks 27-yard field goal six plays later at 3:08.

Dec. 17, 1988 — Cincinnati 20, Washington 17, at Cincinnati; Bengals win toss. Cincinnati's punt returned by Oliphant to Redskins' 16. Grant recovers Williams's fumble at Redskins' 17. Breech kicks 20-yard field goal three plays later at 7:01.

Sept. 24, 1989 — Buffalo 47, Houston 41, at Houston; Oilers win toss. Johnson returns Brady's kickoff 17 yards to Oilers' 19. Oilers drive to Buffalo 25, Zendejas's 37-yard field goal blocked, but Bills offsides and Zendejas's second attempt is wide left. Bills' ball and Kelly completes series of passes, including 28-yard game-winner to Andre Reed, at 8:42.

Oct. 8, 1989 — Miami 13, Cleveland 10, at Miami; Browns win toss. Metcalf returns Stoyanovich's kickoff 20 yards to Browns' 28. Browns drive ball 46 yards in eight plays; Bahr wide left on 44-yard field goal attempt. Dolphins ball. Browns called for pass interference on Marino pass to Banks at Cleveland 47. Two plays later, Banks's 20-yard reception at Browns' 23 sets up winning 35-yard field goal by Stoyanovich at 6:23.

Oct. 22, 1989 — Denver 24, Seattle 21, at Seattle; Seahawks win toss. Treadwell's 56-yard kickoff returned 18 yards by Jefferson to Seahawks' 27. Seahawks drive to Broncos' 22 in 10 plays, but Johnson's 40-yard field goal attempt wide left. Smith intercepts a Krieg pass and returns it 28 yards to Seahawks' 10. Treadwell kicks winning 27-yard field goal at 7:46.

Oct. 29, 1989 — New England 23, Indianapolis 20, at Indianapolis; Patriots win toss. Biasucci kickoff returned 13 yards to Patriots' 23 by Martin. Holding penalty brings ball back to Patriots' 13. After six plays, Feagles punt returned 11 yards by Verdin to Colts' 28. Six plays later, Colts punt to Martin at Patriots' 12. Grogan completes three straight passes to Patriots' 44. Five consecutive runs put New England on Colts' 33. Davis kicks a 51-yard winning field goal for Patriots at 9:46.

Oct. 29, 1989 — Green Bay 23, Detroit 20, at Milwaukee; Lions win toss. Sanders touchback on Jacke kickoff. On first play, Murphy intercepts Lions' Peete and returns it three yards to Lions' 26. Fullwood gains five yards on three plays to set up Jacke's 38-yard field goal at 2:14.

Nov. 5, 1989 — Minnesota 23, Los Angeles Rams 21, at Minneapolis; Rams win toss. Karlis's kick returned 18 yards by Delpino to Rams' 19. Drive stops at Rams' 28. Merriweather blocks Hatcher's punt at 12. Ball rolls out of end zone for safety.

Nov. 19, 1989 — Cleveland 10, Kansas City 10, at Cleveland; Browns win toss. Browns punt three times; Chiefs twice; before Kansas City's Lowery misses 47-yard field goal with 17 seconds remaining in overtime. Kosar's pass intercepted as time expired.

Nov. 26, 1989 — Los Angeles Rams 20, New Orleans 17, at New Orleans; Saints win toss. Lansford's kickoff returned 27 yards to Saints' 30. After four plays, Barnhardt punts to Rams' 15. Saints penalized 35 yards for interference to Rams' 43. Three plays later, Everett hits Anderson with 14-yard pass to Saints' 40, then 26-yarder to put Rams in field goal position. Lansford kicks 31-yard field goal at 6:38.

Dec. 3, 1989 — Los Angeles Raiders 16, Denver 13, at Los Angeles; Broncos win toss. Bell returns Jaeger kickoff 14 yards to Broncos' 18. Broncos' penalized for illegal block to Broncos' 9. Elway completes three passes for two first downs. On third and eight Elway sacked for 10-yard loss. Horan punts, Adams calls for fair catch at Raiders' 29. Dyal's 26-yard reception moves Raiders to Denver 43. Raiders move ball 34 yards in three plays to set up Jaeger's 26-yard field goal at 7:02.

Dec. 10, 1989 — Indianapolis 23, Cleveland 17, at Indianapolis; Browns win toss. Teams trade punts. McNeil returns Colts' punt 42 yards to 42. Seven plays later, Bahr misses 35-yard field goal attempt. Three plays later, Stark punts and McNeil returns ball to 50-yard line. Two plays later, Prior intercepts Kosar's pass at Colts' 42 and returns it 58 yards for touchdown at 10:54.

Dec. 17, 1989 — Cleveland 23, Minnesota 17, at Cleveland; Browns win toss. Browns punt to Vikings' 18. Six plays later, Vikings punt to Browns' 22. Nine plays later, Bahr lines up to attempt 31-yard field goal. Holder Pagel takes snap and passes 14 yards to Waiters for touchdown at 9:30.

Sept. 23, 1990 — Denver 34, Seattle 31, at Denver; Seahawks win toss. Loville returns kickoff 19 yards to Seahawks' 27. Seahawks drive to Broncos' 26, where Johnson misses 44-yard field goal wide right. Broncos take over and Elway completes series of passes to set up Treadwell's 25-yard field goal at 9:14.

Sept. 30, 1990 — Tampa Bay 23, Minnesota 20, at Minnesota; Vikings win toss. Vikings drive to Buccaneers' 31; Igwebuike's 48-yard field goal attempt wide left. Buccaneers drive to Vikings' 43 and punt. Gannon's pass is intercepted at Vikings' 26 by Wayne Haddix. Buccaneers drive to Vikings' 19 to set up Christie's 36-yard field goal at 9:11.

Oct. 7, 1990 — Cincinnati 34, Los Angeles Rams 31, at Anaheim; Rams win toss. Berry returns kickoff to Rams' 21. After 3 plays, English punts and Green downs ball at Bengals' 25. After 3 plays, Johnson punts and Sutton downs ball at Rams' 29-yard line. After 3 plays, English punts and Price signals fair catch at Bengals' 47. Esiason completes series of passes to 26-yard line to set up Breech's 44-yard field goal at 11:56.

Nov. 4, 1990 — Washington 41, Detroit 38, at Detroit; Redskins win toss. Howard downs kickoff on Redskins' 15. After 3 plays, Mojsiejenko punts to Redskins' 45. After 3 plays, Arnold punts to Redskins' 10. Rutledge completes series of passes to set up Lohmiller's 34-yard field goal at 9:10.

Nov. 18, 1990 — Chicago 16, Denver 13, at Denver; Broncos win toss. Ezor returns kickoff to Broncos' 12. Both teams have ball twice and have to punt after each possession. Broncos punt after third possession of overtime and Bailey returns 20 yards to Broncos' 34. Harbaugh completes 10-yard pass to Thornton to set up Butler's 44-yard field goal at 13:14.

Nov. 25, 1990 — Seattle 13, San Diego 10, at San Diego; Chargers win toss. Lewis returns kickoff to Chargers' 22. After 2 plays, Cox fumbles and ball is recovered by Porter at Chargers' 23. After two plays, Johnson kicks 40-yard field goal at 3:01.

Dec. 2, 1990 — Chicago 23, Detroit 17, at Chicago; Lions win toss. Gray returns kickoff to Lions' 35. After 10 plays, Murray misses 35-yard field goal. Bears take possession at Chicago 20. Harbaugh completes 50-yard game-winning pass to Anderson at 10:57.

Dec. 2, 1990 — Seattle 13, Houston 10, at Seattle; Seahawks win toss. Warren returns kickoff to Seahawks' 13. After 5 plays, Donnelly punts to Oilers' 23-yard line. Ford's fumble recovered by Wyman. Seahawks take possession at Oilers' 27. After 2 plays, Johnson kicks 42-yard field goal at 4:25.

Dec. 9, 1990 — Miami 23, Philadelphia 20, at Miami; Eagles win toss. After 11 plays, Feagles punts to Dolphins' 26. After 6 plays, Roby punts to Eagles' 14 and Harris returns to 25. After 3 plays, Feagles punts to Dolphins' 43. Marino completes series of passes to Eagles' 22. Stoyanovich kicks 39-yard field goal at 12:32.

Dec. 9, 1990 — San Francisco 20, Cincinnati 17, at Cincinnati; 49ers win toss. Carter returns kickoff to 49ers' 19. After 10 plays, Cofer kicks 23-yard field goal at 6:12.

Sept. 24, 1991 — Chicago 19, New York Jets 13, at Chicago; Jets win toss. Mathis returns kickoff seven yards to New York's 12. Jets drive to New York 26; Bailey returns punt to Chicago 39. Bears drive to Jets' 44-yard line and punt into the end zone. Jets drive to Bears' 11 where Leahy's 28-yard field goal attempt is wide left. Bears drive from 20 to Jets' 1 where Harbaugh runs for touchdown at 14:42.

Oct. 13, 1991 — Los Angeles Raiders 23, Seattle 20, at Seattle. Seahawks win toss. Seahawks begin on 20. After 5 plays, Tuten punts and Brown signals fair catch at Raiders' 24. After 3 plays, Gossett punts and Land downs ball at Seattle 9. After 1 play, Lott intercepts at Seahawks' 19 to set up Jaeger's game-winning 37-yard field goal at 6:37.

Oct. 20, 1991 — Cleveland 30, San Diego 24, at San Diego; Chargers win toss. After kickoff, Chargers drive to Browns' 45 and punt to Browns' 6 where Hendrickson downs ball. Browns drive to 38 and punt; Taylor fair catches on Chargers' 14. After 3 plays, Brandon intercepts at Chargers' 30 and scores at 5:58.

Oct. 20, 1991 — New England 26, Minnesota 23, at New England; Patriots win toss. Martin returns kickoff 18 yards to New England 22. Patriots drive to Minnesota 19. Staurovsky's 36-yard field goal attempt is wide left. Minnesota drives to the 50 where Newsome punts into end zone. On first play, McMillian intercepts at the 40 for Minnesota. After 2 plays, Marion causes Jordan fumble and Pool recovers at New England 20. New England drives to Minnesota 24 where Staurovsky kicks 42-yard field goal as time expires.

Nov. 3, 1991 — New York Jets 19, Green Bay 16, at New York; Packers win toss. Thompson returns kickoff 30 yards to Packers' 39. Green Bay drives to New York 24 where Jacke's 42-yard field goal attempt is wide right. Jets drive to 50. Aguiar's punt is fumbled by Sikahema and recovered by New York at Packers' 23. After 2 plays, Leahy kicks 37-yard field goal at 9:40.

Nov. 3, 1991 — Washington 16, Houston 13, at Washington; Redskins win toss. Mitchell returns kickoff 9 yards to Washington 14. After 4 plays, Goodburn punts and Givins returns to Houston 31. After 1 play, Moon's pass is intercepted by Green at Oilers' 35. After 3 plays, Lohmiller kicks 41-yard field goal at 4:01.

Nov. 10, 1991 — Houston 26, Dallas 23, at Houston; Oilers win toss. Pinkett returns kickoff 20 yards to Houston 24. After 6 plays, Montgomery punts and Martin returns to Dallas 24. Cowboys drive to Oilers' 24 where Smith fumbles and McDowell recovers at Oilers' 15. Houston drives to Dallas 5 where Del Greco kicks 23-yard field goal at 14:31.

Nov. 10, 1991 — Pittsburgh 33, Cincinnati 27, at Cincinnati; Pittsburgh wins toss. Woodson downs kickoff for touchback. After 3 plays, Stryzinski punts and Barber returns 7 yards to Cincinnati 38. Bengals drive to Pittsburgh 37 where Woods fumbles and Lloyd returns recovery to Cincinnati 44. After 2 plays, O'Donnell passes to Green for 26-yard touchdown at 6:32.

Nov. 24, 1991 — Atlanta 23, New Orleans 20, at New Orleans; Atlanta wins toss. Falcons begin at 20. After 3 plays, Fulhage punts and Fenerty signals fair catch at New Orleans 43. After 3 plays, Barnhardt punts and Thompson downs ball at Atlanta 23. After 3 plays, Fulhage punts and Fenerty fair catches at New Orleans 25. Saints drive to Atlanta 38 where Andersen misses 55-yard field-goal attempt. After 1 play, Rozier fumbles and Martin recovers on 50. Saints drive to Atlanta 38 where Barnhardt punts to Falcons' 2. Atlanta drives to New Orleans 33 where Johnson kicks 50-yard field goal at 13:03.

Nov. 24, 1991 — Miami 16, Chicago 13, at Chicago; Miami wins toss. Butler kicks to Miami 20 where Paige returns kickoff 15 yards to 35. Miami drives to Chicago 9 where Stoyanovich kicks 27-yard field goal at 4:11.

Dec. 8, 1991 — Buffalo 30, Los Angeles Raiders 27, at Los Angeles; Raiders win toss. Daluiso kicks into end zone for touchback. On third play, Kelso intercepts for Buffalo and returns ball to Bills' 36. Bills drive to Los Angeles 24 where Norwood kicks 42-yard field goal at 2:34.

December 8, 1991 — Kansas City 20, San Diego 17, at Kansas City; Chiefs win toss. Carney kicks to Kansas City 10 where Stradford returns 23 yards to 33. After 3 plays, Barker punts to San Diego 4. Chargers drive to 40 where Kidd punts 60 yards into end zone for touchback. Kansas City drives to San Diego 39 where Barker punts 38 yards to 1. After 3 plays, Kidd punts 41 yards to San Diego 42 where Stradford returns 12 yards to 30. Chiefs drive to San Diego 1 where Lowery kicks 18-yard field goal at 11:26.

Dec. 8, 1991 — New England 23, Indianapolis 17, at New England; Indianapolis wins toss. Baumann kicks off to Indianapolis 2 where Martin returns 23 yards to 25. After 3 downs, Stark punts to New England 17 where Henderson returns 8 yards to 25. New England drives to 50 where McCarthy punts and Prior signals fair catch at Indianapolis 15. After 3 plays, Stark punts to New England 40 where Henderson returns 7 yards to 47. After 2 plays, Millen passes to Timpson for 45-yard touchdown at 8:55.

Dec. 22, 1991 — Detroit 17, Buffalo 14, at Buffalo; Detroit wins toss. Daluiso kicks off to Detroit 20 where Dozier returns 15 yards to Lions 35. Lions drive to Bills' 3 where Murray kicks 21-yard field goal at 4:23.

Dec. 22, 1991 — New York Jets 23, Miami 20, at Miami; Jets win toss. Aguiar kicks to Miami's 30 where Logan returns 3 yards to the 33. After 4 downs, Stoyanovich punts to Jets' 15 where Baty returns 8 yards to 23. Jets drive to Miami 12 where Allegre kicks 30-yard field goal at 6:33.

Sept. 6, 1992—Minnesota 23, Green Bay 20, at Lambeau Field. Vikings win toss. Nelson returns kickoff 14 yards to the Minnesota 23. After 5 plays, Newsome punts 49 yards to Green Bay 21 where Brooks returns 12 yards to the 33. After 2 plays, Glenn intercepts pass at the Vikings' 48. On first play, Allen fumbles and Billups recovers at Green Bay 35. After 3 plays, McJulien punts 33 yards to Vikings' 35. Vikings drive to Minnesota 48; Newsome punts 52 yards for touchback. After 3 plays, McJulien punts and Parker returns 10 yards to Green Bay 48. Vikings drive to Packers' 9 where Reveiz kicks 26-yard field goal with 4:40 remaining.

Sept. 13, 1992—Cincinnati 24, Los Angeles Raiders 21, at Riverfront Stadium. Raiders win toss. Land returns kickoff 13 yards but fumbles at Los Angeles's 20; ball recovered by Bengals' Bennett at Raiders' 21. After 1 play, Breech kicks 34-yard field goal with 13:59 remaining.

Sept. 20, 1992—Houston 23, Kansas City 20, at Astrodome. Chiefs win toss. Carter returns kickoff 25 yards to Kansas City 28. On third play of drive, Birden fumbles at Kansas City 34; ball recovered by Houston's D. Smith at Chiefs' 23. After one play, Del Greco kicks 39-yard field goal with 13:05 remaining.

Oct. 11, 1992—Indianapolis 6, New York Jets 3, at Hoosier Dome. Colts win toss. Verdin returns kickoff 33 yards to Colts' 36. Colts drive to Jets' 30 where Biasucci kicks 47-yard field goal with 11:59 remaining.

Nov. 8, 1992—Cincinnati 31, Chicago 28, at Soldier Field. Bears win toss. Lewis returns kickoff 22 yards to Chicago's 29. Bears drive to Chicago's 46 where Gardocki punts; fair catch by Wright at the Cincinnati 17. Bengals drive to Bears' 18 where Breech kicks 36-yard field goal with 6:21 remaining.

Nov. 15, 1992—New England 37, Indianapolis 34, at Hoosier Dome. Colts win toss. Verdin returns kickoff 10 yards to Colts' 20; holding penalty brings ball back to Colts' 10. After two plays, Henderson intercepts pass at Colts' 38 and returns it 9 yards to the 29. In three plays, Patriots drive to 1 where Baumann kicks 18-yard field goal with 11:35 remaining.

Nov. 29, 1992—Indianapolis 16, Buffalo 13, at Hoosier Dome. Colts win toss. Verdin returns kickoff 24 yards to Colts' 22. Colts drive to Buffalo 22 where Biasucci kicks 40-yard field goal with 11:09 remaining.

Nov. 30, 1992—Seattle 16, Denver 13, at Kingdome. Seahawks win toss. Daluiso kicks through end zone for touchback. After three plays, Tuten punts 53 yards to Denver 18 where Marshall returns for no gain. After three plays, Rodriguez punts 29 yards to Seattle 45 where Warren signals fair catch. Seahawks drive to Denver 15 where Kasay's 33-yard field goal attempt misses. Broncos take over at Denver 20. After three plays, Rodriguez punts 43 yards to Seattle 38 where Warren signals for fair catch. After four plays, Tuten punts 39 yards to Denver 4 where Daniels downs punt. After three plays, Rodriguez punts 46 yards to Denver 48 where Warren returns 10 yards to the 38. Seahawks drive to Denver 14 where Kasay kicks 32-yard field goal with 3:50 remaining.

Dec. 27, 1992—Miami 16, New England 13, at Foxboro Stadium. Patriots win toss. Lockwood returns kickoff 15 yards to Patriots' 21. After three plays, McCarthy punts 39 yards to Miami 33 where Miller returns 2 yards to the 35. Miami drives to New England 18 where Stoyanovich kicks 35-yard field goal with 6:43 remaining.

*indicates Monday night game
#indicates Thursday night game

Postseason

Dec. 28, 1958 — Baltimore 23, New York Giants 17, at New York in NFL Championship Game. Giants win toss. Maynard returns kickoff to Giants' 20. Chandler punts and Taseff returns one yard to Colts' 20. Colts win at 8:15 on a one-yard run by Ameche.

Dec. 23, 1962 — Dallas Texans 20, Houston Oilers 17, at Houston in AFL Championship Game. Texans win toss and kick off. Jancik returns kickoff to Oilers' 33. Norton punts and Jackson makes fair catch on Texans' 22. Wilson punts and Jancik makes fair catch on Oilers' 45. Robinson intercepts Blanda's pass and returns 13 yards to Oilers' 47. Wilson's punt rolls dead at Oilers' 12. Hull intercepts Blanda's pass and returns 23 yards to midfield. Texans win at 17:54 on a 25-yard field goal by Brooker.

Dec. 26, 1965 — Green Bay 13, Baltimore 10, at Green Bay in NFL Divisional Playoff Game. Packers win toss. Moore returns kickoff to Packers' 22. Chandler punts and Haymond returns nine yards to Colts' 41. Gilburg punts and Wood makes fair catch at Packers' 21. Chandler punts and Haymond returns one yard to Colts' 41. Michaels misses 47-yard field goal. Packers win at 13:39 on 25-yard field goal by Chandler.

Dec. 25, 1971 — Miami 27, Kansas City 24, at Kansas City in AFC Divisional Playoff Game. Chiefs win toss. Podolak, after a lateral from Buchanan, returns kickoff to Chiefs' 46. Stenerud's 42-yard field goal is blocked. Seiple punts and Podolak makes fair catch at Chiefs' 17. Wilson punts and Scott returns 18 yards to Dolphins' 39. Yepremian misses 62-yard field goal. Scott intercepts Dawson's pass and returns 13 yards to Dolphins' 46. Seiple punts and Podolak loses one yard to Chiefs' 15. Wilson punts and Scott makes fair catch on Dolphins' 30. Dolphins win at 22:40 on a 37-yard field goal by Yepremian.

Dec. 24, 1977 — Oakland 37, Baltimore 31, at Baltimore in AFC Divisional Playoff Game. Colts win toss. Raiders start on own 42 following a punt late in the first overtime. Oakland works way into field-goal range on Stabler's 19-yard pass to Branch at Colts' 26. Four plays later, on the second play of the second overtime, Stabler hits Casper with a 10-yard touchdown pass at 15:43.

Jan. 2, 1982 — San Diego 41, Miami 38, at Miami in AFC Divisional Playoff Game. Chargers win toss. San Diego drives from its 13 to Miami 8. On second-and-goal, Benirschke misses 27-yard field goal attempt wide left at 9:15. Miami has the ball twice and San Diego twice more before the Dolphins get their third possession. Miami drives from the San Diego 46 to Chargers' 17 and on fourth-and-two, von Schamann's 34-yard field goal attempt is blocked by San Diego's Winslow after 11:27. Fouts then completes four of five passes, including a 39-yarder to Joiner that puts the ball on Dolphins' 10. On first down, Benirschke kicks a 29-yard field goal at 13:52. San Diego's winning drive covered 74 yards in six plays.

Jan. 3, 1987 — Cleveland 23, New York Jets 20, at Cleveland in AFC Divisional Playoff Game. Jets win toss. Jets' punt downed at Browns' 26. Moseley's 23-yard field goal attempt is wide right. Teams trade punts. Jets' second punt downed at Browns' 31. First overtime period expires eight plays later with Browns in possession at Jets' 42. Moseley kicks 27-yard field goal four plays into second overtime at 17:02.

Jan. 11, 1987 — Denver 23, Cleveland 20, at Cleveland in AFC Championship Game. Browns win toss. Broncos hold Browns on four downs. Browns' punt returned four yards to Denver's 25. Elway completes 22- and 28-yard passes to set up Karlis's 33-yard field goal nine plays into drive at 5:38.

Jan. 3, 1988 — Houston 23, Seattle 20, at Houston in AFC Wild Card Game. Seahawks win toss. Rodriguez punts to K. Johnson who returns one yard to Houston 15. Zendejas kicks 32-yard field goal 12 plays later at 8:05.

Dec. 31, 1989 — Pittsburgh 26, Houston 23, at Houston in AFC Wild Card Playoff Game. Steelers win toss. Steelers punt to Oilers. Oilers' fumble recovered by Woodson and returned three yards. Four plays and 13 yards later, Anderson kicks a 50-yard field goal at 3:26.

Jan. 7, 1990 — Los Angeles Rams 19, New York Giants 13, at New York in NFC Wild Card Game. Rams win toss. Everett completes two passes to move ball to Giants' 48. White called for pass interference; ball spotted on Giants' 25. Everett hits Anderson with a 30-yard touchdown pass at 1:06.

Jan. 3, 1993—Buffalo 41, Houston 38, at Rich Stadium in AFC Wild Card Game. Houston wins toss. Oilers begin at 20. After 2 plays, Moon's pass is intercepted by Odomes who returns ball 2 yards to Houston 35. After 2 plays, Christie kicks 32-yard field goal with 11:54 remaining.

NFL Postseason Overtime Games (By Length of Game)

Dec. 25, 1971	Miami 27, KANSAS CITY 24	82:40
Dec. 23, 1962	Dallas Texans 20, HOUSTON 17	77:54
Jan. 3, 1987	CLEVELAND 23, New York Jets 20	77:02
Dec. 24, 1977	Oakland 37, BALTIMORE 31	75:43
Jan. 2, 1982	San Diego 41, MIAMI 38	73:52
Dec. 26, 1965	GREEN BAY 13, Baltimore 10	73:39
Dec. 28, 1958	Baltimore 23, N.Y. GIANTS 17	68:15
Jan. 3, 1988	HOUSTON 23, Seattle 20	68:05
Jan. 11, 1987	Denver 23, CLEVELAND 20	65:38
Dec. 31, 1989	Pittsburgh 26, HOUSTON 23	63:26
Jan. 7, 1990	Los Angeles Rams 19, N.Y. GIANTS 13	61:06
Dec. 28, 1958	Baltimore 23, N.Y. GIANTS 17	58:15

Home team in CAPS

Overtime Won-Lost Records, 1974-1992 (Regular Season)

AFC	W	L	T
Buffalo	8	4	0
Cincinnati	10	5	0
Cleveland	11	8	1
Denver	11	7	2
Houston	6	10	0
Indianapolis	6	5	1
Kansas City	4	6	2
Los Angeles Raiders	9	6	0
Miami	7	10	1
New England	5	11	0
New York Jets	8	6	2
Pittsburgh	7	3	1
San Diego	7	9	0
Seattle	4	5	0

NFC	W	L	T
Atlanta	5	7	1
Chicago	9	9	0
Dallas	6	4	0
Detroit	5	7	1
Green Bay	5	8	4
Los Angeles Rams	5	5	1
Minnesota	9	7	2
New Orleans	2	6	0
New York Giants	6	6	1
Philadelphia	4	8	2
Phoenix	3	4	2
San Francisco	4	4	1
Tampa Bay	5	7	1
Washington	9	3	0

Overtime Games By Year (Regular Season)

1992- 9	1982- 4
1991-15	1981-10
1990-10	1980-13
1989-11	1979-12
1988- 9	1978-11
1987-13	1977- 6
1986-16	1976- 5
1985-10	1975- 9
1984- 9	1974- 2
1983-19	

Overtime Game Summary—1974-1992

There have been 193 overtime games in regular-season play since the rule was adopted in 1974 (9 in 1992 season). Breakdown follows:

143 (7) times both teams had at least one possession (74%)

50 (2) times the team which won the toss drove for winning score (35 FG, 15 TD) (26%)

92 (4) times the team which won the toss won the game (48%)

88 (5) times the team which lost the toss won the game (46%)

128 (9) games were decided by a field goal (66%)

51 (0) games were decided by a touchdown (26%)

1 (0) game was decided by a safety (.5%)

13 (0) games ended tied (6.7%). Last time: Nov. 19, 1989, Cleveland 10, Kansas City 10, at Cleveland

Note: The number in parentheses represents the 1992 season total in each category.

Most Overtime Games, Season

5 Green Bay Packers, 1983
4 Denver Broncos, 1985
4 Cleveland Browns, 1989
3 By many teams, last time: Indianapolis Colts, 1992

Longest Consecutive Game Streaks Without Overtime (current)

97 Phoenix Cardinals (last OT game, 12/7/86 vs. Philadelphia)
84 Dallas Cowboys (last OT game, 11/26/87 vs. Minnesota)
78 New York Giants (last OT game, 11/20/88 vs. Philadelphia)

Shortest Overtime Games

0:21 (Chicago 23, Detroit 17; 11/27/80) — only kickoff return for TD
0:30 (Baltimore 29, New England 23; 9/4/83)
0:55 (New York Giants 16, Philadelphia 10; 9/29/85)

There have been 12 overtime postseason games dating back to 1958. In 11 cases, both teams had at least one possession. Last time: 1/3/93; Buffalo 41, Houston 38.

Longest Overtime Games (All Postseason Games)

22:40 Miami 27, Kansas City 24; 12/25/71
17:54 Dallas Texans 20, Houston 17; 12/23/62
17:02 Cleveland 23, New York Jets 20; 1/3/87

There have been 12 postseason overtime games dating back to 1958. Eleven times, both teams had at least one possession. Last postseason overtime: Buffalo Bills 41, Houston Oilers 38, 1/3/93.

Overtime Scoring Summary

128 were decided by a field goal
21 were decided by a touchdown pass
17 were decided by a touchdown run
5 were decided by interceptions (Atlanta 40, New Orleans 34, 9/2/79; Atlanta 47, Green Bay 41, 11/27/83; New York Giants 16, Philadelphia 10, 9/29/85; Indianapolis 23, Cleveland 17, 12/10/89; Cleveland 30, San Diego 24, 10/20/91)
2 were decided on a fake field goal/touchdown pass (Minnesota 22, Chicago 16, 10/16/77; Cleveland 23, Minnesota 17, 12/17/89)
1 was decided by a kickoff return (Chicago 23, Detroit 17, 11/27/80)
1 was decided by a fumble recovery (Baltimore 29, New England 23, 9/4/83)
1 was decided on a fake field goal/touchdown run (Los Angeles Rams 27, Minnesota 21, 12/2/79)
1 was decided on a blocked field goal (Denver 30, San Diego 24, 11/17/85)
1 was decided on a blocked field goal/recovery by kicker (Green Bay 12, Chicago 6, 9/7/80)
1 was decided on a blocked field goal/recovery by kicking team (Philadelphia 23, New York Giants 17, 11/20/88)
1 was decided by a safety (Minnesota 23, Los Angeles Rams 21, 11/5/89)
13 ended tied

Overtime Records

Longest Touchdown Pass

99 Yards — Ron Jaworski to Mike Quick, Philadelphia 23, Atlanta 17 (11/10/85)
50 Yards — Tommy Kramer to Ahmad Rashad, Minnesota 27, Green Bay 21 (9/23/79)
50 Yards — Jim Harbaugh to Neal Anderson, Chicago 23, Detroit 17 (12/2/90)

Longest Touchdown Run

60 Yards — Herschel Walker, Dallas 23, New England 17 (11/15/87)
42 Yards — Eric Dickerson, Los Angeles Rams 26, Tampa Bay 20 (10/5/86)
28 Yards — Marcus Allen, Los Angeles Raiders 37, San Diego 31 (11/20/86)

Longest Field Goal

51 Yards — Greg Davis, New England 23, Indianapolis 20 (10/29/89)
50 Yards — Morten Andersen, New Orleans 20, Philadelphia 17 (12/11/83); Norm Johnson, Atlanta 23, New Orleans 20 (11/24/91)
48 Yards — Eddie Murray, Detroit 27, Atlanta 24 (9/9/84); Mark Moseley, Washington 30, New York Giants 27 (11/15/81)

Longest Touchdown Plays

99 Yards — (Pass) Ron Jaworski to Mike Quick, Philadelphia 23, Atlanta 17 (11/10/85)
60 Yards — (Blocked field goal return) Louis Wright, Denver 30, San Diego 24 (11/17/85)
(Run) Herschel Walker, Dallas 23, New England 17 (11/15/87)
58 Yards — (Interception return) Mike Prior, Indianapolis 23, Cleveland 17 (12/10/89)

NFL Paid Attendance

Year	Regular Season	Average	Postseason	Super Bowl
1992	13,828,887 (224 games)	61,736	815,910 (12)	98,374
1991	13,841,459 (224 games)	61,792	813,247 (12)	63,130
1990#	13,959,896 (224 games)	#62,321	847,543 (12)	73,813
1989	13,625,662 (224 games)	60,829	685,771 (10)	72,919
1988	13,539,848 (224 games)	60,446	658,317 (10)	75,129
1987*	11,406,166 (210 games)	54,315	656,977 (10)	73,302
1986	13,588,551 (224 games)	60,663	734,002 (10)	101,063
1985	13,345,047 (224 games)	59,567	710,768 (10)	73,818
1984	13,398,112 (224 games)	59,813	665,194 (10)	84,059
1983	13,277,222 (224 games)	59,273	675,513 (10)	72,932
1982**	7,367,438 (126 games)	58,472	1,033,153 (16)	103,667
1981	13,606,990 (224 games)	60,745	637,763 (10)	81,270
1980	13,392,230 (224 games)	59,787	624,430 (10)	75,500
1979	13,182,039 (224 games)	58,848	630,326 (10)	103,985
1978	12,771,800 (224 games)	57,017	624,388 (10)	79,641
1977	11,018,632 (196 games)	56,218	534,925 (8)	75,804
1976	11,070,543 (196 games)	56,482	492,884 (8)	103,438
1975	10,213,193 (182 games)	56,116	475,919 (8)	80,187
1974	10,236,322 (182 games)	56,244	438,664 (8)	80,997
1973	10,730,933 (182 games)	58,961	525,433 (8)	71,882
1972	10,445,827 (182 games)	57,395	483,345 (8)	90,182
1971	10,076,035 (182 games)	55,363	483,891 (8)	81,023
1970	9,533,333 (182 games)	52,381	458,493 (8)	79,204
1969	6,096,127 (112 games) NFL	54,430	162,279 (3)	80,562
	2,843,373 (70 games) AFL	40,620	167,088 (3)	
1968	5,882,313 (112 games) NFL	52,521	215,902 (3)	75,377
	2,635,004 (70 games) AFL	37,643	114,438 (2)	
1967	5,938,924 (112 games) NFL	53,026	166,208 (3)	75,546
	2,295,697 (63 games) AFL	36,439	53,330 (1)	
1966	5,337,044 (105 games) NFL	50,829	74,152 (1)	†61,946
	2,160,369 (63 games) AFL	34,291	42,080 (1)	
1965	4,634,021 (98 games) NFL	47,286	100,304 (2)	
	1,782,384 (56 games) AFL	31,828	30,361 (1)	
1964	4,563,049 (98 games) NFL	46,562	79,544 (1)	
	1,447,875 (56 games) AFL	25,855	40,242 (1)	
1963	4,163,643 (98 games) NFL	42,486	45,801 (1)	
	1,208,697 (56 games) AFL	21,584	63,171 (2)	
1962	4,003,421 (98 games) NFL	40,851	64,892 (1)	
	1,147,302 (56 games) AFL	20,487	37,981 (1)	
1961	3,986,159 (98 games) NFL	40,675	39,029 (1)	
	1,002,657 (56 games) AFL	17,904	29,556 (1)	
1960	3,128,296 (78 games) NFL	40,106	67,325 (1)	
	926,156 (56 games) AFL	16,538	32,183 (1)	
1959	3,140,000 (72 games)	43,617	57,545 (1)	
1958	3,006,124 (72 games)	41,752	123,659 (2)	
1957	2,836,318 (72 games)	39,393	119,579 (2)	
1956	2,551,263 (72 games)	35,434	56,836 (1)	
1955	2,521,836 (72 games)	35,026	85,693 (1)	
1954	2,190,571 (72 games)	30,425	43,827 (1)	
1953	2,164,585 (72 games)	30,064	54,577 (1)	
1952	2,052,126 (72 games)	28,502	97,507 (2)	
1951	1,913,019 (72 games)	26,570	57,522 (1)	
1950	1,977,753 (78 games)	25,356	136,647 (3)	
1949	1,391,735 (60 games)	23,196	27,980 (1)	
1948	1,525,243 (60 games)	25,421	36,309 (1)	
1947	1,837,437 (60 games)	30,624	66,268 (2)	
1946	1,732,135 (55 games)	31,493	58,346 (1)	
1945	1,270,401 (50 games)	25,408	32,178 (1)	
1944	1,019,649 (50 games)	20,393	46,016 (1)	
1943	969,128 (40 games)	24,228	71,315 (2)	
1942	887,920 (55 games)	16,144	36,006 (1)	
1941	1,108,615 (55 games)	20,157	55,870 (2)	
1940	1,063,025 (55 games)	19,328	36,034 (1)	
1939	1,071,200 (55 games)	19,476	32,279 (1)	
1938	937,197 (55 games)	17,040	48,120 (1)	
1937	963,039 (55 games)	17,510	15,878 (1)	
1936	816,007 (54 games)	15,111	29,545 (1)	
1935	638,178 (53 games)	12,041	15,000 (1)	
1934	492,684 (60 games)	8,211	35,059 (1)	

Record

*Players' 24-day strike reduced 224-game schedule to 210 games.

**Players' 57-day strike reduced 224-game schedule to 126 games.

†Only Super Bowl that did not sell out.

NFL's 10 Biggest Attendance Weekends

(Paid Count)

Weekend	Games	Attendance
October 16-17, 1988	14	934,211
November 8-9, 1990	14	917,384
November 4-5, 1990	14	916,127
October 29-30, 1989	14	915,401
November 17-18, 1990	14	905,486
October 27-28, 1985	14	902,128
October 12-13, 1980	14	898,223
September 23-24, 1984	14	894,402
November 11-12, 1979	14	890,972
November 26, 29-30, 1992	14	889,784

NFL's 10 Highest Scoring Weekends

Point Total	Date	Weekend
761	October 16-17, 1983	7th
736	October 25-26, 1987	7th
732	November 9-10, 1980	10th
725	November 24, 27-28, 1983	13th
714	September 17-18, 1989	2nd
711	November 26, 29-30, 1987	12th
710	November 28, December 1-2, 1985	13th
696	October 2-3, 1983	5th
693	September 24-25, 1989	3rd
676	September 21-22, 1980	3rd

Top 10 Televised Sports Events Of All-Time

(Based on A.C. Nielsen Figures)

Program	Date	Network	Share	Rating
Super Bowl XVI	1/24/82	CBS	73.0	49.1
Super Bowl XVII	1/30/83	NBC	69.0	48.6
Super Bowl XX	1/26/86	NBC	70.0	48.3
Super Bowl XII	1/15/78	CBS	67.0	47.2
Super Bowl XIII	1/21/79	NBC	74.0	47.1
Super Bowl XVIII	1/22/84	CBS	71.0	46.4
Super Bowl XIX	1/20/85	ABC	63.0	46.4
Super Bowl XIV	1/20/80	CBS	67.0	46.3
Super Bowl XXI	1/25/87	CBS	66.0	45.8
Super Bowl XXVII	1/31/93	NBC	66.0	45.1

Ten Most Watched TV Programs & Estimated Total Number of Viewers

(Based on A.C. Nielsen Figures)

Program	Date	Network	*Total Viewers
Super Bowl XXVII	Jan. 31, 1993	NBC	133,400,000
Super Bowl XX	Jan. 26, 1986	NBC	127,000,000
Super Bowl XXI	Jan. 25, 1987	CBS	122,640,000
M*A*S*H (Special)	Feb. 28, 1983	CBS	121,624,000
Super Bowl XXVI	Jan. 26, 1992	CBS	119,700,000
Super Bowl XIX	Jan. 20, 1985	ABC	115,936,000
Super Bowl XXII	Jan. 31, 1988	ABC	115,000,000
Super Bowl XXV	Jan. 27, 1991	ABC	112,140,000
Super Bowl XXIII	Jan. 22, 1989	NBC	110,230,000
Super Bowl XVI	Jan. 24, 1982	CBS	109,040,000

*Watched some portion of the broadcast

NUMBER-ONE DRAFT CHOICES

Season	Team	Player	Position	College
1993	New England	Drew Bledsoe	QB	Washington State
1992	Indianapolis	Steve Emtman	DT	Washington
1991	Dallas	Russell Maryland	DT	Miami
1990	Indianapolis	Jeff George	QB	Illinois
1989	Dallas	Troy Aikman	QB	UCLA
1988	Atlanta	Aundray Bruce	LB	Auburn
1987	Tampa Bay	Vinny Testaverde	QB	Miami
1986	Tampa Bay	Bo Jackson	RB	Auburn
1985	Buffalo	Bruce Smith	DE	Virginia Tech
1984	New England	Irving Fryar	WR	Nebraska
1983	Baltimore	John Elway	QB	Stanford
1982	New England	Kenneth Sims	DT	Texas
1981	New Orleans	George Rogers	RB	South Carolina
1980	Detroit	Billy Sims	RB	Oklahoma
1979	Buffalo	Tom Cousineau	LB	Ohio State
1978	Houston	Earl Campbell	RB	Texas
1977	Tampa Bay	Ricky Bell	RB	Southern California
1976	Tampa Bay	Lee Roy Selmon	DE	Oklahoma
1975	Atlanta	Steve Bartkowski	QB	California
1974	Dallas	Ed Jones	DE	Tennessee State
1973	Houston	John Matuszak	DE	Tampa
1972	Buffalo	Walt Patulski	DE	Notre Dame
1971	New England	Jim Plunkett	QB	Stanford
1970	Pittsburgh	Terry Bradshaw	QB	Louisiana Tech
1969	Buffalo (AFL)	O.J. Simpson	RB	Southern California
1968	Minnesota	Ron Yary	T	Southern California
1967	Baltimore	Bubba Smith	DT	Michigan State
1966	Atlanta	Tommy Nobis	LB	Texas
	Miami (AFL)	Jim Grabowski	RB	Illinois
1965	New York Giants	Tucker Frederickson	RB	Auburn
	Houston (AFL)	Lawrence Elkins	E	Baylor
1964	San Francisco	Dave Parks	E	Texas Tech
	Boston (AFL)	Jack Concannon	QB	Boston College
1963	Los Angeles	Terry Baker	QB	Oregon State
	Kansas City (AFL)	Buck Buchanan	DT	Grambling
1962	Washington	Ernie Davis	RB	Syracuse
	Oakland (AFL)	Roman Gabriel	QB	North Carolina State
1961	Minnesota	Tommy Mason	RB	Tulane
	Buffalo (AFL)	Ken Rice	G	Auburn
1960	Los Angeles	Billy Cannon	RB	Louisiana State
	(AFL had no formal first pick)			
1959	Green Bay	Randy Duncan	QB	Iowa
1958	Chicago Cardinals	King Hill	QB	Rice
1957	Green Bay	Paul Hornung	HB	Notre Dame
1956	Pittsburgh	Gary Glick	DB	Colorado A&M
1955	Baltimore	George Shaw	QB	Oregon
1954	Cleveland	Bobby Garrett	QB	Stanford
1953	San Francisco	Harry Babcock	E	Georgia
1952	Los Angeles	Bill Wade	QB	Vanderbilt
1951	New York Giants	Kyle Rote	HB	Southern Methodist
1950	Detroit	Leon Hart	E	Notre Dame
1949	Philadelphia	Chuck Bednarik	C	Pennsylvania
1948	Washington	Harry Gilmer	QB	Alabama
1947	Chicago Bears	Bob Fenimore	HB	Oklahoma A&M
1946	Boston	Frank Dancewicz	QB	Notre Dame
1945	Chicago Cardinals	Charley Trippi	HB	Georgia
1944	Boston	Angelo Bertelli	QB	Notre Dame
1943	Detroit	Frank Sinkwich	HB	Georgia
1942	Pittsburgh	Bill Dudley	HB	Virginia
1941	Chicago Bears	Tom Harmon	HB	Michigan
1940	Chicago Cardinals	George Cafego	HB	Tennessee
1939	Chicago Cardinals	Ki Aldrich	C	Texas Christian
1938	Cleveland	Corbett Davis	FB	Indiana
1937	Philadelphia	Sam Francis	FB	Nebraska
1936	Philadelphia	Jay Berwanger	HB	Chicago

Note: From 1947 through 1958, the first selection in the draft was a Bonus pick, awarded to the winner of a random draw. That club, in turn, forfeited its last-round draft choice. The winner of the Bonus choice was eliminated from future draws. The system was abolished after 1958, by which time all clubs had received a Bonus choice.

FIRST-ROUND SELECTIONS

If club had no first-round selection, first player drafted is listed with round in parentheses.

Atlanta Falcons

Year	Player, College, Position
1966	Tommy Nobis, Texas, LB
	Randy Johnson, Texas A&I, QB
1967	Leo Carroll, San Diego State, DE (2)
1968	Claude Humphrey, Tennessee State, DE
1969	George Kunz, Notre Dame, T
1970	John Small, Citadel, LB
1971	Joe Profit, Northeast Louisiana, RB
1972	Clarence Ellis, Notre Dame, DB
1973	Greg Marx, Notre Dame, DT (2)
1974	Gerald Tinker, Kent State, WR (2)
1975	Steve Bartkowski, California, QB
1976	Bubba Bean, Texas A&M, RB
1977	Warren Bryant, Kentucky, T
	Wilson Faumuina, San Jose State, DT
1978	Mike Kenn, Michigan, T
1979	Don Smith, Miami, DE
1980	Junior Miller, Nebraska, TE
1981	Bobby Butler, Florida State, DB
1982	Gerald Riggs, Arizona State, RB
1983	Mike Pitts, Alabama, DE
1984	Rick Bryan, Oklahoma, DT
1985	Bill Fralic, Pittsburgh, T
1986	Tony Casillas, Oklahoma, NT
	Tim Green, Syracuse, LB
1987	Chris Miller, Oregon, QB
1988	Aundray Bruce, Auburn, LB
1989	Deion Sanders, Florida State, DB
	Shawn Collins, Northern Arizona, WR
1990	Steve Broussard, Washington State, RB
1991	Bruce Pickens, Nebraska, DB
	Mike Pritchard, Colorado, WR
1992	Bob Whitfield, Stanford, T
	Tony Smith, Southern Mississippi, RB
1993	Lincoln Kennedy, Washington, T

Buffalo Bills

Year	Player, College, Position
1960	Richie Lucas, Penn State, QB
1961	Ken Rice, Auburn, T
1962	Ernie Davis, Syracuse, RB
1963	Dave Behrman, Michigan State, C
1964	Carl Eller, Minnesota, DE
1965	Jim Davidson, Ohio State, T
1966	Mike Dennis, Mississippi, RB
1967	John Pitts, Arizona State, S
1968	Haven Moses, San Diego State, WR
1969	O.J. Simpson, Southern California, RB
1970	Al Cowlings, Southern California, DE
1971	J. D. Hill, Arizona State, WR
1972	Walt Patulski, Notre Dame, DE
1973	Paul Seymour, Michigan, TE
	Joe DeLamielleure, Michigan State, G
1974	Reuben Gant, Oklahoma State, TE
1975	Tom Ruud, Nebraska, LB
1976	Mario Clark, Oregon, DB
1977	Phil Dokes, Oklahoma State, DT
1978	Terry Miller, Oklahoma State, RB
1979	Tom Cousineau, Ohio State, LB
	Jerry Butler, Clemson, WR
1980	Jim Ritcher, North Carolina State, C
1981	Booker Moore, Penn State, RB
1982	Perry Tuttle, Clemson, WR
1983	Tony Hunter, Notre Dame, TE
	Jim Kelly, Miami, QB
1984	Greg Bell, Notre Dame, RB
1985	Bruce Smith, Virginia Tech, DE
	Derrick Burroughs, Memphis State, DB
1986	Ronnie Harmon, Iowa, RB
	Will Wolford, Vanderbilt, T
1987	Shane Conlan, Penn State, LB
1988	Thurman Thomas, Oklahoma State, RB (2)
1989	Don Beebe, Chadron, Neb., WR (3)
1990	James Williams, Fresno State, DB
1991	Henry Jones, Illinois, DB
1992	John Fina, Arizona, T
1993	Thomas Smith, North Carolina, DB

Chicago Bears

Year	Player, College, Position
1936	Joe Stydahar, West Virginia, T
1937	Les McDonald, Nebraska, E
1938	Joe Gray, Oregon State, B
1939	Sid Luckman, Columbia, QB
	Bill Osmanski, Holy Cross, B
1940	Clyde (Bulldog) Turner, Hardin-Simmons, C
1941	Tom Harmon, Michigan, B
	Norm Standlee, Stanford, B
	Don Scott, Ohio State, B
1942	Frankie Albert, Stanford, B
1943	Bob Steber, Missouri, B
1944	Ray Evans, Kansas, B
1945	Don Lund, Michigan, B
1946	Johnny Lujack, Notre Dame, QB
1947	Bob Fenimore, Oklahoma State, B
	Don Kindt, Wisconsin, B
1948	Bobby Layne, Texas, QB
	Max Bumgardner, Texas, E
1949	Dick Harris, Texas, C
1950	Chuck Hunsinger, Florida, B
	Fred Morrison, Ohio State, B
1951	Bob Williams, Notre Dame, B
	Billy Stone, Bradley, B
	Gene Schroeder, Virginia, E
1952	Jim Dooley, Miami, B
1953	Billy Anderson, Compton (Calif.) J.C., B
1954	Stan Wallace, Illinois, B
1955	Ron Drzewiecki, Marquette, B
1956	Menan (Tex) Schriewer, Texas, E
1957	Earl Leggett, Louisiana State, T
1958	Chuck Howley, West Virginia, G
1959	Don Clark, Ohio State, B
1960	Roger Davis, Syracuse, G
1961	Mike Ditka, Pittsburgh, E
1962	Ronnie Bull, Baylor, RB
1963	Dave Behrman, Michigan State, C
1964	Dick Evey, Tennessee, DT
1965	Dick Butkus, Illinois, LB
	Gale Sayers, Kansas, RB
	Steve DeLong, Tennessee, T
1966	George Rice, Louisiana State, DT
1967	Loyd Phillips, Arkansas, DE
1968	Mike Hull, Southern California, RB
1969	Rufus Mayes, Ohio State, T
1970	George Farmer, UCLA, WR (3)
1971	Joe Moore, Missouri, RB
1972	Lionel Antoine, Southern Illinois, T
	Craig Clemons, Iowa, DB
1973	Wally Chambers, Eastern Kentucky, DE
1974	Waymond Bryant, Tennessee State, LB
	Dave Gallagher, Michigan, DT
1975	Walter Payton, Jackson State, RB
1976	Dennis Lick, Wisconsin, T
1977	Ted Albrecht, California, T
1978	Brad Shearer, Texas, DT (3)
1979	Dan Hampton, Arkansas, DT
	Al Harris, Arizona State, DE
1980	Otis Wilson, Louisville, LB
1981	Keith Van Horne, Southern California, T
1982	Jim McMahon, Brigham Young, QB
1983	Jim Covert, Pittsburgh, T
	Willie Gault, Tennessee, WR
1984	Wilber Marshall, Florida, LB
1985	William Perry, Clemson, DT
1986	Neal Anderson, Florida, RB
1987	Jim Harbaugh, Michigan, QB
1988	Brad Muster, Stanford, RB
	Wendell Davis, Louisiana State, WR
1989	Donnell Woolford, Clemson, DB
	Trace Armstrong, Florida, DE
1990	Mark Carrier, Southern California, DB
1991	Stan Thomas, Texas, T
1992	Alonzo Spellman, Ohio State, DE
1993	Curtis Conway, Southern California, WR

Cincinnati Bengals

Year	Player, College, Position
1968	Bob Johnson, Tennessee, C
1969	Greg Cook, Cincinnati, QB
1970	Mike Reid, Penn State, DT
1971	Vernon Holland, Tennessee State, T
1972	Sherman White, California, DE
1973	Isaac Curtis, San Diego State, WR
1974	Bill Kollar, Montana State, DT
1975	Glenn Cameron, Florida, LB
1976	Billy Brooks, Oklahoma, WR
	Archie Griffin, Ohio State, RB
1977	Eddie Edwards, Miami, DT
	Wilson Whitley, Houston, DT
	Mike Cobb, Michigan State, TE
1978	Ross Browner, Notre Dame, DT
	Blair Bush, Washington, C
1979	Jack Thompson, Washington State, QB
	Charles Alexander, Louisiana State, RB
1980	Anthony Muñoz, Southern California, T
1981	David Verser, Kansas, WR
1982	Glen Collins, Mississippi State, DE
1983	Dave Rimington, Nebraska, C
1984	Ricky Hunley, Arizona, LB
	Pete Koch, Maryland, DE
	Brian Blados, North Carolina, T
1985	Eddie Brown, Miami, WR
	Emanuel King, Alabama, LB
1986	Joe Kelly, Washington, LB
	Tim McGee, Tennessee, WR
1987	Jason Buck, Brigham Young, DE
1988	Rickey Dixon, Oklahoma, DB
1989	Eric Ball, UCLA, RB (2)
1990	James Francis, Baylor, LB
1991	Alfred Williams, Colorado, LB
1992	David Klingler, Houston, QB
	Darryl Williams, Miami, DB
1993	John Copeland, Alabama, DE

Cleveland Browns

Year	Player, College, Position
1950	Ken Carpenter, Oregon State, B
1951	Ken Konz, Louisiana State, B
1952	Bert Rechichar, Tennessee, DB
	Harry Agganis, Boston U., QB
1953	Doug Atkins, Tennessee, DE
1954	Bobby Garrett, Stanford, QB
	John Bauer, Illinois, G
1955	Kurt Burris, Oklahoma, C
1956	Preston Carpenter, Arkansas, B
1957	Jim Brown, Syracuse, RB
1958	Jim Shofner, Texas Christian, DB
1959	Rich Kreitling, Illinois, DE
1960	Jim Houston, Ohio State, DE
1961	Bobby Crespino, Mississippi, TE
1962	Gary Collins, Maryland, WR
	Leroy Jackson, Western Illinois, RB
1963	Tom Hutchinson, Kentucky, WR
1964	Paul Warfield, Ohio State, WR
1965	James Garcia, Purdue, T (2)
1966	Milt Morin, Massachusetts, TE
1967	Bob Matheson, Duke, LB
1968	Marvin Upshaw, Trinity, Tex., DT-DE
1969	Ron Johnson, Michigan, RB
1970	Mike Phipps, Purdue, QB
	Bob McKay, Texas, T
1971	Clarence Scott, Kansas State, CB
1972	Thom Darden, Michigan, DB
1973	Steve Holden, Arizona State, WR
	Pete Adams, Southern California, T
1974	Billy Corbett, Johnson C. Smith, T (2)
1975	Mack Mitchell, Houston, DE
1976	Mike Pruitt, Purdue, RB
1977	Robert Jackson, Texas A&M, LB
1978	Clay Matthews, Southern California, LB
	Ozzie Newsome, Alabama, TE
1979	Willis Adams, Houston, WR
1980	Charles White, Southern California, RB
1981	Hanford Dixon, Southern Mississippi, DB
1982	Chip Banks, Southern California, LB
1983	Ron Brown, Arizona State, WR (2)
1984	Don Rogers, UCLA, DB
1985	Greg Allen, Florida State, RB (2)
1986	Webster Slaughter, San Diego State, WR (2)
1987	Mike Junkin, Duke, LB
1988	Clifford Charlton, Florida, LB
1989	Eric Metcalf, Texas, RB
1990	Leroy Hoard, Michigan, RB (2)
1991	Eric Turner, UCLA, DB
1992	Tommy Vardell, Stanford, RB
1993	Steve Everitt, Michigan, C

Dallas Cowboys

Year	Player, College, Position
1960	None
1961	Bob Lilly, Texas Christian, DT
1962	Sonny Gibbs, Texas Christian, QB (2)
1963	Lee Roy Jordan, Alabama, LB
1964	Scott Appleton, Texas, DT
1965	Craig Morton, California, QB
1966	John Niland, Iowa, G
1967	Phil Clark, Northwestern, DB (3)
1968	Dennis Homan, Alabama, WR
1969	Calvin Hill, Yale, RB
1970	Duane Thomas, West Texas State, RB
1971	Tody Smith, Southern California, DE
1972	Bill Thomas, Boston College, RB
1973	Billy Joe DuPree, Michigan State, TE
1974	Ed (Too Tall) Jones, Tennessee State, DE
	Charley Young, North Carolina State, RB
1975	Randy White, Maryland, LB
	Thomas Henderson, Langston, LB
1976	Aaron Kyle, Wyoming, DB
1977	Tony Dorsett, Pittsburgh, RB
1978	Larry Bethea, Michigan State, DE
1979	Robert Shaw, Tennessee, C
1980	Bill Roe, Colorado, LB (3)
1981	Howard Richards, Missouri, T
1982	Rod Hill, Kentucky State, DB
1983	Jim Jeffcoat, Arizona State, DE
1984	Billy Cannon, Jr., Texas A&M, LB
1985	Kevin Brooks, Michigan, DE
1986	Mike Sherrard, UCLA, WR
1987	Danny Noonan, Nebraska, DT
1988	Michael Irvin, Miami, WR
1989	Troy Aikman, UCLA, QB
1990	Emmitt Smith, Florida, RB
1991	Russell Maryland, Miami, DT
	Alvin Harper, Tennessee, WR
	Kelvin Pritchett, Mississippi, DT
1992	Kevin Smith, Texas A&M, DB
	Robert Jones, East Carolina, LB
1993	Kevin Williams, Miami, WR (2)

Denver Broncos

Year	Player, College, Position
1960	Roger LeClerc, Trinity, Conn., C
1961	Bob Gaiters, New Mexico State, RB
1962	Merlin Olsen, Utah State, DT
1963	Kermit Alexander, UCLA, CB
1964	Bob Brown, Nebraska, T
1965	Dick Butkus, Illinois, LB (2)
1966	Jerry Shay, Purdue, DT
1967	Floyd Little, Syracuse, RB
1968	Curley Culp, Arizona State, DE (2)
1969	Grady Cavness, Texas-El Paso, DB (2)
1970	Bob Anderson, Colorado, RB
1971	Marv Montgomery, Southern California, T
1972	Riley Odoms, Houston, TE
1973	Otis Armstrong, Purdue, RB
1974	Randy Gradishar, Ohio State, LB
1975	Louis Wright, San Jose State, DB
1976	Tom Glassic, Virginia, G
1977	Steve Schindler, Boston College, G
1978	Don Latimer, Miami, DT
1979	Kelvin Clark, Nebraska, T
1980	Rulon Jones, Utah State, DE (2)
1981	Dennis Smith, Southern California, DB
1982	Gerald Willhite, San Jose State, RB
1983	Chris Hinton, Northwestern, G
1984	Andre Townsend, Mississippi, DE (2)
1985	Steve Sewell, Oklahoma, RB
1986	Jim Juriga, Illinois, T (4)
1987	Ricky Nattiel, Florida, WR
1988	Ted Gregory, Syracuse, NT
1989	Steve Atwater, Arkansas, DB
1990	Alton Montgomery, Houston, DB (2)
1991	Mike Croel, Nebraska, LB
1992	Tommy Maddox, UCLA, QB
1993	Dan Williams, Toledo, DE

Detroit Lions

Year	Player, College, Position
1936	Sid Wagner, Michigan State, G
1937	Lloyd Cardwell, Nebraska, B
1938	Alex Wojciechowicz, Fordham, C
1939	John Pingel, Michigan State, B
1940	Doyle Nave, Southern California, B
1941	Jim Thomason, Texas A&M, B
1942	Bob Westfall, Michigan, B
1943	Frank Sinkwich, Georgia, B
1944	Otto Graham, Northwestern, B
1945	Frank Szymanski, Notre Dame, C
1946	Bill Dellastatious, Missouri, B
1947	Glenn Davis, Army, B
1948	Y.A. Tittle, Louisiana State, B
1949	John Rauch, Georgia, B
1950	Leon Hart, Notre Dame, E
	Joe Watson, Rice, C
1951	Dick Stanfel, San Francisco, G (2)
1952	Yale Lary, Texas A&M, B (3)
1953	Harley Sewell, Texas, G
1954	Dick Chapman, Rice, T
1955	Dave Middleton, Auburn, B
1956	Hopalong Cassady, Ohio State, B
1957	Bill Glass, Baylor, G
1958	Alex Karras, Iowa, T
1959	Nick Pietrosante, Notre Dame, B
1960	John Robinson, Louisiana State, S
1961	Danny LaRose, Missouri, T (2)
1962	John Hadl, Kansas, QB
1963	Daryl Sanders, Ohio State, T
1964	Pete Beathard, Southern California, QB
1965	Tom Nowatzke, Indiana, RB
1966	Nick Eddy, Notre Dame, RB (2)
1967	Mel Farr, UCLA, RB
1968	Greg Landry, Massachusetts, QB
	Earl McCullouch, Southern California, WR
1969	Altie Taylor, Utah State, RB (2)
1970	Steve Owens, Oklahoma, RB
1971	Bob Bell, Cincinnati, DT
1972	Herb Orvis, Colorado, DE
1973	Ernie Price, Texas A&I, DE
1974	Ed O'Neil, Penn State, LB
1975	Lynn Boden, South Dakota State, G
1976	James Hunter, Grambling, DB
	Lawrence Gaines, Wyoming, RB
1977	Walt Williams, New Mexico State, DB (2)
1978	Luther Bradley, Notre Dame, DB
1979	Keith Dorney, Penn State, T
1980	Billy Sims, Oklahoma, RB
1981	Mark Nichols, San Jose State, WR
1982	Jimmy Williams, Nebraska, LB
1983	James Jones, Florida, RB
1984	David Lewis, California, TE
1985	Lomas Brown, Florida, T
1986	Chuck Long, Iowa, QB
1987	Reggie Rogers, Washington, DE
1988	Bennie Blades, Miami, DB
1989	Barry Sanders, Oklahoma State, RB
1990	Andre Ware, Houston, QB
1991	Herman Moore, Virginia, WR
1992	Robert Porcher, South Carolina State, DE
1993	Ryan McNeil, Miami, DB (2)

Green Bay Packers

Year	Player, College, Position
1936	Russ Letlow, San Francisco, G
1937	Eddie Jankowski, Wisconsin, B
1938	Cecil Isbell, Purdue, B
1939	Larry Buhler, Minnesota, B
1940	Harold Van Every, Minnesota, B
1941	George Paskvan, Wisconsin, B
1942	Urban Odson, Minnesota, T
1943	Dick Wildung, Minnesota, T
1944	Merv Pregulman, Michigan, G
1945	Walt Schlinkman, Texas Tech, B
1946	Johnny (Strike) Strzykalski, Marquette, B
1947	Ernie Case, UCLA, B
1948	Earl (Jug) Girard, Wisconsin, B
1949	Stan Heath, Nevada, B
1950	Clayton Tonnemaker, Minnesota, C
1951	Bob Gain, Kentucky, T
1952	Babe Parilli, Kentucky, QB
1953	Al Carmichael, Southern California, B
1954	Art Hunter, Notre Dame, T
	Veryl Switzer, Kansas State, B
1955	Tom Bettis, Purdue, G
1956	Jack Losch, Miami, B
1957	Paul Hornung, Notre Dame, B
	Ron Kramer, Michigan, E
1958	Dan Currie, Michigan State, C
1959	Randy Duncan, Iowa, B
1960	Tom Moore, Vanderbilt, RB
1961	Herb Adderley, Michigan State, CB
1962	Earl Gros, Louisiana State, RB
1963	Dave Robinson, Penn State, LB
1964	Lloyd Voss, Nebraska, DT
1965	Donny Anderson, Texas Tech, RB
	Lawrence Elkins, Baylor, E
1966	Jim Grabowski, Illinois, RB
	Gale Gillingham, Minnesota, T
1967	Bob Hyland, Boston College, C
	Don Horn, San Diego State, QB
1968	Fred Carr, Texas-El Paso, LB
	Bill Lueck, Arizona, G
1969	Rich Moore, Villanova, DT
1970	Mike McCoy, Notre Dame, DT
	Rich McGeorge, Elon, TE
1971	John Brockington, Ohio State, RB
1972	Willie Buchanon, San Diego State, DB
	Jerry Tagge, Nebraska, QB
1973	Barry Smith, Florida State, WR
1974	Barty Smith, Richmond, RB
1975	Bill Bain, Southern California, G (2)
1976	Mark Koncar, Colorado, T
1977	Mike Butler, Kansas, DE
	Ezra Johnson, Morris Brown, DE
1978	James Lofton, Stanford, WR
	John Anderson, Michigan, LB
1979	Eddie Lee Ivery, Georgia Tech, RB
1980	Bruce Clark, Penn State, DE
	George Cumby, Oklahoma, LB
1981	Rich Campbell, California, QB
1982	Ron Hallstrom, Iowa, G
1983	Tim Lewis, Pittsburgh, DB
1984	Alphonso Carreker, Florida State, DE
1985	Ken Ruettgers, Southern California, T
1986	Kenneth Davis, Texas Christian, RB (2)
1987	Brent Fullwood, Auburn, RB
1988	Sterling Sharpe, South Carolina, WR
1989	Tony Mandarich, Michigan State, T
1990	Tony Bennett, Mississippi, LB
	Darrell Thompson, Minnesota, RB
1991	Vinnie Clark, Ohio State, DB
1992	Terrell Buckley, Florida State, DB
1993	Wayne Simmons, Clemson, LB
	George Teague, Alabama, DB

Houston Oilers

Year	Player, College, Position
1960	Billy Cannon, Louisiana State, RB
1961	Mike Ditka, Pittsburgh, E
1962	Ray Jacobs, Howard Payne, DT
1963	Danny Brabham, Arkansas, LB
1964	Scott Appleton, Texas, DT
1965	Lawrence Elkins, Baylor, WR
1966	Tommy Nobis, Texas, LB
1967	George Webster, Michigan State, LB
	Tom Regner, Notre Dame, G
1968	Mac Haik, Mississippi, WR (2)
1969	Ron Pritchard, Arizona State, LB
1970	Doug Wilkerson, N. Carolina Central, G
1971	Dan Pastorini, Santa Clara, QB
1972	Greg Sampson, Stanford, DE
1973	John Matuszak, Tampa, DE
	George Amundson, Iowa State, RB
1974	Steve Manstedt, Nebraska, LB (4)
1975	Robert Brazile, Jackson State, LB
	Don Hardeman, Texas A&I, RB
1976	Mike Barber, Louisiana Tech, TE (2)
1977	Morris Towns, Missouri, T
1978	Earl Campbell, Texas, RB
1979	Mike Stensrud, Iowa State, DE (2)
1980	Angelo Fields, Michigan State, T (2)
1981	Michael Holston, Morgan State, WR (3)
1982	Mike Munchak, Penn State, G
1983	Bruce Matthews, Southern California, T
1984	Dean Steinkuhler, Nebraska, T
1985	Ray Childress, Texas A&M, DE
	Richard Johnson, Wisconsin, DB
1986	Jim Everett, Purdue, QB
1987	Alonzo Highsmith, Miami, RB
	Haywood Jeffires, North Carolina St., WR
1988	Lorenzo White, Michigan State, RB
1989	David Williams, Florida, T
1990	Lamar Lathon, Houston, LB
1991	Mike Dumas, Indiana, DB (2)
1992	Eddie Robinson, Alabama State, LB (2)
1993	Brad Hopkins, Illinois, T

Indianapolis Colts

Year	Player, College, Position
1953	Billy Vessels, Oklahoma, B
1954	Cotton Davidson, Baylor, B

1955	George Shaw, Oregon, B
	Alan Ameche, Wisconsin, FB
1956	Lenny Moore, Penn State, B
1957	Jim Parker, Ohio State, G
1958	Lenny Lyles, Louisville, B
1959	Jackie Burkett, Auburn, C
1960	Ron Mix, Southern California, T
1961	Tom Matte, Ohio State, RB
1962	Wendell Harris, Louisiana State, S
1963	Bob Vogel, Ohio State, T
1964	Marv Woodson, Indiana, CB
1965	Mike Curtis, Duke, LB
1966	Sam Ball, Kentucky, T
1967	Bubba Smith, Michigan State, DT
	Jim Detwiler, Michigan, RB
1968	John Williams, Minnesota, G
1969	Eddie Hinton, Oklahoma, WR
1970	Norman Bulaich, Texas Christian, RB
1971	Don McCauley, North Carolina, RB
	Leonard Dunlap, North Texas State, DB
1972	Tom Drougas, Oregon, T
1973	Bert Jones, Louisiana State, QB
	Joe Ehrmann, Syracuse, DT
1974	John Dutton, Nebraska, DE
	Roger Carr, Louisiana Tech, WR
1975	Ken Huff, North Carolina, G
1976	Ken Novak, Purdue, DT
1977	Randy Burke, Kentucky, WR
1978	Reese McCall, Auburn, TE
1979	Barry Krauss, Alabama, LB
1980	Curtis Dickey, Texas A&M, RB
	Derrick Hatchett, Texas, DB
1981	Randy McMillan, Pittsburgh, RB
	Donnell Thompson, North Carolina, DT
1982	Johnie Cooks, Mississippi State, LB
	Art Schlichter, Ohio State, QB
1983	John Elway, Stanford, QB
1984	Leonard Coleman, Vanderbilt, DB
	Ron Solt, Maryland, G
1985	Duane Bickett, Southern California, LB
1986	Jon Hand, Alabama, DE
1987	Cornelius Bennett, Alabama, LB
1988	Chris Chandler, Washington, QB (3)
1989	Andre Rison, Michigan State, WR
1990	Jeff George, Illinois, QB
1991	Shane Curry, Miami, DE (2)
1992	Steve Emtman, Washington, DT
	Quentin Coryatt, Texas A&M, LB
1993	Sean Dawkins, California, WR

Kansas City Chiefs

Year	Player, College, Position
1960	Don Meredith, Southern Methodist, QB
1961	E.J. Holub, Texas Tech, C
1962	Ronnie Bull, Baylor, RB
1963	Buck Buchanan, Grambling, DT
	Ed Budde, Michigan State, G
1964	Pete Beathard, Southern California, QB
1965	Gale Sayers, Kansas, RB
1966	Aaron Brown, Minnesota, DE
1967	Gene Trosch, Miami, DE-DT
1968	Mo Moorman, Texas A&M, G
	George Daney, Texas-El Paso, G
1969	Jim Marsalis, Tennessee State, CB
1970	Sid Smith, Southern California, T
1971	Elmo Wright, Houston, WR
1972	Jeff Kinney, Nebraska, RB
1973	Gary Butler, Rice, TE (2)
1974	Woody Green, Arizona State, RB
1975	Elmore Stephens, Kentucky, TE (2)
1976	Rod Walters, Iowa, G
1977	Gary Green, Baylor, DB
1978	Art Still, Kentucky, DE
1979	Mike Bell, Colorado State, DE
	Steve Fuller, Clemson, QB
1980	Brad Budde, Southern California, G
1981	Willie Scott, South Carolina, TE
1982	Anthony Hancock, Tennessee, WR
1983	Todd Blackledge, Penn State, QB
1984	Bill Maas, Pittsburgh, DT
	John Alt, Iowa, T
1985	Ethan Horton, North Carolina, RB
1986	Brian Jozwiak, West Virginia, T
1987	Paul Palmer, Temple, RB
1988	Neil Smith, Nebraska, DE
1989	Derrick Thomas, Alabama, LB
1990	Percy Snow, Michigan State, LB
1991	Harvey Williams, Louisiana State, RB
1992	Dale Carter, Tennessee, DB
1993	Will Shields, Nebraska, G (3)

Los Angeles Raiders

Year	Player, College, Position
1960	Dale Hackbart, Wisconsin, CB
1961	Joe Rutgens, Illinois, DT
1962	Roman Gabriel, North Carolina State, QB
1963	George Wilson, Alabama, RB (6)
1964	Tony Lorick, Arizona State, RB
1965	Harry Schuh, Memphis State, T
1966	Rodger Bird, Kentucky, S
1967	Gene Upshaw, Texas A&I, G
1968	Eldridge Dickey, Tennessee State, QB
1969	Art Thoms, Syracuse, DT
1970	Raymond Chester, Morgan State, TE
1971	Jack Tatum, Ohio State, S
1972	Mike Siani, Villanova, WR
1973	Ray Guy, Southern Mississippi, P
1974	Henry Lawrence, Florida A&M, T
1975	Neal Colzie, Ohio State, DB
1976	Charles Philyaw, Texas Southern, DT (2)
1977	Mike Davis, Colorado, DB (2)
1978	Dave Browning, Washington, DE (2)
1979	Willie Jones, Florida State, DE (2)
1980	Marc Wilson, Brigham Young, QB
1981	Ted Watts, Texas Tech, DB
	Curt Marsh, Washington, T
1982	Marcus Allen, Southern California, RB
1983	Don Mosebar, Southern California, T
1984	Sean Jones, Northeastern, DE (2)
1985	Jessie Hester, Florida State, WR
1986	Bob Buczkowski, Pittsburgh, DE
1987	John Clay, Missouri, T
1988	Tim Brown, Notre Dame, WR
	Terry McDaniel, Tennessee, DB
	Scott Davis, Illinois, DE
1989	Jeff Francis, Tennessee, QB (6)
1990	Anthony Smith, Arizona, DE
1991	Todd Marinovich, Southern California, QB
1992	Chester McGlockton, Clemson, DE
1993	Patrick Bates, Texas A&M, DB

Los Angeles Rams

Year	Player, College, Position
1937	Johnny Drake, Purdue, B
1938	Corbett Davis, Indiana, B
1939	Parker Hall, Mississippi, B
1940	Ollie Cordill, Rice, B
1941	Rudy Mucha, Washington, C
1942	Jack Wilson, Baylor, B
1943	Mike Holovak, Boston College, B
1944	Tony Butkovich, Illinois, B
1945	Elroy (Crazylegs) Hirsch, Wisconsin, B
1946	Emil Sitko, Notre Dame, B
1947	Herman Wedemeyer, St. Mary's, Calif., B
1948	Tom Keane, West Virginia, B (2)
1949	Bobby Thomason, Virginia Military, B
1950	Ralph Pasquariello, Villanova, B
	Stan West, Oklahoma, G
1951	Bud McFadin, Texas, G
1952	Bill Wade, Vanderbilt, QB
	Bob Carey, Michigan State, E
1953	Donn Moomaw, UCLA, C
	Ed Barker, Washington State, E
1954	Ed Beatty, Cincinnati, C
1955	Larry Morris, Georgia Tech, C
1956	Joe Marconi, West Virginia, B
	Charles Horton, Vanderbilt, B
1957	Jon Arnett, Southern California, B
	Del Shofner, Baylor, E
1958	Lou Michaels, Kentucky, T
	Jim Phillips, Auburn, E
1959	Dick Bass, Pacific, B
	Paul Dickson, Baylor, T
1960	Billy Cannon, Louisiana State, RB
1961	Marlin McKeever, So. California, E-LB
1962	Roman Gabriel, North Carolina State, QB
	Merlin Olsen, Utah State, DT
1963	Terry Baker, Oregon State, QB
	Rufus Guthrie, Georgia Tech, G
1964	Bill Munson, Utah State, QB
1965	Clancy Williams, Washington State, CB
1966	Tom Mack, Michigan, G
1967	Willie Ellison, Texas Southern, RB (2)
1968	Gary Beban, UCLA, QB (2)
1969	Larry Smith, Florida, RB
	Jim Seymour, Notre Dame, WR
	Bob Klein, Southern California, TE
1970	Jack Reynolds, Tennessee, LB
1971	Isiah Robertson, Southern, LB
	Jack Youngblood, Florida, DE
1972	Jim Bertelsen, Texas, RB (2)
1973	Cullen Bryant, Colorado, DB (2)
1974	John Cappelletti, Penn State, RB
1975	Mike Fanning, Notre Dame, DT
	Dennis Harrah, Miami, T
	Doug France, Ohio State, T
1976	Kevin McLain, Colorado State, LB
1977	Bob Brudzinski, Ohio State, LB
1978	Elvis Peacock, Oklahoma, RB
1979	George Andrews, Nebraska, LB
	Kent Hill, Georgia Tech, T
1980	Johnnie Johnson, Texas, DB
1981	Mel Owens, Michigan, LB
1982	Barry Redden, Richmond, RB
1983	Eric Dickerson, Southern Methodist, RB
1984	Hal Stephens, East Carolina, DE (5)
1985	Jerry Gray, Texas, DB
1986	Mike Schad, Queen's University, Canada, T
1987	Donald Evans, Winston-Salem, DE (2)
1988	Gaston Green, UCLA, RB
	Aaron Cox, Arizona State, WR
1989	Bill Hawkins, Miami, DE
	Cleveland Gary, Miami, RB
1990	Bern Brostek, Washington, C
1991	Todd Lyght, Notre Dame, DB
1992	Sean Gilbert, Pittsburgh, DE
1993	Jerome Bettis, Notre Dame, RB

Miami Dolphins

Year	Player, College, Position
1966	Jim Grabowski, Illinois, RB
	Rick Norton, Kentucky, QB
1967	Bob Griese, Purdue, QB
1968	Larry Csonka, Syracuse, RB
	Doug Crusan, Indiana, T
1969	Bill Stanfill, Georgia, DE
1970	Jim Mandich, Michigan, TE (2)
1971	Otto Stowe, Iowa State, WR (2)
1972	Mike Kadish, Notre Dame, DT
1973	Chuck Bradley, Oregon, C (2)
1974	Donald Reese, Jackson State, DE
1975	Darryl Carlton, Tampa, T
1976	Larry Gordon, Arizona State, LB
	Kim Bokamper, San Jose State, LB
1977	A.J. Duhe, Louisiana State, DT
1978	Guy Benjamin, Stanford, QB (2)
1979	Jon Giesler, Michigan, T
1980	Don McNeal, Alabama, DB
1981	David Overstreet, Oklahoma, RB
1982	Roy Foster, Southern California, G
1983	Dan Marino, Pittsburgh, QB
1984	Jackie Shipp, Oklahoma, LB
1985	Lorenzo Hampton, Florida, RB
1986	John Offerdahl, Western Michigan, LB (2)
1987	John Bosa, Boston College, DE
1988	Eric Kumerow, Ohio State, DE
1989	Sammie Smith, Florida State, RB
	Louis Oliver, Florida, DB
1990	Richmond Webb, Texas A&M, T
1991	Randal Hill, Miami, WR
1992	Troy Vincent, Wisconsin, DB
	Marco Coleman, Georgia Tech, LB
1993	O.J. McDuffie, Penn State, WR

Minnesota Vikings

Year	Player, College, Position
1961	Tommy Mason, Tulane, RB
1962	Bill Miller, Miami, WR (3)
1963	Jim Dunaway, Mississippi, T
1964	Carl Eller, Minnesota, DE
1965	Jack Snow, Notre Dame, WR
1966	Jerry Shay, Purdue, DT
1967	Clint Jones, Michigan State, RB
	Gene Washington, Michigan State, WR
	Alan Page, Notre Dame, DT
1968	Ron Yary, Southern California, T
1969	Ed White, California, G (2)
1970	John Ward, Oklahoma State, DT
1971	Leo Hayden, Ohio State, RB
1972	Jeff Siemon, Stanford, LB
1973	Chuck Foreman, Miami, RB
1974	Fred McNeill, UCLA, LB
	Steve Riley, Southern California, T

1975 Mark Mullaney, Colorado State, DE
1976 James White, Oklahoma State, DT
1977 Tommy Kramer, Rice, QB
1978 Randy Holloway, Pittsburgh, DE
1979 Ted Brown, North Carolina State, RB
1980 Doug Martin, Washington, DT
1981 Mardye McDole, Mississippi State, WR (2)
1982 Darrin Nelson, Stanford, RB
1983 Joey Browner, Southern California, DB
1984 Keith Millard, Washington State, DE
1985 Chris Doleman, Pittsburgh, LB
1986 Gerald Robinson, Auburn, DE
1987 D.J. Dozier, Penn State, RB
1988 Randall McDaniel, Arizona State, G
1989 David Braxton, Wake Forest, LB (2)
1990 Mike Jones, Texas A&M, TE (3)
1991 Carlos Jenkins, Michigan State, LB (3)
1992 Robert Harris, Southern University, DE (2)
1993 Robert Smith, Ohio State, RB

New England Patriots

Year	Player, College, Position
1960	Ron Burton, Northwestern, RB
1961	Tommy Mason, Tulane, RB
1962	Gary Collins, Maryland, WR
1963	Art Graham, Boston College, WR
1964	Jack Concannon, Boston College, QB
1965	Jerry Rush, Michigan State, DE
1966	Karl Singer, Purdue, T
1967	John Charles, Purdue, S
1968	Dennis Byrd, North Carolina State, DE
1969	Ron Sellers, Florida State, WR
1970	Phil Olsen, Utah State, DE
1971	Jim Plunkett, Stanford, QB
1972	Tom Reynolds, San Diego State, WR (2)
1973	John Hannah, Alabama, G
	Sam Cunningham, So. California, RB
	Darryl Stingley, Purdue, WR
1974	Steve Corbett, Boston College, G (2)
1975	Russ Francis, Oregon, TE
1976	Mike Haynes, Arizona State, DB
	Pete Brock, Colorado, C
	Tim Fox, Ohio State, DB
1977	Raymond Clayborn, Texas, DB
	Stanley Morgan, Tennessee, WR
1978	Bob Cryder, Alabama, G
1979	Rick Sanford, South Carolina, DB
1980	Roland James, Tennessee, DB
	Vagas Ferguson, Notre Dame, RB
1981	Brian Holloway, Stanford, T
1982	Kenneth Sims, Texas, DT
	Lester Williams, Miami, DT
1983	Tony Eason, Illinois, QB
1984	Irving Fryar, Nebraska, WR
1985	Trevor Matich, Brigham Young, C
1986	Reggie Dupard, Southern Methodist, RB
1987	Bruce Armstrong, Louisville, T
1988	John Stephens, Northwestern St., La., RB
1989	Hart Lee Dykes, Oklahoma State, WR
1990	Chris Singleton, Arizona, LB
	Ray Agnew, North Carolina State, DE
1991	Pat Harlow, Southern California, T
	Leonard Russell, Arizona State, RB
1992	Eugene Chung, Virginia Tech, T
1993	Drew Bledsoe, Washington State, QB

New Orleans Saints

Year	Player, College, Position
1967	Les Kelley, Alabama, RB
1968	Kevin Hardy, Notre Dame, DE
1969	John Shinners, Xavier, G
1970	Ken Burrough, Texas Southern, WR
1971	Archie Manning, Mississippi, QB
1972	Royce Smith, Georgia, G
1973	Derland Moore, Oklahoma, DE (2)
1974	Rick Middleton, Ohio State, LB
1975	Larry Burton, Purdue, WR
	Kurt Schumacher, Ohio State, T
1976	Chuck Muncie, California, RB
1977	Joe Campbell, Maryland, DE
1978	Wes Chandler, Florida, WR
1979	Russell Erxleben, Texas, P-K
1980	Stan Brock, Colorado, T
1981	George Rogers, South Carolina, RB
1982	Lindsay Scott, Georgia, WR
1983	Steve Korte, Arkansas, G (2)
1984	James Geathers, Wichita State, DE
1985	Alvin Toles, Tennessee, LB
1986	Jim Dombrowski, Virginia, T
1987	Shawn Knight, Brigham Young, DT
1988	Craig Heyward, Pittsburgh, RB
1989	Wayne Martin, Arkansas, DE
1990	Renaldo Turnbull, West Virginia, DE
1991	Wesley Carroll, Miami, WR (2)
1992	Vaughn Dunbar, Indiana, RB
1993	Willie Roaf, Louisiana Tech, T
	Irv Smith, Notre Dame, TE

New York Giants

Year	Player, College, Position
1936	Art Lewis, Ohio U., T
1937	Ed Widseth, Minnesota, T
1938	George Karamatic, Gonzaga, B
1939	Walt Neilson, Arizona, B
1940	Grenville Lansdell, Southern California, B
1941	George Franck, Minnesota, B
1942	Merle Hapes, Mississippi, B
1943	Steve Filipowicz, Fordham, B
1944	Billy Hillenbrand, Indiana, B
1945	Elmer Barbour, Wake Forest, B
1946	George Connor, Notre Dame, T
1947	Vic Schwall, Northwestern, B
1948	Tony Minisi, Pennsylvania, B
1949	Paul Page, Southern Methodist, B
1950	Travis Tidwell, Auburn, B
1951	Kyle Rote, Southern Methodist, B
	Jim Spavital, Oklahoma A&M, B
1952	Frank Gifford, Southern California, B
1953	Bobby Marlow, Alabama, B
1954	Ken Buck, Pacific, C (2)
1955	Joe Heap, Notre Dame, B
1956	Henry Moore, Arkansas, B (2)
1957	Sam DeLuca, South Carolina, T (2)
1958	Phil King, Vanderbilt, B
1959	Lee Grosscup, Utah, B
1960	Lou Cordileone, Clemson, G
1961	Bruce Tarbox, Syracuse, G (2)
1962	Jerry Hillebrand, Colorado, LB
1963	Frank Lasky, Florida, T (2)
1964	Joe Don Looney, Oklahoma, RB
1965	Tucker Frederickson, Auburn, RB
1966	Francis Peay, Missouri, T
1967	Louis Thompson, Alabama, DT (4)
1968	Dick Buzin, Penn State, T (2)
1969	Fred Dryer, San Diego State, DE
1970	Jim Files, Oklahoma, LB
1971	Rocky Thompson, West Texas State, WR
1972	Eldridge Small, Texas A&I, DB
	Larry Jacobson, Nebraska, DE
1973	Brad Van Pelt, Michigan State, LB (2)
1974	John Hicks, Ohio State, G
1975	Al Simpson, Colorado State, T (2)
1976	Troy Archer, Colorado, DE
1977	Gary Jeter, Southern California, DT
1978	Gordon King, Stanford, T
1979	Phil Simms, Morehead State, QB
1980	Mark Haynes, Colorado, DB
1981	Lawrence Taylor, North Carolina, LB
1982	Butch Woolfolk, Michigan, RB
1983	Terry Kinard, Clemson, DB
1984	Carl Banks, Michigan State, LB
	William Roberts, Ohio State, T
1985	George Adams, Kentucky, RB
1986	Eric Dorsey, Notre Dame, DE
1987	Mark Ingram, Michigan State, WR
1988	Eric Moore, Indiana, T
1989	Brian Williams, Minnesota, C-G
1990	Rodney Hampton, Georgia, RB
1991	Jarrod Bunch, Michigan, RB
1992	Derek Brown, Notre Dame, TE
1993	Michael Strahan, Texas Southern, DE (2)

New York Jets

Year	Player, College, Position
1960	George Izo, Notre Dame, QB
1961	Tom Brown, Minnesota, G
1962	Sandy Stephens, Minnesota, QB
1963	Jerry Stovall, Louisiana State, S
1964	Matt Snell, Ohio State, RB
1965	Joe Namath, Alabama, QB
	Tom Nowatzke, Indiana, RB
1966	Bill Yearby, Michigan, DT
1967	Paul Seiler, Notre Dame, T
1968	Lee White, Weber State, RB
1969	Dave Foley, Ohio State, T
1970	Steve Tannen, Florida, CB
1971	John Riggins, Kansas, RB
1972	Jerome Barkum, Jackson State, WR
	Mike Taylor, Michigan, LB
1973	Burgess Owens, Miami, DB
1974	Carl Barzilauskas, Indiana, DT
1975	Anthony Davis, Southern California, RB (2)
1976	Richard Todd, Alabama, QB
1977	Marvin Powell, Southern California, T
1978	Chris Ward, Ohio State, T
1979	Marty Lyons, Alabama, DE
1980	Johnny (Lam) Jones, Texas, WR
1981	Freeman McNeil, UCLA, RB
1982	Bob Crable, Notre Dame, LB
1983	Ken O'Brien, Cal-Davis, QB
1984	Russell Carter, Southern Methodist, DB
	Ron Faurot, Arkansas, DE
1985	Al Toon, Wisconsin, WR
1986	Mike Haight, Iowa, T
1987	Roger Vick, Texas A&M, RB
1988	Dave Cadigan, Southern California, T
1989	Jeff Lageman, Virginia, LB
1990	Blair Thomas, Penn State, RB
1991	Browning Nagle, Louisville, QB (2)
1992	Johnny Mitchell, Nebraska, TE
1993	Marvin Jones, Florida State, LB

Philadelphia Eagles

Year	Player, College, Position
1936	Jay Berwanger, Chicago, B
1937	Sam Francis, Nebraska, B
1938	Jim McDonald, Ohio State, B
1939	Davey O'Brien, Texas Christian, B
1940	George McAfee, Duke, B
1941	Art Jones, Richmond, B (2)
1942	Pete Kmetovic, Stanford, B
1943	Joe Muha, Virginia Military, B
1944	Steve Van Buren, Louisiana State, B
1945	John Yonaker, Notre Dame, E
1946	Leo Riggs, Southern California, B
1947	Neill Armstrong, Oklahoma A&M, E
1948	Clyde (Smackover) Scott, Arkansas, B
1949	Chuck Bednarik, Pennsylvania, C
	Frank Tripucka, Notre Dame, B
1950	Harry (Bud) Grant, Minnesota, E
1951	Ebert Van Buren, Louisiana State, B
	Chet Mutryn, Xavier, B
1952	Johnny Bright, Drake, B
1953	Al Conway, Army, B (2)
1954	Neil Worden, Notre Dame, B
1955	Dick Bielski, Maryland, B
1956	Bob Pellegrini, Maryland, C
1957	Clarence Peaks, Michigan State, B
1958	Walt Kowalczyk, Michigan State, B
1959	J.D. Smith, Rice, T (2)
1960	Ron Burton, Northwestern, RB
1961	Art Baker, Syracuse, RB
1962	Pete Case, Georgia, G (2)
1963	Ed Budde, Michigan State, G
1964	Bob Brown, Nebraska, T
1965	Ray Rissmiller, Georgia, T (2)
1966	Randy Beisler, Indiana, DE
1967	Harry Jones, Arkansas, RB
1968	Tim Rossovich, Southern California, DE
1969	Leroy Keyes, Purdue, RB
1970	Steve Zabel, Oklahoma, TE
1971	Richard Harris, Grambling, DE
1972	John Reaves, Florida, QB
1973	Jerry Sisemore, Texas, T
	Charle Young, Southern California, TE
1974	Mitch Sutton, Kansas, DT (3)
1975	Bill Capraun, Miami, T (7)
1976	Mike Smith, Florida, DE (4)
1977	Skip Sharp, Kansas, DB (5)
1978	Reggie Wilkes, Georgia Tech, LB (3)
1979	Jerry Robinson, UCLA, LB
1980	Roynell Young, Alcorn State, DB
1981	Leonard Mitchell, Houston, DE
1982	Mike Quick, North Carolina State, WR
1983	Michael Haddix, Mississippi State, RB
1984	Kenny Jackson, Penn State, WR
1985	Kevin Allen, Indiana, T
1986	Keith Byars, Ohio State, RB
1987	Jerome Brown, Miami, DT
1988	Keith Jackson, Oklahoma, TE
1989	Jessie Small, Eastern Kentucky, LB (2)
1990	Ben Smith, Georgia, DB

1991 Antone Davis, Tennessee, T
1992 Siran Stacy, Alabama, RB (2)
1993 Lester Holmes, Jackson State, T
Leonard Renfro, Colorado, DT

Phoenix Cardinals

Year	Player, College, Position
1936	Jim Lawrence, Texas Christian, B
1937	Ray Buivid, Marquette, B
1938	Jack Robbins, Arkansas, B
1939	Charles (Ki) Aldrich, Texas Christian, C
1940	George Cafego, Tennessee, B
1941	John Kimbrough, Texas A&M, B
1942	Steve Lach, Duke, B
1943	Glenn Dobbs, Tulsa, B
1944	Pat Harder, Wisconsin, B
1945	Charley Trippi, Georgia, B
1946	Dub Jones, Louisiana State, B
1947	DeWitt (Tex) Coulter, Army, T
1948	Jim Spavital, Oklahoma A&M, B
1949	Bill Fischer, Notre Dame, G
1950	Jack Jennings, Ohio State, T (2)
1951	Jerry Groom, Notre Dame, C
1952	Ollie Matson, San Francisco, B
1953	Johnny Olszewski, California, B
1954	Lamar McHan, Arkansas, B
1955	Max Boydston, Oklahoma, E
1956	Joe Childress, Auburn, B
1957	Jerry Tubbs, Oklahoma, C
1958	King Hill, Rice, B
	John David Crow, Texas A&M, B
1959	Bill Stacy, Mississippi State, B
1960	George Izo, Notre Dame, QB
1961	Ken Rice, Auburn, T
1962	Fate Echols, Northwestern, DT
	Irv Goode, Kentucky, C
1963	Jerry Stovall, Louisiana State, S
	Don Brumm, Purdue, DE
1964	Ken Kortas, Louisville, DT
1965	Joe Namath, Alabama, QB
1966	Carl McAdams, Oklahoma, LB
1967	Dave Williams, Washington, WR
1968	MacArthur Lane, Utah State, RB
1969	Roger Wehrli, Missouri, DB
1970	Larry Stegent, Texas A&M, RB
1971	Norm Thompson, Utah, CB
1972	Bobby Moore, Oregon, RB-WR
1973	Dave Butz, Purdue, DT
1974	J. V. Cain, Colorado, TE
1975	Tim Gray, Texas A&M, DB
1976	Mike Dawson, Arizona, DT
1977	Steve Pisarkiewicz, Missouri, QB
1978	Steve Little, Arkansas, K
	Ken Greene, Washington State, DB
1979	Ottis Anderson, Miami, RB
1980	Curtis Greer, Michigan, DE
1981	E. J. Junior, Alabama, LB
1982	Luis Sharpe, UCLA, T
1983	Leonard Smith, McNeese State, DB
1984	Clyde Duncan, Tennessee, WR
1985	Freddie Joe Nunn, Mississippi, LB
1986	Anthony Bell, Michigan State, LB
1987	Kelly Stouffer, Colorado State, QB
1988	Ken Harvey, California, LB
1989	Eric Hill, Louisiana State, LB
	Joe Wolf, Boston College, G
1990	Anthony Thompson, Indiana, RB (2)
1991	Eric Swann, No College, DE
1992	Tony Sacca, Penn State, QB (2)
1993	Garrison Hearst, Georgia, RB
	Ernest Dye, South Carolina, T

Pittsburgh Steelers

Year	Player, College, Position
1936	Bill Shakespeare, Notre Dame, B
1937	Mike Basrak, Duquesne, C
1938	Byron (Whizzer) White, Colorado, B
1939	Bill Patterson, Baylor, B (3)
1940	Kay Eakin, Arkansas, B
1941	Chet Gladchuk, Boston College, C (2)
1942	Bill Dudley, Virginia, B
1943	Bill Daley, Minnesota, B
1944	Johnny Podesto, St. Mary's, Calif., B
1945	Paul Duhart, Florida, B
1946	Felix (Doc) Blanchard, Army, B
1947	Hub Bechtol, Texas, E
1948	Dan Edwards, Georgia, E
1949	Bobby Gage, Clemson, B
1950	Lynn Chandnois, Michigan State, B
1951	Butch Avinger, Alabama, B
1952	Ed Modzelewski, Maryland, B
1953	Ted Marchibroda, St. Bonaventure, B
1954	Johnny Lattner, Notre Dame, B
1955	Frank Varrichione, Notre Dame, T
1956	Gary Glick, Colorado A&M, B
	Art Davis, Mississippi State, B
1957	Len Dawson, Purdue, B
1958	Larry Krutko, West Virginia, B (2)
1959	Tom Barnett, Purdue, B (8)
1960	Jack Spikes, Texas Christian, RB
1961	Myron Pottios, Notre Dame, LB (2)
1962	Bob Ferguson, Ohio State, RB
1963	Frank Atkinson, Stanford, T (8)
1964	Paul Martha, Pittsburgh, S
1965	Roy Jefferson, Utah, WR (2)
1966	Dick Leftridge, West Virginia, RB
1967	Don Shy, San Diego State, RB (2)
1968	Mike Taylor, Southern California, T
1969	Joe Greene, North Texas State, DT
1970	Terry Bradshaw, Louisiana Tech, QB
1971	Frank Lewis, Grambling, WR
1972	Franco Harris, Penn State, RB
1973	J. T. Thomas, Florida State, DB
1974	Lynn Swann, Southern California, WR
1975	Dave Brown, Michigan, DB
1976	Bennie Cunningham, Clemson, TE
1977	Robin Cole, New Mexico, LB
1978	Ron Johnson, Eastern Michigan, DB
1979	Greg Hawthorne, Baylor, RB
1980	Mark Malone, Arizona State, QB
1981	Keith Gary, Oklahoma, DE
1982	Walter Abercrombie, Baylor, RB
1983	Gabriel Rivera, Texas Tech, DT
1984	Louis Lipps, Southern Mississippi, WR
1985	Darryl Sims, Wisconsin, DE
1986	John Rienstra, Temple, G
1987	Rod Woodson, Purdue, DB
1988	Aaron Jones, Eastern Kentucky, DE
1989	Tim Worley, Georgia, RB
	Tom Ricketts, Pittsburgh, T
1990	Eric Green, Liberty, TE
1991	Huey Richardson, Florida, DE
1992	Leon Searcy, Miami, T
1993	Deon Figures, Colorado, DB

San Diego Chargers

Year	Player, College, Position
1960	Monty Stickles, Notre Dame, E
1961	Earl Faison, Indiana, DE
1962	Bob Ferguson, Ohio State, RB
1963	Walt Sweeney, Syracuse, G
1964	Ted Davis, Georgia Tech, LB
1965	Steve DeLong, Tennessee, DE
1966	Don Davis, Cal State-Los Angeles, DT
1967	Ron Billingsley, Wyoming, DE
1968	Russ Washington, Missouri, DT
	Jimmy Hill, Texas A&I, DB
1969	Marty Domres, Columbia, QB
	Bob Babich, Miami, Ohio, LB
1970	Walker Gillette, Richmond, WR
1971	Leon Burns, Long Beach State, RB
1972	Pete Lazetich, Stanford, DE (2)
1973	Johnny Rodgers, Nebraska, WR
1974	Bo Matthews, Colorado, RB
	Don Goode, Kansas, LB
1975	Gary Johnson, Grambling, DT
	Mike Williams, Louisiana State, DB
1976	Joe Washington, Oklahoma, RB
1977	Bob Rush, Memphis State, C
1978	John Jefferson, Arizona State, WR
1979	Kellen Winslow, Missouri, TE
1980	Ed Luther, San Jose State, QB (4)
1981	James Brooks, Auburn, RB
1982	Hollis Hall, Clemson, DB (7)
1983	Billy Ray Smith, Arkansas, LB
	Gary Anderson, Arkansas, WR
	Gill Byrd, San Jose State, DB
1984	Mossy Cade, Texas, DB
1985	Jim Lachey, Ohio State, G
1986	Leslie O'Neal, Oklahoma State, DE
	James FitzPatrick, Southern California, T
1987	Rod Bernstine, Texas A&M, TE
1988	Anthony Miller, Tennessee, WR
1989	Burt Grossman, Pittsburgh, DE
1990	Junior Seau, Southern California, LB
1991	Stanley Richard, Texas, DB
1992	Chris Mims, Tennessee, DE
1993	Darrien Gordon, Stanford, DB

San Francisco 49ers

Year	Player, College, Position
1950	Leo Nomellini, Minnesota, T
1951	Y.A. Tittle, Louisiana State, B
1952	Hugh McElhenny, Washington, B
1953	Harry Babcock, Georgia, E
	Tom Stolhandske, Texas, E
1954	Bernie Faloney, Maryland, B
1955	Dickie Moegle, Rice, B
1956	Earl Morrall, Michigan State, B
1957	John Brodie, Stanford, B
1958	Jim Pace, Michigan, B
	Charlie Krueger, Texas A&M, T
1959	Dave Baker, Oklahoma, B
	Dan James, Ohio State, C
1960	Monty Stickles, Notre Dame, E
1961	Jimmy Johnson, UCLA, CB
	Bernie Casey, Bowling Green, WR
	Bill Kilmer, UCLA, QB
1962	Lance Alworth, Arkansas, WR
1963	Kermit Alexander, UCLA, CB
1964	Dave Parks, Texas Tech, WR
1965	Ken Willard, North Carolina, RB
	George Donnelly, Illinois, DB
1966	Stan Hindman, Mississippi, DE
1967	Steve Spurrier, Florida, QB
	Cas Banaszek, Northwestern, T
1968	Forrest Blue, Auburn, C
1969	Ted Kwalick, Penn State, TE
	Gene Washington, Stanford, WR
1970	Cedrick Hardman, North Texas State, DE
	Bruce Taylor, Boston U., DB
1971	Tim Anderson, Ohio State, DB
1972	Terry Beasley, Auburn, WR
1973	Mike Holmes, Texas Southern, DB
1974	Wilbur Jackson, Alabama, RB
	Bill Sandifer, UCLA, DT
1975	Jimmy Webb, Mississippi State, DT
1976	Randy Cross, UCLA, C (2)
1977	Elmo Boyd, Eastern Kentucky, WR (3)
1978	Ken MacAfee, Notre Dame, TE
	Dan Bunz, Cal State-Long Beach, LB
1979	James Owens, UCLA, WR (2)
1980	Earl Cooper, Rice, RB
	Jim Stuckey, Clemson, DT
1981	Ronnie Lott, Southern California, DB
1982	Bubba Paris, Michigan, T (2)
1983	Roger Craig, Nebraska, RB (2)
1984	Todd Shell, Brigham Young, LB
1985	Jerry Rice, Mississippi Valley State, WR
1986	Larry Roberts, Alabama, DE (2)
1987	Harris Barton, North Carolina, T
	Terrence Flagler, Clemson, RB
1988	Danny Stubbs, Miami, DE (2)
1989	Keith DeLong, Tennessee, LB
1990	Dexter Carter, Florida State, RB
1991	Ted Washington, Louisville, DT
1992	Dana Hall, Washington, DB
1993	Dana Stubblefield, Kansas, DT
	Todd Kelly, Tennessee, DE

Seattle Seahawks

Year	Player, College, Position
1976	Steve Niehaus, Notre Dame, DT
1977	Steve August, Tulsa, G
1978	Keith Simpson, Memphis State, DB
1979	Manu Tuiasosopo, UCLA, DT
1980	Jacob Green, Texas A&M, DE
1981	Ken Easley, UCLA, DB
1982	Jeff Bryant, Clemson, DE
1983	Curt Warner, Penn State, RB
1984	Terry Taylor, Southern Illinois, DB
1985	Owen Gill, Iowa, RB (2)
1986	John L. Williams, Florida, RB
1987	Tony Woods, Pittsburgh, LB
1988	Brian Blades, Miami, WR (2)
1989	Andy Heck, Notre Dame, T
1990	Cortez Kennedy, Miami, DT
1991	Dan McGwire, San Diego State, QB
1992	Ray Roberts, Virginia, T
1993	Rick Mirer, Notre Dame, QB

Tampa Bay Buccaneers

Year	Player, College, Position
1976	Lee Roy Selmon, Oklahoma, DT
1977	Ricky Bell, Southern California, RB
1978	Doug Williams, Grambling, QB
1979	Greg Roberts, Oklahoma, G (2)
1980	Ray Snell, Wisconsin, G
1981	Hugh Green, Pittsburgh, LB
1982	Sean Farrell, Penn State, G
1983	Randy Grimes, Baylor, C (2)
1984	Keith Browner, Southern California, LB (2)
1985	Ron Holmes, Washington, DE
1986	Bo Jackson, Auburn, RB
	Roderick Jones, Southern Methodist, DB
1987	Vinny Testaverde, Miami, QB
1988	Paul Gruber, Wisconsin, T
1989	Broderick Thomas, Nebraska, LB
1990	Keith McCants, Alabama, LB
1991	Charles McRae, Tennessee, T
1992	Courtney Hawkins, Michigan State, WR (2)
1993	Eric Curry, Alabama, DE

Washington Redskins

Year	Player, College, Position
1936	Riley Smith, Alabama, B
1937	Sammy Baugh, Texas Christian, B
1938	Andy Farkas, Detroit, B
1939	I.B. Hale, Texas Christian, T
1940	Ed Boell, New York U., B
1941	Forest Evashevski, Michigan, B
1942	Orban (Spec) Sanders, Texas, B
1943	Jack Jenkins, Missouri, B
1944	Mike Micka, Colgate, B
1945	Jim Hardy, Southern California, B
1946	Cal Rossi, UCLA, B*
1947	Cal Rossi, UCLA, B
1948	Harry Gilmer, Alabama, B
	Lowell Tew, Alabama, B
1949	Rob Goode, Texas A&M, B
1950	George Thomas, Oklahoma, B
1951	Leon Heath, Oklahoma, B
1952	Larry Isbell, Baylor, B
1953	Jack Scarbath, Maryland, B
1954	Steve Meilinger, Kentucky, E
1955	Ralph Guglielmi, Notre Dame, B
1956	Ed Vereb, Maryland, B
1957	Don Bosseler, Miami, B
1958	Mike Sommer, George Washington, B (2)
1959	Don Allard, Boston College, B
1960	Richie Lucas, Penn State, QB
1961	Norman Snead, Wake Forest, QB
	Joe Rutgens, Illinois, DT
1962	Ernie Davis, Syracuse, RB
1963	Pat Richter, Wisconsin, TE
1964	Charley Taylor, Arizona State, RB-WR
1965	Bob Breitenstein, Tulsa, T (2)
1966	Charlie Gogolak, Princeton, K
1967	Ray McDonald, Idaho, RB
1968	Jim Smith, Oregon, DB
1969	Eugene Epps, Texas-El Paso, DB (2)
1970	Bill Brundige, Colorado, DT (2)
1971	Cotton Speyrer, Texas, WR (2)
1972	Moses Denson, Maryland State, RB (8)
1973	Charles Cantrell, Lamar, G (5)
1974	Jon Keyworth, Colorado, TE (6)
1975	Mike Thomas, Nevada-Las Vegas, RB (6)
1976	Mike Hughes, Baylor, G (5)
1977	Duncan McColl, Stanford, DE (4)
1978	Tony Green, Florida, RB (6)
1979	Don Warren, San Diego State, TE (4)
1980	Art Monk, Syracuse, WR
1981	Mark May, Pittsburgh, T
1982	Vernon Dean, San Diego State, DB (2)
1983	Darrell Green, Texas A&I, DB
1984	Bob Slater, Oklahoma, DT (2)
1985	Tory Nixon, San Diego State, DB (2)
1986	Markus Koch, Boise State, DE (2)
1987	Brian Davis, Nebraska, DB (2)
1988	Chip Lohmiller, Minnesota, K (2)
1989	Tracy Rocker, Auburn, DT (3)
1990	Andre Collins, Penn State, LB (2)
1991	Bobby Wilson, Michigan State, DT
1992	Desmond Howard, Michigan, WR
1993	Tom Carter, Notre Dame, DB

**Choice lost due to ineligibility.*

RECORDS

ALL-TIME RECORDS

Compiled by Elias Sports Bureau

The following records reflect all available official information on the National Football League from its formation in 1920 to date. Also included are all applicable records from the American Football League, 1960-69.

Individual Records

Service

Most Seasons

26 George Blanda, Chi. Bears, 1949, 1950-58; Baltimore, 1950; Houston, 1960-66; Oakland, 1967-75
21 Earl Morrall, San Francisco, 1956; Pittsburgh, 1957-58; Detroit, 1958-64; N.Y. Giants, 1965-67; Baltimore, 1968-71; Miami, 1972-76
20 Jim Marshall, Cleveland, 1960; Minnesota, 1961-79

Most Seasons, One Club

19 Jim Marshall, Minnesota, 1961-79
18 Jim Hart, St. Louis, 1966-83
Jeff Van Note, Atlanta, 1969-86
Pat Leahy, N.Y. Jets, 1974-91
17 Lou Groza, Cleveland, 1950-59, 1961-67
Johnny Unitas, Baltimore, 1956-72
John Brodie, San Francisco, 1957-73
Jim Bakken, St. Louis, 1962-78
Mick Tingelhoff, Minnesota, 1962-78

Most Games Played, Career

340 George Blanda, Chi. Bears, 1949, 1950-58; Baltimore, 1950; Houston, 1960-66; Oakland, 1967-75
282 Jim Marshall, Cleveland, 1960; Minnesota, 1961-79
263 Jan Stenerud, Kansas City, 1967-79; Green Bay, 1980-83; Minnesota, 1984-85

Most Consecutive Games Played, Career

282 Jim Marshall, Cleveland, 1960; Minnesota, 1961-79
240 Mick Tingelhoff, Minnesota, 1962-78
234 Jim Bakken, St. Louis, 1962-78

Head Coach

Most Seasons, Head Coach

40 George Halas, Chi. Bears, 1920-29, 1933-42, 1946-55, 1958-67
33 Earl (Curly) Lambeau, Green Bay, 1921-49; Chi. Cardinals, 1950-51; Washington, 1952-53
30 Don Shula, Baltimore, 1963-69; Miami, 1970-92

Most Games Won, Head Coach

318 George Halas, Chi. Bears, 1920-29, 1933-42, 1946-55, 1958-67
300 Don Shula, Baltimore, 1963-69; Miami, 1970-92
250 Tom Landry, Dallas, 1960-88

Most Games Lost, Head Coach

162 Tom Landry, Dallas, 1960-88
148 George Halas, Chi. Bears, 1920-29, 1933-42, 1946-55, 1958-67
Chuck Noll, Pittsburgh, 1969-91
136 Don Shula, Baltimore, 1963-69; Miami, 1970-92

Scoring

Most Seasons Leading League

5 Don Hutson, Green Bay, 1940-44
Gino Cappelletti, Boston, 1961, 1963-66
3 Earl (Dutch) Clark, Portsmouth, 1932; Detroit, 1935-36
Pat Harder, Chi. Cardinals, 1947-49
Paul Hornung, Green Bay, 1959-61
2 Jack Manders, Chi. Bears, 1934, 1937
Gordy Soltau, San Francisco, 1952-53
Doak Walker, Detroit, 1950, 1955
Gene Mingo, Denver, 1960, 1962
Jim Turner, N.Y. Jets, 1968-69
Fred Cox, Minnesota, 1969-70
Chester Marcol, Green Bay, 1972, 1974
John Smith, New England, 1979-80

Most Consecutive Seasons Leading League

5 Don Hutson, Green Bay, 1940-44
4 Gino Cappelletti, Boston, 1963-66
3 Pat Harder, Chi. Cardinals, 1947-49
Paul Hornung, Green Bay, 1959-61

Points

Most Points, Career

2,002 George Blanda, Chi. Bears, 1949, 1950-58; Baltimore, 1950; Houston, 1960-66; Oakland, 1967-75 (9-td, 943-pat, 335-fg)
1,699 Jan Stenerud, Kansas City, 1967-79; Green Bay, 1980-83; Minnesota, 1984-85 (580-pat, 373-fg)
1,470 Pat Leahy, N.Y. Jets, 1974-91 (558-pat, 304-fg)

Most Points, Season

176 Paul Hornung, Green Bay, 1960 (15-td, 41-pat, 15-fg)
161 Mark Moseley, Washington, 1983 (62-pat, 33-fg)
155 Gino Cappelletti, Boston, 1964 (7-td, 38-pat, 25-fg)

Most Points, No Touchdowns, Season

161 Mark Moseley, Washington, 1983 (62-pat, 33-fg)
149 Chip Lohmiller, Washington, 1991 (56-pat, 31-fg)
145 Jim Turner, N.Y. Jets, 1968 (43-pat, 34-fg)

Most Seasons, 100 or More Points

10 Nick Lowery, Kansas City, 1981, 1983-86, 1988-92
7 Jan Stenerud, Kansas City, 1967-71; Green Bay, 1981, 1983
Morten Andersen, New Orleans, 1985-89, 1991-92
6 Gino Cappelletti, Boston, 1961-66
George Blanda, Houston, 1960-61; Oakland, 1967-69, 1973
Bruce Gossett, Los Angeles, 1966-67, 1969; San Francisco, 1970-71, 1973
Pat Leahy, N.Y. Jets, 1978, 1981, 1985, 1988, 1990-91
Gary Anderson, Pittsburgh, 1983-85, 1988, 1991-92

Most Points, Rookie, Season

144 Kevin Butler, Chicago, 1985 (51-pat, 31-fg)
132 Gale Sayers, Chicago, 1965 (22-td)
128 Doak Walker, Detroit, 1950 (11-td, 38-pat, 8-fg)
Cookie Gilchrist, Buffalo, 1962 (15-td, 14-pat, 8-fg)
Chester Marcol, Green Bay, 1972 (29-pat, 33-fg)

Most Points, Game

40 Ernie Nevers, Chi. Cardinals vs. Chi. Bears, Nov. 28, 1929 (6-td, 4-pat)
36 Dub Jones, Cleveland vs. Chi. Bears, Nov. 25, 1951 (6-td)
Gale Sayers, Chicago vs. San Francisco, Dec. 12, 1965 (6-td)
33 Paul Hornung, Green Bay vs. Baltimore, Oct. 8, 1961 (4-td, 6-pat, 1-fg)

Most Consecutive Games Scoring

186 Jim Breech, Oakland, 1979; Cincinnati, 1980-92
151 Fred Cox, Minnesota, 1963-73
133 Garo Yepremian, Miami, 1970-78; New Orleans, 1979

Touchdowns

Most Seasons Leading League

8 Don Hutson, Green Bay, 1935-38, 1941-44
3 Jim Brown, Cleveland, 1958-59, 1963
Lance Alworth, San Diego, 1964-66
2 By many players

Most Consecutive Seasons Leading League

4 Don Hutson, Green Bay, 1935-38, 1941-44
3 Lance Alworth, San Diego, 1964-66
2 By many players

Most Touchdowns, Career

126 Jim Brown, Cleveland, 1957-65 (106-r, 20-p)
125 Walter Payton, Chicago, 1975-87 (110-r, 15-p)
116 John Riggins, N.Y. Jets, 1971-75; Washington, 1976-79, 1981-85 (104-r, 12-p)

Most Touchdowns, Season

24 John Riggins, Washington, 1983 (24-r)
23 O.J. Simpson, Buffalo, 1975 (16-r, 7-p)
Jerry Rice, San Francisco, 1987 (1-r, 22-p)
22 Gale Sayers, Chicago, 1965 (14-r, 6-p, 2-ret)
Chuck Foreman, Minnesota, 1975 (13-r, 9-p)

Most Touchdowns, Rookie, Season

22 Gale Sayers, Chicago, 1965 (14-r, 6-p, 2-ret)
20 Eric Dickerson, L.A. Rams, 1983 (18-r, 2-p)
16 Billy Sims, Detroit, 1980 (13-r, 3-p)

Most Touchdowns, Game

6 Ernie Nevers, Chi. Cardinals vs. Chi. Bears, Nov. 28, 1929 (6-r)
Dub Jones, Cleveland vs. Chi. Bears, Nov. 25, 1951 (4-r, 2-p)
Gale Sayers, Chicago vs. San Francisco, Dec. 12, 1965 (4-r, 1-p, 1-ret)
5 Bob Shaw, Chi. Cardinals vs. Baltimore, Oct. 2, 1950 (5-p)
Jim Brown, Cleveland vs. Baltimore, Nov. 1, 1959 (5-r)
Abner Haynes, Dall. Texans vs. Oakland, Nov. 26, 1961 (4-r, 1-p)
Billy Cannon, Houston vs. N.Y. Titans, Dec. 10, 1961 (3-r, 2-p)
Cookie Gilchrist, Buffalo vs. N.Y. Jets, Dec. 8, 1963 (5-r)
Paul Hornung, Green Bay vs. Baltimore, Dec. 12, 1965 (3-r, 2-p)
Kellen Winslow, San Diego vs. Oakland, Nov. 22, 1981 (5-p)
Jerry Rice, San Francisco vs. Atlanta, Oct. 14, 1990 (5-p)
4 By many players. Last time: Eric Metcalf, Cleveland vs. L.A. Raiders, Sept. 20, 1992 (1-r, 3-p)

Most Consecutive Games Scoring Touchdowns

18 Lenny Moore, Baltimore, 1963-65
14 O.J. Simpson, Buffalo, 1975
13 John Riggins, Washington, 1982-83
George Rogers, Washington, 1985-86
Jerry Rice, San Francisco, 1986-87

Points After Touchdown

Most Seasons Leading League

8 George Blanda, Chi. Bears, 1956; Houston, 1961-62; Oakland, 1967-69, 1972, 1974
4 Bob Waterfield, Cleveland, 1945; Los Angeles, 1946, 1950, 1952
3 Earl (Dutch) Clark, Portsmouth, 1932; Detroit, 1935-36
Jack Manders, Chi. Bears, 1933-35
Don Hutson, Green Bay, 1941-42, 1945

Most Points After Touchdown Attempted, Career

959 George Blanda, Chi. Bears, 1949, 1950-58; Baltimore, 1950; Houston, 1960-66; Oakland, 1967-75
657 Lou Groza, Cleveland, 1950-59, 1961-67
601 Jan Stenerud, Kansas City, 1967-79; Green Bay, 1980-83; Minnesota, 1984-85

Most Points After Touchdown Attempted, Season

70 Uwe von Schamann, Miami, 1984
65 George Blanda, Houston, 1961
63 Mark Moseley, Washington, 1983

Most Points After Touchdown Attempted, Game

10 Charlie Gogolak, Washington vs. N.Y. Giants, Nov. 27, 1966
9 Pat Harder, Chi. Cardinals vs. N.Y. Giants, Oct. 17, 1948; vs. N.Y. Bulldogs, Nov. 13, 1949
Bob Waterfield, Los Angeles vs. Baltimore, Oct. 22, 1950
Bob Thomas, Chicago vs. Green Bay, Dec. 7, 1980
8 By many players

Most Points After Touchdown, Career

943 George Blanda, Chi. Bears, 1949, 1950-58; Baltimore, 1950; Houston, 1960-66; Oakland, 1967-75
641 Lou Groza, Cleveland, 1950-59, 1961-67
580 Jan Stenerud, Kansas City, 1967-79; Green Bay, 1980-83; Minnesota, 1984-85

Most Points After Touchdown, Season

66 Uwe von Schamann, Miami, 1984
64 George Blanda, Houston, 1961
62 Mark Moseley, Washington, 1983

Most Points After Touchdown, Game

9 Pat Harder, Chi. Cardinals vs. N.Y. Giants, Oct. 17, 1948
Bob Waterfield, Los Angeles vs. Baltimore, Oct. 22, 1950
Charlie Gogolak, Washington vs. N.Y. Giants, Nov. 27, 1966
8 By many players

Most Consecutive Points After Touchdown
234 Tommy Davis, San Francisco, 1959-65
221 Jim Turner, N.Y. Jets, 1967-70; Denver, 1971-74
202 Gary Anderson, Pittsburgh, 1983-88
Highest Points After Touchdown Percentage, Career (200 points after touchdown)
99.52 Chip Lohmiller, Washington, 1988-92 (209-208)
99.43 Tommy Davis, San Francisco, 1959-69 (350-348)
99.12 Nick Lowery, New England, 1978; Kansas City, 1980-92 (453-449)
Most Points After Touchdown, No Misses, Season
56 Danny Villanueva, Dallas, 1966
Ray Wersching, San Francisco, 1984
Chip Lohmiller, Washington, 1991
54 Mike Clark, Dallas, 1968
George Blanda, Oakland, 1968
53 Pat Harder, Chi. Cardinals, 1948
Most Points After Touchdown, No Misses, Game
9 Pat Harder, Chi. Cardinals vs. N.Y. Giants, Oct. 17, 1948
Bob Waterfield, Los Angeles vs. Baltimore, Oct. 22, 1950
8 By many players

Field Goals

Most Seasons Leading League
5 Lou Groza, Cleveland, 1950, 1952-54, 1957
4 Jack Manders, Chi. Bears, 1933-34, 1936-37
Ward Cuff, N.Y. Giants, 1938-39, 1943; Green Bay, 1947
Mark Moseley, Washington, 1976-77, 1979, 1982
3 Bob Waterfield, Los Angeles, 1947, 1949, 1951
Gino Cappelletti, Boston, 1961, 1963-64
Fred Cox, Minnesota, 1965, 1969-70
Jan Stenerud, Kansas City, 1967, 1970, 1975
Most Consecutive Seasons Leading League
3 Lou Groza, Cleveland, 1952-54
2 Jack Manders, Chi. Bears, 1933-34
Armand Niccolai, Pittsburgh, 1935-36
Jack Manders, Chi. Bears, 1936-37
Ward Cuff, N.Y. Giants, 1938-39
Clark Hinkle, Green Bay, 1940-41
Cliff Patton, Philadelphia, 1948-49
Gino Cappelletti, Boston, 1963-64
Jim Turner, N.Y. Jets, 1968-69
Fred Cox, Minnesota, 1969-70
Mark Moseley, Washington, 1976-77
Chip Lohmiller, Washington, 1991-92
Pete Stoyanovich, Miami, 1991-92
Most Field Goals Attempted, Career
638 George Blanda, Chi. Bears, 1949, 1950-58; Baltimore, 1950; Houston, 1960-66; Oakland, 1967-75
558 Jan Stenerud, Kansas City, 1967-79; Green Bay, 1980-83; Minnesota, 1984-85
488 Jim Turner, N.Y. Jets, 1964-70; Denver, 1971-79
Most Field Goals Attempted, Season
49 Bruce Gossett, Los Angeles, 1966
Curt Knight, Washington, 1971
48 Chester Marcol, Green Bay, 1972
47 Jim Turner, N.Y. Jets, 1969
David Ray, Los Angeles, 1973
Mark Moseley, Washington, 1983
Most Field Goals Attempted, Game
9 Jim Bakken, St. Louis vs. Pittsburgh, Sept. 24, 1967
8 Lou Michaels, Pittsburgh vs. St. Louis, Dec. 2, 1962
Garo Yepremian, Detroit vs. Minnesota, Nov. 13, 1966
Jim Turner, N.Y. Jets vs. Buffalo, Nov. 3, 1968
7 By many players
Most Field Goals, Career
373 Jan Stenerud, Kansas City, 1967-79; Green Bay, 1980-83; Minnesota, 1984-85
335 George Blanda, Chi. Bears, 1949, 1950-58; Baltimore, 1950; Houston, 1960-66; Oakland, 1967-75
306 Nick Lowery, New England, 1978; Kansas City, 1980-92
Most Field Goals, Season
35 Ali Haji-Sheikh, N.Y. Giants, 1983
34 Jim Turner, N.Y. Jets, 1968
Nick Lowery, Kansas City, 1990
33 Chester Marcol, Green Bay, 1972
Mark Moseley, Washington, 1983
Gary Anderson, Pittsburgh, 1985
Most Field Goals, Rookie, Season
35 Ali Haji-Sheikh, N.Y. Giants, 1983
33 Chester Marcol, Green Bay, 1972
31 Kevin Butler, Chicago, 1985
Most Field Goals, Game
7 Jim Bakken, St. Louis vs. Pittsburgh, Sept. 24, 1967
Rich Karlis, Minnesota vs. L.A. Rams, Nov. 5, 1989 (OT)
6 Gino Cappelletti, Boston vs. Denver, Oct. 4, 1964
Garo Yepremian, Detroit vs. Minnesota, Nov. 13, 1966
Jim Turner, N.Y. Jets vs. Buffalo, Nov. 3, 1968
Tom Dempsey, Philadelphia vs. Houston, Nov. 12, 1972
Bobby Howfield, N.Y. Jets vs. New Orleans, Dec. 3, 1972
Jim Bakken, St. Louis vs. Atlanta, Dec. 9, 1973
Joe Danelo, N.Y. Giants vs. Seattle, Oct. 18, 1981
Ray Wersching, San Francisco vs. New Orleans, Oct. 16, 1983
Gary Anderson, Pittsburgh vs. Denver, Oct. 23, 1988
5 By many players
Most Field Goals, One Quarter
4 Garo Yepremian, Detroit vs. Minnesota, Nov. 13, 1966 (second quarter)
Curt Knight, Washington vs. N.Y. Giants, Nov. 15, 1970 (second quarter)
Roger Ruzek, Dallas vs. N.Y. Giants, Nov. 2, 1987 (fourth quarter)
3 By many players
Most Consecutive Games Scoring Field Goals
31 Fred Cox, Minnesota, 1968-70
28 Jim Turner, N.Y. Jets, 1970; Denver, 1971-72
Chip Lohmiller, Washington, 1988-90
23 Morten Andersen, New Orleans, 1986-88
Most Consecutive Field Goals
24 Kevin Butler, Chicago, 1988-89
23 Mark Moseley, Washington, 1981-82
Tony Zendejas, Houston, 1990; L.A. Rams, 1991
22 Pat Leahy, N.Y. Jets, 1985-86
Longest Field Goal
63 Tom Dempsey, New Orleans vs. Detroit, Nov. 8, 1970
60 Steve Cox, Cleveland vs. Cincinnati, Oct. 21, 1984
Morten Andersen, New Orleans vs. Chicago, Oct. 27, 1991
59 Tony Franklin, Philadelphia vs. Dallas, Nov. 12, 1979
Pete Stoyanovich, Miami vs. N.Y. Jets, Nov. 12, 1989
Highest Field Goal Percentage, Career (100 field goals)
80.80 Pete Stoyanovich, Miami, 1989-92 (125-101)
80.10 Nick Lowery, New England, 1978; Kansas City, 1980-92 (382-306)
78.10 Morten Andersen, New Orleans, 1982-92 (315-246)
Highest Field Goal Percentage, Season (Qualifiers)
100.00 Tony Zendejas, L.A. Rams, 1991 (17-17)
95.24 Mark Moseley, Washington, 1982 (21-20)
Eddie Murray, Detroit, 1988 (21-20)
Eddie Murray, Detroit, 1989 (21-20)
91.89 Nick Lowery, Kansas City, 1990 (37-34)
Most Field Goals, No Misses, Game
7 Rich Karlis, Minnesota vs. L.A. Rams, Nov. 5, 1989 (OT)
6 Gino Cappelletti, Boston vs. Denver, Oct. 4, 1964
Joe Danelo, N.Y. Giants vs. Seattle, Oct. 18, 1981
Ray Wersching, San Francisco vs. New Orleans, Oct. 16, 1983
Gary Anderson, Pittsburgh vs. Denver, Oct. 23, 1988
5 By many players
Most Field Goals, 50 or More Yards, Career
21 Morten Andersen, New Orleans, 1982-92
19 Nick Lowery, New England, 1978; Kansas City, 1980-92
17 Jan Stenerud, Kansas City, 1967-79; Green Bay, 1980-83; Minnesota, 1984-85
Eddie Murray, Detroit, 1980-91; Kansas City, 1992; Tampa Bay, 1992
Most Field Goals, 50 or More Yards, Season
6 Dean Biasucci, Indianapolis, 1988
5 Fred Steinfort, Denver, 1980
Norm Johnson, Seattle, 1986
4 Horst Muhlmann, Cincinnati, 1970
Mark Moseley, Washington, 1977
Nick Lowery, Kansas City, 1980
Raul Allegre, Baltimore, 1983
Kevin Butler, Chicago, 1990
Ken Willis, Dallas, 1991
Norm Johnson, Atlanta, 1992
Most Field Goals, 50 or More Yards, Game
2 Jim Martin, Detroit vs. Baltimore, Oct. 23, 1960
Tom Dempsey, New Orleans vs. Los Angeles, Dec. 6, 1970
Chris Bahr, Cincinnati vs. Houston, Sept. 23, 1979
Nick Lowery, Kansas City vs. Seattle, Sept. 14, 1980
Mark Moseley, Washington vs. New Orleans, Oct. 26, 1980
Fred Steinfort, Denver vs. Seattle, Dec. 21, 1980
Mick Luckhurst, Atlanta vs. Denver, Dec. 5, 1982
Morten Andersen, New Orleans vs. Philadelphia, Dec. 11, 1983
Mick Luckhurst, Atlanta vs. L.A. Rams, Oct. 7, 1984
Paul McFadden, Philadelphia vs. Detroit, Nov. 4, 1984
Nick Lowery, Kansas City vs. New Orleans, Sept. 8, 1985
Pat Leahy, N.Y. Jets vs. New England, Oct. 20, 1985
Tony Zendejas, Houston vs. San Diego, Nov. 24, 1985
Norm Johnson, Seattle vs. L.A. Raiders, Dec. 8, 1986
Raul Allegre, N.Y. Giants vs. Philadelphia, Nov. 15, 1987
Nick Lowery, Kansas City vs. Detroit, Nov. 26, 1987
Dean Biasucci, Indianapolis vs. Miami, Sept. 25, 1988
Paul McFadden, Atlanta vs. Buffalo, Nov. 5, 1989
Kevin Butler, Chicago vs. Minnesota, Sept. 23, 1990
Kevin Butler, Chicago vs. Green Bay, Oct. 7, 1990
Chip Lohmiller, Washington vs. Indianapolis, Dec. 22, 1990
Chip Lohmiller, Washington vs. Dallas, Sept. 9, 1991
John Kasay, Seattle vs. San Diego, October 27, 1991
Fuad Reveiz, Minnesota vs. Tampa Bay, Dec. 8, 1991

Safeties

Most Safeties, Career
4 Ted Hendricks, Baltimore, 1969-73; Green Bay, 1974; Oakland, 1975-81; L.A. Raiders, 1982-83
Doug English, Detroit, 1975-79, 1981-85
3 Bill McPeak, Pittsburgh, 1949-57
Charlie Krueger, San Francisco, 1959-73
Ernie Stautner, Pittsburgh, 1950-63
Jim Katcavage, N.Y. Giants, 1956-68
Roger Brown, Detroit, 1960-66; Los Angeles, 1967-69
Bruce Maher, Detroit, 1960-67; N.Y. Giants, 1968-69
Ron McDole, St. Louis, 1961; Houston, 1962; Buffalo, 1963-70; Washington, 1971-78
Alan Page, Minnesota, 1967-78; Chicago, 1979-81
Lyle Alzado, Denver, 1971-78; Cleveland, 1979-81; L.A. Raiders, 1982-85
Rulon Jones, Denver, 1980-88
Steve McMichael, New England, 1980; Chicago 1981-92
Kevin Greene, L.A. Rams, 1985-92
Burt Grossman, San Diego, 1989-92
2 By many players
Most Safeties, Season
2 Tom Nash, Green Bay, 1932
Roger Brown, Detroit, 1962
Ron McDole, Buffalo, 1964
Alan Page, Minnesota, 1971
Fred Dryer, Los Angeles, 1973
Benny Barnes, Dallas, 1973
James Young, Houston, 1977
Tom Hannon, Minnesota, 1981
Doug English, Detroit, 1983
Don Blackmon, New England, 1985
Tim Harris, Green Bay, 1988

Brian Jordan, Atlanta, 1991
Burt Grossman, San Diego, 1992

Most Safeties, Game
2 Fred Dryer, Los Angeles vs. Green Bay, Oct. 21, 1973

Rushing

Most Seasons Leading League
8 Jim Brown, Cleveland, 1957-61, 1963-65
4 Steve Van Buren, Philadelphia, 1945, 1947-49
O.J. Simpson, Buffalo, 1972-73, 1975-76
Eric Dickerson, L.A. Rams, 1983-84, 1986; Indianapolis, 1988
3 Earl Campbell, Houston, 1978-80

Most Consecutive Seasons Leading League
5 Jim Brown, Cleveland, 1957-61
3 Steve Van Buren, Philadelphia, 1947-49
Jim Brown, Cleveland, 1963-65
Earl Campbell, Houston, 1978-80
2 Bill Paschal, N.Y. Giants, 1943-44
Joe Perry, San Francisco, 1953-54
Jim Nance, Boston, 1966-67
Leroy Kelly, Cleveland, 1967-68
O.J. Simpson, Buffalo, 1972-73; 1975-76
Eric Dickerson, L.A. Rams, 1983-84
Emmitt Smith, Dallas, 1991-92

Attempts

Most Seasons Leading League
6 Jim Brown, Cleveland, 1958-59, 1961, 1963-65
4 Steve Van Buren, Philadelphia, 1947-50
Walter Payton, Chicago, 1976-79
3 Cookie Gilchrist, Buffalo, 1963-64; Denver, 1965
Jim Nance, Boston, 1966-67, 1969
O. J. Simpson, Buffalo, 1973-75
Eric Dickerson, L.A. Rams, 1983, 1986; Indianapolis, 1988

Most Consecutive Seasons Leading League
4 Steve Van Buren, Philadelphia, 1947-50
Walter Payton, Chicago, 1976-79
3 Jim Brown, Cleveland, 1963-65
Cookie Gilchrist, Buffalo, 1963-64; Denver, 1965
O.J. Simpson, Buffalo, 1973-75
2 By many players

Most Attempts, Career
3,838 Walter Payton, Chicago, 1975-87
2,970 Eric Dickerson, L.A. Rams, 1983-87; Indianapolis, 1987-91; L.A. Raiders, 1992
2,949 Franco Harris, Pittsburgh, 1972-83; Seattle, 1984

Most Attempts, Season
407 James Wilder, Tampa Bay, 1984
404 Eric Dickerson, L.A. Rams, 1986
397 Gerald Riggs, Atlanta, 1985

Most Attempts, Rookie, Season
390 Eric Dickerson, L.A. Rams, 1983
378 George Rogers, New Orleans, 1981
335 Curt Warner, Seattle, 1983

Most Attempts, Game
45 Jamie Morris, Washington vs. Cincinnati, Dec. 17, 1988 (OT)
43 Butch Woolfolk, N.Y. Giants vs. Philadelphia, Nov. 20, 1983
James Wilder, Tampa Bay vs. Green Bay, Sept. 30, 1984 (OT)
42 James Wilder, Tampa Bay vs. Pittsburgh, Oct. 30, 1983

Yards Gained

Most Yards Gained, Career
16,726 Walter Payton, Chicago, 1975-87
13,168 Eric Dickerson, L.A. Rams, 1983-87; Indianapolis, 1987-91; L.A. Raiders, 1992
12,739 Tony Dorsett, Dallas, 1977-87; Denver, 1988

Most Seasons, 1,000 or More Yards Rushing
10 Walter Payton, Chicago, 1976-81, 1983-86
8 Franco Harris, Pittsburgh, 1972, 1974-79, 1983
Tony Dorsett, Dallas, 1977-81, 1983-85
7 Jim Brown, Cleveland, 1958-61, 1963-65
Eric Dickerson, L.A. Rams, 1983-86; L.A. Rams-Indianapolis, 1987; Indianapolis, 1988-89

Most Consecutive Seasons, 1,000 or More Yards Rushing
7 Eric Dickerson, L.A. Rams, 1983-86; L.A. Rams-Indianapolis, 1987; Indianapolis, 1988-89
6 Franco Harris, Pittsburgh, 1974-79
Walter Payton, Chicago, 1976-81
5 Jim Taylor, Green Bay, 1960-64
O.J. Simpson, Buffalo, 1972-76
Tony Dorsett, Dallas, 1977-81

Most Yards Gained, Season
2,105 Eric Dickerson, L.A. Rams, 1984
2,003 O.J. Simpson, Buffalo, 1973
1,934 Earl Campbell, Houston, 1980

Most Yards Gained, Rookie, Season
1,808 Eric Dickerson, L.A. Rams, 1983
1,674 George Rogers, New Orleans, 1981
1,605 Ottis Anderson, St. Louis, 1979

Most Yards Gained, Game
275 Walter Payton, Chicago vs. Minnesota, Nov. 20, 1977
273 O.J. Simpson, Buffalo vs. Detroit, Nov. 25, 1976
250 O.J. Simpson, Buffalo vs. New England, Sept. 16, 1973

Most Games, 200 or More Yards Rushing, Career
6 O.J. Simpson, Buffalo, 1969-77; San Francisco, 1978-79
4 Jim Brown, Cleveland, 1957-65
Earl Campbell, Houston, 1978-84; New Orleans, 1984-85
3 Eric Dickerson, L.A. Rams, 1983-87; Indianapolis, 1987-91; L.A. Raiders, 1992
Greg Bell, Buffalo, 1984-87; L.A. Rams, 1987-89; L.A. Raiders, 1990

Most Games, 200 or More Yards Rushing, Season
4 Earl Campbell, Houston, 1980
3 O.J. Simpson, Buffalo, 1973
2 Jim Brown, Cleveland, 1963
O.J. Simpson, Buffalo, 1976
Walter Payton, Chicago, 1977
Eric Dickerson, L.A. Rams, 1984
Greg Bell, L.A. Rams, 1989

Most Consecutive Games, 200 or More Yards Rushing
2 O.J. Simpson, Buffalo, 1973, 1976
Earl Campbell, Houston, 1980

Most Games, 100 or More Yards Rushing, Career
77 Walter Payton, Chicago, 1975-87
64 Eric Dickerson, L.A. Rams, 1983-87; Indianapolis, 1987-91; L.A. Raiders, 1992
58 Jim Brown, Cleveland, 1957-65

Most Games, 100 or More Yards Rushing, Season
12 Eric Dickerson, L.A. Rams, 1984
Barry Foster, Pittsburgh, 1992
11 O.J. Simpson, Buffalo, 1973
Earl Campbell, Houston, 1979
Marcus Allen, L.A. Raiders, 1985
Eric Dickerson, L.A. Rams, 1986
10 Walter Payton, Chicago, 1977, 1985
Earl Campbell, Houston, 1980

Most Consecutive Games, 100 or More Yards Rushing
11 Marcus Allen, L.A. Raiders, 1985-86
9 Walter Payton, Chicago, 1985
7 O.J. Simpson, Buffalo, 1972-73
Earl Campbell, Houston, 1979

Longest Run From Scrimmage
99 Tony Dorsett, Dallas vs. Minnesota, Jan. 3, 1983 (TD)
97 Andy Uram, Green Bay vs. Chi. Cardinals, Oct. 8, 1939 (TD)
Bob Gage, Pittsburgh vs. Chi. Bears, Dec. 4, 1949 (TD)
96 Jim Spavital, Baltimore vs. Green Bay, Nov. 5, 1950 (TD)
Bob Hoernschemeyer, Detroit vs. N.Y. Yanks, Nov. 23, 1950 (TD)

Average Gain

Highest Average Gain, Career (700 attempts)
5.22 Jim Brown, Cleveland, 1957-65 (2,359-12,312)
5.14 Eugene (Mercury) Morris, Miami, 1969-75; San Diego, 1976 (804-4,133)
5.00 Gale Sayers, Chicago, 1965-71 (991-4,956)

Highest Average Gain, Season (Qualifiers)
8.44 Beattie Feathers, Chi. Bears, 1934 (119-1,004)
7.98 Randall Cunningham, Philadelphia 1990 (118-942)
6.87 Bobby Douglass, Chicago, 1972 (141-968)

Highest Average Gain, Game (10 attempts)
17.09 Marion Motley, Cleveland vs. Pittsburgh, Oct. 29, 1950 (11-188)
16.70 Bill Grimes, Green Bay vs. N.Y. Yanks, Oct. 8, 1950 (10-167)
16.57 Bobby Mitchell, Cleveland vs. Washington, Nov. 15, 1959 (14-232)

Touchdowns

Most Seasons Leading League
5 Jim Brown, Cleveland, 1957-59, 1963, 1965
4 Steve Van Buren, Philadelphia, 1945, 1947-49
3 Abner Haynes, Dall. Texans, 1960-62
Cookie Gilchrist, Buffalo, 1962-64
Paul Lowe, L.A. Chargers, 1960; San Diego, 1961, 1965
Leroy Kelly, Cleveland, 1966-68

Most Consecutive Seasons Leading League
3 Steve Van Buren, Philadelphia, 1947-49
Jim Brown, Cleveland, 1957-59
Abner Haynes, Dall. Texans, 1960-62
Cookie Gilchrist, Buffalo, 1962-64
Leroy Kelly, Cleveland, 1966-68

Most Touchdowns, Career
110 Walter Payton, Chicago, 1975-87
106 Jim Brown, Cleveland, 1957-65
104 John Riggins, N.Y. Jets, 1971-75; Washington, 1976-79, 1981-85

Most Touchdowns, Season
24 John Riggins, Washington, 1983
21 Joe Morris, N.Y. Giants, 1985
19 Jim Taylor, Green Bay, 1962
Earl Campbell, Houston, 1979
Chuck Muncie, San Diego, 1981

Most Touchdowns, Rookie, Season
18 Eric Dickerson, L.A. Rams, 1983
15 Ickey Woods, Cincinnati, 1988
14 Gale Sayers, Chicago, 1965
Barry Sanders, Detroit, 1989

Most Touchdowns, Game
6 Ernie Nevers, Chi. Cardinals vs. Chi. Bears, Nov. 28, 1929
5 Jim Brown, Cleveland vs. Baltimore, Nov. 1, 1959
Cookie Gilchrist, Buffalo vs. N.Y. Jets, Dec. 8, 1963
4 By many players

Most Consecutive Games Rushing for Touchdowns
13 John Riggins, Washington, 1982-83
George Rogers, Washington, 1985-86
11 Lenny Moore, Baltimore, 1963-64
10 Greg Bell, L.A. Rams, 1988-89

Passing

Most Seasons Leading League
6 Sammy Baugh, Washington, 1937, 1940, 1943, 1945, 1947, 1949
4 Len Dawson, Dall. Texans; 1962; Kansas City, 1964, 1966, 1968
Roger Staubach, Dallas, 1971, 1973, 1978-79
Ken Anderson, Cincinnati, 1974-75, 1981-82
3 Arnie Herber, Green Bay, 1932, 1934, 1936
Norm Van Brocklin, Los Angeles, 1950, 1952, 1954
Bart Starr, Green Bay, 1962, 1964, 1966

Most Consecutive Seasons Leading League
2 Cecil Isbell, Green Bay, 1941-42
Milt Plum, Cleveland, 1960-61
Ken Anderson, Cincinnati, 1974-75, 1981-82
Roger Staubach, Dallas, 1978-79
Steve Young, San Francisco, 1991-92

Pass Rating

Highest Pass Rating, Career (1,500 attempts)
93.5 Joe Montana, San Francisco, 1979-90; 1992
90.4 Steve Young, Tampa Bay, 1985-86; San Francisco, 1987-92
87.8 Dan Marino, Miami, 1983-92

Highest Pass Rating, Season (Qualifiers)
112.4 Joe Montana, San Francisco, 1989
110.4 Milt Plum, Cleveland, 1960
109.9 Sammy Baugh, Washington, 1945

Highest Pass Rating, Rookie, Season (Qualifiers)
96.0 Dan Marino, Miami, 1983
88.2 Greg Cook, Cincinnati, 1969
84.0 Charlie Conerly, N.Y. Giants, 1948

Attempts

Most Seasons Leading League
4 Sammy Baugh, Washington, 1937, 1943, 1947-48
Johnny Unitas, Baltimore, 1957, 1959-61
George Blanda, Chi. Bears, 1953; Houston, 1963-65
Dan Marino, Miami, 1984, 1986, 1988, 1992
3 Arnie Herber, Green Bay, 1932, 1934, 1936
Sonny Jurgensen, Washington, 1966-67, 1969
2 By many players

Most Consecutive Seasons Leading League
3 Johnny Unitas, Baltimore, 1959-61
George Blanda, Houston, 1963-65
2 By many players

Most Passes Attempted, Career
6,467 Fran Tarkenton, Minnesota, 1961-66, 1972-78; N.Y. Giants, 1967-71
5,604 Dan Fouts, San Diego, 1973-87
5,284 Dan Marino, Miami, 1983-92

Most Passes Attempted, Season
655 Warren Moon, Houston, 1991
623 Dan Marino, Miami, 1986
609 Dan Fouts, San Diego, 1981

Most Passes Attempted, Rookie, Season
439 Jim Zorn, Seattle, 1976
417 Jack Trudeau, Indianapolis, 1986
375 Norm Snead, Washington, 1961

Most Passes Attempted, Game
68 George Blanda, Houston vs. Buffalo, Nov. 1, 1964
66 Chris Miller, Atlanta vs. Detroit, Dec. 24, 1989
63 Rich Gannon, Minnesota vs. New England, Oct. 20, 1991 (OT)

Completions

Most Seasons Leading League
5 Sammy Baugh, Washington, 1937, 1943, 1945, 1947-48
Dan Marino, Miami, 1984-86, 1988, 1992
4 George Blanda, Chi. Bears, 1953; Houston, 1963-65
Sonny Jurgensen, Philadelphia, 1961; Washington, 1966-67, 1969
3 Arnie Herber, Green Bay, 1932, 1934, 1936
Johnny Unitas, Baltimore, 1959-60, 1963
John Brodie, San Francisco, 1965, 1968, 1970
Fran Tarkenton, Minnesota, 1975-76, 1978

Most Consecutive Seasons Leading League
3 George Blanda, Houston, 1963-65
Dan Marino, Miami, 1984-86
2 By many players

Most Passes Completed, Career
3,686 Fran Tarkenton, Minnesota, 1961-66, 1972-78; N.Y. Giants, 1967-71
3,297 Dan Fouts, San Diego, 1973-87
3,128 Dan Marino, Miami, 1983-92

Most Passes Completed, Season
404 Warren Moon, Hosuton, 1991
378 Dan Marino, Miami, 1986
362 Dan Marino, Miami, 1984
Warren Moon, Houston, 1990

Most Passes Completed, Rookie, Season
208 Jim Zorn, Seattle, 1976
204 Jack Trudeau, Indianapolis, 1986
183 Jeff Komlo, Detroit, 1979

Most Passes Completed, Game
42 Richard Todd, N.Y. Jets vs. San Francisco, Sept. 21, 1980
41 Warren Moon, Houston vs. Dallas, Nov. 10, 1991 (OT)
40 Ken Anderson, Cincinnati vs. San Diego, Dec. 20, 1982
Phil Simms, N.Y. Giants vs. Cincinnati, Oct. 13, 1985

Most Consecutive Passes Completed
22 Joe Montana, San Francisco vs. Cleveland (5), Nov. 29, 1987; vs. Green Bay (17), Dec. 6, 1987
20 Ken Anderson, Cincinnati vs. Houston, Jan. 2, 1983
18 Steve DeBerg, Denver vs. L.A. Rams (17), Dec. 12, 1982; vs. Kansas City (1), Dec. 19, 1982
Lynn Dickey, Green Bay vs. Houston, Sept. 4, 1983
Joe Montana, San Francisco vs. L.A. Rams (13), Oct. 28, 1984; vs. Cincinnati (5), Nov. 4, 1984
Don Majkowski, Green Bay vs. New Orleans, Sept. 18, 1989

Completion Percentage

Most Seasons Leading League
8 Len Dawson, Dall. Texans, 1962; Kansas City, 1964-69, 1975
7 Sammy Baugh, Washington, 1940, 1942-43, 1945, 1947-49
5 Joe Montana, San Francisco, 1980-81, 1985, 1987, 1989

Most Consecutive Seasons Leading League
6 Len Dawson, Kansas City, 1964-69
3 Sammy Baugh, Washington, 1947-49
Otto Graham, Cleveland, 1953-55
Milt Plum, Cleveland, 1959-61
2 By many players

Highest Completion Percentage, Career (1,500 attempts)
63.67 Joe Montana, San Francisco, 1979-90, 1992 (4,600-2,929)
60.32 Jim Kelly, Buffalo, 1986-92 (3,024-1,824)
60.29 Steve Young, Tampa Bay, 1985-86; San Francisco, 1987-92 (1,506-908)

Highest Completion Percentage, Season (Qualifiers)
70.55 Ken Anderson, Cincinnati, 1982 (309-218)
70.33 Sammy Baugh, Washington, 1945 (182-128)
70.21 Joe Montana, San Francisco, 1989 (386-271)

Highest Completion Percentage, Rookie, Season (Qualifiers)
58.45 Dan Marino, Miami, 1983 (296-173)
57.14 Jim McMahon, Chicago, 1982 (269-181)
56.07 Fran Tarkenton, Minnesota, 1961 (280-157)

Highest Completion Percentage, Game (20 attempts)
90.91 Ken Anderson, Cincinnati vs. Pittsburgh, Nov. 10, 1974 (22-20)
90.48 Lynn Dickey, Green Bay vs. New Orleans, Dec. 13, 1981 (21-19)
90.00 Steve Young, San Francisco vs. Detroit, Oct. 20, 1991 (20-18)

Yards Gained

Most Seasons Leading League
5 Sonny Jurgensen, Philadelphia, 1961-62; Washington, 1966-67, 1969
Dan Marino, Miami, 1984-86, 1988, 1992
4 Sammy Baugh, Washington, 1937, 1940, 1947-48
Johnny Unitas, Baltimore, 1957, 1959-60, 1963
Dan Fouts, San Diego, 1979-82
3 Arnie Herber, Green Bay, 1932, 1934, 1936
Sid Luckman, Chi. Bears, 1943, 1945-46
John Brodie, San Francisco, 1965, 1968, 1970
John Hadl, San Diego, 1965, 1968, 1971
Joe Namath, N.Y. Jets, 1966-67, 1972

Most Consecutive Seasons Leading League
4 Dan Fouts, San Diego, 1979-82
3 Dan Marino, Miami, 1984-86
2 By many players

Most Yards Gained, Career
47,003 Fran Tarkenton, Minnesota, 1961-66, 1972-78; N.Y. Giants, 1967-71
43,040 Dan Fouts, San Diego, 1973-87
40,239 Johnny Unitas, Baltimore, 1956-72; San Diego, 1973

Most Seasons, 3,000 or More Yards Passing
9 Dan Marino, Miami, 1984-92
7 Joe Montana, San Francisco, 1981, 1983-85, 1987, 1989-90
John Elway, Denver, 1985-91
6 Dan Fouts, San Diego, 1979-81, 1984-86
Boomer Esiason, Cincinnati, 1985-90

Most Yards Gained, Season
5,084 Dan Marino, Miami, 1984
4,802 Dan Fouts, San Diego, 1981
4,746 Dan Marino, Miami, 1986

Most Yards Gained, Rookie, Season
2,571 Jim Zorn, Seattle, 1976
2,507 Dennis Shaw, Buffalo, 1970
2,337 Norm Snead, Washington, 1961

Most Yards Gained, Game
554 Norm Van Brocklin, Los Angeles vs. N.Y. Yanks, Sept. 28, 1951
527 Warren Moon, Houston vs. Kansas City, Dec. 16, 1990
521 Dan Marino, Miami vs. N.Y. Jets, Oct. 23, 1988

Most Games, 400 or More Yards Passing, Career
10 Dan Marino, Miami, 1983-92
7 Joe Montana, San Francisco, 1979-90
6 Dan Fouts, San Diego, 1973-87

Most Games, 400 or More Yards Passing, Season
4 Dan Marino, Miami, 1984
3 Dan Marino, Miami, 1986
2 George Blanda, Houston, 1961
Sonny Jurgensen, Philadelphia, 1961
Joe Namath, N.Y. Jets, 1972
Dan Fouts, San Diego, 1982
Dan Fouts, San Diego, 1985
Phil Simms, N.Y. Giants, 1985
Ken O'Brien, N.Y. Jets, 1986
Bernie Kosar, Cleveland, 1986
Dan Marino, Miami, 1988
Randall Cunningham, Philadelphia, 1989
Joe Montana, San Francisco, 1989
Joe Montana, San Francisco, 1990
Warren Moon, Houston, 1991

Most Consecutive Games, 400 or More Yards Passing
2 Dan Fouts, San Diego, 1982
Dan Marino, Miami, 1984
Phil Simms, N.Y. Giants, 1985

Most Games, 300 or More Yards Passing, Career
51 Dan Fouts, San Diego, 1973-87
44 Dan Marino, Miami, 1983-92
35 Joe Montana, San Francisco, 1979-90, 1992
Warren Moon, Houston, 1984-92

Most Games, 300 or More Yards Passing, Season
9 Dan Marino, Miami, 1984
Warren Moon, Houston, 1990
8 Dan Fouts, San Diego, 1980
7 Dan Fouts, San Diego, 1981
Bill Kenney, Kansas City, 1983
Neil Lomax, St. Louis, 1984
Dan Fouts, San Diego, 1985

Most Consecutive Games, 300 or More Yards Passing, Season
5 Joe Montana, San Francisco, 1982
4 Dan Fouts, San Diego, 1979
Bill Kenney, Kansas City, 1983
Joe Montana, San Francisco, 1990
Warren Moon, Houston, 1990
3 By many players

Longest Pass Completion (All TDs except as noted)
99 Frank Filchock (to Farkas), Washington vs. Pittsburgh, Oct. 15, 1939
George Izo (to Mitchell), Washington vs. Cleveland, Sept. 15, 1963
Karl Sweetan (to Studstill), Detroit vs. Baltimore, Oct. 16, 1966
Sonny Jurgensen (to Allen), Washington vs. Chicago, Sept. 15, 1968
Jim Plunkett (to Branch), L.A. Raiders vs. Washington, Oct. 2, 1983
Ron Jaworski (to Quick), Philadelphia vs. Atlanta, Nov. 10, 1985

98 Doug Russell (to Tinsley), Chi. Cardinals vs. Cleveland, Nov. 27, 1938
Ogden Compton (to Lane), Chi. Cardinals vs. Green Bay, Nov. 13, 1955
Bill Wade (to Farrington), Chicago Bears vs. Detroit, Oct. 8, 1961
Jacky Lee (to Dewveall), Houston vs. San Diego, Nov. 25, 1962
Earl Morrall (to Jones), N.Y. Giants vs. Pittsburgh, Sept. 11, 1966
Jim Hart (to Moore), St. Louis vs. Los Angeles, Dec. 10, 1972 (no TD)
97 Pat Coffee (to Tinsley), Chi. Cardinals vs. Chi. Bears, Dec. 5, 1937
Bobby Layne (to Box), Detroit vs. Green Bay, Nov. 26, 1953
George Shaw (to Tarr), Denver vs. Boston, Sept. 21, 1962
Bernie Kosar (to Slaughter), Cleveland vs. Chicago, Oct. 23, 1989
Steve Young (to Taylor), San Francisco vs. Atlanta, Nov. 3, 1991

Average Gain

Most Seasons Leading League
7 Sid Luckman, Chi. Bears, 1939-43, 1946-47
3 Arnie Herber, Green Bay, 1932, 1934, 1936
Norm Van Brocklin, Los Angeles, 1950, 1952, 1954
Len Dawson, Dall. Texans, 1962; Kansas City, 1966, 1968
Bart Starr, Green Bay, 1966-68

Most Consecutive Seasons Leading League
5 Sid Luckman, Chi. Bears, 1939-43
3 Bart Starr, Green Bay, 1966-68
2 Bernie Masterson, Chi. Bears, 1937-38
Sid Luckman, Chi. Bears, 1946-47
Johnny Unitas, Baltimore, 1964-65
Terry Bradshaw, Pittsburgh, 1977-78
Steve Grogan, New England, 1980-81
Steve Young, San Francisco, 1991-92

Highest Average Gain, Career (1,500 attempts)
8.63 Otto Graham, Cleveland, 1950-55 (1,565-13,499)
8.42 Sid Luckman, Chi. Bears, 1939-50 (1,744-14,686)
8.16 Norm Van Brocklin, Los Angeles, 1949-57; Philadelphia, 1958-60 (2,895-23,611)

Highest Average Gain, Season (Qualifiers)
11.17 Tommy O'Connell, Cleveland, 1957 (110-1,229)
10.86 Sid Luckman, Chi. Bears, 1943 (202-2,194)
10.55 Otto Graham, Cleveland, 1953 (258-2,722)

Highest Average Gain, Rookie, Season (Qualifiers)
9.411 Greg Cook, Cincinnati, 1969 (197-1,854)
9.409 Bob Waterfield, Cleveland, 1945 (171-1,609)
8.36 Zeke Bratkowski, Chi. Bears, 1954 (130-1,087)

Highest Average Gain, Game (20 attempts)
18.58 Sammy Baugh, Washington vs. Boston, Oct. 31, 1948 (24-446)
18.50 Johnny Unitas, Baltimore vs. Atlanta, Nov. 12, 1967 (20-370)
17.71 Joe Namath, N.Y. Jets vs. Baltimore, Sept. 24, 1972 (28-496)

Touchdowns

Most Seasons Leading League
4 Johnny Unitas, Baltimore, 1957-60
Len Dawson, Dall. Texans, 1962; Kansas City, 1963, 1965-66
3 Arnie Herber, Green Bay, 1932, 1934, 1936
Sid Luckman, Chi. Bears, 1943, 1945-46
Y.A. Tittle, San Francisco, 1955; N.Y. Giants, 1962-63
Dan Marino, Miami, 1984-86
2 By many players

Most Consecutive Seasons Leading League
4 Johnny Unitas, Baltimore, 1957-60
3 Dan Marino, Miami, 1984-86
2 By many players

Most Touchdown Passes, Career
342 Fran Tarkenton, Minnesota, 1961-66, 1972-78; N.Y. Giants, 1967-71
290 Johnny Unitas, Baltimore, 1956-72: San Diego, 1973
Dan Marino, Miami, 1983-92
255 Sonny Jurgensen, Philadelphia, 1957-63; Washington, 1964-74

Most Touchdown Passes, Season
48 Dan Marino, Miami, 1984
44 Dan Marino, Miami, 1986
36 George Blanda, Houston, 1961
Y.A. Tittle, N.Y. Giants, 1963

Most Touchdown Passes, Rookie, Season
22 Charlie Conerly, N.Y. Giants, 1948
20 Dan Marino, Miami, 1983
19 Jim Plunkett, New England, 1971

Most Touchdown Passes, Game
7 Sid Luckman, Chi. Bears vs. N.Y. Giants, Nov. 14, 1943
Adrian Burk, Philadelphia vs. Washington, Oct. 17, 1954
George Blanda, Houston vs. N.Y. Titans, Nov. 19, 1961
Y.A. Tittle, N.Y. Giants vs. Washington, Oct. 28, 1962
Joe Kapp, Minnesota vs. Baltimore, Sept. 28, 1969
6 By many players. Last time: Mark Rypien, Washington vs. Atlanta, Nov. 10, 1991

Most Games, Four or More Touchdown Passes, Career
17 Johnny Unitas, Baltimore, 1956-72; San Diego, 1973
Dan Marino, Miami, 1983-92
13 George Blanda, Chi. Bears, 1949, 1950-58; Baltimore, 1950; Houston, 1960-66; Oakland, 1967-75
12 Sonny Jurgensen, Philadelphia, 1957-63; Washington, 1964-74
Fran Tarkenton, Minnesota, 1961-66, 1972-78; N.Y. Giants, 1967-71
Dan Fouts, San Diego, 1973-87

Most Games, Four or More Touchdown Passes, Season
6 Dan Marino, Miami, 1984
5 Dan Marino, Miami, 1986
4 George Blanda, Houston, 1961
Vince Ferragamo, Los Angeles, 1980

Most Consecutive Games, Four or More Touchdown Passes
4 Dan Marino, Miami, 1984
2 By many players

Most Consecutive Games, Touchdown Passes
47 Johnny Unitas, Baltimore, 1956-60
30 Dan Marino, Miami, 1985-87
28 Dave Krieg, Seattle, 1983-85

Had Intercepted

Most Consecutive Passes Attempted, None Intercepted
308 Bernie Kosar, Cleveland, 1990-91
294 Bart Starr, Green Bay, 1964-65
233 Steve DeBerg, Kansas City, 1990

Most Passes Had Intercepted, Career
277 George Blanda, Chi. Bears, 1949, 1950-58; Baltimore, 1950; Houston, 1960-66; Oakland, 1967-75
268 John Hadl, San Diego, 1962-72; Los Angeles, 1973-74; Green Bay, 1974-75; Houston, 1976-77
266 Fran Tarkenton, Minnesota, 1961-66, 1972-78; N.Y. Giants, 1967-71

Most Passes Had Intercepted, Season
42 George Blanda, Houston, 1962
35 Vinny Testaverde, Tampa Bay, 1988
34 Frank Tripucka, Denver, 1960

Most Passes Had Intercepted, Game
8 Jim Hardy, Chi. Cardinals vs. Philadelphia, Sept. 24, 1950
7 Parker Hall, Cleveland vs. Green Bay, Nov. 8, 1942
Frank Sinkwich, Detroit vs. Green Bay, Oct. 24, 1943
Bob Waterfield, Los Angeles vs. Green Bay, Oct. 17, 1948
Zeke Bratkowski, Chicago vs. Baltimore, Oct. 2, 1960
Tommy Wade, Pittsburgh vs. Philadelphia, Dec. 12, 1965
Ken Stabler, Oakland vs. Denver, Oct. 16, 1977
Steve DeBerg, Tampa Bay vs. San Francisco, Sept. 7, 1986
6 By many players

Most Attempts, No Interceptions, Game
63 Rich Gannon, Minnesota vs. New England, Oct. 20, 1991 (OT)
60 Davey O'Brien, Philadelphia vs. Washington, Dec. 1, 1940
57 Joe Montana, San Francisco vs. Atlanta, Oct. 6, 1985

Lowest Percentage, Passes Had Intercepted

Most Seasons Leading League, Lowest Percentage, Passes Had Intercepted
5 Sammy Baugh, Washington, 1940, 1942, 1944-45, 1947
3 Charlie Conerly, N.Y. Giants, 1950, 1956, 1959
Bart Starr, Green Bay, 1962, 1964, 1966
Roger Staubach, Dallas, 1971, 1977, 1979
Ken Anderson, Cincinnati, 1972, 1981-82
Ken O'Brien, N.Y. Jets, 1985, 1987-88
2 By many players

Lowest Percentage, Passes Had Intercepted, Career (1,500 attempts)
2.59 Bernie Kosar, Cleveland, 1985-92 (3,012-78)
2.67 Joe Montana, San Francisco, 1979-90, 1992 (4,600-123)
2.74 Ken O'Brien, N.Y. Jets, 1984-92 (3,465-95)

Lowest Percentage, Passes Had Intercepted, Season (Qualifiers)
0.66 Joe Ferguson, Buffalo, 1976 (151-1)
0.90 Steve DeBerg, Kansas City, 1990 (444-4)
1.16 Steve Bartkowski, Atlanta, 1983 (432-5)

Lowest Percentage, Passes Had Intercepted, Rookie, Season (Qualifiers)
2.03 Dan Marino, Miami, 1983 (296-6)
2.10 Gary Wood, N.Y. Giants, 1964 (143-3)
2.82 Bernie Kosar, Cleveland, 1985 (248-7)

Times Sacked

Times Sacked has been compiled since 1963.

Most Times Sacked, Career
483 Fran Tarkenton, Minnesota, 1961-66, 1972-78; N.Y. Giants, 1967-71
440 Phil Simms, N.Y. Giants, 1979-81, 1983-92
405 Craig Morton, Dallas, 1965-74; N.Y. Giants, 1974-76; Denver, 1977-82

Most Times Sacked, Season
72 Randall Cunningham, Philadelphia, 1986
62 Ken O'Brien, N.Y. Jets, 1985
61 Neil Lomax, St. Louis, 1985

Most Times Sacked, Game
12 Bert Jones, Baltimore vs. St. Louis, Oct. 26, 1980
Warren Moon, Houston vs. Dallas, Sept. 29, 1985
11 Charley Johnson, St. Louis vs. N.Y. Giants, Nov. 1, 1964
Bart Starr, Green Bay vs. Detroit, Nov. 7, 1965
Jack Kemp, Buffalo vs. Oakland, Oct. 15, 1967
Bob Berry, Atlanta vs. St. Louis, Nov. 24, 1968
Greg Landry, Detroit vs. Dallas, Oct. 6, 1975
Ron Jaworski, Philadelphia vs. St. Louis, Dec. 18, 1983
Paul McDonald, Cleveland vs. Kansas City, Sept. 30, 1984
Archie Manning, Minnesota vs. Chicago, Oct. 28, 1984
Steve Pelluer, Dallas vs. San Diego, Nov. 16, 1986
Randall Cunningham, Philadelphia vs. L.A. Raiders, Nov. 30, 1986 (OT)
David Norrie, N.Y. Jets vs. Dallas, Oct. 4, 1987
Troy Aikman, Dallas vs. Philadelphia, Sept. 15, 1991
Bernie Kosar, Cleveland vs. Indianapolis, Sept. 6, 1992
10 By many players

Pass Receiving

Most Seasons Leading League
8 Don Hutson, Green Bay, 1936-37, 1939, 1941-45
5 Lionel Taylor, Denver, 1960-63, 1965
3 Tom Fears, Los Angeles, 1948-50
Pete Pihos, Philadelphia, 1953-55
Billy Wilson, San Francisco, 1954, 1956-57
Raymond Berry, Baltimore, 1958-60
Lance Alworth, San Diego, 1966, 1968-69

Most Consecutive Seasons Leading League
5 Don Hutson, Green Bay, 1941-45
4 Lionel Taylor, Denver, 1960-63
3 Tom Fears, Los Angeles, 1948-50
Pete Pihos, Philadelphia, 1953-55
Raymond Berry, Baltimore, 1958-60

Most Pass Receptions, Career
847 Art Monk, Washington, 1980-92
819 Steve Largent, Seattle, 1976-89
750 Charlie Joiner, Houston, 1969-72; Cincinnati, 1972-75; San Diego, 1976-86
James Lofton, Green Bay, 1978-86; L.A. Raiders, 1987-88; Buffalo, 1989-92

Most Seasons, 50 or More Pass Receptions
10 Steve Largent, Seattle, 1976, 1978-81, 1983-87
9 Art Monk, Washington, 1980-81, 1984-86, 1988-91
James Lofton, Green Bay, 1979-81, 1983-86; Buffalo, 1991-92
8 Gary Clark, Washington, 1985-92
Most Pass Receptions, Season
108 Sterling Sharpe, Green Bay, 1992
106 Art Monk, Washington, 1984
101 Charley Hennigan, Houston, 1964
Most Pass Receptions, Rookie, Season
83 Earl Cooper, San Francisco, 1980
81 Keith Jackson, Philadelphia, 1988
72 Bill Groman, Houston, 1960
Most Pass Receptions, Game
18 Tom Fears, Los Angeles vs. Green Bay, Dec. 3, 1950
17 Clark Gaines, N.Y. Jets vs. San Francisco, Sept. 21, 1980
16 Sonny Randle, St. Louis vs. N.Y. Giants, Nov. 4, 1962
Most Consecutive Games, Pass Receptions
177 Steve Largent, Seattle, 1977-89
150 Ozzie Newsome, Cleveland, 1979-89
148 Art Monk, Washington, 1983-92 (current)

Yards Gained
Most Seasons Leading League
7 Don Hutson, Green Bay, 1936, 1938-39, 1941-44
3 Raymond Berry, Baltimore, 1957, 1959-60
Lance Alworth, San Diego, 1965-66, 1968
Jerry Rice, San Francisco, 1986, 1989-90
2 By many players
Most Consecutive Seasons Leading League
4 Don Hutson, Green Bay, 1941-44
2 By many players
Most Yards Gained, Career
13,821 James Lofton, Green Bay, 1978-86; L.A. Raiders, 1987-88; Buffalo, 1989-92
13,089 Steve Largent, Seattle, 1976-89
12,146 Charlie Joiner, Houston, 1969-72; Cincinnati, 1972-75; San Diego, 1976-86
Most Seasons, 1,000 or More Yards, Pass Receiving
8 Steve Largent, Seattle, 1978-81, 1983-86
7 Lance Alworth, San Diego, 1963-69
Jerry Rice, San Francisco, 1986-92
6 James Lofton, Green Bay, 1980-81, 1983-85; Buffalo, 1991
Most Yards Gained, Season
1,746 Charley Hennigan, Houston, 1961
1,602 Lance Alworth, San Diego, 1965
1,570 Jerry Rice, San Francisco, 1986
Most Yards Gained, Rookie, Season
1,473 Bill Groman, Houston, 1960
1,231 Bill Howton, Green Bay, 1952
1,131 Bill Brooks, Indianapolis, 1986
Most Yards Gained, Game
336 Willie Anderson, L.A. Rams vs. New Orleans, Nov. 26, 1989 (OT)
309 Stephone Paige, Kansas City vs. San Diego, Dec. 22, 1985
303 Jim Benton, Cleveland vs. Detroit, Nov. 22, 1945
Most Games, 200 or More Yards Pass Receiving, Career
5 Lance Alworth, San Diego, 1962-70; Dallas, 1971-72
4 Don Hutson, Green Bay, 1935-45
Charley Hennigan, Houston, 1960-66
3 Don Maynard, N.Y. Giants, 1958; N.Y. Jets, 1960-72; St. Louis, 1973
Wes Chandler, New Orleans, 1978-81; San Diego, 1981-87; San Francisco, 1988
Jerry Rice, San Francisco, 1985-92
Most Games, 200 or More Yards Pass Receiving, Season
3 Charley Hennigan, Houston, 1961
2 Don Hutson, Green Bay, 1942
Gene Roberts, N.Y. Giants, 1949
Lance Alworth, San Diego, 1963
Don Maynard, N.Y. Jets, 1968
Most Games, 100 or More Yards Pass Receiving, Career
50 Don Maynard, N.Y. Giants, 1958; N.Y. Jets, 1960-72; St. Louis, 1973
43 James Lofton, Green Bay, 1978-86; L.A. Raiders, 1987-88; Buffalo, 1989-92
41 Lance Alworth, San Diego, 1962-70; Dallas, 1971-72
Most Games, 100 or More Yards Pass Receiving, Season
10 Charley Hennigan, Houston, 1961
9 Elroy (Crazylegs) Hirsch, Los Angeles, 1951
Bill Groman, Houston, 1960
Lance Alworth, San Diego, 1965
Don Maynard, N.Y. Jets, 1967
Stanley Morgan, New England, 1986
Mark Carrier, Tampa Bay, 1989
8 Charley Hennigan, Houston, 1964
Lance Alworth, San Diego, 1967
Mark Duper, Miami, 1986
Jerry Rice, San Francisco, 1989
Most Consecutive Games, 100 or More Yards Pass Receiving
7 Charley Hennigan, Houston, 1961
Bill Groman, Houston, 1961
6 Raymond Berry, Baltimore, 1960
Pat Studstill, Detroit, 1966
5 Elroy (Crazylegs) Hirsch, Los Angeles, 1951
Bob Boyd, Los Angeles, 1954
Terry Barr, Detroit, 1963
Lance Alworth, San Diego, 1966
Longest Pass Reception (All TDs except as noted)
99 Andy Farkas (from Filchock), Washington vs. Pittsburgh, Oct. 15, 1939
Bobby Mitchell (from Izo), Washington vs. Cleveland, Sept. 15, 1963
Pat Studstill (from Sweetan), Detroit vs. Baltimore, Oct. 16, 1966
Gerry Allen (from Jurgensen), Washington vs. Chicago, Sept. 15, 1968
Cliff Branch (from Plunkett), L.A. Raiders vs. Washington, Oct. 2, 1983
Mike Quick (from Jaworski), Philadelphia vs. Atlanta, Nov. 10, 1985
98 Gaynell Tinsley (from Russell), Chi. Cardinals vs. Cleveland, Nov. 17, 1938
Dick (Night Train) Lane (from Compton), Chi. Cardinals vs. Green Bay, Nov. 13, 1955
John Farrington (from Wade), Chicago vs. Detroit, Oct. 8, 1961
Willard Dewveall (from Lee), Houston vs. San Diego, Nov. 25, 1962
Homer Jones (from Morrall), N.Y. Giants vs. Pittsburgh, Sept. 11, 1966
Bobby Moore (from Hart), St. Louis vs. Los Angeles, Dec. 10, 1972 (no TD)
97 Gaynell Tinsley (from Coffee), Chi. Cardinals vs. Chi. Bears, Dec. 5, 1937
Cloyce Box (from Layne), Detroit vs. Green Bay, Nov. 26, 1953
Jerry Tarr (from Shaw), Denver vs. Boston, Sept. 21, 1962
Webster Slaughter (from Kosar), Cleveland vs. Chicago, Oct. 23, 1989
John Taylor (from Young), San Francisco vs. Atlanta, Nov. 3, 1991

Average Gain
Highest Average Gain, Career (200 receptions)
22.26 Homer Jones, N.Y. Giants, 1964-69; Cleveland, 1970 (224-4,986)
20.83 Buddy Dial, Pittsburgh, 1959-63; Dallas, 1964-66 (261-5,436)
20.24 Harlon Hill, Chicago, 1954-61; Pittsburgh, 1962; Detroit, 1962 (233-4,717)
Highest Average Gain, Season (24 receptions)
32.58 Don Currivan, Boston, 1947 (24-782)
31.44 Bucky Pope, Los Angeles, 1964 (25-786)
28.60 Bobby Duckworth, San Diego, 1984 (25-715)
Highest Average Gain, Game (3 receptions)
60.67 Bill Groman, Houston vs. Denver, Nov. 20, 1960 (3-182)
Homer Jones, N.Y. Giants vs. Washington, Dec. 12, 1965 (3-182)
60.33 Don Currivan, Boston vs. Washington, Nov. 30, 1947 (3-181)
59.67 Bobby Duckworth, San Diego vs. Chicago, Dec. 3, 1984 (3-179)

Touchdowns
Most Seasons Leading League
9 Don Hutson, Green Bay, 1935-38, 1940-44
5 Jerry Rice, San Francisco, 1986-87, 1989-91
3 Lance Alworth, San Diego, 1964-66
Most Consecutive Seasons Leading League
5 Don Hutson, Green Bay, 1940-44
4 Don Hutson, Green Bay, 1935-38
3 Lance Alworth, San Diego, 1964-66
Jerry Rice, San Francisco, 1989-91
Most Touchdowns, Career
103 Jerry Rice, San Francisco, 1985-92
100 Steve Largent, Seattle, 1976-89
99 Don Hutson, Green Bay, 1935-45
Most Touchdowns, Season
22 Jerry Rice, San Francisco, 1987
18 Mark Clayton, Miami, 1984
17 Don Hutson, Green Bay, 1942
Elroy (Crazylegs) Hirsch, Los Angeles, 1951
Bill Groman, Houston, 1961
Jerry Rice, San Francisco, 1989
Most Touchdowns, Rookie, Season
13 Bill Howton, Green Bay, 1952
John Jefferson, San Diego, 1979
12 Harlon Hill, Chi. Bears, 1954
Bill Groman, Houston, 1960
Mike Ditka, Chicago, 1961
Bob Hayes, Dallas, 1965
10 Bill Swiacki, N.Y. Giants, 1948
Bucky Pope, Los Angeles, 1964
Sammy White, Minnesota, 1976
Daryl Turner, Seattle, 1984
Most Touchdowns, Game
5 Bob Shaw, Chi. Cardinals vs. Baltimore, Oct. 2, 1950
Kellen Winslow, San Diego vs. Oakland, Nov. 22, 1981
Jerry Rice, San Francisco vs. Atlanta, Oct. 14, 1990
4 By many players. Last time: Don Beebe, Buffalo vs. Pittsburgh, Sept. 8, 1991
Most Consecutive Games, Touchdowns
13 Jerry Rice, San Francisco, 1986-87
11 Elroy (Crazylegs) Hirsch, Los Angeles, 1950-51
Buddy Dial, Pittsburgh, 1959-60
9 Lance Alworth, San Diego, 1963

Interceptions By
Most Seasons Leading League
3 Everson Walls, Dallas, 1981-82, 1985
2 Dick (Night Train) Lane, Los Angeles, 1952; Chi. Cardinals, 1954
Jack Christiansen, Detroit, 1953, 1957
Milt Davis, Baltimore, 1957, 1959
Dick Lynch, N.Y. Giants, 1961, 1963
Johnny Robinson, Kansas City, 1966, 1970
Bill Bradley, Philadelphia, 1971-72
Emmitt Thomas, Kansas City, 1969, 1974
Ronnie Lott, San Francisco, 1986; L.A. Raiders, 1991
Most Interceptions By, Career
81 Paul Krause, Washington, 1964-67; Minnesota, 1968-79
79 Emlen Tunnell, N.Y. Giants, 1948-58; Green Bay, 1959-61
68 Dick (Night Train) Lane, Los Angeles, 1952-53; Chi. Cardinals, 1954-59; Detroit, 1960-65
Most Interceptions By, Season
14 Dick (Night Train) Lane, Los Angeles, 1952
13 Dan Sandifer, Washington, 1948
Orban (Spec) Sanders, N.Y. Yanks, 1950
Lester Hayes, Oakland, 1980
12 By nine players
Most Interceptions By, Rookie, Season
14 Dick (Night Train) Lane, Los Angeles, 1952
13 Dan Sandifer, Washington, 1948
12 Woodley Lewis, Los Angeles, 1950
Paul Krause, Washington, 1964
Most Interceptions By, Game
4 Sammy Baugh, Washington vs. Detroit, Nov. 14, 1943
Dan Sandifer, Washington vs. Boston, Oct. 31, 1948
Don Doll, Detroit vs. Chi. Cardinals, Oct. 23, 1949
Bob Nussbaumer, Chi. Cardinals vs. N.Y. Bulldogs, Nov. 13, 1949
Russ Craft, Philadelphia vs. Chi. Cardinals, Sept. 24, 1950
Bobby Dillon, Green Bay vs. Detroit, Nov. 26, 1953

Jack Butler, Pittsburgh vs. Washington, Dec. 13, 1953
Austin (Goose) Gonsoulin, Denver vs. Buffalo, Sept. 18, 1960
Jerry Norton, St. Louis vs. Washington, Nov. 20, 1960; vs. Pittsburgh, Nov. 26, 1961
Dave Baker, San Francisco vs. L.A. Rams, Dec. 4, 1960
Bobby Ply, Dall. Texans vs. San Diego, Dec. 16, 1962
Bobby Hunt, Kansas City vs. Houston, Oct. 4, 1964
Willie Brown, Denver vs. N.Y. Jets, Nov. 15, 1964
Dick Anderson, Miami vs. Pittsburgh, Dec. 3, 1973
Willie Buchanon, Green Bay vs. San Diego, Sept. 24, 1978
Deron Cherry, Kansas City vs. Seattle, Sept. 29, 1985

Most Consecutive Games, Passes Intercepted By
8 Tom Morrow, Oakland, 1962-63
7 Paul Krause, Washington, 1964
Larry Wilson, St. Louis, 1966
Ben Davis, Cleveland, 1968
6 Dick (Night Train) Lane, Chi. Cardinals, 1954-55
Will Sherman, Los Angeles, 1954-55
Jim Shofner, Cleveland, 1960
Paul Krause, Minnesota, 1968
Willie Williams, N.Y. Giants, 1968
Kermit Alexander, San Francisco, 1968-69
Mel Blount, Pittsburgh, 1975
Eric Harris, Kansas City, 1980
Lester Hayes, Oakland, 1980
Barry Wilburn, Washington, 1987

Yards Gained

Most Seasons Leading League
2 Dick (Night Train) Lane, Los Angeles, 1952; Chi. Cardinals, 1954
Herb Adderley, Green Bay, 1965, 1969
Dick Anderson, Miami, 1968, 1970

Most Yards Gained, Career
1,282 Emlen Tunnell, N.Y. Giants, 1948-58; Green Bay, 1959-61
1,207 Dick (Night Train) Lane, Los Angeles, 1952-53; Chi. Cardinals, 1954-59; Detroit, 1960-65
1,185 Paul Krause, Washington, 1964-67; Minnesota, 1968-79

Most Yards Gained, Season
349 Charlie McNeil, San Diego, 1961
301 Don Doll, Detroit, 1949
298 Dick (Night Train) Lane, Los Angeles, 1952

Most Yards Gained, Rookie, Season
301 Don Doll, Detroit, 1949
298 Dick (Night Train) Lane, Los Angeles, 1952
275 Woodley Lewis, Los Angeles, 1950

Most Yards Gained, Game
177 Charlie McNeil, San Diego vs. Houston, Sept. 24, 1961
170 Louis Oliver, Miami vs. Buffalo, Oct. 4, 1992
167 Dick Jauron, Detroit vs. Chicago, Nov. 18, 1973

Longest Return (All TDs)
103 Vencie Glenn, San Diego vs. Denver, Nov. 29, 1987
Louis Oliver, Miami vs. Buffalo, Oct. 4, 1992
102 Bob Smith, Detroit vs. Chi. Bears, Nov. 24, 1949
Erich Barnes, N.Y. Giants vs. Dall. Cowboys, Oct. 15, 1961
Gary Barbaro, Kansas City vs. Seattle, Dec. 11, 1977
Louis Breeden, Cincinnati vs. San Diego, Nov. 8, 1981
Eddie Anderson, L.A. Raiders vs. Miami, Dec. 14, 1992
101 Richie Petitbon, Chicago vs Los Angeles, Dec. 9, 1962
Henry Carr, N.Y. Giants vs. Los Angeles, Nov. 13, 1966
Tony Greene, Buffalo vs. Kansas City, Oct. 3, 1976
Tom Pridemore, Atlanta vs. San Francisco, Sept. 20, 1981

Touchdowns

Most Touchdowns, Career
9 Ken Houston, Houston, 1967-72; Washington, 1973-80
7 Herb Adderley, Green Bay, 1961-69; Dallas, 1970-72
Erich Barnes, Chi. Bears, 1958-60; N.Y. Giants, 1961-64; Cleveland, 1965-70
Lem Barney, Detroit, 1967-77
6 Tom Janik, Denver, 1963-64; Buffalo, 1965-68; Boston, 1969-70; New England, 1971
Miller Farr, Denver, 1965; San Diego, 1965-66; Houston, 1967-69; St. Louis, 1970-72; Detroit, 1973
Bobby Bell, Kansas City, 1963-74

Most Touchdowns, Season
4 Ken Houston, Houston, 1971
Jim Kearney, Kansas City, 1972
3 Dick Harris, San Diego, 1961
Dick Lynch, N.Y. Giants, 1963
Herb Adderley, Green Bay, 1965
Lem Barney, Detroit, 1967
Miller Farr, Houston, 1967
Monte Jackson, Los Angeles, 1976
Rod Perry, Los Angeles, 1978
Ronnie Lott, San Francisco, 1981
Lloyd Burruss, Kansas City, 1986
Wayne Haddix, Tampa Bay, 1990
Robert Massey, Phoenix, 1992
2 By many players

Most Touchdowns, Rookie, Season
3 Lem Barney, Detroit, 1967
Ronnie Lott, San Francisco, 1981
2 By many players

Most Touchdowns, Game
2 Bill Blackburn, Chi. Cardinals vs. Boston, Oct. 24, 1948
Dan Sandifer, Washington vs. Boston, Oct. 31, 1948
Bob Franklin, Cleveland vs. Chicago, Dec. 11, 1960
Bill Stacy, St. Louis vs. Dall. Cowboys, Nov. 5, 1961
Jerry Norton, St. Louis vs. Pittsburgh, Nov. 26, 1961
Miller Farr, Houston vs. Buffalo, Dec. 7, 1968
Ken Houston, Houston vs. San Diego, Dec. 19, 1971
Jim Kearney, Kansas City vs. Denver, Oct. 1, 1972
Lemar Parrish, Cincinnati vs. Houston, Dec. 17, 1972
Dick Anderson, Miami vs. Pittsburgh, Dec. 3, 1973
Prentice McCray, New England vs. N.Y. Jets, Nov. 21, 1976
Kenny Johnson, Atlanta vs. Green Bay, Nov. 27, 1983 (OT)
Mike Kozlowski, Miami vs. N.Y. Jets, Dec. 16, 1983
Dave Brown, Seattle vs. Kansas City, Nov. 4, 1984
Lloyd Burruss, Kansas City vs. San Diego, Oct. 19, 1986
Henry Jones, Buffalo vs. Indianapolis, Sept. 20, 1992
Robert Massey, Phoenix vs. Washington, Oct. 4, 1992

Punting

Most Seasons Leading League
4 Sammy Baugh, Washington, 1940-43
Jerrel Wilson, Kansas City, 1965, 1968, 1972-73
3 Yale Lary, Detroit, 1959, 1961, 1963
Jim Fraser, Denver, 1962-64
Ray Guy, Oakland, 1974-75, 1977
Rohn Stark, Baltimore, 1983; Indianapolis, 1985-86
2 By many players

Most Consecutive Seasons Leading League
4 Sammy Baugh, Washington, 1940-43
3 Jim Fraser, Denver, 1962-64
2 By many players

Punts

Most Punts, Career
1,154 Dave Jennings, N.Y. Giants, 1974-84; N.Y. Jets, 1985-87
1,083 John James, Atlanta, 1972-81; Detroit, 1982, Houston, 1982-84
1,072 Jerrel Wilson, Kansas City, 1963-77; New England, 1978

Most Punts, Season
114 Bob Parsons, Chicago, 1981
109 John James, Atlanta, 1978
108 John Teltschik, Philadelphia, 1986
Rick Tuten, Seattle, 1992

Most Punts, Rookie, Season
108 John Teltschik, Philadelphia, 1986
99 Lewis Colbert, Kansas City, 1986
96 Mike Connell, San Francisco, 1978
Chris Norman, Denver, 1984

Most Punts, Game
15 John Teltschik, Philadelphia vs. N.Y. Giants, Dec. 6, 1987 (OT)
14 Dick Nesbitt, Chi. Cardinals vs. Chi. Bears, Nov. 30, 1933
Keith Molesworth, Chi. Bears vs. Green Bay, Dec. 10, 1933
Sammy Baugh, Washington vs. Philadelphia, Nov. 5, 1939
Carl Kinscherf, N.Y. Giants vs. Detroit, Nov. 7, 1943
George Taliaferro, N.Y. Yanks vs. Los Angeles, Sept. 28, 1951
12 By many players. Last time: Bryan Wagner, Cleveland vs. Kansas City, Nov. 19, 1989 (OT)

Longest Punt
98 Steve O'Neal, N.Y. Jets vs. Denver, Sept. 21, 1969
94 Joe Lintzenich, Chi. Bears vs. N.Y. Giants, Nov. 16, 1931
93 Shawn McCarthy, New England vs. Buffalo, Nov. 3, 1991

Average Yardage

Highest Average, Punting, Career (300 punts)
45.10 Sammy Baugh, Washington, 1937-52 (338-15,245)
44.68 Tommy Davis, San Francisco, 1959-69 (511-22,833)
44.29 Yale Lary, Detroit, 1952-53, 1956-64 (503-22,279)

Highest Average, Punting, Season (Qualifiers)
51.40 Sammy Baugh, Washington, 1940 (35-1,799)
48.94 Yale Lary, Detroit, 1963 (35-1,713)
48.73 Sammy Baugh, Washington, 1941 (30-1,462)

Highest Average, Punting, Rookie, Season (Qualifiers)
46.40 Bobby Walden, Minnesota, 1964 (72-3,341)
46.22 Dave Lewis, Cincinnati, 1970 (79-3,651)
45.92 Frank Sinkwich, Detroit, 1943 (12-551)

Highest Average, Punting, Game (4 punts)
61.75 Bob Cifers, Detroit vs. Chi. Bears, Nov. 24, 1946 (4-247)
61.60 Roy McKay, Green Bay vs. Chi. Cardinals, Oct. 28, 1945 (5-308)
59.40 Sammy Baugh, Washington vs. Detroit, Oct. 27, 1940 (5-297)

Punts Had Blocked

Most Consecutive Punts, None Blocked
623 Dave Jennings, N.Y. Giants, 1976-83
619 Ray Guy, Oakland, 1979-81; L.A. Raiders, 1982-86
578 Bobby Walden, Minnesota, 1964-67; Pittsburgh, 1968-72

Most Punts Had Blocked, Career
14 Herman Weaver, Detroit, 1970-76; Seattle, 1977-80
Harry Newsome, Pittsburgh, 1985-89; Minnesota, 1990-92
12 Jerrel Wilson, Kansas City, 1963-77; New England, 1978
Tom Blanchard, N.Y. Giants, 1971-73; New Orleans, 1974-78; Tampa Bay, 1979-81
11 David Lee, Baltimore, 1966-78

Most Punts Had Blocked, Season
6 Harry Newsome, Pittsburgh, 1988
4 Bryan Wagner, Cleveland, 1990
3 By many players

Punt Returns

Most Seasons Leading League
3 Les (Speedy) Duncan, San Diego, 1965-66; Washington, 1971
Rick Upchurch, Denver, 1976, 1978, 1982
2 Dick Christy, N.Y. Titans, 1961-62
Claude Gibson, Oakland, 1963-64
Billy Johnson, Houston, 1975, 1977
Mel Gray, New Orleans, 1987; Detroit, 1991

Punt Returns

Most Punt Returns, Career
282 Billy Johnson, Houston, 1974-80; Atlanta, 1982-87; Washington, 1988
267 J.T. Smith, Washington, 1978; Kansas City, 1978-84; St. Louis, 1985-87; Phoenix, 1988-90
259 Vai Sikahema, St. Louis, 1986-87; Phoenix, 1988-90; Green Bay, 1991; Philadelphia, 1992

Most Punt Returns, Season
70 Danny Reece, Tampa Bay, 1979
62 Fulton Walker, Miami-L.A. Raiders, 1985
58 J. T. Smith, Kansas City, 1979
Greg Pruitt, L.A. Raiders, 1983
Leo Lewis, Minnesota, 1988

Most Punt Returns, Rookie, Season
57 Lew Barnes, Chicago, 1986
54 James Jones, Dallas, 1980
53 Louis Lipps, Pittsburgh, 1984

Most Punt Returns, Game
11 Eddie Brown, Washington vs. Tampa Bay, Oct. 9, 1977
10 Theo Bell, Pittsburgh vs. Buffalo, Dec. 16, 1979
Mike Nelms, Washington vs. New Orleans, Dec. 26, 1982
9 Rodger Bird, Oakland vs. Denver, Sept. 10, 1967
Ralph McGill, San Francisco vs. Atlanta, Oct. 29, 1972
Ed Podolak, Kansas City vs. San Diego, Nov. 10, 1974
Anthony Leonard, San Francisco vs. New Orleans, Oct. 17, 1976
Butch Johnson, Dallas vs. Buffalo, Nov. 15, 1976
Larry Marshall, Philadelphia vs. Tampa Bay, Sept. 18, 1977
Nesby Glasgow, Baltimore vs. Kansas City, Sept. 2, 1979
Mike Nelms, Washington vs. St. Louis, Dec. 21, 1980
Leon Bright, N.Y. Giants vs. Philadelphia, Dec. 11, 1982
Pete Shaw, N.Y. Giants vs. Philadelphia, Nov. 20, 1983
Cleotha Montgomery, L.A. Raiders vs. Detroit, Dec. 10, 1984
Phil McConkey, N.Y. Giants vs. Philadelphia, Dec. 6, 1987 (OT)

Fair Catches

Most Fair Catches, Career
102 Willie Wood, Green Bay, 1960-71
99 Phil McConkey, N.Y. Giants, 1984-88; Green Bay, 1986; San Diego, 1989
98 Leo Lewis, Minnesota, 1981-90, 1991; Cleveland, 1990

Most Fair Catches, Season
27 Leo Lewis, Minnesota, 1989
25 Mark Konecny, Philadelphia, 1988
Phil McConkey, N.Y. Giants, 1988
Chris Warren, Seattle, 1992
24 Ken Graham, San Diego, 1969

Most Fair Catches, Game
7 Lem Barney, Detroit vs. Chicago, Nov. 21, 1976
Bobby Morse, Philadelphia vs. Buffalo, Dec. 27, 1987
6 Jake Scott, Miami vs. Buffalo, Dec. 20, 1970
Greg Pruitt, L.A. Raiders vs. Seattle, Oct. 7, 1984
Phil McConkey, San Diego vs. Kansas City, Dec. 17, 1989
Gerald McNeil, Houston vs. Pittsburgh, Sept. 16, 1990
5 By many players

Yards Gained

Most Seasons Leading League
3 Alvin Haymond, Baltimore, 1965-66; Los Angeles, 1969
2 Bill Dudley, Pittsburgh, 1942, 1946
Emlen Tunnell, N.Y. Giants, 1951-52
Dick Christy, N.Y. Titans, 1961-62
Claude Gibson, Oakland, 1963-64
Rodger Bird, Oakland, 1966-67
J. T. Smith, Kansas City, 1979-80
Vai Sikahema, St. Louis, 1986-87
David Meggett, N.Y. Giants, 1989-90

Most Yards Gained, Career
3,317 Billy Johnson, Houston, 1974-80; Atlanta, 1982-87; Washington, 1988
3,008 Rick Upchurch, Denver, 1975-83
2,894 Vai Sikahema, St. Louis, 1986-87; Phoenix, 1988-90; Green Bay, 1991; Philadelphia, 1992

Most Yards Gained, Season
692 Fulton Walker, Miami-L.A. Raiders, 1985
666 Greg Pruitt, L.A. Raiders, 1983
656 Louis Lipps, Pittsburgh, 1984

Most Yards Gained, Rookie, Season
656 Louis Lipps, Pittsburgh, 1984
655 Neal Colzie, Oakland, 1975
608 Mike Haynes, New England, 1976

Most Yards Gained, Game
207 LeRoy Irvin, Los Angeles vs. Atlanta, Oct. 11, 1981
205 George Atkinson, Oakland vs. Buffalo, Sept. 15, 1968
184 Tom Watkins, Detroit vs. San Francisco, Oct. 6, 1963

Longest Punt Return (All TDs)
98 Gil LeFebvre, Cincinnati vs. Brooklyn, Dec. 3, 1933
Charlie West, Minnesota vs. Washington, Nov. 3, 1968
Dennis Morgan, Dallas vs. St. Louis, Oct. 13, 1974
Terance Mathis, N.Y. Jets vs. Dallas, Nov. 4, 1990
97 Greg Pruitt, L.A. Raiders vs. Washington, Oct. 2, 1983
96 Bill Dudley, Washington vs. Pittsburgh, Dec. 3, 1950

Average Yardage

Highest Average, Career (75 returns)
12.78 George McAfee, Chi. Bears, 1940-41, 1945-50 (112-1,431)
12.75 Jack Christiansen, Detroit, 1951-58 (85-1,084)
12.55 Claude Gibson, San Diego, 1961-62; Oakland, 1963-65 (110-1,381)

Highest Average, Season (Qualifiers)
23.00 Herb Rich, Baltimore, 1950 (12-276)
21.47 Jack Christiansen, Detroit, 1952 (15-322)
21.28 Dick Christy, N.Y. Titans, 1961 (18-383)

Highest Average, Rookie, Season (Qualifiers)
23.00 Herb Rich, Baltimore, 1950 (12-276)
20.88 Jerry Davis, Chi. Cardinals, 1948 (16-334)
20.73 Frank Sinkwich, Detroit, 1943 (11-228)

Highest Average, Game (3 returns)
47.67 Chuck Latourette, St. Louis vs. New Orleans, Sept. 29, 1968 (3-143)
47.33 Johnny Roland, St. Louis vs. Philadelphia, Oct. 2, 1966 (3-142)
45.67 Dick Christy, N.Y. Titans vs. Denver, Sept. 24, 1961 (3-137)

Touchdowns

Most Touchdowns, Career
8 Jack Christiansen, Detroit, 1951-58
Rick Upchurch, Denver, 1975-83
6 Billy Johnson, Houston, 1974-80; Atlanta, 1982-87; Washington, 1988
5 Emlen Tunnell, N.Y. Giants, 1948-58; Green Bay, 1959-61

Most Touchdowns, Season
4 Jack Christiansen, Detroit, 1951
Rick Upchurch, Denver, 1976
3 Emlen Tunnell, N.Y. Giants, 1951
Billy Johnson, Houston, 1975
LeRoy Irvin, Los Angeles, 1981
2 By many players

Most Touchdowns, Rookie, Season
4 Jack Christiansen, Detroit, 1951
2 By seven players

Most Touchdowns, Game
2 Jack Christiansen, Detroit vs. Los Angeles, Oct. 14, 1951; vs. Green Bay, Nov. 22, 1951
Dick Christy, N.Y. Titans vs. Denver, Sept. 24, 1961
Rick Upchurch, Denver vs. Cleveland, Sept. 26, 1976
LeRoy Irvin, Los Angeles vs. Atlanta, Oct. 11, 1981
Vai Sikahema, St. Louis vs. Tampa Bay, Dec. 21, 1986
Todd Kinchen, L.A. Rams vs. Atlanta, Dec. 27, 1992

Kickoff Returns

Most Seasons Leading League
3 Abe Woodson, San Francisco, 1959, 1962-63
2 Lynn Chandnois, Pittsburgh, 1951-52
Bobby Jancik, Houston, 1962-63
Travis Williams, Green Bay, 1967; Los Angeles, 1971

Kickoff Returns

Most Kickoff Returns, Career
275 Ron Smith, Chicago, 1965, 1970-72; Atlanta, 1966-67; Los Angeles, 1968-69; San Diego, 1973; Oakland, 1974
243 Bruce Harper, N.Y. Jets, 1977-84
236 Mel Gray, New Orleans, 1986-88; Detroit, 1989-92

Most Kickoff Returns, Season
60 Drew Hill, Los Angeles, 1981
55 Bruce Harper, N.Y. Jets, 1978, 1979
David Turner, Cincinnati, 1979
Stump Mitchell, St. Louis, 1981
53 Eddie Payton, Minnesota, 1980
Buster Rhymes, Minnesota, 1985

Most Kickoff Returns, Rookie, Season
55 Stump Mitchell, St. Louis, 1981
53 Buster Rhymes, Minnesota, 1985
50 Nesby Glasgow, Baltimore, 1979
Dino Hall, Cleveland, 1979

Most Kickoff Returns, Game
9 Noland Smith, Kansas City vs. Oakland, Nov. 23, 1967
Dino Hall, Cleveland vs. Pittsburgh, Oct. 7, 1979
Paul Palmer, Kansas City vs. Seattle, Sept. 20, 1987
8 George Taliaferro, N.Y. Yanks vs. N.Y. Giants, Dec. 3, 1950
Bobby Jancik, Houston vs. Boston, Dec. 8, 1963
Bobby Jancik, Houston vs. Oakland, Dec. 22, 1963
Mel Renfro, Dallas vs. Green Bay, Nov. 29, 1964
Willie Porter, Boston vs. N.Y. Jets, Sept. 22, 1968
Keith Moody, Buffalo vs. Seattle, Oct. 30, 1977
Brian Baschnagel, Chicago vs. Houston, Nov. 6, 1977
Bruce Harper, N.Y. Jets vs. New England, Oct. 29, 1978
Bruce Harper, N.Y. Jets vs. New England, Sept. 9, 1979
Dino Hall, Cleveland vs. Pittsburgh, Nov. 25, 1979
Terry Metcalf, Washington vs. St. Louis, Sept. 20, 1981
Harlan Huckleby, Green Bay vs. Washington, Oct. 17, 1983
Gary Ellerson, Green Bay vs. St. Louis, Sept. 29, 1985
Bobby Humphery, N.Y. Jets vs. Cincinnati, Dec. 21, 1986
Bobby Joe Edmonds, Seattle vs. L.A. Raiders, Nov. 30, 1987
Joe Cribbs, Miami vs. Pittsburgh, Dec. 18, 1988
Erric Pegram, Atlanta vs. Washington, Nov. 10, 1991
Mel Gray, Detroit vs. Dallas, Nov. 8, 1992
7 By many players

Yards Gained

Most Seasons Leading League
3 Bruce Harper, N.Y. Jets, 1977-79
2 Marshall Goldberg, Chi. Cardinals, 1941-42
Woodley Lewis, Los Angeles, 1953-54
Al Carmichael, Green Bay, 1956-57
Timmy Brown, Philadelphia, 1961, 1963
Bobby Jancik, Houston, 1963, 1966
Ron Smith, Atlanta, 1966-67

Most Yards Gained, Career
6,922 Ron Smith, Chicago, 1965, 1970-72; Atlanta, 1966-67; Los Angeles, 1968-69; San Diego, 1973; Oakland, 1974
5,686 Mel Gray, New Orleans, 1986-88; Detroit, 1989-92
5,538 Abe Woodson, San Francisco, 1958-64; St. Louis, 1965-66

Most Yards Gained, Season
1,345 Buster Rhymes, Minnesota, 1985
1,317 Bobby Jancik, Houston, 1963
1,314 Dave Hampton, Green Bay, 1971

Most Yards Gained, Rookie, Season
1,345 Buster Rhymes, Minnesota, 1985
1,292 Stump Mitchell, St. Louis, 1981
1,245 Odell Barry, Denver, 1964

Most Yards Gained, Game
294 Wally Triplett, Detroit vs. Los Angeles, Oct. 29, 1950
247 Timmy Brown, Philadelphia vs. Dallas, Nov. 6, 1966
244 Noland Smith, Kansas City vs. San Diego, Oct. 15, 1967

Longest Kickoff Return (All TDs)
106 Al Carmichael, Green Bay vs. Chi. Bears, Oct. 7, 1956
Noland Smith, Kansas City vs. Denver, Dec. 17, 1967
Roy Green, St. Louis vs. Dallas, Oct. 21, 1979
105 Frank Seno, Chi. Cardinals vs. N.Y. Giants, Oct. 20, 1946
Ollie Matson, Chi. Cardinals vs. Washington, Oct. 14, 1956
Abe Woodson, San Francisco vs. Los Angeles, Nov. 8, 1959
Timmy Brown, Philadelphia vs. Cleveland, Sept. 17, 1961
Jon Arnett, Los Angeles vs. Detroit, Oct. 29, 1961
Eugene (Mercury) Morris, Miami vs. Cincinnati, Sept. 14, 1969
Travis Williams, Los Angeles vs. New Orleans, Dec. 5, 1971
104 By many players

Average Yardage
Highest Average, Career (75 returns)
30.56 Gale Sayers, Chicago, 1965-71 (91-2,781)
29.57 Lynn Chandnois, Pittsburgh, 1950-56 (92-2,720)
28.69 Abe Woodson, San Francisco, 1958-64; St. Louis, 1965-66 (193-5,538)
Highest Average, Season (Qualifiers)
41.06 Travis Williams, Green Bay, 1967 (18-739)
37.69 Gale Sayers, Chicago, 1967 (16-603)
35.50 Ollie Matson, Chi. Cardinals, 1958 (14-497)
Highest Average, Rookie, Season (Qualifiers)
41.06 Travis Williams, Green Bay, 1967 (18-739)
33.08 Tom Moore, Green Bay, 1960 (12-397)
32.88 Duriel Harris, Miami, 1976 (17-559)
Highest Average, Game (3 returns)
73.50 Wally Triplett, Detroit vs. Los Angeles, Oct. 29, 1950 (4-294)
67.33 Lenny Lyles, San Francisco vs. Baltimore, Dec. 18, 1960 (3-202)
65.33 Ken Hall, Houston vs. N.Y. Titans, Oct. 23, 1960 (3-196)

Touchdowns
Most Touchdowns, Career
6 Ollie Matson, Chi. Cardinals, 1952, 1954-58; L.A. Rams, 1959-62; Detroit, 1963; Philadelphia, 1964
Gale Sayers, Chicago, 1965-71
Travis Williams, Green Bay, 1967-70; Los Angeles, 1971
5 Bobby Mitchell, Cleveland, 1958-61; Washington, 1962-68
Abe Woodson, San Francisco, 1958-64; St. Louis, 1965-66
Timmy Brown, Green Bay, 1959; Philadelphia, 1960-67; Baltimore, 1968
4 Cecil Turner, Chicago, 1968-73
Ron Brown, L.A. Rams, 1984-89, 1991; L.A. Raiders, 1990
Most Touchdowns, Season
4 Travis Williams, Green Bay, 1967
Cecil Turner, Chicago, 1970
3 Verda (Vitamin T) Smith, Los Angeles, 1950
Abe Woodson, San Francisco, 1963
Gale Sayers, Chicago, 1967
Raymond Clayborn, New England, 1977
Ron Brown, L.A. Rams, 1985
2 By many players
Most Touchdowns, Rookie, Season
4 Travis Williams, Green Bay, 1967
3 Raymond Clayborn, New England, 1977
2 By seven players
Most Touchdowns, Game
2 Timmy Brown, Philadelphia vs. Dallas, Nov. 6, 1966
Travis Williams, Green Bay vs. Cleveland, Nov. 12, 1967
Ron Brown, L.A. Rams vs. Green Bay, Nov. 24, 1985

Combined Kick Returns
Most Combined Kick Returns, Career
510 Ron Smith, Chicago, 1965, 1970-72; Atlanta, 1966-67; Los Angeles, 1968-69; San Diego, 1973; Oakland, 1974 (p-235, k-275)
464 Vai Sikahema, St. Louis, 1986-87; Phoenix, 1988-90; Green Bay, 1991; Philadelphia, 1992 (p-259, k-205)
426 Bruce Harper, N.Y. Jets, 1977-84 (p-183, k-243)
Most Combined Kick Returns, Season
100 Larry Jones, Washington, 1975 (p-53, k-47)
97 Stump Mitchell, St. Louis, 1981 (p-42, k-55)
94 Nesby Glasgow, Baltimore, 1979 (p-44, k-50)
Most Combined Kick Returns, Game
13 Stump Mitchell, St. Louis vs. Atlanta, Oct. 18, 1981 (p-6, k-7)
12 Mel Renfro, Dallas vs. Green Bay, Nov. 29, 1964 (p-4, k-8)
Larry Jones, Washington vs. Dallas, Dec. 13, 1975 (p-6, k-6)
Eddie Brown, Washington vs. Tampa Bay, Oct. 9, 1977 (p-11, k-1)
Nesby Glasgow, Baltimore vs. Denver, Sept. 2, 1979 (p-9, k-3)
11 By many players

Yards Gained
Most Yards Returned, Career
8,710 Ron Smith, Chicago, 1965, 1970-72; Atlanta, 1966-67; Los Angeles, 1968-69; San Diego, 1973; Oakland, 1974 (p-1,788, k-6,922)
7,340 Mel Gray, New Orleans, 1986-88; Detroit, 1989-92 (p-1,654, k-5,686)
7,248 Vai Sikahema, St. Louis, 1986-87; Phoenix, 1988-90; Green Bay, 1991; Philadelphia, 1992 (p-2,894, k-4,354)
Most Yards Returned, Season
1,737 Stump Mitchell, St. Louis, 1981 (p-445, k-1,292)
1,658 Bruce Harper, N.Y. Jets, 1978 (p-378, k-1,280)
1,591 Mike Nelms, Washington, 1981 (p-492, k-1,099)
Most Yards Returned, Game
294 Wally Triplett, Detroit vs. Los Angeles, Oct. 29, 1950 (k-294)
Woodley Lewis, Los Angeles vs. Detroit, Oct. 18, 1953 (p-120, k-174)
289 Eddie Payton, Detroit vs. Minnesota, Dec. 17, 1977 (p-105, k-184)
282 Les (Speedy) Duncan, San Diego vs. N.Y. Jets, Nov. 24, 1968 (p-102, k-180)

Touchdowns
Most Touchdowns, Career
9 Ollie Matson, Chi. Cardinals, 1952, 1954-58; Los Angeles, 1959-62; Detroit, 1963; Philadelphia, 1964-66 (p-3, k-6)
8 Jack Christiansen, Detroit, 1951-58 (p-8)
Bobby Mitchell, Cleveland, 1958-61; Washington, 1962-68 (p-3, k-5)
Gale Sayers, Chicago, 1965-71 (p-2, k-6)
Rick Upchurch, Denver, 1975-83 (p-8)
Billy Johnson, Houston, 1974-80; Atlanta, 1982-87; Washington, 1988 (p-6, k-2)
7 Abe Woodson, San Francisco, 1958-64; St. Louis, 1965-66 (p-2, k-5)
Travis Williams, Green Bay, 1967-70; Los Angeles, 1971 (p-1, k-6)
Most Touchdowns, Season
4 Jack Christiansen, Detroit, 1951 (p-4)
Emlen Tunnell, N.Y. Giants, 1951 (p-3, k-1)
Gale Sayers, Chicago, 1967 (p-1, k-3)
Travis Williams, Green Bay, 1967 (k-4)
Cecil Turner, Chicago, 1970 (k-4)
Billy Johnson, Houston, 1975 (p-3, k-1)
Rick Upchurch, Denver, 1976 (p-4)
3 Verda (Vitamin T) Smith, Los Angeles, 1950 (k-3)
Abe Woodson, San Francisco, 1963 (k-3)
Raymond Clayborn, New England, 1977 (k-3)
Billy Johnson, Houston, 1977 (p-2, k-1)
LeRoy Irvin, Los Angeles, 1981 (p-3)
Ron Brown, L.A. Rams, 1985 (k-3)
2 By many players
Most Touchdowns, Game
2 Jack Christiansen, Detroit vs. Los Angeles, Oct. 14, 1951 (p-2); vs. Green Bay, Nov. 22, 1951 (p-2)
Jim Patton, N.Y. Giants vs. Washington, Oct. 30, 1955 (p-1, k-1)
Bobby Mitchell, Cleveland vs. Philadelphia, Nov. 23, 1958 (p-1, k-1)
Dick Christy, N.Y. Titans vs. Denver, Sept. 24, 1961 (p-2)
Al Frazier, Denver vs. Boston, Dec. 3, 1961 (p-1, k-1)
Timmy Brown, Philadelphia vs. Dallas, Nov. 6, 1966 (k-2)
Travis Williams, Green Bay vs. Cleveland, Nov. 12, 1967 (k-2); vs. Pittsburgh, Nov. 2, 1969 (p-1, k-1)
Gale Sayers, Chicago vs. San Francisco, Dec. 3, 1967 (p-1, k-1)
Rick Upchurch, Denver vs. Cleveland, Sept. 26, 1976 (p-2)
Eddie Payton, Detroit vs. Minnesota, Dec. 17, 1977 (p-1, k-1)
LeRoy Irvin, Los Angeles vs. Atlanta, Oct. 11, 1981 (p-2)
Ron Brown, L.A. Rams vs. Green Bay, Nov. 24, 1985 (k-2)
Vai Sikahema, St. Louis vs. Tampa Bay, Dec. 21, 1986 (p-2)

Fumbles
Most Fumbles, Career
118 Dave Krieg, Seattle, 1980-91; Kansas City, 1992
106 Dan Fouts, San Diego, 1973-87
105 Roman Gabriel, Los Angeles, 1962-72; Philadelphia, 1973-77
Most Fumbles, Season
18 Dave Krieg, Seattle, 1989
Warren Moon, Houston, 1990
17 Dan Pastorini, Houston, 1973
Warren Moon, Houston, 1984
Randall Cunningham, Philadelphia, 1989
16 Don Meredith, Dallas, 1964
Joe Cribbs, Buffalo, 1980
Steve Fuller, Kansas City, 1980
Paul McDonald, Cleveland, 1984
Phil Simms, N.Y. Giants, 1985
Most Fumbles, Game
7 Len Dawson, Kansas City vs. San Diego, Nov. 15, 1964
6 Sam Etcheverry, St. Louis vs. N.Y. Giants, Sept. 17, 1961
Dave Krieg, Seattle vs. Kansas City, Nov. 5, 1989
5 Paul Christman, Chi. Cardinals vs. Green Bay, Nov. 10, 1946
Charlie Conerly, N.Y. Giants vs. San Francisco, Dec. 1, 1957
Jack Kemp, Buffalo vs. Houston, Oct. 29, 1967
Roman Gabriel, Philadelphia vs. Oakland, Nov. 21, 1976
Randall Cunningham, Philadelphia vs. L.A. Raiders, Nov. 30, 1986 (OT)
Willie Totten, Buffalo vs. Indianapolis, Oct. 4, 1987
Dave Walter, Cincinnati vs. Seattle, Oct. 11, 1987
Dave Krieg, Seattle vs. San Diego, Nov. 25, 1990 (OT)
Andre Ware, Detroit vs. Green Bay, Dec. 6, 1992

Fumbles Recovered
Most Fumbles Recovered, Career, Own and Opponents'
43 Fran Tarkenton, Minnesota, 1961-66, 1972-78; N.Y. Giants, 1967-71 (43 own)
39 Warren Moon, Houston, 1984-92 (39 own)
38 Jack Kemp, Pittsburgh, 1957; L.A. Chargers, 1960; San Diego, 1961-62; Buffalo, 1962-67, 1969 (38 own)
Dan Fouts, San Diego, 1973-87 (37 own, 1 opp)
Most Fumbles Recovered, Season, Own and Opponents'
9 Don Hultz, Minnesota, 1963 (9 opp)
Dave Krieg, Seattle, 1989 (9 own)
8 Paul Christman, Chi. Cardinals, 1945 (8 own)
Joe Schmidt, Detroit, 1955 (8 opp)
Bill Butler, Minnesota, 1963 (8 own)
Kermit Alexander, San Francisco, 1965 (4 own, 4 opp)
Jack Lambert, Pittsburgh, 1976 (1 own, 7 opp)
Danny White, Dallas, 1981 (8 own)
Dan Marino, Miami, 1988 (7 own, 1 opp)
7 By many players
Most Fumbles Recovered, Game, Own and Opponents'
4 Otto Graham, Cleveland vs. N.Y. Giants, Oct. 25, 1953 (4 own)
Sam Etcheverry, St. Louis vs. N.Y. Giants, Sept. 17, 1961 (4 own)
Roman Gabriel, Los Angeles vs. San Francisco, Oct. 12, 1969 (4 own)
Joe Ferguson, Buffalo vs. Miami, Sept. 18, 1977 (4 own)
Randall Cunningham, Philadelphia vs. L.A. Raiders, Nov. 30, 1986 (OT) (4 own)
3 By many players

Own Fumbles Recovered
Most Own Fumbles Recovered, Career
43 Fran Tarkenton, Minnesota, 1961-66, 1972-78; N.Y. Giants, 1967-71
39 Warren Moon, Houston, 1984-92
38 Jack Kemp, Pittsburgh, 1957; L.A. Chargers, 1960; San Diego, 1961-62; Buffalo, 1962-67, 1969
Most Own Fumbles Recovered, Season
9 Dave Krieg, Seattle, 1989
8 Paul Christman, Chi. Cardinals, 1945

Bill Butler, Minnesota, 1963
Danny White, Dallas, 1981
7 By many players

Most Own Fumbles Recovered, Game
4 Otto Graham, Cleveland vs. N.Y. Giants, Oct. 25, 1953
Sam Etcheverry, St. Louis vs. N.Y. Giants, Sept. 17, 1961
Roman Gabriel, Los Angeles vs. San Francisco, Oct. 12, 1969
Joe Ferguson, Buffalo vs. Miami, Sept. 18, 1977
Randall Cunningham, Philadelphia vs. L.A. Raiders, Nov. 30, 1986 (OT)
3 By many players

Opponents' Fumbles Recovered

Most Opponents' Fumbles Recovered, Career
29 Jim Marshall, Cleveland, 1960; Minnesota, 1961-79
25 Dick Butkus, Chicago, 1965-73
23 Carl Eller, Minnesota, 1964-78; Seattle, 1979
Reggie Williams, Cincinnati, 1976-89
Rickey Jackson, New Orleans, 1981-92

Most Opponents' Fumbles Recovered, Season
9 Don Hultz, Minnesota, 1963
8 Joe Schmidt, Detroit, 1955
7 Alan Page, Minnesota, 1970
Jack Lambert, Pittsburgh, 1976
Ray Childress, Houston, 1988
Rickey Jackson, New Orleans, 1990

Most Opponents' Fumbles Recovered, Game
3 Corwin Clatt, Chi. Cardinals vs. Detroit, Nov. 6, 1949
Vic Sears, Philadelphia vs. Green Bay, Nov. 2, 1952
Ed Beatty, San Francisco vs. Los Angeles, Oct. 7, 1956
Ron Carroll, Houston vs. Cincinnati, Oct. 27, 1974
Maurice Spencer, New Orleans vs. Atlanta, Oct. 10, 1976
Steve Nelson, New England vs. Philadelphia, Oct. 8, 1978
Charles Jackson, Kansas City vs. Pittsburgh, Sept. 6, 1981
Willie Buchanon, San Diego vs. Denver, Sept. 27, 1981
Joey Browner, Minnesota vs. San Francisco, Sept. 8, 1985
Ray Childress, Houston vs. Washington, Oct. 30, 1988
2 By many players

Yards Returning Fumbles

Longest Fumble Run (All TDs)
104 Jack Tatum, Oakland vs. Green Bay, Sept. 24, 1972 (opp)
100 Chris Martin, Kansas City vs. Miami, Oct. 13, 1991 (opp)
99 Don Griffin, San Francisco vs. Chicago, Dec. 23, 1991 (opp)

Touchdowns

Most Touchdowns, Career (Total)
4 Bill Thompson, Denver, 1969-81
Jessie Tuggle, Atlanta, 1987-92
3 Ralph Heywood, Detroit, 1947-48; Boston, 1948; N.Y. Bulldogs, 1949
Leo Sugar, Chi. Cardinals, 1954-59; St. Louis, 1960; Philadelphia, 1961; Detroit, 1962
Bud McFadin, Los Angeles, 1952-56; Denver, 1960-63; Houston, 1964-65
Doug Cline, Houston, 1960-66; San Diego, 1966
Bob Lilly, Dall. Cowboys, 1961-74
Chris Hanburger, Washington, 1965-78
Lemar Parrish, Cincinnati, 1970-77; Washington, 1978-81; Buffalo, 1982
Paul Krause, Washington, 1964-67; Minnesota, 1968-79
Brad Dusek, Washington, 1974-81
David Logan, Tampa Bay, 1979-86; Green Bay, 1987
Thomas Howard, Kansas City, 1977-83; St. Louis, 1984-85
Greg Townsend, L.A. Raiders, 1983-92
Les Miller, San Diego, 1987-90; New Orleans, 1991-92
Chris Martin, New Orleans, 1983; Minnesota, 1984-88; Kansas City, 1989-92
Seth Joyner, Philadelphia, 1986-92
2 By many players

Most Touchdowns, Season (Total)
2 Harold McPhail, Boston, 1934
Harry Ebding, Detroit, 1937
John Morelli, Boston, 1944
Frank Maznicki, Boston, 1947
Fred (Dippy) Evans, Chi. Bears, 1948
Ralph Heywood, Boston, 1948
Art Tait, N.Y. Yanks, 1951
John Dwyer, Los Angeles, 1952
Leo Sugar, Chi. Cardinals, 1957
Doug Cline, Houston, 1961
Jim Bradshaw, Pittsburgh, 1964
Royce Berry, Cincinnati, 1970
Ahmad Rashad, Buffalo, 1974
Tim Gray, Kansas City, 1977
Charles Phillips, Oakland, 1978
Kenny Johnson, Atlanta, 1981
George Martin, N.Y. Giants, 1981
Del Rodgers, Green Bay, 1982
Mike Douglass, Green Bay, 1983
Shelton Robinson, Seattle, 1983
Erik McMillan, N.Y. Jets, 1989
Les Miller, San Diego, 1990
Seth Joyner, Philadelphia, 1991
Robert Goff, New Orleans, 1992

Most Touchdowns, Career (Own recovered)
2 Ken Kavanaugh, Chi. Bears, 1940-41, 1945-50
Mike Ditka, Chicago, 1961-66; Philadelphia, 1967-68; Dallas, 1969-72
Gail Cogdill, Detroit, 1960-68; Baltimore, 1968; Atlanta, 1969-70
Ahmad Rashad, St. Louis, 1972-73; Buffalo, 1974; Minnesota, 1976-82
Jim Mitchell, Atlanta, 1969-79
Drew Pearson, Dallas, 1973-83
Del Rodgers, Green Bay, 1982, 1984; San Francisco, 1987-88

Most Touchdowns, Season (Own recovered)
2 Ahmad Rashad, Buffalo, 1974
Del Rodgers, Green Bay, 1982
1 By many players

Most Touchdowns, Career (Opponents' recovered)
4 Jessie Tuggle, Atlanta, 1987-92
3 Leo Sugar, Chi. Cardinals, 1954-59; St. Louis, 1960; Philadelphia, 1961; Detroit, 1962
Doug Cline, Houston, 1960-66; San Diego, 1966
Bud McFadin, Los Angeles, 1952-56; Denver, 1960-63; Houston, 1964-65
Bob Lilly, Dall. Cowboys, 1961-74
Chris Hanburger, Washington, 1965-78
Paul Krause, Washington, 1964-67; Minnesota, 1968-79
Lemar Parrish, Cincinnati, 1970-77; Washington, 1978-81; Buffalo, 1982
Bill Thompson, Denver, 1969-81
Brad Dusek, Washington, 1974-81
David Logan, Tampa Bay, 1979-86; Green Bay, 1987
Thomas Howard, Kansas City, 1977-83; St. Louis, 1984-85
Greg Townsend, L.A. Raiders, 1983-92
Les Miller, San Diego, 1987-90; New Orleans, 1991-92
Chris Martin, New Orleans, 1983; Minnesota, 1984-88; Kansas City, 1989-92
Seth Joyner, Philadelphia, 1986-92
2 By many players

Most Touchdowns, Season (Opponents' recovered)
2 Harold McPhail, Boston, 1934
Harry Ebding, Detroit, 1937
John Morelli, Boston, 1944
Frank Maznicki, Boston, 1947
Fred (Dippy) Evans, Chi. Bears, 1948
Ralph Heywood, Boston, 1948
Art Tait, N.Y. Yanks, 1951
John Dwyer, Los Angeles, 1952
Leo Sugar, Chi. Cardinals, 1957
Doug Cline, Houston, 1961
Jim Bradshaw, Pittsburgh, 1964
Royce Berry, Cincinnati, 1970
Tim Gray, Kansas City, 1977
Charles Phillips, Oakland, 1978
Kenny Johnson, Atlanta, 1981
George Martin, N.Y. Giants, 1981
Mike Douglass, Green Bay, 1983
Shelton Robinson, Seattle, 1983
Erik McMillan, N.Y. Jets, 1989
Les Miller, San Diego, 1990
Seth Joyner, Philadelphia, 1991
Robert Goff, New Orleans, 1992

Most Touchdowns, Game (Opponents' recovered)
2 Fred (Dippy) Evans, Chi. Bears vs. Washington, Nov. 28, 1948

Combined Net Yards Gained

Rushing, receiving, interception returns, punt returns, kickoff returns, and fumble returns

Most Seasons Leading League
5 Jim Brown, Cleveland, 1958-61, 1964
3 Cliff Battles, Boston, 1932-33; Washington, 1937
Gale Sayers, Chicago, 1965-67
Eric Dickerson, L.A. Rams, 1983-84, 1986
Thurman Thomas, Buffalo, 1989, 1991-92
2 By many players

Most Consecutive Seasons Leading League
4 Jim Brown, Cleveland, 1958-61
3 Gale Sayers, Chicago, 1965-67
2 Cliff Battles, Boston, 1932-33
Charley Trippi, Chi. Cardinals, 1948-49
Timmy Brown, Philadelphia, 1962-63
Floyd Little, Denver, 1967-68
James Brooks, San Diego, 1981-82
Eric Dickerson, L.A. Rams, 1983-84
Thurman Thomas, Buffalo, 1991-92

Attempts

Most Attempts, Career
4,368 Walter Payton, Chicago, 1975-87
3,351 Tony Dorsett, Dallas, 1977-87; Denver, 1988
3,281 Franco Harris, Pittsburgh, 1972-83; Seattle, 1984

Most Attempts, Season
496 James Wilder, Tampa Bay, 1984
449 Marcus Allen, L.A. Raiders, 1985
442 Eric Dickerson, L.A. Rams, 1983

Most Attempts, Rookie, Season
442 Eric Dickerson, L.A. Rams, 1983
395 George Rogers, New Orleans, 1981
390 Joe Cribbs, Buffalo, 1980

Most Attempts, Game
48 James Wilder, Tampa Bay vs. Pittsburgh, Oct. 30, 1983
47 James Wilder, Tampa Bay vs. Green Bay, Sept. 30, 1984 (OT)
46 Gerald Riggs, Atlanta vs. L.A. Rams, Nov. 17, 1985

Yards Gained

Most Yards Gained, Career
21,803 Walter Payton, Chicago, 1975-87
16,326 Tony Dorsett, Dallas, 1977-87; Denver, 1988
15,459 Jim Brown, Cleveland, 1957-65

Most Yards Gained, Season
2,535 Lionel James, San Diego, 1985
2,462 Terry Metcalf, St. Louis, 1975
2,444 Mack Herron, New England, 1974

Most Yards Gained, Rookie, Season
2,317 Tim Brown, L.A. Raiders, 1988
2,272 Gale Sayers, Chicago, 1965
2,212 Eric Dickerson, L.A. Rams, 1983

Most Yards Gained, Game
373 Billy Cannon, Houston vs. N.Y. Titans, Dec. 10, 1961
345 Lionel James, San Diego vs. L.A. Raiders, Nov. 10, 1985 (OT)
341 Timmy Brown, Philadelphia vs. St. Louis, Dec. 16, 1962

Sacks

Sacks have been compiled since 1982.

Most Sacks, Career
126.5 Lawrence Taylor, N.Y. Giants, 1982-92
124 Reggie White, Philadelphia, 1985-92
112 Richard Dent, Chicago, 1983-92

Most Sacks, Season
22 Mark Gastineau, N.Y. Jets, 1984
21 Reggie White, Philadelphia, 1987
Chris Doleman, Minnesota, 1989
20.5 Lawrence Taylor, N.Y. Giants, 1986

Most Sacks, Rookie, Season
12.5 Leslie O'Neal, San Diego, 1986
12 Charles Haley, San Francisco, 1986
11 Vernon Maxwell, Baltimore, 1983

Most Sacks, Game
7 Derrick Thomas, Kansas City vs. Seattle, Nov. 11, 1990
6 Fred Dean, San Francisco vs. New Orleans, Nov. 13, 1983
5.5 William Gay, Detroit vs. Tampa Bay, Sept. 4, 1983

Miscellaneous

Longest Return of Missed Field Goal (All TDs)
101 Al Nelson, Philadelphia vs. Dallas, Sept. 26, 1971
100 Al Nelson, Philadelphia vs. Cleveland, Dec. 11, 1966
Ken Ellis, Green Bay vs. N.Y. Giants, Sept. 19, 1971
99 Jerry Williams, Los Angeles vs. Green Bay, Dec. 16, 1951
Carl Taseff, Baltimore vs. Los Angeles, Dec. 12, 1959
Timmy Brown, Philadelphia vs. St. Louis, Sept. 16, 1962

Team Records

Championships

Most Seasons League Champion
11 Green Bay, 1929-31, 1936, 1939, 1944, 1961-62, 1965-67
9 Chi. Bears, 1921, 1932-33, 1940-41, 1943, 1946, 1963, 1985
6 N.Y. Giants, 1927, 1934, 1938, 1956, 1986, 1990

Most Consecutive Seasons League Champion
3 Green Bay, 1929-31
Green Bay, 1965-67
2 Canton, 1922-23
Chi. Bears, 1932-33
Chi. Bears, 1940-41
Philadelphia, 1948-49
Detroit, 1952-53
Cleveland, 1954-55
Baltimore, 1958-59
Houston, 1960-61
Green Bay, 1961-62
Buffalo, 1964-65
Miami, 1972-73
Pittsburgh, 1974-75
Pittsburgh, 1978-79
San Francisco, 1988-89

Most Times Finishing First, Regular Season (Since 1933)
18 Clev. Browns, 1950-55, 1957, 1964-65, 1967-69, 1971, 1980, 1985-87, 1989
17 N.Y. Giants, 1933-35, 1938-39, 1941, 1944, 1946, 1956, 1958-59, 1961-63, 1986, 1989-90
16 Chi. Bears, 1933-34, 1937, 1940-43, 1946, 1956, 1963, 1984-88, 1990

Most Consecutive Times Finishing First, Regular Season (Since 1933)
7 Los Angeles, 1973-79
6 Cleveland, 1950-55
Dallas, 1966-71
Minnesota, 1973-78
Pittsburgh, 1974-79
5 Oakland, 1972-76
Chicago, 1984-88
San Francisco, 1986-90

Games Won

Most Consecutive Games Won
17 Chi. Bears, 1933-34
16 Chi. Bears, 1941-42
Miami, 1971-73
Miami, 1983-84
15 L.A. Chargers/San Diego, 1960-61
San Francisco, 1989-90

Most Consecutive Games Without Defeat
25 Canton, 1921-23 (won 22, tied 3)
24 Chi. Bears, 1941-43 (won 23, tied 1)
23 Green Bay, 1928-30 (won 21, tied 2)

Most Games Won, Season
15 San Francisco, 1984
Chicago, 1985
14 Miami, 1972
Pittsburgh, 1978
Washington, 1983
Miami, 1984
Chicago, 1986
N.Y. Giants, 1986
San Francisco, 1989
San Francisco, 1990
Washington, 1991
San Francisco, 1992
13 By many teams

Most Consecutive Games Won, Season
14 Miami, 1972
13 Chi. Bears, 1934
12 Minnesota, 1969
Chicago, 1985

Most Consecutive Games Won, Start of Season
14 Miami, 1972, entire season
13 Chi. Bears, 1934, entire season
12 Chicago, 1985

Most Consecutive Games Won, End of Season
14 Miami, 1972, entire season
13 Chi. Bears, 1934, entire season
11 Chi. Bears, 1942, entire season
Cleveland, 1951

Most Consecutive Games Without Defeat, Season
14 Miami, 1972 (won 14)
13 Chi. Bears, 1926 (won 11, tied 2)
Green Bay, 1929 (won 12, tied 1)
Chi. Bears, 1934 (won 13)
Baltimore, 1967 (won 11, tied 2)
12 Canton, 1922 (won 10, tied 2)
Canton, 1923 (won 11, tied 1)
Minnesota, 1969 (won 12)
Chicago, 1985 (won 12)

Most Consecutive Games Without Defeat, Start of Season
14 Miami, 1972 (won 14), entire season
13 Chi. Bears, 1926 (won 11, tied 2)
Green Bay, 1929 (won 12, tied 1), entire season
Chi. Bears, 1934 (won 13), entire season
Baltimore, 1967 (won 11, tied 2)
12 Canton, 1922 (won 10, tied 2), entire season
Canton, 1923 (won 11, tied 1), entire season
Chicago, 1985 (won 12)

Most Consecutive Games Without Defeat, End of Season
14 Miami, 1972 (won 14), entire season
13 Green Bay, 1929 (won 12, tied 1), entire season
Chi. Bears, 1934 (won 13), entire season
12 Canton, 1922 (won 10, tied 2), entire season
Canton, 1923 (won 11, tied 1), entire season

Most Consecutive Home Games Won
27 Miami, 1971-74
20 Green Bay, 1929-32
18 Oakland, 1968-70
Dallas, 1979-81

Most Consecutive Home Games Without Defeat
30 Green Bay, 1928-33 (won 27, tied 3)
27 Miami, 1971-74 (won 27)
23 Chi. Bears, 1923-25 (won 19, tied 6)

Most Consecutive Road Games Won
18 San Francisco, 1988-90
11 L.A. Chargers/San Diego, 1960-61
San Francisco, 1987-88
10 Chi. Bears, 1941-42
Dallas, 1968-69
New Orleans, 1987-88

Most Consecutive Road Games Without Defeat
18 San Francisco, 1988-90 (won 18)
13 Chi. Bears, 1941-43 (won 12, tied 1)
12 Green Bay, 1928-30 (won 10, tied 2)

Most Shutout Games Won or Tied, Season
10 Pottsville, 1926 (won 9, tied 1)
N.Y. Giants, 1927 (won 9, tied 1)
9 Akron, 1921 (won 8, tied 1)
Canton, 1922 (won 7, tied 2)
Frankford, 1926 (won 9)
Frankford, 1929 (won 6, tied 3)
8 By many teams

Most Consecutive Shutout Games Won or Tied
13 Akron, 1920-21 (won 10, tied 3)
7 Pottsville, 1926 (won 6, tied 1)
Detroit, 1934 (won 7)
6 Buffalo, 1920-21 (won 5, tied 1)
Frankford, 1926 (won 6)
Detroit, 1926 (won 4, tied 2)
N.Y. Giants, 1926-27 (won 5, tied 1)

Games Lost

Most Consecutive Games Lost
26 Tampa Bay, 1976-77
19 Chi. Cardinals, 1942-43, 1945
Oakland, 1961-62
18 Houston, 1972-73

Most Consecutive Games Without Victory
26 Tampa Bay, 1976-77 (lost 26)
23 Rochester, 1922-25 (lost 21, tied 2)
Washington, 1960-61 (lost 20, tied 3)
19 Dayton, 1927-29 (lost 18, tied 1)
Chi. Cardinals, 1942-43, 1945 (lost 19)
Oakland, 1961-62 (lost 19)

Most Games Lost, Season
15 New Orleans, 1980
Dallas, 1989
New England, 1990
Indianapolis, 1991
14 By many teams

Most Consecutive Games Lost, Season
14 Tampa Bay, 1976
New Orleans, 1980
Baltimore, 1981
New England, 1990
13 Oakland, 1962
Pittsburgh, 1969
Indianapolis, 1986
12 Tampa Bay, 1977

Most Consecutive Games Lost, Start of Season
14 Tampa Bay, 1976, entire season
New Orleans, 1980

13 Oakland, 1962
Indianapolis, 1986
12 Tampa Bay, 1977

Most Consecutive Games Lost, End of Season
14 Tampa Bay, 1976, entire season
New England, 1990
13 Pittsburgh, 1969
11 Philadelphia, 1936
Detroit, 1942, entire season
Houston, 1972

Most Consecutive Games Without Victory, Season
14 Tampa Bay, 1976 (lost 14), entire season
New Orleans, 1980 (lost 14)
Baltimore, 1981 (lost 14)
New England, 1990 (lost 14)
13 Washington, 1961 (lost 12, tied 1)
Oakland, 1962 (lost 13)
Pittsburgh, 1969 (lost 13)
Indianapolis, 1986 (lost 13)
12 Dall. Cowboys, 1960 (lost 11, tied 1) entire season
Tampa Bay, 1977 (lost 12)

Most Consecutive Games Without Victory, Start of Season
14 Tampa Bay, 1976 (lost 14), entire season
New Orleans, 1980 (lost 14)
13 Washington, 1961 (lost 12, tied 1)
Oakland, 1962 (lost 13)
Indianapolis, 1986 (lost 13)
12 Dall. Cowboys, 1960 (lost 11, tied 1), entire season
Tampa Bay, 1977 (lost 12)

Most Consecutive Games Without Victory, End of Season
14 Tampa Bay, 1976, (lost 14) entire season
New England, 1990 (lost 14)
13 Pittsburgh, 1969 (lost 13)
12 Dall. Cowboys, 1960 (lost 11, tied 1) entire season

Most Consecutive Home Games Lost
14 Dallas, 1988-89
13 Houston, 1972-73
Tampa Bay, 1976-77
11 Oakland, 1961-62
Los Angeles, 1961-63

Most Consecutive Home Games Without Victory
14 Dallas, 1988-89 (lost 14)
13 Houston, 1972-73 (lost 13)
Tampa Bay, 1976-77 (lost 13)
12 Philadelphia, 1936-38 (lost 11, tied 1)

Most Consecutive Road Games Lost
23 Houston, 1981-84
22 Buffalo, 1983-86
19 Tampa Bay, 1983-85
Atlanta, 1988-91

Most Consecutive Road Games Without Victory
23 Houston, 1981-84 (lost 23)
22 Buffalo, 1983-86 (lost 22)
19 Tampa Bay, 1983-85 (lost 19)
Atlanta, 1988-91 (lost 19)

Most Shutout Games Lost or Tied, Season
8 Frankford, 1927 (lost 6, tied 2)
Brooklyn, 1931 (lost 8)
7 Dayton, 1925 (lost 6, tied 1)
Orange, 1929 (lost 4, tied 3)
Frankford, 1931 (lost 6, tied 1)
6 By many teams

Most Consecutive Shutout Games Lost or Tied
8 Rochester, 1922-24 (lost 8)
7 Hammond, 1922-23 (lost 6, tied 1)
6 Providence, 1926-27 (lost 5, tied 1)
Brooklyn, 1942-43 (lost 6)

Tie Games

Most Tie Games, Season
6 Chi. Bears, 1932
5 Frankford, 1929
4 Chi. Bears, 1924
Orange, 1929
Portsmouth, 1932

Most Consecutive Tie Games
3 Chi. Bears, 1932
2 By many teams

Scoring

Most Seasons Leading League
10 Chi. Bears, 1932, 1934-35, 1939, 1941-43, 1946-47, 1956
6 Green Bay, 1931, 1936-38, 1961-62
L.A. Rams, 1950-52, 1957, 1967, 1973
San Francisco, 1953, 1965, 1970, 1987, 1989, 1992
5 Oakland, 1967-69, 1974, 1977
Dallas, 1966, 1968, 1971, 1978, 1980
San Diego, 1963, 1965, 1981-82, 1985

Most Consecutive Seasons Leading League
3 Green Bay, 1936-38
Chi. Bears, 1941-43
Los Angeles, 1950-52
Oakland, 1967-69

Points

Most Points, Season
541 Washington, 1983
513 Houston, 1961
Miami, 1984
485 Washington, 1991

Fewest Points, Season (Since 1932)
37 Cincinnati/St. Louis, 1934
38 Cincinnati, 1933
Detroit, 1942
51 Pittsburgh, 1934
Philadelphia, 1936

Most Points, Game
72 Washington vs. N.Y. Giants, Nov. 27, 1966
70 Los Angeles vs. Baltimore, Oct. 22, 1950
65 Chi. Cardinals vs. N.Y. Bulldogs, Nov. 13, 1949
Los Angeles vs. Detroit, Oct. 29, 1950

Most Points, Both Teams, Game
113 Washington (72) vs. N.Y. Giants (41), Nov. 27, 1966
101 Oakland (52) vs. Houston (49), Dec. 22, 1963
99 Seattle (51) vs. Kansas City (48), Nov. 27, 1983 (OT)

Fewest Points, Both Teams, Game
0 In many games. Last time: N.Y. Giants vs. Detroit, Nov. 7, 1943

Most Points, Shutout Victory, Game
64 Philadelphia vs. Cincinnati, Nov. 6, 1934
62 Akron vs. Oorang, Oct. 29, 1922
60 Rock Island vs. Evansville, Oct. 15, 1922
Chi. Cardinals vs. Rochester, Oct. 7, 1923

Fewest Points, Shutout Victory, Game
2 Green Bay vs. Chi. Bears, Oct. 16, 1932
Chi. Bears vs. Green Bay, Sept. 18, 1938

Most Points Overcome to Win Game
28 San Francisco vs. New Orleans, Dec. 7, 1980 (OT) (trailed 7-35, won 38-35)
25 St. Louis vs. Tampa Bay, Nov. 8, 1987 (trailed 3-28, won 31-28)
24 Philadelphia vs. Washington, Oct. 27, 1946 (trailed 0-24, won 28-24)
Detroit vs. Baltimore, Oct. 20, 1957 (trailed 3-27, won 31-27)
Philadelphia vs. Chi. Cardinals, Oct. 25, 1959 (trailed 0-24, won 28-24)
Denver vs. Boston, Oct. 23, 1960 (trailed 0-24, won 31-24)
Miami vs. New England, Dec. 15, 1974 (trailed 0-24, won 34-27)
Minnesota vs. San Francisco, Dec. 4, 1977 (trailed 0-24, won 28-27)
Denver vs. Seattle, Sept. 23, 1979 (trailed 10-34, won 37-34)
Houston vs. Cincinnati, Sept. 23, 1979 (OT) (trailed 0-24, won 30-27)
L.A. Raiders vs. San Diego, Nov. 22, 1982 (trailed 0-24, won 28-24)
L.A. Raiders vs. Denver, Sept. 26, 1988 (OT) (trailed 0-24, won 30-27)
L.A. Rams vs. Tampa Bay, Dec. 6, 1992 (trailed 3-27, won 31-27)

Most Points Overcome to Tie Game
31 Denver vs. Buffalo, Nov. 27, 1960 (trailed 7-38, tied 38-38)
28 Los Angeles vs. Philadelphia, Oct. 3, 1948 (trailed 0-28, tied 28-28)

Most Points, Each Half
1st: 49 Green Bay vs. Tampa Bay, Oct. 2, 1983
48 Buffalo vs. Miami, Sept. 18, 1966
45 Green Bay vs. Cleveland, Nov. 12, 1967
Indianapolis vs. Denver, Oct. 31, 1988
Houston vs. Cleveland, Dec. 9, 1990
2nd: 49 Chi. Bears vs. Philadelphia, Nov. 30, 1941
48 Chi. Cardinals vs. Baltimore, Oct. 2, 1950
N.Y. Giants vs. Baltimore, Nov. 19, 1950
45 Cincinnati vs. Houston, Dec. 17, 1972

Most Points, Both Teams, Each Half
1st: 70 Houston (35) vs. Oakland (35), Dec. 22, 1963
62 N.Y. Jets (41) vs. Tampa Bay (21), Nov. 17, 1985
59 St. Louis (31) vs. Philadelphia (28), Dec. 16, 1962
2nd: 65 Washington (38) vs. N.Y. Giants (27), Nov. 27, 1966
62 L.A. Raiders (31) vs. San Diego (31), Jan. 2, 1983
58 New England (37) vs. Baltimore (21), Nov. 23, 1980
N.Y. Jets (37) vs. New England (21), Sept. 21, 1987

Most Points, One Quarter
41 Green Bay vs. Detroit, Oct. 7, 1945 (second quarter)
Los Angeles vs. Detroit, Oct. 29, 1950 (third quarter)
37 Los Angeles vs. Green Bay, Sept. 21, 1980 (second quarter)
35 Chi. Cardinals vs. Boston, Oct. 24, 1948 (third quarter)
Green Bay vs. Cleveland, Nov. 12, 1967 (first quarter)
Green Bay vs. Tampa Bay, Oct. 2, 1983 (second quarter)

Most Points, Both Teams, One Quarter
49 Oakland (28) vs. Houston (21), Dec. 22, 1963 (second quarter)
48 Green Bay (41) vs. Detroit (7), Oct. 7, 1945 (second quarter)
Los Angeles (41) vs. Detroit (7), Oct. 29, 1950 (third quarter)
47 St. Louis (27) vs. Philadelphia (20), Dec. 13, 1964 (second quarter)

Most Points, Each Quarter
1st: 35 Green Bay vs. Cleveland, Nov. 12, 1967
31 Buffalo vs. Kansas City, Sept. 13, 1964
28 By seven teams
2nd: 41 Green Bay vs. Detroit, Oct. 7, 1945
37 Los Angeles vs. Green Bay, Sept. 21, 1980
35 Green Bay vs. Tampa Bay, Oct. 2, 1983
3rd: 41 Los Angeles vs. Detroit, Oct. 29, 1950
35 Chi. Cardinals vs. Boston, Oct. 24, 1948
28 By nine teams
4th: 31 Oakland vs. Denver, Dec. 17, 1960
Oakland vs. San Diego, Dec. 8, 1963
Atlanta vs. Green Bay, Sept. 13, 1981
28 By many teams

Most Points, Both Teams, Each Quarter
1st: 42 Green Bay (35) vs. Cleveland (7), Nov. 12, 1967
35 Dall. Texans (21) vs. N.Y. Titans (14), Nov. 11, 1962
Dallas (28) vs. Philadelphia (7), Oct. 19, 1969
Kansas City (21) vs. Seattle (14), Dec. 11, 1977
Detroit (21) vs. L.A. Raiders (14), Dec. 10, 1990
Dallas (21) vs. Atlanta (14), Dec. 22, 1991
34 Los Angeles (21) vs. Baltimore (13), Oct. 22, 1950
Oakland (21) vs. Atlanta (13), Nov. 30, 1975
2nd: 49 Oakland (28) vs. Houston (21), Dec. 22, 1963
48 Green Bay (41) vs. Detroit (7), Oct. 7, 1945
47 St. Louis (27) vs. Philadelphia (20), Dec. 13, 1964
3rd: 48 Los Angeles (41) vs. Detroit (7), Oct. 29, 1950
42 Washington (28) vs. Philadelphia (14), Oct. 1, 1955
41 Green Bay (21) vs. N.Y. Yanks (20), Oct. 8, 1950

4th: 42 Chi. Cardinals (28) vs. Philadelphia (14), Dec. 7, 1947
Green Bay (28) vs. Chi. Bears (14), Nov. 6, 1955
N.Y. Jets (28) vs. Boston (14), Oct. 27, 1968
Pittsburgh (21) vs. Cleveland (21), Oct. 18, 1969
41 Baltimore (27) vs. New England (14), Sept. 18, 1978
New England (27) vs. Baltimore (14), Nov. 23, 1980
40 Chicago (21) vs. Tampa Bay (19), Nov. 19, 1989

Most Consecutive Games Scoring
274 Cleveland, 1950-71
242 San Francisco, 1977-92 (current)
218 Dallas, 1970-85

Touchdowns

Most Seasons Leading League, Touchdowns
13 Chi. Bears, 1932, 1934-35, 1939, 1941-44, 1946-48, 1956, 1965
7 Dallas, 1966, 1968, 1971, 1973, 1977-78, 1980
6 Oakland, 1967-69, 1972, 1974, 1977
San Diego, 1963, 1965, 1979, 1981-82, 1985

Most Consecutive Seasons Leading League, Touchdowns
4 Chi. Bears, 1941-44
Los Angeles, 1949-52
3 Chi. Bears, 1946-48
Baltimore, 1957-59
Oakland, 1967-69
2 By many teams

Most Touchdowns, Season
70 Miami, 1984
66 Houston, 1961
64 Los Angeles, 1950

Fewest Touchdowns, Season (Since 1932)
3 Cincinnati, 1933
4 Cincinnati/St. Louis, 1934
5 Detroit, 1942

Most Touchdowns, Game
10 Philadelphia vs. Cincinnati, Nov. 6, 1934
Los Angeles vs. Baltimore, Oct. 22, 1950
Washington vs. N.Y. Giants, Nov. 27, 1966
9 Chi. Cardinals vs. Rochester, Oct. 7, 1923
Chi. Cardinals vs. N.Y. Giants, Oct. 17, 1948
Chi. Cardinals vs. N.Y. Bulldogs, Nov. 13, 1949
Los Angeles vs. Detroit, Oct. 29, 1950
Pittsburgh vs. N.Y. Giants, Nov. 30, 1952
Chicago vs. San Francisco, Dec. 12, 1965
Chicago vs. Green Bay, Dec. 7, 1980
8 By many teams.

Most Touchdowns, Both Teams, Game
16 Washington (10) vs. N.Y. Giants (6), Nov. 27, 1966
14 Chi. Cardinals (9) vs. N.Y. Giants (5), Oct. 17, 1948
Los Angeles (10) vs. Baltimore (4), Oct. 22, 1950
Houston (7) vs. Oakland (7), Dec. 22, 1963
13 New Orleans (7) vs. St. Louis (6), Nov. 2, 1969
Kansas City (7) vs. Seattle (6), Nov. 27, 1983 (OT)
San Diego (8) vs. Pittsburgh (5), Dec. 8, 1985
N.Y. Jets (7) vs. Miami (6), Sept. 21, 1986 (OT)

Most Consecutive Games Scoring Touchdowns
166 Cleveland, 1957-69
97 Oakland, 1966-73
96 Kansas City, 1963-70

Points After Touchdown

Most Points After Touchdown, Season
66 Miami, 1984
65 Houston, 1961
62 Washington, 1983

Fewest Points After Touchdown, Season
2 Chi. Cardinals, 1933
3 Cincinnati, 1933
Pittsburgh, 1934
4 Cincinnati/St. Louis, 1934

Most Points After Touchdown, Game
10 Los Angeles vs. Baltimore, Oct. 22, 1950
9 Chi. Cardinals vs. N.Y. Giants, Oct. 17, 1948
Pittsburgh vs. N.Y. Giants, Nov. 30, 1952
Washington vs. N.Y. Giants, Nov. 27, 1966
8 By many teams

Most Points After Touchdown, Both Teams, Game
14 Chi. Cardinals (9) vs. N.Y. Giants (5), Oct. 17, 1948
Houston (7) vs. Oakland (7), Dec. 22, 1963
Washington (9) vs. N.Y. Giants (5), Nov. 27, 1966
13 Los Angeles (10) vs. Baltimore (3), Oct. 22, 1950
12 In many games

Field Goals

Most Seasons Leading League, Field Goals
11 Green Bay, 1935-36, 1940-43, 1946-47, 1955, 1972, 1974
8 Washington, 1945, 1956, 1971, 1976-77, 1979, 1982, 1992
7 N.Y. Giants, 1933, 1937, 1939, 1941, 1944, 1959, 1983

Most Consecutive Seasons Leading League, Field Goals
4 Green Bay, 1940-43
3 Cleveland, 1952-54
2 By many teams

Most Field Goals Attempted, Season
49 Los Angeles, 1966
Washington, 1971
48 Green Bay, 1972
47 N.Y. Jets, 1969
Los Angeles, 1973
Washington, 1983

Fewest Field Goals Attempted, Season (Since 1938)
0 Chi. Bears, 1944
2 Cleveland, 1939
Card-Pitt, 1944
Boston, 1946
Chi. Bears, 1947
3 Chi. Bears, 1945
Cleveland, 1945

Most Field Goals Attempted, Game
9 St. Louis vs. Pittsburgh, Sept. 24, 1967
8 Pittsburgh vs. St. Louis, Dec. 2, 1962
Detroit vs. Minnesota, Nov. 13, 1966
N.Y. Jets vs. Buffalo, Nov. 3, 1968
7 By many teams

Most Field Goals Attempted, Both Teams, Game
11 St. Louis (6) vs. Pittsburgh (5), Nov. 13, 1966
Washington (6) vs. Chicago (5), Nov. 14, 1971
Green Bay (6) vs. Detroit (5), Sept. 29, 1974
Washington (6) vs. N.Y. Giants (5), Nov. 14, 1976
10 Denver (5) vs. Boston (5), Nov. 11, 1962
Boston (7) vs. San Diego (3), Sept. 20, 1964
Buffalo (7) vs. Houston (3), Dec. 5, 1965
St. Louis (7) vs. Atlanta (3), Dec. 11, 1966
Boston (7) vs. Buffalo (3), Sept. 24, 1967
Detroit (7) vs. Minnesota (3), Sept. 20, 1971
Washington (7) vs. Houston (3), Oct. 10, 1971
Green Bay (5) vs. St. Louis (5), Dec. 5, 1971
Kansas City (7) vs. Buffalo (3), Dec. 19, 1971
Kansas City (5) vs. San Diego (5), Oct. 29, 1972
Minnesota (6) vs. Chicago (4), Sept. 23, 1973
Cleveland (7) vs. Denver (3), Oct. 19, 1975
Cleveland (5) vs. Denver (5), Oct. 5, 1980
9 In many games

Most Field Goals, Season
35 N.Y. Giants, 1983
34 N.Y. Jets, 1968
Kansas City, 1990
33 Green Bay, 1972
Washington, 1983
Pittsburgh, 1985
New Orleans, 1987
Miami, 1991

Fewest Field Goals, Season (Since 1932)
0 Boston, 1932, 1935
Chi. Cardinals, 1932, 1945
Green Bay, 1932, 1944
N.Y. Giants, 1932
Brooklyn, 1944
Card-Pitt, 1944
Chi. Bears, 1944, 1947
Boston, 1946
Baltimore, 1950
Dallas, 1952

Most Field Goals, Game
7 St. Louis vs. Pittsburgh, Sept. 24, 1967
Minnesota vs. L.A. Rams, Nov. 5, 1989 (OT)
6 Boston vs. Denver, Oct. 4, 1964
Detroit vs. Minnesota, Nov. 13, 1966
N.Y. Jets vs. Buffalo, Nov. 3, 1968
Philadelphia vs. Houston, Nov. 12, 1972
N.Y. Jets vs. New Orleans, Dec. 3, 1972
St. Louis vs. Atlanta, Dec. 9, 1973
N.Y. Giants vs. Seattle, Oct. 18, 1981
San Francisco vs. New Orleans, Oct. 16, 1983
Pittsburgh vs. Denver, Oct. 23, 1988
5 By many teams

Most Field Goals, Both Teams, Game
8 Cleveland (4) vs. St. Louis (4), Sept. 20, 1964
Chicago (5) vs. Philadelphia (3), Oct. 20, 1968
Washington (5) vs. Chicago (3), Nov. 14, 1971
Kansas City (5) vs. Buffalo (3), Dec. 19, 1971
Detroit (4) vs. Green Bay (4), Sept. 29, 1974
Cleveland (5) vs. Denver (3), Oct. 19, 1975
New England (4) vs. San Diego (4), Nov. 9, 1975
San Francisco (6) vs. New Orleans (2), Oct. 16, 1983
Seattle (5) vs. L.A. Raiders (3), Dec. 18, 1988
7 In many games

Most Consecutive Games Scoring Field Goals
31 Minnesota, 1968-70
28 Washington, 1988-90
22 San Francisco, 1988-89

Safeties

Most Safeties, Season
4 Cleveland, 1927
Detroit, 1962
3 By many teams

Most Safeties, Game
3 L.A. Rams vs. N.Y. Giants, Sept. 30, 1984
2 N.Y. Giants vs. Pottsville, Oct. 30, 1927
Chi. Bears vs. Pottsville, Nov. 13, 1927
Detroit vs. Brooklyn, Dec. 1, 1935
N.Y. Giants vs. Pittsburgh, Sept. 17, 1950
N.Y. Giants vs. Washington, Nov. 5, 1961
Chicago vs. Pittsburgh, Nov. 9, 1969
Dallas vs. Philadelphia, Nov. 19, 1972
Los Angeles vs. Green Bay, Oct. 21, 1973
Oakland vs. San Diego, Oct. 26, 1975
Denver vs. Seattle, Jan. 2, 1983
New Orleans vs. Cleveland, Sept. 13, 1987
Buffalo vs. Denver, Nov. 8, 1987

Most Safeties, Both Teams, Game
3 L.A. Rams (3) vs. N.Y. Giants (0), Sept. 30, 1984
2 Chi. Cardinals (1) vs. Frankford (1), Nov. 19, 1927
Chi. Cardinals (1) vs. Cincinnati (1), Nov. 12, 1933
Chi. Bears (1) vs. San Francisco (1), Oct. 19, 1952
Cincinnati (1) vs. Los Angeles (1), Oct. 22, 1972

Chi. Bears (1) vs. San Francisco (1), Sept. 19, 1976
Baltimore (1) vs. Miami (1), Oct. 29, 1978
Atlanta (1) vs. Detroit (1), Oct. 5, 1980
Houston (1) vs. Philadelphia (1), Oct. 2, 1988
(Also see previous record)

First Downs

Most Seasons Leading League
9 Chi. Bears, 1935, 1939, 1941, 1943, 1945, 1947-49, 1955
7 San Diego, 1965, 1969, 1980-83, 1985
6 L.A. Rams, 1946, 1950-51, 1954, 1957, 1973

Most Consecutive Seasons Leading League
4 San Diego, 1980-83
3 Chi. Bears, 1947-49
2 By many teams

Most First Downs, Season
387 Miami, 1984
380 San Diego, 1985
379 San Diego, 1981

Fewest First Downs, Season
51 Cincinnati, 1933
64 Pittsburgh, 1935
67 Philadelphia, 1937

Most First Downs, Game
39 N.Y. Jets vs. Miami, Nov. 27, 1988
Washington vs. Detroit, Nov. 4, 1990 (OT)
38 Los Angeles vs. N.Y. Giants, Nov. 13, 1966
37 Green Bay vs. Philadelphia, Nov. 11, 1962

Fewest First Downs, Game
0 N.Y. Giants vs. Green Bay, Oct. 1, 1933
Pittsburgh vs. Boston, Oct. 29, 1933
Philadelphia vs. Detroit, Sept. 20, 1935
N.Y. Giants vs. Washington, Sept. 27, 1942
Denver vs. Houston, Sept. 3, 1966

Most First Downs, Both Teams, Game
62 San Diego (32) vs. Seattle (30), Sept. 15, 1985
59 Miami (31) vs. Buffalo (28), Oct. 9, 1983 (OT)
Seattle (33) vs. Kansas City (26), Nov. 27, 1983 (OT)
N.Y. Jets (32) vs. Miami (27), Sept. 21, 1986 (OT)
N.Y. Jets (39) vs. Miami (20), Nov. 27, 1988
58 Los Angeles (30) vs. Chi. Bears (28), Oct. 24, 1954
Denver (34) vs. Kansas City (24), Nov. 18, 1974
Atlanta (35) vs. New Orleans (23), Sept. 2, 1979 (OT)
Pittsburgh (36) vs. Cleveland (22), Nov. 25, 1979 (OT)
San Diego (34) vs. Miami (24), Nov. 18, 1984 (OT)
Cincinnati (32) vs. San Diego (26), Sept. 22, 1985

Fewest First Downs, Both Teams, Game
7 Chi. Cardinals (2) vs. Detroit (5), Sept. 15, 1940
9 Pittsburgh (1) vs. Boston (8), Oct. 27, 1935
Boston (4) vs. Brooklyn (5), Nov. 24, 1935
N.Y. Giants (3) vs. Detroit (6), Nov. 7, 1943
Pittsburgh (4) vs. Chi. Cardinals (5), Nov. 11, 1945
N.Y. Bulldogs (1) vs. Philadelphia (8), Sept. 22, 1949
10 N.Y. Giants (4) vs. Washington (6), Dec. 11, 1960

Most First Downs, Rushing, Season
181 New England, 1978
177 Los Angeles, 1973
176 Chicago, 1985

Fewest First Downs, Rushing, Season
36 Cleveland, 1942
Boston, 1944
39 Brooklyn, 1943
40 Philadelphia, 1940
Detroit, 1945

Most First Downs, Rushing, Game
25 Philadelphia vs. Washington, Dec. 2, 1951
23 St. Louis vs. New Orleans, Oct. 5, 1980
21 Cleveland vs. Philadelphia, Dec. 13, 1959
Green Bay vs. Philadelphia, Nov. 11, 1962
Los Angeles vs. New Orleans, Nov. 25, 1973
Pittsburgh vs. Kansas City, Nov. 7, 1976
New England vs. Denver, Nov. 28, 1976
Oakland vs. Green Bay, Sept. 17, 1978

Fewest First Downs, Rushing, Game
0 By many teams. Last time: Tampa Bay vs. Phoenix, Dec. 27, 1992

Most First Downs, Rushing, Both Teams, Game
36 Philadelphia (25) vs. Washington (11), Dec. 2, 1951
31 Detroit (18) vs. Washington (13), Sept. 30, 1951
30 Los Angeles (17) vs. Minnesota (13), Nov. 5, 1961
New Orleans (17) vs. Green Bay (13), Sept. 9, 1979
New Orleans (16) vs. San Francisco (14), Nov. 11, 1979
New England (16) vs. Kansas City (14), Oct. 4, 1981

Fewest First Downs, Rushing, Both Teams, Game
2 Houston (0) vs. Denver (2), Dec. 2, 1962
3 Philadelphia (1) vs. Pittsburgh (2), Oct. 27, 1957
Boston (1) vs. Buffalo (2), Nov. 15, 1964
Los Angeles (0) vs. San Francisco (3), Dec. 6, 1964
Pittsburgh (1) vs. St. Louis (2), Nov. 13, 1966
Seattle (1) vs. New Orleans (2), Sept. 1, 1991
4 In many games

Most First Downs, Passing, Season
259 San Diego, 1985
251 Houston, 1990
250 Miami, 1986

Fewest First Downs, Passing, Season
18 Pittsburgh, 1941
23 Brooklyn, 1942
N.Y. Giants, 1944
24 N.Y. Giants, 1943

Most First Downs, Passing, Game
29 N.Y. Giants vs. Cincinnati, Oct. 13, 1985
27 San Diego vs. Seattle, Sept. 15, 1985
26 Miami vs. Cleveland, Dec. 12, 1988

Fewest First Downs, Passing, Game
0 By many teams. Last time: Houston vs. Kansas City, Oct. 9, 1988

Most First Downs, Passing, Both Teams, Game
43 San Diego (23) vs. Cincinnati (20), Dec. 20, 1982
Miami (24) vs. N.Y. Jets (19), Sept. 21, 1986 (OT)
42 San Francisco (22) vs. San Diego (20), Dec. 11, 1982
41 San Diego (27) vs. Seattle (14), Sept. 15, 1985
Miami (26) vs. Cleveland (15), Dec. 12, 1988

Fewest First Downs, Passing, Both Teams, Game
0 Brooklyn vs. Pittsburgh, Nov. 29, 1942
1 Green Bay (0) vs. Cleveland (1), Sept. 21, 1941
Pittsburgh (0) vs. Brooklyn (1), Oct. 11, 1942
N.Y. Giants (0) vs. Detroit (1), Nov. 7, 1943
Pittsburgh (0) vs. Chi. Cardinals (1), Nov. 11, 1945
N.Y. Bulldogs (0) vs. Philadelphia (1), Sept. 22, 1949
Chicago (0) vs. Buffalo (1), Oct. 7, 1979
2 In many games

Most First Downs, Penalty, Season
42 Chicago, 1987
41 Denver, 1986
39 Seattle, 1978

Fewest First Downs, Penalty, Season
2 Brooklyn, 1940
4 Chi. Cardinals, 1940
N.Y. Giants, 1942, 1944
Washington, 1944
Cleveland, 1952
Kansas City, 1969
5 Brooklyn, 1939
Chi. Bears, 1939
Detroit, 1953
Los Angeles, 1953
Houston, 1982

Most First Downs, Penalty, Game
11 Denver vs. Houston, Oct. 6, 1985
9 Chi. Bears vs. Cleveland, Nov. 25, 1951
Baltimore vs. Pittsburgh, Oct. 30, 1977
N.Y. Jets vs. Houston, Sept. 18, 1988
8 Philadelphia vs. Detroit, Dec. 2, 1979
Cincinnati vs. N.Y. Jets, Oct. 6, 1985
Buffalo vs. Houston, Sept. 20, 1987
Houston vs. Atlanta, Sept. 9, 1990

Fewest First Downs, Penalty, Game
0 By many teams

Most First Downs, Penalty, Both Teams, Game
11 Chi. Bears (9) vs. Cleveland (2), Nov. 25, 1951
Cincinnati (8) vs. N.Y. Jets (3), Oct. 6, 1985
Denver (11) vs. Houston (0), Oct. 6, 1985
Detroit (6) vs. Dallas (5), Nov. 8, 1987
N.Y. Jets (9) vs. Houston (2), Sept. 18, 1988
10 In many games

Net Yards Gained Rushing and Passing

Most Seasons Leading League
12 Chi. Bears, 1932, 1934-35, 1939, 1941-44, 1947, 1949, 1955-56
7 San Diego, 1963, 1965, 1980-83, 1985
6 L.A. Rams, 1946, 1950-51, 1954, 1957, 1973
Baltimore, 1958-60, 1964, 1967, 1976
Dall. Cowboys, 1966, 1968-69, 1971, 1974, 1977

Most Consecutive Seasons Leading League
4 Chi. Bears, 1941-44
San Diego, 1980-83
3 Baltimore, 1958-60
Houston, 1960-62
Oakland, 1968-70
2 By many teams

Most Yards Gained, Season
6,936 Miami, 1984
6,744 San Diego, 1981
6,535 San Diego, 1985

Fewest Yards Gained, Season
1,150 Cincinnati, 1933
1,443 Chi. Cardinals, 1934
1,486 Chi. Cardinals, 1933

Most Yards Gained, Game
735 Los Angeles vs. N.Y. Yanks, Sept. 28, 1951
683 Pittsburgh vs. Chi. Cardinals, Dec. 13, 1958
682 Chi. Bears vs. N.Y. Giants, Nov. 14, 1943

Fewest Yards Gained, Game
−7 Seattle vs. Los Angeles, Nov. 4, 1979
−5 Denver vs. Oakland, Sept. 10, 1967
14 Chi. Cardinals vs. Detroit, Sept. 15, 1940

Most Yards Gained, Both Teams, Game
1,133 Los Angeles (636) vs. N.Y. Yanks (497), Nov. 19, 1950
1,102 San Diego (661) vs. Cincinnati (441), Dec. 20, 1982
1,087 St. Louis (589) vs. Philadelphia (498), Dec. 16, 1962

Fewest Yards Gained, Both Teams, Game
30 Chi. Cardinals (14) vs. Detroit (16), Sept. 15, 1940
136 Chi. Cardinals (50) vs. Green Bay (86), Nov. 18, 1934
154 N.Y. Giants (51) vs. Washington (103), Dec. 11, 1960

Most Consecutive Games, 400 or More Yards Gained
11 San Diego, 1982-83
6 Houston, 1961-62
San Diego, 1981
San Francisco, 1987
5 Chi. Bears, 1947
Philadelphia, 1953
Chi. Bears, 1955
Oakland, 1968
New England, 1981
Cincinnati, 1986

Most Consecutive Games, 300 or More Yards Gained
29 Los Angeles, 1949-51
26 Miami, 1983-85
19 Cleveland, 1978-79
San Diego, 1980-82
San Francisco, 1988-89

Rushing

Most Seasons Leading League
16 Chi. Bears, 1932, 1934-35, 1939-42, 1951, 1955-56, 1968, 1977, 1983-86
7 Buffalo, 1962, 1964, 1973, 1975, 1982, 1991-92
6 Cleveland, 1958-59, 1963, 1965-67
Most Consecutive Seasons Leading League
4 Chi. Bears, 1939-42
Chi. Bears, 1983-86
3 Detroit, 1936-38
San Francisco, 1952-54
Cleveland, 1965-67
2 By many teams

Attempts

Most Rushing Attempts, Season
681 Oakland, 1977
674 Chicago, 1984
671 New England, 1978
Fewest Rushing Attempts, Season
211 Philadelphia, 1982
219 San Francisco, 1982
225 Houston, 1982
Most Rushing Attempts, Game
72 Chi. Bears vs. Brooklyn, Oct. 20, 1935
70 Chi. Cardinals vs. Green Bay, Dec. 5, 1948
69 Chi. Cardinals vs. Green Bay, Dec. 6, 1936
Kansas City vs. Cincinnati, Sept. 3, 1978
Fewest Rushing Attempts, Game
6 Chi. Cardinals vs. Boston, Oct. 29, 1933
7 Oakland vs. Buffalo, Oct. 15, 1963
Houston vs. N.Y. Giants, Dec. 8, 1985
Seattle vs. L.A. Raiders, Nov. 17, 1991
8 Denver vs. Oakland, Dec. 17, 1960
Buffalo vs. St. Louis, Sept. 9, 1984
Detroit vs. San Francisco, Oct. 20, 1991
Most Rushing Attempts, Both Teams, Game
108 Chi. Cardinals (70) vs. Green Bay (38), Dec. 5, 1948
105 Oakland (62) vs. Atlanta (43), Nov. 30, 1975 (OT)
104 Chi. Bears (64) vs. Pittsburgh (40), Oct. 18, 1936
Fewest Rushing Attempts, Both Teams, Game
35 Seattle (15) vs. New Orleans (20), Sept. 1, 1991
36 Houston (15) vs. N.Y. Jets (21), Oct. 13, 1991
37 Atlanta (18) vs. San Francisco (19), Oct. 6, 1985
Houston (11) vs. Philadelphia (26), Dec. 2, 1991

Yards Gained

Most Yards Gained Rushing, Season
3,165 New England, 1978
3,088 Buffalo, 1973
2,986 Kansas City, 1978
Fewest Yards Gained Rushing, Season
298 Philadelphia, 1940
467 Detroit, 1946
471 Boston, 1944
Most Yards Gained Rushing, Game
426 Detroit vs. Pittsburgh, Nov. 4, 1934
423 N.Y. Giants vs. Baltimore, Nov. 19, 1950
420 Boston vs. N.Y. Giants, Oct. 8, 1933
Fewest Yards Gained Rushing, Game
−53 Detroit vs. Chi. Cardinals, Oct. 17, 1943
−36 Philadelphia vs. Chi. Bears, Nov. 19, 1939
−33 Phil-Pitt vs. Brooklyn, Oct. 2, 1943
Most Yards Gained Rushing, Both Teams, Game
595 Los Angeles (371) vs. N.Y. Yanks (224), Nov. 18, 1951
574 Chi. Bears (396) vs. Pittsburgh (178), Oct. 10, 1934
558 Boston (420) vs. N.Y. Giants (138), Oct. 8, 1933
Fewest Yards Gained Rushing, Both Teams, Game
−15 Detroit (−53) vs. Chi. Cardinals (38), Oct. 17, 1943
4 Detroit (−10) vs. Chi. Cardinals (14), Sept. 15, 1940
62 L.A. Rams (15) vs. San Francisco (47), Dec. 6, 1964

Average Gain

Highest Average Gain, Rushing, Season
5.74 Cleveland, 1963
5.65 San Francisco, 1954
5.56 San Diego, 1963
Lowest Average Gain, Rushing, Season
0.94 Philadelphia, 1940
1.45 Boston, 1944
1.55 Pittsburgh, 1935

Touchdowns

Most Touchdowns, Rushing, Season
36 Green Bay, 1962
33 Pittsburgh, 1976
30 Chi. Bears, 1941
New England, 1978
Washington, 1983
Fewest Touchdowns, Rushing, Season
1 Brooklyn, 1934
2 Chi. Cardinals, 1933
Cincinnati, 1933
Pittsburgh, 1934
Philadelphia, 1935
Philadelphia, 1936
Philadelphia, 1937
Philadelphia, 1938
Pittsburgh, 1940
Philadelphia, 1972
3 By many teams
Most Touchdowns, Rushing, Game
7 Los Angeles vs. Atlanta, Dec. 4, 1976
6 By many teams
Most Touchdowns, Rushing, Both Teams, Game
8 Los Angeles (6) vs. N.Y. Yanks (2), Nov. 18, 1951
Chi. Bears (5) vs. Green Bay (3), Nov. 6, 1955
Cleveland (6) vs. Los Angeles (2), Nov. 24, 1957
7 In many games

Passing

Attempts

Most Passes Attempted, Season
709 Minnesota, 1981
667 Houston, 1991
662 San Diego, 1984
Fewest Passes Attempted, Season
102 Cincinnati, 1933
106 Boston, 1933
120 Detroit, 1937
Most Passes Attempted, Game
68 Houston vs. Buffalo, Nov 1, 1964
66 Atlanta vs. Detroit, Dec. 24, 1989
65 San Diego vs. Kansas City, Oct. 19, 1986
Fewest Passes Attempted, Game
0 Green Bay vs. Portsmouth, Oct. 8, 1933
Detroit vs. Cleveland, Sept. 10, 1937
Pittsburgh vs. Brooklyn, Nov. 16, 1941
Pittsburgh vs. Los Angeles, Nov. 13, 1949
Cleveland vs. Philadelphia, Dec. 3, 1950
Most Passes Attempted, Both Teams, Game
104 Miami (55) vs. N.Y. Jets (49), Oct. 18, 1987 (OT)
102 San Francisco (57) vs. Atlanta (45), Oct. 6, 1985
100 Tampa Bay (54) vs. Kansas City (46), Oct. 28, 1984
San Francisco (60) vs. Washington (40), Nov. 17, 1986
Philadelphia (62) vs. Chicago (38), Oct. 2, 1989
Fewest Passes Attempted, Both Teams, Game
4 Chi. Cardinals (1) vs. Detroit (3), Nov. 3, 1935
Detroit (0) vs. Cleveland (4), Sept. 10, 1937
6 Chi. Cardinals (2) vs. Detroit (4), Sept. 15, 1940
8 Brooklyn (2) vs. Philadelphia (6), Oct. 1, 1939

Completions

Most Passes Completed, Season
411 Houston, 1991
401 San Diego, 1984
399 Houston, 1990
Fewest Passes Completed, Season
25 Cincinnati, 1933
33 Boston, 1933
34 Chi. Cardinals, 1934
Detroit, 1934
Most Passes Completed, Game
42 N.Y. Jets vs. San Francisco, Sept. 21, 1980
41 Houston vs. Dallas, Nov. 10, 1991 (OT)
40 Cincinnati vs. San Diego, Dec. 20, 1982
Dallas vs. Detroit, Sept. 15, 1985
N.Y. Giants vs. Cincinnati, Oct. 13, 1985
Fewest Passes Completed, Game
0 By many teams. Last time: Buffalo vs. N.Y. Jets, Sept. 29, 1974
Most Passes Completed, Both Teams, Game
68 San Francisco (37) vs. Atlanta (31), Oct. 6, 1985
66 Cincinnati (40) vs. San Diego (26), Dec. 20, 1982
65 San Diego (33) vs. San Francisco (32), Dec. 11, 1982
San Diego (37) vs. Miami (28), Nov. 18, 1984 (OT)
Houston (41) vs. Dallas (24), Nov. 10, 1991 (OT)
Fewest Passes Completed, Both Teams, Game
1 Chi. Cardinals (0) vs. Philadelphia (1), Nov. 8, 1936
Detroit (0) vs. Cleveland (1), Sept. 10, 1937
Chi. Cardinals (0) vs. Detroit (1), Sept. 15, 1940
Brooklyn (0) vs. Pittsburgh (1), Nov. 29, 1942
2 Chi. Cardinals (0) vs. Detroit (2), Nov. 3, 1935
Buffalo (0) vs. N.Y. Jets (2), Sept. 29, 1974
Chi. Cardinals (0) vs. Green Bay (2), Nov. 18, 1934
3 In seven games

Yards Gained

Most Seasons Leading League, Passing Yardage
10 San Diego, 1965, 1968, 1971, 1978-83, 1985
8 Chi. Bears, 1932, 1939, 1941, 1943, 1945, 1949, 1954, 1964
Washington, 1938, 1940, 1944, 1947-48, 1967, 1974, 1989
7 Houston, 1960-61, 1963-64, 1990-92
Most Consecutive Seasons Leading League, Passing Yardage
6 San Diego, 1978-83
4 Green Bay, 1934-37
3 Miami, 1986-88
Houston, 1990-92
Most Yards Gained, Passing, Season
5,018 Miami, 1984
4,870 San Diego, 1985
4,805 Houston, 1990
Fewest Yards Gained, Passing, Season
302 Chi. Cardinals, 1934
357 Cincinnati, 1933
459 Boston, 1934
Most Yards Gained, Passing, Game
554 Los Angeles vs. N.Y. Yanks, Sept. 28, 1951
530 Minnesota vs. Baltimore, Sept. 28, 1969
521 Miami vs. N.Y. Jets, Oct. 23, 1988

Fewest Yards Gained, Passing, Game
- −53 Denver vs. Oakland, Sept. 10, 1967
- −52 Cincinnati vs. Houston, Oct. 31, 1971
- −39 Atlanta vs. San Francisco, Oct. 23, 1976

Most Yards Gained, Passing, Both Teams, Game
- 884 N.Y. Jets (449) vs. Miami (435), Sept. 21, 1986 (OT)
- 883 San Diego (486) vs. Cincinnati (397), Dec. 20, 1982
- 849 Minnesota (471) vs. Washington (378), Nov. 2, 1986 (OT)

Fewest Yards Gained, Passing, Both Teams, Game
- −11 Green Bay (−10) vs. Dallas (−1), Oct. 24, 1965
- 1 Chi. Cardinals (0) vs. Philadelphia (1), Nov. 8, 1936
- 7 Brooklyn (0) vs. Pittsburgh (7), Nov. 29, 1942

Times Sacked

Most Seasons Leading League, Fewest Times Sacked
- 10 Miami, 1973, 1982-90
- 4 San Diego, 1963-64, 1967-68
  San Francisco, 1964-65, 1970-71
- 3 N.Y. Jets, 1965-66, 1968
  Houston, 1961-62, 1978
  St. Louis, 1974-76
  Washington, 1966-67, 1991

Most Consecutive Seasons Leading League, Fewest Times Sacked
- 9 Miami, 1982-90
- 3 St. Louis, 1974-76
- 2 By many teams

Most Times Sacked, Season
- 104 Philadelphia, 1986
- 72 Philadelphia, 1987
- 70 Atlanta, 1968

Fewest Times Sacked, Season
- 7 Miami, 1988
- 8 San Francisco, 1970
  St. Louis, 1975
- 9 N.Y. Jets, 1966
  Washington, 1991

Most Times Sacked, Game
- 12 Pittsburgh vs. Dallas, Nov. 20, 1966
  Baltimore vs. St. Louis, Oct. 26, 1980
  Detroit vs. Chicago, Dec. 16, 1984
  Houston vs. Dallas, Sept. 29, 1985
- 11 St. Louis vs. N.Y. Giants, Nov. 1, 1964
  Los Angeles vs. Baltimore, Nov. 22, 1964
  Denver vs. Buffalo, Dec. 13, 1964
  Green Bay vs. Detroit, Nov. 7, 1965
  Buffalo vs. Oakland, Oct. 15, 1967
  Denver vs. Oakland, Nov. 5, 1967
  Atlanta vs. St. Louis, Nov. 24, 1968
  Detroit vs. Dallas, Oct. 6, 1975
  Philadelphia vs. St. Louis, Dec. 18, 1983
  Cleveland vs. Kansas City, Sept. 30, 1984
  Minnesota vs. Chicago, Oct. 28, 1984
  Atlanta vs. Cleveland, Nov. 18, 1984
  Dallas vs. San Diego, Nov. 16, 1986
  Philadelphia vs. Detroit, Nov. 16, 1986
  Philadelphia vs. L.A. Raiders, Nov. 30, 1986 (OT)
  L.A. Raiders vs. Seattle, Dec. 8, 1986
  N.Y. Jets vs. Dallas, Oct. 4, 1987
  Philadelphia vs. Chicago, Oct. 4, 1987
  Dallas vs. Philadelphia, Sept. 15, 1991
  Cleveland vs. Indianapolis, Sept. 6, 1992
- 10 By many teams

Most Times Sacked, Both Teams, Game
- 18 Green Bay (10) vs. San Diego (8), Sept. 24, 1978
- 17 Buffalo (10) vs. N.Y. Titans (7), Nov. 23, 1961
  Pittsburgh (12) vs. Dallas (5), Nov. 20, 1966
  Atlanta (9) vs. Philadelphia (8), Dec. 16, 1984
  Philadelphia (11) vs. L.A. Raiders (6), Nov. 30, 1986 (OT)
- 16 Los Angeles (11) vs. Baltimore (5), Nov. 22, 1964
  Buffalo (11) vs. Oakland (5), Oct. 15, 1967

Completion Percentage

Most Seasons Leading League, Completion Percentage
- 11 Washington, 1937, 1939-40, 1942-45, 1947-48, 1969-70
- 9 San Francisco, 1952, 1957-58, 1965, 1981, 1983, 1987, 1989, 1992
- 7 Green Bay, 1936, 1941, 1961-62, 1964, 1966, 1968

Most Consecutive Seasons Leading League, Completion Percentage
- 4 Washington, 1942-45
  Kansas City, 1966-69
- 3 Cleveland, 1953-55
- 2 By many teams

Highest Completion Percentage, Season
- 70.65 Cincinnati, 1982 (310-219)
- 70.19 San Francisco, 1989 (483-339)
- 66.46 San Francisco, 1992 (480-319)

Lowest Completion Percentage, Season
- 22.9 Philadelphia, 1936 (170-39)
- 24.5 Cincinnati, 1933 (102-25)
- 25.0 Pittsburgh, 1941 (168-42)

Touchdowns

Most Touchdowns, Passing, Season
- 49 Miami, 1984
- 48 Houston, 1961
- 46 Miami, 1986

Fewest Touchdowns, Passing, Season
- 0 Cincinnati, 1933
  Pittsburgh, 1945
- 1 Boston, 1932
  Boston, 1933
  Chi. Cardinals, 1934
  Cincinnati/St. Louis, 1934
  Detroit, 1942
- 2 Chi. Cardinals, 1932
  Stapleton, 1932
  Chi. Cardinals, 1935
  Brooklyn, 1936
  Pittsburgh, 1942

Most Touchdowns, Passing, Game
- 7 Chi. Bears vs. N.Y. Giants, Nov. 14, 1943
  Philadelphia vs. Washington, Oct. 17, 1954
  Houston vs. N.Y. Titans, Nov. 19, 1961
  Houston vs. N.Y. Titans, Oct. 14, 1962
  N.Y. Giants vs. Washington, Oct. 28, 1962
  Minnesota vs. Baltimore, Sept. 28, 1969
  San Diego vs. Oakland, Nov. 22, 1981
- 6 By many teams.

Most Touchdowns, Passing, Both Teams, Game
- 12 New Orleans (6) vs. St. Louis (6), Nov. 2, 1969
- 11 N.Y. Giants (7) vs. Washington (4), Oct. 28, 1962
  Oakland (6) vs. Houston (5), Dec. 22, 1963
- 10 San Diego (5) vs. Seattle (5), Sept. 15, 1985
  Miami (6) vs. N.Y. Jets (4), Sept. 21, 1986 (OT)

Passes Had Intercepted

Most Passes Had Intercepted, Season
- 48 Houston, 1962
- 45 Denver, 1961
- 41 Card-Pitt, 1944

Fewest Passes Had Intercepted, Season
- 5 Cleveland, 1960
  Green Bay, 1966
  Kansas City, 1990
  N.Y. Giants, 1990
- 6 Green Bay, 1964
  St. Louis, 1982
- 7 Los Angeles, 1969

Most Passes Had Intercepted, Game
- 9 Detroit vs. Green Bay, Oct. 24, 1943
  Pittsburgh vs. Philadelphia, Dec. 12, 1965
- 8 Green Bay vs. N.Y. Giants, Nov. 21, 1948
  Chi. Cardinals vs. Philadelphia, Sept. 24, 1950
  N.Y. Yanks vs. N.Y. Giants, Dec. 16, 1951
  Denver vs. Houston, Dec. 2, 1962
  Chi. Bears vs. Detroit, Sept. 22, 1968
  Baltimore vs. N.Y. Jets, Sept. 23, 1973
- 7 By many teams. Last time: Green Bay vs. New Orleans, Sept. 14, 1986

Most Passes Had Intercepted, Both Teams, Game
- 13 Denver (8) vs. Houston (5), Dec. 2, 1962
- 11 Philadelphia (7) vs. Boston (4), Nov. 3, 1935
  Boston (6) vs. Pittsburgh (5), Dec. 1, 1935
  Cleveland (7) vs. Green Bay (4), Oct. 30, 1938
  Green Bay (7) vs. Detroit (4), Oct. 20, 1940
  Detroit (7) vs. Chi. Bears (4), Nov. 22, 1942
  Detroit (7) vs. Cleveland (4), Nov. 26, 1944
  Chi. Cardinals (8) vs. Philadelphia (3), Sept. 24, 1950
  Washington (7) vs. N.Y. Giants (4), Dec. 8, 1963
  Pittsburgh (9) vs. Philadelphia (2), Dec 12, 1965
- 10 In many games

Punting

Most Seasons Leading League (Average Distance)
- 7 Denver, 1962-64, 1966-67, 1982, 1988
- 6 Washington, 1940-43, 1945, 1958
  Kansas City, 1968, 1971-73, 1979, 1984
- 4 L.A. Rams, 1946, 1949, 1955-56
  Baltimore/Indianapolis, 1966, 1969, 1983, 1985

Most Consecutive Seasons Leading League (Average Distance)
- 4 Washington, 1940-43
- 3 Cleveland, 1950-52
  Denver, 1962-64
  Kansas City, 1971-73

Most Punts, Season
- 114 Chicago, 1981
- 113 Boston, 1934
  Brooklyn, 1934
- 112 Boston, 1935

Fewest Punts, Season
- 23 San Diego, 1982
- 31 Cincinnati, 1982
- 32 Chi. Bears, 1941

Most Punts, Game
- 17 Chi. Bears vs. Green Bay, Oct. 22, 1933
  Cincinnati vs. Pittsburgh, Oct. 22, 1933
- 16 Cincinnati vs. Portsmouth, Sept. 17, 1933
  Chi. Cardinals vs. Chi. Bears, Nov. 30, 1933
  Chi. Cardinals vs. Detroit, Sept. 15, 1940

Fewest Punts, Game
- 0 By many teams

Most Punts, Both Teams, Game
- 31 Chi. Bears (17) vs. Green Bay (14), Oct. 22, 1933
  Cincinnati (17), vs. Pittsburgh (14), Oct. 22, 1933
- 29 Chi. Cardinals (15) vs. Cincinnati (14), Nov. 12, 1933
  Chi. Cardinals (16) vs. Chi. Bears (13), Nov. 30, 1933
  Chi. Cardinals (16) vs. Detroit (13), Sept. 15, 1940
- 28 Philadelphia (14) vs. Washington (14), Nov. 5, 1939

Fewest Punts, Both Teams, Game
- 0 Buffalo vs. San Francisco, Sept. 13, 1992
- 1 Baltimore (0) vs. Cleveland (1), Nov. 1, 1959
  Dall. Cowboys (0) vs. Cleveland (1), Dec. 3, 1961
  Chicago (0) vs. Detroit (1), Oct. 1, 1972
  San Francisco (0) vs. N.Y. Giants (1), Oct. 15, 1972
  Green Bay (0) vs. Buffalo (1), Dec. 5, 1982
  Miami (0) vs. Buffalo (1), Oct. 12, 1986
  Green Bay (0) vs. Chicago (1), Dec. 17, 1989
- 2 In many games

Average Yardage
Highest Average Distance, Punting, Season
47.6 Detroit, 1961 (56-2,664)
47.0 Pittsburgh, 1961 (73-3,431)
46.9 Pittsburgh, 1953 (80-3,752)
Lowest Average Distance, Punting, Season
32.7 Card-Pitt, 1944 (60-1,964)
33.8 Cincinnati, 1986 (59-1,996)
33.9 Detroit, 1969 (74-2,510)

Punt Returns
Most Seasons Leading League (Average Return)
9 Detroit, 1943-45, 1951-52, 1962, 1966, 1969, 1991
7 Chi. Cardinals/St. Louis, 1948-49, 1955-56, 1959, 1986-87
5 Cleveland, 1958, 1960, 1964-65, 1967
Green Bay, 1950, 1953-54, 1961, 1972
Dall. Texans/Kansas City, 1960, 1968, 1970, 1979-80
Most Consecutive Seasons Leading League (Average Return)
3 Detroit, 1943-45
2 By many teams
Most Punt Returns, Season
71 Pittsburgh, 1976
Tampa Bay, 1979
L.A. Raiders, 1985
67 Pittsburgh, 1974
Los Angeles, 1978
L.A. Raiders, 1984
65 San Francisco, 1976
Fewest Punt Returns, Season
12 Baltimore, 1981
San Diego, 1982
14 Los Angeles, 1961
Philadelphia, 1962
Baltimore, 1982
15 Houston, 1960
Washington, 1960
Oakland, 1961
N.Y. Giants, 1969
Philadelphia, 1973
Kansas City, 1982
Most Punt Returns, Game
12 Philadelphia vs. Cleveland, Dec. 3, 1950
11 Chi. Bears vs. Chi. Cardinals, Oct. 8, 1950
Washington vs. Tampa Bay, Oct. 9, 1977
10 Philadelphia vs. N.Y. Giants, Nov. 26, 1950
Philadelphia vs. Tampa Bay, Sept. 18, 1977
Pittsburgh vs. Buffalo, Dec. 16, 1979
Washington vs. New Orleans, Dec. 26, 1982
Philadelphia vs. Seattle, Dec. 13, 1992 (OT)
Most Punt Returns, Both Teams, Game
17 Philadelphia (12) vs. Cleveland (5), Dec. 3, 1950
16 N.Y. Giants (9) vs. Philadelphia (7), Dec. 12, 1954
Washington (11) vs. Tampa Bay (5), Oct. 9, 1977
15 Detroit (8) vs. Cleveland (7), Sept. 27, 1942
Los Angeles (8) vs. Baltimore (7), Nov. 27, 1966
Pittsburgh (8) vs. Houston (7), Dec. 1, 1974
Philadelphia (10) vs. Tampa Bay (5), Sept. 18, 1977
Baltimore (9) vs. Kansas City (6), Sept. 2, 1979
Washington (10) vs. New Orleans (5), Dec. 26, 1982
L.A. Raiders (8) vs. Cleveland (7), Nov. 16, 1986

Fair Catches
Most Fair Catches, Season
34 Baltimore, 1971
32 San Diego, 1969
30 St. Louis, 1967
Minnesota, 1971
Fewest Fair Catches, Season
0 San Diego, 1975
New England, 1976
Tampa Bay, 1976
Pittsburgh, 1977
Dallas, 1982
1 Cleveland, 1974
San Francisco, 1975
Kansas City, 1976
St. Louis, 1976
San Diego, 1976
L.A. Rams, 1982
St. Louis, 1982
Tampa Bay, 1982
2 By many teams
Most Fair Catches, Game
7 Minnesota vs. Dallas, Sept. 25, 1966
Detroit vs. Chicago, Nov. 21, 1976
Philadelphia vs. Buffalo, Dec. 27, 1987
6 By many teams

Yards Gained
Most Yards, Punt Returns, Season
785 L.A. Raiders, 1985
781 Chi. Bears, 1948
774 Pittsburgh, 1974
Fewest Yards, Punt Returns, Season
27 St. Louis, 1965
35 N.Y. Giants, 1965
37 New England, 1972
Most Yards, Punt Returns, Game
231 Detroit vs. San Francisco, Oct. 6, 1963
225 Oakland vs. Buffalo, Sept. 15, 1968
219 Los Angeles vs. Atlanta, Oct. 11, 1981
Most Yards, Punt Returns, Both Teams, Game
282 Los Angeles (219) vs. Atlanta (63), Oct. 11, 1981
245 Detroit (231) vs. San Francisco (14), Oct. 6, 1963
244 Oakland (225) vs. Buffalo (19), Sept. 15, 1968

Average Yards Returning Punts
Highest Average, Punt Returns, Season
20.2 Chi. Bears, 1941 (27-546)
19.1 Chi. Cardinals, 1948 (35-669)
18.2 Chi. Cardinals, 1949 (30-546)
Lowest Average, Punt Returns, Season
1.2 St. Louis, 1965 (23-27)
1.5 N.Y. Giants, 1965 (24-35)
1.7 Washington, 1970 (27-45)

Touchdowns Returning Punts
Most Touchdowns, Punt Returns, Season
5 Chi. Cardinals, 1959
4 Chi. Cardinals, 1948
Detroit, 1951
N.Y. Giants, 1951
Denver, 1976
3 Washington, 1941
Detroit, 1952
Pittsburgh, 1952
Houston, 1975
Los Angeles, 1981
Most Touchdowns, Punt Returns, Game
2 Detroit vs. Los Angeles, Oct. 14, 1951
Detroit vs. Green Bay, Nov. 22, 1951
Chi. Cardinals vs. Pittsburgh, Nov. 1, 1959
Chi. Cardinals vs. N.Y. Giants, Nov. 22, 1959
N.Y. Titans vs. Denver, Sept. 24, 1961
Denver vs. Cleveland, Sept. 26, 1976
Los Angeles vs. Atlanta, Oct. 11, 1981
St. Louis vs. Tampa Bay, Dec. 21, 1986
L.A. Rams vs. Atlanta, Dec. 27, 1992
Most Touchdowns, Punt Returns, Both Teams, Game
2 Philadelphia (1) vs. Washington (1), Nov. 9, 1952
Kansas City (1) vs. Buffalo (1), Sept. 11, 1966
Baltimore (1) vs. New England (1), Nov. 18, 1979
L.A. Raiders (1) vs. Philadelphia (1), Nov. 30, 1986 (OT)
Cincinnati (1) vs. Green Bay (1), Sept. 20, 1992
(Also see previous record)

Kickoff Returns
Most Seasons Leading League (Average Return)
7 Washington, 1942, 1947, 1962-63, 1973-74, 1981
6 Chicago Bears, 1943, 1948, 1958, 1966, 1972, 1985
5 N.Y. Giants, 1944, 1946, 1949, 1951, 1953
Most Consecutive Seasons Leading League (Average Return)
3 Denver, 1965-67
2 By many teams
Most Kickoff Returns, Season
88 New Orleans, 1980
86 Minnesota, 1984
84 Baltimore, 1981
Fewest Kickoff Returns, Season
17 N.Y. Giants, 1944
20 N.Y. Giants, 1941, 1943
Chi. Bears, 1942
23 Washington, 1942
Most Kickoff Returns, Game
12 N.Y. Giants vs. Washington, Nov. 27, 1966
10 By many teams
Most Kickoff Returns, Both Teams, Game
19 N.Y. Giants (12) vs. Washington (7), Nov. 27, 1966
18 Houston (10) vs. Oakland (8), Dec. 22, 1963
17 Washington (9) vs. Green Bay (8), Oct. 17, 1983
San Diego (9) vs. Pittsburgh (8), Dec. 8, 1985
Detroit (9) vs. Green Bay (8), Nov. 27, 1986
L.A. Raiders (9) vs. Seattle (8), Dec. 18, 1988

Yards Gained
Most Yards, Kickoff Returns, Season
1,973 New Orleans, 1980
1,824 Houston, 1963
1,801 Denver, 1963
Fewest Yards, Kickoff Returns, Season
282 N.Y. Giants, 1940
381 Green Bay, 1940
424 Chicago, 1963
Most Yards, Kickoff Returns, Game
362 Detroit vs. Los Angeles, Oct. 29, 1950
304 Chi. Bears vs. Green Bay, Nov. 9, 1952
295 Denver vs. Boston, Oct. 4, 1964
Most Yards, Kickoff Returns, Both Teams, Game
560 Detroit (362) vs. Los Angeles (198), Oct. 29, 1950
453 Washington (236) vs. Philadelphia (217), Sept. 28, 1947
447 N.Y. Giants (236) vs. Cleveland (211), Dec. 4, 1966

Average Yardage
Highest Average, Kickoff Returns, Season
29.4 Chicago, 1972 (52-1,528)
28.9 Pittsburgh, 1952 (39-1,128)
28.2 Washington, 1962 (61-1,720)
Lowest Average, Kickoff Returns, Season
16.1 Cleveland, 1991 (55-888)
16.26 Philadelphia, 1991 (47-764)
16.27 Chicago, 1990 (54-879)

Touchdowns

Most Touchdowns, Kickoff Returns, Season

4 Green Bay, 1967
Chicago, 1970
3 Los Angeles, 1950
Chi. Cardinals, 1954
San Francisco, 1963
Denver, 1966
Chicago, 1967
New England, 1977
L.A. Rams, 1985
2 By many teams

Most Touchdowns, Kickoff Returns, Game

2 Chi. Bears vs. Green Bay, Sept. 22, 1940
Chi. Bears vs. Green Bay, Nov. 9, 1952
Philadelphia vs. Dallas, Nov. 6, 1966
Green Bay vs. Cleveland, Nov. 12, 1967
L.A. Rams vs. Green Bay, Nov. 24, 1985

Most Touchdowns, Kickoff Returns, Both Teams, Game

2 Washington (1) vs. Philadelphia (1), Nov. 1, 1942
Washington (1) vs. Philadelphia (1), Sept. 28, 1947
Los Angeles (1) vs. Detroit (1), Oct. 29, 1950
N.Y. Yanks (1) vs. N.Y. Giants (1), Nov. 4, 1951 (consecutive)
Baltimore (1) vs. Chi. Bears (1), Oct. 4, 1958
Buffalo (1) vs. Boston (1), Nov. 3, 1962
Pittsburgh (1) vs. Dallas (1), Oct. 30, 1966
St. Louis (1) vs. Washington (1), Sept. 23, 1973 (consecutive)
Atlanta (1) vs. San Francisco (1), Dec. 20, 1987 (consecutive)
Houston (1) vs. Pittsburgh (1), Dec. 4, 1988
(Also see previous record)

Fumbles

Most Fumbles, Season

56 Chi. Bears, 1938
San Francisco, 1978
54 Philadelphia, 1946
51 New England, 1973

Fewest Fumbles, Season

8 Cleveland, 1959
11 Green Bay, 1944
12 Brooklyn, 1934
Detroit, 1943
Cincinnati, 1982
Minnesota, 1982

Most Fumbles, Game

10 Phil-Pitt vs. New York, Oct. 9, 1943
Detroit vs. Minnesota, Nov. 12, 1967
Kansas City vs. Houston, Oct. 12, 1969
San Francisco vs. Detroit, Dec. 17, 1978
9 Philadelphia vs. Green Bay, Oct. 13, 1946
Kansas City vs. San Diego, Nov. 15, 1964
N.Y. Giants vs. Buffalo, Oct. 20, 1975
St. Louis vs. Washington, Oct. 25, 1976
San Diego vs. Green Bay, Sept. 24, 1978
Pittsburgh vs. Cincinnati, Oct. 14, 1979
Cleveland vs. Seattle, Dec. 20, 1981
Cleveland vs. Pittsburgh, Dec. 23, 1990
8 By many teams

Most Fumbles, Both Teams, Game

14 Washington (8) vs. Pittsburgh (6), Nov. 14, 1937
Chi. Bears (7) vs. Cleveland (7), Nov. 24, 1940
St. Louis (8) vs. N.Y. Giants (6), Sept. 17, 1961
Kansas City (10) vs. Houston (4), Oct. 12, 1969
13 Washington (8) vs. Pittsburgh (5), Nov. 14, 1937
Philadelphia (7) vs. Boston (6), Dec. 8, 1946
N.Y. Giants (7) vs. Washington (6), Nov. 5, 1950
Kansas City (9) vs. San Diego (4), Nov. 15, 1964
Buffalo (7) vs. Denver (6), Dec. 13, 1964
N.Y. Jets (7) vs. Houston (6), Sept. 12, 1965
Houston (8) vs. Pittsburgh (5), Dec. 9, 1973
St. Louis (9) vs. Washington (4), Oct. 25, 1976
Cleveland (9) vs. Seattle (4), Dec. 20, 1981
Green Bay (7) vs. Detroit (6), Oct. 6, 1985
12 In many games

Fumbles Lost

Most Fumbles Lost, Season

36 Chi. Cardinals, 1959
31 Green Bay, 1952
29 Chi. Cardinals, 1946
Pittsburgh, 1950

Fewest Fumbles Lost, Season

3 Philadelphia, 1938
Minnesota, 1980
4 San Francisco, 1960
Kansas City, 1982
5 Chi. Cardinals, 1943
Detroit, 1943
N.Y. Giants, 1943
Cleveland, 1959
Minnesota, 1982

Most Fumbles Lost, Game

8 St. Louis vs. Washington, Oct. 25, 1976
Cleveland vs. Pittsburgh, Dec. 23, 1990
7 Cincinnati vs. Buffalo, Nov. 30, 1969
Pittsburgh vs. Cincinnati, Oct. 14, 1979
Cleveland vs. Seattle, Dec. 20, 1981
6 By many teams

Fumbles Recovered

Most Fumbles Recovered, Season, Own and Opponents'

58 Minnesota, 1963 (27 own, 31 opp)
51 Chi. Bears, 1938 (37 own, 14 opp)
San Francisco, 1978 (24 own, 27 opp)
50 Philadelphia, 1987 (23 own, 27 opp)

Fewest Fumbles Recovered, Season, Own and Opponents'

9 San Francisco, 1982 (5 own, 4 opp)
11 Cincinnati, 1982 (5 own, 6 opp)
13 Baltimore, 1967 (5 own, 8 opp)
N.Y. Jets, 1967 (7 own, 6 opp)
Philadelphia, 1968 (6 own, 7 opp)
Miami, 1973 (5 own, 8 opp)
Chicago, 1982 (6 own, 7 opp)
Denver, 1982 (6 own, 7 opp)
Miami, 1982 (5 own, 8 opp)
N.Y. Giants, 1982 (7 own, 6 opp)

Most Fumbles Recovered, Game, Own and Opponents'

10 Denver vs. Buffalo, Dec. 13, 1964 (5 own, 5 opp)
Pittsburgh vs. Houston, Dec. 9, 1973 (5 own, 5 opp)
Washington vs. St. Louis, Oct. 25, 1976 (2 own, 8 opp)
9 St. Louis vs. N.Y. Giants, Sept. 17, 1961 (6 own, 3 opp)
Houston vs. Cincinnati, Oct. 27, 1974 (4 own, 5 opp)
Kansas City vs. Dallas, Nov. 10, 1975 (4 own, 5 opp)
Green Bay vs. Detroit, Oct. 6, 1985 (5 own, 4 opp)
8 By many teams

Most Own Fumbles Recovered, Season

37 Chi. Bears, 1938
28 Pittsburgh, 1987
27 Philadelphia, 1946
Minnesota, 1963

Fewest Own Fumbles Recovered, Season

2 Washington, 1958
3 Detroit, 1956
Cleveland, 1959
Houston, 1982
4 By many teams

Most Opponents' Fumbles Recovered, Season

31 Minnesota, 1963
29 Cleveland, 1951
28 Green Bay, 1946
Houston, 1977
Seattle, 1983

Fewest Opponents' Fumbles Recovered, Season

3 Los Angeles, 1974
4 Philadelphia, 1944
San Francisco, 1982
5 Baltimore, 1982

Most Opponents' Fumbles Recovered, Game

8 Washington vs. St. Louis, Oct. 25, 1976
Pittsburgh vs. Cleveland, Dec. 23, 1990
7 Buffalo vs. Cincinnati, Nov. 30, 1969
Cincinnati vs. Pittsburgh, Oct. 14, 1979
Seattle vs. Cleveland, Dec. 20, 1981
6 By many teams

Touchdowns

Most Touchdowns, Fumbles Recovered, Season, Own and Opponents'

5 Chi. Bears, 1942 (1 own, 4 opp)
Los Angeles, 1952 (1 own, 4 opp)
San Francisco, 1965 (1 own, 4 opp)
Oakland, 1978 (2 own, 3 opp)
4 Chi. Bears, 1948 (1 own, 3 opp)
Boston, 1948 (4 opp)
Denver, 1979 (1 own, 3 opp)
Atlanta, 1981 (1 own, 3 opp)
Denver, 1984 (4 opp)
St. Louis, 1987 (4 opp)
Minnesota, 1989 (4 opp)
Atlanta, 1991 (4 opp)
3 By many teams

Most Touchdowns, Own Fumbles Recovered, Season

2 Chi. Bears, 1953
New England, 1973
Buffalo, 1974
Denver, 1975
Oakland, 1978
Green Bay, 1982
New Orleans, 1983
Cleveland, 1986
Green Bay, 1989

Most Touchdowns, Opponents' Fumbles Recovered, Season

4 Detroit, 1937
Chi. Bears, 1942
Boston, 1948
Los Angeles, 1952
San Francisco, 1965
Denver, 1984
St. Louis, 1987
Minnesota, 1989
Atlanta, 1991
3 By many teams

Most Touchdowns, Fumbles Recovered, Game, Own and Opponents'

2 By many teams

Most Touchdowns, Fumbled Recovered, Game, Both Teams, Own and Opponents'

3 Detroit (2) vs. Minnesota (1), Dec. 9, 1962 (2 own, 1 opp)
Green Bay (2) vs. Dallas (1), Nov. 29, 1964 (3 opp)
Oakland (2) vs. Buffalo (1), Dec. 24, 1967 (3 opp)

Most Touchdowns, Own Fumbles Recovered, Game

1 By many teams

Most Touchdowns, Opponents' Fumbles Recovered, Game

2 Detroit vs. Cleveland, Nov. 7, 1937
Philadelphia vs. N.Y. Giants, Sept. 25, 1938
Chi. Bears vs. Washington, Nov. 28, 1948
N.Y. Giants vs. Pittsburgh, Sept. 17, 1950
Cleveland vs. Dall. Cowboys, Dec. 3, 1961
Cleveland vs. N.Y. Giants, Oct. 25, 1964
Green Bay vs. Dallas, Nov. 29, 1964
San Francisco vs. Detroit, Nov. 14, 1965
Oakland vs. Buffalo, Dec. 24, 1967
N.Y. Giants vs. Green Bay, Sept. 19, 1971
Washington vs. San Diego, Sept. 16, 1973
New Orleans vs. San Francisco, Oct. 19, 1975
Cincinnati vs. Pittsburgh, Oct. 14, 1979
Atlanta vs. Detroit, Oct. 5, 1980
Kansas City vs. Oakland, Oct. 5, 1980
New England vs. Baltimore, Nov. 23, 1980
Denver vs. Green Bay, Oct. 15, 1984
Miami vs. Kansas City, Oct. 11, 1987
St. Louis vs. New Orleans, Oct. 11, 1987
Minnesota vs. Atlanta, Dec. 10, 1989
Philadelphia vs. Phoenix, Nov. 24, 1991
Cincinnati vs. Seattle, Sept. 6, 1992

Most Touchdowns, Opponents' Fumbled Recovered, Game, Both Teams

3 Green Bay (2) vs. Dallas (1), Nov. 29, 1964
Oakland (2) vs. Buffalo (1), Dec. 24, 1967

Turnovers

(Number of times losing the ball on interceptions and fumbles.)

Most Turnovers, Season

63 San Francisco, 1978
58 Chi. Bears, 1947
Pittsburgh, 1950
N.Y. Giants, 1983
57 Green Bay, 1950
Houston, 1962, 1963
Pittsburgh, 1965

Fewest Turnovers, Season

12 Kansas City, 1982
14 N.Y. Giants, 1943
Cleveland, 1959
N.Y. Giants, 1990
16 San Francisco, 1960
Cincinnati, 1982
St. Louis, 1982
Washington, 1982

Most Turnovers, Game

12 Detroit vs. Chi. Bears, Nov. 22, 1942
Chi. Cardinals vs. Philadelphia, Sept. 24, 1950
Pittsburgh vs. Philadelphia, Dec. 12, 1965
11 San Diego vs. Green Bay, Sept. 24, 1978
10 Washington vs. N.Y. Giants, Dec. 4, 1938
Pittsburgh vs. Green Bay, Nov. 23, 1941
Detroit vs. Green Bay, Oct. 24, 1943
Chi. Cardinals vs. Green Bay, Nov. 10, 1946
Chi. Cardinals vs. N.Y. Giants, Nov. 2, 1952
Minnesota vs. Detroit, Dec. 9, 1962
Houston vs. Oakland, Sept. 7, 1963
Washington vs. N.Y. Giants, Dec. 8, 1963
Chicago vs. Detroit, Sept. 22, 1968
St. Louis vs. Washington, Oct. 25, 1976
N.Y. Jets vs. New England, Nov. 21, 1976
San Francisco vs. Dallas, Oct. 12, 1980
Cleveland vs. Seattle, Dec. 20, 1981
Detroit vs. Denver, Oct. 7, 1984

Most Turnovers, Both Teams, Game

17 Detroit (12) vs. Chi. Bears (5), Nov. 22, 1942
Boston (9) vs. Philadelphia (8), Dec. 8, 1946
16 Chi. Cardinals (12) vs. Philadelphia (4), Sept. 24, 1950
Chi. Cardinals (8) vs. Chi. Bears (8), Dec. 7, 1958
Minnesota (10) vs. Detroit (6), Dec. 9, 1962
Houston (9) vs. Kansas City (7), Oct. 12, 1969
15 Philadelphia (8) vs. Chi. Cardinals (7), Oct. 3, 1954
Denver (9) vs. Houston (6), Dec. 2, 1962
Washington (10) vs. N.Y. Giants (5), Dec. 8, 1963
St. Louis (9) vs. Kansas City (6), Oct. 2, 1983

Penalties

Most Seasons Leading League, Fewest Penalties

13 Miami, 1968, 1976-84, 1986, 1990-91
9 Pittsburgh, 1946-47, 1950-52, 1954, 1963, 1965, 1968
6 Boston/New England, 1962, 1964-65, 1973, 1987, 1989

Most Consecutive Seasons Leading League, Fewest Penalties

9 Miami, 1976-84
3 Pittsburgh, 1950-52
2 By many teams

Most Seasons Leading League, Most Penalties

16 Chi. Bears, 1941-44, 1946-49, 1951, 1959-61, 1963, 1965, 1968, 1976
8 Oakland/L.A. Raiders, 1963, 1966, 1968-69, 1975, 1982, 1984, 1991
6 L.A. Rams, 1950, 1952, 1962, 1969, 1978, 1980

Most Consecutive Seasons Leading League, Most Penalties

4 Chi. Bears, 1941-44, 1946-49
3 Chi. Cardinals, 1954-56
Chi. Bears, 1959-61
Houston, 1988-90

Fewest Penalties, Season

19 Detroit, 1937
21 Boston, 1935
24 Philadelphia, 1936

Most Penalties, Season

149 Houston, 1989
144 Buffalo, 1983
143 L.A. Raiders, 1984

Fewest Penalties, Game

0 By many teams. Last time: San Francisco vs. Philadelphia, Nov. 29, 1992

Most Penalties, Game

22 Brooklyn vs. Green Bay, Sept. 17, 1944
Chi. Bears vs. Philadelphia, Nov. 26, 1944
21 Cleveland vs. Chi. Bears, Nov. 25, 1951
20 Tampa Bay vs. Seattle, Oct. 17, 1976

Fewest Penalties, Both Teams, Game

0 Brooklyn vs. Pittsburgh, Oct. 28, 1934
Brooklyn vs. Boston, Sept. 28, 1936
Cleveland vs. Chi. Bears, Oct. 9, 1938
Pittsburgh vs. Philadelphia, Nov. 10, 1940

Most Penalties, Both Teams, Game

37 Cleveland (21) vs. Chi. Bears (16), Nov. 25, 1951
35 Tampa Bay (20) vs. Seattle (15), Oct. 17, 1976
33 Brooklyn (22) vs. Green Bay (11), Sept. 17, 1944

Yards Penalized

Most Seasons Leading League, Fewest Yards Penalized

13 Miami, 1967-68, 1973, 1977-84, 1990-91
8 Boston/Washington, 1935, 1953-54, 1956-58, 1970, 1985
7 Pittsburgh, 1946-47, 1950, 1952, 1962, 1965, 1968

Most Consecutive Seasons Leading League, Fewest Yards Penalized

8 Miami, 1977-84
3 Washington, 1956-58
Boston, 1964-66
2 By many teams

Most Seasons Leading League, Most Yards Penalized

15 Chi. Bears, 1935, 1937, 1939-44, 1946-47, 1949, 1951, 1961-62, 1968
8 Oakland/L.A. Raiders, 1963-64, 1968-69, 1975, 1982, 1984, 1991
6 Buffalo, 1962, 1967, 1970, 1972, 1981, 1983
Houston, 1961, 1985-86, 1988-90

Most Consecutive Seasons Leading League, Most Yards Penalized

6 Chi. Bears, 1939-44
3 Cleveland, 1976-78
Houston, 1988-90
2 By many teams

Fewest Yards Penalized, Season

139 Detroit, 1937
146 Philadelphia, 1937
159 Philadelphia, 1936

Most Yards Penalized, Season

1,274 Oakland, 1969
1,239 Baltimore, 1979
1,209 L.A. Raiders, 1984

Fewest Yards Penalized, Game

0 By many teams. Last time: San Francisco vs. Philadelphia, Nov. 29, 1992

Most Yards Penalized, Game

209 Cleveland vs. Chi. Bears, Nov. 25, 1951
191 Philadelphia vs. Seattle, Dec. 13, 1992 (OT)
190 Tampa Bay vs. Seattle, Oct. 17, 1976

Fewest Yards Penalized, Both Teams, Game

0 Brooklyn vs. Pittsburgh, Oct. 28, 1934
Brooklyn vs. Boston, Sept. 28, 1936
Cleveland vs. Chi. Bears, Oct. 9, 1938
Pittsburgh vs. Philadelphia, Nov. 10, 1940

Most Yards Penalized, Both Teams, Game

374 Cleveland (209) vs. Chi. Bears (165), Nov. 25, 1951
310 Tampa Bay (190) vs. Seattle (120), Oct. 17, 1976
309 Green Bay (184) vs. Boston (125), Oct. 21, 1945

Defense

Scoring

Most Seasons Leading League, Fewest Points Allowed

9 Chi. Bears, 1932, 1936-37, 1942, 1948, 1963, 1985-86, 1988
N.Y. Giants, 1935, 1938-39, 1941, 1944, 1958-59, 1961, 1990
6 Cleveland, 1951, 1953-57
5 Green Bay, 1935, 1947, 1962, 1965-66

Most Consecutive Seasons Leading League, Fewest Points Allowed

5 Cleveland, 1953-57
3 Buffalo, 1964-66
Minnesota, 1969-71
2 By many teams

Fewest Points Allowed, Season (Since 1932)

44 Chi. Bears, 1932
54 Brooklyn, 1933
59 Detroit, 1934

Most Points Allowed, Season

533 Baltimore, 1981
501 N.Y. Giants, 1966
487 New Orleans, 1980

Fewest Touchdowns Allowed, Season (Since 1932)

6 Chi. Bears, 1932
Brooklyn, 1933
7 Detroit, 1934
8 Green Bay, 1932

Most Touchdowns Allowed, Season

68 Baltimore, 1981
66 N.Y. Giants, 1966
63 Baltimore, 1950

First Downs

Fewest First Downs Allowed Season

77 Detroit, 1935
79 Boston, 1935
82 Washington, 1937

Most First Downs Allowed, Season

406 Baltimore, 1981
371 Seattle, 1981
366 Green Bay, 1983

Fewest First Downs Allowed, Rushing, Season
35 Chi. Bears, 1942
40 Green Bay, 1939
41 Brooklyn, 1944

Most First Downs Allowed, Rushing, Season
179 Detroit, 1985
178 New Orleans, 1980
175 Seattle, 1981

Fewest First Downs Allowed, Passing, Season
33 Chi. Bears, 1943
34 Pittsburgh, 1941
Washington, 1943
35 Detroit, 1940
Philadelphia, 1940, 1944

Most First Downs Allowed, Passing, Season
218 San Diego, 1985
216 San Diego, 1981
N.Y. Jets, 1986
214 Baltimore, 1981

Fewest First Downs Allowed, Penalty, Season
1 Boston, 1944
3 Philadelphia, 1940
Pittsburgh, 1945
Washington, 1957
4 Cleveland, 1940
Green Bay, 1943
N.Y. Giants, 1943

Most First Downs Allowed, Penalty, Season
48 Houston, 1985
46 Houston, 1986
43 L.A. Raiders, 1984

Net Yards Allowed Rushing and Passing

Most Seasons Leading League, Fewest Yards Allowed
8 Chi. Bears, 1942-43, 1948, 1958, 1963, 1984-86
6 N.Y. Giants, 1938, 1940-41, 1951, 1956, 1959
Philadelphia, 1944-45, 1949, 1953, 1981, 1991
5 Boston/Washington, 1935-37, 1939, 1946
Minnesota, 1969-70, 1975, 1988-89

Most Consecutive Seasons Leading League, Fewest Yards Allowed
3 Boston/Washington, 1935-37
Chicago, 1984-86
2 By many teams

Fewest Yards Allowed, Season
1,539 Chi. Cardinals, 1934
1,703 Chi. Bears, 1942
1,789 Brooklyn, 1933

Most Yards Allowed, Season
6,793 Baltimore, 1981
6,403 Green Bay, 1983
6,352 Minnesota, 1984

Rushing

Most Seasons Leading League, Fewest Yards Allowed
10 Chi. Bears, 1937, 1939, 1942, 1946, 1949, 1963, 1984-85, 1987-88
7 Detroit, 1938, 1950, 1952, 1962, 1970, 1980-81
Philadelphia, 1944-45, 1947-48, 1953, 1990-91
Dallas, 1966-69, 1972, 1978, 1992
5 N.Y. Giants, 1940, 1951, 1956, 1959, 1986

Most Consecutive Seasons Leading League, Fewest Yards Allowed
4 Dallas, 1966-69
2 By many teams

Fewest Yards Allowed, Rushing, Season
519 Chi. Bears, 1942
558 Philadelphia, 1944
762 Pittsburgh, 1982

Most Yards Allowed, Rushing, Season
3,228 Buffalo, 1978
3,106 New Orleans, 1980
3,010 Baltimore, 1978

Fewest Touchdowns Allowed, Rushing, Season
2 Detroit, 1934
Dallas, 1968
Minnesota, 1971
3 By many teams

Most Touchdowns Allowed, Rushing, Season
36 Oakland, 1961
31 N.Y. Giants, 1980
Tampa Bay, 1986
30 Baltimore, 1981

Passing

Most Seasons Leading League, Fewest Yards Allowed
8 Green Bay, 1947-48, 1962, 1964-68
7 Washington, 1939, 1942, 1945, 1952-53, 1980, 1985
6 Chi. Bears, 1938, 1943-44, 1958, 1960, 1963
Minnesota, 1969-70, 1972, 1975-76, 1989
Pittsburgh, 1941, 1946, 1951, 1955, 1974, 1990
Philadelphia, 1934, 1936, 1940, 1949, 1981, 1991

Most Consecutive Seasons Leading League, Fewest Yards Allowed
5 Green Bay, 1964-68
2 By many teams

Fewest Yards Allowed, Passing, Season
545 Philadelphia, 1934
558 Portsmouth, 1933
585 Chi. Cardinals, 1934

Most Yards Allowed, Passing, Season
4,389 N.Y. Jets, 1986
4,311 San Diego, 1981
4,293 San Diego, 1985

Fewest Touchdowns Allowed, Passing, Season
1 Portsmouth, 1932
Philadelphia, 1934
2 Brooklyn, 1933
Chi. Bears, 1934
3 Chi. Bears, 1932
Green Bay, 1932
Green Bay, 1934
Chi. Bears, 1936
New York, 1939
New York, 1944

Most Touchdowns Allowed, Passing, Season
40 Denver, 1963
38 St. Louis, 1969
37 Washington, 1961
Baltimore, 1981

Sacks

Most Seasons Leading League
5 Oakland/L.A. Raiders, 1966-68, 1982, 1986
4 Boston/New England, 1961, 1963, 1977, 1979
Dallas, 1966, 1968-69, 1978
Dallas/Kansas City, 1960, 1965, 1969, 1990
3 San Francisco, 1967, 1972, 1976
L.A. Rams, 1968, 1970, 1988

Most Consecutive Seasons Leading League
3 Oakland, 1966-68
2 Dallas, 1968-69

Most Sacks, Season
72 Chicago, 1984
71 Minnesota, 1989
70 Chicago, 1987

Fewest Sacks, Season
11 Baltimore, 1982
12 Buffalo, 1982
13 Baltimore, 1981

Most Sacks, Game
12 Dallas vs. Pittsburgh, Nov. 20, 1966
St. Louis vs. Baltimore, Oct. 26, 1980
Chicago vs. Detroit, Dec. 16, 1984
Dallas vs. Houston, Sept. 29, 1985
11 N.Y. Giants vs. St. Louis, Nov. 1, 1964
Baltimore vs. Los Angeles, Nov. 22, 1964
Buffalo vs. Denver, Dec. 13, 1964
Detroit vs. Green Bay, Nov. 7, 1965
Oakland vs. Buffalo, Oct. 15, 1967
Oakland vs. Denver, Nov. 5, 1967
St. Louis vs. Atlanta, Nov. 24, 1968
Dallas vs. Detroit, Oct. 6, 1975
St. Louis vs. Philadelphia, Dec. 18, 1983
Kansas City vs. Cleveland, Sept. 30, 1984
Chicago vs. Minnesota, Oct. 28, 1984
Cleveland vs. Atlanta, Nov. 18, 1984
Detroit vs. Philadelphia, Nov. 16, 1986
San Diego vs. Dallas, Nov. 16, 1986
L.A. Raiders vs. Philadelphia, Nov. 30, 1986 (OT)
Seattle vs. L.A. Raiders, Dec. 8, 1986
Chicago vs. Philadelphia, Oct. 4, 1987
Dallas vs. N.Y. Jets, Oct. 4, 1987
Indianapolis vs. Cleveland, Sept. 6, 1992
10 By many teams

Most Opponents Yards Lost Attempting to Pass, Season
666 Oakland, 1967
583 Chicago, 1984
573 San Francisco, 1976

Fewest Opponents Yards Lost Attempting to Pass, Season
75 Green Bay, 1956
77 N.Y. Bulldogs, 1949
78 Green Bay, 1958

Interceptions By

Most Seasons Leading League
9 N.Y. Giants, 1933, 1937-39, 1944, 1948, 1951, 1954, 1961
8 Green Bay, 1940, 1942-43, 1947, 1955, 1957, 1962, 1965
Chi. Bears, 1935-36, 1941-42, 1946, 1963, 1985, 1990
6 Kansas City, 1966-70, 1974

Most Consecutive Seasons Leading League
5 Kansas City, 1966-70
3 N.Y. Giants, 1937-39
2 By many teams

Most Passes Intercepted By, Season
49 San Diego, 1961
42 Green Bay, 1943
41 N.Y. Giants, 1951

Fewest Passes Intercepted By, Season
3 Houston, 1982
5 Baltimore, 1982
6 Houston, 1972
St. Louis, 1982

Most Passes Intercepted By, Game
9 Green Bay vs. Detroit, Oct. 24, 1943
Philadelphia vs. Pittsburgh, Dec. 12, 1965
8 N.Y. Giants vs. Green Bay, Nov. 21, 1948
Philadelphia vs. Chi. Cardinals, Sept. 24, 1950
N.Y. Giants vs. N.Y. Yanks, Dec. 16, 1951
Houston vs. Denver, Dec. 2, 1962
Detroit vs. Chicago, Sept. 22, 1968
N.Y. Jets vs. Baltimore, Sept. 23, 1973
7 By many teams. Last time: New Orleans vs. Green Bay, Sept. 14, 1986

Most Consecutive Games, One or More Interceptions By
46 L.A. Chargers/San Diego, 1960-63
37 Detroit, 1960-63
36 Boston, 1944-47

Most Yards Returning Interceptions, Season
929 San Diego, 1961
712 Los Angeles, 1952
697 Seattle, 1984
Fewest Yards Returning Interceptions, Season
5 Los Angeles, 1959
37 Dallas, 1989
42 Philadelphia, 1982
Most Yards Returning Interceptions, Game
325 Seattle vs. Kansas City, Nov. 4, 1984
314 Los Angeles vs. San Francisco, Oct. 18, 1964
245 Houston vs. N.Y. Jets, Oct. 15, 1967
Most Touchdowns, Returning Interceptions, Season
9 San Diego, 1961
7 Seattle, 1984
6 Cleveland, 1960
Green Bay, 1966
Detroit, 1967
Houston, 1967
Most Touchdowns Returning Interceptions, Game
4 Seattle vs. Kansas City, Nov. 4, 1984
3 Baltimore vs. Green Bay, Nov. 5, 1950
Cleveland vs. Chicago, Dec. 11, 1960
Philadelphia vs. Pittsburgh, Dec. 12, 1965
Baltimore vs. Pittsburgh, Sept. 29, 1968
Buffalo vs. N.Y. Jets, Sept. 29, 1968
Houston vs. San Diego, Dec. 19, 1971
Cincinnati vs. Houston, Dec. 17, 1972
Tampa Bay vs. New Orleans, Dec. 11, 1977
2 By many teams
Most Touchdowns Returning Interceptions, Both Teams, Game
4 Philadelphia (3) vs. Pittsburgh (1), Dec. 12, 1965
Seattle (4) vs. Kansas City (0), Nov. 4, 1984
3 Los Angeles (2) vs. Detroit (1), Nov. 1, 1953
Cleveland (2) vs. N.Y. Giants (1), Dec. 18, 1960
Pittsburgh (2) vs. Cincinnati (1), Oct. 10, 1983
Kansas City (2) vs. San Diego (1), Oct. 19, 1986
(Also see previous record)

Punt Returns

Fewest Opponents Punt Returns, Season
7 Washington, 1962
San Diego, 1982
10 Buffalo, 1982
11 Boston, 1962
Most Opponents Punt Returns, Season
71 Tampa Bay, 1976, 1977
69 N.Y. Giants, 1953
68 Cleveland, 1974
Fewest Yards Allowed, Punt Returns, Season
22 Green Bay, 1967
34 Washington, 1962
39 Cleveland, 1959
Washington, 1972
Most Yards Allowed, Punt Returns, Season
932 Green Bay, 1949
913 Boston, 1947
906 New Orleans, 1974
Lowest Average Allowed, Punt Returns, Season
1.20 Chi. Cardinals, 1954 (46-55)
1.22 Cleveland, 1959 (32-39)
1.55 Chi. Cardinals, 1953 (44-68)
Highest Average Allowed, Punt Returns, Season
18.6 Green Bay, 1949 (50-932)
18.0 Cleveland, 1977 (31-558)
17.9 Boston, 1960 (20-357)
Most Touchdowns Allowed, Punt Returns, Season
4 New York, 1959
Atlanta, 1992
3 Green Bay, 1949
Chi. Cardinals, 1951
Los Angeles, 1951
Washington, 1952
Dallas, 1952
Pittsburgh, 1959
N.Y. Jets, 1968
Cleveland, 1977
Atlanta, 1986
Tampa Bay, 1986
2 By many teams

Kickoff Returns

Fewest Opponents Kickoff Returns, Season
10 Brooklyn, 1943
13 Denver, 1992
15 Detroit, 1942
Brooklyn, 1944
Most Opponents Kickoff Returns, Season
91 Washington, 1983
89 New England, 1980
88 San Diego, 1981
Fewest Yards Allowed, Kickoff Returns, Season
225 Brooklyn, 1943
254 Denver, 1992
293 Brooklyn, 1944
Most Yards Allowed, Kickoff Returns, Season
2,045 Kansas City, 1966
1,827 Chicago, 1985
1,816 N.Y. Giants, 1963
Lowest Average Allowed, Kickoff Returns, Season
14.3 Cleveland, 1980 (71-1,018)
15.0 Seattle, 1982 (24-361)
15.4 N.Y. Jets, 1991 (60-921)
Highest Average Allowed, Kickoff Returns, Season
29.5 N.Y. Jets, 1972 (47-1,386)
29.4 Los Angeles, 1950 (48-1,411)
29.1 New England, 1971 (49-1,427)
Most Touchdowns Allowed, Kickoff Returns, Season
3 Minnesota, 1963, 1970
Dallas, 1966
Detroit, 1980
Pittsburgh, 1986
2 By many teams

Fumbles

Fewest Opponents Fumbles, Season
11 Cleveland, 1956
Baltimore, 1982
13 Los Angeles, 1956
Chicago, 1960
Cleveland, 1963
Cleveland, 1965
Detroit, 1967
San Diego, 1969
14 Baltimore, 1970
Oakland, 1975
Buffalo, 1982
St. Louis, 1982
San Francisco, 1982
Most Opponents Fumbles, Season
50 Minnesota, 1963
San Francisco, 1978
48 N.Y. Giants, 1980
N.Y. Jets, 1986
47 N.Y. Giants, 1977
Seattle, 1984

Turnovers

(Number of times losing the ball on interceptions and fumbles.)
Fewest Opponents Turnovers, Season
11 Baltimore, 1982
13 San Francisco, 1982
15 St. Louis, 1982
Most Opponents Turnovers, Season
66 San Diego, 1961
63 Seattle, 1984
61 Washington, 1983
Most Opponents Turnovers, Game
12 Chi. Bears vs. Detroit, Nov. 22, 1942
Philadelphia vs. Chi. Cardinals, Sept. 24, 1950
Philadelphia vs. Pittsburgh, Dec. 12, 1965
11 Green Bay vs. San Diego, Sept. 24, 1978
10 N.Y. Giants vs. Washington, Dec. 4, 1938
Green Bay vs. Pittsburgh, Nov. 23, 1941
Green Bay vs. Detroit, Oct. 24, 1943
Green Bay vs. Chi. Cardinals, Nov. 10, 1946
N.Y. Giants vs. Chi. Cardinals, Nov. 2, 1952
Detroit vs. Minnesota, Dec. 9, 1962
Oakland vs. Houston, Sept. 7, 1963
N.Y. Giants vs. Washington, Dec. 8, 1963
Detroit vs. Chicago, Sept. 22, 1968
Washington vs. St. Louis, Oct. 25, 1976
New England vs. N.Y. Jets, Nov. 21, 1976
Dallas vs. San Francisco, Oct. 12, 1980
Seattle vs. Cleveland, Dec. 20, 1981
Denver vs. Detroit, Oct. 7, 1984

1,000 Yards Rushing in a Season

Year	Player, Team	Att.	Yards	Avg.	Long	TD
1992	Emmitt Smith, Dallas[2]	373	1,713	4.6	68	18
	Barry Foster, Pittsburgh	390	1,690	4.3	69	11
	Thurman Thomas, Buffalo[4]	312	1,487	4.8	44	9
	Barry Sanders, Detroit[4]	312	1,352	4.3	55	9
	Lorenzo White, Houston	265	1,226	4.6	44	7
	Terry Allen, Minnesota	266	1,201	4.5	51	13
	Reggie Cobb, Tampa Bay	310	1,171	3.8	25	9
	Harold Green, Cincinnati	265	1,170	4.4	53	2
	Rodney Hampton, N.Y. Giants[2]	257	1,141	4.4	63	14
	Cleveland Gary, L.A. Rams	279	1,125	4.0	63	7
	Herschel Walker, Philadelphia[2]	267	1,070	4.0	38	8
	Chris Warren, Seattle	223	1,017	4.6	52	3
	Ricky Watters, San Francisco	206	1,013	4.9	43	9
1991	Emmitt Smith, Dallas	365	1,563	4.3	75	12
	Barry Sanders, Detroit[3]	342	1,548	4.5	69	16
	Thurman Thomas, Buffalo[3]	288	1,407	4.9	33	7
	Rodney Hampton, N.Y. Giants	256	1,059	4.1	44	10
	Earnest Byner, Washington[3]	274	1,048	3.8	32	5
	Gaston Green, Denver	261	1,037	4.0	63	4
	Christian Okoye, Kansas City[2]	225	1,031	4.6	48	9
1990	Barry Sanders, Detroit[2]	255	1,304	5.1	45	13
	Thurman Thomas, Buffalo[2]	271	1,297	4.8	80	11
	Marion Butts, San Diego	265	1,225	4.6	52	8
	Earnest Byner, Washington[2]	297	1,219	4.1	22	6
	Bobby Humphrey, Denver[2]	288	1,202	4.2	37	7
	Neal Anderson, Chicago[3]	260	1,078	4.1	52	10
	Barry Word, Kansas City	204	1,015	5.0	53	4
	James Brooks, Cincinnati[3]	195	1,004	5.1	56	5
1989	Christian Okoye, Kansas City	370	1,480	4.0	59	12
	*Barry Sanders, Detroit	280	1,470	5.3	34	14
	Eric Dickerson, Indianapolis[7]	314	1,311	4.2	21	7
	Neal Anderson, Chicago[2]	274	1,275	4.7	73	11
	Dalton Hilliard, New Orleans	344	1,262	3.7	40	13
	Thurman Thomas, Buffalo	298	1,244	4.2	38	6
	James Brooks, Cincinnati[2]	221	1,239	5.6	65	7
	*Bobby Humphrey, Denver	294	1,151	3.9	40	7
	Greg Bell, L.A. Rams[3]	272	1,137	4.2	47	15
	Roger Craig, San Francisco[3]	271	1,054	3.9	27	6
	Ottis Anderson, N.Y. Giants[6]	325	1,023	3.1	36	14
1988	Eric Dickerson, Indianapolis[6]	388	1,659	4.3	41	14
	Herschel Walker, Dallas	361	1,514	4.2	38	5
	Roger Craig, San Francisco[2]	310	1,502	4.8	46	9
	Greg Bell, L.A. Rams[2]	288	1,212	4.2	44	16
	*John Stephens, New England	297	1,168	3.9	52	4
	Gary Anderson, San Diego	225	1,119	5.0	36	3
	Neal Anderson, Chicago	249	1,106	4.4	80	12
	Joe Morris, N.Y. Giants[3]	307	1,083	3.5	27	5
	*Ickey Woods, Cincinnati	203	1,066	5.3	56	15
	Curt Warner, Seattle[4]	266	1,025	3.9	29	10
	John Settle, Atlanta	232	1,024	4.4	62	7
	Mike Rozier, Houston	251	1,002	4.0	28	10
1987	Charles White, L.A. Rams	324	1,374	4.2	58	11
	Eric Dickerson, L.A. Rams-Indianapolis[5]	283	1,288	4.6	57	6
1986	Eric Dickerson, L.A. Rams[4]	404	1,821	4.5	42	11
	Joe Morris, N.Y. Giants[2]	341	1,516	4.4	54	14
	Curt Warner, Seattle[3]	319	1,481	4.6	60	13
	*Rueben Mayes, New Orleans	286	1,353	4.7	50	8
	Walter Payton, Chicago[10]	321	1,333	4.2	41	8
	Gerald Riggs, Atlanta[3]	343	1,327	3.9	31	9
	George Rogers, Washington[4]	303	1,203	4.0	42	18
	James Brooks, Cincinnati	205	1,087	5.3	56	5
1985	Marcus Allen, L.A. Raiders[3]	390	1,759	4.6	61	11
	Gerald Riggs, Atlanta[2]	397	1,719	4.3	50	10
	Walter Payton, Chicago[9]	324	1,551	4.8	40	9
	Joe Morris, N.Y. Giants	294	1,336	4.5	65	21
	Freeman McNeil, N.Y. Jets[2]	294	1,331	4.5	69	3
	Tony Dorsett, Dallas[8]	305	1,307	4.3	60	7
	James Wilder, Tampa Bay[2]	365	1,300	3.6	28	10
	Eric Dickerson, L.A. Rams[3]	292	1,234	4.2	43	12
	Craig James, New England	263	1,227	4.7	65	5
	*Kevin Mack, Cleveland	222	1,104	5.0	61	7
	Curt Warner, Seattle[2]	291	1,094	3.8	38	8
	George Rogers, Washington[3]	231	1,093	4.7	35	7
	Roger Craig, San Francisco	214	1,050	4.9	62	9
	Earnest Jackson, Philadelphia[2]	282	1,028	3.6	59	5
	Stump Mitchell, St. Louis	183	1,006	5.5	64	7
	Earnest Byner, Cleveland	244	1,002	4.1	36	8
1984	Eric Dickerson, L.A. Rams[2]	379	2,105	5.6	66	14
	Walter Payton, Chicago[8]	381	1,684	4.4	72	11
	James Wilder, Tampa Bay	407	1,544	3.8	37	13
	Gerald Riggs, Atlanta	353	1,486	4.2	57	13
	Wendell Tyler, San Francisco[3]	246	1,262	5.1	40	7
	John Riggins, Washington[5]	327	1,239	3.8	24	14
	Tony Dorsett, Dallas[7]	302	1,189	3.9	31	6
	Earnest Jackson, San Diego	296	1,179	4.0	32	8
	Ottis Anderson, St. Louis[5]	289	1,174	4.1	24	6
	Marcus Allen, L.A. Raiders[2]	275	1,168	4.2	52	13
	Sammy Winder, Denver	296	1,153	3.9	24	4
	*Greg Bell, Buffalo	262	1,100	4.2	85	7
	Freeman McNeil, N.Y. Jets	229	1,070	4.7	53	5
1983	*Eric Dickerson, L.A. Rams	390	1,808	4.6	85	18
	William Andrews, Atlanta[4]	331	1,567	4.7	27	7
	*Curt Warner, Seattle	335	1,449	4.3	60	13
	Walter Payton, Chicago[7]	314	1,421	4.5	49	6
	John Riggins, Washington[4]	375	1,347	3.6	44	24
	Tony Dorsett, Dallas[6]	289	1,321	4.6	77	8
	Earl Campbell, Houston[5]	322	1,301	4.0	42	12
	Ottis Anderson, St. Louis[4]	296	1,270	4.3	43	5
	Mike Pruitt, Cleveland[4]	293	1,184	4.0	27	10
	George Rogers, New Orleans[2]	256	1,144	4.5	76	5
	Joe Cribbs, Buffalo[3]	263	1,131	4.3	45	3
	Curtis Dickey, Baltimore	254	1,122	4.4	56	4
	Tony Collins, New England	219	1,049	4.8	50	10
	Billy Sims, Detroit[3]	220	1,040	4.7	41	7
	Marcus Allen, L.A. Raiders	266	1,014	3.8	19	9
	Franco Harris, Pittsburgh[8]	279	1,007	3.6	19	5
1981	*George Rogers, New Orleans	378	1,674	4.4	79	13
	Tony Dorsett, Dallas[5]	342	1,646	4.8	75	4
	Billy Sims, Detroit[2]	296	1,437	4.9	51	13
	Wilbert Montgomery, Philadelphia[3]	286	1,402	4.9	41	8
	Ottis Anderson, St. Louis[3]	328	1,376	4.2	28	9
	Earl Campbell, Houston[4]	361	1,376	3.8	43	10
	William Andrews, Atlanta[3]	289	1,301	4.5	29	10
	Walter Payton, Chicago[6]	339	1,222	3.6	39	6
	Chuck Muncie, San Diego[2]	251	1,144	4.6	73	19
	*Joe Delaney, Kansas City	234	1,121	4.8	82	3
	Mike Pruitt, Cleveland[3]	247	1,103	4.5	21	7
	Joe Cribbs, Buffalo[2]	257	1,097	4.3	35	3
	Pete Johnson, Cincinnati	274	1,077	3.9	39	12
	Wendell Tyler, Los Angeles[2]	260	1,074	4.1	69	12
	Ted Brown, Minnesota	274	1,063	3.9	34	6
1980	Earl Campbell, Houston[3]	373	1,934	5.2	55	13
	Walter Payton, Chicago[5]	317	1,460	4.6	69	6
	Ottis Anderson, St. Louis[2]	301	1,352	4.5	52	9
	William Andrews, Atlanta[2]	265	1,308	4.9	33	4
	*Billy Sims, Detroit	313	1,303	4.2	52	13
	Tony Dorsett, Dallas[4]	278	1,185	4.3	56	11
	*Joe Cribbs, Buffalo	306	1,185	3.9	48	11
	Mike Pruitt, Cleveland[2]	249	1,034	4.2	56	6
1979	Earl Campbell, Houston[2]	368	1,697	4.6	61	19
	Walter Payton, Chicago[4]	369	1,610	4.4	43	14
	*Ottis Anderson, St. Louis	331	1,605	4.8	76	8
	Wilbert Montgomery, Philadelphia[2]	338	1,512	4.5	62	9
	Mike Pruitt, Cleveland	264	1,294	4.9	77	9
	Ricky Bell, Tampa Bay	283	1,263	4.5	49	7
	Chuck Muncie, New Orleans	238	1,198	5.0	69	11
	Franco Harris, Pittsburgh[7]	267	1,186	4.4	71	11
	John Riggins, Washington[3]	260	1,153	4.4	66	9
	Wendell Tyler, Los Angeles	218	1,109	5.1	63	9
	Tony Dorsett, Dallas[3]	250	1,107	4.4	41	6
	*William Andrews, Atlanta	239	1,023	4.3	23	3
1978	*Earl Campbell, Houston	302	1,450	4.8	81	13
	Walter Payton, Chicago[3]	333	1,395	4.2	76	11
	Tony Dorsett, Dallas[2]	290	1,325	4.6	63	7
	Delvin Williams, Miami[2]	272	1,258	4.6	58	8
	Wilbert Montgomery, Philadelphia	259	1,220	4.7	47	9
	Terdell Middleton, Green Bay	284	1,116	3.9	76	11
	Franco Harris, Pittsburgh[6]	310	1,082	3.5	37	8
	Mark van Eeghen, Oakland[3]	270	1,080	4.0	34	9
	*Terry Miller, Buffalo	238	1,060	4.5	60	7
	Tony Reed, Kansas City	206	1,053	5.1	62	5
	John Riggins, Washington[2]	248	1,014	4.1	31	5
1977	Walter Payton, Chicago[2]	339	1,852	5.5	73	14
	Mark van Eeghen, Oakland[2]	324	1,273	3.9	27	7
	Lawrence McCutcheon, Los Angeles[4]	294	1,238	4.2	48	7
	Franco Harris, Pittsburgh[5]	300	1,162	3.9	61	11
	Lydell Mitchell, Baltimore[3]	301	1,159	3.9	64	3
	Chuck Foreman, Minnesota[3]	270	1,112	4.1	51	6
	Greg Pruitt, Cleveland[3]	236	1,086	4.6	78	3
	Sam Cunningham, New England	270	1,015	3.8	31	4
	*Tony Dorsett, Dallas	208	1,007	4.8	84	12
1976	O.J. Simpson, Buffalo[5]	290	1,503	5.2	75	8
	Walter Payton, Chicago	311	1,390	4.5	60	13
	Delvin Williams, San Francisco	248	1,203	4.9	80	7
	Lydell Mitchell, Baltimore[2]	289	1,200	4.2	43	5
	Lawrence McCutcheon, Los Angeles[3]	291	1,168	4.0	40	9
	Chuck Foreman, Minnesota[2]	278	1,155	4.2	46	13
	Franco Harris, Pittsburgh[4]	289	1,128	3.9	30	14
	Mike Thomas, Washington	254	1,101	4.3	28	5
	Rocky Bleier, Pittsburgh	220	1,036	4.7	28	5
	Mark van Eeghen, Oakland	233	1,012	4.3	21	3
	Otis Armstrong, Denver[2]	247	1,008	4.1	31	5
	Greg Pruitt, Cleveland[2]	209	1,000	4.8	64	4
1975	O.J. Simpson, Buffalo[4]	329	1,817	5.5	88	16
	Franco Harris, Pittsburgh[3]	262	1,246	4.8	36	10
	Lydell Mitchell, Baltimore	289	1,193	4.1	70	11
	Jim Otis, St. Louis	269	1,076	4.0	30	5
	Chuck Foreman, Minnesota	280	1,070	3.8	31	13
	Greg Pruitt, Cleveland	217	1,067	4.9	50	8
	John Riggins, N.Y. Jets	238	1,005	4.2	42	8
	Dave Hampton, Atlanta	250	1,002	4.0	22	5
1974	Otis Armstrong, Denver	263	1,407	5.3	43	9
	*Don Woods, San Diego	227	1,162	5.1	56	7
	O.J. Simpson, Buffalo[3]	270	1,125	4.2	41	3
	Lawrence McCutcheon, Los Angeles[2]	236	1,109	4.7	23	3
	Franco Harris, Pittsburgh[2]	208	1,006	4.8	54	5
1973	O.J. Simpson, Buffalo[2]	332	2,003	6.0	80	12
	John Brockington, Green Bay[3]	265	1,144	4.3	53	3
	Calvin Hill, Dallas[2]	273	1,142	4.2	21	6
	Lawrence McCutcheon, Los Angeles	210	1,097	5.2	37	2
	Larry Csonka, Miami[3]	219	1,003	4.6	25	5
1972	O.J. Simpson, Buffalo	292	1,251	4.3	94	6
	Larry Brown, Washington[2]	285	1,216	4.3	38	8
	Ron Johnson, N.Y. Giants[2]	298	1,182	4.0	35	9
	Larry Csonka, Miami[2]	213	1,117	5.2	45	6

	Marv Hubbard, Oakland	219	1,100	5.0	39	4
	*Franco Harris, Pittsburgh	188	1,055	5.6	75	10
	Calvin Hill, Dallas	245	1,036	4.2	26	6
	Mike Garrett, San Diego[2]	272	1,031	3.8	41	6
	John Brockington, Green Bay[2]	274	1,027	3.7	30	8
	Eugene (Mercury) Morris, Miami	190	1,000	5.3	33	12
1971	Floyd Little, Denver	284	1,133	4.0	40	6
	*John Brockington, Green Bay	216	1,105	5.1	52	4
	Larry Csonka, Miami	195	1,051	5.4	28	7
	Steve Owens, Detroit	246	1,035	4.2	23	8
	Willie Ellison, Los Angeles	211	1,000	4.7	80	4
1970	Larry Brown, Washington	237	1,125	4.7	75	5
	Ron Johnson, N.Y. Giants	263	1,027	3.9	68	8
1969	Gale Sayers, Chicago[2]	236	1,032	4.4	28	8
1968	Leroy Kelly, Cleveland[3]	248	1,239	5.0	65	16
	*Paul Robinson, Cincinnati	238	1,023	4.3	87	8
1967	Jim Nance, Boston[2]	269	1,216	4.5	53	7
	Leroy Kelly, Cleveland[2]	235	1,205	5.1	42	11
	Hoyle Granger, Houston	236	1,194	5.1	67	6
	Mike Garrett, Kansas City	236	1,087	4.6	58	9
1966	Jim Nance, Boston	299	1,458	4.9	65	11
	Gale Sayers, Chicago	229	1,231	5.4	58	8
	Leroy Kelly, Cleveland	209	1,141	5.5	70	15
	Dick Bass, Los Angeles[2]	248	1,090	4.4	50	8
1965	Jim Brown, Cleveland[7]	289	1,544	5.3	67	17
	Paul Lowe, San Diego[2]	222	1,121	5.0	59	7
1964	Jim Brown, Cleveland[6]	280	1,446	5.2	71	7
	Jim Taylor, Green Bay[5]	235	1,169	5.0	84	12
	John Henry Johnson, Pittsburgh[2]	235	1,048	4.5	45	7
1963	Jim Brown, Cleveland[5]	291	1,863	6.4	80	12
	Clem Daniels, Oakland	215	1,099	5.1	74	3
	Jim Taylor, Green Bay[4]	248	1,018	4.1	40	9
	Paul Lowe, San Diego	177	1,010	5.7	66	8
1962	Jim Taylor, Green Bay[3]	272	1,474	5.4	51	19
	John Henry Johnson, Pittsburgh	251	1,141	4.5	40	7
	*Cookie Gilchrist, Buffalo	214	1,096	5.1	44	13
	Abner Haynes, Dall. Texans	221	1,049	4.7	71	13
	Dick Bass, Los Angeles	196	1,033	5.3	57	6
	Charlie Tolar, Houston	244	1,012	4.1	25	7
1961	Jim Brown, Cleveland[4]	305	1,408	4.6	38	8
	Jim Taylor, Green Bay[2]	243	1,307	5.4	53	15
1960	Jim Brown, Cleveland[3]	215	1,257	5.8	71	9
	Jim Taylor, Green Bay	230	1,101	4.8	32	11
	John David Crow, St. Louis	183	1,071	5.9	57	6
1959	Jim Brown, Cleveland[2]	290	1,329	4.6	70	14
	J. D. Smith, San Francisco	207	1,036	5.0	73	10
1958	Jim Brown, Cleveland	257	1,527	5.9	65	17
1956	Rick Casares, Chi. Bears	234	1,126	4.8	68	12
1954	Joe Perry, San Francisco[2]	173	1,049	6.1	58	8
1953	Joe Perry, San Francisco	192	1,018	5.3	51	10
1949	Steve Van Buren, Philadelphia[2]	263	1,146	4.4	41	11
	Tony Canadeo, Green Bay	208	1,052	5.1	54	4
1947	Steve Van Buren, Philadelphia	217	1,008	4.6	45	13
1934	*Beattie Feathers, Chi. Bears	119	1,004	8.4	82	8

**First year in the league.*

200 Yards Rushing in a Game

Date	Player, Team, Opponent	Att.	Yards	TD
Nov. 24, 1991	Barry Sanders, Detroit vs. Minnesota	23	220	4
Dec. 23, 1990	James Brooks, Cincinnati vs. Houston	20	201	1
Oct. 14, 1990	Barry Word, Kansas City vs. Detroit	18	200	2
Sept. 24, 1990	Thurman Thomas, Buffalo vs. N.Y. Jets	18	214	0
Dec. 24, 1989	Greg Bell, L.A. Rams vs. New England	26	210	1
Sept. 24, 1989	Greg Bell, L.A. Rams vs. Green Bay	28	221	2
Sept. 17, 1989	Gerald Riggs, Washington vs. Philadelphia	29	221	1
Dec. 18, 1988	Gary Anderson, San Diego vs. Kansas City	34	217	1
Nov. 30, 1987	*Bo Jackson, L.A. Raiders vs. Seattle	18	221	2
Nov. 15, 1987	Charles White, L.A. Rams vs. St. Louis	34	213	1
Dec. 7, 1986	Rueben Mayes, New Orleans vs. Miami	28	203	2
Oct. 5, 1986	Eric Dickerson, L.A. Rams vs. Tampa Bay (OT)	30	207	2
Dec. 21, 1985	George Rogers, Washington vs. St. Louis	34	206	1
Dec. 21, 1985	Joe Morris, N.Y. Giants vs. Pittsburgh	36	202	3
Dec. 9, 1984	Eric Dickerson, L.A. Rams vs. Houston	27	215	2
Nov. 18, 1984	*Greg Bell, Buffalo vs. Dallas	27	206	1
Nov. 4, 1984	Eric Dickerson, L.A. Rams vs. St. Louis	21	208	0
Sept. 2, 1984	Gerald Riggs, Atlanta vs. New Orleans	35	202	2
Nov. 27, 1983	*Curt Warner, Seattle vs. Kansas City (OT)	32	207	3
Nov. 6, 1983	James Wilder, Tampa Bay vs. Minnesota	31	219	1
Sept. 18, 1983	Tony Collins, New England vs. N.Y. Jets	23	212	3
Sept. 4, 1983	George Rogers, New Orleans vs. St. Louis	24	206	2
Dec. 21, 1980	Earl Campbell, Houston vs. Minnesota	29	203	1
Nov. 16, 1980	Earl Campbell, Houston vs. Chicago	31	206	0
Oct. 26, 1980	Earl Campbell, Houston vs. Cincinnati	27	202	2
Oct. 19, 1980	Earl Campbell, Houston vs. Tampa Bay	33	203	0
Nov. 26, 1978	*Terry Miller, Buffalo vs. N.Y. Giants	21	208	2
Dec. 4, 1977	*Tony Dorsett, Dallas vs. Philadelphia	23	206	2
Nov. 20, 1977	Walter Payton, Chicago vs. Minnesota	40	275	1
Oct. 30, 1977	Walter Payton, Chicago vs. Green Bay	23	205	2
Dec. 5, 1976	O.J. Simpson, Buffalo vs. Miami	24	203	1
Nov. 25, 1976	O.J. Simpson, Buffalo vs. Detroit	29	273	2
Oct. 24, 1976	Chuck Foreman, Minnesota vs. Philadelphia	28	200	2
Dec. 14, 1975	Greg Pruitt, Cleveland vs. Kansas City	26	214	3
Sept. 28, 1975	O.J. Simpson, Buffalo vs. Pittsburgh	28	227	1
Dec. 16, 1973	O.J. Simpson, Buffalo vs. N.Y. Jets	34	200	1
Dec. 9, 1973	O.J. Simpson, Buffalo vs. New England	22	219	1
Sept. 16, 1973	O.J. Simpson, Buffalo vs. New England	29	250	2
Dec. 5, 1971	Willie Ellison, Los Angeles vs. New Orleans	26	247	1
Dec. 20, 1970	John (Frenchy) Fuqua, Pittsburgh vs. Philadelphia	20	218	2
Nov. 3, 1968	Gale Sayers, Chicago vs. Green Bay	24	205	0
Oct. 30, 1966	Jim Nance, Boston vs. Oakland	38	208	2
Oct. 10, 1964	John Henry Johnson, Pittsburgh vs. Cleveland	30	200	3
Dec. 8, 1963	Cookie Gilchrist, Buffalo vs. N.Y. Jets	36	243	5
Nov. 3, 1963	Jim Brown, Cleveland vs. Philadelphia	28	223	1
Oct. 20, 1963	Clem Daniels, Oakland vs. N.Y. Jets	27	200	2
Sept. 22, 1963	Jim Brown, Cleveland vs. Dallas	20	232	2
Dec. 10, 1961	Billy Cannon, Houston vs. N.Y. Titans	25	216	3
Nov. 19, 1961	Jim Brown, Cleveland vs. Philadelphia	34	237	4
Dec. 18, 1960	John David Crow, St. Louis vs. Pittsburgh	24	203	0
Nov. 15, 1959	Bobby Mitchell, Cleveland vs. Washington	14	232	3
Nov. 24, 1957	*Jim Brown, Cleveland vs. Los Angeles	31	237	4
Dec. 16, 1956	*Tom Wilson, Los Angeles vs. Green Bay	23	223	0
Nov. 22, 1953	Dan Towler, Los Angeles vs. Baltimore	14	205	1
Nov. 12, 1950	Gene Roberts, N.Y. Giants vs. Chi. Cardinals	26	218	2
Nov. 27, 1949	Steve Van Buren, Philadelphia vs. Pittsburgh	27	205	0
Oct. 8, 1933	Cliff Battles, Boston vs. N.Y. Giants	16	215	1

**First year in the league.*

Times 200 or More

57 times by 39 players . . . Simpson 6; Brown, Campbell 4; Bell, Dickerson 3; Payton, Riggs, Rogers 2.

4,000 Yards Passing in a Season

Year	Player, Team	Att.	Comp.	Pct.	Yards	TD	Int.
1992	Dan Marino, Miami[5]	554	330	59.6	4,116	24	16
1991	Warren Moon, Houston[2]	655	404	61.7	4,690	23	21
1990	Warren Moon, Houston	584	362	62.0	4,689	33	13
1989	Don Majkowski, Green Bay	599	353	58.9	4,318	27	20
	Jim Everett, L.A. Rams	518	304	58.7	4,310	29	17
1988	Dan Marino, Miami[4]	606	354	58.4	4,434	28	23
1986	Dan Marino, Miami[3]	623	378	60.7	4,746	44	23
	Jay Schroeder, Washington	541	276	51.0	4,109	22	22
1985	Dan Marino, Miami[2]	567	336	59.3	4,137	30	21
1984	Dan Marino, Miami	564	362	64.2	5,084	48	17
	Neil Lomax, St. Louis	560	345	61.6	4,614	28	16
	Phil Simms, N.Y. Giants	533	286	53.7	4,044	22	18
1983	Lynn Dickey, Green Bay	484	289	59.7	4,458	32	29
	Bill Kenney, Kansas City	603	346	57.4	4,348	24	18
1981	Dan Fouts, San Diego[3]	609	360	59.1	4,802	33	17
1980	Dan Fouts, San Diego[2]	589	348	59.1	4,715	30	24
	Brian Sipe, Cleveland	554	337	60.8	4,132	30	14
1979	Dan Fouts, San Diego	530	332	62.6	4,082	24	24
1967	Joe Namath, N.Y. Jets	491	258	52.5	4,007	26	28

400 Yards Passing in a Game

Date	Player, Team, Opponent	Att.	Comp.	Yards	TD
Sept. 13, 1992	Steve Young, San Francisco vs. Buffalo	37	26	449	3
Sept. 13, 1992	Jim Kelly, Buffalo at San Francisco	33	22	403	3
Nov. 10, 1991	Warren Moon, Houston vs. Dallas (OT)	56	41	432	0
Nov. 10, 1991	Mark Rypien, Washington vs. Atlanta	31	16	442	6
Oct. 13, 1991	Warren Moon, Houston vs. N.Y. Jets	50	35	423	2
Dec. 16, 1990	Warren Moon, Houston vs. Kansas City	45	27	527	3
Nov. 4, 1990	Joe Montana, San Francisco vs. Green Bay	40	25	411	3
Oct. 14, 1990	Joe Montana, San Francisco vs. Atlanta	49	32	476	6
Oct. 7, 1990	Boomer Esiason, Cincinnati vs. L.A. Rams (OT)	45	31	490	3
Dec. 23, 1989	Warren Moon, Houston vs. Cleveland	51	32	414	2
Dec. 11, 1989	Joe Montana, San Francisco vs. L.A. Rams	42	30	458	3
Nov. 26, 1989	Jim Everett, L.A. Rams vs. New Orleans (OT)	51	29	454	1
Nov. 26, 1989	Mark Rypien, Washington vs. Chicago	47	30	401	4
Oct. 2, 1989	Randall Cunningham, Philadelphia vs. Chicago	62	32	401	1
Sept. 24, 1989	Joe Montana, San Francisco vs. Philadelphia	34	25	428	5
Sept. 24, 1989	Dan Marino, Miami vs. N.Y. Jets	55	33	427	3
Sept. 17, 1989	Randall Cunningham, Phil. vs. Washington	46	34	447	5
Dec. 18, 1988	Dave Krieg, Seattle at L.A. Raiders	32	19	410	4
Dec. 12, 1988	Dan Marino, Miami vs. Cleveland	50	30	404	4
Oct. 23, 1988	Dan Marino, Miami vs. N.Y. Jets	60	35	521	3
Oct. 16, 1988	Vinny Testaverde, Tampa Bay at Indianapolis	42	25	469	2
Sept. 11, 1988	Doug Williams, Washington vs. Pittsburgh	52	30	430	2
Nov. 29, 1987	Tom Ramsey, New England vs. Philadelphia	53	34	402	3
Nov. 22, 1987	Boomer Esiason, Cincinnati vs. Pittsburgh	53	30	409	0
Sept. 20, 1987	Neil Lomax, St. Louis vs. San Diego	61	32	457	3
Dec. 21, 1986	Boomer Esiason, Cincinnati vs. N.Y. Jets	30	23	425	5
Dec. 14, 1986	Dan Marino, Miami vs. L.A. Rams (OT)	46	29	403	5
Nov. 23, 1986	Bernie Kosar, Cleveland vs. Pittsburgh (OT)	46	28	414	2
Nov. 17, 1986	Joe Montana, San Francisco vs. Washington	60	33	441	0
Nov. 16, 1986	Dan Marino, Miami vs. Buffalo	54	39	404	4
Nov. 10, 1986	Bernie Kosar, Cleveland vs. Miami	50	32	401	0
Nov. 2, 1986	Tommy Kramer, Minnesota vs. Washington (OT)	35	20	490	4
Nov. 2, 1986	Ken O'Brien, N.Y. Jets vs. Seattle	32	26	431	4
Oct. 27, 1986	Jay Schroeder, Washington vs. N.Y. Giants	40	22	420	1
Oct. 12, 1986	Steve Grogan, New England vs. N.Y. Jets	42	23	401	3
Sept. 21, 1986	Ken O'Brien, N.Y. Jets vs. Miami (OT)	43	29	479	4
Sept. 21, 1986	Dan Marino, Miami vs. N.Y. Jets (OT)	50	30	448	6
Sept. 21, 1986	Tony Eason, New England vs. Seattle	45	26	414	3
Dec. 20, 1985	John Elway, Denver vs. Seattle	42	24	432	1
Nov. 10, 1985	Dan Fouts, San Diego vs. L.A. Raiders (OT)	41	26	436	4
Oct. 13, 1985	Phil Simms, N.Y. Giants vs. Cincinnati	62	40	513	1
Oct. 13, 1985	Dave Krieg, Seattle vs. Atlanta	51	33	405	4
Oct. 6, 1985	Phil Simms, N.Y. Giants vs. Dallas	36	18	432	3
Oct. 6, 1985	Joe Montana, San Francisco vs. Atlanta	57	37	429	5
Sept. 19, 1985	Tommy Kramer, Minnesota vs. Chicago	55	28	436	3
Sept. 15, 1985	Dan Fouts, San Diego vs. Seattle	43	29	440	4
Dec. 16, 1984	Neil Lomax, St. Louis vs. Washington	46	37	468	2
Dec. 9, 1984	Dan Marino, Miami vs. Indianapolis	41	29	404	4
Dec. 2, 1984	Dan Marino, Miami vs. L.A. Raiders	57	35	470	4
Nov. 25, 1984	Dave Krieg, Seattle vs. Denver	44	30	406	3
Nov. 4, 1984	Dan Marino, Miami vs. N.Y. Jets	42	23	422	2
Oct. 21, 1984	Dan Fouts, San Diego vs. L.A. Raiders	45	24	410	3
Sept. 30, 1984	Dan Marino, Miami vs. St. Louis	36	24	429	3
Sept. 2, 1984	Phil Simms, N.Y. Giants vs. Philadelphia	30	23	409	4
Dec. 11, 1983	Bill Kenney, Kansas City vs. San Diego	41	31	411	4
Nov. 20, 1983	Dave Krieg, Seattle vs. Denver	42	31	418	3
Oct. 9, 1983	Joe Ferguson, Buffalo vs. Miami (OT)	55	38	419	5

Oct. 2, 1983	Joe Theismann, Washington vs. L.A. Raiders	39	23	417	3
Sept. 25, 1983	Richard Todd, N.Y. Jets vs. L.A. Rams (OT)	50	37	446	2
Dec. 26, 1982	Vince Ferragamo, L.A. Rams vs. Chicago	46	30	509	3
Dec. 20, 1982	Dan Fouts, San Diego vs. Cincinnati	40	25	435	1
Dec. 20, 1982	Ken Anderson, Cincinnati vs. San Diego	56	40	416	2
Dec. 11, 1982	Dan Fouts, San Diego vs. San Francisco	48	33	444	5
Nov. 21, 1982	Joe Montana, San Francisco vs. St. Louis	39	26	408	3
Nov. 15, 1981	Steve Bartkowski, Atlanta vs. Pittsburgh	50	33	416	2
Oct. 25, 1981	Brian Sipe, Cleveland vs. Baltimore	41	30	444	4
Oct. 25, 1981	David Woodley, Miami vs. Dallas	37	21	408	3
Oct. 11, 1981	Tommy Kramer, Minnesota vs. San Diego	43	27	444	4
Dec. 14, 1980	Tommy Kramer, Minnesota vs. Cleveland	49	38	456	4
Nov. 16, 1980	Doug Williams, Tampa Bay vs. Minnesota	55	30	486	4
Oct. 19, 1980	Dan Fouts, San Diego vs. N.Y. Giants	41	26	444	3
Oct. 12, 1980	Lynn Dickey, Green Bay vs. Tampa Bay (OT)	51	35	418	1
Sept. 21, 1980	Richard Todd, N.Y. Jets vs. San Francisco	60	42	447	3
Oct. 3, 1976	James Harris, Los Angeles vs. Miami	29	17	436	2
Nov. 17, 1975	Ken Anderson, Cincinnati vs. Buffalo	46	30	447	2
Nov. 18, 1974	Charley Johnson, Denver vs. Kansas City	42	28	445	2
Dec. 11, 1972	Joe Namath, N.Y. Jets vs. Oakland	46	25	403	1
Sept. 24, 1972	Joe Namath, N.Y. Jets vs. Baltimore	28	15	496	6
Dec. 21, 1969	Don Horn, Green Bay vs. St. Louis	31	22	410	5
Sept. 28, 1969	Joe Kapp, Minnesota vs. Baltimore	43	28	449	7
Sept. 9, 1968	Pete Beathard, Houston vs. Kansas City	48	23	413	2
Nov. 26, 1967	Sonny Jurgensen, Washington vs. Cleveland	50	32	418	3
Oct. 1, 1967	Joe Namath, N.Y. Jets vs. Miami	39	23	415	3
Sept. 17, 1967	Johnny Unitas, Baltimore vs. Atlanta	32	22	401	2
Nov. 13, 1966	Don Meredith, Dallas vs. Washington	29	21	406	2
Nov. 28, 1965	Sonny Jurgensen, Washington vs. Dallas	43	26	411	3
Oct. 24, 1965	Fran Tarkenton, Minnesota vs. San Francisco	35	21	407	3
Nov. 1, 1964	Len Dawson, Kansas City vs. Denver	38	23	435	6
Oct. 25, 1964	Cotton Davidson, Oakland vs. Denver	36	23	427	5
Oct. 16, 1964	Babe Parilli, Boston vs. Oakland	47	25	422	4
Dec. 22, 1963	Tom Flores, Oakland vs. Houston	29	17	407	6
Nov. 17, 1963	Norm Snead, Washington vs. Pittsburgh	40	23	424	2
Nov. 10, 1963	Don Meredith, Dallas vs. San Francisco	48	30	460	3
Oct. 13, 1963	Charley Johnson, St. Louis vs. Pittsburgh	41	20	428	2
Dec. 16, 1962	Sonny Jurgensen, Philadelphia vs. St. Louis	34	15	419	5
Nov. 18, 1962	Bill Wade, Chicago vs. Dall. Cowboys	46	28	466	2
Oct. 28, 1962	Y.A. Tittle, N.Y. Giants vs. Washington	39	27	505	7
Sept. 15, 1962	Frank Tripucka, Denver vs. Buffalo	56	29	447	2
Dec. 17, 1961	Sonny Jurgensen, Philadelphia vs. Detroit	42	27	403	3
Nov. 19, 1961	George Blanda, Houston vs. N.Y. Titans	32	20	418	7
Oct. 29, 1961	George Blanda, Houston vs. Buffalo	32	18	464	4
Oct. 29, 1961	Sonny Jurgensen, Philadelphia vs. Washington	41	27	436	3
Oct. 13, 1961	Jacky Lee, Houston vs. Boston	41	27	457	2
Dec. 13, 1958	Bobby Layne, Pittsburgh vs. Chi. Cardinals	49	23	409	2
Nov. 8, 1953	Bobby Thomason, Philadelphia vs. N.Y. Giants	44	22	437	4
Oct. 4, 1952	Otto Graham, Cleveland vs. Pittsburgh	49	21	401	3
Sept. 28, 1951	Norm Van Brocklin, Los Angeles vs. N.Y. Yanks	41	27	554	5
Dec. 11, 1949	Johnny Lujack, Chi. Bears vs. Chi. Cardinals	39	24	468	6
Oct. 31, 1948	Sammy Baugh, Washington vs. Boston	24	17	446	4
Oct. 31, 1948	Jim Hardy, Los Angeles vs. Chi. Cardinals	53	28	406	3
Nov. 14, 1943	Sid Luckman, Chi. Bears vs. N.Y. Giants	32	21	433	7

Times 400 or More

109 times by 59 players... Marino 10; Montana 7; Fouts 6; Jurgensen 5; Kramer, Krieg, Moon 4; Esiason, Namath, Simms 3; Anderson, Blanda, Cunningham, Johnson, Kosar, Lomax, Meredith, O'Brien, Rypien, Todd, Williams 2.

1,000 Yards Pass Receiving in a Season

Year	Player, Team	No.	Yards	Avg.	Long	TD
1992	Sterling Sharpe, Green Bay[3]	108	1,461	13.5	76	13
	Michael Irvin, Dallas[2]	78	1,396	17.9	87	7
	Jerry Rice, San Francisco[7]	84	1,201	14.3	80	10
	Andre Rison, Atlanta[2]	93	1,119	12.0	71	11
	Fred Barnett, Philadelphia	67	1,083	16.2	71	6
	Anthony Miller, San Diego[2]	72	1,060	14.7	67	7
	Eric Martin, New Orleans[3]	68	1,041	15.3	52	5
1991	Michael Irvin, Dallas	93	1,523	16.4	66	8
	Gary Clark, Washington[5]	70	1,340	19.1	82	10
	Jerry Rice, San Francisco[6]	80	1,206	15.1	73	14
	Haywood Jeffires, Houston[2]	100	1,181	11.8	44	7
	Michael Haynes, Atlanta	50	1,122	22.4	80	11
	Andre Reed, Buffalo[2]	81	1,113	13.7	55	10
	Drew Hill, Houston[5]	90	1,109	12.3	61	4
	Mark Duper, Miami[4]	70	1,085	15.5	43	5
	James Lofton, Buffalo[6]	57	1,072	18.8	77	8
	Mark Clayton, Miami[5]	70	1,053	15.0	43	12
	Henry Ellard, L.A. Rams[4]	64	1,052	16.4	38	3
	Art Monk, Washington[5]	71	1,049	14.8	64	8
	Irving Fryar, New England	68	1,014	14.9	56	3
	John Taylor, San Francisco[2]	64	1,011	15.8	97	9
	Brian Blades, Seattle[2]	70	1,003	14.3	52	2
1990	Jerry Rice, San Francisco[5]	100	1,502	15.0	64	13
	Henry Ellard, L.A. Rams[3]	76	1,294	17.0	50	4
	Andre Rison, Atlanta	82	1,208	14.7	75	10
	Gary Clark, Washington[4]	75	1,112	14.8	53	8
	Sterling Sharpe, Green Bay[2]	67	1,105	16.5	76	6
	Willie Anderson, L.A. Rams[2]	51	1,097	21.5	55	4
	Haywood Jeffires, Houston	74	1,048	14.2	87	8
	Stephone Paige, Kansas City	65	1,021	15.7	86	5
	Drew Hill, Houston[4]	74	1,019	13.8	57	5
	Anthony Carter, Minnesota[3]	70	1,008	14.4	56	8
1989	Jerry Rice, San Francisco[4]	82	1,483	18.1	68	17
	Sterling Sharpe, Green Bay	90	1,423	15.8	79	12
	Mark Carrier, Tampa Bay	86	1,422	16.5	78	9
	Henry Ellard, L.A. Rams[2]	70	1,382	19.7	53	8
	Andre Reed, Buffalo	88	1,312	14.9	78	9
	Anthony Miller, San Diego	75	1,252	16.7	69	10
	Webster Slaughter, Cleveland	65	1,236	19.0	97	6
	Gary Clark, Washington[3]	79	1,229	15.6	80	9
	Tim McGee, Cincinnati	65	1,211	18.6	74	8
	Art Monk, Washington[4]	86	1,186	13.8	60	8
	Willie Anderson, L.A. Rams	44	1,146	26.0	78	5
	Ricky Sanders, Washington[2]	80	1,138	14.2	68	4
	Vance Johnson, Denver	76	1,095	14.4	69	7
	Richard Johnson, Detroit	70	1,091	15.6	75	8
	Eric Martin, New Orleans[2]	68	1,090	16.0	53	8
	John Taylor, San Francisco	60	1,077	18.0	95	10
	Mervyn Fernandez, L.A. Raiders	57	1,069	18.8	75	9
	Anthony Carter, Minnesota[2]	65	1,066	16.4	50	4
	Brian Blades, Seattle	77	1,063	13.8	60	5
	Mark Clayton, Miami[4]	64	1,011	15.8	78	9
1988	Henry Ellard, L.A. Rams	86	1,414	16.4	68	10
	Jerry Rice, San Francisco[3]	64	1,306	20.4	96	9
	Eddie Brown, Cincinnati	53	1,273	24.0	86	9
	Anthony Carter, Minnesota	72	1,225	17.0	67	6
	Ricky Sanders, Washington	73	1,148	15.7	55	12
	Drew Hill, Houston[3]	72	1,141	15.8	57	10
	Mark Clayton, Miami[3]	86	1,129	13.1	45	14
	Roy Green, Phoenix[3]	68	1,097	16.1	52	7
	Eric Martin, New Orleans	85	1,083	12.7	40	7
	Al Toon, N.Y. Jets[2]	93	1,067	11.5	42	5
	Bruce Hill, Tampa Bay	58	1,040	17.9	42	9
	Lionel Manuel, N.Y. Giants	65	1,029	15.8	46	4
1987	J.T. Smith, St. Louis[2]	91	1,117	12.3	38	8
	Jerry Rice, San Francisco[2]	65	1,078	16.6	57	22
	Gary Clark, Washington[2]	56	1,066	19.0	84	7
	Carlos Carson, Kansas City[3]	55	1,044	19.0	81	7
1986	Jerry Rice, San Francisco	86	1,570	18.3	66	15
	Stanley Morgan, New England[3]	84	1,491	17.8	44	10
	Mark Duper, Miami[3]	67	1,313	19.6	85	11
	Gary Clark, Washington	74	1,265	17.1	55	7
	Al Toon, N.Y. Jets	85	1,176	13.8	62	8
	Todd Christensen, L.A. Raiders[3]	95	1,153	12.1	35	8
	Mark Clayton, Miami[2]	60	1,150	19.2	68	10
	*Bill Brooks, Indianapolis	65	1,131	17.4	84	8
	Drew Hill, Houston[2]	65	1,112	17.1	81	5
	Steve Largent, Seattle[8]	70	1,070	15.3	38	9
	Art Monk, Washington[3]	73	1,068	14.6	69	4
	*Ernest Givins, Houston	61	1,062	17.4	60	3
	Cris Collinsworth, Cincinnati[4]	62	1,024	16.5	46	10
	Wesley Walker, N.Y. Jets[2]	49	1,016	20.7	83	12
	J.T. Smith, St. Louis	80	1,014	12.7	45	6
	Mark Bavaro, N.Y. Giants	66	1,001	15.2	41	4
1985	Steve Largent, Seattle[7]	79	1,287	16.3	43	6
	Mike Quick, Philadelphia[3]	73	1,247	17.1	99	11
	Art Monk, Washington[2]	91	1,226	13.5	53	2
	Wes Chandler, San Diego[4]	67	1,199	17.9	75	10
	Drew Hill, Houston	64	1,169	18.3	57	9
	James Lofton, Green Bay[5]	69	1,153	16.7	56	4
	Louis Lipps, Pittsburgh	59	1,134	19.2	51	12
	Cris Collinsworth, Cincinnati[3]	65	1,125	17.3	71	5
	Tony Hill, Dallas[3]	74	1,113	15.0	53	7
	Lionel James, San Diego	86	1,027	11.9	67	6
	Roger Craig, San Francisco	92	1,016	11.0	73	6
1984	Roy Green, St. Louis[2]	78	1,555	19.9	83	12
	John Stallworth, Pittsburgh[3]	80	1,395	17.4	51	11
	Mark Clayton, Miami	73	1,389	19.0	65	18
	Art Monk, Washington	106	1,372	12.9	72	7
	James Lofton, Green Bay[4]	62	1,361	22.0	79	7
	Mark Duper, Miami[2]	71	1,306	18.4	80	8
	Steve Watson, Denver[3]	69	1,170	17.0	73	7
	Steve Largent, Seattle[6]	74	1,164	15.7	65	12
	Tim Smith, Houston[2]	69	1,141	16.5	75	4
	Stacey Bailey, Atlanta	67	1,138	17.0	61	6
	Carlos Carson, Kansas City[2]	57	1,078	18.9	57	4
	Mike Quick, Philadelphia[2]	61	1,052	17.2	90	9
	Todd Christensen, L.A. Raiders[2]	80	1,007	12.6	38	7
	Kevin House, Tampa Bay[2]	76	1,005	13.2	55	5
	Ozzie Newsome, Cleveland[2]	89	1,001	11.2	52	5
1983	Mike Quick, Philadelphia	69	1,409	20.4	83	13
	Carlos Carson, Kansas City	80	1,351	16.9	50	7
	James Lofton, Green Bay[3]	58	1,300	22.4	74	8
	Todd Christensen, L.A. Raiders	92	1,247	13.6	45	12
	Roy Green, St. Louis	78	1,227	15.7	71	14
	Charlie Brown, Washington	78	1,225	15.7	75	8
	Tim Smith, Houston	83	1,176	14.2	47	6
	Kellen Winslow, San Diego[3]	88	1,172	13.3	46	8
	Earnest Gray, N.Y. Giants	78	1,139	14.6	62	5
	Steve Watson, Denver[2]	59	1,133	19.2	78	5
	Cris Collinsworth, Cincinnati[2]	66	1,130	17.1	63	5
	Steve Largent, Seattle[5]	72	1,074	14.9	46	11
	Mark Duper, Miami	51	1,003	19.7	85	10
1982	Wes Chandler, San Diego[3]	49	1,032	21.1	66	9
1981	Alfred Jenkins, Atlanta[2]	70	1,358	19.4	67	13
	James Lofton, Green Bay[2]	71	1,294	18.2	75	8
	Frank Lewis, Buffalo[2]	70	1,244	17.8	33	4
	Steve Watson, Denver	60	1,244	20.7	95	13
	Steve Largent, Seattle[4]	75	1,224	16.3	57	9
	Charlie Joiner, San Diego[4]	70	1,188	17.0	57	7
	Kevin House, Tampa Bay	56	1,176	21.0	84	9
	Wes Chandler, N.O.-San Diego[2]	69	1,142	16.6	51	6
	Dwight Clark, San Francisco	85	1,105	13.0	78	4
	John Stallworth, Pittsburgh[2]	63	1,098	17.4	55	5
	Kellen Winslow, San Diego[2]	88	1,075	12.2	67	10
	Pat Tilley, St. Louis	66	1,040	15.8	75	3
	Stanley Morgan, New England[2]	44	1,029	23.4	76	6

Year	Player, Team	No.	Yards	Avg.	Long	TD
	Harold Carmichael, Philadelphia[3]	61	1,028	16.9	85	6
	Freddie Scott, Detroit	53	1,022	19.3	48	5
	*Cris Collinsworth, Cincinnati	67	1,009	15.1	74	8
	Joe Senser, Minnesota	79	1,004	12.7	53	8
	Ozzie Newsome, Cleveland	69	1,002	14.5	62	6
	Sammy White, Minnesota	66	1,001	15.2	53	3
1980	John Jefferson, San Diego[3]	82	1,340	16.3	58	13
	Kellen Winslow, San Diego	89	1,290	14.5	65	9
	James Lofton, Green Bay	71	1,226	17.3	47	4
	Charlie Joiner, San Diego[3]	71	1,132	15.9	51	4
	Ahmad Rashad, Minnesota[2]	69	1,095	15.9	76	5
	Steve Largent, Seattle[3]	66	1,064	16.1	67	6
	Tony Hill, Dallas[2]	60	1,055	17.6	58	8
	Alfred Jenkins, Atlanta	57	1,026	18.0	57	6
1979	Steve Largent, Seattle[2]	66	1,237	18.7	55	9
	John Stallworth, Pittsburgh	70	1,183	16.9	65	8
	Ahmad Rashad, Minnesota	80	1,156	14.5	52	9
	John Jefferson, San Diego[2]	61	1,090	17.9	65	10
	Frank Lewis, Buffalo	54	1,082	20.0	55	2
	Wes Chandler, New Orleans	65	1,069	16.4	85	6
	Tony Hill, Dallas	60	1,062	17.7	75	10
	Drew Pearson, Dallas[2]	55	1,026	18.7	56	8
	Wallace Francis, Atlanta	74	1,013	13.7	42	8
	Harold Jackson, New England[3]	45	1,013	22.5	59	7
	Charlie Joiner, San Diego[2]	72	1,008	14.0	39	4
	Stanley Morgan, New England	44	1,002	22.8	63	12
1978	Wesley Walker, N.Y. Jets	48	1,169	24.4	77	8
	Steve Largent, Seattle	71	1,168	16.5	57	8
	Harold Carmichael, Philadelphia[2]	55	1,072	19.5	56	8
	*John Jefferson, San Diego	56	1,001	17.9	46	13
1976	Roger Carr, Baltimore	43	1,112	25.9	79	11
	Cliff Branch, Oakland[2]	46	1,111	24.2	88	12
	Charlie Joiner, San Diego	50	1,056	21.1	81	7
1975	Ken Burrough, Houston	53	1,063	20.1	77	8
1974	Cliff Branch, Oakland	60	1,092	18.2	67	13
	Drew Pearson, Dallas	62	1,087	17.5	50	2
1973	Harold Carmichael, Philadelphia	67	1,116	16.7	73	9
1972	Harold Jackson, Philadelphia[2]	62	1,048	16.9	77	4
	John Gilliam, Minnesota	47	1,035	22.0	66	7
1971	Otis Taylor, Kansas City[2]	57	1,110	19.5	82	7
1970	Gene Washington, San Francisco	53	1,100	20.8	79	12
	Marlin Briscoe, Buffalo	57	1,036	18.2	48	8
	Dick Gordon, Chicago	71	1,026	14.5	69	13
	Gary Garrison, San Diego[2]	44	1,006	22.9	67	12
1969	Warren Wells, Oakland[2]	47	1,260	26.8	80	14
	Harold Jackson, Philadelphia	65	1,116	17.2	65	9
	Roy Jefferson, Pittsburgh[2]	67	1,079	16.1	63	9
	Dan Abramowicz, New Orleans	73	1,015	13.9	49	7
	Lance Alworth, San Diego[7]	64	1,003	15.7	76	4
1968	Lance Alworth, San Diego[6]	68	1,312	19.3	80	10
	Don Maynard, N.Y. Jets[5]	57	1,297	22.8	87	10
	George Sauer, N.Y. Jets[3]	66	1,141	17.3	43	3
	Warren Wells, Oakland	53	1,137	21.5	94	11
	Gary Garrison, San Diego	52	1,103	21.2	84	10
	Roy Jefferson, Pittsburgh	58	1,074	18.5	62	11
	Paul Warfield, Cleveland	50	1,067	21.3	65	12
	Homer Jones, N.Y. Giants[3]	45	1,057	23.5	84	7
	Fred Biletnikoff, Oakland	61	1,037	17.0	82	6
	Lance Rentzel, Dallas	54	1,009	18.7	65	6
1967	Don Maynard, N.Y. Jets[4]	71	1,434	20.2	75	10
	Ben Hawkins, Philadelphia	59	1,265	21.4	87	10
	Homer Jones, N.Y. Giants[2]	49	1,209	24.7	70	13
	Jackie Smith, St. Louis	56	1,205	21.5	76	9
	George Sauer, N.Y. Jets[2]	75	1,189	15.9	61	6
	Lance Alworth, San Diego[5]	52	1,010	19.4	71	9
1966	Lance Alworth, San Diego[4]	73	1,383	18.9	78	13
	Otis Taylor, Kansas City	58	1,297	22.4	89	8
	Pat Studstill, Detroit	67	1,266	18.9	99	5
	Bob Hayes, Dallas[2]	64	1,232	19.3	95	13
	Charlie Frazier, Houston	57	1,129	19.8	79	12
	Charley Taylor, Washington	72	1,119	15.5	86	12
	George Sauer, N.Y. Jets	63	1,081	17.2	77	5
	Homer Jones, N.Y. Giants	48	1,044	21.8	98	8
	Art Powell, Oakland[5]	53	1,026	19.4	46	11
1965	Lance Alworth, San Diego[3]	69	1,602	23.2	85	14
	Dave Parks, San Francisco	80	1,344	16.8	53	12
	Don Maynard, N.Y. Jets[3]	68	1,218	17.9	56	14
	Pete Retzlaff, Philadelphia	66	1,190	18.0	78	10
	Lionel Taylor, Denver[4]	85	1,131	13.3	63	6
	Tommy McDonald, Los Angeles[3]	67	1,036	15.5	51	9
	*Bob Hayes, Dallas	46	1,003	21.8	82	12
1964	Charley Hennigan, Houston[3]	101	1,546	15.3	53	8
	Art Powell, Oakland[4]	76	1,361	17.9	77	11
	Lance Alworth, San Diego[2]	61	1,235	20.2	82	13
	Johnny Morris, Chicago	93	1,200	12.9	63	10
	Elbert Dubenion, Buffalo	42	1,139	27.1	72	10
	Terry Barr, Detroit[2]	57	1,030	18.1	58	9
1963	Bobby Mitchell, Washington[2]	69	1,436	20.8	99	7
	Art Powell, Oakland[3]	73	1,304	17.9	85	16
	Buddy Dial, Pittsburgh[2]	60	1,295	21.6	83	9
	Lance Alworth, San Diego	61	1,205	19.8	85	11
	Del Shofner, N.Y. Giants[4]	64	1,181	18.5	70	9
	Lionel Taylor, Denver[3]	78	1,101	14.1	72	10
	Terry Barr, Detroit	66	1,086	16.5	75	13
	Charley Hennigan, Houston[2]	61	1,051	17.2	83	10
	Sonny Randle, St. Louis[2]	51	1,014	19.9	68	12
	Bake Turner, N.Y. Jets	71	1,009	14.2	53	6
1962	Bobby Mitchell, Washington	72	1,384	19.2	81	11
	Sonny Randle, St. Louis	63	1,158	18.4	86	7
	Tommy McDonald, Philadelphia[2]	58	1,146	19.8	60	10
	Del Shofner, N.Y. Giants[3]	53	1,133	21.4	69	12
	Art Powell, N.Y. Titans[2]	64	1,130	17.7	80	8
	Frank Clarke, Dall. Cowboys	47	1,043	22.2	66	14
	Don Maynard, N.Y. Titans[2]	56	1,041	18.6	86	8
1961	Charley Hennigan, Houston	82	1,746	21.3	80	12
	Lionel Taylor, Denver[2]	100	1,176	11.8	52	4
	Bill Groman, Houston[2]	50	1,175	23.5	80	17
	Tommy McDonald, Philadelphia	64	1,144	17.9	66	13
	Del Shofner, N.Y. Giants[2]	68	1,125	16.5	46	11
	Jim Phillips, Los Angeles	78	1,092	14.0	69	5
	*Mike Ditka, Chicago	56	1,076	19.2	76	12
	Dave Kocourek, San Diego	55	1,055	19.2	76	4
	Buddy Dial, Pittsburgh	53	1,047	19.8	88	12
	R.C. Owens, San Francisco	55	1,032	18.8	54	5
1960	*Bill Groman, Houston	72	1,473	20.5	92	12
	Raymond Berry, Baltimore	74	1,298	17.5	70	10
	Don Maynard, N.Y. Titans	72	1,265	17.6	65	6
	Lionel Taylor, Denver	92	1,235	13.4	80	12
	Art Powell, N.Y. Titans	69	1,167	16.9	76	14
1958	Del Shofner, Los Angeles	51	1,097	21.5	92	8
1956	Bill Howton, Green Bay[2]	55	1,188	21.6	66	12
	Harlon Hill, Chi. Bears[2]	47	1,128	24.0	79	11
1954	Bob Boyd, Los Angeles	53	1,212	22.9	80	6
	*Harlon Hill, Chi. Bears	45	1,124	25.0	76	12
1953	Pete Pihos, Philadelphia	63	1,049	16.7	59	10
1952	*Bill Howton, Green Bay	53	1,231	23.2	90	13
1951	Elroy (Crazylegs) Hirsch, Los Angeles	66	1,495	22.7	91	17
1950	Tom Fears, Los Angeles[2]	84	1,116	13.3	53	7
	Cloyce Box, Detroit	50	1,009	20.2	82	11
1949	Bob Mann, Detroit	66	1,014	15.4	64	4
	Tom Fears, Los Angeles	77	1,013	13.2	51	9
1945	Jim Benton, Cleveland	45	1,067	23.7	84	8
1942	Don Hutson, Green Bay	74	1,211	16.4	73	17

**First year in the league.*

250 Yards Pass Receiving in a Game

Date	Player, Team, Opponent	No.	Yards	TD
Dec. 11, 1989	John Taylor, San Francisco vs. L.A. Rams	11	286	2
Nov. 26, 1989	Willie Anderson, L.A. Rams vs. New Orleans (OT)	15	336	1
Oct. 18, 1987	Steve Largent, Seattle vs. Detroit	15	261	3
Oct. 4, 1987	*Anthony Allen, Washington vs. St. Louis	7	255	3
Dec. 22, 1985	Stephone Paige, Kansas City vs. San Diego	8	309	2
Dec. 20, 1982	Wes Chandler, San Diego vs. Cincinnati	10	260	2
Sept. 23, 1979	*Jerry Butler, Buffalo vs. N.Y. Jets	10	255	4
Nov. 4, 1962	Sonny Randle, St. Louis vs. N.Y. Giants	16	256	1
Oct. 28, 1962	Del Shofner, N.Y. Giants vs. Washington	11	269	1
Oct. 13, 1961	Charley Hennigan, Houston vs. Boston	13	272	1
Oct. 21, 1956	Billy Howton, Green Bay vs. Los Angeles	7	257	2
Dec. 3, 1950	Cloyce Box, Detroit vs. Baltimore	12	302	4
Nov. 22, 1945	Jim Benton, Cleveland vs. Detroit	10	303	1

**First year in the league.*

2,000 Combined Net Yards Gained in a Season

Year	Player, Team	Rushing Att.-Yds.	Pass Rec.	Punt Ret.	Kickoff Ret.	Fum. Runs	Total Yds.
1992	Thurman Thomas, Buffalo	312-1,487	58-626	0-0	0-0	1-0	371-2,113
	Emmitt Smith, Dallas	373-1,713	59-335	0-0	0-0	1-0	433-2,048
	Barry Foster, Pittsburgh	390-1,690	36-344	0-0	0-0	2-(−20)	428-2,014
1991	Thurman Thomas, Buffalo	288-1,407	62-631	0-0	0-0	0-0	350-2,038
1990	Herschel Walker, Minnesota	184-770	35-315	0-0	44-966	4-0	267-2,051
1988	*Tim Brown, L.A. Raiders	14-50	43-725	49-444	41-1,098	7-0	154-2,317
	Roger Craig, San Fran.	310-1,502	76-534	0-0	2-32	2-0	390-2,068
	Eric Dickerson, Indianapolis	388-1,659	36-377	0-0	0-0	1-0	425-2,036
	Herschel Walker, Dallas	361-1,514	53-505	0-0	0-0	3-0	417-2,019
1986	Eric Dickerson, L.A. Rams	404-1,821	26-205	0-0	0-0	2-0	432-2,026
	Gary Anderson, San Diego	127-442	80-871	25-227	24-482	2-0	258-2,022
1985	Lionel James, San Diego	105-516	86-1,027	25-213	36-779	1-0	253-2,535
	Marcus Allen, L.A. Raiders	380-1,759	67-555	0-0	0-0	2-(−6)	449-2,308
	Roger Craig, San Fran.	214-1,050	92-1,016	0-0	0-0	0-0	306-2,066
	Walter Payton, Chicago	324-1,551	49-483	0-0	0-0	1-0	374-2,034
1984	Eric Dickerson, L.A. Rams	379-2,105	21-139	0-0	0-0	4-15	404-2,259
	James Wilder, Tampa Bay	407-1,544	85-685	0-0	0-0	4-0	496-2,229
	Walter Payton, Chicago	381-1,684	45-368	0-0	0-0	1-0	427-2,052
1983	*Eric Dickerson, L.A. Rams	390-1,808	51-404	0-0	0-0	1-0	442-2,212
	William Andrews, Atlanta	331-1,567	59-609	0-0	0-0	2-0	392-2,176
	Walter Payton, Chicago	314-1,421	53-607	0-0	0-0	2-0	369-2,028
1981	*James Brooks, San Diego	109-525	46-329	22-290	40-949	2-0	219-2,093
	William Andrews, Atlanta	289-1,301	81-735	0-0	0-0	0-0	370-2,036
1980	Bruce Harper, N.Y. Jets	45-126	50-634	28-242	49-1,070	3-0	175-2,072
1979	Wilbert Montgomery, Phil.	338-1,512	41-494	0-0	1-6	2-0	382-2,012
1978	Bruce Harper, N.Y. Jets	58-303	13-196	30-378	55-1,280	1-0	157-2,157
1977	Walter Payton, Chicago	339-1,852	27-269	0-0	2-95	5-0	373-2,216
	Terry Metcalf, St. Louis	149-739	34-403	14-108	32-772	1-0	230-2,022
1975	Terry Metcalf, St. Louis	165-816	43-378	23-285	35-960	2-23	268-2,462
	O.J. Simpson, Buffalo	329-1,817	28-426	0-0	0-0	1-0	358-2,243
1974	Mack Herron, New England	231-824	38-474	35-517	28-629	3-0	335-2,444
	Otis Armstrong, Denver	263-1,407	38-405	0-0	16-386	1-0	318-2,198
	Terry Metcalf, St. Louis	152-718	50-377	26-340	20-623	7-0	255-2,058
1973	O.J. Simpson, Buffalo	332-2,003	6-70	0-0	0-0	0-0	338-2,073
1966	Gale Sayers, Chicago	229-1,231	34-447	6-44	23-718	3-0	295-2,440
	Leroy Kelly, Cleveland	209-1,141	32-366	13-104	19-403	0-0	273-2,014
1965	*Gale Sayers, Chicago	166-867	29-507	16-238	21-660	4-0	236-2,272
1963	Timmy Brown, Philadelphia	192-841	36-487	16-152	33-945	2-3	279-2,428
	Jim Brown, Cleveland	291-1,863	24-268	0-0	0-0	0-0	315-2,131
1962	Timmy Brown, Philadelphia	137-545	52-849	6-81	30-831	4-0	229-2,306
	Dick Christy, N.Y. Titans	114-535	62-538	15-250	38-824	2-0	231-2,147
1961	Billy Cannon, Houston	200-948	43-586	9-70	18-439	2-0	272-2,043
1960	*Abner Haynes, Dall. Texans	156-875	55-576	14-215	19-434	4-0	248-2,100

**First year in the league.*

300 Combined Net Yards Gained in a Game

Date	Player, Team, Opponent	No.	Yards	TD
Dec. 11, 1989	John Taylor, San Francisco vs. L.A. Rams	14	321	2
Nov. 26, 1989	Willie Anderson, L.A. Rams vs. New Orleans (OT)	15	336	1
Nov. 28, 1988	Tim Brown, L.A. Raiders vs. San Diego	12	306	1

Dec. 22, 1985	Stephone Paige, Kansas City vs. San Diego	8	309	2
Nov. 10, 1985	Lionel James, San Diego vs. L.A. Raiders (OT)	23	345	0
Sept. 22, 1985	Lionel James, San Diego vs. Cincinnati	20	316	2
Dec. 21, 1975	Walter Payton, Chicago vs. New Orleans	32	300	1
Nov. 23, 1975	Greg Pruitt, Cleveland vs. Cincinnati	28	304	2
Nov. 1, 1970	Eugene (Mercury) Morris, Miami vs. Baltimore	17	302	0
Oct. 4, 1970	O. J. Simpson, Buffalo vs. N.Y. Jets	26	303	2
Dec. 6, 1969	Jerry LeVias, Houston vs. N.Y. Jets	18	329	1
Nov. 2, 1969	Travis Williams, Green Bay vs. Pittsburgh	11	314	3
Dec. 18, 1966	Gale Sayers, Chicago vs. Minnesota	20	339	2
Dec. 12, 1965	Gale Sayers, Chicago vs. San Francisco	17	336	6
Nov. 17, 1963	Gary Ballman, Pittsburgh vs. Washington	12	320	2
Dec. 16, 1962	Timmy Brown, Philadelphia vs. St. Louis	19	341	2
Dec. 10, 1961	Billy Cannon, Houston vs. N.Y. Titans	32	373	5
Nov 19, 1961	Jim Brown, Cleveland vs. Philadelphia	38	313	4
Dec. 3, 1950	Cloyce Box, Detroit vs. Baltimore	13	302	4
Oct. 29, 1950	Wally Triplett, Detroit vs. Los Angeles	11	331	1
Nov. 22, 1945	Jim Benton, Cleveland vs. Detroit	10	303	1

Top 20 Scorers

Player	Years	TD	FG	PAT	TP
George Blanda	26	9	335	943	2,002
Jan Stenerud	19	0	373	580	1,699
Pat Leahy	18	0	304	558	1,470
Jim Turner	16	1	304	521	1,439
Mark Moseley	16	0	300	482	1,382
Jim Bakken	17	0	282	534	1,380
Nick Lowery	14	0	306	449	1,367
Fred Cox	15	0	282	519	1,365
Lou Groza	17	1	234	641	1,349
Chris Bahr	14	0	241	490	1,213
Jim Breech	13	0	224	486	1,158
Gino Cappelletti	11	42	176	350	1,130
Ray Wersching	15	0	222	456	1,122
Eddie Murray	12	0	244	381	1,113
Don Cockroft	13	0	216	432	1,080
Garo Yepremian	14	0	210	444	1,074
Matt Bahr	13	0	221	402	1,065
Bruce Gossett	11	0	219	374	1,031
Gary Anderson	10	0	229	323	1,010
Sam Baker	15	2	179	428	977

Cappelletti's total includes four two-point conversions.

Top 20 Touchdown Scorers

Player	Years	Rush	Rec.	Returns	Total TD
Jim Brown	9	106	20	0	126
Walter Payton	13	110	15	0	125
John Riggins	14	104	12	0	116
Lenny Moore	12	63	48	2	113
Jerry Rice	8	5	103	0	108
Don Hutson	11	3	99	3	105
Steve Largent	14	1	100	0	101
Franco Harris	13	91	9	0	100
Marcus Allen	11	79	18	1	98
Eric Dickerson	10	90	6	0	96
Jim Taylor	10	83	10	0	93
Tony Dorsett	12	77	13	1	91
Bobby Mitchell	11	18	65	8	91
Leroy Kelly	10	74	13	3	90
Charley Taylor	13	11	79	0	90
Don Maynard	15	0	88	0	88
Lance Alworth	11	2	85	0	87
Ottis Anderson	14	81	5	0	86
Paul Warfield	13	1	85	0	86
Tommy McDonald	12	0	84	1	85

Top 20 Rushers

Player	Years	Att.	Yards	Avg.	Long	TD
Walter Payton	13	3,838	16,726	4.4	76	110
Eric Dickerson	10	2,970	13,168	4.4	85	90
Tony Dorsett	12	2,936	12,739	4.3	99	77
Jim Brown	9	2,359	12,312	5.2	80	106
Franco Harris	13	2,949	12,120	4.1	75	91
John Riggins	14	2,916	11,352	3.9	66	104
O.J. Simpson	11	2,404	11,236	4.7	94	61
Ottis Anderson	14	2,562	10,273	4.0	76	81
Earl Campbell	8	2,187	9,407	4.3	81	74
Jim Taylor	10	1,941	8,597	4.4	84	83
Marcus Allen	11	2,090	8,545	4.1	61	79
Joe Perry	14	1,737	8,378	4.8	78	53
Gerald Riggs	10	1,989	8,188	4.1	58	69
Larry Csonka	11	1,891	8,081	4.3	54	64
Freeman McNeil	12	1,798	8,074	4.5	69	38
Roger Craig	10	1,953	8,070	4.1	71	55
James Brooks	12	1,685	7,962	4.7	65	49
Mike Pruitt	11	1,844	7,378	4.0	77	51
Leroy Kelly	10	1,727	7,274	4.2	70	74
George Rogers	7	1,692	7,176	4.2	79	54

Top 20 Combined Yards Gained

Player	Years	Tot.	Rush.	Rec.	Int. Ret.	Punt Ret.	Kickoff Ret.	Fumble Ret.
Walter Payton	13	21,803	16,726	4,538	0	0	539	0
Tony Dorsett	12	16,326	12,739	3,554	0	0	0	33
Jim Brown	9	15,459	12,312	2,499	0	0	648	0
Eric Dickerson	10	15,262	13,168	2,079	0	0	0	15
James Brooks	12	14,910	7,962	3,621	0	565	2,762	0
Franco Harris	13	14,622	12,120	2,287	0	0	233	−18
O.J. Simpson	11	14,368	11,236	2,142	0	0	990	0
James Lofton	15	14,094	246	13,821	0	0	0	27
Bobby Mitchell	11	14,078	2,735	7,954	0	699	2,690	0
John Riggins	14	13,435	11,352	2,090	0	0	0	−7
Steve Largent	14	13,396	83	13,089	0	68	156	0
Ottis Anderson	14	13,364	10,273	3,062	0	0	0	29
Greg Pruitt	12	13,262	5,672	3,069	0	2,007	2,514	0
Drew Hill	13	12,953	19	9,447	0	22	3,460	5
Ollie Matson	14	12,884	5,173	3,285	51	595	3,746	34
Roger Craig	10	12,844	8,070	4,742	0	0	32	0
Marcus Allen	11	12,797	8,545	4,258	0	0	0	−6
Tim Brown	10	12,684	3,862	3,399	0	639	4,781	3
Lenny Moore	12	12,451	5,174	6,039	0	56	1,180	2
Don Maynard	15	12,379	70	11,834	0	132	343	0

Top 20 Passers

Player	Years	Att.	Comp.	Pct. Comp.	Yards	TD	Pct. TD	Int.	Pct. Int.	Avg. Gain	Rating
Joe Montana	13	4,600	2,929	63.7	35,124	244	5.3	123	2.7	7.64	93.5
Steve Young	8	1,506	908	60.3	11,877	76	5.0	42	2.8	7.89	90.4
Dan Marino	10	5,284	3,128	59.2	39,502	290	5.5	165	3.1	7.48	87.8
Jim Kelly	7	3,024	1,824	60.3	23,031	161	5.3	108	3.6	7.62	86.9
Mark Rypien	5	1,888	1,078	57.1	14,414	97	5.1	65	3.4	7.63	84.3
Roger Staubach	11	2,958	1,685	57.0	22,700	153	5.2	109	3.7	7.67	83.4
Neil Lomax	8	3,153	1,817	57.6	22,771	136	4.3	90	2.9	7.22	82.7
Sonny Jurgensen	18	4,262	2,433	57.1	32,224	255	6.0	189	4.4	7.56	82.6
Len Dawson	19	3,741	2,136	57.1	28,711	239	6.4	183	4.9	7.67	82.6
Dave Krieg	13	3,989	2,326	58.3	29,247	210	5.3	160	4.0	7.33	82.1
Ken Anderson	16	4,475	2,654	59.3	32,838	197	4.4	160	3.6	7.34	81.9
Bernie Kosar	8	3,012	1,774	58.9	21,097	111	3.7	78	2.6	7.00	81.8
Boomer Esiason	9	3,378	1,897	56.2	25,671	174	5.2	129	3.8	7.60	81.8
Danny White	13	2,950	1,761	59.7	21,959	155	5.3	132	4.5	7.44	81.7
Warren Moon	9	4,026	2,329	57.8	30,200	175	4.3	145	3.6	7.50	81.0
Ken O'Brien	9	3,465	2,039	58.8	24,386	124	3.6	95	2.7	7.04	81.0
Bart Starr	16	3,149	1,808	57.4	24,718	152	4.8	138	4.4	7.85	80.5
Fran Tarkenton	18	6,467	3,686	57.0	47,003	342	5.3	266	4.1	7.27	80.4
Dan Fouts	15	5,604	3,297	58.8	43,040	254	4.5	242	4.3	7.68	80.2
R. Cunningham	8	2,641	1,464	55.4	18,193	126	4.8	82	3.1	6.89	79.9

1,500 or more attempts. The passing ratings are based on performance standards established for completion percentage, interception percentage, touchdown percentage, and average gain. Passers are allocated points according to how their marks compare with those standards.

Top 20 Pass Receivers

Player	Years	No.	Yards	Avg.	Long	TD
Art Monk	13	847	11,628	13.7	79	63
Steve Largent	14	819	13,089	16.0	74	100
James Lofton	15	750	13,821	18.4	80	75
Charlie Joiner	18	750	12,146	16.2	87	65
Ozzie Newsome	13	662	7,980	12.1	74	47
Charley Taylor	13	649	9,110	14.0	88	79
Don Maynard	15	633	11,834	18.7	87	88
Raymond Berry	13	631	9,275	14.7	70	68
Jerry Rice	8	610	10,273	16.8	96	103
Drew Hill	13	600	9,447	15.7	81	60
Harold Carmichael	14	590	8,985	15.2	85	79
Fred Biletnikoff	14	589	8,974	15.2	82	76
Harold Jackson	16	579	10,372	17.9	79	76
Lionel Taylor	10	567	7,195	12.7	80	45
Wes Chandler	11	559	8,966	16.0	85	56
Roy Green	14	559	8,965	16.0	83	66
Stanley Morgan	14	557	10,716	19.2	76	72
Mark Clayton	10	550	8,643	15.7	78	81
Gary Clark	8	549	8,742	15.9	84	58
Roger Craig	10	547	4,742	8.7	73	16

Top 20 Interceptors

Player	Years	No.	Yards	Avg.	Long	TD
Paul Krause	16	81	1,185	14.6	81	3
Emlen Tunnell	14	79	1,282	16.2	55	4
Dick (Night Train) Lane	14	68	1,207	17.8	80	5
Ken Riley	15	65	596	9.2	66	5
Dick LeBeau	13	62	762	12.3	70	3
Dave Brown	15	62	698	11.3	90	5
Ronnie Lott	12	60	695	11.6	83	5
Emmitt Thomas	13	58	937	16.2	73	5
Bobby Boyd	9	57	994	17.4	74	4
Johnny Robinson	12	57	741	13.0	57	1
Mel Blount	14	57	736	12.9	52	2
Everson Walls	12	57	504	8.8	40	1
Lem Barney	11	56	1,077	19.2	71	7
Pat Fischer	17	56	941	16.8	69	4
Willie Brown	16	54	472	8.7	45	2
Bobby Dillon	8	52	976	18.8	61	5
Jack Butler	9	52	826	15.9	52	4
Larry Wilson	13	52	800	15.4	96	5
Jim Patton	12	52	712	13.7	51	2
Mel Renfro	14	52	626	12.0	90	3

Top 20 Punters

Player	Years	No.	Yards	Avg.	Long	Blk.
Sammy Baugh	16	338	15,245	45.1	85	9
Tommy Davis	11	511	22,833	44.7	82	2
Yale Lary	11	503	22,279	44.3	74	4
Rohn Stark	11	829	36,475	44.0	72	6
Horace Gillom	7	385	16,872	43.8	80	5
Jerry Norton	11	358	15,671	43.8	78	2
Don Chandler	12	660	28,678	43.5	90	4
Sean Landeta	8	493	21,416	43.4	71	3
Reggie Roby	10	555	24,036	43.3	77	3
Jerrel Wilson	16	1,072	46,139	43.0	72	12
Norm Van Brocklin	12	523	22,413	42.9	72	3
Rich Camarillo	12	781	33,426	42.8	76	5
Danny Villanueva	8	488	20,862	42.8	68	2
Tommy Barnhardt	6	310	13,206	42.6	65	2
Bobby Joe Green	14	970	41,317	42.6	75	3
Sam Baker	15	703	29,938	42.6	72	2

Ralf Mojsiejenko	7	413	17,533	42.5	74	5
Harry Newsome	8	593	25,168	42.4	84	14
Bob Waterfield	8	315	13,367	42.4	88	5
Ray Guy	14	1,049	44,493	42.4	74	3

300 or more punts.

Top 20 Punt Returners

Player	Years	No.	Yards	Avg.	Long	TD
George McAfee	8	112	1,431	12.8	74	2
Jack Christiansen	8	85	1,084	12.8	89	8
Claude Gibson	5	110	1,381	12.6	85	3
Bill Dudley	9	124	1,515	12.2	96	3
Rick Upchurch	9	248	3,008	12.1	92	8
Mel Gray	7	137	1,654	12.1	80	3
Billy Johnson	14	282	3,317	11.8	87	6
Mack Herron	3	84	982	11.7	66	0
Billy Thompson	13	157	1,814	11.6	60	0
Brian Mitchell	3	86	978	11.4	84	3
Henry Ellard	9	133	1,509	11.3	83	4
Rodger Bird	3	94	1,063	11.3	78	0
Bosh Pritchard	6	95	1,072	11.3	81	2
Bobby Joe Edmonds	4	105	1,178	11.2	75	1
Vai Sikahema	7	259	2,894	11.2	87	4
Terry Metcalf	6	84	936	11.1	69	1
Bob Hayes	11	104	1,158	11.1	90	3
Floyd Little	9	81	893	11.0	72	2
Louis Lipps	9	112	1,234	11.0	76	3
David Meggett	4	144	1,576	10.9	76	3

75 or more returns.

Top 20 Kickoff Returners

Player	Years	No.	Yards	Avg.	Long	TD
Gale Sayers	7	91	2,781	30.6	103	6
Lynn Chandnois	7	92	2,720	29.6	93	3
Abe Woodson	9	193	5,538	28.7	105	5
Claude (Buddy) Young	6	90	2,514	27.9	104	2
Travis Williams	5	102	2,801	27.5	105	6
Joe Arenas	7	139	3,798	27.3	96	1
Clarence Davis	8	79	2,140	27.1	76	0
Steve Van Buren	8	76	2,030	26.7	98	3
Lenny Lyles	12	81	2,161	26.7	103	3
Eugene (Mercury) Morris	8	111	2,947	26.5	105	3
Bobby Jancik	6	158	4,185	26.5	61	0
Mel Renfro	14	85	2,246	26.4	100	2
Bobby Mitchell	11	102	2,690	26.4	98	5
Ollie Matson	14	143	3,746	26.2	105	6
Alvin Haymond	10	170	4,438	26.1	98	2
Noland Smith	3	82	2,137	26.1	106	1
Al Nelson	9	101	2,625	26.0	78	0
Tim Brown	10	184	4,781	26.0	105	5
Vic Washington	6	129	3,341	25.9	98	1
Dave Hampton	8	113	2,923	25.9	101	3

75 or more returns.

Annual Scoring Leaders

Year	Player, Team	TD	FG	PAT	TP
1992	Pete Stoyanovich, Miami, AFC	0	30	34	124
	Morten Andersen, New Orleans, NFC	0	29	33	120
	Chip Lohmiller, Washington, NFC	0	30	30	120
1991	Chip Lohmiller, Washington, NFC	0	31	56	149
	Pete Stoyanovich, Miami, AFC	0	31	28	121
1990	Nick Lowery, Kansas City, AFC	0	34	37	139
	Chip Lohmiller, Washington, NFC	0	30	41	131
1989	Mike Cofer, San Francisco, NFC	0	29	49	136
	*David Treadwell, Denver, AFC	0	27	39	120
1988	Scott Norwood, Buffalo, AFC	0	32	33	129
	*Mike Cofer, San Francisco, NFC	0	27	40	121
1987	Jerry Rice, San Francisco, NFC	23	0	0	138
	Jim Breech, Cincinnati, AFC	0	24	25	97
1986	Tony Franklin, New England, AFC	0	32	44	140
	Kevin Butler, Chicago, NFC	0	28	36	120
1985	*Kevin Butler, Chicago, NFC	0	31	51	144
	Gary Anderson, Pittsburgh, AFC	0	33	40	139
1984	Ray Wersching, San Francisco, NFC	0	25	56	131
	Gary Anderson, Pittsburgh, AFC	0	24	45	117
1983	Mark Moseley, Washington, NFC	0	33	62	161
	Gary Anderson, Pittsburgh, AFC	0	27	38	119
1982	*Marcus Allen, L.A. Raiders, AFC	14	0	0	84
	Wendell Tyler, L.A. Rams, NFC	13	0	0	78
1981	Ed Murray, Detroit, NFC	0	25	46	121
	Rafael Septien, Dallas, NFC	0	27	40	121
	Jim Breech, Cincinnati, AFC	0	22	49	115
	Nick Lowery, Kansas City, AFC	0	26	37	115
1980	John Smith, New England, AFC	0	26	51	129
	*Ed Murray, Detroit, NFC	0	27	35	116
1979	John Smith, New England, AFC	0	23	46	115
	Mark Moseley, Washington, NFC	0	25	39	114
1978	*Frank Corral, Los Angeles, NFC	0	29	31	118
	Pat Leahy, N.Y. Jets, AFC	0	22	41	107
1977	Errol Mann, Oakland, AFC	0	20	39	99
	Walter Payton, Chicago, NFC	16	0	0	96
1976	Toni Linhart, Baltimore, AFC	0	20	49	109
	Mark Moseley, Washington, NFC	0	22	31	97
1975	O.J. Simpson, Buffalo, AFC	23	0	0	138
	Chuck Foreman, Minnesota, NFC	22	0	0	132
1974	Chester Marcol, Green Bay, NFC	0	25	19	94
	Roy Gerela, Pittsburgh, AFC	0	20	33	93
1973	David Ray, Los Angeles, NFC	0	30	40	130
	Roy Gerela, Pittsburgh, AFC	0	29	36	123
1972	*Chester Marcol, Green Bay, NFC	0	33	29	128
	Bobby Howfield, N.Y. Jets, AFC	0	27	40	121
1971	Garo Yepremian, Miami, AFC	0	28	33	117
	Curt Knight, Washington, NFC	0	29	27	114
1970	Fred Cox, Minnesota, NFC	0	30	35	125
	Jan Stenerud, Kansas City, AFC	0	30	26	116
1969	Jim Turner, N.Y. Jets, AFL	0	32	33	129
	Fred Cox, Minnesota, NFL	0	26	43	121
1968	Jim Turner, N.Y. Jets, AFL	0	34	43	145
	Leroy Kelly, Cleveland, NFL	20	0	0	120
1967	Jim Bakken, St. Louis, NFL	0	27	36	117
	George Blanda, Oakland, AFL	0	20	56	116
1966	Gino Cappelletti, Boston, AFL	6	16	35	119
	Bruce Gossett, Los Angeles, NFL	0	28	29	113
1965	*Gale Sayers, Chicago, NFL	22	0	0	132
	Gino Cappelletti, Boston, AFL	9	17	27	132
1964	Gino Cappelletti, Boston, AFL	7	25	36	#155
	Lenny Moore, Baltimore, NFL	20	0	0	120
1963	Gino Cappelletti, Boston, AFL	2	22	35	113
	Don Chandler, N.Y. Giants, NFL	0	18	52	106
1962	Gene Mingo, Denver, AFL	4	27	32	137
	Jim Taylor, Green Bay, NFL	19	0	0	114
1961	Gino Cappelletti, Boston, AFL	8	17	48	147
	Paul Hornung, Green Bay, NFL	10	15	41	146
1960	Paul Hornung, Green Bay, NFL	15	15	41	176
	*Gene Mingo, Denver, AFL	6	18	33	123
1959	Paul Hornung, Green Bay	7	7	31	94
1958	Jim Brown, Cleveland	18	0	0	108
1957	Sam Baker, Washington	1	14	29	77
	Lou Groza, Cleveland	0	15	32	77
1956	Bobby Layne, Detroit	5	12	33	99
1955	Doak Walker, Detroit	7	9	27	96
1954	Bobby Walston, Philadelphia	11	4	36	114
1953	Gordy Soltau, San Francisco	6	10	48	114
1952	Gordy Soltau, San Francisco	7	6	34	94
1951	Elroy (Crazylegs) Hirsch, Los Angeles	17	0	0	102
1950	*Doak Walker, Detroit	11	8	38	128
1949	Pat Harder, Chi. Cardinals	8	3	45	102
	Gene Roberts, N.Y. Giants	17	0	0	102
1948	Pat Harder, Chi. Cardinals	6	7	53	110
1947	Pat Harder, Chi. Cardinals	7	7	39	102
1946	Ted Fritsch, Green Bay	10	9	13	100
1945	Steve Van Buren, Philadelphia	18	0	2	110
1944	Don Hutson, Green Bay	9	0	31	85
1943	Don Hutson, Green Bay	12	3	36	117
1942	Don Hutson, Green Bay	17	1	33	138
1941	Don Hutson, Green Bay	12	1	20	95
1940	Don Hutson, Green Bay	7	0	15	57
1939	Andy Farkas, Washington	11	0	2	68
1938	Clarke Hinkle, Green Bay	7	3	7	58
1937	Jack Manders, Chi. Bears	5	8	15	69
1936	Earl (Dutch) Clark, Detroit	7	4	19	73
1935	Earl (Dutch) Clark, Detroit	6	1	16	55
1934	Jack Manders, Chi. Bears	3	10	31	79
1933	Ken Strong, N.Y. Giants	6	5	13	64
	Glenn Presnell, Portsmouth	6	6	10	64
1932	Earl (Dutch) Clark, Portsmouth	6	3	10	55

**First year in the league.*
#Cappelletti's total includes a two-point conversion.

Annual Touchdown Leaders

Year	Player, Team	TD	Rush	Pass	Ret.
1992	Emmitt Smith, Dallas, NFC	19	18	1	0
	Thurman Thomas, Buffalo, AFC	12	9	3	0
1991	Barry Sanders, Detroit, NFC	17	16	1	0
	Mark Clayton, Miami, AFC	12	0	12	0
	Thurman Thomas, Buffalo, AFC	12	7	5	0
1990	Barry Sanders, Detroit, NFC	16	13	3	0
	Derrick Fenner, Seattle, AFC	15	14	1	0
1989	Dalton Hilliard, New Orleans, NFC	18	13	5	0
	Christian Okoye, Kansas City, AFC	12	12	0	0
	Thurman Thomas, Buffalo, AFC	12	6	6	0
1988	Greg Bell, L.A. Rams, NFC	18	16	2	0
	Eric Dickerson, Indianapolis, AFC	15	14	1	0
	*Ickey Woods, Cincinnati, AFC	15	15	0	0
1987	Jerry Rice, San Francisco, NFC	23	1	22	0
	Johnny Hector, N.Y. Jets, AFC	11	11	0	0
1986	George Rogers, Washington, NFC	18	18	0	0
	Sammy Winder, Denver, AFC	14	9	5	0
1985	Joe Morris, N.Y. Giants, NFC	21	21	0	0
	Louis Lipps, Pittsburgh, AFC	15	1	12	2
1984	Marcus Allen, L.A. Raiders, AFC	18	13	5	0
	Mark Clayton, Miami, AFC	18	0	18	0
	Eric Dickerson, L.A. Rams, NFC	14	14	0	0
	John Riggins, Washington, NFC	14	14	0	0
1983	John Riggins, Washington, NFC	24	24	0	0
	Pete Johnson, Cincinnati, AFC	14	14	0	0
	*Curt Warner, Seattle, AFC	14	13	1	0
1982	*Marcus Allen, L.A. Raiders, AFC	14	11	3	0
	Wendell Tyler, L.A. Rams, NFC	13	9	4	0
1981	Chuck Muncie, San Diego, AFC	19	19	0	0
	Wendell Tyler, Los Angeles, NFC	17	12	5	0
1980	*Billy Sims, Detroit, NFC	16	13	3	0
	Earl Campbell, Houston, AFC	13	13	0	0
	*Curtis Dickey, Baltimore, AFC	13	11	2	0
	John Jefferson, San Diego, AFC	13	0	13	0
1979	Earl Campbell, Houston, AFC	19	19	0	0
	Walter Payton, Chicago, NFC	16	14	2	0
1978	David Sims, Seattle, AFC	15	14	1	0
	Terdell Middleton, Green Bay, NFC	12	11	1	0
1977	Walter Payton, Chicago, NFC	16	14	2	0
	Nat Moore, Miami, AFC	13	1	12	0
1976	Chuck Foreman, Minnesota, NFC	14	13	1	0
	Franco Harris, Pittsburgh, AFC	14	14	0	0
1975	O.J. Simpson, Buffalo, AFC	23	16	7	0
	Chuck Foreman, Minnesota, NFC	22	13	9	0
1974	Chuck Foreman, Minnesota, NFC	15	9	6	0
	Cliff Branch, Oakland, AFC	13	0	13	0
1973	Larry Brown, Washington, NFC	14	8	6	0
	Floyd Little, Denver, AFC	13	12	1	0
1972	Emerson Boozer, N.Y. Jets, AFC	14	11	3	0
	Ron Johnson, N.Y. Giants, NFC	14	9	5	0
1971	Duane Thomas, Dallas, NFC	13	11	2	0
	Leroy Kelly, Cleveland, AFC	12	10	2	0
1970	Dick Gordon, Chicago, NFC	13	0	13	0
	MacArthur Lane, St. Louis, NFC	13	11	2	0
	Gary Garrison, San Diego, AFC	12	0	12	0
1969	Warren Wells, Oakland, AFL	14	0	14	0
	Tom Matte, Baltimore, NFL	13	11	2	0
	Lance Rentzel, Dallas, NFL	13	0	12	1
1968	Leroy Kelly, Cleveland, NFL	20	16	4	0
	Warren Wells, Oakland, AFL	12	1	11	0
1967	Homer Jones, N.Y. Giants, NFL	14	1	13	0
	Emerson Boozer, N.Y. Jets, AFL	13	10	3	0
1966	Leroy Kelly, Cleveland, NFL	16	15	1	0
	Dan Reeves, Dallas, NFL	16	8	8	0
	Lance Alworth, San Diego, AFL	13	0	13	0
1965	*Gale Sayers, Chicago, NFL	22	14	6	2
	Lance Alworth, San Diego, AFL	14	0	14	0
	Don Maynard, N.Y. Jets, AFL	14	0	14	0
1964	Lenny Moore, Baltimore, NFL	20	16	3	1
	Lance Alworth, San Diego, AFL	15	2	13	0
1963	Art Powell, Oakland, AFL	16	0	16	0
	Jim Brown, Cleveland, NFL	15	12	3	0
1962	Abner Haynes, Dallas, AFL	19	13	6	0
	Jim Taylor, Green Bay, NFL	19	19	0	0
1961	Bill Groman, Houston, AFL	18	1	17	0
	Jim Taylor, Green Bay, NFL	16	15	1	0
1960	Paul Hornung, Green Bay, NFL	15	13	2	0
	Sonny Randle, St. Louis, NFL	15	0	15	0
	Art Powell, N.Y. Titans, AFL	14	0	14	0
1959	Raymond Berry, Baltimore	14	0	14	0
	Jim Brown, Cleveland	14	14	0	0
1958	Jim Brown, Cleveland	18	17	1	0
1957	Lenny Moore, Baltimore	11	3	7	1
1956	Rick Casares, Chi. Bears	14	12	2	0
1955	*Alan Ameche, Baltimore	9	9	0	0
	Harlon Hill, Chi. Bears	9	0	9	0
1954	*Harlon Hill, Chi. Bears	12	0	12	0
1953	Joseph Perry, San Francisco	13	10	3	0
1952	Cloyce Box, Detroit	15	0	15	0
1951	Elroy (Crazylegs) Hirsch, Los Angeles	17	0	17	0
1950	Bob Shaw, Chi. Cardinals	12	0	12	0

1949	Gene Roberts, N.Y. Giants	17	9	8	0
1948	Mal Kutner, Chi. Cardinals	15	1	14	0
1947	Steve Van Buren, Philadelphia	14	13	0	1
1946	Ted Fritsch, Green Bay	10	9	1	0
1945	Steve Van Buren, Philadelphia	18	15	2	1
1944	Don Hutson, Green Bay	9	0	9	0
	Bill Paschal, N.Y. Giants	9	9	0	0
1943	Don Hutson, Green Bay	12	0	11	1
	*Bill Paschal, N.Y. Giants	12	10	2	0
1942	Don Hutson, Green Bay	17	0	17	0
1941	Don Hutson, Green Bay	12	2	10	0
	George McAfee, Chi. Bears	12	6	3	3
1940	John Drake, Cleveland	9	9	0	0
	Richard Todd, Washington	9	4	4	1
1939	Andrew Farkas, Washington	11	5	5	1
1938	Don Hutson, Green Bay	9	0	9	0
1937	Cliff Battles, Washington	7	5	1	1
	Clarke Hinkle, Green Bay	7	5	2	0
	Don Hutson, Green Bay	7	0	7	0
1936	Don Hutson, Green Bay	9	0	8	1
1935	*Don Hutson, Green Bay	7	0	6	1
1934	*Beattie Feathers, Chi. Bears	9	8	1	0
1933	*Charlie (Buckets) Goldenberg, Green Bay	7	4	1	2
	John (Shipwreck) Kelly, Brooklyn	7	2	3	2
	*Elvin (Kink) Richards, N.Y. Giants	7	4	3	0
1932	Earl (Dutch) Clark, Portsmouth	6	3	3	0
	Red Grange, Chi. Bears	6	3	3	0

First year in the league.

Annual Leaders — Most Field Goals Made

Year	Player, Team	Att.	Made	Pct.
1992	Pete Stoyanovich, Miami, AFC	37	30	81.1
	Chip Lohmiller, Washington, NFC	40	30	75.0
1991	Pete Stoyanovich, Miami, AFC	37	31	83.8
	Chip Lohmiller, Washington, NFC	43	31	72.1
1990	Nick Lowery, Kansas City, AFC	37	34	91.9
	Chip Lohmiller, Washington, NFC	40	30	75.0
1989	Rich Karlis, Minnesota, NFC	39	31	79.5
	*David Treadwell, Denver, AFC	33	27	81.8
1988	Scott Norwood, Buffalo, AFC	37	32	86.5
	*Mike Cofer, San Francisco, NFC	38	27	71.1
1987	Morten Andersen, New Orleans, NFC	36	28	77.8
	Dean Biasucci, Indianapolis, AFC	27	24	88.9
	Jim Breech, Cincinnati, AFC	30	24	80.0
1986	Tony Franklin, New England, AFC	41	32	78.0
	Kevin Butler, Chicago, NFC	41	28	68.3
1985	Gary Anderson, Pittsburgh, AFC	42	33	78.6
	Morten Andersen, New Orleans, NFC	35	31	88.6
	*Kevin Butler, Chicago, NFC	37	31	83.8
1984	*Paul McFadden, Philadelphia, NFC	37	30	81.1
	Gary Anderson, Pittsburgh, AFC	32	24	75.0
	Matt Bahr, Cleveland, AFC	32	24	75.0
1983	*Ali Haji-Sheikh, N.Y. Giants, NFC	42	35	83.3
	*Raul Allegre, Baltimore, AFC	35	30	85.7
1982	Mark Moseley, Washington, NFC	21	20	95.2
	Nick Lowery, Kansas City, AFC	24	19	79.2
1981	Rafael Septien, Dallas, NFC	35	27	77.1
	Nick Lowery, Kansas City, AFC	36	26	72.2
1980	*Ed Murray, Detroit, NFC	42	27	64.3
	John Smith, New England, AFC	34	26	76.5
	Fred Steinfort, Denver, AFC	34	26	76.5
1979	Mark Moseley, Washington, NFC	33	25	75.8
	John Smith, New England, AFC	33	23	69.7
1978	*Frank Corral, Los Angeles, NFC	43	29	67.4
	Pat Leahy, N.Y. Jets, AFC	30	22	73.3
1977	Mark Moseley, Washington, NFC	37	21	56.8
	Errol Mann, Oakland, AFC	28	20	71.4
1976	Mark Moseley, Washington, NFC	34	22	64.7
	Jan Stenerud, Kansas City, AFC	38	21	55.3
1975	Jan Stenerud, Kansas City, AFC	32	22	68.8
	Toni Fritsch, Dallas, NFC	35	22	62.9
1974	Chester Marcol, Green Bay, NFC	39	25	64.1
	Roy Gerela, Pittsburgh, AFC	29	20	69.0
1973	David Ray, Los Angeles, NFC	47	30	63.8
	Roy Gerela, Pittsburgh, AFC	43	29	67.4
1972	*Chester Marcol, Green Bay, NFC	48	33	68.8
	Roy Gerela, Pittsburgh, AFC	41	28	68.3
1971	Curt Knight, Washington, NFC	49	29	59.2
	Garo Yepremian, Miami, AFC	40	28	70.0
1970	Jan Stenerud, Kansas City, AFC	42	30	71.4
	Fred Cox, Minnesota, NFC	46	30	65.2
1969	Jim Turner, N.Y. Jets, AFL	47	32	68.1
	Fred Cox, Minnesota, NFL	37	26	70.3
1968	Jim Turner, N.Y. Jets, AFL	46	34	73.9
	Mac Percival, Chicago, NFL	36	25	69.4
1967	Jim Bakken, St. Louis, NFL	39	27	69.2
	Jan Stenerud, Kansas City, AFL	36	21	58.3
1966	Bruce Gossett, Los Angeles, NFL	49	28	57.1
	Mike Mercer, Oakland-Kansas City, AFL	30	21	70.0
1965	Pete Gogolak, Buffalo, AFL	46	28	60.9
	Fred Cox, Minnesota, NFL	35	23	65.7
1964	Jim Bakken, St. Louis, NFL	38	25	65.8
	Gino Cappelletti, Boston, AFL	39	25	64.1
1963	Jim Martin, Baltimore, NFL	39	24	61.5
	Gino Cappelletti, Boston, AFL	38	22	57.9
1962	Gene Mingo, Denver, AFL	39	27	69.2
	Lou Michaels, Pittsburgh, NFL	42	26	61.9
1961	Steve Myhra, Baltimore, NFL	39	21	53.8
	Gino Cappelletti, Boston, AFL	32	17	53.1
1960	Tommy Davis, San Francisco, NFL	32	19	59.4
	*Gene Mingo, Denver, AFL	28	18	64.3
1959	Pat Summerall, New York Giants	29	20	69.0
1958	Paige Cothren, Los Angeles	25	14	56.0
	*Tom Miner, Pittsburgh	28	14	50.0
1957	Lou Groza, Cleveland	22	15	68.2
1956	Sam Baker, Washington	25	17	68.0
1955	Fred Cone, Green Bay	24	16	66.7
1954	Lou Groza, Cleveland	24	16	66.7
1953	Lou Groza, Cleveland	26	23	88.5
1952	Lou Groza, Cleveland	33	19	57.6
1951	Bob Waterfield, Los Angeles	23	13	56.5
1950	*Lou Groza, Cleveland	19	13	68.4
1949	Cliff Patton, Philadelphia	18	9	50.0
	Bob Waterfield, Los Angeles	16	9	56.3
1948	Cliff Patton, Philadelphia	12	8	66.7
1947	Ward Cuff, Green Bay	16	7	43.8
	Pat Harder, Chi. Cardinals	10	7	70.0
	Bob Waterfield, Los Angeles	16	7	43.8
1946	Ted Fritsch, Green Bay	17	9	52.9
1945	Joe Aguirre, Washington	13	7	53.8
1944	Ken Strong, N.Y. Giants	12	6	50.0
1943	Ward Cuff, N.Y. Giants	9	3	33.3
	Don Hutson, Green Bay	5	3	60.0
1942	Bill Daddio, Chi. Cardinals	10	5	50.0
1941	Clarke Hinkle, Green Bay	14	6	42.9
1940	Clarke Hinkle, Green Bay	14	9	64.3
1939	Ward Cuff, N.Y. Giants	16	7	43.8
1938	Ward Cuff, N.Y. Giants	9	5	55.6
	Ralph Kercheval, Brooklyn	13	5	38.5
1937	Jack Manders, Chi. Bears		8	
1936	Jack Manders, Chi. Bears		7	
	Armand Niccolai, Pittsburgh		7	
1935	Armand Niccolai, Pittsburgh		6	
	Bill Smith, Chi. Cardinals		6	
1934	Jack Manders, Chi. Bears		10	
1933	*Jack Manders, Chi. Bears		6	
	Glenn Presnell, Portsmouth		6	
1932	Earl (Dutch) Clark, Portsmouth		3	

First year in the league.

Annual Rushing Leaders

Year	Player, Team	Att.	Yards	Avg.	TD
1992	Emmitt Smith, Dallas, NFC	373	1,713	4.6	18
	Barry Foster, Pittsburgh, AFC	390	1,690	4.3	11
1991	Emmitt Smith, Dallas, NFC	365	1,563	4.3	12
	Thurman Thomas, Buffalo, AFC	288	1,407	4.9	7
1990	Barry Sanders, Detroit, NFC	255	1,304	5.1	13
	Thurman Thomas, Buffalo, AFC	271	1,297	4.8	11
1989	Christian Okoye, Kansas City, AFC	370	1,480	4.0	12
	*Barry Sanders, Detroit, NFC	280	1,470	5.3	14
1988	Eric Dickerson, Indianapolis, AFC	388	1,659	4.3	14
	Herschel Walker, Dallas, NFC	361	1,514	4.2	5
1987	Charles White, L.A. Rams, NFC	324	1,374	4.2	11
	Eric Dickerson, Indianapolis, AFC	223	1,011	4.5	5
1986	Eric Dickerson, L.A. Rams, NFC	404	1,821	4.5	11
	Curt Warner, Seattle, AFC	319	1,481	4.6	13
1985	Marcus Allen, L.A. Raiders, AFC	380	1,759	4.6	11
	Gerald Riggs, Atlanta, NFC	397	1,719	4.3	10
1984	Eric Dickerson, L.A. Rams, NFC	379	2,105	5.6	14
	Earnest Jackson, San Diego, AFC	296	1,179	4.0	8
1983	*Eric Dickerson, L.A. Rams, NFC	390	1,808	4.6	18
	*Curt Warner, Seattle, AFC	335	1,449	4.3	13
1982	Freeman McNeil, N.Y. Jets, AFC	151	786	5.2	6
	Tony Dorsett, Dallas, NFC	177	745	4.2	5
1981	*George Rogers, New Orleans, NFC	378	1,674	4.4	13
	Earl Campbell, Houston, AFC	361	1,376	3.8	10
1980	Earl Campbell, Houston, AFC	373	1,934	5.2	13
	Walter Payton, Chicago, NFC	317	1,460	4.6	6
1979	Earl Campbell, Houston, AFC	368	1,697	4.6	19
	Walter Payton, Chicago, NFC	369	1,610	4.4	14
1978	*Earl Campbell, Houston, AFC	302	1,450	4.8	13
	Walter Payton, Chicago, NFC	333	1,395	4.2	11
1977	Walter Payton, Chicago, NFC	339	1,852	5.5	14
	Mark van Eeghen, Oakland, AFC	324	1,273	3.9	7
1976	O.J. Simpson, Buffalo, AFC	290	1,503	5.2	8
	Walter Payton, Chicago, NFC	311	1,390	4.5	13
1975	O.J. Simpson, Buffalo, AFC	329	1,817	5.5	16
	Jim Otis, St. Louis, NFC	269	1,076	4.0	5
1974	Otis Armstrong, Denver, AFC	263	1,407	5.3	9
	Lawrence McCutcheon, Los Angeles, NFC	236	1,109	4.7	3
1973	O.J. Simpson, Buffalo, AFC	332	2,003	6.0	12
	John Brockington, Green Bay, NFC	265	1,144	4.3	3
1972	O.J. Simpson, Buffalo, AFC	292	1,251	4.3	6
	Larry Brown, Washington, NFC	285	1,216	4.3	8
1971	Floyd Little, Denver, AFC	284	1,133	4.0	6
	*John Brockington, Green Bay, NFC	216	1,105	5.1	4
1970	Larry Brown, Washington, NFC	237	1,125	4.7	5
	Floyd Little, Denver, AFC	209	901	4.3	3
1969	Gale Sayers, Chicago, NFL	236	1,032	4.4	8
	Dickie Post, San Diego, AFL	182	873	4.8	6
1968	Leroy Kelly, Cleveland, NFL	248	1,239	5.0	16
	*Paul Robinson, Cincinnati, AFL	238	1,023	4.3	8
1967	Jim Nance, Boston, AFL	269	1,216	4.5	7
	Leroy Kelly, Cleveland, NFL	235	1,205	5.1	11
1966	Jim Nance, Boston, AFL	299	1,458	4.9	11
	Gale Sayers, Chicago, NFL	229	1,231	5.4	8
1965	Jim Brown, Cleveland, NFL	289	1,544	5.3	17
	Paul Lowe, San Diego, AFL	222	1,121	5.0	7
1964	Jim Brown, Cleveland, NFL	280	1,446	5.2	7
	Cookie Gilchrist, Buffalo, AFL	230	981	4.3	6
1963	Jim Brown, Cleveland, NFL	291	1,863	6.4	12
	Clem Daniels, Oakland, AFL	215	1,099	5.1	3
1962	Jim Taylor, Green Bay, NFL	272	1,474	5.4	19
	*Cookie Gilchrist, Buffalo, AFL	214	1,096	5.1	13
1961	Jim Brown, Cleveland, NFL	305	1,408	4.6	8
	Billy Cannon, Houston, AFL	200	948	4.7	6

Year	Player, Team	Att.	Yards	Avg.	TD
1960	Jim Brown, Cleveland, NFL	215	1,257	5.8	9
	*Abner Haynes, Dall. Texans, AFL	156	875	5.6	9
1959	Jim Brown, Cleveland	290	1,329	4.6	14
1958	Jim Brown, Cleveland	257	1,527	5.9	17
1957	*Jim Brown, Cleveland	202	942	4.7	9
1956	Rick Casares, Chi. Bears	234	1,126	4.8	12
1955	*Alan Ameche, Baltimore	213	961	4.5	9
1954	Joe Perry, San Francisco	173	1,049	6.1	8
1953	Joe Perry, San Francisco	192	1,018	5.3	10
1952	Dan Towler, Los Angeles	156	894	5.7	10
1951	Eddie Price, N.Y. Giants	271	971	3.6	7
1950	*Marion Motley, Cleveland	140	810	5.8	3
1949	Steve Van Buren, Philadelphia	263	1,146	4.4	11
1948	Steve Van Buren, Philadelphia	201	945	4.7	10
1947	Steve Van Buren, Philadelphia	217	1,008	4.6	13
1946	Bill Dudley, Pittsburgh	146	604	4.1	3
1945	Steve Van Buren, Philadelphia	143	832	5.8	15
1944	Bill Paschal, N.Y. Giants	196	737	3.8	9
1943	*Bill Paschal, N.Y. Giants	147	572	3.9	10
1942	*Bill Dudley, Pittsburgh	162	696	4.3	5
1941	Clarence (Pug) Manders, Brooklyn	111	486	4.4	5
1940	Byron (Whizzer) White, Detroit	146	514	3.5	5
1939	*Bill Osmanski, Chicago	121	699	5.8	7
1938	*Byron (Whizzer) White, Pittsburgh	152	567	3.7	4
1937	Cliff Battles, Washington	216	874	4.0	5
1936	*Alphonse (Tuffy) Leemans, N.Y. Giants	206	830	4.0	2
1935	Doug Russell, Chi. Cardinals	140	499	3.6	0
1934	*Beattie Feathers, Chi. Bears	119	1,004	8.4	8
1933	Jim Musick, Boston	173	809	4.7	5
1932	*Cliff Battles, Boston	148	576	3.9	3

First year in the league.

Annual Passing Leaders
(Current rating system implemented in 1973)

Year	Player, Team	Att.	Comp.	Yards	TD	Int.	Rating
1992	Steve Young, San Francisco, NFC	402	268	3,465	25	7	107.0
	Warren Moon, Houston, AFC	346	224	2,521	18	12	89.3
1991	Steve Young, San Francisco, NFC	279	180	2,517	17	8	101.8
	Jim Kelly, Buffalo, AFC	474	304	3,844	33	17	97.6
1990	Jim Kelly, Buffalo, AFC	346	219	2,829	24	9	101.2
	Phil Simms, N.Y. Giants, NFC	311	184	2,284	15	4	92.7
1989	Joe Montana, San Francisco, NFC	386	271	3,521	26	8	112.4
	Boomer Esiason, Cincinnati, AFC	455	258	3,525	28	11	92.1
1988	Boomer Esiason, Cincinnati, AFC	388	223	3,572	28	14	97.4
	Wade Wilson, Minnesota, NFC	332	204	2,746	15	9	91.5
1987	Joe Montana, San Francisco, NFC	398	266	3,054	31	13	102.1
	Bernie Kosar, Cleveland, AFC	389	241	3,033	22	9	95.4
1986	Tommy Kramer, Minnesota, NFC	372	208	3,000	24	10	92.6
	Dan Marino, Miami, AFC	623	378	4,746	44	23	92.5
1985	Ken O'Brien, N.Y. Jets, AFC	488	297	3,888	25	8	96.2
	Joe Montana, San Francisco, NFC	494	303	3,653	27	13	91.3
1984	Dan Marino, Miami, AFC	564	362	5,084	48	17	108.9
	Joe Montana, San Francisco, NFC	432	279	3,630	28	10	102.9
1983	Steve Bartkowski, Atlanta, NFC	432	274	3,167	22	5	97.6
	*Dan Marino, Miami, AFC	296	173	2,210	20	6	96.0
1982	Ken Anderson, Cincinnati, AFC	309	218	2,495	12	9	95.5
	Joe Theismann, Washington, NFC	252	161	2,033	13	9	91.3
1981	Ken Anderson, Cincinnati, AFC	479	300	3,754	29	10	98.5
	Joe Montana, San Francisco, NFC	488	311	3,565	19	12	88.2
1980	Brian Sipe, Cleveland, AFC	554	337	4,132	30	14	91.4
	Ron Jaworski, Philadelphia, NFC	451	257	3,529	27	12	90.9
1979	Roger Staubach, Dallas, NFC	461	267	3,586	27	11	92.4
	Dan Fouts, San Diego, AFC	530	332	4,082	24	24	82.6
1978	Roger Staubach, Dallas, NFC	413	231	3,190	25	16	84.9
	Terry Bradshaw, Pittsburgh, AFC	368	207	2,915	28	20	84.8
1977	Bob Griese, Miami, AFC	307	180	2,252	22	13	88.0
	Roger Staubach, Dallas, NFC	361	210	2,620	18	9	87.1
1976	Ken Stabler, Oakland, AFC	291	194	2,737	27	17	103.7
	James Harris, Los Angeles, NFC	158	91	1,460	8	6	89.8
1975	Ken Anderson, Cincinnati, AFC	377	228	3,169	21	11	94.1
	Fran Tarkenton, Minnesota, NFC	425	273	2,994	25	13	91.7
1974	Ken Anderson, Cincinnati, AFC	328	213	2,667	18	10	95.9
	Sonny Jurgensen, Washington, NFC	167	107	1,185	11	5	94.6
1973	Roger Staubach, Dallas, NFC	286	179	2,428	23	15	94.6
	Ken Stabler, Oakland, AFC	260	163	1,997	14	10	88.5
1972	Norm Snead, N.Y. Giants, NFC	325	196	2,307	17	12	
	Earl Morrall, Miami, AFC	150	83	1,360	11	7	
1971	Roger Staubach, Dallas, NFC	211	126	1,882	15	4	
	Bob Griese, Miami, AFC	263	145	2,089	19	9	
1970	John Brodie, San Francisco, NFC	378	223	2,941	24	10	
	Daryle Lamonica, Oakland, AFC	356	179	2,516	22	15	
1969	Sonny Jurgensen, Washington, NFL	442	274	3,102	22	15	
	*Greg Cook, Cincinnati, AFL	197	106	1,854	15	11	
1968	Len Dawson, Kansas City, AFL	224	131	2,109	17	9	
	Earl Morrall, Baltimore, NFL	317	182	2,909	26	17	
1967	Sonny Jurgensen, Washington, NFL	508	288	3,747	31	16	
	Daryle Lamonica, Oakland, AFL	425	220	3,228	30	20	
1966	Bart Starr, Green Bay, NFL	251	156	2,257	14	3	
	Len Dawson, Kansas City, AFL	284	159	2,527	26	10	
1965	Rudy Bukich, Chicago, NFL	312	176	2,641	20	9	
	John Hadl, San Diego, AFL	348	174	2,798	20	21	
1964	Len Dawson, Kansas City, AFL	354	199	2,879	30	18	
	Bart Starr, Green Bay, NFL	272	163	2,144	15	4	
1963	Y.A. Tittle, N.Y. Giants, NFL	367	221	3,145	36	14	
	Tobin Rote, San Diego, AFL	286	170	2,510	20	17	
1962	Len Dawson, Dall. Texans, AFL	310	189	2,759	29	17	
	Bart Starr, Green Bay, NFL	285	178	2,438	12	9	
1961	George Blanda, Houston, AFL	362	187	3,330	36	22	
	Milt Plum, Cleveland, NFL	302	177	2,416	18	10	
1960	Milt Plum, Cleveland, NFL	250	151	2,297	21	5	
	Jack Kemp, L.A. Chargers, AFL	406	211	3,018	20	25	
1959	Charlie Conerly, N.Y. Giants	194	113	1,706	14	4	
1958	Eddie LeBaron, Washington	145	79	1,365	11	10	
1957	Tommy O'Connell, Cleveland	110	63	1,229	9	8	
1956	Ed Brown, Chi. Bears	168	96	1,667	11	12	
1955	Otto Graham, Cleveland	185	98	1,721	15	8	
1954	Norm Van Brocklin, Los Angeles	260	139	2,637	13	21	
1953	Otto Graham, Cleveland	258	167	2,722	11	9	
1952	Norm Van Brocklin, Los Angeles	205	113	1,736	14	17	
1951	Bob Waterfield, Los Angeles	176	88	1,566	13	10	
1950	Norm Van Brocklin, Los Angeles	233	127	2,061	18	14	
1949	Sammy Baugh, Washington	255	145	1,903	18	14	
1948	Tommy Thompson, Philadelphia	246	141	1,965	25	11	
1947	Sammy Baugh, Washington	354	210	2,938	25	15	
1946	Bob Waterfield, Los Angeles	251	127	1,747	18	17	
1945	Sammy Baugh, Washington	182	128	1,669	11	4	
	Sid Luckman, Chi. Bears	217	117	1,725	14	10	
1944	Frank Filchock, Washington	147	84	1,139	13	9	
1943	Sammy Baugh, Washington	239	133	1,754	23	19	
1942	Cecil Isbell, Green Bay	268	146	2,021	24	14	
1941	Cecil Isbell, Green Bay	206	117	1,479	15	11	
1940	Sammy Baugh, Washington	177	111	1,367	12	10	
1939	*Parker Hall, Cleveland	208	106	1,227	9	13	
1938	Ed Danowski, N.Y. Giants	129	70	848	7	8	
1937	*Sammy Baugh, Washington	171	81	1,127	8	14	
1936	Arnie Herber, Green Bay	173	77	1,239	11	13	
1935	Ed Danowski, N.Y. Giants	113	57	794	10	9	
1934	Arnie Herber, Green Bay	115	42	799	8	12	
1933	*Harry Newman, N.Y. Giants	136	53	973	11	17	
1932	Arnie Herber, Green Bay	101	37	639	9	9	

First year in the league.

Annual Passing Touchdown Leaders

Year	Player, Team	TD
1992	Steve Young, San Francisco, NFC	25
	Dan Marino, Miami, AFC	24
1991	Jim Kelly, Buffalo, AFC	33
	Mark Rypien, Washington, NFC	28
1990	Warren Moon, Houston, AFC	33
	Randall Cunningham, Philadelphia, NFC	30
1989	Jim Everett, L.A. Rams, NFC	29
	Boomer Esiason, Cincinnati, AFC	28
1988	Jim Everett, L.A. Rams, NFC	31
	Boomer Esiason, Cincinnati, AFC	28
	Dan Marino, Miami, AFC	28
1987	Joe Montana, San Francisco, NFC	31
	Dan Marino, Miami, AFC	26
1986	Dan Marino, Miami, AFC	44
	Tommy Kramer, Minnesota, NFC	24
1985	Dan Marino, Miami, AFC	30
	Joe Montana, San Francisco, NFC	27
1984	Dan Marino, Miami, AFC	48
	Neil Lomax, St. Louis, NFC	28
	Joe Montana, San Francisco, NFC	28
1983	Lynn Dickey, Green Bay, NFC	32
	Joe Ferguson, Buffalo, AFC	26
	Brian Sipe, Cleveland, AFC	26
1982	Terry Bradshaw, Pittsburgh, AFC	17
	Dan Fouts, San Diego, AFC	17
	Joe Montana, San Francisco, NFC	17
1981	Dan Fouts, San Diego, AFC	33
	Steve Bartkowski, Atlanta, NFC	30
1980	Steve Bartkowski, Atlanta, NFC	31
	Dan Fouts, San Diego, AFC	30
	Brian Sipe, Cleveland, AFC	30
1979	Steve Grogan, New England, AFC	28
	Brian Sipe, Cleveland, AFC	28
	Roger Staubach, Dallas, NFC	27
1978	Terry Bradshaw, Pittsburgh, AFC	28
	Roger Staubach, Dallas, NFC	25
	Fran Tarkenton, Minnesota, NFC	25
1977	Bob Griese, Miami, AFC	22
	Ron Jaworski, Philadelphia, NFC	18
	Roger Staubach, Dallas, NFC	18
1976	Ken Stabler, Oakland, AFC	27
	Jim Hart, St. Louis, NFC	18
1975	Joe Ferguson, Buffalo, AFC	25
	Fran Tarkenton, Minnesota, NFC	25
1974	Ken Stabler, Oakland, AFC	26
	Jim Hart, St. Louis, NFC	20
1973	Roman Gabriel, Philadelphia, NFC	23
	Roger Staubach, Dallas, NFC	23
	Charley Johnson, Denver, AFC	20
1972	Billy Kilmer, Washington, NFC	19
	Joe Namath, N.Y. Jets, AFC	19
1971	John Hadl, San Diego, AFC	21
	John Brodie, San Francisco, NFC	18
1970	John Brodie, San Francisco, NFC	24
	John Hadl, San Diego, AFC	22
	Daryle Lamonica, Oakland, AFC	22
1969	Daryle Lamonica, Oakland, AFL	34
	Roman Gabriel, Los Angeles, NFL	24
1968	John Hadl, San Diego, AFL	27
	Earl Morrall, Baltimore, NFL	26
1967	Sonny Jurgensen, Washington, NFL	31
	Daryle Lamonica, Oakland, AFL	30
1966	Frank Ryan, Cleveland, NFL	29
	Len Dawson, Kansas City, AFL	26
1965	John Brodie, San Francisco, NFL	30
	Len Dawson, Kansas City, AFL	21
1964	Babe Parilli, Boston, AFL	31
	Frank Ryan, Cleveland, NFL	25
1963	Y.A. Tittle, N.Y. Giants, NFL	36
	Len Dawson, Kansas City, AFL	26
1962	Y.A. Tittle, N.Y. Giants, NFL	33
	Len Dawson, Dallas, AFL	29
1961	George Blanda, Houston, AFL	36

	Sonny Jurgensen, Philadelphia, NFL	32
1960	Al Dorow, N.Y. Titans, AFL	26
	Johnny Unitas, Baltimore, NFL	25
1959	Johnny Unitas, Baltimore	32
1958	Johnny Unitas, Baltimore	19
1957	Johnny Unitas, Baltimore	24
1956	Tobin Rote, Green Bay	18
1955	Tobin Rote, Green Bay	17
	Y.A. Tittle, San Francisco	17
1954	Adrian Burk, Philadelphia	23
1953	Robert Thomason, Philadelphia	21
1952	Jim Finks, Pittsburgh	20
	Otto Graham, Cleveland	20
1951	Bobby Layne, Detroit	26
1950	*George Ratterman, N.Y. Yanks	22
1949	Johnny Lujack, Chicago Bears	23
1948	Tommy Thompson, Philadelphia	25
1947	Sammy Baugh, Washington	25
1946	Sid Luckman, Chicago Bears	17
	Bob Waterfield, Los Angeles	17
1945	Sid Luckman, Chicago Bears	14
	*Bob Waterfield, Cleveland	14
1944	Frank Filchock, Washington	13
1943	Sid Luckman, Chicago Bears	28
1942	Cecil Isbell, Green Bay	24
1941	Cecil Isbell, Green Bay	15
1940	Sammy Baugh, Washington	12
1939	Frank Filchock, Washington	11
1938	Bob Monnett, Green Bay	9
1937	Bernie Masterson, Chicago Bears	9
1936	Arnie Herber, Green Bay	11
1935	Ed Danowski, N.Y. Giants	10
1934	Arnie Herber, Green Bay	8
1933	*Harry Newman, N.Y. Giants	11
1932	Arnie Herber, Green Bay	9

**First year in the league.*

Annual Pass Receiving Leaders

Year	Player, Team	No.	Yards	Avg.	TD
1992	Sterling Sharpe, Green Bay, NFC	108	1,461	13.5	13
	Haywood Jeffires, Houston, AFC	90	913	10.1	9
1991	Haywood Jeffires, Houston, AFC	100	1,181	11.8	7
	Michael Irvin, Dallas, NFC	93	1,523	16.4	8
1990	Jerry Rice, San Francisco, NFC	100	1,502	15.0	13
	Haywood Jeffires, Houston, AFC	74	1,048	14.2	8
	Drew Hill, Houston, AFC	74	1,019	13.8	5
1989	Sterling Sharpe, Green Bay, NFC	90	1,423	15.8	12
	Andre Reed, Buffalo, AFC	88	1,312	14.9	9
1988	Al Toon, N.Y. Jets, AFC	93	1,067	11.5	5
	Henry Ellard, L.A. Rams, NFC	86	1,414	16.4	10
1987	J.T. Smith, St. Louis, NFC	91	1,117	12.3	8
	Al Toon, N.Y. Jets, AFC	68	976	14.4	5
1986	Todd Christensen, L.A. Raiders, AFC	95	1,153	12.1	8
	Jerry Rice, San Francisco, NFC	86	1,570	18.3	15
1985	Roger Craig, San Francisco, NFC	92	1,016	11.0	6
	Lionel James, San Diego, AFC	86	1,027	11.9	6
1984	Art Monk, Washington, NFC	106	1,372	12.9	7
	Ozzie Newsome, Cleveland, AFC	89	1,001	11.2	5
1983	Todd Christensen, L.A. Raiders, AFC	92	1,247	13.6	12
	Roy Green, St. Louis, NFC	78	1,227	15.7	14
	Charlie Brown, Washington, NFC	78	1,225	15.7	8
	Earnest Gray, N.Y. Giants, NFC	78	1,139	14.6	5
1982	Dwight Clark, San Francisco, NFC	60	913	15.2	5
	Kellen Winslow, San Diego, AFC	54	721	13.4	6
1981	Kellen Winslow, San Diego, AFC	88	1,075	12.2	10
	Dwight Clark, San Francisco, NFC	85	1,105	13.0	4
1980	Kellen Winslow, San Diego, AFC	89	1,290	14.5	9
	*Earl Cooper, San Francisco, NFC	83	567	6.8	4
1979	Joe Washington, Baltimore, AFC	82	750	9.1	3
	Ahmad Rashad, Minnesota, NFC	80	1,156	14.5	9
1978	Rickey Young, Minnesota, NFC	88	704	8.0	5
	Steve Largent, Seattle, AFC	71	1,168	16.5	8
1977	Lydell Mitchell, Baltimore, AFC	71	620	8.7	4
	Ahmad Rashad, Minnesota, NFC	51	681	13.4	2
1976	MacArthur Lane, Kansas City, AFC	66	686	10.4	1
	Drew Pearson, Dallas, NFC	58	806	13.9	6
1975	Chuck Foreman, Minnesota, NFC	73	691	9.5	9
	Reggie Rucker, Cleveland, AFC	60	770	12.8	3
	Lydell Mitchell, Baltimore, AFC	60	544	9.1	4
1974	Lydell Mitchell, Baltimore, AFC	72	544	7.6	2
	Charles Young, Philadelphia, NFC	63	696	11.0	3
1973	Harold Carmichael, Philadelphia, NFC	67	1,116	16.7	9
	Fred Willis, Houston, AFC	57	371	6.5	1
1972	Harold Jackson, Philadelphia, NFC	62	1,048	16.9	4
	Fred Biletnikoff, Oakland, AFC	58	802	13.8	7
1971	Fred Biletnikoff, Oakland, AFC	61	929	15.2	9
	Bob Tucker, N.Y. Giants, NFC	59	791	13.4	4
1970	Dick Gordon, Chicago, NFC	71	1,026	14.5	13
	Marlin Briscoe, Buffalo, AFC	57	1,036	18.2	8
1969	Dan Abramowicz, New Orleans, NFL	73	1,015	13.9	7
	Lance Alworth, San Diego, AFL	64	1,003	15.7	4
1968	Clifton McNeil, San Francisco, NFL	71	994	14.0	7
	Lance Alworth, San Diego, AFL	68	1,312	19.3	10
1967	George Sauer, N.Y. Jets, AFL	75	1,189	15.9	6
	Charley Taylor, Washington, NFL	70	990	14.1	9
1966	Lance Alworth, San Diego, AFL	73	1,383	18.9	13
	Charley Taylor, Washington, NFL	72	1,119	15.5	12
1965	Lionel Taylor, Denver, AFL	85	1,131	13.3	6
	Dave Parks, San Francisco, NFL	80	1,344	16.8	12
1964	Charley Hennigan, Houston, AFL	101	1,546	15.3	8
	Johnny Morris, Chicago, NFL	93	1,200	12.9	10
1963	Lionel Taylor, Denver, AFL	78	1,101	14.1	10
	Bobby Joe Conrad, St. Louis, NFL	73	967	13.2	10
1962	Lionel Taylor, Denver, AFL	77	908	11.8	4
	Bobby Mitchell, Washington, NFL	72	1,384	19.2	11
1961	Lionel Taylor, Denver, AFL	100	1,176	11.8	4
	Jim (Red) Phillips, Los Angeles, NFL	78	1,092	14.0	5
1960	Lionel Taylor, Denver, AFL	92	1,235	13.4	12
	Raymond Berry, Baltimore, NFL	74	1,298	17.5	10
1959	Raymond Berry, Baltimore	66	959	14.5	14
1958	Raymond Berry, Baltimore	56	794	14.2	9
	Pete Retzlaff, Philadelphia	56	766	13.7	2
1957	Billy Wilson, San Francisco	52	757	14.6	6
1956	Billy Wilson, San Francisco	60	889	14.8	5
1955	Pete Pihos, Philadelphia	62	864	13.9	7
1954	Pete Pihos, Philadelphia	60	872	14.5	10
	Billy Wilson, San Francisco	60	830	13.8	5
1953	Pete Pihos, Philadelphia	63	1,049	16.7	10
1952	Mac Speedie, Cleveland	62	911	14.7	5
1951	Elroy (Crazylegs) Hirsch, Los Angeles	66	1,495	22.7	17
1950	Tom Fears, Los Angeles	84	1,116	13.3	7
1949	Tom Fears, Los Angeles	77	1,013	13.2	9
1948	*Tom Fears, Los Angeles	51	698	13.7	4
1947	Jim Keane, Chi. Bears	64	910	14.2	10
1946	Jim Benton, Los Angeles	63	981	15.6	6
1945	Don Hutson, Green Bay	47	834	17.7	9
1944	Don Hutson, Green Bay	58	866	14.9	9
1943	Don Hutson, Green Bay	47	776	16.5	11
1942	Don Hutson, Green Bay	74	1,211	16.4	17
1941	Don Hutson, Green Bay	58	738	12.7	10
1940	*Don Looney, Philadelphia	58	707	12.2	4
1939	Don Hutson, Green Bay	34	846	24.9	6
1938	Gaynell Tinsley, Chi. Cardinals	41	516	12.6	1
1937	Don Hutson, Green Bay	41	552	13.5	7
1936	Don Hutson, Green Bay	34	536	15.8	8
1935	*Tod Goodwin, N.Y. Giants	26	432	16.6	4
1934	Joe Carter, Philadelphia	16	238	14.9	4
	Morris (Red) Badgro, N.Y. Giants	16	206	12.9	1
1933	John (Shipwreck) Kelly, Brooklyn	22	246	11.2	3
1932	Ray Flaherty, N.Y. Giants	21	350	16.7	3

**First year in the league.*

Annual Pass Receiving Leaders (Yards)

Year	Player, Team	No.	Yards	Avg.	TD
1992	Sterling Sharpe, Green Bay, NFC	108	1,461	13.5	13
	Anthony Miller, San Diego, AFC	72	1,060	14.7	7
1991	Michael Irvin, Dallas, NFC	93	1,523	16.4	8
	Haywood Jeffires, Houston, AFC	100	1,181	11.8	7
1990	Jerry Rice, San Francisco, NFC	100	1,502	15.0	13
	Haywood Jeffires, Houston, AFC	74	1,048	14.2	8
1989	Jerry Rice, San Francisco, NFC	82	1,483	18.1	17
	Andre Reed, Buffalo, AFC	88	1,312	14.9	9
1988	Henry Ellard, L.A. Rams, NFC	86	1,414	16.4	10
	Eddie Brown, Cincinnati, AFC	53	1,273	24.0	9
1987	J.T. Smith, St. Louis, NFC	91	1,117	12.3	8
	Carlos Carson, Kansas City, AFC	55	1,044	19.0	7
1986	Jerry Rice, San Francisco, NFC	86	1,570	18.3	15
	Stanley Morgan, New England, AFC	84	1,491	17.8	10
1985	Steve Largent, Seattle, AFC	79	1,287	16.3	6
	Mike Quick, Philadelphia, NFC	73	1,247	17.1	11
1984	Roy Green, St. Louis, NFC	78	1,555	19.9	12
	John Stallworth, Pittsburgh, AFC	80	1,395	17.4	11
1983	Mike Quick, Philadelphia, NFC	69	1,409	20.4	13
	Carlos Carson, Kansas City, AFC	80	1,351	16.9	7
1982	Wes Chandler, San Diego, AFC	49	1,032	21.1	9
	Dwight Clark, San Francisco, NFC	60	913	15.2	5
1981	Alfred Jenkins, Atlanta, NFC	70	1,358	19.4	13
	Frank Lewis, Buffalo, AFC	70	1,244	17.8	4
	Steve Watson, Denver, AFC	60	1,244	20.7	13
1980	John Jefferson, San Diego, AFC	82	1,340	16.3	13
	James Lofton, Green Bay, NFC	71	1,226	17.3	4
1979	Steve Largent, Seattle, AFC	66	1,237	18.7	9
	Ahmad Rashad, Minnesota, NFC	80	1,156	14.5	9
1978	Wesley Walker, N.Y. Jets, AFC	48	1,169	24.4	8
	Harold Carmichael, Philadelphia, NFC	55	1,072	19.5	8
1977	Drew Pearson, Dallas, NFC	48	870	18.1	2
	Ken Burrough, Houston, AFC	43	816	19.0	8
1976	Roger Carr, Baltimore, AFC	43	1,112	25.9	11
	*Sammy White, Minnesota, NFC	51	906	17.8	10
1975	Ken Burrough, Houston, AFC	53	1,063	20.1	8
	Mel Gray, St. Louis, NFC	48	926	19.3	11
1974	Cliff Branch, Oakland, AFC	60	1,092	18.2	13
	Drew Pearson, Dallas, NFC	62	1,087	17.5	2
1973	Harold Carmichael, Philadelphia, NFC	67	1,116	16.7	9
	*Isaac Curtis, Cincinnati, AFC	45	843	18.7	9
1972	Harold Jackson, Philadelphia, NFC	62	1,048	16.9	4
	Rich Caster, N.Y. Jets, AFC	39	833	21.4	10
1971	Otis Taylor, Kansas City, AFC	57	1,110	19.5	7
	Gene Washington, San Francisco, NFC	46	884	19.2	4
1970	Gene Washington, San Francisco, NFC	53	1,100	20.8	12
	Marlin Briscoe, Buffalo, AFC	57	1,036	18.2	8
1969	Warren Wells, Oakland, AFL	47	1,260	26.8	14
	Harold Jackson, Philadelphia, NFL	65	1,116	17.2	9
1968	Lance Alworth, San Diego, AFL	68	1,312	19.3	10
	Roy Jefferson, Pittsburgh, NFL	58	1,074	18.5	11
1967	Don Maynard, N.Y. Jets, AFL	71	1,434	20.3	10
	Ben Hawkins, Philadelphia, NFL	59	1,265	21.4	10
1966	Lance Alworth, San Diego, AFL	73	1,383	18.9	13
	Pat Studstill, Detroit, NFL	67	1,266	18.9	5
1965	Lance Alworth, San Diego, AFL	69	1,602	23.2	14
	Dave Parks, San Francisco, NFL	80	1,344	16.8	12
1964	Charley Hennigan, Houston, AFL	101	1,546	15.3	8
	Johnny Morris, Chicago, NFL	93	1,200	12.9	10
1963	Bobby Mitchell, Washington, NFL	69	1,436	20.8	7
	Art Powell, Oakland, AFL	73	1,304	17.8	16

1962	Bobby Mitchell, Washington, NFL	72	1,384	19.2	11
	Art Powell, N.Y. Titans, AFL	64	1,130	17.6	8
1961	Charley Hennigan, Houston, AFL	82	1,746	21.3	12
	Tommy McDonald, Philadelphia, NFL	64	1,144	17.9	13
1960	*Bill Groman, Houston, AFL	72	1,473	20.5	12
	Raymond Berry, Baltimore, NFL	74	1,298	17.5	10
1959	Raymond Berry, Baltimore	66	959	14.5	14
1958	Del Shofner, Los Angeles	51	1,097	21.5	8
1957	Raymond Berry, Baltimore	47	800	17.0	6
1956	Billy Howton, Green Bay	55	1,188	21.6	12
1955	Pete Pihos, Philadelphia	62	864	13.9	7
1954	Bob Boyd, Los Angeles	53	1,212	22.9	6
1953	Pete Pihos, Philadelphia	63	1,049	16.7	10
1952	*Billy Howton, Green Bay	53	1,231	23.2	13
1951	Elroy (Crazylegs) Hirsch, Los Angeles	66	1,495	22.7	17
1950	Tom Fears, Los Angeles	84	1,116	13.3	7
1949	Bob Mann, Detroit	66	1,014	15.4	4
1948	Mal Kutner, Chi. Cardinals	41	943	23.0	14
1947	Mal Kutner, Chi. Cardinals	43	944	21.9	7
1946	Jim Benton, Los Angeles	63	981	15.5	6
1945	Jim Benton, Cleveland	45	1,067	23.7	8
1944	Don Hutson, Green Bay	58	866	14.6	9
1943	Don Hutson, Green Bay	47	776	16.5	11
1942	Don Hutson, Green Bay	74	1,211	16.4	17
1941	Don Hutson, Green Bay	58	738	12.7	10
1940	*Don Looney, Philadelphia	58	707	12.2	4
1939	Don Hutson, Green Bay	34	846	24.9	6
1938	Don Hutson, Green Bay	32	548	17.1	9
1937	*Gaynell Tinsley, Chi. Cardinals	36	675	18.8	5
1936	Don Hutson, Green Bay	34	526	15.5	8
1935	Charley Malone, Boston	22	433	19.7	2
1934	Harry Ebding, Detroit	9	257	28.6	2
1933	*Paul Moss, Pittsburgh	18	383	21.3	2
1932	Johnny Blood (McNally), Green Bay	19	326	17.2	3

**First year in the league.*

Annual Interception Leaders

Year	Player, Team	No.	Yards	TD
1992	Henry Jones, Buffalo, AFC	8	263	2
	Audray McMillian, Minnesota, NFC	8	157	2
1991	Ronnie Lott, L.A. Raiders, AFC	8	52	0
	Ray Crockett, Detroit, NFC	6	141	1
	Deion Sanders, Atlanta, NFC	6	119	1
	*Aeneas Williams, Phoenix, NFC	6	60	0
	Tim McKyer, Atlanta, NFC	6	24	0
1990	*Mark Carrier, Chicago, NFC	10	39	0
	Richard Johnson, Houston, AFC	8	100	1
1989	Felix Wright, Cleveland, AFC	9	91	1
	Eric Allen, Philadelphia, NFC	8	38	0
1988	Scott Case, Atlanta, NFC	10	47	0
	Erik McMillan, N.Y. Jets, AFC	8	168	2
1987	Barry Wilburn, Washington, NFC	9	135	1
	Mike Prior, Indianapolis, AFC	6	57	0
	Mark Kelso, Buffalo, AFC	6	25	0
	Keith Bostic, Houston, AFC	6	−14	0
1986	Ronnie Lott, San Francisco, NFC	10	134	1
	Deron Cherry, Kansas City, AFC	9	150	0
1985	Everson Walls, Dallas, NFC	9	31	0
	Albert Lewis, Kansas City, AFC	8	59	0
	Eugene Daniel, Indianapolis, AFC	8	53	0
1984	Ken Easley, Seattle, AFC	10	126	2
	*Tom Flynn, Green Bay, NFC	9	106	0
1983	Mark Murphy, Washington, NFC	9	127	0
	Ken Riley, Cincinnati, AFC	8	89	2
	Vann McElroy, L.A. Raiders, AFC	8	68	0
1982	Everson Walls, Dallas, NFC	7	61	0
	Ken Riley, Cincinnati, AFC	5	88	1
	Bobby Jackson, N.Y. Jets, AFC	5	84	1
	Dwayne Woodruff, Pittsburgh, AFC	5	53	0
	Donnie Shell, Pittsburgh, AFC	5	27	0
1981	*Everson Walls, Dallas, NFC	11	133	0
	John Harris, Seattle, AFC	10	155	2
1980	Lester Hayes, Oakland, AFC	13	273	1
	Nolan Cromwell, Los Angeles, NFC	8	140	1
1979	Mike Reinfeldt, Houston, AFC	12	205	0
	Lemar Parrish, Washington, NFC	9	65	0
1978	Thom Darden, Cleveland, AFC	10	200	0
	Ken Stone, St. Louis, NFC	9	139	0
	Willie Buchanon, Green Bay, NFC	9	93	1
1977	Lyle Blackwood, Baltimore, AFC	10	163	0
	Rolland Lawrence, Atlanta, NFC	7	138	0
1976	Monte Jackson, Los Angeles, NFC	10	173	3
	Ken Riley, Cincinnati, AFC	9	141	1
1975	Mel Blount, Pittsburgh, AFC	11	121	0
	Paul Krause, Minnesota, NFC	10	201	0
1974	Emmitt Thomas, Kansas City, AFC	12	214	2
	Ray Brown, Atlanta, NFC	8	164	1
1973	Dick Anderson, Miami, AFC	8	163	2
	Mike Wagner, Pittsburgh, AFC	8	134	0
	Bobby Bryant, Minnesota, NFC	7	105	1
1972	Bill Bradley, Philadelphia, NFC	9	73	0
	Mike Sensibaugh, Kansas City, AFC	8	65	0
1971	Bill Bradley, Philadelphia, NFC	11	248	0
	Ken Houston, Houston, AFC	9	220	4
1970	Johnny Robinson, Kansas City, AFC	10	155	0
	Dick LeBeau, Detroit, NFC	9	96	0
1969	Mel Renfro, Dallas, NFL	10	118	0
	Emmitt Thomas, Kansas City, AFL	9	146	1
1968	Dave Grayson, Oakland, AFL	10	195	1
	Willie Williams, N.Y. Giants, NFL	10	103	0
1967	Miller Farr, Houston, AFL	10	264	3
	*Lem Barney, Detroit, NFL	10	232	3
	Tom Janik, Buffalo, AFL	10	222	2
	Dave Whitsell, New Orleans, NFL	10	178	2
	Dick Westmoreland, Miami, AFL	10	127	1
1966	Larry Wilson, St. Louis, NFL	10	180	2
	Johnny Robinson, Kansas City, AFL	10	136	1
	Bobby Hunt, Kansas City, AFL	10	113	0
1965	W.K. Hicks, Houston, AFL	9	156	0
	Bobby Boyd, Baltimore, NFL	9	78	1
1964	Dainard Paulson, N.Y. Jets, AFL	12	157	1
	*Paul Krause, Washington, NFL	12	140	1
1963	Fred Glick, Houston, AFL	12	180	1
	Dick Lynch, N.Y. Giants, NFL	9	251	3
	Roosevelt Taylor, Chicago, NFL	9	172	1
1962	Lee Riley, N.Y. Titans, AFL	11	122	0
	Willie Wood, Green Bay, NFL	9	132	0
1961	Billy Atkins, Buffalo, AFL	10	158	0
	Dick Lynch, N.Y. Giants, NFL	9	60	0
1960	*Austin (Goose) Gonsoulin, Denver, AFL	11	98	0
	Dave Baker, San Francisco, NFL	10	96	0
	Jerry Norton, St. Louis, NFL	10	96	0
1959	Dean Derby, Pittsburgh	7	127	0
	Milt Davis, Baltimore	7	119	1
	Don Shinnick, Baltimore	7	70	0
1958	Jim Patton, N.Y. Giants	11	183	0
1957	*Milt Davis, Baltimore	10	219	2
	Jack Christiansen, Detroit	10	137	1
	Jack Butler, Pittsburgh	10	85	0
1956	Lindon Crow, Chi. Cardinals	11	170	0
1955	Will Sherman, Los Angeles	11	101	0
1954	Dick (Night Train) Lane, Chi. Cardinals	10	181	0
1953	Jack Christiansen, Detroit	12	238	1
1952	*Dick (Night Train) Lane, Los Angeles	14	298	2
1951	Otto Schnellbacher, N.Y. Giants	11	194	2
1950	*Orban (Spec) Sanders, N.Y. Yanks	13	199	0
1949	Bob Nussbaumer, Chi. Cardinals	12	157	0
1948	*Dan Sandifer, Washington	13	258	2
1947	Frank Reagan, N.Y. Giants	10	203	0
	Frank Seno, Boston	10	100	0
1946	Bill Dudley, Pittsburgh	10	242	1
1945	Roy Zimmerman, Philadelphia	7	90	0
1944	*Howard Livingston, N.Y. Giants	9	172	1
1943	Sammy Baugh, Washington	11	112	0
1942	Clyde (Bulldog) Turner, Chi. Bears	8	96	1
1941	Marshall Goldberg, Chi. Cardinals	7	54	0
	*Art Jones, Pittsburgh	7	35	0
1940	Clarence (Ace) Parker, Brooklyn	6	146	1
	Kent Ryan, Detroit	6	65	0
	Don Hutson, Green Bay	6	24	0

**First year in the league.*

Annual Punting Leaders

Year	Player, Team	No.	Avg.	Long
1992	Greg Montgomery, Houston, AFC	53	46.9	66
	Harry Newsome, Minnesota, NFC	72	45.0	84
1991	Reggie Roby, Miami, AFC	54	45.7	64
	Harry Newsome, Minnesota, NFC	68	45.5	65
1990	Mike Horan, Denver, AFC	58	44.4	67
	Sean Landeta, N.Y. Giants, NFC	75	44.1	67
1989	Rich Camarillo, Phoenix, NFC	76	43.4	58
	Greg Montgomery, Houston, AFC	56	43.3	63
1988	Harry Newsome, Pittsburgh, AFC	65	45.4	62
	Jim Arnold, Detroit, NFC	97	42.4	69
1987	Rick Donnelly, Atlanta, NFC	61	44.0	62
	Ralf Mojsiejenko, San Diego, AFC	67	42.9	57
1986	Rohn Stark, Indianapolis, AFC	76	45.2	63
	Sean Landeta, N.Y. Giants, NFC	79	44.8	61
1985	Rohn Stark, Indianapolis, AFC	78	45.9	68
	*Rick Donnelly, Atlanta, NFC	59	43.6	68
1984	Jim Arnold, Kansas City, AFC	98	44.9	63
	*Brian Hansen, New Orleans, NFC	69	43.8	66
1983	Rohn Stark, Baltimore, AFC	91	45.3	68
	*Frank Garcia, Tampa Bay, NFC	95	42.2	64
1982	Luke Prestridge, Denver, AFC	45	45.0	65
	Carl Birdsong, St. Louis, NFC	54	43.8	65
1981	Pat McInally, Cincinnati, AFC	72	45.4	62
	Tom Skladany, Detroit, NFC	64	43.5	74
1980	Dave Jennings, N.Y. Giants, NFC	94	44.8	63
	Luke Prestridge, Denver, AFC	70	43.9	57
1979	*Bob Grupp, Kansas City, AFC	89	43.6	74
	Dave Jennings, N.Y. Giants, NFC	104	42.7	72
1978	Pat McInally, Cincinnati, AFC	91	43.1	65
	*Tom Skladany, Detroit, NFC	86	42.5	63
1977	Ray Guy, Oakland, AFC	59	43.3	74
	Tom Blanchard, New Orleans, NFC	82	42.4	66
1976	Marv Bateman, Buffalo, AFC	86	42.8	78
	John James, Atlanta, NFC	101	42.1	67
1975	Ray Guy, Oakland, AFC	68	43.8	64
	Herman Weaver, Detroit, NFC	80	42.0	61
1974	Ray Guy, Oakland, AFC	74	42.2	66
	Tom Blanchard, New Orleans, NFC	88	42.1	71
1973	Jerrel Wilson, Kansas City, AFC	80	45.5	68
	*Tom Wittum, San Francisco, NFC	79	43.7	62
1972	Jerrel Wilson, Kansas City, AFC	66	44.8	69
	Dave Chapple, Los Angeles, NFC	53	44.2	70
1971	Dave Lewis, Cincinnati, AFC	72	44.8	56
	Tom McNeill, Philadelphia, NFC	73	42.0	64
1970	*Dave Lewis, Cincinnati, AFC	79	46.2	63
	*Julian Fagan, New Orleans, NFC	77	42.5	64
1969	David Lee, Baltimore, NFL	57	45.3	66
	Dennis Partee, San Diego, AFL	71	44.6	62
1968	Jerrel Wilson, Kansas City, AFL	63	45.1	70
	Billy Lothridge, Atlanta, NFL	75	44.3	70
1967	Bob Scarpitto, Denver, AFL	105	44.9	73
	Billy Lothridge, Atlanta, NFL	87	43.7	62

Year	Player, Team	No.	Avg.	Long
1966	Bob Scarpitto, Denver, AFL	76	45.8	70
	*David Lee, Baltimore, NFL	49	45.6	64
1965	Gary Collins, Cleveland, NFL	65	46.7	71
	Jerrel Wilson, Kansas City, AFL	69	45.4	64
1964	*Bobby Walden, Minnesota, NFL	72	46.4	73
	Jim Fraser, Denver, AFL	73	44.2	67
1963	Yale Lary, Detroit, NFL	35	48.9	73
	Jim Fraser, Denver, AFL	81	44.4	66
1962	Tommy Davis, San Francisco, NFL	48	45.6	82
	Jim Fraser, Denver, AFL	55	43.6	75
1961	Yale Lary, Detroit, NFL	52	48.4	71
	Billy Atkins, Buffalo, AFL	85	44.5	70
1960	Jerry Norton, St. Louis, NFL	39	45.6	62
	*Paul Maguire, L.A. Chargers, AFL	43	40.5	61
1959	Yale Lary, Detroit	45	47.1	67
1958	Sam Baker, Washington	48	45.4	64
1957	Don Chandler, N.Y. Giants	60	44.6	61
1956	Norm Van Brocklin, Los Angeles	48	43.1	72
1955	Norm Van Brocklin, Los Angeles	60	44.6	61
1954	Pat Brady, Pittsburgh	66	43.2	72
1953	Pat Brady, Pittsburgh	80	46.9	64
1952	Horace Gillom, Cleveland	61	45.7	73
1951	Horace Gillom, Cleveland	73	45.5	66
1950	*Fred (Curly) Morrison, Chi. Bears	57	43.3	65
1949	*Mike Boyda, N.Y. Bulldogs	56	44.2	61
1948	Joe Muha, Philadelphia	57	47.3	82
1947	Jack Jacobs, Green Bay	57	43.5	74
1946	Roy McKay, Green Bay	64	42.7	64
1945	Roy McKay, Green Bay	44	41.2	73
1944	Frank Sinkwich, Detroit	45	41.0	73
1943	Sammy Baugh, Washington	50	45.9	81
1942	Sammy Baugh, Washington	37	48.2	74
1941	Sammy Baugh, Washington	30	48.7	75
1940	Sammy Baugh, Washington	35	51.4	85
1939	*Parker Hall, Cleveland	58	40.8	80

First year in the league.

Annual Punt Return Leaders

Year	Player, Team	No.	Yards	Avg.	Long	TD
1992	Johnny Bailey, Phoenix, NFC	20	263	13.2	65	0
	Rod Woodson, Pittsburgh, AFC	32	364	11.4	80	1
1991	Mel Gray, Detroit, NFC	25	385	15.4	78	1
	Rod Woodson, Pittsburgh, AFC	28	320	11.4	40	0
1990	Clarence Verdin, Indianapolis, AFC	31	396	12.8	36	0
	*Johnny Bailey, Chicago, NFC	36	399	11.1	95	1
1989	Walter Stanley, Detroit, NFC	36	496	13.8	74	0
	Clarence Verdin, Indianapolis, AFC	23	296	12.9	49	1
1988	John Taylor, San Francisco, NFC	44	556	12.6	95	2
	JoJo Townsell, N.Y. Jets, AFC	35	409	11.7	59	1
1987	Mel Gray, New Orleans, NFC	24	352	14.7	80	0
	Bobby Joe Edmonds, Seattle, AFC	20	251	12.6	40	0
1986	*Bobby Joe Edmonds, Seattle, AFC	34	419	12.3	75	1
	*Vai Sikahema, St. Louis, NFC	43	522	12.1	71	2
1985	Irving Fryar, New England, AFC	37	520	14.1	85	2
	Henry Ellard, L.A. Rams, NFC	37	501	13.5	80	1
1984	Mike Martin, Cincinnati, AFC	24	376	15.7	55	0
	Henry Ellard, L.A. Rams, NFC	30	403	13.4	83	2
1983	*Henry Ellard, L.A. Rams, NFC	16	217	13.6	72	1
	Kirk Springs, N.Y. Jets, AFC	23	287	12.5	76	1
1982	Rick Upchurch, Denver, AFC	15	242	16.1	78	2
	Billy Johnson, Atlanta, NFC	24	273	11.4	71	0
1981	LeRoy Irvin, Los Angeles, NFC	46	615	13.4	84	3
	*James Brooks, San Diego, AFC	22	290	13.2	42	0
1980	J. T. Smith, Kansas City, AFC	40	581	14.5	75	2
	*Kenny Johnson, Atlanta, NFC	23	281	12.2	56	0
1979	John Sciarra, Philadelphia, NFC	16	182	11.4	38	0
	*Tony Nathan, Miami, AFC	28	306	10.9	86	1
1978	Rick Upchurch, Denver, AFC	36	493	13.7	75	1
	Jackie Wallace, Los Angeles, NFC	52	618	11.9	58	0
1977	Billy Johnson, Houston, AFC	35	539	15.4	87	2
	Larry Marshall, Philadelphia, NFC	46	489	10.6	48	0
1976	Rick Upchurch, Denver, AFC	39	536	13.7	92	4
	Eddie Brown, Washington, NFC	48	646	13.5	71	1
1975	Billy Johnson, Houston, AFC	40	612	15.3	83	3
	Terry Metcalf, St. Louis, NFC	23	285	12.4	69	1
1974	Lemar Parrish, Cincinnati, AFC	18	338	18.8	90	2
	Dick Jauron, Detroit, NFC	17	286	16.8	58	0
1973	Bruce Taylor, San Francisco, NFC	15	207	13.8	61	0
	Ron Smith, San Diego, AFC	27	352	13.0	84	2
1972	*Ken Ellis, Green Bay, NFC	14	215	15.4	80	1
	Chris Farasopoulos, N.Y. Jets, AFC	17	179	10.5	65	1
1971	Les (Speedy) Duncan, Washington, NFC	22	233	10.6	33	0
	Leroy Kelly, Cleveland, AFC	30	292	9.7	74	0
1970	Ed Podolak, Kansas City, AFC	23	311	13.5	60	0
	*Bruce Taylor, San Francisco, NFC	43	516	12.0	76	0
1969	Alvin Haymond, Los Angeles, NFL	33	435	13.2	52	0
	*Bill Thompson, Denver, AFL	25	288	11.5	40	0
1968	Bob Hayes, Dallas, NFL	15	312	20.8	90	2
	Noland Smith, Kansas City, AFL	18	270	15.0	80	1
1967	Floyd Little, Denver, AFL	16	270	16.9	72	1
	Ben Davis, Cleveland, NFL	18	229	12.7	52	1
1966	Les (Speedy) Duncan, San Diego, AFL	18	238	13.2	81	1
	Johnny Roland, St. Louis, NFL	20	221	11.1	86	1
1965	Leroy Kelly, Cleveland, NFL	17	265	15.6	67	2
	Les (Speedy) Duncan, San Diego, AFL	30	464	15.5	66	2
1964	Bobby Jancik, Houston, AFL	12	220	18.3	82	1
	Tommy Watkins, Detroit, NFL	16	238	14.9	68	2
1963	Dick James, Washington, NFL	16	214	13.4	39	0
	Claude (Hoot) Gibson, Oakland, AFL	26	307	11.8	85	2
1962	Dick Christy, N.Y. Titans, AFL	15	250	16.7	73	2
	Pat Studstill, Detroit, NFL	29	457	15.8	44	0
1961	Dick Christy, N.Y. Titans, AFL	18	383	21.3	70	2
	Willie Wood, Green Bay, NFL	14	225	16.1	72	2
1960	*Abner Haynes, Dall. Texans, AFL	14	215	15.4	46	0
	Abe Woodson, San Francisco, NFL	13	174	13.4	48	0
1959	Johnny Morris, Chi. Bears	14	171	12.2	78	1
1958	Jon Arnett, Los Angeles	18	223	12.4	58	0
1957	Bert Zagers, Washington	14	217	15.5	76	2
1956	Ken Konz, Cleveland	13	187	14.4	65	1
1955	Ollie Matson, Chi. Cardinals	13	245	18.8	78	2
1954	*Veryl Switzer, Green Bay	24	306	12.8	93	1
1953	Charley Trippi, Chi. Cardinals	21	239	11.4	38	0
1952	Jack Christiansen, Detroit	15	322	21.5	79	2
1951	Claude (Buddy) Young, N.Y. Yanks	12	231	19.3	79	1
1950	*Herb Rich, Baltimore	12	276	23.0	86	1
1949	Verda (Vitamin T) Smith, Los Angeles	27	427	15.8	85	1
1948	George McAfee, Chi. Bears	30	417	13.9	60	1
1947	*Walt Slater, Pittsburgh	28	435	15.5	33	0
1946	Bill Dudley, Pittsburgh	27	385	14.3	52	0
1945	*Dave Ryan, Detroit	15	220	14.7	56	0
1944	*Steve Van Buren, Philadelphia	15	230	15.3	55	1
1943	Andy Farkas, Washington	15	168	11.2	33	0
1942	Merlyn Condit, Brooklyn	21	210	10.0	23	0
1941	Byron (Whizzer) White, Detroit	19	262	13.8	64	0

First year in the league.

Annual Kickoff Return Leaders

Year	Player, Team	No.	Yards	Avg.	Long	TD
1992	Jon Vaughn, New England, AFC	20	564	28.2	100	1
	Deion Sanders, Atlanta, NFC	40	1,067	26.7	99	2
1991	Mel Gray, Detroit, NFC	36	929	25.8	71	0
	Nate Lewis, San Diego, AFC	23	578	25.1	95	1
1990	Kevin Clark, Denver, AFC	20	505	25.3	75	0
	David Meggett, N.Y. Giants, NFC	21	492	23.4	58	0
1989	Rod Woodson, Pittsburgh, AFC	36	982	27.3	84	1
	Mel Gray, Detroit, NFC	24	640	26.7	57	0
1988	*Tim Brown, L.A. Raiders, AFC	41	1,098	26.8	97	1
	Donnie Elder, Tampa Bay, NFC	34	772	22.7	51	0
1987	Sylvester Stamps, Atlanta, NFC	24	660	27.5	97	1
	Paul Palmer, Kansas City, AFC	38	923	24.3	95	2
1986	Dennis Gentry, Chicago, NFC	20	576	28.8	91	1
	*Lupe Sanchez, Pittsburgh, AFC	25	591	23.6	64	0
1985	Ron Brown, L.A. Rams, NFC	28	918	32.8	98	3
	Glen Young, Cleveland, AFC	35	898	25.7	63	0
1984	*Bobby Humphery, N.Y. Jets, AFC	22	675	30.7	97	1
	Barry Redden, L.A. Rams, NFC	23	530	23.0	40	0
1983	Fulton Walker, Miami, AFC	36	962	26.7	78	0
	Darrin Nelson, Minnesota, NFC	18	445	24.7	50	0
1982	*Mike Mosley, Buffalo, AFC	18	487	27.1	66	0
	Alvin Hall, Detroit, NFC	16	426	26.6	96	1
1981	Mike Nelms, Washington, NFC	37	1,099	29.7	84	0
	Carl Roaches, Houston, AFC	28	769	27.5	96	1
1980	Horace Ivory, New England, AFC	36	992	27.6	98	1
	Rich Mauti, New Orleans, NFC	31	798	25.7	52	0
1979	Larry Brunson, Oakland, AFC	17	441	25.9	89	0
	*Jimmy Edwards, Minnesota, NFC	44	1,103	25.1	83	0
1978	Steve Odom, Green Bay, NFC	25	677	27.1	95	1
	*Keith Wright, Cleveland, AFC	30	789	26.3	86	0
1977	*Raymond Clayborn, New England, AFC	28	869	31.0	101	3
	*Wilbert Montgomery, Philadelphia, NFC	23	619	26.9	99	1
1976	*Duriel Harris, Miami, AFC	17	559	32.9	69	0
	Cullen Bryant, Los Angeles, NFC	16	459	28.7	90	1
1975	*Walter Payton, Chicago, NFC	14	444	31.7	70	0
	Harold Hart, Oakland, AFC	17	518	30.5	102	1
1974	Terry Metcalf, St. Louis, NFC	20	623	31.2	94	1
	Greg Pruitt, Cleveland, AFC	22	606	27.5	88	1
1973	Carl Garrett, Chicago, NFC	16	486	30.4	67	0
	*Wallace Francis, Buffalo, AFC	23	687	29.9	101	2
1972	Ron Smith, Chicago, NFC	30	924	30.8	94	1
	*Bruce Laird, Baltimore, AFC	29	843	29.1	73	0
1971	Travis Williams, Los Angeles, NFC	25	743	29.7	105	1
	Eugene (Mercury) Morris, Miami, AFC	15	423	28.2	94	1
1970	Jim Duncan, Baltimore, AFC	20	707	35.4	99	1
	Cecil Turner, Chicago, NFC	23	752	32.7	96	4
1969	Bobby Williams, Detroit, NFL	17	563	33.1	96	1
	*Bill Thompson, Denver, AFL	18	513	28.5	63	0
1968	Preston Pearson, Baltimore, NFL	15	527	35.1	102	2
	*George Atkinson, Oakland, AFL	32	802	25.1	60	0
1967	*Travis Williams, Green Bay, NFL	18	739	41.1	104	4
	*Zeke Moore, Houston, AFL	14	405	28.9	92	1
1966	Gale Sayers, Chicago, NFL	23	718	31.2	93	2
	*Goldie Sellers, Denver, AFL	19	541	28.5	100	2
1965	Tommy Watkins, Detroit, NFL	17	584	34.4	94	0
	Abner Haynes, Denver, AFL	34	901	26.5	60	0
1964	*Clarence Childs, N.Y. Giants, NFL	34	987	29.0	100	1
	Bo Roberson, Oakland, AFL	36	975	27.1	59	0
1963	Abe Woodson, San Francisco, NFL	29	935	32.2	103	3
	Bobby Jancik, Houston, AFL	45	1,317	29.3	53	0
1962	Abe Woodson, San Francisco, NFL	37	1,157	31.3	79	0
	*Bobby Jancik, Houston, AFL	24	826	30.3	61	0
1961	Dick Bass, Los Angeles, NFL	23	698	30.3	64	0
	*Dave Grayson, Dall. Texans, AFL	16	453	28.3	73	0
1960	*Tom Moore, Green Bay, NFL	12	397	33.1	84	0
	Ken Hall, Houston, AFL	19	594	31.3	104	1
1959	Abe Woodson, San Francisco	13	382	29.4	105	1
1958	Ollie Matson, Chi. Cardinals	14	497	35.5	101	2
1957	*Jon Arnett, Los Angeles	18	504	28.0	98	1
1956	*Tom Wilson, Los Angeles	15	477	31.8	103	1
1955	Al Carmichael, Green Bay	14	418	29.9	100	1
1954	Billy Reynolds, Cleveland	14	413	29.5	51	0
1953	Joe Arenas, San Francisco	16	551	34.4	82	0
1952	Lynn Chandnois, Pittsburgh	17	599	35.2	93	2
1951	Lynn Chandnois, Pittsburgh	12	390	32.5	55	0
1950	Verda (Vitamin T) Smith, Los Angeles	22	742	33.7	97	3
1949	*Don Doll, Detroit	21	536	25.5	56	0
1948	*Joe Scott, N.Y. Giants	20	569	28.5	99	1

1947	Eddie Saenz, Washington	29	797	27.5	94	2
1946	Abe Karnofsky, Boston	21	599	28.5	97	1
1945	Steve Van Buren, Philadelphia	13	373	28.7	98	1
1944	Bob Thurbon, Card.-Pitt.	12	291	24.3	55	0
1943	Ken Heineman, Brooklyn	16	444	27.8	69	0
1942	Marshall Goldberg, Chi. Cardinals	15	393	26.2	95	1
1941	Marshall Goldberg, Chi. Cardinals	12	290	24.2	41	0

*First year in the league.

Annual Leaders in Sacks (Since 1982)

Year	Player, Team	Sacks
1992	Clyde Simmons, Phil., NFC	19
	Leslie O'Neal, S.D., AFC	17
1991	Pat Swilling, N.O., NFC	17
	William Fuller, Hou., AFC	15
1990	Derrick Thomas, K.C., AFC	20
	Charles Haley, S.F., NFC	16
1989	Chris Doleman, Minn., NFC	21
	Lee Williams, S.D., AFC	14
1988	Reggie White, Phil., NFC	18
	G. Townsend, Raiders, AFC	11.5
1987	Reggie White, Phil., NFC	21
	Andre Tippett, N.E., AFC	12.5
1986	Lawrence Taylor, N.Y.G., NFC	20.5
	Sean Jones, Raiders, AFC	15.5
1985	Richard Dent, Chi., NFC	17
	Andre Tippett, N.E., AFC	16.5
1984	Mark Gastineau, N.Y.J., AFC	22
	Richard Dent, Chi., NFC	17.5
1983	Mark Gastineau, N.Y.J., AFC	19
	Fred Dean, San Fran., NFC	17.5
1982	Doug Martin, Minn., NFC	11.5
	Jesse Baker, Hou., AFC	7.5

Points Scored

Year	Team	Points
1992	San Francisco, NFC	431
	Buffalo, AFC	381
1991	Washington, NFC	485
	Buffalo, AFC	458
1990	Buffalo, AFC	428
	Philadelphia, NFC	396
1989	San Francisco, NFC	442
	Buffalo, AFC	409
1988	Cincinnati, AFC	448
	L.A. Rams, NFC	407
1987	San Francisco, NFC	459
	Cleveland, AFC	390
1986	Miami, AFC	430
	Minnesota, NFC	398
1985	San Diego, AFC	467
	Chicago, NFC	456
1984	Miami, AFC	513
	San Francisco, NFC	475
1983	Washington, NFC	541
	L.A. Raiders, AFC	442
1982	San Diego, AFC	288
	Dallas, NFC	226
	Green Bay, NFC	226
1981	San Diego, AFC	478
	Atlanta, NFC	426
1980	Dallas, NFC	454
	New England, AFC	441
1979	Pittsburgh, AFC	416
	Dallas, NFC	371
1978	Dallas, NFC	384
	Miami, AFC	372
1977	Oakland, AFC	351
	Dallas, NFC	345
1976	Baltimore, AFC	417
	Los Angeles, NFC	351
1975	Buffalo, AFC	420
	Minnesota, NFC	377
1974	Oakland, AFC	355
	Washington, NFC	320
1973	Los Angeles, NFC	388
	Denver, AFC	354
1972	Miami, AFC	385
	San Francisco, NFC	353
1971	Dallas, NFC	406
	Oakland, AFC	344
1970	San Francisco, NFC	352
	Baltimore, AFC	321
1969	Minnesota, NFL	379
	Oakland, AFL	377
1968	Oakland, AFL	453
	Dallas, NFL	431
1967	Oakland, AFL	468
	Los Angeles, NFL	398
1966	Kansas City, AFL	448
	Dallas, NFL	445
1965	San Francisco, NFL	421
	San Diego, AFL	340
1964	Baltimore, NFL	428
	Buffalo, AFL	400
1963	N.Y. Giants, NFL	448
	San Diego, AFL	399
1962	Green Bay, NFL	415
	Dall. Texans, AFL	389
1961	Houston, AFL	513
	Green Bay, NFL	391
1960	N.Y. Titans, AFL	382
	Cleveland, NFL	362
1959	Baltimore	374
1958	Baltimore	381
1957	Los Angeles	307
1956	Chi. Bears	363
1955	Cleveland	349
1954	Detroit	337
1953	San Francisco	372
1952	Los Angeles	349
1951	Los Angeles	392
1950	Los Angeles	466
1949	Philadelphia	364
1948	Chi. Cardinals	395
1947	Chi. Bears	363
1946	Chi. Bears	289
1945	Philadelphia	272
1944	Philadelphia	267
1943	Chi. Bears	303
1942	Chi. Bears	376
1941	Chi. Bears	396
1940	Washington	245
1939	Chi. Bears	298
1938	Green Bay	223
1937	Green Bay	220
1936	Green Bay	248
1935	Chi. Bears	192
1934	Chi. Bears	286
1933	N.Y. Giants	244
1932	Chicago Bears	160

Total Yards Gained

Year	Team	Yards
1992	San Francisco, NFC	6,195
	Buffalo, AFC	5,893
1991	Buffalo, AFC	6,252
	San Francisco, NFC	5,858
1990	Houston, AFC	6,222
	San Francisco, NFC	5,895
1989	San Francisco, NFC	6,268
	Cincinnati, AFC	6,101
1988	Cincinnati, AFC	6,057
	San Francisco, NFC	5,900
1987	San Francisco, NFC	5,987
	Denver, AFC	5,624
1986	Cincinnati, AFC	6,490
	San Francisco, NFC	6,082
1985	San Diego, AFC	6,535
	San Francisco, NFC	5,920
1984	Miami, AFC	6,936
	San Francisco, NFC	6,366
1983	San Diego, AFC	6,197
	Green Bay, NFC	6,172
1982	San Diego, AFC	4,048
	San Francisco, NFC	3,242
1981	San Diego, AFC	6,744
	Detroit, NFC	5,933
1980	San Diego, AFC	6,410
	Los Angeles, NFC	6,006
1979	Pittsburgh, AFC	6,258
	Dallas, NFC	5,968
1978	New England, AFC	5,965
	Dallas, NFC	5,959
1977	Dallas, NFC	4,812
	Oakland, AFC	4,736
1976	Baltimore, AFC	5,236
	St. Louis, NFC	5,136
1975	Buffalo, AFC	5,467
	Dallas, NFC	5,025
1974	Dallas, NFC	4,983
	Oakland, AFC	4,718
1973	Los Angeles, NFC	4,906
	Oakland, AFC	4,773
1972	Miami, AFC	5,036
	N.Y. Giants, NFC	4,483
1971	Dallas, NFC	5,035
	San Diego, AFC	4,738
1970	Oakland, AFC	4,829
	San Francisco, NFC	4,503
1969	Dallas, NFL	5,122
	Oakland, AFL	5,036
1968	Oakland, AFL	5,696
	Dallas, NFL	5,117
1967	N.Y. Jets, AFL	5,152
	Baltimore, NFL	5,008
1966	Dallas, NFL	5,145
	Kansas City, AFL	5,114
1965	San Francisco, NFL	5,270
	San Diego, AFL	5,188
1964	Buffalo, AFL	5,206
	Baltimore, NFL	4,779
1963	San Diego, AFL	5,153
	N.Y. Giants, NFL	5,024
1962	N.Y. Giants, NFL	5,005
	Houston, AFL	4,971
1961	Houston, AFL	6,288
	Philadelphia, NFL	5,112
1960	Houston, AFL	4,936
	Baltimore, NFL	4,245
1959	Baltimore	4,458
1958	Baltimore	4,539
1957	Los Angeles	4,143
1956	Chi. Bears	4,537
1955	Chi. Bears	4,316
1954	Los Angeles	5,187
1953	Philadelphia	4,811
1952	Cleveland	4,352
1951	Los Angeles	5,506
1950	Los Angeles	5,420
1949	Chi. Bears	4,873
1948	Chi. Cardinals	4,705
1947	Chi. Bears	5,053
1946	Los Angeles	3,793
1945	Washington	3,549
1944	Chi. Bears	3,239
1943	Chi. Bears	4,045
1942	Chi. Bears	3,900
1941	Chi. Bears	4,265
1940	Green Bay	3,400
1939	Chi. Bears	3,988
1938	Green Bay	3,037
1937	Green Bay	3,201
1936	Detroit	3,703
1935	Chi. Bears	3,454
1934	Chi. Bears	3,900
1933	N.Y. Giants	2,973
1932	Chi. Bears	2,755

Yards Rushing

Year	Team	Yards
1992	Buffalo, AFC	2,436
	Philadelphia, NFC	2,388
1991	Buffalo, AFC	2,381
	Minnesota, NFC	2,201
1990	Philadelphia, NFC	2,556
	San Diego, AFC	2,257
1989	Cincinnati, AFC	2,483
	Chicago, NFC	2,287
1988	Cincinnati, AFC	2,710
	San Francisco, NFC	2,523
1987	San Francisco, NFC	2,237
	L.A. Raiders, AFC	2,197
1986	Chicago, NFC	2,700
	Cincinnati, AFC	2,533
1985	Chicago, NFC	2,761
	Indianapolis, AFC	2,439
1984	Chicago, NFC	2,974
	N.Y. Jets, AFC	2,189
1983	Chicago, NFC	2,727
	Baltimore, AFC	2,695
1982	Buffalo, AFC	1,371
	Dallas, NFC	1,313
1981	Detroit, NFC	2,795
	Kansas City, AFC	2,633
1980	Los Angeles, NFC	2,799
	Houston, AFC	2,635
1979	N.Y. Jets, AFC	2,646
	St. Louis, NFC	2,582
1978	New England, AFC	3,165
	Dallas, NFC	2,783
1977	Chicago, NFC	2,811
	Oakland, AFC	2,627
1976	Pittsburgh, AFC	2,971
	Los Angeles, NFC	2,528
1975	Buffalo, AFC	2,974
	Dallas, NFC	2,432
1974	Dallas, NFC	2,454
	Pittsburgh, AFC	2,417
1973	Buffalo, AFC	3,088
	Los Angeles, NFC	2,925
1972	Miami, AFC	2,960
	Chicago, NFC	2,360
1971	Miami, AFC	2,429
	Detroit, NFC	2,376
1970	Dallas, NFC	2,300
	Miami, AFC	2,082
1969	Dallas, NFL	2,276
	Kansas City, AFL	2,220
1968	Chicago, NFL	2,377
	Kansas City, AFL	2,227
1967	Cleveland, NFL	2,139
	Houston, AFL	2,122
1966	Kansas City, AFL	2,274
	Cleveland, NFL	2,166
1965	Cleveland, NFL	2,331
	San Diego, AFL	2,085
1964	Green Bay, NFL	2,276
	Buffalo, AFL	2,040
1963	Cleveland, NFL	2,639
	San Diego, AFL	2,203
1962	Buffalo, AFL	2,480
	Green Bay, NFL	2,460
1961	Green Bay, NFL	2,350
	Dall. Texans, AFL	2,189
1960	St. Louis, NFL	2,356
	Oakland, AFL	2,056
1959	Cleveland	2,149
1958	Cleveland	2,526
1957	Los Angeles	2,142
1956	Chi. Bears	2,468
1955	Chi. Bears	2,388
1954	San Francisco	2,498
1953	San Francisco	2,230
1952	San Francisco	1,905
1951	Chi. Bears	2,408
1950	N.Y. Giants	2,336
1949	Philadelphia	2,607
1948	Chi. Cardinals	2,560
1947	Los Angeles	2,171
1946	Green Bay	1,765
1945	Cleveland	1,714
1944	Philadelphia	1,661
1943	Phil-Pitt	1,730
1942	Chi. Bears	1,881
1941	Chi. Bears	2,263
1940	Chi. Bears	1,818
1939	Chi. Bears	2,043
1938	Detroit	1,893
1937	Detroit	2,074
1936	Detroit	2,885
1935	Chi. Bears	2,096
1934	Chi. Bears	2,847
1933	Boston	2,260
1932	Chi. Bears	1,770

Yards Passing

Leadership in this category has been based on net yards since 1952.

Year	Team	Yards
1992	Houston, AFC	4,029
	San Francisco, NFC	3,880
1991	Houston, AFC	4,621
	San Francisco, NFC	3,997
1990	Houston, AFC	4,805
	San Francisco, NFC	4,177
1989	Washington, NFC	4,349
	Miami, AFC	4,216
1988	Miami, AFC	4,516
	Washington, NFC	4,136
1987	Miami, AFC	3,876
	San Francisco, NFC	3,750
1986	Miami, AFC	4,779
	San Francisco, NFC	4,096
1985	San Diego, AFC	4,870
	Dallas, NFC	3,861
1984	Miami, AFC	5,018
	St. Louis, NFC	4,257
1983	San Diego, AFC	4,661
	Green Bay, NFC	4,365
1982	San Diego, AFC	2,927
	San Francisco, NFC	2,502
1981	San Diego, AFC	4,739
	Minnesota, NFC	4,333
1980	San Diego, AFC	4,531
	Minnesota, NFC	3,688
1979	San Diego, AFC	3,915
	San Francisco, NFC	3,641
1978	San Diego, AFC	3,375
	Minnesota, NFC	3,243
1977	Buffalo, AFC	2,530
	St. Louis, NFC	2,499
1976	Baltimore, AFC	2,933
	Minnesota, NFC	2,855
1975	Cincinnati, AFC	3,241
	Washington, NFC	2,917
1974	Washington, NFC	2,978
	Cincinnati, AFC	2,804
1973	Philadelphia, NFC	2,998
	Denver, AFC	2,519
1972	N.Y. Jets, AFC	2,777
	San Francisco, NFC	2,735
1971	San Diego, AFC	3,134
	Dallas, NFC	2,786
1970	San Francisco, NFC	2,923
	Oakland, AFC	2,865
1969	Oakland, AFL	3,271
	San Francisco, NFL	3,158
1968	San Diego, AFL	3,623
	Dallas, NFL	3,026
1967	N.Y. Jets, AFL	3,845
	Washington, NFL	3,730
1966	N.Y. Jets, AFL	3,464
	Dallas, NFL	3,023
1965	San Francisco, NFL	3,487
	San Diego, AFL	3,103
1964	Houston, AFL	3,527
	Chicago, NFL	2,841
1963	Baltimore, NFL	3,296
	Houston, AFL	3,222
1962	Denver, AFL	3,404
	Philadelphia, NFL	3,385
1961	Houston, AFL	4,392
	Philadelphia, NFL	3,605
1960	Houston, AFL	3,203
	Baltimore, NFL	2,956
1959	Baltimore	2,753
1958	Pittsburgh	2,752
1957	Baltimore	2,388
1956	Los Angeles	2,419

1955	Philadelphia	2,472
1954	Chi. Bears	3,104
1953	Philadelphia	3,089
1952	Cleveland	2,566
1951	Los Angeles	3,296
1950	Los Angeles	3,709
1949	Chi. Bears	3,055
1948	Washington	2,861
1947	Washington	3,336
1946	Los Angeles	2,080
1945	Chi. Bears	1,857
1944	Washington	2,021
1943	Chi. Bears	2,310
1942	Green Bay	2,407
1941	Chi. Bears	2,002
1940	Washington	1,887
1939	Chi. Bears	1,965
1938	Washington	1,536
1937	Green Bay	1,398
1936	Green Bay	1,629
1935	Green Bay	1,449
1934	Green Bay	1,165
1933	N.Y. Giants	1,348
1932	Chi. Bears	1,013

Fewest Points Allowed

Year	Team	Points
1992	New Orleans, NFC	202
	Pittsburgh, AFC	225
1991	New Orleans, NFC	211
	Denver, AFC	235
1990	N.Y. Giants, NFC	211
	Pittsburgh, AFC	240
1989	Denver, AFC	226
	N.Y. Giants, NFC	252
1988	Chicago, NFC	215
	Buffalo, AFC	237
1987	Indianapolis, AFC	238
	San Francisco, NFC	253
1986	Chicago, NFC	187
	Seattle, AFC	293
1985	Chicago, NFC	198
	N.Y. Jets, AFC	264
1984	San Francisco, NFC	227
	Denver, AFC	241
1983	Miami, AFC	250
	Detroit, NFC	286
1982	Washington, NFC	128
	Miami, AFC	131
1981	Philadelphia, NFC	221
	Miami, AFC	275
1980	Philadelphia, NFC	222
	Houston, AFC	251
1979	Tampa Bay, NFC	237
	San Diego, AFC	246
1978	Pittsburgh, AFC	195
	Dallas, NFC	208
1977	Atlanta, NFC	129
	Denver, AFC	148
1976	Pittsburgh, AFC	138
	Minnesota, NFC	176
1975	Los Angeles, NFC	135
	Pittsburgh, AFC	162
1974	Los Angeles, NFC	181
	Pittsburgh, AFC	189
1973	Miami, AFC	150
	Minnesota, NFC	168
1972	Miami, AFC	171
	Washington, NFC	218
1971	Minnesota, NFC	139
	Baltimore, AFC	140
1970	Minnesota, NFC	143
	Miami, AFC	228
1969	Minnesota, NFL	133
	Kansas City, AFL	177
1968	Baltimore, NFL	144
	Kansas City, AFL	170
1967	Los Angeles, NFL	196
	Houston, AFL	199
1966	Green Bay, NFL	163
	Buffalo, AFL	255
1965	Green Bay, NFL	224
	Buffalo, AFL	226
1964	Baltimore, NFL	225
	Buffalo, AFL	242
1963	Chicago, NFL	144
	San Diego, AFL	255
1962	Green Bay, NFL	148
	Dall. Texans, AFL	233
1961	San Diego, AFL	219
	N.Y. Giants, NFL	220
1960	San Francisco, NFL	205
	Dall. Texans, AFL	253
1959	N.Y. Giants	170
1958	N.Y. Giants	183
1957	Cleveland	172
1956	Cleveland	177
1955	Cleveland	218
1954	Cleveland	162
1953	Cleveland	162
1952	Detroit	192
1951	Cleveland	152
1950	Philadelphia	141
1949	Philadelphia	134
1948	Chi. Bears	151
1947	Green Bay	210
1946	Pittsburgh	117
1945	Washington	121
1944	N.Y. Giants	75
1943	Washington	137
1942	Chi. Bears	84
1941	N.Y. Giants	114
1940	Brooklyn	120
1939	N.Y. Giants	85
1938	N.Y. Giants	79
1937	Chi. Bears	100
1936	Chi. Bears	94
1935	Green Bay	96
	N.Y. Giants	96
1934	Detroit	59
1933	Brooklyn	54
1932	Chi. Bears	44

Fewest Total Yards Allowed

Year	Team	Yards
1992	Dallas, NFC	3,931
	Houston, AFC	4,211
1991	Philadelphia, NFC	3,549
	Denver, AFC	4,549
1990	Pittsburgh, AFC	4,115
	N.Y. Giants, NFC	4,206
1989	Minnesota, NFC	4,184
	Kansas City, AFC	4,293
1988	Minnesota, NFC	4,091
	Buffalo, AFC	4,578
1987	San Francisco, NFC	4,095
	Cleveland, AFC	4,264
1986	Chicago, NFC	4,130
	L.A. Raiders, AFC	4,804
1985	Chicago, NFC	4,135
	L.A. Raiders, AFC	4,603
1984	Chicago, NFC	3,863
	Cleveland, AFC	4,641
1983	Cincinnati, AFC	4,327
	New Orleans, NFC	4,691
1982	Miami, AFC	2,312
	Tampa Bay, NFC	2,442
1981	Philadelphia, NFC	4,447
	N.Y. Jets, AFC	4,871
1980	Buffalo, AFC	4,101
	Philadelphia, NFC	4,443
1979	Tampa Bay, NFC	3,949
	Pittsburgh, AFC	4,270
1978	Los Angeles, NFC	3,893
	Pittsburgh, AFC	4,168
1977	Dallas, NFC	3,213
	New England, AFC	3,638
1976	Pittsburgh, AFC	3,323
	San Francisco, NFC	3,562
1975	Minnesota, NFC	3,153
	Oakland, AFC	3,629
1974	Pittsburgh, AFC	3,074
	Washington, NFC	3,285
1973	Los Angeles, NFC	2,951
	Oakland, AFC	3,160
1972	Miami, AFC	3,297
	Green Bay, NFC	3,474
1971	Baltimore, AFC	2,852
	Minnesota, NFC	3,406
1970	Minnesota, NFC	2,803
	N.Y. Jets, AFC	3,655
1969	Minnesota, NFL	2,720
	Kansas City, AFL	3,163
1968	Los Angeles, NFL	3,118
	N.Y. Jets, AFL	3,363
1967	Oakland, AFL	3,294
	Green Bay, NFL	3,300
1966	St. Louis, NFL	3,492
	Oakland, AFL	3,910
1965	San Diego, AFL	3,262
	Detroit, NFL	3,557
1964	Green Bay, NFL	3,179
	Buffalo, AFL	3,878
1963	Chicago, NFL	3,176
	Boston, AFL	3,834
1962	Detroit, NFL	3,217
	Dall. Texans, AFL	3,951
1961	San Diego, AFL	3,726
	Baltimore, NFL	3,782
1960	St. Louis, NFL	3,029
	Buffalo, AFL	3,866
1959	N.Y. Giants	2,843
1958	Chi. Bears	3,066
1957	Pittsburgh	2,791
1956	N.Y. Giants	3,081
1955	Cleveland	2,841
1954	Cleveland	2,658
1953	Philadelphia	2,998
1952	Cleveland	3,075
1951	N.Y. Giants	3,250
1950	Cleveland	3,154
1949	Philadelphia	2,831
1948	Chi. Bears	2,931
1947	Green Bay	3,396
1946	Washington	2,451
1945	Philadelphia	2,073
1944	Philadelphia	1,943
1943	Chi. Bears	2,262
1942	Chi. Bears	1,703
1941	N.Y. Giants	2,368
1940	N.Y. Giants	2,219
1939	Washington	2,116
1938	N.Y. Giants	2,029
1937	Washington	2,123
1936	Boston	2,181
1935	Boston	1,996
1934	Chi. Cardinals	1,539
1933	Brooklyn	1,789

Fewest Rushing Yards Allowed

Year	Team	Yards
1992	Dallas, NFC	1,244
	Buffalo, AFC	1,395
	San Diego, AFC	1,395
1991	Philadelphia, NFC	1,136
	N.Y. Jets, AFC	1,442
1990	Philadelphia, NFC	1,169
	San Diego, AFC	1,515
1989	New Orleans, NFC	1,326
	Denver, AFC	1,580
1988	Chicago, NFC	1,326
	Houston, AFC	1,592
1987	Chicago, NFC	1,413
	Cleveland, AFC	1,433
1986	N.Y. Giants, NFC	1,284
	Denver, AFC	1,651
1985	Chicago, NFC	1,319
	N.Y. Jets, AFC	1,516
1984	Chicago, NFC	1,377
	Pittsburgh, AFC	1,617
1983	Washington, NFC	1,289
	Cincinnati, AFC	1,499
1982	Pittsburgh, AFC	762
	Detroit, NFC	854
1981	Detroit, NFC	1,623
	Kansas City, AFC	1,747
1980	Detroit, NFC	1,599
	Cincinnati, AFC	1,680
1979	Denver, AFC	1,693
	Tampa Bay, NFC	1,873
1978	Dallas, NFC	1,721
	Pittsburgh, AFC	1,774
1977	Denver, AFC	1,531
	Dallas, NFC	1,651
1976	Pittsburgh, AFC	1,457
	Los Angeles, NFC	1,564
1975	Minnesota, NFC	1,532
	Houston, AFC	1,680
1974	Los Angeles, NFC	1,302
	New England, AFC	1,587
1973	Los Angeles, NFC	1,270
	Oakland, AFC	1,470
1972	Dallas, NFC	1,515
	Miami, AFC	1,548
1971	Baltimore, AFC	1,113
	Dallas, NFC	1,144
1970	Detroit, NFC	1,152
	N.Y. Jets, AFC	1,283
1969	Dallas, NFL	1,050
	Kansas City, AFL	1,091
1968	Dallas, NFL	1,195
	N.Y. Jets, AFL	1,195
1967	Dallas, NFL	1,081
	Oakland, AFL	1,129
1966	Buffalo, AFL	1,051
	Dallas, NFL	1,176
1965	San Diego, AFL	1,094
	Los Angeles, NFL	1,409
1964	Buffalo, AFL	913
	Los Angeles, NFL	1,501
1963	Boston, AFL	1,107
	Chicago, NFL	1,442
1962	Detroit, NFL	1,231
	Dall. Texans, AFL	1,250
1961	Boston, AFL	1,041
	Pittsburgh, NFL	1,463
1960	St. Louis, NFL	1,212
	Dall. Texans, AFL	1,338
1959	N.Y. Giants	1,261
1958	Baltimore	1,291
1957	Baltimore	1,174
1956	N.Y. Giants	1,443
1955	Cleveland	1,189
1954	Cleveland	1,050
1953	Philadelphia	1,117
1952	Detroit	1,145
1951	N.Y. Giants	913
1950	Detroit	1,367
1949	Chi. Bears	1,196
1948	Philadelphia	1,209
1947	Philadelphia	1,329
1946	Chi. Bears	1,060
1945	Philadelphia	817
1944	Philadelphia	558
1943	Phil-Pitt	793
1942	Chi. Bears	519
1941	Washington	1,042
1940	N.Y. Giants	977
1939	Chi. Bears	812
1938	Detroit	1,081
1937	Chi. Bears	933
1936	Boston	1,148
1935	Boston	998
1934	Chi. Cardinals	954
1933	Brooklyn	964

Fewest Passing Yards Allowed

Leadership in this category has been based on net yards since 1952.

Year	Team	Yards
1992	New Orleans, NFC	2,470
	Kansas City, AFC	2,537
1991	Philadelphia, NFC	2,413
	Denver, AFC	2,755
1990	Pittsburgh, AFC	2,500
	Dallas, NFC	2,639
1989	Minnesota, NFC	2,501
	Kansas City, AFC	2,527
1988	Kansas City, AFC	2,434
	Minnesota, NFC	2,489
1987	San Francisco, NFC	2,484
	L.A. Raiders, AFC	2,727
1986	St. Louis, NFC	2,637
	New England, AFC	2,978
1985	Washington, NFC	2,746
	Pittsburgh, AFC	2,783
1984	New Orleans, NFC	2,453
	Cleveland, AFC	2,696
1983	New Orleans, NFC	2,691
	Cincinnati, AFC	2,828
1982	Miami, AFC	1,027
	Tampa Bay, NFC	1,384
1981	Philadelphia, NFC	2,696
	Buffalo, AFC	2,870
1980	Washington, NFC	2,171
	Buffalo, AFC	2,282
1979	Tampa Bay, NFC	2,076
	Buffalo, AFC	2,530
1978	Buffalo, AFC	1,960
	Los Angeles, NFC	2,048
1977	Atlanta, NFC	1,384
	San Diego, AFC	1,725
1976	Minnesota, NFC	1,575
	Cincinnati, AFC	1,758
1975	Minnesota, NFC	1,621
	Cincinnati, AFC	1,729
1974	Pittsburgh, AFC	1,466
	Atlanta, NFC	1,572
1973	Miami, AFC	1,290
	Atlanta, NFC	1,430
1972	Minnesota, NFC	1,699
	Cleveland, AFC	1,736
1971	Atlanta, NFC	1,638
	Baltimore, AFC	1,739
1970	Minnesota, NFC	1,438
	Kansas City, AFC	2,010
1969	Minnesota, NFL	1,631
	Kansas City, AFL	2,072
1968	Houston, AFL	1,671
	Green Bay, NFL	1,796
1967	Green Bay, NFL	1,377
	Buffalo, AFL	1,825
1966	Green Bay, NFL	1,959
	Oakland, AFL	2,118
1965	Green Bay, NFL	1,981
	San Diego, AFL	2,168
1964	Green Bay, NFL	1,647
	San Diego, AFL	2,518
1963	Chicago, NFL	1,734
	Oakland, AFL	2,589
1962	Green Bay, NFL	1,746
	Oakland, AFL	2,306
1961	Baltimore, NFL	1,913
	San Diego, AFL	2,363
1960	Chicago, NFL	1,388
	Buffalo, AFL	2,124
1959	N.Y. Giants	1,582
1958	Chi. Bears	1,769
1957	Cleveland	1,300
1956	Cleveland	1,103
1955	Pittsburgh	1,295
1954	Cleveland	1,608
1953	Washington	1,751
1952	Washington	1,580
1951	Pittsburgh	1,687
1950	Cleveland	1,581
1949	Philadelphia	1,607
1948	Green Bay	1,626
1947	Green Bay	1,790
1946	Pittsburgh	939
1945	Washington	1,121
1944	Chi. Bears	1,052
1943	Chi. Bears	980
1942	Washington	1,093
1941	Pittsburgh	1,168
1940	Philadelphia	1,012
1939	Washington	1,116
1938	Chi. Bears	897
1937	Detroit	804

1936 Philadelphia 853
1935 Chi. Cardinals 793
1934 Philadelphia 545
1933 Portsmouth 558

SUPER BOWL RECORDS

Compiled by Elias Sports Bureau

1967: Super Bowl I	1976: Super Bowl X	1985: Super Bowl XIX
1968: Super Bowl II	1977: Super Bowl XI	1986: Super Bowl XX
1969: Super Bowl III	1978: Super Bowl XII	1987: Super Bowl XXI
1970: Super Bowl IV	1979: Super Bowl XIII	1988: Super Bowl XXII
1971: Super Bowl V	1980: Super Bowl XIV	1989: Super Bowl XXIII
1972: Super Bowl VI	1981: Super Bowl XV	1990: Super Bowl XXIV
1973: Super Bowl VII	1982: Super Bowl XVI	1991: Super Bowl XXV
1974: Super Bowl VIII	1983: Super Bowl XVII	1992: Super Bowl XXVI
1975: Super Bowl IX	1984: Super Bowl XVIII	1993: Super Bowl XXVII

Individual Records

Service

Most Games

5 Marv Fleming, Green Bay, 1967-68; Miami, 1972-74
Larry Cole, Dallas, 1971-72, 1976, 1978-79
Cliff Harris, Dallas, 1971-72, 1976, 1978-79
D.D. Lewis, Dallas, 1971-72, 1976, 1978-79
Preston Pearson, Baltimore, 1969; Pittsburgh, 1975; Dallas, 1976, 1978-79
Charlie Waters, Dallas, 1971-72, 1976, 1978-79
Rayfield Wright, Dallas, 1971-72, 1976, 1978-79
4 By many players

Most Games, Winning Team

4 By many players

Most Games, Coach

6 Don Shula, Baltimore, 1969; Miami, 1972-74, 1983, 1985
5 Tom Landry, Dallas, 1971-72, 1976, 1978-79
4 Bud Grant, Minnesota, 1970, 1974-75, 1977
Chuck Noll, Pittsburgh, 1975-76, 1979-80
Joe Gibbs, Washington, 1983-84, 1988, 1992

Most Games, Winning Team, Coach

4 Chuck Noll, Pittsburgh, 1975-76, 1979-80
3 Bill Walsh, San Francisco, 1982, 1985, 1989
Joe Gibbs, Washington, 1983, 1988, 1992
2 Vince Lombardi, Green Bay, 1967-68
Tom Landry, Dallas, 1972, 1978
Don Shula, Miami, 1973-74
Tom Flores, Oakland, 1981; L.A. Raiders, 1984
Bill Parcells, N.Y. Giants, 1987, 1991

Most Games, Losing Team, Coach

4 Bud Grant, Minnesota, 1970, 1974-75, 1977
Don Shula, Baltimore, 1969; Miami, 1972, 1983, 1985
3 Tom Landry, Dallas, 1971, 1976, 1979
Dan Reeves, Denver, 1987-88, 1990
Marv Levy, Buffalo, 1991-93

Scoring

Points

Most Points, Career

24 Franco Harris, Pittsburgh, 4 games (4-td)
Roger Craig, San Francisco, 3 games (4-td)
Jerry Rice, San Francisco, 2 games (4-td)
22 Ray Wersching, San Francisco, 2 games (7-pat, 5-fg)
20 Don Chandler, Green Bay, 2 games (8-pat, 4-fg)

Most Points, Game

18 Roger Craig, San Francisco vs. Miami, 1985 (3-td)
Jerry Rice, San Francisco vs. Denver, 1990 (3-td)
15 Don Chandler, Green Bay vs. Oakland, 1968 (3-pat, 4-fg)
14 Ray Wersching, San Francisco vs. Cincinnati, 1982 (2-pat, 4-fg)
Kevin Butler, Chicago vs. New England, 1986 (5-pat, 3-fg)

Touchdowns

Most Touchdowns, Career

4 Franco Harris, Pittsburgh, 4 games (4-r)
Roger Craig, San Francisco, 3 games (2-r, 2-p)
Jerry Rice, San Francisco, 2 games (4-p)
3 John Stallworth, Pittsburgh, 4 games (3-p)
Lynn Swann, Pittsburgh, 4 games (3-p)
Cliff Branch, Oakland-L.A. Raiders, 3 games (3-p)
Thurman Thomas, Buffalo, 3 games (3-r)

Most Touchdowns, Game

3 Roger Craig, San Francisco vs. Miami, 1985 (1-r, 2-p)
Jerry Rice, San Francisco vs. Denver, 1990 (3-p)
2 Max McGee, Green Bay vs. Kansas City, 1967 (2-p)
Elijah Pitts, Green Bay vs. Kansas City, 1967 (2-r)
Bill Miller, Oakland vs. Green Bay, 1968 (2-p)
Larry Csonka, Miami vs. Minnesota, 1974 (2-r)
Pete Banaszak, Oakland vs. Minnesota, 1977 (2-r)
John Stallworth, Pittsburgh vs. Dallas, 1979 (2-p)
Franco Harris, Pittsburgh vs. Los Angeles, 1980 (2-r)
Cliff Branch, Oakland vs. Philadelphia, 1981 (2-p)
Dan Ross, Cincinnati vs. San Francisco, 1982 (2-p)
Marcus Allen, L.A. Raiders vs. Washington, 1984 (2-r)
Jim McMahon, Chicago vs. New England, 1986 (2-r)
Ricky Sanders, Washington vs. Denver, 1988 (2-p)
Timmy Smith, Washington vs. Denver, 1988 (2-r)
Tom Rathman, San Francisco vs. Denver, 1990 (2-r)
Gerald Riggs, Washington vs. Buffalo, 1992 (2-r)
Michael Irvin, Dallas vs. Buffalo, 1993 (2-p)

Points After Touchdown

Most Points After Touchdown, Career

9 Mike Cofer, San Francisco, 2 games (10 att)
8 Don Chandler, Green Bay, 2 games (8 att)
Roy Gerela, Pittsburgh, 3 games (9 att)
Chris Bahr, Oakland-L.A. Raiders, 2 games (8 att)
7 Ray Wersching, San Francisco, 2 games (7 att)
Lin Elliott, Dallas, 1 game (7 att)

Most Points After Touchdown, Game

7 Mike Cofer, San Francisco vs. Denver, 1990 (8 att)
Lin Elliott, Dallas vs. Buffalo, 1993 (7 att)
6 Ali Haji-Sheikh, Washington vs. Denver, 1988 (6 att)
5 Don Chandler, Green Bay vs. Kansas City, 1967 (5 att)
Roy Gerela, Pittsburgh vs. Dallas, 1979 (5 att)
Chris Bahr, L.A. Raiders vs. Washington, 1984 (5 att)
Ray Wersching, San Francisco vs. Miami, 1985 (5 att)
Kevin Butler, Chicago vs. New England, 1986 (5 att)

Field Goals

Field Goals Attempted, Career

6 Jim Turner, N.Y. Jets-Denver, 2 games
Roy Gerela, Pittsburgh, 3 games
Rich Karlis, Denver, 2 games
5 Efren Herrera, Dallas, 1 game
Ray Wersching, San Francisco, 2 games

Most Field Goals Attempted, Game

5 Jim Turner, N.Y. Jets vs. Baltimore, 1969
Efren Herrera, Dallas vs. Denver, 1978
4 Don Chandler, Green Bay vs. Oakland, 1968
Roy Gerela, Pittsburgh vs. Dallas, 1976
Ray Wersching, San Francisco vs. Cincinnati, 1982
Rich Karlis, Denver vs. N.Y. Giants, 1987
Mike Cofer, San Francisco vs. Cincinnati, 1989

Most Field Goals, Career

5 Ray Wersching, San Francisco, 2 games (5 att)
4 Don Chandler, Green Bay, 2 games (4 att)
Jim Turner, N.Y. Jets-Denver, 2 games (6 att)
Uwe von Schamann, Miami, 2 games (4 att)
3 Mike Clark, Dallas, 2 games (3 att)
Jan Stenerud, Kansas City, 1 game (3 att)
Chris Bahr, Oakland-L.A. Raiders, 2 games (4 att)
Mark Moseley, Washington, 2 games (4 att)
Kevin Butler, Chicago, 1 game (3 att)
Rich Karlis, Denver, 2 games (6 att)
Jim Breech, Cincinnati, 2 games (3 att)
Matt Bahr, Pittsburgh-N.Y. Giants, 2 games (3 att)
Chip Lohmiller, Washington, 1 game (3 att)

Most Field Goals, Game

4 Don Chandler, Green Bay vs. Oakland, 1968
Ray Wersching, San Francisco vs. Cincinnati, 1982
3 Jim Turner, N.Y. Jets vs. Baltimore, 1969
Jan Stenerud, Kansas City vs. Minnesota, 1970
Uwe von Schamann, Miami vs. San Francisco, 1985
Kevin Butler, Chicago vs. New England, 1986
Jim Breech, Cincinnati vs. San Francisco, 1989
Chip Lohmiller, Washington, 1992

Longest Field Goal

48 Jan Stenerud, Kansas City vs. Minnesota, 1970
Rich Karlis, Denver vs. N.Y. Giants, 1987
47 Jim Turner, Denver vs. Dallas, 1978
46 Chris Bahr, Oakland vs. Philadelphia, 1981

Safeties

Most Safeties, Game

1 Dwight White, Pittsburgh vs. Minnesota, 1975
Reggie Harrison, Pittsburgh vs. Dallas, 1976
Henry Waechter, Chicago vs. New England, 1986
George Martin, N.Y. Giants vs. Denver, 1987
Bruce Smith, Buffalo vs. N.Y. Giants, 1991

Rushing

Attempts

Most Attempts, Career

101 Franco Harris, Pittsburgh, 4 games
64 John Riggins, Washington, 2 games
57 Larry Csonka, Miami, 3 games

Most Attempts, Game

38 John Riggins, Washington vs. Miami, 1983
34 Franco Harris, Pittsburgh vs. Minnesota, 1975
33 Larry Csonka, Miami vs. Minnesota, 1974

Yards Gained

Most Yards Gained, Career

354 Franco Harris, Pittsburgh, 4 games
297 Larry Csonka, Miami, 3 games
230 John Riggins, Washington, 2 games

Most Yards Gained, Game

204 Timmy Smith, Washington vs. Denver, 1988
191 Marcus Allen, L.A. Raiders vs. Washington, 1984
166 John Riggins, Washington vs. Miami, 1983

Longest Run From Scrimmage

74 Marcus Allen, L.A. Raiders vs. Washington, 1984 (TD)
58 Tom Matte, Baltimore vs. N.Y. Jets, 1969
Timmy Smith, Washington vs. Denver, 1988 (TD)
49 Larry Csonka, Miami vs. Washington, 1973

Average Gain

Highest Average Gain, Career (20 attempts)

9.6 Marcus Allen, L.A. Raiders, 1 game (20-191)
9.3 Timmy Smith, Washington, 1 game (22-204)
5.3 Walt Garrison, Dallas, 2 games (26-139)

Highest Average Gain, Game (10 attempts)

10.5 Tom Matte, Baltimore vs. N.Y. Jets, 1969 (11-116)
9.6 Marcus Allen, L.A. Raiders vs. Washington, 1984 (20-191)
9.3 Timmy Smith, Washington vs. Denver, 1988 (22-204)

Touchdowns

Most Touchdowns, Career

4 Franco Harris, Pittsburgh, 4 games

3 Thurman Thomas, Buffalo, 3 games
2 Elijah Pitts, Green Bay, 1 game
Jim Kiick, Miami, 3 games
Larry Csonka, Miami, 3 games
Pete Banaszak, Oakland, 2 games
Marcus Allen, L.A. Raiders, 1 game
John Riggins, Washington, 2 games
Jim McMahon, Chicago, 1 game
Timmy Smith, Washington, 1 game
Roger Craig, San Francisco, 3 games
Tom Rathman, San Francisco, 2 games
John Elway, Denver, 3 games
Ottis Anderson, N.Y. Giants, 2 games
Gerald Riggs, Washington, 1 game
Joe Montana, San Francisco, 4 games

Most Touchdowns, Game
2 Elijah Pitts, Green Bay vs. Kansas City, 1967
Larry Csonka, Miami vs. Minnesota, 1974
Pete Banaszak, Oakland vs. Minnesota, 1977
Franco Harris, Pittsburgh vs. Los Angeles, 1980
Marcus Allen, L.A. Raiders vs. Washington, 1984
Jim McMahon, Chicago vs. New England, 1986
Timmy Smith, Washington vs. Denver, 1988
Tom Rathman, San Francisco vs. Denver, 1990
Gerald Riggs, Washington vs. Buffalo, 1992

Passing

Attempts

Most Passes Attempted, Career
122 Joe Montana, San Francisco, 4 games
101 John Elway, Denver, 3 games
98 Roger Staubach, Dallas, 4 games

Most Passes Attempted, Game
58 Jim Kelly, Buffalo vs. Washington, 1992
50 Dan Marino, Miami vs. San Francisco, 1985
38 Ron Jaworski, Philadelphia vs. Oakland, 1981
John Elway, Denver vs. Washington, 1988

Completions

Most Passes Completed, Career
83 Joe Montana, San Francisco, 4 games
61 Roger Staubach, Dallas, 4 games
50 Jim Kelly, Buffalo, 3 games

Most Passes Completed, Game
29 Dan Marino, Miami vs. San Francisco, 1985
28 Jim Kelly, Buffalo vs. Washington, 1992
25 Ken Anderson, Cincinnati vs. San Francisco, 1982

Most Consecutive Completions, Game
13 Joe Montana, San Francisco vs. Denver, 1990
10 Phil Simms, N.Y. Giants vs. Denver, 1987
8 Len Dawson, Kansas City vs. Green Bay, 1967
Joe Theismann, Washington vs. Miami, 1983
Troy Aikman, Dallas vs. Buffalo, 1993

Completion Percentage

Highest Completion Percentage, Career (40 attempts)
68.0 Joe Montana, San Francisco, 4 games (122-83)
63.6 Len Dawson, Kansas City, 2 games (44-28)
63.4 Bob Griese, Miami, 3 games (41-26)

Highest Completion Percentage, Game (20 attempts)
88.0 Phil Simms, N.Y. Giants vs. Denver, 1987 (25-22)
75.9 Joe Montana, San Francisco vs. Denver, 1990 (29-22)
73.5 Ken Anderson, Cincinnati vs. San Francisco, 1982 (34-25)

Yards Gained

Most Yards Gained, Career
1,142 Joe Montana, San Francisco, 4 games
932 Terry Bradshaw, Pittsburgh, 4 games
734 Roger Staubach, Dallas, 4 games

Most Yards Gained, Game
357 Joe Montana, San Francisco vs. Cincinnati, 1989
340 Doug Williams, Washington vs. Denver, 1988
331 Joe Montana, San Francisco vs. Miami, 1985

Longest Pass Completion
80 Jim Plunkett (to King), Oakland vs. Philadelphia, 1981 (TD)
Doug Williams (to Sanders), Washington vs. Denver, 1988 (TD)
76 David Woodley (to Cefalo), Miami vs. Washington, 1983 (TD)
75 Johnny Unitas (to Mackey), Baltimore vs. Dallas, 1971 (TD)
Terry Bradshaw (to Stallworth), Pittsburgh vs. Dallas, 1979 (TD)

Average Gain

Highest Average Gain, Career (40 attempts)
11.10 Terry Bradshaw, Pittsburgh, 4 games (84-932)
9.62 Bart Starr, Green Bay, 2 games (47-452)
9.41 Jim Plunkett, Oakland-L.A. Raiders, 2 games (46-433)

Highest Average Gain, Game (20 attempts)
14.71 Terry Bradshaw, Pittsburgh vs. Los Angeles, 1980 (21-309)
12.80 Jim McMahon, Chicago vs. New England, 1986 (20-256)
12.43 Jim Plunkett, Oakland vs. Philadelphia, 1981 (21-261)

Touchdowns

Most Touchdown Passes, Career
11 Joe Montana, San Francisco, 4 games
9 Terry Bradshaw, Pittsburgh, 4 games
8 Roger Staubach, Dallas, 4 games

Most Touchdown Passes, Game
5 Joe Montana, San Francisco vs. Denver, 1990
4 Terry Bradshaw, Pittsburgh vs. Dallas, 1979
Doug Williams, Washington vs. Denver, 1988
Troy Aikman, Dallas vs. Buffalo, 1993
3 Roger Staubach, Dallas vs. Pittsburgh, 1979
Jim Plunkett, Oakland vs. Philadelphia, 1981
Joe Montana, San Francisco vs. Miami, 1985
Phil Simms, N.Y. Giants vs. Denver, 1987

Had Intercepted

Lowest Percentage, Passes Had Intercepted, Career (40 attempts)
0.00 Jim Plunkett, Oakland-L.A. Raiders, 2 games (46-0)
Joe Montana, San Francisco, 4 games (122-0)
2.13 Bart Starr, Green Bay, 2 games (47-1)
4.00 Dan Marino, Miami, 1 game (50-2)

Most Attempts, Without Interception, Game
36 Joe Montana, San Francisco vs. Cincinnati, 1989
35 Joe Montana, San Francisco vs. Miami, 1985
32 Jeff Hostetler, N.Y. Giants vs. Buffalo, 1991

Most Passes Had Intercepted, Career
7 Craig Morton, Dallas-Denver, 2 games
6 Fran Tarkenton, Minnesota, 3 games
John Elway, Denver, 3 games
Jim Kelly, Buffalo, 3 games
4 Earl Morrall, Baltimore-Miami, 4 games
Roger Staubach, Dallas, 4 games
Terry Bradshaw, Pittsburgh, 4 games
Joe Theismann, Washington, 2 games

Most Passes Had Intercepted, Game
4 Craig Morton, Denver vs. Dallas, 1978
Jim Kelly, Buffalo vs. Washington, 1992
3 By eight players

Pass Receiving

Receptions

Most Receptions, Career
21 Andre Reed, Buffalo, 3 games
20 Roger Craig, San Francisco, 3 games
18 Jerry Rice, San Francisco, 2 games

Most Receptions, Game
11 Dan Ross, Cincinnati vs. San Francisco, 1982
Jerry Rice, San Francisco vs. Cincinnati, 1989
10 Tony Nathan, Miami vs. San Francisco, 1985
9 Ricky Sanders, Washington vs. Denver, 1988

Yards Gained

Most Yards Gained, Career
364 Lynn Swann, Pittsburgh, 4 games
363 Jerry Rice, San Francisco, 2 games
268 John Stallworth, Pittsburgh, 4 games

Most Yards Gained, Game
215 Jerry Rice, San Francisco vs. Cincinnati, 1989
193 Ricky Sanders, Washington vs. Denver, 1988
161 Lynn Swann, Pittsburgh vs. Dallas, 1976

Longest Reception
80 Kenny King (from Plunkett), Oakland vs. Philadelphia, 1981 (TD)
Ricky Sanders (from Williams), Washington vs. Denver, 1988 (TD)
76 Jimmy Cefalo (from Woodley), Miami vs. Washington, 1983 (TD)
75 John Mackey (from Unitas), Baltimore vs. Dallas, 1971 (TD)
John Stallworth (from Bradshaw), Pittsburgh vs. Dallas, 1979 (TD)

Average Gain

Highest Average Gain, Career (8 receptions)
24.4 John Stallworth, Pittsburgh, 4 games (11-268)
23.4 Ricky Sanders, Washington, 2 games (10-234)
22.8 Lynn Swann, Pittsburgh, 4 games (16-364)

Highest Average Gain, Game (3 receptions)
40.33 John Stallworth, Pittsburgh vs. Los Angeles, 1980 (3-121)
40.25 Lynn Swann, Pittsburgh vs. Dallas, 1979 (4-161)
38.33 John Stallworth, Pittsburgh vs. Dallas, 1979 (3-115)

Touchdowns

Most Touchdowns, Career
4 Jerry Rice, San Francisco, 2 games
3 John Stallworth, Pittsburgh, 4 games
Lynn Swann, Pittsburgh, 4 games
Cliff Branch, Oakland-L.A. Raiders, 3 games
2 Max McGee, Green Bay, 2 games
Bill Miller, Oakland, 1 game
Butch Johnson, Dallas, 2 games
Dan Ross, Cincinnati, 1 game
Roger Craig, San Francisco, 3 games
Ricky Sanders, Washington, 2 games
John Taylor, San Francisco, 2 games
Gary Clark, Washington, 2 games
Don Beebe, Buffalo, 2 games
Michael Irvin, Dallas, 1 game

Most Touchdowns, Game
3 Jerry Rice, San Francisco vs. Denver, 1990
2 Max McGee, Green Bay vs. Kansas City, 1967
Bill Miller, Oakland vs. Green Bay, 1968
John Stallworth, Pittsburgh vs. Dallas, 1979
Cliff Branch, Oakland vs. Philadelphia, 1981
Dan Ross, Cincinnati vs. San Francisco, 1982
Roger Craig, San Francisco vs. Miami, 1985
Ricky Sanders, Washington vs. Denver, 1988
Michael Irvin, Dallas vs. Buffalo, 1993

Interceptions By

Most Interceptions By, Career
3 Chuck Howley, Dallas, 2 games
Rod Martin, Oakland-L.A. Raiders, 2 games
2 Randy Beverly, N.Y. Jets, 1 game
Jake Scott, Miami, 3 games
Mike Wagner, Pittsburgh, 3 games
Mel Blount, Pittsburgh, 4 games
Eric Wright, San Francisco, 4 games
Barry Wilburn, Washington, 1 game

Brad Edwards, Washington, 1 game
Thomas Everett, Dallas, 1 game

Most Interceptions By, Game
3 Rod Martin, Oakland vs. Philadelphia, 1981
2 Randy Beverly, N.Y. Jets vs. Baltimore, 1969
Chuck Howley, Dallas vs. Baltimore, 1971
Jake Scott, Miami vs. Washington, 1973
Barry Wilburn, Washington vs. Denver, 1988
Brad Edwards, Washington vs. Buffalo, 1992
Thomas Everett, Dallas vs. Buffalo, 1993

Yards Gained
Most Yards Gained, Career
75 Willie Brown, Oakland, 2 games
63 Chuck Howley, Dallas, 2 games
Jake Scott, Miami, 3 games
60 Herb Adderley, Green Bay-Dallas, 4 games

Most Yards Gained, Game
75 Willie Brown, Oakland vs. Minnesota, 1977
63 Jake Scott, Miami vs. Washington, 1973
60 Herb Adderley, Green Bay vs. Oakland, 1968

Longest Return
75 Willie Brown, Oakland vs. Minnesota, 1977 (TD)
60 Herb Adderley, Green Bay vs. Oakland, 1968 (TD)
55 Jake Scott, Miami vs. Washington, 1973

Touchdowns
Most Touchdowns, Game
1 Herb Adderley, Green Bay vs. Oakland, 1968
Willie Brown, Oakland vs. Minnesota, 1977
Jack Squirek, L.A. Raiders vs. Washington, 1984
Reggie Phillips, Chicago vs. New England, 1986

Punting
Most Punts, Career
17 Mike Eischeid, Oakland-Minnesota, 3 games
15 Larry Seiple, Miami, 3 games
Mike Horan, Denver, 3 games
14 Ron Widby, Dallas, 2 games
Ray Guy, Oakland-L.A. Raiders, 3 games

Most Punts, Game
9 Ron Widby, Dallas vs. Baltimore, 1971
7 By eight players

Longest Punt
63 Lee Johnson, Cincinnati vs. San Francisco, 1989
62 Rich Camarillo, New England vs. Chicago, 1986
61 Jerrel Wilson, Kansas City vs. Green Bay, 1967

Average Yardage
Highest Average, Punting, Career (10 punts)
46.5 Jerrel Wilson, Kansas City, 2 games (11-511)
41.9 Ray Guy, Oakland-L.A. Raiders, 3 games (14-587)
41.3 Larry Seiple, Miami, 3 games (15-620)

Highest Average, Punting, Game (4 punts)
48.5 Jerrel Wilson, Kansas City vs. Minnesota, 1970 (4-194)
46.3 Jim Miller, San Francisco vs. Cincinnati, 1982 (4-185)
45.3 Jerrel Wilson, Kansas City vs. Green Bay, 1967 (7-317)

Punt Returns
Most Punt Returns, Career
6 Willie Wood, Green Bay, 2 games
Jake Scott, Miami, 3 games
Theo Bell, Pittsburgh, 2 games
Mike Nelms, Washington, 1 game
John Taylor, San Francisco, 2 games
5 Dana McLemore, San Francisco, 1 game
4 By eight players

Most Punt Returns, Game
6 Mike Nelms, Washington vs. Miami, 1983
5 Willie Wood, Green Bay vs. Oakland, 1968
Dana McLemore, San Francisco vs. Miami, 1985
4 By six players

Most Fair Catches, Game
3 Ron Gardin, Baltimore vs. Dallas, 1971
Golden Richards, Dallas vs. Pittsburgh, 1976
Greg Pruitt, L.A. Raiders vs. Washington, 1984
Al Edwards, Buffalo vs. N.Y. Giants, 1991
David Meggett, N.Y. Giants vs. Buffalo, 1991

Yards Gained
Most Yards Gained, Career
94 John Taylor, San Francisco, 2 games
52 Mike Nelms, Washington, 1 game
51 Dana McLemore, San Francisco, 1 game

Most Yards Gained, Game
56 John Taylor, San Francisco vs. Cincinnati, 1989
52 Mike Nelms, Washington vs. Miami, 1983
51 Dana McLemore, San Francisco vs. Miami, 1985

Longest Return
45 John Taylor, San Francisco vs. Cincinnati, 1989
34 Darrell Green, Washington vs. L.A. Raiders, 1984
31 Willie Wood, Green Bay vs. Oakland, 1968

Average Yardage
Highest Average, Career (4 returns)
15.7 John Taylor, San Francisco, 2 games (6-94)
10.8 Neal Colzie, Oakland, 1 game (4-43)
10.2 Dana McLemore, San Francisco, 1 game (5-51)

Highest Average, Game (3 returns)
18.7 John Taylor, San Francisco vs. Cincinnati, 1989 (3-56)
12.7 John Taylor, San Francisco vs. Denver, 1990 (3-38)
11.7 Kelvin Martin, Dallas vs. Buffalo, 1993 (3-35)

Touchdowns
Most Touchdowns, Game
None

Kickoff Returns
Most Kickoff Returns, Career
10 Ken Bell, Denver, 3 games
8 Larry Anderson, Pittsburgh, 2 games
Fulton Walker, Miami, 2 games
7 Preston Pearson, Baltimore-Pittsburgh-Dallas, 5 games
Stephen Starring, New England, 1 game

Most Kickoff Returns, Game
7 Stephen Starring, New England vs. Chicago, 1986
6 Darren Carrington, Denver vs. San Francisco, 1990
5 Larry Anderson, Pittsburgh vs. Los Angeles, 1980
Billy Campfield, Philadelphia vs. Oakland, 1981
David Verser, Cincinnati vs. San Francisco, 1982
Alvin Garrett, Washington vs. L.A. Raiders, 1984
Ken Bell, Denver vs. Washington, 1988

Yards Gained
Most Yards Gained, Career
283 Fulton Walker, Miami, 2 games
207 Larry Anderson, Pittsburgh, 2 games
177 Ken Bell, Denver, 3 games

Most Yards Gained, Game
190 Fulton Walker, Miami vs. Washington, 1983
162 Larry Anderson, Pittsburgh vs. Los Angeles, 1980
153 Stephen Starring, New England vs. Chicago, 1986

Longest Return
98 Fulton Walker, Miami vs. Washington, 1983 (TD)
93 Stanford Jennings, Cincinnati vs. San Francisco, 1989 (TD)
67 Rick Upchurch, Denver vs. Dallas, 1978

Average Yardage
Highest Average, Career (4 returns)
35.4 Fulton Walker, Miami, 2 games (8-283)
25.9 Larry Anderson, Pittsburgh, 2 games (8-207)
24.3 Darren Carrington, Denver, 1 game (6-146)

Highest Average, Game (3 returns)
47.5 Fulton Walker, Miami vs. Washington, 1983 (4-190)
32.4 Larry Anderson, Pittsburgh vs. Los Angeles, 1980 (5-162)
31.3 Rick Upchurch, Denver vs. Dallas, 1978 (3-94)

Touchdowns
Most Touchdowns, Game
1 Fulton Walker, Miami vs. Washington, 1983
Stanford Jennings, Cincinnati vs. San Francisco, 1989

Fumbles
Most Fumbles, Career
5 Roger Staubach, Dallas, 4 games
4 Jim Kelly, Buffalo, 3 games
3 Franco Harris, Pittsburgh, 4 games
Terry Bradshaw, Pittsburgh, 4 games
John Elway, Denver, 3 games
Frank Reich, Buffalo, 3 games

Most Fumbles, Game
3 Roger Staubach, Dallas vs. Pittsburgh, 1976
Jim Kelly, Buffalo vs. Washington, 1992
Frank Reich, Buffalo vs. Dallas, 1993
2 Franco Harris, Pittsburgh vs. Minnesota, 1975
Butch Johnson, Dallas vs. Denver, 1978
Terry Bradshaw, Pittsburgh vs. Dallas, 1979
Joe Montana, San Francisco vs. Cincinnati, 1989
John Elway, Denver vs. San Francisco, 1990

Recoveries
Most Fumbles Recovered, Career
2 Jake Scott, Miami, 3 games (1 own, 1 opp)
Fran Tarkenton, Minnesota, 3 games (2 own)
Franco Harris, Pittsburgh, 4 games (2 own)
Roger Staubach, Dallas, 4 games (2 own)
Bobby Walden, Pittsburgh, 2 games (2 own)
John Fitzgerald, Dallas, 4 games (2 own)
Randy Hughes, Dallas, 3 games (2 opp)
Butch Johnson, Dallas, 2 games (2 own)
Mike Singletary, Chicago, 1 game (2 opp)
John Elway, Denver, 3 games (2 own)
Jimmie Jones, Dallas, 1 game (2 opp)

Most Fumbles Recovered, Game
2 Jake Scott, Miami vs. Minnesota, 1974 (1 own, 1 opp)
Roger Staubach, Dallas vs. Pittsburgh, 1976 (2 own)
Randy Hughes, Dallas vs. Denver, 1978 (2 opp)
Butch Johnson, Dallas vs. Denver, 1978 (2 own)
Mike Singletary, Chicago vs. New England, 1986 (2 opp)
Jimmie Jones, Dallas vs. Buffalo, 1993 (2 opp)

Yards Gained
Most Yards Gained, Game
64 Leon Lett, Dallas vs. Buffalo, 1993 (opp)
49 Mike Bass, Washington vs. Miami, 1973 (opp)
37 Mike Hegman, Dallas vs. Pittsburgh, 1979 (opp)

Longest Return
64 Leon Lett, Dallas vs. Buffalo, 1993
49 Mike Bass, Washington vs. Miami, 1973 (TD)
37 Mike Hegman, Dallas vs. Pittsburgh, 1979 (TD)

Touchdowns

Most Touchdowns, Game

1 Mike Bass, Washington vs. Miami, 1973 (opp 49 yds)
Mike Hegman, Dallas vs. Pittsburgh, 1979 (opp 37 yds)
Jimmie Jones, Dallas vs. Buffalo, 1993 (opp 2 yds)
Ken Norton, Dallas vs. Buffalo, 1993 (opp 9 yds)

Combined Net Yards Gained

(Rushing, receiving, interception returns, punt returns, kickoff returns, and fumble returns)

Attempts

Most Attempts, Career

108 Franco Harris, Pittsburgh, 4 games
72 Roger Craig, San Francisco, 3 games
66 John Riggins, Washington, 2 games

Most Attempts, Game

39 John Riggins, Washington vs. Miami, 1983
35 Franco Harris, Pittsburgh vs. Minnesota, 1975
34 Matt Snell, N.Y. Jets vs. Baltimore, 1969

Yards Gained

Most Yards Gained, Career

468 Franco Harris, Pittsburgh, 4 games
410 Roger Craig, San Francisco, 3 games
391 Lynn Swann, Pittsburgh, 4 games

Most Yards Gained, Game

235 Ricky Sanders, Washington vs. Denver, 1988
220 Jerry Rice, San Francisco vs. Cincinnati, 1989
213 Timmy Smith, Washington vs. Denver, 1988

Sacks

Sacks have been compiled since 1983.

Most Sacks, Career

3 Danny Stubbs, San Francisco, 2 games
Leonard Marshall, N.Y. Giants, 2 games
Charles Haley, San Francisco-Dallas, 3 games
2.5 Dexter Manley, Washington, 3 games
2 By seven players

Most Sacks, Game

2 Dwaine Board, San Francisco vs. Miami, 1985
Dennis Owens, New England vs. Chicago, 1986
Otis Wilson, Chicago vs. New England, 1986
Leonard Marshall, N.Y. Giants vs. Denver, 1987
Alvin Walton, Washington vs. Denver, 1988
Charles Haley, San Francisco vs. Cincinnati, 1989
Danny Stubbs, San Francisco vs. Denver, 1990

Team Records

Games, Victories, Defeats

Most Games

6 Dallas, 1971-72, 1976, 1978-79, 1993
5 Miami, 1972-74, 1983, 1985
Washington, 1973, 1983-84, 1988, 1992
4 Minnesota, 1970, 1974-75, 1977
Pittsburgh, 1975-76, 1979-80
Oakland/L.A. Raiders, 1968, 1977, 1981, 1984
Denver, 1978, 1987-88, 1990
San Francisco, 1982, 1985, 1989-90

Most Consecutive Games

3 Miami, 1972-74
Buffalo, 1991-93
2 Green Bay, 1967-68
Dallas, 1971-72
Minnesota, 1974-75
Pittsburgh, 1975-76, 1979-80
Washington, 1983-84
Denver, 1987-88
San Francisco 1989-90

Most Games Won

4 Pittsburgh, 1975-76, 1979-80
San Francisco, 1982, 1985, 1989-90
3 Oakland/L.A. Raiders, 1977, 1981, 1984
Washington, 1983, 1988, 1992
Dallas, 1972, 1978, 1993
2 Green Bay, 1967-68
Miami, 1973-74
N.Y. Giants, 1987, 1991

Most Consecutive Games Won

2 Green Bay, 1967-68
Miami, 1973-74
Pittsburgh, 1975-76, 1979-80
San Francisco, 1989-90

Most Games Lost

4 Minnesota, 1970, 1974-75, 1977
Denver, 1978, 1987-88, 1990
3 Dallas, 1971, 1976, 1979
Miami, 1972, 1983, 1985
Buffalo, 1991-93
2 Washington, 1973, 1984
Cincinnati, 1982, 1989

Most Consecutive Games Lost

3 Buffalo, 1991-93
2 Minnesota, 1974-75
Denver, 1987-88

Scoring

Most Points, Game

55 San Francisco vs. Denver, 1990
52 Dallas vs. Buffalo, 1993
46 Chicago vs. New England, 1986

Fewest Points, Game

3 Miami vs. Dallas, 1972
6 Minnesota vs. Pittsburgh, 1975
7 By four teams

Most Points, Both Teams, Game

69 Dallas (52) vs. Buffalo (17), 1993
66 Pittsburgh (35) vs. Dallas (31), 1979
65 San Francisco (55) vs. Denver (10), 1990

Fewest Points, Both Teams, Game

21 Washington (7) vs. Miami (14), 1973
22 Minnesota (6) vs. Pittsburgh (16), 1975
23 Baltimore (7) vs. N.Y. Jets (16), 1969

Largest Margin of Victory, Game

45 San Francisco vs. Denver, 1990 (55-10)
36 Chicago vs. New England, 1986 (46-10)
35 Dallas vs. Buffalo, 1993 (52-17)

Most Points, Each Half

1st: 35 Washington vs. Denver, 1988
2nd: 30 N.Y. Giants vs. Denver, 1987

Most Points, Each Quarter

1st: 14 Miami vs. Minnesota, 1974
Oakland vs. Philadelphia, 1981
Dallas vs. Buffalo, 1993
2nd: 35 Washington vs. Denver, 1988
3rd: 21 Chicago vs. New England, 1986
4th: 21 Dallas vs. Buffalo, 1993

Most Points, Both Teams, Each Half

1st: 45 Washington (35) vs. Denver (10), 1988
2nd: 44 Buffalo (24) vs. Washington (20), 1992

Fewest Points, Both Teams, Each Half

1st: 2 Minnesota (0) vs. Pittsburgh (2), 1975
2nd: 7 Miami (0) vs. Washington (7), 1973
Denver (0) vs. Washington (7), 1988

Most Points, Both Teams, Each Quarter

1st: 21 Dallas (14) vs. Buffalo (7), 1993
2nd: 35 Washington (35) vs. Denver (0), 1988
3rd: 24 Washington (14) vs. Buffalo (10), 1992
4th: 28 Dallas (14) vs. Pittsburgh (14), 1979

Touchdowns

Most Touchdowns, Game

8 San Francisco vs. Denver, 1990
7 Dallas vs. Buffalo, 1993
6 Washington vs. Denver, 1988

Fewest Touchdowns, Game

0 Miami vs. Dallas, 1972
1 By 16 teams

Most Touchdowns, Both Teams, Game

9 Pittsburgh (5) vs. Dallas (4), 1979
San Francisco (8) vs. Denver (1), 1990
Dallas (7) vs. Buffalo (2), 1993
7 N.Y. Giants (5) vs. Denver (2), 1987
Washington (6) vs. Denver (1), 1988
Washington (4) vs. Buffalo (3), 1992
6 Green Bay (5) vs. Kansas City (1), 1967
Oakland (4) vs. Minnesota (2), 1977
Pittsburgh (4) vs. Los Angeles (2), 1980
L.A. Raiders (5) vs. Washington (1), 1984
San Francisco (5) vs. Miami (1), 1985
Chicago (5) vs. New England (1), 1986

Fewest Touchdowns, Both Teams, Game

2 Baltimore (1) vs. N.Y. Jets (1), 1969
3 In six games

Points After Touchdown

Most Points After Touchdown, Game

7 San Francisco vs. Denver, 1990
Dallas vs. Buffalo, 1993
6 Washington vs. Denver, 1988
5 Green Bay vs. Kansas City, 1967
Pittsburgh vs. Dallas, 1979
L.A. Raiders vs. Washington, 1984
San Francisco vs. Miami, 1985
Chicago vs. New England, 1986

Most Points After Touchdown, Both Teams, Game

9 Pittsburgh (5) vs. Dallas (4), 1979
Dallas (7) vs. Buffalo (2), 1993
8 San Francisco (7) vs. Denver (1), 1990
7 Washington (6) vs. Denver (1), 1988
Washington (4) vs. Buffalo (3), 1992

Fewest Points After Touchdown, Both Teams, Game

2 Baltimore (1) vs. N.Y. Jets (1), 1969
Baltimore (1) vs. Dallas (1), 1971
Minnesota (0) vs. Pittsburgh (2), 1975

Field Goals

Most Field Goals Attempted, Game

5 N.Y. Jets vs. Baltimore, 1969
Dallas vs. Denver, 1978
4 Green Bay vs. Oakland, 1968
Pittsburgh vs. Dallas, 1976
San Francisco vs. Cincinnati, 1982; 1989
Denver vs. N.Y. Giants, 1987

Most Field Goals Attempted, Both Teams, Game

7 N.Y. Jets (5) vs. Baltimore (2), 1969
San Francisco (4) vs. Cincinnati (3), 1989
6 Dallas (5) vs. Denver (1), 1978
5 Green Bay (4) vs. Oakland (1), 1968
Pittsburgh (4) vs. Dallas (1), 1976
Oakland (3) vs. Philadelphia (2), 1981
Denver (4) vs. N.Y. Giants (1), 1987

Fewest Field Goals Attempted, Both Teams, Game

1 Minnesota (0) vs. Miami (1), 1974
San Francisco (0) vs. Denver (1), 1990

2 Green Bay (0) vs. Kansas City (2), 1967
Miami (1) vs. Washington (1), 1973
Dallas (1) vs. Pittsburgh (1), 1979
Dallas (1) vs. Buffalo (1), 1993

Most Field Goals, Game
4 Green Bay vs. Oakland, 1968
San Francisco vs. Cincinnati, 1982
3 N.Y. Jets vs. Baltimore, 1969
Kansas City vs. Minnesota, 1970
Miami vs. San Francisco, 1985
Chicago vs. New England, 1986
Cincinnati vs. San Francisco, 1989
Washington vs. Buffalo, 1992

Most Field Goals, Both Teams, Game
5 Cincinnati (3) vs. San Francisco (2), 1989
4 Green Bay (4) vs. Oakland (0), 1968
San Francisco (4) vs. Cincinnati (0), 1982
Miami (3) vs. San Francisco (1), 1985
Chicago (3) vs. New England (1), 1986
Buffalo (2) vs. N.Y. Giants (2), 1991
Washington (3) vs. Buffalo (1), 1992
3 In eight games

Fewest Field Goals, Both Teams, Game
0 Miami vs. Washington, 1973
Pittsburgh vs. Minnesota, 1975
1 Green Bay (0) vs. Kansas City (1), 1967
Minnesota (0) vs. Miami (1), 1974
Pittsburgh (0) vs. Dallas (1), 1979
Washington (0) vs. Denver (1), 1988
San Francisco (0) vs. Denver (1), 1990

Safeties

Most Safeties, Game
1 Pittsburgh vs. Minnesota, 1975; vs. Dallas, 1976
Chicago vs. New England, 1986
N.Y. Giants vs. Denver, 1987
Buffalo vs. N.Y. Giants, 1991

First Downs

Most First Downs, Game
31 San Francisco vs. Miami, 1985
28 San Francisco vs. Denver, 1990
25 Washington vs. Denver, 1988
Buffalo vs. Washington, 1992

Fewest First Downs, Game
9 Minnesota vs. Pittsburgh, 1975
Miami vs. Washington, 1983
10 Dallas vs. Baltimore, 1971
Miami vs. Dallas, 1972
11 Denver vs. Dallas, 1978

Most First Downs, Both Teams, Game
50 San Francisco (31) vs. Miami (19), 1985
49 Buffalo (25) vs. Washington (24), 1992
47 N.Y. Giants (24) vs. Denver (23), 1987

Fewest First Downs, Both Teams, Game
24 Dallas (10) vs. Baltimore (14), 1971
26 Minnesota (9) vs. Pittsburgh (17), 1975
27 Pittsburgh (13) vs. Dallas (14), 1976

Rushing

Most First Downs, Rushing, Game
16 San Francisco vs. Miami, 1985
15 Dallas vs. Miami, 1972
14 Washington vs. Miami, 1983
San Francisco vs. Denver, 1990

Fewest First Downs, Rushing, Game
1 New England vs. Chicago, 1986
2 Minnesota vs. Kansas City, 1970; vs. Pittsburgh, 1975; vs. Oakland, 1977
Pittsburgh vs. Dallas, 1979
Miami vs. San Francisco, 1985
3 Miami vs. Dallas, 1972
Philadelphia vs. Oakland, 1981

Most First Downs, Rushing, Both Teams, Game
21 Washington (14) vs. Miami (7), 1983
19 Washington (13) vs. Denver (6), 1988
San Francisco (14) vs. Denver (5), 1990
18 Dallas (15) vs. Miami (3), 1972
Miami (13) vs. Minnesota (5), 1974
San Francisco (16) vs. Miami (2), 1985
N.Y. Giants (10) vs. Buffalo (8), 1991

Fewest First Downs, Rushing, Both Teams, Game
8 Baltimore (4) vs. Dallas (4), 1971
Pittsburgh (2) vs. Dallas (6), 1979
9 Philadelphia (3) vs. Oakland (6), 1981
10 Minnesota (2) vs. Kansas City (8), 1970

Passing

Most First Downs, Passing, Game
18 Buffalo vs. Washington, 1992
17 Miami vs. San Francisco, 1985
16 Denver vs. N.Y. Giants, 1987
San Francisco vs. Cincinnati, 1989

Fewest First Downs, Passing, Game
1 Denver vs. Dallas, 1978
2 Miami vs. Washington, 1983
4 Miami vs. Minnesota, 1974

Most First Downs, Passing, Both Teams, Game
32 Miami (17) vs. San Francisco (15), 1985
30 Buffalo (18) vs. Washington (12), 1992
29 Denver (16) vs. N.Y. Giants (13), 1987

Fewest First Downs, Passing, Both Teams, Game
9 Denver (1) vs. Dallas (8), 1978
10 Minnesota (5) vs. Pittsburgh (5), 1975
11 Dallas (5) vs. Baltimore (6), 1971
Miami (2) vs. Washington (9), 1983

Penalty

Most First Downs, Penalty, Game
4 Baltimore vs. Dallas, 1971
Miami vs. Minnesota, 1974
Cincinnati vs. San Francisco, 1982
Buffalo vs. Dallas, 1993
3 Kansas City vs. Minnesota, 1970
Minnesota vs. Oakland, 1977
Buffalo vs. Washington, 1992

Most First Downs, Penalty, Both Teams, Game
6 Cincinnati (4) vs. San Francisco (2), 1982
5 Baltimore (4) vs. Dallas (1), 1971
Miami (4) vs. Minnesota (1), 1974
Buffalo (3) vs. Washington (2), 1992
4 Kansas City (3) vs. Minnesota (1), 1970
Buffalo (4) vs. Dallas (0), 1993

Fewest First Downs, Penalty, Both Teams, Game
0 Dallas vs. Miami, 1972
Miami vs. Washington, 1973
Dallas vs. Pittsburgh, 1976
Miami vs. San Francisco, 1985
1 Green Bay (0) vs. Kansas City (1), 1967
Miami (0) vs. Washington (1), 1983
Cincinnati (0) vs. San Francisco (1), 1989
San Francisco (0) vs. Denver (1), 1990

Net Yards Gained Rushing and Passing

Most Yards Gained, Game
602 Washington vs. Denver, 1988
537 San Francisco vs. Miami, 1985
461 San Francisco vs. Denver, 1990

Fewest Yards Gained, Game
119 Minnesota vs. Pittsburgh, 1975
123 New England vs. Chicago, 1986
156 Denver vs. Dallas, 1978

Most Yards Gained, Both Teams, Game
929 Washington (602) vs. Denver (327), 1988
851 San Francisco (537) vs. Miami (314), 1985
782 Oakland (429) vs. Minnesota (353), 1977

Fewest Yards Gained, Both Teams, Game
452 Minnesota (119) vs. Pittsburgh (333), 1975
481 Washington (228) vs. Miami (253), 1973
Denver (156) vs. Dallas (325), 1978
497 Minnesota (238) vs. Miami (259), 1974

Rushing

Attempts

Most Attempts, Game
57 Pittsburgh vs. Minnesota, 1975
53 Miami vs. Minnesota, 1974
52 Oakland vs. Minnesota, 1977
Washington vs. Miami, 1983

Fewest Attempts, Game
9 Miami vs. San Francisco, 1985
11 New England vs. Chicago, 1986
17 Denver vs. Washington, 1988; vs. San Francisco, 1990

Most Attempts, Both Teams, Game
81 Washington (52) vs. Miami (29), 1983
78 Pittsburgh (57) vs. Minnesota (21), 1975
Oakland (52) vs. Minnesota (26), 1977
77 Miami (53) vs. Minnesota (24), 1974
Pittsburgh (46) vs. Dallas (31), 1976

Fewest Attempts, Both Teams, Game
49 Miami (9) vs. San Francisco (40), 1985
53 Kansas City (19) vs. Green Bay (34), 1967
55 San Francisco (27) vs. Cincinnati (28), 1989

Yards Gained

Most Yards Gained, Game
280 Washington vs. Denver, 1988
276 Washington vs. Miami, 1983
266 Oakland vs. Minnesota, 1977

Fewest Yards Gained, Game
7 New England vs. Chicago, 1986
17 Minnesota vs. Pittsburgh, 1975
25 Miami vs. San Francisco, 1985

Most Yards Gained, Both Teams, Game
377 Washington (280) vs. Denver (97), 1988
372 Washington (276) vs. Miami (96), 1983
338 N.Y. Giants (172) vs. Buffalo (166), 1991

Fewest Yards Gained, Both Teams, Game
168 Buffalo (43) vs. Washington (125), 1992
171 Baltimore (69) vs. Dallas (102), 1971
174 New England (7) vs. Chicago (167), 1986

Average Gain

Highest Average Gain, Game
7.00 L.A. Raiders vs. Washington, 1984 (33-231)
Washington vs. Denver, 1988 (40-280)
6.64 Buffalo vs. N.Y. Giants, 1991 (25-166)
6.22 Baltimore vs. N.Y. Jets, 1969 (23-143)

Lowest Average Gain, Game
0.64 New England vs. Chicago, 1986 (11-7)
0.81 Minnesota vs. Pittsburgh, 1975 (21-17)
2.23 Baltimore vs. Dallas, 1971 (31-69)

Touchdowns

Most Touchdowns, Game
4 Chicago vs. New England, 1986
3 Green Bay vs. Kansas City, 1967

Miami vs. Minnesota, 1974
San Francisco vs. Denver, 1990
2 Oakland vs. Minnesota, 1977
Pittsburgh vs. Los Angeles, 1980
L.A. Raiders vs. Washington, 1984
San Francisco vs. Miami, 1985
N.Y. Giants vs. Denver, 1987
Washington vs. Denver, 1988; vs. Buffalo, 1992
Buffalo vs. N.Y. Giants, 1991

Fewest Touchdowns, Game
0 By 17 teams

Most Touchdowns, Both Teams, Game
4 Miami (3) vs. Minnesota (1), 1974
Chicago (4) vs. New England (0), 1986
San Francisco (3) vs. Denver (1), 1990
3 Green Bay (3) vs. Kansas City (0), 1967
Pittsburgh (2) vs. Los Angeles (1), 1980
L.A. Raiders (2) vs. Washington (1), 1984
N.Y. Giants (2) vs. Denver (1), 1987
Buffalo (2) vs. N.Y. Giants (1), 1991
Washington (2) vs. Buffalo (1), 1992

Fewest Touchdowns, Both Teams, Game
0 Pittsburgh vs. Dallas, 1976
Oakland vs. Philadelphia, 1981
Cincinnati vs. San Francisco, 1989
1 In seven games

Passing
Attempts

Most Passes Attempted, Game
59 Buffalo vs. Washington, 1992
50 Miami vs. San Francisco, 1985
44 Minnesota vs. Oakland, 1977

Fewest Passes Attempted, Game
7 Miami vs. Minnesota, 1974
11 Miami vs. Washington, 1973
14 Pittsburgh vs. Minnesota, 1975

Most Passes Attempted, Both Teams, Game
92 Buffalo (59) vs. Washington (33), 1992
85 Miami (50) vs. San Francisco (35), 1985
70 Baltimore (41) vs. N.Y. Jets (29), 1969

Fewest Passes Attempted, Both Teams, Game
35 Miami (7) vs. Minnesota (28), 1974
39 Miami (11) vs. Washington (28), 1973
40 Pittsburgh (14) vs. Minnesota (26), 1975
Miami (17) vs. Washington (23), 1983

Completions

Most Passes Completed, Game
29 Miami vs. San Francisco, 1985
Buffalo vs. Washington, 1992
26 Denver vs. N.Y. Giants, 1987
25 Cincinnati vs. San Francisco, 1982

Fewest Passes Completed, Game
4 Miami vs. Washington, 1983
6 Miami vs. Minnesota, 1974
8 Miami vs. Washington, 1973
Denver vs. Dallas, 1978

Most Passes Completed, Both Teams, Game
53 Miami (29) vs. San Francisco (24), 1985
48 Denver (26) vs. N.Y. Giants (22), 1987
47 Buffalo (29) vs. Washington (18), 1992

Fewest Passes Completed, Both Teams, Game
19 Miami (4) vs. Washington (15), 1983
20 Pittsburgh (9) vs. Minnesota (11), 1975
22 Miami (8) vs. Washington (14), 1973

Completion Percentage

Highest Completion Percentage, Game (20 attempts)
88.0 N.Y. Giants vs. Denver, 1987 (25-22)
75.0 San Francisco vs. Denver, 1990 (32-24)
73.5 Cincinnati vs. San Francisco, 1982 (34-25)

Lowest Completion Percentage, Game (20 attempts)
32.0 Denver vs. Dallas, 1978 (25-8)
37.9 Denver vs. San Francisco, 1990 (29-11)
38.5 Denver vs. Washington, 1988 (39-15)

Yards Gained

Most Yards Gained, Game
341 San Francisco vs. Cincinnati, 1989
326 San Francisco vs. Miami, 1985
322 Washington vs. Denver, 1988

Fewest Yards Gained, Game
35 Denver vs. Dallas, 1978
63 Miami vs. Minnesota, 1974
69 Miami vs. Washington, 1973

Most Yards Gained, Both Teams, Game
615 San Francisco (326) vs. Miami (289), 1985
583 Denver (320) vs. N.Y. Giants (263), 1987
552 Washington (322) vs. Denver (230), 1988

Fewest Yards Gained, Both Teams, Game
156 Miami (69) vs. Washington (87), 1973
186 Pittsburgh (84) vs. Minnesota (102), 1975
205 Dallas (100) vs. Miami (105), 1972

Times Sacked

Most Times Sacked, Game
7 Dallas vs. Pittsburgh, 1976
New England vs. Chicago, 1986
6 Kansas City vs. Green Bay, 1967
Washington vs. L.A. Raiders, 1984
Denver vs. San Francisco, 1990
5 Dallas vs. Denver, 1978; vs. Pittsburgh, 1979
Cincinnati vs. San Francisco, 1982; 1989
Denver vs. Washington, 1988
Buffalo vs. Washington, 1992

Fewest Times Sacked, Game
0 Baltimore vs. N.Y. Jets, 1969; vs. Dallas, 1971
Minnesota vs. Pittsburgh, 1975
Pittsburgh vs. Los Angeles, 1980
Philadelphia vs. Oakland, 1981
Washington vs. Buffalo, 1992
1 By 11 teams

Most Times Sacked, Both Teams, Game
10 New England (7) vs. Chicago (3), 1986
9 Kansas City (6) vs. Green Bay (3), 1967
Dallas (7) vs. Pittsburgh (2), 1976
Dallas (5) vs. Denver (4), 1978
Dallas (5) vs. Pittsburgh (4), 1979
Cincinnati (5) vs. San Francisco (4), 1989
8 Washington (6) vs. L.A. Raiders (2), 1984

Fewest Times Sacked, Both Teams, Game
1 Philadelphia (0) vs. Oakland (1), 1981
2 Baltimore (0) vs. N.Y. Jets (2), 1969
Baltimore (0) vs. Dallas (2), 1971
Minnesota (0) vs. Pittsburgh (2), 1975
3 In four games

Touchdowns

Most Touchdowns, Game
5 San Francisco vs. Denver, 1990
4 Pittsburgh vs. Dallas, 1979
Washington vs. Denver, 1988
Dallas vs. Buffalo, 1993
3 Dallas vs. Pittsburgh, 1979
Oakland vs. Philadelphia, 1981
San Francisco vs. Miami, 1985
N.Y. Giants vs. Denver, 1987

Fewest Touchdowns, Game
0 By 14 teams

Most Touchdowns, Both Teams, Game
7 Pittsburgh (4) vs. Dallas (3), 1979
5 Washington (4) vs. Denver (1), 1988
San Francisco (5) vs. Denver (0), 1990
Dallas (4) vs. Buffalo (1), 1993
4 Dallas (2) vs. Pittsburgh (2), 1976
Oakland (3) vs. Philadelphia (1), 1981
San Francisco (3) vs. Miami (1), 1985
N.Y. Giants (3) vs. Denver (1), 1987
Washington (2) vs. Buffalo (2), 1992

Fewest Touchdowns, Both Teams, Game
0 N.Y. Jets vs. Baltimore, 1969
Miami vs. Minnesota, 1974
1 In six games

Interceptions By

Most Interceptions By, Game
4 N.Y. Jets vs. Baltimore, 1969
Dallas vs. Denver, 1978
Washington vs. Buffalo, 1992
Dallas vs. Buffalo, 1993
3 By nine teams

Most Interceptions By, Both Teams, Game
6 Baltimore (3) vs. Dallas (3), 1971
5 Washington (4) vs. Buffalo (1), 1992
4 In seven games

Fewest Interceptions By, Both Teams, Game
0 Buffalo vs. N.Y. Giants, 1991
1 Oakland (0) vs. Green Bay (1), 1968
Miami (0) vs. Dallas (1), 1972
Minnesota (0) vs. Miami (1), 1974
N.Y. Giants (0) vs. Denver (1), 1987
San Francisco (1) vs. Cincinnati (0), 1989

Yards Gained

Most Yards Gained, Game
95 Miami vs. Washington, 1973
91 Oakland vs. Minnesota, 1977
89 Pittsburgh vs. Dallas, 1976

Most Yards Gained, Both Teams, Game
95 Miami (95) vs. Washington (0), 1973
91 Oakland (91) vs. Minnesota (0), 1977
89 Pittsburgh (89) vs. Dallas (0), 1976

Touchdowns

Most Touchdowns, Game
1 Green Bay vs. Oakland, 1968
Oakland vs. Minnesota, 1977
L.A. Raiders vs. Washington, 1984
Chicago vs. New England, 1986

Punting

Most Punts, Game
9 Dallas vs. Baltimore, 1971
8 Washington vs. L.A. Raiders, 1984
7 By seven teams

Fewest Punts, Game
2 Pittsburgh vs. Los Angeles, 1980
Denver vs. N.Y. Giants, 1987
3 By 10 teams

Most Punts, Both Teams, Game
15 Washington (8) vs. L.A. Raiders (7), 1984
13 Dallas (9) vs. Baltimore (4), 1971
Pittsburgh (7) vs. Minnesota (6), 1975

12 In three games

Fewest Punts, Both Teams, Game
5 Denver (2) vs. N.Y. Giants (3), 1987
6 Oakland (3) vs. Philadelphia (3), 1981
7 In five games

Average Yardage
Highest Average, Game (4 punts)
48.50 Kansas City vs. Minnesota, 1970 (4-194)
46.25 San Francisco vs. Cincinnati, 1982 (4-185)
45.29 Kansas City vs. Green Bay, 1967 (7-317)

Lowest Average, Game (4 punts)
31.20 Washington vs. Miami, 1973 (5-156)
32.38 Washington vs. L.A. Raiders, 1984 (8-259)
32.40 Oakland vs. Minnesota, 1977 (5-162)

Punt Returns
Most Punt Returns, Game
6 Washington vs. Miami, 1983
5 By five teams

Fewest Punt Returns, Game
0 Minnesota vs. Miami, 1974
Buffalo vs. N.Y. Giants, 1991
Washington vs. Buffalo, 1992
1 By 12 teams

Most Punt Returns, Both Teams, Game
9 Pittsburgh (5) vs. Minnesota (4), 1975
8 Green Bay (5) vs. Oakland (3), 1968
Baltimore (5) vs. Dallas (3), 1971
Washington (6) vs. Miami (2), 1983
7 Green Bay (4) vs. Kansas City (3), 1967
Oakland (4) vs. Minnesota (3), 1977
San Francisco (5) vs. Miami (2), 1985

Fewest Punt Returns, Both Teams, Game
2 Dallas (1) vs. Miami (1), 1972
Denver (1) vs. N.Y. Giants (1), 1987
Buffalo (0) vs. N.Y. Giants (2), 1991
3 Kansas City (1) vs. Minnesota (2), 1970
Minnesota (0) vs. Miami (3), 1974
Washington (1) vs. Denver (2), 1988
Washington (0) vs. Buffalo (3), 1992
4 L.A. Raiders (2) vs. Washington (2), 1984
Chicago (2) vs. New England (2), 1986
Buffalo (1) vs. Dallas (3), 1993

Yards Gained
Most Yards Gained, Game
56 San Francisco vs. Cincinnati, 1989
52 Washington vs. Miami, 1983
51 San Francisco vs. Miami, 1985

Fewest Yards Gained, Game
−1 Dallas vs. Miami, 1972
0 By eight teams

Most Yards Gained, Both Teams, Game
74 Washington (52) vs. Miami (22), 1983
66 San Francisco (51) vs. Miami (15), 1985
61 San Francisco (56) vs. Cincinnati (5), 1989

Fewest Yards Gained, Both Teams, Game
9 Washington (0) vs. Bufffalo (9), 1992
13 Miami (4) vs. Washington (9), 1973
18 Kansas City (0) vs. Minnesota (18), 1970
Washington (0) vs. Denver (18), 1988

Average Return
Highest Average, Game (3 returns)
18.7 San Francisco vs. Cincinnati, 1989 (3-56)
12.7 San Francisco vs. Denver, 1990 (3-38)
11.7 Dallas vs. Buffalo, 1993 (3-35)

Touchdowns
Most Touchdowns, Game
None

Kickoff Returns
Most Kickoff Returns, Game
9 Denver vs. San Francisco, 1990
7 Oakland vs. Green Bay, 1968
Minnesota vs. Oakland, 1977
Cincinnati vs. San Francisco, 1982
Washington vs. L.A. Raiders, 1984
Miami vs. San Francisco, 1985
New England vs. Chicago, 1986
6 By seven teams

Fewest Kickoff Returns, Game
1 N.Y. Jets vs. Baltimore, 1969
L.A. Raiders vs. Washington, 1984
Washington vs. Buffalo, 1992
2 By six teams

Most Kickoff Returns, Both Teams, Game
12 Denver (9) vs. San Francisco (3), 1990
11 Los Angeles (6) vs. Pittsburgh (5), 1980
Miami (7) vs. San Francisco (4), 1985
New England (7) vs. Chicago (4), 1986
10 Oakland (7) vs. Green Bay (3), 1968

Fewest Kickoff Returns, Both Teams, Game
5 N.Y. Jets (1) vs. Baltimore (4), 1969
Miami (2) vs. Washington (3), 1973
Washington (1) vs. Buffalo (4), 1992
6 In three games

Yards Gained
Most Yards Gained, Game
222 Miami vs. Washington, 1983
196 Denver vs. San Francisco, 1990
173 Denver vs. Dallas, 1978

Fewest Yards Gained, Game
16 Washington vs. Buffalo, 1992
17 L.A. Raiders vs. Washington, 1984
25 N.Y. Jets vs. Baltimore, 1969

Most Yards Gained, Both Teams, Game
279 Miami (222) vs. Washington (57), 1983
245 Denver (196) vs. San Francisco (49), 1990
231 Pittsburgh (162) vs. Los Angeles (79), 1980

Fewest Yards Gained, Both Teams, Game
78 Miami (33) vs. Washington (45), 1973
82 Pittsburgh (32) vs. Minnesota (50), 1975
92 San Francisco (40) vs. Cincinnati (52), 1982

Average Gain
Highest Average, Game (3 returns)
44.0 Cincinnati vs. San Francisco, 1989 (3-132)
37.0 Miami vs. Washington, 1983 (6-222)
32.4 Pittsburgh vs. Los Angeles, 1980 (5-162)

Touchdowns
Most Touchdowns, Game
1 Miami vs. Washington, 1983
Cincinnati vs. San Francisco, 1989

Penalties
Most Penalties, Game
12 Dallas vs. Denver, 1978
10 Dallas vs. Baltimore, 1971
9 Dallas vs. Pittsburgh, 1979

Fewest Penalties, Game
0 Miami vs. Dallas, 1972
Pittsburgh vs. Dallas, 1976
Denver vs. San Francisco, 1990
1 Green Bay vs. Oakland, 1968
Miami vs. Minnesota, 1974; vs. San Francisco, 1985
2 By four teams

Most Penalties, Both Teams, Game
20 Dallas (12) vs. Denver (8), 1978
16 Cincinnati (8) vs. San Francisco (8), 1982
14 Dallas (10) vs. Baltimore (4), 1971
Dallas (9) vs. Pittsburgh (5), 1979

Fewest Penalties, Both Teams, Game
2 Pittsburgh (0) vs. Dallas (2), 1976
3 Miami (0) vs. Dallas (3), 1972
Miami (1) vs. San Francisco (2), 1985
4 Denver (0) vs. San Francisco (4), 1990

Yards Penalized
Most Yards Penalized, Game
133 Dallas vs. Baltimore, 1971
122 Pittsburgh vs. Minnesota, 1975
94 Dallas vs. Denver, 1978

Fewest Yards Penalized, Game
0 Miami vs. Dallas, 1972
Pittsburgh vs. Dallas, 1976
Denver vs. San Francisco, 1990
4 Miami vs. Minnesota, 1974
10 Miami vs. San Francisco, 1985
San Francisco vs. Miami, 1985

Most Yards Penalized, Both Teams, Game
164 Dallas (133) vs. Baltimore (31), 1971
154 Dallas (94) vs. Denver (60), 1978
140 Pittsburgh (122) vs. Minnesota (18), 1975

Fewest Yards Penalized, Both Teams, Game
15 Miami (0) vs. Dallas (15), 1972
20 Pittsburgh (0) vs. Dallas (20), 1976
Miami (10) vs. San Francisco (10), 1985
38 Denver (0) vs. San Francisco (38), 1990

Fumbles
Most Fumbles, Game
8 Buffalo vs. Dallas, 1993
6 Dallas vs. Denver, 1978
Buffalo vs. Washington, 1992
5 Baltimore vs. Dallas, 1971

Fewest Fumbles, Game
0 By 10 teams

Most Fumbles, Both Teams, Game
12 Buffalo (8) vs. Dallas (4), 1993
10 Dallas (6) vs. Denver (4), 1978
8 Dallas (4) vs. Pittsburgh (4), 1976

Fewest Fumbles, Both Teams, Game
0 Los Angeles vs. Pittsburgh, 1980
1 Oakland (0) vs. Minnesota (1), 1977
Oakland (0) vs. Philadelphia (1), 1981
Denver (0) vs. Washington (1), 1988
N.Y. Giants (0) vs. Buffalo (1), 1991
2 In four games

Most Fumbles Lost, Game
5 Buffalo vs. Dallas, 1993
4 Baltimore vs. Dallas, 1971
Denver vs. Dallas, 1978
New England vs. Chicago, 1986
2 In many games

Most Fumbles Lost, Both Teams, Game
7 Buffalo (5) vs. Dallas (2), 1993
6 Denver (4) vs. Dallas (2), 1978
New England (4) vs. Chicago (2), 1986
5 Baltimore (4) vs. Dallas (1), 1971

Fewest Fumbles Lost, Both Teams, Game

0 Green Bay vs. Kansas City, 1967
Dallas vs. Pittsburgh, 1976
Los Angeles vs. Pittsburgh, 1980
Denver vs. N.Y. Giants, 1987
Denver vs. Washington, 1988
Buffalo vs. N.Y. Giants, 1991

Most Fumbles Recovered, Game

8 Dallas vs. Denver, 1978 (4 own, 4 opp)
6 Dallas vs. Buffalo, 1993 (1 own, 5 opp)
5 Chicago vs. New England, 1986 (1 own, 4 opp)

Turnovers

(Number of times losing the ball on interceptions and fumbles.)

Most Turnovers, Game

9 Buffalo vs. Dallas, 1993
8 Denver vs. Dallas, 1978
7 Baltimore vs. Dallas, 1971

Fewest Turnovers, Game

0 Green Bay vs. Oakland, 1968
Miami vs. Minnesota, 1974
Pittsburgh vs. Dallas, 1976
Oakland vs. Minnesota, 1977; vs. Philadelphia, 1981
N.Y. Giants vs. Denver, 1987; vs. Buffalo, 1991
San Francisco vs. Denver, 1990
Buffalo vs. N.Y. Giants, 1991
1 By many teams

Most Turnovers, Both Teams, Game

11 Baltimore (7) vs. Dallas (4), 1971
Buffalo (9) vs. Dallas (2), 1993
10 Denver (8) vs. Dallas (2), 1978
8 New England (6) vs. Chicago (2), 1986

Fewest Turnovers, Both Teams, Game

0 Buffalo vs. N.Y. Giants, 1991
1 N.Y. Giants (0) vs. Denver (1), 1987
2 Green Bay (1) vs. Kansas City (1), 1967
Miami (0) vs. Minnesota (2), 1974
Cincinnati (1) vs. San Francisco (1), 1989

POSTSEASON GAME RECORDS

Compiled by Elias Sports Bureau

Throughout this all-time postseason record section, the following abbreviations are used to indicate various levels of postseason games:

SB — Super Bowl (1966 to date)
AFC — AFC Championship Game (1970 to date) or AFL Championship Game (1960-69)
NFC — NFC Championship Game (1970 to date) or NFL Championship Game (1933-69)
AFC-D — AFC Divisional Playoff Game (1970 to date), AFC Second-Round Playoff Game (1982), AFL Inter-Divisional Playoff Game (1969), or special playoff game to break tie for AFL Division Championship (1963, 1968)
NFC-D — NFC Divisional Playoff Game (1970 to date), NFC Second-Round Playoff Game (1982), NFL Conference Championship Game (1967-69), or special playoff game to break tie for NFL Division or Conference Championship (1941, 1943, 1947, 1950, 1952, 1957, 1958, 1965)
AFC-FR — AFC First-Round Playoff Game (1978 to date)
NFC-FR — NFC First-Round Playoff Game (1978 to date)

Year references are to the season following which the postseason game occurred, even if the game was played in the next calendar year.

Postseason Game Composite Standings

	W	L	Pct.	Pts.	OP
Green Bay Packers	13	5	.722	416	259
San Francisco 49ers	17	10	.630	647	495
Pittsburgh Steelers	16	10	.615	585	518
Washington Redskins*	21	14	.600	738	625
Los Angeles Raiders**	20	14	.588	790	606
Dallas Cowboys	24	17	.585	944	738
Detroit Lions	7	5	.583	269	255
Miami Dolphins	16	12	.571	627	557
Buffalo Bills	11	10	.524	491	454
Chicago Bears	13	13	.500	529	490
Denver Broncos	9	9	.500	356	460
Indianapolis Colts***	8	8	.500	285	300
Philadelphia Eagles	8	9	.471	290	288
Kansas City Chiefs****	6	7	.462	199	259
New York Jets	5	6	.455	216	200
Minnesota Vikings	13	16	.448	525	594
New York Giants	13	17	.433	509	539
Houston Oilers	9	12	.429	351	505
Seattle Seahawks	3	4	.429	128	139
Cincinnati Bengals	5	7	.417	246	257
New England Patriots†	4	6	.400	195	258
Los Angeles Rams††	13	20	.394	501	697
Cleveland Browns	10	18	.357	567	650
San Diego Chargers†††	5	9	.357	247	310
Atlanta Falcons	2	4	.333	119	144
Tampa Bay Buccaneers	1	3	.250	41	94
Phoenix Cardinals††††	1	4	.200	81	134
New Orleans Saints	0	4	.000	56	123

**One game played when franchise was in Boston (lost 21-6).*
***24 games played when franchise was in Oakland (won 15, lost 9, 587 points scored, 435 points allowed).*
****15 games played when franchise was in Baltimore (won 8, lost 7, 264 points scored, 262 points allowed).*
*****One game played when franchise was Dallas Texans (won 20-17).*
†Two games played when franchise was in Boston (won 26-8, lost 51-10).
††One game played when franchise was in Cleveland (won 15-14).
†††One game played when franchise was in Los Angeles (lost 24-16).
††††Two games played when franchise was in Chicago (won 28-21, lost 7-0), three games played when franchise was in St. Louis (lost 30-14, lost 35-23, lost 41-16).

Individual Records

Service

Most Games, Career
27 D. D. Lewis, Dallas (SB-5, NFC-9, NFC-D 12, NFC-FR 1)
26 Larry Cole, Dallas (SB-5, NFC-8, NFC-D-12, NFC-FR 1)
25 Charlie Waters, Dallas (SB-5, NFC-9, NFC-D 10, NFC-FR 1)

Scoring

Points

Most Points, Career
115 George Blanda, Chi. Bears-Houston-Oakland, 19 games (49-pat, 22-fg)
102 Franco Harris, Pittsburgh, 19 games (17-td)
96 Matt Bahr, Pittsburgh-Cleveland-N.Y. Giants, 13 games (39-pat, 19-fg)

Most Points, Game
19 Pat Harder, NFC-D: Detroit vs. Los Angeles, 1952 (2-td, 4-pat, 1-fg)
Paul Hornung, NFC: Green Bay vs. N.Y. Giants, 1961 (1-td, 4-pat, 3-fg)
18 By 19 players

Touchdowns

Most Touchdowns, Career
17 Franco Harris, Pittsburgh, 19 games (16-r, 1-p)
13 Jerry Rice, San Francisco, 13 games (13-p)
12 John Riggins, Washington, 9 games (12-r)
John Stallworth, Pittsburgh, 18 games (12-p)

Most Touchdowns, Game
3 Andy Farkas, NFC-D: Washington vs. N.Y. Giants, 1943 (3-r)
Tom Fears, NFC-D: Los Angeles vs. Chi. Bears, 1950 (3-p)
Otto Graham, NFC: Cleveland vs. Detroit, 1954 (3-r)
Gary Collins, NFC: Cleveland vs. Baltimore, 1964 (3-p)
Craig Baynham, NFC-D: Dallas vs. Cleveland, 1967 (2-r, 1-p)
Fred Biletnikoff, AFC-D: Oakland vs. Kansas City, 1968 (3-p)
Tom Matte, NFC: Baltimore vs. Cleveland, 1968 (3-r)
Larry Schreiber, NFC-D: San Francisco vs. Dallas, 1972 (3-r)
Larry Csonka, AFC: Miami vs. Oakland, 1973 (3-r)
Franco Harris, AFC-D: Pittsburgh vs. Buffalo, 1974 (3-r)
Preston Pearson, NFC: Dallas vs. Los Angeles, 1975 (3-p)
Dave Casper, AFC-D: Oakland vs. Baltimore, 1977 (OT) (3-p)
Alvin Garrett, NFC-FR: Washington vs. Detroit, 1982 (3-p)
John Riggins, NFC-D: Washington vs. L.A. Rams, 1983 (3-r)
Roger Craig, SB: San Francisco vs. Miami, 1984 (1-r, 2-p)
Jerry Rice, NFC-D: San Francisco vs. Minnesota, 1988 (3-p)
Jerry Rice, SB: San Francisco vs. Denver, 1989 (3-p)
Kenneth Davis, AFC: Buffalo vs. L.A. Raiders, 1990 (3-r)
Andre Reed, AFC-FR: Buffalo vs. Houston, 1992 (OT) (3-p)

Most Consecutive Games Scoring Touchdowns
8 John Stallworth, Pittsburgh, 1978-83
7 John Riggins, Washington, 1982-84
Marcus Allen, L.A. Raiders, 1982-85
5 Duane Thomas, Dallas, 1970-71
Franco Harris, Pittsburgh, 1974-75
Franco Harris, Pittsburgh, 1977-79
James Lofton, Green Bay-Buffalo, 1982-90

Points After Touchdown

Most Points After Touchdown, Career
49 George Blanda, Chi. Bears-Houston-Oakland, 19 games (49 att)
41 Rafael Septien, L.A. Rams-Dallas, 15 games (41 att)
39 Matt Bahr, Pittsburgh-Cleveland-N.Y. Giants, 13 games (39 att)

Most Points After Touchdown, Game
8 Lou Groza, NFC: Cleveland vs. Detroit, 1954 (8 att)
Jim Martin, NFC: Detroit vs. Cleveland, 1957 (8 att)
George Blanda, AFC-D: Oakland vs. Houston, 1969 (8 att)
7 Danny Villanueva, NFC-D: Dallas vs. Cleveland, 1967 (7 att)
Raul Allegre, NFC-D: N.Y. Giants vs. San Francisco, 1986 (7 att)
Mike Cofer, SB: San Francisco vs. Denver, 1989 (8 att)
Lin Elliott, SB: Dallas vs. Buffalo, 1992 (7 att)
6 George Blair, AFC: San Diego vs. Boston, 1963 (6 att)
Mark Moseley, NFC-D: Washington vs. L.A. Rams, 1983 (6 att)
Uwe von Schamann, AFC: Miami vs. Pittsburgh, 1984 (6 att)
Ali Haji-Sheikh, SB: Washington vs. Denver, 1987 (6 att)
Scott Norwood, AFC: Buffalo vs. L.A. Raiders, 1990 (7 att)

Most Points After Touchdown, No Misses, Career
49 George Blanda, Chi. Bears-Houston-Oakland, 19 games
41 Rafael Septien, L.A. Rams-Dallas, 14 games
39 Matt Bahr, Pittsburgh-Cleveland-N.Y. Giants, 13 games

Field Goals

Most Field Goals Attempted, Career
39 George Blanda, Chi. Bears-Houston-Oakland, 19 games
31 Mark Moseley, Washington-Cleveland, 11 games
26 Roy Gerela, Houston-Pittsburgh, 15 games

Most Field Goals Attempted, Game
6 George Blanda, AFC: Oakland vs. Houston, 1967
David Ray, NFC-D: Los Angeles vs. Dallas, 1973
Mark Moseley, AFC-D: Cleveland vs. N.Y. Jets, 1986 (OT)
Matt Bahr, NFC: N.Y. Giants vs. San Francisco, 1990
Steve Christie, AFC: Buffalo vs. Miami, 1992
5 Jerry Kramer, NFC: Green Bay vs. N.Y. Giants, 1962
Gino Cappelletti, AFC-D: Boston vs. Buffalo, 1963
Pete Gogolak, AFC: Buffalo vs. San Diego, 1965
Jim Turner, SB: N.Y. Jets vs. Baltimore, 1968
Jan Stenerud, AFC-D: Kansas City vs. N.Y. Jets, 1969
George Blanda, AFC-D: Oakland vs. Pittsburgh, 1973
Tony Franklin, AFC-FR: New England vs. N.Y. Jets, 1985
Ed Murray, NFC-D: Detroit vs. San Francisco, 1983
Mark Moseley, NFC: Washington vs. San Francisco, 1983
Tony Franklin, AFC-FR: New England vs. N.Y. Jets, 1985
Tony Zendejas, AFC-FR: Houston vs. Seattle, 1987 (OT)
Chuck Nelson, NFC-D: Minnesota vs. San Francisco, 1987
Luis Zendejas, NFC-D: Philadelphia vs. Chicago, 1988
4 By many players

Most Field Goals, Career
22 George Blanda, Chi. Bears-Houston-Oakland, 19 games
20 Toni Fritsch, Dallas-Houston, 14 games
19 Matt Bahr, Pittsburgh-Cleveland-N.Y. Giants, 13 games

Most Field Goals, Game
5 Chuck Nelson, NFC-D: Minnesota vs. San Francisco, 1987
Matt Bahr, NFC: N.Y. Giants vs. San Francisco, 1990
Steve Christie, AFC: Buffalo vs. Miami, 1992
4 Gino Cappelletti, AFC-D: Boston vs. Buffalo, 1963
George Blanda, AFC: Oakland vs. Houston, 1967
Don Chandler, SB: Green Bay vs. Oakland, 1967
Curt Knight, NFC: Washington vs. Dallas, 1972
George Blanda, AFC-D: Oakland vs. Pittsburgh, 1973
Ray Wersching, SB: San Francisco vs. Cincinnati, 1981
Tony Franklin, AFC-FR: New England vs. N.Y. Jets, 1985
Jess Atkinson, NFC-FR: Washington vs. L.A. Rams, 1986
Luis Zendejas, NFC-D: Philadelphia vs. Chicago, 1988
Gary Anderson, AFC-FR: Pittsburgh vs. Houston, 1989 (OT)
3 By many players

Most Consecutive Field Goals
15 Rafael Septien, Dallas, 1978-82
9 Chuck Nelson, Minnesota, 1987
8 Tony Fritsch, Houston, 1978-79

Longest Field Goal
58 Pete Stoyanovich, AFC-FR: Miami vs. Kansas City, 1990
54 Ed Murray, NFC-D: Detroit vs. San Francisco, 1983
53 Al Del Greco, AFC-FR: Houston vs. N.Y. Jets, 1991

Safeties

Most Safeties, Game
1 Bill Willis, NFC-D: Cleveland vs. N.Y. Giants, 1950
Carl Eller, NFC-D: Minnesota vs. Los Angeles, 1969
George Andrie, NFC-D: Dallas vs. Detroit, 1970
Alan Page, NFC-D: Minnesota vs. Dallas, 1971
Dwight White, SB: Pittsburgh vs. Minnesota, 1974
Reggie Harrison, SB: Pittsburgh vs. Dallas, 1975
Jim Jensen, NFC-D: Dallas vs. Los Angeles, 1976
Ted Washington, AFC: Houston vs. Pittsburgh, 1978
Randy White, NFC-D: Dallas vs. Los Angeles, 1979
Henry Waechter, SB: Chicago vs. New England, 1985
Rulon Jones, AFC-FR: Denver vs. New England, 1986
George Martin, SB: N.Y. Giants vs. Denver, 1986
D.D. Hoggard, AFC: Cleveland vs. Denver, 1987
Bruce Smith, SB: Buffalo vs. N.Y. Giants, 1990
Reggie White, NFC-FR: Philadelphia vs. New Orleans, 1992

Rushing

Attempts

Most Attempts, Career
400 Franco Harris, Pittsburgh, 19 games
302 Tony Dorsett, Dallas, 17 games
251 John Riggins, Washington, 9 games

Most Attempts, Game
38 Ricky Bell, NFC-D: Tampa Bay vs. Philadelphia, 1979
John Riggins, SB: Washington vs. Miami, 1982
37 Lawrence McCutcheon, NFC-D: Los Angeles vs. St. Louis, 1975
John Riggins, NFC-D: Washington vs. Minnesota, 1982
36 John Riggins, NFC: Washington vs. Dallas, 1982
John Riggins, NFC: Washington vs. San Francisco, 1983

Yards Gained

Most Yards Gained, Career
1,556 Franco Harris, Pittsburgh, 19 games
1,383 Tony Dorsett, Dallas, 17 games
996 John Riggins, Washington, 9 games

Most Yards Gained, Game
248 Eric Dickerson, NFC-D: L.A. Rams vs. Dallas, 1985
206 Keith Lincoln, AFC: San Diego vs. Boston, 1963
204 Timmy Smith, SB: Washington vs. Denver, 1987

Most Games, 100 or More Yards Rushing, Career
6 John Riggins, Washington, 9 games
5 Franco Harris, Pittsburgh, 19 games
Marcus Allen, L.A. Raiders, 10 games
4 Larry Csonka, Miami, 12 games
Chuck Foreman, Minnesota, 13 games
Thurman Thomas, Buffalo, 13 games
Emmitt Smith, Dallas, 5 games

Most Consecutive Games, 100 or More Yards Rushing
6 John Riggins, Washington, 1982-83
4 Thurman Thomas, Buffalo, 1990-91
3 Larry Csonka, Miami, 1973-74
Franco Harris, Pittsburgh, 1974-75
Marcus Allen, L.A. Raiders, 1983
Emmitt Smith, Dallas, 1992 (current)

Longest Run From Scrimmage
80 Roger Craig, NFC-D: San Francisco vs. Minnesota, 1988 (TD)
74 Marcus Allen, SB: L.A. Raiders vs. Washington, 1983 (TD)
71 Hugh McElhenny, NFC-D: San Francisco vs. Detroit, 1957
James Lofton, NFC-D: Green Bay vs. Dallas, 1982 (TD)

Average Gain

Highest Average Gain, Career (50 attempts)
6.71 Timmy Smith, Washington, 3 games (51-342)
6.67 Paul Lowe, L.A. Chargers-San Diego, 5 games (57-380)
5.75 Marcus Allen, L.A. Raiders, 10 games (167-961)

Highest Average Gain, Game (10 attempts)
15.90 Elmer Angsman, NFC: Chi. Cardinals vs. Philadelphia, 1947 (10-159)
15.85 Keith Lincoln, AFC: San Diego vs. Boston, 1963 (13-206)
10.90 Bill Osmanski, NFC: Chi. Bears vs. Washington, 1940 (10-109)

Touchdowns

Most Touchdowns, Career
16 Franco Harris, Pittsburgh, 19 games
12 John Riggins, Washington, 9 games
9 Larry Csonka, Miami, 12 games
Tony Dorsett, Dallas, 17 games

Most Touchdowns, Game
3 Andy Farkas, NFC-D: Washington vs. N.Y. Giants, 1943
Otto Graham, NFC: Cleveland vs. Detroit, 1954
Tom Matte, NFC: Baltimore vs. Cleveland, 1968
Larry Schreiber, NFC-D: San Francisco vs. Dallas, 1972
Larry Csonka, AFC: Miami vs. Oakland, 1973
Franco Harris, AFC-D: Pittsburgh vs. Buffalo, 1974
John Riggins, NFC-D: Washington vs. L.A. Rams, 1983
Kenneth Davis, AFC: Buffalo vs. L.A. Raiders, 1990

Most Consecutive Games Rushing for Touchdowns
7 John Riggins, Washington, 1982-84
5 Franco Harris, Pittsburgh, 1974-75
Franco Harris, Pittsburgh, 1977-79
3 By many players

Passing

Passer Rating

Highest Passer Rating, Career (100 attempts)
116.7 Troy Aikman, Dallas, 4 games
104.8 Bart Starr, Green Bay, 10 games
98.2 Joe Montana, San Francisco, 19 games

Attempts

Most Passes Attempted, Career
593 Joe Montana, San Francisco, 19 games
456 Terry Bradshaw, Pittsburgh, 19 games
410 Roger Staubach, Dallas, 20 games

Most Passes Attempted, Game
64 Bernie Kosar, AFC-D: Cleveland vs. N.Y. Jets, 1986 (OT)
58 Jim Kelly, SB: Buffalo vs. Washington, 1991
54 Randall Cunningham, NFC-D: Philadelphia vs. Chicago, 1988
Jim Kelly, AFC-D: Buffalo vs. Cleveland, 1989

Completions

Most Passes Completed, Career
375 Joe Montana, San Francisco, 19 games
261 Terry Bradshaw, Pittsburgh, 19 games
223 Roger Staubach, Dallas, 20 games

Most Passes Completed, Game
36 Warren Moon, AFC-FR: Houston vs. Buffalo, 1992 (OT)
33 Dan Fouts, AFC-D: San Diego vs. Miami, 1981 (OT)
Bernie Kosar, AFC-D: Cleveland vs. N.Y. Jets, 1986 (OT)
32 Neil Lomax, NFC-FR: St. Louis vs. Green Bay, 1982
Danny White, NFC-FR: Dallas vs. L.A. Rams, 1983

Completion Percentage

Highest Completion Percentage, Career (100 attempts)
68.6 Troy Aikman, Dallas, 4 games (105-72)
66.3 Ken Anderson, Cincinnati, 6 games (166-110)
64.3 Warren Moon, Houston, 8 games (308-198)

Highest Completion Percentage, Game (15 completions)
88.0 Phil Simms, SB: N.Y. Giants vs. Denver, 1986 (25-22)
86.7 Joe Montana, NFC: San Francisco vs. L.A. Rams, 1989 (30-26)
84.2 David Woodley, AFC-FR: Miami vs. New England, 1982 (19-16)

Yards Gained

Most Yards Gained, Career
4,758 Joe Montana, San Francisco, 19 games
3,833 Terry Bradshaw, Pittsburgh, 19 games
3,019 John Elway, Denver, 13 games

Most Yards Gained, Game
489 Bernie Kosar, AFC-D: Cleveland vs. N.Y. Jets, 1986 (OT)
433 Dan Fouts, AFC-D: San Diego vs. Miami, 1981 (OT)
421 Dan Marino, AFC: Miami vs. Pittsburgh, 1984

Most Games, 300 or More Yards Passing, Career
5 Dan Fouts, San Diego, 7 games
Joe Montana, San Francisco, 19 games
3 Terry Bradshaw, Pittsburgh, 19 games
Danny White, Dallas, 17 games
Dan Marino, Miami, 10 games
Warren Moon, Houston, 8 games
Jim Kelly, Buffalo, 11 games
2 Daryle Lamonica, Buffalo-Oakland, 13 games
Ken Anderson, Cincinnati, 6 games
Bernie Kosar, Cleveland, 7 games
John Elway, Denver, 13 games

Most Consecutive Games, 300 or More Yards Passing
4 Dan Fouts, San Diego, 1979-81
3 Jim Kelly, Buffalo 1989-90
2 Daryle Lamonica, Oakland, 1968
Ken Anderson, Cincinnati, 1981-82
Terry Bradshaw, Pittsburgh, 1979-82
Joe Montana, San Francisco, 1983-84
Dan Marino, Miami, 1984
Warren Moon, Houston, 1991-92 (current)

Longest Pass Completion
93 Daryle Lamonica (to Dubenion), AFC-D: Buffalo vs. Boston, 1963 (TD)
88 George Blanda (to Cannon), AFC: Houston vs. L.A. Chargers, 1960 (TD)
86 Don Meredith (to Hayes), NFC-D: Dallas vs. Cleveland, 1967 (TD)

Average Gain

Highest Average Gain, Career (100 attempts)
8.66 Troy Aikman, Dallas, 4 games (105-909)
8.45 Joe Theismann, Washington, 10 games (211-1,782)
8.43 Jim Plunkett, Oakland-L.A. Raiders, 10 games (272-2,293)

Highest Average Gain, Game (20 attempts)
14.71 Terry Bradshaw, SB: Pittsburgh vs. Los Angeles, 1979 (21-309)
13.33 Bob Waterfield, NFC-D: Los Angeles vs. Chi. Bears, 1950 (21-280)
13.16 Dan Marino, AFC: Miami vs. Pittsburgh, 1984 (32-421)

Touchdowns

Most Touchdown Passes, Career
39 Joe Montana, San Francisco, 19 games
30 Terry Bradshaw, Pittsburgh, 19 games
24 Roger Staubach, Dallas, 20 games

Most Touchdown Passes, Game
6 Daryle Lamonica, AFC-D: Oakland vs. Houston, 1969
5 Sid Luckman, NFC: Chi. Bears vs. Washington, 1943
Daryle Lamonica, AFC-D: Oakland vs. Kansas City, 1968
Joe Montana, SB: San Francisco vs. Denver, 1989
4 Otto Graham, NFC: Cleveland vs. Los Angeles, 1950
Tobin Rote, NFC: Detroit vs. Cleveland, 1957
Bart Starr, NFC: Green Bay vs. Dallas, 1966
Ken Stabler, AFC-D: Oakland vs. Miami, 1974
Roger Staubach, NFC: Dallas vs. Los Angeles, 1975
Terry Bradshaw, SB: Pittsburgh vs. Dallas, 1978
Don Strock, AFC-D: Miami vs. San Diego, 1981 (OT)

Lynn Dickey, NFC-FR: Green Bay vs. St. Louis, 1982
Dan Marino, AFC: Miami vs. Pittsburgh, 1984
Phil Simms, NFC-D: N.Y. Giants vs. San Francisco, 1986
Doug Williams, SB: Washington vs. Denver, 1987
Jim Kelly, AFC-D: Buffalo vs. Cleveland, 1989
Joe Montana, NFC-D: San Francisco vs. Minnesota, 1989
Warren Moon, AFC-FR: Houston vs. Buffalo, 1992 (OT)
Frank Reich, AFC-FR: Buffalo vs. Houston, 1992 (OT)
Troy Aikman, SB: Dallas vs. Buffalo, 1992

Most Consecutive Games, Touchdown Passes
10 Ken Stabler, Oakland, 1973-77
9 John Elway, Denver, 1984-89
8 Terry Bradshaw, Pittsburgh, 1977-82
Joe Montana, San Francisco, 1981-84
Joe Montana, San Francisco, 1988-90 (current)

Had Intercepted
Lowest Percentage, Passes Had Intercepted, Career (100 attempts)
0.95 Troy Aikman, Dallas, 4 games (105-1)
1.41 Bart Starr, Green Bay, 10 games (213-3)
1.75 Phil Simms, N.Y. Giants, 8 games (228-4)

Most Attempts Without Interception, Game
48 Warren Moon, AFC-FR: Houston vs. Pittsburgh, 1989 (OT)
47 Daryle Lamonica, AFC: Oakland vs. N.Y. Jets, 1968
42 Dan Fouts, AFC-FR: San Diego vs. Pittsburgh, 1982

Most Passes Had Intercepted, Career
26 Terry Bradshaw, Pittsburgh, 19 games
21 Jim Kelly, Buffalo, 11 games
19 Roger Staubach, Dallas, 20 games

Most Passes Had Intercepted, Game
6 Frank Filchock, NFC: N.Y. Giants vs. Chi. Bears, 1946
Bobby Layne, NFC: Detroit vs. Cleveland, 1954
Norm Van Brocklin, NFC: Los Angeles vs. Cleveland, 1955
5 Frank Filchock, NFC: Washington vs. Chi. Bears, 1940
George Blanda, AFC: Houston vs. San Diego, 1961
George Blanda, AFC: Houston vs. Dall. Texans, 1962 (OT)
Y.A. Tittle, NFC: N.Y. Giants vs. Chicago, 1963
Mike Phipps, AFC-D: Cleveland vs. Miami, 1972
Dan Pastorini, AFC: Houston vs. Pittsburgh, 1978
Dan Fouts, AFC-D: San Diego vs. Houston, 1979
Tommy Kramer, NFC-D: Minnesota vs. Philadelphia, 1980
Dan Fouts, AFC-D: San Diego vs. Miami, 1982
Richard Todd, AFC: N.Y. Jets vs Miami, 1982
Gary Danielson, NFC-D: Detroit vs. San Francisco, 1983
Jay Schroeder, AFC: L.A. Raiders vs. Buffalo, 1990
4 By many players

Pass Receiving
Receptions
Most Receptions, Career
75 Jerry Rice, San Francisco, 13 games
73 Cliff Branch, Oakland-L.A. Raiders, 22 games
70 Fred Biletnikoff, Oakland, 19 games

Most Receptions, Game
13 Kellen Winslow, AFC-D: San Diego vs. Miami, 1981 (OT)
Thurman Thomas, AFC-D: Buffalo vs. Cleveland, 1989
12 Raymond Berry, NFC: Baltimore vs. N.Y. Giants, 1958
11 Dante Lavelli, NFC: Cleveland vs. Los Angeles, 1950
Dan Ross, SB: Cincinnati vs. San Francisco, 1981
Franco Harris, AFC-FR: Pittsburgh vs. San Diego, 1982
Steve Watson, AFC-D: Denver vs. Pittsburgh, 1984
John L. Williams, AFC-D: Seattle vs. Cincinnati, 1988
Jerry Rice, SB: San Francisco vs. Cincinnati, 1988
Ernest Givins, AFC-FR: Houston vs. Pittsburgh, 1989 (OT)

Most Consecutive Games, Pass Receptions
22 Drew Pearson, Dallas, 1973-83
18 Paul Warfield, Cleveland-Miami, 1964-74
Cliff Branch, Oakland-L.A. Raiders, 1974-83
17 John Stallworth, Pittsburgh, 1974-84

Yards Gained
Most Yards Gained, Career
1,289 Cliff Branch, Oakland-L.A. Raiders, 22 games
1,180 Jerry Rice, San Francisco, 13 games
1,167 Fred Biletnikoff, Oakland, 19 games

Most Yards Gained, Game
227 Anthony Carter, NFC-D: Minnesota vs. San Francisco, 1987
215 Jerry Rice, SB: San Francisco vs. Cincinnati, 1988
198 Tom Fears, NFC-D: Los Angeles vs. Chi. Bears, 1950

Most Games, 100 or More Yards Receiving, Career
5 John Stallworth, Pittsburgh, 18 games
Jerry Rice, San Francisco, 13 games
Andre Reed, Buffalo, 13 games
4 Fred Biletnikoff, Oakland, 19 games
Dwight Clark, San Francisco, 7 games
Art Monk, Washington, 15 games
3 Tom Fears, L.A. Rams, 6 games
Cliff Branch, Oakland-L.A. Raiders, 22 games
Tony Nathan, Miami, 10 games
Mark Duper, Miami, 10 games
James Lofton, Green Bay-Buffalo, 13 games
Vance Johnson, Denver, 10 games
Ernest Givins, Houston, 9 games

Most Consecutive Games, 100 or More Yards Receiving, Career
3 Tom Fears, Los Angeles, 1950-51
Jerry Rice, San Francisco, 1988-89
2 Lenny Moore, Baltimore, 1958-59
Fred Biletnikoff, Oakland, 1968
Paul Warfield, Miami, 1971
Charlie Joiner, San Diego, 1980-81
Dwight Clark, San Francisco, 1981
Cris Collinsworth, Cincinnati, 1981-82
John Stallworth, Pittsburgh, 1979-82
Wesley Walker, N.Y. Jets, 1982
Charlie Brown, Washington, 1983
Steve Largent, Seattle, 1984-87
Vance Johnson, Denver, 1986-87
Andre Reed, Buffalo, 1989-90
James Lofton, Buffalo, 1990
Ernest Givins, Houston, 1991-92 (current)

Longest Reception
93 Elbert Dubenion (from Lamonica), AFC-D: Buffalo vs. Boston, 1963 (TD)
88 Billy Cannon (from Blanda), AFC: Houston vs. L.A. Chargers, 1960 (TD)
86 Bob Hayes (from Meredith), NFC: Dallas vs. Cleveland, 1967 (TD)

Average Gain
Highest Average Gain, Career (20 receptions)
23.7 Willie Gault, Chicago-L.A. Raiders, 10 games (21-497)
22.8 Harold Jackson, L.A. Rams-New England-Minnesota-Seattle, 14 games (24-548)
20.7 Charlie Brown, Washington, 8 games (31-643)

Highest Average Gain, Game (3 receptions)
46.3 Harold Jackson, NFC: Los Angeles vs. Minnesota, 1974 (3-139)
42.7 Billy Cannon, AFC: Houston vs. L.A. Chargers, 1960 (3-128)
42.0 Lenny Moore, NFC: Baltimore vs. N.Y. Giants, 1959 (3-126)

Touchdowns
Most Touchdowns, Career
13 Jerry Rice, San Francisco, 13 games
12 John Stallworth, Pittsburgh, 18 games
10 Fred Biletnikoff, Oakland, 19 games

Most Touchdowns, Game
3 Tom Fears, NFC-D: Los Angeles vs. Chi. Bears, 1950
Gary Collins, NFC: Cleveland vs. Baltimore, 1964
Fred Biletnikoff, AFC-D: Oakland vs. Kansas City, 1968
Preston Pearson, NFC: Dallas vs. Los Angeles, 1975
Dave Casper, AFC-D: Oakland vs. Baltimore, 1977 (OT)
Alvin Garrett, NFC-FR: Washington vs. Detroit, 1982
Jerry Rice, NFC-D: San Francisco vs. Minnesota, 1988
Jerry Rice, SB: San Francisco vs. Denver, 1989
Andre Reed, AFC-FR: Buffalo vs. Houston, 1992 (OT)

Most Consecutive Games, Touchdown Passes Caught
8 John Stallworth, Pittsburgh, 1978-83
5 James Lofton, Green Bay-Buffalo, 1982-90
4 Lynn Swann, Pittsburgh, 1978-79
Harold Carmichael, Philadelphia, 1978-80
Fred Solomon, San Francisco, 1983-84
Jerry Rice, San Francisco, 1988-89
John Taylor, San Francisco, 1988-89

Interceptions By
Most Interceptions, Career
9 Charlie Waters, Dallas, 25 games
Bill Simpson, Los Angeles-Buffalo, 11 games
Ronnie Lott, San Francisco-L.A. Raiders, 20 games
8 Lester Hayes, Oakland-L.A. Raiders, 13 games
7 Willie Brown, Oakland, 17 games
Dennis Thurman, Dallas, 14 games

Most Interceptions, Game
4 Vernon Perry, AFC-D: Houston vs. San Diego, 1979
3 Joe Laws, NFC: Green Bay vs. N.Y. Giants, 1944
Charlie Waters, NFC-D: Dallas vs. Chicago, 1977
Rod Martin, SB: Oakland vs. Philadelphia, 1980
Dennis Thurman, NFC-D: Dallas vs. Green Bay, 1982
A.J. Duhe, AFC: Miami vs. N.Y. Jets, 1982
2 By many players

Most Consecutive Games, Interceptions
3 Warren Lahr, Cleveland, 1950-51
Ken Gorgal, Cleveland, 1950-53
Joe Schmidt, Detroit, 1954-57
Emmitt Thomas, Kansas City, 1969
Mel Renfro, Dallas, 1970
Rick Volk, Baltimore, 1970-71
Mike Wagner, Pittsburgh, 1975-76
Randy Hughes, Dallas, 1977-78
Vernon Perry, Houston, 1979-80
Lester Hayes, Oakland, 1980
Gerald Small, Miami, 1982
Lester Hayes, L.A. Raiders, 1982-83
Fred Marion, New England, 1985
John Harris, Seattle-Minnesota, 1984-87
Felix Wright, Cleveland, 1987-88
Kurt Gouveia, Washington, 1991

Yards Gained
Most Yards Gained, Career
196 Willie Brown, Oakland, 17 games
187 Ronnie Lott, San Francisco-L.A. Raiders, 20 games
151 Glen Edwards, Pittsburgh-San Diego, 17 games

Most Yards Gained, Game
98 Darrol Ray, AFC-FR: N.Y. Jets vs. Cincinnati, 1982
94 LeRoy Irvin, NFC-FR: L.A. Rams vs. Dallas, 1983
88 Walt Sumner, NFC-D: Cleveland vs. Dallas, 1969

Longest Return
98 Darrol Ray, AFC-FR: N.Y. Jets vs. Cincinnati, 1982 (TD)
94 LeRoy Irvin, NFC-FR: L.A. Rams vs. Dallas, 1983
88 Walt Sumner, NFC-D: Cleveland vs. Dallas, 1969 (TD)

Touchdowns
Most Touchdowns, Career
3 Willie Brown, Oakland, 17 games
2 Lester Hayes, Oakland-L.A. Raiders, 13 games
Ronnie Lott, San Francisco-L.A. Raiders, 20 games
Darrell Green, Washington, 16 games

Most Touchdowns, Game

1 By 53 players. Last time: Eric Allen, NFC-FR: Philadelphia vs. New Orleans, 1992

Punting

Most Punts, Career

111 Ray Guy, Oakland-L.A. Raiders, 22 games
84 Danny White, Dallas, 18 games
73 Mike Eischeid, Oakland-Minnesota, 14 games

Most Punts, Game

14 Dave Jennings, AFC-D: N.Y. Jets vs. Cleveland, 1986 (OT)
12 David Lee, AFC-D: Baltimore vs. Oakland, 1977 (OT)
11 Ken Strong, NFC: N.Y. Giants vs. Chi. Bears, 1933
Jim Norton, AFC: Houston vs. Oakland, 1967
Ode Burrell, AFC-D: Houston vs. Oakland, 1969
Dale Hatcher, NFC: L.A. Rams vs. Chicago, 1985

Longest Punt

76 Ed Danowski, NFC: N.Y. Giants vs. Detroit, 1935
Mike Horan, AFC: Denver vs. Buffalo, 1991
72 Charlie Conerly, NFC-D: N.Y. Giants vs. Cleveland, 1950
Yale Lary, NFC: Detroit vs. Cleveland, 1953
71 Ray Guy, AFC: Oakland vs. San Diego, 1980

Average Yardage

Highest Average, Career (20 punts)

44.5 Rich Camarillo, New England, 6 games (35-1,559)
44.4 Lee Johnson, Cleveland-Cincinnati, 7 games (28-1,244)
43.8 John Kidd, Buffalo-San Diego, 5 games (26-1,139)

Highest Average, Game (4 punts)

56.0 Ray Guy, AFC: Oakland vs. San Diego, 1980 (4-224)
52.5 Sammy Baugh, NFC: Washington vs. Chi. Bears, 1942 (6-315)
51.6 Lee Johnson, AFC-D: Cincinnati vs. L.A. Raiders, 1990 (5-258)

Punt Returns

Most Punt Returns, Career

25 Theo Bell, Pittsburgh-Tampa Bay, 10 games
21 Gerald McNeil, Cleveland-Houston, 8 games
19 Willie Wood, Green Bay, 10 games
Butch Johnson, Dallas-Denver, 18 games
Phil McConkey, N.Y. Giants, 5 games

Most Punt Returns, Game

7 Ron Gardin, AFC-D: Baltimore vs. Cincinnati, 1970
Carl Roaches, AFC-FR: Houston vs. Oakland, 1980
Gerald McNeil, AFC-D: Cleveland vs. N.Y. Jets, 1986 (OT)
Phil McConkey, NFC-D: N.Y. Giants vs. San Francisco, 1986
6 George McAfee, NFC-D: Chi. Bears vs. Los Angeles, 1950
Eddie Brown, NFC-D: Washington vs. Minnesota, 1976
Theo Bell, AFC: Pittsburgh vs. Houston, 1978
Eddie Brown, NFC: Los Angeles vs. Tampa Bay, 1979
John Sciarra, NFC: Philadelphia vs. Dallas, 1980
Kurt Sohn, AFC: N.Y. Jets vs. Miami, 1982
Mike Nelms, SB: Washington vs. Miami, 1982
Anthony Carter, NFC-FR: Minnesota vs. New Orleans, 1987
5 By many players

Yards Gained

Most Yards Gained, Career

237 Anthony Carter, Minnesota, 7 games
221 Neal Colzie, Oakland-Miami-Tampa Bay, 10 games
211 Gerald McNeil, Cleveland-Houston, 8 games

Most Yards Gained, Game

143 Anthony Carter, NFC-FR: Minnesota vs. New Orleans, 1987
141 Bob Hayes, NFC-D: Dallas vs. Cleveland, 1967
102 Charley Trippi, NFC: Chi. Cardinals vs. Philadelphia, 1947

Longest Return

84 Anthony Carter, NFC-FR: Minnesota vs. New Orleans, 1987 (TD)
81 Hugh Gallarneau, NFC-D: Chi. Bears vs. Green Bay, 1941 (TD)
79 Bosh Pritchard, NFC-D: Philadelphia vs. Pittsburgh, 1947 (TD)

Average Yardage

Highest Average, Career (10 returns)

15.8 Anthony Carter, Minnesota, 7 games (15-237)
12.9 Brian Mitchell, Washington, 7 games (11-142)
12.6 Bob Hayes, Dallas, 15 games (12-151)

Highest Average Gain, Game (3 returns)

47.0 Bob Hayes, NFC-D: Dallas vs. Cleveland, 1967 (3-141)
29.0 George (Butch) Byrd, AFC: Buffalo vs. San Diego, 1965 (3-87)
25.3 Bosh Pritchard, NFC-D: Philadelphia vs. Pittsburgh, 1947 (4-101)

Touchdowns

Most Touchdowns

1 Hugh Gallarneau, NFC-D: Chicago Bears vs. Green Bay, 1941
Bosh Pritchard, NFC-D: Philadelphia vs. Pittsburgh, 1947
Charley Trippi, NFC: Chicago Cardinals vs. Philadelphia, 1947
Verda (Vitamin T) Smith, NFC-D: Los Angeles vs. Detroit, 1952
George (Butch) Byrd, AFC: Buffalo vs. San Diego, 1965
Golden Richards, NFC: Dallas vs. Minnesota, 1973
Wes Chandler, AFC-D: San Diego vs. Miami, 1981 (OT)
Shaun Gayle, NFC-D: Chicago vs. N.Y. Giants, 1985
Anthony Carter, NFC-FR: Minnesota vs. New Orleans, 1987
Darrell Green, NFC-D: Washington vs. Chicago, 1987

Kickoff Returns

Most Kickoff Returns, Career

29 Fulton Walker, Miami-L.A. Raiders, 10 games
21 Ken Bell, Denver, 9 games
19 Preston Pearson, Baltimore-Pittsburgh-Dallas, 22 games
James Brooks, San Diego-Cincinnati, 9 games

Most Kickoff Returns, Game

8 Marc Logan, AFC-D: Miami vs. Buffalo, 1990
7 Don Bingham, NFC: Chi. Bears vs. N.Y. Giants, 1956
Reggie Brown, NFC-FR: Atlanta vs. Minnesota, 1982
David Verser, AFC-FR: Cincinnati vs. N.Y. Jets, 1982
Del Rodgers, NFC-D: Green Bay vs. Dallas, 1982
Henry Ellard, NFC-D: L.A. Rams vs. Washington, 1983
Stephen Starring, SB: New England vs. Chicago, 1985
6 By many players

Yards Gained

Most Yards Gained, Career

677 Fulton Walker, Miami-L.A. Raiders, 10 games
481 Carl Garrett, Oakland, 5 games
435 Dennis Gentry, Chicago, 12 games

Most Yards Gained, Game

190 Fulton Walker, SB: Miami vs. Washington, 1982
170 Les (Speedy) Duncan, NFC-D: Washington vs. San Francisco, 1971
169 Carl Garrett, AFC-D: Oakland vs. Baltimore, 1977 (OT)

Longest Return

98 Fulton Walker, SB: Miami vs. Washington, 1982 (TD)
97 Vic Washington, NFC-D: San Francisco vs. Dallas, 1972 (TD)
93 Stanford Jennings, SB: Cincinnati vs. San Francisco, 1988 (TD)

Average Yardage

Highest Average, Career (10 returns)

30.1 Carl Garrett, Oakland, 5 games (16-481)
27.9 George Atkinson, Oakland, 16 games (12-335)
27.7 Eric Metcalf, Cleveland, 2 games (10-277)

Highest Average, Game (3 returns)

56.7 Les (Speedy) Duncan, NFC-D: Washington vs. San Francisco, 1971 (3-170)
51.3 Ed Podolak, AFC-D: Kansas City vs. Miami, 1971 (OT) (3-154)
49.0 Les (Speedy) Duncan, AFC: San Diego vs. Buffalo, 1964 (3-147)

Touchdowns

Most Touchdowns

1 Vic Washington, NFC-D: San Francisco vs. Dallas, 1972
Nat Moore, AFC-D: Miami vs. Oakland, 1974
Marshall Johnson, AFC-D: Baltimore vs. Oakland, 1977 (OT)
Fulton Walker, SB: Miami vs. Washington, 1982
Stanford Jennings, SB: Cincinnati vs. San Francisco, 1988
Eric Metcalf, AFC-D: Cleveland vs. Buffalo, 1989

Fumbles

Most Fumbles, Career

13 Tony Dorsett, Dallas, 17 games
10 Franco Harris, Pittsburgh, 19 games
Terry Bradshaw, Pittsburgh, 19 games
Roger Staubach, Dallas, 20 games
Warren Moon, Houston, 8 games
9 Chuck Foreman, Minnesota, 13 games
Danny White, Dallas, 18 games

Most Fumbles, Game

4 Brian Sipe, AFC-D: Cleveland vs. Oakland, 1980
3 By many players

Recoveries

Most Own Fumbles Recovered, Career

6 John Elway, Denver, 13 games
5 Roger Staubach, Dallas, 20 games
Warren Moon, Houston, 8 games
4 Fran Tarkenton, Minnesota, 11 games

Most Opponents' Fumbles Recovered, Career

4 Cliff Harris, Dallas, 21 games
Harvey Martin, Dallas, 22 games
Ted Hendricks, Baltimore-Oakland-L.A. Raiders, 21 games
Alvin Walton, Washington, 9 games
Monte Coleman, Washington, 21 games
3 Paul Krause, Minnesota, 19 games
Jack Lambert, Pittsburgh, 18 games
Fred Dryer, Los Angeles, 14 games
Charlie Waters, Dallas, 25 games
Jack Ham, Pittsburgh, 16 games
Mike Hegman, Dallas, 16 games
Tom Jackson, Denver, 10 games
Rich Milot, Washington, 13 games
Mike Singletary, Chicago, 12 games
Darryl Grant, Washington, 16 games
Wes Hopkins, Philadelphia, 3 games
Wilber Marshall, Chicago-Washington, 14 games
2 By many players

Most Fumbles Recovered, Game, Own and Opponents'

3 Jack Lambert, AFC: Pittsburgh vs. Oakland, 1975 (3 opp)
Ron Jaworski, NFC-FR: Philadelphia vs. N.Y. Giants, 1981 (3 own)
2 By many players

Yards Gained

Longest Return

93 Andy Russell, AFC-D: Pittsburgh vs. Baltimore, 1975 (opp, TD)
64 Leon Lett, SB: Dallas vs. Buffalo, 1992 (opp)
60 Mike Curtis, NFC-D: Baltimore vs. Minnesota, 1968 (opp, TD)
Hugh Green, NFC-FR: Tampa Bay vs. Dallas, 1982 (opp, TD)

Touchdowns

Most Touchdowns

1 By 22 players

Combined Net Yards Gained

Rushing, receiving, interception returns, punt returns, kickoff returns, and fumble returns.

Attempts

Most Attempts, Career

454 Franco Harris, Pittsburgh, 19 games
350 Tony Dorsett, Dallas, 17 games
275 Chuck Foreman, Minnesota, 13 games
Roger Craig, San Francisco-Minnesota, 17 games

Most Attempts, Game
40 Lawrence McCutcheon, NFC-D: Los Angeles vs. St. Louis, 1975
39 John Riggins, SB: Washington vs. Miami, 1982
38 Ricky Bell, NFC-D: Tampa Bay vs. Philadelphia, 1979
Rob Carpenter, NFC-FR: N.Y. Giants vs. Philadelphia, 1981

Yards Gained

Most Yards Gained, Career
2,060 Franco Harris, Pittsburgh, 19 games
1,786 Tony Dorsett, Dallas, 17 games
1,494 Roger Craig, San Francisco-Minnesota, 17 games
Most Yards Gained, Game
350 Ed Podolak, AFC-D: Kansas City vs. Miami, 1971 (OT)
329 Keith Lincoln, AFC: San Diego vs. Boston, 1963
285 Bob Hayes, NFC-D: Dallas vs. Cleveland, 1967

Sacks

Sacks have been compiled since 1982
Most Sacks, Career
10.5 Richard Dent, Chicago, 10 games
10 Charles Mann, Washington, 17 games
9 Bruce Smith, Buffalo, 13 games
Most Sacks, Game
3.5 Rich Milot, NFC-D: Washington vs. Chicago, 1984
Richard Dent, NFC-D: Chicago vs. N.Y. Giants, 1985
3 Richard Dent, NFC-D: Chicago vs. Washington, 1984
Garin Veris, AFC-FR: New England vs. N.Y. Jets, 1985
Gary Jeter, NFC-D: L.A. Rams vs. Dallas, 1985
Carl Hairston, AFC-D: Cleveland vs. N.Y. Jets, 1986 (OT)
Charles Mann, NFC-D: Washington vs. Chicago, 1987
Kevin Greene, NFC-FR: L.A. Rams vs. Minnesota, 1988
Greg Townsend, AFC-D: L.A. Raiders vs. Cincinnati, 1990
Wilber Marshall, NFC: Washington vs. Detroit, 1991
Fred Stokes, NFC-FR: Washington vs. Minnesota, 1992
Pierce Holt, NFC-D: San Francisco vs. Washington, 1992
Tony Casillas, NFC: Dallas vs. San Francisco, 1992
2.5 Lyle Alzado, AFC-D: L.A. Raiders vs. Pittsburgh, 1983
Jacob Green, AFC-FR: Seattle vs. L.A. Raiders, 1984
Larry Roberts, NFC-D: San Francisco vs. Minnesota, 1988
Leslie O'Neal, AFC-FR: San Diego vs. Kansas City, 1992

Team Records

Games, Victories, Defeats

Most Seasons Participating in Postseason Games
22 Cleveland/L.A. Rams, 1945, 1949-52, 1955, 1967, 1969, 1973-80, 1983-86, 1988-89
Cleveland, 1950-55, 1957-58, 1964-65, 1967-69, 1971-72, 1980, 1982, 1985-89
N.Y. Giants, 1933-35, 1938-39, 1941, 1943-44, 1946, 1950, 1956, 1958-59, 1961-63, 1981, 1984-86, 1989-90
20 Chicago, 1933-34, 1937, 1940-43, 1946, 1950, 1956, 1963, 1977, 1979, 1984-88, 1990-91
Dallas, 1966-73, 1975-83, 1985, 1991-92
Boston/Washington, 1936-37, 1940, 1942-43, 1945, 1971-74, 1976-77, 1982-84, 1986-87, 1990-92
16 Minnesota, 1968-71, 1973-78, 1980, 1982, 1987-89, 1992
Most Consecutive Seasons Participating in Postseason Games
9 Dallas, 1975-83
8 Dallas, 1966-73
Pittsburgh, 1972-79
Los Angeles, 1973-80
San Francisco, 1983-90
6 Cleveland, 1950-55
Oakland, 1972-77
Minnesota, 1973-78
Houston, 1987-92
Most Games
41 Dallas, 1966-73, 1975-83, 1985, 1991-92
35 Boston/Washington, 1936-37, 1940, 1942-43, 1945, 1971-74, 1976-77, 1982-84, 1986-87, 1990-92
34 Oakland/L.A. Raiders, 1967-70, 1973-77, 1980, 1982-85, 1990-91
Most Games Won
24 Dallas, 1967, 1970-73, 1975, 1977-78, 1980-82, 1991-92
21 Washington, 1937, 1942-43, 1972, 1982-83, 1986-87, 1990-92
20 Oakland/L.A. Raiders, 1967-70, 1973-77, 1980, 1982-83, 1990
Most Consecutive Games Won
9 Green Bay, 1961-62, 1965-67
7 Pittsburgh, 1974-76
San Francisco, 1988-90
6 Miami, 1972-73
Pittsburgh, 1978-79
Washington, 1982-83
Most Games Lost
20 L.A. Rams, 1949-50, 1952, 1955, 1967, 1969, 1973-80, 1983-86, 1988-89
18 Cleveland, 1951-53, 1957-58, 1965, 1967-69, 1971-72, 1980, 1982, 1985-89
17 N.Y. Giants, 1933, 1935, 1939, 1941, 1943-44, 1946, 1950, 1958-59, 1961-63, 1981, 1984-85, 1989
Dallas, 1966-70, 1972-73, 1975-76, 1978-83, 1985, 1991
Most Consecutive Games Lost
6 N.Y. Giants, 1939, 1941, 1943-44, 1946, 1950
Cleveland, 1969, 1971-72, 1980, 1982, 1985
5 N.Y. Giants, 1958-59, 1961-63
Los Angeles, 1952, 1955, 1967, 1969, 1973
Denver, 1977-79, 1983-84
Baltimore/Indianapolis, 1971, 1975-77, 1987 (current)
Philadelphia, 1980-81, 1988-90
4 Washington, 1972-74, 1976
Miami, 1974, 1978-79, 1981
Chi. Cardinals/St. Louis, 1948, 1974-75, 1982 (current)
Boston/New England, 1963, 1976, 1978, 1982
New Orleans, 1987, 1990-92 (current)

Scoring

Most Points, Game
73 NFC: Chi. Bears vs. Washington, 1940
59 NFC: Detroit vs. Cleveland, 1957
56 NFC: Cleveland vs. Detroit, 1954
AFC-D: Oakland vs. Houston, 1969
Most Points, Both Teams, Game
79 AFC-D: San Diego (41) vs. Miami (38), 1981 (OT)
AFC-FR: Buffalo (41) vs. Houston (38), 1992 (OT)
78 AFC-D: Buffalo (44) vs. Miami (34), 1990
73 NFC: Chi. Bears (73) vs. Washington (0), 1940
NFC: Detroit (59) vs. Cleveland (14), 1957
AFC: Miami (45) vs. Pittsburgh (28), 1984
Fewest Points, Both Teams, Game
5 NFC-D: Detroit (0) vs. Dallas (5), 1970
7 NFC: Chi. Cardinals (0) vs. Philadelphia (7), 1948
9 NFC: Tampa Bay (0) vs. Los Angeles (9), 1979
Largest Margin of Victory, Game
73 NFC: Chi. Bears vs. Washington, 1940 (73-0)
49 AFC-D: Oakland vs. Houston, 1969 (56-7)
48 AFC: Buffalo vs. L.A. Raiders, 1990 (51-3)
Most Points, Shutout Victory, Game
73 NFC: Chi. Bears vs. Washington, 1940
38 NFC-D: Dallas vs. Tampa Bay, 1981
37 NFC: Green Bay vs. N.Y. Giants, 1961
Most Points Overcome to Win Game
32 AFC-FR: Buffalo vs. Houston, 1992 (trailed 3-35, won 41-38) (OT)
20 NFC-D: Detroit vs. San Francisco, 1957 (trailed 7-27, won 31-27)
18 NFC-D: Dallas vs. San Francisco, 1972 (trailed 3-21, won 30-28)
AFC-D: Miami vs. Cleveland, 1985 (trailed 3-21, won 24-21)
Most Points, Each Half
1st: 41 AFC: Buffalo vs. L.A. Raiders, 1990
38 NFC-D: Washington vs. L.A. Rams, 1983
35 NFC: Cleveland vs. Detroit, 1954
AFC-D: Oakland vs. Houston, 1969
SB: Washington vs. Denver, 1987
2nd: 45 NFC: Chi. Bears vs. Washington, 1940
35 AFC-FR: Buffalo vs.Houston 1992
30 SB: N.Y. Giants vs. Denver, 1986
AFC: Cleveland vs. Denver, 1987
Most Points, Each Quarter
1st: 28 AFC-D: Oakland vs. Houston, 1969
24 AFC-D: San Diego vs. Miami, 1981
21 NFC: Chi. Bears vs. Washington, 1940
AFC: San Diego vs. Boston, 1963
AFC-D: Oakland vs. Kansas City, 1968
AFC: Oakland vs. San Diego, 1980
AFC: Buffalo vs. L.A. Raiders, 1990
2nd: 35 SB: Washington vs. Denver, 1987
26 AFC-D: Pittsburgh vs. Buffalo, 1974
24 NFC-D: Chi. Bears vs. Green Bay, 1941
NFC: Green Bay vs. N. Y. Giants, 1961
3rd: 28 AFC-FR: Buffalo vs. Houston, 1992
26 NFC: Chi. Bears vs. Washington, 1940
21 NFC-D: Dallas vs. Cleveland, 1967
NFC-D: Dallas vs. Tampa Bay, 1981
AFC-D: L.A. Raiders vs. Pittsburgh, 1983
SB: Chicago vs. New England, 1985
NFC-D: N.Y. Giants vs. San Francisco, 1986
AFC: Cleveland vs. Denver, 1987
AFC: Cleveland vs. Denver, 1989
4th 27 NFC: N.Y. Giants vs. Chi. Bears, 1934
26 NFC-FR: Philadelphia vs. New Orleans, 1992
24 NFC: Baltimore vs. N. Y. Giants, 1959
OT: 6 NFC: Baltimore vs. N.Y. Giants, 1958
AFC-D: Oakland vs. Baltimore, 1977
NFC-D: L.A. Rams vs. N.Y. Giants, 1989

Touchdowns

Most Touchdowns, Game
11 NFC: Chi. Bears vs. Washington, 1940
8 NFC: Cleveland vs. Detroit, 1954
NFC: Detroit vs. Cleveland, 1957
AFC-D: Oakland vs. Houston, 1969
SB: San Francisco vs. Denver, 1989
7 AFC: San Diego vs. Boston, 1963
NFC-D: Dallas vs. Cleveland, 1967
NFC-D: N.Y. Giants vs. San Francisco, 1986
AFC: Buffalo vs. L.A. Raiders, 1990
SB: Dallas vs. Buffalo, 1992
Most Touchdowns, Both Teams, Game
11 NFC: Chi. Bears (11) vs. Washington (0), 1940
10 NFC: Detroit (8) vs. Cleveland (2), 1957
AFC-D: Miami (5) vs. San Diego (5), 1981 (OT)
AFC: Miami (6) vs. Pittsburgh (4), 1984
AFC-FR: Buffalo (5) vs. Houston (5), 1992 (OT)
9 NFC: Chi. Bears (6) vs. Washington (3), 1943
NFC: Cleveland (8) vs. Detroit (1), 1954
NFC-D: Dallas (7) vs. Cleveland (2), 1967
AFC-D: Oakland (8) vs. Houston (1), 1969
AFC-D: Oakland (5) vs. Baltimore (4), 1977 (OT)
SB: Pittsburgh (5) vs. Dallas (4), 1978
AFC: Denver (5) vs. Cleveland (4), 1987
SB: San Francisco (8) vs. Denver (1), 1989
AFC-D: Buffalo (5) vs. Miami (4), 1990
SB: Dallas (7) vs. Buffalo (2), 1992
Fewest Touchdowns, Both Teams, Game
0 NFC-D: N.Y. Giants vs. Cleveland, 1950
NFC-D: Dallas vs. Detroit, 1970
NFC: Los Angeles vs. Tampa Bay, 1979

1 NFC: Chi. Cardinals (0) vs. Philadelphia (1), 1948
NFC-D: Cleveland (0) vs. N.Y. Giants (1), 1958
AFC: San Diego (0) vs. Houston (1), 1961
AFC-D: N. Y. Jets (0) vs. Kansas City (1), 1969
NFC-D: Green Bay (0) vs. Washington (1), 1972
NFC-FR: New Orleans (0) vs. Chicago (1), 1990
NFC: N.Y. Giants (0) vs. San Francisco (1), 1990
AFC-FR: L.A. Raiders (0) vs. Kansas City (1), 1991
2 In many games

Points After Touchdown

Most Points After Touchdown, Game
8 NFC: Cleveland vs. Detroit, 1954
NFC: Detroit vs. Cleveland, 1957
AFC-D: Oakland vs. Houston, 1969
7 NFC: Chi. Bears vs. Washington, 1940
NFC-D: Dallas vs. Cleveland, 1967
NFC-D: N.Y. Giants vs. San Francisco, 1986
SB: San Francisco vs. Denver, 1989
SB: Dallas vs. Buffalo, 1992
6 AFC: San Diego vs. Boston, 1963
NFC-D: Washington vs. L.A. Rams, 1983
AFC: Miami vs. Pittsburgh, 1984
SB: Washington vs. Denver, 1987
AFC: Buffalo vs. L.A. Raiders, 1990

Most Points After Touchdown, Both Teams, Game
10 NFC: Detroit (8) vs. Cleveland (2), 1957
AFC-D: Miami (5) vs. San Diego (5), 1981 (OT)
AFC: Miami (6) vs. Pittsburgh (4), 1984
AFC-FR: Buffalo (5) vs. Houston (5), 1992 (OT)
9 NFC: Cleveland (8) vs. Detroit (1), 1954
NFC-D: Dallas (7) vs. Cleveland (2), 1967
AFC-D: Oakland (8) vs. Houston (1), 1969
SB: Pittsburgh (5) vs. Dallas (4), 1978
AFC: Denver (5) vs. Cleveland (4), 1987
AFC-D: Buffalo (5) vs. Miami (4), 1990
SB: Dallas (7) vs. Buffalo (2), 1992
8 In many games

Fewest Points After Touchdown, Both Teams, Game
0 NFC-D: N.Y. Giants vs. Cleveland, 1950
NFC-D: Dallas vs. Detroit, 1970
NFC: Los Angeles vs. Tampa Bay, 1979

Field Goals

Most Field Goals, Game
5 NFC-D: Minnesota vs. San Francisco, 1987
NFC: N.Y. Giants vs. San Francisco, 1990
AFC: Buffalo vs. Miami, 1992
4 AFC-D: Boston vs. Buffalo, 1963
AFC: Oakland vs. Houston, 1967
SB: Green Bay vs. Oakland, 1967
NFC: Washington vs. Dallas, 1972
AFC-D: Oakland vs. Pittsburgh, 1973
SB: San Francisco vs. Cincinnati, 1981
AFC-FR: New England vs. N.Y. Jets, 1985
NFC-FR: Washington vs. L.A. Rams, 1986
NFC-D: Philadelphia vs. Chicago, 1988
AFC-FR: Pittsburgh vs. Houston, 1989 (OT)
3 By many teams

Most Field Goals, Both Teams, Game
7 AFC-FR: Pittsburgh (4) vs. Houston (3), 1989 (OT)
NFC: N.Y. Giants (5) vs. San Francisco (2), 1990
6 NFC-D: Minnesota (5) vs. San Francisco (1), 1987
NFC-D: Philadelphia (4) vs. Chicago (2), 1988
AFC: Buffalo (5) vs. Miami (1), 1992
5 In many games

Most Field Goals Attempted, Game
6 AFC: Oakland vs. Houston, 1967
NFC-D: Los Angeles vs. Dallas, 1973
AFC-D: Cleveland vs. N.Y. Jets, 1986 (OT)
NFC: N.Y. Giants vs. San Francisco, 1990
5 By many teams

Most Field Goals Attempted, Both Teams, Game
9 NFC-D: Philadelphia (5) vs. Chicago (4), 1988
8 NFC-D: Los Angeles (6) vs. Dallas (2), 1973
NFC-D: Detroit (5) vs. San Francisco (3), 1983
AFC-D: Cleveland (6) vs. N.Y. Jets (2), 1986 (OT)
NFC-D: Minnesota (5) vs. San Francisco (3), 1987
AFC-FR: Houston (4) vs. Pittsburgh (4), 1989 (OT)
NFC-FR: Chicago (4) vs. New Orleans (4), 1990
NFC: N.Y. Giants (6) vs. San Francisco (2), 1990
7 In many games

Safeties

Most Safeties, Game
1 By many teams

Most Safeties, Both Teams, Game
1 In many games

First Downs

Most First Downs, Game
34 AFC-D: San Diego vs. Miami, 1981 (OT)
33 AFC-D: Cleveland vs. N.Y. Jets, 1986 (OT)
31 SB: San Francisco vs. Miami, 1984

Fewest First Downs, Game
6 NFC: N.Y. Giants vs. Green Bay, 1961
7 NFC: Green Bay vs. Boston, 1936
NFC-D: Pittsburgh vs. Philadelphia, 1947
NFC: Chi. Cardinals vs. Philadelphia, 1948
NFC: Los Angeles vs. Philadelphia, 1949
NFC-D: Cleveland vs. N. Y. Giants, 1958
AFC-D: Cincinnati vs. Baltimore, 1970
NFC-D: Detroit vs. Dallas, 1970
NFC: Tampa Bay vs. Los Angeles, 1979
8 By many teams

Most First Downs, Both Teams, Game
59 AFC-D: San Diego (34) vs. Miami (25), 1981 (OT)
55 AFC-FR: San Diego (29) vs. Pittsburgh (26), 1982
51 AFC: Buffalo (30) vs. L.A. Raiders (21), 1990

Fewest First Downs, Both Teams, Game
15 NFC: Green Bay (7) vs. Boston (8), 1936
19 NFC: N. Y. Giants (9) vs. Green Bay (10), 1939
NFC: Washington (9) vs. Chi. Bears (10), 1942
20 NFC-D: Cleveland (9) vs. N. Y. Giants (11), 1950

Rushing

Most First Downs, Rushing, Game
19 NFC-FR: Dallas vs. Los Angeles, 1980
18 AFC-D: Miami vs. Cincinnati, 1973
AFC: Miami vs. Oakland, 1973
AFC-D: Pittsburgh vs. Buffalo, 1974
17 AFC-D: Cincinnati vs. Seattle, 1988

Fewest First Downs, Rushing, Game
0 NFC: Los Angeles vs. Philadelphia, 1949
AFC-D: Buffalo vs. Boston, 1963
AFC: Oakland vs. Pittsburgh, 1974
NFC-FR: New Orleans vs. Minnesota, 1987
NFC: L.A. Rams vs. San Francisco, 1989
NFC-D: Chicago vs. N.Y. Giants, 1990
1 By many teams

Most First Downs, Rushing, Both Teams, Game
26 AFC: Buffalo (14) vs. L.A. Raiders (12), 1990
25 NFC-FR: Dallas (19) vs. Los Angeles (6), 1980
23 NFC: Cleveland (15) vs. Detroit (8), 1952
AFC-D: Miami (18) vs. Cincinnati (5), 1973
AFC-D: Pittsburgh (18) vs. Buffalo (5), 1974

Fewest First Downs, Rushing, Both Teams, Game
5 AFC-D: Buffalo (0) vs. Boston (5), 1963
6 NFC: Green Bay (2) vs. Boston (4), 1936
NFC-D: Baltimore (2) vs. Minnesota (4), 1968
AFC-D: Houston (1) vs. Oakland (5), 1969
AFC-FR: N.Y. Jets (1) vs. Houston (5), 1991
7 NFC-D: Washington (2) vs. N. Y. Giants (5), 1943
NFC: Baltimore (3) vs. N. Y. Giants (4), 1959
NFC: Washington (3) vs. Dallas (4), 1972
AFC-FR: N. Y. Jets (3) vs. Buffalo (4), 1981
NFC-D: Detroit (3) vs. Dallas (4), 1991

Passing

Most First Downs, Passing, Game
21 AFC-D: Miami vs. San Diego, 1981 (OT)
AFC-D: San Diego vs. Miami, 1981 (OT)
AFC-D: Cleveland vs. N.Y. Jets, 1986 (OT)
NFC-D: Philadelphia vs. Chicago, 1988
20 NFC-FR: Dallas vs. L.A. Rams, 1983
AFC-D: Buffalo vs. Cleveland, 1989
19 NFC-FR: St. Louis vs. Green Bay, 1982
NFC-FR: Dallas vs. Tampa Bay, 1982
AFC-FR: Pittsburgh vs. San Diego, 1982
AFC-FR: San Diego vs. Pittsburgh, 1982
NFC: Dallas vs. Washington, 1982
NFC-D: Detroit vs. Dallas, 1991

Fewest First Downs, Passing, Game
0 NFC: Philadelphia vs. Chi. Cardinals, 1948
1 NFC-D: N. Y. Giants vs. Washington, 1943
NFC: Cleveland vs. Detroit, 1953
SB: Denver vs. Dallas, 1977
2 By many teams

Most First Downs, Passing, Both Teams, Game
42 AFC-D: Miami (21) vs. San Diego (21), 1981 (OT)
38 AFC-FR: Pittsburgh (19) vs. San Diego (19), 1982
34 NFC-FR: Washington (18) vs. San Francisco (16), 1990

Fewest First Downs, Passing, Both Teams, Game
2 NFC: Philadelphia (0) vs. Chi. Cardinals (2), 1948
4 NFC-D: Cleveland (2) vs. N. Y. Giants (2), 1950
5 NFC: Detroit (2) vs. N. Y. Giants (3), 1935
NFC: Green Bay (2) vs. N. Y. Giants (3), 1939

Penalty

Most First Downs, Penalty, Game
7 AFC-D: New England vs. Oakland, 1976
6 AFC-D: Cleveland vs. N.Y. Jets, 1986 (OT)
5 AFC-FR: Cleveland vs. L. A. Raiders, 1982

Most First Downs, Penalty, Both Teams, Game
9 AFC-D: New England (7) vs. Oakland (2), 1976
8 NFC-FR: Atlanta (4) vs. Minnesota (4), 1982
7 AFC-D: Baltimore (4) vs. Oakland (3), 1977 (OT)

Net Yards Gained Rushing and Passing

Most Yards Gained, Game
610 AFC: San Diego vs. Boston, 1963
602 SB: Washington vs. Denver, 1987
569 AFC: Miami vs. Pittsburgh, 1984

Fewest Yards Gained, Game
86 NFC-D: Cleveland vs. N.Y. Giants, 1958
99 NFC: Chi. Cardinals vs. Philadelphia, 1948
114 NFC-D: N.Y. Giants vs. Washington, 1943

Most Yards Gained, Both Teams, Game
1,036 AFC-D: San Diego (564) vs. Miami (472), 1981 (OT)
1,024 AFC: Miami (569) vs. Pittsburgh (455), 1984
929 SB: Washington (602) vs. Denver (327), 1987

Fewest Yards Gained, Both Teams, Game
331 NFC: Chi. Cardinals (99) vs. Philadelphia (232), 1948
332 NFC-D: N.Y. Giants (150) vs. Cleveland (182), 1950
336 NFC: Boston (116) vs. Green Bay (220), 1936

Rushing
Attempts
Most Attempts, Game
65 NFC: Detroit vs. N.Y. Giants, 1935
61 NFC: Philadelphia vs. Los Angeles, 1949
59 AFC: New England vs. Miami, 1985
Fewest Attempts, Game
9 SB: Miami vs. San Francisco, 1984
10 NFC: L.A. Rams vs. San Francisco, 1989
11 SB: New England vs. Chicago, 1985
AFC-FR: Seattle vs. Houston, 1987 (OT)
NFC: San Francisco vs. N.Y. Giants, 1990
AFC: Miami vs. Buffalo, 1992
Most Attempts, Both Teams, Game
109 NFC: Detroit (65) vs. N.Y. Giants (44), 1935
97 AFC-D: Baltimore (50) vs. Oakland (47), 1977 (OT)
91 NFC: Philadelphia (57) vs. Chi. Cardinals (34), 1948
Fewest Attempts, Both Teams, Game
38 NFC-D: Detroit (16) vs. Dallas (22), 1991
43 AFC-FR: Houston (20) vs. N.Y. Jets (23), 1991
44 NFC-FR: Atlanta (22) vs. New Orleans (22), 1991

Yards Gained
Most Yards Gained, Game
382 NFC: Chi. Bears vs. Washington, 1940
338 NFC-FR: Dallas vs. Los Angeles, 1980
318 AFC: San Diego vs. Boston, 1963
Fewest Yards Gained, Game
7 AFC-D: Buffalo vs. Boston, 1963
SB: New England vs. Chicago, 1985
17 SB: Minnesota vs. Pittsburgh, 1974
18 AFC-D: Seattle vs. Cincinnati, 1988
Most Yards Gained, Both Teams, Game
430 NFC-FR: Dallas (338) vs. Los Angeles (92), 1980
426 NFC: Cleveland (227) vs. Detroit (199), 1952
404 NFC: Chi. Bears (382) vs. Washington (22), 1940
Fewest Yards Gained, Both Teams, Game
90 AFC-D: Buffalo (7) vs. Boston (83), 1963
106 NFC: Boston (39) vs. Green Bay (67), 1936
126 NFC-D: San Francisco (46) vs. Washington (80), 1990

Average Gain
Highest Average Gain, Game
9.94 AFC: San Diego vs. Boston, 1963 (32-318)
9.29 NFC-D: Green Bay vs. Dallas, 1982 (17-158)
7.35 NFC-FR: Dallas vs. Los Angeles, 1980 (46-338)
Lowest Average Gain, Game
0.58 AFC-D: Buffalo vs. Boston, 1963 (12-7)
0.64 SB: New England vs. Chicago, 1985 (11-7)
0.81 SB: Minnesota vs. Pittsburgh, 1974 (21-17)

Touchdowns
Most Touchdowns, Game
7 NFC: Chi. Bears vs. Washington, 1940
5 NFC: Cleveland vs. Detroit, 1954
4 NFC: Detroit vs. N.Y. Giants, 1935
AFC: San Diego vs. Boston, 1963
NFC-D: Dallas vs. Cleveland, 1967
NFC: Baltimore vs. Cleveland, 1968
NFC-D: Dallas vs. Tampa Bay, 1981
AFC-D: L.A. Raiders vs. Pittsburgh, 1983
SB: Chicago vs. New England, 1985
AFC: Buffalo vs. L.A. Raiders, 1990
Most Touchdowns, Both Teams, Game
7 NFC: Chi. Bears (7) vs. Washington (0), 1940
6 NFC: Cleveland (5) vs. Detroit (1), 1954
5 NFC: Chi. Cardinals (3) vs. Philadelphia (2), 1947
AFC: San Diego (4) vs. Boston (1), 1963
AFC-D: Cincinnati (3) vs. Buffalo (2), 1981

Passing
Attempts
Most Attempts, Game
65 AFC-D: Cleveland vs. N.Y. Jets, 1986 (OT)
59 SB: Buffalo vs. Washington, 1991
55 NFC-D: Philadelphia vs. Chicago, 1988
Fewest Attempts, Game
5 NFC: Detroit vs. N.Y. Giants, 1935
6 AFC: Miami vs. Oakland, 1973
7 SB: Miami vs. Minnesota, 1973
Most Attempts, Both Teams, Game
102 AFC-D: San Diego (54) vs. Miami (48), 1981 (OT)
96 AFC: N.Y. Jets (49) vs. Oakland (47), 1968
95 AFC-D: Cleveland (65) vs. N.Y. Jets (30), 1986 (OT)
Fewest Attempts, Both Teams, Game
18 NFC: Detroit (5) vs. N.Y. Giants (13), 1935
23 NFC: Chi. Cardinals (11) vs. Philadelphia (12), 1948
24 NFC-D: Cleveland (9) vs. N.Y. Giants (15), 1950

Completions
Most Completions, Game
36 AFC-FR: Houston vs. Buffalo, 1992 (OT)
34 AFC-D: Cleveland vs. N.Y. Jets, 1986 (OT)
33 AFC-D: San Diego vs. Miami, 1981 (OT)
Fewest Completions, Game
2 NFC: Detroit vs. N.Y. Giants, 1935
NFC: Philadelphia vs. Chi. Cardinals, 1948
3 NFC: N.Y. Giants vs. Chi. Bears, 1941
NFC: Green Bay vs. N.Y. Giants, 1944
NFC: Chi. Cardinals vs. Philadelphia, 1947
NFC: Chi. Cardinals vs. Philadelphia, 1948
NFC-D: Cleveland vs. N.Y. Giants, 1950
NFC-D: N.Y. Giants vs. Cleveland, 1950
NFC: Cleveland vs. Detroit, 1953
AFC: Miami vs. Oakland, 1973
4 NFC: N.Y. Giants vs. Detroit, 1935
NFC-D: N.Y. Giants vs. Washington, 1943
NFC-D: Pittsburgh vs. Philadelphia, 1947
NFC-D: Dallas vs. Detroit, 1970
AFC: Miami vs. Baltimore, 1971
SB: Miami vs. Washington, 1982
AFC-FR: Seattle vs. L.A. Raiders, 1984
Most Completions, Both Teams, Game
64 AFC-D: San Diego (33) vs. Miami (31), 1981 (OT)
57 AFC-FR: Houston (36) vs. Buffalo (21), 1992 (OT)
55 AFC-FR: Pittsburgh (28) vs. San Diego (27), 1982
Fewest Completions, Both Teams, Game
5 NFC: Philadelphia (2) vs. Chi. Cardinals (3), 1948
6 NFC: Detroit (2) vs. N.Y. Giants (4), 1935
NFC-D: Cleveland (3) vs. N.Y. Giants (3), 1950
11 NFC: Green Bay (3) vs. N.Y. Giants (8), 1944
NFC-D: Dallas (4) vs. Detroit (7), 1970

Completion Percentage
Highest Completion Percentage, Game (20 attempts)
88.0 SB: N.Y. Giants vs. Denver, 1986 (25-22)
87.1 NFC: San Francisco vs. L.A. Rams, 1989 (31-27)
80.0 NFC-D: Washington vs. L.A. Rams, 1983 (25-20)
Lowest Completion Percentage, Game (20 attempts)
18.5 NFC: Tampa Bay vs. Los Angeles, 1979 (27-5)
20.0 NFC-D: N.Y. Giants vs. Washington, 1943 (20-4)
25.8 NFC: Chi. Bears vs. Washington, 1937 (31-8)

Yards Gained
Most Yards Gained, Game
483 AFC-D: Cleveland vs. N.Y. Jets, 1986 (OT)
435 AFC: Miami vs. Pittsburgh, 1984
415 AFC-D: San Diego vs. Miami, 1981 (OT)
Fewest Yards Gained, Game
3 NFC: Chi. Cardinals vs. Philadelphia, 1948
7 NFC: Philadelphia vs. Chi. Cardinals, 1948
9 NFC-D: N.Y. Giants vs. Cleveland, 1950
NFC: Cleveland vs. Detroit, 1953
Most Yards Gained, Both Teams, Game
809 AFC-D: San Diego (415) vs. Miami (394), 1981 (OT)
747 AFC: Miami (435) vs. Pittsburgh (312), 1984
666 AFC-D: Cleveland (483) vs. N.Y. Jets (183), 1986 (OT)
Fewest Yards Gained, Both Teams, Game
10 NFC: Chi. Cardinals (3) vs. Philadelphia (7), 1948
38 NFC-D: N.Y. Giants (9) vs. Cleveland (29), 1950
102 NFC-D: Dallas (22) vs. Detroit (80), 1970

Times Sacked
Most Times Sacked, Game
9 AFC: Kansas City vs. Buffalo, 1966
NFC: Chicago vs. San Francisco, 1984
AFC-D: N.Y. Jets vs. Cleveland, 1986 (OT)
8 NFC: Green Bay vs. Dallas, 1967
NFC: Minnesota vs. Washington, 1987
7 NFC-D: Dallas vs. Los Angeles, 1973
SB: Dallas vs. Pittsburgh, 1975
AFC-FR: Houston vs. Oakland, 1980
NFC-D: Washington vs. Chicago, 1984
SB: New England vs. Chicago, 1985
AFC-FR: Kansas City vs. San Diego, 1992
AFC-D: Pittsburgh vs. Buffalo, 1992
Most Times Sacked, Both Teams, Game
13 AFC: Kansas City (9) vs. Buffalo (4), 1966
AFC-D: N.Y. Jets (9) vs. Cleveland (4), 1986 (OT)
12 NFC-D: Dallas (7) vs. Los Angeles (5), 1973
NFC-D: Washington (7) vs. Chicago (5), 1984
NFC: Chicago (9) vs. San Francisco (3), 1984
AFC-FR: Kansas City (7) vs. San Diego (5), 1992
10 AFC-FR: Houston (7) vs. Oakland (3), 1980
NFC-D: N.Y. Giants (6) vs. San Francisco (4), 1984
SB: New England (7) vs. Chicago (3), 1985
Fewest Times Sacked, Both Teams, Game
0 AFC-D: Buffalo vs. Pittsburgh, 1974
AFC-FR: Pittsburgh vs. San Diego, 1982
AFC: Miami vs. Pittsburgh, 1984
AFC-D: Buffalo vs. Miami, 1990
AFC-D: Denver vs. Houston, 1991
1 In many games

Touchdowns
Most Touchdowns, Game
6 AFC-D: Oakland vs. Houston, 1969
5 NFC: Chi. Bears vs. Washington, 1943
NFC: Detroit vs. Cleveland, 1957
AFC-D: Oakland vs. Kansas City, 1968
SB: San Francisco vs. Denver, 1989
4 By many teams
Most Touchdowns, Both Teams, Game
8 AFC-FR: Buffalo (4) vs. Houston (4), 1992 (OT)
7 NFC: Chi. Bears (5) vs. Washington (2), 1943
AFC-D: Oakland (6) vs. Houston (1), 1969
SB: Pittsburgh (4) vs. Dallas (3), 1978
AFC-D: Miami (4) vs. San Diego (3), 1981 (OT)
AFC: Miami (4) vs. Pittsburgh (3), 1984
AFC-D: Buffalo (4) vs. Cleveland (3), 1989
6 NFC-FR: Green Bay (4) vs. St. Louis (2), 1982
AFC: Cleveland (3) vs. Denver (3), 1987
AFC-D: Buffalo (3) vs. Miami (3), 1990

Interceptions By

Most Interceptions By, Game

8 NFC: Chi. Bears vs. Washington, 1940
7 NFC: Cleveland vs. Los Angeles, 1955
6 NFC: Green Bay vs. N.Y. Giants, 1939
NFC: Chi. Bears vs. N.Y. Giants, 1946
NFC: Cleveland vs. Detroit, 1954
AFC: San Diego vs. Houston, 1961
AFC: Buffalo vs. L.A. Raiders, 1990

Most Interceptions By, Both Teams, Game

10 NFC: Cleveland (7) vs. Los Angeles (3), 1955
AFC: San Diego (6) vs. Houston (4), 1961
9 NFC: Green Bay (6) vs. N.Y. Giants (3), 1939
8 NFC: Chi. Bears (8) vs. Washington (0), 1940
NFC: Chi. Bears (6) vs. N.Y. Giants (2), 1946
NFC: Cleveland (6) vs. Detroit (2), 1954
AFC-FR: Buffalo (4) vs. N.Y. Jets (4), 1981
AFC: Miami (5) vs. N.Y. Jets (3), 1982

Yards Gained

Most Yards Gained, Game

138 AFC-FR: N.Y. Jets vs. Cincinnati, 1982
136 AFC: Dall. Texans vs. Houston, 1962 (OT)
130 NFC-D: Los Angeles vs. St. Louis, 1975

Most Yards Gained, Both Teams, Game

156 NFC: Green Bay (123) vs. N.Y. Giants (33), 1939
149 NFC: Cleveland (103) vs. Los Angeles (46), 1955
141 AFC-FR: Buffalo (79) vs. N.Y. Jets (62), 1981

Touchdowns

Most Touchdowns, Game

3 NFC: Chi. Bears vs. Washington, 1940
2 NFC-D: Los Angeles vs. St. Louis, 1975
1 In many games

Punting

Most Punts, Game

14 AFC-D: N.Y. Jets vs. Cleveland, 1986 (OT)
13 NFC: N.Y. Giants vs. Chi. Bears, 1933
AFC-D: Baltimore vs. Oakland, 1977 (OT)
11 AFC: Houston vs. Oakland, 1967
AFC-D: Houston vs. Oakland, 1969
NFC: L.A. Rams vs. Chicago, 1985

Fewest Punts, Game

0 NFC-FR: St. Louis vs. Green Bay, 1982
AFC-FR: N.Y. Jets vs. Cincinnati, 1982
1 NFC-D: Cleveland vs. Dallas, 1969
AFC: Miami vs. Oakland, 1973
AFC-D: Oakland vs. Cincinnati, 1975
AFC-D: Pittsburgh vs. Baltimore, 1976
AFC: Pittsburgh vs. Houston, 1978
NFC-FR: Green Bay vs. St. Louis, 1982
AFC-FR: Miami vs. New England, 1982
AFC-FR: San Diego vs. Pittsburgh, 1982
AFC-D: Cleveland vs. Indianapolis, 1987
AFC-D: Buffalo vs. Miami, 1990
AFC-FR: L.A. Raiders vs. Kansas City, 1991
NFC-FR: Atlanta vs. New Orleans, 1991
NFC-FR: Chicago vs. Dallas, 1991
AFC-D: Houston vs. Denver, 1991
NFC: San Francisco vs. Dallas, 1992
2 In many games

Most Punts, Both Teams, Game

23 NFC: N.Y. Giants (13) vs. Chi. Bears (10), 1933
22 AFC-D: N.Y. Jets (14) vs. Cleveland (8), 1986 (OT)
21 AFC-D: Baltimore (13) vs. Oakland (8), 1977 (OT)
NFC: L.A. Rams (11) vs. Chicago (10), 1985

Fewest Punts, Both Teams, Game

1 NFC-FR: St. Louis (0) vs. Green Bay (1), 1982
2 AFC-FR: N.Y. Jets (0) vs. Cincinnati (2), 1982
3 AFC: Miami (1) vs. Oakland (2), 1973
AFC-FR: San Diego (1) vs. Pittsburgh (2), 1982
AFC-D: Buffalo (1) vs. Miami (2), 1990
AFC-FR: L.A. Raiders (1) vs. Kansas City (2), 1991
AFC-D: Houston (1) vs. Denver (2), 1991

Average Yardage

Highest Average, Punting, Game (4 punts)

56.0 AFC: Oakland vs. San Diego, 1980
52.5 NFC: Washington vs. Chi. Bears, 1942
51.6 AFC-D: Cincinnati vs. L.A. Raiders, 1990

Lowest Average, Punting, Game (4 punts)

24.9 NFC: Washington vs. Chi. Bears, 1937
25.3 AFC-FR: Pittsburgh vs. Houston, 1989
25.5 NFC: Green Bay vs. N.Y. Giants, 1962

Punt Returns

Most Punt Returns, Game

8 NFC: Green Bay vs. N.Y. Giants, 1944
7 By eight teams

Most Punt Returns, Both Teams, Game

13 AFC-FR: Houston (7) vs. Oakland (6), 1980
11 NFC: Green Bay (8) vs. N.Y. Giants (3), 1944
NFC-D: Green Bay (6) vs. Baltimore (5), 1965
10 In many games

Fewest Punt Returns, Both Teams, Game

0 NFC: Chi. Bears vs. N.Y. Giants, 1941
AFC: Boston vs. San Diego, 1963
NFC-FR: Green Bay vs. St. Louis, 1982
AFC-FR: Houston vs. N.Y. Jets, 1991
AFC-D: Denver vs. Houston, 1991
NFC-D: San Francisco vs. Washington, 1992
1 AFC: Miami (0) vs. Pittsburgh (1), 1972
AFC: Cincinnati (0) vs. San Diego (1), 1981
AFC-FR: Cincinnati (0) vs. N.Y. Jets (1), 1982
AFC-FR: San Diego (0) vs. Pittsburgh (1), 1982
NFC-D: Minnesota (0) vs. Washington (1), 1982
AFC: Seattle (0) vs. L.A. Raiders (1), 1983
AFC-D: Pittsburgh (0) vs. Denver (1), 1989
NFC-FR: New Orleans (0) vs. Atlanta (1), 1991
AFC-FR: Buffalo (0) vs. Houston (1), 1992 (OT)
2 In many games

Yards Gained

Most Yards Gained, Game

155 NFC-D: Dallas vs. Cleveland, 1967
150 NFC: Chi. Cardinals vs. Philadelphia, 1947
143 NFC-FR: Minnesota vs. New Orleans, 1987

Fewest Yards Gained, Game

−10 NFC: Green Bay vs. Cleveland, 1965
−9 NFC: Dallas vs. Green Bay, 1966
AFC-D: Kansas City vs. Oakland, 1968
−5 AFC-D: Miami vs. Oakland, 1970
NFC-D: San Francisco vs. Dallas, 1972
NFC: Dallas vs. Washington, 1972

Most Yards Gained, Both Teams, Game

166 NFC-D: Dallas (155) vs. Cleveland (11), 1967
160 NFC: Chi. Cardinals (150) vs. Philadelphia (10), 1947
146 NFC-D: Philadelphia (112) vs. Pittsburgh (34), 1947

Fewest Yards Gained, Both Teams, Game

−9 NFC: Dallas (−9) vs. Green Bay (0), 1966
−6 AFC-D: Miami (−5) vs. Oakland (−1), 1970
−3 NFC-D: San Francisco (−5) vs. Dallas (2), 1972

Touchdowns

Most Touchdowns, Game

1 By 10 teams

Kickoff Returns

Most Kickoff Returns, Game

10 NFC-D: L.A. Rams vs. Washington, 1983
9 NFC: Chi. Bears vs. N.Y. Giants, 1956
AFC: Boston vs. San Diego, 1963
AFC: Houston vs. Oakland, 1967
SB: Denver vs. San Francisco, 1989
AFC-D: Miami vs. Buffalo, 1990
AFC: L.A. Raiders vs. Buffalo, 1990
8 By many teams

Most Kickoff Returns, Both Teams, Game

15 AFC-D: Miami (9) vs. Buffalo (6), 1990
13 NFC-D: Green Bay (7) vs. Dallas (6), 1982
12 In many games

Fewest Kickoff Returns, Both Teams, Game

1 NFC: Green Bay (0) vs. Boston (1), 1936
AFC-FR: San Diego (0) vs. Kansas City (1), 1992
2 NFC-D: Los Angeles (0) vs. Chi. Bears (2), 1950
AFC: Houston (0) vs. San Diego (2), 1961
AFC-D: Oakland (1) vs. Pittsburgh (1), 1972
AFC-D: N.Y. Jets (0) vs. L.A. Raiders (2), 1982
AFC: Miami (1) vs. N.Y. Jets (1), 1982
NFC: N.Y. Giants (0) vs. Washington (2), 1986
3 In many games

Yards Gained

Most Yards Gained, Game

225 NFC: Washington vs. Chi. Bears, 1940
222 SB: Miami vs. Washington, 1982
215 NFC: Los Angeles vs. Cleveland, 1955
AFC: Houston vs. Oakland, 1967

Most Yards Gained, Both Teams, Game

379 AFC-D: Baltimore (193) vs. Oakland (186), 1977 (OT)
321 NFC-D: Dallas (173) vs. Green Bay (148), 1982
318 AFC-D: Miami (183) vs. Oakland (135), 1974

Fewest Yards Gained, Both Teams, Game

5 AFC-FR: San Diego (0) vs. Kansas City (5), 1992
15 NFC: N.Y. Giants (0) vs. Washington (15), 1986
31 NFC-D: Los Angeles (0) vs. Chi. Bears (31), 1950

Touchdowns

Most Touchdowns, Game

1 NFC-D: San Francisco vs. Dallas, 1972
AFC-D: Miami vs. Oakland, 1974
AFC-D: Baltimore vs. Oakland, 1977 (OT)
SB: Miami vs. Washington, 1982
SB: Cincinnati vs. San Francisco, 1988
AFC-D: Cleveland vs. Buffalo, 1989

Penalties

Most Penalties, Game

14 AFC-FR: Oakland vs. Houston, 1980
NFC-D: San Francisco vs. N.Y. Giants, 1981
13 AFC-FR: Houston vs. Cleveland, 1988
AFC-D: Houston vs. Denver, 1991
12 NFC-D: Chi. Bears vs. Green Bay, 1941
AFC-D: Pittsburgh vs. Baltimore, 1976
SB: Dallas vs. Denver, 1977
AFC-FR: N.Y. Jets vs. Cincinnati, 1982

Fewest Penalties, Game

0 NFC: Philadelphia vs. Green Bay, 1960
NFC-D: Detroit vs. Dallas, 1970
AFC-D: Miami vs. Oakland, 1970
SB: Miami vs. Dallas, 1971
NFC-D: Washington vs. Minnesota, 1973

SB: Pittsburgh vs. Dallas, 1975
NFC: San Francisco vs. Chicago, 1988
SB: Denver vs. San Francisco, 1989
AFC-D: L.A. Raiders vs. Cincinnati, 1990
AFC-D: Miami vs. San Diego, 1992
1 By many teams

Most Penalties, Both Teams, Game
22 AFC-FR: Oakland (14) vs. Houston (8), 1980
NFC-D: San Francisco (14) vs. N.Y. Giants (8), 1981
AFC-FR: Houston (13) vs. Cleveland (9), 1988
21 AFC-D: Oakland (11) vs. New England (10), 1976
20 SB: Dallas (12) vs. Denver (8), 1977

Fewest Penalties, Both Teams, Game
1 AFC-D: L.A. Raiders (0) vs. Cincinnati (1), 1990
2 NFC: Washington (1) vs. Chi. Bears (1), 1937
NFC-D: Washington (0) vs. Minnesota (2), 1973
SB: Pittsburgh (0) vs. Dallas (2), 1975
3 AFC: Miami (1) vs. Baltimore (2), 1971
NFC: San Francisco (1) vs. Dallas (2), 1971
SB: Miami (0) vs. Dallas (3), 1971
AFC-D: Pittsburgh (1) vs. Oakland (2), 1972
AFC-D: Miami (1) vs. Cincinnati (2), 1973
SB: Miami (1) vs. San Francisco (2), 1984
NFC: San Francisco (0) vs. Chicago (3), 1988

Yards Penalized

Most Yards Penalized, Game
145 NFC-D: San Francisco vs. N.Y. Giants, 1981
133 SB: Dallas vs. Baltimore, 1970
128 NFC-D: Chi. Bears vs. Green Bay, 1941

Fewest Yards Penalized, Game
0 By 10 teams

Most Yards Penalized, Both Teams, Game
206 NFC-D: San Francisco (145) vs. N.Y. Giants (61), 1981
193 AFC-FR: Houston (118) vs. Cleveland (75), 1988
192 AFC-D: Denver (104) vs. Pittsburgh (88), 1978

Fewest Yards Penalized, Both Teams, Game
5 AFC-D: L.A. Raiders (0) vs. Cincinnati (5), 1990
9 NFC-D: Washington (0) vs. Minnesota (9), 1973
15 SB: Miami (0) vs. Dallas (15), 1971

Fumbles

Most Fumbles, Game
8 SB: Buffalo vs. Dallas, 1992
6 By 11 teams

Most Fumbles, Both Teams, Game
12 AFC: Houston (6) vs. Pittsburgh (6), 1978
SB: Buffalo (8) vs. Dallas (4), 1992
10 NFC: Chi. Bears (5) vs. N.Y. Giants (5), 1934
SB: Dallas (6) vs. Denver (4), 1977
9 NFC-D: San Francisco (6) vs. Detroit (3), 1957
NFC-D: San Francisco (5) vs. Dallas (4), 1972
NFC: Dallas (5) vs. Philadelphia (4), 1980

Most Fumbles Lost, Game
5 SB: Buffalo vs. Dallas, 1992
4 NFC: N.Y. Giants vs. Baltimore, 1958 (OT)
AFC: Kansas City vs. Oakland, 1969
SB: Baltimore vs. Dallas, 1970
AFC: Pittsburgh vs. Oakland, 1975
SB: Denver vs. Dallas, 1977
AFC: Houston vs. Pittsburgh, 1978
AFC: Miami vs. New England, 1985
SB: New England vs. Chicago, 1985
NFC-FR: L.A. Rams vs. Washington, 1986
3 By many teams

Fewest Fumbles, Both Teams, Game
0 NFC: Green Bay vs. Cleveland, 1965
AFC-D: Houston vs. San Diego, 1979
NFC-D: Dallas vs. Los Angeles, 1979
SB: Los Angeles vs. Pittsburgh, 1979
AFC-D: Buffalo vs. Cincinnati, 1981
NFC-D: San Francisco vs. Washington, 1990
1 In many games

Recoveries

Most Total Fumbles Recovered, Game
8 SB: Dallas vs. Denver, 1977 (4 own, 4 opp)
7 NFC: Chi. Bears vs. N.Y. Giants, 1934 (5 own, 2 opp)
NFC-D: San Francisco vs. Detroit, 1957 (4 own, 3 opp)
NFC-D: San Francisco vs. Dallas, 1972 (4 own, 3 opp)
AFC: Pittsburgh vs. Houston, 1978 (3 own, 4 opp)
6 AFC: Houston vs. San Diego, 1961 (4 own, 2 opp)
AFC-D: Cleveland vs. Baltimore, 1971 (4 own, 2 opp)
AFC-D: Cleveland vs. Oakland, 1980 (5 own, 1 opp)
NFC: Philadelphia vs. Dallas, 1980 (3 own, 3 opp)
SB: Dallas vs. Buffalo, 1992 (1 own, 5 opp)

Most Own Fumbles Recovered, Game
5 NFC: Chi. Bears vs. N.Y. Giants, 1934
AFC-D: Cleveland vs. Oakland, 1980
4 By many teams

Turnovers

(Numbers of times losing the ball on interceptions and fumbles.)

Most Turnovers, Game
9 NFC: Washington vs. Chi. Bears, 1940
NFC: Detroit vs. Cleveland, 1954
AFC: Houston vs. Pittsburgh, 1978
SB: Buffalo vs. Dallas, 1992
8 NFC: N.Y. Giants vs. Chi. Bears, 1946
NFC: Los Angeles vs. Cleveland, 1955
NFC: Cleveland vs. Detroit, 1957
SB: Denver vs. Dallas, 1977
NFC-D: Minnesota vs. Philadelphia, 1980
7 AFC: Houston vs. San Diego, 1961
SB: Baltimore vs. Dallas, 1970
AFC: Pittsburgh vs. Oakland, 1975
NFC-D: Chicago vs. Dallas, 1977
NFC: Los Angeles vs. Dallas, 1978
AFC-D: San Diego vs. Miami, 1982
AFC: Buffalo vs. L.A. Raiders, 1990

Fewest Turnovers, Game
0 By many teams

Most Turnovers, Both Teams, Game
14 AFC: Houston (9) vs. Pittsburgh (5), 1978
13 NFC: Detroit (9) vs. Cleveland (4), 1954
AFC: Houston (7) vs. San Diego (6), 1961
12 AFC: Pittsburgh (7) vs. Oakland (5), 1975

Fewest Turnovers, Both Teams, Game
0 SB: Buffalo vs. N.Y. Giants, 1990
1 AFC-D: Baltimore (0) vs. Cincinnati (1), 1970
AFC-D: Pittsburgh (0) vs. Buffalo (1), 1974
AFC: Oakland (0) vs. Pittsburgh (1), 1976
NFC-D: Minnesota (0) vs. Washington (1), 1982
NFC-D: Chicago (0) vs. N.Y. Giants (1), 1985
SB: N.Y. Giants (0) vs. Denver (1), 1986
NFC: Washington (0) vs. Minnesota (1), 1987
AFC-D: Cincinnati (0) vs. L.A. Raiders (1), 1990
NFC: N.Y. Giants (0) vs. San Francisco (1), 1990
2 In many games

AFC-NFC PRO BOWL RECORDS

Compiled by Elias Sports Bureau

Individual Records

Service

Most Games

10 Lawrence Taylor, N.Y. Giants, 1982-91
Ronnie Lott, San Francisco, 1982-85, 1987-91; L.A. Raiders 1992
Mike Singletary, Chicago, 1984-93
9 *Ken Houston, Houston, 1971-73; Washington, 1974-79
Joe Greene, Pittsburgh, 1971-77, 1979-80
Jack Lambert, Pittsburgh, 1976-84
Walter Payton, Chicago, 1977-81, 1984-87
Harry Carson, N.Y. Giants, 1979-80, 1982-88
Mike Webster, Pittsburgh, 1979-86, 1988
**Anthony Muñoz, Cincinnati, 1982-87, 1989-90, 1992
8 Tom Mack, Los Angeles, 1971-76, 1978-79
*Franco Harris, Pittsburgh, 1973-76, 1978-81
Lemar Parrish, Cincinnati, 1971-72, 1975-77; Washington, 1978, 1980-81
Art Shell, Oakland, 1973-79, 1981
Ted Hendricks, Baltimore, 1972-74; Green Bay, 1975; Oakland, 1981-82; L.A. Raiders, 1983-84
*John Hannah, New England, 1977, 1979-83, 1985-86
*Randy White, Dallas, 1978, 1980-86
*Mike Haynes, New England, 1978-81, 1983; L.A. Raiders, 1985-87
James Lofton, Green Bay, 1979, 1981-86; Buffalo 1992
Mike Munchak, Houston, 1985-86, 1988-93
*Also selected, but did not play, in one additional game
**Also selected, but did not play, in two additional games

Scoring

Points

Most Points, Career

37 Morten Andersen, New Orleans, 1986-89, 1991, 1993 (13-pat, 8-fg)
30 Jan Stenerud, Kansas City, 1971-72, 1976; Green Bay, 1985 (6-pat, 8-fg)
26 Nick Lowery, Kansas City, 1982, 1991, 1993 (5 pat, 7 fg)

Most Points, Game

18 John Brockington, Green Bay, 1973 (3-td)
15 Garo Yepremian, Miami, 1974 (5-fg)
14 Jan Stenerud, Kansas City, 1972 (2-pat, 4-fg)

Touchdowns

Most Touchdowns, Career

3 John Brockington, Green Bay, 1972-74 (2-r, 1-p)
Earl Campbell, Houston, 1979-82, 1984 (3-r)
Chuck Muncie, New Orleans, 1980; San Diego, 1982-83 (3-r)
William Andrews, Atlanta, 1981-84 (1-r, 2-p)
Marcus Allen, L.A. Raiders, 1983, 1985-86, 1988 (2-r, 1-p)
2 By 13 players

Most Touchdowns, Game

3 John Brockington, Green Bay, 1973 (2-r, 1-p)
2 Mel Renfro, Dallas, 1971 (2-ret)
Earl Campbell, Houston, 1980 (2-r)
Chuck Muncie, New Orleans, 1980 (2-r)
William Andrews, Atlanta, 1984 (2-p)
Herschel Walker, Dallas, 1989 (2-r)
Johnny Johnson, Phoenix, 1991 (2-r)

Points After Touchdown

Most Points After Touchdown, Career

13 Morten Andersen, New Orleans, 1986-89, 1991, 1993 (13 att)
6 Chester Marcol, Green Bay, 1973, 1975 (6 att)
Mark Moseley, Washington, 1980, 1983 (7 att)
Ali Haji-Sheikh, N.Y. Giants, 1984 (6 att)
Jan Stenerud, Kansas City, 1971-72, 1976; Green Bay, 1985 (6 att)

Most Points After Touchdown, Game

6 Ali Haji-Sheikh, N.Y. Giants, 1984 (6 att)
4 Chester Marcol, Green Bay, 1973 (4 att)
Mark Moseley, Washington, 1980 (5 att)
Morten Andersen, New Orleans, 1986 (4 att), 1989 (4 att)

Field Goals

Most Field Goals Attempted, Career

15 Jan Stenerud, Kansas City, 1971-72, 1976; Green Bay, 1985
Morten Andersen, New Orleans, 1986-89, 1991, 1993
10 Nick Lowery, Kansas City, 1982, 1991, 1993

Most Field Goals Attempted, Game

6 Jan Stenerud, Kansas City, 1972
Eddie Murray, Detroit, 1981
Mark Moseley, Washington, 1983
5 Garo Yepremian, Miami, 1974
4 Jan Stenerud, Kansas City, 1976
Nick Lowery, Kansas City, 1991, 1993
Morten Andersen, New Orleans, 1993

Most Field Goals, Career

8 Jan Stenerud, Kansas City, 1971-72, 1976; Green Bay, 1985
Morten Andersen, New Orleans, 1986-89, 1991, 1993
7 Nick Lowery, Kansas City, 1982, 1991, 1993

Most Field Goals, Game

5 Garo Yepremian, Miami, 1974 (5 att)
4 Jan Stenerud, Kansas City, 1972 (6 att)
Eddie Murray, Detroit, 1981 (6 att)
3 Nick Lowery, Kansas City, 1991 (4 att)
Nick Lowery, Kansas City, 1993 (4 att)

Longest Field Goal

51 Morten Andersen, New Orleans, 1989
48 Jan Stenerud, Kansas City, 1972
Jeff Jaeger, L.A. Raiders, 1992
43 Gary Anderson, Pittsburgh, 1984
Nick Lowery, Kansas City, 1991

Safeties

Most Safeties, Game

1 Art Still, Kansas City, 1983
Mark Gastineau, N.Y. Jets, 1985
Greg Townsend, L.A. Raiders, 1992

Rushing

Attempts

Most Attempts, Career

81 Walter Payton, Chicago, 1977-81, 1984-87
68 O.J. Simpson, Buffalo, 1973-77
63 Eric Dickerson, L.A. Rams, 1984-85, 1987; Indianapolis, 1988-90

Most Attempts, Game

19 O.J. Simpson, Buffalo, 1974
17 Marv Hubbard, Oakland, 1974
16 O.J. Simpson, Buffalo, 1973
Marcus Allen, L.A. Raiders, 1986

Yards Gained

Most Yards Gained, Career

368 Walter Payton, Chicago, 1977-81, 1984-87
356 O.J. Simpson, Buffalo, 1973-77
220 Earl Campbell, Houston, 1979-82, 1984

Most Yards Gained, Game

112 O. J. Simpson, Buffalo, 1973
104 Marv Hubbard, Oakland, 1974
85 Neal Anderson, Chicago, 1989

Longest Run From Scrimmage

41 Lawrence McCutcheon, Los Angeles, 1976
32 Randall Cunningham, Philadelphia, 1989
30 O.J. Simpson, Buffalo, 1975

Average Gain

Highest Average Gain, Career (20 attempts)

5.81 Marv Hubbard, Oakland, 1972-74 (36-209)
5.71 Wilbert Montgomery, Philadelphia, 1979-80 (21-120)
5.36 Larry Csonka, Miami, 1971-72, 1975 (22-118)

Highest Average Gain, Game (10 attempts)

7.00 O.J. Simpson, Buffalo, 1973 (16-112)
Ottis Anderson, St. Louis, 1981 (10-70)
6.91 Walter Payton, Chicago, 1985 (11-76)
6.90 Earl Campbell, Houston, 1980 (10-69)

Touchdowns

Most Touchdowns, Career

3 Earl Campbell, Houston, 1979-82, 1984
Chuck Muncie, New Orleans, 1980; San Diego, 1982-83
2 John Brockington, Green Bay, 1972-74
O.J. Simpson, Buffalo, 1973-77
Walter Payton, Chicago, 1977-81, 1984-87
Marcus Allen, L.A. Raiders, 1983, 1985-86, 1988
Herschel Walker, Dallas, 1988-89
Johnny Johnson, Phoenix, 1991

Most Touchdowns, Game

2 John Brockington, Green Bay, 1973
Earl Campbell, Houston, 1980
Chuck Muncie, New Orleans, 1980
Herschel Walker, Dallas, 1989
Johnny Johnson, Phoenix, 1991

Passing

Attempts

Most Attempts, Career

120 Dan Fouts, San Diego, 1980-84, 1986
88 Bob Griese, Miami, 1971-72, 1974-75, 1977, 1979
60 Warren Moon, Houston, 1989-93

Most Attempts, Game

32 Bill Kenney, Kansas City, 1984
Steve Young, San Francisco, 1993
30 Dan Fouts, San Diego, 1983
28 Jim Hart, St. Louis, 1976

Completions

Most Completions, Career

63 Dan Fouts, San Diego, 1980-84, 1986
44 Bob Griese, Miami, 1971-72, 1974-75, 1977, 1979
33 Ken Anderson, Cincinnati, 1976-77, 1982-83

Most Completions, Game

21 Joe Theismann, Washington, 1984
18 Steve Young, San Francisco, 1993
17 Dan Fouts, San Diego, 1983

Completion Percentage

Highest Completion Percentage, Career (40 attempts)

68.9 Joe Theismann, Washington, 1983-84 (45-31)
64.4 Jim Kelly, Buffalo, 1988, 1991-92 (45-29)
58.9 Ken Anderson, Cincinnati, 1976-77, 1982-83 (56-33)

Highest Completion Percentage, Game (10 attempts)

90.0 Archie Manning, New Orleans, 1980 (10-9)
77.8 Joe Theismann, Washington, 1984 (27-21)
72.2 Jim Everett, L.A. Rams, 1991 (18-13)

Yards Gained
Most Yards Gained, Career
890 Dan Fouts, San Diego, 1980-84, 1986
554 Bob Griese, Miami, 1971-72, 1974-75, 1977, 1979
398 Ken Anderson, Cincinnati, 1976-77, 1982-83
Most Yards Gained, Game
274 Dan Fouts, San Diego, 1983
242 Joe Theismann, Washington, 1984
212 Phil Simms, N.Y. Giants, 1986
Longest Completion
64 Dan Pastorini, Houston (to Burrough, Houston), 1976 (TD)
59 Randall Cunningham, Philadelphia (to Jackson, Philadelphia [19 yards] lateral to Byner, Washington [40 yards]), 1991
57 James Harris, Los Angeles (to Gray, St. Louis), 1975
Ken Anderson, Cincinnati (to G. Pruitt, Cleveland), 1977

Average Gain
Highest Average Gain, Career (40 attempts)
8.02 Jim Kelly, Buffalo, 1988, 1991-92 (45-361)
7.91 Randall Cunningham, Philadelphia, 1989-91 (44-348)
7.64 Joe Theismann, Washington, 1983-84 (45-344)
Highest Average Gain, Game (10 attempts)
15.27 Randall Cunningham, Philadelphia, 1991 (11-168)
11.40 Ken Anderson, Cincinnati, 1977 (10-114)
11.20 Archie Manning, New Orleans, 1980 (10-112)

Touchdowns
Most Touchdowns, Career
3 Joe Theismann, Washington, 1983-84
Joe Montana, San Francisco, 1982, 1984-85, 1988
Phil Simms, N.Y. Giants, 1986
Jim Kelly, Buffalo, 1988, 1991-92
2 James Harris, Los Angeles, 1975
Mike Boryla, Philadelphia, 1976
Ken Anderson, Cincinnati, 1976-77, 1982-83
Mark Rypien, Washington, 1990, 1992
Most Touchdowns, Game
3 Joe Theismann, Washington, 1984
Phil Simms, N.Y. Giants, 1986
2 James Harris, Los Angeles, 1975
Mike Boryla, Philadelphia, 1976
Ken Anderson, Cincinnati, 1977
Jim Kelly, Buffalo, 1991
Mark Rypien, Washington, 1992

Had Intercepted
Most Passes Had Intercepted, Career
8 Dan Fouts, San Diego, 1980-84, 1986
6 Jim Hart, St. Louis, 1975-78
5 Ken Stabler, Oakland, 1974-75, 1978
Most Passes Had Intercepted, Game
5 Jim Hart, St. Louis, 1977
4 Ken Stabler, Oakland, 1974
3 Dan Fouts, San Diego, 1986
Mark Rypien, Washington, 1990
Steve Young, San Francisco, 1993
Most Attempts, Without Interception, Game
27 Joe Theismann, Washington, 1984
Phil Simms, N.Y. Giants, 1986
26 John Brodie, San Francisco, 1971
Danny White, Dallas, 1983
21 Roman Gabriel, Philadelphia, 1974
Dan Marino, Miami, 1985

Percentage, Passes Had Intercepted
Lowest Percentage, Passes Had Intercepted, Career (40 attempts)
0.00 Joe Theismann, Washington, 1983-84 (45-0)
2.13 Dave Krieg, Seattle, 1985, 1989-90 (47-1)
2.22 Jim Kelly, Buffalo, 1988, 1991-92 (45-1)

Pass Receiving
Receptions
Most Receptions, Career
20 Jerry Rice, San Francisco, 1987-88, 1990-93
18 Walter Payton, Chicago, 1977-81, 1984-87
17 Steve Largent, Seattle, 1979, 1982, 1985-88
Most Receptions, Game
8 Steve Largent, Seattle, 1986
Michael Irvin, Dallas, 1992
Andre Rison, Atlanta, 1993
7 John Stallworth, Pittsburgh, 1983
Jerry Rice, San Francisco, 1992
6 John Stallworth, Pittsburgh, 1980
Kellen Winslow, San Diego, 1982
Gary Clark, Washington, 1991

Yards Gained
Most Yards Gained, Career
287 Jerry Rice, San Francisco, 1987-88, 1990-93
236 Steve Largent, Seattle, 1979, 1982, 1985-88
226 Wes Chandler, New Orleans, 1980; San Diego, 1983-84, 1986
Most Yards Gained, Game
125 Michael Irvin, Dallas, 1992
114 Wes Chandler, San Diego, 1986
96 Ken Burrough, Houston, 1976
Longest Reception
64 Ken Burrough, Houston (from Pastorini, Houston), 1976 (TD)
59 Keith Jackson, Philadelphia (19 yards) lateral to Earnest Byner, Washington (40 yards) (from Cunningham, Philadelphia), 1991
57 Mel Gray, St. Louis (from Harris, Los Angeles), 1975
Greg Pruitt, Cleveland (from Anderson, Cincinnati), 1977

Touchdowns
Most Touchdowns, Career
2 Mel Gray, St. Louis, 1975-78
Cliff Branch, Oakland, 1975-78
Terry Metcalf, St. Louis, 1975-76, 1978
Tony Hill, Dallas, 1979-80, 1986
William Andrews, Atlanta, 1981-84
James Lofton, Green Bay, 1979, 1981-86; Buffalo 1992
Jimmie Giles, Tampa Bay, 1981-83, 1986
Michael Irvin, Dallas, 1992-93
Most Touchdowns, Game
2 William Andrews, Atlanta, 1984

Interceptions By
Most Interceptions By, Career
4 Everson Walls, Dallas, 1982-84, 1986
3 Ken Houston, Houston, 1971-73; Washington, 1974-79
Jack Lambert, Pittsburgh, 1976-84
Ted Hendricks, Baltimore, 1972-74; Green Bay, 1975; Oakland, 1981-82; L.A. Raiders, 1983-84
Mike Haynes, New England, 1978-81, 1983; L.A. Raiders, 1985-87
2 By eight players
Most Interceptions By, Game
2 Mel Blount, Pittsburgh, 1977
Everson Walls, Dallas, 1982, 1983
LeRoy Irvin, L.A. Rams, 1986
David Fulcher, Cincinnati, 1990

Yards Gained
Most Yards Gained, Career
77 Ted Hendricks, Baltimore, 1972-74; Green Bay, 1975; Oakland, 1981-82; L.A. Raiders, 1983-84
51 Jerry Gray, L.A. Rams, 1987-90
48 Joey Browner, Minnesota, 1986-90
Most Yards Gained, Game
65 Ted Hendricks, Baltimore, 1973
51 Jerry Gray, L.A. Rams, 1990
48 Joey Browner, Minnesota, 1986
Longest Gain
65 Ted Hendricks, Baltimore, 1973
51 Jerry Gray, L.A. Rams, 1990 (TD)
48 Joey Browner, Minnesota, 1986 (TD)

Touchdowns
Most Touchdowns, Game
1 Bobby Bell, Kansas City, 1973
Nolan Cromwell, L.A. Rams, 1984
Joey Browner, Minnesota, 1986
Jerry Gray, L.A. Rams, 1990
Mike Johnson, Cleveland, 1990
Junior Seau, San Diego, 1993

Punting
Most Punts, Career
33 Ray Guy, Oakland, 1974-79, 1981
23 Rohn Stark, Indianapolis, 1986-87, 1991, 1993
19 Dave Jennings, N.Y. Giants, 1979-81, 1983
Most Punts, Game
10 Reggie Roby, Miami, 1985
9 Tom Wittum, San Francisco, 1974
Rohn Stark, Indianapolis, 1987
8 Jerrel Wilson, Kansas City, 1971
Tom Skladany, Detroit, 1982
Longest Punt
64 Tom Wittum, San Francisco, 1974
61 Reggie Roby, Miami, 1985
60 Ron Widby, Dallas, 1972

Average Yardage
Highest Average, Career (10 punts)
45.25 Jerrel Wilson, Kansas City, 1971-73 (16-724)
44.79 Reggie Roby, Miami, 1985, 1990 (14-627)
44.65 Rohn Stark, Indianapolis, 1986-87, 1991, 1993 (23-1,027)
Highest Average, Game (4 punts)
49.57 Jim Arnold, Detroit, 1988 (7-347)
49.00 Ray Guy, Oakland, 1974 (4-196)
47.75 Bob Grupp, Kansas City, 1980 (4-191)

Punt Returns
Most Punt Returns, Career
13 Rick Upchurch, Denver, 1977, 1979-80, 1983
11 Vai Sikahema, St. Louis, 1987-88
10 Mike Nelms, Washington, 1981-83
Most Punt Returns, Game
7 Vai Sikahema, St. Louis, 1987
6 Henry Ellard, L.A. Rams, 1985
Gerald McNeil, Cleveland, 1988
5 Rick Upchurch, Denver, 1980
Mike Nelms, Washington, 1981
Carl Roaches, Houston, 1982
Johnny Bailey, Phoenix, 1993
Most Fair Catches, Game
2 Jerry Logan, Baltimore, 1971
Dick Anderson, Miami, 1974
Henry Ellard, L.A. Rams, 1985

Yards Gained
Most Yards Gained, Career
183 Billy Johnson, Houston, 1976, 1978; Atlanta, 1984
138 Rick Upchurch, Denver, 1977, 1979-80, 1983
Mel Renfro, Dallas, 1971-72, 1974
119 Mike Nelms, Washington, 1981-83

Most Yards Gained, Game
159 Billy Johnson, Houston, 1976
138 Mel Renfro, Dallas, 1971
117 Wally Henry, Philadelphia, 1980
Longest Punt Return
90 Billy Johnson, Houston, 1976 (TD)
86 Wally Henry, Philadelphia, 1980 (TD)
82 Mel Renfro, Dallas, 1971 (TD)

Touchdowns
Most Touchdowns, Game
2 Mel Renfro, Dallas, 1971
1 Billy Johnson, Houston, 1976
Wally Henry, Philadelphia, 1980

Kickoff Returns
Most Kickoff Returns, Career
10 Rick Upchurch, Denver, 1977, 1979-80, 1983
Greg Pruitt, Cleveland, 1974-75, 1977-78; L.A. Raiders, 1984
8 Mike Nelms, Washington, 1981-83
7 Mel Gray, Detroit, 1991-92
Most Kickoff Returns, Game
6 Greg Pruitt, L.A. Raiders, 1984
5 Les (Speedy) Duncan, Washington, 1972
Ron Smith, Chicago, 1973
Herb Mul-Key, Washington, 1974
Mel Gray, Detroit, 1991
4 By six players

Yards Gained
Most Yards Gained, Career
309 Greg Pruitt, Cleveland, 1974-75, 1977-78; L.A. Raiders, 1984
222 Rick Upchurch, Denver, 1977, 1979-80, 1983
175 Les (Speedy) Duncan, Washington, 1972
Most Yards Gained, Game
192 Greg Pruitt, L.A. Raiders, 1984
175 Les (Speedy) Duncan, Washington, 1972
152 Ron Smith, Chicago, 1973
Longest Kickoff Return
62 Greg Pruitt, L.A. Raiders, 1984
61 Eugene (Mercury) Morris, Miami, 1972
55 Ron Smith, Chicago, 1973

Touchdowns
Most Touchdowns, Game
None

Fumbles
Most Fumbles, Career
6 Dan Fouts, San Diego, 1980-84, 1986
4 Lawrence McCutcheon, Los Angeles, 1974-78
Franco Harris, Pittsburgh, 1973-76, 1978-81
Jay Schroeder, Washington, 1987
Vai Sikahema, St. Louis, 1987-88
3 O.J. Simpson, Buffalo, 1973-77
William Andrews, Atlanta, 1981-84
Joe Montana, San Francisco, 1982, 1984-85, 1988
Walter Payton, Chicago, 1977-81, 1984-87
Neil Lomax, St. Louis, 1985, 1988
Jim Kelly, Buffalo, 1988, 1991-92
Most Fumbles, Game
4 Jay Schroeder, Washington, 1987
3 Dan Fouts, San Diego, 1982
Vai Sikahema, St. Louis, 1987
2 By 11 players

Recoveries
Most Fumbles Recovered, Career
3 Harold Jackson, Philadelphia, 1973; Los Angeles, 1974, 1976, 1978 (3-own)
Dan Fouts, San Diego, 1980-84, 1986 (3-own)
Randy White, Dallas, 1978, 1980-86 (3-opp)
2 By many players
Most Fumbles Recovered, Game
2 Dick Anderson, Miami, 1974 (1-own, 1-opp)
Harold Jackson, Los Angeles, 1974 (2-own)
Dan Fouts, San Diego, 1982 (2-own)
Joey Browner, Minnesota, 1990 (2-opp)

Yardage
Longest Fumble Return
83 Art Still, Kansas City, 1985 (TD, opp)
51 Phil Villapiano, Oakland, 1974 (opp)
37 Sam Mills, New Orleans, 1988 (opp)

Touchdowns
Most Touchdowns, Game
1 Art Still, Kansas City, 1985
Keith Millard, Minnesota, 1990

Sacks
Sacks have been compiled since 1983.
Most Sacks, Career
9.5 Reggie White, Philadelphia, 1987-93
9 Howie Long, L.A. Raiders, 1984-88, 1990, 1993
7 Mark Gastineau, N.Y. Jets, 1983-86
Most Sacks, Game
4 Mark Gastineau, N.Y. Jets, 1985
Reggie White, Philadelphia, 1987
3 Richard Dent, Chicago, 1985
Bruce Smith, Buffalo, 1991
2 By many players

Team Records

Scoring
Most Points, Game
45 NFC, 1984
Fewest Points, Game
3 AFC, 1984, 1989
Most Points, Both Teams, Game
64 NFC (37) vs. AFC (27), 1980
Fewest Points, Both Teams, Game
16 NFC (6) vs. AFC (10), 1987

Touchdowns
Most Touchdowns, Game
6 NFC, 1984
Fewest Touchdowns, Game
0 AFC, 1971, 1974, 1984, 1989
NFC, 1987, 1988
Most Touchdowns, Both Teams, Game
8 AFC (4) vs. NFC (4), 1973
NFC (5) vs. AFC (3), 1980
Fewest Touchdowns, Both Teams, Game
1 AFC (0) vs. NFC (1), 1974
NFC (0) vs. AFC (1), 1987
NFC (0) vs. AFC (1), 1988

Points After Touchdown
Most Points After Touchdown, Game
6 NFC, 1984
Most Points After Touchdown, Both Teams, Game
7 NFC (4) vs. AFC (3), 1973
NFC (4) vs. AFC (3), 1980
NFC (4) vs. AFC (3), 1986

Field Goals
Most Field Goals Attempted, Game
6 AFC, 1972
NFC, 1981, 1983
Most Field Goals Attempted, Both Teams, Game
9 NFC (6) vs. AFC (3), 1983
Most Field Goals, Game
5 AFC, 1974
Most Field Goals, Both Teams, Game
7 AFC (5) vs. NFC (2), 1974

Net Yards Gained Rushing And Passing
Most Yards Gained, Game
472 NFC, 1993
Fewest Yards Gained, Game
114 AFC, 1993
Most Yards Gained, Both Teams, Game
811 AFC (466) vs. NFC (345), 1983
Fewest Yards Gained, Both Teams, Game
424 AFC (202) vs. NFC (222), 1987

Rushing
Attempts
Most Attempts, Game
50 AFC, 1974
Fewest Attempts, Game
15 AFC, 1989
Most Attempts, Both Teams, Game
80 AFC (50) vs. NFC (30), 1974
Fewest Attempts, Both Teams, Game
48 AFC (20) vs. NFC (28), 1991

Yards Gained
Most Yards Gained, Game
224 NFC, 1976
Fewest Yards Gained, Game
28 NFC, 1992
Most Yards Gained, Both Teams, Game
425 NFC (224) vs. AFC (201), 1976
Fewest Yards Gained, Both Teams, Game
131 NFC (28) vs. AFC (103), 1992

Touchdowns
Most Touchdowns, Game
3 NFC, 1989, 1991
Most Touchdowns, Both Teams, Game
4 AFC (2) vs. NFC (2), 1973
AFC (2) vs. NFC (2), 1980

Passing
Attempts
Most Attempts, Game
55 NFC, 1993
Fewest Attempts, Game
17 NFC, 1972
Most Attempts, Both Teams, Game
94 AFC (50) vs. NFC (44), 1983
Fewest Attempts, Both Teams, Game
42 NFC (17) vs. AFC (25), 1972

Completions
Most Completions, Game
32 NFC, 1993
Fewest Completions, Game
7 NFC, 1972, 1982
Most Completions, Both Teams, Game
55 AFC (31) vs. NFC (24), 1983

Fewest Completions, Both Teams, Game
18 NFC (7) vs. AFC (11), 1972

Yards Gained
Most Yards Gained, Game
387 AFC, 1983
Fewest Yards Gained, Game
42 NFC, 1982
Most Yards Gained, Both Teams, Game
608 AFC (387) vs. NFC (221), 1983
Fewest Yards Gained, Both Teams, Game
215 NFC (89) vs. AFC (126), 1972

Times Sacked
Most Times Sacked, Game
9 NFC, 1985
Fewest Times Sacked, Game
0 NFC, 1971
Most Times Sacked, Both Teams, Game
17 NFC (9) vs. AFC (8), 1985
Fewest Times Sacked, Both Teams, Game
4 AFC (2) vs. NFC (2), 1978

Touchdowns
Most Touchdowns, Game
4 NFC, 1984
Most Touchdowns, Both Teams, Game
5 NFC (3) vs. AFC (2), 1986

Interceptions By
Most Interceptions By, Game
6 AFC, 1977
Most Interceptions By, Both Teams, Game
7 AFC (6) vs. NFC (1), 1977

Yards Gained
Most Yards Gained, Game
78 NFC, 1986
Most Yards Gained, Both Teams, Game
99 NFC (64) vs. AFC (35), 1975

Touchdowns
Most Touchdowns, Game
1 AFC, 1973, 1990, 1993
NFC, 1984, 1986, 1990

Punting
Most Punts, Game
10 AFC, 1985
Fewest Punts, Game
0 NFC, 1989
Most Punts, Both Teams, Game
16 AFC (10) vs. NFC (6), 1985
Fewest Punts, Both Teams, Game
4 NFC (1) vs. AFC (3), 1992

Average Yardage
Highest Average, Game
50.50 AFC, 1991 (2-101)

Punt Returns
Most Punt Returns, Game
7 NFC, 1985, 1987
Fewest Punt Returns, Game
0 AFC, 1984, 1989
Most Punt Returns, Both Teams, Game
11 NFC (7) vs. AFC (4), 1985
Fewest Punt Returns, Both Teams, Game
3 AFC (0) vs. NFC (3), 1984
AFC (0) vs. NFC (3), 1989
NFC (1) vs. AFC (2), 1991
NFC (2) vs. AFC (1), 1992

Yards Gained
Most Yards Gained, Game
177 AFC, 1976
Fewest Yards Gained, Game
−1 NFC, 1991
Most Yards Gained, Both Teams, Game
263 AFC (177) vs. NFC (86), 1976
Fewest Yards Gained, Both Teams, Game
16 AFC (0) vs. NFC (16), 1984

Touchdowns
Most Touchdowns, Game
2 NFC, 1971

Kickoff Returns
Most Kickoff Returns, Game
7 AFC, 1984
Fewest Kickoff Returns, Game
1 NFC, 1971, 1984
AFC, 1988, 1991
Most Kickoff Returns, Both Teams, Game
10 AFC (5) vs. NFC (5), 1976
AFC (5) vs. NFC (5), 1986
Fewest Kickoff Returns, Both Teams, Game
5 NFC (2) vs. AFC (3), 1979
AFC (1) vs. NFC (4), 1988
NFC (2) vs. AFC (3), 1992

Yards Gained
Most Yards Gained, Game
215 AFC, 1984
Fewest Yards Gained, Game
6 NFC, 1971
Most Yards Gained, Both Teams, Game
293 NFC (200) vs. AFC (93), 1972
Fewest Yards Gained, Both Teams, Game
99 NFC (48) vs. AFC (51), 1987

Touchdowns
Most Touchdowns, Game
None

Fumbles
Most Fumbles, Game
10 NFC, 1974
Most Fumbles, Both Teams, Game
15 NFC (10) vs. AFC (5), 1974

Recoveries
Most Fumbles Recovered, Game
10 NFC, 1974 (6 own, 4 opp)
Most Fumbles Lost, Game
4 AFC, 1974, 1988
NFC, 1974

Yards Gained
Most Yards Gained, Game
87 AFC, 1985

Touchdowns
Most Touchdowns, Game
1 AFC, 1985
NFC, 1990

Turnovers
(Number of times losing the ball on interceptions and fumbles.)
Most Turnovers, Game
8 AFC, 1974
Fewest Turnovers, Game
0 AFC, 1991
NFC, 1991
Most Turnovers, Both Teams, Game
12 AFC (8) vs. NFC (4), 1974
Fewest Turnovers, Both Teams, Game
0 AFC vs. NFC, 1991

RULES

1993 NFL Roster of Officials

Jerry Seeman, Director of Officiating
Jack Reader, Assistant Director of Officiating
Leo Miles, Supervisor of Officials
Ron DeSouza, Supervisor of Officials

No.	Name	Position	College
25	Alderton, John	Line Judge	Portland State
115	Ancich, Hendi	Umpire	Harbor College
81	Anderson, Dave	Line Judge	Salem College
34	Austin, Gerald	Referee	Western Carolina
22	Baetz, Paul	Back Judge	Heidelberg
91	Baker, Ken	Back Judge	Eastern Illinois
26	Baltz, Mark	Head Linesman	Ohio University
55	Barnes, Tom	Line Judge	Minnesota
56	Baynes, Ron	Line Judge	Auburn
32	Bergman, Jeff	Line Judge	Robert Morris
17	Bergman, Jerry	Head Linesman	Duquesne
7	Blum, Ron	Referee	Marin College
90	Borgard, Mike	Side Judge	St. Louis
110	Botchan, Ron	Umpire	Occidental
101	Boylston, Bob	Umpire	Alabama
31	Brown, Chad	Umpire	East Texas State
94	Carey, Mike	Side Judge	Santa Clara
39	Carlsen, Don	Side Judge	Cal State-Chico
63	Carollo, Bill	Side Judge	Wisconsin
43	Cashion, Red	Referee	Texas A&M
24	Clymer, Roy	Back Judge	New Mexico State
45	Coleman, George	Back Judge	Bishop College
65	Coleman, Walt	Line Judge	Arkansas
27	Conway, Al	Umpire	Army
71	Coukart, Ed	Umpire	Northwestern
61	Creed, Dick	Side Judge	Louisville
75	Daopoulos, Jim	Back Judge	Kentucky
78	Demmas, Art	Umpire	Vanderbilt
113	Dorkowski, Don	Field Judge	Cal State-Los Angeles
74	Duke, James	Line Judge	Howard
57	Fiffick, Ed	Umpire	Marquette
47	Fincken, Tom	Side Judge	Kansas State
111	Frantz, Earnie	Head Linesman	No College
50	Gereb, Neil	Umpire	California
72	Gierke, Terry	Head Linesman	Portland State
15	Glass, Bama	Line Judge	Colorado
3	Golmont, Van	Side Judge	Miami
19	Green, Scott	Field Judge	Delaware
23	Grier, Johnny	Referee	University of D.C.
96	Hakes, Don	Field Judge	Bradley
104	Hamer, Dale	Referee	California, Pa.
42	Hamilton, Dave	Umpire	Utah
44	Hampton, Donnie	Field Judge	Georgia
105	Hantak, Dick	Referee	Southeast Missouri
54	Hayward, George	Head Linesman	Missouri Western
85	Hochuli, Ed	Back Judge	Texas-El Paso
114	Johnson, Tom	Head Linesman	Miami, Ohio
97	Jones, Nathan	Side Judge	Lewis & Clark
106	Jury, Al	Back Judge	San Bernardino Valley
107	Kearney, Jim	Back Judge	Pennsylvania
67	Keck, John	Umpire	Cornell College
86	Kukar, Bernie	Referee	St. John's
120	Lane, Gary	Referee	Missouri
18	Lewis, Bob	Field Judge	No College
49	Look, Dean	Side Judge	Michigan State
98	Lovett, Bill	Back Judge	Maryland
59	Luckett, Phil	Field Judge	Texas-El Paso
82	Mallette, Pat	Field Judge	Nebraska
9	Markbreit, Jerry	Referee	Illinois
38	Maurer, Bruce	Line Judge	Ohio State
48	McCarter, Gordon	Referee	Western Reserve
95	McElwee, Bob	Referee	Navy
35	McGrath, Bob	Head Linesman	Western Kentucky
41	McKenzie, Dick	Line Judge	Ashland
64	McPeters, Lloyd	Line Judge	Oklahoma State
76	Merrifield, Ed	Field Judge	Missouri
80	Millis, Timmie	Back Judge	Millsaps
117	Montgomery, Ben	Line Judge	Morehouse
36	Moore, Bob	Back Judge	Dayton
60	Moore, Tommy	Side Judge	Stephen F. Austin
20	Nemmers, Larry	Referee	Upper Iowa
51	Orem, Dale	Line Judge	Louisville
77	Orr, Don	Field Judge	Vanderbilt
10	Phares, Ron	Head Linesman	Virginia Tech
79	Pointer, Aaron	Head Linesman	Pacific Lutheran
92	Poole, Jim	Back Judge	San Diego State
58	Quinby, Bill	Side Judge	Iowa
5	Quirk, Jim	Line Judge	Delaware
83	Reels, Richard	Field Judge	No College
53	Reynolds, Bill	Line Judge	West Chester State
68	Richard, Louis	Back Judge	Southwest Louisiana
30	Riggs, Dennis	Umpire	Bellarmine
121	Rivers, Sanford	Head Linesman	Youngstown State
46	Robison, John	Field Judge	Utah
33	Roe, Howard	Referee	Wichita State
21	Schleyer, John	Head Linesman	Millersville
122	Schmitz, Bill	Field Judge	Colorado State
109	Semon, Sid	Head Linesman	Southern California
118	Sifferman, Tom	Back Judge	Seattle
73	Skelton, Bobby	Field Judge	Alabama
29	Slavin, Howard	Side Judge	Southern California
119	Spitler, Ron	Side Judge	Panhandle State
88	Steenson, Scott	Back Judge	North Texas State
62	Stewart, Charles	Line Judge	Long Beach State
103	Stuart, Rex	Umpire	Appalachian State
4	Toole, Doug	Side Judge	Utah State
37	Upson, Larry	Field Judge	Prince George C.C.
93	Vaughan, Jack	Field Judge	Mississippi State
52	Veteri, Tony	Head Linesman	Manhattan College
100	Wagner, Bob	Umpire	Penn State
28	Wedge, Don	Side Judge	Ohio Wesleyan
87	Weidner, Paul	Head Linesman	Cincinnati
89	Wells, Gordon	Umpire	Occidental
123	White, Tom	Referee	Temple
99	Williams, Banks	Back Judge	Houston
8	Williams, Dale	Head Linesman	Cal St.-Northridge
16	Wyant, David	Side Judge	Virginia

Numerical Roster

No.	Name	Position
3	Van Golmont	SJ
4	Doug Toole	SJ
5	Jim Quirk	LJ
7	Ron Blum	R
8	Dale Williams	HL
9	Jerry Markbreit	R
10	Ron Phares	HL
15	Bama Glass	LJ
16	David Wyant	SJ
17	Jerry Bergman	HL
18	Bob Lewis	FJ
19	Scott Green	FJ
20	Larry Nemmers	R
21	John Schleyer	HL
22	Paul Baetz	BJ
23	Johnny Grier	R
24	Roy Clymer	BJ
25	John Alderton	LJ
26	Mark Baltz	HL
27	Al Conway	U
28	Don Wedge	SJ
29	Howard Slavin	SJ
30	Dennis Riggs	U
31	Chad Brown	U
32	Jeff Bergman	LJ
33	Howard Roe	R
34	Gerry Austin	R
35	Bob McGrath	HL
36	Bob Moore	BJ
37	Larry Upson	FJ
38	Bruce Maurer	LJ
39	Don Carlsen	SJ
41	Dick McKenzie	LJ
42	Dave Hamilton	U
43	Red Cashion	R
44	Donnie Hampton	FJ
45	George Coleman	BJ
46	John Robison	FJ
47	Tom Fincken	SJ
48	Gordon McCarter	R
49	Dean Look	SJ
50	Neil Gereb	U
51	Dale Orem	LJ
52	Tony Veteri	HL
53	Bill Reynolds	LJ
54	George Hayward	HL
55	Tom Barnes	LJ
56	Ron Baynes	LJ
57	Ed Fiffick	U
58	Bill Quinby	SJ
59	Phil Luckett	FJ
60	Tommy Moore	SJ
61	Dick Creed	SJ
62	Charles Stewart	LJ
63	Bill Carollo	SJ
64	Lloyd McPeters	LJ
65	Walt Coleman	LJ
67	John Keck	U
68	Louis Richard	BJ
71	Ed Coukart	U
72	Terry Gierke	HL
73	Bobby Skelton	FJ
74	James Duke	LJ
75	Jim Daopoulos	BJ
76	Ed Merrifield	FJ
77	Don Orr	FJ
78	Art Demmas	U
79	Aaron Pointer	HL
80	Timmie Millis	BJ
81	Dave Anderson	LJ
82	Pat Mallette	FJ
83	Richard Reels	FJ
85	Ed Hochuli	BJ
86	Bernie Kukar	R
87	Paul Weidner	HL
88	Scott Steenson	BJ
89	Gordon Wells	U
90	Mike Borgard	SJ
91	Ken Baker	BJ
92	Jim Poole	BJ
93	Jack Vaughan	FJ
94	Mike Carey	SJ
95	Bob McElwee	R
96	Don Hakes	FJ
97	Nathan Jones	SJ
98	Bill Lovett	BJ
99	Banks Williams	BJ
100	Bob Wagner	U
101	Bob Boylston	U
103	Rex Stuart	U
104	Dale Hamer	R
105	Dick Hantak	R
106	Al Jury	BJ
107	Jim Kearney	BJ
109	Sid Semon	HL
110	Ron Botchan	U
111	Earnie Frantz	HL
113	Don Dorkowski	FJ
114	Tom Johnson	HL
115	Hendi Ancich	U
117	Ben Montgomery	LJ
118	Tom Sifferman	BJ
119	Ron Spitler	SJ
120	Gary Lane	R
121	Sanford Rivers	HL
122	Bill Schmitz	FJ
123	Tom White	R

1993 Officials at a Glance

Referees

Gerry Austin, No. **34,** Western Carolina, associate superintendent, county schools, 12th year.
Ron Blum, No. **7,** Marin College, professional golfer, 9th year.
Red Cashion, No. **43,** Texas A&M, chairman, insurance company, 22nd year.
Johnny Grier, No. **23,** University of D.C., planning engineer, 13th year.
Dale Hamer, No. **104,** California (Pa.) University, consultant, 16th year.
Dick Hantak, No. **105,** Southeast Missouri, educator, 16th year.
Ed Hochuli, No. **85,** Texas-El Paso, attorney, 4th year.
Bernie Kukar, No. **86,** St. John's, sales representative, employees benefit plan, 10th year.
Gary Lane, No. **120,** Missouri, vice president, medical supplies, former NFL player, 12th year.
Jerry Markbreit, No. **9,** Illinois, trade and barter manager, 18th year.
Gordon McCarter, No. **48,** Western Reserve, retired sales manager, 27th year.
Bob McElwee, No. **95,** Navy, owner, heavy construction firm, 18th year.
Larry Nemmers, No. **20,** Upper Iowa, high school principal, 9th year.
Howard Roe, No. **33,** Wichita State, director, administration and finance, 10th year.
Tom White, No. **123,** Temple, president, athletic sportswear, 5th year.

Umpires

Hendi Ancich, No. **115,** Harbor, longshoreman, 12th year.
Ron Botchan, No. **110,** Occidental, college professor, former AFL player, 14th year.
Bob Boylston, No. **101,** Alabama, stockbroker, 16th year.
Chad Brown, No. **31,** East Texas State, director, intramural/sports clubs, 2nd year.
Al Conway, No. **27,** Army, director of manufacturing, 25th year.
Ed Coukart, No. **71,** Northwestern, president, commercial bank, 5th year.
Art Demmas, No. **78,** Vanderbilt, Southern coordinator, National Football Foundation and College Hall of Fame, 26th year.
Ed Fiffick, No. **57,** Marquette, podiatric physician, 15th year.
Neil Gereb, No. **50,** California, project manager, aircraft company, 13th year.
Dave Hamilton, No. **42,** Utah, chief rehabilitation therapy services, 19th year.
John Keck, No. **67,** Cornell, petroleum distributor, 22nd year.
Dennis Riggs, No. **30,** Bellarmine, president, community foundation, 6th year.
Rex Stuart, No. **103,** Appalachian State, insurance agent, 10th year.
Bob Wagner, No. **100,** Penn State, executive director, cardiovascular institute, 9th year.
Gordon Wells, No. **89,** Occidental, college department chairman, 22nd year.

Head Linesmen

Mark Baltz, No. **26,** Ohio University, manufacturer's representative, 5th year.
Jerry Bergman, No. **17,** Duquesne, executive director, pension fund, 28th year.
Earnie Frantz, No. **111,** no college, vice president and manager, insurance company, 13th year.
Terry Gierke, No. **72,** Portland State, real estate broker, 13th year.
George Hayward, No. **54,** Missouri Western, vice president and manager, warehouse company, 3rd year.
Tom Johnson, No. **114,** Miami, Ohio, educator, president, security company, 12th year.
Bob McGrath, No. **35,** Western Kentucky, sales representative, fund raiser, 1st year.
Ron Phares, No. **10,** Virginia Tech, president, construction company, 9th year.
Aaron Pointer, No. **79,** Pacific Lutheran, park department administrator, 7th year.
Sanford Rivers, No. **121,** Youngstown State, assistant vice president, school administration, 5th year.
John Schleyer, No. **21,** Millersville, medical sales, 4th year.
Sid Semon, No. **109,** Southern California, chairman, physical education department, 16th year.
Tony Veteri, No. **52,** Manhattan, director of athletics, 2nd year.
Paul Weidner, No. **87,** Cincinnati, marketing manager, 8th year.
Dale Williams, No. **8,** Cal State-Northridge, owner, coin-op laundromats, 14th year.

Line Judges

John Alderton, No. **25,** Portland State, vice president, insurance, 5th year.
Dave Anderson, No. **81,** Salem, insurance executive, 10th year.
Tom Barnes, No. **55,** Minnesota, manufacturing representative, 8th year.
Ron Baynes, No. **56,** Auburn, school administrator, coach, 7th year.
Jeff Bergman, No. **32,** Robert Morris, president and chief executive officer, medical services, 3rd year.
Walt Coleman, No. **65,** Arkansas, president, dairy processor, 5th year.
James Duke, No. **74,** Howard, ward manager, department of recreation and parks, 1st year.
Bama Glass, No. **15,** Colorado, agent, insurance/financial services, 15th year.
Bruce Maurer, No. **38,** Ohio State, administrator and associate director, recreational sports, 7th year.
Dick McKenzie, No. **41,** Ashland, financial services, 16th year.
Lloyd McPeters, No. **64,** Oklahoma State, business insurance sales, 1st year.
Ben Montgomery, No. **117,** Morehouse, school administrator, 12th year.
Dale Orem, No. **51,** Louisville, executive director, community foundation, 14th year.
Jim Quirk, No. **5,** Delaware, vice president, government securities, 6th year.
Bill Reynolds, No. **53,** West Chester State, retired teacher, 19th year.
Charles Stewart, No. **62,** Long Beach State, administrative deputy director, 2nd year.

Back Judges

Paul Baetz, No. **22,** Heidelberg, financial consultant, 16th year.
Ken Baker, No. **91,** Eastern Illinois, optician, surgical ophthalmic technician, 3rd year.
Roy Clymer, No. **24,** New Mexico State, district marketing manager, gas company, 14th year.
George Coleman, No. **45,** Bishop College, executive director, YMCA, 1st year.
Jim Daopoulos, No. **75,** Kentucky, mortgage broker, 5th year.
Al Jury, No. **106,** San Bernardino Valley, state traffic officer, 16th year.
Jim Kearney, No. **107,** Pennsylvania, marketing manager, 16th year.
Bill Lovett, No. **98,** Maryland, managing partner, financial sales, 4th year.
Timmie Millis, No. **80,** Millsaps, financial investigative consultant, 5th year.
Bob Moore, No. **36,** Dayton, attorney, 10th year.
Jim Poole, No. **92,** San Diego State, college professor, 19th year.
Louis Richard, No. **68,** Southwestern Louisiana, sales manager, 8th year.
Tom Sifferman, No. **118,** Seattle, manufacturer's representative, 8th year.
Scott Steenson, No. **88,** North Texas State, real estate broker, 3rd year.
Banks Williams, No. **99,** Houston, consultant, 16th year.

Side Judges

Mike Borgard, No. **90,** St. Louis, president/owner, advertising specialties, 4th year.
Mike Carey, No. **94,** Santa Clara, marketing manager, 4th year.
Don Carlsen, No. **39,** Cal State-Chico, budget analyst, comptroller, 5th year.
Bill Carollo, No. **63,** Wisconsin, marketing executive, 5th year.
Richard Creed, No. **61,** Louisville, manager, real estate, 16th year.
Tom Fincken, No. **47,** Emporia State, educator, 10th year.
Van Golmont, No. **3,** Miami, regional manager, marketing development, 3rd year.
Nathan Jones, No. **97,** Lewis and Clark, high school principal, 17th year.
Dean Look, No. **49,** Michigan State, director, medical manufacturing, former AFL player, 21st year.
Tommy Moore, No. **60,** Stephen F. Austin, marketing, manufacturing representative, 2nd year.
Bill Quinby, No. **58,** Iowa, retired athletic director, 16th year.
Howard Slavin, No. **29,** Southern California, attorney, 7th year.
Ron Spitler, No. **119,** Panhandle State, owner, service center, 12th year.
Doug Toole, No. **4,** Utah State, physical therapist, orthopedic and sports medicine, 6th year.
Don Wedge, No. **28,** Ohio Wesleyan, executive account manager, 22nd year.
David Wyant, No. **16,** Virginia, research scientist, 3rd year.

Field Judges

Don Dorkowski, No. **113,** Cal State Los Angeles, department head, health and safety, 8th year.
Scott Green, No. **19,** Delaware, vice president, government relations, 3rd year.
Don Hakes, No. **96,** Bradley, retired educator, 17th year.
Donnie Hampton, No. **44,** Georgia, mortgage banker, 6th year.
Bob Lewis, No. **18,** no college, retired U.S. government specialist, 18th year.
Phil Luckett, No. **59,** Texas-El Paso, computer program analyst, federal civil services, 3rd year.
Pat Mallette, No. **82,** Nebraska, real estate broker, 25th year.
Ed Merrifield, No. **76,** Missouri, sales representative, 19th year.
Don Orr, No. **77,** Vanderbilt, mechanical contractor, 23rd year.
Richard Reels, No. **83,** no college, director of security, court services, 1st year.
John Robison, No. **46,** Utah, high school teacher, 6th year.
Bill Schmitz, No. **122,** Colorado State, general sales manager, 5th year.
Bobby Skelton, No. **73,** Alabama, industrial representative, 9th year.
Larry Upson, No. **37,** Prince George City College, senior personnel management specialist, 3rd year.
Jack Vaughan, No. **93,** Mississippi State, financial services, 18th year.

1

TOUCHDOWN, FIELD GOAL, or SUCCESSFUL TRY
Both arms extended above head.

2

SAFETY
Palms together above head.

3

FIRST DOWN
Arm pointed toward defensive team's goal.

4

CROWD NOISE, DEAD BALL, or NEUTRAL ZONE ESTABLISHED
One arm above head with an open hand
With fist closed: **Fourth Down.**

5

BALL ILLEGALLY TOUCHED, KICKED, or BATTED
Fingertips tap both shoulders.

6

TIME OUT
Hands crisscrossed above head. Same signal followed by placing one hand on top of cap: **Referee's Time Out.** Same signal followed by arm swung at side: **Touchback.**

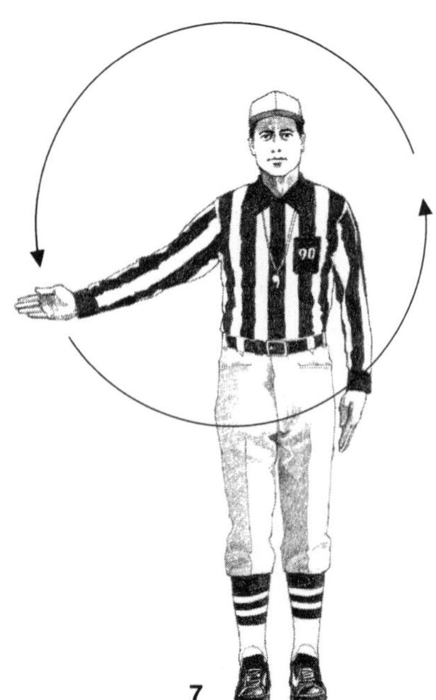

7

NO TIME OUT or TIME IN WITH WHISTLE
Full arm circled to simulate moving clock.

8

DELAY OF GAME, ILLEGAL SUBSTITUTIO[N] or EXCESS TIME OUT
Folded arms.

9

FALSE START, ILLEGAL SHIFT, ILLEGAL FORMATION, or KICKOFF or SAFETY KICK OUT OF BOUNDS
orearms rotated over and over in front of body.

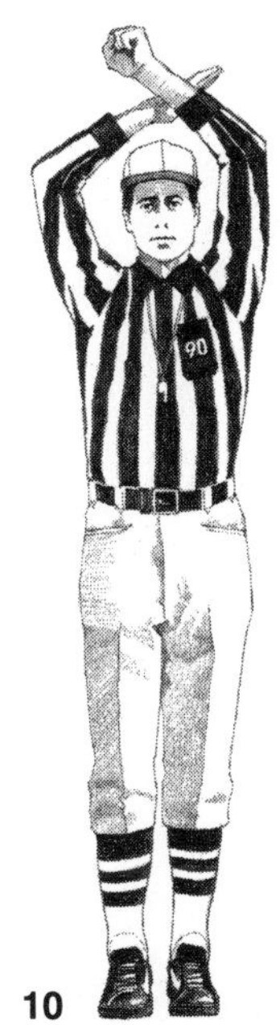

10

PERSONAL FOUL
One wrist striking the other above head. Same signal followed by swinging leg: **Roughing Kicker.** Same signal followed by raised arm swinging forward: **Roughing Passer.** Same signal followed by hand striking back of calf: **Clipping.**

11

HOLDING
Grasping one wrist, the fist clenched, in front of chest.

12

ILLEGAL USE OF HANDS, ARMS, or BODY
Grasping one wrist, the hand open and facing forward, in front of chest.

13

PENALTY REFUSED, INCOMPLETE PASS, PLAY OVER, or MISSED GOAL
Hands shifted in horizontal plane.

14

PASS JUGGLED INBOUNDS AND CAUGHT OUT OF BOUNDS
Hands up and down in front of chest (following incomplete pass signal).

15

ILLEGAL FORWARD PASS
One hand waved behind back followed by loss of down signal (23).

16

INTENTIONAL GROUNDING OF PASS
Parallel arms waved in a diagonal plane across body. Followed by loss of down signal (23).

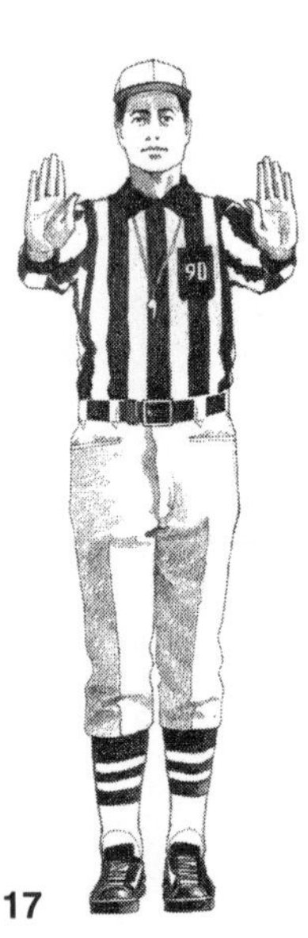

17

INTERFERENCE WITH FORWARD PASS or FAIR CATCH
Hands open and extended forward from shoulders with hands vertical.

18

INVALID FAIR CATCH SIGNAL
One hand waved above head.

19

INELIGIBLE RECEIVER or INELIGIBLE MEMBER OF KICKING TEAM DOWNFIELD
Right hand touching top of cap.

20

ILLEGAL CONTACT
One open hand extended forward.

21

OFFSIDE or ENCROACHING
Hands on hips.

22

ILLEGAL MOTION AT SNAP
Horizontal arc with one hand.

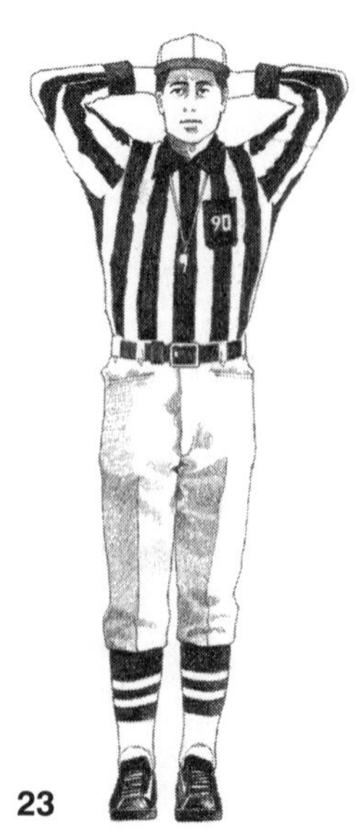

23

LOSS OF DOWN
Both hands held behind head.

24

CRAWLING, INTERLOCKING INTERFERENCE, PUSHING, or HELPING RUNNER
Pushing movement of hands to front with arms downward.

TOUCHING A FORWARD PASS or SCRIMMAGE KICK
Diagonal motion of one hand across another.

UNSPORTSMANLIKE CONDUCT
Arms outstretched, palms down. (Same signal means continuous action fouls are disregarded.) Chop block.

ILLEGAL CUT or BLOCKING BELOW THE WAIST
Hands striking front of thigh preceded by personal foul signal (10).

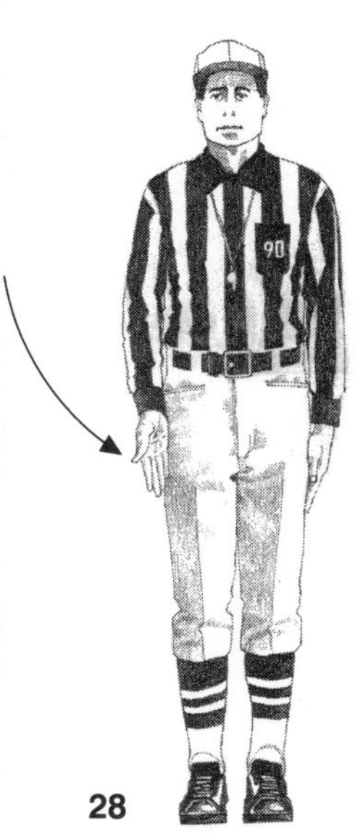

ILLEGAL CRACKBACK
Strike of an open right hand against the right mid-thigh preceded by personal foul signal (10).

PLAYER DISQUALIFIED
Ejection signal.

TRIPPING
Repeated action of right foot in back of left heel.

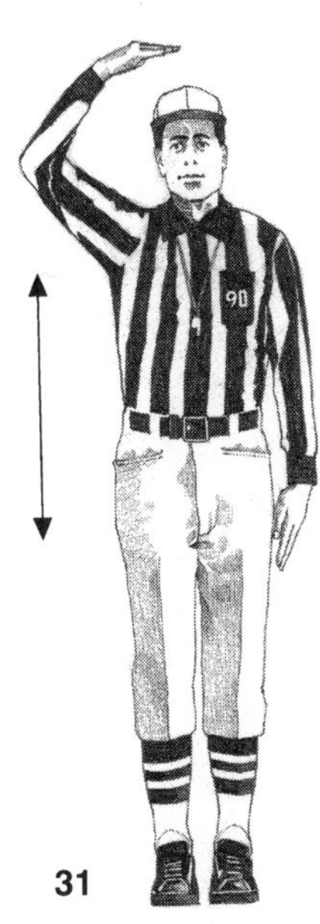

UNCATCHABLE FORWARD PASS
Palm of right hand held parallel to ground above head and moved back and forth.

NFL Digest of Rules

This Digest of Rules of the National Football League has been prepared to aid players, fans, and members of the press, radio, and television media in their understanding of the game.

It is not meant to be a substitute for the official rule book. In any case of conflict between these explanations and the official rules, the rules always have precedence.

In order to make it easier to coordinate the information in this digest the topics discussed generally follow the order of the rule book.

Officials' Jurisdictions, Positions, and Duties

Referee — General oversight and control of game. Gives signals for all fouls and is final authority for rule interpretations. Takes a position in backfield 10 to 12 yards behind line of scrimmage, favors right side (if quarterback is right-handed passer). Determines legality of snap, observes deep back(s) for legal motion. On running play, observes quarterback during and after handoff, remains with him until action has cleared away, then proceeds downfield, checking on runner and contact behind him. When runner is downed, Referee determines forward progress from wing official and, if necessary, adjusts final position of ball.

On pass plays, drops back as quarterback begins to fade back, picks up legality of blocks by near linemen. Changes to complete concentration on quarterback as defenders approach. Primarily responsible to rule on possible roughing action on passer and if ball becomes loose, rules whether ball is free on a fumble or dead on an incomplete pass.

During kicking situations, Referee has primary responsibility to rule on kicker's actions and whether or not any subsequent contact by a defender is legal.

Umpire — Primary responsibility to rule on players' equipment, as well as their conduct and actions on scrimmage line. Lines up approximately four to five yards downfield, varying position from in front of weakside tackle to strongside guard. Looks for possible false start by offensive linemen. Observes legality of contact by both offensive linemen while blocking and by defensive players while they attempt to ward off blockers. Is prepared to call rule infractions if they occur on offense or defense. Moves forward to line of scrimmage when pass play develops in order to insure that interior linemen do not move illegally downfield. If offensive linemen indicate screen pass is to be attempted, Umpire shifts his attention toward screen side, picks up potential receiver in order to insure that he will legally be permitted to run his pattern and continues to rule on action of blockers. Umpire is to assist in ruling on incomplete or trapped passes when ball is thrown overhead or short.

Head Linesman — Primarily responsible for ruling on offside, encroachment, and actions pertaining to scrimmage line prior to or at snap. Keys on closest setback on his side of the field. On pass plays, Linesman is responsible to clear this receiver approximately seven yards downfield as he moves to a point five yards beyond the line. Linesman's secondary responsibility is to rule on any illegal action taken by defenders on any delay receiver moving downfield. Has full responsibility for ruling on sideline plays on his side, e.g., pass receiver or runner in or out of bounds. Together with Referee, Linesman is responsible for keeping track of number of downs and is in charge of mechanics of his chain crew in connection with its duties.

Linesman must be prepared to assist in determining forward progress by a runner on play directed toward middle or into his side zone. He, in turn, is to signal Referee or Umpire what forward point ball has reached. Linesman is also responsible to rule on legality of action involving any receiver who approaches his side zone. He is to call pass interference when the infraction occurs and is to rule on legality of blockers and defenders on plays involving ball carriers, whether it is entirely a running play, a combination pass and run, or a play involving a kick.

Line Judge — Straddles line of scrimmage on side of field opposite Linesman. Keeps time of game as a backup for clock operator. Along with Linesman is responsible for offside, encroachment, and actions pertaining to scrimmage line prior to or at snap. Line Judge keys on closest setback on his side of field. Line Judge is to observe his receiver until he moves at least seven yards downfield. He then moves toward backfield side, being especially alert to rule on any back in motion and on flight of ball when pass is made (he must rule whether forward or backward). Line Judge has primary responsibility to rule whether or not passer is behind or beyond line of scrimmage when pass is made. He also assists in observing actions by blockers and defenders who are on his side of field. After pass is thrown, Line Judge directs attention toward activities that occur in back of Umpire. During punting situations, Line Judge remains at line of scrimmage to be sure that only the end men move downfield until kick has been made. He also rules whether or not the kick crossed line and then observes action by members of the kicking team who are moving downfield to cover the kick.

Back Judge — Operates on same side of field as Line Judge, 20 yards deep. Keys on wide receiver on his side. Concentrates on path of end or back, observing legality of his potential block(s) or of actions taken against him. Is prepared to rule from deep position on holding or illegal use of hands by end or back or on defensive infractions committed by player guarding him. Has primary responsibility to make decisions involving sideline on his side of field, e.g., pass receiver or runner in or out of bounds.

Back Judge makes decisions involving catching, recovery, or illegal touching of a loose ball beyond line of scrimmage; rules on plays involving pass receiver, including legality of catch or pass interference; assists in covering actions of runner, including blocks by teammates and that of defenders; calls clipping on punt returns; and, together with Field Judge, rules whether or not field goal attempts are successful.

Side Judge — Operates on same side of field as Linesman, 20 yards deep. Keys on wide receiver on his side. Concentrates on path of end or back, observing legality of his potential block(s) or of actions taken against him. Is prepared to rule from deep position on holding or illegal use of hands by end or back or on defensive infractions committed by player guarding him. Has primary responsibility to make decisions involving sideline on his side of field, e.g., pass receiver or runner in or out of bounds.

Side Judge makes decisions involving catching, recovery, or illegal touching of a loose ball beyond line of scrimmage; rules on plays involving pass receiver, including legality of catch or pass interference; assists in covering actions of runner, including blocks by teammates and that of defenders; and calls clipping on punt returns. On punts, field goals, and point after touchdown attempts, he becomes a double umpire.

Field Judge — Takes a position 25 yards downfield. In general, favors the tight end's side of field. Keys on tight end, concentrates on his path and observes legality of tight end's potential block(s) or of actions taken against him. Is prepared to rule from deep position on holding or illegal use of hands by end or back or on defensive infractions committed by player guarding him.

Field Judge times interval between plays on 40/25-second clock plus intermission between two periods of each half; makes decisions involving catching, recovery, or illegal touching of a loose ball beyond line of scrimmage; is responsible to rule on plays involving end line; calls pass interference, fair catch infractions, and clipping on kick returns; and, together with Back Judge, rules whether or not field goals and conversions are successful.

Definitions

1. **Chucking:** Warding off an opponent who is in front of a defender by contacting him with a quick extension of arm or arms, followed by the return of arm(s) to a flexed position, thereby breaking the original contact.
2. **Clipping:** Throwing the body across the back of an opponent's leg or hitting him from the back below the waist while moving up from behind unless the opponent is a runner or the action is in close line play.
3. **Close Line Play:** The area between the positions normally occupied by the offensive tackles, extending three yards on each side of the line of scrimmage.
4. **Crackback:** Eligible receivers who take or move to a position more than two yards outside the tackle may not block an opponent below the waist if they then move back inside to block.
5. **Dead Ball:** Ball not in play.
6. **Double Foul:** A foul by each team during the same down.
7. **Down:** The period of action that starts when the ball is put in play and ends when it is dead.
8. **Encroachment:** When a player enters the neutral zone and makes contact with an opponent before the ball is snapped.
9. **Fair Catch:** An unhindered catch of a kick by a member of the receiving team who must raise one arm a full length above his head while the kick is in flight.
10. **Foul:** Any violation of a playing rule.
11. **Free Kick:** A kickoff, kick after a safety, or kick after a fair catch. It may be a placekick, dropkick, or punt, except a punt may not be used on a kickoff.
12. **Fumble:** The loss of possession of the ball.
13. **Game Clock:** Scoreboard game clock.
14. **Impetus:** The action of a player that gives momentum to the ball.
15. **Live Ball:** A ball legally free kicked or snapped. It continues in play until the down ends.
16. **Loose Ball:** A live ball not in possession of any player.
17. **Muff:** The touching of a loose ball by a player in an unsuccessful attempt to obtain possession.
18. **Neutral Zone:** The space the length of a ball between the two scrimmage lines. The offensive team and defensive team must remain behind their end of the ball.
    Exception: The offensive player who snaps the ball.
19. **Offside:** A player is offside when any part of his body is beyond his scrimmage or free kick line when the ball is snapped.
20. **Own Goal:** The goal a team is guarding.
21. **Play Clock:** 40/25 second clock.
22. **Pocket Area:** Applies from a point two yards outside of either offensive tackle and includes the tight end if he drops off the line of scrimmage to pass protect. Pocket extends longitudinally behind the line back to offensive team's own end line.
23. **Possession:** When a player controls the ball throughout the act of clearly touching both feet, or any other part of his body other than his hand(s), to the ground inbounds.
24. **Post-Possession Foul:** A foul by the receiving team that occurs after a ball is legally kicked from scrimmage prior to possession changing. The ball must cross the line of scrimmage and the receiving team must retain possession of the kicked ball.
25. **Punt:** A kick made when a player drops the ball and kicks it while it is in flight.
26. **Safety:** The situation in which the ball is dead on or behind a team's own goal if the impetus comes from a player on that team. Two points are scored for the opposing team.
27. **Shift:** The movement of two or more offensive players at the same time before the snap.
28. **Striking:** The act of swinging, clubbing, or propelling the arm or forearm in contacting an opponent.
29. **Sudden Death:** The continuation of a tied game into sudden death overtime in which the team scoring first (by safety, field goal, or touchdown) wins.
30. **Touchback:** When a ball is dead on or behind a team's own goal line, provided the impetus came from an opponent and provided it is not a touchdown or a missed field goal.

31. **Touchdown:** When any part of the ball, legally in possession of a player inbounds, is on, above, or over the opponent's goal line, provided it is not a touchback.
32. **Unsportsmanlike Conduct:** Any act contrary to the generally understood principles of sportsmanship.

Summary of Penalties

Automatic First Down

1. Awarded to offensive team on all defensive fouls with these exceptions:
   (a) Offside.
   (b) Encroachment.
   (c) Delay of game.
   (d) Illegal substitution.
   (e) Excessive time out(s).
   (f) Incidental grasp of facemask.
   (g) Prolonged, excessive or premeditated celebrations by individual players or groups of players.
   (h) Running into the kicker.

Loss of Down (No yardage)

1. Second forward pass behind the line.
2. Forward pass strikes ground, goal post, or crossbar.
3. Forward pass goes out of bounds.
4. Forward pass is first touched by eligible receiver who has gone out of bounds and returned.
5. Forward pass touches or is caught by an ineligible receiver on or behind line.
6. Forward pass thrown from behind line of scrimmage after ball once crossed the line.

Five Yards

1. Defensive holding or illegal use of hands (automatic first down).
2. Delay of game.
3. Encroachment.
4. Too many time outs.
5. False start.
6. Illegal formation.
7. Illegal shift.
8. Illegal motion.
9. Illegal substitution.
10. First onside kickoff out of bounds between goal lines and not touched.
11. Invalid fair catch signal.
12. More than 11 players on the field at snap for either team.
13. Less than seven men on offensive line at snap.
14. Offside.
15. Failure to pause one second after shift or huddle.
16. Running into kicker.
17. More than one man in motion at snap.
18. Grasping facemask of opponent.
19. Player out of bounds at snap.
20. Ineligible member(s) of kicking team going beyond line of scrimmage before ball is kicked.
21. Illegal return.
22. Failure to report change of eligibility.
23. Prolonged, excessive or premeditated celebrations by individual players or groups of players.
24. Loss of team time out(s) or five-yard penalty on the defense for excessive crowd noise.
25. Ineligible player downfield during passing down.

10 Yards

1. Offensive pass interference.
2. Holding, illegal use of hands, arms, or body by offense.
3. Tripping by a member of either team.
4. Helping the runner.
5. Deliberately batting or punching a loose ball.
6. Deliberately kicking a loose ball.

15 Yards

1. Chop block.
2. Clipping below the waist.
3. Fair catch interference.
4. Illegal crackback block by offense.
5. Piling on (automatic first down).
6. Roughing the kicker (automatic first down).
7. Roughing the passer (automatic first down).
8. Twisting, turning, or pulling an opponent by the facemask.
9. Unnecessary roughness.
10. Unsportsmanlike conduct.
11. Delay of game at start of either half.
12. Illegal blocking below the waist.
13. A tackler using his helmet to butt, spear, or ram an opponent.
14. Any player who uses the top of his helmet unnecessarily.
15. A punter, placekicker, or holder who simulates being roughed by a defensive player.
16. A defender who takes a running start from beyond the line of scrimmage in an attempt to block a field goal or point after touchdown and lands on players.

Five Yards and Loss of Down

1. Forward pass thrown from beyond line of scrimmage.

10 Yards and Loss of Down

1. Intentional grounding of forward pass (safety if passer is in own end zone). If foul occurs more than 10 yards behind line, play results in loss of down at spot of foul.

15 Yards and Loss of Coin Toss Option

1. Team's late arrival on the field prior to scheduled kickoff.
2. Captains not appearing for coin toss.

15 Yards (and disqualification if flagrant)

1. Striking opponent with fist.
2. Kicking or kneeing opponent.
3. Striking opponent on head or neck with forearm, elbow, or hands whether or not the initial contact is made below the neck area.
4. Roughing kicker.
5. Roughing passer.
6. Malicious unnecessary roughness.
7. Unsportsmanlike conduct.
8. Palpably unfair act. (Distance penalty determined by the Referee after consultation with other officials.)

15 Yards and Automatic Disqualification

1. Using a helmet as a weapon.

Suspension From Game

1. Illegal equipment. (Player may return after one down when legally equipped.)

Touchdown

1. When Referee determines a palpably unfair act deprived a team of a touchdown. (Example: Player comes off bench and tackles runner apparently en route to touchdown.)

Field

1. Sidelines and end lines are out of bounds. The goal line is actually in the end zone. A player with the ball in his possession scores when the ball is on, above, or over the goal line.
2. The field is rimmed by a white border, a minimum six feet wide, along the sidelines. All of this is out of bounds.
3. The hashmarks (inbound lines) are 70 feet, 9 inches from each sideline.
4. Goal posts must be single-standard type, offset from the end line and painted bright gold. The goal posts must be 18 feet, 6 inches wide and the top face of the crossbar must be 10 feet above the ground. Vertical posts extend at least 30 feet above the crossbar. A ribbon 4 inches by 42 inches long is to be attached to the top of each post. The actual goal is the plane extending indefinitely above the crossbar and between the outer edges of the posts.
5. The field is 360 feet long and 160 feet wide. The end zones are 30 feet deep. The line used in try-for-point plays is two yards out from the goal line.
6. Chain crew members and ball boys must be uniformly identifiable.
7. All clubs must use standardized sideline markers. Pylons must be used for goal line and end line markings.
8. End zone markings and club identification at 50 yard line must be approved by the Commissioner to avoid any confusion as to delineation of goal lines, sidelines, and end lines.

Ball

1. The home club must have 24 balls available for testing by the Referee one hour before game time. In case of bad weather, a playable ball is to be substituted on request of the offensive team captain.

Coin Toss

1. The toss of coin will take place within three minutes of kickoff in center of field. The toss will be called by the visiting captain. The winner may choose one of two privileges and the loser gets the other:
   (a) Receive or kick
   (b) Goal his team will defend
2. Immediately prior to the start of the second half, the captains of both teams must inform the officials of their respective choices. The loser of the original coin toss gets first choice.

Timing

1. The stadium game clock is official. In case it stops or is operating incorrectly, the Line Judge takes over the official timing on the field.
2. Each period is 15 minutes. The intermission between the periods is two minutes. Halftime is 12 minutes, unless otherwise specified.
3. On charged team time outs, the Field Judge starts watch and blows whistle after 1 minute 50 seconds, unless television does not utilize the time for commercial. In this case the length of the time out is reduced to 40 seconds.
4. Referee may allow two minutes for injured player and three minutes for equipment repair.
5. Each team is allowed three time outs each half.
6. Time between plays will be 40 seconds from the end of a given play until the snap of the ball for the next play, or a 25-second interval after certain administrative stoppages and game delays.
7. Clock will start running when ball is snapped following all changes of team possession.
8. With the exception of the last two minutes of the first half and the last five minutes of the second half, the game clock will be restarted following a kickoff return, a player going out of bounds on a play from scrimmage, or after declined penalties when appropriate on the referee's signal.
9. Consecutive team time outs can be taken by opposing teams but the length of the second time out will be reduced to 40 seconds.
10. When, in the judgment of the Referee, the level of crowd noise prevents the offense from hearing its signals, he can institute a series of procedures which can result in a loss of team time outs or a five-yard penalty against the defensive team.

Sudden Death

1. The sudden death system of determining the winner shall prevail when score is tied at the end of the regulation playing time of all NFL games. The team scoring first during overtime play shall be the winner and the game automatically ends upon any score (by safety, field goal, or touchdown) or when a score is awarded by Referee for a palpably unfair act.
2. At the end of regulation time the Referee will immediately toss coin at center of field in accordance with rules pertaining to the usual pregame toss. The captain of the visiting team will call the toss.
3. Following a three-minute intermission after the end of the regulation game, play will be continued in 15-minute periods or until there is a score. There is a two-minute intermission between subsequent periods. The teams change goals at the start of each period. Each team has three time outs and general provisions for play in the last two minutes of a half shall prevail. Disqualified players are not allowed to return.
   Exception: In preseason and regular season games there shall be a maximum of 15 minutes of sudden death with two time outs instead of three. General provisions for play in the last two minutes of a half will be in force.

Timing in Final Two Minutes of Each Half

1. On kickoff, clock does not start until the ball has been legally touched by player of either team in the field of play. (In all other cases, clock starts with kickoff.)
2. A team cannot buy an excess time out for a penalty. However, a fourth time out is allowed without penalty for an injured player, who must be removed immediately. A fifth time out or more is allowed for an injury and a five-yard penalty is assessed if the clock was running. Additionally, if the clock was running and the score is tied or the team in possession is losing, the ball cannot be put in play for at least 10 seconds on the fourth or more time out. The half or game can end while those 10 seconds are run off on the clock.
3. If the defensive team is behind in the score and commits a foul when it has no time outs left in the final 30 seconds of either half, the offensive team can decline the penalty for the foul and have the time on the clock expire.
4. Fouls that occur in the last five minutes of the fourth quarter as well as the last two minutes of the first half will result in the clock starting on the snap.

Try-for-Point

1. After a touchdown, the scoring team is allowed a try-for-point during one scrimmage down. The ball may be spotted anywhere between the inbounds lines, two or more yards from the goal line. The successful conversion counts one point, whether by run, kick, or pass.
2. The defensive team never can score on a try-for-point. As soon as defense gets possession, or the kick is blocked, the ball is dead.
3. Any distance penalty for fouls committed by the defense that prevent the try from being attempted can be enforced on the succeeding kickoff. Any foul committed on a successful try will result in a distance penalty being assessed on the ensuing kickoff.
4. Only the fumbling player may advance a fumble during a try-for-point.

Players-Substitutions

1. Each team is permitted 11 men on the field at the snap.
2. Unlimited substitution is permitted. However, players may enter the field only when the ball is dead. Players who have been substituted for are not permitted to linger on the field. Such lingering will be interpreted as unsportsmanlike conduct.
3. Players leaving the game must be out of bounds on their own side, clearing the field between the end lines, before a snap or free kick. If player crosses end line leaving field, it is delay of game (five-yard penalty).
4. Substitutes who remain in the game must move onto the field as far as the inside of the field numerals before moving to a wide position.

Kickoff

1. The kickoff shall be from the kicking team's 35 yard line at the start of each half and after a field goal and try-for-point. A kickoff is one type of free kick.
2. Either a one-, two-, or three-inch tee may be used (no tee permitted for field goal or try-for-point plays). The ball is put in play by a placekick or dropkick.
3. If the kickoff clears the opponent's goal posts it is not a field goal.
4. A kickoff is illegal unless it travels 10 yards OR is touched by the receiving team. Once the ball is touched by the receiving team it is a free ball. Receivers may recover and advance. Kicking team may recover but NOT advance UNLESS receiver had possession and lost the ball.
5. When a kickoff goes out of bounds between the goal lines without being touched by the receiving team, the ball belongs to the receivers 30 yards from the spot of the kick or at the out-of-bounds spot unless the ball went out-of-bounds the first time an onside kick was attempted. In this case the kicking team is to be penalized five yards and the ball must be kicked again.
6. When a kickoff goes out of bounds between the goal lines and is touched last by receiving team, it is receiver's ball at out-of-bounds spot.

Free Kick

1. In addition to a kickoff, the other free kicks are a kick after a safety and a kick after a fair catch. In both cases, a dropkick, placekick, or punt may be used (a punt may not be used on a kickoff).
2. On a free kick after a fair catch, captain of receiving team has the option to put ball in play by punt, dropkick, or placekick without a tee, or by snap. If the placekick or dropkick goes between the uprights a field goal is scored.
3. On a free kick after a safety, the team scored upon puts ball in play by a punt, dropkick, or placekick without tee. No score can be made on a free kick following a safety, even if a series of penalties places team in position. (A field goal can be scored only on a play from scrimmage or a free kick after a fair catch.)

Field Goal

1. All field goals attempted and missed from scrimmage line beyond the 20 yard line will result in the defensive team taking possession of the ball at the scrimmage line. On any field goal attempted and missed from scrimmage line inside the 20 yard line, ball will revert to defensive team at the 20 yard line.

Safety

1. The important factor in a safety is impetus. Two points are scored for the opposing team when the ball is dead on or behind a team's own goal line if the impetus came from a player on that team.

Examples of Safety:

(a) Blocked punt goes out of kicking team's end zone. Impetus was provided by punting team. The block only changes direction of ball, not impetus.
(b) Ball carrier retreats from field of play into his own end zone and is downed. Ball carrier provides impetus.
(c) Offensive team commits a foul and spot of enforcement is behind its own goal line.
(d) Player on receiving team muffs punt and, trying to get ball, forces or illegally kicks it into end zone where he or a teammate recovers. He has given new impetus to the ball.

Examples of Non-Safety:

(a) Player intercepts a pass with both feet inbounds in the field of play and his momentum carries him into his own end zone. Ball is put in play at spot of interception.
(b) Player intercepts a pass in his own end zone and is downed. Impetus came from passing team, not from defense. (Touchback)
(c) Player passes from behind his own goal line. Opponent bats down ball in end zone. (Incomplete pass)

Measuring

1. The forward point of the ball is used when measuring.

Position of Players at Snap

1. Offensive team must have at least seven players on line.
2. Offensive players, not on line, must be at least one yard back at snap. (**Exception:** player who takes snap.)
3. No interior lineman may move after taking or simulating a three-point stance.
4. No player of either team may invade neutral zone before snap.
5. No player of offensive team may charge or move, after assuming set position, in such manner as to lead defense to believe snap has started.
6. If a player changes his eligibility, the Referee must alert the defensive captain after player has reported to him.
7. All players of offensive team must be stationary at snap, except one back who may be in motion parallel to scrimmage line or backward (not forward).
8. After a shift or huddle all players on offensive team must come to an absolute stop for at least one second with no movement of hands, feet, head, or swaying of body.
9. Quarterbacks can be called for a false start penalty (five yards) if their actions are judged to be an obvious attempt to draw an opponent offside.

Use of Hands, Arms, and Body

1. No player on offense may assist a runner except by blocking for him. There shall be no interlocking interference.
2. A runner may ward off opponents with his hands and arms but no other player on offense may use hands or arms to obstruct an opponent by grasping with hands, pushing, or encircling any part of his body during a block. Hands (open or closed) can be thrust forward to initially contact an opponent on or outside the opponent's frame, but the blocker must work to bring his hands on or inside the frame.
   Note: Pass blocking: Hand(s) thrust forward that slip outside the body of the defender will be legal if blocker worked to bring them back inside. Hand(s) or arm(s) that encircle a defender – i.e., hook an opponent – are to be considered illegal and officials are to call a foul for holding.
   Blocker cannot use his hands or arms to push from behind, hang onto, or encircle an opponent in a manner that restricts his movement as the play develops.
3. Hands cannot be thrust forward above the frame to contact an opponent on the neck, face or head.
   Note: The frame is defined as the part of the opponent's body below the neck that is presented to the blocker.
4. A defensive player may not tackle or hold an opponent other than a runner. Otherwise, he may use his hands, arms, or body only:
   (a) To defend or protect himself against an obstructing opponent.
   Exception: An eligible receiver is considered to be an obstructing opponent ONLY to a point five yards beyond the line of scrimmage unless the player who receives the snap clearly demonstrates no further intention to pass the ball. Within this five-yard zone, a defensive player may make contact with an eligible receiver that may be maintained as long as it is continuous and unbroken. The defensive player cannot use his hands or arms to push from behind, hang onto, or encircle an eligible receiver in a manner that restricts movement as the play develops. Beyond this five-yard limitation, a defender may use his hands or arms ONLY to defend or protect himself against impend-

ing contact caused by a receiver. In such reaction, the defender may not contact a receiver who attempts to take a path to evade him.
   (b) To push or pull opponent out of the way on line of scrimmage.
   (c) In actual attempt to get at or tackle runner.
   (d) To push or pull opponent out of the way in a legal attempt to recover a loose ball.
   (e) During a legal block on an opponent who is not an eligible pass receiver.
   (f) When legally blocking an eligible pass receiver above the waist.
   Exception: Eligible receivers lined up within two yards of the tackle, whether on or immediately behind the line, may be blocked below the waist at or behind the line of scrimmage. NO eligible receiver may be blocked below the waist after he goes beyond the line.
   Note: Once the quarterback hands off or pitches the ball to a back, or if the quarterback leaves the pocket area, the restrictions on the defensive team relative to the offensive receivers will end, provided the ball is not in the air.
5. A defensive player must not contact an opponent above the shoulders with the palm of his hand except to ward him off on the line. This exception is permitted only if it is not a repeated act against the same opponent during any one contact. In all other cases the palms may be used on head, neck, or face only to ward off or push an opponent in legal attempt to get at the ball.
6. Any offensive player who pretends to possess the ball or to whom a teammate pretends to give the ball may be tackled provided he is crossing his scrimmage line between the ends of a normal tight offensive line.
7. An offensive player who lines up more than two yards outside his own tackle or a player who, at the snap, is in a backfield position and subsequently takes a position more than two yards outside a tackle may not clip an opponent anywhere nor may he contact an opponent below the waist if the blocker is moving toward the ball and if contact is made within an area five yards on either side of the line.
8. A player of either team may block at any time provided it is not pass interference, fair catch interference, or unnecessary roughness.
9. A player may not bat or punch:
   (a) A loose ball (in field of play) toward his opponent's goal line or in any direction in either end zone.
   (b) A ball in player possession or attempt to get possession.
   Exception: A forward or backward pass may be batted, tipped, or deflected in any direction at any time by either the offense or the defense.
   Note: A pass in flight that is controlled or caught may only be thrown backward.
10. No player may deliberately kick any ball except as a punt, dropkick, or placekick.

Forward Pass

1. A forward pass may be touched or caught by any eligible receiver. All members of the defensive team are eligible. Eligible receivers on the offensive team are players on either end of line (other than center, guard, or tackle) or players at least one yard behind the line at the snap. A T-formation quarterback is not eligible to receive a forward pass during a play from scrimmage.
   Exception: T-formation quarterback becomes eligible if pass is previously touched by an eligible receiver.
2. An offensive team may make only one forward pass during each play from scrimmage (Loss of down).
3. The passer must be behind his line of scrimmage (Loss of down and five yards, enforced from the spot of pass).
4. Any eligible offensive player may catch a forward pass. If a pass is touched by one offensive player and touched or caught by a second eligible offensive player, pass completion is legal. Further, all offensive players become eligible once a pass is touched by an eligible receiver or any defensive player.
5. The rules concerning a forward pass and ineligible receivers:
   (a) If ball is touched accidentally by an ineligible receiver on or behind his line: loss of down.
   (b) If ineligible receiver is illegally downfield: loss of five yards.
   (c) If touched or caught (intentionally or accidentally) by ineligible receiver beyond the line: loss of 10 yards or loss of down.
6. The player who first controls and continues to maintain control of a pass will be awarded the ball even though his opponent later establishes joint control of the ball.
7. Any forward pass becomes incomplete and ball is dead if:
   (a) Pass hits the ground or goes out of bounds.
   (b) Hits the goal post or the crossbar of either team.
   (c) Is caught by offensive player after touching ineligible receiver.
   (d) An illegal pass is caught by the passer.
8. A forward pass is complete when a receiver clearly touches the ground with both feet inbounds while in possession of the ball. If a receiver would have landed inbounds with both feet but is carried or pushed out of bounds while maintaining possession of the ball, pass is complete at the out-of-bounds spot.
9. If an eligible receiver goes out of bounds accidentally or is forced out by a defender and returns to catch a pass, the play is regarded as a pass caught out of bounds. (Loss of down, no yardage.)
10. On a fourth down pass — when the offensive team is inside the opposition's 20 yard line — an incomplete pass results in a loss of down at the line of scrimmage.
11. If a personal foul is committed by the defense prior to the completion of a pass, the penalty is 15 yards from the spot where ball becomes dead.
12. If a personal foul is committed by the offense prior to the completion of a pass, the penalty is 15 yards from the previous line of scrimmage.

Intentional Grounding of Forward Pass

1. Intentional grounding of a forward pass is a foul: loss of down and 10 yards from previous spot if passer is in the field of play or loss of down at the spot of the foul if it occurs more than 10 yards behind the line or safety if passer is in his own end zone when ball is released.
2. Intentional grounding will be called when a passer, facing an imminent loss of yardage due to pressure from the defense, throws a forward pass without a realistic chance of completion.
3. Intentional grounding will not be called when a passer, while out of the pocket and facing an imminent loss of yardage, throws a pass that lands beyond the line of scrimmage, even if no offensive player(s) have a realistic chance to catch the ball (including if the ball lands out of bounds over the sideline or end line).

Protection of Passer

1. By interpretation, a pass begins when the passer — with possession of ball — starts to bring his hand forward. If ball strikes ground after this action has begun, play is ruled an incomplete pass. If passer loses control of ball prior to his bringing his hand forward, play is ruled a fumble.
2. No defensive player may run into a passer of a legal forward pass after the ball has left his hand (15 yards). The Referee must determine whether opponent had a reasonable chance to stop his momentum during an attempt to block the pass or tackle the passer while he still had the ball.
3. No defensive player who has an unrestricted path to the quarterback may hit him flagrantly in the area of the knee(s) when approaching in any direction.
4. Officials are to blow the play dead as soon as the quarterback is clearly in the grasp and control of any tackler, and his safety is in jeopardy.

Pass Interference

1. There shall be no interference with a forward pass thrown from behind the line. The restriction for the passing team starts with the snap. The restriction on the defensive team starts when the ball leaves the passer's hand. Both restrictions end when the ball is touched by anyone.
2. The penalty for defensive pass interference is an automatic first down at the spot of the foul. If interference is in the end zone, it is first down for the offense on the defense's 1 yard line. If previous spot was inside the defense's 1 yard line, penalty is half the distance to the goal line.
3. The penalty for offensive pass interference is 10 yards from the previous spot.
4. It is pass interference by either team when any player movement beyond the offensive line significantly hinders the progress of an eligible player or such player's opportunity to catch the ball during a legal forward pass. When players are competing for position to make a play on the ball, any contact by hands, arms or body shall be considered incidental unless prohibited. Prohibited conduct shall be when a player physically restricts or impedes the opponent in such a manner that is visually evident and materially affects the opponent's opportunity to gain position or retain his position to catch the ball. If a player has gained position, he shall not be considered to have impeded or restricted his opponent in a prohibited manner if all of his actions are a bona fide effort to go to and catch the ball. Provided an eligible player is not interfered with in such a manner, the following exceptions to pass interference will prevail:
   (a) If neither player is looking for the ball and there is incidental contact in the act of moving to the ball that does not materially affect the route of an eligible player, there is no interference. If there is any question whether the incidental contact materially affects the route, the ruling shall be no interference.
   Note: Inadvertent tripping is not a foul in this situation.
   (b) Any eligible player looking for and intent on playing the ball who initiates contact, however severe, while attempting to move to the spot of completion or interception will not be called for interference.
   (c) Any eligible player who makes contact, however severe, with one or more eligible players while looking for and making a genuine attempt to catch or bat a reachable ball, will not be called for interference.
   (d) It must be remembered that defensive players have as much right to the ball as offensive eligible receivers.
   (e) Pass interference by the defense is not to be called when the forward pass is clearly uncatchable.
   (f) Note: There is no defensive pass interference behind the line.

Backward Pass

1. Any pass not forward is regarded as a backward pass or lateral. A pass parallel to the line is a backward pass. A runner may pass backward at any time. Any player on either team may catch the pass or recover the ball after it touches the ground.
2. A backward pass that strikes the ground can be recovered and advanced by either team.
3. A backward pass caught in the air can be advanced by either team.
4. A backward pass in flight may not be batted forward by an offensive player.

Fumble

1. The distinction between a fumble and a muff should be kept in mind in considering rules about fumbles. A fumble is the loss of possession of the ball. A muff is the touching of a loose ball by a player in an unsuccessful attempt to obtain possession.
2. A fumble may be advanced by any player on either team regardless of whether recovered before or after ball hits the ground.

Kicks From Scrimmage

1. Any kick from scrimmage must be made from behind the line to be legal.
2. Any punt or missed field goal that touches a goal post is dead.
3. During a kick from scrimmage, only the end men, as eligible receivers on the line of scrimmage at the time of the snap, are permitted to go beyond the line before the ball is kicked.
   Exception: An eligible receiver who, at the snap, is aligned or in motion behind the line and more than one yard outside the end man on his side of the line, clearly making him the outside receiver, REPLACES that end man as the player eligible to go downfield after the snap. All other members of the kicking team must remain at the line of scrimmage until the ball has been kicked.
4. Any punt that is blocked and does not cross the line of scrimmage can be recovered and advanced by either team. However, if offensive team recovers it must make the yardage necessary for its first down to retain possession if punt was on fourth down.
5. The kicking team may never advance its own kick even though legal recovery is made beyond the line of scrimmage. Possession only.
6. A member of the receiving team may not run into or rough a kicker who kicks from behind his line unless contact is:
   (a) Incidental to and after he had touched ball in flight.
   (b) Caused by kicker's own motions.
   (c) Occurs during a quick kick, or a kick made after a run, or after kicker recovers a loose ball. Ball is loose when kicker muffs snap or snap hits ground.
   (d) Defender is blocked into kicker.
   The penalty for running into the kicker is 5 yards. For roughing the kicker: 15 yards, an automatic first down and disqualification if flagrant.
7. If a member of the kicking team attempting to down the ball on or inside opponent's 5 yard line carries the ball into the end zone, it is a touchback.
8. Fouls during a punt are enforced from the previous spot (line of scrimmage).
   Exception: Illegal touching, illegal fair catch, invalid fair catch signal, and fouls by the receiving team during loose ball after ball is kicked.
9. While the ball is in the air or rolling on the ground following a punt or field goal attempt and receiving team commits a foul before gaining possession, receiving team will retain possession and will be penalized for its foul.
10. It will be illegal for a defensive player to jump or stand on any player, or be picked up by a teammate or to use a hand or hands on a teammate to gain additional height in an attempt to block a kick (Penalty 15 yards, unsportsmanlike conduct).
11. A punted ball remains a kicked ball until it is declared dead or in possession of either team.
12. Any member of the punting team may down the ball anywhere in the field of play. However, it is illegal touching (Official's time out and receiver's ball at spot of illegal touching). This foul does not offset any foul by receivers during the down.
13. Defensive team may advance all kicks from scrimmage (including unsuccessful field goal) whether or not ball crosses defensive team's goal line. Rules pertaining to kicks from scrimmage apply until defensive team gains possession.

Fair Catch

1. The member of the receiving team must raise one arm a full length above his head and wave it from side to side while kick is in flight. (Failure to give proper sign: receivers' ball five yards behind spot of signal.) **Note:** It is legal for the receiver to shield his eyes from the sun by raising one hand no higher than the helmet.
2. No opponent may interfere with the fair catcher, the ball, or his path to the ball. Penalty: 15 yards from spot of foul and fair catch is awarded.
3. A player who signals for a fair catch is not required to catch the ball. However, if a player signals for a fair catch, he may not block or initiate contact with any player on the kicking team until the ball touches a player. Penalty: snap 15 yards behind spot of foul.
4. If ball hits ground or is touched by member of kicking team in flight, fair catch signal is off and all rules for a kicked ball apply.
5. Any undue advance by a fair catch receiver is delay of game. No specific distance is specified for undue advance as ball is dead at spot of catch. If player comes to a reasonable stop, no penalty. For violation, five yards.
6. If time expires while ball is in play and a fair catch is awarded, receiving team may choose to extend the period with one free kick down. However, placekicker may not use tee.

Foul on Last Play of Half or Game

1. On a foul by defense on last play of half or game, the down is replayed if penalty is accepted.
2. On a foul by the offense on last play of half or game, the down is not replayed and the play in which the foul is committed is nullified.
   Exception: Fair catch interference, foul following change of possession, illegal touching. No score by offense counts.
3. On double foul on last play of half or game, down is replayed.

Spot of Enforcement of Foul

1. There are four basic spots at which a penalty for a foul is enforced:
   (a) Spot of foul: The spot where the foul is committed.
   (b) Previous spot: The spot where the ball was put in play.
   (c) Spot of snap, pass, fumble, return kick, or free kick: The spot where the act connected with the foul occurred.
   (d) Succeeding spot: The spot where the ball next would be put in play if no distance penalty were to be enforced.
   Exception: If foul occurs after a touchdown and before the whistle for a try-for-point, succeeding spot is spot of next kickoff.
2. All fouls committed by offensive team behind the line of scrimmage and in the field of play shall be penalized from the previous spot.
3. When spot of enforcement for fouls involving defensive holding or illegal use of hands by the defense is behind the line of scrimmage, any penalty yardage to be assessed on that play shall be measured from the line if the foul occurred beyond the line.

Double Foul

1. If there is a double foul during a down in which there is a change of possession, the team last gaining possession may keep the ball unless its foul was committed prior to the change of possession.
2. If double foul occurs after a change of possession, the defensive team retains the ball at the spot of its foul or dead ball spot.
3. If one of the fouls of a double foul involves disqualification, that player must be removed, but no penalty yardage is to be assessed.
4. If the kickers foul during a kick before possession changes and the receivers foul after possession changes, the receivers will retain the ball after enforcment of its foul.

Penalty Enforced on Following Kickoff

1. When a team scores by touchdown, field goal, extra point, or safety and either team commits a personal foul, unsportsmanlike conduct, or obvious unfair act during the down, the penalty will be assessed on the following kickoff.

Procedures to Terminate or Temporarily Delay Completion of a Game

The National Football League holds to the position that all games should be played to their conclusion. However, if in the opinion of appropriate League authorities, it is impossible to begin or continue a game due to an emergency, or a game is deemed to be imminently threatened by any such emergency—e.g., severely inclement weather, lightning, flooding, power failure, interference by spectators, or other non-participants—then the following procedures will serve as guidelines for the Commissioner and/or his duly appointed representatives. The Commissioner will have the power to review the circumstances of each emergency and to adjust the following procedures in whatever manner he deems appropriate. If, in the Commissioner's opinion, it is reasonable to project that the resumption of an interrupted game would not change its ultimate result, he will be empowered to terminate the game.

1. The League employees vested with the authority to define emergencies under these procedures are the Commissioner, his representatives, and the game Referee. In cases where neither the Commissioner nor his representatives are present, the referee shall have sole authority, but he must make every effort to contact the Commissioner or representative for consultation. In all cases of significant delay, the League authorities will consult with the management of the participating clubs.
2. If, due to an emergency, a regular-season or postseason game is not started at its scheduled time and cannot be played at any later time that same day, the game, nevertheless, must be played on a subsequent date to be determined by the Commissioner.
3. If there is deemed to be a threat of an emergency (e.g., incoming tropical storm) that may occur during the playing of a game, the starting time of such game will not be moved to an earlier time unless there is clearly sufficient time to make an orderly change.
4. If an interrupted regular-season or postseason game cannot be completed on the same day, such game will be rescheduled by the Commissioner and resumed at that point.
5. In instances which require the Commissioner to reschedule a regular-season game, he will make every effort to set the game for no later than two days after its originally scheduled date, and if possible, at its original site. If unable to do so, he will schedule it at the nearest available facility. If it is impossible to schedule the game within two days after its original date, the Commissioner will attempt to schedule it on the Tuesday of the next calendar week in which the two involved clubs play other clubs no earlier than Sunday.
6. If an emergency interrupts a postseason game and such game cannot be resumed on that same date, the Commissioner will make every effort to arrange for its completion as soon as possible. If unable to schedule the game at the same site, he will select an appropriate alternate site. He will terminate the game short of completion only if in his judgment the continuation of the game would not be normally expected to alter the ultimate outcome.
7. In all instances where a game is resumed after interruption, the resumption will begin at the point at which the game was interrupted. The referee will call time out when it is necessary to declare an emergency interruption, and he will make a record of the team possessing the ball, position of the ball on the field, down, distance, time remaining in the period, and any other pertinent information required for an efficient and equitable resumption of play.

Note: In recent history, only two games, both preseason, have been terminated. In 1976, the Chicago College All-Star game was terminated due to thunderstorms with the Steelers leading the All-Stars 24-0, and the 1980 Pro Football Hall of Fame Game at Canton, Ohio, was called with 5:29 remaining due to severe thunder and lightning with the Chargers and Packers tied 0-0.

NOTES

NOTES

NOTES

NOTES

NOTES

NOTES